Official 1999
National Football League

Record & Fact Book

A National Football League Book.
Workman Publishing Co., New York.

National Football League
280 Park Avenue, New York, N.Y. 10017 (212) 450-2000. NFL Internet Address: http://nfl.com

Printed in the United States of America.

A National Football League Book.

Compiled by the NFL Communications Department and Seymour Siwoff, Elias Sports Bureau.

Edited by Chris McCloskey, NFL Communications Department, and Matt Marini, NFLP Publishing. Layout by William Tham. Proofread by Joe Velazquez, Greg Solomon, and John Fawaz. Print managing by Dick Falk, Tina Dahl, and Lawson Desrochers. Cover design by Helen Choy Whang and Samantha Kang. Typesetting by Cynthia Jolissaint.
Statistics by Elias Sports Bureau.
Produced by NFL Properties, Inc., Publishing Group, Los Angeles.

Cover photograph by E.B. Graphics.

Workman Publishing Co.
708 Broadway, New York, N.Y. 10003
Manufactured in the United States of America.
First printing, July 1999.
10 9 8 7 6 5 4 3 2 1

1999 SCHEDULE AND NOTE CALENDAR

(All times local except American Bowl game, which is EDT.)
Nationally televised games in parentheses.

	Saturday, August 7	Indianapolis _____ at Chicago _____	7:00
		Oakland _____ at St. Louis _____	7:00
		American Bowl at Sydney, Australia	
		Denver _____ vs. San Diego _____	(FOX) 9:00
	Monday, August 9	AFC-NFC Pro Football Hall of Fame Game at Canton, Ohio	
		Cleveland _____ vs. Dallas _____	(ABC) 8:00
PRESEASON/FIRST WEEK	Thursday, August 12	San Diego _____ at San Francisco _____	5:00
Open Date:		Baltimore _____ at Philadelphia _____	8:00
St. Louis	Friday, August 13	Detroit _____ at Atlanta _____	7:30
		Carolina _____ at Jacksonville _____	7:30
		Chicago _____ at Pittsburgh _____	7:30
		Washington _____ at New England _____	7:30
		New Orleans _____ at Miami _____	7:30
		New York Giants _____ at Minnesota _____	(ESPN) 7:00
	Saturday, August 14	Cleveland _____ at Tampa Bay _____	8:00
		New York Jets _____ at Green Bay _____	(CBS) 7:00
		Cincinnati _____ at Indianapolis _____	7:00
		Arizona _____ at Denver _____	7:00
		Buffalo _____ at Seattle _____	6:00
	Sunday, August 15	Dallas _____ at Oakland _____	1:00
		Tennessee _____ at Kansas City _____	7:30
PRESEASON/SECOND WEEK	Thursday, August 19	Seattle _____ at San Francisco _____	(ESPN) 5:00
Open Date:	Friday, August 20	Pittsburgh _____ at Carolina _____	8:00
Oakland		Cincinnati _____ at Detroit _____	7:00
		Philadelphia _____ at New York Jets _____	7:30
		Buffalo _____ at Washington _____	8:00
		Tennessee _____ at Arizona _____	7:00
	Saturday, August 21	Jacksonville _____ at New York Giants _____	7:00
		Minnesota _____ at Cleveland _____	7:00
		Baltimore _____ at Atlanta _____	7:30
		Indianapolis _____ at New Orleans _____	7:00
		Dallas _____ at New England _____	(ESPN) 8:00
		St. Louis _____ at Chicago _____	7:00
		Tampa Bay _____ at Kansas City _____	7:30
		Miami _____ at San Diego _____	8:00
	Monday, August 23	Denver _____ vs. Green Bay _____ at Madison, Wisconsin	(ABC) 7:00
PRESEASON/THIRD WEEK	Thursday, August 26	Kansas City _____ at Jacksonville _____	(CBS) 8:00
Open Date:		Philadelphia _____ at Minnesota _____	7:00
Indianapolis	Friday, August 27	Atlanta _____ at Tennessee _____	(ESPN) 7:00
	Saturday, August 28	Detroit _____ at Miami _____	7:00
		Buffalo _____ at Cincinnati _____	7:30
		Carolina _____ at Baltimore _____	7:30
		Washington _____ at Pittsburgh _____	7:30
		Chicago _____ at Cleveland _____	8:00
		Green Bay _____ at New Orleans _____	7:00
		New England _____ at Tampa Bay _____	8:00
		New York Jets _____ at New York Giants _____	8:00
		San Diego _____ at St. Louis _____	7:00
		Arizona _____ at Seattle _____	7:00
	Sunday, August 29	Denver _____ at Dallas _____	(FOX) 7:00
	Monday, August 30	San Francisco _____ at Oakland _____	(ABC) 5:00

1999 SCHEDULE AND NOTE CALENDAR

PRESEASON/FOURTH WEEK	**Thursday, September 2**	St. Louis ____ at Detroit ____	7:00
Open Date:		Cleveland ____ at Philadelphia ____	7:30
Chicago		New Orleans ____ at Tennessee ____	7:00
		New England ____ at Carolina ____	8:00
		Miami ____ at Green Bay ____	7:00
		Seattle ____ at Indianapolis ____	7:00
		Jacksonville ____ at Dallas ____	8:00
	Friday, September 3	New York Giants ____ at Baltimore ____	12:00
		Atlanta ____ at Cincinnati ____	7:30
		Minnesota ____ at New York Jets ____	7:30
		Tampa Bay ____ at Washington ____	8:00
		San Francisco ____ at Denver ____	7:00
		Oakland ____ at Arizona ____	7:00
		Kansas City ____ at San Diego ____	8:00
	Saturday, September 4	Pittsburgh ____ at Buffalo ____	7:30

KICKOFF WEEKEND	**Sunday, September 12**	Arizona ____ at Philadelphia ____	1:00
Open Date:	**(FOX-TV National Weekend)**	Baltimore ____ at St. Louis ____	12:00
San Diego		Buffalo ____ at Indianapolis ____	12:00
		Carolina ____ at New Orleans ____	12:00
		Cincinnati ____ at Tennessee ____	12:00
		Dallas ____ at Washington ____	1:00
		Kansas City ____ at Chicago ____	12:00
		New England ____ at New York Jets ____	1:00
		Oakland ____ at Green Bay ____	12:00
		Detroit ____ at Seattle ____	1:15
		Minnesota ____ at Atlanta ____	4:15
		New York Giants ____ at Tampa Bay ____	4:15
		San Francisco ____ at Jacksonville ____	4:15
		Pittsburgh ____ at Cleveland ____	(ESPN) 8:20
	Monday, September 13	Miami ____ at Denver ____	(ABC) 7:00

SECOND WEEK	**Sunday, September 19**	Arizona ____ at Miami ____	1:00
Open Date:	**(CBS-TV National Weekend)**	Green Bay ____ at Detroit ____	1:00
St. Louis		Indianapolis ____ at New England ____	1:00
		Jacksonville ____ at Carolina ____	1:00
		Oakland ____ at Minnesota ____	12:00
		Pittsburgh ____ at Baltimore ____	1:00
		San Diego ____ at Cincinnati ____	1:00
		Seattle ____ at Chicago ____	12:00
		Tampa Bay ____ at Philadelphia ____	1:00
		Washington ____ at New York Giants ____	1:00
		New Orleans ____ at San Francisco ____	1:05
		Cleveland ____ at Tennessee ____	3:15
		Denver ____ at Kansas City ____	3:15
		New York Jets ____ at Buffalo ____	(ESPN) 8:20
	Monday, September 20	Atlanta ____ at Dallas ____	(ABC) 8:00

THIRD WEEK	**Sunday, September 26**	Atlanta ____ at St. Louis ____	12:00
Open Dates:	**(FOX-TV National Weekend)**	Cincinnati ____ at Carolina ____	1:00
Dallas, Miami, New Orleans		Cleveland ____ at Baltimore ____	1:00
		Denver ____ at Tampa Bay ____	1:00
		Detroit ____ at Kansas City ____	12:00
		Philadelphia ____ at Buffalo ____	1:00
		Seattle ____ at Pittsburgh ____	1:00
		Washington ____ at New York Jets ____	1:00
		Indianapolis ____ at San Diego ____	1:05
		Tennessee ____ at Jacksonville ____	4:05
		Chicago ____ at Oakland ____	1:15
		Minnesota ____ at Green Bay ____	3:15
		New York Giants ____ at New England ____	(ESPN) 8:20
	Monday, September 27	San Francisco ____ at Arizona ____	(ABC) 6:00

1999 SCHEDULE AND NOTE CALENDAR

FOURTH WEEK Open Dates: Detroit, Green Bay, Indianapolis	Sunday, October 3 (CBS-TV National Weekend)	Arizona ____ at Dallas ____	12:00
		Baltimore ____ at Atlanta ____	1:00
		Jacksonville ____ at Pittsburgh ____	1:00
		New England ____ at Cleveland ____	1:00
		New Orleans ____ at Chicago ____	12:00
		New York Jets ____ at Denver ____	2:15
		Philadelphia ____ at New York Giants ____	1:00
		St. Louis ____ at Cincinnati ____	1:00
		Tampa Bay ____ at Minnesota ____	12:00
		Carolina ____ at Washington ____	4:05
		Kansas City ____ at San Diego ____	1:15
		New York Jets ____ at Denver ____	2:15
		Tennessee ____ at San Francisco ____	1:15
		Oakland ____ at Seattle ____	(ESPN) 5:20
	Monday, October 4	Buffalo ____ at Miami ____	(ABC) 9:00
FIFTH WEEK Open Dates: Carolina, Seattle, Washington	Sunday, October 10 (CBS-TV National Weekend)	Atlanta ____ at New Orleans ____	12:00
		Chicago ____ at Minnesota ____	12:00
		Cincinnati ____ at Cleveland ____	1:00
		Dallas ____ at Philadelphia ____	1:00
		New England ____ at Kansas City ____	12:00
		Pittsburgh ____ at Buffalo ____	1:00
		San Diego ____ at Detroit ____	1:00
		San Francisco ____ at St. Louis ____	12:00
		New York Giants ____ at Arizona ____	1:05
		Baltimore ____ at Tennessee ____	3:15
		Denver ____ at Oakland ____	1:15
		Miami ____ at Indianapolis ____	3:15
		Tampa Bay ____ at Green Bay ____	(ESPN) 7:20
	Monday, October 11	Jacksonville ____ at New York Jets ____	(ABC) 9:00
SIXTH WEEK Open Dates: Baltimore, Kansas City, Tampa Bay	Sunday, October 17 (FOX-TV National Weekend)	Cleveland ____ at Jacksonville ____	1:00
		Indianapolis ____ at New York Jets ____	1:00
		Miami ____ at New England ____	1:00
		Minnesota ____ at Detroit ____	1:00
		Oakland ____ at Buffalo ____	1:00
		Philadelphia ____ at Chicago ____	12:00
		Pittsburgh ____ at Cincinnati ____	1:00
		St. Louis ____ at Atlanta ____	1:00
		Tennesee ____ at New Orleans ____	12:00
		Seattle ____ at San Diego ____	1:05
		Carolina ____ at San Francisco ____	1:15
		Green Bay ____ at Denver ____	2:15
		Washington ____ at Arizona ____	(ESPN) 5:20
	Monday, October 18	Dallas ____ at New York Giants ____	(ABC) 9:00
SEVENTH WEEK Open Dates: Arizona, Jacksonville, Tennessee	Thursday, October 21	Kansas City ____ at Baltimore ____	(ESPN) 8:20
	Sunday, October 24 (CBS-TV National Weekend)	Cincinnati ____ at Indianapolis ____	12:00
		Cleveland ____ at St. Louis ____	12:00
		Denver ____ at New England ____	1:00
		Detroit ____ at Carolina ____	1:00
		New Orleans ____ at New York Giants ____	1:00
		Philadelphia ____ at Miami ____	1:00
		San Francisco ____ at Minnesota ____	12:00
		Washington ____ at Dallas ____	12:00
		Green Bay ____ at San Diego ____	1:05
		Buffalo ____ at Seattle ____	1:15
		New York Jets ____ at Oakland ____	1:15
	Monday, October 25	Atlanta ____ at Pittsburgh ____	(ABC) 9:00

EIGHTH WEEK	**Sunday, October 31**	Buffalo ____ at Baltimore ____	1:00
Open Dates:	**(FOX-TV National Weekend)**	Carolina ____ at Atlanta ____	1:00
New York Jets, Pittsburgh,		Chicago ____ at Washington ____	1:00
San Francisco		Cleveland ____ at New Orleans ____	12:00
		Dallas ____ at Indianapolis ____	1:00
		Jacksonville ____ at Cincinnati ____	1:00
		New York Giants ____ at Philadelphia ____	1:00
		St. Louis ____ at Tennessee ____	12:00
		San Diego ____ at Kansas City ____	12:00
		Miami ____ at Oakland ____	1:05
		New England ____ at Arizona ____	2:05
		Minnesota ____ at Denver ____	2:15
		Tampa Bay ____ at Detroit ____	(ESPN) 8:20
	Monday, November 1	Seattle ____ at Green Bay ____	(ABC) 8:00
NINTH WEEK	**Sunday, November 7**	Arizona ____ at New York Jets ____	1:00
Open Dates:	**(CBS-TV National Weekend)**	Baltimore ____ at Cleveland ____	1:00
New England, New York Giants,		Buffalo ____ at Washington ____	1:00
Oakland		Chicago ____ at Green Bay ____	12:00
		Jacksonville ____ at Atlanta ____	1:00
		Kansas City ____ at Indianapolis ____	1:00
		Philadelphia ____ at Carolina ____	1:00
		St. Louis ____ at Detroit ____	1:00
		Tampa Bay ____ at New Orleans ____	3:05
		Cincinnati ____ at Seattle ____	1:15
		Denver ____ at San Diego ____	1:15
		Pittsburgh ____ at San Francisco ____	1:15
		Tennessee ____ at Miami ____	(ESPN) 8:20
	Monday, November 8	Dallas ____ at Minnesota ____	(ABC) 8:00
TENTH WEEK	**Sunday, November 14**	Carolina ____ at St. Louis ____	12:00
Open Date:	**(FOX-TV National Weekend)**	Cleveland ____ at Pittsburgh ____	1:00
Atlanta		Indianapolis ____ at New York Giants ____	1:00
		Kansas City ____ at Tampa Bay ____	1:00
		Miami ____ at Buffalo ____	1:00
		Minnesota ____ at Chicago ____	12:00
		San Francisco ____ at New Orleans ____	12:00
		Tennessee ____ at Cincinnati ____	1:00
		Washington ____ at Philadelphia ____	1:00
		Baltimore ____ at Jacksonville ____	4:05
		San Diego ____ at Oakland ____	1:05
		Detroit ____ at Arizona ____	2:15
		Green Bay ____ at Dallas ____	3:15
		Denver ____ at Seattle ____	(ESPN) 5:20
	Monday, November 15	New York Jets ____ at New England ____	(ABC) 9:00
ELEVENTH WEEK	**Sunday, November 21**	Atlanta ____ at Tampa Bay ____	1:00
Open Date:	**(FOX-TV National Weekend)**	Buffalo ____ at New York Jets ____	1:00
Minnesota		Carolina ____ at Cleveland ____	1:00
		Detroit ____ at Green Bay ____	12:00
		Indianapolis ____ at Philadelphia ____	1:00
		New England ____ at Miami ____	1:00
		Pittsburgh ____ at Tennessee ____	12:00
		Seattle ____ at Kansas City ____	12:00
		Baltimore ____ at Cincinnati ____	4:05
		Chicago ____ at San Diego ____	1:15
		Dallas ____ at Arizona ____	2:15
		New York Giants ____ at Washington ____	4:15
		St. Louis ____ at San Francisco ____	1:15
		New Orleans ____ at Jacksonville ____	(ESPN) 8:20
	Monday, November 22	Oakland ____ at Denver ____	(ABC) 7:00

1999 SCHEDULE AND NOTE CALENDAR

Week	Date	Game	Time
TWELFTH WEEK	**Thursday, November 25**	Chicago _____ at Detroit _____	(FOX) 12:40
Open Date:	**(CBS-TV National Weekend)**	Miami _____ at Dallas _____	(CBS) 3:15
Denver	**Sunday, November 28**	Arizona _____ at New York Giants _____	1:00
		Cincinnati _____ at Pittsburgh _____	1:00
		Jacksonville _____ at Baltimore _____	1:00
		New England _____ at Buffalo _____	1:00
		New Orleans _____ at St. Louis _____	12:00
		Philadelphia _____ at Washington _____	1:00
		San Diego _____ at Minnesota _____	12:00
		Tennessee _____ at Cleveland _____	1:00
		Tampa Bay _____ at Seattle _____	1:05
		Kansas City _____ at Oakland _____	1:15
		New York Jets _____ at Indianapolis _____	4:15
		Atlanta _____ at Carolina _____	(ESPN) 8:20
	Monday, November 29	Green Bay _____ at San Francisco _____	(ABC) 6:00

Week	Date	Game	Time
THIRTEENTH WEEK	**Thursday, December 2**	Pittsburgh _____ at Jacksonville _____	(ESPN) 8:20
Open Date:	**Sunday, December 5**	Green Bay _____ at Chicago _____	12:00
Buffalo	**(CBS-TV National Weekend)**	Indianapolis _____ at Miami _____	1:00
		New Orleans _____ at Atlanta _____	1:00
		New York Jets _____ at New York Giants _____	1:00
		Philadelphia _____ at Arizona _____	2:05
		St. Louis _____ at Carolina _____	1:00
		San Francisco _____ at Cincinnati _____	1:00
		Tennessee _____ at Baltimore _____	1:00
		Washington _____ at Detroit _____	1:00
		Philadelphia _____ at Arizona _____	2:05
		Cleveland _____ at San Diego _____	1:15
		Kansas City _____ at Denver _____	2:15
		Seattle _____ at Oakland _____	1:15
		Dallas _____ at New England _____	(ESPN) 8:20
	Monday, December 6	Minnesota _____ at Tampa Bay _____	(ABC) 9:00

Week	Date	Game	Time
FOURTEENTH WEEK	**Thursday, December 9**	Oakland _____ at Tennessee _____	(ESPN) 7:20
Open Date:	**Sunday, December 12**	Arizona _____ at Washington _____	1:00
Chicago	**(FOX-TV National Weekend)**	Baltimore _____ at Pittsburgh _____	1:00
		Carolina _____ at Green Bay _____	12:00
		Cleveland _____ at Cincinnati _____	1:00
		Detroit _____ at Tampa Bay _____	1:00
		New England _____ at Indianapolis _____	1:00
		New York Giants _____ at Buffalo _____	1:00
		Philadelphia _____ at Dallas _____	12:00
		St. Louis _____ at New Orleans _____	12:00
		Miami _____ at New York Jets _____	4:05
		San Diego _____ at Seattle _____	1:05
		Atlanta _____ at San Francisco _____	1:15
		Minnesota _____ at Kansas City _____	(ESPN) 7:20
	Monday, December 13	Denver _____ at Jacksonville _____	(ABC) 9:00

Week	Date	Game	Time
FIFTEENTH WEEK	**Saturday, December 18**	Pittsburgh _____ at Kansas City _____	(CBS) 11:40
Open Date:	**(CBS-TV National Weekend)**	San Francisco _____ at Carolina _____	(FOX) 4:15
Cincinnati	**Sunday, December 19**	Atlanta _____ at Tennessee _____	12:00
		Detroit _____ at Chicago _____	12:00
		Jacksonville _____ at Cleveland _____	1:00
		New England _____ at Philadelphia _____	1:00
		New Orleans _____ at Baltimore _____	1:00
		New York Giants _____ at St. Louis _____	12:00
		San Diego _____ at Miami _____	1:00
		Washington _____ at Indianapolis _____	1:00
		Tampa Bay _____ at Oakland _____	1:05
		New York Jets _____ at Dallas _____	3:15
		Seattle _____ at Denver _____	2:15
		Buffalo _____ at Arizona _____	(ESPN) 6:20
	Monday, December 20	Green Bay _____ at Minnesota _____	(ABC) 8:00

SIXTEENTH WEEK Open Date: Philadelphia			
	Friday, December 24	Dallas _____ at New Orleans _____	(FOX) 2:05
	Saturday, December 25	Denver _____ at Detroit _____	(CBS) 4:15
	Sunday, December 26 (FOX-TV National Weekend)	Arizona _____ at Atlanta _____	1:00
		Buffalo _____ at New England _____	1:00
		Carolina _____ at Pittsburgh _____	1:00
		Chicago _____ at St. Louis _____	12:00
		Cincinnati _____ at Baltimore _____	1:00
		Indianapolis _____ at Cleveland _____	1:00
		Jacksonville _____ at Tennessee _____	12:00
		Minnesota _____ at New York Giants _____	1:00
		Kansas City _____ at Seattle _____	1:05
		Oakland _____ at San Diego _____	1:05
		Green Bay _____ at Tampa Bay _____	4:15
		Washington _____ at San Francisco _____	(ESPN) 5:20
	Monday, December 27	New York Jets _____ at Miami _____	(ABC) 9:00

SEVENTEENTH WEEK Open Date: Cleveland			
	Sunday, January 2 (CBS-TV National Weekend)	Arizona _____ at Green Bay _____	12:00
		Baltimore _____ at New England _____	1:00
		Cincinnati _____ at Jacksonville _____	1:00
		Detroit _____ at Minnesota _____	12:00
		Indianapolis _____ at Buffalo _____	1:00
		New Orleans _____ at Carolina _____	1:00
		Oakland _____ at Kansas City _____	12:00
		St. Louis _____ at Philadelphia _____	1:00
		Seattle _____ at New York Jets _____	1:00
		Tampa Bay _____ at Chicago _____	12:00
		New York Giants _____ at Dallas _____	3:05
		Miami _____ at Washington _____	4:15
		San Diego _____ at Denver _____	2:15
		Tennessee _____ at Pittsburgh _____	4:15
	Monday, January 3	San Francisco _____ at Atlanta _____	(ABC) 9:00

Wild Card Playoff Games

Site Priorities

Three Wild Card teams (division non-champions with best three records) from each conference and the division champion with the third-best record in each conference will enter the first round of the playoffs. The division champion with the third-best record will play host to the Wild Card team with the third-best record. The Wild Card team with the best record will play host to the Wild Card team with the second-best record. There are no restrictions on intra-division games.

Saturday, January 8, 2000

American Football Conference

_______________ at _______________ (ABC)

National Football Conference

_______________ at _______________ (ABC)

Sunday, January 9, 2000

American Football Conference

_______________ at _______________ (CBS)

National Football Conference

_______________ at _______________ (FOX)

Divisional Playoff Games

Site Priorities

In each conference, the two division champions with the highest won-lost-tied percentage during the regular season will play host to the Wild Card winners. The division champion with the best record in each conference is assured of playing the lowest seeded Wild Card survivor. There are no restrictions on intra-division games.

Saturday, January 15, 2000

American Football Conference

_______________ at _______________ (CBS)

National Football Conference

_______________ at _______________ (FOX)

Sunday, January 16, 2000

American Football Conference

_______________ at _______________ (CBS)

National Football Conference

_______________ at _______________ (FOX)

1999 SCHEDULE AND NOTE CALENDAR

Championship Games **Site Priorities for Championship Games** The home teams will be the surviving playoff winners with the best won-lost-tied percentage during the regular season. A Wild Card team cannot play host unless two Wild Card teams are in the game, in which case the Wild Card team that was seeded highest in the first round of the playoffs will be the home team.	**Sunday, January 23, 2000**	American Football Conference __________ at __________ (CBS) National Football Conference __________ at __________ (FOX)
Super Bowl XXXIV	**Sunday, January 30, 2000**	Super Bowl XXXIV at Georgia Dome, Atlanta, Georgia __________ vs. __________(ABC)
AFC-NFC Pro Bowl	**Sunday, February 6, 2000**	AFC-NFC Pro Bowl at Honolulu, Hawaii AFC __________ vs. NFC __________(ABC)

POSTSEASON AND NATIONALLY TELEVISED GAMES

POSTSEASON GAMES

Saturday, January 8	AFC and NFC Wild Card Playoffs (ABC)
Sunday, January 9	AFC and NFC Wild Card Playoffs (CBS and FOX)
Saturday, January 15	AFC and NFC Divisional Playoffs (CBS and FOX)
Sunday, January 16	AFC and NFC Divisional Playoffs (CBS and FOX)
Sunday, January 23	AFC and NFC Championship Games (CBS and FOX)
Sunday, January 30	Super Bowl XXXIV at Georgia Dome in Atlanta, Georgia (ABC)
Sunday, February 6	AFC-NFC Pro Bowl in Honolulu, Hawaii (ABC)

1999 NATIONALLY TELEVISED GAMES

Regular Season

Sunday, September 12	Minnesota at Atlanta (day, FOX)
	Pittsburgh at Cleveland (night, ESPN)
Monday, September 13	Miami at Denver (night, ABC)
Sunday, September 19	Denver at Kansas City (day, CBS)
	New York Jets at Buffalo (night, ESPN)
Monday, September 20	Atlanta at Dallas (night, ABC)
Sunday, September 26	Minnesota at Green Bay (day, FOX)
	New York Giants at New England (night, ESPN)
Monday, September 27	San Francisco at Arizona (night, ABC)
Sunday, October 3	New York Jets at Denver (day, CBS)
	Oakland at Seattle (night, ESPN)
Monday, October 4	Buffalo at Miami (night, ABC)
Sunday, October 10	Denver at Oakland (day, CBS)
	Tampa Bay at Green Bay (night, ESPN)
Monday, October 11	Jacksonville at New York Jets (night, ABC)
Sunday, October 17	Green Bay at Denver (day, FOX)
	Washington at Arizona (night, ESPN)
Monday, October 18	Dallas at New York Giants (night, ABC)
Thursday, October 21	Kansas City at Baltimore (night, ESPN)
Sunday, October 24	New York Jets at Oakland (day, CBS)
Monday, October 25	Atlanta at Pittsburgh (night, ABC)
Sunday, October 31	Minnesota at Denver (day, FOX)
	Tampa Bay at Detroit (night, ESPN)
Monday, November 1	Seattle at Green Bay (night, ABC)
Sunday, November 7	Pittsburgh at San Francisco (day, CBS)
	Tennessee at Miami (night, ESPN)
Monday, November 8	Dallas at Minnesota (night, ABC)
Sunday, November 14	Green Bay at Dallas (day, FOX)
	Denver at Seattle (night, ESPN)
Monday, November 15	New York Jets at New England (night, ABC)
Sunday, November 21	Dallas at Arizona (day, FOX)
	New Orleans at Jacksonville (night, ESPN)
Monday, November 22	Oakland at Denver (night, ABC)
Thursday, November 25	Chicago at Detroit (day, FOX)
	Miami at Dallas (day, CBS)
Sunday, November 28	Kansas City at Oakland (day, CBS)
	Atlanta at Carolina (night, ESPN)
Monday, November 29	Green Bay at San Francisco (night, ABC)
Thursday, December 2	Pittsburgh at Jacksonville (night, ESPN)
Sunday, December 5	Kansas City at Denver (day, CBS)
	Dallas at New England (night, ESPN)
Monday, December 6	Minnesota at Tampa Bay (night, ABC)
Thursday, December 9	Oakland at Tennessee (night, ESPN)
Sunday, December 12	Atlanta at San Francisco (day, FOX)
	Minnesota at Kansas City (night, ESPN)
Monday, December 13	Denver at Jacksonville (night, ABC)
Saturday, December 18	Pittsburgh at Kansas City (day, CBS)
	San Francisco at Carolina (day, FOX)
Sunday, December 19	New York Jets at Dallas (day, CBS)
	Buffalo at Arizona (night, ESPN)
Monday, December 20	Green Bay at Minnesota (night, ABC)
Friday, December 24	Dallas at New Orleans (day, FOX)
Saturday, December 25	Denver at Detroit (day, CBS)
Sunday, December 26	Green Bay at Tampa Bay (day, FOX)
	Washington at San Francisco (night, ESPN)
Monday, December 27	New York Jets at Miami (night, ABC)
Sunday, January 2	San Diego at Denver (day, CBS)
Monday, January 3	San Francisco at Atlanta (night, ABC)

NATIONAL PRIMETIME TELEVISION GAMES AT A GLANCE

(All times Eastern; Sunday and Thursday on ESPN, Monday on ABC; all on CBS radio)

Sunday, September 12	Pittsburgh at Cleveland (ESPN)	8:20
Monday, September 13	Miami at Denver (ABC)	9:00
Sunday, September 19	New York Jets at Buffalo (ESPN)	8:20
Monday, September 20	Atlanta at Dallas (ABC)	9:00
Sunday, September 26	New York Giants at New England (ESPN)	8:20
Monday, September 27	San Francisco at Arizona (ABC)	9:00
Sunday, October 3	Oakland at Seattle (ESPN)	8:20
Monday, October 4	Buffalo at Miami (ABC)	9:00
Sunday, October 10	Tampa Bay at Green Bay (ESPN)	8:20
Monday, October 11	Jacksonville at New York Jets (ABC)	9:00
Sunday, October 17	Washington at Arizona (ESPN)	8:20
Monday, October 18	Dallas at New York Giants (ABC)	9:00
Thursday, October 21	Kansas City at Baltimore (ESPN)	8:20
Monday, October 25	Atlanta at Pittsburgh (ABC)	9:00
Sunday, October 31	Tampa Bay at Detroit (ESPN)	8:20
Monday, November 1	Seattle at Green Bay (ABC)	9:00
Sunday, November 7	Tennessee at Miami (ESPN)	8:20
Monday, November 8	Dallas at Minnesota (ABC)	9:00
Sunday, November 14	Denver at Seattle (ESPN)	8:20
Monday, November 15	New York Jets at New England (ABC)	9:00
Sunday, November 21	New Orleans at Jacksonville (ESPN)	8:20
Monday, November 22	Oakland at Denver (ABC)	9:00
Sunday, November 28	Atlanta at Carolina (ESPN)	8:20
Monday, November 29	Green Bay at San Francisco (ABC)	9:00
Thursday, December 2	Pittsburgh at Jacksonville (ESPN)	8:20
Sunday, December 5	Dallas at New England (ESPN)	8:20
Monday, December 6	Minnesota at Tampa Bay (ABC)	9:00
Thursday, December 9	Oakland at Tennessee (ESPN)	8:20
Sunday, December 12	Minnesota at Kansas City (ESPN)	8:20
Monday, December 13	Denver at Jacksonville (ABC)	9:00
Sunday, December 19	Buffalo at Arizona (ESPN)	8:20
Monday, December 20	Green Bay at Minnesota (ABC)	9:00
Sunday, December 26	Washington at San Francisco (ESPN)	8:20
Monday, December 27	New York Jets at Miami (ABC)	9:00
Monday, January 3	San Francisco at Atlanta (ABC)	9:00

IMPORTANT DATES

1999

July 6	Claiming period of 24 hours begins in waiver system. All waiver requests for the rest of the year are no-recall and no-withdrawal.
Mid-July	Training camps open. Veteran players cannot be required to report earlier than 15 days prior to club's first preseason game or July 15, whichever is later.
July 15	Signing period ends at 4 P.M., Eastern Time, for Unrestricted Free Agents to whom June 1 tender was made by Old Club, and for Transition Players, and Franchise Players who are eligible to recieve Offer Sheets. After this date and through 4 P.M., Eastern Time, on November 16, Old Club has exclusive negotiating rights to these players.
August 7	American Bowl, Sydney, Australia: Denver vs. San Diego.
August 9	Hall of Fame Game, Canton, Ohio: Cleveland vs. Dallas.
August 13	If a drafted rookie has not signed with his club by this date, he may not be traded to any other club in 1999.
August 13	Deadline for players under contract to report in order to earn a season of free agency credit.
August 31	Roster cutdown to maximum of 60 players on Active List by 4 P.M., Eastern Time.
September 5	Roster cutdown to maximum of 53 players on Active/Inactive List by 4 P.M., Eastern Time. Clubs may dress minimum of 42 and maximum of 45 players and third quarterback for each regular-season and postseason game.
September 6	After 4 P.M., Eastern Time, clubs may establish a Practice Squad of five players by signing free agents who do not have an accrued season of free-agency credit or who were on the Active/Inactive List for less than nine regular season games during their only Accrued Season(s).
September 10	All clubs are required to identify their 49-player Active List by 7:00 P.M., Eastern Time, on this Friday and thereafter on each Friday before a regular-season Sunday game. No later than one hour and 30 minutes prior to kickoff, clubs must identify their 45-player Active List and third quarterback, if any.
September 12-13	Regular season opens.
September 28	Priority on multiple waiver claims is now based on the current season's standing.
October 19	All trading ends at 4 P.M., Eastern Time.
October 20	Players with at least four previous pension-credited seasons are subject to the waiver system for the remainder of the regular season and postseason.
November 2-3	NFL Fall Meeting, Chicago, Illinois.
November 16	Deadline for clubs to sign by 4 P.M., Eastern Time, their Franchise and Transition players. If still unsigned after this date, such players are prohibited from playing in NFL in 1999.
November 16	Deadline for clubs to sign by 4 P.M., Eastern Time, their Unrestricted and Restricted Free Agents to whom June 1 tender was made. If still unsigned after this date, such players are prohibited from playing in NFL in 1999.
November 16	Deadline for clubs to sign drafted players by 4 P.M., Eastern Time. If such players remain unsigned, they are prohibited from playing in NFL in 1999.
December 4	Deadline for reinstatement of players in Reserve List categories of Retired, Did Not Report, Exclusive Rights, and of players who were placed on Reserve/Left Squad in a previous season.
December 31	Deadline for waiver requests in 1999, except for "special waiver requests" which have a 10-day claiming period, with termination or assignment delayed until after the Super Bowl.

2000

Early-January	Clubs may begin signing free-agent players for the 2000 season.
January 8-9	Wild Card Playoff Games.
January 15-16	Divisional Playoff Games.
January 23	AFC and NFC Championship Games.
January 30	Super Bowl XXXIV, Georgia Dome, Atlanta, Georgia.
February 6	AFC-NFC Pro Bowl, Honolulu, Hawaii.
February 24	Waiver system begins for 2000. Players with at least four previous pension-credited seasons that a club desires to terminate are not subject to the waiver system until after the trading deadline.
Mid-February	Deadline for clubs to designate Franchise and Transition Players.
February 24-28	Combine Timing and Testing, RCA Dome, Indianapolis, Indiana.
March 1	Expiration date of all player contracts due to expire in 2000.
March 2	Free Agency period begins.
March 2	Trading period begins for 2000 after expiration of all 1999 contracts.
March 26-31	NFL Annual Meeting, Palm Beach, Florida.
*April 10	Deadline for signing of Offer Sheets by Restricted Free Agents.
*April 15-16	Annual player selection meeting, New York, New York.
May 23-24	NFL Spring Meeting, Baltimore, Maryland.
*June 1	Deadline for Old Club to send tender to its unsigned Restricted Free Agents or to extend Qualifying Offer, whichever is greater, in order to retain rights.
*June 1	Deadline for Old Club to send tender to its unsigned Unrestricted Free Agents to retain rights if player is not signed by another club by July 15.
*July 29	Hall of Fame Game, Canton, Ohio.
*September 3-4	Regular season opens.
*December 30-31	Wild Card Playoff Games.

2001

*January 6-7	Divisional Playoff Games.
*January 14	AFC and NFC Championship Games.
*January 28	Super Bowl XXXV, Raymond James Stadium, Tampa, Florida.

2002

*January 27	Super Bowl XXXVI, Louisiana Superdome, New Orleans, Louisiana.

**Tentatively scheduled.*

The NFL is online to provide fans and media quick and easy access to all the latest professional football information.

NFL.COM—(http://nfl.com)

NFL.com, the league's year-round home page on the Internet, enters its fourth season in cyberspace. The site continues to provide NFL information during the regular season, postseason, and offseason, including:

NEWS/STATS: Up-to-the-minute news from around the league, plus game previews, injury reports, and player and team stats.

TEAM AREAS: Customized areas for all 31 clubs featuring updated rosters, depth carts, and all the latest news from the teams.

GAMEDAY COVERAGE: Live game coverage with play-by-play, scores, and statistics, including graphical drive charts and comprehensive Java scoreboard that does not require reloading to get the latest information. Also includes "Player Tracker," which instantaneously updates individual player statistics.

VIDEO HIGHLIGHTS: The site will showcase NFL Films video highlights of the previous week's games as well as upcoming matchups. Video will also support feature stories and team highlight clips from every game last season.

PLAY FOOTBALL: An interactive area dedicated to the league's younger fans featuring live chats with NFL players, educational and interactive games and activities, plus information on players and teams.

SUPERBOWL.COM—(http://superbowl.com)

Look for superbowl.com in late December for complete coverage of the playoffs and Super Bowl XXXIV. The multimedia site follows all postseason action and features audio and video clips of past Super Bowls.

During the week leading up to Super Bowl XXXIV, the site will go 'live' from Atlanta, providing coverage of events, press conferences, and chats with Super Bowl players and coaches.

On Super Bowl Sunday, superbowl.com will showcase a live Internet cybercast, complete with online commentators calling the action. The site also features digital photos from the game, live public address audio and press-box announcements, and live audio from foreign broadcasts.

NFLeurope.COM—(http://nfleurope.com)

The official site of NFL Europe League provides in-depth information on the six teams and their players, streaming video of one game each weekend, live audio broadcasts of all games, and weekly video highlights of game action. In addition, the site includes collectible online player trading cards of the league's Players of the Week, weekly player diaries from NFL allocated players, as well as a complete league stats package.

NFL PLAYER SITES

Following are addresses for some current and former NFL players who have their own websites:

Reidel Anthony, Buccaneers (www.85rmp.com)
Darren Bennett, Chargers (www.nflaussie.com)
Doug Brien, Saints (www.kicking.com)
Derrick Brooks, Buccaneers (www.hit55.com)
Robert Brooks, Packers (www.robertbrooks.com)
Santana Dotson, Packers (www.santanadotson.com)
Brett Favre, Packers (www.favre4.com)
Jim Flanigan, Bears (www.jimflanigan.com)
Scott Frost, Jets (www.scottfrost.com)
Kent Graham, Giants (kentgraham.com)
Mike Hollis, Jaguars (mikehollis.com)
Charlie Jones, Chargers (www.82mph.com)
Jim Kelly, Bills (www.jimkelly.com)
Shaun King, Buccaneers (www.shaunking.com)
Bronzell Miller, Chargers (www.bronzell.com)
Jerry Rice, 49ers (www.sportsline.com/u/jrice/)
Warren Sapp, Buccaneers (www.big99.com)
Junior Seau, Chargers (www.juniorseau.org/)
Jason Sehorn, Giants (www.sehornscorner.com)
Terrance Shaw, Chargers (www.run29.com)
Fran Tarkenton, Vikings-Giants (www.tarkenton.com)
Fred Taylor, Jaguars (www.run28.com)
Mike Utley, Lions (www.imageone.com/mikeutley/)

OFFICIAL NFL TEAM SITES

In addition to a dedicated area on NFL.COM, several teams have created their own Web sites, which have separate URLs, and are hot linked from NFL.COM.

Arizona Cardinals (www.azcardinals.com)
Atlanta Falcons (www.atlantafalcons.com)
Baltimore Ravens (www.baltimoreravens.com)
Buffalo Bills (www.buffalobills.com)
Chicago Bears (www.chicagobears.com)
Cleveland Browns (www.clevelandbrowns.com)
Dallas Cowboys (www.dallascowboys.com)
Denver Broncos (www.denverbroncos.com)
Detroit Lions (www.detroitlions.com)
Green Bay Packers (www.packers.com)
Jacksonville Jaguars (www.jaguars.com)
Indianapolis Colts (www.colts.com)
Kansas City Chiefs (www.kcchiefs.com)
Miami Dolphins (www.dolphinsendzone.com)
Minnesota Vikings (www.vikings.com)
New England Patriots (www.patriots.com)
New York Giants (www.giants.com)
New York Jets (www.newyorkjets.com)
Oakland Raiders (www.raiders.com)
Philadelphia Eagles (www.eaglesnet.com)
St. Louis Rams (www.stlouisrams.com)
San Francisco 49ers (www.sf49ers.com)
Seattle Seahawks (www.seahawks.com)
Washington Redskins (www.redskins.com)

1999 SCHEDULING FORMULA

Each 1999 team schedule is based on a "common-opponent" formula initiated for the 1978 season and most recently modified in 1995. Under the common-opponent format, all teams in a division play at least 10 of their 16 games the following season against common opponents. It is not a position scheduling format in which the strong play the strong and the weak play the weak.

In creating a schedule, the NFL seeks an easily understood and balanced formula that provides both competitive equality and a variety of opponents. Under the rotation scheduling system in effect from 1970-77, non-division opponents were determined by a pre-set formula. This often resulted in competitive imbalances.

With common opponents as the basis for scheduling, a more competitive and equitable method of determining division champions and postseason playoff representatives has developed. Teams battling for a division title are playing approximately two-thirds of their games against common opponents.

In 1987, NFL owners passed a bylaw proposal designed to modify the common-opponent scheduling format and create greater equity. And in 1995, with the addition of two expansion teams, the 1987 changes were modified to include fifth-place teams in the common-opponent scheduling format for each division. The following chart shows a history of the pairings in non-division games within the conference since the change to a common-opponent format in 1978:

Prior Year's Finish in Division	Current Pairings in Non-Division Games Within Conference	Previous Pairings 1987-94	Previous Pairings 1978-86
1	1-1-2-3	1-1-2-3	1-1-4-4
2	1-2-2-4	1-2-2-4	2-2-3-3
3	1-3-3-5	1-3-3-4	2-2-3-3
4	2-4-4-5	2-3-4-4	1-1-4-4
5	3-4-5-5		

With the addition of Cleveland as the League's 31st franchise, some modifications to the scheduling formula were necessary to accomodate a new six-team division (AFC Central).

Under the common-opponent format, schedules of all NFL teams are figured according to the following formula. (The reference point for the figuring is the team's final division standing. Ties in divisions are broken according to the tie-breaking procedures outlined on page 25.)

A. Divisional Games

Each team will play home-and-home with the other teams in its division (8 games for all divisions except for teams in the AFC Central which will each have 10 divisional games).

B. Intraconference Games

1. Each team in all divisions except the AFC Central will play four nondivision conference opponents based on the previous season's standings, as shown below.

2. Teams that finished first and second in the AFC Central in the previous season's standings will play two nondivision conference opponents, and teams that finished third, fourth, fifth, and sixth will each play three nondivision conference opponents, as shown below:

Prior Year's Finish in Division	NFC Teams	AFC East/West (alternating years)	AFC Central
1	1-1-2-3	1-1-2-3/1-1-2-4	1-1
2	1-2-2-4	1-2-2-5/1-2-2-3	2-2
3	1-3-3-5	2-3-3-4/1-3-3-5	3-3-4
4	2-4-4-5	1-4-4-6/3-4-4-5	3-4-4
5	3-4-5-5	4-5-5-6/2-5-5-6	3-5-5
6			4-5-5

C. Interconference Games

1. Continuing the current rotation, teams from each division of one conference will play teams from a division of the other conference, as follows:

1999	NFC-E vs. AFC-E	NFC-C vs. AFC-W	NFC-W vs. AFC-C
2000	NFC-E vs. AFC-C	NFC-C vs. AFC-E	NFC-W vs. AFC-W
2001	NFC-E vs. AFC-W	NFC-C vs. AFC-C	NFC-W vs. AFC-E

2. Each team in all divisions except the AFC Central will play four games against teams of a division of the other conference, as is done currently. The NFL will continue the rotation of interconference opponents, including rotation of home and away sites, for games between teams of the NFC and teams from the AFC East and AFC West that provides for all teams from NFC divisions to play all teams from the AFC East and AFC West four times in 15 years, two home and two away.

3. Beginning in 1999, teams that finished first and second in the AFC Central in the previous season will play four games against teams of a division of the other conference, and teams that finished third, fourth, fifth, and sixth will each play three games against teams of a division of the other conference, based on the standings from the previous season as shown below. For preparation of the 1999 schedule, Cleveland was assigned the schedule of the sixth-place team.

Prior Year's Finish In Division	AFC Central Schedule vs. NFC Division	NFC Division Schedule vs. AFC Central
1	1-2-3-4	1-2-3-4
2	1-2-3-5	1-2-3-5
3	1-2-4	1-2-4-6
4	1-3-5	1-3-5-6
5	2-4-5	2-4-5-6
6	3-4-5	

1999 NFL Standings

AFC

EAST (AE)

1 ________
2 ________
3 ________
4 ________
5 ________

CENTRAL (AC)

1 ________
2 ________
3 ________
4 ________
5 ________
6 ________

WEST (AW)

1 ________
2 ________
3 ________
4 ________
5 ________

NFC

EAST (NE)

1 ________
2 ________
3 ________
4 ________
5 ________

CENTRAL (NC)

1 ________
2 ________
3 ________
4 ________
5 ________

WEST (NW)

1 ________
2 ________
3 ________
4 ________
5 ________

A Team's 2000 Schedule

____
Team Name

OPPONENTS

1 ________
2 ________
3 ________
4 ________
5 ________
6 ________
7 ________
8 ________
9 ________
10 ________
11 ________
12 ________
13 ________
14 ________
15 ________
16 ________

2000 Non-Divisional Opponent Breakdown

Intraconference Games

American Football Conference

AFC East

	Home	Away
AE1	AC 1	AW 1
	AW 4	AW 2
AE2	AC 2	AW 2
	AW 3	AW 1
AE3	AC 3	AW 3
	AW 1	AC 5
AE4	AC 4	AW 4
	AW 5	AC 3
AE5	AC 5	AW 5
	AW 2	AC 6

AFC Central

	Home	Away
AC1	AW1	AE 1
AC2	AW 2	AE 2
AC3	AW 3	AE 3
	AE 4	
AC4	AW 4	AE 4
		AW 3
AC5	AW 5	AE 5
	AE 3	
AC 6	AE 5	AW 5
		AW 4

AFC West

	Home	Away
AW1	AE 1	AC 1
	AE 2	AE 3
AW2	AE 2	AC 2
	AE 1	AE 5
AW3	AE 3	AC 3
	AC 4	AE 2
AW4	AE 4	AC 4
	AC 6	AE 1
AW5	AE 5	AC 5
	AC 6	AE 4

National Football Conference

NFC East

	Home	Away
NE1	NC 1	NW 1
	NW 2	NC 3
NE2	NC 2	NW 2
	NW 4	NC 1
NE3	NC 3	NW 3
	NW 1	NC 5
NE4	NC 4	NW 4
	NW 5	NC 2
NE5	NC 5	NW 5
	NW 3	NC 4

NFC Central

	Home	Away
NC1	NW 1	NE 1
	NE 2	NW 3
NC2	NW 2	NE 2
	NE 4	NW 1
NC3	NW 3	NE 3
	NE 1	NW 5
NC4	NW 4	NE 4
	NE 5	NW 2
NC5	NW 5	NE 5
	NE 3	NW 4

NFC West

	Home	Away
NW1	NE 1	NC 1
	NC 2	NE 3
NW2	NE 2	NC 2
	NC 4	NE 1
NW3	NE 3	NC 3
	NC 1	NE 5
NW4	NE 4	NC 4
	NC 5	NE 2
NW5	NE 5	NC 5
	NC 3	NE 4

Interconference Games

BUF	CHI	MIN
	GB	TB
IND	DET	CHI
	MIN	GB
MIA	GB	DET
	TB	MIN
NE	MIN	CHI
	TB	DET
NYJ	CHI	GB
	DET	TB

AC1	NE 1	NE 2
	NE 4	NE 3
AC2	NE 2	NE 1
	NE 3	NE 5
AC3	NE 2	NE 1
		NE 4
AC4	NE 1	NE 3
	NE 5	
AC5	NE 4	NE 2
		NE 5
AC6	NE 3	NE 4
	NE 5	

DEN	ATL	NO
	SF	STL
KC	CAR	ATL
	STL	SF
OAK	ATL	NO
	CAR	SF
SD	NO	CAR
	SF	STL
SEA	NO	ATL
	STL	CAR

NE1	AC 2	AC 1
	AC 3	AC 4
NE2	AC 1	AC 2
	AC 5	AC 3
NE3	AC 1	AC 2
	AC 4	AC 6
NE4	AC 3	AC 1
	AC 6	AC 5
NE5	AC 2	AC 4
	AC 5	AC 6

CHI	IND	BUF
	NE	NYJ
DET	MIA	IND
	NE	NYJ
GB	IND	BUF
	NYJ	MIA
MIN	BUF	IND
	MIA	NE
TB	BUF	MIA
	NYJ	NE

ATL	KC	DEN
	SEA	OAK
CAR	SD	KC
	SEA	OAK
NO	DEN	SD
	OAK	SEA
STL	DEN	KC
	SD	SEA
SF	KC	DEN
	OAK	SD

NFL PASSER RATING SYSTEM

The NFL rates its passers for statistical purposes against a fixed performance standard based on statistical achievements of all qualified pro passers since 1960. The current system replaced one that rated passers in relation to their position in a total group based on various criteria. The current system, which was adopted in 1973, removes inequities that existed in the former method and, at the same time, provides a means of comparing passing performances from one season to the next.

It is important to remember that the system is used to rate **passers,** not **quarterbacks.** Statistics do not reflect leadership, play-calling, and other intangible factors that go into making a successful professional quarterback. Four categories are used as a basis for compiling a rating:

—Percentage of completions per attempt
—Average yards gained per attempt
—Percentage of touchdown passes per attempt
—Percentage of interceptions per attempt

The **average** standard, is 1.000. The bottom is .000. To earn a 2.000 rating, a passer must perform at exceptional levels, i.e., 70 percent in completions, 10 percent in touchdowns, 1.5 percent in interceptions, and 11 yards average gain per pass attempt. The **maximum** a passer can receive in any category is 2.375.

For example, to gain a 2.375 in completion percentage, a passer would have to complete 77.5 percent of his passes. The NFL record is 70.55 by Ken Anderson (Cincinnati, 1982). To earn a 2.375 in percentage of touchdowns, a passer would have to achieve a percentage of 11.9. The record is 13.9 by Sid Luckman (Chicago, 1943). To gain 2.375 in percentage of interceptions, a passer would have to go the entire season without an interception. The 2.375 figure in average yards is 12.50, compared with the NFL record of 11.17 by Tommy O'Connell (Cleveland, 1957).

In order to make the rating more understandable, the point rating is then converted into a scale of 100. In rare cases, where statistical performance has been superior, it is possible for a passer to surpass a 100 rating. For example, take Steve Young's record-setting season in 1994 when he completed 324 of 461 passes for 3,969 yards, 35 touchdowns, and 10 interceptions. The four calculations would be:

—**Percentage of Completions**—324 of 461 is 70.28 percent. Subtract 30 from the completion percentage (40.28) and multiply the result by 0.05. The result is a point rating of **2.014**.
Note: If the result is less than zero (Comp. Pct. less than 30.0), award zero points. If the results are greater than 2.375 (Comp. Pct. greater than 77.5), award 2.375.

—**Average Yards Gained Per Attempt**—3,969 yards divided by 461 attempts is 8.61. Subtract three yards from yards-per-attempt (5.61) and multiply the result by 0.25. The result is **1.403**.
Note: If the result is less than zero (yards per attempt less than 3.0), award zero points. If the result is greater than 2.375 (yards per attempt greater than 12.5), award 2.375 points.

—**Percentage of Touchdown Passes**—35 touchdowns in 461 attempts is 7.59 percent. Multiply the touchdown percentage by 0.2. The result is **1.518**.
Note: If the result is greater than 2.375 (touchdown percentage greater than 11.875), award 2.375.

—**Percentage of Interceptions**—10 interceptions in 461 attempts is 2.17 percent. Multiply the interception percentage by 0.25 (0.542) and subtract the number from 2.375. The result is **1.833**.
Note: If the result is less than zero (interception percentage greater than 9.5), award zero points.

The sum of the four steps is (2.014 + 1.403 + 1.518 + 1.833) **6.768**. The sum is then divided by six (1.128) and multiplied by 100. In this case, the result is **112.8**. This same formula can be used to determine a passer rating for any player who attempts at least one pass.

The following is a list of qualifying passers who had a single-season passer rating of 100 or higher:

Player, Team	Season	Rating	Att.	Comp.	Pct.	Yds.	Avg.	TD	TD Pct.	Int.	Int. Pct.
Steve Young, San Francisco	1994	112.8	461	324	70.2	3,969	8.61	35	7.6	10	2.2
Joe Montana, San Francisco	1989	112.4	386	271	70.2	3,521	9.12	26	6.7	8	2.1
Milt Plum, Cleveland	1960	110.4	250	151	60.4	2,297	9.19	21	8.4	5	2.0
Sammy Baugh, Washington	1945	109.9	182	128	70.3	1,669	9.17	11	6.0	4	2.2
Dan Marino, Miami	1984	108.9	564	362	64.2	5,084	9.01	48	8.5	17	3.0
Sid Luckman, Chicago Bears	1943	107.5	202	110	54.5	2,194	10.86	28	13.9	12	5.9
Steve Young, San Francisco	1992	107.0	402	268	66.7	3,465	8.62	25	6.2	7	1.7
Randall Cunningham, Minnesota	1998	106.0	425	259	60.9	3,704	8.72	34	8.0	10	2.4
Bart Starr, Green Bay	1966	105.0	251	156	62.2	2,257	8.99	14	5.6	3	1.2
Roger Staubach, Dallas	1971	104.8	211	126	59.7	1,882	8.92	15	7.1	4	1.9
Y.A. Tittle, N.Y. Giants	1963	104.8	367	221	60.2	3,145	8.57	36	9.8	14	3.8
Steve Young, San Francisco	1997	104.7	356	241	67.7	3,029	8.51	19	5.3	6	1.7
Bart Starr, Green Bay	1968	104.3	171	109	63.7	1,617	9.46	15	8.8	8	4.7
Ken Stabler, Oakland	1976	103.4	291	194	66.7	2,737	9.41	27	9.3	17	5.8
Joe Montana, San Francisco	1984	102.9	432	279	64.6	3,630	8.40	28	6.5	10	2.3
Charlie Conerly, N.Y. Giants	1959	102.7	194	113	58.2	1,706	8.79	14	7.2	4	2.1
Bert Jones, Baltimore	1976	102.5	343	207	60.3	3,104	9.05	24	7.0	9	2.6
Joe Montana, San Francisco	1987	102.1	398	266	66.8	3,054	7.67	31	7.8	13	3.3
Steve Young, San Francisco	1991	101.8	279	180	64.5	2,517	9.02	17	6.1	8	2.9
Len Dawson, Kansas City	1966	101.7	284	159	56.0	2,527	8.90	26	9.2	10	3.5
Vinny Testaverde, N.Y. Jets	1998	101.6	421	259	61.5	3,256	7.73	29	6.9	7	1.7
Steve Young, San Francisco	1993	101.5	462	314	68.0	4,023	8.71	29	6.3	16	3.5
Jim Kelly, Buffalo	1990	101.2	346	219	63.3	2,829	8.18	24	6.9	9	2.6
Steve Young, San Francisco	1998	101.1	517	322	62.3	4,170	8.07	36	7.0	12	2.3
Chris Chandler, Atlanta	1998	100.9	327	190	58.1	3,154	9.65	25	7.6	12	3.7
Jim Harbaugh, Indianapolis	1995	100.7	314	200	63.7	2,575	8.20	17	5.4	5	1.6

WAIVERS

The waiver system is a procedure by which player contracts or NFL rights to players are made available by a club to other clubs in the League. During the procedure, the 30 other clubs either file claims to obtain the players or waive the opportunity to do so—thus the term "waiver." Claiming clubs are assigned players on a priority based on the inverse of won-and-lost standing. The claiming period is three business days from the beginning of the League Year through April 30, 10 days from May 1 through the last business day before July 4, and 24 hours after July 4 through the conclusion of the regular season. If a player passes through waivers unclaimed, he becomes a free agent. All waivers are no recall and no withdrawal. Under the Collective Bargaining Agreement, from the beginning of the waiver system each year through the trading deadline (October 19, 1999), any veteran who has acquired four years of pension credit is not subject to the waiver system if the club desires to release him. After the trading deadline, such players are subject to the waiver system.

ACTIVE/INACTIVE LIST

The Active/Inactive List is the principal status for players participating for a club. It consists of all players under contract who are eligible for preseason, regular-season, and postseason games. Teams are permitted to open training camp with no more than 80 players under contract and thereafter must meet two mandatory roster reductions prior to the season opener. Teams will be permitted an Active List of 45 players and an Inactive List of eight players for each regular-season and postseason game. Provided that a club has two quarterbacks on its 45-player Active List, a third quarterback from its Inactive List is permitted to dress for the game, but if he enters the game during the first three quarters, the other two quarterbacks are thereafter prohibited from playing. Teams also are permitted to establish Practice Squads of up to five players who are eligible to participate in practice, but these players remain free agents and are eligible to sign with any other team in the league.

August 31 ....Roster reduction to 60 players
September 5........Roster reduction to 53 players
September 6........Teams establish a Practice Squad of up to five players

In addition to the squad limits described above, the overall roster limit of 80 players remains in effect throughout the regular season and postseason. The overall limit is applicable to players on a team's Active, Inactive, and Exempt Lists, players on the Practice Squad, and players on the Reserve List as Injured, Physically Unable to Perform, Non-Football Illness/Injury, and Suspended by Club.

RESERVE LIST

The Reserve List is a status for players who, for reasons of injury, retirement, military service, or other circumstances, are not immediately available for participation with a club. Players on Reserve/Injured are not eligible to practice or return to the Active/Inactive List in the same season that they are placed on Reserve. Players in the category of Reserve/Retired, Reserve/Did Not Report, Reserve/Exclusive Rights, and players who were placed in the category of Reserve/Left Squad in a previous season may not be reinstated during the period from 30 days before the end of the regular season through the postseason.

TRADES

Unrestricted trading between the AFC and NFC is allowed in 1999 through October 19, after which trading will end until 2000.

ANNUAL ACTIVE PLAYER LIMITS

NFL

Year(s)	Limit
1991-99	45**
1985-90	45
1983-84	49
1982	45†-49
1978-81	45
1975-77	43
1974	47
1964-73	40
1963	37
1961-62	36
1960	38
1959	36
1957-58	35
1951-56	33
1949-50	32
1948	35
1947	35*-34
1945-46	33
1943-44	28
1940-42	33
1938-39	30
1936-37	25
1935	24
1930-34	20
1926-29	18
1925	16

**45 plus a third quarterback
† 45 for first two games
* 35 for first three games

AFL

Year(s)	Limit
1966-69	40
1965	38
1964	34
1962-63	33
1960-61	35

NFL FREE AGENCY MOVEMENT

The following chart details veteran free agents who signed with new teams:

	1993	1994	1995	1996	1997	1998
Unrestricted	108	121	171	99	85	110
Restricted	8	7	6	4	2	4
Transition	4	4	2	2	2	1
Franchise	1	0	0	0	0	2
TOTALS	121	132	179	105	89	117

NFL ACTIVE STATISTICAL LEADERS

TOP ACTIVE PASSERS

1,000 or more attempts

	Yrs.	Att.	Comp.	Pct. Comp.	Yards	TD	Pct. TD	Had Int.	Pct. Int.	Rating Pts.
1. Steve Young, S.F.	14	4,065	2,622	64.5	32,678	229	5.6	103	2.5	97.6
2. Brett Favre, G.B.	8	3,757	2,318	61.7	26,803	213	5.7	118	3.1	89.0
3. Dan Marino, Mia.	16	7,989	4,763	59.6	58,913	408	5.1	235	2.9	87.3
4. Mark Brunell, Jac.	5	1,719	1,038	60.4	12,512	72	4.2	43	2.5	86.3
5. Troy Aikman, Dal.	10	4,011	2,479	61.8	28,346	141	3.5	115	2.9	82.8
6. Neil O'Donnell, *	8	2,862	1,650	57.7	19,026	104	3.6	57	2.0	81.6
7. Randall Cunningham, Minn.	13	3,875	2,177	56.2	27,082	190	4.9	119	3.1	81.6
8. Dave Krieg, Tenn.	19	5,311	3,105	58.5	38,147	261	4.9	199	3.7	81.5
9. Warren Moon, K.C.	15	6,786	3,972	58.5	49,097	290	4.3	232	3.4	81.0
10. Chris Chandler, Atl.	11	2,587	1,494	57.8	18,526	119	4.6	90	3.5	80.9
11. Jeff Hostetler, *	12	2,338	1,357	58.0	16,430	94	4.0	71	3.0	80.5
12. Jeff George, Minn.	9	3,402	1,971	57.9	23,229	124	3.6	92	2.7	79.7
13. Scott Mitchell, Balt.	8	2,091	1,184	56.6	14,452	91	4.4	66	3.2	79.4
14. Jeff Blake, Cin.	6	1,841	1,029	55.9	12,504	77	4.2	51	2.8	79.4
15. Jim Harbaugh, S.D.	12	3,282	1,933	58.9	22,111	111	3.4	93	2.8	78.7
16. Erik Kramer, Chi.	9	2,158	1,239	57.4	14,549	90	4.2	69	3.2	78.6
17. Steve McNair, Tenn.	4	1,130	634	56.1	7,659	38	3.4	28	2.5	78.0
18. Steve Beuerlein, Car.	10	2,044	1,126	55.1	14,566	84	4.1	69	3.4	77.3
19. Drew Bledsoe, N.E.	6	3,382	1,887	55.8	21,981	128	3.8	102	3.0	75.7
20. Rich Gannon, Oak.	10	1,758	1,000	56.9	11,158	66	3.8	54	3.1	75.6
21. Wade Wilson, Oak.	17	2,428	1,391	57.3	17,283	99	4.1	102	4.2	75.6
22. Vinny Testaverde, NYJ	12	4,598	2,559	55.7	32,479	204	4.4	190	4.1	75.5
23. Steve Bono, Car.	13	1,700	934	54.9	10,439	62	3.6	42	2.5	75.3
24. Craig Erickson, Mia.	6	1,092	591	54.1	7,625	41	3.8	38	3.5	74.3
25. Bubby Brister, Den.	12	2,172	1,185	54.6	14,276	81	3.7	74	3.4	73.2
26. John Friesz, Sea.	8	1,343	734	54.7	8,633	45	3.4	41	3.1	72.9
27. Gus Frerotte, Det.	5	1,422	744	52.3	9,769	48	3.4	44	3.1	72.7
28. Rodney Peete, Wash.	10	1,937	1,108	57.2	13,579	59	3.0	77	4.0	72.6
29. Tony Banks, Balt.	3	1,263	685	54.2	8,333	36	2.9	42	3.3	70.4
30. Billy Joe Tolliver, N.O.	8	1,439	752	52.3	8,844	52	3.6	48	3.3	69.4

TOP ACTIVE SCORERS

(number in parentheses represents 2-point conversions scored)

	Yrs.	TD	FG	PAT	TP
1. Gary Anderson, Minn.	17	0	420	585	1,845
2. Morten Andersen, Atl.	17	0	401	558	1,761
3. Norm Johnson, Pitt.	17	0	348	613	1,657
4. Al Del Greco, Tenn.	15	0	299	463	1,360
5. Pete Stoyanovich, K.C.	10	0	246	349	1,087
6. Jerry Rice, S.F.	14	175	0	(4)	1,058
7. Jeff Jaeger, Chi.	11	0	227	314	995
8. Greg Davis, *	12	0	224	290	962
9. Steve Christie, Buff.	9	0	221	294	957
10. John Carney, S.D.	11	0	214	250	892
11. Chris Jacke, Ariz.	9	0	183	312	861
12. Emmitt Smith, Dal.	9	134	0	(1)	806
13. John Kasay, Car.	8	0	186	216	774
14. Matt Stover, Balt.	8	0	174	246	768
15. Jason Hanson, Det.	7	0	168	247	751
16. Jason Elam, Den.	6	0	157	259	730
17. Barry Sanders, Det.	10	109	0	0	654
18. Cris Carter, Minn.	12	102	0	(5)	622
19. Doug Pelfrey, Cin.	6	0	135	174	579
20. Cary Blanchard, Wash.	5	0	131	151	544
21. Chris Boniol, Phil.	5	0	117	166	517
22. Andre Reed, Buff.	14	86	0	0	516
Thurman Thomas, Buff.	11	86	0	0	516
24. Michael Husted, Oak.	6	0	117	151	502
25. Andre Rison, K.C.	10	78	0	(1)	470
26. Doug Brien, N.O.	5	0	98	166	460
27. Mike Hollis, Jac.	4	0	102	140	446
Ricky Watters, Sea.	7	74	0	(1)	446
29. Tim Brown, Oak.	11	73	0	(1)	440
30. Todd Peterson, Sea.	5	0	94	149	431

TOP ACTIVE RUSHERS

	Yrs.	Att.	Yards	TD
1. Barry Sanders, Det.	10	3,062	15,269	99
2. Emmitt Smith, Dal.	9	2,914	12,566	125
3. Thurman Thomas, Buff.	11	2,813	11,786	65
4. Ricky Watters, Sea.	7	1,947	7,873	65
5. Jerome Bettis, Pitt.	6	1,807	7,372	34
6. Chris Warren, Dal.	9	1,618	6,997	48
7. Terry Allen, *	7	1,684	6,881	60
8. Terrell Davis, Den.	4	1,343	6,413	56
9. Marshall Faulk, St.L.	5	1,389	5,320	42
10. Curtis Martin, NYJ	4	1,327	5,086	40
11. Garrison Hearst, S.F.	6	1,166	4,939	14
12. Natrone Means, S.D.	6	1,297	4,938	41
13. Randall Cunningham, Minn.	13	728	4,741	33
14. Adrian Murrell, Ariz.	6	1,134	4,489	23
15. Harold Green, *	9	1,151	4,365	13
16. Craig Heyward, *	11	1,031	4,301	30
17. Robert Smith, Minn.	6	895	4,282	23
18. Steve Young, S.F.	14	711	4,182	43
19. Gary Brown, NYG	7	977	4,123	21
20. Jamal Anderson, Atl.	5	973	4,063	27
21. Eddie George, Tenn.	3	1,040	4,061	19
22. Edgar Bennett, Chi.	6	1,109	3,964	21
23. Harvey Williams, Oak.	8	1,021	3,952	20
24. Napoleon Kaufman, Oak.	4	747	3,579	10
25. Leroy Hoard, Minn.	9	870	3,409	26
26. Byron (Bam) Morris, K.C.	5	854	3,395	32
27. Keith Byars, NYJ	13	865	3,109	23
28. Errict Rhett, Balt.	5	867	3,033	24
29. Karim Abdul-Jabbar, Mia.	3	860	2,968	32
30. Anthony Johnson, Car.	9	763	2,782	8

TOP ACTIVE PASS RECEIVERS

	Yrs.	No.	Yards	TD
1. Jerry Rice, S.F.	14	1,139	17,612	164
2. Andre Reed, Buff.	14	889	12,559	85
3. Cris Carter, Minn.	12	834	10,447	101
4. Michael Irvin, Dal.	11	740	11,737	62
5. Andre Rison, K.C.	10	681	9,381	78
6. Tim Brown, Oak.	11	680	9,600	69
7. Herman Moore, Det.	8	610	8,467	57
Keith Byars, NYJ	13	610	5,661	31
9. Rob Moore, Ariz.	9	591	8,747	44
10. Brian Blades, *	11	581	7,620	34
11. Mark Carrier, *	12	569	8,763	48
12. Webster Slaughter, Balt.	12	563	8,111	44
13. Larry Centers, Ariz.	9	535	4,539	19
14. Shannon Sharpe, Den.	9	529	6,759	44
15. Eric Metcalf, Ariz.	10	526	5,420	31
16. Terance Mathis, Atl.	9	477	6,332	48
17. Carl Pickens, Cin.	7	473	6,150	57
18. Tony Martin, Mia.	9	463	7,087	48
19. Ben Coates, N.E.	8	458	5,101	48
20. Quinn Early, Buff.	11	454	6,365	40
21. Thurman Thomas, Buff.	11	453	4,304	21
22. Ricky Proehl, St.L.	9	433	5,702	33
23. Emmitt Smith, Dal.	9	415	2,609	9
24. Mike Pritchard, Sea.	8	396	4,812	24
25. Jeff Graham, S.D.	8	378	5,486	19
26. Chris Calloway, Atl.	9	359	5,088	29
27. O. J. McDuffie, Mia.	6	358	4,415	27
28. Eric Green, NYJ	9	355	4,353	34
29. Michael Jackson, Balt.	8	353	5,393	46
Ricky Watters, Sea.	7	353	3,141	9

TOP ACTIVE INTERCEPTORS

	Yrs.	No.	Yards	TD
1. Eugene Robinson, Atl.	14	53	755	1
2. Rod Woodson, Balt.	12	47	968	7
Darrell Green, Wash.	16	47	553	6
4. Eric Allen, Oak.	11	44	629	5
5. Deion Sanders, Dal.	10	41	1,094	8
6. Aeneas Williams, Ariz.	8	39	546	6
7. Tim McDonald, S.F.	12	38	622	4
8. Cris Dishman, K.C.	11	37	455	2
9. Tyrone Braxton, Den.	12	36	617	4
10. Terry McDaniel, *	11	35	667	6
Mike Prior, *	13	35	440	1
12. LeRoy Butler, G.B.	9	34	508	1
James Hasty, K.C.	11	34	404	2
14. Darren Perry, S.D.	7	32	574	1
Greg Jackson, *	10	32	329	2
16. Merton Hanks, S.F.	8	31	380	2
17. Terrell Buckley, Mia.	7	29	449	3
18. Ray Buchanan, Atl.	6	28	509	3
Mark Carrier, Det.	9	28	324	1
20. Darryll Lewis, Tenn.	8	27	540	5
Eric Turner, Oak.	8	27	426	3
Ray Crockett, Den.	10	27	407	2
Eric Davis, Car.	9	27	365	4
Mark Collins, Sea.	13	27	343	2
25. Darryl Williams, Sea.	7	25	598	3
Keith Lyle, St.L.	5	25	317	0
27. Steve Atwater, NYJ	10	24	408	1
Willie Clay, N.E.	7	24	405	2
Dwayne Harper, S.D.	11	24	337	0
Seth Joyner, *	13	24	307	2

TOP ACTIVE PUNT RETURNERS

40 or more punt returns

	Yrs.	No.	Yards	Avg.	TD
1. Karl Williams, T.B.	3	69	954	13.8	2
2. Darrien Gordon, Den.	5	177	2,329	13.2	6
3. Jermaine Lewis, Balt.	3	96	1,181	12.3	4
4. Reggie Barlow, Jac.	3	79	967	12.2	1
5. Desmond Howard, *	7	164	1,981	12.1	6
6. Brian Mitchell, Wash.	9	277	3,144	11.4	7
7. Darrell Green, Wash.	16	51	576	11.3	0
8. Deion Sanders, Dal.	10	152	1,629	10.7	5
9. Winslow Oliver, Car.	3	110	1,173	10.7	1
10. Terrell Buckley, Mia.	7	68	723	10.6	1
11. David Meggett, NYJ	10	349	3,708	10.6	7
12. David Palmer, Minn.	5	140	1,484	10.6	2
13. Eddie Kennison, N.O.	3	103	1,085	10.5	3
14. Jeff Burris, Ind.	5	100	1,045	10.5	0
15. Leon Johnson, NYJ	2	80	822	10.3	1
16. Tim Brown, Oak.	11	304	3,106	10.2	2
17. Kevin Williams, Buff.	6	172	1,744	10.1	3
18. Joey Galloway, Sea.	4	76	769	10.1	4
19. Charles Jordan, Sea.	5	53	533	10.1	0
20. Amani Toomer, NYG	3	100	1,005	10.1	3
21. Tamarick Vanover, K.C.	4	130	1,303	10.0	2
22. Eric Metcalf, Ariz.	10	281	2,804	10.0	9
23. Glyn Milburn, Chi.	6	218	2,166	9.9	1
24. Troy Brown, N.E.	6	66	651	9.9	0
25. Eric Guliford, N.O.	5	134	1,300	9.7	1
26. Corey Sawyer, Cin.	5	50	482	9.6	1
27. Dale Carter, Den.	7	83	787	9.5	2
28. Andre Hastings, N.O.	6	110	1,036	9.4	1
29. Anthony Parker, T.B.	9	46	431	9.4	0
30. Mark Seay, Clev.	5	51	477	9.4	0

TOP ACTIVE KICKOFF RETURNERS

40 or more kickoff returns

	Yrs.	No.	Yards	Avg.	TD
1. Terry Fair, Det.	1	51	1,428	28.0	2
2. Tremain Mack, Cin.	2	45	1,165	25.9	1
3. Reggie Barlow, Jac.	3	40	1,014	25.4	1
4. John Avery, Mia.	1	43	1,085	25.2	0
5. Tim Brown, Oak.	11	49	1,235	25.2	1
6. Eric Guliford, N.O.	5	66	1,660	25.2	1
7. Tamarick Vanover, K.C.	4	168	4,213	25.1	4
8. Michael Bates, Car.	6	204	5,046	24.7	2
9. Tyrone Hughes, *	6	283	6,999	24.7	3
10. Byron Hanspard, Atl.	1	40	987	24.7	2
11. Allen Rossum, Phil.	1	44	1,080	24.5	0
12. Derrick Cullors, N.E.	2	60	1,471	24.5	1
13. Glyn Milburn, Chi.	6	277	6,742	24.3	2
14. Robert Brooks, G.B.	7	51	1,237	24.3	2
15. Duce Staley, Phil.	2	48	1,158	24.1	0
16. Reidel Anthony, T.B.	2	71	1,710	24.1	0
17. Vaughn Hebron, Den.	5	158	3,802	24.1	1
18. Roell Preston, *	4	126	3,016	23.9	2
19. Napoleon Kaufman, Oak.	4	47	1,120	23.8	1
20. Tony Smith, *	3	61	1,453	23.8	1
21. Aaron Glenn, NYJ	5	81	1,926	23.8	1
22. Kevin Williams, Buff.	6	250	5,933	23.7	1
23. Corey Harris, Balt.	7	150	3,543	23.6	1
24. Thomas Lewis, S.D.	4	53	1,237	23.3	1
25. Tony Horne, St.L.	1	56	1,306	23.3	1
26. Steve Broussard, Balt.	9	175	4,060	23.2	1
27. Andre Coleman, Pitt.	5	193	4,466	23.1	4
28. David Dunn, Pitt.	4	125	2,886	23.1	1
29. Brian Mitchell, Wash.	9	378	8,693	23.0	2
30. O.J. McDuffie, Mia.	6	91	2,086	22.9	0

TOP ACTIVE QUARTERBACK SACKERS

	Yrs.	No.
1. Bruce Smith, Buff.	14	164.0
2. Kevin Greene, Car.	14	148.0
3. Chris Doleman, S.F.	14	142.5
4. Leslie O'Neal, K.C.	12	127.0
5. Derrick Thomas, K.C.	10	119.5
6. Clyde Simmons, Chi.	13	114.0
7. Pat Swilling, Oak.	12	107.5
8. William Fuller, S.D.	13	100.5
9. Neil Smith, Den.	11	98.0
10. Charles Haley, *	11	97.5
11. John Randle, Minn.	9	96.0
12. Ken Harvey, Wash.	11	89.0
13. Henry Thomas, N.E.	12	86.0
14. Wayne Martin, N.O.	10	78.0
15. Trace Armstrong, Mia.	10	74.5
16. Bryce Paup, Jac.	9	72.0
17. Cornelius Bennett, Ind.	12	63.5
18. Michael Sinclair, Sea.	7	60.5
19. Alfred Williams, Den.	8	55.5
20. Greg Lloyd, *	11	54.5
21. Seth Joyner, *	13	52.0
22. Robert Porcher, Det.	7	51.5
23. Danny Stubbs, *	10	51.5
24. Phil Hansen, Buff.	8	50.5
Cortez Kennedy, Sea.	9	50.5
26. Rob Burnett, Balt.	9	50.0
27. Chuck Smith, Atl.	7	48.5
28. Broderick Thomas, Dal.	9	47.5
29. Jeff Lageman, Jac.	10	47.0
Michael Strahan, NYG	6	47.0

TOP ACTIVE PUNTERS

50 or more punts

	Yrs.	No.	Avg.	LG
1. Darren Bennett, S.D.	4	343	44.7	66
2. Matt Turk, Wash.	4	326	44.2	69
3. Leo Araguz, Oak.	3	204	44.0	64
4. Tom Rouen, Den.	6	386	43.7	76
5. Craig Hentrich, Tenn.	5	358	43.6	71
6. Kyle Richardson, Balt.	2	109	43.6	67
7. Sean Landeta, Phil.	14	926	43.6	74
8. Tom Tupa, NYJ	10	366	43.5	73
9. Rick Tuten, St.L.	10	709	43.5	73
10. Reggie Roby, *	16	992	43.3	77
11. Brad Maynard, NYG	2	212	42.9	63
12. Bryan Barker, Jac.	9	640	42.7	67
13. Todd Sauerbrun, Chi.	4	243	42.7	72
14. Tommy Barnhardt, T.B.	12	729	42.6	65
15. Lee Johnson, N.E.	14	984	42.6	70
16. Josh Miller, Pitt.	3	200	42.6	73
17. Toby Gowin, Dal.	2	163	42.5	72
18. Mark Royals, N.O.	10	728	42.5	69
19. Chris Gardocki, Clev.	8	512	42.5	72
20. Tom Hutton, *	4	349	42.4	63
21. John Jett, Det.	6	403	42.3	60
22. Brian Hansen, *	14	1,048	42.3	73
23. Mike Horan, *	14	977	42.2	75
24. Mitch Berger, Minn.	4	241	42.1	67
25. Jeff Feagles, Sea.	11	896	41.7	77
26. Scott Player, Ariz.	1	81	41.7	67
27. Louie Aguiar, K.C.	8	631	41.6	71
28. Ken Walter, Car.	2	162	41.6	62
29. John Kidd, *	15	957	41.5	67
30. Klaus Wilmsmeyer, Mia.	6	398	41.0	63

** Free agent; subject to developments.*

COACHES RECORDS

ACTIVE COACHES' CAREER RECORDS (Order Based on Career Victories)

Start of 1999 Season			Regular Season				Postseason				Career			
Coach	Team(s)	Yrs.	Won	Lost	Tied	Pct.	Won	Lost	Tied	Pct.	Won	Lost	Tied	Pct.
Dan Reeves	Denver Broncos, New York Giants, Atlanta Falcons	18	162	117	1	.580	10	8	0	.556	172	125	1	.579
Bill Parcells	New York Giants, New England Patriots, New York Jets	14	130	92	1	.585	11	6	0	.647	141	98	1	.590
Mike Ditka	Chicago Bears, New Orleans Saints	13	118	82	0	.590	6	6	0	.500	124	88	0	.585
George Seifert	San Francisco 49ers, Carolina Panthers	8	98	30	0	.766	10	5	0	.667	108	35	0	.755
Jim Mora	New Orleans Saints, Indianapolis Colts	12	96	87	0	.525	0	4	0	.000	96	91	0	.513
Mike Holmgren	Green Bay Packers, Seattle Seahawks	7	75	37	0	.670	9	5	0	.643	84	42	0	.667
Jimmy Johnson	Dallas Cowboys, Miami Dolphins	8	71	57	0	.555	8	3	0	.727	79	60	0	.568
Bill Cowher	Pittsburgh Steelers	7	71	41	0	.634	5	6	0	.455	76	47	0	.618
Dennis Green	Minnesota Vikings	7	71	41	0	.634	2	6	0	.250	73	47	0	.608
Dick Vermeil	Philadelphia Eagles, St. Louis Rams	9	63	70	0	.474	3	4	0	.429	66	74	0	.471
Bobby Ross	San Diego Chargers, Detroit Lions	7	61	51	0	.545	3	4	0	.429	64	55	0	.538
Mike Shanahan	Los Angeles Raiders, Denver Broncos	6	55	29	0	.655	7	1	0	.875	62	30	0	.674
Bruce Coslet	New York Jets, Cincinnati Bengals	7	43	62	0	.410	0	1	0	.000	43	63	0	.406
Tom Coughlin	Jacksonville Jaguars	4	35	29	0	.547	3	3	0	.500	38	32	0	.543
Jeff Fisher	Houston Oilers/Tennessee Oilers-Titans	4	32	38	0	.457	0	0	0	.000	32	38	0	.457
Norv Turner	Washington Redskins	5	32	47	1	.406	0	0	0	.000	32	47	1	.406
Ray Rhodes	Philadelphia Eagles, Green Bay Packers	4	29	34	1	.461	1	2	0	.333	30	36	1	.455
Steve Mariucci	San Francisco 49ers	2	25	7	0	.781	2	2	0	.500	27	9	0	.750
Wade Phillips	New Orleans Saints, Denver Broncos, Buffalo Bills	3	27	25	0	.519	0	2	0	.000	27	27	0	.500
Pete Carroll	New York Jets, New England Patriots	3	25	23	0	.521	1	2	0	.333	26	25	0	.510
Tony Dungy	Tampa Bay Buccaneers	3	24	24	0	.500	1	1	0	.500	25	25	0	.500
Vince Tobin	Arizona Cardinals	3	20	28	0	.417	1	1	0	.500	21	29	0	.420
Jim Fassel	New York Giants	2	18	13	1	.578	0	1	0	.000	18	14	1	.561
Chan Gailey	Dallas Cowboys	1	10	6	0	.625	0	1	0	.000	10	7	0	.588
Jon Gruden	Oakland Raiders	1	8	8	0	.500	0	0	0	.000	8	8	0	.500
Brian Billick	Baltimore Ravens	0	0	0	0	.000	0	0	0	.000	0	0	0	.000
Gunther Cunningham	Kansas City Chiefs	0	0	0	0	.000	0	0	0	.000	0	0	0	.000
Dick Jauron	Chicago Bears	0	0	0	0	.000	0	0	0	.000	0	0	0	.000
Chris Palmer	Cleveland Browns	0	0	0	0	.000	0	0	0	.000	0	0	0	.000
Andy Reid	Philadelphia Eagles	0	0	0	0	.000	0	0	0	.000	0	0	0	.000
Mike Riley	San Diego Chargers	0	0	0	0	.000	0	0	0	.000	0	0	0	.000

COACHES WITH 100 CAREER VICTORIES (Order Based on Career Victories)

Start of 1999 Season			Regular Season				Postseason				Career			
Coach	Team(s)	Yrs.	Won	Lost	Tied	Pct.	Won	Lost	Tied	Pct.	Won	Lost	Tied	Pct.
Don Shula	Baltimore Colts, Miami Dolphins	33	328	156	6	.676	19	17	0	.528	347	173	6	.665
George Halas	Chicago Bears	40	318	148	31	.671	6	3	0	.667	324	151	31	.671
Tom Landry	Dallas Cowboys	29	250	162	6	.605	20	16	0	.556	270	178	6	.601
Earl (Curly) Lambeau	Green Bay Packers, Chicago Cardinals, Washington Redskins	33	226	132	22	.624	3	2	0	.600	229	134	22	.623
Chuck Noll	Pittsburgh Steelers	23	193	148	1	.566	16	8	0	.667	209	156	1	.572
Chuck Knox	Los Angeles Rams, Buffalo Bills, Seattle Seahawks	22	186	147	1	.558	7	11	0	.389	193	158	1	.550
Dan Reeves	Denver Broncos, New York Giants, Atlanta Falcons	18	162	117	1	.580	10	8	0	.556	172	125	1	.579
Paul Brown	Cleveland Browns, Cincinnati Bengals	21	166	100	6	.621	4	8	0	.333	170	108	6	.609
Bud Grant	Minnesota Vikings	18	158	96	5	.620	10	12	0	.455	168	108	5	.607
Marv Levy	Kansas City Chiefs, Buffalo Bills	17	143	112	0	.561	11	8	0	.579	154	120	0	.562
Steve Owen	New York Giants	23	151	100	17	.595	2	8	0	.200	153	108	17	.581
Marty Schottenheimer	Cleveland Browns, Kansas City Chiefs	15	145	85	1	.630	5	11	0	.313	150	96	1	.609
Bill Parcells	New York Giants, New England Patriots, New York Jets	14	130	92	1	.585	11	6	0	.647	141	98	1	.590
Joe Gibbs	Washington Redskins	12	124	60	0	.674	16	5	0	.762	140	65	0	.683
Hank Stram	Kansas City Chiefs, New Orleans Saints	17	131	97	10	.571	5	3	0	.625	136	100	10	.573
Weeb Ewbank	Baltimore Colts, New York Jets	20	130	129	7	.502	4	1	0	.800	134	130	7	.507
Mike Ditka	Chicago Bears, New Orleans Saints	13	118	82	0	.590	6	6	0	.500	124	88	0	.585
Sid Gillman	Los Angeles Rams, Los Angeles-San Diego Chargers, Houston Oilers	18	122	99	7	.550	1	5	0	.167	123	104	7	.541
George Allen	Los Angeles Rams, Washington Redskins	12	116	47	5	.705	2	7	0	.222	118	54	5	.681
Don Coryell	St. Louis Cardinals, San Diego Chargers	14	111	83	1	.572	3	6	0	.333	114	89	1	.561
John Madden	Oakland Raiders	10	103	32	7	.750	9	7	0	.563	112	39	7	.731
George Seifert	San Francisco 49ers, Carolina Panthers	8	98	30	0	.766	10	5	0	.667	108	35	0	.755
Ray (Buddy) Parker	Chicago Cardinals, Detroit Lions, Pittsburgh Steelers	15	104	75	9	.577	3	1	0	.750	107	76	9	.581
Vince Lombardi	Green Bay Packers, Washington Redskins	10	96	34	6	.728	9	1	0	.900	105	35	6	.740
Tom Flores	Oakland-Los Angeles Raiders, Seattle Seahawks	12	97	87	0	.527	8	3	0	.727	105	90	0	.538
Bill Walsh	San Francisco 49ers	10	92	59	1	.609	10	4	0	.714	102	63	1	.617

Active coaches in bold.

The **Denver Broncos** need to win their first four home games to pass the Green Bay Packers (25) and Miami Dolphins (27) for the most consecutive wins at home in NFL history. The Broncos have won 24 straight at Denver's Mile High Stadium.

Denver also needs five victories to reach 300 regular-season wins.

The **Dallas Cowboys** need six victories to reach 350 regular-season wins.

The **Miami Dolphins** need one victory to reach 300 regular-season wins.

The **Oakland Raiders** need 10 victories to reach 350 regular-season wins.

Head coach **Jim Mora**, Indianapolis, needs four victories to become only the fifth active coach and twenty-seventh all-time to reach 100 in a career.

Head coach **Bill Parcells**, New York Jets, needs nine victories to become only the second active coach and thirteenth all-time to reach 150 in a career.

Barry Sanders, Detroit, needs 1,458 rushing yards to pass Walter Payton (16,726) and become the league's all-time leader. Sanders has 15,269 rushing yards in 10 seasons.

He needs one rushing touchdown to become the sixth player in NFL history with 100 in a career.

Sanders also can extend his NFL record of 10 straight 1,000-yard rushing seasons to 11.

Terrell Davis, Denver, needs 1,000 rushing yards to join Eric Dickerson, Tony Dorsett, and Barry Sanders as the only players in NFL history to rush for 1,000 yards in each of their first five seasons.

Corey Dillon, Cincinnati, needs 1,000 rushing yards to become the eleventh player all-time to rush for 1,000 yards in each of his first three seasons.

Emmitt Smith, Dallas, needs 12 touchdowns to pass Marcus Allen (145) and become second all-time with 146 career touchdowns. Smith has scored 134 touchdowns in nine seasons.

Smith needs 694 rushing yards to pass Tony Dorsett (12,739) and Eric Dickerson (13,259) for third all-time. Smith has rushed for 12,566 yards in nine seasons.

He also can become the second player all-time to rush for 1,000 yards in nine consecutive seasons.

Troy Aikman, Dallas, needs 1,654 passing yards to become the twenty-second player all-time to reach 30,000 career passing yards. Aikman has 28,346 passing yards in 10 seasons.

Drew Bledsoe, New England, needs to lead the league in attempts to tie Sammy Baugh, George Blanda, and Johnny Unitas for second all-time with four seasons leading the league.

Brett Favre, Green Bay, needs to start his first eight games to pass Ron Jaworski (116) for the most consecutive starts by a quarterback since 1970. Favre has started 109 consecutive regular-season games.

Favre can join Johnny Unitas, Len Dawson, and Steve Young as the only players to lead the league in touchdown passes four times.

He also can join Dan Marino (9) as the only players in league history with at least eight consecutive 3,000-yard passing seasons.

Dave Krieg, Tennessee, will play in his twentieth career season, tying Jim Marshall and Jackie Slater for the third-most seasons in NFL history.

Dan Marino, Miami, needs 1,087 passing yards to become the first player all-time to reach 60,000 in a career. Marino has 58,913 passing yards in 16 seasons.

Marino needs 11 attempts to become the first player all-time to reach 8,000 in a career. He has 7,989 in 16 seasons.

He also needs eight victories to become the first quarterback all-time to reach 150 career victories as a starter.

Tim Brown, Oakland, needs 400 receiving yards to become the sixteenth player all-time with 10,000 career receiving yards. Brown has 9,600 receiving yards in 11 seasons.

Cris Carter, Minnesota, needs 1,000 receiving yards to tie Lance Alworth, Henry Ellard, and Michael Irvin for third place all-time with seven career 1,000-yard seasons.

Carter needs 66 receptions to become the third player all-time to reach 900 career receptions (see Reed note). He has 834 catches in 12 seasons.

He also needs nine touchdowns to become the eighth player all-time to reach 110 career touchdowns.

Carter needs 553 receiving yards to become the eleventh player all-time to reach 11,000 career receiving yards. He has 10,447 receiving yards in 12 seasons.

Michael Irvin, Dallas, needs 263 receiving yards to become the eighth player all-time to reach 12,000 in a career. He also needs 985 yards to pass Don Maynard (11,834), Irving Fryar (11,983), Charlie Joiner (12,146), Andre Reed (12,559), and Art Monk (12,721) into fifth place all-time (see Reed note). Irvin has 11,737 receiving yards in 11 seasons.

Irvin needs 60 receptions to become the seventh player all-time with 800 career receptions. He has 740 catches in 11 seasons.

Andre Reed, Buffalo, needs 11 receptions to become the third player all-time to reach 900 career receptions (see Carter note). He has 889 catches in 14 seasons.

Reed needs 531 receiving yards to pass Art Monk (12,721) and Steve Largent (13,089) and take over fourth place all-time (see Irvin note). He has 12,559 receiving yards in 14 seasons.

Shannon Sharpe, Denver, needs 13 catches to pass Kellen Winslow (541) for second place all-time in receptions by a tight end. Sharpe has 529 catches in nine seasons.

Keenan McCardell and **Jimmy Smith**, Jacksonville, each need 1,000 receiving yards to become only the second duo all-time to post three straight 1,000-yard receiving seasons.

John Randle, Minnesota, needs 10 sacks to move into second place all-time with eight straight 10-sack seasons. Randle has at least 10 sacks in each of the last seven seasons (see B. Smith note).

Bruce Smith, Buffalo, needs 10 sacks to move into second place all-time with eight straight 10-sack seasons. Smith has at least 10 sacks in each of the last seven seasons (see Randle note).

Eugene Robinson, Atlanta, needs four interceptions to tie four players for ninth place all-time with 57 career interceptions. Robinson has 53 interceptions in 14 seasons.

Deion Sanders, Dallas, needs one interception return for a touchdown to tie Ken Houston for most all-time with nine. Sanders has eight interception-return touchdowns in 10 seasons.

Morten Andersen, Atlanta, needs to play in four games to pass Gary Anderson (261) and Jan Stenerud (263) and move into fourth place in games played. Andersen has played in 260 games in 17 seasons (see Anderson note).

Gary Anderson, Minnesota, needs 158 points to pass George Blanda (2,002) as the all-time scoring leader in NFL history. Anderson has scored 1,845 points in 17 seasons.

Anderson can extend his NFL record of 40 consecutive field goals made.

He also needs to play in three games to pass Jan Stenerud (263) and move into fourth place in games played. Anderson has played in 261 games in 17 seasons (see Andersen note).

Al Del Greco, Tennessee, needs one field goal to become the twelfth player in NFL history to kick 300. He has 299 field goals in 15 seasons.

DRAFT LIST FOR 1999

64th Annual NFL Draft, April 17-18, 1999
*Denotes Compensatory Selection

ARIZONA CARDINALS
1. David Boston—8 , WR, Ohio State, from San Diego
   L.J. Shelton—21, T, Eastern Michigan
2. Johnny Rutledge—51, LB, Florida
3. Tom Burke—83, DE, Wisconsin
4. Joel Makovicka—116, RB, Nebraska
5. Paris Johnson—155, DB, Miami, Ohio
   *Yusuf Scott—168, G, Arizona
6. Jacoby Rhinehart—190, DB, Southern Methodist
   *Melvin Bradley—202, LB, Arkansas
   *Dennis McKinley—206, RB, Mississippi State
7. Choice to Pittsburgh
   *Chris Greisen—239, QB, Northwest Missouri State

ATLANTA FALCONS
1. Patrick Kerney—30, DE, Virginia
2. Reggie Kelly—42, TE, Mississippi State, from Baltimore
   Choice to San Diego
3. Jeff Paulk—92, RB, Arizona State
4. Johndale Carty—126, DB, Utah State
5. Eugene Baker—164, WR, Kent State
6. Jeff Kelly—198, LB, Kansas State, from San Francisco
   Eric Thigpen—200, DB, Iowa
7. Todd McClure—237, C, Louisiana State
   *Rondel Menendez—247, WR, Eastern Kentucky

BALTIMORE RAVENS
1. Chris McAlister—10, DB, Arizona
2. Choice to Atlanta
3. Choice to Miami through Detroit
4. Brandon Stokley—105, WR, Southwestern Louisiana
   *Edwin Mulitalo—129, G, Arizona
5. Choice to St. Louis
6. Choice to New England
7. Anthony Poindexter—216, DB, Virginia

BUFFALO BILLS
1. Antoine Winfield—23, DB, Ohio State
2. Peerless Price—53, WR, Tennessee
3. Shawn Bryson—86, RB, Tennessee
4. Keith Newman—119, LB, North Carolina
   Bobby Collins—122, TE, North Alabama, from Green Bay
5. Jay Foreman—156, LB, Nebraska
6. Armon Hatcher—194, DB, Oregon State
7. Sheldon Jackson—230, TE, Nebraska
   *Bryce Fisher—248, DE, Air Force

CAROLINA PANTHERS
1. Choice to New Orleans through Washington
2. Chris Terry—34, T, Georgia, from Indianapolis
   Mike Rucker—38, DE, Nebraska
3. Choice to Denver
4. Hannibal Navies—100, LB, Colorado
5. Choice to Seattle through Dallas
6. Robert Daniel—175, DE, Northwestern State, La.
7. Tony Booth—211, DB, James Madison

CHICAGO BEARS
1. Choice to Washington
   Cade McNown—12, QB, UCLA, from New Orleans through Washington
2. Choice to Washington
   Russell Davis—48, DT, North Carolina, from Oakland
3. Rex Tucker—66, G, Texas A&M
   D'Wayne Bates—71, WR, Northwestern, from New Orleans through Washington
   Marty Booker—78, WR, Northeast Louisiana, from Oakland
4. Choice to Oakland
   Warrick Holdman—106, LB, Texas A&M, from Washington
   Rosevelt Colvin—111, DE, Purdue, from Oakland
5. Choice to San Diego
   Jerry Wisne—143, G, Notre Dame, from Washington
   Khari Samuel—144, LB, Massachusetts, from New Orleans through Washington
   Jerry Azumah—147, RB, New Hampshire, from Kansas City
6. Choice to Cleveland
   Rashard Cook—184, DB, Southern California, from Cleveland
7. Choice to Green Bay
   Sulecio Sanford—221, WR, Middle Tennessee State, from Cleveland
   Jim Finn—253, RB, Pennsylvania, from Cleveland

CINCINNATI BENGALS
1. Akili Smith—3, QB, Oregon
2. Charles Fisher—33, DB, West Virginia
3. Cory Hall—65, DB, Fresno State
4. Craig Yeast—98, WR, Kentucky
5. Nick Williams—135, RB, Miami
6. Kelly Gregg—173, DT, Oklahoma
7. Tony Coats—209, G, Washington
   *Scott Covington—245, QB, Miami
   *Donald Broomfield—249, DT, Clemson

CLEVELAND BROWNS
1. Tim Couch—1, QB, Kentucky
2. Kevin Johnson—32, WR, Syracuse
   Rahim Abdullah—45, LB, Clemson
3. Daylon McCutcheon—62, DB, Southern California
   Marquis Smith—76, DB, California
4. Choice to Indianapolis through San Francisco
   Choice to San Francisco
   Wali Rainer—124, LB, Virginia, from San Francisco
5. Choice to Miami through San Francisco
   Darrin Chiaverini—148, WR, Colorado
6. Choice to Seattle
   Marcus Spriggs—174, DT, Troy State, from Chicago
   Choice to Chicago
   Kendall Ogle—187, LB, Maryland, from Seattle
   James Dearth—191, TE, Tarleton State, from New England through Seattle
7. Madre Hill—207, RB, Arkansas
   Choice to Chicago
   Choice to Chicago

DALLAS COWBOYS
1. Ebenezer Ekuban—20, DE, North Carolina, from New England through Seattle
   Choice to Seattle
2. Solomon Page—55, T, West Virginia
3. Dat Nguyen—85, LB, Texas A&M
4. Wane McGarity—118, WR, Texas
   *Peppi Zellner—132, DE, Fort Valley State
5. Choice to Denver
6. Mar Tay Jenkins—193, WR, Nebraska-Omaha
7. Mike Lucky—229, TE, Arizona
   *Kelvin Garmon—243, G, Baylor

DENVER BRONCOS
1. Al Wilson—31, LB, Tennessee
2. Montae Reagor—58, DE, Texas Tech, from San Francisco
   Lennie Friedman—61, G, Duke
3. Chris Watson—67, DB, Eastern Illinois, from Carolina
   Travis McGriff—93, WR, Florida
4. Olandis Gary—127, RB, Georgia
5. David Bowens—158, DE, Western Illinois, from Dallas
   Choice to Washington
   *Darwin Brown—167, DB, Texas Tech
6. Desmond Clark—179, TE, Wake Forest, from New Orleans through Washington
   Choice to Philadelphia
   *Chad Plummer—204, WR, Cincinnati
7. Billy Miller—218, WR, Southern California, from New Orleans through Washington
   Justin Swift—238, TE, Kansas State

DETROIT LIONS
1. Chris Claiborne—9, LB, Southern California
   Aaron Gibson—27, T, Wisconsin, from San Francisco through Miami
2. Choice to Miami
3. Jared DeVries—70, DE, Iowa
4. Sedrick Irvin—103, RB, Michigan State
5. Tyree Talton—137, DB, Northern Iowa, from Philadelphia
   Choice to Miami
6. Clint Kriewaldt—177, LB, Wisconsin-Stevens Point
7. Mike Pringley—215, DE, North Carolina

GREEN BAY PACKERS
1. Antuan Edwards—25, DB, Clemson
2. Fred Vinson—47, DB, Vanderbilt, from Seattle
   Choice exercised in 1998 Supplemental Draft, Mike Wahle, T, Navy
3. Mike McKenzie—87, DB, Memphis
   *Cletidus Hunt—94, DT, Kentucky State
4. Choice to Buffalo
   *Aaron Brooks—131, QB, Virginia
   *Josh Bidwell—133, P, Oregon
5. DeMond Parker—159, RB, Oklahoma
   Craig Heimburger—163, C, Missouri, from Minnesota through Pittsburgh and Oakland
6. Dee Miller—196, WR, Ohio State
   *Scott Curry—203, T, Montana
7. Chris Akins—212, DB, Arkansas-Pine Bluff, from St. Louis
   Donald Driver—213, WR, Alcorn State, from Chicago
   Choice to Miami through Detroit

INDIANAPOLIS COLTS
1. Edgerrin James—4, RB, Miami
2. Choice to Carolina
   Mike Peterson—36, LB, Florida, from St. Louis
3. Brandon Burlsworth—63, G, Arkansas
4. Paul Miranda—96, DB, Central Florida, from Cleveland through San Francisco
   Choice to San Francisco
5. Choice to Pittsburgh
   Brad Scioli—138, DE, Penn State, from St. Louis
6. Choice to San Francisco
7. Hunter Smith—210, P, Notre Dame
   *Corey Terry—250, LB, Tennessee

JACKSONVILLE JAGUARS
1. Fernando Bryant—26, DB, Alabama
2. Larry Smith—56, DT, Florida State
3. Anthony Cesario—88, G, Colorado State
4. Kevin Landolt—121, DT, West Virginia
5. Jason Craft—160, DB, Colorado State
6. Emarlos Leroy—182, DT, Georgia, from Kansas City through Tampa Bay
   Choice to Tampa Bay
7. Choice to Tampa Bay
   *Dee Moronkola—242, DB, Washington State
   *Chris White—246, DE, Southern

DRAFT LIST FOR 1999

KANSAS CITY CHIEFS
1. John Tait—14, T, Brigham Young
2. Choice to Miami
   Mike Cloud—54, RB, Boston College, from Miami
3. Gary Stills—75, LB, West Virginia
   Larry Atkins—84, DB, UCLA, from Miami
4. Larry Parker—108, WR, Southern California
5. Choice to Chicago
6. Choice to Jacksonville through Tampa Bay
7. Eric King—220, G, Richmond

MIAMI DOLPHINS
1. Choice to San Francisco
2. James Johnson—39, RB, Mississippi State, from Detroit
   Rob Konrad—43, RB, Syracuse, from Kansas City
   Choice to Kansas City
3. Grey Ruegamer—72, C, Arizona State, from Baltimore through Detroit
   Choice to Kansas City
4. Choice to Minnesota
5. Cecil Collins—134, RB, McNeese State, from Cleveland through San Francisco
   Bryan Jones—142, LB, Oregon State, from Detroit
   Choice to San Francisco
6. Brent Bartholomew—192, P, Ohio State
7. Choice to New York Giants
   Jermaine Haley—232, DT, Butte J.C., from Green Bay through Detroit
   *Joe Wong—244, T, Brigham Young

MINNESOTA VIKINGS
1. Daunte Culpepper—11, QB, Central Florida, from Washington
   Dimitrius Underwood—29, DE, Michigan State
2. Jim Kleinsasser—44, TE, North Dakota, from Pittsburgh
   Choice to Pittsburgh
3. Choice to New England
4. Kenny Wright—120, DB, Northwestern State, La., from Miami
   Jay Humphrey—125, T, Texas
5. Choice to Green Bay through Pittsburgh and Oakland
   *Chris Jones—169, LB, Clemson
6. Talance Sawyer—185, DE, Nevada-Las Vegas, from Tampa Bay through Baltimore
   Antico Dalton—199, LB, Hampton
7. Noel Scarlett—236, DT, Langston

NEW ENGLAND PATRIOTS
1. Damien Woody—17, C, Boston College, from Seattle
   Choice to Dallas through Seattle
   Andy Katzenmoyer—28, LB, Ohio State, from New York Jets
2. Kevin Faulk—46, RB, Louisiana State, from Tennessee
   Choice to Tennessee
3. Choice to Seattle
   Tony George—91, DB, Florida, from Minnesota
4. Choice to Tennessee
5. Derrick Fletcher—154, G, Baylor
6. Marcus Washington—180, DB, Colorado, from Baltimore
   Choice to Cleveland through Seattle
7. Michael Bishop—227, QB, Kansas State
   *Sean Morey—241, WR, Brown

NEW ORLEANS SAINTS
1. Ricky Williams—5, RB, Texas, from Carolina through Washington
   Choice to Chicago through Washington
2. Choice to St. Louis
3. Choice to Chicago through Washington
4. Choice to Washington
5. Choice to Chicago through Washington
6. Choice to Denver through Washington
7. Choice to Denver through Washington

NEW YORK GIANTS
1. Luke Petitgout—19, T, Notre Dame
2. Joe Montgomery—49, RB, Ohio State
3. Dan Campbell—79, TE, Texas A&M
4. Sean Bennett—112, RB, Northwestern
5. Mike Rosenthal—149, T, Notre Dame
6. Lyle West—189, DB, San Jose State
   *Andre Weathers—205, DB, Michigan
7. Ryan Hale—225, DT, Arkansas
   O.J. Childress—231, LB, Clemson, from Miami

NEW YORK JETS
1. Choice to New England
2. Randy Thomas—57, G, Mississippi State
3. David Loverne—90, T, San Jose State
4. Jason Wiltz—123, DT, Nebraska
5. Jermaine Jones—162, DB, Northwestern State, La.
6. Marc Megna—183, LB, Richmond, from Pittsburgh
   J.P. Machado—197, G, Illinois
7. Ryan Young—223, T, Kansas State, from Seattle
   J.J. Syvrud—235, DE, Jamestown

OAKLAND RAIDERS
1. Matt Stinchcomb—18, T, Georgia
2. Tony Bryant—40, DE, Florida State, from Washington through Chicago
   Choice to Chicago
3. Choice to Chicago
4. Dameane Douglas—102, WR, California, from Chicago
   Choice to Chicago
5. Eric Barton—146, LB, Maryland, from Pittsburgh
   Roderick Coleman—153, LB, East Carolina
6. Daren Yancey—188, DT, Brigham Young
7. Jo Juan Armour—224, LB, Miami, Ohio

PHILADELPHIA EAGLES
1. Donovan McNabb—2, QB, Syracuse
2. Barry Gardner—35, LB, Northwestern
3. Doug Brzezinski—64, G, Boston College
4. John Welbourn—97, T, California
   *Damon Moore—128, DB, Ohio State
   *Na Brown—130, WR, North Carolina
5. Choice to Detroit
6. Cecil Martin—172, RB, Wisconsin
   Troy Smith—201, WR, East Carolina, from Denver
7. Jed Weaver—208, TE, Oregon
   *Pernell Davis—251, DT, Alabama-Birmingham

PITTSBURGH STEELERS
1. Troy Edwards—13, WR, Louisiana Tech
2. Choice to Minnesota
   Scott Shields—59, DB, Weber State, from Minnesota
3. Joey Porter—73, LB, Colorado State, from Washington through Minnesota
   Kris Farris—74, T, UCLA
   *Amos Zereoue—95, RB, West Virginia
4. Aaron Smith—109, DE, Northern Colorado
5. Jerame Tuman—136, TE, Michigan, from Indianapolis
   Choice to Oakland
   *Malcolm Johnson—166, WR, Notre Dame
6. Choice to New York Jets
7. Antonio Dingle—214, DT, Virginia, from San Diego
   Chad Kelsay—219, LB, Nebraska
   Kris Brown—228, K, Nebraska, from Arizona

ST. LOUIS RAMS
1. Torry Holt—6, WR, North Carolina State
2. Choice to Indianapolis
   Dre' Bly—41, DB, North Carolina, from New Orleans
3. Richard Coady—68, DB, Texas A&M
4. Joe Germaine—101, QB, Ohio State
5. Choice to Indianapolis
   Cameron Spikes—145, G, Texas A&M, from Baltimore
6. Lionel Barnes—176, DE, Northeast Louisiana
7. Choice to Green Bay
   *Rodney Williams—252, P, Georgia Tech

SAN DIEGO CHARGERS
1. Choice to Arizona
2. Choice exercised in 1998 Supplemental Draft
   Jamal Williams, DT, Oklahoma State
   Jermaine Fazande—60, RB, Oklahoma, from Atlanta
3. Steve Heiden—69, TE, South Dakota State
4. Jason Perry—104, DB, North Carolina State
5. Adrian Dingle—139, DE, Clemson, from Chicago
   Reggie Nelson—141, G, McNeese State
6. Tyrone Bell—178, DB, North Alabama
7. Choice to Pittsburgh

SAN FRANCISCO 49ERS
1. Reggie McGrew—24, DT, Florida, from Miami
   Choice to Detroit through Miami
2. Choice to Denver
3. Chike Okeafor—89, DE, Purdue
4. Anthony Parker—99, DB, Weber State, from Indianapolis
   Pierson Prioleau—110, DB, Virginia Tech, from Cleveland
   Choice to Cleveland
5. Terry Jackson—157, RB, Florida, from Miami
   Tyrone Hopson—161, T, Eastern Kentucky
6. Tai Streets—171, WR, Michigan, from Indianapolis
   Choice to Atlanta
7. Kory Minor—234, LB, Notre Dame

SEATTLE SEAHAWKS
1. Choice to New England
   Lamar King—22, DE, Saginaw Valley, from Dallas
2. Choice to Green Bay
3. Brock Huard—77, QB, Washington
   Karsten Bailey—82, WR, Auburn, from New England
4. Antonio Cochran—115, DE, Georgia
5. Floyd Wedderburn—140, T, Penn State, from Carolina through Dallas
   Charlie Rogers—152, WR, Georgia Tech
6. Steve Johnson—170, DB, Tennessee, from Cleveland
   Choice to Cleveland
7. Choice to New York Jets

TAMPA BAY BUCCANEERS
1. Anthony McFarland—15, DT, Louisiana State
2. Shaun King—50, QB, Tulane
3. Martin Gramatica—80, K, Kansas State
4. Dexter Jackson—113, DB, Florida State
5. John McLaughlin—150, DE, California
6. Choice to Minnesota through Baltimore
   Lamarr Glenn—195, RB, Florida State, from Jacksonville
7. Robert Hunt—226, G, Virginia
   Autry Denson—233, RB, Notre Dame, from Jacksonville
   *Darnell McDonald—240, WR, Kansas State

TENNESSEE TITANS
1. Jevon Kearse—16, DE, Florida
2. Choice to New England
   John Thornton—52, DT, West Virginia, from New England
3. Zach Piller—81, G, Florida
4. Brad Ware—114, DB, Auburn
   Donald Mitchell—117, DB, Southern Methodist, from New England
5. Kevin Daft—151, QB, California-Davis
6. Darran Hall—186, WR, Colorado State
7. Phil Glover—222, LB, Utah

WASHINGTON REDSKINS
1. Champ Bailey—7, DB, Georgia, from Chicago
   Choice to Minnesota
2. Jon Jansen—37, T, Michigan, from Chicago
   Choice to Oakland through Chicago
3. Choice to Pittsburgh through Minnesota
4. Choice to Chicago
   Nate Stimson—107, LB, Georgia Tech, from New Orleans
5. Choice to Chicago
   Derek Smith—165, T, Virginia Tech, from Denver
6. Jeff Hall—181, K, Tennessee
7. Tim Alexander—217, WR, Oregon State

DRAFT LIST

NUMBER OF PLAYERS DRAFTED—1999

BY POSITION:

Defensive Backs	45
Linebackers	33
Wide Receivers	32
Running Backs	26
Defensive Ends	26
Tackles	19
Defensive Tackles	18
Guards	18
Quarterbacks	13
Tight Ends	12
Centers	4
Punters	4
Kickers	3

BY COLLEGE:

Florida	8
Ohio State	8
Nebraska	7
Notre Dame	7
Clemson	6
Georgia	6
Kansas State	6
North Carolina	6
Tennessee	6
Texas A&M	6
Virginia	6
West Virginia	6
Southern California	5
Arizona	4
Arkansas	4
California	4
Colorado State	4
Florida State	4
Michigan	4
Mississippi State	4
Boston College	3
Brigham Young	3
Colorado	3
Georgia Tech	3
Louisiana State	3
Miami	3
Northwestern	3
Northwestern State, La.	3
Oklahoma	3
Oregon	3
Oregon State	3
Syracuse	3
Texas	3
UCLA	3
Wisconsin	3
Arizona State	2
Auburn	2
Baylor	2
Central Florida	2
East Carolina	2
Eastern Kentucky	2
Iowa	2
Kentucky	2
Maryland	2
McNeese State	2
Miami, Ohio	2
Michigan State	2
North Alabama	2
North Carolina State	2
Northeast Louisiana	2
Penn State	2
Purdue	2
Richmond	2
San Jose State	2
Southern Methodist	2
Texas Tech	2
Virginia Tech	2
Washington	2
Weber State	2
Air Force	1
Alabama	1
Alabama-Birmingham	1
Alcorn State	1
Arkansas-Pine Bluff	1
Brown	1
Butte J.C.	1
California-Davis	1
Cincinnati	1
Duke	1
Eastern Illinois	1
Eastern Michigan	1
Fort Valley State	1
Fresno State	1
Hampton	1
Illinois	1
James Madison	1
Jamestown	1
Kent State	1
Kentucky State	1
Langston	1
Louisiana Tech	1
Massachusetts	1
Memphis	1
Middle Tennessee State	1
Missouri	1
Montana	1
Nebraska-Omaha	1
Nevada-Las Vegas	1
New Hampshire	1
North Dakota	1
Northern Colorado	1
Northern Iowa	1
Northwest Missouri State	1
Pennsylvania	1
Saginaw Valley	1
South Dakota State	1
Southern	1
Southwestern Louisiana	1
Tarleton State	1
Troy State	1
Tulane	1
Utah	1
Utah State	1
Vanderbilt	1
Wake Forest	1
Washington State	1
Western Illinois	1
Wisconsin-Stevens Point	1

BY CONFERENCE:

SEC	37
Big 12	33
ACC	31
Big 10	27
Pac 10	27
Big East	17
Independent	17
WAC	15
Southland	6
Atlantic 10	5
Conference USA	5
MAC	4
North Central Intercollegiate Athletic	4
Ohio Valley	4
Big Sky	3
SWAC	3
Gateway	2
Gulf South	2
Ivy	2
Southern Intercollegiate Athletic	2
Big West	1
Lone Star	1
MEAC	1
Mid-America Intercollegiate Athletic Assoc.	1
Midwest Intercollegiate Football	1
North Dakota College Athletic	1
Wisconsin Intercollegiate Athletic	1

UNDERCLASSMEN AND THE DRAFT

Year	Entered	Drafted	In Top 10
1989	25	12	3
1990	38	18	5
1991	33	22	2
1992	48	25	5
1993	46	24	5
1994	42	26	6
1995	42	22	2
1996	47	21	4
1997	44	27	7
1998	41	20	3
1999	35	27	5

The following procedures will be used to break standings ties for postseason playoffs and to determine regular-season schedules. NOTE: Tie games count as one-half win and one-half loss for both clubs.

TO BREAK A TIE WITHIN A DIVISION

If, at the end of the regular season, two or more clubs in the same division finish with identical won-lost-tied percentages, the following steps will be taken until a champion is determined.

TWO CLUBS

1. Head-to-head (best won-lost-tied percentage in games between the clubs).
2. Best won-lost-tied percentage in games played within the division.
3. Best won-lost-tied percentage in games played within the conference.
4. Best won-lost-tied percentage in common games, if applicable.
5. Best net points in division games.
6. Best net points in all games.
7. Strength of schedule.
8. Best net touchdowns in all games.
9. Coin toss.

THREE OR MORE CLUBS

(Note: If two clubs remain tied after third or other clubs are eliminated during any step, tie breaker reverts to step 1 of the two-club format).

1. Head-to-head (best won-lost-tied percentage in games among the clubs).
2. Best won-lost-tied percentage in games played within the division.
3. Best won-lost-tied percentage in games played within the conference.
4. Best won-lost-tied percentage in common games.
5. Best net points in division games.
6. Best net points in all games.
7. Strength of schedule.
8. Best net touchdowns in all games.
9. Coin toss.

TO BREAK A TIE FOR THE WILD-CARD TEAM

If it is necessary to break ties to determine the three Wild-Card clubs from each conference, the following steps will be taken.

1. If the tied clubs are from the same division, apply division tie breaker.
2. If the tied clubs are from different divisions, apply the following steps.

TWO CLUBS

1. Head-to-head, if applicable.
2. Best won-lost-tied percentage in games played within the conference.
3. Best won-lost-tied percentage in common games, minimum of four.
4. Best average net points in conference games.
5. Best net points in all games.
6. Strength of schedule.
7 Best net touchdowns in all games.
8. Coin toss.

THREE OR MORE CLUBS

(Note: If two clubs remain tied after third or other clubs are eliminated, tie breaker reverts to step 1 of applicable two-club format.)

1. Apply division tie breaker to eliminate all but the highest ranked club in each division prior to proceeding to step 2. The original seeding within a division upon application of the division tie breaker remains the same for all subsequent applications of the procedure that are necessary to identify the three Wild-Card participants.
2. Head-to-head sweep. (Applicable only if one club has defeated each of the others or if one club has lost to each of the others.)
3. Best won-lost-tied percentage in games played within the conference.
4. Best won-lost-tied percentage in common games, minimum of four.
5. Best average net points in conference games.
6. Best net points in all games.
7. Strength of schedule.
8. Best net touchdowns in all games.
9. Coin toss.

When the first Wild-Card team has been identified, the procedure is repeated to name the second Wild-Card, i.e., eliminate all but the highest-ranked club in each division prior to proceeding to step 2, and repeated a third time, if necessary, to identify the third Wild Card. In situations where three or more teams from the same division are involved in the procedure, the original seeding of the teams remains the same for subsequent applications of the tie breaker if the top-ranked team in that division qualifies for a Wild-Card berth.

OTHER TIE-BREAKING PROCEDURES

1. Only one club advances to the playoffs in any tie-breaking step. Remaining tied clubs revert to the first step of the applicable division or Wild-Card tie breakers. As an example, if two clubs remain tied in any tie-breaker step after all other clubs have been eliminated, the procedure reverts to step one of the two-club format to determine the winner. When one club wins the tie breaker, all other clubs revert to step 1 of the applicable two-club or three-club format.
2. In comparing division and conference records or records against common opponents among tied teams, the best won-lost-tied percentage is the deciding factor since teams may have played an unequal number of games.
3. To determine home-field priority among division titlists, apply Wild-Card tie breakers.
4. To determine home-field priority for Wild-Card qualifiers, apply division tie breakers (if teams are from the same division) or Wild-Card tie breakers (if teams are from different divisions).

TIE-BREAKING PROCEDURE FOR SELECTION MEETING

If two or more clubs are tied in the selection order, the strength-of-schedule tie breaker is applied, subject to the following exceptions for playoff clubs:

1. The Super Bowl winner is last and the Super Bowl loser next-to-last.
2. Any non-Super Bowl playoff club involved in a tie shall be assigned priority within its segment below that of non-playoff clubs and in the order that the playoff clubs exited from the playoffs. Thus, within a tied segment a playoff club that loses in the Wild-Card game will have priority over a playoff club that loses in the Divisional playoff game, which in turn will have priority over a club that loses in the Conference Championship game. If two tied clubs exited the playoffs in the same round, the tie is broken by strength of schedule.

If any ties cannot be broken by strength of schedule, the divisional or conference tie breakers, whichever are applicable, are applied. Any ties that still exist are broken by a coin flip.

INSTANT REPLAY

For the 1999 season, the NFL will employ a system of Referee Replay Review to aid officiating.

Prior to the two-minute warning of each half, a Coaches' Challenge System will be in effect. After the two-minute warning, and throughout any overtime period, a Referee Review will be initiated by a Replay Assistant from a Replay Booth.

The following procedures will be used:

REVIEWS BY REFEREE: All Replay Reviews will be conducted by the Referee on a field-level monitor after consultation with the other covering official(s), prior to review. A decision will be reversed only when the Referee has *indisputable visual evidence* available to him that warrants the change.

COACHES' CHALLENGE: In each game, a team will be permitted a maximum of two challenges that will initiate Referee Replay reviews. Each challenge will require the use of a team timeout. If a challenge is upheld, the timeout will be restored to the challenging team. A challenge will never be restored. No challenges will be recognized from a team that has exhausted its timeouts.

REPLAY ASSISTANT'S REQUEST FOR REVIEW: After the two-minute warning of each half, and throughout any overtime period, any review will be initiated by a Replay Assistant. There is no limit to the number of reviews that may be initiated by the Replay Assistant. His ability to initiate a review will be unrelated to the number of timeouts that either team has remaining, and no timeout will be charged for any review initiated by the Replay Assistant.

TIME LIMIT: Each review will be a maximum of 90 seconds in length, timed from when the Referee begins his review of the replay at the field-level monitor.

REVIEWABLE PLAYS: The Replay System will cover the following play situations only:

A) PLAYS GOVERNED BY SIDELINE, GOAL LINE, END ZONE, AND END LINE:
1. Scoring plays, including a runner breaking the plane of the goal line.
2. Pass complete/incomplete/intercepted at sideline, goal line, end zone, and end line.
3. Runner/receiver in or out of bounds.
4. Recovery of loose ball in or out of bounds.

B) PASSING PLAYS:
1. Pass ruled complete/incomplete/intercepted in the field of play.
2. Touching of a forward pass by an ineligible receiver.
3. Touching of a forward pass by a defensive player.
4. Quarterback (Passer) forward pass or fumble.
5. Illegal forward pass beyond line of scrimmage.
6. Illegal forward pass after change of possession.
7. Forward or backward pass thrown from behind line of scrimmage.

C) OTHER DETECTABLE INFRACTIONS:
1. Runner ruled not down by defensive contact.
2. Forward progress with respect to first down.
3. Touching of a kick.
4. Number of players on the field.

INSTANT REPLAY HISTORY

From 1986-1991, a limited system of Instant Replay was used on a year-by-year basis. Replay was also experimented with during the 1996 and 1998 preseasons.

Following are the results of both systems:

REGULAR SEASON, 1986-1991

Year	Games	Reversals	Plays Closely Reviewed
1986	224	38	374
1987	210	57	490
1988	224	53	537
1989	224	65	492
1990	224	73	504
1991	224	90	570
TOTAL	1,330	376	2,967

PRESEASON, 1996, 1998

Year	Games	Reversals	Challenges
1996	10	3	13
1998	10	3	10
TOTAL	20	6	23

VOTING SUMMARY, 1986-1992, 1997-99

Year	Yes	No	Abstain	Votes Needed
1986	23	4	1	21 of 28
1987	21	7	0	21 of 28
1988	23	5	0	21 of 28
1989	24	4	0	21 of 28
1990	21	7	0	21 of 28
1991	21	7	0	21 of 28
1992	17	11	0	21 of 28
1997	20	10	0	23 of 30
1998	21	9	0	23 of 30
1999	28	3	0	23 of 31

TEAMS VOTING AGAINST INSTANT REPLAY, 1997-1999

1997	1998	1999
Arizona	Arizona	Arizona
Buffalo	Buffalo	Cincinnati
Chicago	Chicago	New York Jets
Cincinnati	Cincinnati	
Dallas	Kansas City	
Kansas City	New York Giants	
New York Giants	Oakland	
New York Jets	Tampa Bay	
Oakland	San Diego	
Tampa Bay		

The AFC

BALTIMORE RAVENS

American Football Conference
Central Division
Team Colors: Black, Purple, and Metallic Gold
11001 Owings Mills Boulevard
Owings Mills, Maryland 21117
Telephone: (410) 654-6200

CLUB OFFICIALS

Owner: Arthur B. Modell
President: David Modell
Vice President/Public Relations: Kevin Byrne
Vice President/Sales and Marketing: David Cope
Vice President/Player Personnel: Ozzie Newsome
Vice President/Administration: Pat Moriarty
Treasurer: Luis Perez
Director of Ticket Operations: Roy Sommerhof
Director of Operations/Information: Bob Eller
Director of Publications/Assistant Director of Public Relations: Francine Lubera
Director of Player Development: Earnest Byner
Director of Broadcasting: Lisa Bercu
Director of Pro Personnel: James Harris
Director of College Scouting: Phil Savage
Assistant Director of Pro Personnel and College Scouting: John Wooten
Scouts: Eric DeCosta, George Kokinis, Ron Marciniak, T.J. McCreight, Terry McDonough, Vince Newsome, Art Perkins, Ellis Rainsberger
Head Trainer: Bill Tessendorf
Facilities Manager: Chuck Cusick
Equipment Manager: Ed Carroll
Video Director: Jon Dube
Stadium: PSINet Stadium • **Capacity:** 69,354
1101 Russell Street
Baltimore, Maryland 21230
Playing Surface: SportGrass
Training Camp: Western Maryland College
2 College Hill
Westminster, Maryland 21157

RECORD HOLDERS

INDIVIDUAL RECORDS—CAREER

Category	Name	Performance
Rushing (Yds.)	Byron (Bam) Morris, 1996-97	1,511
Passing (Yds.)	Vinny Testaverde, 1996-97	7,148
Passing (TDs)	Vinny Testaverde, 1996-97	51
Receiving (No.)	Michael Jackson, 1996-98	183
Receiving (Yds.)	Michael Jackson, 1996-98	2,596
Interceptions	Antonio Langham, 1996-97	8
Punting (Avg.)	Kyle Richardson, 1998	43.9
Punt Return (Avg.)	Jermaine Lewis, 1996-98	12.3
Kickoff Return (Avg.)	Corey Harris, 1998	27.6
Field Goals	Matt Stover, 1996-98	66
Touchdowns (Tot.)	Michael Jackson, 1996-98	18
	Derrick Alexander, 1996-97	18
Points	Matt Stover, 1996-98	288

INDIVIDUAL RECORDS—SINGLE SEASON

Category	Name	Performance
Rushing (Yds.)	Priest Holmes, 1998	1,008
Passing (Yds.)	Vinny Testaverde, 1996	4,177
Passing (TDs)	Vinny Testaverde, 1996	33
Receiving (No.)	Michael Jackson, 1996	76
Receiving (Yds.)	Michael Jackson, 1996	1,201
Interceptions	Rod Woodson, 1998	6
Punting (Avg.)	Kyle Richardson, 1998	43.9
Punt Return (Avg.)	Jermaine Lewis, 1997	15.6
Kickoff Return (Avg.)	Corey Harris, 1998	27.6
Field Goals	Matt Stover, 1997	26
Touchdowns (Tot.)	Michael Jackson, 1996	14
Points	Matt Stover, 1997	110

INDIVIDUAL RECORDS—SINGLE GAME

Category	Name	Performance
Rushing (Yds.)	Priest Holmes, 11-22-98	227
Passing (Yds.)	Vinny Testaverde, 10-27-96	429
Passing (TDs)	Vinny Testaverde, 10-20-96	4
Receiving (No.)	Priest Holmes, 10-11-98	13
Receiving (Yds.)	Derrick Alexander, 12-1-96	198
Interceptions	Many times	2
	Last time by Rod Woodson, 9-13-98	
Field Goals	Matt Stover, 9-21-97	5
Touchdowns (Tot.)	Michael Jackson, 12-22-96	3
	Jermaine Lewis, 12-7-97	3
Points	Michael Jackson, 12-22-96	18
	Matt Stover, 9-21-97	18
	Jermaine Lewis, 12-7-97	18

1999 SCHEDULE

PRESEASON

Aug. 12	at Philadelphia	8:00
Aug. 21	at Atlanta	7:30
Aug. 28	**Carolina**	7:30
Sept. 3	**New York Giants**	12:00

REGULAR SEASON

Sept. 12	at St. Louis	12:00
Sept. 19	**Pittsburgh**	1:00
Sept. 26	**Cleveland**	1:00
Oct. 3	at Atlanta	1:00
Oct. 10	at Tennessee	3:15
Oct. 17	Open Date	
Oct. 21	**Kansas City** (Thurs.)	8:20
Oct. 31	**Buffalo**	1:00
Nov. 7	at Cleveland	1:00
Nov. 14	at Jacksonville	4:05
Nov. 21	at Cincinnati	4:05
Nov. 28	**Jacksonville**	1:00
Dec. 5	**Tennessee**	1:00
Dec. 12	at Pittsburgh	1:00
Dec. 19	**New Orleans**	1:00
Dec. 26	**Cincinnati**	1:00
Jan. 2	at New England	1:00

COACHING HISTORY

(16-31-1)

1996-98 Ted Marchibroda 16-31-1

PSINet STADIUM

N

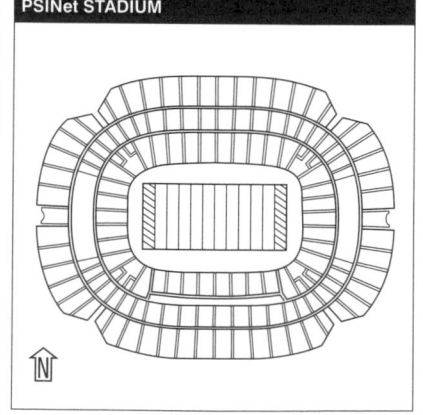

1998 TEAM RECORD

PRESEASON (4-0)

Date	Result		Opponent
8/8	W	19-14	Chicago
8/15	W	33-0	at New York Jets
8/24	W	23-6	Philadelphia
8/28	W	14-6	at New York Giants

REGULAR SEASON (6-10)

Date	Result		Opponent	Att.
9/6	L	13-20	Pittsburgh	68,847
9/13	W	24-10	at New York Jets	70,063
9/20	L	10-24	at Jacksonville	67,069
9/27	W	31-24	Cincinnati	68,154
10/11	L	8-12	Tennessee	68,561
10/18	L	6-16	at Pittsburgh	58,620
10/25	L	10-28	at Green Bay	59,860
11/1	L	19-45	Jacksonville	68,915
11/8	W	13-10	Oakland	69,037
11/15	L	13-14	at San Diego	54,388
11/22	W	20-13	at Cincinnati	52,571
11/29	W	38-31	Indianapolis	68,898
12/6	L	14-16	at Tennessee	31,124
12/13	L	28-38	Minnesota	69,074
12/20	L	3-24	at Chicago	40,853
12/27	W	19-10	Detroit	68,045

SCORE BY PERIODS

Ravens	79	63	41	86	—	269
Opponents	96	104	85	50	—	335

ATTENDANCE

Home 549,531 Away 434,548 Total 984,079
Single-game home record, 69,074 (12/13/98)
Single-season home record, 549,531 (1998)

1998 TEAM STATISTICS

	Ravens	Opp.
Total First Downs	243	298
Rushing	86	90
Passing	140	180
Penalty	17	28
Third Down: Made/Att	64/207	93/237
Third Down Pct.	30.9	39.2
Fourth Down: Made/Att	6/15	4/11
Fourth Down Pct.	40.0	36.4
Total Net Yards	4,498	5,297
Avg. Per Game	281.1	331.1
Total Plays	926	1,050
Avg. Per Play	4.9	5.0
Net Yards Rushing	1,629	1,705
Avg. Per Game	101.8	106.6
Total Rushes	408	472
Net Yards Passing	2,869	3,592
Avg. Per Game	179.3	224.5
Sacked/Yards Lost	41/283	39/286
Gross Yards	3,152	3,878
Att./Completions	477/272	539/316
Completion Pct.	57.0	58.6
Had Intercepted	15	17
Punts/Avg.	92/42.9	86/42.5
Net Punting Avg.	92/38.3	86/33.6
Penalties/Yards Lost	113/909	122/1,013
Fumbles/Ball Lost	31/15	17/6
Touchdowns	29	37
Rushing	7	12
Passing	16	20
Returns	6	5
Avg. Time of Possession	28:04	31:56

1998 INDIVIDUAL STATISTICS

Passing	Att.	Comp.	Yds.	Pct.	TD	Int.	Tkld.	Rate
Harbaugh	293	164	1,839	56.0	12	11	23/145	72.9
Zeier	181	107	1,312	59.1	4	3	18/138	82.0
W. Richardson	2	1	1	50.0	0	0	0/0	56.3
Holmes	1	0	0	0.0	0	1	0/0	0.0
Ravens	477	272	3,152	57.0	16	15	41/283	75.2
Opponents	539	316	3,878	58.6	20	17	39/286	80.1

SCORING	TD R	TD P	TD Rt	PAT	FG	Saf	PTS
Stover	0	0	0	24/24	21/28	0	87
J. Lewis	0	6	2	0/0	0/0	0	48
Holmes	7	0	0	0/0	0/0	0	42
Turner	0	5	0	0/0	0/0	0	34
Johnson	0	1	1	0/0	0/0	0	12
Potts	0	2	0	0/0	0/0	0	12
Woodson	0	0	2	0/0	0/0	0	12
Green	0	1	0	0/0	0/0	0	6
Harris	0	0	1	0/0	0/0	0	6
Roe	0	1	0	0/0	0/0	0	6
Burnett	0	0	0	0/0	0/0	1	2
Ravens	7	16	6	24/24	21/28	2	269
Opponents	12	20	5	35/35	26/30	0	335

2-Point conversions: Turner 2.
Team 2-5, Opponents 0-2.

RUSHING	Att.	Yds.	Avg.	LG	TD
Holmes	233	1,008	4.3	56	7
Rhett	44	180	4.1	46	0
Harbaugh	40	172	4.3	15	0
Potts	36	115	3.2	33	0
Graham	35	109	3.1	12	0
J. Lewis	5	20	4.0	9	0
Zeier	11	17	1.5	7	0
Cotton	2	8	4.0	7	0
K. Richardson	1	0	0.0	0	0
W. Richardson	1	0	0.0	0	0
Ravens	408	1,629	4.0	56	7
Opponents	472	1,705	3.6	68t	12

RECEIVING	No.	Yds.	Avg.	LG	TD
Holmes	43	260	6.0	25	0
J. Lewis	41	784	19.1	73t	6
M. Jackson	38	477	12.6	53	0
Green	34	422	12.4	56	1
Turner	32	512	16.0	66t	5
Potts	30	168	5.6	18	2
Kinchen	13	110	8.5	24	0
Johnson	12	159	13.3	35	1
Rhett	11	65	5.9	16	0
Roe	8	115	14.4	27	1
Graham	5	41	8.2	14	0
Yarborough	4	39	9.8	18	0
Atkins	1	0	0.0	0	0
Ravens	272	3,152	11.6	73t	16
Opponents	316	3,878	12.3	78t	20

INTERCEPTIONS	No.	Yds.	Avg.	LG	TD
Woodson	6	108	18.0	60t	2
Starks	5	3	0.6	2	0
Staten	3	25	8.3	14	0
R. Lewis	2	25	12.5	26	0
Jenkins	1	0	0.0	0	0
Ravens	17	161	9.5	60t	2
Opponents	15	148	9.9	43	0

PUNTING	No.	Yds.	Avg.	In 20	LG
K. Richardson	90	3,948	43.9	25	67
Ravens	92	3,948	42.9	25	67
Opponents	86	3,653	42.5	21	69

PUNT RETURNS	No.	FC	Yds.	Avg.	LG	TD
J. Lewis	32	10	405	12.7	87t	2
Roe	9	2	87	9.7	19	0
Thompson	1	0	43	43.0	43	0
Johnson	1	0	6	6.0	6	0
Ravens	43	12	541	12.6	87t	2
Opponents	40	24	284	7.1	71t	1

KICKOFF RETURNS	No.	Yds.	Avg.	LG	TD
Harris	35	965	27.6	95t	1
Johnson	16	399	24.9	97t	1
J. Lewis	6	145	24.2	37	0
Graham	3	52	17.3	22	0
Roe	2	40	20.0	27	0
Kinchen	2	33	16.5	21	0
Cotton	2	33	16.5	18	0
Holmes	2	30	15.0	19	0
Potts	1	3	3.0	3	0
Ravens	69	1,700	24.6	97t	2
Opponents	57	1,168	20.5	97t	2

FIELD GOALS	1-19	20-29	30-39	40-49	50+
Stover	0/0	6/6	5/5	10/17	0/0
Ravens	0/0	6/6	5/5	10/17	0/0
Opponents	0/0	8/9	6/6	11/12	1/3

SACKS	No.
McCrary	14.5
Boulware	8.5
J. Jones	5.5
R. Lewis	3.0
Burnett	2.5
Brady	1.0
Harris	1.0
Sharper	1.0
Staten	1.0
Washington	1.0
Ravens	39.0
Opponents	41.0

1999 DRAFT CHOICES

Round	Name	Pos.	College
1	Chris McAlister	DB	Arizona
4	Brandon Stokley	WR	Southwestern Louisiana
	Edwin Mulitalo	G	Arizona
7	Anthony Poindexter	DB	Virginia

BALTIMORE RAVENS

1999 VETERAN ROSTER

No.	Name	Pos.	Ht.	Wt.	Birthdate	NFL Exp.	College	Hometown	How Acq.	'98 Games/ Starts
74	Atkins, James	G-T	6-6	306	1/28/70	6	Southwestern Louisiana	Amite, La.	FA-'98	9/6
12	t- Banks, Tony	QB	6-4	215	4/5/73	4	Michigan State	San Diego, Calif.	T(StL)-'99	14/14*
2	Bentley, Scott	K	6-0	203	4/10/74	2	Florida State	Aurora, Colo.	W(TB)-'99	0*
69	Blackshear, Jeff	G-T	6-6	323	3/29/69	7	Northeast Louisiana	Fort Pierce, Fla.	T(Sea)-'96	16/16
58	Boulware, Peter	LB	6-4	255	12/18/74	3	Florida State	Columbia, S.C.	D1-'97	16/16
31	Broussard, Steve	RB	5-7	201	2/22/67	10	Washington State	Los Angeles, Calif.	FA-'99	15/0*
51	Brown, Cornell	LB	6-0	240	3/15/75	3	Virginia Tech	Lynchburg, Va.	D6-'97	16/1
90	Burnett, Rob	DE	6-4	280	8/27/67	10	Syracuse	Selden, N.Y.	D5-'90	16/16
92	Chase, Martin	DT	6-2	295	12/19/74	2	Oklahoma	Lawton, Okla.	D5a-'98	0*
23	Cotton, Kenyon	RB	6-0	255	2/23/74	3	Southwestern Louisiana	Minden, La.	FA-'97	12/0
91	Dalton, Lional	DT	6-1	320	2/21/75	2	Eastern Michigan	Detroit, Mich.	FA-'98	2/0
86	DeLong, Greg	TE	6-4	250	4/3/73	5	North Carolina	Orefield, Pa.	UFA(Minn)-'99	15/6*
29	Evans, Chuck	RB	6-1	245	4/16/67	7	Clark	Augusta, Ga.	UFA(Minn)-'99	16/8*
62	Flynn, Mike	G-T	6-3	295	6/15/74	2	Maine	Springfield, Mass.	FA-'97	3/0
71	Folau, Spencer	T	6-5	300	4/5/73	3	Idaho	Redwood City, Calif.	FA-'96	3/3
34	Graham, Jay	RB	5-11	220	7/14/75	3	Tennessee	Concord, N.C.	D3-'97	5/1
67	Harrison, Chris	GT	6-3	290	2/25/72	3	Virginia	Washington, D.C.	FA-'99	0*
20	Herring, Kim	S	5-11	210	9/10/75	3	Penn State	Solon, Ohio	D2b-'97	7/7
33	Holmes, Priest	RB	5-'9	205	10/7/73	3	Texas	San Antonio, Tex.	FA-'97	16/13
87	Ismail, Qadry	WR	6-0	195	11/8/70	7	Syracuse	Wilkes-Barre, Pa.	FA-'99	10/1*
25	† Jenkins, De Ron	CB	5-11	190	11/14/73	4	Tennessee	St. Louis, Mo.	D2-'96	16/7
85	Johnson, Patrick	WR	5-10	180	8/10/76	2	Oregon	Redlands, Calif.	D2-'98	13/0
57	Kopp, Jeff	LB	6-3	244	7/8/71	5	Southern California	Danville, Calif.	FA-'98	7/0
84	Lewis, Jermaine	WR	5-7	172	10/16/74	4	Maryland	Lanham, Md.	D5-'96	13/13
52	Lewis, Ray	LB	6-1	240	5/15/75	4	Miami	Lakeland, Fla.	D1b-'96	14/14
61	t- Lindsay, Everett	G-T	6-4	302	9/18/70	6	Mississippi	Raleigh, N.C.	T(Minn)-'99	16/3*
54	McCloud, Tyrus	LB	6-1	250	11/23/74	3	Louisville	Ft. Lauderdale, Fla.	D4b-'97	7/2
99	McCrary, Michael	DE	6-4	270	7/7/70	7	Wake Forest	Falls Church, Va.	UFA(Sea)-'97	16/16
60	Mitchell, Jeff	C	6-4	300	1/29/74	3	Florida	Clearwater, Fla.	D5-'97	11/10
19	t- Mitchell, Scott	QB	6-6	230	1/2/68	10	Utah	Springville, Utah	T(Det)-'99	2/2*
27	Moore, Stevon	S	5-11	210	2/9/67	11	Mississippi	Wiggins, Miss.	PB(Mia)-'92	16/16
89	Ofodile, A.J.	TE	6-6	260	10/9/73	3	Missouri	Detroit, Mich.	FA-'96	5/0
75	Ogden, Jonathan	G-T	6-8	318	7/31/74	4	UCLA	Washington, D.C.	D1a-'96	13/13
53	Peters, Tyrell	LB	6-0	230	8/4/74	3	Oklahoma	Norman, Okla.	FA-'97	10/0
81	Pierce, Aaron	TE	6-5	250	9/8/69	7	Washington	Seattle, Wash.	FA-'99	0*
80	t- Purnell, Lovett	TE	6-3	245	4/7/72	4	West Virginia	Seaford, Del.	T(NE)-'99	16/5*
32	Rhett, Errict	RB	5-11	210	12/11/70	6	Florida	Hollywood, Fla.	T(TB)-'98	13/2
5	Richardson, Kyle	P	6-2	190	3/2/73	2	Arkansas State	Farmington, Mo.	FA-'98	16/0
14	Richardson, Wally	QB	6-4	225	2/11/74	3	Penn State	Sumter, S.C.	D7b-'97	1/0
30	Robertson, Rob	RB	5-11	223	11/6/75	2	Northwestern State, La.	Baton Rouge, La.	FA-'98	0*
76	Robinson, Kareem	DE	6-4	250	7/1/76	2	Tennessee-Chattanooga	Nashville, Tenn.	FA-'98	0*
83	Roe, James	WR	6-1	187	8/23/73	4	Norfolk State	Richmond, Va.	D6b-'96	10/3
77	Sapp, Bob	G-T	6-4	303	9/22/73	3	Washington	Colorado Springs, Colo.	FA-'99	0*
55	Sharper, Jamie	LB	6-3	240	11/23/74	3	Virginia	Richmond, Va.	D2a-'97	16/16
98	Siragusa, Tony	DT	6-3	320	5/14/67	10	Pittsburgh	Kenilworth, N.J.	UFA(Ind)-'97	15/15
96	Smith, Fernando	DE	6-6	277	8/2/71	6	Jackson State	Flint, Mich.	FA-'99	15/0*
22	Starks, Duane	CB	5-10	170	5/23/74	2	Miami	Miami Beach, Fla.	D1-'98	16/8
41	Staten, Ralph	S	6-3	205	12/3/74	3	Alabama	Wilmer, Ala.	D7c-'97	15/3
3	Stover, Matt	K	5-11	178	1/27/68	10	Louisiana Tech	Dallas, Tex.	PB(NYG)-'91	16/0
70	Swayne, Harry	T	6-5	295	2/2/65	13	Rutgers	Philadelphia, Pa.	UFA(Den)-'99	16/16*
37	Thompson, Bennie	S	6-0	214	2/10/63	10	Grambling State	New Orleans, La.	UFA(NO)-'94	16/0
38	Trapp, James	CB	6-0	195	12/28/69	7	Clemson	Lawton, Okla.	FA-'99	16/0*
88	Turner, Floyd	WR	5-11	199	5/29/66	10	Northwestern State, La.	Metairie, La	FA-'98	16/3
44	Vinson, Tony	RB	6-1	229	3/13/71	3	Towson	Newport News, Va.	FA-'97	0*
82	Wainright, Frank	TE	6-3	250	10/10/67	9	Northern Colorado	Arvada, Colo.	UFA(Mia)-'99	16/1*
93	Washington, Keith	DE	6-4	270	12/18/72	5	Nevada-Las Vegas	Dallas, Tex.	FA-'97	16/0
79	Webster, Larry	DE-DT	6-5	288	1/18/69	7	Maryland	Elkton, Md.	FA-'95	15/1
21	Williams, John	CB-S	5-7	180	7/26/74	2	Southern	Hammond, La.	FA-'97	16/0
72	Williams, Sammy	T	6-5	318	12/14/74	2	Oklahoma	Harvey, Ill.	D6b-'98	0*
26	Woodson, Rod	CB	6-0	200	3/10/65	13	Purdue	Fort Wayne, Ind.	FA-'98	16/16

* Banks played 14 games with St. Louis in '98; Bentley last active with Denver in '97; Broussard played 15 games with Seattle; Chase, Robertson, Robinson, Vinson, and S. Williams missed '98 season because of injury; DeLong played 15 games with Minnesota; Evans and Lindsay played 16 games with Minnesota; Harrison inactive for 2 games with Detroit; Ismail played 10 games with New Orleans; Mitchell played 2 games with Detroit; Pierce last active with N.Y. Giants in '97; Purnell played 16 games with New England; Sapp inactive for 10 games with Minnesota; Smith played 15 games with Jacksonville; Swayne played 16 games with Denver; Trapp played 16 games with Oakland; Wainright played 16 games with Miami.

† Restricted free agent; subject to developments.

t- Ravens traded for Banks (St. Louis), Lindsay (Minnesota), Mitchell (Detroit), Purnell (New England).

Traded—QB Jim Harbaugh (14 games in '98) to San Diego, QB Eric Zeier (10) to Tampa Bay.

Players lost through free agency (8): T Orlando Brown (Clev; 13 games in '98), DE Mike Frederick (NYJ; 10), TE Eric Green (NYJ; 12), DT James Jones (Det; 16), G Sale Isaia (Ind; 0), TE Brian Kinchen (Car; 16), RB Roosevelt Potts (Mia; 16), G Wally Williams (NO; 13).

Also played with Ravens in '98—G Ben Cavil (16 games), DE Paul Frase (11), S Corey Harris (16), WR Michael Jackson (13), TE Harper LeBel (5), LB Jerry Olsavsky (9), WR Ryan Yarborough (6).

COACHING STAFF

Head Coach,
Brian Billick

Pro Career: Brian Billick became the second head coach in Baltimore Ravens' history on January 19, 1999. Billick, the highly successful offensive coordinator for the Minnesota Vikings the last five years (1994-98), directed a Vikings' attack that set a variety of NFL and club records. He was the architect of a Minnesota offense that broke the NFL record for most points scored in a season (556), surpassing the old mark (541) set by the 1983 Washington Redskins. The 1998 Vikings ranked second in the NFL with a team-record 6,264 total yards and first in the league with 4,328 passing yards. Billick joined the Vikings in 1992 as tight ends coach. Named offensive coordinator three games into the 1993 season, the Vikings' production increased dramatically—from 264.8 yards per game throughout the first six weeks of the season to a 323.3-yard average over the final 10 games. In Billick's first full season as offensive coordinator in 1994, the Vikings finished second in the NFL in passing yards (4,324), and won the NFC Central. In 1995, the Vikings failed to qualify for the postseason, but the offense scored a club-record 412 points and gained 5,938 yards. The 1996 Minnesota team qualified for a wild-card berth in the playoffs with a 9-7 mark. The Vikings once again made the playoffs in 1997, qualifying as a wild card with a 9-7 record.

Background: Prior to his appointment with the Vikings, Billick was a Stanford assistant from 1989-1991 under Vikings' head coach Dennis Green. Billick spent three seasons as offensive coordinator at Utah State (1986-88). Billick coached receivers, tight ends, and quarterbacks at San Diego State from 1981-85 and held a dual responsibility as recruiting coordinator. He began his coaching career as an assistant at Redlands in 1977 and spent the following year (1978) as a graduate assistant at Brigham Young where he worked with tight ends and the offensive line. Following that season, Billick was assistant director of public relations for the San Francisco 49ers in 1979-1980.

Personal: Born February 28, 1954 in Fairborne, Ohio, Billick earned All-Western Athletic Conference honors and was a honorable mention All-America in 1976 as a tight end at Brigham Young. Played linebacker at Air Force as a freshman before transferring to Brigham Young. In 1977, Billick was drafted by the 49ers in the eleventh round, was released, and had a brief stint with the Dallas Cowboys, but did not play. He and his wife Kim have two daughters—Aubree and Keegan.

ASSISTANT COACHES

Matt Cavanaugh, offensive coordinator; born October 27, 1956, Youngstown, Ohio, lives in Owings Mills, Md. Quarterback Pittsburgh 1974-77. Pro quarterback New England Patriots 1978-1982, San Francisco 49ers 1983-85, Philadelphia Eagles 1986-89, New York Giants 1990-91. College coach: Pittsburgh 1993. Pro coach: Arizona Cardinals 1994-95, San Francisco 49ers 1996, Chicago Bears 1997-98, joined Ravens in 1999.

Jim Colletto, offensive line; born October 2, 1944, San Francisco, lives in Owings Mills, Md. Fullback-linebacker UCLA 1964-67. No pro playing experience. College coach: UCLA 1967-68, Brown 1969, Xavier 1970-71, Pacific 1972-74, Cal State-Fullerton 1975-79 (head coach), UCLA 1980-1981, Purdue 1982-84, Arizona State 1985-87, Ohio State 1988-1990, Purdue 1991-96 (head coach), Notre Dame 1997-98. Pro coach: Joined Ravens in 1999.

Jack Del Rio, Jr., linebackers; born April 4, 1963, Castro Valley, Calif., lives in Reisterstown, Md. Linebacker Southern California 1981-84. Pro linebacker New Orleans Saints 1985-86, Kansas City Chiefs 1987-88, Dallas Cowboys 1989-1991, Minnesota Vikings 1992-95. Pro coach: New Orleans Saints 1997-98, joined Ravens in 1999.

Jeff Friday, strength and conditioning; born October 11, 1966, Milwaukee, Wis., lives in Owings Mills, Md. Attended Wisconsin-Milwaukee. No college or pro playing experience. College coach: Illinois State 1991-92, Northwestern 1992-95. Pro coach: Minnesota Vikings 1996-98, joined Ravens in 1999.

Wade Harman, tight ends-asst. offensive line; born October 1, 1963, Corydon, Iowa, lives in Woodensburg, Md. Linebacker Drake 1985, Utah State 1986. No pro playing experience. College coach: Utah State 1987-1991, Pacific 1992-95, Morningside 1996. Pro coach: Minnesota Vikings 1997-98, joined Ravens in 1999.

Donnie Henderson, asst. defensive backs; born May 17, 1957, Baltimore, lives in Owings Mills, Md. Defensive back Utah State 1978-79. No pro playing experience. College coach: Utah State 1983-88, Idaho 1989-1990, California 1992-97, Houston 1998. Pro coach: Joined Ravens in 1999.

Milt Jackson, wide receivers; born October 16, 1943, Groesbeck, Texas, lives in Owings Mills, Md. Free safety Tulsa 1965-66. Pro defensive back San Francisco 49ers 1967. College coach: Oregon State 1973, Rice 1974, Califronia 1975-76, Oregon 1977-78, UCLA 1979. Pro coach: San Francisco 49ers 1980-82, Buffalo Bills 1983-84, Philadelphia Eagles 1985, Houston Oilers 1986-88, Indianapolis Colts 1989-1991, Los Angeles Rams 1992-93, Atlanta Falcons 1994-96, New York Giants 1997, Seattle Seahawks 1998, joined Ravens in 1999.

Marvin Lewis, defensive coordinator; born September 23, 1958, McDonald, Pa., lives in Finksburg, Md. Linebacker Idaho State 1977-1980. No pro playing experience. College coach: Idaho State 1981-84, Long Beach State 1985-86, New Mexico 1987-89, Pittsburgh 1990-91. Pro coach: Pittsburgh Steelers 1992-95, joined Ravens in 1996.

Chip Morton, asst. strength and conditioning; born November 27, 1962, Hamden, Conn., lives in Owings Mills, Md. Attended North Carolina. No college or pro playing experience. College coach: Ohio State 1985-86, Penn State 1987-1992. Pro coach: San Diego Chargers 1992-94, Carolina Panthers 1995-98, joined Ravens in 1999.

Russ Purnell, special teams; born June 12, 1948, Chicago, lives in Owings Mills, Md. Center Orange Coast (Calif.) J.C. 1966-67, Whittier College 1968-69. No pro playing experience. College coach: Whittier College 1970-71, Southern California 1982-84. Pro coach: Seattle Seahawks 1986-1994, Tennessee Oilers 1995, joined Ravens in 1999.

Rex Ryan, defensive line; born December 13, 1962, Ardmore, Okla., lives in Ellicott City, Md. Defensive end Southwest Oklahoma State 1983-86. No pro playing experience. College coach: Eastern Kentucky 1987-88, New Mexico Highlands 1989, Morehead State 1990-93, Cincinnati 1996-97, Oklahoma 1998. Pro coach: Arizona Cardinals 1994-95, joined Ravens in 1999.

Steve Shafer, defensive backs, asst. to the head coach; born December 8, 1940, Glendale, Calif., lives in Owings Mills, Md. Quarterback-defensive back Utah State 1961-62. Pro defensive back British Columbia Lions (CFL) 1963-67. College coach: San Mateo (Calif.) J.C. 1968-1974 (head coach 1973-74), San Diego State 1975-1982, 1994. Pro coach: Los Angeles Rams 1983-1990, Tampa Bay Buccaneers 1991-93, Oakland Raiders 1995-97, Carolina Panthers 1998, joined Ravens in 1999.

Matt Simon, running backs; born December 6, 1953, Akron, Ohio, lives in Owings Mills, Md. Linebacker Eastern New Mexico 1972-75. No pro playing experience. College coach: Washington 1982-1991, New Mexico 1992-94, North Texas 1994-97 (head coach). Pro coach: Denver Broncos 1998, joined Ravens in 1999.

Mike Smith, defensive assistant; born June 13, 1959, Chicago, lives in Owings Mills, Md. Linebacker East Tennessee 1977-1980. No pro playing experience. College coach: San Diego State 1982-85, Morehead State 1986, Tennessee Tech 1987-1998. Pro coach: Joined Ravens in 1999.

1999 FIRST-YEAR ROSTER

Name	Pos.	Ht.	Wt.	Birthdate	College	Hometown	How Acq.
Bowman, Mike (1)	WR	6-2	200	9/16/74	Valdosta State	Gainsville, Fla.	FA-'98
Chamblin, Cory	CB-S	5-11	188	5/29/77	Tennessee Tech	Birmingham, Ala.	FA
Derricott, Jermaine	S	6-0	218	2/8/76	South Carolina State	Norway, S.C.	FA
Douglas, Marques	DE	6-2	270	3/5/77	Howard	Greensboro, N.C.	FA
Dyson, Brandon (1)	G-T	6-4	290	5/31/76	Utah State	Bountiful, Utah	FA-'98
Fitzpatrick, Larry (1)	DT	6-4	275	8/17/76	Illinois State	Detroit, Mich.	FA-'98
Francis, Cory	DT	6-1	310	5/27/76	North Carolina Central	Raeford, N.C.	FA
Hill, Brad	P	6-0	200	3/20/76	Tulane	Memphis, Tenn.	FA
Huff, Ramon	WR	6-2	195	10/1/76	Savannah State	Savannah, Ga.	FA
Jackson, Brad (1)	LB	6-0	230	1/11/75	Cincinnati	Akron, Ohio	FA-'98
Maas, Jason	QB	6-2	205	11/19/75	Oregon	Beaver Falls, Wis.	FA
McAlister, Chris	CB	6-1	206	6/14/77	Arizona	Pasadena, Calif.	D1
Mitchell, Tywan	WR	6-5	220	12/10/75	Mankato State	Crete, Ill.	FA
Mulitalo, Edwin	G-T	6-3	328	9/1/74	Arizona	Daly City, Calif.	D4b
Nord, Kendrick (1)	WR	6-2	210	4/28/72	Grambling State	Mobile, Ala.	FA
Poindexter, Anthony	S	6-0	210	7/28/76	Virginia	Forest, Va.	D7
Preston, Charles	DE	6-5	270	4/19/75	Hampton	Washington, D.C.	FA
Roberts, Cleve	T	6-6	300	1/5/75	Troy State	Buhler, Kan.	FA
Savoy, Phil (1)	WR	6-2	195	2/16/75	Colorado	Washington, D.C.	FA-'98
Sieh, Thomas	RB	5-8	212	11/20/75	Texas Southern	Staten Island, N.Y.	FA
Snell, Ben (1)	RB	6-2	225	7/24/76	Ohio Northern	Canton, Ohio	FA-'98
Stokley, Brandon	WR	5-11	197	6/23/76	Southwestern Louisiana	Lafayette, La.	D4a
Wilkerson, Fred	CB	6-2	200	5/7/76	Northwestern	Detroit, Mich.	FA
Wright, Antron	LB	6-1	240	6/28/75	Bethune-Cookman	Miami, Fla.	FA

The term NFL Rookie is defined as a player who is in his first season of professional football and has not been on the roster of another professional football team for any regular-season or postseason games. A Rookie is designated by an "R" on NFL rosters. Players who have been active in another professional football league or players who have NFL experience, including either preseason training camp or being on an Active List or Inactive List, or on Reserve/Injured or Reserve/Physically Unable to Perform for fewer than six regular-season games, are termed NFL First-Year Players. An NFL First-Year Player is designated by a "1" on NFL rosters. Thereafter, a player is credited with an additional year of experience for each season in which he accumulates six games on the Active List or Inactive List, or on Reserve/Injured or Reserve/Physically Unable to Perform.

NOTES

BUFFALO BILLS

American Football Conference
Eastern Division
Team Colors: Royal Blue, Scarlet Red, and White
One Bills Drive
Orchard Park, New York 14127-2296
Telephone: (716) 648-1800

CLUB OFFICIALS

President: Ralph C. Wilson, Jr.
Exec. V.P./General Manager: John Butler
Executive Vice President/Administration: Bill Duffy
Corporate V.P.: Linda Bogdan
Treasurer: Jeffrey C. Littmann
Vice President/Communications: Scott Berchtold
Vice President/Business Development and Marketing: Russ Brandon
Vice President/Business Operations: Bill Munson
Director of Business Operations: Jim Overdorf
Director of Player Personnel: Dwight Adams
Director of Pro Personnel: A.J. Smith
Director of Merchandising: Christy Wilson Hofmann
Director of Marketing Communications: Marc Honan
Director of Guest Services and Event Management: Jan Eberle
Director of Ticket Sales: Jerry Foran
Director of Public/Community Relations: Denny Lynch
Director of Stadium Operations: George Koch
Engineering and Operations Manager: Joseph Frandina
Director of Security: Bill Bambach
Ticket Director: June Foran
Media Relations Coordinator: Mark Dalton
Equipment Manager: Dave Hojnowski
Asst. Equipment Manager: Randy Ribbeck
Strength/Conditioning Coordinator: Rusty Jones
Conditioning Assistant: Rich Gray
Trainers: Bud Carpenter, Melvin Lewis, Greg McMillen
Video Director: Henry Kunttu
Video Assistant: Matt Werder
Scouts: Brad Forsyth, Tom Gibbons, Joe Haering, Doug Majeski, Buddy Nix, Bob Ryan, George (Chink) Sengel, Jim Shofner, David G. Smith, David W. Smith, Bob Williams
Stadium: Ralph Wilson Stadium
•**Capacity:** 75,300 (approx.)
One Bills Drive
Orchard Park, New York 14127-2296
Playing Surface: AstroTurf
Training Camp: Fredonia State University
Fredonia, New York 14063

1999 SCHEDULE

PRESEASON

Aug. 14	at Seattle	6:00
Aug. 20	at Washington	8:00
Aug. 28	at Cincinnati	7:30
Sept. 4	**Pittsburgh**	7:30

REGULAR SEASON

Sept. 12	at Indianapolis	12:00
Sept. 19	**New York Jets**	8:20
Sept. 26	**Philadelphia**	1:00
Oct. 4	at Miami (Mon.)	9:00
Oct. 10	**Pittsburgh**	1:00
Oct. 17	**Oakland**	1:00
Oct. 24	at Seattle	1:15
Oct. 31	at Baltimore	1:00
Nov. 7	at Washington	1:00
Nov. 14	**Miami**	1:00
Nov. 21	at New York Jets	1:00
Nov. 28	**New England**	1:00
Dec. 5	Open Date	
Dec. 12	**New York Giants**	1:00
Dec. 19	at Arizona	6:20
Dec. 26	at New England	1:00
Jan. 2	**Indianapolis**	1:00

RECORD HOLDERS

INDIVIDUAL RECORDS—CAREER

Category	Name	Performance
Rushing (Yds.)	Thurman Thomas, 1988-1998	11,786
Passing (Yds.)	Jim Kelly, 1986-1996	35,467
Passing (TDs)	Jim Kelly, 1986-1996	237
Receiving (No.)	Andre Reed, 1985-1998	889
Receiving (Yds.)	Andre Reed, 1985-1998	12,559
Interceptions	George (Butch) Byrd, 1964-1970	40
Punting (Avg.)	Paul Maguire, 1964-1970	42.1
Punt Return (Avg.)	Clifford Hicks, 1990-92	12.2
Kickoff Return (Avg.)	O.J. Simpson, 1969-1977	30.0
Field Goals	Steve Christie, 1992-98	183
Touchdowns (Tot.)	Andre Reed, 1985-1998	86
	Thurman Thomas, 1988-1998	86
Points	Steve Christie, 1992-98	794

INDIVIDUAL RECORDS—SINGLE SEASON

Category	Name	Performance
Rushing (Yds.)	O.J. Simpson, 1973	2,003
Passing (Yds.)	Jim Kelly, 1991	3,844
Passing (TDs)	Jim Kelly, 1991	33
Receiving (No.)	Andre Reed, 1994	90
Receiving (Yds.)	Eric Moulds, 1998	1,368
Interceptions	Billy Atkins, 1961	10
	Tom Janik, 1967	10
Punting (Avg.)	Billy Atkins, 1961	44.5
Punt Return (Avg.)	Keith Moody, 1977	13.1
Kickoff Return (Avg.)	Ed Rutkowski, 1963	30.2
Field Goals	Steve Christie, 1998	33
Touchdowns (Tot.)	O.J. Simpson, 1975	23
Points	Steve Christie, 1998	140

INDIVIDUAL RECORDS—SINGLE GAME

Category	Name	Performance
Rushing (Yds.)	O.J. Simpson, 11-25-76	273
Passing (Yds.)	Joe Ferguson, 10-9-83	419
Passing (TDs)	Jim Kelly, 9-8-91	6
Receiving (No.)	Andre Reed, 11-20-94	15
Receiving (Yds.)	Jerry Butler, 9-23-79	255
Interceptions	Many times	3
	Last time by Jeff Nixon, 9-7-80	
Field Goals	Steve Christie, 10-20-96	6
Touchdowns (Tot.)	Cookie Gilchrist, 12-8-63	5

COACHING HISTORY

(291-309-8)

1960-61	Buster Ramsey	11-16-1
1962-65	Lou Saban	38-18-3
1966-68	Joe Collier*	13-17-1
1968	Harvey Johnson	1-10-1
1969-70	John Rauch	7-20-1
1971	Harvey Johnson	1-13-0
1972-76	Lou Saban**	32-29-1
1976-77	Jim Ringo	3-20-0
1978-82	Chuck Knox	38-38-0
1983-85	Kay Stephenson***	10-26-0
1985-86	Hank Bullough****	4-17-0
1986-97	Marv Levy	123-78-0
1998	Wade Phillips	10-7-0

*Released after two games in 1968
**Resigned after five games in 1976
***Released after four games in 1985
****Released after nine games in 1986

RALPH WILSON STADIUM

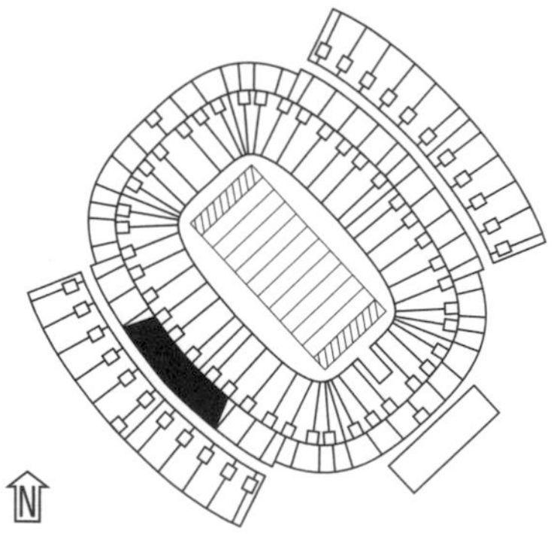

1998 TEAM RECORD

PRESEASON (2-2)

Date	Result		Opponent
8/8	L	13-24	at Pittsburgh
8/14	L	7-12	Carolina
8/21	W	17-9	at Chicago
8/28	W	27-17	Washington

REGULAR SEASON (10-6)

Date	Result		Opponent	Att.
9/6	L	14-16	at San Diego	64,037
9/13	L	7-13	at Miami	73,097
9/20	L	33-34	St. Louis	65,199
10/4	W	26-21	San Francisco	76,615
10/11	W	31-24	at Indianapolis	52,938
10/18	W	17-16	Jacksonville	77,635
10/25	W	30-14	at Carolina	64,050
11/1	W	30-24	Miami	79,011
11/8	L	12-34	at New York Jets	75,403
11/15	W	13-10	New England	72,020
11/22	W	34-11	Indianapolis	49,032
11/29	L	21-25	at New England	58,304
12/6	W	33-20	at Cincinnati	54,359
12/13	W	44-21	Oakland	62,002
12/19	L	10-17	New York Jets	79,056
12/27	W	45-33	at New Orleans	39,707

POSTSEASON (0-1)

Date	Result		Opponent	Att.
1/2	L	17-24	at Miami	72,698

SCORE BY PERIODS

Bills	67	139	95	99	0	— 400
Opponents	40	97	70	126	0	— 333

ATTENDANCE

Home 560,570 Away 481,895 Total 1,042,465
Single-game home record, 80,368 (10/4/92)
Single-season home record, 635,889 (1991)

1998 TEAM STATISTICS

	Bills	Opp.
Total First Downs	319	283
Rushing	115	79
Passing	176	168
Penalty	28	36
Third Down: Made/Att	97/219	80/207
Third Down Pct.	44.3	38.6
Fourth Down: Made/Att	3/8	10/18
Fourth Down Pct.	37.5	55.6
Total Net Yards	5,541	4,691
Avg. Per Game	346.3	293.2
Total Plays	1,033	950
Avg. Per Play	5.4	4.9
Net Yards Rushing	2,161	1,493
Avg. Per Game	135.1	93.3
Total Rushes	531	375
Net Yards Passing	3,380	3,198
Avg. Per Game	211.3	199.9
Sacked/Yards Lost	41/241	43/276
Gross Yards	3,621	3,474
Att./Completions	461/269	532/294
Completion Pct.	58.4	55.3
Had Intercepted	14	18
Punts/Avg.	69/41.8	77/44.9
Net Punting Avg.	69/33.2	77/37.5
Penalties/Yards Lost	123/993	104/836
Fumbles/Ball Lost	17/6	21/13
Touchdowns	43	39
Rushing	13	11
Passing	28	27
Returns	2	1
Avg. Time of Possession	32:26	27:34

1998 INDIVIDUAL STATISTICS

Passing	Att.	Comp.	Yds.	Pct.	TD	Int.	Tkld.	Rate
Flutie	354	202	2,711	57.1	20	11	12/78	87.4
R. Johnson	107	67	910	62.6	8	3	29/163	102.9
Bills	461	269	3,621	58.4	28	14	41/241	91.0
Opponents	532	294	3,474	55.3	27	18	43/276	78.2

SCORING	TD R	TD P	TD Rt	PAT	FG	Saf	PTS
Christie	0	0	0	41/41	33/41	0	140
Moulds	0	9	0	0/0	0/0	0	54
A. Smith	8	0	0	0/0	0/0	0	48
Riemersma	0	6	0	0/0	0/0	0	36
Reed	0	5	0	0/0	0/0	0	30
Gash	0	3	0	0/0	0/0	0	18
Thomas	2	1	0	0/0	0/0	0	18
L. Johnson	0	2	0	0/0	0/0	0	12
Early	0	1	0	0/0	0/0	0	6
Flutie	1	0	0	0/0	0/0	0	6
Hansen	0	0	1	0/0	0/0	0	6
R. Johnson	1	0	0	0/0	0/0	0	6
Linton	1	0	0	0/0	0/0	0	6
Northern	0	0	1	0/0	0/0	0	6
K. Williams	0	1	0	0/0	0/0	0	6
Washington	0	0	0	0/0	0/0	1	2
Bills	13	28	2	41/41	33/41	1	400
Opponents	11	27	1	28/28	21/26	0	333

2-Point conversions: None.
Team 0-2, Opponents 4-11.

RUSHING	Att.	Yds.	Avg.	LG	TD
A. Smith	300	1,124	3.7	30	8
Thomas	93	381	4.1	17t	2
Flutie	48	248	5.2	23	1
Linton	45	195	4.3	20	1
R. Johnson	24	123	5.1	32	1
K. Williams	5	46	9.2	28	0
Gash	11	32	2.9	11	0
Holmes	2	8	4.0	5	0
C. Williams	2	5	2.5	3	0
Van Pelt	1	-1	-1.0	-1	0
Bills	531	2,161	4.1	32	13
Opponents	375	1,493	4.0	46	11

RECEIVING	No.	Yds.	Avg.	LG	TD
Moulds	67	1,368	20.4	84t	9
Reed	63	795	12.6	67t	5
K. Williams	29	392	13.5	55	1
Thomas	26	220	8.5	26	1
Riemersma	25	288	11.5	28	6
Early	19	217	11.4	37	1
Gash	19	165	8.7	20	3
L. Johnson	14	146	10.4	27	2
A. Smith	5	11	2.2	9	0
Linton	1	10	10.0	10	0
Holmes	1	9	9.0	9	0
Bills	269	3,621	13.5	84t	28
Opponents	294	3,474	11.8	72t	27

INTERCEPTIONS	No.	Yds.	Avg.	LG	TD
Schulz	6	48	8.0	24	0
Jones	3	0	0.0	0	0
Jackson	2	27	13.5	27	0
Cowart	2	23	11.5	23	0
Irvin	1	43	43.0	43	0
Northern	1	40	40.0	40t	1
Martin	1	23	23.0	23	0
T. Smith	1	0	0.0	0	0
Washington	1	0	0.0	0	0
Bills	18	204	11.3	43	1
Opponents	14	65	4.6	18	0

PUNTING	No.	Yds.	Avg.	In 20	LG
Mohr	69	2,882	41.8	18	57
Bills	69	2,882	41.8	18	57
Opponents	77	3,459	44.9	13	69

PUNT RETURNS	No.	FC	Yds.	Avg.	LG	TD
K. Williams	37	11	369	10.0	73	0
Bills	37	11	369	10.0	73	0
Opponents	32	17	374	11.7	75t	1

KICKOFF RETURNS	No.	Yds.	Avg.	LG	TD
K. Williams	47	1,059	22.5	46	0
Gash	3	41	13.7	17	0
L. Johnson	3	18	6.0	16	0
Cummings	1	21	21.0	21	0
Holmes	1	20	20.0	20	0
Riemersma	1	9	9.0	9	0
Bills	56	1,168	20.9	46	0
Opponents	77	1,638	21.3	55	0

FIELD GOALS	1-19	20-29	30-39	40-49	50+
Christie	1/1	10/12	12/14	9/11	1/3
Bills	1/1	10/12	12/14	9/11	1/3
Opponents	0/0	7/7	5/7	8/11	1/1

SACKS	No.
B. Smith	10.0
Hansen	7.5
Price	5.0
Rogers	4.5
Washington	4.5
Wiley	3.5
P. Williams	3.5
Northern	2.0
Smedley	2.0
Simmons	0.5
Bills	43.0
Opponents	41.0

1999 DRAFT CHOICES

Round	Name	Pos.	College
1	Antoine Winfield	DB	Ohio State
2	Peerless Price	WR	Tennessee
3	Shawn Bryson	RB	Tennessee
4	Keith Newman	LB	North Carolina
	Bobby Collins	TE	North Alabama
5	Jay Foreman	LB	Nebraska
6	Armon Hatcher	DB	Oregon State
7	Sheldon Jackson	TE	Nebraska
	Bryce Fisher	DE	Air Force

BUFFALO BILLS

1999 VETERAN ROSTER

No.	Name	Pos.	Ht.	Wt.	Birthdate	NFL Exp.	College	Hometown	How Acq.	'98 Games/ Starts
76	Albright, Ethan	G-T	6-5	283	5/1/71	5	North Carolina	Greensboro, N.C.	FA-'96	16/0
96	Brandenburg, Dan	LB	6-3	240	2/16/73	3	Indiana State	Rensselaer, Ind.	D7a-'96	16/1
79	Brown, Ruben	G	6-3	304	2/13/72	5	Pittsburgh	Lynchburg, Va.	D1-'95	13/13
2	Christie, Steve	K	6-0	185	11/13/67	10	William & Mary	Oakville, Canada	PB(TB)-'92	16/0
63	Conaty, Bill	G-T	6-2	306	3/8/73	3	Virginia Tech	Pennsauken, N.J.	FA-'97	16/1
56	Cowart, Sam	LB	6-2	239	2/26/75	2	Florida State	Jacksonville, Fla.	D2-'98	16/11
51	Cummings, Joe	LB	6-2	242	6/8/74	3	Wyoming	Missoula, Mont.	FA-'98	9/2
70	Fina, John	T	6-4	300	3/11/69	8	Arizona	Tucson, Ariz.	D1-'92	14/14
7	Flutie, Doug	QB	5-10	175	10/23/62	6	Boston College	Natick, Mass.	FA-'98	13/10
33	Gash, Sam	RB	6-0	235	3/7/69	8	Penn State	Hendersonville, N.C.	FA-'98	16/12
25	Greer, Donovan	DB	5-9	178	9/11/74	3	Texas A&M	Alief, Tex.	FA-'98	11/2
90	Hansen, Phil	DE	6-5	278	5/20/68	9	North Dakota State	Oakes, N.D.	D2-'91	15/15
77	Hicks, Robert	T	6-7	338	11/17/74	2	Mississippi State	Atlanta, Ga.	D3-'98	10/2
52	Holecek, John	LB	6-2	242	5/7/72	5	Illinois	Steger, Ill.	D5-'95	13/13
27	Irvin, Ken	CB	5-10	186	7/11/72	5	Memphis	Rome, Ga.	D4a-'95	16/16
11	Johnson, Rob	QB	6-4	214	3/18/73	5	Southern California	Newport Beach, Calif.	T(Jac)-'98	8/6
20	Jones, Henry	S	5-11	197	12/29/67	9	Illinois	St. Louis, Mo.	D1-'91	16/16
46	# Kerner, Marlon	CB	5-10	190	3/8/73	5	Ohio State	Columbus, Ohio	D3a-'95	1/0
35	Linton, Jonathan	RB	6-0	248	10/7/74	2	North Carolina	Catasauqua, Pa.	D5-'98	14/0
89	Loud, Kamil	WR	6-0	190	6/25/76	2	Cal Poly-SLO	El Cerrito, Calif.	D7b-'98	5/0
21	Martin, Manny	S	5-11	184	7/31/69	4	Alabama State	Miami, Fla.	FA-'96	14/4
9	Mohr, Chris	P	6-5	215	5/11/66	10	Alabama	Thomson, Ga.	FA-'91	16/0
98	Moran, Sean	DT	6-3	275	6/5/73	4	Colorado State	Aurora, Colo.	D4-'96	10/2
80	Moulds, Eric	WR	6-0	204	7/17/73	4	Mississippi State	Lucedale, Miss.	D1-'96	16/15
74	Nails, Jamie	T	6-6	354	3/3/75	3	Florida A&M	Baxley, Ga.	D4-'97	16/3
99	Northern, Gabe	LB	6-3	240	6/8/74	4	Louisiana State	Baton Rouge, La.	D2-'96	16/16
60	Ostroski, Jerry	G	6-4	310	7/12/70	5	Tulsa	Collegeville, Pa.	FA-'93	16/16
72	Panos, Joe	G	6-2	293	1/24/71	6	Wisconsin	Brookfield, Ill.	FA-'98	16/16
58	Perry, Marlo	LB	6-4	250	8/25/72	6	Jackson State	Forest, Miss.	D3a-'94	16/1
22	Porter, Daryl	CB	5-9	190	1/16/74	2	Boston College	Fort Lauderdale, Fla.	FA-'98	2/0
91	Price, Shawn	DE	6-5	285	3/28/70	7	Pacific	Woodland Hills, Calif.	FA-'96	14/2
83	Reed, Andre	WR	6-2	190	1/29/64	15	Kutztown State	Allentown, Pa.	D4a-'85	15/13
85	Riemersma, Jay	TE	6-5	254	5/17/73	3	Michigan	Zeeland, Mich.	D7b-'96	16/4
59	Rogers, Sam	LB	6-3	245	5/30/70	6	Colorado	Pontiac, Mich.	D2c-'94	15/15
24	Schulz, Kurt	S	6-1	208	12/12/68	8	Eastern Washington	Yakima, Wash.	D7-'92	12/12
40	Smedley, Eric	CB-S	5-11	199	7/23/73	4	Indiana	Charleston, W. Va.	D7c-'96	16/0
23	Smith, Antowain	RB	6-2	224	3/14/72	3	Houston	Montgomery, Ala.	D1-'97	16/14
78	Smith, Bruce	DE	6-4	273	6/18/63	15	Virginia Tech	Norfolk, Va.	D1a-85	15/15
28	Smith, Thomas	CB	5-11	188	12/5/70	7	North Carolina	Gates, N.C.	D1-'93	14/14
69	Spriggs, Marcus	T	6-3	295	5/17/74	3	Houston	Hattiesburg, Miss.	D6-'97	1/0
87	Stocz, Eric	TE	6-4	265	5/25/74	3	Westminster	Cortland, Ohio	FA-'99	0*
34	Thomas, Thurman	RB	5-10	198	5/16/66	12	Oklahoma State	Missouri City, Tex.	D2-'88	14/3
10	Van Pelt, Alex	QB	6-0	220	5/1/70	5	Pittsburgh	Pittsburgh, Pa.	FA-'94	1/0
92	Washington, Ted	NT	6-4	325	4/13/68	9	Louisville	Tampa, Fla.	FA-'95	16/16
75	Wiley, Marcellus	DE	6-5	271	11/30/74	3	Columbia	Los Angeles, Calif.	D2-'97	16/3
82	Williams, Kevin	WR	5-9	195	1/25/71	7	Miami	Dallas, Tex.	FA-'98	16/0
93	Williams, Pat	DT	6-3	270	10/24/72	3	Texas A&M	Monroe, La.	FA-'97	14/0
61	Zeigler, Dusty	C-G	6-5	298	9/27/73	4	Notre Dame	Rincon, Ga.	D6b-'96	16/16

* Stocz missed '98 season because of injury.

\# Unrestricted free agent; subject to developments.

Retired—Mark Pike, 14-year DE-LB, 13 games in '98.

Players lost through free agency (1): TE Lonnie Johnson (KC; 16 games in '98).

Also played with Bills in '98—WR Quinn Early (16 games), K Cole Ford (1), CB Ray Hill (4), RB Darick Holmes (3), CB Ray Jackson (14), LB Wayne Simmons (6), RB Clarence Williams (2), TE Duane Young (5).

COACHING STAFF

Head Coach,
Wade Phillips

Pro Career: Became the eleventh head coach in Bills history on January 5, 1998, after having served as the club's defensive coordinator since 1995. In his first season, led the Bills to a 10-6 record and a return to the playoffs following a one-year hiatus. Enjoyed the best season of any first-year coach in Bills history, both in number of victories and turnaround in wins and losses. Has been a NFL coach for 23 years, which includes a two-year stint as the head coach of the Denver Broncos in 1993-94. He led them to a wild-card playoff spot in 1993. Began his pro coaching career in 1976 with the Houston Oilers, where he remained until 1980. Then accepted the position of defensive coordinator for the New Orleans Saints (1981-85) and served as the head coach for the final four games of the 1985 season. Served as the defensive coordinator for the Philadelphia Eagles (1986-88) before joining the Broncos' staff in 1989 and serving as the defensive coordinator through the 1992 season. During the 1990 preseason, Phillips assumed the capacity of interim head coach. No pro playing experience. Career record: 27-27.

Background: Linebacker at Houston 1966-68. Coached at his alma mater in 1969. Served as the head coach at Orange (Texas) High in 1970-72. Moved to Oklahoma State as an assistant in 1973-74. Later served as an assistant at Kansas in 1975.

Personal: Born June 21, 1947. Is the son of former NFL coaching legend O.A. (Bum) Phillips. Has two children, daughter Tracy and a son Wesley, who plays quarterback at Texas-El Paso. He and his wife, Laurie, reside in East Amherst, New York.

ASSISTANT COACHES

Max Bowman, asst. to the head coach-tight ends; born September 18, 1945, Colorado Springs, Colo., lives in East Amherst, N.Y. Attended Nyack College. No college or pro playing experience. College coach: Westchester C.C. 1972-78, Lees McRae College 1979, Boston College 1980, Kent State 1981, Texas-El Paso 1982-85, Greenville College 1986 1993. Pro coach: West Virginia Rockets (AFL) 1981, joined Bills in 1998.

Bill Bradley, defensive backs; born January 14, 1947, Paletine, Texas, lives in Orchard Park, N.Y. Quarterback-defensive back-punter-kicker-returner-holder Texas 1966-68. Pro safety-punter-returner-holder Philadelphia Eagles 1969-1977, St. Louis Cardinals 1978. College coach: Texas 1987. Pro coach: San Antonio Gunslingers (USFL) 1983-84, Memphis Showboats (USFL) 1985, Calgary Stampeders (CFL) 1988-1990, San Antonio Riders (WLAF) 1991-92, Sacramento Gold Miners (CFL) 1993-94, San Antonio Texans (CFL) 1995, Toronto Argonauts (CFL) 1996-97, joined Bills in 1998.

Ted Cottrell, defensive coordinator; born June 13, 1947, Chester, Pa., lives in Orchard Park, N.Y. Linebacker Delaware Valley College 1966-68. Pro linebacker Atlanta Falcons 1969-1970, Winnipeg Blue Bombers (CFL) 1971. College coach: Rutgers 1973-1980, 1983. Pro coach: Kansas City Chiefs 1981-82, New Jersey Generals (USFL) 1983-84, Buffalo Bills 1986-89, Arizona Cardinals 1990-94, rejoined Bills in 1995.

Bruce DeHaven, special teams; born September 6, 1952, Trousdale, Kan., lives in East Aurora, N.Y. Attended Southwestern (Kan.) College. No college or pro playing experience. College coach: Kansas 1979-1981, New Mexico State 1982. Pro coach: New Jersey Generals (USFL) 1983, Pittsburgh Maulers (USFL) 1984, Orlando Renegades (USFL) 1985, joined Bills in 1987.

Bishop Harris, running backs; born November 23, 1941, Phoenix City, Ala., lives in Buffalo. Running back-defensive back North Carolina College 1960-63. No pro playing experience. College coach: Duke 1972-75, North Carolina State 1977-79, Louisiana State 1980-83, Notre Dame 1984-85, Minnesota 1986-1990, North Carolina Central 1991-92 (head coach). Pro coach: Denver Broncos 1993-94, Oakland Raiders 1995-97, joined Bills in 1998.

Charlie Joiner, receivers; born October 14, 1947, Many, La., lives in Orchard Park, N.Y. Wide receiver Grambling 1965-68. Pro defensive back-wide receiver Houston Oilers 1969-1972, Cincinnati Bengals 1972-75, San Diego Chargers 1976-1986. Inducted into Pro Football Hall of Fame 1996. Pro coach: San Diego Chargers 1987-1991, joined Bills in 1992.

Rusty Jones, strength and conditioning; born August 14, 1953, Berwick, Maine, lives in Hamburg, N.Y. Attended Springfield College. No college or pro playing experience. College coach: Springfield College 1978-79. Pro coach: Pittsburgh Maulers (USFL) 1983-84, joined Bills in 1985.

Chuck Lester, linebackers; born May 18, 1955, Chicago, lives in Orchard Park, N.Y. Linebacker Oklahoma 1974. No pro playing experience. College coach: Iowa State 1980-81, Oklahoma 1982-84. Pro coach: Kansas City Chiefs 1984-86 (scout), joined Bills in 1987.

John Levra, defensive line; born October 2, 1937, Arma, Kan., lives in Hamburg, N.Y. Guard-linebacker Pittsburg State 1963-65. No pro playing experience. College coach: New Mexico Highlands 1966-1970, Stephen F. Austin 1971-74, Kansas 1975-78, North Texas State 1979. Pro coach: British Columbia Lions (CFL) 1980, New Orleans Saints 1981-85, Chicago Bears 1986-1992, Denver Broncos 1993-94, Minnesota Vikings 1995, joined Bills in 1998.

Carl Mauck, offensive line; born July 7, 1947, McLeansboro, Ill., lives in Orchard Park, N.Y. Linebacker-center Southern Illinois 1966-68. Pro center Baltimore Colts 1969, Miami Dolphins 1970, San Diego Chargers 1971-74, Houston Oilers 1975-1981. Pro coach: New Orleans Saints 1982-85, Kansas City Chiefs 1986-88, Tampa Bay Buccaneers 1991, San Diego Chargers 1992-95, Arizona Cardinals 1996-97, joined Bills in 1998.

Joe Pendry, offensive coordinator; born August 5, 1947. Matheny, W. Va., lives in Orchard Park, N.Y. Tight end West Virginia 1966-67. No pro playing experience. College coach: West Virginia 1967-1974, 1976-77, Kansas State 1975, Pittsburgh 1978-79, Michigan State 1980-81. Pro coach: Philadelphia Stars (USFL) 1983, Pittsburgh Maulers (USFL) 1984 (head coach), Cleveland Browns 1985-88, Kansas City Chiefs 1989-1992, Chicago Bears 1993-94, Carolina Panthers 1995-97, joined Bills in 1998.

Turk Schonert, quarterbacks; born January 15, 1957, Torrance, Calif., lives in Lancaster, N.Y. Quarterback Stanford 1975-79. Pro quarterback Cincinnati Bengals 1980-85, Atlanta Falcons 1986, Cincinnati Bengals 1987-89. Pro coach: Tampa Bay Buccaneers 1992-95, joined Bills in 1998.

1999 FIRST-YEAR ROSTER

Name	Pos.	Ht.	Wt.	Birthdate	College	Hometown	How Acq.
Akins, Tony	WR	5-9	181	3/10/77	Northeast Louisiana	Starkville, Miss.	FA
Allen, Reginald	WR	5-11	176	9/11/76	Central Michigan	Flint, Mich.	FA
Bryson, Shawn	RB	6-0	235	11/30/76	Tennessee	Franklin, N.C.	D3
Carpenter, Keion	S	5-11	205	10/31/77	Virginia Tech	Baltimore, Md.	FA
Carter, Zach	DT	6-3	290	12/29/75	South Dakota State	Spearfish, S.D.	FA
Cawley, Mike (1)	QB	6-1	205	8/28/72	James Madison	Pittsburgh, Pa.	FA
Cleveland, Kendall	RB	6-0	227	12/3/75	Louisiana State	Orange, Tex.	FA
Collins, Bobby	TE	6-4	249	8/20/76	North Alabama	York, Ala.	D4b
Edwards, Brian	RB	6-1	223	6/6/76	East Tennessee State	Ocala, Fla.	FA
Fisher, Bryce	DT	6-2	251	5/12/77	Air Force	Renton, Wash.	D7b
Foreman, Jay	LB	6-1	237	12/18/76	Nebraska	Eden Prairie, Minn.	D5
Gordon, Lennox	RB	5-11	194	4/9/78	New Mexico	Higley, Ariz.	FA
Gray, Anthony	RB	6-0	228	10/1/74	West New Mexico	Hayward, Calif.	FA
Guest, Craig (1)	LB	6-1	242	12/10/75	Buffalo	North Haven, Conn.	FA
Hamilton, Mercedes	G	6-3	322	2/26/75	Tennessee	Waynesboro, Ga.	FA
Hatcher, Armon	S	6-0	212	7/15/76	Oregon State	Diamond Bar, Calif.	D6
Hill, Raion	S	6-0	200	9/2/76	Louisiana State	Marrero, La.	FA
Holmes, Jaret (1)	K	6-0	203	3/3/76	Auburn	Clinton, Miss.	FA
Hulsey, Corey	G	6-5	367	7/26/77	Clemson	Lula, Ga.	FA
Jackson, Sheldon	TE	6-3	237	7/24/76	Nebraska	Diamond Bar, Calif.	D7a
Kushner, Bill (1)	P	6-0	203	1/13/70	Boston College	San Diego, Calif.	FA
McDaniel, Jeremy	WR	6-0	197	5/2/76	Arizona	New Bern, N.C.	FA
Meyers, Andy	G	6-5	303	9/3/75	UCLA	Fontana, Calif.	FA
Mudge, David (1)	T	6-7	293	10/22/74	Michigan State	Whitby, Canada	FA
Newman, Keith	LB	6-2	243	1/19/77	North Carolina	Tampa, Fla.	D4a
Price, Peerless	WR	5-10	180	10/27/76	Tennessee	Dayton, Ohio	D2
Renfro, Dusty	LB	6-0	239	11/5/76	Texas	Cleburne, Tex.	FA
Ross, Jerry (1)	TE	6-4	248	9/11/74	Pittsburg State	Cherokee, Kan.	FA
Scott, Robert	WR	6-2	207	1/3/76	Utah State	Fontana, Calif.	FA
Talamaivao, Pene	DT	6-3	301	6/14/75	Utah	Pomona, Calif.	FA
Tellison, A.C. (1)	WR	6-3	210	9/5/71	Miami	Bay City, Tex.	FA
Winfield, Antoine	CB	5-8	180	6/24/77	Ohio State	Akron, Ohio	D1

The term NFL Rookie is defined as a player who is in his first season of professional football and has not been on the roster of another professional football team for any regular-season or postseason games. A Rookie is designated by an "R" on NFL rosters. Players who have been active in another professional football league or players who have NFL experience, including either preseason training camp or being on an Active List or Inactive List, or on Reserve/Injured or Reserve/Physically Unable to Perform for fewer than six regular-season games, are termed NFL First-Year Players. An NFL First-Year Player is designated by a "1" on NFL rosters. Thereafter, a player is credited with an additional year of experience for each season in which he accumulates six games on the Active List or Inactive List, or on Reserve/Injured or Reserve/Physically Unable to Perform.

NOTES

CINCINNATI BENGALS

American Football Conference
Central Division
Team Colors: Black, Orange, and White
One Bengals Drive
Cincinnati, Ohio 45204
Telephone: (513) 621-3550

CLUB OFFICIALS

President: Michael Brown
Vice President: Pete Brown
Executive Vice President: Katherine Blackburn
Vice President: Paul H. Brown
Vice President: John Sawyer
Chairman of the Board: Austin E. Knowlton
Director of Stadium Development: Troy Blackburn
Stadium Project Manager: Mark Horton
Director of Community Affairs: Jeff Berding
Stadium Construction Manager: Eric J. Brown
Administration Assistant: Jan Sutton
Business Manager: Bill Connelly
Business Manager's Assistant: Terri Stewart
Chief Financial Officer: Bill Scanlon
Controller: Johanna Kappner
Director of Corporate Sales and Marketing: Vince Cicero
Corporate Sales Executives: Michael Alford, Tony Kountz, Brian Sells
Corporate Sponsorship Coordinator: Jennifer Benjamin
Group Sales Coordinator: Kevin Lane
Public Relations Director: Jack Brennan
Assistant Public Relations Director: Patrick J. Combs
Public Relations Assistant: Inky Studley
Ticket Manager: Paul Kelly
Ticket Office: Tim Kelly, JoAnn Meyer
Director of Pro/College Personnel: Jim Lippincott
Scouting: Duke Tobin
Personnel Assistant: Debbie LaRocco
Equipment Manager: Tom Gray
Athletic Trainer: Paul Sparling
Assistant Athletic Trainer: Billy Brooks
Assistant Athletic Trainer/Assistant Equipment Manager: Rob Recker
Video Director: Travis Brammer
Assistant Video Director: Andy Fineberg
Assistant to the Coaching Staff: Sandy Schick
Receptionist: Teri Moratschek
Stadium: Cinergy Field •**Capacity:** 60,389
200 Cinergy Field
Cincinnati, Ohio 45202
Playing Surface: AstroTurf-8
Training Camp: Georgetown College
Georgetown, Kentucky 40324

RECORD HOLDERS

INDIVIDUAL RECORDS—CAREER

Category	Name	Performance
Rushing (Yds.)	James Brooks, 1984-1991	6,447
Passing (Yds.)	Ken Anderson, 1971-1986	32,838
Passing (TDs)	Ken Anderson, 1971-1986	197
Receiving (No.)	Carl Pickens, 1992-98	473
Receiving (Yds.)	Isaac Curtis, 1973-1984	7,101
Interceptions	Ken Riley, 1969-1983	65
Punting (Avg.)	Dave Lewis, 1970-73	43.8
Punt Return (Avg.)	Mitchell Price, 1990-93	10.4
Kickoff Return (Avg.)	Tremain Mack, 1998	25.9
Field Goals	Jim Breech, 1980-1992	225
Touchdowns (Tot.)	Pete Johnson, 1977-1983	70
Points	Jim Breech, 1980-1992	1,151

INDIVIDUAL RECORDS—SINGLE SEASON

Category	Name	Performance
Rushing (Yds.)	James Brooks, 1989	1,239
Passing (Yds.)	Boomer Esiason, 1986	3,959
Passing (TDs)	Ken Anderson, 1981	29
Receiving (No.)	Carl Pickens, 1996	100
Receiving (Yds.)	Eddie Brown, 1988	1,273
Interceptions	Ken Riley, 1976	9
Punting (Avg.)	Dave Lewis, 1970	46.2
Punt Return (Avg.)	Lemar Parrish, 1974	18.8
Kickoff Return (Avg.)	Tremain Mack, 1998	25.9
Field Goals	Doug Pelfrey, 1995	29
Touchdowns (Tot.)	Carl Pickens, 1995	17
Points	Doug Pelfrey, 1995	121

INDIVIDUAL RECORDS—SINGLE GAME

Category	Name	Performance
Rushing (Yds.)	Corey Dillon, 12-4-97	246
Passing (Yds.)	Boomer Esiason, 10-7-90	490
Passing (TDs)	Boomer Esiason, 12-21-86	5
	Boomer Esiason, 10-29-89	5
Receiving (No.)	Carl Pickens, 10-11-98	13
Receiving (Yds.)	Eddie Brown, 11-6-88	216
Interceptions	Many times	3
	Last time by David Fulcher, 12-17-89	
Field Goals	Doug Pelfrey, 11-6-94	6
Touchdowns (Tot.)	Larry Kinnebrew, 10-28-84	4
	Corey Dillon, 12-4-97	4
Points	Larry Kinnebrew, 10-28-84	24
	Corey Dillon, 12-4-97	24

1999 SCHEDULE

PRESEASON

Aug. 14	at Indianapolis	7:00
Aug. 20	at Detroit	7:00
Aug. 28	**Buffalo**	7:30
Sept. 3	**Atlanta**	7:30

REGULAR SEASON

Sept. 12	at Tennessee	12:00
Sept. 19	**San Diego**	1:00
Sept. 26	at Carolina	1:00
Oct. 3	**St. Louis**	1:00
Oct. 10	at Cleveland	1:00
Oct. 17	**Pittsburgh**	1:00
Oct. 24	at Indianapolis	12:00
Oct. 31	**Jacksonville**	1:00
Nov. 7	at Seattle	1:15
Nov. 14	**Tennessee**	1:00
Nov. 21	**Baltimore**	4:05
Nov. 28	at Pittsburgh	1:00
Dec. 5	**San Francisco**	1:00
Dec. 12	**Cleveland**	1:00
Dec. 19	Open Date	
Dec. 26	at Baltimore	1:00
Jan. 2	at Jacksonville	1:00

CINERGY FIELD

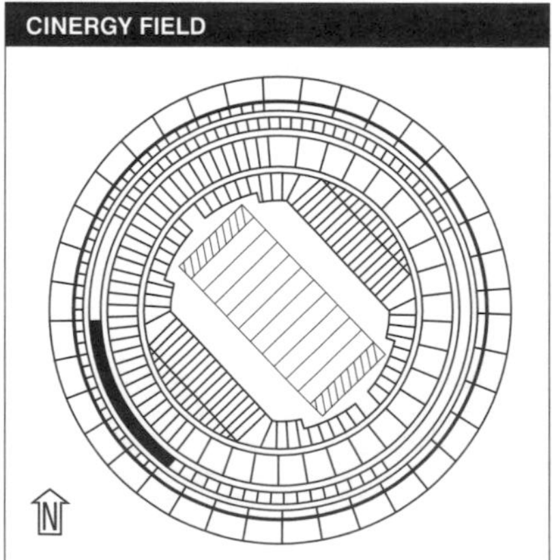

COACHING HISTORY

(215-264-1)

1968-75	Paul Brown	55-59-1
1976-78	Bill Johnson*	18-15-0
1978-79	Homer Rice	8-19-0
1980-83	Forrest Gregg	34-27-0
1984-91	Sam Wyche	64-68-0
1992-96	Dave Shula**	19-52-0
1996-98	Bruce Coslet	17-24-0

* Resigned after five games in 1978
** Released after seven games in 1996

1998 TEAM RECORD

PRESEASON (1-3)

Date	Result		Opponent
8/8	L	17-24	at New York Giants
8/17	L	27-30	Indianapolis
8/22	W	33-19	Detroit
8/28	L	0-17	at Atlanta

REGULAR SEASON (3-13)

Date	Result		Opponent	Att.
9/6	L	14-23	Tennessee	55,848
9/13	W	34-28	at Detroit (OT)	66,354
9/20	L	6-13	Green Bay	56,346
9/27	L	24-31	at Baltimore	68,154
10/11	W	25-20	Pittsburgh	59,979
10/18	L	14-44	at Tennessee	33,288
10/25	L	10-27	at Oakland	40,089
11/1	L	26-33	Denver	59,974
11/8	L	11-24	at Jacksonville	67,040
11/15	L	3-24	at Minnesota	64,232
11/22	L	13-20	Baltimore	52,571
11/29	L	17-34	Jacksonville	55,432
12/6	L	20-33	Buffalo	54,359
12/13	L	26-39	at Indianapolis	55,179
12/20	W	25-24	at Pittsburgh	52,017
12/27	L	0-35	Tampa Bay	49,826

(OT) Overtime

SCORE BY PERIODS

Bengals	26	90	66	80	6	—	268
Opponents	113	143	99	97	0	—	452

ATTENDANCE

Home 444,335   Away 446,353   Total 890,688
Single-game home record, 60,284 (10/17/71)
Single-season home record, 473,288 (1990)

1998 TEAM STATISTICS

	Bengals	Opp.
Total First Downs	271	310
Rushing	92	142
Passing	148	152
Penalty	31	16
Third Down: Made/Att	76/224	89/200
Third Down Pct.	33.9	44.5
Fourth Down: Made/Att	11/29	4/9
Fourth Down Pct.	37.9	44.4
Total Net Yards	4,824	5,763
Avg. Per Game	301.5	360.2
Total Plays	979	992
Avg. Per Play	4.9	5.8
Net Yards Rushing	1,639	2,612
Avg. Per Game	102.4	163.3
Total Rushes	405	558
Net Yards Passing	3,185	3,151
Avg. Per Game	199.1	196.9
Sacked/Yards Lost	53/360	28/199
Gross Yards	3,545	3,350
Att./Completions	521/307	406/233
Completion Pct.	58.9	57.4
Had Intercepted	12	13
Punts/Avg.	81/44.2	64/44.5
Net Punting Avg.	81/35.2	34/39.6
Penalties/Yards Lost.	69/620	127/1,012
Fumbles/Ball Lost	21/10	12/7
Touchdowns	31	53
Rushing	7	23
Passing	20	23
Returns	4	7
Avg. Time of Possession	28:31	31:29

1998 INDIVIDUAL STATISTICS

Passing	Att.	Comp.	Yds.	Pct.	TD	Int.	Tkld.	Rate
O'Donnell	343	212	2,216	61.8	15	4	30/217	90.2
Blake	93	51	739	54.8	3	3	15/79	78.2
Justin	63	34	426	54.0	1	3	7/60	60.7
Kresser	21	10	164	47.6	1	2	0/0	50.6
Pelfrey	1	0	0	0.0	0	0	0/0	39.6
Dillon	0	0	0	—	0	0	1/4	—
Bengals	521	307	3,545	58.9	20	12	53/360	82.7
Opponents	406	233	3,350	57.4	23	13	28/199	89.8

SCORING	TD R	TD P	TD Rt	PAT	FG	Saf	PTS
Pelfrey	0	0	0	21/21	19/27	0	78
Scott	0	7	0	0/0	0/0	0	42
Pickens	0	5	0	0/0	0/0	0	32
Dillon	4	1	0	0/0	0/0	0	30
Gibson	0	3	1	0/0	0/0	0	24
Bennett	2	0	0	0/0	0/0	0	12
Battaglia	0	1	0	0/0	0/0	0	6
Hundon	0	1	0	0/0	0/0	0	6
Mack	0	0	1	0/0	0/0	0	6
McGee	0	1	0	0/0	0/0	0	6
Milne	1	0	0	0/0	0/0	0	6
Sawyer	0	0	1	0/0	0/0	0	6
Shade	0	0	1	0/0	0/0	0	6
Williams	0	1	0	0/0	0/0	0	6
Justin	0	0	0	0/0	0/0	0	2
Bengals	7	20	4	21/21	19/27	0	268
Opponents	23	23	7	51/51	27/31	0	452

2-Point conversions: Justin, Pickens.
Team 2-9, Opponents 1-2.

RUSHING	Att.	Yds.	Avg.	LG	TD
Dillon	262	1,130	4.3	66	4
Bennett	77	243	3.2	17	2
Blake	15	103	6.9	18	0
Bieniemy	17	56	3.3	9	0
Milne	10	41	4.1	10	1
O'Donnell	13	34	2.6	10	0
Scott	2	10	5.0	8	0
Gibson	1	9	9.0	9	0
Blair	1	4	4.0	4	0
Carter	2	4	2.0	4	0
Pickens	2	4	2.0	4	0
Justin	1	2	2.0	2	0
Costello	1	0	0.0	0	0
Kresser	1	-1	-1.0	-1	0
Bengals	405	1,639	4.0	66	7
Opponents	558	2,612	4.7	67t	23

RECEIVING	No.	Yds.	Avg.	LG	TD
Pickens	82	1,023	12.5	67t	5
Scott	51	817	16.0	70t	7
Dillon	28	178	6.4	41	1
Bieniemy	27	153	5.7	15	0
Milne	26	124	4.8	18	0
McGee	22	363	16.5	40	1
Gibson	19	258	13.6	76t	3
Hundon	10	112	11.2	17	1
Battaglia	10	47	4.7	16	1
Bennett	8	153	19.1	55	0
Jackson	7	165	23.6	47	0
Williams	6	81	13.5	19t	1
Carter	6	25	4.2	8	0
Bush	4	39	9.8	18	0
Blair	1	7	7.0	7	0
Bengals	307	3,545	11.5	76t	20
Opponents	233	3,350	14.4	73t	23

INTERCEPTIONS	No.	Yds.	Avg.	LG	TD
Shade	3	33	11.0	32	0
Hawkins	3	21	7.0	12	0
Ambrose	2	0	0.0	0	0
Sawyer	1	58	58.0	58t	1
B. Simmons	1	18	18.0	18	0
Ross	1	11	11.0	11	0
Copeland	1	3	3.0	3	0
Randolph	1	0	0.0	0	0
Bengals	13	144	11.1	58t	1
Opponents	12	206	17.2	56	1

PUNTING	No.	Yds.	Avg.	In 20	LG
Johnson	69	3,083	44.7	14	69
Costello	10	495	49.5	0	73
Bengals	81	3,578	44.2	14	73
Opponents	64	2,850	44.5	29	72

PUNT RETURNS	No.	FC	Yds.	Avg.	LG	TD
Gibson	27	19	218	8.1	65t	1
Williams	2	3	16	8.0	10	0
Bengals	29	22	234	8.1	65t	1
Opponents	36	15	503	14.0	87t	1

KICKOFF RETURNS	No.	Yds.	Avg.	LG	TD
Mack	45	1,165	25.9	97t	1
Gibson	17	372	21.9	30	0
Bieniemy	5	87	17.4	22	0
Bennett	3	61	20.3	21	0
Battaglia	1	5	5.0	5	0
Williams	1	20	20.0	20	0
Bengals	72	1,710	23.8	97t	1
Opponents	46	1,199	26.1	51	0

FIELD GOALS	1-19	20-29	30-39	40-49	50+
Pelfrey	1/1	4/4	6/7	6/10	2/5
Bengals	1/1	4/4	6/7	6/10	2/5
Opponents	0/1	5/6	12/12	8/10	2/2

SACKS	No.
Wilson	6.0
C. Simmons	5.0
Bankston	4.5
B. Simmons	3.0
Foley	2.0
Spikes	2.0
Bell	1.0
Hawkins	1.0
Purvis	1.0
Shade	1.0
Langford	0.5
Thompson	0.5
Tumulty	0.5
Bengals	28.0
Opponents	53.0

1999 DRAFT CHOICES

Round	Name	Pos.	College
1	Akili Smith	QB	Oregon
2	Charles Fisher	DB	West Virginia
3	Cory Hall	DB	Fresno State
4	Craig Yeast	WR	Kentucky
5	Nick Williams	RB	Miami
6	Kelly Gregg	DT	Oklahoma
7	Tony Coats	G	Washington
	Scott Covington	QB	Miami
	Donald Broomfield	DT	Clemson

CINCINNATI BENGALS

1999 VETERAN ROSTER

No.	Name	Pos.	Ht.	Wt.	Birthdate	NFL Exp.	College	Hometown	How Acq.	'98 Games/ Starts
33	# Ambrose, Ashley	CB	5-10	185	9/17/70	8	Mississippi Valley State	New Orleans, La.	UFA(Ind)-'96	15/15
71	Anderson, Willie	T	6-5	340	7/11/75	4	Auburn	Whistler, Ala.	D1-'96	16/16
90	Bankston, Michael	DE	6-5	285	3/12/70	8	Sam Houston State	Elm Grove, Tex.	UFA(Ariz)-'98	16/16
89	Battaglia, Marco	TE	6-3	252	1/25/73	4	Rutgers	Queens, N.Y.	D2-'96	16/0
40	Bell, Myron	S	5-11	203	9/15/71	6	Michigan State	Toledo, Ohio	UFA(Pitt)-'98	16/1
36	Bennett, Brandon	RB	5-11	220	2/3/73	2	South Carolina	Greer, S.C.	FA-'98	14/1
66	Blackman, Ken	G	6-6	320	11/8/72	4	Illinois	Abilene, Tex.	D3-'96	8/8
37	Blackmon, Roosevelt	CB	6-1	185	9/10/74	2	Morris Brown	Belle Glade, Fla.	W(GB)-'98	15/0*
8	Blake, Jeff	QB	6-0	210	12/4/70	8	East Carolina	Sanford, Fla.	W(NYJ)-'94	8/2
74	Braham, Rich	G	6-4	305	11/6/70	6	West Virginia	Morgantown, W. Va.	W(Ariz)-'94	12/12
65	# Brilz, Darrick	C	6-3	300	2/14/64	13	Oregon State	Pinole, Calif.	UFA(Sea)-'94	16/16
88	Bush, Steve	TE-RB	6-3	258	7/4/74	3	Arizona State	Paradise Valley, Ariz.	FA-'97	12/2
32	Carter, Ki-Jana	RB	5-10	222	9/12/73	5	Penn State	Westerville, Ohio	D1-'95	1/0
16	Clayton, Alonzo	WR	6-1	194	10/5/74	2	Northern Iowa	Fort Dodge, Iowa	FA-'98	0*
92	Copeland, John	DE	6-3	280	9/20/70	7	Alabama	Lanette, Ala.	D1-'93	5/0
98	Curtis, Canute	LB	6-2	256	8/4/74	3	West Virginia	Amityville, N.Y.	FA-'98	5/0
73	DeMarco, Brian	G	6-7	323	4/9/72	5	Michigan State	Lorain, Ohio	UFA(Jac)-'99	16/9*
28	Dillon, Corey	RB	6-1	225	10/24/75	3	Washington	Seattle, Wash.	D2-'97	15/15
95	Foley, Steve	LB	6-3	260	9/9/75	2	Northeast Louisiana	Little Rock, Ark.	D3a-'98	10/1
50	Francis, James	LB	6-5	257	8/4/68	10	Baylor	Houston, Tex.	D1-'90	14/14
99	Gibson, Oliver	NT	6-2	290	3/15/72	5	Notre Dame	Romeoville, Ill.	UFA(Pitt)-'99	16/0*
63	Goff, Mike	G	6-5	316	1/6/76	2	Iowa	Peru, Ill.	D3b-'98	10/5
91	Granville, Billy	LB	6-3	252	3/11/74	3	Duke	Lawrenceville, N.J.	FA-'97	16/0
46	Groce, Clif	RB	5-11	245	7/30/72	3	Texas A&M	College Station, Tex.	W(NE)-'98	0*
62	Gutierrez, Brock	G-C	6-3	304	9/25/73	3	Central Michigan	Charlotte, Mich.	FA-'98	1/0
27	Hawkins, Artrell	CB	5-10	190	11/24/75	2	Cincinnati	Johnstown, Pa.	D2-'98	16/16
85	Hundon, James	WR	6-1	173	4/9/71	3	Portland State	Daly City, Calif.	FA-'96	9/3
80	Jackson, Willie	WR	6-1	212	8/16/71	6	Florida	Gainesville, Fla.	FA-'98	8/0
60	Jones, Rod	T	6-4	325	1/11/74	4	Kansas	Detroit, Mich.	D7-'96	6/2
94	Langford, Jevon	DE	6-3	290	2/16/74	4	Oklahoma State	Washington, D.C.	D4-'96	14/1
34	Mack, Tremain	S	6-0	193	11/21/74	3	Miami	Tyler, Tex.	D4-'97	12/0
24	Mathias, Ric	CB	5-10	180	12/10/75	2	Wisconsin-La Crosse	Monroe, Wis.	FA-'98	3/0
82	McGee, Tony	TE	6-3	250	4/21/71	7	Michigan	Terre Haute, Ind.	D2-'93	16/16
44	Milne, Brian	RB	6-3	254	1/7/73	4	Penn State	Waterford, Pa.	W(Ind)-'96	14/14
31	Myers, Greg	S	6-1	202	9/30/72	4	Colorado State	Windsor, Colo.	D5-'96	16/16
64	Payne, Rod	C	6-4	305	6/14/74	3	Michigan	Miami, Fla.	D3-'97	6/0
9	Pelfrey, Doug	K	5-11	185	9/25/70	7	Kentucky	Edgewood, Ky.	D8-'93	16/0
81	# Pickens, Carl	WR	6-2	206	3/23/70	8	Tennessee	Murphy, N.C.	D2-'92	16/16
97	Purvis, Andre	DE	6-4	310	7/14/73	3	North Carolina	Jacksonville, N.C.	D5-'97	9/0
20	Randolph, Thomas	CB	5-9	185	10/5/70	6	Kansas State	Norfolk, Va.	UFA(NYG)-'98	16/1
57	Ross, Adrian	LB	6-2	244	2/19/75	2	Colorado State	Elk Grove, Calif.	FA-'98	14/1
77	Sargent, Kevin	T	6-6	300	3/31/69	8	Eastern Washington	Bremerton, Wash.	FA-'92	16/16
23	Sawyer, Corey	CB	5-11	177	10/4/71	6	Florida State	Key West, Fla.	D4-'94	3/0
86	Scott, Darnay	WR	6-1	205	7/7/72	6	San Diego State	St. Louis, Mo.	D2-'94	13/13
68	Shaw, Scott	G	6-3	303	6/2/74	2	Michigan State	Sterling Heights, Mich.	FA-'98	2/0
56	Simmons, Brian	LB	6-3	233	6/21/75	2	North Carolina	New Bern, N.C.	D1b-'98	14/12
51	Spikes, Takeo	LB	6-2	230	12/17/76	2	Auburn	Sandersville, Ga.	D1a-'98	16/16
52	Sprotte, Jimmy	LB	6-3	235	10/2/74	2	Arizona	Lakeside, Ariz.	FA-'98	5/0
70	Steele, Glen	DE	6-4	295	10/4/74	2	Michigan	Ligonier, Ind.	D4-'98	10/0
58	Terry, Tim	LB	6-3	248	7/26/74	2	Temple	Hempstead, N.Y.	FA-'98	0*
59	Truitt, Greg	LS	6-0	235	12/8/65	6	Penn State	Sarasota, Fla.	FA-'94	11/0
53	Tumulty, Tom	LB	6-3	247	2/11/73	4	Pittsburgh	Penn Hills, Pa.	D6-'96	4/4
67	von Oelhoffen, Kimo	NT	6-4	305	1/30/71	6	Boise State	Kaunakakai, Hawaii	D6a-'94	16/16
87	Williams, Stepfret	WR	6-0	170	6/14/73	4	Northeast Louisiana	Minden, La.	W(Dall)-'98	5/0
55	Wilson, Reinard	LB	6-2	261	12/17/73	3	Florida State	Lake City, Fla.	D1-'97	16/15
42	Wright, Lawrence	S	6-1	211	9/6/73	2	Florida	Miami, Fla.	FA-'98	0*
45	# Zellars, Ray	RB	5-11	233	3/25/73	5	Notre Dame	Pittsburgh, Pa.	W(NO)-'98	11/7*

* Blackmon played 3 games with Green Bay and 12 games with Cincinnati in '98; Clayton missed '98 season because of injury; DeMarco played 16 games with Jacksonville; Gibson played 16 games with Pittsburgh; Groce inactive for 1 game with New England and inactive for 1 game with Cincinnati; Terry and Wright last active with Cincinnati in '97; Zellars played 11 games with New Orleans and inactive for 2 games with Cincinnati.

\# Unrestricted free agent; subject to developments.

Players lost through free agency (4): RB Eric Bieniemy (Phil; 16 games in '98), G-T Anthony Brown (Pitt; 16), DE Clyde Simmons (Chi; 16), S Sam Shade (Wash; 16).

Also played with Bengals in '98—RB Michael Blair (2 games), P Brad Costello (3), WR David Dunn (1), WR Damon Gibson (16), P-K Lee Johnson (13), QB Paul Justin (5), QB Eric Kresser (2), DB Kelvin Moore (4), QB Neil O'Donnell (13), NT Mike Thompson (10).

COACHING STAFF

Head Coach,
Bruce Coslet

Pro Career: Coslet is entering his third full season as head coach of the Cincinnati Bengals. He was named the franchise's seventh head coach seven games into the 1996 season, leading the team to a 7-2 record during the final nine games after its 1-6 start. The Bengals started 1-7 in 1997, but again rebounded to finish 7-9. Cincinnati finished 3-13 in 1998. This is the second head coaching position held by Coslet, who was head coach of the New York Jets for four season from 1990-93. Coslet began his coaching career as an assistant coach with the San Francisco 49ers in 1980. He joined the Bengals as an assistant coach in 1981. Coslet coached with Cincinnati for nine seasons from 1981-89, including four as offensive coordinator from 1986-89, before becoming head coach of the Jets. After four seasons with the Jets, he again returned to Cincinnati as offensive coordinator in 1994, and retained that position until his promotion to head coach in 1996. Coslet played tight end for the Bengals for eight seasons from 1969-1976. Career record: 43-63.

Background: Coslet is a native of Oakdale, Calif., and played football for Joint H.S. He was a tight end for the University of the Pacific from 1965-67.

Personal: Born August 5, 1946, Coslet and his wife, Kathy, live in Cincinnati and have two children, son J.J., and daughter Amy.

ASSISTANT COACHES

Paul Alexander, offensive line; born February 12, 1960, Rochester, N.Y., lives in Cincinnati. Tackle Cortland State 1979-1981. No pro playing experience. College coach: Penn State 1982-84, Michigan 1985-86, Central Michigan 1987-1991. Pro coach: New York Jets 1992-93, joined Bengals in 1994.

Jim Anderson, running backs; born March 27, 1948, Harrisburg, Pa., lives in Cincinnati. Linebacker-defensive end California Western 1967-1970. No pro playing experience. College coach: California Western 1970-71, Scottsdale (Ariz.) Community College 1973, Nevada-Las Vegas 1974-75, Southern Methodist 1976-1980, Stanford 1981-83. Pro coach: Joined Bengals in 1984.

Ken Anderson, offensive coordinator; born February 15, 1949, Batavia, Ill., lives in Highland Heights, Ky. Quarterback Augustana (Ill.) 1967-1970. Pro quarterback Cincinnati Bengals 1971-1986. Pro coach: Joined Bengals in 1992.

Louie Cioffi, defensive staff assistant; born September 21, 1973, Greenlawn, N.Y., lives in Cincinnati. Attended SUNY-Stony Brook. No college or pro playing experience. College coach: C.W. Post 1995-96. Pro coach: New York Jets 1993-94, joined Bengals in 1997.

Mark Duffner, linebackers; born July 19, 1953, Annandale, Va., lives in Cincinnati. Defensive lineman William & Mary 1973-74. No pro playing experience. College coach: Ohio State 1975-76, Cincinnati 1977-1980, Holy Cross 1981-1991 (head coach 1986-1991), Maryland 1992-96 (head coach). Pro coach: Joined Bengals in 1997.

Ray Horton, defensive backs; born April 12, 1960, Tacoma, Wash., lives in Cincinnati. Defensive back Washington 1979-1982. Pro defensive back Cincinnati Bengals 1983-88, Dallas Cowboys 1989-1992. Pro coach: Washington Redskins 1994-96, joined Bengals in 1997.

Tim Krumrie, defensive line; born May 20, 1960, Menomonie, Wis., lives in Cincinnati. Defensive tackle Wisconsin 1979-1982. Pro defensive tackle Cincinnati Bengals 1983-1994. Pro coach: Joined Bengals in 1995.

Dick LeBeau, asst. head coach-defensive coordinator; born September 9, 1937, London, Ohio, lives in Cincinnati. Offensive-defensive back Ohio State 1954-57. Pro cornerback Detroit Lions 1959-1972. Pro coach: Philadelphia Eagles 1973-75, Green Bay Packers 1976-79, Cincinnati Bengals 1980-1991, Pittsburgh Steelers 1992-96, rejoined Bengals in 1997.

1999 FIRST-YEAR ROSTER

Name	Pos.	Ht.	Wt.	Birthdate	College	Hometown	How Acq.
Ainsworth, Greg	WR	6-1	192	8/12/75	Oregon State	Duarte, Calif.	FA
Basnight, Michael	RB	6-1	230	9/3/77	North Carolina A&T	Norfolk, Va.	FA
Broomfield, Donald	DE	6-3	295	6/10/76	Clemson	Olustee, Fla.	D7c
Cleary, Anthony	RB	6-0	255	10/6/76	Shippensburg	Chambersburg, Pa.	FA
Coats, Tony	G	6-6	305	10/5/75	Washington	Port Orchard, Wash.	D7a
Costello, Brad (1)	P	6-1	230	12/12/74	Boston	Moorestown, N.J.	FA-'98
Covington, Scott	QB	6-2	217	1/17/76	Miami	Laguna Niguel, Calif.	D7b
Doughty, Mike (1)	T	6-7	315	2/18/75	Notre Dame	Lakeville, Minn.	FA-'98
Dow, Marcus	NT	6-0	295	1/16/76	North Carolina	Thomasville, N.C.	FA
Fisher, Charles	CB	6-0	185	2/2/76	West Virginia	Aliquippa, Pa.	D2
Gregg, Kelly	NT	6-0	285	11/1/76	Oklahoma	Edmond, Okla.	D6
Hall, Cory	S	6-0	205	12/5/76	Fresno State	Bakersfield, Calif.	D3
Hampton, Louis	LB	6-2	245	6/8/76	Houston	Killeen, Tex.	FA
Hanley, Brien	T	6-2	325	11/2/75	Kansas State	Coffeyville, Kan.	FA
Heath, Rodney (1)	CB	5-10	170	10/2974	Minnesota	Cincinnati, Ohio	FA
Jackson, Quincy	WR	6-0	187	4/2/77	Alabama	Brundidge, Ala.	FA
Jennings, John	TE	6-4	250	7/25/75	Belhaven College	Taylorsville, Miss.	FA
Krause, Greg	G	6-3	285	4/4/76	New Hampshire	Bedford, N.H.	FA
Kresser, Eric (1)	QB	6-2	223	2/6/73	Marshall	Palm Beach Gardens, Fla.	FA-'98
Moore, Kelvin (1)	S	6-0	203	3/7/75	Morgan State	Los Angeles, Calif.	FA-'98
Murphy, Terry	WR	6-0	180	8/25/75	Pittsburgh	Los Angeles, Calif.	FA
Noisy, Geoff	WR	6-0	195	1/31/76	Nevada	Irvine, Calif.	FA
Parks, Marcus	CB	5-10	185	7/27/76	Sam Houston State	Corsicana, Tex.	FA
Pegues, Chad	NT	6-0	291	12/13/76	Illinois State	Gainesville, Tex.	FA
Peterson, Ben	LB	6-3	250	3/28/77	Pittsburg State	Clay Center, Kan.	FA
Schorejs, Derek	K	5-11	210	5/14/73	Bowling Green	Westerville, Ohio	FA
Shelley, Jason (1)	WR	6-1	191	8/4/74	Central State, Ohio	Sparks, Nev.	FA
Smith, Akili	QB	6-3	220	8/21/75	Oregon	San Diego, Calif.	D1
Uhl, Brian	C	6-3	296	12/31/75	Cincinnati	Cincinnati, Ohio	FA
Vaughn, Damian (1)	TE	6-4	252	6/14/75	Miami, Ohio	Orrville, Ohio	FA-'98
Williams, Nick	RB	6-1	267	3/30/77	Miami	Farmington Hills, Mich.	D5
Yeast, Craig	WR	5-7	160	11/20/76	Kentucky	Harrodsburg, Ky.	D4

The term NFL Rookie is defined as a player who is in his first season of professional football and has not been on the roster of another professional football team for any regular-season or postseason games. A Rookie is designated by an "R" on NFL rosters. Players who have been active in another professional football league or players who have NFL experience, including either preseason training camp or being on an Active List or Inactive List, or on Reserve/Injured or Reserve/Physically Unable to Perform for fewer than six regular-season games, are termed NFL First-Year Players. An NFL First-Year Player is designated by a "1" on NFL rosters. Thereafter, a player is credited with an additional year of experience for each season in which he accumulates six games on the Active List or Inactive List, or on Reserve/Injured or Reserve/Physically Unable to Perform.

NOTES

Steve Mooshagian, wide receivers; born March 27, 1959, Downey, Calif., lives in Cincinnati. Wide receiver Cerritos College 1978-79, Fresno State 1980-81. No pro playing experience. College coach: Fresno State 1985-1994, Fresno City College 1995 (head coach), Nevada 1996, Pittsburgh 1997-98. Pro coach: Joined Bengals in 1999.

Al Roberts, special teams; born January 6, 1944, Fresno, Calif., lives in Cincinnati. Running back Washington 1964-65, Puget Sound 1967-68. No pro playing experience. College coach: Washington 1977-1982, 1996, Purdue 1986-87. Pro coach: Los Angeles Express (USFL) 1983-84, Houston Oilers 1984-85, Philadelphia Eagles 1988-1990, New York Jets 1991-93, Arizona Cardinals 1994-95, joined Bengals in 1997.

Frank Verducci, tight ends; born March 17, 1957, Glen Ridge, N.J., lives in Cincinnati. Tight end-fullback U.S. Merchant Marine Academy-Kings Port 1975. No pro playing experience. College coach: Colorado State 1980, Maryland 1981-83, Northern Illinois 1984, Iowa 1985-86, 1989-1998, Northwestern 1987-88. Pro coach: Joined Bengals in 1999.

Kim Wood, strength; born July 12, 1945, Barrington, Ill., lives in Cincinnati. Running back Wisconsin 1965-68. No pro playing experience. Pro coach: Joined Bengals in 1975.

CLEVELAND BROWNS

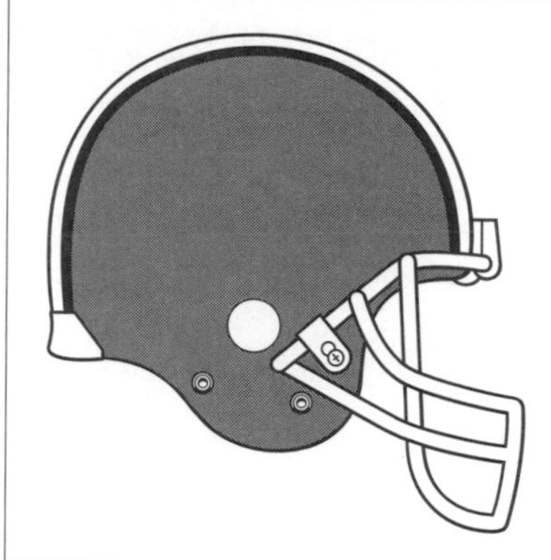

American Football Conference
Central Division
Team Colors: Brown, Orange, and White
76 Lou Groza Blvd.
Berea, Ohio 44017
Telephone: (440) 891-5000

CLUB OFFICIALS

Owner and Chairman: Alfred Lerner
President and Chief Executive Officer: Carmen Policy
Vice President, Director of Football Operations: Dwight Clark
Vice President, Chief Administrative Officer: Kofi Bonner
Vice President of Finance & Treasurer: Doug Jacobs
Vice President, Director of Stadium Operations and Security: Lew Merletti
Vice President, Director of Communications & Public Affairs: Alex Martins
Assistant Director of Football Operations & General Counsel: Lal Heneghan
Director of Player Personnel: Joe Collins
Director of College Scouting: Phil Neri
Pro Personnel Coordinator: Keith Kidd
Business Manager: Bill Hampton
Executive Director of Marketing: Bruce Popko
Director of Ticket Sales: Mike Jennings
Stadium Operations Manager: Bill Squires
Director, Cleveland Browns Foundation: Judge George White
Director of Publicity/Media Relations: Todd Stewart
Director of Publications/Internet: Dan Arthur
Coordinator of Publicity/Media Relations: Ken Mather
Coordinator of Publications/Internet: Amy Gretsinger
Browns Backers Coordinator: Krystal Thomas
Facilities Manager: Greg Hipp
Head Athletic Trainer: Mike Colello
Equipment Manager: Bobby Monica
Video Director: Pat Dolan
Head Groundskeeper: Chris Powell
Stadium: Cleveland Browns Stadium • **Capacity:** 72,000
1085 West 3rd Street
Cleveland, Ohio 44114
Playing Surface: Grass
Headquarters/Training Camp:
76 Lou Groza Boulevard
Berea, Ohio 44017

1999 SCHEDULE

PRESEASON

Aug. 9	vs. Dallas at Canton, Ohio	8:00
Aug. 14	at Tampa Bay	8:00
Aug. 21	**Minnesota**	7:00
Aug. 28	**Chicago**	8:00
Sept. 2	at Philadelphia	7:30

REGULAR SEASON

Sept. 12	**Pittsburgh**	8:20
Sept. 19	at Tennessee	3:15
Sept. 26	at Baltimore	1:00
Oct. 3	**New England**	1:00
Oct. 10	**Cincinnati**	1:00
Oct. 17	at Jacksonville	1:00
Oct. 24	at St. Louis	12:00
Oct. 31	at New Orleans	12:00
Nov. 7	**Baltimore**	1:00
Nov. 14	at Pittsburgh	1:00
Nov. 21	**Carolina**	1:00
Nov. 28	**Tennessee**	1:00
Dec. 5	at San Diego	1:15
Dec. 12	at Cincinnati	1:00
Dec. 19	**Jacksonville**	1:00
Dec. 26	**Indianapolis**	1:00
Jan. 2	Open Date	

RECORD HOLDERS

INDIVIDUAL RECORDS—CAREER

Category	Name	Performance
Rushing (Yds.)	Jim Brown, 1957-1965	12,312
Passing (Yds.)	Brian Sipe, 1974-1983	23,713
Passing (TDs)	Brian Sipe, 1974-1983	154
Receiving (No.)	Ozzie Newsome, 1978-1990	662
Receiving (Yds.)	Ozzie Newsome, 1978-1990	7,980
Interceptions	Thom Darden, 1972-74, 1976-1981	45
Punting (Avg.)	Horace Gillom, 1950-56	43.8
Punt Return (Avg.)	Greg Pruitt, 1973-1981	11.8
Kickoff Return (Avg.)	Greg Pruitt, 1973-1981	26.3
Field Goals	Lou Groza, 1950-59, 1961-67	234
Touchdowns (Tot.)	Jim Brown, 1957-1965	126
Points	Lou Groza, 1950-59, 1961-67	1,349

INDIVIDUAL RECORDS—SINGLE SEASON

Category	Name	Performance
Rushing (Yds.)	Jim Brown, 1963	1,863
Passing (Yds.)	Brian Sipe, 1980	4,132
Passing (TDs)	Brian Sipe, 1980	30
Receiving (No.)	Ozzie Newsome, 1983	89
	Ozzie Newsome, 1984	89
Receiving (Yds.)	Webster Slaughter, 1989	1,236
Interceptions	Thom Darden, 1978	10
Punting (Avg.)	Gary Collins, 1965	46.7
Punt Return (Avg.)	Leroy Kelly, 1965	15.6
Kickoff Return (Avg.)	Billy Reynolds, 1954	29.5
Field Goals	Matt Stover, 1995	29
Touchdowns (Tot.)	Jim Brown, 1965	21
Points	Jim Brown, 1965	126

INDIVIDUAL RECORDS—SINGLE GAME

Category	Name	Performance
Rushing (Yds.)	Jim Brown, 11-24-57	237
	Jim Brown, 11-19-61	237
Passing (Yds.)	Bernie Kosar, 1-3-87	489
Passing (TDs)	Frank Ryan, 12-12-64	5
	Bill Nelsen, 11-2-69	5
	Brian Sipe, 10-7-79	5
Receiving (No.)	Ozzie Newsome, 10-14-84	14
Receiving (Yds.)	Ozzie Newsome, 10-14-84	191
Interceptions	Many times	3
	Last time by Frank Minnifield, 11-22-87	
Field Goals	Don Cockroft, 10-19-75	5
Touchdowns (Tot.)	Dub Jones, 11-25-51	*6
Points	Dub Jones, 11-25-51	36

*NFL Record

COACHING HISTORY

(385-285-10)

1950-62	Paul Brown	115-49-5
1963-70	Blanton Collier	79-38-2
1971-74	Nick Skorich	30-26-2
1975-77	Forrest Gregg*	18-23-0
1977	Dick Modzelewski	0-1-0
1978-84	Sam Rutigliano**	47-52-0
1984-88	Marty Schottenheimer	46-31-0
1989-90	Bud Carson***	12-14-1
1990	Jim Shofner	1-6-0
1991-95	Bill Belichick	37-45-0

*Resigned after 13 games in 1977
**Released after eight games in 1984
***Released after nine games in 1990

CLEVELAND BROWNS STADIUM

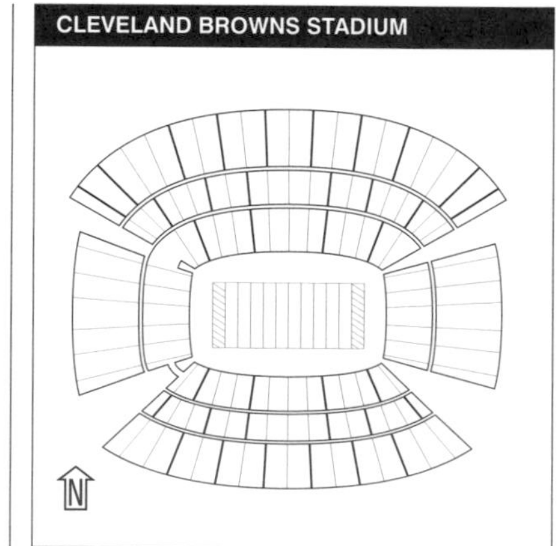

AGREEMENT BETWEEN THE NFL AND THE CITY OF CLEVELAND

The 1996 agreement between the city of Cleveland and the NFL guaranteed the Browns franchise would return to Cleveland in a new state-of-the-art stadium in 1999.

The agreement held the following key points:
• The Cleveland Browns franchise will remain in Cleveland and will resume play in the 1999 season.
• The tradition and records, including the Browns' name, trademarks, colors, history, playing records, trophies, and memorabilia, will remain in Cleveland as property of the Cleveland Browns franchise.
• The new stadium will be owned by the city of Cleveland and will have a 30-year lease with the Browns. A provision in the lease stipulates the Browns will be responsible for operating the stadium.

CHRONOLOGY OF BROWNS RETURN

June 12, 1996
The city of Cleveland and the NFL announce the terms of a historic public-private partnership that continues the Browns franchise in Cleveland and guarantees a new state-of-the-art stadium in Cleveland in 1999.
May 15, 1997
At the site of the new Cleveland Browns Stadium, NFL President Neil Austrian, Cleveland Mayor Michael R. White, and local officials officially break ground for the new home of the Browns.
March 23, 1998
At a league meeting in Orlando, NFL owners agree that the Cleveland Browns will be an expansion team in 1999.
July 23, 1998
Alfred Lerner and Carmen Policy announce they will submit an application to the National Football League to purchase the new Cleveland Browns expansion team.
September 8, 1998
The NFL awards the Cleveland Browns to Alfred Lerner and Carmen Policy.
October 23, 1998
The NFL formerly transfers ownership of the Cleveland Browns to Alfred Lerner and Carmen Policy.
November 30, 1998
Dwight Clark named vice president, director of football operations.
December 17, 1998
First players come aboard as Cleveland Browns agree to terms with the following free agents: WR Corey Bridges, DL Darion Conner, QB John Dutton, TE Aaron Laing, DL Chris Maumalanga, RB John Henry Mills, DL Albert Reese.
January 21, 1999
Chris Palmer named head coach.
February 9, 1999
Cleveland Browns select 37 players in the expansion draft including Detroit Lions offensive lineman Jim Pyne with the first pick.
March 26-28, 1999
Cleveland Browns return to the field for the first time as the team holds its first mini-camp in the club's indoor practice facility in Berea, Ohio. The Browns hold five practices over three days.
March 28, 1999
Cleveland Browns announce all Permanent Seat Licenses, suites and Dawg Pound seats at the new Cleveland Browns Stadium are sold out.
April 17-18, 1999
Cleveland Browns select 11 players over the two-day NFL draft including University of Kentucky quarterback Tim Couch with the first overall selection.

PLAYER ACCESS PLAN

The expansion Cleveland Browns acquired players four ways:
1) Free Agents—The Browns were allowed to sign previously terminated free agents. From December 17 (12 days before the applicable date for the other NFL teams) until the end of the 1998 regular season, Cleveland could sign a maximum of 10 free agents (not under contract to other teams) to 1999 contracts.
2) Expansion Draft—Each of the existing 30 NFL clubs was required to submit a list of five veteran players for selection by the Browns. Each club could put forward only one player who was placed on injured reserved after the start of the 1998 regular season and one player who had 10 or more years of free agency experience. Neither punters nor kickers could be part of the list. The Browns had three minutes to select a player and were required to select between 30 and 42 players or a fewer number of players with total salaries of 38 percent of the salary cap. The existing clubs had two minutes to recall one player from its list after one of its players was selected. After a second player was selected from a club, that club could pull back both of its remaining players.
3) NFL Draft—The Browns were designated 28 choices in the NFL Draft encompassing the 1999 and 2000 seasons, 14 in 1999 and 14 in 2000. If the Browns make the playoffs in 1999, the team will not have extra picks in 2000.

In the 1999 draft, the Browns were allocated the first pick in each of the seven rounds and an additional seven picks allocated in the following manner: one selection in rounds two, three, four, five, six, and seven after all teams with a 1998 regular-season winning percentage of less than .500; the final selection in round seven.

In the 2000 draft, Cleveland will receive one regular selection per round based on its 1999 record, the same as all other clubs. The Browns will also receive seven additional picks in the 2000 draft, unless they make the playoffs in 1999, in which case they will receive no extra picks. These additional picks will vary based on Cleveland's 1999 win-loss percentage and will be allocated in the following manner based on the 2000 draft order: If Cleveland's normal selection is between 1-7, the Browns receive one extra pick in rounds three, four, and five and two extra picks in rounds six and seven. If Cleveland's normal selection is between 8-13, the Browns receive one extra pick in rounds four and five, two extra picks in round six and three extra picks in round seven. If Cleveland's normal selection is between 14-19, the Browns receive one extra pick in round five, two extra picks in round six and four extra picks in round seven.

The first extra Cleveland selection in any round will fall 16 slots below the club's original choice in that round, but no lower than the end of the round, after any regular compensatory selections.

In 1998 and 1999 Cleveland was prohibited from trading any draft picks to acquire or obtain the contractual release of any non-player personnel (i.e. coach, general manager).
4) Restricted and Unrestricted Free Agents—The Browns were eligible to sign both restricted and unrestricted free agents during this year's veteran free agency period. They had the same access to veteran free agents as the other clubs.

During the period from February 12 until July 15th, however, the Browns' roster had to include at least 30 players acquired from the expansion draft or a fewer number of players acquired in the draft with total salaries of at least 38 percent of the 1999 salary cap. Any of these players who are released after June 1 are entitled to a supplemental expansion bonus equal to the player's minimum Collective Bargaining Agreement salary even if he subsequently signs with another team.

ALL-TIME LEADERS

PASSER RATING (minimum 1,000 attempts)	Att.	Comp.	Yds.	TD	Int.	Rating
Plum, Milt	1,083	627	8,914	66	39	89.9
Kosar, Bernie	3,150	1,853	21,904	116	81	81.6
Ryan, Frank	1,755	907	13,361	134	88	81.4
Graham, Otto	1,565	872	13,499	88	94	78.2
Sipe, Brian	3,439	1,944	23,713	154	149	74.8
Nelsen, Bill	1,314	689	9,725	71	71	72.1
Phipps, Mike	1,317	633	7,700	40	81	51.0

SCORING	Pts.
Groza, Lou	1,349
Cockroft, Don	1,080
Brown, Jim	756
Bahr, Matt	677
Kelly, Leroy	540
Stover, Matt	480
Collins, Gary	420
Renfro, Ray	330
Mack, Kevin	324
Warfield, Paul	318

RUSHING	Att.	Yds.	TD
Brown, Jim	2,359	12,312	106
Kelly, Leroy	1,727	7,274	74
Pruitt, Mike	1,593	6,540	47
Pruitt, Greg	1,158	5,496	25
Mack, Kevin	1,291	5,123	46
Byner, Earnest	862	3,364	27
Green, Ernie	668	3,204	15
Mitchell, Bobby	423	2,297	16
Miller, Cleo	546	2,286	16
Metcalf, Eric	592	2,229	11

RECEIVING	No.	Yds.	TD
Newsome, Ozzie	662	7,980	47
Collins, Gary	331	5,299	70
Pruitt, Greg	323	3,022	17
Brennan, Brian	315	4,148	19
Rucker, Reggie	310	4,953	32
Slaughter, Webster	305	4,834	27
Metcalf, Eric	297	2,732	15
Renfro, Ray	281	5,508	50
Byner, Earnest	276	2,630	10
Morin, Milt	271	4,208	16
Warfield, Paul	271	5,210	52

RECEIVING YARDAGE	Yds.	No.	TD
Newsome, Ozzie	7,980	662	47
Renfro, Ray	5,508	281	50
Collins, Gary	5,299	331	70
Warfield, Paul	5,210	271	52
Rucker, Reggie	4,953	310	32
Slaughter, Webster	4,834	305	27
Logan, Dave	4,247	262	24
Morin, Milt	4,208	271	16
Brennan, Brian	4,148	315	19
Lavelli, Dante	3,908	244	33

INTERCEPTIONS	No.	Yds.	TD
Darden, Thom	45	820	2
Lahr, Warren	40	530	5
Scott, Clarence	39	407	2
Konz, Ken	30	392	4
Parrish, Bernie	29	557	3
Fichtner, Ross	27	581	3
Howell, Mike	27	252	0
Dixon, Hanford	26	225	0
James, Tommy	26	208	0
Wright, Felix	26	469	2

PUNT RETURNS (minimum 50 returns)	No.	Yds.	Avg.	TD
Pruitt, Greg	56	659	11.8	0
Mitchell, Bobby	54	607	11.2	3
Metcalf, Eric	127	1,341	10.6	5
Kelly, Leroy	94	990	10.5	3
McNeil, Gerald	161	1,545	9.6	1
Konz, Ken	68	556	8.2	1
Hall, Dino	111	901	8.1	0
Brennan, Brian	55	435	7.9	1
Wright, Keith	78	467	6.0	0
Reynolds, Billy	67	363	5.4	0

KICKOFF RETURNS (minimum 50 returns)	No.	Yds.	Avg.	TD
Pruitt, Greg	58	1,523	26.3	1
Roberts, Walt	62	1,608	25.9	0
Wright, Keith	70	1,767	25.2	0
Mitchell, Bobby	62	1,550	25.0	3
Lefear, Billy	60	1,461	24.4	0
Young, Glen	87	2,079	23.9	0
Kelly, Leroy	76	1,784	23.5	0
Baldwin, Randy	82	1,872	22.8	1
Hall, Dino	151	3,185	21.1	0
McNeil, Gerald	64	1,301	20.3	1

OTHER PERSONNEL RULES

Roster Size—The Browns have an off-season roster limit of 90 (rest of NFL 80), the first cutdown (August 31) must be to 65 (others 60), the final cutdown (September 5) to 56 (others 53), an active/inactive roster limit of 56 through the third week of the regular season (others 53).
Waiver Priorities—Through week three of the 1999 regular season, Cleveland will have waiver priority and thereafter waiver rights will be based on its 1999 record, the same as all other teams.

1999 DRAFT CHOICES

Round	Name	Pos.	College
1	Tim Couch	QB	Kentucky
2	Kevin Johnson	WR	Syracuse
	Rahim Abdullah	LB	Clemson
3	Daylon McCutcheon	DB	Southern California
	Marquis Smith	DB	California
4	Wali Rainer	LB	Virginia
5	Darrin Chiaverini	WR	Colorado
6	Marcus Spriggs	DT	Troy State
	Kendall Ogle	LB	Maryland
	James Dearth	TE	Tarleton State
7	Madre Hill	RB	Arkansas

HALL OF FAMERS

Jim Brown	RB	Inducted 1971
Paul Brown	Coach	Inducted 1967
Len Ford	DE	Inducted 1976
Frank Gatski	C	Inducted 1985
Otto Graham	QB	Inducted 1965
Lou Groza	T-K	Inducted 1974
Leroy Kelly	RB	Inducted 1994
Dante Lavelli	E	Inducted 1975
Mike McCormack	T	Inducted 1984
Bobby Mitchell	RB	Inducted 1983
Marion Motley	RB	Inducted 1968
Ozzie Newsome	TE	Inducted 1999
Paul Warfield	WR	Inducted 1983
Bill Willis	G	Inducted 1977

CLEVELAND BROWNS

1999 VETERAN ROSTER

No.	Name	Pos.	Ht.	Wt.	Birthdate	NFL Exp.	College	Hometown	How Acq.	'98 Games/ Starts
94	Alexander, Derrick	DE	6-4	286	11/13/73	5	Florida State	Jacksonville, Fla.	UFA(Minn)-'99	16/16*
93	Ball, Jerry	DT	6-1	320	12/15/64	13	Southern Methodist	Beaumont, Tex.	UFA(Minn)-'99	16/16*
92	Barker, Roy	DE	6-5	290	2/14/69	8	North Carolina	Long Island, N.Y.	T(SF)-'99	16/16*
28	Blackwell, Kory	CB-S	5-11	185	8/3/72	2	Massachusetts	Queens, N.Y.	ED(NYG)-'99	5/0*
27	Blair, Michael	RB	5-11	245	11/26/74	2	Ball State	South Holland, Ill.	ED(GB)-'99	13/0*
74	Bobo, Orlando	G	6-3	299	2/9/74	3	Northeast Louisiana	West Point, Miss.	ED(Minn)-'99	4/0*
75	Brown, Lomas	T	6-4	290	3/30/63	15	Florida	Miami, Fla.	UFA(Ariz)-'99	16/16*
77	Brown, Orlando	T	6-7	350	12/12/70	7	South Carolina State	Washington, D.C.	UFA(Balt)-'99	13/13*
70	Buckey, Jeff	T	6-5	305	8/7/74	4	Stanford	Bakersfield, Calif.	ED(Mia)-'99	7/0*
30	Butler, Duane	CB-S	6-1	203	11/29/73	3	Illinois State	Trotwood, Ohio	ED(Minn)-'99	14/0*
63	Cavil, Ben	G	6-2	310	1/31/72	3	Oklahoma	Galveston, Tex.	ED(Balt)-'99	16/6*
11	Detmer, Ty	QB	6-0	194	10/30/67	8	Brigham Young	San Antonio, Tex.	T(SF)-'99	16/1*
26	Devine, Kevin	CB-S	5-9	179	12/11/74	3	California	West Covina, Calif.	ED(Jac)-'99	5/0*
44	Edwards, Marc	RB	6-0	229	11/17/74	2	Notre Dame	Norwood, Ohio	T(SF)-'99	16/10*
47	Forbes, Marlon	CB-S	6-1	215	12/25/71	4	Penn State	Long Island, N.Y.	ED(Chi)-'99	16/2*
24	Fuller, Corey	CB-S	5-10	217	5/1/71	5	Florida State	Tallahassee, Fla.	UFA(Minn)-'99	16/16*
17	Gardocki, Chris	P	6-1	200	2/7/70	9	Clemson	Stone Mountain, Ga.	UFA(Ind)-'99	16/0*
81	Gibson, Damon	WR	5-9	184	2/25/75	2	Iowa	Houston, Tex.	ED(Cin)-'99	16/0*
61	Gordon, Steve	C	6-3	288	4/15/69	2	California	Grass Valley, Calif.	ED(SF)-'99	13/1*
66	Holland, Darius	DT	6-5	320	11/10/73	5	Colorado	Las Cruces, N.M.	UFA(Det)-'99	16/4*
31	Jackson, Raymond	CB-S	5-10	189	2/17/73	4	Colorado State	Denver, Colo.	ED(Buff)-'99	14/0*
51	Jones, Lenoy	LB	6-1	235	9/25/74	4	Texas Christian	Groesbeck, Tex.	ED(Tenn)-'99	9/0*
67	Jurkovic, John	DT	6-2	301	8/18/67	9	Eastern Illinois	Calumet City, Ill.	UFA(Jac)-'99	16/16*
42	Kirby, Terry	RB	6-1	213	1/20/70	7	Virginia	Yorktown, Va.	UFA(SF)-'99	9/0*
97	Kuehl, Ryan	DT	6-5	290	1/18/72	2	Virginia	Bethesda, Md.	FA-'99	0*
57	Kyle, Jason	LB	6-3	242	5/12/72	5	Arizona State	Tempe, Ariz.	ED(Sea)-'99	16/0*
86	Laing, Aaron	TE	6-4	260	7/19/71	4	New Mexico State	Houston, Tex.	FA-'99	0*
38	Langham, Antonio	CB-S	6-0	184	7/31/72	6	Alabama	Town Creek, Ala.	ED(SF)-'99	11/6*
96	Manuel, Rod	DE	6-5	295	10/8/74	3	Oklahoma	Fort Worth, Tex.	ED(Pitt)-'99	2/0*
87	Marsh, Curtis	WR	6-2	210	11/24/70	4	Utah	Panorama City, Calif.	FA-'99	0*
91	Maumalanga, Chris	DT	6-3	300	12/15/71	3	Kansas	Torrance, Calif.	FA-'99	0*
99	McCormack, Hurvin	DT	6-5	284	4/6/72	6	Indiana	Brooklyn, N.Y.	ED(Dall)-'99	16/1*
21	McPhail, Jerris	RB	5-11	198	6/26/72	4	East Carolina	Clinton, N.C.	ED(Det)-'99	3/0*
22	McTyer, Tim	CB-S	5-11	181	12/14/75	3	Brigham Young	Los Angeles, Calif.	ED(Phil)-'99	16/1*
95	Miller, Jamir	LB	6-5	266	11/19/73	6	UCLA	Oakland, Calif.	UFA(Ariz)-'99	16/16*
20	Moore, Ronald	RB	5-10	220	1/26/70	7	Pittsburg State	Spencer, Okla.	ED(Mia)-'99	1/0*
23	Pope, Marquez	CB-S	5-11	193	10/29/70	8	Fresno State	Nashville, Tenn.	UFA(SF)-'99	6/3*
71	Pyne, Jim	G	6-2	297	11/23/71	6	Virginia Tech	Wallingford, Conn.	ED(Det)-'99	16/16*
98	Reese, Albert	DT	6-6	280	4/29/73	2	Grambling State	Prichard, Ala.	FA-'99	0*
79	Rehberg, Scott	T	6-8	330	11/17/73	3	Central Michigan	Kalamazoo, Mich.	ED(NE)-'99	2/0*
89	Ross, Jermaine	WR	6-0	189	4/27/71	4	Purdue	Jeffersonville, Ind.	FA-'99	0*
40	Saleh, Tarek	RB	6-0	240	11/7/74	3	Wisconsin	Fairfield, Conn.	ED(Car)-'99	11/1*
34	Sanders, Brandon	CB-S	5-9	185	6/10/73	4	Arizona	La Mesa, Calif.	ED(NYG)-'99	13/0*
80	Seay, Mark	WR	6-0	180	4/11/67	6	Long Beach State	San Bernardino, Calif.	FA-'99	0*
25	Shaw, Sedrick	RB	6-0	214	11/16/73	3	Iowa	Austin, Tex.	T(NE)-'99	13/1*
6	Shepherd, Leslie	WR	5-11	186	11/3/69	6	Temple	Forestville, Md.	UFA(Wash)-'99	16/16*
82	Smith, Irv	TE	6-3	262	10/13/71	7	Notre Dame	Pemberton, N.J.	T(SF)-'99	16/8*
54	Spielman, Chris	LB	6-0	247	10/11/65	11	Ohio State	Massillon, Ohio	T(Buff)-'99	0*
37	Stokes, Eric	CB-S	5-11	200	12/18/73	3	Nebraska	Lincoln, Neb.	ED(Sea)-'99	4/0*
53	Thierry, John	LB	6-4	265	9/4/71	6	Alcorn State	Opelousas, La.	UFA(Chi)-'99	16/9*
65	Thompson, Mike	DT	6-4	295	12/22/71	3	Wisconsin	Portage, Wis.	ED(Cin)-'99	9/0*
69	Wiggins, Paul	T	6-3	305	8/17/73	3	Oregon	Portland, Ore.	ED(Wash)-'99	1/0*
39	Williams, Clarence	RB	6-1	286	1/20/75	2	Florida State	Crescent City, Fla.	ED(Buff)-'99	3/0*
36	Williams, Gerome	CB-S	6-2	210	7/9/73	3	Houston	Houston, Tex.	ED(SD)-'99	16/0*
90	Williams, James	LB	6-0	246	10/10/68	9	Mississippi State	Natchez, Miss.	ED(SF)-'99	15/0*
64	Wohlabaugh, Dave	C	6-3	292	4/13/72	5	Syracuse	Hamburg, N.Y.	UFA(NE)-'99	16/16*

* D. Alexander played 16 games with Minnesota in '98; Ball played 16 games with Minnesota; Barker played 16 games with San Francisco; Blackwell played 5 games with N.Y. Giants; Blair played 13 games with Green Bay; Bobo played 4 games with Minnesota; L. Brown played 16 games with Arizona; O. Brown played 13 games with Baltimore; Buckey played 7 games with Miami; Butler played 14 games with Minnesota; Cavil played 16 games with Baltimore; Detmer played 16 games with San Francisco; Devine played 5 games with Jacksonville; Edwards played 16 games with San Francisco; Forbes played 16 games with Chicago; Fuller played 16 games with Minnesota; Gardocki played 16 games with Indianapolis; Gibson played 16 games with Cincinnati; Gordon played 13 games with San Francisco; Holland played 16 games with Detroit; Jackson played 14 games with Buffalo; Jones played 9 games with Tennessee; Jurkovic played 16 games with Jacksonville; Kirby played 9 games with San Francisco; Kuehl last active with Washington in '97; Kyle played 16 games with Seattle; Laing inactive for 1 game with St. Louis; Langham played 11 games with San Francisco; Manuel played 2 games with Pittsburgh; Marsh last active with Pittsburgh in '97; Maumalanga last active with Chicago and St. Louis in '97; McCormack played 16 games with Dallas; McPhail played 3 games with Detroit; McTyer played 16 games with Philadelphia; Miller played 16 games with Arizona; Moore played 1 game with Miami; Pope played 6 games with San Francisco; Pyne played 16 games with Detroit; Reese last active with San Francisco in '97; Rehberg played 2 games with New England; Ross last active with Jacksonville in '97; Saleh played 11 games with Carolina; Sanders played 13 games with N.Y. Giants; Seay played 12 games with Philadelphia in '97; Shaw played 13 games with New England; Shepherd played 16 games with Washington; Smith played 16 games with San Francisco; Spielman last active with Buffalo in '97; Stokes played 4 games with Seattle; Thierry played 16 games with Chicago; Thompson played 9 games with Cincinnati; P. Wiggins played 1 game with Washington; C. Williams played 3 games with Buffalo; G. Williams played 16 games with San Diego; J. Williams played 15 games with San Francisco; Wohlabaugh played 16 games with New England.

COACHING STAFF

Head Coach,
Chris Palmer

Pro Career: Named head coach of Browns on January 21, 1999, coming to Cleveland from Jacksonville where he served as offensive coordinator and helped guide the Jaguars to the playoffs in each of the last two seasons. Jacksonville captured the AFC Central Division title with an 11-5 regular season record in 1998 and defeated New England 25-10 in an AFC Wild Card Game. Jacksonville posted an identical 11-5 record in 1997 before losing at eventual Super Bowl XXXII champion Denver in a Wild Card Game. Palmer coached with the New England Patriots from 1993-96. He coached the team's wide receivers from 1993-95 and was the quarterbacks coach in 1996 when the Patriots captured the AFC Championship and earned a berth in Super Bowl XXXI. Palmer served as wide receivers coach for the Houston Oilers from 1990-92 and helped Houston lead the NFL in passing offense each season. Palmer was the offensive line coach for the Canadian Football League's Montreal Concordes in 1983 and served as receivers coach in 1984 and quarterbacks coach/offensive coordinator in 1985 for the United States Football League's New Jersey Generals.
Background: Quarterback at Southern Connecticut State 1968-1971. No pro playing experience. Began coaching career as assistant coaching the defensive line and wide receivers at the Connecticut from 1972-74. Wide receivers coach at Lehigh in 1975. Offensive coordinator at Colgate from 1976-1982. Head coach at the New Haven in 1986-87 and posted consecutive 8-2 marks. Head coach at Boston University in 1988-89. Career college head coaching record: 24-18.
Personal: Born September 23, 1949, Mt. Kisco, N.Y. Received bachelor's and master's degrees from Southern Connecticut State. Chris and his wife, Donna, reside in Cleveland. They have a son, Mark (2/24/77) and a daughter, Kristin (9/22/80).

ASSISTANT COACHES

Clarence Brooks, defensive line; born May 20, 1951, New York, N.Y., lives in Cleveland. Guard Massachusetts 1970-73. No pro playing experience. College coach: Massachusetts 1976-1980, Syracuse 1981-89, Arizona 1990-92. Pro coach: Chicago Bears 1993-98, joined Browns in 1999.
Jerry Butler, wide receivers; born October 12, 1957, Ware Shoals, S.C., lives in Cleveland. Wide receiver Clemson 1975-78. Pro wide receiver Buffalo Bills 1979-1987. Pro coach: Joined Browns in 1999.
Keith Butler, linebackers; born May 16, 1956, Anniston, Ala., lives in Cleveland. Linebacker Memphis 1974-77. Pro linebacker Seattle 1978-1987. College coach: Memphis 1990-97, Arkansas State 1998. Pro coach: Joined Browns in 1999.
Billy Davis, defensive quality control; born November 5, 1965, Youngstown, Ohio, lives in Cleveland. Quarterback Cincinnati 1984-88. No pro playing experience. College coach: Michigan State 1990-91. Pro coach: Pittsburgh Steelers 1992-94, Carolina Panthers 1995-1998, joined Browns in 1999.
Jerry Holmes, defensive backfield; born December 22, 1957, Hampton, Va., lives in Cleveland. Defensive back Chowon (N.J.) J.C. 1976-77, West Virginia 1978-79. Pro defensive back New York Jets 1980-83, 1986-87, Pittsburgh Maulers (USFL) 1984, New Jersey Generals (USFL) 1985, Detroit Lions 1988-89, Green Bay Packers 1990-91. College coach: Hampton 1992-94, West Virginia 1995-98. Pro coach: Joined Browns in 1999.
John Hufnagel, quarterbacks; born September 13, 1951, Pittsburgh, lives in Cleveland. Quarterback Penn State 1969-1972. Pro quarterback Denver Broncos 1973-75, Calgary Stampeders (CFL) 1976-79, Saskatchewan Roughriders (CFL) 1980-83, 1987; Winnipeg Blue Bombers (CFL) 1984-85. Pro coach: Saskatchewan Roughriders (CFL) 1988, Calgary Stampeders (CFL) 1989-1995, New Jersey Red Dogs (Arena League) 1997-1998, joined Browns in 1999.
Tim Jorgensen, strength; born April 21, 1955, St. Louis, Mo., lives in Cleveland. Guard Southwest Missouri State 1974-76. No pro playing experience. College coach: Southwest Missouri State 1977-78, Alabama 1979, Louisiana State 1980-83. Pro coach: Philadelphia Eagles 1984-86, Atlanta Falcons 1987-1998, joined Browns in 1999.
Mark Michaels, special teams quality control; born August 15, 1963, Kingston, Pa., lives in Cleveland. Linebacker Connecticut 1982-85. No pro playing experience. College coach: New Haven 1987-1990, Brown 1994-97, Massachusetts 1998. Pro coach: Helsinki Roosters (Finnish Maple League) 1991, Utah Pioneers (Professional Spring Football League) 1992, joined Browns in 1999.
Bob Palcic, offensive line; born July 2, 1948, Gowanda, N.Y., lives in Cleveland. Linebacker Dayton 1968-1970. No pro playing experience. College coach: Dayton 1974-75, Ball State 1976-77, Wisconsin 1978-1981, Arizona 1984-85, Ohio State 1986-1991, Southern California 1992, UCLA 1993. Pro coach: Atlanta Falcons 1994-96, Detroit Lions 1997-98, joined Browns in 1999.
Ray Perkins, tight ends; born November 6, 1941, Mount Olive, Miss., lives in Cleveland. Wide receiver Alabama 1964-66. Pro wide receiver Baltimore Colts 1967-1971. College coach: Mississippi State 1973, Alabama 1983-86 (head coach), Arkansas State 1992 (head coach). Pro coach: New England Patriots 1974-77, 1993-1996, San Diego Chargers 1978, New York Giants 1979-1982 (head coach), Tampa Bay Buccaneers 1987-1990 (head coach), Oakland Raiders 1997, joined Browns in 1999.
Dick Portee, running backs; born April 20, 1942, Decatur, Ill., lives in Cleveland. Defensive back Eastern Illinois 1960-63. No pro playing experience. College coach: Illinois State 1969-1976, Cornell 1977-1981, Maryland 1982-89, North Carolina State 1990-98. Pro coach: Joined Browns in 1999.
Bob Slowik, defensive coordinator; born May 16, 1954, Pittsburgh, lives in Cleveland. Cornerback Delaware 1973-76. No pro playing experience. College coach: Delaware 1978, Florida 1979-1982, Drake 1983, Rutgers 1984-89, East Carolina 1990-1991. Pro coach: Dallas Cowboys 1992, Chicago Bears 1993-98, joined Browns in 1999.
Aril Smith, asst. strength coach; born January 27, 1959, Philadelphia, lives in Cleveland. Defensive line Millersville 1978-1981. No pro playing experience. College coach: Millersville 1993-98. Pro coach: Joined Browns in 1999.
Tony Sparano, offensive quality control; born October 7, 1961, West Haven, Conn., lives in Cleveland. Center 1978-1981. No pro playing experience. College coach: New Haven 1984-87, 1994-98 (head coach 1994-98), Boston 1988-93. Pro coach: Joined Browns in 1999.
Ken Whisenhunt, special teams; born February 28, 1962, Atlanta, lives in Cleveland. Tight end Georgia Tech 1980-84. Pro tight end Atlanta Falcons 1985-88, Washington Redskins 1989-1990, New York Jets 1991-1993. College coach: Vanderbilt 1995-96. Pro coach: Baltimore Ravens 1997-98, joined Browns in 1999.

1999 FIRST-YEAR ROSTER

Name	Pos.	Ht.	Wt.	Birthdate	College	Hometown	How Acq.
Abdullah, Rahim	LB	6-5	233	3/22/76	Clemson	Jacksonville, Fla.	D2b
Baron, Jim (1)	DE	6-3	264	6/8/73	Virginia Tech	Blacksburg, Va.	W(Chi)
Bateman, Eric (1)	G	6-7	315	12/28/73	Brigham Young	Camarillo, Calif.	FA
Beauchamp, Tim	DE	6-2	271	3/18/77	Florida	Oak Hill, Fla.	FA
Bridges, Corey (1)	WR	5-7	178	6/30/74	South Carolina	Newnan, Ga.	FA
Bundren, Jim (1)	C	6-3	303	10/6/74	Clemson	Wilmington, Del.	ED(NYJ)
Campbell, Mark	TE	6-6	253	12/6/75	Michigan	Clawson, Mich.	FA
Chiaverini, Darrin	WR	6-1	205	10/12/77	Colorado	Orange County, Calif.	D5
Collins, Ryan (1)	TE	6-6	259	11/1/75	St. Thomas	Minneapolis, Minn.	FA
Comstock, Kris	OT	6-8	304	12/4/75	Kentucky	Apopka, Fla.	FA
Cook, Mike	QB	6-2	203	3/19/76	William & Mary	Lancaster, Penn.	FA
Cortez, Jose	K	5-11	205	5/27/75	Oregon State	Van Nuys, Calif.	FA
Couch, Tim	QB	6-4	227	7/31/77	Kentucky	Hyden, Ky.	D1
Dawson, Phil (1)	K	5-11	190	1/23/75	Texas	Dallas, Tex.	FA(NE)
Dearth, James	TE	6-3	269	1/22/76	Tarleton State	Scurry, Tex.	D6c
Duff, Bill (1)	DT	6-3	285	2/24/74	Tennessee	Delran, N.J.	FA
Dutton, John (1)	QB	6-4	225	9/20/75	Nevada	Fallbrook, Calif.	FA
Girard, Sylvain	WR	6-1	198	10/3/75	Concordia, Canada	Chicoutimi, Quebec, Canada	FA
Hanson, Chris	P	6-1	214	10/25/76	Marshall	Senioa, Ga.	FA
Hill, Madre	RB	5-11	199	1/2/76	Arkansas	Malvern, Ark.	D7
Johnson, Kevin	WR	5-10	188	7/15/75	Syracuse	Hamilton Township, N.J.	D2a
Kight, Danny (1)	K	6-0	200	8/18/71	Augusta State	Atlanta, Ga.	W(TB)
McClellion, Central	CB	5-10	191	9/15/75	Ohio State	Delray Beach, Fla.	FA
McCutcheon, Daylon	CB	5-8	180	12/9/76	Southern California	La Puente, Calif.	D3a
Menard, David	LB	6-2	245	3/8/77	New Haven	Attleboro, Mass.	FA
Miller, Arnold	DE	6-3	239	1/3/75	Louisiana State	New Orleans, La.	FA
Nastasi, Joseph	WR	5-10	190	9/27/75	Penn State	Woodbury, Pa.	FA
Neal, Randy (1)	LB	6-3	245	10/29/72	Virginia	Hackensack, N.J.	FA
Ogle, Kendall	LB	6-0	231	11/25/75	Maryland	Hillside, N.J.	D6b
Powell, Ronnie	WR	5-10	174	11/3/74	Northwestern State, La.	Hope, Ark.	FA
Rainer, Wali	LB	6-2	235	4/19/77	Virginia	Charlotte, N.C.	D4
Rasheed, Dawud	RB	5-10	226	1/22/77	Duke	Birmingham, Ala.	FA
Rogers, Tyrone	DE	6-5	240	10/11/76	Alabama State	Montgomery, Ala.	FA
Rudzinski, Jerry	LB	6-1	226	7/16/75	Ohio State	Centerville, Ohio	FA
Smith, Ed (1)	TE	6-4	253	6/5/69	No College	Trenton, N.J.	W(Atl)
Smith, Marquis	S	6-2	213	1/13/75	California	San Diego, Calif.	D3b
Spriggs, Marcus	DT	6-4	314	7/26/76	Troy State	Washington, D.C.	D6a
Swanson, Pete (1)	T	6-5	307	3/26/74	Stanford	San Bento, Calif.	ED(KC)
Tarver, Hurley (1)	CB-S	6-0	180	11/30/75	Oklahoma Central State	Fort Worth, Tex.	FA
Taylor, Ryan	LB	6-2	230	12/11/76	Auburn	Dublin, Ga.	FA
Thomas, Malcolm (1)	RB	5-8	205	5/15/74	Syracuse	Jacksonville, Fla.	FA
Zahursky, Steve (1)	G	6-6	305	9/2/76	Kent State	Euclid, Ohio	FA

The term NFL Rookie is defined as a player who is in his first season of professional football and has not been on the roster of another professional football team for any regular-season or postseason games. A Rookie is designated by an "R" on NFL rosters. Players who have been active in another professional football league or players who have NFL experience, including either preseason training camp or being on an Active List or Inactive List, or on Reserve/Injured or Reserve/Physically Unable to Perform for fewer than six regular-season games, are termed NFL First-Year Players. An NFL First-Year Player is designated by a "1" on NFL rosters. Thereafter, a player is credited with an additional year of experience for each season in which he accumulates six games on the Active List or Inactive List, or on Reserve/Injured or Reserve/Physically Unable to Perform.

NOTES

DENVER BRONCOS

American Football Conference
Western Division
Team Colors: Orange, Broncos Navy Blue, and White
13655 Broncos Parkway
Englewood, Colorado 80112
Telephone: (303) 649-9000

CLUB OFFICIALS

President-Chief Executive Officer: Pat Bowlen
Vice President of Football Operations/Head Coach: Mike Shanahan
Vice President of Business Operations: Joe Ellis
Vice President of Administration: John Beake
General Manager: Neal Dahlen
Director of Pro Scouting: Jack Elway
Director of College Scouting: Ted Sundquist
Director of Salary Cap and Football Finance Administration: Dave Blando
Chief Financial Officer: Allen Fears
Senior Director of Ticket Operations/Business Development: Rick Nichols
Executive Assistant to the President: Yolanda Saltus
Senior Director of Media Relations: Jim Saccomano
Director of Stadium Operations: Gail Stuckey
Senior Director of Operations: Bill Harpole
Senior Director of Marketing: Greg Carney
Director of Special Services: Fred Fleming
Director of Player Relations: Bill Thompson
Community Relations Coordinator: Steve Sewell
Trainer: Steve Antonopulos
Equipment Manager: Doug West
Video Director: Kent Erickson
Stadium: Denver Mile High Stadium
•**Capacity:** 76,082
1900 West Eliot
Denver, Colorado 80204
Playing Surface: Grass (PAT)
Training Camp: University of Northern Colorado
Greeley, Colorado 80639

1999 SCHEDULE

PRESEASON

Aug. 7	vs. San Diego at Sydney, Australia	7:00
Aug. 14	**Arizona**	7:00
Aug. 23	vs. Green Bay at Madison, Wisconsin	7:00
Aug. 29	at Dallas	7:00
Sept. 3	**San Francisco**	7:00

REGULAR SEASON

Sept. 13	**Miami** (Mon.)	7:00
Sept. 19	at Kansas City	3:15
Sept. 26	at Tampa Bay	1:00
Oct. 3	**New York Jets**	2:15
Oct. 10	at Oakland	1:15
Oct. 17	**Green Bay**	2:15
Oct. 24	at New England	1:00
Oct. 31	**Minnesota**	2:15
Nov. 7	at San Diego	1:15
Nov. 14	at Seattle	5:20
Nov. 22	**Oakland** (Mon.)	7:00
Nov. 28	Open Date	
Dec. 5	**Kansas City**	2:15
Dec. 13	at Jacksonville (Mon.)	9:00
Dec. 19	**Seattle**	2:15
Dec. 25	at Detroit (Sat.)	4:15
Jan. 2	**San Diego**	2:15

RECORD HOLDERS

INDIVIDUAL RECORDS—CAREER

Category	Name	Performance
Rushing (Yds.)	Terrell Davis, 1995-98	6,413
Passing (Yds.)	John Elway, 1983-1998	51,475
Passing (TDs)	John Elway, 1983-1998	300
Receiving (No.)	Lionel Taylor, 1960-66	543
Receiving (Yds.)	Lionel Taylor, 1960-66	6,872
Interceptions	Steve Foley, 1976-1986	44
Punting (Avg.)	Jim Fraser, 1962-64	45.2
Punt Return (Avg.)	Darrien Gordon, 1997-98	12.5
Kickoff Return (Avg.)	Abner Haynes, 1965-66	26.3
Field Goals	Jason Elam, 1993-98	157
Touchdowns (Tot.)	Terrell Davis, 1995-98	61
Points	Jim Turner, 1971-79	742

INDIVIDUAL RECORDS—SINGLE SEASON

Category	Name	Performance
Rushing (Yds.)	Terrell Davis, 1998	2,008
Passing (Yds.)	John Elway, 1993	4,030
Passing (TDs)	John Elway, 1997	27
Receiving (No.)	Lionel Taylor, 1961	100
Receiving (Yds.)	Steve Watson, 1981	1,244
Interceptions	Goose Gonsoulin, 1960	11
Punting (Avg.)	Tom Rouen, 1998	46.9
Punt Return (Avg.)	Floyd Little, 1967	16.9
Kickoff Return (Avg.)	Bill Thompson, 1969	28.5
Field Goals	Jason Elam, 1995	31
Touchdowns (Tot.)	Terrell Davis, 1998	23
Points	Terrell Davis, 1998	138

INDIVIDUAL RECORDS—SINGLE GAME

Category	Name	Performance
Rushing (Yds.)	Terrell Davis, 9-21-97	215
Passing (Yds.)	Frank Tripucka, 9-15-62	447
Passing (TDs)	Frank Tripucka, 10-28-62	5
	John Elway, 11-18-84	5
Receiving (No.)	Lionel Taylor, 11-29-64	13
	Bobby Anderson, 9-30-73	13
Receiving (Yds.)	Lionel Taylor, 11-27-60	199
Interceptions	Goose Gonsoulin, 9-18-60	*4
	Willie Brown, 11-15-64	*4
Field Goals	Gene Mingo, 10-6-63	5
	Rich Karlis, 11-20-83	5
	Jason Elam, 9-3-95	5
Touchdowns (Tot.)	Many times	3
	Last time by Terrell Davis, 11-24-97	
Points	Gene Mingo, 12-10-60	21

*NFL Record

COACHING HISTORY

(311-286-10)

1960-61	Frank Filchock	7-20-1
1962-64	Jack Faulkner*	9-22-1
1964-66	Mac Speedie**	6-19-1
1966	Ray Malavasi	4-8-0
1967-71	Lou Saban***	20-42-3
1971	Jerry Smith	2-3-0
1972-76	John Ralston	34-33-3
1977-80	Robert (Red) Miller	42-25-0
1981-92	Dan Reeves	117-79-1
1993-94	Wade Phillips	16-17-0
1995-98	Mike Shanahan	54-18-0

*Released after four games in 1964
**Resigned after two games in 1966
***Resigned after nine games in 1971

DENVER MILE HIGH STADIUM

1998 TEAM RECORD

PRESEASON (3-1)

Date	Result		Opponent
8/8	W	20-13	at St. Louis
8/14	W	17-10	New Orleans
8/24	W	34-31	Green Bay
8/29	L	13-16	at Tennessee

REGULAR SEASON (14-2)

Date	Result		Opponent	Att.
9/7	W	27-21	New England	74,745
9/13	W	42-23	Dallas	75,013
9/20	W	34-17	at Oakland	56,578
9/27	W	38-16	at Washington	71,880
10/4	W	41-16	Philadelphia	73,218
10/11	W	21-16	at Seattle	66,258
10/25	W	37-24	Jacksonville	75,217
11/1	W	33-26	at Cincinnati	59,974
11/8	W	27-10	San Diego	74,925
11/16	W	30-7	at Kansas City	78,100
11/22	W	40-14	Oakland	75,325
11/29	W	31-16	at San Diego	66,532
12/6	W	35-31	Kansas City	74,962
12/13	L	16-20	at New York Giants	72,336
12/21	L	21-31	at Miami	74,363
12/27	W	28-21	Seattle	74,057

POSTSEASON (3-0)

Date	Result		Opponent	Att.
1/9	W	38-3	Miami	75,729
1/17	W	23-10	New York Jets	75,482
1/31	W	34-19	vs. Atlanta, in Miami	74,803

SCORE BY PERIODS

Broncos	144	156	64	137	0	—	501
Opponents	54	87	58	110	0	—	309

ATTENDANCE

Home 597,462 Away 546,021 Total 1,143,483
Single-game home record, 76,089 (10/26/86)
Single-season home record, 598,224 (1981)

1998 TEAM STATISTICS

	Broncos	Opp.
Total First Downs	347	283
Rushing	135	80
Passing	186	183
Penalty	26	20
Third Down: Made/Att	90/207	88/225
Third Down Pct.	43.5	39.1
Fourth Down: Made/Att	4/10	10/19
Fourth Down Pct.	40.0	52.6
Total Net Yards	6,092	4,935
Avg. Per Game	380.8	308.4
Total Plays	1,041	999
Avg. Per Play	5.9	4.9
Net Yards Rushing	2,468	1,287
Avg. Per Game	154.3	80.4
Total Rushes	525	356
Net Yards Passing	3,624	3,648
Avg. Per Game	226.5	228.0
Sacked/Yards Lost	25/184	47/335
Gross Yards	3,808	3,983
Att./Completions	491/290	596/345
Completion Pct.	59.1	57.9
Had Intercepted	14	19
Punts/Avg.	67/46.2	88/42.4
Net Punting Avg.	67/37.6	88/36.1
Penalties/Yards Lost	115/1,023	113/865
Fumbles/Ball Lost	17/6	28/11
Touchdowns	62	38
Rushing	26	8
Passing	32	28
Returns	4	2
Avg. Time of Possession	32:08	27:52

1998 INDIVIDUAL STATISTICS

Passing	Att.	Comp.	Yds.	Pct.	TD	Int.	Tkld.	Rate
Elway	356	210	2,806	59.0	22	10	18/135	93.0
Brister	131	78	986	59.5	10	3	7/49	99.0
Griese	3	1	2	33.3	0	1	0/0	2.8
R. Smith	1	1	14	100.0	0	0	0/0	118.8
Broncos	491	290	3,808	59.1	32	14	25/184	93.5
Opponents	596	345	3,983	57.9	28	19	47/335	80.5

SCORING	TD R	TD P	TD Rt	PAT	FG	Saf	PTS
Davis	21	2	0	0/0	0/0	0	138
Elam	0	0	0	58/58	23/27	0	127
McCaffrey	0	10	0	0/0	0/0	0	62
Sharpe	0	10	0	0/0	0/0	0	60
R. Smith	0	6	1	0/0	0/0	0	42
Griffith	0	3	0	0/0	0/0	0	18
Hebron	1	0	1	0/0	0/0	0	12
Loville	2	0	0	0/0	0/0	0	12
Brister	1	0	0	0/0	0/0	0	6
Crockett	0	0	1	0/0	0/0	0	6
Elway	1	0	0	0/0	0/0	0	6
Gordon	0	0	1	0/0	0/0	0	6
Green	0	1	0	0/0	0/0	0	6
Rouen	0	0	0	0/1	0/0	0	0
Broncos	26	32	4	58/59	23/27	0	501
Opponents	8	28	2	31/31	14/20	2	309

2-Point conversions: McCaffrey.
Team 1-3, Opponents 2-7.

RUSHING	Att.	Yds.	Avg.	LG	TD
Davis	392	2,008	5.1	70	21
Loville	53	161	3.0	12	2
Brister	19	102	5.4	38t	1
Elway	37	94	2.5	16	1
R. Smith	6	63	10.5	37	0
Hebron	9	31	3.4	8	1
Griffith	4	13	3.3	16	0
Rouen	1	0	0.0	0	0
Griese	4	-4	-1.0	0	0
Broncos	525	2,468	4.7	70	26
Opponents	356	1,287	3.6	45	8

RECEIVING	No.	Yds.	Avg.	LG	TD
R. Smith	86	1,222	14.2	58	6
McCaffrey	64	1,053	16.5	48	10
Sharpe	64	768	12.0	38t	10
Davis	25	217	8.7	35	2
Green	16	194	12.1	50	1
Griffith	15	97	6.5	15	3
Nash	4	76	19.0	31	0
Carswell	4	51	12.8	15	0
Chamberlain	3	35	11.7	16	0
D. Smith	3	24	8.0	16	0
Loville	2	29	14.5	17	0
Hebron	2	5	2.5	3	0
Armour	1	23	23.0	23	0
Elway	1	14	14.0	14	0
Broncos	290	3,808	13.1	58	32
Opponents	345	3,983	11.5	75t	28

INTERCEPTIONS	No.	Yds.	Avg.	LG	TD
Gordon	4	125	31.3	55t	1
Crockett	3	105	35.0	80t	1
Johnson	2	79	39.5	45	0
Romanowski	2	22	11.0	18	0
Cadrez	2	11	5.5	6	0
Braxton	1	72	72.0	72	0
Coghill	1	20	20.0	20	0
Atwater	1	4	4.0	4	0
N. Smith	1	2	2.0	2	0
Pryce	1	1	1.0	1	0
Mobley	1	-2	-2.0	-2	0
Broncos	19	439	23.1	80t	2
Opponents	14	270	19.3	94t	2

PUNTING	No.	Yds.	Avg.	In 20	LG
Rouen	66	3,097	46.9	14	76
Broncos	67	3,097	46.2	14	76
Opponents	88	3,733	42.4	22	69

PUNT RETURNS	No.	FC	Yds.	Avg.	LG	TD
Gordon	34	6	379	11.1	44	0
Coghill	3	2	20	6.7	8	0
Paul	1	0	0	0.0	0	0
Broncos	38	8	399	10.5	44	0
Opponents	43	2	381	8.9	39	0

KICKOFF RETURNS	No.	Yds.	Avg.	LG	TD
Hebron	46	1,216	26.4	95t	1
Loville	6	105	17.5	25	0
D. Smith	3	51	17.0	21	0
Burns	2	17	8.5	17	0
Tanuvasa	1	13	13.0	13	0
Broncos	58	1,402	24.2	95t	1
Opponents	89	2,006	22.5	91	0

FIELD GOALS	1-19	20-29	30-39	40-49	50+
Elam	0/0	3/3	13/14	4/6	3/4
Broncos	0/0	3/3	13/14	4/6	3/4
Opponents	1/1	6/7	3/5	3/4	1/3

SACKS	No.
Pryce	8.5
Tanuvasa	8.5
Romanowski	7.5
Cadrez	4.0
N. Smith	4.0
Hasselbach	3.0
Williams	3.0
Lodish	2.0
Traylor	2.0
Washington	2.0
Johnson	1.0
Mobley	1.0
Crockett	0.5
Broncos	47.0
Opponents	25.0

1999 DRAFT CHOICES

Round	Name	Pos.	College
1	Al Wilson	LB	Tennessee
2	Montae Reagor	DE	Texas Tech
	Lennie Friedman	G	Duke
3	Chris Watson	DB	Eastern Illinois
	Travis McGriff	WR	Florida
4	Olandis Gary	RB	Georgia
5	David Bowens	DE	Western Illinois
	Darwin Brown	DB	Texas Tech
6	Desmond Clark	TE	Wake Forest
	Chad Plummer	WR	Cincinnati
7	Billy Miller	WR	Southern California
	Justin Swift	TE	Kansas State

DENVER BRONCOS

1999 VETERAN ROSTER

No.	Name	Pos.	Ht.	Wt.	Birthdate	NFL Exp.	College	Hometown	How Acq.	'98 Games/ Starts
79	Banks, Chris	G	6-1	300	4/4/73	2	Kansas	Lexington, Mo.	FA-'98	4/0
75	Berti, Tony	T	6-6	300	6/21/72	5	Colorado	Thornton, Colo.	UFA(Sea)-'99	0*
34	Braxton, Tyrone	S	5-11	190	12/17/64	13	North Dakota State	Madison, Wis.	FA-'95	16/6
6	Brister, Bubby	QB	6-3	205	8/15/62	13	Northeast Louisiana	Monroe, La.	FA-'97	7/4
11	Brohm, Jeff	QB	6-1	205	4/24/71	5	Louisville	Louisville, Ky.	FA-'99	0*
73	Brown, Cyron	DE	6-5	265	6/28/75	2	Western Illinois	Chicago, Ill.	FA-'98	4/0
26	Brown, Eric	S	6-0	210	3/20/75	2	Mississippi State	San Antonio, Tex.	D2-'98	11/10
59	Cadrez, Glenn	LB	6-3	240	1/2/70	8	Houston	El Centro, Calif.	FA-'95	16/15
89	Carswell, Dwayne	TE	6-3	260	1/18/72	5	Liberty	Jacksonville, Fla.	FA-'94	16/1
40	Carter, Dale	CB	6-1	188	11/28/69	8	Tennessee	Covington, Ga.	UFA(KC)-'99	11/9*
86	Chamberlain, Byron	TE	6-1	242	10/17/71	4	Wayne State	Fort Worth, Tex.	D7b-'95	16/0
46	Christopherson, Ryan	RB	5-11	246	7/26/72	3	Wyoming	Sioux Falls, S.D.	FA-'99	0*
9	Clements, Chuck	QB	6-3	211	9/29/73	2	Houston	Huntsville, Tex.	FA-'99	0*
48	Coghill, George	S	6-0	210	3/30/70	3	Wake Forest	Fredricksburg, Va.	FA-'97	9/0
39	Crockett, Ray	CB	5-10	184	1/5/67	11	Baylor	Dallas, Tex.	UFA(Det)-'94	16/16
30	Davis, Terrell	RB	5-11	210	10/28/72	5	Georgia	San Diego, Calif.	D6b-'95	16/16
63	Diaz-Infante, David	G	6-3	295	3/31/64	4	San Jose State	San Jose, Calif.	FA-'96	10/0
55	Dumas, Troy	LB	6-3	242	9/30/72	4	Nebraska	Cheyenne, Wyo.	FA-'99	0*
1	Elam, Jason	K	5-11	200	3/8/70	7	Hawaii	Ft. Walton Beach, Fla.	D3b-'93	16/0
52	Elliott, Matt	C	6-3	295	10/1/68	6	Michigan	Carmel, Ind.	FA-'99	0*
14	Griese, Brian	QB	6-3	215	3/18/75	2	Michigan	Miami, Fla.	D3-'98	1/0
29	Griffith, Howard	RB	6-0	230	11/17/67	7	Illinois	Chicago, Ill.	UFA(Car)-'97	14/13
96	Hasselbach, Harald	DE	6-6	285	9/22/67	6	Washington	Tsawassen, B.C., Canada	FA-'94	16/3
20	James, Tory	CB	6-1	195	5/18/73	4	Louisiana State	New Orleans, La.	D2-'96	16/0
25	Johnson, Darrius	CB	5-9	185	9/17/72	4	Oklahoma	Terrell, Tex.	D4b-'96	16/2
60	Jones, K.C.	C	6-1	275	3/28/74	3	Miami	Midland, Tex.	FA-'97	0*
77	Jones, Tony	T	6-5	291	5/24/66	12	Western Carolina	Royston, Ga.	T(Balt)-'97	16/16
76	Kohn, Tim	T	6-5	310	12/6/73	2	Iowa State	Wadsworth, Ill.	FA-'99	0*
78	Lepsis, Matt	T	6-4	290	1/13/74	2	Colorado	Conroe, Tex.	FA-'97	16/0
97	Lodish, Mike	DT	6-3	270	8/11/67	10	UCLA	Birmingham, Mich.	UFA(Buff)-'96	15/1
31	Loville, Derek	RB	5-10	210	7/4/68	9	Oregon	San Francisco, Calif.	UFA(SF)-'97	16/0
37	Lynn, Anthony	RB	6-3	230	12/21/68	6	Texas Tech	McKinney, Tex.	UFA(SF)-'97	16/0
87	McCaffrey, Ed	WR	6-5	215	8/17/68	9	Stanford	Allentown, Pa.	UFA(SF)-'95	15/15
33	McElroy, Leeland	RB	5-9	212	6/25/74	3	Texas A&M	Beaumont, Tex.	FA-'99	0*
12	Miller, Chris	QB	6-2	212	8/9/65	10	Oregon	Eugene, Ore.	FA-'99	0*
51	Mobley, John	LB	6-1	236	10/10/73	4	Kutztown	Chester, Pa.	D1-'96	16/15
66	Nalen, Tom	C	6-2	286	5/13/71	6	Boston College	Foxboro, Mass.	D7c-'94	16/16
82	Nash, Marcus	WR	6-3	195	2/1/76	2	Tennessee	Tulsa, Okla.	D1-'98	8/0
62	Neil, Dan	G	6-2	281	10/21/73	3	Texas	Cypress Creek, Tex.	D3-'97	16/16
28	Paul, Tito	CB	6-0	195	12/7/71	5	Ohio State	Osceola, Fla.	FA-'98	16/0
93	Pryce, Trevor	DT	6-5	295	8/3/75	3	Clemson	Winter Park, Fla.	D1-'97	16/15
68	Reeves, Carl	DE	6-4	270	12/17/71	5	North Carolina State	Durham, N.C.	UFA(Chi)-'99	11/0*
53	Romanowski, Bill	LB	6-4	245	4/2/66	12	Boston College	Vernon, Conn.	UFA(Phil)-'96	16/16
16	Rouen, Tom	P	6-3	225	6/9/68	7	Colorado	Hinsdale, Ill.	FA-'93	16/0
58	Russ, Steve	LB	6-4	245	9/16/72	3	Air Force	Stetsonville, Wis.	D7a-'95	0*
69	Schlereth, Mark	G	6-3	287	1/25/66	11	Idaho	Anchorage, Alaska	UFA(Wash)-'95	16/16
84	Sharpe, Shannon	TE	6-2	230	6/26/68	10	Savannah State	Glennville, Ga.	D7-'90	16/16
42	Smith, Detron	RB	5-9	230	2/25/74	4	Texas A&M	Dallas, Tex.	D3a-'96	15/2
90	Smith, Neil	DE	6-4	270	4/10/66	12	Nebraska	New Orleans, La.	UFA(KC)-'97	14/14
80	Smith, Rod	WR	6-0	200	5/15/70	5	Missouri Southern	Texarkana, Ark.	FA-'94	16/16
98	Tanuvasa, Maa	DT	6-2	270	11/6/70	6	Hawaii	Mililani, Hawaii	FA-'95	16/16
70	Teague, Trey	T	6-5	285	12/27/74	2	Tennessee	Jackson, Tenn.	D7a-'98	0*
94	Traylor, Keith	DT	6-2	304	9/3/69	8	Central State, Okla.	Little Rock, Ark.	UFA(KC)-'97	15/14
71	Tuten, Melvin	T	6-6	305	11/11/71	3	Syracuse	Washington, D.C.	FA-'99	0*
50	Ulmer, Artie	LB	6-3	247	7/30/73	2	Valdosta State	Rincon, Ga.	FA-'99	0*
57	Ward, Ronnie	LB	6-0	230	2/11/74	2	Kansas	St. Louis, Mo.	FA-'99	0*
54	Wayne, Nate	LB	6-0	230	1/12/75	2	Mississippi	Macon, Miss.	D7b-'98	1/0
91	Williams, Alfred	DE	6-6	265	11/6/68	9	Colorado	Houston, Tex.	UFA(SF)-'96	10/0

* Berti inactive for 5 games with Seattle and missed 11 games because of injury with San Diego in '98; Brohm missed '98 season because of injury with Tampa Bay; Carter played 11 games with Kansas City; Christopherson last active with Arizona in '96; Clements last active with N.Y. Jets in '97; Dumas last active with St. Louis in '97; Elliott missed '98 season because of injury with Atlanta; K.C. Jones inactive for 12 games; Kohn last active with Oakland in '97; McElroy last active with Arizona in '97; Miller last active with St. Louis in '95; Reeves played in 11 games with Chicago; Russ missed '98 season because of injury; Teague inactive for 16 games; Tuten last active with Cincinnati in '96; Ulmer last active with Minnesota in '97; Ward last active with Miami in '97.

Retired—John Elway, 16-year quarterback, 13 games in '98.

Players lost through free agency (3): LB Keith Burns (Chi; 16 games in '98), T Harry Swayne (Balt; 16), DE Marvin Washington (SF; 16).

Also played with Broncos in '98—WR Justin Armour (8 games), S Steve Atwater (16), CB Darrien Gordon (16), WR Willie Green (15), RB Vaughn Hebron (15), DE Ernest Jones (1), LB Seth Joyner (16).

COACHING STAFF

Head Coach,
Mike Shanahan

Pro Career: Became the eleventh head coach in Broncos history on January 31, 1995, coming to Denver from the 1994 world champion San Francisco 49ers, where he served as offensive coordinator from 1992-94. Mike Shanahan led the Broncos to back-to-back Super Bowl championships in 1997 and 1998, becoming just the fifth head coach to accomplish that feat. Shanahan has led Denver to seven postseason wins in the last two seasons, the highest two-year total in history. His 1997 Broncos became just the second Wild Card team to win the Super Bowl, and they became the first AFC team to capture the NFL crown in 14 years. In 1996 Shanahan led the Broncos to a 13-3 record and the AFC Western Division title, tying the club record for wins in a season and leading the NFL in total offense. In 1995 he improved the Broncos to an 8-8 mark. During his NFL career, Shanahan has been a part of teams that have played in nine AFC or NFC Championship Games, in addition to his six Super Bowl appearances, five with Denver and Super Bowl XXIX with San Francisco. In his 24 seasons coaching in the NFL and at the college level, Shanahan's teams have participated in postseason playoffs or bowl games 18 times. A driving force behind the Broncos' offense for all three of the team's Super Bowl appearances in the 1980s (following the '86, '87, and '89 seasons), he first came to Denver in 1984 as wide receivers coach. Shanahan was Broncos' offensive coordinator from 1985-87, and returned to Denver as quarterbacks coach on October 16, 1989, after serving as head coach of the Los Angeles Raiders in 1988 and through the first four games of the 1989 season. His record with the Raiders was 8-12. Career record: 62-30.

Background: Shanahan began his coaching career at Oklahoma in 1975-76, also coaching at Northern Arizona (1977), Eastern Illinois (1978), and Minnesota (1979), before moving on to Florida (1980-83). During his tenure on the college level, Shanahan's teams had a combined record of 77-29-3 (.720), including national championship seasons at Oklahoma in 1975 and at Eastern Illinois.

Personal: Shanahan was born in Oak Park, Illinois, on August 24, 1952. He attended East Leyden High School in Franklin Park and was a wishbone quarterback-defensive back at Eastern Illinois, graduating in 1974 with a degree in physical education and a master's degree in 1975. Mike and his wife, Peggy, have two children, son Kyle and daughter Krystal.

ASSISTANT COACHES

Frank Bush, linebackers; born January 10, 1963, Athens, Ga., lives in Englewood, Colo. Linebacker North Carolina State 1981-84. Pro linebacker Houston Oilers 1985-86. Pro coach: Houston Oilers 1992-94, joined Broncos in 1995.

Barney Chavous, asst. offensive line-assistant strength and conditioning; born March 22, 1951, Aiken, S.C., lives in Englewood, Colo. Defensive end South Carolina State 1969-1972. Pro defensive end Denver Broncos 1973-1985. Pro coach: Joined Broncos in 1989.

Rick Dennison, special teams; born June 22, 1958, in Kalispell, Mont., lives in Englewood, Colo. Tight end Colorado State 1976-79. Pro linebacker Denver Broncos 1982-1990. Pro coach: Joined Broncos in 1995.

Ed Donatell, defensive backs; born February 4, 1957, Akron, Ohio, lives in Littleton, Colo. Safety Glenville State 1975-78. No pro playing experience. College coach: Kent State 1979-1980, Washington 1981-82, Pacific 1983-85, Idaho 1986-88, Cal State-Fullerton 1989. Pro coach: New York Jets 1990-94, joined Broncos in 1995.

George Dyer, defensive line; born May 4, 1940, Alhambra, Calif., lives in Aurora, Colo. Center-linebacker U.C. Santa Barbara 1961-63. No pro playing experience. College coach: Humboldt State 1964-66, Coalinga (Calif.) J.C. 1967 (head coach), Portland State 1968-1971, Idaho 1972, San Jose State 1973, Michigan State 1977-79, Arizona State 1980-81. Pro coach: Winnipeg Blue Bombers (CFL) 1974-76, Buffalo Bills 1982, Seattle Seahawks 1983-1991, Los Angeles Rams 1992-94, joined Broncos in 1995.

Alex Gibbs, asst. head coach-offensive line; born February 11, 1941, Morganton, N.C., lives in Greenwood Village, Colo. Running back-defensive back Davidson College 1959-1963. No pro playing experience. College coach: Duke 1969-1970, Kentucky 1971-72, West Virginia 1973-74, Ohio State 1975-78, Auburn 1979-1981, Georgia 1982-83. Pro coach: Denver Broncos 1984-87, Los Angeles Raiders 1988-89, San Diego Chargers 1990-91, Indianapolis Colts 1992, Kansas City Chiefs 1993-94, rejoined Broncos in 1995.

Mike Heimerdinger, wide receivers; born October 13, 1952, DeKalb, Ill., lives in Englewood, Colo. Wide receiver Eastern Illinois 1970-74. No pro playing experience. College coach: Florida 1980, Air Force 1981, North Texas State 1982, Florida 1983-87, Cal State-Fullerton 1988, Rice 1989-1993, Duke 1994. Pro coach: Joined Broncos in 1995.

Gary Kubiak, offensive coordinator-quarterbacks; born August 15, 1961, Houston, Tex., lives in Englewood, Colo. Quarterback Texas A&M 1979-1982. Pro quarterback Denver Broncos 1983-1991. College coach: Texas A&M 1992-93. Pro coach: San Francisco 49ers 1994, joined Broncos in 1995.

Pat McPherson, offensive assistant; born April 15, 1969, Santa Clara, Calif., live in Englewood, Colo. Linebacker Santa Clara 1991-92. No pro playing experience. Pro coach: Joined Broncos in 1998.

Brian Pariani, tight ends; born July 2, 1965, San Francisco, lives in Castle Pines, Colo. No college or pro playing experience. College coach: UCLA 1989. Pro coach: San Francisco 49ers 1991-94, joined Broncos in 1995.

Ricky Porter, asst. strength and conditioning; born January 14, 1960, Sylacaga, Ala., lives in Englewood, Colo. Running back Slippery Rock 1978-1981. Pro running back Detroit Lions 1982, Baltimore Colts 1983, Memphis Showboats (USFL) 1985, Montreal Alouettes (CFL) 1986-87, Buffalo Bills 1987. College coach: Slippery Rock 1990-91, Kent 1992-93. Pro coach: Tampa Bay Buccaneers 1996, joined Broncos in 1997.

Greg Robinson, defensive coordinator; born October 9, 1951, Los Angeles, Calif., lives in Aurora, Colo. Linebacker-tight end Pacific 1972-74. No pro playing experience. College coach: Pacific 1975-76, Cal State-Fullerton 1977-79, North Carolina State 1980-81, UCLA 1982-89. Pro coach: New York Jets 1990-94, joined Broncos in 1995.

Greg Saporta, asst. strength and conditioning; born February 2, 1957, New York, N.Y., lives in Englewood, Colo. Wide receiver Buffalo State 1977-79. No pro playing experience. College coach: Florida 1981-88, 1993-94, North Carolina 1989-1992. Pro coach: Joined Broncos in 1995.

Rick Smith, defensive assistant; born September 3, 1969, Petersburg, Va., lives in Aurora, Colo. Safety Purdue 1987-1991. No pro playing experience. College coach: Purdue 1992-95. Pro coach: Joined Broncos in 1996.

John Teerlinck, pass rush specialist; born April 9, 1951, Rochester, N.Y., lives in Englewood, Colo. Defensive lineman Western Illinois 1970-73. Pro defensive tackle San Diego Chargers 1974-76. College coach: Iowa Lakes J.C. 1977, Eastern Illinois 1978-79, Illinois 1980-82. Pro coach: Chicago Blitz (USFL) 1983, Arizona Wranglers/Outlaws (USFL) 1984-85, Cleveland Browns 1989-1990, Los Angeles Rams 1991, Minnesota Vikings 1992-94, Detroit Lions 1995-96, joined Broncos in 1997.

Terry Tumey, defensive assistant; born October 29, 1965, Tulsa, Okla., lives in Parker, Colo. Defensive lineman UCLA 1983-1987. No pro playing experience. College coach: UCLA 1993-1998. Pro coach: joined Broncos in 1999.

Bobby Turner, running backs; born May 6, 1949, East Chicago, Ind., lives in Englewood, Colo. Defensive back Indiana State 1968-1971. No pro playing experience. College coach: Indiana State 1975-1982, Fresno State 1983-88, Ohio State 1989-1990, Purdue 1991-94. Pro coach: Joined Broncos in 1995.

Rich Tuten, strength and conditioning; born December 30, 1953, Columbia, S.C., lives in Englewood, Colo. Nose guard Clemson 1976-78. No pro playing experience. College coach: Florida 1979-1988, 1993-94, North Carolina 1989-1992. Pro coach: Joined Broncos in 1995.

1999 FIRST-YEAR ROSTER

Name	Pos.	Ht.	Wt.	Birthdate	College	Hometown	How Acq.
Alexander, Curtis (1)	RB	6-0	204	6/11/74	Alabama	Memphis, Tenn.	D4-'98
Baker, Jeff	P-K	6-2	185	2/18/77	Western Illinois	Lakewood, Colo.	FA
Bowens, David	LB	6-2	255	7/3/77	Western Illinois	Pontiac, Mich.	D5a
Brown, Darwin	CB	5-10	170	7/6/77	Texas Tech	Tyler, Tex.	D5b
Clark, Desmond	TE	6-3	255	4/20/77	Wake Forest	Lakeland, Fla.	D6a
Coleman, Herb (1)	DE	6-4	300	9/4/71	Trinity	Chicago, Ill.	FA
Cooper, Andre (1)	WR	6-2	210	6/21/75	Florida State	Jacksonville, Fla.	FA-'98
Crosland, Ben (1)	DE	6-4	269	4/29/74	Utah State	Kemmerer, Wyo.	FA
Doering, Chris (1)	WR	6-4	195	5/19/73	Florida	Gainesville, Fla.	FA
Finn, Dan (1)	G	6-3	300	8/23/76	Northern Arizona	Mesa, Ariz.	FA
Friedman, Lennie	G	6-3	300	10/13/76	Duke	West Milford, N.J.	D2b
Gary, Olandis	RB	5-11	218	5/18/75	Georgia	Washington, D.C.	D4
Gizzi, Chris (1)	LB	6-0	230	3/8/75	Air Force	Cleveland, Ohio	FA-'98
Johnson, Taj (1)	WR	6-2	195	1/9/75	San Diego State	Ardmore, Okla.	FA
Maumau, Viliami (1)	DT	6-2	302	4/3/75	Colorado	Honolulu, Hawaii	FA
McGriff, Travis	WR	5-8	182	6/24/76	Florida	Gainesville, Fla.	D3b
Miller, Billy	WR	6-3	215	4/24/77	Southern California	Westlake Village, Calif.	D7a
Moore, Jason (1)	CB	5-10	191	1/15/76	San Diego State	San Bernardino, Calif.	FA
Noel, Tori (1)	S	6-0	200	2/17/75	Tennessee	Memphis, Tenn.	FA-'98
Plummer, Chad	WR	6-3	223	11/30/75	Cincinnati	Tallahassee, Fla.	D6b
Reagor, Montae	DE	6-2	256	6/29/77	Texas Tech	Waxahachie, Tex.	D2a
Suttle, Jason (1)	CB	5-10	182	12/2/74	Wisconsin	Burnsville, Minn.	FA
Swift, Justin	TE	6-4	264	8/14/75	Kansas State	Overland Park, Kan.	D7b
Thomas, Dave (1)	LB	6-3	225	1/12/76	Eastern Illinois	Lookout Mtn., Tenn.	FA
Thomas, Marvin (1)	DE	6-5	264	10/19/73	Memphis	Minette, Ala.	FA
Trout, Brad (1)	DB	6-2	209	1/22/75	Valdosta State	Miami, Fla.	FA
Turner, Shawn (1)	WR	6-1	200	5/18/73	Utah State	Nampa, Idaho	FA
Watson, Chris	CB	6-1	192	6/30/77	Eastern Illinois	Chicago, Ill.	D3a
Wilson, Al	LB	6-0	240	6/21/77	Tennessee	Jackson, Tenn.	D1

The term NFL Rookie is defined as a player who is in his first season of professional football and has not been on the roster of another professional football team for any regular-season or postseason games. A Rookie is designated by an "R" on NFL rosters. Players who have been active in another professional football league or players who have NFL experience, including either preseason training camp or being on an Active List or Inactive List, or on Reserve/Injured or Reserve/Physically Unable to Perform for fewer than six regular-season games, are termed NFL First-Year Players. An NFL First-Year Player is designated by a "1" on NFL rosters. Thereafter, a player is credited with an additional year of experience for each season in which he accumulates six games on the Active List or Inactive List, or on Reserve/Injured or Reserve/Physically Unable to Perform.

INDIANAPOLIS COLTS

American Football Conference
Eastern Division
Team Colors: Royal Blue and White
P.O. Box 535000
Indianapolis, Indiana 46253
Telephone: (317) 297-2658

CLUB OFFICIALS

Owner and CEO: James Irsay
President: Bill Polian
Vice Chairman and COO: Michael G. Chernoff
Senior Vice President: Bob Terpening
Senior Vice President-Administration: Pete Ward
Vice President-Sales and Marketing: Ray Compton
Vice President-Finance: Kurt Humphrey
Vice President-Public Relations: Craig Kelley
Director of Football Operations: Dom Anile
Director of Pro Player Personnel: Clyde Powers
Director of College Scouting: George Boone
Director of Pro Scouting: Chris Polian
Director of Player Development: Steve Champlin
Director of Sponsorship Sales: Jay Souers
Director of Business Development: Tom Zupancic
Director of Ticket Operations: Larry Hall
Director of Ticket Sales: Greg Hylton
Director of Community Development/Player Relations: Bill Brooks
Director of Community Relations and Promotions: Nicole Duncan
Assistant Director of Public Relations: Ryan Robinson
Equipment Manager: Jon Scott
Video Director: Marty Heckscher
Head Trainer: Hunter Smith
Assistant Equipment Manager: Mike Mays
Assistant Trainers: Dave Hammer, Dave Walston
Assistant Video Director: John Starliper
Purchasing Administrator: Dave Filar
Stadium: RCA Dome • **Capacity:** 56,637
100 South Capitol Avenue
Indianapolis, Indiana 46225
Playing Surface: AstroTurf
Training Camp: Rose-Hulman Institute
5500 Wabash Avenue
Terre Haute, Indiana 47803

1999 SCHEDULE

PRESEASON

Aug. 7	at Chicago	7:00
Aug. 14	**Cincinnati**	7:00
Aug. 21	at New Orleans	7:00
Sept. 2	**Seattle**	7:00

REGULAR SEASON

Sept. 12	**Buffalo**	12:00
Sept. 19	at New England	1:00
Sept. 26	at San Diego	1:05
Oct. 3	Open Date	
Oct. 10	**Miami**	3:15
Oct. 17	at New York Jets	1:00
Oct. 24	**Cincinnati**	12:00
Oct. 31	**Dallas**	1:00
Nov. 7	**Kansas City**	1:00
Nov. 14	at New York Giants	1:00
Nov. 21	at Philadelphia	1:00
Nov. 28	**New York Jets**	4:15
Dec. 5	at Miami	1:00
Dec. 12	**New England**	1:00
Dec. 19	**Washington**	1:00
Dec. 26	at Cleveland	1:00
Jan. 2	at Buffalo	1:00

RECORD HOLDERS

INDIVIDUAL RECORDS—CAREER

Category	Name	Performance
Rushing (Yds.)	Lydell Mitchell, 1972-77	5,487
Passing (Yds.)	Johnny Unitas, 1956-1972	39,768
Passing (TDs)	Johnny Unitas, 1956-1972	287
Receiving (No.)	Raymond Berry, 1955-1967	631
Receiving (Yds.)	Raymond Berry, 1955-1967	9,275
Interceptions	Bob Boyd, 1960-68	57
Punting (Avg.)	Chris Gardocki, 1994-98	44.8
Punt Return (Avg.)	Ron Gardin, 1970-71	13.5
Kickoff Return (Avg.)	Jim Duncan, 1969-1971	32.5
Field Goals	Dean Biasucci 1984, 1986-1994	176
Touchdowns (Tot.)	Lenny Moore, 1956-1967	113
Points	Dean Biasucci, 1984, 1986-1994	783

INDIVIDUAL RECORDS—SINGLE SEASON

Category	Name	Performance
Rushing (Yds.)	Eric Dickerson, 1988	1,659
Passing (Yds.)	Peyton Manning, 1998	3,739
Passing (TDs)	Johnny Unitas, 1959	32
Receiving (No.)	Marshall Faulk, 1998	86
Receiving (Yds.)	Raymond Berry, 1960	1,298
Interceptions	Tom Keane, 1953	11
Punting (Avg.)	Rohn Stark, 1985	45.9
Punt Return (Avg.)	Clarence Verdin, 1989	12.9
Kickoff Return (Avg.)	Jim Duncan, 1970	35.4
Field Goals	Cary Blanchard, 1996	36
Touchdowns (Tot.)	Lenny Moore, 1964	20
Points	Cary Blanchard, 1996	135

INDIVIDUAL RECORDS—SINGLE GAME

Category	Name	Performance
Rushing (Yds.)	Norm Bulaich, 9-19-71	198
Passing (Yds.)	Johnny Unitas, 9-17-67	401
Passing (TDs)	Gary Cuozzo, 11-14-65	5
	Gary Hogeboom, 10-4-87	5
Receiving (No.)	Lydell Mitchell, 12-15-74	13
	Joe Washington, 9-2-79	13
Receiving (Yds.)	Raymond Berry, 11-10-57	224
Interceptions	Many times	3
	Last time by Mike Prior, 12-20-92	
Field Goals	Many times	5
	Last time by Cary Blanchard, 9-21-97	
Touchdowns (Tot.)	Many times	4
	Last time by Eric Dickerson, 10-31-88	
Points	Many times	24
	Last time by Eric Dickerson, 10-31-88	

RCA DOME

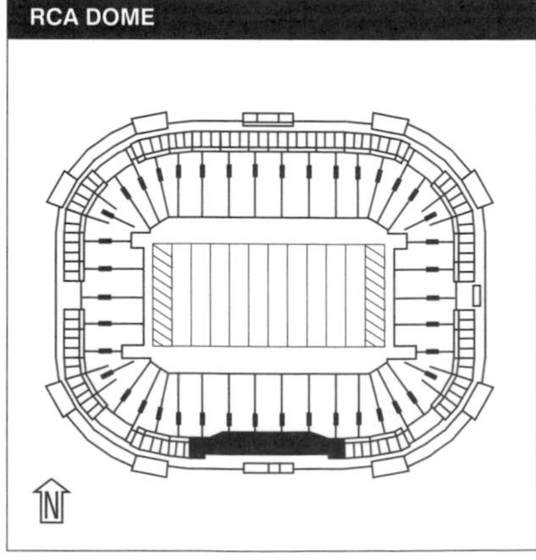

COACHING HISTORY

BALTIMORE 1953-1983
(323-351-7)

1953	Keith Molesworth	3-9-0
1954-62	Weeb Ewbank	61-52-1
1963-69	Don Shula	73-26-4
1970-72	Don McCafferty*	26-11-1
1972	John Sandusky	4-5-0
1973-74	Howard Schnellenberger**	4-13-0
1974	Joe Thomas	2-9-0
1975-79	Ted Marchibroda	41-36-0
1980-81	Mike McCormack	9-23-0
1982-84	Frank Kush***	11-28-1
1984	Hal Hunter	0-1-0
1985-86	Rod Dowhower****	5-24-0
1986-91	Ron Meyer#	36-36-0
1991	Rick Venturi	1-10-0
1992-95	Ted Marchibroda	32-35-0
1996-97	Lindy Infante	12-21-0
1998	Jim Mora	3-13-0

*Released after five games in 1972
**Released after three games in 1974
***Resigned after 15 games in 1984
****Released after 13 games in 1986
#Released after five games in 1991

1998 TEAM RECORD

PRESEASON (2-2)

Date	Result		Opponent
8/8	L	21-24	at Seattle
8/17	W	30-27	at Cincinnati
8/22	L	3-33	San Diego
8/27	W	20-17	Detroit

REGULAR SEASON (3-13)

Date	Result		Opponent	Att.
9/6	L	15-24	Miami	60,587
9/13	L	6-29	at New England	60,068
9/20	L	6-44	at New York Jets	66,321
9/27	L	13-19	New Orleans (OT)	48,480
10/4	W	17-12	San Diego	51,988
10/11	L	24-31	Buffalo	52,938
10/18	L	31-34	at San Francisco	68,486
11/1	L	16-21	New England	58,056
11/8	L	14-27	at Miami	73,400
11/15	W	24-23	New York Jets	55,520
11/22	L	11-34	at Buffalo	49,032
11/29	L	31-38	at Baltimore	68,898
12/6	L	21-28	at Atlanta	61,141
12/13	W	39-26	Cincinnati	55,179
12/20	L	23-27	at Seattle	58,703
12/27	L	19-27	Carolina	58,182

(OT) Overtime

SCORE BY PERIODS

Colts	105	69	47	89	0	—	310
Opponents	60	170	61	147	6	—	444

ATTENDANCE

Home 440,930 Away 506,049 Total 946,979
Single-game home record, 61,139 (10/20/97)
Single-season home record, 481,305 (1984)

1998 TEAM STATISTICS

	Colts	Opp.
Total First Downs	298	341
Rushing	77	131
Passing	190	181
Penalty	31	29
Third Down: Made/Att	71/202	89/208
Third Down Pct.	35.1	42.8
Fourth Down: Made/Att	4/10	3/9
Fourth Down Pct.	40.0	33.3
Total Net Yards	5,116	5,836
Avg. Per Game	319.8	364.8
Total Plays	982	1,043
Avg. Per Play	5.2	5.6
Net Yards Rushing	1,486	2,570
Avg. Per Game	92.9	160.6
Total Rushes	384	544
Net Yards Passing	3,630	3,266
Avg. Per Game	226.9	204.1
Sacked/Yards Lost	22/109	38/231
Gross Yards	3,739	3,497
Att./Completions	576/326	461/275
Completion Pct.	56.6	59.7
Had Intercepted	28	8
Punts/Avg.	79/45.4	68/44.6
Net Punting Avg.	79/37.1	68/36.6
Penalties/Yards Lost	106/853	108/917
Fumbles/Ball Lost	10/5	29/11
Touchdowns	33	52
Rushing	7	20
Passing	26	27
Returns	0	5
Avg. Time of Possession	27:47	32:13

1998 INDIVIDUAL STATISTICS

Passing	Att.	Comp.	Yds.	Pct.	TD	Int.	Tkld.	Rate
Manning	575	326	3,739	56.7	26	28	22/109	71.2
Small	1	0	0	0.0	0	0	0/0	39.6
Colts	576	326	3,739	56.6	26	28	22/109	71.1
Opponents	461	275	3,497	59.7	27	8	38/231	95.7

SCORING	TD R	TD P	TD Rt	PAT	FG	Saf	PTS
Vanderjagt	0	0	0	23/23	27/31	0	104
Faulk	6	4	0	0/0	0/0	0	60
Harrison	0	7	0	0/0	0/0	0	44
Small	0	7	0	0/0	0/0	0	42
Pollard	0	4	0	0/0	0/0	0	28
Warren	1	1	0	0/0	0/0	0	12
Dilger	0	1	0	0/0	0/0	0	8
Green	0	1	0	0/0	0/0	0	6
Pathon	0	1	0	0/0	0/0	0	6
Colts	7	26	0	23/23	27/31	0	310
Opponents	20	27	5	44/45	28/37	0	444

2-Point conversions: Pollard 2, Dilger, Harrison. Team 4-10, Opponents 2-6.

RUSHING	Att.	Yds.	Avg.	LG	TD
Faulk	324	1,319	4.1	68t	6
Manning	15	62	4.1	15	0
Warren	25	61	2.4	14	1
Elias	8	24	3.0	8	0
Heyward	6	15	2.5	8	0
Crockett	2	5	2.5	5	0
Small	1	2	2.0	2	0
Pathon	3	-2	-0.7	4	0
Colts	384	1,486	3.9	68t	7
Opponents	544	2,570	4.7	51	20

RECEIVING	No.	Yds.	Avg.	LG	TD
Faulk	86	908	10.6	78t	4
Harrison	59	776	13.2	61t	7
Pathon	50	511	10.2	45	1
Small	45	681	15.1	53	7
Dilger	31	303	9.8	27	1
Pollard	24	309	12.9	44t	4
Green	15	177	11.8	25	1
Warren	11	44	4.0	12	1
Elias	1	11	11.0	11	0
Heyward	1	9	9.0	9	0
Banta	1	7	7.0	7	0
Greene	1	2	2.0	2	0
Crockett	1	1	1.0	1	0
Colts	326	3,739	11.5	78t	26
Opponents	275	3,497	12.7	82t	27

INTERCEPTIONS	No.	Yds.	Avg.	LG	TD
Clark	1	30	30.0	30	0
Montgomery	1	22	22.0	22	0
Belser	1	19	19.0	19	0
Blackmon	1	14	14.0	14	0
Alexander	1	12	12.0	12	0
M. Barber	1	0	0.0	0	0
Burris	1	0	0.0	0	0
Poole	1	0	0.0	0	0
Colts	8	97	12.1	30	0
Opponents	28	353	12.6	59t	2

PUNTING	No.	Yds.	Avg.	In 20	LG
Gardocki	79	3,583	45.4	23	62
Colts	79	3,583	45.4	23	62
Opponents	68	3,032	44.6	21	73

PUNT RETURNS	No.	FC	Yds.	Avg.	LG	TD
Bailey	19	4	176	9.3	33	0
Poole	12	6	107	8.9	16	0
McGuire	2	1	4	2.0	4	0
Belser	1	0	53	53.0	53	0
Colts	34	11	340	10.0	53	0
Opponents	42	16	451	10.7	40	0

KICKOFF RETURNS	No.	Yds.	Avg.	LG	TD
Bailey	34	759	22.3	44	0
Elias	14	317	22.6	29	0
Warren	8	152	19.0	26	0
Hetherington	5	71	14.2	20	0
McGuire	4	75	18.8	28	0
Clark	3	38	12.7	15	0
Dilger	1	14	14.0	14	0
Pollard	1	4	4.0	4	0
Morrison	1	2	2.0	2	0
Colts	71	1,432	20.2	44	0
Opponents	65	1,688	26.0	99t	1

FIELD GOALS	1-19	20-29	30-39	40-49	50+
Vanderjagt	1/1	8/8	4/4	8/9	6/9
Colts	1/1	8/8	4/4	8/9	6/9
Opponents	1/1	12/13	5/5	8/12	2/6

SACKS	No.
E. Johnson	8.0
McCoy	6.0
Berry	4.0
Whittington	4.0
Chester	3.0
M. Barber	2.0
Montgomery	2.0
Tuinei	2.0
Belser	1.0
Blackmon	1.0
Chorak	1.0
Fontenot	1.0
Morrison	1.0
Shello	1.0
M. Thomas	1.0
Colts	38.0
Opponents	22.0

1999 DRAFT CHOICES

Round	Name	Pos.	College
1	Edgerrin James	RB	Miami
2	Mike Peterson	LB	Florida
3	Brandon Burlsworth	G	Arkansas
4	Paul Miranda	DB	Central Florida
5	Brad Scioli	DE	Penn State
7	Hunter Smith	P	Notre Dame
	Corey Terry	LB	Tennessee

INDIANAPOLIS COLTS

1999 VETERAN ROSTER

No.	Name	Pos.	Ht.	Wt.	Birthdate	NFL Exp.	College	Hometown	How Acq.	'98 Games/ Starts
83	Banta, Bradford	TE	6-6	260	12/14/70	6	Southern California	Baton Rouge, La.	D4-'94	16/0
53	Barber, Michael	LB	6-0	254	11/9/71	5	Clemson	Edgemore, S.C.	W(Sea)-'98	12/6
29	Belser, Jason	S	5-9	196	5/28/70	8	Oklahoma	Kansas City, Mo.	D8a-'92	16/16
97	Bennett, Cornelius	LB	6-3	240	8/25/65	13	Alabama	Birmingham, Ala.	FA-'99	16/16*
57	Berry, Bertrand	LB	6-3	250	8/15/75	3	Notre Dame	Houston, Tex.	D3-'97	16/12
26	Blevins, Tony	S	6-0	165	1/29/75	2	Kansas	Rockford, Ill.	W(SF)-'98	3/0
92	Bratzke, Chad	DE	6-5	275	9/15/71	6	Eastern Kentucky	Brandon, Fla.	UFA(NYG)-'99	16/16*
20	Burris, Jeff	S	6-0	190	6/7/72	6	Notre Dame	Rock Hill, S.C.	UFA(Buff)-'98	14/14
15	Case, Stoney	QB	6-3	201	7/7/72	5	New Mexico	Odessa, Tex.	UFA(Ariz)-'99	0*
64	Chester, Larry	DE-DT	6-2	305	10/17/75	2	Temple	Hammond, La.	FA-'98	14/2
93	Chorak, Jason	LB	6-3	253	9/23/74	2	Washington	Vashon, Wash.	FA-'98	8/0
27	Clark, Rico	CB-S	5-10	181	6/6/74	3	Louisville	Decatur, Ga.	FA-'97	16/0
37	Cota, Chad	CB-S	6-1	198	8/8/71	5	Oregon	Ashland, Ore.	UFA(NO)-'99	16/16*
87	Dawson, Lake	WR	6-2	207	1/2/72	5	Notre Dame	Federal Way, Wash.	FA-'99	0*
85	Dilger, Ken	TE	6-5	259	2/2/71	5	Illinois	Mariah Hill, Ind.	D2-'95	16/16
23	Elias, Keith	RB	5-9	203	2/3/72	5	Princeton	Virginia Beach, Va.	FA-'98	13/0
78	Glenn, Tarik	T	6-5	335	5/25/76	3	California	Oakland, Calif.	D1-'97	16/16
84	Green, E.G.	WR	5-11	190	6/28/75	2	Florida State	Fort Walton Beach, Fla.	D3-'98	11/0
44	# Greene, Scott	RB	5-10	240	6/1/72	4	Michigan State	Canandaigua, N.Y.	FA-'98	5/0
88	Harrison, Marvin	WR	6-0	181	8/25/72	4	Syracuse	Philadelphia, Pa.	D1-'96	12/12
94	Hobgood-Chittick, Nate	DE-DT	6-3	290	11/30/74	2	North Carolina	New Haven, Conn.	FA-'98	0*
13	Holcomb, Kelly	QB	6-2	212	7/9/73	3	Middle Tennessee State	Fayetteville, Tenn.	FA-'96	0*
44	Holmes, Derick	RB	6-0	237	7/1/71	5	Portland State	Pasadena, Calif.	UFA(GB)-'99	14/4*
69	Isaia, Sale	G-T	6-3	330	6/13/72	5	UCLA	Oceanside, Calif.	UFA(Balt)-'99	0*
74	Jackson, Waverly	T	6-2	310	12/19/72	2	Virginia Tech	South Hill, Va.	FA-'98	6/2
62	Johnson, Ellis	DT	6-2	292	10/30/73	5	Florida	Wildwood, Fla.	D1-'95	16/16
60	Johnson, Jason	C	6-3	290	2/6/74	2	Kansas State	Gladstone, Mo.	FA-'98	14/0
91	Jordan, Antony	LB	6-3	240	12/19/74	2	Vanderbilt	Sewell, N.J.	D5b-'98	15/3
96	King, Shawn	DE	6-3	290	6/24/72	5	Northeast Louisiana	West Monroe, La.	UFA(Car)-'99	0*
58	Leeuwenburg, Jay	C-G	6-3	290	6/18/69	8	Colorado	St. Louis, Mo.	UFA(Chi)-'96	16/16
79	Mandarich, Tony	G	6-5	307	9/23/66	8	Michigan State	Ontario, Canada	FA-'96	10/10
18	Manning, Peyton	QB	6-5	230	3/24/76	2	Tennessee	New Orleans, La.	D1-'98	16/16
61	McCoy, Tony	DT	6-1	289	6/10/69	8	Florida	Orlando, Fla.	D4b-'92	14/13
40	McElroy, Ray	CB-S	5-11	207	7/31/72	5	Eastern Illinois	Bellwood, Ill.	D4-'95	16/0
11	McGuire, Kaipo	WR	5-10	174	1/16/74	3	Brigham Young	Honolulu, Hawaii	FA-'98	1/0
76	McKinney, Steve	G	6-4	302	10/15/75	2	Texas A&M	Houston, Tex.	D4-'98	16/16
73	Meadows, Adam	T	6-5	299	1/25/74	3	Georgia	Powder Springs, Ga.	D2-'97	14/14
34	Montgomery, Monty	CB-S	5-11	197	12/8/73	3	Houston	Gladewater,Tex.	D4-'97	16/5
72	Moore, Larry	G	6-2	312	6/1/75	2	Brigham Young	San Diego, Calif.	FA-'98	6/5
86	Pathon, Jerome	WR	6-0	187	12/16/75	2	Washington	Capetown, South Africa	D2-'98	16/15
81	Pollard, Marcus	TE	6-4	257	2/8/72	5	Bradley	Valley, Ala.	FA-'95	16/11
38	Poole, Tyrone	CB	5-8	188	2/3/72	5	Fort Valley State	Lagrange, Ga.	T(Car)-'98	15/15
41	Reddick, Nakia	CB-S	5-11	200	9/29/74	2	Central Florida	Miami, Fla.	FA-'98	0*
56	Royal, Andre	LB	6-2	220	12/1/72	5	Alabama	North Port, Ala.	T(NO)-'98	13/9
90	Thomas, Mark	DE	6-5	265	5/6/69	8	North Carolina State	Lilburn, Ga.	W(Chi)-'98	4/1
75	Tuinei, Van	DE-DT	6-4	275	2/16/71	3	Arizona	Garden Grove, Calif.	FA-'98	12/0
12	† Vanderjagt, Mike	P-K	6-5	210	3/24/70	2	West Virginia	Oakville, Ontario, Canada	FA-'98	14/0
95	Whittington, Bernard	DE	6-5	280	8/20/71	6	Indiana	St. Louis, Mo.	FA-'94	15/11

* Bennett played 16 games with Atlanta in '98; Bratzke played 16 games with N.Y. Giants; Case inactive for 16 games with Arizona; Cota played 16 games with New Orleans; Dawson last active with Kansas City in '97; Hobgood-Chittick inactive for 5 games; Holcomb inactive for 16 games; Holmes played 3 games with Buffalo and 11 games with Green Bay; Isaia missed '98 season because of injury with Baltimore; King missed '98 season because of injury with Carolina; Reddick inactive for 16 games.

Unrestricted free agent; subject to developments.

† Restricted free agent; subject to developments.

Traded—RB Marshall Faulk (16 games in '98) to St. Louis.

Players lost to free agency (5): LB Elijah Alexander (Clev; 13 games in '98), CB-S Tim Hauck (Phil; 16), P Chris Gardocki (Clev; 16), WR Torrance Small (Phil; 16), DT Jeff Zgonina (StL; 2).

Also played with Colts in '98—CB-S Billy Austin (1 game), WR Aaron Bailey (9), CB Robert Blackmon (15), DE Steven Conley (1), RB Zack Crockett (2), DE Al Fontenot (7), DE Dan Footman (3), CB-S Tim Hauck (16), LB Jeff Herrod (10), RB Chris Hetherington (14), RB Craig Heyward (4), LB Rob Holmberg (3), DE-DT Steve Martin (4), CB-S Ray McElroy (16), CB-S Monty Montgomery (16), LB Steve Morrison (16), G Tom Myslinski (4), WR Freddie Scott (1), DE-DT Kendel Shello (6), LB Ratcliff Thomas (5), RB Lamont Warren (12).

COACHING STAFF

Head Coach,
Jim Mora

Pro Career: Jim Mora joined the Colts as their seventeenth head coach on January 12, 1998. He led the Colts to a 3-13 record in his first season. Mora spent 1986-1996 as head coach at New Orleans, amassing a 93-74 regular-season record and four playoff appearances. In 1996, Mora stood as the most tenured coach with the same team in all of professional sports, and he had won more games than the previous nine Saints coaches combined. Mora is one of only 20 head coaches in NFL history who has had 10 or more consecutive seasons of service with the same team. Mora produced 91 victories during his first 10 seasons, a total exceeded by only eight other coaches in NFL history. Mora's 96 career wins rank fifth among active coaches, and he stands to become the twenty-seventh coach to produce 100 career victories. His 1991 Saints squad went 11-5, earning the only division title in club history. Prior to his stint with New Orleans, Mora directed the Philadelphia/Baltimore Stars of the USFL from 1983-85. Mora forged a 48-13-1 record and led the Stars to two titles in three league-championship-game appearances. Mora began his pro coaching career in 1978 as defensive line coach with Seattle. In 1982, he was defensive coordinator at New England. Career record: 96-91.

Background: Played tight end and defensive end at Occidental College. Assistant coach at Occidental from 1960-63 and head coach from 1964-66. Linebacker coach at Stanford in 1967. Defensive assistant at Colorado from 1968-1973. Linebacker coach at UCLA in 1974. Defensive coordinator at Washington from 1975-77. Received bachelor's degree in physical education from Occidental in 1957. Also holds master's degree in education from Southern California.

Personal: Born May 24, 1935, in Glendale, Calif. Jim and his wife, Connie, live in Indianapolis, and have three sons—Michael, Stephen, and Jim (defensive coordinator with San Francisco 49ers).

ASSISTANT COACHES

Bruce Arians, quarterbacks; born October 3, 1952, Paterson, N.J., lives in Indianapolis. Quarterback Virginia Tech 1971-74. No pro playing experience. College coach: Virginia Tech 1975-77, Mississippi State 1978-1980, 1993-95, Alabama 1981-82, 1997, Temple 1983-88 (head coach). Pro coach: Kansas City Chiefs 1989-1992, New Orleans Saints 1996, joined Colts in 1998.

George Catavolos, asst. head coach-defensive backs; born May 8, 1945, Chicago, lives in Indianapolis. Defensive back Purdue 1964-67. No pro playing experience. College coach: Purdue 1967-68, 1971-76, Middle Tennessee State 1969, Louisville 1970, Kentucky 1977-1981, Tennessee 1982-83. Pro coach: Indianapolis Colts 1984-1993, Carolina Panthers 1995-97, rejoined Colts in 1998.

Vic Fangio, defensive coordinator; born August 22, 1958, Dunmore, Pa., lives in Indianapolis. Attended East Stroudsburg. No pro playing experience. College coach: North Carolina 1993. Pro coach: Philadelphia/Baltimore Stars (USFL) 1984-85, New Orleans Saints 1986-1994, Carolina Panthers 1995-98, joined Colts 1999.

Todd Grantham, defensive line; born September 13, 1966, Pulaski, Va., lives in Indianapolis. Attended Virginia Tech. No college or pro playing experience. College coach: Virginia Tech 1990-95, Michigan State 1996-98. Pro coach: Joined Colts in 1999.

Gene Huey, running backs; born July 20, 1947, Uniontown, Pa., lives in Indianapolis. Defensive back-wide receiver Wyoming 1966-69. No pro playing experience. College coach: Wyoming 1970-74, New Mexico 1975-77, Nebraska 1978-1986, Arizona State 1987, Ohio State 1988-1991. Pro coach: Joined Colts in 1992.

Tony Marciano, tight ends; born June 14, 1956, Scranton, Pa., lives in Indianapolis. Attended Indiana (Pa.) No college or pro playing experience. College coach: Texas Christian 1978-1980, Southern Methodist 1981-86, Brown 1987-88, Richmond 1989-1990, Kent State 1991-92. Pro coach: Toronto Argonauts (CFL) 1994, Calgary Stampeders (CFL) 1995-97, joined Colts in 1998.

Tom Moore, offensive coordinator; born November 7, 1938, Owatanna, Minn., lives in Indianapolis. Quarterback Iowa 1957-1960. No pro playing experience. College coach: Iowa 1961-62, Dayton 1965-68, Wake Forest 1969, Georgia Tech 1970-71, Minnesota 1972-73, 1975-76. Pro coach: New York Stars (WFL) 1974, Pittsburgh Steelers 1977-1989, Minnesota Vikings 1990-93, Detroit Lions 1994-96, New Orleans Saints 1997, joined Colts in 1998.

Howard Mudd, offensive line; born February 10, 1942, Midland, Mich., lives in Indianapolis. Guard Hillsdale (Mich.) College 1960-63. Pro offensive lineman San Francisco 49ers 1964-69, Chicago Bears 1969-1970. College coach: California 1972-73. Pro coach: San Diego Chargers 1974-76, San Francisco 49ers 1977, Seattle Seahawks 1978-1982, 1993-97, Cleveland Browns 1983-88, Kansas City Chiefs 1989-1992, joined Colts in 1998.

Mike Murphy, linebackers; born September 25, 1944, New York, N.Y., lives in Indianapolis. Guard-linebacker Huron (S.D.) 1963-66. No pro playing experience. College coach: Vermont 1970-73, Idaho State 1974-76, Western Illinois 1977-78. Pro coach: Saskatchewan Roughriders (CFL) 1979-1983, Chicago Blitz (USFL) 1984, Detroit Lions 1985-89, Arizona Cardinals 1990-93, Seattle Seahawks 1995-97, joined Colts in 1998.

Jay Norvell, receivers; born March 28, 1963, Madison, Wis., lives in Indianapolis. Defensive back Iowa 1982-85. Pro defensive back Chicago Bears 1987. College coach: Iowa 1986, Northern Iowa 1988, Wisconsin 1989-1993, Iowa State 1995-97. Pro coach: Joined Colts in 1998.

John Pagano, defensive assistant; born March 30, 1967, Boulder, Colo., lives in Indianapolis. Linebacker Mesa State College 1985-88. No pro playing experience. College coach: Mesa State College 1989, Nevada-Las Vegas 1990-91, Louisiana Tech 1994, Mississippi 1995. Pro coach: New Orleans Saints 1996-97, joined Colts in 1998.

Kevin Spencer, special teams; born November 2, 1953, Queens, N.Y., lives in Indianapolis. Attended Springfield (Mass.) College. No college or pro playing experience. College coach: SUNY 1975-76, Cornell 1979-1980, Ithaca 1981-86, Wesleyan 1987-1990. Pro coach: Cleveland Browns 1991-94, Oakland Raiders 1995-97, joined Colts in 1998.

Jon Torine, strength and conditioning; born November 16, 1973, Livingston, N.J., lives in Indianapolis. Linebacker Springfield (Mass.) College 1991. No pro playing experience. Pro coach: Buffalo Bills 1995-97, joined Colts in 1998.

1999 FIRST-YEAR ROSTER

Name	Pos.	Ht.	Wt.	Birthdate	College	Hometown	How Acq.
Anders, David	T	6-7	310	9/9/75	Eastern Washington	Paseo, Wash.	FA
Armour, Phillip	C	6-3	218	12/9/76	North Texas State	Denton, Tex.	FA
Austin, Billy (1)	CB-S	5-10	195	3/8/75	New Mexico	Washington, D.C.	FA-'98
Blackman, Jon (1)	G-T	6-6	265	10/8/75	Purdue	Yorkville, Ill.	FA-'98
Calicchio, Lonny (1)	P	6-2	250	10/24/72	Mississippi	Plantation, Fla.	FA
Caswell, Wes	WR	5-8	186	1/4/75	Tulsa	Tulsa, Okla.	FA
Davis, Joel (1)	G-T	6-5	310	4/6/73	Army	Binghamton, N.Y.	FA
Eberly, Chris	RB	5-10	225	12/25/75	Penn State	Mount Holly, N.J.	FA
Fassel, John	WR	6-4	189	1/10/74	Weber State	Morris, N.J.	FA
Gall, Chris	RB	6-0	231	4/4/76	Indiana	River Forest, Ill.	FA
James, Edgerrin	RB	6-0	216	8/1/78	Miami	Immokalee, Fla.	D1
Jones, Isaac	WR	6-0	190	12/7/75	Purdue	Philadelphia, Pa.	FA
Keur, Joshua	TE	6-4	283	9/14/76	Michigan State	Muskegon, Mich.	FA
Kirby, Charles (1)	RB	6-1	247	11/27/74	Virginia	Fayetteville, N.C.	FA-'98
Kubiak, Jim (1)	QB	6-2	218	5/12/72	Navy	Buffalo, N.Y.	FA
Kuykendall, Joe	TE	6-5	267	8/28/77	Oregon State	San Jose, Calif.	FA
Miller, Craig	CB-S	5-11	199	10/4/77	Utah State	Bakersfield, Calif.	FA
Miranda, Paul	CB-S	5-10	184	5/2/76	Central Florida	Thomasville, Ga.	D4
Muhammad, Steve	CB-S	5-10	180	10/19/73	Fresno State	Los Angeles, Calif.	FA
Nwokorie, Chuckie	DE	6-2	286	7/10/75	Purdue	Lafayette, Ind.	FA
Olsen, Eric	K	5-9	192	4/12/77	Army	Fort Lauderdale, Fla.	FA
Pearsall, Melvin (1)	TE	6-1	248	2/3/75	Florida State	Lake Wales, Fla.	FA
Peterson, Mike	LB	6-2	229	6/17/76	Florida	Gainesville, Fla.	D2
Prentiss, Kevin	WR-KR	5-7	160	11/9/76	Mississippi State	Vicksburg, Miss.	FA
Ridder, Tim	G-T	6-7	301	12/17/76	Notre Dame	Omaha, Neb.	FA
Robinson, Roderick	QB	6-2	230	5/17/76	Arkansas-Pine Bluff	Memphis, Tenn.	FA
Rogers, Ron (1)	LB	6-1	246	4/20/75	Georgia Tech	Dublin, Ga.	FA-'98
Sanford, Kio (1)	WR	5-10	180	1/8/75	Kentucky	Lexington, Ky.	FA-'98
Sartin, Trey (1)	T	6-7	322	3/19/75	Liberty	Charlotte, N.C.	FA-'98
Saturday, Jeff	C	6-2	298	6/8/75	North Carolina	Tucker, Ga.	FA
Scioli, Brad	DE	6-3	277	9/6/76	Penn State	Bridgeport, Pa.	D5
Shields, Paul	RB	6-1	238	1/31/76	Arizona	Mesa, Ariz.	FA
Smart, Kirby	CB-S	5-10	192	12/23/75	Georgia	Bainbridge, Ga.	FA
Smith, Hunter	P	6-2	212	8/9/77	Notre Dame	Sherman, Tex.	D7a
Snellings, Paul	T	6-5	286	11/5/75	Georgia	LaGrange, Ga.	FA
Terry, Corey	LB	6-3	258	3/6/76	Tennessee	Warrenton, N.C.	D7b
Thomas, Scott	CB-S	6-2	203	1/31/75	Azusa Pacific	Norwalk, Calif.	FA
Wilkins, Terrence	KR	5-8	179	7/29/75	Virginia	Washington, D.C.	FA

The term NFL Rookie is defined as a player who is in his first season of professional football and has not been on the roster of another professional football team for any regular-season or postseason games. A Rookie is designated by an "R" on NFL rosters. Players who have been active in another professional football league or players who have NFL experience, including either preseason training camp or being on an Active List or Inactive List, or on Reserve/Injured or Reserve/Physically Unable to Perform for fewer than six regular-season games, are termed NFL First-Year Players. An NFL First-Year Player is designated by a "1" on NFL rosters. Thereafter, a player is credited with an additional year of experience for each season in which he accumulates six games on the Active List or Inactive List, or on Reserve/Injured or Reserve/Physically Unable to Perform.

NOTES

JACKSONVILLE JAGUARS

American Football Conference
Central Division
Team Colors: Teal, Black, and Gold
ALLTEL Stadium
One ALLTEL Stadium Place
Jacksonville, Florida 32202
Telephone: (904) 633-6000

CLUB OFFICIALS

Chairman and Chief Executive Officer: Wayne Weaver
Senior Vice President/Football Operations: Michael Huyghue
Senior Vice President/Marketing: Dan Connell
Vice President/Chief Financial Officer: Bill Prescott
Vice President, Administration/General Counsel: Paul Vance
Executive Director of Communications: Dan Edwards
Director of Player Personnel: Rick Reiprish
Director of Pro Scouting: Fran Foley
Director of College Scouting: Rick Mueller
Director of Finance: Kim Dodson
Director of Facilities: Jeff Cannon
Director of Football Administration: Skip Richardson
Director of Information Technology: Bruce Swindell
Director of Broadcasting: Jennifer Kumik
Director of Corporate Sponsorship: Macky Weaver
Director of Special Events: Roddy White
Director of Player Development/Staff Counsel: Quentin Williams
Head Athletic Trainer: Michael Ryan
Video Director: Mike Perkins
Equipment Manager: Drew Hampton

Chair & Chief Executive Officer, Jaguars Foundation: Delores Barr Weaver
President, Jaguars Foundation: Dr. Gregory Gross
Stadium: ALLTEL Stadium • **Capacity:** 73,000
One ALLTEL Stadium Place
Jacksonville, Florida 32202
Playing Surface: Grass
Training Camp: ALLTEL Stadium
One ALLTEL Stadium Place
Jacksonville, Florida 32202

RECORD HOLDERS

INDIVIDUAL RECORDS—CAREER

Category	Name	Performance
Rushing (Yds.)	James Stewart, 1995-98	2,020
Passing (Yds.)	Mark Brunell, 1995-98	12,417
Passing (TDs)	Mark Brunell, 1995-98	72
Receiving (No.)	Jimmy Smith, 1995-98	265
Receiving (Yds.)	Jimmy Smith, 1995-98	4,038
Interceptions	Chris Hudson 1996-98	8
Punting (Avg.)	Bryan Barker, 1995-98	44.4
Punt Return (Avg.)	Reggie Barlow, 1997-98	12.2
Kickoff Return (Avg.)	Reggie Barlow, 1997-98	25.4
Field Goals	Mike Hollis, 1995-98	102
Touchdowns (Tot.)	James Stewart, 1995-98	25
Points	Mike Hollis, 1995-98	446

INDIVIDUAL RECORDS—SINGLE SEASON

Category	Name	Performance
Rushing (Yds.)	Fred Taylor, 1998	1,223
Passing (Yds.)	Mark Brunell, 1996	4,367
Passing (TDs)	Mark Brunell, 1998	20
Receiving (No.)	Keenan McCardell, 1996, 1997	85
Receiving (Yds.)	Jimmy Smith, 1997	1,324
Interceptions	Deon Figures, 1997	5
Punting (Avg.)	Bryan Barker, 1998	45.0
Punt Return (Avg.)	Reggie Barlow, 1998	12.9
Kickoff Return (Avg.)	Reggie Barlow, 1998	24.9
Field Goals	Mike Hollis, 1997	31
Touchdowns (Tot.)	Fred Taylor, 1998	17
Points	Mike Hollis, 1997	134

INDIVIDUAL RECORDS—SINGLE GAME

Category	Name	Performance
Rushing (Yds.)	Fred Taylor, 12-6-98	183
Passing (Yds.)	Mark Brunell, 9-22-96	432
Passing (TDs)	Mark Brunell, 11-29-98	4
Receiving (No.)	Keenan McCardell, 10-20-96	16
Receiving (Yds.)	Keenan McCardell, 10-20-96	232
Interceptions	Deon Figures, 8-31-97	2
Field Goals	Mike Hollis, 12-1-96, 11-30-97	5
Touchdowns (Tot.)	James Stewart, 10-12-97	5
Points	James Stewart, 10-12-97	30

1999 SCHEDULE

PRESEASON

Aug. 13	**Carolina**	7:30
Aug. 21	at New York Giants	7:00
Aug. 26	**Kansas City**	8:00
Sept. 2	at Dallas	8:00

REGULAR SEASON

Sept. 12	**San Francisco**	4:15
Sept. 19	at Carolina	1:00
Sept. 26	**Tennessee**	4:05
Oct. 3	at Pittsburgh	1:00
Oct. 11	at New York Jets (Mon.)	9:00
Oct. 17	**Cleveland**	1:00
Oct. 24	Open Date	
Oct. 31	at Cincinnati	1:00
Nov. 7	at Atlanta	1:00
Nov. 14	**Baltimore**	4:05
Nov. 21	**New Orleans**	8:20
Nov. 28	at Baltimore	1:00
Dec. 2	**Pittsburgh** (Thurs.)	8:20
Dec. 13	**Denver** (Mon.)	9:00
Dec. 19	at Cleveland	1:00
Dec. 26	at Tennessee	12:00
Jan. 2	**Cincinnati**	1:00

COACHING HISTORY

(38-32-0)

1995-98	Tom Coughlin	38-32-0

ALLTEL STADIUM

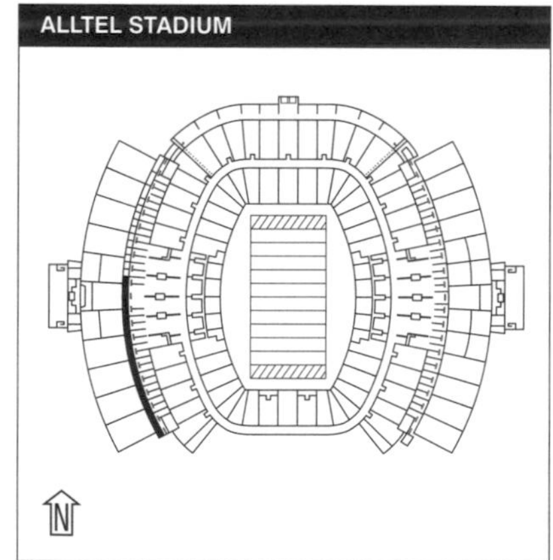

1998 TEAM RECORD

PRESEASON (2-2)

Date	Result		Opponent
8/8	L	27-30	at Carolina
8/14	W	24-10	N.Y. Giants
8/22	L	21-22	at Kansas City
8/27	W	42-20	Dallas

REGULAR SEASON (11-5)

Date	Result		Opponent	Att.
9/6	W	24-23	at Chicago	55,614
9/13	W	21-16	Kansas City	69,821
9/20	W	24-10	Baltimore	67,069
9/27	W	27-22	at Tennessee	34,656
10/12	W	28-21	Miami	74,051
10/18	L	16-17	at Buffalo	77,635
10/25	L	24-37	at Denver	75,217
11/1	W	45-19	at Baltimore	68,915
11/8	W	24-11	Cincinnati	67,040
11/15	W	29-24	Tampa Bay	72,974
11/22	L	15-30	at Pittsburgh	59,124
11/29	W	34-17	at Cincinnati	55,432
12/6	W	37-22	Detroit	70,717
12/13	L	13-16	Tennessee	65,657
12/20	L	10-50	at Minnesota	64,363
12/28	W	21-3	Pittsburgh	74,143

POSTSEASON (1-1)

Date	Result		Opponent	Att.
1/3	W	25-10	New England	71,139
1/10	L	24-34	at New York Jets	76,469

SCORE BY PERIODS

Jaguars	100	127	81	84	0	— 392
Opponents	42	138	53	105	0	— 338

ATTENDANCE

Home 561,472 Away 490,956 Total 1,052,428
Single-game home record, 74,143 (12/28/98)
Single-season home record, 561,472 (1998)

1998 TEAM STATISTICS

	Jaguars	Opp.
Total First Downs	287	309
Rushing	111	108
Passing	153	178
Penalty	23	23
Third Down: Made/Att	94/220	81/222
Third Down Pct.	42.7	36.5
Fourth Down: Made/Att	4/8	10/20
Fourth Down Pct.	50.0	50.0
Total Net Yards	5,214	5,559
Avg. Per Game	325.9	347.4
Total Plays	989	1,057
Avg. Per Play	5.3	5.3
Net Yards Rushing	2,102	2,000
Avg. Per Game	131.4	125
Total Rushes	487	450
Net Yards Passing	3,112	3,559
Avg. Per Game	194.5	222.4
Sacked/Yards Lost	39/231	30/209
Gross Yards	3,343	3,768
Att./Completions	463/269	577/325
Completion Pct.	58.1	56.3
Had Intercepted	12	13
Punts/Avg.	85/45.0	78/43.5
Net Punting Avg.	85/38.5	78/34.0
Penalties/Yards Lost	121/898	109/953
Fumbles/Ball Lost	18/8	25/17
Touchdowns	47	36
Rushing	19	9
Passing	24	23
Returns	4	4
Avg. Time of Possession	28:59	31:01

1998 INDIVIDUAL STATISTICS

Passing	Att.	Comp.	Yds.	Pct.	TD	Int.	Tkld.	Rate
Brunell	354	208	2,601	58.8	20	9	28/172	89.9
Quinn	64	34	387	53.1	2	3	9/49	62.4
Martin	45	27	355	60.0	2	0	2/10	99.8
Jaguars	463	269	3,343	58.1	24	12	39/231	87.1
Opponents	577	325	3,768	56.3	23	13	30/209	80.1

SCORING	TD R	TD P	TD Rt	PAT	FG	Saf	PTS
Hollis	0	0	0	45/45	21/26	0	108
F. Taylor	14	3	0	0/0	0/0	0	102
J. Smith	0	8	0	0/0	0/0	0	48
McCardell	0	6	0	0/0	0/0	0	38
D. Jones	0	4	0	0/0	0/0	0	24
Stewart	2	1	0	0/0	0/0	0	18
Mitchell	0	2	0	0/0	0/0	0	12
Banks	1	0	0	0/0	0/0	0	6
Barlow	0	0	1	0/0	0/0	0	6
Beasley	0	0	1	0/0	0/0	0	6
Darius	0	0	1	0/0	0/0	0	6
Quinn	1	0	0	0/0	0/0	0	6
Shelton	1	0	0	0/0	0/0	0	6
Whitted	0	0	1	0/0	0/0	0	6
Jaguars	19	24	4	45/45	21/26	0	392
Opponents	9	23	4	30/30	30/35	0	338

2-Point conversions: McCardell.
Team 1-2, Opponents 1-6.

RUSHING	Att.	Yds.	Avg.	LG	TD
F. Taylor	264	1,223	4.6	77t	14
Stewart	53	217	4.1	30	2
Brunell	49	192	3.9	18	0
Banks	26	140	5.4	51	1
G. Jones	39	121	3.1	21	0
Shelton	30	95	3.2	16	1
Quinn	11	77	7.0	17	1
Howard	7	16	2.3	5	0
Whitted	3	13	4.3	16	0
Martin	5	8	1.6	6	0
Jaguars	487	2,102	4.3	77t	19
Opponents	450	2,000	4.4	61	9

RECEIVING	No.	Yds.	Avg.	LG	TD
J. Smith	78	1,182	15.2	72t	8
McCardell	64	892	13.9	67t	6
F. Taylor	44	421	9.6	78t	3
Mitchell	38	363	9.6	38	2
Barlow	11	168	15.3	31	0
Shelton	10	79	7.9	19	0
D. Jones	8	90	11.3	31t	4
Stewart	6	42	7.0	19	1
Banks	4	20	5.0	10	0
Whitted	2	61	30.5	55	0
G. Jones	1	9	9.0	9	0
Moore	1	9	9.0	9	0
Crockett	1	4	4.0	4	0
Howard	1	3	3.0	3	0
Jaguars	269	3,343	12.4	78t	24
Opponents	325	3,768	11.6	79t	23

INTERCEPTIONS	No.	Yds.	Avg.	LG	TD
Beasley	3	35	11.7	34	0
Hudson	3	10	3.3	8	0
Hardy	2	40	20.0	24	0
Davis	2	34	17.0	34	0
Devine	1	0	0.0	0	0
Figures	1	0	0.0	0	0
Thomas	1	0	0.0	0	0
Jaguars	13	119	9.2	34	0
Opponents	12	216	18.0	78t	3

PUNTING	No.	Yds.	Avg.	In 20	LG
Barker	85	3,824	45.0	28	65
Jaguars	85	3,824	45.0	28	65
Opponents	78	3,395	43.5	17	67

PUNT RETURNS	No.	FC	Yds.	Avg.	LG	TD
Barlow	43	14	555	12.9	85t	1
Logan	2	0	26	13.0	17	0
Jaguars	45	14	581	12.9	85t	1
Opponents	40	11	332	8.3	25	0

KICKOFF RETURNS	No.	Yds.	Avg.	LG	TD
Barlow	30	747	24.9	91	0
Logan	18	414	23.0	53	0
Banks	5	133	26.6	65	0
D. Jones	2	-1	-0.5	0	0
Mitchell	2	27	13.5	14	0
G. Jones	1	21	21.0	21	0
McCardell	1	15	15.0	15	0
Fordham	1	0	0.0	0	0
Sadowski	1	0	0.0	0	0
Moore	0	10	—	10	0
Jaguars	61	1,366	22.4	91	0
Opponents	76	1,858	24.4	88t	1

FIELD GOALS	1-19	20-29	30-39	40-49	50+
Hollis	1/1	8/10	8/9	4/5	0/1
Jaguars	1/1	8/10	8/9	4/5	0/1
Opponents	1/1	7/7	12/12	7/11	3/4

SACKS	No.
Smeenge	7.5
Paup	6.5
Brackens	3.5
Pritchett	3.0
White	3.0
F. Smith	2.0
Hardy	1.5
Boyer	1.0
Wynn	1.0
Davis	0.5
Jurkovic	0.5
Jaguars	30.0
Opponents	39.0

1999 DRAFT CHOICES

Round	Name	Pos.	College
1	Fernando Bryant	DB	Alabama
2	Larry Smith	DT	Florida State
3	Anthony Cesario	G	Colorado State
4	Kevin Landolt	DT	West Virginia
5	Jason Craft	DB	Colorado State
6	Emarlos Leroy	DT	Georgia
7	Dee Moronkola	DB	Washington State
	Chris White	DE	Southern

JACKSONVILLE JAGUARS

1999 VETERAN ROSTER

No.	Name	Pos.	Ht.	Wt.	Birthdate	NFL Exp.	College	Hometown	How Acq.	'98 Games/ Starts
22	Banks,Tavian	RB	5-10	194	2/17/74	2	Iowa	Bettendorf, Iowa	D4a-'98	6/1
4	Barker, Bryan	P	6-2	201	6/28/64	10	Santa Clara	Orinda, Calif.	UFA(Phil)-'95	16/0
84	Barlow, Reggie	WR	6-0	190	1/22/73	4	Alabama State	Montgomery, Ala.	D4-'96	16/2
21	Beasley, Aaron	CB	6-0	202	7/7/73	4	West Virginia	Pottstown, Pa.	D3-'96	16/15
71	Boselli, Tony	T	6-7	324	4/17/72	5	Southern California	Boulder, Colo.	D1a-'95	15/15
52	Boyer, Brant	LB	6-1	232	6/27/71	5	Arizona	Hooper, Utah	FA-'96	11/0
90	Brackens, Tony	DE	6-4	260	12/26/74	4	Texas	Fairfield, Tex.	D2a-'96	12/8
80	Brady, Kyle	TE	6-6	268	1/14/72	5	Penn State	New Cumberland, Pa.	UFA(NYJ)-'99	16/16*
8	Brunell, Mark	QB	6-1	211	9/17/70	7	Washington	Santa Maria, Calif.	T(GB)-'95	13/13
62	Coleman, Ben	G-T	6-5	323	5/18/71	7	Wake Forest	South Hill, Va.	W(Ariz)-'95	16/16
75	Curry, Eric	DE	6-6	269	2/3/70	7	Alabama	Thomasville, Ga.	FA-'98	11/0
20	Darius, Donovin	S	6-1	213	8/12/75	2	Syracuse	Camden, N.J.	D1b-'98	14/14
11	Fiedler, Jay	QB	6-2	224	12/29/71	4	Dartmouth	Oceanside, N.Y.	FA-'99	5/0*
27	Figures, Deon	CB	6-0	192	1/20/70	7	Colorado	Bellflower, Calif.	UFA(Pitt)-'97	16/5
78	Fordham, Todd	G-T	6-5	308	10/9/73	3	Florida State	Tifton, Ga.	FA-'97	11/1
7	Furrer, Will	QB	6-3	221	2/5/68	6	Virginia Tech	Pullman, Wash.	FA-'98	0*
85	Griffith, Rich	TE	6-5	261	7/31/69	6	Arizona	Tucson, Ariz.	FA-'95	7/0
54	Hamilton, James	LB	6-5	245	4/17/74	3	North Carolina	Hamlet, N.C.	D3-'97	7/0
51	Hardy, Kevin	LB	6-4	250	7/24/73	4	Illinois	Evansville, Ind.	D1-'96	16/16
1	Hollis, Mike	K	5-7	175	5/5/72	5	Idaho	Spokane, Wash.	FA-'95	16/0
24	Howard, Chris	RB	5-10	223	5/5/75	2	Michigan	River Ridge, La.	FA-'98	8/0
67	Ingram, Steve	G	6-4	315	5/8/71	4	Maryland	Greenbelt, Md.	FA-'99	0*
88	Jones, Damon	TE	6-5	265	9/18/74	3	Southern Illinois	Evanston, Ill.	D5-'97	16/7
43	Jones, George	RB	5-9	212	12/31/73	3	San Diego State	Greenville, S.C.	FA-'98	12/0
37	Lake, Carnell	S	6-1	210	7/15/67	11	UCLA	Inglewood, Calif.	UFA(Pitt)-'99	16/16*
32	Logan, Mike	CB-S	6-0	205	9/15/74	3	West Virginia	McKeesport, Pa.	D2-'97	15/0
53	Mason, Eddie	LB	6-0	223	1/9/72	3	North Carolina	Siler City, N.C.	FA-'98	4/0
87	McCardell, Keenan	WR	6-1	183	1/6/70	8	Nevada-Las Vegas	Houston, Tex.	UFA(Balt)-'96	15/15
55	McManus, Tom	LB	6-2	256	7/30/70	5	Boston College	Edgewater, Fla.	FA-'95	16/4
81	Moore, Will	WR	6-1	186	2/21/70	4	Texas Southern	Dallas, Tex.	FA-'97	16/0
65	Neujahr, Quentin	C	6-4	297	1/30/71	5	Kansas State	Ulysses, Neb.	RFA(Balt)-'98	16/16
95	Paup, Bryce	LB	6-5	248	2/29/68	10	Northern Iowa	Jefferson, Iowa	UFA(Buff)-'98	16/16
91	Payne, Seth	DT	6-4	293	2/12/75	3	Cornell	Victor, N.Y.	D4-'97	6/1
12	Quinn, Jonathan	QB	6-5	245	2/27/75	2	Middle Tenn. State	Nashville, Tenn.	D3-'98	4/2
58	Schwartz, Bryan	LB	6-4	256	12/5/71	5	Augustana, S.D.	St. Lawrence, S.D.	D2b-'95	13/12
72	Searcy, Leon	T	6-4	322	12/21/69	8	Miami	Washington, D.C.	UFA(Pitt)-'96	15/15
31	Shelton, Daimon	RB	6-0	251	9/15/72	3	Sacramento State	Fresno, Calif.	D6-'97	14/8
99	Smeenge, Joel	DE	6-6	270	4/1/68	10	Western Michigan	Grand Rapids, Mich.	UFA(NO)-'95	16/14
82	Smith, Jimmy	WR	6-1	207	2/9/69	7	Jackson State	Jackson, Miss.	FA-'95	16/15
33	Stewart, James	RB	6-1	224	12/27/71	5	Tennessee	Morristown, Tenn.	D1b-'95	3/3
23	Taylor, Cordell	CB	5-11	187	12/22/73	2	Hampton, Virginia	Norfolk, Va.	D2-'98	11/0
28	Taylor, Fred	RB	6-0	226	1/27/76	2	Florida	Belle Glade, Fla.	D1a-'98	15/12
41	Thomas, Dave	CB	6-3	213	8/25/68	7	Tennessee	Miami, Fla.	ED16(Dall)-'95	14/12
98	Threats, Jabbar	DE	6-5	256	4/26/75	3	Michigan State	Springfield, Ohio	FA-'97	2/0
76	Tylski, Rich	G-C	6-5	305	2/27/71	4	Utah State	San Diego, Calif.	W(NE)-'95	12/8
66	Wade, John	C-G	6-5	294	1/25/75	2	Marshall	Harrisonburg, Va.	D5-'98	5/0
96	Walker, Gary	DT	6-2	295	2/28/73	5	Auburn	Lavonia, Ga.	UFA(Tenn)-'99	16/16*
86	Whitted, Alvis	WR	5-11	179	9/4/74	2	North Carolina State	Hillsborough, N.C.	D7a-'98	16/0
72	Wiegert, Zach	G	6-4	310	8/16/72	5	Nebraska	Fremont, Neb.	FA-'99	12/12*
92	Williams, Lamanzer	DE	6-4	267	11/17/74	2	Minnesota	Ypsilanti, Mich.	D6a-'98	2/0
97	Wynn, Renaldo	DE	6-3	291	9/3/74	3	Notre Dame	Chicago, Ill.	D1-'97	15/15

* Brady played 16 games for N.Y. Jets in '98; Fiedler played 5 games for Minnesota; Furrer inactive for 2 games; Ingram last active with Tampa Bay in '97; Lake played 16 games for Pittsburgh; Walker played 16 games for Tennessee; Wiegert played 12 games for St. Louis.

Players lost through free agency (9): RB Zack Crockett (Oak; 10 games in '98); S Travis Davis (Pitt; 16); G-T Brian DeMarco (Cin; 16); S Chris Hudson (Chi; 13); DT John Jurkovic (Clev; 16); TE Pete Mitchell (NYG; 16); DT Kelvin Pritchett (Det; 15); TE Troy Sadowski (Wash; 5); DE Fernando Smith (Balt; 15).

Also played with Jaguars in '98—CB Kevin Devine (5 games), LB Jeff Kopp (6), DE Jeff Lageman (1), QB Jamie Martin (4), CB-S Blaine McElmurry (2), G-T Jeff Novak (4), S Tawambi Settles (7), LB Erik Storz (1).

COACHING STAFF

Head Coach,
Tom Coughlin

Pro Career: Under Tom Coughlin, the Jaguars became the only expansion team in NFL history to advance to the playoffs three times in their first four seasons. After a 4-12 inaugural season, Coughlin's team went 9-7 in year two on the way to the AFC Championship Game, and 11-5, and into the playoffs each of the last two seasons. En route to the 1996 AFC Championship Game, the Jaguars became the first visiting team to win a playoff game at Buffalo's Rich Stadium, and only the second to win a playoff game at Denver's Mile High Stadium. Coughlin became the first head coach of the Jaguars on February 21, 1994, following a successful three seasons as head coach at Boston College. A veteran of nearly 30 years in coaching, including 17 at the collegiate level and seven as an NFL assistant, Coughlin previously coached wide receivers for the Philadelphia Eagles (1984-85), Green Bay Packers (1986-87), and New York Giants (1988-1990). He was a member of the Giants' Super Bowl XXV champion coaching staff prior to being named head coach at Boston College in 1991. In three seasons at Boston College, he turned a struggling program into a top-20 team, posting a 21-13-1 record. His final season at Boston College was highlighted by eight consecutive wins, including a 41-39 victory over top-ranked Notre Dame, and a 9-3 finish. Despite an 0-2 start to the season, Boston College ranked thirteenth in the *Associated Press* poll and twelfth in the *USA Today/CNN* coaches poll at the end of the 1993 season. Coughlin's previous 14 seasons as a college coach were at Rochester Institute of Technology 1970-73 (head coach), Syracuse 1974-1980, and Boston College 1981-83. No pro playing experience. Career record: 38-32.

Background: Played wingback for Syracuse from 1965-67 under legendary coach Ben Schwartzwalder, along with teammates Larry Csonka and Floyd Little. Received Syracuse 1967 Orange Key Award as outstanding scholar athlete, and graduated in 1968 with bachelor's degree in education. Received master's degree in education from Syracuse in 1969.

Personal: Born August 31, 1947, Waterloo, N.Y. Was standout scholastic star for Waterloo Central High School. Tom and his wife, Judy, reside in Jacksonville. They have two daughters, Keli and Katie, and two sons, Tim and Brian.

ASSISTANT COACHES

John Bonamego, asst. special teams, born August 14, 1963, Waynesboro, Pa., lives in Jacksonville. Wide reciever-quarterback Central Michigan 1985-86. No pro playing experience. College coach: Maine 1988-1991, Lehigh 1992, Army 1993-98. Pro coach: Joined Jaguars in 1999.

Dom Capers, defensive coordinator; born August 5, 1950, Cambridge, Ohio, lives in Jacksonville. Defensive back Mount Union College 1968-1971. No pro playing experience. College coach: Kent State 1972-74, Hawaii 1975-76, San Jose State 1977, California 1978-79, Tennessee 1980-81, Ohio State 1982-83. Pro coach: Baltimore/Philadelphia Stars (USFL) 1984-85, New Orleans Saints 1986-1991, Pittsburgh Steelers 1992-94, Carolina Panthers 1995-98 (head coach), joined Jaguars in 1999.

Pete Carmichael, wide receivers; born March 4, 1941, North Plainfield, N.J., lives in Jacksonville. Quarterback Dayton 1961, Montclair State College 1962-63. No pro playing experience. College coach: Virginia Military 1965-66, New Hampshire 1967, Boston College 1968-1972, 1981-1993, Trenton State College 1973 (head coach), Columbia 1974-77, Merchant Marine Academy 1977-1980 (head coach). Pro coach: Joined Jaguars in 1995.

Perry Fewell, secondary; born November 7, 1962, Gastonia, N.C., lives in Jacksonville. Defensive back Lenoir-Rhyne 1981-84. No pro playing experience. College coach: Army 1987, 1992-94, Kent State 1988-1991, Vanderbilt 1995-97. Pro coach: Joined Jaguars in 1998.

1999 FIRST-YEAR ROSTER

Name	Pos.	Ht.	Wt.	Birthdate	College	Hometown	How Acq.
Bollers, Trevor	RB	6-0	255	9/24/74	Iowa	Edmonton, Alberta, Canada	FA
Bryant, Fernando	CB	5-10	180	3/26/77	Alabama	Murfreesboro, Tenn.	D1
Calhoun, Matt (1)	RB	6-0	250	12/31/73	Ohio State	Heath, Ohio	FA
Cesario, Anthony	G	6-6	312	8/19/76	Colorado State	Pueblo, Colo.	D3
Clyburn, James (1)	DT	6-2	303	8/17/74	North Carolina A&T	Winston-Salem, N.C.	FA
Craft, Jason	CB	5-9	175	2/13/76	Colorado State	Denver, Colo.	D5
Douglas, Rome	T	6-5	292	10/12/76	Southern California	Clairmont, Calif.	FA
Dunn, Damon (1)	WR	5-9	181	3/15/76	Stanford	Arlington, Tex.	FA
Jackson, Lenzie	WR	6-0	188	6/17/77	Arizona State	Milpitas, Calif.	FA
Jenkins, Nakia (1)	WR	6-1	210	6/29/75	Utah State	Belle Glade, Fla.	FA
Kehl, Ed	DE	6-4	302	8/3/72	Brigham Young	Sandy, Utah	FA
Kempfert, David (1)	C	6-4	295	5/11/74	Montana	Missoula, Mont.	FA
Landolt, Kevin	DT	6-5	300	10/25/75	West Virginia	Burlington, N.J.	D4
Leroy, Emarlos	DT	6-2	298	7/31/75	Georgia	Albany, Ga.	D6
Lindsey, Steve (1)	K	6-0	170	11/25/74	Mississippi	Hattiesburg, Miss.	FA
Lowe, Reggie (1)	LB	6-2	240	6/14/75	Troy State	Phenix City, Ala.	FA
Mack, Stacey	RB	6-1	232	6/26/75	Temple	Orlando, Fla.	FA
McElmurry, Blaine (1)	S	6-0	193	10/23/73	Montana	Helena, Mont.	FA-'98
Mitchell, Anthony	S	6-0	198	12/13/74	Tuskegee	Atlanta, Ga.	FA
Moronkola, Dee	CB	5-9	203	7/1/77	Washington State	Richmond, Calif.	D7a
Myricks, Dary	DT	6-2	290	9/27/76	The Citadel	Jackson, Ga.	FA
Nevadomsky, Jason (1)	LB	6-2	240	11/8/75	UCLA	Fullerton, Calif.	FA
Nori, Mark (1)	G	6-4	299	1/1/74	Boston College	Germantown, Pa.	FA-'98
Quayle, Cam (1)	TE	6-7	255	9/24/72	Weber State	Ogden, Utah	FA
Reado, Jarvis	OT	6-5	302	8/13/75	Tennessee	Marrero, La.	FA
Smith, Larry	DT	6-4	290	12/4/74	Florida State	Folkston, Ga.	D2
Storz, Erik (1)	LB	6-2	234	6/24/75	Boston College	Rockaway, N.J.	FA-'98
Taylor, Tory	WR	5-9	181	9/12/76	Connecticut	Winter Garden, Fla.	FA
Thomas, Mark (1)	TE	6-4	248	4/26/76	North Carolina State	Smithfield, N.C.	FA
White, Chris	DE	6-3	280	9/28/76	Southern	Shreveport, La.	D7b

The term NFL Rookie is defined as a player who is in his first season of professional football and has not been on the roster of another professional football team for any regular-season or postseason games. A Rookie is designated by an "R" on NFL rosters. Players who have been active in another professional football league or players who have NFL experience, including either preseason training camp or being on an Active List or Inactive List, or on Reserve/Injured or Reserve/Physically Unable to Perform for fewer than six regular-season games, are termed NFL First-Year Players. An NFL First-Year Player is designated by a "1" on NFL rosters. Thereafter, a player is credited with an additional year of experience for each season in which he accumulates six games on the Active List or Inactive List, or on Reserve/Injured or Reserve/Physically Unable to Perform.

NOTES

Greg Finnegan, asst. strength and conditioning; born February 21, 1969, Toledo, Ohio, lives in Jacksonville. Center Cornell 1988-1992. No pro playing experience. College coach: Kansas State 1993, Boston College 1994-97. Pro coach: Joined Jaguars in 1998.

Fred Hoaglin, tight ends; born January 28, 1944, Alliance, Ohio, lives in Jacksonville. Center Pittsburgh 1962-65. Pro center Cleveland Browns 1966-1972, Baltimore Colts 1973, Houston Oilers 1974-75, Seattle Seahawks 1976. Pro coach: Detroit Lions 1978-1984, New York Giants 1985-1992, New England Patriots 1993-96, joined Jaguars in 1997.

Jerald Ingram, running backs; born December 24, 1960, Beaver, Pa., lives in Jacksonville. Fullback Michigan 1979-1984. No pro playing experience. College coach: Ball State 1985-1990, Boston College 1991-93. Pro coach: Joined Jaguars in 1995.

Mike Maser, offensive line; born March 2, 1947, Clayton, N.Y., lives in Jacksonville. Guard Buffalo 1967-1970. No pro playing experience. College coach: Marshall 1973, Bluefield State College 1974-78, Maine 1979-1980, Boston College 1981-1993. Pro coach: Joined Jaguars in 1995.

John McNulty, quality control; born May 29, 1968, Scranton, Pa., lives in Jacksonville. Safety Penn State 1987-1990. No pro playing experience. College coach: Michigan 1991-94, Connecticut 1995-97. Pro coach: Joined Jaguars in 1998.

Jerry Palmieri, strength and conditioning; born October 30, 1958, Englewood, N.J., lives in Jacksonville. No college or pro playing experience. College coach: Oklahoma State 1984-87, Kansas State 1988-1992, Boston College 1993-94. Pro coach: Joined Jaguars in 1995.

Larry Pasquale, special teams coordinator; born April 21, 1941, Brooklyn, N.Y., lives in Jacksonville. Quarterback Bridgeport 1961-63. No pro playing experience. College coach: Slippery Rock State 1967, Boston University 1968, Navy 1969-1970, Massachusetts 1971-75, Idaho State 1976. Pro coach: Montreal Alouettes (CFL) 1977-78, Detroit Lions 1979, New York Jets 1980-89, San Diego Chargers 1990-91, Philadelphia Eagles 1992-94, joined Jaguars in 1995.

John Pease, defensive line; born October 14, 1943, Pittsburgh, lives in Jacksonville. Wingback Utah 1963-64. No pro playing experience. College coach: Fullerton, Calif., J.C. 1970-73, Long Beach State 1974-76, Utah 1977, Washington 1978-1983. Pro coach: Philadelphia/Baltimore Stars (USFL) 1983-85, New Orleans Saints 1986-1994, joined Jaguars in 1995.

Bob Petrino, quarterbacks; born March 10, 1961, Lewiston, Mont., lives in Jacksonville. Quarterback Carroll College 1979-1982. No pro playing experience. College coach: Carroll College 1983, 1985-86, Weber State 1984, 1987-88, Idaho 1989-1991, Arizona State 1992-93, Nevada 1994, Utah State 1995-97, Louisville 1998. Pro coach: Joined Jaguars in 1999.

Lucious Selmon, outside linebackers; born March 15, 1951, Muskogee, Okla., lives in Jacksonville. Defensive tackle Oklahoma 1970-73. Pro defensive tackle Memphis Southmen (WFL) 1974-75. College coach: Oklahoma 1976-1994. Pro coach: Joined Jaguars in 1995.

Steve Szabo, inside linebackers; born September 11, 1943, Chicago, lives in Jacksonville. Halfback/defensive back Navy 1961-64. No pro playing experience. College coach: Johns Hopkins 1969, Toledo 1970, Iowa 1971-73, Syracuse 1974-76, Iowa State 1977-78, Ohio State 1979-1981, Western Michigan 1982-84, Edinboro 1985-87 (head coach), Northern Iowa 1988, Colorado State 1989-1990, Boston College 1991-93. Pro coach: Joined Jaguars in 1995.

KANSAS CITY CHIEFS

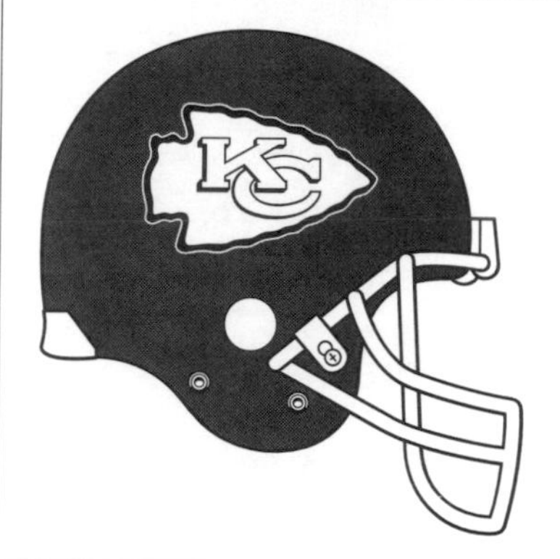

American Football Conference
Western Division
Team Colors: Red, Gold, and White
One Arrowhead Drive
Kansas City, Missouri 64129
Telephone: (816) 920-9300

CLUB OFFICIALS

Founder: Lamar Hunt
Chairman of the Board: Jack Steadman
President/General Manager and Chief Executive Officer: Carl Peterson
Executive Vice President, Assistant General Manager: Dennis Thum
Senior Vice President: Dennis Watley
Secretary: Jim Seigfreid
Director of Finance/Treasurer: Dale Young
Director of Public Relations: Bob Moore
Vice President of Sales and Marketing: Wallace Bennett
Director of Player Personnel: Terry Bradway
Director of Pro Personnel: John Schneider
Director of College Scouting: Chuck Cook
Director of Operations: Steve Schneider
Director of Development: Ken Blume
Assistant Directors of Public Relations: Jim Carr, Pete Moris
Director of Corporate Sales: Anita Bailey
Director of Advertising, Sales and Hospitality: Gary Spani
Community Relations Manager: Brenda Sniezek
Director of Ticket Operations: Doug Hopkins
Equipment Manager: Mike Davidson
Asst. Equipment Managers: Allen Wright, Chris Shropshire
Trainer: Dave Kendall
Assistant Trainer: Bud Epps
Director of Video Operations: John Wuehrmann
Manager of Video Operations: Mike Kirk
Video Assistant: Todd Weger
Stadium: Arrowhead Stadium • **Capacity:** 79,451
One Arrowhead Drive
Kansas City, Missouri 64129
Playing Surface: Grass
Training Camp: University of Wisconsin-River Falls
River Falls, Wisconsin 54022

1999 SCHEDULE

PRESEASON

Aug. 15	**Tennessee**	7:30
Aug. 21	**Tampa Bay**	7:30
Aug. 26	at Jacksonville	8:00
Sept. 3	at San Diego	8:00

REGULAR SEASON

Sept. 12	at Chicago	12:00
Sept. 19	**Denver**	3:15
Sept. 26	**Detroit**	12:00
Oct. 3	at San Diego	1:15
Oct. 10	**New England**	12:00
Oct. 17	Open Date	
Oct. 21	at Baltimore (Thurs.)	8:20
Oct. 31	**San Diego**	12:00
Nov. 7	at Indianapolis	1:00
Nov. 14	at Tampa Bay	1:00
Nov. 21	**Seattle**	12:00
Nov. 28	at Oakland	1:15
Dec. 5	at Denver	2:15
Dec. 12	**Minnesota**	7:20
Dec. 18	**Pittsburgh** (Sat.)	11:40
Dec. 26	at Seattle	1:05
Jan. 2	**Oakland**	12:00

RECORD HOLDERS

INDIVIDUAL RECORDS—CAREER

Category	Name	Performance
Rushing (Yds.)	Christian Okoye, 1987-1992	4,897
Passing (Yds.)	Len Dawson, 1962-1975	28,507
Passing (TDs)	Len Dawson, 1962-1975	237
Receiving (No.)	Henry Marshall, 1976-1987	416
Receiving (Yds.)	Otis Taylor, 1965-1975	7,306
Interceptions	Emmitt Thomas, 1966-1978	58
Punting (Avg.)	Jerrel Wilson, 1963-1977	43.5
Punt Return (Avg.)	Noland Smith, 1967-69	11.1
Kickoff Return (Avg.)	Noland Smith, 1967-69	26.8
Field Goals	Nick Lowery, 1980-1993	329
Touchdowns (Tot.)	Otis Taylor, 1965-1975	60
Points	Nick Lowery, 1980-1993	1,466

INDIVIDUAL RECORDS—SINGLE SEASON

Category	Name	Performance
Rushing (Yds.)	Christian Okoye, 1989	1,480
Passing (Yds.)	Bill Kenney, 1983	4,348
Passing (TDs)	Len Dawson, 1964	30
Receiving (No.)	Carlos Carson, 1983	80
Receiving (Yds.)	Carlos Carson, 1983	1,351
Interceptions	Emmitt Thomas, 1974	12
Punting (Avg.)	Jerrel Wilson, 1965	46.0
Punt Return (Avg.)	Abner Haynes, 1960	15.4
Kickoff Return (Avg.)	Dave Grayson, 1962	29.7
Field Goals	Nick Lowery, 1990	34
Touchdowns (Tot.)	Abner Haynes, 1962	19
Points	Nick Lowery, 1990	139

INDIVIDUAL RECORDS—SINGLE GAME

Category	Name	Performance
Rushing (Yds.)	Barry Word, 10-14-90	200
Passing (Yds.)	Len Dawson, 11-1-64	435
Passing (TDs)	Len Dawson, 11-1-64	6
Receiving (No.)	Ed Podolak, 10-7-73	12
Receiving (Yds.)	Stephone Paige, 12-22-85	309
Interceptions	Bobby Ply, 10-16-62	*4
	Bobby Hunt, 12-4-64	*4
	Deron Cherry, 9-29-85	*4
Field Goals	Many times	5
	Last time by Nick Lowery, 9-21-93	
Touchdowns (Tot.)	Abner Haynes, 11-26-61	5
Points	Abner Haynes, 11-26-61	30

*NFL Record

COACHING HISTORY

DALLAS TEXANS 1960-62
(314-273-12)

1960-74	Hank Stram	129-79-10
1975-77	Paul Wiggin*	11-24-0
1977	Tom Bettis	1-6-0
1978-82	Marv Levy	31-42-0
1983-86	John Mackovic	30-35-0
1987-88	Frank Gansz	8-22-1
1989-98	Marty Schottenheimer	104-65-1

*Released after seven games in 1977

ARROWHEAD STADIUM

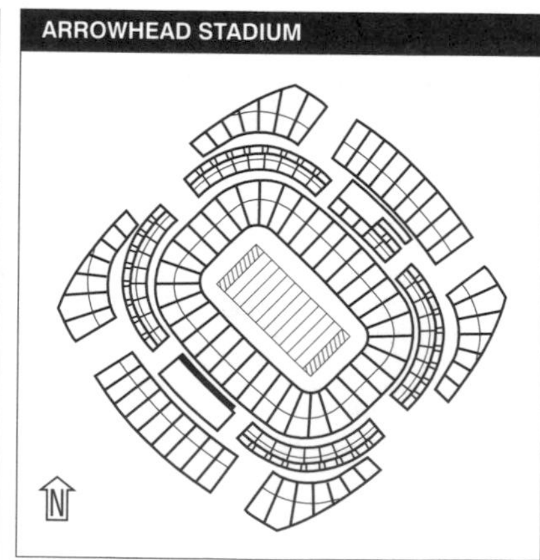

1998 TEAM RECORD

PRESEASON (2-3)

Date	Result		Opponent
8/1	L	24-27	Green Bay
8/8	W	17-13	at Tampa Bay
8/15	L	0-34	at Minnesota
8/22	W	22-21	Jacksonville
8/28	L	6-10	St. Louis

REGULAR SEASON (7-9)

Date	Result		Opponent	Att.
9/6	W	28-8	Oakland	78,945
9/13	L	16-21	at Jacksonville	69,821
9/20	W	23-7	San Diego	73,730
9/27	W	24-21	at Philadelphia	66,675
10/4	W	17-6	Seattle	66,418
10/11	L	10-40	at New England	59,749
10/26	L	13-20	Pittsburgh	79,431
11/1	L	17-20	New York Jets	65,104
11/8	L	12-24	at Seattle	66,251
11/16	L	7-30	Denver	78,100
11/22	L	37-38	at San Diego	59,894
11/29	W	34-24	Arizona	69,613
12/6	L	31-35	at Denver	74,962
12/13	W	20-17	Dallas	77,697
12/20	L	7-28	at New York Giants	66,040
12/26	W	31-24	at Oakland	52,679

SCORE BY PERIODS

Chiefs	77	67	105	78	0	—	327
Opponents	101	100	65	97	0	—	363

ATTENDANCE

Home 589,038 Away 516,071 Total 1,105,109
Single-game home record, 82,094 (11/5/72)
Single-season home record, 620,180 (1995)

1998 TEAM STATISTICS

	Chiefs	Opp.
Total First Downs	289	321
Rushing	103	119
Passing	153	146
Penalty	33	56
Third Down: Made/Att	70/220	69/204
Third Down Pct.	31.8	33.8
Fourth Down: Made/Att	13/25	6/12
Fourth Down Pct.	52.0	50.0
Total Net Yards	4,808	4,854
Avg. Per Game	300.5	303.4
Total Plays	1,012	1,010
Avg. Per Play	4.8	4.8
Net Yards Rushing	1,548	1,869
Avg. Per Game	96.8	116.8
Total Rushes	433	491
Net Yards Passing	3,260	2,985
Avg. Per Game	203.8	186.6
Sacked/Yards Lost	36/212	40/268
Gross Yards	3,472	3,253
Att./Completions	543/305	479/259
Completion Pct.	56.2	54.1
Had Intercepted	18	13
Punts/Avg.	77/42.3	77/42.2
Net Punting Avg.	77/34.3	77/36.0
Penalties/Yards Lost	158/1,304	138/1,292
Fumbles/Ball Lost	35/14	36/20
Touchdowns	35	44
Rushing	19	22
Passing	15	17
Returns	1	5
Avg. Time of Possession	29:53	30:07

1998 INDIVIDUAL STATISTICS

Passing	Att.	Comp.	Yds.	Pct.	TD	Int.	Tkld.	Rate
Gannon	354	206	2,305	58.2	10	6	25/155	80.1
Grbac	188	98	1,142	52.1	5	12	11/57	53.1
Hughes	1	1	25	100.0	0	0	0/0	118.8
Chiefs	543	305	3,472	56.2	15	18	36/212	70.9
Opponents	479	259	3,253	54.1	17	13	40/268	76.0

SCORING	TD R	TD P	TD Rt	PAT	FG	Saf	PTS
Stoyanovich	0	0	0	34/34	27/32	0	115
Morris	8	0	0	0/0	0/0	0	48
Bennett	5	1	0	0/0	0/0	0	36
Rison	0	5	0	0/0	0/0	0	30
Alexander	0	4	0	0/0	0/0	0	24
Anders	1	2	0	0/0	0/0	0	18
Gannon	3	0	0	0/0	0/0	0	18
Gonzalez	0	2	0	0/0	0/0	0	12
Richardson	2	0	0	0/0	0/0	0	12
Thomas	0	0	1	0/0	0/0	1	8
Horn	0	1	0	0/0	0/0	0	6
Chiefs	19	15	1	34/34	27/32	1	327
Opponents	22	17	5	43/43	18/30	0	363

2-Point conversions: None.
Team 0-1, Opponents 1-1.

RUSHING	Att.	Yds.	Avg.	LG	TD
Bennett	148	527	3.6	26	5
Morris	129	481	3.7	38	8
Anders	58	230	4.0	20	1
Gannon	44	168	3.8	21	3
Shehee	22	57	2.6	10	0
Richardson	20	45	2.3	6	2
Grbac	7	27	3.9	10	0
Rison	2	12	6.0	11	0
Vanover	2	1	0.5	2	0
Horn	1	0	0.0	0	0
Chiefs	433	1,548	3.6	38	19
Opponents	491	1,869	3.8	72t	22

RECEIVING	No.	Yds.	Avg.	LG	TD
Anders	64	462	7.2	29	2
Gonzalez	59	621	10.5	32	2
Alexander	54	992	18.4	65	4
Rison	40	542	13.6	80t	5
Lockett	19	281	14.8	38	0
Bennett	16	91	5.7	14	1
Horn	14	198	14.1	57	1
Popson	13	90	6.9	17	0
Morris	12	95	7.9	29	0
Shehee	10	73	7.3	14	0
Richardson	2	13	6.5	15	0
Hughes	1	10	10.0	10	0
Shields	1	4	4.0	4	0
Chiefs	305	3,472	11.4	80t	15
Opponents	259	3,253	12.6	58	17

INTERCEPTIONS	No.	Yds.	Avg.	LG	TD
Hasty	4	42	10.5	21	0
McMillian	3	48	16.0	21	0
Woods	2	47	23.5	28	0
Davis	2	27	13.5	27	0
Carter	2	23	11.5	23	0
Chiefs	13	187	14.4	28	0
Opponents	18	189	10.5	43t	3

PUNTING	No.	Yds.	Avg.	In 20	LG
Aguiar	75	3,226	43.0	20	59
Stoyanovich	1	29	29.0	1	29
Chiefs	77	3,255	42.3	21	59
Opponents	77	3,248	42.2	26	61

PUNT RETURNS	No.	FC	Yds.	Avg.	LG	TD
Vanover	27	11	264	9.8	37	0
Lockett	7	1	36	5.1	16	0
Hughes	2	0	10	5.0	11	0
Horn	1	0	6	6.0	6	0
Richardson	1	0	0	0.0	0	0
Chiefs	38	12	316	8.3	37	0
Opponents	41	11	513	12.5	85t	1

KICKOFF RETURNS	No.	Yds.	Avg.	LG	TD
Vanover	41	956	23.3	62	0
Horn	11	233	21.2	37	0
Shehee	4	72	18.0	20	0
Manusky	3	20	6.7	12	0
Parten	2	22	11.0	22	0
Anders	1	16	16.0	16	0
Ransom	1	0	0.0	0	0
Chiefs	63	1,319	20.9	62	0
Opponents	69	1,374	19.9	65	0

FIELD GOALS	1-19	20-29	30-39	40-49	50+
Stoyanovich	2/2	9/9	9/9	5/10	2/2
Chiefs	2/2	9/9	9/9	5/10	2/2
Opponents	0/0	6/7	9/15	3/6	0/2

SACKS	No.
Thomas	12.0
Edwards	6.0
Davis	4.5
O'Neal	4.5
Barndt	3.5
Favors	2.0
Tongue	2.0
Hasty	1.0
Johnson	1.0
McGlockton	1.0
Williams	0.5
Chiefs	40.0
Opponents	36.0

1999 DRAFT CHOICES

Round	Name	Pos.	College
1	John Tait	T	Brigham Young
2	Mike Cloud	RB	Boston College
3	Gary Stills	LB	West Virginia
	Larry Atkins	DB	UCLA
4	Larry Parker	WR	Southern California
7	Eric King	G	Richmond

KANSAS CITY CHIEFS

1999 VETERAN ROSTER

No.	Name	Pos.	Ht.	Wt.	Birthdate	NFL Exp.	College	Hometown	How Acq.	'98 Games/ Starts
48	Adams, Vashone	S	5-10	201	9/12/73	4	Eastern Michigan	Aurora, Colo.	FA-'98	0*
5	Aguiar, Louie	P	6-2	218	6/30/66	9	Utah State	Livermore, Calif.	FA-'94	16/0
82	Alexander, Derrick	WR	6-2	198	11/6/71	6	Michigan	Detroit, Mich.	UFA(Balt)-'98	15/14
38	Anders, Kimble	RB	5-11	225	9/10/66	9	Houston	Galveston, Tex.	FA-'91	16/15
71	Barndt, Tom	DT	6-3	301	3/14/72	4	Pittsburgh	Mentor, Ohio	D6b-'95	16/16
30	Bennett, Donnell	RB	6-0	235	9/14/72	6	Miami	Ft. Lauderdale, Fla.	D2-'94	16/10
43	Bolden, Juran	CB	6-2	201	6/27/74	4	Mississippi Delta	Tampa, Fla.	FA-'99	6/0*
93	Browning, John	DE	6-4	295	9/30/73	4	West Virginia	Miami, Fla.	D3-'96	8/8
53	Chung, Eugene	C	6-5	311	6/14/69	6	Virginia Tech	Vienna, Va.	FA-'99	0*
15	Collins, Todd	QB	6-4	224	11/5/71	5	Michigan	Walpole, Mass.	W(Buff)-'98	0*
41	Crawford, Keith	WR	6-2	195	11/21/70	6	Howard Payne	Palestine, Tex.	FA-'98	8/0
69	Criswell, Jeff	T	6-7	294	3/7/64	12	Graceland College	Searsboro, Iowa	UFA(NYJ)-'95	14/14
11	Dar Dar, Kirby	WR	5-9	192	3/27/72	3	Syracuse	Tampa, Fla.	FA-'99	2/0*
26	Dishman, Cris	CB	6-0	195	8/13/65	12	Purdue	Louisville, Ky.	FA-'99	16/16*
52	Dixon, Ernest	LB	6-1	240	10/17/71	6	South Carolina	Fort Mill, S.C.	FA-'98	1/0
90	Dixon, Ronnie	DT	6-3	310	5/10/71	6	Cincinnati	Clinton, N.C.	FA-'98	4/0
59	Edwards, Donnie	LB	6-2	236	4/6/73	4	UCLA	Chula Vista, Calif.	D4-'96	15/15
54	Favors, Greg	LB	6-1	236	9/30/74	2	Mississippi State	Atlanta, Ga.	D4-'98	16/4
55	George, Ron	LB	6-2	241	3/20/70	7	Stanford	Heidelberg, West Germany	FA-'98	16/0
88	Gonzalez, Tony	TE	6-4	250	2/27/76	3	California	Huntington Beach, Calif.	D1-'97	16/16
23	Gray, Carlton	CB	6-0	200	6/26/71	7	UCLA	Cincinnati, Ohio	FA-'99	14/3*
18	Grbac, Elvis	QB	6-5	232	8/13/70	7	Michigan	Cleveland, Ohio	UFA(SF)-'97	8/6
61	Grunhard, Tim	C	6-2	307	5/17/68	10	Notre Dame	Chicago, Ill.	D2-'90	16/16
40	Hasty, James	CB	6-0	208	5/23/65	12	Washington State	Seattle, Wash.	UFA(NYJ)-'95	16/14
98	Hicks, Eric	DE	6-6	261	6/17/76	2	Maryland	Erie, Pa.	FA-'98	3/0
56	Hollinquest, Lamont	LB	6-3	250	10/24/70	6	Southern California	Downey, Calif.	UFA (GB)-'99	14/2*
84	Horn, Joe	WR	6-1	199	1/16/72	4	Itawamba J.C.	Fayetteville, N.C.	D5-'96	16/1
83	Johnson, Lonnie	TE	6-3	240	2/14/71	6	Florida State	Miami, Fla.	UFA(Buff)-'99	16/16*
31	Kidd, Carl	S	6-1	200	6/14/73	3	Arkansas	Pine Bluff, Ark.	FA-'99	0*
81	Lockett, Kevin	WR	6-0	188	9/8/74	3	Kansas State	Tulsa, Okla.	D2-'97	13/3
94	Manuel, Sean	TE	6-2	245	12/1/73	2	New Mexico State	El Sobrante, Calif.	FA-'98	0*
51	Manusky, Greg	LB	6-1	235	8/12/66	12	Colgate	Dallas, Pa.	FA-'94	16/1
75	McGlockton, Chester	DT	6-4	320	9/16/69	8	Clemson	Whiteville, N.C.	RFA(Oak)-'98	10/9
1	Moon, Warren	QB	6-3	213	11/18/56	16	Washington	Los Angeles, Calif.	FA-'99	10/10*
39	Morris, Byron (Bam)	RB	6-0	248	1/13/72	6	Texas Tech	Cooper, Tex.	T(Chi)-'98	10/5*
91	O'Neal, Leslie	DE	6-4	275	5/7/64	14	Oklahoma State	Little Rock, Ark.	FA-'98	16/13
62	Parker, Glenn	G-T	6-5	305	4/22/66	10	Arizona	Huntington Beach, Calif.	FA-'97	15/15
74	Parks, Nate	T	6-5	303	10/24/74	2	Stanford	Durham, Calif.	D7-'97	0*
73	Parrish, James	T	6-5	292	5/19/68	5	Temple	Dundalk, Md.	FA-'99	0*
97	† Parten, Ty	DT	6-5	295	10/13/69	5	Arizona	Scottsdale, Ariz.	FA-'97	16/6
53	Patton, Marvcus	LB	6-2	236	5/1/67	10	UCLA	Lawndale, Calif.	UFA(Wash)-'99	16/16*
48	Popson, Ted	TE	6-4	245	9/10/66	6	Portland State	Truckee, Calif.	FA-'97	12/1
95	Ransom, Derrick	DT	6-3	291	9/13/76	2	Cincinnati	Indianapolis, Ind.	D6-'98	7/0
49	Richardson, Tony	RB	6-1	230	12/17/71	5	Auburn	Daleville, Ala.	FA-'95	14/1
66	Riley, Victor	T	6-5	321	11/4/74	2	Auburn	Swansea, S.C.	D1-'98	16/15
89	Rison, Andre	WR	6-1	195	3/18/67	11	Michigan State	Flint, Mich.	FA-'97	14/13
85	Roche, Brian	TE	6-5	255	5/5/73	4	San Jose State	LaVerne, Calif.	FA-'98	4/1
22	Shehee, Rashaan	RB	5-10	205	6/20/75	2	Washington	Bakersfield, Calif.	D3-'98	16/0
68	Shields, Will	G	6-3	310	9/15/71	7	Nebraska	Lawton, Okla.	D3-'93	16/16
77	Smith, Artie	DT	6-5	305	5/15/70	6	Louisiana Tech	Stillwater, Okla.	UFA(Dall)-'99	16/0*
65	† Smith, Jeff	C-G	6-3	322	5/25/73	4	Tennessee	Deactur, Tenn.	D7b-'96	11/3
70	Spears, Marcus	T	6-4	320	9/28/71	6	Northwestern State, La.	Scotlandville, La.	FA-'97	12/0
10	Stoyanovich, Pete	K	5-11	191	4/28/67	11	Indiana	Dearborn Heights, Mich.	T(Mia)-'96	16/0
79	Szott, Dave	G	6-4	293	12/12/67	10	Penn State	Clifton, N.J.	D7-'90	1/1
58	Thomas, Derrick	LB	6-3	247	1/1/67	11	Alabama	Miami, Fla.	D1-'89	15/10
25	Tongue, Reggie	S	6-0	205	4/11/73	4	Oregon State	Fairbanks, Alaska	D2-'96	15/15
87	Vanover, Tamarick	WR	5-11	220	2/25/74	5	Florida State	Tallahassee, Fla.	D3a-'95	12/0
27	Walker, Bracy	S	6-0	204	6/11/70	6	North Carolina	Fayetteville, N.C.	FA-'98	8/0
44	Warfield, Eric	CB	6-0	192	3/3/76	2	Nebraska	Texarkana, Ark.	D7a-'98	12/0
92	Williams, Dan	DE	6-4	290	12/15/69	6	Toledo	Ypsilanti, Mich.	FA-'97	0*
29	Williams, Robert	CB	5-10	177	5/29/77	2	North Carolina	Shelby, N.C.	D5-'98	16/1
57	Willis, Donald	G	6-3	330	7/15/73	3	North Carolina A&T	Lompoc, Calif.	FA-'99	0*
21	Woods, Jerome	S	6-2	207	3/17/73	4	Memphis	Memphis, Tenn.	D1-'96	16/16

* Adams and Manuel missed '98 season because of injury; Bolden played 6 games with Carolina in '98; Chung last active with Indianapolis in '97; Collins inactive for 13 games; Dar Dar played 2 games with Miami; Dishman and Patton played 16 games with Washington; Gray played 14 games with N.Y. Giants; Hollinquest played 14 games with Green Bay; Johnson played 16 games with Buffalo; Kidd last active with Oakland in '96; Moon played 10 games with Seattle; Morris played 2 games with Chicago and 8 with Kansas City; Parks and D. Williams last active with Kansas City in '97; Parrish last active with Chicago in '96; A. Smith played 16 games with Dallas; Willis last active with New Orleans in '96.

† Restricted free agent; subject to developments.

Players lost through free agency (3): CB Dale Carter (Den; 11 games in '98), QB Rich Gannon (Oak; 12), LB Pellom McDaniels (Atl; 11).

Also played with Chiefs in '98—CB Bucky Brooks (6 games), LB Anthony Davis (16), DT Darius Holland (6), WR Danan Hughes (16), S Melvin Johnson (7), CB Jason Kasier (1), CB Mark McMillian (16), T Ricky Siglar (4), LB Wayne Simmons (10), G Ralph Tamm (16), TE Willy Tate (1), LB Jerrott Willard (1).

COACHING STAFF

Head Coach,
Gunther Cunningham

Pro Career: The Kansas City Chiefs ushered in a new chapter in franchise history on January 22, 1999, appointing Cunningham the eighth head coach in the illustrious history of the franchise, which celebrates its fortieth anniversary this season. Cunningham is regarded as one of the game's most dynamic and talented coaches. A noted teacher, tactician, and motivator, he enters his thirty-first season in the coaching ranks and his eighteenth in the NFL. He ascends to the Chiefs' head coaching position after spending the previous four campaigns (1995-98) as Kansas City's defensive coordinator. Since his arrival in 1995, the Chiefs have twice (1995 and 1997) led the league in scoring defense. During that span, Kansas City permitted an AFC-low 17.8 points per contest. His Chiefs defenses were opportunistic, accumulating 127 takeaways while scoring 77 points on 10 touchdowns and 4 safeties. His Kansas City defensive units put constant pressure on the opposition's passer, producing 172 sacks from 1995-98 to rank third in the AFC and sixth in the NFL. He brought his expertise to the Chiefs after logging four seasons (1991-94) with the Raiders. He served as the Raiders' linebackers coach in 1991, as defensive coordinator the next two seasons, and defensive line coach in 1994. Prior to joining the Raiders, he spent six years (1985-1990) as the Chargers' defensive line coach. He began his NFL coaching career as the defensive line coach of the Baltimore Colts in 1982, staying there for three seasons. He originally entered the pro ranks in the CFL, coaching the defensive line and linebackers for the Hamilton Tiger-Cats in 1981.

Background: Cunningham graduated from Oregon, where he was a linebacker and placekicker from 1966-68. He was a college assistant coach at Oregon (1969-1971), Arkansas (1972), Stanford (1973-76), and California (1977-1980).

Personal: Born June 19, 1946, in Munich, West Germany, he is just the fourth foreign-born head coach in the NFL's 80-year history. Gunther and his wife, Rene, live in Overland Park, Kansas, with their daughter, Natalie, and son, Adam.

ASSISTANT COACHES

Dave Adolph, asst. head coach-linebackers; born June 6, 1937, Akron, Ohio, lives in Overland Park, Kan. Guard-linebacker Akron 1955-58. No pro playing experience. College coach: Akron 1963-64, Connecticut 1965-68, Kentucky 1969-1972, Illinois 1973-76, Ohio State 1977-78. Pro coach: Cleveland Browns 1979-1984, 1986-88, San Diego Chargers 1985, 1995-96, Los Angeles Raiders 1989-1991, Kansas City Chiefs 1992-94, Oakland Raiders 1997-98, rejoined Chiefs in 1999.

Frank Cignetti, Jr., offensive assistant-quality control; born October 4, 1965, Pittsburgh, lives in Kansas City, Mo. Defensive back Indiana (Pa.) 1984-87. No pro playing experience. College coach: Pittsburgh 1989, Indiana (Pa.) 1990-98. Pro coach: Joined Chiefs in 1999.

Jeff Fish, asst. strength and conditioning; born June 6, 1966, Ithaca, N.Y., lives in Lee's Summit, Mo. Wide receiver Western Carolina 1986-89. No pro playing experience. College coach: Western Michigan 1989-1991, Clemson 1991-93, Kent State 1993-95, Tulsa 1995-97. Pro coach: Tampa Bay Buccaneers 1997 (intern), joined Chiefs in 1998.

Jeff Hurd, strength and conditioning; born April 24, 1958, Pomona, Calif., lives in Overland Park, Kan. Attended Fort Hays State. No college or pro playing experience. College coach: Fort Hays State 1984, Delta State 1985, Clemson 1986, Western Michigan 1987-1993, Tulsa 1994. Pro coach: Jacksonville Jaguars 1995-97, joined Chiefs in 1998.

Bob Karmelowicz, defensive line; born July 22, 1949, New Britain, Conn., lives in Lenexa, Kan. Nose tackle Bridgeport 1968-1971. No pro playing experience. College coach: Arizona State 1974-78, Massachusetts 1979-1980, Texas-El Paso 1980-81, Illinois 1982-86, Washington State 1987-88, Miami 1989-1991. Pro coach: Cincinnati Bengals 1992-93, Washington Redskins 1994-96, joined Chiefs in 1997.

Al Lavan, running backs; born September 13, 1946, Pierce, Fla., lives in Overland Park, Kan. Defensive back Colorado State 1965-67. Pro defensive back Philadelphia Eagles 1968, Atlanta Falcons 1969-1970. College coach: Colorado State 1972, Louisville 1973, Iowa State 1974, Georgia Tech 1977-78, Stanford 1979, Washington 1992-95. Pro coach: Atlanta Falcons 1975-76, Dallas Cowboys 1980-88, San Francisco 49ers 1989-1990, Baltimore Ravens 1996-98, joined Chiefs in 1999.

Richard Mann, wide receivers; born April 20, 1947, Aliquippa, Pa., lives in Kansas City, Mo. Wide receiver Arizona State 1966-68. No pro playing experience. College coach: Arizona State 1974-79, Louisville 1980-81. Pro coach: Baltimore/Indianapolis Colts 1982-84, Cleveland Browns 1985-93, New York Jets 1994-96, Baltimore Ravens 1997-98, joined Chiefs in 1999.

Jimmy Raye, offensive coordinator; born March 26, 1946, Fayetteville, N.C., lives in Kansas City, Mo. Quarterback Michigan State 1965-67. Pro defensive back Philadelphia Eagles 1969. College coach: Michigan State 1971-75, Wyoming 1976. Pro coach: San Francisco 49ers 1977, Detroit Lions 1978-79, Atlanta Falcons 1980-82, 1987-89, Los Angeles Rams 1983-84, 1991, Tampa Bay Buccaneers 1985-86, New England Patriots 1990, joined Chiefs in 1992.

Tom Rossley, quarterbacks; born August 9, 1946, Painesville, Ohio, lives in Overland Park, Kan. Wide receiver Cincinnati 1966-68. No pro playing experience. College coach: Arkansas 1972, Rice 1976, 1978-1981, Cincinnati 1977, Holy Cross 1986-87, Southern Methodist 1988-89, 1991-96 (head coach). Pro coach: Montreal Concorde (CFL) 1982-84, San Antonio Gunslingers (USFL) 1985, Denver Dynamite (Arena) 1987, Atlanta Falcons 1990, Chicago Bears 1997-98, joined Chiefs in 1999.

Keith Rowen, tight ends; born September 2, 1952, New York, N.Y., lives in Overland Park, Kan. Offensive tackle Stanford 1972-74. No pro playing experience. College coach: Stanford 1974-75, Long Beach State 1977-78, Arizona 1979-1982. Pro coach: Boston/New Orleans Breakers (USFL) 1983-84, Cleveland Browns 1984, Indianapolis Colts 1985-88, New England Patriots 1989, Atlanta Falcons 1990-93, Minnesota Vikings 1994-96, Oakland Raiders 1997-98, joined Chiefs in 1999.

Kurt Schottenheimer, defensive coordinator; born October 1, 1949, McDonald, Pa., lives in Leawood, Kan. Defensive back Miami 1969-1970. No pro playing experience. College coach: William Patterson 1974, Michigan State 1978-1982, Tulane 1983, Louisiana State 1984-85, Notre Dame 1986. Pro coach: Cleveland Browns 1987-88, joined Chiefs in 1989.

Mike Solari, offensive line; born January 16, 1955, Daly City, Calif., lives in Leawood, Kan. Offensive lineman San Diego State 1975-76. No pro playing experience. College coach: Mira Vista (Calif.) J.C. 1977-78, U.S. International 1979, Boise State 1980, Cincinnati 1990-91. Pro coach: Dallas Cowboys 1987-88, Phoenix Cardinals 1989, San Francisco 49ers 1992-96, joined Chiefs in 1997.

Mike Stock, special teams; born September 29, 1939, Barberton, Ohio, lives in Overland Park, Kan. Fullback Northwestern 1957-1960. Pro running back Saskatchewan Roughriders (CFL) 1961. College coach: Northwestern 1961, Buffalo 1966-67, Navy 1968, Notre Dame 1969-1974, Wisconsin 1975-78, Eastern Michigan 1979-1983 (head coach), Notre Dame 1984-86, Ohio State 1992-94. Pro coach: Cincinnati Bengals 1987-1991, joined Chiefs in 1995.

Darvin Wallis, defensive assistant-quality control; born February 14, 1949, Ft. Branch, Ind., lives in Overland Park, Kan. Defensive end Arizona 1970-71. No pro playing experience. College coach: Adams State 1976-77, Tulane 1978-79, Mississippi 1980-81. Pro coach: Cleveland Browns 1982-88, joined Chiefs in 1989.

Ron Zook, defensive backs; born April 28, 1954, Ashland, Ohio, lives in Overland Park, Kan. Defensive back Miami (Ohio) 1972-75. No pro playing experience. College coach: Murray State 1978-1980, Cincinnati 1981-82, Kansas 1983, Tennessee 1984-86, Virginia Tech 1987, Ohio State 1988-1990, Florida 1991-95. Pro coach: Pittsburgh Steelers 1996-98, joined Chiefs in 1999.

1999 FIRST-YEAR ROSTER

Name	Pos.	Ht.	Wt.	Birthdate	College	Hometown	How Acq.
Atkins, Larry	S	6-3	215	7/21/75	UCLA	Venice, Calif.	D3b
Cloud, Mike	RB	5-10	204	7/1/75	Boston College	Portsmouth, R.I.	D2
Condie, Brandon	TE	6-3	238	7/4/73	Brigham Young	Sandy, Utah	FA
Fleming, Sean (1)	P-K	6-3	205	3/19/70	Wyoming	Vancouver, B.C., Canada	FA
Haslip, Ken	CB	5-10	171	5/17/76	Southern California	Pasadena, Calif.	FA
Haynes, Jesse (1)	RB	5-9	206	8/8/72	Northwest Missouri State	Ft. Worth, Tex.	FA-'98
Hoffman, Jim (1)	DT	6-4	280	12/14/72	Arizona	Spring Valley, Calif.	FA
Jones, Reggie (1)	WR	6-0	187	5/5/71	Louisiana State	Kansas City, Mo.	FA-'98
Kaiser, Jason (1)	S	6-0	190	11/9/73	Culver-Stockton	Highland Ranch, Colo.	FA-'98
King, Eric	G	6-4	290	7/27/75	Richmond	Pittsburgh, Pa.	D7
Kubik, Brad (1)	G	6-3	292	3/31/75	Southwest Missouri State	Springfield, Mo.	FA-'98
Maslowski, Mike (1)	LB	6-1	246	7/11/74	Wisconsin-La Crosse	Thorp, Wis.	FA
McWashington, Shawn (1)	WR	5-9	180	1/24/75	Washington State	Seattle, Wash.	FA
Parker, Larry	WR	6-1	200	7/14/76	Southern California	Bakersfield, Calif.	D4
Pollack, Fred (1)	G	6-1	321	2/27/74	Nebraska	Omaha, Neb.	FA-'98
Rice-Locket, Terry (1)	LB	6-2	258	3/15/75	Louisville	St. Louis, Mo.	FA
Rosenstiel, Bob (1)	TE	6-3	240	2/7/74	Eastern Illinois	Junction City, Ore.	FA-'98
Shay, Brian	RB	5-8	213	2/22/77	Emporia State	Paola, Kan.	FA
Stills, Gary	LB	6-2	238	7/11/74	West Virginia	Trenton, N.J.	D3a
Tait, John	T	6-6	311	1/26/75	Brigham Young	Tempe, Ariz.	D1
Thornton, Burt (1)	WR	6-2	215	1/30/72	Purdue	Akron, Ohio	FA
White, Ted	QB	6-2	226	3/31/75	Howard	Baton Rouge, La.	FA
Williams, Sean (1)	CB	5-11	180	6/11/75	Ohio	Cleveland, Ohio	FA
Word, Mark	DE	6-4	258	11/23/75	Jacksonville State	Miami, Fla.	FA

The term NFL Rookie is defined as a player who is in his first season of professional football and has not been on the roster of another professional football team for any regular-season or postseason games. A Rookie is designated by an "R" on NFL rosters. Players who have been active in another professional football league or players who have NFL experience, including either preseason training camp or being on an Active List or Inactive List, or on Reserve/Injured or Reserve/Physically Unable to Perform for fewer than six regular-season games, are termed NFL First-Year Players. An NFL First-Year Player is designated by a "1" on NFL rosters. Thereafter, a player is credited with an additional year of experience for each season in which he accumulates six games on the Active List or Inactive List, or on Reserve/Injured or Reserve/Physically Unable to Perform.

MIAMI DOLPHINS

American Football Conference
Eastern Division
Team Colors: Aqua, Coral, Blue, and White
7500 S.W. 30th Street
Davie, Florida 33314
Telephone: (954) 452-7000

CLUB OFFICIALS

Owner/Chairman of the Board: H. Wayne Huizenga
President/Chief Operating Officer: Eddie J. Jones
General Manager/Head Coach: Jimmy Johnson
Vice President-Administration: Bryan Wiedmeier
Vice President-Finance: Jill R. Strafaci
Director of Football Operations: Bob Ackles
Director of Pro Personnel: Tom Heckert
Director of College Scouting: Tom Braatz
Vice President-Media Relations: Harvey Greene
Media Relations Coordinator: Neal Gulkis
Director of Publications: Scott Stone
Vice President-Sales and Marketing: Bob Reif
Senior Director-Marketing: David Evans
Senior Director-Information Systems: Burt Gilner
Community Relations Director: Fudge Browne
Vice President-Ticket Sales: Bill Galante
Head Athletic Trainer: Kevin O'Neill
Equipment Manager: Tony Egues
Stadium: Pro Player Stadium • **Capacity:** 75,192
2269 N.W. 199th Street
Miami, Florida 33056
Playing Surface: Grass (PAT)
Training Camp: Nova University
7500 S.W. 30th Street
Davie, Florida 33314

1999 SCHEDULE

PRESEASON

Aug. 13	**New Orleans**	7:30
Aug. 21	at San Diego	8:00
Aug. 28	**Detroit**	7:00
Sept. 2	at Green Bay	7:00

REGULAR SEASON

Sept. 13	at Denver (Mon.)	7:00
Sept. 19	**Arizona**	1:00
Sept. 26	Open Date	
Oct. 4	**Buffalo** (Mon.)	9:00
Oct. 10	at Indianapolis	3:15
Oct. 17	at New England	1:00
Oct. 24	**Philadelphia**	1:00
Oct. 31	at Oakland	1:05
Nov. 7	**Tennessee**	8:20
Nov. 14	at Buffalo	1:00
Nov. 21	**New England**	1:00
Nov. 25	at Dallas (Thurs.)	3:15
Dec. 5	**Indianapolis**	1:00
Dec. 12	at New York Jets	4:05
Dec. 19	**San Diego**	1:00
Dec. 27	**New York Jets** (Mon.)	9:00
Jan. 2	at Washington	4:15

RECORD HOLDERS

INDIVIDUAL RECORDS—CAREER

Category	Name	Performance
Rushing (Yds.)	Larry Csonka, 1968-1974, 1979	6,737
Passing (Yds.)	Dan Marino, 1983-1998	*58,913
Passing (TDs)	Dan Marino, 1983-1998	*408
Receiving (No.)	Mark Clayton, 1983-1992	550
Receiving (Yds.)	Mark Duper, 1982-1992	8,869
Interceptions	Jake Scott, 1970-75	35
Punting (Avg.)	John Kidd, 1994-97	44.2
Punt Return (Avg.)	Freddie Solomon, 1975-77	11.4
Kickoff Return (Avg.)	Mercury Morris, 1969-1975	26.5
Field Goals	Pete Stoyanovich, 1989-1995	176
Touchdowns (Tot.)	Mark Clayton, 1983-1992	82
Points	Garo Yepremian, 1970-78	830

INDIVIDUAL RECORDS—SINGLE SEASON

Category	Name	Performance
Rushing (Yds.)	Delvin Williams, 1978	1,258
Passing (Yds.)	Dan Marino, 1984	*5,084
Passing (TDs)	Dan Marino, 1984	*48
Receiving (No.)	O.J. McDuffie, 1998	90
Receiving (Yds.)	Mark Clayton, 1984	1,389
Interceptions	Dick Westmoreland, 1967	10
Punting (Avg.)	John Kidd, 1996	46.3
Punt Return (Avg.)	Freddie Solomon, 1975	12.3
Kickoff Return (Avg.)	Duriel Harris, 1976	32.9
Field Goals	Pete Stoyanovich, 1991	31
Touchdowns (Tot.)	Mark Clayton, 1984	18
Points	Pete Stoyanovich, 1992	124

INDIVIDUAL RECORDS—SINGLE GAME

Category	Name	Performance
Rushing (Yds.)	Mercury Morris, 9-30-73	197
Passing (Yds.)	Dan Marino, 10-23-88	521
Passing (TDs)	Bob Griese, 11-24-77	6
	Dan Marino, 9-21-86	6
Receiving (No.)	Jim Jensen, 11-6-88	12
Receiving (Yds.)	Mark Duper, 11-10-85	217
Interceptions	Dick Anderson, 12-3-73	*4
Field Goals	Garo Yepremian, 9-26-71	5
Touchdowns (Tot.)	Paul Warfield, 12-15-73	4
	Mark Ingram, 11-27-94	4
Points	Paul Warfield, 12-15-73	24
	Mark Ingram, 11-27-94	24

*NFL Record

COACHING HISTORY

(317-209-4)

1966-69	George Wilson	15-39-2
1970-95	Don Shula	274-147-2
1996-98	Jimmy Johnson	28-23-0

PRO PLAYER STADIUM

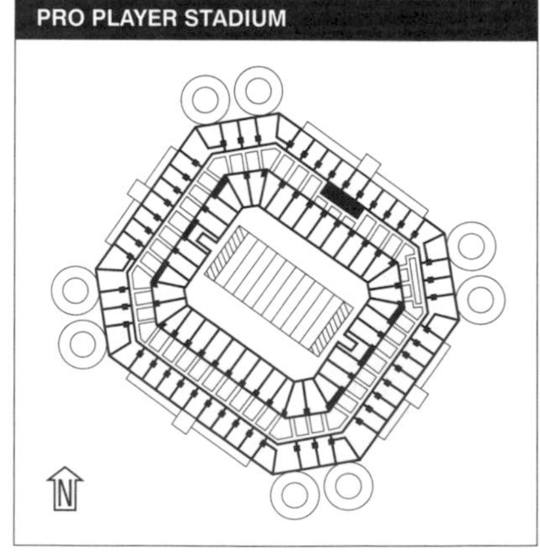

1998 TEAM RECORD

PRESEASON (4-0)

Date	Result		Opponent
8/8	W	19-16	at Washington
8/13	W	14-13	Tampa Bay
8/23	W	21-20	at San Francisco
8/28	W	21-7	Green Bay

REGULAR SEASON (10-6)

Date	Result		Opponent	Att.
9/6	W	24-15	at Indianapolis	60,587
9/13	W	13-7	Buffalo	73,097
9/20	W	21-0	Pittsburgh	73,948
10/4	L	9-20	at New York Jets	75,257
10/12	L	21-28	at Jacksonville	74,051
10/18	W	14-0	St. Louis	65,418
10/25	W	12-9	New England (OT)	73,973
11/1	L	24-30	at Buffalo	79,011
11/8	W	27-14	Indianapolis	73,400
11/15	W	13-9	at Carolina	67,887
11/23	L	23-26	at New England	58,729
11/29	W	30-10	New Orleans	73,216
12/6	W	27-17	at Oakland	61,254
12/13	L	16-21	New York Jets	74,369
12/21	W	31-21	Denver	74,363
12/27	L	16-38	at Atlanta	69,754

(OT) Overtime

POSTSEASON (1-1)

Date	Result		Opponent	Att.
1/2	W	24-17	Buffalo	72,698
1/9	L	3-38	at Denver	75,729

SCORE BY PERIODS

Dolphins	54	115	61	88	3	— 321
Opponents	51	70	44	100	0	— 265

ATTENDANCE

Home 516,366 Away 546,530 Total 1,062,896
Single-game home record, 75,283 (10/27/96)
Single-season home record, 574,811 (1997)

1998 TEAM STATISTICS

	Dolphins	Opp.
Total First Downs	269	257
Rushing	73	75
Passing	176	148
Penalty	20	34
Third Down: Made/Att	81/226	70/213
Third Down Pct.	35.8	32.9
Fourth Down: Made/Att	6/12	6/11
Fourth Down Pct.	50.0	54.5
Total Net Yards	4,930	4,435
Avg. Per Game	308.1	277.2
Total Plays	1,028	944
Avg. Per Play	4.8	4.7
Net Yards Rushing	1,535	1,511
Avg. Per Game	95.9	94.4
Total Rushes	458	395
Net Yards Passing	3,395	2,924
Avg. Per Game	212.2	182.8
Sacked/Yards Lost	24/187	45/270
Gross Yards	3,582	3,194
Att./Completions	546/316	504/252
Completion Pct.	57.9	50.0
Had Intercepted	16	29
Punts/Avg.	97/41.9	88/45.3
Net Punting Avg.	97/35.5	88/36.2
Penalties/Yards Lost	106/864	97/875
Fumbles/Ball Lost	25/12	25/7
Touchdowns	37	28
Rushing	10	6
Passing	23	17
Returns	4	5
Avg. Time of Possession	32:10	27:50

1998 INDIVIDUAL STATISTICS

Passing	Att.	Comp.	Yds.	Pct.	TD	Int.	Tkld.	Rate
Marino	537	310	3,497	57.7	23	15	23/178	80.0
Huard	9	6	85	66.7	0	1	1/9	57.4
Dolphins	546	316	3,582	57.9	23	16	24/187	79.5
Opponents	504	252	3,194	50.0	17	29	45/270	57.4

SCORING	TD R	TD P	TD Rt	PAT	FG	Saf	PTS
Mare	0	0	0	33/34	22/27	0	99
Gadsden	0	7	0	0/0	0/0	0	42
McDuffie	0	7	0	0/0	0/0	0	42
Abdul-Jabbar	6	0	0	0/0	0/0	0	36
L. Thomas	0	5	0	0/0	0/0	0	30
Avery	2	1	0	0/0	0/0	0	18
Drayton	0	3	0	0/0	0/0	0	18
Z. Thomas	0	0	2	0/0	0/0	0	12
Buckley	0	0	1	0/0	0/0	0	6
Ro. Jones	0	0	1	0/0	0/0	0	6
Marino	1	0	0	0/0	0/0	0	6
Pritchett	1	0	0	0/0	0/0	0	6
Dolphins	10	23	4	33/34	22/27	0	321
Opponents	6	17	5	24/24	23/32	0	265

2-Point conversions: None.
Team 0-3, Opponents 2-4.

RUSHING	Att.	Yds.	Avg.	LG	TD
Abdul-Jabbar	270	960	3.6	45	6
Avery	143	503	3.5	44	2
Parmalee	8	20	2.5	10	0
Pritchett	6	19	3.2	11	1
Moore	4	12	3.0	4	0
McDuffie	3	11	3.7	5	0
Lusk	1	7	7.0	7	0
Doxzon	2	6	3.0	3	0
Marino	21	-3	-0.1	10	1
Dolphins	458	1,535	3.4	45	10
Opponents	395	1,511	3.8	77t	6

RECEIVING	No.	Yds.	Avg.	LG	TD
McDuffie	90	1,050	11.7	61t	7
Gadsden	48	713	14.9	50	7
L. Thomas	43	603	14.0	56t	5
Drayton	30	334	11.1	35	3
Perry	25	255	10.2	46	0
Parmalee	21	221	10.5	23	0
Abdul-Jabbar	21	102	4.9	18	0
Pritchett	17	97	5.7	24	0
Avery	10	67	6.7	19t	1
Jacquet	8	122	15.3	29	0
Jordan	2	17	8.5	9	0
Moore	1	1	1.0	1	0
Dolphins	316	3,582	11.3	61t	23
Opponents	252	3,194	12.7	62t	17

INTERCEPTIONS	No.	Yds.	Avg.	LG	TD
Buckley	8	157	19.6	61	1
Madison	8	114	14.3	35	0
Walker	4	12	3.0	7	0
Z. Thomas	3	21	7.0	17t	2
Ro. Jones	2	14	7.0	14t	1
Surtain	2	1	0.5	1	0
Wilson	1	0	0.0	0	0
Gardener	1	-1	-1.0	-1	0
Dolphins	29	318	11.0	61	4
Opponents	16	365	22.8	87	2

PUNTING	No.	Yds.	Avg.	In 20	LG
Wilmsmeyer	93	3,949	42.5	23	57
Mare	3	115	38.3	1	43
Dolphins	97	4,064	41.9	24	57
Opponents	88	3,986	45.3	26	73

PUNT RETURNS	No.	FC	Yds.	Avg.	LG	TD
Buckley	29	3	354	12.2	35	0
McDuffie	12	8	141	11.8	39	0
Jordan	5	4	47	9.4	24	0
Dolphins	46	15	542	11.8	39	0
Opponents	43	17	339	7.9	40	0

KICKOFF RETURNS	No.	Yds.	Avg.	LG	TD
Avery	43	1,085	25.2	55	0
Marion	6	109	18.2	28	0
Jacquet	4	103	25.8	37	0
Dolphins	53	1,297	24.5	55	0
Opponents	56	1,227	21.9	95t	1

FIELD GOALS	1-19	20-29	30-39	40-49	50+
Mare	0/0	12/13	5/5	5/7	0/2
Dolphins	0/0	12/13	5/5	5/7	0/2
Opponents	0/1	8/8	5/6	8/15	2/2

SACKS	No.
Armstrong	10.5
Taylor	9.0
Bromell	8.0
Ro. Jones	5.0
Rodgers	2.5
Burton	2.0
Mixon	2.0
Z. Thomas	2.0
Gardener	1.0
Jackson	1.0
Madison	1.0
Dolphins	45.0
Opponents	24.0

1999 DRAFT CHOICES

Round	Name	Pos.	College
2	James Johnson	RB	Mississippi State
	Rob Konrad	RB	Syracuse
3	Grey Ruegamer	C	Arizona State
5	Cecil Collins	RB	McNeese State
	Bryan Jones	LB	Oregon State
6	Brent Bartholomew	P	Ohio State
7	Jermaine Haley	DT	Butte J.C.
	Joe Wong	T	Brigham Young

MIAMI DOLPHINS

1999 VETERAN ROSTER

No.	Name	Pos.	Ht.	Wt.	Birthdate	NFL Exp.	College	Hometown	How Acq.	'98 Games/ Starts
33	Abdul-Jabbar, Karim	RB	5-10	205	6/28/74	4	UCLA	Los Angeles, Calif.	D3b-'96	15/15
93	Armstrong, Trace	DE	6-4	270	10/5/65	11	Florida	Birmingham, Ala.	T(Chi)-'95	16/0
20	Avery, John	RB	5-9	190	1/11/76	2	Mississippi	Asheville, N.C.	D1-'98	16/0
48	Barber, Kantroy	RB	6-1	245	10/4/73	3	West Virginia	Miami, Fla.	FA-'98	0*
60	Bock, John	G	6-3	298	2/11/71	5	Indiana State	Crystal Lake, Ill.	FA-'96	16/6
95	Bowens, Tim	DT	6-4	315	2/7/73	5	Mississippi	Okolona, Miss.	D1-'94	16/16
57	Brigance, O.J.	LB	6-0	236	9/29/69	4	Rice	Sugarland, Tex.	FA-'96	16/0
91	Bromell, Lorenzo	DE	6-6	265	9/23/75	2	Clemson	Georgetown, S.C.	D4-'98	14/0
76	Brown, James	T	6-6	330	11/30/70	7	Virginia State	Philadelphia, Pa.	T(NYJ)-'96	16/16
27	Buckley, Terrell	CB	5-10	180	6/7/71	8	Florida State	Pascagoula, Miss.	T(GB)-'95	16/16
58	Burroughs, Sammie	LB	6-0	227	6/21/73	4	Florida State	Pomona, Calif.	FA-'99	0*
75	Burton, Shane	DT	6-6	305	1/18/74	4	Tennessee	Catawba, N.C.	D5b-'96	15/0
56	Crawford, Mike	LB	6-1	245	10/29/74	3	Nevada	Zephyr Cover, Nev.	D6c-'97	0*
63	Dixon, Mark	G	6-4	300	11/26/70	2	Virginia	Jamestown, N.C.	FA-'98	11/10
65	Donnalley, Kevin	G	6-5	305	6/10/68	9	North Carolina	Raleigh, N.C.	UFA(Tenn)-'98	14/14
17	Doxzon, Todd	WR	6-0	186	3/28/75	2	Iowa State	Sioux City, Iowa	FA-'98	9/0
84	Drayton, Troy	TE	6-3	270	6/29/70	7	Penn State	Steelton, Pa.	T(StL)-'96	15/15
7	Erickson, Craig	QB	6-2	213	5/17/69	8	Miami	West Palm Beach, Fla.	FA-'96	0*
86	Gadsden, Oronde	WR	6-2	218	8/20/71	2	Winston-Salem State	Charleston, S.C.	FA-'98	16/12
92	Gardener, Daryl	DT	6-6	315	2/25/73	4	Baylor	Lawton, Okla.	D1-'96	16/16
66	t- Gogan, Kevin	G	6-7	330	11/2/64	13	Washington	San Francisco, Calif.	T(SF)-'99	16/16*
82	Green, Willie	WR	6-4	191	4/2/66	10	Mississippi	Athens, Ga.	FA-'99	16/0*
87	Green, Yatil	WR	6-2	205	11/25/73	3	Miami	Lake City, Fla.	D1-'97	0*
51	Harris, Anthony	LB	6-1	240	1/25/73	4	Auburn	Fort Pierce, Fla.	FA-'96	5/0
28	Hill, Ray	CB	6-0	182	8/7/75	2	Michigan State	Detroit, Mich.	W(Buff)-'98	6/0*
50	Hollier, Dwight	LB	6-2	242	4/21/69	8	North Carolina	Hampton, Va.	D4-'92	16/0
11	Huard, Damon	QB	6-3	215	7/9/73	3	Washington	Puyallup, Wash.	FA-'97	2/0
53	Izzo, Larry	LB	5-10	228	9/26/74	4	Rice	Houston, Tex.	FA-'96	13/0
38	Jackson, Calvin	CB	5-9	195	10/28/72	5	Auburn	Ft. Lauderdale, Fla.	FA-'95	16/15
88	Jacquet, Nate	WR	6-0	173	9/2/75	3	San Diego State	Duarte, Calif.	W(Ind)-'98	15/0
25	Jeffries, Greg	CB	5-9	185	10/16/71	7	Virginia	High Point, N.C.	UFA(Det)-'99	15/3*
52	Jones, Robert	LB	6-3	250	9/27/69	8	East Carolina	Blackstone, Va.	FA-'98	16/16
29	Madison, Sam	CB	5-11	185	4/23/74	3	Louisville	Monticello, Fla.	D2-'97	16/16
10	Mare, Olindo	K	5-10	190	6/6/73	3	Syracuse	Cooper City, Fla.	FA-'97	16/0
13	Marino, Dan	QB	6-4	228	9/15/61	17	Pittsburgh	Pittsburgh, Pa.	D1-'83	16/16
31	Marion, Brock	S	5-11	197	6/11/70	7	Nevada	Bakersfield, Calif.	UFA(Dall)-'98	16/16
80	Martin, Tony	WR	6-1	181	9/5/65	10	Mesa, Colo.	Miami, Fla.	FA-'99	16/16*
81	McDuffie, O.J.	WR	5-10	195	12/2/69	7	Penn State	Gate Mills, Ohio	D1-'93	16/16
79	Mixon, Kenny	DE	6-4	273	5/31/75	2	Louisiana State	Pineville, La.	D2b-'98	16/16
96	Owens, Rich	DE	6-6	281	5/22/72	5	Lehigh	Philadelphia, Pa.	UFA(Wash)-'99	0*
30	Parmalee, Bernie	RB	5-11	210	9/16/67	8	Ball State	Jersey City, N.J.	FA-'92	15/0
89	Perry, Ed	TE	6-4	255	9/1/74	3	James Madison	Richmond, Va.	D6d-'97	14/5
40	Potts, Roosevelt	RB	6-0	250	1/8/71	6	Northeast Louisiana	Rayville, La.	UFA(Balt)-'99	16/15*
36	Pritchett, Stanley	RB	6-1	242	12/12/73	4	South Carolina	College Park, Ga.	D4b-'96	16/12
70	Rayam, Thomas	T	6-7	345	1/3/68	3	Alabama	Orlando, Fla.	FA-'99	0*
59	Rodgers, Derrick	LB	6-1	227	10/14/71	3	Arizona State	New Orleans, La.	D3b-'97	16/16
61	Ruddy, Tim	C	6-3	300	4/27/72	6	Notre Dame	Dunmore, Pa.	D2b-'94	16/16
15	Shannon, Larry	WR	6-4	215	2/2/75	2	East Carolina	Starke, Fla.	D3b-'98	0*
68	Sheldon, Mike	T	6-4	305	6/8/73	3	Grand Valley State	Villa Park, Ill.	FA-'97	9/2
74	Smith, Brent	G	6-5	315	11/21/73	3	Mississippi State	Pontotoc, Miss.	D3d-'97	8/7
9	Steagall, Derrick	WR	6-0	207	1/21/74	2	Georgia Tech	Newnan, Ga.	FA-'98	0*
21	Stewart, Rayna	S	5-10	200	6/18/73	4	Northern Arizona	Chatsworth, Calif.	FA-'98	14/0
67	Stokes, Barry	T	6-4	315	12/20/73	2	Eastern Michigan	Flint, Mich.	FA-'98	3/0
23	Surtain, Patrick	CB	5-11	197	6/19/76	2	Southern Mississippi	New Orleans, La.	D2a-'98	16/0
72	Tanner, Barron	DT	6-3	312	9/14/73	3	Oklahoma	Athens, Tex.	D5a-'97	13/0
99	Taylor, Jason	DE	6-6	260	9/1/74	3	Akron	Woodland Hills, Pa.	D3a-'97	16/15
85	Thomas, Lamar	WR	6-1	175	2/12/70	7	Miami	Gainesville, Fla.	FA-'96	16/2
54	Thomas, Zach	LB	5-11	235	9/1/73	4	Texas Tech	Pampa, Tex.	D5c-'96	16/16
45	Walker, Brian	S	6-1	198	5/31/72	4	Washington State	Colorado Springs, Colo.	FA-'97	16/0
78	Webb, Richmond	T	6-6	318	1/11/67	10	Texas A&M	Dallas, Tex.	D1-'90	9/9
42	t- Wheatley, Tyrone	RB	6-0	235	1/19/72	5	Michigan	Inkster, Mich.	T(NYG)-'99	5/0*
24	Wilson, Jerry	CB	5-10	187	7/17/73	5	Southern	Lake Charles, La.	FA-'96	16/0
37	Wimberly, Marcus	S	5-11	192	7/8/74	2	Miami	Memphis, Tenn.	FA-'99	0*
22	Wooden, Shawn	S	5-11	205	10/23/73	4	Notre Dame	Abington, Pa.	D6-'96	2/1

* Barber last active with Carolina in '97; Burroughs missed '98 season because of injury with Colts; Crawford, Y. Green, Shannon, Steagall missed '98 season because of injury; Erickson inactive for 7 games; Gogan played 16 games with San Francisco in '98; W. Green played 16 games with Denver; Hill played 4 games with Buffalo; Jeffries played 15 games with Detroit; Martin played 16 games with Atlanta; Owens was inactive for 16 games with Washington; Potts played 16 games with Baltimore; Rayam last active with Cincinnati in '93; Wheatley played 5 games with N.Y. Giants; Wimberly last active with Atlanta in '97.

† Restricted free agent; subject to developments.

t- Dolphins traded for Gogan (San Francisco) and Wheatley (N.Y. Giants).

Players lost through free agency (2): TE Frank Wainright (Balt; 16 games in '98), P Klaus Wilmsmeyer (Car; 16).

Also played with the Dolphins in '98—T Jeff Buckey (7 games), WR Horace Copeland (2), WR Kirby Dar Dar (3), WR Charles Jordan (3), TE Hendrick Lusk (3), RB Ron Moore (1), DE Daniel Stubbs (5), WR Iheanyi Uwaezuoke (4).

COACHING STAFF

Head Coach,
Jimmy Johnson

Pro Career: Begins his ninth season as an NFL head coach and his fourth with the Miami Dolphins. He has led the Dolphins to a 27-21 regular-season record in his previous three seasons with two playoff appearances, reaching the AFC divisional round in 1998. Named general manager/head coach of the Dolphins on January 11, 1996, becoming the third head coach in club history. Became the first, and one of only two head coaches ever in football history, to win both a Super Bowl title (Dallas Cowboys - 1992 and 1993) and a national collegiate championship (University of Miami - 1987). Served as head coach of the Cowboys from 1989 through 1993. One of only five men in NFL history to coach consecutive Super Bowl winners, winning Super Bowl XXVII in 1992 and following that with a victory in Super Bowl XXVIII in 1993. In his five years in Dallas, Johnson led the Cowboys to two NFL championships, with their first title in 1992 coming just three years after the franchise produced a 1-15 mark in 1989. In addition, Johnson's postseason winning percentage of .727 (8-3 record) is tied for fourth in NFL history among coaches with five of more postseason wins, behind only Vince Lombardi's mark of .900 (9-1), Mike Shanahan's percentage of .875 (7-1), and Joe Gibbs's mark of .762 (16-5). Career record: 79-60.

Background: At the University of Miami (1984-88), Johnson led the Hurricanes to a 52-9 (.853) record, including a 44-4 mark over the final four seasons. His Hurricane teams also captured two Orange Bowl titles, a national championship in 1987, and two number-two finishes (1986, 1988). In his first head coaching job, Johnson took over a losing program at Oklahoma State in 1979 and brought it to national prominence, compiling a 29-25 record in five seasons, including two bowl appearances. Johnson was named Big Eight Coach of the Year following his first season. Served as assistant head coach/defensive coordinator at Pittsburgh (1977-78), defensive coordinator at Arkansas (1973-76), defensive line coach at Oklahoma (1970-72), defensive coordinator at Iowa State (1968-69), assistant coach at Wichita State (1967), and defensive line coach at Louisiana Tech (1965). Before beginning his coaching career, Johnson was an All-Southwest Conference defensive lineman at Arkansas and helped lead the Razorbacks to the 1964 national championship. A three-year letterman, Johnson was named to Arkansas' All-Decade Team of the 1960s.

Personal: Born July 16, 1943, in Port Arthur, Texas. Lives in Miami. He has two sons, Brent and Chad.

ASSISTANT COACHES

Doug Blevins, kicking; born August 3, 1963, Abingdon, Va., lives in Vero Beach, Fla. No college or pro playing experience. College coach: Tennessee 1982-83, Emory & Henry College 1984-85, East Tennessee State 1986-87. Pro coach: World League kicking coordinator 1995-97, joined Dolphins in 1997.

Paul Boudreau, offensive line; born December 30, 1949, Arlington, Mass., lives in Miami. Offensive lineman Boston College 1971-73. No pro playing experience. College coach: Boston College 1974-75, Maine 1976-78, Dartmouth 1979-1981, Navy 1982. Pro coach: Edmonton Eskimos (CFL) 1983-86, New Orleans Saints 1987-1993, Detroit Lions 1994-96, New England Patriots 1997-98, joined Dolphins in 1999.

Kippy Brown, offensive coordinator; born March 6, 1955, Sweetwater, Tenn., lives in Plantation, Fla. Quarterback Memphis State 1974-77. No pro playing experience. College coach: Memphis State 1978-80, Louisville 1982, Tennessee 1983-89, 1993-94. Pro coach: New York Jets 1990-92, Tampa Bay Buccaneers 1995, joined Dolphins in 1996.

Joel Collier, running backs; born December 25, 1963, Buffalo, lives in Plantation, Fla. Linebacker Northern Colorado 1984-87. No pro playing experience. College coach: Syracuse 1988-89. Pro coach: Tampa Bay Buccaneers 1990, New England Patriots 1991-93, joined Dolphins in 1994.

Robert Ford, wide receivers; born June 21, 1951, Belton, Texas, lives in Pembroke Pines, Fla. Wide receiver Houston 1970-72. No pro playing experience. College coach: Western Illinois 1974-76, New Mexico 1977-79, Oregon State 1980-1981, Mississippi State 1982-83, Kansas 1986, Texas Tech 1987-88, Texas A&M 1989-1990. Pro coach: Houston Gamblers (USFL) 1985, Dallas Cowboys 1991-97, joined Dolphins in 1998.

John Gamble, strength and conditioning; born June 26, 1957, Richmond, Va., lives in Weston, Fla. Linebacker Hampton Institute 1975-78. No pro playing experience. College coach: Virginia 1982-1993. Pro coach: Joined Dolphins in 1994.

Cary Godette, defensive line; born March 20, 1954, New Bern, N.C., lives in Plantation, Fla. Defensive end East Carolina 1973-76. No pro playing experience. College coach: East Carolina 1977-79, 1990-1991, Wyoming 1980-82, Cincinnati 1983-88, Georgia Tech 1992-93, North Carolina State 1994. Pro coach: Carolina Panthers 1995, joined Dolphins in 1996.

George Hill, defensive coordinator-linebackers; born April 28, 1933, Bay Village, Ohio, lives in Plantation, Fla. Tackle-fullback Denison 1954-57. No pro playing experience. College coach: Findlay 1959, Denison 1960-64, Cornell 1965, Duke 1966-1970, Ohio State 1971-78. Pro coach: Philadelphia Eagles 1979-1984, Indianapolis Colts 1985-88, joined Dolphins in 1989.

Pat Jones, tight ends; born November 4, 1947, Memphis, Tenn., lives in Ft. Lauderdale, Fla. Nose guard Arkansas Tech 1965, linebacker-nose guard Arkansas 1966-67. No pro playing experience. College coach: Arkansas 1974-75, Southern Methodist 1976-77, Pittsburgh 1978, Oklahoma State 1979-1994 (head coach 1984-1994). Pro coach: Joined Dolphins in 1996.

Bill Lewis, defensive nickel package; born August 5, 1941, Bristol, Pa., lives in Ft. Lauderdale, Fla. Quarterback East Stroudsburg State 1959-1962. No pro playing experience. College coach: East Stroudsburg State 1963-65, Pittsburgh 1966-68, Wake Forest 1969-1970, Georgia Tech 1971-72, 1992-94 (head coach), Arkansas 1973-76, Wyoming 1977-79, Georgia 1980-88, East Carolina 1989-1991 (head coach). Pro coach: Joined Dolphins in 1996.

Rich McGeorge, assistant offensive line; born September 14, 1948, Roanoke, Va., lives in Plantation, Fla. Tight end Elon College 1966-69. Pro tight end Green Bay Packers 1970-78. College coach: Duke 1981-82, 1987-89, Florida 1990-92. Pro coach: Birmingham Stallions (USFL) 1983-84, Tampa Bay Bandits (USFL) 1985, joined Dolphins in 1993.

Mel Phillips, secondary; born January 6, 1942, Shelby, N.C., lives in Miami Lakes, Fla. Defensive back-running back North Carolina A&T 1964-65. Pro defensive back San Francisco 49ers 1966-1977. Pro coach: Detroit Lions 1980-84, joined Dolphins in 1985.

Brad Roll, asst. strength and conditioning; born July 4, 1958, Houston, lives in Ft. Lauderdale, Fla. Center Blinn (Tex.) J.C. 1976-77, Stephen F. Austin 1978-79. No pro playing experience. College coach: Stephen F. Austin 1980, Southwestern Louisiana 1981-86, Kansas 1987-88, Miami 1989-1992. Pro coach: Tampa Bay Buccaneers 1993-95, joined Dolphins in 1996.

Larry Seiple, quarterbacks; born February 14, 1945, Allentown, Pa., lives in Pembroke Pines, Fla. Running back-receiver-punter Kentucky 1964-66. Pro punter-tight end-receiver-running back Miami Dolphins 1966-1977. College coach: Miami 1978-79. Pro coach: Detroit Lions 1980-84, Tampa Bay Buccaneers 1985-86, joined Dolphins in 1988.

Randy Shannon, defensive assistant; born February 24, 1966, Miami, lives in Miami. Linebacker Miami 1985-88. Pro linebacker Dallas Cowboys 1989-1990. College coach: Miami 1991-97. Pro coach: Joined Dolphins in 1998.

Dave Wannstedt, asst. head coach; born May 21, 1952, Pittsburgh, lives in Miami. Offensive lineman Pittsburgh 1970-73. No pro playing experience. College coach: Pittsburgh 1975-78, Oklahoma State 1979-1982, Southern California 1983-85, Miami 1986-88. Pro coach: Dallas Cowboys 1989-1992, Chicago Bears (head coach) 1993-98, joined Dolphins in 1999.

Mike Westhoff, special teams; born January 10, 1948, Pittsburgh, lives in Plantation, Fla. Center-linebacker Wichita State 1967-69. No pro playing experience. College coach: Indiana 1974-75, Dayton 1976, Indiana State 1977, Northwestern 1978-1980, Texas Christian 1981. Pro coach: Baltimore/Indianapolis Colts 1982-84, Arizona Outlaws (USFL) 1985, joined Dolphins in 1986.

1999 FIRST-YEAR ROSTER

Name	Pos.	Ht.	Wt.	Birthdate	College	Hometown	How Acq.
Bartholomew, Brent	P	6-2	210	10/22/76	Ohio State	Apopka, Fla.	D6
Brady, Rickey (1)	TE	6-4	265	11/19/70	Oklahoma	Putnam City, Okla.	FA
Burley, Siaha	WR	5-10	163	7/16/77	Central Florida	Mesa, Ariz.	FA
Collins, Cecil	RB	5-10	209	11/19/76	McNeese State	Leesville, La.	D5a
Darden, Travis	DT	6-1	280	9/3/76	East Carolina	Kelford, N.C.	FA
Davis, Eric	DE	6-3	260	2/3/75	Georgia Southern	Albany, Ga.	FA
Gallery, Nick (1)	P	6-4	245	2/15/75	Iowa	Winthrop, Iowa	FA
Glasgow, Justin	G	6-5	308	5/17/77	Kansas	Lawton, Okla.	FA
Gonzalez, Dan (1)	QB	6-3	214	9/20/74	East Carolina	Neptune, N.J.	FA-'98
Johnson, J.J.	RB	6-1	235	4/20/74	Mississippi State	Mobile, Ala.	D2a
Johnson, Juan (1)	RB	6-1	210	1/28/76	Utah	Hunter, Utah	FA
Jones, Bryan	LB	6-4	217	12/21/75	Oregon State	San Luis Obispo, Calif.	D5b
Konrad, Rob	RB	6-3	260	11/12/76	Syracuse	Andover, Mass.	D2b
Leatherwood, Frank	TE	6-2	259	8/15/77	Appalachian State	Clyde, N.C.	FA
Mitchell, Jackie	S	6-0	198	5/30/76	Southern	Winston-Salem, N.C.	FA
Pope, O'Lester	G	6-5	354	8/24/75	Southern Mississippi	Utica, Miss.	FA
Reader, Jamie (1)	RB	5-11	233	5/4/74	Akron	Monessen, Pa.	FA
Ruegamer, Grey	G	6-5	304	6/1/76	Arizona State	Las Vegas, Nev.	D3
Simpson, Antoine (1)	DT	6-2	305	12/7/76	Houston	LaPorte, Tex.	FA
Stevenson, Derik	LB	6-4	235	3/31/74	Brigham Young	Diamond Bar, Calif.	FA
Wong, Joe	G	6-6	313	2/24/76	Brigham Young	Honolulu, Hawaii	D7b
Young Marshall (1)	K	5-10	195	3/13/74	Texas-El Paso	The Woodlands, Tex.	FA

The term NFL Rookie is defined as a player who is in his first season of professional football and has not been on the roster of another professional football team for any regular-season or postseason games. A Rookie is designated by an "R" on NFL rosters. Players who have been active in another professional football league or players who have NFL experience, including either preseason training camp or being on an Active List or Inactive List, or on Reserve/Injured or Reserve/Physically Unable to Perform for fewer than six regular-season games, are termed NFL First-Year Players. An NFL First-Year Player is designated by a "1" on NFL rosters. Thereafter, a player is credited with an additional year of experience for each season in which he accumulates six games on the Active List or Inactive List, or on Reserve/Injured or Reserve/Physically Unable to Perform.

NOTES

NEW ENGLAND PATRIOTS

American Football Conference
Eastern Division
Team Colors: Blue, Red, Silver, and White
Foxboro Stadium
60 Washington Street
Foxboro, Massachusetts 02035
Telephone: (508) 543-8200

CLUB OFFICIALS

Owner/Chief Executive Officer: Robert K. Kraft
Vice President-Owner's Representative: Jonathan A. Kraft
Vice President-Business Operations: Andrew Wasynczuk
Vice President of Player Personnel: Bobby Grier
Vice President of Marketing and Broadcast Sales: Daniel A. Kraft
Vice President-Finance: James Hausmann
Vice President of Player Development and Community Affairs: Donald Lowery
Dir. of Marketing & Special Events: Lou Imbriano
Director of Media Relations: Stacey James
Director of Football Operations: Ken Deininger
Controller: Jim Nolan
Director of Pro Scouting: Dave Uyrus
Director of Ticketing: Mike Nichols
General Manager of Foxboro Stadium: Dan Murphy
Building Services Manager: Bernie Reinhart
Head Trainer: Ron O'Neil
Equipment Manager: Don Brocher
Video Director: Jimmy Dee
Stadium: Foxboro Stadium • **Capacity:** 60,292
60 Washington Street
Foxboro, Massachusetts 02035
Playing Surface: Grass
Training Camp: Bryant College
Route 7
Smithfield, Rhode Island 02917

1999 SCHEDULE

PRESEASON

Aug. 13	**Washington**	7:30
Aug. 21	**Dallas**	8:00
Aug. 28	at Tampa Bay	8:00
Sept. 2	at Carolina	8:00

REGULAR SEASON

Sept. 12	at New York Jets	1:00
Sept. 19	**Indianapolis**	1:00
Sept. 26	**New York Giants**	8:20
Oct. 3	at Cleveland	1:00
Oct. 10	at Kansas City	12:00
Oct. 17	**Miami**	1:00
Oct. 24	**Denver**	1:00
Oct. 31	at Arizona	2:05
Nov. 7	Open Date	
Nov. 15	**New York Jets** (Mon.)	9:00
Nov. 21	at Miami	1:00
Nov. 28	at Buffalo	1:00
Dec. 5	**Dallas**	8:20
Dec. 12	at Indianapolis	1:00
Dec. 19	at Philadelphia	1:00
Dec. 26	**Buffalo**	1:00
Jan. 2	**Baltimore**	1:00

RECORD HOLDERS

INDIVIDUAL RECORDS—CAREER

Category	Name	Performance
Rushing (Yds.)	Sam Cunningham, 1973-79, 1981-82	5,453
Passing (Yds.)	Steve Grogan, 1975-1990	26,886
Passing (TDs)	Steve Grogan, 1975-1990	182
Receiving (No.)	Stanley Morgan, 1977-1989	534
Receiving (Yds.)	Stanley Morgan, 1977-1989	10,352
Interceptions	Raymond Clayborn, 1977-1989	36
Punting (Avg.)	Tom Tupa, 1996-97	44.7
Punt Return (Avg.)	Mack Herron, 1973-75	12.0
Kickoff Return (Avg.)	Allen Carter, 1975-76	27.2
Field Goals	Gino Cappelletti, 1960-1970	176
Touchdowns (Tot.)	Stanley Morgan, 1977-1989	68
Points	Gino Cappelletti, 1960-1970	1,130

INDIVIDUAL RECORDS—SINGLE SEASON

Category	Name	Performance
Rushing (Yds.)	Curtis Martin, 1995	1,487
Passing (Yds.)	Drew Bledsoe, 1994	4,555
Passing (TDs)	Vito (Babe) Parilli, 1964	31
Receiving (No.)	Ben Coates, 1994	96
Receiving (Yds.)	Stanley Morgan, 1986	1,491
Interceptions	Ron Hall, 1964	11
Punting (Avg.)	Tom Tupa, 1997	45.8
Punt Return (Avg.)	Mack Herron, 1974	14.8
Kickoff Return (Avg.)	Raymond Clayborn, 1977	31.0
Field Goals	Tony Franklin, 1986	32
Touchdowns (Tot.)	Curtis Martin, 1996	17
Points	Gino Cappelletti, 1964	155

INDIVIDUAL RECORDS—SINGLE GAME

Category	Name	Performance
Rushing (Yds.)	Tony Collins, 9-18-83	212
Passing (Yds.)	Drew Bledsoe, 11-13-94	426
Passing (TDs)	Vito (Babe) Parilli, 11-15-64	5
	Vito (Babe) Parilli, 10-15-67	5
	Steve Grogan, 9-9-79	5
Receiving (No.)	Ben Coates, 11-27-94	12
Receiving (Yds.)	Terry Glenn, 12-6-98	193
Interceptions	Many times	3
	Last time by Roland James, 10-23-83	
Field Goals	Gino Cappelletti, 10-4-64	6
Touchdowns (Tot.)	Many times	3
	Last time by Curtis Martin, 11-3-96	
Points	Gino Cappelletti, 12-18-65	28

COACHING HISTORY

BOSTON 1960-1970
(274-314-9)

1960-61	Lou Saban*	7-12-0
1961-68	Mike Holovak	53-47-9
1969-70	Clive Rush**	5-16-0
1970-72	John Mazur***	9-21-0
1972	Phil Bengtson	1-4-0
1973-78	Chuck Fairbanks****	46-41-0
1978	Hank Bullough-Ron Erhardt#	0-1-0
1979-81	Ron Erhardt	21-27-0
1982-84	Ron Meyer##	18-16-0
1984-89	Raymond Berry	51-41-0
1990	Rod Rust	1-15-0
1991-92	Dick MacPherson	8-24-0
1993-96	Bill Parcells	34-34-0
1997-98	Pete Carroll	20-15-0

*Released after five games in 1961
**Released after seven games in 1970
***Resigned after nine games in 1972
****Suspended for final regular-season game in 1978
#Co-coaches
##Released after eight games in 1984

FOXBORO STADIUM

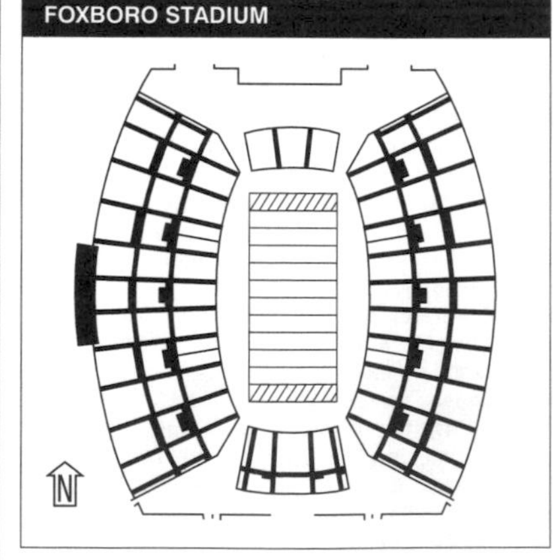

NEW ENGLAND PATRIOTS

1998 TEAM RECORD

PRESEASON (3-2)

Date	Result		Opponent
8/2	L	13-14	at San Francisco
8/9	L	0-28	Minnesota
8/17	W	21-3	vs. Dallas at Mexico City
8/22	W	20-17	at Washington
8/29	W	24-7	Philadelphia

REGULAR SEASON (9-7)

Date	Result		Opponent	Att.
9/7	L	21-27	at Denver	74,745
9/13	W	29-6	Indianapolis	60,068
9/20	W	27-16	Tennessee	59,973
10/4	W	30-27	at New Orleans	56,172
10/11	W	40-10	Kansas City	59,749
10/19	L	14-24	New York Jets	60,062
10/25	L	9-12	at Miami (OT)	73,973
11/1	W	21-16	at Indianapolis	58,056
11/8	L	10-41	Atlanta	59,790
11/15	L	10-13	at Buffalo	72,020
11/23	W	26-23	Miami	58,729
11/29	W	25-21	Buffalo	58,304
12/6	W	23-9	at Pittsburgh	58,632
12/13	L	18-32	at St. Louis	48,946
12/20	W	24-21	San Francisco	59,153
12/27	L	10-31	at New York Jets	74,302

(OT) Overtime

POSTSEASON (0-1)

Date	Result		Opponent	Att.
1/3	L	10-25	at Jacksonville	71,139

SCORE BY PERIODS

Patriots	60	116	62	99	0	—	337
Opponents	64	111	67	84	3	—	329

ATTENDANCE

Home 475,828 Away 516,576 Total 992,404
Single-game home record, 61,457 (12/5/71)
Single-season home record, 482,572 (1986)

1998 TEAM STATISTICS

	Patriots	Opp.
Total First Downs	281	305
Rushing	68	76
Passing	184	208
Penalty	29	21
Third Down: Made/Att	90/237	98/230
Third Down Pct.	38.0	42.6
Fourth Down: Made/Att	10/21	4/14
Fourth Down Pct.	47.6	28.6
Total Net Yards	5,140	5,182
Avg. Per Game	321.3	323.9
Total Plays	999	1,053
Avg. Per Play	5.1	4.9
Net Yards Rushing	1,480	1,547
Avg. Per Game	92.5	96.7
Total Rushes	403	447
Net Yards Passing	3,660	3,635
Avg. Per Game	228.8	227.2
Sacked/Yards Lost	40/344	36/222
Gross Yards	4,004	3,857
Att./Completions	556/295	570/336
Completion Pct.	53.1	58.9
Had Intercepted	17	24
Punts/Avg.	74/44.5	73/42.5
Net Punting Avg.	74/35.4	73/34.9
Penalties/Yards Lost	108/853	104/787
Fumbles/Ball Lost	20/7	16/7
Touchdowns	35	36
Rushing	9	8
Passing	23	26
Returns	3	2
Avg. Time of Possession	28:34	31:26

1998 INDIVIDUAL STATISTICS

Passing	Att.	Comp.	Yds.	Pct.	TD	Int.	Tkld.	Rate
Bledsoe	481	263	3,633	54.7	20	14	36/295	80.9
Zolak	75	32	371	42.7	3	3	4/49	54.9
Patriots	556	295	4,004	53.1	23	17	40/344	77.4
Opponents	570	336	3,857	58.9	26	24	36/222	77.1

SCORING	TD R	TD P	TD Rt	PAT	FG	Saf	PTS
Vinatieri	0	0	0	32/32	31/39	0	127
Edwards	9	3	0	0/0	0/0	0	72
Coates	0	6	0	0/0	0/0	0	36
Glenn	0	3	0	0/0	0/0	0	18
Simmons	0	3	0	0/0	0/0	0	18
Brisby	0	2	0	0/0	0/0	0	12
Jefferson	0	2	0	0/0	0/0	0	12
Purnell	0	2	0	0/0	0/0	0	12
Brown	0	1	0	0/0	0/0	0	6
Cullors	0	1	0	0/0	0/0	0	6
Law	0	0	1	0/0	0/0	0	6
Milloy	0	0	1	0/0	0/0	0	6
Thomas	0	0	1	0/0	0/0	0	6
Patriots	9	23	3	32/32	31/39	0	337
Opponents	8	26	2	30/30	27/32	0	329

2-Point conversions: Vinatieri.
Team 1-3, Opponents 1-6.

RUSHING	Att.	Yds.	Avg.	LG	TD
Edwards	291	1,115	3.8	53	9
S. Shaw	48	236	4.9	71	0
Cullors	18	48	2.7	15	0
Bledsoe	28	44	1.6	10	0
Floyd	6	22	3.7	10	0
Jefferson	1	15	15.0	15	0
T. Carter	2	3	1.5	3	0
Zolak	5	0	0.0	4	0
Glenn	2	-1	-0.5	7	0
Tupa	2	-2	-1.0	-1	0
Patriots	403	1,480	3.7	71	9
Opponents	447	1,547	3.5	34t	8

RECEIVING	No.	Yds.	Avg.	LG	TD
Coates	67	668	10.0	33	6
Glenn	50	792	15.8	86t	3
Edwards	35	331	9.5	46	3
Jefferson	34	771	22.7	61t	2
Simmons	23	474	20.6	63t	3
Brown	23	346	15.0	52	1
T. Carter	18	166	9.2	49	0
Cullors	14	146	10.4	43	1
Purnell	12	92	7.7	22	2
Brisby	7	96	13.7	27	2
S. Shaw	6	30	5.0	11	0
Ellard	5	86	17.2	19	0
Floyd	1	6	6.0	6	0
Patriots	295	4,004	13.6	86t	23
Opponents	336	3,857	11.5	84t	26

INTERCEPTIONS	No.	Yds.	Avg.	LG	TD
Law	9	133	14.8	59t	1
Milloy	6	54	9.0	30t	1
Clay	3	19	6.3	19	0
Israel	3	13	4.3	12	0
Thomas	1	24	24.0	24t	1
Canty	1	12	12.0	12	0
Whigham	1	0	0.0	0	0
Patriots	24	255	10.6	59t	3
Opponents	17	197	11.6	36	0

PUNTING	No.	Yds.	Avg.	In 20	LG
Tupa	74	3,294	44.5	13	64
Patriots	74	3,294	44.5	13	64
Opponents	73	3,100	42.5	20	58

PUNT RETURNS	No.	FC	Yds.	Avg.	LG	TD
Brown	17	8	225	13.2	39	0
Canty	16	7	170	10.6	36	0
Clay	0	2	0	—	—	0
Patriots	33	17	395	12.0	39	0
Opponents	43	8	493	11.5	76	0

KICKOFF RETURNS	No.	Yds.	Avg.	LG	TD
Cullors	45	1,085	24.1	68	0
Canty	11	198	18.0	29	0
Sullivan	2	14	7.0	9	0
Bruschi	1	4	4.0	4	0
Eaton	1	13	13.0	13	0
S. Shaw	1	16	16.0	16	0
Whigham	1	0	0.0	0	0
Patriots	62	1,330	21.5	68	0
Opponents	71	1,335	18.8	37	0

FIELD GOALS	1-19	20-29	30-39	40-49	50+
Vinatieri	3/3	8/8	9/14	9/12	2/2
Patriots	3/3	8/8	9/14	9/12	2/2
Opponents	0/0	9/9	8/11	8/10	2/2

SACKS	No.
Thomas	6.5
Eaton	6.0
Slade	4.0
McGinest	3.5
Spires	3.0
Bruschi	2.0
Israel	2.0
Johnson	2.0
Mitchell	2.0
Sullivan	2.0
Canty	1.0
C. Carter	1.0
Milloy	1.0
Patriots	36.0
Opponents	40.0

1999 DRAFT CHOICES

Round	Name	Pos.	College
1	Damien Woody	C	Boston College
	Andy Katzenmoyer	LB	Ohio State
2	Kevin Faulk	RB	Louisiana State
3	Tony George	DB	Florida
5	Derrick Fletcher	G	Baylor
6	Marcus Washington	DB	Colorado
7	Michael Bishop	QB	Kansas State
	Sean Morey	WR	Brown

NEW ENGLAND PATRIOTS

1999 VETERAN ROSTER

No.	Name	Pos.	Ht.	Wt.	Birthdate	NFL Exp.	College	Hometown	How Acq.	'98 Games/ Starts
67	Andersen, Jason	C	6-6	312	9/3/75	2	Brigham Young	San Jose, Calif.	D7-'98	0*
78	Armstrong, Bruce	T	6-4	295	9/7/65	13	Louisville	Miami, Fla.	D1-'87	16/16
86	Bartrum, Mike	TE	6-5	245	6/23/70	6	Marshall	Pomeroy, Ohio	T(GB)-'96	16/0
11	Bledsoe, Drew	QB	6-5	233	2/14/72	7	Washington State	Walla Walla, Wash.	D1-'93	14/14
82	Brisby, Vincent	WR	6-3	193	1/25/71	7	Northeast Louisiana	Houston, Tex.	D2c-'93	6/1
80	Brown, Troy	WR	5-10	190	7/2/71	7	Marshall	Blackville, S.C.	D8-'93	10/0
54	† Bruschi, Tedy	LB	6-1	245	6/9/73	4	Arizona	Roseville, Calif.	D3-'96	16/7
26	Canty, Chris	CB	5-9	185	3/30/76	3	Kansas State	Voorhees, N.J.	D1-'97	16/9
42	Carter, Chris	S	6-1	201	9/27/74	3	Texas	Tyler, Tex.	D3b-'97	16/0
30	Carter, Tony	RB	6-0	230	8/23/72	6	Minnesota	Columbus, Ohio	UFA(Chi)-'98	11/7
32	Clay, Willie	S	5-10	200	9/5/70	8	Georgia Tech	Pittsburgh, Pa.	FA-'96	16/16
87	Coates, Ben	TE	6-5	245	8/16/69	9	Livingstone College	Greenwood, S.C.	D5b-'91	14/14
99	Crawford, Vernon	LB	6-4	245	6/25/74	3	Florida State	Texas City, Tex.	D5-'97	16/1
29	Cullors, Derrick	RB	6-0	195	12/26/72	3	Murray State	Dallas, Tex.	FA-'97	16/0
61	Denson, Damon	G	6-4	305	2/8/75	3	Michigan	Pittsburgh, Pa.	D4a-'97	11/4
90	Eaton, Chad	DT	6-5	300	4/6/72	3	Washington State	Puyallup, Wash.	FA-'96	15/14
47	Edwards, Robert	RB	5-11	218	10/2/74	2	Georgia	Tennille, Ga.	D1a-'98	16/15
66	Ellis, Ed	T	6-7	340	10/13/75	3	Buffalo	Hamden, Conn.	D4b-'97	7/0
37	Floyd, Chris	RB	6-0	231	6/23/75	2	Michigan	Detroit, Mich.	D3a-'98	16/2
17	Friesz, John	QB	6-4	223	6/19/67	10	Idaho	Missoula, Mont.	UFA(Sea)-'99	5/1*
88	Glenn, Terry	WR	5-11	185	7/23/74	4	Ohio State	Columbus, Ohio	D1-'96	10/9
63	† Irwin, Heath	G	6-4	300	6/27/73	4	Colorado	Boulder, Colo.	D4a-'96	13/3
21	Israel, Steve	CB	5-11	194	3/16/69	8	Pittsburgh	Haddon Heights, N.J.	UFA(SF)-'97	11/7
84	Jefferson, Shawn	WR	5-11	180	2/22/69	9	Central Florida	Jacksonville, Fla.	FA-'96	16/16
10	Johnson, Lee	P	6-2	200	11/27/61	15	Brigham Young	Conroe, Tex.	FA-'99	13/0*
52	Johnson, Ted	LB	6-3	240	12/4/72	5	Colorado	Alameda, Calif.	D2-'95	13/13
34	Jones, Tebucky	CB	6-2	216	10/6/74	2	Syracuse	New Britain, Conn.	D1b-'98	16/0
18	Ladd, Anthony	WR	6-1	193	12/23/73	2	Cincinnati	Homestead, Fla.	FA-'98	3/0
68	Lane, Max	G	6-6	305	2/22/71	6	Navy	Norborne, Mo.	D6b-'94	16/11
24	Law, Ty	CB	5-11	200	2/10/74	5	Michigan	Aliquippa, Pa.	D1-'95	16/16
55	McGinest, Willie	DE	6-5	255	12/11/71	6	Southern California	Long Beach, Calif.	D1-'94	9/8
50	Merkerson, Ron	LB	6-2	247	8/30/75	2	Colorado	Clarksville, Tenn.	D5-'98	0*
36	Milloy, Lawyer	S	6-0	208	11/14/73	4	Washington	Tacoma, Wash.	D2-'96	16/16
98	Mitchell, Brandon	DT	6-3	289	6/19/75	3	Texas A&M	Abbeville, La.	D2-'97	7/1
58	Moore, Marty	LB	6-1	244	3/19/71	6	Kentucky	Fort Thomas, Ky.	D7b-'94	14/2
77	Moss, Zefross	T	6-6	325	8/17/66	11	Alabama State	Holt, Ala.	UFA(Det)-'97	14/14
75	Rheams, Leonta	DT	6-2	280	8/1/76	2	Houston	Tyler, Tex.	D4-'98	6/0
71	Rucci, Todd	G	6-5	296	7/14/70	7	Penn State	Upper Darby, Pa.	D2b-'93	16/16
51	Russ, Bernard	LB	6-1	238	11/4/73	2	West Virginia	Utica, N.Y.	FA-'97	1/0
83	Rutledge, Rod	TE	6-5	262	8/12/75	2	Alabama	Birmingham, Ala.	D2b-'98	16/4
44	Shaw, Harold	RB	6-0	228	9/3/74	2	Southern Mississippi	Magee, Miss.	D6-'98	11/0
81	Simmons, Tony	WR	6-1	206	12/8/74	2	Wisconsin	Chicago, Ill.	D2a-'98	11/6
53	Slade, Chris	LB	6-5	245	1/30/71	7	Virginia	Newport News, Va.	D2a-'93	15/15
94	Spires, Greg	DE	6-1	260	8/12/74	2	Florida State	Cape Coral, Fla.	D3b-'98	15/1
93	Stuckey, Shawn	LB	6-0	229	10/22/75	2	Troy State	Daleville, Ala.	FA-'98	6/0
74	† Sullivan, Chris	DE	6-4	279	3/14/73	4	Boston College	North Attleboro, Mass.	D4b-'96	15/10
95	Thomas, Henry	DT	6-2	277	1/12/65	13	Louisiana State	Houston, Tex.	FA-'97	16/15
4	Vinatieri, Adam	K	6-0	200	12/28/72	4	South Dakota State	Rapid City, S.D.	FA-'96	16/0
27	Warren, Lamont	RB	5-11	202	1/4/73	6	Colorado	Los Angeles, Calif.	FA-'99	12/2*
25	Whigham, Larry	S	6-2	205	6/23/72	6	Northeast Louisiana	Hattiesburg, Miss.	FA-'94	16/0

* Andersen inactive for 9 games in '98; Friesz played 5 games with Seattle; L. Johnson played 13 games with Cincinnati; Merkerson was missed '98 season because of injury; Warren played 12 games with Indianapolis.

† Restricted free agent; subject to developments.

Traded—TE Lovett Purnell (16 games in '98) to Baltimore.

Players lost to free agency (5): LB Todd Collins (StL; 12 games), P Tom Tupa (NYJ; 16), DT Mark Wheeler (Phil; 16), C David Wohlabaugh (Clev; 16), QB Scott Zolak (NYJ; 6).

Also played with the Patriots in '98—DE Ferric Collins (14 games), LB Dana Cottrell (2), WR Henry Ellard (5), CB Steve Lofton (6), T Scott Rehberg (2), RB Sedrick Shaw (13).

COACHING STAFF

Head Coach,
Pete Carroll

Pro Career: Pete Carroll was named the thirteenth head coach in franchise history on February 3, 1997. In his first year, he directed the Patriots to a 10-6 overall record and claimed the AFC Eastern Division title. It was the first time in the club's 38-year history that they had won back-to-back division titles. In 1998, the Patriots qualified for the playoffs for the third consecutive year, another franchise first. When Carroll joined the Patriots, he brought an attacking defensive philosophy with him. Since his arrival, the Patriots have intercepted a conference-leading 43 passes and set, then tied, the franchise record for the fewest fumbles surrendered in a season (7). Prior to joining the Patriots, he served two seasons as the defensive coordinator for the San Francisco 49ers. Carroll joined the 49ers after five seasons with the New York Jets. His tenure in New York began in 1990 when he was named defensive coordinator. During the next four years, he established a reputation for being one of the game's most innovative defensive minds. In 1994, the Jets named Carroll their ninth head coach in franchise history. That year, the Jets were in contention for the AFC East title through the season's first 11 games. Despite the early success the Jets enjoyed that year, Carroll was relieved of his duties after just one rebuilding season. He began his NFL coaching career in 1984 with the Buffalo Bills. The following year, he joined Bud Grant's staff in Minnesota and spent the next five seasons (1985-89) as the defensive backs coach for the Vikings. Career record: 26-25.

Background: Carroll began his coaching career at Pacific in 1974 at the age of 22. He coached three seasons at Pacific before moving on, gaining coaching experience at Arkansas (1977), Iowa State (1978) and Ohio State (1979) before settling in at North Carolina State in 1980. For the next three seasons (1980-82), Carroll directed the Wolfpack's defense before returning to his alma mater for one year as the assistant head coach in 1983.

Personal: Carroll was born September 15, 1951 in San Francisco, Calif. He was a football standout at Redwood High School prior to a stellar collegiate career at the University of the Pacific, where he twice earned All-Pacific Coast Conference honors as a defensive back. He had a tryout with the Hawaiians of the World Football League before pursuing a coaching career. He and his wife, Glena, live in Medfield, Mass. and have two sons, Brennan and Nathan and a daughter, Jaime.

ASSISTANT COACHES

Jeff Davidson, offensive assistant-offensive line; born October 3, 1967, Akron, Ohio, lives in Franklin, Mass. Offensive lineman Ohio State 1986-89. Pro offensive lineman Denver Broncos 1990-92, New Orleans Saints 1994. Pro coach: New Orleans Saints 1995-96, joined Patriots in 1997.

Ivan Fears, wide receivers; born November 15, 1954, Portsmouth, Va., lives in Foxboro, Mass. Running back William & Mary 1973-75. No pro playing experience. College coach: William & Mary 1977-1980, Syracuse 1981-1990. Pro coach: New England Patriots 1991-92, Chicago Bears 1993-98, rejoined Patriots in 1999.

Ray Hamilton, defensive line; born January 20, 1951, Omaha, Neb., lives in Sharon, Mass. Nose tackle Oklahoma 1969-1972. Pro nose tackle-defensive end New England Patriots 1973-81. College coach: Tennessee 1992. Pro coach: New England Patriots 1985-89, Tampa Bay Buccaneers 1991, Los Angeles Raiders 1993-94, New York Jets 1995-96, rejoined Patriots in 1997.

Ron Lynn, defensive backs; born December 6, 1944, Youngstown, Ohio, lives in Dover, Mass. Quarterback-defensive back Mt. Union (Ohio) 1962-65. No pro playing experience. College coach: Toledo 1966, Mt. Union (Ohio) 1967-1973, Kent State 1974-76, San Jose State 1977-78, Pacific 1979, California 1980-82. Pro coach: Oakland Invaders (USFL) 1983-85, San Diego Chargers 1986-1991, Cincinnati Bengals 1992-93, Washington Redskins 1994-96, joined Patriots in 1997.

Johnny Parker, strength and conditioning; born February 1, 1947, Greenville, S.C., lives in Foxboro, Mass. Attended Mississippi. No college or pro playing experience. College coach: South Carolina 1974-76, Indiana 1977-79, Louisiana State 1980, Mississippi 1981-83. Pro coach: New York Giants 1984-1992, joined Patriots in 1993.

Bo Pelini, linebackers; born December 13, 1967, Youngstown, Ohio, lives in Attleboro, Mass. Defensive back Ohio State 1986-1990. No pro playing experience. College coach: Iowa 1991-92. Pro coach: San Francisco 49ers 1994-96, joined Patriots in 1997.

Jack Reilly, quarterbacks; born May 22, 1945, Boston, Mass., lives in Foxboro, Mass. Quarterback Washington State 1963, Santa Monica (Calif.) J.C. 1964, Long Beach State 1965-66. No pro playing experience. College coach: El Camino (Calif.) J.C. 1980-84 (head coach 1981-84), Utah 1985-89. Pro coach: San Diego Chargers 1990-93, Los Angeles Raiders 1994, St. Louis Rams 1995-96, Dallas Cowboys 1997, joined Patriots in 1998.

Dante Scarnecchia, special teams; born February 15, 1948, Los Angeles, lives in Wrentham, Mass. Center-guard California Western 1968-1970. No pro playing experience. College coach: California Western (now U.S. International) 1970-72, Iowa State 1973, Southern Methodist 1975-76, 1980-81, Pacific 1977-78, Northern Arizona 1979. Pro coach: New England Patriots 1982-89, Indianapolis Colts 1990, rejoined Patriots in 1991.

Brad Seely, special teams; born September 6, 1956, Vinton, Iowa, lives in Wrentham, Mass. Tackle-guard South Dakota State 1974-77. No pro playing experience. College coach: Colorado State 1980, Southern Methodist 1981, North Carolina State 1982, Pacific 1983, Oklahoma State 1984-88. Pro coach: Indianapolis Colts 1989-1993, New York Jets 1994, Carolina Panthers 1995-98, joined Patriots in 1999.

Steve Sidwell, defensive coordinator; born August 30, 1944, Winfield, Kan., lives in Wrentham, Mass. Linebacker Colorado 1962-65. No pro playing experience. College coach: Colorado 1966-1973, Nevada-Las Vegas 1974-75, Southern Methodist 1976-1981. Pro coach: New England Patriots 1982-84, Indianapolis Colts 1985, New Orleans Saints 1986-1994, Houston Oilers 1995-96, rejoined Patriots in 1997.

Carl Smith, tight ends, born April 26, 1948, Wasco, Calif., lives in Franklin, Mass. Defensive back Cal Poly-SLO 1968-1970. No pro playing experience. College coach: Cal Poly-SLO 1974-78, Lamar 1979-1981, North Carolina State 1982. Pro coach: Philadelphia/Baltimore Stars (USFL) 1983-85, New Orleans Saints 1986-1996, joined Patriots in 1997.

DeWayne Walker, defensive assistant-secondary; born December 3, 1960, Los Angeles, lives in Foxboro, Mass. Cornerback Pasadena C.C. 1978-79, Minnesota 1980-81. Pro cornerback Edmonton Eskimos (CFL) 1982, Oakland Invaders (USFL) 1984, Arizona Outlaws (USFL) 1985. College coach: Mt. San Antonio J.C. 1988-1992, Utah State 1993, Brigham Young 1994, Oklahoma State 1995, California 1996-97. Pro coach: Joined Patriots in 1998.

Kirby Wilson, running backs; born August 24, 1961, Los Angeles, lives in Franklin, Mass. Running back-wide receiver Pasadena C.C. 1979-1980, wide receiver-kick returner Illinois 1981-82. Pro defensive back-kick returner Winnipeg (CFL) 1983, Toronto (CFL) 1984. College coach: Pasadena C.C. 1985, L.A. Southwest C.C. 1989-1990, Southern Illinois 1991-92, Wyoming 1993-94, Iowa State 1995-96. Pro coach: Joined Patriots in 1997.

Ernie Zampese, offensive coordinator; born March 12, 1936, Santa Barbara, Calif., lives in Foxboro, Mass. Halfback Southern California 1956-58. No pro playing experience. College coach: Hancock (Calif.) J.C. 1962-65, Cal Poly-SLO 1966, San Diego State 1967-1975. Pro coach: San Diego Chargers 1976, 1979-1986, Los Angeles Rams 1987-1993, Dallas Cowboys 1994-97, joined Patriots in 1998.

1999 FIRST-YEAR ROSTER

Name	Pos.	Ht.	Wt.	Birthdate	College	Hometown	How Acq.
Bishop, Michael	QB	6-0	195	5/15/76	Kansas State	Willis, Tex.	D7a
Bray, Jason	CB	5-10	188	3/7/78	Auburn	LaGrange, Ga.	FA
Cohens, Willie	DE	6-2	264	11/21/76	Florida	Starke, Fla.	FA
Collins, Daniel	G	6-4	300	7/27/76	Boston College	Raynham, Mass.	FA
Cottrell, Dana (1)	LB	6-3	244	1/11/74	Syracuse	Billerica, Mass.	FA-'98
Crawford, Tarren (1)	G	6-6	319	9/23/77	Central State, Ohio	Baltimore, Md.	FA
Faulk, Kevin	RB	5-8	197	6/15/76	Louisiana State	Carencro, La.	D2
Fletcher, Derrick	G-T	6-6	348	9/9/75	Baylor	Aldine, Tex.	D5
George, Tony	S	5-11	200	8/10/75	Florida	Cincinnati, Ohio	D3
Gilliard, Cory (1)	S	5-10	210	10/10/74	Ball State	Bronx, N.Y.	FA
Grier, James (1)	DT	6-4	327	12/20/74	Mississippi State	Macon, Ga.	FA
Hamilton, Kadar (1)	S	5-10	200	8/24/76	Stanford	Los Angeles, Calif.	FA
Johnson, Garrett	DT	6-3	294	12/31/75	Illinois	Belleville, Ill.	FA
Karim, Nafis	WR	5-11	192	3/1/76	Florida	Marietta, Ga.	FA
Katzenmoyer, Andy	LB	6-3	264	12/2/77	Ohio State	Westerville, Ohio	D1b
Lumpkin, John	TE	6-7	274	12/31/75	Ohio State	Dayton, Ohio	FA
Mack, Kendall	T	6-4	322	7/18/75	Auburn	Pineville, S.C.	FA
Mackey, Chad (1)	WR	6-0	224	3/21/74	Louisiana Tech	Longview, Tex.	FA
Manley, James (1)	DT	6-3	320	7/11/74	Vanderbilt	Birmingham, Ala.	FA
Martin, Tim	DE	6-4	274	4/12/76	Tulsa	Claremore, Okla.	FA
McCall, Jon	DT	6-2	281	7/19/77	Central Michigan	Troy, Mich.	FA
Morey, Sean	WR	5-11	190	2/26/76	Brown	Marshfield, Mass.	D7b
Murphy, Jim (1)	QB	6-4	230	2/23/75	Northeastern	Reading, Mass.	FA
Reem, Matt (1)	T	6-6	270	12/23/72	Minnesota	Minneapolis, Minn.	FA
Serwanga, Kato (1)	CB	5-11	192	7/23/76	California	Sacramento, Calif.	FA-'98
Shepard, Derrick (1)	DT	6-2	300	5/29/75	Georgia Tech	Dayton, Ohio	FA
Smith, Devon	TE	6-4	243	1/17/76	North Carolina State	Ahoskie, N.C.	FA
Warren, Brent (1)	G-T	6-5	338	2/10/75	Syracuse	Brockton, Mass.	FA
Washington, Marcus	CB-S	6-1	217	2/26/75	Colorado	Colorado Springs, Colo.	D6
Woody, Damien	C	6-3	319	11/3/77	Boston College	Beaverdam, Va.	D1a

The term NFL Rookie is defined as a player who is in his first season of professional football and has not been on the roster of another professional football team for any regular-season or postseason games. A Rookie is designated by an "R" on NFL rosters. Players who have been active in another professional football league or players who have NFL experience, including either preseason training camp or being on an Active List or Inactive List, or on Reserve/Injured or Reserve/Physically Unable to Perform for fewer than six regular-season games, are termed NFL First-Year Players. An NFL First-Year Player is designated by a "1" on NFL rosters. Thereafter, a player is credited with an additional year of experience for each season in which he accumulates six games on the Active List or Inactive List, or on Reserve/Injured or Reserve/Physically Unable to Perform.

NEW YORK JETS

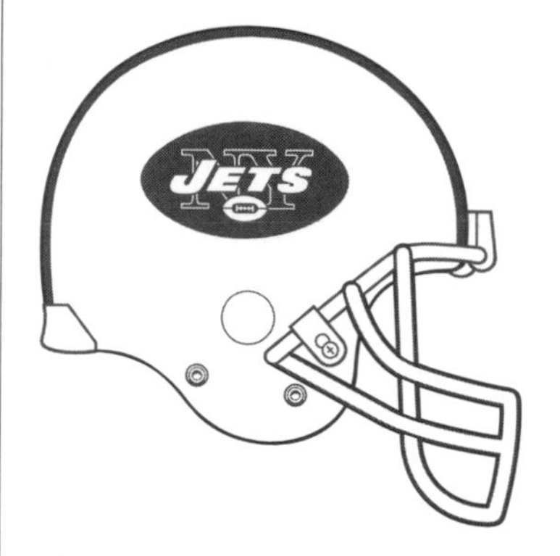

American Football Conference
Eastern Division
Team Colors: Green and White
1000 Fulton Avenue
Hempstead, New York 11550
Telephone: (516) 560-8100

CLUB OFFICIALS

President: Steve Gutman
Chief Football Operations Officer: Bill Parcells
Director of Player Personnel: Dick Haley
Director of Pro Personnel: Scott Pioli
Director of Player Contract Negotiations: Mike Tannenbaum
Director of Player Development: Carl Banks
Director of Security: Steve Yarnell
Treasurer and Chief Financial Officer: Michael Gerstle
Executive Director of Business Operations: Bob Parente
Director of Public Relations: Frank Ramos
Director of Operations: Mike Kensil
Talent Scouts: Trent Baalke, Joey Clinkscales, Michael Davis, Sid Hall, Jesse Kaye, Bob Schmitz, Lionel Vital
Director of Team Travel: Kevin Coyle
College Scouting Coordinator: John Griffin
Asst. Director of Public Relations: Douglas Miller
Public Relations Assistants: Sharon Czark, Danny Ferrauiloa, Berj Najarian
Coordinator of Special Projects: Ken Ilchuk
Controller: Mike Minarczyk
Director of Marketing: Mark Riccio
Senior Marketing Manager: Beth Conroy
Accountant: Dawn Aponte
Director of Computer Technology: Hal Masure
Manager of Football Computer Operations: Christine Haefling
Director of Network Operations: Thomas Murphy
Director of Ticket Operations: John Buschhorn
Assistant Director of Ticket Operations: Carol Anne Coppola
Assistant Director of Operations: Kathy Reade
Head Athletic Trainer: David Price
Assistant Athletic Trainer: John Mellody
Equipment Manager: Bill Hampton
Equipment Director: Clay Hampton
Assistant Equipment Manager: Gus Granneman
Video Director: John Seiter
Football Video Director: Jim Pons
Assistant Video Director: Jim Space
Stadium: Giants Stadium • **Capacity:** 78,739
East Rutherford, New Jersey 07073
Playing Surface: AstroTurf
Training Center: 1000 Fulton Avenue
Hempstead, New York 11550

RECORD HOLDERS

INDIVIDUAL RECORDS—CAREER

Category	Name	Performance
Rushing (Yds.)	Freeman McNeil, 1981-1992	8,074
Passing (Yds.)	Joe Namath, 1965-1976	27,057
Passing (TDs)	Joe Namath, 1965-1976	170
Receiving (No.)	Don Maynard, 1960-1972	627
Receiving (Yds.)	Don Maynard, 1960-1972	11,732
Interceptions	Bill Baird, 1963-69	34
Punting (Avg.)	Curley Johnson, 1961-68	42.8
Punt Return (Avg.)	Dick Christy, 1961-63	16.2
Kickoff Return (Avg.)	Bobby Humphery, 1984-89	22.8
Field Goals	Pat Leahy, 1974-1991	304
Touchdowns (Tot.)	Don Maynard, 1960-1972	88
Points	Pat Leahy, 1974-1991	1,470

INDIVIDUAL RECORDS—SINGLE SEASON

Category	Name	Performance
Rushing (Yds.)	Freeman McNeil, 1985	1,331
Passing (Yds.)	Joe Namath, 1967	4,007
Passing (TDs)	Vinny Testaverde, 1998	29
Receiving (No.)	Al Toon, 1988	93
Receiving (Yds.)	Don Maynard, 1967	1,434
Interceptions	Dainard Paulson, 1964	12
Punting (Avg.)	Curley Johnson, 1965	45.3
Punt Return (Avg.)	Dick Christy, 1961	21.3
Kickoff Return (Avg.)	Bobby Humphery, 1984	30.7
Field Goals	Jim Turner, 1968	34
Touchdowns (Tot.)	Art Powell, 1960	14
	Don Maynard, 1965	14
	Emerson Boozer, 1972	14
Points	Jim Turner, 1968	145

INDIVIDUAL RECORDS—SINGLE GAME

Category	Name	Performance
Rushing (Yds.)	Adrian Murrell, 10-27-96	199
Passing (Yds.)	Joe Namath, 9-24-72	496
Passing (TDs)	Joe Namath, 9-24-72	6
Receiving (No.)	Clark Gaines, 9-21-80	17
Receiving (Yds.)	Don Maynard, 11-17-68	228
Interceptions	Many times.	3
	Last time by Marcus Turner, 11-20-94	
Field Goals	Jim Turner, 11-3-68	6
	Bobby Howfield, 12-3-72	6
Touchdowns (Tot.)	Wesley Walker, 9-21-86	4
Points	Wesley Walker, 9-21-86	24

1999 SCHEDULE

PRESEASON

Aug. 14	at Green Bay	7:00
Aug. 20	**Philadelphia**	7:30
Aug. 28	at New York Giants	8:00
Sept. 3	**Minnesota**	7:30

REGULAR SEASON

Sept. 12	**New England**	1:00
Sept. 19	at Buffalo	8:20
Sept. 26	**Washington**	1:00
Oct. 3	at Denver	2:15
Oct. 11	**Jacksonville** (Mon.)	9:00
Oct. 17	**Indianapolis**	1:00
Oct. 24	at Oakland	1:15
Oct. 31	Open Date	
Nov. 7	**Arizona**	1:00
Nov. 15	at New England (Mon.)	9:00
Nov. 21	**Buffalo**	1:00
Nov. 28	at Indianapolis	4:15
Dec. 5	at New York Giants	1:00
Dec. 12	**Miami**	4:05
Dec. 19	at Dallas	3:15
Dec. 27	at Miami (Mon.)	9:00
Jan. 2	**Seattle**	1:00

COACHING HISTORY

New York Titans 1960-62
(258-327-8)

1960-61	Sammy Baugh	14-14-0
1962	Clyde (Bulldog) Turner	5-9-0
1963-73	Weeb Ewbank	73-78-6
1974-75	Charley Winner*	9-14-0
1975	Ken Shipp	1-4-0
1976	Lou Holtz**	3-10-0
1976	Mike Holovak	0-1-0
1977-82	Walt Michaels	41-49-1
1983-89	Joe Walton	54-59-1
1990-93	Bruce Coslet	26-39-0
1994	Pete Carroll	6-10-0
1995-96	Rich Kotite	4-28-0
1997-98	Bill Parcells	22-12-0

*Released after nine games in 1975
**Resigned after 13 games in 1976

GIANTS STADIUM

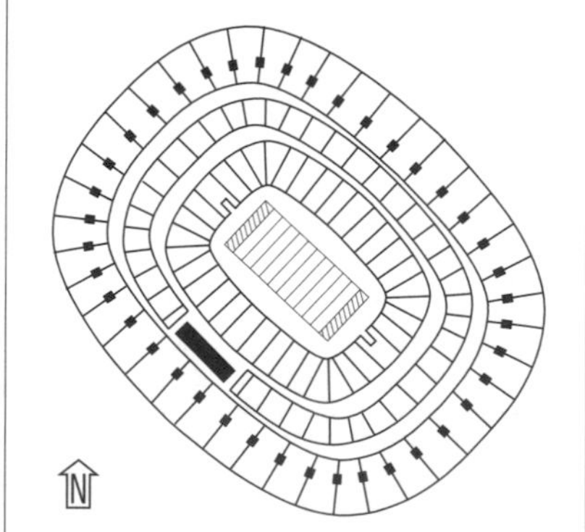

1998 TEAM RECORD

PRESEASON (3-1)

Date	Result		Opponent
8/6	W	29-15	at Philadelphia
8/15	L	0-33	Baltimore
8/20	W	27-23	N.Y. Jets
8/28	W	24-7	at Chicago

REGULAR SEASON (12-4)

Date	Result		Opponent	Att.
9/6	L	30-36	at San Francisco (OT)	64,419
9/13	L	10-24	Baltimore	70,063
9/20	W	44-6	Indianapolis	66,321
10/4	W	20-9	Miami	75,257
10/11	L	10-30	at St. Louis	55,938
10/19	W	24-14	at New England	60,062
10/25	W	28-3	Atlanta	71,573
11/1	W	20-17	at Kansas City	65,104
11/8	W	34-12	Buffalo	75,403
11/15	L	23-24	at Indianapolis	55,520
11/22	W	24-3	at Tennessee	37,084
11/29	W	48-21	Carolina	71,501
12/6	W	32-31	Seattle	72,200
12/13	W	21-16	at Miami	74,369
12/19	W	17-10	at Buffalo	79,056
12/27	W	31-10	New England	74,302

(OT) Overtime

POSTSEASON (1-1)

Date	Result		Opponent	Att.
1/10	W	34-24	Jacksonville	76,469
1/17	L	10-23	at Denver	75,482

SCORE BY PERIODS

Jets	78	125	101	112	0	—	416
Opponents	75	63	54	68	6	—	266

ATTENDANCE

Home 576,620 Away 491,552 Total 1,068,172
Single-game home record, 75,606 (11/27/94)
Single-season home record, 576,620 (1998)

1998 TEAM STATISTICS

	Jets	Opp.
Total First Downs	338	263
Rushing	99	87
Passing	207	150
Penalty	32	26
Third Down: Made/Att	103/224	79/222
Third Down Pct.	46.0	35.6
Fourth Down: Made/Att	9/16	12/22
Fourth Down Pct.	56.3	54.5
Total Net Yards	5,715	4,699
Avg. Per Game	357.2	293.7
Total Plays	1,057	980
Avg. Per Play	5.4	4.8
Net Yards Rushing	1,879	1,659
Avg. Per Game	117.4	103.7
Total Rushes	500	400
Net Yards Passing	3,836	3,040
Avg. Per Game	239.8	190.0
Sacked/Yards Lost	25/196	36/259
Gross Yards	4,032	3,299
Att./Completions	532/318	544/285
Completion Pct.	59.8	52.4
Had Intercepted	13	21
Punts/Avg.	65/40.6	85/42.2
Net Punting Avg.	65/34.6	85/36.1
Penalties/Yards Lost	85/651	109/967
Fumbles/Ball Lost	23/11	25/9
Touchdowns	49	30
Rushing	12	11
Passing	33	16
Returns	4	3
Avg. Time of Possession	32:17	27:43

1998 INDIVIDUAL STATISTICS

Passing	Att.	Comp.	Yds.	Pct.	TD	Int.	Tkld.	Rate
Testaverde	421	259	3,256	61.5	29	7	19/140	101.6
Foley	108	58	749	53.7	4	6	5/49	64.9
Lucas	3	1	27	33.3	0	0	0/0	67.4
L. Johnson	0	0	0	—	0	0	1/7	—
Jets	532	318	4,032	59.8	33	13	25/196	94.0
Opponents	544	285	3,299	52.4	16	21	36/259	64.7

SCORING	TD R	TD P	TD Rt	PAT	FG	Saf	PTS
Hall	0	0	0	45/46	25/35	0	120
K. Johnson	1	10	0	0/0	0/0	0	66
Martin	8	1	0	0/0	0/0	0	54
Chrebet	0	8	0	0/0	0/0	0	48
Brady	0	5	0	0/0	0/0	0	30
L. Johnson	2	2	0	0/0	0/0	0	24
Ward	0	4	0	0/0	0/0	0	24
Byars	0	3	0	0/0	0/0	0	18
Cascadden	0	0	1	0/0	0/0	0	6
Glenn	0	0	1	0/0	0/0	0	6
Gordon	0	0	1	0/0	0/0	0	6
J. Henderson	0	0	1	0/0	0/0	0	6
Testaverde	1	0	0	0/0	0/0	0	6
Cox	0	0	0	0/0	0/0	1	2
Jets	12	33	4	45/46	25/35	1	416
Opponents	11	16	3	26/27	20/25	0	266

2-Point conversions: None.
Team 0-3, Opponents 0-2.

RUSHING	Att.	Yds.	Avg.	LG	TD
Martin	369	1,287	3.5	60t	8
L. Johnson	41	185	4.5	40	2
Sowell	40	164	4.1	33	0
Testaverde	24	104	4.3	25	1
K. Johnson	2	60	30.0	35t	1
Byars	4	34	8.5	13	0
Meggett	7	24	3.4	18	0
Lucas	5	23	4.6	16	0
Ward	2	7	3.5	4	0
Anderson	1	2	2.0	2	0
Foley	5	-11	-2.2	-1	0
Jets	500	1,879	3.8	60t	12
Opponents	400	1,659	4.1	96t	11

RECEIVING	No.	Yds.	Avg.	LG	TD
K. Johnson	83	1,131	13.6	41t	10
Chrebet	75	1,083	14.4	63t	8
Martin	43	365	8.5	23	1
Brady	30	315	10.5	35	5
Byars	26	258	9.9	29	3
Ward	25	477	19.1	71t	4
L. Johnson	13	222	17.1	82t	2
Sowell	10	59	5.9	13	0
Van Dyke	5	40	8.0	15	0
Baxter	3	50	16.7	23	0
Anderson	3	12	4.0	7	0
Meggett	1	15	15.0	15	0
Spence	1	5	5.0	5	0
Jets	318	4,032	12.7	82t	33
Opponents	285	3,299	11.6	70t	16

INTERCEPTIONS	No.	Yds.	Avg.	LG	TD
Glenn	6	23	3.8	26	0
Green	4	99	24.8	87	0
Mickens	3	10	3.3	10	0
Smith	2	34	17.0	32	0
Williams	1	34	34.0	34	0
Gordon	1	31	31.0	31t	1
J. Henderson	1	21	21.0	21	0
Lewis	1	11	11.0	11	0
Brown	1	0	0.0	0	0
P. Johnson	1	0	0.0	0	0
Jets	21	263	12.5	87	1
Opponents	13	234	18.0	61	2

PUNTING	No.	Yds.	Avg.	In 20	LG
B. Hansen	31	1,233	39.8	6	62
Kidd	28	1,166	41.6	8	57
Gallery	6	238	39.7	2	49
Jets	65	2,637	40.6	16	62
Opponents	85	3,587	42.2	20	64

PUNT RETURNS	No.	FC	Yds.	Avg.	LG	TD
L. Johnson	29	12	203	7.0	23	0
Ward	8	3	72	9.0	20	0
Meggett	5	0	40	8.0	18	0
Frost	1	0	0	0.0	0	0
Jets	43	15	315	7.3	23	0
Opponents	30	13	309	10.3	69t	1

KICKOFF RETURNS	No.	Yds.	Avg.	LG	TD
Glenn	24	585	24.4	62	0
L. Johnson	16	366	22.9	37	0
Williams	11	230	20.9	31	0
Ward	3	60	20.0	23	0
Baxter	1	8	8.0	8	0
Brady	1	20	20.0	20	0
Meggett	1	16	16.0	16	0
Jets	57	1,285	22.5	62	0
Opponents	60	1,370	22.8	47	0

FIELD GOALS	1-19	20-29	30-39	40-49	50+
Hall	0/0	9/9	9/13	6/10	1/3
Jets	0/0	9/9	9/13	6/10	1/3
Opponents	1/1	5/7	5/5	6/8	3/4

SACKS	No.
Lewis	7.0
Cox	6.0
Pleasant	6.0
Cascadden	5.0
Ferguson	4.0
Logan	2.5
Lyle	1.5
Green	1.0
J. Henderson	1.0
P. Johnson	1.0
Jets	36.0
Opponents	25.0

1999 DRAFT CHOICES

Round	Name	Pos.	College
2	Randy Thomas	G	Mississippi State
3	David Loverne	T	San Jose State
4	Jason Wiltz	DT	Nebraska
5	Jermaine Jones	DB	Northwestern State, La.
6	Marc Megna	LB	Richmond
	J.P. Machado	G	Illinois
7	Ryan Young	T	Kansas State
	J.J. Syvrud	DE	Jamestown

NEW YORK JETS

1999 VETERAN ROSTER

No.	Name	Pos.	Ht.	Wt.	Birthdate	NFL Exp.	College	Hometown	How Acq.	'98 Games/ Starts
20	Anderson, Richie	RB	6-2	230	9/13/71	7	Penn State	Sandy Spring, Md.	D6-'93	8/1
27	Atwater, Steve	S	6-3	217	10/28/66	11	Arkansas	St. Louis, Mo.	FA-'99	16/16*
84	Baxter, Fred	TE	6-3	265	6/14/71	7	Auburn	Brundidge, Ala.	D5a-'93	14/2
66	Bernstein, Alex	G	6-3	325	8/11/75	2	Amherst	Edina, Minn.	FA-'98	0*
97	Boose, Dorian	DE	6-5	292	1/29/74	2	Washington State	Tacoma, Wash.	D2-'98	12/0
44	Brown, Corwin	S	6-1	205	4/25/70	7	Michigan	Chicago, Ill.	FA-'97	16/1
53	Cascadden, Chad	LB	6-1	240	5/14/72	5	Wisconsin	Chippewa Falls, Wis.	FA-'95	13/4
80	Chrebet, Wayne	WR	5-10	185	8/14/73	5	Hofstra	Garfield, N.J.	FA-'95	16/15
42	Coleman, Marcus	CB-S	6-2	210	5/24/74	4	Texas Tech	Dallas, Tex.	D5-'96	14/0
51	Cox, Bryan	LB	6-4	250	2/17/68	9	Western Illinois	E. St. Louis, Mo.	FA-'98	16/10
49	Dailey, Casey	LB	6-3	249	6/11/75	2	Northwestern	Covina, Calif.	D5a-'98	0*
78	Day, Terry	DE	6-4	290	9/18/74	2	Mississippi State	Pickens, Miss.	D4a-'97	0*
76	Elliott, John	T	6-7	308	4/1/65	12	Michigan	Lake Ronkonkoma, N.Y.	UFA(NYG)-'96	16/16
69	Fabini, Jason	T	6-7	312	8/25/74	2	Cincinnati	Ft. Wayne, Ind.	D4-'98	16/16
58	Farrior, James	LB	6-2	242	1/6/75	3	Virginia	Ettrick, Va.	D1-'97	12/2
72	Ferguson, Jason	DT	6-3	305	11/28/74	3	Georgia	Nettleton, Miss.	D7b-'97	16/16
94	Frederick, Mike	DE	6-5	280	8/6/72	5	Virginia	Langhorne, Pa.	UFA(Balt)-'99	10/0*
47	Frost, Scott	S	6-3	219	1/4/75	2	Nebraska	Lincoln, Neb.	D3a-'98	13/0
67	Gisler, Mike	C-G	6-4	295	8/26/69	7	Houston	Runge, Tex.	UFA(NE)-'98	16/0
31	Glenn, Aaron	CB-KR	5-9	185	7/16/72	6	Texas A&M	Aldine, Tex.	D1-'94	13/13
54	Gordon, Dwayne	LB	6-1	240	11/2/69	7	New Hampshire	LaGrangeville, N.Y.	FA-'97	16/4
86	Green, Eric	TE	6-5	285	6/22/67	10	Liberty	Savannah, Ga.	UFA(Balt)-'99	12/12*
21	Green, Victor	S	5-11	205	12/8/69	7	Akron	Americus, Ga.	FA-'93	16/16
9	Hall, John	K	6-3	223	3/17/74	3	Wisconsin	Port Charlotte, Fla.	FA-'97	16/0
92	Hamilton, Bobby	DE	6-5	280	1/7/71	5	Southern Mississippi	Columbia, Miss.	FA-'96	16/1
75	Hansen, Carl	DT	6-5	280	1/25/76	2	Stanford	Houston, Tex.	FA-'98	5/0
30	Hayes, Chris	S	6-0	206	5/7/72	3	Washington State	San Bernardino, Calif.	T(GB)-'97	15/0
50	Holmberg, Rob	LB	6-3	230	5/6/71	6	Penn State	Mt. Pleasant, Pa.	FA-'98	9/0
65	Hudson, John	C-G	6-2	270	1/29/68	10	Auburn	Paris, Tenn.	UFA(Phil)-'96	16/0
71	Jenkins, Kerry	T-G	6-5	310	9/6/73	2	Troy State	Tuscaloosa, Ala.	FA-'97	16/0
19	Johnson, Keyshawn	WR	6-3	210	7/22/72	4	Southern California	Los Angeles, Calif.	D1-'96	16/16
32	Johnson, Leon	RB	6-0	215	7/13/74	3	North Carolina	Morgantown, N.C.	D4b-'97	12/2
55	Jones, Marvin	LB	6-2	250	6/28/72	7	Florida State	Miami, Fla.	D1-'93	0*
60	Karczewski, Doug	G-T	6-5	300	2/6/75	2	Virginia	Gathersburg, Md.	D5b-'98	0*
57	Lewis, Mo	LB	6-3	258	10/21/69	9	Georgia	Peachtree, Ga.	D3-'91	16/16
93	Logan, Ernie	DT-DE	6-3	290	5/18/68	8	East Carolina	Fayetteville, N.C.	UFA(Jac)-'97	16/12
6	Lucas, Ray	QB	6-3	214	8/6/72	3	Rutgers	Harrison, N.J.	FA-'97	15/0
95	Lyle, Rick	DE-DT	6-5	290	2/26/71	6	Missouri	Hickman Milla, Mo.	FA-'97	16/16
28	Martin, Curtis	RB	5-11	210	5/1/73	5	Pittsburgh	Pittsburgh, Pa.	RFA(NE)-'98	15/15
68	Mawae, Kevin	C	6-4	305	1/23/71	6	Louisiana State	Leesville, La.	UFA(Sea)-'98	16/16
24	Mickens, Ray	CB-KR	5-8	184	1/4/73	4	Texas A&M	El Paso, Tex.	D3-'96	16/4
37	Mitchell, Johnny	TE	6-3	241	1/20/71	5	Nebraska	Chicago, Ill.	FA-'99	0*
64	Norgard, Erik	G	6-1	290	11/4/65	10	Colorado	Arlington, Wash.	UFA(Tenn)-'99	1/1*
70	# O'Dwyer, Matt	G	6-5	300	9/1/72	5	Northwestern	Lincolnshire, Ill.	D2-'95	16/16
99	Ogbogu, Eric	DE	6-4	280	7/18/75	2	Maryland	Irvington, N.Y.	D6a-'98	12/0
56	Phifer, Roman	LB	6-2	240	3/5/68	9	UCLA	Pineville, N.C.	UFA(StL)-'99	13/13*
98	Pleasant, Anthony	DE	6-5	280	1/27/68	10	Tennessee State	Century, Fla.	FA-'98	16/15
45	Smith, Otis	CB	5-11	195	10/22/65	10	Missouri	New Orleans, La.	UFA(NE)-'97	16/16
33	Sowell, Jerald	FB	6-0	248	1/21/74	3	Tulane	Baker, La.	W(GB)-'97	16/2
82	Spence, Blake	TE	6-4	249	6/20/75	2	Oregon	San Juan Capistrano, Calif.	D5c-'98	5/0
16	Testaverde, Vinny	QB	6-5	238	11/13/63	13	Miami	Floral Park, N.Y.	FA-'98	14/13
7	Tupa, Tom	P	6-4	220	2/6/66	11	Ohio State	Cleveland, Ohio	UFA(NE)-'99	16/0*
89	Ward, Dedric	WR-KR	5-9	184	9/29/74	3	Northern Iowa	Cedar Rapids, Iowa	D3-'97	16/4
23	Williams, Kevin	S-CB	6-0	190	8/4/75	2	Oklahoma State	Pine Bluff, Ark.	D3b-'98	15/6
11	Zolak, Scott	QB	6-5	235	12/13/67	9	Maryland	Monongahela, Pa.	UFA(NE)-'99	5/1*

* Atwater played 16 games with Denver in '98; Bernstein inactive for 13 games; Dailey and Jones missed '98 season because of injury; Day on the non-football injury list in '98; Frederick played 10 games with Baltimore; Green played 12 games with Baltimore; Karczewski inactive for 14 games; Mitchell last active with Dallas in '96; Norgard played 1 game with Tennessee; Phifer played 13 games with St. Louis; Tupa played 16 games with New England; Zolak played 5 games with New England.

Traded—QB Glenn Foley (5 games in '98) to Seattle; WR Alex Van Dyke (16) to Pittsburgh.

Retired—LB Pepper Johnson 13-year linebacker, 16 games in '98.

\# Unrestricted free agent, subject to developments.

Players lost through free agency (1): TE Kyle Brady (Jac; 16 games in '98).

Also played for Jets in '98—G Todd Burger (16 games), RB Keith Byars (13), P Nick Gallery (1), P Brian Hansen (7), CB-S Jerome Henderson (13), P John Kidd (8), RB David Meggett (2), LB Craig Powell (2).

COACHING STAFF

Head Coach and Chief Football Operations Officer, Bill Parcells

Pro Career: On February 11, 1997, Parcells was named the Jets' eleventh head coach. Parcells came to the Jets after having led the New England Patriots to the 1996 AFC championship and an appearance in Super Bowl XXXI against the Green Bay Packers. In just two years with the Jets, Parcells has guided the Jets to a 21-11 regular-season record (sixth best in the NFL over that course of time) and became just the third NFL coach in league history to guide three different franchises into postseason play. In addition, Parcells is the first coach in NFL history to take a 1-15 team to a division title two years later. With the Jets, Parcells is 22-12, including the 1998 AFC Championship Game loss at Denver. He trails only Atlanta's Dan Reeves for most career regular-season wins (130) among active coaches, and his 141 career victories rank thirteenth in NFL history. Throughout the course of his four-year Patriots career, Parcells had a 34-34 record, including 2-2 in the postseason. Parcells made his NFL coaching debut with the Patriots as the linebackers coach on Ron Erhardt's staff in 1980. He accepted the same position on the New York Giants' staff in 1981 and was named the Giants' head coach in 1983. In eight seasons at the helm of the Giants, Parcells led his teams to two Super Bowl championships. His first title came in 1986, with a 39-20 win over the Denver Broncos. Four years later, the Giants claimed another victory over the Buffalo Bills in Super Bowl XXV. On May 15, 1991, Parcells resigned from the Giants because of health reasons. During his two years away from coaching, Parcells served as a studio analyst in 1991 and as a color commentator in 1992 for NBC Sports. Career record: 141-98-1.

Background: Linebacker at Wichita State 1961-63. College assistant Hastings (Neb.) 1964, Wichita State 1965, Army 1966-69, Florida State 1970-72, Vanderbilt 1973-74, Texas Tech 1975-77, Air Force 1978 (head coach).

Personal: Born August 22, 1941, Englewood, N.J. Bill and his wife, Judy, live in Sea Girt, N.J., and have three daughters—Suzy, Jill, and Dallas.

ASSISTANT COACHES

Bill Belichick, asst. head coach-defensive backs; born April 16, 1952, Nashville, Tenn., lives on Long Island, N.Y. Center-tight end Wesleyan 1971-74. No pro playing experience. Pro coach: Baltimore Colts 1975, Detroit Lions 1976-77, Denver Broncos 1978, New York Giants 1979-1990, Cleveland Browns 1991-95 (head coach), New England Patriots 1996, joined Jets in 1997.

Maurice Carthon, running backs; born April 24, 1961, Chicago, lives on Long Island, N.Y. Running back Arkansas State 1979-1982. Pro running back New Jersey Generals (USFL) 1983-85, New York Giants 1985-1991, Indianapolis Colts 1992. Pro coach: New England Patriots 1994-96, joined Jets in 1997.

Romeo Crennel, defensive line; born June 18, 1947, Lynchburgh, Va., lives on Long Island, N.Y. Defensive-offensive tackle, linebacker Western Kentucky 1966-69. No pro playing experience. College coach: Western Kentucky 1970-74, Texas Tech 1975-77, Mississippi 1978-79, Georgia Tech 1980. Pro coach: New York Giants 1981-1992, New England Patriots 1993-96, joined Jets in 1997.

Al Groh, linebackers; born July 13, 1944, New York, N.Y., lives on Long Island, N.Y. Defensive end Virginia 1964-67. No pro playing experience. College coach: Army 1968-69, Virginia 1970-72, North Carolina 1973-77, Air Force 1978-79, Texas Tech 1980, Wake Forest 1981-86 (head coach), South Carolina 1988. Pro coach: Atlanta Falcons 1987, New York Giants 1989-1991, Cleveland Browns 1992, New England Patriots 1993-96, joined Jets in 1997.

Todd Haley, wide receivers; born February 28, 1967, Atlanta, lives on Long Island, N.Y. Attended Florida and Miami. No college or pro playing experience. Pro coach: Joined Jets in 1997.

Dan Henning, quarterbacks; born June 21, 1942, Bronx, N.Y., lives on Long Island, N.Y. Quarterback William & Mary 1962-64. Pro quarterback San Diego Chargers 1964, 1966-67. College coach: Florida State 1968-1970, 1974, Virginia Tech 1971, 1973, Boston College 1994-96 (head coach). Pro coach: Houston Oilers 1972, New York Jets 1976-78, Miami Dolphins 1979-1980, Washington Redskins 1981-82, 1987-88, Atlanta Falcons 1983-86 (head coach), San Diego Chargers 1989-1991 (head coach), Detroit Lions 1992-93, Buffalo Bills 1997, rejoined Jets in 1998.

Pat Hodgson, tight ends; born January 30, 1944, Columbus, Ga., lives on Long Island, N.Y. Tight end Georgia 1963-65. Pro tight end Washington Redskins 1966, Minnesota Vikings 1967. College coach: Georgia 1968-1970, 1972-77, Florida State 1971, Texas Tech 1978. Pro coach: San Diego Chargers 1978, New York Giants 1979-1987, Pittsburgh Steelers 1992-95, joined Jets in 1996.

John Lott, strength and conditioning; born May 9, 1964 in Denton, Texas, lives on Long Island, N.Y. Offensive lineman North Texas State 1983-86. Offensive lineman Pittsburgh Steelers 1987. College coach: North Texas State 1989, Houston 1990-96. Pro coach: Joined Jets in 1997.

Eric Mangini, defensive assistant-quality control; born January 19, 1971, Hartford, Conn., lives on Long Island, N.Y. Defensive tackle Wesleyan 1990-93. No pro playing experience. Pro coach: Baltimore Ravens 1996, joined Jets in 1997.

Bill Muir, offensive line; born October 26, 1942, Pittsburgh, lives on Long Island, N.Y. Tackle Susquehanna 1962-64. No pro playing experience. College coach: Susquehanna 1965, Delaware Valley 1966-67, Rhode Island 1970-71, Idaho State 1972-73, Southern Methodist 1976-77. Pro coach: Orlando (Continental Football League) 1968-69, Houston-Shreveport Steamer (WFL) 1975, New England Patriots 1982-88, Indianapolis Colts 1989-1991, Philadelphia Eagles 1992-94, joined Jets in 1995.

Mike Sweatman, special teams; born October 23, 1947, Kansas City, Mo., lives on Long Island, N.Y. Linebacker Kansas 1964-67. No pro playing experience. College coach: Kansas 1973-74, 1979-1982, Tulsa 1977-78, Tennessee 1983. Pro coach: Minnesota Vikings 1984, New York Giants 1985-1992, New England Patriots 1993-96, joined Jets in 1997.

Charlie Weis, offensive coordinator-F-backs; born March 30, 1956, Trenton, N.J., lives on Long Island, N.Y. Attended Notre Dame. No college or pro playing experience. College coach: South Carolina 1985-88. Pro coach: New York Giants 1990-92, New England Patriots 1993-96, joined Jets in 1997.

1999 FIRST-YEAR ROSTER

Name	Pos.	Ht.	Wt.	Birthdate	College	Hometown	How Acq.
Adderley, James	WR	6-2	195	12/13/76	Bethune-Cookman	Ft. Lauderdale, Fla.	FA
Bell, Geno (1)	DT	6-3	290	6/3/75	Arkansas	Columbia, S.C.	FA-'98
Brazzell, Chris (1)	WR	6-2	198	5/22/76	Angelo State	Alice, Tex.	D6b-'98
Collins, Odell	RB	6-2	240	11/4/73	Georgia	Athens, Ga.	FA
Conti, Eddie	WR	5-8	175	8/14/75	Delaware	Ocean, N.J.	FA
Farmer, Robert (1)	RB	5-11	217	3/4/74	Notre Dame	Bolingbrook, Ill.	FA-'97
Foreman, Shawn	WR	6-1	210	6/3/75	West Virginia	Chesapeake, Va.	FA
Hart, Lawrence (1)	TE	6-4	268	9/19/76	Southern	Shreveport, La.	D7-'98
Johnson, Dirk (1)	P	6-0	205	6/1/75	Northern Colorado	Montrose, Colo.	FA
Johnson, Olrick	LB	6-0	250	8/20/77	Florida A&M	Miami, Fla.	FA
Jones, Jermaine	CB-KR	5-8	173	7/25/76	Northwestern State, La.	Morgan City, La.	D5
Ledyard, Courtney	LB	6-2	240	3/9/77	Michigan State	Cleveland, Ohio	FA
Lee, Delphrine	CB	5-10	190	1/19/76	McNeese State	New Orleans, La.	FA
Lotysz, Greg	T	6-6	320	4/9/74	North Dakota	Thunder Bay, Ont., Canada	FA
Loverne, David	G	6-3	299	5/22/76	San Jose State	Concord, Calif.	D3
Machado, J.P.	G	6-4	295	1/6/76	Illinois	Monmouth, Ill.	D6b
Megna, Marc	LB	6-2	250	7/30/76	Richmond	Fall River, Mass.	D6a
Mills, Jason	T	6-5	315	7/18/76	Tulsa	Topeka, Kan.	FA
Musso, Brian (1)	WR-KR	6-0	190	9/11/75	Northwestern	Hinsdale, Ill.	FA-'98
Poles, Jason	S	6-3	220	4/20/75	Syracuse	Glassboro, N.J.	FA
Syvrud, J.J.	LB	6-3	265	5/10/77	Jamestown	Rock Springs, Wyo.	D7b
Thomas, Randy	G	6-4	301	1/19/76	Mississippi State	East Point, Ga.	D2
Wiggins, Jermaine	TE	6-2	250	1/18/75	Georgia	East Boston, Mass.	FA
Wiltz, Jason	DT	6-4	308	11/23/76	Nebraska	New Orleans, La.	D4
Young, Ryan	T	6-5	337	6/28/76	Kansas State	St. Louis, Mo.	D7a

The term NFL Rookie is defined as a player who is in his first season of professional football and has not been on the roster of another professional football team for any regular-season or postseason games. A Rookie is designated by an "R" on NFL rosters. Players who have been active in another professional football league or players who have NFL experience, including either preseason training camp or being on an Active List or Inactive List, or on Reserve/Injured or Reserve/Physically Unable to Perform for fewer than six regular-season games, are termed NFL First-Year Players. An NFL First-Year Player is designated by a "1" on NFL rosters. Thereafter, a player is credited with an additional year of experience for each season in which he accumulates six games on the Active List or Inactive List, or on Reserve/Injured or Reserve/Physically Unable to Perform.

NOTES

OAKLAND RAIDERS

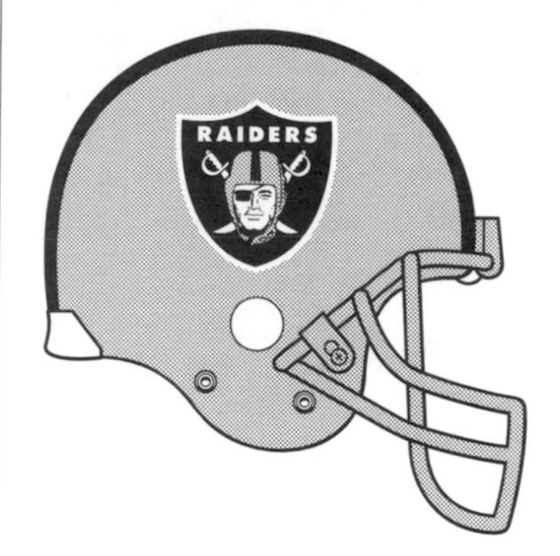

American Football Conference
Western Division
Team Colors: Silver and Black
1220 Harbor Bay Parkway
Alameda, California 94502
Telephone: (510) 864-5000

CLUB OFFICIALS

President of the General Partner: Al Davis
Chief Executive: Amy Trask
Executive Assistant: Al LoCasale
Senior Assistant: Bruce Allen
Personnel Executive: Chet Franklin, Michael Lombardi
Legal Affairs: Jeff Birren, Roxanne Kosarzycki
Finance: Marc Badain, Tom Blanda, Ron Lavelle, Derek Person
Senior Administrator: Morris Bradshaw
Senior Executive: John Herrera
Public Relations: Mike Taylor
Broadcasting & Multi-Media: Bill Zagger
Public Relations Assistant: Craig Long
Special Projects: Jim Otto
Bussiness Affairs: Scott Fink
Ticket Operations: Peter Eiges
Trainers: H. Rod Martin, Scott Touchet, Mark Mayer
Equipment Manager: Bob Romanski
Video Director: Dave Nash
Stadium: Network Associates Coliseum
•**Capacity:** 63,142
Playing Surface: Grass
Training Camp: Napa Valley Marriott
Napa, California 94558

1999 SCHEDULE

PRESEASON

Aug. 7	at St. Louis	7:00
Aug. 15	**Dallas**	1:00
Aug. 30	**San Francisco**	5:00
Sept. 3	at Arizona	7:00

REGULAR SEASON

Sept. 12	at Green Bay	12:00
Sept. 19	at Minnesota	12:00
Sept. 26	**Chicago**	1:15
Oct. 3	at Seattle	5:20
Oct. 10	**Denver**	1:15
Oct. 17	at Buffalo	1:00
Oct. 24	**New York Jets**	1:15
Oct. 31	**Miami**	1:05
Nov. 7	Open Date	
Nov. 14	**San Diego**	1:05
Nov. 22	at Denver (Mon.)	7:00
Nov. 28	**Kansas City**	1:15
Dec. 5	**Seattle**	1:15
Dec. 9	at Tennessee (Thurs.)	7:20
Dec. 19	**Tampa Bay**	1:05
Dec. 26	at San Diego	1:05
Jan. 2	at Kansas City	12:00

RECORD HOLDERS

INDIVIDUAL RECORDS—CAREER

Category	Name	Performance
Rushing (Yds.)	Marcus Allen, 1982-1992	8,545
Passing (Yds.)	Ken Stabler, 1970-79	19,078
Passing (TDs)	Ken Stabler, 1970-79	150
Receiving (No.)	Tim Brown, 1988-1998	680
Receiving (Yds.)	Tim Brown, 1988-1998	9,600
Interceptions	Willie Brown, 1967-1978	39
	Lester Hayes, 1977-1986	39
Punting (Avg.)	Leo Araguz, 1996-98	44.0
Punt Return (Avg.)	Claude Gibson, 1963-65	12.6
Kickoff Return (Avg.)	Jack Larscheid, 1960-61	28.4
Field Goals	Chris Bahr, 1980-88	162
Touchdowns (Tot.)	Marcus Allen, 1982-1992	98
Points	George Blanda, 1967-1975	863

INDIVIDUAL RECORDS—SINGLE SEASON

Category	Name	Performance
Rushing (Yds.)	Marcus Allen, 1985	1,759
Passing (Yds.)	Jeff George, 1997	3,917
Passing (TDs)	Daryle Lamonica, 1969	34
Receiving (No.)	Tim Brown 1997	104
Receiving (Yds.)	Tim Brown, 1997	1,408
Interceptions	Lester Hayes, 1980	13
Punting (Avg.)	Ray Guy, 1973	45.3
Punt Return (Avg.)	Claude Gibson, 1964	14.4
Kickoff Return (Avg.)	Harold Hart, 1975	30.5
Field Goals	Jeff Jaeger, 1993	35
Touchdowns (Tot.)	Marcus Allen, 1984	18
Points	Jeff Jaeger, 1993	132

INDIVIDUAL RECORDS—SINGLE GAME

Category	Name	Performance
Rushing (Yds.)	Napoleon Kaufman, 10-19-97	227
Passing (Yds.)	Jeff Hostetler, 10-31-93	424
Passing (TDs)	Tom Flores, 12-22-63	6
	Daryle Lamonica, 10-19-69	6
Receiving (No.)	Tim Brown, 12-21-97	14
Receiving (Yds.)	Art Powell, 12-22-63	247
Interceptions	Many times	3
	Last time by Terry McDaniel, 10-9-94	
Field Goals	Jeff Jaeger, 12-11-94	5
Touchdowns (Tot.)	Art Powell, 12-22-63	4
	Marcus Allen, 9-24-84	4
	Harvey Williams, 11-16-97	4
Points	Art Powell, 12-22-63	24
	Marcus Allen, 9-24-84	24
	Harvey Williams, 11-16-97	24

COACHING HISTORY

OAKLAND 1960-1981
LOS ANGELES 1982-1994
(361-244-11)

1960-61	Eddie Erdelatz*	6-10-0
1961-62	Marty Feldman**	2-15-0
1962	Red Conkright	1-8-0
1963-65	Al Davis	23-16-3
1966-68	John Rauch	35-10-1
1969-78	John Madden	112-39-7
1979-87	Tom Flores	91-56-0
1988-89	Mike Shanahan***	8-12-0
1989-94	Art Shell	56-41-0
1995-96	Mike White	15-17-0
1997	Joe Bugel	4-12-0
1998	Jon Gruden	8-8-0

*Released after two games in 1961
**Released after five games in 1962
***Released after four games in 1989

NETWORK ASSOCIATES COLISEUM

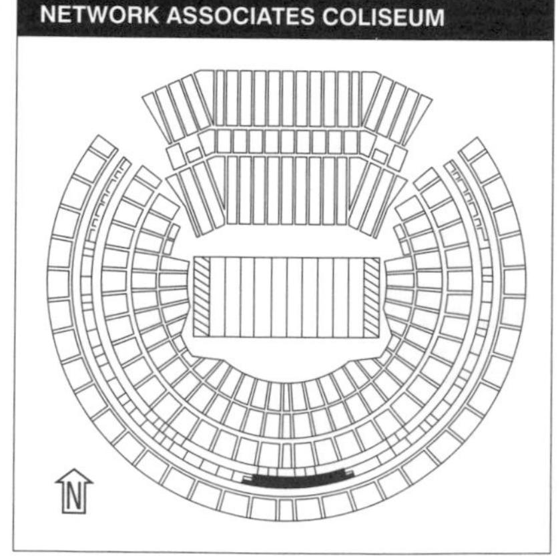

1998 TEAM RECORD

PRESEASON (2-2)

Date	Result		Opponent
8/8	W	16-3	at Dallas
8/16	W	27-21	at Green Bay
8/24	L	7-41	Tampa Bay
8/29	L	14-21	Arizona

REGULAR SEASON (8-8)

Date	Result		Opponent	Att.
9/6	L	8-28	at Kansas City	78,945
9/13	W	20-17	New York Giants	40,545
9/20	L	17-34	Denver	56,578
9/27	W	13-12	at Dallas	63,544
10/4	W	23-20	at Arizona	52,178
10/11	W	7-6	San Diego	42,467
10/25	W	27-10	Cincinnati	40,089
11/1	W	31-18	at Seattle	66,246
11/8	L	10-13	at Baltimore	69,037
11/15	W	20-17	Seattle	51,527
11/22	L	14-40	at Denver	75,325
11/29	L	19-29	Washington	41,409
12/6	L	17-27	Miami	61,254
12/13	L	21-44	at Buffalo	62,002
12/20	W	17-10	at San Diego	60,716
12/26	L	24-31	Kansas City	52,679

SCORE BY PERIODS

Raiders	51	92	66	79	0	—	288
Opponents	88	101	74	93	0	—	356

ATTENDANCE

Home 386,548 Away 527,993 Total 914,541
Single-game home record, 61,523 (9/8/97)
Single-season home record, 398,915 (1996)

1998 TEAM STATISTICS

	Raiders	Opp.
Total First Downs	273	273
Rushing	89	95
Passing	156	150
Penalty	28	28
Third Down: Made/Att	71/225	59/224
Third Down Pct.	31.6	26.3
Fourth Down: Made/Att.	6/13	9/20
Fourth Down Pct.	46.2	45.0
Total Net Yards	4,815	4,550
Avg. Per Game	300.9	284.4
Total Plays	1,035	1,020
Avg. Per Play	4.7	4.5
Net Yards Rushing	1,727	1,674
Avg. Per Game	107.9	104.6
Total Rushes	449	482
Net Yards Passing	3,088	2,876
Avg. Per Game	193	179.8
Sacked/Yards Lost	67/446	41/258
Gross Yards	3,534	3,134
Att./Completions	519/282	497/291
Completion Pct.	54.3	58.6
Had Intercepted	25	21
Punts/Avg.	98/43.4	96/44.8
Net Punting Avg.	98/33.4	96/36.6
Penalties/Yards Lost.	127/986	115/921
Fumbles/Ball Lost	38/18	26/14
Touchdowns	34	38
Rushing	6	8
Passing	21	22
Returns	7	8
Avg. Time of Possession	28:51	31:09

1998 INDIVIDUAL STATISTICS

Passing	Att.	Comp.	Yds.	Pct.	TD	Int.	Tkld.	Rate
Hollas	260	135	1,754	51.9	10	16	36/207	60.6
George	169	93	1,186	55.0	4	5	22/162	72.7
Wilson	88	52	568	59.1	7	4	9/77	85.8
Araguz	1	1	-1	100.0	0	0	0/0	79.2
H. Williams	1	1	27	100.0	0	0	0/0	118.8
Raiders	519	282	3,534	54.3	21	25	67/446	69.2
Opponents	497	291	3,134	58.6	22	21	41/258	74.3

SCORING	TD R	TD P	TD Rt	PAT	FG	Saf	PTS
Davis	0	0	0	31/31	17/27	0	82
T. Brown	0	9	0	0/0	0/0	0	54
Jett	0	6	0	0/0	0/0	0	36
Dudley	0	5	0	0/0	0/0	0	32
Howard	0	0	2	0/0	0/0	0	12
Kaufman	2	0	0	0/0	0/0	0	12
H. Williams	2	0	0	0/0	0/0	0	12
Ashmore	0	0	1	0/0	0/0	0	6
Hollas	1	0	0	0/0	0/0	0	6
Johnstone	0	0	1	0/0	0/0	0	6
Jordan	1	0	0	0/0	0/0	0	6
Lewis	0	0	1	0/0	0/0	0	6
Mickens	0	1	0	0/0	0/0	0	6
Turner	0	0	1	0/0	0/0	0	6
Woodson	0	0	1	0/0	0/0	0	6
Raiders	6	21	7	31/31	17/27	0	288
Opponents	8	22	8	36/36	28/37	3	356

2-Point conversions: Dudley. Team 1-3, Opponents 1-2.

RUSHING	Att.	Yds.	Avg.	LG	TD
Kaufman	217	921	4.2	80t	2
H. Williams	128	496	3.9	25t	2
Jordan	47	159	3.4	23	1
Hollas	29	120	4.1	14	1
Wilson	7	24	3.4	12	0
Ritchie	9	23	2.6	14	0
Jett	1	3	3.0	3	0
George	8	2	0.3	8	0
Dudley	1	-2	-2.0	-2	0
T. Brown	1	-7	-7.0	-7	0
Araguz	1	-12	-12.0	-12	0
Raiders	449	1,727	3.8	80t	6
Opponents	482	1,674	3.5	45	8

RECEIVING	No.	Yds.	Avg.	LG	TD
T. Brown	81	1,012	12.5	49	9
Jett	45	882	19.6	75t	6
Dudley	36	549	15.3	32	5
Ritchie	29	225	7.8	31	0
H. Williams	26	173	6.7	15	0
Kaufman	25	191	7.6	39	0
Mickens	24	346	14.4	32	1
D. Brown	7	89	12.7	27	0
Shedd	3	50	16.7	21	0
Jordan	3	2	0.7	2	0
Howard	2	16	8.0	10	0
Folston	1	-1	-1.0	-1	0
Raiders	282	3,534	12.5	75t	21
Opponents	291	3,134	10.8	55	22

INTERCEPTIONS	No.	Yds.	Avg.	LG	TD
Woodson	5	118	23.6	46t	1
Allen	5	59	11.8	22	0
Turner	3	108	36.0	94t	1
Lewis	2	74	37.0	74t	1
Walker	2	28	14.0	28	0
Newman	2	17	8.5	11	0
Wooden	1	14	14.0	14	0
Harvey	1	2	2.0	2	0
Raiders	21	420	20.0	94t	3
Opponents	25	435	17.4	80t	5

PUNTING	No.	Yds.	Avg.	In 20	LG
Araguz	98	4,256	43.4	29	64
Raiders	98	4,256	43.4	29	64
Opponents	96	4,300	44.8	29	76

PUNT RETURNS	No.	FC	Yds.	Avg.	LG	TD
Howard	45	13	541	12.0	75t	2
T. Brown	3	1	23	7.7	8	0
Brooks	1	0	0	0.0	0	0
Prior	1	0	0	0.0	0	0
Raiders	50	14	564	11.3	75t	2
Opponents	53	12	787	14.8	73	1

KICKOFF RETURNS	No.	Yds.	Avg.	LG	TD
Howard	49	1,040	21.2	42	0
Branch	5	70	14.0	27	0
R. Williams	4	63	15.8	21	0
Shedd	2	32	16.0	21	0
Amey	1	0	0.0	0	0
Morton	1	3	3.0	3	0
Raiders	62	1,208	19.5	42	0
Opponents	60	1,388	23.1	59	0

FIELD GOALS	1-19	20-29	30-39	40-49	50+
Davis	0/0	5/6	5/8	6/11	1/2
Raiders	0/0	5/6	5/8	6/11	1/2
Opponents	1/1	7/7	11/12	8/15	1/2

SACKS	No.
Johnstone	11.0
Russell	10.0
Harvey	4.0
Biekert	3.0
Jackson	3.0
Maryland	2.0
Swilling	2.0
Wooden	2.0
Folston	1.0
Harris	1.0
Lewis	1.0
Turner	1.0
Raiders	41.0
Opponents	67.0

1999 DRAFT CHOICES

Round	Name	Pos.	College
1	Matt Stinchcomb	T	Georgia
2	Tony Bryant	DE	Florida State
4	Dameane Douglas	WR	California
5	Eric Barton	LB	Maryland
	Roderick Coleman	LB	East Carolina
6	Daren Yancey	DT	Brigham Young
7	JoJuan Armour	LB	Miami, Ohio

OAKLAND RAIDERS

1999 VETERAN ROSTER

No.		Name	Pos.	Ht.	Wt.	Birthdate	NFL Exp.	College	Hometown	How Acq.	'98 Games/ Starts
21		Allen, Eric	CB	5-10	180	11/22/65	12	Arizona State	San Diego, Calif.	T(NO)-'98	10/10
92		Amey, Vincent	DE	6-3	300	9/9/75	2	Arizona State	Union City, Calif.	D7-'98	4/1
2		Araguz, Leo	P	5-11	190	1/18/70	4	Stephen F. Austin	Harlington, Tex.	FA-'96	16/0
73		Ashmore, Darryl	G	6-7	310	11/1/69	8	Northwestern	Peoria, Ill.	UFA(Wash)-'98	15/4
4		Barnes, Pat	QB	6-3	215	2/23/75	3	California	Trabuco Hills, Calif.	FA-'98	0*
58		Bellisari, Greg	LB	6-0	230	6/21/75	2	Ohio State	Boca Raton, Fla.	FA-'99	2/0*
54		Biekert, Greg	LB	6-2	240	3/14/69	7	Colorado	Longmont, Colo.	D7-'93	16/16
27		Branch, Calvin	S	5-11	195	5/8/74	3	Colorado State	Spring, Tex.	D6-'97	16/0
33		Brooks, Bucky	CB	6-0	195	1/22/71	5	North Carolina	Raleigh, N.C.	FA-'98	6/0
86	#	Brown, Derek	TE	6-6	265	3/31/70	8	Notre Dame	Fairfax, Va.	UFA(Jac)-'98	16/4
81		Brown, Tim	WR	6-0	195	7/22/66	12	Notre Dame	Dallas, Tex.	D1-'88	16/16
20		Carter, Perry	CB	6-0	195	8/5/71	3	Southern Mississippi	Magnolia, Miss.	FA-'96	6/0
79		Collins, Mo	T	6-4	320	9/22/76	2	Florida	Charlotte, N.C.	D1-'98	16/11
32		Crockett, Zack	RB	6-2	245	12/2/72	5	Florida State	Pompano Beach, Fla.	UFA(Jac)-'99	12/2*
68		Cunningham, Rick	G-T	6-7	315	1/4/69	9	Texas A&M	Beverly Hills, Calif.	FA-'96	12/0
7	#	Davis, Greg	K	6-0	220	10/20/65	12	The Citadel	Rome, Ga.	FA-'98	16/0
71		Davis, Isaac	G	6-3	315	4/8/72	5	Arkansas	Malvern, Ark.	FA-'99	0*
64		DiNapoli, Gennaro	G	6-3	300	5/25/75	2	Virginia Tech	Cazenovia, N.Y.	D4-'98	0*
83		Dudley, Rickey	TE	6-6	255	7/15/72	4	Ohio State	Hendersonville, Tex.	D1-'96	16/15
95		Faumui, Ta'ase	DT	6-3	285	3/19/71	3	Hawaii	Honolulu, Hawaii	FA-'99	0*
55		Folston, James	LB	6-3	240	8/14/71	6	Northeast Louisiana	Cocoa, Fla.	D2-'94	16/5
12		Gannon, Rich	QB	6-3	210	12/20/65	12	Delaware	Philadelphia, Pa.	UFA(KC)-'99	12/10*
74	#	Graham, Derrick	G	6-4	340	3/18/67	10	Appalachian State	Groveland, Fla.	UFA(Sea)-'98	12/12
77		Harlow, Pat	T	6-6	295	3/16/69	9	Southern California	Norco, Calif.	T(NE)-'96	5/5
93		Harris, James	DE	6-6	285	5/13/68	6	Temple	East St. Louis, Ill.	FA-'98	16/16
52		Harvey, Richard	LB	6-6	235	9/11/66	10	Tulane	Pasagoula, Miss.	FA-'98	16/16
49		Hinton, Marcus	TE	6-4	265	12/27/71	2	Alcorn State	Wiggins, Miss.	FA-'99	0*
12	#	Hollas, Donald	QB	6-3	215	11/22/67	7	Rice	Rosenberg, Tex.	FA-'97	12/6
80		Howard, Desmond	WR	5-10	185	5/15/70	8	Michigan	Cleveland, Ohio	UFA(GB)-'97	15/1
5		Husted, Michael	K	6-0	200	6/16/70	7	Virginia	Hampton, Va.	FA-'99	16/0*
90		Jackson, Grady	DT	6-2	315	1/21/73	3	Knoxville	Greensboro, Ala.	D6-'97	15/1
82		Jett, James	WR	5-10	165	12/28/70	7	West Virginia	Kearneysville, W. Va.	FA-'93	16/16
51		Johnstone, Lance	DE	6-4	250	6/11/73	4	Temple	Philadelphia, Pa.	D2-'96	16/15
88		Jones, Chris T.	WR	6-3	210	8/7/71	4	Miami	West Palm Beach, Fla.	UFA(Phil)-'99	0*
28		Jordon, Randy	RB	5-11	215	6/6/70	6	North Carolina	Manson, N.C.	FA-'98	16/0
26		Kaufman, Napoleon	RB	5-9	180	6/7/73	5	Washington	Lompoc, Calif.	D1-'95	13/13
72		Kennedy, Lincoln	T	6-6	330	2/12/71	7	Washington	San Diego, Calif.	T(Atl)-'96	16/16
29		Lewis, Albert	S	6-2	205	10/6/60	17	Grambling State	Mansfield, La.	UFA(KC)-'94	15/12
70		Malamala, Siupeli	T	6-5	305	1/15/69	7	Washington	Kailau, Hawaii	FA-'99	0*
67		Maryland, Russell	DT	6-1	295	3/22//69	9	Miami	Chicago, Ill.	UFA(Dall)-'96	15/15
85		Mickens, Terry	WR	6-1	200	2/21/71	6	Florida A&M	Tallahassee, Fla.	UFA(GB)-'98	16/2
31		Mincy, Charles	S	6-0	195	12/16/69	9	Washington	Los Angeles, Calif.	FA-'99	16/16*
30		Newman, Anthony	S	6-0	215	11/25/65	12	Oregon	Beaverton, Ore.	UFA(NO)-'98	11/11
98		Osborne, Chuck	DT	6-2	290	11/2/73	4	Arizona	Canyon Country, Calif.	FA-'98	6/0
41	#	Riddick, Louis	S	6-2	215	3/15/69	7	Pittsburgh	Perkasie, Pa.	FA-'98	15/3
40		Ritchie, Jon	RB	6-1	250	9/4/74	2	Stanford	Mechanicsburg, Pa.	D3-'98	15/10
63		Robbins, Barret	C	6-3	315	8/26/73	5	Texas Christian	Houston, Tex.	D2-'95	16/16
96		Russell, Darrell	DT	6-5	320	5/27/76	3	Southern California	San Diego, Calif.	D1-'97	16/16
84		Shedd, Kenny	WR	5-10	165	2/14/71	5	Northern Iowa	Davenport, Iowa	FA-'96	15/0
75		Shello, Kendel	DE	6-3	295	11/24/73	3	Southern	New Iberia, La.	FA-'99	6/1*
9		Shuler, Heath	QB	6-3	230	12/31/71	5	Tennessee	Bryson City, N.C.	FA-'99	0*
78		Skrepenak, Greg	G	6-7	340	1/31/70	7	Michigan	Wilkes-Barre, Pa.	FA-'99	0*
56	#	Swilling, Pat	DE	6-3	250	10/25/64	13	Georgia Tech	Toccoa, Ga.	FA-'95	16/0
62		Treu, Adam	C	6-5	300	6/24/74	3	Nebraska	Lincoln, Neb.	D3-'97	16/0
42		Turner, Eric	S	6-1	215	9/20/68	9	UCLA	Ventura, Calif.	FA-'97	6/6
47		Walker, Derrick	TE	6-0	250	6/23/67	9	Michigan	Chicago Heights, Ill.	FA-'99	0*
38		Walker, Marquis	CB	5-10	175	7/6/72	4	Southeast Missouri	St Louis, Mo.	FA-'98	16/7
11		Ware, Andre	QB	6-2	200	7/31/68	5	Houston	Dickinson, Tex.	FA-'99	0*
66	#	Wilkerson, Bruce	G	6-5	315	7/28/64	13	Tennessee	Knoxville, Tenn.	FA-'98	0*
22		Williams, Harvey	RB	6-2	220	4/22/67	9	Louisiana State	Hempstead, Tex.	UFA(KC)-'94	16/3
34		Williams, Jemaine	RB	6-0	235	7/3/72	2	Houston	Greenville, N.C.	FA-'98	10/0
89		Williams, Rodney	WR	6-0	195	8/15/73	2	Arizona	Palmdale, Calif.	FA-'98	1/0
16		Wilson, Wade	QB	6-3	210	2/1/59	19	East Texas State	Dallas, Tex.	FA-'98	5/3
76		Wisniewski, Steve	G	6-4	305	4/7/67	11	Penn State	Houston, Tex.	D2-'89	16/16
24		Woodson, Charles	CB	6-1	200	10/7/76	2	Michigan	Fremont, Ohio	D1-'98	16/16

* Barnes inactive for 6 games in '98; Bellisari played 2 games with Tampa Bay in '98; Crockett played 2 games with Indianapolis and 10 games with Jacksonville; I. Davis was inactive for 5 games with Minnesota; DiNapoli was inactive for 12 games; Faumui last active with Oakland in '97; Gannon played 12 games with Kansas City; Hinton last active with Oakland in '96; Husted played 16 games with Tampa Bay; Jones last active with Philadelphia in '97; Malamala inactive for 3 games with N.Y. Jets; Mincy played 16 games with Tampa Bay; Shello played 6 games with Indianapolis; Shuler inactive for 8 games with New Orleans; Skrepenak last active with Carolina in '97; D. Walker last active with Kansas City in '97; Ware last active with Detroit in '93; Wilkerson inactive for 7 games.

Unrestricted free agent; subject to development.

Players lost through free agency (3): QB Jeff George (Minn; 8 games in '98), LB Mike Morton (GB; 16), CB James Trapp (Balt; 16).

Also played with Raiders in '98—TE Jeremy Brigham (2 games), DE Aundray Bruce (1), LB Ernest Dixon (3), LB John Henry Mills (5), S Anthony Prior (4), LB Aaron Wallace (4).

COACHING STAFF

Head Coach,
Jon Gruden

Pro career: Became the twelfth head coach in Raiders history on January 22, 1998, after seven seasons as an NFL assistant coach. Guided Raiders to an 8-8 record as a 35-year-old rookie head coach in 1998. Gruden's teams reached the postseason five times during his assistant coaching tenure. Spent the last three years as offensive coordinator for the Philadelphia Eagles on Ray Rhodes's staff. The Eagles were 26-21-1 during this 1995-97 period, including playoff appearances after both the 1995 and 1996 seasons. In 1997, the Eagles ranked second in passing, fifth in rushing and third in total offense in the NFC. In 1996, they led the NFC in passing, were second in rushing and led the NFC in total offense. In 1995—his first season as an NFL offensive coordinator—the Eagles finished fourth in the league in rushing. He served as an offensive assistant to Green Bay Packers head coach Mike Holmgren in 1992, then spent the 1993 and 1994 campaigns as Green Bay's receivers coach. Gruden spent the 1991 season as wide receivers coach at the University of Pittsburgh under coach Paul Hackett. In 1990, he was an offensive assistant to head coach George Seifert with the San Francisco 49ers, working with offensive coordinator Holmgren. The 49ers were an NFL best 14-2 that season. Career record: 8-8.

Background: Quarterback at Dayton 1983-85, while earning bachelor's degree in communications. Won the prestigious Lt. Andy Zulli Memorial Award given annually "to the senior player who best exemplifies the qualities of sportsmanship and character." Dayton had a 24-7 record in Gruden's three varsity seasons there.

Personal: Born August 17, 1963, in Sandusky, Ohio. Gruden and his wife Cindy have two sons, Jon II, 4, and Michael, 1. His father, Jim, is a scout for the San Francisco 49ers and formerly served as an assistant coach under John McKay with the Tampa Bay Buccaneers from 1982-83. His brother Jay, who played in the Arena Football League, served as offensive coordinator of that league's Nashville team and is presently offensive coordinator of the Arena League's 1998 champion Orlando Predators.

1999 FIRST-YEAR ROSTER

Name	Pos.	Ht.	Wt.	Birthdate	College	Hometown	How Acq.
Armour, JoJuan	LB	5-11	220	7/10/76	Miami, Ohio	Toledo, Ohio	D7
Barnes, Marlon	RB	5-10	215	3/13/76	Colorado	Millington, Tenn.	FA
Barton, Eric	LB	6-2	245	9/29/77	Maryland	Alexandria, Va.	D5
Battle, James	WR	6-2	200	6/8/76	Oregon State	Pittsburg, Calif.	FA
Brigham, Marques	RB	5-11	205	4/26/77	Wyoming	Aurora, Colo.	FA
Brooks, Bobby (1)	LB	6-2	235	3/3/76	Fresno State	Vallejo, Calif.	FA
Bryant, Tony	DE	6-4	270	9/3/76	Florida State	Marathon, Fla.	D2
Cipa, Mike	C	6-4	300	5/8/76	Central Michigan	Rochester, Mich.	FA
Coleman, Roderick	LB	6-2	260	8/16/76	East Carolina	Philadelphia, Pa.	D5
Dalan, Aaron	T	6-7	325	10/19/75	Washington	Sequim, Wash.	FA
Douglas, Dameane	WR	6-0	195	3/15/76	California	Hanford, Calif.	D4
Dreisbach, Scott	QB	6-3	215	12/16/75	Michigan	Mishawaka, Ind.	FA
Eafon, Kelvin	RB	5-11	215	11/18/74	Arizona	Dallas, Tex.	FA
Freedman, Mitch	S	6-0	215	11/30/75	Arizona State	Phoenix, Ariz.	FA
Harris, Johnnie	S	6-2	210	8/21/72	Mississippi State	Chicago, Ill.	FA
Martucci, Nick	DE	6-4	255	4/19/77	Lehigh	Bangor, Pa.	FA
Maxwell, Howard	WR	6-1	200	10/7/72	New Mexico Highlands	Chester, Pa.	FA
Mustafa, Isiah (1)	WR	6-2	200	2/11/74	Arizona State	Oxnard, Calif.	FA
Palmer, Randy	TE	6-4	235	11/12/75	Texas A&M-Kingsville	Pleasonton, Tex.	FA
Rainville, Rob	G	6-4	325	9/6/76	Washington State	Lewiston, Idaho	FA
Ray, Marcus	S	5-11	215	8/14/76	Michigan	Columbus, Ohio	FA
Rutherford, Reynard (1)	RB	6-0	215	5/15/73	California	Benecia, Calif.	FA-'98
Smith, Travian (1)	LB	6-4	240	8/26/75	Oklahoma	Tatum, Tex.	D5-'98
Spann, Creig	WR	6-0	190	8/8/75	Arizona State	Phoenix, Ariz.	FA
Stinchcomb, Matt	T	6-6	310	6/3/77	Georgia	Lilburn, Ga.	D1
Sword, Sam	LB	6-1	240	12/9/74	Michigan	Saginaw, Mich.	FA
Taves, Josh (1)	DE	6-7	280	5/13/72	Northeastern	Yarmouth, Mass.	FA
Williams, K.D. (1)	LB	6-0	235	4/22/73	Henderson	Tampa, Fla.	FA
Yancey, Daren	DT	6-6	310	12/21/73	Brigham Young	Blackfoot, Idaho	D6

The term NFL Rookie is defined as a player who is in his first season of professional football and has not been on the roster of another professional football team for any regular-season or postseason games. A Rookie is designated by an "R" on NFL rosters. Players who have been active in another professional football league or players who have NFL experience, including either preseason training camp or being on an Active List or Inactive List, or on Reserve/Injured or Reserve/Physically Unable to Perform for fewer than six regular-season games, are termed NFL First-Year Players. An NFL First-Year Player is designated by a "1" on NFL rosters. Thereafter, a player is credited with an additional year of experience for each season in which he accumulates six games on the Active List or Inactive List, or on Reserve/Injured or Reserve/Physically Unable to Perform.

ASSISTANT COACHES

Fred Biletnikoff, wide receivers; born February 23, 1943, Erie, Pa., lives in San Ramon, Calif. Wide receiver Florida State 1962-64. Pro wide receiver Oakland Raiders 1965-1978, Montreal Alouettes (CFL) 1980. Inducted into Pro Football Hall of Fame in 1988. College coach: Palomar (Calif.) J.C. 1983, Diablo Valley (Calif.) J.C. 1984, 1986. Pro coach: Oakland Invaders (USFL) 1985, Calgary Stampeders (CFL) 1987-88, joined Raiders in 1989.

Chuck Bresnahan, defensive backs; born September 8, 1960, Springfield, Mass., lives in Alameda, Calif. Linebacker Navy 1979-1982. No pro playing experience. College coach: Navy 1983, 1986, Georgia Tech 1987-1991, Maine 1992-93. Pro coach: Cleveland Browns 1994-95, Indianapolis Colts 1996-97, joined Raiders in 1998.

Willie Brown, squad development; born December 2, 1940, Yazoo City, Miss., lives in Tracy, Calif. Defensive back Grambling 1959-1962. Pro defensive back Denver Broncos 1963-66, Oakland Raiders 1967-78. Inducted into Pro Football Hall of Fame in 1984. College coach: Long Beach State 1990-91 (head coach 1991). Pro coach: Oakland/Los Angeles Raiders 1979-1988, rejoined Raiders in 1995.

Bill Callahan, offensive coordinator-offensive line; born July 31, 1956, Chicago, lives in Danville, Calif. Quarterback Illinois-Benedictine 1975-77. No pro playing experience. College coach: Illinois 1980-86, Northern Arizona 1987-88, Southern Illinois 1989, Wisconsin 1990-94. Pro coach: Philadelphia Eagles 1995-97, joined Raiders in 1998.

Jim Erkenbeck, tight ends; born September 10, 1933, Los Angeles, lives in Alameda, Calif. Linebacker-end San Diego State 1949-1951. No pro playing experience. College coach: San Diego State 1961-63, Grossmont (Calif.) J.C. 1964-67 (head coach), Utah State 1968, Washington State 1969-1971, California 1972-76. Pro coach: Winnipeg Blue Bombers (CFL) 1977, Montreal Alouettes (CFL) 1978-1981, Calgary Stampeders (CFL) 1982, Philadelphia/Baltimore Stars (USFL) 1983-85, New Orleans Saints 1986, Dallas Cowboys 1987-88, Kansas City Chiefs 1989-1991, 1995-98, Los Angeles Rams 1992-94, joined Raiders in 1999.

Frank Gansz, Jr., special teams; born August 8, 1962, Greenville, S.C, lives Alameda, Calif. Defensive back The Citadel 1981-84. No pro playing experience. College coach: Kansas 1987, Pittsburgh 1988-89, Army 1990-91, Houston 1993-97. Pro coach: New York-New Jersey Knights (WLAF) 1992, joined Raiders in 1998.

Garrett Giemont, strength and conditioning; born August 31, 1957, Fullerton, Calif., lives in San Francisco. Attended Fullerton College. No college or pro playing experience. Pro coach: Los Angeles Rams 1990-91, joined Raiders in 1995.

Woodrow Lowe, defense; born June 9, 1954, Columbus, Ga., lives in Antioch, Calif. Linebacker Alabama 1973-75. Pro linebacker San Diego Chargers 1976-1986. Pro coach: Kansas City Chiefs 1995-98, joined Raiders in 1999.

Don Martin, quality control-defense; born September 17, 1949, Carrollton, Mo., lives Oakland. Running back Yale 1968-1970. Pro defensive back New England Patriots 1973, Kansas City Chiefs 1975, Tampa Bay Buccaneers 1976. College coach: Yale 1981-1996. Pro coach: Joined Raiders in 1998.

John Morton, offensive assistant; born September 24, 1969, Pontiac, Mich., lives in Castro Valley, Calif. Wide receiver Western Michigan 1991-92, Grand Rapids C.C. 1989-1990. Pro wide receiver Los Angeles Raiders 1993-94, Toronto Argonauts (CFL) 1995-96, Frankfurt Galaxy (WLAF) 1997. Pro coach: Joined Raiders in 1998.

Skip Peete, running backs, born January 30, 1963, Mesa, Ariz., lives in Alameda, Calif. Wide receiver Arizona 1981-82, Kansas 1984-85. Pro wide receiver New York Jets 1987. College coach: Pittsburgh 1988-92, Michigan State 1993-94, Rutgers 1995, UCLA 1996-97. Pro coach: Joined Raiders in 1998.

Robin Ross, linebackers; born August 17, 1954, Huntington Beach, Calif., lives in Alameda, Calif. Offensive lineman Rio Hondo C.C. 1973-74, Washington State 1975-76. No pro playing experience. College coach: Long Beach State 1977-1983, Cincinnati 1984-85, Washington State 1986, Iowa State 1987-1993, Western Washington 1994-95, Fresno State 1996, Oregon 1997-98. Pro coach: Joined Raiders in 1999.

David Shaw, quality control-offense; born July 31, 1972, San Diego, lives in Alameda, Calif. Wide receiver Stanford 1990-94. No pro playing experience. College coach: Western Washington 1995-96. Pro coach: Philadelphia Eagles 1997, joined Raiders in 1998.

Willie Shaw, defensive coordinator; born January 11, 1944, Glenmora, La., lives in Union City, Calif. Cornerback New Mexico 1966-68. No pro playing experience. College coach: San Diego C.C. 1970-73, Stanford 1974-76, 1989-1991, Long Beach State 1977-78, Oregon 1979, Arizona State 1980-84. Pro coach: Detroit Lions 1985-88, Minnesota Vikings 1992-93, San Diego Chargers 1994, St. Louis Rams 1995-96, New Orleans Saints 1997, joined Raiders in 1998.

Gary Stevens, quarterbacks; born March 19, 1943, Cleveland, lives in Alameda, Calif. Running back John Carroll 1963-65. No pro playing experience. College coach: Louisville 1971-74, Kent State 1975, West Virginia 1976-79, Miami 1980-88. Pro coach: Miami Dolphins 1989-1997, joined Raiders in 1998.

Mike Waufle, defensive line; born June 27, 1954, Hornell, N.Y., lives in Oakland. Defensive lineman Bakersfield J.C. 1975-76, Utah State 1977-78. No pro playing experience. College coach: Alfred 1979, Utah State 1980-84, Fresno State 1985-88, UCLA 1989, Oregon State 1990-91, California 1992-97. Pro coach: Joined Raiders in 1998.

PITTSBURGH STEELERS

American Football Conference
Central Division
Team Colors: Black and Gold
Three Rivers Stadium
300 Stadium Circle
Pittsburgh, Pennsylvania 15212
Telephone: (412) 323-0300

CLUB OFFICIALS

President: Daniel M. Rooney
Vice President/General Counsel: Arthur J. Rooney II
Vice President: John R. McGinley
Vice President: Arthur J. Rooney, Jr.
Administration Advisor: Charles H. Noll
Communications Coordinator: Ron Wahl
Public Relations/Media Manager: David Lockett
Director of Business: Mark Hart
Business Relations Coordinator: Dan Ferens
Business Accounting Coordinator: Jim Ellenberger
Director of Football Operations: Tom Donahoe
College Personnel Coordinator: Max McCartney
College Scouts: Mark Gorscak, Phil Kreidler, Bob Lane, Dan Rooney
Office/Ticket Coordinator: Geraldine R. Glenn
Ticket Manager: Brian Bonifate
Marketing Coordinator: Mark Fuhrman
Player Development Coordinator: Anthony Griggs
Trainers: John Norwig, Ryan Grove
Equipment Manager: Rodgers Freyvogel
Stadium: Three Rivers Stadium • **Capacity:** 59,600
300 Stadium Circle
Pittsburgh, Pennsylvania 15212
Playing Surface: AstroTurf
Training Camp: St. Vincent College
Latrobe, Pennsylvania 15650

1999 SCHEDULE

PRESEASON

Aug. 13	**Chicago**	7:30
Aug. 20	at Carolina	8:00
Aug. 28	**Washington**	7:30
Sept. 4	at Buffalo	7:30

REGULAR SEASON

Sept. 12	at Cleveland	8:20
Sept. 19	at Baltimore	1:00
Sept. 26	**Seattle**	1:00
Oct. 3	**Jacksonville**	1:00
Oct. 10	at Buffalo	1:00
Oct. 17	at Cincinnati	1:00
Oct. 25	**Atlanta** (Mon.)	9:00
Oct. 31	Open Date	
Nov. 7	at San Francisco	1:15
Nov. 14	**Cleveland**	1:00
Nov. 21	at Tennessee	12:00
Nov. 28	**Cincinnati**	1:00
Dec. 2	at Jacksonville (Thurs.)	8:20
Dec. 12	**Baltimore**	1:00
Dec. 18	at Kansas City (Sat.)	11:40
Dec. 26	**Carolina**	1:00
Jan. 2	**Tennessee**	4:15

RECORD HOLDERS

INDIVIDUAL RECORDS—CAREER

Category	Name	Performance
Rushing (Yds.)	Franco Harris, 1972-1983	11,950
Passing (Yds.)	Terry Bradshaw, 1970-1983	27,989
Passing (TDs)	Terry Bradshaw, 1970-1983	212
Receiving (No.)	John Stallworth, 1974-1987	537
Receiving (Yds.)	John Stallworth, 1974-1987	8,723
Interceptions	Mel Blount, 1970-1983	57
Punting (Avg.)	Bobby Joe Green, 1960-61	45.7
Punt Return (Avg.)	Bobby Gage, 1949-1950	14.9
Kickoff Return (Avg.)	Lynn Chandnois, 1950-56	29.6
Field Goals	Gary Anderson, 1982-1994	309
Touchdowns (Tot.)	Franco Harris, 1972-1983	100
Points	Gary Anderson, 1982-1994	1,343

INDIVIDUAL RECORDS—SINGLE SEASON

Category	Name	Performance
Rushing (Yds.)	Barry Foster, 1992	1,690
Passing (Yds.)	Terry Bradshaw, 1979	3,724
Passing (TDs)	Terry Bradshaw, 1978	28
Receiving (No.)	Yancey Thigpen, 1995	85
Receiving (Yds.)	Yancey Thigpen, 1997	1,398
Interceptions	Mel Blount, 1975	11
Punting (Avg.)	Bobby Joe Green, 1961	47.0
Punt Return (Avg.)	Bobby Gage, 1949	16.0
Kickoff Return (Avg.)	Lynn Chandnois, 1952	35.2
Field Goals	Norm Johnson, 1995	34
Touchdowns (Tot.)	Louis Lipps, 1985	15
Points	Norm Johnson, 1995	141

INDIVIDUAL RECORDS—SINGLE GAME

Category	Name	Performance
Rushing (Yds.)	John Fuqua, 12-20-70	218
Passing (Yds.)	Bobby Layne, 12-3-58	409
Passing (TDs)	Terry Bradshaw, 11-15-81	5
	Mark Malone, 9-8-85	5
Receiving (No.)	Courtney Hawkins, 11-1-98	14
Receiving (Yds.)	Buddy Dial, 10-22-61	235
Interceptions	Jack Butler, 12-13-53	*4
Field Goals	Gary Anderson, 10-23-88	6
Touchdowns (Tot.)	Ray Mathews, 10-17-54	4
	Roy Jefferson, 11-3-68	4
Points	Ray Mathews, 10-17-54	24
	Roy Jefferson, 11-3-68	24

*NFL Record

COACHING HISTORY

Pittsburgh Pirates 1933-1940
(446-459-20)

1933	Forrest (Jap) Douds	3-6-2
1934	Luby DiMelio	2-10-0
1935-36	Joe Bach	10-14-0
1937-39	Johnny (Blood) McNally*	6-19-0
1939-40	Walt Kiesling	3-13-3
1941	Bert Bell**	0-2-0
	Aldo (Buff) Donelli***	0-5-0
1941-44	Walt Kiesling****	13-20-2
1945	Jim Leonard	2-8-0
1946-47	Jock Sutherland	13-10-1
1948-51	Johnny Michelosen	20-26-2
1952-53	Joe Bach	11-13-0
1954-56	Walt Kiesling	14-22-0
1957-64	Raymond (Buddy) Parker	51-48-6
1965	Mike Nixon	2-12-0
1966-68	Bill Austin	11-28-3
1969-91	Chuck Noll	209-156-1
1992-98	Bill Cowher	76-47-0

*Released after three games in 1939
**Resigned after two games in 1941
***Released after five games in 1941
****Co-coach with Earle (Greasy) Neale in Philadelphia-Pittsburgh merger in 1943 and with Phil Handler in Chicago Cardinals-Pittsburgh merger in 1944

THREE RIVERS STADIUM

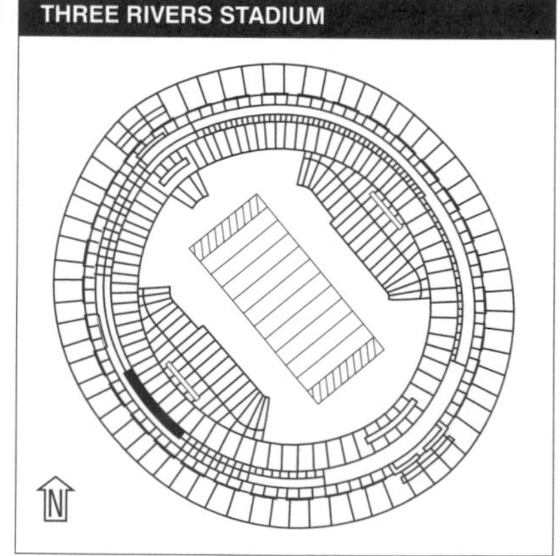

1998 TEAM RECORD

PRESEASON (3-2)

Date	Result		Opponent
8/1	L	6-30	at Tampa Bay
8/8	W	24-13	Buffalo
8/14	L	17-21	at Philadelphia
8/22	W	28-22	Atlanta
8/29	W	38-24	Carolina

REGULAR SEASON (7-9)

Date	Result		Opponent	Att.
9/6	W	20-13	at Baltimore	68,847
9/13	W	17-12	Chicago	59,084
9/20	L	0-21	at Miami	73,948
9/27	W	13-10	Seattle	58,413
10/11	L	20-25	at Cincinnati	59,979
10/18	W	16-6	Baltimore	58,620
10/26	W	20-13	at Kansas City	79,431
11/1	L	31-41	Tennessee	58,222
11/9	W	27-20	Green Bay	60,507
11/15	L	14-23	at Tennessee	41,104
11/22	W	30-15	Jacksonville	59,124
11/26	L	16-19	at Detroit (OT)	78,139
12/6	L	9-23	New England	58,632
12/13	L	3-16	at Tampa Bay	65,335
12/20	L	24-25	Cincinnati	52,017
12/28	L	3-21	at Jacksonville	74,143

(OT) Overtime

SCORE BY PERIODS

Steelers	40	86	70	67	0	—	263
Opponents	24	112	63	101	3	—	303

ATTENDANCE

Home 464,619 Away 540,926 Total 1,005,545
Single-game home record, 60,608 (12/18/94)
Single-season home record, 466,944 (1996)

1998 TEAM STATISTICS

	Steelers	Opp.
Total First Downs	268	266
Rushing	106	88
Passing	135	155
Penalty	27	23
Third Down: Made/Att	87/224	89/236
Third Down Pct.	38.8	37.7
Fourth Down: Made/Att	3/15	8/18
Fourth Down Pct.	20.0	44.4
Total Net Yards	4,586	4,963
Avg. Per Game	286.6	310.2
Total Plays	1,014	1,002
Avg. Per Play	4.5	5.0
Net Yards Rushing	2,034	1,642
Avg. Per Game	127.1	102.6
Total Rushes	490	479
Net Yards Passing	2,552	3,321
Avg. Per Game	159.5	207.6
Sacked/Yards Lost	35/229	41/238
Gross Yards	2,781	3,559
Att./Completions	489/274	482/268
Completion Pct.	56.0	55.6
Had Intercepted	20	16
Punts/Avg.	82/43.5	76/45.8
Net Punting Avg.	82/36.8	76/38.9
Penalties/Yards Lost	79/691	106/854
Fumbles/Ball Lost	18/12	28/13
Touchdowns	26	30
Rushing	8	8
Passing	13	17
Returns	5	5
Avg. Time of Possession	30:20	29:40

1998 INDIVIDUAL STATISTICS

Passing	Att.	Comp.	Yds.	Pct.	TD	Int.	Tkld.	Rate
Stewart	458	252	2,560	55.0	11	18	33/211	62.9
Tomczak	30	21	204	70.0	2	2	2/18	83.2
Ward	1	1	17	100.0	0	0	0/0	118.8
Steelers	489	274	2,781	56.0	13	20	35/229	64.3
Opponents	482	268	3,559	55.6	17	16	41/238	77.1

SCORING	TD R	TD P	TD Rt	PAT	FG	Saf	PTS
N. Johnson	0	0	0	21/21	26/31	0	99
C. Johnson	0	7	0	0/0	0/0	0	46
Bettis	3	0	0	0/0	0/0	0	18
Fuamatu-Ma'afala	2	1	0	0/0	0/0	0	18
Bruener	0	2	0	0/0	0/0	0	12
Stewart	2	0	0	0/0	0/0	0	12
Washington	0	0	2	0/0	0/0	0	12
Blackwell	0	1	0	0/0	0/0	0	8
Coleman	0	1	0	0/0	0/0	0	6
Hawkins	0	1	0	0/0	0/0	0	6
Huntley	1	0	0	0/0	0/0	0	6
Lake	0	0	1	0/0	0/0	0	6
McAfee	0	0	1	0/0	0/0	0	6
Oldham	0	0	1	0/0	0/0	0	6
George	0	0	0	2/2	0/1	0	2
Steelers	8	13	5	23/23	26/32	0	263
Opponents	8	17	5	23/24	32/41	0	303

2-Point conversions: C. Johnson 2, Blackwell. Team 3-3, Opponents 2-6.

RUSHING	Att.	Yds.	Avg.	LG	TD
Bettis	316	1,185	3.8	42	3
Stewart	81	406	5.0	56	2
Huntley	55	242	4.4	48	1
McAfee	18	111	6.2	14	0
Hawkins	10	41	4.1	14	0
Fuamatu-Ma'afala	7	30	4.3	10t	2
Ward	1	13	13.0	13	0
C. Johnson	1	4	4.0	4	0
Witman	1	2	2.0	2	0
Steelers	490	2,034	4.2	56	8
Opponents	479	1,642	3.4	37t	8

RECEIVING	No.	Yds.	Avg.	LG	TD
Hawkins	66	751	11.4	53	1
C. Johnson	65	815	12.5	55t	7
Blackwell	32	297	9.3	24t	1
Bruener	19	157	8.3	20	2
Bettis	16	90	5.6	26	0
Ward	15	246	16.4	45	0
Witman	13	74	5.7	15	0
Dunn	9	87	9.7	24	0
Fuamatu-Ma'afala	9	84	9.3	26t	1
Lester	9	46	5.1	9	0
McAfee	9	27	3.0	11	0
Coleman	4	49	12.3	13t	1
Lyons	3	19	6.3	11	0
Huntley	3	18	6.0	7	0
Stewart	1	17	17.0	17	0
Bishop	1	4	4.0	4	0
Steelers	274	2,781	10.1	55t	13
Opponents	268	3,559	13.3	86t	17

INTERCEPTIONS	No.	Yds.	Avg.	LG	TD
Washington	5	178	35.6	78t	2
Lake	4	33	8.3	27	1
Perry	2	69	34.5	40	0
Holmes	1	36	36.0	36	0
Oldham	1	14	14.0	14	0
Emmons	1	2	2.0	2	0
Flowers	1	2	2.0	2	0
Kirkland	1	1	1.0	1	0
Steelers	16	335	20.9	78t	3
Opponents	20	169	8.5	33	2

PUNTING	No.	Yds.	Avg.	In 20	LG
Miller	81	3,530	43.6	12	73
Stewart	1	35	35.0	0	35
Steelers	82	3,565	43.5	12	73
Opponents	76	3,482	45.8	13	71

PUNT RETURNS	No.	FC	Yds.	Avg.	LG	TD
Hawkins	15	8	175	11.7	47	0
Coleman	10	3	53	5.3	12	0
Arnold	4	1	19	4.8	8	0
Blackwell	4	4	22	5.5	13	0
Steelers	33	16	269	8.2	47	0
Opponents	30	18	310	10.3	46	0

KICKOFF RETURNS	No.	Yds.	Avg.	LG	TD
Dunn	21	525	25.0	44	0
Blackwell	20	382	19.1	43	0
Huntley	6	119	19.8	26	0
Arnold	3	78	26.0	31	0
Lyons	2	-4	-2.0	6	0
Gibson	1	9	9.0	9	0
McAfee	1	10	10.0	25	0
Roye	1	0	0.0	0	0
Bruener	0	-7	—	-7	0
Steelers	55	1,112	20.2	44	0
Opponents	64	1,212	18.9	53	0

FIELD GOALS	1-19	20-29	30-39	40-49	50+
N. Johnson	0/0	10/10	5/5	11/14	0/2
George	0/0	0/0	0/1	0/0	0/0
Steelers	0/0	10/10	5/6	11/14	0/2
Opponents	1/1	9/9	9/10	12/17	1/4

SACKS	No.
Gildon	11.0
Henry	4.0
Emmons	3.5
Harrison	3.5
Roye	3.5
D. Jones	3.0
Kirkland	2.5
Vrabel	2.5
Gibson	2.0
Holmes	1.5
Flowers	1.0
Lake	1.0
Steed	1.0
Oldham	0.5
Perry	0.5
Steelers	41.0
Opponents	35.0

1999 DRAFT CHOICES

Round	Name	Pos.	College
1	Troy Edwards	WR	Louisiana Tech
2	Scott Shields	DB	Weber State
3	Joey Porter	LB	Colorado State
	Kris Farris	T	UCLA
	Amos Zereoue	RB	West Virginia
4	Aaron Smith	DE	Northern Colorado
5	Jerame Tuman	TE	Michigan
	Malcolm Johnson	WR	Notre Dame
7	Antonio Dingle	DT	Virginia
	Chad Kelsay	LB	Nebraska
	Kris Brown	K	Nebraska

PITTSBURGH STEELERS

1999 VETERAN ROSTER

No.	Name	Pos.	Ht.	Wt.	Birthdate	NFL Exp.	College	Hometown	How Acq.	'98 Games/ Starts
36	Bettis, Jerome	RB	5-11	250	2/16/72	7	Notre Dame	Detroit, Mich.	T(StL)-'96	15/15
80	Bishop, Harold	TE	6-5	250	4/8/70	5	Louisiana State	Tuscaloosa, Ala.	FA-'98	7/1
89	Blackwell, Will	WR	6-0	190	7/6/75	3	San Diego State	Capitol Heights, Md.	D2-'97	16/1
60	Brown, Anthony	T	6-5	315	11/6/72	5	Utah	Salt Lake City, Utah	UFA(Cin)-'99	16/5*
29	Brown, Lance	CB-S	6-2	203	2/2/72	4	Indiana	Jacksonville, Fla.	FA-'97	16/0
87	Bruener, Mark	TE	6-4	261	9/16/72	5	Washington	Aberdeen, Wash.	D1-'95	16/16
78	Conrad, Chris	T	6-6	310	5/27/75	2	Fresno State	Fullerton, Calif.	D3a-'98	6/1
27	Davis, Travis	S	6-0	209	1/10/73	4	Notre Dame	Harbor City, Calif.	UFA(Jac)-'99	16/16*
63	Dawson, Dermontti	C	6-2	292	6/17/65	12	Kentucky	Lexington, Ky.	D2-'88	16/16
62	Duffy, Roger	G-C	6-3	299	7/16/67	10	Penn State	Canton, Ohio	UFA(NYJ)-'98	16/4
83	Dunn, David	WR	6-2	220	6/10/72	5	Fresno State	San Diego, Calif.	UFA(Cin)-'98	10/0
51	Emmons, Carlos	LB	6-5	250	9/3/73	4	Arkansas State	Greenwood, Miss.	D7-'96	15/14
65	Faneca, Alan	G	6-4	315	12/7/76	2	Louisiana State	New Orleans, La.	D1-'98	16/12
57	Fiala, John	LB	6-2	235	11/25/73	2	Washington	Kirkland, Wash.	FA-'98	16/0
41	Flowers, Lee	S	6-0	211	1/14/73	5	Georgia Tech	Columbia, S.C.	D5a-'95	16/16
45	Fuamatu-Ma'afala, Chris	RB	5-11	252	3/4/77	2	Utah	Honolulu, Hawaii	D6a-'98	12/0
72	Gandy, Wayne	T	6-5	310	2/10/71	6	Auburn	Haines City, Fla.	UFA(StL)-'99	16/16*
92	Gildon, Jason	LB	6-3	255	7/31/72	6	Oklahoma State	Altus, Okla.	D3a-'99	16/16
7	Gonzalez, Pete	QB	6-1	217	7/4/74	2	Pittsburgh	Miami, Fla.	FA-'98	0*
74	Harrison, Nolan	DE	6-5	291	1/25/69	9	Indiana	Chicago, Ill.	UFA(Oak)-'97	9/7
88	Hawkins, Courtney	WR	5-9	190	12/12/69	8	Michigan State	Flint, Mich.	UFA(TB)-'97	15/14
76	Henry, Kevin	DE	6-4	285	10/23/68	7	Mississippi State	Mound Bayou, Miss.	D4-'93	16/16
50	Holmes, Earl	LB	6-2	250	4/28/73	4	Florida A&M	Tallahassee, Fla.	D4a-'96	14/14
33	Huntley, Richard	RB	5-11	225	9/18/72	3	Winston Salem State	Monroe, N.C.	FA-'98	16/1
35	King, Carlos	RB	6-0	230	11/27/73	2	North Carolina State	Booneville, N.C.	D4b-'98	0*
99	Kirkland, Levon	LB	6-1	270	2/17/69	8	Clemson	Lamar, S.C.	D2-'92	16/16
85	Lyons, Mitch	TE	6-5	268	5/13/70	7	Michigan State	Grand Rapids, Mich.	UFA(Atl)-'97	15/0
4	Miller, Josh	P	6-3	219	7/14/70	4	Arizona	East Brunswick, N.J.	FA-'96	16/0
24	Oldham, Chris	S	5-9	200	10/26/68	9	Oregon	Sacramento, Calif.	UFA(Ariz)-'95	16/1
71	Roye, Orpheus	DE	6-4	288	1/21/74	4	Florida State	Miami Springs, Fla.	D6a-'96	16/9
30	Scott, Chad	CB-S	6-1	192	9/6/74	3	Maryland	Capitol Heights, Md.	D1-'97	0*
82	Shaw, Bobby	WR	6-0	186	4/23/75	2	California	San Francisco, Calif.	UFA(Sea)-'98	0*
23	Simmons, Jason	CB	5-8	186	3/30/76	2	Arizona State	Inglewood, Calif.	D5-'98	6/0
94	Staat, Jeremy	DE	6-5	300	10/10/76	2	Arizona State	Bakersfield, Calif.	D2-'98	6/0
68	Stai, Brenden	G	6-4	310	3/30/72	5	Nebraska	Anaheim, Calif.	D3-'95	16/16
93	Steed, Joel	NT	6-2	308	2/17/69	8	Colorado	Denver, Colo.	D3-'92	16/16
67	Stephens, Jamain	T	6-6	330	1/9/74	4	North Carolina A&T	Lumberton, N.C.	D1-'96	11/10
10	Stewart, Kordell	QB	6-1	211	10/16/72	5	Colorado	Marrero, La.	D2-'95	16/16
73	Strzelczyk, Justin	G-T	6-6	309	8/18/68	10	Maine	Seneca, N.Y.	D11-'90	7/7
66	Sweeney, Jim	C-G	6-4	297	8/8/62	16	Pittsburgh	Pittsburgh, Pa.	FA-'96	8/1
18	Tomczak, Mike	QB	6-1	210	10/23/62	15	Ohio State	Calumet City, Ill.	UFA(Clev)-'93	16/0
26	Townsend, Deshea	CB	5-10	175	9/8/75	2	Alabama	Batesville, Miss.	D4a-'98	12/0
84	t- Van Dyke, Alex	WR	6-0	205	7/24/74	4	Nevada	Sacramento, Calif.	T(NYJ)-'99	16/0*
56	Vrabel, Mike	LB	6-4	250	8/14/75	3	Ohio State	Stow, Ohio	D3b-'97	11/0
86	Ward, Hines	WR	6-0	197	3/8/76	2	Georgia	Rex, Ga.	D3b-'98	16/0
20	Washington, Dewayne	CB	6-0	193	12/27/72	6	North Carolina State	Durham, N.C.	UFA(Minn)-'98	16/16
38	Witman, Jon	RB	6-1	240	6/1/72	4	Penn State	Wrightsville, Pa.	D3b-'96	16/9

* Brown played 16 games with Cincinnati in '98; Davis started 16 games with Jacksonville; Gandy played 16 games with St. Louis; Gonzalez inactive for 16 games; King inactive for 7 games; Scott missed '98 season because of injury; Shaw inactive for 5 games; Van Dyke played 16 games with N.Y. Jets.

t- Steelers traded for Van Dyke (N.Y. Jets).

Traded—WR Jahine Arnold, 3 games in '98, to Green Bay.

Players lost through free agency (5): DE-DT Oliver Gibson (Cin; 16 games in '98), WR Charles Johnson (Phil; 16), LB Donta Jones (Car; 16), Carnell Lake (Jac; 16), Darren Perry (SD; 14).

Also played with Steelers in '98—LB Steve Conley (4), T Chris Conrad (2), P-K Matt George (1), CB-S John Jenkins (1), K Norm Johnson (15), RB Tim Lester (9), DE Rod Manuel (2), RB Fred McAfee (14), S Bo Orlando (11), C Mark Rodenhauser (16), T Will Wolford (13).

COACHING STAFF

Head Coach,
Bill Cowher

Pro Career: Begins his eighth season as the fifteenth head coach in Steelers' history, replacing Chuck Noll on January 21, 1992. In 1995, at age 38, he became the youngest coach to lead his team to a Super Bowl. Cowher is only the second coach in NFL history to lead his team to the playoffs in each of his first six seasons as head coach, the other coach is Pro Football Hall of Fame member Paul Brown. During Cowher's 14-year coaching career, teams he has been associated with have made the postseason 12 times. Began his NFL career as a free-agent linebacker with the Philadelphia Eagles in 1979, and then signed with the Cleveland Browns the following year. Cowher played three seasons (1980-82) in Cleveland before being traded back to the Eagles, where he played two more years (1983-84). Cowher began his coaching career in 1985 at age 28 under Marty Schottenheimer with the Browns. He was the Browns' special teams coach in 1985-86 and secondary coach in 1987-88 before following Schottenheimer to the Kansas City Chiefs in 1989 as defensive coordinator. Career record: 76-47.
Background: Excelled in football, basketball, and track for Carlynton High in Crafton, Pa. Was a three-year starter at linebacker for North Carolina State, serving as captain and earning team MVP honors as a senior. Graduated in 1979 with education degree.
Personal: Born in Pittsburgh, on May 8, 1957. His wife Kaye, also a North Carolina State graduate, played professional basketball for the New York Stars of the Women's Professional Basketball League with twin sister Faye. Bill and Kaye live in Pittsburgh and have three daughters—Meagan Lyn, Lauren Marie, and Lindsay Morgan.

ASSISTANT COACHES

Mike Archer, linebackers; born July 26, 1953, State College, Pa., lives in Pittsburgh. Safety/punter Miami 1972-75. No pro playing experience. College coach: Miami 1978-1983, Louisiana State 1984-1990 (head coach 1987-1990), Virginia 1991-92, Kentucky 1993-95. Pro coach: Joined Steelers in 1996.
Bob Bratkowski, receivers; born December 22, 1995, San Angelo, Tex., lives in Pittsburgh. Wide receiver Washington State. No pro playing experience. College coach: Missouri 1978-1980, Weber State 1981-85, Wyoming 1986, Washington State 1987-88, Miami 1989-1991. Pro coach: Seattle Seahawks 1992-98, joined Steelers in 1999.
Kevin Gilbride, offensive coordinator; born August 27, 1951, North Haven, Conn., lives in Pittsburgh. Quarterback/tight end Southern Connecticut State 1971-73. No pro playing experience. College coach: Idaho State 1974-75, Tufts 1976-77, American International 1978-79, Southern Connecticut 1980-84, East Carolina 1987-88. Pro coach: Ottawa Rough Riders (CFL) 1985-86, Houston Oilers 1989-1994, Jacksonville Jaguars 1995-96, San Diego Chargers 1997-98, joined Steelers in 1999.
Jim Haslett, defensive coordinator; born December 9, 1955, Pittsburgh, lives in Pittsburgh. Defensive end Indiana (Pa.) 1975-78. Linebacker Buffalo Bills 1979-1986, New York Jets 1987. College coach: Buffalo 1988-1990. Pro coach: Sacramento Surge (World League) 1991-92, Los Angeles Raiders 1993-94, New Orleans Saints 1995-96, joined Steelers in 1997.
Jay Hayes, special teams, born March 3, 1960, South Fayette, Pa., lives in Pittsburgh. Defensive end Idaho 1980-81. Pro defensive end/linebacker Michigan Panthers (USFL) 1984, Memphis Showboats (USFL) 1985. College coach: Notre Dame 1988-1991, California 1992-94, Wisconsin 1995-98. Pro coach: Joined Steelers in 1999.
Dick Hoak, running backs; born December 8, 1939, Jeannette, Pa., lives in Greensburg, Pa. Halfback-quarterback Penn State 1958-1960. Pro running back Pittsburgh Steelers 1961-1970. Pro coach: Joined Steelers in 1972.
Tim Lewis, defensive backs; born December 18, 1961, Quakertown, Pa., lives in Pittsburgh. Defensive back Pittsburgh 1979-1982. Pro cornerback Green Bay Packers 1983-86. College coach: Texas A&M 1987-88, Southern Methodist 1989-1992, Pittsburgh 1993-94. Pro coach: Joined Steelers in 1995.
John Mitchell, defensive line; born October 14, 1951, Mobile, Ala., lives in Pittsburgh. Defensive end Eastern Arizona J.C. 1969-1970, Alabama 1971-72. No pro playing experience. College coach: Alabama 1973-76, Arkansas 1977-1982, Temple 1986, Louisiana State 1987-1990. Pro coach: Birmingham Stallions (USFL) 1983-85, Cleveland Browns 1991-93, joined Steelers in 1994.
Mike Mularkey, tight ends; born November 19, 1961, Ft. Lauderdale, Fla., lives in Pittsburgh. Tight end Florida 1979-1982. Pro tight end Minnesota Vikings 1983-88, Pittsburgh Steelers 1989-1991. College coach: Concordia 1993. Pro coach: Tampa Bay Buccaneers 1994-95, joined Steelers in 1996.
Kent Stephenson, offensive line; born February 4, 1942, Anita, Iowa, lives in Pittsburgh. Guard-nose tackle Northern Iowa 1962-64. No pro playing experience. College coach: Wayne State 1965-68, North Dakota 1969-1971, Southern Methodist 1972-73, Iowa 1974-76, Oklahoma State 1977-78, Kansas 1979-1982. Pro coach: Michigan Panthers (USFL) 1983-84, Seattle Seahawks 1985-1991, joined Steelers in 1992.

1999 FIRST-YEAR ROSTER

Name	Pos.	Ht.	Wt.	Birthdate	College	Hometown	How Acq.
Brown, Ernie (1)	DE-DT	6-3	295	3/14/71	Syracuse	Pittsburgh, Pa.	FA
Brown, Kris	K	5-10	204	12/23/76	Nebraska	Southlake, Tex.	D7c
Carroll, Kevin	RB	6-0	245	5/26/76	West Georgia	Stockbridge, Ga.	FA
Cotten, Bobbie	LB	6-1	250	8/10/75	North Carolina State	Windsor, Va.	FA
Cushing, Matt (1)	TE	6-3	258	7/2/75	Illinois	Chicago, Ill.	FA
D'Amato, Tony	LB	6-0	242	11/16/76	Utah State	Long Beach, Calif.	FA
Davenport, Matt	K	5-10	171	6/8/77	Wisconsin	Mission Viejo, Calif.	FA
Dingle, Antonio	NT	6-2	315	10/7/76	Virginia	Fayetteville, N.C.	D7a
Farris, Kris	T	6-8	322	3/26/77	UCLA	Mission Viejo, Calif.	D3b
Fisher, Stephen	CB	5-10	183	5/20/76	North Carolina	New Bern, N.C.	FA
George, John	WR	5-10	166	7/7/75	Southern	LaFayette, La.	FA
Harper, Matt (1)	DE	6-4	273	4/28/74	Texas Christian	McKinney, Tex.	FA-'98
Homer, Kevin	LB	6-2	241	1/21/76	Chadron State	Casper, Wyo.	FA
Jenkins, Marcus	G	6-3	282	9/12/75	Central Florida	St. Petersburg, Fla.	FA
Johnson, Malcolm	WR	6-5	215	8/27/77	Notre Dame	Washington, D.C.	D5b
Joseph, Terrance (1)	CB-S	6-2	221	2/14/75	Tulsa	Midwest City, Okla.	FA-'98
Kelsay, Chad	LB	6-2	252	4/9/77	Nebraska	Auburn, Neb.	D7b
Kollar, Todd (1)	G-T	6-4	290	8/6/76	Youngstown State	North Lima, Ohio	FA
Lomax, Greg	RB	5-9	195	8/7/75	Akron	Monongahela, Pa.	FA
Olson, Ryan (1)	LB	6-2	255	6/27/75	Colorado	Wheat Ridge, Colo.	D6-'98
Orlandini, Tony (1)	G	6-5	310	8/13/75	Pittsburgh	West Wyoming, Pa.	FA-'98
Porter, Joey	LB	6-2	240	3/22/77	Colorado State	Bakersfield, Calif.	D3a
Scales, Shawn (1)	WR	5-11	193	3/5/73	Virginia Tech	Arlington, Va.	FA-'98
Shields, Scott	S	6-4	228	3/29/76	Weber State	San Diego, Calif.	D2
Smith, Aaron	DE	6-5	281	4/9/76	Northern Colorado	Colorado Springs, Colo.	D4
Torrance, Homer	S	5-11	210	2/1/75	South Carolina	Oakland, Fla.	FA
Tuman, Jerame	TE	6-3	250	3/24/76	Michigan	Liberal, Kan.	D5a
Wright, Anthony	QB	6-1	195	2/14/76	South Carolina	Vanceboro, N.C.	FA
Zereoue, Amos	RB	5-8	202	10/8/76	West Virginia	Hempstead, N.Y.	D3c

The term NFL Rookie is defined as a player who is in his first season of professional football and has not been on the roster of another professional football team for any regular-season or postseason games. A Rookie is designated by an "R" on NFL rosters. Players who have been active in another professional football league or players who have NFL experience, including either preseason training camp or being on an Active List or Inactive List, or on Reserve/Injured or Reserve/Physically Unable to Perform for fewer than six regular-season games, are termed NFL First-Year Players. An NFL First-Year Player is designated by a "1" on NFL rosters. Thereafter, a player is credited with an additional year of experience for each season in which he accumulates six games on the Active List or Inactive List, or on Reserve/Injured or Reserve/Physically Unable to Perform.

NOTES

SAN DIEGO CHARGERS

American Football Conference
Western Division
Team Colors: Navy Blue, White, and Gold
Qualcomm Stadium
P.O. Box 609609
San Diego, California 92160-9609
Telephone: (619) 874-4500

CLUB OFFICIALS

Chairman of the Board: Alex G. Spanos
President-Vice Chairman: Dean A. Spanos
Executive Vice President: Michael A. Spanos
General Manager: Bobby Beathard
Vice President-Finance: Jeremiah T. Murphy
Chief Financial and Administrative Officer: Jeanne Bonk
Director of Player Personnel: Billy Devaney
Director of Pro Personnel: Greg Gaines
Coordinator of Football Operations: Ed McGuire
Director of Sales & Marketing: Lynn Abramson
Business Manager: John Hinek
Director of Public Relations: Bill Johnston
Director of Ticket Sales & Guest Relations: Jerry McBurney
Director of Video Operations: Brian Duddy
Head Trainer: James Collins
Equipment Manager: Sid Brooks
Stadium: Qualcomm Stadium • **Capacity:** 71,000
9449 Friars Road
San Diego, California 92108
Playing Surface: Grass
Training Camp: University of California-San Diego
Third College
La Jolla, California 92037

1999 SCHEDULE

PRESEASON

Aug. 7	vs. Denver at Sydney, Australia	6:00
Aug. 12	at San Francisco	5:00
Aug. 21	**Miami**	8:00
Aug. 28	at St. Louis	7:00
Sept. 3	**Kansas City**	8:00

REGULAR SEASON

Sept. 12	Open Date	
Sept. 19	at Cincinnati	1:00
Sept. 26	**Indianapolis**	1:05
Oct. 3	**Kansas City**	1:15
Oct. 10	at Detroit	1:00
Oct. 17	**Seattle**	1:05
Oct. 24	**Green Bay**	1:05
Oct. 31	at Kansas City	12:00
Nov. 7	**Denver**	1:15
Nov. 14	at Oakland	1:05
Nov. 21	**Chicago**	1:15
Nov. 28	at Minnesota	12:00
Dec. 5	**Cleveland**	1:15
Dec. 12	at Seattle	1:05
Dec. 19	at Miami	1:00
Dec. 26	**Oakland**	1:05
Jan. 2	at Denver	2:15

RECORD HOLDERS

INDIVIDUAL RECORDS—CAREER

Category	Name	Performance
Rushing (Yds.)	Paul Lowe, 1960-67	4,963
Passing (Yds.)	Dan Fouts, 1973-1987	43,040
Passing (TDs)	Dan Fouts, 1973-1987	254
Receiving (No.)	Charlie Joiner, 1976-1986	586
Receiving (Yds.)	Lance Alworth, 1962-1970	9,585
Interceptions	Gill Byrd, 1983-1992	42
Punting (Avg.)	Darren Bennett, 1995-98	44.7
Punt Return (Avg.)	Darrien Gordon, 1993-96	13.6
Kickoff Return (Avg.)	Leslie (Speedy) Duncan, 1964-1970	25.3
Field Goals	John Carney, 1990-98	212
Touchdowns (Tot.)	Lance Alworth, 1962-1970	83
Points	John Carney, 1990-98	880

INDIVIDUAL RECORDS—SINGLE SEASON

Category	Name	Performance
Rushing (Yds.)	Natrone Means, 1994	1,350
Passing (Yds.)	Dan Fouts, 1981	4,802
Passing (TDs)	Dan Fouts, 1981	33
Receiving (No.)	Tony Martin, 1995	90
Receiving (Yds.)	Lance Alworth, 1965	1,602
Interceptions	Charlie McNeil, 1961	9
Punting (Avg.)	Darren Bennett, 1996	45.6
Punt Return (Avg.)	Leslie (Speedy) Duncan, 1965	15.5
Kickoff Return (Avg.)	Keith Lincoln, 1962	28.4
Field Goals	John Carney, 1994	34
Touchdowns (Tot.)	Chuck Muncie, 1981	19
Points	John Carney, 1994	135

INDIVIDUAL RECORDS—SINGLE GAME

Category	Name	Performance
Rushing (Yds.)	Gary Anderson, 12-18-88	217
Passing (Yds.)	Dan Fouts, 10-19-80, 12-11-82	444
Passing (TDs)	Dan Fouts, 11-22-81	6
Receiving (No.)	Kellen Winslow, 10-7-84	15
Receiving (Yds.)	Wes Chandler, 12-20-82	260
Interceptions	Many times	3
	Last time by Dwayne Harper, 11-27-95	
Field Goals	John Carney, 9-5-93, 9-18-93	6
	Greg Davis, 10-5-97	6
Touchdowns (Tot.)	Kellen Winslow, 11-22-81	5
Points	Kellen Winslow, 11-22-81	30

COACHING HISTORY

Los Angeles 1960
(289-298-11)

1960-69	Sid Gillman*	83-51-6
1969-70	Charlie Waller	9-7-3
1971	Sid Gillman**	4-6-0
1971-73	Harland Svare***	7-17-2
1973	Ron Waller	1-5-0
1974-78	Tommy Prothro****	21-39-0
1978-86	Don Coryell#	72-60-0
1986-88	Al Saunders	17-22-0
1989-91	Dan Henning	16-32-0
1992-96	Bobby Ross	50-36-0
1997-98	Kevin Gilbride##	6-16-0
1998	June Jones	3-7-0

*Retired after nine games in 1969
**Resigned after 10 games in 1971
***Resigned after eight games in 1973
****Resigned after four games in 1978
#Resigned after eight games in 1986
##Released after six games in 1998

QUALCOMM STADIUM

N

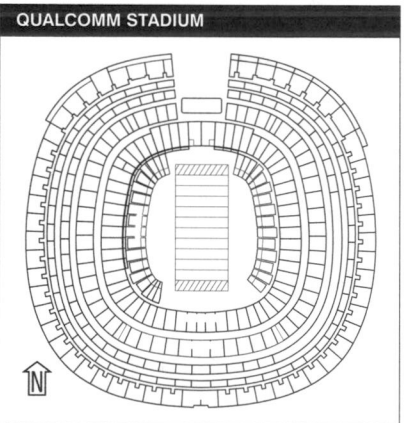

1998 TEAM RECORD

PRESEASON (3-1)

Date	Result		Opponent
8/8	W	27-21	San Francisco
8/15	W	41-27	St. Louis
8/22	W	33-3	at Indianapolis
8/28	L	28-42	at Minnesota

REGULAR SEASON (5-11)

Date	Result		Opponent	Att.
9/6	W	16-14	Buffalo	64,037
9/13	W	13-7	at Tennessee	41,089
9/20	L	7-23	at Kansas City	73,730
9/27	L	16-34	New York Giants	55,672
10/4	L	12-17	at Indianapolis	51,988
10/11	L	6-7	at Oakland	42,467
10/18	W	13-10	Philadelphia	56,967
10/25	L	20-27	Seattle	58,512
11/8	L	10-27	at Denver	74,925
11/15	W	14-13	Baltimore	54,388
11/22	W	38-37	Kansas City	59,894
11/29	L	16-31	Denver	66,532
12/6	L	20-24	at Washington	65,713
12/13	L	17-38	at Seattle	62,690
12/20	L	10-17	Oakland	60,716
12/27	L	13-16	at Arizona	71,670

SCORE BY PERIODS

Chargers	39	66	58	78	0	—	241
Opponents	94	101	71	76	0	—	342

ATTENDANCE

Home 476,718 Away 484,272 Total 960,990
Single-game home record, 66,532 (11/29/98)
Single-season home record, 479,842 (1994)

1998 TEAM STATISTICS

	Chargers	Opp.
Total First Downs	272	256
Rushing	95	72
Passing	146	149
Penalty	31	35
Third Down: Made/Att	78/237	68/227
Third Down Pct.	32.9	30.0
Fourth Down: Made/Att	8/17	6/13
Fourth Down Pct.	47.1	46.2
Total Net Yards	4,592	4,208
Avg. Per Game	287.0	263.0
Total Plays	1,063	991
Avg. Per Play	4.3	4.2
Net Yards Rushing	1,728	1,140
Avg. Per Game	108.0	71.3
Total Rushes	460	422
Net Yards Passing	2,864	3,068
Avg. Per Game	179.0	191.8
Sacked/Yards Lost	37/251	39/246
Gross Yards	3,115	3,314
Att./Completions	566/261	530/271
Completion Pct.	46.1	51.1
Had Intercepted	34	20
Punts/Avg.	95/43.9	103/44.1
Net Punting Avg.	95/36.8	103/36.0
Penalties/Yards Lost	137/1,229	120/1,005
Fumbles/Ball Lost	33/17	21/7
Touchdowns	23	38
Rushing	11	12
Passing	11	21
Returns	1	5
Avg. Time of Possession	31:17	28:44

1998 INDIVIDUAL STATISTICS

Passing	Att.	Comp.	Yds.	Pct.	TD	Int.	Tkld.	Rate
Whelihan	320	149	1,803	46.6	8	19	15/111	48.0
Leaf	245	111	1,289	45.3	2	15	22/140	39.0
Fletcher	1	1	23	100.0	1	0	0/0	158.3
Chargers	566	261	3,115	46.1	11	34	37/251	44.9
Opponents	530	271	3,314	51.1	21	20	39/246	68.2

SCORING	TD R	TD P	TD Rt	PAT	FG	Saf	PTS
Carney	0	0	0	19/19	26/30	0	97
Fletcher	5	0	0	0/0	0/0	0	30
Means	5	0	0	0/0	0/0	0	30
F. Jones	0	3	0	0/0	0/0	0	20
C. Jones	0	3	0	0/0	0/0	0	18
Ricks	0	2	0	0/0	0/0	0	12
Still	0	2	0	0/0	0/0	0	12
Stephens	1	0	0	0/0	0/0	0	6
Thelwell	0	1	0	0/0	0/0	0	6
J. Williams	0	0	1	0/0	0/0	0	6
Whelihan	0	0	0	0/0	0/0	0	2
Chargers	11	11	1	19/19	26/30	1	241
Opponents	12	21	5	37/37	25/34	0	342

2-Point conversions: F. Jones, Whelihan. Team 2-4, Opponents 1-1.

RUSHING	Att.	Yds.	Avg.	LG	TD
Means	212	883	4.2	72t	5
Fletcher	153	543	3.5	21	5
Stephens	35	122	3.5	12	1
Leaf	27	80	3.0	20	0
C. Jones	4	39	9.8	14	0
Whelihan	18	38	2.1	13	0
Bynum	11	23	2.1	14	0
Chargers	460	1,728	3.8	72t	11
Opponents	422	1,140	2.7	25	12

RECEIVING	No.	Yds.	Avg.	LG	TD
F. Jones	57	602	10.6	28	3
C. Jones	46	699	15.2	56	3
Still	43	605	14.1	67	2
Ricks	30	450	15.0	39t	2
Fletcher	30	188	6.3	22	0
Thelwell	16	268	16.8	55	1
Means	16	91	5.7	22	0
Slaughter	8	93	11.6	31	0
Bynum	4	27	6.8	12	0
W. Davis	4	23	5.8	8	0
Burke	3	32	10.7	17	0
Hartley	2	28	14.0	17	0
Stephens	2	9	4.5	5	0
Chargers	261	3,115	11.9	67	11
Opponents	271	3,314	12.2	81t	21

INTERCEPTIONS	No.	Yds.	Avg.	LG	TD
G. Jackson	6	50	8.3	25	0
Harrison	3	42	14.0	21	0
Dimry	3	38	12.7	30	0
Hand	2	47	23.5	30	0
Shaw	2	0	0.0	0	0
J. Williams	1	14	14.0	14t	1
Harper	1	12	12.0	12	0
Spencer	1	0	0.0	0	0
Turner	1	0	0.0	0	0
Chargers	20	203	10.2	30	1
Opponents	34	512	15.1	43t	2

PUNTING	No.	Yds.	Avg.	In 20	LG
Bennett	95	4,174	43.9	27	65
Chargers	95	4,174	43.9	27	65
Opponents	103	4,546	44.1	24	63

PUNT RETURNS	No.	FC	Yds.	Avg.	LG	TD
Rachal	32	8	387	12.1	56	0
Gaiter	13	6	155	11.9	49	0
Chargers	45	14	542	12.0	56	0
Opponents	49	18	515	10.5	74t	1

KICKOFF RETURNS	No.	Yds.	Avg.	LG	TD
Bynum	19	345	18.2	30	0
Stephens	16	349	21.8	36	0
Gaiter	16	295	18.4	33	0
Rachal	11	192	17.5	25	0
Fletcher	3	71	23.7	36	0
C. Jones	2	25	12.5	17	0
Burke	1	5	5.0	5	0
Hartley	1	11	11.0	11	0
Jacox	1	0	0.0	0	0
Chargers	70	1,293	18.5	36	0
Opponents	54	1,484	27.5	101t	1

FIELD GOALS	1-19	20-29	30-39	40-49	50+
Carney	0/0	11/12	5/5	8/10	2/3
Chargers	0/0	11/12	5/5	8/10	2/3
Opponents	1/1	5/6	10/12	6/11	3/4

SACKS	No.
Hand	6.0
Johnson	5.5
Harrison	4.0
Coleman	3.5
Seau	3.5
Fuller	3.0
Dixon	2.5
Mims	2.0
Parrella	1.5
Bush	1.0
Dumas	1.0
Mohring	1.0
Tovar	1.0
Turner	1.0
Gouveia	0.5
Chargers	39.0
Opponents	37.0

1999 DRAFT CHOICES

Round	Name	Pos.	College
2	Jermaine Fazande	RB	Oklahoma
3	Steve Heiden	TE	South Dakota State
4	Jason Perry	DB	North Carolina State
5	Adrian Dingle	DE	Clemson
	Reggie Nelson	G	McNeese State
6	Tyrone Bell	DB	North Alabama

SAN DIEGO CHARGERS

1999 VETERAN ROSTER

No.		Name	Pos.	Ht.	Wt.	Birthdate	NFL Exp.	College	Hometown	How Acq.	'98 Games/ Starts
2		Bennett, Darren	P	6-5	235	1/9/65	5	No College	Perth, Australia	FA-'95	16/0
50		Binn, David	C	6-3	250	2/6/72	6	California	San Mateo, Calif.	FA-'94	15/0
69		Bordelon, Ben	T	6-6	305	4/9/74	2	Louisiana State	Mathews, La.	FA-'97	0*
25		Bradford, Paul	CB	5-8	185	4/20/74	3	Portland State	Palo Alto, Calif.	D5b-'97	0*
83		Burke, John	TE	6-3	250	9/7/71	6	Virginia Tech	Elizabeth, N.J.	FA-'98	10/6
58		Bush, Lew	LB	6-2	245	12/2/69	7	Washington State	Tacoma, Wash.	D4b-'93	10/10
43		Bynum, Kenny	RB	5-11	191	5/29/74	3	South Carolina State	Gainesville, Fla.	D5a-'97	10/0
3		Carney, John	K	5-11	175	4/20/64	10	Notre Dame	West Palm Beach, Fla.	FA-'90	16/0
90	#	Coleman, Marco	DE	6-3	267	12/18/69	8	Georgia Tech	Dayton, Ohio	UFA(Mia)-'96	16/16
89		Davis, Wendell	TE	6-2	246	10/24/75	2	Temple	Escatawpa, Miss.	FA-'98	11/7
27		Dimry, Charles	CB	6-0	176	1/31/66	12	Nevada-Las Vegas	Oceanside, Calif.	UFA(Phil)-'98	16/15
51		Dixon, Gerald	LB	6-3	250	6/20/69	8	South Carolina	Rock Hill, S.C.	UFA(Cin)-'98	16/6
38		Dumas, Michael	S	6-0	198	3/18/69	8	Indiana	Lowell, Mich.	FA-'97	3/3
6		Ethridge, Ray	WR	5-10	180	12/12/68	3	Pasadena City College	San Diego, Calif.	FA-'99	0*
41		Fletcher, Terrell	RB	5-8	196	9/14/73	5	Wisconsin	St. Louis, Mo.	D2b-'95	12/5
72		Fontenot, Al	DE	6-4	287	9/17/70	7	Baylor	Houston, Tex.	UFA(Ind)-'99	7/5
67		Fortin, Roman	C-G	6-5	297	2/26/67	10	San Diego State	Ventura, Calif.	FA-'98	16/16
85		Gaiter, Tony	WR-KR	5-8	170	7/15/74	3	Miami	Miami, Fla.	FA-'98	5/0
81		Graham, Jeff	WR	6-2	206	2/14/69	9	Ohio State	Dayton, Ohio	FA-'99	15/15*
53		Hamilton, Michael	LB	6-2	245	12/3/73	3	North Carolina A&T	Greenville, S.C.	D3-'97	13/0
96		Hand, Norman	DT	6-3	313	9/4/72	5	Mississippi	Walterboro, S.C.	W(Mia)-'97	16/16
4	t-	Harbaugh, Jim	QB	6-3	215	1/23/63	13	Michigan	Palo Alto, Calif.	T(Balt)-'99	14/12*
28		Harper, Dwayne	CB	5-11	175	3/29/66	12	South Carolina State	Orangeburg, S.C.	UFA(Sea)-'94	1/1
37		Harrison, Rodney	S	6-1	207	12/15/72	6	Western Illinois	Chicago Heights, Ill.	D5b-'94	16/16
59		Haskins, Jon	LB	6-2	245	10/6/75	2	Stanford	Sarasota, Fla.	FA-'99	2/0
54		Hill, Eric	LB	6-2	265	11/14/66	11	Louisiana State	Galveston, Tex.	UFA(StL)-'99	15/15*
91		Ifeanyichukwu, Israel	DE	6-3	260	11/21/70	2	Southern California	Lagos, Nigeria	FA-'98	0*
65		Jackson, John	T	6-6	297	1/4/65	12	Eastern Kentucky	Cincinnati, Ohio	UFA(Pitt)-'98	16/16
64		Jacox, Kendyl	G	6-2	330	6/10/75	2	Kansas State	Dallas, Tex.	FA-'98	16/6
25		Johnson, Melvin	S	6-0	205	4/15/72	5	Kentucky	Cincinnati, Ohio	FA-'99	7/1*
99		Johnson, Raylee	DE	6-3	272	6/1/70	7	Arkansas	Fordyce, Ark.	D4a-'93	16/3
82		Jones, Charlie	WR	5-8	175	12/1/72	4	Fresno State	Lemoore, Calif.	D4-'96	16/11
88		Jones, Freddie	TE	6-4	255	9/16/74	3	North Carolina	Landover, Md.	D2-'97	16/16
16		Leaf, Ryan	QB	6-5	235	5/15/76	2	Washington State	Great Falls, Mont.	D1-'98	10/9
36		Lee, Lloyd	S	6-2	215	8/10/76	2	Dartmouth	Bloomington, Minn.	FA-'98	8/0
84		Lewis, Thomas	WR	6-1	195	1/10/72	5	Indiana	Akron, Ohio	FA-'99	0*
44		McCrary, Fred	RB	6-0	235	9/19/72	3	Mississippi State	Naples, Fla.	FA-'99	0*
20		Means, Natrone	RB	5-10	245	4/26/72	7	North Carolina	Harrisburg, N.C.	UFA(Jac)-'98	10/10
78		Miller, Bronzell	DE	6-4	275	10/12/71	2	Utah	Seattle, Wash.	FA-'99	0*
94		Mims, Chris	DE-DT	6-5	300	9/29/70	8	Tennessee	Los Angeles, Calif.	FA-'98	6/0
98		Mohring, Michael	DE-DT	6-5	295	3/22/74	3	Pittsburgh	West Chester, Pa.	FA-'97	10/0
70		Parker, Vaughn	T	6-3	300	6/5/71	6	UCLA	Buffalo, N.Y.	D2b-'94	6/6
97		Parrella, John	DT	6-3	300	11/22/69	7	Nebraska	Topeka, Kan.	FA-'94	16/16
39		Perry, Darren	S	5-11	199	1/29/68	8	Penn State	Chesapeake, Va.	UFA(Pitt)-'99	14/14*
79		Price, Marcus	G-T	6-6	321	3/3/72	3	Louisiana State	Port Arthur, Tex.	FA-'97	10/0
49		Pupunu, Al	TE	6-2	260	10/17/69	7	Weber State	Salt Lake City, Utah	FA-'99	9/0*
33		Raymond, Corey	CB	5-11	185	7/28/69	6	Louisiana State	New Iberia, La.	FA-'99	0*
86		Ricks, Mikhael	WR	6-5	237	11/14/74	2	Stephen F. Austin	Anahuac, Tex.	D2-'98	16/9
74		Roundtree, Raleigh	T	6-4	295	8/31/75	3	South Carolina State	Augusta, Ga.	D4-'97	15/5
26		Rusk, Reggie	CB	5-10	190	12/19/72	2	Kentucky	Texas City, Tex.	FA-'98	0*
55		Seau, Junior	LB	6-3	250	1/19/69	10	Southern California	Oceanside, Calif.	D1-'90	16/16
29		Shaw, Terrance	CB	5-11	190	11/11/73	5	Stephen F. Austin	Marshall, Tex.	D2a-'95	13/13
95		Sienkiewicz, Troy	DT	6-5	300	5/27/72	5	New Mexico State	Alamogordo, N.M.	D6a-'95	7/0
57		Simien, Tracy	LB	6-1	250	5/21/67	8	Texas Christian	Sweeny, Tex.	FA-'99	0*
22		Spencer, Jimmy	CB	5-10	185	3/29/69	8	Florida	Belle Glade, Fla.	FA-'98	15/4
34		Stephens, Tremayne	RB	5-11	206	4/16/76	2	North Carolina State	Greer, S.C.	FA-'98	13/1
80	†	Still, Bryan	WR	5-11	174	6/3/74	4	Virginia Tech	Richmond, Va.	D2a-'96	14/9
73		Taylor, Aaron	G	6-4	305	11/14/72	6	Notre Dame	Concord, Calif.	UFA(GB)-'98	15/15
87		Thelwell, Ryan	WR	6-2	188	4/6/73	2	Minnesota	London, Ontario, Canada	FA-'98	6/3
21		Turner, Scott	CB	5-10	180	2/26/72	5	Illinois	Richardson, Tex.	FA-'98	16/1
77		Walker, Bruce	DT	6-4	310	7/8/72	2	UCLA	Compton, Calif.	FA-'99	0*
5		Whelihan, Craig	QB	6-5	220	4/15/71	5	Pacific	San Jose, Calif.	D6c-'95	10/7
76		Williams, Jamal	DT	6-3	305	4/28/76	2	Oklahoma State	Washington, D.C.	D2(Supp)-'98	9/0

* Bordelon last active with San Diego in '97; Bradford missed '98 season because of injury; Ethridge last active with Baltimore in '97; Fontenot played 7 games with Indianapolis; Graham played 15 games with Philadelphia in '98; Harbaugh played 14 games with Baltimore; Hill played 15 games with St. Louis; Ifeanyichukwu last active with San Francisco in '96; M. Johnson played 7 games with Kansas City; Lewis last active with the N.Y. Giants in '97; McCrary last active with New Orleans in '97; Miller last active with Jacksonville in '95; Perry played 14 games with Pittsburgh; Pupunu played 9 games with N.Y. Giants; Raymond last active with Detroit in '97; Rusk last active with Seattle and Tampa Bay in '97; Simien last active with Kansas City in '97; Walker last active with New England in '95.

\# Unrestricted free agent; subject to developments.

† Restricted free agent; subject to developments.

t- Chargers traded for Harbaugh (Baltimore).

Retired—William Fuller, 14-year defensive end, 13 games in '98.

Players lost through free agency (2): G-T Raleigh McKenzie (GB; 16 games in '98); LB Steve Tovar (Car; 16).

Also played with the Chargers in '98—LB James Burgess (16 games), CB Willie Clark (5), S Dedrick Dodge (8), LB Kurt Gouveia (14), TE Frank Hartley (16), S Greg Jackson (16), C Marc Raab (1), WR Latario Rachal (11), WR Webster Slaughter (10), S Gerome Williams (16).

COACHING STAFF

Head Coach,
Mike Riley

Pro Career: Mike Riley was named the twelfth head coach in Chargers history on January 10, 1999. Riley has 24 years of coaching experience. He has spent eight seasons as a head coach, including two on the collegiate level (Oregon State 1997-98), four in the Canadian Football League (Winnipeg 1987-1990) and two in the World League (San Antonio 1991-92). While coach at Winnipeg, the Blue Bombers posted a record of 40-32 and two Grey Cup championships. Riley was named the CFL's coach of the year following the 1988 and 1990 seasons. He also spent three seasons (1983-85) as Winnipeg's secondary coach, winning the 1984 Grey Cup championship. Riley led the San Antonio Riders to a record of 11-9 in two World League seasons. His career professional record is 51-41.

Background: Collegiately, Riley won two national championships, one as a player and one as a coach, and three bowl games. Riley spent two seasons (1997-98) as the head coach at Oregon State, where he led the Beavers to their best record in 27 years. Riley served as assistant head coach and offensive coordinator-quarterbacks coach at Southern California (1993-96). In 1986, Riley was the defensive coordinator and secondary coach at Northern Colorado. Riley was a coach at Linfield College (1977-1982) in McMinnville, Oregon, winning the 1982 NAIA championship. Riley served as a graduate assistant at Whitworth College (1976) in Spokane, Washington, and began his coaching career as a graduate assistant at California (1975). As a high school athlete, he helped lead Corvallis High to state championships in football, basketball, and baseball as a senior. In college, he played defensive back under Paul (Bear) Bryant at Alabama (1971-74). During that period, the Crimson Tide won the 1973 national crown. Riley graduated from Alabama (1975) with a bachelor's degree in social science and earned his master's degree from Whitworth (1977).

Personal: Born July 6, 1953 in Wallace, Idaho. Mike and his wife, Dee, have two children—Matthew and Kate.

ASSISTANT COACHES

DelVaughn Alexander, offensive assistant; born July 16, 1971, Los Angeles, lives in San Diego. Wide receiver Southern California 1993-94. No pro playing experience. College coach: Southern California 1995-97, Nevada-Las Vegas 1998. Pro coach: Joined Chargers in 1999.

Mark Banker, defensive coverage; born January 15, 1956, in Plymouth, Mass., lives in San Diego. Running back Springfield College 1975-77. No pro playing experience. College coach: Springfield 1978-1980, Cal State-Northridge 1981-1994, Hawaii 1995, Southern California 1996, Oregon State 1997-98. Pro coach: Joined Chargers in 1999.

Joe Bugel, offensive line; born March 10, 1940, Pittsburgh, lives in San Diego. Guard-linebacker Western Kentucky 1960-63. No pro playing experience. College coach: Western Kentucky 1964-68, Navy 1969-1972, Iowa State 1973, Ohio State 1974. Pro coach: Detroit Lions 1975-76, Houston Oilers 1977-1980, Washington Redskins 1981-89, Phoenix Cardinals 1990-93 (head coach), Oakland Raiders 1995-97 (head coach 1997), joined Chargers in 1998.

Geep Chryst, quarterbacks-offensive coordinator; born June 25, 1962, Madison, Wisc., lives in San Diego. Linebacker Princeton 1981-84. Pro linebacker Orlando Thunder (World League) 1992. College coach: Wisconsin-Platteville 1987, Wisconsin 1988-1990. Pro coach: Orlando Thunder (World League) 1991, Chicago Bears 1991-95, Arizona Cardinals 1996-98, joined Chargers in 1999.

Paul Chryst, tight ends; born November 17, 1965, in Madison, Wisc., lives in San Diego. Quarterback-linebacker-tight end-holder Wisconsin 1986-88. No pro playing experience. College coach: West Virginia 1989-1990, Wisconsin-Platteville 1993, Illinois State 1995, Oregon State 1997-98. Pro coach: San Antonio Riders (World League) 1991-92, Edmonton Eskimos (CFL) 1993, Ottawa Rough Riders (CFL) 1994, Saskatchewan Roughriders (CFL) 1996, joined Chargers in 1999.

John Hastings, strength and conditioning; born July 5, 1964, in Newport News, Va., lives in San Marcos, Calif. No college or pro playing experience. Pro coach: Joined Chargers in 1990.

Kevin Lempa, defensive assistant; born July 17, 1952, in Jersey City, N.J., lives in San Diego. Wide receiver Southern Connecticut State 1970-73. No pro playing experience. College coach: Southern Connecticut State 1974-75, Wesleyan 1976, Maine 1977-1980, Boston College 1981-1990, Dartmouth 1991-96. Pro coach: Joined Chargers in 1997.

Wayne Nunnely, defensive line; born March 29, 1952, Los Angeles, lives in San Diego. Fullback Nevada-Las Vegas 1972-75. No pro playing experience. College coach: Nevada-Las Vegas 1976, 1982-89 (head coach 1986-89), Cal Poly-Pomona 1977-78, Cal State-Fullerton 1979, Pacific 1980-81, Southern California 1991-92, UCLA 1993-94. Pro coach: New Orleans Saints 1995-96, joined Chargers in 1997.

Joe Pascale, defensive coordinator; born April 4, 1946, New York, N.Y., lives in San Diego. Linebacker Connecticut 1963-66. No pro playing experience. College coach: Connecticut 1967-68, Rhode Island 1969-1973, Idaho State 1974-76 (head coach 1976), Princeton 1977-79. Pro coach: Montreal Alouettes (CFL) 1980-81, Ottawa Rough Riders (CFL) 1982-83, New Jersey Generals (USFL) 1984-85, St. Louis/Phoenix Cardinals 1986-1993, Cincinnati Bengals 1994-96, joined Chargers in 1997.

Rod Perry, secondary; born September 11, 1953, Fresno, Calif., lives in San Diego. Defensive back Colorado 1972-74. Pro cornerback Los Angeles Rams 1975-1982, Cleveland Browns 1983-84. College coach: Columbia 1985, Fresno City College 1986, Fresno State 1987-88. Pro coach: Seattle Seahawks 1989-1991, Los Angeles Rams 1992-94, Houston Oilers 1995-96, joined Chargers in 1997.

Bruce Read, special teams; born January 26, 1962, in Santa Rosa, Calif., lives in San Diego. No college or pro playing experience. College coach: Oregon Institute of Technology 1980, Portland State 1981-84, Montana 1985-1996, Oregon State 1997-98. Pro coach: Joined Chargers in 1999.

Mike Sanford, wide receivers; born April 20, 1955, in Los Altos, Calif., lives in San Diego. Quarterback-safety Southern California 1973-76. No pro playing experience. College coach: Southern California 1977, 1989-1996, San Diego City College 1978, Army 1979-1980, Virginia Military Institute 1981-82, Long Beach State 1983-86, Purdue 1987-88, Notre Dame 1997-98. Pro coach: Joined Chargers in 1999.

Johnny Thomas, special teams assistant; born August 3, 1964, in Houston, lives in San Diego. Pro cornerback Washington Redskins 1987-88, 1990-94, San Diego Chargers 1989, 1997, Cleveland Browns 1995, Philadelphia Eagles 1996. Pro coach: Joined Chargers in 1999.

Jim Vechiarella, linebackers; born February 20, 1937, Youngstown, Ohio, lives in San Diego. Linebacker Youngstown State 1955-57. No pro playing experience. College coach: Youngstown State 1964-1974, Southern Illinois 1976-77, Tulane 1978-1980. Pro coach: Charlotte (WFL) 1975, Los Angeles Rams 1981-82, Kansas City Chiefs 1983-85, New York Jets 1986-89, 1995-96, Cleveland Browns 1990, Philadelphia Eagles 1991-94, joined Chargers in 1997.

Ollie Wilson, running backs; born March 3, 1951, Worcester, Mass., lives in San Diego. Wide receiver Springfield 1971-73. No pro playing experience. College coach: Springfield 1975, Northeastern 1976-1982, California 1983-1990. Pro coach: Atlanta Falcons 1991-96, joined Chargers in 1997.

1999 FIRST-YEAR ROSTER

Name	Pos.	Ht.	Wt.	Birthdate	College	Hometown	How Acq.
Alexander, Rod (1)	WR	6-0	195	10/30/71	Northern Arizona	San Diego, Calif.	FA
Austin, Rick	G	6-1	307	9/13/76	San Diego State	Rialto, Calif.	FA
Baker, Jeff (1)	QB	6-3	215	3/2/75	Wisconsin-La Crosse	West Bend, Wis.	FA-'98
Bell, Tyrone	CB	6-2	210	10/20/74	North Alabama	West Point, Miss.	D6
Brown, Fakhir	CB	5-11	192	9/21/77	Grambling State	Detroit, Mich.	FA
Brown, Larry	TE	6-5	270	9/1/76	Georgia	Decatur, Ga.	FA
Brown, Wilbert	G	6-2	310	5/9/77	Houston	Hooks, Tex.	FA
Bryant, John	LB	6-1	230	5/1/73	Central Florida	Ft. Lauderdale, Fla.	FA
Chappell, Brett	RB	5-11	209	2/22/76	Western Carolina	Rosman, N.C.	FA
Clark, Brian (1)	S	6-2	210	5/5/74	Hofstra	Toms River, N.J.	FA
Davis, Reggie	TE	6-3	233	9/3/76	Washington	Long Beach, Calif.	FA
Dingle, Adrian	DE	6-3	272	6/25/77	Clemson	Holly Hill, S.C.	D5a
Fazande, Jermaine	RB	6-0	262	1/14/75	Oklahoma	New Orleans, La.	D2
Gartung, Matt	T	6-5	302	5/26/76	Oregon State	Strathmore, Calif.	FA
Graham, DeMingo (1)	G-T	6-3	310	9/10/73	Hofstra	Newark, N.J.	FA-'98
Harden, Cedric (1)	DE	6-6	260	10/18/74	Florida A&M	Atlanta, Ga.	D5-'98
Heiden, Steve	TE	6-4	256	9/21/76	South Dakota State	Brookings, S.D.	D3
Ivory, Clifford (1)	CB	5-11	183	8/1/75	Troy State	Quitman, Ga.	D6-'98
Keith, Dwight	DE	6-4	272	5/26/72	No College	Millbrook, Ala.	FA
Knipper, Chris	T	6-5	315	11/27/75	Iowa	Dyersville, Iowa	FA
Mitchell, Deon	WR	5-10	180	4/30/76	Northern Illinois	Ft. Wayne, Ind.	FA
Moore, Craig	G	6-3	330	12/29/76	Mississippi State	Immokalee, Fla.	FA
Nelson, Reggie	G	6-4	310	6/23/76	McNeese State	Alexandria, La.	D5b
Parker, Sirr	WR	5-11	196	10/31/77	Texas A&M	Los Angeles, Calif.	FA
Perry, Jason	S	6-0	200	8/1/76	North Carolina State	Passaic, N.J.	D4
Reed, Robert	WR	6-1	203	1/14/75	Lambuth	Oxford, Miss.	FA
Reeves, John	LB	6-3	236	2/23/75	Purdue	Bradenton, Fla.	FA
Rodgers, Anthony (1)	WR	6-3	190	12/11/73	Cal State-Northridge	Los Angeles, Calif.	FA-'98
Ruff, Orlando	LB	6-3	247	9/28/76	Furman	Winnsboro, S.C.	FA
Taylor, Tyrone (1)	WR	5-9	175	9/29/76	Cal State-Sacramento	Pittsburg, Calif.	FA

The term NFL Rookie is defined as a player who is in his first season of professional football and has not been on the roster of another professional football team for any regular-season or postseason games. A Rookie is designated by an "R" on NFL rosters. Players who have been active in another professional football league or players who have NFL experience, including either preseason training camp or being on an Active List or Inactive List, or on Reserve/Injured or Reserve/Physically Unable to Perform for fewer than six regular-season games, are termed NFL First-Year Players. An NFL First-Year Player is designated by a "1" on NFL rosters. Thereafter, a player is credited with an additional year of experience for each season in which he accumulates six games on the Active List or Inactive List, or on Reserve/Injured or Reserve/Physically Unable to Perform.

SEATTLE SEAHAWKS

American Football Conference
Western Division
Team Colors: Blue, Green, and Silver
11220 N.E. 53rd Street
Kirkland, Washington 98033
Telephone: (425) 827-9777

CLUB OFFICIALS

Chairman: Paul Allen
Vice Chair: Bert Kolde
President: Bob Whitsitt
Executive VP of Football Operations/
General Manager & Head Coach: Mike Holmgren
Sr. Vice President: Mike Reinfeldt
Sr. VP/Marketing: Harry Hutt
VP/CFO: Nathaniel (Buster) Brown
VP/Community Outreach, I.S., Facilities: Mike Flood
VP/General Counsel: Richard Leigh
VP/Ticket Sales & Services: Duane McLean
VP/Football Operations: Randy Mueller
VP/Corporate Sales: Scott Patrick
VP/Communications: Gary Wright
Director of Player Personnel: John Dorsey
Director of College Scouting: Don Deisch
Director of Pro Scouting: Will Lewis
Director of Public Relations: Dave Pearson
Asst. Director of Public Relations: Steve Wright
Director of Community Outreach: Sandy Gregory
Director of Player Programs: Nesby Glasgow
Director of Publications: Vernon Cheek
Director of Corporate Sales: Doug Smith
Director of Broadcasting: Mike Wacker
Director of Vendor Sales: Kevin Williams
Director Ticket Operations/Customer Service:
Chuck Arnold
Assistant to the GM: Gary Reynolds
Administrative Assistant/Football Operations:
Bill Nayes
Video Director Football: Thom Fermstad
Head AthleticTrainer: Paul Federici
Equipment Manager: Erik Kennedy
Stadium: Kingdome • **Capacity:** 66,400
201 South King Street
Seattle, Washington 98104
Playing Surface: AstroTurf
Training Camp: Eastern Washington University
Cheney, Washington 99004

1999 SCHEDULE

PRESEASON

Aug. 14	**Buffalo**	6:00
Aug. 19	at San Francisco	5:00
Aug. 28	**Arizona**	7:00
Sept. 2	at Indianapolis	7:00

REGULAR SEASON

Sept. 12	**Detroit**	1:15
Sept. 19	at Chicago	12:00
Sept. 26	at Pittsburgh	1:00
Oct. 3	**Oakland**	5:20
Oct. 10	Open Date	
Oct. 17	at San Diego	1:05
Oct. 24	**Buffalo**	1:15
Nov. 1	at Green Bay (Mon.)	8:00
Nov. 7	**Cincinnati**	1:15
Nov. 14	**Denver**	5:20
Nov. 21	at Kansas City	12:00
Nov. 28	**Tampa Bay**	1:05
Dec. 5	at Oakland	1:15
Dec. 12	**San Diego**	1:05
Dec. 19	at Denver	2:15
Dec. 26	**Kansas City**	1:05
Jan. 2	at New York Jets	1:00

RECORD HOLDERS

INDIVIDUAL RECORDS—CAREER

Category	Name	Performance
Rushing (Yds.)	Chris Warren, 1990-97	6,706
Passing (Yds.)	Dave Krieg, 1980-1991	26,132
Passing (TDs)	Dave Krieg, 1980-1991	195
Receiving (No.)	Steve Largent, 1976-1989	819
Receiving (Yds.)	Steve Largent, 1976-1989	13,089
Interceptions	Dave Brown, 1976-1986	50
Punting (Avg.)	Rick Tuten, 1991-97	43.8
Punt Return (Avg.)	Paul Johns, 1981-84	11.4
Kickoff Return (Avg.)	Steve Broussard, 1995-98	23.2
Field Goals	Norm Johnson, 1982-1990	159
Touchdowns (Tot.)	Steve Largent, 1976-1989	101
Points	Norm Johnson, 1982-1990	810

INDIVIDUAL RECORDS—SINGLE SEASON

Category	Name	Performance
Rushing (Yds.)	Chris Warren, 1994	1,545
Passing (Yds.)	Warren Moon, 1997	3,678
Passing (TDs)	Dave Krieg, 1984	32
Receiving (No.)	Brian Blades, 1994	81
Receiving (Yds.)	Steve Largent, 1985	1,287
Interceptions	John Harris, 1981	10
	Kenny Easley, 1984	10
Punting (Avg.)	Rick Tuten, 1995	45.0
Punt Return (Avg.)	Bobby Joe Edmonds, 1987	12.6
Kickoff Return (Avg.)	Steve Broussard, 1995	24.7
Field Goals	Todd Peterson, 1996	28
Touchdowns (Tot.)	Chris Warren, 1995	16
Points	Todd Peterson, 1996	111

INDIVIDUAL RECORDS—SINGLE GAME

Category	Name	Performance
Rushing (Yds.)	Curt Warner, 11-27-83	207
Passing (Yds.)	Dave Krieg, 11-20-83	418
Passing (TDs)	Dave Krieg, 12-2-84, 9-15-85, 11-28-88	5
	Warren Moon, 10-26-97	5
Receiving (No.)	Steve Largent, 10-18-87	15
Receiving (Yds.)	Steve Largent, 10-18-87	261
Interceptions	Kenny Easley, 9-3-84	3
	Eugene Robinson, 12-6-92	3
	Darryl Williams, 9-21-97	3
Field Goals	Norm Johnson, 9-20-87, 12-18-88	5
Touchdowns (Tot.)	Daryl Turner, 9-15-85	4
	Curt Warner, 12-11-88	4
Points	Daryl Turner, 9-15-85	24

COACHING HISTORY

(167-196-0)

1976-82	Jack Patera*	35-59-0
1982	Mike McCormack	4-3-0
1983-91	Chuck Knox	83-67-0
1992-94	Tom Flores	14-34-0
1995-98	Dennis Erickson	31-33-0

*Released after two games in 1982

KINGDOME

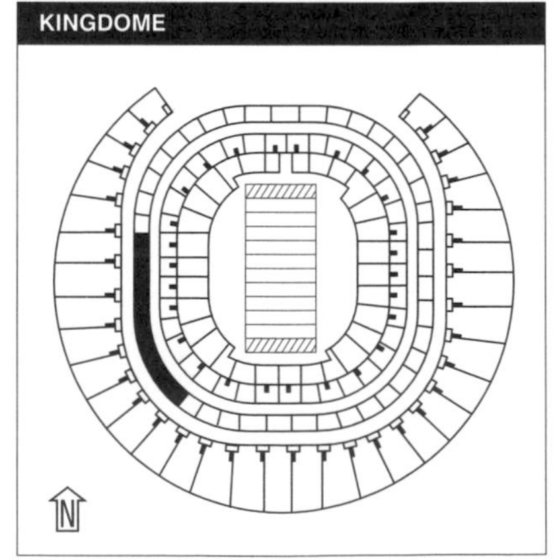

1998 TEAM RECORD

PRESEASON (4-1)

Date	Result		Opponent
7/31	W	20-19	at Dallas
8/8	W	24-21	Indianapolis
8/15	L	21-24	vs. San Francisco at Vancouver, Canada
8/22	W	31-24	at Arizona
8/28	W	21-20	San Francisco

REGULAR SEASON (8-8)

Date	Result		Opponent	Att.
9/6	W	38-0	at Philadelphia	66,418
9/13	W	33-14	Arizona	57,678
9/20	W	24-14	Washington	63,336
9/27	L	10-13	at Pittsburgh	58,413
10/4	L	6-17	at Kansas City	66,418
10/11	L	16-21	Denver	66,258
10/25	W	27-20	at San Diego	58,512
11/1	L	18-31	Oakland	66,246
11/8	W	24-12	Kansas City	66,251
11/15	L	17-20	at Oakland	51,527
11/22	L	22-30	at Dallas	64,142
11/29	W	20-18	Tennessee	59,048
12/6	L	31-32	at New York Jets	72,200
12/13	W	38-17	San Diego	62,690
12/20	W	27-23	Indianapolis	58,703
12/27	L	21-28	at Denver	74,057

SCORE BY PERIODS

Seahawks	107	91	75	99	0	—	372
Opponents	71	73	61	105	0	—	310

ATTENDANCE

Home 500,210 Away 511,687 Total 1,011,897

Single-game home record, 66,264 (10/26/97, 11/23/97)

Single-season home record, 514,984 (1992)

1998 TEAM STATISTICS

	Seahawks	Opp.
Total First Downs	267	337
Rushing	92	111
Passing	144	197
Penalty	31	29
Third Down: Made/Att	54/195	92/236
Third Down Pct.	27.7	39.0
Fourth Down: Made/Att	6/17	8/20
Fourth Down Pct.	35.3	40.0
Total Net Yards	4,626	5,689
Avg. Per Game	289.1	355.6
Total Plays	940	1,137
Avg. Per Play	4.9	5.0
Net Yards Rushing	1,626	1,999
Avg. Per Game	101.6	124.9
Total Rushes	426	487
Net Yards Passing	3,000	3,690
Avg. Per Game	187.5	230.6
Sacked/Yards Lost	34/219	53/282
Gross Yards	3,219	3,972
Att./Completions	480/273	597/343
Completion Pct.	56.9	57.5
Had Intercepted	18	24
Punts/Avg.	81/44.0	78/43.6
Net Punting Avg.	81/36.5	78/36.0
Penalties/Yards Lost	117/914	130/1,157
Fumbles/Ball Lost	30/16	34/18
Touchdowns	45	35
Rushing	11	13
Passing	21	18
Returns	13	4
Avg. Time of Possession	27:05	32:55

1998 INDIVIDUAL STATISTICS

Passing	Att.	Comp.	Yds.	Pct.	TD	Int.	Tkld.	Rate
Moon	258	145	1,632	56.2	11	8	22/140	76.6
Kitna	172	98	1,177	57.0	7	8	11/72	72.3
Friesz	49	29	409	59.2	2	2	1/7	82.8
Watters	1	1	1	100.0	1	0	0/0	118.8
Seahawks	480	273	3,219	56.9	21	18	34/219	76.4
Opponents	597	343	3,972	57.5	18	24	53/282	71.0

SCORING	TD R	TD P	TD Rt	PAT	FG	Saf	PTS
Peterson	0	0	0	41/41	19/24	0	98
Galloway	0	10	2	0/0	0/0	0	72
Watters	9	0	0	0/0	0/0	0	56
Pritchard	0	3	0	0/0	0/0	0	20
Springs	0	0	3	0/0	0/0	0	18
Fauria	0	2	0	0/0	0/0	0	12
McKnight	0	2	0	0/0	0/0	0	12
Smith	0	0	2	0/0	0/0	0	12
Strong	0	2	0	0/0	0/0	0	12
Adams	0	0	1	0/0	0/0	0	6
Broussard	0	0	1	0/0	0/0	0	6
Crumpler	0	1	0	0/0	0/0	0	6
Green	1	0	0	0/0	0/0	0	6
Kennedy	0	0	1	0/0	0/0	0	6
Kitna	1	0	0	0/0	0/0	0	6
May	0	1	0	0/0	0/0	0	6
McDaniel	0	0	1	0/0	0/0	0	6
Simmons	0	0	1	0/0	0/0	0	6
W. Williams	0	0	1	0/0	0/0	0	6
Seahawks	11	21	13	41/41	19/24	0	372
Opponents	13	18	4	31/31	23/30	0	310

2-Point conversions: Pritchard, Watters. Team 2-4, Opponents 0-4.

RUSHING	Att.	Yds.	Avg.	LG	TD
Watters	319	1,239	3.9	39t	9
Green	35	209	6.0	64	1
Kitna	20	67	3.4	21	1
Strong	15	47	3.1	9	0
Galloway	9	26	2.9	14	0
Pritchard	1	17	17.0	17	0
Moon	16	10	0.6	9	0
Friesz	5	5	1.0	8	0
Broussard	5	4	0.8	3	0
R. Brown	1	2	2.0	2	0
Seahawks	426	1,626	3.8	64	11
Opponents	487	1,999	4.1	70	13

RECEIVING	No.	Yds.	Avg.	LG	TD
Galloway	65	1,047	16.1	81t	10
Pritchard	58	742	12.8	50t	3
Watters	52	373	7.2	24	0
Fauria	37	377	10.2	25	2
McKnight	21	346	16.5	59t	2
Blades	15	184	12.3	47	0
Strong	8	48	6.0	11t	2
Crumpler	6	52	8.7	16	1
Broussard	4	21	5.3	16	0
May	3	7	2.3	5	1
Green	3	2	0.7	3	0
Mili	1	20	20.0	20	0
Seahawks	273	3,219	11.8	81t	21
Opponents	343	3,972	11.6	80t	18

INTERCEPTIONS	No.	Yds.	Avg.	LG	TD
Springs	7	142	20.3	56t	2
Smith	3	56	18.7	26t	2
D. Williams	3	41	13.7	28	0
Bellamy	3	40	13.3	24	0
W. Williams	2	36	18.0	28t	1
McDaniel	1	43	43.0	43t	1
Simmons	1	36	36.0	36t	1
Adams	1	25	25.0	25t	1
Wells	1	25	25.0	25	0
C. Brown	1	11	11.0	11	0
Collins	1	0	0.0	0	0
Seahawks	24	455	19.0	56t	8
Opponents	18	220	12.2	74t	2

PUNTING	No.	Yds.	Avg.	In 20	LG
Feagles	81	3,568	44.0	27	59
Seahawks	81	3,568	44.0	27	59
Opponents	78	3,397	43.6	23	61

PUNT RETURNS	No.	FC	Yds.	Avg.	LG	TD
Galloway	25	5	251	10.0	74t	2
Joseph	15	5	182	12.1	66	0
Harris	1	0	-5	-5.0	-5	0
Seahawks	41	10	428	10.4	74t	2
Opponents	33	15	369	11.2	63t	1

KICKOFF RETURNS	No.	Yds.	Avg.	LG	TD
Broussard	29	781	26.9	90t	1
Green	27	620	23.0	57	0
R. Brown	4	44	11.0	19	0
Joseph	2	49	24.5	24	0
Fauria	1	0	0.0	0	0
Wilson	1	16	16.0	16	0
Seahawks	64	1,510	23.6	90t	1
Opponents	68	1,311	19.3	35	0

FIELD GOALS	1-19	20-29	30-39	40-49	50+
Peterson	0/0	7/7	4/5	5/5	3/7
Seahawks	0/0	7/7	4/5	5/5	3/7
Opponents	0/0	10/10	6/7	6/11	1/2

SACKS	No.
Sinclair	16.5
C. Brown	7.5
Daniels	6.5
LaBounty	6.0
Smith	5.0
Adams	2.0
Kennedy	2.0
Collins	1.5
Bellamy	1.0
Logan	1.0
Parker	1.0
Seahawks	53.0
Opponents	34.0

1999 DRAFT CHOICES

Round	Name	Pos.	College
1	Lamar King	DE	Saginaw Valley
3	Brock Huard	QB	Washington
	Karsten Bailey	WR	Auburn
4	Antonio Cochran	DE	Georgia
5	Floyd Wedderburn	T	Penn State
	Charlie Rogers	WR	Georgia Tech
6	Steve Johnson	DB	Tennessee

SEATTLE SEAHAWKS

1999 VETERAN ROSTER

No.	Name	Pos.	Ht.	Wt.	Birthdate	NFL Exp.	College	Hometown	How Acq.	'98 Games/ Starts
98	Adams, Sam	DT	6-3	300	6/13/73	6	Texas A&M	Houston, Tex.	D1-'94	16/11
75	Ballard, Howard	T	6-6	325	11/3/63	12	Alabama A&M	Ashland, Ala.	UFA(Buff)-'94	16/16
63	Beede, Frank	G	6-4	296	5/1/73	4	Panhandle State	Antioch, Calif.	FA-'96	0*
20	Bellamy, Jay	S	5-11	199	7/8/72	6	Rutgers	Aberdeen, N.J.	FA-'94	16/16
89	Blades, Brian	WR	5-11	190	7/24/65	12	Miami	Ft. Lauderdale, Fla.	D2-'88	16/6
60	Bloedorn, Greg	C	6-6	278	11/15/72	3	Cornell	Elmhurst, Ill.	FA-'98	0*
94	Brown, Chad	LB	6-2	240	7/12/70	7	Colorado	Altadena, Calif.	UFA(Pitt)-'97	16/16
34	Brown, Reggie	RB	6-0	244	6/26/73	4	Fresno State	Detroit, Mich.	D3b-'96	15/1
55	Butler, Hillary	LB	6-2	244	1/5/71	2	Washington	San Francisco, Calif.	FA-'98	7/0
25	Collins, Mark	S	5-10	196	1/16/64	13	California-Fullerton	San Bernardino, Calif.	FA-'98	9/0
93	Daniels, Phillip	DE	6-5	263	3/4/73	4	Georgia	Donalsonville, Ga.	D4a-'96	16/15
81	Dawkins, Sean	WR	6-4	218	2/3/71	7	California	Sunnyvale, Calif.	UFA(NO)-'99	15/15*
86	Fauria, Christian	TE	6-4	245	9/22/71	5	Colorado	Encino, Calif.	D2-'95	16/15
10	Feagles, Jeff	P	6-1	207	8/7/66	12	Miami	Anaheim, Calif.	UFA(Ariz)-'98	16/0
13	t- Foley, Glenn	QB	6-2	220	10/10/70	6	Boston College	Cherry Hill, N.J.	T(NYJ)-'99	5/3*
84	Galloway, Joey	WR	5-11	188	11/20/71	5	Ohio State	Bellaire, Ohio	D1-'95	16/16
53	Glover, Kevin	C	6-2	282	6/17/63	15	Maryland	Columbia, Md.	UFA(Det)-'98	8/8
62	Gray, Chris	G	6-4	305	6/19/70	7	Auburn	Birmingham, Ala.	UFA(Chi)-'98	15/8
35	Gray, Oscar	RB	6-1	255	8/7/72	2	Arkansas	Houston, Tex.	FA-'99	0*
30	Green, Ahman	RB	6-0	213	2/16/77	2	Nebraska	Omaha, Neb.	D3-'98	16/0
68	Habib, Brian	G	6-7	299	12/2/64	12	Washington	Ellensburg, Wash.	UFA(Den)-'98	16/16
71	Jones, Walter	T	6-5	300	1/19/74	3	Florida State	Aliceville, Ala.	D1b-'97	16/16
28	Joseph, Kerry	S	6-2	205	10/4/73	3	McNeese State	New Iberia, La.	FA-'98	16/0
66	Kendall, Pete	G	6-5	292	7/9/73	4	Boston College	Weymouth, Mass.	D1-'96	16/16
96	Kennedy, Cortez	DT	6-3	306	8/23/68	10	Miami	Wilson, Ark.	D1a-'90	15/15
7	Kitna, Jon	QB	6-2	217	9/21/72	3	Central Washington	Tacoma, Wash.	FA-'96	6/5
99	LaBounty, Matt	DE	6-4	275	1/3/69	7	Oregon	Novato, Calif.	T(GB)-'96	16/1
56	Logan, James	LB	6-2	225	12/6/72	5	Memphis	Opp, Ala.	W(Cin)-'95	4/1
88	May, Deems	TE	6-4	263	3/6/69	8	North Carolina	Lexington, N.C.	UFA(SD)-'97	16/1
26	McGill, Lenny	CB	6-1	202	5/31/71	6	Arizona State	Escondido, Calif.	FA-'99	10/0*
82	McKnight, James	WR	6-1	198	6/17/72	5	Liberty	Apopka, Fla.	FA-'94	14/3
49	Mili, Itula	TE	6-4	265	4/20/73	2	Brigham Young	Laie, Hawaii	D6-'97	7/0
50	Myles, DeShone	LB	6-2	235	10/31/74	2	Nevada	Las Vegas, Nev.	D4-'98	12/7
97	Parker, Riddick	DT	6-3	274	11/20/72	3	North Carolina	Southampton, Va.	FA-'96	8/0
2	Peterson, Todd	K	5-10	171	2/4/70	5	Georgia	Valdosta, Ga.	FA-'95	16/0
85	Pritchard, Mike	WR	5-10	193	10/26/69	9	Colorado	Las Vegas, Nev.	FA-'96	16/16
51	Simmons, Anthony	LB	6-0	230	6/7/76	2	Clemson	Spartanburg, S.C.	D1-'98	12/4
70	Sinclair, Michael	DE	6-4	267	1/31/68	8	Eastern New Mexico	Beaumont, Tex.	D6-'91	16/16
59	Smith, Darrin	LB	6-1	230	4/15/70	7	Miami	Miami, Fla.	UFA(Phil)-'98	13/12
24	Springs, Shawn	CB	6-0	195	3/11/75	3	Ohio State	Silver Springs, Md.	D1a-'97	16/16
38	Strong, Mack	RB	6-0	235	9/11/71	6	Georgia	Columbus, Ga.	FA-'93	16/5
22	† Thomas, Fred	CB	5-9	172	9/11/73	4	Tennessee-Martin	Bruce, Miss.	D2-'96	15/2
32	Watters, Ricky	RB	6-1	217	4/7/69	9	Notre Dame	Harrisburg, Pa.	UFA(Phil)-'98	16/16
74	Weiner, Todd	T	6-4	300	9/16/75	2	Kansas State	Coral Springs, Fla.	D2-'98	6/0
33	Williams, Darryl	S	6-0	202	1/8/70	8	Miami	Hialeah, Fla.	UFA(Cin)-'96	16/16
79	Williams, Grant	T	6-7	323	5/10/74	4	Louisiana Tech	Clinton, Miss.	FA-'96	16/0
27	Williams, Willie	CB	5-9	180	12/26/70	7	Western Carolina	Columbia, S.C.	UFA(Pitt)-'97	14/14
83	Wilson, Robert	WR	5-11	176	6/23/74	3	Florida A&M	Monticello, Fla.	FA-'97	16/0

* Beede missed '98 season because of injury; Bloedorn and Gray last active with Seattle in '97; Dawkins played 15 games with New Orleans in '98; Foley played 5 games with N.Y. Jets; McGill played 10 games with Carolina.

† Restricted free agent; subject to developments.

t- Seahawks traded for Foley (N.Y. Jets).

Players lost through free agency (3): Tony Berti (Den; 12 games in '98), Carlester Crumpler (Minn; 11), Dean Wells (Car; 9).

Also played with Seattle in '98—RB Steve Broussard (15 games), DE Mike Croel (12), QB John Friesz (6), G Andrew Greene (4), WR Ronnie Harris (2), LB Jason Kyle (16), CB Terry McDaniel (9), QB Warren Moon (10), DT Dan Saleaumua (11), WR Bobby Shaw (1), S Eric Stokes (4).

COACHING STAFF

Executive Vice President of Football Operations/ General Manager & Head Coach, Mike Holmgren

Pro Career: Named to his current position as the Seahawks' executive vice president of football operations/general manager and head coach on January 8, 1999. In addition to his coaching duties, Holmgren oversees all facets of the team's football operations, including scouting, personnel, salary cap, player negotiations, as well as regular coaching responsibilities. Holmgren takes control of the Seahawks following one of the most successful coaching stints in league history as the head coach of the Green Bay Packers (1992-98). Holmgren posted a 75-37 (.670) regular-season record, a 9-5 (.643) postseason mark, and two Super Bowl appearances, including a 35-21 victory over the New England Patriots in Super Bowl XXXI. By winning at least one game in five consecutive postseasons (1993-97) Holmgren joined John Madden (1973-77) as the only coaches in league history to accomplish that feat. From 1995-98, Holmgren's Packers posted an NFL-best 48-16 (.750) record and finished first in the NFC Central Division three times. By taking the Packers to six consecutive postseasons (1993-98), Holmgren established a franchise record, with a team that had recorded just two winning seasons in the 19 years before he was hired. In 13 NFL seasons (1992-98 head coach Green Bay, 1986-1991 assistant coach San Francisco) Holmgren's teams have posted a 146-60-1 (.708) record, hit double digits in the victory column 10 times, made the postseason 12 times, won three Super Bowls (XXIII, XXIV, and XXXI), and reached another (Super Bowl XXXII). Holmgren's 1996 team that won the Super Bowl led the NFL in scoring with a club-record 456 points and also led the league in defensive scoring, a feat that had not been accomplished since 1972. Before becoming the Packers' head coach, Holmgren served as an assistant coach of the San Francisco 49ers from 1986-1991. He coached the quarterbacks from 1986-88, under head coach Bill Walsh, and was the team's offensive coordinator from 1989-1991, under George Seifert. Career record: 84-42.

Background: Quarterback at Southern California (1966-69) and was drafted by the St. Louis Cardinals in the eighth round of the 1970 NFL draft. He served as an assistant coach at San Francisco State (1981) and Brigham Young (1982-85) before his tenure with the 49ers. Earned his bachelor of science degree in business finance at Southern California (1970).

Personal: Born June 15, 1948, in San Francisco. He and his wife, Kathy, live in Mercer Island, Wash. and have four daughters—Calla, Jenny, Emily, and Gretchen.

ASSISTANT COACHES

Larry Brooks, defensive line; born June 10, 1950, Prince George, Va., lives in Kirkland, Wash. Defensive lineman Virginia State 1968-1971. Pro defensive tackle Los Angeles Rams 1972-1982. College coach: Virginia State 1992-93. Pro coach: Los Angeles Rams 1983-1990, Green Bay Packers 1994-98, joined Seahawks in 1999.

Jerry Colquitt, offensive quality control; born June 28, 1972, Oak Ridge, Tenn., lives in Kirkland, Wash. Quarterback Tennessee 1991-94. Quarterback Frankfurt Galaxy (NFL Europe) 1997. College coach: Tennessee 1996-98. Pro coach: Joined Seahawks in 1999.

Nolan Cromwell, wide receivers; born January 30, 1955, Smith Center, Kan., lives in Bellevue, Wash. Quarterback-safety Kansas 1973-76. Pro defensive back Los Angeles Rams 1977-1987. Pro coach: Los Angeles Rams 1991, Green Bay Packers 1992-98, joined Seahawks in 1999.

Ken Flajole, defensive backs; born October 4, 1954, Seattle, lives in Kirkland, Wash. Linebacker Wenatchee (Wash.) Valley C.C. 1973-74, Pacific Lutheran 1975-76. No pro playing experience. College coach: Pacific Lutheran 1977-78, Washington 1979, Montana 1980-85, Texas-El Paso 1986-88, Missouri 1989-1993, Richmond 1994, Hawaii 1995, Nevada 1996-97. Pro coach: Green Bay Packers 1998, joined Seahawks in 1999.

Kent Johnston, strength and conditioning; born February 21, 1956, Mexia, Texas, lives in Bellevue, Wash. Defensive back Stephen F. Austin 1974-77. No pro playing experience. College coach: Northwestern State (La.) 1979, Northeast Louisiana 1980-81, Alabama 1983-86. Pro coach: Tampa Bay Buccaneers 1987-1991, Green Bay Packers 1992-98, joined Seahawks in 1999.

Jim Lind, linebackers; born Novemeber 11, 1947, Isle, Minn., lives in Bellevue, Wash. Linebacker Bethel College 1965-66, defensive back Bemidji State 1971-72. No pro playing experience. College coach: St. Cloud State 1977-78, St. John's (Minn.) 1979-1980, Brigham Young 1981-82, Minnesota-Morris 1983-86 (head coach), Wisconsin-Eau Claire 1987-1991 (head coach). Pro coach: Green Bay Packers 1992-98, joined Seahawks in 1999.

Clayton Lopez, defensive quality control; born May 26, 1971, Los Angeles, lives in Kirkland, Wash. Safety Nevada 1991-94. No pro playing experience. College coach: Nevada 1995-98. Pro coach: Joined Seahawks in 1999.

Tom Lovat, asst. head coach-offensive line; born December 28, 1938, Bingham, Utah, lives in Bellevue, Wash. Guard-linebacker Utah 1958-1960. No pro playing experience. College coach: Utah 1967, 1972-76 (head coach 1974-76), Idaho State 1968-1970, Stanford 1977-79, Wyoming 1989. Pro coach: Saskatchewan Roughriders (CFL) 1971, Green Bay Packers 1980, 1992-98, St. Louis/Phoenix Cardinals 1981-84, 1990-91, Indianapolis Colts 1985-88, joined Seahawks in 1999.

Stump Mitchell, running backs; born March 15, 1959, St. Mary's, Ga., lives in Kirkland, Wash. Tailback The Citadel 1977-1980. Running back St. Louis/Phoenix Cardinals 1981-89. College coach: Morgan State 1995-98 (head coach 1996-98). Pro coach: San Antonio Rough Riders (WLAF) 1991, joined Seahawks in 1999.

Pete Rodriguez, special teams coordinator; born July 25, 1940, Chicago, lives in Kirkland, Wash. Guard-linebacker Denver 1959-1960, Western State (Colo.) 1961-63. No pro playing experience. College coach: Western State (Colo.) 1964, Arizona 1968-69, Western Illinois 1970-73, 1979-1982 (head coach), Florida State 1974-75, Iowa State 1976-78, Northern Iowa 1986. Pro coach: Michigan Panthers (USFL) 1983-84, Denver Gold (USFL) 1985, Jacksonville Bulls (USFL) 1986, Ottawa Rough Riders (CFL) 1987, Los Angeles Raiders 1988-89, Phoenix Cardinals 1990-93, Washington Redskins 1994-97, joined Seahawks in 1998.

Mike Sheppard, quarterbacks; born October 29, 1951, Tulsa, Okla., lives in Redmond, Wash. Wide receiver Cal Lutheran 1969-1972. No pro playing experience. College coach: Cal Lutheran 1974-76, Brigham Young 1977-78, U.S. International 1979, Idaho State 1980-81, Long Beach State 1982, 1984-86 (head coach), New Mexico 1987-1991 (head coach), California 1992. Pro coach: Cleveland Browns/Baltimore Ravens 1993-96, San Diego Chargers 1997-98, joined Seahawks in 1999.

Mike Sherman, offensive coordinator-tight ends; born December 19, 1954, Norwood, Mass., lives in Kirkland, Wash. Linebacker-offensive guard-tackle Central Connecticut State 1974, 1976-77. No pro playing experience. College coach: Pittsburgh 1981-82, Tulane 1983-84, Holy Cross 1985-88, Texas A&M 1989-1993, 1995-96, UCLA 1994. Pro coach: Green Bay Packers 1997-98, joined Seahawks in 1999.

Fritz Shurmur, defensive coordinator; born July 15, 1932, Riverview, Mich., lives in Bellevue, Wash. Center-linebacker Albion 1950-53. No pro playing experience. College coach: Albion 1954-1961, Wyoming 1962-1974 (head coach 1971-74). Pro coach: Detroit Lions 1975-77, New England Patriots 1978-1981, Los Angeles Rams 1982-1990, Phoenix Cardinals 1991-93, Green Bay Packers 1994-98, joined Seahawks in 1999.

1999 FIRST-YEAR ROSTER

Name	Pos.	Ht.	Wt.	Birthdate	College	Hometown	How Acq.
Amundson, Josh	LB	6-1	241	8/2/75	Wyoming	Twin Falls, Idaho	FA
Bailey, Karsten	WR	5-10	201	4/26/77	Auburn	Newnan, Ga.	D3b
Black, Michael (1)	RB	5-11	206	5/3/74	Washington State	Los Angeles, Calif.	FA-'98
Brown, DeAuntae (1)	CB	5-10	195	4/28/74	Central State, Ohio	Detroit, Mich.	FA
Cochran, Antonio	DE	6-4	297	6/21/76	Georgia	Montezuma, Ga.	D4
Corbett, Mondell	G	6-2	308	2/11/77	East Carolina	Yanceyville, N.C.	FA
Eloms, Joey (1)	CB	5-10	183	4/4/76	Indiana	Fort Wayne, Ind.	FA-'98
French, Rufus	TE	6-3	257	3/15/78	Mississippi	Amory, Miss.	FA
Frier, T.J.	DT	6-2	307	8/17/77	Memphis	Newbern, Tenn.	FA
Goolsby, Brian	RB	6-1	251	12/31/76	Kansas State	Dodge City, Kan.	FA
Hickl, Matt	CB-S	6-1	201	9/26/75	Texas-Kingsville	Friendswood, Tex.	FA
Hill, James	TE	6-3	246	10/25/74	Abilene Christian	Riverhead, N.Y.	FA
Hinton, Jay	RB	5-11	203	2/28/76	Morgan State	Phoenix, Ariz.	FA
Holmes, Gary	DT	6-6	320	3/1/76	Washington State	Lacey, Wash.	FA
Huard, Brock	QB	6-5	228	4/15/76	Washington	Puyallup, Wash.	D3a
Jackson, Chris (1)	WR	6-1	203	2/26/75	Washington State	Santa Ana, Calif.	FA
Jenkins, Michael (1)	WR	6-3	191	8/25/74	Hampton	Portsmouth, Va.	FA-'98
Johnson, Steve	CB	5-10	178	3/24/76	Tennessee	Powder Springs, Ga.	D6
King, Lamar	DE	6-3	294	8/10/75	Saginaw Valley	Boston, Mass.	D1
Kohl, Jamie	K	5-11	211	7/11/77	Iowa State	Wauhesha, Wis.	FA
Kreinhagen, Kevin	QB	6-2	219	9/15/76	Indianapolis	Seymour, Idaho	FA
McBride, Tod	S	6-1	210	1/26/76	UCLA	Walnut, Calif.	FA
McCoy, Mike (1)	QB	6-3	200	4/1/72	Utah	Novato, Calif.	FA
McEndoo, Jason (1)	C	6-5	315	2/25/75	Washington State	Cosmopolis, Wash.	D7-'98
Moorman, Brian	P	6-1	170	2/5/76	Pittsburg State	Sedgwick, Kan.	FA
Nance, Jonathan	DE	6-4	257	2/18/75	Washington State	Miami, Fla.	FA
Rogers, Brian	LB	6-2	239	8/25/76	Oregon State	Missouri City, Tex.	FA
Rogers, Charlie	WR	5-9	179	6/19/76	Georgia Tech	Cliffwood, N.J.	D5b
Strey, Derek (1)	LB	6-2	247	10/26/74	Eastern Washington	Port Orchard, Wash.	FA-'98
Thomas, Kevin	DT	6-2	310	3/28/74	Delta State	Hammond, La.	FA
Wedderburn, Floyd	T	6-5	333	5/5/76	Penn State	Upper Darby, Pa.	D5a

The term NFL Rookie is defined as a player who is in his first season of professional football and has not been on the roster of another professional football team for any regular-season or postseason games. A Rookie is designated by an "R" on NFL rosters. Players who have been active in another professional football league or players who have NFL experience, including either preseason training camp or being on an Active List or Inactive List, or on Reserve/Injured or Reserve/Physically Unable to Perform for fewer than six regular-season games, are termed NFL First-Year Players. An NFL First-Year Player is designated by a "1" on NFL rosters. Thereafter, a player is credited with an additional year of experience for each season in which he accumulates six games on the Active List or Inactive List, or on Reserve/Injured or Reserve/Physically Unable to Perform

TENNESSEE TITANS

American Football Conference
Central Division
Team Colors: Navy, Titans Blue, Red, Silver
460 Great Circle Road
Nashville, Tennessee 37228
Telephone: (615) 565-4000

CLUB OFFICIALS

President: K.S. (Bud) Adams, Jr.
Executive Assistant to President: Thomas S. Smith
Executive V.P./General Manager: Floyd Reese
Executive Vice President: Don MacLachlan
Vice President/General Counsel: Steve Underwood
Vice President/Finance: Jackie Curley
Vice President/Community Affairs: Bob Hyde
Director of Player Personnel: Rich Snead
Director of College Scouting: Glenn Cumbee
Director of Sales and Operations: Stuart Spears
Asst. General Counsel: Elza Bullock
Asst. Dir. of Sales and Operations: Chad Bottorff
Director of Broadcasting: Mike Keith
Director of Marketing: Ralph Ockenfels
Director of Media Relations: Tony Wyllie
Asst. Dir. of Media Relations: Robbie Bohren
Director of Security: Steve Berk
Director of Ticket Operations: Marty Collins
Director of Player Programs: Al Smith
Director of Cheerleading and Entertainment: Meeka Gabriel
Stadium Operations Manager: Bill Dickerson
Head Trainer: Brad Brown
Assistant Trainers: Don Moseley, Geoff Kaplan
Equipment Manager: Paul Noska
Video Coordinator: Ken Sparacino
Stadium: NFL Stadium •**Capacity:** 67,000
One Titans Way
Nashville, Tennessee 37213
Playing Surface: Natural Grass
Training Camp: Baptist Sports Park
7640 Highway 70 South
Nashville, Tennessee 37221

1999 SCHEDULE

PRESEASON

Aug. 15	at Kansas City	7:30
Aug. 20	at Arizona	7:00
Aug. 27	**Atlanta**	7:00
Sept. 2	**New Orleans**	7:00

REGULAR SEASON

Sept. 12	**Cincinnati**	12:00
Sept. 19	**Cleveland**	3:15
Sept. 26	at Jacksonville	4:05
Oct. 3	at San Francisco	1:15
Oct. 10	**Baltimore**	3:15
Oct. 17	at New Orleans	12:00
Oct. 24	Open Date	
Oct. 31	**St. Louis**	12:00
Nov. 7	at Miami	8:20
Nov. 14	at Cincinnati	1:00
Nov. 21	**Pittsburgh**	12:00
Nov. 28	at Cleveland	1:00
Dec. 5	at Baltimore	1:00
Dec. 9	**Oakland** (Thurs.)	7:20
Dec. 19	**Atlanta**	12:00
Dec. 26	**Jacksonville**	12:00
Jan. 2	at Pittsburgh	4:15

RECORD HOLDERS

INDIVIDUAL RECORDS—CAREER

Category	Name	Performance
Rushing (Yds.)	Earl Campbell, 1978-1984	8,574
Passing (Yds.)	Warren Moon, 1984-1993	33,685
Passing (TDs)	Warren Moon, 1984-1993	196
Receiving (No.)	Ernest Givins, 1986-1994	542
Receiving (Yds.)	Ernest Givins, 1986-1994	7,935
Interceptions	Jim Norton, 1960-68	45
Punting (Avg.)	Craig Hentrich, 1998	47.2
Punt Return (Avg.)	Billy Johnson, 1974-1980	13.2
Kickoff Return (Avg.)	Bobby Jancik, 1962-67	26.5
Field Goals	Al Del Greco, 1991-98	198
Touchdowns (Tot.)	Earl Campbell, 1978-1984	73
Points	Al Del Greco, 1991-98	836

INDIVIDUAL RECORDS—SINGLE SEASON

Category	Name	Performance
Rushing (Yds.)	Earl Campbell, 1980	1,934
Passing (Yds.)	Warren Moon, 1991	4,690
Passing (TDs)	George Blanda, 1961	36
Receiving (No.)	Charley Hennigan, 1964	101
Receiving (Yds.)	Charley Hennigan, 1961	1,746
Interceptions	Fred Glick, 1963	12
	Mike Reinfeldt, 1979	12
Punting (Avg.)	Craig Hentrich, 1998	47.2
Punt Return (Avg.)	Billy Johnson, 1977	15.4
Kickoff Return (Avg.)	Ken Hall, 1960	31.3
Field Goals	Al Del Greco, 1998	36
Touchdowns (Tot.)	Earl Campbell, 1979	19
Points	Al Del Greco, 1998	136

INDIVIDUAL RECORDS—SINGLE GAME

Category	Name	Performance
Rushing (Yds.)	Billy Cannon, 12-10-61	216
	Eddie George, 8-31-97	216
Passing (Yds.)	Warren Moon, 12-16-90	527
Passing (TDs)	George Blanda, 11-19-61	*7
Receiving (No.)	Charley Hennigan, 10-13-61	13
	Haywood Jeffires, 10-13-91	13
Receiving (Yds.)	Charley Hennigan, 10-13-61	272
Interceptions	Many times	3
	Last time by Marcus Robertson, 11-21-93	
Field Goals	Roy Gerela, 9-28-69	5
Touchdowns (Tot.)	Billy Cannon, 12-10-61	5
Points	Billy Cannon, 12-10-61	30

*NFL Record

COACHING HISTORY

HOUSTON 1960-1996
(276-320-6)

1960-61	Lou Rymkus*	12-7-1
1961	Wally Lemm	10-0-0
1962-63	Frank (Pop) Ivy	17-12-0
1964	Sammy Baugh	4-10-0
1965	Hugh Taylor	4-10-0
1966-70	Wally Lemm	28-40-4
1971	Ed Hughes	4-9-1
1972-73	Bill Peterson**	1-18-0
1973-74	Sid Gillman	8-15-0
1975-80	O.A. (Bum) Phillips	59-38-0
1981-83	Ed Biles***	8-23-0
1983	Chuck Studley	2-8-0
1984-85	Hugh Campbell****	8-22-0
1985-89	Jerry Glanville	35-35-0
1990-94	Jack Pardee#	44-35-0
1994-98	Jeff Fisher	32-38-0

* Released after five games in 1961
** Released after five games in 1973
*** Resigned after six games in 1983
**** Released after 14 games in 1985
\# Released after 10 games in 1994

NFL STADIUM

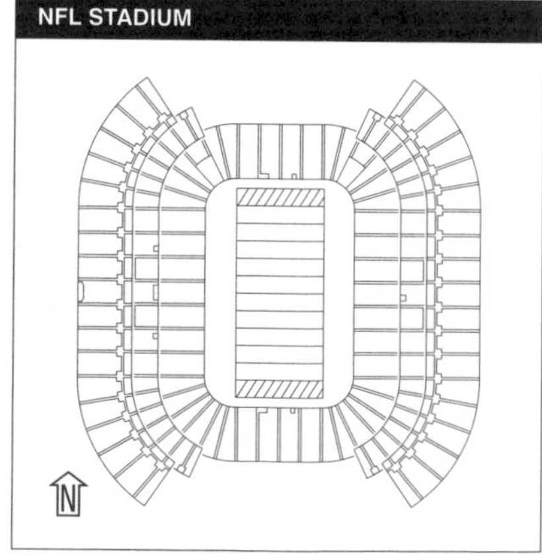

1998 TEAM RECORD

PRESEASON (3-1)

Date	Result		Opponent
8/7	W	31-16	at Atlanta
8/15	L	24-27	Washington
8/22	W	26-24	at New Orleans
8/29	W	16-13	Denver

REGULAR SEASON (8-8)

Date	Result		Opponent	Att.
9/6	W	23-14	at Cincinnati	55,848
9/13	L	7-13	San Diego	41,089
9/20	L	16-27	at New England	59,973
9/27	L	22-27	Jacksonville	34,656
10/11	W	12-8	at Baltimore	68,561
10/18	W	44-14	Cincinnati	33,288
10/25	L	20-23	Chicago	40,089
11/1	W	41-31	at Pittsburgh	58,222
11/8	W	31-22	at Tampa Bay	65,054
11/15	W	23-14	Pittsburgh	41,104
11/22	L	3-24	New York Jets	37,084
11/29	L	18-20	at Seattle	59,048
12/6	W	16-14	Baltimore	31,124
12/13	W	16-13	at Jacksonville	65,657
12/20	L	22-30	at Green Bay	59,888
12/26	L	16-26	Minnesota	41,121

SCORE BY PERIODS

Oilers	54	112	71	93	0	— 330
Opponents	58	69	87	106	0	— 320

ATTENDANCE

Home 299,555 Away 492,251 Total 791,806
Single-game home record, 64,934 (9/6/92)
Single-season home record, 482,726 (1991)

1998 TEAM STATISTICS

	Oilers	Opp.
Total First Downs	308	279
Rushing	118	81
Passing	171	170
Penalty	19	28
Third Down: Made/Att	84/210	76/201
Third Down Pct.	40	37.8
Fourth Down: Made/Att	4/11	3/16
Fourth Down Pct.	36.4	18.8
Total Net Yards	5,261	5,121
Avg. Per Game	328.8	320.1
Total Plays	1,016	955
Avg. Per Play	5.2	5.4
Net Yards Rushing	1,970	1,610
Avg. Per Game	123.1	100.6
Total Rushes	462	414
Net Yards Passing	3,291	3,511
Avg. Per Game	205.7	219.4
Sacked/Yards Lost	35/191	30/172
Gross Yards	3,482	3,683
Att./Completions	519/305	511/319
Completion Pct.	58.8	62.4
Had Intercepted	10	12
Punts/Avg.	69/47.2	74/43.1
Net Punting Avg.	69/39.2	74/37.2
Penalties/Yards Lost	126/1,135	93/704
Fumbles/Ball Lost	25/9	11/7
Touchdowns	32	34
Rushing	12	9
Passing	16	24
Returns	4	1
Avg. Time of Possession	31:41	28:20

1998 INDIVIDUAL STATISTICS

Passing	Att.	Comp.	Yds.	Pct.	TD	Int.	Tkld.	Rate
McNair	492	289	3,228	58.7	15	10	33/176	80.1
Krieg	21	12	199	57.1	0	0	2/15	89.2
S. Matthews	3	2	24	66.7	0	0	0/0	91.0
Archie	2	1	18	50.0	1	0	0/0	120.8
Hentrich	1	1	13	100.0	0	0	0/0	118.8
Oilers	519	305	3,482	58.8	16	10	35/191	81.3
Opponents	511	319	3,683	62.4	24	12	30/172	90.0

SCORING	TD R	TD P	TD Rt	PAT	FG	Saf	PTS
Del Greco	0	0	0	28/28	36/39	0	136
E. George	5	1	0	0/0	0/0	0	38
McNair	4	0	0	0/0	0/0	0	24
Davis	0	3	0	0/0	0/0	0	18
Mason	0	3	0	0/0	0/0	0	18
Thigpen	0	3	0	0/0	0/0	0	18
Bowden	0	0	2	0/0	0/0	0	12
Dyson	0	2	0	0/0	0/0	0	12
Harris	0	2	0	0/0	0/0	0	12
Thomas	2	0	0	0/0	0/0	0	12
Wycheck	0	2	0	0/0	0/0	0	12
Archie	1	0	0	0/0	0/0	0	6
Marts	0	0	1	0/0	0/0	0	6
Roan	0	0	1	0/0	0/0	0	6
Hentrich	0	0	0	0/0	0/1	0	0
Oilers	12	16	4	28/28	36/40	0	330
Opponents	9	24	1	29/29	25/30	2	320

2-Point conversions: E. George. Team 1-4, Opponents 4-5.

RUSHING	Att.	Yds.	Avg.	LG	TD
E. George	348	1,294	3.7	37t	5
McNair	77	559	7.3	71t	4
Thomas	24	100	4.2	21	2
Archie	6	24	4.0	20	1
Dyson	1	4	4.0	4	0
Stepnoski	1	0	0.0	0	0
Hentrich	1	-1	-1.0	-1	0
Krieg	3	-1	-.3	0	0
Sanders	1	-9	-9.0	-9	0
Oilers	462	1,970	4.3	71t	12
Opponents	414	1,610	3.9	66	9

RECEIVING	No.	Yds.	Avg.	LG	TD
Wycheck	70	768	11.0	38	2
Harris	43	412	9.6	32	2
Thigpen	38	493	13.0	55	3
E. George	37	310	8.4	29	1
Davis	32	461	14.4	38	3
Mason	25	333	13.3	47	3
Dyson	21	263	12.5	45t	2
Roan	13	93	7.2	16	0
Byrd	6	71	11.8	18	0
Thomas	6	55	9.2	20	0
Sanders	5	136	27.2	46	0
Archie	5	25	5.0	7	0
Kent	4	62	15.5	23	0
Oilers	305	3,482	11.4	55	16
Opponents	319	3,683	11.5	76t	24

INTERCEPTIONS	No.	Yds.	Avg.	LG	TD
Lewis	4	40	10.0	33	0
D. Walker	2	6	3.0	6	0
Marts	1	27	27.0	27t	1
Bishop	1	13	13.0	13	0
Robinson	1	11	11.0	11	0
Bowden	1	1	1.0	1t	1
Jackson	1	0	0.0	0	0
Robertson	1	0	0.0	0	0
Oilers	12	98	8.2	33	2
Opponents	10	88	8.8	34	1

PUNTING	No.	Yds.	Avg.	In 20	LG
Hentrich	69	3,258	47.2	18	71
Oilers	69	3,258	47.2	18	71
Opponents	74	3,190	43.1	25	67

PUNT RETURNS	No.	FC	Yds.	Avg.	LG	TD
Mason	31	11	228	7.4	25	0
Archie	7	6	52	7.4	22	0
Oilers	38	17	280	7.4	25	0
Opponents	34	16	332	9.8	43	0

KICKOFF RETURNS	No.	Yds.	Avg.	LG	TD
Archie	42	913	21.7	50	0
Mason	8	154	19.3	26	0
Thomas	3	64	21.3	39	0
Harris	1	3	3.0	3	0
Roan	1	4	4.0	11	0
Wycheck	1	10	10.0	10	0
Oilers	56	1,148	20.5	50	0
Opponents	55	1,114	20.3	47	0

FIELD GOALS	1-19	20-29	30-39	40-49	50+
Del Greco	1/1	8/8	15/15	12/15	0/0
Hentrich	0/0	0/0	0/0	0/1	0/0
Oilers	1/1	8/8	15/15	12/16	0/0
Opponents	1/1	7/7	7/10	9/9	1/3

SACKS	No.
Marts	4.0
Evans	3.5
Robinson	3.5
Bishop	3.0
Holmes	2.5
Cook	2.0
Lyons	2.0
Rolle	2.0
Bowden	1.5
Ford	1.5
Jackson	1.5
Lewis	1.0
Salave'a	1.0
G. Walker	1.0
Oilers	30.0
Opponents	35.0

1999 DRAFT CHOICES

Round	Name	Pos.	College
1	Jevon Kearse	DE	Florida
2	John Thornton	DT	West Virginia
3	Zach Piller	G	Florida
4	Brad Ware	DB	Auburn
	Donald Mitchell	DB	Southern Methodist
5	Kevin Daft	QB	California-Davis
6	Darran Hall	WR	Colorado State
7	Phil Glover	LB	Utah

TENNESSEE TITANS

1999 VETERAN ROSTER

No.	Name	Pos.	Ht.	Wt.	Birthdate	NFL Exp.	College	Hometown	How Acq.	'98 Games/ Starts
22	† Archie, Mike	RB	5-8	204	10/14/72	4	Penn State	Sharon, Pa.	D7-'96	16/0
23	Bishop, Blaine	S	5-9	203	7/24/70	7	Ball State	Indianapolis, Ind.	D8-'93	13/13
58	Bowden, Joe	LB	5-11	235	2/25/70	8	Oklahoma	Mesquite, Tex.	D5a-'92	16/16
83	Byrd, Isaac	WR	6-1	188	11/16/74	3	Kansas	St. Louis, Mo.	FA-'97	4/3
28	Byrd, Israel	DB	5-11	184	2/1/71	4	Utah State	St. Louis, Mo.	FA-'99	0*
3	Del Greco, Al	K	5-10	202	3/2/62	16	Auburn	Coral Gables, Fla.	FA-'91	16/0
33	† Dorsett, Anthony	CB	5-11	200	9/14/73	4	Pittsburgh	Dallas, Tex.	D6-'96	16/0
87	Dyson, Kevin	WR	6-1	201	6/23/75	2	Utah	Clearfield, Utah	D1-'98	13/9
91	Evans, Josh	DT-DE	6-2	288	9/6/72	5	Alabama-Birmingham	West Shawmut, Ala.	FA-'95	14/11
97	Fisk, Jason	DT	6-3	295	9/4/72	5	Stanford	Davis, Calif.	UFA(Minn)-'99	16/0*
92	Ford, Henry	DT	6-3	295	10/30/71	6	Arkansas	Ft. Worth, Tex.	D1-'94	13/5
27	George, Eddie	RB	6-3	240	9/24/73	4	Ohio State	Philadelphia, Pa.	D1-'96	16/16
26	George, Spencer	RB	5-9	200	10/28/73	2	Rice	Beaumont, Tex.	FA-'98	5/0
88	Harris, Jackie	TE	6-4	250	1/4/68	10	Northeast Louisiana	Pine Bluff, Ark.	UFA(TB)-'98	16/16
15	Hentrich, Craig	P-K	6-3	205	5/18/71	6	Notre Dame	Alton, Ill.	UFA(GB)-'98	16/0
99	Holmes, Kenny	DE	6-4	270	10/24/73	3	Miami	Vero Beach, Fla.	D1-'97	14/11
72	Hopkins, Brad	T	6-3	305	9/5/70	7	Illinois	Moline, Ill.	D1-'97	13/13
24	Jackson, Steve	CB	5-8	188	4/8/69	9	Purdue	Houston, Tex.	D3A-'91	14/4
96	Jones, Mike	DT-DE	6-4	280	8/25/69	9	North Carolina State	Columbia, S.C.	UFA(StL)-'99	16/15*
86	Kent, Joey	WR	6-1	191	4/23/74	3	Tennessee	Huntsville, Ala.	D2-'97	10/0
50	† Killens, Terry	LB	6-1	235	3/24/74	4	Penn State	Cincinnati, Ohio	D3-'96	16/1
66	Layman, Jason	G	6-5	310	7/29/73	4	Tennessee	Sevierville, Tenn.	D2b-'96	16/15
29	Lewis, Darryll	CB	5-9	188	12/16/68	9	Arizona	La Puente, Calif.	D2b-'91	16/15
60	Long, Kevin	C	6-5	295	5/2/75	2	Florida State	Summerville, S.C.	D7-'98	16/2
98	Lyons, Pratt	DT-DE	6-5	295	9/17/74	3	Troy State	Fort Worth, Tex.	D4b-'97	16/12
51	Marts, Lonnie	LB	6-2	250	11/10/68	10	Tulane	New Orleans, La.	UFA(TB)-'97	16/15
85	Mason, Derrick	WR	5-10	188	1/17/74	3	Michigan State	Detroit, Mich.	D4a-'97	16/0
76	Mathews, Jason	T	6-5	304	2/9/71	6	Texas A&M	Orange, Tex.	FA-'98	3/0
74	Matthews, Bruce	G-C	6-5	305	8/8/61	17	Southern California	Arcadia, Calif.	D1-'83	16/16
11	† Matthews, Steve	QB	6-3	228	10/13/70	4	Memphis State	Tullahoma, Tenn.	W(Jac)-'98	1/0
38	McCullough, George	CB	5-10	187	2/18/75	2	Baylor	Galveston, Tex.	D5-'97	7/0
9	McNair, Steve	QB	6-2	225	2/14/73	5	Alcorn State	Mt. Olive, Miss.	D1-'95	16/16
41	Neal, Lorenzo	RB	5-11	240	12/27/70	7	Fresno State	Fresno, Calif.	UFA(TB)-'99	16/1*
75	Olson, Benji	G	6-3	315	6/5/75	2	Washington	Port Orchard, Wash.	D5-'98	13/1
35	Phenix, Perry	S	5-11	210	11/14/74	2	Southern Mississippi	Dallas, Tex.	FA-'98	15/3
61	Pilgrim, Evan	G	6-4	305	8/14/72	5	Brigham Young	Pittsburgh, Calif.	FA-'98	3/0
80	Roan, Michael	TE-HB	6-3	250	8/29/72	5	Wisconsin	Iowa City, Iowa	D4-'95	16/1
90	Roberson, James	DE	6-3	275	5/3/71	4	Florida State	Lake Wales, Fla.	FA-'96	10/5
31	Robertson, Marcus	S	5-11	205	10/2/69	9	Iowa State	Pasadena, Calif.	D4b-'91	12/12
55	Robinson, Eddie	LB	6-1	243	4/13/70	8	Alabama State	New Orleans, La	FA-'98	16/16
21	Rolle, Samari	CB	6-0	175	8/10/76	2	Florida State	Miami, Fla.	D2-'98	15/1
69	† Runyan, Jon	T	6-7	320	11/27/73	4	Michigan	Flint, Mich.	D4b-'96	16/16
95	Salave'a, Joe	DT	6-3	290	3/23/75	2	Arizona	San Diego, Calif.	D4-'98	13/0
81	Sanders, Chris	WR	6-1	188	5/8/72	5	Ohio State	Denver, Colo.	D3a-'95	14/1
73	Sanderson, Scott	T	6-6	295	7/25/74	3	Washington State	Concord, Calif.	D3b-'97	16/3
37	Sidney, Dainon	CB	6-0	188	5/30/75	2	Alabama-Birmingham	Atlanta, Ga.	D3-'98	16/1
56	Stallings, Dennis	LB	6-0	240	5/25/74	3	Illinois	East St. Louis, Ill.	D6-'97	15/0
82	Thigpen, Yancey	WR	6-1	203	8/15/69	8	Winston-Salem State	Rocky Mt., N.C.	UFA(Pitt)-'98	9/8
20	Thomas, Rodney	RB	5-10	210	3/30/73	5	Texas A&M	Groveton, Tex.	D3b-'95	11/0
25	Walker, Denard	CB	6-1	190	8/9/73	3	Louisiana State	Garland, Tex.	D3a-'97	16/16
52	Wortham, Barron	LB	5-11	245	11/1/69	6	Texas-El Paso	Everman, Tex.	D6b-'94	13/0
89	Wycheck, Frank	TE-HB	6-3	250	10/14/71	7	Maryland	Philadelphia, Pa.	W(Wash)-'95	16/16

* Israel Byrd last active with New Orleans in '96; Fisk played 16 games with Minnesota in '98; Jones played 16 games with St. Louis; Neal played 16 games with Tampa Bay.

† Restricted free agent; subject to developments.

Players lost through free agency (3): DE Anthony Cook (Wash; 13 games in '98), C Mark Stepnoski (Dall; 13), DT Gary Walker (Jac; 16).

Also played with Tennessee in '98—WR Willie Davis (13 games), LB Lenoy Jones (9), QB Dave Krieg (5), G Erik Norgard (1).

COACHING STAFF

Head Coach,
Jeff Fisher

Pro Career: Officially named as franchise's fifteenth head coach on January 5, 1995. Was elevated to head coach-defensive coordinator on November 14, 1994, after head coach Jack Pardee and assistant head coach-offense Kevin Gilbride were relieved of their duties. Took over a 1-9 team and guided them through the final six games of the season, picking up his first victory against the New York Jets in the season finale. Originally joined the franchise on February 9, 1994, as defensive coordinator after spending two seasons as defensive backs coach for the San Francisco 49ers (1992-93). Prior to stint with the 49ers, worked as defensive coordinator for the Los Angeles Rams (1991). From 1986-1990, was an assistant for Buddy Ryan's Philadelphia Eagles, serving as defensive backs coach from 1986-88 before becoming the NFL's youngest defensive coordinator in 1989. Drafted by Chicago in seventh round in 1981, spent five seasons as a cornerback and kick returner for the Bears (1981-85). Did not play in Bears' 1985 Super Bowl championship season after being placed on injured reserve with an ankle injury. That season he assisted defensive coordinator Buddy Ryan. Career record: 32-38.

Background: Played at Southern California (1977-1980) for John Robinson in a star-studded defensive backfield that included Ronnie Lott, Dennis Smith, and Joey Browner. Member of the USC team that won the national championship in 1978. Also served as the Trojans' backup placekicker and was a Pac-10 All-Academic selection in 1980.

Personal: Born February 25, 1958, in Culver City, Calif. Jeff and his wife, Juli, have three children, sons Brandon and Trenton, and daughter Tara. The family resides in Franklin, Tenn.

ASSISTANT COACHES

Bart Andrus, quarterbacks; born March 30, 1958, Logan, Utah, lives in Franklin, Tenn. Quarterback Montana 1978-1981. No pro playing experience. College coach: Humboldt State 1986-89, Montana State 1990-91, Southern Utah 1993-95, Rocky Mountain College 1996 (head coach). Pro coach: Joined Titans/Oilers in 1997.

O'Neill Gilbert, linebackers; born March 29, 1965, Monroe, La., lives in Franklin, Tenn. Linebacker Texas A&M 1985-88. Pro linebacker San Francisco 49ers 1990, Montreal Machine (WFL) 1991. College coach: Navarro (Texas) J.C. 1991, Nevada-Las Vegas 1992-94, Illinois 1995-96. Pro coach: Joined Titans/Oilers in 1997.

Jerry Gray, defensive backs; born December 16, 1962, Lubbock, Texas, lives in Franklin, Tenn. Defensive back Texas 1981-84. Pro safety-cornerback Los Angeles Rams 1985-1991, Houston Oilers 1992, Tampa Bay Buccaneers 1993. College coach: Southern Methodist 1995-96. Pro coach: Joined Titians/Oilers in 1997.

George Henshaw, asst. head coach; born January 22, 1948, Richmond, Va., lives in Nashville. Defensive tackle West Virginia 1967-69. No pro playing experience. College coach: West Virginia 1970-75, Florida State 1976-1982, Alabama 1983-86, Tulsa 1987 (head coach). Pro coach: Denver Broncos 1988-1992, New York Giants 1993-96, joined Titans/Oilers in 1997.

Alan Lowry, special teams; born November 21, 1950, Miami, Okla., lives in Franklin, Tenn. Defensive back-quarterback Texas 1970-72. No pro playing experience. College coach: Virginia Tech 1974, Wyoming 1975, Texas 1977-1981. Pro coach: Dallas Cowboys 1982-1990, Tampa Bay Buccaneers 1991, San Francisco 49ers 1992-95, joined Titans/Oilers in 1996.

Mike Munchak, offensive line; born March 5, 1960, Scranton, Pa., lives in Brentwood, Tenn. Guard-tackle Penn State 1979-1981. Pro guard Houston Oilers 1982-1993. Pro coach: Joined Titans/Oilers in 1994.

Jim Schwartz, defensive assistant-quality control; born June 2, 1966, Baltimore, lives in Nashville. Linebacker Georgetown 1984-88. No pro playing experience. College coach: Maryland 1989, Minnesota 1990, North Carolina Central 1991, Colgate 1992. Pro coach: Cleveland Browns/Baltimore Ravens 1995-98, joined Titans in 1999.

Sherman Smith, running backs; born November 1, 1954, Youngstown, Ohio, lives in Franklin, Tenn. Quarterback Miami (Ohio) 1972-75. Pro running back Seattle Seahawks 1976-1982, San Diego Chargers 1983-84. College coach: Miami (Ohio) 1990-91, Illinois 1992-94. Pro coach: Joined Titans/Oilers in 1995.

Les Steckel, offensive coordinator; born July 1, 1946, North Hampton, Pa., lives in Brentwood, Tenn. Running back Kansas 1964-68. No pro playing experience. College coach: Colorado 1972-76, 1991-92, Navy 1977, Brown 1989. Pro coach: San Francisco 49ers 1978, Minnesota Vikings 1979-1984 (head coach 1984), New England Patriots 1985-88, Denver Broncos 1993-94, joined Titans/Oilers in 1995.

Steve Walters, wide receivers; born June 16, 1948, Jonesboro, Ark., lives in Nashville. Quarterback-defensive back Arkansas 1967-1970. No pro playing experience. College coach: Tampa 1973, Northeastern Louisana 1974-75, Morehead State 1976, Tulsa 1977-78, Memphis State 1979, Southern Methodist 1980-81, Alabama 1985. Pro coach: New England Patriots 1982-84, 1997-98, New Orleans 1986-1996, joined Titans in 1999.

Jim Washburn, defensive line; born December 2, 1949, Shelby, N.C., lives in Nashville. Offensive lineman Gardner-Webb 1969-1973. No pro playing experience. College coach: Southern Methodist 1976, Lees McRae J.C. 1977-78, Livingston 1979, New Mexico 1980-82, South Carolina 1983-88, Purdue 1989, Arkansas 1994-97, Houston 1998. Pro coach: London Monarchs (WLAF) 1991, Charlotte Rage (AFL) 1993, joined Titans in 1999.

Steve Watterson, strength and rehabilitation; born November 27, 1956, Newport, R.I., lives in Brentwood, Tenn. Attended Rhode Island. No college or pro playing experience. Pro coach: Philadelphia Eagles 1984-85, joined Titans/Oilers in 1986.

Gregg Williams, defensive coordinator; born July 15, 1958, Excelsior Springs, Mo., lives in Franklin, Tenn. Quarterback Northeast Missouri State 1976-79. No pro playing experience. College coach: Houston 1988-89. Pro coach: Joined Titans/Oilers in 1990.

1999 FIRST-YEAR ROSTER

Name	Pos.	Ht.	Wt.	Birthdate	College	Hometown	How Acq.
Adams, Ben	G	6-5	315	12/27/75	Texas	La Mirada, Calif.	FA
Battle, Albrey	DT	6-2	293	10/21/76	Arizona State	Poway, Calif.	FA
Bloom, Jason	P	6-6	185	1/31/77	New Mexico	Baltimore, Md.	FA
Bradley, Josh (1)	TE	6-6	270	3/27/74	Louisiana Tech	Oak Grove, La.	FA-'98
Bryant, Aaron	TE	6-4	275	11/3/76	Samford	Brentwood, Tenn.	FA
Bryant, Maurice (1)	WR	6-0	195	10/8/73	Houston	Houston, Tex.	FA
Burnett, Everett	WR	6-1	196	12/10/76	Kansas State	St. Louis, Mo.	FA
Caliandro, Matt	DE	6-5	250	3/26/77	Albany	Valley Stream, N.Y.	FA
Cameron, Delaunta	LB	6-2	237	7/2/75	Georgia Tech	Arlington, Va.	FA
Church, Tony (1)	TE	6-5	251	3/2/74	Wisconsin-Oshkosh	Black Creek, Wis.	FA
Daft, Kevin	QB	6-1	184	11/19/75	California-Davis	Tustin, Calif.	D5
Gamble, Jason	C	6-3	300	9/12/75	Clemson	Wichita, Kan.	FA
Gilbert, Lonnie (1)	G	6-2	290	8/27/75	North Carolina State	Miami, Fla.	FA-'98
Glover, Phil	LB	5-11	239	12/17/75	Utah	Las Vegas, Nev.	D7
Gould, Garett	RB	6-2	238	5/30/76	Michigan State	Troy, Mich.	FA
Hall, Darran	WR-KR	5-8	166	9/8/75	Colorado State	San Diego, Calif.	D6
Kearse, Jevon	DE	6-4	260	9/3/76	Florida	Ft. Myers, Fla.	D1
Mitchell, Donald	CB-S	5-9	185	12/14/76	Southern Methodist	Beaumont, Tex.	D4b
Page, Craig	C	6-3	300	1/17/76	Georgia Tech	Jupiter, Fla.	FA
Piller, Zach	G	6-5	332	5/2/76	Florida	Tallahassee, Fla.	D3
Rafferty, Ian	T	6-5	300	9/2/76	North Carolina State	Summerville, S.C.	FA
Sigler, Kelvin	S	6-1	186	6/20/76	Alabama	Mobile, Ala.	FA
Stroshine, David	LB	6-2	225	6/3/76	Weber State	Orem, Utah	FA
Sutton, Mike (1)	DE	6-4	265	4/21/75	Louisiana State	Fliell, La.	FA-'98
Thornton, John	DT	6-2	304	10/2/76	West Virginia	Philadelphia, Pa.	D2
Ward, Chris (1)	DE-DT	6-3	275	2/4/74	Kentucky	Atlanta, Ga.	FA-'98
Ware, Brad	S	6-1	207	3/26/78	Auburn	Powder Springs, Ga.	D4a

The term NFL Rookie is defined as a player who is in his first season of professional football and has not been on the roster of another professional football team for any regular-season or postseason games. A Rookie is designated by an "R" on NFL rosters. Players who have been active in another professional football league or players who have NFL experience, including either preseason training camp or being on an Active List or Inactive List, or on Reserve/Injured or Reserve/Physically Unable to Perform for fewer than six regular-season games, are termed NFL First-Year Players. An NFL First-Year Player is designated by a "1" on NFL rosters. Thereafter, a player is credited with an additional year of experience for each season in which he accumulates six games on the Active List or Inactive List, or on Reserve/Injured or Reserve/Physically Unable to Perform.

NOTES

The NFC

ARIZONA CARDINALS

National Football Conference
Eastern Division
Team Colors: Cardinal Red, Black, and White
P.O. Box 888
Phoenix, Arizona 85001-0888
Telephone: (602) 379-0101

CLUB OFFICIALS

President: William V. Bidwill
Vice President: Larry Wilson
Vice Chairman: Thomas J. Guilfoil
Treasurer and Chief Financial Officer: Charley Schlegel
Vice President: William V. Bidwill, Jr.
Vice President/General Counsel: Michael Bidwill
General Manager: Bob Ferguson
Assistant to the President: Rod Graves
Public Relations Director: Paul Jensen
Media Coordinator: Greg Gladysiewski
Publications/Internet Coordinator: Luke Sacks
Director-NFL Programs & Community Outreach: Garth Jax
Director of Players Programs: Earl Edwards
Director of Community Relations: Adele Harris
Director of Marketing: Joe Castor
Business Manager: Steve Walsh
Ticket Manager: Steve Bomar
Trainer: John Omohundro
Assistant Trainers: Jim Shearer, Jeff Herndon
Equipment Manager: Mark Ahlemeier
Assistant Equipment Manager: Steve Christensen
Stadium: Sun Devil Stadium • **Capacity:** 73,273
Fifth Street
Tempe, Arizona 85287
Playing Surface: Grass
Training Camp: Northern Arizona University
Flagstaff, Arizona 86011

1999 SCHEDULE

PRESEASON

Aug. 14	at Denver	7:00
Aug. 20	**Tennessee**	7:00
Aug. 28	at Seattle	7:00
Sept. 3	**Oakland**	7:00

REGULAR SEASON

Sept. 12	at Philadelphia	1:00
Sept. 19	at Miami	1:00
Sept. 27	**San Francisco** (Mon.)	6:00
Oct. 3	at Dallas	12:00
Oct. 10	**New York Giants**	1:05
Oct. 17	**Washington**	5:20
Oct. 24	Open Date	
Oct. 31	**New England**	2:05
Nov. 7	at New York Jets	1:00
Nov. 14	**Detroit**	2:15
Nov. 21	**Dallas**	2:15
Nov. 28	at New York Giants	1:00
Dec. 5	**Philadelphia**	2:05
Dec. 12	at Washington	1:00
Dec. 19	**Buffalo**	6:20
Dec. 26	at Atlanta	1:00
Jan. 2	at Green Bay	12:00

RECORD HOLDERS

INDIVIDUAL RECORDS—CAREER

Category	Name	Performance
Rushing (Yds.)	Ottis Anderson, 1979-1986	7,999
Passing (Yds.)	Jim Hart, 1966-1983	34,639
Passing (TDs)	Jim Hart, 1966-1983	209
Receiving (No.)	Larry Centers, 1990-98	535
Receiving (Yds.)	Roy Green, 1979-1990	8,497
Interceptions	Larry Wilson, 1960-1972	52
Punting (Avg.)	Jerry Norton, 1959-1961	44.9
Punt Return (Avg.)	Charley Trippi, 1947-1955	13.7
Kickoff Return (Avg.)	Ollie Matson, 1952, 1954-58	28.5
Field Goals	Jim Bakken, 1962-1978	282
Touchdowns (Tot.)	Roy Green, 1979-1990	70
Points	Jim Bakken, 1962-1978	1,380

INDIVIDUAL RECORDS—SINGLE SEASON

Category	Name	Performance
Rushing (Yds.)	Ottis Anderson, 1979	1,605
Passing (Yds.)	Neil Lomax, 1984	4,614
Passing (TDs)	Charley Johnson, 1963	28
	Neil Lomax, 1984	28
Receiving (No.)	Larry Centers, 1995	101
Receiving (Yds.)	Rob Moore, 1997	1,584
Interceptions	Bob Nussbaumer, 1949	12
Punting (Avg.)	Jerry Norton, 1960	45.6
Punt Return (Avg.)	John (Red) Cochran, 1949	20.9
Kickoff Return (Avg.)	Ollie Matson, 1958	35.5
Field Goals	Greg Davis, 1995	30
Touchdowns (Tot.)	John David Crow, 1962	17
Points	Jim Bakken, 1967	117
	Neil O'Donoghue, 1984	117

INDIVIDUAL RECORDS—SINGLE GAME

Category	Name	Performance
Rushing (Yds.)	LeShon Johnson, 9-22-96	214
Passing (Yds.)	Boomer Esiason, 11-10-96 (OT)	522
Passing (TDs)	Jim Hardy, 10-2-50	6
	Charley Johnson, 9-26-65, 11-2-69	6
Receiving (No.)	Sonny Randle, 11-4-62	16
Receiving (Yds.)	Sonny Randle, 11-4-62	256
Interceptions	Bob Nussbaumer, 11-13-49	*4
	Jerry Norton, 11-20-60	*4
	Kwamie Lassiter, 12-27-98	*4
Field Goals	Jim Bakken, 9-24-67	*7
Touchdowns (Tot.)	Ernie Nevers, 11-28-29	*6
Points	Ernie Nevers, 11-28-29	*40

*NFL Record

COACHING HISTORY

Chicago 1920-1959, St. Louis 1960-1987
(419-575-39)

1920-22	John (Paddy) Driscoll	17-8-4
1923-24	Arnold Horween	13-8-1
1925-26	Norman Barry	16-8-2
1927	Guy Chamberlin	3-7-1
1928	Fred Gillies	1-5-0
1929	Dewey Scanlon	6-6-1
1930	Ernie Nevers	5-6-2
1931	LeRoy Andrews*	0-1-0
1931	Ernie Nevers	5-3-0
1932	Jack Chevigny	2-6-2
1933-34	Paul Schissler	6-15-1
1935-38	Milan Creighton	16-26-4
1939	Ernie Nevers	1-10-0
1940-42	Jimmy Conzelman	8-22-3
1943-45	Phil Handler**	1-29-0
1946-48	Jimmy Conzelman	27-10-0
1949	Phil Handler-Buddy Parker***	2-4-0
1949	Raymond (Buddy) Parker	4-1-1
1950-51	Earl (Curly) Lambeau****	7-15-0
1951	Phil Handler-Cecil Isbell#	1-1-0
1952	Joe Kuharich	4-8-0
1953-54	Joe Stydahar	3-20-1
1955-57	Ray Richards	14-21-1
1958-61	Frank (Pop) Ivy##	17-29-2
1961	Chuck Drulis-Ray Prochaska-Ray Willsey###	2-0-0
1962-65	Wally Lemm	27-26-3
1966-70	Charley Winner	35-30-5
1971-72	Bob Hollway	8-18-2
1973-77	Don Coryell	42-29-1
1978-79	Bud Wilkinson####	9-20-0
1979	Larry Wilson	2-1-0
1980-85	Jim Hanifan	39-50-1
1986-89	Gene Stallings@	23-34-1
1989	Hank Kuhlmann	0-5-0
1990-93	Joe Bugel	20-44-0
1994-95	Buddy Ryan	12-20-0
1996-98	Vince Tobin	21-29-0

* Resigned after one game in 1931
** Co-coach with Walt Kiesling in Chicago Cardinals-Pittsburgh merger in 1944
*** Co-coaches for first six games in 1949
**** Resigned after 10 games in 1951
\# Co-coaches
\## Resigned after 12 games in 1961
\### Co-coaches
\#### Released after 13 games in 1979
@ Released after 11 games in 1989

SUN DEVIL STADIUM

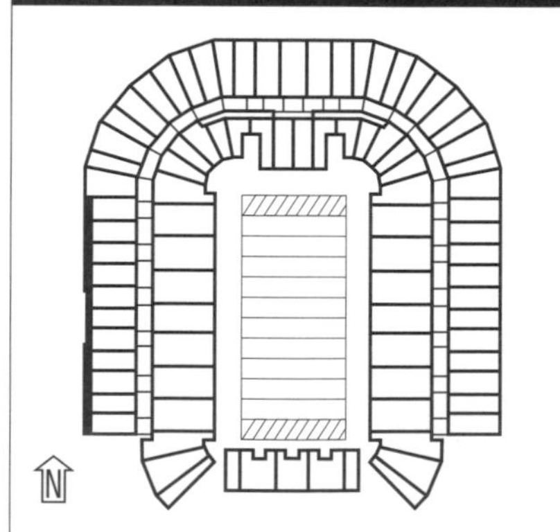

1998 TEAM RECORD

PRESEASON (2-2)

Date	Result		Opponent
8/7	L	10-13	at Detroit (OT)
8/14	W	27-24	Chicago
8/22	L	24-31	Seattle
8/29	W	21-14	at Oakland

REGULAR SEASON (9-7)

Date	Result		Opponent	Att.
9/6	L	10-38	at Dallas	63,602
9/13	L	14-33	at Seattle	57,678
9/20	W	17-3	Philadelphia	36,717
9/27	W	20-17	at St. Louis	55,832
10/4	L	20-23	Oakland	52,178
10/11	W	20-7	Chicago	47,860
10/18	L	7-34	at New York Giants	70,456
11/1	W	17-15	at Detroit	66,087
11/8	W	29-27	Washington	43,159
11/15	L	28-35	Dallas	69,923
11/22	W	45-42	at Washington	66,435
11/29	L	24-34	at Kansas City	69,613
12/6	L	19-23	New York Giants	46,128
12/13	W	20-17	at Philadelphia (OT)	62,176
12/20	W	19-17	New Orleans	51,617
12/27	W	16-13	San Diego	71,670

(OT) Overtime

POSTSEASON (1-1)

Date	Result		Opponent	Att.
1/2	W	20-7	at Dallas	62,969
1/10	L	21-41	at Minnesota	63,760

SCORE BY PERIODS

Cardinals	61	99	69	93	3	—	325
Opponents	61	127	68	122	0	—	378

ATTENDANCE

Home 419,252 Away 511,879 Total 931,131
Single-game home record, 73,025 (9/19/93)
Single-season home record, 497,330 (1994)

1998 TEAM STATISTICS

	Cardinals	Opp.
Total First Downs	315	321
Rushing	98	117
Passing	179	177
Penalty	38	27
Third Down: Made/Att	76/218	78/210
Third Down Pct.	34.9	37.1
Fourth Down: Made/Att	10/18	11/18
Fourth Down Pct.	55.6	61.1
Total Net Yards	5,109	5,265
Avg. Per Game	319.3	329.1
Total Plays	1052	1049
Avg. Per Play	4.9	5.0
Net Yards Rushing	1,627	1,989
Avg. Per Game	101.7	124.3
Total Rushes	450	492
Net Yards Passing	3,482	3,276
Avg. Per Game	217.6	204.8
Sacked/Yards Lost	50/286	39/250
Gross Yards	3,768	3,526
Att./Completions	552/326	518/299
Completion Pct.	59.1	57.7
Had Intercepted	20	20
Punts/Average	82/41.2	75/43.9
Net Punting Avg.	82/35.9	75/38.7
Penalties/Yards	88/758	114/954
Fumbles/Ball Lost	30/16	31/19
Touchdowns	36	44
Rushing	18	18
Passing	17	21
Returns	1	5
Avg. Time of Possession	29:15	30:45

1998 INDIVIDUAL STATISTICS

Passing	Att.	Comp.	Yds.	Pct.	TD	Int.	Tkld.	Rating
Plummer	547	324	3,737	59.2	17	20	49/280	75.0
D. Brown	5	2	31	40.0	0	0	1/6	61.3
Cardinals	552	326	3,768	59.1	17	20	50/286	74.9
Opponents	518	299	3,526	57.7	21	20	39/250	76.0

SCORING	TD R	TD P	TD Rt	PAT	FG	Saf	PTS
Nedney	0	0	0	30/30	13/19	0	69
Murrell	8	2	0	0/0	0/0	0	60
Bates	6	0	0	0/0	0/0	0	36
Jacke	0	0	0	6/6	10/14	0	36
Rob Moore	0	5	0	0/0	0/0	0	30
McWilliams	0	4	0	0/0	0/0	0	24
Plummer	4	0	0	0/0	0/0	0	24
Sanders	0	3	0	0/0	0/0	0	18
Centers	0	2	0	0/0	0/0	0	12
Bennett	0	0	1	0/0	0/0	0	6
Gedney	0	1	0	0/0	0/0	0	6
Cardinals	18	17	1	36/36	23/33	2	325
Opponents	18	21	5	40/41	24/30	0	378

2-Pt. Conversions: None.
Team 0-0, Opponents 1-3.

RUSHING	Att.	Yds.	Avg.	LG	TD
Murrell	274	1,042	3.8	32	8
Plummer	51	217	4.3	27	4
Bates	60	165	2.8	15	6
Centers	31	110	3.5	14	0
Pittman	29	91	3.1	11	0
D. Brown	1	2	2.0	2	0
Sanders	4	0	0.0	7	0
Cardinals	450	1,627	3.6	32	18
Opponents	492	1,989	4.0	30t	18

RECEIVING	No.	Yds.	Avg.	LG	TD
Sanders	89	1,145	12.9	42	3
Centers	69	559	8.1	54	2
Rob Moore	67	982	14.7	57	5
Metcalf	31	324	10.5	29	0
McWilliams	26	284	10.9	26	4
Gedney	22	271	12.3	32	1
Murrell	18	169	9.4	30	2
Brock	2	12	6.0	7	0
Bates	1	14	14.0	14	0
Anderson	1	8	8.0	8	0
Cardinals	326	3,768	11.6	57	17
Opponents	299	3,526	11.8	87t	21

INTERCEPTIONS	No.	Yds.	Avg.	LG	TD
Lassiter	8	80	10.0	29	0
McKinnon	5	25	5.0	17	0
Bennett	2	100	50.0	70t	1
Chavous	2	0	0.0	0	0
Williams	1	15	15.0	15	0
McCombs	1	14	14.0	14	0
McCleskey	1	1	1.0	1	0
Cardinals	20	235	11.8	70t	1
Opponents	20	373	18.7	56t	4

PUNTING	No.	Yds.	Avg.	In 20	LG
Player	81	3,378	41.7	12	67
Cardinals	82	3,378	41.2	12	67
Opponents	75	3,296	43.9	26	64

PUNT RETURNS	No.	FC	Yds.	Avg.	LG	TD
Metcalf	43	7	295	6.9	24	0
Cardinals	43	7	295	6.9	24	0
Opponents	38	21	313	8.2	43	0

KICKOFF RETURNS	No.	Yds.	Avg.	LG	TD
Metcalf	57	1,218	21.4	59	0
Pittman	4	84	21.0	22	0
Gedney	2	12	6.0	7	0
Cardinals	63	1,314	20.9	59	0
Opponents	56	1,200	21.4	62	0

FIELD GOALS	1-19	20-29	30-39	40-49	50+
Nedney	0/0	6/6	1/1	5/8	1/4
Jacke	0/0	3/3	5/6	1/3	1/2
Cardinals	0/0	9/9	6/7	6/11	2/6
Opponents	2/2	8/8	5/8	4/5	5/7

SACKS	No.
Rice	10.0
M. Smith	9.0
Wadsworth	5.0
Swann	4.0
Miller	3.0
McKinnon	2.0
Knight	1.0
Maddox	1.0
Sapp	1.0
Tillman	1.0
Williams	1.0
Wilson	1.0
Cardinals	39.0
Opponents	50.0

1999 DRAFT CHOICES

Round	Name	Pos.	College
1	David Boston	WR	Ohio State
	L.J. Shelton	T	Eastern Michigan
2	Johnny Rutledge	LB	Florida
3	Tom Burke	DE	Wisconsin
4	Joel Makovicka	RB	Nebraska
5	Paris Johnson	DB	Miami, Ohio
	Yusuf Scott	G	Arizona
6	Jacoby Rhinehart	DB	Southern Methodist
	Melvin Bradley	LB	Arkansas
	Dennis McKinley	RB	Mississippi State
7	Chris Greisen	QB	Northwest Missouri State

ARIZONA CARDINALS

1999 VETERAN ROSTER

No.		Name	Pos.	Ht.	Wt.	Birthdate	NFL Exp.	College	Hometown	How Acq.	'98 Games/ Starts
82		Anderson, Ronnie	WR	6-1	189	2/27/74	2	Allegheny College	Hunting Valley, Ohio	W(GB)-'98	4/0
24		Bates, Mario	RB	6-1	217	1/16/73	6	Arizona State	Tucson, Ariz.	UFA(NO)-'98	16/1
28	†	Bennett, Tommy	DB	6-2	219	2/19/73	4	UCLA	San Diego, Calif.	FA-'96	16/16
7		Brown, Dave	QB	6-5	230	2/25/70	8	Duke	Summit, N.J.	UFA(NYG)-'98	1/0
37		Centers, Larry	RB	6-0	225	6/1/68	10	Stephen F. Austin	Tatum, Tex.	D5-'90	16/12
25		Chavous, Corey	DB	6-0	204	1/15/76	2	Vanderbilt	Aiken, S.C.	D2a-'98	16/5
79		Clark, Jon	T	6-6	345	4/11/73	4	Temple	Philadelphia, Pa.	UFA(Chi)-'98	6/0
65		Clement, Anthony	T	6-7	355	4/10/76	2	Southwestern Louisiana	Lafayette, La.	D2b-'98	1/0
92		Cousins, Jomo	DE	6-5	277	9/2/74	2	Florida A&M	Seneca Valley, Calif.	D7a-'98	0*
72		Daniels, Jerome	T	6-5	350	9/13/74	2	Northeastern	Hartford, Conn.	FA-'97	8/5
69		DeGraffenreid, Allen	G	6-4	293	6/3/74	2	Vanderbilt	Kansas City, Mo.	FA-'97	5/0
62		Devlin, Mike	C	6-2	318	11/16/69	7	Iowa	Blacksburg, Va.	UFA(Buff)-'96	15/3
64	†	Dexter, James	T	6-7	319	3/3/73	4	South Carolina	Springfield, Va.	D5-'96	16/16
67		Dishman, Chris	G	6-3	320	2/27/74	3	Nebraska	Cozad, Neb.	D4-'97	12/11
76		Drake, Jerry	DE	6-5	310	7/9/69	4	Hastings College	Kingston, N.Y.	FA-'95	1/1
59		Fredrickson, Rob	LB	6-4	240	5/13/71	6	Michigan State	St. Joseph, Mich.	UFA(Det)-'99	16/16*
84		Gedney, Chris	TE	6-5	250	8/9/70	7	Syracuse	Liverpool, N.Y.	UFA(Chi)-'97	16/3
54	†	Graham, Aaron	C	6-4	293	5/22/73	4	Nebraska	Denton, Tex.	D4-'96	14/13
80		Hardy, Terry	TE	6-4	266	5/31/76	2	Southern Mississippi	Montgomery, Ala.	D5-'98	9/0
48		Hayes, Jarius	RB-TE	6-3	266	3/27/73	3	North Alabama	Muscle Shoals, Ala.	FA-'98	16/0
70		Holmes, Lester	G	6-4	315	9/27/69	7	Jackson State	Tylertown, Miss.	UFA(Oak)-'98	16/16
29		Howard, Ty	CB	5-9	185	11/30/73	3	Ohio State	Columbus, Ohio	D3-'97	9/0
13		Jacke, Chris	K	6-0	205	3/12/66	10	Texas-El Paso	Richmond, Va.	FA-'98	4/0
73		Joyce, Matt	G	6-7	313	3/30/72	4	Richmond	St. Petersubrg, Fla.	FA-'96	11/0
86		Junkin, Trey	TE	6-2	258	1/23/61	17	Louisiana Tech	North Little Rock, Ark.	W(Oak)-'96	16/0
22		Knight, Tom	CB	5-11	196	12/29/74	3	Iowa	Marlton, N.J.	D1-'97	8/5
42		Lassiter, Kwamie	S	6-0	202	12/3/69	5	Kansas	Newport News, Va.	FA-'95	16/6
53		Maddox, Mark	LB	6-1	233	3/23/68	9	Northern Michigan	Milwaukee, Wis.	UFA(Buff)-'98	14/3
44		McCleskey, J.J.	CB	5-8	184	4/10/70	6	Tennessee	Knoxville, Tenn.	W(NO)-'96	12/0
50		McCombs, Tony	LB	6-2	246	8/24/74	3	Eastern Kentucky	Hopkinsville, Ky.	D6b-'97	14/13
57	†	McKinnon, Ronald	LB	6-0	240	9/20/73	4	North Alabama	Elba, Ala.	FA-'96	13/13
87	†	McWilliams, Johnny	TE	6-4	271	12/14/72	4	Southern California	Ontario, Calif.	D3-'96	16/15
21	#	Metcalf, Eric	WR	5-10	188	1/23/68	11	Texas	Seattle, Wash.	T(SD)-'98	16/3
85		Moore, Rob	WR	6-3	203	9/27/68	10	Syracuse	Hempstead, N.Y.	T(NYJ)-'95	16/16
27		Murrell, Adrian	RB	5-11	214	10/16/70	7	West Virginia	Wahaiwa, Hawaii	T(NYJ)-'97	15/14
6		Nedney, Joe	K	6-4	215	3/22/73	4	San Jose State	San Jose, Calif.	FA-'97	12/0
96		Ottis, Brad	DT	6-5	281	8/2/72	6	Wayne State	Fremont, Neb.	FA-'96	0*
32		Pittman, Michael	RB	6-0	214	8/14/75	2	Fresno State	San Diego, Calif.	D4-'98	15/0
10		Player, Scott	P	6-0	220	12/17/69	2	Florida State	St. Augustine, Fla.	FA-'98	16/0
16		Plummer, Jake	QB	6-2	197	12/19/74	3	Arizona State	Boise, Idaho	D2-'97	16/16
97		Rice, Simeon	DE	6-5	260	2/24/74	4	Illinois	Chicago, Ill.	D1-'96	16/16
81		Sanders, Frank	WR	6-2	197	2/17/73	5	Auburn	Fort Lauderdale, Fla.	D2-'95	16/16
55	†	Sapp, Patrick	LB	6-4	258	5/11/73	4	Clemson	Jacksonville, Fla.	T(SD)-'98	16/1
78		Simpson, Carl	DE	6-2	292	4/18/70	7	Florida State	Baxley, Ga.	FA-'98	13/1
93		Smith, Mark	DE	6-4	290	8/28/74	3	Auburn	Vicksburg, Miss.	D7-'97	14/13
98		Swann, Eric	DE	6-5	313	8/16/70	9	No College	Swann Station, N.C.	D1-'91	7/5
91		Swinger, Rashod	DT	6-2	286	11/27/74	2	Rutgers	Manalapan, N.J.	FA-'97	16/11
40		Tillman, Pat	S	5-11	204	11/6/76	2	Arizona State	San Jose, Calif.	D7c-'98	16/10
90		Wadsworth, Andre	DE	6-4	278	10/19/74	2	Florida State	Miami, Fla.	D1-'98	16/15
52		Walz, Zack	LB	6-4	228	2/13/76	2	Dartmouth	San Jose, Calif.	D6-'98	16/0
66		West, Derek	T	6-8	312	3/28/72	4	Colorado	Denver, Colo.	FA-'99	0*
35		Williams, Aeneas	CB	5-11	202	1/29/68	9	Southern	New Orleans, La.	D3-'90	16/16
94		Wilson, Bernard	DT	6-3	318	8/17/70	7	Tennessee State	Nashville, Tenn.	W(TB)-'94	16/3

* Cousins inactive for 8 games in '98; Fredrickson played 16 games with Detroit; Ottis missed '98 season because of injury; West last active with Indianapolis in '97.

† Restricted free agent; subject to developments.

Unrestricted free agent; subject to developments.

Players lost through free agency (3): T Lomas Brown (Clev; 16), QB Stoney Case (Ind; 0), LB Jamir Miller (Clev; 16).

Also played with Cardinals in '98—WR Fred Brock (12 games), CB J.B. Brown (15), LB Terry Irving (6), CB Dell McGee (3).

COACHING STAFF

Head Coach,
Vince Tobin

Pro Career: Named Cardinals' head coach on February 7, 1996. Became thirty-third coach in the history of the franchise dating back to 1920. A 9-7 regular-season mark in 1998 translated into the team's first playoff appearance since 1982 and first postseason victory since 1947—a span of 51 years. The "Cardiac Cards" recorded seven victories by three points or less, won their first-round playoff contest 20-7 at Dallas, and logged eight wins against NFC opponents—the most by a Cardinals' team in 22 seasons. In his first season, Arizona rebounded from an 0-3 start to claim a 7-4 record in its final 11 games and remain in playoff contention until the final week of the season. Arizona improved from twenty-fourth (1995) to twelfth in offense, from twenty-sixth (1995) to twenty-first in defense, and forged the club's first winning November (3-1) since 1987. As a defensive coordinator of the Indianapolis Colts from 1994-95, oversaw a defense that was a principal reason Indianapolis finished 9-7 during the 1995 regular season before defeating San Diego (35-20) and Kansas City (10-7) in the first two rounds of postseason play. Tobin earned credit for rebuilding a Colts' defense he inherited that ranked last in overall defense in 1993. Tobin's first unit improved to twentieth in 1994 and tied for seventh with Carolina in 1995 at 314.2 yards per game. In four seasons prior to Tobin's arrival, the Colts' defense finished twenty-fourth or lower against the run. In 1994, Tobin's first Indianapolis defense ranked twelfth against the rush, then improved to sixth in 1995 at 91.1 yards per game, the second-lowest figure in club history. It also was just the third time in Colts history the opposition averaged less than 100 yards per game on the ground. Over the past two seasons, Tobin's defensive unit did not allow an individual to rush for 100 yards in 24 consecutive games (final 13 games in 1994, first 11 games in 1995). His 1994 Colts' defense also boasted the lowest red-zone touchdown percentage (40) in the NFL and did not allow a touchdown at home in the final 12 quarters of the season. Tobin previously served as defensive coordinator of the Chicago Bears (1986-1992), tutoring a Bears' defense that set an NFL record for fewest points allowed in a 16-game season (187 in 1986). His 1986 Chicago unit topped the league by allowing just 258 yards per contest. The 1987 Bears surrendered the league's fewest points (215) and sported the best rushing defense (82.9). Tobin also earned victories over Tampa Bay and Washington as Chicago's interim head coach for Mike Ditka. Tobin's other coaching stops have been with the USFL Philadelphia/Baltimore Stars (1983-85), the CFL British Columbia Lions (1977-1982), and his alma mater, the University of Missouri (1967-1976). Tobin's defensive units in the CFL ranked second overall during his six seasons, while his defensive schemes in the USFL helped the Stars rank first defensively in 1983 and 1984 and second in 1985 while allowing the fewest points all three seasons. The Stars reached the league championship game each season, winning the final two times. Career record: 21-29.

Background: Tobin played defensive back at Missouri from 1961-64. He joined the Missouri coaching staff as a defensive assistant from 1967-1976, serving the final six years as defensive coordinator. Tobin owns a bachelor's degree in education and a master's degree in guidance and counseling.

Personal: Born September 29, 1943, in Burlington Junction, Missouri. He and his wife, Kathy, have two children—son Ryan and daughter Shannon.

ASSISTANT COACHES

Alan Everest, special teams; born August 22, 1950, Santa Barbara, Calif., lives in Phoenix. Safety Southern Methodist 1970-71. No pro playing experience. College coach: Southern Methodist 1972, North Texas State 1973-74, Cameron (Okla.) 1974-75, U.S. International 1981-87. Pro coach: Arkansas Miners (PSFL) 1991-92, Birmingham Barracudas (CFL) 1995, joined Cardinals in 1996.

John Garrett, quarterbacks; born March 2, 1965, Danville, Pa., lives in Phoenix. Wide reciever Columbia 1983-84, Princeton 1987. Pro wide receiver Cincinnati Bengals 1989, San Antonio Riders (World League) 1991. Pro coach: Cincinnati Bengals 1995-98, joined Cardinals in 1999.

Joe Greene, defensive line; born September 24, 1946, Temple, Tex., lives in Phoenix. Defensive tackle North Texas State 1966-68. Pro defensive tackle Pittsburgh Steelers 1969-1981. Inducted into Pro Football Hall of Fame in 1987. Pro coach: Pittsburgh Steelers 1987-1991, Miami Dolphins 1992-95, joined Cardinals in 1996.

Larry Marmie, defensive backs; born October 17, 1942, Barnesville, Ohio, lives in Phoenix. Quarterback Eastern Kentucky 1962-65. No pro playing experience. College coach: Eastern Kentucky 1967-68, 1972-76, Morehead State 1968-1971, Tulsa 1977-78, North Carolina 1979-1982, Tennessee 1983-84, 1992-94, Arizona State 1988-1991 (head coach), UCLA 1995. Pro coach: Joined Cardinals in 1996.

Dave McGinnis, defensive coordinator; born August 7, 1951, Independence, Kan., lives in Phoenix. Defensive back Texas Christian 1970-72. No pro playing experience. College coach: Texas Christian 1973-74, 1982, Missouri 1975-77, Indiana State 1978-1981, Kansas State 1983-85. Pro coach: Chicago Bears 1986-1995, joined Cardinals in 1996.

Glenn Pires, linebackers; born September 13, 1958, New Bedford, Mass., lives in Phoenix. Linebacker Springfield College 1978-1980. No pro playing experience. College coach: Syracuse 1983-84, Dartmouth 1985-88, Michigan State 1989-1995. Pro coach: Joined Cardinals in 1996.

Vic Rapp, wide receivers; born December 23, 1935, Marionville, Mo., lives in Phoenix. Running back Southwest Missouri State 1954-57. No pro playing experience. Pro coach: Edmonton Eskimos (CFL) 1972-76, British Columbia Lions (CFL) 1977-1982 (head coach), Houston Oilers 1983, Los Angeles Rams 1984, Tampa Bay Buccaneers 1985-86, Detroit Lions 1987, Chicago Bears 1989-1992, joined Cardinals in 1996.

Bob Rogucki, strength and conditioning; born September 27, 1953, Clarksburg, W. Va., lives in Phoenix. No college or pro playing experience. College coach: Penn State 1981, Weber State 1982, Army 1983-89. Pro coach: Joined Cardinals in 1990.

Johnny Roland, running backs; born May 21, 1943, Corpus Christi, Tex., lives in Phoenix. Running back Missouri 1961-65. Pro running back St. Louis Cardinals 1966-1972, New York Giants 1973. College coach: Notre Dame 1975. Pro coach: Green Bay Packers 1974, Philadelphia Eagles 1976-78, Chicago Bears 1983-1992, New York Jets 1993-94, St. Louis Rams 1995-96, joined Cardinals in 1997.

Marc Trestman, offensive coordinator; born January 15, 1956, Minneapolis, Minn., lives in Phoenix. Quarterback Minnesota 1975-77, Moorhead (Minn.) State 1978. Pro quarterback Minnesota Vikings 1979. College coach: Miami 1981-84. Pro coach: Minnesota Vikings 1985-86, 1990-1991, Tampa Bay Buccaneers 1987, Cleveland Browns 1988-89, San Francisco 49ers 1995-96, Detroit Lions 1997, joined Cardinals in 1998.

George Warhop, offensive line; born September 19, 1961, Riverside, Calif., lives in Phoenix. Guard Mt. San Jacinto (Calif.) J.C. 1979-80. Pro center Cincinnati Bengals 1981-82. College coach: Cincinnati 1983, Kansas 1984-86, Vanderbilt 1987-89, New Mexico 1990, Southern Methodist 1993, Boston College 1994-95. Pro coach: London Monarchs (World League) 1991-92, St. Louis Rams 1996-97, joined Cardinals in 1998.

1999 FIRST-YEAR ROSTER

Name	Pos.	Ht.	Wt.	Birthdate	College	Hometown	How Acq.
Boston, David	WR	6-1	215	8/19/78	Ohio State	Humble, Tex.	D1a
Bradley, Melvin	LB	6-1	269	8/15/76	Arkansas	Barton, Ark.	D6b
Brown, Rod	RB	5-11	247	2/28/74	North Carolina State	Litonia, Ga.	D6a-'97
Burke, Thomas	DE	6-2	264	10/12/76	Wisconsin	Poplar, Wis.	D3
Carpenter, Chad (1)	WR	5-11	198	7/17/73	Washington State	Ontario, Ore.	D5-'97
Carpenter, Jim	WR	6-0	185	10/30/76	Texas-El Paso	Fort Lauderdale, Fla.	FA
Collins, Aaron	LB	6-0	237	7/19/75	Penn State	Cinnaminson, N.J.	FA-'98
Dozier, Joey	RB	6-0	226	2/23/77	New Mexico State	Topeka, Kan.	FA
Drake, Kevin (1)	WR	6-3	187	1/2/75	Alabama-Birmingham	Gardendale, Ala.	FA-'98
Falcon, Dan	DT	6-1	248	2/19/76	Western Michigan	Highland Park, Ill.	FA
Fleming, Antonio (1)	G	6-3	309	2/6/74	Georgia	Calhoun County, Ga.	FA-'98
Greisen, Chris	QB	6-3	223	7/2/76	Northwest Missouri State	Sturgeon Bay, Wis.	D7
Hamler, Tony (1)	WR	6-1	180	12/20/75	Morehouse	Miami, Fla.	FA
Houzah, Terry	LB	6-2	246	6/26/76	Mississippi Valley State	Rolling Fork, Miss.	FA
Johnson, Paris	S	6-2	213	1/18/76	Miami, Ohio	Chicago, Ill.	D5a
Kelenic, Joe	DT	6-3	286	11/3/75	Northern Michigan	New Berlin, Wis.	FA
Leigh, Graham	QB	6-2	212	5/10/75	New Mexico	Mesa, Ariz.	FA
Lucas, Justin	CB	5-10	194	7/15/76	Albilene Christian	Victoria, Tex.	FA
Makovicka, Joel	RB	5-10	247	10/6/75	Nebraska	Brainard, Neb.	D4
McCullough, Andy (1)	WR	6-3	210	11/11/75	Tennessee	Dayton, Ohio	FA-'98
McKinley, Dennis	RB	6-1	241	11/3/76	Mississippi State	Weir, Miss.	D6c
Moten, Mike (1)	DE	6-5	266	3/12/74	Florida	Daytona Beach, Fla.	FA-'98
Rhinehart, Coby	CB	5-10	187	2/7/77	Southern Methodist	Dallas, Tex.	D6a
Riles, Nate	CB	5-10	177	2/13/74	Ohio Northern	Akron, Ohio	FA
Roberts, Jeff	P	6-3	207	6/1/76	Fresno State	Ben Lomond, Calif.	FA-'98
Rutledge, Johnny	LB	6-2	245	1/4/77	Florida	Belle Glade, Fla.	D2
Scott, Yusuf	G	6-2	324	11/30/76	Arizona	LaPorte, Tex.	D5b
Shelton, L.J.	T	6-6	341	3/21/76	Eastern Michigan	Rochester Hills, Mich.	D1b
Thompson, Ricky	CB	6-0	182	7/15/77	Oklahoma State	Hubbard, Tex.	FA
Williams, Aaron	DE	6-4	255	7/26/74	Indiana	Brampton, Ontario, Canada	FA
Williams, Clerence	RB	5-9	202	5/16/77	Michigan	Detroit, Mich.	FA
Williams, Damon	WR	6-2	217	10/30/77	Nevada-Las Vegas	Culver City, Calif.	FA

The term NFL Rookie is defined as a player who is in his first season of professional football and has not been on the roster of another professional football team for any regular-season or postseason games. A Rookie is designated by an "R" on NFL rosters. Players who have been active in another professional football league or players who have NFL experience, including either preseason training camp or being on an Active List or Inactive List, or on Reserve/Injured or Reserve/Physically Unable to Perform for fewer than six regular-season games, are termed NFL First-Year Players. An NFL First-Year Player is designated by a "1" on NFL rosters. Thereafter, a player is credited with an additional year of experience for each season in which he accumulates six games on the Active List or Inactive List, or on Reserve/Injured or Reserve/Physically Unable to Perform.

NOTES

ATLANTA FALCONS

National Football Conference
Western Division
Team Colors: Black, Red, Silver, and White
One Falcon Place
Suwanee, Georgia 30024
Telephone: (770) 945-1111

CLUB OFFICIALS

President: Taylor Smith
Executive Vice President/Football Operations & Head Coach: Dan Reeves
Executive Vice President of Administration: Jim Hay
General Manager: Harold Richardson
Vice President of Football Operations: Ron Hill
Vice President of Finance, CFO: Kevin Anthony
Vice President of Corporate Development: Tommy Nobis
Controller: Wallace Norman
Administrative Asst./Finance: John Knox
Vice President of Administration: Rob Jackson
Sales & Marketing: Todd Marble, Jan Zeller
Special Events: Spencer Treadwell
Director of Public Relations: Aaron Salkin
Asst. Director of Public Relations: Frank Kleha
Director of Ticket Operations: Jack Ragsdale
Director of Community Relations: Carol Breeding
Player Programs Coordinator: Billy (White Shoes) Johnson
Director of Information Systems: Randy Kopp
Special Assistant to President: Jerry Rhea
Director of Player Personnel/Pro: Chuck Connor
Director of Player Personnel/College: Reed Johnson
Area Scouts: Ken Blair, Melvin Bratton, Dick Corrick, Boyd Dowler, Elbert Dubenion, Bill Groman, Bob Harrison
National Scout: Mike Hagen
Assistant to Vice President of Football Operations: Les Snead
Head Athletic Trainer: Ron Medlin
Assistant Athletic Trainer: Harold King
Video Director: Tom Atcheson
Equipment Manager: Brian Boigner
Senior Director/Gameday Coordinator: Horace Daniel
Stadium: Georgia Dome • **Capacity:** 71,228
One Georgia Dome Drive
Atlanta, Georgia 30313
Playing Surface: Artificial turf
Training Camp: Furman University
3000 Poinsett Highway
Greenville, South Carolina 29613

1999 SCHEDULE

PRESEASON

Aug. 13	**Detroit**	7:30
Aug. 21	**Baltimore**	7:30
Aug. 27	at Tennessee	7:00
Sept. 3	at Cincinnati	7:30

REGULAR SEASON

Sept. 12	**Minnesota**	4:15
Sept. 20	at Dallas (Mon.)	8:00
Sept. 26	at St. Louis	12:00
Oct. 3	**Baltimore**	1:00
Oct. 10	at New Orleans	12:00
Oct. 17	**St. Louis**	1:00
Oct. 25	at Pittsburgh (Mon.)	9:00
Oct. 31	**Carolina**	1:00
Nov. 7	**Jacksonville**	1:00
Nov. 14	Open Date	
Nov. 21	at Tampa Bay	1:00
Nov. 28	at Carolina	8:20
Dec. 5	**New Orleans**	1:00
Dec. 12	at San Francisco	1:15
Dec. 19	at Tennessee	12:00
Dec. 26	**Arizona**	1:00
Jan. 3	**San Francisco** (Mon.)	9:00

RECORD HOLDERS

INDIVIDUAL RECORDS—CAREER

Category	Name	Performance
Rushing (Yds.)	Gerald Riggs, 1982-88	6,631
Passing (Yds.)	Steve Bartkowski, 1975-1985	23,468
Passing (TDs)	Steve Bartkowski, 1975-1985	154
Receiving (No.)	Andre Rison, 1990-94	423
Receiving (Yds.)	Alfred Jenkins, 1975-1983	6,257
Interceptions	Rolland Lawrence, 1973-1980	39
Punting (Avg.)	Rick Donnelly, 1985-89	42.6
Punt Return (Avg.)	Al Dodd, 1973-74	11.8
Kickoff Return (Avg.)	Tim Dwight, 1998	27.0
Field Goals	Mick Luckhurst, 1981-87	115
Touchdowns (Tot.)	Andre Rison, 1990-94	56
Points	Mick Luckhurst, 1981-87	558

INDIVIDUAL RECORDS—SINGLE SEASON

Category	Name	Performance
Rushing (Yds.)	Jamal Anderson, 1998	1,846
Passing (Yds.)	Jeff George, 1995	4,143
Passing (TDs)	Steve Bartkowski, 1980	31
Receiving (No.)	Terance Mathis, 1994	111
Receiving (Yds.)	Alfred Jenkins, 1981	1,358
Interceptions	Scott Case, 1988	10
Punting (Avg.)	Billy Lothridge, 1968	44.3
Punt Return (Avg.)	Al Dodd, 1974	12.7
Kickoff Return (Avg.)	Sylvester Stamps, 1987	27.5
Field Goals	Morten Andersen, 1995	31
Touchdowns (Tot.)	Jamal Anderson, 1998	16
Points	Morten Andersen, 1995	122

INDIVIDUAL RECORDS—SINGLE GAME

Category	Name	Performance
Rushing (Yds.)	Gerald Riggs, 9-2-84	202
Passing (Yds.)	Steve Bartkowski, 11-15-81	416
Passing (TDs)	Wade Wilson, 12-13-92	5
Receiving (No.)	William Andrews, 11-15-81	15
Receiving (Yds.)	Terance Mathis, 12-13-98	198
Interceptions	Many times Last time by Ray Buchanan, 12-7-97	2
Field Goals	Norm Johnson, 11-13-94	6
Touchdowns (Tot.)	Many times Last time by Jamal Anderson, 11-1-98	3
Points	Norm Johnson, 11-13-94	20

COACHING HISTORY

(200-301-5)

1966-68	Norb Hecker*	4-26-1
1968-74	Norm Van Brocklin**	37-49-3
1974-76	Marion Campbell***	6-19-0
1976	Pat Peppler	3-6-0
1977-82	Leeman Bennett	47-44-0
1983-86	Dan Henning	22-41-1
1987-89	Marion Campbell****	11-32-0
1989	Jim Hanifan	0-4-0
1990-93	Jerry Glanville	28-38-0
1994-96	June Jones	19-30-0
1997-98	Dan Reeves	23-12-0

*Released after three games in 1968
**Released after eight games in 1974
***Released after five games in 1976
****Retired after 12 games in 1989

GEORGIA DOME

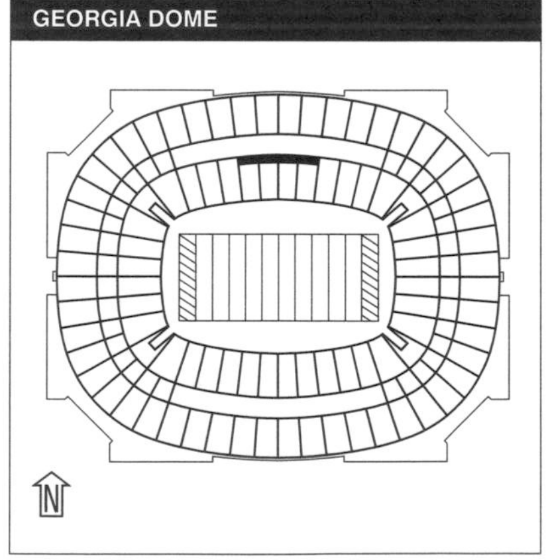

1998 TEAM RECORD

PRESEASON (2-2)

Date	Result		Opponent
8/7	L	16-31	Tennessee
8/14	W	7-3	at Detroit
8/22	L	22-28	vs. Pittsburgh at Morgantown, W. Va.
8/28	W	17-0	Cincinnati

REGULAR SEASON (14-2)

Date	Result		Opponent	Att.
9/6	W	19-14	at Carolina	65,129
9/13	W	17-12	Philadelphia	46,456
9/27	L	20-31	at San Francisco	62,296
10/4	W	51-23	Carolina	50,724
10/11	W	34-20	at New York Giants	71,173
10/18	W	31-23	New Orleans	60,774
10/25	L	3-28	at New York Jets	71,573
11/1	W	37-15	St. Louis	37,996
11/8	W	41-10	at New England	59,790
11/15	W	31-19	San Francisco	69,828
11/22	W	20-13	Chicago	60,804
11/29	W	21-10	at St. Louis	47,971
12/6	W	28-21	Indianapolis	61,141
12/13	W	27-17	at New Orleans	61,678
12/20	W	24-17	at Detroit	67,143
12/27	W	38-16	Miami	69,754

POSTSEASON (2-1)

Date	Result		Opponent	Att.
1/9	W	20-18	San Francisco	70,262
1/17	W	30-27	at Minnesota (OT)	64,060
1/31	L	19-34	vs. Denver at Miami	74,803

Overtime (OT)

SCORE BY PERIODS

Falcons	114	91	106	131	0	—	442
Opponents	60	95	76	58	0	—	289

ATTENDANCE

Home 457,477 Away 506,753 Total 964,230
Single-game home record, 70,089 (10/29/95)
Single-season home record, 553,979 (1992)

1998 TEAM STATISTICS

	Falcons	Opp.
Total First Downs	319	267
Rushing	111	65
Passing	175	172
Penalty	33	30
Third Down: Made/Att	83/199	72/201
Third Down Pct.	41.7	35.8
Fourth Down: Made/Att	1/3	9/19
Fourth Down Pct.	33.3	47.4
Total Net Yards	5,487	4,734
Avg. Per Game	342.9	295.9
Total Plays	993	950
Avg. Per Play	5.5	5.0
Net Yards Rushing	2,101	1,203
Avg. Per Game	131.3	75.2
Total Rushes	516	361
Net Yards Passing	3,386	3,531
Avg. Per Game	211.6	220.7
Sacked/Yards Lost	53/358	38/275
Gross Yards	3,744	3,806
Att./Completions	424/237	551/311
Completion Pct.	55.9	56.4
Had Intercepted	15	19
Punts/Avg.	74/40.0	80/42.8
Net Punting Avg.	74/36.6	80/37.5
Penalties/Yards Lost	116/841	118/858
Fumbles/Ball Lost	24/9	37/25
Touchdowns	53	35
Rushing	18	7
Passing	28	22
Returns	7	6
Avg. Time of Possession	33:10	26:50

1998 INDIVIDUAL STATISTICS

Passing	Att.	Comp.	Yds.	Pct.	TD	Int.	Tkld.	Rate
Chandler	327	190	3,154	58.1	25	12	45/283	100.9
DeBerg	59	30	369	50.8	3	1	6/60	80.4
Graziani	33	16	199	48.5	0	2	2/15	42.4
J. Anderson	2	0	0	0.0	0	0	0/0	39.6
Dwight	2	1	22	50.0	0	0	0/0	89.6
Martin	1	0	0	0.0	0	0	0/0	39.6
Falcons	424	237	3,744	55.9	28	15	53/358	92.7
Opponents	551	311	3,806	56.4	22	19	38/275	76.8

SCORING	TD R	TD P	TD Rt	PAT	FG	Saf	PTS
Andersen	0	0	0	51/52	23/28	0	120
J. Anderson	14	2	0	0/0	0/0	0	98
Mathis	0	11	0	0/0	0/0	0	66
Martin	0	6	0	0/0	0/0	0	36
Santiago	0	5	0	0/0	0/0	0	30
Christian	2	1	0	0/0	0/0	0	18
Chandler	2	0	0	0/0	0/0	0	12
Dwight	0	1	1	0/0	0/0	0	12
Bradford	0	0	1	0/0	0/0	1	8
A. Edwards	0	0	1	0/0	0/0	0	6
Kinchen	0	1	0	0/0	0/0	0	6
Kozlowski	0	1	0	0/0	0/0	0	6
Robinson	0	0	1	0/0	0/0	0	6
C. Smith	0	0	1	0/0	0/0	0	6
Tuggle	0	0	1	0/0	0/0	0	6
White	0	0	1	0/0	0/0	0	6
Falcons	18	28	7	51/52	23/28	1	442
Opponents	7	22	6	28/31	15/20	1	289

2-Point conversions: J. Anderson.
Team 1-1, Opponents 2-4.

RUSHING	Att.	Yds.	Avg.	LG	TD
J. Anderson	410	1,846	4.5	48	14
Chandler	36	121	3.4	19	2
Oxendine	18	50	2.8	21	0
Green	20	37	1.9	6	0
Christian	8	21	2.6	6	2
Graziani	4	21	5.3	12	0
Dwight	8	19	2.4	7	0
Downs	1	4	4.0	4	0
E. Williams	2	-2	-1.0	2	0
Mathis	1	-6	-6.0	-6	0
DeBerg	8	-10	-1.3	2	0
Falcons	516	2,101	4.1	48	18
Opponents	361	1,203	3.3	32	7

RECEIVING	No.	Yds.	Avg.	LG	TD
Martin	66	1,181	17.9	62	6
Mathis	64	1,136	17.8	78t	11
Santiago	27	428	15.9	62t	5
J. Anderson	27	319	11.8	27	2
Christian	19	214	11.3	39	1
Kinchen	11	157	14.3	32	1
Kozlowski	10	103	10.3	25	1
Dwight	4	94	23.5	44t	1
Downs	4	31	7.8	11	0
Green	2	34	17.0	28	0
Chandler	1	22	22.0	22	0
Harris	1	14	14.0	14	0
Oxendine	1	11	11.0	11	0
Falcons	237	3,744	15.8	78t	28
Opponents	311	3,806	12.2	82t	22

INTERCEPTIONS	No.	Yds.	Avg.	LG	TD
Buchanan	7	102	14.6	34	0
Robinson	4	36	9.0	25t	1
Bradford	3	11	3.7	11t	1
White	2	36	18.0	36	0
Booker	1	27	27.0	27	0
Brooking	1	12	12.0	12	0
Sauer	1	0	0.0	0	0
Falcons	19	224	11.8	36	2
Opponents	15	224	14.9	63t	2

PUNTING	No.	Yds.	Avg.	In 20	LG
Stryzinski	74	2,963	40.0	25	55
Falcons	74	2,963	40.0	25	55
Opponents	80	3,427	42.8	19	60

PUNT RETURNS	No.	FC	Yds.	Avg.	LG	TD
Dwight	31	13	263	8.5	23	0
Kinchen	6	5	38	6.3	9	0
Harris	1	6	-1	-1.0	-1	0
Buchanan	1	0	4	4.0	4	0
Mathis	1	0	0	0.0	0	0
Falcons	40	24	304	7.6	23	0
Opponents	20	29	112	5.6	37	0

KICKOFF RETURNS	No.	Yds.	Avg.	LG	TD
Dwight	36	973	27.0	93t	1
E. Williams	7	132	18.9	28	0
Green	1	24	24.0	24	0
Harris	1	16	16.0	16	0
Kozlowski	1	12	12.0	12	0
Falcons	46	1,157	25.2	93t	1
Opponents	69	1,613	23.4	102t	1

FIELD GOALS	1-19	20-29	30-39	40-49	50+
Andersen	0/1	8/9	7/7	6/9	2/2
Falcons	0/1	8/9	7/7	6/9	2/2
Opponents	0/0	5/5	6/6	4/7	0/2

SACKS	No.
Archambeau	10.0
C. Smith	8.5
Dronett	6.5
Hall	4.5
Tuggle	3.0
Fuller	2.0
Bennett	1.0
Crockett	1.0
A. Edwards	1.0
Burrough	0.5
Falcons	38.0
Opponents	53.0

1999 DRAFT CHOICES

Round	Name	Pos.	College
1	Patrick Kerney	DE	Virginia
2	Reggie Kelly	TE	Mississippi State
3	Jeff Paulk	RB	Arizona State
4	Johndale Carty	DB	Utah State
5	Eugene Baker	WR	Kent State
6	Jeff Kelly	LB	Kansas State
	Eric Thigpen	DB	Iowa
7	Todd McClure	C	Louisiana State
	Rondel Menendez	WR	Eastern Kentucky

ATLANTA FALCONS

1999 VETERAN ROSTER

No.	Name	Pos.	Ht.	Wt.	Birthdate	NFL Exp.	College	Hometown	How Acq.	'98 Games/ Starts
5	Andersen, Morten	K	6-2	222	8/19/60	18	Michigan State	Struer, Denmark	FA-'95	16/0
32	Anderson, Jamal	RB	5-11	235	9/30/72	6	Utah	Victoria, Tex.	D7-'94	16/16
92	Archambeau, Lester	DE	6-5	275	6/27/67	10	Stanford	Ft. Lauderdale, Fla.	T(GB)-'93	15/15
47	Bayne, Chris	S	6-1	215	3/22/75	3	Fresno State	Monroeville, Penn.	D7-'97	10/0
65	Bishop, Greg	G	6-5	315	5/2/71	7	Pacific	Wilson, N.C.	UFA(NYG)-'99	16/16*
20	Booker, Michael	CB	6-2	200	4/27/75	3	Nebraska	Red Bank, N.J.	D1-'97	14/6
23	Bradford, Ronnie	CB	5-10	195	10/1/70	7	Colorado	Oceanside, Calif.	UFA(Ariz)-'97	14/11
56	Brooking, Keith	LB	6-2	242	10/30/75	2	Georgia Tech	Milton, Fla.	D1-'98	15/0
27	Brown, Omar	S	5-10	200	3/28/75	2	North Carolina	Detroit, Mich.	D4-'98	2/0
34	Buchanan, Ray	CB	5-9	185	9/29/71	7	Louisville	Minot, N.D.	UFA(Ind)-'97	16/16
80	Calloway, Chris	WR	5-10	188	3/29/68	10	Michigan	Desoto, Tex.	FA-'99	16/16*
25	Carter, Marty	S	6-1	210	12/17/69	9	Middle Tennessee State	LaGrange, Ga.	UFA(Chi)-'99	16/16*
12	Chandler, Chris	QB	6-4	225	10/12/65	12	Washington	York, Pa.	T(Hou)-'97	14/14
44	Christian, Bob	RB	5-11	232	11/14/68	7	Northwestern	Chester, Va.	UFA(Car)-'97	14/10
68	Collins, Calvin	G-C	6-2	305	1/5/74	3	Texas A&M	Griffin, Ga.	D6-'97	16/16
94	Crockett, Henri	LB	6-2	238	10/28/74	3	Florida State	Pompano Beach, Fla.	D4-'97	10/10
45	Downs, Gary	RB	6-1	218	6/6/72	6	North Carolina State	El Camino, Calif.	FA-'97	16/1
75	Dronett, Shane	DT	6-6	298	1/12/71	8	Texas	Arkadelphia, Ark.	FA-'97	16/16
83	Dwight, Tim	WR-KR	5-8	180	7/13/75	2	Iowa	Chicago, Ill.	D4-'98	12/0
29	Fuller, Randy	CB	5-10	184	6/2/70	6	Tennessee State	East Orange, N.J.	UFA(Pitt)-'98	13/0
87	German, Jammi	WR	6-1	192	7/4/74	2	Miami	Hartford, Conn.	D3-'98	6/0
13	Graziani, Tony	QB	6-2	215	12/23/73	3	Oregon	Florissant, Mo.	D7-'97	4/1
98	Hall, Travis	DT	6-5	298	8/3/72	5	Brigham Young	Miami, Fla.	D6-'95	14/13
64	Hallen, Bob	C-G	6-4	305	3/9/75	2	Kent State	La Grange, Tex.	D2-'98	12/0
54	Hamilton, Ruffin	LB	6-1	235	3/2/71	4	Tulane	Sartell, Minn.	FA-'97	16/0
24	Hanspard, Byron	RB	5-10	200	1/23/76	3	Texas Tech	Santa Cruz, Calif.	D2-'97	0*
82	Harris, Ronnie	WR	5-11	185	6/4/70	5	Oregon	Senoia, Ga.	FA-'98	6/0
95	Jasper, Ed	DT	6-2	305	1/18/73	3	Texas A&M	Tarpon Springs, Fla.	FA-'99	7/0*
7	Kanell, Danny	QB	6-3	220	11/21/73	4	Florida State	Baton Rouge, La.	FA-'99	10/10*
85	Kozlowski, Brian	TE	6-3	250	10/4/70	6	Connecticut	San Antonio, Tex.	FA-'97	16/4
99	Kuberski, Bob	DT	6-4	300	4/5/71	5	Navy	Galveston, Tex.	UFA(GB)-'99	16/0*
37	Lane, Eric	RB	6-2	235	3/17/74	2	Tennessee	Beaumont, Tex.	FA-'99	0*
81	Mathis, Terance	WR	5-10	186	6/7/67	10	New Mexico	Omaha, Neb.	UFA(NYJ)-'94	16/16
22	McBurrows, Gerald	S	5-11	205	10/7/73	5	Kansas	Carson, Calif.	UFA(StL)-'99	10/0*
77	McDaniels, Pellom	DE	6-3	295	2/21/68	7	Oregon State	Jackson, Tenn.	UFA(KC)-'99	11/2*
28	Oxendine, Ken	RB	6-0	230	10/4/75	2	Virginia Tech	Houston, Tex.	D7-'98	9/0
76	Portilla, Jose	T	6-6	315	9/11/72	2	Arizona	Daytona Beach, Fla.	FA-'98	16/0
41	Robinson, Eugene	S	6-1	200	5/28/63	15	Colgate	Chicago, Ill.	UFA(GB)-'98	16/16
74	Salaam, Ephraim	T	6-7	310	6/19/76	2	San Diego State	Stone Mountain, Ga.	D7-'98	16/16
88	Santiago, O.J.	TE	6-7	264	4/4/74	3	Kent State	Granada Hills, Calif.	D3-'97	16/16
52	Sauer, Craig	LB	6-1	235	12/13/72	4	Minnesota	Iowa City, Iowa	D6-'96	16/6
67	Schreiber, Adam	C-G	6-4	295	2/20/62	16	Texas	Hearne, Tex.	UFA(NYG)-'97	16/0
90	Smith, Chuck	DE	6-2	262	12/21/69	8	Tennessee	Rochester, N.Y.	D2-'92	16/16
4	Stryzinski, Dan	P	6-2	200	5/15/65	10	Indiana	Ft. Myers, Fla.	UFA(TB)-'95	16/0
93	Swayda, Shawn	DE	6-5	297	9/4/74	2	Arizona State	Aberdeen, Miss.	FA-'98	5/0
59	Talley, Ben	LB	6-3	245	7/14/72	4	Tennessee	Athens, Ga.	FA-'98	8/0
26	Thibodeaux, Keith	CB	5-11	189	5/16/74	2	Northwestern State, La.	Charlotte, N.C.	FA-'99	0*
61	Tobeck, Robbie	C-G	6-4	298	3/6/70	6	Washington State	Phoenix, Ariz.	FA-'93	16/16
58	Tuggle, Jessie	LB	5-11	230	4/4/65	13	Valdosta State	Pompano Beach, Fla.	FA-'87	16/16
70	Whitfield, Bob	T	6-5	315	10/18/71	8	Stanford	Albany, Ga.	D1a-'92	16/16
21	Williams, Elijah	CB	5-10	182	8/20/75	2	Florida	Kenai, Alaska	D6-'98	15/0
69	Williams, Gene	G	6-2	320	10/14/68	9	Iowa State	Chester, Pa.	T(Clev)-'95	16/16

* Bishop and Calloway played 16 games with N.Y. Giants in '98; Carter played 16 games with Chicago; Hanspard missed the '98 season because of injury; Jasper played 7 games with Philadelphia; Kanell played 10 games with N.Y. Giants; Kuberski played 16 games with Green Bay; Lane was last active with N.Y. Giants in '97; McBurrows played 10 games with St. Louis; McDaniels played 11 games with Kansas City; Thibodeaux was last active with Washington in '97.

Players lost to free agency (3): DE John Burrough (Min; 16 games in '98), S Devin Bush (StL; 13), DE Antonio Edwards (Car; 15), WR Todd Kincher (Car; 11).

Also played with Falcons in '98—CB Darren Anderson (5 games), LB Cornelius Bennett (16), CB Juran Bolden (3), QB Steve DeBerg (8), RB Harold Green (6), WR Tony Martin (16), DT Esera Tuaolo (13), S William White (16), C Dave Widell (1).

COACHING STAFF

Head Coach,
Dan Reeves

Pro Career: The NFL's winningest active coach with 172 career wins, head coach Dan Reeves led the Falcons to their first-ever Super Bowl appearance last season after capturing the NFC title. In only his second season with Atlanta since taking over on January 20, 1997, Reeves led the Falcons to the NFC West title with a 14-2 record and a franchise record 442 points. Reeves was named Coach of the Year in 1998 for the fifth time in his coaching career after the Falcons improved from a 7-9 finish in 1997. Reeves had been the head coach of the New York Giants from 1993-96. Prior to that, he compiled a 117-79-1 record as head coach of the Denver Broncos from 1981-1992, earning NFL Coach of the Year honors in 1982, 1988, and 1991. He led the Broncos to three Super Bowl berths, four AFC Championship games, five AFC West Division titles, and eight winning seasons. In his first year in New York, he earned NFL Coach of the Year honors for a fourth time, taking the Giants from 6-10 to an 11-5 mark, including a wild-card playoff victory. Overall, Reeves has accumulated eleven winning seasons as head coach, participated in 46 playoff games and nine Super Bowls as an NFL player, assistant coach, and head coach. He is one of three coaches (Bill Parcells and Don Shula) to guide two different franchises to the Super Bowl. Reeves, whose teams have won at least 10 games nine different times, was very successful at Mile High Stadium, where he compiled a 72-21 (.774) record. His Broncos teams finished in first place five times and in second place three times in the AFC West. In 1984, Denver set a club record with 10 straight wins en route to a then franchise-best 13-win season. The following season (1985), the Broncos set a club record for total offense and points scored. In 1986, they started out 6-0 and established thirty-five team and individual club marks. Career record: 172-125-1.

Background: Prior to obtaining his first NFL head coaching job in 1981, Reeves had been a member of the Dallas Cowboys coaching staff since 1970, spending a total of 16 years under Tom Landry as a player and coach. In 1977 he was named offensive coordinator of Landry's staff. Reeves began his pro career as a free agent running back for Dallas in 1965. Prior to that he was a quarterback at South Carolina from 1962-64, passing for 2,561 yards and 16 TD's. He totaled 3,376 yards during his career with the Gamecocks, leading to his induction into the school's hall of fame in 1978. Reeves later was inducted into the state of Georgia Sports Hall of Fame.

Personal: Born January 19, 1944, Americus, Ga. Dan and his wife, Pam, live in Atlanta, and have three children—Dana, Laura, and Lee.

ASSISTANT COACHES

Marvin Bass, assistant to head coach-pro personnel; born August 28, 1919, Norfolk, Va., lives in Suwanee, Ga. Tackle William & Mary 1940-42. No pro playing experience. College coach: William & Mary 1944-48, 1950-51 (head coach), North Carolina 1949, 1953-55, South Carolina 1956-59, 1961-65, Georgia Tech 1960, Richmond 1963. Pro coach: Washington Redskins 1952, Montreal Beavers (Continental League) 1966-67, Montreal Alouettes (CFL) 1968, Buffalo Bills 1969-71, Birmingham Americans (WFL) 1974-75, Denver Broncos 1982-92. Joined Falcons in 1997.

Don Blackmon, linebackers; born March 14, 1958, Pompano Beach, Fla., lives in Suwanee, Ga. Linebacker Tulsa 1977-80. Pro linebacker New England Patriots 1981-87. Pro coach: New England Patriots 1988-90, Cleveland Browns 1991-92, New York Giants 1993-96, joined Falcons in 1997.

Rich Brooks, assistant head coach-defensive coordinator; born August 10, 1941, Forest, Calif., lives in Duluth, Ga. Tailback, defensive back, and quarterback Oregon State 1959-62. No pro playing experience. College coach: Oregon State 1965-69, 1973, UCLA 1970, 1976, Oregon 1977-94 (head coach). Pro coach: Los Angeles Rams 1971-72, San Francisco 49ers 1974-75, St. Louis Rams 1995-96 (head coach), joined Falcons in 1997.

Jack Burns, quarterbacks, born January 3, 1949, Tampa, Fla., lives in Suwanee, Ga. Safety Florida, 1967-70. No pro playing experience. College coach: Florida 1971-73, 1975, Louisville 1974, 1985-88, Texas 1976, Vanderbilt 1977-78, Auburn 1979-80. Pro coach: Tampa Bay Bandits (USFL) 1983, Washington Redskins 1989-91, Minnesota Vikings 1992-93, joined Falcons in 1997.

Rocky Colburn, asst. strength and conditioning; born May 24, 1963, Dallas, Ore., lives in Lawrenceville, Ga. Safety Alabama 1981-83. No pro playing experience. College coach: Alabama 1984, 1987-92, Samford 1986. Pro coach: Joined Falcons 1999.

James Daniel, tight ends; born January 17, 1953, Wetumpka, Ala., lives in Suwanee, Ga. Offensive guard Alabama State 1970-73. No pro playing experience. College coach: Auburn 1981-92. Pro coach: New York Giants 1993-96, joined Falcons in 1997.

Joe DeCamillis, special teams; born June 29, 1965, Arvada, Colo., lives in Alpharetta, Ga. No college or pro playing experience. College coach: Wyoming 1988. Pro coach: Denver Broncos 1989, Miami Dolphins 1990, New York Giants 1993-96, joined Falcons in 1997.

Bill Kollar, defensive line; born November 27, 1952, Warren, Ohio, lives in Duluth, Ga. Defensive end Montana State 1971-74. Pro defensive end Cincinnati Bengals 1974-76, Tampa Bay Buccaneers 1977-81. College coach: Illinois 1985-87, Purdue 1988-89. Pro coach: Tampa Bay Buccaneers 1984, joined Falcons in 1990.

Ron Meeks, secondary; born August 27, 1954, Jacksonville, Fla., lives in Suwanee, Ga. Defensive back Arkansas State 1975-76. Pro defensive back Hamilton Tiger-Cats (CFL) 1977-79, Ottawa Rough Riders (CFL) 1979, Toronto Argonauts (CFL) 1980-81. College coach: Arkansas State 1984-85, Miami 1986-87, New Mexico State 1988, Fresno State 1989-90. Pro coach: Dallas Cowboys 1991, Cincinnati Bengals 1992-96, joined Falcons in 1997.

Al Miller, strength and conditioning; born August 29, 1947, El Dorado, Ark., lives in Alpharetta, Ga. Wide receiver Northeast Louisiana 1965-69. No pro playing experience. College coach: Northwestern State (La.) 1974-78, Mississippi State 1980, Northeast Louisiana 1981, Alabama 1982-84. Pro coach: Denver Broncos 1987-92, New York Giants 1993-96, joined Falcons in 1997.

George Sefcik, offensive coordinator-running backs; born December 27, 1939, Cleveland, Ohio, lives in Suwanee, Ga. Halfback Notre Dame 1959-61. No pro playing experience. College coach: Notre Dame 1963-68, Kentucky 1969-72. Pro coach: Baltimore Colts 1973-74, Cleveland Browns 1975-77, 1989-90, Cincinnati Bengals 1978-83, Green Bay Packers 1984-87, Kansas City Chiefs 1988, New York Giants 1991-96, joined Falcons in 1997.

Art Shell, offensive line; born November 26, 1946, Charleston, S.C., lives in Lawrenceville, Ga. Offensive-defensive tackle Maryland State 1965-67. Pro offensive tackle Oakland/Los Angeles Raiders 1968-82. Inducted into Pro Football Hall of Fame 1989. Pro coach: Los Angeles Raiders 1983-94 (head coach 1989-94), Kansas City Chiefs 1995-96, joined Falcons in 1997.

Warren "Rennie" Simmons, wide receivers; born February 25, 1942, Poughkeepsie, N.Y., lives in Gainesville, Ga. Center San Diego State 1961-65. No pro playing experience. College coach: Cal State-Fullerton 1974-78, Cerritos (Calif.) J.C. 1978-80, Vanderbilt 1995. Pro coach: Washington Redskins 1981-93, Los Angeles Rams 1994, Houston Oilers 1996, joined Falcons in 1997.

Ed West, offensive quality control; born August 2, 1961, Leighton, Ala., lives in Woodstock, Ga. Tight end Auburn 1980-83. Pro tight end Green Bay Packers 1984-94, Philadelphia Eagles 1995-96, Atlanta Falcons 1997. Pro coach: Joined Falcons in 1998.

Brian Xanders, defensive quality control; born April 10, 1971, East Stroudsburg, Pa., lives in Atlanta. Linebacker Florida State 1989-92. No pro playing experience. Pro coach: Joined Falcons in 1997.

1999 FIRST-YEAR ROSTER

Name	Pos.	Ht.	Wt.	Birthdate	College	Hometown	How Acq.
Allen, Corey (1)	WR	6-1	199	4/4/76	Georgia	Riverdale, Ga.	FA
Ayanbadejo, Brendon	LB	6-2	234	9/6/76	UCLA	Santa Cruz, Calif.	FA
Baker, Eugene	WR	6-0	167	3/18/76	Kent State	Monroeville, Pa.	D5
Barnes, Octavus (1)	WR	6-2	200	11/1/74	North Carolina	Wilson, N.C.	FA-'98
Bishop, Octavious	T	6-5	330	5/31/75	Texas	Jackson, Tenn.	FA
Bonner, Sherdrick (1)	QB	6-4	228	10/19/68	Cal. State-Northridge	Los Angeles, Calif.	FA-'98
Carty, Johndale	S	6-0	196	8/27/77	Utah State	Miami, Fla.	D4
Ekiyor, Emil (1)	DE	6-4	265	12/25/73	Central Florida	Daytona Beach, Fla.	FA
Garcia, James	P	6-2	200	4/7/76	Kansas State	Victoria, Tex.	FA
Gardner, Derrick	CB	6-0	185	3/10/77	California	Oakland, Calif.	FA
Green, Lamont	LB	6-3	230	1/10/76	Florida State	Miami, Fla.	FA
Harris, Eric (1)	WR	6-2	207	3/3/73	Gardner-Webb	Red Bank, N.J.	FA
Hookfin, Steve	RB	6-1	210	3/5/77	Ohio	Arkadelphia, Ark.	FA
Huff, Ben (1)	DT	6-4	275	2/21/75	Michigan	Charlotte, N.C.	FA-'98
Kelly, Jeff	LB	5-11	234	12/13/75	Kansas State	La Grange, Tex.	D6
Kelly, Reggie	TE	6-3	251	2/22/77	Mississippi State	Aberdeen, Miss.	D2
Kerney, Patrick	DE	6-5	262	12/30/76	Virginia	Trenton, N.J.	D1
McClure, Todd	C	6-1	283	2/16/77	Louisiana State	Baton Rouge, La.	D7
Menendez, Rondel	WR	5-9	178	5/18/75	Eastern Kentucky	Louisville, Ky.	D7
Monroe, Rod (1)	TE	6-4	244	7/30/75	Cincinnati	Hearne, Tex.	FA-'98
Nichols, Ben	G	6-6	305	9/9/74	Colorado	Springfield, Mo.	FA
Paulk, Jeff	RB	6-0	252	4/26/76	Arizona State	Phoenix, Ariz.	D3
Studdard, Greg (1)	T	6-6	300	9/6/74	Sam Houston State	Lodi, Calif.	FA-'98
Thigpen, Eric	S	6-0	191	6/19/76	Iowa	Thornridge, Ill.	D6
Watts, Kenny	G	6-4	303	9/8/76	Utah State	Bellflower, Calif.	FA
Williams, Brett (1)	DE	6-4	263	10/15/73	Clemson	Albany, Ga.	FA-'98

The term NFL Rookie is defined as a player who is in his first season of professional football and has not been on the roster of another professional football team for any regular-season or postseason games. A Rookie is designated by an "R" on NFL rosters. Players who have been active in another professional football league or players who have NFL experience, including either preseason training camp or being on an Active List or Inactive List, or on Reserve/Injured or Reserve/Physically Unable to Perform for fewer than six regular-season games, are termed NFL First-Year Players. An NFL First-Year Player is designated by a "1" on NFL rosters. Thereafter, a player is credited with an additional year of experience for each season in which he accumulates six games on the Active List or Inactive List, or on Reserve/Injured or Reserve/Physically Unable to Perform.

NOTES

CAROLINA PANTHERS

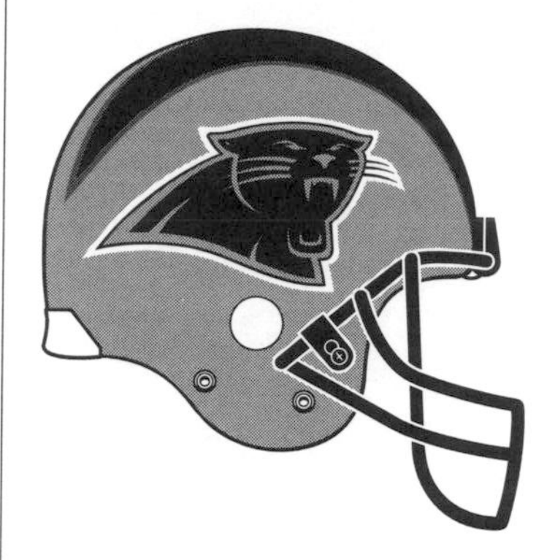

National Football Conference
Western Division
Team Colors: Black, Panther Blue, and Silver
800 South Mint Street
Charlotte, North Carolina 28202-1502
Telephone: (704) 358-7000

CLUB OFFICIALS

Founder/Owner: Jerry Richardson
President: Mark Richardson
President Carolina Stadium Corp.: Jon Richardson
Director of Player Personnel: Jack Bushofsky
Director of Football Operations: Marty Hurney
Director of Marketing and Sponsorships: Charles Waddell
Counsel: Richard M. Thigpen
Chief Financial Officer: Dave Olsen
Controller: Lisa Garber
Pro Scouts: Hal Hunter, Mark Koncz
College Scouts: Hal Athon, Joe Bushofsky, Matt Malaspina, Jeff Morrow, Tony Softli
Director of Communications: Charlie Dayton
Media Relations Assistant: Lex Sant
Communications and Marketing Assistant: Bruce Speight
Director of Ticket Sales: Phil Youtsey
Assistant Ticket Manager: Kati Hynes
Director of Player Relations: Donnie Shell
Director of Community Relations/Family Programs: B.J. Harrison Waymer
Director of Special Events: Leslie Matz
Director of Information Systems: Roger Goss
Systems: Trevor Baker, Dave Carpenter
Football Systems: Rob Rogers
Video Director: Mark Hobbs
Assistant Video Director: Jeff Mueller
Head Trainer: John Kasik
Assistant Trainers: Al Shuford, Dan Ruiz
Equipment Manager: Jackie Miles
Assistant Equipment Manager: Don Toner
Director of Football and Stadium Security: Gene Brown
Director of Facilities: Tom Fellows
Stadium Operations Manager: Rick Skaar
Office Manager: Jackie Jeffries
Stadium: Ericsson Stadium • **Capacity:** 73,250
Charlotte, North Carolina 28202-1502
Playing Surface: Grass
Training Camp: Wofford College
Spartanburg, South Carolina
29303

RECORD HOLDERS

INDIVIDUAL RECORDS—CAREER

Category	Name	Performance
Rushing (Yds.)	Anthony Johnson, 1995-98	1,723
Passing (Yds.)	Kerry Collins, 1995-98	8,306
Passing (Tds)	Kerry Collins, 1995-98	47
Receiving (No.)	Mark Carrier, 1995-98	176
Receiving (Yds.)	Mark Carrier, 1995-98	2,547
Interceptions	Eric Davis, 1996-98	15
Punting (Avg.)	Ken Walter, 1997-98	41.6
Punt Return (Avg.)	Winslow Oliver, 1996-98	10.7
Kickoff Return (Avg.)	Michael Bates, 1996-98	27.0
Field Goals	John Kasay, 1995-98	104
Touchdowns (Tot.)	Wesley Walls, 1996-98	21
Points	John Kasay, 1995-98	433

INDIVIDUAL RECORDS—SINGLE SEASON

Category	Name	Performance
Rushing (Yds.)	Anthony Johnson, 1996	1,120
Passing (Yds.)	Kerry Collins, 1995	2,717
Passing (Tds)	Steve Beuerlein, 1998	17
Receiving (No.)	Raghib Ismail, 1998	69
Receiving (Yds.)	Raghib Ismail, 1998	1,024
Interceptions	Brett Maxie, 1995	6
Punting (Avg.)	Ken Walter, 1997	42.4
Punt Return (Avg.)	Winslow Oliver, 1996	11.5
Kickoff Return (Avg.)	Michael Bates, 1996	30.2
Field Goals	John Kasay, 1996	37
Touchdowns (Tot.)	Wesley Walls, 1996	10
Points	John Kasay, 1996	145

INDIVIDUAL RECORDS—SINGLE GAME

Category	Name	Performance
Rushing (Yds.)	Fred Lane, 11-2-97	147
Passing (Yds.)	Kerry Collins, 11-26-95	335
Passing (Tds)	Kerry Collins, 11-26-95, 10-13-96, 12-8-96, 10-4-98	3
	Steve Beuerlein, 11-24-96, 10-11-98, 12-6-98	3
Receiving (No.)	Willie Green, 11-3-96	9
	Muhsin Muhammad, 9-13-98	9
Receiving (Yds.)	Muhsin Muhammad, 9-13-98	192
Interceptions	Many times	2
	Last time by Jeff Brady, 9-27-98	
Field Goals	John Kasay, 9-1-96, 9-8-96	5
Touchdowns (Tot.)	Fred Lane, 11-2-97	3
Points	Fred Lane, 11-2-97	18

1999 SCHEDULE

PRESEASON

Aug. 13	at Jacksonville	7:30
Aug. 20	**Pittsburgh**	8:00
Aug. 28	at Baltimore	7:30
Sept. 2	**New England**	8:00

REGULAR SEASON

Sept. 12	at New Orleans	12:00
Sept. 19	**Jacksonville**	1:00
Sept. 26	**Cincinnati**	1:00
Oct. 3	at Washington	4:05
Oct. 10	Open Date	
Oct. 17	at San Francisco	1:15
Oct. 24	**Detroit**	1:00
Oct. 31	at Atlanta	1:00
Nov. 7	**Philadelphia**	1:00
Nov. 14	at St. Louis	12:00
Nov. 21	at Cleveland	1:00
Nov. 28	**Atlanta**	8:20
Dec. 5	**St. Louis**	1:00
Dec. 12	at Green Bay	12:00
Dec. 18	**San Francisco** (Sat.)	4:15
Dec. 26	at Pittsburgh	1:00
Jan. 2	**New Orleans**	1:00

ERICSSON STADIUM

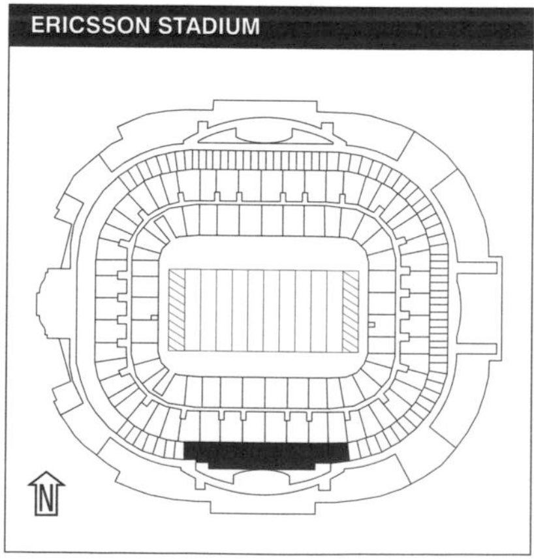

COACHING HISTORY

(31-35-0)

1995-98	Dom Capers	31-35-0

1998 TEAM RECORD

PRESEASON (2-2)

Date	Result		Opponent
8/8	W	30-27	Jacksonville
8/14	W	12-7	at Buffalo
8/22	L	22-25	Minnesota
8/29	L	24-38	at Pittsburgh

REGULAR SEASON (4-12)

Date	Result		Opponent	Att.
9/6	L	14-19	Atlanta	65,129
9/13	L	14-19	at New Orleans	51,915
9/27	L	30-37	Green Bay	69,723
10/4	L	23-51	at Atlanta	50,724
10/11	L	20-27	at Dallas	64,181
10/18	L	13-16	at Tampa Bay	63,600
10/25	L	14-30	Buffalo	64,050
11/1	W	31-17	New Orleans	62,514
11/8	L	23-25	at San Francisco	68,572
11/15	L	9-13	Miami	67,887
11/22	W	24-20	at St. Louis	50,716
11/29	L	21-48	at New York Jets	71,501
12/6	L	28-31	San Francisco (OT)	63,332
12/13	L	25-28	Washington	46,940
12/20	W	20-13	St. Louis	50,047
12/27	W	27-19	at Indianapolis	58,182

(OT) Overtime

SCORE BY PERIODS

Panthers	60	108	61	107	0	— 336
Opponents	84	117	128	81	3	— 413

ATTENDANCE

Home 489,622 Away 479,391 Total 969,013
Single-game home record, 76,136 (12/10/95)
Single-season home record, 553,382 (1996)

1998 TEAM STATISTICS

	Panthers	Opp.
Total First Downs	261	315
Rushing	68	95
Passing	171	197
Penalty	22	23
Third Down: Made/Att	80/216	88/211
Third Down Pct.	37.0	41.7
Fourth Down: Made/Att	10/21	5/9
Fourth Down Pct.	47.6	55.6
Total Net Yards	4,780	5,842
Avg. Per Game	298.8	365.1
Total Plays	966	1,029
Avg. Per Play	4.9	5.7
Net Yards Rushing	1,458	2,133
Avg. Per Game	91.1	133.3
Total Rushes	405	491
Net Yards Passing	3,322	3,709
Avg. Per Game	207.6	231.8
Sacked/Yards Lost	54/302	37/228
Gross Yards	3,624	3,937
Att./Completions	507/292	501/298
Completion Pct.	57.6	59.5
Had Intercepted	18	19
Punts/Avg.	77/40.7	71/44.0
Net Punting Avg.	77/38.1	71/35.2
Penalties/Yards Lost	113/931	110/892
Fumbles/Ball Lost	39/17	24/14
Touchdowns	40	46
Rushing	11	14
Passing	25	30
Returns	4	2
Avg. Time of Possession	28:10	31:50

1998 INDIVIDUAL STATISTICS

Passing	Att.	Comp.	Yds.	Pct.	TD	Int.	Tkld.	Rate
Beuerlein	343	216	2,613	63.0	17	12	44/251	88.2
Collins	162	76	1,011	46.9	8	5	10/51	70.8
Floyd	1	0	0	0.0	0	1	0/0	0.0
Walter	1	0	0	0.0	0	0	0/0	39.6
Panthers	507	292	3,624	57.6	25	18	54/302	81.5
Opponents	501	298	3,937	59.5	30	19	37/228	88.6

SCORING	TD R	TD P	TD Rt	PAT	FG	Saf	PTS
Kasay	0	0	0	35/37	19/26	0	92
Ismail	0	8	0	0/0	0/0	0	48
Muhammad	0	6	0	0/0	0/0	0	38
Lane	5	0	0	0/0	0/0	0	30
Walls	0	5	0	0/0	0/0	0	30
Biakabutuka	3	1	0	0/0	0/0	0	24
Floyd	3	1	0	0/0	0/0	0	24
Carrier	0	2	0	0/0	0/0	0	12
E. Davis	0	0	2	0/0	0/0	0	12
Bates	0	0	1	0/0	0/0	0	6
Broughton	0	1	0	0/0	0/0	0	6
Johnson	0	1	0	0/0	0/0	0	6
Stone	0	0	1	0/0	0/0	0	6
Collins	0	0	0	0/0	0/0	0	2
Panthers	11	25	4	35/37	19/26	0	336
Opponents	14	30	2	41/43	30/31	2	413

2-Point conversions: Collins, Muhammad. Team 2-3, Opponents 1-3.

RUSHING	Att.	Yds.	Avg.	LG	TD
Lane	205	717	3.5	31	5
Biakabutuka	101	427	4.2	41	3
Johnson	36	135	3.8	21	0
Floyd	28	71	2.5	7	3
Ismail	3	42	14.0	36	0
Collins	7	40	5.7	16	0
Beuerlein	22	26	1.2	13	0
Walter	3	0	0.0	0	0
Panthers	405	1,458	3.6	41	11
Opponents	491	2,133	4.3	71t	14

RECEIVING	No.	Yds.	Avg.	LG	TD
Ismail	69	1,024	14.8	62	8
Muhammad	68	941	13.8	72t	6
Walls	49	506	10.3	30	5
Johnson	27	242	9.0	38t	1
Floyd	24	123	5.1	20	1
Carrier	19	301	15.8	42	2
Lane	12	85	7.1	16	0
Biakabutuka	8	138	17.3	42	1
Broughton	6	142	23.7	68t	1
Carruth	4	59	14.8	47	0
Hayes	3	62	20.7	35	0
Stone	1	7	7.0	7	0
Mangum	1	5	5.0	5	0
Collins	1	-11	-11.0	-11	0
Panthers	292	3,624	12.4	72t	25
Opponents	298	3,937	13.2	82t	30

INTERCEPTIONS	No.	Yds.	Avg.	LG	TD
E. Davis	5	81	16.2	56t	2
Brady	4	85	21.3	43	0
Evans	2	18	9.0	18	0
Greene	2	18	9.0	18	0
Smith	1	43	43.0	43	0
Veland	1	24	24.0	24	0
Barrow	1	10	10.0	10	0
Minter	1	7	7.0	7	0
McGill	1	6	6.0	6	0
Lloyd	1	3	3.0	3	0
Panthers	19	295	15.5	56t	2
Opponents	18	179	9.9	41	0

PUNTING	No.	Yds.	Avg.	In 20	LG
Walter	77	3,131	40.7	20	59
Panthers	77	3,131	40.7	20	59
Opponents	71	3,125	44.0	14	60

PUNT RETURNS	No.	FC	Yds.	Avg.	LG	TD
Oliver	44	11	464	10.5	35	0
Panthers	44	11	464	10.5	35	0
Opponents	20	36	94	4.7	24	0

KICKOFF RETURNS	No.	Yds.	Avg.	LG	TD
Bates	59	1,480	25.1	99t	1
Stone	9	252	28.0	45	0
Johnson	2	12	6.0	9	0
Oliver	2	43	21.5	25	0
Brady	1	8	8.0	8	0
Floyd	1	22	22.0	22	0
Jensen	1	9	9.0	9	0
Saleh	1	8	8.0	8	0
Panthers	76	1,834	24.1	99t	1
Opponents	65	1,439	22.1	93t	1

FIELD GOALS	1-19	20-29	30-39	40-49	50+
Kasay	0/0	5/5	4/5	6/9	4/7
Panthers	0/0	5/5	4/5	6/9	4/7
Opponents	0/0	10/10	7/7	12/12	1/2

SACKS	No.
Greene	15.0
Gilbert	6.0
Barrow	4.0
Brady	4.0
Terry	2.0
E. Davis	1.0
Fox	1.0
Jones	1.0
Lloyd	1.0
McGill	1.0
Peter	1.0
Panthers	37.0
Opponents	54.0

1999 DRAFT CHOICES

Round	Name	Pos.	College
2	Chris Terry	T	Georgia
	Mike Rucker	DE	Nebraska
4	Hannibal Navies	LB	Colorado
6	Robert Daniel	DE	Northwestern State, La.
7	Tony Booth	DB	James Madison

CAROLINA PANTHERS

1999 VETERAN ROSTER

No.	Name	Pos.	Ht.	Wt.	Birthdate	NFL Exp.	College	Hometown	How Acq.	'98 Games/ Starts
46	Alexander, Brent	S	5-11	196	7/10/71	6	Tennessee State	Gallatin, Tenn.	UFA(Ariz)-'98	16/16
56	Barrow, Mike	LB	6-2	236	4/19/70	7	Miami	Homestead, Fla.	UFA(Hou)-'97	16/16
82	Bates, Michael	WR	5-10	189	12/19/69	7	Arizona	Tucson, Ariz.	FA-'96	14/0
7	Beuerlein, Steve	QB	6-3	220	3/7/65	13	Notre Dame	Anaheim, Calif.	UFA(Jac)-'96	12/12
21	Biakabutuka, Tshimanga	RB	6-0	215	1/24/74	4	Michigan	Lonqueuil, Que., Canada	D1-'96	10/3
79	Bohlinger, Rob	G-T	6-9	310	6/14/75	2	Wyoming	Maple Grove, Minn.	FA-'98	13/1
12	Bono, Steve	QB	6-4	212	5/11/62	15	UCLA	Norristown, Pa.	UFA(StL)-'99	6/2*
52	# Brady, Jeff	LB	6-1	243	11/9/68	9	Kentucky	Newport, Ky.	FA-'98	16/16
84	Broughton, Luther	TE	6-2	248	11/30/74	3	Furman	Huger, S.C.	FA-'97	16/4
66	Campbell, Mathew	T	6-4	300	7/14/72	5	South Carolina	North Augusta, S.C.	FA-'95	10/10
89	Carruth, Rae	WR	5-11	194	1/20/74	3	Colorado	Sacramento, Calif.	D1-'97	2/1
57	Conley, Steven	LB	6-5	240	1/18/72	3	Arkansas	Chicago, Ill.	FA-'99	3/0*
76	† Davidds-Garrido, Norberto	T	6-6	313	10/4/72	4	Southern California	La Puente, Calif.	D4a-'96	16/16
25	Davis, Eric	CB	5-11	185	1/26/68	10	Jacksonville State	Anniston, Ala.	UFA(SF)-'96	16/16
34	† Dulaney, Mike	RB	6-0	245	9/9/70	4	North Carolina	Kingsport, Tenn.	FA-'98	8/0
96	Edwards, Antonio	DE	6-3	271	3/10/70	7	Valdosta State	Moultrie, Ga.	UFA(Atl)-'99	15/0*
98	England, Eric	DT	6-3	270	4/25/71	4	Texas A&M	Sugarland, Tex.	FA-'99	0*
33	Evans, Doug	CB	6-1	190	5/13/70	7	Louisiana Tech	Haynesville, La.	UFA(GB)-'98	9/7
40	Floyd, William	RB	6-1	230	2/17/72	6	Florida State	St. Petersburg, Fla.	UFA(SF)-'98	16/13
65	Garcia, Frank	G	6-1	295	1/28/72	5	Washington	Phoenix, Ariz.	D4-'95	14/14
94	Gilbert, Sean	DE-DT	6-5	318	4/10/70	6	Pittsburgh	Aliquippa, Pa.	FA-'98	16/16
44	# Gray, Derwin	CB-S	5-11	210	4/9/71	7	Brigham Young	San Antonio,Tex.	UFA(Ind)-'98	3/0
91	Greene, Kevin	LB	6-3	247	7/31/62	15	Auburn	Granite City, Ill.	FA-'98	15/15
81	Hayes, Donald	WR	6-4	208	7/13/75	2	Wisconsin	Madison, Wis.	D4-'98	7/0
45	Hetherington, Chris	RB	6-3	249	11/27/72	4	Yale	North Branford, Conn.	FA-'99	14/1*
83	Jeffers, Patrick	WR	6-3	218	2/2/73	4	Virginia	Fort Worth, Tex.	RFA(Dall)-'98	8/1*
53	Jensen, Jerry	LB	6-0	235	2/26/75	2	Washington	Everett, Wash.	D5-'98	10/0
23	Johnson, Anthony	RB	6-0	225	10/15/67	10	Notre Dame	South Bend, Ind.	W(Chi)-'95	16/2
75	Jones, Clarence	T	6-6	300	5/6/68	9	Maryland	Brooklyn, N.Y.	UFA(NO)-'99	14/14*
52	Jones, Donta	LB	6-2	235	8/27/72	5	Nebraska	Promfet, Md.	UFA(Pitt)-'99	16/3*
59	Jones, Ernest	LB	6-2	255	4/1/71	5	Oregon	Utica, N.Y.	W(NO)-'98	7/0
4	Kasay, John	K	5-10	198	10/27/69	9	Georgia	Athens, Ga.	UFA(Sea)-'95	16/0
88	Kinchen, Brian	TE	6-2	240	8/6/65	12	Louisiana State	Baton Rouge, La.	UFA(Balt)-'99	16/5*
80	Kinchen, Todd	WR	5-11	187	1/7/69	8	Louisiana State	Baton Rouge, La.	FA-'99	11/0*
64	Lacina, Corbin	G	6-4	308	11/2/70	6	Augustana	Woodbury, Minn.	UFA(Buff)-'98	10/10
32	Lane, Fred	RB	5-10	205	9/6/75	3	Lane College	Franklin, Tenn.	FA-'97	14/11
8	Lewis, Jeff	QB	6-2	211	4/17/73	3	Northern Arizona	Phoenix, Ariz.	T(Den)-'99	0*
95	# Lloyd, Greg	LB	6-2	228	5/26/65	13	Fort Valley State	Miami, Fla.	FA-'98	16/13
29	Lofton, Steve	CB	5-9	177	11/26/68	8	Texas A&M	Alto, Tex.	W(NE)-'98	10/7
27	Lyons, Lamar	S	6-3	210	3/25/73	2	Washington	Santa Monica, Calif.	FA-'99	0*
86	Mangum, Kris	TE	6-4	249	8/15/73	2	Mississippi	Magee, Miss.	D7-'97	8/0
68	Marrow, Mitch	DE-DT	6-4	285	7/16/75	2	Pennsylvania	Harrison, N.Y.	D3b-'98	0*
69	# Miller, Les	DE	6-7	305	3/1/65	12	Fort Hayes State	Arkansas City, Kan.	FA-'96	14/3
30	Minter, Mike	S	5-10	188	1/15/74	3	Nebraska	Lawton, Okla.	D2-'97	6/4
90	† Morabito, Tim	NT	6-3	296	10/12/73	4	Boston College	Garnerville, N.Y.	W(Cin)-'97	9/9
87	Muhammad, Muhsin	WR	6-2	217	5/5/73	4	Michigan State	Lansing, Mich.	D2-'96	16/16
28	Mullen, Roderick	CB-S	6-1	202	12/5/72	5	Grambling State	St. Francisville, La.	UFA(GB)-'99	0*
20	Oliver, Winslow	RB	5-7	180	3/3/73	4	New Mexico	Houston, Tex.	D3a-'96	16/0
97	Peter, Jason	DE	6-4	295	9/13/74	2	Nebraska	Locust, N.J.	D1-'98	14/11
61	Redmon, Anthony	G	6-5	308	4/9/71	6	Auburn	Brewton, Ala.	FA-'98	10/4
54	Reid, Spencer	LB	6-1	247	2/8/76	2	Brigham Young	Pago Pago, American Samoa	FA-'98	16/0
39	Richardson, Damien	S	6-1	210	4/3/76	2	Arizona State	Fresno, Calif.	D6-'98	14/7
38	Scurlock, Mike	S	5-10	200	2/26/72	5	Arizona	Tucson, Ariz.	UFA(StL)-'99	16/0*
67	Stoltenberg, Bryan	C	6-1	300	8/25/72	4	Colorado	Sugarland, Tex.	FA-'98	14/10
80	# Stone, Dwight	WR	6-0	195	1/28/64	13	Middle Tennessee State	Florala, Ala.	UFA(Pitt)-'95	16/0
26	Swift, Michael	CB	5-10	165	2/28/74	3	Austin Peay	Tiptonville, Tenn.	FA-'98	0*
50	Tatum, Kinnon	LB	6-0	222	7/19/75	3	Notre Dame	Fayetteville, N.C.	D3-'97	15/0
71	Terry, Rick	DE	6-4	300	4/5/74	3	North Carolina	Lexington, N.C.	W(NYJ)-'98	7/3
58	Tovar, Steve	LB	6-3	244	4/25/70	7	Ohio State	Elyria, Ohio	UFA(SD)-'99	16/2*
83	Turner, Jim	WR	6-4	212	11/13/75	2	Syracuse	Jacksonville, Fla.	D7b-'98	0*
15	Uwaezuoke, Iheanyi	WR	6-2	198	7/24/73	4	California	Westlake, Calif.	FA-'99	11/0*
72	# Villa, Danny	C	6-5	308	9/21/64	12	Arizona State	Nogales, Ariz.	FA-'98	7/0
85	Walls, Wesley	TE	6-5	250	2/26/66	11	Mississippi	Pontotoc, Miss.	UFA(NO)-'96	14/14
13	Walter, Ken	P	6-1	195	8/15/72	3	Kent State	Euclid, Ohio	FA-'96	16/0
95	Wells, Dean	LB	6-3	248	6/20/70	7	Kentucky	Louisville, Ky.	UFA(Sea)-'99	9/8*
37	Wheeler, Leonard	CB	6-0	198	1/15/69	8	Troy State	Toccoa, Ga.	FA-'98	16/0
99	Wiley, Chuck	DE-DT	6-5	282	3/6/75	2	Louisiana State	Baton Rouge, La.	D3a-'98	0*
17	Wilmsmeyer, Klaus	P	6-2	205	12/14/67	7	Louisville	Mississauga, Ont., Canada	UFA(Mia)-'99	16/0*
73	Wilson, Jamie	G-T	6-6	300	6/6/73	3	Marshall	Gloucester, Va.	FA-'97	0*

* Bono played 6 games with St. Louis in '98; Conley played 1 game with Indianapolis and 2 games with Pittsburgh; Edwards played 15 games with Atlanta; England last active with Tennessee in '97; Hetherington played 14 games with Indianapolis; Jeffers played 8 games with Dallas; C. Jones played 14 games with New Orleans; D. Jones played 16 games with Pittsburgh; B. Kinchen played 16 games with Baltimore; T. Kinchen played 11 games with Atlanta; Lewis, Marrow, Mullen, Swift, Turner, Wiley, and Wilson missed '98 season because of injury; Lyons last active with Baltimore in '97; Scurlock played 16 games with St. Louis; Tovar played 16 games with San Diego; Uwaezuoke played 7 games with San Francisco and 4 games with Miami; Wells played 9 games with Seattle; Wilmsmeyer played 16 games with Miami.

Unrestricted free agent; subject to developments.

† Restricted free agent; subject to developments.

Players lost through free agency (5): T Blake Brockermeyer (Chi; 14 games in '98), WR Raghib Ismail (Dall; 16), DE Shawn King (Ind; 0), QB Shane Matthews (Chi; 0), CB Lenny McGill (Sea; 10).

Also played with Panthers in '98—CB Juran Bolden (6 games), WR Mark Carrier (16), QB Kerry Collins (4), DE Mike Fox (16), C Paul Janus (5), LB Tarek Saleh (11), DE Don Sasa (2), C-G Steve Scifres (1), T Ricky Siglar (1), CB Rod Smith (6), CB-S Ryan Sutter (1), S Tony Veland (15).

COACHING STAFF

Head Coach,
George Seifert

Pro Career: After a two-year hiatus from coaching, Seifert became the second coach in Carolina Panthers history on January 4, 1999. Ranks first all-time among NFL head coaches with a .755 winning percentage and reached both 50 and 75 victories faster than any head coach in League history. One of nine head coaches to win two Super Bowls. Coached on all five of San Francisco's Super Bowl championship teams, earning one ring as secondary coach (1981), two as defensive coordinator (1984, 1988), and two as head coach (1989, 1994). Ranks as 49ers' all-time leader with 98 regular-season victories and 108 total wins. Directed 49ers teams that boasted the NFL's best record in 1989, 1990, 1992, and 1994. Guided 49ers to club-record five NFC championship appearances and tied Bill Walsh's club mark with six NFC West titles. Named 49ers head coach in 1989 and became second rookie head coach to win Super Bowl while posting 17 total victories. Appointed San Francisco's defensive coordinator in 1983 after joining 49ers as secondary coach in 1980. No pro playing experience. Career record: 108-35.

Background: Linebacker at University of Utah (1960-62). Served a six-month tour of duty with the U.S. Army following graduation. Returned to Utah as a graduate assistant in 1964. Named head coach at Westminster College in Salt Lake City in 1965. Assistant at Iowa (1966), Oregon (1967-1971), and Stanford (1972-74). Left Stanford to become head coach at Cornell (1975-76). Joined Bill Walsh's staff at Stanford in 1977 and helped the Cardinal to a two-year mark of 17-7, including victories in the Sun and Bluebonnet Bowls. Received bachelor's degree in zoology (1963) and master's degree in physical education (1966) from Utah.

Personal: Born January 22, 1940, in San Francisco. He and his wife, Linda, have two children—Eve and Jason—and live in Los Altos, Calif.

ASSISTANT COACHES

Don Breaux, tight ends; born August 3, 1940, Jennings, La., lives in Charlotte. Quarterback McNeese State 1959-1961. Pro quarterback Denver Broncos 1963, San Diego Chargers 1964-65. College coach: Florida State 1966-67, Arkansas 1968-1971, 1977-1980, Florida 1973-74, Texas 1975-76. Pro coach: Houston Oilers 1972, Washington Redskins 1981-1993, New York Jets 1994, joined Panthers in 1995.

Jacob Burney, defensive line; born January 24, 1959, Chattanooga, Tenn., lives in Charlotte. Defensive tackle Tennessee-Chattanooga 1977-1980. No pro playing experience. College coach: New Mexico 1983-86, Tulsa 1987, Mississippi State 1988, Wisconsin 1989, UCLA 1990-92, Tennessee 1993. Pro coach: Cleveland Browns/Baltimore Ravens 1994-98, joined Panthers in 1999.

Chick Harris, running backs; born September 21, 1945, Durham, N.C., lives in Charlotte. Running back Northern Arizona 1966-69. No pro playing experience. College coach: Colorado State 1970-72, Long Beach State 1973-74, Washington 1975-1980. Pro coach: Buffalo Bills 1981-82, Seattle Seahawks 1983-1991, Los Angeles Rams 1992-94, joined Panthers in 1995.

Gill Haskell, offensive coordinator; born September 24, 1943, San Francisco, lives in Charlotte. Defensive back San Francisco State 1961, 1963-65. No pro playing experience. College coach: Southern California 1978-1982. Pro coach: Los Angeles Rams 1983-1991, Green Bay Packers 1992-97, joined Panthers in 1998.

John Marshall, defensive coordinator; born October 2, 1945, Arroyo Grande, Calif., lives in Charlotte. Linebacker Washington State 1964. No pro playing experience. College coach: Oregon 1970-76, Southern California 1977-79. Pro coach: Green Bay Packers 1980-82, Atlanta Falcons 1983-85, Indianapolis Colts 1986-88, San Francisco 49ers 1989-1998, joined Panthers in 1999.

Sam Mills, linebackers; born June 3, 1959, Neptune, N.J., lives in Charlotte. Linebacker Montclair State 1977-1980. Pro linebacker Philadelphia/Baltimore Stars (USFL) 1983-85, New Orleans Saints 1986-1994, Carolina Panthers 1995-97. Pro coach: Joined Panthers in 1999.

Bill Musgrave, quarterbacks; born November 11, 1967, Grand Junction, Colo., lives in Charlotte. Quarterback Oregon 1987-1990. Pro quarterback San Francisco 49ers 1991-94, Denver Broncos 1995-96. Pro coach: Oakland Raiders 1997, Philadelphia Eagles 1998, joined Panthers in 1999.

Scott O'Brien, special teams; born June 25, 1957, Superior, Wis., lives in Charlotte. Defensive end Wisconsin-Superior 1975-78. Pro defensive end Green Bay Packers 1979, Toronto Argonauts (CFL) 1979. College coach: Wisconsin-Superior 1980-82, Nevada-Las Vegas 1983-85, Rice 1986, Pittsburgh 1987-1990. Pro coach: Cleveland Browns/Baltimore Ravens 1991-98, joined Panthers in 1999.

Alvin Reynolds, defensive quality control; born June 24, 1959, Pineville, La., lives in Charlotte. Safety Indiana State 1978-1981. No pro playing experience. College coach: Indiana State 1982-1992. Pro coach: Denver Broncos 1993-95, Baltimore Ravens 1996-98, joined Panthers in 1999.

Greg Roman, offensive quality control; born August 19, 1972, lives in Charlotte. Defensive line-linebacker John Carroll 1990-94. No pro playing experience. Pro coach: Joined Panthers in 1999.

Darrin Simmons, special teams quality control-asst. strength and conditioning; born April 9, 1973, Elkhart, Kan., lives in Charlotte. Punter Kansas 1993-95. No pro playing experience. College coach: Kansas 1996, Minnesota 1997. Pro coach: Baltimore Ravens 1998, joined Panthers in 1999.

Jerry Simmons, strength and conditioning; born June 15, 1954, Elkhart, Kan., lives in Charlotte. Linebacker Fort Hays State 1976-77. No pro playing experience. College coach: Fort Hays State 1978, Clemson 1980, Rice 1981-82, Southern California 1983-87. Pro coach: New England Patriots 1988-1990, Cleveland Browns/Baltimore Ravens 1991-98, joined Panthers in 1999.

Bob Valesente, defensive backs, born July 19, 1940, Seneca Falls, N.Y., lives in Charlotte. Running back-defensive back Ithaca College 1958-1961. No pro playing experience. College coach: Cornell 1964-1974, Cincinnati 1975-76, Arizona 1977-79, Mississippi State 1980-81, Kansas 1984-87 (head coach 1986-87), Maryland 1988, Pittsburgh 1989. Pro coach: Baltimore Colts 1982-83, Pittsburgh Steelers 1990-91, Green Bay Packers 1992-98, joined Panthers in 1999.

Richard Williamson, wide receivers; born April 13, 1941, Ft. Deposit, Ala., lives in Charlotte. Receiver Alabama 1961-62. No pro playing experience. College coach: Alabama 1963-67, 1970-71, Arkansas 1968-69, 1972-74, Memphis State 1975-1980 (head coach). Pro coach: Kansas City Chiefs 1983-86, Tampa Bay Buccaneers 1987-1991 (interim head coach final three games of 1990, head coach 1991), Cincinnati Bengals 1992-94, joined Panthers in 1995.

Tony Wise, offensive line, born December 28, 1951, Albany, N.Y., lives in Charlotte. Offensive lineman Ithaca College 1971-72. No pro playing experience. College coach: Albany State 1973, Bridgeport 1974, Central Connecticut State 1975, Washington State 1976, Pittsburgh 1977-78, Oklahoma State 1979-1983, Syracuse 1984, Miami 1985-88. Pro coach: Dallas Cowboys 1989-1992, Chicago Bears 1993-98, joined Panthers in 1999.

1999 FIRST-YEAR ROSTER

Name	Pos.	Ht.	Wt.	Birthdate	College	Hometown	How Acq.
Best, Dan	T	6-5	290	6/2/76	Western Carolina	Faison, N.C.	FA
Booth, Tony	CB	6-1	195	8/3/75	James Madison	Richmond, Va.	D7
Broughton, Vernon (1)	DE	6-5	293	2/26/71	Fayetteville State	Huger, S.C.	FA
Burden, John	WR	6-2	207	4/2/76	Northwestern	Orlando, Fla.	FA
Cook, Horace	LB	6-1	248	7/29/75	Morris Brown	Atlanta, Ga.	FA
Craig, Dameyune (1)	QB	6-1	200	4/19/74	Auburn	Prichard, Ala.	FA
Cramer, Paul	K	5-11	185	2/29/72	Clarion	Greenville, Pa.	FA
Daniel, Robert	DE	6-6	275	10/19/75	Northwestern State, La.	Dallas, Tex.	D6
Darby, Chartric (1)	DT	6-0	250	10/22/75	South Carolina State	North, S.C.	FA
Deligianis, Harry (1)	DT	6-4	304	8/4/75	Youngstown State	Ashtabula, Ohio	FA
Egbuniwe, Chike (1)	LB	6-1	236	12/15/74	Duke	Dallas, Tex.	FA
Flowe, Jeffrey	T	6-6	310	12/24/75	Wake Forest	Charlotte, N.C.	FA
Heidelburg, Daryle (1)	WR	5-11	180	1/29/75	Jackson State	Miami, Fla.	FA
Janus, Paul (1)	G-T	6-4	294	3/17/75	Northwestern	Edgerton, Wis.	FA
Lies, Michael	G	6-3	309	9/8/75	Kansas	Witchita, Kan.	FA
Lytle, Matt	QB	6-4	225	9/4/75	Pittsburgh	Wyomissing, Pa.	FA
Manuel, Sam (1)	LB	6-2	235	12/1/73	New Mexico State	Sobrante, Calif.	FA
Navies, Hannibal	LB	6-2	240	7/19/77	Colorado	Oakland, Calif.	D4
Nesbit, Jamar	C	6-4	330	12/17/76	South Carolina	Summerville, S.C.	FA
Rucker, Micheal	DE	6-5	258	2/28/75	Nebraska	St. Joseph, Mo.	D2b
Slappey, Andre	DL	6-5	302	12/28/75	Albany State, Ga.	Americus, Ga.	FA
Snider, Matt	RB	6-2	235	1/26/76	Richmond	Wynnewood, Pa.	FA
Sutter, Ryan (1)	S	6-1	203	9/14/74	Colorado	Fort Collins, Colo.	FA
Terry, Chris	T	6-5	295	8/8/75	Georgia	Jacksonville, Fla.	D2a

The term NFL Rookie is defined as a player who is in his first season of professional football and has not been on the roster of another professional football team for any regular-season or postseason games. A Rookie is designated by an "R" on NFL rosters. Players who have been active in another professional football league or players who have NFL experience, including either preseason training camp or being on an Active List or Inactive List, or on Reserve/Injured or Reserve/Physically Unable to Perform for fewer than six regular-season games, are termed NFL First-Year Players. An NFL First-Year Player is designated by a "1" on NFL rosters. Thereafter, a player is credited with an additional year of experience for each season in which he accumulates six games on the Active List or Inactive List, or on Reserve/Injured or Reserve/Physically Unable to Perform.

NOTES

CHICAGO BEARS

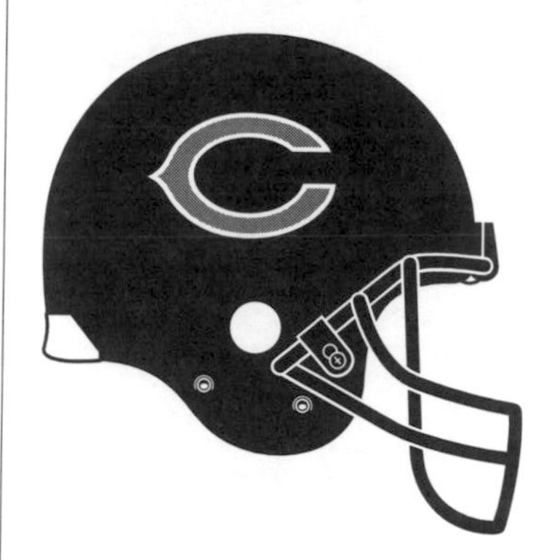

National Football Conference
Central Division
Team Colors: Navy Blue, Orange, and White
Halas Hall at Conway Park
1000 Football Drive
Lake Forest, Illinois 60045
Telephone: (847) 295-6600

CLUB OFFICIALS

Chairman Emeritus: Edward W. McCaskey
Chairman of the Board: Michael B. McCaskey
President and CEO: Ted Phillips
Secretary: Virginia H. McCaskey
Vice President: Tim McCaskey
Director of Business Operations: Jim Miller
Director Player Development: Brian McCaskey
Vice President of Player Personnel: Mark Hatley
Director of Pro Personnel: Rick Spielman
Director of College Scouting: Bill Rees
Director of Administration: Bill McGrane
Ticket Manager: George McCaskey
Director of Community Relations: Pat McCaskey
Director of Marketing/Communications: Ken Valdiserri
Manager of Promotions: John Bostrom
Manager of Sales: Jack Trompeter
Director of Public Relations: Bryan Harlan
Asst. Directors of Public Relations: Phil Handler, Scott Hagel
Computer Systems: Greg Gershuny
Controller: Kris Voska
Video Director: Dean Pope
Head Athletic Trainer: Tim Bream
Assistant Trainers: Eric Sugarman, Bobby Slatter
Physical Development Coordinator: Russ Riederer
Assistant Physical Development Coordinator: Steve Little
Head Equipment Manager: Tony Medlin
Quality Control: Eric Studesville, Chuck Bullough
Assistant Equipment Managers: Carl Piekarski, Steve Bierer
Scouts: Marty Barrett, Glenn Schembechler, George Paton, Jeff Shiver, Pat Roberts, Phil Emery, John Paul Young
Stadium: Soldier Field • **Capacity:** 66,944
425 McFetridge Place
Chicago, Illinois 60605
Playing Surface: Grass
Training Camp: University of Wisconsin-Platteville
Platteville, Wisconsin 53818

1999 SCHEDULE

PRESEASON

Aug. 7	**Indianapolis**	7:00
Aug. 13	at Pittsburgh	7:30
Aug. 21	**St. Louis**	7:00
Aug. 28	at Cleveland	8:00

REGULAR SEASON

Sept. 12	**Kansas City**	12:00
Sept. 19	**Seattle**	12:00
Sept. 26	at Oakland	1:15
Oct. 3	**New Orleans**	12:00
Oct. 10	at Minnesota	12:00
Oct. 17	**Philadelphia**	12:00
Oct. 24	at Tampa Bay	1:00
Oct. 31	at Washington	1:00
Nov. 7	at Green Bay	12:00
Nov. 14	**Minnesota**	12:00
Nov. 21	at San Diego	1:15
Nov. 25	at Detroit (Thurs.)	12:40
Dec. 5	**Green Bay**	12:00
Dec. 12	Open Date	
Dec. 19	**Detroit**	12:00
Dec. 26	at St. Louis	12:00
Jan. 2	**Tampa Bay**	12:00

RECORD HOLDERS

INDIVIDUAL RECORDS—CAREER

Category	Name	Performance
Rushing (Yds.)	Walter Payton, 1975-1987	*16,726
Passing (Yds.)	Sid Luckman, 1939-1950	14,686
Passing (TDs)	Sid Luckman, 1939-1950	137
Receiving (No.)	Walter Payton, 1975-1987	492
Receiving (Yds.)	Johnny Morris, 1958-1967	5,059
Interceptions	Gary Fencik, 1976-1987	38
Punting (Avg.)	George Gulyanics, 1947-1952	44.5
Punt Return (Avg.)	Ray (Scooter) McLean, 1940-47	14.8
Kickoff Return (Avg.)	Gale Sayers, 1965-1971	30.6
Field Goals	Kevin Butler, 1985-1995	243
Touchdowns (Tot.)	Walter Payton, 1975-1987	125
Points	Kevin Butler, 1985-1995	1,116

INDIVIDUAL RECORDS—SINGLE SEASON

Category	Name	Performance
Rushing (Yds.)	Walter Payton, 1977	1,852
Passing (Yds.)	Erik Kramer, 1995	3,838
Passing (TDs)	Erik Kramer, 1995	29
Receiving (No.)	Johnny Morris, 1964	93
Receiving (Yds.)	Jeff Graham, 1995	1,301
Interceptions	Mark Carrier, 1990	10
Punting (Avg.)	Bobby Joe Green, 1963	46.5
Punt Return (Avg.)	Harry Clark, 1943	15.8
Kickoff Return (Avg.)	Gale Sayers, 1967	37.7
Field Goals	Kevin Butler, 1985	31
Touchdowns (Tot.)	Gale Sayers, 1965	22
Points	Kevin Butler, 1985	144

INDIVIDUAL RECORDS—SINGLE GAME

Category	Name	Performance
Rushing (Yds.)	Walter Payton, 11-20-77	*275
Passing (Yds.)	Johnny Lujack, 12-11-49	468
Passing (TDs)	Sid Luckman, 11-14-43	*7
Receiving (No.)	Jim Keane, 10-23-49	14
Receiving (Yds.)	Harlon Hill, 10-31-54	214
Interceptions	Many times	3
	Last time by Mark Carrier, 12-9-90	
Field Goals	Roger LeClerc, 12-3-61	5
	Mac Percival, 10-20-68	5
Touchdowns (Tot.)	Gale Sayers, 12-12-65	*6
Points	Gale Sayers, 12-12-65	36

*NFL Record

COACHING HISTORY

Decatur Staleys 1920,
Chicago Staleys 1921
(620-432-42)

1920-29	George Halas	84-31-19
1930-32	Ralph Jones	24-10-7
1933-42	George Halas*	88-24-4
1942-45	Hunk Anderson-Luke Johnsos**	24-12-2
1946-55	George Halas	76-43-2
1956-57	John (Paddy) Driscoll	14-10-1
1958-67	George Halas	76-53-6
1968-71	Jim Dooley	20-36-0
1972-74	Abe Gibron	11-30-1
1975-77	Jack Pardee	20-23-0
1978-81	Neill Armstrong	30-35-0
1982-92	Mike Ditka	112-68-0
1993-98	Dave Wannstedt	41-57-0

*Retired after five games to enter U.S. Navy
**Co-coaches

SOLDIER FIELD

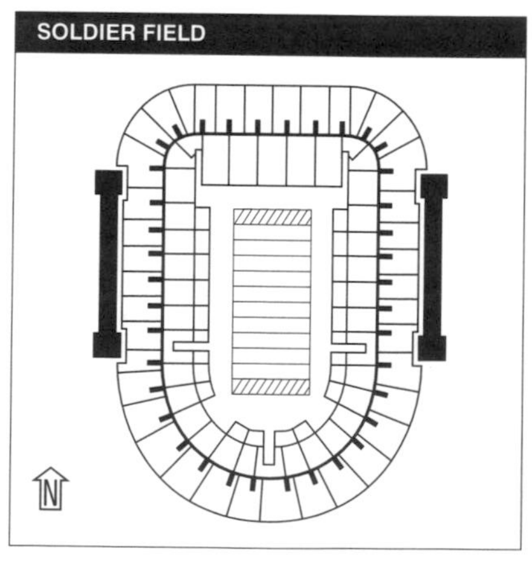

1998 TEAM RECORD

PRESEASON (0-4)

Date	Result		Opponent
8/8	L	14-19	at Baltimore
8/14	L	24-27	at Arizona
8/21	L	9-17	Buffalo
8/28	L	7-24	New York Jets

REGULAR SEASON (4-12)

Date	Result		Opponent	Att.
9/6	L	23-24	Jacksonville	55,614
9/13	L	12-17	at Pittsburgh	59,084
9/20	L	15-27	at Tampa Bay	64,328
9/27	L	28-31	Minnesota	57,783
10/4	W	31-27	Detroit	55,562
10/11	L	7-20	at Arizona	47,860
10/18	W	13-12	Dallas	59,201
10/25	W	23-20	at Tennessee	40,089
11/8	L	12-20	St. Louis	50,263
11/15	L	3-26	at Detroit	63,152
11/22	L	13-20	at Atlanta	60,804
11/29	L	17-31	Tampa Bay	51,938
12/6	L	22-48	at Minnesota	64,247
12/13	L	20-26	at Green Bay	59,813
12/20	W	24-3	Baltimore	40,853
12/27	L	13-16	Green Bay	58,393

SCORE BY PERIODS

Bears	51	95	53	77	0	—	276
Opponents	61	104	116	87	0	—	368

ATTENDANCE

Home 429,607 Away 459,377 Total 888,984
Single-game home record, 66,900 (9/5/93)
Single-season home record, 495,484 (1986)

1998 TEAM STATISTICS

	Bears	Opp.
Total First Downs	264	300
Rushing	89	121
Passing	154	155
Penalty	21	24
Third Down: Made/Att	75/215	80/196
Third Down Pct.	34.9	40.8
Fourth Down: Made/Att	11/25	3/6
Fourth Down Pct.	44.0	50.0
Total Net Yards	4,766	5,103
Avg. Per Game	297.9	318.9
Total Plays	979	963
Avg. Per Play	4.9	5.3
Net Yards Rushing	1,713	1,875
Avg. Per Game	107.1	117.2
Total Rushes	454	479
Net Yards Passing	3,053	3,228
Avg. Per Game	190.8	201.8
Sacked/Yards Lost	31/224	28/173
Gross Yards	3,277	3,401
Att./Completions	494/284	456/292
Completion Pct.	57.5	64.0
Had Intercepted	13	14
Punts/Avg.	80/42.6	72/42.8
Net Punting Avg.	80/36.5	72/35.7
Penalties/Yards Lost	86/714	102/852
Fumbles/Ball Lost	29/21	33/14
Touchdowns	30	42
Rushing	9	12
Passing	16	27
Returns	5	3
Avg. Time of Possession	29:26	30:34

1998 INDIVIDUAL STATISTICS

Passing	Att.	Comp.	Yds.	Pct.	TD	Int.	Tkld.	Rate
Kramer	250	151	1,823	60.4	9	7	10/71	83.1
Stenstrom	196	112	1,252	57.1	4	6	19/137	70.4
Moreno	43	19	166	44.2	1	0	2/16	62.7
Bennett	2	1	18	50.0	1	0	0/0	120.8
Horan	2	1	18	50.0	1	0	0/0	120.8
Conway	1	0	0	0.0	0	0	0/0	39.6
Bears	494	284	3,277	57.5	16	13	31/224	77.5
Opponents	456	292	3,401	64.0	27	14	28/173	93.5

SCORING	TD R	TD P	TD Rt	PAT	FG	Saf	PTS
Jaeger	0	0	0	27/28	21/26	0	90
Engram	0	5	0	0/0	0/0	0	30
Penn	0	3	0	0/0	0/0	0	20
Conway	0	3	0	0/0	0/0	0	18
Milburn	0	0	3	0/0	0/0	0	18
J. Allen	1	1	0	0/0	0/0	0	12
Bennett	2	0	0	0/0	0/0	0	12
Chancey	2	0	0	0/0	0/0	0	12
Stenstrom	2	0	0	0/0	0/0	0	12
Wetnight	0	2	0	0/0	0/0	0	12
Bownes	0	1	0	0/0	0/0	0	6
Hallock	1	0	0	0/0	0/0	0	6
W. Harris	0	0	1	0/0	0/0	0	6
Kramer	1	0	0	0/0	0/0	0	6
S. Lee	0	0	1	0/0	0/0	0	6
M. Robinson	0	1	0	0/0	0/0	0	6
Thierry	0	0	0	0/0	0/0	1	2
Bears	9	16	5	27/28	21/26	2	276
Opponents	12	27	3	36/38	26/31	0	368

2-Point conversions: Penn. Team 1-2, Opponents 1-4.

RUSHING	Att.	Yds.	Avg.	LG	TD
Bennett	173	611	3.5	43	2
Enis	133	497	3.7	29	0
J. Allen	58	270	4.7	57	1
Chancey	29	122	4.2	14	2
Stenstrom	18	79	4.4	14	2
Conway	5	48	9.6	29	0
Hallock	13	41	3.2	14	1
Kramer	13	17	1.3	8	1
Moreno	4	9	2.3	9	0
Milburn	4	8	2.0	3	0
Morris	3	8	2.7	6	0
Engram	1	3	3.0	3	0
Bears	454	1,713	3.8	57	9
Opponents	479	1,875	3.9	50	12

RECEIVING	No.	Yds.	Avg.	LG	TD
Engram	64	987	15.4	79t	5
Conway	54	733	13.6	47	3
Penn	31	448	14.5	37	3
Bennett	28	209	7.5	31	0
Hallock	25	166	6.6	16	0
Wetnight	23	168	7.3	30	2
Mayes	21	217	10.3	22	0
Chancey	11	102	9.3	15	0
J. Allen	8	77	9.6	33	1
Enis	6	20	3.3	7	0
Bownes	5	69	13.8	44	1
M. Robinson	4	44	11.0	20t	1
Milburn	4	37	9.3	13	0
Hall	0	0	—	—	0
Bears	284	3,277	11.5	79t	16
Opponents	292	3,401	11.6	98t	27

INTERCEPTIONS	No.	Yds.	Avg.	LG	TD
W. Harris	4	41	10.3	26	1
Collins	3	29	9.7	28	0
T. Carter	2	20	10.0	19	0
Minter	1	17	17.0	17	0
Thierry	1	14	14.0	14	0
Parrish	1	8	8.0	8	0
Cousin	1	0	0.0	0	0
S. Harris	1	0	0.0	0	0
Bears	14	129	9.2	28	1
Opponents	13	146	11.2	33t	1

PUNTING	No.	Yds.	Avg.	In 20	LG
Horan	64	2,643	41.3	12	57
Sauerbrun	15	741	49.4	6	71
Jaeger	1	27	27.0	0	27
Bears	80	3,411	42.6	18	71
Opponents	72	3,084	42.8	20	68

PUNT RETURNS	No.	FC	Yds.	Avg.	LG	TD
Milburn	25	15	291	11.6	93t	1
Bears	25	15	291	11.6	93t	1
Opponents	38	19	349	9.2	53	1

KICKOFF RETURNS	No.	Yds.	Avg.	LG	TD
Milburn	62	1,550	25.0	94t	2
Chancey	2	18	9.0	18	0
Bownes	1	19	19.0	19	0
Wiegmann	1	8	8.0	8	0
Bears	66	1,595	24.2	94t	2
Opponents	55	1,097	19.9	40	0

FIELD GOALS	1-19	20-29	30-39	40-49	50+
Jaeger	2/2	8/9	9/10	1/4	1/1
Bears	2/2	8/9	9/10	1/4	1/1
Opponents	2/2	12/12	3/4	7/10	2/3

SACKS	No.
Flanigan	8.5
Thomas	4.5
Thierry	3.5
Wells	3.0
S. Lee	2.0
Grasmanis	1.0
S. Harris	1.0
McDonald	1.0
Minter	1.0
Parrish	1.0
Reeves	1.0
B. Robinson	0.5
Bears	28.0
Opponents	31.0

1999 DRAFT CHOICES

Round	Name	Pos.	College
1	Cade McNown	QB	UCLA
2	Russell Davis	DT	North Carolina
3	Rex Tucker	G	Texas A&M
	D'Wayne Bates	WR	Northwestern
	Marty Booker	WR	Northeast Louisiana
4	Warrick Holdman	LB	Texas A&M
	Rosevelt Colvin	DE	Purdue
5	Jerry Wisne	G	Notre Dame
	Khari Samuel	LB	Massachusetts
	Jerry Azumah	RB	New Hampshire
6	Rashard Cook	DB	Southern California
7	Sulecio Sanford	WR	Middle Tennessee State
	Jim Finn	RB	Pennsylvania

CHICAGO BEARS

1999 VETERAN ROSTER

No.	Name	Pos.	Ht.	Wt.	Birthdate	NFL Exp.	College	Hometown	How Acq.	'98 Games/ Starts
20	Allen, James	RB	5-10	215	3/28/75	2	Oklahoma	Wynnewood, Okla.	FA-'97	6/2
84	Allred, John	TE	6-4	249	9/9/74	2	Southern California	Del Mar, Calif.	D2-'97	4/0
95	Anderson, Dunstan	DE	6-3	265	12/31/70	2	Tulsa	Fort Worth, Tex.	FA-'99	0*
36	Austin, Ray	S	5-11	198	12/21/74	3	Tennessee	Lawton, Okla.	W(NYJ)-'98	12/0
30	Bell, Ricky	CB	5-10	194	10/2/74	3	North Carolina State	Columbia, S.C.	W(Jac)-'97	14/0
32	Bennett, Edgar	RB	6-0	218	2/15/69	8	Florida State	Jacksonville, Fla.	UFA(GB)-'98	16/13
82	Bownes, Fabien	WR	5-11	190	2/29/72	3	Western Illinois	Aurora, Ill.	FA-'95	16/0
78	Brockermeyer, Blake	T	6-4	305	4/11/73	5	Texas	Arlington Heights, Tex.	UFA(Car)-'99	14/14*
94	Burns, Keith	LB	6-2	245	5/16/72	6	Oklahoma State	Alexandria, Va.	UFA(Den)-'99	16/0*
25	Carter, Tom	CB	6-0	189	9/5/72	7	Notre Dame	St. Petersburg, Fla.	RFA(Wash)-'97	4/4
38	Chancey, Robert	RB	6-0	250	9/7/72	3	No College	Millbrook, Ala.	W(SD)-'98	16/1
52	Collins, Andre	LB	6-1	240	5/4/68	10	Penn State	Riverside, N.J.	UFA(Cin)-'98	16/2
80	Conway, Curtis	WR	6-0	194	3/13/71	7	Southern California	Hawthorn, Calif.	D1-'93	15/15
21	Cousin, Terry	CB	5-9	182	4/11/75	3	South Carolina	Miami Beach, Fla.	FA-'97	16/12
90	Duff, Jamal	DE	6-7	285	3/11/72	5	San Diego State	Tustin, Calif.	UFA(Wash)-'99	13/3*
81	Engram, Bobby	WR	5-10	192	1/7/73	4	Penn State	Camden, S.C.	D2-'96	16/16
44	Enis, Curtis	RB	6-0	242	6/15/76	2	Penn State	Union City, Ohio	D1-'98	9/1
99	Flanigan, Jim	DT	6-2	288	8/27/71	6	Notre Dame	Green Bay, Wis.	D3-'94	16/16
93	Grasmanis, Paul	DT	6-2	298	8/2/74	4	Notre Dame	Jenison, Mich.	D4-'96	15/0
53	Hall, Lemanski	LB	6-0	235	11/24/70	5	Alabama	Valley, Ala.	T(Tenn)-'98	15/0
49	Hallock, Ty	RB	6-2	256	4/30/71	6	Michigan State	Greenville, Mich.	UFA(Jac)-'98	16/10
55	Harris, Sean	LB	6-3	248	2/25/72	5	Arizona	Magnet, Ariz.	D3a-'95	16/14
27	Harris, Walt	CB	5-11	195	8/10/74	4	Mississippi State	LaGrange, Ga.	D1-'96	14/14
64	Heck, Andy	T	6-6	298	1/1/67	11	Notre Dame	Fairfax, Va.	RFA(Sea)-'94	14/14
74	Herndon, Jimmy	T	6-8	318	8/30/73	4	Houston	Baytown, Tex.	T(Jac)-'97	9/2
47	Hudson, Chris	S	5-10	199	10/6/71	5	Colorado	Houston, Tex.	UFA(Jac)-'99	13/13*
67	Huntington, Greg	G	6-3	308	9/22/70	6	Penn State	Cincinnati, Ohio	FA-'97	2/0
1	Jaeger, Jeff	K	5-11	190	11/26/64	13	Washington	Kent, Wash.	FA-'96	16/0
12	Kramer, Erik	QB	6-1	204	11/6/64	11	North Carolina State	Burbank, Calif.	UFA(Det)-'94	8/8
57	Kreutz, Olin	C	6-2	300	6/9/77	2	Washington	Honolulu, Hawaii	D3-'98	9/1
65	Mannelly, Patrick	T	6-5	285	4/18/75	2	Duke	Atlanta, Ga.	D6b-'98	16/0
9	Matthews, Shane	QB	6-3	196	6/1/70	6	Florida	Pascagoula, Miss.	FA-'99	0*
85	Mayes, Alonzo	TE	6-4	259	6/4/75	2	Oklahoma State	Oklahoma City, Okla.	D4-'98	16/16
54	McDonald, Ricardo	LB	6-2	248	11/8/69	8	Pittsburgh	Paterson, N.J.	UFA(Cin)-'98	15/14
24	Milburn, Glyn	RB	5-8	174	2/19/71	7	Stanford	Santa Monica, Calif.	T(GB)-'98	16/1
15	Miller, Jim	QB	6-2	210	2/9/71	5	Michigan State	Waterford, Mich.	FA-'98	0*
92	Minter, Barry	LB	6-2	242	1/28/70	7	Tulsa	Mt. Pleasant, Tex.	T(Dall)-'93	16/16
4	Moreno, Moses	QB	6-1	205	9/5/75	2	Colorado State	Chula Vista, Calif.	D7b-'98	2/1
37	Parrish, Tony	S	5-10	206	11/23/75	2	Washington	Huntington Beach, Calif.	D2-'98	16/16
86	Penn, Chris	WR	6-0	198	4/20/71	6	Tulsa	Lenapah, Okla.	T(KC)-'97	14/1
75	Perry, Todd	G	6-5	308	11/28/70	7	Kentucky	Elizabethtown, Ky.	D4a-'93	16/16
98	Robinson, Bryan	DE-DT	6-4	283	6/22/74	3	Fresno State	Toledo, Ohio	FA-'98	11/5
88	Robinson, Marcus	WR	6-3	215	2/27/75	2	South Carolina	Ft. Valley, Ga.	D4b-'97	3/0
16	Sauerbrun, Todd	P-K	5-10	209	1/4/73	5	West Virginia	Setauket, N.Y.	D2b-'95	3/0
59	Schwantz, Jim	LB	6-2	240	1/23/70	6	Purdue	Arlington Heights, Ill.	W(SF)-'98	16/0
96	Simmons, Clyde	DE	6-5	287	8/4/64	14	Western Carolina	Wilmington, N.C.	UFA(Cin)-'99	16/16*
29	Smith, Frankie	CB	5-9	182	10/8/68	7	Baylor	Groesbeck, Tex.	FA-'98	15/0
58	Villarrial, Chris	C	6-4	310	6/9/73	4	Indiana, Pa.	Hershey, Pa.	D5-'96	16/16
97	Wells, Mike	DT	6-3	310	1/6/71	6	Iowa	Arnold, Mo.	UFA(Det)-'98	16/16
89	Wetnight, Ryan	TE	6-2	236	11/5/70	7	Stanford	Fresno, Calif.	FA-'93	15/4
60	Wiegmann, Casey	C	6-3	295	7/20/75	4	Iowa	Parkersburg, Iowa	W(NYJ)-'97	16/15
71	Williams, James	T	6-7	340	3/29/68	9	Cheyney State, Pa.	Allerdice, Pa.	FA-'91	16/16

* Anderson last active with Miami in '97; Brockermeyer played 14 games with Carolina; Burns played 16 games with Denver; Duff played 13 games with Washington; Hudson played 14 games with Jacksonville; Matthews inactive for 4 games with Carolina; Miller last active with Atlanta in '97; Simmons played 16 games with Cincinnati.

Players lost through free agency (3): S Marty Carter (Atl; 16 games in '98), DE Carl Reeves (Den; 11), DE John Thierry (Clev; 16).

Also played with Bears in '98—LB Chris Draft (1 game), S Marlon Forbes (16), CB Randy Hillard (9), P Mike Horan (13), DE Shawn Lee (15), S John Mangum (3), RB Byron (Bam) Morris (3), QB Steve Stenstrom (7), DE Mark Thomas (10).

COACHING STAFF

Head Coach,
Dick Jauron

Pro Career: Named eleventh head coach in franchise history on January 24, 1999. As Jacksonville's inaugural defensive coordinator, he was instrumental in the success of the Jaguars, which included three playoff berths in the franchise's first four seasons and a run to the 1996 AFC Championship Game. Jauron coached defensive backs for nine years in Green Bay (1986-1994) before moving to Jacksonville. His coaching career started in Buffalo in 1985. Jauron played eight years as a defensive back in the NFL with the Detroit Lions and Cincinnati Bengals, earning a trip to the 1975 Pro Bowl.

Background: Played running back at Yale from 1970-72 where he still holds the school's career rushing mark with 2,947 yards. Drafted by the Detroit Lions in the fourth round of the 1973 draft. Played defensive back for Detroit from 1973-77 and was named to the Pro Bowl after the 1974 season. Joined Cincinnati in 1978 and played with the Bengals until retiring in 1980. Spent several years away from NFL before joining the Buffalo Bills' coaching staff in 1985. Moved to Green Bay the following season and served as the defensive backs coach under three different head coaches (Forrest Greg, 1986-87; Lindy Infante, 1988-91; Mike Holmgren, 1992-94). Jauron accepted the defensive coordinator post with the expansion Jacksonville Jaguars in 1995 and helped lead the team to three consecutive playoff berths after their opening season.

Personal: Born October 7, 1950, Peoria, Ill. Dick and his wife Gail live in Lake Forest, Ill. and have two daughters—Kacy and Amy.

ASSISTANT COACHES

Keith Armstrong, special teams; born December 15, 1963, Trenton, N.J., lives in Round Lake Beach, Ill. Running back–defensive back Temple 1983-86. No pro playing experience. College coach: Temple 1986, Miami 1987-88, Akron 1989, Oklahoma State 1990-92, Notre Dame 1993. Pro coach: Atlanta Falcons 1994-96, joined Bears in 1997.

Vance Bedford, defensive backs; born August 20, 1958, Houston, Tex. Defensive back Texas 1977-79, 1981. Pro defensive back St. Louis Cardinals 1982, Oklahoma Outlaws (USFL) 1984. College coach: Navarro (Tex.) J.C. 1986, Colorado State 1987-1992, Oklahoma State 1993-94, Michigan 1995-98. Pro coach: Joined Bears in 1999.

Greg Blache, defensive coordinator; born March 9, 1949, New Orleans, lives in Lake Bluff, Ill. Attended Notre Dame. No college or pro playing experience. College coach: Notre Dame 1973-75, 1981-83, Tulane 1976-1980, Southern 1986, Kansas 1987. Pro coach: Jacksonville Bulls (USFL) 1984-85, Green Bay Packers 1988-1993, Indianapolis Colts 1994-98, joined Bears in 1999.

Jim Bollman, tight ends; born December 1, 1954, Ashtabula, Ohio, lives in Lake Bluff, Ill. Offensive lineman Ohio 1973-76. No pro playing experience. College coach: Miami (Ohio) 1977-1982, North Carolina State 1983-85, Youngstown State 1986-1990, Virginia 1991-94, Michigan State 1995-97. Pro coach: Philadelphia Eagles 1998, joined Bears in 1999.

Mike Borich, wide receivers; born December 8, 1966, South Jordan, Utah, lives in Grayslake, Ill. Wide receiver Snow J.C. 1986-87, Western Illinois 1988-89. No pro playing experience. College coach: New Hampshire 1989-1991, Northeastern 1992-94, Louisiana Tech 1995-98. Pro coach: Joined Bears in 1999.

Gary Crowton, offensive coordinator; born June 14, 1957, Provo, Utah, lives in Gurnee, Ill. Quarterback Snow J.C. 1975-77, Colorado State 1978. No pro playing experience. College coach: Brigham Young 1982, Snow J.C. 1983-86, Western Illinois 1987, New Hampshire 1988-1990, Boston College 1991-93, Georgia Tech 1994, Louisiana Tech 1995-98 (head coach 1996-98). Pro coach: Joined Bears in 1999.

Dale Lindsey, linebackers; born January 18, 1943, Bedford, Ind., lives in Lake Bluff, Ill. Linebacker Western Kentucky 1961-64. Pro linebacker Cleveland Browns 1965-1973. College coach: Southern Methodist 1988-89. Pro coach: Green Bay Packers 1986-87, New England Patriots 1990, Tampa Bay Buccaneers 1991, San Diego Chargers 1994-96, Washington Redskins 1997-98, joined Bears in 1999.

Earle Mosley, running backs; born December 20, 1946, Darby, Pa., lives in Buffalo Grove, Ill. Defensive back West Chester State 1970-72. No pro playing experience. College coach: West Chester State 1979, Rutgers 1980-83, Northwestern 1984-87, Temple 1988-1991, Notre Dame 1992-96, Stanford 1997-98. Pro coach: Joined Bears in 1999.

Rex Norris, defensive line; born December 10, 1939, Tipton, Ind., lives in Libertyville, Ill. Linebacker San Angelo (Tex.) J.C. 1959-1960, East Texas State 1961-62. No pro playing experience. College coach: Navarro (Tex.) J.C. 1970-71, Texas A&M 1972, Oklahoma 1973-1983, Arizona State 1984, Florida 1988-89, Tennessee 1990-91, Texas 1992-93. Pro coach: Detroit Lions 1985-87, Denver Broncos 1994, Tennessee Oilers 1995-98, joined Bears in 1999.

John Shoop, quarterbacks; born August 1, 1969, Pittsburgh, lives in Libertyville, Ill. Quarterback University of the South 1987-1990. No pro playing experience. College coach: Dartmouth 1991, Vanderbilt 1992-94. Pro coach: Carolina Panthers 1995-98, joined Bears in 1999.

Bob Wylie, offensive line; born February 16, 1951, West Warwick, R.I., lives in Lake Bluff, Ill. Linebacker Colorado 1969-1971. No pro playing experience. College coach: Brown 1980-82, Holy Cross 1983-84, Ohio 1985-87, Colorado State 1988-89, Cincinnati 1996. Pro coach: New York Jets 1990-91, Tampa Bay Buccaneers 1992-95, Cincinnati Bengals 1997-98, joined Bears in 1999.

1999 FIRST-YEAR ROSTER

Name	Pos.	Ht.	Wt.	Birthdate	College	Hometown	How Acq.
Allen, Tremayne (1)	RB	6-2	244	8/9/74	Florida	Nashville, Tenn.	FA-'97
Anderson, Curtis (1)	S	6-0	203	9/29/73	Pittsburgh	Lynchburg, Va.	FA
Anderson, Ken (1)	DT	6-3	306	10/4/75	Arkansas	Shreveport, La.	FA-'98
Azumah, Jerry	CB-S	5-10	195	9/1/77	New Hampshire	Worcester, Mass.	D5c
Banks, Shawn (1)	LB	6-1	228	10/14/72	Texas Tech	Dallas, Tex.	FA
Bates, D'Wayne	WR	6-2	215	12/4/75	Northwestern	Aiken, S.C.	D3b
Booker, Marty	WR	5-11	218	7/31/76	Northeast Louisiana	Jonesboro, La.	D3c
Brooks, Macey (1)	WR	6-5	220	2/2/75	James Madison	Hampton, Va.	FA-'98
Chambers, Marlon	TE	6-8	275	7/21/74	Louisiana Tech	Corpus Christi, Tex.	FA
Coleman, Quincy (1)	CB-S	5-10	182	7/23/75	Jackson State	Birmingham, Ala.	FA-'98
Colvin, Rosevelt	DE	6-0	252	9/5/77	Purdue	Indianapolis, Ind.	D4a
Cook, Rashard	S	5-11	197	4/18/77	Southern California	San Diego, Calif.	D6
Davis, Russell	DE-DT	6-4	300	3/28/75	North Carolina	Fayetteville, N.C.	D2
Dolan, Chris (1)	P	5-11	221	11/22/70	East Texas State	Jacksonville, Tex.	FA
Draft, Chris (1)	LB	5-11	222	2/26/76	Stanford	Placentia, Calif.	D6-'98
Early, Michael	G	6-2	280	6/2/77	Norfolk State	Brunswick, Ga.	FA
Ferguson, Nick (1)	CB	5-10	187	11/27/73	Georgia Tech	Miami, Fla.	FA
Finn, Jim	RB	5-10	238	12/9/76	Pennsylvania	Fair Lawn, N.J.	D7b
Fleming, Joe (1)	DT	6-3	280	12/5/71	New Hampshire	Wellesley, Mass.	FA
Hernandez, Adam (1)	G	6-3	310	11/14/76	Yale	Potomac, Md.	FA-'98
Holdman, Warrick	LB	6-1	233	11/22/75	Texas A&M	Alief, Tex.	D4a
Jefferson, Love	RB	6-3	261	2/15/76	Washington State	Garden Grove, Calif.	FA
McNown, Cade	QB	6-1	213	1/12/77	UCLA	West Linn, Ore.	D1
Mitchell, Derrell (1)	RB	5-8	190	9/16/71	Texas Tech	Miami, Fla.	FA
O'Neal, Heron (1)	CB	6-2	195	2/9/75	Western Michigan	Chicago, Ill.	FA
Overhauser, Chad (1)	T	6-4	316	6/17/75	UCLA	Sacramento, Calif.	D7a-'98
Palmer, Dan (1)	G	6-4	290	8/24/73	Air Force	Anderson, S.C.	FA
Palmer, Emile (1)	DT	6-3	320	4/5/73	Syracuse	Cheverly, Md.	FA
Samuel, Khari	LB	6-3	242	10/14/76	Massachusetts	Framingham, Mass.	D5b
Sanford, Sulecio	WR	5-10	190	3/23/76	Middle Tennessee State	Milledgeville, Ga.	D7a
Spiller, Derrick	TE	6-3	257	9/8/77	Texas A&M	LeMarque, Tex.	FA
Stecker, Aaron	RB	5-11	205	11/13/75	Western Illinois	Green Bay, Wis.	FA
Tucker, Rex	G-T	6-5	285	12/20/76	Texas A&M	Midland, Tex.	D3a
Washington, Damon	RB	5-11	193	2/20/77	Colorado State	San Diego, Calif.	FA
Williams, Greg (1)	CB-S	5-10	191	3/12/76	North Carolina	Bolingbrook, Ill.	FA
Wisne, Jerry	G	6-6	306	7/28/76	Notre Dame	Tulsa, Okla.	D5a

The term NFL Rookie is defined as a player who is in his first season of professional football and has not been on the roster of another professional football team for any regular-season or postseason games. A Rookie is designated by an "R" on NFL rosters. Players who have been active in another professional football league or players who have NFL experience, including either preseason training camp or being on an Active List or Inactive List, or on Reserve/Injured or Reserve/Physically Unable to Perform for fewer than six regular-season games, are termed NFL First-Year Players. An NFL First-Year Player is designated by a "1" on NFL rosters. Thereafter, a player is credited with an additional year of experience for each season in which he accumulates six games on the Active List or Inactive List, or on Reserve/Injured or Reserve/Physically Unable to Perform.

NOTES

DALLAS COWBOYS

National Football Conference
Eastern Division
Team Colors: Royal Blue, Metallic Silver Blue, and White
Cowboys Center
One Cowboys Parkway
Irving, Texas 75063
Telephone: (972) 556-9900

CLUB OFFICIALS

Owner/President/General Manager: Jerry Jones
Executive Vice President-Player Personnel: Stephen Jones
Vice President/Marketing: George Hays
Vice President/Director of Marketing and Special Events: Charlotte Anderson
Vice President/Legal Operations: Jerry Jones, Jr.
Public Relations Director: Rich Dalrymple
Assistant Director of Public Relations: Brett Daniels
Director of College and Pro Scouting: Larry Lacewell
Director of Operations: Bruce Mays
Director of Human Resources: Vincent Thompson
Treasurer: Robert Nunez
Ticket Manager: Carol Padgett
Trainer: Jim Maurer
Equipment Manager: Mike McCord
Video Director: Robert Blackwell
Cheerleader Director: Kelli Finglass
Stadium: Texas Stadium • **Capacity:** 65,675
Irving, Texas 75062
Playing Surface: Sportfield Turf
Training Camp: Midwestern State University
Wichita Falls, Texas 76308

1999 SCHEDULE

PRESEASON

Aug. 9	vs. Cleveland at Canton, Ohio	8:00
Aug. 15	at Oakland	1:00
Aug. 21	at New England	8:00
Aug. 29	**Denver**	7:00
Sept. 2	**Jacksonville**	8:00

REGULAR SEASON

Sept. 12	at Washington	1:00
Sept. 20	**Atlanta** (Mon.)	8:00
Sept. 26	Open Date	
Oct. 3	**Arizona**	12:00
Oct. 10	at Philadelphia	1:00
Oct. 18	at N.Y. Giants (Mon.)	9:00
Oct. 24	**Washington**	12:00
Oct. 31	at Indianapolis	1:00
Nov. 8	at Minnesota (Mon.)	8:00
Nov. 14	**Green Bay**	3:15
Nov. 21	at Arizona	2:15
Nov. 25	**Miami** (Thurs.)	3:15
Dec. 5	at New England	8:20
Dec. 12	**Philadelphia**	12:00
Dec. 19	**New York Jets**	3:15
Dec. 24	at New Orleans (Fri.)	2:05
Jan. 2	**New York Giants**	3:05

RECORD HOLDERS

INDIVIDUAL RECORDS—CAREER

Category	Name	Performance
Rushing (Yds.)	Emmitt Smith, 1990-98	12,566
Passing (Yds.)	Troy Aikman, 1989-1998	28,346
Passing (TDs)	Danny White, 1976-1988	155
Receiving (No.)	Michael Irvin, 1988-1998	740
Receiving (Yds.)	Michael Irvin, 1988-1998	11,737
Interceptions	Mel Renfro, 1964-1977	52
Punting (Avg.)	Mike Saxon, 1985-1992	41.5
Punt Return (Avg.)	Bob Hayes, 1965-1974	11.1
Kickoff Return (Avg.)	Mel Renfro, 1964-1977	26.4
Field Goals	Rafael Septien, 1978-1986	162
Touchdowns (Tot.)	Emmitt Smith, 1990-98	134
Points	Rafael Septien, 1978-1986	874

INDIVIDUAL RECORDS—SINGLE SEASON

Category	Name	Performance
Rushing (Yds.)	Emmitt Smith, 1995	1,773
Passing (Yds.)	Danny White, 1983	3,980
Passing (TDs)	Danny White, 1983	29
Receiving (No.)	Michael Irvin, 1995	111
Receiving (Yds.)	Michael Irvin, 1995	1,603
Interceptions	Everson Walls, 1981	11
Punting (Avg.)	Sam Baker, 1962	45.4
Punt Return (Avg.)	Bob Hayes, 1968	20.8
Kickoff Return (Avg.)	Mel Renfro, 1965	30.0
Field Goals	Richie Cunningham, 1997	34
Touchdowns (Tot.)	Emmitt Smith, 1995	*25
Points	Emmitt Smith, 1995	150

INDIVIDUAL RECORDS—SINGLE GAME

Category	Name	Performance
Rushing (Yds.)	Emmitt Smith, 10-31-93	237
Passing (Yds.)	Don Meredith, 11-10-63	460
Passing (TDs)	Many times	5
	Last time by Danny White, 10-30-83	
Receiving (No.)	Lance Rentzel, 11-19-67	13
Receiving (Yds.)	Bob Hayes, 11-13-66	246
Interceptions	Herb Adderley, 9-26-71	3
	Lee Roy Jordan, 11-4-73	3
	Dennis Thurman, 12-13-81	3
Field Goals	Chris Boniol, 11-18-96	*7
Touchdowns (Tot.)	Many times	4
	Last time by Emmitt Smith, 9-4-95	
Points	Many times	24
	Last time by Emmitt Smith, 9-4-95	

*NFL Record

COACHING HISTORY

(376-248-6)

1960-88	Tom Landry	270-178-6
1989-93	Jimmy Johnson	51-37-0
1994-97	Barry Switzer	45-26-0
1998	Chan Gailey	10-7-0

TEXAS STADIUM

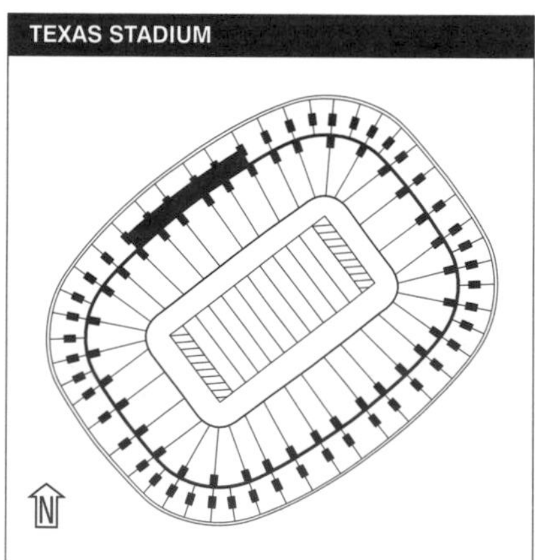

1998 TEAM RECORD

PRESEASON (0-5)

Date	Result		Opponent
7/31	L	19-20	Seattle
8/8	L	3-16	Oakland
8/17	L	3-21	vs. New England at Mexico City
8/22	L	14-22	at St. Louis
8/27	L	20-42	at Jacksonville

REGULAR SEASON (10-6)

Date	Result		Opponent	Att.
9/6	W	38-10	Arizona	63,602
9/13	L	23-42	at Denver	75,013
9/21	W	31-7	at New York Giants	78,039
9/27	L	12-13	Oakland	63,544
10/4	W	31-10	at Washington	72,284
10/11	W	27-20	Carolina	64,181
10/18	L	12-13	at Chicago	59,201
11/2	W	34-0	at Philadelphia	67,002
11/8	W	16-6	New York Giants	64,316
11/15	W	35-28	at Arizona	69,923
11/22	W	30-22	Seattle	64,142
11/26	L	36-46	Minnesota	64,366
12/6	L	3-22	at New Orleans	65,065
12/13	L	17-20	at Kansas City	77,697
12/20	W	13-9	Philadelphia	62,722
12/27	W	23-7	Washington	63,565

POSTSEASON (0-1)

Date	Result		Opponent	Att.
1/2	L	7-20	Arizona	62,969

SCORE BY PERIODS

Cowboys	72	124	80	105	0	—	381
Opponents	77	82	66	50	0	—	275

ATTENDANCE

Home 510,438 Away 564,224 Total 1,074,662
Single-game home record, 65,180 (11/12/95)
Single-season home record, 518,167 (1995)

1998 TEAM STATISTICS

	Cowboys	Opp.
Total First Downs	308	276
Rushing	125	84
Passing	154	162
Penalty	29	30
Third Down: Made/Att	76/206	71/210
Third Down Pct.	36.9	33.8
Fourth Down: Made/Att	8/12	5/20
Fourth Down Pct.	66.7	25.0
Total Net Yards	5,450	5,164
Avg. Per Game	340.6	322.8
Total Plays	992	988
Avg. Per Play	5.5	5.2
Net Yards Rushing	2,014	1,619
Avg. Per Game	125.9	101.2
Total Rushes	499	401
Net Yards Passing	3,436	3,545
Avg. Per Game	214.8	221.6
Sacked/Yards Lost	19/110	34/222
Gross Yards	3,546	3,767
Att./Completions	474/279	553/290
Completion Pct.	58.9	52.4
Had Intercepted	8	14
Punts/Avg.	78/42.8	85/42.4
Net Punting Avg.	78/36.6	85/35.0
Penalties/Yards Lost	129/1,106	120/917
Fumbles/Ball Lost	18/7	23/12
Touchdowns	42	32
Rushing	21	10
Passing	17	21
Returns	4	1
Avg. Time of Possession	31:50	28:10

1998 INDIVIDUAL STATISTICS

Passing	Att.	Comp.	Yds.	Pct.	TD	Int.	Tkld.	Rate
Aikman	315	187	2,330	59.4	12	5	9/58	88.5
Garrett	158	91	1,206	57.6	5	3	10/52	84.5
Quinn	1	1	10	100.0	0	0	0/0	108.3
Cowboys	474	279	3,546	58.9	17	8	19/110	87.2
Opponents	553	290	3,767	52.4	21	14	34/222	76.3

SCORING	TD R	TD P	TD Rt	PAT	FG	Saf	PTS
Cunningham	0	0	0	40/40	29/35	0	127
E. Smith	13	2	0	0/0	0/0	0	90
Warren	4	1	0	0/0	0/0	0	30
Mills	0	4	0	0/0	0/0	0	24
B. Davis	0	3	0	0/0	0/0	0	18
Sanders	0	0	3	0/0	0/0	0	18
Aikman	2	0	0	0/0	0/0	0	12
Bjornson	1	1	0	0/0	0/0	0	12
Jeffers	0	2	0	0/0	0/0	0	12
LaFleur	0	2	0	0/0	0/0	0	12
Wheaton	0	0	1	0/0	0/0	1	8
Irvin	0	1	0	0/0	0/0	0	6
Johnston	0	1	0	0/0	0/0	0	6
S. Williams	1	0	0	0/0	0/0	0	6
Cowboys	21	17	4	40/40	29/35	1	381
Opponents	10	21	1	29/30	16/19	1	275

2-Point conversions: None.
Team 0-2, Opponents 2-2.

RUSHING	Att.	Yds.	Avg.	LG	TD
E. Smith	319	1,332	4.2	32	13
Warren	59	291	4.9	49	4
S. Williams	64	220	3.4	24	1
Aikman	22	69	3.1	23	2
Gowin	1	33	33.0	33	0
Johnston	8	17	2.1	6	0
B. Davis	4	15	3.8	8	0
Garrett	11	14	1.3	5	0
Ogden	1	12	12.0	12	0
Mills	3	9	3.0	5	0
Bjornson	1	7	7.0	7t	1
Irvin	1	1	1.0	1	0
Quinn	5	-6	-1.2	-1	0
Cowboys	499	2,014	4.0	49	21
Opponents	401	1,619	4.0	63t	10

RECEIVING	No.	Yds.	Avg.	LG	TD
Irvin	74	1,057	14.3	51	1
B. Davis	39	691	17.7	80t	3
Mills	28	479	17.1	43t	4
E. Smith	27	175	6.5	24	2
LaFleur	20	176	8.8	24	2
Jeffers	18	330	18.3	67t	2
Johnston	18	60	3.3	9	1
Bjornson	15	218	14.5	43	1
Warren	13	66	5.1	15	1
S. Williams	11	104	9.5	30	0
Ogden	8	63	7.9	12	0
Sanders	7	100	14.3	55	0
Clay	1	27	27.0	27	0
Cowboys	279	3,546	12.7	80t	17
Opponents	290	3,767	13.0	89t	21

INTERCEPTIONS	No.	Yds.	Avg.	LG	TD
Sanders	5	153	30.6	71t	1
K. Smith	2	31	15.5	22	0
Mathis	2	0	0.0	0	0
Wheaton	1	41	41.0	41	0
Coakley	1	18	18.0	18	0
Reese	1	6	6.0	6	0
Woodson	1	1	1.0	1	0
Godfrey	1	0	0.0	0	0
Cowboys	14	250	17.9	71t	1
Opponents	8	121	15.1	30	1

PUNTING	No.	Yds.	Avg.	In 20	LG
Gowin	77	3,342	43.4	31	65
Cowboys	78	3,342	42.8	31	65
Opponents	85	3,604	42.4	22	65

PUNT RETURNS	No.	FC	Yds.	Avg.	LG	TD
Sanders	24	8	375	15.6	69t	2
Hughes	10	3	93	9.3	35	0
Mathis	2	1	3	1.5	5	0
Warren	2	1	11	5.5	6	0
K. Smith	1	0	11	11.0	11	0
Cowboys	39	13	493	12.6	69t	2
Opponents	34	13	210	6.2	18	0

KICKOFF RETURNS	No.	Yds.	Avg.	LG	TD
Mathis	25	621	24.8	42	0
Hughes	11	274	24.9	36	0
Warren	5	90	18.0	23	0
S. Williams	4	103	25.8	40	0
Ogden	3	65	21.7	28	0
B. Davis	1	10	10.0	10	0
LaFleur	1	12	12.0	12	0
Sanders	1	16	16.0	16	0
Stoutmire	0	0	—	—	0
Cowboys	51	1,191	23.4	42	0
Opponents	69	1,274	18.5	44	0

FIELD GOALS	1-19	20-29	30-39	40-49	50+
Cunningham	1/1	9/9	8/11	10/11	1/3
Cowboys	1/1	9/9	8/11	10/11	1/3
Opponents	0/0	6/6	5/5	3/6	2/2

SACKS	No.
Pittman	6.0
McCormack	5.0
Lett	4.0
Ellis	3.0
Godfrey	3.0
Myers	3.0
Woodson	3.0
Coakley	2.0
Teague	2.0
Hennings	1.0
Mathis	1.0
Stoutmire	1.0
Cowboys	34.0
Opponents	19.0

1999 DRAFT CHOICES

Round	Name	Pos.	College
1	Ebenezer Ekuban	DE	North Carolina
2	Solomon Page	T	West Virginia
3	Dat Nguyen	LB	Texas A&M
4	Wane McGarity	WR	Texas
	Peppi Zellner	DE	Fort Valley State
6	Mar Tay Jenkins	WR	Nebraska-Omaha
7	Mike Lucky	TE	Arizona
	Kelvin Garmon	G	Baylor

DALLAS COWBOYS

1999 VETERAN ROSTER

No.	Name	Pos.	Ht.	Wt.	Birthdate	NFL Exp.	College	Hometown	How Acq.	'98 Games/ Starts
76	Adams, Flozell	G-T	6-7	335	5/18/75	2	Michigan State	Bellwood, Ill.	D2-'98	16/12
8	Aikman, Troy	QB	6-4	226	11/21/66	11	UCLA	Henryetta, Okla.	D1-'89	11/11
73	Allen, Larry	G-T	6-3	326	11/27/71	6	Sonoma State	Napa, Calif.	D2-'94	16/16
91	Benson, Darren	DT	6-7	308	8/25/74	5	Trinity Valley	Memphis, Tenn.	SD3-'95	0*
86	Bjornson, Eric	TE	6-4	236	12/15/71	5	Washington	Oakland, Calif.	D4a-'95	16/4
65	Childress, Freddie	G	6-4	335	9/17/66	3	Arkansas	West Helena, Ark.	FA-'99	0*
83	Clay, Hayward	TE	6-3	260	7/5/73	3	Texas A&M	Snyder, Tex.	W(Chi)-'98	3/2
52	Coakley, Dexter	LB	5-10	228	10/20/72	3	Appalachian State	Mt. Pleasant, S.C.	D3a-'97	16/16
51	Coryatt, Quentin	LB	6-3	250	8/1/70	8	Texas A&M	St. Croix, Virgin Islands	FA-'99	0*
3	Cunningham, Richie	K	5-10	167	8/18/70	3	Southwestern Louisiana	Houma, La.	FA-'97	16/0
87	Davis, Billy	WR	6-1	203	7/6/72	5	Pittsburgh	El Paso, Tex.	FA-'95	16/11
99	Davis, Nathan	DT	6-5	312	2/6/74	3	Indiana	Richmond, Ind.	FA-'98	0*
98	Ellis, Greg	DE	6-6	286	8/14/75	2	North Carolina	Wendell, N.C.	D1-'98	16/16
17	Garrett, Jason	QB	6-2	195	3/28/66	7	Princeton	Chagrin, Ohio	FA-'93	8/5
56	† Godfrey, Randall	LB	6-2	245	4/6/73	4	Georgia	Valdosta, Ga.	D2b-'96	16/16
4	Gowin, Toby	P	5-10	167	3/30/75	3	North Texas	Jacksonville, Tex.	FA-'97	16/0
54	Hambrick, Darren	LB	6-2	227	8/30/75	2	South Carolina	Pasco, Fla.	D5a-'98	14/0
70	# Hellestrae, Dale	G-C	6-5	291	7/11/62	15	Southern Methodist	Scottsdale, Ariz.	T(Raid)-'90	16/0
58	Hemsley, Nate	LB	6-0	228	5/15/74	2	Syracuse	Delran, N.J.	FA-'97	3/0
95	Hennings, Chad	DT	6-6	291	10/20/65	8	Air Force	Elberon, Iowa	D11-'88	16/16
66	Hutson, Tony	G-T	6-3	306	3/13/74	3	Northeast Oklahoma State	Houston, Tex.	FA-'97	10/1
88	Irvin, Michael	WR	6-2	207	3/5/66	12	Miami	Ft. Lauderdale, Fla.	D1-'88	16/15
81	Ismail, Raghib	WR	5-11	175	11/18/69	7	Notre Dame	Wilkes Barre, Pa.	UFA(Car)-'99	16/15*
48	Johnston, Daryl	RB	6-2	242	2/10/66	11	Syracuse	Youngstown, N.Y.	D2-'89	16/13
63	Kiselak, Michael	C-G	6-3	295	3/9/67	2	Maryland	Pine Bush, N.Y.	FA-'98	15/7
89	LaFleur, David	TE	6-7	272	1/29/74	3	Louisiana State	Westlake, La.	D1-'97	13/13
78	Lett, Leon	DT	6-6	290	10/12/68	9	Emporia State	Fairhope, Ala.	D7-'91	16/15
23	Mathis, Kevin	CB	5-9	179	4/29/74	3	Texas A&M-Commerce	Gainsville, Tex.	FA-'97	13/4
67	McIver, Everett	G	6-5	330	8/5/70	6	Elizabeth City State	Fayetteville, N.C.	UFA(Mia)-'98	6/6
80	Mills, Ernie	WR	5-11	196	10/28/68	9	Florida	Dunnellon, Fla.	FA-'98	11/1
27	Mobley, Singor	S	5-11	195	10/12/72	3	Washington State	Tacoma, Wash.	FA-'97	16/0
94	Myers, Michael	DE-DT	6-2	275	1/20/76	2	Alabama	Vicksburg, Miss.	D4-'98	16/1
61	# Newton, Nate	G	6-3	318	12/20/61	14	Florida A&M	Orlando, Fla.	FA-'86	16/16
82	Ogden, Jeff	WR	6-0	190	2/22/75	2	Eastern Washington	Snohomish, Wash.	FA-'98	16/0
97	Pittman, Kavika	DE	6-6	267	2/9/74	4	McNeese State	Leesville, La.	D2a-'96	15/15
11	Quinn, Mike	QB	6-4	217	4/15/74	3	Stephen F. Austin	Houston, Tex.	W(Ind)-'98	3/0
43	Reese, Izell	S	6-2	196	5/7/74	2	Alabama-Birmingham	Dothan, Ala.	D6-'98	16/0
71	Ross, Oliver	T	6-4	300	9/27/74	2	Iowa State	Los Angeles, Calif.	D5b-'98	2/0
21	Sanders, Deion	CB-WR	6-1	195	8/9/67	11	Florida State	Fort Myers, Fla.	UFA(SF)-'95	11/11
50	† Shiver, Clay	C	6-2	283	12/7/72	4	Florida State	Tifton, Ga.	D3a-'96	14/9
22	Smith, Emmitt	RB	5-9	214	5/15/69	10	Florida	Escambia, Fla.	D1-'90	16/16
26	Smith, Kevin	CB	5-11	190	4/7/70	8	Texas A&M	Orange, Tex.	D1a-'92	14/14
57	Smith, Myron	LB	6-1	225	3/28/75	2	Louisiana Tech	Corsicana, Tex.	FA-'98	0*
53	Stepnoski, Mark	C	6-2	265	1/20/67	11	Pittsburgh	Erie, Pa.	UFA(Tenn)-'99	13/13*
24	Stoutmire, Omar	S	5-11	201	7/9/74	3	Fresno State	Long Beach, Calif.	D7-'97	16/12
45	Sualua, Nicky	RB	5-11	260	4/16/75	3	Ohio State	Santa Ana, Calif.	D4c-'97	16/0
31	Teague, George	S	6-1	206	2/18/71	7	Alabama	Montgomery, Ala.	FA-'98	16/5
51	# Thomas, Broderick	DE-LB	6-4	254	2/20/67	11	Nebraska	Houston, Tex.	FA-'96	0*
59	Thomas, Robert	LB	6-1	260	12/1/74	2	Henderson State	Jacksonville, Ark.	FA-'98	16/0
50	Tolbert, Brandon	LB	6-3	230	4/6/75	2	Georgia	Villa Rica, Ga.	FA-'98	0*
42	Warren, Chris	RB	6-2	236	1/24/68	10	Ferrum	Burke, Va.	FA-'98	9/0
30	Wheaton, Kenny	S	5-10	195	3/8/75	3	Oregon	Phoenix, Ariz.	D3c-'97	15/1
25	Williams, Charlie	CB-S	6-0	207	2/2/72	5	Bowling Green	Detroit, Mich.	D3-'95	15/3
79	Williams, Erik	T	6-6	328	9/7/68	9	Central State, Ohio	Philadelphia, Pa.	D3c-'91	15/15
20	# Williams, Sherman	RB	5-8	202	8/13/73	5	Alabama	Mobile, Ala.	FA-'98	16/2
28	Woodson, Darren	S	6-1	219	4/25/69	8	Arizona State	Phoenix, Ariz.	D2b-'92	16/15

* Benson, Coryatt, and Thomas missed '98 season because of injury; Childress last active with Cleveland in '92; N. Davis inactive for 11 games; Ismail played 16 games with Carolina in '98; M. Smith inactive for 8 games; Stepnoski played 13 games with Tennessee; Tolbert inactive for 3 games.

\# Unrestricted free agent; subject to developments.

† Restricted free agent; subject to developments.

Players lost through free agency (2): WR Patrick Jeffers (Carolina; 8 games in '98), DT Artie Smith (KC; 16).

Also played with Cowboys in '98—DT Antonio Anderson (5 games), CB Larry Brown (4), QB Daniel Gonzalez (0), CB Tyrone Hughes (4), DE Hurvin McCormack (16), LB Fred Strickland (16).

COACHING STAFF

Head Coach,
Chan Gailey

Pro Career: Chan Gailey became the fourth head coach in Cowboys history on February 12, 1998, after four seasons with the Pittsburgh Steelers. In his first season in Dallas, Gailey guided the Cowboys to a 10-6 record and their sixth NFC East title in the last seven seasons. In 10 seasons as an NFL assistant coach with Pittsburgh and Denver, Gailey appeared in four Super Bowls, six AFC Championship Games, and was part of seven division winning teams. Gailey was the Pittsburgh offensive coordinator (1996-97) after having served two years (1994-95) as the team's wide receivers coach. Gailey's other NFL experience came during a six-year stint (1985-1990) with the Denver Broncos. In his first season with the Broncos, Gailey served as a defensive assistant and special teams coach. The following year he coached special teams-tight ends and in 1987 he was in charge of the tight ends-wide receivers. He took over the quarterback coaching duties in 1988. In 1989, Gailey's first season as the Broncos' offensive coordinator, the Broncos earned a berth in Super Bowl XXIV. Sandwiched between his two NFL tours of duty were head coaching stops in the World League with the Birmingham Fire (1991-92) and at Samford University (1993). Gailey is the first former World League head coach to take on NFL head coaching responsibilities. Career record: 10-7.

Background: Gailey was a quarterback at Florida from 1970-73. He received his bachelor's degree in physical education in 1974 and began his coaching career as a graduate assistant at Florida (1974-75). He then served as the secondary coach at Troy State (1976-78), and four years at the Air Force Academy (1979-1982). He returned to Troy State as the head coach (1983-84) and captured the NCAA Division II Championship in 1984. He posted a 36-18-1 (.664) record in his three head coaching stops (five seasons).

Personal: Born in Gainesville, Ga., on January 5, 1952. Was a standout at Americus, (Georgia) High School. Chan and his wife, Laurie, have two sons, Tate and Andrew.

1999 FIRST-YEAR ROSTER

Name	Pos.	Ht.	Wt.	Birthdate	College	Hometown	How Acq.
Billups, Terry (1)	CB	5-9	179	2/9/75	North Carolina	Orlando, Fla.	FA-'98
Brooks, Kevin	CB	5-9	174	12/20/73	South Carolina	Jacksonville, Fla.	FA
Brymer, Chris (1)	C-G	6-3	300	11/29/74	Southern California	Apple Valley, Calif.	FA
Ekuban, Ebenezer	DE	6-3	281	5/29/76	North Carolina	Riverdale, Md.	D1
Fortney, Denny (1)	C	6-3	265	12/27/74	Miami	Waynesboro, Pa.	FA-'98
Garmon, Kelvin	G	6-2	329	10/26/76	Baylor	Haltom, Tex.	D7b
Gustin, Billy	S	6-1	188	1/27/76	Purdue	Fort Lauderdale, Fla.	FA
Hawthorne, Duane	CB	5-10	165	8/26/76	Northern Illinois	St. Louis, Mo.	FA
Jenkins, MarTay	WR	5-11	203	2/28/75	Nebraska-Omaha	Des Moines, Iowa	D6
Lethridge, Zebbie (1)	WR	6-0	201	1/31/75	Texas Tech	Lubbock, Tex.	FA-'98
Lindstrom, Gabe	P	6-4	220	5/25/76	Toledo	Bisbee, Ariz.	FA
Lucky, Mike	TE	6-6	273	11/23/75	Arizona	Antioch, Calif.	D7a
Manns, Denvis	RB	5-8	197	7/21/76	New Mexico State	Lufkin, Tex.	FA
McCalla, LaDouphyous	CB	5-8	185	1/1/76	Rice	Tyler, Tex.	FA
McCann, David (1)	RB	5-10	230	7/27/75	Murray State	Elizabethtown, Ky.	FA
McCarty, Chance (1)	DE	6-3	265	8/29/75	Texas Christian	Fort Worth, Tex.	FA
McGarity, Wane	WR	5-8	191	9/30/76	Texas	San Antonio, Tex.	D4a
Morgan, Beau (1)	RB	5-10	192	8/4/75	Air Force	Carrollton, Tex.	FA-'97
Neufeld, Ryan	TE	6-4	240	11/22/75	UCLA	Morgan Hill, Calif.	FA
Newkirk, Robert	DT	6-3	290	3/6/77	Michigan State	Belle Glade, Fla.	FA
Nguyen, Dat	LB	5-11	231	9/25/75	Texas A&M	Rockport, Tex.	D3
Noble, Brandon (1)	DT	6-2	285	4/10/74	Penn State	Virginia Beach, Va.	FA
Page Solomon	T	6-4	306	2/27/76	West Virginia	Pittsburgh, Pa.	D2
Painter, Zac	CB-S	5-9	205	3/24/76	Arkansas	Jonesboro, Ark.	FA
Pearsall, Grant	S	6-0	197	11/7/75	Southern California	Orange, Calif.	FA
Phipps, Joe	LB	6-1	220	11/1/75	Texas Christian	Diboll, Tex.	FA
Powell, Billy	WR	6-1	196	6/25/75	Rutgers	Rockville, Md.	FA
Ricard, Alan	RB	6-0	235	1/17/77	Northeast Louisiana	Amite, La.	FA
Scott, Earl (1)	G-C	6-3	290	8/31/73	Arkansas	Fayetteville, Ark.	FA
Simmons, Sam	DE	6-6	279	1/2/75	Arkansas-Pine Bluff	Atlanta, Ga.	FA
Smith, Myron (1)	LB	6-1	225	3/28/75	Louisiana Tech	Corsicana, Tex.	FA-'98
Smith, Tarik (1)	RB	5-10	204	4/16/75	California	Agoura, Calif.	D7a-'98
Tucker, Jason (1)	WR	6-1	182	6/24/76	Texas Christian	Waco, Tex.	FA
Turner, Omar	CB	5-10	195	4/7/75	Montana State	Duncanville, Tex.	FA
Waters, Brian	RB	6-2	277	2/18/77	North Texas	Waxahachie, Tex.	FA
Washington, John (1)	WR	5-10	170	7/8/74	Texas Christian	Longview, Tex.	FA
Wilkins, Greg	DT	6-3	305	11/1/73	Langston	Chicago, Ill.	FA
Winn, Brad	G-T	6-5	350	7/26/76	North Texas	Austin, Tex.	FA
Zellner, Peppi	DE	6-5	251	3/14/75	Fort Valley State	Forsythe, Ga.	D4b

The term NFL Rookie is defined as a player who is in his first season of professional football and has not been on the roster of another professional football team for any regular-season or postseason games. A Rookie is designated by an "R" on NFL rosters. Players who have been active in another professional football league or players who have NFL experience, including either preseason training camp or being on an Active List or Inactive List, or on Reserve/Injured or Reserve/Physically Unable to Perform for fewer than six regular-season games, are termed NFL First-Year Players. An NFL First-Year Player is designated by a "1" on NFL rosters. Thereafter, a player is credited with an additional year of experience for each season in which he accumulates six games on the Active List or Inactive List, or on Reserve/Injured or Reserve/Physically Unable to Perform.

ASSISTANT COACHES

Joe Avezzano, special teams; born November 17, 1943, Yonkers, N.Y., lives in Coppell, Texas. Guard Florida State 1961-65. Pro center Boston Patriots 1966. College coach: Florida State 1968, Iowa State 1969-1972, Pittsburgh 1973-76, Tennessee 1977-79, Oregon State 1980-84 (head coach), Texas 1985-88. Pro coach: Joined Cowboys in 1990.

Bill Bates, special teams defensive assistant; born June 6, 1961, Knoxville, Tenn., lives in Plano, Texas. Defensive back Tennessee 1979-1982. Pro defensive back Dallas Cowboys 1983-1997. Pro coach: Joined Cowboys in 1998.

Jim Bates, defensive line; born May 31, 1946, Pontiac, Mich., lives in Irving, Texas. Linebacker Tennessee 1964-67. No pro playing experience. College coach: Tennessee 1968, Southern Mississippi 1972, Villanova 1973-74, Kansas State 1975-76, West Virginia 1977, Texas Tech 1978-1983, Tennessee 1989, Florida 1990. Pro coach: San Antonio Gunslingers (USFL) 1984-85 (head coach 1985), Arizona Outlaws (USFL) 1986, Detroit Drive (AFL) 1988, Cleveland Browns 1991-93, 1995, Atlanta Falcons 1994, joined Cowboys in 1996.

Dave Campo, defensive coordinator; born July 18, 1947, New London, Conn., lives in Coppell, Texas. Defensive back Central Connecticut State 1967-1970. No pro playing experience. College coach: Central Connecticut State 1971-72, Albany State 1973, Bridgeport 1974, Pittsburgh 1975, Washington State 1976, Boise State 1977-79, Oregon State 1980, Weber State 1981-82, Iowa State 1983, Syracuse 1984-86, Miami 1987-88. Pro coach: Joined Cowboys in 1989.

George Edwards, linebackers; born January 16, 1967, Siler City, N.C., lives in Coppell, Texas. Linebacker Duke 1986-89. No pro playing experience. College coach: Florida 1990-91, Appalachian State 1992-95, Duke 1996, Georgia 1997. Pro coach: Joined Cowboys in 1998.

Wayne (Buddy) Geis, quarterbacks; born September 16, 1946, Altoona, Pa., lives in Irving, Texas. Wide receiver Northern Arizona 1965. No pro playing experience. College coach: Arizona 1974-76, Tulane 1977-1982, Memphis State 1986-87, Duke 1993, Tulane 1994. Pro coach: Jacksonville Bulls (USFL) 1984-85, Green Bay Packers 1988-1991, Memphis Mad Dogs (CFL) 1995, Indianapolis Colts 1996-97, joined Cowboys in 1998.

Steve Hoffman, kickers-research and development; born September 8, 1958, Camden, N.J., lives in Irving, Texas. Quarterback-running back-wide receiver Dickinson College 1979-1982. Pro punter Washington Federals (USFL) 1983. College coach: Miami 1985-87. Pro coach: Joined Cowboys in 1989.

Hudson Houck, offensive line; born January 7, 1943, Los Angeles, lives in Irving, Texas. Center Southern California 1962-64. No pro playing experience. College coach: Southern California 1970-72, 1976-1982, Stanford 1973-75. Pro coach: Los Angeles Rams 1983-1991, Seattle Seahawks 1992, joined Cowboys in 1993.

Jim Jeffcoat, defensive line assistant; born April 1, 1961, Cliffwood, N.J., lives in Irving, Texas. Defensive end Arizona State 1979-1982. Pro defensive end Dallas Cowboys 1983-1994, Buffalo Bills 1995-97. Pro coach: Joined Cowboys in 1998.

Joe Juraszek, strength and conditioning; born June 8, 1958, Chicago, lives in Coppell, Texas. Linebacker-defensive end New Mexico 1976-1980. No pro playing experience. College coach: Oklahoma 1981-86, 1993-96, Texas Tech 1987-1992. Pro coach: Joined Cowboys in 1997.

Les Miles, tight ends; born November 10, 1953, Elyria, Ohio, lives in Irving, Texas. Guard Michigan 1972-75. No pro playing experience. College coach: Colorado 1982-86, Michigan 1987-1994, Oklahoma State 1995-97. Pro coach: Joined Cowboys in 1998.

Dwain Painter, wide receivers; born February 13, 1942, Monroeville, Pa., lives in Coppell, Texas. Quarterback-defensive back Rutgers 1961-64. No pro playing experience. College coach: San Jose State 1971-72, College of San Mateo 1973, BYU 1974-75, UCLA 1976-78, Northern Arizona 1979-1981 (head coach), Georgia Tech 1982-85, Texas. 1986, Illinois 1987. Pro coach: Pittsburgh Steelers 1988-1991, Indianapolis Colts 1992-93, San Diego Chargers 1994-96, Denver Broncos 1997, joined Cowboys in 1998.

Clancy Pendergast, defensive assistant; born November 29, 1967, Phoenix, lives in Irving, Texas. No college or pro playing experience. College coach: Mississippi State 1991, Southern California 1992, Oklahoma 1993-94. Pro coach: Houston Oilers 1995, joined Cowboys in 1996.

Tommie Robinson, offensive assistant; born April 4, 1963, Phenix City, Ala., lives in Fort Worth, Texas. Defensive back Troy State 1981-84. No pro playing experience. College coach: Arkansas 1991, Utah State 1992-93, Texas Christian 1994-97. Pro coach: Joined Cowboys in 1998.

Clarence Shelmon, running backs; born September 17, 1952, Bossier City, La., lives in Coppell, Texas. Running back Houston 1971-75. No pro playing experience. College coach: Army 1978-1980, Indiana 1981-83, Arizona 1984-86, Southern California 1987-1990. Pro coach: Los Angeles Rams 1991, Seattle Seahawks 1992-97, joined Cowboys in 1998.

Mike Zimmer, defensive backs; born June 5, 1956, Peoria, Ill., lives in Colleyville, Texas. Quarterback-linebacker Illinois State 1974-76. No pro playing experience. College coach: Missouri 1979-1980, Weber State 1981-88, Washington State 1989-1993. Pro coach: Joined Cowboys in 1994.

DETROIT LIONS

National Football Conference
Central Division
Team Colors: Honolulu Blue and Silver
Pontiac Silverdome
1200 Featherstone Road
Pontiac, Michigan 48342
Telephone: (248) 335-4131

CLUB OFFICIALS

Chairman and President: William Clay Ford
Vice Chairman: William Clay Ford, Jr.
Executive Vice President and Chief Operating Officer: Chuck Schmidt
Vice President of Player Personnel: Ron Hughes
Vice President of Communications, Sales and Marketing: Bill Keenist
Vice President of Football Administration: Larry Lee
Vice President of Finance and Chief Financial Officer: Tom Lesnau
Vice President of Stadium Development and Salary Cap Director: Tom Lewand
Secretary: David Hempstead
Director of Pro Scouting: Kevin Colbert
Scouts: Russ Bolinger, Chad Henry, Scott McEwen, Lance Newmark, Jim Owens, Charlie Sanders, Sheldon White
Director of Media Relations: Mike Murray
Executive Director of Marketing: Steve Harms
Director of Box Office Operations: Mark Graham
Director of Ticket Sales and Customer Service: Jennifer Manzo
Director of Broadcast Services: Bryan Bender
Director of Community Relations and Detroit Lions Charities: Tim Pendell
Head Athletic Trainer: Kent Falb
Equipment Manager: Dan Jaroshewich
Video Director: Steve Hermans
Stadium: Pontiac Silverdome •**Capacity:** 80,311
1200 Featherstone Road
Pontiac, Michigan 48342
Playing Surface: AstroTurf
Training Camp: Saginaw Valley State University
University Center, Michigan 48710

1999 SCHEDULE

PRESEASON

Aug. 13	at Atlanta	7:30
Aug. 20	**Cincinnati**	7:00
Aug. 28	at Miami	7:00
Sept. 2	**St. Louis**	7:00

REGULAR SEASON

Sept. 12	at Seattle	1:15
Sept. 19	**Green Bay**	1:00
Sept. 26	at Kansas City	12:00
Oct. 3	Open Date	
Oct. 10	**San Diego**	1:00
Oct. 17	**Minnesota**	1:00
Oct. 24	at Carolina	1:00
Oct. 31	**Tampa Bay**	8:20
Nov. 7	**St. Louis**	1:00
Nov. 14	at Arizona	2:15
Nov. 21	at Green Bay	12:00
Nov. 25	**Chicago** (Thurs.)	12:40
Dec. 5	**Washington**	1:00
Dec. 12	at Tampa Bay	1:00
Dec. 19	at Chicago	12:00
Dec. 25	**Denver** (Sat.)	4:15
Jan. 2	at Minnesota	12:00

RECORD HOLDERS

INDIVIDUAL RECORDS—CAREER

Category	Name	Performance
Rushing (Yds.)	Barry Sanders, 1989-1998	15,269
Passing (Yds.)	Bobby Layne, 1950-58	15,710
Passing (TDs)	Bobby Layne, 1950-58	118
Receiving (No.)	Herman Moore, 1991-98	610
Receiving (Yds.)	Herman Moore, 1991-98	8,467
Interceptions	Dick LeBeau, 1959-1972	62
Punting (Avg.)	Yale Lary, 1952-53, 1956-1964	44.3
Punt Return (Avg.)	Jack Christiansen, 1951-58	12.8
Kickoff Return (Avg.)	Pat Studstill, 1961-67	25.7
Field Goals	Eddie Murray, 1980-1991	243
Touchdowns (Tot.)	Barry Sanders, 1989-1998	109
Points	Eddie Murray, 1980-1991	1,113

INDIVIDUAL RECORDS—SINGLE SEASON

Category	Name	Performance
Rushing (Yds.)	Barry Sanders, 1997	2,053
Passing (Yds.)	Scott Mitchell, 1995	4,338
Passing (TDs)	Scott Mitchell, 1995	32
Receiving (No.)	Herman Moore, 1995	*123
Receiving (Yds.)	Herman Moore, 1995	1,686
Interceptions	Don Doll, 1950	12
	Jack Christiansen, 1953	12
Punting (Avg.)	Yale Lary, 1963	48.9
Punt Return (Avg.)	Jack Christiansen, 1952	21.5
Kickoff Return (Avg.)	Tom Watkins, 1965	34.4
Field Goals	Jason Hanson, 1993	34
Touchdowns (Tot.)	Barry Sanders, 1991	17
Points	Jason Hanson, 1995	132

INDIVIDUAL RECORDS—SINGLE GAME

Category	Name	Performance
Rushing (Yds.)	Barry Sanders, 11-13-94	237
Passing (Yds.)	Scott Mitchell, 11-23-95	410
Passing (TDs)	Gary Danielson, 12-9-78	5
Receiving (No.)	Herman Moore, 12-4-95	14
Receiving (Yds.)	Cloyce Box, 12-3-50	302
Interceptions	Don Doll, 10-23-49	*4
Field Goals	Garo Yepremian, 11-13-66	6
Touchdowns (Tot.)	Dutch Clark, 10-22-34	4
	Cloyce Box, 12-3-50	4
	Barry Sanders, 11-24-91	4
Points	Dutch Clark, 10-22-34	24
	Cloyce Box, 12-3-50	24
	Barry Sanders, 11-24-91	24

*NFL Record

COACHING HISTORY

Portsmouth Spartans 1930-33
(447-466-32)

1930	Hal (Tubby) Griffen	5-6-3
1931-36	George (Potsy) Clark	49-20-6
1937-38	Earl (Dutch) Clark	14-8-0
1939	Elmer (Gus) Henderson	6-5-0
1940	George (Potsy) Clark	5-5-1
1941-42	Bill Edwards*	4-9-1
1942	John Karcis	0-8-0
1943-47	Charles (Gus) Dorais	20-31-2
1948-50	Alvin (Bo) McMillin	12-24-0
1951-56	Raymond (Buddy) Parker	50-24-2
1957-64	George Wilson	55-45-6
1965-66	Harry Gilmer	10-16-2
1967-72	Joe Schmidt	43-35-7
1973	Don McCafferty	6-7-1
1974-76	Rick Forzano**	15-17-0
1976-77	Tommy Hudspeth	11-13-0
1978-84	Monte Clark	43-63-1
1985-88	Darryl Rogers***	18-40-0
1988-96	Wayne Fontes	67-71-0
1997-98	Bobby Ross	14-19-0

* Released after three games in 1942
** Resigned after four games in 1976
*** Released after 11 games in 1988

PONTIAC SILVERDOME

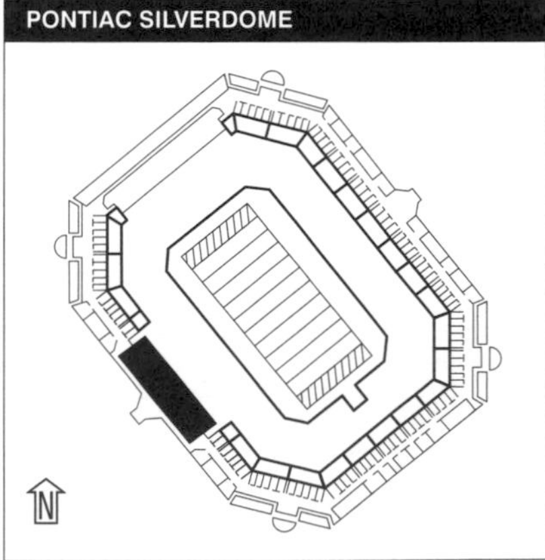

1998 TEAM RECORD

PRESEASON (1-3)

Date	Result		Opponent
8/7	W	13-10	Arizona
8/14	L	3-7	Atlanta
8/22	L	19-33	at Cincinnati
8/27	L	17-20	at Indianapolis

REGULAR SEASON (5-11)

Date	Result		Opponent	Att.
9/6	L	19-38	at Green Bay	60,102
9/13	L	28-34	Cincinnati (OT)	66,354
9/20	L	6-29	at Minnesota	63,107
9/28	W	27-6	Tampa Bay	74,724
10/4	L	27-31	at Chicago	55,562
10/15	W	27-20	Green Bay	77,932
10/25	L	13-34	Minnesota	77,885
11/1	L	15-17	Arizona	66,087
11/8	L	9-10	at Philadelphia	66,785
11/15	W	26-3	Chicago	63,152
11/22	W	28-25	at Tampa Bay	64,265
11/26	W	19-16	Pittsburgh (OT)	78,139
12/6	L	22-37	at Jacksonville	70,717
12/14	L	13-35	at San Francisco	68,585
12/20	L	17-24	Atlanta	67,143
12/27	L	10-19	at Baltimore	68,045

(OT) Overtime

SCORE BY PERIODS

Lions	57	88	72	86	3	—	306
Opponents	64	114	74	120	6	—	378

ATTENDANCE

Home 571,416 Away 517,168 Total 1,088,584
Single-game home record, 80,441 (12/20/81)
Single-season home record, 622,593 (1980)

1998 TEAM STATISTICS

	Lions	Opp.
Total First Downs	278	308
Rushing	94	113
Passing	160	167
Penalty	24	28
Third Down: Made/Att	72/211	89/217
Third Down Pct.	34.1	41.0
Fourth Down: Made/Att	10/20	5/7
Fourth Down Pct.	50.0	71.4
Total Net Yards	5,085	5,117
Avg. Per Game	317.8	319.8
Total Plays	975	1,004
Avg. Per Play	5.2	5.1
Net Yards Rushing	1,955	2,102
Avg. Per Game	122.2	131.4
Total Rushes	441	487
Net Yards Passing	3,130	3,015
Avg. Per Game	195.6	188.4
Sacked/Yards Lost	45/268	43/261
Gross Yards	3,398	3,276
Att./Completions	489/274	474/284
Completion Pct.	56.0	59.9
Had Intercepted	13	12
Punts/Avg.	82/42.8	81/42.7
Net Punting Avg.	82/35.5	81/36.9
Penalties/Yards Lost	121/1,019	98/791
Fumbles/Ball Lost	17/12	27/9
Touchdowns	32	43
Rushing	12	15
Passing	17	23
Returns	3	5
Avg. Time of Possession	29:22	30:38

1998 INDIVIDUAL STATISTICS

Passing	Att.	Comp.	Yds.	Pct.	TD	Int.	Tkld.	Rate
Batch	303	173	2,178	57.1	11	6	37/222	83.5
Reich	110	63	768	57.3	5	4	4/18	78.9
Mitchell	75	38	452	50.7	1	3	4/28	57.2
Jett	1	0	0	0.0	0	0	0/0	39.6
Lions	489	274	3,398	56.0	17	13	45/268	78.2
Opponents	474	284	3,276	59.9	23	12	43/261	86.4

SCORING	TD R	TD P	TD Rt	PAT	FG	Saf	PTS
Hanson	0	0	0	27/29	29/33	0	114
Vardell	6	1	0	0/0	0/0	0	42
Moore	0	5	0	0/0	0/0	0	30
Sanders	4	0	0	0/0	0/0	0	24
Crowell	0	3	0	0/0	0/0	0	18
Chryplewicz	0	2	0	0/0	0/0	0	12
Fair	0	0	2	0/0	0/0	0	12
Morton	0	2	0	0/0	0/0	0	12
Batch	1	0	0	0/0	0/0	0	6
T. Boyd	0	1	0	0/0	0/0	0	6
Rasby	0	1	0	0/0	0/0	0	6
Rivers	1	0	0	0/0	0/0	0	6
Schlesinger	0	1	0	0/0	0/0	0	6
Sloan	0	1	0	0/0	0/0	0	6
Westbrook	0	0	1	0/0	0/0	0	6
Lions	12	17	3	27/29	29/33	0	306
Opponents	15	23	5	41/41	25/30	1	378

2-Point conversions: None.
Team 0-3, Opponents 1-1.

RUSHING	Att.	Yds.	Avg.	LG	TD
Sanders	343	1,491	4.3	73t	4
Batch	41	229	5.6	17	1
Rivers	19	102	5.4	36t	1
Vardell	18	37	2.1	17	6
Crowell	1	35	35.0	35	0
Mitchell	7	30	4.3	17	0
Schlesinger	5	17	3.4	5	0
Morton	1	11	11.0	11	0
Reich	6	3	0.5	5	0
Lions	441	1,955	4.4	73t	12
Opponents	487	2,102	4.3	57t	15

RECEIVING	No.	Yds.	Avg.	LG	TD
Moore	82	983	12.0	36	5
Morton	69	1,028	14.9	98t	2
Sanders	37	289	7.8	44	0
Crowell	25	464	18.6	68t	3
Rasby	15	119	7.9	17	1
Vardell	14	143	10.2	31	1
Sloan	11	146	13.3	33	1
Stablein	7	80	11.4	15	0
T. Boyd	4	52	13.0	19	1
Chryplewicz	4	20	5.0	8	2
Rivers	3	58	19.3	38	0
Schlesinger	3	16	5.3	8t	1
Lions	274	3,398	12.4	98t	17
Opponents	284	3,276	11.5	84t	23

INTERCEPTIONS	No.	Yds.	Avg.	LG	TD
Westbrook	3	49	16.3	34t	1
Carrier	3	33	11.0	33	0
Rice	3	25	8.3	25	0
Jamison	1	21	21.0	21	0
Jordan	1	4	4.0	4	0
Fredrickson	1	0	0.0	0	0
Lions	12	132	11.0	34t	1
Opponents	13	198	15.2	79t	2

PUNTING	No.	Yds.	Avg.	In 20	LG
Jett	66	2,892	43.8	17	60
Kidd	13	520	40.0	1	54
Hanson	3	94	31.3	1	36
Lions	82	3,506	42.8	19	60
Opponents	81	3,460	42.7	26	67

PUNT RETURNS	No.	FC	Yds.	Avg.	LG	TD
Fair	30	15	189	6.3	23	0
T. Boyd	4	0	11	2.8	3	0
Abrams	2	1	12	6.0	16	0
Stablein	0	3	0	—	—	0
Lions	36	19	212	5.9	23	0
Opponents	47	20	471	10.0	65t	1

KICKOFF RETURNS	No.	Yds.	Avg.	LG	TD
Fair	51	1,428	28.0	105t	2
T. Boyd	8	163	20.4	26	0
McPhail	6	71	11.8	20	0
Rivers	2	15	7.5	9	0
Vardell	1	23	23.0	23	0
Jamison	0	0	—	0	0
Lions	68	1,700	25.0	105t	2
Opponents	49	1,196	24.4	100t	1

FIELD GOALS	1-19	20-29	30-39	40-49	50+
Hanson	0/0	8/8	7/7	13/15	1/3
Lions	0/0	8/8	7/7	13/15	1/3
Opponents	0/0	6/6	11/12	7/9	1/3

SACKS	No.
Porcher	11.5
Scroggins	6.5
S. Boyd	4.0
Rice	3.5
Abrams	3.0
Aldridge	3.0
Elliss	3.0
Fredrickson	2.5
Owens	2.5
Waldroup	1.5
Fair	1.0
Lions	43.0
Opponents	45.0

1999 DRAFT CHOICES

Round	Name	Pos.	College
1	Chris Claiborne	LB	Southern California
	Aaron Gibson	T	Wisconsin
3	Jared DeVries	DE	Iowa
4	Sedrick Irvin	RB	Michigan State
5	Ty Talton	DB	Northern Iowa
6	Clint Kriewaldt	LB	Wisconsin-Stevens Point
7	Mike Pringley	DE	North Carolina

DETROIT LIONS

1999 VETERAN ROSTER

No.	Name	Pos.	Ht.	Wt.	Birthdate	NFL Exp.	College	Hometown	How Acq.	'98 Games/ Starts
24	Abrams, Kevin	CB	5-8	175	2/28/74	3	Syracuse	Tampa, Fla.	D2b-'97	16/7
55	Aldridge, Allen	LB	6-1	255	5/30/72	6	Houston	Missouri City, Tex.	UFA(Den)-'98	16/15
35	Bailey, Robert	CB	5-9	174	9/3/68	9	Miami	Miami, Fla.	FA-'97	16/0
10	Batch, Charlie	QB	6-2	216	12/5/74	2	Eastern Michigan	Homestead, Pa.	D2b-'98	12/12
79	Beverly, Eric	C	6-3	279	3/28/74	2	Miami, Ohio	Bedford Heights, Ohio	FA-'97	16/0
65	Blaise, Kerlin	G	6-5	306	12/25/74	2	Miami	Orlando, Fla.	FA-'98	0*
57	Boyd, Stephen	LB	6-0	247	8/22/72	5	Boston College	Valley Stream, N.Y.	D5a-'95	13/12
76	Brooks, Barrett	T	6-4	320	5/5/72	5	Kansas State	St. Louis, Mo.	UFA(Phil)-'99	16/1*
39	Campbell, Lamar	CB	5-11	182	8/29/76	2	Wisconsin	Chester, Pa.	FA-'98	12/0
27	Carrier, Mark	S	6-1	192	4/28/68	10	Southern California	Long Beach, Calif.	FA-'97	13/13
81	Chryplewicz, Pete	TE	6-5	253	4/27/74	3	Notre Dame	Sterling Heights, Mich.	D5a-'97	16/2
77	Compton, Mike	G	6-6	297	9/18/70	7	West Virginia	Richland, Va.	D3b-'93	16/16
82	Crowell, Germane	WR	6-3	213	9/13/76	2	Virginia	Winston-Salem, N.C.	D2a-'98	14/2
94	Elliss, Luther	DT	6-5	291	3/22/73	5	Utah	Mancos, Colo.	D1-'95	16/16
23	Fair, Terry	CB	5-9	185	7/20/76	2	Tennessee	Phoenix, Ariz.	D1-'98	14/10
12	Frerotte, Gus	QB	6-3	240	8/3/71	6	Tulsa	Ford City, Pa.	FA-'99	3/2*
4	Hanson, Jason	K	5-11	183	6/17/70	8	Washington State	Spokane, Wash.	D2b-'92	16/0
64	Hartings, Jeff	G	6-3	283	9/7/72	4	Penn State	St. Henry, Ohio	D1b-'96	13/13
18	Jett, John	P	6-0	199	11/11/68	7	East Carolina	Reedville, Va.	UFA(Dall)-'97	14/0
70	Johnson, Andre	T	6-5	314	8/25/73	4	Penn State	Southampton, N.Y.	FA-'97	3/0
98	Jones, James	DT	6-2	290	2/6/69	9	Northern Iowa	Davenport, Iowa	UFA(Balt)-'99	16/16*
99	Jordan, Richard	LB	6-1	245	12/1/74	3	Missouri Southern	Vian, Okla.	D7c-'97	16/4
67	Kirschke, Travis	DT	6-3	286	9/6/74	3	UCLA	Yorba Linda, Calif.	FA-'97	0*
52	Kowalkowski, Scott	LB	6-2	228	8/23/68	9	Notre Dame	Orchard Lake, Mich.	FA-'94	15/0
84	Moore, Herman	WR	6-3	210	10/20/69	9	Virginia	Danville, Va.	D1-'91	15/15
87	Morton, Johnnie	WR	6-0	190	10/7/71	6	Southern California	Torrance, Calif.	D1-'94	16/16
26	Olivo, Brock	RB	6-0	226	6/24/76	2	Missouri	Washington, Mo.	FA-'98	1/0
59	O'Neill, Kevin	LB	6-2	239	4/14/75	2	Bowling Green	Twinsburg, Ohio	FA-'98	11/0
90	Owens, Dan	DT	6-3	290	3/16/67	10	Southern California	Whittier, Calif.	UFA(Atl)-'98	11/11
91	Porcher, Robert	DE	6-3	283	7/30/69	8	South Carolina State	Wando, S.C.	D1-'92	16/16
93	Pritchett, Kelvin	DT	6-3	301	10/24/69	9	Mississippi	Atlanta, Ga.	UFA(Jac)-'99	15/9*
75	Ramirez, Tony	T	6-6	296	1/26/73	3	Northern Colorado	Lincoln, Neb.	D6-'97	16/7
89	Rasby, Walter	TE	6-3	247	9/7/72	6	Wake Forest	Washington, N.C.	UFA(Car)-'98	16/16
36	Reece, Travis	RB	6-3	252	4/3/75	2	Michigan State	Detroit, Mich.	FA-'98	3/0
28	Rice, Ron	S	6-1	206	11/9/72	5	Eastern Michigan	Detroit, Mich.	FA-'95	16/16
34	Rivers, Ron	RB	5-8	205	11/13/71	5	Fresno State	Highland, Calif.	FA-'94	15/0
72	Roberts, Ray	T	6-6	308	6/3/69	8	Virginia	Asheville, N.C.	UFA(Sea)-'96	16/16
74	Roque, Juan	T	6-8	333	1/6/74	3	Arizona State	Ontario, Calif.	D2a-'97	0*
54	Russell, Matt	LB	6-2	245	7/5/73	3	Colorado	Belleville, Ill.	D4-'97	0*
20	Sanders, Barry	RB	5-8	203	7/16/68	11	Oklahoma State	Wichita, Kan.	D1-'89	16/16
30	Schlesinger, Cory	RB	6-0	230	6/23/72	5	Nebraska	Duncan, Neb.	D6b-'95	15/2
80	Scott, Freddie	WR	5-10	189	8/26/74	3	Penn State	Southfield, Mich.	FA-'99	1/0*
97	Scroggins, Tracy	LB	6-2	255	9/11/69	8	Tulsa	Checotah, Okla.	D2a-'92	11/3
62	Semple, Tony	G	6-5	305	12/20/70	6	Memphis	Lincoln, Ill.	D5-'94	16/3
86	Sloan, David	TE	6-6	254	6/8/72	5	New Mexico	Tollhouse, Calif.	D3-'95	10/2
83	Stablein, Brian	WR	6-1	193	4/14/70	6	Ohio State	Erie, Pa.	FA-'98	10/0
42	Stewart, Ryan	S	6-1	207	9/30/73	4	Georgia Tech	Moncks Corner, S.C.	D3-'96	16/0
29	Supernaw, Kywin	S	6-1	206	6/2/75	2	Indiana	Claremore, Okla.	FA-'98	2/0
96	Taylor, Henry	DT	6-2	295	11/29/75	2	South Carolina	Barnwell, S.C.	FA-'98	1/0
32	Westbrook, Bryant	CB	6-0	199	12/19/74	3	Texas	Oceanside, Calif.	D1-'97	16/16

* Blaise inactive for 16 games; Brooks played 16 games with Philadelphia in '98; Frerotte played 3 games with Washington; Jones played 16 games with Baltimore; Kirschke, Russell, and Roque missed '98 season because of injury; Pritchett played 15 games with Jacksonville; Scott played 1 game with Indianapolis.

Traded—QB Scott Mitchell (2 games in '98) to Baltimore.

Retired—Frank Reich, 14-year quarterback, 6 games in '98; George Jamison, 13-year linebacker, 14 games.

Players lost to free agency (4): LB Rob Fredrickson (Ariz; 16 games in '98), DT Darius Holland (Clev; 10), CB Greg Jeffries (Mia; 15), RB Tommy Vardell (SF; 14).

Also played with Lions in '98—WR Tommie Boyd (8 games), DE Mike Chalenski (10), TE Kevin Hickman (3), P John Kidd (2), RB Jerris McPhail (3), C Jim Pyne (16), DT Don Sasa (2), DT Marc Spindler (15), T Larry Tharpe (16), DE Marvin Thomas (4), DE Kerwin Waldroup (13).

COACHING STAFF

Head Coach,
Bobby Ross

Pro Career: Named the Lions' head coach January 13, 1997. In his first season with the Lions, Ross guided the club to victories in five of its final six games to earn a NFC wild-card berth. Joined the Lions following five seasons as the head coach of the San Diego Chargers. Led the Chargers to a 50-36 record, three playoff appearances in five years, including two AFC Western Division titles, the club's first AFC championship, and an appearance in Super Bowl XXIX. Began coaching career with Chiefs' special teams and defense in 1978-79 and offensive backs in 1980-81. No pro playing experience. Career record: 64-55.

Background: Played quarterback and defensive back for Virginia Military Institute (1956-58). Began coaching career at VMI in 1965. Moved on as an assistant at William & Mary (1967-1970), Rice (1971), and Maryland (1972). Head coach at The Citadel (1973-77). Compiled 39-19-1 record at Maryland (1982-86) as he led the Terrapins to three Atlantic Coast Conference titles and made four bowl game appearances in five seasons. Guided Georgia Tech (1987-1991) to first ACC title in school history. Under Ross, the Yellow Jackets won first national championship as country's only undefeated team (11-0-1) in 1990. Named consensus national coach of the year in 1990. Career collegiate record: 94-76-2.

Personal: Born December 23, 1935, Richmond, Va. Bobby and wife, Alice, live in West Bloomfield, Mich. and have five children—Chris, Kevin, Robbie, Mary, and Teresa.

ASSISTANT COACHES

Brian Baker, defensive line; born June 20, 1962, Baltimore, lives in Rochester, Mich. Linebacker Maryland 1980-83. No pro playing experience. College coach: Maryland 1984-85, Army 1986, Georgia Tech 1987-1995. Pro coach: San Diego Chargers 1996, joined Lions in 1997.

Don Clemons, defensive assistant; born February 15, 1954, Newark, N.J., lives in Rochester, Mich. Defensive end Muhlenberg College 1973-76. No pro playing experience. College coach: Kutztown State 1977-78, New Mexico 1979, Arizona State 1980-84. Pro coach: Joined Lions in 1985.

Sylvester Croom, offensive coordinator; born September 25, 1954, Tuscaloosa, Ala., lives in Rochester, Mich. Center Alabama 1971-74. Pro center New Orleans Saints 1975. College coach: Alabama 1976-1986. Pro coach: Tampa Bay Buccaneers 1987-1990, Indianapolis Colts 1991, San Diego Chargers 1992-96, joined Lions in 1997.

Frank Falks, running backs; born March 9, 1943, Tampa, lives in Rochester Hills, Mich. Linebacker Joplin (Mo.) J.C. 1963-64, Parsons College 1965-66. No pro playing experience. College coach: Parsons College 1967-69, Kansas State 1970-72, Arkansas 1973-77, Wyoming 1978-79, San Diego State 1980, Oklahoma State 1981-82, Southern California 1983-86, Arizona State 1987-1991, Ohio State 1992-93. Pro coach: San Diego Chargers 1994-96, joined Lions in 1997.

Robert Graf, asst. strength and conditioning; born January 25, 1967, Wichita Falls, Tex., lives in Auburn Hills, Mich. No college or pro playing experience. College coach: Texas A&M 1990-91, 1993-98. Pro coach: Joined Lions in 1999.

Jack Henry, offensive line; born March 14, 1946, Wilmerding, Pa., lives in Rochester Hills, Mich. Linebacker Penn State 1964-65, guard Indiana (Pa.) University 1967-68. No pro playing experience. College coach: West Virginia 1970, 1978-79, Edinboro 1973, Louisville 1974, Millersville 1975-76, Southern Illinois 1977, Appalachian State 1980, Wake Forest 1981-85, Indiana (Pa.) University 1986-89, Pittsburgh 1993-95. Pro coach: Pittsburgh Steelers 1990-91, San Diego Chargers 1996, joined Lions in 1997.

Bert Hill, strength and conditioning; born January 25, 1958, Montgomery, Ala., lives in Rochester Hills, Mich. Linebacker Marion (Ala.) Military Institute 1976-77, Wichita State 1978. No pro playing experience. College coach: Nicholls State 1981-82, Auburn 1983, Texas A&M 1984-88, Ohio State 1989. Pro coach: Joined Lions in 1990.

Stan Kwan, offense and special teams assistant; born November 2, 1967, Phoenix, lives in Rochester Hills, Mich. No college or pro playing experience. Pro coach: San Diego Chargers 1991-96, joined Lions in 1997.

John Misciagna, quality control-offense & administrative assistant; born December 11, 1954, Brooklyn, N.Y., lives in Auburn Hills, Mich. Guard Dickinson College 1973-76. No pro playing experience. College coach: Indiana (Pa.) University 1977, Columbia 1978-79, Maryland 1980-88, Georgia Tech 1989-1991. Pro coach: San Diego Chargers 1992-96, joined Lions in 1997.

Gary Moeller, linebackers; born January 26, 1941, Lima, Ohio, lives in Ann Arbor, Mich. Center-linebacker Ohio State 1960-62. No pro playing experience. College coach: Miami (Ohio) 1967-68, Michigan 1969-1976, 1980-1994 (head coach 1990-94), Illinois 1977-79 (head coach). Pro coach: Cincinnati Bengals 1995-96, joined Lions in 1997.

Dennis Murphy, quality control-defense; born October 22, 1940, Endicott, N.Y., lives in Rochester, Mich. Tight end-defensive lineman Notre Dame 1959-1961. No pro playing experience. College coach: Notre Dame 1968-1974, Colgate 1975, Holy Cross 1976-77, Eastern Michigan 1978-1981, Maryland 1982-1991, Navy 1992-93. Pro coach: San Diego Chargers 1994-96, joined Lions in 1997.

Larry Peccatiello, defensive coordinator; born December 21, 1937, Newark, N.J., lives in Rochester, Mich. Receiver William & Mary 1955-58. No pro playing experience. College coach: William & Mary 1961-68, Navy 1969-1970, Rice 1971. Pro coach: Houston Oilers 1972-75, Seattle Seahawks 1976-1980, Washington Redskins 1981-1993, Cincinnati Bengals 1994-96, joined Lions in 1997.

Chuck Priefer, special teams; born July 26, 1944, Cleveland, lives in Rochester Hills, Mich. No college or pro playing experience. College coach: Miami (Ohio) 1977, North Carolina 1978-1983, Kent State 1986, Georgia Tech 1987-1991. Pro coach: Green Bay Packers 1984-85, San Diego Chargers 1992-96, joined Lions in 1997.

Richard Selcer, defensive backs; born August 22, 1937, Cincinnati, lives in Rochester, Mich. Running back Notre Dame 1955-58. No pro playing experience. College coach: Xavier 1962-64, 1970-71 (head coach), Cincinnati 1965-66, Brown 1967-69, Wisconsin 1972-74, Kansas State 1975-77, Southwestern Louisiana 1978-1980. Pro coach: Houston Oilers 1981-83, Cincinnati Bengals 1984-1991, Los Angeles/St. Louis Rams 1992-96, joined Lions in 1997.

Danny Smith, tight ends; born November 7, 1953, Pittsburgh, lives in Rochester Hills, Mich. Defensive back Edinboro State 1972-75. No pro playing experience. College coach: Edinboro State 1976, Clemson 1979, William & Mary 1980-83, The Citadel 1984-86, Georgia Tech 1987-1994. Pro coach: Philadelphia Eagles 1995-98, joined Lions in 1999.

Jerry Sullivan, wide receivers; born July 13, 1944, Miami, lives in Rochester Hills, Mich. Quarterback Florida State 1963-64. No pro playing experience. College coach: Kansas State 1971-72, Texas Tech 1973-75, South Carolina 1976-1982, Indiana 1983, Louisiana State 1984-1990, Ohio State 1991. Pro coach: San Diego Chargers 1992-96, joined Lions in 1997.

Jim Zorn, quarterbacks; born May 10, 1953, Whittier, Calif., lives in Bloomfield Hills, Mich. Quarterback Cal Poly-Pomona 1973-75. Pro quarterback Seattle Seahawks 1976-1984, Green Bay Packers 1985, Winnipeg Blue Bombers (CFL) 1986, Tampa Bay Buccaneers 1987. College coach: Boise State 1989-1991, Utah State 1992-94, Minnesota 1995-96. Pro coach: Seattle Seahawks 1997, joined Lions in 1998.

1999 FIRST-YEAR ROSTER

Name	Pos.	Ht.	Wt.	Birthdate	College	Hometown	How Acq.
Claiborne, Chris	LB	6-3	250	7/26/78	Southern California	Riverside, Calif.	D1a
Codia, Nikia	S	6-2	206	1/20/76	Baylor	Cleburne, Tex.	FA
Daniel, Darryl	WR	5-11	188	1/24/76	Syracuse	Lancaster, Pa.	FA
DeVries, Jared	DE	6-4	280	6/11/76	Iowa	Aplington, Iowa	D3
Dorsey, Charles	DT	6-1	289	8/7/74	Auburn	Ft. Lauderdale, Fla.	FA
Douglas, Henry	WR	5-11	167	3/3/73	North Carolina A&T	Southern Pines, N.C.	FA
Gibson, Aaron	T	6-4	375	9/27/77	Wisconsin	Indianapolis, Ind.	D1b
Gowins, Brian	K	5-9	171	6/3/76	Northwestern	Birmingham, Ala.	FA
Hall, Jay	WR	5-10	191	1/11/76	Miami, Ohio	Cincinnati, Ohio	FA
Hall, Joey	LB	6-0	235	6/10/77	Appalachian State	Augusta, Ga.	FA
Hart, Donnie	WR	6-0	192	12/11/76	Texas Tech	Wolfforth, Tex.	FA
Irvin, Sedrick	RB	5-11	217	3/30/78	Michigan State	Miami, Fla.	D4
Johnson, Demetrius	CB	5-9	187	8/13/76	Eastern Michigan	Detroit, Mich.	FA
Kanu, Sorie	S	5-10	193	7/11/77	Michigan State	Alexandria, Va.	FA
Kriewaldt, Clint	LB	6-1	235	3/17/76	Wisconsin-Stevens Point	Shiocton, Wis.	D6
Morgan, Dwayne (1)	G	6-4	315	5/3/74	Clemson	Griffin, Ga.	FA
Nash, Phil	CB	6-0	192	6/19/74	Syracuse	Clearwater, Fla.	FA
Offutt, Jeremy	C	6-4	294	10/28/75	Oklahoma State	Paris, Tex.	FA
Pearson, Pepe (1)	RB	5-10	208	12/11/75	Ohio State	Euclid, Ohio	W(Clev)
Pope, Daniel	P	5-10	195	3/28/75	Alabama	Alpharetta, Ga.	FA
Powlus, Ron (1)	QB	6-1	225	7/16/74	Notre Dame	Berwick, Pa.	FA
Pringley, Mike	DE	6-4	270	5/22/76	North Carolina	Linden, N.J.	D7
Rubin, Marek	T	6-6	312	3/21/77	Yale	Delran, N.J.	FA
Sauter, Cory (1)	QB	6-4	218	11/21/74	Minnesota	Hutchinson, Minn.	FA
Spicer, Paul (1)	DE	6-4	260	8/18/75	Saginaw Valley	Indianapolis, Ind.	FA
Talton, Ty	S	5-11	200	5/10/76	Northern Iowa	Beloit, Wis.	D5
Taylor, Kerry	TE	6-2	256	1/24/77	Massachusetts	Mansfield, Mass.	FA
Thomas, Corey (1)	WR	6-0	164	6/6/75	Duke	Wilson, N.C.	FA-'98
Thorp, Deron (1)	T	6-8	324	8/31/73	Nevada	Santa Clara, Calif.	FA-'98
Tuipala, Joe	LB	6-0	237	9/13/76	San Diego State	Ridgecrest, Calif.	FA
Williams, Undre (1)	WR	5-9	165	2/11/75	Florida A&M	Macon, Ga.	FA

The term NFL Rookie is defined as a player who is in his first season of professional football and has not been on the roster of another professional football team for any regular-season or postseason games. A Rookie is designated by an "R" on NFL rosters. Players who have been active in another professional football league or players who have NFL experience, including either preseason training camp or being on an Active List or Inactive List, or on Reserve/Injured or Reserve/Physically Unable to Perform for fewer than six regular-season games, are termed NFL First-Year Players. An NFL First-Year Player is designated by a "1" on NFL rosters. Thereafter, a player is credited with an additional year of experience for each season in which he accumulates six games on the Active List or Inactive List, or on Reserve/Injured or Reserve/Physically Unable to Perform.

GREEN BAY PACKERS

National Football Conference
Central Division
Team Colors: Dark Green, Gold, and White
1265 Lombardi Avenue
Green Bay, Wisconsin 54304
Telephone: (920) 496-5700

CLUB OFFICIALS

President and CEO: Bob Harlan
Vice President: John Fabry
Secretary: Peter Platten
Treasurer: John Underwood
Exec. V.P. and General Manager: Ron Wolf
Senior Vice President of Administration: John Jones
Vice President-General Counsel: Lance Lopes
Vice President of Personnel: Ken Herock
Exec. Assistant to the President: Phil Pionek
Exec. Director of Public Relations: Lee Remmel
Associate Director of Public Relations: Jeff Blumb
Assistant Director of Public Relations/Travel Coordinator: Aaron Popkey
Public Relations Assistants: Christian Johnson, Paula Martin
Exec. Director of Player Programs and Community Affairs: Gill Byrd
Director of Family Programs: Sherry Schuldes
Director of Marketing: Jeff Cieply
Ticket Director: Mark Wagner
Director of Administrative Affairs: Mark Schiefelbein
Director of Finance: Vicki Vannieuwenhoven
Director of Accounting: Duke Copp
Director of Computer Services: Wayne Wichlacz
Corporate Security Officer: Jerry Parins
Director of Player Finance-Football Operations: Andrew Brandt
Director of Player Personnel: Ted Thompson
Director of Pro Personnel: Reggie McKenzie
College Scouts: Lee Gissendaner, Brian Gutekunst, Shaun Herock, Alonzo Highsmith, Scot McCloughan, Sam Seale, Red Cochran
Scouting Coordinator: Danny Mock
Strength and Conditioning Assistant: Mark Lovat
Administrative Assistant-Football: Matt Klein
Video Director: Al Treml
Head Trainer: Pepper Burruss
Equipment Manager: Gordon (Red) Batty
Stadium Supervisor: Ted Eisenreich
Fields Coordinator: Allen Johnson
Stadium: Lambeau Field • **Capacity:** 60,890
1265 Lombardi Avenue
Green Bay, Wisconsin 54304
Playing Surface: Grass
Training Camp: St. Norbert College
De Pere, Wisconsin 54115

RECORD HOLDERS

INDIVIDUAL RECORDS—CAREER

Category	Name	Performance
Rushing (Yds.)	Jim Taylor, 1958-1966	8,207
Passing (Yds.)	Brett Favre, 1992-98	26,803
Passing (TDs)	Brett Favre, 1992-98	213
Receiving (No.)	Sterling Sharpe, 1988-1994	595
Receiving (Yds.)	James Lofton, 1978-1986	9,656
Interceptions	Bobby Dillon, 1952-59	52
Punting (Avg.)	Craig Hentrich, 1994-97	42.8
Punt Return (Avg.)	Desmond Howard, 1996	15.1
Kickoff Return (Avg.)	Travis Williams, 1967-1970	26.7
Field Goals	Chris Jacke, 1989-1996	173
Touchdowns (Tot.)	Don Hutson, 1935-1945	105
Points	Don Hutson, 1935-1945	823

INDIVIDUAL RECORDS—SINGLE SEASON

Category	Name	Performance
Rushing (Yds.)	Jim Taylor, 1962	1,474
Passing (Yds.)	Lynn Dickey, 1983	4,458
Passing (TDs)	Brett Favre, 1996	39
Receiving (No.)	Sterling Sharpe, 1993	112
Receiving (Yds.)	Robert Brooks, 1995	1,497
Interceptions	Irv Comp, 1943	10
Punting (Avg.)	Craig Hentrich, 1997	45.0
Punt Return (Avg.)	Billy Grimes, 1950	19.1
Kickoff Return (Avg.)	Travis Williams, 1967	*41.1
Field Goals	Chester Marcol, 1972	33
Touchdowns (Tot.)	Jim Taylor, 1962	19
Points	Paul Hornung, 1960	*176

INDIVIDUAL RECORDS—SINGLE GAME

Category	Name	Performance
Rushing (Yds.)	Dorsey Levens, 11-23-97	190
Passing (Yds.)	Lynn Dickey, 10-12-80	418
Passing (TDs)	Many times	5
	Last time by Brett Favre, 9-27-98	
Receiving (No.)	Don Hutson, 11-22-42	14
Receiving (Yds.)	Bill Howton, 10-21-56	257
Interceptions	Bobby Dillon, 11-26-53	*4
	Willie Buchanon, 9-24-78	*4
Field Goals	Chris Jacke, 11-11-90, 10-14-96	5
Touchdowns (Tot.)	Paul Hornung, 12-12-65	5
Points	Paul Hornung, 10-8-61	33

*NFL Record

1999 SCHEDULE

PRESEASON

Aug. 14	**New York Jets**	7:00
Aug. 23	vs. Denver at Madison, Wisconsin	7:00
Aug. 28	at New Orleans	7:00
Sept. 2	**Miami**	7:00

REGULAR SEASON

Sept. 12	**Oakland**	12:00
Sept. 19	at Detroit	1:00
Sept. 26	**Minnesota**	3:15
Oct. 3	Open Date	
Oct. 10	**Tampa Bay**	7:20
Oct. 17	at Denver	2:15
Oct. 24	at San Diego	1:05
Nov. 1	**Seattle** (Mon.)	8:00
Nov. 7	**Chicago**	12:00
Nov. 14	at Dallas	3:15
Nov. 21	**Detroit**	12:00
Nov. 29	at San Francisco (Mon.)	6:00
Dec. 5	at Chicago	12:00
Dec. 12	**Carolina**	12:00
Dec. 20	at Minnesota (Mon.)	8:00
Dec. 26	at Tampa Bay	4:15
Jan. 2	**Arizona**	12:00

COACHING HISTORY

(573-455-36)

1921-49	Earl (Curly) Lambeau	212-106-21
1950-53	Gene Ronzani*	14-31-1
1953	Hugh Devore- Ray (Scooter) McLean**	0-2-0
1954-57	Lisle Blackbourn	17-31-0
1958	Ray (Scooter) McLean	1-10-1
1959-67	Vince Lombardi	98-30-4
1968-70	Phil Bengtson	20-21-1
1971-74	Dan Devine	25-28-4
1975-83	Bart Starr	53-77-3
1984-87	Forrest Gregg	25-37-1
1988-91	Lindy Infante	24-40-0
1992-98	Mike Holmgren	84-42-0

*Resigned after 10 games in 1953
**Co-coaches

LAMBEAU FIELD

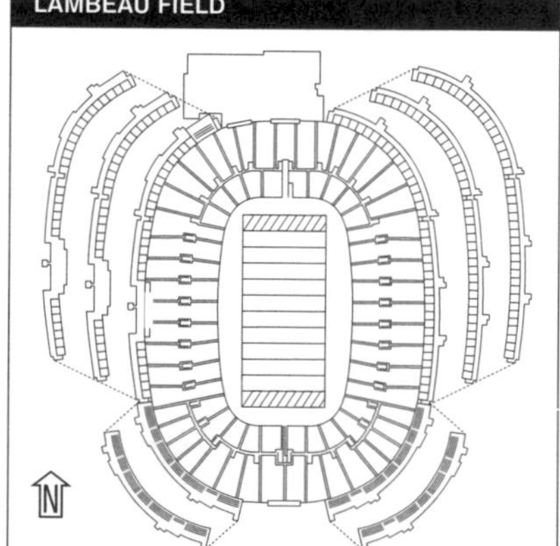

1998 TEAM RECORD

PRESEASON (2-3)

Date	Result		Opponent
8/1	W	27-24	vs. Kansas City at Tokyo, Japan
8/8	W	31-7	New Orleans
8/16	L	21-27	Oakland
8/24	L	31-34	at Denver
8/28	L	7-21	at Miami

REGULAR SEASON (11-5)

Date	Result		Opponent	Att.
9/6	W	38-19	Detroit	60,102
9/13	W	23-15	Tampa Bay	60,124
9/20	W	13-6	at Cincinnati	56,346
9/27	W	37-30	at Carolina	69,723
10/5	L	24-37	Minnesota	59,849
10/15	L	20-27	at Detroit	77,932
10/25	W	28-10	Baltimore	59,860
11/1	W	36-22	San Francisco	59,794
11/9	L	20-27	at Pittsburgh	60,507
11/15	W	37-3	at New York Giants	76,272
11/22	L	14-28	at Minnesota	64,471
11/29	W	24-16	Philadelphia	59,862
12/7	L	22-24	at Tampa Bay	65,497
12/13	W	26-20	Chicago	59,813
12/20	W	30-22	Tennessee	59,888
12/27	W	16-13	at Chicago	58,393

POSTSEASON (0-1)

Date	Result		Opponent	Att.
1/3	L	27-30	at San Francisco	66,506

SCORE BY PERIODS

Packers	107	89	73	139	0	—	408
Opponents	70	100	57	92	0	—	319

ATTENDANCE

Home 479,292 Away 529,141 Total 1,008,433
Single-game home record, 60,766 (9/1/97)
Single-season home record, 482,988 (1996)

1998 TEAM STATISTICS

	Packers	Opp.
Total First Downs	329	246
Rushing	93	67
Passing	210	166
Penalty	26	13
Third Down: Made/Att	99/218	92/233
Third Down Pct.	45.4	39.5
Fourth Down: Made/Att	5/13	5/17
Fourth Down Pct.	38.5	29.4
Total Net Yards	5,636	4,507
Avg. Per Game	352.3	281.7
Total Plays	1,061	980
Avg. Per Play	5.3	4.6
Net Yards Rushing	1,526	1,442
Avg. Per Game	95.4	90.1
Total Rushes	447	390
Net Yards Passing	4,110	3,065
Avg. Per Game	256.9	191.6
Sacked/Yards Lost	39/230	50/336
Gross Yards	4,340	3,401
Att./Completions	575/361	540/296
Completion Pct.	62.8	54.8
Had Intercepted	23	13
Punts/Avg.	65/42.9	90/43.6
Net Punting Avg.	65/37.1	90/37.2
Penalties/Yards Lost	88/681	94/828
Fumbles/Ball Lost	27/11	20/10
Touchdowns	46	36
Rushing	7	7
Passing	33	23
Returns	6	6
Avg. Time of Possession	31:37	28:23

1998 INDIVIDUAL STATISTICS

Passing	Att.	Comp.	Yds.	Pct.	TD	Int.	Tkld.	Rate
Favre	551	347	4,212	63.0	31	23	38/223	87.8
Pederson	24	14	128	58.3	2	0	1/7	100.7
Packers	575	361	4,340	62.8	33	23	39/230	88.3
Opponents	540	296	3,401	54.8	23	13	50/336	78.2

SCORING	TD R	TD P	TD Rt	PAT	FG	Saf	PTS
Longwell	0	0	0	41/43	29/33	0	128
Freeman	0	14	0	0/0	0/0	0	86
T. Davis	0	7	0	0/0	0/0	0	42
Chmura	0	4	0	0/0	0/0	0	24
Brooks	0	3	0	0/0	0/0	0	18
Henderson	2	1	0	0/0	0/0	0	18
Mayes	0	3	0	0/0	0/0	0	18
Preston	0	0	3	0/0	0/0	0	18
McKenzie	0	0	2	0/0	0/0	0	12
Butler	0	0	1	0/0	0/0	0	6
Favre	1	0	0	0/0	0/0	0	6
R. Harris	1	0	0	0/0	0/0	0	6
Holmes	1	0	0	0/0	0/0	0	6
Jervey	1	0	0	0/0	0/0	0	6
Levens	1	0	0	0/0	0/0	0	6
Schroeder	0	1	0	0/0	0/0	0	6
Packers	7	33	6	41/43	29/33	1	408
Opponents	7	23	6	28/30	23/27	0	319

2-Point conversions: Freeman.
Team 1-3, Opponents 3-6.

RUSHING	Att.	Yds.	Avg.	LG	TD
Holmes	93	386	4.2	13	1
Levens	115	378	3.3	50	1
Jervey	83	325	3.9	16	1
R. Harris	79	228	2.9	14	1
Favre	40	133	3.3	35	1
Henderson	23	70	3.0	9	2
Freeman	3	5	1.7	10	0
Blair	2	3	1.5	2	0
Brooks	1	2	2.0	2	0
Pederson	8	-4	-0.5	1	0
Packers	447	1526	3.4	50	7
Opponents	390	1442	3.7	73t	7

RECEIVING	No.	Yds.	Avg.	LG	TD
Freeman	84	1,424	17.0	84t	14
Chmura	47	554	11.8	25t	4
Henderson	37	241	6.5	15	1
Schroeder	31	452	14.6	46	1
Brooks	31	420	13.5	30t	3
Mayes	30	394	13.1	33t	3
Levens	27	162	6.0	17	0
Holmes	19	179	9.4	24	0
T. Davis	18	250	13.9	60t	7
R. Harris	10	68	6.8	12	0
Thomason	9	89	9.9	22	0
Jervey	9	33	3.7	11	0
Bradford	3	27	9.0	18	0
Preston	2	23	11.5	13	0
Blair	2	13	6.5	10	0
Copeland	2	11	5.5	12	0
Packers	361	4,340	12.0	84t	33
Opponents	296	3,401	11.5	68t	23

INTERCEPTIONS	No.	Yds.	Avg.	LG	TD
T. Williams	5	40	8.0	15	0
Butler	3	3	1.0	3	0
McKenzie	1	33	33.0	33t	1
Newsome	1	26	26.0	26	0
Terrell	1	9	9.0	9	0
Prior	1	0	0.0	0	0
R. Smith	1	0	0.0	0	0
Packers	13	111	8.5	33t	1
Opponents	23	312	13.6	58t	3

PUNTING	No.	Yds.	Avg.	In 20	LG
Landeta	65	2,788	42.9	30	72
Packers	65	2,788	42.9	30	72
Opponents	90	3,920	43.6	17	62

PUNT RETURNS	No.	FC	Yds.	Avg.	LG	TD
Preston	44	17	398	9.0	71t	1
Schroeder	2	0	5	2.5	3	0
Mayes	1	0	9	9.0	9	0
Prior	1	4	0	0.0	0	0
Packers	48	21	412	8.6	71t	1
Opponents	27	14	237	8.8	95t	1

KICKOFF RETURNS	No.	Yds.	Avg.	LG	TD
Preston	57	1,497	26.3	101t	2
Bradford	2	33	16.5	24	0
McKenzie	1	17	17.0	17	0
Packers	60	1,547	25.8	101t	2
Opponents	74	1,807	24.4	101t	2

FIELD GOALS	1-19	20-29	30-39	40-49	50+
Longwell	1/1	6/6	13/15	9/10	0/1
Packers	1/1	6/6	13/15	9/10	0/1
Opponents	2/2	8/8	6/7	6/9	1/1

SACKS	No.
White	16.0
Holliday	8.0
McKenzie	8.0
Butler	4.0
Booker	3.0
S. Dotson	3.0
B. Harris	2.0
B. Williams	2.0
Koonce	1.0
Lyon	1.0
Terrell	1.0
Waddy	1.0
Packers	50.0
Opponents	39.0

1999 DRAFT CHOICES

Round	Name	Pos.	College
1	Antuan Edwards	DB	Clemson
2	Fred Vinson	DB	Vanderbilt
	Mike Wahle	T	Navy
3	Mike McKenzie	DB	Memphis
	Cletidus Hunt	DT	Kentucky State
4	Aaron Brooks	QB	Virginia
	Josh Bidwell	P	Oregon
5	DeMonn Parker	RB	Oklahoma
	Craig Heimburger	G	Missouri
6	Dee Miller	WR	Ohio State
	Scott Curry	T	Montana
7	Chris Akins	DB	Arkansas-Pine Bluff
	Donald Driver	WR	Alcorn State

GREEN BAY PACKERS

1999 VETERAN ROSTER

No.	Name	Pos.	Ht.	Wt.	Birthdate	NFL Exp.	College	Hometown	How Acq.	'98 Games/ Starts
70	Andruzzi, Joe	G	6-3	310	8/23/75	3	Southern Connecticut State	Staten Island, N.Y.	FA-'97	15/1
88	t- Arnold, Jahine	WR	6-0	180	6/19/73	4	Fresno State	Cupertino, Calif.	T(Pitt)-'99	3/0*
96	Booker, Vaughn	DE	6-5	300	2/24/68	6	Cincinnati	Cincinnati, Ohio	T(KC)-'98	16/4
85	Bradford, Corey	WR	6-1	197	12/8/75	2	Jackson State	Clinton, La.	D5-'98	8/0
18	Brice, Will	P	6-4	225	10/24/74	2	Virginia	Lancaster, S.C.	FA-'99	0*
87	Brooks, Robert	WR	6-0	180	6/23/70	8	South Carolina	Greenwood, S.C.	D3-'92	12/12
93	Brown, Gilbert	DT	6-2	350	2/22/71	7	Kansas	Detroit, Mich.	W(Minn)-'93	16/16
91	Brown, Jonathan	DE	6-4	265	11/28/75	2	Tennessee	Tulsa, Okla.	D3-'98	4/0
36	Butler, LeRoy	S	6-0	198	7/19/68	10	Florida State	Jacksonville, Fla.	D2-'90	16/16
89	Chmura, Mark	TE	6-5	255	2/22/69	8	Boston College	South Deerfield, Mass.	D6-'92	15/14
45	Cooks, Kerry	S	5-11	202	3/28/74	2	Iowa	Irving, Tex.	W(Minn)-'98	9/0
73	Davis, Antone	T	6-5	320	2/28/67	8	Tennessee	Ft. Valley, Ga.	FA-'99	0*
60	Davis, Rob	C-G	6-3	290	12/10/68	4	Shippensburg	Greenbelt, Md.	FA-'97	16/0
81	Davis, Tyrone	TE	6-4	252	6/30/72	4	Virginia	Halifax, Va.	FA-'97	13/1
72	Dotson, Earl	T	6-4	315	12/17/70	7	Texas A&I	Beaumont, Tex.	D3-'93	16/16
71	Dotson, Santana	DT	6-5	286	12/19/69	8	Baylor	Houston, Tex.	UFA(TB)-'96	16/16
4	Favre, Brett	QB	6-2	230	10/10/69	9	Southern Mississippi	Kiln, Miss.	T(Atl)-'92	16/16
58	Flanagan, Mike	C	6-5	290	11/10/73	4	UCLA	Sacramento, Calif.	D3a-'96	2/0
86	Freeman, Antonio	WR	6-1	198	5/27/72	5	Virginia Tech	Baltimore, Md.	D3d-'95	15/15
55	Harris, Bernardo	LB	6-2	248	10/15/71	5	North Carolina	Chapel Hill, N.C.	FA-'95	16/16
33	Henderson, William	RB	6-1	245	2/19/71	5	North Carolina	Chester, Va.	D3b-'95	16/10
90	Holliday, Vonnie	DE	6-5	296	12/11/75	2	North Carolina	Camden, S.C.	D1-'98	12/12
48	Kitts, Jim	RB	6-1	245	12/28/72	3	Ferrum	Chesapeake, Va.	FA-'98	2/0
53	Koonce, George	LB	6-1	245	10/15/68	8	East Carolina	Vanceboro, N.C.	FA-'92	14/14
25	Levens, Dorsey	RB	6-1	228	5/21/70	6	Georgia Tech	Syracuse, N.Y.	D5b-'94	7/4
49	Lewis, Rod	TE	6-5	260	6/9/71	5	Arizona	Dallas, Tex.	FA-'99	0*
57	London, Antonio	LB	6-2	238	4/14/71	7	Alabama	Tullahoma, Tenn.	FA-'98	1/0
8	Longwell, Ryan	K	6-0	192	8/16/74	3	California	Bend, Ore.	W(SF)-'97	16/0
98	Lyon, Billy	DT	6-5	295	12/10/73	2	Marshall	Erlanger, Ky.	FA-'98	4/0
29	Manning, Brian	WR	5-11	186	4/22/75	2	Stanford	Kansas City, Mo.	FA-'98	3/0
80	† Mayes, Derrick	WR	6-0	205	1/28/74	4	Notre Dame	Indianapolis, Ind.	D2-'96	10/6
43	McGarrahan, Scott	S	6-1	197	2/12/74	2	New Mexico	Arlington, Tex.	D6a-'98	15/0
95	† McKenzie, Keith	DE	6-3	264	10/17/73	4	Ball State	Highland Park, Mich.	D7b-'96	16/0
63	McKenzie, Raleigh	G-C	6-2	285	2/8/63	15	Tennessee	Knoxville, Tenn.	UFA(SD)-'99	0*
77	Michels, John	T	6-7	300	3/19/73	4	Southern California	La Jolla, Calif.	D1-'96	0*
12	Mirer, Rick	QB	6-3	212	3/19/70	7	Notre Dame	Goshen, Ind.	FA-'98	0*
50	Morton, Mike	LB	6-4	235	3/28/75	5	North Carolina	Kannapolis, N.C.	UFA(Oak)-'99	16/0*
31	Moss, Brent	RB	5-8	225	1/30/72	2	Wisconsin	Racine, Wis.	FA-'99	0*
21	Newsome, Craig	CB	6-0	190	8/10/71	5	Arizona State	Rialto, Calif.	D1-'95	13/13
62	Rivera, Marco	G	6-4	305	4/26/72	4	Penn State	Elmont, N.Y.	D6-'96	15/15
84	Schroeder, Bill	WR	6-3	200	1/9/71	4	Wisconsin-La Crosse	Sheboygan, Wis.	FA-'97	13/3
42	Sharper, Darren	S	6-2	210	11/3/75	3	William & Mary	Richmond, Va.	D2-'97	16/16
99	Smith, Jermaine	DT	6-3	298	2/3/72	2	Georgia	Augusta, Ga.	D4-'97	0*
83	Thomason, Jeff	TE	6-5	255	12/30/69	7	Oregon	Newport Beach, Calif.	FA-'95	16/2
78	Verba, Ross	T	6-4	302	10/31/73	3	Iowa	West Des Moines, Iowa	D1-'97	16/16
54	Waddy, Jude	LB	6-2	220	9/12/75	2	William & Mary	Suitland, Md.	FA-'98	13/0
68	Wahle, Mike	T	6-6	306	3/29/77	2	Navy	Lake Arrowhead, Calif.	SD2-'98	1/0
35	Watson, Edwin	RB	6-0	225	9/29/76	2	Purdue	Pontiac, Mich.	D7-'98	0*
51	Williams, Brian	LB	6-1	245	12/17/72	5	Southern California	Dallas, Tex.	D3c-'95	16/15
37	Williams, Tyrone	CB	5-11	192	5/31/73	4	Nebraska	Bradenton, Fla.	D3b-'96	16/16
52	Winters, Frank	C	6-3	300	1/23/64	13	Western Illinois	Union City, N.J.	PB(KC)-'92	13/13

Arnold played in 3 games for Pittsburgh in '98; Brice last active with St. Louis in '97; A. Davis last active with Atlanta in '97; James played 1 game for Seattle; Lewis last active with Tennessee in '97; R. McKenzie played 16 games for San Diego; Michels, Smith, and Watson missed the '98 season because of injury; Mirer inactive for 16 games; Morton played 16 games for Oakland; Moss last active with St. Louis in '95.

Unrestricted free agent; subject to developments.

† Restricted free agent; subject to developments.

t- Packers traded for Arnold (Pittsburgh).

Retired—Reggie White, 14-year defensive end, 16 games in '98.

Players lost through free agency (8): LB Lamont Hollinquest (KC; 14 games in '98), RB Darick Holmes (Ind; 11), RB Travis Jervey (SF; 8), DT Bob Kuberski (Atl; 16), P Sean Landeta (Phil; 16), CB-S Roderick Mullen (Car; 0), QB Doug Pederson (Phil; 12), G Adam Timmerman (StL; 16).

Also played with Packers in '98—CB Roosevelt Blackmon (3 games), RB Michael Blair (11), CB Juran Bolden (3), WR Russell Copeland (3), C Jeff Dellenbach (16), TE Scott Galbraith (1), RB Raymont Harris (8), WR-KR Roell Preston (16), S Mike Prior (16), CB Rod Smith (8), S Pat Terrell (16), T Matt Willig (16).

COACHING STAFF

Head Coach,
Ray Rhodes

Pro Career: Named the twelfth head coach in Packers history January 11, 1999. Spent the previous four seasons (1995-98) as head coach of the Philadelphia Eagles. Is the only head coach in Eagles history to lead the team to the playoffs in each of his first two seasons. Overcame a 1-3 start his initial year to post a 10-6 regular-season record, register a wild-card playoff victory, and earn consensus recognition as NFL coach of the year. Also finished 10-6 during his second season in Philadelphia. His teams have participated in the playoffs in all but five seasons of an 18-year pro coaching career. Was an assistant coach on all five championship teams of the San Francisco 49ers (1981, 1984, 1988-89, 1994). Reshaped 49ers' defense in lone season as San Francisco defensive coordinator (1994). Had spent the two previous years (1992-93) as Green Bay's defensive coordinator. Took the Packers to a second-place defensive ranking in 1993 as the team made its first postseason appearance in more than a decade, and sent a pair of defenders to the Pro Bowl for the first time in 15 years. Joined Bill Walsh's San Francisco staff as assistant defensive backs coach in 1981 immediately upon his retirement as a player. Was promoted to defensive backs coach the following year, serving in that role for the 49ers for the next 10 seasons (1982-1991). Career record: 30-36-1.

Background: Running back at Texas Christian (1969-1970), then transferred to Tulsa (1972-73), where he was converted to wide receiver and defensive back. Drafted in 1974 by the New York Giants in the tenth round. Played wide receiver for the Giants during his first three NFL seasons, leading all NFC receivers in yards per catch (20.7) in 1975. Moved to defense by the Giants in 1977, he won a starting cornerback job. In 1980, he was traded to the San Francisco 49ers in a two-for-two player exchange that also included current Tampa Bay Buccaneers head coach Tony Dungy. Made 51 receptions for 980 yards and 7 touchdowns during a seven-year NFL career (1974-1980). He also intercepted 8 passes.

Personal: Born October 20, 1950, in Mexia, Texas. He and his wife, Carmen, live in Green Bay and have four daughters—Detra, Candra, Tynesha, and Raven.

ASSISTANT COACHES

Charlie Baggett, wide receivers; born January 21, 1953, Fayetteville, N.C., lives in Green Bay. Quarterback Michigan State 1973-75. No pro playing experience. College coach: Bowling Green 1977-1980, Minnesota 1981-82, Michigan State 1983-1992, 1995-98. Pro coach: Houston Oilers 1993-94, joined Packers in 1999.

Larry Beightol, offensive line; born November 21, 1942, Pittsburgh, lives in Green Bay. Guard-linebacker Catawba College 1960-63. No pro playing experience. College coach: William & Mary 1968-1971, North Carolina State 1972-75, Auburn 1976, Arkansas 1977-78, 1980-82, Louisiana Tech 1979 (head coach), Missouri 1983-84. Pro coach: Atlanta Falcons 1985-86, Tampa Bay Buccaneers 1987-88, San Diego Chargers 1989, New York Jets 1990-94, Houston Oilers 1995, Miami Dolphins 1996-98, joined Packers in 1999.

Johnny Holland, linebackers; born March 11, 1965, Belleville, Texas, lives in Green Bay. Linebacker Texas A&M 1983-86. Pro linebacker Green Bay Packers 1987-1993. Pro coach: Joined Packers in 1995.

Jeff Jagodzinski, tight ends; born October 12, 1963, Milwaukee, Wis., lives in Green Bay. Running back Wisconsin-Whitewater 1981-84. No pro playing experience. College coach: Wisconsin-Whitewater 1985, Northern Illinois 1986, Louisiana State 1987-88, East Carolina 1989-1996, Boston College 1997-98. Pro coach: Joined Packers in 1999.

Chuck Knox, Jr., defensive assistant-quality control; born February 19, 1965, Englewood, N.J., lives in Green Bay. Running back Arizona 1984-88. No pro playing experience. Pro coach: Los Angeles Rams 1993-94, Philadelphia Eagles 1995-98, joined Packers in 1999.

Sherman Lewis, offensive coordinator; born June 29, 1942, Louisville, Ky., lives in Green Bay. Running back Michigan State 1960-63. Pro running back Toronto Argonauts (CFL) 1964-65, New York Jets 1966. College coach: Michigan State 1969-1982. Pro coach: San Francisco 49ers 1983-1991, joined Packers in 1992.

Mike McCarthy, quarterbacks; born November 10, 1963, Pittsburgh, lives in Green Bay. Tight end Salem (W. Va.) College 1982, Scottsdale (Ariz.) C.C. 1984, Baker 1985-86. No pro playing experience. College coach: Fort Hays State 1987-88, Pittsburgh 1989-1992. Pro coach: Kansas City Chiefs 1993-98, joined Packers in 1999.

Steve Ortmayer, special teams; born February 13, 1944, Painesville, Ohio, lives in Green Bay. Center Vanderbilt 1962, La Verne College 1963, 1965-66. No pro playing experience. College coach: Colorado 1967-1973, Georgia Tech 1974. Pro coach: Kansas City Chiefs 1975-77, Oakland/Los Angeles Raiders 1978-1986, 1990-94, San Diego Chargers 1987-89 (director of football operations), St. Louis Rams 1995-96 (vice president-football operations), joined Packers in 1999.

Barry Rubin, strength and conditioning; born June 25, 1957, Monroe, La., lives in Green Bay. Running back-punter Louisiana State 1976-77, tight end-punter Northwestern (La.) State 1978-1980. No pro playing experience. College coach: Northeast Louisiana 1981-83, 1987-1990, 1994, Louisiana State 1984-85. Pro coach: Joined Packers in 1995.

Harry Sydney, running backs; born June 26, 1959, Petersburg, Va., lives in Green Bay. Quarterback-running back Kansas 1978-1981. Pro running back Denver Gold (USFL) 1983-84, Memphis Showboats (USFL) 1985, Montreal Alouettes (CFL) 1986, San Francisco 49ers 1987-1991, Green Bay Packers 1992. Pro coach: Joined Packers in 1994.

Emmitt Thomas, defensive coordinator; born June 3, 1943, Angleton, Texas, lives in Green Bay. Quarterback-wide receiver Bishop (Texas) College 1963-65. Pro defensive back Kansas City Chiefs 1966-1978. College coach: Central Missouri State 1979-1980. Pro coach: St. Louis Cardinals 1981-85, Washington Redskins 1986-1994, Philadelphia Eagles 1995-98, joined Packers in 1999.

Mike Trgovac, defensive line; born February 27, 1959, Youngstown, Ohio, lives in De Pere, Wis. Defensive lineman Michigan 1977-1980. No pro playing experience. College coach: Michigan 1984-85, Ball State 1986-88, Navy 1989, Colorado State 1990-91, Notre Dame 1992-94. Pro coach: Philadelphia Eagles 1995-98, joined Packers in 1999.

Joe Vitt, defensive backs; born August 23, 1954, Syracuse, N.Y., lives in Green Bay. Linebacker Towson State 1973-75. No pro playing experience. Pro coach: Baltimore Colts 1979-1981, Seattle Seahawks 1982-1991, Los Angeles Rams 1992-94, Philadelphia Eagles 1995-98, joined Packers in 1999.

Lionel Washington, asst. defensive backs; born October 21, 1960, New Orleans, lives in Green Bay. Defensive back Tulane 1979-1982. Pro defensive back St. Louis Cardinals 1983-86, Los Angeles/Oakland Raiders 1987-1994, 1997, Denver Broncos 1995-96. Pro coach: Joined Packers in 1999.

Ken Zampese, offensive assistant-quality control; born July 19, 1967, Santa Maria, Calif., lives in De Pere, Wis. Wide receiver San Diego 1985-88. No pro playing experience. College coach: San Diego 1989, Southern California 1990-91, Northern Arizona 1992-95, Miami (Ohio) 1996-97. Pro coach: Philadelphia Eagles 1998, joined Packers in 1999.

1999 FIRST-YEAR ROSTER

Name	Pos.	Ht.	Wt.	Birthdate	College	Hometown	How Acq.
Akins, Chris	S	5-11	194	11/29/76	Arkansas-Pine Bluff	Little Rock, Ark.	D7a
Artmore, Rodney (1)	S	6-0	208	6/14/74	Baylor	Galveston, Tex.	FA
Bidwell, Josh	P	6-3	229	3/13/76	Oregon	Winston, Ore.	D4b
Brooks, Aaron	QB	6-4	203	3/24/76	Virginia	Newport News, Va.	D4a
Burns, Howard	DT	6-3	290	9/25/75	Lane College	Franklin, Tenn.	FA
Carter, Daryl (1)	LB	6-2	240	2/24/75	Wisconsin	Milwaukee, Wis.	FA
Collins, Alphonso	TE	6-2	274	8/14/74	East Carolina	Thomson, Ga.	FA
Curry, Scott	T	6-5	294	12/25/75	Montana	Valier, Mont.	D6b
Davis, Zola	WR	6-0	183	1/16/75	South Carolina	Charleston, S.C.	FA
Dixon, Andre	CB	6-1	205	12/4/75	Northeastern	Philadelphia, Pa.	FA
Driver, Donald	WR	6-0	174	2/2/75	Alcorn State	Houston, Tex.	D7b
Edwards, Antuan	CB	6-1	208	5/26/77	Clemson	Starkville, Miss.	D1
Garrett, Grant	C	6-3	301	8/11/76	Arkansas	Pearcy, Ark.	FA
Goodson, Tyrone (1)	WR	6-2	190	2/24/74	Auburn	Brooksville, Fla.	FA
Hasselbeck, Matt (1)	QB	6-4	217	9/25/75	Boston College	Norfolk, Mass.	FA
Heimburger, Craig	G	6-2	314	2/3/77	Missouri	Belleville, Ill.	D5b
Humphrey, Deon	LB	6-3	233	5/7/76	Florida State	Lake Worth, Fla.	FA
Hunt, Cletidus	DT	6-4	300	1/2/76	Kentucky State	Memphis, Tenn.	D3b
Ivey, Pat (1)	DE	6-4	275	12/27/72	Missouri	Detroit, Mich.	FA
McAda, Ronnie (1)	QB	6-3	205	12/6/73	Army	Mesquite, Tex.	D7c-'97
McCullar, Kevin	LB	6-3	241	9/25/76	Texas Tech	Irving, Tex.	FA
McKenzie, Mike	CB	6-0	193	4/26/76	Memphis	Miami, Fla.	D3a
Miller, Dee	WR	6-0	194	12/4/75	Ohio State	Springfield, Ohio	D6a
Mitchell, Basil	RB	5-10	199	9/7/75	Texas Christian	Mt. Pleasant, Tex.	FA
Mosley, Denorse (1)	CB	6-0	195	2/15/75	Edinboro	Pahokee, Fla.	FA
Nelson, Jim (1)	RB	6-1	235	4/16/75	Penn State	Pomfret, Md.	FA-'98
Newell, Mike	C	6-4	296	7/22/76	Colorado State	Littleton, Colo.	FA
Palmer, Pat (1)	WR	6-2	181	7/13/75	Northwestern State, La.	Port Arthur, Tex.	FA
Parker, DeMonn	RB	5-10	190	12/24/76	Oklahoma	Tulsa, Okla.	D5a
Reed, Chris (1)	DE	6-4	279	5/8/76	Abilene Christian	Port Arthur, Tex.	FA
Vaughn, Michael	WR	6-0	190	1/27/77	Alabama	Clarksdale, Miss.	FA
Vinson, Fred	CB	5-11	177	4/2/77	Vanderbilt	North Augusta, S.C.	D2
Williams, Keith	CB	5-11	202	5/16/73	St. Cloud State	Escondido, Calif.	FA

The term NFL Rookie is defined as a player who is in his first season of professional football and has not been on the roster of another professional football team for any regular-season or postseason games. A Rookie is designated by an "R" on NFL rosters. Players who have been active in another professional football league or players who have NFL experience, including either preseason training camp or being on an Active List or Inactive List, or on Reserve/Injured or Reserve/Physically Unable to Perform for fewer than six regular-season games, are termed NFL First-Year Players. An NFL First-Year Player is designated by a "1" on NFL rosters. Thereafter, a player is credited with an additional year of experience for each season in which he accumulates six games on the Active List or Inactive List, or on Reserve/Injured or Reserve/Physically Unable to Perform.

MINNESOTA VIKINGS

National Football Conference
Central Division
Team Colors: Purple, Gold, and White
9520 Viking Drive
Eden Prairie, Minnesota 55344
Telephone: (612) 828-6500

CLUB OFFICIALS

Owner: Red McCombs
President: Gary Woods
Head Coach/Vice President of Football Operations: Dennis Green
Executive V.P. & General Manager: Tim Connolly
Vice President/Player Personnel: Frank Gilliam
Assistant General Manager/National Scouting: Jerry Reichow
Assistant General Manager/Pro Personnel: Paul Wiggin
Senior Football Administrator: Russ Ball
Director of Football Administration: Rob Brzezinski
Director of Research and Development: Mike Eayrs
Director of Public Relations: Bob Hagan
Director of Marketing and Sales: Terri Huml
Director of Corporate Sales: Kernal Buhler
Director of Finance: Nick Valentine
Director of Operations: Breck Spinner
Director of Ticket Sales: Phil Huebner
Equipment Manager: Dennis Ryan
Trainer: Fred Zamberletti
Video Director: Larry Kohout
Stadium: Hubert H. Humphrey Metrodome
•**Capacity:** 64,121
500 11th Avenue South
Minneapolis, Minnesota 55415
Playing Surface: AstroTurf
Training Camp: Minnesota State-Mankato
Mankato, Minnesota 56001

1999 SCHEDULE

PRESEASON

Aug. 13	**New York Giants**	7:00
Aug. 21	at Cleveland	7:00
Aug. 26	**Philadelphia**	7:00
Sept. 3	at New York Jets	7:30

REGULAR SEASON

Sept. 12	at Atlanta	4:15
Sept. 19	**Oakland**	12:00
Sept. 26	at Green Bay	3:15
Oct. 3	**Tampa Bay**	12:00
Oct. 10	**Chicago**	12:00
Oct. 17	at Detroit	1:00
Oct. 24	**San Francisco**	12:00
Oct. 31	at Denver	2:15
Nov. 8	**Dallas** (Mon.)	8:00
Nov. 14	at Chicago	12:00
Nov. 21	Open Date	
Nov. 28	**San Diego**	12:00
Dec. 6	at Tampa Bay (Mon.)	9:00
Dec. 12	at Kansas City	7:20
Dec. 20	**Green Bay** (Mon.)	8:00
Dec. 26	at New York Giants	1:00
Jan. 2	**Detroit**	12:00

RECORD HOLDERS

INDIVIDUAL RECORDS—CAREER

Category	Name	Performance
Rushing (Yds.)	Chuck Foreman, 1973-79	5,879
Passing (Yds.)	Fran Tarkenton, 1961-66, 1972-78	33,098
Passing (TDs)	Fran Tarkenton, 1961-66, 1972-78	239
Receiving (No.)	Cris Carter, 1990-98	745
Receiving (Yds.)	Cris Carter, 1990-98	8,997
Interceptions	Paul Krause, 1968-79	53
Punting (Avg.)	Harry Newsome, 1990-93	43.8
Punt Return (Avg.)	David Palmer, 1994-98	10.6
Kickoff Return (Avg.)	Charlie West, 1968-73	25.5
Field Goals	Fred Cox, 1963-77	282
Touchdowns (Tot.)	Cris Carter, 1990-98	82
Points	Fred Cox, 1963-77	1,365

INDIVIDUAL RECORDS—SINGLE SEASON

Category	Name	Performance
Rushing (Yds.)	Robert Smith, 1997	1,266
Passing (Yds.)	Warren Moon, 1994	4,264
Passing (TDs)	Randall Cunningham, 1998	34
Receiving (No.)	Cris Carter, 1994, 1995	122
Receiving (Yds.)	Cris Carter, 1995	1,371
Interceptions	Paul Krause, 1975	10
Punting (Avg.)	Bobby Walden, 1964	46.4
Punt Return (Avg.)	David Palmer, 1995	13.2
Kickoff Return (Avg.)	John Gilliam, 1972	26.3
Field Goals	Gary Anderson, 1998	35
Touchdowns (Tot.)	Chuck Foreman, 1975	22
Points	Gary Anderson, 1998	164

INDIVIDUAL RECORDS—SINGLE GAME

Category	Name	Performance
Rushing (Yds.)	Chuck Foreman, 10-24-76	200
Passing (Yds.)	Tommy Kramer, 11-2-86	490
Passing (TDs)	Joe Kapp, 9-28-69	*7
Receiving (No.)	Rickey Young, 12-16-79	15
Receiving (Yds.)	Sammy White, 11-7-76	210
Interceptions	Many Times	3
	Last time by Jack Del Rio, 12-5-93	
Field Goals	Rich Karlis, 11-5-89	*7
Touchdowns (Tot.)	Chuck Foreman, 12-20-75	4
	Ahmad Rashad, 9-2-79	4
Points	Chuck Foreman, 12-20-75	24
	Ahmad Rashad, 9-2-79	24

*NFL Record

VIKINGS COACHING HISTORY

(328-265-9)

1961-66	Norm Van Brocklin	29-51-4
1967-83	Bud Grant	161-99-5
1984	Les Steckel	3-13-0
1985	Bud Grant	7-9-0
1986-91	Jerry Burns	55-46-0
1992-98	Dennis Green	73-47-0

METRODOME

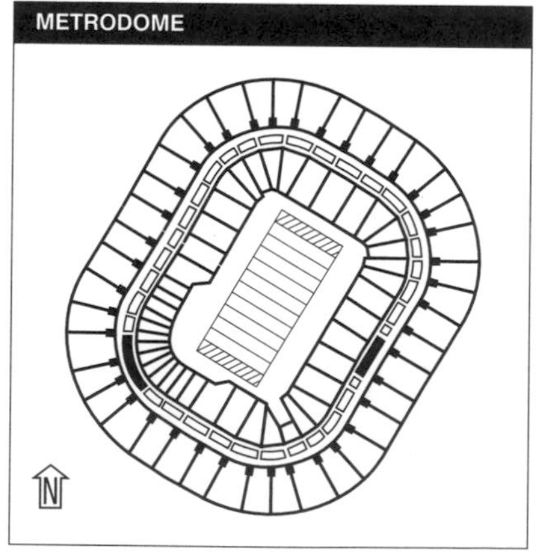

1998 TEAM RECORD

PRESEASON (4-0)

Date	Result		Opponent
8/9	W	28-0	at New England
8/15	W	34-0	Kansas City
8/22	W	25-22	at Carolina (OT)
8/28	W	42-28	San Diego

REGULAR SEASON (15-1)

Date	Result		Opponent	Att.
9/6	W	31-7	Tampa Bay	62,538
9/13	W	38-31	at St. Louis	56,234
9/20	W	29-6	Detroit	63,107
9/27	W	31-28	at Chicago	57,783
10/5	W	37-24	at Green Bay	59,849
10/18	W	41-7	Washington	64,004
10/25	W	34-13	at Detroit	77,885
11/1	L	24-27	at Tampa Bay	64,979
11/8	W	31-24	New Orleans	63,779
11/15	W	24-3	Cincinnati	64,232
11/22	W	28-14	Green Bay	64,471
11/26	W	46-36	at Dallas	64,366
12/6	W	48-22	Chicago	64,247
12/13	W	38-28	at Baltimore	69,074
12/20	W	50-10	Jacksonville	64,363
12/26	W	26-16	at Tennessee	41,121

POSTSEASON (1-1)

Date	Result		Opponent	Att.
1/10	W	41-21	Arizona	63,760
1/17	L	27-30	Atlanta (OT)	64,060

(OT) Overtime

SCORE BY PERIODS

Vikings	135	138	139	144	0	—	556
Opponents	50	93	58	95	0	—	296

ATTENDANCE

Home 510,741 Away 491,291 Total 1,002,032
Single-game home record, 64,471 (11/22/98)
Single-season home record, 510,741 (1998)

1998 TEAM STATISTICS

	Vikings	Opp.
Total First Downs	335	300
Rushing	98	102
Passing	210	171
Penalty	27	27
Third Down: Made/Att	107/208	69/203
Third Down Pct.	51.4	34.0
Fourth Down: Made/Att	3/3	17/32
Fourth Down Pct.	100.0	53.1
Total Net Yards	6,264	5,066
Avg. Per Game	391.5	316.6
Total Plays	1,008	997
Avg. Per Play	6.2	5.1
Net Yards Rushing	1,936	1,614
Avg. Per Game	121.0	100.9
Total Rushes	450	404
Net Yards Passing	4,328	3,452
Avg. Per Game	270.5	215.8
Sacked/Yards Lost	25/164	38/247
Gross Yards	4,492	3,699
Att./Completions	533/327	555/320
Completion Pct.	61.4	57.7
Had Intercepted	16	19
Punts/Avg.	55/44.7	74/42.6
Net Punting Avg.	55/37.0	74/36.6
Penalties/Yards Lost	116/1,045	132/1,167
Fumbles/Ball Lost	10/4	21/15
Touchdowns	64	35
Rushing	17	12
Passing	41	17
Returns	6	6
Avg. Time of Possession	29:58	30:02

1998 INDIVIDUAL STATISTICS

Passing	Att.	Comp.	Yds.	Pct.	TD	Int.	Tkld.	Rate
Cunningham	425	259	3,704	60.9	34	10	20/132	106.0
Johnson	101	65	747	64.4	7	5	4/30	89.0
Fiedler	7	3	41	42.9	0	1	0/0	22.6
Palmer	0	0	0	—	0	0	1/2	—
Vikings	533	327	4,492	61.4	41	16	25/164	101.5
Opponents	555	320	3,699	57.7	17	19	38/247	73.8

SCORING	TD R	TD P	TD Rt	PAT	FG	Saf	PTS
Anderson	0	0	0	59/59	35/35	0	164
R. Moss	0	17	0	0/0	0/0	0	106
Carter	0	12	0	0/0	0/0	0	72
Hoard	9	1	0	0/0	0/0	0	60
R. Smith	6	2	0	0/0	0/0	0	48
Glover	0	5	0	0/0	0/0	0	30
J. Reed	0	4	0	0/0	0/0	0	24
Hitchcock	0	0	3	0/0	0/0	0	18
Rudd	0	0	2	0/0	0/0	0	12
Cunningham	1	0	0	0/0	0/0	0	8
Evans	1	0	0	0/0	0/0	0	6
Palmer	0	0	1	0/0	0/0	0	6
Vikings	17	41	6	59/59	35/35	1	556
Opponents	12	17	6	31/31	17/19	0	296

2-Point conversions: R. Moss 2, Cunningham. Team 3-5, Opponents 2-4.

RUSHING	Att.	Yds.	Avg.	LG	TD
R. Smith	249	1,187	4.8	74t	6
Hoard	115	479	4.2	50t	9
Cunningham	32	132	4.1	22	1
Evans	23	67	2.9	12	1
Palmer	10	52	5.2	15	0
Johnson	12	15	1.3	6	0
Morrow	3	7	2.3	8	0
R. Moss	1	4	4.0	4	0
Carter	1	-1	-1.0	-1	0
Fiedler	4	-6	-1.5	-1	0
Vikings	450	1,936	4.3	74t	17
Opponents	404	1,614	4.0	50	12

RECEIVING	No.	Yds.	Avg.	LG	TD
Carter	78	1,011	13.0	54t	12
R. Moss	69	1,313	19.0	61t	17
Glover	35	522	14.9	36	5
J. Reed	34	474	13.9	56t	4
R. Smith	28	291	10.4	67t	2
Hoard	22	198	9.0	24t	1
Palmer	18	185	10.3	33	0
Hatchette	15	216	14.4	25	0
Evans	12	84	7.0	14	0
DeLong	8	58	7.3	17	0
Goodwin	3	16	5.3	9	0
Walsh	2	46	23.0	25	0
M. Williams	1	64	64.0	64	0
Tate	1	17	17.0	17	0
Cunningham	1	-3	-3.0	-3	0
Vikings	327	4,492	13.7	67t	41
Opponents	320	3,699	11.6	80t	17

INTERCEPTIONS	No.	Yds.	Avg.	LG	TD
Hitchcock	7	242	34.6	79t	3
Griffith	5	25	5.0	17	0
Fuller	4	36	9.0	26	0
Thomas	2	27	13.5	27	0
Gray	1	11	11.0	11	0
Vikings	19	341	17.9	79t	3
Opponents	16	221	13.8	91t	1

PUNTING	No.	Yds.	Avg.	In 20	LG
Berger	55	2,458	44.7	17	67
Vikings	55	2,458	44.7	17	67
Opponents	74	3,155	42.6	23	59

PUNT RETURNS	No.	FC	Yds.	Avg.	LG	TD
Palmer	28	18	289	10.3	53	0
R. Moss	1	2	0	0.0	0	0
Vikings	29	20	289	10.0	53	0
Opponents	27	12	325	12.0	71t	1

KICKOFF RETURNS	No.	Yds.	Avg.	LG	TD
Palmer	50	1,176	23.5	88t	1
Tate	2	43	21.5	23	0
M. Williams	2	19	9.5	12	0
Vikings	54	1,238	22.9	88t	1
Opponents	73	2,008	27.5	101t	4

FIELD GOALS	1-19	20-29	30-39	40-49	50+
Anderson	1/1	11/11	9/9	12/12	2/2
Vikings	1/1	11/11	9/9	12/12	2/2
Opponents	0/0	3/3	6/6	7/9	1/1

SACKS	No.
Randle	10.5
Alexander	7.5
E. McDaniel	7.0
Clemons	2.5
Rudd	2.0
Fisk	1.5
Wong	1.5
Colinet	1.0
Fuller	1.0
Gray	1.0
T. Williams	1.0
Thomas	0.5
Vikings	38.0
Opponents	25.0

1999 DRAFT CHOICES

Round	Name	Pos.	College
1	Daunte Culpepper	QB	Central Florida
	Dimitrius Underwood	DE	Michigan State
2	Jim Kleinsasser	TE	North Dakota
4	Kenny Wright	DB	Northwestern State, La.
	Jay Humphrey	T	Texas
5	Chris Jones	LB	Clemson
6	Talance Sawyer	DE	Nevada-Las Vegas
	Antico Dalton	LB	Hampton
7	Noel Scarlett	DT	Langston

MINNESOTA VIKINGS

1999 VETERAN ROSTER

No.	Name	Pos.	Ht.	Wt.	Birthdate	NFL Exp.	College	Hometown	How Acq.	'98 Games/ Starts
1	Anderson, Gary	K	5-11	179	7/16/59	18	Syracuse	Durban, South Africa	UFA(SF)-'98	16/0
30	Banks, Antonio	CB	5-10	195	3/12/73	2	Virginia Tech	Newport News, Va.	FA-'98	4/0
38	Bass, Anthony	CB-S	6-1	203	3/27/75	2	Bethune Cookman	St. Alban, W. Va.	FA-'98	3/0
56	Bercich, Pete	LB	6-1	239	12/23/71	5	Notre Dame	Joliet, Ill.	D7-'94	15/1
17	Berger, Mitch	P	6-2	217	6/24/72	4	Colorado	Vancouver, B.C.,Canada	FA-'96	16/0
75	Birk, Matt	T	6-4	310	7/23/76	2	Harvard	St. Paul, Minn.	D6-'98	7/0
18	Bland, Tony	WR	6-3	213	12/12/72	2	Florida A&M	St. Petersburg, Fla.	FA-'98	1/0
8	Bouman, Todd	QB	6-2	211	8/1/72	2	St. Cloud State	Ruthton, Minn.	FA-'97	0*
91	Burrough, John	DE	6-5	275	5/17/72	5	Wyoming	Pinedale, Wyo.	FA-'99	16/3*
80	Carter, Cris	WR	6-3	214	11/25/65	13	Ohio State	Middletown, Ohio	W(Phil)-'90	16/16
62	Christy, Jeff	C	6-3	285	2/3/69	7	Pittsburgh	Freeport, Pa.	FA-'93	16/16
92	Clemons, Duane	DE	6-5	272	5/23/74	4	California	Riverside, Calif.	D1-'96	16/3
99	Colinet, Stalin	DE	6-6	284	7/19/74	3	Boston College	New York, N.Y.	D3-'97	11/3
87	Crumpler, Carlester	TE	6-6	260	9/5/71	6	East Carolina	Greenville, N.C.	UFA(Sea)-'99	11/1*
7	Cunningham, Randall	QB	6-4	215	3/27/63	14	Nevada-Las Vegas	Santa Barbara, Calif.	FA-'97	15/14
25	Darden, Tony	CB	5-11	190	8/11/75	2	Texas Tech	San Antonio, Tex.	D7b-'98	0*
71	Dixon, David	G	6-5	352	1/5/69	6	Arizona State	Aukland, New Zealand	FA-'94	16/16
59	Edwards, Dixon	LB	6-1	237	3/25/68	9	Michigan State	Cincinnati, Ohio	UFA(Dall)-'96	14/15
3	George, Jeff	QB	6-4	215	12/8/67	9	Illinois	Indianapolis, Ind.	UFA(Oak)-'99	8/7*
82	Glover, Andrew	TE	6-6	252	8/12/67	9	Grambling State	Gonzales, La.	UFA(Oak)-'97	16/12
23	Gray, Torrian	S	6-0	200	3/18/74	3	Virginia Tech	Lakeland, Fla.	D2-'97	9/1
24	Griffith, Robert	S	5-11	195	11/30/70	6	San Diego State	San Diego, Calif.	FA-'94	16/16
95	Harrison, Martin	DE	6-5	285	9/20/67	8	Washington	Bellevue, Wash.	FA-'99	0*
89	Hatchette, Matthew	WR	6-2	198	5/1/74	3	Langston	Cleveland, Ohio	D7b-'97	5/0
37	Hitchcock, Jimmy	CB	5-10	187	11/9/70	5	North Carolina	Concord, N.C.	T(NE)-'98	16/16
44	Hoard, Leroy	RB	5-11	224	5/15/68	10	Michigan	New Orleans, La.	FA-'96	16/1
63	Jenkins, Trezelle	T	6-7	354	3/13/73	4	Michigan	Chicago, Ill.	FA-'99	0*
76	Liwienski, Chris	G-T	6-5	308	8/2/75	2	Indiana	Sterling Heights, Mich.	FA-'98	1/0
53	Mays, Kivuusama	LB	6-3	250	1/7/75	2	North Carolina	San Antonio, Tex.	D4-'98	16/0
58	McDaniel, Ed	LB	5-11	230	2/23/69	8	Clemson	Battesburgh, S.C.	D5-'92	16/16
64	McDaniel, Randall	G	6-3	287	12/19/64	12	Arizona State	Avondale, Ariz.	D1-'88	16/16
34	McDonald, Ramos	CB	5-11	194	4/30/76	2	New Mexico	Texarkana, Tex.	D3-'98	15/0
54	Miller, Corey	LB	6-2	252	10/25/68	9	South Carolina	Pageland, S.C.	FA-'99	0*
45	Mills, John Henry	RB	6-0	222	10/31/69	7	Wake Forest	Tallahassee, Fla.	FA-'99	5/0*
68	Morris, Mike	C	6-5	272	2/22/61	13	Northeastern Missouri State	Centerville, Iowa	FA-'91	16/0
33	Morrow, Harold	RB	5-11	217	2/24/73	4	Auburn	Maplesville, Ala.	W(Dall)-'96	11/0
84	Moss, Randy	WR	6-4	202	2/13/77	2	Marshall	Rand, W. Va.	D1-'98	16/11
22	Palmer, David	RB	5-8	173	11/19/72	6	Alabama	Birmingham, Ala.	D2a-'94	16/0
93	Randle, John	DT	6-1	283	12/12/67	10	Texas A&I	Hearne, Tex.	FA-'90	16/16
86	Reed, Jake	WR	6-3	216	9/28/67	9	Grambling State	Covington, Ga.	D3b-'91	11/11
57	Rudd, Dwayne	LB	6-2	238	2/3/76	3	Alabama	South Panola, Miss.	D1-'97	15/15
26	Smith, Robert	RB	6-2	212	3/4/72	7	Ohio State	Euclid, Ohio	D1-'93	14/14
73	Steussie, Todd	T	6-6	316	12/1/70	6	California	Canoga Park, Calif.	D1b-'94	15/15
77	Stringer, Korey	T	6-4	335	5/8/74	5	Ohio State	Warren, Ohio	D1b-'95	14/14
83	Tate, Robert	WR	5-10	186	10/19/73	3	Cincinnati	Harrisburg, Pa.	D6-'97	15/1
42	Thomas, Orlando	S	6-1	214	10/21/72	5	Southwest Louisiana	Crowley, La.	D2a-'95	16/16
81	Walsh, Chris	WR	6-1	199	12/12/68	7	Stanford	Concord, Calif.	FA-'94	15/0
21	Williams, Moe	RB	6-1	200	7/26/74	4	Kentucky	Columbus, Ga.	D3-'96	12/1
94	Williams, Tony	DT	6-1	285	7/9/75	3	Memphis	Germantown, Tenn.	D5-'97	14/9
52	Wong, Kailee	LB	6-2	257	5/23/76	2	Stanford	Eugene, Ore.	D2-'98	15/0
72	Wyman, Devin	DT	6-7	290	8/29/73	4	Kentucky State	East Palo Alto, Calif.	FA-'99	0*

* Bouman inactive for 16 games; Burrough played 16 games with Atlanta in '98; Crumpler played 12 games with Seattle; Darden inactive for 7 games; George played 7 games with Oakland; Harrison last active with Seattle in '97; Jenkins last active with Kansas City in '97; Miller and Wyman missed '98 season because of injury; Mills played 5 games with Oakland.

Traded—QB Brad Johnson (4 games in '98) to Washington; G-T Everett Lindsay (16) to Baltimore.

Players lost to free agency (8): DE Derrick Alexander (Clev; 16 games in '98), DT Jerry Ball (Clev; 16), TE Greg DeLong (Balt; 15), RB Chuck Evans (Balt; 16), QB Jay Fiedler (Jac; 5), DT Jason Fisk (Tenn; 16), CB Corey Fuller (Clev; 16), TE Hunter Goodwin (Mia; 15).

Also played with the Vikings in '98—G-T Orlando Bobo (4 games), S Greg Briggs (2), CB Duane Butler (14), LB Bobby Houston (8), CB-S Anthony Phillips (2).

COACHING STAFF

Head Coach
Dennis Green

Pro Career: Named the fifth head coach in Vikings history on January 10, 1992, Green is one of only seven people in the history of the league to lead his team to the playoffs in each of his first three seasons as an NFL head coach. He has led Vikings to playoffs six of his seven seasons at the helm, including three NFC Central titles. The 1998 Vikings posted an NFL-best 15-1 record and scored a league-record 556 points. Dennis was named Maxwell Club coach of the year and *Sports Illustrated* co-coach of the year following the 1998 season. In 1997, Green became the second winningest coach in franchise history. He also led Minnesota to its biggest come-from-behind playoff win, 23-22 over the Giants on December 27, 1997. In 1994, NFL Commissioner Paul Tagliabue appointed Green to the league's Competition Committee. In 1992, Green led the Vikings to a 11-5 record and first division title under a first-year head coach. He earned NFL coach of the year honors from the Washington Touchdown Club and NFC coach of the year honors from *United Press International* and *College & Pro Football Newsweekly*. As receivers coach at San Francisco from 1986-88, Green developed Pro Bowl players Jerry Rice and John Taylor. Green's first pro coaching opportunity came as special teams coach for the 49ers in 1979. Green briefly played defensive back with British Columbia (CFL) in 1971. Career record: 73-47.

Background: A running back at Iowa from 1968-1970, Green began his coaching career as a graduate assistant for Iowa in 1972. He coached running backs and receivers at Dayton in 1973, then running backs and receivers at Iowa from 1974-76. Green worked with running backs at Stanford in 1977-78. He returned to Stanford as offensive coordinator in 1980, then was head coach at Northwestern from 1981-85. Green was named Big Ten coach of the year in 1982. As head coach at Stanford from 1989-1991, he led the school to the 1991 Aloha Bowl, its first bowl game since 1986.

Personal: Born February 17, 1949 in Harrisburg, Pa., Green earned his degree in recreation from Iowa. He and his wife, Marie, live in Minnetonka, Minn. with their daughter Vanessa. Green also has a daughter, Patti, and a son, Jeremy.

ASSISTANT COACHES

Hubbard Alexander, wide receivers; born February 14, 1939, Winston-Salem, N.C., lives in Eden Prairie, Minn. Center Tennessee State 1958-1961. No pro playing experience. College coach: Tennessee State 1962-63, Vanderbilt 1974-78, Miami 1979-1988. Pro coach: Dallas Cowboys 1989-1997, joined Vikings in 1998.

Dave Atkins, tight ends; born May 18, 1949, Victoria, Texas, lives in Eden Prairie, Minn. Running back Texas-El Paso 1970-72. Pro running back San Francisco 49ers 1973, Honolulu Hawaiians (WFL) 1974, San Diego Chargers 1975. College coach: Texas-El Paso 1979-1980, San Diego State 1981-85. Pro coach: Philadelphia Eagles 1986-1992, New England Patriots 1993, Arizona Cardinals 1994-95, New Orleans Saints 1996, joined Vikings in 1997.

Dean Dalton, quality control; born July 27, 1963, Platteville, Wis., lives in Eden Prairie, Minn. Defensive back Air Force Academy 1981-82, Western Illinois 1983-84. College coach: Western Illinois 1984-85, Wisconsin 1986-87, Texas Southern 1988-89, Purdue 1990. Pro coach: Joined Vikings in 1999.

Foge Fazio, defensive coordinator; born February 28, 1939, Dawmont, W. Va., lives in Eden Prairie, Minn. Linebacker-center Pittsburgh 1957-1960. No pro playing experience. College coach: Boston University 1967, Harvard 1968, Pittsburgh 1969-1972, 1977-1985 (head coach 1982-85), Cincinnati 1973-76, Notre Dame 1986-87. Pro coach: Atlanta Falcons 1988-89, New York Jets 1990-94, joined Vikings in 1995.

Carl Hargrave, running backs; born November 8, 1954, Frankfurt, Germany, lives in Eden Prairie, Minn. Defensive back Upper Iowa 1972-75. No pro playing experience. College coach: Upper Iowa 1977-1980, Northwestern 1981-85, Pittsburgh 1986, Houston 1987-1991, Iowa 1992-93. Pro coach: Joined Vikings in 1994.

John Kasper, asst. strength and conditioning; born May 13, 1968, Oaklawn, Ill., lives in Lakeville, Minn. Free safety Waldorf J.C. 1987-88, Upper Iowa 1990-91. No pro playing experience. College coach: Central Missouri State 1993-95. Pro coach: Joined Vikings in 1999.

Tom Olivadotti, inside linebackers; born September 22, 1945, Long Branch, N.J., lives in Eden Prairie, Minn. Defensive back-wide receiver Upsala 1963-66. No pro playing experience. College coach: Princeton 1975-77, Boston College 1978-79, Miami 1980-83. Pro coach: Cleveland Browns 1985-86, Miami Dolphins 1987-1995, joined Vikings in 1996.

Andre Patterson, defensive line; born June 12, 1960, Richmond, Calif., lives in Eden Prairie, Minn. Offensive lineman Contra Costa J.C. 1978-1980, Montana 1981. No pro playing experience. College coach: Montana 1982, Weber State 1988, Western Washington 1989, Cornell 1990, Washington State 1992-93, Cal Poly-San Luis Obispo 1994-96 (head coach). Pro coach: New England Patriots 1997, joined Vikings in 1998.

Ray Sherman, offensive coordinator; born November 27, 1951, Berkeley, Calif., lives in Eden Prairie, Minn. Wide receiver Lancey (Calif.) J.C. 1969-1970, Fresno State 1971-72. Pro defensive back Green Bay Packers 1973. College coach: San Jose State 1974, California 1975, 1981, Michigan State 1976-77, Wake Forest 1978-1980, Purdue 1982-85, Georgia 1986-87. Pro coach: Houston Oilers 1988-89, Atlanta Falcons 1990, San Francisco 49ers 1991-93, New York Jets 1994, Minnesota Vikings 1995-97, Pittsburgh Steelers 1998, rejoined Vikings in 1999.

Richard Solomon, defensive backs; born December 8, 1949, New Orleans, lives in Eden Prairie, Minn. Running back-defensive back Iowa 1970-73. No pro playing experience. College coach: Dubuque 1973-75, Southern Illinois 1976, Iowa 1977-78, Syracuse 1979, Illinois 1980-86. Pro coach: New York Giants 1987-1991 (scout), joined Vikings in 1992.

Mike Tice, offensive line; born February 2, 1959, Bayshore, N.Y., lives in Eden Prairie, Minn. Quarterback Maryland 1977-1980. Pro tight end Seattle Seahawks 1981-88, 1990-91, Washington Redskins 1989, Minnesota Vikings 1992-93, 1995. Pro coach: Joined Vikings in 1996.

Trent Walters, outside linebackers; born November 20, 1943, Knoxville, Tenn., lives in Eden Prairie, Minn. Defensive back Indiana 1963-65. Pro defensive back Edmonton Eskimos (CFL) 1966-67. College coach: Indiana 1968-1971, Louisville 1972, 1986-1990, Indiana 1973-1980, Washington 1981-83, Pittsburgh 1985, Texas A&M 1991-93. Pro coach: Cincinnati Bengals 1984, joined Vikings in 1994.

Steve Wetzel, strength and conditioning; born May 11, 1963, Washington, D.C., lives in Eden Prairie, Minn. Attended Slippery Rock. No college or pro playing experience. College coach: Maryland 1985-89, George Mason 1990. Pro coach: Washington Redskins 1990-91, joined Vikings in 1992.

Alex Wood, quarterbacks; born March 14, 1955, Massillion, Ohio, lives in Eden Prarie, Minn. Running back Iowa 1974-77. No pro playing experience. College coach: Iowa 1978, Kent 1979-1980, Southern Illinois 1981, Southern 1982-84, Wyoming 1985-86, Washington State 1987-88, Miami 1989-1992, Wake Forest 1993-94, James Madison (head coach) 1995-98. Pro coach: Joined Vikings in 1999.

Gary Zauner, special teams; born November 2, 1950, Milwaukee, Wis., lives in Eden Prairie, Minn. Kicker Wisconsin-LaCrosse 1968-1972. No pro playing experience. College coach: Brigham Young 1979-1980, San Diego State 1981-86, New Mexico 1987-88, Long Beach State 1990-91. Pro coach: Joined Vikings in 1994.

1999 FIRST-YEAR ROSTER

Name	Pos.	Ht.	Wt.	Birthdate	College	Hometown	How Acq.
Abernathy, Chad	T	6-5	302	7/2/76	Arkansas	Mountain View, Ark.	FA
Cercone, Matt	TE	6-5	255	11/30/75	Arizona State	Bakersfield, Calif.	FA
Cooper, Kevin	WR	6-3	195	2/20/76	Mississippi State	Batesville, Miss.	FA
Culpepper, Daunte	QB	6-4	255	1/28/77	Central Florida	Ocala, Fla.	D1a
Dalton, Antico	LB	6-1	242	12/31/75	Hampton	Eden, N.C.	D6b
Davis, Robert (1)	CB	5-9	198	8/6/72	Vanderbilt	Nashville, Tenn.	FA-'98
Hardin, Travis	T	6-8	309	4/12/75	Kentucky State	Coldwater, Miss.	FA
Hinsley, Ken	P-K	6-3	214	6/8/76	Western Carolina	Palm City, Fla.	FA
Humphrey, Jay	T	6-6	322	6/20/76	Texas	Richardson, Tex.	D4b
Johnson, MacArthur (1)	WR	6-0	191	7/16/75	Howard	Jacksonville, Fla.	FA
Jones, Chris	LB	5-10	229	9/30/76	Clemson	Monroe, Ga.	D5
Kleinsasser, Jim	TE	6-3	272	1/31/77	North Dakota	Carrington, N.D.	D2
McCullough, Carl (1)	RB	6-2	223	11/14/73	Wisconsin	St. Paul, Minn.	FA
Moore, Cory	RB	6-3	235	1/12/76	Bethune-Cookman	Richardson, Tex.	FA
Morgan, Don	S	5-11	190	9/18/75	Nevada	Stockton, Calif.	FA
Moss, Eric (1)	G-T	6-4	311	9/25/74	Ohio State	Belle, W. Va.	FA-'97
Oats, Jami	CB	5-10	171	10/17/76	South Carolina State	Gainsville, Fla.	FA
Rogers, Chris	CB	5-10	190	1/3/77	Howard	Largo, Md.	FA
Sawyer, Talance	DE	6-2	252	6/14/76	Nevada-Las Vegas	Bastrop, La.	D6a
Scarlett, Noel	NT	6-3	320	1/21/74	Langston	Ft. Lauderdale, Fla.	D7
Souder, James	S	5-11	208	1/29/77	Bethune-Cookman	Newark, N.J.	FA
Underwood, Dimitrius	DE	6-6	276	3/29/77	Michigan State	Fayetteville, N.C.	D1b
Withrow, Cory (1)	C	6-2	281	4/5/75	Washington State	Spokane, WA	FA
Wright, Kenny	CB	6-1	200	9/14/77	Northwestern State, La.	Ruston, La.	D4a

The term NFL Rookie is defined as a player who is in his first season of professional football and has not been on the roster of another professional football team for any regular-season or postseason games. A Rookie is designated by an "R" on NFL rosters. Players who have been active in another professional football league or players who have NFL experience, including either preseason training camp or being on an Active List or Inactive List, or on Reserve/Injured or Reserve/Physically Unable to Perform for fewer than six regular-season games, are termed NFL First-Year Players. An NFL First-Year Player is designated by a "1" on NFL rosters. Thereafter, a player is credited with an additional year of experience for each season in which he accumulates six games on the Active List or Inactive List, or on Reserve/Injured or Reserve/Physically Unable to Perform.

NOTES

NEW ORLEANS SAINTS

National Football Conference
Western Division
Team Colors: Old Gold, Black, and White
5800 Airline Drive
Metairie, Louisiana 70003
Telephone: (504) 733-0255

CLUB OFFICIALS

Owner: Tom Benson
President, General Manager, & Chief Operating Officer: Bill Kuharich
Assistant General Manager and Vice President of Football Operations: Charles Bailey
Senior Vice President of Marketing & Administration: Greg Suit
Director of College Scouting: Bruce Lemmerman
Treasurers: Bruce Broussard, Dennis Lauscha
Comptroller: Charleen Sharpe
Director of Corporate Sales: Greg Seeling
Director of Media and Public Relations: Greg Bensel
Assistant Director of Media and Public Relations: Robert Gunn
Director of Player Programs: Maurice Hurst
Data Processing Manager: Jay Romig
Director of Travel/Entertainment/Special Projects: Barra Birrcher
Club Level Manager/Marketing Assistant: Scott Sidwell
Salary Cap Consultant: Terry O'Neil
Player Personnel Scouts: Matt Boockmeier, Hokie Gajan, Cornell Gowdy, Tim Heffelfinger, Tom Mariono, Grant Neill
Director of Ticket Sales: Jasen Feyerherm
Head Athletic Trainer: Dean Kleinschmidt
Equipment Manager: Dan Simmons
Video Director: Joe Malota
Facilities Manager: Terry Ashburn
Stadium: Louisiana Superdome
•**Capacity:** 70,200
1500 Poydras Street
New Orleans, Louisiana 70112
Playing Surface: AstroTurf
Training Camp: University of Wisconsin-La Crosse
La Crosse, Wisconsin 54601

1999 SCHEDULE

PRESEASON

Aug. 13	at Miami	7:30
Aug. 21	**Indianapolis**	7:00
Aug. 28	**Green Bay**	7:00
Sept. 2	at Tennessee	7:00

REGULAR SEASON

Sept. 12	**Carolina**	12:00
Sept. 19	at San Francisco	1:05
Sept. 26	Open Date	
Oct. 3	at Chicago	12:00
Oct. 10	**Atlanta**	12:00
Oct. 17	**Tennessee**	12:00
Oct. 24	at New York Giants	1:00
Oct. 31	**Cleveland**	12:00
Nov. 7	**Tampa Bay**	3:05
Nov. 14	**San Francisco**	12:00
Nov. 21	at Jacksonville	8:20
Nov. 28	at St. Louis	12:00
Dec. 5	at Atlanta	1:00
Dec. 12	**St. Louis**	12:00
Dec. 19	at Baltimore	1:00
Dec. 24	**Dallas** (Fri.)	2:05
Jan. 2	at Carolina	1:00

RECORD HOLDERS

INDIVIDUAL RECORDS—CAREER

Category	Name	Performance
Rushing (Yds.)	George Rogers, 1981-84	4,267
Passing (Yds.)	Archie Manning, 1971-1982	21,734
Passing (TDs)	Archie Manning, 1971-1982	115
Receiving (No.)	Eric Martin, 1985-1993	532
Receiving (Yds.)	Eric Martin, 1985-1993	7,854
Interceptions	Dave Waymer, 1980-89	37
Punting (Avg.)	Mark Royals, 1997	45.9
Punt Return (Avg.)	Mel Gray, 1986-88	13.4
Kickoff Return (Avg.)	Walter Roberts, 1967	26.3
Field Goals	Morten Andersen, 1982-1994	302
Touchdowns (Tot.)	Dalton Hilliard, 1986-1993	53
Points	Morten Andersen, 1982-1994	1,318

INDIVIDUAL RECORDS—SINGLE SEASON

Category	Name	Performance
Rushing (Yds.)	George Rogers, 1981	1,674
Passing (Yds.)	Jim Everett, 1995	3,970
Passing (TDs)	Jim Everett, 1995	26
Receiving (No.)	Eric Martin, 1988	85
Receiving (Yds.)	Eric Martin, 1989	1,090
Interceptions	Dave Whitsell, 1967	10
Punting (Avg.)	Mark Royals, 1997-98	45.7
Punt Return (Avg.)	Mel Gray, 1987	14.7
Kickoff Return (Avg.)	Don Shy, 1969	27.9
	Mel Gray, 1986	27.9
Field Goals	Morten Andersen, 1985	31
Touchdowns (Tot.)	Dalton Hilliard, 1989	18
Points	Morten Andersen, 1987	121

INDIVIDUAL RECORDS—SINGLE GAME

Category	Name	Performance
Rushing (Yds.)	George Rogers, 9-4-83	206
Passing (Yds.)	Archie Manning, 12-7-80	377
Passing (TDs)	Billy Kilmer, 11-2-69	6
Receiving (No.)	Tony Galbreath, 9-10-78	14
Receiving (Yds.)	Wes Chandler, 9-2-79	205
Interceptions	Tommy Myers, 9-3-78	3
	Dave Waymer, 10-6-85	3
	Reggie Sutton, 10-18-87	3
	Gene Atkins, 12-22-91	3
Field Goals	Many times	5
	Last time by Morten Andersen, 12-11-94	
Touchdowns (Tot.)	Many times	3
	Last time by Mario Bates, 12-4-94	
Points	Many times	18
	Last time by Mario Bates, 12-4-94	

COACHING HISTORY

(189-292-5)

1967-70	Tom Fears*	13-34-2
1970-72	J.D. Roberts	7-25-3
1973-75	John North**	11-23-0
1975	Ernie Hefferle	1-7-0
1976-77	Hank Stram	7-21-0
1978-80	Dick Nolan***	15-29-0
1980	Dick Stanfel	1-3-0
1981-85	O.A. (Bum) Phillips****	27-42-0
1985	Wade Phillips	1-3-0
1986-96	Jim Mora#	93-78-0
1996	Rick Venturi	1-7-0
1997-98	Mike Ditka	12-20-0

*Released after seven games in 1970
**Released after six games in 1975
***Released after 12 games in 1980
****Resigned after 12 games in 1985
#Resigned after 8 games in 1996

LOUISIANA SUPERDOME

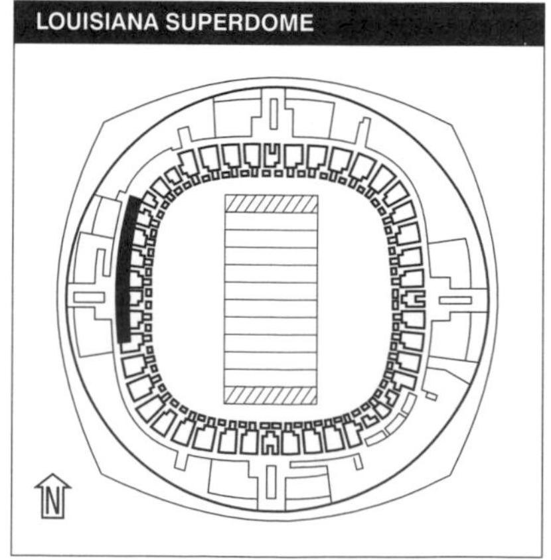

1998 TEAM RECORD

PRESEASON (1-3)

Date	Result		Opponent
8/8	L	7-31	at Green Bay
8/14	L	10-17	at Denver
8/22	L	24-26	Tennessee
8/29	W	10-6	Tampa Bay

REGULAR SEASON (6-10)

Date	Result		Opponent	Att.
9/6	W	24-17	at St. Louis	56,943
9/13	W	19-14	Carolina	51,915
9/27	W	19-13	at Indianapolis (OT)	48,480
10/4	L	27-30	New England	56,172
10/11	L	0-31	San Francisco	62,811
10/18	L	23-31	at Atlanta	60,774
10/25	W	9-3	Tampa Bay	52,695
11/1	L	17-31	at Carolina	62,514
11/8	L	24-31	at Minnesota	63,779
11/15	W	24-3	St. Louis	46,430
11/22	L	20-31	at San Francisco	68,429
11/29	L	10-30	at Miami	73,216
12/6	W	22-3	Dallas	65,065
12/13	L	17-27	Atlanta	61,678
12/20	L	17-19	at Arizona	51,617
12/27	L	33-45	Buffalo	39,707

(OT) Overtime

SCORE BY PERIODS

Saints	50	125	41	83	6	—	305
Opponents	74	126	74	85	0	—	359

ATTENDANCE

Home 436,473 Away 485,752 Total 922,225
Single-game home record, 70,940 (9/2/79)
Single-season home record, 548,728 (1992)

1998 TEAM STATISTICS

	Saints	Opp.
Total First Downs	258	326
Rushing	67	86
Passing	165	208
Penalty	26	32
Third Down: Made/Att	77/215	99/226
Third Down Pct.	35.8	43.8
Fourth Down: Made/Att	6/17	4/9
Fourth Down Pct.	35.3	44.4
Total Net Yards	4,463	5,668
Avg. Per Game	278.9	354.3
Total Plays	966	1,053
Avg. Per Play	4.6	5.4
Net Yards Rushing	1,325	1,700
Avg. Per Game	82.8	106.3
Total Rushes	374	467
Net Yards Passing	3,138	3,968
Avg. Per Game	196.1	248.0
Sacked/Yards Lost	57/376	47/288
Gross Yards	3,514	4,256
Att./Completions	535/278	539/328
Completion Pct.	52.0	60.9
Had Intercepted	19	21
Punts/Avg.	90/45.4	75/43.5
Net Punting Avg.	90/35.8	75/36.7
Penalties/Yards Lost	121/928	132/1,164
Fumbles/Ball Lost	28/14	24/11
Touchdowns	35	40
Rushing	6	13
Passing	19	24
Returns	10	3
Avg. Time of Possession	28:03	31:57

1998 INDIVIDUAL STATISTICS

Passing	Att.	Comp.	Yds.	Pct.	TD	Int.	Tkld.	Rate
Tolliver	199	110	1,427	55.3	8	4	11/88	83.1
Collins	191	94	1,202	49.2	4	10	21/140	54.5
Wuerffel	119	62	695	52.1	5	5	23/131	66.3
Hobert	23	11	170	47.8	1	0	2/17	87.2
L. Smith	2	1	20	50.0	1	0	0/0	125.0
Craver	1	0	0	0.0	0	0	0/0	39.6
Saints	535	278	3,514	52.0	19	19	57/376	69.8
Opponents	539	328	4,256	60.9	24	21	47/288	84.3

SCORING	TD R	TD P	TD Rt	PAT	FG	Saf	PTS
Brien	0	0	0	31/31	20/22	0	91
Cleeland	0	6	0	0/0	0/0	0	36
Craver	2	2	1	0/0	0/0	0	30
Bech	0	3	0	0/0	0/0	0	18
Hastings	0	3	0	0/0	0/0	0	18
L. Smith	1	2	0	0/0	0/0	0	18
Knight	0	0	2	0/0	0/0	0	12
Poole	0	2	0	0/0	0/0	0	12
Collins	1	0	0	0/0	0/0	0	6
T. Davis	1	0	0	0/0	0/0	0	6
Dawkins	0	1	0	0/0	0/0	0	6
Drakeford	0	0	1	0/0	0/0	0	6
Fields	0	0	1	0/0	0/0	0	6
J. Johnson	0	0	1	0/0	0/0	0	6
Kelly	0	0	1	0/0	0/0	0	6
Kei. Mitchell	0	0	1	0/0	0/0	0	6
Robbins	0	0	1	0/0	0/0	0	6
Weary	0	0	1	0/0	0/0	0	6
Zellars	1	0	0	0/0	0/0	0	6
Martin	0	0	0	0/0	0/0	1	2
Wuerffel	0	0	0	0/0	0/0	0	0
Saints	6	19	10	31/31	20/22	2	305
Opponents	13	24	3	39/39	26/33	0	359

2-Point conversions: None.
Team 0-3, Opponents 1-1.

RUSHING	Att.	Yds.	Avg.	LG	TD
L. Smith	138	457	3.3	33	1
Craver	45	180	4.0	25	2
Zellars	56	162	2.9	15t	1
T. Davis	55	143	2.6	14	1
Perry	30	122	4.1	19	0
Collins	23	113	4.9	20	1
Wuerffel	11	60	5.5	18	0
Tolliver	11	43	3.9	16	0
Hastings	3	32	10.7	16	0
Hobert	2	13	6.5	14	0
Saints	374	1,325	3.5	33	6
Opponents	467	1,700	3.6	61t	13

RECEIVING	No.	Yds.	Avg.	LG	TD
Cleeland	54	684	12.7	53	6
Dawkins	53	823	15.5	64t	1
Hastings	35	455	13.0	89t	3
Craver	33	214	6.5	49	2
Poole	24	509	21.2	82t	2
L. Smith	24	249	10.4	35t	2
T. Davis	16	99	6.2	19	0
Bech	14	264	18.9	72t	3
Guliford	10	124	12.4	24	0
Zellars	10	50	5.0	14	0
Farquhar	1	13	13.0	13	0
Slutzker	1	10	10.0	10	0
Wilcox	1	10	10.0	10	0
T. Johnson	1	8	8.0	8	0
Perry	1	2	2.0	2	0
Saints	278	3,514	12.6	89t	19
Opponents	328	4,256	13.0	81t	24

INTERCEPTIONS	No.	Yds.	Avg.	LG	TD
Knight	6	171	28.5	91t	2
Drakeford	4	76	19.0	32t	1
Cota	4	16	4.0	9	0
Kelly	2	104	52.0	79t	1
Weary	2	64	32.0	63t	1
Molden	2	35	17.5	24	0
Glover	1	0	0.0	0	0
Falcons	21	466	22.2	91t	5
Opponents	19	186	9.8	56t	3

PUNTING	No.	Yds.	Avg.	In 20	LG
Royals	88	4,017	45.6	26	64
Brien	2	72	36.0	0	37
Saints	90	4,089	45.4	26	64
Opponents	75	3,263	43.5	18	64

PUNT RETURNS	No.	FC	Yds.	Avg.	LG	TD
Hastings	22	17	307	14.0	76	0
Guliford	10	7	101	10.1	40	0
Saints	32	24	408	12.8	76	0
Opponents	53	5	649	12.2	55	0

KICKOFF RETURNS	No.	Yds.	Avg.	LG	TD
Ismail	28	590	21.1	39	0
Guliford	18	431	23.9	34	0
Craver	7	212	30.3	100t	1
Little	4	64	16.0	20	0
T. Davis	2	21	10.5	19	0
Bech	1	20	20.0	20	0
Hastings	1	16	16.0	16	0
Tomich	1	0	0.0	0	0
Saints	62	1,354	21.8	100t	1
Opponents	52	1,128	21.7	51	0

FIELD GOALS	1-19	20-29	30-39	40-49	50+
Brien	0/0	7/7	3/3	6/6	4/6
Saints	0/0	7/7	3/3	6/6	4/6
Opponents	1/1	5/5	11/12	6/10	3/5

SACKS	No.
Glover	10.0
J. Johnson	7.0
Fields	6.0
Tomich	6.0
Martin	3.0
Kei. Mitchell	2.5
Kev. Mitchell	2.5
Cherry	2.0
Cota	2.0
Hewitt	2.0
Aleaga	1.0
Bordano	1.0
Robbins	1.0
Wilson	1.0
Saints	47.0
Opponents	57.0

1999 DRAFT CHOICE

Round	Name	Pos.	College
1	Ricky Williams	RB	Texas

NEW ORLEANS SAINTS

1999 VETERAN ROSTER

No.	Name	Pos.	Ht.	Wt.	Birthdate	NFL Exp.	College	Hometown	How Acq.	'98 Games/ Starts
69	Ackerman, Tom	C-G	6-3	296	9/6/72	4	Eastern Washington	Nooksack, Wash.	D5b-'96	15/10
54	Aleaga, Ink	LB	6-1	251	4/4/73	3	Washington	Honolulu, Hawaii	FA-'97	15/3
89	Bech, Brett	WR	6-1	201	8/20/71	3	Louisiana State	Slidell, La.	FA-'96	16/0
56	Bordano, Chris	LB	6-1	248	12/30/74	2	Southern Methodist	San Antonio, Tex.	D6-'98	16/6
10	Brien, Doug	K	6-0	180	11/24/70	6	California	Danville, Calif.	FA-'95	16/0
30	† Cherry, Je'Rod	DB	6-1	208	5/30/73	4	California	Berkeley, Calif.	D2-'96	14/0
85	Cleeland, Cameron	TE	6-4	272	8/15/75	2	Washington	Sedro Woolley, Wash.	D2-'98	16/16
66	Cocozzo, Joe	G	6-4	295	8/7/70	6	Michigan	Mechanicsville, N.Y.	FA-'99	0*
32	Craver, Aaron	RB	6-0	232	12/18/68	9	Fresno State	Compton, Calif.	UFA(SD)-'98	16/10
28	Davis, Troy	RB	5-7	191	9/14/75	3	Iowa State	Miami, Fla.	D3-'97	14/2
15	Dawsey, Lawrence	WR	6-0	198	11/16/67	8	Florida State	Dothan, Ala.	FA-'99	0*
22	Drakeford, Tyronne	CB	5-11	185	6/21/71	6	Virginia Tech	Camden, S.C.	UFA(SF)-'98	16/15
87	† Farquhar, John	TE	6-6	278	3/22/72	4	Duke	Menlo Park, Calif.	FA-'97	5/0
55	Fields, Mark	LB	6-2	244	11/9/72	5	Washington State	Cerritos, Calif.	D1-'95	15/15
60	Floyd, Malcom	WR	6-0	194	12/29/72	5	Fresno State	Sacramento, Calif.	FA-'99	0*
62	Fontenot, Jerry	C	6-3	300	11/21/66	11	Texas A&M	Lafayette, La.	UFA(Chi)-'97	4/4
46	Gammon, Kendall	C	6-4	265	10/23/68	8	Pittsburg State	Rose Hill, Kan.	FA-'96	16/0
97	Glover, La'Roi	DT	6-2	285	7/4/74	4	San Diego State	San Diego, Calif.	W(Oak)-'97	16/15
	Halapin, Mike	T	6-5	310	7/1/73	3	Pittsburgh	Vandergrift, Pa.	FA-'99	0*
70	Hamiter, Uhuru	DE	6-4	280	3/14/73	2	Delaware State	Philadelphia, Pa.	W(Phil)-'98	0*
88	Hastings, Andre	WR	6-1	190	11/7/71	7	Georgia	Morrow, Ga.	UFA(Pitt)-'97	16/12
23	Hewitt, Chris	S	6-0	210	7/22/74	3	Cincinnati	Englewood, N.J.	FA-'97	16/2
76	Hills, Keno	G-T	6-6	305	6/13/73	4	Southwestern Louisiana	Tampa, Fla.	D6a-'96	12/1
12	Hobert, Billy Joe	QB	6-3	230	1/8/71	7	Washington	Puyallup, Wash.	FA-'97	1/1
86	Hughes, Danan	WR	6-2	211	12/11/70	7	Iowa	Bayonne, N.J.	UFA-'99(KC)	16/0*
19	Johnson, Alonzo	WR	5-11	186	4/18/73	2	Central State, Ohio	Tuscaloosa, Ala.	FA-'98	1/0
94	Johnson, Joe	DE	6-4	270	7/11/72	6	Louisville	St. Louis, Mo.	D1-'94	16/16
80	† Johnson, Tony	TE	6-5	255	2/5/72	4	Alabama	Como, Miss.	FA-'96	11/0
44	Kelly, Rob	S	6-0	199	6/21/74	3	Ohio State	Newark, Ohio	D2a-'97	16/3
82	Kennison, Eddie	WR	6-0	195	1/20/73	4	Louisiana State	Lake Charles, La.	T(StL)-'99	16/13*
29	Knight, Sammy	S	6-0	205	9/10/75	3	Southern California	Riverside, Calif.	FA-'97	14/13
21	Little, Earl	DB	6-0	191	3/10/73	2	Miami	Miami, Fla.	FA-'97	16/0
93	Martin, Wayne	DT	6-5	275	10/26/65	11	Arkansas	Cherry Valley, Ark.	D1-89	16/16
59	Mitchell, Keith	LB	6-2	245	7/24/74	3	Texas A&M	Garland, Tex.	FA-'97	16/15
50	Mitchell, Kevin	LB	6-1	250	1/1/71	6	Syracuse	Harrisburg, Pa.	UFA(SF)-'98	8/8
25	Molden, Alex	CB	5-10	190	8/4/73	4	Oregon	Colorado Springs, Colo.	D1-'96	16/15
65	Naeole, Chris	G	6-3	313	12/25/74	3	Colorado	Kaaawa, Hawaii	D1-'97	16/16
33	Perry, Wilmont	RB	6-1	235	2/24/75	2	Livingstone College	Franklinton, N.C.	D5-'98	6/2
37	Philyaw, Dino	RB	5-10	205	10/30/70	3	Oregon	Dudley, N.C.	FA-'99	0*
75	Pittman, Julian	DT	6-4	294	4/22/75	2	Florida State	Niceville, Fla.	D4b-'98	2/0
83	Poole, Keith	WR	6-0	193	6/18/74	3	Arizona State	Clovis, Calif.	D4b-'97	15/4
77	Roaf, William	T	6-5	312	4/18/70	7	Louisiana Tech	Pine Bluff, Ark.	D1a-'93	15/15
95	Robbins, Austin	DT	6-6	290	3/1/71	6	North Carolina	Washington, D.C.	T(Oak)-'96	16/1
3	Royals, Mark	P	6-5	220	6/22/65	10	Appalachian State	Mathews, Va.	UFA(Det)-'97	16/0
99	Sagapolutele, Pio	DT	6-6	302	11/28/69	9	San Diego State	Honolulu, Hawaii	UFA(NE)-'97	0*
	Scifres, Steve	T	6-4	300	1/22/72	3	Wyoming	Colorado Springs, Colo.	FA-'99	1/0*
84	Slutzker, Scott	TE	6-4	240	12/20/72	4	Iowa	Hasbrouck Heights, N.J.	T(Ind)-'98	3/0
91	Smith, Brady	DE	6-5	260	6/5/73	4	Colorado State	Barrington, Ill.	D3-'96	14/5
36	Smith, Lamar	RB	5-11	225	11/29/70	6	Houston	Fort Wayne, Ind.	UFA(Sea)-'98	14/9
52	Smith, Vinson	LB	6-2	247	7/3/65	12	East Carolina	Statesville, N.C.	FA-'98	15/0
11	Tolliver, Billy Joe	QB	6-1	217	2/7/66	10	Texas Tech	Boyd, Tex.	FA-'98	7/4
90	Tomich, Jared	DE	6-2	272	4/24/74	3	Nebraska	St. John, Ind.	D2b-'97	16/11
68	Turley, Kyle	T	6-5	300	9/24/75	2	San Diego State	Moreno Valley, Calif.	D1-'98	15/15
98	Warner, Ron	LB	6-2	252	9/26/75	2	Kansas	Independence, Kan.	D7b-'98	1/0
24	Weary, Fred	CB	5-10	181	4/12/74	2	Florida	Jacksonville, Fla.	D4a-'98	14/1
51	Williams, Armon	LB	6-6	233	8/13/73	2	Arizona	Tempe, Ariz.	FA-'99	0*
63	Williams, Wally	C-G	6-2	321	2/19/71	7	Florida A&M	Tallahassee, Fla.	UFA(Balt)-'99	13/13*
92	† Wilson, Troy	DE	6-4	257	11/22/70	4	Pittsburg State	Shawnee Heights, Kan.	W(SF)-'98	15/0
7	Wuerffel, Danny	QB	6-1	208	5/27/74	3	Florida	Ft. Walton, Fla.	D4a-'97	5/4
14	Yarborough, Ryan	WR	6-2	195	4/26/71	6	Wyoming	Park Forest, Ill.	UFA(Balt)-'99	6/1*

* Cocozzo last active with San Diego in '97; Dawsey last active with N.Y. Giants in '96; Floyd last active with St. Louis in '97; Halapin last active with Tennessee in '97; Hamiter inactive for 15 games in '98; Hughes played 16 games with Kansas City; Kennison played 16 games with St. Louis; Philyaw last active with Carolina in '96; Sagapolutele missed '98 season because of injury; Scifres played 1 game with Carolina; A. Williams last active with Tennessee; W. Williams played 13 games with Baltimore; Yarborough played 6 games with Baltimore.

Unrestricted free agent; subject to developments.

† Restricted free agent; subject to developments.

Players lost through free agency (5): QB Kerry Collins (NYG; 7 games in '98), S Chad Cota (Ind; 16), WR Sean Dawkins (Sea; 15), T Clarence Jones (Car; 14), C-G Andy McCollum (StL; 16).

Also played with the Saints in '98—LB Don Davis (4), WR Eric Guliford (5), WR Qadry Ismail (10), LB Brian Jones (1), T Ricky Siglar (1), RB Ray Zellars (11).

COACHING STAFF

Head Coach,
Mike Ditka

Pro Career: Named the twelfth head coach in Saints history in January, 1997. Entering the 1999 season, Ditka ranks third among all active coaches with 124 career victories. He is one of just two people (Tom Flores) to have won a Super Bowl ring as a head coach, assistant coach, and player. All three of Ditka's Super Bowl triumphs have taken place in New Orleans. Came to New Orleans after a four-year stint as a broadcaster with NBC. Was head coach of the Chicago Bears for eleven seasons (1982-1992). The Bears won the NFC Central Division five consecutive seasons (1984-88) and reached the playoffs seven times during his tenure. The 1985 Bears finished with a 15-1 record and won Super Bowl XX. Ditka began his pro coaching career as an assistant with the Dallas Cowboys (1973-1981), and won Super Bowl XII. As a NFL player, Ditka earned rookie of the year honors after being chosen in the first round with the fifth overall pick of the 1961 draft by the Chicago Bears. Also played for Philadelphia (1967-68) and Dallas (1969-1972). Dallas won Super Bowl VI at Tulane Stadium and Ditka caught a 7-yard touchdown pass from Roger Staubach. Career record: 124-88.
Background: Played tight end at Pittsburgh (1958-1960), where he earned all-America honors his senior season. Also played defensive end, linebacker, and ranked among the nation's top punters. Attended Aliquippa High School, where he lettered in football, baseball, and basketball.
Personal: Born October 18, 1939, in Carneige, Pa. Mike and his wife, Diana, live in Metairie, La., and have four children—sons Mike, Mark, and Matthew, and daughter Megan.

ASSISTANT COACHES

Danny Abramowicz, offensive coordinator; born July 13, 1945, Steubenville, Ohio, lives in New Orleans. Wide receiver Xavier 1964-66. Wide receiver New Orleans 1967-1972, San Francisco 49ers 1973-74. No college coaching experience. Pro coach: Chicago Bears 1992-96, joined Saints in 1997.
Bobby April, special teams; born April 15, 1953, New Orleans, lives in Mandeville, La. Linebacker-defensive end Nicholls State 1972-75. College coach: Southern Mississippi 1978, Tulane 1979, Arizona 1980-86, Southern California 1987-1990. Pro coach: Atlanta Falcons 1991-93, Pittsburgh Steelers 1994-95 , joined Saints in 1996.
Tom Clements, quarterbacks; born June 18, 1953, McKees Rocks, Pa., lives in Harahan, La. Quarterback Notre Dame 1972-74. Pro quarterback Ottawa Rough Riders (CFL) 1975-78, Saskatchewan Roughriders (CFL) 1979, Hamilton Tiger-Cats (CFL) 1979, 1981-83, Kansas City Chiefs 1980, Winnipeg Blue Bombers (CFL) 1983-87. College coach: Notre Dame 1992-95. Pro coach: Joined Saints in 1996.
Walt Corey, defensive line; born May 9, 1938, Latrobe, Pa., lives in River Ridge, La. Defensive end Miami 1956-59. Pro linebacker Dallas Texans/Kansas City Chiefs 1960-66. College coach: Utah State 1967-69, Miami 1970, Coast Guard Academy 1995. Pro coach: Kansas City Chiefs 1971-74, 1978-1986, Cleveland Browns 1975-77, Buffalo Bills 1987-1994, joined Saints in 1997.
Judd Garrett, offensive assistant; born June 25, 1967, Abington, Pa., lives in La Place, La. Running back Princeton 1987-89. Pro running back London Monarchs (WLAF) 1991-92, Dallas Cowboys 1993, Las Vegas Posse (CFL) 1994, San Antonio Texans (CFL) 1995. College coach: Princeton 1990. Pro coach: Joined Saints in 1997.
Rodney Holman, offensive assistant/tight ends; born April 20, 1960, Ypsilanti, Mich., lives in Kenner, La. Tight end Tulane 1978-1981. Pro tight end Cincinnati Bengals 1982-1992, Detroit Lions 1993-95. Pro coach: Joined Saints in 1998.
Harold Jackson, wide receivers; born January 6, 1946, Hattiesburg, Miss., lives in River Ridge, La. Wide receiver Jackson State 1964-67. Pro wide receiver Los Angeles Rams 1968, 1973-77, Philadelphia Eagles 1969-1972, New England Patriots 1978-1981, Seattle Seahawks 1983. College coach: North Carolina Central 1990, Virginia Union 1994 (head coach), Benedict College 1995-96 (head coach). Pro coach: New England Patriots 1985-89, New Orleans Night (Arena League) 1991, Tampa Bay Buccaneers 1992-93, joined Saints in 1997.
Rickey Jackson, defensive assistant-pass rush; born March 20, 1958, Pahokee, Fla., lives in Kenner, La. Linebacker Pittsburgh 1977-1980. Pro linebacker New Orleans Saints 1981-1993, San Francisco 49ers 1994-95. Pro coach: Joined Saints in 1998.
Ned James, defensive assistant-linebackers; born January 18, 1964, Syracuse, N.Y., lives in Metairie, La. Quarterback New Mexico 1985-86. Pro quarterback Montreal Alouettes (CFL) 1987, Dallas Texans (Arena League) 1990. College coach: Arizona State 1987, Long Beach State 1988, Texas Christian 1989-1990, Winona State 1992-94. Pro coach: Seattle Seahawks 1995-97, joined Saints in 1998.
Lary Kuharich, running backs; born December 20, 1945, Middletown, N.Y., lives in Metairie, La. Halfback-defensive back Boston College 1964-68. College coach: Boston State 1970-74, Rhode Island 1975, Temple 1977-1980, Illinois State 1981, California 1982-83. Pro coach: Hamilton Tiger-Cats (CFL) 1976, San Antonio Gunslingers (USFL) 1984, Oakland Invaders (USFL) 1985, Calgary Stampeders (CFL) 1986-89, British Columbia Lions (CFL) 1990, Tampa Bay Storm (Arena League) 1991-94, Scottish Claymores (WLAF) 1995, Connecticut Coyotes (Arena League) 1996, New York CityHawks (Arena League) 1997, joined Saints in 1998.
Carlos Mainord, defensive backs; born Aug. 26, 1944, Greenville, Texas, lives in Kenner, La. Linebacker Navarro (Texas) J.C. 1962-63, McMurry College 1964-65. No pro playing experience. College coach: McMurry College 1966-68, Texas Tech 1969, 1983-85, 1987-1992, Ranger (Texas) J.C. 1970-71, 1972-77 (head coach), Rice 1978-1982, Miami 1986. Pro coach: Chicago Bears 1993-98, joined Saints in 1999.
Bill Meyers, offensive line; born Oct. 8, 1946, Chippewa Falls, Wis., lives in Bellevue, Wash. Tackle Stanford 1970-71. No pro playing experience. College coach: California 1972-73, 1977-78, Santa Clara 1974-76, Notre Dame 1979-1981, Missouri 1985-86, Pittsburgh 1987-1992. Pro coach: Green Bay Packers 1982-83, Pittsburgh Steelers 1984, Oakland Raiders 1993, Seattle Seahawks 1998, joined Saints in 1999.
Dan Neal, tight ends; born August 30, 1949, Corbin, Ky., lives in Harahan, La. Center Kentucky 1969-1972. Pro center Baltimore Colts 1973-74, Chicago Bears 1975-1983. College coach: Western Illinois 1996. Pro coach: Philadelphia Eagles 1986-1991, Arizona Cardinals 1994-95, joined Saints in 1997.
Markus Paul, asst. strength & conditioning; born April 1, 1966, in Orlando, Fla., lives in Metairie, La. Safety Syracuse 1984-88. Pro safety Chicago Bears 1989-1993, Tampa Bay Buccaneers 1993. No college coaching experience. Pro coach: Joined Saints in 1998.
Rick Venturi, asst. head coach-linebackers; born February 23, 1946, Taylorville, Ill., lives in Destrehan, La. Quarterback-defensive back Northwestern 1965-67. No pro playing experience. College coach: Northwestern 1968-1972, 1978-1980 (head coach), Purdue 1973-76, Illinois 1977. Pro coach: Hamilton Tiger-Cats (CFL) 1981, Indianapolis Colts 1982-1993 (interim head coach for final 11 games of 1991), Cleveland Browns 1994-95, joined Saints in 1996 (interim head coach for final eight games of 1996).
Mike Woicik, strength and conditioning; born September 26, 1956, Baltimore, lives in Kenner, La. Attended Boston College. No college or pro playing experience. College coach: Springfield College 1978-79, Syracuse 1980-89. Pro coach: Dallas Cowboys 1990-96, joined Saints in 1997.
Zaven Yaralian, defensive coordinator; born February 5, 1952, Syria, lives in Metairie, La. Cornerback Nebraska 1972-73. Pro cornerback Green Bay Packers 1974, Philadelphia Bell (WFL) 1975. College coach: Nebraska 1975, Washington State 1976-77, Missouri 1978-1982, Florida 1983-87, Colorado 1988-89. Pro coach: Chicago Bears 1990-92, New York Giants 1993-96, joined Saints in 1997.

1999 FIRST-YEAR ROSTER

Name	Pos.	Ht.	Wt.	Birthdate	College	Hometown	How Acq.
Brown, Cuncho	TE	6-4	271	11/2/76	Penn State	Winston-Salem, N.C.	FA
Burroughs, Justin	C	6-5	292	5/22/76	North Carolina State	Charlotte, N.C.	FA
Clarke, Phil	LB	6-0	241	1/19/77	Pittsburgh	Miami, Fla.	FA
Cobbs, Anthony (1)	CB	6-0	191	1/9/74	UCLA	Long Beach, Calif.	FA-'97
Coley, Marvin	DE-DT	6-3	284	2/27/76	North Alabama	Pahokee, Fla.	FA
Cummings, Chris	CB	5-9	185	1/5/74	Louisiana State	Dothan, Ala.	FA
Delhomme, Jake (1)	QB	6-2	205	1/10/75	Southwestern Louisiana	Lafayette, La.	FA-'97
Ernest, Justin	DT	6-3	284	12/17/72	Eastern Kentucky	Orange, Calif.	FA
Franklin, P.J.	WR	5-10	180	9/28/77	Tulane	Amite, La.	FA
Gumina, Scott (1)	S	5-11	204	11/26/71	Mississippi State	River Ridge, La.	FA
Jones, Carlos (1)	CB	5-11	180	8/31/73	Miami	Marrero, La.	FA
Joseph, Gana	S	6-0	212	4/20/77	Oklahoma	Miami, Fla.	FA
Leshinski, Ron (1)	RB-TE	6-2	248	3/6/74	Army	Vermillion, Ohio	FA-'97
Lillibridge, Marc (1)	LB	6-1	245	2/18/72	Iowa State	Marion, Iowa	FA-'98
Lurtsema, Rob (1)	DE	6-5	276	10/28/74	Wisconsin	Burnsville, Minn.	FA-'98
Maranto, Tony (1)	CB	5-11	200	7/28/76	Northwestern State	Port Allen, La.	FA
Nord, Rick	G	6-6	310	6/17/75	Louisville	Louisville, Ky.	FA
Powell, Marvin	RB	6-2	235	6/6/76	Southern California	Van Nuys, Calif.	FA
Ridgley, Troy (1)	DT	6-3	300	10/28/70	Norte Dame	Ambridge, Pa.	FA-'98
Schau, Thomas	C	6-5	290	12/30/75	Illinois	Bloomington, Ill.	FA
Spragan, Donnie	LB	6-4	240	7/12/76	Stanford	Union City, Calif.	FA
Stevens, L.C.	WR	6-4	218	12/31/74	North Carolina	Clinton, N.C.	FA
Terrell, Daryl (1)	T	6-5	296	1/25/75	Southern Mississippi	Vossburg, Miss.	FA-'98
Twyner, Gunnard (1)	WR	5-10	183	7/14/73	Western Illinois	Bettendorf, Iowa	FA-'97
Whitehead, William (1)	LB	6-3	285	1/26/73	Auburn	Tuskegee, Ala.	FA
Wilcox, Josh (1)	TE	6-3	255	6/5/74	Oregon	Junction City, Ore.	FA-'98
Williams, Ricky	RB	5-10	236	5/21/77	Texas	San Diego, Calif	D-1
Williams, Tashe (1)	T	6-4	295	9/23/72	Northern Colorado	Colorado Springs, Colo.	FA

The term NFL Rookie is defined as a player who is in his first season of professional football and has not been on the roster of another professional football team for any regular-season or postseason games. A Rookie is designated by an "R" on NFL rosters. Players who have been active in another professional football league or players who have NFL experience, including either preseason training camp or being on an Active List or Inactive List, or on Reserve/Injured or Reserve/Physically Unable to Perform for fewer than six regular-season games, are termed NFL First-Year Players. An NFL First-Year Player is designated by a "1" on NFL rosters. Thereafter, a player is credited with an additional year of experience for each season in which he accumulates six games on the Active List or Inactive List, or on Reserve/Injured or Reserve/Physically Unable to Perform.

NEW YORK GIANTS

National Football Conference
Eastern Division
Team Colors: Blue, Red, and White
Giants Stadium
East Rutherford, New Jersey 07073
Telephone: (201) 935-8111

CLUB OFFICIALS

President/Co-CEO: Wellington T. Mara
Chairman/Co-CEO: Preston Robert Tisch
Executive Vice President/General Counsel: John K. Mara, Esq.
Treasurer: Jonathan Tisch
Vice President-General Manager: Ernie Accorsi
Vice President-Player Personnel: Tom Boisture
Vice President-Chief Financial Officer: John Pasquali
Vice President-Marketing: Rusty Hawley
Vice-President-Communications: Pat Hanlon
Assistant General Manager: Rick Donohue
Director of Player Personnel: Marv Sunderland
Director of Pro Personnel: David Gettleman
Assistant Director of Pro Personnel: Jerry Reese
Director of College Scouting: Jerry Shay
Director of Research and Development: Raymond J. Walsh, Jr.
Director of Player Development: Greg Gabriel
Pro Personnel Assistant: Geoff Mazza
Director of Promotion: Frank Mara
Ticket Manager: John Gorman
Director of Administration: Jim Phelan
Controller: Christine Procops
Director of Community Relations: Allison Stangeby
Director of Sales: Dan Lynch
Assistant Director of Marketing: Bill Smith
Director of Creative Services: Doug Murphy
Assistant Director of Community and Media Relations: Peter John-Baptiste
Assistant Director of Communications: Avis Roper
Head Athletic Trainer: Ronnie Barnes
Assistant Athletic Trainers: John Johnson, Steve Kennelly, Byron Hansen
Equipment Manager: Ed Wagner, Jr.
Stadium: Giants Stadium • **Capacity:** 79,469
East Rutherford, New Jersey 07073
Playing Surface: AstroTurf
Training Camp: University at Albany
1400 Washington Avenue
Albany, N.Y. 12222

1999 SCHEDULE

PRESEASON

Aug. 13	at Minnesota	7:00
Aug. 21	**Jacksonville**	7:00
Aug. 28	**New York Jets**	8:00
Sept. 3	at Baltimore	12:00

REGULAR SEASON

Sept. 12	at Tampa Bay	4:15
Sept. 19	**Washington**	1:00
Sept. 26	at New England	8:20
Oct. 3	**Philadelphia**	1:00
Oct. 10	at Arizona	1:05
Oct. 18	**Dallas** (Mon.)	9:00
Oct. 24	**New Orleans**	1:00
Oct. 31	at Philadelphia	1:00
Nov. 7	Open Date	
Nov. 14	**Indianapolis**	1:00
Nov. 21	at Washington	4:15
Nov. 28	**Arizona**	1:00
Dec. 5	**New York Jets**	1:00
Dec. 12	at Buffalo	1:00
Dec. 19	at St. Louis	12:00
Dec. 26	**Minnesota**	1:00
Jan. 2	at Dallas	3:05

RECORD HOLDERS

INDIVIDUAL RECORDS—CAREER

Category	Name	Performance
Rushing (Yds.)	Rodney Hampton, 1990-97	6,897
Passing (Yds.)	Phil Simms, 1979-1993	33,462
Passing (TDs)	Phil Simms, 1979-1993	199
Receiving (No.)	Joe Morrison, 1959-1972	395
Receiving (Yds.)	Frank Gifford, 1952-1960, 1962-64	5,434
Interceptions	Emlen Tunnell, 1948-1958	74
Punting (Avg.)	Don Chandler, 1956-1964	43.8
Punt Return (Avg.)	David Meggett, 1989-1994	11.0
Kickoff Return (Avg.)	Rocky Thompson, 1971-72	27.2
Field Goals	Pete Gogolak, 1966-1974	126
Touchdowns (Tot.)	Frank Gifford, 1952-1960, 1962-64	78
Points	Pete Gogolak, 1966-1974	646

INDIVIDUAL RECORDS—SINGLE SEASON

Category	Name	Performance
Rushing (Yds.)	Joe Morris, 1986	1,516
Passing (Yds.)	Phil Simms, 1984	4,044
Passing (TDs)	Y.A. Tittle, 1963	36
Receiving (No.)	Earnest Gray, 1983	78
Receiving (Yds.)	Homer Jones, 1967	1,209
Interceptions	Otto Schnellbacher, 1951	11
	Jim Patton, 1958	11
Punting (Avg.)	Don Chandler, 1959	46.6
Punt Return (Avg.)	Merle Hapes, 1942	15.5
Kickoff Return (Avg.)	John Salscheider, 1949	31.6
Field Goals	Ali Haji-Sheikh, 1983	35
Touchdowns (Tot.)	Joe Morris, 1985	21
Points	Ali Haji-Sheikh, 1983	127

INDIVIDUAL RECORDS—SINGLE GAME

Category	Name	Performance
Rushing (Yds.)	Gene Roberts, 11-12-50	218
Passing (Yds.)	Phil Simms, 10-13-85	513
Passing (TDs)	Y.A. Tittle, 10-28-62	*7
Receiving (No.)	Mark Bavaro, 10-13-85	12
Receiving (Yds.)	Del Shofner, 10-28-62	269
Interceptions	Many times	3
	Last time by Terry Kinard, 9-27-87	
Field Goals	Joe Danelo, 10-18-81	6
Touchdowns (Tot.)	Ron Johnson, 10-2-72	4
	Earnest Gray, 9-7-80	4
	Rodney Hampton, 9-24-95	4
Points	Ron Johnson, 10-2-72	24
	Earnest Gray, 9-7-80	24
	Rodney Hampton, 9-24-95	24

*NFL Record

COACHING HISTORY

(545-456-33)

1925	Bob Folwell	8-4-0
1926	Joe Alexander	8-4-1
1927-28	Earl Potteiger	15-8-3
1929-30	LeRoy Andrews*	24-5-1
1930	Benny Friedman-Steve Owen	2-0-0
1931-53	Steve Owen	153-108-17
1954-60	Jim Lee Howell	55-29-4
1961-68	Allie Sherman	57-54-4
1969-73	Alex Webster	29-40-1
1974-76	Bill Arnsparger**	7-28-0
1976-78	John McVay	14-23-0
1979-82	Ray Perkins	24-35-0
1983-90	Bill Parcells	85-52-1
1991-92	Ray Handley	14-18-0
1993-96	Dan Reeves	32-34-0
1997-98	Jim Fassel	18-14-1

*Released after 15 games in 1930
**Released after seven games in 1976

GIANTS STADIUM

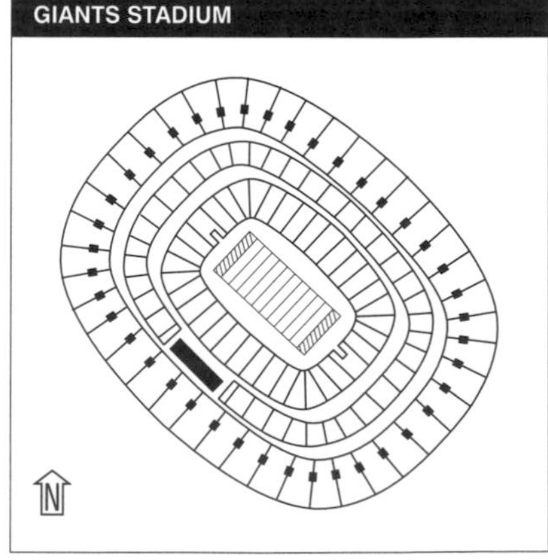

1998 TEAM RECORD

PRESEASON (1-3)

Date	Result		Opponent
8/8	W	24-17	Cincinnati
8/14	L	10-24	at Jacksonville
8/20	L	23-27	at New York Jets
8/28	L	6-14	Baltimore

REGULAR SEASON (8-8)

Date	Result		Opponent	Att.
9/6	W	31-24	Washington	76,629
9/13	L	17-20	at Oakland	40,545
9/21	L	7-31	Dallas	78,039
9/27	W	34-16	at San Diego	55,672
10/4	L	3-20	at Tampa Bay	64,989
10/11	L	20-34	Atlanta	71,173
10/18	W	34-7	Arizona	70,456
11/1	L	14-21	at Washington	67,976
11/8	L	6-16	at Dallas	64,316
11/15	L	3-37	Green Bay	76,272
11/22	W	20-0	Philadelphia	65,763
11/30	L	7-31	at San Francisco	68,212
12/6	W	23-19	at Arizona	46,128
12/13	W	20-16	Denver	72,336
12/20	W	28-7	Kansas City	66,040
12/27	W	20-10	at Philadelphia	66,596

SCORE BY PERIODS

Giants	81	67	86	53	0	—	287
Opponents	72	89	78	70	0	—	309

ATTENDANCE

Home 576,708 Away 474,434 Total 1,051,142
Single-game home record, 78,039 (9/21/98)
Single-season home record, 599,570 (1990)

1998 TEAM STATISTICS

	Giants	Opp.
Total First Downs	263	286
Rushing	104	103
Passing	129	163
Penalty	30	20
Third Down: Made/Att	70/229	88/234
Third Down Pct.	30.6	37.6
Fourth Down: Made/Att	8/18	7/18
Fourth Down Pct.	44.4	38.9
Total Net Yards	4,455	5,171
Avg. Per Game	278.4	323.2
Total Plays	1,016	1,051
Avg. Per Play	4.4	4.9
Net Yards Rushing	1,889	2,004
Avg. Per Game	118.1	125.3
Total Rushes	474	476
Net Yards Passing	2,566	3,167
Avg. Per Game	160.4	197.9
Sacked/Yards Lost	35/256	54/336
Gross Yards	2,822	3,503
Att./Completions	507/265	521/282
Completion Pct.	52.3	54.1
Had Intercepted	15	19
Punts/Avg.	101/45.2	88/42.1
Net Punting Avg.	101/37.8	88/36.5
Penalties/Yards Lost	124/946	124/967
Fumbles/Ball Lost	17/9	25/7
Touchdowns	32	34
Rushing	10	13
Passing	18	17
Returns	4	4
Avg. Time of Possession	28:21	31:39

1998 INDIVIDUAL STATISTICS

Passing	Att.	Comp.	Yds.	Pct.	TD	Int.	Tkld.	Rate
Kanell	299	160	1,603	53.5	11	10	22/172	67.3
Graham	205	105	1,219	51.2	7	5	12/75	70.8
Cherry	1	0	0	0.0	0	0	1/9	39.6
Maynard	1	0	0	0.0	0	0	0/0	39.6
Toomer	1	0	0	0.0	0	0	0/0	39.6
Giants	507	265	2,822	52.3	18	15	35/256	68.3
Opponents	521	282	3,503	54.1	17	19	54/336	70.9

SCORING	TD R	TD P	TD Rt	PAT	FG	Saf	PTS
Daluiso	0	0	0	32/32	21/27	0	95
Calloway	0	6	0	0/0	0/0	0	36
Brown	5	0	0	0/0	0/0	0	30
Toomer	0	5	0	0/0	0/0	0	30
Way	3	1	0	0/0	0/0	0	24
Barber	0	3	0	0/0	0/0	0	18
Ellsworth	0	0	2	0/0	0/0	0	12
Graham	2	0	0	0/0	0/0	0	12
Hilliard	0	2	0	0/0	0/0	0	12
Patten	0	1	1	0/0	0/0	0	12
Strahan	0	0	1	0/0	0/0	0	6
Giants	10	18	4	32/32	21/27	0	287
Opponents	13	17	4	34/34	23/30	1	309

2-Point conversions: None.
Team 0-0, Opponents 0-0.

RUSHING	Att.	Yds.	Avg.	LG	TD
Brown	247	1,063	4.3	45	5
Way	113	432	3.8	21	3
Barber	52	166	3.2	23	0
Graham	27	138	5.1	23	2
Wheatley	14	52	3.7	15	0
Kanell	15	36	2.4	10	0
Comella	1	6	6.0	6	0
Hilliard	1	4	4.0	4	0
Cherry	3	-3	-1.0	-1	0
Maynard	1	-5	-5.0	-5	0
Giants	474	1,889	4.0	45	10
Opponents	476	2,004	4.2	80t	13

RECEIVING	No.	Yds.	Avg.	LG	TD
Calloway	62	812	13.1	36	6
Hilliard	51	715	14.0	50	2
Barber	42	348	8.3	87t	3
Way	31	131	4.2	16	1
Toomer	27	360	13.3	37t	5
Cross	13	90	6.9	22	0
Brown	13	36	2.8	12	0
Patten	11	119	10.8	39t	1
Jurevicius	9	146	16.2	59	0
Haase	2	33	16.5	27	0
Graham	1	16	16.0	16	0
Alford	1	11	11.0	11	0
Comella	1	3	3.0	3	0
Pupunu	1	2	2.0	2	0
Giants	265	2,822	10.6	87t	18
Opponents	282	3,503	12.4	80t	17

INTERCEPTIONS	No.	Yds.	Avg.	LG	TD
Ellsworth	5	92	18.4	43t	2
Sparks	4	25	6.3	12	0
S. Williams	2	6	3.0	6	0
Armstead	2	4	2.0	4	0
Gray	1	36	36.0	36	0
Strahan	1	24	24.0	24t	1
C. Hamilton	1	17	17.0	17	0
Garnes	1	13	13.0	13	0
M. Buckley	1	0	0.0	0	0
Lincoln	1	0	0.0	0	0
Giants	19	217	11.4	43t	3
Opponents	15	232	15.5	71t	2

PUNTING	No.	Yds.	Avg.	In 20	LG
Maynard	101	4,566	45.2	33	63
Giants	101	4,566	45.2	33	63
Opponents	88	3,701	42.1	24	65

PUNT RETURNS	No.	FC	Yds.	Avg.	LG	TD
Toomer	35	22	252	7.2	39	0
Giants	35	22	252	7.2	39	0
Opponents	53	11	587	11.1	59t	1

KICKOFF RETURNS	No.	Yds.	Avg.	LG	TD
Patten	43	928	21.6	90t	1
Barber	14	250	17.9	32	0
Toomer	4	66	16.5	31	0
Palelei	3	14	4.7	13	0
Wheatley	1	16	16.0	16	0
Comella	1	12	12.0	12	0
Giants	66	1,286	19.5	90t	1
Opponents	51	1,234	24.2	66	0

FIELD GOALS	1-19	20-29	30-39	40-49	50+
Daluiso	2/2	5/5	6/8	7/11	1/1
Giants	2/2	5/5	6/8	7/11	1/1
Opponents	2/2	6/6	9/12	6/10	0/0

SACKS	No.
Strahan	15.0
Bratzke	11.0
K. Hamilton	7.0
Armstead	5.0
Jones	4.0
Harris	3.5
Wooten	3.0
M. Buckley	1.5
Galyon	1.0
Gray	1.0
C. Hamilton	1.0
Peter	1.0
Giants	54.0
Opponents	35.0

1999 DRAFT CHOICES

Round	Name	Pos.	College
1	Luke Petitgout	T	Notre Dame
2	Joe Montgomery	RB	Ohio State
3	Dan Campbell	TE	Texas A&M
4	Sean Bennett	RB	Northwestern
5	Mike Rosenthal	T	Notre Dame
6	Lyle West	DB	San Jose State
	Andre Weathers	DB	Michigan
7	Ryan Hale	DT	Arkansas
	O.J. Childress	LB	Clemson

NEW YORK GIANTS

1999 VETERAN ROSTER

No.	Name	Pos.	Ht.	Wt.	Birthdate	NFL Exp.	College	Hometown	How Acq.	'98 Games/ Starts
80	Alford, Brian	WR	6-1	190	6/7/75	2	Purdue	Oak Park, Mich.	D3-'98	2/0
98	Armstead, Jessie	LB	6-1	240	10/26/70	7	Miami	Dallas, Tex.	D8-'93	16/16
21	Barber, Tiki	RB	5-10	205	4/7/75	3	Virginia	Roanoke, Va.	D2-'97	16/4
82	Brock, Fred	WR	5-11	181	11/15/74	3	Southern Mississippi	Montgomery, Ala.	FA-'99	12/0*
33	Brown, Gary	RB	5-11	230	7/1/69	8	Penn State	Williamsport, Pa.	UFA(SD)-'98	16/11
28	Buckley, Curtis	S	6-0	182	9/25/70	7	East Texas State	Silsbee, Tex.	W(SF)-'98	14/0*
55	Buckley, Marcus	LB	6-3	240	2/3/71	7	Texas A&M	Ft. Worth, Tex.	D3-'93	14/12
18	Cherry, Mike	QB	6-3	225	12/15/73	3	Murray State	Texarkana, Ark.	D6-'97	1/0
5	Collins, Kerry	QB	6-5	240	12/30/72	5	Penn State	Lebanon, Pa.	UFA(NO)-'99	11/11*
58	† Colman, Doug	LB	6-2	250	6/4/73	4	Nebraska	Somers Point, N.J.	D6-'96	16/0
34	Comella, Greg	RB	6-1	240	7/29/75	2	Stanford	Wellesley, Mass.	FA-'98	16/0
87	Cross, Howard	TE	6-5	275	8/8/67	11	Alabama	Huntsville, Ala.	D6-'89	16/16
3	Daluiso, Brad	K	6-2	215	12/31/67	9	UCLA	San Diego, Calif.	FA-'93	16/0
43	† Ellsworth, Percy	S	6-2	225	10/19/74	4	Virginia	Drewryville, Va.	FA-'96	16/9
69	Engler, Derek	G	6-5	300	7/11/74	3	Wisconsin	St. Paul, Minn.	FA-'97	11/0
52	Galyon, Scott	LB	6-2	245	3/23/74	4	Tennessee	Seymour, Tenn.	D6-'96	10/1
20	Garnes, Sam	S	6-3	225	7/12/74	3	Cincinnati	Bronx, N.Y.	D5-'97	11/11
74	Gragg, Scott	T	6-8	325	2/28/72	5	Montana	Silverton, Ore.	D2-'95	16/16
10	Graham, Kent	QB	6-5	240	11/1/68	8	Ohio State	Wheaton, Ill.	UFA(Ariz)-'98	11/6
89	Haase, Andy	TE	6-4	260	7/10/74	2	Northern Colorado	Odessa, Wash.	FA-'98	7/1
41	† Hamilton, Conrad	CB	5-10	195	11/5/74	4	Eastern New Mexico	Alamogordo, N.M.	D7-'96	16/15
75	Hamilton, Keith	DT	6-6	300	5/25/71	8	Pittsburgh	Lynchburg, Va.	D4-'92	16/16
97	Harris, Robert	DT	6-4	300	6/13/69	8	Southern	Riviera Beach, Fla.	RFA(Minn)-'95	10/10
88	Hilliard, Ike	WR	5-11	195	4/5/76	3	Florida	Patterson, La.	D1-'97	16/16
79	† Holsey, Bernard	DE	6-2	295	12/10/73	4	Duke	Cave Spring, Ga.	FA-'96	16/0
23	Johnson, LeShon	RB	6-0	214	1/15/71	5	Northern Illinois	Haskell, Okla.	UFA(Ariz)-'98	0*
94	Jones, Cedric	DE	6-4	275	4/30/74	4	Oklahoma	Houston, Tex.	D1-'96	16/1
84	Jurevicius, Joe	WR	6-5	230	12/23/74	2	Penn State	Chadron, Ohio	D2-'98	14/1
9	Maynard, Brad	P	6-1	190	2/9/74	3	Ball State	Atlanta, Ind.	D3-'97	16/0
76	Miller, Nate	T	6-3	310	10/8/71	5	Louisiana State	Tuscaloosa, Ala.	FA-'98	0*
83	Mitchell, Pete	TE	6-2	240	10/9/71	5	Boston College	Royal Oak, Mich.	UFA(Jac)-'99	16/16*
51	Monty, Pete	LB	6-2	250	7/3/74	3	Wisconsin	Fort Collins, Colo.	D4-'97	11/0
70	Myles, Toby	T	6-4	310	7/23/75	2	Jackson State	Jackson, Miss.	D5-'98	0*
72	† Oben, Roman	T	6-4	310	10/9/72	4	Louisville	Washington, D.C.	D3-'96	16/16
85	Patten, David	WR	5-9	180	8/19/74	3	West Carolina	Hopkins, S.C.	FA-'97	12/0
99	Peter, Christian	DT	6-3	300	10/5/72	3	Nebraska	Locust, N.J.	FA-'97	16/6
91	Phillips, Ryan	LB	6-4	252	2/7/74	3	Idaho	Auburn, Wash.	D3-'97	16/3
52	Scott, Lance	C	6-3	300	2/15/72	5	Utah	Salt Lake City, Utah	FA-'97	16/16
31	Sehorn, Jason	CB	6-2	210	4/15/71	6	Southern California	Mt. Shasta, Calif.	D2-'94	0*
22	Sparks, Phillippi	CB	5-11	195	4/15/69	8	Arizona State	Glendale, Calif.	D2-'92	13/13
65	Stone, Ron	G	6-5	325	7/20/71	7	Boston College	Roxbury, Mass.	RFA(Dall)-'96	14/14
92	Strahan, Michael	DE	6-4	280	11/21/71	7	Texas Southern	Westbury, Tex.	D2-'93	16/15
81	† Toomer, Amani	WR	6-3	202	9/8/74	4	Michigan	Berkeley, Calif.	D2-'96	16/0
30	Way, Charles	FB	6-0	250	12/27/72	5	Virginia	Philadelphia, Pa.	D6-'95	16/15
62	Whittle, Jason	G	6-6	300	3/7/75	2	Southwestern Missouri	Springfield, Mo.	FA-'98	1/0
90	Widmer, Corey	LB	6-3	255	12/25/68	8	Montana State	Bozeman, Mont.	D7-'92	16/15
59	Williams, Brian	C	6-5	315	6/8/66	11	Minnesota	Mt. Lebanon, Pa.	D1-'89	0*
96	Williams, George	DT	6-3	295	12/8/75	2	North Carolina State	Roseboro, N.C.	FA-'98	2/0
36	Williams, Shaun	S	6-2	215	10/10/76	2	UCLA	Encino, Calif.	D1-'98	13/0
29	Wooten, Tito	S	6-0	195	12/12/71	6	Northeast Louisiana	Goldsboro, N.C.	D4(Supp)-'94	14/13

* Brock played 12 games with Arizona in '98; Buckley played 8 games with San Francisco; Collins played 4 games with Carolina and 7 games with New Orleans; Johnson, Sehorn and Williams missed '98 season because of injury; Miller inactive for 2 games; Mitchell played 16 games for Jacksonville; Myles inactive for 12 games.

† Restricted free agent; subject to developments.

Players lost to free agency (3): G Greg Bishop (Atl; 16 games in '98), DE Chad Bratzke (Ind; 16), TE Al Pupunu (SD; 9).

Also played with Giants in '98—CB Kory Blackwell (5 games), WR Chris Calloway (16), CB Carlton Gray (14), QB Danny Kanell (10), CB Jeremy Lincoln (16), G Lonnie Palelei (9), G Jerry Reynolds (12), S Brandon Sanders (13), RB Tyrone Wheatley (5), S Rodney Young (2).

COACHING STAFF

Head Coach,
Jim Fassel

Pro Career: Was named the fifteenth head coach in Giants history on January 15, 1997. Enters his third season as head coach of the Giants. The Giants finished 8-8 by winning five of their last six games, which included a 20-16 victory over the previously undefeated and eventual Super Bowl champion Denver Broncos. In 1997, Fassel led his squad to a 10-5-1 record and a berth in the playoffs while capturing the NFC East title. Fassel was named coach of the year by 11 media outlets, including *The Sporting News*. The Giants became the fifteenth team in NFL history to finish in first place in their division the season after finishing last. The Giants finished with a 7-0-1 division record and became the first team ever to go undefeated in NFC Eastern Division play. Fassel entered the NFL with the Giants in 1991 as quarterbacks coach, then as offensive coordinator in 1992. Fassel spent two campaigns as assistant head coach/offensive coordinator for the Denver Broncos in 1993 and 1994. He spent the 1995 season as quarterbacks coach for the Oakland Raiders and was the offensive coordinator and quarterbacks coach for the Arizona Cardinals in 1996. Fassel has been credited with an ability to develop quarterbacks, including John Elway, Kent Graham, and Boomer Esiason. Career record: 18-14-1.

Background: A former collegiate quarterback, Fassel began coaching in 1973 at his alma mater, Fullerton College, then was a player-coach for the Hawaii Hawaiians of the World Football League in 1974. He coached quarterbacks and receivers at Utah in 1976, then served seven seasons as offensive coordinator at both Weber State (1977-78) and Stanford (1979-1983). At Stanford, Fassel was credited with recruiting and coaching Elway. Fassel entered the pro arena in 1984 as offensive coordinator for the New Orleans Breakers of the USFL, then returned to Utah as the school's head coach from 1985-89 where he recruited and coached current Baltimore Ravens quarterback Scott Mitchell, who set 10 NCAA records under Fassel's tutelage.

Personal: A native of Anaheim, California, Fassel was a standout quarterback at Anaheim High School before leading Fullerton College to the junior college national championship in 1967. He also played collegiately at Southern California with Seattle Seahawks head coach Mike Holmgren and at Long Beach State. He was drafted by the Chicago Bears in the seventh round of the 1972 NFL draft and played briefly with Chicago, the Houston Oilers, and San Diego Chargers. Born August 31, 1949 in Anaheim, Fassel and his wife, Kitty, have four children—John, Brian, Jana, and Mike.

ASSISTANT COACHES

Dave Brazil, defensive quality control; born March 25, 1936, Detroit, lives in East Rutherford, N.J. No college or pro playing experience. College coach: Holy Cross 1968, Tulsa 1969-1970, Eastern Michigan 1971-73, Boston College 1980, Kent State 1981-82. Pro coach: Detroit Wheels (WFL) 1974, Chicago Wind (WFL) 1975, Kansas City Chiefs 1984-88, Pittsburgh Steelers 1989-1991, joined Giants in 1992.

John Dunn, strength and conditioning; born July 22, 1956, Hillsdale, N.Y., lives in Wayne, N.J. Guard Penn State 1974-77. No pro playing experience. College coach: Penn State 1978. Pro coach: Washington Redskins 1984-86, Los Angeles Raiders 1987-89, San Diego Chargers 1990-96, joined Giants in 1997.

John Fox, defensive coordinator; born February 8, 1955, Virginia Beach, Va., lives in Wayne, N.J. Defensive back San Diego State 1975-77. No pro playing experience. College coach: U.S. International 1979, Boise State 1980, Long Beach State 1981, Utah 1982, Kansas 1983, 1985, Iowa State 1984, Pittsburgh 1986-88. Pro coach: Los Angeles Express (USFL) 1985, Pittsburgh Steelers 1989-1991, San Diego Chargers 1992-93, Los Angeles/Oakland Raiders 1994-95, St. Louis Rams 1996, joined Giants in 1997.

Mike Gillhamer, offensive assistant; born February 20, 1954, Oakland, lives in Somerset, N.J. Defensive back Humboldt State. No pro playing experience. College coach: College of the Sequoias 1979-1983, Weber State 1984, Utah 1985-89, San Jose State 1990-93, Nevada 1994-95, Rutgers 1996. Pro coach: Joined Giants in 1997.

Mike Haluchak, linebackers; born November 28, 1949, Concord, Calif., lives in Cedar Grove, N.J. Linebacker Southern California 1967-1970. No pro playing experience. College coach: Southern California 1976-77, Cal State-Fullerton 1978, Pacific 1979-1980, California 1981, North Carolina State 1982. Pro coach: Oakland Invaders (USFL) 1983-85, San Diego Chargers 1986-1991, Cincinnati Bengals 1992-93, Washington Redskins 1994-96, joined Giants in 1997.

Johnnie Lynn, defensive backs; born December 19, 1956, Los Angeles, lives in Wayne, N.J. Defensive back UCLA 1975-78. Pro defensive back New York Jets 1979-1986. College coach: Arizona 1988-1993. Pro coach: Tampa Bay Buccaneers 1994-95, San Francisco 49ers 1996, joined Giants in 1997.

Larry MacDuff, special teams; born June 22, 1948, Clinton, Iowa, lives in Mundham, N.J. Defensive end Fullerton C.C. 1966-67, Oklahoma 1968-69. No pro playing experience. College coach: Fullerton C.C. 1970, 1974-79, Stanford 1980-83, Hawaii 1984-86, Arizona 1987-1996. Pro coach: Joined Giants in 1997.

Denny Marcin, defensive line; born April 24, 1942, Cleveland, lives in Wayne, N.J. Defensive and offensive line Miami (Ohio) 1961-64. No pro playing experience. College coach: Miami (Ohio) 1974-77, North Carolina 1978-1987, Illinois 1988-1996. Pro coach: Joined Giants in 1997.

Jim McNally, offensive line; born December 13, 1943, Buffalo, lives in Cedar Grove, N.J. Guard Buffalo 1961-65. No pro playing experience. College coach: Buffalo 1966-1970, Marshall 1971-74, Boston College 1975-77, Wake Forest 1978-79. Pro coach: Cincinnati Bengals 1980-1994, Carolina Panthers 1995-98, joined Giants in 1999.

Sean Payton, quarterbacks; born December 29, 1963, San Mateo, Calif., lives in Wayne, N.J. Quarterback Eastern Illinois 1982-86. Pro quarterback Ottawa Rough Riders (CFL) 1987, Chicago Bears 1987. College coach: San Diego State 1988-89, 1992-93, Indiana State 1990-91, Miami (Ohio) 1994-95, Illinois 1996. Pro coach: Philadelphia Eagles 1997-98, joined Giants in 1999.

Dick Rehbein, tight ends-asst. offensive line; born November 22, 1955, Green Bay, lives in Wayne, N.J. Center Ripon 1973-77. No pro playing experience. Pro coach: Green Bay Packers 1979-1983, Los Angeles Express (USFL) 1984, Minnesota Vikings 1984-1991, joined Giants in 1992.

Jimmy Robinson, wide receivers; born January 3, 1953, Atlanta, lives in Wayne, N.J. Wide receiver Georgia Tech 1972-74. Pro wide receiver Atlanta Falcons 1975, New York Giants 1976-79, San Francisco 49ers 1980, Denver Broncos 1981. College coach: Georgia Tech 1986-89. Pro coach: Memphis Showboats (USFL) 1984-85, Atlanta Falcons 1990-93, Indianapolis Colts 1994-97, joined Giants in 1998.

Jim Skipper, offensive coordinator-running backs; born January 23, 1949, Breaux Bridge, La., lives in Clifton, N.J. Defensive back Whittier College 1971-72. No pro playing experience. College coach: Cal Poly-Pomona 1974-76, San Jose State 1977-78, Pacific 1979, Oregon 1980-82. Pro coach: Philadelphia/Baltimore Stars (USFL) 1983-85, New Orleans Saints 1986-1995, Arizona Cardinals 1996, joined Giants in 1997.

Craig Stoddard, asst. strength and conditioning; born February 8, 1972, North Tarrytown, N.Y., lives in Hackensack, N.J. Linebacker Springfield College 1990-93. No pro playing experience. College coach: Penn State 1995-96. Pro coach: San Diego Chargers 1994, joined Giants in 1997.

1999 FIRST-YEAR ROSTER

Name	Pos.	Ht.	Wt.	Birthdate	College	Hometown	How Acq.
Ardoin, Ty	S	6-0	195	4/5/77	Texas Tech	Galveston, Tex.	FA
Bennett, Sean	RB	6-1	222	11/9/75	Northwestern	Evansville, Ind.	D4
Buck, Steve	QB	6-4	210	2/25/76	Weber State	Alta Loma, Calif.	FA
Campbell, Dan	TE	6-5	263	4/13/76	Texas A&M	Glen Rose, Tex.	D3
Cheatham, Kenny	WR	6-2	211	8/11/76	Nebraska	Phoenix, Ariz.	FA
Childress, O.J.	LB	6-1	244	12/6/76	Clemson	Hermitage, Tenn.	D7b
Council, Keith (1)	DT	6-6	285	12/3/74	Hampton	Orlando, Fla.	FA-'98
Curry, Ray	WR	5-9	170	9/3/76	Toledo	Detroit, Mich.	FA
Davis, Greg	C	6-4	330	3/21/76	Texas Christian	Kingsville, Tex.	FA
Derrick, Greg	DE	6-5	270	10/10/76	North Carolina State	Lexington, S.C.	FA
Dragos, Scott (1)	TE	6-2	255	10/28/75	Boston College	Old Rochester, Mass.	FA-'98
Estes, Charles (1)	DE	6-3	265	9/30/75	Army	Georgetown, Ky.	FA-'97
Ferrara, Frank	DE	6-3	273	12/25/75	Rhode Island	Brooklyn, N.Y.	FA
Hale, Ryan	DT	6-4	298	6/10/75	Arkansas	Rodgers, Ark.	D7a
Kiernan, Scott	G	6-3	307	8/16/74	Syracuse	Cos Cob, Conn.	FA
Konopka, Steve	DT	6-4	299	5/12/76	Central Connecticut	West Hartford, Conn.	FA
Lauta, Dan	T	6-4	296	4/4/76	Buffalo State	Amherst, N.Y.	FA
Levingston, Bashir	CB	5-9	174	10/2/76	Eastern Washington	Seaside, Calif.	FA
Montgomery, Joe	RB	5-10	228	6/8/76	Ohio State	Robbins, Ill.	D2
Ortiz, Chris	WR	6-2	193	9/25/74	Southern Connecticut	Waterbury, Conn.	FA
Petitgout, Luke	G	6-6	315	6/16/76	Notre Dame	Georgetown, Del.	D1
Pollack, Todd (1)	TE	6-4	255	12/10/74	Boston College	Rye, N.Y.	FA
Pukenas, Bryan	C	6-4	302	6/26/76	West Virginia	Bordentown, N.J.	FA
Rosenthal, Mike	T	6-7	310	6/10/77	Notre Dame	Granger, Ind.	D5
Sanders, Kenny	LB	6-1	237	11/6/76	Tennessee-Chattanooga	Lanett, Ala.	FA
Simmons, Rasheed	DE	6-5	244	9/17/75	Maryland	Edison, N.J.	FA
Stephens, Cedric	CB	5-9	186	3/4/76	Oklahoma	Dallas, Tex.	FA
Stephens, Reggie	CB	5-9	194	2/21/75	Rutgers	Santa Cruz, Calif.	FA
Suggs, Kelvin	CB	6-1	189	1/7/76	East Carolina	Kinston, N.C.	FA
Tarplin, Jessie	LB	6-2	251	2/18/77	Georgia Tech	Decatur, Ga.	FA
Weathers, Andre	CB	6-0	189	8/6/76	Michigan	Flint, Mich.	D6b
West, Lyle	S	6-0	210	12/20/76	San Jose State	Fremont, Calif.	D6a

The term NFL Rookie is defined as a player who is in his first season of professional football and has not been on the roster of another professional football team for any regular-season or postseason games. A Rookie is designated by an "R" on NFL rosters. Players who have been active in another professional football league or players who have NFL experience, including either preseason training camp or being on an Active List or Inactive List, or on Reserve/Injured or Reserve/Physically Unable to Perform for fewer than six regular-season games, are termed NFL First-Year Players. An NFL First-Year Player is designated by a "1" on NFL rosters. Thereafter, a player is credited with an additional year of experience for each season in which he accumulates six games on the Active List or Inactive List, or on Reserve/Injured or Reserve/Physically Unable to Perform.

PHILADELPHIA EAGLES

National Football Conference
Eastern Division
Team Colors: Midnight Green, Silver, Black, and White
Veterans Stadium
3501 South Broad Street
Philadelphia, Pennsylvania 19148
Telephone: (215) 463-2500

CLUB OFFICIALS

Owner/Chief Executive Officer: Jeffrey Lurie
Executive Vice President: Joe Banner
Director of Football Operations: Tom Modrak
Senior Vice President-Special Projects: Mimi Box
Senior Vice President, Marketing and Administration: Len Komoroski
Vice President, Sales: Scott O'Neil
Vice President, Corporate Sales: Dave Rowan
Executive Director of Eagles Youth Partnership: Sarah Helfman
Chief Financial Officer: Don Smolenski
Pro Scouting Coordinator: Mike McCartney
Director of College Scouting: John Goeller
Director of Administration: Vicki Chatley
Director of Public Relations: Ron Howard
Assistant Directors of Public Relations: Derek Boyko, Rich Burg
Director, Broadcasting/Exec. Producer Eagles Television Network: Rob Alberino
Director of Premium Services: Jason Gonella
Ticket Manager: Leo Carlin
Director of Merchandise: Steve Strawbridge
Director of Advertising and Promotions: Kim Babiak
Office Manager/Travel Coordinator: Tracey Bucher
Director of Security: Anthony (Butch) Buchanico
Director of Penthouse Operations: Christiana Noyalas
Head Athletic Trainer: Rick Burkholder
Asst. Athletic Trainers: Scottie Patton, Chris Peduzzi
Video Director: Mike Dougherty
Equipment Manager: Angelo Ortiz
Stadium: Veterans Stadium • **Capacity:** 65,352
3501 South Broad Street
Philadelphia, Pennsylvania 19148
Playing Surface: AstroTurf-8
Training Camp: Lehigh University
Bethlehem, Pennsylvania 18015

1999 SCHEDULE

PRESEASON

Aug. 12	**Baltimore**	8:00
Aug. 20	at New York Jets	7:30
Aug. 26	at Minnesota	7:00
Sept. 2	**Cleveland**	7:30

REGULAR SEASON

Sept. 12	**Arizona**	1:00
Sept. 19	**Tampa Bay**	1:00
Sept. 26	at Buffalo	1:00
Oct. 3	at New York Giants	1:00
Oct. 10	**Dallas**	1:00
Oct. 17	at Chicago	12:00
Oct. 24	at Miami	1:00
Oct. 31	**New York Giants**	1:00
Nov. 7	at Carolina	1:00
Nov. 14	**Washington**	1:00
Nov. 21	**Indianapolis**	1:00
Nov. 28	at Washington	1:00
Dec. 5	at Arizona	2:05
Dec. 12	at Dallas	12:00
Dec. 19	**New England**	1:00
Dec. 26	Open Date	
Jan. 2	**St. Louis**	1:00

RECORD HOLDERS

INDIVIDUAL RECORDS—CAREER

Category	Name	Performance
Rushing (Yds.)	Wilbert Montgomery, 1977-1984	6,538
Passing (Yds.)	Ron Jaworski, 1977-1986	26,963
Passing (TDs)	Ron Jaworski, 1977-1986	175
Receiving (No.)	Harold Carmichael, 1971-1983	589
Receiving (Yds.)	Harold Carmichael, 1971-1983	8,978
Interceptions	Bill Bradley, 1969-1976	34
	Eric Allen, 1988-1994	34
Punting (Avg.)	Joe Muha, 1946-1950	42.9
Punt Return (Avg.)	Steve Van Buren, 1944-1951	13.9
Kickoff Return (Avg.)	Steve Van Buren, 1944-1951	26.7
Field Goals	Paul McFadden, 1984-87	91
Touchdowns (Tot.)	Harold Carmichael, 1971-1983	79
Points	Bobby Walston, 1951-1962	881

INDIVIDUAL RECORDS—SINGLE SEASON

Category	Name	Performance
Rushing (Yds.)	Wilbert Montgomery, 1979	1,512
Passing (Yds.)	Randall Cunningham, 1988	3,808
Passing (TDs)	Sonny Jurgensen, 1961	32
Receiving (No.)	Irving Fryar, 1996	88
Receiving (Yds.)	Mike Quick, 1983	1,409
Interceptions	Bill Bradley, 1971	11
Punting (Avg.)	Joe Muha, 1948	47.2
Punt Return (Avg.)	Steve Van Buren, 1944	15.3
Kickoff Return (Avg.)	Al Nelson, 1972	29.1
Field Goals	Paul McFadden, 1984	30
Touchdowns (Tot.)	Steve Van Buren, 1945	18
Points	Paul McFadden, 1984	116

INDIVIDUAL RECORDS—SINGLE GAME

Category	Name	Performance
Rushing (Yds.)	Steve Van Buren, 11-27-49	205
Passing (Yds.)	Randall Cunningham, 9-17-89	447
Passing (TDs)	Adrian Burk, 10-17-54	*7
Receiving (No.)	Don Looney, 12-1-40	14
Receiving (Yds.)	Tommy McDonald, 12-10-60	237
Interceptions	Russ Craft, 9-24-50	*4
Field Goals	Tom Dempsey, 11-12-72	6
Touchdowns (Tot.)	Many times. Last time by Irving Fryar, 10-20-96	4
Points	Bobby Walston, 10-17-54	25

*NFL Record

COACHING HISTORY

(400-479-25)

1933-35	Lud Wray	9-21-1
1936-40	Bert Bell	10-44-2
1941-50	Earle (Greasy) Neale*	66-44-5
1951	Alvin (Bo) McMillin**	2-0-0
1951	Wayne Millner	2-8-0
1952-55	Jim Trimble	25-20-3
1956-57	Hugh Devore	7-16-1
1958-60	Lawrence (Buck) Shaw	20-16-1
1961-63	Nick Skorich	15-24-3
1964-68	Joe Kuharich	28-41-1
1969-71	Jerry Williams***	7-22-2
1971-72	Ed Khayat	8-15-2
1973-75	Mike McCormack	16-25-1
1976-82	Dick Vermeil	57-51-0
1983-85	Marion Campbell****	17-29-1
1985	Fred Bruney	1-0-0
1986-90	Buddy Ryan	43-38-1
1991-94	Rich Kotite	37-29-0
1995-98	Ray Rhodes	30-36-1

*Co-coach with Walt Kiesling in Philadelphia-Pittsburgh merger in 1943
**Retired after two games in 1951
***Released after three games in 1971
****Released after 15 games in 1985

VETERANS STADIUM

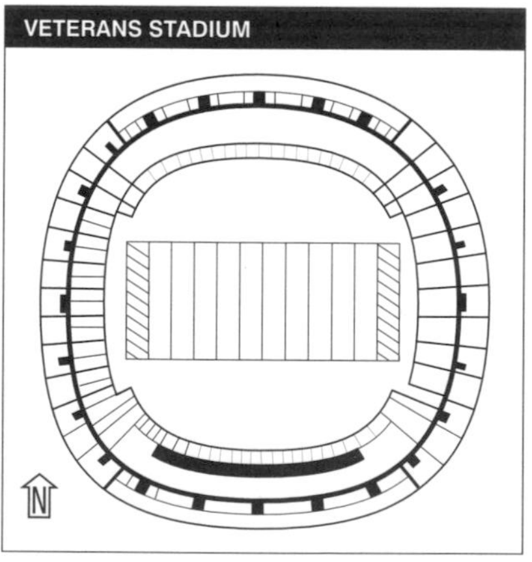

1998 TEAM RECORD

PRESEASON (1-3)

Date	Result		Opponent
8/6	L	15-29	New York Jets
8/14	W	21-17	Pittsburgh
8/24	L	6-23	at Baltimore
8/29	L	7-24	at New England

REGULAR SEASON (3-13)

Date	Result		Opponent	Att.
9/6	L	0-38	Seattle	66,418
9/13	L	12-17	at Atlanta	46,456
9/20	L	3-17	at Arizona	36,717
9/27	L	21-24	Kansas City	66,675
10/4	L	16-41	at Denver	73,218
10/11	W	17-12	Washington	66,183
10/18	L	10-13	at San Diego	56,967
11/2	L	0-34	Dallas	67,002
11/8	W	10-9	Detroit	66,785
11/15	L	3-28	at Washington	67,704
11/22	L	0-20	at New York Giants	65,763
11/29	L	16-24	at Green Bay	59,862
12/3	W	17-14	St. Louis	66,155
12/13	L	17-20	Arizona (OT)	62,176
12/20	L	9-13	at Dallas	62,722
12/27	L	10-20	New York Giants	66,596

(OT) Overtime

SCORE BY PERIODS

Eagles	33	47	24	57	0	—	161
Opponents	85	53	94	109	3	—	344

ATTENDANCE

Home 527,990 Away 469,409 Total 997,399
Single-game home record, 72,111 (11/1/81)
Single-season home record, 557,325 (1980)

1998 TEAM STATISTICS

	Eagles	Opp.
Total First Downs	259	286
Rushing	86	125
Passing	141	133
Penalty	32	28
Third Down: Made/Att	80/240	85/230
Third Down Pct.	33.3	37.0
Fourth Down: Made/Att	7/23	7/12
Fourth Down Pct.	30.4	58.3
Total Net Yards	4,188	5,136
Avg. Per Game	261.8	321.0
Total Plays	1,017	1,019
Avg. Per Play	4.1	5.0
Net Yards Rushing	1,775	2,416
Avg. Per Game	110.9	151.0
Total Rushes	427	528
Net Yards Passing	2,413	2,720
Avg. Per Game	150.8	170.0
Sacked/Yards Lost	56/317	42/281
Gross Yards	2,730	3,001
Att./Completions	534/282	449/249
Completion Pct.	52.8	55.5
Had Intercepted	18	9
Punts/Avg.	104/41.7	85/42.5
Net Punting Avg.	104/34.9	85/37.3
Penalties/Yards Lost	102/852	113/904
Fumbles/Ball Lost	20/8	20/8
Touchdowns	17	39
Rushing	10	18
Passing	7	18
Returns	0	3
Avg. Time of Possession	29:24	30:36

1998 INDIVIDUAL STATISTICS

Passing	Att.	Comp.	Yds.	Pct.	TD	Int.	Tkld.	Rate
Hoying	224	114	961	50.9	0	9	35/185	45.6
Detmer	181	97	1,011	53.6	5	5	5/29	67.7
Peete	129	71	758	55.0	2	4	16/103	64.7
Eagles	534	282	2,730	52.8	7	18	56/317	57.7
Opponents	449	249	3,001	55.5	18	9	42/281	81.2

SCORING	TD R	TD P	TD Rt	PAT	FG	Saf	PTS
Boniol	0	0	0	15/17	14/21	0	57
Staley	5	1	0	0/0	0/0	0	36
Garner	4	0	0	0/0	0/0	0	24
Fryar	0	2	0	0/0	0/0	0	12
Graham	0	2	0	0/0	0/0	0	12
Peete	1	0	0	0/0	0/0	0	6
Sinceno	0	1	0	0/0	0/0	0	6
Solomon	0	1	0	0/0	0/0	0	6
Eagles	10	7	0	15/17	14/21	1	161
Opponents	18	18	3	36/37	24/32	0	344

2-Point conversions: None.
Team 0-0, Opponents 1-2.

RUSHING	Att.	Yds.	Avg.	LG	TD
Staley	258	1,065	4.1	64t	5
Garner	96	381	4.0	40	4
Turner	20	94	4.7	19	0
Hoying	22	84	3.8	11	0
Walker	12	55	4.6	20	0
Fryar	3	46	15.3	32	0
Peete	5	30	6.0	19t	1
Detmer	7	20	2.9	8	0
Jells	2	9	4.5	13	0
Hankton	1	-4	-4.0	-4	0
Dunn	1	-5	-5.0	-5	0
Eagles	427	1,775	4.2	64t	10
Opponents	528	2,416	4.6	64	18

RECEIVING	No.	Yds.	Avg.	LG	TD
Staley	57	432	7.6	33	1
Fryar	48	556	11.6	61t	2
Graham	47	600	12.8	45	2
Turner	34	232	6.8	18	0
Solomon	21	193	9.2	20	1
Garner	19	110	5.8	21	0
Copeland	18	221	12.3	20	0
Dunn	18	132	7.3	21	0
Fontenot	8	90	11.3	19	0
Sinceno	3	42	14.0	22	1
Jells	2	53	26.5	37	0
Walker	2	35	17.5	33	0
J. Johnson	2	14	7.0	9	0
Jordan	2	9	4.5	8	0
Miller	1	11	11.0	11	0
Eagles	282	2,730	9.7	61t	7
Opponents	249	3,001	12.1	59	18

INTERCEPTIONS	No.	Yds.	Avg.	LG	TD
Dawkins	2	39	19.5	30	0
Vincent	2	29	14.5	29	0
Zordich	2	18	9.0	14	0
Caldwell	1	33	33.0	33	0
W. Thomas	1	21	21.0	21	0
McTyer	1	18	18.0	18	0
Eagles	9	158	17.6	33	0
Opponents	18	319	17.7	70t	2

PUNTING	No.	Yds.	Avg.	In 20	LG
Hutton	104	4,339	41.7	21	61
Eagles	104	4,339	41.7	21	61
Opponents	85	3,616	42.5	29	71

PUNT RETURNS	No.	FC	Yds.	Avg.	LG	TD
Rossum	22	7	187	8.5	25	0
Solomon	11	12	100	9.1	40	0
A. Harris	1	0	-2	-2.0	-2	0
Eagles	34	19	285	8.4	40	0
Opponents	61	9	511	8.4	69t	1

KICKOFF RETURNS	No.	Yds.	Avg.	LG	TD
Rossum	44	1,080	24.5	54	0
Walker	8	150	18.8	28	0
Copeland	3	52	17.3	23	0
Hayden	1	22	22.0	22	0
Staley	1	19	19.0	19	0
Hankton	1	18	18.0	18	0
Turner	1	15	15.0	15	0
Brooks	1	7	7.0	7	0
Eagles	60	1,363	22.7	54	0
Opponents	40	764	19.1	61	0

FIELD GOALS	1-19	20-29	30-39	40-49	50+
Boniol	3/3	3/3	4/5	3/9	1/1
Eagles	3/3	3/3	4/5	3/9	1/1
Opponents	0/0	7/7	6/8	11/13	0/4

SACKS	No.
Douglas	12.5
Wallace	6.0
H. Thomas	5.0
Jefferson	4.0
B. Johnson	2.5
Darling	2.0
W. Thomas	2.0
Whiting	1.5
Caldwell	1.0
Dawkins	1.0
J. Harris	1.0
Martin	1.0
Rossum	1.0
Vincent	1.0
McTyer	0.5
Eagles	42.0
Opponents	56.0

1999 DRAFT CHOICES

Round	Name	Pos.	College
1	Donovan McNabb	QB	Syracuse
2	Barry Gardner	LB	Northwestern
3	Doug Brzezinski	G	Boston College
4	John Welbourn	T	California
	Damon Moore	DB	Ohio State
	Na Brown	WR	North Carolina
6	Cecil Martin	RB	Wisconsin
	Troy Smith	WR	East Carolina
7	Jed Weaver	TE	Oregon
	Pernell Davis	DT	Alabama-Birmingham

PHILADELPHIA EAGLES

1999 VETERAN ROSTER

No.	Name	Pos.	Ht.	Wt.	Birthdate	NFL Exp.	College	Hometown	How Acq.	'98 Games/ Starts
55	Alexander, Patrise	LB	6-1	244	10/23/72	4	Southwestern Louisiana	Galveston, Tex.	FA-'99	1/0*
86	Asher, Jamie	TE	6-3	245	10/31/72	5	Louisville	Indianapolis, Ind.	UFA(Wash)-'99	9/6*
62	# Beckles, Ian	G	6-1	310	7/20/67	10	Indiana	Montreal, Que., Canada	UFA(TB)-'97	16/16
33	Bieniemy, Eric	RB	5-7	205	8/15/69	9	Colorado	LaPuente, Calif.	UFA(Cin)-'99	10/0*
18	Boniol, Chris	K	5-11	167	12/9/71	6	Louisiana Tech	Alexandria, La.	RFA(Dall)-'95	16/0
27	Bostic, James	RB	5-11	225	3/13/72	3	Auburn	Ft. Lauderdale, Fla.	FA-'98	2/0
56	Caldwell, Mike	LB	6-2	237	8/31/71	7	Middle Tennessee State	Oak Ridge, Tenn.	UFA(Ariz)-'98	16/8
66	Crafts, Jerry	T-G	6-5	334	1/6/68	6	Louisville	Tulsa, Okla.	FA-'97	1/0
26	Cunningham, T.J.	S	6-0	197	10/24/72	2	Colorado	Aurora, Col.	FA-'99	0*
57	Darling, James	LB	6-0	250	12/29/74	3	Washington State	Kettle Falls, Wash.	D2-'97	12/8
20	Dawkins, Brian	S	5-11	200	10/13/73	4	Clemson	Jacksonville, Fla.	D2b-'96	14/14
10	Detmer, Koy	QB	6-1	195	7/5/73	3	Colorado	San Antonio, Tex.	D7a-'97	8/5
53	Douglas, Hugh	LB-DE	6-2	280	8/23/71	5	Central State, Ohio	Mansfield, Ohio	T(NYJ)-'98	15/13
87	† Dunn, Jason	TE	6-4	257	11/15/73	4	Eastern Kentucky	Harrodsburg, Ky.	D2a-'96	10/10
61	Everitt, Steve	C	6-5	310	8/21/70	7	Michigan	Miami, Fla.	UFA(Balt)-'97	13/13
85	Fontenot, Chris	TE	6-3	250	7/11/74	2	McNeese State	Iota, La.	UFA(KC)-'98	5/3
63	Gaines, Wendell	G	6-5	315	1/17/72	3	Oklahoma State	Frederick, Okla.	FA-'98	0*
97	# Hall, Rhett	DT	6-2	276	12/5/68	9	California	Morgan Hill, Calif.	UFA(SF)-'95	2/0
82	Hankton, Karl	WR	6-2	202	7/24/70	3	Trinity College	Wayne, Pa.	FA-'98	10/0
31	Harris, Al	CB	6-1	185	12/7/74	2	Texas A&M-Kingsville	Pompano Beach, Fla.	W(TB)-'98	16/7
90	Harris, Jon	DE	6-7	300	6/9/74	3	Virginia	Inwood, N.Y.	D1-'97	16/4
48	Harris, Kenny	S	6-1	203	4/27/75	2	North Carolina State	Durham, N.C.	FA-'99	0*
45	Hauck, Tim	S	5-10	187	12/20/66	10	Montana	Big Timber, Mont.	UFA(Indy)-'99	16/7*
24	Hayden, Aaron	RB	6-0	216	4/13/73	5	Tennessee	Detroit, Mich.	W(GB)-'98	1/0
69	Hegamin, George	G-T	6-7	331	2/14/73	6	North Carolina State	Camden, N.J.	UFA(Dall)-'98	16/6
47	Howard, Dana	LB	6-1	244	2/25/72	4	Illinois	East St. Louis, Mo.	FA-'99	0*
7	† Hoying, Bobby	QB	6-3	221	9/20/72	4	Ohio State	St. Henry, Ohio	D3-'96	8/7
4	# Hutton, Tom	P-K	6-1	193	7/8/72	5	Tennessee	Memphis, Tenn.	FA-'95	16/0
79	Jefferson, Greg	DE	6-3	280	8/31/71	5	Central Florida	Bartow, Fla.	D3a-'95	15/14
83	Jells, Dietrich	WR	5-10	185	4/11/72	4	Pittsburgh	Erie, Pa.	T(NE)-'98	9/0
94	Johnson, Bill	DT	6-4	305	12/8/68	8	Michigan State	Chicago, Ill.	UFA(StL)-'98	13/13
81	Johnson, Charles	WR	6-0	200	1/3/72	6	Colorado	San Bernardino, Calif.	UFA(Pitt)-'99	16/16*
88	Jordan, Andrew	TE	6-4	254	6/21/72	5	Western Carolina	Charlotte, N.C.	FA-'98	3/0
6	Landeta, Sean	P	6-0	200	1/6/62	15	Towson State	Towson, Md.	UFA(GB)-'99	16/0*
28	Love, Clarence	CB	5-10	181	6/16/76	2	Toledo	Jackson, Mich.	D4b-'98	6/0
59	Mamula, Mike	LB-DE	6-4	252	8/14/73	5	Boston College	Lackawanna, N.Y.	D1-'95	0*
35	# Marshall, Anthony	S	6-1	212	9/16/70	6	Louisiana State	Mobile, Ala.	FA-'98	16/0
73	Martin, Steve	DT	6-4	303	5/31/74	4	Missouri	Jefferson City, Mo.	W(Ind)-'98	13/3*
71	Mayberry, Jermane	G-T	6-4	325	8/29/73	4	Texas A&M-Kingsville	Floresville, Tex.	D1-'96	15/10
65	Miller, Bubba	C-G	6-1	305	1/24/73	4	Tennessee	Franklin, Tenn.	FA-'96	15/4
77	Palelei, Lonnie	G	6-3	310	10/15/70	6	Nevada-Las Vegas	Blue Springs, Mo.	UFA(NYG)-'99	9/0*
14	Pederson, Doug	QB	6-3	216	1/31/68	7	Northeast Louisiana	Ferndale, Wash.	UFA(GB)-'99	12/0
39	Reed, Michael	RB	6-0	215	1/6/75	2	Washington	Tacoma, Wash.	FA-'98	4/0
58	Reese, Ike	LB	6-2	222	10/16/73	2	Michigan State	Cincinnati, Ohio	D5-'98	16/0
25	Rossum, Allen	CB-KR	5-8	178	10/22/75	2	Notre Dame	Dallas, Tex.	D3b-'98	15/2
89	Sinceno, Kaseem	TE	6-4	259	3/26/76	2	Syracuse	Liberty, N.Y.	FA-'98	10/0
80	Small, Torrance	WR	6-3	209	9/4/70	8	Alcorn State	Tampa, Fla.	UFA(Ind)-'99	16/4*
16	Smith, Eric	WR	5-11	183	9/15/71	2	Louisiana State	Vero Beach, Fla.	FA-'99	0*
22	Staley, Duce	RB	5-11	220	2/27/75	3	South Carolina	Columbia, S.C.	D3-'97	16/13
21	Taylor, Bobby	CB	6-3	216	12/28/73	5	Notre Dame	Longview, Tex.	D2a-'95	11/10
78	Thomas, Hollis	DT	6-0	306	1/10/74	4	Northern Illinois	St. Louis, Mo.	FA-'96	12/12
72	Thomas, Tra	T	6-7	349	11/20/74	2	Florida State	Deland, Fla.	D1-'98	16/16
51	Thomas, William	LB	6-2	223	8/13/68	9	Texas A&M	Amarillo, Tex.	D4-'91	16/16
54	Trotter, Jeremiah	LB	6-0	261	1/20/77	2	Stephen F. Austin	Hooks, Tex.	D3a-'98	8/0
34	Turner, Kevin	RB	6-1	231	6/12/69	8	Alabama	Prattville, Ala.	RFA(NE)-'95	16/15
68	Unutoa, Morris	C	6-1	284	3/10/71	4	Brigham Young	Carson, Calif.	FA-'96	16/0
23	Vincent, Troy	CB	6-0	194	6/8/70	8	Wisconsin	Trenton, N.J.	RFA(Mia)-'96	13/13
29	Walker, Corey	RB	5-10	188	6/4/73	3	Arkansas State	Memphis, Tenn.	FA-'97	14/0
96	Wallace, Al	DE	6-5	258	3/25/74	2	Maryland	Delray Beach, Fla.	FA-'97	15/0
91	Wheeler, Mark	DT	6-3	285	4/1/70	8	Texas A&M	San Marcos, Tex.	FA-'99	10/2*
98	Whiting, Brandon	DT	6-3	278	7/30/76	2	California	Long Beach, Calif.	D4a-'98	16/5
50	Willis, James	LB	6-2	237	9/2/72	7	Auburn	Huntsville, Ala.	FA-'95	16/16
37	Woodson, Sean	S	6-1	214	8/27/74	2	Jackson State	Jackson, Miss.	FA-'98	0*
36	# Zordich, Michael	S	6-1	212	10/12/63	13	Penn State	Youngstown, Ohio	UFA(Ariz)-'94	16/16

* Alexander played 1 game with Washington in '98; Asher played 9 games with Washington; Bieniemy played 16 games with Cincinnati; Cunningham last active with Seattle in '96; Gaines last active with Arizona in '95; K. Harris last active with Arizona in '97; Hauck played 16 games with Indianapolis; Howard last active with Chicago in '96; C. Johnson played 16 games with Pittsburgh; Landeta played 16 games with Green Bay; Mamula missed '98 season because of injury; Martin played 4 games with Indianapolis; Palelei played 9 games with N.Y. Giants; Small played 16 games witih Indianapolis; E. Smith last active with Chicago in '97; Wheeler played 10 games with New England; Woodson last active with Buffalo in '97.

Unrestricted free agent; subject to developments.

† Restricted free agent; subject to developments.

Players lost through free agency (1): T Barrett Brooks (16 games).

Also played with Eagles in '98—T Richard Cooper (15 games), WR Russell Copeland (11), LB Ray Farmer (2), WR Irving Fryar (16), RB Charlie Garner (10), WR Jeff Graham (15), DT Edward Jasper (7), TE Jimmie Johnson (3), TE Chad Lewis (2), S Tim McTyer (16), QB Rodney Peete (5), DT Henry Slay (3), WR Freddie Solomon (16), S Matt Stevens (7).

COACHING STAFF

Head Coach,
Andy Reid

Pro Career: Andy Reid became the twentieth head coach in franchise history on January 11, 1999. Reid joins the Eagles after spending the last seven seasons with the Green Bay Packers. With Green Bay, Reid helped the Packers reach the playoffs six consecutive times from 1993-98. During that span, Green Bay defeated the New England Patriots in Super Bowl XXXI and reached the NFL's title game again the following year. During the Packers' remarkable run, Reid played a significant role in helping put together that club's renowned offensive attack. Indeed, Reid put his signature on nearly every part of the Packers' offense while coaching three different positions and assisting head coach Mike Holmgren and offensive coordinator Sherman Lewis with their game-planning duties. Prior to being the quarterbacks coach in 1997-98, Reid served as the Packers' tight ends and assistant offensive line coach.

Background: Quality pass-blocking offensive lines, in both the Division I and II ranks, have been Reid's hallmark since launching his coaching career at San Francisco State in 1983. The school led the nation in passing offense and total offense for three consecutive years (1983-85) while he served as the school's offensive coordinator, offensive line coach, and strength coach. Reid moved to Northern Arizona as offensive line coach in 1986, to Texas-El Paso for two seasons (1987-88), and coached at Missouri from 1989-1991. Reid's coaching career began at his alma mater, Brigham Young, as a graduate assistant under LaVell Edwards in 1982. Reid first met Holmgren, who was a member of BYU's coaching staff, when Reid was an offensive tackle and guard on three Cougars Holiday Bowl teams. Reid went on to earn three varsity football letters, graduating with a bachelor's degree in physical education. He also received a master's degree in professional leadership in physical education and athletics.

Personal: Born in Los Angeles on March 19, 1958, Reid and his wife Tammy have five children—Garrett, Britt, Crosby, Drew Ann, and Spencer.

ASSISTANT COACHES

Tommy Brasher, defensive line; born Dec. 30, 1940, El Dorado, Ark., lives in Philadelphia. Linebacker Arkansas 1962-63. No pro playing experience. College coach: Arkansas 1970, Virginia Tech 1971, Northeast Louisiana 1974, 1976, Southern Methodist 1977-1981. Pro coach: Shreveport Steamer (WFL) 1975, New England Patriots 1982-84, Philadelphia Eagles 1985, Atlanta Falcons 1986-89, Tampa Bay Buccaneers 1990, Seattle Seahawks 1992-98, rejoined Eagles in 1999.

Juan Castillo, offensive line; born October 8, 1959, Port Isabel, Tex., lives in Moorestown, N.J. Linebacker Texas A&I (now Texas A&M-Kingsville) 1978-1980. Pro linebacker San Antonio Gunslingers (USFL) 1984-85. College coach: Texas A&M-Kingsville 1982-85, 1990-94. Pro coach: Joined Eagles in 1995.

Brad Childress, quarterbacks; born June 27, 1956, Aurora, Ill., lives in Philadelphia. Eastern Illinois 1975-78. No pro playing experience. College coach: Illinois 1978-1984, Northern Arizona 1986-89, Utah 1990, Wisconsin 1991-98. Pro coach: Indianapolis Colts 1985, joined Eagles in 1999.

Dave Culley, wide receivers; born September 17, 1955, Sparta, Tenn., lives in Philadelphia. Quarterback Vanderbilt 1973-77. No pro playing experience. College coach: Austin Peay 1978, Vanderbilt 1979-1981, Middle Tennessee State 1982, Tennessee-Chattanooga 1983, Western Kentucky 1984, Southwestern Louisiana 1985-88, Texas-El Paso 1989-1990, Texas A&M 1991-93. Pro coach: Tampa Bay Buccaneers 1994-95, Pittsburgh Steelers 1996-1998, joined Eagles in 1999.

Rod Dowhower, offensive coordinator; born April 15, 1943, Ord, Neb., lives in Philadelphia. Quarterback San Diego State 1963-65. No pro playing experience. College coach: San Diego State 1966-1972, UCLA 1974-75, Boise State 1976, Stanford 1977-79 (head coach 1979), Vanderbilt 1995-96 (head coach). Pro coach: St. Louis Cardinals 1973, 1982-84, Denver Broncos 1980-1981, Indianapolis Colts 1985-86 (head coach), Atlanta Falcons 1987-89, Washington Redskins 1990-93, New York Giants 1997-98, joined Eagles in 1999.

Leslie Frazier, defensive backs; born April 3, 1959, Columbus, Miss., lives in Philadelphia. Defensive back Alcorn State 1979-1980. Pro defensive back Chicago Bears 1981-86. College coach: Trinity (Ill.) College 1988-1996 (head coach), Illinois 1997-98. Pro coach: Joined Eagles in 1999.

John Harbaugh, special teams; born September 23, 1962, Perrysburg, Ohio, lives in Philadelphia. Defensive back Miami (Ohio) 1980-83. No pro playing experience. College coach: Western Michigan 1984-86, Pittsburgh 1987, Morehead State 1988, Cincinnati 1989-1996, Indiana 1997. Pro coach: Joined Eagles in 1998.

Jim Johnson, defensive coordinator; born May 26, 1941, Maywood, Ill., lives in Philadelphia. Quarterback Missouri 1959-1962. Pro tight end Buffalo Bills 1963-64. College coach: Missouri Southern 1967-68 (head coach), Drake 1969-1972, Indiana 1973-76, Notre Dame 1977-1980. Pro coach: Oklahoma Outlaws (USFL) 1984, Jacksonville Bulls (USFL) 1985, Phoenix Cardinals 1986-1993, Indianapolis Colts 1994-97, Seattle Seahawks 1998, joined Eagles in 1999.

Tom Melvin, offensive assistant-quality control; born October 1, 1961, Redwood City, Ca., lives in Philadelphia. Offensive lineman San Francisco State 1982-83. No pro playing experience. College coach: San Francisco State 1984-85, Northern Arizona 1986-87, California-Santa Barbara 1988-1990, Occidental College 1991-98. Pro coach: Joined Eagles in 1999.

Ron Rivera, linebackers; born January 7, 1962, Fort Ord, Calif., lives in Philadelphia. Linebacker California 1980-83. Pro linebacker Chicago Bears 1984-1992. Pro coach: Chicago Bears 1997-98, joined Eagles in 1999.

Pat Shurmur, tight ends-asst. offensive line; born April 14, 1965, Dearborn Heights, Mich., lives in Philadelphia. Center Michigan State 1983-87. No pro playing experience. College coach: Michigan State 1988-1997, Stanford 1998. Pro coach: Joined Eagles in 1999.

Steve Spagnuolo, defensive asistant-quality control; born December 21, 1959, Witinsville, Mass., lives in Philadelphia. Wide receiver Springfield College 1979-1981. No pro playing experience. College coach: Massachusetts 1982-83, Lafayette 1984-86, Connecticut 1987-1991, Maine 1993, Rutgers 1994-95, Bowling Green 1996-97. Pro coach: Barcelona Dragons (World League) 1992, Frankfurt Galaxy (NFL Europe) 1998, joined Eagles in 1999.

Ted Williams, running backs; born November 17, 1943, Lyons, Tex., lives in Siclerville, N.J. No college or pro playing experience. College coach: UCLA 1980-89, Washington State 1991-93, Arizona 1994. Pro coach: Joined Eagles in 1995.

Mike Wolf, strength and conditioning; born May 15, 1965, Allentown, Pa., lives in Marlton, N.J. Center Penn State 1983-87. No pro playing experience. College coach: Vanderbilt 1988-89, Lehigh 1990, Penn State 1991. Pro coach: Minnesota Vikings 1992-94, joined Eagles in 1995.

1999 FIRST-YEAR ROSTER

Name	Pos.	Ht.	Wt.	Birthdate	College	Hometown	How Acq.
Akers, David (1)	K	5-10	180	12/9/74	Louisville	Lexington, Ky.	FA
Bostic, Jason	CB	5-9	181	6/30/76	Georgia Tech	Lauderhill, Fla.	FA
Brown, Na	WR	6-0	187	2/22/77	North Carolina	Reidsville, N.C.	D4c
Brzezinski, Doug	G	6-4	305	3/11/76	Boston College	Detroit, Mich.	D3
Cantrell, Barry (1)	P	6-1	180	11/2/76	Fordham	Margate, Fla.	FA
Coleman, Fred (1)	WR	6-1	190	1/31/75	Washington	Tyler, Tex.	FA
Cook, Brian	G	6-6	290	4/10/76	Delaware	New Providence, N.J.	FA
Cotton, Kotto	WR	6-0	182	4/17/73	Arkansas	North Little Rock, Ark.	FA
Davis, Pernell	DT	6-2	320	5/19/76	Alabama-Birmingham	Birmingham, Ala.	D7b
Edwards, Eric	CB	5-11	180	3/6/75	Oregon	Pasco, Wash.	FA
Gardner, Barry	LB	6-0	248	12/13/76	Northwestern	Harvey, Ill.	D2
Hogg, Matt (1)	T	6-5	306	12/27/74	Youngstown State	Slippery Rock, Pa.	FA
Kacmarynski, Mark (1)	RB	6-1	230	2/2/74	Central College, Iowa	West Bend, Iowa.	FA
McKenzie, Kevin (1)	WR	5-9	187	9/20/75	Washington State	Long Beach, Ca.	FA-'98
McNabb, Donovan	QB	6-2	226	11/25/76	Syracuse	Mt. Carmel, Ill.	D1
Mallard, Deshone	CB	5-10	188	1/22/76	Southern Mississippi	Jackson, Miss.	FA
Martin, Cecil	RB	6-0	235	7/8/75	Wisconsin	Evanston, Ill.	D6a
Martino, Tony (1)	P	6-0	190	6/9/66	Kent State	Kelowna, B.C., Canada	FA
Middleton, Harvey (1)	WR	5-11	186	4/20/75	Georgia Tech	Jamestown, S.C.	FA-'98
Moore, Damon	S	5-11	215	9/15/76	Ohio State	Fostoria, Ohio	D4b
Rountree, Glenn (1)	G	6-3	304	11/24/73	Clemson	Suffolk, Va.	FA
Schau, Ryan	G	6-6	300	12/30/75	Illinois	Bloomington, Ill.	FA
Slay, Henry (1)	DT	6-2	290	4/28/75	West Virginia	Elyria, Ohio	FA-'98
Smith, Troy	WR	6-2	193	7/30/77	East Carolina	Greenville, N.C.	D6b
Spencer, Jamie	RB	6-1	245	1/21/77	Notre Dame	Monroe, La.	FA
Thomas, Melvin (1)	G	6-3	322	6/11/75	Colorado	New Orleans, La.	D7b-'98
Weaver, Jed	TE	6-4	246	8/11/76	Oregon	Redmond, Ore.	D7a
Welbourn, John	T-G	6-5	318	3/30/76	California	Palos Verdes, Calif.	D4a
Williams, Gerald	WR	6-3	197	10/7/76	Oklahoma	Decatur, Ga.	FA

The term NFL Rookie is defined as a player who is in his first season of professional football and has not been on the roster of another professional football team for any regular-season or postseason games. A Rookie is designated by an "R" on NFL rosters. Players who have been active in another professional football league or players who have NFL experience, including either preseason training camp or being on an Active List or Inactive List, or on Reserve/Injured or Reserve/Physically Unable to Perform for fewer than six regular-season games, are termed NFL First-Year Players. An NFL First-Year Player is designated by a "1" on NFL rosters. Thereafter, a player is credited with an additional year of experience for each season in which he accumulates six games on the Active List or Inactive List, or on Reserve/Injured or Reserve/Physically Unable to Perform.

NOTES

ST. LOUIS RAMS

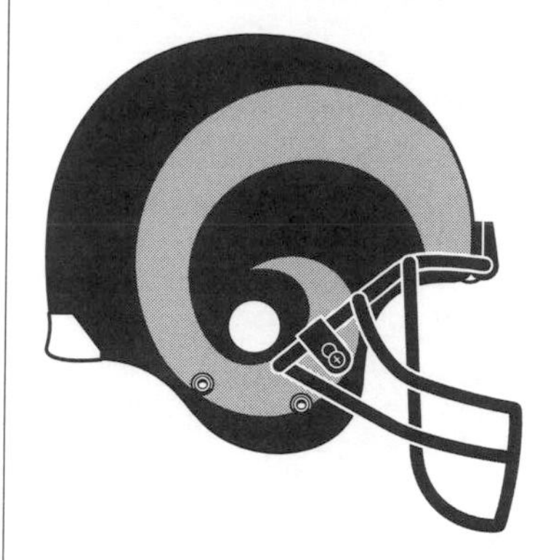

National Football Conference
Western Division
Team Colors: Royal Blue, Gold, and White
One Rams Way
St. Louis, Missouri 63045
Telephone: (314) 982-7267

CLUB OFFICIALS

Owner/Chairman: Georgia Frontiere
Owner/Vice Chairman: Stan Kroenke
President: John Shaw
President-Football Operations and Head Coach: Dick Vermeil
Executive Vice President: Jay Zygmunt
Senior Vice President-Administration and General Counsel: Bob Wallace
Treasurer: Jeff Brewer
Vice President-Finance: Adrian Barr-Bracy
Vice President-Player Personnel: Charley Armey
Vice President-Media and Community Relations: Marshall Klein
Vice President-Football Operations: Lynn Stiles
Vice President-Marketing: Phil Thomas
Vice President-Sales: Brian Ulione
Director-College Scouting: John Becker
Vice President/Player Relations and Football General Counsel: Kevin Warren
Director of Ticket Operations: Michael T. Naughton
Director of Operations: John Oswald
Director of Public Relations: Rick Smith
Assistant Director of Public Relations: Duane Lewis
Head Trainer: Jim Anderson
Assistant Trainers: Dake Walden, Ron DuBuque
Equipment Manager: Todd Hewitt
Scouts: Kevin McCabe, Lawrence McCutcheon, David Razzano, Paul Russell, Harley Sewell, Howard Tippett
Stadium: Trans World Dome at America's Center
•**Capacity:** 66,000
701 Convention Plaza
St. Louis, Missouri 63101
Playing Surface: AstroTurf
Training Camp: Western Illinois University
Thompson Hall
Macomb, Illinois 61455

1999 SCHEDULE

PRESEASON

Aug. 7	**Oakland**	7:00
Aug. 21	at Chicago	7:00
Aug. 28	**San Diego**	7:00
Sept. 2	at Detroit	7:00

REGULAR SEASON

Sept. 12	**Baltimore**	12:00
Sept. 19	Open Date	
Sept. 26	**Atlanta**	12:00
Oct. 3	at Cincinnati	1:00
Oct. 10	**San Francisco**	12:00
Oct. 17	at Atlanta	1:00
Oct. 24	**Cleveland**	12:00
Oct. 31	at Tennessee	12:00
Nov. 7	at Detroit	1:00
Nov. 14	**Carolina**	12:00
Nov. 21	at San Francisco	1:15
Nov. 28	**New Orleans**	12:00
Dec. 5	at Carolina	1:00
Dec. 12	at New Orleans	12:00
Dec. 19	**New York Giants**	12:00
Dec. 26	**Chicago**	12:00
Jan. 2	at Philadelphia	1:00

RECORD HOLDERS

INDIVIDUAL RECORDS—CAREER

Category	Name	Performance
Rushing (Yds.)	Eric Dickerson, 1983-87	7,245
Passing (Yds.)	Jim Everett, 1986-1993	23,758
Passing (TDs)	Roman Gabriel, 1962-1972	154
Receiving (No.)	Henry Ellard, 1983-1993	593
Receiving (Yds.)	Henry Ellard, 1983-1993	9,761
Interceptions	Ed Meador, 1959-1970	46
Punting (Avg.)	Danny Villanueva, 1960-64	44.2
Punt Return (Avg.)	Henry Ellard, 1983-1992	11.3
Kickoff Return (Avg.)	Tom Wilson, 1956-1961	27.1
Field Goals	Mike Lansford, 1982-1990	158
Touchdowns (Tot.)	Eric Dickerson, 1983-87	58
Points	Mike Lansford, 1982-1990	789

INDIVIDUAL RECORDS—SINGLE SEASON

Category	Name	Performance
Rushing (Yds.)	Eric Dickerson, 1984	*2,105
Passing (Yds.)	Jim Everett, 1989	4,310
Passing (TDs)	Jim Everett, 1988	31
Receiving (No.)	Isaac Bruce, 1995	119
Receiving (Yds.)	Isaac Bruce, 1995	1,781
Interceptions	Dick (Night Train) Lane, 1952	*14
Punting (Avg.)	Danny Villanueva, 1962	45.5
Punt Return (Avg.)	Woodley Lewis, 1952	18.5
Kickoff Return (Avg.)	Verda (Vitamin T) Smith, 1950	33.7
Field Goals	David Ray, 1973	30
Touchdowns (Tot.)	Eric Dickerson, 1983	20
Points	David Ray, 1973	130

INDIVIDUAL RECORDS—SINGLE GAME

Category	Name	Performance
Rushing (Yds.)	Eric Dickerson, 1-4-86	248
Passing (Yds.)	Norm Van Brocklin, 9-28-51	*554
Passing (TDs)	Many times	5
	Last time by Jim Everett, 9-25-88	
Receiving (No.)	Tom Fears, 12-3-50	*18
Receiving (Yds.)	Willie Anderson, 11-26-89	*336
Interceptions	Many times	3
	Last time by Keith Lyle, 12-15-96	
Field Goals	Bob Waterfield, 12-9-51	5
Touchdowns (Tot.)	Bob Shaw, 12-11-49	4
	Elroy (Crazylegs) Hirsch, 9-28-51	4
	Harold Jackson, 10-14-73	4
Points	Bob Shaw, 12-11-49	24
	Elroy (Crazylegs) Hirsch, 9-28-51	24
	Harold Jackson, 10-14-73	24

*NFL Record

COACHING HISTORY

Cleveland 1937-1945, Los Angeles 1946-1994
(433-411-20)

1937-38	Hugo Bezdek*	1-13-0
1938	Art Lewis	4-4-0
1939-42	Earl (Dutch) Clark	16-26-2
1944	Aldo (Buff) Donelli	4-6-0
1945-46	Adam Walsh	16-5-1
1947	Bob Snyder	6-6-0
1948-49	Clark Shaughnessy	14-8-3
1950-52	Joe Stydahar**	19-9-0
1952-54	Hamp Pool	23-11-2
1955-59	Sid Gillman	28-32-1
1960-62	Bob Waterfield***	9-24-1
1962-65	Harland Svare	14-31-3
1966-70	George Allen	49-19-4
1971-72	Tommy Prothro	14-12-2
1973-77	Chuck Knox	57-20-1
1978-82	Ray Malavasi	43-36-0
1983-91	John Robinson	79-74-0
1992-94	Chuck Knox	15-33-0
1995-96	Rich Brooks	13-19-0
1997-98	Dick Vermeil	9-23-0

*Released after three games in 1938
**Resigned after one game in 1952
***Resigned after eight games in 1962

TRANS WORLD DOME

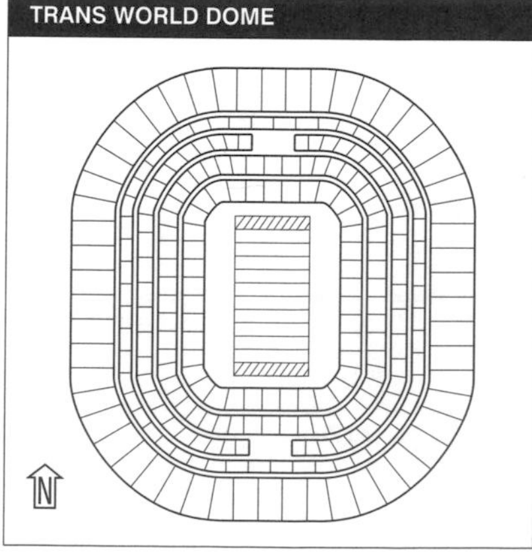

1998 TEAM RECORD

PRESEASON (2-2)

Date	Result		Opponent
8/8	L	13-20	Denver
8/15	L	27-41	at San Diego
8/22	W	22-14	Dallas
8/28	W	10-6	at Kansas City

REGULAR SEASON (4-12)

Date	Result		Opponent	Att.
9/6	L	17-24	New Orleans	56,943
9/13	L	31-38	Minnesota	56,234
9/20	W	34-33	at Buffalo	65,199
9/27	L	17-20	Arizona	55,832
10/11	W	30-10	New York Jets	55,938
10/18	L	0-14	at Miami	65,418
10/25	L	10-28	San Francisco	58,563
11/1	L	15-37	at Atlanta	37,996
11/8	W	20-12	at Chicago	50,263
11/15	L	3-24	at New Orleans	46,430
11/22	L	20-24	Carolina	50,716
11/29	L	10-21	Atlanta	47,971
12/3	L	14-17	at Philadelphia	66,155
12/13	W	32-18	New England	48,946
12/20	L	13-20	at Carolina	50,047
12/27	L	19-38	at San Francisco	68,386

SCORE BY PERIODS

Rams	37	91	72	85	0	—	285
Opponents	116	107	80	75	0	—	378

ATTENDANCE

Home 431,143 Away 449,894 Total 881,037
Single-game home record, 66,030 (12/14/97)
Single-season home record, 518,468 (1997)

1998 TEAM STATISTICS

	Rams	Opp.
Total First Downs	281	282
Rushing	81	92
Passing	164	161
Penalty	36	29
Third Down: Made/Att	77/222	83/221
Third Down Pct.	34.7	37.6
Fourth Down: Made/Att	9/16	3/9
Fourth Down Pct.	56.3	33.3
Total Net Yards	4,472	4,880
Avg. Per Game	279.5	305.0
Total Plays	998	1,004
Avg. Per Play	4.5	4.9
Net Yards Rushing	1,385	2,049
Avg. Per Game	86.6	128.1
Total Rushes	395	479
Net Yards Passing	3,087	2,831
Avg. Per Game	192.9	176.9
Sacked/Yards Lost	47/294	50/349
Gross Yards	3,381	3,180
Att./Completions	556/314	475/256
Completion Pct.	56.5	53.9
Had Intercepted	18	16
Punts/Avg.	95/44.2	92/41.6
Net Punting Avg.	95/35.3	92/35.8
Penalties/Yards Lost	111/945	112/915
Fumbles/Ball Lost	32/15	16/7
Touchdowns	32	43
Rushing	17	11
Passing	12	28
Returns	3	4
Avg. Time of Possession	28:59	31:01

1998 INDIVIDUAL STATISTICS

Passing	Att.	Comp.	Yds.	Pct.	TD	Int.	Tkld.	Rate
Banks	408	241	2,535	59.1	7	14	41/237	68.6
Bono	136	69	807	50.7	5	4	6/57	69.1
Warner	11	4	39	36.4	0	0	0/0	47.2
Tuten	1	0	0	0.0	0	0	0/0	39.6
Rams	556	314	3,381	56.5	12	18	47/294	68.2
Opponents	475	256	3,180	53.9	28	16	50/349	80.5

SCORING	TD R	TD P	TD Rt	PAT	FG	Saf	PTS
Wilkins	0	0	0	25/26	20/26	0	85
Lee	2	2	0	0/0	0/0	0	26
G. Hill	4	0	0	0/0	0/0	0	24
Banks	3	0	0	0/0	0/0	0	20
Proehl	0	3	0	0/0	0/0	0	20
Henley	3	0	0	0/0	0/0	0	18
Hakim	1	1	0	0/0	0/0	0	12
Harris	0	2	0	0/0	0/0	0	12
Holcombe	2	0	0	0/0	0/0	0	12
Kennison	0	1	1	0/0	0/0	0	12
Moore	2	0	0	0/0	0/0	0	12
Bruce	0	1	0	0/0	0/0	0	6
Horne	0	0	1	0/0	0/0	0	6
McNeil	0	0	1	0/0	0/0	0	6
Robinson	0	1	0	0/0	0/0	0	6
R. Williams	0	1	0	0/0	0/0	0	6
Bono	0	0	0	0/0	0/0	0	2
Rams	17	12	3	25/26	20/26	0	285
Opponents	11	28	4	40/40	24/27	2	378

2-Point conversions: Banks, Bono, Lee, Proehl. Team 4-6, Opponents 2-3.

RUSHING	Att.	Yds.	Avg.	LG	TD
Henley	88	313	3.6	22	3
G. Hill	40	240	6.0	46	4
Holcombe	98	230	2.3	12	2
Lee	44	175	4.0	38	2
Banks	40	156	3.9	19	3
Moore	55	137	2.5	18	2
Harris	14	38	2.7	15	0
Bruce	1	30	30.0	30	0
Hakim	2	30	15.0	34t	1
Proehl	1	14	14.0	14	0
Bono	10	13	1.3	7	0
Kennison	2	9	4.5	9	0
Rams	395	1,385	3.5	46	17
Opponents	479	2,049	4.3	74t	11

RECEIVING	No.	Yds.	Avg.	LG	TD
Lee	64	667	10.4	44	2
Proehl	60	771	12.9	47	3
Henley	35	252	7.2	43	0
Bruce	32	457	14.3	80t	1
Thomas	20	287	14.4	42	0
Hakim	20	247	12.4	22	1
Kennison	17	234	13.8	45	1
R. Williams	15	144	9.6	33	1
Conwell	15	105	7.0	13	0
Harris	12	57	4.8	8	2
Moore	9	60	6.7	14	0
Armstrong	6	54	9.0	20	0
Holcombe	6	34	5.7	14	0
G. Hill	1	6	6.0	6	0
Robinson	1	4	4.0	4t	1
Flannery	1	2	2.0	2	0
Rams	314	3,381	10.8	80t	12
Opponents	256	3,180	12.4	68t	28

INTERCEPTIONS	No.	Yds.	Avg.	LG	TD
Lyght	3	30	10.0	17	0
Lyle	3	20	6.7	20	0
Jenkins	2	31	15.5	25	0
McCleon	2	29	14.5	15	0
Mike A. Jones	2	13	6.5	13	0
Phifer	1	41	41.0	41	0
McNeil	1	37	37.0	37t	1
Agnew	1	0	0.0	0	0
E. Hill	1	0	0.0	0	0
Rams	16	201	12.6	41	1
Opponents	18	194	10.8	32t	1

PUNTING	No.	Yds.	Avg.	In 20	LG
Tuten	95	4,202	44.2	16	64
Rams	95	4,202	44.2	16	64
Opponents	92	3,825	41.6	24	66

PUNT RETURNS	No.	FC	Yds.	Avg.	LG	TD
Kennison	40	25	415	10.4	71t	1
Horne	1	0	0	0.0	0	0
Rams	41	25	415	10.1	71t	1
Opponents	58	15	652	11.2	72t	1

KICKOFF RETURNS	No.	Yds.	Avg.	LG	TD
Horne	56	1,306	23.3	102t	1
Fletcher	5	72	14.4	20	0
Thomas	4	79	19.8	24	0
Henley	1	13	13.0	13	0
Mike D. Jones	1	2	2.0	2	0
Clemons	1	0	0.0	0	0
Rams	68	1,472	21.6	102t	1
Opponents	47	1,020	21.7	55	0

FIELD GOALS	1-19	20-29	30-39	40-49	50+
Wilkins	0/0	4/5	8/8	5/7	3/6
Rams	0/0	4/5	8/8	5/7	3/6
Opponents	1/1	8/9	8/8	4/6	3/3

SACKS	No.
Carter	12.0
Farr	7.0
Phifer	6.5
Agnew	5.0
Jenkins	3.0
Mike A. Jones	3.0
Wistrom	3.0
Mike D. Jones	2.5
Clemons	2.0
Lyght	1.5
E. Hill	1.0
Lyle	1.0
J. Williams	1.0
Wright	1.0
Little	0.5
Rams	50.0
Opponents	47.0

1999 DRAFT CHOICES

Round	Name	Pos.	College
1	Torry Holt	WR	North Carolina State
2	Dre' Bly	DB	North Carolina
3	Richard Coady	DB	Texas A&M
4	Joe Germaine	QB	Ohio State
5	Cameron Spikes	G	Texas A&M
6	Lionel Barnes	DE	Northeast Louisiana
7	Rodney Williams	P	Georgia Tech

ST. LOUIS RAMS

1999 VETERAN ROSTER

No.	Name	Pos.	Ht.	Wt.	Birthdate	NFL Exp.	College	Hometown	How Acq.	'98 Games/ Starts
99	Agnew, Ray	DT	6-3	285	12/9/67	10	North Carolina State	Winston-Salem, N.C.	UFA(NYG)-'98	16/12
20	Allen, Taje	CB	5-10	185	11/6/73	3	Texas	Lubbock, Tex.	D5-'97	16/0
77	Brooks, Ethan	G-T	6-6	299	4/27/72	4	Williams	Simsbury, Conn.	FA-'97	15/0
80	Bruce, Isaac	WR	6-0	188	11/10/72	6	Memphis	Ft. Lauderdale, Fla.	D2a-'94	5/5
23	Bush, Devin	S	5-11	210	7/3/73	5	Florida State	Miami, Fla.	UFA(Atl)-'99	13/0*
24	Carpenter, Ron	S	6-1	188	1/20/70	3	Miami, Ohio	Cincinnati, Ohio	FA-'98	6/0
93	Carter, Kevin	DE	6-5	280	9/21/73	5	Florida	Tallahassee, Fla.	D1-'95	16/16
69	Chanoine, Roger	T	6-4	295	9/11/76	2	Temple	Linden, N.J.	FA-'98	0*
56	Clemons, Charlie	LB	6-2	255	7/4/72	3	Georgia	Griffin, Ga.	FA-'97	16/0
54	Collins, Todd	LB	6-2	248	5/27/70	7	Carson-Newman	New Market, Tenn.	UFA(NE)-'99	12/10*
84	Conwell, Ernie	TE	6-1	265	8/17/72	4	Washington	Kent, Wash.	D2b-'96	7/7
75	Farr, D'Marco	DT	6-1	280	6/9/71	6	Washington	Richmond, Calif.	FA-'94	16/16
28	t- Faulk, Marshall	RB	5-10	211	2/26/73	6	San Diego State	New Orleans, La.	T(Ind)-'99	16/15*
63	Flannery, John	C	6-3	304	1/13/69	8	Syracuse	Pottsville, Pa.	UFA (Dall)-'98	16/16
59	Fletcher, London	LB	6-0	241	5/19/75	2	John Carroll	Cleveland, Ohio	FA-'98	16/1
10	Green, Trent	QB	6-3	215	7/9/70	6	Indiana	St. Louis, Mo.	UFA(Wash)-'99	15/14*
60	† Gruttadauria, Mike	C	6-3	297	12/6/72	4	Central Florida	Tarpon Springs, Fla.	FA-'96	11/2
81	Hakim, Az-Zahir	WR	5-10	178	6/3/77	2	San Diego State	Los Angeles, Calif.	D4a-'98	9/4
33	† Harris, Derrick	RB	6-0	252	9/18/72	4	Miami	Angleton, Tex.	D6a-'96	16/14
26	Henley, June	RB	5-10	226	9/4/75	2	Kansas	Columbus, Ohio	FA-'97	11/3
55	Hesse, Jon	LB	6-3	247	6/6/73	2	Nebraska	Lincoln, Neb.	FA-'98	6/0
39	Hiles, Van	S	6-0	198	11/1/75	2	Kentucky	Baton Rouge, La.	FA-'99	0*
27	Hill, Greg	RB	5-11	212	2/23/72	6	Texas A&M	Dallas, Tex.	UFA(KC)-'98	2/2
25	Holcombe, Robert	RB	5-11	220	12/11/75	2	Illinois	Mesa, Ariz.	D2-'98	13/6
82	Horne, Tony	WR	5-9	173	3/21/76	2	Clemson	Rockingham, N.C.	FA-'98	16/0
46	Jacoby, Mitch	TE	6-4	260	12/8/73	3	Northern Illinois	Fredonia, Wis.	FA-'98	5/0
22	Jenkins, Billy	S	5-10	205	7/8/74	3	Howard	Albuquerque, N.M.	FA-'97	16/13
52	Jones, Mike	LB	6-1	240	4/15/69	9	Missouri	Kansas City, Mo.	UFA(Oak)-'97	16/15
31	Lee, Amp	RB	5-11	200	10/1/71	8	Florida State	Chipley, Fla.	FA-'97	14/2
34	Levitt, Chad	RB	6-1	242	11/21/75	2	Cornell	Wyncote, Pa.	FA-'99	0*
49	Lewis, Chad	TE	6-6	252	10/5/71	2	Brigham Young	Orem, Utah	FA-'98	2/0*
41	Lyght, Todd	CB	6-0	190	2/9/69	9	Notre Dame	Flint, Mich.	D1-'91	16/16
35	Lyle, Keith	S	6-2	210	4/17/72	6	Virginia	Vienna, Va.	D3a-'94	16/16
21	McCleon, Dexter	CB	5-10	200	10/9/73	3	Clemson	Meridian, Miss.	D2-'97	15/6
64	McCollum, Andy	G	6-4	295	6/2/70	6	Toledo	Akron, Ohio	UFA(NO)-'99	16/5*
73	† Miller, Fred	T	6-7	315	2/6/73	4	Baylor	Houston, Tex.	D5-'96	15/15
61	Nutten, Tom	G	6-4	285	6/8/71	3	Western Michigan	Magog, Quebec, Canada	FA-'98	5/2
76	Pace, Orlando	T	6-7	320	11/4/75	3	Ohio State	Sandusky, Ohio	D1-'97	16/16
87	Proehl, Ricky	WR	6-0	190	3/7/68	10	Wake Forest	Hillsborough, N.J.	UFA(Chi)-'98	16/11
94	Robinson, Jeff	DE	6-4	275	2/20/70	7	Idaho	Spokane, Wash.	UFA(Den)-'97	16/0
95	Sears, Corey	DT	6-2	293	4/15/73	2	Mississippi State	Converse, Tex.	FA-'98	4/0
51	Styles, Lorenzo	LB	6-1	245	1/31/74	5	Ohio State	Columbus, Ohio	FA-'97	7/3
83	# Thomas, J.T.	WR	5-10	180	7/11/71	5	Arizona State	San Bernardino, Calif.	D7d-'95	16/0
30	Thompson, David	RB	5-8	200	1/13/75	3	Oklahoma State	Okmulgee, Okla.	FA-'97	1/0
62	Timmerman, Adam	G	6-4	300	8/14/71	5	South Dakota State	Cherokee, Iowa	UFA(GB)-'99	16/16*
50	Tucker, Ryan	C	6-5	305	6/12/75	3	Texas Christian	Midland, Tex.	D4-'97	5/0
11	Tuten, Rick	P	6-2	221	1/5/65	10	Florida State	Ocala, Fla.	UFA(Sea)-'98	16/0
67	Verstegen, Mike	G	6-6	311	10/24/71	4	Wisconsin	Appleton, Wis.	FA-'99	0*
13	Warner, Kurt	QB	6-2	220	6/22/71	2	Northern Iowa	Burlington, Iowa	FA-'98	1/0
14	Wilkins, Jeff	K	6-2	205	4/19/72	6	Youngstown State	Austintown, Ohio	RFA(SF)-'97	16/0
96	Williams, Jay	DE	6-3	280	10/13/71	4	Wake Forest	Washington, D.C.	FA-'96	16/1
86	Williams, Roland	TE	6-5	269	4/27/75	2	Syracuse	Rochester, N.Y.	D4b-'98	13/9
98	Wistrom, Grant	DE	6-4	267	7/3/76	2	Nebraska	Webb City, Mo.	D1-'98	13/0
32	Wright, Toby	S	5-11	212	11/19/70	6	Nebraska	Phoenix, Ariz.	D2b-'94	3/3
90	Zgonina, Jeff	DT	6-2	300	5/24/70	6	Purdue	Chicago, Ill.	UFA(Ind)-'99	2/0*

* Bush played 13 games with Atlanta in '98; Chanoine missed '98 season because of injury; Collins played 12 games for New England; Faulk played 16 games for Indianapolis; Green played 15 games for Washington; Hiles last active with Chicago in '97; Levitt last active with Oakland in '97; Lewis played 2 games with Philadelphia; McCollum played 16 games with New Orleans; Timmerman played 16 games with Green Bay; Verstegen last active with New Orleans in '97; Zgonina played 2 games with Indianapolis.

\# Unrestricted free agents; subject to developments.

† Restricted free agents; subject to developments.

t- Rams traded for Faulk (Indianapolis).

Traded—QB Tony Banks (14 games in '98) to Baltimore; WR Eddie Kennison (16) to New Orleans.

Players lost through free agency (5): QB Steve Bono (Car; 6 games in '98), DE Mike A. Jones (Tenn; 16), S Gerald McBurrows (Atl; 10), LB Roman Phifer (NYJ; 13), S Mike Scurlock (Car; 16).

Also played with Rams in '98—TE Tyji Armstrong (12 games), T Wayne Gandy (16), LB Eric Hill (15), LB Leonard Little (6), CB Ryan McNeil (16), RB Jerald Moore (11), DT Joe Phillips (13), LB Phillip Ward (2), G Zach Wiegert (13), DE Jay Williams (1).

COACHING STAFF

Head Coach,
Dick Vermeil

Pro Career: Named twentieth head coach of the Rams on January 22, 1997. Was designated the first special teams coach in NFL history in 1969 for the Los Angeles Rams. After one year of coaching in college, he returned to the Rams as the quarterbacks coach from 1971-73. In 1976, he was named head coach of the Philadelphia Eagles. In 1978, he led the Eagles to their first playoff appearance in eighteen seasons. In 1980, he led the Eagles to Super Bowl XV before losing to the Oakland Raiders. He concluded his stint in Philadelphia in 1982 after piloting the Eagles to four playoff appearances in seven seasons. Career record: 66-74.

Background: Played quarterback at San Jose State from 1956-57 after transferring from Napa Junior College. Began his head coaching career in 1959 at Delmar High School in San Jose, California. He became head coach at Hillsdale High School in San Mateo, California, then moved to College of San Mateo in 1963. The following year he became head coach at Napa College. He was at Stanford for four years beginning in 1965. Became the offensive coordinator at UCLA in 1970, and was named head coach at UCLA in 1974. In 1975, the Bruins capped off an improbable season by upsetting top-ranked Ohio State in the Rose Bowl. Has been named coach of the year on four levels: high school, junior college, Division I, and NFL. Is the only coach who has guided his team to a Super Bowl and a Rose Bowl.

Personal: Born October 30, 1936, in Calistoga, Calif. Graduated from San Jose State with a bachelor of science degree in physical education (1958) and with a master's degree in physical education (1959). Vermeil and his wife, Carol, reside in St. Charles, Mo., and have three children and ten grandchildren.

ASSISTANT COACHES

Steve Brown, secondary; born March 20, 1960, Sacramento, Calif., lives in Wildhorse, Mo. Defensive back Oregon 1978-1982. Pro cornerback Houston Oilers 1983-1990. Pro coach: Joined Rams in 1995.

John Bunting, defensive coordinator; born July 15, 1950, Portland, Maine, lives in St. Louis. Linebacker North Carolina 1968-1971. Pro linebacker Philadelphia Eagles 1972-1982, Philadelphia Stars (USFL) 1983-84. College coach: Brown 1986, Rowan College 1987-1992 (head coach 1988-1992). Pro coach: Baltimore Stars (USFL) 1985, Kansas City Chiefs 1993-96, joined Rams in 1997.

Chris Clausen, strength and conditioning coordinator; born February 21, 1958, Evergreen Park, Ill., lives in St. Louis. Cornerback Indiana 1976-79. No pro playing experience. College coach: San Diego State 1987-88. Pro coach: San Diego Chargers 1989-1991, joined Rams in 1992.

Frank Gansz, special teams-offensive assistant; born November 22, 1938, Altoona, Pa., lives in Chesterfield, Mo. Guard-linebacker Navy 1957-59. No pro playing experience. College coach: Air Force 1964-66, Colgate 1968, Navy 1969-1972, Oklahoma State 1973, 1975, Army 1974, UCLA 1976-77. Pro coach: San Francisco 49ers 1978, Cincinnati Bengals 1979-1980, Kansas City Chiefs 1981-82, 1986-88 (head coach 1987-88), Philadelphia Eagles 1983-85, Detroit Lions 1989-1993, Atlanta Falcons 1994-96, joined Rams in 1997.

Peter Giunta, asst. head coach-defensive coordinator; born August 11, 1956, Salem, Mass., lives in Chesterfield, Mo. Running back-defensive back Northeastern 1974-77. No pro playing experience. College coach: Penn State 1981-83, Brown 1984-87, Lehigh 1988-1990. Pro coach: Philadelphia Eagles 1991-94, New York Jets 1995-96, joined Rams in 1997.

Carl Hairston, defensive line; born December 15, 1952, Martinsville, Va., lives in Chesterfield, Mo. Defensive end Maryland-Eastern Shore 1972-75. Pro defensive end Philadelphia Eagles 1976-1983, Cleveland Browns 1984-89, Phoenix Cardinals 1990. Pro coach: Kansas City Chiefs 1995-96, joined Rams in 1997.

Jim Hanifan, offensive line; born September 21, 1933, Compton, Calif., lives in St. Charles, Mo. Tight end California 1952-54. Pro tight end Toronto Argonauts (USFL) 1955. College coach: Yuba City J.C. (Calif.) 1959-1961, Glendale J.C. (Calif.) 1964-65, Utah 1966-69, California 1970-71, San Diego State 1972. Pro coach: St. Louis Cardinals 1973-78, 1980-85 (head coach), San Diego Chargers 1979, Atlanta Falcons 1987-89, Washington Redskins 1990-96, joined Rams in 1997.

Todd Howard, defensive assistant; born February 18, 1965, Bryan, Tex., lives in St. Louis. Linebacker Texas A&M 1983-86. Pro linebacker Kansas City Chiefs 1987-88, Barcelona Dragons (WLAF) 1991-92. College coach: Texas A&M 1991-93, Grinnell (Iowa) 1994-97. Pro coach: Joined Rams in 1998.

Dana LeDuc, strength and conditioning, born March 22, 1953, Tacoma, Wash., lives in St. Charles, Mo. No college or pro playing experience. College coach: Texas 1977-1992, Miami 1993-94. Pro coach: Seattle Seahawks 1995-98, joined Rams in 1999.

Mike Martz, offensive coordinator; born May 13, 1951, Sioux Falls, S.D, lives in Wildwood, Mo. No college or pro playing experience. College coach: San Diego Mesa 1974, 1976-77, San Jose State 1975, Santa Ana College 1978, Fresno State 1979, Pacific 1980-81, Arizona State 1983-1991. Pro coach: Los Angeles/St. Louis Rams 1992-96, Washington Redskins 1997-98, rejoined Rams 1999.

John Matsko, offensive line; born February 2, 1951, Cleveland, lives in Lake St. Louis, Mo. Fullback Kent State 1970-73. No pro playing experience. College coach Kent State 1973, Miami (Ohio) 1974-75, 1977, North Carolina 1978-1984, Navy 1985, Arizona 1986, Southern California 1987-1991. Pro coach: Phoenix Cardinals 1992-93, New Orleans Saints 1994-96, New York Giants 1997-98, joined Rams in 1999.

Wilbert Montgomery, running backs; born September 16, 1954, Greenville, Miss., lives in Chesterfield, Mo. Running back Abilene Christian 1973-76. Pro running back Philadelphia Eagles 1977-1984, Detroit Lions 1985-86. Pro coach: Joined Rams in 1997.

John Ramsdell, quarterbacks; born August 16, 1954, Lafayette, Ind., lives in Chesterfield, Mo. Running back Springfield (Mass.) College 1972-75. No pro playing experience. College coach: San Francisco State 1976-77, Long Beach State 1978, Pacific 1979-1982, Oregon 1983-1994. Pro coach: Joined Rams in 1995.

Al Saunders, receivers, born February 1, 1947, London, England, lives in St. Louis. Defensive back San Jose State 1966-68. No pro playing experience. College coach: Southern California 1970-71, Missouri 1972, Utah State 1973-75, California 1976-1981, Tennessee 1982. Pro coach San Diego Chargers 1983-88 (head coach 1986-88), Kansas City Chiefs 1989-1998, joined Rams in 1999.

Lynn Stiles, vice president football operations-tight ends; born April 12, 1941, Kermit, Tex., lives in Chesterfield, Mo. Guard Utah 1960-62. No pro playing experience. College coach: Utah 1963-65, Iowa 1966-1970, UCLA 1971-75, San Jose State 1976-78 (head coach). Pro coach: Philadelphia Eagles 1979-1981, San Francisco 49ers 1987-1991, joined Rams in 1997.

Mike White, asst. head coach; born January 4, 1936, Berkeley, Calif., lives in Clayton, Mo. Wide receiver California 1955-57. No pro playing experience. College coach: California 1958-1963, 1972-1977 (head coach 1972-77), Stanford 1964-1971, Illinois 1980-87 (head coach). Pro coach: San Francisco 49ers 1978-79, Los Angeles-Oakland Raiders 1990-96 (head coach 1995-96), joined Rams in 1997.

1999 FIRST-YEAR ROSTER

Name	Pos.	Ht.	Wt.	Birthdate	College	Hometown	How Acq.
Barnes, Lionel	DE	6-4	264	4/19/76	Northeast Lousiana	Suffolk, England	D6
Bly, Dre'	CB	5-9	197	5/22/77	North Carolina	Chesapeake, Va.	D2
Chatham, Matt	LB	6-4	242	6/28/77	South Dakota	Sioux City, Iowa	FA
Coady, Rich	S	6-0	203	1/26/76	Texas A&M	Dallas, Tex.	D3
Cody, Mac (1)	WR	5-11	182	8/7/72	Memphis	St. Louis, Mo.	FA
Copeland, Jeremaine	WR	6-1	200	2/19/77	Tennessee	Harriman, Tenn.	FA
Crosby, Clifton	CB	5-9	172	9/17/74	Maryland	Erie, Pa.	FA
Frohbieter, Todd	LB	6-2	248	3/7/75	Arkansas State	Richardson, Tex.	FA
Germaine, Joe	QB	6-0	203	8/11/75	Ohio State	Mesa, Ariz.	D4
Hodgins, James	RB	5-11	230	4/30/77	San Jose State	San Jose, Calif.	FA
Holt, Torry	WR	6-0	190	6/5/76	North Carolina State	Greensboro, N.C.	D1
Jones, Daniel	WR	5-10	185	10/18/76	Utah	Blythe, Calif.	FA
Jones, Willie	T	6-6	372	12/17/75	Grambling State	Belle Glade, Fla.	FA
Knox, Kevin (1)	WR	6-2	194	1/30/71	Florida State	Niceville, Fla.	FA
Lewis, Derek	TE	6-1	250	4/2/77	Texas	New Orleans, La.	FA
Love, Marvin	CB	5-8	167	12/2/75	Kentucky	Oakland, Calif.	FA
McKinney, Jeremy (1)	G-T	6-5	301	1/6/76	Iowa	Brighton, Colo.	FA
Munch, John (1)	LB	6-3	218	1/7/76	Illinois Wesleyan	Genoa, Ill.	FA
Ornstein, Gus	QB	6-3	218	11/23/74	Rowan College	Tenafly, N.J.	FA
Pelshak, Troy	LB	6-2	242	3/6/77	North Carolina A&T	Charlotte, N.C.	FA
Rowe, Joe (1)	CB	6-0	195	12/8/73	Virginia	Emporia, Va.	FA
Sellers, Donald (1)	WR	6-0	195	12/30/74	New Mexico	Birmingham, Ala.	FA
Singh, Bobby	G	6-2	316	11/21/75	Portland State	Richmond, B.C., Canada	FA
Small, Tony	WR	6-1	220	4/26/77	Georgia	Jacksonville, Fla.	FA
Smith, Robert	LB	6-4	240	11/14/74	Cumberland College	Sumpter, S.C.	FA
Spikes, Cameron	G	6-2	310	11/6/76	Texas A&M	Bryan, Tex.	D5
Troy, Damon	CB	6-1	203	8/27/76	Rowan	Whitesboro, N.J.	FA
Ward, Phillip (1)	LB	6-3	235	11/11/74	UCLA	Compton, Calif.	FA
Weaver, Alton	DT	6-3	296	10/2/75	Oklahoma State	Houston, Tex.	FA
Williams, Rodney	P	6-0	189	4/25/77	Georgia Tech	Decatur, Ga.	D7
Wofford, Steve	RB	5-10	180	1/12/77	Southern	Bakersfield, Calif.	FA
Young, Glenn (1)	DE	6-3	251	9/10/75	Vanderbilt	Detroit, Mich.	FA

The term NFL Rookie is defined as a player who is in his first season of professional football and has not been on the roster of another professional football team for any regular-season or postseason games. A Rookie is designated by an "R" on NFL rosters. Players who have been active in another professional football league or players who have NFL experience, including either preseason training camp or being on an Active List or Inactive List, or on Reserve/Injured or Reserve/Physically Unable to Perform for fewer than six regular-season games, are termed NFL First-Year Players. An NFL First-Year Player is designated by a "1" on NFL rosters. Thereafter, a player is credited with an additional year of experience for each season in which he accumulates six games on the Active List or Inactive List, or on Reserve/Injured or Reserve/Physically Unable to Perform.

NOTES

SAN FRANCISCO 49ERS

National Football Conference
Western Division
Team Colors: Forty Niners Gold and Cardinal
4949 Centennial Boulevard
Santa Clara, California 95054
Telephone: (408) 562-4949

CLUB OFFICIALS

Vice President: Dr. John York
Vice President/General Manager: Bill Walsh
Vice President/CFO: Keith Lenhart
Vice President/Director of Football Administration: John McVay
Vice President/Director of 49ers Foundation: Lisa DeBartolo
Director of Player Personnel: Terry Donahue
Pro Personnel Director: Bill McPherson
Director of Communications and Marketing: Rodney Knox
Director of Public Relations: Kirk Reynolds
Ticket Manager: Lynn Carrozzi
Director of Stadium Operations: Murlan (Mo) Fowell
Video Director: Robert Yanagi
Trainer: Lindsy McLean
Equipment Manager: Kevin Lartigue
Stadium: 3Com Park • **Capacity:** 70,140
San Francisco, California 94124
Playing Surface: Grass
Training Camp: University of the Pacific
Stockton, California 95211

1999 SCHEDULE

PRESEASON

Aug. 12	**San Diego**	5:00
Aug. 19	**Seattle**	5:00
Aug. 30	at Oakland	5:00
Sept. 3	at Denver	7:00

REGULAR SEASON

Sept. 12	at Jacksonville	4:15
Sept. 19	**New Orleans**	1:05
Sept. 27	at Arizona (Mon.)	6:00
Oct. 3	**Tennessee**	1:15
Oct. 10	at St. Louis	12:00
Oct. 17	**Carolina**	1:15
Oct. 24	at Minnesota	12:00
Oct. 31	Open Date	
Nov. 7	**Pittsburgh**	1:15
Nov. 14	at New Orleans	12:00
Nov. 21	**St. Louis**	1:15
Nov. 29	**Green Bay** (Mon.)	6:00
Dec. 5	at Cincinnati	1:00
Dec. 12	**Atlanta**	1:15
Dec. 18	at Carolina (Sat.)	4:15
Dec. 26	**Washington**	5:20
Jan. 3	at Atlanta (Mon.)	9:00

RECORD HOLDERS

INDIVIDUAL RECORDS—CAREER

Category	Name	Performance
Rushing (Yds.)	Joe Perry, 1950-1960, 1963	7,344
Passing (Yds.)	Joe Montana, 1979-1992	35,124
Passing (TDs)	Joe Montana, 1979-1992	244
Receiving (No.)	Jerry Rice, 1985-1998	*1,139
Receiving (Yds.)	Jerry Rice, 1985-1998	*17,612
Interceptions	Ronnie Lott, 1981-1990	51
Punting (Avg.)	Tommy Davis, 1959-1969	44.7
Punt Return (Avg.)	Dana McLemore, 1982-87	10.8
Kickoff Return (Avg.)	Abe Woodson, 1958-1964	29.4
Field Goals	Ray Wersching, 1977-1987	190
Touchdowns (Tot.)	Jerry Rice, 1985-1998	*175
Points	Jerry Rice, 1985-1998	1,058

INDIVIDUAL RECORDS—SINGLE SEASON

Category	Name	Performance
Rushing (Yds.)	Roger Craig, 1988	1,502
Passing (Yds.)	Steve Young, 1998	4,170
Passing (TDs)	Steve Young, 1998	36
Receiving (No.)	Jerry Rice, 1995	122
Receiving (Yds.)	Jerry Rice, 1995	*1,848
Interceptions	Dave Baker, 1960	10
	Ronnie Lott, 1986	10
Punting (Avg.)	Tommy Davis, 1965	45.8
Punt Return (Avg.)	Dana McLemore, 1982	22.3
Kickoff Return (Avg.)	Joe Arenas, 1953	34.4
Field Goals	Jeff Wilkins, 1996	30
Touchdowns (Tot.)	Jerry Rice, 1987	23
Points	Jerry Rice, 1987	138

INDIVIDUAL RECORDS—SINGLE GAME

Category	Name	Performance
Rushing (Yds.)	Garrison Hearst, 12-14-98	198
Passing (Yds.)	Joe Montana, 10-14-90	476
Passing (TDs)	Joe Montana, 10-14-90	6
Receiving (No.)	Jerry Rice, 11-20-94	16
Receiving (Yds.)	Jerry Rice, 12-18-95	289
Interceptions	Dave Baker, 12-4-60	*4
Field Goals	Ray Wersching, 10-16-83	6
	Jeff Wilkins, 9-29-96	6
Touchdowns (Tot.)	Jerry Rice, 10-14-90	5
Points	Jerry Rice, 10-14-90	30

*NFL Record

COACHING HISTORY

(417-307-13)

1950-54	Lawrence (Buck) Shaw	33-25-2
1955	Norman (Red) Strader	4-8-0
1956-58	Frankie Albert	19-17-1
1959-63	Howard (Red) Hickey*	27-27-1
1963-67	Jack Christiansen	26-38-3
1968-75	Dick Nolan	56-56-5
1976	Monte Clark	8-6-0
1977	Ken Meyer	5-9-0
1978	Pete McCulley**	1-8-0
1978	Fred O'Connor	1-6-0
1979-88	Bill Walsh	102-63-1
1989-96	George Seifert	108-35-0
1997-98	Steve Mariucci	27-9-0

*Resigned after three games in 1963
**Released after nine games in 1978

3COM PARK

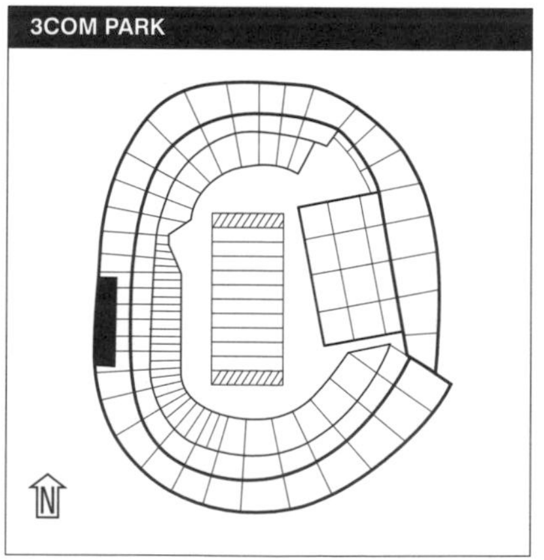

1998 TEAM RECORD

PRESEASON (2-3)

Date	Result		Opponent
8/2	W	14-13	New England
8/8	L	21-27	at San Diego
8/15	W	24-21	vs. Seattle at Vancouver, Canada
8/23	L	20-21	Miami
8/28	L	20-21	at Seattle

REGULAR SEASON (12-4)

Date	Result		Opponent	Att.
9/6	W	36-30	New York Jets (OT)	64,419
9/14	W	45-10	at Washington	76,798
9/27	W	31-20	Atlanta	62,296
10/4	L	21-26	at Buffalo	76,615
10/11	W	31-0	at New Orleans	62,811
10/18	W	34-31	Indianapolis	68,486
10/25	W	28-10	at St. Louis	58,563
11/1	L	22-36	at Green Bay	59,794
11/8	W	25-23	Carolina	68,572
11/15	L	19-31	at Atlanta	69,828
11/22	W	31-20	New Orleans	68,429
11/30	W	31-7	New York Giants	68,212
12/6	W	31-28	at Carolina (OT)	63,332
12/14	W	35-13	Detroit	68,585
12/20	L	21-24	at New England	59,153
12/27	W	38-19	St. Louis	68,386

(OT) Overtime

POSTSEASON (1-1)

Date	Result		Opponent	Att.
1/3	W	30-27	Green Bay	66,506
1/9	L	18-20	at Atlanta	70,262

SCORE BY PERIODS

49ers	79	163	116	112	9	— 479
Opponents	98	70	30	130	0	— 328

ATTENDANCE

Home 537,385 Away 526,894 Total 1,064,279
Single-game home record, 69,014 (11/13/94)
Single-season home record, 537,385 (1998)

1998 TEAM STATISTICS

	49ers	Opp.
Total First Downs	381	297
Rushing	129	91
Passing	223	178
Penalty	29	28
Third Down: Made/Att	96/211	73/213
Third Down Pct.	45.5	34.3
Fourth Down: Made/Att	4/9	7/17
Fourth Down Pct.	44.4	41.2
Total Net Yards	6,800	5,343
Avg. Per Game	425.0	333.9
Total Plays	1,100	1,012
Avg. Per Play	6.2	5.3
Net Yards Rushing	2,544	1,610
Avg. Per Game	159.0	100.6
Total Rushes	491	395
Net Yards Passing	4,256	3,733
Avg. Per Game	266.0	233.3
Sacked/Yards Lost	53/254	51/259
Gross Yards	4,510	3,992
Att./Completions	556/347	566/294
Completion Pct.	62.4	51.9
Had Intercepted	15	21
Punts/Avg.	69/41.1	83/42.1
Net Punting Avg.	69/34.1	83/35.3
Penalties/Yards Lost	133/1,156	101/800
Fumbles/Ball Lost	22/15	24/12
Touchdowns	61	39
Rushing	19	13
Passing	41	25
Returns	1	1
Avg. Time of Possession	31:52	28:08

1998 INDIVIDUAL STATISTICS

Passing	Att.	Comp.	Yds.	Pct.	TD	Int.	Tkld.	Rate
S. Young	517	322	4,170	62.3	36	12	48/234	101.1
Detmer	38	24	312	63.2	4	3	5/20	91.1
Kirby	1	1	28	100.0	1	0	0/0	158.3
49ers	556	347	4,510	62.4	41	15	53/254	101.2
Opponents	566	294	3,992	51.9	25	21	51/259	74.0

SCORING	TD R	TD P	TD Rt	PAT	FG	Saf	PTS
Richey	0	0	0	49/51	18/27	0	103
Owens	1	14	0	0/0	0/0	0	92
Rice	0	9	0	0/0	0/0	0	58
Hearst	7	2	0	0/0	0/0	0	56
Stokes	0	8	0	0/0	0/0	0	48
S. Young	6	0	0	0/0	0/0	0	36
Smith	0	5	0	0/0	0/0	0	30
Edwards	1	2	0	0/0	0/0	0	18
Kirby	3	0	0	0/0	0/0	0	18
Clark	0	1	0	0/0	0/0	0	8
Levy	1	0	0	0/0	0/0	0	6
McQuarters	0	0	1	0/0	0/0	0	6
49ers	19	41	1	49/51	18/27	0	479
Opponents	13	25	1	35/38	19/32	1	328

2-Point conversions: Rice 2, Clark, Hearst, Owens. Team 5-9, Opponents 0-1.

RUSHING	Att.	Yds.	Avg.	LG	TD
Hearst	310	1,570	5.1	96t	7
S. Young	70	454	6.5	24	6
Kirby	48	258	5.4	31t	3
Levy	25	112	4.5	21t	1
Edwards	22	94	4.3	32	1
Owens	4	53	13.3	21t	1
Detmer	8	7	0.9	10	0
Roby	1	0	0.0	0	0
Druckenmiller	3	-4	-1.3	-1	0
49ers	491	2,544	5.2	96t	19
Opponents	395	1,610	4.1	65t	13

RECEIVING	No.	Yds.	Avg.	LG	TD
Rice	82	1,157	14.1	75t	9
Owens	67	1,097	16.4	79t	14
Stokes	63	770	12.2	33t	8
Hearst	39	535	13.7	81t	2
Smith	25	266	10.6	25t	5
Edwards	22	218	9.9	47t	2
Kirby	16	134	8.4	25	0
Levy	15	64	4.3	13	0
Clark	12	124	10.3	23	1
Uwaezuoke	3	67	22.3	35	0
Harris	2	67	33.5	42	0
Beasley	1	11	11.0	11	0
49ers	347	4,510	13.0	81t	41
Opponents	294	3,992	13.6	80t	25

INTERCEPTIONS	No.	Yds.	Avg.	LG	TD
Walker	4	78	19.5	36	0
Hanks	4	37	9.3	37	0
Bronson	4	34	8.5	28	0
McDonald	4	22	5.5	18	0
Tubbs	1	7	7.0	7	0
Woodall	1	4	4.0	4	0
Langham	1	0	0.0	0	0
Pope	1	0	0.0	0	0
Barker	1	-4	-4.0	-4	0
49ers	21	178	8.5	37	0
Opponents	15	304	20.3	43	0

PUNTING	No.	Yds.	Avg.	In 20	LG
Roby	60	2,511	41.9	14	66
Howard	9	324	36.0	2	45
49ers	69	2,835	41.1	16	66
Opponents	83	3,492	42.1	20	64

PUNT RETURNS	No.	FC	Yds.	Avg.	LG	TD
McQuarters	47	10	406	8.6	72t	1
49ers	47	10	406	8.6	72t	1
Opponents	36	15	341	9.5	53	0

KICKOFF RETURNS	No.	Yds.	Avg.	LG	TD
Levy	22	383	17.4	30	0
Kirby	17	340	20.0	33	0
McQuarters	17	339	19.9	45	0
Smith	2	35	17.5	23	0
Richie	1	11	11.0	11	0
49ers	59	1,108	18.8	45	0
Opponents	67	1,296	19.3	47	0

FIELD GOALS	1-19	20-29	30-39	40-49	50+
Richey	0/0	9/10	3/4	6/13	0/0
49ers	0/0	9/10	3/4	6/13	0/0
Opponents	1/1	4/4	7/10	6/11	1/6

SACKS	No.
Doleman	15.0
Barker	12.0
B. Young	9.5
Bryant	5.0
McDonald	4.0
Norton	2.0
Peterson	1.0
Tubbs	1.0
Buckner	0.5
Hanks	0.5
Posey	0.5
49ers	51.0
Opponents	53.0

1999 DRAFT CHOICES

Round	Name	Pos.	College
1	Reggie McGrew	DT	Florida
3	Chike Okeafor	DE	Purdue
4	Anthony Parker	DB	Weber State
	Pierson Prioleau	DB	Virginia Tech
5	Terry Jackson	RB	Florida
	Tyrone Hopson	T	Eastern Kentucky
6	Tai Streets	WR	Michigan
7	Kory Minor	LB	Notre Dame

SAN FRANCISCO 49ERS

1999 VETERAN ROSTER

No.	Name	Pos.	Ht.	Wt.	Birthdate	NFL Exp.	College	Hometown	How Acq.	'98 Games/ Starts
40	Beasley, Fred	RB	6-0	220	9/18/74	2	Auburn	Montgomery, Ala.	D6-'98	16/0
78	Bonham, Shane	DT	6-2	286	10/18/70	6	Tennessee	Fairbanks, Alaska	UFA(Det)-'98	8/0
31	Bronson, Zack	S	6-1	191	1/28/74	3	McNeese State	Jasper, Tex.	FA-'97	11/1
65	Brown, Ray	G	6-5	318	12/12/62	14	Arkansas State	Marion, Ark.	UFA(Wash)-'96	16/16
90	Bryant, Junior	DT	6-4	278	1/16/71	5	Notre Dame	Omaha, Neb.	FA-'93	16/16
99	Buckner, Brentson	DE	6-2	305	9/30/71	6	Clemson	Columbus, Ga.	UFA(Cin)-'98	13/0
85	Clark, Greg	TE	6-4	251	4/7/72	3	Stanford	Bountiful, Utah	D3-'97	13/9
67	Dalman, Chris	C	6-3	297	3/15/70	7	Stanford	Salinas, Calif.	D6-'93	15/15
63	Deese, Derrick	T	6-3	289	5/17/70	8	Southern California	Culver City, Calif.	FA-'92	16/16
56	Doleman, Chris	DE	6-5	289	10/16/61	15	Pittsburgh	York, Pa.	UFA(Atl)-'96	16/16
14	Druckenmiller, Jim	QB	6-4	241	9/19/72	3	Virginia Tech	Allentown, Pa.	D1-'97	2/0
10	Edge, Shayne	P	5-11	175	8/21/71	3	Florida	Newton County, Ga.	FA-'99	0*
86	Fann, Chad	TE	6-3	256	6/7/70	6	Florida A&M	Jacksonville, Fla.	FA-'97	12/0
74	Fiore, Dave	T	6-4	288	8/10/74	4	Hofstra	Waldwick, N.J.	FA-'98	9/3
59	Givens, Reggie	LB	6-0	234	10/3/71	2	Penn State	Emporia, Va.	FA-'98	16/0
36	Hanks, Merton	S	6-2	181	3/12/68	9	Iowa	Dallas, Tex.	D5-'91	16/16
88	Harris, Mark	WR	6-4	201	4/28/70	3	Stanford	Brigham City, Utah	FA-'97	10/0
20	Hearst, Garrison	RB	5-11	219	1/4/71	7	Georgia	Lincolnton, Ga.	UFA(Cin)-'97	16/16
27	Jervey, Travis	RB	6-0	222	5/5/72	5	Citadel	Columbia, S.C.	FA-'99	11/11*
89	LaChapelle, Sean	WR	6-3	217	7/29/70	3	UCLA	Napa, Calif.	FA-'99	0*
32	Levy, Chuck	RB	6-0	206	1/7/72	4	Arizona	Lynwood, Calif.	FA-'96	12/0
46	McDonald, Tim	S	6-2	219	1/6/65	13	Southern California	Fresno, Calif.	UFA(Phx)-'93	16/16
21	McQuarters, R.W.	CB	5-9	198	12/21/76	2	Oklahoma State	Tulsa, Okla.	D1-'98	16/7
62	Newberry, Jeremy	C	6-5	315	3/23/76	2	California	Antioch, Calif.	D2-'98	0*
51	Norton Jr., Ken	LB	6-2	254	9/29/66	12	UCLA	Los Angeles, Calif.	UFA(Dall)-'94	16/16
69	Ostrowski, Phil	G	6-4	291	9/23/75	2	Penn State	Wilkes-Barre, Pa.	D5-'98	0*
81	† Owens, Terrell	WR	6-3	217	12/7/73	4	Tennessee-Chattanooga	Alexander City, Ala.	D3-'96	16/10
50	Peterson, Anthony	LB	6-1	232	1/23/72	6	Notre Dame	Monogahela, Pa.	T(Chi)-'98	16/1
96	Posey, Jeff	DE	6-4	240	8/14/75	2	Southern Mississippi	Bassfield, Miss.	FA-'98	16/0
80	Rice, Jerry	WR	6-2	196	10/13/62	15	Mississippi Valley State	Crawford, Miss.	D1-'85	16/16
7	Richey, Wade	K	6-4	200	5/19/76	2	Louisiana State	Lafayette, La.	FA-'98	16/0
93	Richie, David	DT	6-4	280	9/26/73	3	Washington	Orange, Calif.	T(Den)-'98	8/0
71	Ruhman, Chris	T	6-5	321	12/19/74	2	Texas A&M	Houston, Tex.	D3-'98	6/0
30	Schulters, Lance	S	6-2	195	5/27/75	2	Hofstra	Brooklyn, N.Y.	D4-'98	15/0
83	Stokes, J.J.	WR	6-4	223	10/6/72	5	UCLA	San Diego, Calif.	D1-'95	16/11
55	Tubbs, Winfred	LB	6-4	260	9/24/70	6	Texas	Fairfield, Tex.	UFA(NO)-'98	16/15
44	Vardell, Tommy	RB	6-2	230	2/20/69	8	Stanford	El Cajon, Calif.	FA-'99	14/9*
38	Walker, Darnell	CB	5-8	167	1/17/70	7	Oklahoma	St. Louis, Mo.	FA-'97	16/16
95	Washington, Marvin	DE	6-6	285	10/22/65	11	Idaho	Denver, Colo.	FA-'99	16/0*
98	Wilkins, Gabe	DE	6-5	315	9/1/71	6	Gardner-Webb	Cowpens, S.C.	UFA(GB)-'98	8/4
54	Woodall, Lee	LB	6-1	224	10/31/69	6	West Chester	Carlisle, Pa.	D6b-'94	15/15
97	Young, Bryant	DT	6-3	291	1/27/72	6	Notre Dame	Chicago Heights, Ill.	D1-'94	12/12
8	Young, Steve	QB	6-2	215	10/11/61	15	Brigham Young	Greenwich, Conn.	T(TB)-'87	15/15

* Edge last active with Pittsburgh in '96; Jervey played 11 games with Green Bay in '98; LaChapelle last active with Kansas City in '97; Newberry inactive for 7 games; Ostrowski inactive for 16 games; Vardell played 14 games with Detroit; Washington played 16 games with Denver.

† Restricted free agent; subject to developments.

Traded—DE Roy Barker (16 games in '98) to Cleveland; QB Ty Detmer (16) to Cleveland; RB Marc Edwards (16) to Cleveland; G Kevin Gogan (16) to Miami; TE Irv Smith (16) to Cleveland.

Retired—Kirk Scrafford, 9-year tackle, 9 games in '98.

Players lost through free agency (2): RB Terry Kirby (Clev; 9 games in '98), CB Marquez Pope (Clev; 6).

Also played with 49ers in '98—S Tony Blevins (2 games), T Jamie Brown (8), S Curtis Buckley (8), C Steve Gordon (13), DE Charles Haley (2), G Tim Hanshaw (16), P Eddie Howard (2), LB Randy Kirk (16), CB Antonio Langham (11), CB Tyrone Legette (7), LB Randy Neal (1), P Reggie Roby (14), WR Iheanyi Uwaezuoeke (7), LB James Williams (15).

COACHING STAFF

Head Coach,
Steve Mariucci

Pro Career: Became the thirteenth head coach in 49ers history on January 16, 1997. One of thirteen head coaches since the NFL-AFL merger in 1970 to lead his team to a division title in his first season. He established an NFL mark for consecutive wins by a rookie head coach with an 11-game winning streak. He served as the quarterbacks coach of the Green Bay Packers from 1992-95. His first pro position was in 1985 when he was the receivers coach for the USFL's Orlando Renegades. Later that fall, he had a brief stint with the Los Angeles Rams as quality control coach. Career record: 27-9.

Background: Three-time All-America quarterback at Northern Michigan. Began his coaching career at his alma mater (1978-79), and moved to Cal State-Fullerton (1980-82), and Louisville (1983-84). Joined the Southern California staff in 1986, then moved to California in 1987. In 1990-91, he served as the Bears' offensive coordinator. Became the head coach at California in 1996 and guided the squad to a 5-0 start and a berth in the Aloha Bowl.

Personal: Born November 4, 1955, in Iron Mountain, Mich. He and his wife, Gayle, have four children—Tyler, Adam, Stephen, and Brielle—and live in Saratoga, Calif.

ASSISTANT COACHES

Jerry Attaway, physical development; born January 3, 1946, Susanville, Calif., lives in San Jose, Calif. Defensive back Yuba, Calif. J.C. 1964-65, UC Davis 1967. No pro playing experience. College coach: UC Davis 1970-71, Idaho 1972-74, Utah State 1975-77, Southern California 1978-1982. Pro coach: Joined 49ers in 1983.

Mike Barnes, strength development; born March 13, 1966, Rochester, N.Y., lives in Pleasanton, Calif. No college or pro playing experience. College coach: Texas A&M 1990, California 1991-93. Pro coach: Joined 49ers in 1994.

Tom Batta, tight ends, born October 6, 1942, in Youngstown, Ohio, lives in Santa Clara, Calif. Offensive-defensive lineman Kent State 1961-63. No pro playing experience. College coach: Akron 1973, Colorado 1974-78, Kansas 1979-1982, North Carolina State 1983. Pro coach: Minnesota Vikings 1984-1993, Indianapolis Colts 1994-97, Pittsburgh Steelers 1998, joined 49ers in 1999.

Christopher Beake, defensive quality control; born September 10, 1972, Highlands Ranch, Colo., lives in Santa Clara, Calif. Quarterback Air Force 1991-92. No pro playing experience. College coach: Air Force 1994-95. Pro coach: Joined 49ers in 1999.

Dwaine Board, defensive line; born November 29, 1956, Rocky Mount, Va., lives in Redwood City, Calif. Defensive lineman North Carolina A&T 1974-77. Pro defensive lineman San Francisco 49ers 1979-1987, New Orleans Saints 1988. Pro coach: Joined 49ers in 1991.

Greg Brown, secondary; born October 10, 1957, Denver, lives in Santa Clara, Calif. Defensive back Texas-El Paso 1980. No pro playing experience. College coach: Wyoming 1987-88, Purdue 1989-1990, Colorado 1991-93. Pro coach: Tampa Bay Buccaneers 1984-86, Atlanta Falcons 1994, San Diego Chargers 1995-96, Tennessee Oilers 1997-98, joined 49ers in 1999.

Larry Kirksey, wide receivers; born January 6, 1951, Harlan, Ky., lives in Pleasanton, Calif. Wide receiver Eastern Kentucky 1970-72. No pro playing experience. College coach: Miami (Ohio) 1974-76, Kentucky 1977-1981, Kansas 1982, Kentucky State 1983 (head coach), Florida 1984-88, Pittsburgh 1989, Alabama 1990-93. Pro coach: Joined 49ers in 1994.

Greg Knapp, offensive assistant-quarterback; born March 5, 1963, Long Beach, Calif., lives in Santa Clara, Calif. Quarterback Cal State-Sacramento 1982-85. No pro playing experience. College coach: Cal State-Sacramento 1986-1994. Pro coach: Joined 49ers in 1995.

Brett Maxie, defensive assistant-secondary; born January 13, 1962, Dallas, lives in Santa Clara, Calif. Safety Texas Southern 1980-85. Pro safety New Orleans Saints 1985-1993, Atlanta Falcons 1994, Carolina Panthers 1995-96, San Francisco 49ers 1997. Pro coach: Carolina Panthers 1998, joined 49ers in 1999.

Bobb McKittrick, offensive line; born December 29, 1935, Baker, Ore., lives in San Mateo, Calif. Guard Oregon State 1955-57. No pro playing experience. College coach: Oregon State 1961-64, UCLA 1965-1970. Pro coach: Los Angeles Rams 1971-72, San Diego Chargers 1974-78, joined 49ers in 1979.

Jim Mora, defensive coordinator; born November 19, 1961, Los Angeles, lives in Sunnyvale, Calif. Defensive back Washington 1980-83. No pro playing experience. College coach: Washington 1984. Pro coach: San Diego Chargers 1985-1991, New Orleans Saints 1992-96, joined 49ers in 1997.

Marty Mornhinweg, offensive coordinator; born March 29, 1962, Edmond, Okla., lives in Pleasanton, Calif. Quarterback Montana 1980-84. No pro playing experience. College coach: Montana 1985, Texas-El Paso 1986-87, Northern Arizona 1988, 1994, Southeast Missouri State 1989-1990, Missouri 1991-93. Pro coach: Green Bay Packers 1995-96, joined 49ers in 1997.

Pat Morris, offensive line; born April 7, 1954, Cleveland, lives in Mountain View, Calif. Offensive lineman Southern California 1972-75. No pro playing experience. College coach: Southern California 1976-77, 1983-86, Northern Arizona 1978, Minnesota 1979-1982, Michigan State 1987-1994, Stanford 1995-96. Pro coach: Joined 49ers in 1997.

Tom Rathman, running backs; born October 7, 1962, Grand Island, Neb., lives in Redwood City, Calif. Running back Nebraska 1983-85. Pro running back San Francisco 49ers 1986-1993, Los Angeles Raiders 1994. College coach: Menlo College 1996. Pro coach: Joined 49ers in 1997.

Richard Smith, linebackers; born October 17, 1955, Los Angeles, lives in Santa Clara, Calif. Offensive lineman Rio Hondo J.C. 1975-76, Fresno State 1977-78. No pro playing experience. College coach: Rio Hondo J.C. 1979-1980, Cal State-Fullerton 1981-83, California 1984-86, Arizona 1987. Pro coach: Houston Oilers 1988-1992, Denver Broncos 1993-96, joined 49ers in 1997.

George Stewart, special teams; born December 29, 1958, Little Rock, Ark., lives in Santa Clara, Calif. Guard Arkansas 1977-1980. No pro playing experience. College coach: Minnesota 1984-85, Notre Dame 1986-88. Pro coach: Pittsburgh Steelers 1989-1991, Tampa Bay Buccaneers 1992-95, joined 49ers in 1996.

Andy Sugarman, offensive quality control; born May 23, 1972, San Francisco, lives in Mountain View, Calif. No college or pro playing experience. College coach: California 1990-97. Pro coach: Joined 49ers in 1998.

1999 FIRST-YEAR ROSTER

Name	Pos.	Ht.	Wt.	Birthdate	College	Hometown	How Acq.
Anderson, Morris	WR	6-1	194	2/22/77	Baylor	Tyler, Tex.	FA
Bell, Shonn (1)	TE	6-5	257	10/25/74	Clinch Valley College	Stuarts Draft, Va.	FA
Croff, Tim	DT	6-2	283	11/7/76	Carson-Newman	Phoenix, Ariz.	FA
Dercher, Dan	T	6-5	293	6/2/76	Kansas	Kansas City, Kan.	FA
Dumas, James	CB-S	5-10	191	9/13/75	Edinboro	Columbus, Ohio	FA
Eason, Curtis (1)	DT	6-2	292	4/16/76	East Tennessee State	Jacksonville, Fla.	FA-'98
Freeman, Chris	LB	6-2	230	5/23/75	Clark	LaGrange, Ga.	FA
Garcia, Jeff (1)	QB	6-1	195	2/24/70	San Jose State	Gilroy, Calif.	FA
Garcia, Mark	QB	6-3	220	5/7/76	Ohio State	Modesto, Calif.	FA
Grieb, Mike	TE	6-3	248	2/25/76	UCLA	Torrance, Calif.	FA
Griffin, Damon	WR	5-9	186	6/14/76	Ohio State	Los Angeles, Calif.	FA
Hannah, Tito	LB	6-3	232	7/13/76	South Carolina State	Marion, S.C.	FA
Herndon, Kelly	CB	5-10	180	11/3/76	Toledo	Bedford, Ohio	FA
Hopson, Tyronne	T	6-2	305	5/28/76	Eastern Kentucky	Hopkinsville, Ky.	D5a
Jackson, Terry	RB	6-0	218	1/10/76	Florida	Gainesville, Fla.	D5a
Jones, Toya	S	6-1	199	10/28/76	UCLA	Victoria, Tex.	FA
Kapp, Anthony	T	6-4	320	9/6/75	Mississippi State	Toms River, N.J.	FA
Keneley, Matt (1)	DT	6-5	295	12/1/73	Southern California	Santa Ana, Calif.	FA
Kimbrough, Jamie	RB	5-7	198	7/10/77	Fresno State	Dayton, Ohio	FA
Kobdish, Josh	T	6-6	301	1/29/76	Fresno State	Bakersfield, Calif.	FA
Ledford, Dwayne	T	6-3	295	11/2/76	East Carolina	Morgantown, S.C.	FA
Lerum, Karl (1)	WR	6-2	200	7/23/74	Pacific Lutheran	Puyallup, Wash.	FA-'98
Malveaux, Kelly (1)	CB	5-9	175	5/11/76	Arizona	Long Beach, Calif.	FA-'98
Matock, Marc	DT	6-3	287	11/30/75	Southern California	Salinas, Calif.	FA
McElroy, Jim (1)	WR	5-10	155	9/15/76	UCLA	Los Angeles, Calif.	FA
McGrew, Reggie	DT	6-1	301	12/16/76	Florida	Mayo, Fla.	D1
Minor, Kory	LB	6-0	247	12/14/76	Notre Dame	LaPuente, Calif.	D7
O'Sullivan, Dennis	DT	6-3	285	1/28/76	Tulane	Suffern, N.Y.	FA
Okeafor, Chike	DE	6-4	248	3/27/76	Purdue	West Lafayette, Ind.	D3
Owens, Patterson	DE	6-5	273	11/15/75	Houston	Mobile, Ala.	FA
Parker, Anthony	CB	6-1	200	12/4/75	Weber State	Denver, Colo.	D4a
Prioleau, Pierson	CB	5-10	191	8/6/77	Virginia Tech	Charleston, S.C.	D4b
Roscoe, James	DE	6-3	275	9/25/75	Clark	Ft. Lauderdale, Fla.	FA
Rubio, Angel (1)	DT	6-2	307	4/12/75	Southeast Missouri State	Modesto, Calif.	T(Pitt)-'98
Sailer, Chris	K	5-8	190	1/9-77	UCLA	Burbank, Calif.	FA
Scissum, Ed (1)	RB	6-0	229	1/5/76	Alabama	Attalla, Ala.	FA-'98
Serwanga, Wasswa	CB	5-11	196	7/23/76	UCLA	Kampala, Uganda	FA
Smith, Brian	LB	6-1	252	2/25/78	Alabama-Birmingham	Floyd County, Ga.	FA
Stanley, Chad	P	6-3	205	1/29/76	Stephen F. Austin	Pittsburg, Tex.	FA
Streets, Tai	WR	6-1	193	4/20/77	Michigan	Matteson, Ill.	D6
Strickland, Vernon (1)	LB	6-4	252	4/9/73	Georgia Tech	Newnan, Ga.	FA-'98
Tenner, Jason	DT	6-5	275	8/17/77	Villanova	Stanford, Calif.	FA
Walendy, Craig	RB	6-1	229	7/11/77	UCLA	New Brunswick, N.J.	FA
Wesley, Joe	LB	6-1	229	11/10/76	Louisiana State	Jackson, Miss.	FA
Wilson, Geoff	T	6-6	292	2/10/76	Stanford	Slidell, La.	FA
Wilson, Sam	CB	5-11	175	6/20/76	Fresno State	Los Angeles, Calif.	FA
Zalenka, Joe	C	6-3	280	3/9/76	Wake Forest	Cleveland, Ohio	FA

The term NFL Rookie is defined as a player who is in his first season of professional football and has not been on the roster of another professional football team for any regular-season or postseason games. A Rookie is designated by an "R" on NFL rosters. Players who have been active in another professional football league or players who have NFL experience, including either preseason training camp or being on an Active List or Inactive List, or on Reserve/Injured or Reserve/Physically Unable to Perform for fewer than six regular-season games, are termed NFL First-Year Players. An NFL First-Year Player is designated by a "1" on NFL rosters. Thereafter, a player is credited with an additional year of experience for each season in which he accumulates six games on the Active List or Inactive List, or on Reserve/Injured or Reserve/Physically Unable to Perform.

TAMPA BAY BUCCANEERS

National Football Conference
Central Division
Team Colors: Buccaneer Red, Pewter, Black, and Orange
One Buccaneer Place
Tampa, Florida 33607
Telephone: (813) 870-2700

CLUB OFFICIALS

Owner/President: Malcolm Glazer
Executive Vice President: Bryan Glazer
Executive Vice President: Joel Glazer
Executive Vice President: Edward Glazer
General Manager: Rich McKay
Director of Player Personnel: Jerry Angelo
Director of College Scouting: Tim Ruskell
Director of Football Administration: John Idzik
Executive Director of the Glazer Family Foundation: Veronica (Roni) Costello
Director of Communications: Reggie Roberts
Director of Marketing: George Woods
Director of Premium Seating: Jim Overton
Director of Community Relations: Stephanie Waller
Director of Player Programs: Kevin Winston
Director of Human Resources: Maureen Borek
Director of Security: Andre Trescastro
College Scouts: Mike Ackerley, Joe DiMarzo, Jr., Dennis Hickey, Ruston Webster, Mike Yowarsky
Pro Personnel Assistant: Lloyd Richards, Jr.
Director of Ticketing and Customer Relations: Mike Newquist
Communications Manager: Scott Smith
Communications Coordinator: Cater Toole
Trainer: Todd Toriscelli
Director of Rehabilitation/Assistant Trainer: Mark Shermansky
Assistant Trainer: Keith Abrams
Equipment Manager: Darin Kerns
Assistant Equipment Manager: Mark Meschede
Video Director: Dave Levy
Assistant Video Director: Pat Brazil
Stadium: Raymond James Stadium
•**Capacity:** 66,321
Tampa, Florida 33607
Playing Surface: Grass
Training Camp: University of Tampa
Tampa, Florida 33606

1999 SCHEDULE

PRESEASON

Aug. 14	**Cleveland**	8:00
Aug. 21	at Kansas City	7:30
Aug. 28	**New England**	8:00
Sept. 3	at Washington	8:00

REGULAR SEASON

Sept. 12	**New York Giants**	4:15
Sept. 19	at Philadelphia	1:00
Sept. 26	**Denver**	1:00
Oct. 3	at Minnesota	12:00
Oct. 10	at Green Bay	7:20
Oct. 17	Open Date	
Oct. 24	**Chicago**	1:00
Oct. 31	at Detroit	8:20
Nov. 7	at New Orleans	3:05
Nov. 14	**Kansas City**	1:00
Nov. 21	**Atlanta**	1:00
Nov. 28	at Seattle	1:05
Dec. 6	**Minnesota** (Mon.)	9:00
Dec. 12	**Detroit**	1:00
Dec. 19	at Oakland	1:05
Dec. 26	**Green Bay**	4:15
Jan. 2	at Chicago	12:00

COACHING HISTORY

(120-241-1)

1976-84	John McKay	45-91-1
1985-86	Leeman Bennett	4-28-0
1987-90	Ray Perkins*	19-41-0
1990-91	Richard Williamson	4-15-0
1992-95	Sam Wyche	23-41-0
1996-98	Tony Dungy	25-25-0

*Released after 13 games in 1990

RECORD HOLDERS

INDIVIDUAL RECORDS—CAREER

Category	Name	Performance
Rushing (Yds.)	James Wilder, 1981-89	5,957
Passing (Yds.)	Vinny Testaverde, 1987-1992	14,820
Passing (TDs)	Vinny Testaverde, 1987-1992	77
Receiving (No.)	James Wilder, 1981-89	430
Receiving (Yds.)	Mark Carrier, 1987-1992	5,018
Interceptions	Cedric Brown, 1976-1984	29
Punting (Avg.)	Tommy Barnhardt, 1996-98	42.6
Punt Return (Avg.)	Karl Williams, 1996-98	13.8
Kickoff Return (Avg.)	Reidel Anthony, 1997-98	24.1
Field Goals	Michael Husted, 1993-98	117
Touchdowns (Tot.)	James Wilder, 1981-89	46
Points	Michael Husted, 1993-98	502

INDIVIDUAL RECORDS—SINGLE SEASON

Category	Name	Performance
Rushing (Yds.)	James Wilder, 1984	1,544
Passing (Yds.)	Doug Williams, 1981	3,563
Passing (TDs)	Trent Dilfer, 1997, 1998	21
Receiving (No.)	Mark Carrier, 1989	86
Receiving (Yds.)	Mark Carrier, 1989	1,422
Interceptions	Cedric Brown, 1981	9
Punting (Avg.)	Tommy Barnhardt, 1996	43.1
Punt Return (Avg.)	Karl Williams, 1996	21.1
Kickoff Return (Avg.)	Karl Williams, 1996	27.4
Field Goals	Michael Husted, 1996	25
Touchdowns (Tot.)	James Wilder, 1984	13
Points	Donald Igwebuike, 1989	99

INDIVIDUAL RECORDS—SINGLE GAME

Category	Name	Performance
Rushing (Yds.)	James Wilder, 11-6-83	219
Passing (Yds.)	Doug Williams, 11-16-80	486
Passing (TDs)	Steve DeBerg, 9-13-87	5
Receiving (No.)	James Wilder, 9-15-85	13
Receiving (Yds.)	Mark Carrier, 12-6-87	212
Interceptions	Many times Last time by John Lynch, 12-13-98	2
Field Goals	Many times Last time by Michael Husted, 11-17-96	4
Touchdowns (Tot.)	Jimmie Giles, 10-20-85	4
Points	Jimmie Giles, 10-20-85	24

RAYMOND JAMES STADIUM

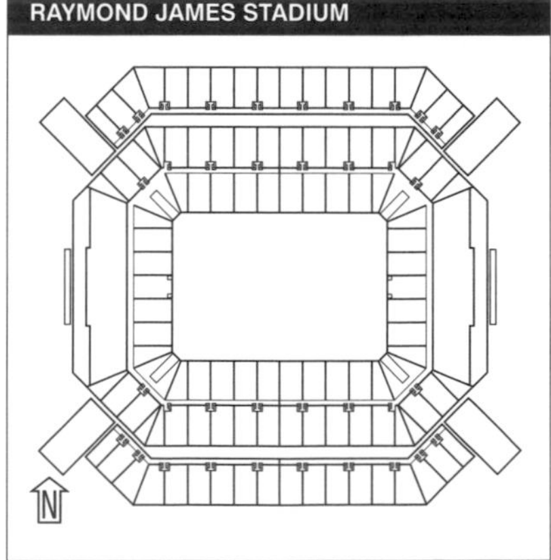

1998 TEAM RECORD

PRESEASON (2-3)

Date	Result		Opponent
8/1	W	30-6	vs. Pittsburgh at Canton, Ohio
8/8	L	13-17	vs. Kansas City at Norman, Okla.
8/13	L	13-14	at Miami
8/24	W	41-7	at Oakland
8/28	L	6-10	at New Orleans

REGULAR SEASON (8-8)

Date	Result		Opponent	Att.
9/6	L	7-31	at Minnesota	62,538
9/13	L	15-23	at Green Bay	60,124
9/20	W	27-15	Chicago	64,328
9/28	L	6-27	at Detroit	74,724
10/4	W	20-3	New York Giants	64,989
10/18	W	16-13	Carolina	63,600
10/25	L	3-9	at New Orleans	52,695
11/1	W	27-24	Minnesota	64,979
11/8	L	22-31	Tennessee	65,054
11/15	L	24-29	at Jacksonville	72,974
11/22	L	25-28	Detroit	64,265
11/29	W	31-17	at Chicago	51,938
12/7	W	24-22	Green Bay	65,497
12/13	W	16-3	Pittsburgh	65,335
12/19	L	16-20	at Washington	66,309
12/27	W	35-0	at Cincinnati	49,826

SCORE BY PERIODS

Buccaneers	61	101	49	103	0	—	314
Opponents	78	71	57	89	0	—	295

ATTENDANCE

Home 518,047 Away 491,128 Total 1,009,175
Single-game home record, 73,523 (12/7/97)
Single-season home record, 545,980 (1979)

1998 TEAM STATISTICS

	Buccaneers	Opp.
Total First Downs	262	244
Rushing	111	75
Passing	139	148
Penalty	12	21
Third Down: Made/Att	93/230	64/202
Third Down Pct.	40.4	31.7
Fourth Down: Made/Att	6/14	3/14
Fourth Down Pct.	42.9	21.4
Total Net Yards	4,754	4,345
Avg. Per Game	297.1	271.6
Total Plays	1,000	925
Avg. Per Play	4.8	4.7
Net Yards Rushing	2,148	1,583
Avg. Per Game	134.3	98.9
Total Rushes	523	415
Net Yards Passing	2,606	2,762
Avg. Per Game	162.9	172.6
Sacked/Yards Lost	28/181	37/252
Gross Yards	2,787	3,014
Att./Completions	449/234	473/274
Completion Pct.	52.1	57.9
Had Intercepted	18	12
Punts/Avg.	81/41.2	87/42.0
Net Punting Avg.	81/35.3	87/34.4
Penalties/Yards Lost	99/840	88/669
Fumbles/Ball Lost	23/13	28/14
Touchdowns	36	31
Rushing	12	12
Passing	21	15
Returns	3	4
Avg. Time of Possession	31:58	28:02

1998 INDIVIDUAL STATISTICS

Passing	Att.	Comp.	Yds.	Pct.	TD	Int.	Tkld.	Rate
Dilfer	429	225	2,729	52.4	21	15	27/172	74.0
Walsh	19	9	58	47.4	0	3	1/9	14.7
Alstott	1	0	0	0.0	0	0	0/0	39.6
Buccaneers	449	234	2,787	52.1	21	18	28/181	70.3
Opponents	473	274	3,014	57.9	15	12	37/252	76.9

SCORING	TD R	TD P	TD Rt	PAT	FG	Saf	PTS
Husted	0	0	0	29/30	21/28	0	92
Alstott	8	1	0	0/0	0/0	0	54
Anthony	0	7	0	0/0	0/0	0	44
Moore	0	4	0	0/0	0/0	0	24
Green	0	2	1	0/0	0/0	0	18
Dilfer	2	0	0	0/0	0/0	0	12
Dunn	2	0	0	0/0	0/0	0	12
Emanuel	0	2	0	0/0	0/0	0	12
Hunter	0	1	0	0/0	0/0	0	8
R. Barber	0	0	1	0/0	0/0	0	6
J. Davis	0	1	0	0/0	0/0	0	6
Mincy	0	0	1	0/0	0/0	0	6
Neal	0	1	0	0/0	0/0	0	6
Thomas	0	1	0	0/0	0/0	0	6
Williams	0	1	0	0/0	0/0	0	6
Hape	0	0	0	0/0	0/0	0	2
Buccaneers	12	21	3	29/30	21/28	0	314
Opponents	12	15	4	29/29	26/30	1	295

2-Point conversions: Anthony, Hape, Hunter. Team 3-6, Opponents 0-2.

RUSHING	Att.	Yds.	Avg.	LG	TD
Dunn	245	1,026	4.2	50	2
Alstott	215	846	3.9	37	8
Dilfer	40	141	3.5	17	2
Anthony	4	43	10.8	32	0
Neal	5	25	5.0	12	0
Ellison	9	24	2.7	10	0
Husted	1	20	20.0	20	0
Green	3	12	4.0	18	0
Emanuel	1	11	11.0	11	0
Buccaneers	523	2,148	4.1	50	12
Opponents	415	1,583	3.8	71t	12

RECEIVING	No.	Yds.	Avg.	LG	TD
Anthony	51	708	13.9	79t	7
Dunn	44	344	7.8	31	0
Emanuel	41	636	15.5	62t	2
Moore	24	255	10.6	44t	4
Alstott	22	152	6.9	26	1
Williams	21	252	12.0	29t	1
Green	14	251	17.9	64t	2
Neal	5	14	2.8	5	1
Hunter	4	73	18.3	45t	1
Hape	4	27	6.8	11	0
Thomas	2	63	31.5	50t	1
J. Davis	2	12	6.0	11	1
Buccaneers	234	2,787	11.9	79t	21
Opponents	274	3,014	11.0	61	15

INTERCEPTIONS	No.	Yds.	Avg.	LG	TD
Mincy	4	58	14.5	22t	1
R. Barber	2	67	33.5	56	0
Lynch	2	29	14.5	17	0
Upshaw	1	26	26.0	26	0
Brooks	1	25	25.0	25	0
Kelly	1	4	4.0	4	0
Abraham	1	3	3.0	3	0
Buccaneers	12	212	17.7	56	1
Opponents	18	192	10.7	38	2

PUNTING	No.	Yds.	Avg.	In 20	LG
Barnhardt	81	3,340	41.2	19	55
Buccaneers	81	3,340	41.2	19	55
Opponents	87	3,655	42.0	29	71

PUNT RETURNS	No.	FC	Yds.	Avg.	LG	TD
Green	30	9	453	15.1	95t	1
Williams	10	6	83	8.3	18	0
R. Barber	1	0	23	23.0	23t	1
Buccaneers	41	15	559	13.6	95t	2
Opponents	38	23	302	7.9	93t	1

KICKOFF RETURNS	No.	Yds.	Avg.	LG	TD
Anthony	46	1,118	24.3	60	0
Green	10	229	22.9	44	0
Dunn	1	25	25.0	25	0
Ellison	1	19	19.0	19	0
Alstott	1	8	8.0	8	0
Buccaneers	59	1,399	23.7	60	0
Opponents	62	1,333	21.5	105t	1

FIELD GOALS	1-19	20-29	30-39	40-49	50+
Husted	0/1	7/7	8/12	5/7	1/1
Buccaneers	0/1	7/7	8/12	5/7	1/1
Opponents	0/0	10/11	8/8	5/8	3/3

SACKS	No.
Culpepper	9.0
Sapp	7.0
Upshaw	7.0
R. Barber	3.0
Jackson	3.0
Lynch	2.0
White	2.0
Gooch	1.0
Nickerson	1.0
Parker	1.0
Quarles	1.0
Buccaneers	37.0
Opponents	28.0

1999 DRAFT CHOICES

Round	Name	Pos.	College
1	Anthony McFarland	DT	Louisiana State
2	Shaun King	QB	Tulane
3	Martin Gramatica	K	Kansas State
4	Dexter Jackson	DB	Florida State
5	John McLaughlin	DE	California
6	Lamarr Glenn	RB	Florida State
7	Robert Hunt	G	Virginia
	Autry Denson	RB	Notre Dame
	Darnell McDonald	WR	Kansas State

TAMPA BAY BUCCANEERS

1999 VETERAN ROSTER

No.	Name	Pos.	Ht.	Wt.	Birthdate	NFL Exp.	College	Hometown	How Acq.	'98 Games/ Starts
27	Abdullah, Rabih	RB	6-1	219	4/27/75	2	Lehigh	Roselle, N.J.	FA-'98	0*
21	Abraham, Donnie	CB	5-10	184	10/8/73	4	East Tennessee State	Orangeburg, S.C.	D3-'96	13/13
72	Ahanotu, Chidi	DE	6-2	285	10/11/70	7	California	Berkeley, Calif.	D6-'93	4/4
40	Alstott, Mike	RB	6-1	255	12/21/73	4	Purdue	Joliet, Ill.	D2-'96	16/16
85	Anthony, Reidel	WR	5-11	177	10/20/76	3	Florida	Glades Central, Fla.	D1b-'97	15/13
80	Barber, Ronde	CB	5-10	180	4/7/75	3	Virginia	Roanoke, Va.	D3b-'97	16/9
55	Brooks, Derrick	LB	6-0	229	4/18/73	5	Florida State	Pensacola, Fla.	D1b-'95	16/16
98	Cannida, James	DT	6-2	285	1/3/75	2	Nevada	Fremont, Calif.	D6a-'98	10/0
77	Culpepper, Brad	DT	6-1	270	5/8/69	8	Florida	Tallahassee, Fla.	W(Minn)-'94	16/16
58	Davis, Don	LB	6-1	240	12/17/72	4	Kansas	Olathe, Kan.	W(NO)-'98	9/0*
80	Davis, John	TE	6-4	262	5/14/73	4	Emporia State	Jasper, Tex.	FA-'97	16/0
64	Diaz, Jorge	G	6-4	315	11/15/73	4	Texas A&M-Kingsville	Katy, Tex.	FA-'96	12/12
12	Dilfer, Trent	QB	6-4	237	3/13/72	6	Fresno State	Aptos, Calif.	D1-'94	16/16
65	Dogins, Kevin	C-G	6-1	298	12/7/72	3	Texas A&M-Kingsville	Eagle Lake, Tex.	FA-'96	6/4
59	Duncan, Jamie	LB	6-0	228	7/20/75	2	Vanderbilt	Wilmington, Del.	D3-'98	14/6
28	Dunn, Warrick	RB	5-8	178	1/5/75	3	Florida State	Baton Rouge, La.	D1a-'97	16/14
87	Emanuel, Bert	WR	5-10	175	10/26/70	6	Rice	Langham Creek, Tex.	UFA(Atl)-'98	11/11
35	Emanuel, Charles	DB	6-0	196	6/3/73	2	West Virginia	Stuart, Fla.	FA-'99	0*
50	Gooch, Jeff	LB	5-11	219	10/31/74	4	Austin Peay State	Nashville, Tenn.	FA-'96	16/16
81	Green, Jacquez	WR	5-9	170	1/15/76	2	Florida	Fort Valley, Ga.	D2a-'98	12/1
74	Gruber, Paul	T	6-5	293	2/24/65	12	Wisconsin	Prairie du Sac, Wis.	D1-'88	16/16
82	Hape, Patrick	TE	6-4	247	6/6/74	3	Alabama	Killen, Ala.	D5-'97	16/2
97	Jackson, Tyoka	DE-DT	6-2	274	11/22/71	5	Penn State	Washington, D.C.	FA-'96	16/12
78	Jones, Marcus	DT	6-6	265	8/15/73	4	North Carolina	Jacksonville, N.C.	D1b-'96	15/0
25	Kelly, Brian	CB	5-11	190	1/14/76	2	Southern California	Aurora, Colo.	D2b-'98	16/3
47	Lynch, John	S	6-2	216	9/25/71	7	Stanford	Solana Beach, Calif.	D3-'93	15/15
61	Mayberry, Tony	C	6-4	282	12/8/67	10	Wake Forest	Springfield, Va.	D4b-'90	16/16
73	Middleton, Frank	G	6-3	340	10/25/74	3	Arizona	Beaumont, Tex.	D3a-'97	16/16
96	Mix, Bryant	DE-DT	6-3	295	7/28/72	4	Alcorn State	Water Valley, Miss.	FA-'98	0*
83	Moore, Dave	TE	6-2	246	11/11/69	7	Pittsburgh	Succasunna, N.J.	FA-'92	16/16
18	Myers, Shannon	WR	6-1	171	6/16/73	2	Lenoir-Rhyne	Salisbury, N.C.	FA-'99	0*
56	Nickerson, Hardy	LB	6-2	225	9/1/65	13	California	Compton, Calif.	UFA(Pitt)-'93	10/10
70	† Odom, Jason	T	6-5	306	3/31/74	4	Florida	Bartow, Fla.	D4a-'96	15/15
57	Palmer, Mitch	LB-LS	6-4	250	9/2/73	2	Colorado State	San Diego, Calif.	FA-'98	16/0
69	Pierson, Pete	T	6-5	315	2/4/71	5	Washington	Portland, Ore.	D5-'94	16/0
53	Quarles, Shelton	LB	6-1	223	9/11/71	3	Vanderbilt	Whites Creek, Tenn.	FA-'97	16/0
24	Robinson, Damien	S	6-2	205	12/22/73	3	Iowa	Dallas, Tex.	FA-'97	7/0
99	Sapp, Warren	DT	6-2	291	12/19/72	5	Miami	Apopka, Fla.	D1a-'95	16/16
51	Singleton, Alshermond	LB	6-2	213	8/7/75	3	Temple	Irvington, N.J.	D4-'97	15/0
30	Smith, Shevin	S	5-11	195	6/17/75	2	Florida State	Miami, Fla.	D6b-'98	3/0
91	Upshaw, Regan	DE	6-4	261	8/12/75	4	California	Pittsburg, Calif.	D1a-'96	16/16
33	Vance, Eric	S	6-2	215	7/14/75	2	Vanderbilt	Hurst, Tex.	FA-'98	3/1
75	Washington, Todd	C-G	6-3	325	7/19/76	2	Virginia Tech	Melfa, Va.	D4-'98	4/0
94	White, Steve	DE	6-2	261	10/25/73	4	Tennessee	Memphis, Tenn.	FA-'96	16/0
86	Williams, Karl	WR	5-10	179	4/10/71	4	Texas A&M-Kingsville	Garland, Tex.	FA-'96	13/6
71	Wunsch, Jerry	T	6-6	334	1/21/74	3	Wisconsin	Wausau, Wis.	D2-'97	16/1
31	Young, Floyd	CB	6-0	178	11/23/75	3	Texas A&M-Kingsville	New Orleans, La.	FA-'97	11/0
15	t- Zeier, Eric	QB	6-1	205	9/6/72	5	Georgia	Marietta, Ga.	T(Balt)-'99	10/4*

* Abdullah inactive for 16 games in '98; D. Davis played 4 games with New Orleans and 5 games with Tampa Bay; C. Emanuel last active with Philadelphia in '97; Mix was inactive for 9 games; Myers last active with Miami in '95; Zeier played 10 games with Baltimore.

† Restricted free agents; subject to developments.

t- Buccaneers traded for Zeier (Baltimore).

Retired—Anthony Parker, 9-year cornerback, 11 games played in '98.

Also played with Buccaneers in '98—P Tommy Barnhardt (16 games), LB Greg Bellisari (2), S Tony Bouie (16) RB Jerry Ellison (16), WR Brice Hunter (10), K Michael Husted (16), DT Jason Maniecki (3), QB Scott Milanovich (0), S Charles Mincy (16), RB Lorenzo Neal (16), WR Robb Thomas (7), QB Steve Walsh (5).

COACHING STAFF

Head Coach,
Tony Dungy

Pro Career: After 15 years as an NFL assistant coach, Dungy was named as the Buccaneers' sixth head coach on January 22, 1996, when he signed a six-year contract. In 1998, the Buccaneers finished with an 8-8 record, marking the first time the club had consecutive non-losing seasons since 1981-82. In just his second season as head coach, Dungy's 1997 Buccaneers matched a franchise record with a 10-6 campaign that also featured a wild-card playoff victory over the Detroit Lions. Under Dungy's guidance in 1997, Tampa Bay continued improving on 1996's strong finish in which it won five of its last eight games, completing one of the largest single-season turnarounds in club history. Joined Tampa Bay after serving as Minnesota Vikings' defensive coordinator from 1992-95. Helped the Vikings' defense lead NFL with 95 interceptions during his four years in Minnesota. Prior to going to Vikings, spent 1989-1991 as defensive backs coach for Kansas City Chiefs. Also worked eight years as an assistant coach for the Pittsburgh Steelers under Chuck Noll as a defensive assistant (1981), defensive backs coach (1982-83), and as defensive coordinator (1984-88). At 25, was NFL's youngest assistant coach when hired by Steelers in 1981, then became league's youngest coordinator at age of 28. Began coaching career as defensive backs coach at University of Minnesota in 1980. As an NFL player, signed with Pittsburgh as a free agent in 1977 and played safety for Steelers for two seasons (1977-78). Had 9 interceptions (second in AFC with 6 in 1978) in 30 games for Pittsburgh and played in Super Bowl XIII victory over Dallas Cowboys. Had unusual distinction of making and throwing an interception in same 1977 game against Houston Oilers. Traded to San Francisco 49ers during 1979 training camp and played 15 games for 49ers. Was traded again prior to 1980 season to New York Giants in multi-player deal that sent current Green Bay Packers head coach Ray Rhodes to 49ers. Career record: 25-25.

Background: Starred as quarterback at University of Minnesota from 1973-76. Finished career as school's all-time leader in attempts, completions, passing yards, and touchdown passes. Left Minnesota in fourth place in Big Ten history in total offense. Two-time team most valuable player, played in Hula Bowl, East-West Shrine Game, and Japan Bowl. Attended Parkside High School in Jackson, Michigan.

Personal: Born October 6, 1955, in Jackson, Michigan. Tony and his wife, Lauren, have three children including daughter Tiara (13), and sons James (11) and Eric (6). The family resides in Tampa.

ASSISTANT COACHES

Mark Asanovich, strength and conditioning; born May 20, 1959, Duluth, Minn., lives in Tampa. No college or pro playing experience. College coach: Ohio State 1985, Citadel 1986. Pro coach: Minnesota Vikings 1995, joined Buccaneers in 1996.

Wendell Avery, offensive assistant; born October 20, 1956, Corpus Christi, Tex., lives in Tampa. Quarterback Minnesota 1975-79. No pro playing experience. College coach: McCalister College (Minn.) 1982-83, Winona State 1990-91, Alabama A&M 1992-93, Savannah State 1994-96 (head coach, 1995-96), Fort Valley State 1998. Pro coach: Joined Buccaneers in 1999.

Clyde Christensen, quarterbacks; born January 28, 1958, Corvine, Calif., lives in Tampa. Quarterback Fresno (Calif.) J.C. 1975, North Carolina 1976-78. No pro playing experience. College coach: East Tennessee State 1980-82, Temple 1983-85, East Carolina 1986-88, Holy Cross 1989-90, South Carolina 1991, Maryland 1992-93, Clemson 1994-95. Pro coach: Joined Buccaneers in 1996.

Herman Edwards, assistant head coach/defensive backs; born April 27, 1954, Monmouth, N.J., lives in Tampa. Defensive back California 1972, 1974, Monterrey Peninsula (Calif.) J.C. 1973, San Diego State 1975-76. Pro defensive back Philadelphia Eagles 1977-85, Los Angeles Rams 1986, Atlanta Falcons 1986. College coach. San Jose State 1987-89. Pro coach: Kansas City Chiefs 1992-94 (scout 1990-91, 1995), joined Buccaneers in 1996.

Chris Foerster, offensive line; born October 12, 1961, Milwaukee, Wis., lives in Tampa. Center Colorado State 1979-82. No pro playing experience. College coach: Colorado State 1983-87, Stanford 1988-91, Minnesota 1992. Pro coach: Minnesota Vikings 1993-95, joined Buccaneers in 1996.

Monte Kiffin, defensive coordinator; born February 29, 1940, Lexington, Neb., lives in Tampa. Offensive/defensive tackle Nebraska 1959-63. Pro defensive end Winnipeg Blue Bombers (CFL) 1965. College coach: Nebraska 1966-76, Arkansas 1977-79, North Carolina State 1980-82 (head coach). Pro coach: Green Bay Packers 1983, Buffalo Bills 1984-85, Minnesota Vikings 1986-89, 1991-94, New York Jets 1990, New Orleans Saints 1995, joined Buccaneers in 1996.

Aaron Komarek, asst. strength and conditioning; born July 17, 1971, St. Paul, Minn., lives in Tampa. Attended Minnesota. No college or pro playing experience. Pro coach: Minnesota Vikings 1993-95, joined Buccaneers in 1996.

Joe Marciano, special teams; born February 10, 1954, Scranton, Pa., lives in Tampa. Quarterback Temple 1972-75. No pro playing experience. College coach: East Stroudsburg 1977, Rhode Island 1978-79, Villanova 1980, Penn State 1981, Temple 1982. Pro coach: Philadelphia/Baltimore Stars (USFL) 1983-85, New Orleans Saints 1986-95, joined Buccaneers in 1996.

Rod Marinelli, defensive line; born July 13, 1949, Rosemead, Calif., lives in Tampa. Offensive/defensive tackle Utah 1968, offensive tackle California Lutheran 1970-72 (military service 1969-70). No pro playing experience. College coach: Utah State 1976-82, California 1983-91, Arizona State 1992-94, Southern California 1995. Pro coach: Joined Buccaneers in 1996.

Tony Nathan, running backs; born December 14, 1956, Birmingham, Ala., lives in Tampa. Running back Alabama 1975-78. Pro running back Miami Dolphins 1979-87. Pro coach: Miami Dolphins 1988-95, joined Buccaneers in 1996.

Kevin O'Dea, defensive assistant; born June 9, 1960, Williamsport, Va., lives in Tampa. Defensive back/wide receiver Lock Haven 1982-85. No pro playing experience. College coach: Lock Haven 1986, Cornell 1987, Virginia 1988-90, Penn State 1991-93. Pro coach: San Diego Chargers 1994-95, joined Buccaneers in 1996.

Mike Shula, offensive coordinator; born June 3, 1965, Baltimore, Md., lives in Tampa. Quarterback Alabama 1983-86. Pro quarterback Tampa Bay Buccaneers 1987. Pro coach: Tampa Bay Buccaneers 1988-90, Miami Dolphins 1991-92, Chicago Bears 1993-95, rejoined Buccaneers in 1996.

Lovie Smith, linebackers; born May 8, 1958, Gladewater, Tex., lives in Tampa. Linebacker Tulsa 1976-79. No pro playing experience. College coach: Tulsa 1983-86, Wisconsin 1987, Arizona State 1988-91, Kentucky 1992, Tennessee 1993-94, Ohio State 1995. Pro coach: Joined Buccaneers in 1996.

Ricky Thomas, tight ends; born March 29, 1965, London, England, lives in Tampa. Safety Alabama 1983-86. Pro safety Seattle Seahawks 1987. College coach: Kentucky 1996, Gardner-Webb 1996. Pro coach: Joined Buccaneers in 1997.

Charlie Williams, wide receivers; born January 31, 1958, Long Beach, Calif., lives in Tampa. Defensive back Long Beach City College 1977-78, Colorado State 1979-80. No pro playing experience. College coach: Colorado State 1981, Long Beach City College 1984-85, New Mexico State 1986-87, Texas Christian 1988-91, Minnesota 1992, Miami 1993-95. Pro coach: Joined Buccaneers in 1996.

1999 FIRST-YEAR ROSTER

Name	Pos.	Ht.	Wt.	Birthdate	College	Hometown	How Acq.
Bailey, Ronald (1)	CB	5-11	187	2/14/75	Georgia	Charlton County, Ga.	FA
Bonner, Patrick	QB	6-1	195	2/19/76	Florida A&M	Ft. Lauderdale, Fla.	FA
Curry, DeMarcus	T	6-5	322	4/30/75	Auburn	Columbus, Ga.	FA
DeGroh, Eric	C	6-4	324	4/16/77	West Virginia	Huron, Ohio	FA
Denson, Autry	RB	5-10	202	12/8/76	Notre Dame	Lauderhill, Fla.	D7b
DiCosmo, Anthony	WR	6-3	221	8/8/77	Boston College	Fair Lawn, N.J.	FA
Donaldson, Cedric (1)	CB	5-9	180	2/12/76	Louisiana State	Provine, Miss.	FA
Elezovic, Peter (1)	K	5-11	187	6/28/71	Michigan	Detroit, Mich.	FA
Feazell, Juaquin	DT	6-3	275	10/15/75	Michigan	Ft. Valley, Ga.	FA
Freeman, Jason	TE	6-3	248	11/14/76	Oklahoma	Muskogee, Okla.	FA
Gibbs, Stanakeane	LB	5-11	226	4/22/75	Syracuse	Orange, N.J.	FA
Glenn, Lamarr	RB	6-1	235	12/11/75	Florida State	Daytona Beach, Fla.	D6
Gramatica, Martin	K	5-8	180	11/27/75	Kansas State	LaBelle, Fla.	D3
Howard, Bobbie	LB	5-10	230	6/14/77	Notre Dame	Belle, W. Va.	FA
Howard, Eddie (1)	P	6-1	203	10/6/72	Idaho	Covina, Calif.	FA
Hughes, Ralph (1)	DE	6-4	256	10/26/75	Georgia Tech	Montgomery, Ala.	FA
Humphrey, John	RB	5-10	195	12/30/75	Texas A&M-Kingsville	Galveston, Tex.	FA
Hunt, Robert	G-T	6-2	290	7/22/75	Virginia	Newport News, Va.	D7a
Jackson, Dexter	S	6-0	189	7/28/77	Florida State	Quincy, Fla.	D4
King, Shaun	QB	6-0	221	5/29/77	Tulane	St. Petersburg, Fla.	D2
Langley, Aron	P	6-0	187	5/31/76	Wyoming	Longmont, Colo.	FA
Malveaux, Felman (1)	WR	6-0	179	8/20/73	Michigan	Hamshire, Tex.	FA
Marshall, Lemar	S	6-2	203	12/17/76	Michigan State	Cincinnati, Ohio	FA
McDonald, Darnell	WR	6-3	190	5/26/76	Kansas State	Fairfax, Va.	D7c
McFarland, Anthony	DT	6-0	292	12/18/77	Louisiana State	Winnsboro, La.	D1
McLaughlin, John	LB	6-3	247	11/13/75	California	Newhall, Calif.	D5
McLeod, Kevin (1)	RB	6-0	242	10/17/74	Auburn	Clarkston, Ga.	FA
Micus, Dillon	WR	5-11	194	10/11/75	Northern Colorado	Mullen, Hawaii	FA
O'Connor, Drew	WR	6-3	211	2/2/76	Maine	Plainfield, N.J.	FA
Oster, Scott	G	6-2	341	9/24/77	Temple	Plhiladelphia, Pa.	FA
Saunders, Troy	CB	5-10	185	4/25/76	Florida State	Miami, Fla.	FA
Smith, Landon	RB	5-11	245	8/6/76	Cincinnati	Madison, Miss.	FA
Spearman, Andray	G	6-3	287	11/12/75	South Carolina	Greenwood, S.C.	FA
Vandervelt, Jamie (1)	T	6-5	298	4/23/74	Wisconsin	Waukesha, Wis.	FA

The term NFL Rookie is defined as a player who is in his first season of professional football and has not been on the roster of another professional football team for any regular-season or postseason games. A Rookie is designated by an "R" on NFL rosters. Players who have been active in another professional football league or players who have NFL experience, including either preseason training camp or being on an Active List or Inactive List, or on Reserve/Injured or Reserve/Physically Unable to Perform for fewer than six regular-season games, are termed NFL First-Year Players. An NFL First-Year Player is designated by a "1" on NFL rosters. Thereafter, a player is credited with an additional year of experience for each season in which he accumulates six games on the Active List or Inactive List, or on Reserve/Injured or Reserve/Physically Unable to Perform.

WASHINGTON REDSKINS

National Football Conference
Eastern Division
Team Colors: Burgundy and Gold
Redskin Park
P.O. Box 17247
Washington, D.C. 20041
Telephone: (703) 478-8900

CLUB OFFICIALS

Owner: Daniel M. Snyder
Controller: Mark Francis
General Manager: Charley Casserly
Assistant General Manager: Bobby Mitchell
Director of Player Development: Joe Mendes
Director of College Scouting: George Saimes
Scouts: Gene Bates, Larry Bryan, Scott Cohen, Mike Maccagnan, Miller McCalmon, Joel Patten, Dave Sears
Coordinator of Scouting: Chuck Banker
Scouting Administrator: Ray Wright
Director of Public Relations: Mike McCall
Director of Media Relations: Chris Helein
Publications/Internet Director: Scott McKeen
Community Relations Director: Wendy Brinker
Director of Administration: Barry Asimos
Director of Marketing: John Wagner
Video Director: Donnie Schoenmann
Asst. Video Director: Hugh McPhillips
Ticket Manager: Jeff Ritter
Vice President-Stadium Operations: Jeff Klein
Head Trainer: Bubba Tyer
Assistant Trainers: Al Bellamy, Kevin Bastin
Equipment Manager: Jay Brunetti
Asst. Equipment Manager: Jeff Parsons
Stadium: Jack Kent Cooke Stadium
•**Capacity:** 80,116
Raljon, Maryland 20785-4236
Playing Surface: Grass
Training Camp: Frostburg State University
Frostburg, Maryland 21532-1099

1999 SCHEDULE

PRESEASON

Aug. 13	at New England	7:30
Aug. 20	**Buffalo**	8:00
Aug. 28	at Pittsburgh	7:30
Sept. 3	**Tampa Bay**	8:00

REGULAR SEASON

Sept. 12	**Dallas**	1:00
Sept. 19	at New York Giants	1:00
Sept. 26	at New York Jets	1:00
Oct. 3	**Carolina**	4:05
Oct. 10	Open Date	
Oct. 17	at Arizona	5:20
Oct. 24	at Dallas	12:00
Oct. 31	**Chicago**	1:00
Nov. 7	**Buffalo**	1:00
Nov. 14	at Philadelphia	1:00
Nov. 21	**New York Giants**	4:15
Nov. 28	**Philadelphia**	1:00
Dec. 5	at Detroit	1:00
Dec. 12	**Arizona**	1:00
Dec. 19	at Indianapolis	1:00
Dec. 26	at San Francisco	5:20
Jan. 2	**Miami**	4:15

RECORD HOLDERS

INDIVIDUAL RECORDS—CAREER

Category	Name	Performance
Rushing (Yds.)	John Riggins, 1976-79, 1981-85	7,472
Passing (Yds.)	Joe Theismann, 1974-1985	25,206
Passing (TDs)	Sammy Baugh, 1937-1952	187
Receiving (No.)	Art Monk, 1980-1993	888
Receiving (Yds.)	Art Monk, 1980-1993	12,028
Interceptions	Darrell Green, 1983-1998	47
Punting (Avg.)	Sammy Baugh, 1937-1952	*45.1
Punt Return (Avg.)	Johnny Williams, 1952-53	12.8
Kickoff Return (Avg.)	Bobby Mitchell, 1962-68	28.5
Field Goals	Mark Moseley, 1974-1986	263
Touchdowns (Tot.)	Charley Taylor, 1964-1977	90
Points	Mark Moseley, 1974-1986	1,206

INDIVIDUAL RECORDS—SINGLE SEASON

Category	Name	Performance
Rushing (Yds.)	Terry Allen, 1996	1,353
Passing (Yds.)	Jay Schroeder, 1986	4,109
Passing (TDs)	Sonny Jurgensen, 1967	31
Receiving (No.)	Art Monk, 1984	106
Receiving (Yds.)	Bobby Mitchell, 1963	1,436
Interceptions	Dan Sandifer, 1948	13
Punting (Avg.)	Sammy Baugh, 1940	*51.4
Punt Return (Avg.)	Johnny Williams, 1952	15.3
Kickoff Return (Avg.)	Mike Nelms, 1981	29.7
Field Goals	Mark Moseley, 1983	33
Touchdowns (Tot.)	John Riggins, 1983	24
Points	Mark Moseley, 1983	161

INDIVIDUAL RECORDS—SINGLE GAME

Category	Name	Performance
Rushing (Yds.)	Gerald Riggs, 9-17-89	221
Passing (Yds.)	Sammy Baugh, 10-31-43	446
Passing (TDs)	Sammy Baugh, 10-31-43, 11-23-47	6
	Mark Rypien, 11-10-91	6
Receiving (No.)	Art Monk, 12-15-85	13
	Kelvin Bryant, 12-7-86	13
	Art Monk, 11-4-90	13
Receiving (Yds.)	Anthony Allen, 10-4-87	255
Interceptions	Sammy Baugh, 11-14-43	*4
	Dan Sandifer, 10-31-48	*4
Field Goals	Many times	5
	Last time by Chip Lohmiller, 10-25-92	
Touchdowns (Tot.)	Dick James, 12-17-61	4
	Larry Brown, 12-16-73	4
Points	Dick James, 12-17-61	24
	Larry Brown, 12-16-73	24

*NFL Record

COACHING HISTORY

Boston 1932-36
(482-424-27)

1932	Lud Wray	4-4-2
1933-34	William (Lone Star) Dietz	11-11-2
1935	Eddie Casey	2-8-1
1936-42	Ray Flaherty	56-23-3
1943	Arthur (Dutch) Bergman	7-4-1
1944-45	Dudley DeGroot	14-6-1
1946-48	Glen (Turk) Edwards	16-18-1
1949	John Whelchel*	3-3-1
1949-51	Herman Ball**	4-16-0
1951	Dick Todd	5-4-0
1952-53	Earl (Curly) Lambeau	10-13-1
1954-58	Joe Kuharich	26-32-2
1959-60	Mike Nixon	4-18-2
1961-65	Bill McPeak	21-46-3
1966-68	Otto Graham	17-22-3
1969	Vince Lombardi	7-5-2
1970	Bill Austin	6-8-0
1971-77	George Allen	69-35-1
1978-80	Jack Pardee	24-24-0
1981-92	Joe Gibbs	140-65-0
1993	Richie Petitbon	4-12-0
1994-98	Norv Turner	32-47-1

JACK KENT COOKE STADIUM

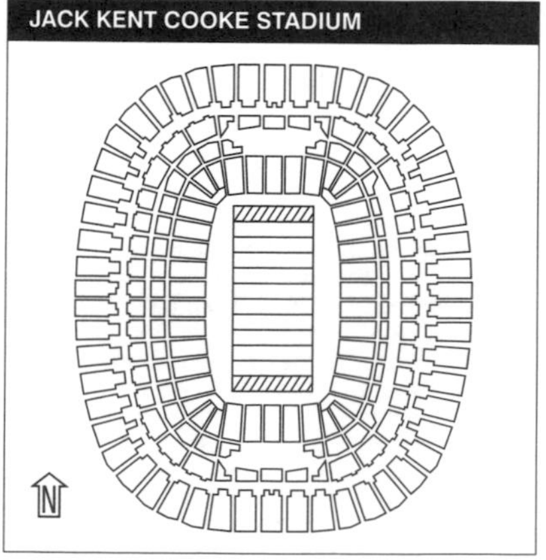

*Released after seven games in 1949
**Released after three games in 1951

1998 TEAM RECORD

PRESEASON (1-3)

Date	Result		Opponent
8/8	L	16-19	Miami
8/15	W	27-24	at Tennessee
8/22	L	17-20	New England
8/28	L	17-27	at Buffalo

REGULAR SEASON (6-10)

Date	Result		Opponent	Att.
9/6	L	24-31	at New York Giants	76,629
9/14	L	10-45	San Francisco	76,798
9/20	L	14-24	at Seattle	63,336
9/27	L	16-38	Denver	71,880
10/4	L	10-31	Dallas	72,284
10/11	L	12-17	at Philadelphia	66,183
10/18	L	7-41	at Minnesota	64,004
11/1	W	21-14	New York Giants	67,976
11/8	L	27-29	at Arizona	43,159
11/15	W	28-3	Philadelphia	67,704
11/22	L	42-45	Arizona	66,435
11/29	W	29-19	at Oakland	41,409
12/6	W	24-20	San Diego	65,713
12/13	W	28-25	at Carolina	46,940
12/19	W	20-16	Tampa Bay	66,309
12/27	L	7-23	at Dallas	63,565

SCORE BY PERIODS

Redskins	94	80	57	88	0	— 319
Opponents	92	133	93	103	0	— 421

ATTENDANCE

Home 555,099 Away 465,225 Total 1,020,324
Single-game home record, 78,270 (9/14/97)
Single-season home record, 605,592 (1997)

1998 TEAM STATISTICS

	Redskins	Opp.
Total First Downs	295	303
Rushing	84	127
Passing	186	152
Penalty	25	24
Third Down: Made/Att	68/215	88/231
Third Down Pct.	31.6	38.1
Fourth Down: Made/Att	5/15	6/15
Fourth Down Pct.	33.3	40.0
Total Net Yards	5,010	5,354
Avg. Per Game	313.1	334.6
Total Plays	1,027	1,057
Avg. Per Play	4.9	5.1
Net Yards Rushing	1,685	2,436
Avg. Per Game	105.3	152.3
Total Rushes	401	531
Net Yards Passing	3,325	2,918
Avg. Per Game	207.8	182.4
Sacked/Yards Lost	61/399	33/194
Gross Yards	3,724	3,112
Att./Completions	565/304	493/281
Completion Pct.	53.8	57.0
Had Intercepted	14	13
Punts/Avg.	97/43.5	92/43.1
Net Punting Avg.	97/38.9	92/35.2
Penalties/Yards Lost	112/975	96/824
Fumbles/Ball Lost	27/15	17/8
Touchdowns	40	50
Rushing	15	24
Passing	24	21
Returns	1	5
Avg. Time of Possession	28:34	31:26

1998 INDIVIDUAL STATISTICS

Passing	Att.	Comp.	Yds.	Pct.	TD	Int.	Tkld.	Rate
T. Green	509	278	3,441	54.6	23	11	49/338	81.8
Frerotte	54	25	283	46.3	1	3	12/61	45.5
Mitchell	2	1	0	50.0	0	0	0/0	56.3
Redskins	565	304	3,724	53.8	24	14	61/399	78.2
Opponents	493	281	3,112	57.0	21	13	33/194	79.1

SCORING	TD R	TD P	TD Rt	PAT	FG	Saf	PTS
Blanchard	0	0	0	30/31	11/17	0	63
Shepherd	1	8	0	0/0	0/0	0	56
Hicks	8	0	0	0/0	0/0	0	48
Westbrook	0	6	0	0/0	0/0	0	36
S. Alexander	0	4	0	0/0	0/0	0	24
Mitchell	2	0	1	0/0	0/0	0	18
Allen	2	0	0	0/0	0/0	0	12
Connell	0	2	0	0/0	0/0	0	12
Davis	0	2	0	0/0	0/0	0	12
T. Green	2	0	0	0/0	0/0	0	12
Blanton	0	0	0	4/4	2/4	0	10
Bowie	0	1	0	0/0	0/0	0	6
Thrash	0	1	0	0/0	0/0	0	6
Akers	0	0	0	2/2	0/2	0	2
Boutte	0	0	0	0/0	0/0	1	2
Redskins	15	24	1	36/37	13/23	1	319
Opponents	24	21	5	46/46	23/28	1	421

2-Point conversions: Shepherd.
Team 1-3, Opponents 2-4.

RUSHING	Att.	Yds.	Avg.	LG	TD
Allen	148	700	4.7	45	2
Hicks	122	433	3.5	28	8
Mitchell	39	208	5.3	22	2
T. Green	42	117	2.8	13	2
Davis	34	109	3.2	12	0
Shepherd	6	91	15.2	29	1
Frerotte	3	20	6.7	20	0
Westbrook	1	11	11.0	11	0
Bowie	4	8	2.0	4	0
M. Turk	2	-12	-6.0	0	0
Redskins	401	1,685	4.2	45	15
Opponents	531	2,436	4.6	55	24

RECEIVING	No.	Yds.	Avg.	LG	TD
Westbrook	44	736	16.7	75t	6
Mitchell	44	306	7.0	24	0
Shepherd	43	712	16.6	43t	8
S. Alexander	37	383	10.4	33	4
Connell	28	451	16.1	61	2
Asher	28	294	10.5	28	0
Davis	21	263	12.5	30	2
Allen	17	128	7.5	17	0
Thomas	14	173	12.4	25	0
Thrash	10	163	16.3	28	1
Bowie	7	53	7.6	17	1
Hicks	4	23	5.8	9	0
Sellers	3	18	6.0	8	0
Ellard	2	29	14.5	19	0
T. Green	2	-8	-4.0	0	0
Redskins	304	3,724	12.3	75t	24
Opponents	281	3,112	11.1	63	21

INTERCEPTIONS	No.	Yds.	Avg.	LG	TD
L. Evans	3	77	25.7	54	0
D. Green	3	36	12.0	36	0
Dishman	2	60	30.0	49	0
Jones	1	9	9.0	9	0
Campbell	1	4	4.0	4	0
Wilkinson	1	4	4.0	4	0
Barber	1	0	0.0	0	0
Richard	1	0	0.0	0	0
Redskins	13	190	14.6	54	0
Opponents	14	169	12.1	55t	2

PUNTING	No.	Yds.	Avg.	In 20	LG
M. Turk	93	4,103	44.1	33	69
Blanchard	3	113	37.7	1	43
Redskins	97	4,216	43.5	34	69
Opponents	92	3,966	43.1	20	64

PUNT RETURNS	No.	FC	Yds.	Avg.	LG	TD
Mitchell	44	18	506	11.5	47	0
Redskins	44	18	506	11.5	47	0
Opponents	32	16	261	8.2	40	0

KICKOFF RETURNS	No.	Yds.	Avg.	LG	TD
Mitchell	59	1,337	22.7	101t	1
Thrash	6	129	21.5	39	0
Sellers	2	33	16.5	14	0
Asher	1	8	8.0	8	0
Burnett	1	5	5.0	5	0
Jenkins	1	0	0.0	0	0
Redskins	70	1,512	21.6	101t	1
Opponents	61	1,569	25.7	90t	2

FIELD GOALS	1-19	20-29	30-39	40-49	50+
Blanchard	0/0	2/2	6/8	2/5	1/2
Blanton	0/0	0/0	1/2	1/2	0/0
Akers	0/0	0/0	0/0	0/2	0/0
Redskins	0/0	2/2	7/10	3/9	1/2
Opponents	1/1	10/11	5/6	7/9	0/1

SACKS	No.
Wilkinson	7.5
Lang	7.0
Duff	3.0
Kalu	3.0
M. Patton	3.0
Boutte	2.0
Harvey	2.0
Stubblefield	1.5
L. Evans	1.0
Jones	1.0
Kinney	1.0
Pounds	0.5
D. Smith	0.5
Redskins	33.0
Opponents	61.0

1999 DRAFT CHOICES

Round	Name	Pos.	College
1	Champ Bailey	DB	Georgia
2	Jon Jansen	T	Michigan
4	Nate Stimson	LB	Georgia Tech
5	Derek Smith	T	Virginia Tech
6	Jeff Hall	K	Tennessee
7	Tim Alexander	WR	Oregon State

WASHINGTON REDSKINS

1999 VETERAN ROSTER

No.	Name	Pos.	Ht.	Wt.	Birthdate	NFL Exp.	College	Hometown	How Acq.	'98 Games/ Starts
80	Alexander, Stephen	WR	6-4	246	11/7/75	2	Oklahoma	Chickasha, Okla.	D2-'98	15/5
74	Badger, Brad	G	6-4	298	1/11/75	3	Stanford	Corvalis, Ore.	D5d-'97	16/16
59	Barber, Shawn	LB	6-2	224	1/14/75	2	Richmond	Richmond, Va.	D4-'98	16/1
17	Blanchard, Cary	K	6-1	232	11/5/68	8	Oklahoma State	Hurst, Tex.	FA-'98	13/0
93	Boutte, Marc	DT	6-4	307	7/26/69	8	Louisiana State	Lake Charles, La.	FA-'94	13/1
47	Bowie, Larry	RB	6-0	249	3/21/73	4	Georgia	Anniston, Ala.	FA-'96	5/4
78	Brown, Doug	DT	6-7	290	9/29/74	2	Simon Fraser	Coquittlam, B.C. Canada	FA-'98	10/8
73	Brown, Jamie	T	6-8	318	4/24/72	5	Florida A&M	Miami, Fla.	UFA(SF)-'99	8/5*
56	Burnett, Chester	LB	5-10	238	4/15/75	2	Arizona	Denver, Colo.	FA-'98	5/0
61	Burns, Lamont	G	6-4	305	3/16/74	2	East Carolina	Greensboro, N.C.	FA-'98	0*
83	Connell, Albert	WR	6-0	179	5/13/74	3	Texas A&M	Brooklyn, N.Y.	D4-'97	14/5
5	Conway, Brett	K	6-2	192	3/8/75	3	Penn State	Liburn, Ga.	FA-'98	6/0
75	Cook, Anthony	DE	6-3	295	5/30/72	5	South Carolina State	Bennettsville, S.C.	UFA(Tenn)-'99	13/3*
41	Crutchfield, Buddy	CB	6-0	196	3/7/76	2	North Carolina Central	Raleigh, N.C.	FA-'98	2/0
48	Davis, Stephen	RB	6-0	234	3/1/74	4	Auburn	Spartanburg, S.C.	D4-'96	16/12
25	Denton, Tim	CB-S	5-11	182	2/2/73	2	Sam Houston	Galveston, Tex.	FA-'98	16/0
27	Evans, Greg	S	6-1	208	6/28/71	3	Texas Christian	San Antonio, Tex.	FA-'98	13/0
35	Evans, Leomont	S	6-1	202	7/12/74	4	Clemson	Abbeville, S.C.	D5-'96	16/13
60	Fischer, Mark	C	6-3	293	7/29/74	2	Purdue	Cincinnati, Ohio	D5-'98	6/0
28	Green, Darrell	CB	5-8	184	2/15/60	17	Texas A&I	Houston, Tex.	D1-'83	16/16
57	Harvey, Ken	LB	6-2	237	5/6/65	12	California	Austin, Tex.	UFA(Ariz)-'94	11/9
20	Hicks, Skip	RB	6-0	230	10/13/74	2	UCLA	Burkburnett, Tex.	D3-'98	9/5
91	Hoelscher, David	DT	6-5	285	11/27/75	2	Eastern Kentucky	Versailles, Ohio	FA-'98	1/0
88	Jenkins, James	TE	6-2	249	8/17/67	9	Rutgers	Staten Island, N.Y.	FA-'91	16/4
14	t- Johnson, Brad	QB	6-5	224	9/13/68	8	Florida State	Black Mountain, N.C.	T(Minn)-'99	4/2*
77	Johnson, Tre'	G	6-2	326	8/30/71	6	Temple	Peekskill, N.Y.	D2-'94	10/10
54	Jones, Greg	LB	6-4	238	5/22/74	3	Colorado	Denver, Colo.	D2-'97	16/5
72	Kalu, Ndukwe	DE	6-3	246	8/3/75	3	Rice	San Antonio, Tex.	FA-'99	13/1
97	Kinney, Kelvin	DE	6-6	264	12/31/72	4	Virginia State	Montgomery, W. Va.	D6-'96	14/12
90	Lang, Kenard	DE	6-4	277	1/31/75	3	Miami	Orlando, Fla.	D1-'97	16/16
85	Lusk, Henry	TE	6-2	250	5/8/72	3	Utah	Carmel, Calif.	FA-'99	3/1*
69	Milstead, Rod	G	6-2	290	11/10/69	8	Delaware State	Bryan's Road, Md.	FA-'98	14/11
30	Mitchell, Brian	RB	5-10	221	8/18/68	10	Southwestern Louisiana	Plaquemine, La.	D5-'90	16/0
68	Patton, Joe	G	6-5	309	1/5/72	6	Alabama A&M	Birmingham, Ala.	D3b-'94	11/10
16	t- Peete, Rodney	QB	6-0	225	3/16/66	11	Southern California	Tucson, Ariz.	T(Phil)-'99	5/4*
51	Ponds, Antwaune	LB	6-2	252	6/29/75	2	Syracuse	Jacksonville, Fla.	D7b-'98	3/0
31	Pounds, Darryl	CB	5-10	189	7/21/72	5	Nicholls State	Ft. Worth, Tex.	D3-'95	16/3
67	Pourdanesh, Shar	T	6-6	312	7/19/70	4	Nevada	Teheran, Iran	FA-'96	16/15
52	Raymer, Cory	C	6-2	289	3/3/73	5	Wisconsin	Fond du Lac, Wis.	D2-'95	16/16
98	Russell, Twan	LB	6-1	219	4/25/74	3	Miami	Ft. Lauderdale, Fla.	D5c-'97	3/0
46	Sadowski, Troy	TE	6-5	252	12/8/65	10	Georgia	Woodstock, Ga.	FA-'99	5/0*
45	Sellers, Mike	RB	6-3	260	7/21/75	2	Walla Walla	Lacey, Wash.	FA-'98	14/1
29	Shade, Sam	S	6-1	201	6/14/73	5	Alabama	Birmingham, Ala.	UFA(Cin)-'99	16/15*
63	Sims, Keith	G	6-3	318	6/17/67	9	Iowa State	Warren, N.J.	FA-'98	4/0
50	Smith, Derek	LB	6-2	239	1/18/75	3	Arizona State	American Fork, Utah	D3-'97	16/15
23	Stevens, Matt	S	6-0	206	6/15/73	4	Appalachian State	Chapel Hill, N.C.	FA-'98	3/0
55	Strickland, Fred	LB	6-2	251	8/15/66	12	Purdue	Wanaque, N.J.	UFA(Dall)-'99	16/15*
94	Stubblefield, Dana	DT	6-2	315	11/14/70	7	Kansas	Cleves, Ohio	UFA(SF)-'98	7/7
89	Thomas, Chris	WR	6-2	190	7/16/71	4	Cal Poly-San Luis Obispo	Burbank, Calif.	FA-'97	14/0
87	Thrash, James	WR	6-0	200	4/28/75	3	Missouri Southern	Wewoka, Okla.	FA-'97	10/1
66	Turk, Dan	C	6-4	290	6/25/62	15	Wisconsin	Greenfield, Wis.	FA-'97	16/0
1	Turk, Matt	P	6-5	237	6/16/68	5	Wisconsin-Whitewater	Greenfield, Wis.	FA-'95	16/0
79	Vickers, Kipp	T	6-2	298	8/27/69	4	Miami	Tarpon Springs, Fla.	FA-'99	0*
11	Weldon, Casey	QB	6-1	206	2/3/69	8	Florida State	Tallahassee, Fla.	FA-'98	0*
82	Westbrook, Michael	WR	6-3	220	7/7/72	5	Colorado	Detroit, Mich.	D1-'95	11/10
95	Wilkinson, Dan	DT	6-5	313	3/13/73	6	Ohio State	Dayton, Ohio	T(Cin)-'98	16/16
22	Williams, Jamel	S	5-11	205	12/22/73	3	Nebraska	Gary, Ind.	D5a-'97	16/0

* J. Brown played 8 games with San Francisco in '98; Burns inactive for 4 games; Cook played 13 games with Tennessee; B. Johnson played 4 games with Minnesota; Lusk played 3 games with Miami; Peete played 5 games with Philadelphia; Sadowski played 5 games with Jacksonville; Shade played 16 games with Cincinnati; Strickland played 16 games with Dallas; Vickers inactive for 5 games; Weldon inactive for 13 games.

t– Redskins traded for Johnson (Minnesota), Peete (Philadelphia).

Players lost to free agency (6): TE Jamie Asher (Phil; 9 games in '98), DE Jamal Duff (Chi; 13), QB Trent Green (StL; 15), DE Rich Owens (Mia; 0), LB Marcus Patton (KC; 16), WR Leslie Shephard (Cle; 16).

Also played with Redskins in '98—K David Akers (1 game), LB Patrise Alexander (1), RB Terry Allen (10), C-G-T Michael Batiste (6), K Scott Blanton (2), S Jesse Campbell (3), CB Cris Dishman (16), T Troy Drake (11), WR Henry Ellard (2), QB Gus Frerotte (3), RB Jim Kitts (3), RB Le'Shai Maston (1), S Stanley Richard (15), T Paul Wiggins (1).

COACHING STAFF

Head Coach,
Norv Turner

Pro Career: Enters his sixth season as head coach of the Washington Redskins after serving three years as the Dallas Cowboys' offensive coordinator. Turner guided the Cowboys' prolific offense during back-to-back Super Bowl championship seasons. He inherited a Cowboys' offense that finished twenty-eighth in total offense in 1990, and a year later improved to ninth. The Cowboys finished fourth in the league offensively in 1992-93. In three seasons under Turner, quarterback Troy Aikman compiled a 91.7 rating, and running back Emmitt Smith won three consecutive NFL rushing titles. Prior to joining the Cowboys, Turner coached six seasons (1985-1990) with the Los Angeles Rams where he oversaw the passing game. Quarterback Jim Everett enjoyed his best seasons under Turner, while Willie Anderson led the NFL in yards per catch in 1989 and 1990, and Henry Ellard was the league's leading receiver in 1988. Career record: 32-47-1.

Background: Turner played quarterback for three seasons at the University of Oregon (1972-74). He began his coaching career as a graduate assistant at Oregon in 1975. A year later, he moved to the University of Southern California, where he coached from 1976-1984.

Personal: Born May 17, 1952, in LeJeune, N.C. Turner and his wife, Nancy, live in Oakton, Va., and have three children—Scott, Stephanie, and Drew.

ASSISTANT COACHES

Jason Arapoff, asst. conditioning; born July 8, 1965, Weymouth, Mass., lives in Centreville, Va. Defensive back Springfield College 1985-88. No pro playing experience. Pro coach: Joined Redskins in 1992.

Rubin Carter, defensive line; born December 12, 1952, Ft. Lauderdale, Fla., lives in Laurel, Md. Defensive tackle Miami 1970-74. Pro defensive tackle Denver Broncos 1975-1986. College coach: Howard 1989-1993, San Jose State 1995-96, Maryland 1997-98. Pro coach: Denver Broncos 1987-88, joined Redskins in 1999.

Jeff FitzGerald, defensive assistant-linebackers; born April 18, 1960, Burbank, Calif., lives in Reston, Va. Attended Oregon State. No college or pro playing experience. College coach: Cincinnati 1985-86, Alabama 1987-89, San Diego State 1994-97. Pro coach: Tampa Bay Buccaneers 1990-93, joined Redskins in 1998.

Russ Grimm, offensive line; born May 2, 1959, Scottdale, Pa., lives in Fairfax, Va. Guard-center Pittsburgh 1977-1980. Pro guard Washington Redskins 1981-1991. Pro coach: Joined Redskins in 1992.

Tom Hayes, defensive backs; born March 26, 1949, Keokuk, Iowa, lives in Ashburn, Va. Defensive back Iowa 1968-1971. No pro playing experience. College coach: Coe College 1973, Iowa 1977-78, Cal State-Fullerton 1979, UCLA 1980-88, Texas A&M 1989, Oklahoma 1990-94. Pro coach: Joined Redskins in 1995.

Bobby Jackson, running game coordinator; born February 16, 1940, Forsyth, Ga., lives in Sterling, Va. Linebacker-running back Samford 1959-1962. No pro playing experience. College coach: Florida State 1965-69, Kansas State 1970-74, Louisville 1975-76, Tennessee 1977-1982. Pro coach: Atlanta Falcons 1983-86, San Diego Chargers 1987-1991, Phoenix Cardinals 1992-93, joined Redskins in 1994.

Earl Leggett, defensive line; born March 5, 1935, Jacksonville, lives in Leesburg, Va. Defensive tackle Hinds J.C. 1953-54, Louisiana State 1955-56. Pro defensive tackle Chicago Bears 1957-1965, Los Angeles Rams 1966, New Orleans Saints 1967-68. College coach: Nicholls State 1971, Texas Christian 1972-73. Pro coach: Southern California Sun (WFL) 1974-75, Seattle Seahawks 1976-77, San Francisco 49ers 1978, Oakland/Los Angeles Raiders 1980-88, 1991-92, Denver Broncos 1989-1990, New York Giants 1993-96, joined Redskins in 1997.

LeCharls McDaniel, special teams; born October 15, 1958, Fort Bragg, N.C., lives in Ashburn, Va. Cornerback Cal Poly-San Luis Obispo 1976-1980. Pro defensive back Washington Redskins 1981-82, New York Giants 1983. College coach: Hartnell College (Calif.) 1984-89, Cal Poly-San Luis Obispo 1992, San Diego State 1994-95. Pro coach: San Diego Chargers 1990-1991, Phoenix Cardinals 1993, joined Redskins in 1997.

Mike Nolan, defensive coordinator-linebackers; born March 7, 1959, Baltimore, lives in Oakton, Va. Free safety Oregon 1977-1980. No pro playing experience. College coach: Oregon 1981, Stanford 1982-83, Rice 1984-85, Louisiana State 1986. Pro coach: Denver Broncos 1987-1992, New York Giants 1993-96, joined Redskins in 1997.

Rich Olson, quarterbacks; born July 7, 1948, Wilmington, Calif., lives in Herndon, Va. Quarterback-free safety Washington State 1968-69. No pro playing experience. College coach: Washington State 1970, Fresno State 1976, Southern California 1977, Southern Methodist 1978-1980, Arkansas 1981-83, Fresno State 1984-1991, Miami 1992-94. Pro coach: Seattle Seahawks 1995-98, joined Redskins in 1999.

Michael Pope, tight ends; born March 15, 1942, Monroe, N.C., lives in Ashburn, Va. Quarterback Lenoir Rhyne 1962-64. No pro playing experience. College coach: Florida State 1970-74, Texas Tech 1975-77, Mississippi 1978-1982. Pro coach: New York Giants 1983-1991, Cincinnati Bengals 1992-93, New England Patriots 1994-96, joined Redskins in 1997.

Dan Riley, strength; born October 19, 1949, Syracuse, N.Y., lives in Ashburn, Va. Attended Keene State. No college or pro playing experience. College coach: Army 1973-76, Penn State 1977-1981. Pro coach: Joined Redskins in 1982.

Terry Robiskie, passing game coordinator; born November 12, 1954, New Orleans, lives in Clifton, Va. Running back Louisiana State 1973-76. Pro running back Oakland Raiders 1977-79, Miami Dolphins 1980-81. Pro coach: Los Angeles Raiders 1982-1993, joined Redskins in 1994.

Ed Sidwell, offensive assistant; born January 11, 1967, Belleville, Ill., lives in McClean, Va. Attended Ohio State. No college or pro playing experience. College coach: Ohio State 1988-1993. Pro coach: San Antonio Texans (CFL) 1995, Houston Oilers 1996, joined Redskins in 1997.

1999 FIRST-YEAR ROSTER

Name	Pos.	Ht.	Wt.	Birthdate	College	Hometown	How Acq.
Alexander, Kevin (1)	WR	5-9	183	1/10/74	Utah State	Placentia, Calif.	FA
Alexander, Tim	WR	6-0	186	10/14/74	Oregon State	Sarasota, Fla.	D7
Bailey, Champ	CB	6-1	184	6/22/78	Georgia	Folkston, Ga.	D1
Ball, Raphael (1)	CB	5-10	179	12/9/74	Ball State	Forest Park, Ohio	FA
Collins, Leroy	RB	5-11	200	4/5/76	Louisville	Hudson, N.Y.	FA
Colquitt, Travis	P	6-1	210	7/16/71	Marshall	Salem, Va.	FA
Dukes, Chad (1)	RB	6-0	230	12/29/71	Pittsburgh	Albany, N.Y.	FA
Hall, Jeff	K	5-11	190	7/30/76	Tennessee	Winchester, Tenn.	FA
Ham, Derrick	DE	6-5	275	3/23/75	Miami	Merritt Island, Fla.	FA
Hamilton, Malcolm (1)	LB	6-1	235	12/31/72	Baylor	Odessa, Tex.	FA-'98
Jansen, Jon	T	6-6	302	1/28/76	Michigan	Clawson, Mich.	FA
Lord, Junior (1)	WR	6-1	197	3/11/76	Guilford	Greenwich, Conn.	FA
Miller, Norman (1)	RB	5-10	189	8/16/74	Texas A&M-Kingsville	Sacramento, Calif.	FA-'98
Mitchell, Kenny	WR	6-3	211	9/4/77	Arizona State	Peoria, Ariz.	FA
Paci, John (1)	QB	6-3	212	9/19/72	Indiana	Huntington, N.Y.	FA
Peoples, Kevin	S	6-2	210	7/28/74	North Carolina Central	Fayetteville, N.C.	FA
Pesak, Kevin (1)	RB	6-2	222	4/18/75	Sam Houston	Alvin, Tex.	FA
Powell, Ozell (1)	T	6-5	316	11/17/73	Alabama	Greenville, Ala.	FA
Smith, Derek	G-T	6-6	309	14/13/76	Virginia Tech	Shennandoah Jct., W Va.	D5
Smith, Tyrone (1)	CB	5-11	193	9/29/72	Baylor	Houston, Tex.	FA
Stimson, Nate	LB	6-2	253	3/4/76	Georgia Tech	Palm Beach, Fla.	D4
Streater, Rahmaan (1)	DE	6-5	263	4/23/75	Richmond	Alexandria, Va.	FA
Tardio, Robert	TE	6-5	245	3/17/77	Boston College	Franklin Lakes, N.J.	FA
Thompson, Derrius	WR	6-2	215	7/5/77	Baylor	Cedar Hill, Tex.	FA
Walker, Rod	DT	6-4	305	2/4/76	Troy State	Milton, Fla.	FA
Webster, Mike	G	6-6	281	5/31/76	Kentucky	Independence, Ky.	FA
Williams, Nigel	WR	6-3	217	8/16/71	No College	Pointe Claire, Que., Canada	FA

The term NFL Rookie is defined as a player who is in his first season of professional football and has not been on the roster of another professional football team for any regular-season or postseason games. A Rookie is designated by an "R" on NFL rosters. Players who have been active in another professional football league or players who have NFL experience, including either preseason training camp or being on an Active List or Inactive List, or on Reserve/Injured or Reserve/Physically Unable to Perform for fewer than six regular-season games, are termed NFL First-Year Players. An NFL First-Year Player is designated by a "1" on NFL rosters. Thereafter, a player is credited with an additional year of experience for each season in which he accumulates six games on the Active List or Inactive List, or on Reserve/Injured or Reserve/Physically Unable to Perform.

NOTES

1998 Season in Review

TRADES

1998 INTERCONFERENCE TRADES

Defensive back **Melvin Johnson** from Tampa Bay to Kansas City for Chiefs' unannounced selection in 1999 (4/20).

Defensive back **Jimmy Hitchcock** from New England to Minnesota for Vikings' third-round selection in 1999. New England selected defensive back **Tony George** (Florida) (4/20).

Defensive end **Vaughn Booker** from Kansas City to Green Bay for defensive tackle **Darius Holland** (5/13).

Wide receiver **Tony Martin** from San Diego to Atlanta for Falcons' second-round selection in 1999. San Diego selected running back **Jermaine Fazande** (Oklahoma) (6/4).

Defensive tackle **Shawn Lee** from San Diego to Chicago for Bears' fifth-round selection in 1999. San Diego selected defensive end **Adrian Dingle** (Clemson) (6/9).

Defensive back **Tyrone Poole** from Carolina to Indianapolis for Colts' second-round selection in 1999. Carolina selected tackle **Chris Terry** (Georgia) (7/23).

Punter **Brian Hansen** from New York Jets to Green Bay for past considerations (8/17).

Tight end **Kendall Watkins** from Denver to Dallas for Cowboys' fifth-round selection in 1999. Denver selected defensive end **David Bowens** (Western Illinois) (8/19).

Kicker **Brett Conway** from Green Bay to New York Jets for Jets' unannounced selection (8/21).

Defensive end **Angel Rubio** from Pittsburgh to San Francisco for past considerations (8/24).

Center **Steve Gordon** and defensive end **David Richie** from Denver to San Francisco for past considerations (8/25).

Defensive tackle **Artie Smith** from New England to Dallas for past considerations (8/25).

Defensive back **J.B. Brown** from Pittsburgh to Arizona for Cardinals' seventh-round selection in 1999. Pittsburgh selected kicker **Kris Brown** (Nebraska) (8/25).

Wide receiver **Patrick Jeffers** from Denver to Dallas for past considerations (8/30).

Linebacker **Seth Joyner** from Denver to Green Bay for past considerations (8/30).

Tight end **Scott Slutzker** from Indianapolis to New Orleans for linebacker **Andre Royal** (8/30).

Wide receiver **Dietrich Jells** from New England to Philadelphia for Eagles' seventh-round selection in 2000 (8/30).

Defensive tackle **Mike Jones** from New England to St. Louis for Rams' fifth-round selection in 2000 (8/30).

Linebacker **Lemanski Hall** from Tennessee to Chicago for Bears' seventh-round selection in 2000 (9/1).

Running back **Darick Holmes** from Buffalo to Green Bay for Packers' fourth-round selection in 1999. Buffalo selected tight end **Bobby Collins** (North Alabama) (9/29).

1999 INTERCONFERENCE TRADES

Running back **Tyrone Wheatley** from New York Giants to Miami for Dolphins' seventh-round selection in 1999. New York selected linebacker **O.J. Childress** (Clemson) (2/12).

Defensive end **Roy Barker** and tight end **Irv Smith** from San Francisco to Cleveland for past considerations (2/12).

Seattle's second-round choice in 1999 to Green Bay for past considerations (2/23).

Quarterback **Ty Detmer** from San Francisco to Cleveland for Browns' fourth- and fifth-round selections in 1999. San Francisco selected defensive back **Pierson Prioleau** (Virginia Tech) and traded the fifth-round selection acquired from Cleveland to Miami (2/26).

Quarterback **Jeff Lewis** from Denver to Carolina for Panthers' third-round selection in 1999. Denver selected defensive back **Chris Watson** (Eastern Illinois) (3/2).

Guard **Kevin Gogan** from San Francisco to Miami for Dolphins' fifth-round selection in 1999. San Francisco selected running back **Terry Jackson** (Florida) (3/2).

Quarterback **Scott Mitchell** from Detroit to Baltimore for Ravens' third-round selection in 1999 and unannounced selection. Detroit traded the third-round selection acquired from Baltimore to Miami (3/22).

Wide receiver **Jahine Arnold** from Pittsburgh to Green Bay for past considerations (4/6).

Running back **Marshall Faulk** from Indianapolis to St. Louis for second- and fifth-round selections in 1999. Indianapolis selected linebacker **Mike Peterson** (Florida) and defensive end **Brad Scioli** (Penn State) (4/15).

Seattle's first-round selection in 1999 to Dallas for Cowboys' first- and fifth-round selections in 1999. Dallas selected defensive end **Ebenezer Ekuban** (North Carolina). Seattle selected defensive end **Lamar King** (Saginaw Valley) and tackle **Floyd Wedderburn** (Penn State) (4/17).

Miami's first-round selection in 1999 to San Francisco for 49ers' first- and fifth-round selections in 1999. San Francisco selected defensive tackle **Reggie McGrew** (Florida). Miami traded the first-round selection acquired from San Francisco to Detroit and with the fifth-round pick selected running back **Cecil Collins** (McNeese State) (4/17).

Miami's first-round selection in 1999 to Detroit for Lions' second-, third-, and fifth-round selections in 1999. Detroit selected tackle **Aaron Gibson** (Wisconsin). Miami selected running back **James Johnson** (Mississippi State), center **Grey Ruegamer** (Arizona State), and linebacker **Bryan Jones** (Oregon State) (4/17).

Chicago's second- and fourth-round selections in 1999 to Oakland for Raiders' second-, third-, and fourth-round selections in 1999. Oakland selected defensive end **Tony Bryant** (Florida State) and wide receiver **Dameane Douglas** (California). Chicago selected defensive tackle **Russell Davis** (North Carolina), wide receiver **Marty Booker** (Northeast Louisiana), and defensive end **Rosevelt Colvin** (Purdue) (4/17).

Baltimore's second-round selection in 1999 to Atlanta for Falcons' first-round selection in 2000. Atlanta selected tight end **Reggie Kelly** (Mississippi State) (4/17).

Quarterback **Eric Zeier** from Baltimore to Tampa Bay for Buccaneers' sixth-round selection in 1999. Baltimore traded the sixth-round selection acquired from Tampa Bay to Minnesota (4/17).

Quarterback **Tony Banks** from St. Louis to Baltimore for Ravens' fifth-round selection in 1999 and seventh-round selection in 2000. St. Louis selected guard **Cameron Spikes** (Texas A&M) (4/17).

Pittsburgh's second-round selection in 1999 to Minnesota for Vikings' second-, third-, and fifth-round selections in 1999. Minnesota selected tight end **Jim Kleinsasser** (North Dakota). Pittsburgh selected defensive back **Scott Shields** (Weber State), linebacker **Joey Porter** (Colorado State), and traded the fifth-round selection acquired from Minnesota to Oakland (4/17).

Miami's third-round selection in 1999 to Detroit for Lions' third- and seventh-round selections in 1999. Detroit selected defensive end **Jared DeVries** (Iowa). Miami selected center **Grey Ruegamer** (Arizona State) and defensive tackle **Jermaine Haley** (Butte J.C.) (4/17).

Running back **Marc Edwards** from San Francisco to Cleveland for Browns' fourth-round selection in 1999. San Francisco traded the fourth-round selection acquired from Cleveland to Indianapolis (4/18).

San Francisco's fourth-round selection in 1999 to Indianapolis for Colts' fourth- and sixth-round selections in 1999. Indianapolis selected defensive back **Paul Miranda** (Central Florida). San Francisco selected defensive back **Anthony Parker** (Weber State) and wide receiver **Tai Streets** (Michigan) (4/18).

Oakland's fifth-round selection in 1999 to Green Bay for Packers' sixth-round selection in 1999 and past considerations. Green Bay selected center **Craig Heimburger** (Missouri). Oakland selected defensive tackle **Daren Yancey** (Brigham Young) (4/18).

Denver's fifth-round selection in 1999 to Washington for Redskins' sixth- and seventh-round selections in 1999. Washington selected tackle **Derek Smith** (Virginia Tech). Denver selected tight end **Desmond Clark** (Wake Forest) and wide receiver **Billy Miller** (Southern California) (4/18).

Chicago's sixth-round selection in 1999 to Cleveland for Browns' sixth- and seventh-round selections in 1999. Cleveland selected defensive tackle **Marcus Spriggs** (Troy State). Chicago selected defensive back **Rashard Cook** (Southern California) and wide receiver **Sulecio Sanford** (Middle Tennessee) (4/18).

Tampa Bay's sixth-round selection in 1999 to Jacksonville for Jaguars' sixth- and seventh-round selections in 1999. Jacksonville selected defensive tackle **Emarlos Leroy** (Georgia). Tampa Bay selected running back **Lamarr Glenn** (Florida State) and running back **Autry Denson** (Notre Dame) (4/18).

Tackle **Everett Lindsay** from Minnesota to Baltimore for Ravens' sixth-round selection in 1999. Minnesota selected defensive end **Talance Sawyer** (Nevada-Las Vegas) (4/18).

Cleveland's two seventh-round selections in 1999 to Chicago for Bears' seventh-round selection in 1999. Chicago selected wide receiver **Sulecio Sanford** (Middle Tennessee) and running back **Jim Finn** (Pennsylvania). Cleveland selected running back **Madre Hill** (Arkansas) (4/18).

1998 AFC TRADES

Linebacker **Steve Conley** from Pittsburgh to Indianapolis for Colts' fifth-round selection in 1999. Pittsburgh selected tight end **Jerame Tuman** (Michigan) (8/30).

1999 AFC TRADES

Linebacker **Chris Spielman** from Buffalo to Cleveland for past considerations (2/16).

Quarterback **Glenn Foley** from New York Jets to Seattle for Seahawks' seventh-round selection in 1999. New York selected tackle **Ryan Young** (Kansas State) (3/19).

Quarterback **Jim Harbaugh** from Baltimore to San Diego for Chargers' unannounced selection (3/22).

Wide receiver **Alex Van Dyke** from New York Jets to Pittsburgh for Steelers' sixth-round selection in 1999. New York selected linebacker **Marc Megna** (Richmond) (3/25).

Tight end **Lovett Purnell** from New England to Baltimore for Ravens' sixth-round selection in 1999. New England selected defensive back **Marcus Washington** (Colorado) (3/30).

Seattle's first-round selection in 1999 to New England for Patriots' first-, third-, and sixth-round selections in 1999. New England selected center **Damien Woody** (Boston College). Seattle traded the first-round selection acquired from New England to Dallas. Seattle selected wide receiver **Karsten Bailey** (Auburn) and traded the sixth-round selection acquired from New England to Cleveland (4/17).

Kansas City's second-round selection in 1999 to Miami for Dolphins' second- and third-round selections in 1999, and sixth-round selection in 2000. Miami selected running back **Rob Konrad** (Syracuse). Kansas City selected running back **Mike Cloud** (Boston College) and defensive back **Larry Atkins** (UCLA) (4/17).

Tennessee's second-round selection in 1999 to New England for Patriots' second- and fourth-round selections in 1999. New England selected running back **Kevin Faulk** (Louisiana State). Tennessee selected defensive tackle **John Thorton** (West Virginia) and defensive back **Donald Mitchell** (Southern Methodist) (4/17).

Pittsburgh's two fifth-round selections in 1999 to

Oakland for Raiders' third-round selection in 2000. Oakland selected linebacker **Eric Barton** (Maryland) and traded the second fifth-round selection acquired from Pittsburgh to Green Bay (4/18).

Cleveland's sixth-round selection to Seattle for Seahawks' two sixth-round selections. Seattle selected defensive back **Steve Johnson** (Tennessee). Cleveland selected linebacker **Kendall Ogle** (Maryland) and tight end **James Dearth** (Tarleton State) (4/18).

1998 NFC TRADES

Running back **Glyn Milburn** from Detroit to Green Bay for Packers' unannounced selection (4/23).

Tight end **Aaron Laing** from St. Louis to Green Bay for Packers' unannounced selection in 1999 (8/13).

Running back **Glyn Milburn** from Green Bay to Chicago for Bears' seventh-round selection in 1999 (8/30). Green Bay selected wide receiver **Donald Driver** (Alcorn State) (8/30).

Center **Mike Flanigan** from Green Bay to Carolina for Panthers' unannounced selection (8/31).

1999 NFC TRADES

Quarterback **Brad Johnson** from Minnesota to Washington for Redskins first- and third-round selections in 1999. Minnesota selected quarterback **Daunte Culpepper** (Central Florida) and traded the third-round selection acquired from Washington to Pittsburgh (2/16).

Wide receiver **Eddie Kennison** from St. Louis to New Orleans for Saints second-round selection in 1999. St. Louis selected defensive back **Dre' Bly** (North Carolina) (2/18).

Washington's first-round selection in 1999 to New Orleans for Saints' first-, third-, fourth-, fifth-, sixth-, and seventh-round selections in 1999, and first- and third-round selections in 2000. New Orleans selected running back **Ricky Williams** (Texas). Washington traded the first-, third-, and fifth-round selections in 1999 and third-round selection in 2000 acquired from New Orleans to Chicago. Washington selected linebacker **Nate Stimson** (Georgia Tech) and traded the sixth- and seventh-round selections in 1999 acquired from New Orleans to Denver (4/17).

Chicago's first-round selection in 1999 to Washington for Redskins' first-, third-, fourth-, and fifth-round selections in 1999, and third-round selection in 2000. Washington selected cornerback **Champ Bailey** (Georgia). Chicago selected quarterback **Cade McNown** (UCLA), wide receiver **D'Wayne Bates** (Northwestern), linebacker **Warrick Holdman** (Texas A&M), and guard **Jerry Wisne** (Notre Dame) (4/17).

Chicago's second-round selection in 1999 to Washington for Redskins' second- and fifth-round selections in 1999. Washington selected tackle **Jon Jansen** (Michigan). Chicago traded the second-round selection acquired from Washington to Oakland and selected linebacker **Khari Samuel** (Massachusetts) (4/17).

Philadelphia's fifth-round selection in 1999 to Detroit for Lions' fourth-round selection in 2000. Detroit selected defensive back **Tyree Talton** (Northern Iowa) (4/18).

PRESEASON FINAL STANDINGS

AMERICAN FOOTBALL CONFERENCE

Eastern Division

	W	L	T	Pct.	Pts.	OP
Miami	4	0	0	1.000	75	56
N.Y. Jets	3	1	0	.750	80	78
New England	3	2	0	.600	78	69
Buffalo	2	2	0	.500	64	62
Indianapolis	2	2	0	.500	74	101

Central Division

	W	L	T	Pct.	Pts.	OP
Baltimore	4	0	0	1.000	89	26
Tennessee	3	1	0	.750	97	80
Pittsburgh	3	2	0	.600	113	110
Jacksonville	2	2	0	.500	114	82
Cincinnati	1	3	0	.250	77	90

Western Division

	W	L	T	Pct.	Pts.	OP
Seattle	4	1	0	.800	117	108
Denver	3	1	0	.750	84	70
San Diego	3	1	0	.750	129	93
Oakland	2	2	0	.500	64	86
Kansas City	2	3	0	.400	69	105

NATIONAL FOOTBALL CONFERENCE

Eastern Division

	W	L	T	Pct.	Pts.	OP
Arizona	2	2	0	.500	82	82
N.Y. Giants	1	3	0	.250	63	82
Philadelphia	1	3	0	.250	49	93
Washington	1	3	0	.250	77	90
Dallas	0	5	0	.000	59	121

Central Division

	W	L	T	Pct.	Pts.	OP
Minnesota	4	0	0	1.000	129	50
Green Bay	2	3	0	.400	117	113
Tampa Bay	2	3	0	.400	103	54
Detroit	1	3	0	.250	52	70
Chicago	0	4	0	.000	54	87

Western Division

	W	L	T	Pct.	Pts.	OP
Atlanta	2	2	0	.500	62	62
Carolina	2	2	0	.500	88	97
St. Louis	2	2	0	.500	72	81
San Francisco	2	3	0	.400	99	103
New Orleans	1	3	0	.250	51	80

AFC PRESEASON RECORDS—TEAM BY TEAM

Eastern Division

BUFFALO (2-2)

13	at Pittsburgh	24
7	Carolina	12
17	at Chicago	9
27	Washington	17
64		62

INDIANAPOLIS (2-2)

21	at Seattle	24
30	at Cincinnati	27
3	San Diego	33
20	Detroit	17
74		101

MIAMI (4-0)

19	at Washington	16
14	Tampa Bay	13
21	at San Francisco	20
21	Green Bay	7
75		56

NEW ENGLAND (3-2)

13	at San Francisco	14
0	Minnesota	28
21	vs. Dallas (a)	3
20	at Washington	17
24	Philadelphia	7
78		69

N.Y. JETS (3-1)

29	at Philadelphia	15
0	Baltimore	33
27	N.Y. Giants	23
24	at Chicago	7
80		78

Central Division

BALTIMORE (4-0)

19	Chicago	14
33	at N.Y. Jets	0
23	Philadelphia	6
14	at N.Y. Giants	6
89		26

CINCINNATI (1-3)

17	at N.Y. Giants	24
27	Indianapolis	30
33	Detroit	19
0	at Atlanta	17
77		90

JACKSONVILLE (2-2)

27	at Carolina	30
24	N.Y. Giants	10
21	at Kansas City	22
42	Dallas	20
114		82

PITTSBURGH (3-2)

6	vs. Tampa Bay (c)	30
24	Buffalo	13
17	at Philadelphia	21
28	vs. Atlanta (e)	22
38	Carolina	24
113		110

TENNESSEE (3-1)

31	at Atlanta	16
24	Washington	27
26	at New Orleans	24
16	Denver	13
97		80

Western Division

DENVER (3-1)

20	at St. Louis	13
17	New Orleans	10
34	Green Bay	31
13	at Tennessee	16
84		70

KANSAS CITY (2-3)

24	vs. Green Bay (OT) (b)	27
17	vs. Tampa Bay (d)	13
0	at Minnesota	34
22	Jacksonville	21
6	St. Louis	10
69		105

OAKLAND (2-2)

16	at Dallas	3
27	at Green Bay	21
7	Tampa Bay	41
14	Arizona	21
64		86

SAN DIEGO (3-1)

27	San Francisco	21
41	St. Louis	27
33	at Indianapolis	3
28	at Minnesota	42
129		93

SEATTLE (4-1)

20	at Dallas	19
24	Indianapolis	21
21	vs. San Francisco (f)	24
31	at Arizona	24
21	San Francisco	20
117		108

NFC PRESEASON RECORDS—TEAM BY TEAM

Eastern Division

ARIZONA (2-2)

10	at Detroit (OT)	13
27	Chicago	24
24	Seattle	31
21	at Oakland	14
82		82

DALLAS (0-5)

19	Seattle	20
3	Oakland	16
3	vs. New England (a)	21
14	at St. Louis	22
20	at Jacksonville	42
59		121

N.Y. GIANTS (1-3)

24	Cincinnati	17
10	at Jacksonville	24
23	at N.Y. Jets	27
6	Baltimore	14
63		82

PHILADELPHIA (1-3)

15	N.Y. Jets	29
21	Pittsburgh	17
6	at Baltimore	23
7	at New England	24
49		93

WASHINGTON (1-3)

16	Miami	19
27	at Tennessee	24
17	New England	20
17	at Buffalo	27
77		90

Central Division

CHICAGO (0-4)

14	at Baltimore	19
24	at Arizona	27
9	Buffalo	17
7	N.Y. Jets	24
54		87

DETROIT (1-3)

13	Arizona (OT)	10
3	Atlanta	7
19	at Cincinnati	33
17	at Indianapolis	20
52		70

GREEN BAY (2-3)

27	vs. Kansas City (OT)(b)	24
31	New Orleans	7
21	Oakland	27
31	at Denver	34
7	at Miami	21
117		113

MINNESOTA (4-0)

28	at New England	0
34	Kansas City	0
25	at Carolina (OT)	22
42	San Diego	28
129		50

TAMPA BAY (2-3)

30	vs. Pittsburgh (c)	6
13	vs. Kansas City (d)	17
13	at Miami	14
41	at Oakland	7
6	at New England	10
103		54

Western Division

ATLANTA (2-2)

16	Tennessee	31
7	at Detroit	3
22	vs. Pittsburgh (e)	28
17	Cincinnati	0
62		62

CAROLINA (2-2)

30	Jacksonville	27
12	at Buffalo	7
22	Minnesota (OT)	25
24	at Pittsburgh	38
88		97

NEW ORLEANS (1-3)

7	at Green Bay	31
10	at Denver	17
24	Tennessee	26
10	Tampa Bay	6
51		80

ST. LOUIS (2-2)

13	Denver	20
27	at San Diego	41
22	Dallas	14
10	at Kansas City	6
72		81

SAN FRANCISCO (2-3)

14	New England	13
21	at San Diego	27
24	vs. Seattle (f)	21
20	Miami	21
20	at Seattle	21
99		103

(OT) denotes overtime
(a) American Bowl at Mexico City, Mexico
(b) American Bowl at Tokyo, Japan
(c) Pro Football Hall of Fame Game at Canton, Ohio
(d) at Norman, Oklahoma
(e) at Morgantown, West Virginia
(f) American Bowl at Vancouver, Canada

1998 NFL STANDINGS/RESULTS

FINAL STANDINGS

AMERICAN FOOTBALL CONFERENCE

Eastern Division	W	L	T	Pct.	Pts.	OP
*New York Jets	12	4	0	.750	416	266
#Miami	10	6	0	.625	321	265
#Buffalo	10	6	0	.625	400	333
#New England	9	7	0	.563	337	329
Indianapolis	3	13	0	.188	310	444
Central Division						
*Jacksonville	11	5	0	.688	392	338
Tennessee	8	8	0	.500	330	320
Pittsburgh	7	9	0	.438	263	303
Baltimore	6	10	0	.375	269	335
Cincinnati	3	13	0	.188	268	452
Western Division						
*Denver	14	2	0	.875	501	309
Oakland	8	8	0	.500	288	356
Seattle	8	8	0	.500	372	310
Kansas City	7	9	0	.438	327	363
San Diego	5	11	0	.313	241	342

NATIONAL FOOTBALL CONFERENCE

Eastern Division	W	L	T	Pct.	Pts.	OP
*Dallas	10	6	0	.625	381	275
#Arizona	9	7	0	.563	325	378
New York Giants	8	8	0	.500	287	309
Washington	6	10	0	.375	319	421
Philadelphia	3	13	0	.188	161	344
Central Division						
*Minnesota	15	1	0	.938	556	296
#Green Bay	11	5	0	.688	408	319
Tampa Bay	8	8	0	.500	314	295
Detroit	5	11	0	.313	306	378
Chicago	4	12	0	.250	276	368
Western Division						
*Atlanta	14	2	0	.875	442	289
#San Francisco	12	4	0	.750	479	328
New Orleans	6	10	0	.375	305	359
Carolina	4	12	0	.250	336	413
St. Louis	4	12	0	.250	285	378

*Division Champion; #Wild Card Team

Miami finished ahead of Buffalo based on better net division points (6 to Bills' 0). Oakland finished ahead of Seattle based on head-to-head sweep (2-0). Carolina finished ahead of St. Louis based on head-to-head sweep (2-0).

WILD CARD PLAYOFFS
AFC
MIAMI 24, Buffalo 17
JACKSONVILLE 25, New England 10
NFC
Arizona 20, DALLAS 7
SAN FRANCISCO 30, Green Bay 27

DIVISIONAL PLAYOFFS
AFC
DENVER 38, Miami 3
N.Y. JETS 34, Jacksonville 24
NFC
ATLANTA 20, San Francisco 18
MINNESOTA 41, Arizona 21

CHAMPIONSHIP GAMES
AFC
DENVER 23, N.Y. Jets 10
NFC
Atlanta 30, MINNESOTA 27 (OT)

SUPER BOWL XXXIII
Denver (AFC) 34, Atlanta (NFC) 19, at Pro Player Stadium, Miami, Florida

AFC-NFC PRO BOWL
AFC 23, NFC 10, at Aloha Stadium, Honolulu, Hawaii

Home teams in playoff games are indicated in CAPS.

AFC SEASON RECORDS—TEAM BY TEAM

BALTIMORE (6-10)

13	PITTSBURGH	20
24	at N.Y. Jets	10
10	at Jacksonville	24
31	CINCINNATI	24
8	TENNESSEE	12
6	at Pittsburgh	16
10	at Green Bay	28
19	JACKSONVILLE	45
13	OAKLAND	10
13	at San Diego	14
20	at Cincinnati	13
38	INDIANAPOLIS	31
14	at Tennessee	16
28	MINNESOTA	38
3	at Chicago	24
19	DETROIT	10
269		335

BUFFALO (10-6)

14	at San Diego	16
7	at Miami	13
33	ST. LOUIS	34
26	SAN FRANCISCO	21
31	at Indianapolis	24
17	JACKSONVILLE	16
30	at Carolina	14
30	MIAMI	24
12	at N.Y. Jets	34
13	NEW ENGLAND	10
34	INDIANAPOLIS	11
21	at New England	25
33	at Cincinnati	20
44	OAKLAND	21
10	N.Y. JETS	17
45	at New Orleans	33
400		333

CINCINNATI (3-13)

14	TENNESSEE	23
34	at Detroit (OT)	28
6	GREEN BAY	13
24	at Baltimore	31
25	PITTSBURGH	20
14	at Tennessee	44
10	at Oakland	27
26	DENVER	33
11	at Jacksonville	24
3	at Minnesota	24
13	BALTIMORE	20
17	JACKSONVILLE	34
20	BUFFALO	33
26	at Indianapolis	39
25	at Pittsburgh	24
0	TAMPA BAY	35
268		452

DENVER (14-2)

27	NEW ENGLAND	21
42	DALLAS	23
34	at Oakland	17
38	at Washington	16
41	PHILADELPHIA	16
21	at Seattle	16
37	JACKSONVILLE	24
33	at Cincinnati	26
27	SAN DIEGO	10
30	at Kansas City	7
40	OAKLAND	14
31	at San Diego	16
35	KANSAS CITY	31
16	at N.Y. Giants	20
21	at Miami	31
28	SEATTLE	21
501		309

INDIANAPOLIS (3-13)

15	MIAMI	24
6	at New England	29
6	at N.Y. Jets	44
13	NEW ORLEANS (OT)	19
17	SAN DIEGO	12
24	BUFFALO	31
31	at San Francisco	34
16	NEW ENGLAND	21
14	at Miami	27
24	N.Y. JETS	23
11	at Buffalo	34
31	at Baltimore	38
21	at Atlanta	28
39	CINCINNATI	26
23	at Seattle	27
19	CAROLINA	27
310		444

JACKSONVILLE (11-5)

24	at Chicago	23
21	KANSAS CITY	16
24	BALTIMORE	10
27	at Tennessee	22
28	MIAMI	21
16	at Buffalo	17
24	at Denver	37
45	at Baltimore	19
24	CINCINNATI	11
29	TAMPA BAY	24
15	at Pittsburgh	30
34	at Cincinnati	17
37	DETROIT	22
13	TENNESSEE	16
10	at Minnesota	50
21	PITTSBURGH	3
392		338

KANSAS CITY (7-9)

28	OAKLAND	8
16	at Jacksonville	21
23	SAN DIEGO	7
24	at Philadelphia	21
17	SEATTLE	6
10	at New England	40
13	PITTSBURGH	20
17	N.Y. JETS	20
12	at Seattle	24
7	DENVER	30
37	at San Diego	38
34	ARIZONA	24
31	at Denver	35
20	DALLAS	17
7	at N.Y. Giants	28
31	at Oakland	24
327		363

MIAMI (10-6)

24	at Indianapolis	15
13	BUFFALO	7
21	PITTSBURGH	0
9	at N.Y. Jets	20
21	at Jacksonville	28
14	ST. LOUIS	0
12	NEW ENGLAND (OT)	9
24	at Buffalo	30
27	INDIANAPOLIS	14
13	at Carolina	9
23	at New England	26
30	NEW ORLEANS	10
27	at Oakland	17
16	N.Y. JETS	21
31	DENVER	21
16	at Atlanta	38
321		265

NEW ENGLAND (9-7)

21	at Denver	27
29	INDIANAPOLIS	6
27	TENNESSEE	16
30	at New Orleans	27
40	KANSAS CITY	10
14	N.Y. JETS	24
9	at Miami (OT)	12
21	at Indianapolis	16
10	ATLANTA	41
10	at Buffalo	13
26	MIAMI	23
25	BUFFALO	21
23	at Pittsburgh	9
18	at St. Louis	32
24	SAN FRANCISCO	21
10	at N.Y. Jets	31
337		329

N.Y. JETS (12-4)

30	at San Francisco (OT)	36
10	BALTIMORE	24
44	INDIANAPOLIS	6
20	MIAMI	9
10	at St. Louis	30
24	at New England	14
28	ATLANTA	3
20	at Kansas City	17
34	BUFFALO	12
23	at Indianapolis	24
24	at Tennessee	3
48	CAROLINA	21
32	SEATTLE	31
21	at Miami	16
17	at Buffalo	10
31	NEW ENGLAND	10
416		266

OAKLAND (8-8)

8	at Kansas City	28
20	N.Y. GIANTS	17
17	DENVER	34
13	at Dallas	12
23	at Arizona	20
7	SAN DIEGO	6
27	CINCINNATI	10
31	at Seattle	18
10	at Baltimore	13
20	SEATTLE	17
14	at Denver	40
19	WASHINGTON	29
17	MIAMI	27
21	at Buffalo	44
17	at San Diego	10
24	KANSAS CITY	31
288		356

PITTSBURGH (7-9)

20	at Baltimore	13
17	CHICAGO	12
0	at Miami	21
13	SEATTLE	10
20	at Cincinnati	25
16	BALTIMORE	6
20	at Kansas City	13
31	TENNESSEE	41
27	GREEN BAY	20
14	at Tennessee	23
30	JACKSONVILLE	15
16	at Detroit (OT)	19
9	NEW ENGLAND	23
3	at Tampa Bay	16
24	CINCINNATI	25
3	at Jacksonville	21
263		303

SAN DIEGO (5-11)

16	BUFFALO	14
13	at Tennessee	7
7	at Kansas City	23
16	N.Y. GIANTS	34
12	at Indianapolis	17
6	at Oakland	7
13	PHILADELPHIA	10
20	SEATTLE	27
10	at Denver	27
14	BALTIMORE	13
38	KANSAS CITY	37
16	DENVER	31
20	at Washington	24
17	at Seattle	38
10	OAKLAND	17
13	at Arizona	16
241		342

SEATTLE (8-8)

38	at Philadelphia	0
33	ARIZONA	14
24	WASHINGTON	14
10	at Pittsburgh	13
6	at Kansas City	17
16	DENVER	21
27	at San Diego	20
18	OAKLAND	31
24	KANSAS CITY	12
17	at Oakland	20
22	at Dallas	30
20	TENNESSEE	18
31	at N.Y. Jets	32
38	SAN DIEGO	17
27	INDIANAPOLIS	23
21	at Denver	28
372		310

TENNESSEE (8-8)

23	at Cincinnati	14
7	SAN DIEGO	13
16	at New England	27
22	JACKSONVILLE	27
12	at Baltimore	8
44	CINCINNATI	14
20	CHICAGO	23
41	at Pittsburgh	31
31	at Tampa Bay	22
23	PITTSBURGH	14
3	N.Y. JETS	24
18	at Seattle	20
16	BALTIMORE	14
16	at Jacksonville	13
22	at Green Bay	30
16	MINNESOTA	26
330		320

(OT) denotes overtime

NFC SEASON RECORDS—TEAM BY TEAM

ARIZONA (9-7)

Pts	Opponent	Opp
10	at Dallas	38
14	at Seattle	33
17	PHILADELPHIA	3
20	at St. Louis	17
20	OAKLAND	23
20	CHICAGO	7
7	at N.Y. Giants	34
17	at Detroit	15
29	WASHINGTON	27
28	DALLAS	35
45	at Washington	42
24	at Kansas City	34
19	N.Y. GIANTS	23
20	at Philadelphia (OT)	17
19	NEW ORLEANS	17
16	SAN DIEGO	13
325		378

ATLANTA (14-2)

Pts	Opponent	Opp
19	at Carolina	14
17	PHILADELPHIA	12
20	at San Francisco	31
51	CAROLINA	23
34	at N.Y. Giants	20
31	NEW ORLEANS	23
3	at N.Y. Jets	28
37	ST. LOUIS	15
41	at New England	10
31	SAN FRANCISCO	19
20	CHICAGO	13
21	at St. Louis	10
28	INDIANAPOLIS	21
27	at New Orleans	17
24	at Detroit	17
38	MIAMI	16
442		289

CAROLINA (4-12)

Pts	Opponent	Opp
14	ATLANTA	19
14	at New Orleans	19
30	GREEN BAY	37
23	at Atlanta	51
20	at Dallas	27
13	at Tampa Bay	16
14	BUFFALO	30
31	NEW ORLEANS	17
23	at San Francisco	25
9	MIAMI	13
24	at St. Louis	20
21	at N.Y. Jets	48
28	SAN FRANCISCO (OT)	31
25	WASHINGTON	28
20	ST. LOUIS	13
27	at Indianapolis	19
336		413

CHICAGO (4-12)

Pts	Opponent	Opp
23	JACKSONVILLE	24
12	at Pittsburgh	17
15	at Tampa Bay	27
28	MINNESOTA	31
31	DETROIT	27
7	at Arizona	20
13	DALLAS	12
23	at Tennessee	20
12	ST. LOUIS	20
3	at Detroit	26
13	at Atlanta	20
17	TAMPA BAY	31
22	at Minnesota	48
20	at Green Bay	26
24	BALTIMORE	3
13	GREEN BAY	16
276		368

(OT) denotes overtime

DALLAS (10-6)

Pts	Opponent	Opp
38	ARIZONA	10
23	at Denver	42
31	at N.Y. Giants	7
12	OAKLAND	13
31	at Washington	10
27	CAROLINA	20
12	at Chicago	13
34	at Philadelphia	0
16	N.Y. GIANTS	6
35	at Arizona	28
30	SEATTLE	22
36	MINNESOTA	46
3	at New Orleans	22
17	at Kansas City	20
13	PHILADELPHIA	9
23	WASHINGTON	7
381		275

DETROIT (5-11)

Pts	Opponent	Opp
19	at Green Bay	38
28	CINCINNATI (OT)	34
6	at Minnesota	29
27	TAMPA BAY	6
27	at Chicago	31
27	GREEN BAY	20
13	MINNESOTA	34
15	ARIZONA	17
9	at Philadelphia	10
26	CHICAGO	3
28	at Tampa Bay	25
19	PITTSBURGH (OT)	16
22	at Jacksonville	37
13	at San Francisco	35
17	ATLANTA	24
10	at Baltimore	19
306		378

GREEN BAY (11-5)

Pts	Opponent	Opp
38	DETROIT	19
23	TAMPA BAY	15
13	at Cincinnati	6
37	at Carolina	30
24	MINNESOTA	37
20	at Detroit	27
28	BALTIMORE	10
36	SAN FRANCISCO	22
20	at Pittsburgh	27
37	at N.Y. Giants	3
14	at Minnesota	28
24	PHILADELPHIA	16
22	at Tampa Bay	24
26	CHICAGO	20
30	TENNESSEE	22
16	at Chicago	13
408		319

MINNESOTA (15-1)

Pts	Opponent	Opp
31	TAMPA BAY	7
38	at St. Louis	31
29	DETROIT	6
31	at Chicago	28
37	at Green Bay	24
41	WASHINGTON	7
34	at Detroit	13
24	at Tampa Bay	27
31	NEW ORLEANS	24
24	CINCINNATI	3
28	GREEN BAY	14
46	at Dallas	36
48	CHICAGO	22
38	at Baltimore	28
50	JACKSONVILLE	10
26	at Tennessee	16
556		296

NEW ORLEANS (6-10)

Pts	Opponent	Opp
24	at St. Louis	17
19	CAROLINA	14
19	at Indianapolis (OT)	13
27	NEW ENGLAND	30
0	SAN FRANCISCO	31
23	at Atlanta	31
9	TAMPA BAY	3
17	at Carolina	31
24	at Minnesota	31
24	ST. LOUIS	3
20	at San Francisco	31
10	at Miami	30
22	DALLAS	3
17	ATLANTA	27
17	at Arizona	19
33	BUFFALO	45
305		359

N.Y. GIANTS (8-8)

Pts	Opponent	Opp
31	WASHINGTON	24
17	at Oakland	20
7	DALLAS	31
34	at San Diego	16
3	at Tampa Bay	20
20	ATLANTA	34
34	ARIZONA	7
14	at Washington	21
6	at Dallas	16
3	GREEN BAY	37
20	PHILADELPHIA	0
7	at San Francisco	31
23	at Arizona	19
20	DENVER	16
28	KANSAS CITY	7
20	at Philadelphia	10
287		309

PHILADELPHIA (3-13)

Pts	Opponent	Opp
0	SEATTLE	38
12	at Atlanta	17
3	at Arizona	17
21	KANSAS CITY	24
16	at Denver	41
17	WASHINGTON	12
10	at San Diego	13
0	DALLAS	34
10	DETROIT	9
3	at Washington	28
0	at N.Y. Giants	20
16	at Green Bay	24
17	ST. LOUIS	14
17	ARIZONA (OT)	20
9	at Dallas	13
10	N.Y. GIANTS	20
161		344

ST. LOUIS (4-12)

Pts	Opponent	Opp
17	NEW ORLEANS	24
31	MINNESOTA	38
34	at Buffalo	33
17	ARIZONA	20
30	N.Y. JETS	10
0	at Miami	14
10	SAN FRANCISCO	28
15	at Atlanta	37
20	at Chicago	12
3	at New Orleans	24
20	CAROLINA	24
10	ATLANTA	21
14	at Philadelphia	17
32	NEW ENGLAND	18
13	at Carolina	20
19	at San Francisco	38
285		378

SAN FRANCISCO (12-4)

Pts	Opponent	Opp
36	N.Y. JETS (OT)	30
45	at Washington	10
31	ATLANTA	20
21	at Buffalo	26
31	at New Orleans	0
34	INDIANAPOLIS	31
28	at St. Louis	10
22	at Green Bay	36
25	CAROLINA	23
19	at Atlanta	31
31	NEW ORLEANS	20
31	N.Y. GIANTS	7
31	at Carolina (OT)	28
35	DETROIT	13
21	at New England	24
38	ST. LOUIS	19
479		328

TAMPA BAY (8-8)

Pts	Opponent	Opp
7	at Minnesota	31
15	at Green Bay	23
27	CHICAGO	15
6	at Detroit	27
20	N.Y. GIANTS	3
16	CAROLINA	13
3	at New Orleans	9
27	MINNESOTA	24
22	TENNESSEE	31
24	at Jacksonville	29
25	DETROIT	28
31	at Chicago	17
24	GREEN BAY	22
16	PITTSBURGH	3
16	at Washington	20
35	at Cincinnati	0
314		295

WASHINGTON (6-10)

Pts	Opponent	Opp
24	at N.Y. Giants	31
10	SAN FRANCISCO	45
14	at Seattle	24
16	DENVER	38
10	DALLAS	31
12	at Philadelphia	17
7	at Minnesota	41
21	N.Y. GIANTS	14
27	at Arizona	29
28	PHILADELPHIA	3
42	ARIZONA	45
29	at Oakland	19
24	SAN DIEGO	20
28	at Carolina	25
20	TAMPA BAY	16
7	at Dallas	23
319		421

Attendance figures as they appear in the following, and in the club-by-club sections starting on page 28, are turnstile counts and not paid attendance. Paid attendance totals are on page 242.

FIRST WEEK SUMMARIES

AMERICAN FOOTBALL CONFERENCE

Eastern Division	W	L	T	Pct.	Pts.	OP
Miami	1	0	0	1.000	24	15
Buffalo	0	1	0	.000	14	46
Indianapolis	0	1	0	.000	15	24
New England	0	1	0	.000	21	27
N.Y. Jets	0	1	0	.000	30	36
Central Division						
Jacksonville	1	0	0	1.000	24	23
Pittsburgh	1	0	0	1.000	20	13
Tennessee	1	0	0	1.000	23	14
Baltimore	0	1	0	.000	13	20
Cincinnati	0	1	0	.000	14	23
Western Division						
Denver	1	0	0	1.000	27	21
Kansas City	1	0	0	1.000	28	8
San Diego	1	0	0	1.000	16	14
Seattle	1	0	0	1.000	38	0
Oakland	0	1	0	.000	8	28

NATIONAL FOOTBALL CONFERENCE

Eastern Division	W	L	T	Pct.	Pts.	OP
Dallas	1	0	0	1.000	38	10
N.Y. Giants	1	0	0	1.000	31	24
Arizona	0	1	0	.000	10	38
Philadelphia	0	1	0	.000	0	38
Washington	0	1	0	.000	24	31
Central Division						
Green Bay	1	0	0	1.000	38	19
Minnesota	1	0	0	1.000	31	7
Chicago	0	1	0	.000	23	24
Detroit	0	1	0	.000	19	38
Tampa Bay	0	1	0	.000	7	31
Western Division						
Atlanta	1	0	0	1.000	19	14
New Orleans	1	0	0	1.000	24	17
San Francisco	1	0	0	1.000	36	30
Carolina	0	1	0	.000	14	19
St. Louis	0	1	0	.000	17	24

SUNDAY, SEPTEMBER 6

DALLAS 38, ARIZONA 10—at Texas Stadium, attendance 63,602. Troy Aikman threw 2 touchdown passes and ran for a career-high 2 scores as the Cowboys defeated the Cardinals. The game was scoreless until late in the first half when Dallas scored on consecutive possessions, capped by Aikman's 30-yard touchdown pass to Ernie Mills with 2:49 left in the half. Jake Plummer and Rob Moore hooked up for 41- and 27-yard pass plays to set up Joe Nedney's 22-yard field goal to start the second half, but Aikman scored on the ensuing drive to give the Cowboys a 21-3 lead. Tommy Bennett's 30-yard interception return led to Plummer's 1-yard run late in the third quarter, but Dallas responded with an 80-yard drive that culminated with Aikman's 7-yard touchdown pass to Billy Davis. Arizona failed to cross midfield in the fourth quarter, and Dallas scored twice in the final 20 seconds, as Kenny Wheaton scored on Eric Metcalf's fumble to end the scoring. Aikman was 22 of 32 for 256 yards and 2 touchdowns, with 2 interceptions. Emmitt Smith carried 28 times for 122 rushing yards. Irvin had 9 catches for 119 yards. Plummer was 14 of 33 for 166 yards. The Cowboys had more than twice as many first downs (30-13), total yards (439-205), and the Cardinals were 0-for-10 in third-down situations.

Arizona	0	0	10	0	—	10
Dallas	0	14	7	17	—	38

Dall — Aikman 1 run (Cunningham kick)
Dall — Mills 30 pass from Aikman (Cunningham kick)
Ariz — FG Nedney 22
Dall — Aikman 2 run (Cunningham kick)
Ariz — Plummer 1 run (Nedney kick)
Dall — Davis 7 pass from Aikman (Cunningham kick)
Dall — FG Cunningham 25
Dall — Wheaton 15 fumble return (Cunningham kick)

ATLANTA 19, CAROLINA 14—at Ericsson Stadium, attendance 65,129. Chris Chandler passed for 2 touchdowns as the Falcons discreetly began their march to Super Bowl XXXIII. Ray Buchanan's interception near the goal line preserved a scoreless tie and kick-started a 98-yard drive capped by Chandler's 11-yard touchdown pass to Terance Mathis. With the score tied 7-7, Jerry Jensen's punt snap sailed over Ken Walter's head. Walter fell on the ball in the end zone for a safety, and Chandler fired a 44-yard touchdown pass to Tim Dwight later in the quarter to stretch the Falcons' lead to 16-7. Carolina responded quickly as Michael Bates returned the ensuing kickoff 45 yards and Collins threw a 56-yard touchdown pass to Raghib Ismail on the next play. The punting game let the Panthers down again as Juran Bolden blocked Walter's punt in the fourth quarter, setting up Morten Andersen's 43-yard field goal with 8:46 remaining. Collins's Hail Mary pass fell incomplete in the end zone as time expired. Chandler was 17 of 33 for 268 yards and 2 touchdowns, with 3 interceptions. Collins was 21 of 37 for 270 yards and 2 touchdowns, with 1 interception.

Atlanta	0	7	9	3	—	19
Carolina	0	7	7	0	—	14

Atl — Mathis 11 pass from Chandler (Andersen kick)
Car — Walls 6 pass from Collins (Kasay kick)
Atl — Safety, Walters fell on punt snap in end zone
Atl — Dwight 44 pass from Chandler (Andersen kick)
Car — Ismail 56 pass from Collins (Kasay kick)
Atl — FG Andersen 43

SAN DIEGO 16, BUFFALO 14—at Qualcomm Stadium, attendance 64,037. John Carney's 54-yard field goal bounced off the left upright but went through with 4:30 left, and Steve Christie missed a 39-yard field goal with three seconds remaining to make Ryan Leaf's NFL debut a success. The Chargers led 3-0 at halftime when Leaf fired a 67-yard pass to Bryan Still on the first play of the second half to set up the tandem's 6-yard touchdown. Doug Flutie replaced an injured Rob Johnson and promptly threw a 43-yard touchdown pass to Andre Reed to cut the deficit to 10-7. Trailing 13-7, Christie missed a 21-yard field goal, but Henry Jones's second interception moments later set up Flutie's 5-yard touchdown pass to Reed with 9:05 left in the game to give Buffalo a 14-13 lead. Leaf guided the Chargers to Carney's third field goal with 4:30 left to retake the lead. A 36-yard pass interference penalty helped keep the Bills' final drive alive, but Christie's 39-yard field goal sailed wide left. Leaf was 16 of 31 for 192 yards and 1 touchdown, with 2 interceptions. Still had 6 catches for 128 yards. Johnson was 8 of 14 for 75 yards, with 1 interception. Flutie, in his first NFL game since 1989, was 12 of 20 for 158 yards and 2 touchdowns, with 1 interception.

Buffalo	0	0	7	7	—	14
San Diego	3	0	10	3	—	16

SD — FG Carney 48
SD — Still 6 pass from Leaf (Carney kick)
Buff — Reed 43 pass from Flutie (Christie kick)
SD — FG Carney 47
Buff — Reed 5 pass from Flutie (Christie kick)
SD — FG Carney 54

GREEN BAY 38, DETROIT 19—at Lambeau Field, attendance 60,102. Brett Favre passed for 2 touchdowns as the Packers won their 24th consecutive home game. Trailing 3-0, the Lions went for a first down on fourth-and-1 from their own 41 during their first drive of the season. Scott Mitchell attempted a quarterback sneak, fumbled, and LeRoy Butler scampered 32 yards for a touchdown. The Packers led 17-3 late in the first half, but Jason Hanson's field goal just before halftime and Mitchell's 25-yard touchdown pass to Herman Moore 2:21 into the second half pulled the Lions to within five points. After an exchange of punts, the Packers pounded out an 18-play, 85-yard drive that lasted 9:34 and culminated with Favre's 6-yard touchdown pass to Antonio Freeman. Terry Fair returned the ensuing kickoff 101 yards to end the third quarter, but Roell Preston responded with a 100-yard kickoff return, marking the first time since 1987 the NFL had consecutive kickoffs returned for touchdowns, to give the Packers a 31-19 lead. The Lions got no closer than the Packers' 40 the remainder of the game. Favre was 24 of 32 for 277 yards and 2 touchdowns. Freeman had 4 receptions for 110 yards. Mitchell was 23 of 44 for 248 yards and 1 touchdown, with 1 interception. Moore had 9 catches for 100 yards. The Packers' defense stopped Barry Sanders NFL record streak of 100-yard rushing games at 14. Sanders had 17 carries for 70 yards.

Detroit	3	3	13	0	—	19
Green Bay	10	7	7	14	—	38

GB — FG Longwell 32
GB — Butler 32 fumble return (Longwell kick)
Det — FG Hanson 47
GB — Levens 4 run (Longwell kick)
Det — FG Hanson 43
Det — Moore 25 pass from Mitchell (pass failed)
GB — Freeman 6 pass from Favre (Longwell kick)
Det — Fair 101 kickoff return (Hanson kick)
GB — Preston 100 kickoff return (Longwell kick)
GB — Freeman 84 pass from Favre (Longwell kick)

JACKSONVILLE 24, CHICAGO 23—at Soldier Field, attendance 55,614. Mark Brunell threw a touchdown pass to Jimmy Smith with 29 seconds left. The Jaguars turned the ball over three times in the first half, twice setting up Jeff Jaeger field goals and once throwing an interception near the Bears' goal-line, and allowed a 89-yard kickoff return for a touchdown by Glyn Milburn to trail 13-7 at halftime. The Bears let the Jaguars back in the game when Jaeger missed a 42-yard field-goal attempt early in the third quarter, and Bryan Schwartz recovered Ty Hallock's fumble at the Bears' 27 later in the quarter to set up James Stewart's 7-yard touchdown run. Chris Hudson's fumble recovery on the Bears' next play from scrimmage led to Mike Hollis's field goal and a 17-13 Jacksonville lead. The Bears scored a touchdown and, on their next possession, reached the Jaguars' 1, but Erik Kramer's third-down pass fell incomplete and Chicago settled for Jaeger's 19-yard field goal to take a 23-17 lead with 4:08 to play. Brunell engineered a 12-play, 86-yard drive, capped by his 4-yard touchdown pass to Smith to take the lead. Kramer's Hail Mary pass fell incomplete in the end zone as time expired. Brunell was 22 of 35 for 207 yards and 2 touchdowns, with 2 interceptions. Stewart had 26 carries for 115 yards. Kramer was 16 of 27 for 189 yards.

Jacksonville	0	7	7	10	—	24
Chicago	3	10	0	10	—	23

Chi — FG Jaeger 45
Jac — Stewart 3 pass from Brunell (Hollis kick)
Chi — Milburn 89 kickoff return (Jaeger kick)
Chi — FG Jaeger 35
Jac — Stewart 7 run (Hollis kick)
Jac — FG Hollis 23
Chi — Bennett 1 run (Jaeger kick)
Chi — FG Jaeger 19
Jac — Smith 4 pass from Brunell (Hollis kick)

MIAMI 24, INDIANAPOLIS 15—at RCA Dome, attendance 60,587. Terrell Buckley grabbed 2 interceptions, 1 of which he returned for a touchdown and the other set up a score, as the Dolphins defeated Indianapolis. With the score tied 3-3, Dan Marino fired a 44-yard touchdown pass to Oronde Gadsden and Karim Abdul-Jabbar scored 27 seconds later following Buckley's 12-yard interception return to the Colts' 4 to give Miami a 17-3 lead. Two field goals by Mike Vanderjagt cut the deficit to 17-9, and the Colts regained possession at their own 4-yard line following a punt with 1:32 left. However, Buckley intercepted Peyton Manning two plays later and raced into the end zone to ice the game. Marino was 13 of 24 for 135 yards and 1 touchdown. Abdul-Jabbar rushed 23 times for 108 yards. Manning was 21 of 37 for 302 yards and 1 touchdown, with 3 interceptions in his NFL debut. Marvin Harrison had 5 catches for 102 yards.

Miami	3	14	0	7	—	24
Indianapolis	0	3	0	12	—	15

Mia — FG Mare 22
Ind — FG Vanderjagt 51
Mia — Gadsden 44 pass from Marino (Mare kick)
Mia — Abdul-Jabbar 4 run (Mare kick)
Ind — FG Vanderjagt 27
Ind — FG Vanderjagt 20
Mia — Buckley 21 interception return (Mare kick)
Ind — Harrison 6 pass from Manning (pass failed)

NEW ORLEANS 24, ST. LOUIS 17—at Trans World Dome, attendance 56,943. Running back Lamar Smith threw a touchdown pass and ran for another as the Saints turned both Rams' turnovers into touchdowns for their first-ever season-opening road win. Joe Johnson's 5-yard fumble return three minutes into the game gave the Saints a quick lead. Smith capped the Saints' next possession with a 20-yard halfback-option touchdown pass to Andre Hastings. After Doug Brien's field goal gave New Orleans a 17-0 lead, Sammy Knight's interception led to Billy Joe Hobert's 35-yard touchdown pass to Smith on the next play to give the Saints a 24-0 lead with 4:45 left in the first half. The Rams, who had not crossed midfield with any of their first seven possessions, drove 83 yards and scored when Jerald Moore recovered his own fumble in the end zone in the half's final minute. Eddie Kennison's 32-yard punt return led to Tony Banks's 15-yard touchdown pass to Kennison midway through the third quarter, and Billy Jenkins, Jr.'s interception in the Rams' end zone spurred an 82-yard drive capped by Jeff Wilkins's 34-yard field goal with 1:26 remaining. The Rams reached the Saints' 40 in the final seconds, but La'Roi Glover sacked Banks to end the game. Hobert was 11 of 23 for 170 yards and 1 touchdown. Banks was 29 of 44 for 298 yards and 1 touchdown, with 1 interception. Isaac Bruce had 10 catches for 131 yards.

New Orleans	14	10	0	0	—	24
St. Louis	0	7	7	3	—	17

NO — Johnson 5 fumble return (Brien kick)
NO — Hastings 20 pass from Smith (Brien kick)
NO — FG Brien 36
NO — Smith 35 pass from Hobert (Brien kick)
StL — J. Moore recovered fumble in end zone (Wilkins kick)
StL — Kennison 15 pass from Banks (Wilkins kick)
StL — FG Wilkins 34

SAN FRANCISCO 36, N.Y. JETS 30 (OT)—at 3Com Park, attendance 64,419. Garrison Hearst scored on a 96-yard touchdown run in overtime to give the 49ers a thrilling Kickoff Weekend victory. Glenn Foley threw 2 second-quarter touchdown passes, the second a 6-yard touchdown pass to Wayne Chrebet 33 seconds before halftime, to give the Jets a 17-14 lead. Foley and Keyshawn Johnson broke a 17-17 tie with a 21-yard scoring play, but the 49ers responded with a 68-yard drive, capped by Steve Young's 14-yard touchdown pass to Jerry Rice. However, the Jets maintained a 24-23 lead as Wade Richey's extra point attempt was blocked, and Richey missed a 47-yard field-goal attempt on the 49ers' next possession. After Hall's 32-yard field goal with 3:46 left, Young threw a 35-yard pass to Hearst and a 31-yard scoring pass to J.J. Stokes with 1:26 left to give the 49ers a 30-27 lead. Undaunted, the Jets drove 60 yards, capped by Hall's 31-yard field goal as time expired, sending the game to overtime. The Jets won the coin toss, but were unable to move the ball beyond midfield on either two of their overtime possessions. Nick Gallery's 49-yard punt was downed at the 49ers' 4, but Hearst raced a club-record 96 yards down the right sideline and dove into the end zone just ahead of Mo Lewis. Young was 26 of 46 for 363 yards and 3 touchdowns, with 1 interception. Hearst carried 20 times for 187 yards. Stokes had 7 receptions for 111 yards. Foley was 30 of 58 for 415 yards and 3 touchdowns, with 1 interception. Johnson had 9 receptions for 126 yards. The teams combined for 1,022 total yards.

N.Y. Jets	3	14	7	6	0	—	30
San Francisco	7	7	9	7	6	—	36

NYJ — FG Hall 24
SF — Hearst 5 run (Richey kick)
NYJ — Johnson 41 pass from Foley (Hall kick)
SF — Stokes 6 pass from Young (Richey kick)
NYJ — Chrebet 6 pass from Foley (Hall kick)
SF — FG Richey 22
NYJ — Johnson 21 pass from Foley (Hall kick)
SF — Rice 14 pass from Young (kick blocked)
NYJ — FG Hall 32
SF — Stokes 31 pass from Young (Richey kick)
NYJ — FG Hall 31
SF — Hearst 96 run

PITTSBURGH 20, BALTIMORE 13—at NFL Stadium at Camden Yards, attendance 68,847. Kordell Stewart passed for 1 touchdown and ran for another as the Steelers took advantage of the Ravens' special teams to spoil the debut of Baltimore's new stadium. With the score tied 3-3, Ralph Staten and Duane Starks intercepted Stewart passes, giving the Ravens the ball at the Steelers' 48 and 40 on consecutive possessions. But Matt Stover missed 42-yard field-goal attempts to end both scoring opportunities. Stover missed a 45-yard field-goal attempt to conclude the Ravens' first drive of the second half. Norm Johnson capped the ensuing drive with a 49-yard field goal, and a low snap as the Ravens attempted to punt on their next possession gave the Steelers the ball at the Ravens' 5, setting up Stewart's touchdown run. Pittsburgh scored on its next possession as well, with Charles Johnson's touchdown grab giving the Steelers a 20-3 lead with 10:00 left. Following a Stover field goal, Eric Zeier, who replaced injured Jim Harbaugh, fired a 64-yard touchdown pass to Jermaine Lewis to cut the deficit to 20-13 with 2:48 remaining, but Baltimore got no closer. Stewart was 14 of 27 for 240 yards and 1 touchdown, with 2 interceptions. Harbaugh was 4 of 7 for 33 yards and Zeier was 16 of 27 for 240 yards and 1 touchdown.

Pittsburgh	3	0	10	7	—	20
Baltimore	3	0	0	10	—	13

Pitt — FG N. Johnson 27
Balt — FG Stover 41
Pitt — FG N. Johnson 49
Pitt — Stewart 1 run (N. Johnson kick)
Pitt — C. Johnson 20 pass from Stewart (N. Johnson kick)
Balt — FG Stover 25
Balt — J. Lewis 64 pass from Zeier (Stover kick)

SEATTLE 38, PHILADELPHIA 0—at Veterans Stadium, attendance 66,418. Joey Galloway caught 2 touchdown passes as the Seahawks recorded their first shutout since 1986. Shawn Springs's 42-yard interception return for a touchdown midway through the first quarter started the scoring for Seattle. Sam Adams recovered Bobby Hoying's fumble on the next play, and Moon promptly threw a 25-yard touchdown pass to Galloway to give Seattle 2 touchdowns within 56 seconds. The Seahawks scored on their first 2 possessions of the second half, both via Moon's arm, to take a 28-0 lead with 8:54 left in the third quarter. Rookie Ahman Green's 64-yard run in the fourth quarter led to his 6-yard scoring scamper to finish the scoring. The Eagles did not cross midfield until their final possession, but Darrin Smith recovered Kevin Turner's fumble at the Seahawks' 31 with 1:08 left to preserve the shutout. The Seahawks outgained the Eagles, 406-174 yards. Moon was 13 of 21 for 204 yards and 3 touchdowns. Galloway had 6 catches for 142 yards, while Green had 6 carries for 100 yards. Hoying was 9 of 23 for 63 yards, with 1 interception.

Seattle	14	0	17	7	—	38
Philadelphia	0	0	0	0	—	0

Sea — Springs 42 interception return (Peterson kick)
Sea — Galloway 25 pass from Moon (Peterson kick)
Sea — Strong 11 pass from Moon (Peterson kick)
Sea — Galloway 35 pass from Moon (Peterson kick)
Sea — FG Peterson 42
Sea — Green 6 run (Peterson kick)

MINNESOTA 31, TAMPA BAY 7—at Hubert H. Humphrey Metrodome, attendance 62,538. Rookie Randy Moss made an impressive splash by catching touchdown passes of 48 and 31 yards en route to the Vikings' victory. Brad Johnson's 1-yard scoring pass to Cris Carter was quickly followed by John Randle's fumble recovery at the Vikings' 33. Johnson hit Moss with a 48-yard bomb three plays later to give Minnesota a 14-0 lead. After Michael Husted missed a 41-yard field-goal attempt, Johnson and Moss hooked up on a 31-yard scoring play to give Minnesota a 21-0 lead. The Buccaneers reached the Vikings' 14 just before halftime, but Trent Dilfer's fourth-and-3 pass fell incomplete. Charles Mincy's 22-yard interception return set up Dilfer's 3-yard touchdown pass to Lorenzo Neal, but the Vikings responded with a 12-play drive, keyed by a running-into-the-punter penalty, to set up Gary Anderson's field goal. The Buccaneers failed to cross midfield in the fourth quarter, and Jimmy Hitchcock's 38-yard interception return led to Johnson's fourth touchdown pass. Johnson was 15 of 25 for 189 yards and 4 touchdowns, with 1 interception. Dilfer was 17 of 25 for 207 yards and 1 touchdown.

Tampa Bay	0	0	7	0	—	7
Minnesota	14	7	0	10	—	31

Minn — Carter 1 pass from Johnson (Anderson kick)
Minn — Moss 48 pass from Johnson (Anderson kick)
Minn — Moss 31 pass from Johnson (Anderson kick)
TB — Neal 3 pass from Dilfer (Husted kick)
Minn — FG Anderson 43
Minn — Carter 18 pass from Johnson (Anderson kick)

TENNESSEE 23, CINCINNATI 14—at Cinergy Field, attendance 55,848. The Oilers drove into Bengals' territory on 8 of their first 10 possessions, leading to 3 Al Del Greco field goals, 2 touchdowns, and controlling the clock for nearly 34 minutes, to defeat Cincinnati. Trailing 7-3, the Oilers capped a 66-yard drive with Steve McNair's 8-yard touchdown pass to Willie Davis. After each team drove in excess of 80 yards for third-quarter touchdowns, Dave Krieg replaced the injured McNair and completed a 55-yard pass to Yancey Thigpen to set up Del Greco's second field goal and give Tennessee a 20-14 lead with 14:56 remaining. Marcus Roberton's interception at the Bengals' 37 midway through the final quarter led to Del Greco's third field goal, and Kenny Holmes's sack on fourth-and-1 from the Oilers' 11 with 1:27 left clinched the Oilers' victory. McNair was 10 of 21 for 135 yards and 1 touchdown. Krieg was 7 of 13 for 129 yards. O'Donnell was 24 of 32 for 200 yards and 1 touchdown, with 1 interception.

Tennessee	3	7	7	6	—	23
Cincinnati	7	0	7	0	—	14

Tenn — FG Del Greco 38
Cin — Scott 23 pass from O'Donnell (Pelfrey kick)
Tenn — Davis 8 pass from McNair (Del Greco kick)
Tenn — George 3 run (Del Greco kick)
Cin — Dillon 3 run (Pelfrey kick)
Tenn — FG Del Greco 31
Tenn — FG Del Greco 48

N.Y. GIANTS 31, WASHINGTON 24—at Giants Stadium, attendance 76,629. The Giants forced 3 second-half turnovers that all led to touchdowns en route to defeating the Redskins. A 37-yard punt return by Brian Mitchell led to the Redskins first touchdown, but Danny Kanell's 45-yard pass to Ike Hilliard set up Chris Calloway's 5-yard touchdown catch with 28 seconds left in the first half to tie the game 10-10. Conrad Hamilton's 17-yard interception return to the Redskins' 2 was immediatley cashed in by Charles Way, and Michael Strahan's 24-yard interception return for a touchdown less than a minute later gave the Giants a 24-10 lead with 12:07 left in the third quarter. Trent Green replaced Gus Frerotte and threw a 62-yard pass to Michael Westbrook to set up Larry Bowie's scoring catch, but Keith Hamilton's fumble recovery at the Redskins' 22 late in the quarter was promptly turned into a 22-yard scoring pass from Kanell to Amani Toomer. Jesse Campbell's interception led to Green's 1-yard touchdown pass to Stephen Alexander with 6:16 left, but the Redskins did not drive beyond the Giants' 38 the remainder of the game. Kanell was 15 of 28 for 159 yards and 2 touchdowns, with 1 interception. Frerotte was 8 of 12 for 93 yards and 1 touchdown, with 2 interceptions, while Green was 17 of 25 for 208 yards and 2 touchdowns.

Washington	7	3	7	7	—	24
N.Y. Giants	0	10	21	0	—	31

Wash — Shepherd 17 pass from Frerotte (Blanton kick)
NYG — FG Daluiso 35
Wash — FG Blanton 46
NYG — Calloway 5 pass from Kanell (Daluiso kick)
NYG — Way 2 run (Daluiso kick)
NYG — Strahan 24 interception return (Daluiso kick)
Wash — Bowie 4 pass from Green (Blanton kick)
NYG — Toomer 22 pass from Kanell (Daluiso kick)
Wash — Alexander 1 pass from Green (Blanton kick)

1998 WEEK BY WEEK

SUNDAY NIGHT, SEPTEMBER 6

KANSAS CITY 28, OAKLAND 8—at Arrowhead Stadium, attendance 78,945. Derrick Thomas recorded 6 sacks, including 1 for a safety, and Pete Stoyanovich kicked 4 field goals for the Chiefs. The Chiefs scored on their first three possessions, and four of their first five, as the Raiders fumbled three times in their own territory, twice by Desmond Howard, to set up Elvis Grbac's 30-yard touchdown pass to Andre Rison and 2 first-half Pete Stoyanovich field goals to take a 20-0 halftime lead. Stoyanovich made a third field goal, and Greg Davis missed his second of the game, before the Raiders put together a 12-play, 81-yard drive to get on the scoreboard late in the third quarter. After Stoyanovich's fourth field goal, Thomas sacked Jeff George in the end zone to finish the scoring. Both teams had 18 first downs, but the Raiders fumbled 7 times, losing 5, while the Chiefs did not commit a turnover. Grbac was 12 of 23 for 130 yards and 1 touchdown. Donnell Bennett rushed 24 times for 115 yards. George completed 19 of 31 passes for 270 yards.

Oakland	0	0	8	0	—	8
Kansas City	17	3	3	5	—	28

KC — Bennett 1 run (Stoyanovich kick)
KC — Rison 30 pass from Grbac (Stoyanovich kick)
KC — FG Stoyanovich 28
KC — FG Stoyanovich 19
KC — FG Stoyanovich 49
Oak — Williams 2 run (Dudley pass from Hollas)
KC — FG Stoyanovich 33
KC — Safety, George sacked by Thomas in end zone

MONDAY NIGHT, SEPTEMBER 7

DENVER 27, NEW ENGLAND 21—at Mile High Stadium, attendance 74,745. Terrell Davis scored 2 touchdowns as the Broncos began their journey to defend their Super Bowl XXXII title. Special teams were the difference early, as Adam Vinatieri missed a 39-yard field goal and had a 37-yard attempt blocked while the Broncos scored on three of their first four possessions to take a 17-0 lead. The Patriots scored touchdowns on two of their next three possessions, with Drew Bledsoe's 24-yard touchdown pass to Troy Brown culminating the opening drive of the second half, to cut the deficit to 17-14. Jason Elam answered with a field goal, and Darrien Gordon's 30-yard punt return set up Davis's second touchdown with 10:51 remaining to give Denver a 27-14 edge. The Patriots drove 90 yards to cut the deficit to 27-21 with 1:59 left, but Ed McCaffrey recovered the ensuing onside kick to ice the game. John Elway was 22 of 34 for 257 yards and 1 touchdown. Bledsoe was 20 of 32 for 289 yards and 2 touchdowns.

New England	0	7	7	7	—	21
Denver	10	7	3	7	—	27

Den — FG Elam 53
Den — Sharpe 12 pass from Elway (Elam kick)
Den — Davis 9 run (Elam kick)
NE — Edwards 1 run (Vinatieri kick)
NE — Brown 24 pass from Bledsoe (Vinatieri kick)
Den — FG Elam 42
Den — Davis 1 run (Elam kick)
NE — Brisby 10 pass from Bledsoe (Vinatieri kick)

SECOND WEEK SUMMARIES

AMERICAN FOOTBALL CONFERENCE

Eastern Division	W	L	T	Pct.	Pts.	OP
Miami	2	0	0	1.000	37	22
New England	1	1	0	.500	50	33
Buffalo	0	2	0	.000	21	29
Indianapolis	0	2	0	.000	21	53
N.Y. Jets	0	2	0	.000	40	60
Central Division						
Jacksonville	2	0	0	1.000	45	39
Pittsburgh	2	0	0	1.000	37	25
Baltimore	1	1	0	.500	37	30
Cincinnati	1	1	0	.500	48	51
Tennessee	1	1	0	.500	30	27
Western Division						
Denver	2	0	0	1.000	69	44
San Diego	2	0	0	1.000	29	21
Seattle	2	0	0	1.000	71	14
Kansas City	1	1	0	.500	44	29
Oakland	1	1	0	.500	28	45

NATIONAL FOOTBALL CONFERENCE

Eastern Division	W	L	T	Pct.	Pts.	OP
Dallas	1	1	0	.500	61	52
N.Y. Giants	1	1	0	.500	48	44
Arizona	0	2	0	.000	24	71
Philadelphia	0	2	0	.000	12	55
Washington	0	2	0	.000	34	76
Central Division						
Green Bay	2	0	0	1.000	61	34
Minnesota	2	0	0	1.000	69	38
Chicago	0	2	0	.000	35	41
Detroit	0	2	0	.000	47	72
Tampa Bay	0	2	0	.000	22	54
Western Division						
Atlanta	2	0	0	1.000	36	26
New Orleans	2	0	0	1.000	43	31
San Francisco	2	0	0	1.000	81	40
Carolina	0	2	0	.000	28	38
St. Louis	0	2	0	.000	48	62

SUNDAY, SEPTEMBER 13

SEATTLE 33, ARIZONA 14—at Kingdome, attendance 57,678. Willie Williams and Shawn Springs each returned interceptions for touchdowns as the Seahawks improved to 2-0. Williams raced across the goal line 20 seconds after Todd Peterson's 51-yard field goal to stake the Seahawks to a 10-0 lead. The Cardinals failed to cross midfield again until the opening drive of the second half, when Adrian Murrell pierced the end zone. After Warren Moon's second touchdown pass gave Seattle a 26-7 lead, Springs returned an interception for a touchdown for the second consecutive week to stretch the advantage to 33-7 with 12:03 left. Moon was 14 of 23 for 146 yards and 2 touchdowns. Watters rushed 22 times for 105 yards. Jake Plummer was 22 of 36 for 204 yards and 1 touchdown, with 3 interceptions.

Arizona	0	0	7	7	—	14
Seattle	10	10	0	13	—	33

Sea — FG Peterson 51
Sea — Williams 28 interception return (Peterson kick)
Sea — Strong 4 pass from Moon (Peterson kick)
Sea — FG Peterson 22
Ariz — Murrell 4 run (Nedney kick)
Sea — Galloway 9 pass from Moon (run failed)
Sea — Springs 56 interception return (Peterson kick)
Ariz — Gedney 23 pass from Plummer (Nedney kick)

BALTIMORE 24, N.Y. JETS 10—at Giants Stadium, attendance 70,063. Rod Woodson had 2 interceptions, 1 of which he returned for the game-clinching touchdown, as the Ravens defeated the Jets. Jermaine Lewis's 69-yard punt return for a touchdown opend the scoring, but the Jets drove 83 yards to tie the game on Glenn Foley's 4-yard scoring pass. The Jets reached the Ravens' 3 late in the half, but Curtis Martin gained just 2 yards on 4 carries to stifle the drive. The Ravens' offense responded with a 99-yard drive, capped by Eric Zeier's 20-yard touchdown pass to Eric Green with 21 seconds left in the half. Woodson's 16-yard interception return early in the second half led to Matt Stover's 29-yard field goal. The Jets answered with John Hall's 20-yard field goal to cut the deficit to 17-10, but Woodson's 60-yard interception return with 8:44 left increased the Ravens' lead to 24-10, and Deron Jenkins's interception in the end zone stifled the Jets' final scoring opportunity. Zeier was 13 of 20 for 173 yards and 1 touchdown. Foley was 22 of 32 for 247 yards and 1 touchdown, with 3 interceptions.

Baltimore	7	7	3	7	—	24
N.Y. Jets	7	0	3	0	—	10

Balt — Lewis 69 punt return (Stover kick)
NYJ — Johnson 4 pass from Foley (Hall kick)
Balt — Green 20 pass from Zeier (Stover kick)
Balt — FG Stover 29
NYJ — FG Hall 20
Balt — Woodson 60 interception return (Stover kick)

MIAMI 13, BUFFALO 7—at Pro Player Stadium, attendance 73,097. The Dolphins permitted just 187 total yards and recorded 8 sacks to stifle the Bills' offense and improve to 2-0. Each team punted five times before exchanging touchdown passes in the final 5:20 of the first half. The Dolphins drove 80 yards late in the third quarter to set up Olindo Mare's 33-yard field goal, and Patrick Surtain's interception, the game's lone turnover, led to Mare's second boot with 12:29 to play. The Bills' failed to cross midfield with either of their final two possessions. Dan Marino was 14 of 26 for 159 yards and 1 touchdown. Rob Johnson was 10 of 18 for 134 yards and 1 touchdown, with 1 interception.

Buffalo	0	7	0	0	—	7
Miami	0	7	3	3	—	13

Buff — Moulds 28 pass from Johnson (Christie kick)
Mia — Thomas 17 pass from Marino (Mare kick)
Mia — FG Mare 33
Mia — FG Mare 27

NEW ORLEANS 19, CAROLINA 14—at Louisiana Superdome, attendance 51,915. Ray Zellars's 15-yard touchdown run with 9:15 remaining enabled the Saints to start 2-0 for the first time in five years. The Saints took a 7-0 lead three plays into the game on Danny Wuerffel's 64-yard touchdown pass to Sean Dawkins. John Kasay missed a 45-yard field goal late in the first quarter, but Carolina tied the game when William Floyd capped a 75-yard drive with a touchdown run and took a 14-10 lead just before halftime on Kerry Collins's 17-yard pass to Muhsin Muhammad. Collins and Muhammad hooked up for a 59-yard pass early in the second half, but Chad Cota's interception in the end zone ended the drive. Doug Brien's 56-yard field goal late in the third quarter cut the Saints' deficit to 14-13, and, following a punt, runs of 27 and 26 yards by Lamar Smith set up Zellars's winning scamper. The Panthers reached the Saints' 12, but Floyd was stopped for no gain on third-and-1, and Collins's fourth-down pass to Wesley Walls fell incomplete. Carolina failed to cross midfield in its final two possessions. Wuerffel was 13 of 18 for 145 yards and 1 touchdown. Dawkins had 5 receptions for 110 yards. Collins was 15 of 34 for 251 yards and 1 touchdown, with 1 interception. Muhammad had 9 receptions for 192 yards, and Fred Lane had 18 carries for 100 yards.

Carolina	0	14	0	0	—	14
New Orleans	7	3	3	6	—	19

NO — Dawkins 64 pass from Wuerffel (Brien kick)
Car — Floyd 1 run (Kasay kick)
NO — FG Brien 46
Car — Muhammad 17 pass from Collins (Kasay kick)
NO — FG Brien 56
NO — Zellars 15 run (pass failed)

PITTSBURGH 17, CHICAGO 12—at Three Rivers Stadium, attendance 59,084. Jerome Bettis rushed for 131 yards, and Carnell Lake intercepted a pass in the final minute to give the Steelers a 2-0 start. The Bears got on the board with Erik Kramer's 54-yard touchdown pass to Bobby Engram, but the Bears missed the extra point. On the ensuing possession Jerome Bettis's 42-yard run keyed an 83-yard drive and led to his go-ahead touchdown run. Tom Carter's interception at the Steelers' 43 with 29 seconds left in the half enabled Jeff Jaeger to kick a 19-yard field goal to give the Bears a 9-7 halftime lead. The Steelers scored 10 points within 2:17 of the third quarter, with Jason Gildon's fumble recovery at the Bears' 27 leading to Kordell Stewart's 13-yard touchdown pass to Andre Coleman. Jaeger added a field goal early in the fourth quarter, and the Bears drove to the Steelers' 16 with 44 seconds left, but Lake intercepted Kramer to ice the game. Stewart was 17 of 30 for 137 yards and 1 touchdown, with 1 interception. Kramer was 18 of 33 for 194 yards and 1 touchdown, with 1 interception.

Chicago	0	9	0	3	—	12
Pittsburgh	0	7	10	0	—	17

Chi — Engram 54 pass from Kramer (kick failed)
Pitt — Bettis 1 run (N. Johnson kick)
Chi — FG Jaeger 19
Pitt — FG N. Johnson 49
Pitt — Coleman 13 pass from Stewart (N. Johnson kick)
Chi — FG Jaeger 36

CINCINNATI 34, DETROIT 28 (OT)—at Pontiac Silverdome, attendance 66,354. Corey Sawyer's 53-yard interception return in overtime capped a seesaw battle. Neil O'Donnell threw 70- and 36-yard touchdown passes to Darnay Scott in the first half, but the Lions responded with

80-yard drives following each Bengals score. Barry Sanders's 67-yard run on the second half's second play gave Detroit its first lead, but O'Donnell's 38-yard pass to Tony McGee set up Corey Dillon's 18-yard game-tying run. The Bengals retook the lead 28-21 on Damon Gibson's 65-yard punt return, but Doug Pelfrey missed a 35-yard field goal and the Lions drove 75 yards to tie the game on Sanders's third touchdown run with 1:52 remaining. The Lions forced a punt, but Ashley Ambrose intercepted Scott Mitchell's pass at the Lions' 31 with 35 seconds left. However, Pelfrey missed a 48-yard field-goal attempt, sending the game to overtime. Sawyer intercepted a sideline pass by Mitchell four plays into the overtime and scurried untouched down the sideline for the winning points. O'Donnell was 25 of 36 for 303 yards and 2 touchdowns. Scott had 5 catches for 130 yards. Mitchell was 15 of 31 for 204 yards, with 2 interceptions. Sanders carried 26 times for 185 yards and 3 touchdowns.

Cincinnati	7	7	7	7	6	—	34
Detroit	7	7	7	7	0	—	28

Cin — Scott 70 pass from O'Donnell (Pelfrey kick)
Det — Vardell 1 run (Hanson kick)
Cin — Scott 36 pass from O'Donnell (Pelfrey kick)
Det — Sanders 2 run (Hanson kick)
Det — Sanders 67 run (Hanson kick)
Cin — Dillon 18 run (Pelfrey kick)
Cin — Gibson 65 punt return (Pelfrey kick)
Det — Sanders 5 run (Hanson kick)
Cin — Sawyer 53 interception return

DENVER 42, DALLAS 23—at Mile High Stadium, attendance 75,013. Terrell Davis rushed for 191 yards and 3 touchdowns as the Broncos compiled 35 first-half points in defeating the Cowboys. The Broncos scored touchdowns on all five of their first-half possessions, highlighted by Davis's 63- and 59-yard scoring runs on consecutive Broncos plays from scrimmage late in the first quarter to take a 21-7 lead. The Cowboys scored on their next two possessions, but John Elway capped an 80-yard drive with a 1-yard touchdown run just before halftime to take a 35-17 lead into intermission. Denver outgained the Cowboys 379-209 in total yards in the first half. Toby Gowin's 33-yard run on a fake punt set up the second of Richie Cunningham's three field goals, but Davis's 3-yard touchdown run culminated another 80-yard drive midway through the final quarter to complete the scoring. The Broncos drove at least 80 yards on five of their six scoring possessions. Elway was 16 of 22 for 268 yards and 2 touchdowns. Ed McCaffrey had 5 receptions for 117 yards. Troy Aikman was 5 of 12 for 88 yards and 1 touchdown before leaving the game with an injured collarbone.

Dallas	7	10	3	3	—	23
Denver	21	14	0	7	—	42

Den — Sharpe 38 pass from Elway (Elam kick)
Dall — Mills 36 pass from Aikman (Cunningham kick)
Den — Davis 63 run (Elam kick)
Den — Davis 59 run (Elam kick)
Dall — Smith 4 run (Cunningham kick)
Den — Sharpe 23 pass from Elway (Elam kick)
Dall — FG Cunningham 30
Den — Elway 1 run (Elam kick)
Dall — FG Cunningham 54
Dall — FG Cunningham 26
Den — Davis 3 run (Elam kick)

JACKSONVILLE 21, KANSAS CITY 16—at ALLTEL Stadium, attendance 69,821. James Stewart rushed for 103 yards and 1 touchdown as the Jaguars won at home for the sixteenth time in their last eighteen games. The Chiefs punted to conclude each of their first four possessions. Reggie Barlow returned one of those punts for a touchdown, and Mark Brunell threw a 17-yard touchdown pass to Jimmy Smith early in the second quarter to give Jacksonville a 14-0 lead. Pete Stoyanovich booted 2 field goals in the final 1:05 of the first half, but Tavian Banks's 65-yard kickoff return to begin the second half set up Stewart's 1-yard plunge to put the Jaguars ahead 21-6. Mike Hollis missed 37- and 21-yard field goals, allowing Kimble Anders's touchdown run to cut the deficit to 21-16 with 3:39 left, but Stewart and Fred Taylor ran out the clock. Brunell was 11 of 18 for 126 yards and 1 touchdown. Rich Gannon was 23 of 37 for 263 yards.

Kansas City	0	6	3	7	—	16
Jacksonville	7	7	7	0	—	21

Jac — Barlow 85 punt return (Hollis kick)
Jac — Smith 17 pass from Brunell (Hollis kick)
KC — FG Stoyanovich 36
KC — FG Stoyanovich 43
Jac — Stewart 1 run (Hollis kick)
KC — FG Stoyanovich 29
KC — Anders 3 run (Stoyanovich kick)

MINNESOTA 38, ST. LOUIS 31—at Trans World Dome, attendance 56,234. Orladon Thaoms stopped Tony Banks at the 1-yard line as time expired as the Vikings held off the Rams' comeback attempt. Interceptions in Rams territory by Torrian Gray and Robert Griffith set up 10 first-half points, and along with Robert Smith's 2 touchdown runs, staked the Vikings to a 24-10 halftime lead. Mike D. Jones returned a Brad Johnson fumble 38 yards to the Vikings' 14 midway through the third quarter, setting up Greg Hill's 5-yard scoring jaunt. Eddie Kennison returned a punt 71 yards for a touchdown less than two minutes later to tie the game. The Vikings drove 60 yards in seven plays to retake the lead on Leroy Hoard's touchdown run, but the Rams tied the game less than one minute later on Tony Banks's 80-yard touchdown pass to Isaac Bruce. Jimmy Hitchcock's interception at the Rams' 45 with less than four minutes left set up Cris Carter's 19-yard touchdown catch from Randall Cunningham, who had entered the game for the injured Johnson, with 2:09 left. The Rams reached the Vikings' 9 with six seconds remaining, but Banks scrambled for the end zone and was stopped short by Thomas and a host of Vikings defenders at the 1-yard line as time expired. Johnson was 18 of 31 for 208 yards and 1 touchdown, with 2 interceptions. Smith had 23 carries for 179 yards. Banks was 25 of 45 for 283 yards and 1 touchdown, with 4 interceptions. Bruce had 11 receptions for 192 yards.

Minnesota	14	10	7	7	—	38
St. Louis	0	10	14	7	—	31

Minn — Smith 24 run (Anderson kick)
Minn — Glover 3 pass from Johnson (Anderson kick)
StL — Hill 1 run (Wilkins kick)
Minn — FG Anderson 24
StL — FG Wilkins 53
Minn — Smith 74 run (Anderson kick)
StL — Hill 5 run (Wilkins kick)
StL — Kennison 71 punt return (Wilkins kick)
Minn — Hoard 1 run (Anderson kick)
StL — Bruce 80 pass from Banks (Wilkins kick)
Minn — Carter 19 pass from Cunningham (Anderson kick)

OAKLAND 20, N.Y. GIANTS 17—at Oakland-Alameda County Coliseum, attendance 40,545. Greg Davis kicked a 26-yard field goal with 1:58 remaining to give Jon Gruden his first victory. Napoleon Kaufman raced 80 yards for a touchdown on the first play from scrimmage, but the Giants responded with a 77-yard drive capped by Danny Kanell's 10-yard touchdown pass to Ike Hilliard. Each team punted six times before Davis broke the tie with a 41-yard field goal as the half expired. David Patten's 49-yard kickoff return to begin the second half sparked the Giants to take a 14-10 lead on Kanell's scoring pass to Chris Calloway. Desmond Howard's ensuing 42-yard kickoff return led to Jeff George's 22-yard touchdown pass to Tim Brown, but Marcus Buckley's recovery of Jon Ritchie's fumble set up Brad Daluiso's game-tying field goal late in the third quarter. However, Daluiso missed a 40-yard field-goal attempt, and Davis converted from 26 yards with 1:58 to play. Eric Turner's interception at midfield stifled the Giants' final threat. George was 25 of 44 for 303 yards and 1 touchdown. Brown had 6 catches for 127 yards, and Kaufman rushed 20 times for 139 yards. Kanell was 23 of 33 for 188 yards and 2 touchdowns, with 1 interception.

N.Y. Giants	7	0	10	0	—	17
Oakland	7	3	7	3	—	20

Oak — Kaufman 80 run (Davis kick)
NYG — Hilliard 10 pass from Kanell (Daluiso kick)
Oak — FG Davis 41
NYG — Calloway 20 pass from Kanell (Daluiso kick)
Oak — Brown 22 pass from George (Davis kick)
NYG — FG Daluiso 43
Oak — FG Davis 26

ATLANTA 17, PHILADELPHIA 12—at Georgia Dome, attendance 46,456. Atlanta improved to 2-0 for the first time since 1986 by defeating the Eagles. The Falcons failed to run a play inside the Eagles' 35 in their first five possessions, but Chris Boniol missed a field goal and had an extra point blocked, limiting the Eagles lead to 9-0. The Falcons needed just four plays to get on the board in the second half, capped by Chris Chandler's 19-yard pass to Brian Kozlowski. After forcing a punt, the Falcons drove 46 yards to take a 14-9 lead on Jamal Anderson's 1-yard burst. Bobby Hoying's 38-yard pass to Jeff Graham set up Boniol's 42-yard field goal, but the Falcons responded with an 11-play drive that culminated with Morten Andersen's 23-yard field goal and gave the Falcons a 17-12 lead with 7:31 left. The Eagles failed to cross midfield with their final two possessions. Chandler was 14 of 26 for 196 yards and 1 touchdown. Hoying was 24 of 35 for 232 yards.

Philadelphia	6	3	0	3	—	12
Atlanta	0	0	14	3	—	17

Phil — Staley 1 run (kick blocked)
Phil — FG Boniol 24
Atl — Kozlowski 19 pass from Chandler (Andersen kick)
Atl — Anderson 1 run (Andersen kick)
Phil — FG Boniol 42
Atl — FG Andersen 23

SAN DIEGO 13, TENNESSEE 7—at Vanderbilt Stadium, attendance 41,089. Natrone Means scored the go-ahead touchdown in the third quarter, and the Chargers' defense kept the Oilers from crossing midfield in the second half to improve to 2-0. The Chargers used 11- and 14-play drives to set up John Carney field goals to take a 6-0 lead. The Oilers responded with a 14-play, 80-yard drive just before halftime, with Steve McNair's 15-yard touchdown pass to Frank Wycheck giving Tennessee a 7-6 halftime lead. Carney missed a 51-yard field goal early in the second half, but the Chargers drove 72 yards on their next drive, keyed by Ryan Leaf's 34-yard pass to Mikhael Ricks and 20-yard scramble, to take a 13-7 lead on Means's 1-yard run around right end. McNair's fourth-and-5 pass from the Oilers' 49 fell incomplete with 1:34 left to ice the game. Leaf was 13 of 24 for 179 yards. McNair was 20 of 34 for 193 yards and 1 touchdown.

San Diego	3	3	7	0	—	13
Tennessee	0	7	0	0	—	7

SD — FG Carney 48
SD — FG Carney 23
Tenn — Wycheck 15 pass from McNair (Del Greco kick)
SD — Means 1 run (Carney kick)

GREEN BAY 23, TAMPA BAY 15—at Lambeau Field, attendance 60,124. Brett Favre passed for 2 touchdowns as the Packers defeated the Buccaneers for the fifteenth time in seventeen games. Following Ryan Longwell's 38-yard field goal, Santana Dotson sacked Trent Dilfer and forced him to fumble. Vonnie Holliday recovered at the Buccaneers' 14, setting up Favre's 10-yard touchdown pass to Tyrone Davis en route to a 20-0 halftime lead. Favre's 38-yard scoring pass to Antonio Freeman extended Green Bay's lead to 27-0 before Jacquez Green spoiled the shutout with a 95-yard punt return midway through the fourth quarter. The Buccaneers drove deep into Packers territory three times prior to scoring on offense, but Dilfer fumbled at the Packers' 15- and 21-yard lines and Steve Walsh had a pass intercepted in the end zone before Dilfer capped an 84-yard drive with a 2-yard touchdown pass to Dave Moore. Favre was 22 of 33 for 237 yards and 2 touchdowns. Dilfer was 20 of 36 for 211 yards and 1 touchdown.

Tampa Bay	0	0	0	15	—	15
Green Bay	10	6	0	7	—	23

GB — FG Longwell 38
GB — Davis 10 pass from Favre (Longwell kick)
GB — FG Longwell 27
GB — FG Longwell 20
GB — Freeman 38 pass from Favre (Longwell kick)
TB — Green 95 punt return (Hape pass from Dilfer)
TB — Moore 2 pass from Dilfer (Husted kick)

SUNDAY NIGHT, SEPTEMBER 13

NEW ENGLAND 29, INDIANAPOLIS 6—at Foxboro Stadium, attendance 60,068. Ty Law had 2 interceptions, one of which he returned 59 yards for a touchdown, as the Patriots' defense forced 4 turnovers to defeat the Colts. Wilie Clay recovered a Peyton Manning fumble inside the Colts' 5, setting up the first of 3 Adam Vinatieri field goals. Law's touchdown came less than three minutes later, and Law intercepted a pass in the Patriots' end zone early in the second quarter to thwart the Colts. Drew Bledsoe threw a 3-yard touchdown pass to Terry Glenn to cap the Patriots' initial possession of the second half to give New England a 22-0 lead, and Robert Edwards had receptions of 39 and 24 yards before scoring on a 1-yard run in the fourth quarter's opening minute. Bledsoe was 15 of 29 for 218 yards and 1 touchdown. Manning was 21 of 33 for 188 yards and 1 touchdown, with 3 interceptions. Marshall Faulk rushed 29 times for 127 yards.

Indianapolis	0	0	0	6	—	6
New England	10	6	6	7	—	29

NE — FG Vinatieri 19
NE — Law 59 interception return (Vinatieri kick)
NE — FG Vinatieri 23
NE — FG Vinatieri 52
NE — Glenn 3 pass from Bledsoe (pass failed)
NE — Edwards 1 run (Vinatieri kick)
Ind — Small 3 pass from Manning (pass failed)

MONDAY NIGHT, SEPTEMBER 14

SAN FRANCISCO 45, WASHINGTON 10—at Jack Kent Cooke Stadium, attendance 76,798. Steve Young passed for 303 yards and 3 touchdowns to defeat the Redskins for the seventh consecutive time. Trent Green, making his first career start, guided the Redskins on a 8-play, 86-yard drive on their first possession and threw a 9-yard touchdown pass to Leslie Shepherd. The 49ers scored on their next three possessions, the second set up by Merton Hanks's fumble recovery and the third drive sparked by Young's 57-yard pass to Jerry Rice. The 49ers scored on four consecutive second-half possessions as San Francisco accumulated 504 total yards in the victory. Young was 21 of 32 for 303 yards and 3 touchdowns. Garrison Hearst had 22 carries for 138 yards. Green was 14 fo 25 for 201 yards and 1 touchdown, with 1 interception. Michael Westbrook had 5 catches for 109 yards.

San Francisco	7	14	7	17	—	45
Washington	7	3	0	0	—	10

Wash — Shepherd 9 pass from Green (Blanton kick)
SF — Owens 20 pass from Young (Richey kick)
SF — Young 3 run (Richey kick)
Wash — FG Blanton 37
SF — Smith 16 pass from Young (Richey kick)
SF — Edwards 2 pass from Young (Richey kick)
SF — Hearst 5 run (Richey kick)
SF — FG Richey 22
SF — Levy 21 run (Richey kick)

THIRD WEEK SUMMARIES

AMERICAN FOOTBALL CONFERENCE						
Eastern Division	**W**	**L**	**T**	**Pct.**	**Pts.**	**OP**
Miami	3	0	0	1.000	58	22
New England	2	1	0	.667	77	49
N.Y. Jets	1	2	0	.333	84	66
Buffalo	0	3	0	.000	54	63
Indianapolis	0	3	0	.000	27	97
Central Division						
Jacksonville	3	0	0	1.000	69	49
Pittsburgh	2	1	0	.667	37	46
Baltimore	1	2	0	.333	47	54
Cincinnati	1	2	0	.333	54	64
Tennessee	1	2	0	.333	46	54
Western Division						
Denver	3	0	0	1.000	103	61
Seattle	3	0	0	1.000	95	28
Kansas City	2	1	0	.667	67	36
San Diego	2	1	0	.667	36	44
Oakland	1	2	0	.333	45	79

NATIONAL FOOTBALL CONFERENCE						
Eastern Division	**W**	**L**	**T**	**Pct.**	**Pts.**	**OP**
Dallas	2	1	0	.667	92	59
Arizona	1	2	0	.333	41	74
N.Y. Giants	1	2	0	.333	55	75
Philadelphia	0	3	0	.000	15	72
Washington	0	3	0	.000	48	100
Central Division						
Green Bay	3	0	0	1.000	74	40
Minnesota	3	0	0	1.000	98	44
Tampa Bay	1	2	0	.333	49	69
Chicago	0	3	0	.000	50	68
Detroit	0	3	0	.000	53	101
Western Division						
Atlanta	2	0	0	1.000	36	26
New Orleans	2	0	0	1.000	43	31
San Francisco	2	0	0	1.000	81	40
St. Louis	1	2	0	.333	82	95
Carolina	0	2	0	.000	28	38

SUNDAY, SEPTEMBER 20

JACKSONVILLE 24, BALTIMORE 10—at ALLTEL Stadium, attendance 67,069. The first half featured 11 punts and 2 big plays, a 52-yard touchdown run by Fred Taylor and a 56-yard scoring pass from Eric Zeier to Jermaine Lewis, and the teams went into the locker room tied 10-10. Mark Brunell kept the big-play theme alive with a 72-yard touchdown pass to Jimmy Smith two plays into the second half to give Jacksonville a 17-10 lead. After forcing a punt, the Jaguars drove 80 yards in 14 plays, capped by Brunell's 1-yard touchdown pass to Damon Jones. Rod Woodson blocked Mike Hollis's 25-yard field goal late in the third quarter, but the Ravens only drove into Jaguars' territory once in the second half. Brunell was 25 of 34 for 376 yards and 2 touchdowns. Taylor, who replaced injured James Stewart on the Jaguars' second play, rushed 23 times for 128 yards. Zeier was 13 of 25 for 189 yards and 1 touchdown, with 1 interception.

Baltimore	3	7	0	0	—	10
Jacksonville	7	3	14	0	—	24

Jac — Taylor 52 run (Hollis kick)
Balt — FG Stover 25
Balt — Lewis 56 pass from Zeier (Stover kick)
Jac — FG Hollis 34
Jac — Smith 72 pass from Brunell (Hollis kick)
Jac — Jones 1 pass from Brunell (Hollis kick)

TAMPA BAY 27, CHICAGO 15—at Raymond James Stadium, attendance 64,328. The Buccaneers roared back from a 15-0 halftime deficit to score 27 unanswered second-half points to defeat the Bears. The Bears used Glyn Milburn's 93-yard punt return and John Thierry's sack of Trent Dilfer for a safety to take a 15-0 halftime lead. Chicago could have led by more, but the Bears failed to convert fumbles recovered at the Buccaneers' 37 and 20 into points. Jeff Jaeger missed a 29-yard field goal, and Ryan Wetnight fumbled at the Buccaneers' 6. The Buccaneers scored touchdowns on their first 4 second-half drives. Tampa Bay began the second half with a 14-play, 8:59 drive capped by Trent Dilfer's 13-yard touchdown pass. Dilfer then threw a 44-yard scoring pass to Dave Moore; Warrick Dunn scampered 43 yards to give Tampa Bay a 21-15 lead; and John Lynch's fumble recovery led to Mike Alstott's 2-yard touchdown run with 5:44 left. Dilfer was 12 of 18 for 147 yards and 2 touchdowns. Alstott had 20 carries for 103 yards. Erik Kramer was 19 of 32 for 169 yards.

Chicago	10	5	0	0	—	15
Tampa Bay	0	0	13	14	—	27

Chi — FG Jaeger 26
Chi — Milburn 93 punt return (Jaeger kick)
Chi — Safety, Dilfer sacked by Thierry in end zone
Chi — FG Jaeger 52
TB — Anthony 13 pass from Dilfer (pass failed)
TB — Moore 44 pass from Dilfer (Husted kick)
TB — Dunn 43 run (Hunter pass from Dilfer)
TB — Alstott 2 run (pass failed)

DENVER 34, OAKLAND 17—at Oakland-Alameda County Coliseum, attendance 56,578. Ray Crockett intercepted 2 passes, and Bubby Brister came off the bench to give the undefeated Broncos a 3-0 record. The Broncos led 7-3 and were driving for more points when John Elway was forced to leave the game with an injured hamstring. Brister's first pass was intercepted by Eric Turner and returned 94 yards for a touchdown. The Broncos responded by scoring twice in the final 2:11 of the first half, the second score set up by Bill Romanowski's interception, to take a 17-10 lead. Crockett's first interception led to Brister's 13-yard touchdown pass to Ed McCaffrey, but Darrien Gordon's muffed punt late in the third quarter resulted in Jeff George's 11-yard touchdown pass to Rickey Dudley to cut the lead to 24-17. Following Jason Elam's second field goal, the Raiders drove into Denver territory, but Crockett returned his second interception of the game 80 yards for a touchdown to thwart the rally. Brister was 10 of 17 for 140 yards and 2 touchdowns, with 1 interception. George was 16 of 28 for 188 yards and 1 touchdown, with 3 interceptions. Jett had 5 receptions for 116 yards.

Denver	7	10	7	10	—	34
Oakland	0	10	7	0	—	17

Den — McCaffrey 1 pass from Elway (Elam kick)
Oak — FG Davis 44
Oak — Turner 94 interception return (Davis kick)
Den — FG Elam 35
Den — Griffith 3 pass from Brister (Elam kick)
Den — McCaffrey 13 pass from Brister (Elam kick)
Oak — Dudley 11 pass from George (Davis kick)
Den — FG Elam 35
Den — Crockett 80 interception return (Elam kick)

MINNESOTA 29, DETROIT 6—at Hubert H. Humphrey Metrodome, attendance 63,107. Gary Anderson kicked 5 field goals as the Vikings ruined rookie Charlie Batch's NFL debut. Batch guided the Lions to scoring drives on their first two possessions, converting numerous third-down opportunities, to take a 6-0 lead. Anderson booted 2 field goals to tie the game 6-6 at halftime, and the Vikings scored on their first 4 possessions of the second half. A 44-yard punt return by David Palmer set up Randy Moss's touchdown catch and 2 turnovers in Lions' territory, during a decisive 3:00 stretch spanning the end of the third quarter and beginning of the final quarter and capped by Leroy Hoard's 11-yard touchdown run, gave Minnesota a 26-6 advantage. Randall Cunningham, making his first start of the season for the injured Brad Johnson, was 20 of 35 for 220 yards and 1 touchdown. Batch was 20 of 40 for 160 yards, with 2 interceptions. Anderson finished the day second on the NFL's all-time scoring list with 1,713 points.

Detroit	3	3	0	0	—	6
Minnesota	0	6	13	10	—	29

Det — FG Hanson 37
Det — FG Hanson 49
Minn — FG Anderson 27
Minn — FG Anderson 28
Minn — Moss 5 pass from Cunningham (Anderson kick)
Minn — FG Anderson 42
Minn — FG Anderson 29
Minn — Hoard 11 run (Anderson kick)
Minn — FG Anderson 34

GREEN BAY 13, CINCINNATI 6—at Cinergy Field, attendance 56,346. Brett Favre passed for 274 yards and 1 touchdown as the Packers' defense limited the Bengals to just 7 first downs to remain undefeated. Both teams scored on their initial possessions, as Favre's 16-yard touchdown pass to Robert Brooks capped a 78-yard drive. The Packers led 10-3 late in the first half when Jeff Blake completed a 41-yard pass to Darnay Scott to the Packers' 4. Corey Dillon gained 3 yards on the next play, but Dillon and Blake were stopped on rushing attempts on second and third downs, forcing Cincinnati to settle for Doug Pelfrey's 19-yard field goal as the half expired. Ryan Longwell's 35-yard field goal increased the Packers lead to seven points late in the third quarter, and the Bengals were unable to cross the Packers' 48 in the game's final quarter. Favre was 23 of 35 for 274 yards and 1 touchdown, with 1 interception. Neil O'Donnell was 16 of 30 for 151 yards.

Green Bay	7	3	0	3	—	13
Cincinnati	3	3	0	0	—	6

Cin — FG Pelfrey 37
GB — Brooks 16 pass from Favre (Longwell kick)
GB — FG Longwell 30
Cin — FG Pelfrey 19
GB — FG Longwell 35

N.Y. JETS 44, INDIANAPOLIS 6—at Giants Stadium, attendance 79,469. Vinny Tesaverde threw 4 touchdown passes, and Leon Johnson secored 3 times as the Jets won their first game of the season. Johnson turned a screen pass into an 82-yard touchdown on the Jets' third play to begin the scoring. The Jets scored on three consecutive second-quarter possessions, the first of which was set up by Aaron Glenn's interception and the last of which was capped by Johnson's 16-yard scamper, to give the Jets a 27-0 lead. Testaverde's fourth touchdown pass culminated the opening drive of the second half and gave the Jets a 34-3 lead. The Colts drove into Jets' territory four times in the second half, but scored just 3 points. The Jets amassed 302 rushing yards, led by Curtis Martin's 23 carries for 144 yards. Testaverde was 12 of 21 for 203 yards and 4 touchdowns, with 1 interception. Manning was 20 of 44 for 193 yards, with 2 interceptions.

Indianapolis	0	3	3	0	—	6
N.Y. Jets	7	20	7	10	—	44

NYJ — L. Johnson 82 pass from Testaverde (Hall kick)
NYJ — Brady 1 pass from Testaverde (Hall kick)
NYJ — Chrebet 8 pass from Testaverde (Hall kick)
NYJ — L. Johnson 16 run (kick blocked)
Ind — FG Vanderjagt 43
NYJ — K. Johnson 11 pass from Testaverde (Hall kick)
Ind — FG Vanderjagt 24
NYJ — FG Hall 36
NYJ — L. Johnson 1 run (Hall kick)

MIAMI 21, PITTSBURGH 0—at Pro Player Stadium, attendance 73,948. The Dolphins' defense intercepted 3 passes, 2 of which were turned into 14 Miami points, as the Dolphins recorded their first shutout in six seasons. Norm Johnson missed a 47-yard field-goal attempt early in the second quarter for the Steelers. The Dolphins drove 64 yards midway through the quarter and cracked the scoreboard on Karim Abdul-Jabbar's 3-yard run. Sam Madison's interception and return to the Steelers' 24 two plays later set up Dan Marino's 8-yard touchdown pass to Lamar Thomas to stake Miami to a 14-0 lead. Zach Thomas's 17-yard interception return for a touchdown finished the scoring as neither team ran a play inside the opponents' 36-yard line in the second half. Marino was 14 of 22 for 113 yards and 1 touchdown. Abdul-Jabbar had 33 carries for 108 yards. Kordell Stewart was 11 of 35 for 82 yards, with 3 interceptions. The Dolphins limited the Steelers to 200 total yards.

Pittsburgh	0	0	0	0	—	0
Miami	0	14	7	0	—	21

Mia — Abdul-Jabbar 3 run (Mare kick)
Mia — L. Thomas 8 pass from Marino (Mare kick)
Mia — Z. Thomas 17 interception return (Mare kick)

ST. LOUIS 34, BUFFALO 33—at Rich Stadium, attendance 65,199. One week after being stopped at the 1-yard line as time expired, Tony Banks scrambled 2 yards into the end zone with 11 seconds remaining to give the Rams their first victory. Trailing 7-3 in the second quarter, the Rams needed just three plays to drive 98 yards, capped by Greg Hill's 12-yard scoring run. The Bills responded with a 67-yard scoring drive, with Andre Reed catching a 13-yard touchdown pass in the final minute of the half to take a 14-10 lead. Thurman Thomas's 14-yard touchdown run kick started the second half, and Kurt Schulz's interception on the next play was promptly cashed in by the Bills courtesy of Rob Johnson's 16-yard touchdown pass to Jay Riemersma to take a 28-10 lead. Schulz intercepted another pass, but Antowain Smith fumbled two plays later and Jeff Wilkins converted the turnover into a field goal. Dexter McCleon then intercepted a pass and returned it to the Bills' 28, setting up Tony Banks's 23-yard touchdown pass to Amp Lee to cut the deficit to 28-20. Following a Steve Christie field goal, Eddie Kennison's 37-yard punt return set up Hill's second touchdown with 10:32 remaining. Chris Mohr's 57-yard punt on the next possession bounced out of bounds at the Rams' 1, and Ted Washington tackled Hill in the end zone on the following play for a safety to give Buffalo a 33-28 lead with 8:19 to play. The Rams' defense forced another punt, and Banks led the Rams on a 11-play, 80-yard drive, capped by his 2-yard scramble on first and goal with 11 seconds left. Banks was 13 of 27 for 235 yards and 1 touchdown, with 2 interceptions. Hill had 19 carries for 158 yards. Johnson was 18 of 28 for 231 yards and 3 touchdowns, with 1 interception. Smith rushed 22 times for 118 yards.

St. Louis	0	10	10	14	—	34
Buffalo	7	7	14	5	—	33

Buff — Gash 5 pass from Johnson (Christie kick)
StL — FG Wilkins 27
StL — Hill 12 run (Wilkins kick)
Buff — Reed 13 pass from Johnson (Christie kick)
Buff — Thomas 14 run (Christie kick)
Buff — Riemersma 16 pass from Johnson (Christie kick)
StL — FG Wilkins 25
StL — Lee 23 pass from Banks (Wilkins kick)
Buff — FG Christie 36
StL — Hill 1 run (Lee run)
Buff — Safety, Washington tackled Hill in end zone
STL — Banks 2 run (run failed)

KANSAS CITY 23, SAN DIEGO 7—at Arrowhead Stadium, attendance 73,730. The Chiefs scored on their first four possessions and forced the Chargers into 5 turnovers in their initial seven drives in a steady rain to hand San Diego its first loss of the year. Derrick Thomas and Donnie Edwards recovered Ryan Leaf fumbles in Chargers' territory to set 2 of Pete Stoyanovich's 3 first-half field goals. Dale Carter's 23-yard interception return on the first play following Stoyanovich's third field goal set up Rich Gannon's 44-yard touchdown pass to Andre Rison to give Kansas City a 16-0 less than 11 minutes into the game. Leaf lost 3 fumbles and threw 2 interceptions in a first half that saw the Chargers limited to just 57 yards on nine possessions. Latario Rachal's muffed punt and a 36-yard pass interference penalty set up Donnell Bennett's 1-yard scoring plunge early in the third quarter to give the Chiefs a 23-0 lead. Natrone Means chugged 72 yards through the mud for the Chargers' lone points. Gannon was 10 of 29 for 144 yards and 1 touchdown. Leaf was 1 of 15 for 4 yards, with 2 interceptions. The Chiefs had more first downs (16-7), total yards (243-147), and enjoyed an advantage in time of possession (39:05-20:55).

San Diego	0	0	7	0	—	7
Kansas City	6	10	7	0	—	23

KC — FG Stoyanovich 35
KC — FG Stoyanovich 31
KC — FG Stoyanovich 33
KC — Rison 44 pass from Gannon (Stoyanovich kick)
KC — Richardson 1 run (Stoyanovich kick)
SD — Means 72 run (Carney kick)

NEW ENGLAND 27, TENNESSEE 16—at Foxboro Stadium, attendance 59,973. Drew Bledsoe threw a 51-yard touchdown pass to Terry Glenn, and Lawyer Milloy scored on an interception return less than 20 seconds later as the Patriots avoided slipping below .500. The teams were tied 3-3 when Al Del Greco booted a 26-yard field goal with 1:57 left in the first half. The Patriots promptly drove 65 yards to set up Adam Vinatieri's game-tying 41-yard field goal as the half expired. The Patriots again allowed the Oilers to take the lead on Steve McNair's 22-yard touchdown pass to Eddie George, only to tie the game on Robert Edwards's 7-yard run on the ensuing drive. Derrick Mason's 12-yard punt return set up Del Greco's third field goal early in the fourth quarter, but Bledsoe fired a 51-yard touchdown pass to Glenn with 4:25 remaining to take a 20-16 lead, and Milloy intercepted a pass two plays later and scored to increase the lead to 27-16 with 4:06 left. The Oilers reached the Patriots' 28, but Ty Law intercepted McNair to thwart Tennessee's final threat. Bledsoe was 18 of 30 for 250 yards and 1 touchdown. Glenn had 4 receptions for 102 yards. McNair was 28 of 38 for 202 yards and 1 touchdown, with 2 interceptions. George rushed 23 times for 100 yards.

Tennessee	3	3	7	3	—	16
New England	3	3	7	14	—	27

Tenn — FG Del Greco 34
NE — FG Vinatieri 43
Tenn — FG Del Greco 26
NE — FG Vinatieri 41
Tenn — George 22 pass from McNair (Del Greco kick)
NE — Edwards 7 run (Vinatieri kick)
Tenn — FG Del Greco 45
NE — Glenn 51 pass from Bledsoe (Vinatieri kick)
NE — Milloy 30 interception return (Vinatieri kick)

SEATTLE 24, WASHINGTON 14—at Kingdome, attendance 63,336. Steve Broussard returned the opening kickoff 90 yards for a touchdown, and the Seahawks' defense forced 3 turnovers to improve their record to 3-0 for the first time since 1986. Following Broussard's game-opening theatrics, the Redskins tied the game on Trent Green's 36-yard touchdown pass to Michael Westbrook. Both kickers struggled in the second quarter, with David Akers missing from 48 and 49 yards and Todd Peterson misfiring from 52, before Peterson drilled a 32-yard field goal just before halftime. Darrin Smith's interception two plays into the second half led to Ricky Watters's touchdown run, and Watters's 33-yard third-down scamper set up Warren Moon's 21-yard touchdown pass to Mike Pritchard midway through the third quarter to give Seattle a 24-7 lead. The Redskins were twice stopped on downs, at the Seahawks' 34 and 5-yard lines, and Terry Allen lost a fumble at the Seahawks' 11 in the final 22 minutes before Green and Westbrook hooked up for their second touchdown with 31 seconds left. The Redskins outgained the Seahawks (465-299). Moon was 16 of 33 for 141 yards and 1 touchdown. Watters had 24 carries for 136 yards. Green was 27 of 54 for 383 yards and 2 touchdowns, with 2 interceptions. Westbrook had 7 receptions for 132 yards.

Washington	7	0	0	7	—	14
Seattle	7	3	14	0	—	24

Sea — Broussard 90 kickoff return (Peterson kick)
Wash — Westbrook 36 pass from Green (Akers kick)
Sea — FG Peterson 32
Sea — Watters 13 run (Peterson kick)
Sea — Pritchard 21 pass from Moon (Peterson kick)
Wash — Westbrook 26 pass from Green (Akers kick)

SUNDAY NIGHT, SEPTEMBER 20

ARIZONA 17, PHILADELPHIA 3—at Sun Devil Stadium, attendance 39,782. Adrian Murrell rushed for 145 yards and 1 touchdown as the Cardinals broke into the victory column. The game was scoreless for three quarters, the first time that had happened since October 30, 1988, before Chris Boniol capped an 18-play, 74-yard drive with a field goal 40 seconds into the final quarter. Joe Nedney promptly tied the game with a 47-yard boot, and Ronald McKinnon forced Rodney Peete to fumble moments later. Simeon Rice returned the fumble to the Eagles' 18, and Jake Plummer threw a 7-yard touchdown pass to Johnny McWilliams with 7:19 left to give Arizona a 10-3 lead. The Eagles chose to punt on fourth-and-5 from the Cardinals' 40 with 5:00 left, and Murrell capped the 86-yard game-clinching drive with a 25-yard touchdown run. Plummer was 21 of 35 for 137 yards and 1 touchdown. Peete was 13 of 23 for 145 yards.

Philadelphia	0	0	0	3	—	3
Arizona	0	0	0	17	—	17

Phil — FG Boniol 29
Ariz — FG Nedney 47
Ariz — McWilliams 7 pass from Plummer (Nedney kick)
Ariz — Murrell 25 run (Nedney kick)

MONDAY NIGHT, SEPTEMBER 21

DALLAS 31, N.Y. GIANTS 7—at Giants Stadium, attendance 78,039. Deion Sanders returned a punt and interception for a touchdown and set up a third touchdown with a reception as the Cowboys moved into first place in the NFC East. The Giants had to punt following each of their first six possessions, with Sanders returning the fourth punt 59 yards for the game's first points. The Giants tied the game with 3:54 left in the half on Danny Kanell's 36-yard touchdown pass to Amani Toomer, but three plays later Billy Davis took a quick pass from Jason Garrett and streaked 80 yards for the go-ahead touchdown. Kevin Mathis's interception near midfield two plays later led to Richie Cunningham's 40-yard field goal and a 17-7 halftime lead. Sanders caught a 55-yard pass from Garrett to set up Sherman Williams's 18-yard touchdown run early in the third quarter. Sanders capped his performance with a 71-yard interception return for a score with 2:25 left in the game. Garrett, who made his third career start because of Troy Aikman's injury, was 12 of 28 for 222 yards and 1 touchdown. Kanell was 25 of 45 for 228 yards and 1 touchdown, with 2 interceptions.

Dallas	0	17	7	7	—	31
N.Y. Giants	0	7	0	0	—	7

Dall — Sanders 59 punt return (Cunningham kick)
NYG — Tommer 36 pass from Kanell (Daluiso kick)
Dall — Davis 80 pass from Garrett (Cunningham kick)
Dall — FG Cunningham 40
Dall — Sh. Williams 18 run (Cunningham kick)
Dall — Sanders 71 interception return (Cunningham kick)

FOURTH WEEK SUMMARIES

AMERICAN FOOTBALL CONFERENCE

Eastern Division	W	L	T	Pct.	Pts.	OP
Miami	3	0	0	1.000	58	22
New England	2	1	0	.667	77	49
N.Y. Jets	1	2	0	.333	84	66
Buffalo	0	3	0	.000	54	63
Indianapolis	0	4	0	.000	40	116
Central Division						
Jacksonville	4	0	0	1.000	96	71
Pittsburgh	3	1	0	.750	50	56
Baltimore	2	2	0	.500	78	78
Cincinnati	1	3	0	.250	78	95
Tennessee	1	3	0	.250	52	78
Western Division						
Denver	4	0	0	1.000	141	77
Seattle	3	1	0	.750	105	41
Kansas City	3	1	0	.750	91	57
Oakland	2	2	0	.500	58	91
San Diego	2	2	0	.500	52	78

NATIONAL FOOTBALL CONFERENCE

Eastern Division	W	L	T	Pct.	Pts.	OP
Dallas	2	2	0	.500	104	72
Arizona	2	2	0	.500	61	91
N.Y. Giants	2	2	0	.500	89	91
Philadelphia	0	4	0	.000	36	96
Washington	0	4	0	.000	64	138
Central Division						
Green Bay	4	0	0	1.000	111	70
Minnesota	4	0	0	1.000	129	72
Detroit	1	3	0	.250	80	107
Tampa Bay	1	3	0	.250	55	96
Chicago	0	4	0	.000	78	99
Western Division						
San Francisco	3	0	0	1.000	112	60
New Orleans	3	0	0	1.000	62	44
Atlanta	2	1	0	.667	56	57
St. Louis	1	3	0	.250	99	115
Carolina	0	3	0	.000	58	75

SUNDAY, SEPTEMBER 27

ARIZONA 20, ST. LOUIS 17—at Trans World Dome, attendance 55,832. Joe Nedney's fourth-quarter field goal gave the Cardinals a victory in their first game as a visitor in St. Louis. Nedney missed a 48-yard field goal on the Cardinals' opening drive, allowing the Rams to score first on Robert Holcombe's 5-yard touchdown run. Arizona responded by scoring on each of their next three possessions, the second of which followed a 45-yard missed field goal by Jeff Wilkins, to take a 17-7 lead on Adrian Murrell's 4-yard scoring jaunt with 1:05 remaining in the half. A 15-yard unnecessary roughness penalty by Eric Swann set up Wilkins's 57-yard field goal as the half expired. Keith Lyle intercepted a pass at the Rams' 16 to thwart a Cardinals' drive early in the final quarter, and Tony Banks's 42-yard pass to J.T. Thomas set up Holcombe's second touchdown to tie the game with 9:52 left. A 43-yard pass interference penalty on Dexter McCleon set up Nedney's 29-yard field goal with 4:04 left to retake the lead. The Rams were forced to punt after three plays, and the Cardinals ran the final 3:03 off the clock. Jake Plummer was 21 of 31 for 211 yards and 1 touchdown, with 1 interception. Banks was 15 of 26 for 171 yards.

Arizona	0	17	0	3	—	20
St. Louis	7	3	0	7	—	17

StL — Holcombe 5 run (Wilkins kick)
Ariz — FG Nedney 22
Ariz — F. Sanders 13 pass from Plummer (Nedney kick)
Ariz — Murrell 4 run (Nedney kick)
StL — FG Wilkins 57
StL — Holcombe 4 run (Wilkins kick)
Ariz — FG Nedney 29

SAN FRANCISCO 31, ATLANTA 20—at 3Com Park, attendance 62,296. Steve Young threw 3 touchdown passes, including 1 to Jerry Rice just 43 seconds into the game, as the 49ers kept pace with the undefeated Saints. The 49ers led 14-7 when Zack Bronson intercepted a long pass at the 49ers' 7 to thwart a Falcons' drive, and Young scrambled for 18 yards on a fourth-and-1 play to set up his second touchdown pass. In all, the 49ers scored on their first four possessions to take a 24-7 lead. Young and Rice connected for a 26-yard touchdown just before halftime to give San Francisco a 31-7 lead. A 42-yard run by Jamal Anderson set up his 4-yard touchdown run early in the fourth quarter, and Anderson's 18-yard run set up another touchdown with 7:23 to play. Tim McDonald intercepted a Chandler pass at the 49ers' 45 with 3:19 left, and the 49ers ran out the clock. Young was 28 of 39 for 387 yards and 3 touchdowns, with 1 interception. Rice had 8 receptions for 162 yards, and his 27 career touchdowns against the Falcons set an NFL record for touchdowns against one club, breaking Marcus Allen's record against the Chargers. Chandler was 16 of 38 for 254 yards and 2 touchdowns, with 3 interceptions. Mathis had 7 catches for 130 yards.

Atlanta	7	0	0	13	—	20
San Francisco	14	17	0	0	—	31

SF — Rice 66 pass from Young (Richey kick)
SF — Edwards 7 run (Richey kick)
Atl — Mathis 49 pass from Chandler (Andersen kick)
SF — Stokes 3 pass from Young (Richey kick)
SF — FG Richey 31
SF — Rice 26 pass from Young (Richey kick)
Atl — Anderson 4 run (Andersen kick)
Atl — Mathis 31 pass from Chandler (kick blocked)

DENVER 38, WASHINGTON 16—at Jack Kent Cooke Stadium, attendance 71,880. Bubby Brister threw 2 touchdown passes as the Broncos won without John Elway as their starting quarterback for the first time since 1989. A 37-yard reverse by Rod Smith set up Brister's 19-yard touchdown pass to Ed McCaffrey to begin the scoring. Newly-signed Cary Blanchard missed a 44-yard field goal on the Redskins' ensuing possession. Denver responded with a field goal by Jason Elam and, less than three minutes later, a 55-yard interception return by Darrien Gordon for a touchdown to give the Broncos a 17-0 lead. Terry Allen's 5-yard run capped a 79-yard drive, and the Redskins reached the Broncos' 25 in the half's closing moments, but Trevor Pryce's interception thwarted Washington and Denver led 17-7 at halftime. Vaughn Hebron's 44-yard kickoff return was a prelude to a big second half. The Broncos scored on three of their first four possessions, capped by Derek Loville's 1-yard touchdown run with 8:18 remaining to give Denver a 38-10 lead. Brister was 16 of 24 for 180 yards and 2 touchdowns. Davis rushed 21 times for 119 yards. Trent Green was 19 of 31 for 252 yards and 1 touchdown, with 2 interceptions.

Denver	7	10	14	7	—	38
Washington	0	7	3	6	—	16

Den — McCaffrey 19 pass from Brister (Elam kick)
Den — FG Elam 37
Den — Gordon 55 interception return (Elam kick)
Wash — Allen 5 run (Blanchard kick)
Den — Davis 42 run (Elam kick)
Den — Griffith 14 pass from Brister (Elam kick)
Wash — FG Blanchard 37
Den — Loville 1 run (Elam kick)
Wash — Westbrook 75 pass from Green (pass failed)

GREEN BAY 37, CAROLINA 30—at Ericsson Stadium, attendance 69,723. Brett Favre passed for 388 yards and 5 touchdowns as Green Bay fought off a late Panthers rally to give the Packers their first 4-0 record since 1966. Leading 3-0, the first of Jeff Brady's 2 interceptions set up Kerry Collins's 5-yard touchdown pass to Raghib (Rocket) Ismail to give Carolina a 10-0 lead 4:43 into the game. Favre capped consecutive drives with touchdown passes in a six-minute stretch, but Eric Davis intercepted a Favre pass and returned it for a touchdown midway through the second quarter to give the Panthers a 17-13 lead. The Panthers stopped the Packers on downs for the second time in the half, setting up John Kasay's second field goal, but the Packers needed just 6 plays to cover 62 yards and tie the game on Favre's scoring toss to Tyrone Davis. The Panthers gained a total of 3 yards on their first 19 plays from scrimmage in the second half, but trailed just 30-23 following Brady's second interception and Kasay's third field goal. Favre responded by throwing his fifth touchdown pass of the game, but the Panthers cut the deficit to 37-30 with 4:17 remaining and got the ball back on their own 35 with 2:00 left. Carolina reached the Packers' 5 with two seconds left, but Collins's lob pass in the end zone was batted down as time expired. Favre was 27 of 45 for 388 yards and 5 touchdowns, with 3 interceptions. Collins was 20 of 53 for 188 yards and 2 touchdowns, with 1 interception.

Green Bay	6	14	10	7	—	37
Carolina	10	10	0	10	—	30

Car — FG Kasay 42
Car — Ismail 5 pass from Collins (Kasay kick)
GB — Chmura 25 pass from Favre (kick failed)
GB — Mayes 21 pass from Favre (Longwell kick)
Car — E. Davis 16 interception return (Kasay kick)
Car — FG Kasay 42
GB — T. Davis 20 pass from Favre (Longwell kick)
GB — Mayes 4 pass from Favre (Longwell kick)
GB — FG Longwell 41
Car — FG Kasay 56
GB — Mayes 33 pass from Favre (Longwell kick)
Car — Muhammad 15 pass from Collins (Kasay kick)

JACKSONVILLE 27, TENNESSEE 22—at Vanderbilt Stadium, attendance 34,656. Fred Taylor rushed for 116 yards and 1 touchdown in his first NFL start to give the Jaguars their first 4-0 start in franchise history. The Oilers scored on their first four possessions to claim a 19-7 lead midway through the second quarter. Eddie Robinson's interception moments after Steve McNair's second touchdown pass gave the Oilers a chance to expand their lead. However, Tyrone Davis intercepted McNair and returned the ball 34 yards to set up Mark Brunell's 7-yard touchdown pass to Keenan McCardell just before halftime. Taylor's 49-yard run on the first play of the second half led to his 1-yard touchdown run and gave the Jaguars a 21-19 lead. Blaine Bishop recovered Jimmy Smith's fumble at midfield to set up Al Del Greco's 32-yard field goal and allow the Oilers to retake the lead. Mike Hollis kicked field goals on consecutive fourth-quarter possessions, the second of which gave the Jaguars a 27-22 lead with 1:56 left. Dave Krieg, who replaced an injured McNair, fumbled in the Oilers' last possession, and Renaldo Wynn recovered to ice the game. Brunell was 17 of 28 for 155 yards and 2 touchdowns, with 2 interceptions. McNair was 16 of 30 for 198 yards and 2 touchdowns, with 2 interceptions.

Jacksonville	7	7	7	6	—	27
Tennessee	10	9	3	0	—	22

Tenn — FG Del Greco 34
Jac — Jones 5 pass from Brunell (Hollis kick)
Tenn — Thigpen 38 pass from McNair (Del Greco kick)
Tenn — FG Del Greco 32
Tenn — Thigpen 18 pass from McNair (run failed)
Jac — McCardell 7 pass from Brunell (Hollis kick)
Jac — Taylor 1 run (Hollis kick)
Tenn — FG Del Greco 32
Jac — FG Hollis 18
Jac — FG Hollis 36

KANSAS CITY 24, PHILADELPHIA 21—at Veterans Stadium, attendance 66,675. Donnell Bennett scored 3 touchdowns as the Chiefs scored 17 unanswered fourth-quarter points to defeat the Eagles. Pete Stoyanovich missed a 40-yard field goal on the game's opening possession, and the Eagles capitalized with the first of Duce Staley's 3 touchdowns. The Chiefs responded as Bennett capped a 73-yard drive with a touchdown. Tied at halftime, Staley capped a 72-yard drive, which consumed more than half the third quarter, with a 3-yard run. Staley was stopped on fourth-and-1 at the Chiefs' 46 on the Eagles' next possession, seemingly changing the game's momentum. Stoyanovich converted a 21-yard field goal with 11:38 to play and, after the Eagles failed to get a first down and punted, Rich Gannon threw a 57-yard pass to Joe Horn to set up Bennett's second touchdown with 8:41 remaining to give the Chiefs a 17-14 lead. Mark McMillian's interception and 12-yard return to the Chiefs' 43 set up Bennett's final touchdown with 3:06 to play. Rodney Peete threw a 17-yard touchdown pass to Staley with 1:01 remaining, but the Chiefs ran out the clock. Gannon was 17 of 25 for 262 yards. Peete was 21 of 36 for 260 yards and 1 touchdown, with 1 interception.

Kansas City	0	7	0	17	—	24
Philadelphia	7	0	7	7	—	21

Phil — Staley 5 run (Boniol kick)
KC — Bennett 1 run (Stoyanovich kick)
Phil — Staley 3 run (Boniol kick)
KC — FG Stoyanovich 21
KC — Bennett 7 run (Stoyanovich kick)
KC — Bennett 5 run (Stoyanovich kick)
Phil — Staley 17 pass from Peete (Boniol kick)

MINNESOTA 31, CHICAGO 28—at Soldier Field, attendance 57,783. Both Randall Cunningham and Erik Kramer threw 4 touchdown passes, but Gary Anderson's 50-yard field goal was the difference as the Vikings improved their record to 4-0. Each team scored on their first possession, and the Vikings took advantage of a 20-yard punt by Mike Horan to take a 10-7 lead on Anderson's 50-yard field goal, but Kramer threw 2 touchdown passes in a 5:44 stretch late in the first half to take a 21-10 lead into the locker room. David Palmer's 53-yard punt return set up Cunningham's second touchdown pass early in the third quarter. The Bears drove to the Vikings' 10, but Corey Fuller intercepted a Kramer pass to thwart the drive, and Cris Carter caught a 35-yard touchdown pass four plays later to give Minnesota a 24-21 lead. The Vikings extended the lead early in the fourth quarter on Randy Moss's 44-yard touchdown catch. Kramer's fourth touchdown pass, with 1:53 left, cut the deficit to three points, but the onside kick went out of bounds and the Vikings ran out the clock. Cunningham was 16 of 25 for 275 yards and 4 touchdowns. Kramer was 25 of 39 for 372 yards and 4 touchdowns, with 1 interception. Bobby Engram had 6 catches for 123 yards.

Minnesota	7	3	14	7	—	31
Chicago	7	14	0	7	—	28

Minn — Smith 67 pass from Cunningham (Anderson kick)
Chi — Engram 33 pass from Kramer (Jaeger kick)
Minn — FG Anderson 50
Chi — Penn 23 pass from Kramer (Jaeger kick)
Chi — Engram 4 pass from Kramer (Jaeger kick)
Minn — Glover 19 pass from Cunningham (Anderson kick)
Minn — Carter 35 pass from Cunningham (Anderson kick)
Minn — Moss 44 pass from Cunningham (Anderson kick)
Chi — Wetnight 19 pass from Kramer (Jaeger kick)

NEW ORLEANS 19, INDIANAPOLIS 13 (OT)—at RCA Dome, attendance 48,480. The Saints scored in the final minute of regulation, and Cameron Cleeland's touchdown catch in overtime gave New Orleans its first 3-0 record since 1993. Each team intercepted a pass in the opponents' territory to set up first-half field goals as the Colts took a 6-3 halftime lead. Chad Cota's interception near midfield set up Doug Brien's game-tying field goal in the third quarter, but the Colts retook the lead on the first play of the fourth quarter when Peyton Manning threw a 78-yard touchdown pass to Marshall Faulk. The Saints got the ball on their own 4-yard line with 2:49 left trailing 13-6. On fourth-and-17, Danny Wuerffel completed a 44-yard pass to Sean Dawkins, which was followed by Andre Hastings's touchdown catch on the next play to tie the game with 41 seconds left. Tyronne Drakeford's interception and 23-yard return to the Colts' 36 was cashed in two plays later when Wuerffel found Cleeland open. Cleeland raced down the right sideline for the final points 6:10 into overtime. Wuerffel was 12 of 27 for 153 yards and 2 touchdowns, with 1 interception. Lamar Smith rushed 24 times for a career-high 157 yards. Manning was 19 of 32 for 309 yards and 1 touchdown, with 3 interceptions. Marshall Faulk had 6 receptions for 128 yards.

New Orleans	0	3	3	7	6	—	19
Indianapolis	3	3	0	7	0	—	13

Ind — FG Vanderjagt 52
Ind — FG Vanderjagt 19
NO — FG Brien 22
NO — FG Brien 20
Ind — Faulk 78 pass from Manning (Vanderjagt kick)
NO — Hastings 15 pass from Wuerffel (Brien kick)
NO — Cleeland 33 pass from Wuerffel

N.Y. GIANTS 34, SAN DIEGO 16—at Qualcomm Stadium, attendance 55,672. Percy Ellsworth returned 1 of his 2 interceptions for a touchdown, and the Giants turned 4 interceptions into 21 points en route to breaking a seven-game losing streak on the West Coast. After Gary Brown's 4-yard run capped a 70-yard drive, the Giants took advantage of interceptions by Carlton Gray and Ellsworth, both in Giants' territory, to thwart drives and set up touchdowns for the Giants to take a 21-0 lead midway through the second quarter. John Carney booted 3 field goals on consecutive possessions to cut the deficit to 21-9, but Ellsworth swiped Ryan Leaf's third-and-10 pass and scampered 20 yards into the end zone. Craig Whelihan replaced Leaf and threw a 41-yard touchdown pass to Charlie Jones on their next drive, but Cedric Jones sacked Whelihan on fourth down midway through the final quarter to quell any threat. Danny Kanell was 17 of 33 for 208 yards and 1 touchdown, with 1 interception. Leaf was 15 of 34 for 193 yards, with 4 interceptions. Whelihan was 6 of 15 for 97 yards and 1 touchdown.

N.Y. Giants	14	7	7	6	—	34
San Diego	0	6	10	0	—	16

NYG — Brown 4 run (Daluiso kick)
NYG — Calloway 25 pass from Kanell (Daluiso kick)
NYG — Way 1 run (Daluiso kick)
SD — FG Carney 41
SD — FG Carney 46
SD — FG Carney 34
NYG — Ellsworth 20 interception return (Daluiso kick)
SD — C. Jones 41 pass from Whelihan (Carney kick)
NYG — FG Daluiso 32
NYG — FG Daluiso 19

OAKLAND 13, DALLAS 12—at Texas Stadium, attendance 63,544. James Jett caught a deflected pass for a 75-yard touchdown to give the Raiders a 3-0 record at Texas Stadium. With the score tied 3-3 in the second quarter, Jeff George threw a long pass to Jett. Kevin Smith deflected the ball into Jett's hands, who proceeded to run the remaining distance for a 75-yard touchdown to give Oakland a 10-3 lead. The Cowboys drove to the Raiders' 7 in the third quarter, but Charles Woodson's interception at the goal line thwarted the drive. Dallas had another chance to score but Richie Cunningham missed a 37-yard field goal early in the fourth quarter, and Greg Davis converted from 38 yards with 10:47 remaining to increase the Raiders lead to 13-3. After a pair of punts, Billy Davis broke a tackle after catching a pass and raced 55 yards to the Raiders' 1 to set up Emmitt Smith's scoring plunge with 5:49 left. The Cowboys forced Oakland to punt, but Eric Turner intercepted Jason Garrett's long pass for a touchback with 1:31 remaining. Punter Leo Araguz stepped out of the end zone with two seconds left for the game's final points. George was 12 of 20 for 171 yards and 1 touchdown. Napoleon Kaufman rushed 24 times for 116 yards. Garrett was 18 of 33 for 222 yards, with 2 interceptions.

Oakland	3	7	0	3	—	13
Dallas	0	3	0	9	—	12

Oak — FG Davis 30
Dall — FG Cunningham 40
Oak — Jett 75 pass from George (Davis kick)
Oak — FG Davis 38
Dall — E. Smith 1 run (Cunningham kick)
Dall — Safety, Araguz ran out of end zone

PITTSBURGH 13, SEATTLE 10—at Three Rivers Stadium, attendance 58,413. Jerome Bettis rushed for 138 yards, and good special teams play, lifted the Steelers past the Seahawks. Late in the first quarter, Hines Ward tipped a punt back into play and Lance Brown downed the ball at the Seahawks' 1. Brown recovered Mike Pritchard's fumble moments later to set up Norm Johnson's first field goal. The Seahawks struck back immediately, using Warren Moon's 40-yard pass to Joey Galloway to get in position to take a 7-3 lead on Moon's 14-yard touchdown pass to Christian Fauria. The Steelers responded with a 13-play, 82-yard drive that consumed 8:13 and was capped by Chris Fuamatu-Ma'afala's 10-yard scoring run to give Pittsburgh a 10-7 halftime edge. Johnson missed a 42-yard field-goal attempt early in the second half, but Chris Oldham recovered Mack Strong's fumble moments later to set up Johnson's second field goal. The Seahawks once again responded with points on the board, courtesy of Todd Peterson's 47-yard field goal. However, Peterson's 52-yard attempt midway through the fourth quarter sailed wide right, and, in the Seahawks final possession, Moon's fourth-and-11pass fell incomplete. Kordell Stewart was 16 of 25 for 108 yards. Moon was 14 of 27 for 183 yards and 1 touchdown, with 1 interception.

Seattle	0	7	3	0	—	10
Pittsburgh	3	7	3	0	—	13

Pitt — FG N. Johnson 33
Sea — Fauria 14 pass from Moon (Peterson kick)
Pitt — Fuamata-Ma'afala 10 run (N. Johnson kick)
Pitt — FG N. Johnson 25
Sea — FG Peterson 47

SUNDAY NIGHT, SEPTEMBER 27

BALTIMORE 31, CINCINNATI 24—at NFL Stadium at Camden Yards, attendance 68,154. Priest Holmes rushed for 173 yards and 2 touchdowns in his first NFL start, and Jermaine Lewis scored on 2 long touchdown plays to lead the Ravens. Baltimore scored on its first three possessions, taking a 21-0 lead on Eric Zeier's 73-yard bomb to Lewis with 12:27 left in the second quarter. Deron Jenkins's fourth-down pass interference penalty set up Doug Pelfrey's field goal, and Michael Bankston's fumble recovery at the Ravens' 39 set up Neil O'Donnell's touchdown pass 17 seconds before halftime to cut the deficit to 21-10. The Bengals immediately cut the deficit to four points when Tremain Mack returned the second half's opening kickoff for a touchdown. Lewis responded later in the quarter with an 87-yard punt return, but Cincinnati pulled to within 28-24 on Carl Pickens's second touchdown catch, a 67-yard bomb from Jeff Blake, who had replaced an injured O'Donnell. The Ravens responded with an 11-play drive, with a fourth-down run by Errict Rhett, to set up Matt Stover's 46-yard field goal with 5:15 remaining. The Bengals reached the Ravens' 32 with 1:46 to play, but Rod Woodson knocked down Blake's fourth-and-1 pass to secure the victory. Zeier was 15 of 20 for 254 yards and 1 touchdown. Lewis had 4 receptions for 122 yards. O'Donnell was 13 of 19 for 100 yards and 1 touchdown. Pickens had 7 catches for 120 yards.

Cincinnati	0	10	7	7	—	24
Baltimore	14	7	7	3	—	31

Balt — Holmes 3 run (Stover kick)
Balt — Holmes 15 run (Stover kick)
Balt — Lewis 73 pass from Zeier (Stover kick)
Cin — FG Pelfrey 48
Cin — Pickens 1 pass from O'Donnell (Pelfrey kick)
Cin — Mack 97 kickoff return (Pelfrey kick)
Balt — Lewis 87 punt return (Stover kick)
Cin — Pickens 67 pass from Blake (Pelfrey kick)
Balt — FG Stover 46

MONDAY NIGHT, SEPTEMBER 28

DETROIT 27, TAMPA BAY 6—at Pontiac Silverdome, attendance 74,724. The Lions' defense allowed just 6 first downs, and Bryant Westbrook returned an interception 34 yards for a touchdown en route to their first victory. Leading 6-3, Westbrook intercepted a Trent Dilfer pass on the second half's third play and raced untouched into the end zone. On the Lions' next possession, Barry Sanders exploded for a 44-yard run to set up Charlie Batch's first NFL touchdown to give Detroit a 20-3 lead. Tampa Bay produced just 2 second-half first downs, and its lone points of the half were set up by Terry Fair's fumbled punt. But Fair redeemed himself with a 105-yard kickoff return with 10:19

left to end the scoring. Batch was 14 of 23 for 115 yards. Sanders rushed 27 times for 131 yards. Dilfer was 12 of 30 for 120 yards, with 1 interception.

Tampa Bay	0	3	0	3	—	6
Detroit	0	6	14	7	—	27

Det — FG Hanson 27
Det — FG Hanson 25
TB — FG Husted 43
Det — Westbrook 34 interception return (Hanson kick)
Det — Batch 1 run (Hanson kick)
TB — FG Husted 47
Det — Fair 105 kickoff return (Hanson kick)

FIFTH WEEK SUMMARIES

AMERICAN FOOTBALL CONFERENCE

Eastern Division	W	L	T	Pct.	Pts.	OP
New England	3	1	0	.750	107	76
Miami	3	1	0	.750	67	42
N.Y. Jets	2	2	0	.500	104	75
Buffalo	1	3	0	.250	80	84
Indianapolis	1	4	0	.200	57	128
Central Division						
Jacksonville	4	0	0	1.000	96	71
Pittsburgh	3	1	0	.750	50	56
Baltimore	2	2	0	.500	78	78
Cincinnati	1	3	0	.250	78	95
Tennessee	1	3	0	.250	52	78
Western Division						
Denver	5	0	0	1.000	182	93
Kansas City	4	1	0	.800	108	63
Oakland	3	2	0	.600	81	111
Seattle	3	2	0	.600	111	58
San Diego	2	3	0	.400	64	95

NATIONAL FOOTBALL CONFERENCE

Eastern Division	W	L	T	Pct.	Pts.	OP
Dallas	3	2	0	.600	135	82
Arizona	2	3	0	.400	81	114
N.Y. Giants	2	3	0	.400	92	111
Philadelphia	0	5	0	.000	52	137
Washington	0	5	0	.000	74	169
Central Division						
Minnesota	5	0	0	1.000	166	96
Green Bay	4	1	0	.800	135	107
Tampa Bay	2	3	0	.400	75	99
Chicago	1	4	0	.200	109	126
Detroit	1	4	0	.200	107	138
Western Division						
Atlanta	3	1	0	.750	107	80
New Orleans	3	1	0	.750	89	74
San Francisco	3	1	0	.750	133	86
St. Louis	1	3	0	.250	99	115
Carolina	0	4	0	.000	81	126

SUNDAY, OCTOBER 4

ATLANTA 51, CAROLINA 23—at Georgia Dome, attendance 50,724. Jamal Anderson rushed for 117 yards and 1 touchdown, and the Falcons set an NFL record by scoring 3 touchdowns in a 48-second span to move into a tie for first place. Tim Dwight left little doubt about the game by scampering 93 yards with the game's opening kickoff for a touchdown. John Kasay missed a 54-yard field goal on the ensuing possession, and the Falcons' needed just five plays to retaliate, taking a 14-0 lead on Chris Chandler's 30-yard touchdown pass to Tony Martin. Leading 14-3, Ray Buchanan halted a Panthers' drive with an end zone interception, and Morten Andersen added a field goal late in the half to give Atlanta a 17-3 lead. William White recovered Luther Broughton's fumble at the Falcons' 22 to thwart Carolina's first drive of the second half. The Falcons marched 78 yards in 11 plays, capped by Bob Christian's 1-yard run, to take a 24-3 lead with 6:27 left in the third quarter. Travis Hall recovered Fred Lane's fumble at the Panthers' 26 on Carolina' first play, and Chandler threw a 26-yard touchdown pass to O.J. Santiago on the next play with 6:01 left. Muhsin Muhammad fumbled after his reception on the Panthers' next play, and White raced into the end zone with the loose ball to give Atlanta a 38-3 lead with 5:39 remaining in the quarter. The Panthers scored on their next three possessions, two of the drives lasting 42 and 41 seconds, to cut the deficit to 45-23, but Collins fumbled and threw an interception deep in Atlanta territory to set up 2 late Morten Andersen field goals. Chandler was 12 of 20 for 189 yards and 2 touchdowns, with 2 interceptions, and caught a 22-yard pass from Dwight to set up Andersen's first field goal. Collins was 20 of 38 for 302 yards and 3 touchdowns, with 2 interceptions. The Falcons' defense forced 6 turnovers.

Carolina	3	0	6	14	—	23
Atlanta	14	3	21	13	—	51

Atl — Dwight 93 kickoff return (Andersen kick)
Atl — Martin 30 pass from Chandler (Andersen kick)
Car — FG Kasay 28
Atl — FG Andersen 23
Atl — Christian 1 run (Andersen kick)
Atl — Santiago 26 pass from Chandler (Andersen kick)
Atl — White 18 fumble return (Andersen kick)
Car — Walls 24 pass from Collins (kick blocked)
Car — Carrier 5 pass from Collins (pass failed)
Atl — Anderson 20 run (Andersen kick)
Car — Muhammad 72 pass from Collins (Collins run)
Atl — FG Andersen 25
Atl — FG Andersen 28

DALLAS 31, WASHINGTON 10—at Jack Kent Cooke Stadium, attendance 72,284. Emmitt Smith and Chris Warren each rushed for more than 100 yards as the Cowboys moved into first place in the NFC East. Ken Harvey's recovery of Jason Garrett's fumble near midfield led to Trent Green's 40-yard touchdown pass to Leslie Shepherd midway through the first quarter. The Cowboys scored on their next three possessions in a span of 5:23, the second of which was set up by Deion Sanders's 21-yard interception return to the Redskins' 22, and capped by Ernie Mills's 43-yard touchdown catch to take a 17-7 lead. The Redskins responded with an 11-play drive that culminated with Cary Blanchard's field goal, but Washington failed to drive inside the Cowboys' 35 its remaining six possessions. The Cowboys took a 24-10 lead on the opening drive of the second half, and Warren carried 10 times for 96 yards on an 11-play drive in the waning moments to finalize the scoring. Garrett was 14 of 17 for 169 yards and 1 touchdown. Smith rushed 28 times for 120 yards, while Warren had 14 carries for 104 yards. It marked the first time since 1978, and the third time in franchise history, the Cowboys' had two 100-yard rushers in a game. Green was 13 of 29 for 193 yards and 1 touchdown, with 1 interception.

Dallas	3	14	7	7	—	31
Washington	7	3	0	0	—	10

Wash — Shepherd 40 pass from Green (Blanchard kick)
Dall — FG Cunningham 42
Dall — E. Smith 3 run (Cunningham kick)
Dall — Mills 43 pass from Garrett (Cunningham kick)
Wash — FG Blanchard 31
Dall — Warren 6 run (Cunningham kick)
Dall — Warren 6 run (Cunningham kick)

CHICAGO 31, DETROIT 27—at Soldier Field, attendance 66,944. Erik Kramer threw 2 touchdown passes and ran for another as the Bears scored 2 touchdowns in the final five minutes to snap their four-game losing streak. Greg Jeffries's recovery of Kramer's fumble at the Bears' 17 in the opening moments led to Jason Hanson's 28-yard field goal. After being pinned deep by a punt, Charlie Batch threw a 98-yard touchdown pass to Johnnie Morton on third down to give the Lions a 10-0 lead. Detroit led 17-10 when the Bears fumbled away their next two possessions at their own 41- and 29-yard line, respectively, setting up 10 more Lions' points. Trailing 27-10, Chicago scored touchdowns on its next three possessions, driving 75 and 72 yards to cut the deficit to 27-24, and then relying on Chris Penn's 37-yard catch to the Lions' 1 to set up Kramer's winning run with 1:50 left. The Lions reached the Bears' 41, but Batch's fourth-and-3 pass fell incomplete. Kramer was 26 of 37 for 275 yards and 2 touchdowns. Penn had 6 receptions for 106 yards. Edgar Bennett rushed for 88 yards and completed the first pass attempt of his career for a touchdown. Batch was 16 of 31 for 268 yards and 2 touchdowns. The Bears won despite losing 5 fumbles, 3 of which were recovered by Stephen Boyd.

Detroit	10	0	17	0	—	27
Chicago	0	10	0	21	—	31

Det — FG Hanson 28
Det — Morton 98 pass from Batch (Hanson kick)
Chi — Robinson 20 pass from Kramer (Jaeger kick)
Chi — FG Jaeger 23
Det — Chryplewicz 3 pass from Batch (Hanson kick)
Det — Vardell 1 run (Hanson kick)
Det — FG Hanson 43
Chi — Penn 18 pass from Bennett (Jaeger kick)
Chi — Bownes 6 pass from Kramer (Jaeger kick)
Chi — Kramer 1 run (Jaeger kick)

N.Y. JETS 20, MIAMI 9—at Giants Stadium, attendance 75,257. Curtis Martin rushed 36 times for 108 yards and 1 touchdown as the Jets handed the Dolphins their first defeat. Trailing 3-0, the Jets got great field position because of a penalty on Bernie Parmalee and capitalized with Vinny Testaverde's 10-yard touchdown pass to Keyshawn Johnson. Shane Burton recovered Testaverde's fumble at the Dolphins' 24 on the next drive, but John Hall's 47-yard field goal with 22 seconds left in the half increased the Jets lead to 10-3 at intermission. Victor Green grabbed the first of his 2 interceptions midway through the third quarter, and the Jets converted a fourth-and-1 situation with a 16-yard pass to Keith Byars to set up Martin's touchdown run. Troy Drayton's touchdown catch with 5:42 left cut the deficit to 17-9, but Olindo Mare attempted to run in the 2-point conversion and was stopped. The Jets went on a game-clinching 11-play, 68-yard drive, capped by Hall's second field goal with just 48 seconds to play. Testaverde was 19 of 32 for 185 yards and 1 touchdown. Byars, who had 6 catches for 71 yards, became the NFL's all-time reception leader among running backs. Marino was 13 of 31 for 121 yards and 1 touchdown, with 2 interceptions. The Dolphins only were in Jets' territory twice the entire game. The Jets had more first downs (22-11), total yards (289-153), and time of possession (37:04-22:56).

Miami	3	0	0	6	—	9
N.Y. Jets	0	10	7	3	—	20

Mia — FG Mare 46
NYJ — Johnson 10 pass from Testaverde (Hall kick)
NYJ — FG Hall 47
NYJ — Martin 6 run (Hall kick)
Mia — Drayton 2 pass from Marino (run failed)
NYJ — FG Hall 25

NEW ENGLAND 30, NEW ORLEANS 27—at Louisiana Superdome, attendance 56,172. Adam Vinatieri kicked a 27-yard field goal with three seconds left as the Patriots held off the previously undefeated Saints in Mike Ditka's 200th game as a head coach. The Patriots drove into Saints' territory on all six of their first-half possessions, including inside the Saints' 25 five times, but scored just three times while throwing 2 interceptions and fumbling once. The fumble by Drew Bledsoe was taken 63 yards for a touchdown by Keith Mitchell. Faced with third-and-goal from the Patriots' 1 with three seconds left in the half and trailing 17-7, the Saints went for and got a touchdown on Danny Wuerffel's pass to Cameron Cleeland. Henry Thomas returned an interception 24 yards for his first touchdown since 1989 to give the Patriots a 24-14 lead. Leading 27-17, Bledsoe was intercepted by Tyronne Drakeford at the Saints' 5. Wuerffel's 7-yard touchdown pass to Lamar Smith thirteen plays later cut the deficit to 27-24 with 7:30 to play. Tom Tupa's punt from the Saints' 44 bounced near the goal line where Larry Whigham and Tebucky Jones attempted to keep the ball in play. The Saints' Earl Little touched the ball in the end zone, so Andre Hastings grabbed it and raced 75 yards before being pushed out of bounds by Tupa with 2:00 left. Doug Brien kicked a field goal to tie the game with 1:32 left, but Bledsoe completed 4 consecutive passes covering 62 yards to put Vinatieri in position for the winning boot. Bledsoe was 21 of 35 for 317 yards and 1 touchdown, with 3 interceptions. Terry Glenn had 4 receptions for 105 yards. Wuerffel was 35 of 47 for 278 yards and 2 touchdowns, with 2 interceptions.

New England	3	14	10	3	—	30
New Orleans	0	14	3	10	—	27

NE — FG Vinatieri 34
NO — Mitchell 63 fumble return (Brien kick)
NE — Brisby 6 pass from Bledsoe (Vinatieri kick)
NE — Edwards 8 run (Vinatieri kick)

NO — Cleeland 1 pass from Wuerffel (Brien kick)
NE — Thomas 24 interception return (Vinatieri kick)
NO — FG Brien 21
NE — FG Vinatieri 49
NO — Smith 7 pass from Wuerffel (Brien kick)
NO — FG Brien 37
NE — FG Vinatieri 27

TAMPA BAY 20, N.Y. GIANTS 3—at Raymond James Stadium, attendance 64,989. The Buccaneers' defense allowed just 135 yards, 8 first downs, and forced 3 turnovers to improve to 2-0 at home. Charles Mincy's 22-yard interception return 1:34 into the game set the tone for the day. Michael Husted added a field goal after Regan Upshaw's interception stopped the Giants at the Buccaneers' 21. Trailing 10-0 late in the third quarter, the Giants attempted a fake field goal on fourth-and-7 from the Buccaneers' 27, but holder Brad Maynard's pass fell incomplete. However, Chad Bratzke recovered Trent Dilfer's fumble at the Buccaneers' 10 three plays later to set up Brad Daluiso's field goal. The Buccaneers responded with a 13-play, 61-yard drive that consumed 8:18 and was capped by Husted' field goal with 5:02 remaining to take a 13-3 lead. Ronde Barber's interception two plays later set up Mike Alstott's touchdown with 1:54 left. Dilfer was 12 of 20 for 85 yards, with 1 interception. Kanell was 10 of 27 for 83 yards, with 3 interceptions.

N.Y. Giants	0	0	0	3	—	3
Tampa Bay	10	0	0	10	—	20

TB — Mincy 22 interception return (Husted kick)
TB — FG Husted 35
NYG — FG Daluiso 22
TB — FG Husted 26
TB — Alstott 1 run (Husted kick)

OAKLAND 23, ARIZONA 20—at Sun Devil Stadium, attendance 53,240. The Raiders capitalized on 4 Cardinals' turnovers to win their second consecutive road game. Kwamie Lassiter's interception stalled the Raiders' opening drive and led to Jake Plummer's 2-yard touchdown pass to Johnny McWilliams. Following 2 Greg Davis field goals, the second of which was sparked by a 43-yard punt return by Desmond Howard, the Cardinals used a 59-yard kickoff return by Eric Metcalf to set up Plummer's 13-yard touchdown pass to Rob Moore. Three Cardinals' turnovers in a nine-minute stretch of the second quarter led to 17 Raiders' points: Metcalf's fumbled punt return was recovered at the Cardinals' 36 to set up Davis's third field goal; Charles Woodson's 46-yard interception return for a touchdown gave Oakland a 16-14 lead; and Marquis Walker's interception return to the Cardinals' 4 led to Donald Hollas's 1-yard touchdown. Robert McKinnon recovered Hollas's fumble at the Raiders' 16 late in the third quarter, but on the next play Plummer was intercepted by Eric Allen in the end zone. The Cardinals got 2 field goals from Joe Nedney on their next two possessions, the latter with 8:16 left, to cut the deficit to 23-20. The Raiders consumed more than six minutes on their next drive, but Andre Wadsworth forced Hollas to fumble and J.B. Brown recovered at the Cardinals' 31 with 1:50 left. The Cardinals reached the Raiders' 38 with five seconds remaining, but instead of trying for the tying field goal Arizona ran a short sideline route and Metcalf could not get out of bounds in time on the 2-yard reception to stop the clock from expiring. Hollas, who replaced an injured Jeff George in the first half, was 12 of 22 for 104 yards. Plummer was 23 of 39 for 208 yards and 2 touchdowns, with 3 interceptions. Frank Sanders had 10 receptions for 118 yards.

Oakland	6	17	0	0	—	23
Arizona	7	7	0	6	—	20

Ariz — McWilliams 2 pass from Plummer (Nedney kick)
Oak — FG Davis 51
Oak — FG Davis 40
Ariz — Moore 13 pass from Plummer (Nedney kick)
Oak — FG Davis 34
Oak — Woodson 46 interception return (Davis kick)
Oak — Hollas 1 run (Davis kick)
Ariz — FG Nedney 41
Ariz — FG Nedney 29

DENVER 41, PHILADELPHIA 16—at Mile High Stadium, attendance 73,218. Terrell Davis rushed for 168 yards and 2 touchdowns and Bubby Brister threw 4 touchdown passes as the Broncos scored on their first four possessions to remain unbeaten. Brister's 48-yard pass to Ed McCaffrey and 16-yard third-down pass to Rod Smith set up Davis's 20-yard jaunt 2:48 into the game. Davis's 22-yard run set up Brister's 8-yard touchdown pass to Smith. Following another punt, Davis's 57-yard run led to Brister's 9-yard touchdown pass to Shannon Sharpe. Tory James recovered Allen Rossum's fumble on the ensuing kickoff, and Davis scored six plays later to give Denver a 28-0 lead with 1:11 left in the first quarter. William Thomas blocked Tom Rouen's punt out of the end zone for a safety late in the first half, but Darrius Johnson intercepted Bobby Hoying's pass on the Eagles' first play after the free kick. Johnson returned the ball 45 yards to the Eagles' 12, and Brister found McCaffrey in the end zone to give Denver a 35-2 halftime lead. Smith's touchdown catch with 5:17 left in the third quarter extended the lead to 41-2. Brister was 16 of 29 for 203 yards and 4 touchdowns, with 1 interception. Hoying was 11 of 24 for 96 yards, with 1 interception. The Broncos had more first downs (22-12), total yards (423-157), and time of possession (35:44-24:16).

Philadelphia	0	2	0	14	—	16
Denver	28	7	6	0	—	41

Den — Davis 20 run (Elam kick)
Den — R. Smith 8 pass from Brister (Elam kick)
Den — Sharpe 9 pass from Brister (Elam kick)
Den — Davis 1 run (Elam kick)
Phil — Safety, Rouen punt blocked out of end zone
Den — McCaffrey 12 pass from Brister (Elam kick)
Den — R. Smith 31 pass from Brister (kick failed)
Phil — Garner 3 run (Boniol kick)
Phil — Garner 3 run (Boniol kick)

INDIANAPOLIS 17, SAN DIEGO 12—at RCA Dome, attendance 51,988. Elijah Alexander recovered a fumble and grabbed an interception as the Colts won their first game in a battle of the top two picks of the 1998 draft. Alexander's 12-yard interception return to the Chargers' 44 led to first-pick Peyton Manning's 19-yard touchdown pass to Marshall Faulk, and Ken Dilger took the extra point attempt around left end for two points to take an 8-0 lead. Alexander's fumble recovery on the next possession set up Mike Vanderjagt's 48-yard field goal. John Carney made 2 of 3 field-goal attempts to cut the halftime deficit to 11-6. Natrone Means's fumble at the Chargers' 36 set up a 51-yard field goal for Vanderjagt with 6:14 left to take a 14-6 lead. The Chargers drove 80 yards and scored on Means's 1-yard run with 1:48 to play, but Webster Slaughter's reception was shy of the end zone, thus denying the 2-point conversion. Dilger returned the ensuing onsides kick to the Chargers' 25, and Vanderjagt kicked a 40-yard field goal with 1:14 left. Alexander tackled Freddie Jones on fourth down to ice the game. Manning was 12 of 23 for 137 yards and 1 touchdown, with 1 interception. Ryan Leaf, the second pick of the 1998 draft, was 12 of 23 also, for 160 yards, with 1 interception. Means had 31 carries for 130 yards.

San Diego	0	6	0	6	—	12
Indianapolis	11	0	0	6	—	17

Ind — Faulk 19 pass from Manning (Dilger run)
Ind — FG Vanderjagt 48
SD — FG Carney 50
SD — FG Carney 25
Ind — FG Vanderjagt 51
SD — Means 1 run (pass failed)
Ind — FG Vanderjagt 40

BUFFALO 26, SAN FRANCISCO 21—at Rich Stadium, attendance 76,615. The Bills forced 4 turnovers, recorded 4 sacks, and took advantage of the 49ers' NFL record-tying 22 penalties en route to knocking San Francisco from the ranks of the unbeaten. The Bills set the tone early as Rob Johnson's 50-yard pass to Eric Moulds on the game's first play led to Steve Christie's field goal. Thomas Smith recovered Garrison Hearst's fumble at the 49ers' 30 later in the quarter, and Antowain Smith scored four plays later. R.W. McQuarters fumbled on the ensuing kickoff, and Kamil Laud recovered at the 49ers' 34. Johnson's 5-yard scoring pass to Quinn Early moments later staked the Bills to a 17-0 lead. Christie kicked a field goal just before halftime and added a 38-yard boot late in the third quarter after Marcellus Wiley returned a Steve Young fumble 16 yards to the 49ers' 44. The 49ers' had not been inside the Bills' 30 all day but scored on their final three possessions, the last coming with 1:03 left, and Jeff Posey recovered the ensuing onsides kick. However, Curtis Buckley was offsides so the 49ers had to rekick and Thurman Thomas recovered to ice the game. Johnson was 19 of 27 for 254 yards and 1 touchdown. Young was 23 of 38 for 329 yards and 3 touchdowns, with 1 interception.

San Francisco	0	0	0	21	—	21
Buffalo	10	10	3	3	—	26

Buff — FG Christie 24
Buff — Smith 6 run (Christie kick)
Buff — Early 5 pass from Johnson (Christie kick)
Buff — FG Christie 19
Buff — FG Christie 38
SF — Edwards 47 pass from Young (Rice pass from Young)
Buff — FG Christie 45
SF — Smith 9 pass from Young (pass failed)
SF — Stokes 21 pass from Young (Richey kick)

SUNDAY NIGHT, OCTOBER 4

KANSAS CITY 17, SEATTLE 6—at Arrowhead Stadium, attendance 66,418. Andre Rison caught an 80-yard bomb from Rich Gannon to help the Chiefs win in a torrential downpour that delayed the game for 54 minutes. Phillip Daniels's recovery of Gannon's fumble at the Chiefs' 16 1:05 into the game led to Todd Peterson's field goal. With the score tied 3-3 and 7:10 left in the second quarter, the game was halted because of severe lightning and nearly of five inches of rain on the field that forced the teams to run 26 consecutive running plays. John Friesz replaced Warren Moon once play resumed, and Dale Carter intercepted Friesz and returned the ball to the Seahawks' 32. A 15-yard facemask penalty on the return gave the Chiefs the ball at the Seahawks' 17, and Gannon scored six plays later to take a 10-3 lead. Darrin Smith's fumble recovery at the Chiefs' 7 early in the third quarter only netted a Seattle field goal to cut the deficit to 10-6. Rison's touchdown reception broke open the game late in the third quarter. The Seahawks twice drove deep into Chiefs' territory in the fourth quarter, but Peterson missed a 38-yard field goal and Jon Kitna, the Seahawks' third quarterback of the game, was intercepted by James Hasty at the Chiefs' 2. Gannon was 12 of 19 for 142 yards and 1 touchdown. Seattle's three quarterbacks were a combined 11 of 33 for 94 yards, with 2 interceptions. The Chiefs, who committed 5 of the game's 9 turnovers, defeated the Seahawks for the fourteenth time in 15 games. Darryl Williams had 3 fumble recoveries for the Seahawks.

Seattle	3	0	3	0	—	6
Kansas City	3	7	7	0	—	17

Sea — FG Peterson 22
KC — FG Stoyanovich 22
KC — Gannon 4 run (Stoyanovich kick)
Sea — FG Peterson 28
KC — Rison 80 pass from Gannon (Stoyanovich kick)

MONDAY NIGHT, OCTOBER 5

MINNESOTA 37, GREEN BAY 24—at Lambeau Field, attendance 59,849. Randy Moss had 5 receptions for 190 yards as Randall Cunningham threw for 442 yards and 4 touchdowns to snap the Packers' 25-game home winning streak. Gary Anderson's 33-yard field goal capped a 7:00 drive on the Vikings' first possession. The Packers responded with a field goal, but the Vikings needed just 5 plays to drive 80 yards, the last 56 coming on Jake Reed's touchdown catch. Roell Preston's second kickoff return for a touchdown of the season tied the game 10-10, but the Vikings scored 4 plays later on Moss's 52-yard scoring grab. William Henderson was stopped on fourth-and-1 at the Vikings' 35, and Cunningham's 41-yard bomb to Moss set up Robert Smith's 24-yard touchdown catch to take a 24-10 lead. Anderson began the second half with a field goal, and Robert Griffith intercepted Brett Favre in the end zone to thwart a Packers' drive. Cunningham's 46-yard bomb to Moss set up Anderson's third field goal. Four plays after Griffith's second interception of the half stopped another Favre drive, Moss caught a 44-yard bomb to extend the Vikings' lead to 37-10 with 10:16 to play. Doug Pederson engineered 2 late touchdown drives for the Packers. Cunningham was 20 of 32 for 442 yards and 4 touchdowns. Along with Moss, Cris Carter had 8 catches for 119 yards. Favre was 13 of 23 for 114 yards, with 3 interceptions. Pederson was 10 of 16 for 103 yards and 2 touchdowns. The Vikings registered 545 total yards.

Minnesota	3	21	3	10	—	37
Green Bay	0	10	0	14	—	24

Minn — FG Anderson 33
GB — FG Longwell 40
Minn — Reed 56 pass from Cunningham (Anderson kick)
GB — Preston 101 kickoff return (Longwell kick)
Minn — Moss 52 pass from Cunningham (Anderson kick)
Minn — Smith 24 pass from Cunningham (Anderson kick)
Minn — FG Anderson 25
Minn — FG Anderson 19
Minn — Moss 44 pass from Cunningham (Anderson kick)
GB — Davis 11 pass from Pederson (Longwell kick)
GB — Schroeder 16 pass from Pederson (Longwell kick)

SIXTH WEEK SUMMARIES

AMERICAN FOOTBALL CONFERENCE

Eastern Division	W	L	T	Pct.	Pts.	OP
New England	4	1	0	.800	147	86
Miami	3	2	0	.600	88	70
Buffalo	2	3	0	.400	111	108
N.Y. Jets	2	3	0	.400	114	105
Indianapolis	1	5	0	.167	81	159
Central Division						
Jacksonville	5	0	0	1.000	124	92
Pittsburgh	3	2	0	.600	70	81
Cincinnati	2	2	0	.500	103	115
Baltimore	2	3	0	.400	86	90
Tennessee	2	3	0	.400	80	89
Western Division						
Denver	6	0	0	1.000	203	109
Kansas City	4	2	0	.667	118	103
Oakland	4	2	0	.667	88	117
Seattle	3	3	0	.500	127	79
San Diego	2	4	0	.333	70	102

NATIONAL FOOTBALL CONFERENCE

Eastern Division	W	L	T	Pct.	Pts.	OP
Dallas	4	2	0	.667	162	102
Arizona	3	3	0	.500	101	121
N.Y. Giants	2	4	0	.333	112	145
Philadelphia	1	5	0	.167	69	149
Washington	0	6	0	.000	86	186
Central Division						
Minnesota	5	0	0	1.000	166	96
Green Bay	4	1	0	.800	135	107
Tampa Bay	2	3	0	.400	75	99
Detroit	1	4	0	.200	107	138
Chicago	1	5	0	.167	116	146
Western Division						
Atlanta	4	1	0	.800	141	100
San Francisco	4	1	0	.800	164	86
New Orleans	3	2	0	.600	89	105
St. Louis	2	3	0	.400	129	125
Carolina	0	5	0	.000	101	153

SUNDAY, OCTOBER 11

BUFFALO 31, INDIANAPOLIS 24—at RCA Dome, attendance 52,938. Doug Flutie replaced an injured Rob Johnson and guided the Bills on four consecutive scoring drives in the second half to spearhead a comeback victory. Mike Vanderjagt concluded all four Colts' possessions with field goals to give Indianapolis a 12-7 halftime lead. Larry Chester knocked Johnson out of the game with a first-quarter sack, setting the stage for Flutie. The 5-foot, 10-inch backup threw a 6-yard touchdown pass to Kevin Williams to cap a 59-yard third-quarter drive to give the Bills a 14-12 lead. The Bills' defense forced a punt, and Antowain Smith scored from 4 yards. Two plays later, Ted Washington's interception set up another Smith touchdown with 11:04 to play. Another punt set up Steve Christie's 39-yard field goal with 5:20 remaining. Peyton Manning threw 2 touchdown passes, the second to Marvin Harrison with six seconds left, but Jay Riemersma recovered the onsides kick to ice the game. Flutie was 23 of 28 for 213 yards and 2 touchdowns. Smith rushed for 130 yards. Manning was 20 of 41 for 235 yards and 2 touchdowns, with 2 interceptions.

Buffalo	0	7	7	17	—	31
Indianapolis	6	6	0	12	—	24

Ind — FG Vanderjagt 22
Ind — FG Vanderjagt 33
Ind — FG Vanderjagt 43
Buff — Riemersma 7 pass from Flutie (Christie kick)
Ind — FG Vanderjagt 41
Buff — Williams 6 pass from Flutie (Christie kick)
Buff — Smith 4 run (Christie kick)
Buff — Smith 1 run (Christie kick)
Buff — FG Christie 39
Ind — Small 3 pass from Manning (pass failed)
Ind — Harrison 25 pass from Manning (pass failed)

DALLAS 27, CAROLINA 20—at Texas Stadium, attendance 64,181. Emmitt Smith rushed for 112 yards and 1 touchdown ,and Kevin Mathis had 2 key fumble recoveries as the Cowboys improved to 4-0 against NFC opponents. Trailing 3-0, the Panthers put together impressive back-to-back touchdown drives, both ending with Steve Beuerlein scoring passes to Raghib Ismail, to take a 14-3 lead. The Cowboys drove 93 yards following the second touchdown to cut the lead to 14-10 on Jason Garrett's 18-yard pass to Ernie Mills. Early in the third quarter, Mathis recovered William Floyd's fumble at the Panthers' 2, setting up Garrett's scoring pass to Chris Warren to retake the lead. Garrett's 30-yard pass to Michael Irvin on the next possession led to Smith's touchdown. The Panthers were driving when Ismail had a 35-yard catch but fumbled at the Cowboys' 21. Mathis recovered again, and Richie Cunningham booted his second field goal. Rod Smith's fumble recovery and a 40-yard pass interference penalty on Darren Woodson led to Floyd's touchdown, but Chad Hennings blocked the extra-point attempt to maintain a seven-point edge for the Cowboys. The Panthers got the ball back two more times, but Deion Sanders thwarted the first possession with an interception, and Beuerlein's desperation heave at the end of the game sailed out of the end zone. Garrett was 14 of 22 for 287 yards and 2 touchdowns. Irvin had 6 catches for 146 yards. Beuerlein was 22 of 32 for 286 yards and 3 touchdowns, with 1 interception. Ismail had 6 receptions for 117 yards.

Carolina	7	7	0	6	—	20
Dallas	3	7	14	3	—	27

Dall — FG Cunningham 27
Car — Ismail 35 pass from Beuerlein (Kasay kick)
Car — Ismail 16 pass from Beuerlein (Kasay kick)
Dall — Mills 18 pass from Garrett (Cunningham kick)
Dall — Warren 6 pass from Garrett (Cunningham kick)
Dall — Smith 2 run (Cunningham kick)
Dall — FG Cunningham 38
Car — Floyd 3 pass from Beuerlein (kick blocked)

ARIZONA 20, CHICAGO 7—at Sun Devil Stadium, attendance 50,495. Mario Bates scored 2 touchdowns, and Ronald McKinnon intercepted 3 passes as the Cardinals forced 8 of the game's 13 turnovers. The Cardinals scored 13 points off of 4 first-half Bears' turnovers, as the Bears got no closer to the end zone than the Cardinals' 42, to take a 17-0 halftime lead. The Cardinals turned the ball over on their first 2 possessions of the second half, and the Bears drove to the Cardinals' 10, but Eric Swann sacked Erik Kramer and forced him to fumble. Mark Smith recovered the ball to thwart the drive. Joe Nedney added his second field goal after McKinnon forced Ty Hallock to fumble early in the fourth quarter. Kramer threw a 79-yard touchdown pass to Bobby Engram on third-and-6 with 2:30 left to avoid the shutout. Jake Plummer was 18 of 25 for 157 yards, with 2 interceptions. Bates had 2 touchdowns on just 3 carries. Kramer was 16 of 28 for 247 yards and 1 touchdown, with 4 interceptions.

Chicago	0	0	0	7	—	7
Arizona	3	14	0	3	—	20

Ariz — FG Nedney 49
Ariz — Bates 2 run (Nedney kick)
Ariz — Bates 2 run (Nedney kick)
Ariz — FG Nedney 40
Chi — Engram 79 pass from Kramer (Jaeger kick)

DENVER 21, SEATTLE 16—at Kingdome, attendance 66,258. Terrell Davis rushed for 208 yards and 1 touchdown as the Broncos remained unbeaten. The Broncos scored twice in the first quarter, the second coming one play after a 36-yard punt return by Darrien Gordon, to take a 14-0 lead. The Seahawks punted to conclude all seven of their first-half possessions, scoring their lone points on Darrin Smith's interception return in the first minute of the second quarter. Seattle put together a 14-play, 65-yard drive to begin the second half, but had to settle for Todd Peterson's 23-yard field goal. Gordon's 25-yard punt return set up Davis's touchdown 1:04 into the final quarter. Mike Pritchard's touchdown catch six plays later cut the deficit to 21-16 with 10:34 remaining, but Ricky Watters was stopped on the 2-point conversion attempt. The Seahawks' defense forced a punt, and Seattle drove to the Broncos' 28 but Glenn Cadrez intercepted John Friesz's third-down pass with 1:49 left. Davis dashed the Seahawks' final hopes by streaking 70 yards to the Seahawks' 5 on third-and-3 to ice the game. John Elway was 13 of 27 for 185 yards and 2 touchdowns, with 2 interceptions. Rod Smith had 8 catches for 136 yards. Warren Moon, who played the first three quarters before leaving with injured ribs, was 15 of 32 for 154 yards. Friesz was 6 of 8 for 109 yards and 1 touchdown, with 1 interception.

Denver	14	0	0	7	—	21
Seattle	0	7	3	6	—	16

Den — R. Smith 50 pass from Elway (Elam kick)
Den — Sharpe 29 pass from Elway (Elam kick)
Sea — D. Smith 23 interception return (Peterson kick)
Sea — FG Peterson 23
Den — Davis 2 run (Elam kick)
Sea — Pritchard 50 pass from Friesz (run failed)

NEW ENGLAND 40, KANSAS CITY 10—at Foxboro Stadium, attendance 59,749. Drew Bledsoe threw 3 touchdown passes, and the Patriots scored on seven consecutive possessions en route to their fourth consecutive victory. Henry Thomas recovered Donnell Bennett's fumble at the Chiefs' 40 to set up Robert Edwards's first-quarter touchdown. The Chiefs went for a first down on fourth-and-1 from their own 48, but Tony Richardson was stopped and Adam Vinatieri's field goal moments later gave the Patriots a 10-0 lead. A punt gave the Patriots the ball at midfield, leading to Bledsoe's scoring pass to Edwards. The Chiefs again went for it on fourth-and-6 from the Patriots' 36, but Elvis Grbac's pass was incomplete. The Chiefs' defense held the Patriots, but Ron George was penalized for roughing the kicker, setting up Ben Coates's first touchdown of the day. After another punt, Vinatieri tacked a field goal onto the board as the half expired, giving New England a 27-0 lead. The Patriots scored on their first 2 possessions of the second half to take a 37-0 lead with 3:24 left in the third quarter. Bledsoe was 17 of 26 for 226 yards and 3 touchdowns. Edwards rushed for 104 yards. Grbac was 14 of 29 for 144 yards and 1 touchdown, with 1 interception. The Patriots had more first downs (31-9) and total yards (438-134).

Kansas City	0	0	7	3	—	10
New England	7	20	10	3	—	40

NE — Edwards 1 run (Vinatieri kick)
NE — FG Vinatieri 32
NE — Edwards 15 pass from Bledsoe (Vinatieri kick)
NE — Coates 2 pass from Bledsoe (Vinatieri kick)
NE — FG Vinatieri 38
NE — Coates 11 pass from Bledsoe (Vinatieri kick)
NE — FG Vinatieri 27
KC — Alexander 8 pass from Grbac (Stoyanovich kick)
KC — FG Stoyanovich 33
NE — FG Vinatieri 20

ST. LOUIS 30, N.Y. JETS 10—at Trans World Dome, attendance 65,437. Amp Lee caught a team-high 6 passes and rushed for 53 yards and 2 touchdowns as the Jets tallied just 177 total yards and committed 5 turnovers. After

John Hall's field goal midway through the first quarter, the Jets' defense forced a punt. Todd Lyght blitzed and sacked Glenn Foley deep in Rams' territory, forcing him to fumble. Mike D. Jones recovered the ball, setting up Tony Banks's 7-yard scoring pass to Derrick Harris. Eric Hill's end zone interception thwarted a Jets' drive and led to Jeff Wilkins's first field goal. Mo Lewis recovered Banks's fumble late in the half, but fumbled the ball right back to the Rams and Orlando Pace. Lee scored eight plays later to give the Rams a 17-3 halftime lead. Leading 20-3, Dexter McCleon's interception of Foley's pass at the Jets' 20 set up Wilkins's third field goal, and Vinny Testaverde's fumble at the Jets' 12 on the next possession led to Lee's second touchdown. Banks was 18 of 24 for 171 yards and 1 touchdown. Foley was 5 of 15 for 76 yards, with 2 interceptions before being replaced by Testaverde, who completed 9 of 18 passes for 96 yards and 1 touchdown. The Jets, without injured Curtis Martin, rushed for just 53 yards as the Rams maintained possession for 38:59.

N.Y. Jets	3	0	0	7	—	10
St. Louis	7	10	6	7	—	30

NYJ — FG Hall 54
StL — Harris 7 pass from Banks (Wilkins kick)
StL — FG Wilkins 52
StL — Lee 1 run (Wilkins kick)
StL — FG Wilkins 30
StL — FG Wilkins 34
StL — Lee 3 run (Wilkins kick)
NYJ — L. Johnson 17 pass from Testaverde (Hall kick)

CINCINNATI 25, PITTSBURGH 20—at Cinergy Field, attendance 59,979. Neil O'Donnell deked spiking the ball and instead threw a 25-yard touchdown pass to Carl Pickens with 20 seconds left as the Bengals upset the Steelers. The Steelers led 10-3 and were driving for more points when Sam Shade forced Richard Huntley to fumble, and Greg Myers recovered the ball at the Bengals' 13 with 2:08 left in the half. The Bengals promptly drove 87 yards to score a touchdown on Darnay Scott's 44-yard catch, but a poor snap led to a failed 2-point conversion attempt and allowed the Steelers to maintain a 10-9 lead at halftime. Huntley atoned for his fumble with a touchdown run to cap the opening drive of the second half, but the Bengals answered with Doug Pelfrey's field goal to cut the deficit to 17-12. Scott capped a 4-play, 60-yard drive with a 30-yard touchdown catch to give the Bengals a 18-17 lead early in the fourth quarter. After an exchange of punts, Norm Johnson booted a 40-yard field goal with 1:56 left to allow the Steelers to retake the lead 20-18. The Bengals faced fourth-and-12 when O'Donnell threw a 50-yard bomb to Pickens to keep the final drive alive. Two runs by Corey Dillon got the Bengals to the 25 where, pretending to stop the clock, O'Donnell faked spiking the ball thus freezing the Steelers' defenders. Pickens ran downfield and, despite interference by Dewayne Washington, caught the winning pass. O'Donnell was 20 of 26 for 298 yards and 3 touchdowns. Pickens had 13 catches for 204 yards. Stewart was 13 of 22 for 151 yards, and rushed 7 times for 103 yards.

Pittsburgh	0	10	7	3	—	20
Cincinnati	0	9	3	13	—	25

Pitt — FG N. Johnson 40
Pitt — Bettis 13 run (N. Johnson kick)
Cin — FG Pelfrey 44
Cin — Scott 44 pass from O'Donnell (pass failed)
Pitt — Huntley 9 run (N. Johnson kick)
Cin — FG Pelfrey 48
Cin — Scott 30 pass from O'Donnell (pass failed)
Pitt — FG N. Johnson 40
Cin — Pickens 25 pass from O'Donnell (Pelfrey kick)

OAKLAND 7, SAN DIEGO 6—at Oakland-Alameda County Coliseum, attendance 42,467. Leo Araguz punted an NFL-record 16 times, and the Raiders recorded just 6 first downs but still managed to improve their record to 4-2. In the first half the Chargers twice drove deep into Raiders' territory, but Terry Wooden's interception stopped one drive and John Carney's field goal after Latario Rachal's 56-yard punt return gave San Diego a 3-0 halftime lead. The Raiders went three-and-out in their first nine possessions of the second half (and 14 times in all), but trailed just 6-0 after Carney's 48-yard field goal. Faced with third-and-10 from their own 32, 39-year-old Wade Wilson, who had entered the game two possessions earlier, threw a bomb to James Jett for a 68-yard touchdown with 1:28 left. The Chargers got the ball at their own 47 following a facemask penalty on the kickoff return, but Craig Whelihan's pass to Natrone Means on fourth-and-6 from the Raiders' 38 went for 5 yards. Donald Hollas was 12 of 35 for 101 yards, with 1 interception. Wilson was 1 of 7 for 68 yards and 1 touchdown. Ryan Leaf was 7 of 18 for 78 yards, with 3 interceptions before being replaced by Whelihan, who was 3 of 6 for 19 yards, with 1 interception. The defenses permitted just 15 first downs and 354 total yards, as the offenses converted only 7 of 38 third-down opportunities.

San Diego	0	3	0	3	—	6
Oakland	0	0	0	7	—	7

SD — FG Carney 39
SD — FG Carney 48
Oak — Jett 68 pass from Wilson (Davis kick)

SAN FRANCISCO 31, NEW ORLEANS 0—at Louisiana Superdome, attendance 62,811. Steve Young threw 3 touchdown passes and tied an NFL record with his fifth consecutive 300-yard game as the 49ers rebounded from their loss to the Bills. While the 49ers' defense forced the Saints to punt each of their first five possessions, the 49ers' offense scored three times to take a 13-0 lead. Roy Barker's interception at the Saints' 18 with 1:38 left in the half set up Young's touchdown pass to Terrell Owens just 10 seconds before halftime. Young's 33-yard touchdown pass to Garrison Hearst capped the second half's opening drive and gave the 49ers a 28-0 lead. The 49ers permitted just 2 first downs in the Saints' first nine possessions and outgained the Saints 459-167 yards. Chris Doleman had 4 sacks. Young was 21 of 40 for 309 yards and 3 touchdowns. Danny Wuerffel was 9 of 21 for 95 yards, with 1 interception before being replaced for the final drive by Billy Joe Tolliver.

San Francisco	7	14	10	0	—	31
New Orleans	0	0	0	0	—	0

SF — Clark 1 pass from Young (Richey kick)
SF — FG Richey 42
SF — FG Richey 37
SF — Owens 6 pass from Young (Hearst pass from Young)
SF — Hearst 33 pass from Young (Richey kick)
SF — FG Richey 43

TENNESSEE 12, BALTIMORE 8—at NFL Stadium at Camden Yards, attendance 68,561. Steve McNair scrambled 40 yards for a touchdown, and the Oilers relied on defense and special teams to win in Baltimore. The Ravens got on the board in the game's opening minutes when Rob Burnett sacked McNair for a safety. McNair atoned for the safety by scrambling for a touchdown, but Eddie George was stopped on the 2-point conversion attempt. On the ensuing possession Terry Killens blocked Kyle Richardson's punt to set up the first of 2 Al Del Greco field goals. The Ravens responded after Del Greco's second boot with field goals by Matt Stover on consecutive possessions to cut the lead to 12-8. Rod Woodson intercepted McNair at the Ravens' 20 with 4:23 to play, but the Ravens had to punt. After Baltimore's defense forced a punt, the Ravens drove to the Oilers' 29, but Eric Zeier's pass for the end zone was intercepted by Blaine Bishop as time expired. The Oilers won despite committing 13 penalties. McNair was 17 of 29 for 207 yards, with 1 interception. George had 30 carries for 121 yards. Zeier was 25 of 44 for 249 yards, with 1 interception. Running back Priest Holmes had 13 receptions for 98 yards.

Tennessee	6	3	3	0	—	12
Baltimore	2	0	3	3	—	8

Balt — Safety, Burnett sacked McNair in end zone
Tenn — McNair 40 run (run failed)
Tenn — FG Del Greco 26
Tenn — FG Del Greco 29
Balt — FG Stover 21
Balt — FG Stover 45

PHILADELPHIA 17, WASHINGTON 12—at Veterans Stadium, attendance 66,183. Newly inserted quarterback Rodney Peete ran for 1 touchdown and threw for another to give the Eagles their first victory of the season against the winless Redskins. Peete's touchdown run came after Brandon Whiting returned a fumble to the Redskins' 21. Despite being in Eagles' territory on four of their seven first-half possessions, the Redskins could manage just a field goal by Cary Blanchard, with Blanchard missing from 47 yards and 2 fumbles ending the other drives. Blanchard cut the deficit to 10-6 late in the third quarter, but the Eagles responded with a 15-play, 75-yard drive, capped by Peete's 3-yard touchdown pass to Kaseem Sinceno to take a 17-6 lead with 8:32 left. Chris Boniol missed a 48-yard field-goal attempt with 4:36 remaining, and Brian Mitchell scored less than two minutes later to cut the deficit to 17-12. The Redskins got the ball back but Jamie Asher was stopped 1 yard shy of a first down near midfield with 17 seconds left. Peete was 15 of 28 for 121 yards and 1 touchdown, with 1 interception. Trent Green started and was 12 of 21 for 115 yards, with 1 interception. Gus Frerotte came in midway through the third quarter and was 7 of 16 for 73 yards.

Washington	0	3	3	6	—	12
Philadelphia	7	3	0	7	—	17

Phil — Peete 19 run (Boniol kick)
Wash — FG Blanchard 46
Phil — FG Boniol 44
Wash — FG Blanchard 34
Phil — Sinceno 3 pass from Peete (Boniol kick)
Wash — Mitchell 1 run (run failed)

SUNDAY NIGHT, OCTOBER 11

ATLANTA 34, N.Y. GIANTS 20—at Giants Stadium, attendance 71,173. Chris Chandler threw 2 touchdown passes and ran for another as Dan Reeves beat his old team. Conrad Hamilton's fumble recovery at the Falcons' 36 set up Brad Daluiso's field goal less than five minutes into the game. The Falcons responded with a 4-play drive for a touchdown and scored early in the second quarter when Antonio Edwards knocked the ball out of Danny Kanell's hand and caught it in the air for a touchdown to take a 14-6 lead. Kanell threw a 39-yard touchdown pass to David Patten just before halftime to cut the deficit to 14-13, but the Falcons scored on four of their first five possessions of the second half, three on drives in excess of 70 yards, to pull away. Chandler was 14 of 27 for 266 yards and 2 touchdowns. Jamal Anderson rushed for 110 yards. Kanell was 11 of 21 for 100 yards and 1 touchdown. Kent Graham came in late and was 11 of 16 for 105 yards. The Falcons held the ball for 34:49, outgained the Giants 381-266 total yards, and recorded 6 sacks.

Atlanta	7	7	10	10	—	34
N.Y. Giants	6	7	0	7	—	20

NYG — FG Daluiso 46
Atl — Martin 36 pass from Chandler (Andersen kick)
NYG — FG Daluiso 45
Atl — Edwards 2 fumble return (Andersen kick)
NYG — Patten 39 pass from Kanell (Daluiso kick)
Atl — FG Andersen 26
Atl — Mathis 55 pass from Chandler (Andersen kick)
Atl — Chandler 1 run (Andersen kick)
Atl — FG Andersen 32
NYG — Graham 5 run (Daluiso kick)

MONDAY NIGHT, OCTOBER 12

JACKSONVILLE 28, MIAMI 21—at ALLTEL Stadium, attendance 74,051. Keenan McCardell caught 2 fourth-quarter touchdown passes, and Fred Taylor scored twice as the Jaguars remained one of the NFL's three unbeaten teams. Taylor sprinted 77 yards on the first play from scrimmage and added a 2-yard run early in the second quarter to give Jacksonville a 14-0 lead. The Dolphins drove 69 yards in nearly seven minutes to cut the deficit to 14-7, and Mike Hollis missed a 45-yard field-goal attempt as the half expired. Miami scored on its first two drives of the second half to take a 21-14 lead, but the Dolphins got pinned deep in their own territory and gave the Jaguars the ball at the Dolphins' 40 following a punt. Mark Brunell threw a 23-yard touchdown pass to McCardell four plays later to tie the game with 11:55 left. The Dolphins reached the Jaguars' 36, but Olindo Mare's 54-yard field-goal attempt sailed wide right on fourth-and-5 with 2:44 to play. Brunell promptly threw a 56-yard bomb to McCardell on the next play to retake the lead, and Tony Brackens forced and recovered Dan Marino's fumble at the Jaguars' 48 in the final moments to ensure the victory. Brunell was 12 of 18 for 213 yards and 2 touchdowns, with 1 interception. Marino was 30 of 49 for 323 yards and 2 touchdowns, with 1 interception.

Miami	0	7	14	0	—	21
Jacksonville	7	7	0	14	—	28

Jac — Taylor 77 run (Hollis kick)
Jac — Taylor 2 run (Hollis kick)
Mia — Drayton 2 pass from Marino (Mare kick)
Mia — Abdul-Jabbar 1 run (Mare kick)
Mia — Drayton 15 pass from Marino (Mare kick)
Jac — McCardell 23 pass from Brunell (Hollis kick)
Jac — McCardell 56 pass from Brunell (Hollis kick)

SEVENTH WEEK SUMMARIES

AMERICAN FOOTBALL CONFERENCE

Eastern Division	W	L	T	Pct.	Pts.	OP
Miami	4	2	0	.667	102	70
New England	4	2	0	.667	161	110
Buffalo	3	3	0	.500	128	124
N.Y. Jets	3	3	0	.500	138	119
Indianapolis	1	6	0	.143	112	193
Central Division						
Jacksonville	5	1	0	.833	140	109
Pittsburgh	4	2	0	.667	86	87
Tennessee	3	3	0	.500	124	103
Cincinnati	2	4	0	.333	117	159
Baltimore	2	4	0	.333	92	106
Western Division						
Denver	6	0	0	1.000	203	109
Kansas City	4	2	0	.667	118	103
Oakland	4	2	0	.667	88	117
Seattle	3	3	0	.500	127	79
San Diego	3	4	0	.429	83	112

NATIONAL FOOTBALL CONFERENCE

Eastern Division	W	L	T	Pct.	Pts.	OP
Dallas	4	3	0	.571	174	115
Arizona	3	4	0	.429	108	155
N.Y. Giants	3	4	0	.429	146	152
Philadelphia	1	6	0	.143	79	162
Washington	0	7	0	.000	93	227
Central Division						
Minnesota	6	0	0	1.000	207	103
Green Bay	4	2	0	.667	155	134
Tampa Bay	3	3	0	.500	91	112
Detroit	2	4	0	.333	134	158
Chicago	2	5	0	.143	129	158
Western Division						
Atlanta	5	1	0	.833	172	123
San Francisco	5	1	0	.833	198	117
New Orleans	3	3	0	.500	112	136
St. Louis	2	4	0	.333	129	139
Carolina	0	6	0	.000	114	169

THURSDAY, OCTOBER 15

DETROIT 27, GREEN BAY 20—at Pontiac Silverdome, attendance 77,932. Barry Sanders rushed for 155 yards and 1 touchdown, and Mark Carrier intercepted 2 passes as the Lions defeated the Packers in the Pontiac Silverdome for the fifth time in six seasons. The Packers scored on their first two drives to take a 10-0 lead, but rookie Charlie Batch completed all 4 of his pass attempts on the Lions' ensuing drive en route to Jason Hanson's 25-yard field goal. Carrier's 33-yard interception return two plays later led to Batch's game-tying 3-yard touchdown pass to Pete Chryplewicz. Roell Preston's 47-yard kickoff return to begin the second half set up Ryan Longwell's 40-yard field goal to allow the Packers to retake the lead, 13-10. The Lions drove to the Packers' 2 late in the third quarter, but Tommy Vardell fumbled the ball away. Faced with third-and-9 to begin the fourth quarter, Lions rookie Germane Crowell made a one-handed catch of Batch's pass and outran the coverage for a 68-yard touchdown. After the Lions' defense forced a punt, Sanders scampered 73 yards for a touchdown to put Detroit ahead 24-13 with 8:05 to play. George Jamison's 21-yard interception return thwarted the Packers' next drive and set up Hanson's second field goal with 2:08 remaining. The Packers scored with three seconds left, and Preston recovered the onsides kick near midfield, but Favre's Hail Mary pass fell incomplete in the end zone as time expired. Batch was 16 of 19 for 218 yards and 2 touchdowns. Favre was 22 of 43 for 300 yards and 2 touchdowns, with 3 interceptions for the third consecutive game. Antonio Freeman had 6 receptions for 126 yards and 2 touchdown catches.

Green Bay	10	0	3	7	—	20
Detroit	0	10	0	17	—	27

GB — Freeman 67 pass from Favre (Longwell kick)
GB — FG Longwell 28
Det — FG Hanson 25
Det — Chryplewicz 3 pass from Batch (Hanson kick)
GB — FG Longwell 40
Det — Crowell 68 pass from Batch (Hanson kick)
Det — Sanders 73 run (Hanson kick)
Det — FG Hanson 36
GB — Freeman 14 pass from Favre (Longwell kick)

SUNDAY, OCTOBER 18

N.Y. GIANTS 34, ARIZONA 7—at Giants Stadium, attendance 70,456. Danny Kanell threw 3 touchdown passes and Gary Brown rushed for 108 yards as the Giants beat the Cardinals in Giants Stadium for the fourteenth time in the last 15 seasons. The Giants strung together consecutive 11-play drives, both kept alive by third-down pass interference penalties, to take an early 14-0 lead. Jake Plummer threw a 14-yard touchdown pass to Johnny McWilliams to cut the deficit to 14-7, but the Giants extended their lead after Daluiso, who missed a 33-yard field-goal attempt, made a 26-yard field goal as the half expired. Percy Ellsworth's interception at the Cardinals' 40 early in the second half led to Daluiso's second field goal, and, following a Cardinals punt, Danny Kanell completed an 80-yard drive with a 19-yard touchdown pass to Chris Calloway. Scott Galyon recovered Plummer's fumble on the ensuing possession, leading to Kanell's 18-yard scoring pass to Amani Toomer. Kanell was 22 of 36 for 259 yards and 3 touchdowns. Plummer was 12 of 21 for 139 yards and 1 touchdown, with 2 interceptions. The Giants gained twice as many yards as the Cardinals (390-194) and forced 3 turnovers while committing none.

Arizona	0	7	0	0	—	7
N.Y. Giants	7	10	10	7	—	34

NYG — Way 1 pass from Kanell (Daluiso kick)
NYG — Brown 1 run (Daluiso kick)
Ariz — McWilliams 14 pass from Plummer (Nedney kick)
NYG — FG Daluiso 26
NYG — FG Daluiso 34
NYG — Calloway 19 pass from Kanell (Daluiso kick)
NYG — Toomer 18 pass from Kanell (Daluiso kick)

PITTSBURGH 16, BALTIMORE 6—at Three Rivers Stadium, attendance 58,620. Norm Johnson kicked 3 field goals, and the Steelers defense forced 5 turnovers and recorded 7 sacks to defeat the Ravens. Lee Flowers recovered Priest Holmes's fumble at the Ravens' 40 two plays into the game, setting up Johnson's first field goal. Matt Stover added 2 field goals, the second of which came after James Jones recovered Richard Huntley's fumble at the Steelers' 35 just before halftime to give the Ravens a 6-3 lead at intermission. The Steelers retook the lead three plays into the second half as Kordell Stewart fired a 55-yard touchdown pass to Charles Johnson. The Ravens drove deep into Steelers territory, but Dewayne Washington intercepted Eric Zeier's pass at the Steelers' 4 to thwart a late third-quarter drive. Duane Starks returned the favor by intercepting a Stewart pass at the Ravens' 17 on the ensuing possession. Johnson's second field goal with 3:09 left increased the lead to seven points, and, after Chris Oldham recovered Jermaine Lewis's fumble on the ensuing kickoff, Johnson put the game out of reach with a 40-yard boot with 2:09 to play. Stewart was 12 of 27 for 196 yards and 1 touchdown, with 1 interception. Zeier was 17 of 26 for 173 yards, with 1 interception.

Baltimore	3	3	0	0	—	6
Pittsburgh	3	0	7	6	—	16

Pitt — FG N. Johnson 41
Balt — FG Stover 41
Balt — FG Stover 40
Pitt — C. Johnson 55 pass from Stewart (N. Johnson kick)
Pitt — FG N. Johnson 42
Pitt — FG N. Johnson 40

TAMPA BAY 16, CAROLINA 13—at Raymond James Stadium, attendance 63,600. Trent Dilfer scored 1 touchdown and threw the game-winning scoring pass to Karl Williams with 1:39 remaining to give the Buccaneers a comeback victory. Tampa Bay had the game's first scoring threat, but Les Miller recovered Dilfer's fumble at the Panthers' 8 early in the second quarter. John Kasay's 20-yard field goal capped a 6:18 second-half opening drive to give the Panthers a 6-3 lead. Doug Evans's interception on the ensuing possession led to Fred Lane's 1-yard touchdown run late in the third quarter. After an exchange of punts, the Buccaneers drove 80 yards in 14 plays in 7:30, capped by Dilfer's 1-yard run with 5:05 remaining. The Panthers could get just one first down and had to punt with 2:47 remaining. Dilfer needed just 1:08 to put the go-ahead points on the board, but Michael Husted missed the extra point wide left. Trailing by three points, Kasay made a 52-yard field goal, but the play was whistled dead before the ball was snapped because of an offsides penalty. Attempting a 47-yard field-goal attempt, Kasay's kick sailed wide left. Dilfer was 21 of 31 for 219 yards and 1 touchdown, with 1 interception. Steve Beuerlein was 22 of 31 for 234 yards.

Carolina	0	3	10	0	—	13
Tampa Bay	0	3	0	13	—	16

Car — FG Kasay 53
TB — FG Husted 33
Car — FG Kasay 20
Car — Lane 1 run (Kasay kick)
TB — Dilfer 1 run (Husted kick)
TB — K. Williams 29 pass from Dilfer (kick failed)

TENNESSEE 44, CINCINNATI 14—at Vanderbilt Stadium, attendance 33,288. Steve McNair passed for 277 yards, and the Oilers scored on their first six possessions to post their highest point total since 1991 and record their first-ever victory in Nashville. After a 72-yard, game-opening 4:50 drive ended with running back Mike Archie throwing to Jackie Harris for a touchdown, the Oilers took 9:28 off the clock with a 66-yard drive that culminated in Al Del Greco's 35-yard field goal. Tennessee held the ball for 7:22 on its next possession, with McNair scoring on a 1-yard run, and Del Greco added a 38-yard field goal just before halftime to take a 20-0 lead. The Oilers outgained the Bengals 304-72 in the first half, and held the ball for 22:24 of the half. Following another Del Greco field goal, Joe Bowden returned a Neil O'Donnell fumble for a touchdown to give the Oilers a 30-0 lead less than five minutes into the third quarter. After Corey Dillon broke the ice for the Bengals, the Oilers used a 50-yard kickoff return by Archie to set up McNair's 45-yard touchdown bomb to Kevin Dyson on the next play. McNair was 16 of 21 for 277 yards and 1 touchdown. Eddie George rushed for 107 yards, while Chris Sanders had 3 receptions for 101 yards as the Oilers rolled up 515 total yards. O'Donnell was 11 of 22 for 192 yards and 1 touchdown. Dillon rushed for 124 yards.

Cincinnati	0	0	7	7	—	14
Tennessee	7	13	17	7	—	44

Tenn — Harris 18 pass from Archie (Del Greco kick)
Tenn — FG Del Greco 35
Tenn — McNair 1 run (Del Greco kick)
Tenn — FG Del Greco 38
Tenn — FG Del Greco 42
Tenn — Bowden 12 fumble return (Del Greco kick)
Cin — Dillon 12 run (Pelfrey kick)
Tenn — Dyson 45 pass from McNair (Del Greco kick)
Cin — Gibson 76 pass from O'Donnell (Pelfrey kick)
Tenn — Thomas 1 run (Del Greco kick)

CHICAGO 13, DALLAS 12—at Soldier Field, attendance 59,201. Jeff Jaeger kicked a 29-yard field goal with 11 seconds left as the Bears defeated the Cowboys. Randall Godfrey recovered Edgar Bennett's fumble at the Bears' 14 to set up the first of 2 first-half field goals by Richie Cunningham. The Bears only got as close to the end zone as the Cowboys' 39 in the first half. Erik Kramer's 31-yard pass to Bobby Engram led to his 13-yard scoring pass to Chris Penn midway through the third quarter, marking the Bears' first points after having been outscored 61-0 in the third quarter in 1998. Dexter Coakley intercepted Kramer's tipped pass in the third quarter and returned it for a touchdown. However, an illegal block by Kavika Pittman spotted the ball at midfield and led to Jason Garrett's 1-yard touchdown pass to David LaFleur in the final minute of the third quarter. But Garrett's 2-point conversion pass attempt to

Michael Irvin fell incomplete, giving the Cowboys just a 12-7 lead. The Bears drove 6:36 to set up Jaeger's first field goal, and, after forcing a punt, drove 4:50, with 2 key passes to Alonzo Mayes, to set up the winning boot with 11 seconds left. Kramer was 18 of 30 for 233 yards and 1 touchdown, with 1 interception. Garrett was 14 of 26 for 136 yards and 1 touchdown, with 1 interception.

Dallas	3	3	6	0	—	12
Chicago	0	0	7	6	—	13

Dall — FG Cunningham 23
Dall — FG Cunningham 23
Chi — Penn 13 pass from Kramer (Jaeger kick)
Dall — LaFleur 1 pass from Garrett (pass failed)
Chi — FG Jaeger 22
Chi — FG Jaeger 29

SAN FRANCISCO 34, INDIANAPOLIS 31—at 3Com Park, attendance 68,486. Steve Young threw 2 touchdown passes and ran for 2 more, and Wade Richey kicked a game-winning 24-yard field goal with five seconds left as the 49ers scored 17 unanswered fourth-quarter points to defeat the Colts. After Richey missed a field goal to begin the game, Marshall Faulk raced 65 yards for a touchdown on the Colts' first play from scrimmage. Marvin Harrison then caught a 4-yard touchdown pass two plays after Jason Belser returned a punt 53 yards to the 49ers' 7, and added a 6-yard catch to complete an 84-yard drive and give the Colts a 21-0 lead. The 49ers scored on their last three possessions of the half, the last two scores coming after penalties wiped out Colts' interceptions in the end zone. Harrison scored from 61 yards in the third quarter, and the Colts increased their lead to 31-17 on Mike Vanderjagt's field goal. Belser recovered Terrell Owens's fumble to stall the 49ers' next drive, but the Colts had to punt. Young finished a 10-play, 91-yard drive with a 1-yard touchdown run with 9:58 remaining, but a bad snap on the extra point kept the 49ers behind by eight points. The Colts went three and out, and Young's 23-yard scramble cut the deficit to two points, and Young then found Rice for the game-tying 2-point conversion with 5:52 remaining. The Colts drove to the 49ers' 36, but Vanderjagt's 53-yard field-goal attempt was short with 1:13 to play. A 27-yard pass interference penalty on Tyrone Poole set up Richey's winning boot. Young was 33 of 51 for 331 yards, thus setting an NFL record with his sixth consecutive 300-yard game. J.J. Stokes had 9 receptions for 110 yards. Rice caught a 10-yard pass in the first quarter to tie Art Monk's NFL record of 183 consecutive games with a reception. Peyton Manning was 18 of 30 for 231 yards and 3 touchdowns. The 49ers amassed 36 first downs.

Indianapolis	14	7	10	0	—	31
San Francisco	0	17	0	17	—	34

Ind — Faulk 65 run (Vanderjagt kick)
Ind — Harrison 4 pass from Manning (Vanderjagt kick)
Ind — Harrison 6 pass from Manning (Vanderjagt kick)
SF — FG Richey 43
SF — Stokes 3 pass from Young (Richey kick)
SF — Owens 10 pass from Young (Richey kick)
Ind — Harrison 61 pass from Manning (Vanderjagt kick)
Ind — FG Vanderjagt 38
SF — Young 1 run (bad snap)
SF — Young 23 run (Rice pass from Young)
SF — FG Richey 24

BUFFALO 17, JACKSONVILLE 16—at Rich Stadium, attendance 77,635. Doug Flutie bootlegged around left end on fourth-and-goal with 13 seconds left to give the Bills a victory over the undefeated Jaguars. It took the Jaguars 16 plays and 10:27 to march 69 yards on the game-opening drive, with Tavian Banks posting the points on the board. After an exchange of punts, Flutie threw a 12-yard scoring pass to Eric Moulds to tie the game. Mike Hollis's field goal as the half ended gave Jacksonville a 10-7 halftime lead. Tony Brackens recovered Antowain Smith's fumble on the opening drive of the second half, setting up Hollis's second field goal. An exchange of field goals gave the Jaguars a 16-10 lead heading into the fourth quarter. The Bills got the ball at their own 30 following a punt with 1:50 left. Two catches and 2 rushes by Thurman Thomas got the Bills to the Jaguars' 39 with 39 seconds left. Flutie then threw deep down the left side to Moulds, who was ruled down at the Jaguars' 1. After three incompletions, Flutie was supposed to pitch the ball to Thomas, but Thomas failed to hear the audible so Flutie ran untouched into the end zone. Flutie, who was starting for injured Rob Johnson, completed 18 of 39 passes for 228 yards and 1 touchdown. Mark Brunell was 16 of 28 for 119 yards.

Jacksonville	7	3	6	0	—	16
Buffalo	0	7	3	7	—	17

Jac — Banks 1 run (Hollis kick)
Buff — Moulds 12 pass from Flutie (Christie kick)
Jac — FG Hollis 35
Jac — FG Hollis 23
Buff — FG Christie 24
Jac — FG Hollis 27
Buff — Flutie 1 run (Christie kick)

ATLANTA 31, NEW ORLEANS 23—at Georgia Dome, attendance 60,774. Jamal Anderson rushed for 132 yards and 1 touchdown as the Falcons matched their best start since 1986. After both teams took in excess of seven minutes to score on their opening drives, Anderson streaked 31 yards for a go-ahead touchdown. After the Falcons' defense forced a punt, Chris Chandler threw a 45-yard touchdown pass to Tony Martin on the first play to take a 17-7 lead. The Saints cut the deficit to three on Billy Joe Tolliver's 64-yard touchdown pass to Keith Poole, and knocked Chandler out of the game just before halftime when sacked by Mark Fields. The Saints trimmed the lead to one when Wayne Martin sacked DeBerg in the end zone for a safety in the third quarter, but DeBerg's 26-yard pass to Terance Mathis on third-and-3 set up his 8-yard scoring toss to Bob Christian. It was DeBerg's first touchdown pass since 1993. Three plays later, Eugene Robinson returned an interception, the 50th of his career, for a touchdown for the first time in his career. After Tolliver and Poole hooked up again, this time for 82 yards with 3:19 left, the Falcons got two first downs to run out the clock. Chandler was 7 of 10 for 129 yards and 1 touchdown, while the 44-year-old DeBerg was 7 of 10 for 60 yards and 1 touchdown. Martin had 7 receptions for 116 yards. Tolliver was 14 of 29 for 261 yards and 2 touchdowns, with 3 interceptions. Poole had 3 catches for 154 yards.

New Orleans	0	14	2	7	—	23
Atlanta	3	14	0	14	—	31

Atl — FG Andersen 22
NO — Smith 5 run (Brien kick)
Atl — Anderson 31 run (Andersen kick)
Atl — Martin 45 pass from Chandler (Andersen kick)
NO — Poole 64 pass from Tolliver (Brien kick)
NO — Safety, Martin sacked DeBerg in end zone
Atl — Christian 8 pass from DeBerg (Andersen kick)
Atl — Robinson 25 interception return (Andersen kick)
NO — Poole 82 pass from Tolliver (Brien kick)

SAN DIEGO 13, PHILADELPHIA 10—at Qualcomm Stadium, attendance 56,967. John Carney kicked 2 field goals to help give June Jones a victory in his first game as Chargers coach. Carney's 23-yard field goal capped a game-opening 64-yard drive. Chris Boniol missed a 42-yard field-goal attempt but made a 35-yard boot in the second quarter to tie the game 3-3 at halftime. Natrone Means scored on the Chargers' only possession of the third quarter to take a 10-3 lead. Charles Dimry thwarted an Eagles scoring attempt with an interception in the end zone late in the third quarter, but the Eagles forced a punt and drove 51 yards in six plays to tie the game on Charlie Garner's 12-yard run with 11:32 left. The Eagles forced another punt, but fourth-year defensive tackle Norman Hand recorded his first career interception, returning it 18 yards to the Eagles' 17 to set up Carney's go-ahead boot with 7:18 to play. The Eagles reached the Chargers' 31 in the final moments, but Russell Copeland fumbled and Junior Seau recovered the ball with 1:54 left to seal the victory. Ryan Leaf was 9 of 19 for 83 yards. Means rushed for 112 yards in 21 carries. Rodney Peete was 22 of 39 for 232 yards, with 2 inteceptions. The Chargers won despite recording just 168 yards and 11 first downs. Hugh Douglas recorded 4.5 of the Eagles' 6 sacks.

Philadelphia	0	3	0	7	—	10
San Diego	3	0	7	3	—	13

SD — FG Carney 23
Phil — FG Boniol 35
SD — Means 14 run (Carney kick)
Phil — Garner 12 run (Boniol kick)
SD — FG Carney 26

MIAMI 14, ST. LOUIS 0—at Pro Player Stadium, attendance 65,418. Dan Marino threw 2 touchdown passes and the Dolphins' defense recorded back-to-back shutouts at home for the first time in franchise history. Billy Jenkins, Jr.'s interception at the Rams' 25 halted a Dolphins first-quarter drive, but Terrell Buckley's 31-yard punt return led to a 46-yard drive that culminated with Marino's 1-yard touchdown pass to Oronde Gadsden with six seconds left in the half. A 19-yard touchdown pass from Marino to John Avery ended an 80-yard drive and gave the Dolphins a 14-0 lead with 10:21 left. The Rams reached the Dolphins' 20, but Tony Banks's fourth-down pass fell incomplete with 6:12 remaining. Patrick Surtain then intercepted a Banks pass at the Dolphins' 29 with 4:03 left, and punt returner Tony Horne fumbled away the Rams' last chance with 1:48 to play. Marino was 14 of 26 for 114 yards and 2 touchdowns, with 1 interception. Banks was 14 of 29 for 143 yards, with 1 interception. The Dolphins' defense permitted just 204 yards and recorded 4 sacks.

St. Louis	0	0	0	0	—	0
Miami	0	7	0	7	—	14

Mia — Gadsden 1 pass from Marino (Mare kick)
Mia — Avery 19 pass from Marino (Mare kick)

MINNESOTA 41, WASHINGTON 7—at Hubert H. Humphrey Metrodome, attendance 64,004. Randall Cunnigham passed for 259 yards and 2 touchdowns and the Vikings' defense recorded 5 sacks and allowed just 177 total yards to remain unbeaten. Terry Allen scored one play after Darryl Pounds recovered a punt that deflected off blocker Randy Moss. The Redskins got no closer than the Vikings' 31 the remainder of the game, with that second-quarter drive ending in Cary Blanchard's missed 49-yard field-goal attempt. The Vikings scored on successive first-quarter drives, and took a 21-7 halftime lead on Cunningham's 1-yard touchdown pass to Cris Carter just 14 seconds before halftime to culminate a 61-yard drive that took just 59 seconds. Corey Fuller's third-quarter interception led to Gary Anderson's first field goal and the Vikings pulled away by scoring on all three of their fourth-quarter possessions. Cunningham was 20 of 34 for 259 yards and 2 touchdowns. Robert Smith rushed for 103 yards, while Carter had 5 catches for 109 yards. Gus Frerotte, in his first start since week 1, was 10 of 26 for 117 yards, with 1 interception. The Vikings' defense held the Redskins to just 9 first downs and permitted them to convert just 2 of 14 third-down opportunities.

Washington	7	0	0	0	—	7
Minnesota	14	7	3	17	—	41

Wash — Allen 2 run (Blanchard kick)
Minn — Glover 11 pass from Cunningham (Anderson kick)
Minn — Hoard 1 run (Anderson kick)
Minn — Carter 1 pass from Cunningham (Anderson kick)
Minn — FG Anderson 49
Minn — Smith 19 run (Anderson kick)
Minn — FG Anderson 46
Minn — Hoard 1 run (Anderson kick)

MONDAY NIGHT, OCTOBER 19

N.Y. JETS 24, NEW ENGLAND 14—at Foxboro Stadium, attendance 60,062. Vinnty Testaverde threw 3 touchdown passes as Bill Parcells defeated his former team. Testaverde's 1-yard scoring pass to Kyle Brady capped their game-opening drive. The Patriots responded with a 76-yard drive that finished with rookie Robert Edwards setting an NFL record by scoring a touchdown in each of his first six games. The Jets got into scoring position again, but Chad Eaton blocked Jeff Hall's 38-yard field-goal attempt and the Patriots drove 77 yards to take a 14-7 lead on Drew Bledsoe's 6-yard touchdown pass to Lovett Purnell. Leading 14-10, the Patriots drove deep into Jets territory late in the third quarter, but Aaron Glenn intercepted Bledsoe's pass in the end zone to thwart the drive. Testaverde then proceeded to march the Jets 80 yards in 17 plays, capped by his second short scoring toss to Brady to retake the lead with 8:54 left. The Jets' defense forced a punt, and Testaverde hit Dedric Ward down the right sideline for a 43-yard touchdown with 3:29 to play to clinch the win. Testaverde was 22 of 32 for 294 yards and 3 touchdowns. Curtis Martin rushed for 107 yards. Bledsoe was 18 of 30 for 206 yards and 1 touchdown, with 1 interception.

N.Y. Jets	7	3	0	14	—	24
New England	7	7	0	0	—	14

NYJ — Brady 1 pass from Testaverde (Hall kick)
NE — Edwards 1 run (Vinatieri kick)
NE — Purnell 6 pass from Bledsoe (Vinatieri kick)
NYJ — FG Hall 23
NYJ — Brady 1 pass from Testaverde (Hall kick)
NYJ — Ward 43 pass from Testaverde (Hall kick)

EIGHTH WEEK SUMMARIES

AMERICAN FOOTBALL CONFERENCE

Eastern Division	**W**	**L**	**T**	**Pct.**	**Pts.**	**OP**
Miami	5	2	0	.714	114	79
Buffalo	4	3	0	.571	158	138
New England	4	3	0	.571	170	122
N.Y. Jets	4	3	0	.571	166	122
Indianapolis	1	6	0	.143	112	193
Central Division						
Jacksonville	5	2	0	.714	164	146
Pittsburgh	5	2	0	.714	106	100
Tennessee	3	4	0	.429	144	126
Baltimore	2	5	0	.286	102	134
Cincinnati	2	5	0	.286	127	186
Western Division						
Denver	7	0	0	1.000	240	133
Oakland	5	2	0	.714	115	127
Kansas City	4	3	0	.571	131	123
Seattle	4	3	0	.571	154	99
San Diego	3	5	0	.375	103	139

NATIONAL FOOTBALL CONFERENCE

Eastern Division	**W**	**L**	**T**	**Pct.**	**Pts.**	**OP**
Dallas	4	3	0	.571	174	115
Arizona	3	4	0	.429	108	155
N.Y. Giants	3	4	0	.429	146	152
Philadelphia	1	6	0	.143	79	162
Washington	0	7	0	.000	93	227
Central Division						
Minnesota	7	0	0	1.000	241	116
Green Bay	5	2	0	.714	183	144
Tampa Bay	3	4	0	.429	94	121
Chicago	3	5	0	.375	152	178
Detroit	2	5	0	.286	147	192
Western Division						
San Francisco	6	1	0	.857	226	127
Atlanta	5	2	0	.714	175	151
New Orleans	4	3	0	.429	121	139
St. Louis	2	5	0	.286	139	167
Carolina	0	7	0	.000	128	199

SUNDAY, OCTOBER 25

N.Y. JETS 28, ATLANTA 3—at Giants Stadium, attendance 71,573. Curtis Martin rushed for 101 yards and 1 touchdown, and Vinny Testaverde passed for 2 touchdowns as the Jets defeated the Falcons and 44-year-old quarterback Steve DeBerg. Martin had 8 carries on a 13-play, 86-yard drive and capped it with a 2-yard touchdown run. Victor Green sacked DeBerg on the first play of the second quarter, forcing him to fumble. Jerome Henderson scooped up the bouncing ball and raced 53 yards for a touchdown. Lester Archambeau sacked Testaverde on fourth-and-8, giving the Falcons the ball at their own 47 with 37 seconds left in the half to set up Morten Andersen's 53-yard field goal as the half expired. The Jets forced a punt to start the second half, and the offense marched 65 yards in 10 plays, culminated by Testaverde's 12-yard touchdown pass to Keyshawn Johnson. Mo Lewis's interception return to the Falcons' 40 three plays later set up Testaverde's 22-yard touchdown pass to Keith Byars. The Falcons got no closer than the Jets' 39 the remainder of the game. Testaverde was 16 of 29 passes for 206 yards and 2 touchdowns. DeBerg, who became the oldest quarterback to start an NFL game, was 9 of 20 for 117 yards, with 1 interception before leaving after Lewis's pick. Tony Graziani replaced DeBerg and was 7 of 14 for 86 yards, with 1 interception.

Atlanta	0	3	0	0	—	3
N.Y. Jets	7	7	14	0	—	28

NYJ — Martin 2 run (Hall kick)
NYJ — Henderson 53 fumble return (Hall kick)
Atl — FG Andersen 53
NYJ — K. Johnson 12 pass from Testaverde (Hall kick)
NYJ — Byars 22 pass from Testaverde (Hall kick)

GREEN BAY 28, BALTIMORE 10—at Lambeau Field, attendance 59,860. Brett Favre threw 2 touchdown passes and ran for another score as the Packers broke a two-game losing streak. Roell Preston's 71-yard punt return 1:47 into the game began the scoring for the Packers. The Packers forced the Ravens to punt on all eight of their first-half possessions, but led just 14-0 at intermission. Favre's 44-yard pass to Antonio Freeman set up his 28-yard scoring pass to Robert Brooks four plays into the third quarter. Corey Harris's 52-yard kickoff return set up Matt Stover's field goal to cut the deficit to 21-3. However, LeRoy Butler intercepted Jim Harbaugh at the Ravens' 27 moments later, and Favre scored on a 4-yard run to put the Packers ahead 28-3. Harbaugh replaced Eric Zeier at halftime and guided the Ravens to all 10 of their points. Favre was 22 of 41 for 260 yards and 2 touchdowns, with 2 interceptions. Freeman had 9 receptions for 103 yards. Harbaugh was 9 of 20 for 174 yards and 1 touchdown, with 2 interceptions. Zeier was 8 of 19 for 34 yards. The Ravens converted just 2 of 15 third-down opportunities.

Baltimore	0	0	3	7	—	10
Green Bay	14	0	14	0	—	28

GB — Preston 71 punt return (Longwell kick)
GB — Freeman 4 pass from Favre (Longwell kick)
GB — Brooks 28 pass from Favre (Longwell kick)
Balt — FG Stover 38
GB — Favre 4 run (Longwell kick)
Balt — Lewis 46 pass from Harbaugh (Stover kick)

CHICAGO 23, TENNESSEE 20—at Vanderbilt Stadium, attendance 40,089. Jeff Jaeger kicked his third field goal with 1:03 remaining, and Jim Flanigan blocked Craig Hentrich's potential game-tying field goal with 14 seconds left as the Bears won their first road game of the season. Barry Minter recovered Chris Sanders's fumble and returned it 10 yards to the Oilers' 1 three minutes into the game to set up Robert Chancey's first NFL touchdown. The Oilers put together 83- and 79-yard drives in the first half, sandwiched around a Jaeger field goal, to tie the game 10-10 at halftime. Ricky Bell recovered Mike Archie's fumble on the second half's opening kickoff, and Ty Hallock scored five plays later to give the Bears a 17-10 lead. Edgar Bennett's 17-yard run later in the quarter led to Jaeger's second field goal and a 20-10 lead. The Oilers responded with a long drive, but Marty Carter stopped Michael Roan at the Bears' 1 and forced Al Del Greco to kick a field goal. After Jaeger missed a 34-yard field-goal attempt, the Oilers swiftly marched 76 yards, capped by Rodney Thomas's game-tying 7-yard touchdown run with 3:44 remaining. Erik Kramer completed 2 key passes to Curtis Conway to set up Jaeger's go-ahead kick with 1:03 left. The Oilers drove to the Bears' 31 and faced fourth-and-3 with 21 seconds left. Hentrich, normally the punter, is the Oilers' long kicker and had his first field-goal attempt of the season blocked by Flanigan. The kick would not have counted if it were successful because Del Greco ran onto the field as a twelfth man. Kramer was 13 of 24 for 144 yards. McNair was 18 of 29 for 187 yards and 1 touchdown, with 1 interception. Eddie George rushed for 137 yards.

Chicago	7	3	10	3	—	23
Tennessee	0	10	0	10	—	20

Chi — Chancey 1 run (Jaeger kick)
Tenn — FG Del Greco 29
Chi — FG Jaeger 39
Tenn — Mason 13 pass from McNair (Del Greco kick)
Chi — Hallock 6 run (Jaeger kick)
Chi — FG Jaeger 26
Tenn — FG Del Greco 19
Tenn — Thomas 7 run (Del Greco kick)
Chi — FG Jaeger 33

OAKLAND 27, CINCINNATI 10—at Oakland-Alameda County Coliseum, attendance 40,089. Napoleon Kaufman rushed for 143 yards, and the Raiders' top-ranked defense limited the Bengals to 170 yards and forced 3 turnovers as Oakland surpassed its win total for the 1997 season. Mike Morton recovered Damon Gibson's muffed punt at the Bengals' 20, setting up Donald Hollas's 19-yard touchdown pass to Tim Brown late in the first quarter. The Bengals put together a 95-yard drive, capped by Neil O'Donnell's 17-yard touchdown pass to Corey Dillon, to tie the game. Hollas hit James Jett with a 39-yard bomb five plays later to retake the lead. Darrell Russell sacked O'Donnell and forced him to fumble moments later. Lance Johnstone scooped up the loose ball and rumbled 40 yards for a touchdown and a 21-7 halftime lead. Doug Pelfrey booted a field goal on the Bengals' second possession of the second half, but Cincinnati's offense could only muster 15 total yards in its final four possessions as the Raiders added 2 Greg Davis field goals. Hollas was 9 of 21 for 173 yards and 2 touchdowns. O'Donnell was 16 of 26 for 137 yards and 1 touchdown. The Raiders won their fourth consecutive game for the first time since 1991.

Cincinnati	0	7	3	0	—	10
Oakland	7	14	3	3	—	27

Oak — Brown 19 pass from Hollas (Davis kick)
Cin — Dillon 17 pass from O'Donnell (Pelfrey kick)
Oak — Jett 39 pass from Hollas (Davis kick)
Oak — Johnstone 40 fumble return (Davis kick)
Cin — FG Pelfrey 51
Oak — FG Davis 22
Oak — FG Davis 48

DENVER 37, JACKSONVILLE 24—at Mile High Stadium, attendance 75,217. Terrell Davis rushed for 136 yards and 3 touchdowns, and Jason Elam tied a 28-year-old NFL record by making a 63-yard field goal as the Broncos remained unbeaten. With the score tied 3-3, John Elway threw a 41-yard touchdown pass to Ed McCaffrey on the first play of the second quarter. Brunell fumbled a snap at the Broncos' 10 moments later, and Davis scored his first touchdown to put Denver ahead 17-3. Reggie Barlow returned the ensuing kickoff 91 yards to set up Brunell's 4-yard touchdown pass to Fred Taylor, but the Broncos responded with a 10-play drive, keyed by Elway's 35-yard pass to Davis, and capped by Davis's 1-yard run. The Broncos reached the Jaguars' 40 but faced fourth-and-3. The play clock expired with three seconds left in the half. The Jaguars' accepted the delay of game penalty, moving the ball back to the Jaguars' 45. Elam's 63-yard field goal split the uprights with about five feet to spare as the half expired. The kick tied Tom Dempsey's NFL record and gave Denver a 27-10 lead. Mike Hollis missed a 51-yard field-goal attempt on the Jaguars' first possession of the second half, but Brunell connected with Damon Jones from 31 yards to pull within 27-17. Davis sealed the Jaguars' fate with a 37-yard scoring run down the left sideline early in the fourth quarter. Elway was 21 of 35 for 295 yards and 1 touchdown. Davis became just the third player to rush for more than 1,000 yards (he finished the game with 1,001) in the season's first seven games, matching O.J. Simpson and Jim Brown's mark. Brunell was 28 of 46 for 353 yards and 3 touchdowns. Keenan McCardell had 9 receptions for 113 yards, while Jimmy Smith hauled in 8 passes for 121 yards.

Jacksonville	3	7	7	7	—	24
Denver	3	24	0	10	—	37

Den — FG Elam 31
Jac — FG Hollis 45
Den — McCaffrey 41 pass from Elway (Elam kick)
Den — Davis 4 run (Elam kick)
Jac — Taylor 4 pass from Brunell (Hollis kick)
Den — Davis 1 run (Elam kick)
Den — FG Elam 63
Jac — D. Jones 31 pass from Brunell (Hollis kick)
Den — Davis 37 run (Elam kick)
Jac — Mitchell 2 pass from Brunell (Hollis kick)
Den — FG Elam 32

MINNESOTA 34, DETROIT 13—at Pontiac Silverdome, attendance 77,885. Randall Cunningham threw 2 touchdown passes, and Robert Smith rushed for 134 yards and 1 touchdown as the Vikings remained the NFC's lone unbeaten team. The Lions scored on three consecutive first-half possessions, capped by Jason Hanson's 48-yard field goal as the first half expired, to take a 13-10 halftime edge. The Vikings' defense forced the Lions to punt away the second half's opening possession, and Gary Anderson's second field goal tied the game. After another Lions' punt, Bryant Westbrook was flagged for a 59-yard pass interference penalty, one of 14 penalties committed by the Lions, to give the Vikings the ball at the Lions' 5. After a penalty, Cunningham threw a 10-yard touchdown pass to Cris Carter to give Minnesota a 20-13 lead. Four plays after a third consecutive punt, Smith scampered 57 yards for a touchdown. Westbrook intercepted Cunningham at the Vikings' 29 with 4:50 left, but Jimmy Hitchcock intercepted Charlie Batch's pass two plays later and raced 79 yards to finish the scoring. Cunningham was 17 of 30 for 190 yards and 2 touchdowns, with 2 interceptions. Batch was 20 of 37 for 231 yards and 1 touchdown, with 1 interception.

Minnesota	0	10	17	7	—	34
Detroit	3	10	0	0	—	13

Det — FG Hanson 47
Minn — Reed 11 pass from Cunningham (Anderson kick)
Det — Morton 1 pass from Batch (Hanson kick)
Minn — FG Anderson 35
Det — FG Hanson 48
Minn — FG Anderson 44
Minn — Carter 10 pass from Cunningham (Anderson kick)
Minn — Smith 57 run (Anderson kick)
Minn — Hitchcock 79 interception return (Anderson kick)

MIAMI 12, NEW ENGLAND 9 (OT)—at Pro Player Stadium, attendance 73,973. Olindo Mare booted 4 field goals, including the game winner on the Dolphins' first possession of overtime, as Miami snapped a four-game losing streak to the Patriots and moved into first place in the AFC East. Mare made a 48-yard field goal, and Adam Vinatieri missed a 45-yard attempt in the second quarter to give the Dolphins a 3-0 halftime lead. Ty Law's interception at the Dolphins' 29 set up Vinatieri's tying field goal in the third quarter. Drew Bledsoe threw a 36-yard third-down pass to Shawn Jefferson, and the Patriots got a 38-yard pass interference penalty called on Terrell Buckley, to lead to Vinatieri's second field goal with 9:10 remaining. John Avery's 32-yard kickoff return allowed Mare to tie the game 6-6 with 5:07 left. Rookie Tony Simmons caught a 47-yard, third-down pass on the next possession to set up Vinatieri's 36-yard boot with 2:13 left. Avery returned the ensuing kickoff 37 yards, and Dan Marino threw a 28-yard pass to Oronde Gadsden, as Mare tied the game with 49 seconds left. The Patriots knelt-out the clock to send the game to overtime, but they never got the ball back as the Dolphins got a third-down pass interference call on Law and a 25-yard pass from Marino to O.J. McDuffie to set up Mare's winning boot. Marino was 23 of 42 for 279 yards, with 3 interceptions. Bledsoe was 13 of 33 for 240 yards, with 1 interception. Jefferson had 4 catches for 116 yards.

New England	0	0	3	6	0	—	9
Miami	0	3	0	6	3	—	12

Mia — FG Mare 48
NE — FG Vinatieri 41
NE — FG Vinatieri 30
Mia — FG Mare 38
NE — FG Vinatieri 36
Mia — FG Mare 25
Mia — FG Mare 43

SAN FRANCISCO 28, ST. LOUIS 10—at Trans World Dome, attendance 58,563. Darnell Walker intercepted 2 passes, and Jerry Rice set an NFL record as the 49ers defeated the Rams for the sixteenth consecutive time. Walker intercepted a Tony Banks pass on the game's first play, and Steve Young threw a 12-yard touchdown pass to Rice on the next play to give the 49ers a 7-0 lead 27 seconds into the game. With the touchdown catch, Rice caught a pass in an NFL record 184th consecutive game. The play also marked Young's 79th touchdown pass to Rice, tying the NFL record of Dan Marino and Mark Clayton. Walker's 23-yard interception return to the Rams' 35 later in the quarter led to Young's 2-yard scoring pass to Irv Smith. Jeff Wilkins's 46-yard field goal in the half's final minute cut the intermission deficit to 14-3. Faced with third-and-10 on their own 25-yard line late in the third quarter, Terrell Owens took a short Young pass and turned it into a 48-yard gain. On the next play, Young lofted a 27-yard touchdown pass to Owens. The Rams responded with a 13-play, 83-yard drive, capped by Banks's 6-yard scoring run to cut the deficit to 21-10 with 11:44 remaining. On the ensuing kickoff, Wilkins recovered his own onsides kick. However, Banks mishandled the Shotgun snap on the first play, and Ken Norton, Jr. returned the fumble to the Rams' 21. Owens, on his first NFL carry, ran 21 yards on a reverse on the next play to finish the scoring. Young was 13 of 24 for 227 yards and 3 touchdowns, with 2 interceptions. Banks was 15 of 35 for 121 yards, with 3 interceptions. The 49ers' defense recorded 8 sacks, limited the Rams to 168 yards, and forced 4 turnovers.

San Francisco	14	0	7	7	—	28
St. Louis	0	3	0	7	—	10

SF — Rice 12 pass from Young (Richey kick)
SF — Smith 2 pass from Young (Richey kick)
StL — FG Wilkins 46
SF — Owens 27 pass from Young (Richey kick)
StL — Banks 6 run (Wilkins kick)
SF — Owens 21 run (Richey kick)

SEATTLE 27, SAN DIEGO 20—at Qualcomm Stadium, attendance 58,512. Joey Galloway scored 2 long touchdowns, and the Seahawks' defense held off a late Chargers rally to snap a three-game losing skid. John Friesz, playing for injured Warren Moon, threw a 81-yard bomb to Galloway to open the scoring. After a John Carney field goal, Steve Broussard returned the ensuing kickoff 78 yards to set up Todd Peterson's 40-yard boot. The Seahawks' defense then forced a punt, and Galloway returned it 74 yards for a touchdown and a 17-3 lead. The Chargers answered with a 12-play drive, capped by Ryan Leaf's 5-yard touchdown pass to Mikhael Ricks with 33 seconds left in the half. A 28-yard pass interference penalty on Fred Thomas gave the Chargers the ball at the Seahawks' 5, setting up Natrone Means's game-tying touchdown run midway through the third quarter. The Seahawks added a second field goal by Peterson, and then, on their next possession, Friesz threw a 41-yard pass to Galloway, in which it was ruled he wrestled the ball away from Terrance Shaw, to the Chargers' 2. Shaw was ejected for disputing the play. Ricky Watters's touchdown run on the next play gave the Seahawks a 27-17 lead with 8:43 remaining. Willie Williams intercepted Leaf on the Chargers' ensuing drive, but Dan Saleaumua was called for offsides, enabling Carney to kick his second field goal with 4:16 remaining. The Chargers got the ball back on their own 20 with 2:43 to play and used 17- and 23-yard passes to Charlie Jones to help get to the Seahawks' 3 with 11 seconds left, but Leaf threw 3 consecutive incompletions as the clock expired. Friesz was 14 of 21 for 234 yards and 1 touchdown. Leaf was 25 of 52 for 281 yards and 1 touchdown. The Seahawks had 274 total yards of offense, but had 284 return yards.

Seattle	7	10	3	7	—	27
San Diego	0	10	7	3	—	20

Sea — Galloway 81 pass from Friesz (Peterson kick)
SD — FG Carney 21
Sea — FG Peterson 40
Sea — Galloway 74 punt return (Peterson kick)
SD — Ricks 5 pass from Leaf (Carney kick)
SD — Means 1 run (Carney kick)
Sea — FG Peterson 23
Sea — Watters 1 run (Peterson kick)
SD — FG Carney 45

NEW ORLEANS 9, TAMPA BAY 3—at Louisiana Superdome, attendance 52,695. Doug Brien booted 3 field goals and Sammy Knight had an interception and fumble recovery as the Saints snapped a three-game losing streak. Jacquez Green's 55-yard punt return gave the Buccaneers the ball at the Saints' 25 for their first possession, but Patrick Hape fumbled at the Saints' 5 and Knight recovered. Knight's interception early in the second quarter set up Brien's 46-yard field goal for the first half's only points. Reidel Anthony's 32-yard kickoff return to start the second half led to Michael Husted's 52-yard game-tying field goal. The Saints responded as Billy Joe Tolliver completed a 26-yard pass to Keith Poole to put Brien in position for his second field goal and a 6-3 lead. Tolliver fumbled on the Saints' next possession, and Jeff Gooch recovered at the Saints' 20. But Husted missed a 32-yard field-goal attempt, and then missed a 48-yard field-goal attempt early in the fourth quarter. Brien made a 41-yard field goal to put the Saints ahead 9-3 with 7:15 remaining. The Buccaneers reached Saints' territory one last time, but Chad Cota intercepted Trent Dilfer's pass at the Saints' 26 with 1:41 to play. Tolliver was 20 of 32 for 216 yards. Difler was 20 of 44 for 186 yards, with 2 interceptions. Both teams were held to less than 60 rushing yards, and each converted just 4 of 16 third-down opportunities.

Tampa Bay	0	0	3	0	—	3
New Orleans	0	3	3	3	—	9

NO — FG Brien 46
TB — FG Husted 52
NO — FG Brien 50
NO — FG Brien 41

SUNDAY NIGHT, OCTOBER 25

BUFFALO 30, CAROLINA 14—at Ericsson Stadium, attendance 64,050. Doug Flutie passed for a career-high 282 yards and 2 touchdowns as the Bills won their fourth consecutive game. The Bills scored on their initial drive when Flutie's pass bounced off Doug Evans's hands into Eric Moulds for a 20-yard touchdown. The Panthers cut the deficit to 10-7 in the second quarter when Flutie threw an 82-yard bomb to Moulds three plays later to give the Bills a 17-7 halftime lead. Steve Christie booted a field goal on the Bills' first possession of the second half, and Sam Cowart forced Steve Beuerlein to fumble a few plays later. Bruce Smith recovered the ball at the Panthers' 40, and Thurman Thomas scampered 17 yards for a touchdown three plays later to put the Bills up 27-7. Flutie, who was starting for the second consecutive week in place of injured Rob Johnson, completed 18 of 22 passes for 2 touchdowns, with 1 interception. Moulds had 5 receptions for 145 yards. Beuerlein was 22 of 39 for 286 yards and 1 touchdown, with 2 interceptions. Mark Carrier had 5 catches for 100 yards and a late touchdown.

Buffalo	10	7	10	3	—	30
Carolina	0	7	0	7	—	14

Buff — Moulds 20 pass from Flutie (Christie kick)
Buff — FG Christie 42
Car — Floyd 1 run (Kasay kick)
Buff — Moulds 82 pass from Flutie (Christie kick)
Buff — FG Christie 47
Buff — Thomas 17 run (Christie kick)
Buff — FG Christie 44
Car — Carrier 8 pass from Beuerlein (Kasay kick)

MONDAY NIGHT, OCTOBER 26

PITTSBURGH 20, KANSAS CITY 13—at Arrowhead Stadium, attendance 79,431. Jerome Bettis rushed for 119 yards, his sixth consecutive 100-yard rushing game on Monday Night Football, as the Steelers moved into a tie for first place in the AFC Central. Standing in his own end zone in the first quarter, Louie Aguiar had the first punt blocked of his 8-year career. Lance Brown blocked the punt, and Fred McAfee recovered it for a touchdown. Leading 7-6 just before halftime, the Steelers used 11-, 12-, and 13-yard runs by McAfee to set up Norm Johnson's 34-yard field goal as the half expired. Joe Horn ran the opening kickoff of the second half back for a touchdown, but a penalty negated the score. After allowing another Johnson field goal midway through the third quarter, the Chiefs responded with a 65-yard pass from Elvis Grbac to Derrick Alexander to set up Grbac's 2-yard touchdown pass to Andre Rison to tie the game. However, Pittsburgh answered with a 14-play, 60-yard drive capped by Kordell Stewart's 5-yard touchdown pass to Charles Johnson with 10:05 remaining. The Chiefs had three possessions the remainder of the game: One saw a 43-yard pass bounce off Andre Rison's facemask in the end zone; the second possession was thwarted by Carnell Lake's interception with 4:28 left; and, after getting the ball back with 1:04 left, Jason Gildon forced Grbac to fumble on the first play and Lee Flowers recovered. Stewart was 11 of 22 for 82 yards and 1 touchdown. Grbac was 15 of 36 for 224 yards and 1 touchdown, with 2 interceptions.

Pittsburgh	7	3	3	7	—	20
Kansas City	3	3	7	0	—	13

Pitt — McAfee recovered blocked punt in end zone
KC — FG Stoyanovich 20
KC — FG Stoyanovich 28
Pitt — FG N. Johnson 34
Pitt — FG N. Johnson 22
KC — Rison 2 pass from Grbac (Stoyanovich kick)
Pitt — C. Johnson 5 pass from Stewart (N. Johnson kick)

NINTH WEEK SUMMARIES

AMERICAN FOOTBALL CONFERENCE

Eastern Division	W	L	T	Pct.	Pts.	OP
Buffalo	5	3	0	.625	188	162
Miami	5	3	0	.625	138	109
New England	5	3	0	.625	191	138
N.Y. Jets	5	3	0	.625	186	139
Indianapolis	1	7	0	.125	128	214
Central Division						
Jacksonville	6	2	0	.750	209	165
Pittsburgh	5	3	0	.625	137	141
Tennessee	4	4	0	.500	185	157
Baltimore	2	6	0	.250	121	179
Cincinnati	2	6	0	.250	153	219
Western Division						
Denver	8	0	0	1.000	273	159
Oakland	6	2	0	.750	146	145
Kansas City	4	4	0	.500	148	143
Seattle	4	4	0	.500	172	130
San Diego	3	5	0	.375	103	139

NATIONAL FOOTBALL CONFERENCE

Eastern Division	W	L	T	Pct.	Pts.	OP
Dallas	5	3	0	.625	208	115
Arizona	4	4	0	.500	125	170
N.Y. Giants	3	5	0	.375	160	173
Philadelphia	1	7	0	.125	79	196
Washington	1	7	0	.125	114	241
Central Division						
Minnesota	7	1	0	.875	265	143
Green Bay	6	2	0	.750	219	166
Tampa Bay	4	4	0	.500	121	145
Chicago	3	5	0	.375	152	178
Detroit	2	6	0	.250	160	209
Western Division						
San Francisco	6	2	0	.750	248	163
Atlanta	6	2	0	.750	212	166
New Orleans	4	4	0	.500	138	170
St. Louis	2	6	0	.250	154	204
Carolina	1	7	0	.125	159	216

SUNDAY, NOVEMBER 1

ARIZONA 17, DETROIT 15—at Pontiac Silverdome, attendance 66,087. Joe Nedney booted a 53-yard field goal with 2:46 left and the Cardinals forced 6 turnovers to have a .500 record at the season's midpoint for the first time since 1991. The Cardinals blew two scoring chances as Jake Plummer fumbled at the Lions' 12 and Nedney had a field goal blocked in the first quarter, but Plummer's 16-yard touchdown pass to Frank Sanders gave the Cardinals a 7-6 halftime lead. The Lions drove into Cardinals' territory five times during the first half, but Charlie Batch threw 2 interceptions from the Cardinals' 40, 3 in all during the half, and fumbled at the Cardinals' 48. Frank Reich guided the Lions to Jason Hanson's third field goal, but Plummer responded four plays later with a 36-yard touchdown pass to Rob Moore. Detroit took a 15-14 lead with 9:29 left on Tommy Vardell's touchdown run, but Barry Sanders was stopped on the 2-point conversion attempt. Nedney's field goal gave the Cardinals a 17-15 lead, and Mark Smith sacked Reich and forced him to fumble, leading to Tony McCombs's fumble recovery with 1:57 left to ice the game. Plummer was 15 of 25 for 198 yards and 2 touchdowns, with 1 interception. Moore had 5 receptions for 107 yards. Batch was 10 of 17 for 71 yards, with 3 interceptions, while Reich was 10 of 15 for 119 yards. Sanders rushed for 107 yards. Johnnie Morton had 7 catches for 115 yards.

Arizona	0	7	7	3	—	17
Detroit	0	6	3	6	—	15

Det — FG Hanson 28
Ariz — Sanders 16 pass from Plummer (Nedney kick)
Det — FG Hanson 47
Det — FG Hanson 44
Ariz — Moore 36 pass from Plummer (Nedney kick)
Det — Vardell 1 run (run failed)
Ariz — FG Nedney 53

DENVER 33, CINCINNATI 26—at Cinergy Field, attendance 59,974. Terrell Davis rushed for 149 yards and 2 touchdowns, including the game-winner with 58 seconds left, and Vaughn Hebron made 2 key special-teams plays in the final 6:00 as the Broncos came from behind to become the first 8-0 team since the 1991 Redskins. Tied 3-3 late in the first quarter, Corey Dillon fumbled a handoff at the Broncos' 3, and Bill Romanowski recovered to stall the Bengals' drive. After splitting another pair of field goals, the Bengals hit pay dirt on their fourth drive of the first half to penetrate inside the Broncos' 20, as Neil O'Donnell hit Damon Gibson with a 17-yard pass 57 seconds before halftime to take a 12-6 lead. The Broncos appeared to regroup at halftime, and John Elway threw 33 yards to Ed McCaffrey to set up his 17-yard touchdown pass to Willie Green 3:40 into the second half. Doug Pelfrey missed a 52-yard field goal, but Sam Shade's interception moments later sparked a 60-yard drive that enabled the Bengals to retake the lead 18-13 on James Hundon's touchdown catch with 12:00 left. The Broncos retook the lead on Davis's 2-yard run with 7:05 remaining. Lee Johnson punted the ball out of bounds at the Broncos' 21, but a penalty on Steve Bush forced Johnson to rekick. Hebron took advantage and blocked Johnson's second punt, and Elway threw a scoring pass to McCaffrey two plays later to extend the lead to 26-18 with 5:04 left. The Bengals hurried downfield as O'Donnell completed 2 key third-down passes and eventually found Marco Battaglia for a touchdown and Carl Pickens for the 2-point conversion to tie the game with 2:54 left. Hebron ran the ensuing kickoff back 38 yards, Elway completed a 30- and 14-yard passes to McCaffrey, and Davis scored with 58 seconds left. Tremain Mack returned the ensuing kickoff 61 yards to the Broncos' 32, but Cincinnati lost 7 yards and O'Donnell's fourth-down pass sailed out of bounds. Elway was 15 of 26 for 213 yards and 2 touchdowns, with 1 interception. McCaffrey had 7 receptions for 133 yards. O'Donnell was 20 of 37 for 257 yards and 3 touchdowns. Dillon had 35 carries for 110 yards.

Denver	3	3	7	20	—	33
Cincinnati	3	9	0	14	—	26

Cin — FG Pelfrey 25
Den — FG Elam 33
Cin — FG Pelfrey 23
Den — FG Elam 37
Cin — Gibson 17 pass from O'Donnell (dropped hold)
Den — Green 17 pass from Elway (Elam kick)
Cin — Hundon 11 pass from O'Donnell (pass failed)
Den — Davis 2 run (run failed)
Den — McCaffrey 25 pass from Elway (Elam kick)
Cin — Battaglia 1 pass from O'Donnell (Pickens pass from O'Donnell)
Den — Davis 5 run (Elam kick)

JACKSONVILLE 45, BALTIMORE 19—at NFL Stadium at Camden Yards, attendance 68,915. Fred Taylor scored 2 touchdowns, and the Jaguars tallied touchdowns on their first four possessions en route to a club-record 42-point first half. Mark Brunell completed a 6-play, 76-yard drive with a 37-yard scoring pass to Jimmy Smith midway through the first quarter. Following a 73-yard Ravens touchdown drive that tied the game, the Jaguars scored 23 seconds later as Taylor outran the secondary on a 78-yard scoring pass from Brunell. Joel Smeenge's recovery of Eric Green's fumble at the Ravens' 25 set up Taylor's touchdown run, and Bryan Schwartz's recovery of Roosevelt Potts's fumble led to Daimon Shelton's touchdown to give the Jaguars a 28-7 lead with 9:33 left in the first half. Alvis Whitted blocked Kyle Richardson's punt and returned it for a touchdown with 4:03 left in the half, and Donovin Darius recovered Green's second fumble and raced 83 yards for a touchdown. Brunell was 13 of 20 for 237 yards and 2 touchdowns, with 1 interception. Jim Harbaugh was 27 of 34 for 243 yards and 3 touchdowns, with 1 interception. The Jaguars' defense forced 5 turnovers.

Jacksonville	14	28	0	3	—	45
Baltimore	7	6	0	6	—	19

Jac — Smith 37 pass from Brunell (Hollis kick)
Balt — Lewis 6 pass from Harbaugh (Stover kick)
Jac — Taylor 78 pass from Brunell (Hollis kick)
Jac — Taylor 1 run (Hollis kick)
Jac — Shelton 2 run (Hollis kick)
Jac — Whitted 24 blocked punt return (Hollis kick)
Jac — Darius 83 fumble return (Hollis kick)
Balt — Turner 5 pass from Harbaugh (pass failed)
Jac — FG Hollis 33
Balt — Johnson 3 pass from Harbaugh (pass failed)

BUFFALO 30, MIAMI 24—at Rich Stadium, attendance 79,011. Doug Flutie's threw 3 touchdown passes, and the Bills' scored the game's final 16 points to win their third straight home game against a division leader and move into a share of the AFC East lead. Leading 7-0, the Dolphins went for it on fourth-and-1 from their own 36, only to have Karim Abdul-Jabbar thrown for a 2-yard loss. Flutie threw a touchdown pass to Jay Riemersma seven plays later to tie the game. Flutie and Riemersma joined forces again, this time to tie the game 14-14 1:02 before halftime. John Avery's leap over the pile capped a 9-play, 71-yard drive to begin the second half, and Terrell Buckley's fumble recovery at the Bills' 28 set up Olindo Mare's field goal 1:21 into the final quarter to take a 24-14 lead. Four plays later Flutie hit Eric Moulds streaking down the left side for a 48-yard touchdown, and Ted Washington forced Dan Marino to fumble two plays later. Phil Hansen recovered the ball at the Dolphins' 13 to set up Steve Christie's tying field goal with 9:54 left. The Bills forced a punt and methodically drove 54 yards, taking 6:19 off the clock, capped by Christie's go-ahead field goal with 1:58 left. The Dolphins immediately lost the ball on downs, and Christie added his third field goal with 23 seconds left. Avery returned the ensuing kickoff 55 yards to the Bills' 45, and Marino completed a Hail Mary pass to O.J. McDuffie at the Bills' 4, but the Dolphins were out of time outs and the clock expired. Flutie was 15 of 26 for 206 yards and 3 touchdowns, with 1 interception. Marino was 15 of 27 for 196 yards and 1 touchdown.

Miami	7	7	7	3	—	24
Buffalo	0	14	0	16	—	30

Mia — Gadsden 12 pass from Marino (Mare kick)
Buff — Riemersma 1 pass from Flutie (Christie kick)
Mia — Abdul-Jabbar 1 run (Mare kick)
Buff — Riemersma 16 pass from Flutie (Christie kick)
Mia — Avery 1 run (Mare kick)
Mia — FG Mare 38
Buff — Moulds 48 pass from Flutie (Christie kick)
Buff — FG Christie 22
Buff — FG Christie 36
Buff — FG Christie 25

TAMPA BAY 27, MINNESOTA 24—at Raymond James Stadium, attendance 64,979. Mike Alstott rushed for 128 yards and 1 touchdown while Warrick Dunn added 115 yards and a score as the Buccaneers remained unbeaten in their new stadium while also handing the Vikings their first loss. The Buccaneers had a game-opening 13-play, 65-yard drive that consumed 7:15 and was capped by Dunn's 10-yard run. Randall Cunningham completed all 4 of his pass attempts on the ensuing drive, with Robert Smith tying the game. Tampa Bay responded with another 13-play touchdown drive, this one covering 80 yards and lasting 7:14, with Reidel Anthony doing the scoring honors. Not to be outdone, the Vikings drove 90 yards in 6:31, with Jake Reed hauling in Cunningham's 44-yard scoring bomb to tie the game 14-14. Each side kicked a field goal in the final 36 seconds of the half, and the Vikings scored on a 9-play, 75-yard drive to begin the second half to take a 24-17 lead. The string of scoring possessions ended as Trent Dilfer's fourth-and-goal pass from the Vikings' 5 fell incomplete. Derrick Brooks intercepted Cunningham at the Vikings' 23 to set up Michael Husted's field goal with 11:47 left. The Buccaneers' defense then forced the game's first punt with 9:37 left, and Alstott capped a 7-play, 43-yard drive with a scoring run of 6 yards with 5:48 remaining to take a 27-24 lead. The Vikings punted again with 3:04 left, but the Buccaneers ran out the clock. Dilfer was 11 of 22 for 132 yards and 1 touchdown. The Buccaneers rushed 41 times for a team-record 246 yards and did not punt. Cunningham was 21 of 25 for 291 yards and 2 touchdowns, with 1 interception. Reed had 6 catches for 117 yards.

Minnesota	7	10	7	0	—	24
Tampa Bay	7	10	0	10	—	27

TB — Dunn 10 run (Husted kick)
Minn — Smith 9 run (Anderson kick)
TB — Anthony 12 pass from Dilfer (Husted kick)
Minn — Reed 44 pass from Cunningham (Anderson kick)
TB — FG Husted 29
Minn — FG Anderson 44

Minn — Reed 1 pass from Cunningham (Anderson kick)
TB — FG Husted 38
TB — Alstott 6 run (Husted kick)

NEW ENGLAND 21, INDIANAPOLIS 16—at RCA Dome, attendance 58,056. Drew Bledsoe threw 2 touchdown passes, and Lawyer Milloy intercepeted 2 passes in the final 1:55 as the Patriots snapped a two-game losing skid. After each team strung together 9-play scoring drives in the first quarter, the Patriots broke the 7-7 tie with Robert Edwards's 1-yard touchdown run to cap a 10-play, 81-yard drive early in the second quarter. The Colts relied on Mike Vanderjagt's foot for a 49-yard field goal to cut the deficit to 14-10 as the half expired. Robert Blackmon's interception at the Colts' 5 denied the Patriots a scoring opportunity in the third quarter, but Tony Simmons hauled in Bledsoe's bomb for a 63-yard touchdown on the Patriots' next drive to take a 21-10 lead. The Colts drove 93 yards, as Peyton Manning completed 9 of 13 passes, to cut the deficit to 21-16 on a 15-yard scoring pass to Marcus Pollard with 3:40 remaining. The Colts forced two late punts, but Milloy intercepted Manning with 1:55 and 44 seconds left, both near midfield, to secure the victory. Bledsoe was 22 of 35 for 306 yards and 2 touchdowns, with 1 interception. Coates had 10 receptions for 109 yards, while Simmons had 109 receiving yards in 4 catches. Manning was 30 of 52 for 278 yards and 2 touchdowns, with 2 interceptions. Marshall Faulk had 9 catches for 119 yards.

New England	7	7	0	7	—	21
Indianapolis	7	3	0	6	—	16

NE — Coates 2 run (Vinatieri kick)
Ind — Warren 4 pass from Manning (Vanderjagt kick)
NE — Edwards 1 run (Vinatieri kick)
Ind — FG Vanderjagt 49
NE — Simmons 63 pass from Bledsoe (Vinatieri kick)
Ind — Pollard 15 pass from Manning (run failed)

CAROLINA 31, NEW ORLEANS 17—at Ericsson Stadium, attendance 62,514. Steve Beuerlein threw 2 touchdown passes, and Fred Lane rushed for 101 yards and 1 touchdown as the Panthers' defense forced 4 turnovers en route to their first victory of the season. The Panthers set the tone for the game with a 17-play, 73-yard drive that consumed the first 9:38 off the clock, saw Fred Lane get 9 yards on a fourth-and-1 run, and finished with Beuerlein's 1-yard scoring pass to Muhsin Muhammad. Eric Davis gave Carolina a 14-0 lead with a 56-yard interception return, and the Panthers led 17-3 when Keith Mitchell recovered Lane's fumble at the Saints' 24 in the half's waning moments. Juran Bolden recovered Qadry Ismail's fumble at the Saints' 20 on the second half's opening kickoff, setting up Lane's touchdown run to give the Panthers a 24-3 lead. Billy Joe Tolliver guided the Saints 67 yards for a touchdown, but the Panthers responded with a 7-play drive, capped by Beuerlein's touchdown pass to Raghib Ismail with 9:37 to play. Micheal Barrow's end zone interception stalled the Saints' next drive, and thus their scoring drive in the final moments ended the scoring. Beuerlein was 13 of 17 for 132 yards and 2 touchdowns, with 1 interception. Tolliver was 24 of 48 for 325 yards and 2 touchdowns, with 2 interceptions. Sean Dawkins had 6 receptions for 102 yards.

New Orleans	0	3	0	14	—	17
Carolina	7	10	7	7	—	31

Car — Muhammad 1 pass from Beuerlein (Kasay kick)
Car — Davis 56 interception return (Kasay kick)
NO — FG Brien 49
Car — FG Kasay 54
Car — Lane 5 run (Kasay kick)
NO — Cleeland 2 pass from Tolliver (Brien kick)
Car — Ismail 33 pass from Beuerlein (Kasay kick)
NO — Bech 6 pass from Tolliver (Brien kick)

WASHINGTON 21, N.Y. GIANTS 14—at Jack Kent Cooke Stadium, attendance 67,976. Trent Green threw 1 touchdown pass and ran for another as the Redskins' defense permitted just 10 first downs and forced 11 punts to win their first game of the season. Green completed all 4 of his pass attempts to set up his 1-yard touchdown run late in the first quarter. David Patten returned the ensuing kickoff 90 yards for a touchdown to tie the game, but the Redskins marched 11 plays and 69 yards to retake the lead on Green's touchdown pass to Stephen Davis. The Redskins opened the second half with a 79-yard drive, capped by Skip Hicks's first NFL touchdown. The Giants used a 46-yard pass from Danny Kanell to Ike Hilliard to set up Hilliard's 11-yard touchdown catch late in the third quarter to cut the deficit to 21-14, but New York failed to drive into Redskins' territory the remainder of the game. Green was 21 of 31 for 225 yards and 1 touchdown. Kanell was 17 of 32 for 151 yards and 1 touchdown.

N.Y. Giants	7	0	7	0	—	14
Washington	7	7	7	0	—	21

Wash — Green 1 run (Blanchard kick)
NYG — Patten 90 kickoff return (Daluiso kick)
Wash — Davis 12 pass from Green (Blanchard kick)
Wash — Hicks 4 run (Blanchard kick)
NYG — Hilliard 11 pass from Kanell (Daluiso kick)

N.Y. JETS 20, KANSAS CITY 17—at Arrowhead Stadium, attendance 65,104. John Hall made a 32-yard field goal as time expired to give the Jets a victory in the rain. Tony Richardson plowed into the end zone from 2 yards out to put the Chiefs on the board late in the first quarter. Vinny Testaverde's 56-yard pass to Wayne Chrebet set up Hall's first field goal, and Corwin Brown intercepted an Elvis Grbac pass at the Jets' 1 to halt a drive. Late in the second quarter Dwayne Gordon intercepted a Grbac pass and returned it 31 yards for a touchdown. The Jets led 10-7 at halftime despite 2 missed field goals by Hall. Pete Sotyanovich's field goal tied the game midway through the third quarter, but Grbac was thwarted again when Pepper Johnson intercepted his pass at the Jets' 20 late in the third quarter. However, Anthony Davis intercepted Testaverde and returned the ball 27 yards to the Chiefs' 8. Donnell Bennett scored three plays later to give the Chiefs a 17-10 lead 1:17 into the final quarter. Aaron Glenn promptly returned the ensuing kickoff 62 yards, and Testaverde tied the game with a 20-yard pass to Kyle Brady 50 seconds after Bennett's touchdown. Louie Aguiar's 25-yard punt to the Chiefs' 43 with 1:50 left gave the Jets great field position and set up Hall's winning kick. Testaverde was 20 of 34 for 260 yards and 1 touchdown, with 1 interception. Chrebet had 6 catches for 101 yards. Grbac was 13 of 28 for 120 yards, with 3 interceptions.

N.Y. Jets	0	10	0	10	—	20
Kansas City	7	0	3	7	—	17

KC — Richardson 2 run (Stoyanovich kick)
NYJ — FG Hall 20
NYJ — Gordon 31 interception return (Hall kick)
KC — FG Stoyanovich 42
KC — Bennett 1 run (Stoyanovich kick)
NYJ — Brady 20 pass from Testaverde (Hall kick)
NYJ — FG Hall 32

ATLANTA 37, ST. LOUIS 15—at Georgia Dome, attendance 37,996. Jamal Anderson rushed for 172 yards and scored 3 touchdowns as the Falcons improved to 6-2 for the first time in team history. The Falcons scored on their first three possessions, with two 4-play drives culminating in Anderson touchdowns, to take a 17-0 lead 12:25 into the game. The Rams, who had to punt five of their first six possessions, scored on Ryan McNeil's 37-yard interception return to cut the deficit to 17-7. However, Atlanta scored on its final two drives of the half, with Chris Chandler's 18-yard touchdown pass to Tony Martin giving Atlanta a 27-7 halftime lead. The Falcons outgained the Rams 303-83 in the first half. Chandler was 12 of 26 for 236 yards and 2 touchdowns, with 1 interception. Tony Banks was 23 of 37 for 221 yards and 1 touchdown.

St. Louis	0	7	0	8	—	15
Atlanta	17	10	7	3	—	37

Atl — Anderson 9 pass from Chandler (Andersen kick)
Atl — FG Andersen 23
Atl — Anderson 12 run (Andersen kick)
StL — McNeil 37 interception return (Wilkins kick)
Atl — FG Andersen 22
Atl — Martin 18 pass from Chandler (Andersen kick)
Atl — Anderson 4 run (Andersen kick)
StL — Williams 1 pass from Banks (Banks run)
Atl — FG Andersen 43

GREEN BAY 36, SAN FRANCISCO 22—at Lambeau Field, attendance 59,794. The Packers scored 16 points in the first 5:16 but then had to tally the game's final 17 points to defeat the 49ers for the fifth consecutive time. Brett Favre fired an 80-yard touchdown pass to Antonio Freeman on the game's first play to give Green Bay a 7-0 lead. Randy Kirk then snapped the ball over Reggie Roby and through the end zone for a safety. The Packers were forced to punt, but Pat Terrell's interception at the Packers' 31 led to Favre's 30-yard touchdown pass to Robert Brooks to put the Packers up 16-0. The 49ers responded with a 15-play, 75-yard drive, and in the second quarter added a 10-play, 70-yard scoring drive, and Lee Woodall intercepted Favre in the end zone just before halftime to keep San Francisco within six points. Zack Bronson's interception led to Garrison Hearst's 30-yard romp, but Ty Detmer dropped the snap for the extra point, keeping the game tied. Tim McDonald intercepted Favre two plays later, and Wade Richey gave the 49ers their first lead. Richey, however, hit the left upright with a 47-yard attempt late in the third quarter, and Ryan Longwell tied the game with 13:14 left. After forcing a punt, Favre and Freeman hooked up for a 68-yard touchdown to retake the lead. Keith McKenzie then sacked Steve Young, forcing him to fumble. Santana Dotson recovered at the 49ers' 11, and Travis Jervey scored on the next play with 9:30 left. Favre was 15 of 28 for 279 yards and 3 touchdowns, with 3 interceptions. Freeman had 7 catches for 193 yards. Young was 24 of 39 for 186 yards and 1 touchdown, with 1 interception, and also broke Jack Kemp's record by recording the 41st rushing touchdown of his career. The Packers' defense recorded 9 sacks, 3 by Reggie White.

San Francisco	6	7	9	0	—	22
Green Bay	16	3	0	17	—	36

GB — Freeman 80 pass from Favre (Longwell kick)
GB — Safety, 49ers punt snap sailed out of end zone
GB — Brooks 30 pass from Favre (Longwell kick)
SF — Rice 12 pass from Young (kick blocked)
GB — FG Longwell 26
SF — Young 1 run (Richey kick)
SF — Hearst 30 run (dropped snap)
SF — FG Richey 20
GB — FG Longwell 45
GB — Freeman 62 pass from Favre (Longwell kick)
GB — Jervey 11 run (Longwell kick)

TENNESSEE 41, PITTSBURGH 31—at Three Rivers Stadium, attendance 58,222. Steve McNair threw 3 touchdown passes, and Eddie George rushed for 153 yards and 1 touchdown as the Oilers scored on six of their first seven possessions to beat the Steelers in Pittsburgh for just the second time this decade. The Oilers consumed 6:51, 8:03, and 4:50 off the clock in their three first-half scoring drives to take a 17-7 halftime lead. The Steelers missed a field goal on their first drive of the second half, but the Pittsburgh defense forced a punt. However, Darryll Lewis's 33-yard interception return set up Al Del Greco's second field goal, and Denard Walker's 6-yard interception return moments later led to George's 37-yard touchdown run. The Oilers' defense then stopped the Steelers on their own 29 to regain possession, and McNair threw a 29-yard touchdown pass to Willie Davis three plays later to give Tennessee a 34-7 lead 13 seconds into the fourth quarter. After Stewart threw a touchdown pass to Courtney Hawkins, the Steelers got the ball back only to watch Lonnie Marts intercept Stewart and return the pass 27 yards for a touchdown. Mike Tomczak entered the game and drove the Steelers to 2 touchdowns in the final nine minutes. McNair was 13 of 21 for 167 yards and 3 touchdowns. George recorded his fourth consecutive 100-yard rushing game. Stewart was 23 of 32 for 230 yards and 2 touchdowns, with 3 interceptions, while Tomczak was 15 of 17 for 117 yards and 2 touchdowns in the fourth quarter. Hawkins had a club-record 14 receptions for 147 yards and 1 touchdown, with Charles Johnson adding 9 catches for 115 yards and 2 touchdowns.

Tennessee	3	14	10	14	—	41
Pittsburgh	0	7	0	24	—	31

Tenn — FG Del Greco 43
Tenn — Wycheck 2 pass from McNair (Del Greco kick)
Pitt — C. Johnson 9 pass from Stewart (N. Johnson kick)
Tenn — Dyson 6 pass from McNair (Del Greco kick)
Tenn — FG Del Greco 32
Tenn — George 37 run (Del Greco kick)
Tenn — Davis 29 pass from McNair (Del Greco kick)
Pitt — Hawkins 3 pass from Stewart (C. Johnson pass from Stewart)
Tenn — Marts 27 interception return (Del Greco kick)
Pitt — C. Johnson 37 pass from Tomczak (C. Johnson pass from Tomczak)
Pitt — C. Johnson 2 pass from Tomczak (Blackwell pass from Tomczak)

SUNDAY NIGHT, NOVEMBER 1

OAKLAND 31, SEATTLE 18—at Kingdome, attendance 66,246. Donald Hollas passed for 2 touchdowns, and the Raiders' defense forced 5 turnovers that led to 17 points as the Raiders won their fifth consecutive game. Desmond Howard's 35-yard kickoff return after Todd Peterson's field goal set up Hollas's 28-yard scoring pass to Tim Brown. However, Willie Williams intercepted Hollas at the Seahawks' 19 to halt a drive, and, after the Raiders were stopped on downs at the Seahawks' 29, Carlester Crumpler caught a touchdown pass from Warren Moon to give Seattle a 10-7 halftime lead. The Raiders scored twice in the first 4:45 of the second half, with Hollas's 47-yard third-and-11 pass to Jett setting up his touchdown pass to Rickey Dudley, and Albert Lewis streaking 74 yards with an interception return moments later, to take a 21-10 lead. Seattle cut the deficit to 21-18 on its next possession, but fumbled the next three times it had the ball, with Ronnie Harris's fumbled punt at the 5-yard line being recovered by Kenny Shedd to the Seahawks' 1. Jon Ritchie fumbled two plays later, but Darryl Ashmore picked up the ball and stepped into the end zone to complete the scoring. Hollas was 12 of 22 for 237 yards and 2 touchdowns, with 1 interception. Moon was 29 of 39 for 275 yards and 1 touchdown, with 1 interception.

Oakland	7	0	14	10	—	31
Carolina	3	7	8	0	—	18

Sea — FG Peterson 38
Oak — Brown 28 pass from Hollas (Davis kick)
Sea — Crumpler 1 pass from Moon (Peterson kick)
Oak — Dudley 27 pass from Hollas (Davis kick)
Oak — Lewis 74 interception return (Davis kick)
Sea — Watters 1 run (Pritchard pass from Moon)
Oak — FG Davis 35
Oak — Ashmore 1 fumble return (Davis kick)

MONDAY NIGHT, NOVEMBER 2

DALLAS 34, PHILADELPHIA 0—at Veterans Stadium, attendance 67,002. In his first game since September 13, Troy Aikman threw 2 touchdown passes, and Deion Sanders returned a punt for a touchdown and added an interception as the Cowboys remained in first place in the NFC East. The Cowboys converted 2 third downs and 1 fourth down on their opening drive, but had to settle for Richie Cunningham's field goal. An injury to Rodney Peete forced the Eagles to put Bobby Hoying in late in the first quarter. On Hoying's first play, Hoying and Charlie Garner misconnected on the handoff and Kavika Pittman recovered the fumble at the Eagles' 9. Aikman, who had suffered a fractured left collarbone in week 2, threw a touchdown pass to Michael Irvin two plays later. The Eagles responded with their longest drive into Cowboy territory of the night, but Jason Dunn slipped running his route and Darren Woodson intercepted his pass at the Cowboys' 11. After punting away from Sanders for the entire half, Sanders took Tommy Hutton's punt and rocketed 69 yards for a touchdown. The Cowboys scored on their first three possessions of the second half, the last of which was set up by Sanders's 21-yard interception return. Aikman was 14 of 26 for 171 yards and 2 touchdowns. Smith had 23 carries for 101 yards and an electrifying, broken-field 15-yard touchdown run. Hoying was 13 of 39 for 124 yards, with 2 interceptions.

Dallas	10	7	10	7	—	34
Philadelphia	0	0	0	0	—	0

Dall — FG Cunningham 33
Dall — Irvin 10 pass from Aikman (Cunningham kick)
Dall — Sanders 69 punt return (Cunningham kick)
Dall — LaFleur 9 pass from Aikman (Cunningham kick)
Dall — FG Cunningham 25
Dall — Smith 15 run (Cunningham kick)

TENTH WEEK SUMMARIES

AMERICAN FOOTBALL CONFERENCE

Eastern Division	W	L	T	Pct.	Pts.	OP
N.Y. Jets	6	3	0	.667	220	151
Miami	6	3	0	.667	165	123
Buffalo	5	4	0	.556	200	196
New England	5	4	0	.556	201	179
Indianapolis	1	8	0	.111	142	241
Central Division						
Jacksonville	7	2	0	.778	233	176
Pittsburgh	6	3	0	.667	164	161
Tennessee	5	4	0	.556	216	179
Baltimore	3	6	0	.333	134	189
Cincinnati	2	7	0	.222	164	243
Western Division						
Denver	9	0	0	1.000	300	169
Oakland	6	3	0	.667	156	158
Seattle	5	4	0	.556	196	142
Kansas City	4	5	0	.444	160	167
San Diego	3	6	0	.333	113	166

NATIONAL FOOTBALL CONFERENCE

Eastern Division	W	L	T	Pct.	Pts.	OP
Dallas	6	3	0	.667	224	121
Arizona	5	4	0	.556	154	197
N.Y. Giants	3	6	0	.333	166	189
Philadelphia	2	7	0	.222	89	205
Washington	1	8	0	.111	141	270
Central Division						
Minnesota	8	1	0	.889	296	167
Green Bay	6	3	0	.667	239	193
Tampa Bay	4	5	0	.444	143	176
Chicago	3	6	0	.333	164	198
Detroit	2	7	0	.222	171	219
Western Division						
Atlanta	7	2	0	.778	253	176
San Francisco	7	2	0	.778	273	186
New Orleans	4	5	0	.444	162	201
St. Louis	3	6	0	.333	174	216
Carolina	1	8	0	.111	182	241

SUNDAY, NOVEMBER 8

ATLANTA 41, NEW ENGLAND 10—at Foxboro Stadium, attendance 59,790. The Falcons defense recorded 6 sacks and forced 5 turnovers as the Falcons kept pace with the San Francisco 49ers in the NFC West. The Falcons scored on three of their first four possessions, the second of which was set up by John Burrough's fumble recovery at the Patriots' 16, to take a 21-3 lead. Midway through the second quarter, the Patriots drove to the Falcons' 13 and faced fourth-and-2. Lester Archambeau sacked Bledsoe for a 16-yard loss and forced him to fumble. Chuck Smith scooped up the ball and rumbled 71 yards to stake the Falcons to a 28-3 lead. Eugene Robinson and Keith Brooking each intercepted passes in Falcons' territory to stop second-half drives by New England. Chris Chandler was 15 of 22 for 240 yards and 2 touchdowns, with 2 interceptions. Jamal Anderson rushed 32 times for 104 yards and 2 touchdowns. Terance Mathis had 8 catches for 117 yards. Bledsoe was 19 of 34 for 229 yards and 1 touchdown, with 1 interception.

Atlanta	14	14	3	10	—	41
New England	3	0	7	0	—	10

Atl — Anderson 1 run (Andersen kick)
Atl — Santiago 7 pas from Chandler (Andersen kick)
NE — FG Vinatieri 40
Atl — Anderson 10 run (Andersen kick)
Atl — Smith 71 fumble return (Andersen kick)
Atl — FG Andersen 40
NE — Coates 2 pass from Bledsoe (Vinatieri kick)
Atl — Santiago 22 pass from Chandler (Andersen kick)
Atl — FG Andersen 32

N.Y. JETS 34, BUFFALO 12—at Giants Stadium, attendance 75,403. In the first battle of Heisman Trophy quarterbacks since 1977, Vinny Testaverde threw 3 touchdown passes as the Jets snapped the Bills' five-game winning streak. The Bills ran plays inside the Jets' 40 in five of their six first-half possessions, yet settled for 3 Steve Christie field goals and punted twice. The Jets trailed 9-7 before John Hall made a 49-yard field goal with 27 seconds left in the half. Otis Smith intercepted Doug Flutie two plays later, setting up Hall's 43-yard field goal as the half expired to give the Jets a 13-9 lead. After Testaverde's second touchdown pass gave the Jets a 20-9 advantage, Chrisite booted his fourth field goal to keep the game close. However, Testaverde capped an 11-play drive with a touchdown pass to Wayne Chrebet, and Ray Mickens's interception at the Bills' 46 three plays later set up Curtis Martin's 6-yard scoring run midway through the final quarter. Testaverde was 22 of 331 for 258 yards and 3 touchdowns, with 1 interception. Flutie was 12 of 30 for 154 yards, with 2 interceptions.

Buffalo	3	6	3	0	—	12
N.Y. Jets	7	6	7	14	—	34

Buff — FG Christie 40
NYJ — K. Johnson 25 pass from Testaverde (Hall kick)
Buff — FG Christie 37
Buff — FG Christie 44
NYJ — FG Hall 49
NYJ — FG Hall 43
NYJ — Ward 36 pass from Testaverde (Hall kick)
Buff — FG Christie 21
NYJ — Chrebet 12 pass from Testaverde (Hall kick)
NYJ — Martin 6 run (Hall kick)

SAN FRANCISCO 25, CAROLINA 23—at 3Com Park, attendance 68,572. Wade Richey kicked a 46-yard field goal with 33 seconds left as the 49ers stormed back from a 16-0 deficit behind reserve Ty Detmer to remain tied for first in the NFC West despite committing 6 turnovers. The Panthers drove deep into 49ers territory on each of their first five possessions, scoring four times and having a field goal blocked, to take a 16-0 lead. After throwing interceptions on two of the 49ers first three drives, Detmer threw a 36-yard touchdown pass to Terrell Owens just before halftime to cut the lead to 16-7. The same pair connected on a 5-yard scoring play to open the second half, and after Kasay missed a 51-yard field-goal attempt, Detmer threw a 29-yard touchdown pass to J.J. Stokes late in the third quarter to give the 49ers a 22-16 lead. Eric Davis recovered Jerry Rice's fumble near midfield with 10:46 left, and William Floyd scored five minutes later to give the Panthers a 23-22 lead. The 49ers responded with a 12-play, 62-yard drive capped by Richey's kick. In an attempt to avoid kicking deep to Michael Bates, the 49ers decided to squib their kickoff. But Anthony Johnson grabbed the ball at midfield and returned it 3 yards to the 49ers' 47 with 30 seconds left, but Kasay's game-winning 57-yard field-goal attempt fell short as time expired. Detmer, who was playing for injured Steve Young, was 21 of 35 for 268 yards and 3 touchdowns, with 3 interceptions. Steve Beuerlein was 25 of 41 for 265 yards and 1 touchdown.

Carolina	3	13	0	7	—	23
San Francisco	0	7	15	3	—	25

Car — FG Kasay 50
Car — FG Kasay 42
Car — Ismail 20 pass from Beuerlein (Kasay kick)
Car — FG Kasay 41
SF — Owens 36 pass from Detmer (Richey kick)
SF — Owens 5 pass from Detmer (Richey kick)
SF — Stokes 29 pass from Detmer (Owens pass from Detmer)
Car — Floyd 2 run (Kasay kick)
SF — FG Richey 46

JACKSONVILLE 24, CINCINNATI 11—at ALLTEL Stadium, attendance 67,040. Fred Taylor rushed for 118 yards and 1 touchdown as the Jaguars maintained their one-game lead in the AFC Central. Mark Brunell's 55-yard pass to Alvis Whitted set up Taylor's touchdown less than five minutes into the game. Jacksonville scored on its next two possessions as well to take a 17-0 lead. The Bengals threatened to score midway through the second quarter, reaching the Jaguars' 4, but Joel Smeenge stripped Corey Dillon of the ball. Aaron Beasley recovered it and scampered 90 yards for a touchdown and a 24-0 lead. The Bengals reached the Jaguars' 3 on their next drive, but consecutive incompletions from Neil O'Donnell on third and fourth down ended the threat. Reserve Paul Justin's touchdown pass came with just 1:55 left, and Reggie Barlow recovered the ensuing onside kick to clinch the victory. Brunell was 5 of 12 for 111 yards and 1 touchdown before leaving with an injury. O'Donnell was 17 of 30 for 128 yards, with 1 interception, while Justin was 7 of 10 for 107 yards and 1 touchdown.

Cincinnati	0	0	3	8	—	11
Jacksonville	10	14	0	0	—	24

Jac — Taylor 1 run (Hollis kick)
Jac — FG Hollis 39
Jac — Smith 18 pass from Brunell (Hollis kick)
Jac — Beasley 90 fumble return (Hollis kick)
Cin — FG Pelfrey 50
Cin — Gibson 9 pass from Justin (Justin run)

PHILADELPHIA 10, DETROIT 9—at Veterans Stadium, attendance 66,785. Charlie Garner rushed for 129 yards and 1 touchdown and the Eagles' defense permitted just 9 first downs to give Philadelphia its second victory. Garner's 40-yard scamper set up his own 3-yard scoring run early in the second quarter, but the Lions answered on the ensuing drive with a 41-yard field goal by Jason Hanson. Hanson drilled a 48-yard field goal in the third quarter, and a 44-yard run by Barry Sanders set up Hanson's go-ahead 35-yard boot in the opening minute of the final quarter. The Eagles responded quickly as Allen Rossum's 36-yard kickoff return led to Chris Boniol's 39-yard field goal with 10:48 left. After an exchange of punts, the Lions reached the Eagles' 34 with 37 seconds left, but a false start penalty on third-and-2, and then an incompletion, forced Hanson to attempt a 58-yard field goal, which fell short. Bobby Hoying was 15 of 21 for 97 yards. Charlie Batch was 14 of 27 for 146 yards. Sanders rushed 20 times for 140 yards.

Detroit	0	3	3	3	—	9
Philadelphia	0	7	0	3	—	10

Phil — Garner 3 run (Boniol kick)
Det — FG Hanson 41
Det — FG Hanson 48
Det — FG Hanson 35
Phil — FG Boniol 39

MIAMI 27, INDIANAPOLIS 14—at Pro Player Stadium, attendance 73,400. O.J. McDuffie had 9 catches for 132 yards and 2 touchdowns as the Dolphins took a 27-0 lead and held on to defeat the Colts. While the Colts did not run a play inside the Dolphins' 49 during the first half, the Dolphins strung together drives of 80, 96, and 75 yards and turned Sam Madison's interception into a field goal to take a 20-0 halftime lead. Terrell Buckley's interception and return to the Colts' 44 set up John Avery's 8-yard touchdown run to give Miami a 27-0 lead with 14:11 remaining in the game. The Colts scored 2 late touchdowns and reached the Dolphins' 23 in the final minute before being stopped on downs. Dan Marino was 18 of 27 for 207 yards and 2 touchdowns, with 1 interception. Avery had 21 carries for 100 yards. Peyton Manning was 22 of 42 for 140 yards and 1 touchdown, with 2 interceptions.

Indianapolis	0	0	0	14	—	14
Miami	7	13	0	7	—	27

Mia — McDuffie 61 pass from Marino (Mare kick)
Mia — McDuffie 6 pass from Marino (Mare kick)
Mia — FG Mare 21
Mia — FG Mare 23
Mia — Avery 8 run (Mare kick)
Ind — Faulk 6 run (Pollard pass from Manning)
Ind — Dilger 9 pass from Manning (pass failed)

SEATTLE 24, KANSAS CITY 12—at Kingdome, attendance 66,251. Ricky Watters rushed for 105 yards and 2 touchdowns as the Seahawks moved ahead of the Chiefs in the AFC West standings. Leading 7-3, Shawn Springs's 22-yard interception return to the Chiefs' 6 set up Watters's second touchdown of the first quarter and gave Seattle a 14-3 lead. After Pete Stoyanovich missed a 43-yard attempt, Warren Moon's 45-yard pass to Joey Galloway set up Todd Peterson's 38-yard field goal to give Seattle a 17-6 advantage, and Darrin Smith's 26-yard interception return for a touchdown 11 seconds later gave the Seahawks a commanding lead. The Chiefs drove into Seahawks' territory three times in the second half, but failed to pierce the end zone until just three seconds remained in the game. The Chiefs limited the Seahawks to just 202 total yards, but committed a team-record 17 penalties and committed 4 turnovers to stifle their attack. Moon was 12 of 20 for 108 yards, with 2 interceptions. Elvis Grbac was 12 of 18 for 109 yards, with 2 interceptions, while replacement Rich Gannon was 20 of 32 for 177 yards, with 1 interception.

Kansas City	3	3	0	6	—	12
Seattle	14	10	0	0	—	24

KC — FG Stoyanovich 53
Sea — Watters 1 run (Peterson kick)
Sea — Watters 1 run (Peterson kick)
KC — FG Stoyanovich 38
Sea — FG Peterson 38
Sea — Smith 26 interception return (Peterson kick)
KC — Gannon 1 run (pass failed)

MINNESOTA 31, NEW ORLEANS 24—at Hubert H. Humphrey Metrodome, attendance 63,779. Robert Smith rushed for 137 yards and 1 touchdown, and Leroy Hoard scored twice as the Vikings held off the Saints. Minnesota had drives of 94 yards and 70 yards to take a 10-0 lead with 1:37 left in the half. Aaron Craver fumbled the ensuing kickoff return, and Harold Morrow's return to the Saints' 4 set up Hoard's first touchdown. Craver redeemed himself, however, by returning the following kickoff 100 yards for a touchdown. After Doug Brien's field goal cut the deficit to 17-10, Robert Smith raced 61 yards for a touchdown on the next play from scrimmage to give the Vikings a 24-10 lead. Billy Joe Tolliver's 49-yard pass to Craver set up a 9-yard touchdown by the tandem to cut the deficit to seven points. The Vikings were about to increase their lead early in the fourth quarter when Sammy Knight intercepted Brad Johnson's deflected pass and bolted 94 yards untouched to tie the game. The Vikings proceeded to march 81 yards in 11 plays on the ensuing drive to retake the lead on Hoard's second touchdown with 3:43 left. The Saints could not cross midfield on their final drive. The Vikings outgained the Saints 465-190 yards. Johnson, who replaced an injured Randall Cunningham, was 28 of 38 for 316 yards and 1 touchdown, with 2 interceptions. Tolliver was 11 of 16 for 168 yards and 1 touchdown.

New Orleans	0	7	10	7	—	24
Minnesota	7	10	7	7	—	31

Minn — Carter 14 pass from Johnson (Anderson kick)
Minn — FG Anderson 28
Minn — Hoard 4 run (Anderson kick)
NO — Craver 100 kickoff return (Brien kick)
NO — FG Brien 20
Minn — Smith 61 run (Anderson kick)
NO — Craver 9 pass from Tolliver (Brien kick)
NO — Knight 91 interception return (Brien kick)
Minn — Hoard 1 run (Anderson kick)

DALLAS 16, N.Y. GIANTS 6—at Texas Stadium, attendance 64,316. Troy Aikman threw a touchdown pass midway through the fourth quarter to give Dallas a three-game lead over the Giants. Each kicker made 2 first-half field goals, but Richie Cunningham missed from 38 yards, allowing the game to be tied 6-6 at halftime. Aikman and Mills hooked up on a 32-yard third-down pass to set up Cunningham's third field goal, and the same tandem connected on a 27-yard third-down pass to the Giants' 1 to set up Eric Bjornson's scoring grab with 8:44 left in the game. The Giants were forced to punt on their next possession, and Dallas ran off the final 6:01 to preserve the victory. Aikman was 16 of 23 for 161 yards and 1 touchdown. Emmitt Smith rushed 29 times for 163 yards. Danny Kanell was 12 of 24 for 139 yards. Gary Brown had 15 carries for 119 rushing yards.

N.Y. Giants	3	3	0	0	—	6
Dallas	3	3	3	7	—	16

Dall — FG Cunningham 37
NYG — FG Daluiso 32
Dall — FG Cunningham 40
NYG — FG Daluiso 23
Dall — FG Cunningham 19
Dall — Bjornson 2 pass from Aikman (Cunningham kick)

BALTIMORE 13, OAKLAND 10—at NFL Stadium at Camden Yards, attendance 69,037. Matt Stover kicked a fourth-quarter field goal, and Duane Starks intercepted a Hail Mary pass in the end zone as time expired to give the Ravens their first-ever victory in the month of November. Stover missed a 41-yard field-goal attempt in the first quarter, but Rod Woodson put the Ravens on the board first with an 18-yard interception return late in the quarter. Donald Hollas, who had replaced an injured Jeff George in the first quarter, guided the Raiders on a 9-play, 69-yard game-tying drive early in the fourth quarter, but Jim Harbaugh threw a 28-yard pass to Jermaine Lewis on the next play from scrimmage and Priest Holmes had a 25-yard run to set up Stover's go-ahead field goal with 9:14 remaining. The Raiders only had two possessions the rest of the game, with Hollas's desperation pass intercepted in the end zone on the game's final play. Harbaugh was 10 of 17 for 102 yards, with 1 interception. Rickey Dudley had 6 receptions for 105 yards. Hollas was 17 of 26 for 249 yards and 1 touchdown, with 2 interceptions.

Oakland	0	3	0	7	—	10
Baltimore	7	3	0	3	—	13

Balt — Woodson 18 interception return (Stover kick)
Oak — FG Davis 23
Balt — FG Stover 30
Oak — Dudley 5 pass from Hollas (Davis kick)
Balt — FG Stover 30

ST. LOUIS 20, CHICAGO 12—at Soldier Field, attendance 50,263. Tony Banks threw 1 touchdown pass and ran for another as the Rams defense held off a late rally to snap a three-game losing streak. Each team had 70-yard scoring drives on their opening possession, and the Rams broke the tie with 58 seconds left in the half on Banks's scoring run. Field goals on three consecutive drives, 2 by Jeff Wilkins, gave the Rams a 20-10 lead with 11:06 left. Tony Parrish recovered Eddie Kennison's fumble at the Rams' 33 with 4:24 remaining, but Keith Lyle intercepted Steve Stenstrom's pass at the Rams' 6 two plays later. Following a Bears' defensive stand, Gerald McBurrows was called for holding in the end zone while blocking for punter Rick Tuten. The safety cut the lead to 20-12, and Bobby Engram's 48-yard catch put the Bears at the Rams' 20 with 1:22 left. An 11-yard run by Edgar Bennett got the Bears to the Rams' 9, but Stenstrom threw 4 consecutive incompletions. Banks was 24 of 31 for 202 yards and 1 touchdown. Stenstrom was 15 of 25 for 154 yards and 1 touchdown, with 1 interception.

St. Louis	0	14	3	3	—	20
Chicago	7	0	3	2	—	12

Chi — Conway 4 pass from Stenstrom (Jaeger kick)
StL — Proehl 3 pass from Banks (Wilkins kick)
StL — Banks 7 run (Wilkins kick)
StL — FG Wilkins 24
Chi — FG Jaeger 31
StL — FG Wilkins 33
Chi — Safety, McBurrows called for holding in the end zone

DENVER 27, SAN DIEGO 10—at Mile High Stadium, attendance 74,925. Terrell Davis scored 2 touchdowns as Bubby Brister guided the undefeated Broncos to victory. The Broncos scored on their last four possessions of the first half, and Darrien Gordon's 36-yard interception return to the Chargers' 7 set up Brister's 7-yard touchdown pass to Ed McCaffrey to give Denver a 27-0 lead late in the third quarter. To that point of the game, the Broncos' defense limited the Chargers to just 2 first downs on nine possessions. The Chargers marched 92 yards on their next drive to score, and reached the Broncos' 1 with 4:00 left, but Natrone Means fumbled and Bill Romanowski recovered to stifle the comeback. Brister was 20 of 33 for 229 yards and 2 touchdowns, with 1 interception. McCaffrey had 9 receptions for 133 yards. Craig Whelihan, who replaced Ryan Leaf in the third quarter, was 13 of 23 for 113 yards and 1 touchdown.

San Diego	0	0	0	10	—	10
Denver	7	13	7	0	—	27

Den — Davis 4 pass from Brister (Elam kick)
Den — FG Elam 31
Den — Davis 24 run (Elam kick)
Den — FG Elam 26
Den — McCaffrey 7 pass from Brister (Elam kick)

SD — F. Jones 14 pass from Whelihan (Whelihan run)
SD — Safety, Brister fumbled ball out of the end zone

ARIZONA 29, WASHINGTON 27—at Sun Devil Stadium, attendance 45,950. Joe Nedney kicked a 47-yard field goal with two seconds remaining to give the Cardinals a 5-4 record for the first time since 1988. The Redskins scored touchdowns on their final two possessions of the half to take a 17-7 lead. Trailing 17-14, Jake Plummer completed all 4 of his pass attempts on an 11-play, 60-yard drive capped by Bates's second touchdown to give Arizona a 21-17 lead with 12:34 remaining. Pinned on the Redskins' 4-yard line moments later, punter Matt Turk missed the snap, which resulted in an Arizona safety. The Cardinals ran 7:39 off the clock following the free kick and took a 26-17 lead on Nedney's 26-yard field goal with 3:09 left. The Redskins needed just seven plays to drive 80 yards and cut the deficit to 26-24 on Trent Green's 35-yard touchdown pass to Leslie Shepherd. Stephen Davis recovered the ensuing onside kick for the Redskins, and Cary Blanchard drilled a 54-yard field goal with 35 seconds left to give Washington the lead. Plummer completed 4 of 5 passes, including an 18-yard pass to Frank Sanders, to set up Nedney's heroics. Plummer was 22 of 30 for 186 yards and 1 touchdown. Adrian Murrell rushed 23 times for 107 yards. Green was 17 of 33 for 183 yards and 1 touchdown.

Washington	3	14	0	10	—	27
Arizona	0	7	7	15	—	29

Wash — FG Blanchard 34
Wash — Hicks 2 run (Blanchard kick)
Ariz — Bates 1 run (Nedney kick)
Wash — Mitchell 6 run (Blanchard kick)
Ariz — Centers 4 pass from Plummer (Nedney kick)
Ariz — Bates 1 run (Nedney kick)
Ariz — Safety, Turk missed snap and ball went out of end zone
Ariz — FG Nedney 26
Wash — Shepherd 35 pass from Green (Blanchard kick)
Wash — FG Blanchard 54
Ariz — FG Nedney 47

SUNDAY NIGHT, NOVEMBER 8

TENNESSEE 31, TAMPA BAY 22—at Raymond James Stadium, attendance 65,054. Steve McNair's 71-yard touchdown run with 1:46 left gave the Oilers their fourth victory in five games and handed the Buccaneers their first loss at Raymond James Stadium. In the first half, the Buccaneers outgained the Oilers 289-110 and scored on four of their five possessions to take a 16-3 lead into the locker room. Eddie George's 14-yard touchdown run on the second half's opening drive cut the deficit to six points, and George's 30-yard run on the Oilers' next possession set up Mike Archie's touchdown and gave Tennessee a 17-16 edge. Early in the fourth quarter, Anthony Dorsett downed Craig Hentrich's 50-yard punt at the Buccaneers' 1, setting up Joe Bowden's 1-yard interception return for a touchdown on the next play to give Tennessee a 24-16 lead. The Buccaneers regrouped and marched 79 yards in 14 plays and scored on Trent Dilfer's 10-yard pass to Reidel Anthony with 3:32 to play. However, Dilfer's potential game-tying 2-point conversion pass to Bert Emanuel fell incomplete. The Oilers faced third-and-8 from their own 29 with 2:00 left when McNair avoided Tyoka Jackson in the backfield and scrambled 71 yards for the game-clinching touchdown. McNair was 9 of 16 for 123 yards. George rushed 27 times for 134 yards. Dilfer was 20 of 38 for 294 yards and 2 touchdowns, with 1 interception. Emanuel had 5 receptions for 106 yards.

Tennessee	3	0	14	14	—	31
Tampa Bay	3	13	0	6	—	22

TB — FG Husted 46
Tenn — FG Del Greco 45
TB — FG Husted 30
TB — Emanuel 58 pass from Dilfer (Husted kick)
Tenn — George 14 run (Del Greco kick)
Tenn — Archie 7 run (Del Greco kick)
Tenn — Bowden 1 interception return (Del Greco kick)
TB — Anthony 10 pass from Dilfer (pass failed)
Tenn — McNair 71 run (Del Greco kick)

MONDAY NIGHT, NOVEMBER 9

PITTSBURGH 27, GREEN BAY 20—at Three Rivers Stadium, attendance 60,507. Kordell Stewart passed for 1 touchdown and ran for another as the Steelers took a 27-point lead and held off a late rally to defeat the Packers. The Steelers scored on their first five possessions, taking advantage of Ryan Longwell's missed 51-yard field goal on the Packers' first drive and Dewayne Washington's interception at the Packers' 46 to open the second half, en route to a 27-0 lead. The Packers responded with a field goal, but were stopped on downs at their own 39 early in the fourth quarter and the Steelers drove to the Packers' 4. Faced with third-and-goal, the Steelers sent Mike Tomczak into the game and lined up Stewart as a wide receiver. The play backfired, however, as Reggie White sacked Tomczak and forced him to fumble. Keith McKenzie scooped up the ball and raced 88 yards for a touchdown to cut the lead to 27-9. The Steelers punted after three plays, and Raymont Harris capped a 74-yard drive with a touchdown to cut the deficit to 27-17. Jeff Thomason recovered the ensuing onside kick with 4:52 left. Longwell kicked a 37-yard field goal with 2:40 remaining, but Mark Bruener recovered the onside kick. Jerome Bettis gained 12 yards on a third-and-5 run with 2:00 left to clinch the victory. Stewart was 15 of 22 for 231 yards and 1 touchdown. Bettis rushed for 100 yards, marking the seventh consecutive time he reached the century mark on *Monday Night Football*. Brett Favre was 22 of 39 for 234 yards, with 1 interception.

Green Bay	0	0	3	17	—	20
Pittsburgh	14	10	3	0	—	27

Pitt — C. Johnson 8 pass from Stewart (N. Johnson kick)
Pitt — Stewart 1 run (N. Johnson kick)
Pitt — FG N. Johnson 45
Pitt — Fuamatu-Ma'afala 5 run (N. Johnson kick)
Pitt — FG N. Johnson 21
GB — FG Longwell 42
GB — McKenzie 88 fumble return (pass failed)
GB — Harris 2 run (Freeman pass from Favre)
GB — FG Longwell 37

ELEVENTH WEEK SUMMARIES

AMERICAN FOOTBALL CONFERENCE

Eastern Division	W	L	T	Pct.	Pts.	OP
Miami	7	3	0	.700	178	132
Buffalo	6	4	0	.600	213	206
N.Y. Jets	6	4	0	.600	243	175
New England	5	5	0	.500	211	192
Indianapolis	2	8	0	.200	166	264
Central Division						
Jacksonville	8	2	0	.800	262	200
Pittsburgh	6	4	0	.600	178	184
Tennessee	6	4	0	.600	239	193
Baltimore	3	7	0	.300	147	203
Cincinnati	2	8	0	.200	167	267
Western Division						
Denver	10	0	0	1.000	330	176
Oakland	7	3	0	.700	176	175
Seattle	5	5	0	.500	213	162
Kansas City	4	6	0	.400	167	197
San Diego	4	6	0	.400	127	179

NATIONAL FOOTBALL CONFERENCE

Eastern Division	W	L	T	Pct.	Pts.	OP
Dallas	7	3	0	.700	259	149
Arizona	5	5	0	.500	182	232
N.Y. Giants	3	7	0	.300	169	226
Philadelphia	2	8	0	.200	92	233
Washington	2	8	0	.200	169	273
Central Division						
Minnesota	9	1	0	.900	320	170
Green Bay	7	3	0	.700	276	196
Tampa Bay	4	6	0	.400	167	205
Chicago	3	7	0	.300	167	224
Detroit	3	7	0	.300	197	222
Western Division						
Atlanta	8	2	0	.800	284	195
San Francisco	7	3	0	.700	292	217
New Orleans	5	5	0	.500	186	204
St. Louis	3	7	0	.300	177	240
Carolina	1	9	0	.100	191	254

SUNDAY, NOVEMBER 15

SAN DIEGO 14, BALTIMORE 13—at Qualcomm Stadium, attendance 54,388. The Chargers defense recorded 6 sacks, intercepted 2 passes, and limited the Ravens to 8 first downs to improve to 3-2 at home. One of the Ravens' 2 first-half first downs set up Matt Stover's 42-yard field goal. The Ravens defense did not let the Chargers run a play inside their own 40-yard line in the first half, but Craig Whelihan's 47-yard touchdown pass to Charlie Jones gave San Diego a 7-3 halftime lead. Jim Harbaugh's 58-yard touchdown pass to Jermaine Lewis gave the Ravens a 10-7 lead, but the Chargers responded with a 16-play, 69-yard drive, capped by Terrell Fletcher's 3-yard scoring run. Greg Jackson's interception at the Chargers' 10 thwarted the ensuing drive, and Lewis's 35-yard punt return set up Stover's second field goal with 3:49 remaining. The Ravens failed to get a first down on their final possession. Whelihan was 15 of 42 for 172 yards and 1 touchdown. Harbaugh was 12 of 33 for 150 yards and 1 touchdown, with 1 interception.

Baltimore	0	3	7	3	—	13
San Diego	0	7	0	7	—	14

Balt — FG Stover 42
SD — C. Jones 47 pass from Whelihan (Carney kick)
Balt — Lewis 58 pass from Harbaugh (Stover kick)
SD — Fletcher 3 run (Carney kick)
Balt — FG Stover 42

MINNESOTA 24, CINCINNATI 3—at Metrodome, attendance 64,232. Randall Cunningham ran for 1 touchdown and threw for another as the Vikings maintained a 2-game lead over the Green Bay Packers in the NFC Central. The Vikings scored a touchdown on their only drive inside Bengals' territory in the first half, while the Bengals could only muster a Doug Pelfrey field goal out of three first half-possessions inside Vikings' territory. An Artrell Hawkins interception at the Bengals' 12 put a halt to the Vikings drive midway through the third quarter, but John Randle forced Neil O'Donnell to fumble moments later. Dwayne Rudd scooped up the loose ball and raced 63 yards for his first NFL touchdown. Gary Anderson booted a 32-yard field goal on the Vikings' next possession, and one play after Jimmy Hitchcock intercepted a pass to stop a drive, Cunningham threw a 61-yard touchdown bomb to Randy Moss to ice the game. Cunningham was 13 of 20 for 224 yards and 1 touchdown, with 2 interceptions. Neil O'Donnell was 10 of 17 for 77 yards.

Cincinnati	0	3	0	0	—	3
Minnesota	7	0	7	10	—	24

Minn — Cunningham 3 run (Anderson kick)
Cin — FG Pelfrey 37
Minn — Rudd 63 fumble return (Anderson kick)
Minn — FG Anderson 32
Minn — Moss 61 pass from Cunningham (Anderson kick)

DALLAS 35, ARIZONA 28—at Sun Devil Stadium, attendance 71,670. The Cowboys sprinted to a 28-0 lead but had to withstand a furious Cardinals' rally to take a two-game lead in the NFC East. The Cowboys scored touchdowns on four out of five possessions during a stretch of the first half, with the second and fourth tallies set up by Arizona turnovers, to take a 28-0 lead with 3:29 remaining in the half. The Cardinals scored just before halftime and marched 60 yards to begin the second half to cut the deficit to 28-14. The Cowboys, buoyed by Troy Aikman's 43-yard pass to Billy Davis, took a 35-14 lead on their next possession when Emmitt Smith scored his third touchdown. The Cardinals drove 73 yards on their next drive to slash the lead to 35-21, and reached the Cowboys' 16 on their following possession, but turned the ball over on downs with 6:51 remaining. Not deterred, the Cardinals' defense forced a punt, and Jake Plummer guided the offense on an 8-play, 70-yard drive to trim the lead to 35-28 with 3:09 left. After another punt, the Cardinals began their final drive from their own 22 with 52 seconds left. Plummer's 57-yard pass to Rob Moore to the Cowboys' 5 set up two plays in the final nine seconds, but both pass attempts into the end zone fell incomplete. Aikman was 14 of 18 for 208 yards and 1 touchdown. Smith had 26 carries for 118 yards. Plummer was 31 of 56 for 465 yards and 3 touchdowns, with 1 interception. Frank Sanders had 11 receptions for 190 yards.

Dallas	14	14	7	0	—	35
Arizona	0	7	14	7	—	28

Dall — Warren 3 run (Cunningham kick)
Dall — Johnston 1 pass from Aikman (Cunningham kick)

Dall — E. Smith 1 run (Cunningham kick)
Dall — E. Smith 1 run (Cunningham kick)
Ariz — Sanders 2 pass from Plummer (Nedney kick)
Ariz — Bates 2 run (Nedney kick)
Dall — E. Smith 3 run (Cunningham kick)
Ariz — Moore 3 pass from Plummer (Nedney kick)
Ariz — Murrell 7 pass from Plummer (Nedney kick)

GREEN BAY 37, N.Y. GIANTS 3—at Giants Stadium, attendance 76,272. Brett Favre passed for 2 touchdowns, and Darick Holmes rushed for 111 yards as the Packers' defense permitted just 9 first downs and 127 total yards. The Packers led just 10-3 following Brad Daluiso's field goal with 4:15 left in the half, but Favre threw his second touchdown pass of the half to Tyrone Davis and Ryan Longwell made his second field goal, both set up by Giants' turnovers, to give the Packers a 20-3 halftime lead. Roell Preston's 66-yard kickoff return to begin the second half led to Longwell's third field goal, and a 73-yard drive on their next possession was capped by William Henderson's 7-yard run to give the Packers a 30-3 lead. Favre was 21 of 33 for 267 yards and 2 touchdowns. Danny Kanell was 8 of 20 for 88 yards, with 2 interceptions.

Green Bay	7	13	10	7	—	37
N.Y. Giants	0	3	0	0	—	3

GB — T. Davis 2 pass from Favre (Longwell kick)
GB — FG Longwell 39
NYG — FG Daluiso 24
GB — T. Davis 60 pass from Favre (Longwell kick)
GB — FG Longwell 24
GB — FG Longwell 31
GB — Henderson 7 run (Longwell kick)
GB — Holmes 2 run (Longwell kick)

MIAMI 13, CAROLINA 9—at Ericsson Stadium, attendance 67,887. The Dolphins moved into first place in the AFC East by limiting the Panthers to just 210 yards. The Dolphins drove 92 yards with the game's opening kickoff, capped by Karim Abdul-Jabbar's 1-yard plunge. The Panthers benefited from a 39-yard kickoff return by Michael Bates and, two possessions later, an 18-yard interception return by Kevin Greene to the Dolphins' 15, to set up 2 John Kasay field goals. The Dolphins led 10-6 when the Panthers were confronted with third-and-1 on the Dolphins' 17 with the opening possession of the second half, but William Floyd and Tim Biakabutuka were both stopped for no gain. Bracey Walker's interception at the Dolphins' 40 two drives later set up Olindo Mare's second field goal to give Miami a 13-6 lead with 14:12 left. A short punt set up Kasay's third field goal with 8:45 remaining, but Walker thwarted another drive with his second interception at the Dolphins' 35 with 5:03 left, and Dan Marino completed a 5-yard pass to Oronde Gadsden on fourth-and-3 from the Panthers' 33 with 1:51 left to ice the game. Marino was 14 of 21 for 140 yards, with 1 interception. Abdul-Jabbar rushed 25 times for 127 yards. Steve Beuerlein was 17 of 30 for 160 yards, with 2 interceptions.

Miami	7	3	0	3	—	13
Carolina	3	3	0	3	—	9

Mia — Abdul-Jabbar 1 run (Mare kick)
Car — FG Kasay 32
Car — FG Kasay 27
Mia — FG Mare 24
Mia — FG Mare 22
Car — FG Kasay 43

BUFFALO 13, NEW ENGLAND 10—at Rich Stadium, attendance 72,020. Doug Flutie passed for 1 touchdown, and the Bills' defense limited the Patriots to just 11 first downs to remain a game behind Miami in the AFC East. Each team had 3 field-goal attempts in the first half, with Steve Christie making 2 of his attempts to give the Bills a 6-3 halftime lead. Willie Clay's interception in the end zone stopped Buffalo's first drive of the second half, but Flutie threw a 10-yard touchdown pass to Jay Riemersma on their next possession to take a 13-3 lead. Drew Bledsoe answered with a 37-yard scoring pass to Tony Simmons, and Lawyer Milloy's interception in the end zone with 4:41 left kept the Patriots within three points. The Patriots reached the Bills' 34 with 1:46 remaining, but Bledsoe threw 4 consecutive incompletions. Flutie was 14 of 26 for 178 yards and 1 touchdown, with 2 interceptions. Bledsoe was 12 of 31 for 180 yards and 1 touchdown.

New England	0	3	0	7	—	10
Buffalo	3	3	7	0	—	13

Buff — FG Christie 31
Buff — FG Christie 20
NE — FG Vinatieri 38
Buff — Riemersma 10 pass from Flutie (Christie kick)
NE — Simmons 37 pass from Bledsoe (Vinatieri kick)

INDIANAPOLIS 24, N.Y. JETS 23—at RCA Dome, attendance 55,520. Peyton Manning threw a 14-yard touchdown pass to Marcus Pollard with 24 seconds left as the Colts snapped the Jets' four-game winning streak. The Jets scored on four consecutive possessions, with John Hall's 25-yard field goal 22 seconds before halftime giving the Jets a 16-10 lead. With one second left in the half, Mike Vanderjagt attempted what would have been an NFL-record 64-yard field goal. The kick fell short and was caught four yards deep in the end zone by Aaron Glenn, who returned it an NFL-record 104 yards for a touchdown to give the Jets a 23-10 halftime lead. Manning's 38-yard touchdown pass to Marvin Harrison cut the deficit to six points, and Hall missed a 47-yard attempt late in the third quarter. Following a punt, the Colts gained possession at their own 20 with 3:04 remaining. Manning converted two third-and-1 situations with rushes of 3 and 4 yards to keep the drive alive and set the stage for Pollard's winning catch. Al Fontenot recovered Vinny Testaverde's fumble at the Jets' 45 with six seconds remaining to clinch the victory. Manning was 26 of 44 for 276 yards and 3 touchdowns, with 2 interceptions. Harrison had 9 receptions for 128 yards. Testaverde was 12 of 28 for 249 yards and 1 touchdown, with 1 interception. Curtis Martin rushed 28 times for 134 yards, while Keyshawn Johnson had 5 catches for 107 yards.

N.Y. Jets	3	20	0	0	—	23
Indianapolis	10	0	7	7	—	24

Ind — FG Vanderjagt 31
NYJ — FG Hall 37
Ind — Small 3 pass from Manning (Vanderjagt kick)
NYJ — Chrebet 63 pass from Testaverde (Hall kick)
NYJ — FG Hall 40
NYJ — FG Hall 25
NYJ — Glenn 104 return of attempted field goal (Hall kick)
Ind — Harrison 38 pass from Manning (Vanderjagt kick)
Ind — Pollard 14 pass from Manning (Vanderjagt kick)

WASHINGTON 28, PHILADELPHIA 3—at Jack Kent Cooke Stadium, attendance 57,704. Skip Hicks rushed for 3 touchdowns, and the Redskins' defense permitted just 9 first downs and intercepted 3 passes en route to their second victory. Dan Wilkinson's interception and 4-yard return to the Eagles' 10 set up Hicks's first touchdown late in the first quarter. Hollis Thomas's fumble recovery at the Redskins' 9 allowed the Eagles to cut the deficit to 7-3, but 13- and 16-yard runs by Brian Mitchell set up Hicks's second touchdown just 22 seconds before halftime. Trent Green threw a 56-yard bomb to Albert Connell for a touchdown in the third quarter, and Cris Dishman's interception return to the Eagles' 1 led to Hicks's final points. Green was 14 of 33 for 169 yards and 1 touchdown. Bobby Hoying was 16 of 34 for 118 yards, with 2 interceptions.

Philadelphia	0	3	0	0	—	3
Washington	7	7	7	7	—	28

Wash — Hicks 1 run (Blanchard kick)
Phil — FG Boniol 19
Wash — Hicks 1 run (Blanchard kick)
Wash — Connell 56 pass from Green (Blanchard kick)
Wash — Hicks 5 run (Blanchard kick)

TENNESSEE 23, PITTSBURGH 14—at Vanderbilt Stadium, attendance 41,104. The Oilers scored 10 points in the final three seconds to win their third consecutive game. The Steelers drove deep into Oilers' territory 4 times in the first half, piercing the end zone with 2 Kordell Stewart touchdown passes, but were stopped on downs on their first possession, and Matt George, who was replacing the injured Norm Johnson, had a field goal blocked. Al Del Greco's 24-yard field goal just before halftime cut the deficit to 14-13. The Steelers drove into Oilers' territory 4 more times in the second half, but had to punt 3 times and, faced with fourth-and-1 from the Oilers' 25 with 4:15 remaining, Stewart was stopped on downs. Steve McNair's third-and-10 31-yard pass to Frank Wycheck, and third-and-5 19-yard pass to Derrick Mason set up Del Greco's go-ahead field goal with three seconds left. The Steelers began to lateral the kickoff return as time expired, but Will Blackwell's toss bounced into the end zone and Michael Roan recovered for a touchdown. McNair was 19 of 31 for 234 yards and 1 touchdown, with 1 interception. Stewart was 22 of 28 for 239 yards and 2 touchdowns.

Pittsburgh	0	14	0	0	—	14
Tennessee	3	10	0	10	—	23

Tenn — FG Del Greco 46
Pitt — Bruener 10 pass from Stewart (George kick)
Tenn — Davis 25 pass from McNair (Del Greco kick)
Pitt — Fuamata-Ma'afala 26 pass from Stewart (George kick)
Tenn — FG Del Greco 24
Tenn — FG Del Greco 22
Tenn — Roan recovered fumble in end zone (Del Greco kick)

NEW ORLEANS 24, ST. LOUIS 3—at Louisiana Superdome, attendance 46,430. The Saints forced 3 turnovers and returned 2 for touchdowns to even their record. Kerry Collins, making his first start for the Saints, completed 5 of 7 passes on the game's opening drive, capped by his 10-yard touchdown pass to Cam Cleeland, to give the Saints a 7-0 lead. Tyronne Drakeford's 32-yard interception return for a touchdown three plays later gave the Saints a 14-0 lead. Leading 14-3, Doug Brien kicked a 26-yard field goal, and one play after the ensuing kickoff, Austin Robbins recovered a Tony Banks fumble in the end zone to give the Saints a 24-3 lead with 2:08 left in the half. Wilkins missed a 53-yard field-goal attempt as the half expired, and the Rams got no closer than the Saints' 37 in the second half. Collins was 13 of 26 for 150 yards and 1 touchdown. Banks was 24 of 37 for 246 yards, with 2 interceptions.

St. Louis	3	0	0	0	—	3
New Orleans	14	10	0	0	—	24

NO — Cleeland 10 pass from Collins (Brien kick)
NO — Drakeford 32 interception return (Brien kick)
StL — FG Wilkins 33
NO — FG Brien 26
NO — Robbins recovered fumble in end zone (Brien kick)

ATLANTA 31, SAN FRANCISCO 19—at Georgia Dome, attendance 69,828. Jamal Anderson rushed for 100 yards and scored twice as the Falcons took sole possession of first place in the NFC West for the first time this late in the season since 1980. Neither team threatened on their first four possessions before Anderson capped an 80-yard drive with a 10-yard touchdown run. The 49ers responded with field goals just before halftime and to begin the second half, but the Falcons answered with 17 points in a stretch of 1:54. After Morten Andersen's field goal, Ray Buchanan intercepted a pass on the next play from scrimmage and returned it to the 49ers' 1, setting up Anderson's second touchdown. Two plays later, Shane Dronett sacked Steve Young, Jessie Tuggle scooped up the ball and scored his NFL record fifth touchdown on a fumble recovery. Young threw two long touchdown passes, the second to Jerry Rice with 3:09 remaining to cut the deficit to 24-19, but Chris Chandler threw a 78-yard scoring pass to Terance Mathis two plays later to clinch the victory. Chandler was 12 of 21 for 198 yards and 1 touchdown. Young was 21 of 40 for 342 yards and 2 touchdowns, with 1 interception. Rice had 10 receptions for 169 yards.

San Francisco	0	3	3	13	—	19
Atlanta	0	7	3	21	—	31

Atl — Anderson 10 run (Andersen kick)
SF — FG Richey 24
SF — FG Richey 28
Atl — FG Andersen 37
Atl — Anderson 2 run (Andersen kick)
Atl — Tuggle 1 fumble return (Andersen kick)
SF — Owens 54 pass from Young (run failed)
SF — Rice 65 pass from Young (Richey kick)

Atl — Mathis 78 pass from Chandler (Andersen kick)

OAKLAND 20, SEATTLE 17—at Network Associates Coliseum, attendance 51,527. Greg Davis's 38-yard field goal with 21 seconds left gave the Raiders a two-game lead in the AFC West standings over the Seahawks. Joey Galloway and Desmond Howard's punt returns for touchdowns cancelled each other out, but Dean Wells' 25-yard interception return to the Raiders' 11 set up Todd Peterson's 22-yard field goal, Davis missed a 30-yard field-goal attempt, to give the Seahawks a 10-7 halftime lead. The Seahawks' defense stopped Donald Hollas on consecutive sneak attempts at the Seahawks' 1 to turn the ball over on downs midway through the third quarter, allowing Seattle to maintain its lead. Hollas and Rickey Dudley connected on passes of 20 and 31 yard's to set up Davis's 26-yard field goal to tie the game. On their next possession, Harvey Williams scored the go-ahead 25-yard touchdown run with 3:50 remaining. The Seahawks drove downfield, and one play after Ricky Watters's successful fourth-and-1 carry, Warren Moon threw a 12-yard touchdown pass to Christian Fauria with 1:01 left to tie the game 17-17. Hollas completed all 3 of his pass attempts and benefited from a roughing-the-passer penalty to set up Davis's winning boot. Hollas was 20 of 31 for 266 yards, with 2 interceptions. Moon was 17 of 33 for 220 yards and 1 touchdown, with 3 interceptions.

Seattle	7	3	0	7	—	17
Oakland	0	7	0	13	—	20

Sea — Galloway 56 punt return (Peterson kick)
Sea — FG Peterson 22
Oak — Howard 63 punt return (Davis kick)
Oak — FG Davis 26
Oak — Williams 25 run (Davis kick)
Sea — Fauria 12 pass from Moon (Peterson kick)
Oak — FG Davis 38

JACKSONVILLE 29, TAMPA BAY 24—at ALLTEL Stadium, attendance 72,974. Fred Taylor's 70-yard touchdown run, his third of the day, with 2:40 left lifted the Jaguars to their third consecutive victory. Touchdown runs by Taylor on consecutive possessions gave Jacksonville a 14-3 lead early in the second quarter. Trent Dilfer responded with touchdown passes on two of the Buccaneers' next three drives, the second coming with 24 seconds left in the half, to give Tampa Bay a 17-14 edge. Mike Hollis kicked his third field goal of the second half, but, because of Dilfer's 79-yard touchdown pass to Reidel Anthony, the Buccaneers led 24-23 with 3:27 to play. The Jaguars forced a punt, and Taylor scampered 70 yards for a touchdown on the next play to give Jacksonville a 29-24 lead. Aaron Beasley intercepted Dilfer's fourth-down pass moments later to secure the victory. Mark Brunell was 22 of 37 for 248 yards. Taylor had 20 carries for 128 yards. Dilfer was 9 of 23 for 189 yards and 3 touchdowns, with 2 interceptions. Anthony had 2 catches for 126 yards.

Tampa Bay	3	14	0	7	—	24
Jacksonville	7	7	6	9	—	29

Jac — Taylor 6 run (Hollis kick)
TB — FG Husted 34
Jac — Taylor 3 run (Hollis kick)
TB — Anthony 47 pass from Dilfer (Husted kick)
TB — Davis 1 pass from Dilfer (Husted kick)
Jac — FG Hollis 31
Jac — FG Hollis 27
TB — Anthony 79 pass from Dilfer (Husted kick)
Jac — FG Hollis 34
Jac — Taylor 70 run (run failed)

SUNDAY NIGHT, NOVEMBER 15

DETROIT 26, CHICAGO 3—at Pontiac Silverdome, attendance 63,152. Tommy Vardell scored 3 touchdowns as the Lions scored on three consecutive possessions before halftime. Jason Hanson's 24-yard field goal splitting the uprights just nine seconds before halftime gave Detroit a 17-3 halftime lead. Vardell's 1-yard run late in the third quarter capped a 79-yard drive, and Hanson's 25-yard field goal culminated a 89-yard drive for the game's final points. The Bears had a couple of other scoring opportunities, but failed to convert. Charlie Batch was 16 of 21 for 253 yards and 1 touchdown. Johnnie Morton had 5 catches for 109 yards. Barry Sanders rushed 24 times for 114 yards. Stenstrom was 13 of 25 for 159 yards.

Chicago	0	3	0	0	—	3
Detroit	7	10	6	3	—	26

Det — Vardell 12 pass from Batch (Hanson kick)
Chi — FG Jaeger 31
Det — Vardell 3 run (Hanson kick)
Det — FG Hanson 24
Det — Vardell 1 run (kick blocked)
Det — FG Hanson 25

MONDAY NIGHT, NOVEMBER 16

DENVER 30, KANSAS CITY 7—at Arrowhead Stadium, attendance 78,100. Terrell Davis rushed for 111 yards and 1 touchdown as the Broncos became just the sixteenth team to begin a season with a 10-0 record. A 38-yard scramble by Bubby Brister and Davis's 41-yard jaunt capped Denver's first two drives and staked the Broncos to a 14-0 lead just 7:36 into the game. The Chiefs drove 87 yards for a touchdown midway through the second quarter, but Jason Elam added field goals on the Broncos' next three possessions to increase the lead to 23-7. Bill Romanowski's interception at the Broncos' 16 stopped one drive, and the Chiefs were stopped twice on downs in the fourth quarter, including once at the Broncos' 10. Brister was 13 of 23 for 180 yards. Gannon was 26 of 39 for 224 yards and 1 touchdown, with 1 interception. Kimble Anders had 10 receptions for 75 yards.

Denver	14	6	3	7	—	30
Kansas City	0	7	0	0	—	7

Den — Brister 38 run (Elam kick)
Den — Davis 41 run (Elam kick)
KC — Anders 3 pass from Gannon (Stoyanovich kick)
Den — FG Elam 42
Den — FG Elam 46
Den — FG Elam 35
Den — Loville 2 run (Elam kick)

TWELFTH WEEK SUMMARIES

AMERICAN FOOTBALL CONFERENCE

Eastern Division	**W**	**L**	**T**	**Pct.**	**Pts.**	**OP**
Buffalo	7	4	0	.636	247	217
Miami	7	4	0	.636	201	158
N.Y. Jets	7	4	0	.636	267	178
New England	6	5	0	.545	237	215
Indianapolis	2	9	0	.182	177	298
Central Division						
Jacksonville	8	3	0	.727	277	230
Pittsburgh	7	4	0	.636	208	199
Tennessee	6	5	0	.545	242	217
Baltimore	4	7	0	.364	167	216
Cincinnati	2	9	0	.182	180	287
Western Division						
Denver	11	0	0	1.000	370	190
Oakland	7	4	0	.636	190	215
San Diego	5	6	0	.455	165	216
Seattle	5	6	0	.455	235	192
Kansas City	4	7	0	.364	204	235

NATIONAL FOOTBALL CONFERENCE

Eastern Division	**W**	**L**	**T**	**Pct.**	**Pts.**	**OP**
Dallas	8	3	0	.727	289	171
Arizona	6	5	0	.545	227	274
N.Y. Giants	4	7	0	.364	189	226
Philadelphia	2	9	0	.182	92	253
Washington	2	9	0	.182	211	318
Central Division						
Minnesota	10	1	0	.909	348	184
Green Bay	7	4	0	.636	290	224
Chicago	4	7	0	.364	180	244
Detroit	4	7	0	.364	225	247
Tampa Bay	4	7	0	.364	192	233
Western Division						
Atlanta	9	2	0	.818	304	208
San Francisco	8	3	0	.727	323	237
New Orleans	5	6	0	.455	206	235
St. Louis	3	8	0	.273	197	264
Carolina	2	9	0	.182	215	274

SUNDAY, NOVEMBER 22

ARIZONA 45, WASHINGTON 42—at Jack Kent Cooke Stadium, attendance 63,435. Jake Plummer rushed for 3 touchdowns and threw for 2 more as the Cardinals held off the Redskins. Arizona led 31-0 with 4:05 left in the first half, driving 80, 58, and 70 yards for the last three touchdowns. Ten of the points were set up by Brian Mitchell's muffed punt return and Bernard Wilson's blocked field goal. The Redskins responded with a fury. Trailing 38-20 late in the third quarter following Trent Green's third touchdown pass to Michael Westbrook, Lemont Evans successfully recovered an onside kick, and Green threw his fourth touchdown pass five plays later. Evans intercepted Plummer to halt the Cardinals' next drive, and Skip Hicks scored nine plays later to cut the deficit to 38-35 with 9:18 left. Plummer's third touchdown run, on a fourth-and-goal quarterback sneak, increased the Cardinals lead to 45-35 with 3:49 remaining. Green countered with a 2-yard run of his own with 1:46 left, giving the Redskins a touchdown on each of their last six possessions. Pat Tillman recovered the ensuing onside kick, but Dan Wilkinson stuffed Michael Bates on fourth-and-1 at the Redskins' 31 with 1:16 left. However, Kwamie Lassiter denied the Redskins the biggest regular-season comeback in NFL history by intercepting Green's tipped pass at the Redskins' 47 with 1:02 left. Plummer was 17 of 28 for 251 yards and 2 touchdowns, with 1 interception. Green was 30 of 49 for 382 yards and 4 touchdowns, with 1 interception. Westbrook had 10 catches for 135 yards, while Leslie Shepherd had 7 receptions for 107 yards.

Arizona	17	14	7	7	—	45
Washington	0	6	21	15	—	42

Ariz — FG Nedney 26
Ariz — McWilliams 6 pass from Plummer (Nedney kick)
Ariz — Plummer 1 run (Nedney kick)
Ariz — Murrell 13 run (Nedney kick)
Ariz — Plummer 10 run (Nedney kick)
Wash — Westbrook 15 pass from Green (kick failed)
Wash — Westbrook 12 pass from Green (Blanchard kick)
Ariz — Centers 9 pass from Plummer (Nedney kick)
Wash — Westbrook 11 pass from Green (Blanchard kick)
Wash — Shepherd 16 pass from Green (Blanchard kick)
Wash — Hicks 5 run (Shepherd pass from Green)
Ariz — Plummer 1 run (Nedney kick)
Wash — Green 2 run (Blanchard kick)

BALTIMORE 20, CINCINNATI 13—at Cinergy Field, attendance 52,571. Priest Holmes set an NFL season-high mark with 227 rushing yards as the Ravens handed the Bengals their sixth consecutive defeat. The Ravens scored on three of their last four drives of the first half, capped by Holmes's 1-yard plunge, to take a 17-3 halftime lead. Trailing 17-6, Thomas Randolph's interception at the Bengals' 44 set up Brandon Bennett's 2-yard touchdown run late in the third quarter to cut the lead to four points. However, Ray Lewis intercepted Paul Justin's pass on the Bengals' next possession, setting up Matt Stover's second field goal with 13:13 to play, and after a punt the Ravens ran the final 8:27 off the clock to preserve the victory. Jim Harbaugh was 9 of 18 for 92 yards and 1 touchdown, with 1 interception. Justin was 18 of 32 for 202 yards, with 2 interceptions.

Baltimore	7	10	0	3	—	20
Cincinnati	0	3	10	0	—	13

Balt — Potts 12 pass from Harbaugh (Stover kick)
Balt — FG Stover 34
Cin — FG Pelfrey 40
Balt — Holmes 1 run (Stover kick)
Cin — FG Pelfrey 34
Cin — Bennett 2 run (Pelfrey kick)
Balt — FG Stover 23

CAROLINA 24, ST. LOUIS 20—at Trans World Dome, attendance 71,670. Mark Carrier forced a game-saving turnover, and the Panthers' defense kept the Rams out of the end zone in the game's final moments to win their first road game. The Panthers scored on three consecutive possessions, 2 on Steve Beuerlein touchdown passes to Wesley Walls, to take a 17-0 lead. The Rams scored just before halftime and on their first drive of the second half to pull within three points. Fred Lane's touchdown on the first play of the fourth quarter extended the Panthers' lead, but the Rams kicked field goals to cap their next two drives to cut the deficit to 24-20 with 6:07 left. On Carolina's next possession, Roman Phifer intercepted Beuerlein's pass at the Panthers' 41 and headed for the end zone. Carrier chased Phifer and knocked the ball out of his hands at the Panthers' 5. Frank Garcia recovered the ball in the end zone for a touchback with 2:41 left. The Rams forced a punt and reached the Panthers' 14 with five seconds remaining, but Steve Bono's pass to Amp Lee fell incomplete as time expired. Beuerlein was 21 of 26 for 211 yards and 2 touchdowns, with 1 interception. Bono was 16 of 33 for 221 yards and 1 touchdown.

Carolina	7	10	0	7	—	24
St. Louis	0	7	7	6	—	20

Car — Walls 1 pass from Beuerlein (Kasay kick)
Car — Walls 13 pass from Beuerlein (Kasay kick)
Car — FG Kasay 35
StL — Robinson 4 pass from Bono (Wilkins kick)
StL — Moore 7 run (Wilkins kick)
Car — Lane 1 run (Kasay kick)
StL — FG Wilkins 39
StL — FG Wilkins 41

ATLANTA 20, CHICAGO 13—at Georgia Dome, attendance 60,804. The Falcons scored the game's final 17 points over the course of the final 16 minutes, 45 seconds to defeat the Bears. Ray Buchanan's interception at the Falcons' 24 stopped a Bears drive and led to Morten Andersen's 50-yard field goal. The Bears scored 13 points during a 4:45 stretch spanning the second and third quarters, with Jeff Jaeger's second field goal following a 61-yard kickoff return by Glyn Milburn and Shawn Lee's 15-yard fumble return keyed by Jim Flanigan's sack forcing Chris Chandler to fumble. The Falcons regrouped, and Chandler capped consecutive drives with touchdown passes, the second an 11-yard pass to Todd Kinchen with 9:32 left to tie the game 17-17. Faced with third-and-19 from the Bears' 24 with 3:20 to play, Chuck Smith forced Steve Stenstrom to fumble. Cornelius Bennett recovered, and Andersen made the go-ahead 44-yard field goal with 1:58 left. Ronnie Bradford's interception at the Bears' 44 secured the comeback. Chandler was 18 of 27 for 272 yards and 2 touchdowns. Tony Martin had 6 receptions for 100 yards. Stenstrom was 7 of 18 for 109 yards, with 2 interceptions.

Chicago	0	3	10	0	—	13
Atlanta	0	3	7	10	—	20

Atl — FG Andersen 50
Chi — FG Jaeger 35
Chi — FG Jaeger 32
Chi — Lee 15 fumble return (Jaeger kick)
Atl — Mathis 13 pass from Chandler (Andersen kick)
Atl — Kinchen 11 pass from Chandler (Andersen kick)
Atl — FG Andersen 44

DETROIT 28, TAMPA BAY 25—at Raymond James Stadium, attendance 64,265. Ron Rice's interception in the end zone with 2:12 remaining stifled a Buccaneers' comeback attempt to give the Lions their second consecutive victory. The Lions scored on their first two possessions, and Ron Rivers's 36-yard touchdown run late in the second quarter gave Detroit a 21-7 lead. The Buccaneers answered with a 12-play, 80-yard drive capped by Trent Dilfer's 8-yard touchdown pass to Dave Moore just before halftime. Tampa Bay cut the deficit to 21-17, but Richard Jordan's interception at the Buccaneers' 22 set up Tommy Vardell's 1-yard touchdown on the first play of the fourth quarter to increase the lead. The Buccaneers needed just eight plays to score, and Dilfer's 2-point conversion pass to Reidel Anthony pulled Tampa Bay to within three points with 10:42 left. Tampa Bay was in scoring position when Rice intercepted Dilfer's tipped third-down pass for a touchback with 2:12 left, and the Lions all but ran out the clock. Charlie Batch was 14 of 23 for 195 yards and 2 touchdowns. Dilfer was 16 of 30 for 283 yards and 2 touchdowns, with 2 interceptions.

Detroit	14	7	0	7	—	28
Tampa Bay	0	14	3	8	—	25

Det — Crowell 53 pass from Batch (Hanson kick)
Det — Rasby 3 pass from Batch (Hanson kick)
TB — Green 44 pass from Dilfer (Husted kick)
Det — Rivers 36 run (Hanson kick)
TB — Moore 8 pass from Dilfer (Husted kick)
TB — FG Husted 33
Det — Vardell 1 run (Hanson kick)
TB — Alstott 5 run (Anthony pass from Dilfer)

MINNESOTA 28, GREEN BAY 14—at Metrodome, attendance 64,471. Randall Cunningham passed for 2 touchdowns, including a game-clinching 49-yard bomb to Randy Moss, and the Vikings' defense forced 3 turnovers to help sweep the Packers. Tony Williams's recovery of Brett Favre's fumble four plays into the game set up Gary Anderson's first field goal, and Jimmy Hitchcock's 58-yard interception return for a touchdown late in the first quarter helped stake the Vikings to a 13-0 lead. The Packers got on the board as Tyrone Davis capped an 80-yard drive with a 12-yard touchdown catch, but the Vikings stormed downfield and Cunningham's 4-yard touchdown pass to Cris Carter with 24 seconds remaining in the half gave Minnesota a 20-7 edge. Davis's second touchdown catch with 7:31 left in the game culminated a 71-yard drive, but Cunningham's bomb to Moss with 3:17 left sealed the victory. Cunningham was 20 of 30 for 264 yards and 2 touchdowns, with 1 interception. Moss had 8 receptions for 153 yards. Favre was 31 of 39 for 303 yards and 2 touchdowns, with 1 interception.

Green Bay	0	7	0	7	—	14
Minnesota	10	10	0	8	—	28

Minn — FG Anderson 35
Minn — Hitchcock 58 interception return (Anderson kick)
Minn — FG Anderson 29
GB — T. Davis 12 pass from Favre (Longwell kick)
Minn — Carter 4 pass from Cunningham (Anderson kick)
GB — T. Davis 2 pass from Favre (Longwell kick)
Minn — Moss 49 pass from Cunningham (Cunningham run)

BUFFALO 34, INDIANAPOLIS 11—at Rich Stadium, attendance 49,032. Doug Flutie passed for 2 touchdowns as the Bills reeled off 34 unanswered points to defeat the Colts. Trailing 3-0, Ken Irvin intercepted a pass and returned it 43 yards to the Colts' 1, setting up Sam Gash's touchdown catch. The Bills scored on their next three possessions as well, capped by Steve Christie's 35-yard field goal one second before halftime to take a 24-3 lead. The Bills added a field goal to begin the second half, and on the ensuing drive, Buffalo's defense stopped the Colts on four plays from inside the Bills' 2. A muffed punt return by Aaron Bailey set up Antowain Smith's touchdown to give Buffalo a 34-3 lead. Flutie was 20 of 28 for 230 yards and 2 touchdowns. Smith rushed for 107 yards, while Reed had 6 receptions for 108 yards. Peyton Manning was 14 of 29 for 164 yards and 1 touchdown, with 2 interceptions. Marshall Faulk had 8 receptions for 102 yards.

Indianapolis	3	0	0	8	—	11
Buffalo	0	24	3	7	—	34

Ind — FG Vanderjagt 27
Buff — Gash 1 pass from Flutie (Christie kick)
Buff — Smith 4 run (Christie kick)
Buff — Reed 67 pass from Flutie (Christie kick)
Buff — FG Christie 35
Buff — FG Christie 24
Buff — Smith 5 run (Christie kick)
Ind — Harrison 30 pass from Manning (Harrison pass from Manning)

PITTSBURGH 30, JACKSONVILLE 15—at Three Rivers Stadium, attendance 59,124. Dewayne Washington tied an NFL record by returning 2 interceptions for touchdowns as the Steelers pulled within one game of the Jaguars in the AFC Central standings. Washington's first interception came midway through the first quarter and was the highlight of a first half in which the Jaguars only ran one play inside the Steelers' 40. Trailing 13-0, the Jaguars drove 90 yards with their first possession of the second half, capped by Taylor's 2-yard run, to cut the deficit to 13-7. The Steelers scored on their next two drives, with Kordell Stewart's 9-yard touchdown pass to Mark Bruener giving the Steelers a seemingly safe 23-7 lead with 8:59 to play in the game. The Jaguars scored less than two minutes later on Mark Brunell's 33-yard pass to Jimmy Smith, and Brunell's 2-point conversion pass pulled Jacksonville to within eight points. The Jaguars reached the Steelers' 32 with 50 seconds remaining, but Washington secured the victory by intercepting Brunell for the second time and racing 78 yards for the game's final points. Stewart was 25 of 36 for 208 yards and 1 touchdown. Brunell was 18 of 42 for 212 yards and 1 touchdown, with 3 interceptions.

Jacksonville	0	0	7	8	—	15
Pittsburgh	7	6	3	14	—	30

Pitt — Washington 52 interception return (N. Johnson kick)
Pitt — FG N. Johnson 38
Pitt — FG N. Johnson 29
Jac — Taylor 2 run (Hollis kick)
Pitt — FG N. Johnson 41
Pitt — Bruener 9 pass from Stewart (N. Johnson kick)
Jac — J. Smith 33 pass from Brunell (McCardell pass from Brunell)
Pitt — Washington 78 interception return (N. Johnson kick)

SAN DIEGO 38, KANSAS CITY 37—at Qualcomm Stadium, attendance 59,894. Craig Whelihan's 1-yard touchdown pass to Charlie Jones with nine seconds remaining clinched a furious comeback as the Chargers scored 17 points in the final 8:01 to defeat the Chiefs. The Chargers scored on their first three possessions to take a 17-7 lead, but the Chiefs scored the next 27 points, 1 touchdown and 2 field goals of which were set up by San Diego turnovers in their own territory. Byron (Bam) Morris's third touchdown of the game gave the Chiefs a 34-17 lead with 11:46 to play. Terrell Fletcher's 4-yard run capped a 91-yard Chargers drive, but Pete Stoyanovich's third field goal gave Kansas City a 37-24 lead with 5:28 remaining. Whelihan's 55-yard pass to Ryan Thelwell set up his 25-yard fourth-and-13 touchdown pass to Freddie Jones with 4:14 left. Stoyanovich's 46-yard field-goal attempt sailed wide left with 51 seconds left and gave the Chargers the ball, and 2 James Hasty pass interference penalties, including 1 in the end zone, gave the Chargers the ball at the Chiefs' 1 with 16 seconds left. After an incomplete pass, Whelihan and Charlie Jones connected for the winning points. The game marked the first time since 1993 that the Chargers had scored 5 touchdowns in a game. Whelihan was 19 of 37 for 279 yards and 2 touchdowns, with 1 interception. Rich Gannon was 20 of 33 for 304 yards and 1 touchdown, with 1 interception. Derrick Alexander had 5 receptions for 173 yards.

Kansas City	7	7	13	10	—	37
San Diego	7	10	0	21	—	38

SD — Fletcher 4 run (Carney kick)
KC — Alexander 35 pass from Gannon (Stoyanovich kick)
SD — Stephens 2 run (Carney kick)
SD — FG Carney 31
KC — Morris 2 run (Stoyanovich kick)
KC — Morris 1 run (Stoyanovich kick)
KC — FG Stoyanovich 27
KC — FG Stoyanovich 42
KC — Morris 3 run (Stoyanovich kick)
SD — Fletcher 4 run (Carney kick)
KC — FG Stoyanovich 50
SD — F. Jones 25 pass from Whelihan (Carney kick)
SD — C. Jones 1 pass from Whelihan (Carney kick)

N.Y. JETS 24, TENNESSEE 3—at Vanderbilt Stadium, attendance 37,064. Vinny Testaverde passed for 2 touchdowns as the Jets matched the Bills and Dolphins atop the AFC East standings. Neither team drove inside the opponents' 15 in the first half, and John Hall missed a 38-yard field goal, allowing the score to be tied 3-3 at the half. The Jets drove 58, 78, and 53 yards on their first three drives of the second half, capped by Curtis Martin's 31-yard scamper, to take a 24-3 lead with 9:00 left. The Jets' defense contained the Oilers on their own end of the field throughout the second half. Testaverde was 21 of 33 for 237 yards and 2 touchdowns. Martin rushed 27 times for 123 yards. Steve McNair was 13 of 24 for 137 yards.

N.Y. Jets	0	3	7	14	—	24
Tennessee	0	3	0	0	—	3

NYJ — FG Hall 43
Tenn — FG Del Greco 34
NYJ — K. Johnson 3 pass from Testaverde (Hall kick)
NYJ — Byars 2 pass from Testaverde (Hall kick)
NYJ — Martin 31 run (Hall kick)

DENVER 40, OAKLAND 14—at Mile High Stadium, attendance 69,828. John Elway passed for 3 touchdowns as the Broncos improved to 11-0. The Broncos' defense did not allow the Raiders inside Denver's 40 during Oakland's first four possessions. The Broncos' offense capitalized, taking a 17-0 lead. Oakland scored the next 14 points and trailed by just three points following Donald Hollas's 14-yard touchdown pass to James Jett with 5:06 left in the third quarter. Jason Elam's 23-yard field goal gave the Broncos a six-point lead with 13:37 to play, and Ray Crockett intercepted Hollas four plays later. Elway threw a 28-yard touchdown pass to Rod Smith less than a minute later to give Denver a 26-14 lead, and interceptions by Neil Smith and Tyrone Braxton set up 2 more touchdowns in the final five minutes. Elway was 17 of 25 for 197 yards and 3 touchdowns. Davis rushed 31 times for 162 yards. Hollas was 20 of 35 for 270 yards and 2 touchdowns, with 3 interceptions.

Oakland	0	7	7	0	—	14
Denver	3	14	0	23	—	40

Den — FG Elam 33
Den — Sharpe 7 pass from Elway (Elam kick)
Den — T. Davis 1 run (Elam kick)
Oak — Dudley 29 pass from Hollas (Davis kick)
Oak — Jett 14 pass from Hollas (Davis kick)
Den — FG Elam 23
Den — R. Smith 28 pass from Elway (pass failed)
Den — Griffith 3 pass from Elway (Elam kick)
Den — Hebron 3 run (Elam kick)

N.Y. GIANTS 20, PHILADELPHIA 0—at Giants Stadium, attendance 65,763. Phillippi Sparks intercepted 2 passes, and the Eagles crossed midfield just twice as the Giants' recorded their first shutout since 1990. Brad Daluiso's 40-yard field goal gave the Giants a 3-0 halftime lead. An unnecessary roughness penalty on Mike Caldwell led to Gary Brown's 4-yard touchdown run, and Daluiso added a second field goal with 11:04 left to give the Giants a 13-0 lead. The Eagles threatened on their next possession, but Phillippi Sparks's interception in the end zone with 6:49 left stifled the drive, and Kent Graham added a late touchdown pass to Tiki Barber following Sparks's second interception. Graham was 10 of 21 for 153 yards and 1 touchdown, with 1 interception. Bobby Hoying was 14 of 28 for 161 yards, with 2 interceptions.

Philadelphia	0	0	0	0	—	0
N.Y. Giants	3	0	7	10	—	20

NYG — FG Daluiso 40
NYG — Brown 4 run (Daluiso kick)
NYG — FG Daluiso 49
NYG — Barber 8 pass from Graham (Daluiso kick)

DALLAS 30, SEATTLE 22—at Texas Stadium, attendance 64,142. Troy Aikman passed for 2 touchdowns as the Cowboys won their fourth consecutive game. The Cowboys scored on their first two possessions and led 13-7 when Kevin Smith thwarted a Seahawks drive with an interception at the Cowboys' 10 with 2:20 left in the half. However, Sam Adams intercepted a pass two plays later and rumbled 25 yards into the end zone to give Seattle a 14-13 lead. Richie Cunningham's third field goal of the half split the uprights as time expired to give the Cowboys a 16-14 lead. Dallas put together drives of 81 and 61 yards to increase their advantage to 30-16 with 7:04 remaining. The Seahawks answered with a 68-yard scoring drive and forced a punt to get the ball back. However, Kevin Smith knocked away Warren Moon's fourth-and-3 pass to Joey Galloway at the Cowboys' 39 with 2:31 left, and Sherman Williams gained 2 yards on third-and-1 to enable Dallas to run out the clock. Aikman was 28 of 42 for 296 yards and 2 touchdowns, with 1 interception. Moon was 15 of 28 for 201 yards and 2 touchdowns, with 1 interception.

Seattle	0	14	0	8	—	22
Dallas	10	6	0	14	—	30

Dall — FG Cunningham 47
Dall — E. Smith 8 pass from Aikman (Cunningham kick)
Sea — Galloway 44 pass from Moon (Peterson kick)
Dall — FG Cunningham 44
Sea — Adams 25 interception return (Peterson kick)
Dall — FG Cunningham 28
Dall — Davis 18 pass from Aikman (Cunningham kick)
Dall — Warren 1 run (Cunningham kick)
Sea — McKnight 5 pass from Moon (Watters run)

SUNDAY NIGHT, NOVEMBER 22

SAN FRANCISCO 31, NEW ORLEANS 20—at 3Com Park, attendance 63,152. Steve Young threw 4 touchdown passes as the 49ers defeated the Saints for the sixth consecutive time. The 49ers committed turnovers on three of their first four possessions to fall behind 13-0. However, Sean Dawkins fumbled on the first play following the third turnover, and Tim McDonald recovered at the 49ers' 26. The 49ers proceeded to score touchdowns on their next four drives, highlighted by Young's 81-yard bomb to Garrison Hearst on the second half's second play and culminated by Young's 8-yard touchdown pass to Jerry Rice following Dawkins's second fumble, to take a 28-13 lead with 11:54 left in the third quarter. Leading 31-13 early in the fourth quarter, the 49ers' defense stopped the Saints on third-and-goal and fourth-and-goal from the 49ers' 1 and did not allow another touchdown until just 1:22 was left in the game. Young was 22 of 31 for 290 yards and 4 touchdowns, with 1 interception. Hearst had 4 receptions for 103 yards. Collins was 22 of 44 for 328 yards, with 2 interceptions.

New Orleans	10	3	0	7	—	20
San Francisco	0	14	17	0	—	31

NO — FG Brien 47
NO — Collins 1 run (Brien kick)
SF — Owens 8 pass from Young (Richey kick)
SF — Owens 8 pass from Young (Richey kick)
NO — FG Brien 22
SF — Hearst 81 pass from Young (Richey kick)
SF — Rice 8 pass from Young (Richey kick)
SF — FG Richey 45
NO — Craver 1 run (Brien kick)

MONDAY NIGHT, NOVEMBER 23

NEW ENGLAND 26, MIAMI 23—at Foxboro Stadium, attendance 58,729. Drew Bledsoe threw a 25-yard touchdown pass to Shawn Jefferson with 29 seconds remaining to lift the Patriots to a hard-earned AFC East victory. With the score tied 7-7, Sam Madison's 31-yard interception return to the Patriots' 37 set up Dan Marino's second touchdown pass of the half to Oronde Gadsden, and the Dolphins took a 14-10 lead into the locker room. Madison's second interception, this one early in the third quarter, gave the Dolphins the ball at the Patriots' 35. However, Ferric Collons stuffed Karim Abdul-Jabbar for a 3-yard loss on fourth-and-1, leading to Adam Vinatieri's field goal moments later to cut the deficit to 14-13. Vinatieri's fourth field goal gave the Patriots a 19-17 lead with 9:01 left, but the Dolphins answered with an 8-play touchdown drive, capped by Abdul-Jabbar's 4-yard run, to take a 23-19 lead with 3:22 remaining. Bledsoe guided the Patriots on a game-winning 80-yard drive, highlighted by 2 fourth-down completions to Jefferson and capped by the duo's 25-yard touchdown one play after the second successful fourth-down conversion. Bledsoe, who fractured his finger during the winning drive, was 28 of 54 for 423 yards and 2 touchdowns, with 2 interceptions. Jefferson had 6 receptions for 131 yards. Marino was 24 of 38 for 289 yards and 2 touchdowns, with 1 interception. Both rushing defenses were strong, as the Patriots gained just 2.2 yards per carry, while Miami was limited to 1.7 yards per rush.

Miami	7	7	3	6	—	23
New England	7	3	6	10	—	26

Mia — Gadsden 35 pass from Marino (Mare kick)
NE — Coates 8 pass from Bledsoe (Vinatieri kick)
Mia — Gadsden 11 pass from Marino (Mare kick)
NE — FG Vinatieri 25
NE — FG Vinatieri 44
Mia — FG Mare 21
NE — FG Vinatieri 45
NE — FG Vinatieri 24
Mia — Abdul-Jabbar 4 run (pass failed)
NE — Jefferson 25 pass from Bledsoe (Vinatieri kick)

THIRTEENTH WEEK SUMMARIES

AMERICAN FOOTBALL CONFERENCE

Eastern Division	**W**	**L**	**T**	**Pct.**	**Pts.**	**OP**
N.Y. Jets	8	4	0	.667	315	199
Miami	8	4	0	.667	231	168
Buffalo	7	5	0	.583	268	242
New England	7	5	0	.583	262	236
Indianapolis	2	10	0	.167	208	336
Central Division						
Jacksonville	9	3	0	.750	311	247
Pittsburgh	7	5	0	.583	224	218
Tennessee	6	6	0	.500	260	237
Baltimore	5	7	0	.417	205	247
Cincinnati	2	10	0	.167	197	321
Western Division						
Denver	12	0	0	1.000	401	206
Oakland	7	5	0	.583	209	244
Seattle	6	6	0	.500	255	210
Kansas City	5	7	0	.417	238	259
San Diego	5	7	0	.417	181	247

NATIONAL FOOTBALL CONFERENCE

Eastern Division	**W**	**L**	**T**	**Pct.**	**Pts.**	**OP**
Dallas	8	4	0	.667	325	217
Arizona	6	6	0	.500	251	308
N.Y. Giants	4	8	0	.333	196	257
Washington	3	9	0	.250	240	337
Philadelphia	2	10	0	.167	108	277
Central Division						
Minnesota	11	1	0	.917	394	220
Green Bay	8	4	0	.667	314	240
Detroit	5	7	0	.417	244	263
Tampa Bay	5	7	0	.417	223	250
Chicago	3	9	0	.250	197	275
Western Division						
Atlanta	10	2	0	.833	325	218
San Francisco	9	3	0	.750	354	244
New Orleans	5	7	0	.417	216	265
St. Louis	3	9	0	.250	207	285
Carolina	2	10	0	.167	236	322

THURSDAY, NOVEMBER 26

MINNESOTA 46, DALLAS 36—at Texas Stadium, attendance 64,366. Randall Cunningham passed for 4 touchdowns, including 3 bombs to Randy Moss that each exceeded 50 yards, as the Vikings won their fourth consecutive game. The Cowboys kicked field goals to conclude their first two possessions, but the Vikings scored touchdowns on their first three possessions, needing just 10 plays to cover 218 yards. Minnesota took a 21-6 lead when Cunningham and Moss connected on a 56-yard touchdown on the first play following David Palmer's 44-yard kickoff return. Troy Aikman responded with a 67-yard touchdown pass to Patrick Jeffers with 2:32 left in the half, but Gary Anderson's field goal with sixteen seconds remaining gave the Vikings a 24-12 halftime lead. Emmitt Smith's 2-yard touchdown run capped the opening drive of the second half, but the Vikings needed just five plays to stretch their lead on Leroy Hoard's scoring run. Izell Reese's interception at the Vikings' 39 set up Richie Cunningham's 47-yard field goal, but Cunningham and Moss hooked up three plays later for the tandem's third touchdown to give the Vikings a 39-22 lead. After Smith's second touchdown, Cunningham threw an incomplete pass on third-and-13 with 8:00 remaining. However, Charlie Williams was penalized for pass interference, and on the next play Hoard raced 50 yards for a touchdown. Smith's third touchdown, with 1:06 remaining, tied him with Marcus Allen for the most career rushing touchdowns (123). Randall Cunningham was 17 of 35 for 359 yards and 4 touchdowns, with 1 interception. Moss had 3 receptions for 163 yards, while Cris Carter had 7 catches for 135 yards. Aikman was 34 of 57 for 455 yards and 1 touchdown. Michael Irvin had 10 catches for 137 yards. The Cowboys lost despite having more first downs (31-21), total yards (513-471), and time of possession (38:03-21:57).

Minnesota	21	3	15	7	—	46
Dallas	6	6	10	14	—	36

Minn — Moss 51 pass from Ra. Cunningham (Anderson kick)
Dall — FG Ri. Cunningham 30
Minn — Carter 54 pass from Ra. Cunningham (Anderson kick)
Dall — FG Ri. Cunningham 46
Minn — Moss 56 pass from Ra. Cunningham (Anderson kick)

Dall — Jeffers 67 pass from Aikman (pass failed)
Minn — FG Anderson 45
Dall — E. Smith 2 run (Ri. Cunningham kick)
Minn — Hoard 12 run (Moss pass from Ra. Cunningham)
Dall — FG Ri. Cunningham 47
Minn — Moss 56 pass from Ra. Cunningham (Anderson kick)
Dall — E. Smith 1 run (Ri. Cunningham kick)
Minn — Hoard 50 run (Anderson kick)
Dall — E. Smith 4 run (Ri. Cunningham kick)

DETROIT 19, PITTSBURGH 16 (OT)—at Pontiac Silverdome, attendance 78,139. Jason Hanson kicked a 42-yard field goal, his fourth of the game, in overtime to give the Lions their third consecutive victory. Norm Johnson kicked 2 first-half field goals, the second set up by Chris Oldham's fumble recovery at the Lions' 44, to give the Steelers a 6-3 halftime lead. Trailing 13-3, Hanson made a 52-yard field goal, missed from 43 yards on the next drive, and Charlie Batch threw a 21-yard touchdown pass to Herman Moore to tie the game 13-13 with 6:36 remaining. On the ensuing kickoff, Scott Kowalkowski recovered Richard Huntley's fumble at the Steelers' 9, setting up Hanson's fourth field goal. Johnson capped a 15-play, 74-yard drive with a 25-yard field goal with one second left to send the game to overtime. The Lions won the coin toss despite the Steelers' insistence that Jerome Bettis had correctly called tails. Television replays were inconclusive. Detroit wasted little time, as Batch completed a 28-yard pass to Herman Moore, and Oldham was flagged for a facemask penalty on third-and-11. Hanson booted his winning kick moments later. Batch was 16 of 23 for 236 yards and 1 touchdown. Moore had 8 receptions for 148 yards. Stewart was 21 of 36 for 225 yards and 1 touchdown, with 1 interception.

Pittsburgh	0	6	7	3	0	—	16
Detroit	0	3	3	10	3	—	19

Pitt — FG N. Johnson 30
Pitt — FG N. Johnson 38
Det — FG Hanson 45
Pitt — Blackwell 24 pass from Stewart (N. Johnson kick)
Det — FG Hanson 52
Det — Moore 21 pass from Batch (Hanson kick)
Det — FG Hanson 35
Pitt — FG N. Johnson 25
Det — FG Hanson 42

SUNDAY, NOVEMBER 29

KANSAS CITY 34, ARIZONA 24—at Arrowhead Stadium, attendance 69,613. Rich Gannon passed for 3 touchdowns as the Chiefs snapped a six-game losing streak. James Hasty's 21-yard interception return to the Cardinals' 4 set up Kansas City's first touchdown, and Tamarick Vanover's 62-yard kickoff return led to the second score as the Chiefs took a 14-3 lead. Jake Plummer threw a touchdown pass to Rob Moore and Joe Nedney missed a 50-yard field-goal attempt at the end of the half. Leading 14-10, the Chiefs scored the first 10 points of the second half, but the Cardinals scored on successive possessions to cut the deficit to 31-24 on Mario Bates's 1-yard run with 6:07 remaining. Gannon threw 18- and 25-yard passes to Alexander to set up Stoyanovich's 18-yard field goal with 1:57 to play, and Mark McMillian intercepted Plummer three plays later to clinch the victory. Gannon was 21 of 28 for 231 yards and 3 touchdowns, with 1 interception. Alexander had 6 catches for 116 yards. Plummer was 20 of 37 for 250 yards and 1 touchdown, with 2 interceptions. Sanders had 6 receptions for 100 yards.

Arizona	0	10	7	7	—	24
Kansas City	7	7	10	10	—	34

KC — Morris 2 run (Stoyanovich kick)
Ariz — FG Nedney 37
KC — Bennett 2 pass from Gannon (Stoyanovich kick)
Ariz — Moore 10 pass from Plummer (Nedney kick)
KC — Alexander 30 pass from Gannon (Stoyanovich kick)
KC — FG Stoyanovich 37
Ariz — Murrell 4 run (Nedney kick)
KC — Alexander 15 pass from Gannon (Stoyanovich kick)
Ariz — Bates 1 run (Nedney kick)
KC — FG Stoyanovich 18

ATLANTA 21, ST. LOUIS 10—at Trans World Dome, attendance 47,971. Jamal Anderson rushed for 188 yards and 1 touchdown as the Falcons clinched their first playoff berth since 1995. Atlanta led 3-0 when Keith Lyle's interception at the Rams' 25 thwarted a Falcons drive late in the first half, but Jeff Wilkins missed a 61-yard field-goal attempt as the half expired. Tony Horne returned the second half's opening kickoff 102 yards to give the Rams their first lead. Playing without injured Chris Chandler, 44-year-old Steve DeBerg replaced Tony Graziani and guided the Falcons to a field goal and, two possessions later, threw a 27-yard touchdown pass to Terance Mathis to give Atlanta a 14-7 lead. The Rams responded with a 12-play drive for a field goal and, after an exchange of punts, had the Falcons trapped in a third-and-9 situation from the Rams' 27. Anderson answered the call at the game's key moment, bursting through the Rams' secondary for a 27-yard touchdown to give Atlanta a 21-10 lead with 3:13 remaining. Horne returned the ensuing kickoff 66 yards, but the Rams failed to make a first down, and Wilkins missed a 48-yard field-goal attempt. DeBerg was 5 of 12 for 75 yards and 1 touchdown. Tony Banks was 10 of 21 for 95 yards, and Steve Bono was 6 of 13 for 54 yards.

Atlanta	3	0	11	7	—	21
St. Louis	0	0	7	3	—	10

Atl — FG Andersen 42
StL — Horne 102 kickoff return (Wilkins kick)
Atl — FG Andersen 32
Atl — Mathis 27 pass from DeBerg (Anderson run)
StL — FG Wilkins 39
Atl — Anderson 27 run (Andersen kick)

NEW ENGLAND 25, BUFFALO 21—at Foxboro Stadium, attendance 58,304. Drew Bledsoe threw a 1-yard touchdown pass to Ben Coates with no time remaining as the Patriots recorded a miraculous comeback for the second consecutive week. Steve Christie missed a 35-yard field-goal attempt, and Bledsoe threw 2 touchdown passes early in the second quarter to stake the Patriots to a 14-0 lead. Trailing 14-3, Doug Flutie completed a 55-yard pass to Kevin Williams just before halftime to set up Christie's 26-yard boot as the half expired. Flutie threw an 84-yard touchdown pass to Eric Moulds on the Bills' second play of the second half, but the 2-point conversion attempt fell incomplete. After an exchange of field goals, the Bills took their first lead 21-17, on Flutie's 4-yard touchdown pass to Andre Reed with 6:14 remaining. The Patriots regained possession following a punt at their own 18 with 1:52 left. Bledsoe completed a 10-yard pass to Shawn Jefferson on fourth-and-9 to reach the Bills' 26 wih 6 seconds left. With time for one play, Bledsoe lofted a pass into the end zone. Henry Jones was flagged for pass interference, giving the Patriots the ball on the Bills' 1 with no time on the clock. Bledsoe lobbed a touch pass to Coates in the back of the end zone. The Bills thought the game was over and went to the locker room, which allowed Adam Vinatieri to have the ball snapped directly to him and run into the end zone for a 2-point conversion. Bledsoe was 28 of 43 for 246 yards and 3 touchdowns, with 1 interception. Flutie was 21 of 39 for 339 yards and 2 touchdowns. Moulds had 8 receptions for 177 yards.

Buffalo	0	6	9	6	—	21
New England	0	14	3	8	—	25

NE — Edwards 2 pass from Bledsoe (Vinatieri kick)
NE — Cullors 12 pass from Bledsoe (Vinatieri kick)
Buff — FG Christie 34
Buff — FG Christie 26
Buff — Moulds 84 pass from Flutie (pass failed)
NE — FG Vinatieri 44
Buff — FG Christie 22
Buff — Reed 4 pass from Flutie (pass failed)
NE — Coates 1 pass from Bledsoe (Vinatieri run)

N.Y. JETS 48, CAROLINA 21—at Giants Stadium, attendance 71,501. The Jets scored on seven consecutive possessions, and nine of their first ten, to remain even in the AFC East standings with the Dolphins. The Panthers took a 7-3 lead late in the first quarter, but Curtis Martin's 60-yard touchdown run two plays later began a 35-point run by the Jets. Leading 22-7 at halftime, Aaron Glenn's 26-yard interception return to the Panthers' 30 set up Martin's second touchdown, and a sack by Bryan Cox for a safety 21 seconds later gave the Jets a 31-7 lead. The Panthers got no closer than 20 points the remainder of the game. Vinny Testaverde was 16 of 21 for 255 yards and 2 touchdowns. Wayne Chrebet had 7 receptions for 107 yards. Steve Beuerlein was 13 of 23 for 169 yards. The Jets outgained the Panthers (456-216).

Carolina	7	0	7	7	—	21
N.Y. Jets	10	12	19	7	—	48

NYJ — FG Hall 30
Car — Lane 1 run (Kasay kick)
NYJ — Martin 60 run (Hall kick)
NYJ — FG Hall 37
NYJ — K. Johnson 35 run (pass failed)
NYJ — FG Hall 26
NYJ — Martin 1 run (Hall kick)
NYJ — Safety, Beuerlein sacked by Cox in end zone
NYJ — Chrebet 36 pass from Testaverde (Hall kick)
Car — Walls 2 pass from Beuerlein (Kasay kick)
NYJ — FG Hall 38
Car — Lane 2 run (Kasay kick)
NYJ — Chrebet 21 pass from Testaverde (Hall kick)

BALTIMORE 38, INDIANAPOLIS 31—at NFL Stadium at Camden Yards, attendance 68,898. Priest Holmes rushed for 103 yards and 2 touchdowns as the Ravens won their second consecutive game with a comeback victory. The Colts punted just once in their first seven possessions. Marshall Faulk's 68-yard touchdown run on the Colts' third possession gave Indianapolis a 17-3 lead. The Colts had a chance to increase the lead, but Rod Woodson blocked Mike Vanderjagt's 52-yard field-goal attempt, and Jim Harbaugh threw a 15-yard touchdown pass to James Roe. The Colts marched 77 yards on their ensuing drive to score again, but Corey Harris's 49-yard kickoff return in the half's final minute enabled Matt Stover to make a 48-yard field goal as time expired, trimming the deficit to 24-13. Trailing 31-21 late in the third quarter, Harris returned a kickoff 47 yards to set up Harbaugh's touchdown pass to Floyd Turner. The Ravens forced a punt, and Holmes scampered 36 yards for a touchdown two plays later to give Baltimore its first lead. Stover's 47-yard field goal on their next possession increased the Ravens lead to 38-31 with 2:49 left, and Ralph Staten's interception at the Ravens' 20 secured the victory. Harbaugh was 16 of 25 for 198 yards and 2 touchdowns. Peyton Manning was 27 of 42 for 357 yards and 3 touchdowns, with 1 interception. Faulk had 17 carries for 92 yards, and Torrance Small had 9 receptions for 153 yards.

Indianapolis	17	7	7	0	—	31
Baltimore	3	10	8	17	—	38

Ind — FG Vanderjagt 53
Balt — FG Stover 43
Ind — Faulk 34 pass from Manning (Vanderjagt kick)
Ind — Faulk 68 run (Vanderjagt kick)
Balt — Roe 15 pass from Harbaugh (Stover kick)
Ind — Small 24 pass from Manning (Vanderjagt kick)
Balt — FG Stover 48
Balt — Holmes 2 run (Turner pass from Harbaugh)
Ind — Pathon 5 pass from Manning (Vanderjagt kick)
Balt — Turner 22 pass from Harbaugh (Stover kick)
Balt — Holmes 36 run (Stover kick)
Balt — FG Stover 47

JACKSONVILLE 34, CINCINNATI 17—at Cinergy Field, attendance 55,432. Mark Brunell passed for 4 touchdowns as the Jaguars held-off Cincinnati to hand the Bengals their seventh consecutive defeat. The Jaguars' benefitted from Doug Pelfrey's missed 42-yard field-goal attempt, Kevin Hardy's interception at the Bengals' 11, and Mike Logan's fumble recovery at Cincinnati's 24-yard line to claim a 17-0 lead midway through the second quarter. The Bengals scored twice in the final 3:48 of the first half, with Doug Pelfrey's 30-yard field goal splitting the uprights as the half expired, to trim the deficit to 17-10. Corey Dillon's 61-yard run set up Neil O'Donnell's 7-yard touchdown pass to Tony McGee to cut the lead to 20-17. However, the Jaguars drove 80 and 83 yards for touchdowns on their next two possessions, and Chris Hudson's interception at the Jaguars' 15 and Hardy's fumble recovery at the Jaguars' 28 thwarted Cincinnati. Brunell was 19 of 35 for 244 yards and 4 touchdowns. Jimmy Smith had 7 receptions for 110 yards. O'Donnell was 20 of 36 for 203 yards and 1 touchdown, with 1 interception. Dillon had 16 carries for 107 yards.

Jacksonville	7	10	10	7	—	34
Cincinnati	0	10	7	0	—	17

Jac — Smith 21 pass from Brunell (Hollis kick)
Jac — McCardell 8 pass from Brunell (Hollis kick)
Jac — FG Hollis 23
Cin — Milne 1 run (Pelfrey kick)
Cin — FG Pelfrey 30
Jac — FG Hollis 47
Cin — McGee 7 pass from O'Donnell (Pelfrey kick)
Jac — McCardell 3 pass from Brunell (Hollis kick)
Jac — Jones 1 pass from Brunell (Hollis kick)

MIAMI 30, NEW ORLEANS 10—at Pro Player Stadium, attendance 73,216. Dan Marino threw his 400th career touchdown pass, and the Dolphins' defense forced 4 turnovers, recorded 6 sacks, and permitted just 175 yards en route to defeating the Saints. With the score tied 3-3 in the second quarter, Rob Kelly returned an interception 79 yards for a touchdown to give the Saints a 10-3 lead. The Dolphins responded with the first of 3 Marino-to-O.J. McDuffie touchdown passes to tie the game. Sam Madison's interception on the next play set up Olindo Mare's 32-yard field goal just before halftime. The Dolphins scored on three of their first four second-half possessions to put the game out of reach as the Saints failed to run a play in Miami territory after intermission. Marino was 22 of 40 for 255 yards and 3 touchdowns, with 1 interception. McDuffie had 9 receptions for 102 yards. Kerry Collins was 9 of 24 for 110 yards, with 3 interceptions.

New Orleans	3	7	0	0	—	10
Miami	0	13	3	14	—	30

NO — FG Brien 43
Mia — FG Mare 27
NO — Kelly 79 interception return (Brien kick)
Mia — McDuffie 22 pass from Marino (Mare kick)
Mia — FG Mare 32
Mia — FG Mare 34
Mia — McDuffie 7 pass from Marino (Mare kick)
Mia — McDuffie 9 pass from Marino (Mare kick)

GREEN BAY 24, PHILADELPHIA 16—at Lambeau Field, attendance 59,862. Darick Holmes rushed for a career-high 163 yards and Brett Favre passed for 2 touchdowns as the Packers held off the Eagles. Troy Vincent's interception in the end zone thwarted Green Bay's second drive, but the Eagles failed to record a first down on their first five possessions. Trailing 10-0, the Eagles responded with a 78-yard touchdown drive, capped by Koy Detmer's 16-yard touchdown pass to Jeff Graham just 28 seconds before halftime, only to have Vaughn Booker block the extra-point attempt. Detmer and Graham joined forces to culminate the Eagles' 79-yard drive to begin the second half to give Philadelphia a 13-10 lead. Favre and Antonio Freeman responded with a 33-yard touchdown pass to retake the lead. Chris Boniol's field goal with 8:41 left in the game trimmed the deficit to 17-16, but Henderson crashed into the end zone with 3:00 remaining and the Eagles punted with 2:00 left. Faced with second-and-5, Holmes gained 6 yards to secure the victory. Favre was 20 of 33 for 321 yards and 2 touchdowns, with 2 interceptions. Bill Schroeder had 5 receptions for 128 yards. Detmer was 22 of 36 for 185 yards and 2 touchdowns.

Philadelphia	0	6	7	3	—	16
Green Bay	0	10	7	7	—	24

GB — FG Longwell 30
GB — Henderson 1 pass from Favre (Longwell kick)
Phil — Graham 16 pass from Detmer (kick blocked)
Phil — Graham 4 pass from Detmer (Boniol kick)
GB — Freeman 33 pass from Favre (Longwell kick)
Phil — FG Boniol 34
GB — Henderson 3 run (Longwell kick)

TAMPA BAY 31, CHICAGO 17—at Soldier Field, attendance 51,938. The Buccaneers won the battle of turnovers and special teams to hand the Bears their fourth consecutive defeat. Brad Culpepper recovered Moses Moreno's fumble at the Bears' 19, setting up Tampa Bay's first touchdown. Andre Collins's interception at the Buccaneers' 23 set up Ryan Wetnight's 26-yard touchdown on a fake field-goal shovel pass, and Wetnight's fumble recovery on the ensuing kickoff led to Moreno's 21-yard touchdown pass to Curtis Conway to give the Bears 14 points in a 53-second span. Late in the half, with the line of scrimmage the Bears' 18, Mike Horan's punt was deflected by Jeff Gooch. Ronde Barber scooped up the bouncing ball and raced 23 yards into the end zone for a touchdown to tie the game. Trent Dilfer added a 45-yard Hail Mary touchdown pass to Brice Hunter on the last play of the first half to give the Buccaneers a lead. Donnie Abraham's fumble recovery at the Bears' 29 and Jacquez Green's 17-yard punt return set up 2 Tampa Bay scores to increase the Buccaneers lead to 31-14. Dilfer was 13 of 22 for 153 yards and 3 touchdowns, with 1 interception. Moreno was 18 of 41 for 153 yards and 1 touchdown.

Tampa Bay	7	14	10	0	—	31
Chicago	0	14	0	3	—	17

TB — Alstott 5 pass from Dilfer (Husted kick)
Chi — Wetnight 26 pass from Horan (Jaeger kick)
Chi — Conway 21 pass from Moreno (Jaeger kick)
TB — Barber 23 punt return (Husted kick)
TB — Hunter 45 pass from Dilfer (Husted kick)
TB — Anthony 14 pass from Dilfer (Husted kick)
TB — FG Husted 28
Chi — FG Jaeger 33

SEATTLE 20, TENNESSEE 18—at Kingdome, attendance 59,048. Todd Peterson's 48-yard field goal with one second left lifted the Seahawks to a stunning victory. Denard Walker's interception in the end zone kept the Seahawks out of the end zone and helped the Oilers take a 6-3 halftime lead. The Seahawks drove deep into Oilers' territory to begin the second half, but Perry Phenix forced Christian Fauria to fumble at the Oilers' 1. Joe Bowden recovered to help Tennessee maintain the lead. However, Jon Kitna and Joey Galloway connected on a 7-yard scoring play on Seattle's next possession to give the Seahawks a 10-6 lead. Leading 10-9, Kitna threw a 55-yard touchdown pass to James McKnight to give the Seahawks a 17-9 lead with 11:04 remaining. Steve McNair's 3-yard run cut the deficit to 17-15 with 4:59 left, but Eddie George was stopped on the 2-point conversion attempt. The Oilers forced a punt, and Al Del Greco kicked a 42-yard field goal with 33 seconds left to give Tennessee an 18-17 lead. Kitna completed a 13-yard pass to Mike Pritchard with six seconds left, allowing Peterson to convert from 48 yards for the victory. Kitna was 24 of 39 for 298 yards and 2 touchdowns, with 1 interception. McNair was 18 of 34 for 199 yards.

Tennessee	3	3	0	12	—	18
Seattle	0	3	7	10	—	20

Tenn — FG Del Greco 26
Tenn — FG Del Greco 30
Sea — FG Peterson 50
Sea — Galloway 7 pass from Kitna (Peterson kick)
Tenn — FG Del Greco 43
Sea — McKnight 55 pass from Kitna (Peterson kick)
Tenn — McNair 3 run (run failed)
Tenn — FG Del Greco 42
Sea — FG Peterson 48

WASHINGTON 29, OAKLAND 19—at Network Associates Coliseum, attendance 41,409. Trent Green passed for 3 touchdowns as the Redskins handed the Raiders their second consecutive defeat. The Redskins led 7-0 and reached the Raiders' 9, but Stephen Alexander fumbled and Louis Riddick recovered in the end zone for a touchback. The Raiders tied the game and reached the Redskins' 16 late in the first quarter, but Harvey Williams fumbled and Derek Smith recovered to thwart the rally. Later in the half, Shawn Barber's interception near midfield set up Green's 43-yard touchdown pass to Leslie Shepherd that was deflected by Marquis Walker. Brian Mitchell's 45-yard punt return led to Cary Blanchard's 28-yard field goal just before halftime to give the Redskins a 17-7 lead. Faced with third-and-4 on their own 8, Donald Hollas, who at halftime replaced an ineffective Jeff George, was sacked in the end zone for a safety, and Green's touchdown pass to Alexander six plays later increased the advantage to 26-7. Green was 16 of 31 for 224 yards and 3 touchdowns. Stephen Davis had 7 receptions for 110 yards. Hollas was 16 of 29 for 134 yards and 2 touchdowns, with 1 interception.

Washington	7	10	2	10	—	29
Oakland	7	0	0	12	—	19

Wash — Davis 19 pass from Green (Blanchard kick)
Oak — Kaufman 23 run (Davis kick)
Wash — Shepherd 43 pass from Green (Blanchard kick)
Wash — FG Blanchard 28
Wash — Safety, Hollas sacked by Boutte in end zone
Wash — Alexander 2 pass from Green (Blanchard kick)
Oak — Mickens 12 pass from Hollas (pass failed)
Wash — FG Blanchard 47
Oak — Brown 2 pass from Hollas (pass failed)

SUNDAY NIGHT, NOVEMBER 29

DENVER 31, SAN DIEGO 16—at Qualcomm Stadium, attendance 66,532. John Elway passed for 4 touchdowns as the Broncos became just the fourth team to open a season with a 12-0 record. Darrien Gordon's 17-yard interception return to the Chargers' 22 led to the first of Elway's 2 touchdown passes to Ed McCaffrey to give Denver a 14-3 lead. With Denver leading 14-10, Gordon recovered Kenny Bynum's fumble at the Broncos' 5 to stifle a Chargers threat. Elway threw 3 interceptions on the Broncos' next three possessions, but the Chargers responded with 2 interceptions, the second by John Mobley, to set up Elway's 13-yard touchdown pass to Rod Smith just before halftime. The Broncos scored on their first two drives of the second half as well, capped by Elway's 18-yard touchdown pass to Shannon Sharpe, to take a 31-10 lead with 14:46 left. Elway was 19 of 34 for 239 yards and 4 touchdowns, with 3 interceptions. Rod Smith had 8 receptions for 101 yards. Whelihan was 30 of 53 for 304 yards and 1 touchdown, with 5 interceptions.

Denver	14	7	7	3	—	31
San Diego	10	0	0	6	—	16

SD — FG Carney 27
Den — McCaffrey 15 pass from Elway (Elam kick)
Den — McCaffrey 37 pass from Elway (Elam kick)
SD — Fletcher 13 run (Carney kick)
Den — Smith 13 pass from Elway (Elam kick)
Den — Sharpe 18 pass from Elway (Elam kick)
Den — FG Elam 34
SD — Still 47 pass from Whelihan (pass failed)

MONDAY NIGHT, NOVEMBER 30

SAN FRANCISCO 31, N.Y. GIANTS 7—at 3Com Park, attendance 68,212. Garrison Hearst rushed for 166 yards and Steve Young passed for 2 touchdowns to help the 49ers win their club-record fifteenth consecutive home game. The Giants scored first, needing just four plays to cover 80 yards, keyed by Kent Graham's 48-yard pass to Ike Hilliard, and capped by Gary Brown's 11-yard run. After Wade Richey missed a 41-yard field goal, Young threw a 79-yard touchdown pass to Terrell Owens to tie the game. Richey missed another field goal, but the 49ers drove 90 yards in 13 plays to take the lead on Irv Smith's touchdown catch 28 seconds before halftime. R.W. McQuarter's 26-yard punt return led to Terry Kirby's 7-yard scoring run midway through the third quarter. Brad Daluiso then missed a 43-yard field-goal attempt and, on the following possession, had a 42-yard attempt blocked by Jeff Bryant. Richey's 39-yard field goal with 10:07 left increased the lead, and Hearst's 70-yard run closed out the scoring. Bryant Young suffered a season-ending injury in the fourth quarter for the 49ers. Steve Young was 19 of 33 for 253 yards and 2 touchdowns. Owens had 5 receptions for 140 yards. Graham was 21 of 41 for 237 yards, with 1 interception. Hilliard had 6 catches for 141 yards.

N.Y. Giants	7	0	0	0	—	7
San Francisco	7	7	7	10	—	31

NYG — Brown 11 run (Daluiso kick)
SF — Owens 79 pass from Young (Richey kick)
SF — Smith 1 pass from Young (Richey kick)
SF — Kirby 7 run (Richey kick)
SF — FG Richey 39
SF — Hearst 70 run (Richey kick)

FOURTEENTH WEEK SUMMARIES

AMERICAN FOOTBALL CONFERENCE

Eastern Division	W	L	T	Pct.	Pts.	OP
N.Y. Jets	9	4	0	.692	347	230
Miami	9	4	0	.692	258	185
Buffalo	8	5	0	.615	301	262
New England	8	5	0	.615	285	245
Indianapolis	2	11	0	.154	229	364
Central Division						
Jacksonville	10	3	0	.769	348	269
Pittsburgh	7	6	0	.538	233	241
Tennessee	7	6	0	.538	276	251
Baltimore	5	8	0	.385	219	263
Cincinnati	2	11	0	.154	217	354
Western Division						
Denver	13	0	0	1.000	436	237
Oakland	7	6	0	.538	226	271
Seattle	6	7	0	.462	286	242
Kansas City	5	8	0	.385	269	294
San Diego	5	8	0	.385	201	271

NATIONAL FOOTBALL CONFERENCE

Eastern Division	W	L	T	Pct.	Pts.	OP
Dallas	8	5	0	.615	328	239
Arizona	6	7	0	.462	270	331
N.Y. Giants	5	8	0	.385	219	276
Washington	4	9	0	.308	264	357
Philadelphia	3	10	0	.231	125	291
Central Division						
Minnesota	12	1	0	.923	442	242
Green Bay	8	5	0	.615	336	264
Tampa Bay	6	7	0	.462	247	272
Detroit	5	8	0	.385	266	300
Chicago	3	10	0	.231	219	323
Western Division						
Atlanta	11	2	0	.846	353	239
San Francisco	10	3	0	.769	385	272
New Orleans	6	7	0	.462	238	268
St. Louis	3	10	0	.231	221	302
Carolina	2	11	0	.154	264	353

THURSDAY, DECEMBER 3

PHILADELPHIA 17, ST. LOUIS 14—at Veterans Stadium, attendance 66,155. Koy Detmer passed for 2 touchdowns as the Eagles spoiled Dick Vermeil's return to the City of Brotherly Love. Vermeil had guided the Eagles to Super Bowl XV following the 1980 season. Michael Zordich's interception at the Rams' 23 set up Detmer's first touchdown pass. The Rams trailed 10-0 before 2 Jeff Wilkins field goals, the second coming with just 17 seconds remaining in the half, to cut the deficit to four points. Detmer's 61-yard touchdown pass to Irving Fryar staked the Eagles to a 17-6 lead, and Chris Boniol lined up for a 46-yard field-goal attempt early in the fourth quarter. However, Kevin Carter blocked the field-goal attempt, and June Henley scored seven plays later to cut the Eagles' lead to 17-14 with 11:04 remaining. Wilkins's game-tying 52-yard field-goal attempt sailed wide left with 4:15 left, but the Rams got the ball back and reached their own 48-yard line with 12 seconds left. On fourth-and-2, Tony Banks completed a pass to J.T. Thomas, who nearly split the secondary before being tackled by Tim McTyer in bounds at the Eagles' 35. The Rams were out of time outs, and the clock expired. Detmer was 17 of 33 for 169 yards and 2 touchdowns, with 1 interception. Banks was 22 of 37 for 255 yards, with 1 interception.

St. Louis	0	6	0	8	—	14
Philadelphia	10	0	7	0	—	17

Phil — Solomon 7 pass from Detmer (Boniol kick)
Phil — FG Boniol 50
StL — FG Wilkins 46
StL — FG Wilkins 20
Phil — Fryar 61 pass from Detmer (Boniol kick)
StL — Henley 1 run (Proehl pass from Banks)

SUNDAY, DECEMBER 6

TENNESSEE 16, BALTIMORE 14—at Vanderbilt Stadium, attendance 31,124. Al Del Greco kicked 3 field goals as the Oilers snapped a two-game losing streak. The Oilers scored on their first three possessions to take a 13-0 halftime lead. The Ravens scored on their second play of the second half to cut the deficit to 13-7. Del Greco added a third field goal with 3:34 remaining, but Jim Harbaugh and Floyd Turner hooked up for the second time to cut the deficit to 16-14 with 1:46 remaining. The Ravens got the ball back at their 18 with 1:18 left, but Steve Jackson thwarted the comeback attempt with an interception at the Oilers' 37. McNair was 25 of 44 for 213 yards, with 1 interception. Harbaugh was 15 of 28 for 214 yards and 2 touchdowns, with 1 interception. Turner had 4 receptions for 108 yards.

Baltimore	0	0	7	7	—	14
Tennessee	10	3	0	3	—	16

Tenn — FG Del Greco 48
Tenn — George 2 run (Del Greco kick)
Tenn — FG Del Greco 48
Balt — Turner 66 pass from Harbaugh (Stover kick)
Tenn — FG Del Greco 33
Balt — Turner 20 pass from Harbaugh (Stover kick)

BUFFALO 33, CINCINNATI 20—at Cinergy Field, attendance 54,359. Eric Moulds had 6 receptions for a career-high 196 yards as the Bills handed the Bengals their eighth consecutive defeat. The Bills took a 10-0 lead after two possessions, but Brian Simmons's interception and 18-yard return to the Bills' 3 set up Neil O'Donnell's touchdown pass to Darnay Scott. O'Donnell and Carl Pickens teamed up less than five minutes later to give the Bengals a 13-10 lead. The Bills scored the game's next 23 points, as Moulds began and ended the run with touchdown catches, the second of which was set up by Sam Cowart's interception at the Bills' 18 to thwart a Bengals drive, to forge a 33-13 lead with 12:12 remaining. Flutie was 18 of 30 for 319 yards and 2 touchdowns, with 3 interceptions. O'Donnell was 19 of 31 for 168 yards and 2 touchdowns, with 1 interception.

Buffalo	10	10	6	7	—	33
Cincinnati	0	13	0	7	—	20

Buff — Smith 1 run (Christie kick)
Buff — FG Christie 20
Cin — Scott 8 pass from O'Donnell (bad snap)
Cin — Pickens 3 pass from O'Donnell (Pelfrey kick)
Buff — Moulds 70 pass from Flutie (Christie kick)
Buff — FG Christie 52
Buff — FG Christie 46
Buff — FG Christie 34
Buff — Moulds 30 pass from Flutie (Christie kick)
Cin — Dillon 3 run (Pelfrey kick)

NEW ORLEANS 22, DALLAS 3—at Louisiana Superdome, attendance 65,065. Kerry Collins passed for 2 touchdowns and the Saints' defense limited the Cowboys to just 8 rushing yards en route to their third consecutive home victory. The game began ominously for the Cowboys when Troy Aikman was pressured into an intentional grounding penalty in the end zone for a safety just 55 seconds into the game. Kevin Mathis's interception at the Saints' 16 late in the quarter, however, did set up Richie Cunningham's 33-yard field goal for the Cowboys' lone lead. The Saints' offense exploded for four consecutive scoring drives, highlighted by Collins's 89-yard touchdown pass to Andre Hastings, and capped by 2 Doug Brien 53-yard field goals, to take a 22-3 lead with 8:41 remaining in the third quarter. The Cowboys tallied just 6 first downs and 82 total yards in their first nine possessions before driving 83 yards but being stopped on downs at the Saints' 2 with 1:59 left in the game. Collins was 16 of 28 for 239 yards and 2 touchdowns, with 1 interception. Hastings had 4 receptions for 122 yards. Aikman was 16 of 32 for 192 yards.

Dallas	3	0	0	0	—	3
New Orleans	2	17	3	0	—	22

NO — Safety, Aikman penalized for intentional grounding in end zone
Dall — FG Cunningham 33
NO — Craver 4 pass from Collins (Brien kick)
NO — Hastings 89 pass from Collins (Brien kick)
NO — FG Brien 53
NO — FG Brien 53

JACKSONVILLE 37, DETROIT 22—at ALLTEL Stadium, attendance 70,717. Reserve Jamie Martin passed for 2 touchdowns and Fred Taylor rushed for 183 yards to give the Jaguars a three-game lead in the AFC Central. Mark Brunell was injured on the opening series, but Martin did not waste any time. His first pass, a 67-yard touchdown strike to Keenan McCardell, came just two plays following Jason Hanson's missed 47-yard field goal. The Jaguars scored on three of their next four possessions to take a 24-6 lead. Charlie Batch's 27-yard scoring pass to Germane Crowell with 35 seconds left in the half, and Hanson's 45-yard boot to cap the second half's opening drive, cut the deficit to 24-16. However, the Jaguars scored on their next three possessions, the second keyed by 2 third-down conversion runs by Taylor and capped by his 11-yard scoring jaunt, en route to victory. Martin was 15 of 23 for 228 yards and 2 touchdowns. Jimmy Smith had 7 catches for 112 yards. Batch was 14 of 33 for 250 yards and 2 touchdowns. Barry Sanders rushed 18 times for 103 yards. Herman Moore had 7 receptions for 116 yards.

Detroit	3	10	3	6	—	22
Jacksonville	14	10	3	10	—	37

Jac — McCardell 67 pass from Martin (Hollis kick)
Jac — Taylor 1 run (Hollis kick)
Det — FG Hanson 34
Jac — FG Hollis 44
Det — FG Hanson 24
Jac — Smith 11 pass from Martin (Hollis kick)
Det — Crowell 27 pass from Batch (Hanson kick)
Det — FG Hanson 45
Jac — FG Hollis 43
Jac — Taylor 11 run (Hollis kick)
Det — Moore 20 pass from Batch (pass failed)
Jac — FG Hollis 30

ATLANTA 28, INDIANAPOLIS 21—at Georgia Dome, attendance 61,141. Chris Chandler passed for 2 touchdowns and ran for another as the Falcons held off the Colts. The Colts jumped out to a 14-0 lead less than ten minutes into the game, but Chandler's 40-yard touchdown pass to Tony Martin five plays later cut the deficit in half. Marshall Faulk's 3-yard touchdown run put the Colts ahead 21-7, but the Falcons scored twice in the final 1:21 of the first half to tie the game. Ray Buchanan intercepted Peyton Manning on the first play of the second half gave Atlanta the ball at the Colts' 14, setting up Chandler's 3-yard touchdown pass to Terance Mathis. Chuck Smith's recovery of Faulk's fumble at the Falcons' 34 early in the fourth quarter stopped Indianapolis' final threat, as Atlanta's offense ran the final 6:33 off the clock. Chandler was 20 of 28 for 297 yards and 2 touchdowns, with 1 interception. Jamal Anderson rushed 30 times for 122 yards, and Martin had 7 catches for 140 yards. Manning was 19 of 27 for 159 yards and 2 touchdowns, with 2 interceptions.

Indianapolis	14	7	0	0	—	21
Atlanta	7	14	7	0	—	28

Ind — Faulk 11 pass from Manning (Vanderjagt kick)
Ind — Small 30 pass from Manning (Vanderjagt kick)
Atl — Martin 40 pass from Chandler (Andersen kick)
Ind — Faulk 3 run (Vanderjagt kick)
Atl — Anderson 1 run (Andersen kick)
Atl — Chandler 3 run (Andersen kick)
Atl — Mathis 3 pass from Chandler (Andersen kick)

DENVER 35, KANSAS CITY 31—at Mile High Stadium, attendance 74,962. John Elway passed for 400 yards and 2 touchdowns, including a 24-yard scoring pass to Shannon Sharpe with 3:34 remaining, to climax the Broncos' comeback and enable their perfect season to continue. The Chiefs scored on three consecutive first-quarter possessions to claim a 21-7 lead. However, the Broncos scored twice and drove to the Chiefs' 14 just before halftime only to have Mark McMillian intercept a pass in the end zone to keep the game tied 21-21 at intermission. The

Broncos were about to take the lead in the third quarter when Terrell Davis fumbled at the Chiefs' 2 and Leslie O'Neal recovered in the end zone for a touchback. The Chiefs responded by scoring on their next two possessions, taking a 31-21 lead on Pete Stoyanovich's 20-yard field goal with 8:25 to play in the game. Vaughn Hebron's 42-yard kickoff return and Willie Green's 50-yard reception set up Davis's third touchdown and, after a punt, the Broncos needed just five plays to navigate the final 50 yards, capped by Sharpe's touchdown catch. The Chiefs drove to the Broncos' 36, but Rich Gannon threw 3 consecutive incompletions before Alfred Williams sacked him on fourth down to secure the victory. Elway was 22 of 32 for 400 yhards and 2 touchdowns, with 1 interception. Rod Smith had 8 catches for 165 yards. Ed McCaffrey had 6 receptions for 103 yards. Gannon was 27 of 43 for 240 yards and 3 touchdowns.

Kansas City	21	0	7	3	—	31
Denver	7	14	0	14	—	35

KC — Rison 26 pass from Gannon (Stoyanovich kick)
KC — Anders 11 pass from Gannon (Stoyanovich kick)
Den — Davis 1 run (Elam kick)
KC — Morris 1 run (Stoyanovich kick)
Den — Davis 1 run (Elam kick)
Den — McCaffrey 13 pass from Elway (Elam kick)
KC — Horn 26 pass from Gannon (Stoyanovich kick)
KC — FG Stoyanovich 20
Den — Davis 1 run (Elam kick)
Den — Sharpe 24 pass from Elway (Elam kick)

MIAMI 27, OAKLAND 17—at Network Associates Coliseum, attendance 61,254. The Dolphins' defense grabbed 6 interceptions and recorded 8 sacks to defeat the Raiders. The Raiders failed to convert two early scoring opportunities, as Greg Davis missed a 48-yard field-goal attempt and, following a blocked punt, Sam Madison intercepted Donald Hollas's pass in the end zone for a touchback. The Dolphins scored 17 points in 1:50. Olindo Mare's field goal was followed three plays later by Zach Thomas's interception of a screen pass and return 1 yard for a touchdown, and Dwight Hollier's fumble recovery on the ensuing kickoff to set up Dan Marino's 19-yard touchdown pass to Oronde Gadsden. Davis converted from 40 yards, but Robert Jones's interception and 14-yard touchdown return just before halftime staked the Dolphins to a 24-3 lead. Marino was 22 of 33 for 170 yards and 1 touchdown. Hollas was 12 of 31 for 152 yards and 1 touchdown, with 6 interceptions. Tim Brown had 9 catches for 104 yards.

Miami	17	7	0	3	—	27
Oakland	0	3	7	7	—	17

Mia — FG Mare 25
Mia — Thomas 1 interception return (Mare kick)
Mia — Gadsden 19 pass from Marino (Mare kick)
Oak — FG Davis 40
Mia — Jones 14 interception return (Mare kick)
Oak — Brown 7 pass from Hollas (Davis kick)
Mia — FG Mare 47
Oak — Brown 2 pass from Wilson (Davis kick)

NEW ENGLAND 23, PITTSBURGH 9—at Three Rivers Stadium, attendance 58,632. The Patriots' defense forced 3 second-half turnovers en route to their third consecutive victory. The Patriots led 6-0 after two possessions and were looking for more points when Levon Kirkland intercepted a pass at the Steelers' 17 to stifle the drive. Drew Bledsoe redeemed himself with an 86-yard touchdown pass later in the quarter. Norm Johnson's 26-yard field goal with seven seconds left in the half cut the deficit to 13-6 at intermission. Chris Oldham's interception early in the second half led to Johnson's third field goal. Ty Law's interception and 10-yard return to the Steelers' 18 set up Vinatieri's third field goal to give the Patriots a 16-9 lead with 12:55 left. Lawyer Milloy recovered Jerome Bettis's fumble two plays later, and Robert Edwards scored from 4 yards with 9:20 left to secure the lead. The Steelers threatened late, but Steve Israel's interception at the Patriots' 6 with 1:51 left iced the game. Bledsoe was 21 of 34 for 327 yards and 1 touchdown, with 3 interceptions. Glenn had 9 receptions for 193 yards. Stewart was 21 of 45 for 206 yards, with 2 interceptions.

New England	3	10	0	10	—	23
Pittsburgh	0	6	3	0	—	9

NE — FG Vinatieri 21
NE — FG Vinatieri 29
Pitt — FG N. Johnson 49
NE — Glenn 86 pass from Bledsoe (Vinatieri kick)
Pitt — FG N. Johnson 26
Pitt — FG N. Johnson 43
NE — FG Vinatieri 35
NE — Edwards 4 run (Vinatieri kick)

N.Y. GIANTS 23, ARIZONA 19—at Sun Devil Stadium, attendance 46,128. The Giants' defense forced 3 turnovers and twice kept the Cardinals from scoring inside their own 10-yard line to pull within one game of Arizona in the NFC East. The Cardinals scored on three consecutive first-half possessions to take a 17-7 lead. Shaun Williams's 9-yard interception return to the Cardinals' 45 with 21 seconds left in the half set up Brad Daluiso's momentum-turning 51-yard field goal as the half expired. The Giants scored on their first two possessions of the second half to take a 20-17 lead. The Cardinals quickly drove to the Giants' 1, but Arizona lost 3 yards on the next two plays and Jeremy Lincoln intercepted Jake Plummer's third-down pass in the end zone for a touchback. Daluiso added a third field goal to increase the lead, but Plummer drove the Cardinals to the Giants' 6, where his fourth-down pass fell incomplete with 1:54 remaining. Brad Maynard took a safety with 17 seconds left to finish the scoring. Kent Graham was 8 of 23 for 144 yards and 1 touchdown, with 2 interceptions. Gary Brown rushed 25 times for 124 yards. Plummer was 18 of 40 for 263 yards and 1 touchdown, with 2 interceptions.

N.Y. Giants	7	3	10	3	—	23
Arizona	14	3	0	2	—	19

Ariz — Murrell 20 pass from Plummer (Jacke kick)
NYG — Barber 87 pass from Graham (Daluiso kick)
Ariz — Murrell 8 run (Jacke kick)
Ariz — FG Jacke 21
NYG — FG Daluiso 51
NYG — FG Daluiso 28
NYG — Way 8 run (Daluiso kick)
NYG — FG Daluiso 45
Ariz — Safety, Maynard ran out of end zone

WASHINGTON 24, SAN DIEGO 20—at Jack Kent Cooke Stadium, attendance 65,713. Leslie Shepherd's 20-yard touchdown catch with 1:54 remaining lifted the Redskins past the Chargers. The Chargers scored on their first three possessions, but were just tied 14-14 because Brian Mitchell returned a kickoff 101 yards for a touchdown following one of the scores. Dan Wilkinson recovered Craig Whelihan's fumble at the Redskins' 39 with 56 seconds left in the half set up Cary Blanchar's 35-yard field goal to give the Redskins a 17-14 halftime lead. John Carney made 2 of 3 second-half field-goal attempts to stake the Chargers to a 20-17 lead with 4:31 left. After an exchange of punts, the Redskins got the ball at the Chargers' 44 with 2:34 remaining. Washington needed just three plays to retake the lead on Trent Green's 20-yard scoring pass to Shepherd, and Leomont Evans's interception at the Chargers' 24 with 44 seconds left secured the victory. Green was 18 of 37 for 235 yards and 2 touchdowns, with 1 interception. Whelihan was 20 of 37 for 212 yards, with 1 interception. Terrell Fletcher rushed 34 times for 122 yards.

San Diego	3	11	3	3	—	20
Washington	7	10	0	7	—	24

SD — FG Carney 32
Wash — Thrash 25 pass from Green (Blanchard kick)
SD — FG Carney 27
Wash — Mitchell 101 kickoff return (Blanchard kick)
SD — F. Jones 23 pass from Fletcher (F. Jones pass from Fletcher)
Wash — FG Blanchard 35
SD — FG Carney 40
SD — FG Carney 25
Wash — Shepherd 20 pass from Green (Blanchard kick)

SAN FRANCISCO 31, CAROLINA 28 (OT)—at Ericsson Stadium, attendance 63,332. Wade Richey's 23-yard field goal in overtime lifted the 49ers into the playoffs for the seventh consecutive season. Each team scored on its first possession, and the 49ers used Terry Kirby's 28-yard halfback option pass to Terrell Owens to score on their second to take a 14-7 lead. The Panthers had a chance to tie in the second quarter, but William Floyd fumbled and Winfred Tubbs recovered at the 49ers' 1. The 49ers took a 28-7 lead on Garrison Hearst's 71-yard touchdown run five plays into the second half. The Panthers scored on three consecutive possessions, with Tim Biakabutuka's 10-yard touchdown run tying the game with 6:20 remaining, and had a chance to win but John Kasay's 47-yard field-goal attempt sailed wide right with 22 seconds left. The Panthers won the overtime coin toss and Floyd returned the kickoff to the Panthers' 36. However, Steve Beuerlein fumbled three plays later and Chris Doleman recovered at the Panthers' 30. Young's 17-yard bootleg set up Richey's winning kick. Young was 19 of 31 for 213 yards and 2 touchdowns, with 1 interception. Hearst carried 20 times for 139 yards. Beuerlein was 18 of 33 for 235 yards and 3 touchdowns, with 1 interception.

San Francisco	7	14	7	0	3	—	31
Carolina	7	0	7	14	0	—	28

Car — Muhammad 12 pass from Beuerlein (Kasay kick)
SF — Stokes 2 pass from Young (Richey kick)
SF — Owens 28 pass from Kirby (Richey kick)
SF — Stokes 33 pass from Young (Richey kick)
SF — Hearst 71 run (Richey kick)
Car — Johnson 38 pass from Beuerlein (Kasay kick)
Car — Ismail 40 pass from Beuerlein (Kasay kick)
Car — Biakabatuka 10 run (Kasay kick)
SF — FG Richey 23

N.Y. JETS 32, SEATTLE 31—at Kingdome, attendance 72,200. Vinny Testaverde scored on a 5-yard touchdown run with 20 seconds remaining to lift the Jets to victory. Joey Galloway had touchdown catches of 57 and 70 yards within a three-minute span to take a 14-7 lead. Chad Brown's recovery of Kyle Brady's fumble near midfield set up Ricky Watters's 39-yard touchdown run and Anthony Simmons's 36-yard interception return for a touchdown less than two minutes into the second half gave the Seahawks a 28-13 lead. The Jets put together touchdown drives of 65 and 76 yards, sandwiched around a Todd Peterson 50-yard field goal, to cut the deficit to 31-26 with 12:22 remaining. The Jets reached the Seahawks' 20, but Testaverde's fourth-and-9 pass to Dedric Ward netted just 5 yards with 4:55 left. The Jets' defense held Watters to 1 yard on third-and-2 to force another punt, and the Jets reached the Seahawks' 5 with 30 seconds left. Faced with a fourth-and-goal situation, Testaverde attempted a quarterback sneak, and was awarded a touchdown after the officials consulted. Testaverde was 42 of 63 for 418 yards and 2 touchdowns, with 1 interception. Keyshawn Johnson had 9 receptions for 114 yards. Kitna was 17 of 24 for 278 yards and 2 touchdowns, with 2 interceptions.

Seattle	14	7	10	0	—	31
N.Y. Jets	7	6	6	13	—	32

NYJ — Byars 3 pass from Testaverde (Hall kick)
Sea — Galloway 70 pass from Kitna (Peterson kick)
Sea — Galloway 57 pass from Kitna (Peterson kick)
NYJ — FG Hall 20
Sea — Watters 39 run (Peterson kick)
NYJ — FG Hall 20
Sea — Simmons 36 interception return (Peterson kick)
NYJ — Martin 1 run (pass failed)
Sea — FG Peterson 50
NYJ — K. Johnson 16 pass from Testaverde (Hall kick)
NYJ — Testaverde 5 run (run failed)

SUNDAY NIGHT, DECEMBER 6

MINNESOTA 48, CHICAGO 22—at Hubert H. Humphrey Metrodome, attendance 64,247. Randall Cunningham passed for 4 touchdowns, including 3 to Randy Moss, as the Vikings clinched the NFC Central Division title. The Vikings' defense limited the Bears to just 14 yards on 20 first-half plays. Meanwhile, the Vikings offense scored on five of their six first-half possessions en route to a 27-0 lead. All three touchdown drives were in excess of 75 yards. Trailing 34-7 in the third quarter, the Bears reached the Vikings' 10 on five of their last six possessions, but were scored just twice. The key turnover was when Dwyane Rudd scooped up Steve Stenstrom's fumble and raced 94 yards for a touchdown to give Minnesota 48-14 lead with 5:46 remaining. Cunningham was 21 of 31 for 349 yards and 4 touchdowns, with 1 interception. Moss had 8 receptions for 106 yards. Stenstrom was 25 of 42 for 303 yards and 1 touchdown, with 1 interception. Bobby Engram had 9 catches for 140 yards.

Chicago	0	0	14	8	—	22
Minnesota	14	13	7	14	—	48

Minn — Moss 6 pass from Cunningham (Anderson kick)
Minn — Hoard 24 pass from Cunningham (Anderson kick)
Minn — FG Anderson 30
Minn — FG Anderson 20
Minn — Moss 3 pass from Cunningham (Anderson kick)
Chi — Engram 47 pass from Stenstrom (Jaeger kick)
Minn — Moss 34 pass from Cunningham (Anderson kick)
Chi — Bennett 5 run (Jaeger kick)
Minn — Hoard 8 run (Anderson kick)
Minn — Rudd 94 fumble return (Anderson kick)
Chi — Stenstrom 4 run (Penn pass from Stenstrom)

MONDAY NIGHT, DECEMBER 7

TAMPA BAY 24, GREEN BAY 22—at Raymond James Stadium, attendance 65,497. Trent Dilfer passed for 2 touchdowns and ran for another as the Buccaneers snapped a six-game losing streak to the Packers. Trailing 3-0, Dilfer completed nearly identical touchdown passes to Bert Emanuel and Jacquez Green on consecutive possessions to stake Tampa Bay to a 14-3 lead. Tyrone Williams's interception late in the third quarter set up Ryan Longwell's third field goal and cut the deficit to 17-9. and Brett Favre tossed a 4-yard touchdown pass to Mark Chmura. However, Favre's 2-point conversion pass fell incomplete, denying the Packers a chance to tie the game. The Packers once again forced a punt, but Derrick Mayes fumbled and Donnie Abraham recovered at the Buccaneers' 47. Dilfer scored eleven plays later to give Tampa Bay a 24-15 lead with 6:01 left. The Packers responded with an 80-yard drive to cut the deficit to two points with 2:20 left, and the Packers got the ball back for one last attempt, but Warren Sapp and Brad Culpepper sacked Favre as time expired. Dilfer was 9 of 22 for 181 yards and 2 touchdowns, with 1 interception. Favre was 29 of 41 for 262 yards and 2 touchdowns.

Green Bay	3	3	3	13	—	22
Tampa Bay	7	7	3	7	—	24

GB — FG Longwell 33
TB — Green 64 pass from Dilfer (Husted kick)
TB — Emanuel 62 pass from Dilfer (Husted kick)
GB — FG Longwell 36
TB — FG Husted 46
GB — FG Longwell 35
GB — Chmura 4 pass from Favre (pass failed)
TB — Dilfer 6 run (Husted kick)
GB — Chmura 1 pass from Favre (Longwell kick)

FIFTEENTH WEEK SUMMARIES

AMERICAN FOOTBALL CONFERENCE

Eastern Division	W	L	T	Pct.	Pts.	OP
N.Y. Jets	10	4	0	.714	368	246
Buffalo	9	5	0	.643	345	283
Miami	9	5	0	.643	274	206
New England	8	6	0	.571	303	277
Indianapolis	3	11	0	.154	268	390
Central Division						
Jacksonville	10	4	0	.714	361	285
Tennessee	8	6	0	.571	292	264
Pittsburgh	7	7	0	.500	236	257
Baltimore	5	9	0	.357	247	301
Cincinnati	2	12	0	.143	243	393
Western Division						
Denver	13	1	0	.929	452	257
Seattle	7	7	0	.500	324	259
Oakland	7	7	0	.500	247	315
Kansas City	6	8	0	.429	289	311
San Diego	5	9	0	.357	218	309

NATIONAL FOOTBALL CONFERENCE

Eastern Division	W	L	T	Pct.	Pts.	OP
Dallas	8	6	0	.571	345	259
Arizona	7	7	0	.500	290	348
N.Y. Giants	6	8	0	.429	239	292
Washington	5	9	0	.357	292	382
Philadelphia	3	11	0	.154	142	311
Central Division						
Minnesota	13	1	0	.929	480	270
Green Bay	9	5	0	.643	362	284
Tampa Bay	7	7	0	.500	263	275
Detroit	5	9	0	.357	279	335
Chicago	3	11	0	.154	239	349
Western Division						
Atlanta	12	2	0	.857	382	256
San Francisco	11	3	0	.786	420	285
New Orleans	6	8	0	.429	255	295
St. Louis	4	10	0	.286	253	320
Carolina	2	12	0	.143	289	381

SUNDAY, DECEMBER 13

ARIZONA 20, PHILADELPHIA 17 (OT)—at Veterans Stadium, attendance 62,176. Chris Jacke's 32-yard field goal in overtime lifted the Cardinals back to the .500 mark. Tommy Bennett's 70-yard interception return for a touchdown staked the Cardinals to an early 10-0 lead. After Duce Staley's 30-yard scoring run ct the deficit to 10-7, the Cardinals were about to score again. However, Adrian Murrell fumbled and James Willis recovered at the Eagles' 7. Philadelphia drove 92 yards in 12 plays, tying the game with Chris Boniol's field goal with one second left in the half. The Cardinals threatened twice on their first two second-half possessions, but Mario Bates was stopped on fourth-and-1 from the Eagles' 11 and Troy Vincent intercepted a Jake Plummer pass at the Eagles' 15. Irving Fryar's over-the-shoulder 26-yard touchdown catch on a post-pattern with 12:58 remaining in the game forged the Eagles in front for the first time. The Cardinals responded with a 10-play scoring drive to tie the game with 8:14 left. Each team had golden opportunities to win the game in the final three minutes of regulation, but Boniol pushed a 33-yard field-goal attempt wide right with 2:29 remaining and Jacke missed a 34-yard field-goal attempt with seven seconds left to force overtime. The Cardinals won the toss and drove downfield on the strength of 30 and 16-yard catches by Rob Moore to set up Jacke's winning 32-yard field goal.

Arizona	10	0	0	7	3	—	20
Philadelphia	0	10	0	7	0	—	17

Ariz — FG Jacke 28
Ariz — Bennett 70 interception return (Jacke kick)
Phil — Staley 30 run (Boniol kick)
Phil — FG Boniol 19
Phil — Fryar 26 pass from Detmer (Boniol kick)
Ariz — Moore 9 pass from Plummer (Jacke kick)
Ariz — FG Jacke 32

ATLANTA 27, NEW ORLEANS 17—at Louisiana Superdome, attendance 61,678. Chris Chandler and Terance Mathis hooked up for 2 touchdowns as the Falcons won their seventh consecutive game. The Saints reached the Falcons' 35 on their opening possession, but Kerry Collins fumbled and Eugene Robinson recovered. Bob Christian pierced the goal line five plays later to put Atlanta ahead, and Chandler's 62-yard touchdown pass to Mathis on the ensuing possession staked the Falcons to a quick 14-0 lead. The Saints' defense scored twice, on Fred Weary's 63-yard interception return and Mark Fields's 36-yard fumble return, in a six minute stretch spanning halftime to cut the Falcons' lead to 17-14 early in the third quarter. Doug Brien's 36-yard field goal cut the Atlanta lead to three points with 8:34 remaining, but Mathis and Chandler hooked up for a similar slant pass, this time covering 63 yards, to stretch Atlanta's lead to 27-17. The Saints reached the Falcons' 29, but Billy Joe Tolliver's fourth-down pass fell incomplete to dash the Saints' hopes. Chandler was 19 of 28 for 345 yards and 2 touchdowns, with 2 interceptions. Mathis had 6 catches for 198 yards, while Tony Martin had 8 receptions for 109 yards. Jamal Anderson rushed 27 times for 148 yards. Collins was 6 of 14 for 87 yards, with 3 interceptions. Tolliver was 12 of 23 for 82 yards in a relief role.

Atlanta	14	3	0	10	—	27
New Orleans	0	7	7	3	—	17

Atl — Christian 1 run (Andersen kick)
Atl — Mathis 62 pass from Chandler (Andersen kick)
NO — Weary 63 interception return (Brien kick)
Atl — FG Andersen 49
NO — Fields 36 fumble return (Brien kick)
Atl — FG Andersen 33
NO — FG Brien 36
Atl — Mathis 63 pass from Chandler (Andersen kick)

GREEN BAY 26, CHICAGO 20—at Lambeau Field, attendance 59,813. Brett Favre passed for 2 touchdowns as the Packers defeated the Bears for the ninth consecutive time. Edgar Bennett's 43-yard run against his former team set up Steve Stenstrom's quarterback sneak to give the Bears a quick 7-0 lead. The Packers' defense limited the Bears to just 58 yards on their next six possessions, but the Bears took a 13-9 lead on Walt Harris's 13-yard interception return for a touchdown early in the third quarter. Favre guided the Packers on scoring drives of 67, 71, and 64 yards on their next three possessions to take a 26-13 lead with 3:57 to play. Glyn Milburn returned the ensuing kickoff 94 yards for a touchdown to cut the deficit to seven points, and the Bears got the ball back and reached the Packers' 25 with 1:05 remaining. However, Stenstrom was sacked on three consecutive plays to end the Bears' hope of an upset. Favre was 26 of 42 for 290 yards and 2 touchdowns, with 2 interceptions. Antonio Freeman had 8 receptions for 103 yards, and Dorsey Levens rushed 15 times for 105 yards. Stenstrom was 16 of 28 for 126 yards.

Chicago	7	6	0	7	—	20
Green Bay	3	6	7	10	—	26

Chi — Stenstrom 1 run (Jaeger kick)
GB — FG Longwell 35
GB — FG Longwell 43
GB — FG Longwell 40
Chi — Harris 13 interception return (pass failed)
GB — Chmura 6 pas from Favre (Longwell kick)
GB — Freeman 13 pass from Favre (Longwell kick)
GB — FG Longwell 24
Chi — Milburn 94 kickoff return (Jaeger kick)

INDIANAPOLIS 39, CINCINNATI 26—at RCA Dome, attendance 55,179. Peyton Manning passed for 3 touchdowns and Marshall Faulk rushed for 115 yards and 2 scores as the Colts handed the Bengals their ninth consecutive defeat. Aaron Bailey set up the Colts' first two scores with 18- and 33-yard punt returns, and touchdown drives of 81 and 62 yards in the second quarter staked the Colts to a 24-6 halftime lead. Cincinnati trailed 31-12 early in the fourth quarter when Corey Dillon was stopped for no gain on fourth-and-1 from the Bengals' 31, and Manning completed his third touchdown pass moments later to secure the victory. Manning was 17 of 26 for 210 yards and 3 touchdowns. Jeff Blake was 16 of 29 for 180 yards and 1 touchdown.

Cincinnati	3	3	6	14	—	26
Indianapolis	10	14	7	8	—	39

Ind — Faulk 16 run (Vanderjagt kick)
Ind — FG Vanderjagt 50
Cin — FG Pelfrey 41
Ind — Faulk 1 run (Vanderjagt kick)
Cin — FG Pelfrey 26
Ind — Green 11 pass from Manning (Vanderjagt kick)
Cin — Pickens 6 pass from Blake (pass failed)
Ind — Small 16 pass from Manning (Vanderjagt kick)
Ind — Small 16 pass from Manning (Pollard pass from Manning)
Cin — Bennett 5 run (Pelfrey kick)
Cin — St. Williams 19 pass from Kresser (Pelfrey kick)

KANSAS CITY 20, DALLAS 17—at Arrowhead Stadium, attendance 77,697. Byron (Bam) Morris rushed for 137 yrads and 1 touchdown as the Chiefs denied the Cowboys the opportunity to clinch the NFC East title. With the score tied 3-3 in the third quarter, Greg Manusky recovered Tyrone Hughes's fumbled punt at midfield. Morris scored eleven plays later to give the Chiefs a 10-3 lead. James Hasty then intercepted a Troy Aikman pass on the Cowboys' next play from scrimmage, setting up Rich Gannon's 9-yard touchdown run to put the Chiefs ahead 17-10 late in the third quarter. Aikman threw touchdown passes on the Cowboys' next two possessions, but Pete Stoyanovich added a 43-yard field goal in between Dallas' points, to hold a 20-17 lead with 2:48 left. The Cowboys eschewed the onside kick, and Morris had a 17-yard run on third-and-3 with 1:48 remaining to secure the victory. Gannon was 19 of 41 for 200 yards. Aikman was 18 of 35 for 199 yards and 2 touchdowns, with 1 interception.

Dallas	0	3	0	14	—	17
Kansas City	3	0	14	3	—	20

KC — FG Stoyanovich 24
Dall — FG Cunningham 32
KC — Morris 1 run (Stoyanovich kick)
KC — Gannon 9 run (Stoyanovich kick)
Dall — Jeffers 28 pass from Aikman (Cunningham kick)
KC — FG Stoyanovich 43
Dall — Smith 8 pass from Aikman (Cunningham kick)

N.Y. GIANTS 20, DENVER 16—at Giants Stadium, attendance 72,336. Kent Graham completed a 37-yard touchdown pass to Amani Toomer with 48 seconds remaining to hand the Broncos their first defeat of the season. Graham's 21-yard touchdown pass to Tiki Barber just 45 seconds before halftime capped a 15-play, 80-yard drive and gave the Giants a 10-6 lead at intermission. Denver trailed 10-9 early in the fourth quarter when Shaun Williams's interception at the Giants' 37 stopped the Broncos and led to Brad Daluiso's 19-yard field goal with 7:36 remaining in the game. Typical of their perfect season, the Broncos drove 76 yards to promptly take a 16-13 lead on Terrell Davis's 27-yard run with 4:08 left. Graham's 36-yard pass to Chris Calloway put the Giants back into Denver territory, but Gary Brown fumbled on the next play. Bill Romanowski recovered with 3:36 left, but Howard Griffith was dropped for a 5-yard loss on third-and-3 with 2:00 remaining, forcing Tom Rouen to punt. Rouen's 51-yard punt pinned the Giants back to their own 14, but Graham scrambled for 23 yards and later completed a third-down pass to Joe Jurevicius for a first down with 57 seconds left. On the next play, Graham lofted a pass to the back of the end zone, where a streaking Toomer clutched the ball. The Broncos reached the Giants' 30 with five seconds left, but Elway's Hail Mary pass fell incomplete as time expired. Graham was 21 of 33 for 265 yards and 2 touchdowns. Brown rushed 18 times for 112 yards. Elway was 19 of 36 for 180 yards, with 1 interception. Davis rushed 28 times for 147 yards.

Denver	3	3	3	7	—	16
N.Y. Giants	3	7	0	10	—	20

Den — FG Elam 24
NYG — FG Daluiso 36
Den — FG Elam 38
NYG — Barber 21 pass from Graham (Daluiso kick)
Den — FG Elam 30
NYG — FG Daluiso 19
Den — Davis 27 run (Elam kick)
NYG — Toomer 37 pass from Graham (Daluiso kick)

MINNESOTA 38, BALTIMORE 28—at NFL Stadium at Camden Yards, attendance 69,074. Gary Anderson kicked 6 field goals in the game, and set an NFL record with 36 consecutive field goals, as the Vikings won their sixth successive game. Corey Harris and Patrick Johnson each returned a kickoff for a touchdown following each of Anderson's first 2 field goals to give Baltimore a 14-6 lead. Following Johnson's score, David Palmer returned the ensuing kickoff 88 yards for a touchdown. The three returns in one game set an NFL record. Anderson added 2 more field goals in the second quarter as the Vikings took a 25-14 halftime lead. The Ravens committed turnovers on their first two plays of the second half, a fumble recovery by Ed McDaniel at the Ravens' 27 and Corey Fuller's interception at the Ravens' 28, to give Minnesota 10 quick points and a 35-14 lead. The Ravens scored on each of their last two possessions, but Chris Walsh recovered the onside kick with 2:06 left to secure the victory. Cunningham was 32 of 55 for 345 yards and 2 touchdowns, with 1 interception. Cris Carter had 11 receptions for 85 yards. Jim Harbaugh was 16 of 26 for 212 yards and 1 touchdown, with 1 interception. Floyd Turner had 10 catches for 147 yards.

Minnesota	12	13	10	3	—	38
Baltimore	14	0	0	14	—	28

Minn — FG Anderson 43
Balt — Harris 95 kickoff return (Stover kick)
Minn — FG Anderson 31
Balt — Johnson 97 kickoff return (Stover kick)
Minn — Palmer 88 kickoff return (pass failed)
Minn — FG Anderson 45
Minn — Moss 17 pass from Cunningham (Anderson kick)
Minn — FG Anderson 24
Minn — FG Anderson 46
Minn — Carter 11 pass from Cunningham (Anderson kick)
Balt — Turner 42 pass from Harbaugh (bad snap)
Minn — FG Anderson 20
Balt — Holmes 2 run (Turner pass from Harbaugh)

ST. LOUIS 32, NEW ENGLAND 18—at Trans World Dome, attendance 48,946. Az-Zahir Hakim and June Henly each scored 2 touchdowns as the Rams snapped a four-game losing streak. The Rams scored on their first two possessions, but were stopped on downs in Patriots' territory each of the next two possessions. Robert Edwards had rushes of 53 and 36 yards to set up 2 Adam Vinatieri field goals, but Henley's first touchdown stretched the Rams lead to 17-6. Two turnovers by Steve Bono in the final three minutes of the half, a fumble and interception, led to 9 New England points and cut the deficit to 17-15 at halftime. Adam Vinatieri capped a 13-play, 79-yard drive to open the second half with a field goal to give New England its first lead. The Rams responded with touchdowns on each of their next two possessions, and the Patriots' were stopped on downs at the Rams' 6 with 4:33 remaining in the game to ice the victory for St. Louis. Bono was 11 of 22 for 122 yards, with 1 interception. Bledsoe was 11 of 35 for 176 yards and 1 touchdown, with 1 interception.

New England	3	12	3	0	—	18
St. Louis	10	7	15	0	—	32

StL — FG Wilkins 48
StL — Hakim 9 pass from Banks (Wilkins kick)
NE — FG Vinatieri 37
NE — FG Vinatieri 41
StL — Henley 1 run (Wilkins kick)
NE — Purnell 16 pass from Bledsoe (pass failed)
NE — FG Vinatieri 55
NE — FG Vinatieri 17
StL — Hakim 34 run (Bono run)
StL — Henley 1 run (Wilkins kick)

BUFFALO 44, OAKLAND 21—at Rich Stadium, attendance 62,002. The Bills scored on six successive possessions to hand the Raiders their first consecutive defeat. Kevin Williams's 73-yard punt return set up Doug Flutie's 2-yard touchdown pass to Lonnie Johnson to stake the Bills to a 17-0 lead. The Raiders responded with a 12-play, 65-yard drive capped by Wade Wilson's 18-yard touchdown pass to Rickey Dudley, but Williams's 29-yard kickoff return set up Steve Christie's field goal in the half's waning seconds to give Buffalo a 21-7 lead. Buffalo scored 3 times in a 3:18 stretch of the third quarter, the second set up by Phil Hansen's fumble recovery at the Raiders' 19 and the third tallybeing posted on the board by Hansen's 13-yard fumble return moments later, to take a 37-7 lead. Flutie was 17 of 26 for 184 yards and 2 touchdowns. Wilson was 16 of 26 for 131 yards and 2 touchdowns, with 2 interceptions.

Oakland	0	7	7	7	—	21
Buffalo	3	17	17	7	—	44

Buff — FG Christie 32
Buff — Riemersma 13 pass from Flutie (Christie kick)
Buff — L. Johnson 2 pass from Flutie (Christie kick)
Oak — Dudley 18 pass from Wilson (Davis kick)
Buff — FG Christie 49
Buff — Smith 5 run (Christie kick)
Buff — FG Christie 32
Buff — Hansen 13 fumble return (Christie kick)
Oak — Howard 75 punt return (Christie kick)
Buff — Northern 40 interception return (Christie kick)
Oak — Brown 30 pass from Wilson (Davis kick)

TAMPA BAY 16, PITTSBURGH 3—at Raymond James Stadium, attendance 65,335. Michael Husted kicked 3 field goals and the Buccaneers' defense forced 5 second-half turnovers en route to their third consecutive victory. The Steelers drove 66 yards with the opening kickoff and scored when Norm Johnson's 27-yard field goal sailed through the uprights. Then the Buccaneers' defense stiffened, allowing the Steelers to cross midfield once in their last eleven possessions. The Buccaneers led 6-3 in the third quarter when Warren Sapp recovered Mike Tomczak's fumble at the Steelers' 7. Mike Alstott scored two plays later to give Tampa Bay a 13-3 lead, and Husted's third field goal with 1:57 remaining closed out the scoring. Dilfer was 9 of 18 for 111 yards. Stewart was 9 of 21 for 88 yards, with 3 interceptions.

Pittsburgh	3	0	0	0	—	3
Tampa Bay	3	3	7	3	—	16

Pitt — FG N. Johnson 27
TB — FG Husted 39
TB — FG Husted 37
TB — Alstott 3 run (Husted kick)
TB — FG Husted 21

SEATTLE 38, SAN DIEGO 17—at Kingdome, attendance 62,690. The Seahawks intercepted a club-record 7 passes, and set an NFL record with their eleventh and twelfth return touchdowns of the season en route to defeating the Chargers. Trailing 7-0, Jamal Williams intercepted a Jon Kitna pass and returned it 14 yards for the tying touchdown. Terry McDaniel's 43-yard interception return for a score allowed the Seahawks to retake the lead late in the first quarter. Darryl Williams's interception at the Chargers' 27 set up Ricky Watters's 1-yard run, but Norman Hand's 30-yard interception return led to Terrell Fletcher's 1-yard scoring run just before halftime to cut the deficit to 21-14. Darryl Williams's second interception led to Joey Galloway's 9-yard scoring catch, but John Carney kicked a field goal and Greg Jackson intercepted a Kitna pass to give the Chargers the ball at their 47 down 28-17. However, Ryan Leaf, who had replaced Craig Whelihan, fumbled and Cortez Kennedy returned the ball 39 yards for a touchdown to give Seattle a 35-17 lead. Kitna was 16 of 31 for 140 yards and 1 touchdown, with 3 interceptions. Whelihan was 8 of 28 for 142 yards, with 5 interceptions. Leaf was 9 of 14 for 93 yards, with 2 interceptions.

San Diego	7	7	0	3	—	17
Seattle	14	7	7	10	—	38

Sea — Kitna 2 run (Peterson kick)
SD — Williams 14 interception return (Carney kick)
Sea — McDaniel 43 interception return (Peterson kick)
Sea — Watters 1 run (Peterson kick)
SD — Fletcher 1 run (Carney kick)
Sea — Galloway 9 pass from Kitna (Peterson kick)
SD — FG Carney 21
Sea — Kennedy 39 fumble return (Peterson kick)
Sea — FG Peterson 29

TENNESSEE 16, JACKSONVILLE 13—at ALLTEL Stadium, attendance 65,657. Al Del Greco's 41-yard field goal with four seconds remaining to keep the Oilers' playoff hopes alive. The Jaguars scored twice in a 1:07 span of the first quarter, the second score set up by Bryan Schwartz's fumble recovery at the Oilers' 22, to take a quick 10-0 lead. The Oilers' defense permitted just 1 first down during the Jaguars' next five possessions and Tennessee's offense put together scoring drives of 55 and 32 yards to tie the game. Darryll Lewis thwarted a Jaguars' drive late in the third quarter with an interception in the end zone for a touchback. The teams then exchanged field goals and punts, giving the Oilers the ball at their own 24 in a tied game with 2:19 remaining. Steve McNair completed 3 short passes and scrambled twice, including a 12-yard run to the Jaguars' 28, to set up Del Greco's winning boot. McNair was 22 of 39 for 232 yards and 1 touchdown, with 1 interception. Jamie Martin started for the injured Mark Brunell and was 6 of 11 for 71 yards before being injured. His replacement, Jonathan Quinn, was 12 of 18 for 107 yards, with 1 interception.

	1	2	3	4		Final
Tennessee	0	10	0	6	—	16
Jacksonville	10	0	0	3	—	13

Jac — FG Hollis 21
Jac — Taylor 1 run (Hollis kick)
Tenn — Harris 4 pass from McNair (Del Greco kick)
Tenn — FG Del Greco 28
Tenn — FG Del Greco 30
Jac — FG Hollis 29
Tenn — FG Del Greco 41

WASHINGTON 28, CAROLINA 25—at Ericsson Stadium, attendance 46,940. Trent Green passed for 2 touchdowns and Skip Hicks scored twice as the Redskins held off the Panthers. The Panthers loss was their ninth defeat by seven or fewer points, tying an NFL record. The Redskins scored on their first possession, and Muhsin Muhammad appeared ready to tie the game two plays later when he caught a long pass and raced towards the end zone. Cris Dishman knocked the ball away from Muhammad at the Redskins' 5 and it rolled through the end zone for a touchback. The Redskins scored on their next two drives to take a 21-3 lead. Trailing 21-10 late in the half, Michael Bates blocked Matt Turk's punt and Dwight Stone recovered in the end zone for a touchdown to finish the scoring of a wild first half. Green drove the Redskins 82 yards on their first possession of the second half to claim a 28-17 lead, but Tim Biakabutuka's 2-yard run and Beuerlein's 2-point conversion pass to Muhammad cut the deficit to 28-25 with 12:38 left. The Panthers were driving for the tie or lead when Stanley Richard intercepted Beuerlein's pass at the Redskins' 8 with 3:16 to play. Carolina got the ball for one more chance, but Darrell Green intercepted Beuerlein at the Redskins' 41 to secure the victory. Trent Green was 23 of 42 for 257 yards and 2 touchdowns. Albert Connell had 8 receptions for 116 yards. Beuerlein was 16 of 25 for 264 yards and 1 touchdown, with 2 interceptions. Muhammad had 7 receptions for 118 yards, while Biakabutuka rushed 17 times for 103 yards.

	1	2	3	4		Final
Washington	14	7	7	0	—	28
Carolina	3	14	0	8	—	25

Wash — Connell 16 pass from Green (Blanchard kick)
Wash — Hicks 4 run (Blanchard kick)
Car — FG Kasay 26
Wash — Hicks 5 run (Blanchard kick)
Car — Biakabutuka 29 pass from Beuerlein (Kasay kick)
Car — Stone recovered blocked punt in end zone (Kasay kick)
Wash — Alexander 17 pass from Green (Blanchard kick)
Car — Biakabutuka 2 run (Muhammad pass from Beuerlein)

SUNDAY NIGHT, DECEMBER 13

N.Y. JETS 21, MIAMI 16—at Pro Player Stadium, attendance 74,369. Vinny Testaverde passed for 232 yards and 1 touchdown as the Jets positioned themselves for a great chance to win their first-ever AFC East title. The Jets put together three sustained drives in the first three quarters, getting 2 touchdowns and 1 missed field goal out of the opportunities. Miami recorded 10 first downs on its first eight possessions, 5 of which came on a late first-quarter drive to set up Olindo Mare's 24-yard field goal. Leading 14-3 with 9:25 remaining, the Jets reached the Dolphins' 6 and were about to put the game away. Terrell Buckley thwarted the Jets' plans by intercepting Testaverde's pass and returning it 61 yards. Dan Marino threw a 3-yard touchdown pass to O.J. McDuffie five plays later, and suddenly the Dolphins trailed just 14-10 with 6:25 remaining in the game. Buckley forced Curtis Martin to fumble and Trace Armstrong recovered at the Dolphins' 30 to thwart another Jets' drive, but Chad Cascadden sacked Marino, forced him to fumble, and scurried 23 yards for a touchdown with 1:51 left. The Dolphins scored with three seconds left, but Leon Johnson recovered the onside kick to ice the game. Testaverde was 17 of 29 for 232 yards and 1 touchdown, with 1 interception. Wayne Chrebet had 5 receptions for 105 yards. Marino was 30 of 57 for 321 yards and 1 touchdown, with 1 interception. McDuffie had 11 receptions for 105 yards.

	1	2	3	4		Final
N.Y. Jets	7	0	7	7	—	21
Miami	3	0	0	13	—	16

Mia — FG Mare 24
NYJ — Chrebet 12 pass from Testaverde (Hall kick)
NYJ — Martin 9 run (Hall kick)
Mia — McDuffie 3 pass from Marino (Mare kick)
NYJ — Cascadden 23 fumble return (Hall kick)
Mia — Pritchett 1 run (pass failed)

MONDAY NIGHT, DECEMBER 14

SAN FRANCISCO 35, DETROIT 13—at 3Com Park, attendance 68,585. Garrison Hearst rushed for a club-record 198 yards and the 49ers rushed for a club-record 328 yards to wear down and defeat the Lions. The 49ers drove 80 and 73 yards to take a 14-0 lead, but the Lions drove to the 49ers' 1. However, Frank Reich threw consecutive incompletions on third and fourth down. The 49ers then drove the length of the field, capped by Steve Young's 1-yard touchdown pass to Terrell Owens, to take a 21-0 lead with 1:06 left. The Lions once again reached the 49ers' 1, but Merton Hanks intercepted Reich's pass in the end zone for a touchback with ten seconds left in the half. The 49ers drove 70 yards for a touchdown on their first possession of the second half to take a commanding 28-0 lead. Young was 12 of 18 for 82 yards and 1 touchdown, with 1 interception. Reich was 18 of 35 for 281 yards and 2 touchdowns, with 2 interceptions.

	1	2	3	4		Final
Detroit	0	0	0	13	—	13
San Francisco	7	14	7	7	—	35

SF — Hearst 5 run (Richey kick)
SF — Kirby 1 run (Richey kick)
SF — Owens 1 pass from Young (Richey kick)
SF — Young 9 run (Richey kick)
Det — Moore 24 pass from Reich (kick blocked)
SF — Kirby 31 run (Richey kick)
Det — Sloan 3 pass from Reich (Hanson kick)

SIXTEENTH WEEK SUMMARIES

AMERICAN FOOTBALL CONFERENCE

Eastern Division	W	L	T	Pct.	Pts.	OP
N.Y. Jets	11	4	0	.733	385	256
Miami	10	5	0	.667	305	227
Buffalo	9	6	0	.600	355	300
New England	9	6	0	.600	327	298
Indianapolis	3	12	0	.200	291	417
Central Division						
Jacksonville	10	5	0	.667	371	335
Tennessee	8	7	0	.533	314	294
Pittsburgh	7	8	0	.467	260	282
Baltimore	5	10	0	.333	250	325
Cincinnati	3	12	0	.200	268	417
Western Division						
Denver	13	2	0	.867	473	288
Seattle	8	7	0	.533	351	282
Oakland	8	7	0	.533	264	325
Kansas City	6	9	0	.400	296	339
San Diego	5	10	0	.333	228	326

NATIONAL FOOTBALL CONFERENCE

Eastern Division	W	L	T	Pct.	Pts.	OP
Dallas	9	6	0	.600	358	268
Arizona	8	7	0	.533	309	365
N.Y. Giants	7	8	0	.467	267	299
Washington	6	9	0	.400	312	398
Philadelphia	3	12	0	.200	151	324
Central Division						
Minnesota	14	1	0	.933	530	280
Green Bay	10	5	0	.667	392	306
Tampa Bay	7	8	0	.467	279	295
Detroit	5	10	0	.333	296	359
Chicago	4	11	0	.267	263	352
Western Division						
Atlanta	13	2	0	.867	404	273
San Francisco	11	4	0	.733	441	309
New Orleans	6	9	0	.400	272	314
St. Louis	4	11	0	.267	266	340
Carolina	3	12	0	.200	309	394

SATURDAY, DECEMBER 19

N.Y. JETS 17, BUFFALO 10—at Rich Stadium, attendance 79,056. Vinny Testaverde threw 2 touchdown passes as the Jets won their first AFC Eastern Division title. Wayne Chrebet's 7-yard touchdown catch capped the Jets' first possession, but it was the Jets only drive of the half beyond the Bills' 45. Buffalo drove into Jets' territory during five of its six first-half possessions, but a fumble, punt, being stopped on downs, and a missed field goal thwarted the Bills' efforts. Only Doug Flutie's 25-yard touchdown pass to Thurman Thomas put the Bills on the board to tie the game 7-7. Each team's opening drive of the second half ended with a field goal, but Testaverde quickly broke the 10-10 tie with a 71-yard touchdown pass to Dedric Ward. Victor Green's diving interception at the Jets' 17 ended Buffalo's best fourth-quarter threat, and Testaverde connected for 7 yards on a third-and-6 pass with Keyshawn Johnson with 41 seconds left to ice the game. Testaverde was 14 of 23 for 184 yards and 2 touchdowns. Doug Flutie was 14 for 38 for 220 yards and 1 touchdown, with 1 interception. Eric Moulds had 4 receptions for 107 yards.

	1	2	3	4		Final
N.Y. Jets	7	0	10	0	—	17
Buffalo	0	7	3	0	—	10

NYJ — Chrebet 7 pass from Testaverde (Hall kick)
Buff — Thomas 25 pass from Flutie (Christie kick)
NYJ — FG Hall 48
Buff — FG Christie 44
NYJ — Ward 71 pass from Testaverde (Hall kick)

WASHINGTON 20, TAMPA BAY 16—at Jack Kent Cooke Stadium, attendance 66,309. Trent Green's 15-yard touchdown pass to Stephen Alexander with 5:49 remaining capped a 13-point fourth quarter as the Redskins shocked the Buccaneers. The Buccaneers scored on three of their first five possessions, with Charles Mincy's interception setting up Michael Husted's 42-yard field goal to give Tampa Bay a 13-7 halftime lead. Jacquez Green's 25-yard punt return set up Husted's 24-yard field goal to give the Buccaneers a 16-7 lead midway through the third quarter. Trent Green's 61-yard pass to Albert Connell led to Cary Blanchard's 26-yard field goal, and 10- and 16-yard passes to Alexander set up Blanchard's 35-yard boot with 6:06 left. Mike Sellers recovered Jacquez Green's fumble on the ensuing kickoff, and Alexander's scoring catch on the next play gave the Redskins their only lead. Greg Jones and Darrell Green each intercepted Trent Dilfer in the closing minutes. Trent Green was 16 of 33 for 191 yards and 1 touchdown, with 1 interception. Dilfer was 14 of 34 for 100 yards and 1 touchdown, with 2 interceptions.

	1	2	3	4		Final
Tampa Bay	7	6	3	0	—	16
Washington	7	0	0	13	—	20

TB — Moore 8 pass from Dilfer (Husted kick)
Wash — Shepherd 16 run (Blanchard kick)
TB — FG Husted 20
TB — FG Husted 42
TB — FG Husted 24
Wash — FG Blanchard 26
Wash — FG Blanchard 35
Wash — Alexander 15 pass from T. Green (Blanchard kick)

SUNDAY, DECEMBER 20

ATLANTA 24, DETROIT 17—at Pontiac Silverdome, attendance 67,143. Jamal Anderson scored 2 touchdowns as the Falcons recorded a comeback victory to win just their second NFC West title. Detroit led 7-0 when Barry Sanders fumbled deep in Lions' territory. Chuck Smith recovered the ball, and Chris Chandler threw an 8-yard touchdown pass to Anderson two plays later to tie the game. Atlanta led 10-7 when Frank Reich capped a 57-yard drive with a 2-yard scoring pass to Herman Moore with just 29 seconds left in the half to give Detroit a 14-10 lead. Jason Hanson's 30-yard field goal ended an 8:54, 15-play drive late in the third quarter, but the Falcons scored on the ensuing possession to tie the game 17-17 on Chandler's 27-yard touchdown pass to Terance Mathis. Anderson's 26-yard run on third-and-4 to the Lions' 1 set up his second touchdown to give Atlanta a 24-17 lead with 6:57 to play. Eugene Robinson's interception with 1:39 remaining sealed the victory. Chandler was 11 of 19 for 146 yards and 2 touchdowns. Anderson had 30 carries for 147 yards. Frank Reich was 15 of 26 for 148 yards and 2 touchdowns, with 2 interceptions.

	1	2	3	4		Final
Atlanta	7	3	0	14	—	24
Detroit	7	7	3	0	—	17

Det — Boyd 18 pass from Reich (Hanson kick)
Atl — Anderson 8 pass from Chandler (Andersen kick)
Atl — FG Andersen 34
Det — Moore 2 pass from Reich (Hanson kick)
Det — FG Hanson 30
Atl — Mathis 27 pass from Chandler (Andersen kick)
Atl — Anderson 1 run (Andersen kick)

CHICAGO 24, BALTIMORE 3—at Soldier Field, attendance 40,853. Rookie James Allen, who had rushed for a combined 47 yards in his first five NFL games, rushed for 163 yards in his first career start as the Bears broke a six-game losing streak. Allen's 57-yard run set up his own 1-yard plunge to give the Bears a 10-0 lead early in the second quarter. Allen's 54-yard scamper moments later was followed by Steve Stenstrom's 16-yard touchdown pass to Curtis Conway. Late in the half, Stenstrom's 47-yard pass to Conway keyed an 82-yard drive that was capped by Robert Chancey's 4-yard touchdown run five seconds before halftime to give the Bears a 24-0 halftime lead. Matt Stover's 27-yard field goal on the opening drive of the second half put the Ravens on the scoreboard, but Baltimore drove no further than the Bears' 41 the remainder of the game. Stenstrom was 19 of 28 for 202 yards and 1 touchdown. Jim Harbaugh was 20 of 35 for 185 yards, with 1 interception. The Bears compiled more than twice as many (391-176) total yards.

Baltimore	0	0	3	0	—	3
Chicago	3	21	0	0	—	24

Chi — FG Jaeger 20
Chi — Allen 1 run (Jaeger kick)
Chi — Conway 16 pass from Stenstrom (Jaeger kick)
Chi — Chancey 4 run (Jaeger kick)
Balt — FG Stover 27

CINCINNATI 25, PITTSBURGH 24—at Three Rivers Stadium, attendance 52,017. Doug Pelfrey kicked 4 field goals and Jeff Blake passed for 367 yards as the Bengals snapped a nine-game losing streak and knocked the Steelers out of playoff contention. The Bengals led 3-0 early in the second quarter when Reinard Wilson sacked Kordell Stewart near midfield. Stewart fumbled, and Sam Shade scooped up the ball and scampered 55 yards for a touchdown. Carnell Lake's 15-yard interception return for a touchdown cut the deficit to 13-7, but Pelfrey's 43-yard field goal as the half expired gave Cincinnati a 16-7 halftime lead. David Dunn returned the second half's opening kickoff 36 yards, but fumbled. Chris Oldham returned it for a touchdown, and Jerome Bettis's 4-yard touchdown run following Pelfrey's missed 53-yard field goal gave Pittsburgh its first lead. However, the Bengals retook the lead 19 seconds later on Jeff Blake's 61-yard touchdown pass to Darnay Scott. The Bengals gave the Steelers some chances early in the fourth quarter when Pelfrey missed a 46-yard field goal and Damon Gibson fumbled a punt at the Bengals' 10-yard line. Pittsburgh settled for Norm Johnson's 22-yard field goal with 10:17 left to take a 24-22 lead, but the Bengals responded with a 12-play, 62-yard drive, capped by Pelfrey's fourth field goal to take a 25-24 lead with 5:12 remaining. Artrell Hawkins's interception with 17 seconds remaining clinched the Bengals' victory. Blake was 20 of 36 for 367 yards and 1 touchdown, with 1 interception. Scott had 7 catches for 152 yards, while Brandon Bennett added 3 catches for 119 yards. Stewart was 5 of 13 for 30 yards before being replaced by Mike Tomczak, who was 5 of 11 for 77 yards, with 1 interception. Bettis rushed for 104 yards. The Bengals outgained the Steelers by 272 yards (483-211).

Cincinnati	3	13	6	3	—	25
Pittsburgh	0	7	14	3	—	24

Cin — FG Pelfrey 33
Cin — Shade 55 fumble return (Pelfrey kick)
Cin — FG Pelfrey 37
Pitt — Lake 15 interception return (N. Johnson kick)
Cin — FG Pelfrey 43
Pitt — Oldham 54 fumble return (N. Johnson kick)
Pitt — Bettis 4 run (N. Johnson kick)
Cin — Scott 61 pass from Blake (bad snap)
Pitt — FG N. Johnson 22
Cin — FG Pelfrey 21

SEATTLE 27, INDIANAPOLIS 23—at Kingdome, attendance 58,703. Ricky Watters rushed for 178 yards, and his 33-yard scoring scamper started a 17-point outburst in the game's final 10 minutes as the Seahawks held on to defeat the Colts. Mike Vanderjagt's 32-yard field goal as the half expired tied the game 10-10. The Colts scored on their first three possessions of the second half to take a 23-10 lead with 13:17 to play. A 17-yard scramble by Jon Kitna on third-and-14 keyed a drive that culminated with Watters's touchdown jaunt. Marshall Faulk fumbled moments later, and Shawn Springs scooped up the ball and scooted 14 yards for the go-ahead touchdown with 7:36 remaining. Watters's 38-yard run on the Seahawks' next possession set up Peterson's 30-yard field goal with 1:57 to play. The Colts roared back, using Peyton Manning's arm and a 27-yard pass interference penalty on Terry McDaniel to reach the Seahawks' 7 with 56 seconds left. However, Manning threw 4 consecutive incompletions, and Seattle was victorious. Kitna was 16 of 29 for 177 yards and 1 touchdown. Manning was 23 of 39 for 335 yards and 1 touchdown, with 1 interception. Torrance Small had 3 receptions for 120 yards.

Indianapolis	7	3	10	3	—	23
Seattle	7	3	0	17	—	27

Ind — Warren 4 run (Vanderjagt kick)
Sea — Galloway 3 pass from Kitna (Peterson kick)
Sea — FG Peterson 42
Ind — FG Vanderjagt 32
Ind — FG Vanderjagt 48
Ind — Pollard 1 pass from Manning (Vanderjagt kick)
Ind — FG Vanderjagt 20
Sea — Watters 33 run (Peterson kick)
Sea — Springs 14 fumble return (Peterson kick)
Sea — FG Peterson 30

N.Y. GIANTS 28, KANSAS CITY 7—at Giants Stadium, attendance 66,040. Gary Brown rushed for 103 yards and 1 touchdown as the Giants used 4 interceptions to win their third consecutive game. Percy Ellsworth's 43-yard interception return three plays into the game set the tone for the afternoon. The Giants marched 83 yards on their first possession, scoring on Kent Graham's 12-yard touchdown pass to Amani Toomer to give the Giants a 14-0 lead 8:39 into the game. The Chiefs failed to pass the Giants' 43 on any of their first nine possessions, including Byron (Bam) Morris being stopped on fourth-and-1 from the Chiefs' 44 midway through the second quarter, leading to Brown's 1-yard touchdown run to give the Giants a 21-0 lead. The Chiefs drove deep into Giants' territory their final three possessions, but scored just the first time, stopped by an interception and on downs in their other two attempts. Graham was 16 of 33 for 167 yards and 1 touchdown. Elvis Grbac was 11 of 20 for 160 yards and 1 touchdown, with 2 interceptions. Rich Gannon was 7 of 16 passes for 79 yards, with 2 interceptions.

Kansas City	0	0	7	0	—	7
N.Y. Giants	14	7	7	0	—	28

NYG — Ellsworth 43 interception return (Daluiso kick)
NYG — Toomer 12 pass from Graham (Daluiso kick)
NYG — Brown 1 run (Daluiso kick)
NYG — Graham 6 run (Daluiso kick)
KC — Gonzalez 4 pass from Grbac (Stoyanovich kick)

ARIZONA 19, NEW ORLEANS 17—at Sun Devil Stadium, attendance 51,617. Jake Plummer piloted another daring comeback, and Chris Jacke booted through the exclamation point as time expired to keep the Cardinals in the playoff chase while eliminating the Saints. Sammy Knight's 39-yard interception return for a touchdown staked the Saints to a 7-3 lead. The Cardinals drove deep into Saints' territory four times in the first half. But Jacke made only 2 of 3 field goals and the Cardinals turned the ball over when Alex Molden stripped Frank Sanders of the ball at the Saints' 1 and Chad Cota recovered to secure a 10-6 halftime lead. The Saints drove to the Cardinals' 23, but Patrick Sapp forced Kerry Collins to fumble. Jamir Miller recovered, and Adrian Murrell scooted 29 yards for a touchdown seven plays later to give Arizona a 13-10 lead. The Cardinals defense stiffened as Bernard Wilson blocked Doug Brien's 54-yard field-goal attempt and a slew of defenders stopped Aaron Craver on fourth-and-1 from the Cardinals' 9 with 10:50 to play. Jacke added a 46-yard field goal on the ensuing drive to give Arizona a 16-10 lead, but the Saints marched 75 yards in 14 plays to retake the lead on Collins's 13-yard scoring toss to Cameron Cleeland with 1:21 remaining. With elimination from playoff contention facing the loser, the Cardinals began on their own 8-yard line. Plummer promptly fired 25- and 28-yard strikes to Sanders to reach the Saints' 39, and his 21-yard scramble a few plays later set up Jacke's heroics. Arizona compiled 513 yards and 28 first downs. Plummer was 32 of 44 for 394 yards, with 1 interception. Sanders has 10 receptions for 138 yards. Collins was 25 of 43 for 265 yards and 1 touchdown.

New Orleans	0	10	0	7	—	17
Arizona	3	3	7	6	—	19

Ariz — FG Jacke 21
NO — Knight 39 interception return (Brien kick)
Ariz — FG Jacke 38
NO — FG Brien 28
Ariz — Murrell 29 run (Jacke kick)
Ariz — FG Jacke 46
NO — Cleeland 13 pass from Collins (Brien kick)
Ariz — FG Jacke 36

OAKLAND 17, SAN DIEGO 10—at Qualcomm Stadium, attendance 60,716. Wade Wilson threw 2 touchdown passes as the Raiders snapped a four-game losing streak. John Carney missed a 46-yard field-goal attempt on the Chargers' opening possession, but converted from 28 yards to give San Diego a 3-0 lead. The Raiders scored on their next two possessions, both capped by Wade Wilson touchdown passes, to take a 14-3 lead. Trailing 17-3, the Chargers reached the Raiders' 25 following a Greg Jackson interception late in the third quarter, but Craig Whelihan threw consecutive incompletions to turn the ball over on downs. Whelihan connected on a 39-yard touchdown pass to Mikhael Ricks on San Diego's next drive to cut the deficit to 17-10. Greg Davis missed a 35-yard field-goal attempt midway through the fourth quarter, but Whelihan and the Chargers were stopped on downs at the Raiders' 42. The Chargers defense forced a punt, and Tony Gaiter returned it 49 yards to the Raiders' 37 with 2:42 to play. However, Anthony Newman intercepted Whelihan on the next play. Wilson was 14 of 25 for 167 yards and 2 touchdowns, with 2 interceptions. Whelihan was 19 of 39 for 251 yards and 1 touchdown, with 2 interceptions.

Oakland	0	14	3	0	—	17
San Diego	3	0	7	0	—	10

SD — FG Carney 28
Oak — Jett 45 pass from Wilson (Davis kick)
Oak — T. Brown 12 pass from Wilson (Davis kick)
Oak — FG Davis 25
SD — Ricks 39 pass from Whelihan (Carney kick)

DALLAS 13, PHILADELPHIA 9—at Texas Stadium, attendance 62,722. A little trickery helped the Cowboys clinch their sixth NFC East title in seven seasons. Chris Boniol's 21-yard field goal capped the Eagles' opening drive, but Eric Bjornson's 7-yard touchdown run off a fake field goal two possessions later gave Dallas a 7-3 lead. Each team missed a long field-goal attempt in the half's final minute, enabling the Cowboys to maintain their four-point lead at intermission. Michael Zordich's 14-yard interception return to the Cowboys' 31 led to Boniol's second field goal, but Troy Aikman's 27-yard pass to Hayward Clay set up Richie Cunningham's 42-yard field goal. Moments later, Kevin Smith's 9-yard interception return to the Eagles' 30 set up Cunningham's 41-yard boot to give Dallas a 13-6 lead. Jon Harris recovered an Emmitt Smith fumble near midfield late in the third quarter, but the Eagles had to settle for Boniol's 39-yard field goal with 12:02 to play. The Eagles reached the Cowboys' 12 on their next drive, but on fourth-and-2, Koy Detmer completed a 1-yard pass to Andrew Jordan to turn the ball over on downs with 3:10 left. The Eagles got the ball back one last time, but Freddie Solomon was unable to pull in Detmer's bomb at the goal line, and Philadephia turned the ball over on downs two plays later. The Cowboys won despite recording just 11 first downs and 248 total yards. Aikman was 10 of 23 for 120 yards, with 1 interception. Emmitt Smith had 25 carries for 110 yards. Detmer was 24 of 43 for 231 yards, with 1 interception.

Philadelphia	3	0	3	3	—	9
Dallas	7	0	6	0	—	13

Phil — FG Boniol 21
Dall — Bjornson 7 run (Cunningham kick)
Phil — FG Boniol 41
Dall — FG Cunningham 42
Dall — FG Cunningham 41
Phil — FG Boniol 39

CAROLINA 20, ST. LOUIS 13—at Ericsson Stadium, attendance 50,047. Steve Beuerlein passed for 2 touchdowns as the Panthers scored 10 points in the final three minutes to record a comeback victory against the Rams. The Rams grabbed an early 10-0 lead and had the ball at midfield looking for more points when Eric Davis intercepted Steve Bono's pass. Tim Biakabutuka's 41-yard run set up Beuerlein's 3-yard touchdown pass to Muhsin Muhammad to cut the deficit to 10-7 at halftime. Each team had third-quarter drives in excess of six minutes that led to field goals. Trailing 13-10, Beuerlein found Luther Broughton open down the left sideline. Broughton stiff-armed Roman Phifer en route to a 68-yard touchdown with 2:44 to play to give Carolina its first lead. Amp Lee fumbled on the next play from scrimmage, and Leonard Wheeler recovered at the Rams' 23 to set up John Kasay's 37-yard field goal with 1:04 remaining. Mike Minter intercepted Bono on the next play from scrimmage to ensure the Panthers' victory. Beuerlein was 15 of 25 for 193 yards and 2 touchdowns. Bono, who started in place of injured Tony Banks, was 20 of 37 for 163 yards and 1 touchdown, with 2 interceptions.

St. Louis	3	7	3	0	—	13
Carolina	0	7	3	10	—	20

StL — FG Wilkins 43
StL — Harris 1 pass from Bono (Wilkins kick)
Car — Muhammad 3 pass from Beuerlein (Kasay kick)
StL — FG Wilkins 38
Car — FG Kasay 32
Car — Broughton 68 pass from Beuerlein (Kasay kick)
Car — FG Kasay 37

NEW ENGLAND 24, SAN FRANCISCO 21—at Foxboro Stadium, attendance 59,153. Adam Vinatieri's 35-yard field goal with three seconds left gave Scott Zolak his first victory as a starting quarterback since 1992. The Patriots led 7-0 in the second quarter when Steve Young threw a 75-yard touchdown pass to Jerry Rice only to be matched moments later on Zolak's 61-yard touchdown pass to Shawn Jefferson. Tim McDonald's interception return to the Patriots' 22 set up Terrell Owens's tying touchdown grab, and holder Ty Detmer turned a mishandled snap into a 25-yard touchdown pass to Irv Smith as the half expired to give the 49ers their first lead. Willie Clay's interception near midfield set up Robert Edwards's game-tying 5-yard touchdown run with 7:34 remaining. Troy Brown had a 14-yard punt return to the Patriots' 41 with 1:48 left and Edwards carried four times to get the Patriots in field-goal position for Vinatieri's winning boot. Zolak was 14 of 30 for 205 yards and 2 touchdowns, with 2 interceptions. The Patriots' defense recorded 5 sacks. Young was 18 of 23 for 267 yards and 2 touchdowns, with 2 interceptions. Rice had 5 catches for 115 yards, while Garrison Hearst carried 27 times for 107 yards.

San Francisco	0	21	0	0	—	21
New England	7	7	0	10	—	24

NE — Edwards 19 pass from Zolak (Vinatieri kick)
SF — Rice 75 pass from Young (Richey kick)
NE — Jefferson 61 pass from Zolak (Vinatieri kick)
SF — Owens 7 pass from Young (Richey kick)
SF — Smith 25 pass from Detmer (Richey kick)
NE — Edwards 5 run (Vinatieri kick)
NE — FG Vinatieri 35

GREEN BAY 30, TENNESSEE 22—at Lambeau Field, attendance 59,888. Brett Favre and Antonio Freeman hooked up for 3 touchdowns as the Packers hurt the Oilers' playoff hopes. Favre and Freeman wasted little time, connecting on the third play of the game for a 57-yard touchdown. The tandem scored two possessions later and, clinging to a 14-7 lead late in the half, hit paydirt from 32 yards out just before halftime to give the Packers a 21-7 halftime lead. The Packers drove into Oilers territory in five of their six second-half possessions, yet came away with just 3 field goals. Steve McNair's third touchdown pass, along with Eddie George's 2-point conversion, cut the deficit to 30-22 with 53 seconds left, but Mike Prior recovered the ensuing onside kick to secure the victory. Favre was 14 of 22 for 253 yards and 3 touchdowns. Freeman had 7 receptions for 186 yards. McNair was 29 of 49 for 263 yards and 3 touchdowns, with 1 interception.

Tennessee	0	7	7	8	—	22
Green Bay	14	7	3	6	—	30

GB — Freeman 57 pass from Favre (Longwell kick)
GB — Freeman 68 pass from Favre (Longwell kick)
Tenn — Mason 25 pass from McNair (Del Greco kick)
GB — Freeman 32 pass from Favre (Longwell kick)
GB — FG Longwell 38
Tenn — Thigpen 30 pass from McNair (Del Greco kick)
GB — FG Longwell 40
GB — FG Longwell 40
Tenn — Mason 3 pass from McNair (George run)

SUNDAY NIGHT, DECEMBER 20

MINNESOTA 50, JACKSONVILLE 10—at Metrodome, attendance 64,363. Randall Cunningham passed for 3 touchdowns and the Vikings scored 17 points during a 48-second outburst early in the fourth quarter to defeat the Jaguars. The Vikings led 6-0 when Orlando Thomas intercepted Jonathan Quinn's pass near midfield. Cunningham's 13-yard touchdown pass to Andrew Glover moments later gave Minnesota a 12-0 lead, which was cut to 12-3 by Mike Hollis's 25-yard field goal as the half expired. A flea-flicker on the second half's second play produced a 43-yard touchdown catch by Randy Moss to give the Vikings a 19-3 edge. Glover's second touchdown catch capped an 11-play drive a few possessions later, and Brad Johnson's 1-yard touchdown pass to Cris Carter was Carter's 100th career touchdown catch and gave Minnesota a 33-3 lead with 12:38 to play. After another Anderson field goal on the next drive, Jimmy Hitchcock's interception and 30-yard touchdown return on the next play gave the Vikings a 43-3 lead. Bobby Houston's fumble recovery and return to the Jaguars' 1 on the next play from scrimmage set up Charles Evans's touchdown on the following play. Quinn tossed a touchdown pass to Pete Mitchell with 2:56 remaining. Cunningham was 16 of 30 for 210 yards and 3 touchdowns. Robert Smith carried 19 times for 101 yards. Quinn was 12 of 27 for 88 yards and 1 touchdown, with 2 interceptions. Fred Taylor had 23 carries for 105 yards.

Jacksonville	0	3	0	7	—	10
Minnesota	3	9	14	24	—	50

Minn — FG Anderson 48
Minn — FG Anderson 53
Minn — Glover 13 pass from Cunningham (pass failed)
Jac — FG Hollis 25
Minn — Moss 43 pass from Cunningham (Anderson kick)
Minn — Glover 14 pass from Cunningham (Anderson kick)
Minn — Carter 1 pass from Johnson (Anderson kick)
Minn — FG Anderson 44
Minn — Hitchcock 30 interception return (Anderson kick)
Minn — Evans 1 run (Anderson kick)
Jac — Mitchell 1 pass from Quinn (Hollis kick)

MONDAY NIGHT, DECEMBER 21

MIAMI 31, DENVER 21—at Pro Player Stadium, attendance 74,363. In his first matchup with John Elway since 1985, Dan Marino passed for 355 yards and 4 touchdowns as the Dolphins clinched the AFC's final playoff berth. It seemed to be the Broncos night when, leading 3-0, Olindo Mare missed a 28-yard field-goal attempt and, moments later, a scrambling Elway fumbled into the end zone, only to have Rod Smith recover the ball for a touchdown and 10-0 lead. Marino threw a 9-yard touchdown pass to Lamar Thomas with 54 seconds left in the half, but Jason Elam gave Denver a 13-7 halftime lead with a 44-yard boot as the half expired. Elam missed a 43-yard field-goal attempt to open the second half, and Marino struck quickly with a 56-yard scoring pass to Thomas. The same duo connected less than five minutes later to give Miami a 21-13 lead. Sam Madison's 35-yard interception return to the Broncos' 6 set up Marino's fourth touchdown pass with 8:15 remaining to give the Dolphins a 28-13 advantage. On the ensuing kickoff, Vaughn Hebron recorded the Broncos' first kickoff return for a touchdown since 1972, a span of 1,362 kickoffs. However, Jerry Wilson's interception at the Broncos' 44 with 3:17 to play set up Mare's 42-yard field goal to ice the game. Marino was 23 of 38 for 355 yards and 4 touchdowns, with 1 interception. Thomas had 6 receptions for 136 yards. Elway was 13 of 36 for 151 yards, with 2 interceptions.

Denver	3	10	0	8	—	21
Miami	0	7	14	10	—	31

Den — FG Elam 52
Den — R. Smith recovered fumble in end zone (Elam kick)
Mia — Thomas 9 pass from Marino (Mare kick)
Den — FG Elam 44
Mia — Thomas 56 pass from Marino (Mare kick)
Mia — Thomas 17 pass from Marino (Mare kick)
Mia — Gadsden 8 pass from Marino (Mare kick)
Den — Hebron 95 kickoff return (McCaffrey pass from Brister)
Mia — FG Mare 42

SEVENTEENTH WEEK SUMMARIES

AMERICAN FOOTBALL CONFERENCE

Eastern Division	**W**	**L**	**T**	**Pct.**	**Pts.**	**OP**
N.Y. Jets	12	4	0	.750	416	266
Miami	10	6	0	.625	321	265
Buffalo	10	6	0	.625	400	333
New England	9	7	0	.563	337	329
Indianapolis	3	13	0	.188	310	444
Central Division						
Jacksonville	11	5	0	.688	392	338
Tennessee	8	8	0	.500	330	320
Pittsburgh	7	9	0	.438	263	303
Baltimore	6	10	0	.375	269	335
Cincinnati	3	13	0	.188	268	452
Western Division						
Denver	14	2	0	.875	501	309
Seattle	8	8	0	.500	372	310
Oakland	8	8	0	.500	288	356
Kansas City	7	9	0	.438	327	363
San Diego	5	11	0	.313	241	342

NATIONAL FOOTBALL CONFERENCE

Eastern Division	**W**	**L**	**T**	**Pct.**	**Pts.**	**OP**
Dallas	10	6	0	.625	381	275
Arizona	9	7	0	.563	325	378
N.Y. Giants	8	8	0	.500	287	309
Washington	6	10	0	.375	319	421
Philadelphia	3	13	0	.188	161	344
Central Division						
Minnesota	15	1	0	.938	556	296
Green Bay	11	5	0	.688	408	319
Tampa Bay	8	8	0	.500	314	295
Detroit	5	11	0	.313	306	378
Chicago	4	12	0	.250	276	368
Western Division						
Atlanta	14	2	0	.875	442	289
San Francisco	12	4	0	.750	479	328
New Orleans	6	10	0	.375	305	359
Carolina	4	12	0	.250	336	413
St. Louis	4	12	0	.250	285	378

SATURDAY, DECEMBER 26

KANSAS CITY 31, OAKLAND 24—at Network Associates Coliseum, attendance 52,679. Byron (Bam) Morris rushed for 96 yards and 2 touchdowns as the Chiefs overcame an early 14-0 deficit to deny the Raiders their first winning season since 1994. Wade Wilson's touchdown pass to Tim Brown gave Oakland a 7-0 lead, and Charles Woodson's interception moments later led to Randy Jordan's 10-yard scoring run. Morris's first touchdown culminated a 64-yard march on the ensuing drive. Morris and Elvis Grbac hooked up for a 29-yard pass play on the Chiefs' first possession of the second half, setting up Morris's tying touchdown run. Greg Davis kicked a field goal to cap the Raiders' next possession, but Wilson was forced to leave the game because of a groin injury during the drive. Grbac's 37-yard pass to Derrick Alexander set up Pete Stoyanovich's tying field goal, and Leslie O'Neal stripped reserve Donald Hollas of the ball less than three minutes later. Derrick Thomas scooped up the fumble and gave the Chiefs their first defensive touchdown of the season and their first lead of the game. Hollas also left because of an injury, and Jeff George guided the Raiders to a game-tying touchdown with 9:17 left. Grbac responded with a 20-yard touchdown pass to Tony Gonzalez with 5:56 remaining, and the Raiders got no closer than the Chiefs' 40 in their final two possessions. Grbac was 20 of 32 for 254 yards and 1 touchdown, with 2 interceptions. Wilson was 13 of 18 for 127 yards and 1 touchdown, Hollas was 4 of 6 for 60 yards, and George was 9 of 18 for 138 yards and 1 touchdown. Brown had 10 catches for 140 yards to record his sixth consecutive 1,000-receiving yard season.

Kansas City	0	7	17	7	—	31
Oakland	14	0	3	7	—	24

Oak — T. Brown 13 pass from Wilson (Davis kick)
Oak — Jordan 10 run (Davis kick)
KC — Morris 1 run (Stoyanovich kick)
KC — Morris 1 run (Stoyanovich kick)
Oak — FG Davis 44
KC — FG Stoyanovich 30
KC — Thomas 44 fumble return (Stoyanovich kick)
Oak — Jett 15 pass from George (Davis kick)
KC — Gonzalez 20 pass from Grbac (Stoyanovich kick)

MINNESOTA 26, TENNESSEE 16—at Vanderbilt Stadium, attendance 41,121. Randall Cunningham passed for 2 touchdowns as the Vikings set the NFL record for most points in a season and became just the third club to have a 15-1 record. Tennessee led 6-5 midway into the second quarter when Steve McNair completed a 23-yard pass to Kevin Dyson and 26-yard pass to Jackie Harris to set up Eddie George's 2-yard scoring burst. Trailing 13-8 at halftime, the Vikings, who needed 12 points to break the 1983 Washington Redskins record, drove downfield to open the second half and broke the mark on Cunningham's 5-yard touchdown pass to Randy Moss. Moss's one-handed 2-point conversion catch gave Minnesota a 16-13 lead. The Oilers responded with Al Del Greco's third field goal to tie the game, but Cunningham fired a 38-yard scoring pass to Cris Carter three minutes later to give the Vikings a 23-16 lead. The Oilers didn't drive beyond the Vikings' 49 in their final four possessions, and Gary Anderson's 30-yard field goal with 1:03 left iced the game. Anderson became the first kicker in NFL history to finish a season without a missed field goal (35-35) or extra point (59-59). Cunningham was 23 of 35 for 235 yards and 1 touchdown, with 2 interceptions. McNair was 16 of 33 for 261 yards. This was Tennessee's last game as the Oilers, having changed its name to Titans for the 1999 season.

Minnesota	2	6	15	3	—	26
Tennessee	3	10	3	0	—	16

Minn — Safety, McNair penalized for intentional grounding in end zone
Tenn — FG Del Greco 36
Minn — FG Anderson 39
Tenn — FG Del Greco 33
Tenn — George 2 run (Del Greco kick)
Minn — FG Anderson 23
Minn — Moss 5 pass from Cunningham (Moss pass from Cunningham)
Tenn — FG Del Greco 45
Minn — Carter 38 pass from Cunningham (Anderson kick)
Minn — FG Anderson 30

SUNDAY, DECEMBER 27

BUFFALO 45, NEW ORLEANS 33—at Superdome, attendance 39,707. Rob Johnson threw 3 touchdown passes as the Bills jumped out to a 28-0 lead but had to endure a fierce comeback attempt before defeating the Saints. Bruce Smith's 18-yard fumble return to the Saints' 1 set up Antowain Smith's 1-yard touchdown run 35 seconds into the game. Johnson and Eric Moulds connected on a 66-yard scoring play less than three minutes into the game, and Kurt Schulz's interception at the Saints' 49 led to Johnson's 12-yard touchdown run and a 21-0 Bills lead 8:47 into the game. After punting on their fourth possession, Johnson capped an 81-yard drive with a scoring toss to Sam Gash to take a 28-0 lead. Billy Joe Tolliver replaced starter Kerry Collins, and the Saints scored on three consecutive possessions spanning the second and third quarters to cut the deficit to 31-21. However, the Saints attempted an onside kick, and Joe Cummings returned it 21 yards to the Saints' 33 to set up Rob Johnson's scoring pass to Lonnie Johnson on the first play of the final quarter. Emanuel Martin's 23-yard interception return led to Jonathan Linton's touchdown with 6:39 left to give Buffalo a 45-21 lead. After Aaron Craver's touchdown cut the lead to 45-27 with 1:57 remaining, Rob Kelly recovered the ensuing onside kick. Tolliver threw a 72-yard touchdown pass to Brett Bech on the next play, cutting the Saints deficit to 12 points with 1:44 left. Bech recovered the Saints' third onside kick of the half, and the Saints drove to the Bills' 14 but Tolliver threw four consecutive incompletions to end the comeback attempt. Johnson was 12 of 18 for 216 yards and 3 touchdowns. Collins was 3 of 12 for 23 yards, with 1 interception, while Tolliver completed 23 of 41 passes for 296 yards and 3 touchdowns, with 1 interception. Cameron Cleeland had 10 catches for 112 yards and Bech had 4 receptions for 113 yards.

Buffalo	21	7	3	14	—	45
New Orleans	0	14	7	12	—	33

Buff — Smith 1 run (Christie kick)
Buff — Moulds 66 pass from R. Johnson (Christie kick)
Buff — R. Johnson 12 run (Christie kick)
Buff — Gash 1 pass from R. Johnson (Christie kick)
NO — Davis 1 run (Brien kick)
NO — Cleeland 5 pass from Tolliver (Brien kick)
Buff — FG Christie 35
NO — Bech 10 pass from Tolliver (Brien kick)
Buff — L. Johnson 23 pass from R. Johnson (Christie kick)
Buff — Linton 8 run (Christie kick)
NO — Craver 1 run (pass failed)
NO — Bech 72 pass from Tolliver (pass failed)

CAROLINA 27, INDIANAPOLIS 19—at RCA Dome, attendance 58,182. Michael Bates's 99-yard kickoff return spurred a second-half comeback as the Panthers were victorious. The Colts used a 46-yard pass from Peyton Manning to Torrance Small to set up the first of Mike Vanderjagt's 3 first-half field goals. Monty Montgomery's fumble recovery at the Panthers' 15 led to the second, and after Manning's 44-yard touchdown pass to Marcus Pollard, Vanderjagt's 47-yard boot with one second left in the half gave the Colts a 16-6 lead. Bates changed the game's momentum by breaking three tackles en route to his 99-yard return to begin the second half. After a punt, Steve Beuerlein's 46-yard pass to Raghib Ismail set up Tim Biakabutuka's touchdown run to give the Panthers a 20-16 lead. Vanderjagt's fourth field goal cut the deficit to one point late in the third quarter, but Beuerlein and Ismail capped a 9-play, 80-yard drive with a 5-yard scoring play with 3:16 left. Eric Davis intercepted Manning at the Panthers' 46 with 1:58 remaining, but the Colts received another chance following Ken Walter's fumbled punt snap, giving Indianapolis the ball at the Panthers' 37 with 55 seconds left. However, Lenny McGill intercepted Manning on third down to ice the game. Beuerlein was 12 of 21 for 178 yards and 1 touchdown, with 1 interception. Manning was 17 of 34 for 225 yards and 1 touchdown, with 2 interceptions.

Carolina	3	3	14	7	—	27
Indianapolis	3	13	3	0	—	19

Car — FG Kasay 44
Ind — FG Vanderjagt 22
Ind — FG Vanderjagt 28
Ind — Pollard 44 pass from Manning (Vanderjagt kick)
Car — FG Kasay 27
Ind — FG Vanderjagt 47
Car — Bates 99 kickoff return (Kasay kick)
Car — Biakabutuka 5 run (Kasay kick)
Ind — FG Vanderjagt 42
Car — Ismail 5 pass from Beuerlein (Kasay kick)

BALTIMORE 19, DETROIT 10—at NFL Stadium at Camden Yards, attendance 68,045. Priest Holmes rushed for 132 yards, and the Ravens' defense limited the Lions to just 236 total yards and 11 first downs in Ted Marchibroda's final game. Tony Siragusa's fumble recovery at the Lions' 2 set up Holmes's 1-yard touchdown. A 13-play, 97-yard drive in the second quarter resulted in Jim Harbaugh's 11-yard touchdown pass to Roosevelt Potts. After not driving beyond the Ravens' 47 with their first five possessions, the Lions got a 39-yard field goal from Jason Hanson just before halftime. Detroit reached the Ravens' 16 in the third quarter, but Tommy Vardell was stopped by Cornell Brown and Lional Dalton on fourth and-1. The Lions did find the end zone with their next possession, scoring on Frank Reich's 8-yard touchdown pass to Cory Schlesinger with 13:25 left. After an exchange of punts, Matt Stover booted a 30-yard field goal with 5:03 left to finish the scoring. Harbaugh was 17 of 26 for 141 yards and 1 touchdown. Reich, who started in place of injured Charlie Batch, was 18 of 29 for 195 yards and 1 touchdown. Herman Moore had 10 catches for 120 yards.

Detroit	0	3	0	7	—	10
Baltimore	9	7	0	3	—	19

Balt — Safety, Roberts penalized for holding in end zone
Balt — Holmes 1 run (Stover kick)
Balt — Potts 11 pass from Harbaugh (Stover kick)
Det — FG Hanson 39
Det — Schlesinger 8 pass from Reich (Hanson kick)
Balt — FG Stover 30

GREEN BAY 16, CHICAGO 13—at Soldier Field, attendance 58,393. Ryan Longwell booted an 18-yard field goal with 9:49 left as the Packers defeated the Bears for the tenth consecutive time. Keith McKenzie's 28-yard interception return gave the Packers an early lead, but Andre Collins's interception return to the Packers' 17 set up Steve Stenstrom's 14-yard touchdown pass to James Allen two plays later to tie the game. Jeff Jaeger and Ryan Longwell each missed field goals, but Jaeger's 29-yard field goal culminated a 73-yard scoring drive and gave the Bears a 10-7 halftime lead. The Bears' defense limited the Packers to just 72 yards in the first half. The Packers drove 71 yards to open the second half, with Brett Favre's 8-yard scoring pass to Antonio Freeman giving the Packers the lead. Longwell missed the extra point, and Tony Parrish's 8-yard interception return to the Packers' 28 set up Jaeger's tying boot late in the third quarter. The Packers reached the Bears' 1 on the ensuing possession, but Dorsey Levens was twice stopped for no gain, leading to Longwell's winning kick. Lemanski Hall recovered Doug Pederson's fumble and returned it to the Bears' 49 with 2:45 left, but with 1:01 left from the Packers' 33, LeRoy Butler sacked Stenstrom, forced him to fumble, and recovered the ball to ensure the victory. Favre was 16 of 22 for 153 yards and 1 touchdown, with 2 interceptions. Stenstrom was 17 of 30 for 199 yards and 1 touchdown, with 2 interceptions.

Green Bay	7	0	6	3	—	16
Chicago	7	3	3	0	—	13

GB — McKenzie 28 interception return (Longwell kick)
Chi — Allen 14 pass from Stenstrom (Jaeger kick)
Chi — FG Jaeger 29
GB — Freeman 8 pass from Favre (kick failed)
Chi — FG Jaeger 21
GB — FG Longwell 18

ATLANTA 38, MIAMI 16—at Georgia Dome, attendance 69,754. Jamal Anderson rushed for 103 yards and 1 touchdown as the Falcons scored 3 touchdowns in the first seven minutes to rout the Dolphins. Chris Chandler threw a 62-yard touchdown pass to O.J. Santiago on the game's first play and, after a punt and 53-yard pass to Tony Martin, hooked up with Santiago from 2 yards to give Atlanta a 14-0 lead 3:52 into the game. Chandler injured his ankle on the second touchdown pass and did not return. Ronnie Bradford intercepted a Dan Marino pass and scampered 11 yards into the end zone to give the Falcons a 21-0 lead. The Dolphins drove inside the Falcons' 20 three times before intermission, but scored just once because of Oronde Gadsden's fumble at the Falcons' 9 and Michael Booker's interception in the end zone. Travis Hall recovered Ron Moore's fumble three plays into the second half, and backup Steve DeBerg fired a 35-yard touchdown pass to Tony Martin on the next play. John Avery fumbled less than two minutes later, and Anderson rumbled 36 yards for a touchdown on the following play to give Atlanta a 38-6 lead with 12:24 left in the third quarter. Chandler was 3 for 3 for 118 yards and 2 touchdowns. DeBerg was 5 for 10 for 85 yards and 1 touchdown. Martin had 3 catches for 105 yards. Marino, who was 21 of 36 for 320 yards and 1 touchdown, with 2 interceptions, recorded his first rushing touchdown since 1994. Rich Brooks filled in for coach Dan Reeves, who was recovering from quadruple bypass surgery that occurred 13 days earlier.

Miami	0	6	10	0	—	16
Atlanta	21	3	14	0	—	38

Atl — Santiago 62 pass from Chandler (Andersen kick)

Atl — Santiago 2 pass from Chandler (Andersen kick)
Atl — Bradford 11 interception return (Andersen kick)
Mia — McDuffie 12 pass from Marino (kick blocked)
Atl — FG Andersen 35
Atl — Martin 35 pass from DeBerg (Andersen kick)
Atl — Anderson 36 run (Andersen kick)
Mia — Marino 3 run (Mare kick)
Mia — FG Mare 26

N.Y. JETS 31, NEW ENGLAND 10—at Giants Stadium, attendance 74,302. Vinny Testaverde equaled his career high with 4 touchdown passes as the Jets reached the 12-win plateau for the first time. John Hall's 36-yard field goal capped a game-opening 15-play, 82-yard drive. After a punt, Testaverde's 4-yard touchdown pass to Kyle Brady gave the Jets a 10-0 lead, and Ray Mickens's fumble recovery at the Patriots' 33 set up Testaverde's 8-yard touchdown pass to Curtis Martin. The Patriots had run just five plays, but the Jets had a 17-0 lead. Adam Vinatieri's field goal capped the ensuing possession, but the Patriots recorded just 1 first down on their next five possessions, and the Jets scored on their first two possessions of the second half, the second of which was a 15-play, 96-yard drive, to take a 31-3 lead. Scott Zolak's 44-yard touchdown pass to Tony Simmons with 1:31 left finished the scoring. Testaverde was 17 of 27 for 179 yards and 4 touchdowns, with 1 interception. Martin carried 29 times for 102 yards. Zolak, who played for injured Drew Bledsoe, was 14 of 31 for 127 yards and 1 touchdown.

New England	0	3	0	7	—	10
N.Y. Jets	3	14	7	7	—	31

NYJ — FG Hall 36
NYJ — Brady 4 pass from Testaverde (Hall kick)
NYJ — Martin 8 pass from Testaverde (Hall kick)
NE — FG Vinatieri 19
NYJ — Ward 17 pass from Testaverde (Hall kick)
NYJ — K. Johnson 24 pass from Testaverde (Hall kick)
NE — Simmons 44 pass from Zolak (Vinatieri kick)

N.Y. GIANTS 20, PHILADELPHIA 10—at Veterans Stadium, attendance 66,596. The Giants won their fourth consecutive game to close out the season. Each team scored on consecutive possessions in the first half, with Duce Staley's 64-yard touchdown run being the difference in the 10-6 halftime score. The Giants strung together a 12-play, 77-yard drive late in the third quarter, capped by Kent Graham's 5-yard touchdown pass to Chris Calloway. Sam Garnes thwarted the Eagles' next drive with an interception at the Giants' 6. Graham and Calloway combined to culminate the ensuing possession with an 18-yard scoring play to give the Giants a 20-10 lead with 5:42 left. The Eagles drove to the Giants' 7, where Koy Detmer's fourth down pass fell incomplete with 2:14 left to secure the Giants' victory. Graham was 15 of 26 for 133 yards and 2 touchdowns. Gary Brown had 25 carries for 112 yards. Detmer was 13 of 27 for 151 yards, with 1 interception. The Giants' defense permitted just 11 first downs.

N.Y. Giants	3	3	7	7	—	20
Philadelphia	0	10	0	0	—	10

NYG — FG Daluiso 43
Phil — Staley 64 run (Boniol kick)
NYG — FG Daluiso 33
Phil — FG Boniol 19
NYG — Calloway 5 pass from Graham (Daluiso kick)
NYG — Calloway 18 pass from Graham (Daluiso kick)

SAN FRANCISCO 38, ST. LOUIS 19—at 3Com Park, attendance 68,386. Steve Young passed for 2 touchdowns and ran for another as the 49ers defeated the Rams for the seventeenth consecutive time. Tony Horne's 31-yard kickoff return to begin the game set up Steve Bono's 5-yard touchdown pass to Ricky Proehl to give the Rams an early lead. The 49ers scored on their next two possessions, with Young's 4-yard touchdown pass to Jerry Rice giving the 49ers a 10-7 lead. The 49ers then exploded for 17 points in a span of less than seven minutes of the third quarter, highlighted by R.W. McQuarters's 72-yard punt return for his first NFL touchdown, and capped by Young's 16-yard scoring scramble to take a 28-7 lead. Bono threw 2 touchdown passes to cut the deficit to 31-19, but Greg Clark recovered the ensuing onside kick and Young found Terrell Owens open for a 24-yard touchdown with 3:38 left to finish the scoring. Young was 22 of 32 for 288 yards and 2 touchdowns. Bono was 15 of 30 for 240 yards and 3 touchdowns, with 1 interception. Proehl had 7 catches for 100 yards.

St. Louis	7	0	0	12	—	19
San Francisco	3	7	18	10	—	38

StL — Proehl 5 pass from Bono (Wilkins kick)
SF — FG Richey 20
SF — Rice 4 pass from Young (Richey kick)
SF — FG Richey 26
SF — McQuarters 72 punt return (Clark pass from Young)
SF — Young 16 run (Richey kick)
StL — Lee 25 pass from Bono (kick failed)
SF — FG Richey 44
StL — Proehl 17 pass from Bono (pass failed)
SF — Owens 24 pass from Young (Richey kick)

ARIZONA 16, SAN DIEGO 13—at Sun Devil Stadium, attendance 71,670. Chris Jacke drilled a 52-yard field goal as time expired to vault the Cardinals into the postseason for the first time since 1982. The victory also gave the Cardinals their first winning season since 1984. The Cardinals took a 10-0 lead, with Jacke's 37-yard field goal being set up by the first of Kwamie Lassiter's NFL record-tying 4 interceptions. After intercepting a pass to end the half, Lassiter's third interception, midway through the third quarter, stopped the Chargers at the Cardinals' 12. Jacke missed a 45-yard field-goal attempt, but Simeon Rice's fumble recovery at the Chargers' 27 a few plays later led to Jacke's 36-yard field goal and gave Arizona a 13-3 lead. John Carney's 26-yard field goal cut the deficit to 13-6 with 9:46 left in the game. Lassiter's fourth interception, at the Cardinals' 7, was returned 29 yards with 4:21 remaining, but Jacke missed a 42-yard field goal with 1:55 left. The Chargers took advantage and tied the game on Craig Whelihan's 30-yard fourth-and-20 scoring strike to Ryan Thelwell with 16 seconds left. Eric Metcalf returned the ensuing kickoff 46 yards to the Chargers' 44 with seven seconds left. Jake Plummer took four seconds to throw a 10-yard pass to Frank Sanders, thus setting up Jacke's heroics. Plummer was 20 of 41 for 274 yards. Sanders had 8 receptions for 106 yards. Whelihan was 16 of 40 for 214 yards and 1 touchdown, with 4 interceptions. Terrell Fletcher carried 23 times for 127 yards.

San Diego	0	3	0	10	—	13
Arizona	7	3	3	3	—	16

Ariz — Murrell 4 run (Jacke kick)
Ariz — FG Jacke 37
SD — FG Carney 31
Ariz — FG Jacke 36
SD — FG Carney 26
SD — Thelwell 30 pass from Whelihan (Carney kick)
Ariz — FG Jacke 52

DENVER 28, SEATTLE 21—at Mile High Stadium, attendance 74,057. Terrell Davis rushed for 178 yards to become the fourth running back in NFL history to surpass the 2,000-rushing yard mark for a season as the Broncos defeated Seattle. The Seahawks drove 67 yards following Jason Elam's missed field goal to take a 7-0 lead on the strength of Ricky Watters's 4-yard run. The Broncos' defense stymied the Seahawks into six consecutive scoreless possessions, while the offense drove 85, 85, 74, and 88 yards for touchdowns, 2 on touchdown passes from John Elway to Shannon Sharpe, to take a 28-7 lead with 11:45 left. The Seahawks strung together two touchdowns in the final six minutes, the second coming on Watters's first-ever touchdown pass with 1:32 remaining. However, Derek Loville recovered the ensuing onside kick to seal the victory. Elway was 26 of 36 for 338 yards and 4 touchdowns. Davis finished the season with 2,008 yards, passing the 2,000-yard mark on a 15-yard run with 8:52 remaining in the game. Jon Kitna was 22 of 37 for 242 yards and 1 touchdown, with 1 interception.

Seattle	7	0	0	14	—	21
Denver	0	14	7	7	—	28

Sea — Watters 4 run (Peterson kick)
Den — R. Smith 33 pass from Elway (Elam kick)
Den — Sharpe 17 pass from Elway (Elam kick)
Den — Davis 2 pass from Elway (Elam kick)
Den — Sharpe 1 pass from Elway (Elam kick)
Sea — Pritchard 7 pass from Kitna (Peterson kick)
Sea — May 1 pass from Watters (Peterson kick)

TAMPA BAY 35, CINCINNATI 0—at Cinergy Field, attendance 49,826. Mike Alstott rushed for 3 touchdowns as the Buccaneers accumulated their highest point total since week one of the 1990 season. The Buccaneers needed to win, have the Giants defeat the Eagles, and the Cardinals lose to the Chargers. The Giants won, but so did Arizona, thus denying the Buccaneers a postseason berth. After scoring on a 50-yard pass play from Trent Dilfer to Robb Thomas five plays into the game, the Buccaneers had possession inside the Bengals' 20 five more times during the first half, three of the possessions set up by special-teams gaffes: a bad punt snap at the Bengals' 8; a fumbled kickoff return by Eric Bieniemy at the Bengals' 31; and Don Davis's blocked punt at the Bengals' 4, to take a 28-0 halftime lead. The Bengals drove into Buccaneers' territory just once in the first half, but Doug Pelfrey missed a 40-yard field-goal attempt on the Bengals' first drive. The Bengals were thwarted twice in the second half, once being stopped on downs at the Buccaneers' 7 and the second time falling prey to Ronde Barber goal-line interception and 56-yard return to set up Alstott's final touchdown plunge. Dilfer was 10 of 16 for 111 yards and 2 touchdowns, with 1 interception. Paul Justin was 4 of 10 for 74 yards before being replaced by Eric Kresser, who was 7 of 17 for 102 yards, with 2 interceptions.

Tampa Bay	14	14	0	7	—	35
Cincinnati	0	0	0	0	—	0

TB — Thomas 50 pass from Dilfer (Husted kick)
TB — Alstott 1 run (Husted kick)
TB — Alstott 1 run (Husted kick)
TB — Anthony 4 pass from Dilfer (Husted kick)
TB — Alstott 3 run (Husted kick)

SUNDAY NIGHT, DECEMBER 27

DALLAS 23, WASHINGTON 7—at Texas Stadium, attendance 63,565. Emmitt Smith scored twice as he set an NFL record for career rushing touchdowns as the Cowboys became the first NFC East team to have an 8-0 record against its divisional opponents. Each team drove into the opposition's territory in five of their six first-half possessions, but the Redskins scored just once, turning the ball over twice, while the Cowboys scored four times en route to a 20-7 halftime edge. Smith passed Marcus Allen on the all-time list with a 1-yard run 2:20 into the second quarter for his 124th career rushing touchdown. The Cowboys' defense limited the Redskins to just 3 first downs in their five second-half possessions and did not permit them to cross the Cowboys' 42. Troy Aikman was 10 of 15 for 184 yards. Trent Green was 21 of 35 for 223 yards and 1 touchdown, with 1 interception.

Washington	7	0	0	0	—	7
Dallas	3	17	0	3	—	23

Dall — FG Cunningham 34
Wash — Shepherd 6 pass from Green (Blanchard kick)
Dall — E. Smith 1 run (Cunningham kick)
Dall — E. Smith 26 run (Cunningham kick)
Dall — FG Cunningham 23
Dall — FG Cunningham 26

MONDAY NIGHT, DECEMBER 28

JACKSONVILLE 21, PITTSBURGH 3—at ALLTEL Stadium, attendance 74,143. The Jaguars prepared for the playoffs by handing the Steelers their fifth consecutive loss and their first non winning record since 1991. The Steelers drove into Jaguars' territory on each of their first 3 possessions, but fumbled and missed a field goal before settling for a 24-yard field goal. A 40-yard pass interference penalty set up rookie quarterback Jonathan Quinn's first career touchdown run, and Quinn's 64-yard pass to Keenan McCardell on the next possession led to Fred Taylor's 9-yard touchdown grab. Quinn's 42-yard pass to Jimmy Smith in the third quarter led to Taylor's 12-yard scamper and a 21-3 Jaguars lead. Kordell Stewart had three potential touchdown passes dropped in the end zone, including two on back-to-back plays in the fourth quarter to turn the ball over on downs. Quinn was 10 of 19 for 192 yards and 1 touchdown. Stewart was 17 of 37 for 174 yards, with 2 interceptions. Jerome Bettis rushed for 139 yards, marking his eighth consecutive 100-yard rushing game on *Monday Night Football*.

Pittsburgh	0	3	0	0	—	3
Jacksonville	0	14	7	0	—	21

Pitt — FG N. Johnson 24
Jac — Quinn 15 run (Hollis kick)
Jac — Taylor 9 pass from Quinn (Hollis kick)
Jac — Taylor 12 run (Hollis kick)

EIGHTEENTH WEEK SUMMARIES
SATURDAY, JANUARY 2
AFC WILD CARD PLAYOFF GAME

MIAMI 24, BUFFALO 17—at Pro Player Stadium, attendance 72,698. Trace Armstrong sacked Doug Flutie and forced him to fumble at the Dolphins' 3-yard line with nine seconds left to preserve Miami's first postseason victory in four seasons. Flutie completed a 65-yard pass to Eric Moulds on the game's first play, but Terrell Buckley stripped Moulds and Brock Marion recovered. Olindo Mare kicked field goals to finish each of the Dolphins' first 2 possessions. Following the second score, Mare attempted an onside kick, but Buffalo's Dan Brandenburg recovered the ball. Flutie's 37-yard pass to Moulds set up Thurman Thomas's touchdown run to give Buffalo a 7-6 lead. The Bills drove to the Dolphins' 6 late in the half, but Marion intercepted Flutie's pass in the end zone. Dan Marino's 52-yard Hail Mary pass was caught by Oronde Gadsden at the Bills' 9 with six seconds left, but Mare's 26-yard field-goal attempt hit the right upright as the half expired. Karim Abdul-Jabbar's 3-yard run, and Stanley Pritchett's 2-point conversion jaunt, gave the Dolphins a 14-7 lead with 2:32 left in the quarter. However, Flutie's 23-yard pass to Moulds set up the pair's 32-yard touchdown connection to tie the game in the quarter's final minute. Mare's 23-yard field goal gave the Dolphins a 17-14 lead with 9:45 left, and Jerry Wilson forced Andre Reed to fumble and Buckley recovered at the Dolphins' 44 with 8:02 left. The Dolphins burned 4:20 off the clock and scored on Marino's 11-yard touchdown pass to Lamar Thomas. On the following drive, Buffalo reached the Dolphins' 1, but a personal foul penalty on Reed pushed the Bills back and they settled for Steve Christie's field goal with 1:33 left to cut the deficit to 24-17. Sam Madison bobbled the ensuing onsides kick, and Buffalo's Curt Schulz recovered at the Bills' 31. The Bills drove to the Dolphins' 5 with 17 seconds left before Shane Burton recovered the fumble that Armstrong forced. Marino was 23 of 34 for 235 yards and 1 touchdown, with 1 interception. Flutie was 21 of 36 for 360 yards and 1 touchdown, with 1 interception. Moulds, who had 9 catches, set an NFL playoff record with 240 receiving yards.

Buffalo	0	7	7	3	—	17
Miami	3	3	8	10	—	24

Mia — FG Mare 31
Mia — FG Mare 40
Buff — Thomas 1 run (Christie kick)
Mia — Abdul-Jabbar 3 run (Pritchett run)
Buff — Moulds 32 pass from Flutie (Christie kick)
Mia — FG Mare 23
Mia — Thomas 12 pass from Marino (Mare kick)
Buff — FG Christie 33

NFC WILD CARD PLAYOFF GAME

ARIZONA 20, DALLAS 7—at Texas Stadium, attendance 62,969. Jake Plummer passed for 2 touchdowns and Aeneas Williams had 2 interceptions as the Cardinals won a postseason game for the first time since 1947. Richie Cunningham missed a 36-yard field goal in the latter part of the first quarter, and Plummer immediately seized the opportunity, firing a 59-yard pass to Frank Sanders. Three plays later, Plummer threw a shovel pass to Adrian Murrell, who scooted into the end zone to give Arizona a 7-0 lead. The Cowboys drove deep into Cardinals' territory, but Mark Maddox stopped Emmitt Smith on fourth-and-1 at the Cardinals' 7. Chris Jacke kicked a field goal 19 seconds before halftime, and Murrell raced 74 yards on the second play of the second half, setting up Plummer's 3-yard toss to Larry Centers to give the Cardinals a 17-0 lead 1:16 into the third quarter. Williams's second interception at the Cowboys' 37 set up Jacke's second field goal 2:05 into the final quarter. The Cardinals' defense twice stopped Dallas on fourth-down attempts before Troy Aikman's 6-yard pass to Billy Davis averted the shutout with 3:33 remaining. Larry Centers recovered the ensuing onsides kick, and Tommy Bennett intercepted an Aikman pass with 48 seconds remaining to secure the victory. Plummer was 19 of 36 for 213 yards, 2 touchdowns, with 2 interceptions. Aikman was 22 of 49 for 191 yards, 1 touchdown, with 3 interceptions.

Arizona	7	3	7	3	—	20
Dallas	0	0	0	7	—	7

Ariz — Murrell 12 pass from Plummer (Jacke kick)
Ariz — FG Jacke 37
Ariz — Centers 3 pass from Plummer (Jacke kick)
Ariz — FG Jacke 46
Dall — Davis 6 pass from Aikman (Cunningham kick)

SUNDAY, JANUARY 3
AFC WILD CARD PLAYOFF GAME

JACKSONVILLE 25, NEW ENGLAND 10—at Foxboro Stadium, attendance 71,139. Fred Taylor rushed for 162 yards, the most in the postseason by a rookie since Timmy Smith in Super Bowl XXII, and scored a touchdown as the Jaguars reached the divisional playoffs for the second time in the franchise's four seasons. The Jaguars scored on two of their first three possessions, the second keyed by Taylor's 46-yard run, to take a 6-0 lead. Taylor reversed field on a 21-yard gain before sprinting 13 yards for a touchdown in the second quarter to give the Jaguars a 12-0 halftime lead. The Jaguars' defense forced 7 punts in the first half, as Jacksonville had more first downs (12-1) and total yards (199-54). The Patriots retaliated with a 17-play, 85-yard scoring drive that took 8:48 off the clock on their first possession of the second half, capped by Robert Edwards's 1-yard run. Adam Vinatieri's field goal on the next drive cut the deficit to 12-10, but Mark Brunell, who missed the previous three games with an ankle injury, needed just six plays to respond, lofting a 37-yard touchdown pass to a diving Jimmy Smith to give the Jaguars a 19-10 lead with 12:24 remaining in the game. Tony Brackens recovered a fumble and sacked Scott Zolak on fourth down to set up 2 late Mike Hollis field goals as the Patriots never crossed midfield the remainder of the game. Brunell was 14 of 34 for 161 yards and 1 touchdown. Zolak, who started in place of injured Drew Bledsoe, was 21 of 44 for 190 yards, with 1 interception. The Jaguars' defense limited the Patriots to 35 rushing yards on 19 carries.

New England	0	0	7	3	—	10
Jacksonville	6	6	0	13	—	25

Jac — FG Hollis 35
Jac — FG Hollis 24
Jac — Taylor 13 run (run failed)
NE — Edwards 1 run (Vinatieri kick)
NE — FG Vinatieri 27
Jac — Smith 37 pass from Brunell (Hollis kick)
Jac — FG Hollis 34
Jac — FG Hollis 21

NFC WILD CARD PLAYOFF GAME

SAN FRANCISCO 30, GREEN BAY 27—at 3Com Park, attendance 66,506. With eight seconds left and no timeouts remaining, Steve Young fired a 25-yard strike to Terrell Owens to give the 49ers a victory against the Packers in stunning fashion. Darren Sharper forced Owens to fumble at the Packers' 47 on the game's third play. Pat Terrell recovered the ball, leading to Ryan Longwell's first field goal. Merton Hanks forced Dorsey Levens to fumble later in the quarter, and Chris Doleman recovered. Greg Clark caught a touchdown pass from Steve Young three plays later to give the 49ers a 7-3 lead. Brett Favre threw a 2-yard touchdown pass to Antonio Freeman on the next drive, but R.W. McQuarter's 19-yard punt return set up Wade Richey's tying field goal midway through the second quarter. Randy Kirk recovered Roell Preston's muffed punt at the 49ers' 18, but George Koonce intercepted a Young pass two plays later and the Packers proceeded to drive 83 yards to take a 17-10 lead on Levens's touchdown run. Recently signed free-agent Charles Haley pressured Favre into throwing an early second-half interception, returned 17 yards by Lee Woodall to the Packers' 33. From there, Young threw his second touchdown pass of the game to Clark to tie the score. Three field goals on successive possessions, 2 by Richey, gave the 49ers a 23-20 lead with 6:12 to play. Darnell Walker intercepted Favre at the Packers' 43, but the 49ers were forced to punt giving Green Bay the ball at their own 11 with 4:19 remaining. Favre threw a 47-yard pass to Corey Bradford, and a few plays later lofted a 15-yard scoring pass to Freeman to give the Packers a 27-23 lead with 1:56 to play. The 49ers drove to the Packers' 25 with eight seconds left and no timeouts, when Young fired a 25-yard strike to Owens, who was belted by Terrell and Sharper but held on for the winning points. Young, who completed 7 of 9 passes on the game-winning 76-yard drive, was 18 of 32 for 182 yards and 3 touchdowns, with 2 interceptions. Garrison Hearst had 22 carries for 128 yards. Favre was 20 of 35 for 292 yards and 2 touchdowns, with 2 interceptions. Levens had 27 carries for 116 yards.

Green Bay	3	14	0	10	—	27
San Francisco	7	3	10	10	—	30

GB — FG Longwell 23
SF — Clark 1 pass from Young (Richey kick)
GB — Freeman 2 pass from Favre (Longwell kick)
SF — FG Richey 34
GB — Levens 2 run (Longwell kick)
SF — Clark 8 pass from Young (Richey kick)
SF — FG Richey 48
GB — FG Longwell 37
SF — FG Richey 40
GB — Freeman 15 pass from Favre (Longwell kick)
SF — Owens 25 pass from Young (Richey kick)

NINETEENTH WEEK SUMMARIES
SATURDAY, JANUARY 9
NFC DIVISIONAL PLAYOFF GAME

ATLANTA 20, SAN FRANCISCO 18—at Georgia Dome, attendance 70,262. Jamal Anderson rushed for 113 yards and 2 touchdowns as the Falcons won just their third playoff game in club history. Tim Dwight's 36-yard punt return midway through the first quarter set up Anderson's first touchdown run, and Anderson carried 4 times for 52 yards on a 7-play, 82-yard second-quarter drive, capped by a 34-yard scamper, to give Atlanta a 14-0 lead. The 49ers scored twice in the final 1:10 of the half, with Steve Young's 34-yard pass to Chuck Levy on third-and-23 setting up Jerry Rice's 17-yard touchdown catch, and Junior Bryant's interception leading to Wade Richey's 36-yard field goal as the half expired. Eugene Robinson stopped a 49ers' drive late in the third quarter by intercepting a pass at the Falcons' 3 and returning it 77 yards, being denied a touchdown by Terry Kirby's tackle. Atlanta settled for Morten Andersen's 29-yard field goal, and Andersen tacked three more points on the board less than six minutes later following William White's interception. The 49ers responded with a 13-play, 87-yard drive, capped by Young's 8-yard run with 2:57 remaining. A high snap on the extra-point attempt prompted holder Ty Detmer to roll out and throw a 2-point conversion pass to Greg Clark to cut the deficit to 20-18. The 49ers' onside kick hopped out of bounds, and San Francisco did not gain possession until getting the ball on their own 4-yard line with 38 seconds left. The 49ers' hopes ended when White intercepted Young at the 49ers' 35 as time expired. Chris Chandler was 13 of 19 for 169 yards, with 1 interception. Young was 23 of 37 for 289 yards and 1 touchdown, with 3 interceptions.

San Francisco	0	10	0	8	—	18
Atlanta	7	7	3	3	—	20

Atl — Anderson 2 run (Andersen kick)
Atl — Anderson 34 run (Andersen kick)
SF — Rice 17 pass from Young (Richey kick)
SF — FG Richey 36
Atl — FG Andersen 29
Atl — FG Andersen 32
SF — Young 8 run (Clark pass from Detmer)

AFC DIVISIONAL PLAYOFF GAME

DENVER 38, MIAMI 3—at Mile High Stadium, attendance 75,729. Terrell Davis rushed for 199 yards and 2 touchdowns and the Broncos' defense limited Miami to just 14 rushing yards as Denver began its quest to repeat as Super Bowl champions. The Broncos scored on their first three possessions, driving 92 and 66 yards in the first quarter and, following an Olindo Mare field goal, marching 87 yards to a third touchdown in the second quarter to take a 21-3 lead at halftime. Davis rushed for more yards (129) than the Dolphins had gained (119) at intermission. Davis scampered 62 yards on the first play of the second half to set up Jason Elam's field goal to give Denver a 24-

3 lead. The Dolphins drove into Broncos' territory three times in the second half, but Bill Romanowski and Darrius Johnson each recorded interceptions and Neil Smith recovered Oronde Gadsden's fumble and rumbled 79 yards for the game's final points. John Elway was 14 of 23 for 182 yards and 1 touchdown. Dan Marino was 26 of 37 for 243 yards, with 2 interceptions. O.J. McDuffie had 9 receptions for 118 yards.

Miami	0	3	0	0	—	3
Denver	14	7	3	14	—	38

Den — Davis 1 run (Elam kick)
Den — Davis 20 run (Elam kick)
Mia — FG Mare 22
Den — Loville 11 run (Elam kick)
Den — FG Elam 32
Den — R. Smith 28 pass from Elway (Elam kick)
Den — N. Smith 79 fumble return (Elam kick)

SUNDAY, JANUARY 10
AFC DIVISIONAL PLAYOFF GAME

N.Y. JETS 34, JACKSONVILLE 24—at Giants Stadium, attendance 78,817. Keyshawn Johnson caught a touchdown pass, rushed for a touchdown, and intercepted a pass to seal the Jets' first postseason victory since 1986. The Jets needed just seven plays on the game's opening drive to reach the end zone, courtesy of Vinny Testaverde's 21-yard pass to Johnson, to take a 7-0 lead. A 13-play drive set up John Hall's 52-yard field goal to give the Jets a 10-0 lead, and Otis Smith's interception on the Jaguars' first play after the field goal gave the Jets the ball at their own 40. Ten plays later, from the Jaguars' 22, Curtis Martin fumbled, and Chris Hudson recovered the ball. Hudson ran into Jets' territory and attempted a lateral, recovered by Johnson at the Jets' 35. The Jets then took 11 plays to march 65 yards, capped by Johnson's 10-yard reverse run to take a 17-0 lead with 33 seconds left in the half. The Jets had run 34 of the last 35 plays from scrimmage. The Jaguars got on the scoreboard, as Jimmy Smith caught Mark Brunell's 52-yard bomb as the half expired. Corwin Brown's interception in the opening minutes of the second half set up Martin's 1-yard touchdown run, but Reggie Barlow's 88-yard kickoff return led to Brunell's 3-yard touchdown pass to Keenan McCardell to cut the deficit to 24-10. Martin scored again on the next drive, but the Jaguars used Brunell's second touchdown pass to Smith to cut the lead to 31-21, and then used Wayne Chrebet's fumble to set up Mike Hollis's 37-yard field goal with 6:38 left. Donovin Darius halted the Jets' next drive with an interception in the end zone, but he stepped out and was tackled at the Jets' 1 with 2:24 left. The Jaguars failed to get a first down, and Hall iced the game with a 30-yard field goal with 24 seconds left. In the final seconds, Brunell's Hail Mary pass was picked off by Johnson, who finished with 9 receptions for 121 yards, with a touchdown, interception , and fumble recovery. Testaverde was 24 of 36 for 284 yards and 1 touchdown, with 1 interception. Martin rushed 36 times for 124 yards, while Johnson had 9 receptions for 121 yards. Brunell was 12 of 31 for 156 yards and 3 touchdowns, with 3 interceptions. Smith had 5 catches for 104 yards.

Jacksonville	0	7	7	10	—	24
N.Y. Jets	7	10	14	3	—	34

NYJ — K. Johnson 21 pass from Testaverde (Hall kick)
NYJ — FG Hall 52
NYJ — K. Johnson 10 run (Hall kick)
Jac — Smith 52 pass from Brunell (Hollis kick)
NYJ — Martin 1 run (Hall kick)
Jac — McCardell 3 pass from Brunell (Hollis kick)
NYJ — Martin 1 run (Hall kick)
Jac — Smith 19 pass from Brunell (Hollis kick)
Jac — FG Hollis 37
NYJ — FG Hall 30

NFC DIVISIONAL PLAYOFF GAME

MINNESOTA 41, ARIZONA 21—at Metrodome, attendance 63,760. Randall Cunningham threw 3 touchdown passes, and Leroy Hoard scored 3 times, as the Vikings reached the NFC Championship Game for the first time since 1987. The Vikings consumed nearly half of the first quarter during a 13-play, 80-yard game-opening drive capped by Hoard's 1-yard plunge. After a Cardinals' punt, the Vikings were set to score again, but Aeneas Williams intercepted a pass in the end zone. However, Jake Plummer threw interceptions on consecutive plays, leading to a Vikings' touchdown and a field goal. The Vikings led 17-0 before the Cardinals recorded a first down. The clubs exchanged touchdowns, with Hoard's second coming with just 24 seconds left in the half, as Minnesota took a 24-7 lead into the locker room. The Cardinals used the first 7:35 of the third quarter to drive 80 yards, capped by Mario Bates's second touchdown run. However, David Palmer's 38-yard kickoff return set up Gary Anderson's 20-yard field goal and, after Antonio Banks recovered Plummer's fumble at the Cardinals' 10, Cunningham threw a 2-yard scoring pass to Randy Moss to give Minnesota a 34-14 lead late in the third quarter. Eric Metcalf's 36-yard punt return set up Bates's third touchdown, with 11:45 left, but the Vikings went on a 12-play, 73-yard drive that consumed more than seven minutes and culminated with Hoard's third touchdown with 4:23 left. Cunningham was 17 of 27 for 236 yards and 3 touchdowns, with 1 interception. Robert Smith had 19 carries for 124 yards. Plummer was 23 of 41 for 242 yards, with 2 interceptions.

Arizona	0	7	7	7	—	21
Minnesota	7	17	10	7	—	41

Minn — Hoard 1 run (Anderson kick)
Minn — Glover 15 pass from Cunningham (Anderson kick)
Minn — FG Anderson 34
Ariz — Bates 1 run (Jacke kick)
Minn — Hoard 16 pass from Cunningham (Anderson kick)
Ariz — Bates 1 run (Jacke kick)
Minn — FG Anderson 20
Minn — Moss 2 pass from Cunningham (Anderson kick)
Ariz — Bates 1 run (Jacke kick)
Minn — Hoard 6 run (Anderson kick)

TWENTIETH WEEK SUMMARIES
SUNDAY, JANUARY 17, 1999
NFC CHAMPIONSHIP PLAYOFF GAME

ATLANTA 30, MINNESOTA 27 (OT)—at Metrodome, attendance 64,060. Chris Chandler passed for 3 touchdowns, and Morten Andersen made a 38-yard field goal 11:52 into overtime to catapult the Falcons into their first Super Bowl. The Falcons drove 12 plays to score on their opening possession, but Minnesota retaliated by scoring on their first four possessions. First, Randall Cunningham capped a 5-play drive with a 31-yard touchdown pass to Randy Moss. Fumbles by Harold Green and O.J. Santiago led to Gary Anderson's 29-yard field goal and Cunningham's 1-yard sneak. Following a punt, Anderson, who did not miss a field-goal or extra-point attempt all season, made a 35-yard field goal to give the Vikings a 20-7 lead with 2:45 left in the half. The Vikings' defense forced another punt and started at their own 18 with 1:17 left in the half. After 2 incompletions, Chuck Smith stripped Cunningham of the ball, and Travis Hall recovered. Chandler fired a 14-yard scoring strike to Terance Mathis on the next play to cut the deficit to 20-14 at halftime. Andersen's field goal cut the Vikings' lead to three points midway through the third quarter, but the Vikings used a 15-play, 82-yard drive, culminated by Cunningham's 5-yard touchdown pass to Matthew Hatchette, to take a 27-17 lead with 13:41 left. Chandler's 70-yard pass to Tony Martin set up Andersen's second field goal with 11:02 left, and Cunningham's fumble, recovered by Shane Dronett at the Vikings' 30, kept the Falcons' hopes alive. However, trailing 27-20 and faced with fourth-and-4 from the Vikings' 24 with 6:13 left, Chandler threw an incomplete pass. The Vikings held onto the ball for the next four minutes, but Anderson's 38-yard field-goal attempt failed, his first miss in 122 attempts. Chandler promptly drove the Falcons downfield, with the big play being a 29-yard pass to Ronnie Harris, and on second-and-10 from the Vikings' 16 with 57 seconds left, Chandler found Mathis just beyond the goal-line for the game-tying touchdown. After a scramble and incomplete pass, Cunningham took a knee and the game went to overtime. Minnesota won the toss, but couldn't move beyond midfield with either one of its two possessions. Following the second overtime punt, the Falcons began at the their 9, and Chandler found Santiago for 15- and 26-yard gains to move into Vikings' territory. A scramble by Chandler and a 9-yard run by Jamal Anderson set up Andersen's winning kick. Chandler was 27 of 43 for 340 yards and 3 touchdowns. Martin had 5 catches for 129 yards. Cunningham was 29 of 48 for 266 yards and 2 touchdowns. This was the first championship game to go to overtime since the 1986 AFC Championship Game.

Atlanta	7	7	3	10	3	—	30
Minnesota	7	13	0	7	0	—	27

Atl — J. Anderson 5 pass from Chandler (Andersen kick)
Minn — Moss 31 pass from Cunningham (G. Anderson kick)
Minn — FG G. Anderson 29
Minn — Cunningham 1 run (Anderson kick)
Minn — FG G. Anderson 35
Atl — Mathis 14 pass from Chandler (Andersen kick)
Atl — FG Andersen 27
Minn — Hatchette 5 pass from Cunningham (G. Anderson kick)
Atl — FG Andersen 24
Atl — Mathis 16 pass from Chandler (Andersen kick)
Atl — FG Andersen 38

AFC CHAMPIONSHIP PLAYOFF GAME

DENVER 23, N.Y. JETS 10—at Mile High Stadium, attendance 75,482. In John Elway's final game in Denver, Terrell Davis rushed for 167 yards, and the Broncos forced 6 Jets' turnovers en route to scoring the game's final 23 points to capture their second consecutive AFC title. The game was played in a strong wind, with the wind chill dipping to 18 degrees and causing special teams problems for both sides. John Hall missed a 42-yard field goal on the game's opening drive, but the Jets kept the game scoreless by forcing Elway to throw an incomplete pass on fourth-and-goal from the Jets' 1 late in the first quarter. Tom Rouen dropped the ball while attempting to punt early in the second quarter, resulting in a 9-yard loss and giving the Jets the ball at the Broncos' 43. However, Keith Byars fumbled on the ensuing possession. Hall ended the half with a 32-yard field goal to give the Jets a 3-0 lead going into the locker room. Blake Spence blocked Rouen's punt early in the second half, and Fred Baxter recovered the ball at the Broncos' 1. Curtis Martin crashed into the end zone on the next play to give the Jets a 10-0 lead with 11:56 left in the third quarter. Elway, who had passed for just 33 yards in the first half, threw a 47-yard pass to Ed McCaffrey on the first play of the next drive, and then found Howard Griffith two plays later for a touchdown. A strong wind knocked Jason Elam's next kickoff to the ground near the Jets' 25. James Farrior momentarily recovered the bouncing ball, but he fumbled and Keith Burns's recovery gave the Broncos the ball at the Jets' 31. Elam's field goal tied the game with 8:23 left, and, after forcing a punt, Elam gave the Broncos the lead with 2:58 left in the quarter. The Broncos' defense forced another punt, and Darrien Gordon returned it 36 yards, setting up Davis's 31-yard touchdown run to give the Broncos 20 points in a span of 11:38. Gordon intercepted Vinny Testaverde twice in the final five minutes, the first of which led to Elam's final field goal. Elway was 13 of 34 for 173 yards and 1 touchdown. Testaverde was 31 of 52 for 356 yards, with 2 interceptions. Wayne Chrebet had 8 receptions for 121 yards.

N.Y. Jets	0	3	7	0	—	10
Denver	0	0	20	3	—	23

NYJ — FG Hall 32
NYJ — Martin 1 run (Hall kick)
Den — Griffith 11 pass from Elway (Elam kick)
Den — FG Elam 44
Den — FG Elam 48
Den — Davis 31 run (Elam kick)
Den — FG Elam 35

TWENTY-FIRST WEEK SUMMARY
SUNDAY, JANUARY 31, 1999
SUPER BOWL XXXIII

DENVER 34, ATLANTA 19—at Pro Player Stadium, attendance 74,803. John Elway, in his last game, passed for 336 yards and ran for a touchdown to earn most valuable player honors as the Broncos became the first AFC team to win consecutive Super Bowls since the Steelers won XIII and XIV. A 25-yard pass interference penalty on Ray Crockett assisted the Falcons' 10-play, 48-yard game-opening drive that was capped by Morten Andersen's 32-yard field goal. Elway's third-down 41-yard pass to Rod Smith kept alive Denver's ensuing drive and led to Howard Griffith's 1-yard touchdown run. Ronnie Bradford's interception and return to the Broncos' 35 late in the first quarter gave Atlanta excellent field position. However, Jamal Anderson was stopped for no gain on third-and-1 and thrown for a 2-yard loss on fourth down. Denver capitalized on its defensive effort by tacking three points on the board with Jason Elam's 26-yard field goal. The Falcons responded by driving to the Broncos' 8, but Andersen's 26-yard field-goal attempt sailed wide right and on the next play, Elway fired an 80-yard touchdown pass to Smith to turn a possible 10-6 game into a 17-3 Broncos lead. Andersen's 28-yard field goal and 2 Elam misses on the Broncos' first two second-half possessions gave Atlanta an opportunity to climb back into the game. However, Darrien Gordon dashed the Falcons' hopes with interceptions on consecutive possessions inside the Broncos' 20 to stop drives and set up Broncos touchdowns. Gordon returned the first interception, on a tipped pass, 58 yards to the Falcons' 24 to set up Griffith's second touchdown five plays later, and picked the second pass off at the Broncos' 2 and returned it 50 yards. Terrell Davis turned a short pass into a 39-yard gain, and Elway scored two plays later to give Denver a 31-6 lead. Tim Dwight returned the ensuing kickoff for a touchdown, and, after an Elam field goal, the Falcons offense scored with 2:04 remaining on Chandler's 3-yard pass to Tony Martin. Byron Chamberlain recovered the ensuing onside kick, but, Tyrone Braxton recovered Anderson's fumble at the Falcons' 33 with 1:30 remaining to ice the game. The Falcons drove inside the Broncos' 30 seven times, but tallied just 1 touchdown and 2 field goals during the opportunities, throwing 2 interceptions, missing 1 field goal, and turning the ball over on downs the other 4 possessions. Elway was 18 of 29 for 336 yards and 1 touchdown, with 1 interception. Davis had 25 carries for 102 yards. Smith had 5 receptions for 152 yards. Chandler was 19 of 35 for 219 yards and 1 touchdown, with 3 interceptions.

Denver	7	10	0	17	—	34
Atlanta	3	3	0	13	—	19

Atl — FG Andersen 32
Den — Griffith 1 run (Elam kick)
Den — FG Elam 26
Den — R. Smith 80 pass from Elway (Elam kick)
Atl — FG Andersen 28
Den — Griffith 1 run (Elam kick)
Den — Elway 3 run (Elam kick)
Atl — Dwight 94 kickoff return (Andersen kick)
Den — FG Elam 37
Atl — Mathis 3 pass from Chandler (pass failed)

TWENTY-SECOND WEEK SUMMARY
SUNDAY, FEBRUARY 7, 1999
1999 PRO BOWL GAME

AFC 23, NFC 10—at Aloha Stadium, attendance 50,075. John Elway, appearing in uniform on a football field for possibly the final time, drove the AFC to its initial touchdown and then watched a strong defensive effort as the AFC won the Pro Bowl for the third consecutive season. Elway capped a game-opening 61-yard drive with a touchdown pass to Sam Gash. The AFC led 10-3 late in the first half when Deion Sanders intercepted a Vinny Testaverde pass at the NFC's 10 and raced downfield, only to be caught by Ed McCaffrey at the AFC 3-yard line as the half expired. The NFC drove into AFC territory early in the second half, but Ty Law thwarted the NFC's spirits with a 67-yard interception return for a touchdown to give the AFC a 17-3 lead. The NFC reached the end zone three minutes later as Emmitt Smith scored, but the AFC responded with a field goal on its ensuing possession and Jason Elam's third field goal with 1:02 remaining finished the scoring. Elway played just one drive and was 4 of 5 for 55 yards and 1 touchdown. Keyshawn Johnson had 7 catches for 87 yards and shared the player-of-the-game honors with Law. Chandler completed 9 of 25 passes for 133 yards en route to leading the NFC to its only touchdown. Randy Moss had 7 catches for 108 yards.

NFC	3	0	7	0	—	10
AFC	7	3	10	3	—	23

AFC — Gash 3 pass from Elway (Elam kick)
NFC — FG Anderson 23
AFC — FG Elam 23
AFC — Law 67 interception return (Elam kick)
NFC — E. Smith 3 run (Anderson kick)
AFC — FG Elam 46
AFC — FG Elam 26

1998 PRO FOOTBALL AWARDS

	NFL	AFC	NFC
PRO FOOTBALL WRITERS OF AMERICA			
Most Valuable Player	Terrell Davis		
Rookie of the Year		Charles Woodson	Randy Moss
Coach of the Year	Dan Reeves		
ASSOCIATED PRESS			
Most Valuable Player	Terrell Davis		
Offensive Player of the Year	Terrell Davis		
Defensive Player of the Year	Reggie White		
Offensive Rookie of the Year	Randy Moss		
Defensive Rookie of the Year	Charles Woodson		
Coach of the Year	Dan Reeves		
THE SPORTING NEWS			
Player of the Year	Terrell Davis		
Rookie of the Year	Randy Moss		
Coach of the Year	Dan Reeves		
FOOTBALL NEWS			
Player of the Year		Terrell Davis	Randall Cunningham
Coach of the Year	Dan Reeves		
Rookie of the Year	Randy Moss		
PRO FOOTBALL WEEKLY			
Most Valuable Player	Terrell Davis		
Defensive Most Valuable Player	Reggie White		
Offensive Rookie of the Year	Randy Moss		
Defensive Rookie of the Year	Charles Woodson		
Coach of the Year	Dan Reeves		
Assistant Coach of the Year	Brian Billick		
Golden Toe	Gary Anderson		
Comeback Player of the Year	Doug Flutie		
Executive of the Year	Minnesota Vikings front office		
FOOTBALL DIGEST			
Player of the Year	Terrell Davis		
Defensive Player of the Year	Junior Seau		
Offensive Rookie of the Year	Randy Moss		
Defensive Rookie of the Year	Charles Woodson		
Coach of the Year	Dan Reeves		
SPORTS ILLUSTRATED			
Player of the Year	Marshall Faulk		
Coach of the Year	(tie) Dan Reeves, Mike Shanahan, Dennis Green		
Rookie of the Year	Randy Moss		
USA TODAY			
Coach of the Year		Bill Parcells	Dan Reeves
COLLEGE AND PRO FOOTBALL NEWSWEEKLY			
Offensive Player of the Year	Randall Cunningham		
Defensive Player of the Year	Zach Thomas		
Offensive Rookie of the Year	Randy Moss		
Defensive Rookie of the Year		Charles Woodson	Vonnie Holliday
Coach of the Year	Dan Reeves		
Rookie Coach of the Year	Chan Gailey		
MAXWELL CLUB PLAYER OF THE YEAR (Bert Bell Trophy)	Randall Cunningham		
MAXWELL CLUB COACH OF THE YEAR (Earle "Greasy" Neale Trophy)	Dennis Green		
MILLER LITE PLAYER OF THE YEAR	Randall Cunningham		
SPRINT NFL MAN OF THE YEAR	Dan Marino		
SUPER BOWL MOST VALUABLE PLAYER (Pete Rozelle Trophy)	John Elway		
AFC-NFC PRO BOWL PLAYER OF THE GAME (Dan McGuire Award)	(tie) Keyshawn Johnson, Ty Law		

1998 PLAYERS OF THE WEEK/MONTH

1998 AFC PLAYERS OF THE WEEK

Week	Offense		Defense		Special Teams	
Week 1	RB	James Stewart, Jacksonville	LB	Derrick Thomas, Kansas City	K	John Carney, San Diego
Week 2	RB	Terrell Davis, Denver	CB	Rod Woodson, Baltimore	PR-KR	Reggie Barlow, Jacksonville
Week 3	RB	Fred Taylor, Jacksonville	CB	Ray Crockett, Denver	K	Pete Stoyanovich, Kansas City
Week 4	RB	Priest Holmes, Baltimore	LB	Levon Kirkland, Pittsburgh	PR	Jermaine Lewis, Baltimore
Week 5	RB	Terrell Davis, Denver	DE	Bruce Smith, Buffalo	K	Adam Vinatieri, New England
Week 6	WR	Carl Pickens, Cincinnati	S	Blaine Bishop, Tennessee	P	Leo Araguz, Oakland
Week 7	QB	Vinny Testaverde, New York Jets	DT	Norman Hand, San Diego	PR-KR	Mike Archie, Tennessee
Week 8	RB	Terrell Davis, Denver	LB	Mo Lewis, New York Jets	K	Jason Elam, Denver
Week 9	QB	Doug Flutie, Buffalo	S	Lawyer Milloy, New England	KR	Vaughn Hebron, Denver
Week 10	RB	Eddie George, Tennessee	DE	Michael McCrary, Baltimore	P	Craig Hentrich, Tennessee
Week 11	QB	Peyton Manning, Indianapolis	LB	Robert Jones, Miami	CB-KR	Aaron Glenn, New York Jets
Week 12	QB	Drew Bledsoe, New England	CB	Dewayne Washington, Pittsburgh	K	Adam Vinatieri, New England
Week 13	QB	Jon Kitna, Seattle	CB	Darrien Gordon, Denver	K	John Hall, New York Jets
Week 14	QB	John Elway, Denver	DT	Chad Eaton, New England	K	Steve Christie, Buffalo
Week 15	RB	Marshall Faulk, Indianapolis	LB	Bryan Cox, New York Jets	K	Al Del Greco, Tennessee
Week 16	QB	Dan Marino, Miami	S	Willie Clay, New England	KR	Vaughn Hebron, Denver
Week 17	RB	Terrell Davis, Denver	DE	Anthony Pleasant, New York Jets	P	Bryan Barker, Jacksonville

1998 AFC PLAYERS OF THE MONTH

Month	Offense		Defense		Special Teams	
September	RB	Terrell Davis, Denver	LB	Zach Thomas, Miami	PR	Jermaine Lewis, Baltimore
October	RB	Terrell Davis, Denver	CB	Eric Allen, Oakland	K	Adam Vinatieri, New England
November	QB	Vinny Testaverde, New York Jets	LB	Chad Brown, Seattle	P	Craig Hentrich, Tennessee
December	QB	Vinny Testaverde, New York Jets	LB	Robert Jones, Miami	K	Steve Christie, Buffalo

1998 NFC PLAYERS OF THE WEEK

Week	Offense		Defense		Special Teams	
Week 1	RB	Garrison Hearst, San Francisco	DE	Michael Strahan, New York Giants	KR	Roell Preston, Green Bay
Week 2	QB	Steve Young, San Francisco	DE	Reggie White, Green Bay	PR	Jacquez Green, Tampa Bay
Week 3	RB	Greg Hill, St. Louis	DE	Simeon Rice, Arizona	K	Gary Anderson, Minnesota
			WR-CB-PR	Deion Sanders, Dallas (PRIME TIME AWARD)		
Week 4	QB	Randall Cunningham, Minnesota	LB	Mark Fields, New Orleans	KR	Terry Fair, Detroit
Week 5	QB	Randall Cunningham, Minnesota	DT	Jim Flanigan, Chicago	KR	Tim Dwight, Atlanta
Week 6	QB	Chris Chandler, Atlanta	LB	Ronald McKinnon, Arizona	K	Morten Andersen, Atlanta
Week 7	QB	Steve Young, San Francisco	S	Mark Carrier, Detroit	K	Jeff Jaeger, Chicago
Week 8	RB	Robert Smith, Minnesota	DE	Roy Barker, San Francisco	P	Mark Royals, New Orleans
Week 9	RB	Jamal Anderson, Atlanta	DE	Reggie White, Green Bay	P	Matt Turk, Washington
Week 10	RB	Emmitt Smith, Dallas	DE	Chuck Smith, Atlanta	K	Joe Nedney, Arizona
Week 11	QB	Charlie Batch, Detroit	CB	Ray Buchanan, Atlanta	P	Mitch Berger, Minnesota
Week 12	WR	Randy Moss, Minnesota	CB	Phillippi Sparks, New York Giants	P	Mitch Berger, Minnesota
Week 13	WR	Randy Moss, Minnesota	CB	Darrell Green, Washington	CB	Ronde Barber, Tampa Bay
Week 14	QB	Randall Cunningham, Minnesota	DT	La'Roi Glover, New Orleans	KR-PR	Brian Mitchell, Washington
Week 15	QB	Kent Graham, New York Giants	S	Tommy Bennett, Arizona	K	Gary Anderson, Minnesota
Week 16	WR	Antonio Freeman, Green Bay	S	Percy Ellsworth, New York Giants	K	Chris Jacke, Arizona
Week 17	QB	Steve Young, San Francisco	S	Kwamie Lassiter, Arizona	KR	Michael Bates, Carolina

1998 NFC PLAYERS OF THE MONTH

Month	Offense		Defense		Special Teams	
September	QB	Steve Young, San Francisco	DE	Reggie White, Green Bay	KR	Terry Fair, Detroit
October	QB	Randall Cunningham, Minnesota	DE	Hugh Douglas, Philadelphia	KR-PR	Roell Preston, Green Bay
November	RB	Jamal Anderson, Atlanta	LB	Stephen Boyd, Detroit	P	Mitch Berger, Minnesota
December	QB	Chris Chandler, Atlanta	DT	John Randle, Minnesota	K	Gary Anderson, Minnesota

1998 PLAYOFF PLAYERS OF THE WEEK

Round	Offense		Defense		Special Teams	
Wild Card	RB	Fred Taylor, Jacksonville	CB	Aeneas Williams, Arizona	K	Wade Richey, San Francisco
Divisional	WR	Keyshawn Johnson, New York Jets	S	Robert Griffith, Minnesota	K	John Hall, New York Jets
Championship	QB	Chris Chandler, Atlanta	LB	Bill Romanowski, Denver	K	Morten Andersen, Atlanta

1998 ROOKIES OF THE MONTH

Month	Offense		Defense	
September	RB	Fred Taylor, Jacksonville (Florida)	DE	Vonnie Holliday, Green Bay (North Carolina)
October	QB	Charlie Batch, Detroit (Eastern Michigan)	LB	Sam Cowart, Buffalo (Florida State)
November	WR	Randy Moss, Minnesota (Marshall)	S	Donovin Darius, Jacksonville (Syracuse)
December	RB	Fred Taylor, Jacksonville (Florida)	CB	Charles Woodson, Oakland (Michigan)

1998 PFW/PFWA ALL-PRO TEAM

Selected by Pro Football Weekly *and the Professional Football Writers of America*

Offense

Randy Moss, Minnesota	Wide Receiver
Antonio Freeman, Green Bay	Wide Receiver
Shannon Sharpe, Denver	Tight End
Tony Boselli, Jacksonville	Tackle
Larry Allen, Dallas	Tackle
Randall McDaniel, Minnesota	Guard
Bruce Matthews, Tennessee	Guard
Dermontti Dawson, Pittsburgh	Center
Randall Cunningham, Minnesota	Quarterback
Jamal Anderson, Atlanta	Running Back
Terrell Davis, Denver	Running Back

Defense

Reggie White, Green Bay	End
Michael Strahan, New York Giants	End
John Randle, Minnesota	Tackle
Darrell Russell, Oakland	Tackle
Chad Brown, Seattle	Linebacker
Mo Lewis, New York Jets	Linebacker
Junior Seau, San Diego	Linebacker
Ty Law, New England	Cornerback
Deion Sanders, Dallas	Cornerback
LeRoy Butler, Green Bay	Safety
Rodney Harrison, San Diego	Safety

Specialists

Gary Anderson, Minnesota	Kicker
Craig Hentrich, Tennessee	Punter
Terry Fair, Detroit	Kickoff Returner
Roell Preston, Green Bay	Kickoff Returner
Deion Sanders, Dallas	Punt Returner
Bennie Thompson, Baltimore	Special Teams Player

1998 ASSOCIATED PRESS ALL-PRO TEAM

Selected by the Associated Press

Offense

Antonio Freeman, Green Bay	Wide Receiver
Randy Moss, Minnesota	Wide Receiver
Shannon Sharpe, Denver	Tight End
Larry Allen, Dallas	Tackle
Tony Boselli, Jacksonville	Tackle
Randall McDaniel, Minnesota	Guard
Bruce Matthews, Tennessee	Guard
Dermontti Dawson, Pittsburgh	Center
Randall Cunningham, Minnesota	Quarterback
Jamal Anderson, Atlanta	Running Back
Terrell Davis, Denver	Running Back
Mike Alstott, Tampa Bay	Fullback

Defense

Michael Strahan, New York Giants	End
Reggie White, Green Bay	End
John Randle, Minnesota	Tackle
Darrell Russell, Oakland	Tackle
Chad Brown, Seattle	Linebacker
Mo Lewis, N.Y. Jets	Linebacker
Junior Seau, San Diego	Linebacker
Zach Thomas, Miami	Linebacker
Deion Sanders, Dallas	Cornerback
Ty Law, New England	Cornerback
LeRoy Butler, Green Bay	Safety
Rodney Harrison, San Diego	Safety

Specialists

Gary Anderson, Minnesota	Kicker
Craig Hentrich, Tennessee	Punter
Jermaine Lewis, Baltimore	Kickoff Returner

1998 ALL-NFL TEAM

Selected by the Associated Press, Pro Football Weekly, *and the Professional Football Writers of America*

Offense

Randy Moss, Minnesota (AP, PFW)	Wide Receiver
Antonio Freeman, Green Bay (AP, PFW)	Wide Receiver
Shannon Sharpe, Denver (AP, PFW)	Tight End
Tony Boselli, Jacksonville (AP, PFW)	Tackle
Larry Allen, Dallas (AP, PFW)	Tackle
Randall McDaniel, Minnesota (AP, PFW)	Guard
Bruce Matthews, Tennessee (AP, PFW)	Guard
Dermontti Dawson, Pittsburgh (AP, PFW)	Center
Randall Cunningham, Minnesota (AP, PFW)	Quarterback
Terrell Davis, Denver (AP, PFW)	Running Back
Jamal Anderson, Atlanta (AP, PFW)	Running Back
Mike Alstott, Tampa Bay (AP)	Fullback

Defense

Reggie White, Green Bay (AP, PFW)	End
Michael Strahan, New York Giants (AP, PFW)	End
John Randle, Minnesota (AP, PFW)	Tackle
Darrell Russell, Oakland (AP, PFW)	Tackle
Chad Brown, Seattle (AP, PFW)	Linebacker
Mo Lewis, New York Jets (AP, PFW)	Linebacker
Junior Seau, San Diego (AP, PFW)	Linebacker
Zach Thomas, Miami (AP)	Linebacker
Ty Law, New England (AP, PFW)	Cornerback
Deion Sanders, Dallas (AP, PFW)	Cornerback
Rodney Harrison, San Diego (AP, PFW)	Safety
LeRoy Butler, Green Bay (AP, PFW)	Safety

Specialists

Gary Anderson, Minnesota (AP, PFW)	Kicker
Craig Hentrich, Tennessee (AP, PFW)	Punter
Jermaine Lewis, Baltimore (AP)	Kick Returner
Terry Fair, Detroit (PFW)	Kickoff Returner
Roell Preston, Green Bay (PFW)	Kickoff Returner
Deion Sanders, Dallas (PFW)	Punt Returner
Bennie Thompson, Baltimore (PFW)	Special Teams Player

1998 ALL-PRO TEAMS

1998 FOOTBALL NEWS ALL-AFC TEAM

Selected by Football News

Offense

Ed McCaffrey, Denver	Wide Receiver
Eric Moulds, Buffalo	Wide Receiver
Shannon Sharpe, Denver	Tight End
Tony Boselli, Jacksonville	Tackle
Jonathan Ogden, Baltimore	Tackle
Ruben Brown, Buffalo	Guard
Bruce Matthews, Tennessee	Guard
Dermontti Dawson, Pittsburgh	Center
Vinny Testaverde, New York Jets	Quarterback
Marshall Faulk, Indianapolis	Running Back
Terrell Davis, Denver	Running Back

Defense

Michael Sincair, Seattle	End
Michael McCrary, Baltimore	End
Darrell Russell, Oakland	Tackle
Ted Washington, Buffalo	Tackle
Chad Brown, Seattle	Linebacker
Mo Lewis, New York Jets	Linebacker
Junior Seau, San Diego	Linebacker
Sam Madison, Miami	Cornerback
Ty Law, New England	Cornerback
Rodney Harrison, San Diego	Safety
Lawyer Milloy, New England	Safety

Specialists

Jason Elam, Denver	Kicker
Craig Hentrich, Tennessee	Punter
Corey Harris, Baltimore	Kickoff Returner
Jermaine Lewis, Baltimore	Punt Returner

1998 FOOTBALL NEWS ALL-NFC TEAM

Selected by Football News

Offense

Antonio Freeman, Green Bay	Wide Receiver
Randy Moss, Minnesota	Wide Receiver
Wesley Walls, Carolina	Tight End
Larry Allen, Dallas	Tackle
William Roaf, New Orleans	Tackle
Randall McDaniel, Minnesota	Guard
Kevin Gogan, San Francisco	Guard
Jeff Christy, Minnesota	Center
Randall Cunningham, Minnesota	Quarterback
Jamal Anderson, Atlanta	Running Back
Garrison Hearst, San Francisco	Running Back

Defense

Michael Strahan, New York Giants	End
Reggie White, Green Bay	End
John Randle, Minnesota	Tackle
La'Roli Glover, New Orleans	Tackle
Derrick Brooks, Tampa Bay	Linebacker
Dwayne Rudd, Minnesota	Linebacker
Jessie Tuggle, Atlanta	Linebacker
Deion Sanders, Dallas	Cornerback
Ray Buchanan, Atlanta	Cornerback
LeRoy Butler, Green Bay	Safety
Eugene Robinson, Atlanta	Safety

Specialists

Gary Anderson, Minnesota	Kicker
Matt Turk, Washington	Punter
Terry Fair, Detroit	Kickoff Returner
Deion Sanders, Dallas	Punt Returner

1998 PFW/PFWA ALL-ROOKIE TEAM

Selected by Pro Football Weekly *and the Professional Football Writers of America*

Offense

Randy Moss, Minnesota	Wide Receiver
Jerome Pathon, Indianapolis	Wide Receiver
Cam Cleeland, New Orleans	Tight End
Jason Fabini, New York Jets	Tackle
Ephraim Salaam, Atlanta	Tackle
Kyle Turley, New Orleans	Guard
Steve McKinney, Indianapolis	Guard
Kevin Long, Tennessee	Center
Peyton Manning, Indianapolis	Quarterback
Fred Taylor, Jacksonville	Running Back
Robert Edwards, New England	Running Back

Defense

Vonnie Holliday, Green Bay	End
Andre Wadsworth, Arizona	End
Brandon Whiting, Philadelphia	Tackle
Larry Chester, Indianapolis	Tackle
Takeo Spikes, Cincinnati	Linebacker
Sam Cowart, Buffalo	Linebacker
Anthony Simmons, Seattle	Linebacker
Charles Woodson, Oakland	Cornerback
Terry Fair, Detroit	Cornerback
Donovan Darius, Jacksonville	Safety
Tony Parrish, Chicago	Safety

Specialists

Mike Vanderjagt, Indianapolis	Kicker
Brad Costello, Cincinnati	Punter
Terry Fair, Detroit	Kickoff Returner
Jacquez Green, Tampa Bay	Punt Returner
Tim Dwight, Atlanta	Special Teams Player

TEN BEST RUSHING PERFORMANCES, 1998

	Att.	Yards	TD
1. Priest Holmes Baltimore vs. Cincinnati, Nov. 22	36	227	1
2. Terrell Davis Denver vs. Seattle, Oct. 11	30	208	1
3. Garrison Hearst San Francisco vs. Detroit, Dec. 14	24	198	1
4. Robert Edwards New England vs. St. Louis, Dec. 13	24	196	0
5. Marshall Faulk Indianapolis vs. Baltimore, Nov. 29	17	192	1
6. Terrell Davis Denver vs. Dallas, Sept. 13	23	191	3
7. Jamal Anderson Atlanta vs. St. Louis, Nov. 29	31	188	1
8. Garrison Hearst San Francisco vs. N.Y. Jets, Sept. 6	20	187	2
9. Barry Sanders Detroit vs. Cincinnati, Sept. 13	26	185	3
10. Fred Taylor Jacksonville vs. Detroit, Dec. 6	32	183	2

100-YARD RUSHING PERFORMANCES, 1998

First Week

Garrison Hearst, San Francisco — 187 yards vs. N.Y. Jets
Emmitt Smith, Dallas — 124 yards vs. Arizona
Donnell Bennett, Kansas City — 115 yards vs. Oakland
James Stewart, Jacksonville — 115 yards vs. Chicago
Karim Abdul-Jabbar, Miami — 108 yards vs. Indianapolis
Ahman Green, Seattle — 100 yards vs. Philadelphia

Second Week

Terrell Davis, Denver — 191 yards vs. Dallas
Barry Sanders, Detroit — 185 yards vs. Cincinnati
Robert Smith, Minnesota — 179 yards vs. St. Louis
Napoleon Kaufman, Oakland — 139 yards vs. N.Y. Giants
Garrison Hearst, San Francisco — 138 yards vs. Washington
Jerome Bettis, Pittsburgh — 131 yards vs. Chicago
Marshall Faulk, Indianapolis — 127 yards vs. New England
Ricky Watters, Seattle — 105 yards vs. Arizona
James Stewart, Jacksonville — 103 yards vs. Kansas City
Fred Lane, Carolina — 100 yards vs. New Orleans

Third Week

Natrone Means, San Diego — 165 yards vs. Kansas City
Greg Hill, St. Louis — 158 yards vs. Buffalo
Adrian Murrell, Arizona — 145 yards vs. Philadelphia
Curtis Martin, N.Y. Jets — 144 yards vs. Indianapolis
Ricky Watters, Seattle — 136 yards vs. Washington
Fred Taylor, Jacksonville — 128 yards vs. Baltimore
Antowain Smith, Buffalo — 118 yards vs. St. Louis
Karim Abdul-Jabbar, Miami — 108 yards vs. Pittsburgh
Terrell Davis, Denver — 104 yards vs. Oakland
Mike Alstott, Tampa Bay — 103 yards vs. Chicago
Eddie George, Tennessee — 100 yards vs. New England

Fourth Week

Priest Holmes, Baltimore — 173 yards vs. Cincinnati
Lamar Smith, New Orleans — 157 yards vs. Indianapolis
Jerome Bettis, Pittsburgh — 138 yards vs. Seattle
Barry Sanders, Detroit — 131 yards vs. Tampa Bay
Jamal Anderson, Atlanta — 123 yards vs. San Francisco
Terrell Davis, Denver — 119 yards vs. Washington
Corey Dillon, Cincinnati — 116 yards vs. Baltimore
Napoleon Kaufman, Oakland — 116 yards vs. Dallas
Fred Taylor, Jacksonville — 116 yards vs. Tennessee

Fifth Week

Terrell Davis, Denver — 168 yards vs. Philadelphia
Natrone Means, San Diego — 130 yards vs. Indianapolis
Emmitt Smith, Dallas — 120 yards vs. Washington
Jamal Anderson, Atlanta — 117 yards vs. Carolina
Curtis Martin, N.Y. Jets — 108 yards vs. Miami
Chris Warren, Dallas — 104 yards vs. Washington

Sixth Week

Terrell Davis, Denver — 208 yards vs. Seattle
Antowain Smith, Buffalo — 130 yards vs. Indianapolis
Eddie George, Tennessee — 121 yards vs. Baltimore
Emmitt Smith, Dallas — 112 yards vs. Carolina
Jamal Anderson, Atlanta — 110 yards vs. N.Y. Giants
Robert Edwards, New England — 104 yards vs. Kansas City
Kordell Stewart, Pittsburgh — 103 yards vs. Cincinnati
Natrone Means, San Diego — 101 yards vs. Oakland

Seventh Week

Barry Sanders, Detroit — 155 yards vs. Green Bay
Jamal Anderson, Atlanta — 132 yards vs. New Orleans
Corey Dillon, Cincinnati — 124 yards vs. Tennessee
Natrone Means, San Diego — 112 yards vs. Philadelphia
Gary Brown, N.Y. Giants — 108 yards vs. Arizona
Eddie George, Tennessee — 107 yards vs. Cincinnati
Curtis Martin, N.Y. Jets — 107 yards vs. New England
Robert Edwards, New England — 104 yards vs. N.Y. Jets
Marshall Faulk, Indianapolis — 103 yards vs. San Francisco
Robert Smith, Minnesota — 103 yards vs. Washington

Eighth Week

Napoleon Kaufman, Oakland — 143 yards vs. Cincinnati
Eddie George, Tennessee — 137 yards vs. Chicago
Terrell Davis, Denver — 136 yards vs. Jacksonville
Robert Smith, Minnesota — 134 yards vs. Detroit
Barry Sanders, Detroit — 127 yards vs. Minnesota
Jerome Bettis, Pittsburgh — 119 yards vs. Kansas City
Curtis Martin, N.Y. Jets — 101 yards vs. Atlanta

Ninth Week

Jamal Anderson, Atlanta — 172 yards vs. St. Louis
Eddie George, Tennessee — 153 yards vs. Pittsburgh
Terrell Davis, Denver — 149 yards vs. Cincinnati
Mike Alstott, Tampa Bay — 128 yards vs. Minnesota
Warrick Dunn, Tampa Bay — 115 yards vs. Minnesota
Corey Dillon, Cincinnati — 110 yards vs. Denver
Barry Sanders, Detroit — 107 yards vs. Arizona
Fred Lane, Carolina — 101 yards vs. New Orleans
Emmitt Smith, Dallas — 101 yards vs. Philadelphia

Tenth Week

Emmitt Smith, Dallas — 163 yards vs. N.Y. Giants
Barry Sanders, Detroit — 140 yards vs. Philadelphia
Robert Smith, Minnesota — 137 yards vs. New Orleans
Eddie George, Tennessee — 134 yards vs. Tampa Bay
Charlie Garner, Philadelphia — 129 yards vs. Detroit
Gary Brown, N.Y. Giants — 119 yards vs. Dallas
Fred Taylor, Jacksonville — 118 yards vs. Cincinnati
Adrian Murrell, Arizona — 107 yards vs. Washington
Ricky Watters, Seattle — 105 yards vs. Kansas City
Jamal Anderson, Atlanta — 104 yards vs. New England
John Avery, Miami — 100 yards vs. Indianapolis
Jerome Bettis, Pittsburgh — 100 yards vs. Green Bay

Eleventh Week

Curtis Martin, N.Y. Jets — 134 yards vs. Indianapolis
Fred Taylor, Jacksonville — 128 yards vs. Tampa Bay
Karim Abdul-Jabbar, Miami — 127 yards vs. Carolina
Emmitt Smith, Dallas — 118 yards vs. Arizona
Barry Sanders, Detroit — 114 yards vs. Chicago
Terrell Davis, Denver — 111 yards vs. Kansas City
Darick Holmes, Green Bay — 111 yards vs. N.Y. Giants
Warrick Dunn, Tampa Bay — 107 yards vs. Jacksonville
Jamal Anderson, Atlanta — 100 yards vs. San Francisco

1998 BEST PERFORMANCES

Twelfth Week

Priest Holmes, Baltimore	227 yards vs. Cincinnati
Terrell Davis, Denver	162 yards vs. Oakland
Curtis Martin, N.Y. Jets	123 yards vs. Tennessee
Antowain Smith, Buffalo	107 yards vs. Indianapolis
Thirteenth Week	
Marshall Faulk, Indianapolis	192 yards vs. Baltimore
Jamal Anderson, Atlanta	188 yards vs. St. Louis
Garrison Hearst, San Francisco	166 yards vs. N.Y. Giants
Darick Holmes, Green Bay	163 yards vs. Philadelphia
Napoleon Kaufman, Oakland	152 yards vs. Washington
Curtis Martin, N.Y. Jets	110 yards vs. Carolina
Corey Dillon, Cincinnati	107 yards vs. Jacksonville
Priest Holmes, Baltimore	103 yards vs. Indianapolis
Fourteenth Week	
Fred Taylor, Jacksonville	183 yards vs. Detroit
Garrison Hearst, San Francisco	139 yards vs. Carolina
Gary Brown, N.Y. Giants	124 yards vs. Arizona
Jamal Anderson, Atlanta	122 yards vs. Indianapolis
Terrell Fletcher, San Diego	122 yards vs. Washington
Barry Sanders, Detroit	102 yards vs. Jacksonville
Fifteenth Week	
Garrison Hearst, San Francisco	198 yards vs. Detroit
Robert Edwards, New England	196 yards vs. St. Louis
Adrian Murrell, Arizona	174 yards vs. Philadelphia
Jamal Anderson, Atlanta	148 yards vs. New Orleans
Terrell Davis, Denver	147 yards vs. N.Y. Giants
Duce Staley, Philadelphia	141 yards vs. Arizona
Byron (Bam) Morris, Kansas City	137 yards vs. Dallas
Marshall Faulk, Indianapolis	115 yards vs. Cincinnati
Gary Brown, N.Y. Giants	112 yards vs. Denver
Dorsey Levens, Green Bay	105 yards vs. Chicago
Tshimanga Biakabutuka, Carolina	103 yards vs. Washington
Sixteenth Week	
Ricky Watters, Seattle	178 yards vs. Indianapolis
James Allen, Chicago	163 yards vs. Baltimore
Jamal Anderson, Atlanta	147 yards vs. Detroit
Emmitt Smith, Dallas	110 yards vs. Philadelphia
Garrison Hearst, San Francisco	107 yards vs. New England
Fred Taylor, Jacksonville	105 yards vs. Minnesota
Jerome Bettis, Pittsburgh	104 yards vs. Cincinnati
Gary Brown, N.Y. Giants	103 yards vs. Kansas City
Robert Edwards, New England	101 yards vs. San Francisco
Robert Smith, Minnesota	101 yards vs. Jacksonville
Seventeenth Week	
Terrell Davis, Denver	178 yards vs. Seattle
Jerome Bettis, Pittsburgh	139 yards vs. Jacksonville
Priest Holmes, Baltimore	132 yards vs. Detroit
Terrell Fletcher, San Diego	127 yards vs. Arizona
Gary Brown, N.Y. Giants	112 yards vs. Philadelphia
Tshimanga Biakabutuka, Carolina	104 yards vs. Indianapolis
Jamal Anderson, Atlanta	103 yards vs. Miami
Curtis Martin, N.Y. Jets	102 yards vs. New England

Times 100 or More (144)
Anderson, 12; Davis, 11; Martin, Sanders, 8; E. Smith, 7; Bettis, Brown, George, Hearst, Taylor, 6; R. Smith, 5; Dillon, Edwards, Faulk, Holmes, Kaufman, Means, Watters, 4; Abdul-Jabbar, Murrell, A. Smith, 3; Alstott, Biakabutuka, Dunn, Fletcher, Holmes, Lane, Stewart, 2.

TEN BEST PASSING PERFORMANCES, 1998

		Att.	Comp.	Yards	TD
1.	Jake Plummer Arizona vs. Dallas, Nov. 15	56	31	465	3
2.	Troy Aikman Dallas vs. Minnesota, Nov. 26	34	57	455	1
3.	Randall Cunningham Minnesota vs. Green Bay, Oct. 5	32	20	442	4
4.	Drew Bledsoe New England vs. Miami, Nov. 23	54	28	423	2
5.	Vinny Testaverde N.Y. Jets vs. Seattle, Dec. 6	63	42	418	2
6.	Glenn Foley N.Y. Jets vs. San Francisco, Sept. 6	58	30	415	3
7.	John Elway Denver vs. Kansas City, Dec. 6	32	22	400	2
8.	Jake Plummer Arizona vs. New Orleans, Dec. 20	44	32	394	0
9.	Brett Favre Green Bay vs. Carolina, Sept. 27	45	27	388	5
10.	Steve Young San Francisco vs. Atlanta, Sept. 27	39	28	387	3

300-YARD PASSING PERFORMANCES, 1998

First Week	
Glenn Foley, N.Y. Jets	415 yards vs. San Francisco
Steve Young, San Francisco	363 yards vs. N.Y. Jets
Peyton Manning, Indianapolis	302 yards vs. Miami
Second Week	
Jeff George, Oakland	303 yards vs. N.Y. Giants
Neil O'Donnell, Cincinnati	303 yards vs. Detroit
Steve Young, San Francisco	303 yards vs. Washington
Third Week	
Trent Green, Washington	383 yards vs. Seattle
Mark Brunell, Jacksonville	376 yards vs. Baltimore
Fourth Week	
Brett Favre, Green Bay	388 yards vs. Carolina
Steve Young, San Francisco	387 yards vs. Atlanta
Erik Kramer, Chicago	373 yards vs. Minnesota
Peyton Manning, Indianapolis	309 yards vs. New Orleans
Fifth Week	
Randall Cunningham, Minnesota	442 yards vs. Green Bay
Steve Young, San Francisco	329 yards vs. Buffalo
Drew Bledsoe, New England	317 yards vs. New Orleans
Kerry Collins, Carolina	302 yards vs. Atlanta
Sixth Week	
Dan Marino, Miami	323 yards vs. Jacksonville
Steve Young, San Francisco	309 yards vs. New Orleans
Seventh Week	
Steve Young, San Francisco	331 yards vs. Indianapolis
Brett Favre, Green Bay	300 yards vs. Detroit
Eighth Week	
Mark Brunell, Jacksonville	353 yards vs. Denver
Ninth Week	
Billy Joe Tolliver, New Orleans	325 yards vs. Carolina
Drew Bledsoe, New England	306 yards vs. Indianapolis
Tenth Week	
Brad Johnson, Minnesota	316 yards vs. New Orleans
Eleventh Week	
Jake Plummer, Arizona	465 yards vs. Dallas
Steve Young, San Francisco	342 yards vs. Atlanta

Twelfth Week

Drew Bledsoe, New England	423 yards vs. Miami
Trent Green, Washington	382 yards vs. Arizona
Kerry Collins, New Orleans	328 yards vs. San Francisco
Rich Gannon, Kansas City	304 yards vs. San Diego
Brett Favre, Green Bay	303 yards vs. Minnesota
Thirteenth Week	
Troy Aikman, Dallas	455 yards vs. Minnesota
Randall Cunningham, Minnesota	359 yards vs. Dallas
Peyton Manning, Indianapolis	357 yards vs. Baltimore
Doug Flutie, Buffalo	339 yards vs. New England
Brett Favre, Green Bay	321 yards vs. Philadelphia
Craig Whelihan, San Diego	304 yards vs. Denver
Fourteenth Week	
Vinny Testaverde, N.Y. Jets	418 yards vs. Seattle
John Elway, Denver	400 yards vs. Kansas City
Randall Cunningham, Minnesota	349 yards vs. Chicago
Drew Bledsoe, New England	327 yards vs. Pittsburgh
Doug Flutie, Buffalo	319 yards vs. Cincinnati
Steve Stenstrom, Chicago	303 yards vs. Minnesota
Fifteenth Week	
Chris Chandler, Atlanta	345 yards vs. New Orleans
Randall Cunningham, Minnesota	345 yards vs. Baltimore
Dan Marino, Miami	321 yards vs. N.Y. Jets
Sixteenth Week	
Jake Plummer, Arizona	394 yards vs. New Orleans
Jeff Blake, Cincinnati	367 yards vs. Pittsburgh
Dan Marino, Miami	355 yards vs. Denver
Peyton Manning, Indianapolis	335 yards vs. Seattle
Seventeenth Week	
John Elway, Denver	338 yards vs. Seattle
Dan Marino, Miami	320 yards vs. Atlanta

Times 300 or More (52)
Young, 7; Bledsoe, Cunningham, Favre, Manning, 4; Marino, 3; Brunell, Collins, Elway, Flutie, Green, Plummer, 2.

TEN BEST RECEIVING PERFORMANCES, 1998

		No.	Yards	TD
1.	Carl Pickens Cincinnati vs. Pittsburgh, Oct. 11	13	204	1
2.	Terance Mathis Atlanta vs. New Orleans, Dec. 13	6	198	2
3.	Eric Moulds Buffalo vs. Cincinnati, Dec. 6	6	196	2
4.	Antonio Freeman Green Bay vs. San Francisco, Nov. 1	7	193	2
	Terry Glenn New England vs. Pittsburgh, Dec. 6	9	193	1
6.	Isaac Bruce St. Louis vs. Minnesota, Sept. 13	11	192	1
7.	Muhsin Muhammad Carolina vs. New Orleans, Sept. 13	9	192	1
8.	Randy Moss Minnesota vs. Green Bay, Oct. 5	5	190	2
9.	Antonio Freeman Green Bay vs. Tennessee, Dec. 20	7	186	3
10.	Eric Moulds Buffalo vs. New England, Nov. 29	8	177	1

100-YARD RECEIVING PERFORMANCES, 1998

First Week

Joey Galloway, Seattle	142 yards vs. Philadelphia
Isaac Bruce, St. Louis	131 yards vs. New Orleans
Bryan Still, San Diego	128 yards vs. Buffalo
Keyshawn Johnson, N.Y. Jets	126 yards vs. San Francisco
Wayne Chrebet, N.Y. Jets	125 yards vs. San Francisco
Michael Irvin, Dallas	119 yards vs. Arizona
Raghib Ismail, Carolina	119 yards vs. Atlanta
J.J. Stokes, San Francisco	111 yards vs. N.Y. Jets
Antonio Freeman, Green Bay	110 yards vs. Detroit
Marvin Harrison, Indianapolis	102 yards vs. Miami
Herman Moore, Detroit	100 yards vs. Green Bay
Second Week	
Isaac Bruce, St. Louis	192 yards vs. Minnesota
Muhsin Muhammad, Carolina	192 yards vs. New Orleans
Darnay Scott, Cincinnati	130 yards vs. Detroit
Tim Brown, Oakland	127 yards vs. N.Y. Giants
Ed McCaffrey, Denver	117 yards vs. Dallas
Sean Dawkins, New Orleans	110 yards vs. Carolina
Michael Westbrook, Washington	109 yards vs. San Francisco
Third Week	
Michael Westbrook, Washington	132 yards vs. Seattle
Jermaine Lewis, Baltimore	117 yards vs. Jacksonville
James Jett, Oakland	116 yards vs. Denver
Jimmy Smith, Jacksonville	116 yards vs. Baltimore
Keenan McCardell, Jacksonville	108 yards vs. Baltimore
Terry Glenn, New England	102 yards vs. Tennessee
Fourth Week	
Jerry Rice, San Francisco	162 yards vs. Atlanta
Joey Galloway, Seattle	139 yards vs. Pittsburgh
Terance Mathis, Atlanta	130 yards vs. San Francisco
Marshall Faulk, Indianapolis	128 yards vs. New Orleans
Bobby Engram, Chicago	123 yards vs. Minnesota
Jermaine Lewis, Baltimore	122 yards vs. Cincinnati
Carl Pickens, Cincinnati	120 yards vs. Baltimore
Garrison Hearst, San Francisco	105 yards vs. Atlanta
Bryan Still, San Diego	104 yards vs. N.Y. Giants
Michael Westbrook, Washington	104 yards vs. Denver
Yancey Thigpen, Tennessee	102 yards vs. Jacksonville

1998 BEST PERFORMANCES

Fifth Week

Randy Moss, Minnesota	190 yards vs. Green Bay
Johnnie Morton, Detroit	138 yards vs. Chicago
Cris Carter, Minnesota	119 yards vs. Green Bay
Frank Sanders, Arizona	118 yards vs. Oakland
Chris Penn, Chicago	106 yards vs. Detroit
Terry Glenn, New England	105 yards vs. New Orleans
Muhsin Muhammad, Carolina	104 yards vs. Atlanta

Sixth Week

Carl Pickens, Cincinnati	204 yards vs. Pittsburgh
Michael Irvin, Dallas	146 yards vs. Carolina
Bobby Engram, Chicago	142 yards vs. Arizona
Rod Smith, Denver	136 yards vs. Seattle
Raghib Ismail, Carolina	117 yards vs. Dallas
Ernie Mills, Dallas	110 yards vs. Carolina

Seventh Week

Keith Poole, New Orleans	154 yards vs. Atlanta
Antonio Freeman, Green Bay	126 yards vs. Detroit
Tony Martin, Atlanta	116 yards vs. New Orleans
J.J. Stokes, San Francisco	110 yards vs. Indianapolis
Cris Carter, Minnesota	109 yards vs. Washington
Chris Sanders, Tennessee	101 yards vs. Cincinnati

Eighth Week

Eric Moulds, Buffalo	145 yards vs. Carolina
Joey Galloway, Seattle	130 yards vs. San Diego
Jimmy Smith, Jacksonville	121 yards vs. Denver
Terrell Owens, San Francisco	120 yards vs. St. Louis
Shawn Jefferson, New England	116 yards vs. Miami
Keenan McCardell, Jacksonville	113 yards vs. Denver
Antonio Freeman, Green Bay	103 yards vs. Baltimore
Mark Carrier, Carolina	100 yards vs. Buffalo

Ninth Week

Antonio Freeman, Green Bay	193 yards vs. San Francisco
Courtney Hawkins, Pittsburgh	147 yards vs. Tennessee
Ed McCaffrey, Denver	133 yards vs. Cincinnati
Marshall Faulk, Indianapolis	119 yards vs. New England
Jake Reed, Minneapolis	117 yards vs. Tampa Bay
Charles Johnson, Pittsburgh	115 yards vs. Tennessee
Johnnie Morton, Detroit	115 yards vs. Arizona
Ben Coates, New England	109 yards vs. Indianapolis
Tony Simmons, New England	109 yards vs. Indianapolis
Rob Moore, Arizona	107 yards vs. Detroit
Sean Dawkins, New Orleans	102 yards vs. Carolina
Wayne Chrebet, N.Y. Jets	101 yards vs. Kansas City

Tenth Week

Ed McCaffrey, Denver	133 yards vs. San Diego
O.J. McDuffie, Miami	132 yards vs. Indianapolis
Terance Mathis, Atlanta	117 yards vs. New England
Bert Emanuel, Tampa Bay	106 yards vs. Tennessee
Ricky Dudley, Oakland	105 yards vs. Baltimore

Eleventh Week

Frank Sanders, Arizona	190 yards vs. Dallas
Jerry Rice, San Francisco	169 yards vs. Atlanta
Marvin Harrison, Indianapolis	128 yards vs. N.Y. Jets
Reidel Anthony, Tampa Bay	126 yards vs. Jacksonville
Wayne Chrebet, N.Y. Jets	112 yards vs. Indianapolis
Johnnie Morton, Detroit	109 yards vs. Chicago
Keyshawn Johnson, N.Y. Jets	107 yards vs. Indianapolis

Twelfth Week

Derrick Alexander, Kansas City	173 yards vs. San Diego
Randy Moss, Minnesota	153 yards vs. Green Bay
Sean Dawkins, New Orleans	148 yards vs. San Francisco
Michael Westbrook, Washington	135 yards vs. Arizona
Shawn Jefferson, New England	131 yards vs. Miami
Keyshawn Johnson, N.Y. Jets	112 yards vs. Tennessee
Andre Reed, Buffalo	108 yards vs. Indianapolis
Leslie Shepherd, Washington	107 yards vs. Arizona
Garrison Hearst, San Francisco	103 yards vs. New Orleans
Marshall Faulk, Indianapolis	102 yards vs. Buffalo
Tony Martin, Atlanta	100 yards vs. Chicago

Thirteenth Week

Eric Moulds, Buffalo	177 yards vs. New England
Randy Moss, Minnesota	163 yards vs. Dallas
Torrance Small, Indianapolis	153 yards vs. Baltimore
Herman Moore, Detroit	148 yards vs. Pittsburgh
Ike Hilliard, N.Y. Giants	141 yards vs. San Francisco
Terrell Owens, San Francisco	140 yards vs. N.Y. Giants
Michael Irvin, Dallas	137 yards vs. Minnesota
Cris Carter, Minnesota	135 yards vs. Dallas
Bill Schroeder, Green Bay	128 yards vs. Philadelphia
Derrick Alexander, Kansas City	116 yards vs. Arizona
James McKnight, Seattle	113 yards vs. Tennessee
Stephen Davis, Washington	110 yards vs. Oakland
Jimmy Smith, Jacksonville	110 yards vs. Cincinnati
Wayne Chrebet, N.Y. Jets	107 yards vs. Carolina
Terry Glenn, New England	104 yards vs. Buffalo
O.J. McDuffie, Miami	102 yards vs. New Orleans
Rod Smith, Denver	101 yards vs. San Diego
Frank Sanders, Arizona	100 yards vs. Kansas City

Fourteenth Week

Eric Moulds, Buffalo	196 yards vs. Cincinnati
Terry Glenn, New England	193 yards vs. Pittsburgh
Rod Smith, Denver	165 yards vs. Kansas City
Bobby Engram, Chicago	140 yards vs. Minnesota
Tony Martin, Atlanta	140 yards vs. Indianapolis
Joey Galloway, Seattle	127 yards vs. N.Y. Jets
Andre Hastings, New Orleans	122 yards vs. Dallas
Herman Moore, Detroit	116 yards vs. Jacksonville
Keyshawn Johnson, N.Y. Jets	114 yards vs. Seattle
Jimmy Smith, Jacksonville	112 yards vs. Detroit
Floyd Turner, Baltimore	108 yards vs. Tennessee
Randy Moss, Minnesota	106 yards vs. Chicago
Tim Brown, Oakland	104 yards vs. Miami
Ed McCaffrey, Denver	103 yards vs. Kansas City

Fifteenth Week

Terance Mathis, Atlanta	198 yards vs. New Orleans
Floyd Turner, Baltimore	147 yards vs. Minnesota
Muhsin Muhammad, Carolina	118 yards vs. Washington
Albert Connell, Washington	116 yards vs. Carolina
Tony Martin, Atlanta	109 yards vs. New Orleans
Rob Moore, Arizona	109 yards vs. Philadelphia
Wayne Chrebet, N.Y. Jets	105 yards vs. Miami
O.J. McDuffie, Miami	105 yards vs. N.Y. Jets
Antonio Freeman, Green Bay	103 yards vs. Chicago
Jimmy Smith, Jacksonville	103 yards vs. Tennessee

Sixteenth Week

Antonio Freeman, Green Bay	186 yards vs. Tennessee
Darnay Scott, Cincinnati	152 yards vs. Pittsburgh
Frank Sanders, Arizona	138 yards vs. New Orleans
Lamar Thomas, Miami	136 yards vs. Denver
Torrance Small, Indianapolis	120 yards vs. Seattle
Brandon Bennett, Cincinnati	119 yards vs. Pittsburgh
Jerry Rice, San Francisco	115 yards vs. New England
Eric Moulds, Buffalo	107 yards vs. N.Y. Jets
James Jett, Oakland	106 yards vs. San Diego

Seventeenth Week

Rod Smith, Denver	158 yards vs. Seattle
Oronde Gadsden, Miami	153 yards vs. Atlanta
Tim Brown, Oakland	140 yards vs. Kansas City
Herman Moore, Detroit	120 yards vs. Baltimore
Brett Bech, New Orleans	113 yards vs. Buffalo
Cam Cleeland, New Orleans	112 yards vs. Buffalo
Raghib Ismail, Carolina	109 yards vs. Indianapolis
Frank Sanders, Arizona	106 yards vs. San Diego
Tony Martin, Atlanta	105 yards vs. Miami
Ricky Proehl, St. Louis	100 yards vs. San Francisco

Times 100 or More (158)

Freeman, 6; Chrebet, Martin, Sanders, J. Smith, 5; Galloway, Glenn, Johnson, McCaffrey, Moore, Moss, Moulds, R. Smith, Westbrook, 4; Brown, Carter, Dawkins, Engram, Faulk, Irvin, Ismail, Mathis, McDuffie, Morton, Muhammad, Rice, 3; Alexander, Bruce, Harrison, Hearst, Jefferson, Jett, Lewis, McCardell, Moore, Owens, Pickens, Scott, Small, Still, Stokes, Turner, 2.

TOP QUARTERBACK SACK PERFORMANCES, 1998

(2.5 or More Sacks Per Game Needed to Qualify)

First Week

Derrick Thomas, Kansas City	6.0 vs. Oakland
Kevin Greene, Carolina	3.0 vs. Atlanta
Rodney Harrison, San Diego	3.0 vs. Buffalo
Michael Sinclair, Seattle	2.5 vs. Philadelphia

Second Week

Reggie White, Green Bay	3.0 vs. Tampa Bay
Michael Sinclair, Seattle	2.5 vs. Arizona

Third Week

None

Fourth Week

Chris Doleman, San Francisco	2.5 vs. Atlanta

Fifth Week

Jim Flanigan, Chicago	3.0 vs. Detroit

Sixth Week

Chris Doleman, San Francisco	4.0 vs. New Orleans
Norman Hand, San Diego	3.0 vs. Oakland

Seventh Week

Hugh Douglas, Philadelphia	4.5 vs. San Diego
Reggie White, Green Bay	2.5 vs. Detroit

Eighth Week

Roy Barker, San Francisco	4.0 vs. St. Louis
Tracy Scroggins, Detroit	2.5 vs. Minnesota

Ninth Week

Reggie White, Green Bay	3.0 vs. San Francisco

Tenth Week

Michael McCrary, Baltimore	4.0 vs. Oakland
Chris Doleman, San Francisco	3.5 vs. Carolina
Lester Archambeau, Atlanta	2.5 vs. New England
Hugh Douglas, Philadelphia	2.5 vs. Detroit
Donta Jones, Pittsburgh	2.5 vs. Green Bay

Eleventh Week

La'Roi Glover, New Orleans	3.0 vs. St. Louis

Twelfth Week

Kevin Carter, St. Louis	3.0 vs. Carolina

Thirteenth Week

None

Fourteenth Week

Chad Eaton, New England	3.0 vs. Pittsburgh
Pat Williams, Buffalo	3.0 vs. Cincinnati
Trace Armstrong, Miami	2.5 vs. Oakland

Fifteenth Week

Henry Thomas, New England	3.0 vs. St. Louis

Sixteenth Week

Robert Porcher, Detroit	2.5 vs. Atlanta

Seventeenth Week

Shawn Price, Buffalo	2.5 vs. New Orleans

1998 TEAM STATISTICS

AMERICAN FOOTBALL CONFERENCE OFFENSE

	Balt.	Buff.	Cin.	Den.	Ind.	Jac.	K.C.	Mia.	N.E.	NYJ	Oak.	Pitt.	S.D.	Sea.	Tenn.
First Downs	243	319	271	347	298	287	289	269	281	338	273	268	272	267	308
Rushing	86	115	92	135	77	111	103	73	68	99	89	106	95	92	118
Passing	140	176	148	186	190	153	153	176	184	207	156	135	146	144	171
Penalty	17	28	31	26	31	23	33	20	29	32	28	27	31	31	19
Rushes	408	531	405	525	384	487	433	458	403	500	449	490	460	426	462
Net Yds. Gained	1629	2161	1639	2468	1486	2102	1548	1535	1480	1879	1727	2034	1728	1626	1970
Avg. Gain	4.0	4.1	4.0	4.7	3.9	4.3	3.6	3.4	3.7	3.8	3.8	4.2	3.8	3.8	4.3
Avg. Yds. per Game	101.8	135.1	102.4	154.3	92.9	131.4	96.8	95.9	92.5	117.4	107.9	127.1	108.0	101.6	123.1
Passes Attempted	477	461	521	491	576	463	543	546	556	532	519	489	566	480	519
Completed	272	269	307	290	326	269	305	316	295	318	282	274	261	273	305
% Completed	57.0	58.4	58.9	59.1	56.6	58.1	56.2	57.9	53.1	59.8	54.3	56.0	46.1	56.9	58.8
Total Yds. Gained	3152	3621	3545	3808	3739	3343	3472	3582	4004	4032	3534	2781	3115	3219	3482
Times Sacked	41	41	53	25	22	39	36	24	40	25	67	35	37	34	35
Yds. Lost	283	241	360	184	109	231	212	187	344	196	446	229	251	219	191
Net Yds. Gained	2869	3380	3185	3624	3630	3112	3260	3395	3660	3836	3088	2552	2864	3000	3291
Avg. Yds. per Game	179.3	211.3	199.1	226.5	226.9	194.5	203.8	212.2	228.8	239.8	193.0	159.5	179.0	187.5	205.7
Net Yds. per Pass Play	5.54	6.73	5.55	7.02	6.07	6.20	5.63	5.96	6.14	6.89	5.27	4.87	4.75	5.84	5.94
Yds. Gained per Comp.	11.59	13.46	11.55	13.13	11.47	12.43	11.38	11.34	13.57	12.68	12.53	10.15	11.93	11.79	11.42
Combined Net Yds. Gained	4498	5541	4824	6092	5116	5214	4808	4930	5140	5715	4815	4586	4592	4626	5261
% Total Yds. Rushing	36.2	39.0	34.0	40.5	29.0	40.3	32.2	31.1	28.8	32.9	35.9	44.4	37.6	35.1	37.4
% Total Yds. Passing	63.8	61.0	66.0	59.5	71.0	59.7	67.8	68.9	71.2	67.1	64.1	55.6	62.4	64.9	62.6
Avg. Yds. per Game	281.1	346.3	301.5	380.8	319.8	325.9	300.5	308.1	321.3	357.2	300.9	286.6	287.0	289.1	328.8
Ball Control Plays	926	1033	979	1041	982	989	1012	1028	999	1057	1035	1014	1063	940	1016
Avg. Yds. per Play	4.9	5.4	4.9	5.9	5.2	5.3	4.8	4.8	5.1	5.4	4.7	4.5	4.3	4.9	5.2
Avg. Time of Poss.	28:04	32:26	28:31	32:08	27:47	28:59	29:53	32:10	28:34	32:17	28:51	30:20	31:17	27:05	31:41
Third Down Efficiency	30.9	44.3	33.9	43.5	35.1	42.7	31.8	35.8	38.0	46.0	31.6	38.8	32.9	27.7	40.0
Had Intercepted	15	14	12	14	28	12	18	16	17	13	25	20	34	18	10
Yds. Opp. Returned	148	65	206	270	353	216	189	365	197	234	435	169	512	220	88
Ret. by Opp. for TD	0	0	1	2	2	3	3	2	0	2	5	2	2	2	1
Punts	92	69	81	67	79	85	77	97	74	65	98	82	95	81	69
Yds. Punted	3948	2882	3578	3097	3583	3824	3255	4064	3294	2637	4256	3565	4174	3568	3258
Avg. Yds. per Punt	42.9	41.8	44.2	46.2	45.4	45.0	42.3	41.9	44.5	40.6	43.4	43.5	43.9	44.0	47.2
Punt Returns	43	37	29	38	34	45	38	46	33	43	50	33	45	41	38
Yds. Returned	541	369	234	399	340	581	316	542	395	315	564	269	542	428	280
Avg. Yds. per Return	12.6	10.0	8.1	10.5	10.0	12.9	8.3	11.8	12.0	7.3	11.3	8.2	12.0	10.4	7.4
Returned for TD	2	0	1	0	0	1	0	0	0	0	2	0	0	2	0
Kickoff Returns	69	56	72	58	71	61	63	53	62	57	62	55	70	64	56
Yds. Returned	1700	1168	1710	1402	1432	1366	1319	1297	1330	1285	1208	1112	1293	1510	1148
Avg. Yds. per Return	24.6	20.9	23.8	24.2	20.2	22.4	20.9	24.5	21.5	22.5	19.5	20.2	18.5	23.6	20.5
Returned for TD	2	0	1	1	0	0	0	0	0	0	0	0	0	1	0
Fumbles	31	17	21	17	10	18	35	25	20	23	38	18	33	30	25
Lost	15	6	10	6	5	8	14	12	7	11	18	12	17	16	9
Out of Bounds	2	1	1	2	1	0	3	1	1	1	2	1	0	0	1
Own Rec. for TD	0	0	0	1	0	0	0	0	0	0	1	1	0	0	0
Opp. Rec. by	5	13	7	11	11	17	20	7	7	9	14	13	7	18	7
Opp. Rec. for TD	0	1	1	0	0	2	1	0	0	2	1	0	0	2	2
Penalties	113	123	69	115	106	121	158	106	108	85	127	79	137	117	126
Yds. Penalized	909	993	620	1023	853	898	1304	864	853	651	986	691	1229	914	1135
Total Points Scored	269	400	268	501	310	392	327	321	337	416	288	263	241	372	330
Total TDs	29	43	31	62	33	47	35	37	35	49	34	26	23	45	32
TDs Rushing	7	13	7	26	7	19	19	10	9	12	6	8	11	11	12
TDs Passing	16	28	20	32	26	24	15	23	23	33	21	13	11	21	16
TDs on Ret. and Rec.	6	2	4	4	0	4	1	4	3	4	7	5	1	13	4
Extra Point Kicks	24	41	21	58	23	45	34	33	32	45	31	23	19	41	28
Extra Point Kicks Att.	24	41	21	59	23	45	34	34	32	46	31	23	19	41	28
2Pt Conversions	2	0	2	1	4	1	0	0	1	0	1	3	2	2	1
2Pt Conversions Att.	5	2	9	3	10	2	1	3	3	3	3	3	4	4	4
Safeties	2	1	0	0	0	0	1	0	0	1	0	0	1	0	0
Field Goals Made	21	33	19	23	27	21	27	22	31	25	17	26	26	19	36
Field Goals Attempted	28	41	27	27	31	26	32	27	39	35	27	32	30	24	40
% Successful	75.0	80.5	70.4	85.2	87.1	80.8	84.4	81.5	79.5	71.4	63.0	81.3	86.7	79.2	90.0

AMERICAN FOOTBALL CONFERENCE DEFENSE

	Balt.	Buff.	Cin.	Den.	Ind.	Jac.	K.C.	Mia.	N.E.	NYJ	Oak.	Pitt.	S.D.	Sea.	Tenn.
First Downs	298	283	310	283	341	309	321	257	305	263	273	266	256	337	279
Rushing	90	79	142	80	131	108	119	75	76	87	95	88	72	111	81
Passing	180	168	152	183	181	178	146	148	208	150	150	155	149	197	170
Penalty	28	36	16	20	29	23	56	34	21	26	28	23	35	29	28
Rushes	472	375	558	356	544	450	491	395	447	400	482	479	422	487	414
Net Yds. Gained	1705	1493	2612	1287	2570	2000	1869	1511	1547	1659	1674	1642	1140	1999	1610
Avg. Gain	3.6	4.0	4.7	3.6	4.7	4.4	3.8	3.8	3.5	4.1	3.5	3.4	2.7	4.1	3.9
Avg. Yds. per Game	106.6	93.3	163.3	80.4	160.6	125.0	116.8	94.4	96.7	103.7	104.6	102.6	71.3	124.9	100.6
Passes Attempted	539	532	406	596	461	577	479	504	570	544	497	482	530	597	511
Completed	316	294	233	345	275	325	259	252	336	285	291	268	271	343	319
% Completed	58.6	55.3	57.4	57.9	59.7	56.3	54.1	50.0	58.9	52.4	58.6	55.6	51.1	57.5	62.4
Total Yds. Gained	3878	3474	3350	3983	3497	3768	3253	3194	3857	3299	3134	3559	3314	3972	3683
Times Sacked	39	43	28	47	38	30	40	45	36	36	41	41	39	53	30
Yds. Lost	286	276	199	335	231	209	268	270	222	259	258	238	246	282	172
Net Yds. Gained	3592	3198	3151	3648	3266	3559	2985	2924	3635	3040	2876	3321	3068	3690	3511
Avg. Yds. per Game	224.5	199.9	196.9	228.0	204.1	222.4	186.6	182.8	227.2	190.0	179.8	207.6	191.8	230.6	219.4
Net Yds. per Pass Play	6.21	5.56	7.26	5.67	6.55	5.86	5.75	5.33	6.00	5.24	5.35	6.35	5.39	5.68	6.49
Yds. Gained per Comp.	12.27	11.82	14.38	11.54	12.72	11.59	12.56	12.67	11.48	11.58	10.77	13.28	12.23	11.58	11.55
Combined Net Yds. Gained	5297	4691	5763	4935	5836	5559	4854	4435	5182	4699	4550	4963	4208	5689	5121
% Total Yds. Rushing	32.2	31.8	45.3	26.1	44.0	36.0	38.5	34.1	29.9	35.3	36.8	33.1	27.1	35.1	31.4
% Total Yds. Passing	67.8	68.2	54.7	73.9	56.0	64.0	61.5	65.9	70.1	64.7	63.2	66.9	72.9	64.9	68.6
Avg. Yds. per Game	331.1	293.2	360.2	308.4	364.8	347.4	303.4	277.2	323.9	293.7	284.4	310.2	263.0	355.6	320.1
Ball Control Plays	1050	950	992	999	1043	1057	1010	944	1053	980	1020	1002	991	1137	955
Avg. Yds. per Play	5.0	4.9	5.8	4.9	5.6	5.3	4.8	4.7	4.9	4.8	4.5	5.0	4.2	5.0	5.4
Avg. Time of Poss.	31:56	27:34	31:29	27:52	32:13	31:01	30:07	27:50	31:26	27:43	31:09	29:40	28:44	32:55	28:20
Third Down Efficiency	39.2	38.6	44.5	39.1	42.8	36.5	33.8	32.9	42.6	35.6	26.3	37.7	30.0	39.0	37.8
Intercepted By	17	18	13	19	8	13	13	29	24	21	21	16	20	24	12
Yds. Returned By	161	204	144	439	97	119	187	318	255	263	420	335	203	455	98
Returned for TD	2	1	1	2	0	0	0	4	3	1	3	3	1	8	2
Punts	86	77	64	88	68	78	77	88	73	85	96	76	103	78	74
Yds. Punted	3653	3459	2850	3733	3032	3395	3248	3986	3100	3587	4300	3482	4546	3397	3190
Avg. Yds. per Punt	42.5	44.9	44.5	42.4	44.6	43.5	42.2	45.3	42.5	42.2	44.8	45.8	44.1	43.6	43.1
Punt Returns	40	32	36	43	42	40	41	43	43	30	53	30	49	33	34
Yds. Returned	284	374	503	381	451	332	513	339	493	309	787	310	515	369	332
Avg. Yds. per Return	7.1	11.7	14.0	8.9	10.7	8.3	12.5	7.9	11.5	10.3	14.8	10.3	10.5	11.2	9.8
Returned for TD	1	1	1	0	0	0	1	0	0	1	1	0	1	1	0
Kickoff Returns	57	77	46	89	65	76	69	56	71	60	60	64	54	68	55
Yds. Returned	1168	1638	1199	2006	1688	1858	1374	1227	1335	1370	1388	1212	1484	1311	1114
Avg. Yds. per Return	20.5	21.3	26.1	22.5	26.0	24.4	19.9	21.9	18.8	22.8	23.1	18.9	27.5	19.3	20.3
Returned for TD	2	0	0	0	1	1	0	1	0	0	0	0	1	0	0
Fumbles	17	21	12	28	29	25	36	25	16	25	26	28	21	34	11
Lost	6	13	7	11	11	17	20	7	7	9	14	13	7	18	7
Out of Bounds	3	2	0	0	0	1	3	0	1	1	2	2	2	0	1
Own Rec. for TD	0	0	1	0	0	0	0	1	0	0	0	0	0	1	0
Opp. Rec. by	15	6	10	6	5	8	14	12	7	11	18	11	17	16	9
Opp. Rec. for TD	1	0	4	0	1	0	0	1	2	0	2	3	1	0	0
Penalties	122	104	127	113	108	109	138	97	104	109	115	106	120	130	93
Yds. Penalized	1013	836	1012	865	917	953	1292	875	787	967	921	854	1005	1157	704
Total Points Scored	335	333	452	309	444	338	363	265	329	266	356	303	342	310	320
Total TDs	37	39	53	38	52	36	44	28	36	30	38	30	38	35	34
TDs Rushing	12	11	23	8	20	9	22	6	8	11	8	8	12	13	9
TDs Passing	20	27	23	28	27	23	17	17	26	16	22	17	21	18	24
TDs on Ret. and Rec.	5	1	7	2	5	4	5	5	2	3	8	5	5	4	1
Extra Point Kicks	35	28	51	31	44	30	43	24	30	26	36	23	37	31	29
Extra Point Kicks Att.	35	28	51	31	45	30	43	24	30	27	36	24	37	31	29
2Pt Conversions	0	4	1	2	2	1	1	2	1	0	1	2	1	0	4
2Pt Conversions Att.	2	11	2	7	6	6	1	4	6	2	2	6	1	4	5
Safeties	0	0	0	2	0	0	0	0	0	0	3	0	0	0	2
Field Goals Made	26	21	27	14	28	30	18	23	27	20	28	32	25	23	25
Field Goals Attempted	30	26	31	20	37	35	30	32	32	25	37	41	34	30	30
% Successful	86.7	80.8	87.1	70.0	75.7	85.7	60.0	71.9	84.4	80.0	75.7	78.0	73.5	76.7	83.3

1998 TEAM STATISTICS

NATIONAL FOOTBALL CONFERENCE OFFENSE

	Ariz.	Atl.	Car.	Chi.	Dall.	Det.	G.B.	Minn.	N.O.	NYG	Phil.	St.L.	S.F.	T.B.	Wash.
First Downs	315	319	261	264	308	278	329	335	258	263	259	281	381	262	295
Rushing	98	111	68	89	125	94	93	98	67	104	86	81	129	111	84
Passing	179	175	171	154	154	160	210	210	165	129	141	164	223	139	186
Penalty	38	33	22	21	29	24	26	27	26	30	32	36	29	12	25
Rushes	450	516	405	454	499	441	447	450	374	474	427	395	491	523	401
Net Yds. Gained	1627	2101	1458	1713	2014	1955	1526	1936	1325	1889	1775	1385	2544	2148	1685
Avg. Gain	3.6	4.1	3.6	3.8	4.0	4.4	3.4	4.3	3.5	4.0	4.2	3.5	5.2	4.1	4.2
Avg. Yds. per Game	101.7	131.3	91.1	107.1	125.9	122.2	95.4	121.0	82.8	118.1	110.9	86.6	159.0	134.3	105.3
Passes Attempted	552	424	507	494	474	489	575	533	535	507	534	556	556	449	565
Completed	326	237	292	284	279	274	361	327	278	265	282	314	347	234	304
% Completed	59.1	55.9	57.6	57.5	58.9	56.0	62.8	61.4	52.0	52.3	52.8	56.5	62.4	52.1	53.8
Total Yds. Gained	3768	3744	3624	3277	3546	3398	4340	4492	3514	2822	2730	3381	4510	2787	3724
Times Sacked	50	53	54	31	19	45	39	25	57	35	56	47	53	28	61
Yds. Lost	286	358	302	224	110	268	230	164	376	256	317	294	254	181	399
Net Yds. Gained	3482	3386	3322	3053	3436	3130	4110	4328	3138	2566	2413	3087	4256	2606	3325
Avg. Yds. per Game	217.6	211.6	207.6	190.8	214.8	195.6	256.9	270.5	196.1	160.4	150.8	192.9	266.0	162.9	207.8
Net Yds. per Pass Play	5.78	7.10	5.92	5.82	6.97	5.86	6.69	7.76	5.30	4.73	4.09	5.12	6.99	5.46	5.31
Yds. Gained per Comp.	11.56	15.80	12.41	11.54	12.71	12.40	12.02	13.74	12.64	10.65	9.68	10.77	13.00	11.91	12.25
Combined Net Yds. Gained	5109	5487	4780	4766	5450	5085	5636	6264	4463	4455	4188	4472	6800	4754	5010
% Total Yds. Rushing	31.8	38.3	30.5	35.9	37.0	38.4	27.1	30.9	29.7	42.4	42.4	31.0	37.4	45.2	33.6
% Total Yds. Passing	68.2	61.7	69.5	64.1	63.0	61.6	72.9	69.1	70.3	57.6	57.6	69.0	62.6	54.8	66.4
Avg. Yds. per Game	319.3	342.9	298.8	297.9	340.6	317.8	352.3	391.5	278.9	278.4	261.8	279.5	425.0	297.1	313.1
Ball Control Plays	1052	993	966	979	992	975	1061	1008	966	1016	1017	998	1100	1000	1027
Avg. Yds. per Play	4.9	5.5	4.9	4.9	5.5	5.2	5.3	6.2	4.6	4.4	4.1	4.5	6.2	4.8	4.9
Avg. Time of Poss.	29:15	33:10	28:10	29:26	31:50	29:22	31:37	29:58	28:03	28:21	29:24	28:59	31:52	31:58	28:34
Third Down Efficiency	34.9	41.7	37.0	34.9	36.9	34.1	45.4	51.4	35.8	30.6	33.3	34.7	45.5	40.4	31.6
Had Intercepted	20	15	18	13	8	13	23	16	19	15	18	18	15	18	14
Yds. Opp. Returned	373	224	179	146	121	198	312	221	186	232	319	194	304	192	169
Ret. by Opp. for TD	4	2	0	1	1	2	3	1	3	2	2	1	0	2	2
Punts	82	74	77	80	78	82	65	55	90	101	104	95	69	81	97
Yds. Punted	3378	2963	3131	3411	3342	3506	2788	2458	4089	4566	4339	4202	2835	3340	4216
Avg. Yds. per Punt	41.2	40.0	40.7	42.6	42.8	42.8	42.9	44.7	45.4	45.2	41.7	44.2	41.1	41.2	43.5
Punt Returns	43	40	44	25	39	36	48	29	32	35	34	41	47	41	44
Yds. Returned	295	304	464	291	493	212	412	289	408	252	285	415	406	559	506
Avg. Yds. per Return	6.9	7.6	10.5	11.6	12.6	5.9	8.6	10.0	12.8	7.2	8.4	10.1	8.6	13.6	11.5
Returned for TD	0	0	0	1	2	0	1	0	0	0	0	1	1	2	0
Kickoff Returns	63	46	76	66	51	68	60	54	62	66	60	68	59	59	70
Yds. Returned	1314	1157	1834	1595	1191	1700	1547	1238	1354	1286	1363	1472	1108	1399	1512
Avg. Yds. per Return	20.9	25.2	24.1	24.2	23.4	25.0	25.8	22.9	21.8	19.5	22.7	21.6	18.8	23.7	21.6
Returned for TD	0	1	1	2	0	2	2	1	1	1	0	1	0	0	1
Fumbles	30	24	39	29	18	17	27	10	28	17	20	32	22	23	27
Lost	16	9	17	21	7	12	11	4	14	9	8	15	15	13	15
Out of Bounds	1	2	2	1	2	1	6	1	3	1	1	1	1	3	2
Own Rec. for TD	0	0	0	0	0	0	0	0	0	0	0	0	0	0	0
Opp. Rec. by	19	25	14	14	12	9	10	15	11	7	8	7	12	14	7
Opp. Rec. for TD	0	4	0	1	1	0	2	2	4	0	0	0	0	0	0
Penalties	88	116	113	86	128	121	88	116	121	124	102	111	133	99	112
Yds. Penalized	758	841	931	714	1106	1019	681	1045	928	946	852	945	1156	840	975
Total Points Scored	325	442	336	276	381	306	408	556	305	287	161	285	479	314	319
Total TDs	36	53	40	30	42	32	46	64	35	32	17	32	61	36	40
TDs Rushing	18	18	11	9	21	12	7	17	6	10	10	17	19	12	15
TDs Passing	17	28	25	16	17	17	33	41	19	18	7	12	41	21	24
TDs on Ret. and Rec.	1	7	4	5	4	3	6	6	10	4	0	3	1	3	1
Extra Point Kicks	36	51	35	27	40	27	41	59	31	32	15	25	49	29	36
Extra Point Kicks Att.	36	52	37	28	40	29	43	59	31	32	17	26	51	30	37
2Pt Conversions	0	1	2	1	0	0	1	3	0	0	0	4	5	3	1
2Pt Conversions Att.	0	1	3	2	2	3	3	5	3	0	0	6	9	6	3
Safeties	2	1	0	2	1	0	1	1	2	0	1	0	0	0	1
Field Goals Made	23	23	19	21	29	29	29	35	20	21	14	20	18	21	13
Field Goals Attempted	33	28	26	26	35	33	33	35	22	27	21	26	27	28	23
% Successful	69.7	82.1	73.1	80.8	82.9	87.9	87.9	100.0	90.9	77.8	66.7	76.9	66.7	75.0	56.5

NATIONAL FOOTBALL CONFERENCE DEFENSE

	Ariz.	Atl.	Car.	Chi.	Dall.	Det.	G.B.	Minn.	N.O.	NYG	Phil.	St.L.	S.F.	T.B.	Wash.
First Downs	321	267	315	300	276	308	246	300	326	286	286	282	297	244	303
Rushing	117	65	95	121	84	113	67	102	86	103	125	92	91	75	127
Passing	177	172	197	155	162	167	166	171	208	163	133	161	178	148	152
Penalty	27	30	23	24	30	28	13	27	32	20	28	29	28	21	24
Rushes	492	361	491	479	401	487	390	404	467	476	528	479	395	415	531
Net Yds. Gained	1989	1203	2133	1875	1619	2102	1442	1614	1700	2004	2416	2049	1610	1583	2436
Avg. Gain	4.0	3.3	4.3	3.9	4.0	4.3	3.7	4.0	3.6	4.2	4.6	4.3	4.1	3.8	4.6
Avg. Yds. per Game	124.3	75.2	133.3	117.2	101.2	131.4	90.1	100.9	106.3	125.3	151.0	128.1	100.6	98.9	152.3
Passes Attempted	518	551	501	456	553	474	540	555	539	521	449	475	566	473	493
Completed	299	311	298	292	290	284	296	320	328	282	249	256	294	274	281
% Completed	57.7	56.4	59.5	64.0	52.4	59.9	54.8	57.7	60.9	54.1	55.5	53.9	51.9	57.9	57.0
Total Yds. Gained	3526	3806	3937	3401	3767	3276	3401	3699	4256	3503	3001	3180	3992	3014	3112
Times Sacked	39	38	37	28	34	43	50	38	47	54	42	50	51	37	33
Yds. Lost	250	275	228	173	222	261	336	247	288	336	281	349	259	252	194
Net Yds. Gained	3276	3531	3709	3228	3545	3015	3065	3452	3968	3167	2720	2831	3733	2762	2918
Avg. Yds. per Game	204.8	220.7	231.8	201.8	221.6	188.4	191.6	215.8	248.0	197.9	170.0	176.9	233.3	172.6	182.4
Net Yds. per Pass Play	5.88	5.99	6.89	6.67	6.04	5.83	5.19	5.82	6.77	5.51	5.54	5.39	6.05	5.42	5.55
Yds. Gained per Comp.	11.79	12.24	13.21	11.65	12.99	11.54	11.49	11.56	12.98	12.42	12.05	12.42	13.58	11.00	11.07
Combined Net Yds. Gained	5265	4734	5842	5103	5164	5117	4507	5066	5668	5171	5136	4880	5343	4345	5354
% Total Yds. Rushing	37.8	25.4	36.5	36.7	31.4	41.1	32.0	31.9	30.0	38.8	47.0	42.0	30.1	36.4	45.5
% Total Yds. Passing	62.2	74.6	63.5	63.3	68.6	58.9	68.0	68.1	70.0	61.2	53.0	58.0	69.9	63.6	54.5
Avg. Yds. per Game	329.1	295.9	365.1	318.9	322.8	319.8	281.7	316.6	354.3	323.2	321.0	305.0	333.9	271.6	334.6
Ball Control Plays	1049	950	1029	963	988	1004	980	997	1053	1051	1019	1004	1012	925	1057
Avg. Yds. per Play	5.0	5.0	5.7	5.3	5.2	5.1	4.6	5.1	5.4	4.9	5.0	4.9	5.3	4.7	5.1
Avg. Time of Poss.	30:45	26:50	31:50	30:34	28:10	30:38	28:23	30:02	31:57	31:39	30:36	31:01	28:08	28:02	31:26
Third Down Efficiency	37.1	35.8	41.7	40.8	33.8	41.0	39.5	34.0	43.8	37.6	37.0	37.6	34.3	31.7	38.1
Intercepted By	20	19	19	14	14	12	13	19	21	19	9	16	21	12	13
Yds. Returned By	235	224	295	129	250	132	111	341	466	217	158	201	178	212	190
Returned for TD	1	2	2	1	1	1	1	3	5	3	0	1	0	1	0
Punts	75	80	71	72	85	81	90	74	75	88	85	92	83	87	92
Yds. Punted	3296	3427	3125	3084	3604	3460	3920	3155	3263	3701	3616	3825	3492	3655	3966
Avg. Yds. per Punt	43.9	42.8	44.0	42.8	42.4	42.7	43.6	42.6	43.5	42.1	42.5	41.6	42.1	42.0	43.1
Punt Returns	38	20	20	38	34	47	27	27	53	53	61	58	36	38	32
Yds. Returned	313	112	94	349	210	471	237	325	649	587	511	652	341	302	261
Avg. Yds. per Return	8.2	5.6	4.7	9.2	6.2	10.0	8.8	12.0	12.2	11.1	8.4	11.2	9.5	7.9	8.2
Returned for TD	0	0	0	1	0	1	1	1	0	1	1	1	0	1	0
Kickoff Returns	56	69	65	55	69	49	74	73	52	51	40	47	67	62	61
Yds. Returned	1200	1613	1439	1097	1274	1196	1807	2008	1128	1234	764	1020	1296	1333	1569
Avg. Yds. per Return	21.4	23.4	22.1	19.9	18.5	24.4	24.4	27.5	21.7	24.2	19.1	21.7	19.3	21.5	25.7
Returned for TD	0	1	1	0	0	1	2	4	0	0	0	0	0	1	2
Fumbles	31	37	24	33	23	27	20	21	24	25	20	16	24	28	17
Lost	19	25	14	14	12	9	10	15	11	7	8	7	12	14	8
Out of Bounds	3	2	0	4	3	3	2	0	3	2	2	1	1	0	1
Own Rec. for TD	0	0	0	0	0	0	0	0	0	0	0	0	0	0	0
Opp. Rec. by	16	9	16	21	7	12	11	4	14	9	8	15	15	13	15
Opp. Rec. for TD	1	3	1	1	0	1	0	0	0	1	0	2	1	0	0
Penalties	114	118	110	102	120	98	94	132	132	124	113	112	101	88	95
Yds. Penalized	954	858	892	852	917	791	828	1167	1164	967	904	915	800	669	824
Total Points Scored	378	289	413	368	275	378	319	296	359	309	344	378	328	295	421
Total TDs	44	35	46	42	32	43	36	35	40	34	39	43	39	31	50
TDs Rushing	18	7	14	12	10	15	7	12	13	13	18	11	13	12	24
TDs Passing	21	22	30	27	21	23	23	17	24	17	18	28	25	15	21
TDs on Ret. and Rec.	5	6	2	3	1	5	6	6	3	4	3	4	1	4	5
Extra Point Kicks	40	28	41	36	29	41	28	31	39	34	36	40	35	29	46
Extra Point Kicks Att.	41	31	43	38	30	41	30	31	39	34	37	40	38	29	46
2Pt Conversions	1	2	1	1	2	1	3	2	1	0	1	2	0	0	2
2Pt Conversions Att.	3	4	3	4	2	1	6	4	1	0	2	3	1	2	4
Safeties	0	1	2	0	1	1	0	0	0	1	0	2	1	1	1
Field Goals Made	24	15	30	26	16	25	23	17	26	23	24	24	19	26	23
Field Goals Attempted	30	20	31	31	19	30	27	19	33	30	32	27	32	30	28
% Successful	80.0	75.0	96.8	83.9	84.2	83.3	85.2	89.5	78.8	76.7	75.0	88.9	59.4	86.7	82.1

1998 TEAM STATISTICS

AFC, NFC, AND NFL SUMMARY

	AFC Offense Total	AFC Offense Average	AFC Defense Total	AFC Defense Average	NFC Offense Total	NFC Offense Average	NFC Defense Total	NFC Defense Average	NFL Total	NFL Average
First Downs	4330	288.7	4381	292.1	4408	293.9	4357	290.5	8738	291.3
Rushing	1459	97.3	1434	95.6	1438	95.9	1463	97.5	2897	96.6
Passing	2465	164.3	2515	167.7	2560	170.7	2510	167.3	5025	167.5
Penalty	406	27.1	432	28.8	410	27.3	384	25.6	816	27.2
Rushes	6821	454.7	6772	451.5	6747	449.8	6796	453.1	13568	452.3
Net Yds. Gained	27012	1800.8	26318	1754.5	27081	1805.4	27775	1851.7	54093	1803.1
Avg. Gain	—	4.0	—	3.9	—	4.0	—	4.1	—	4.0
Avg. Yds. per Game	—	112.6	—	109.7	—	112.8	—	115.7	—	112.7
Passes Attempted	7739	515.9	7825	521.7	7750	516.7	7664	510.9	15489	516.3
Completed	4362	290.8	4412	294.1	4404	293.6	4354	290.3	8766	292.2
% Completed	—	56.4	—	56.4	—	56.8	—	56.8	—	56.6
Total Yds. Gained	52429	3495.3	53215	3547.7	53657	3577.1	52871	3524.7	106086	3536.2
Times Sacked	554	36.9	586	39.1	653	43.5	621	41.4	1207	40.2
Yds. Lost	3683	245.5	3751	250.1	4019	267.9	3951	263.4	7702	256.7
Net Yds. Gained	48746	3249.7	49464	3297.6	49638	3309.2	48920	3261.3	98384	3279.5
Avg. Yds. per Game	—	203.1	—	206.1	—	206.8	—	203.8	—	205.0
Net Yds. per Pass Play	—	5.88	—	5.88	—	5.91	—	5.90	—	5.89
Yds. Gained per Comp.	—	12.02	—	12.06	—	12.18	—	12.14	—	12.10
Combined Net Yds. Gained	75758	5050.5	75782	5052.1	76719	5114.6	76695	5113.0	152477	5082.6
% Total Yds. Rushing	—	35.7	—	34.7	—	35.3	—	36.2	—	35.5
% Total Yds. Passing	—	64.3	—	65.3	—	64.7	—	63.8	—	64.5
Avg. Yds. per Game	—	315.7	—	315.8	—	319.7	—	319.6	—	317.7
Ball Control Plays	15114	1007.6	15183	1012.2	15150	1010.0	15081	1005.4	30264	1008.8
Avg. Yds. per Play	—	5.0	—	5.0	—	5.1	—	5.1	—	5.0
Third Down Efficiency	—	36.9	—	37.1	—	37.8	—	37.6	—	37.4
Interceptions	266	17.7	268	17.9	243	16.2	241	16.1	509	17.0
Yds. Returned	3667	244.5	3698	246.5	3370	224.7	3339	222.6	7037	234.6
Returned for TD	27	1.8	31	2.1	26	1.7	22	1.5	53	1.8
Punts	1211	80.7	1211	80.7	1230	82.0	1230	82.0	2441	81.4
Yds. Punted	52983	3532.2	52958	3530.5	52564	3504.3	52589	3505.9	105547	3518.2
Avg. Yds. per Punt	—	43.8	—	43.7	—	42.7	—	42.8	—	43.2
Punt Returns	593	39.5	589	39.3	578	38.5	582	38.8	1171	39.0
Yds. Returned	6115	407.7	6292	419.5	5591	372.7	5414	360.9	11706	390.2
Avg. Yds. per Return	—	10.3	—	10.7	—	9.7	—	9.3	—	10.0
Returned for TD	8	0.5	8	0.5	8	0.5	8	0.5	16	0.5
Kickoff Returns	929	61.9	967	64.5	928	61.9	890	59.3	1857	61.9
Yds. Returned	20280	1352.0	21372	1424.8	21070	1404.7	19978	1331.9	41350	1378.3
Avg. Yds. per Return	—	21.8	—	22.1	—	22.7	—	22.4	—	22.3
Returned for TD	5	0.3	6	0.4	13	0.9	12	0.8	18	0.6
Fumbles	361	24.1	354	23.6	363	24.2	370	24.7	724	24.1
Lost	166	11.1	167	11.1	186	12.4	185	12.3	352	11.7
Out of Bounds	17	1.1	18	1.2	28	1.9	27	1.8	45	1.5
Own Rec. for TD	3	0.2	3	0.2	0	0.0	0	0.0	3	0.1
Opp. Rec.	166	11.1	165	11.0	184	12.3	185	12.3	350	11.7
Opp. Rec. for TD	12	0.8	15	1.0	14	0.9	11	0.7	26	0.9
Penalties	1690	112.7	1695	113.0	1658	110.5	1653	110.2	3348	111.6
Yds. Penalized	13923	928.2	14158	943.9	13737	915.8	13502	900.1	27660	922.0
Total Points Scored	5035	335.7	5065	337.7	5180	345.3	5150	343.3	10215	340.5
Total TDs	561	37.4	568	37.9	596	39.7	589	39.3	1157	38.6
TDs Rushing	177	11.8	180	12.0	202	13.5	199	13.3	379	12.6
TDs Passing	322	21.5	326	21.7	336	22.4	332	22.1	658	21.9
TDs on Ret. and Rec.	62	4.1	62	4.1	58	3.9	58	3.9	120	4.0
Extra Point Kicks	498	33.2	498	33.2	533	35.5	533	35.5	1031	34.4
Extra Point Kicks Att.	501	33.4	501	33.4	548	36.5	548	36.5	1049	35.0
2Pt Conversions	20	1.3	22	1.5	21	1.4	19	1.3	41	1.4
2Pt Conversions Att.	59	3.9	65	4.3	46	3.1	40	2.7	105	3.5
Safeties	6	0.4	7	0.5	12	0.8	11	0.7	18	0.6
Field Goals Made	373	24.9	367	24.5	335	22.3	341	22.7	708	23.6
Field Goals Attempted	466	31.1	470	31.3	423	28.2	419	27.9	889	29.6
% Successful	—	80.0	—	78.1	—	79.2	—	81.4	—	79.6

CLUB LEADERS

	Offense	Defense
First Downs	S.F. 381	T.B. 244
Rushing	Den. 135	Atl. 65
Passing	S.F. 223	Phil. 133
Penalty	Ariz. 38	G.B. 13
Rushes	Buff. 531	Den. 356
Net Yds. Gained	S.F. 2544	S.D. 1140
Avg. Gain	S.F. 5.2	S.D. 2.7
Passes Attempted	Ind. 576	Cin. 406
Completed	G.B. 361	Cin. 233
% Completed	G.B. 62.8	Mia. 50.0
Total Yds. Gained	S.F. 4510	Phil. 3001
Times Sacked	Dall. 19	N.Y.G. 54
Yds. Lost	Ind. 109	St.L. 349
Net Yds. Gained	Minn. 4328	Phil. 2720
Net Yds. per Pass Play	Minn. 7.76	G.B. 5.19
Yds. Gained per Comp.	Atl. 15.80	Oak. 10.77
Combined Net Yds. Gained	S.F. 6800	S.D. 4208
% Total Yds. Rushing	T.B. 45.2	Atl. 25.4
% Total Yds. Passing	G.B. 72.9	Phil. 53.0
Ball Control Plays	S.F. 1100	T.B. 925
Avg. Yds. per Play	Minn. 6.2	S.D. 4.3
Avg. Time of Poss.	Atl. 33:10	—
Third Down Efficiency	Minn. 51.4	Oak. 26.3
Interceptions	—	Mia. 29
Yds. Returned	—	N.O. 466
Returned for TD	—	Sea. 8
Punts	Phil. 104	—
Yds. Punted	N.Y.G. 4566	—
Avg. Yds. per Punt	Tenn. 47.2	—
Punt Returns	Oak. 50	Atl. & Car. 20
Yds. Returned	Jac. 581	Car. 94
Avg. Yds. per Return	T.B. 13.6	Car. 4.7
Returned for TD	five tied 2	—
Kickoff Returns	Car. 76	Phil. 40
Yds. Returned	Car. 1834	Phil. 764
Avg. Yds. per Return	G.B. 25.8	Dall. 18.5
Returned for TD	four tied 2	—
Total Points Scored	Minn. 556	Mia. 265
Total TDs	Minn. 64	Mia. 28
TDs Rushing	Den. 26	Mia. 6
TDs Passing	Minn. & S.F. 41	T.B. 15
TDs on Ret. and Rec.	Sea. 13	four tied 1
Extra Points	Minn. 59	Pitt. 23
2-Point Conversions	S.F. 5	—
Safeties	four tied 2	—
Field Goals Made	Tenn. 36	Den. 14
Field Goals Attempted	Buff. 41	Dall. & Minn. 19
% Successful	Minn. 100.0	S.F. 59.4

NFL CLUB RANKINGS BY YARDS

	Offense			Defense		
	Total	Rush	Pass	Total	Rush	Pass
Arizona	13	21	8	21	20	17
Atlanta	7	6	11	8	2	21
Baltimore	26	20	25	22	17	24
Buffalo	6	3	12	6	5	14
Carolina	20	28	14	30	26	28
Chicago	21	17	23	14	19	15
Cincinnati	17	19	17	28	30	12
Dallas	8	8	9	18	12	22
Denver	3	2	7	11	3	26
Detroit	14	10	19	15	25	8
Green Bay	5	25	3	4	4	10
Indianapolis	12	26	6	29	29	16
Jacksonville	10	5	20	25	22	23
Kansas City	19	23	16	9	18	7
Miami	16	24	10	3	6	6
Minnesota	2	11	*1	13	11	19
New England	11	27	5	20	7	25
New Orleans	28	30	18	26	16	30
N.Y. Giants	29	12	28	19	23	13
N.Y. Jets	4	13	4	7	14	9
Oakland	18	16	21	5	15	4
Philadelphia	30	14	30	17	27	*1
Pittsburgh	25	7	29	12	13	18
St. Louis	27	29	22	10	24	3
San Diego	24	15	26	*1	*1	11
San Francisco	*1	*1	2	23	9T	29
Seattle	23	22	24	27	21	27
Tampa Bay	22	4	27	2	8	2
Tennessee	9	9	15	16	9T	20
Washington	15	18	13	24	28	5

T = Tied for position
* = League Leader

AFC TAKEAWAYS/GIVEAWAYS

	Takeaways			Giveaways			Net
	Int	Fum	Total	Int	Fum	Total	Diff.
Buffalo	18	13	31	14	6	20	+11
Denver	19	11	30	14	6	20	+10
Jacksonville	13	17	30	12	8	20	+10
Miami	29	7	36	16	12	28	+8
Seattle	24	18	42	18	16	34	+8
New England	24	7	31	17	7	24	+7
N.Y. Jets	21	9	30	13	11	24	+6
Kansas City	13	20	33	18	14	32	+1
Tennessee	12	7	19	10	9	19	0
Cincinnati	13	7	20	12	10	22	-2
Pittsburgh	16	13	29	20	12	32	-3
Baltimore	17	6	23	15	15	30	-7
Oakland	21	14	35	25	18	43	-8
Indianapolis	8	11	19	28	5	33	-14
San Diego	20	7	27	34	17	51	-24

NFC TAKEAWAYS/GIVEAWAYS

	Takeaways			Giveaways			Net
	Int	Fum	Total	Int	Fum	Total	Diff.
Atlanta	19	25	44	15	9	24	+20
Minnesota	19	15	34	16	4	20	+14
Dallas	14	12	26	8	7	15	+11
Arizona	20	19	39	20	16	36	+3
San Francisco	21	12	33	15	15	30	+3
N.Y. Giants	19	7	26	15	9	24	+2
New Orleans	21	11	32	19	14	33	-1
Carolina	19	14	33	18	17	35	-2
Detroit	12	9	21	13	12	25	-4
Tampa Bay	12	14	26	18	13	31	-5
Chicago	14	14	28	13	21	34	-6
Washington	13	8	21	14	15	29	-8
Philadelphia	9	8	17	18	8	26	-9
St. Louis	16	7	23	18	15	33	-10
Green Bay	13	10	23	23	11	34	-11

1998 INDIVIDUAL STATISTICS—SCORING

SCORING

Points

NFC: 164—Gary Anderson, Minnesota
AFC: 140—Steve Christie, Buffalo

Touchdowns

AFC: 23—Terrell Davis, Denver
NFC: 17—Randy Moss, Minnesota

Extra Points

NFC: 59—Gary Anderson, Minnesota
AFC: 58—Jason Elam, Denver

Field Goals

AFC: 36—Al Del Greco, Tennessee
NFC: 35—Gary Anderson, Minnesota

Field Goal Attempts

AFC: 41—Steve Christie, Buffalo
NFC: 35—Gary Anderson, Minnesota
Richie Cunningham, Dallas

Longest Field Goal

AFC: 63—Jason Elam, Denver vs. Jacksonville, October 25
NFC: 57—Jeff Wilkins, St. Louis vs. Arizona, September 27

Most Points, Game

AFC: 22—Charles Johnson, Pittsburgh vs. Tennessee, November 1 (3-TD, 2-2pt)
NFC: 20—Randy Moss, Minnesota at Dallas, November 26 (3-TD, 2pt)
Gary Anderson, Minnesota at Baltimore, December 13 (6-FG, 2-XP)

AFC: BALTIMORE: 87, Matt Stover; BUFFALO: 140, Steve Christie; CINCINNATI: 78, Doug Pelfrey; DENVER: 138, Terrell Davis; INDIANAPOLIS: 104, Mike Vanderjag; JACKSONVILLE: 108, Mike Hollis; KANSAS CITY: 115, Pete Stoyanovich; MIAMI: 99, Olindo Mare; NEW ENGLAND: 127, Adam Vinatieri; N.Y. JETS: 120, John Hall; OAKLAND: 82, Greg Davis; PITTSBURGH: 99, Norm Johnson; SAN DIEGO: 97, John Carney; SEATTLE: 98, Todd Peterson; TENNESSEE: 136, Al Del Greco.

NFC: ARIZONA: 69, Joe Nedney; ATLANTA: 120, Morten Andersen; CAROLINA: 92, John Kasay; CHICAGO: 90, Jeff Jaeger; DALLAS: 127, Richie Cunningham; DETROIT: 114, Jason Hanson; GREEN BAY: 128, Ryan Longwell; MINNESOTA: 164, Gary Anderson; NEW ORLEANS: 91, Doug Brien; N.Y. GIANTS: 95, Brad Daluiso; PHILADELPHIA: 57, Chris Boniol; ST. LOUIS: 85, Jeff Wilkins; SAN FRANCISCO: 103, Wade Richey; TAMPA BAY: 92, Michael Husted; WASHINGTON: 63, Cary Blanchard.

Team Champion

AFC: 556—Minnesota
NFC: 501—Denver

AFC SCORING—TEAM

	TD	TDR	TDP	TDM	Extra Pt. Made	Kicks Att.	2-Point Made	Tries Att.	FG	FGA	SAF	PTS
Denver	62	26	32	4	58	59	1	3	23	27	0	501
N.Y. Jets	49	12	33	4	45	46	0	3	25	35	1	416
Buffalo	43	13	28	2	41	41	0	2	33	41	1	400
Jacksonville	47	19	24	4	45	45	1	2	21	26	0	392
Seattle	45	11	21	13	41	41	2	4	19	24	0	372
New England	35	9	23	3	32	32	1	3	31	39	0	337
Tennessee	32	12	16	4	28	28	1	4	36	40	0	330
Kansas City	35	19	15	1	34	34	0	1	27	32	1	327
Miami	37	10	23	4	33	34	0	3	22	27	0	321
Indianapolis	33	7	26	0	23	23	4	10	27	31	0	310
Oakland	34	6	21	7	31	31	1	3	17	27	0	288
Baltimore	29	7	16	6	24	24	2	5	21	28	2	269
Cincinnati	31	7	20	4	21	21	2	9	19	27	0	268
Pittsburgh	26	8	13	5	23	23	3	3	26	32	0	263
San Diego	23	11	11	1	19	19	2	4	26	30	1	241
AFC Total	561	177	322	62	498	501	20	59	373	466	6	5035
AFC Average	37.4	11.8	21.5	4.1	33.2	33.4	1.3	3.9	24.9	31.1	0.4	335.7

NFC SCORING—TEAM

	TD	TDR	TDP	TDM	Extra Pt. Made	Kicks Att.	2-Point Made	Tries Att.	FG	FGA	SAF	PTS
Minnesota	64	17	41	6	59	59	3	5	35	35	1	556
San Francisco	61	19	41	1	49	51	5	9	18	27	0	479
Atlanta	53	18	28	7	51	52	1	1	23	28	1	442
Green Bay	46	7	33	6	41	43	1	3	29	33	1	408
Dallas	42	21	17	4	40	40	0	2	29	35	1	381
Carolina	40	11	25	4	35	37	2	3	19	26	0	336
Arizona	36	18	17	1	36	36	0	0	23	33	2	325
Washington	40	15	24	1	36	37	1	3	13	23	1	319
Tampa Bay	36	12	21	3	29	30	3	6	21	28	0	314
Detroit	32	12	17	3	27	29	0	3	29	33	0	306
New Orleans	35	6	19	10	31	31	0	3	20	22	2	305
N.Y. Giants	32	10	18	4	32	32	0	0	21	27	0	287
St. Louis	32	17	12	3	25	26	4	6	20	26	0	285
Chicago	30	9	16	5	27	28	1	2	21	26	2	276
Philadelphia	17	10	7	0	15	17	0	0	14	21	1	161
NFC Total	596	202	336	58	533	548	21	46	335	423	12	5180
NFC Average	39.7	13.5	22.4	3.9	35.5	36.5	1.4	3.1	22.3	28.2	0.8	345.3
League Total	1157	379	658	120	1031	1049	41	105	708	889	18	10215
League Average	38.6	12.6	21.9	4.0	34.4	35.0	1.4	3.5	23.6	29.6	0.6	340.5

NFL TOP TEN SCORERS—NONKICKERS

	TD	TDR	TDP	TDM	2-PT	PTS
Davis, Terrell, Den.	23	21	2	0	0	138
Moss, Randy, Min.	17	0	17	0	2	106
Taylor, Fred, Jac.	17	14	3	0	0	102
Anderson, Jamal, Atl.	16	14	2	0	1	98
Owens, Terrell, S.F.	15	1	14	0	1	92
Smith, Emmitt, Dal.	15	13	2	0	0	90
Freeman, Antonio, G.B.	14	0	14	0	1	86
Carter, Cris, Min.	12	0	12	0	0	72
Edwards, Robert, N.E.	12	9	3	0	0	72
Galloway, Joey, Sea.	12	0	10	2	0	72

NFL TOP TEN SCORERS—KICKERS

	XP	XPA	FG	FGA	PTS
Anderson, Gary, Min.	59	59	35	35	164
Christie, Steve, Buf.	41	41	33	41	140
Del Greco, Al, Ten.	28	28	36	39	136
Longwell, Ryan, G.B.	41	43	29	33	128
Cunningham, Richie, Dal.	40	40	29	35	127
Elam, Jason, Den.	58	58	23	27	127
Vinatieri, Adam, N.E.	33	33	31	39	127
Andersen, Morten, Atl.	51	52	23	28	120
Hall, John, NY-J	45	46	25	35	120
Stoyanovich, Pete, K.C.	34	34	27	32	115

AFC SCORERS—INDIVIDUAL

Kickers

	XP	XPA	FG	FGA	PTS
Christie, Steve, Buf.	41	41	33	41	140
Del Greco, Al, Ten.	28	28	36	39	136
Elam, Jason, Den.	58	58	23	27	127
Vinatieri, Adam, N.E.	32†	32	31	39	127
Hall, John, NY-J	45	46	25	35	120
Stoyanovich, Pete, K.C.	34	34	27	32	115
Hollis, Mike, Jac.	45	45	21	26	108
Vanderjagt, Mike, Ind.	23	23	27	31	104
Johnson, Norm, Pit.	21	21	26	31	99
Mare, Olindo, Mia.	33	34	22	27	99
Peterson, Todd, Sea.	41	41	19	24	98
Carney, John, S.D.	19	19	26	30	97
Stover, Matt, Bal.	24	24	21	28	87
Davis, Greg, Oak.	31	31	17	27	82
Pelfrey, Doug, Cin.	21	21	19	27	78
George, Matt, Pit.	2	2	0	1	2
Hentrich, Craig, Ten.	0	0	0	1	0
Rouen, Tom, Den.	0	1	0	0	0

† *Scored two-point extra point; Vinatieri was 32-32 in kicking extra points.*

Nonkickers

	TD	TDR	TDP	TDM	2-PT	PTS
Davis, Terrell, Den.	23	21	2	0	0	138
Taylor, Fred, Jac.	17	14	3	0	0	102
Edwards, Robert, N.E.	12	9	3	0	0	72
Galloway, Joey, Sea.	12	0	10	2	0	72
Johnson, Keyshawn, NY-J	11	1	10	0	0	66
McCaffrey, Ed, Den.	10	0	10	0	1	62
Faulk, Marshall, Ind.	10	6	4	0	0	60
Sharpe, Shannon, Den.	10	0	10	0	0	60
Watters, Ricky, Sea.	9	9	0	0	1	56
Brown, Tim, Oak.	9	0	9	0	0	54
Martin, Curtis, NY-J	9	8	1	0	0	54
Moulds, Eric, Buf.	9	0	9	0	0	54
Chrebet, Wayne, NY-J	8	0	8	0	0	48
Lewis, Jermaine, Bal.	8	0	6	2	0	48
Morris, Bam, K.C.	8	8	0	0	0	48
Smith, Antowain, Buf.	8	8	0	0	0	48
Smith, Jimmy, Jac.	8	0	8	0	0	48
Johnson, Charles, Pit.	7	0	7	0	2	46
Harrison, Marvin, Ind.	7	0	7	0	1	44
Gadsden, Oronde, Mia.	7	0	7	0	0	42
Holmes, Priest, Bal.	7	7	0	0	0	42
McDuffie, O. J., Mia.	7	0	7	0	0	42
Scott, Darnay, Cin.	7	0	7	0	0	42
Small, Torrance, Ind.	7	0	7	0	0	42
Smith, Rod, Den.	7	0	6	1	0	42
George, Eddie, Ten.	6	5	1	0	1	38
McCardell, Keenan, Jac.	6	0	6	0	1	38
Abdul-Jabbar, Karim, Mia.	6	6	0	0	0	36
Bennett, Donnell, K.C.	6	5	1	0	0	36
Coates, Ben, N.E.	6	0	6	0	0	36
Jett, James, Oak.	6	0	6	0	0	36
Riemersma, Jay, Buf.	6	0	6	0	0	36
Turner, Floyd, Bal.	5	0	5	0	2	34
Dudley, Rickey, Oak.	5	0	5	0	1	32
Pickens, Carl, Cin.	5	0	5	0	1	32
Brady, Kyle, NY-J	5	0	5	0	0	30
Dillon, Corey, Cin.	5	4	1	0	0	30
Fletcher, Terrell, S.D.	5	5	0	0	0	30
Means, Natrone, S.D.	5	5	0	0	0	30
Reed, Andre, Buf.	5	0	5	0	0	30
Rison, Andre, K.C.	5	0	5	0	0	30
Thomas, Lamar, Mia.	5	0	5	0	0	30
Pollard, Marcus, Ind.	4	0	4	0	2	28
Alexander, Derrick, K.C.	4	0	4	0	0	24
Gibson, Damon, Cin.	4	0	3	1	0	24
Johnson, Leon, NY-J	4	2	2	0	0	24
Jones, Damon, Jac.	4	0	4	0	0	24
McNair, Steve, Ten.	4	4	0	0	0	24
Ward, Dedric, NY-J	4	0	4	0	0	24
Jones, Freddie, S.D.	3	0	3	0	1	20
Pritchard, Mike, Sea.	3	0	3	0	1	20
Anders, Kimble, K.C.	3	1	2	0	0	18
Avery, John, Mia.	3	2	1	0	0	18
Bettis, Jerome, Pit.	3	3	0	0	0	18
Byars, Keith, NY-J	3	0	3	0	0	18
Davis, Willie, Ten.	3	0	3	0	0	18
Drayton, Troy, Mia.	3	0	3	0	0	18
Fuamatu-Ma'afala, Chris, Pit.	3	2	1	0	0	18
Gannon, Rich, K.C.	3	3	0	0	0	18
Gash, Sam, Buf.	3	0	3	0	0	18
Glenn, Terry, N.E.	3	0	3	0	0	18
Griffith, Howard, Den.	3	0	3	0	0	18
Jones, Charlie, S.D.	3	0	3	0	0	18
Mason, Derrick, Ten.	3	0	3	0	0	18
Simmons, Tony, N.E.	3	0	3	0	0	18
Springs, Shawn, Sea.	3	0	0	3	0	18
Stewart, James, Jac.	3	2	1	0	0	18
Thigpen, Yancey, Ten.	3	0	3	0	0	18
Thomas, Thurman, Buf.	3	2	1	0	0	18
Bennett, Brandon, Cin.	2	2	0	0	0	12
Bowden, Joe, Ten.	2	0	0	2	0	12
Brisby, Vincent, N.E.	2	0	2	0	0	12
Bruener, Mark, Pit.	2	0	2	0	0	12
Dyson, Kevin, Ten.	2	0	2	0	0	12
Fauria, Christian, Sea.	2	0	2	0	0	12
Gonzalez, Tony, K.C.	2	0	2	0	0	12
Harris, Jackie, Ten.	2	0	2	0	0	12
Hebron, Vaughn, Den.	2	1	0	1	0	12
Howard, Desmond, Oak.	2	0	0	2	0	12
Jefferson, Shawn, N.E.	2	0	2	0	0	12
Johnson, Lonnie, Buf.	2	0	2	0	0	12
Johnson, Pat, Bal.	2	0	1	1	0	12
Kaufman, Napoleon, Oak.	2	2	0	0	0	12
Loville, Derek, Den.	2	2	0	0	0	12
McKnight, James, Sea.	2	0	2	0	0	12
Mitchell, Pete, Jac.	2	0	2	0	0	12
Potts, Roosevelt, Bal.	2	0	2	0	0	12
Purnell, Lovett, N.E.	2	0	2	0	0	12
Richardson, Tony, K.C.	2	2	0	0	0	12
Ricks, Mikhael, S.D.	2	0	2	0	0	12
Smith, Darrin, Sea.	2	0	0	2	0	12
Stewart, Kordell, Pit.	2	2	0	0	0	12
Still, Bryan, S.D.	2	0	2	0	0	12
Strong, Mack, Sea.	2	0	2	0	0	12
Thomas, Rodney, Ten.	2	2	0	0	0	12
Thomas, Zach, Mia.	2	0	0	2	0	12
Warren, Lamont, Ind.	2	1	1	0	0	12
Washington, Dewayne, Pit.	2	0	0	2	0	12
Williams, Harvey, Oak.	2	2	0	0	0	12
Woodson, Rod, Bal.	2	0	0	2	0	12
Wycheck, Frank, Ten.	2	0	2	0	0	12
Blackwell, Will, Pit.	1	0	1	0	1	8
Dilger, Ken, Ind.	1	0	1	0	1	8
Thomas, Derrick, K.C.	1	0	0	1	0	*8
Adams, Sam, Sea.	1	0	0	1	0	6
Archie, Mike, Ten.	1	1	0	0	0	6
Ashmore, Darryl, Oak.	1	0	0	1	0	6
Banks, Tavian, Jac.	1	1	0	0	0	6
Barlow, Reggie, Jac.	1	0	0	1	0	6
Battaglia, Marco, Cin.	1	0	1	0	0	6
Beasley, Aaron, Jac.	1	0	0	1	0	6
Brister, Bubby, Den.	1	1	0	0	0	6
Broussard, Steve, Sea.	1	0	0	1	0	6
Brown, Troy, N.E.	1	0	1	0	0	6

1998 INDIVIDUAL STATISTICS—SCORING

	TD	TDR	TDP	TDM	2-PT	PTS
Buckley, Terrell, Mia.	1	0	0	1	0	6
Cascadden, Chad, NY-J	1	0	0	1	0	6
Coleman, Andre, Pit.	1	0	1	0	0	6
Crockett, Ray, Den.	1	0	0	1	0	6
Crumpler, Carlester, Sea.	1	0	1	0	0	6
Cullors, Derrick, N.E.	1	0	1	0	0	6
Darius, Donovin, Jac.	1	0	0	1	0	6
Early, Quinn, Buf.	1	0	1	0	0	6
Elway, John, Den.	1	1	0	0	0	6
Flutie, Doug, Buf.	1	1	0	0	0	6
Glenn, Aaron, NY-J	1	0	0	1	0	6
Gordon, Darrien, Den.	1	0	0	1	0	6
Gordon, Dwayne, NY-J	1	0	0	1	0	6
Green, Ahman, Sea.	1	1	0	0	0	6
Green, Eric, Bal.	1	0	1	0	0	6
Green, E.G., Ind.	1	0	1	0	0	6
Green, Willie, Den.	1	0	1	0	0	6
Hansen, Phil, Buf.	1	0	0	1	0	6
Harris, Corey, Bal.	1	0	0	1	0	6
Hawkins, Courtney, Pit.	1	0	1	0	0	6
Henderson, Jerome, NY-J	1	0	0	1	0	6
Hollas, Donald, Oak.	1	1	0	0	0	6
Horn, Joe, K.C.	1	0	1	0	0	6
Hundon, James, Cin.	1	0	1	0	0	6
Huntley, Richard, Pit.	1	1	0	0	0	6
Johnson, Rob, Buf.	1	1	0	0	0	6
Johnstone, Lance, Oak.	1	0	0	1	0	6
Jones, Robert, Mia.	1	0	0	1	0	6
Jordan, Randy, Oak.	1	1	0	0	0	6
Kennedy, Cortez, Sea.	1	0	0	1	0	6
Kitna, Jon, Sea.	1	1	0	0	0	6
Lake, Carnell, Pit.	1	0	0	1	0	6
Law, Ty, N.E.	1	0	0	1	0	6
Lewis, Albert, Oak.	1	0	0	1	0	6
Linton, Jonathan, Buf.	1	1	0	0	0	6
Mack, Tremain, Cin.	1	0	0	1	0	6
Marino, Dan, Mia.	1	1	0	0	0	6
Marts, Lonnie, Ten.	1	0	0	1	0	6
May, Deems, Sea.	1	0	1	0	0	6
McAfee, Fred, Pit.	1	0	0	1	0	6
McDaniel, Terry, Sea.	1	0	0	1	0	6
McGee, Tony, Cin.	1	0	1	0	0	6
Mickens, Terry, Oak.	1	0	1	0	0	6
Milloy, Lawyer, N.E.	1	0	0	1	0	6
Milne, Brian, Cin.	1	1	0	0	0	6
Northern, Gabe, Buf.	1	0	0	1	0	6
Oldham, Chris, Pit.	1	0	0	1	0	6
Pathon, Jerome, Ind.	1	0	1	0	0	6
Pritchett, Stanley, Mia.	1	1	0	0	0	6
Quinn, Jonathan, Jac.	1	1	0	0	0	6
Roan, Michael, Ten.	1	0	0	1	0	6
Roe, James, Bal.	1	0	1	0	0	6
Sawyer, Corey, Cin.	1	0	0	1	0	6
Shade, Sam, Cin.	1	0	0	1	0	6
Shelton, Daimon, Jac.	1	1	0	0	0	6
Simmons, Anthony, Sea.	1	0	0	1	0	6
Stephens, Tremayne, S.D.	1	1	0	0	0	6
Testaverde, Vinny, NY-J	1	1	0	0	0	6
Thelwell, Ryan, S.D.	1	0	1	0	0	6
Thomas, Henry, N.E.	1	0	0	1	0	6
Turner, Eric, Oak.	1	0	0	1	0	6
Whitted, Alvis, Jac.	1	0	0	1	0	6
Williams, Jamal, S.D.	1	0	0	1	0	6
Williams, Kevin, Buf.	1	0	1	0	0	6
Williams, Stepfret, Cin.	1	0	1	0	0	6
Williams, Willie, Sea.	1	0	0	1	0	6
Woodson, Charles, Oak.	1	0	0	1	0	6
Burnett, Rob, Bal.	0	0	0	0	0	*2
Cox, Bryan, NY-J	0	0	0	0	0	*2
Justin, Paul, Cin.	0	0	0	0	1	2
Washington, Ted, Buf.	0	0	0	0	0	*2
Whelihan, Craig, S.D.	0	0	0	0	1	2

** Safety*
Team safety credited to Baltimore, San Diego.

NFC SCORERS—INDIVIDUAL
Kickers

	XP	XPA	FG	FGA	PTS
Anderson, Gary, Min.	59	59	35	35	164
Longwell, Ryan, G.B.	41	43	29	33	128
Cunningham, Richie, Dal.	40	40	29	35	127
Andersen, Morten, Atl.	51	52	23	28	120
Hanson, Jason, Det.	27	29	29	33	114
Richey, Wade, S.F.	49	51	18	27	103
Daluiso, Brad, NY-G	32	32	21	27	95
Husted, Michael, T.B.	29	30	21	28	92
Kasay, John, Car.	35	37	19	26	92
Brien, Doug, N.O.	31	31	20	22	91
Jaeger, Jeff, Chi.	27	28	21	26	90
Wilkins, Jeff, St.L	25	26	20	26	85
Nedney, Joe, Ariz	30	30	13	19	69
Blanchard, Cary, Was.	30	31	11	17	63
Boniol, Chris, Phi.	15	17	14	21	57
Jacke, Chris, Ariz	6	6	10	14	36
Blanton, Scott, Was.	4	4	2	4	10
Akers, David, Was.	2	2	0	2	2

Nonkickers

	TD	TDR	TDP	TDM	2-PT	PTS
Moss, Randy, Min.	17	0	17	0	2	106
Anderson, Jamal, Atl.	16	14	2	0	1	98
Owens, Terrell, S.F.	15	1	14	0	1	92
Smith, Emmitt, Dal.	15	13	2	0	0	90
Freeman, Antonio, G.B.	14	0	14	0	1	86
Carter, Cris, Min.	12	0	12	0	0	72
Mathis, Terance, Atl.	11	0	11	0	0	66
Hoard, Leroy, Min.	10	9	1	0	0	60
Murrell, Adrian, Ariz	10	8	2	0	0	60
Rice, Jerry, S.F.	9	0	9	0	2	58
Hearst, Garrison, S.F.	9	7	2	0	1	56
Shepherd, Leslie, Was.	9	1	8	0	1	56
Alstott, Mike, T.B.	9	8	1	0	0	54
Hicks, Skip, Was.	8	8	0	0	0	48
Ismail, Raghib, Car.	8	0	8	0	0	48
Smith, Robert, Min.	8	6	2	0	0	48
Stokes, J.J., S.F.	8	0	8	0	0	48
Anthony, Reidel, T.B.	7	0	7	0	1	44
Davis, Tyrone, G.B.	7	0	7	0	0	42
Vardell, Tommy, Det.	7	6	1	0	0	42
Muhammad, Muhsin, Car.	6	0	6	0	1	38
Bates, Mario, Ariz	6	6	0	0	0	36
Calloway, Chris, NY-G	6	0	6	0	0	36
Cleeland, Cameron, N.O.	6	0	6	0	0	36
Martin, Tony, Atl.	6	0	6	0	0	36
Staley, Duce, Phi.	6	5	1	0	0	36
Westbrook, Michael, Was.	6	0	6	0	0	36
Young, Steve, S.F.	6	6	0	0	0	36
Brown, Gary, NY-G	5	5	0	0	0	30
Craver, Aaron, N.O.	5	2	2	1	0	30
Engram, Bobby, Chi.	5	0	5	0	0	30
Glover, Andrew, Min.	5	0	5	0	0	30
Lane, Fred, Car.	5	5	0	0	0	30
Moore, Herman, Det.	5	0	5	0	0	30
Moore, Rob, Ariz	5	0	5	0	0	30
Santiago, O.J., Atl.	5	0	5	0	0	30
Smith, Irv, S.F.	5	0	5	0	0	30
Toomer, Amani, NY-G	5	0	5	0	0	30
Walls, Wesley, Car.	5	0	5	0	0	30
Warren, Chris, Dal.	5	4	1	0	0	30
Lee, Amp, St.L	4	2	2	0	1	26
Alexander, Stephen, Was.	4	0	4	0	0	24
Biakabutuka, Tim, Car.	4	3	1	0	0	24
Chmura, Mark, G.B.	4	0	4	0	0	24
Floyd, William, Car.	4	3	1	0	0	24
Garner, Charlie, Phi.	4	4	0	0	0	24
Hill, Greg, St.L	4	4	0	0	0	24
McWilliams, Johnny, Ariz	4	0	4	0	0	24
Mills, Ernie, Dal.	4	0	4	0	0	24
Moore, Dave, T.B.	4	0	4	0	0	24
Plummer, Jake, Ariz	4	4	0	0	0	24
Reed, Jake, Min.	4	0	4	0	0	24
Sanders, Barry, Det.	4	4	0	0	0	24
Way, Charles, NY-G	4	3	1	0	0	24
Banks, Tony, St.L	3	3	0	0	1	20
Penn, Chris, Chi.	3	0	3	0	1	20
Proehl, Ricky, St.L	3	0	3	0	1	20
Barber, Tiki, NY-G	3	0	3	0	0	18
Bech, Brett, N.O.	3	0	3	0	0	18
Brooks, Robert, G.B.	3	0	3	0	0	18
Christian, Bob, Atl.	3	2	1	0	0	18
Conway, Curtis, Chi.	3	0	3	0	0	18
Crowell, Germane, Det.	3	0	3	0	0	18

1998 INDIVIDUAL STATISTICS—SCORING

	TD	TDR	TDP	TDM	2-PT	PTS
Davis, Billy, Dal.	3	0	3	0	0	18
Edwards, Marc, S.F.	3	1	2	0	0	18
Green, Jacquez, T.B.	3	0	2	1	0	18
Hastings, Andre, N.O.	3	0	3	0	0	18
Henderson, William, G.B.	3	2	1	0	0	18
Henley, June, St.L	3	3	0	0	0	18
Hitchcock, Jimmy, Min.	3	0	0	3	0	18
Kirby, Terry, S.F.	3	3	0	0	0	18
Mayes, Derrick, G.B.	3	0	3	0	0	18
Milburn, Glyn, Chi.	3	0	0	3	0	18
Mitchell, Brian, Was.	3	2	0	1	0	18
Preston, Roell, G.B.	3	0	0	3	0	18
Sanders, Deion, Dal.	3	0	0	3	0	18
Sanders, Frank, Ariz	3	0	3	0	0	18
Smith, Lamar, N.O.	3	1	2	0	0	18
Aikman, Troy, Dal.	2	2	0	0	0	12
Allen, James, Chi.	2	1	1	0	0	12
Allen, Terry, Was.	2	2	0	0	0	12
Bennett, Edgar, Chi.	2	2	0	0	0	12
Bjornson, Eric, Dal.	2	1	1	0	0	12
Carrier, Mark, Car.	2	0	2	0	0	12
Centers, Larry, Ariz	2	0	2	0	0	12
Chancey, Robert, Chi.	2	2	0	0	0	12
Chandler, Chris, Atl.	2	2	0	0	0	12
Chryplewicz, Pete, Det.	2	0	2	0	0	12
Connell, Albert, Was.	2	0	2	0	0	12
Davis, Eric, Car.	2	0	0	2	0	12
Davis, Stephen, Was.	2	0	2	0	0	12
Dilfer, Trent, T.B.	2	2	0	0	0	12
Dunn, Warrick, T.B.	2	2	0	0	0	12
Dwight, Tim, Atl.	2	0	1	1	0	12
Ellsworth, Percy, NY-G	2	0	0	2	0	12
Emanuel, Bert, T.B.	2	0	2	0	0	12
Fair, Terry, Det.	2	0	0	2	0	12
Fryar, Irving, Phi.	2	0	2	0	0	12
Graham, Jeff, Phi.	2	0	2	0	0	12
Graham, Kent, NY-G	2	2	0	0	0	12
Green, Trent, Was.	2	2	0	0	0	12
Hakim, Az-Zahir, St.L	2	1	1	0	0	12
Harris, Derrick, St.L	2	0	2	0	0	12
Hilliard, Ike, NY-G	2	0	2	0	0	12
Holcombe, Robert, St.L	2	2	0	0	0	12
Jeffers, Patrick, Dal.	2	0	2	0	0	12
Kennison, Eddie, St.L	2	0	1	1	0	12
Knight, Sammy, N.O.	2	0	0	2	0	12
LaFleur, David, Dal.	2	0	2	0	0	12
McKenzie, Keith, G.B.	2	0	0	2	0	12
Moore, Jerald, St.L	2	2	0	0	0	12
Morton, Johnnie, Det.	2	0	2	0	0	12
Patten, David, NY-G	2	0	1	1	0	12
Poole, Keith, N.O.	2	0	2	0	0	12
Rudd, Dwayne, Min.	2	0	0	2	0	12
Stenstrom, Steve, Chi.	2	2	0	0	0	12
Wetnight, Ryan, Chi.	2	0	2	0	0	12
Bradford, Ronnie, Atl.	1	0	0	1	0	*8
Clark, Greg, S.F.	1	0	1	0	1	8
Collins, Kerry, Car.-N.O.	1	1	0	0	1	8
Cunningham, Randall, Min.	1	1	0	0	1	8
Hunter, Brice, T.B.	1	0	1	0	1	8
Wheaton, Kenny, Dal.	1	0	0	1	0	*8
Barber, Ronde, T.B.	1	0	0	1	0	6
Batch, Charlie, Det.	1	1	0	0	0	6
Bates, Michael, Car.	1	0	0	1	0	6
Bennett, Tommy, Ariz	1	0	0	1	0	6
Bowie, Larry, Was.	1	0	1	0	0	6
Bownes, Fabien, Chi.	1	0	1	0	0	6
Boyd, Tommie, Det.	1	0	1	0	0	6
Broughton, Luther, Car.	1	0	1	0	0	6
Bruce, Isaac, St.L	1	0	1	0	0	6
Butler, LeRoy, G.B.	1	0	0	1	0	6
Davis, John, T.B.	1	0	1	0	0	6
Davis, Troy, N.O.	1	1	0	0	0	6
Dawkins, Sean, N.O.	1	0	1	0	0	6
Drakeford, Tyronne, N.O.	1	0	0	1	0	6
Edwards, Antonio, Atl.	1	0	0	1	0	6
Evans, Chuck, Min.	1	1	0	0	0	6
Favre, Brett, G.B.	1	1	0	0	0	6
Fields, Mark, N.O.	1	0	0	1	0	6
Gedney, Chris, Ariz	1	0	1	0	0	6
Hallock, Ty, Chi.	1	1	0	0	0	6
Harris, Raymont, G.B.	1	1	0	0	0	6
Harris, Walt, Chi.	1	0	0	1	0	6
Holmes, Darick, G.B.	1	1	0	0	0	6
Horne, Tony, St.L	1	0	0	1	0	6
Irvin, Michael, Dal.	1	0	1	0	0	6
Jervey, Travis, G.B.	1	1	0	0	0	6
Johnson, Anthony, Car.	1	0	1	0	0	6
Johnson, Joe, N.O.	1	0	0	1	0	6
Johnston, Daryl, Dal.	1	0	1	0	0	6
Kelly, Rob, N.O.	1	0	0	1	0	6
Kinchen, Todd, Atl.	1	0	1	0	0	6
Kozlowski, Brian, Atl.	1	0	1	0	0	6
Kramer, Erik, Chi.	1	1	0	0	0	6
Lee, Shawn, Chi.	1	0	0	1	0	6
Levens, Dorsey, G.B.	1	1	0	0	0	6
Levy, Chuck, S.F.	1	1	0	0	0	6
McNeil, Ryan, St.L	1	0	0	1	0	6
McQuarters, R.W., S.F.	1	0	0	1	0	6
Mincy, Charles, T.B.	1	0	0	1	0	6
Mitchell, Keith, N.O.	1	0	0	1	0	6
Neal, Lorenzo, T.B.	1	0	1	0	0	6
Palmer, David, Min.	1	0	0	1	0	6
Peete, Rodney, Phi.	1	1	0	0	0	6
Rasby, Walter, Det.	1	0	1	0	0	6
Rivers, Ron, Det.	1	1	0	0	0	6
Robbins, Austin, N.O.	1	0	0	1	0	6
Robinson, Eugene, Atl.	1	0	0	1	0	6
Robinson, Jeff, St.L	1	0	1	0	0	6
Robinson, Marcus, Chi.	1	0	1	0	0	6
Schlesinger, Cory, Det.	1	0	1	0	0	6
Schroeder, Bill, G.B.	1	0	1	0	0	6
Sinceno, Kaseem, Phi.	1	0	1	0	0	6
Sloan, David, Det.	1	0	1	0	0	6
Smith, Chuck, Atl.	1	0	0	1	0	6
Solomon, Freddie, Phi.	1	0	1	0	0	6
Stone, Dwight, Car.	1	0	0	1	0	6
Strahan, Michael, NY-G	1	0	0	1	0	6
Thomas, Robb, T.B.	1	0	1	0	0	6
Thrash, James, Was.	1	0	1	0	0	6
Tuggle, Jessie, Atl.	1	0	0	1	0	6
Weary, Fred, N.O.	1	0	0	1	0	6
Westbrook, Bryant, Det.	1	0	0	1	0	6
White, William, Atl.	1	0	0	1	0	6
Williams, Karl, T.B.	1	0	1	0	0	6
Williams, Roland, St.L	1	0	1	0	0	6
Williams, Sherman, Dal.	1	1	0	0	0	6
Zellars, Ray, N.O.	1	1	0	0	0	6
Bono, Steve, St.L	0	0	0	0	1	2
Boutte, Marc, Was.	0	0	0	0	0	*2
Hape, Patrick, T.B.	0	0	0	0	1	2
Martin, Wayne, N.O.	0	0	0	0	0	*2
Thierry, John, Chi.	0	0	0	0	0	*2

** Safety*

Team safety credited to Arizona (2), Chicago, Green Bay, Minnesota, New Orleans, Philadelphia

FIELD GOALS

Field Goal Percentage
- **NFC:** 1.000—Gary Anderson, Minnesota
- **AFC:** .923—Al Del Greco, Tennessee

Field Goals
- **AFC:** 36—Al Del Greco, Tennessee
- **NFC:** 35—Gary Anderson, Minnesota

Field Goal Attempts
- **AFC:** 41—Steve Christie, Buffalo
- **NFC:** 35—Gary Anderson, Minnesota
  Richie Cunningham, Dallas

Longest Field Goal
- **AFC:** 63—Jason Elam, Denver vs. Jacksonville, October 25
- **NFC:** 57—Jeff Wilkins, St. Louis vs. Arizona, September 27

Average Yards Made
- **NFC:** 38.5—John Kasay, Carolina
- **AFC:** 37.2—Jason Elam, Denver

1998 INDIVIDUAL STATISTICS—FIELD GOALS

AFC FIELD GOALS—TEAM

	FG	FGA	Pct.	Long
Tennessee	36	40	.900	48
Indianapolis	27	31	.871	53
San Diego	26	30	.867	54
Denver	23	27	.852	63
Kansas City	27	32	.844	53
Miami	22	27	.815	48
Pittsburgh	26	32	.813	49
Jacksonville	21	26	.808	47
Buffalo	33	41	.805	52
New England	31	39	.795	55
Seattle	19	24	.792	51
Baltimore	21	28	.750	48
N.Y. Jets	25	35	.714	54
Cincinnati	19	27	.704	51
Oakland	17	27	.630	51
AFC Total	373	466	—	63
AFC Average	24.9	31.1	.800	—

NFC FIELD GOALS—TEAM

	FG	FGA	Pct.	Long
Minnesota	35	35	1.000	53
New Orleans	20	22	.909	56
Detroit	29	33	.879	51
Green Bay	29	33	.879	45
Dallas	29	35	.829	54
Atlanta	23	28	.821	53
Chicago	21	26	.808	52
N.Y. Giants	21	27	.778	51
St. Louis	20	26	.769	57
Tampa Bay	21	28	.750	52
Carolina	19	26	.731	56
Arizona	23	33	.697	53
Philadelphia	14	21	.667	50
San Francisco	18	27	.667	46
Washington	13	23	.565	54
NFC Total	335	423	—	57
NFC Average	22.3	28.2	.792	—
League Total	708	889	—	63
League Average	23.6	29.6	.796	—

AFC FIELD GOALS—INDIVIDUAL

	1-19 Yards	20-29 Yards	30-39 Yards	40-49 Yards	50 or Longer	Totals	Avg. Yds. Att.	Avg. Yds. Made	Avg. Yds. Miss	Long
Del Greco, Al, Ten.	1-1	8-8	15-15	12-15	0-0	36-39	35.8	35.2	43.3	48
	1.000	1.000	1.000	.800	—	.923				
Vanderjagt, Mike, Ind.	1-1	8-8	4-4	8-9	6-9	27-31	39.0	37.1	52.0	53
	1.000	1.000	1.000	.889	.667	.871				
Carney, John, S.D.	0-0	11-12	5-5	8-10	2-3	26-30	35.7	34.9	41.0	54
	—	.917	1.000	.800	.667	.867				
Elam, Jason, Den.	0-0	3-3	13-14	4-6	3-4	23-27	38.3	37.2	44.3	63
	—	1.000	.929	.667	.750	.852				
Stoyanovich, Pete, K.C.	2-2	9-9	9-9	5-10	2-2	27-32	34.6	32.7	44.6	53
	1.000	1.000	1.000	.500	1.000	.844				
Johnson, Norm, Pit.	0-0	10-10	5-5	11-14	0-2	26-31	36.8	34.6	48.2	49
	—	1.000	1.000	.786	.000	.839				
Mare, Olindo, Mia.	0-0	12-13	5-5	5-7	0-2	22-27	33.6	31.2	44.4	48
	—	.923	1.000	.714	.000	.815				
Hollis, Mike, Jac.	1-1	8-10	8-9	4-5	0-1	21-26	32.5	31.8	35.8	47
	1.000	.800	.889	.800	.000	.808				
Christie, Steve, Buf.	1-1	10-12	12-14	9-11	1-3	33-41	35.0	33.9	39.5	52
	1.000	.833	.857	.818	.333	.805				
Vinatieri, Adam, N.E.	3-3	8-8	9-14	9-12	2-2	31-39	35.4	34.2	40.0	55
	1.000	1.000	.643	.750	1.000	.795				
Peterson, Todd, Sea.	0-0	7-7	4-5	5-5	3-7	19-24	38.5	35.6	49.4	51
	—	1.000	.800	1.000	.429	.792				
Stover, Matt, Bal.	0-0	6-6	5-5	10-17	0-0	21-28	37.5	35.6	43.4	48
	—	1.000	1.000	.588	—	.750				
Hall, John, NY-J	0-0	9-9	9-13	6-10	1-3	25-35	36.4	33.4	43.7	54
	—	1.000	.692	.600	.333	.714				
Pelfrey, Doug, Cin.	1-1	4-4	6-7	6-10	2-5	19-27	39.1	36.2	46.1	51
	1.000	1.000	.857	.600	.400	.704				
Davis, Greg, Oak.	0-0	5-6	5-8	6-11	1-2	17-27	37.3	35.6	40.2	51
	—	.833	.625	.545	.500	.630				
Nonqualifiers										
George, Matt, Pit.	0-0	0-0	0-1	0-0	0-0	0-1	36.0	—	36.0	0
	—	—	.000	—	—	.000				
Hentrich, Craig, Ten.	0-0	0-0	0-0	0-1	0-0	0-1	49.0	—	49.0	0
	—	—	—	.000	—	.000				
AFC Totals	10-10	118-125	114-133	108-153	23-45	373-466	36.3	34.6	43.3	63
	1.000	.944	.857	.706	.511	.800				
League Totals	20-22	219-230	216-254	206-296	47-87	708-889	36.6	34.9	43.3	63
	.909	.952	.850	.696	.540	.796				

Leader based on percentage, minimum 16 field-goal attempts

NFC FIELD GOALS—INDIVIDUAL

	1-19 Yards	20-29 Yards	30-39 Yards	40-49 Yards	50 or Longer	Totals	Avg. Yds. Att.	Avg. Yds. Made	Avg. Yds. Miss	Long
Anderson, Gary, Min.	1-1	11-11	9-9	12-12	2-2	35-35	35.6	35.6	—	53
	1.000	1.000	1.000	1.000	1.000	1.000				
Brien, Doug, N.O.	0-0	7-7	3-3	6-6	4-6	20-22	39.0	37.6	53.5	56
	—	1.000	1.000	1.000	.667	.909				
Hanson, Jason, Det.	0-0	8-8	7-7	13-15	1-3	29-33	39.2	37.7	50.3	51
	—	1.000	1.000	.867	.333	.879				
Longwell, Ryan, G.B.	1-1	6-6	13-15	9-10	0-1	29-33	35.4	34.1	44.3	45
	1.000	1.000	.867	.900	.000	.879				
Cunningham, Richie, Dal.	1-1	9-9	8-11	10-11	1-3	29-35	36.1	34.3	44.7	54
	1.000	1.000	.727	.909	.333	.829				
Andersen, Morten, Atl.	0-1	8-9	7-7	6-9	2-2	23-28	34.9	34.4	37.4	53
	.000	.889	1.000	.667	1.000	.821				
Jaeger, Jeff, Chi.	2-2	8-9	9-10	1-4	1-1	21-26	32.0	30.3	39.2	52
	1.000	.889	.900	.250	1.000	.808				
Daluiso, Brad, NY-G	2-2	5-5	6-8	7-11	1-1	21-27	35.7	34.5	39.7	51
	1.000	1.000	.750	.636	1.000	.778				
Wilkins, Jeff, St.L	0-0	4-5	8-8	5-7	3-6	20-26	40.4	38.1	48.0	57
	—	.800	1.000	.714	.500	.769				
Husted, Michael, T.B.	0-1	7-7	8-12	5-7	1-1	21-28	34.8	34.6	35.1	52
	.000	1.000	.667	.714	1.000	.750				
Kasay, John, Car.	0-0	5-5	4-5	6-9	4-7	19-26	40.9	38.5	47.6	56
	—	1.000	.800	.667	.571	.731				
Nedney, Joe, Ariz	0-0	6-6	1-1	5-8	1-4	13-19	39.8	36.0	48.0	53
	—	1.000	1.000	.625	.250	.684				
Boniol, Chris, Phi.	3-3	3-3	4-5	3-9	1-1	14-21	36.2	32.5	43.7	50
	1.000	1.000	.800	.333	1.000	.667				
Richey, Wade, S.F.	0-0	9-10	3-4	6-13	0-0	18-27	35.2	32.2	41.3	46
	—	.900	.750	.462	—	.667				
Blanchard, Cary, Was.	0-0	2-2	6-8	2-5	1-2	11-17	39.1	37.0	42.8	54
	—	1.000	.750	.400	.500	.647				
Nonqualifiers										
Jacke, Chris, Ariz	0-0	3-3	5-6	1-3	1-2	10-14	37.1	34.7	43.0	52
	—	1.000	.833	.333	.500	.714				
Blanton, Scott, Was.	0-0	0-0	1-2	1-2	0-0	2-4	41.0	41.5	40.5	46
	—	—	.500	.500	—	.500				
Akers, David, Was.	0-0	0-0	0-0	0-2	0-0	0-2	48.5	—	48.5	0
	—	—	—	.000	—	.000				
NFC Totals	10-12	101-105	102-121	98-143	24-42	335-423	36.9	35.2	43.3	57
	.833	.962	.843	.685	.571	.792				
League Totals	20-22	219-230	216-254	206-296	47-87	708-889	36.6	34.9	43.3	63
	.909	.952	.850	.696	.540	.796				

Leader based on percentage, minimum 16 field-goal attempts

RUSHING

Yards
AFC: 2008—Terrell Davis, Denver
NFC: 1846—Jamal Anderson, Atlanta

Yards, Game
AFC: 227—Priest Holmes, Baltimore at Cincinnati, November 22 (36 attempts, TD)
NFC: 198—Garrison Hearst, San Francisco vs. Detroit, December 14 (24 attempts, TD)

Longest
NFC: 96—Garrison Hearst, San Francisco vs. N.Y. Jets, September 6 - TD
AFC: 80—Napoleon Kaufman, Oakland vs. N.Y. Giants, September 13 - TD

Attempts
NFC: 410—Jamal Anderson, Atlanta
AFC: 392—Terrell Davis, Denver

Attempts, Game
AFC: 37—Natrone Means, San Diego at Oakland, October 11 (101 yards)
NFC: 35—Fred Lane, Carolina vs. New Orleans, November 1 (101 yards - TD)

Yards Per Attempt
AFC: 5.2—Terrell Davis, Denver
NFC: 5.1—Garrison Hearst, San Francisco

Touchdowns
AFC: 21—Terrell Davis, Denver
NFC: 14—Jamal Anderson, Atlanta

Team Leaders, Yards
AFC: BALTIMORE: 1008, Priest Holmes; BUFFALO: 1124, Antowain Smith; CINCINNATI: 1130, Corey Dillon; DENVER: 2008, Terrell Davis; INDIANAPOLIS: 1319, Marshall Faulk; JACKSONVILLE: 1223, Fred Taylor; KANSAS CITY: 527, Donnell Bennett; MIAMI: 960, Karim Abdul-Jabbar; NEW ENGLAND: 1115, Robert Edwards; N.Y. JETS: 1287, Curtis Martin; OAKLAND: 921, Napoleon Kaufman; PITTSBURGH: 1185, Jerome Bettis; SAN DIEGO: 883, Natrone Means; SEATTLE: 1239, Ricky Watters; TENNESSEE: 1294, Eddie George.
NFC: ARIZONA: 1042, Adrian Murrell; ATLANTA: 1846, Jamal Anderson; CAROLINA: 717, Fred Lane; CHICAGO: 611, Edgar Bennett; DALLAS: 1332, Emmitt Smith; DETROIT: 1491, Barry Sanders; GREEN BAY: 386, Darick Holmes; MINNESOTA: 1187, Robert Smith; NEW ORLEANS: 457, Lamar Smith; N.Y. GIANTS: 1063, Gary Brown; PHILADELPHIA: 1065, Duce Staley; ST. LOUIS: 313, June Henley; SAN FRANCISCO: 1570, Garrison Hearst; TAMPA BAY: 1026, Warrick Dunn; WASHINGTON: 700, Terry Allen.

Team Champion
NFC: 2544—San Francisco
AFC: 2468—Denver

1998 INDIVIDUAL STATISTICS—RUSHING

AFC RUSHING—TEAM

	Att.	Yards	Avg.	Long	TD
Denver	525	2468	4.7	70	26
Buffalo	531	2161	4.1	32	13
Jacksonville	487	2102	4.3	77t	19
Pittsburgh	490	2034	4.2	56	8
Tennessee	462	1970	4.3	71t	12
N.Y. Jets	500	1879	3.8	60t	12
San Diego	460	1728	3.8	72t	11
Oakland	449	1727	3.8	80t	6
Cincinnati	405	1639	4.0	66	7
Baltimore	408	1629	4.0	56	7
Seattle	426	1626	3.8	64	11
Kansas City	433	1548	3.6	38	19
Miami	458	1535	3.4	45	10
Indianapolis	384	1486	3.9	68t	7
New England	403	1480	3.7	71	9
AFC Total	6821	27012	4.0	80t	177
AFC Average	454.7	1800.8	4.0	—	11.8

NFC RUSHING—TEAM

	Att.	Yards	Avg.	Long	TD
San Francisco	491	2544	5.2	96t	19
Tampa Bay	523	2148	4.1	50	12
Atlanta	516	2101	4.1	48	18
Dallas	499	2014	4.0	49	21
Detroit	441	1955	4.4	73t	12
Minnesota	450	1936	4.3	74t	17
N.Y. Giants	474	1889	4.0	45	10
Philadelphia	427	1775	4.2	64t	10
Chicago	454	1713	3.8	57	9
Washington	401	1685	4.2	45	15
Arizona	450	1627	3.6	32	18
Green Bay	447	1526	3.4	50	7
Carolina	405	1458	3.6	41	11
St. Louis	395	1385	3.5	46	17
New Orleans	374	1325	3.5	33	6
NFC Total	6747	27081	4.0	96t	202
NFC Average	449.8	1805.4	4.0	—	13.5
League Total	13568	54093	—	96t	379
League Average	452.3	1803.1	4.0	—	12.6

NFL TOP TEN RUSHERS

	Att.	Yards	Avg.	Long	TD
Davis, Terrell, Den.	392	2008	5.1	70	21
Anderson, Jamal, Atl.	410	1846	4.5	48	14
Hearst, Garrison, S.F.	310	1570	5.1	96t	7
Sanders, Barry, Det.	343	1491	4.3	73t	4
Smith, Emmitt, Dal.	319	1332	4.2	32	13
Faulk, Marshall, Ind.	324	1319	4.1	68t	6
George, Eddie, Ten.	348	1294	3.7	37t	5
Martin, Curtis, NY-J	369	1287	3.5	60t	8
Watters, Ricky, Sea.	319	1239	3.9	39t	9
Taylor, Fred, Jac.	264	1223	4.6	77t	14

AFC RUSHERS—INDIVIDUAL

	Att.	Yards	Avg.	Long	TD
Davis, Terrell, Den.	392	2008	5.1	70	21
Faulk, Marshall, Ind.	324	1319	4.1	68t	6
George, Eddie, Ten.	348	1294	3.7	37t	5
Martin, Curtis, NY-J	369	1287	3.5	60t	8
Watters, Ricky, Sea.	319	1239	3.9	39t	9
Taylor, Fred, Jac.	264	1223	4.6	77t	14
Bettis, Jerome, Pit.	316	1185	3.8	42	3
Dillon, Corey, Cin.	262	1130	4.3	66	4
Smith, Antowain, Buf.	300	1124	3.7	30	8
Edwards, Robert, N.E.	291	1115	3.8	53	9
Holmes, Priest, Bal.	233	1008	4.3	56	7
Abdul-Jabbar, Karim, Mia.	270	960	3.6	45	6
Kaufman, Napoleon, Oak.	217	921	4.2	80t	2
Means, Natrone, S.D.	212	883	4.2	72t	5
McNair, Steve, Ten.	77	559	7.3	71t	4
Fletcher, Terrell, S.D.	153	543	3.5	21	5
Bennett, Donnell, K.C.	148	527	3.6	26	5
Avery, John, Mia.	143	503	3.5	44	2
Williams, Harvey, Oak.	128	496	3.9	25t	2
Morris, Bam, Chi.-K.C.	132	489	3.7	38	8
Stewart, Kordell, Pit.	81	406	5.0	56	2
Thomas, Thurman, Buf.	93	381	4.1	17t	2
Flutie, Doug, Buf.	48	248	5.2	23	1
Bennett, Brandon, Cin.	77	243	3.2	17	2
Huntley, Richard, Pit.	55	242	4.4	48	1
Shaw, Sedrick, N.E.	48	236	4.9	71	0
Anders, Kimble, K.C.	58	230	4.0	20	1
Stewart, James, Jac.	53	217	4.1	30	2
Green, Ahman, Sea.	35	209	6.0	64	1
Linton, Jonathan, Buf.	45	195	4.3	20	1
Brunell, Mark, Jac.	49	192	3.9	18	0
Johnson, Leon, NY-J	41	185	4.5	40	2
Rhett, Errict, Bal.	44	180	4.1	46	0
Harbaugh, Jim, Bal.	40	172	4.3	15	0
Gannon, Rich, K.C.	44	168	3.8	21	3
Sowell, Jerald, NY-J	40	164	4.1	33	0
Loville, Derek, Den.	53	161	3.0	12	2
Jordan, Randy, Oak.	47	159	3.4	23	1
Banks, Tavian, Jac.	26	140	5.4	51	1
Johnson, Rob, Buf.	24	123	5.1	32	1
Stephens, Tremayne, S.D.	35	122	3.5	12	1
Jones, George, Jac.	39	121	3.1	21	0
Hollas, Donald, Oak.	29	120	4.1	14	1
Potts, Roosevelt, Bal.	36	115	3.2	33	0
McAfee, Fred, Pit.	18	111	6.2	14	0
Graham, Jay, Bal.	35	109	3.1	12	0
Testaverde, Vinny, NY-J	24	104	4.3	25	1
Blake, Jeff, Cin.	15	103	6.9	18	0
Brister, Bubby, Den.	19	102	5.4	38t	1
Thomas, Rodney, Ten.	24	100	4.2	21	2
Shelton, Daimon, Jac.	30	95	3.2	16	1
Elway, John, Den.	37	94	2.5	16	1
Leaf, Ryan, S.D.	27	80	3.0	20	0
Quinn, Jonathan, Jac.	11	77	7.0	17	1
Kitna, Jon, Sea.	20	67	3.4	21	1
Smith, Rod, Den.	6	63	10.5	37	0
Manning, Peyton, Ind.	15	62	4.1	15	0
Warren, Lamont, Ind.	25	61	2.4	14	1
Johnson, Keyshawn, NY-J	2	60	30.0	35t	1
Shehee, Rashaan, K.C.	22	57	2.6	10	0
Bieniemy, Eric, Cin.	17	56	3.3	9	0
Cullors, Derrick, N.E.	18	48	2.7	15	0
Strong, Mack, Sea.	15	47	3.1	9	0
Williams, Kevin, Buf.	5	46	9.2	28	0
Richardson, Tony, K.C.	20	45	2.3	6	2
Bledsoe, Drew, N.E.	28	44	1.6	10	0
Hawkins, Courtney, Pit.	10	41	4.1	14	0
Milne, Brian, Cin.	10	41	4.1	10	1
Jones, Charlie, S.D.	4	39	9.8	14	0
Whelihan, Craig, S.D.	18	38	2.1	13	0
Byars, Keith, NY-J	4	34	8.5	13	0
O'Donnell, Neil, Cin.	13	34	2.6	10	0
Gash, Sam, Buf.	11	32	2.9	11	0
Hebron, Vaughn, Den.	9	31	3.4	8	1
Fuamatu-Ma'afala, Chris, Pit.	7	30	4.3	10t	2
Grbac, Elvis, K.C.	7	27	3.9	10	0
Galloway, Joey, Sea.	9	26	2.9	14	0
Archie, Mike, Ten.	6	24	4.0	20	1
Elias, Keith, Ind.	8	24	3.0	8	0
Meggett, David, NY-J	7	24	3.4	18	0
Wilson, Wade, Oak.	7	24	3.4	12	0
Bynum, Kenny, S.D.	11	23	2.1	14	0
Lucas, Ray, NY-J	5	23	4.6	16	0
Ritchie, Jon, Oak.	9	23	2.6	14	0
Floyd, Chris, N.E.	6	22	3.7	10	0
Lewis, Jermaine, Bal.	5	20	4.0	9	0
Parmalee, Bernie, Mia.	8	20	2.5	10	0
Pritchett, Stanley, Mia.	6	19	3.2	11	1
Pritchard, Mike, Sea.	1	17	17.0	17	0
Zeier, Eric, Bal.	11	17	1.5	7	0
Howard, Chris, Jac.	7	16	2.3	5	0
Heyward, Craig, Ind.	6	15	2.5	8	0
Jefferson, Shawn, N.E.	1	15	15.0	15	0
Griffith, Howard, Den.	4	13	3.3	16	0
Ward, Hines, Pit.	1	13	13.0	13	0
Whitted, Alvis, Jac.	3	13	4.3	16	0
Moore, Ronald, Mia.	4	12	3.0	4	0
Rison, Andre, K.C.	2	12	6.0	11	0
McDuffie, O. J., Mia.	3	11	3.7	5	0
Moon, Warren, Sea.	16	10	0.6	9	0
Scott, Darnay, Cin.	2	10	5.0	8	0
Gibson, Damon, Cin.	1	9	9.0	9	0

1998 INDIVIDUAL STATISTICS—RUSHING

	Att.	Yards	Avg.	Long	TD
Cotton, Kenyon, Bal.	2	8	4.0	7	0
Martin, Jamie, Jac.	5	8	1.6	6	0
Lusk, Henry, Mia.	1	7	7.0	7	0
Ward, Dedric, NY-J	2	7	3.5	4	0
Doxzon, Todd, Mia.	2	6	3.0	3	0
Crockett, Zack, Ind.	2	5	2.5	5	0
Friesz, John, Sea.	5	5	1.0	8	0
Williams, Clarence, Buf.	2	5	2.5	3	0
Broussard, Steve, Sea.	5	4	0.8	3	0
Carter, Ki-Jana, Cin.	2	4	2.0	4	0
Dyson, Kevin, Ten.	1	4	4.0	4	0
Johnson, Charles, Pit.	1	4	4.0	4	0
Pickens, Carl, Cin.	2	4	2.0	4	0
Carter, Tony, N.E.	2	3	1.5	3	0
Jett, James, Oak.	1	3	3.0	3	0
Anderson, Richie, NY-J	1	2	2.0	2	0
Brown, Reggie, Sea.	1	2	2.0	2	0
George, Jeff, Oak.	8	2	0.3	8	0
Justin, Paul, Cin.	1	2	2.0	2	0
Small, Torrance, Ind.	1	2	2.0	2	0
Witman, Jon, Pit.	1	2	2.0	2	0
Vanover, Tamarick, K.C.	2	1	0.5	2	0
Costello, Brad, Cin.	1	0	0.0	0	0
Horn, Joe, K.C.	1	0	0.0	0	0
Richardson, Kyle, Bal.	1	0	0.0	0	0
Richardson, Wally, Bal.	1	0	0.0	0	0
Rouen, Tom, Den.	1	0	0.0	0	0
Stepnoski, Mark, Ten.	1	0	0.0	0	0
Zolak, Scott, N.E.	5	0	0.0	4	0
Glenn, Terry, N.E.	2	-1	-0.5	7	0
Hentrich, Craig, Ten.	1	-1	-1.0	-1	0
Kresser, Eric, Cin.	1	-1	-1.0	-1	0
Krieg, Dave, Ten.	3	-1	-0.3	0	0
Van Pelt, Alex, Buf.	1	-1	-1.0	-1	0
Dudley, Rickey, Oak.	1	-2	-2.0	-2	0
Pathon, Jerome, Ind.	3	-2	-0.7	4	0
Tupa, Tom, N.E.	2	-2	-1.0	-1	0
Marino, Dan, Mia.	21	-3	-0.1	10	1
Griese, Brian, Den.	4	-4	-1.0	0	0
Brown, Tim, Oak.	1	-7	-7.0	-7	0
Sanders, Chris, Ten.	1	-9	-9.0	-9	0
Foley, Glenn, NY-J	5	-11	-2.2	-1	0
Araguz, Leo, Oak.	1	-12	-12.0	-12	0

t = Touchdown
Leader based on most yards gained

NFC RUSHERS—INDIVIDUAL

	Att.	Yards	Avg.	Long	TD
Anderson, Jamal, Atl.	410	1846	4.5	48	14
Hearst, Garrison, S.F.	310	1570	5.1	96t	7
Sanders, Barry, Det.	343	1491	4.3	73t	4
Smith, Emmitt, Dal.	319	1332	4.2	32	13
Smith, Robert, Min.	249	1187	4.8	74t	6
Staley, Duce, Phi.	258	1065	4.1	64t	5
Brown, Gary, NY-G	247	1063	4.3	45	5
Murrell, Adrian, Ariz	274	1042	3.8	32	8
Dunn, Warrick, T.B.	245	1026	4.2	50	2
Alstott, Mike, T.B.	215	846	3.9	37	8
Lane, Fred, Car.	205	717	3.5	31	5
Allen, Terry, Was.	148	700	4.7	45	2
Bennett, Edgar, Chi.	173	611	3.5	43	2
Enis, Curtis, Chi.	133	497	3.7	29	0
Hoard, Leroy, Min.	115	479	4.2	50t	9
Smith, Lamar, N.O.	138	457	3.3	33	1
Young, Steve, S.F.	70	454	6.5	24	6
Hicks, Skip, Was.	122	433	3.5	28	8
Way, Charles, NY-G	113	432	3.8	21	3
Biakabutuka, Tim, Car.	101	427	4.2	41	3
Holmes, Darick, Buf.-G.B.	95	394	4.1	13	1
Garner, Charlie, Phi.	96	381	4.0	40	4
Levens, Dorsey, G.B.	115	378	3.3	50	1
Jervey, Travis, G.B.	83	325	3.9	16	1
Henley, June, St.L	88	313	3.6	22	3
Warren, Chris, Dal.	59	291	4.9	49	4
Allen, James, Chi.	58	270	4.7	57	1
Kirby, Terry, S.F.	48	258	5.4	31t	3
Hill, Greg, St.L	40	240	6.0	46	4
Holcombe, Robert, St.L	98	230	2.3	12	2
Batch, Charlie, Det.	41	229	5.6	17	1
Harris, Raymont, G.B.	79	228	2.9	14	1
Williams, Sherman, Dal.	64	220	3.4	24	1

	Att.	Yards	Avg.	Long	TD
Plummer, Jake, Ariz	51	217	4.3	27	4
Mitchell, Brian, Was.	39	208	5.3	22	2
Craver, Aaron, N.O.	45	180	4.0	25	2
Lee, Amp, St.L	44	175	4.0	38	2
Barber, Tiki, NY-G	52	166	3.2	23	0
Bates, Mario, Ariz	60	165	2.8	15	6
Zellars, Ray, N.O.	56	162	2.9	15t	1
Banks, Tony, St.L	40	156	3.9	19	3
Collins, Kerry, Car.-N.O.	30	153	5.1	20	1
Davis, Troy, N.O.	55	143	2.6	14	1
Dilfer, Trent, T.B.	40	141	3.5	17	2
Graham, Kent, NY-G	27	138	5.1	23	2
Moore, Jerald, St.L	55	137	2.5	18	2
Johnson, Anthony, Car.	36	135	3.8	21	0
Favre, Brett, G.B.	40	133	3.3	35	1
Cunningham, Randall, Min.	32	132	4.1	22	1
Chancey, Robert, Chi.	29	122	4.2	14	2
Perry, Wilmont, N.O.	30	122	4.1	19	0
Chandler, Chris, Atl.	36	121	3.4	19	2
Green, Trent, Was.	42	117	2.8	13	2
Levy, Chuck, S.F.	25	112	4.5	21t	1
Centers, Larry, Ariz	31	110	3.5	14	0
Davis, Stephen, Was.	34	109	3.2	12	0
Rivers, Ron, Det.	19	102	5.4	36t	1
Edwards, Marc, S.F.	22	94	4.3	32	1
Turner, Kevin, Phi.	20	94	4.7	19	0
Pittman, Michael, Ariz	29	91	3.1	11	0
Shepherd, Leslie, Was.	6	91	15.2	29	1
Hoying, Bobby, Phi.	22	84	3.8	11	0
Stenstrom, Steve, Chi.	18	79	4.4	14	2
Floyd, William, Car.	28	71	2.5	7	3
Henderson, William, G.B.	23	70	3.0	9	2
Aikman, Troy, Dal.	22	69	3.1	23	2
Evans, Chuck, Min.	23	67	2.9	12	1
Wuerffel, Danny, N.O.	11	60	5.5	18	0
Walker, Corey, Phi.	12	55	4.6	20	0
Owens, Terrell, S.F.	4	53	13.3	21t	1
Palmer, David, Min.	10	52	5.2	15	0
Wheatley, Tyrone, NY-G	14	52	3.7	15	0
Oxendine, Ken, Atl.	18	50	2.8	21	0
Conway, Curtis, Chi.	5	48	9.6	29	0
Fryar, Irving, Phi.	3	46	15.3	32	0
Anthony, Reidel, T.B.	4	43	10.8	32	0
Tolliver, Billy Joe, N.O.	11	43	3.9	16	0
Ismail, Raghib, Car.	3	42	14.0	36	0
Hallock, Ty, Chi.	13	41	3.2	14	1
Harris, Derrick, St.L	14	38	2.7	15	0
Green, Harold, Atl.	20	37	1.9	6	0
Vardell, Tommy, Det.	18	37	2.1	17	6
Kanell, Danny, NY-G	15	36	2.4	10	0
Crowell, Germane, Det.	1	35	35.0	35	0
Gowin, Toby, Dal.	1	33	33.0	33	0
Hastings, Andre, N.O.	3	32	10.7	16	0
Bruce, Isaac, St.L	1	30	30.0	30	0
Hakim, Az-Zahir, St.L	2	30	15.0	34t	1
Mitchell, Scott, Det.	7	30	4.3	17	0
Peete, Rodney, Phi.	5	30	6.0	19t	1
Beuerlein, Steve, Car.	22	26	1.2	13	0
Neal, Lorenzo, T.B.	5	25	5.0	12	0
Ellison, Jerry, T.B.	9	24	2.7	10	0
Christian, Bob, Atl.	8	21	2.6	6	2
Graziani, Tony, Atl.	4	21	5.3	12	0
Detmer, Koy, Phi.	7	20	2.9	8	0
Frerotte, Gus, Was.	3	20	6.7	20	0
Husted, Michael, T.B.	1	20	20.0	20	0
Dwight, Tim, Atl.	8	19	2.4	7	0
Johnston, Daryl, Dal.	8	17	2.1	6	0
Kramer, Erik, Chi.	13	17	1.3	8	1
Schlesinger, Cory, Det.	5	17	3.4	5	0
Davis, Billy, Dal.	4	15	3.8	8	0
Johnson, Brad, Min.	12	15	1.3	6	0
Garrett, Jason, Dal.	11	14	1.3	5	0
Proehl, Ricky, St.L	1	14	14.0	14	0
Bono, Steve, St.L	10	13	1.3	7	0
Hobert, Billy Joe, N.O.	2	13	6.5	14	0
Green, Jacquez, T.B.	3	12	4.0	18	0
Ogden, Jeff, Dal.	1	12	12.0	12	0
Emanuel, Bert, T.B.	1	11	11.0	11	0
Morton, Johnnie, Det.	1	11	11.0	11	0
Westbrook, Michael, Was.	1	11	11.0	11	0
Jells, Dietrich, Phi.	2	9	4.5	13	0
Kennison, Eddie, St.L	2	9	4.5	9	0

1998 INDIVIDUAL STATISTICS—PASSING

	Att.	Yards	Avg.	Long	TD
Mills, Ernie, Dal.	3	9	3.0	5	0
Moreno, Moses, Chi.	4	9	2.3	9	0
Bowie, Larry, Was.	4	8	2.0	4	0
Milburn, Glyn, Chi.	4	8	2.0	3	0
Bjornson, Eric, Dal.	1	7	7.0	7t	1
Blair, Michael, G.B.-Cin.-G.B.	3	7	2.3	4	0
Detmer, Ty, S.F.	8	7	0.9	10	0
Morrow, Harold, Min.	3	7	2.3	8	0
Comella, Greg, NY-G	1	6	6.0	6	0
Freeman, Antonio, G.B.	3	5	1.7	10	0
Downs, Gary, Atl.	1	4	4.0	4	0
Hilliard, Ike, NY-G	1	4	4.0	4	0
Moss, Randy, Min.	1	4	4.0	4	0
Engram, Bobby, Chi.	1	3	3.0	3	0
Reich, Frank, Det.	6	3	0.5	5	0
Brooks, Robert, G.B.	1	2	2.0	2	0
Brown, Dave, Ariz	1	2	2.0	2	0
Irvin, Michael, Dal.	1	1	1.0	1	0
Roby, Reggie, S.F.	1	0	0.0	0	0
Sanders, Frank, Ariz	4	0	0.0	7	0
Walter, Ken, Car.	3	0	0.0	0	0
Carter, Cris, Min.	1	-1	-1.0	-1	0
Williams, Elijah, Atl.	2	-2	-1.0	2	0
Cherry, Mike, NY-G	3	-3	-1.0	-1	0
Druckenmiller, Jim, S.F.	3	-4	-1.3	-1	0
Hankton, Karl, Phi.	1	-4	-4.0	-4	0
Pederson, Doug, G.B.	8	-4	-0.5	1	0
Dunn, Jason, Phi.	1	-5	-5.0	-5	0
Maynard, Brad, NY-G	1	-5	-5.0	-5	0
Fiedler, Jay, Min.	4	-6	-1.5	-1	0
Mathis, Terance, Atl.	1	-6	-6.0	-6	0
Quinn, Mike, Dal.	5	-6	-1.2	-1	0
DeBerg, Steve, Atl.	8	-10	-1.2	2	0
Turk, Matt, Was.	2	-12	-6.0	0	0

t = Touchdown
Leader based on most yards gained

PASSING

Highest Rating
NFC: 106.0—Randall Cunningham, Minnesota
AFC: 101.6—Vinny Testaverde, N.Y. Jets

Completion Percentage
NFC: 63.0—Brett Favre, Green Bay
AFC: 61.8—Neil O'Donnell, Cincinnati

Attempts
AFC: 575—Peyton Manning, Indianapolis
NFC: 551—Brett Favre, Green Bay

Completions
NFC: 347—Brett Favre, Green Bay
AFC: 326—Peyton Manning, Indianapolis

Yards
NFC: 4212—Brett Favre, Green Bay
AFC: 3739—Peyton Manning, Indianapolis

Yards, Game
NFC: 465—Jake Plummer, Arizona vs. Dallas, November 15 (31-56, 3 TD)
AFC: 423—Drew Bledsoe, New England vs. Miami, November 23 (28-54, 2 TD)

Longest
NFC: 98—Charlie Batch (to Johnnie Morton), Detroit at Chicago, October 4 - TD
AFC: 86—Drew Bledsoe (to Terry Glenn), New England at Pittsburgh, December 6 - TD

Yards Per Attempt
NFC: 9.65—Chris Chandler, Atlanta
AFC: 7.88—John Elway, Denver

Touchdown Passes
NFC: 36—Steve Young, San Francisco
AFC: 29—Vinny Testaverde, N.Y. Jets

Touchdown Passes, Game
NFC: 5—Brett Favre, Green Bay at Carolina, September 27 (27-45, 388 yards)
AFC: 4—by many

Lowest Interception Percentage
AFC: 1.2—Neil O'Donnell, Cincinnati
NFC: 1.6—Troy Aikman, Dallas

Team Champion (Most Net Yards)
NFC: 4328—Minnesota
AFC: 3836—N.Y. Jets

AFC PASSING—TEAM

	Att.	Comp.	Pct. Comp.	Gross Yards	Sacked	Yds. Lost	Net Yards	Yds./ Att.	Yds./ Comp.	TD	Pct. TD	Long	Int.	Pct. Int.
N.Y. Jets	532	318	59.8	4032	25	196	3836	7.58	12.68	33	6.20	82t	13	2.4
New England	556	295	53.1	4004	40	344	3660	7.20	13.57	23	4.14	86t	17	3.1
Denver	491	290	59.1	3808	25	184	3624	7.76	13.13	32	6.52	58	14	2.9
Indianapolis	576	326	56.6	3739	22	109	3630	6.49	11.47	26	4.51	78t	28	4.9
Buffalo	461	269	58.4	3621	41	241	3380	7.85	13.46	28	6.07	84t	14	3.0
Miami	546	316	57.9	3582	24	187	3395	6.56	11.34	23	4.21	61t	16	2.9
Cincinnati	521	307	58.9	3545	53	360	3185	6.80	11.55	20	3.84	76t	12	2.3
Oakland	519	282	54.3	3534	67	446	3088	6.81	12.53	21	4.05	75t	25	4.8
Tennessee	519	305	58.8	3482	35	191	3291	6.71	11.42	16	3.08	55	10	1.9
Kansas City	543	305	56.2	3472	36	212	3260	6.39	11.38	15	2.76	80t	18	3.3
Jacksonville	463	269	58.1	3343	39	231	3112	7.22	12.43	24	5.18	78t	12	2.6
Seattle	480	273	56.9	3219	34	219	3000	6.71	11.79	21	4.38	81t	18	3.8
Baltimore	477	272	57.0	3152	41	283	2869	6.61	11.59	16	3.35	73t	15	3.1
San Diego	566	261	46.1	3115	37	251	2864	5.50	11.93	11	1.94	67	34	6.0
Pittsburgh	489	274	56.0	2781	35	229	2552	5.69	10.15	13	2.66	55t	20	4.1
AFC Total	7739	4362	—	52429	554	3683	48746	—	—	322	—	86t	266	—
AFC Average	515.9	290.8	56.4	3495.3	36.9	245.5	3249.7	6.77	12.02	21.5	4.2	—	17.7	3.4

NFC PASSING—TEAM

	Att.	Comp.	Pct. Comp.	Gross Yards	Sacked	Yds. Lost	Net Yards	Yds./ Att.	Yds./ Comp.	TD	Pct. TD	Long	Int.	Pct. Int.
San Francisco	556	347	62.4	4510	53	254	4256	8.11	13.00	41	7.37	81t	15	2.7
Minnesota	533	327	61.4	4492	25	164	4328	8.43	13.74	41	7.69	67t	16	3.0
Green Bay	575	361	62.8	4340	39	230	4110	7.55	12.02	33	5.74	84t	23	4.0
Arizona	552	326	59.1	3768	50	286	3482	6.83	11.56	17	3.08	57	20	3.6
Atlanta	424	237	55.9	3744	53	358	3386	8.83	15.80	28	6.60	78t	15	3.5
Washington	565	304	53.8	3724	61	399	3325	6.59	12.25	24	4.25	75t	14	2.5
Carolina	507	292	57.6	3624	54	302	3322	7.15	12.41	25	4.93	72t	18	3.6
Dallas	474	279	58.9	3546	19	110	3436	7.48	12.71	17	3.59	80t	8	1.7
New Orleans	535	278	52.0	3514	57	376	3138	6.57	12.64	19	3.55	89t	19	3.6
Detroit	489	274	56.0	3398	45	268	3130	6.95	12.40	17	3.48	98t	13	2.7
St. Louis	556	314	56.5	3381	47	294	3087	6.08	10.77	12	2.16	80t	18	3.2
Chicago	494	284	57.5	3277	31	224	3053	6.63	11.54	16	3.24	79t	13	2.6
N.Y. Giants	507	265	52.3	2822	35	256	2566	5.57	10.65	18	3.55	87t	15	3.0
Tampa Bay	449	234	52.1	2787	28	181	2606	6.21	11.91	21	4.68	79t	18	4.0
Philadelphia	534	282	52.8	2730	56	317	2413	5.11	9.68	7	1.31	61t	18	3.4
NFC Total	7750	4404	—	53657	653	4019	49638	—	—	336	—	98t	243	—
NFC Average	516.7	293.6	56.8	3577.1	43.5	267.9	3309.2	6.92	12.18	22.4	4.3	—	16.2	3.1
League Total	15489	8766	—	106086	1207	7702	98384	—	—	658	—	98t	509	—
League Average	516.3	292.2	56.6	3536.2	40.2	256.7	3279.5	6.85	12.10	21.9	4.2	—	17.0	3.3

Leader based on net yards

NFL TOP TEN PASSERS

	Att.	Comp.	Pct. Comp.	Yds.	Avg. Gain	TD	Pct. TD	Long	Int.	Pct. Int.	Sack	Yds. Lost	Rating Points
Cunningham, Randall, Min.	425	259	60.9	3704	8.72	34	8.0	67t	10	2.4	20	132	106.0
Testaverde, Vinny, NY-J	421	259	61.5	3256	7.73	29	6.9	82t	7	1.7	19	140	101.6
Young, Steve, S.F.	517	322	62.3	4170	8.07	36	7.0	81t	12	2.3	48	234	101.1
Chandler, Chris, Atl.	327	190	58.1	3154	9.65	25	7.6	78t	12	3.7	45	283	100.9
Elway, John, Den.	356	210	59.0	2806	7.88	22	6.2	58	10	2.8	18	135	93.0
O'Donnell, Neil, Cin.	343	212	61.8	2216	6.46	15	4.4	76t	4	1.2	30	217	90.2
Brunell, Mark, Jac.	354	208	58.8	2601	7.35	20	5.6	78t	9	2.5	28	172	89.9
Aikman, Troy, Dal.	315	187	59.4	2330	7.40	12	3.8	67t	5	1.6	9	58	88.5
Beuerlein, Steve, Car.	343	216	63.0	2613	7.62	17	5.0	68t	12	3.5	44	251	88.2
Favre, Brett, G.B.	551	347	63.0	4212	7.64	31	5.6	84t	23	4.2	38	223	87.8

AFC PASSING—INDIVIDUAL

	Att.	Comp.	Pct. Comp.	Yds.	Avg. Gain	TD	Pct. TD	Long	Int.	Pct. Int.	Sack	Yds. Lost	Rating Points
Testaverde, Vinny, NY-J	421	259	61.5	3256	7.73	29	6.9	82t	7	1.7	19	140	101.6
Elway, John, Den.	356	210	59.0	2806	7.88	22	6.2	58	10	2.8	18	135	93.0
O'Donnell, Neil, Cin.	343	212	61.8	2216	6.46	15	4.4	76t	4	1.2	30	217	90.2
Brunell, Mark, Jac.	354	208	58.8	2601	7.35	20	5.6	78t	9	2.5	28	172	89.9
Flutie, Doug, Buf.	354	202	57.1	2711	7.66	20	5.6	84t	11	3.1	12	78	87.4
Bledsoe, Drew, N.E.	481	263	54.7	3633	7.55	20	4.2	86t	14	2.9	36	295	80.9
McNair, Steve, Ten.	492	289	58.7	3228	6.56	15	3.0	47	10	2.0	33	176	80.1
Gannon, Rich, K.C.	354	206	58.2	2305	6.51	10	2.8	80t	6	1.7	25	155	80.1
Marino, Dan, Mia.	537	310	57.7	3497	6.51	23	4.3	61t	15	2.8	23	178	80.0
Moon, Warren, Sea.	258	145	56.2	1632	6.33	11	4.3	45	8	3.1	22	140	76.6
Harbaugh, Jim, Bal.	293	164	56.0	1839	6.28	12	4.1	66t	11	3.8	23	145	72.9
Manning, Peyton, Ind.	575	326	56.7	3739	6.50	26	4.5	78t	28	4.9	22	109	71.2
Stewart, Kordell, Pit.	458	252	55.0	2560	5.59	11	2.4	55t	18	3.9	33	211	62.9
Hollas, Donald, Oak.	260	135	51.9	1754	6.75	10	3.8	47	16	6.2	36	207	60.6
Whelihan, Craig, S.D.	320	149	46.6	1803	5.63	8	2.5	55	19	5.9	15	111	48.0
Leaf, Ryan, S.D.	245	111	45.3	1289	5.26	2	0.8	67	15	6.1	22	140	39.0
Nonqualifiers													
Johnson, Rob, Buf.	107	67	62.6	910	8.50	8	7.5	66t	3	2.8	29	163	102.9
Martin, Jamie, Jac.	45	27	60.0	355	7.89	2	4.4	67t	0	0.0	2	10	99.8
Brister, Bubby, Den.	131	78	59.5	986	7.53	10	7.6	48	3	2.3	7	49	99.0
Krieg, Dave, Ten.	21	12	57.1	199	9.48	0	0.0	55	0	0.0	2	15	89.2
Wilson, Wade, Oak.	88	52	59.1	568	6.45	7	8.0	68t	4	4.5	9	77	85.8
Tomczak, Mike, Pit.	30	21	70.0	204	6.80	2	6.7	42	2	6.7	2	18	83.2
Friesz, John, Sea.	49	29	59.2	409	8.35	2	4.1	81t	2	4.1	1	7	82.8
Zeier, Eric, Bal.	181	107	59.1	1312	7.25	4	2.2	73t	3	1.7	18	138	82.0
Blake, Jeff, Cin.	93	51	54.8	739	7.95	3	3.2	67t	3	3.2	15	79	78.2
George, Jeff, Oak.	169	93	55.0	1186	7.02	4	2.4	75t	5	3.0	22	162	72.7
Kitna, Jon, Sea.	172	98	57.0	1177	6.84	7	4.1	70t	8	4.7	11	72	72.3
Foley, Glenn, NY-J	108	58	53.7	749	6.94	4	3.7	48	6	5.6	5	49	64.9
Quinn, Jonathan, Jac.	64	34	53.1	387	6.05	2	3.1	64	3	4.7	9	49	62.4
Justin, Paul, Cin.	63	34	54.0	426	6.76	1	1.6	41	3	4.8	7	60	60.7
Zolak, Scott, N.E.	75	32	42.7	371	4.95	3	4.0	61t	3	4.0	4	49	54.9
Grbac, Elvis, K.C.	188	98	52.1	1142	6.07	5	2.7	65	12	6.4	11	57	53.1
Kresser, Eric, Cin.	21	10	47.6	164	7.81	1	4.8	37	2	9.5	0	0	50.6
Fewer than 10 attempts													
Araguz, Leo, Oak.	1	1	100.0	-1	-1.00	0	0.0	-1	0	0.0	0	0	79.2
Archie, Mike, Ten.	2	1	50.0	18	9.00	1	50.0	18t	0	0.0	0	0	120.8
Dillon, Corey, Cin.	0	0	—	0	—	0	—	—	0	—	1	4	—

1998 INDIVIDUAL STATISTICS—PASSING

	Att.	Comp.	Pct. Comp.	Yds.	Avg. Gain	TD	Pct. TD	Long	Int.	Pct. Int.	Sack	Yds. Lost	Rating Points
Fletcher, Terrell, S.D.	1	1	100.0	23	23.00	1	100.0	23t	0	0.0	0	0	158.3
Griese, Brian, Den.	3	1	33.3	2	0.67	0	0.0	2	1	33.3	0	0	2.8
Hentrich, Craig, Ten.	1	1	100.0	13	13.00	0	0.0	13	0	0.0	0	0	118.8
Holmes, Priest, Bal.	1	0	0.0	0	0.00	0	0.0	0	1	100.0	0	0	0.0
Huard, Damon, Mia.	9	6	66.7	85	9.44	0	0.0	24	1	11.1	1	9	57.4
Hughes, Danan, K.C.	1	1	100.0	25	25.00	0	0.0	25	0	0.0	0	0	118.8
Johnson, Leon, NY-J	0	0	—	0	—	0	—	—	0	—	1	7	—
Lucas, Ray, NY-J	3	1	33.3	27	9.00	0	0.0	27	0	0.0	0	0	67.4
Matthews, Steve, Ten.	3	2	66.7	24	8.00	0	0.0	13	0	0.0	0	0	91.0
Pelfrey, Doug, Cin.	1	0	0.0	0	0.00	0	0.0	0	0	0.0	0	0	39.6
Richardson, Wally, Bal.	2	1	50.0	1	0.50	0	0.0	1	0	0.0	0	0	56.3
Small, Torrance, Ind.	1	0	0.0	0	0.00	0	0.0	0	0	0.0	0	0	39.6
Smith, Rod, Den.	1	1	100.0	14	14.00	0	0.0	14	0	0.0	0	0	118.8
Ward, Hines, Pit.	1	1	100.0	17	17.00	0	0.0	17	0	0.0	0	0	118.8
Watters, Ricky, Sea.	1	1	100.0	1	1.00	1	100.0	1t	0	0.0	0	0	118.8
Williams, Harvey, Oak.	1	1	100.0	27	27.00	0	0.0	27	0	0.0	0	0	118.8

t = Touchdown
Leader based on rating points, minimum 224 attempts

NFC PASSING—INDIVIDUAL

	Att.	Comp.	Pct. Comp.	Yds.	Avg. Gain	TD	Pct. TD	Long	Int.	Pct. Int.	Sack	Yds. Lost	Rating Points
Cunningham, Randall, Min.	425	259	60.9	3704	8.72	34	8.0	67t	10	2.4	20	132	106.0
Young, Steve, S.F.	517	322	62.3	4170	8.07	36	7.0	81t	12	2.3	48	234	101.1
Chandler, Chris, Atl.	327	190	58.1	3154	9.65	25	7.6	78t	12	3.7	45	283	100.9
Aikman, Troy, Dal.	315	187	59.4	2330	7.40	12	3.8	67t	5	1.6	9	58	88.5
Beuerlein, Steve, Car.	343	216	63.0	2613	7.62	17	5.0	68t	12	3.5	44	251	88.2
Favre, Brett, G.B.	551	347	63.0	4212	7.64	31	5.6	84t	23	4.2	38	223	87.8
Batch, Charlie, Det.	303	173	57.1	2178	7.19	11	3.6	98t	6	2.0	37	222	83.5
Kramer, Erik, Chi.	250	151	60.4	1823	7.29	9	3.6	79t	7	2.8	10	71	83.1
Green, Trent, Was.	509	278	54.6	3441	6.76	23	4.5	75t	11	2.2	49	338	81.8
Plummer, Jake, Ariz	547	324	59.2	3737	6.83	17	3.1	57	20	3.7	49	280	75.0
Dilfer, Trent, T.B.	429	225	52.4	2729	6.36	21	4.9	79t	15	3.5	27	172	74.0
Banks, Tony, St.L	408	241	59.1	2535	6.21	7	1.7	80t	14	3.4	41	237	68.6
Kanell, Danny, NY-G	299	160	53.5	1603	5.36	11	3.7	46	10	3.3	22	172	67.3
Collins, Kerry, Car.-N.O.	353	170	48.2	2213	6.27	12	3.4	89t	15	4.2	31	191	62.0
Hoying, Bobby, Phi.	224	114	50.9	961	4.29	0	0.0	38	9	4.0	35	185	45.6
Nonqualifiers													
Pederson, Doug, G.B.	24	14	58.3	128	5.33	2	8.3	29	0	0.0	1	7	100.7
Detmer, Ty, S.F.	38	24	63.2	312	8.21	4	10.5	36t	3	7.9	5	20	91.1
Johnson, Brad, Min.	101	65	64.4	747	7.40	7	6.9	48t	5	5.0	4	30	89.0
Hobert, Billy Joe, N.O.	23	11	47.8	170	7.39	1	4.3	35t	0	0.0	2	17	87.2
Garrett, Jason, Dal.	158	91	57.6	1206	7.63	5	3.2	80t	3	1.9	10	52	84.5
Tolliver, Billy Joe, N.O.	199	110	55.3	1427	7.17	8	4.0	82t	4	2.0	11	88	83.1
DeBerg, Steve, Atl.	59	30	50.8	369	6.25	3	5.1	35t	1	1.7	6	60	80.4
Reich, Frank, Det.	110	63	57.3	768	6.98	5	4.5	41	4	3.6	4	18	78.9
Graham, Kent, NY-G	205	105	51.2	1219	5.95	7	3.4	87t	5	2.4	12	75	70.8
Stenstrom, Steve, Chi.	196	112	57.1	1252	6.39	4	2.0	48	6	3.1	19	137	70.4
Bono, Steve, St.L	136	69	50.7	807	5.93	5	3.7	47	4	2.9	6	57	69.1
Detmer, Koy, Phi.	181	97	53.6	1011	5.59	5	2.8	61t	5	2.8	5	29	67.7
Wuerffel, Danny, N.O.	119	62	52.1	695	5.84	5	4.2	64t	5	4.2	23	131	66.3
Peete, Rodney, Phi.	129	71	55.0	758	5.88	2	1.6	25	4	3.1	16	103	64.7
Moreno, Moses, Chi.	43	19	44.2	166	3.86	1	2.3	21t	0	0.0	2	16	62.7
Mitchell, Scott, Det.	75	38	50.7	452	6.03	1	1.3	44	3	4.0	4	28	57.2
Warner, Kurt, St.L	11	4	36.4	39	3.55	0	0.0	21	0	0.0	0	0	47.2
Frerotte, Gus, Was.	54	25	46.3	283	5.24	1	1.9	22	3	5.6	12	61	45.5
Graziani, Tony, Atl.	33	16	48.5	199	6.03	0	0.0	32	2	6.1	2	15	42.4
Walsh, Steve, T.B.	19	9	47.4	58	3.05	0	0.0	12	3	15.8	1	9	14.7
Fewer than 10 attempts													
Alstott, Mike, T.B.	1	0	0.0	0	0.00	0	0.0	0	0	0.0	0	0	39.6
Anderson, Jamal, Atl.	2	0	0.0	0	0.00	0	0.0	0	0	0.0	0	0	39.6
Bennett, Edgar, Chi.	2	1	50.0	18	9.00	1	50.0	18t	0	0.0	0	0	120.8
Brown, Dave, Ariz	5	2	40.0	31	6.20	0	0.0	19	0	0.0	1	6	61.3
Cherry, Mike, NY-G	1	0	0.0	0	0.00	0	0.0	0	0	0.0	1	9	39.6
Conway, Curtis, Chi.	1	0	0.0	0	0.00	0	0.0	0	0	0.0	0	0	39.6
Craver, Aaron, N.O.	1	0	0.0	0	0.00	0	0.0	0	0	0.0	0	0	39.6
Dwight, Tim, Atl.	2	1	50.0	22	11.00	0	0.0	22	0	0.0	0	0	89.6
Fiedler, Jay, Min.	7	3	42.9	41	5.86	0	0.0	19	1	14.3	0	0	22.6
Floyd, William, Car.	1	0	0.0	0	0.00	0	0.0	0	1	100.0	0	0	0.0
Horan, Mike, Chi.	2	1	50.0	18	9.00	1	50.0	18t	0	0.0	0	0	120.8
Jett, John, Det.	1	0	0.0	0	0.00	0	0.0	0	0	0.0	0	0	39.6
Kirby, Terry, S.F.	1	1	100.0	28	28.00	1	100.0	28t	0	0.0	0	0	158.3
Martin, Tony, Atl.	1	0	0.0	0	0.00	0	0.0	0	0	0.0	0	0	39.6
Maynard, Brad, NY-G	1	0	0.0	0	0.00	0	0.0	0	0	0.0	0	0	39.6
Mitchell, Brian, Was.	2	1	50.0	0	0.00	0	0.0	0	0	0.0	0	0	56.3
Palmer, David, Min.	0	0	—	0	—	0	—	—	0	—	1	2	—
Quinn, Mike, Dal.	1	1	100.0	10	10.00	0	0.0	10	0	0.0	0	0	108.3
Smith, Lamar, N.O.	2	1	50.0	20	10.00	1	50.0	20t	0	0.0	0	0	125.0
Toomer, Amani, NY-G	1	0	0.0	0	0.00	0	0.0	0	0	0.0	0	0	39.6
Tuten, Rick, St.L	1	0	0.0	0	0.00	0	0.0	0	0	0.0	0	0	39.6
Walter, Ken, Car.	1	0	0.0	0	0.00	0	0.0	0	0	0.0	0	0	39.6

t = Touchdown
Leader based on rating points, minimum 224 attempts

PASS RECEIVING

Receptions
AFC: 90—O.J. McDuffie, Miami
NFC: 89—Frank Sanders, Arizona

Recptions, Game
AFC: 14—Courtney Hawkins, Pittsburgh vs. Tennessee, November 1 (147 yards - TD)
NFC: 11—Isaac Bruce, St. Louis vs. Minnesota, September 13 (192 yards - TD)
Frank Sanders, Arizona vs. Dallas, November 15 (190 yards - TD)
Cris Carter, Minnesota at Baltimore, December 13 (85 yards - TD)

Yards
NFC: 1424—Antonio Freeman, Green Bay
AFC: 1368—Eric Moulds, Buffalo

Yards, Game
AFC: 204—Carl Pickens, Cincinnati vs. Pittsburgh, October 11 (13 receptions - TD)
NFC: 198—Terance Mathis, Atlanta at New Orleans, December 13 (6 receptions - 2 TD)

Longest
NFC: 98—Johnnie Morton (from Charlie Batch), Detroit at Chicago, October 4 - TD
AFC: 86—Terry Glenn (from Drew Bledsoe), New England at Pittsburgh, December 6 - TD

Yards Per Reception
AFC: 22.7—Shawn Jefferson, New England
NFC: 19.0—Randy Moss, Minnesota

Touchdowns
NFC: 17—Randy Moss, Minnesota
AFC: 10—Joey Galloway, Seattle
Keyshawn Johnson, N.Y. Jets
Ed McCaffrey, Denver
Shannon Sharpe, Denver

Team Leaders, Receptions
AFC: BALTIMORE: 43, Priest Holmes; BUFFALO: 67, Eric Moulds; CINCINNATI: 82, Carl Pickens; DENVER: 86, Rod Smith; INDIANAPOLIS, 86: Marshall Faulk; JACKSONVILLE, 78: Jimmy Smith; KANSAS CITY, 64: Kimble Anders; MIAMI: 90, O. J. McDuffie; NEW ENGLAND, 67: Ben Coates; N.Y. JETS: 83, Keyshawn Johnson; OAKLAND: 81, Tim Brown; PITTSBURGH: 66, Courtney Hawkins; SAN DIEGO: 57, Freddie Jones; SEATTLE: 65, Joey Galloway; TENNESSEE: 70, Frank Wycheck.
NFC: ARIZONA: 89, Frank Sanders ; ATLANTA: 66, Tony Martin ; CAROLINA: 69, Raghib Ismail ; CHICAGO: 64, Bobby Engram ; DALLAS: 74, Michael Irvin ; DETROIT: 82, Herman Moore ; GREEN BAY: 84, Antonio Freeman ; MINNESOTA: 78, Cris Carter ; NEW ORLEANS, 54: Cameron Cleeland ; N.Y. GIANTS: 62, Chris Calloway ; PHILADELPHIA, 57: Duce Staley ; ST. LOUIS: 64, Amp Lee ; TAMPA BAY: 51, Reidel Anthony ; WASHINGTON: 44, Brian Mitchell, Michael Westbrook.

NFL TOP TEN PASS RECEIVERS

	No.	Yards	Avg.	Long	TD
McDuffie, O. J., Mia.	90	1050	11.7	61t	7
Sanders, Frank, Ariz	89	1145	12.9	42	3
Faulk, Marshall, Ind.	86	908	10.6	78t	4
Smith, Rod, Den.	86	1222	14.2	58	6
Freeman, Antonio, G.B.	84	1424	17.0	84t	14
Johnson, Keyshawn, NY-J	83	1131	13.6	41t	10
Moore, Herman, Det.	82	983	12.0	36	5
Pickens, Carl, Cin.	82	1023	12.5	67t	5
Rice, Jerry, S.F.	82	1157	14.1	75t	9
Brown, Tim, Oak.	81	1012	12.5	49	9

NFL TOP TEN RECEIVERS BY YARDS

	Yards	No.	Avg.	Long	TD
Freeman, Antonio, G.B.	1424	84	17.0	84t	14
Moulds, Eric, Buf.	1368	67	20.4	84t	9
Moss, Randy, Min.	1313	69	19.0	61t	17
Smith, Rod, Den.	1222	86	14.2	58	6
Smith, Jimmy, Jac.	1182	78	15.2	72t	8
Martin, Tony, Atl.	1181	66	17.9	62	6
Rice, Jerry, S.F.	1157	82	14.1	75t	9
Sanders, Frank, Ariz	1145	89	12.9	42	3
Mathis, Terance, Atl.	1136	64	17.8	78t	11
Johnson, Keyshawn, NY-J	1131	83	13.6	41t	10

AFC RECEIVERS—INDIVIDUAL

	No.	Yards	Avg.	Long	TD
McDuffie, O. J., Mia.	90	1050	11.7	61t	7
Smith, Rod, Den.	86	1222	14.2	58	6
Faulk, Marshall, Ind.	86	908	10.6	78t	4
Johnson, Keyshawn, NY-J	83	1131	13.6	41t	10
Pickens, Carl, Cin.	82	1023	12.5	67t	5
Brown, Tim, Oak.	81	1012	12.5	49	9
Smith, Jimmy, Jac.	78	1182	15.2	72t	8
Chrebet, Wayne, NY-J	75	1083	14.4	63t	8
Wycheck, Frank, Ten.	70	768	11.0	38	2
Moulds, Eric, Buf.	67	1368	20.4	84t	9
Coates, Ben, N.E.	67	668	10.0	33	6
Hawkins, Courtney, Pit.	66	751	11.4	53	1
Galloway, Joey, Sea.	65	1047	16.1	81t	10
Johnson, Charles, Pit.	65	815	12.5	55t	7
McCaffrey, Ed, Den.	64	1053	16.5	48	10
McCardell, Keenan, Jac.	64	892	13.9	67t	6
Sharpe, Shannon, Den.	64	768	12.0	38t	10
Anders, Kimble, K.C.	64	462	7.2	29	2
Reed, Andre, Buf.	63	795	12.6	67t	5
Harrison, Marvin, Ind.	59	776	13.2	61t	7
Gonzalez, Tony, K.C.	59	621	10.5	32	2
Pritchard, Mike, Sea.	58	742	12.8	50t	3
Jones, Freddie, S.D.	57	602	10.6	28	3
Alexander, Derrick, K.C.	54	992	18.4	65	4
Watters, Ricky, Sea.	52	373	7.2	24	0
Scott, Darnay, Cin.	51	817	16.0	70t	7
Glenn, Terry, N.E.	50	792	15.8	86t	3
Pathon, Jerome, Ind.	50	511	10.2	45	1
Gadsden, Oronde, Mia.	48	713	14.9	50	7
Jones, Charlie, S.D.	46	699	15.2	56	3
Jett, James, Oak.	45	882	19.6	75t	6
Small, Torrance, Ind.	45	681	15.1	53	7
Taylor, Fred, Jac.	44	421	9.6	78t	3
Still, Bryan, S.D.	43	605	14.1	67	2
Thomas, Lamar, Mia.	43	603	14.0	56t	5
Harris, Jackie, Ten.	43	412	9.6	32	2
Martin, Curtis, NY-J	43	365	8.5	23	1
Holmes, Priest, Bal.	43	260	6.0	25	0
Lewis, Jermaine, Bal.	41	784	19.1	73t	6
Rison, Andre, K.C.	40	542	13.6	80t	5
Thigpen, Yancey, Ten.	38	493	13.0	55	3
Jackson, Michael, Bal.	38	477	12.6	53	0
Mitchell, Pete, Jac.	38	363	9.6	38	2
Fauria, Christian, Sea.	37	377	10.2	25	2
George, Eddie, Ten.	37	310	8.4	29	1
Dudley, Rickey, Oak.	36	549	15.3	32	5
Edwards, Robert, N.E.	35	331	9.5	46	3
Jefferson, Shawn, N.E.	34	771	22.7	61t	2
Green, Eric, Bal.	34	422	12.4	56	1
Turner, Floyd, Bal.	32	512	16.0	66t	5
Davis, Willie, Ten.	32	461	14.4	38	3
Blackwell, Will, Pit.	32	297	9.3	24t	1
Dilger, Ken, Ind.	31	303	9.8	27	1
Ricks, Mikhael, S.D.	30	450	15.0	39t	2
Drayton, Troy, Mia.	30	334	11.1	35	3
Brady, Kyle, NY-J	30	315	10.5	35	5
Fletcher, Terrell, S.D.	30	188	6.3	22	0
Potts, Roosevelt, Bal.	30	168	5.6	18	2
Williams, Kevin, Buf.	29	392	13.5	55	1
Ritchie, Jon, Oak.	29	225	7.8	31	0
Dillon, Corey, Cin.	28	178	6.4	41	1
Bieniemy, Eric, Cin.	27	153	5.7	15	0
Byars, Keith, NY-J	26	258	9.9	29	3
Thomas, Thurman, Buf.	26	220	8.5	26	1
Williams, Harvey, Oak.	26	173	6.7	15	0
Milne, Brian, Cin.	26	124	4.8	18	0
Ward, Dedric, NY-J	25	477	19.1	71t	4
Mason, Derrick, Ten.	25	333	13.3	47	3
Riemersma, Jay, Buf.	25	288	11.5	28	6
Perry, Ed, Mia.	25	255	10.2	46	0
Davis, Terrell, Den.	25	217	8.7	35	2
Kaufman, Napoleon, Oak.	25	191	7.6	39	0
Mickens, Terry, Oak.	24	346	14.4	32	1
Pollard, Marcus, Ind.	24	309	12.9	44t	4
Simmons, Tony, N.E.	23	474	20.6	63t	3
Brown, Troy, N.E.	23	346	15.0	52	1
McGee, Tony, Cin.	22	363	16.5	40	1
McKnight, James, Sea.	21	346	16.5	59t	2
Dyson, Kevin, Ten.	21	263	12.5	45t	2
Parmalee, Bernie, Mia.	21	221	10.5	23	0
Abdul-Jabbar, Karim, Mia.	21	102	4.9	18	0

1998 INDIVIDUAL STATISTICS—RECEIVING

	No.	Yards	Avg.	Long	TD
Lockett, Kevin, K.C.	19	281	14.8	38	0
Gibson, Damon, Cin.	19	258	13.6	76t	3
Early, Quinn, Buf.	19	217	11.4	37	1
Gash, Sam, Buf.	19	165	8.7	20	3
Bruener, Mark, Pit.	19	157	8.3	20	2
Carter, Tony, N.E.	18	166	9.2	49	0
Pritchett, Stanley, Mia.	17	97	5.7	24	0
Thelwell, Ryan, S.D.	16	268	16.8	55	1
Green, Willie, Den.	16	194	12.1	50	1
Bennett, Donnell, K.C.	16	91	5.7	14	1
Means, Natrone, S.D.	16	91	5.7	22	0
Bettis, Jerome, Pit.	16	90	5.6	26	0
Ward, Hines, Pit.	15	246	16.4	45	0
Blades, Brian, Sea.	15	184	12.3	47	0
Green, E.G., Ind.	15	177	11.8	25	1
Griffith, Howard, Den.	15	97	6.5	15	3
Horn, Joe, K.C.	14	198	14.1	57	1
Cullors, Derrick, N.E.	14	146	10.4	43	1
Johnson, Lonnie, Buf.	14	146	10.4	27	2
Johnson, Leon, NY-J	13	222	17.1	82t	2
Kinchen, Brian, Bal.	13	110	8.5	24	0
Roan, Michael, Ten.	13	93	7.2	16	0
Popson, Ted, K.C.	13	90	6.9	17	0
Witman, Jon, Pit.	13	74	5.7	15	0
Johnson, Pat, Bal.	12	159	13.3	35	1
Morris, Bam, K.C.	12	95	7.9	29	0
Purnell, Lovett, N.E.	12	92	7.7	22	2
Barlow, Reggie, Jac.	11	168	15.3	31	0
Rhett, Errict, Bal.	11	65	5.9	16	0
Warren, Lamont, Ind.	11	44	4.0	12	1
Hundon, James, Cin.	10	112	11.2	17	1
Shelton, Daimon, Jac.	10	79	7.9	19	0
Shehee, Rashaan, K.C.	10	73	7.3	14	0
Avery, John, Mia.	10	67	6.7	19t	1
Sowell, Jerald, NY-J	10	59	5.9	13	0
Battaglia, Marco, Cin.	10	47	4.7	16	1
Dunn, David, Pit.	9	87	9.7	24	0
Fuamatu-Ma'afala, Chris, Pit.	9	84	9.3	26t	1
Lester, Tim, Pit.	9	46	5.1	9	0
McAfee, Fred, Pit.	9	27	3.0	11	0
Bennett, Brandon, Cin.	8	153	19.1	55	0
Jacquet, Nate, Mia.	8	122	15.3	29	0
Roe, James, Bal.	8	115	14.4	27	1
Slaughter, Webster, S.D.	8	93	11.6	31	0
Jones, Damon, Jac.	8	90	11.3	31t	4
Strong, Mack, Sea.	8	48	6.0	11t	2
Jackson, Willie, Cin.	7	165	23.6	47	0
Brisby, Vincent, N.E.	7	96	13.7	27	2
Brown, Derek, Oak.	7	89	12.7	27	0
Williams, Stepfret, Cin.	6	81	13.5	19t	1
Byrd, Isaac, Ten.	6	71	11.8	18	0
Thomas, Rodney, Ten.	6	55	9.2	20	0
Crumpler, Carlester, Sea.	6	52	8.7	16	1
Stewart, James, Jac.	6	42	7.0	19	1
Shaw, Sedrick, N.E.	6	30	5.0	11	0
Carter, Ki-Jana, Cin.	6	25	4.2	8	0
Sanders, Chris, Ten.	5	136	27.2	46	0
Graham, Jay, Bal.	5	41	8.2	14	0
Van Dyke, Alex, NY-J	5	40	8.0	15	0
Archie, Mike, Ten.	5	25	5.0	7	0
Smith, Antowain, Buf.	5	11	2.2	9	0
Nash, Marcus, Den.	4	76	19.0	31	0
Kent, Joey, Ten.	4	62	15.5	23	0
Carswell, Dwayne, Den.	4	51	12.8	15	0
Coleman, Andre, Pit.	4	49	12.3	13t	1
Bush, Steve, Cin.	4	39	9.8	18	0
Yarborough, Ryan, Bal.	4	39	9.8	18	0
Bynum, Kenny, S.D.	4	27	6.8	12	0
Davis, Wendell, S.D.	4	23	5.8	8	0
Broussard, Steve, Sea.	4	21	5.3	16	0
Banks, Tavian, Jac.	4	20	5.0	10	0
Baxter, Fred, NY-J	3	50	16.7	23	0
Shedd, Kenny, Oak.	3	50	16.7	21	0
Chamberlain, Byron, Den.	3	35	11.7	16	0
Burke, John, S.D.	3	32	10.7	17	0
Smith, Detron, Den.	3	24	8.0	16	0
Lyons, Mitch, Pit.	3	19	6.3	11	0
Huntley, Richard, Pit.	3	18	6.0	7	0
Anderson, Richie, NY-J	3	12	4.0	7	0
May, Deems, Sea.	3	7	2.3	5	1
Green, Ahman, Sea.	3	2	0.7	3	0
Jordan, Randy, Oak.	3	2	0.7	2	0
Whitted, Alvis, Jac.	2	61	30.5	55	0
Loville, Derek, Den.	2	29	14.5	17	0
Hartley, Frank, S.D.	2	28	14.0	17	0
Jordan, Charles, Mia.	2	17	8.5	9	0
Howard, Desmond, Oak.	2	16	8.0	10	0
Richardson, Tony, K.C.	2	13	6.5	15	0
Stephens, Tremayne, S.D.	2	9	4.5	5	0
Crockett, Zack, Ind.-Jac.	2	5	2.5	4	0
Hebron, Vaughn, Den.	2	5	2.5	3	0
Armour, Justin, Den.	1	23	23.0	23	0
Mili, Itula, Sea.	1	20	20.0	20	0
Stewart, Kordell, Pit.	1	17	17.0	17	0
Meggett, David, NY-J	1	15	15.0	15	0
Elway, John, Den.	1	14	14.0	14	0
Elias, Keith, Ind.	1	11	11.0	11	0
Hughes, Danan, K.C.	1	10	10.0	10	0
Linton, Jonathan, Buf.	1	10	10.0	10	0
Heyward, Craig, Ind.	1	9	9.0	9	0
Jones, George, Jac.	1	9	9.0	9	0
Moore, Will, Jac.	1	9	9.0	9	0
Banta, Brad, Ind.	1	7	7.0	7	0
Floyd, Chris, N.E.	1	6	6.0	6	0
Spence, Blake, NY-J	1	5	5.0	5	0
Bishop, Harold, Pit.	1	4	4.0	4	0
Shields, Will, K.C.	1	4	4.0	4	0
Howard, Chris, Jac.	1	3	3.0	3	0
Greene, Scott, Ind.	1	2	2.0	2	0
Moore, Ronald, Mia.	1	1	1.0	1	0
Atkins, James, Bal.	1	0	0.0	0	0
Folston, James, Oak.	1	-1	-1.0	-1	0

t = Touchdown
Leader based on receptions

NFC RECEIVERS—INDIVIDUAL

	No.	Yards	Avg.	Long	TD
Sanders, Frank, Ariz	89	1145	12.9	42	3
Freeman, Antonio, G.B.	84	1424	17.0	84t	14
Rice, Jerry, S.F.	82	1157	14.1	75t	9
Moore, Herman, Det.	82	983	12.0	36	5
Carter, Cris, Min.	78	1011	13.0	54t	12
Irvin, Michael, Dal.	74	1057	14.3	51	1
Moss, Randy, Min.	69	1313	19.0	61t	17
Morton, Johnnie, Det.	69	1028	14.9	98t	2
Ismail, Raghib, Car.	69	1024	14.8	62	8
Centers, Larry, Ariz	69	559	8.1	54	2
Muhammad, Muhsin, Car.	68	941	13.8	72t	6
Owens, Terrell, S.F.	67	1097	16.4	79t	14
Moore, Rob, Ariz	67	982	14.7	57	5
Martin, Tony, Atl.	66	1181	17.9	62	6
Mathis, Terance, Atl.	64	1136	17.8	78t	11
Engram, Bobby, Chi.	64	987	15.4	79t	5
Lee, Amp, St.L	64	667	10.4	44	2
Stokes, J.J., S.F.	63	770	12.2	33t	8
Calloway, Chris, NY-G	62	812	13.1	36	6
Proehl, Ricky, St.L	60	771	12.9	47	3
Staley, Duce, Phi.	57	432	7.6	33	1
Conway, Curtis, Chi.	54	733	13.6	47	3
Cleeland, Cameron, N.O.	54	684	12.7	53	6
Dawkins, Sean, N.O.	53	823	15.5	64t	1
Hilliard, Ike, NY-G	51	715	14.0	50	2
Anthony, Reidel, T.B.	51	708	13.9	79t	7
Walls, Wesley, Car.	49	506	10.3	30	5
Fryar, Irving, Phi.	48	556	11.6	61t	2
Graham, Jeff, Phi.	47	600	12.8	45	2
Chmura, Mark, G.B.	47	554	11.8	25t	4
Westbrook, Michael, Was.	44	736	16.7	75t	6
Dunn, Warrick, T.B.	44	344	7.8	31	0
Mitchell, Brian, Was.	44	306	7.0	24	0
Shepherd, Leslie, Was.	43	712	16.6	43t	8
Barber, Tiki, NY-G	42	348	8.3	87t	3
Emanuel, Bert, T.B.	41	636	15.5	62t	2
Davis, Billy, Dal.	39	691	17.7	80t	3
Hearst, Garrison, S.F.	39	535	13.7	81t	2
Alexander, Stephen, Was.	37	383	10.4	33	4
Sanders, Barry, Det.	37	289	7.8	44	0
Henderson, William, G.B.	37	241	6.5	15	1
Glover, Andrew, Min.	35	522	14.9	36	5
Hastings, Andre, N.O.	35	455	13.0	89t	3
Henley, June, St.L	35	252	7.2	43	0
Reed, Jake, Min.	34	474	13.9	56t	4

1998 INDIVIDUAL STATISTICS—RECEIVING

	No.	Yards	Avg.	Long	TD
Turner, Kevin, Phi.	34	232	6.8	18	0
Craver, Aaron, N.O.	33	214	6.5	49	2
Bruce, Isaac, St.L	32	457	14.3	80t	1
Schroeder, Bill, G.B.	31	452	14.6	46	1
Penn, Chris, Chi.	31	448	14.5	37	3
Brooks, Robert, G.B.	31	420	13.5	30t	3
Metcalf, Eric, Ariz	31	324	10.5	29	0
Way, Charles, NY-G	31	131	4.2	16	1
Mayes, Derrick, G.B.	30	394	13.1	33t	3
Mills, Ernie, Dal.	28	479	17.1	43t	4
Connell, Albert, Was.	28	451	16.1	61	2
Asher, Jamie, Was.	28	294	10.5	28	0
Smith, Robert, Min.	28	291	10.4	67t	2
Bennett, Edgar, Chi.	28	209	7.5	31	0
Santiago, O.J., Atl.	27	428	15.9	62t	5
Toomer, Amani, NY-G	27	360	13.3	37t	5
Anderson, Jamal, Atl.	27	319	11.8	27	2
Johnson, Anthony, Car.	27	242	9.0	38t	1
Smith, Emmitt, Dal.	27	175	6.5	24	2
Levens, Dorsey, G.B.	27	162	6.0	17	0
McWilliams, Johnny, Ariz	26	284	10.9	26	4
Crowell, Germane, Det.	25	464	18.6	68t	3
Smith, Irv, S.F.	25	266	10.6	25t	5
Hallock, Ty, Chi.	25	166	6.6	16	0
Poole, Keith, N.O.	24	509	21.2	82t	2
Moore, Dave, T.B.	24	255	10.6	44t	4
Smith, Lamar, N.O.	24	249	10.4	35t	2
Floyd, William, Car.	24	123	5.1	20	1
Wetnight, Ryan, Chi.	23	168	7.3	30	2
Gedney, Chris, Ariz	22	271	12.3	32	1
Edwards, Marc, S.F.	22	218	9.9	47t	2
Hoard, Leroy, Min.	22	198	9.0	24t	1
Alstott, Mike, T.B.	22	152	6.9	26	1
Davis, Stephen, Was.	21	263	12.5	30	2
Williams, Karl, T.B.	21	252	12.0	29t	1
Mayes, Alonzo, Chi.	21	217	10.3	22	0
Solomon, Freddie, Phi.	21	193	9.2	20	1
Thomas, J.T., St.L	20	287	14.4	42	0
Hakim, Az-Zahir, St.L	20	247	12.4	22	1
Copeland, Russell, Phi.-G.B.	20	232	11.6	20	0
Holmes, Darick, Buf.-G.B.	20	188	9.4	24	0
LaFleur, David, Dal.	20	176	8.8	24	2
Carrier, Mark, Car.	19	301	15.8	42	2
Christian, Bob, Atl.	19	214	11.3	39	1
Garner, Charlie, Phi.	19	110	5.8	21	0
Jeffers, Patrick, Dal.	18	330	18.3	67t	2
Davis, Tyrone, G.B.	18	250	13.9	60t	7
Palmer, David, Min.	18	185	10.3	33	0
Murrell, Adrian, Ariz	18	169	9.4	30	2
Dunn, Jason, Phi.	18	132	7.3	21	0
Johnston, Daryl, Dal.	18	60	3.3	9	1
Kennison, Eddie, St.L	17	234	13.8	45	1
Allen, Terry, Was.	17	128	7.5	17	0
Kirby, Terry, S.F.	16	134	8.4	25	0
Davis, Troy, N.O.	16	99	6.2	19	0
Bjornson, Eric, Dal.	15	218	14.5	43	1
Hatchette, Matthew, Min.	15	216	14.4	25	0
Williams, Roland, St.L	15	144	9.6	33	1
Rasby, Walter, Det.	15	119	7.9	17	1
Conwell, Ernie, St.L	15	105	7.0	13	0
Levy, Chuck, S.F.	15	64	4.3	13	0
Bech, Brett, N.O.	14	264	18.9	72t	3
Green, Jacquez, T.B.	14	251	17.9	64t	2
Thomas, Chris, Was.	14	173	12.4	25	0
Vardell, Tommy, Det.	14	143	10.2	31	1
Cross, Howard, NY-G	13	90	6.9	22	0
Warren, Chris, Dal.	13	66	5.1	15	1
Brown, Gary, NY-G	13	36	2.8	12	0
Clark, Greg, S.F.	12	124	10.3	23	1
Lane, Fred, Car.	12	85	7.1	16	0
Evans, Chuck, Min.	12	84	7.0	14	0
Harris, Derrick, St.L	12	57	4.8	8	2
Kinchen, Todd, Atl.	11	157	14.3	32	1
Sloan, David, Det.	11	146	13.3	33	1
Patten, David, NY-G	11	119	10.8	39t	1
Williams, Sherman, Dal.	11	104	9.5	30	0
Chancey, Robert, Chi.	11	102	9.3	15	0
Thrash, James, Was.	10	163	16.3	28	1
Guliford, Eric, N.O.	10	124	12.4	24	0
Kozlowski, Brian, Atl.	10	103	10.3	25	1
Harris, Raymont, G.B.	10	68	6.8	12	0
Zellars, Ray, N.O.	10	50	5.0	14	0
Jurevicius, Joe, NY-G	9	146	16.2	59	0
Thomason, Jeff, G.B.	9	89	9.9	22	0
Moore, Jerald, St.L	9	60	6.7	14	0
Jervey, Travis, G.B.	9	33	3.7	11	0
Biakabutuka, Tim, Car.	8	138	17.3	42	1
Fontenot, Chris, Phi.	8	90	11.3	19	0
Allen, James, Chi.	8	77	9.6	33	1
Ogden, Jeff, Dal.	8	63	7.9	12	0
DeLong, Greg, Min.	8	58	7.3	17	0
Ellard, Henry, N.E.-Was.	7	115	16.4	19	0
Sanders, Deion, Dal.	7	100	14.3	55	0
Stablein, Brian, Det.	7	80	11.4	15	0
Bowie, Larry, Was.	7	53	7.6	17	1
Broughton, Luther, Car.	6	142	23.7	68t	1
Armstrong, Tyji, St.L	6	54	9.0	20	0
Holcombe, Robert, St.L	6	34	5.7	14	0
Enis, Curtis, Chi.	6	20	3.3	7	0
Bownes, Fabien, Chi.	5	69	13.8	44	1
Neal, Lorenzo, T.B.	5	14	2.8	5	1
Dwight, Tim, Atl.	4	94	23.5	44t	1
Hunter, Brice, T.B.	4	73	18.3	45t	1
Carruth, Rae, Car.	4	59	14.8	47	0
Boyd, Tommie, Det.	4	52	13.0	19	1
Robinson, Marcus, Chi.	4	44	11.0	20t	1
Milburn, Glyn, Chi.	4	37	9.3	13	0
Downs, Gary, Atl.	4	31	7.8	11	0
Hape, Patrick, T.B.	4	27	6.8	11	0
Hicks, Skip, Was.	4	23	5.8	9	0
Chryplewicz, Pete, Det.	4	20	5.0	8	2
Uwaezuoke, Iheanyi, S.F.	3	67	22.3	35	0
Hayes, Donald, Car.	3	62	20.7	35	0
Rivers, Ron, Det.	3	58	19.3	38	0
Sinceno, Kaseem, Phi.	3	42	14.0	22	1
Bradford, Corey, G.B.	3	27	9.0	18	0
Blair, Michael, G.B.-Cin.-G.B.	3	20	6.7	10	0
Sellers, Mike, Was.	3	18	6.0	8	0
Goodwin, Hunter, Min.	3	16	5.3	9	0
Schlesinger, Cory, Det.	3	16	5.3	8t	1
Harris, Mark, S.F.	2	67	33.5	42	0
Thomas, Robb, T.B.	2	63	31.5	50t	1
Jells, Dietrich, Phi.	2	53	26.5	37	0
Walsh, Chris, Min.	2	46	23.0	25	0
Walker, Corey, Phi.	2	35	17.5	33	0
Green, Harold, Atl.	2	34	17.0	28	0
Haase, Andy, NY-G	2	33	16.5	27	0
Preston, Roell, G.B.	2	23	11.5	13	0
Johnson, Jimmie, Phi.	2	14	7.0	9	0
Brock, Fred, Ariz	2	12	6.0	7	0
Davis, John, T.B.	2	12	6.0	11	1
Jordan, Andrew, Phi.	2	9	4.5	8	0
Green, Trent, Was.	2	-8	-4.0	0	0
Williams, Moe, Min.	1	64	64.0	64	0
Clay, Hayward, Dal.	1	27	27.0	27	0
Chandler, Chris, Atl.	1	22	22.0	22	0
Tate, Robert, Min.	1	17	17.0	17	0
Graham, Kent, NY-G	1	16	16.0	16	0
Bates, Mario, Ariz	1	14	14.0	14	0
Harris, Ronnie, Atl.	1	14	14.0	14	0
Farquhar, John, N.O.	1	13	13.0	13	0
Alford, Brian, NY-G	1	11	11.0	11	0
Beasley, Fred, S.F.	1	11	11.0	11	0
Miller, Bubba, Phi.	1	11	11.0	11	0
Oxendine, Ken, Atl.	1	11	11.0	11	0
Slutzker, Scott, N.O.	1	10	10.0	10	0
Wilcox, Josh, N.O.	1	10	10.0	10	0
Anderson, Ronnie, Ariz	1	8	8.0	8	0
Johnson, Tony, N.O.	1	8	8.0	8	0
Stone, Dwight, Car.	1	7	7.0	7	0
Hill, Greg, St.L	1	6	6.0	6	0
Mangum, Kris, Car.	1	5	5.0	5	0
Robinson, Jeff, St.L	1	4	4.0	4t	1
Comella, Greg, NY-G	1	3	3.0	3	0
Flannery, John, St.L	1	2	2.0	2	0
Perry, Wilmont, N.O.	1	2	2.0	2	0
Pupunu, Alfred, NY-G	1	2	2.0	2	0
Cunningham, Randall, Min.	1	-3	-3.0	-3	0
Collins, Kerry, Car.	1	-11	-11.0	-11	0

t = Touchdown
Leader based on receptions

1998 INDIVIDUAL STATISTICS—INTERCEPTIONS

INTERCEPTIONS

Interceptions
- **AFC:** 9—Ty Law, New England
- **NFC:** 8—Kwamie Lassiter, Arizona

Interceptions, Game
- **NFC:** 4—Kwamie Lassiter, Arizona vs. San Diego, December 27
- **AFC:** 2—by many

Yards
- **NFC:** 242—Jimmy Hitchcock, Minnesota
- **AFC:** 178—Dewayne Washington, Pittsburgh

Longest
- **AFC:** 94—Eric Turner, Oakland vs. Denver, September 20 - TD
- **NFC:** 91—Sammy Knight, New Orleans at Minnesota, November 8 - TD

Touchdowns
- **NFC:** 3—Jimmy Hitchcock, Minnesota
- **AFC:** 2—Darrin Smith, Seattle
  Shawn Springs, Seattle
  Zach Thomas, Miami
  Dewayne Washington, Pittsburgh
  Rod Woodson, Baltimore

Team Leaders, Interceptions

AFC: BALTIMORE: 6, Rod Woodson; BUFFALO: 6, Kurt Schulz; CINCINNATI: 3, Artrell Hawkins, Sam Shade; DENVER: 4, Darrien Gordon; INDIANAPOLIS: 1, Elijah Alexander, Mike Barber ,Jason Belser, Robert Blackmon, Jeff Burris, Rico Clark, Monty Montgomery, Tyrone Poole; JACKSONVILLE: 3, Aaron Beasley, Chris Hudson; KANSAS CITY: 4, James Hasty; MIAMI: 8, Terrell Buckley, Sam Madison; NEW ENGLAND: 9, Ty Law; N.Y. JETS: 6, Aaron Glenn; OAKLAND: 5, Eric Allen, Charles Woodson; PITTSBURGH: 5, Dewayne Washington; SAN DIEGO: 6, Greg Jackson ; SEATTLE: 7, Shawn Springs; TENNESSEE: 4, Darryll Lewis.

NFC: ARIZONA: 8, Kwamie Lassiter; ATLANTA: 7, Ray Buchanan; CAROLINA: 5, Eric Davis; CHICAGO: 4, Walt Harris; DALLAS: 5, Deion Sanders; DETROIT: 3, Mark Carrier, Ron Rice, Bryant Westbrook; GREEN BAY: 5, Tyrone Williams; MINNESOTA: 7, Jimmy Hitchcock; NEW ORLEANS: 6, Sammy Knight; N.Y. GIANTS: 5, Percy Ellsworth; PHILADELPHIA: 2, Brian Dawkins, Troy Vincent, Mike Zordich; ST. LOUIS: 3, Todd Lyght, Keith Lyle; SAN FRANCISCO: 4, Zack Bronson, Merton Hanks, Tim McDonald, Darnell Walker; TAMPA BAY: 4, Charles Mincy; WASHINGTON: 3, Leomont Evans, Darrell Green.

Team Champion
- **AFC:** 29—Miami
- **NFC:** 21—New Orleans
  San Francisco

AFC INTERCEPTIONS—TEAM

	No.	Yards	Avg.	Long	TD
Miami	29	318	11.0	61	4
New England	24	255	10.6	59t	3
Seattle	24	455	19.0	56t	8
N.Y. Jets	21	263	12.5	87	1
Oakland	21	420	20.0	94t	3
San Diego	20	203	10.2	30	1
Denver	19	439	23.1	80t	2
Buffalo	18	204	11.3	43	1
Baltimore	17	161	9.5	60t	2
Pittsburgh	16	335	20.9	78t	3
Cincinnati	13	144	11.1	58t	1
Jacksonville	13	119	9.2	34	0
Kansas City	13	187	14.4	28	0
Tennessee	12	98	8.2	33	2
Indianapolis	8	97	12.1	30	0
AFC Total	268	3698	13.8	94t	31
AFC Average	17.9	246.5	13.8	—	2.1

NFC INTERCEPTIONS—TEAM

	No.	Yards	Avg.	Long	TD
New Orleans	21	466	22.2	91t	5
San Francisco	21	178	8.5	37	0
Arizona	20	235	11.8	70t	1
Atlanta	19	224	11.8	36	2
Carolina	19	295	15.5	56t	2
Minnesota	19	341	17.9	79t	3
N.Y. Giants	19	217	11.4	43t	3
St. Louis	16	201	12.6	41	1
Chicago	14	129	9.2	28	1
Dallas	14	250	17.9	71t	1
Green Bay	13	111	8.5	33t	1
Washington	13	190	14.6	54	0
Detroit	12	132	11.0	34t	1
Tampa Bay	12	212	17.7	56	1
Philadelphia	9	158	17.6	33	0
NFC Total	241	3339	13.9	91t	22
NFC Average	16.1	222.6	13.9	—	1.5
League Total	509	7037	—	94t	53
League Average	17.0	234.6	13.8	—	1.8

NFL TOP TEN INTERCEPTORS

	No.	Yards	Avg.	Long	TD
Law, Ty, N.E.	9	133	14.8	59t	1
Buckley, Terrell, Mia.	8	157	19.6	61	1
Lassiter, Kwamie, Ariz	8	80	10.0	29	0
Madison, Sam, Mia.	8	114	14.3	35	0
Buchanan, Ray, Atl.	7	102	14.6	34	0
Hitchcock, Jimmy, Min.	7	242	34.6	79t	3
Springs, Shawn, Sea.	7	142	20.3	56t	2
Glenn, Aaron, NY-J	6	23	3.8	26	0
Jackson, Greg, S.D.	6	50	8.3	25	0
Knight, Sammy, N.O.	6	171	28.5	91t	2
Milloy, Lawyer, N.E.	6	54	9.0	30t	1
Schulz, Kurt, Buf.	6	48	8.0	24	0
Woodson, Rod, Bal.	6	108	18.0	60t	2

AFC INTERCEPTIONS—INDIVIDUAL

	No.	Yards	Avg.	Long	TD
Law, Ty, N.E.	9	133	14.8	59t	1
Buckley, Terrell, Mia.	8	157	19.6	61	1
Madison, Sam, Mia.	8	114	14.3	35	0
Springs, Shawn, Sea.	7	142	20.3	56t	2
Woodson, Rod, Bal.	6	108	18.0	60t	2
Milloy, Lawyer, N.E.	6	54	9.0	30t	1
Jackson, Greg, S.D.	6	50	8.3	25	0
Schulz, Kurt, Buf.	6	48	8.0	24	0
Glenn, Aaron, NY-J	6	23	3.8	26	0
Washington, Dewayne, Pit.	5	178	35.6	78t	2
Woodson, Charles, Oak.	5	118	23.6	46t	1
Allen, Eric, Oak.	5	59	11.8	22	0
Starks, Duane, Bal.	5	3	0.6	2	0
Gordon, Darrien, Den.	4	125	31.3	55t	1
Green, Victor, NY-J	4	99	24.8	87	0
Hasty, James, K.C.	4	42	10.5	21	0
Lewis, Darryll, Ten.	4	40	10.0	33	0
Lake, Carnell, Pit.	4	33	8.3	27	1
Walker, Brian, Mia.	4	12	3.0	7	0
Turner, Eric, Oak.	3	108	36.0	94t	1
Crockett, Ray, Den.	3	105	35.0	80t	1
Smith, Darrin, Sea.	3	56	18.7	26t	2
McMillian, Mark, K.C.	3	48	16.0	21	0
Harrison, Rodney, S.D.	3	42	14.0	21	0
Williams, Darryl, Sea.	3	41	13.7	28	0
Bellamy, Jay, Sea.	3	40	13.3	24	0
Dimry, Charles, S.D.	3	38	12.7	30	0
Beasley, Aaron, Jac.	3	35	11.7	34	0
Shade, Sam, Cin.	3	33	11.0	32	0
Staten, Ralph, Bal.	3	25	8.3	14	0
Hawkins, Artrell, Cin.	3	21	7.0	12	0
Thomas, Zach, Mia.	3	21	7.0	17t	2
Clay, Willie, N.E.	3	19	6.3	19	0
Israel, Steve, N.E.	3	13	4.3	12	0
Hudson, Chris, Jac.	3	10	3.3	8	0
Mickens, Ray, NY-J	3	10	3.3	10	0
Jones, Henry, Buf.	3	0	0.0	0	0
Johnson, Darrius, Den.	2	79	39.5	45	0
Lewis, Albert, Oak.	2	74	37.0	74t	1

1998 INDIVIDUAL STATISTICS—INTERCEPTIONS

	No.	Yards	Avg.	Long	TD
Perry, Darren, Pit.	2	69	34.5	40	0
Hand, Norman, S.D.	2	47	23.5	30	0
Woods, Jerome, K.C.	2	47	23.5	28	0
Hardy, Kevin, Jac.	2	40	20.0	24	0
Williams, Willie, Sea.	2	36	18.0	28t	1
Davis, Travis, Jac.	2	34	17.0	34	0
Smith, Otis, NY-J	2	34	17.0	32	0
Walker, Marquis, Oak.	2	28	14.0	28	0
Davis, Anthony, K.C.	2	27	13.5	27	0
Jackson, Raymond, Buf.	2	27	13.5	27	0
Lewis, Ray, Bal.	2	25	12.5	26	0
Carter, Dale, K.C.	2	23	11.5	23	0
Cowart, Sam, Buf.	2	23	11.5	23	0
Romanowski, Bill, Den.	2	22	11.0	18	0
Newman, Anthony, Oak.	2	17	8.5	11	0
Jones, Robert, Mia.	2	14	7.0	14t	1
Cadrez, Glenn, Den.	2	11	5.5	6	0
Walker, Denard, Ten.	2	6	3.0	6	0
Surtain, Patrick, Mia.	2	1	0.5	1	0
Ambrose, Ashley, Cin.	2	0	0.0	0	0
Shaw, Terrance, S.D.	2	0	0.0	0	0
Braxton, Tyrone, Den.	1	72	72.0	72	0
Sawyer, Corey, Cin.	1	58	58.0	58t	1
Irvin, Ken, Buf.	1	43	43.0	43	0
McDaniel, Terry, Sea.	1	43	43.0	43t	1
Northern, Gabe, Buf.	1	40	40.0	40t	1
Holmes, Earl, Pit.	1	36	36.0	36	0
Simmons, Anthony, Sea.	1	36	36.0	36t	1
Williams, Kevin, NY-J	1	34	34.0	34	0
Gordon, Dwayne, NY-J	1	31	31.0	31t	1
Clark, Rico, Ind.	1	30	30.0	30	0
Marts, Lonnie, Ten.	1	27	27.0	27t	1
Adams, Sam, Sea.	1	25	25.0	25t	1
Wells, Dean, Sea.	1	25	25.0	25	0
Thomas, Henry, N.E.	1	24	24.0	24t	1
Martin, Emanuel, Buf.	1	23	23.0	23	0
Montgomery, Monty, Ind.	1	22	22.0	22	0
Henderson, Jerome, NY-J	1	21	21.0	21	0
Coghill, George, Den.	1	20	20.0	20	0
Belser, Jason, Ind.	1	19	19.0	19	0
Simmons, Brian, Cin.	1	18	18.0	18	0
Blackmon, Robert, Ind.	1	14	14.0	14	0
Oldham, Chris, Pit.	1	14	14.0	14	0
Williams, Jamal, S.D.	1	14	14.0	14t	1
Wooden, Terry, Oak.	1	14	14.0	14	0
Bishop, Blaine, Ten.	1	13	13.0	13	0
Alexander, Elijah, Ind.	1	12	12.0	12	0
Canty, Chris, N.E.	1	12	12.0	12	0
Harper, Dwayne, S.D.	1	12	12.0	12	0
Brown, Chad, Sea.	1	11	11.0	11	0
Lewis, Mo, NY-J	1	11	11.0	11	0
Robinson, Eddie, Ten.	1	11	11.0	11	0
Ross, Adrian, Cin.	1	11	11.0	11	0
Atwater, Steve, Den.	1	4	4.0	4	0
Copeland, John, Cin.	1	3	3.0	3	0
Emmons, Carlos, Pit.	1	2	2.0	2	0
Flowers, Lethon, Pit.	1	2	2.0	2	0
Harvey, Richard, Oak.	1	2	2.0	2	0
Smith, Neil, Den.	1	2	2.0	2	0
Bowden, Joe, Ten.	1	1	1.0	1t	1
Kirkland, Levon, Pit.	1	1	1.0	1	0
Pryce, Trevor, Den.	1	1	1.0	1	0
Barber, Mike, Ind.	1	0	0.0	0	0
Brown, Corwin, NY-J	1	0	0.0	0	0
Burris, Jeff, Ind.	1	0	0.0	0	0
Collins, Mark, Sea.	1	0	0.0	0	0
Devine, Kevin, Jac.	1	0	0.0	0	0
Figures, Deon, Jac.	1	0	0.0	0	0
Jackson, Steve, Ten.	1	0	0.0	0	0
Jenkins, DeRon, Bal.	1	0	0.0	0	0
Johnson, Pepper, NY-J	1	0	0.0	0	0
Poole, Tyrone, Ind.	1	0	0.0	0	0
Randolph, Thomas, Cin.	1	0	0.0	0	0
Robertson, Marcus, Ten.	1	0	0.0	0	0
Smith, Thomas, Buf.	1	0	0.0	0	0
Spencer, Jimmy, S.D.	1	0	0.0	0	0
Thomas, Dave, Jac.	1	0	0.0	0	0
Turner, Scott, S.D.	1	0	0.0	0	0
Washington, Ted, Buf.	1	0	0.0	0	0
Whigham, Larry, N.E.	1	0	0.0	0	0
Wilson, Jerry, Mia.	1	0	0.0	0	0
Gardener, Daryl, Mia.	1	-1	-1.0	-1	0
Mobley, John, Den.	1	-2	-2.0	-2	0

t = Touchdown
Leader based on interceptions

NFC INTERCEPTIONS—INDIVIDUAL

	No.	Yards	Avg.	Long	TD
Lassiter, Kwamie, Ariz	8	80	10.0	29	0
Hitchcock, Jimmy, Min.	7	242	34.6	79t	3
Buchanan, Ray, Atl.	7	102	14.6	34	0
Knight, Sammy, N.O.	6	171	28.5	91t	2
Sanders, Deion, Dal.	5	153	30.6	71t	1
Ellsworth, Percy, NY-G	5	92	18.4	43t	2
Davis, Eric, Car.	5	81	16.2	56t	2
Williams, Tyrone, G.B.	5	40	8.0	15	0
Griffith, Robert, Min.	5	25	5.0	17	0
McKinnon, Ronald, Ariz	5	25	5.0	17	0
Brady, Jeff, Car.	4	85	21.3	43	0
Walker, Darnell, S.F.	4	78	19.5	36	0
Drakeford, Tyronne, N.O.	4	76	19.0	32t	1
Mincy, Charles, T.B.	4	58	14.5	22t	1
Harris, Walt, Chi.	4	41	10.3	26	1
Hanks, Merton, S.F.	4	37	9.3	37	0
Fuller, Corey, Min.	4	36	9.0	26	0
Robinson, Eugene, Atl.	4	36	9.0	25t	1
Bronson, Zack, S.F.	4	34	8.5	28	0
Sparks, Phillippi, NY-G	4	25	6.3	12	0
McDonald, Tim, S.F.	4	22	5.5	18	0
Cota, Chad, N.O.	4	16	4.0	9	0
Evans, Leomont, Was.	3	77	25.7	54	0
Westbrook, Bryant, Det.	3	49	16.3	34t	1
Green, Darrell, Was.	3	36	12.0	36	0
Carrier, Mark, Det.	3	33	11.0	33	0
Lyght, Todd, St.L	3	30	10.0	17	0
Collins, Andre, Chi.	3	29	9.7	28	0
Rice, Ron, Det.	3	25	8.3	25	0
Lyle, Keith, St.L	3	20	6.7	20	0
Bradford, Ronnie, Atl.	3	11	3.7	11t	1
Butler, LeRoy, G.B.	3	3	1.0	3	0
Kelly, Rob, N.O.	2	104	52.0	79t	1
Bennett, Tommy, Ariz	2	100	50.0	70t	1
Barber, Ronde, T.B.	2	67	33.5	56	0
Weary, Fred, N.O.	2	64	32.0	63t	1
Dishman, Cris, Was.	2	60	30.0	49	0
Smith, Rod, Car.-G.B.	2	43	21.5	43	0
Dawkins, Brian, Phi.	2	39	19.5	30	0
White, William, Atl.	2	36	18.0	36	0
Molden, Alex, N.O.	2	35	17.5	24	0
Jenkins, Billy, St.L	2	31	15.5	25	0
Smith, Kevin, Dal.	2	31	15.5	22	0
Lynch, John, T.B.	2	29	14.5	17	0
McCleon, Dexter, St.L	2	29	14.5	15	0
Vincent, Troy, Phi.	2	29	14.5	29	0
Thomas, Orlando, Min.	2	27	13.5	27	0
Carter, Tom, Chi.	2	20	10.0	19	0
Evans, Doug, Car.	2	18	9.0	18	0
Greene, Kevin, Car.	2	18	9.0	18	0
Zordich, Mike, Phi.	2	18	9.0	14	0
Jones, Mike A., St.L	2	13	6.5	13	0
Williams, Shaun, NY-G	2	6	3.0	6	0
Armstead, Jessie, NY-G	2	4	2.0	4	0
Chavous, Corey, Ariz	2	0	0.0	0	0
Mathis, Kevin, Dal.	2	0	0.0	0	0
Phifer, Roman, St.L	1	41	41.0	41	0
Wheaton, Kenny, Dal.	1	41	41.0	41	0
McNeil, Ryan, St.L	1	37	37.0	37t	1
Gray, Carlton, NY-G	1	36	36.0	36	0
Caldwell, Mike, Phi.	1	33	33.0	33	0
McKenzie, Keith, G.B.	1	33	33.0	33t	1
Booker, Michael, Atl.	1	27	27.0	27	0
Newsome, Craig, G.B.	1	26	26.0	26	0
Upshaw, Regan, T.B.	1	26	26.0	26	0
Brooks, Derrick, T.B.	1	25	25.0	25	0
Strahan, Michael, NY-G	1	24	24.0	24t	1
Veland, Tony, Car.	1	24	24.0	24	0
Jamison, George, Det.	1	21	21.0	21	0
Thomas, William, Phi.	1	21	21.0	21	0
Coakley, Dexter, Dal.	1	18	18.0	18	0
McTyer, Tim, Phi.	1	18	18.0	18	0
Hamilton, Conrad, NY-G	1	17	17.0	17	0
Minter, Barry, Chi.	1	17	17.0	17	0
Williams, Aeneas, Ariz	1	15	15.0	15	0

1998 INDIVIDUAL STATISTICS—PUNTING

	No.	Yards	Avg.	Long	TD
McCombs, Tony, Ariz	1	14	14.0	14	0
Thierry, John, Chi.	1	14	14.0	14	0
Garnes, Sam, NY-G	1	13	13.0	13	0
Brooking, Keith, Atl.	1	12	12.0	12	0
Gray, Torrian, Min.	1	11	11.0	11	0
Barrow, Micheal, Car.	1	10	10.0	10	0
Jones, Greg, Was.	1	9	9.0	9	0
Terrell, Pat, G.B.	1	9	9.0	9	0
Parrish, Tony, Chi.	1	8	8.0	8	0
Minter, Mike, Car.	1	7	7.0	7	0
Tubbs, Winfred, S.F.	1	7	7.0	7	0
McGill, Lenny, Car.	1	6	6.0	6	0
Reese, Izell, Dal.	1	6	6.0	6	0
Campbell, Jesse, Was.	1	4	4.0	4	0
Jordan, Richard, Det.	1	4	4.0	4	0
Kelly, Brian, T.B.	1	4	4.0	4	0
Wilkinson, Dan, Was.	1	4	4.0	4	0
Woodall, Lee, S.F.	1	4	4.0	4	0
Abraham, Donnie, T.B.	1	3	3.0	3	0
Lloyd, Greg, Car.	1	3	3.0	3	0
McCleskey, J. J., Ariz	1	1	1.0	1	0
Woodson, Darren, Dal.	1	1	1.0	1	0
Agnew, Ray, St.L	1	0	0.0	0	0
Barber, Shawn, Was.	1	0	0.0	0	0
Buckley, Marcus, NY-G	1	0	0.0	0	0
Cousin, Terry, Chi.	1	0	0.0	0	0
Fredrickson, Rob, Det.	1	0	0.0	0	0
Glover, La'Roi, N.O.	1	0	0.0	0	0
Godfrey, Randall, Dal.	1	0	0.0	0	0
Harris, Sean, Chi.	1	0	0.0	0	0
Hill, Eric, St.L	1	0	0.0	0	0
Langham, Antonio, S.F.	1	0	0.0	0	0
Lincoln, Jeremy, NY-G	1	0	0.0	0	0
Pope, Marquez, S.F.	1	0	0.0	0	0
Prior, Mike, G.B.	1	0	0.0	0	0
Richard, Stanley, Was.	1	0	0.0	0	0
Sauer, Craig, Atl.	1	0	0.0	0	0
Barker, Roy, S.F.	1	-4	-4.0	-4	0

t = Touchdown
Leader based on interceptions

PUNTING

Average Yards Per Punt
AFC: 47.2—Craig Hentrich, Tennessee
NFC: 45.6—Mark Royals, New Orleans

Net Average Yards Per Punt
AFC: 39.2—Craig Hentrich, Tennessee
NFC: 39.0—Matt Turk, Washington

Longest
AFC: 76—Tom Rouen, Denver at Oakland, September 20
NFC: 72—Sean Landeta, Green Bay at Cincinnati, September 20

Punts
NFC: 104—Tom Hutton, Philadelphia
AFC: 98—Leo Araguz, Oakland

Punts, Game
AFC: 16—Leo Araguz, Oakland vs. San Diego, October 11 (709 yards)
NFC: 11—Brad Maynard, N.Y. Giants at Washington, November 1 (497 yards)

Team Champion
AFC: 47.2—Tennessee
NFC: 45.4—New Orleans

AFC PUNTING—TEAM

	Total Punts	Yards	Long	Avg.	TB	Blk.	Opp. Ret.	Ret. Yds.	In 20	Net. Avg.
Tennessee	69	3258	71	47.2	11	0	34	332	18	39.2
Denver	67	3097	76	46.2	10	1	43	381	14	37.6
Indianapolis	79	3583	62	45.4	10	0	42	451	23	37.1
Jacksonville	85	3824	65	45.0	11	0	40	332	28	38.5
New England	74	3294	64	44.5	9	0	43	493	13	35.4
Cincinnati	81	3578	73	44.2	11	2	36	503	14	35.2
Seattle	81	3568	59	44.0	12	0	33	369	27	36.5
San Diego	95	4174	65	43.9	8	0	49	515	27	36.8
Pittsburgh	82	3565	73	43.5	12	0	30	310	35	36.8
Oakland	98	4256	64	43.4	10	0	53	787	29	33.4
Baltimore	92	3948	67	42.9	7	2	40	284	25	38.3
Kansas City	77	3255	59	42.3	5	1	41	513	21	34.3
Miami	97	4064	57	41.9	14	1	43	339	24	35.5
Buffalo	69	2882	57	41.8	11	0	32	374	18	33.2
N.Y. Jets	65	2637	62	40.6	4	0	30	309	16	34.6
AFC Total	1211	52983	76	—	145	7	589	6292	332	—
AFC Average	80.7	3532.2	—	43.8	9.7	0.5	39.3	419.5	22.1	36.2

NFC PUNTING—TEAM

	Total Punts	Yards	Long	Avg.	TB	Blk.	Opp. Ret.	Ret. Yds.	In 20	Net. Avg.
New Orleans	90	4089	64	45.4	11	0	53	649	26	35.8
N.Y. Giants	101	4566	63	45.2	8	0	53	587	33	37.8
Minnesota	55	2458	67	44.7	5	0	27	325	17	37.0
St. Louis	95	4202	64	44.2	10	0	58	652	16	35.3
Washington	97	4216	69	43.5	9	1	32	261	34	38.9
Green Bay	65	2788	72	42.9	7	0	27	237	30	37.1
Dallas	78	3342	65	42.8	14	1	34	210	31	36.6
Detroit	82	3506	60	42.8	6	0	47	471	19	35.5
Chicago	80	3411	71	42.6	7	0	38	349	18	36.5
Philadelphia	104	4339	61	41.7	10	0	61	511	21	34.9
Tampa Bay	81	3340	55	41.2	9	0	38	302	19	35.3
Arizona	82	3378	67	41.2	6	1	38	313	12	35.9
San Francisco	69	2835	66	41.1	7	0	36	341	16	34.1
Carolina	77	3131	59	40.7	5	0	20	94	20	38.1
Atlanta	74	2963	55	40.0	7	0	20	112	25	36.6
NFC Total	1230	52564	72	—	121	3	582	5414	337	—
NFC Average	82.0	3504.3	—	42.7	8.1	0.2	38.7	360.9	22.5	36.4
League Total	2441	105547	76	—	266	10	1171	11706	669	—
League Average	81.4	3518.2	—	43.2	8.9	0.3	39.0	390.2	22.3	36.3

1998 INDIVIDUAL STATISTICS—PUNTING

NFL TOP TEN PUNTERS

	No.	Yards	Long	Avg.	Total Punts	TB	Blk.	Opp. Ret.	Ret. Yds.	In 20	Net. Avg.
Hentrich, Craig, Ten.	69	3258	71	47.2	69	11	0	34	332	18	39.2
Rouen, Tom, Den.	66	3097	76	46.9	67	10	1	43	381	14	37.6
Royals, Mark, N.O.	88	4017	64	45.6	88	10	0	52	649	26	36.0
Gardocki, Chris, Ind.	79	3583	62	45.4	79	10	0	42	451	23	37.1
Maynard, Brad, NY-G	101	4566	63	45.2	101	8	0	53	587	33	37.8
Barker, Bryan, Jac.	85	3824	65	45.0	85	11	0	40	332	28	38.5
Berger, Mitch, Min.	55	2458	67	44.7	55	5	0	27	325	17	37.0
Johnson, Lee, Cin.	69	3083	69	44.7	70	8	1	31	428	14	35.6
Tupa, Tom, N.E.	74	3294	64	44.5	74	9	0	43	493	13	35.4
Tuten, Rick, St.L	95	4202	64	44.2	95	10	0	58	652	16	35.3

AFC PUNTERS—INDIVIDUAL

	No.	Yards	Long	Avg.	Total Punts	TB	Blk.	Opp. Ret.	Ret. Yds.	In 20	Net. Avg.
Hentrich, Craig, Ten.	69	3258	71	47.2	69	11	0	34	332	18	39.2
Rouen, Tom, Den.	66	3097	76	46.9	67	10	1	43	381	14	37.6
Gardocki, Chris, Ind.	79	3583	62	45.4	79	10	0	42	451	23	37.1
Barker, Bryan, Jac.	85	3824	65	45.0	85	11	0	40	332	28	38.5
Johnson, Lee, Cin.	69	3083	69	44.7	70	8	1	31	428	14	35.6
Tupa, Tom, N.E.	74	3294	64	44.5	74	9	0	43	493	13	35.4
Feagles, Jeff, Sea.	81	3568	59	44.0	81	12	0	33	369	27	36.5
Bennett, Darren, S.D.	95	4174	65	43.9	95	8	0	49	515	27	36.8
Richardson, Kyle, Bal.	90	3948	67	43.9	92	7	2	40	284	25	38.3
Miller, Josh, Pit.	81	3530	73	43.6	81	12	0	30	310	34	36.8
Araguz, Leo, Oak.	98	4256	64	43.4	98	10	0	53	787	29	33.4
Aguiar, Louie, K.C.	75	3226	59	43.0	76	5	1	41	513	20	34.4
Wilmsmeyer, Klaus, Mia.	93	3949	57	42.5	94	13	1	43	339	23	35.6
Mohr, Chris, Buf.	69	2882	57	41.8	69	11	0	32	374	18	33.2
Kidd, John, Det.-NY-J	41	1686	57	41.1	41	2	0	20	159	9	36.3
Nonqualifiers											
Hansen, Brian, NY-J	31	1233	62	39.8	31	2	0	15	178	6	32.7
Costello, Brad, Cin.	10	495	73	49.5	11	3	1	5	75	0	32.7
Gallery, Nick, NY-J	6	238	49	39.7	6	0	0	3	38	2	33.3
Mare, Olindo, Mia.	3	115	43	38.3	3	1	0	0	0	1	31.7
Stewart, Kordell, Pit.	1	35	35	35.0	1	0	0	0	0	1	35.0
Stoyanovich, Pete, K.C.	1	29	29	29.0	1	0	0	0	0	1	29.0

Leader based on average, minimum 40 punts

NFC PUNTERS—INDIVIDUAL

	No.	Yards	Long	Avg.	Total Punts	TB	Blk.	Opp. Ret.	Ret. Yds.	In 20	Net. Avg.
Royals, Mark, N.O.	88	4017	64	45.6	88	10	0	52	649	26	36.0
Maynard, Brad, NY-G	101	4566	63	45.2	101	8	0	53	587	33	37.8
Berger, Mitch, Min.	55	2458	67	44.7	55	5	0	27	325	17	37.0
Tuten, Rick, St.L	95	4202	64	44.2	95	10	0	58	652	16	35.3
Turk, Matt, Was.	93	4103	69	44.1	94	9	1	31	260	33	39.0
Jett, John, Det.	66	2892	60	43.8	66	6	0	38	398	17	36.0
Gowin, Toby, Dal.	77	3342	65	43.4	78	14	1	34	210	31	36.6
Landeta, Sean, G.B.	65	2788	72	42.9	65	7	0	27	237	30	37.1
Roby, Reggie, S.F.	60	2511	66	41.9	60	6	0	34	332	14	34.3
Hutton, Tom, Phi.	104	4339	61	41.7	104	10	0	61	511	21	34.9
Player, Scott, Ariz	81	3378	67	41.7	82	6	1	38	313	12	35.9
Horan, Mike, Chi.	64	2643	57	41.3	64	4	0	33	299	12	35.4
Barnhardt, Tommy, T.B.	81	3340	55	41.2	81	9	0	38	302	19	35.3
Walter, Ken, Car.	77	3131	59	40.7	77	5	0	20	94	20	38.1
Stryzinski, Dan, Atl.	74	2963	55	40.0	74	7	0	20	112	25	36.6
Nonqualifiers											
Sauerbrun, Todd, Chi.	15	741	71	49.4	15	3	0	5	50	6	42.1
Howard, Eddie, S.F.	9	324	45	36.0	9	1	0	2	9	2	32.8
Blanchard, Cary, Was.	3	113	43	37.7	3	0	0	1	1	1	37.3
Hanson, Jason, Det.	3	94	36	31.3	3	0	0	1	7	1	29.0
Brien, Doug, N.O.	2	72	37	36.0	2	1	0	1	0	0	26.0
Jaeger, Jeff, Chi.	1	27	27	27.0	1	0	0	0	0	0	27.0

Leader based on average, minimum 40 punts

1998 INDIVIDUAL STATISTICS—PUNT RETURNS

PUNT RETURNS

Yards Per Return
- NFC: 15.6—Deion Sanders, Dallas
- AFC: 12.9—Reggie Barlow, Jacksonville

Yards
- AFC: 555—Reggie Barlow, Jacksonville
- NFC: 506—Brian Mitchell, Washington

Yards, Game
- AFC: 134—Reggie Barlow, Jacksonville vs. Kansas City, September 13 (3 returns - TD)
- NFC: 106—Glyn Milburn, Chicago at Tampa Bay, September 20 (2 returns - TD)

Longest
- NFC: 95—Jacquez Green, Tampa Bay at Green Bay, September 13 - TD
- AFC: 87—Jermaine Lewis, Baltimore vs. Cincinnati, September 27 - TD

Returns
- NFC: 47—R.W. McQuarters, San Francisco
- AFC: 45—Desmond Howard, Oakland

Returns, Game
- AFC: 8—Desmond Howard, Oakland vs. San Diego, October 11 (76 yards)
  Latario Rachal, San Diego at Oakland, October 11 (105 yards)
- NFC: 8—Terry Fair, Detroit at Philadelphia, November 8 (43 yards)

Fair Catches
- NFC: 25—Eddie Kennison, St. Louis
- AFC: 19—Damon Gibson, Cincinnati

Touchdowns
- AFC: 2—Joey Galloway, Seattle
  Desmond Howard, Oakland
  Jermaine Lewis, Baltimore
- NFC: 2—Deion Sanders, Dallas

Team Champion
- NFC: 13.6—Tampa Bay
- AFC: 12.9—Jacksonville

AFC PUNT RETURNS—TEAM

	No.	FC	Yards	Avg.	Long	TD
Jacksonville	45	14	581	12.9	85t	1
Baltimore	43	12	541	12.6	87t	2
San Diego	45	14	542	12.0	56	0
New England	33	17	395	12.0	39	0
Miami	46	15	542	11.8	39	0
Oakland	50	14	564	11.3	75t	2
Denver	38	8	399	10.5	44	0
Seattle	41	10	428	10.4	74t	2
Indianapolis	34	11	340	10.0	53	0
Buffalo	37	11	369	10.0	73	0
Kansas City	38	12	316	8.3	37	0
Pittsburgh	33	16	269	8.2	47	0
Cincinnati	29	22	234	8.1	65t	1
Tennessee	38	17	280	7.4	25	0
N.Y. Jets	43	15	315	7.3	23	0
AFC Total	593	208	6115	10.3	87t	8
AFC Average	39.5	13.9	407.7	10.3	—	0.5

NFC PUNT RETURNS—TEAM

	No.	FC	Yards	Avg.	Long	TD
Tampa Bay	41	15	559	13.6	95t	2
New Orleans	32	24	408	12.8	76	0
Dallas	39	13	493	12.6	69t	2
Chicago	25	15	291	11.6	93t	1
Washington	44	18	506	11.5	47	0
Carolina	44	11	464	10.5	35	0
St. Louis	41	25	415	10.1	71t	1
Minnesota	29	20	289	10.0	53	0
San Francisco	47	10	406	8.6	72t	1
Green Bay	48	21	412	8.6	71t	1
Philadelphia	34	19	285	8.4	40	0
Atlanta	40	24	304	7.6	23	0
N.Y. Giants	35	22	252	7.2	39	0
Arizona	43	7	295	6.9	24	0
Detroit	36	19	212	5.9	23	0
NFC Total	578	263	5591	9.7	95t	8
NFC Average	38.5	17.5	372.7	9.7	—	0.5
League Total	1171	471	11706	—	95t	16
League Average	39.0	15.7	390.2	10.0	—	0.5

NFL TOP TEN PUNT RETURNERS

	No.	FC	Yards	Avg.	Long	TD
Sanders, Deion, Dal.	24	8	375	15.6	69t	2
Green, Jacquez, T.B.	30	9	453	15.1	95t	1
Hastings, Andre, N.O.	22	17	307	14.0	76	0
Barlow, Reggie, Jac.	43	14	555	12.9	85t	1
Lewis, Jermaine, Bal.	32	10	405	12.7	87t	2
Buckley, Terrell, Mia.	29	3	354	12.2	35	0
Rachal, Latario, S.D.	32	8	387	12.1	56	0
Howard, Desmond, Oak.	45	13	541	12.0	75t	2
Milburn, Glyn, Chi.	25	15	291	11.6	93t	1
Mitchell, Brian, Was.	44	18	506	11.5	47	0

AFC—INDIVIDUAL PUNT RETURNERS

	No.	FC	Yards	Avg.	Long	TD
Barlow, Reggie, Jac.	43	14	555	12.9	85t	1
Lewis, Jermaine, Bal.	32	10	405	12.7	87t	2
Buckley, Terrell, Mia.	29	3	354	12.2	35	0
Rachal, Latario, S.D.	32	8	387	12.1	56	0
Howard, Desmond, Oak.	45	13	541	12.0	75t	2
Gordon, Darrien, Den.	34	6	379	11.1	44	0
Galloway, Joey, Sea.	25	5	251	10.0	74t	2
Williams, Kevin, Buf.	37	11	369	10.0	73	0
Vanover, Tamarick, K.C.	27	11	264	9.8	37	0
Gibson, Damon, Cin.	27	19	218	8.1	65t	1
Mason, Derrick, Ten.	31	11	228	7.4	25	0
Johnson, Leon, NY-J	29	12	203	7.0	23	0
Nonqualifiers						
Bailey, Aaron, Ind.	19	4	176	9.3	33	0
Brown, Troy, N.E.	17	8	225	13.2	39	0
Canty, Chris, N.E.	16	7	170	10.6	36	0
Joseph, Kerry, Sea.	15	5	182	12.1	66	0
Hawkins, Courtney, Pit.	15	8	175	11.7	47	0
Gaiter, Tony, S.D.	13	6	155	11.9	49	0
McDuffie, O. J., Mia.	12	8	141	11.8	39	0
Poole, Tyrone, Ind.	12	6	107	8.9	16	0
Coleman, Andre, Pit.	10	3	53	5.3	12	0
Roe, James, Bal.	9	2	87	9.7	19	0
Ward, Dedric, NY-J	8	3	72	9.0	20	0
Archie, Mike, Ten.	7	6	52	7.4	22	0
Lockett, Kevin, K.C.	7	1	36	5.1	16	0
Jordan, Charles, Mia.	5	4	47	9.4	24	0
Meggett, David, NY-J	5	0	40	8.0	18	0
Blackwell, Will, Pit.	4	4	22	5.5	13	0
Arnold, Jahine, Pit.	4	1	19	4.8	8	0
Brown, Tim, Oak.	3	1	23	7.7	8	0
Coghill, George, Den.	3	2	20	6.7	8	0
Logan, Mike, Jac.	2	0	26	13.0	17	0
Williams, Stepfret, Cin.	2	3	16	8.0	10	0
Hughes, Danan, K.C.	2	0	10	5.0	11	0
McGuire, Kaipo, Ind.	2	1	4	2.0	4	0
Belser, Jason, Ind.	1	0	53	53.0	53	0
Thompson, Bennie, Bal.	1	0	43	43.0	43	0
Horn, Joe, K.C.	1	0	6	6.0	6	0
Johnson, Pat, Bal.	1	0	6	6.0	6	0
Brooks, Bucky, Oak.	1	0	0	0.0	0	0
Frost, Scott, NY-J	1	0	0	0.0	0	0
Paul, Tito, Den.	1	0	0	0.0	0	0
Prior, Anthony, Oak.	1	0	0	0.0	0	0
Richardson, Tony, K.C.	1	0	0	0.0	0	0
Clay, Willie, N.E.	0	2	0	—	—	0

t = Touchdown
Leader based on average return, minimum 20 returns

1998 INDIVIDUAL STATISTICS—KICKOFF RETURNS

NFC—INDIVIDUAL PUNT RETURNERS

	No.	FC	Yards	Avg.	Long	TD
Sanders, Deion, Dal.	24	8	375	15.6	69t	2
Green, Jacquez, T.B.	30	9	453	15.1	95t	1
Hastings, Andre, N.O.	22	17	307	14.0	76	0
Milburn, Glyn, Chi.	25	15	291	11.6	93t	1
Mitchell, Brian, Was.	44	18	506	11.5	47	0
Oliver, Winslow, Car.	44	11	464	10.5	35	0
Kennison, Eddie, St.L	40	25	415	10.4	71t	1
Palmer, David, Min.	28	18	289	10.3	53	0
Preston, Roell, G.B.	44	17	398	9.0	71t	1
McQuarters, R.W., S.F.	47	10	406	8.6	72t	1
Rossum, Allen, Phi.	22	7	187	8.5	25	0
Dwight, Tim, Atl.	31	13	263	8.5	23	0
Toomer, Amani, NY-G	35	22	252	7.2	39	0
Metcalf, Eric, Ariz.	43	7	295	6.9	24	0
Fair, Terry, Det.	30	15	189	6.3	23	0
Nonqualifiers						
Solomon, Freddie, Phi.	11	12	100	9.1	40	0
Guliford, Eric, N.O.	10	7	101	10.1	40	0
Hughes, Tyrone, Dal.	10	3	93	9.3	35	0
Williams, Karl, T.B.	10	6	83	8.3	18	0
Kinchen, Todd, Atl.	6	5	38	6.3	9	0
Boyd, Tommie, Det.	4	0	11	2.8	3	0
Abrams, Kevin, Det.	2	1	12	6.0	16	0
Warren, Chris, Dal.	2	1	11	5.5	6	0
Schroeder, Bill, G.B.	2	0	5	2.5	3	0
Mathis, Kevin, Dal.	2	1	3	1.5	5	0
Harris, Ronnie, Sea.-Atl.	2	6	-6	-3.0	-1	0
Barber, Ronde, T.B.	1	0	23	23.0	23t	1
Smith, Kevin, Dal.	1	0	11	11.0	11	0
Mayes, Derrick, G.B.	1	0	9	9.0	9	0
Buchanan, Ray, Atl.	1	0	4	4.0	4	0
Horne, Tony, St.L	1	0	0	0.0	0	0
Mathis, Terance, Atl.	1	0	0	0.0	0	0
Moss, Randy, Min.	1	2	0	0.0	0	0
Prior, Mike, G.B.	1	4	0	0.0	0	0
Harris, Al, Phi.	1	0	-2	-2.0	-2	0
Stablein, Brian, Det.	0	3	0	—	—	0

t = Touchdown
Leader based on average return, minimum 20 returns

KICKOFF RETURNS

Yards Per Return
NFC: 28.0—Terry Fair, Detroit
AFC: 27.6—Corey Harris, Baltimore

Yards
NFC: 1550—Glyn Milburn, Chicago
AFC: 1216—Vaughn Hebron, Denver

Yards, Game
NFC: 256—Roell Preston, Green Bay vs. Minnesota, October 5 (8 returns)
AFC: 243—Corey Harris, Baltimore vs. Minnesota, December 13 (8 returns)

Longest
NFC: 105—Terry Fair, Detroit vs. Tampa Bay, September 28 - TD
AFC: 97—Tremain Mack, Cincinnati at Baltimore, September 27 - TD
Pat Johnson, Baltimore vs. Minnesota, December 13 - TD

Returns
NFC: 62—Glyn Milburn, Chicago
AFC: 49—Desmond Howard, Oakland

Returns, Game
NFC: 9—Michael Bates, Carolina at Atlanta, October 4 (200 yards)
AFC: 8—Corey Harris, Baltimore vs. Minnesota, December 13 (243 yards)

Touchdowns
NFC: 2—Terry Fair, Detroit
Glyn Milburn, Chicago
Roell Preston, Green Bay
AFC: 1—Steve Broussard, Seattle
Corey Harris, Baltimore
Vaughn Hebron, Denver
Pat Johnson, Baltimore
Tremain Mack, Cincinnati

Team Champion
NFC: 25.8 Green Bay
AFC: 24.6 Baltimore

AFC KICKOFF RETURNS—TEAM

	No.	Yards	Avg.	Long	TD
Baltimore	69	1700	24.6	97t	2
Miami	53	1297	24.5	55	0
Denver	58	1402	24.2	95t	1
Cincinnati	72	1710	23.8	97t	1
Seattle	64	1510	23.6	90t	1
N.Y. Jets	57	1285	22.5	62	0
Jacksonville	61	1366	22.4	91	0
New England	62	1330	21.5	68	0
Kansas City	63	1319	20.9	62	0
Buffalo	56	1168	20.9	46	0
Tennessee	56	1148	20.5	50	0
Pittsburgh	55	1112	20.2	44	0
Indianapolis	71	1432	20.2	44	0
Oakland	62	1208	19.5	42	0
San Diego	70	1293	18.5	36	0
AFC Total	929	20280	21.8	97t	5
AFC Average	61.9	1352.0	21.8	—	0.3

NFC KICKOFF RETURNS—TEAM

	No.	Yards	Avg.	Long	TD
Green Bay	60	1547	25.8	101t	2
Atlanta	46	1157	25.2	93t	1
Detroit	68	1700	25.0	105t	2
Chicago	66	1595	24.2	94t	2
Carolina	76	1834	24.1	99t	1
Tampa Bay	59	1399	23.7	60	0
Dallas	51	1191	23.4	42	0
Minnesota	54	1238	22.9	88t	1
Philadelphia	60	1363	22.7	54	0
New Orleans	62	1354	21.8	100t	1
St. Louis	68	1472	21.6	102t	1
Washington	70	1512	21.6	101t	1
Arizona	63	1314	20.9	59	0
N.Y. Giants	66	1286	19.5	90t	1
San Francisco	59	1108	18.8	45	0
NFC Total	928	21070	22.7	105t	13
NFC Average	61.9	1404.7	22.7	—	0.9
League Total	1857	41350	—	105t	18
League Average	61.9	1378.3	22.3	—	0.6

NFL TOP TEN KICKOFF RETURNERS

	No.	Yards	Avg.	Long	TD
Fair, Terry, Det.	51	1428	28.0	105t	2
Harris, Corey, Bal.	35	965	27.6	95t	1
Dwight, Tim, Atl.	36	973	27.0	93t	1
Broussard, Steve, Sea.	29	781	26.9	90t	1
Hebron, Vaughn, Den.	46	1216	26.4	95t	1
Preston, Roell, G.B.	57	1497	26.3	101t	2
Mack, Tremain, Cin.	45	1165	25.9	97t	1
Avery, John, Mia.	43	1085	25.2	55	0
Bates, Michael, Car.	59	1480	25.1	99t	1
Dunn, David, Pit.	21	525	25.0	44	0
Milburn, Glyn, Chi.	62	1550	25.0	94t	2

1998 INDIVIDUAL STATISTICS—KICKOFF RETURNS

AFC KICKOFF RETURNERS—INDIVIDUAL

	No.	Yards	Avg.	Long	TD
Harris, Corey, Bal.	35	965	27.6	95t	1
Broussard, Steve, Sea.	29	781	26.9	90t	1
Hebron, Vaughn, Den.	46	1216	26.4	95t	1
Mack, Tremain, Cin.	45	1165	25.9	97t	1
Avery, John, Mia.	43	1085	25.2	55	0
Dunn, David, Pit.	21	525	25.0	44	0
Barlow, Reggie, Jac.	30	747	24.9	91	0
Glenn, Aaron, NY-J	24	585	24.4	62	0
Cullors, Derrick, N.E.	45	1085	24.1	68	0
Vanover, Tamarick, K.C.	41	956	23.3	62	0
Green, Ahman, Sea.	27	620	23.0	57	0
Williams, Kevin, Buf.	47	1059	22.5	46	0
Bailey, Aaron, Ind.	34	759	22.3	44	0
Archie, Mike, Ten.	42	913	21.7	50	0
Howard, Desmond, Oak.	49	1040	21.2	42	0
Blackwell, Will, Pit.	20	382	19.1	43	0
Nonqualifiers					
Bynum, Kenny, S.D.	19	345	18.2	30	0
Logan, Mike, Jac.	18	414	23.0	53	0
Gibson, Damon, Cin.	17	372	21.9	30	0
Johnson, Pat, Bal.	16	399	24.9	97t	1
Johnson, Leon, NY-J	16	366	22.9	37	0
Stephens, Tremayne, S.D.	16	349	21.8	36	0
Gaiter, Tony, S.D.	16	295	18.4	33	0
Elias, Keith, Ind.	14	317	22.6	29	0
Horn, Joe, K.C.	11f	233	21.2	37	0
Williams, Kevin, NY-J	11	230	20.9	31	0
Canty, Chris, N.E.	11	198	18.0	29	0
Rachal, Latario, S.D.	11	192	17.5	25	0
Mason, Derrick, Ten.	8	154	19.3	26	0
Warren, Lamont, Ind.	8	152	19.0	26	0
Lewis, Jermaine, Bal.	6	145	24.2	37	0
Huntley, Richard, Pit.	6	119	19.8	26	0
Marion, Brock, Mia.	6	109	18.2	28	0
Loville, Derek, Den.	6	105	17.5	25	0
Banks, Tavian, Jac.	5	133	26.6	65	0
Bieniemy, Eric, Cin.	5	87	17.4	22	0
Hetherington, Chris, Ind.	5	71	14.2	20	0
Branch, Calvin, Oak.	5	70	14.0	27	0
Jacquet, Nate, Mia.	4	103	25.8	37	0
McGuire, Kaipo, Ind.	4	75	18.8	28	0
Shehee, Rashaan, K.C.	4	72	18.0	20	0
Williams, Rodney, Oak.	4	63	15.8	21	0
Brown, Reggie, Sea.	4	44	11.0	19	0
Arnold, Jahine, Pit.	3	78	26.0	31	0
Fletcher, Terrell, S.D.	3	71	23.7	36	0
Thomas, Rodney, Ten.	3	64	21.3	39	0
Bennett, Brandon, Cin.	3	61	20.3	21	0
Ward, Dedric, NY-J	3	60	20.0	23	0
Graham, Jay, Bal.	3	52	17.3	22	0
Smith, Detron, Den.	3	51	17.0	21	0
Gash, Sam, Buf.	3	41	13.7	17	0
Clark, Rico, Ind.	3	38	12.7	15	0
Manusky, Greg, K.C.	3	20	6.7	12	0
Johnson, Lonnie, Buf.	3	18	6.0	16	0
Joseph, Kerry, Sea.	2	49	24.5	24	0
Roe, James, Bal.	2	40	20.0	27	0
Cotton, Kenyon, Bal.	2	33	16.5	18	0
Kinchen, Brian, Bal.	2	33	16.5	21	0
Shedd, Kenny, Oak.	2	32	16.0	21	0
Holmes, Priest, Bal.	2	30	15.0	19	0
Mitchell, Pete, Jac.	2	27	13.5	14	0
Jones, Charlie, S.D.	2	25	12.5	17	0
Parten, Ty, K.C.	2	22	11.0	22	0
Burns, Keith, Den.	2	17	8.5	17	0
Sullivan, Chris, N.E.	2	14	7.0	9	0
Jones, Damon, Jac.	2	-1	-0.5	0	0
Lyons, Mitch, Pit.	2	-4	-2.0	6	0
Cummings, Joe, Buf.	1	21	21.0	21	0
Jones, George, Jac.	1	21	21.0	21	0
Brady, Kyle, NY-J	1	20	20.0	20	0
Holmes, Darick, Buf.	1	20	20.0	20	0
Williams, Stepfret, Cin.	1	20	20.0	20	0
Anders, Kimble, K.C.	1	16	16.0	16	0
Meggett, David, NY-J	1	16	16.0	16	0
Shaw, Sedrick, N.E.	1	16	16.0	16	0
Wilson, Robert, Sea.	1	16	16.0	16	0
McCardell, Keenan, Jac.	1	15	15.0	15	0
Dilger, Ken, Ind.	1	14	14.0	14	0
Eaton, Chad, N.E.	1	13	13.0	13	0
Tanuvasa, Maa, Den.	1	13	13.0	13	0
Hartley, Frank, S.D.	1	11	11.0	11	0
McAfee, Fred, Pit.	1	10	10.0	25	0
Wycheck, Frank, Ten.	1	10	10.0	10	0
Gibson, Oliver, Pit.	1	9	9.0	9	0
Riemersma, Jay, Buf.	1	9	9.0	9	0
Baxter, Fred, NY-J	1	8	8.0	8	0
Battaglia, Marco, Cin.	1	5	5.0	5	0
Burke, John, S.D.	1	5	5.0	5	0
Bruschi, Tedy, N.E.	1	4	4.0	4	0
Pollard, Marcus, Ind.	1	4	4.0	4	0
Roan, Michael, Ten.	1	4	4.0	11	0
Harris, Jackie, Ten.	1	3	3.0	3	0
Morton, Mike, Oak.	1	3	3.0	3	0
Potts, Roosevelt, Bal.	1	3	3.0	3	0
Morrison, Steve, Ind.	1	2	2.0	2	0
Amey, Vincent, Oak.	1	0	0.0	0	0
Fauria, Christian, Sea.	1	0	0.0	0	0
Fordham, Todd, Jac.	1	0	0.0	0	0
Jacox, Kendyl, S.D.	1	0	0.0	0	0
Ransom, Derrick, K.C.	1f	0	0.0	0	0
Roye, Orpheus, Pit.	1	0	0.0	0	0
Sadowski, Troy, Jac.	1	0	0.0	0	0
Whigham, Larry, N.E.	1	0	0.0	0	0
Moore, Will, Jac.	0	10	—	10	0
Bruener, Mark, Pit.	0	-7	—	-7	0

t = Touchdown
f = Fair Catch
Leader based on average return, minimum 20 returns

NFC KICKOFF RETURNERS—INDIVIDUAL

	No.	Yards	Avg.	Long	TD
Fair, Terry, Det.	51	1428	28.0	105t	2
Dwight, Tim, Atl.	36f	973	27.0	93t	1
Preston, Roell, G.B.	57	1497	26.3	101t	2
Bates, Michael, Car.	59	1480	25.1	99t	1
Milburn, Glyn, Chi.	62	1550	25.0	94t	2
Mathis, Kevin, Dal.	25	621	24.8	42	0
Rossum, Allen, Phi.	44	1080	24.5	54	0
Anthony, Reidel, T.B.	46	1118	24.3	60	0
Palmer, David, Min.	50	1176	23.5	88t	1
Horne, Tony, St.L	56	1306	23.3	102t	1
Mitchell, Brian, Was.	59	1337	22.7	101t	1
Patten, David, NY-G	43	928	21.6	90t	1
Metcalf, Eric, Ariz	57	1218	21.4	59	0
Ismail, Qadry, N.O.	28	590	21.1	39	0
Levy, Chuck, S.F.	22	383	17.4	30	0
Nonqualifiers					
Guliford, Eric, N.O.	18	431	23.9	34	0
Kirby, Terry, S.F.	17	340	20.0	33	0
McQuarters, R.W., S.F.	17	339	19.9	45	0
Barber, Tiki, NY-G	14	250	17.9	32	0
Hughes, Tyrone, Dal.	11	274	24.9	36	0
Green, Jacquez, T.B.	10	229	22.9	44	0
Stone, Dwight, Car.	9	252	28.0	45	0
Boyd, Tommie, Det.	8	163	20.4	26	0
Walker, Corey, Phi.	8	150	18.8	28	0
Craver, Aaron, N.O.	7	212	30.3	100t	1
Williams, Elijah, Atl.	7	132	18.9	28	0
Thrash, James, Was.	6	129	21.5	39	0
McPhail, Jerris, Det.	6	71	11.8	20	0
Warren, Chris, Dal.	5	90	18.0	23	0
Fletcher, London, St.L	5	72	14.4	20	0
Williams, Sherman, Dal.	4	103	25.8	40	0
Pittman, Michael, Ariz	4	84	21.0	22	0
Thomas, J.T., St.L	4	79	19.8	24	0
Toomer, Amani, NY-G	4	66	16.5	31	0
Little, Earl, N.O.	4	64	16.0	20	0
Ogden, Jeff, Dal.	3	65	21.7	28	0
Copeland, Russell, Phi.	3	52	17.3	23	0
Palelei, Lonnie, NY-G	3	14	4.7	13	0
Oliver, Winslow, Car.	2	43	21.5	25	0
Tate, Robert, Min.	2	43	21.5	23	0
Smith, Irv, S.F.	2	35	17.5	23	0
Bradford, Corey, G.B.	2	33	16.5	24	0
Sellers, Mike, Was.	2	33	16.5	14	0
Davis, Troy, N.O.	2	21	10.5	19	0
Williams, Moe, Min.	2	19	9.5	12	0
Chancey, Robert, Chi.	2	18	9.0	18	0
Rivers, Ron, Det.	2	15	7.5	9	0
Gedney, Chris, Ariz	2	12	6.0	7	0
Johnson, Anthony, Car.	2	12	6.0	9	0

	No.	Yards	Avg.	Long	TD
Dunn, Warrick, T.B.	1	25	25.0	25	0
Green, Harold, Atl.	1	24	24.0	24	0
Vardell, Tommy, Det.	1	23	23.0	23	0
Floyd, William, Car.	1	22	22.0	22	0
Hayden, Aaron, Phi.	1	22	22.0	22	0
Bech, Brett, N.O.	1	20	20.0	20	0
Bownes, Fabien, Chi.	1	19	19.0	19	0
Ellison, Jerry, T.B.	1	19	19.0	19	0
Staley, Duce, Phi.	1	19	19.0	19	0
Hankton, Karl, Phi.	1	18	18.0	18	0
McKenzie, Keith, G.B.	1	17	17.0	17	0
Harris, Ronnie, Atl.	1	16	16.0	16	0
Hastings, Andre, N.O.	1	16	16.0	16	0
Sanders, Deion, Dal.	1	16	16.0	16	0
Wheatley, Tyrone, NY-G	1	16	16.0	16	0
Turner, Kevin, Phi.	1	15	15.0	15	0
Henley, June, St.L	1	13	13.0	13	0
Comella, Greg, NY-G	1	12	12.0	12	0
Kozlowski, Brian, Atl.	1	12	12.0	12	0
LaFleur, David, Dal.	1	12	12.0	12	0
Richie, David, S.F.	1f	11	11.0	11	0
Davis, Billy, Dal.	1	10	10.0	10	0
Jensen, Jerry, Car.	1	9	9.0	9	0
Alstott, Mike, T.B.	1	8	8.0	8	0
Asher, Jamie, Was.	1	8	8.0	8	0
Brady, Jeff, Car.	1	8	8.0	8	0
Saleh, Tarek, Car.	1	8	8.0	8	0
Wiegmann, Casey, Chi.	1	8	8.0	8	0
Brooks, Barrett, Phi.	1	7	7.0	7	0
Burnett, Chester, Was.	1	5	5.0	5	0
Jones, Mike D., St.L	1	2	2.0	2	0
Clemons, Charlie, St.L	1	0	0.0	0	0
Jenkins, James, Was.	1	0	0.0	0	0
Tomich, Jared, N.O.	1	0	0.0	0	0

t = Touchdown
f = Fair Catch
Leader based on average return, minimum 20 returns

FUMBLES

Most Fumbles
NFC: 14—Trent Green, Washington
AFC: 10—Donald Hollas, Oakland

Most Fumbles, Game
NFC: 6—Brett Favre, Green Bay at Tampa Bay, December 7
AFC: 4—Jeff George, Oakland at Kansas City, September 6
Ryan Leaf, San Diego at Kansas City, September 20

Own Fumbles Recovered
NFC: 8—Tony Banks, St. Louis
AFC: 4—Drew Bledsoe, New England
Doug Flutie, Buffalo
Rich Gannon, Kansas City
Eddie George, Tennessee
Donald Hollas, Oakland
Jon Kitna, Seattle

Most Own Fumbles Recovered, Game
AFC: 2—by many
NFC: 2—by many

Opponents' Fumbles Recovered
AFC: 4—Chris Oldham, Pittsburgh
Bryan Schwartz, Jacksonville
NFC: 4—Travis Hall, Atlanta
Simeon Rice, Arizona

Most Opponents' Fumbles Recovered, Game
AFC: 3—Darryl Williams, Seattle at Kansas City, October 4
NFC: 3—Stephen Boyd, Detroit at Chicago, October 4

Yards
NFC: 157—Dwayne Rudd, Minnesota
AFC: 120—Aaron Beasley, Jacksonville

Longest
NFC: 94—Dwayne Rudd, Minnesota vs. Chicago, December 6 - TD
AFC: 90—Aaron Beasley, Jacksonville vs. Cincinnati, November 8 - TD

AFC FUMBLES—TEAM

	Fum.	Own Rec.	Fum. OB	TD	Opp. Rec.	TD	Fum. Yards	Tot. Rec.
Indianapolis	10	4	1	0	11	0	27	15
Buffalo	17	10	1	0	13	1	40	23
Denver	17	9	2	1	11	0	-25	20
Jacksonville	18	10	0	0	17	2	212	27
Pittsburgh	18	6	1	1	13	0	53	19
New England	20	12	1	0	7	0	5	19
Cincinnati	21	10	1	0	7	1	93	17
N.Y. Jets	23	11	1	0	9	2	86	20
Miami	25	12	1	0	7	0	-8	19
Tennessee	25	15	1	0	7	2	20	22
Seattle	30	14	0	0	18	2	40	32
Baltimore	31	14	2	0	5	0	-48	19
San Diego	33	16	0	0	7	0	-18	23
Kansas City	35	18	3	0	20	1	69	38
Oakland	38	18	2	1	14	1	79	32
AFC Total	361	179	17	3	166	12	625	345
AFC Average	24.1	11.9	1.1	0.2	11.1	0.8	41.7	23.0

NFC FUMBLES—TEAM

	Fum.	Own Rec.	Fum. OB	TD	Opp. Rec.	TD	Fum. Yards	Tot. Rec.
Minnesota	10	5	1	0	15	2	197	20
Detroit	17	4	1	0	9	0	-1	13
N.Y. Giants	17	7	1	0	7	0	0	14
Dallas	18	9	2	0	12	1	-7	21
Philadelphia	20	11	1	0	8	0	22	19
San Francisco	22	6	1	0	12	0	7	18
Tampa Bay	23	7	3	0	14	0	10	21
Atlanta	24	13	2	0	25	4	120	38
Green Bay	27	10	6	0	10	2	127	20
Washington	27	10	2	0	7	0	-8	17
New Orleans	28	11	3	0	11	4	93	22
Chicago	29	7	1	0	14	1	13	21
Arizona	30	13	1	0	19	0	56	32
St. Louis	32	16	1	0	7	0	26	23
Carolina	39	21	2	0	14	0	5	35
NFC Total	363	150	28	0	184	14	660	334
NFC Average	24.2	10.0	1.9	0.0	12.3	0.9	44.0	22.3
League Total	724	329	45	3	350	26	1285	679
League Average	24.1	11.0	1.5	0.1	11.7	0.9	42.8	22.6

Fum OB = Fumbled out of bounds, includes fumbled through the end zone.

AFC TOUCHDOWNS ON FUMBLE RECOVERIES

1—Ashmore, Darryl, Oak.; 1—Beasley, Aaron, Jac.; 1—Bowden, Joe, Ten.; 1—Cascadden, Chad, NYJ; 1—Darius, Donovin, Jac.; 1—Hansen, Phil, Buf.; 1—Henderson, Jerome, NYJ; 1—Johnstone, Lance, Oak.; 1—Kennedy, Cortez, Sea.; 1—Oldham, Chris, Pit.; 1—Roan, Michael, Ten.; 1—Shade, Sam, Cin.; 1—Smith, Rod, Den.; 1—Springs, Shawn, Sea.; 1—Thomas, Derrick, K.C.

NFC TOUCHDOWNS ON FUMBLE RECOVERIES

2—Rudd, Dwayne, Min.; 1—Butler, LeRoy, G.B.; 1—Edwards, Antonio, Atl.; 1—Fields, Mark, N.O.; 1—Johnson, Joe, N.O.; 1—Lee, Shawn, Chi.; 1—McKenzie, Keith, G.B.; 1—Mitchell, Keith, N.O.; 1—Robbins, Austin, N.O.; 1—Smith, Chuck, Atl.; 1—Tuggle, Jessie, Atl.; 1—Wheaton, Kenny, Dal.; 1—White, William, Atl.

1998 INDIVIDUAL STATISTICS—FUMBLES

AFC FUMBLES—INDIVIDUAL

	Fum.	Own Rec.	Opp. Rec.	Yards	Tot. Rec.
Abdul-Jabbar, Karim, Mia	2	1	0	0	1
Adams, Sam, Sea	0	0	1	0	1
Aguiar, Louie, K.C	0	0	1	0	1
Albright, Ethan, Buf	0	0	1	0	1
Alexander, Elijah, Ind	0	0	2	0	2
Anders, Kimble, K.C	6	1	0	0	1
Anderson, Willie, Cin	0	1	0	0	1
Archie, Mike, Ten	3	0	0	0	0
Armstrong, Bruce, N.E	0	3	0	0	3
Armstrong, Trace, Mia	0	0	1	2	1
Ashmore, Darryl, Oak	0	1	0	1	1
Avery, John, Mia	5	2	0	0	2
Bailey, Aaron, Ind	2	1	0	0	1
Ballard, Howard, Sea	0	1	1	0	2
Banks, Tavian, Jac	2	1	0	0	1
Bankston, Michael, Cin	0	0	1	5	1
Banta, Brad, Ind	0	0	1	0	1
Barlow, Reggie, Jac	1	1	0	0	1
Barndt, Tom, K.C	0	0	2	0	2
Battaglia, Marco, Cin	1	3	0	0	3
Baxter, Fred, NY-J	0	1	0	0	1
Beasley, Aaron, Jac	0	0	1	120	1
Bellamy, Jay, Sea	0	0	2	0	2
Belser, Jason, Ind	0	0	1	0	1
Bennett, Brandon, Cin	1	1	0	0	1
Bennett, Darren, S.D	1	1	0	0	1
Bennett, Donnell, K.C	4	0	0	0	0
Bettis, Jerome, Pit	2	0	0	0	0
Biekert, Greg, Oak	0	0	1	0	1
Bieniemy, Eric, Cin	1	0	0	0	0
Bishop, Blaine, Ten	0	0	1	0	1
Blackwell, Will, Pit	1	0	0	0	0
Blades, Brian, Sea	1	0	0	0	0
Blair, Michael, Cin	1	1	0	0	1
Blake, Jeff, Cin	1	0	0	0	0
Bledsoe, Drew, N.E	9	4	0	-10	4
Boselli, Tony, Jac	0	1	0	2	1
Boulware, Peter, Bal	0	0	1	0	1
Bowden, Joe, Ten	0	0	2	17	2
Brackens, Tony, Jac	0	0	3	8	3
Brady, Kyle, NY-J	1	0	0	0	0
Branch, Calvin, Oak	1	1	0	0	1
Brister, Bubby, Den	2	1	0	-1	1
Bromell, Lorenzo, Mia	0	0	1	0	1
Brooks, Bucky, Oak	1	0	0	0	0
Broussard, Steve, Sea	1	1	0	0	1
Brown, Chad, Sea	0	0	1	0	1
Brown, Corwin, NY-J	0	0	1	16	1
Brown, Derek, Oak	0	1	0	0	1
Brown, Eric, Den	0	0	1	0	1
Brown, Lance, Pit	0	0	2	1	2
Brown, Tim, Oak	3	2	0	0	2
Brunell, Mark, Jac	3	2	0	-1	2
Buckley, Terrell, Mia	1	1	1	0	2
Burger, Todd, NY-J	0	2	0	0	2
Burnett, Rob, Bal	0	0	1	0	1
Burns, Keith, Den	1	1	0	0	1
Burton, Shane, Mia	0	0	1	0	1
Bynum, Kenny, S.D	3	2	0	0	2
Byrd, Isaac, Ten	0	1	0	0	1
Canty, Chris, N.E	2	0	0	0	0
Cascadden, Chad, NY-J	0	0	2	23	2
Clay, Willie, N.E	0	0	1	3	1
Coleman, Andre, Pit	1	0	0	0	0
Coleman, Marco, S.D	0	0	2	0	2
Crockett, Zack, Ind	1	0	0	0	0
Cullors, Derrick, N.E	1	0	0	0	0
Daniels, Phillip, Sea	0	0	2	0	2
Darius, Donovin, Jac	0	0	1	83	1
Davis, Terrell, Den	2	1	0	0	1
Davis, Travis, Jac	0	0	1	0	1
Davis, Wendell, S.D	0	1	0	0	1
Dawson, Dermontti, Pit	1	0	0	-25	0
Dillon, Corey, Cin	2	0	0	0	0
Dixon, Mark, Mia	0	2	0	0	2
Donnalley, Kevin, Mia	0	1	0	0	1
Dudley, Rickey, Oak	1	0	0	0	0
Dunn, David, Pit	1	0	0	0	0
Eaton, Chad, N.E	0	0	1	2	1
Edwards, Donnie, K.C	0	0	1	0	1
Edwards, Robert, N.E	5	2	0	0	2
Elway, John, Den	7	2	0	-18	2
Emmons, Carlos, Pit	0	0	1	0	1
Farrior, James, NY-J	0	0	1	0	1
Faulk, Marshall, Ind	3	2	0	13	2
Fauria, Christian, Sea	1	1	0	0	1
Favors, Greg, K.C	0	1	0	41	1
Fletcher, Terrell, S.D	1	2	0	21	2
Flowers, Lethon, Pit	0	0	2	0	2
Flutie, Doug, Buf	3	4	0	-13	4
Foley, Glenn, NY-J	1	0	0	0	0
Fontenot, Al, Ind	0	0	1	0	1
Ford, Henry, Ten	0	0	1	0	1
Fordham, Todd, Jac	0	1	0	0	1
Frost, Scott, NY-J	1	0	0	0	0
Gadsden, Oronde, Mia	2	0	0	0	0
Gaiter, Tony, S.D	1	0	0	0	0
Galloway, Joey, Sea	1	0	0	0	0
Gannon, Rich, K.C	9	4	0	-15	4
George, Eddie, Ten	7	4	1	0	5
George, Jeff, Oak	7	1	0	-6	1
George, Ron, K.C	0	0	1	0	1
Gibson, Damon, Cin	3	1	0	0	1
Gildon, Jason, Pit	0	0	1	0	1
Glenn, Aaron, NY-J	1	1	0	0	1
Gonzalez, Tony, K.C	3	0	0	0	0
Gordon, Darrien, Den	1	0	1	0	1
Granville, Billy, Cin	0	0	1	0	1
Grbac, Elvis, K.C	1	0	1	0	1
Green, Ahman, Sea	1	1	0	0	1
Green, Eric, Bal	4	0	0	0	0
Green, Victor, NY-J	0	0	1	0	1
Greer, Donovan, Buf	0	0	1	18	1
Griese, Brian, Den	1	0	0	-1	0
Habib, Brian, Sea	0	2	0	0	2
Hamilton, Michael, S.D	0	0	1	0	1
Hansen, Phil, Buf	0	0	3	13	3
Harbaugh, Jim, Bal	7	3	0	-7	3
Hardy, Kevin, Jac	0	0	1	0	1
Harlow, Pat, Oak	0	2	0	0	2
Harris, Corey, Bal	2	1	0	0	1
Harris, James, Oak	0	0	1	1	1
Hasty, James, K.C	0	0	1	0	1
Hawkins, Artrell, Cin	0	0	1	25	1
Hawkins, Courtney, Pit	1	1	0	0	1
Hebron, Vaughn, Den	0	1	0	0	1
Henderson, Jerome, NY-J	1	0	1	53	1
Hetherington, Chris, Ind	1	0	0	0	0
Hicks, Eric, K.C	0	1	0	0	1
Hollas, Donald, Oak	10	4	0	0	4
Hollier, Dwight, Mia	0	0	1	0	1
Holmes, Priest, Bal	3	1	0	1	1
Horn, Joe, K.C	2	2	1	-8	3
Howard, Desmond, Oak	4	0	0	0	0
Hudson, Chris, Jac	0	0	1	0	1
Hughes, Danan, K.C	0	1	1	0	2
Huntley, Richard, Pit	5	0	0	0	0
Jackson, Grady, Oak	0	0	1	2	1
Jackson, Greg, S.D	0	1	0	0	1
Jackson, Michael, Bal	1	0	0	0	0
James, Tory, Den	0	0	1	0	1
Jefferson, Shawn, N.E	0	1	0	0	1
Jenkins, DeRon, Bal	0	1	0	0	1
Jett, James, Oak	0	1	0	4	1
Johnson, Leon, NY-J	3	3	0	0	3
Johnson, Lonnie, Buf	1	0	0	0	0
Johnson, Pat, Bal	1	0	0	0	0
Johnson, Pepper, NY-J	0	0	1	0	1
Johnson, Rob, Buf	2	1	0	-1	1
Johnstone, Lance, Oak	0	0	1	40	1
Jones, Charlie, S.D	1	0	0	0	0
Jones, Damon, Jac	1	0	0	0	0
Jones, Freddie, S.D	1	0	0	0	0
Jones, James, Bal	0	0	1	0	1
Jones, Tebucky, N.E	0	1	0	0	1
Jordan, Charles, Mia	2	1	0	0	1
Jordan, Randy, Oak	1	0	0	0	0
Joseph, Kerry, Sea	1	0	0	0	0
Kaufman, Napoleon, Oak	2	1	0	0	1
Kennedy, Cortez, Sea	0	0	1	39	1
Kennedy, Lincoln, Oak	0	1	0	27	1

1998 INDIVIDUAL STATISTICS—FUMBLES

	Fum.	Own Rec.	Opp. Rec.	Yards	Tot. Rec.
Kitna, Jon, Sea	6	4	0	-10	4
Krieg, Dave, Ten	3	1	0	-2	1
LaBounty, Matt, Sea	1	0	1	13	1
Lake, Carnell, Pit	0	0	1	-2	1
Law, Ty, N.E	0	0	1	17	1
Layman, Jason, Ten	0	1	0	0	1
Leaf, Ryan, S.D	8	2	0	-18	2
LeBel, Harper, Bal	1	0	0	-31	0
Leeuwenburg, Jay, Ind	0	1	0	0	1
Lewis, Jermaine, Bal	3	3	0	0	3
Lewis, Mo, NY-J	1	0	1	0	1
Linton, Jonathan, Buf	0	1	0	0	1
Lockett, Kevin, K.C	2	2	0	0	2
Logan, Mike, Jac	1	0	1	2	1
Loud, Kamil, Buf	0	0	1	0	1
Mack, Tremain, Cin	2	1	0	0	1
Manning, Peyton, Ind	3	0	0	0	0
Manusky, Greg, K.C	0	0	2	7	2
Marino, Dan, Mia	9	2	0	-9	2
Marion, Brock, Mia	0	0	1	2	1
Martin, Curtis, NY-J	5	1	0	0	1
Martin, Emanuel, Buf	0	0	1	0	1
Mason, Derrick, Ten	1	1	0	0	1
Matthews, Bruce, Ten	0	1	0	0	1
McCaffrey, Ed, Den	1	0	0	0	0
McEndoo, Jason, Sea	1	0	0	-4	0
McGlockton, Chester, K.C	0	0	1	0	1
McNair, Steve, Ten	5	3	0	-7	3
Means, Natrone, S.D	2	1	0	0	1
Mickens, Ray, NY-J	0	0	1	0	1
Mickens, Terry, Oak	0	1	1	3	2
Milloy, Lawyer, N.E	0	0	1	0	1
Milne, Brian, Cin	0	1	0	0	1
Mitchell, Jeff, Bal	1	0	0	-11	0
Mitchell, Pete, Jac	0	1	0	0	1
Mobley, John, Den	0	0	1	0	1
Montgomery, Monty, Ind	0	0	2	14	2
Moon, Warren, Sea	8	1	0	-12	1
Moore, Marty, N.E	0	0	1	0	1
Moore, Ronald, Mia	1	0	0	0	0
Morris, Bam, K.C	3	1	0	0	1
Morton, Mike, Oak	0	0	2	0	2
Myers, Greg, Cin	0	0	1	0	1
Myles, DeShone, Sea	0	0	1	0	1
O'Donnell, Neil, Cin	6	1	0	-2	1
Oldham, Chris, Pit	0	1	4	79	5
O'Neal, Leslie, K.C	0	0	2	0	2
Parker, Glenn, K.C	0	1	0	0	1
Parmalee, Bernie, Mia	2	1	1	0	2
Parrella, John, S.D	0	0	1	0	1
Parten, Ty, K.C	0	0	1	0	1
Paul, Tito, Den	1	0	1	0	1
Perry, Darren, Pit	1	0	1	0	1
Phenix, Perry, Ten	0	0	1	18	1
Pickens, Carl, Cin	2	0	0	0	0
Potts, Roosevelt, Bal	4	2	0	0	2
Prior, Anthony, Oak	1	0	0	0	0
Pritchard, Mike, Sea	1	0	0	0	0
Pritchett, Stanley, Mia	0	1	0	0	1
Quinn, Jonathan, Jac	3	0	0	0	0
Rachal, Latario, S.D	4	1	0	0	1
Richardson, Kyle, Bal	0	1	0	0	1
Richardson, Tony, K.C	0	1	0	0	1
Richardson, Wally, Bal	1	0	0	0	0
Ricks, Mikhael, S.D	1	0	0	0	0
Riddick, Louis, Oak	0	0	1	0	1
Riemersma, Jay, Buf	0	0	1	0	1
Riley, Victor, K.C	0	1	0	0	1
Rison, Andre, K.C	1	1	0	0	1
Ritchie, Jon, Oak	2	0	0	0	0
Roan, Michael, Ten	1	0	1	0	1
Romanowski, Bill, Den	0	0	3	0	3
Rouen, Tom, Den	1	0	0	-15	0
Roundtree, Raleigh, S.D	0	1	0	0	1
Ruddy, Tim, Mia	1	0	0	-3	0
Russell, Darrell, Oak	0	0	1	0	1
Sanders, Chris, Ten	1	0	0	0	0
Schulz, Kurt, Buf	0	0	1	9	1
Schwartz, Bryan, Jac	0	0	4	0	4
Seau, Junior, S.D	0	0	2	0	2
Shade, Sam, Cin	0	0	2	55	2
Shaw, Sedrick, N.E	2	1	0	-7	1
Shedd, Kenny, Oak	0	0	2	4	2
Shehee, Rashaan, K.C	2	0	0	0	0
Shello, Kendel, Ind	0	0	1	0	1
Shields, Will, K.C	0	1	0	0	1
Simmons, Brian, Cin	0	0	1	22	1
Simmons, Wayne, K.C	0	0	2	17	2
Siragusa, Tony, Bal	0	0	1	0	1
Smeenge, Joel, Jac	0	0	1	0	1
Smith, Antowain, Buf	5	2	0	0	2
Smith, Bruce, Buf	0	0	2	18	2
Smith, Darrin, Sea	0	0	2	0	2
Smith, Fernando, Jac	0	0	1	0	1
Smith, Jimmy, Jac	2	2	0	0	2
Smith, Rod, Den	0	2	0	11	2
Smith, Thomas, Buf	0	0	1	0	1
Sowell, Jerald, NY-J	2	0	0	0	0
Springs, Shawn, Sea	0	1	1	14	2
Staten, Ralph, Bal	1	0	0	0	0
Stephens, Tremayne, S.D	1	0	0	0	0
Stepnoski, Mark, Ten	2	1	0	-6	1
Stewart, James, Jac	2	0	0	-11	0
Stewart, Kordell, Pit	3	2	0	0	2
Strong, Mack, Sea	2	1	0	0	1
Stuckey, Shawn, N.E	0	0	1	0	1
Swayne, Harry, Den	0	1	0	0	1
Swilling, Pat, Oak	0	0	1	0	1
Tanuvasa, Maa, Den	0	0	2	-1	2
Taylor, Aaron, S.D	0	1	0	0	1
Taylor, Fred, Jac	3	1	0	9	1
Testaverde, Vinny, NY-J	7	3	0	-6	3
Thomas, Dave, Jac	0	0	1	0	1
Thomas, Derrick, K.C	0	0	2	27	2
Thomas, Fred, Sea	0	0	1	0	1
Thomas, Henry, N.E	0	0	1	0	1
Tomczak, Mike, Pit	2	0	0	0	0
Tongue, Reggie, K.C	0	0	1	0	1
Traylor, Keith, Den	0	0	1	0	1
Truitt, Greg, Cin	1	0	0	-12	0
Tuinei, Van, Ind	0	0	1	0	1
Vanover, Tamarick, K.C	2	0	0	0	0
Walker, Marquis, Oak	0	0	1	3	1
Wallace, Aaron, Oak	0	0	1	0	1
Washington, Dewayne, Pit	0	1	1	0	2
Watters, Ricky, Sea	4	1	0	0	1
Whelihan, Craig, S.D	9	3	0	-21	3
Whittington, Bernard, Ind	0	0	2	0	2
Wiley, Marcellus, Buf	0	0	1	15	1
Williams, Darryl, Sea	0	0	3	0	3
Williams, Gerome, S.D	0	0	1	0	1
Williams, Harvey, Oak	3	1	0	0	1
Williams, John, Bal	0	0	1	0	1
Williams, Kevin, Buf	3	2	0	0	2
Williams, Rodney, Oak	1	0	0	0	0
Williams, Wally, Bal	0	1	0	0	1
Williams, Willie, Sea	0	0	1	0	1
Wilson, Wade, Oak	1	0	0	0	0
Wolford, Will, Pit	0	1	0	0	1
Wooden, Terry, Oak	0	1	0	0	1
Wycheck, Frank, Ten	2	2	0	0	2
Wynn, Renaldo, Jac	0	0	1	0	1
Zeier, Eric, Bal	2	1	0	0	1
Zeigler, Dusty, Buf	3	0	0	-19	0
Zolak, Scott, N.E	1	0	0	0	0

Yards includes aborted plays, own recoveries, and opponents' recoveries.

NFC FUMBLES—INDIVIDUAL

	Fum.	Own Rec.	Opp. Rec.	Yards	Tot. Rec.
Abraham, Donnie, T.B.	0	0	2	0	2
Abrams, Kevin, Det	0	0	1	7	1
Adams, Flozell, Dal	0	1	0	0	1
Agnew, Ray, St.L	0	0	1	0	1
Aikman, Troy, Dal	3	0	0	-20	0
Aldridge, Allen, Det	0	0	1	0	1
Alexander, Brent, Car	0	1	0	12	1
Alexander, Stephen, Was	2	0	0	0	0
Allen, James, Chi	1	2	0	0	2
Allen, Terry, Was	4	1	0	0	1
Alstott, Mike, T.B	5	0	0	0	0

1998 INDIVIDUAL STATISTICS—FUMBLES

	Fum.	Own Rec.	Opp. Rec.	Yards	Tot. Rec.
Anderson, Jamal, Atl	5	1	0	0	1
Anderson, Ronnie, Ariz	0	1	0	0	1
Andruzzi, Joseph, G.B	0	1	0	0	1
Anthony, Reidel, T.B	0	1	0	0	1
Archambeau, Lester, Atl	0	0	2	0	2
Asher, Jamie, Was	0	1	0	0	1
Ball, Jerry, Min	0	0	1	0	1
Banks, Tony, St.L	10	8	0	-23	8
Barber, Tiki, NY-G	1	0	0	0	0
Barrow, Micheal, Car	0	0	2	0	2
Batch, Charlie, Det	2	0	0	0	0
Bates, Michael, Car	1	0	0	0	0
Beckles, Ian, Phi	0	2	0	0	2
Bell, Ricky, Chi	0	0	1	0	1
Bellisari, Greg, T.B	0	0	1	0	1
Bennett, Cornelius, Atl	0	0	2	10	2
Bennett, Edgar, Chi	2	1	0	0	1
Beuerlein, Steve, Car	13	5	0	-19	5
Biakabutuka, Tim, Car	1	0	0	0	0
Bohlinger, Rob, Car	0	1	0	0	1
Bolden, Juran, Car	0	0	1	0	1
Bono, Steve, St.L	4	0	0	-11	0
Booker, Michael, Atl	1	0	1	5	1
Bouie, Tony, T.B	0	0	1	0	1
Boyd, Stephen, Det	0	1	3	1	4
Bradford, Corey, G.B	1	0	0	0	0
Bradford, Ronnie, Atl	0	0	1	0	1
Brady, Jeff, Car	1	1	0	0	1
Bratzke, Chad, NY-G	0	0	1	0	1
Brock, Fred, Ariz	0	0	1	19	1
Brockermeyer, Blake, Car	0	2	0	0	2
Broughton, Luther, Car	1	1	0	0	1
Brown, Gary, NY-G	1	1	0	0	1
Brown, J.B., Ariz	0	0	1	0	1
Buckley, Marcus, NY-G	0	0	1	0	1
Buckner, Brentson, S.F	0	0	1	0	1
Burrough, John, Atl	0	0	1	0	1
Butler, LeRoy, G.B	0	0	2	32	2
Calloway, Chris, NY-G	1	0	0	0	0
Campbell, Jesse, Was	1	0	0	0	0
Carrier, Mark, Det	1	0	0	0	0
Carter, Marty, Chi	0	0	2	0	2
Centers, Larry, Ariz	1	0	0	0	0
Chancey, Robert, Chi	2	0	0	0	0
Chandler, Chris, Atl	6	1	0	-4	1
Chmura, Mark, G.B	1	0	0	0	0
Christian, Bob, Atl	1	0	2	0	2
Chryplewicz, Pete, Det	1	0	0	0	0
Cleeland, Cameron, N.O	1	2	0	7	2
Coakley, Dexter, Dal	0	0	1	0	1
Collins, Calvin, Atl	0	1	0	0	1
Collins, Kerry, Car.-N.O	13	2	0	-9	2
Comella, Greg, NY-G	0	1	0	0	1
Conway, Curtis, Chi	1	0	1	0	1
Cooks, Kerry, G.B	0	1	0	0	1
Copeland, Russell, Phi	1	0	0	0	0
Cota, Chad, N.O	0	0	1	0	1
Cousin, Terry, Chi	0	0	2	0	2
Craver, Aaron, N.O	2	1	0	0	1
Cross, Howard, NY-G	2	0	0	0	0
Crowell, Germane, Det	1	0	0	0	0
Culpepper, Brad, T.B	0	0	1	0	1
Cunningham, Randall, Min	2	0	0	0	0
Davidds-Garrido, Norbert, Car.	0	1	0	0	1
Davis, Billy, Dal	1	1	0	0	1
Davis, Eric, Car	0	0	1	0	1
Davis, Troy, N.O	1	0	0	0	0
Davis, Tyrone, G.B	1	0	0	0	0
Dawkins, Brian, Phi	0	0	1	0	1
Dawkins, Sean, N.O	2	0	0	0	0
DeBerg, Steve, Atl	2	1	0	0	1
Deese, Derrick, S.F	0	1	0	0	1
Dellenbach, Jeff, G.B	0	2	0	0	2
Detmer, Koy, Phi	1	0	0	0	0
Detmer, Ty, S.F	1	0	0	0	0
Devlin, Mike, Ariz	0	1	0	0	1
Dexter, James, Ariz	0	2	0	0	2
Dilfer, Trent, T.B	9	2	0	-5	2
Dishman, Chris, Ariz	0	1	0	0	1
Dixon, David, Min	0	1	0	0	1
Doleman, Chris, S.F	0	0	2	0	2
Dotson, Santana, G.B	0	0	1	0	1
Dronett, Shane, Atl	0	0	1	0	1
Dunn, Jason, Phi	1	1	0	0	1
Dunn, Warrick, T.B	1	1	0	0	1
Dwight, Tim, Atl	3	0	0	0	0
Edwards, Antonio, Atl	0	0	1	2	1
Edwards, Dixon, Min	0	0	1	0	1
Ellis, Greg, Dal	0	0	1	2	1
Ellison, Jerry, T.B	0	0	2	0	2
Elliss, Luther, Det	0	0	1	0	1
Engram, Bobby, Chi	1	0	0	0	0
Enis, Curtis, Chi	1	0	0	0	0
Evans, Greg, Was	0	1	0	0	1
Fair, Terry, Det	5	1	0	0	1
Farr, D'Marco, St.L	0	0	1	18	1
Favre, Brett, G.B	8	3	0	-1	3
Fields, Mark, N.O	0	0	1	36	1
Fisk, Jason, Min	0	0	1	0	1
Flanigan, Jim, Chi	0	0	1	0	1
Flannery, John, St.L	2	0	0	-5	0
Fletcher, London, St.L	1	0	0	0	0
Floyd, William, Car	1	1	0	0	1
Fuller, Randy, Atl	0	0	2	0	2
Galyon, Scott, NY-G	0	0	1	0	1
Garcia, Frank, Car	0	1	1	2	2
Garner, Charlie, Phi	1	0	0	0	0
Garrett, Jason, Dal	4	0	0	-17	0
Gedney, Chris, Ariz	1	0	0	0	0
Godfrey, Randall, Dal	0	0	1	0	1
Gooch, Jeff, T.B	0	0	1	0	1
Goodwin, Hunter, Min	0	1	0	0	1
Gragg, Scott, NY-G	0	1	0	0	1
Graham, Kent, NY-G	2	0	0	-3	0
Gray, Torrian, Min	0	0	1	14	1
Green, Harold, Atl	1	0	0	0	0
Green, Jacquez, T.B	5	2	0	0	2
Green, Trent, Was	14	4	0	0	4
Greene, Kevin, Car	0	0	1	2	1
Guliford, Eric, N.O	1	1	0	0	1
Hakim, Az-Zahir, St.L	1	0	0	0	0
Hall, Lemanski, Chi	0	0	1	5	1
Hall, Travis, Atl	0	0	4	0	4
Hallock, Ty, Chi	3	0	1	0	1
Hamilton, Conrad, NY-G	0	0	1	0	1
Hamilton, Keith, NY-G	0	0	1	0	1
Hanks, Merton, S.F	0	0	1	0	1
Hape, Patrick, T.B	1	0	0	0	0
Harris, Al, Phi	1	0	0	0	0
Harris, Derrick, St.L	1	2	0	0	2
Harris, Jon, Phi	0	0	1	0	1
Harris, Raymont, G.B	3	0	0	0	0
Harris, Ronnie, Sea.-Atl	2	1	0	0	1
Harris, Walt, Chi	0	0	1	0	1
Harvey, Ken, Was	0	0	1	0	1
Hastings, Andre, N.O	0	1	0	0	1
Hearst, Garrison, S.F	4	1	0	0	1
Henderson, William, G.B	1	0	0	0	0
Henley, June, St.L	1	1	0	0	1
Hennings, Chad, Dal	0	0	1	0	1
Hilliard, Ike, NY-G	2	0	0	0	0
Hitchcock, Jimmy, Min	0	0	1	1	1
Hoard, Leroy, Min	1	1	0	0	1
Holliday, Vonnie, G.B	0	0	2	0	2
Holmes, Darick, G.B	1	1	0	0	1
Horne, Tony, St.L	1	0	0	0	0
Houston, Bobby, Min	0	0	1	14	1
Hoying, Bobby, Phi	6	2	0	-2	2
Hughes, Tyrone, Dal	1	0	0	0	0
Irvin, Michael, Dal	1	0	0	0	0
Ismail, Qadry, N.O	2	0	0	0	0
Ismail, Raghib, Car	2	1	0	0	1
Jeffries, Greg, Det	0	0	1	0	1
Jenkins, James, Was	0	1	0	0	1
Jensen, Jerry, Car	1	0	0	-20	0
Johnson, Anthony, Car	3	1	0	0	1
Johnson, Brad, Min	1	0	0	0	0
Johnson, Joe, N.O	0	0	1	5	1
Jones, Cedric, NY-G	0	0	1	0	1
Jones, Clarence, N.O	0	1	0	0	1
Jones, Marcus, T.B	0	0	1	0	1
Jones, Mike D., St.L	0	0	2	43	2

1998 INDIVIDUAL STATISTICS—FUMBLES

	Fum.	Own Rec.	Opp. Rec.	Yards	Tot. Rec.
Kanell, Danny, NY-G	6	1	0	0	1
Kelly, Brian, T.B	1	0	1	15	1
Kennison, Eddie, St.L	4	1	0	0	1
Kinchen, Todd, Atl	2	0	0	0	0
Kirk, Randy, S.F	1	0	0	-18	0
Kiselak, Mike, Dal	0	1	0	0	1
Knight, Sammy, N.O	0	0	2	3	2
Koonce, George, G.B	0	0	1	4	1
Kowalkowski, Scott, Det	0	0	1	0	1
Kramer, Erik, Chi	3	0	0	0	0
Lacina, Corbin, Car	0	1	0	0	1
LaFleur, David, Dal	1	0	0	0	0
Lane, Fred, Car	4	0	0	0	0
Lassiter, Kwamie, Ariz	0	0	1	0	1
Lee, Amp, St.L	3	0	0	0	0
Lee, Shawn, Chi	0	0	1	15	1
Lloyd, Greg, Car	0	0	1	6	1
Lynch, John, T.B	0	0	1	0	1
Maddox, Mark, Ariz	0	0	1	0	1
Marshall, Anthony, Phi	0	0	1	0	1
Martin, Wayne, N.O	0	0	1	0	1
Mathis, Kevin, Dal	2	2	2	6	4
Mathis, Terance, Atl	0	2	0	0	2
Mayes, Alonzo, Chi	2	0	0	0	0
Mayes, Derrick, G.B	1	0	0	0	0
Mays, Kivuusama, Min	0	0	1	0	1
McBurrows, Gerald, St.L	0	1	0	0	1
McCollum, Andy, N.O	0	1	0	0	1
McCombs, Tony, Ariz	0	0	1	0	1
McCormack, Hurvin, Dal	0	0	1	0	1
McDaniel, Ed, Min	0	0	2	5	2
McDonald, Tim, S.F	0	0	2	0	2
McKenzie, Keith, G.B	0	0	3	88	3
McKinnon, Ronald, Ariz	1	0	2	0	2
McNeil, Ryan, St.L	0	0	1	0	1
McQuarters, R.W., S.F	4	2	0	0	2
McTyer, Tim, Phi	0	1	0	0	1
Metcalf, Eric, Ariz	5	2	0	0	2
Milburn, Glyn, Chi	1	0	0	0	0
Miller, Jamir, Ariz	0	0	2	0	2
Miller, Les, Car	1	0	3	8	3
Minter, Barry, Chi	0	0	1	11	1
Mitchell, Brian, Was	3	0	0	0	0
Mitchell, Keith, N.O	0	0	3	63	3
Mitchell, Scott, Det	1	0	0	-9	0
Mobley, Singor, Dal	0	1	0	0	1
Moore, Dave, T.B	1	0	0	0	0
Moore, Jerald, St.L	3	2	0	0	2
Moreno, Moses, Chi	2	0	0	-4	0
Morrow, Harold, Min	0	0	1	0	1
Moss, Randy, Min	2	0	0	0	0
Muhammad, Muhsin, Car	2	1	0	0	1
Murrell, Adrian, Ariz	6	1	0	0	1
Naeole, Chris, N.O	0	1	0	0	1
Nickerson, Hardy, T.B	0	0	1	0	1
Norton, Ken, S.F	0	0	3	12	3
Ogden, Jeff, Dal	1	0	0	0	0
Oliver, Winslow, Car	1	0	0	0	0
Owens, Terrell, S.F	1	0	1	13	1
Oxendine, Ken, Atl	1	0	0	0	0
Pace, Orlando, St.L	0	0	1	0	1
Palelei, Lonnie, NY-G	1	0	0	0	0
Palmer, David, Min	2	1	0	0	1
Parrish, Tony, Chi	1	0	2	-2	2
Pederson, Doug, G.B	1	0	0	-2	0
Peete, Rodney, Phi	1	0	0	0	0
Penn, Chris, Chi	1	0	0	0	0
Perry, Wilmont, N.O	1	0	0	0	0
Peter, Jason, Car	0	0	1	0	1
Phifer, Roman, St.L	1	0	0	0	0
Pittman, Kavika, Dal	0	0	2	7	2
Pittman, Michael, Ariz	1	0	1	0	1
Plummer, Jake, Ariz	12	3	0	-2	3
Portilla, Jose, Atl	0	1	0	0	1
Pounds, Darryl, Was	0	0	1	0	1
Pourdanesh, Shar, Was	1	1	0	-4	1
Preston, Roell, G.B	7	1	0	0	1
Prior, Mike, G.B	1	0	0	0	0
Randle, John, Min	0	0	1	0	1
Raymer, Cory, Was	0	1	0	0	1
Reich, Frank, Det	2	1	0	0	1
Rice, Jerry, S.F	2	0	0	0	0
Rice, Simeon, Ariz	0	0	4	39	4
Richard, Stanley, Was	0	0	1	0	1
Richardson, Damien, Car	0	0	1	0	1
Robbins, Austin, N.O	0	0	1	0	1
Robinson, Eugene, Atl	0	0	2	16	2
Rossum, Allen, Phi	4	2	1	0	3
Rudd, Dwayne, Min	0	0	3	157	3
Ruhman, Chris, S.F	0	1	0	0	1
Sanders, Barry, Det	3	1	0	0	1
Sanders, Deion, Dal	1	1	0	0	1
Sanders, Frank, Ariz	3	2	0	0	2
Santiago, O.J., Atl	1	1	0	0	1
Sapp, Warren, T.B	0	0	1	0	1
Schroeder, Bill, G.B	1	0	0	0	0
Schwantz, Jim, Chi	0	1	0	0	1
Scott, Lance, NY-G	1	1	0	-1	1
Sellers, Mike, Was	0	0	1	0	1
Sinceno, Kaseem, Phi	1	0	0	0	0
Smith, Chuck, Atl	0	1	3	71	4
Smith, Derek, Was	0	0	1	0	1
Smith, Emmitt, Dal	3	1	0	0	1
Smith, Lamar, N.O	4	0	0	0	0
Smith, Mark, Ariz	0	0	1	0	1
Smith, Robert, Min	1	0	0	0	0
Smith, Rod, Car	0	0	1	35	1
Staley, Duce, Phi	2	2	0	0	2
Stenstrom, Steve, Chi	6	1	0	-9	1
Stoutmire, Omar, Dal	0	0	1	0	1
Talley, Ben, Atl	0	1	0	0	1
Tatum, Kinnon, Car	0	1	0	0	1
Terrell, Pat, G.B	0	0	1	6	1
Thomas, Chris, Was	0	0	1	0	1
Thomas, Hollis, Phi	0	0	1	0	1
Thomas, Tra, Phi	0	1	0	0	1
Tobeck, Robbie, Atl	0	1	0	1	1
Tolliver, Billy Joe, N.O	3	0	0	-13	0
Tomich, Jared, N.O	0	0	1	0	1
Tuaolo, Esera, Atl	0	0	1	0	1
Tubbs, Winfred, S.F	0	0	1	0	1
Tuggle, Jessie, Atl	0	0	1	1	1
Turk, Dan, Was	1	0	0	-4	0
Turk, Matt, Was	1	0	0	0	0
Turner, Kevin, Phi	1	0	0	0	0
Vardell, Tommy, Det	1	0	0	0	0
Villarrial, Chris, Chi	0	1	0	0	1
Wadsworth, Andre, Ariz	0	0	3	0	3
Waldroup, Kerwin, Det	0	0	1	0	1
Walter, Ken, Car	2	2	0	-20	2
Walz, Zack, Ariz	0	0	1	0	1
Warren, Chris, Dal	0	1	0	0	1
Way, Charles, NY-G	0	2	0	0	2
Wetnight, Ryan, Chi	1	0	0	0	0
Wheaton, Kenny, Dal	0	0	2	15	2
Wheeler, Leonard, Car	0	0	1	0	1
White, Steve, T.B	0	0	1	0	1
White, William, Atl	0	0	1	18	1
Whiting, Brandon, Phi	0	0	1	24	1
Widmer, Corey, NY-G	0	0	1	4	1
Wiegert, Zach, St.L	0	1	0	0	1
Wiegmann, Casey, Chi	1	1	0	-3	1
Wilkinson, Dan, Was	0	0	1	0	1
Williams, Gene, Atl	0	1	0	0	1
Williams, Moe, Min	1	1	0	0	1
Williams, Tony, Min	0	0	1	6	1
Willig, Matt, G.B	0	1	0	0	1
Willis, James, Phi	0	0	1	0	1
Wistrom, Grant, St.L	0	0	1	4	1
Wuerffel, Danny, N.O	1	1	0	0	1
Young, Bryant, S.F	0	0	1	0	1
Young, Floyd, T.B	0	1	0	0	1
Young, Steve, S.F	9	1	0	0	1
Zellars, Ray, N.O.	2	0	0	0	0
Zordich, Mike, Phi	0	0	1	0	1

Yards includes aborted plays, own recoveries, and opponents' recoveries.

1998 INDIVIDUAL STATISTICS—SACKS

SACKS

Most Sacks
AFC: 16.5—Michael Sinclair, Seattle
NFC: 16.0—Reggie White, Green Bay

Most Sacks, Game
AFC: 6.0—Derrick Thomas, Kansas City vs. Oakland, September 6
NFC: 4.5—Hugh Douglas, Philadelphia at San Diego, October 18

Team Champion
NFC: 54—N.Y. Giants
AFC: 53—Seattle

Team Leaders, Sacks
AFC—BALTIMORE: 14.5, Michael McCrary; BUFFALO: 10, Bruce Smith; CINCINNATI: 6, Reinard Wilson; DENVER: 8.5, Trevor Pryce, Maa Tanuvasa; INDIANAPOLIS: 8, Ellis Johnson; JACKSONVILLE: 7.5, Joel Smeenge; KANSAS CITY: 12, Derrick Thomas; MIAMI: 10.5, Trace Armstrong; NEW ENGLAND: 6.5, Henry Thomas; N.Y. JETS: 7, Mo Lewis; OAKLAND: 11, Lance Johnstone; PITTSBURGH: 11, Jason Gildon; SAN DIEGO: 6, Norman Hand; SEATTLE: 16.5, Mike Sinclair; TENNESSEE: 4, Lonnie Marts
NFC—ARIZONA: 10, Simeon Rice; ATLANTA: 10, Lester Archambeau; CAROLINA: 15, Kevin Greene; CHICAGO: 8.5, Jim Flanigan; DALLAS: 6, Kavika Pittman; DETROIT: 11.5, Robert Porcher; GREEN BAY: 16, Reggie White; MINNESOTA: 10.5, John Randle; NEW ORLEANS: 10, La'Roi Glover; N.Y. GIANTS: 15, Mike Strahan; PHILADELPHIA: 12.5, Hugh Douglas; ST. LOUIS: 12, Kevin Carter; SAN FRANCISCO: 15, Chris Doleman; TAMPA BAY: 9, Brad Culpepper; WASHINGTON: 7.5, Dan Wilkinson

AFC SACKS—TEAM

	Sacks	Yards
Seattle	53	282
Denver	47	335
Miami	45	270
Buffalo	43	276
Oakland	41	258
Pittsburgh	41	238
Kansas City	40	268
Baltimore	39	286
San Diego	39	246
Indianapolis	38	231
New England	36	222
N.Y. Jets	36	259
Jacksonville	30	209
Tennessee	30	172
Cincinnati	28	199
AFC Total	586	3751
AFC Average	39.1	250.1

NFC SACKS—TEAM

	Sacks	Yards
N.Y. Giants	54	336
San Francisco	51	259
Green Bay	50	336
St. Louis	50	349
New Orleans	47	288
Detroit	43	261
Philadelphia	42	281
Arizona	39	250
Atlanta	38	275
Minnesota	38	247
Carolina	37	228
Tampa Bay	37	252
Dallas	34	222
Washington	33	194
Chicago	28	173
NFC Total	621	3951
NFC Average	41.4	263.4
League Total	1207	7702
League Average	40.2	256.7

SACKS—TOP TEN LEADERS

Sinclair, Michael, Sea.	16.5
White, Reggie, G.B.	16.0
Doleman, Chris, S.F.	15.0
Greene, Kevin, Car.	15.0
Strahan, Michael, NY-G	15.0
McCrary, Michael, Bal.	14.5
Douglas, Hugh, Phi.	12.5
Barker, Roy, S.F.	12.0
Carter, Kevin, St.L	12.0
Thomas, Derrick, K.C.	12.0

AFC SACKS—INDIVIDUAL

Sinclair, Michael, Sea.	16.5
McCrary, Michael, Bal.	14.5
Thomas, Derrick, K.C.	12.0
Gildon, Jason, Pit.	11.0
Johnstone, Lance, Oak.	11.0
Armstrong, Trace, Mia.	10.5
Russell, Darrell, Oak.	10.0
Smith, Bruce, Buf.	10.0
Taylor, Jason, Mia.	9.0
Boulware, Peter, Bal.	8.5
Pryce, Trevor, Den.	8.5
Tanuvasa, Maa, Den.	8.5
Bromell, Lorenzo, Mia.	8.0
Johnson, Ellis, Ind.	8.0
Brown, Chad, Sea.	7.5
Hansen, Phil, Buf.	7.5
Romanowski, Bill, Den.	7.5
Smeenge, Joel, Jac.	7.5
Lewis, Mo, NY-J	7.0
Daniels, Phillip, Sea.	6.5
Paup, Bryce, Jac.	6.5
Thomas, Henry, N.E.	6.5
Cox, Bryan, NY-J	6.0
Eaton, Chad, N.E.	6.0
Edwards, Donnie, K.C.	6.0
Hand, Norman, S.D.	6.0
LaBounty, Matt, Sea.	6.0
McCoy, Tony, Ind.	6.0
Pleasant, Anthony, NY-J	6.0
Wilson, Reinard, Cin.	6.0
Johnson, Raylee, S.D.	5.5
Jones, James, Bal.	5.5
Thomas, Mark, Chi.-Ind.	5.5
Cascadden, Chad, NY-J	5.0
Jones, Robert, Mia.	5.0
Price, Shawn, Buf.	5.0
Simmons, Clyde, Cin.	5.0
Smith, Darrin, Sea.	5.0
Bankston, Michael, Cin.	4.5
Davis, Anthony, K.C.	4.5
O'Neal, Leslie, K.C.	4.5
Rogers, Sam, Buf.	4.5
Washington, Ted, Buf.	4.5
Berry, Bert, Ind.	4.0
Cadrez, Glenn, Den.	4.0
Ferguson, Jason, NY-J	4.0
Harrison, Rodney, S.D.	4.0
Harvey, Richard, Oak.	4.0
Henry, Kevin, Pit.	4.0
Marts, Lonnie, Ten.	4.0
Slade, Chris, N.E.	4.0
Smith, Neil, Den.	4.0
Whittington, Bernard, Ind.	4.0
Barndt, Tom, K.C.	3.5
Brackens, Tony, Jac.	3.5
Coleman, Marco, S.D.	3.5
Emmons, Carlos, Pit.	3.5
Evans, Josh, Ten.	3.5
Harrison, Nolan, Pit.	3.5
McGinest, Willie, N.E.	3.5
Robinson, Eddie, Ten.	3.5
Roye, Orpheus, Pit.	3.5
Seau, Junior, S.D.	3.5
Wiley, Marcellus, Buf.	3.5
Williams, Pat, Buf.	3.5
Biekert, Greg, Oak.	3.0
Bishop, Blaine, Ten.	3.0
Chester, Larry, Ind.	3.0
Fuller, William, S.D.	3.0
Hasselbach, Harald, Den.	3.0
Jackson, Grady, Oak.	3.0
Jones, Donta, Pit.	3.0
Lewis, Ray, Bal.	3.0
Pritchett, Kelvin, Jac.	3.0
Simmons, Brian, Cin.	3.0
Spires, Greg, N.E.	3.0
White, Jose, Jac.	3.0
Williams, Alfred, Den.	3.0
Burnett, Rob, Bal.	2.5
Dixon, Gerald, S.D.	2.5
Holmes, Kenny, Ten.	2.5
Kirkland, Levon, Pit.	2.5
Logan, Ernie, NY-J	2.5
Rodgers, Derrick, Mia.	2.5
Vrabel, Mike, Pit.	2.5
Adams, Sam, Sea.	2.0
Barber, Mike, Ind.	2.0
Bruschi, Tedy, N.E.	2.0
Burton, Shane, Mia.	2.0

Player	Sacks
Cook, Anthony, Ten.	2.0
Favors, Greg, K.C.	2.0
Foley, Steve, Cin.	2.0
Gibson, Oliver, Pit.	2.0
Israel, Steve, N.E.	2.0
Johnson, Ted, N.E.	2.0
Kennedy, Cortez, Sea.	2.0
Lodish, Mike, Den.	2.0
Lyons, Pratt, Ten.	2.0
Maryland, Russell, Oak.	2.0
Mims, Chris, S.D.	2.0
Mitchell, Brandon, N.E.	2.0
Mixon, Kenny, Mia.	2.0
Montgomery, Monty, Ind.	2.0
Northern, Gabe, Buf.	2.0
Rolle, Samari, Ten.	2.0
Smedley, Eric, Buf.	2.0
Smith, Fernando, Jac.	2.0
Spikes, Takeo, Cin.	2.0
Sullivan, Chris, N.E.	2.0
Swilling, Pat, Oak.	2.0
Thomas, Zach, Mia.	2.0
Tongue, Reggie, K.C.	2.0
Traylor, Keith, Den.	2.0
Tuinei, Van, Ind.	2.0
Washington, Marvin, Den.	2.0
Wooden, Terry, Oak.	2.0
Bowden, Joe, Ten.	1.5
Collins, Mark, Sea.	1.5
Ford, Henry, Ten.	1.5
Hardy, Kevin, Jac.	1.5
Holmes, Earl, Pit.	1.5
Jackson, Steve, Ten.	1.5
Lyle, Rick, NY-J	1.5
Parrella, John, S.D.	1.5
Bell, Myron, Cin.	1.0
Bellamy, Jay, Sea.	1.0
Belser, Jason, Ind.	1.0
Blackmon, Robert, Ind.	1.0
Boyer, Brant, Jac.	1.0
Brady, Donny, Bal.	1.0
Bush, Lewis, S.D.	1.0
Canty, Chris, N.E.	1.0
Carter, Chris, N.E.	1.0
Chorak, Jason, Ind.	1.0
Dumas, Mike, S.D.	1.0
Flowers, Lethon, Pit.	1.0
Folston, James, Oak.	1.0
Fontenot, Al, Ind.	1.0
Gardener, Daryl, Mia.	1.0
Green, Victor, NY-J	1.0
Harris, Corey, Bal.	1.0
Harris, James, Oak.	1.0
Hasty, James, K.C.	1.0
Hawkins, Artrell, Cin.	1.0
Henderson, Jerome, NY-J	1.0
Jackson, Calvin, Mia.	1.0
Johnson, Darrius, Den.	1.0
Johnson, Melvin, K.C.	1.0
Johnson, Pepper, NY-J	1.0
Lake, Carnell, Pit.	1.0
Lewis, Albert, Oak.	1.0
Lewis, Darryll, Ten.	1.0
Logan, James, Sea.	1.0
Madison, Sam, Mia.	1.0
McGlockton, Chester, K.C.	1.0
Milloy, Lawyer, N.E.	1.0
Mobley, John, Den.	1.0
Mohring, Mike, S.D.	1.0
Morrison, Steve, Ind.	1.0
Parker, Riddick, Sea.	1.0
Purvis, Andre, Cin.	1.0
Salave'a, Joe, Ten.	1.0
Shade, Sam, Cin.	1.0
Sharper, Jamie, Bal.	1.0
Shello, Kendel, Ind.	1.0
Staten, Ralph, Bal.	1.0
Steed, Joel, Pit.	1.0
Tovar, Steve, S.D.	1.0
Turner, Eric, Oak.	1.0
Turner, Scott, S.D.	1.0
Walker, Gary, Ten.	1.0
Washington, Keith, Bal.	1.0
Wynn, Renaldo, Jac.	1.0
Crockett, Ray, Den.	0.5
Davis, Travis, Jac.	0.5
Gouveia, Kurt, S.D.	0.5
Jurkovic, John, Jac.	0.5
Langford, Jevon, Cin.	0.5
Oldham, Chris, Pit.	0.5
Perry, Darren, Pit.	0.5
Simmons, Wayne, K.C.-Buf.	0.5
Thompson, Mike, Cin.	0.5
Tumulty, Tom, Cin.	0.5
Williams, Robert, K.C.	0.5

NFC SACKS—INDIVIDUAL

Player	Sacks
White, Reggie, G.B.	16.0
Doleman, Chris, S.F.	15.0
Greene, Kevin, Car.	15.0
Strahan, Michael, NY-G	15.0
Douglas, Hugh, Phi.	12.5
Barker, Roy, S.F.	12.0
Carter, Kevin, St.L	12.0
Porcher, Robert, Det.	11.5
Bratzke, Chad, NY-G	11.0
Randle, John, Min.	10.5
Archambeau, Lester, Atl.	10.0
Glover, La'Roi, N.O.	10.0
Rice, Simeon, Ariz	10.0
Young, Bryant, S.F.	9.5
Culpepper, Brad, T.B.	9.0
Smith, Mark, Ariz	9.0
Flanigan, Jim, Chi.	8.5
Smith, Chuck, Atl.	8.5
Holliday, Vonnie, G.B.	8.0
McKenzie, Keith, G.B.	8.0
Alexander, Derrick, Min.	7.5
Wilkinson, Dan, Was.	7.5
Farr, D'Marco, St.L	7.0
Hamilton, Keith, NY-G	7.0
Johnson, Joe, N.O.	7.0
Lang, Kenard, Was.	7.0
McDaniel, Ed, Min.	7.0
Sapp, Warren, T.B.	7.0
Upshaw, Regan, T.B.	7.0
Dronett, Shane, Atl.	6.5
Phifer, Roman, St.L	6.5
Scroggins, Tracy, Det.	6.5
Fields, Mark, N.O.	6.0
Gilbert, Sean, Car.	6.0
Pittman, Kavika, Dal.	6.0
Tomich, Jared, N.O.	6.0
Wallace, Al, Phi.	6.0
Agnew, Ray, St.L	5.0
Armstead, Jessie, NY-G	5.0
Bryant, Junior, S.F.	5.0
McCormack, Hurvin, Dal.	5.0
Thomas, Hollis, Phi.	5.0
Wadsworth, Andre, Ariz	5.0
Hall, Travis, Atl.	4.5
Barrow, Micheal, Car.	4.0
Boyd, Stephen, Det.	4.0
Brady, Jeff, Car.	4.0
Butler, LeRoy, G.B.	4.0
Jefferson, Greg, Phi.	4.0
Jones, Cedric, NY-G	4.0
Lett, Leon, Dal.	4.0
McDonald, Tim, S.F.	4.0
Swann, Eric, Ariz	4.0
Harris, Robert, NY-G	3.5
Rice, Ron, Det.	3.5
Thierry, John, Chi.	3.5
Abrams, Kevin, Det.	3.0
Aldridge, Allen, Det.	3.0
Barber, Ronde, T.B.	3.0
Booker, Vaughn, G.B.	3.0
Dotson, Santana, G.B.	3.0
Duff, Jamal, Was.	3.0
Ellis, Greg, Dal.	3.0
Elliss, Luther, Det.	3.0
Godfrey, Randall, Dal.	3.0
Jackson, Tyoka, T.B.	3.0
Jenkins, Billy, St.L	3.0
Jones, Mike A., St.L	3.0
Kalu, Ndukwe, Was.	3.0
Martin, Wayne, N.O.	3.0
Miller, Jamir, Ariz	3.0
Myers, Michael, Dal.	3.0
Patton, Marvcus, Was.	3.0
Tuggle, Jessie, Atl.	3.0
Wells, Mike, Chi.	3.0
Wistrom, Grant, St.L	3.0
Woodson, Darren, Dal.	3.0
Wooten, Tito, NY-G	3.0
Clemons, Duane, Min.	2.5
Fredrickson, Rob, Det.	2.5
Johnson, Bill, Phi.	2.5
Jones, Mike D., St.L	2.5
Mitchell, Keith, N.O.	2.5
Mitchell, Kevin, N.O.	2.5
Owens, Dan, Det.	2.5
Boutte, Marc, Was.	2.0
Cherry, Je'Rod, N.O.	2.0
Clemons, Charlie, St.L	2.0
Coakley, Dexter, Dal.	2.0
Cota, Chad, N.O.	2.0
Darling, James, Phi.	2.0
Fuller, Randy, Atl.	2.0
Harris, Bernardo, G.B.	2.0
Harvey, Ken, Was.	2.0
Hewitt, Chris, N.O.	2.0
Lee, Shawn, Chi.	2.0
Lynch, John, T.B.	2.0
McKinnon, Ronald, Ariz	2.0
Norton, Ken, S.F.	2.0
Rudd, Dwayne, Min.	2.0
Teague, George, Dal.	2.0
Terry, Rick, Car.	2.0
Thomas, William, Phi.	2.0
White, Steve, T.B.	2.0
Williams, Brian, G.B.	2.0
Buckley, Marcus, NY-G	1.5
Fisk, Jason, Min.	1.5
Lyght, Todd, St.L	1.5
Stubblefield, Dana, Was.	1.5
Waldroup, Kerwin, Det.	1.5
Whiting, Brandon, Phi.	1.5
Wong, Kailee, Min.	1.5
Aleaga, Ink, N.O.	1.0
Bennett, Cornelius, Atl.	1.0
Bordano, Chris, N.O.	1.0
Caldwell, Mike, Phi.	1.0
Colinet, Stalin, Min.	1.0
Crockett, Henri, Atl.	1.0
Davis, Eric, Car.	1.0
Dawkins, Brian, Phi.	1.0
Edwards, Antonio, Atl.	1.0
Evans, Leomont, Was.	1.0
Fair, Terry, Det.	1.0
Fox, Mike, Car.	1.0
Fuller, Corey, Min.	1.0
Galyon, Scott, NY-G	1.0
Gooch, Jeff, T.B.	1.0
Grasmanis, Paul, Chi.	1.0
Gray, Carlton, NY-G	1.0
Gray, Torrian, Min.	1.0
Hamilton, Conrad, NY-G	1.0
Harris, Jon, Phi.	1.0
Harris, Sean, Chi.	1.0
Hennings, Chad, Dal.	1.0
Hill, Eric, St.L	1.0
Jones, Ernest, Car.	1.0
Jones, Greg, Was.	1.0
Kinney, Kelvin, Was.	1.0
Knight, Tom, Ariz	1.0
Koonce, George, G.B.	1.0
Lloyd, Greg, Car.	1.0
Lyle, Keith, St.L	1.0
Lyon, Billy, G.B.	1.0
Maddox, Mark, Ariz	1.0
Martin, Steve, Phi.	1.0
Mathis, Kevin, Dal.	1.0
McDonald, Ricardo, Chi.	1.0
McGill, Lenny, Car.	1.0
Minter, Barry, Chi.	1.0
Nickerson, Hardy, T.B.	1.0
Parker, Anthony, T.B.	1.0
Parrish, Tony, Chi.	1.0
Peter, Christian, NY-G	1.0
Peter, Jason, Car.	1.0
Peterson, Tony, S.F.	1.0
Quarles, Shelton, T.B.	1.0
Reeves, Carl, Chi.	1.0
Robbins, Austin, N.O.	1.0
Rossum, Allen, Phi.	1.0
Sapp, Patrick, Ariz	1.0
Stoutmire, Omar, Dal.	1.0
Terrell, Pat, G.B.	1.0
Tillman, Pat, Ariz	1.0
Tubbs, Winfred, S.F.	1.0
Vincent, Troy, Phi.	1.0
Waddy, Jude, G.B.	1.0
Williams, Aeneas, Ariz	1.0
Williams, Jay, St.L	1.0
Williams, Tony, Min.	1.0
Wilson, Bernard, Ariz	1.0
Wilson, Troy, N.O.	1.0
Wright, Toby, St.L	1.0
Buckner, Brentson, S.F.	0.5
Burrough, John, Atl.	0.5
Hanks, Merton, S.F.	0.5
Little, Leonard, St.L	0.5
McTyer, Tim, Phi.	0.5
Posey, Jeff, S.F.	0.5
Pounds, Darryl, Was.	0.5
Robinson, Bryan, Chi.	0.5
Smith, Derek, Was.	0.5
Thomas, Orlando, Min.	0.5

1998 ATTENDANCE

1998 NFL PAID ATTENDANCE BREAKDOWN

	Games	Attendance	Average
NFL Preseason Total	64	3,553,735	55,527
NFL Regular-Season Total	240	15,364,873	64,020
NFL Postseason Total	12	822,885	68,574
NFL All Games	316	19,741,493	62,473

ONE MILLION PLUS CLUB

During the 1998 season, 22 clubs drew a combined home and away paid attendance of more than 1 million. The Kansas City Chiefs drew an NFL-leading 1,160,272 fans in 1998.

Team	Total Paid Home Attendance	Total Paid Visiting Attendance	Total Paid Attendance
Kansas City	629,209	531,063	1,160,272
Denver	597,481	554,796	1,152,277
New York Jets	623,878	509,993	1,133,871
Miami	581,784	546,275	1,128,059
New York Giants	623,593	477,567	1,101,160
Detroit	571,381	523,496	1,094,877
Washington	599,553	489,555	1,089,108
San Francisco	546,507	539,940	1,086,447
Dallas	497,685	573,065	1,070,750
Carolina	574,116	490,809	1,064,925
Jacksonville	564,156	497,262	1,061,418
Buffalo	560,378	499,779	1,060,157
Seattle	491,050	537,091	1,028,141
San Diego	535,261	490,153	1,025,414
Philadelphia	519,162	501,518	1,020,680
Baltimore	541,504	476,308	1,017,812
Green Bay	479,292	537,519	1,016,811
Tampa Bay	506,363	509,683	1,016,046
New England	480,005	532,958	1,012,963
Pittsburgh	477,608	534,681	1,012,289
Minnesota	505,150	500,824	1,005,974
Atlanta	455,726	545,393	1,001,119

For complete year-by-year attendance records, see page 383.

Inside the Numbers

RECORDS FOR NFL TEAMS FOR MOST POINTS IN A GAME (REGULAR SEASON ONLY)

***Note:** When the record has been achieved more than once, only the most recent game is shown; summaries are listed in alphabetical order by conference. Bold face indicates team holding record.*

BALTIMORE RAVENS
November 29, 1998, at Baltimore

Indianapolis	17	7	7	0	— 31
Baltimore	3	10	8	17	— 38

TDs: Balt—Priest Holmes 2, James Roe, Floyd Turner; Ind—Marshall Faulk 2, Jerome Pathon, Torrance Small. TD Passes: Balt—Jim Harbaugh 2; Ind—Peyton Manning 3. FGs: Balt—Matt Stover 3; Ind—Mike Vanderjagt.

BUFFALO BILLS
September 18, 1966, at Buffalo

Miami	3	7	0	14	— 24
Buffalo	21	27	3	7	— 58

TDs: Buff—Bobby Burnett 2, Butch Byrd 2, Jack Spikes 2, Bobby Crockett, Jack Kemp; Mia—Dave Kocourek, Bo Roberson, John Roderick. TD Passes: Buff—Jack Kemp, Daryle Lamonica; Mia—George Wilson 3. FGs: Buff—Booth Lusteg; Mia—Gene Mingo.

CINCINNATI BENGALS
December 17, 1989, at Cincinnati

Houston	0	0	0	7	— 7
Cincinnati	21	10	21	9	— 61

TDs: Cin—Eddie Brown 2, Eric Ball, James Brooks, Ira Hillary, Rodney Holman, Tim McGee, Craig Taylor; Hou—Lorenzo White. TD Passes: Cin—Boomer Esiason 4, Erik Wilhelm. FGs: Cin—Jim Breech 2.

CLEVELAND BROWNS
November 7, 1954, at Cleveland

Washington	0	3	0	0	— 3
Cleveland	13	14	21	14	— 62

TDs: Clev—Darrell Brewster 2, Mo Bassett, Ken Gorgal, Otto Graham, Dub Jones, Dante Lavelli, Curley Morrison. TD Passes: Clev—George Ratterman 3, Otto Graham. FGs: Clev—Lou Groza 2; Wash—Vic Janowicz.

DENVER BRONCOS
October 6, 1963, at Denver

San Diego	13	7	0	14	— 34
Denver	3	14	9	24	— 50

TDs: Den—Lionel Taylor 2, Goose Gonsoulin, Gene Prebola, Donnie Stone; SD—Keith Lincoln 2, Lance Alworth, Paul Lowe, Jacque MacKinnon. TD Passes: Den—John McCormick 3; SD—Tobin Rote 3, John Hadl 2. FGs: Den—Gene Mingo 5.

INDIANAPOLIS COLTS
December 12, 1976, at Baltimore

Buffalo	3	3	7	7	— 20
Baltimore Colts	7	13	28	10	— 58

TDs: Balt—Roger Carr, Raymond Chester, Glenn Doughty, Roosevelt Leaks, Derrel Luce, Lydell Mitchell, Howard Stevens; Buff—Bob Chandler, O.J. Simpson. TD Passes: Balt—Bert Jones 3; Buff—Gary Marangi. FGs: Balt—Toni Linhart 3; Buff—George Jakowenko 2.

JACKSONVILLE JAGUARS
November 1, 1998, at Baltimore

Jacksonville	14	28	0	3	— 45
Baltimore	7	6	0	6	— 19

TDs: Jac—Fred Taylor 2, Donovin Darius, Daimon Shelton, Jimmy Smith, Alvis Whitted; Balt—Pat Johnson, Jermaine Lewis, Floyd Turner. TD Passes: Jac—Mark Brunell 2; Balt—Jim Harbaugh 3. FGs: Jac—Mike Hollis.

KANSAS CITY CHIEFS
September 7, 1963, at Denver

Kansas City	14	14	21	10	— 59
Denver	0	7	0	0	— 7

TDs: KC—Chris Burford 2, Frank Jackson 2, Dave Grayson, Abner Haynes, Sherrill Headrick, Curtis McClinton; Den—Lionel Taylor. TD Passes: KC—Len Dawson 4, Curtis McClinton; Den—Mickey Slaughter. FG: KC—Tommy Brooker.

MIAMI DOLPHINS
November 24, 1977, at St. Louis

Miami	14	14	20	7	— 55
St. Louis Cardinals	7	0	0	7	— 14

TDs: Mia—Nat Moore 3, Gary Davis, Duriel Harris, Leroy Harris, Benny Malone, Andre Tillman; StL—Ike Harris, Terry Metcalf. TD Passes: Mia—Bob Griese 6; StL—Jim Hart.

NEW ENGLAND PATRIOTS
September 9, 1979, at New England

New York Jets	3	0	0	0	— 3
New England	14	21	7	14	— 56

TDs: NE—Harold Jackson 3, Stanley Morgan 2, Allan Clark, Andy Johnson, Don Westbrook. TD Passes: NE—Steve Grogan 5, Tom Owen. FG: NYJ—Pat Leahy.

NEW YORK JETS
November 17, 1985, at New York

Tampa Bay	14	7	7	0	— 28
New York Jets	17	24	14	7	— 62

TDs: NYJ—Mickey Shuler 3, Johnny Hector 2, Tony Paige, Al Toon, Wesley Walker; TB—James Wilder 2, Kevin House, Calvin Magee. TD Passes: NYJ—Ken O'Brien 5; TB—Steve DeBerg 2. FGs: NYJ—Pat Leahy 2.

OAKLAND RAIDERS
December 22, 1963, at Oakland

Houston	14	21	14	0	— 49
Oakland	7	28	7	10	— 52

TDs: Oak—Art Powell 4, Clem Daniels, Claude Gibson, Ken Herock; Hou—Willard Dewveall 2, Dave Smith 2, Charley Hennigan, Bob McLeod, Charley Tolar. TD Passes: Oak—Tom Flores 6; Hou—George Blanda 5. FG: Oak—Mike Mercer.

PITTSBURGH STEELERS
November 30, 1952, at Pittsburgh

New York Giants	0	0	7	0	— 7
Pittsburgh	14	14	7	28	— 63

TDs: Pitt—Lynn Chandnois 2, Dick Hensley 2, Jack Butler, George Hays, Ray Mathews, Ed Modzelewski, Elbie Nickel; NYG—Bill Stribling. TD Passes: Pitt—Jim Finks 4, Gary Kerkorian; NYG—Tom Landry.

SAN DIEGO CHARGERS
December 22, 1963, at San Diego

Denver	7	10	3	0	— 20
San Diego	10	16	10	22	— 58

TDs: SD—Paul Lowe 2, Chuck Allen, Bobby Jackson, Dave Kocourek, Keith Lincoln, Jacque MacKinnon; Den—Billy Joe, Donnie Stone. TD Passes: SD—John Hadl, Tobin Rote; Den—Don Breaux. FGs: SD—George Blair 3; Den—Gene Mingo 2.

SEATTLE SEAHAWKS
October 30, 1977, at Seattle

Buffalo	3	0	7	7	— 17
Seattle	14	28	7	7	— 56

TDs: Sea—Steve Largent 2, Duke Fergerson, Al Hunter, David Sims, Sherman Smith, Don Testerman, Jim Zorn; Buff—Joe Ferguson, John Kimbrough. TD Passes: Sea—Jim Zorn 4; Buff—Joe Ferguson. FG: Buff—Carson Long.

TENNESSEE OILERS
December 9, 1990, at Houston

Cleveland	0	7	7	0	— 14
Houston Oilers	14	31	7	6	— 58

TDs: Hou—Lorenzo White 4, Ernest Givins, Leonard Harris, Tony Jones, Terry Kinard; Clev—Eric Metcalf 2. TD Passes: Hou—Warren Moon 2, Cody Carlson; Clev—Bernie Kosar. FG: Hou—Teddy Garcia.

ARIZONA CARDINALS
November 13, 1949, at New York

Chicago Cardinals	7	31	14	13	— 65
New York Bulldogs	7	0	6	7	— 20

TDs: Chi—Red Cochran 2, Pat Harder 2, Bill Dewell, Mel Kutner, Bob Ravensburg, Vic Schwall, Charlie Trippi; NY—Joe Golding, Frank Muehlheuser, Johnny Rauch. TD Passes: Chi—Paul Christman 3, Jim Hardy 3; NY—Bobby Layne. FG: Chi—Pat Harder.

ATLANTA FALCONS
September 16, 1973, at New Orleans

Atlanta	0	24	21	17	— 62
New Orleans	0	0	7	0	— 7

TDs: Atl—Ken Burrow 2, Eddie Ray 2, Wes Chesson, Tom Hayes, Art Malone, Joe Profit; NO—Bill Butler. TD Passes: Atl—Dick Shiner 3, Bob Lee; NO—Archie Manning. FGs: Atl—Nick Mike-Mayer 2.

CAROLINA PANTHERS
October 13, 1996, at Carolina

St. Louis	0	13	0	0	— 13
Carolina	14	14	10	7	— 45

TDs: Car—Wesley Walls 2, Kevin Greene, Muhsin Muhammad, Michael Bates, Dino Philyaw; StL—Anthony Parker, Eddie Kennison. TD Passes: Car—Kerry Collins 3; StL—Tony Banks. FG: Car—John Kasay.

CHICAGO BEARS
December 7, 1980, at Chicago

Green Bay	0	7	0	0	— 7
Chicago	0	28	13	20	— 61

TDs: Chi—Walter Payton 3, Brian Baschnagel, Robin Earl, Roland Harper, Willie McClendon, Len Walterscheid, Rickey Watts; GB—James Lofton. TD Passes: Chi—Vince Evans 3; GB—Lynn Dickey.

DALLAS COWBOYS
October 12, 1980, at Dallas

San Francisco	0	7	0	7	— 14
Dallas	14	24	14	7	— 59

TDs: Dall—Drew Pearson 3, Ron Springs 2, Tony Dorsett, Billy Joe DuPree, Robert Newhouse; SF—Dwight Clark 2. TD Passes: Dall—Danny White 4; SF—Steve DeBerg 2. FG: Dall—Rafael Septien.

DETROIT LIONS
November 27, 1997, at Detroit

Chicago	14	6	0	0	— 20
Detroit	3	14	17	21	— 55

TDs: Det—Herman Moore, Johnnie Morton, Ron Rivers, Barry Sanders 3, Tracy Scroggins; Chi—Raymont Harris, Ricky Proehl. TD Passes: Det—Scott Mitchell 2; Chi—Erik Kramer. FGs: Det—Jason Hanson 2; Chi—Jeff Jaeger 2.

GREEN BAY PACKERS
October 7, 1945, at Milwaukee

Detroit	0	7	7	7	— 21
Green Bay	0	41	9	7	— 57

TDs: GB—Don Hutson 4, Charley Brock, Irv Comp, Ted Fritsch, Clyde Goodnight; Det—Chuck Fenenbock, John Greene, Bob Westfall. TD Passes: GB—Tex McKay 4, Lou Brock, Irv Comp; Det—Dave Ryan.

MINNESOTA VIKINGS
October 18, 1970, at Minnesota

Dallas	3	3	0	7	— 13
Minnesota	14	20	17	3	— 54

TDs: Minn—Clint Jones 2, Ed Sharockman 2, John Beasley, Dave Osborn; Dall—Calvin Hill. TD Pass: Minn—Gary Cuozzo. FGs: Minn—Fred Cox 4; Dall—Mike Clark 2.

NEW ORLEANS SAINTS
November 21, 1976, at Seattle

New Orleans	3	17	28	3	— 51
Seattle	6	0	7	14	— 27

TDs: NO—Bobby Douglass 2, Tony Galbreath, Chuck Muncie, Tom Myers, Elex Price; Sea—Sherman Smith 2, Steve Largent, Jim Zorn. TD Pass: Sea—Bill Munson. FGs: NO—Rich Szaro 3.

NEW YORK GIANTS
November 26, 1972, at New York

Philadelphia	3	7	0	0	— 10
New York Giants	14	24	10	14	— 62

TDs: NYG—Don Herrmann 2, Ron Johnson 2, Bob Tucker 2, Randy Johnson; Phil—Harold Jackson. TD Passes: NYG—Norm Snead 3, Randy Johnson 2; Phil—John Reaves. FGs: NYG—Pete Gogolak 2; Phil—Tom Dempsey.

PHILADELPHIA EAGLES
November 6, 1934, at Philadelphia

Cincinnati Reds	0	0	0	0	— 0
Philadelphia	26	6	12	20	— 64

TDs: Phil—Joe Carter 3, Swede Hanson 3, Marvin Ellstrom, Roger Kirkman, Ed Matesic, Ed Storm. TD Passes: Phil—Ed Matesic 2, Albert Weiner 2, Marvin Elstrom.

ST. LOUIS RAMS
October 22, 1950, at Los Angeles

Baltimore	13	0	7	7	— 27
Los Angeles Rams	21	14	14	21	— 70

TDs: LA—Bob Boyd 2, Vitamin T. Smith 2, Tom Fears, Elroy (Crazylegs) Hirsch, Dick Hoerner, Ralph

Pasquariello, Dan Towler, Bob Waterfield; Balt—Chet Mutryn 2, Adrian Burk, Billy Stone. TD Passes: LA—Norm Van Brocklin 2, Bob Waterfield 2, Glenn Davis; Balt—Adrian Burk 3.

SAN FRANCISCO 49ERS
October 18, 1992, at San Francisco

Atlanta	7	3	0	7	— 17
San Francisco	21	21	14	0	— 56

TDs: SF—Jerry Rice 3, Ricky Watters 3, Brent Jones, Tom Rathman; Atl—Michael Haynes, Jason Phillips. TD Passes: SF—Steve Young 3; Atl—Chris Miller, Wade Wilson. FG: Atl—Norm Johnson.

TAMPA BAY BUCCANEERS
September 13, 1987, at Tampa Bay

Atlanta	0	3	0	7	— 10
Tampa Bay	14	13	7	14	— 48

TDs: TB—Gerald Carter 2, Cliff Austin, Steve Bartalo, Mark Carrier, Phil Freeman, Calvin Magee; Atl—Stacey Bailey. TD Passes: TB—Steve DeBerg 5; Atl—Scott Campbell. FG: Atl—Mick Luckhurst.

WASHINGTON REDSKINS
November 27, 1966, at Washington

New York Giants	0	14	14	13	— 41
Washington	13	21	14	24	— 72

TDs: Wash—A.D. Whitfield 3, Brig Owens 2, Charley Taylor 2, Rickie Harris, Joe Don Looney, Bobby Mitchell; NYG—Allen Jacobs, Homer Jones, Dan Lewis, Joe Morrison, Aaron Thomas, Gary Wood. TD Passes: Wash—Sonny Jurgensen 3; NYG—Gary Wood 2, Tom Kennedy. FG: Wash—Charlie Gogolak.

TEAMS THAT FINISHED IN FIRST PLACE IN THEIR DIVISION THE SEASON AFTER FINISHING IN LAST PLACE

Season	Team	Record	Previous Season
1967	Houston	9-4-1	*3-11-0
1968	Minnesota	8-6-0	3- 8-3
1970	Cincinnati	8-6-0	4- 9-1
1970	San Francisco	10-3-1	4- 8-2
1972	Green Bay	10-4-0	4- 8-2
1975	Baltimore	10-4-0	2-12-0
1979	Tampa Bay	10-6-0	5-11-0
1981	Cincinnati	12-4-0	6-10-0
1987	Indianapolis	9-6-0	3-13-0
1988	Cincinnati	12-4-0	4-11-0
1990	Cincinnati	9-7-0	8- 8-0
1991	Denver	12-4-0	5-11-0
1992	San Diego	11-5-0	4-12-0
1993	Detroit	10-6-0	5-11-0
1997	N.Y. Giants	10-5-1	6-10-0

**tied for last place*

RECORDS OF NFL TEAMS, 1989-1998

AFC	W	L	T	Pct.	Division Titles	Playoff Berths	Postseason Record	Super Bowl Record
Kansas City	101	58	1	.634	3	7	3-7	0-0
Buffalo	101	59	0	.631	5	8	10-8	0-4
Denver	99	61	0	.619	4	6	10-4	2-1
Pittsburgh	96	64	0	.600	5	7	6-7	0-1
Miami	94	66	0	.588	2	6	4-6	0-0
Jacksonville	35	29	0	.547	1	3	3-3	0-0
Tennessee	84	76	0	.525	2	5	1-5	0-0
Oakland	82	78	0	.513	1	3	2-3	0-0
San Diego	72	88	0	.450	2	3	3-3	0-1
Cleveland	48	63	1	.433	1	2	2-2	0-0
Seattle	68	92	0	.425	0	0	0-0	0-0
New England	65	95	0	.406	2	4	3-4	0-1
Indianapolis	61	99	0	.381	0	2	2-2	0-0
N.Y. Jets	61	99	0	.381	1	2	1-2	0-0
Cincinnati	56	104	0	.350	1	1	1-1	0-0
Baltimore	16	31	1	.344	0	0	0-0	0-0

Oakland totals include L.A. Raiders, 1989-94
Tennessee totals include Houston, 1989-96

NFC	W	L	T	Pct.	Division Titles	Playoff Berths	Postseason Record	Super Bowl Record
San Francisco	123	37	0	.769	7	9	12-7	2-0
Green Bay	95	65	0	.594	3	6	9-5	1-1
Minnesota	95	65	0	.594	4	7	2-7	0-0
Dallas	94	66	0	.588	6	7	12-4	3-0
N.Y. Giants	88	71	1	.553	3	4	4-3	1-0
Philadelphia	86	73	1	.541	0	5	2-5	0-0
Washington	79	80	1	.497	1	3	5-2	1-0
Detroit	78	82	0	.488	2	5	1-5	0-0
New Orleans	77	83	0	.481	1	3	0-3	0-0
Carolina	30	34	0	.469	1	1	1-1	0-0
Chicago	73	87	0	.456	1	3	2-3	0-0
Atlanta	70	90	0	.438	1	3	3-3	0-1
Tampa Bay	61	99	0	.381	0	1	1-1	0-0
Arizona	57	103	0	.356	0	1	1-1	0-0
St. Louis	56	104	0	.350	0	1	2-1	0-0

Arizona totals include Phoenix, 1989-93
St. Louis totals include L.A. Rams, 1989-94

HOME RECORDS, 1989-1998

AFC	W-L-T	Pct.	NFC	W-L-T	Pct.
Denver	63-17-0	.788	San Francisco	67-13-0	.838
Kansas City	62-18-0	.775	Green Bay	60-20-0	.750
Buffalo	60-20-0	.750	Minnesota	55-25-0	.688
Pittsburgh	60-20-0	.750	Dallas	53-27-0	.663
Jacksonville	23- 9-0	.719	Philadelphia	52-28-0	.650
Miami	54-26-0	.675	Detroit	50-30-0	.625
Tennessee	47-33-0	.588	N.Y. Giants	50-30-0	.625
Oakland	46-34-0	.575	Atlanta	48-32-0	.600
San Diego	41-39-0	.513	Washington	45-34-1	.569
Seattle	40-40-0	.500	Chicago	45-35-0	.563
Cleveland	27-28-1	.491	Carolina	17-15-0	.531
Baltimore	11-12-1	.479	New Orleans	42-38-0	.525
Cincinnati	37-43-0	.463	Tampa Bay	40-40-0	.500
New England	37-43-0	.463	Arizona	35-45-0	.438
Indianapolis	36-44-0	.450	St. Louis	32-48-0	.400
New York Jets	32-48-0	.400			

Arizona totals include Phoenix, 1989-93
Oakland totals include L.A. Raiders, 1989-94
St. Louis totals include L.A. Rams, 1989-94
Tennessee totals include Houston, 1989-96

ROAD RECORDS, 1989-1998

AFC	W-L-T	Pct.	NFC	W-L-T	Pct.
Buffalo	41-39-0	.513	San Francisco	56-24-0	.700
Miami	40-40-0	.500	Dallas	41-39-0	.513
Kansas City	39-40-1	.494	Minnesota	40-40-0	.500
Tennessee	37-43-0	.463	N.Y. Giants	38-41-1	.481
Denver	36-44-0	.450	Green Bay	35-45-0	.438
Oakland	36-44-0	.450	New Orleans	35-45-0	.438
Pittsburgh	36-44-0	.450	Philadelphia	34-45-1	.431
San Diego	31-49-0	.388	Washington	34-46-0	.425
Cleveland	21-35-0	.375	Carolina	13-19-0	.406
Jacksonville	12-20-0	.375	Chicago	28-52-0	.350
New York Jets	29-51-0	.363	Detroit	28-52-0	.350
New England	28-52-0	.350	St. Louis	24-56-0	.300
Seattle	28-52-0	.350	Arizona	22-58-0	.275
Indianapolis	25-55-0	.313	Atlanta	22-58-0	.275
Cincinnati	19-61-0	.238	Tampa Bay	21-59-0	.263
Baltimore	5-19-0	.208			

Arizona totals include Phoenix, 1989-93
Oakland totals include L.A. Raiders, 1989-94
St. Louis totals include L.A. Rams, 1989-94
Tennessee totals include Houston, 1989-96

RECORDS BY MONTHS, 1989-1998

AFC	Sept. W-L-T	Oct. W-L-T	Nov. W-L-T	Dec. W-L-T	Total W-L-T	Pct.
Kansas City	29-12	20-17	27-14-1	25-15	101- 58-1	.634
Buffalo	26-11	26-12	28-16	21-20	101- 59-0	.631
Denver	29-12	23-13	29-13	18-23	99- 61-0	.619
Pittsburgh	21-18	25-13	28-15	22-18	96- 64-0	.600
Miami	25-11	25-15	25-18	19-22	94- 66-0	.588
Jacksonville	9- 8	7- 9	10- 6	9- 6	35- 29-0	.547
Tennessee	17-22	22-16	22-20	23-18	84- 76-0	.525
Oakland	19-22	25-12	18-23	20-21	82- 78-0	.513
San Diego	19-22	15-23	20-21	18-22	72- 88-0	.450
Cleveland	15-12	15-12	8-19-1	10-20	48- 63-1	.433
Seattle	16-24	18-21	15-25	19-22	68- 92-0	.425
New England	15-22	12-28	19-23	19-22	65- 95-0	.406
Indianapolis	11-26	17-23	13-29	20-21	61- 99-0	.381
N.Y. Jets	14-26	14-25	22-19	11-29	61- 99-0	.381
Cincinnati	12-26	8-31	16-26	20-21	56-104-0	.350
Baltimore	7- 6	2- 8	3-10-1	4- 7	16- 31-1	.344

Oakland totals include L.A. Raiders, 1989-94
Tennessee totals include Houston, 1989-96
September totals include August
December totals include January

NFC	Sept. W-L-T	Oct. W-L-T	Nov. W-L-T	Dec. W-L-T	Total W-L-T	Pct.
San Francisco	29-10	30- 8	32-10	32- 9	123- 37-0	.769
Green Bay	23-18	19-16	27-15	26-16	95- 65-0	.594
Minnesota	25-16	21-15	24-18	25-16	95- 65-0	.594
Dallas	21-17	25-14	27-18	21-17	94- 66-0	.588

	Sept. W-L-T	Oct. W-L-T	Nov. W-L-T	Dec. W-L-T	Total W-L-T	Pct.
N.Y. Giants	23-16	21-17	20-22-1	24-16	88- 71-1	.553
Philadelphia	19-19	24-14	21-21-1	22-19	86- 73-1	.541
Washington	21-18	17-21	16-26-1	25-15	79- 80-1	.497
Detroit	19-23	16-19	20-24	23-16	78- 82-0	.488
New Orleans	18-22	19-19	20-21	20-21	77- 83-0	.481
Carolina	5-10	7- 9	9- 9	9- 6	30- 34-0	.469
Chicago	19-22	22-14	18-25	14-26	73- 87-0	.456
Atlanta	12-27	16-22	25-17	17-24	70- 90-0	.438
Tampa Bay	17-24	12-25	16-26	16-24	61- 99-0	.381
Arizona	13-26	13-26	16-27	15-24	57- 103-0	.356
St. Louis	20-20	9-28	12-30	15-26	56- 104-0	.350

Arizona totals include Phoenix, 1989-93
St. Louis totals include L.A. Rams, 1989-94
September totals include August
December totals include January

TAKEAWAYS/GIVEAWAYS IN 1989-1998

AFC	Takeaways Int.	Fum.	Total	Giveaways Int.	Fum.	Total	Net.Diff.
Kansas City	174	179	353	130	124	254	99
Pittsburgh	208	156	364	158	143	301	63
Jacksonville	53	57	110	56	42	98	12
Denver	167	136	303	158	137	295	8
N.Y. Jets	175	144	319	178	141	319	0
Buffalo	190	137	327	187	142	329	-2
San Diego	201	113	314	197	122	319	-5
Miami	173	118	291	163	138	301	-10
Cincinnati	163	124	287	160	138	298	-11
Cleveland	116	87	203	124	100	224	-21
Tennessee	181	142	323	173	171	344	-21
Baltimore	49	24	73	51	45	96	-23
Seattle	167	151	318	198	145	343	-25
Indianapolis	139	126	265	176	123	299	-34
New England	172	136	308	202	141	343	-35
Oakland	146	126	272	178	136	314	-42

Oakland totals include L.A. Raiders, 1989-94
Tennessee totals include Houston, 1989-96

NFC	Takeaways Int.	Fum.	Total	Giveaways Int.	Fum.	Total	Net.Diff.
N.Y. Giants	189	125	314	127	110	237	77
San Francisco	201	131	332	134	130	264	68
Minnesota	205	138	343	175	114	289	54
Philadelphia	201	152	353	167	150	317	36
Washington	198	122	320	182	107	289	31
Dallas	142	121	263	142	117	259	4
Green Bay	183	126	309	180	135	315	-6
Atlanta	163	144	307	185	130	315	-8
Chicago	178	132	310	173	146	319	-9
Carolina	73	57	130	78	62	140	-10
Detroit	166	127	293	178	132	310	-17
New Orleans	169	158	327	195	150	345	-18
Tampa Bay	151	144	295	212	125	337	-42
St. Louis	176	120	296	191	153	344	-48
Arizona	162	146	308	223	150	373	-65

Arizona totals include Phoenix, 1989-93
St. Louis totals include L.A. Rams, 1989-94

BEST TAKEAWAY/GIVEAWAY DIFFERENTIAL, SEASON

+43 Washington, 1983
+26 Kansas City, 1990
+25 N.Y. Giants, 1997

HIGH AND LOW SINGLE-GAME YARDAGE TOTALS, 1989-1998

Most Total Yards, Game
676 Washington vs. Detroit, Nov. 4, 1990 (OT)
615 Arizona vs. Washington, Nov. 10, 1996 (OT)
598 San Francisco vs. Buffalo, Sept. 13, 1992
590 San Francisco vs. Atlanta, Oct. 18, 1992
584 Cincinnati vs. Houston, Dec. 17, 1989

Fewest Total Yards, Game
53 Pittsburgh vs. Cleveland, Sept. 10, 1989
62 Seattle vs. Dallas, Oct. 11, 1992
82 Denver vs. Philadelphia, Sept. 20, 1992
87 Seattle vs. Philadelphia, Dec. 13, 1992 (OT)
89 Philadelphia vs. Washington, Sept. 30, 1991
Seattle vs. Kansas City, Dec. 24, 1995

Most Yards Rushing, Game
328 San Francisco vs. Detroit, Dec. 14, 1998
315 Buffalo vs. Atlanta, Nov. 22, 1992
310 Kansas City vs. Detroit, Oct. 14, 1990
304 Philadelphia vs. New England, Nov. 4, 1990
302 N.Y. Jets vs. Indianapolis, Sept. 20, 1998

Fewest Yards Rushing, Game
1 Tampa Bay vs. Washington, Oct. 22, 1989
4 Indianapolis vs. Detroit, Sept. 22, 1991
Buffalo vs. Tennessee, Nov. 23, 1997
6 N.Y. Giants vs. L.A. Rams, Nov. 12, 1989
8 Oakland vs. Kansas City, Dec. 3, 1995
Dallas vs. New Orleans, Dec. 6, 1998

Most Yards Passing, Game
507 Arizona vs. Washington, Nov. 10, 1996 (OT)
505 Houston vs. Kansas City, Dec. 16, 1990
483 Cincinnati vs. L.A. Rams, Oct. 7, 1990 (OT)
482 Washington vs. Detroit, Nov. 4, 1990 (OT)
475 San Francisco vs. L.A. Rams, Nov. 28, 1993

Fewest Yards Passing, Game
-19 San Diego vs. Kansas City, Sept. 20, 1998
Philadelphia vs. Seattle, Sept. 6, 1998
12 Carolina vs. Buffalo, Sept. 10, 1995
13 Seattle vs. Oakland, Dec. 22, 1996
15 New England vs. Atlanta, Nov. 29, 1992

NFL INDIVIDUAL LEADERS, 1989-1998

Points		Touchdowns		Field Goals	
1,118	Gary Anderson	134	Emmitt Smith	255	Gary Anderson
1,105	Morten Andersen	122	Jerry Rice	250	Morten Andersen
1,087	Pete Stoyanovich	109	Barry Sanders	246	Pete Stoyanovich
1,021	Norm Johnson	93	Cris Carter	233	Al Del Greco
1,000	Al Del Greco	84	Thurman Thomas	227	Norm Johnson

Rushes		Rushing Yards		Rushing TDs	
3,062	Barry Sanders	15,269	Barry Sanders	125	Emmitt Smith
2,914	Emmitt Smith	12,566	Emmitt Smith	99	Barry Sanders
2,606	Thurman Thomas	10,905	Thurman Thomas	65	Ricky Watters
1,947	Ricky Watters	7,873	Ricky Watters	63	Thurman Thomas
1,824	Rodney Hampton	7,372	Jerome Bettis	62	Marcus Allen

Attempts		Completions		Passing Yards	
4,889	Dan Marino	2,913	Warren Moon	35,057	Dan Marino
4,809	Warren Moon	2,897	Dan Marino	34,428	Warren Moon
4,596	John Elway	2,681	John Elway	33,331	John Elway
4,011	Troy Aikman	2,479	Troy Aikman	28,346	Troy Aikman
3,967	Vinny Testaverde	2,318	Brett Favre	28,211	Steve Young

TD Passes		Receptions		Reception Yards	
213	Brett Favre	875	Jerry Rice	12,731	Jerry Rice
212	Dan Marino	790	Cris Carter	11,083	Michael Irvin
212	Warren Moon	708	Michael Irvin	9,602	Cris Carter
205	Steve Young	681	Andre Rison	9,463	Andre Reed
198	John Elway	660	Andre Reed	9,455	Irving Fryar

Receiving TDs		Interceptions		Sacks	
115	Jerry Rice	44	Eugene Robinson	122.5	Reggie White
93	Cris Carter	42	Rod Woodson	120.0	Chris Doleman
78	Andre Rison	41	Deion Sanders	119.5	Bruce Smith
64	Tim Brown	39	Eric Allen	119.5	Derrick Thomas
64	Sterling Sharpe	39	Aeneas Williams	118.5	Kevin Greene

NFL GAMES IN WHICH A TEAM HAS SCORED 60 OR MORE POINTS

(Home team in capitals)

Regular Season
WASHINGTON 72, New York Giants 41 .... November 27, 1966
LOS ANGELES RAMS 70, Baltimore 27 .... October 22, 1950
Chicago Cardinals 65, NEW YORK BULLDOGS 20 .... November 13, 1949
LOS ANGELES RAMS 65, Detroit 24 .... October 29, 1950
PHILADELPHIA 64, Cincinnati 0 .... November 6, 1934
CHICAGO CARDINALS 63, New York Giants 35 .... October 17, 1948
AKRON 62, Oorang 0 .... October 29, 1922
PITTSBURGH 62, New York Giants 7 .... November 30, 1952
CLEVELAND 62, New York Giants 14 .... December 6, 1953
CLEVELAND 62, Washington 3 .... November 7, 1954
NEW YORK GIANTS 62, Philadelphia 10 .... November 26, 1972
Atlanta 62, NEW ORLEANS 7 .... September 16, 1973
NEW YORK JETS 62, Tampa Bay 28 .... November 17, 1985
CHICAGO 61, San Francisco 20 .... December 12, 1965
Cincinnati 61, HOUSTON 17 .... December 17, 1972
CHICAGO 61, Green Bay 7 .... December 7, 1980
CINCINNATI 61, Houston 7 .... December 17, 1989
ROCK ISLAND 60, Evansville 0 .... October 15, 1922
CHICAGO CARDINALS 60, Rochester 0 .... October 7, 1923

Postseason
Chicago Bears 73, WASHINGTON 0 .... December 8, 1940

YOUNGEST AND OLDEST PLAYERS IN NFL IN 1998

10 Youngest Players	Birthdate	Games	Starts	Position
Olin Kreutz, Chicago	6/9/77	9	1	C
Az-zahir Hakim, St. Louis	6/3/77	9	4	WR
Robert Williams, Kansas City	5/29/77	16	1	DB
Mike Wahle, Green Bay	3/29/77	1	0	G
Chris Fuamatu-Ma'afala, Pittsburgh	3/4/77	12	0	RB
Ahman Green, Seattle	2/16/77	16	0	RB
Randy Moss, Minnesota	2/13/77	16	11	WR
Jeremiah Trotter, Philadelphia	1/20/77	8	0	LB
R.W. McQuarters, San Francisco	12/21/76	16	7	CB
Takeo Spikes, Cincinnati	12/17/76	16	16	LB

10 Oldest Players	Birthdate	Games	Starts	Position
Steve DeBerg, Atlanta	1/19/54	8	1	QB
Warren Moon, Seattle	11/18/56	10	10	QB
Dave Krieg, Tennessee	10/20/58	5	0	QB
Wade Wilson, Oakland	2/1/59	5	3	QB
Mike Horan, Chicago	2/1/59	13	0	P
Gary Anderson, Minnesota	7/16/59	16	0	K
Darrell Green, Washington	2/15/60	16	16	CB
Norm Johnson, Pittsburgh	5/31/60	15	0	K
John Elway, Denver	6/28/60	13	12	QB
Morten Andersen, Atlanta	8/19/60	16	0	K

YOUNGEST AND OLDEST REGULAR STARTERS BY POSITION IN 1998

Minimum: 8 Games Started

	Youngest		Oldest	
QB	5/15/76	Ryan Leaf, S.D.	11/18/56	Warren Moon, Sea.
RB	6/27/76	Fred Taylor, Jac.	10/14/63	Keith Byars, NY-J
WR	2/13/77	Randy Moss, Minn.	9/28/62	Irving Fryar, Phil.
TE	2/27/76	Tony Gonzalez, K.C.	2/26/66	Wesley Walls, Car.
C	7/20/75	Casey Wiegmann, Chi.	6/17/63	Kevin Glover, Sea.
G	12/7/76	Alan Faneca, Pitt.	8/8/61	Bruce Matthews, Tenn.
T	9/22/76	Mo Collins, Oak.	2/8/63	Raleigh McKenzie, S.D.
DE	12/11/75	Vonnie Holliday, G.B.	10/16/61	Chris Doleman, S.F.
DT	5/27/76	Darrell Russell, Oak.	12/15/64	Jerry Ball, Minn.
LB	12/17/76	Takeo Spikes, Cin.	7/31/62	Kevin Green, Car.
CB	10/7/76	Charles Woodson, Oak.	2/15/60	Darrell Green, Wash.
S	11/6/76	Pat Tillman, Ariz.	10/6/60	Albert Lewis, Oak.

EMMITT SMITH'S CAREER RUSHING VS. EACH OPPONENT

Opponent	Games	Rushes	Yards	Yards Per Rush	Yards Per Game	TD
Arizona	18	374	1,618	4.3	89.9	23
Atlanta	6	114	586	5.1	97.7	7
Buffalo	1	15	25	1.7	25.0	1
Carolina	2	23	115	5.0	57.5	1
Chicago	4	67	322	4.8	80.5	1
Cincinnati	3	56	222	4.0	74.0	1
Cleveland	2	58	224	3.9	112.0	1
Denver	3	72	269	3.7	89.7	3
Detroit	3	64	276	4.3	92.0	4
Green Bay	6	139	567	4.1	94.5	6
Indianapolis	2	51	205	4.0	102.5	2
Jacksonville	1	24	75	3.1	75.0	1
Kansas City	3	56	193	3.4	64.3	2
Miami	2	38	125	3.3	62.5	0
Minnesota	3	57	298	5.2	99.3	6
New England	1	27	85	3.1	85.0	0
New Orleans	4	81	277	3.4	69.3	2
N.Y. Giants	17	332	1,541	4.6	90.6	14
N.Y. Jets	2	35	146	4.2	73.0	0
Oakland	3	79	321	4.1	107.0	7
Philadelphia	18	419	1,967	4.7	109.3	12
Pittsburgh	3	89	349	3.9	116.3	2
St. Louis	2	40	134	3.4	67.0	1
San Diego	2	24	70	2.9	35.0	2
San Francisco	6	110	422	3.8	70.3	4
Seattle	2	39	152	3.9	76.0	2
Tampa Bay	2	39	169	4.3	84.5	1
Tennessee	3	49	161	3.3	53.7	1
Washington	16	343	1,652	4.8	103.3	18
Totals	140	2,914	12,566	4.3	89.8	125

Arizona totals include eight games vs. Phoenix
Oakland totals include one game vs. L.A. Raiders
St. Louis totals include two games vs. L.A. Rams
Tennessee totals include two games vs. Houston

BARRY SANDERS'S CAREER RUSHING VS. EACH OPPONENT

Opponent	Games	Rushes	Yards	Yards Per Rush	Yards Per Game	TD
Arizona	4	83	415	5.0	103.8	2
Atlanta	8	169	681	4.0	85.1	5
Baltimore	1	19	41	2.2	41.0	0
Buffalo	3	70	260	3.7	86.7	2
Chicago	19	368	1,846	5.0	97.2	12
Cincinnati	3	73	450	6.2	150.0	5
Cleveland	3	76	389	5.1	129.7	4
Dallas	3	79	357	4.5	119.0	0
Denver	1	23	147	6.4	147.0	1
Green Bay	19	384	2,059	5.4	108.4	7
Indianapolis	2	54	395	7.3	197.5	4
Jacksonville	2	40	178	4.5	89.0	2
Kansas City	2	36	167	4.6	83.5	2
Miami	3	74	332	4.5	110.7	1
Minnesota	19	363	1,858	5.1	97.8	11
New England	2	50	279	5.6	139.5	2
New Orleans	5	75	307	4.1	61.4	2
N.Y. Giants	5	89	424	4.8	84.8	2
N.Y. Jets	3	66	425	6.4	141.7	3
Oakland	2	34	212	6.2	106.0	2
Philadelphia	2	36	189	5.3	94.5	2
Pittsburgh	4	67	236	3.5	59.0	1
St. Louis	2	52	148	2.8	74.0	1
San Diego	1	16	51	3.2	51.0	2
San Francisco	6	107	452	4.2	75.3	2
Seattle	3	47	258	5.5	86.0	2
Tampa Bay	19	392	2,195	5.6	115.5	14
Tennessee	3	60	199	3.3	66.3	4
Washington	4	60	319	5.3	79.8	2
Totals	153	3,062	15,269	5.0	99.8	99

Arizona totals include two games vs. Phoenix
Oakland totals include one game vs. L.A. Raiders
St. Louis totals include two games vs. L.A. Rams
Tennessee totals include three games vs. Houston

THURMAN THOMAS'S CAREER RUSHING VS. EACH OPPONENT

Opponent	Games	Rushes	Yards	Yards Per Rush	Yards Per Game	TD
Arizona	1	26	112	4.3	112.0	0
Atlanta	3	51	264	5.2	88.0	1
Carolina	2	29	110	3.8	55.0	2
Chicago	3	37	151	4.1	50.3	1
Cincinnati	5	74	334	4.5	66.8	1
Cleveland	2	40	144	3.6	72.0	2
Dallas	2	47	126	2.7	63.0	1
Denver	6	93	390	4.2	65.0	3
Detroit	2	30	131	4.4	65.5	0
Green Bay	4	85	330	3.9	82.5	2
Indianapolis	20	304	1,230	4.0	61.5	7
Jacksonville	2	15	60	4.0	30.0	0
Kansas City	5	76	213	2.8	42.6	1
Miami	20	364	1,620	4.5	81.0	8
Minnesota	3	48	199	4.1	66.3	1
New England	22	400	1,804	4.5	82.0	10
New Orleans	2	40	155	3.9	77.5	2
N.Y. Giants	3	79	279	3.5	93.0	2
N.Y. Jets	22	349	1,590	4.6	72.3	7
Oakland	6	84	376	4.5	62.7	3
Philadelphia	3	53	174	3.3	58.0	1
Pittsburgh	6	118	510	4.3	85.0	1
St. Louis	4	77	369	4.8	92.3	4
San Francisco	4	43	174	4.0	43.5	1
Seattle	4	68	216	3.2	54.0	0
Tampa Bay	2	24	55	2.3	27.5	0
Tennessee	7	103	434	4.2	62.0	2
Washington	3	56	236	4.2	78.7	2
Totals	168	2,813	11,786	4.2	70.2	65

Arizona totals include one game vs. Phoenix
Oakland totals include five games vs. L.A. Raiders
St. Louis totals include two games vs. L.A. Rams
Tennessee totals include six games vs. Houston

INSIDE THE NUMBERS

DAN MARINO'S CAREER PASSING VS. EACH OPPONENT

Opponent	Games	Att.	Cmp.	Pct.	Yards	Avg. Gain	TD	Int.	Sacked
Arizona	3	84	56	66.7	812	9.67	7	0	3/21
Atlanta	4	166	96	57.8	1,216	7.33	5	8	3/15
Baltimore	1	27	19	70.4	189	7.00	0	0	0/0
Buffalo	29	957	592	61.9	7,302	7.63	49	33	40/333
Carolina	1	21	14	66.7	140	6.67	0	1	1/9
Chicago	5	156	81	51.9	1,129	7.24	8	5	12/78
Cincinnati	6	219	143	65.3	1,680	7.67	11	2	6/47
Cleveland	6	205	126	61.5	1,661	8.10	11	5	4/33
Dallas	4	142	78	54.9	1,033	7.27	7	4	4/36
Denver	2	81	48	59.3	745	9.20	7	1	3/25
Detroit	4	152	89	58.6	1,016	6.68	4	3	4/28
Green Bay	6	218	133	61.0	1,568	7.19	12	7	6/37
Indianapolis	31	954	575	60.3	6,831	7.16	49	16	27/172
Jacksonville	1	49	30	61.2	323	6.59	2	1	2/16
Kansas City	7	243	142	58.4	1,687	6.94	12	4	4/35
Minnesota	2	91	49	53.8	695	7.64	5	6	1/5
New England	29	1,024	607	59.3	7,374	7.20	42	45	28/207
New Orleans	4	145	87	60.0	905	6.24	8	3	6/42
N.Y. Giants	2	60	30	50.0	324	5.40	1	4	4/25
N.Y. Jets	28	1,033	608	58.9	8,141	7.88	69	31	40/245
Oakland	10	347	196	56.5	2,356	6.79	18	11	11/90
Philadelphia	3	127	72	56.7	987	7.77	6	2	5/45
Pittsburgh	10	306	193	63.1	2,195	7.17	13	10	10/68
St. Louis	5	182	112	61.5	1,309	7.19	13	6	4/24
San Diego	5	202	128	63.4	1,534	7.59	11	3	6/42
San Francisco	4	144	84	58.3	942	6.54	5	5	8/56
Seattle	2	68	40	58.8	504	7.41	3	4	3/25
Tampa Bay	4	154	98	63.6	1,110	7.21	9	1	1/10
Tennessee	9	291	161	55.3	2,025	6.96	11	11	13/88
Washington	4	141	76	53.9	1,180	8.37	10	3	2/7
Totals	231	7,989	4,763	59.6	58,913	7.37	408	235	261/1,864

Arizona totals include one game vs. St. Louis, one game vs. Phoenix
Indianapolis totals include two games vs. Baltimore Colts
Oakland totals include seven games vs. L.A. Raiders
St. Louis totals include three games vs. L.A. Rams
Tennessee totals include eight games vs. Houston

BRETT FAVRE'S CAREER PASSING VS. EACH OPPONENT

Opponent	Games	Att.	Cmp.	Pct.	Yards	Avg. Gain	TD	Int.	Sacked
Atlanta	2	87	62	71.3	597	6.86	3	2	4/26
Baltimore	1	41	22	53.7	260	6.34	2	2	1/8
Buffalo	2	58	34	58.6	370	6.38	5	1	1/9
Carolina	2	79	45	59.0	644	8.15	8	4	5/26
Chicago	14	430	271	63.0	3,264	7.59	30	14	24/149
Cincinnati	3	117	76	65.0	902	7.71	6	2	9/68
Cleveland	2	61	43	70.5	433	7.10	3	0	4/22
Dallas	5	190	112	58.9	1,123	5.91	10	2	9/75
Denver	2	70	40	57.1	515	7.36	5	5	1/4
Detroit	14	488	309	63.3	3,698	7.58	26	21	26/178
Indianapolis	1	25	18	72.0	363	14.52	3	2	3/29
Jacksonville	1	30	20	66.7	202	6.73	2	1	2/9
Kansas City	2	83	47	56.6	527	6.35	3	4	8/50
Miami	2	88	55	62.5	615	6.99	4	1	5/20
Minnesota	13	390	236	60.5	2,561	6.57	20	16	30/188
New England	2	81	48	59.3	533	6.58	4	2	5/42
New Orleans	2	62	39	62.9	458	7.39	5	0	8/39
N.Y. Giants	3	102	62	60.8	687	6.74	4	3	6/37
N.Y. Jets	1	28	20	71.4	183	6.54	2	0	1/11
Oakland	1	28	14	50.0	190	6.79	1	0	2/9
Philadelphia	6	207	115	55.6	1,527	7.38	10	9	11/61
Pittsburgh	3	90	59	65.6	745	8.28	4	1	7/44
St. Louis	7	219	130	59.4	1,471	6.72	10	10	15/124
San Diego	2	56	35	62.5	377	6.73	3	2	4/49
San Francisco	2	89	43	48.3	674	7.57	4	5	4/22
Seattle	1	34	20	58.8	209	6.15	4	0	2/7
Tampa Bay	14	467	310	66.4	3,267	7.00	28	6	29/135
Tennessee	2	52	33	63.5	408	7.85	4	1	5/11
Washington	1	5	0	0.0	0	0.00	0	2	1/11
Totals	113	3,757	2,318	61.7	26,803	7.13	213	118	232/1,463

Oakland totals include one game vs. L.A. Raiders
St. Louis totals include four games vs. L.A. Rams
Tennessee totals include one game vs. Houston

WARREN MOON'S CAREER PASSING VS. EACH OPPONENT

Opponent	Games	Att.	Cmp.	Pct.	Yards	Avg. Gain	TD	Int.	Sacked
Arizona	5	174	98	56.3	1,296	7.45	11	4	12/101
Atlanta	5	194	111	57.2	1,429	7.37	11	6	12/55
Baltimore	1	19	12	63.2	140	7.37	1	1	3/23
Buffalo	8	206	117	56.8	1,528	7.42	7	9	12/94
Carolina	1	34	19	55.9	209	6.15	2	1	4/17
Chicago	8	281	168	59.8	2,019	7.19	9	8	19/141
Cincinnati	20	649	383	59.0	4,902	7.55	37	22	37/310
Cleveland	19	590	336	56.9	4,315	7.31	25	22	42/314
Dallas	5	177	104	58.8	1,259	7.11	6	5	21/148
Denver	6	198	113	57.1	1,409	7.12	9	3	14/93
Detroit	7	223	142	63.7	1,824	8.18	9	8	12/95
Green Bay	6	222	126	56.8	1,291	5.82	8	10	14/133
Indianapolis	8	293	184	62.8	2,426	8.28	14	8	15/97
Kansas City	12	352	217	61.6	2,614	7.43	13	11	36/251
Miami	6	148	102	68.9	1,236	8.35	8	6	11/112
Minnesota	3	95	58	61.1	592	6.23	2	2	14/106
New England	4	136	76	55.9	946	6.96	6	4	5/41
New Orleans	7	248	144	58.1	1,746	7.04	11	6	16/107
N.Y. Giants	4	142	84	59.2	1,008	7.10	4	4	8/56
N.Y. Jets	5	192	125	65.1	1,500	7.81	8	7	10/86
Oakland	7	254	142	55.9	1,908	7.51	13	11	21/165
Philadelphia	2	67	37	55.2	466	6.96	3	0	4/36
Pittsburgh	21	648	364	56.2	4,604	7.10	25	30	46/334
St. Louis	5	193	109	56.5	1,424	7.38	4	9	11/81
San Diego	8	280	149	53.2	1,910	6.82	11	9	13/87
San Francisco	6	192	109	56.8	1,359	7.08	14	8	16/98
Seattle	4	145	87	60.0	970	6.69	5	6	6/44
Tampa Bay	6	216	132	61.1	1,498	6.94	7	7	9/63
Tennessee	2	83	55	66.3	549	6.61	2	2	3/30
Washington	4	135	69	51.1	720	5.33	5	3	7/51
Totals	205	6,786	3,972	58.5	49,097	7.24	290	232	453/3,369

Arizona totals include one game vs. St. Louis, one game vs. Phoenix
Oakland totals include four games vs. L.A. Raiders
St. Louis totals include four games vs. L.A. Rams
Tennessee totals include one game vs. Houston

TROY AIKMAN'S CAREER PASSING VS. EACH OPPONENT

Opponent	Games	Att.	Cmp.	Pct.	Yards	Avg. Gain	TD	Int.	Sacked
Arizona	18	472	300	63.6	3,914	8.29	19	13	20/131
Atlanta	4	93	67	72.0	943	10.14	8	3	3/19
Buffalo	2	78	44	56.4	461	5.91	0	5	2/11
Carolina	1	26	14	53.8	180	6.92	1	0	4/42
Chicago	3	84	43	51.2	414	4.93	2	2	6/41
Cincinnati	3	108	62	57.4	833	7.71	5	5	2/23
Cleveland	2	73	45	61.6	462	6.33	3	2	4/20
Denver	3	78	48	61.5	515	6.60	6	1	2/9
Detroit	3	106	70	66.0	765	7.22	3	3	4/30
Green Bay	6	182	127	69.8	1,381	7.59	4	4	7/44
Indianapolis	2	55	38	69.1	429	7.80	2	0	2/14
Jacksonville	1	32	21	65.6	262	8.19	2	0	2/24
Kansas City	3	93	60	64.5	583	6.27	5	3	4/29
Miami	3	117	86	73.5	805	6.88	5	2	1/4
Minnesota	3	124	77	62.1	909	7.33	3	0	2/13
New England	1	28	16	57.1	169	6.04	0	2	3/25
New Orleans	4	116	69	59.5	724	6.24	1	4	6/64
N.Y. Giants	19	477	317	66.5	3,399	7.13	16	11	21/129
N.Y. Jets	2	67	46	68.7	501	7.48	2	5	6/40
Oakland	2	49	35	71.4	461	9.41	1	0	6/31
Philadelphia	18	453	238	52.5	2,608	5.76	13	16	47/296
Pittsburgh	2	62	40	64.5	540	8.71	5	1	0/0
St. Louis	3	103	58	56.3	754	7.32	7	2	4/25
San Diego	2	59	34	57.6	415	7.03	1	1	6/39
San Francisco	6	179	103	57.5	1,155	6.45	3	8	14/97
Seattle	2	65	43	66.2	469	7.22	2	3	2/7
Tampa Bay	2	53	30	56.6	332	6.26	2	2	5/38
Tennessee	3	106	65	61.3	844	7.96	4	4	8/38
Washington	17	473	283	59.8	3,119	6.59	16	13	34/244
Totals	140	4,011	2,479	61.8	28,346	7.07	141	115	227/1,527

Arizona totals include eight games vs. Phoenix
Oakland totals include one game vs. L.A. Raiders
St. Louis totals include three games vs. L.A. Rams
Tennessee totals include two games vs. Houston

STEVE YOUNG'S CAREER PASSING VS. EACH OPPONENT

Opponent	Games	Att.	Cmp.	Pct.	Yards	Avg. Gain	TD	Int.	Sacked
Arizona	5	131	69	52.7	885	6.76	5	2	10/71
Atlanta	19	519	342	65.9	4,784	9.22	37	15	31/184
Buffalo	5	162	100	61.7	1,380	8.52	7	5	17/105
Carolina	6	203	134	66.0	1,582	7.79	10	5	15/53
Chicago	6	136	75	55.1	993	7.30	8	3	9/52
Cincinnati	2	55	32	58.2	453	8.24	2	5	5/29
Cleveland	3	34	19	55.9	274	8.06	0	3	1/8
Dallas	6	108	71	65.7	887	8.21	6	2	11/53
Denver	3	66	42	63.6	626	9.48	4	3	3/19
Detroit	10	236	161	68.2	1,846	7.82	14	4	16/116
Green Bay	6	148	83	56.1	854	5.77	3	7	33/231
Indianapolis	3	116	75	64.7	811	6.99	4	3	13/53
Kansas City	4	81	54	66.7	617	7.62	2	4	13/78
Miami	1	27	19	70.4	220	8.15	2	1	0/0
Minnesota	10	268	174	64.9	2,218	8.28	14	9	30/139
New England	4	104	77	74.0	973	9.36	10	4	12/63
New Orleans	19	447	297	66.4	3,411	7.63	27	5	53/305
N.Y. Giants	6	120	72	60.0	759	6.33	5	1	8/50
N.Y. Jets	3	89	54	60.7	708	7.96	6	1	3/17
Oakland	2	67	37	55.2	525	7.84	4	3	4/20
Philadelphia	5	115	73	63.5	805	7.00	5	3	9/59
Pittsburgh	3	72	48	66.7	493	6.85	6	3	4/21
St. Louis	17	417	279	66.9	3,568	8.56	28	7	28/146
San Diego	4	101	73	72.3	911	9.02	7	1	9/50
Seattle	2	18	11	61.1	136	7.56	1	0	0/0
Tampa Bay	5	95	66	69.5	883	9.29	8	0	5/28
Tennessee	3	30	16	53.3	187	6.23	0	2	2/10
Washington	4	100	69	69.0	889	8.89	4	2	7/33
Totals	166	4,065	2,622	64.5	32,678	8.04	229	103	350/1,992

Arizona totals include two games vs. St. Louis, three games vs. Phoenix
Oakland totals include two games vs. L.A. Raiders
St. Louis totals include 12 games vs. L.A. Rams
Tennessee totals include three games vs. Houston

JERRY RICE'S CAREER RECEIVING VS. EACH OPPONENT

Opponent	Games	Rec.	Yards	Yds./Rec.	Yds./Game	TD
Arizona	5	25	465	18.6	93.0	5
Atlanta	25	158	2,481	15.7	99.2	25
Baltimore	1	6	58	9.7	58.0	1
Buffalo	4	14	158	11.3	39.5	1
Carolina	6	45	611	13.6	101.8	1
Chicago	5	24	424	17.7	84.8	7
Cincinnati	4	23	351	15.3	87.8	2
Cleveland	3	19	275	14.5	91.7	4
Dallas	7	43	671	15.6	95.9	4
Denver	4	19	306	16.1	76.5	2
Detroit	9	42	559	13.3	62.1	2
Green Bay	6	37	576	15.6	96.0	7
Indianapolis	4	22	414	78.8	103.5	5
Kansas City	3	13	178	13.7	59.3	2
Miami	3	18	304	16.9	101.3	5
Minnesota	9	50	874	17.5	97.1	10
New England	5	24	409	17.0	81.8	6
New Orleans	26	129	1,857	14.4	71.4	14
N.Y. Giants	8	37	550	14.9	68.8	5
N.Y. Jets	4	21	351	16.7	87.8	3
Oakland	4	18	362	20.1	90.5	2
Philadelphia	6	31	490	15.8	81.7	5
Pittsburgh	4	27	278	10.3	69.5	4
St. Louis	26	142	2,247	15.8	86.4	20
San Diego	3	27	465	17.2	155.0	4
Seattle	3	14	272	19.4	90.7	4
Tampa Bay	8	47	710	15.1	88.8	10
Tennessee	4	28	274	9.8	68.5	2
Washington	7	36	642	17.8	91.7	2
Totals	206	1,139	17,612	15.5	85.5	164

Arizona totals include one game vs. St. Louis, four games vs. Phoenix
Oakland totals include four games vs. L.A. Raiders
St. Louis totals include 20 games vs. L.A. Rams
Tennessee totals include four games vs. Houston

ANDRE REED'S CAREER RECEIVING VS. EACH OPPONENT

Opponent	Games	Rec.	Yards	Yds./Rec.	Yds./Game	TD
Arizona	2	0	0	—	0.0	0
Atlanta	2	9	170	18.9	85.0	1
Carolina	2	2	17	8.5	8.5	0
Chicago	4	16	185	11.6	46.3	0
Cincinnati	7	24	344	14.3	49.1	2
Cleveland	5	25	347	13.9	69.4	2
Dallas	2	6	46	7.7	23.0	0
Denver	7	34	478	14.1	68.3	3
Detroit	3	15	184	12.3	61.3	2
Green Bay	3	21	249	11.9	83.0	3
Indianapolis	26	119	1,656	13.9	63.7	15
Jacksonville	2	6	57	9.5	28.5	0
Kansas City	7	36	557	15.5	79.6	5
Miami	26	120	1,708	14.2	65.7	10
Minnesota	4	18	247	13.7	61.8	0
New England	24	100	1,600	16.0	66.7	8
New Orleans	3	8	74	9.3	24.7	0
N.Y. Giants	3	12	233	19.4	77.7	2
N.Y. Jets	27	102	1,339	13.1	49.6	12
Oakland	6	33	476	14.4	79.3	1
Philadelphia	4	17	183	10.8	45.8	3
Pittsburgh	8	33	389	11.8	48.6	3
St. Louis	3	14	170	12.1	56.7	2
San Diego	3	16	232	14.5	77.3	2
San Francisco	2	20	259	13.0	129.5	0
Seattle	3	6	123	20.5	41.0	1
Tampa Bay	3	8	119	14.9	39.7	0
Tennessee	10	49	756	15.4	75.6	6
Washington	4	20	361	18.1	90.3	2
Totals	205	889	12,559	14.1	61.3	85

Arizona totals include one game vs. St. Louis, one game vs. Phoenix
Oakland totals include five games vs. L.A. Raiders
St. Louis totals include two games vs. L.A. Rams
Tennessee totals include nine games vs. Houston

MICHAEL IRVIN'S CAREER RECEIVING VS. EACH OPPONENT

Opponent	Games	Rec.	Yards	Yds./Rec.	Yds./Game	TD
Arizona	20	81	1,483	18.3	74.2	8
Atlanta	8	41	660	16.1	82.5	3
Buffalo	1	8	115	14.4	115.0	0
Carolina	2	8	213	26.6	106.5	1
Chicago	3	16	213	13.3	71.0	1
Cincinnati	4	24	431	18.0	107.8	1
Cleveland	3	18	248	13.8	82.7	1
Denver	3	18	237	13.2	79.0	2
Detroit	3	16	304	19.0	101.3	1
Green Bay	7	38	633	16.7	90.4	4
Indianapolis	1	7	112	16.0	112.0	0
Jacksonville	1	3	57	19.0	57.0	0
Kansas City	3	18	214	11.9	71.3	1
Miami	2	15	217	14.5	108.5	1
Minnesota	4	28	411	14.7	102.8	2
New England	1	6	76	12.7	76.0	0
New Orleans	6	22	342	15.5	57.0	0
N.Y. Giants	18	75	1,107	14.8	61.5	4
N.Y. Jets	2	10	184	18.4	92.0	2
Oakland	3	16	252	15.8	84.0	1
Philadelphia	19	63	1,039	16.5	54.7	5
Pittsburgh	4	26	522	20.1	130.5	4
St. Louis	2	10	239	23.9	119.5	2
San Diego	1	7	103	14.7	103.0	0
San Francisco	7	43	508	11.8	72.6	3
Seattle	2	14	211	15.1	105.5	0
Tampa Bay	2	2	42	21.0	21.0	1
Tennessee	4	16	259	16.2	64.8	3
Washington	19	91	1,305	14.3	68.7	11
Totals	155	740	11,737	15.9	75.7	62

Arizona totals include 10 games vs. Phoenix
Oakland totals include one game vs. L.A. Raiders
St. Louis totals include two games vs. L.A. Rams
Tennessee totals include three games vs. Houston

INSIDE THE NUMBERS

HERMAN MOORE'S CAREER RECEIVING VS. EACH OPPONENT

Opponent	Games	Rec.	Yards	Yds./Rec.	Yds./Game	TD
Arizona	4	16	238	14.9	59.5	1
Atlanta	6	32	629	19.7	104.8	7
Baltimore	1	10	120	12.0	120.0	0
Buffalo	3	17	310	18.2	103.3	1
Chicago	16	77	1,021	13.3	63.8	5
Cincinnati	2	12	172	14.3	86.0	0
Cleveland	2	11	177	16.1	88.5	0
Dallas	3	12	156	13.0	52.0	1
Green Bay	16	72	970	13.5	60.6	10
Indianapolis	2	2	16	8.0	8.0	0
Jacksonville	2	12	175	14.6	87.5	1
Kansas City	1	7	84	12.0	84.0	0
Miami	3	11	133	12.1	44.3	1
Minnesota	15	77	1,146	14.9	76.4	7
New England	2	10	141	14.1	70.5	0
New Orleans	2	15	153	10.2	76.5	1
N.Y. Giants	3	20	243	12.2	81.0	2
N.Y. Jets	2	10	109	10.9	54.5	0
Oakland	1	10	109	10.9	109.0	2
Philadelphia	2	9	111	12.3	55.5	0
Pittsburgh	3	23	350	15.2	116.7	2
St. Louis	1	6	120	20.0	120.0	0
San Diego	1	3	39	13.0	39.0	0
San Francisco	7	34	441	13.0	63.0	5
Seattle	2	14	153	10.9	76.5	3
Tampa Bay	12	64	820	12.8	68.3	4
Tennessee	2	9	193	21.4	96.5	3
Washington	3	15	138	9.2	46.0	1
Totals	119	610	8,467	13.9	71.2	57

Arizona totals include two games vs. Phoenix
St. Louis totals include one game vs. L.A. Rams
Tennessee totals include two games vs. Houston

CRIS CARTER'S CAREER RECEIVING VS. EACH OPPONENT

Opponent	Games	Rec.	Yards	Yds./Rec.	Yds./Game	TD
Arizona	12	53	774	14.6	64.5	11
Atlanta	3	13	254	19.5	84.7	5
Baltimore	1	11	85	7.7	85.0	1
Buffalo	3	18	242	13.4	80.7	2
Carolina	2	9	108	12.0	54.0	3
Chicago	19	107	1,164	10.9	61.3	5
Cincinnati	4	25	310	12.4	77.5	3
Cleveland	3	12	166	13.8	55.3	0
Dallas	7	29	387	13.3	55.3	6
Denver	5	20	259	13.0	51.8	3
Detroit	18	82	898	11.0	49.9	7
Green Bay	17	85	977	11.5	57.5	8
Indianapolis	1	5	89	17.8	89.0	3
Jacksonville	1	4	27	6.8	27.0	1
Kansas City	3	14	177	12.6	59.0	3
Miami	2	7	81	11.6	40.5	3
Minnesota	2	5	30	6.0	15.0	1
New England	4	24	276	11.5	69.0	1
New Orleans	7	37	433	11.7	61.9	4
N.Y. Giants	9	19	329	17.3	36.6	2
N.Y. Jets	3	18	219	12.2	73.0	2
Oakland	4	21	257	12.2	64.3	1
Philadelphia	2	11	209	19.0	104.5	3
Pittsburgh	2	9	140	15.6	70.0	2
St. Louis	4	12	165	13.8	41.3	1
San Diego	2	9	122	13.6	61.0	0
San Francisco	7	31	283	9.1	40.4	5
Seattle	3	12	217	18.1	72.3	1
Tampa Bay	19	83	1,058	12.7	55.7	8
Tennessee	4	23	289	12.6	72.3	4
Washington	8	26	422	16.2	52.8	2
Totals	181	834	10,447	12.5	57.7	101

Arizona totals include two games vs. St. Louis, six games vs. Phoenix
Oakland totals include three games vs. L.A. Raiders
St. Louis totals include three games vs. L.A. Rams
Tennessee totals include three games vs. Houston

MORTEN ANDERSEN'S CAREER KICKING VS. EACH OPPONENT

Opponent	Games	FG	FGA	FG%	Long FG	XP	XPA	Pts.
Arizona	11	18	18	100.0	52	28	29	82
Atlanta	25	40	51	78.4	49	56	58	176
Buffalo	4	7	11	63.6	50	7	7	28
Carolina	8	16	18	88.9	51	14	14	62
Chicago	6	5	8	62.5	60	14	14	29
Cincinnati	5	5	8	62.5	49	17	17	32
Cleveland	4	7	8	87.5	53	7	7	28
Dallas	10	18	24	75.0	54	17	17	71
Denver	4	4	8	50.0	55	14	15	26
Detroit	9	10	16	62.5	50	18	18	48
Green Bay	6	10	11	90.9	52	15	15	45
Indianapolis	3	3	5	60.0	46	11	11	20
Jacksonville	1	1	2	50.0	46	2	2	5
Kansas City	4	4	5	80.0	50	7	7	19
Miami	5	5	7	71.4	35	15	15	30
Minnesota	9	15	17	88.2	47	15	15	60
New England	6	10	12	83.3	54	16	16	46
New Orleans	8	18	23	78.3	55	19	19	73
N.Y. Giants	8	15	17	88.2	45	15	15	60
N.Y. Jets	6	10	11	90.9	53	12	12	42
Oakland	5	7	9	77.8	51	11	11	32
Philadelphia	10	18	22	81.8	56	19	19	73
Pittsburgh	5	7	9	77.8	50	9	9	30
St. Louis	31	49	57	86.0	51	78	80	225
San Diego	4	3	7	42.9	35	9	9	18
San Francisco	33	51	62	82.3	59	51	53	204
Seattle	4	6	7	85.7	47	8	8	26
Tampa Bay	14	23	31	74.2	50	32	32	101
Tennessee	5	8	12	66.7	47	11	11	35
Washington	7	8	14	57.1	45	11	11	35
Totals	260	401	510	78.6	60	558	556	1,761

Arizona totals include five games vs. St. Louis, four games vs. Phoenix
Oakland totals include four games vs. L.A. Raiders
St. Louis totals include 23 games vs. L.A. Rams
Tennessee totals include five games vs. Houston

STARTING RECORDS OF ACTIVE NFL QUARTERBACKS

Minimum: 10 starts

Player	W - L - T	Pct.
Brett Favre	74 - 35	.679
Steve Bono	28 - 14	.667
Doug Flutie	16 - 8	.667
Steve Young	92 - 48	.657
Brad Johnson	15 - 8	.652
Elvis Grbac	16 - 9	.640
Randall Cunningham	77 - 46 -1	.625
Dan Marino	142 - 87	.620
Jeff Hostetler	51 - 32	.614
Mike Tomczak	41 - 27	.603
Troy Aikman	83 - 57	.593
Mark Brunell	31 - 22	.585
Kordell Stewart	18 - 14	.563
Drew Bledsoe	50 - 39	.562
Dave Krieg	98 - 77	.560
Rich Gannon	31 - 27	.534
Neil O'Donnell	49 - 43	.533
Ty Detmer	10 - 9	.526
Steve McNair	20 - 18	.526
Steve Walsh	20 - 18	.526
Danny Kanell	10 - 9 -1	.525
Wade Wilson	36 - 33	.522
Rodney Peete	37 - 35	.514
Warren Moon	102 -100	.505
Bubby Brister	37 - 38	.493
Chris Chandler	48 - 50	.490
Kerry Collins	24 - 25	.490
Jim Harbaugh	60 - 63	.488
Jake Plummer	12 - 13	.480
Trent Dilfer	31 - 35	.470
Scott Mitchell	30 - 34	.469
Steve Beuerlein	30 - 35	.462
Erik Kramer	29 - 34	.460
Dave Brown	23 - 30	.434
Trent Green	6 - 8	.429
Gus Frerotte	19 - 26 -1	.424
Vinny Testaverde	60 - 84 -1	.417
Charlie Batch	5 - 7	.417
Kent Graham	10 - 14	.417
Todd Collins	7 - 10	.412
Jeff Blake	22 - 32	.407
Craig Erickson	14 - 21	.400
Steve DeBerg	53 - 86 -1	.382
Rick Mirer	20 - 34	.370
Heath Shuler	8 - 14	.364
Eric Zeier	4 - 7	.364
Billy Joe Tolliver	14 - 26	.350
Jeff George	37 - 70	.346
John Friesz	13 - 25	.342
Tony Banks	14 - 29	.326
Billy Joe Hobert	3 - 7	.300
Paul Justin	3 - 7	.300
Bobby Hoying	3 - 9 -1	.269
Frank Reich	5 - 15	.250
Peyton Manning	3 - 13	.188
Craig Whelihan	2 - 12	.143

ALL-TIME RANKINGS OF PLAYERS IN FOUR CATEGORIES THAT DETERMINE NFL PASSER RATING

Minimum: 1,500 Attempts

COMPLETION PERCENTAGE	Pct.	Att.	Comp.
Steve Young	64.50	4,065	2,622
Joe Montana	63.24	5,391	3,409
Troy Aikman	61.81	4,011	2,479
Brett Favre	61.70	3,757	2,318
Mark Brunell	60.38	1,719	1,038
Jim Kelly	60.14	4,779	2,874
Ken Stabler	59.85	3,793	2,270
Danny White	59.69	2,950	1,761
Dan Marino	59.62	4,763	7,989
Ken Anderson	59.31	4,475	2,654

AVERAGE YARDS PER PASS	Avg.	Att.	Yards
Otto Graham	8.63	1,565	13,499
Sid Luckman	8.42	1,744	14,686
Norm Van Brocklin	8.16	2,895	23,611
Steve Young	8.04	4,065	32,678
Ed Brown	7.85	1,987	15,600
Bart Starr	7.85	3,149	24,718
Johnny Unitas	7.76	5,186	40,239
Earl Morrall	7.74	2,689	20,809
Dan Fouts	7.68	5,604	43,040
Len Dawson	7.67	3,741	28,711

TOUCHDOWN PERCENTAGE	Pct.	Att.	TD
Sid Luckman	7.86	1,744	137
Frank Ryan	6.99	2,133	149
Len Dawson	6.39	3,741	239
Daryle Lamonica	6.31	2,601	164
Sammy Baugh	6.24	2,995	187
Charley Conerly	6.11	2,833	173
Bob Waterfield	6.00	1,617	97
Earl Morrall	5.99	2,689	161
Sonny Jurgensen	5.98	4,262	255
Norm Van Brocklin	5.98	2,895	173

INTERCEPTION PERCENTAGE	Pct.	Att.	Int.
Neil O'Donnell	1.99	2,862	57
Steve Bono	2.47	1,700	42
Mark Brunell	2.50	1,719	43
Steve Young	2.53	4,065	103
Joe Montana	2.58	5,391	139
Bernie Kosar	2.59	3,365	87
Jeff George	2.70	3,402	92
Ken O'Brien	2.72	3,602	98
Jeff Blake	2.77	1,841	51
Jim Harbaugh	2.83	3,282	93

HIGHEST NFL POSTSEASON PASSER RATINGS (MINIMUM: 150 ATTEMPTS)

	Games	Att.	Comp.	Pct.	Yds.	Avg. Gain	TD	Int.	Rating
Bart Starr	10	213	130	61.0	1,753	8.23	15	3	104.8
Joe Montana	23	734	460	62.7	5,772	7.86	45	21	95.6
Ken Anderson	6	166	110	66.3	1,321	7.96	9	6	93.5
Joe Theismann	10	211	128	60.7	1,782	8.45	11	7	91.4
Brett Favre	14	449	270	60.1	3,390	7.55	25	12	91.1
Troy Aikman	15	464	298	64.2	3,563	7.68	23	16	89.8
Steve Young	22	471	292	62.0	3,326	7.06	20	13	85.8
Warren Moon	10	403	259	64.3	2,870	7.12	17	14	84.9
Ken Stabler	13	351	203	57.8	2,641	7.52	19	13	84.2
Bernie Kosar	10	270	152	56.3	1,953	7.23	16	10	83.5

HIGHEST NFL POSTSEASON PASSER RATINGS, ACTIVE PLAYERS (MINIMUM: 150 ATTEMPTS)

	Games	Att.	Comp.	Pct.	Yds.	Avg. Gain	TD	Int.	Rating
Brett Favre	14	449	270	60.1	3,390	7.55	25	12	91.1
Troy Aikman	15	464	298	64.2	3,563	7.68	23	16	89.8
Steve Young	22	471	292	62.0	3,326	7.06	20	13	85.8
Warren Moon	10	403	259	64.3	2,870	7.12	17	14	84.9
Dan Marino	16	632	357	56.5	4,219	6.68	30	22	78.3
Wade Wilson	7	185	99	53.5	1,322	7.15	7	6	75.6
Neil O'Donnell	7	273	158	57.9	1,690	6.19	9	8	74.9
Randall Cunningham	10	365	192	52.6	2,426	6.65	12	9	74.3
Dave Krieg	12	282	144	51.1	1,895	6.72	11	9	72.3
Mark Rypien	8	234	126	53.8	1,776	7.54	8	10	72.2

INSIDE THE NUMBERS

NFL INDIVIDUAL LEADERS OVER RECENT SEASONS

Points

Last 2 Seasons		Last 3 Seasons		Last 4 Seasons	
289	Gary Anderson	404	Gary Anderson	502	Gary Anderson
253	Richie Cunningham	380	Al Del Greco	494	Al Del Greco
251	Jason Elam	362	Adam Vinatieri	492	Jason Elam
249	Al Del Greco	360	Jason Elam	464	Steve Christie
248	Ryan Longwell	359	Mike Hollis	452	Norm Johnson

Touchdowns

Last 2 Seasons		Last 3 Seasons		Last 4 Seasons	
38	Terrell Davis	53	Terrell Davis	61	Terrell Davis
26	Jamal Anderson	35	Cris Carter	59	Emmitt Smith
26	Antonio Freeman	35	Antonio Freeman	52	Cris Carter
25	Cris Carter	34	Emmitt Smith	46	Curtis Martin
24	Joey Galloway	33	Karim Abdul-Jabbar	41	three tied

Field Goals

Last 2 Seasons		Last 3 Seasons		Last 4 Seasons	
64	Gary Anderson	95	Al Del Greco	122	Al Del Greco
63	Richie Cunningham	89	Gary Anderson	112	Steve Christie
63	Al Del Greco	83	Adam Vinatieri	111	Gary Anderson
57	Steve Christie	82	Mike Hollis	105	Norm Johnson
56	Adam Vinatieri	81	Steve Christie	104	John Kasay

Rushes

Last 2 Seasons		Last 3 Seasons		Last 4 Seasons	
761	Terrell Davis	1,106	Terrell Davis	1,343	Terrell Davis
705	Eddie George	1,040	Eddie George	1,327	Curtis Martin
700	Jamal Anderson	1,011	Jerome Bettis	1,299	Barry Sanders
691	Jerome Bettis	985	Barry Sanders	1,294	Ricky Watters
678	Barry Sanders	959	Curtis Martin	1,284	Emmitt Smith

Rushing Yards

Last 2 Seasons		Last 3 Seasons		Last 4 Seasons	
3,758	Terrell Davis	5,296	Terrell Davis	6,597	Barry Sanders
3,544	Barry Sanders	5,097	Barry Sanders	6,413	Terrell Davis
2,850	Jerome Bettis	4,281	Jerome Bettis	5,383	Emmitt Smith
2,848	Jamal Anderson	4,061	Eddie George	5,086	Curtis Martin
2,693	Eddie George	3,903	Jamal Anderson	5,033	Ricky Watters

Rushing TDs

Last 2 Seasons		Last 3 Seasons		Last 4 Seasons	
36	Terrell Davis	49	Terrell Davis	56	Terrell Davis
21	Karim Abdul-Jabbar	32	Karim Abdul-Jabbar	54	Emmitt Smith
21	Jamal Anderson	29	Emmitt Smith	40	Curtis Martin
17	Emmitt Smith	29	Ricky Watters	40	Ricky Watters
16	Antowain Smith	27	Terry Allen	37	Terry Allen
16	Ricky Watters			37	Barry Sanders

Passes

Last 2 Seasons		Last 3 Seasons		Last 4 Seasons	
1,085	Dan Marino	1,626	Drew Bledsoe	2,262	Drew Bledsoe
1,064	Brett Favre	1,607	Brett Favre	2,177	Brett Favre
1,003	Drew Bledsoe	1,458	Dan Marino	1,940	Dan Marino
907	Steve McNair	1,440	Vinny Testaverde	1,866	John Elway
898	Kordell Stewart	1,346	Mark Brunell	1,832	Vinny Testaverde

Completions

Last 2 Seasons		Last 3 Seasons		Last 4 Seasons	
651	Brett Favre	976	Brett Favre	1,335	Brett Favre
629	Dan Marino	950	Drew Bledsoe	1,273	Drew Bledsoe
577	Drew Bledsoe	855	Vinny Testaverde	1,159	Dan Marino
563	Steve Young	850	Dan Marino	1,096	Vinny Testaverde
530	Vinny Testaverde	825	Mark Brunell	1,093	John Elway

Passing Yards

Last 2 Seasons		Last 3 Seasons		Last 4 Seasons	
8,079	Brett Favre	11,978	Brett Favre	16,391	Brett Favre
7,339	Drew Bledsoe	11,425	Drew Bledsoe	14,932	Drew Bledsoe
7,277	Dan Marino	10,404	Vinny Testaverde	13,740	Dan Marino
7,199	Steve Young	10,249	Mark Brunell	13,739	John Elway
6,441	John Elway	10,072	Dan Marino	13,287	Vinny Testaverde

Touchdown Passes

Last 2 Seasons		Last 3 Seasons		Last 4 Seasons	
66	Brett Favre	105	Brett Favre	143	Brett Favre
55	Steve Young	80	Vinny Testaverde	101	John Elway
49	John Elway	75	Drew Bledsoe	97	Vinny Testaverde
48	Drew Bledsoe	75	John Elway	89	Steve Young
47	Vinny Testaverde	69	Steve Young	88	Drew Bledsoe

Receptions

Last 2 Seasons		Last 3 Seasons		Last 4 Seasons	
186	Herman Moore	292	Herman Moore	415	Herman Moore
185	Tim Brown	275	Tim Brown	385	Cris Carter
167	Cris Carter	263	Cris Carter	364	Tim Brown
166	O.J. McDuffie	243	Jimmy Smith	333	Carl Pickens
165	Antonio Freeman	240	O.J. McDuffie	324	Michael Irvin

Reception Yards

Last 2 Seasons		Last 3 Seasons		Last 4 Seasons	
2,667	Antonio Freeman	3,750	Jimmy Smith	5,258	Herman Moore
2,566	Rob Moore	3,600	Antonio Freeman	4,866	Tim Brown
2,506	Jimmy Smith	3,582	Rob Moore	4,802	Michael Irvin
2,420	Tim Brown	3,572	Herman Moore	4,614	Cris Carter
2,402	Rod Smith	3,524	Tim Brown	4,489	Rob Moore

Receiving Touchdowns

Last 2 Seasons		Last 3 Seasons		Last 4 Seasons	
26	Antonio Freeman	35	Cris Carter	52	Cris Carter
25	Cris Carter	35	Antonio Freeman	39	Carl Pickens
22	Joey Galloway	29	Joey Galloway	36	Antonio Freeman
22	Terrell Owens	26	Tony Martin	36	Joey Galloway
18	three tied	26	Terrell Owens	36	Herman Moore

Interceptions

Last 2 Seasons		Last 3 Seasons		Last 4 Seasons	
12	Ray Buchanan	20	Keith Lyle	23	Keith Lyle
12	Terrell Buckley	18	Terrell Buckley	21	Willie Clay
12	Ty Law	16	Darryl Williams	20	Darryll Lewis
11	four tied	15	four tied	19	Terrell Buckley
				19	Merton Hanks
				19	Aeneas Williams

Sacks

Last 2 Seasons		Last 3 Seasons		Last 4 Seasons	
29.0	Michael Strahan	41.5	Michael Sinclair	49.0	Kevin Greene
28.5	Michael Sinclair	40.0	Kevin Greene	48.0	John Randle
27.0	Chris Doleman	38.0	Chris Doleman	48.0	Bruce Smith
27.0	Reggie White	37.5	John Randle	47.5	Reggie White
26.0	John Randle	37.5	Bruce Smith	47.0	Chris Doleman
				47.0	Michael Sinclair

NFL TEAM LEADERS OVER RECENT SEASONS

Highest Won-Lost Percentage

Last 2 Seasons		Last 3 Seasons		Last 4 Seasons	
.813	Denver	.813	Denver	.750	Green Bay
.781	San Francisco	.771	Green Bay	.750	San Francisco
.750	Green Bay	.771	San Francisco	.734	Denver
.750	Minnesota	.688	Minnesota	.656	Kansas City
.688	Jacksonville	.646	Jacksonville	.641	Minnesota

Most Points

Last 2 Seasons		Last 3 Seasons		Last 4 Seasons	
973	Denver	1,364	Denver	1,752	Denver
910	Minnesota	1,286	Green Bay	1,709	San Francisco
854	San Francisco	1,252	San Francisco	1,690	Green Bay
830	Green Bay	1,208	Minnesota	1,620	Minnesota
786	Jacksonville	1,124	New England	1,433	Atlanta

Most Total Yards

Last 2 Seasons		Last 3 Seasons		Last 4 Seasons	
11,964	Denver	17,755	Denver	23,795	Denver
11,912	San Francisco	17,418	San Francisco	23,505	San Francisco
11,618	Minnesota	16,822	Minnesota	22,760	Minnesota
11,250	Green Bay	16,785	Green Bay	22,535	Green Bay
10,883	Detroit	16,398	Jacksonville	22,009	Detroit

Most Rushing Yards

Last 2 Seasons		Last 3 Seasons		Last 4 Seasons	
4,846	Denver	7,208	Denver	9,203	Denver
4,513	Pittsburgh	6,812	Pittsburgh	8,664	Pittsburgh
4,513	San Francisco	6,360	San Francisco	7,998	Tennessee
4,419	Detroit	6,334	Tennessee	7,982	Detroit
4,384	Tennessee	6,229	Detroit	7,950	Kansas City

Most Passing Yards

Last 2 Seasons		Last 3 Seasons		Last 4 Seasons	
7,815	Green Bay	11,512	Green Bay	15,834	Green Bay
7,641	Minnesota	11,299	Minnesota	15,666	San Francisco
7,399	San Francisco	11,111	New England	15,504	Minnesota
7,210	New England	11,058	San Francisco	14,940	Miami
7,187	Miami	10,926	Jacksonville	14,702	New England

*Fewest Turnovers

Last 2 Seasons		Last 3 Seasons		Last 4 Seasons	
38	Dallas	67	Dallas	90	Dallas
40	Jacksonville	69	Cincinnati	97	Kansas City
41	Denver	70	Jacksonville	98	Jacksonville
42	Minnesota	72	Miami	101	Cincinnati
43	N.Y. Giants	73	Denver	102	San Francisco
		73	New England	103	Detroit

*Fewest Points Allowed

Last 2 Seasons		Last 3 Seasons		Last 4 Seasons	
553	N.Y. Jets	811	Green Bay	1,108	San Francisco
558	Tampa Bay	839	Dallas	1,125	Green Bay
574	N.Y. Giants	850	San Francisco	1,130	Dallas
589	Dallas	851	Tampa Bay	1,136	Kansas City
592	Miami	867	Pittsburgh	1,186	Tampa Bay

Last 2 Seasons		Last 3 Seasons		Last 4 Seasons	
***Fewest Total Yards Allowed**					
8,973	Tampa Bay	13,490	Green Bay	18,415	San Francisco
9,334	Green Bay	13,787	Tampa Bay	18,591	Pittsburgh
9,356	San Francisco	14,017	San Francisco	18,645	Green Bay
9,374	San Diego	14,030	Pittsburgh	19,106	Dallas
9,544	Buffalo	14,062	Dallas	19,268	Philadelphia
***Fewest Rushing Yards Allowed**					
2,838	San Diego	4,375	Pittsburgh	5,534	San Francisco
2,869	Atlanta	4,421	Denver	5,696	Pittsburgh
2,960	Pittsburgh	4,473	San Francisco	6,094	Tennessee
2,976	San Francisco	4,568	Tennessee	6,249	Green Bay
3,090	Denver	4,593	San Diego	6,284	San Diego
***Fewest Passing Yards Allowed**					
5,643	Philadelphia	8,622	Philadelphia	11,438	Philadelphia
5,736	Washington	8,698	Tampa Bay	12,145	Dallas
5,773	Tampa Bay	8,756	Green Bay	12,396	Green Bay
6,016	Green Bay	8,873	Dallas	12,452	Washington
6,067	Dallas	9,184	Washington	12,565	N.Y. Jets
Most Opponents' Turnovers					
74	San Francisco	108	San Francisco	142	San Francisco
72	Atlanta	105	N.Y. Giants	137	Pittsburgh
71	Seattle	103	Pittsburgh	137	St. Louis
70	N.Y. Giants	103	Seattle	136	Minnesota
67	Kansas City	101	St. Louis	136	N.Y. Giants

**Baltimore excluded from last-four-seasons' list; Cleveland excluded from all lists.*

RECORDS OF TEAMS ON OPENING DAY, 1933-1998

AFC	W	L	T	Pct.	Longest W Strk.	Longest L Strk.	Current Streak
Jacksonville	3	1	0	.750	3	1	W-3
Denver	25	13	1	.658	4	4	W-4
Kansas City	23	16	0	.590	7	4	W-1
Cleveland	26	20	0	.565	5	5	L-1
San Diego	22	17	0	.564	6	6	W-1
Miami	18	14	1	.563	7	5	W-7
Oakland	21	18	0	.538	5	5	L-3
Pittsburgh	31	29	4	.517	4	3	W-1
Tennessee	20	19	0	.513	4	3	W-2
Indianapolis	23	23	1	.500	8	8	L-2
Cincinnati	15	16	0	.484	4	4	L-1
New England	18	21	0	.462	6	3	L-1
Buffalo	16	23	0	.410	6	5	L-2
N.Y. Jets	16	23	0	.410	3	5	L-1
Baltimore	1	2	0	.333	1	2	L-2
Seattle	6	17	0	.261	3	8	W-1

NFC	W	L	T	Pct.	Longest W Strk.	Longest L Strk.	Current Streak
Dallas	29	9	1	.763	17	3	W-2
N.Y. Giants	37	25	4	.597	4	3	W-2
Chicago	38	27	1	.585	9	6	L-2
Minnesota	21	16	1	.568	4	3	W-3
St. Louis	33	28	0	.541	5	6	L-1
Green Bay	34	29	3	.540	5	6	W-3
San Francisco	25	23	1	.521	5	3	W-1
Detroit	33	31	2	.516	7	4	L-1
Atlanta	17	16	0	.515	5	3	W-1
Washington	31	31	4	.500	6	5	L-1
Arizona	26	38	1	.406	6	7	L-7
Philadelphia	26	38	1	.406	5	9	L-2
Tampa Bay	9	14	0	.391	3	5	L-1
Carolina	1	3	0	.250	1	2	L-2
New Orleans	8	24	0	.250	1	6	W-1

Kansas City totals include Dallas Texans, 1960-62.
Oakland totals include L.A. Raiders, 1982-94.
San Diego totals include L.A. Chargers, 1960.
Indianapolis totals include Baltimore, 1953-83.
Tennessee totals include Houston, 1960-96.
New England totals include Boston, 1960-70.
St. Louis totals include Cleveland, 1937-42 and 1944-45, and L.A. Rams, 1946-94.
Detroit totals include Portsmouth, 1933.
Arizona totals include Chi. Cardinals, 1933-59, St. Louis, 1960-87, and Phoenix, 1988-93.
NOTE: All tied games occurred prior to 1972, when calculation of ties in percentages as half-win, half-loss was begun.

OLDEST INDIVIDUAL SINGLE-SEASON OR SINGLE-GAME RECORDS IN NFL RECORD & FACT BOOK

Regular-Season Records That Have Not Been Surpassed or Tied

Most Points, Game—40, Ernie Nevers, Chi. Cardinals vs. Chi. Bears, Nov. 28, 1929 (6-td, 4-pat)

Most Touchdowns Rushing, Game—6, Ernie Nevers, Chi. Cardinals vs. Chi. Bears, Nov. 28, 1929

Highest Punting Average, Season (Qualifiers)—51.40, Sammy Baugh, Washington, 1940 (35-1,799)

Highest Punting Average, Game (minimum: 4 punts)—61.75, Bob Cifers, Detroit vs. Chi. Bears, Nov. 24, 1946 (4-247)

Highest Average Gain, Pass Receptions, Season (minimum: 24 receptions)—32.58, Don Currivan, Boston, 1947 (24-782)

Highest Average Gain, Passing, Game (minimum: 20 passes)—18.58, Sammy Baugh, Washington vs. Boston, Oct. 31, 1948 (24-446)

Most Touchdowns, Fumble Recoveries, Game—2, Fred (Dippy) Evans, Chi. Bears vs. Washington, Nov. 28, 1948

Most Yards Gained, Intercepted Passes, Rookie, Season—301, Don Doll, Detroit, 1949

Most Passes Had Intercepted, Game—8, Jim Hardy, Chi. Cardinals vs. Philadelphia, Sept. 24, 1950

Highest Average Gain, Rushing, Game (minimum: 10 attempts)—17.09, Marion Motley, Cleveland vs. Pittsburgh, Oct. 29, 1950 (11-188)

Highest Kickoff Return Average, Game (minimum: 3 returns)—73.50, Wally Triplett, Detroit vs. Los Angeles, Oct. 29, 1950 (4-294)

Most Pass Receptions, Game—18, Tom Fears, Los Angeles vs. Green Bay, Dec. 3, 1950

Highest Punt Return Average, Season (Qualifiers)—23.00, Herb Rich, Baltimore, 1950 (12-276)

Highest Punt Return Average, Rookie, Season (Qualifiers)—23.00, Herb Rich, Baltimore, 1950 (12-276)

Most Yards Passing, Game—554, Norm Van Brocklin, Los Angeles vs. N.Y. Yanks, Sept. 28, 1951

Most Touchdowns, Punt Returns, Rookie, Season—4, Jack Christiansen, Detroit, 1951

Most Interceptions By, Season—14, Dick (Night Train) Lane, Los Angeles, 1952

Most Interceptions By, Rookie, Season—14, Dick (Night Train) Lane, Los Angeles, 1952

Highest Average Gain, Passing, Season (Qualifiers)—11.17, Tommy O'Connell, Cleveland, 1957 (110-1,229)

Most Points, Season—176, Paul Hornung, Green Bay, 1960 (15-td, 41-pat,15-fg)

Most Yards Gained, Pass Receptions, Rookie, Season—1,473, Bill Groman, Houston, 1960

INSIDE THE NUMBERS

RETIRED UNIFORM NUMBERS IN NFL

AFC

Baltimore:	None	
Buffalo:	None	
Cincinnati:	Bob Johnson	54
Cleveland:	Otto Graham	14
	Jim Brown	32
	Ernie Davis	45
	Don Fleming	46
	Lou Groza	76
Denver:	Frank Tripucka	18
	Floyd Little	44
Indianapolis:	Johnny Unitas	19
	Buddy Young	22
	Lenny Moore	24
	Art Donovan	70
	Jim Parker	77
	Raymond Berry	82
	Gino Marchetti	89
Jacksonville	None	
Kansas City:	Jan Stenerud	3
	Len Dawson	16
	Abner Haynes	28
	Stone Johnson	33
	Mack Lee Hill	36
	Willie Lanier	63
	Bobby Bell	78
	Buck Buchanan	86
Miami:	Bob Griese	12
New England:	Gino Cappelletti	20
	Mike Haynes	40
	Steve Nelson	57
	John Hannah	73
	Jim Hunt	79
	Bob Dee	89
New York Jets:	Joe Namath	12
	Don Maynard	13
Oakland:	None	
Pittsburgh:	None	
San Diego:	Dan Fouts	14
Seattle:	"Fans/the twelfth man"	12
	Steve Largent	80
Tennessee:	Earl Campbell	34
	Jim Norton	43
	Mike Munchak	63
	Elvin Bethea	65

NFC

Arizona:	Larry Wilson	8
	Stan Mauldin	77
	J.V. Cain	88
	Marshall Goldberg	99
Atlanta:	Steve Bartowski	10
	William Andrews	31
	Jeff Van Note	57
	Tommy Nobis	60
Carolina	None	
Chicago:	Bronko Nagurski	3
	George McAfee	5
	George Halas	7
	Willie Galimore	28
	Walter Payton	34
	Gale Sayers	40
	Brian Piccolo	41
	Sid Luckman	42
	Dick Butkus	51
	Bill Hewitt	56
	Bill George	61
	Bulldog Turner	66
	Red Grange	77
Dallas:	None	
Detroit:	Dutch Clark	7
	Bobby Layne	22
	Doak Walker	37
	Joe Schmidt	56
	Chuck Hughes	85
	Charlie Sanders	88
Green Bay:	Tony Canadeo	3
	Don Hutson	14
	Bart Starr	15
	Ray Nitschke	66
Minnesota:	Fran Tarkenton	10
	Paul Krause	22
	Alan Page	88
New Orleans:	Jim Taylor	31
	Doug Atkins	81
New York Giants:	Ray Flaherty	1
	Tuffy Leemans	4
	Mel Hein	7
	Phil Simms	11
	Y.A. Tittle	14
	Al Blozis	32
	Joe Morrison	40
	Charlie Conerly	42
	Ken Strong	50
	Lawrence Taylor	56
Philadelphia:	Steve Van Buren	15
	Tom Brookshier	40
	Pete Retzlaff	44
	Chuck Bednarik	60
	Al Wistert	70
	Jerome Brown	99
St. Louis:	Bob Waterfield	7
	Merlin Olsen	74
	Jackie Slater	78
San Francisco:	John Brodie	12
	Joe Montana	16
	Joe Perry	34
	Jimmy Johnson	37
	Hugh McElhenny	39
	Charlie Krueger	70
	Leo Nomellini	73
	Dwight Clark	87
Tampa Bay:	Lee Roy Selmon	63
Washington:	Sammy Baugh	33

1998 NFL SCORE BY QUARTERS

AFC Offense	1	2	3	4	OT	PTS
Denver	144	156	64	137	0	501
N.Y. Jets	78	125	101	112	0	416
Buffalo	67	139	95	99	0	400
Jacksonville	100	127	81	84	0	392
Seattle	107	91	75	99	0	372
New England	60	116	62	99	0	337
Tennessee	54	112	71	93	0	330
Kansas City	77	67	105	78	0	327
Miami	54	115	61	88	3	321
Indianapolis	105	69	47	89	0	310
Oakland	51	92	66	79	0	288
Baltimore	79	63	41	86	0	269
Cincinnati	26	90	66	80	6	268
Pittsburgh	40	86	70	67	0	263
San Diego	39	66	58	78	0	241

NFC Offense	1	2	3	4	OT	PTS
Minnesota	135	138	139	144	0	556
San Francisco	79	163	116	112	9	479
Atlanta	114	91	106	131	0	442
Green Bay	107	89	73	139	0	408
Dallas	72	124	80	105	0	381
Carolina	60	108	61	107	0	336
Arizona	61	99	69	93	3	325
Washington	94	80	57	88	0	319
Tampa Bay	61	101	49	103	0	314
Detroit	57	88	72	86	3	306
New Orleans	50	125	41	83	6	305
N.Y. Giants	81	67	86	53	0	287
St. Louis	37	91	72	85	0	285
Chicago	51	95	53	77	0	276
Philadelphia	33	47	24	57	0	161

AFC Defense	1	2	3	4	OT	PTS
Miami	51	70	44	100	0	265
New York Jets	75	63	54	68	6	266
Pittsburgh	24	112	63	101	3	303
Denver	54	87	58	110	0	309
Seattle	71	73	61	105	0	310
Tennessee	58	69	87	106	0	320
New England	64	111	67	84	3	329
Buffalo	40	97	70	126	0	333
Baltimore	96	104	85	50	0	335
Jacksonville	42	138	53	105	0	338
San Diego	94	101	71	76	0	342
Oakland	88	101	74	93	0	356
Kansas City	101	100	65	97	0	363
Indianapolis	60	170	61	147	6	444
Cincinnati	113	143	99	97	0	452

NFC Defense	1	2	3	4	OT	PTS
Dallas	77	82	66	50	0	275
Atlanta	60	95	76	58	0	289
Tampa Bay	78	71	57	89	0	295
Minnesota	50	93	58	95	0	296
New York Giants	72	89	78	70	0	309
Green Bay	70	100	57	92	0	319
San Francisco	98	70	30	130	0	328
Philadelphia	85	53	94	109	3	344
New Orleans	74	126	74	85	0	359
Chicago	61	104	116	87	0	368
Arizona	61	127	68	122	0	378
Detroit	64	114	74	120	6	378
St. Louis	116	107	80	75	0	378
Carolina	84	117	128	81	3	413
Washington	92	133	93	103	0	421
NFL Totals	2,173	3,020	2,161	2,831	30	10,215

TEAM LEADERS

Offense	Most Scored	Fewest Scored
1st Quarter	144 Denver	26 Cincinnati
2nd Quarter	163 San Francisco	47 Philadelphia
3rd Quarter	139 Minnesota	24 Philadelphia
4th Quarter	144 Minnesota	53 N.Y. Giants

Defense	Most Allowed	Fewest Allowed
1st Quarter	116 St. Louis	24 Pittsburgh
2nd Quarter	170 Indianapolis	53 Philadelphia
3rd Quarter	128 Carolina	30 San Francisco
4th Quarter	147 Indianapolis	50 Baltimore Dallas

LARGEST TRADES IN NFL HISTORY

(Based on number of players or draft choices involved)

18—October 13, 1989—RB Herschel Walker from the Dallas Cowboys to Minnesota. Dallas also traded its third-round choice in 1990, its tenth-round choice in 1990, and its third-round choice in 1991 to Minnesota. Minnesota traded LB Jesse Solomon, LB David Howard, CB Issiac Holt, and DE Alex Stewart along with its first-round choice in 1990, its second-round choice in 1990, its sixth-round choice in 1990, its first-round choice in 1991, its second-round choice in 1991, its first-round choice in 1992, its second-round choice in 1992, and its third-round choice in 1992 to Dallas. Minnesota traded RB Darrin Nelson to Dallas, which traded Nelson to San Diego for the Chargers' fifth-round choice in 1990, which Dallas then sent to Minnesota.

15—March 26, 1953—T Mike McCormack, DT Don Colo, LB Tom Catlin, DB John Petitbon, and G Herschell Forester from Baltimore to Cleveland for DB Don Shula, DB Bert Rechichar, DB Carl Taseff, LB Ed Sharkey, E Gern Nagler, QB Harry Agganis, T Dick Batten, T Stu Sheets, G Art Spinney, and G Elmer Willhoite.

15—January 28, 1971—LB Marlin McKeever, first- and third-round choices in 1971, and third-, fourth-, fifth-, sixth-, and seventh-round choices in 1972 from Washington to the Los Angeles Rams for LB Maxie Baughan, LB Jack Pardee, LB Myron Pottios, RB Jeff Jordan, G John Wilbur, DT Diron Talbert, and a fifth-round choice in 1971.

12—June 13, 1952—Selection rights to Les Richter from the Dallas Texans to the Los Angeles Rams for RB Dick Hoerner, DB Tom Keane, DB George Sims, C Joe Reid, HB Billy Baggett, T Jack Halliday, FB Dick McKissack, LB Vic Vasicek, E Richard Wilkins, C Aubrey Phillips, and RB Dave Anderson.

10—March 23, 1959—HB Ollie Matson from the Chicago Cardinals to the Los Angeles Rams for T Frank Fuller, DE Glenn Holtzman, T Ken Panfil, DT Art Hauser, E John Tracey, FB Larry Hickman, HB Don Brown, the Rams second-round choice in 1960, and a player to be delivered during the 1959 training camp.

10—October 31, 1987—RB Eric Dickerson from the Los Angeles Rams to Indianapolis. The rights to LB Cornelius Bennett from Indianapolis to Buffalo. Indianapolis running back Owen Gill and the Colts' first- and second-round choices in 1988 and second-round choice in 1989, plus Bills running back Greg Bell and Buffalo's first-round choice in 1988 and first- and second-round choices in 1989 to the Rams.

OTHER SIGNIFICANT TRADES

March 21, 1967—QB Fran Tarkenton from Minnesota to the New York Giants for the Giants' first- and second-round selections in 1967, first-round selection in 1968, and second-round selection in 1969.

January 27, 1972—QB Fran Tarkenton from the New York Giants to Minnesota for QB Norm Snead, WR Bob Grim, RB Vince Clements, and the Vikings' first-round selection in 1972 and second-round selection in 1973.

June 8, 1973—QB Roman Gabriel from Los Angeles to Philadelphia for WR Harold Jackson, RB Tony Baker, the Eagles' first-round selection in 1974, and the Eagles' first- and third-round selections in 1975.

October 22, 1974—QB John Hadl from Los Angeles to Green Bay for the Packers' first- and third-round selections in 1975, Baltimore's second-round selection in 1975, and the Packers' first- and second-round selections in 1976.

April 5, 1976—QB Jim Plunkett from New England to San Francisco for the 49ers' first-round selection in 1976, Houston's first-round selection in 1976, the 49ers' first- and second-round selections in 1977, and QB Tom Owen.

April 17, 1999—Washington's first-round selection in 1999 (fifth overall) to New Orleans for the Saints first-round selection in 1999 (12th overall); third-round, fourth-round, fifth-round, sixth-round, and seventh-round selections in 1999; and first-round and third-round selections in 2000. The Saints drafted Texas RB Ricky Williams.

INSIDE THE NUMBERS

GREATEST COMEBACKS IN NFL HISTORY

(Most Points Overcome To Win Game)

REGULAR SEASON GAMES

FROM 28 POINTS BEHIND TO WIN:
December 7, 1980, at San Francisco

New Orleans	14	21	0	0	0	— 35
San Francisco	0	7	14	14	3	— 38

NO — Harris 33 pass from Manning (Ricardo kick)
NO — Childs 21 pass from Manning (Ricardo kick)
NO — Holmes 1 run (Ricardo kick)
SF — Solomon 57 punt return (Wersching kick)
NO — Holmes 1 run (Ricardo kick)
NO — Harris 41 pass from Manning (Ricardo kick)
SF — Montana 1 run (Wersching kick)
SF — Clark 71 pass from Montana (Wersching kick)
SF — Solomon 14 pass from Montana (Wersching kick)
SF — Elliott 7 run (Wersching kick)
SF — FG Wersching 36

	N.O.	S.F.
First Downs	27	24
Total Yards	519	430
Yards Rushing	143	176
Yards Passing	376	254
Turnovers	3	0

FROM 26 POINTS BEHIND TO WIN:
September 21, 1997, at Buffalo

Indianapolis	14	12	0	9	— 35
Buffalo	0	10	6	21	— 37

Ind — Bailey 10 pass from Harbaugh (Blanchard kick)
Ind — Faulk 10 run (Blanchard kick)
Ind — FG Blanchard 39
Ind — FG Blanchard 36
Ind — FG Blanchard 49
Ind — FG Blanchard 22
Buff — Johnson 16 pass from Collins (Christie kick)
Buff — FG Christie 27
Buff — A. Smith 15 run (2-pt attempt failed)
Ind — FG Blanchard 25
Buff — Early 4 pass from Collins (Christie kick)
Buff — A. Smith 1 run (Christie kick)
Buff — A. Smith 54 run (Christie kick)
Ind — Harrison 2 pass from Justin (2-pt attempt failed)

	Ind.	Buff.
First Downs	17	25
Total Yards	322	393
Yards Rushing	124	163
Yards Passing	198	230
Turnovers	1	5

FROM 25 POINTS BEHIND TO WIN:
November 8, 1987, at St. Louis

Tampa Bay	7	7	14	0	— 28
St. Louis	0	3	0	28	— 31

TB — Carrier 5 pass from DeBerg (Igwebuike kick)
TB — Carter 3 pass from DeBerg (Igwebuike kick)
StL — FG Gallery 31
TB — Smith 34 pass from DeBerg (Igwebuike kick)
TB — Smith 3 run (Igwebuike kick)
StL — Awalt 4 pass from Lomax (Gallery kick)
StL — Noga 23 fumble recovery (Gallery kick)
StL — J. Smith 11 pass from Lomax (Gallery kick)
StL — J. Smith 17 pass from Lomax (Gallery kick)

	T.B.	St.L.
First Downs	26	26
Total Yards	377	415
Yards Rushing	83	137
Yards Passing	294	278
Turnovers	1	2

FROM 24 POINTS BEHIND TO WIN:
October 27, 1946, at Washington

Philadelphia	0	0	14	14	— 28
Washington	10	14	0	0	— 24

Wash — Rosato 2 run (Poillon kick)
Wash — FG Poillon 28
Wash — Rosato 4 run (Poillon kick)
Wash — Lapka recovered fumble in end zone (Poillon kick)
Phil — Steele 1 run (Lio kick)
Phil — Pritchard 45 pass from Thompson (Lio kick)
Phil — Steinke 7 pass from Thompson (Lio kick)
Phil — Ferrante 30 pass from Thompson (Lio kick)

	Phil.	Wash.
First Downs	14	8
Total Yards	262	127
Yards Rushing	34	66
Yards Passing	228	61
Turnovers	6	3

FROM 24 POINTS BEHIND TO WIN:
October 20, 1957, at Detroit

Baltimore	7	14	6	0	— 27
Detroit	0	3	7	21	— 31

Balt — Mutscheller 15 pass from Unitas (Rechichar kick)
Det — FG Martin 47
Balt — Moore 72 pass from Unitas (Rechichar kick)
Balt — Mutscheller 52 pass from Unitas (Rechichar kick)
Balt — Moore 4 pass from Unitas (kick failed)
Det — Junker 14 pass from Rote (Layne kick)
Det — Cassady 26 pass from Layne (Layne kick)
Det — Johnson 1 run (Layne kick)
Det — Cassady 29 pass from Layne (Layne kick)

	Balt.	Det.
First Downs	15	20
Total Yards	322	369
Yards Rushing	117	178
Yards Passing	205	191
Turnovers	6	4

FROM 24 POINTS BEHIND TO WIN:
October 25, 1959, at Minneapolis

Philadelphia	0	0	21	7	— 28
Chicago Cardinals	7	10	7	0	— 24

Cardinals — Crow 10 pass from Roach (Conrad kick)
Cardinals — J. Hill 77 blocked field goal return (Conrad kick)
Cardinals — FG Conrad 15
Cardinals — Lane 37 interception return (Conrad kick)
Phil — Barnes 1 run (Walston kick)
Phil — McDonald 29 pass from Van Brocklin (Walston kick)
Phil — Barnes 2 run (Walston kick)
Phil — McDonald 22 pass from Van Brocklin (Walston kick)

	Phil.	Cardinals
First Downs	22	14
Total Yards	399	313
Yards Rushing	168	163
Yards Passing	231	150
Turnovers	2	6

FROM 24 POINTS BEHIND TO WIN:
October 23, 1960, at Denver

Boston	10	7	7	0	— 24
Denver	0	0	14	17	— 31

Bos — FG Cappelletti 12
Bos — Colclough 10 pass from Songin (Cappelletti kick)
Bos — Wells 6 pass from Songin (Cappelletti kick)
Bos — Miller 47 pass from Songin (Cappelletti kick)
Den — Carmichael 21 pass from Tripucka (Mingo kick)
Den — Jessup 19 pass from Tripucka (Mingo kick)
Den — Carmichael 35 lateral from Taylor, pass from Tripucka (Mingo kick)
Den — Taylor 8 pass from Tripucka (Mingo kick)
Den — FG Mingo 9

	Bos.	Den.
First Downs	19	16
Total Yards	434	326
Yards Rushing	211	65
Yards Passing	223	261
Turnovers	7	4

FROM 24 POINTS BEHIND TO WIN:
December 15, 1974, at Miami

New England	21	3	0	3	— 27
Miami	0	17	7	10	— 34

NE — Hannah recovered fumble in end zone (J. Smith kick)
NE — Sanders 23 interception return (J. Smith kick)
NE — Herron 4 pass from Plunkett (J. Smith kick)
NE — FG J. Smith 46
Mia — Nottingham 1 run (Yepremian kick)
Mia — Baker 37 pass from Morrall (Yepremian kick)
Mia — FG Yepremian 28
Mia — Baker 46 pass from Morrall (Yepremian kick)
NE — FG J. Smith 34
Mia — Nottingham 2 run (Yepremian kick)
Mia — FG Yepremian 40

	N.E.	Mia.
First Downs	18	18
Total Yards	333	333
Yards Rushing	114	61
Yards Passing	219	272
Turnovers	3	4

FROM 24 POINTS BEHIND TO WIN:
December 4, 1977, at Minnesota

San Francisco	0	10	14	3	— 27
Minnesota	0	0	7	21	— 28

SF — Delvin Williams 2 run (Wersching kick)
SF — FG Wersching 31
SF — Dave Williams 80 kickoff return (Wersching kick)
SF — Delvin Williams 5 run (Wersching kick)
Minn — McClanahan 15 pass from Lee (Cox kick)
Minn — Rashad 8 pass from Kramer (Cox kick)
Minn — Tucker 9 pass from Kramer (Cox kick)
SF — FG Wersching 31
Minn — S. White 69 pass from Kramer (Cox kick)

	S.F.	Minn.
First Downs	19	18
Total Yards	243	309
Yards Rushing	196	52
Yards Passing	47	257
Turnovers	2	5

FROM 24 POINTS BEHIND TO WIN:
September 23, 1979, at Denver

Seattle	10	10	14	0	— 34
Denver	0	10	21	6	— 37

Sea — FG Herrera 28
Sea — Doornink 5 run (Herrera kick)
Den — FG Turner 27
Sea — Doornink 5 run (Herrera kick)
Den — Armstrong 2 run (Turner kick)
Sea — FG Herrera 22
Sea — McCullum 13 pass from Zorn (Herrera kick)
Sea — Smith 1 run (Herrera kick)
Den — Studdard 2 pass from Morton (Turner kick)
Den — Moses 11 pass from Morton (Turner kick)
Den — Upchurch 35 pass from Morton (Turner kick)
Den — Lytle 1 run (kick failed)

	Sea.	Den.
First Downs	22	23
Total Yards	350	344
Yards Rushing	153	90
Yards Passing	197	254
Turnovers	4	3

FROM 24 POINTS BEHIND TO WIN:
September 23, 1979, at Cincinnati

Houston	0	10	17	0	3	—30
Cincinnati	14	10	0	3	0	—27

Cin — Johnson 1 run (Bahr kick)
Cin — Alexander 2 run (Bahr kick)
Cin — Johnson 1 run (Bahr kick)
Cin — FG Bahr 52
Hou — Burrough 35 pass from Pastorini (Fritsch kick)
Hou — FG Fritsch 33
Hou — Campbell 8 run (Fritsch kick)
Hou — Caster 22 pass from Pastorini (Fritsch kick)
Hou — FG Fritsch 47
Cin — FG Bahr 55
Hou — FG Fritsch 29

	Hou.	Cin.
First Downs	19	21
Total Yards	361	265
Yards Rushing	177	165
Yards Passing	184	100
Turnovers	3	2

FROM 24 POINTS BEHIND TO WIN:
November 22, 1982, at Los Angeles

San Diego	10	14	0	0 — 24
L.A. Raiders	0	7	14	7 — 28

SD — FG Benirschke 19
SD — Scales 29 pass from Fouts (Benirschke kick)
SD — Muncie 2 run (Benirschke kick)
SD — Muncie 1 run (Benirschke kick)
Raiders — Christensen 1 pass from Plunkett (Bahr kick)
Raiders — Allen 3 run (Bahr kick)
Raiders — Allen 6 run (Bahr kick)
Raiders — Hawkins 1 run (Bahr kick)

	S.D.	Raiders
First Downs	26	23
Total Yards	411	326
Yards Rushing	72	181
Yards Passing	339	145
Turnovers	4	2

FROM 24 POINTS BEHIND TO WIN:
September 26, 1988, at Denver

L.A. Raiders	0	0	14	13	3 — 30
Denver	7	17	0	3	0 — 27

Den — Dorsett 1 run (Karlis kick)
Den — Dorsett 1 run (Karlis kick)
Den — Sewell 7 pass from Elway (Karlis kick)
Den — FG Karlis 39
Raiders — Smith 40 pass from Schroeder (Bahr kick)
Raiders — Smith 42 pass from Schroeder (Bahr kick)
Raiders — FG Bahr 28
Raiders — Allen 4 run (Bahr kick)
Den — FG Karlis 25
Raiders — FG Bahr 44
Raiders — FG Bahr 35

	Raiders	Den.
First Downs	20	23
Total Yards	363	398
Yards Rushing	128	189
Yards Passing	235	209
Turnovers	1	5

FROM 24 POINTS BEHIND TO WIN:
December 6, 1992, at Tampa

L.A. Rams	0	3	21	7 — 31
Tampa Bay	6	21	0	0 — 27

TB — FG Murray 34
TB — FG Murray 47
TB — Armstrong 81 pass from Testaverde (Murray kick)
TB — Jones 26 fumble recovery (Murray kick)
Rams — FG Zendejas 18
TB — Carrier 10 pass from Testaverde (Murray kick)
Rams — Anderson 40 pass from Everett (Zendejas kick)
Rams — Chadwick 27 pass from Everett (Zendejas kick)
Rams — Lang 1 run (Zendejas kick)
Rams — Carter 8 pass from Everett (Zendejas kick)

	Rams	T.B.
First Downs	21	16
Total Yards	405	313
Yards Rushing	63	150
Yards Passing	342	163
Turnovers	3	3

POSTSEASON GAMES

FROM 32 POINTS BEHIND TO WIN:
AFC First-Round Playoff Game
January 3, 1993, at Buffalo

Houston	7	21	7	3	0 — 38
Buffalo	3	0	28	7	3 — 41

Hou — Jeffires 3 pass from Moon (Del Greco kick)
Buff — FG Christie 36
Hou — Slaughter 7 pass from Moon (Del Greco kick)
Hou — Duncan 26 pass from Moon (Del Greco kick)
Hou — Jeffires 27 pass from Moon (Del Greco kick)
Hou — McDowell 58 interception return (Del Greco kick)
Buff — Davis 1 run (Christie kick)
Buff — Beebe 38 pass from Reich (Christie kick)
Buff — Reed 26 pass from Reich (Christie kick)
Buff — Reed 18 pass from Reich (Christie kick)
Buff — Reed 17 pass from Reich (Christie kick)
Hou — FG Del Greco 26
Buff — FG Christie 32

	Hou.	Buff.
First Downs	27	19
Total Yards	429	366
Yards Rushing	82	98
Yards Passing	347	268
Turnovers	2	1

FROM 20 POINTS BEHIND TO WIN:
Western Conference Playoff Game
December 22, 1957, at San Francisco

Detroit	0	7	14	10 — 31
San Francisco	14	10	3	0 — 27

SF — Owens 34 pass from Tittle (Soltau kick)
SF — McElhenny 47 pass from Tittle (Soltau kick)
Det — Junker 4 pass from Rote (Martin kick)
SF — Wilson 12 pass from Tittle (Soltau kick)
SF — FG Soltau 25
SF — FG Soltau 10
Det — Tracy 2 run (Martin kick)
Det — Tracy 58 run (Martin kick)
Det — Gedman 3 run (Martin kick)
Det — FG Martin 14

	Det.	S.F.
First Downs	22	20
Total Yards	324	351
Yards Rushing	129	127
Yards Passing	195	224
Turnovers	5	4

FROM 18 POINTS BEHIND TO WIN:
NFC Divisional Playoff Game
December 23, 1972, at San Francisco

Dallas	3	10	0	17 — 30
San Francisco	7	14	7	0 — 28

SF — Washington 97 kickoff return (Gossett kick)
Dall — FG Fritsch 37
SF — Schreiber 1 run (Gossett kick)
SF — Schreiber 1 run (Gossett kick)
Dall — FG Fritsch 45
Dall — Alworth 28 pass from Morton (Fritsch kick)
SF — Schreiber 1 run (Gossett kick)
Dall — FG Fritsch 27
Dall — Parks 20 pass from Staubach (Fritsch kick)
Dall — Sellers 10 pass from Staubach (Fritsch kick)

	Dall.	S.F.
First Downs	22	13
Total Yards	402	255
Yards Rushing	165	105
Yards Passing	237	150
Turnovers	5	3

FROM 18 POINTS BEHIND TO WIN:
AFC Divisional Playoff Game
January 4, 1986, at Miami

Cleveland	7	7	7	0 — 21
Miami	3	0	14	7 — 24

Mia — FG Reveiz 51
Clev — Newsome 16 pass from Kosar (Bahr kick)
Clev — Byner 21 run (Bahr kick)
Clev — Byner 66 run (Bahr kick)
Mia — Moore 6 pass from Marino (Reveiz kick)
Mia — Davenport 31 run (Reveiz kick)
Mia — Davenport 1 run (Reveiz kick)

	Clev.	Mia.
First Downs	17	20
Total Yards	313	330
Yards Rushing	251	92
Yards Passing	62	238
Turnovers	1	1

RECORDS OF NFL TEAMS SINCE 1970 AFL-NFL MERGER

AFC	W - L - T	Pct.	Division Titles	Playoff Berths	Post-season Record	Super Bowl Record
Miami	284-154-2	.648	11	18	18-16	2-3
Oakland	263-171-6	.606	9	15	18-12	3-0
Pittsburgh	263-176-1	.599	14	18	21-14	4-1
Denver	256-178-6	.589	9	13	16-11	2-4
Jacksonville**	35- 29-0	.547	1	3	3-3	0-0
Kansas City	219-214-7	.506	4	9	3-9	0-0
Cleveland+	194-195-3	.499	6	10	4-10	0-0
Buffalo	212-226-2	.484	7	12	12-12	0-4
New England	204-236-0	.464	4	9	6-9	0-2
Cincinnati	203-237-0	.461	5	7	5-7	0-2
Seattle*	164-192-0	.461	1	4	3-4	0-0
San Diego	196-239-5	.451	5	7	6-7	0-1
Tennessee	197-241-2	.450	2	10	7-10	0-0
N.Y. Jets	183-255-2	.418	1	6	4-6	0-0
Indianapolis	180-258-2	.411	5	8	6-7	1-0
Baltimore***	16- 31-1	.344	0	0	0-0	0-0

NFC	W - L - T	Pct.	Division Titles	Playoff Berths	Post-season Record	Super Bowl Record
Dallas	277-163-0	.630	15	21	31-16	5-3
San Francisco	273-164-3	.624	16	19	24-14	5-0
Minnesota	261-177-2	.595	13	19	13-19	0-3
Washington	257-181-2	.587	5	13	18-10	3-2
St. Louis	229-207-4	.525	8	14	10-14	0-1
Chicago	219-220-1	.499	6	10	7-9	1-0
Green Bay	207-225-8	.479	4	8	10-7	1-1
Philadelphia	207-226-7	.478	2	10	5-10	0-1
N.Y. Giants	207-230-3	.474	4	8	10-6	2-0
Carolina**	30- 34-0	.469	1	1	1-1	0-0
Detroit	198-238-4	.454	3	8	1-8	0-0
Atlanta	184-252-4	.422	2	6	4-6	0-1
Arizona	183-251-6	.422	2	4	1-4	0-0
New Orleans	177-259-4	.406	1	4	0-4	0-0
Tampa Bay*	118-237-1	.333	2	4	2-4	0-0

*entered NFL in 1976.
**entered NFL in 1995.
***entered NFL in 1996.
+ Did not play 1996-98.
Oakland totals include L.A. Raiders, 1982-94.
Tennessee totals include Houston, 1970-96.
Indianapolis totals include Baltimore, 1970-83.
St. Louis totals include L.A. Rams, 1970-94.
Arizona totals include St. Louis, 1970-87, and Phoenix, 1988-93.
Tie games before 1972 are not calculated in won-lost percentage.
In 1982, because of players' strike, the divisional format was abandoned; L.A. Raiders and Washington won regular-season conference titles, not included in "Division Titles" totals listed above. Sixteen teams were awarded playoff berths, included in totals listed above.

INSIDE THE NUMBERS

LONGEST WINNING STREAKS SINCE 1970

Regular-Season Games

16	Miami, 1971-73	(1 in 1971, 14 in 1972, 1 in 1973)
16	Miami, 1983-84	(5 in 1983, 11 in 1984)
15	San Francisco, 1989-90	(5 in 1989, 10 in 1990)
14	Oakland, 1976-77	(10 in 1976, 4 in 1977)
14	Denver, 1997-98	(1 in 1997, 13 in 1998)
13	Minnesota, 1974-75	(3 in 1974, 10 in 1975)
13	Chicago, 1984-85	(1 in 1984, 12 in 1985)
13	N.Y. Giants, 1989-90	(3 in 1989, 10 in 1990)
12	Washington, 1990-91	(1 in 1990, 11 in 1991)
11	Pittsburgh, 1975	
11	Baltimore, 1975-76	(9 in 1975, 2 in 1976)
11	Chicago, 1986-87	(7 in 1986, 4 in 1987)
11	Houston, 1993	
11	San Francisco, 1997	
10	Miami, 1973	
10	Pittsburgh, 1976-77	(9 in 1976, 1 in 1977)
10	Denver, 1984	
10	San Francisco, 1994	

NFL PLAYOFF APPEARANCES BY SEASONS

Team	Number of Seasons in Playoffs
Dallas	25
N.Y. Giants	24
Cleveland	23
St. Louis	22
Chicago	21
Minnesota	21
San Francisco	20
Green Bay	19
Washington	19
Pittsburgh	19
Miami	18
Oakland	18
Buffalo	16
Tennessee	15
Philadelphia	14
Denver	13
Detroit	13
Indianapolis	13
Kansas City	13
San Diego	12
New England	10
N.Y. Jets	8
Cincinnati	7
Arizona	6
Atlanta	6
New Orleans	4
Seattle	4
Tampa Bay	4
Jacksonville	3
Carolina	1

TEAMS IN SUPER BOWL CONTENTION, 1978-1998

	With 3 Weeks to Play	With 2 Weeks to Play	With 1 Week to Play
1998	22	19	14
1997	22	18	14
1996	23	21	13
1995	*27	21	*18
1994	25	*22	15
1993	20	18	16
1992	20	16	14
1991	20	18	13
1990	23	20	15
1989	21	18	17
1988	21	18	15
1987	19	19	15
1986	19	17	14
1985	21	18	13
1984	18	14	13
1983	24	19	15
1982	20	17	16
1981	21	20	16
1980	20	14	12
1979	19	15	13
1978	20	17	12

*NFL Record

GAMES DECIDED BY 7 POINTS OR LESS AND 3 POINTS OR LESS (1970-1998)

	Games Decided by 7 Points or Less	Games Decided by 3 Points or Less
1970	59 of 182 (32.4%)	34 of 182 (18.7%)
1971	76 of 182 (41.8%)	35 of 182 (19.2%)
1972	71 of 182 (39.0%)	38 of 182 (20.9%)
1973	60 of 182 (32.9%)	28 of 182 (15.4%)
1974	91 of 182 (50.0%)	37 of 182 (20.3%)
1975	62 of 182 (34.1%)	35 of 182 (19.2%)
1976	73 of 196 (37.2%)	38 of 196 (19.4%)
1977	85 of 196 (43.4%)	36 of 196 (18.4%)
1978	108 of 224 (48.2%)	49 of 224 (21.9%)
1979	104 of 224 (46.4%)	51 of 224 (22.8%)
1980	108 of 224 (48.2%)	58 of 224 (25.9%)
1981	91 of 224 (40.6%)	**60 of 224 (26.8%)
1982	61 of 126 (48.4%)	33 of 126 (26.2%)
1983	106 of 224 (47.3%)	54 of 224 (24.1%)
1984	95 of 224 (42.4%)	58 of 224 (25.9%)
1985	87 of 224 (38.8%)	38 of 224 (17.0%)
1986	106 of 224 (47.3%)	48 of 224 (21.4%)
1987	99 of 210 (47.1%)	40 of 210 (19.0%)
1988	113 of 224 (50.4%)	62 of 224 (27.7%)
1989	107 of 224 (47.8%)	55 of 224 (24.6%)
1990	97 of 224 (43.3%)	54 of 224 (24.1%)
1991	112 of 224 (50.0%)	57 of 224 (25.4%)
1992	88 of 224 (39.3%)	**48 of 224 (21.4%)
1993	*105 of 224 (46.9%)	53 of 224 (23.7%)
1994	115 of 224 (51.3%)	60 of 224 (26.8%)
1995	115 of 240 (47.9%)	61 of 240 (25.4%)
1996	109 of 240 (45.4%)	47 of 240 (19.6%)
1997	111 of 240 (46.3%)	67 of 240 (27.9%)
1998	113 of 240 (47.1%)	50 of 240 (20.8%)

*Week record: Dec. 11-13, 1993 (Week 15), 12 of 14 games (86%) decided by 7 points or less.

**Week record: Nov. 8-9, 1981 (Week 10), 8 of 14 games (57%), and Nov. 15-16, 1992 (Week 11), 8 of 14 games (57%) decided by 3 points or less.

1998 RECORDS OF TEAMS IN CLOSE GAMES

AFC	Overall Record	Decided by 8 Pts. or Less	Decided By 3 Pts. or Less
Baltimore	6-10	4-4	1-2
Buffalo	10-6	5-5	2-2
Cincinnati	3-13	3-4	1-0
Denver	14-2	5-1	0-0
Indianapolis	3-13	2-8	1-1
Jacksonville	11-5	5-2	1-2
Kansas City	7-9	3-5	2-2
Miami	10-6	3-4	1-1
New England	9-7	5-3	3-2
N.Y. Jets	12-4	4-2	2-1
Oakland	8-8	6-2	5-1
Pittsburgh	7-9	5-3	1-2
San Diego	5-11	5-6	4-2
Seattle	8-8	3-6	1-3
Tennessee	8-8	3-5	2-2

NFC	Overall Record	Decided by 8 Pts. or Less	Decided By 3 Pts. or Less
Arizona	9-7	7-3	7-1
Atlanta	14-2	6-0	0-0
Carolina	4-12	3-9	0-4
Chicago	4-12	3-7	2-3
Dallas	10-6	4-3	0-3
Detroit	5-11	3-5	2-2
Green Bay	11-5	7-3	1-1
Minnesota	15-1	3-1	1-1
New Orleans	6-10	4-4	0-2
N.Y. Giants	8-8	3-2	0-1
Philadelphia	3-13	3-6	2-3
St. Louis	4-12	2-6	1-2
San Francisco	12-4	4-2	3-1
Tampa Bay	8-8	3-5	3-1
Washington	6-10	4-4	1-2

SUPER BOWL CHAMPIONS WHO DID NOT MAKE PLAYOFFS THE FOLLOWING YEAR

N.Y. Giants—Super Bowl XXV champions did not make playoffs in the 1991 season.

Washington—Super Bowl XXII champions did not make playoffs in the 1988 season.

N.Y. Giants—Super Bowl XXI champions did not make playoffs in the 1987 season.

San Francisco—Super Bowl XVI champions did not make playoffs in the 1982 season.

Oakland—Super Bowl XV champions did not make playoffs in the 1981 season.

Pittsburgh—Super Bowl XIV champions did not make playoffs in the 1980 season.

Kansas City—Super Bowl IV champions did not make playoffs in the 1970 season.

Green Bay—Super Bowl II champions did not make playoffs in the 1968 season.

NON-DIVISION WINNERS THAT PLAYED IN SUPER BOWL

1997	Denver Broncos (Defeated Green Bay, 31-24)	Super Bowl XXXII
1992	Buffalo Bills (Lost to Dallas, 52-17)	Super Bowl XXVII
1985	New England Patriots (Lost to Chicago, 46-10)	Super Bowl XX
1980	Oakland Raiders (Defeated Philadelphia, 27-10)	Super Bowl XV
1975	Dallas Cowboys (Lost to Pittsburgh, 21-17)	Super Bowl X
1969	Kansas City Chiefs (Defeated Minnesota, 23-7)	Super Bowl IV

TEAMS AT OR UNDER .500 IN POSTSEASON PLAY

1991	New York Jets	8-8
1990	New Orleans Saints	8-8
1985	Cleveland Browns	8-8
1982	Cleveland Browns	4-5
1982	Detroit Lions	4-5
1969	Houston Oilers	6-6-2

COLDEST NFL GAMES ON RECORD

-13 degrees (-48 degree wind chill)—December 31, 1967, Lambeau Field, Green Bay, Wisconsin, NFL Championship (Green Bay 21, Dallas 17)

-9 degrees (-59 degree wind chill)—January 10, 1982, Riverfront Stadium, Cincinnati, Ohio, AFC Championship (Cincinnati 27, San Diego 7)

0 degrees (-32 degree wind chill)—January 15, 1994, Rich Stadium, Orchard Park, New York, AFC Divisional Playoff (Buffalo 29, Los Angeles Raiders 23)

1 degree (wind chill not recorded)—January 4, 1981, Cleveland Stadium, Cleveland, Ohio, AFC Divisional Playoff (Oakland 14, Cleveland 12)

ALL-TIME REGULAR-SEASON RECORDS OF CURRENT NFL TEAMS

AFC

BALTIMORE RAVENS

	All Games			Home Games			Road Games		
Season	W	L	T	W	L	T	W	L	T
1996	4	12		4	4		0	8	
1997	6	9	1	3	4	1	3	5	
1998	6	10		4	4		2	6	
	16	31	1	11	12	1	5	19	

BUFFALO BILLS

	All Games			Home Games			Road Games		
Season	W	L	T	W	L	T	W	L	T
1960	5	8	1	3	4		2	4	1
1961	6	8		2	5		4	3	
1962	7	6	1	3	3	1	4	3	
1963	7	6	1	4	2	1	3	4	
1964	12	2		6	1		6	1	
1965	10	3	1	5	2		5	1	1
1966	9	4	1	4	2	1	5	2	
1967	4	10		2	5		2	5	
1968	1	12	1	1	6		0	6	1
1969	4	10		4	3		0	7	
1970	3	10	1	1	6		2	4	1

Season	All Games W	L	T	Home Games W	L	T	Road Games W	L	T
1971	1	13		1	6		0	7	
1972	4	9	1	2	4	1	2	5	
1973	9	5		5	2		4	3	
1974	9	5		5	2		4	3	
1975	8	6		3	4		5	2	
1976	2	12		1	6		1	6	
1977	3	11		1	6		2	5	
1978	5	11		4	4		1	7	
1979	7	9		3	5		4	4	
1980	11	5		6	2		5	3	
1981	10	6		7	1		3	5	
1982	4	5		4	1		0	4	
1983	8	8		3	5		5	3	
1984	2	14		2	6		0	8	
1985	2	14		2	6		0	8	
1986	4	12		3	5		1	7	
1987	7	8		4	4		3	4	
1988	12	4		8	0		4	4	
1989	9	7		6	2		3	5	
1990	13	3		8	0		5	3	
1991	13	3		7	1		6	2	
1992	11	5		6	2		5	3	
1993	12	4		6	2		6	2	
1994	7	9		4	4		3	5	
1995	10	6		6	2		4	4	
1996	10	6		7	1		3	5	
1997	6	10		4	4		2	6	
1998	10	6		6	2		4	4	
	277	295	8	159	128	4	118	167	4

CINCINNATI BENGALS

Season	All Games W	L	T	Home Games W	L	T	Road Games W	L	T
1968	3	11		2	5		1	6	
1969	4	9	1	4	3		0	6	1
1970	8	6		5	2		3	4	
1971	4	10		3	4		1	6	
1972	8	6		4	3		4	3	
1973	10	4		7	0		3	4	
1974	7	7		4	3		3	4	
1975	11	3		6	1		5	2	
1976	10	4		6	1		4	3	
1977	8	6		5	2		3	4	
1978	4	12		3	5		1	7	
1979	4	12		4	4		0	8	
1980	6	10		3	5		3	5	
1981	12	4		6	2		6	2	
1982	7	2		4	0		3	2	
1983	7	9		4	4		3	5	
1984	8	8		5	3		3	5	
1985	7	9		5	3		2	6	
1986	10	6		6	2		4	4	
1987	4	11		1	7		3	4	
1988	12	4		8	0		4	4	
1989	8	8		5	3		3	5	
1990	9	7		5	3		4	4	
1991	3	13		3	5		0	8	
1992	5	11		3	5		2	6	
1993	3	13		3	5		0	8	
1994	3	13		2	6		1	7	
1995	7	9		3	5		4	4	
1996	8	8		6	2		2	6	
1997	7	9		6	2		1	7	
1998	3	13		1	7		2	6	
	210	257	1	132	102		78	155	1

CLEVELAND BROWNS

Season	All Games W	L	T	Home Games W	L	T	Road Games W	L	T
1950	10	2		5	1		5	1	
1951	11	1		6	0		5	1	
1952	8	4		4	2		4	2	
1953	11	1		6	0		5	1	
1954	9	3		5	1		4	2	
1955	9	2	1	5	1		4	1	1
1956	5	7		1	5		4	2	
1957	9	2	1	6	0		3	2	1
1958	9	3		4	2		5	1	
1959	7	5		3	3		4	2	
1960	8	3	1	4	2		4	1	1
1961	8	5	1	4	3		4	2	1
1962	7	6	1	4	2	1	3	4	
1963	10	4		5	2		5	2	
1964	10	3	1	5	1	1	5	2	
1965	11	3		5	2		6	1	
1966	9	5		5	2		4	3	
1967	9	5		6	1		3	4	
1968	10	4		5	2		5	2	
1969	10	3	1	5	1	1	5	2	
1970	7	7		4	3		3	4	
1971	9	5		4	3		5	2	
1972	10	4		4	3		6	1	
1973	7	5	2	5	1	1	2	4	1
1974	4	10		3	4		1	6	
1975	3	11		3	4		0	7	
1976	9	5		6	1		3	4	
1977	6	8		2	5		4	3	
1978	8	8		5	3		3	5	
1979	9	7		5	3		4	4	
1980	11	5		6	2		5	3	
1981	5	11		3	5		2	6	
1982	4	5		2	2		2	3	
1983	9	7		6	2		3	5	
1984	5	11		2	6		3	5	
1985	8	8		5	3		3	5	
1986	12	4		6	2		6	2	
1987	10	5		5	2		5	3	
1988	10	6		6	2		4	4	
1989	9	6	1	5	2	1	4	4	
1990	3	13		2	6		1	7	
1991	6	10		3	5		3	5	
1992	7	9		4	4		3	5	
1993	7	9		4	4		3	5	
1994	11	5		6	2		5	3	
1995	5	11		3	5		2	6	
	374	266	10	202	117	5	172	149	5

DENVER BRONCOS

Season	All Games W	L	T	Home Games W	L	T	Road Games W	L	T
1960	4	9	1	2	4	1	2	5	
1961	3	11		2	5		1	6	
1962	7	7		3	4		4	3	
1963	2	11	1	2	5		0	6	1
1964	2	11	1	2	4	1	0	7	
1965	4	10		2	5		2	5	
1966	4	10		3	4		1	6	
1967	3	11		1	6		2	5	
1968	5	9		3	4		2	5	
1969	5	8	1	4	2	1	1	6	
1970	5	8	1	3	3	1	2	5	
1971	4	9	1	2	4	1	2	5	
1972	5	9		3	4		2	5	
1973	7	5	2	3	3	1	4	2	1
1974	7	6	1	3	3	1	4	3	
1975	6	8		5	2		1	6	
1976	9	5		6	1		3	4	
1977	12	2		6	1		6	1	
1978	10	6		6	2		4	4	
1979	10	6		6	2		4	4	
1980	8	8		4	4		4	4	
1981	10	6		8	0		2	6	
1982	2	7		1	4		1	3	
1983	9	7		6	2		3	5	
1984	13	3		7	1		6	2	
1985	11	5		6	2		5	3	
1986	11	5		7	1		4	4	
1987	10	4	1	7	1		3	3	1
1988	8	8		6	2		2	6	
1989	11	5		6	2		5	3	
1990	5	11		4	4		1	7	
1991	12	4		7	1		5	3	
1992	8	8		7	1		1	7	
1993	9	7		5	3		4	4	
1994	7	9		4	4		3	5	
1995	8	8		6	2		2	6	
1996	13	3		8	0		5	3	
1997	12	4		8	0		4	4	
1998	14	2		8	0		6	2	
	295	275	10	182	102	7	113	173	3

INDIANAPOLIS COLTS*

Season	All Games W	L	T	Home Games W	L	T	Road Games W	L	T
1953	3	9		2	4		1	5	
1954	3	9		2	4		1	5	
1955	5	6	1	4	1	1	1	5	
1956	5	7		4	2		1	5	
1957	7	5		4	2		3	3	
1958	9	3		6	0		3	3	
1959	9	3		4	2		5	1	
1960	6	6		4	2		2	4	
1961	8	6		5	2		3	4	
1962	7	7		3	4		4	3	
1963	8	6		4	3		4	3	
1964	12	2		7	1		5	1	
1965	10	3	1	5	2		5	1	1
1966	9	5		5	2		4	3	
1967	11	1	2	6	0	1	5	1	1
1968	13	1		6	1		7	0	
1969	8	5	1	4	2	1	4	3	
1970	11	2	1	5	1	1	6	1	
1971	10	4		5	2		5	2	
1972	5	9		2	5		3	4	
1973	4	10		3	4		1	6	
1974	2	12		0	7		2	5	
1975	10	4		5	2		5	2	
1976	11	3		6	1		5	2	
1977	10	4		6	1		4	3	
1978	5	11		2	6		3	5	
1979	5	11		3	5		2	6	
1980	7	9		2	6		5	3	
1981	2	14		1	7		1	7	
1982	0	8	1	0	3	1	0	5	
1983	7	9		3	5		4	4	
1984	4	12		2	6		2	6	
1985	5	11		4	4		1	7	
1986	3	13		1	7		2	6	
1987	9	6		4	4		5	2	
1988	9	7		6	2		3	5	
1989	8	8		6	2		2	6	
1990	7	9		3	5		4	4	
1991	1	15		0	8		1	7	
1992	9	7		4	4		5	3	
1993	4	12		2	6		2	6	
1994	8	8		5	3		3	5	
1995	9	7		5	3		4	4	
1996	9	7		6	2		3	5	
1997	3	13		2	6		1	7	
1998	3	13		3	5		0	8	
	313	342	7	171	156	5	142	186	2

includes Baltimore Colts (1953-83).

JACKSONVILLE JAGUARS

Season	All Games W	L	T	Home Games W	L	T	Road Games W	L	T
1995	4	12		2	6		2	6	
1996	9	7		7	1		2	6	
1997	11	5		7	1		4	4	
1998	11	5		7	1		4	4	
	35	29		23	9		12	20	

KANSAS CITY CHIEFS*

Season	All Games W	L	T	Home Games W	L	T	Road Games W	L	T
1960	8	6		5	2		3	4	
1961	6	8		4	3		2	5	
1962	11	3		6	1		5	2	
1963	5	7	2	4	3		1	4	2
1964	7	7		4	3		3	4	
1965	7	5	2	5	2		2	3	2
1966	11	2	1	4	2	1	7	0	
1967	9	5		4	3		5	2	
1968	12	2		6	1		6	1	
1969	11	3		6	1		5	2	
1970	7	5	2	4	1	2	3	4	
1971	10	3	1	7	0		3	3	1
1972	8	6		3	4		5	2	
1973	7	5	2	5	1	1	2	4	1
1974	5	9		1	6		4	3	
1975	5	9		3	4		2	5	
1976	5	9		1	6		4	3	
1977	2	12		1	6		1	6	
1978	4	12		3	5		1	7	

	All Games			Home Games			Road Games		
Season	W	L	T	W	L	T	W	L	T
1979	7	9		3	5		4	4	
1980	8	8		3	5		5	3	
1981	9	7		5	3		4	4	
1982	3	6		2	2		1	4	
1983	6	10		5	3		1	7	
1984	8	8		5	3		3	5	
1985	6	10		5	3		1	7	
1986	10	6		6	2		4	4	
1987	4	11		3	4		1	7	
1988	4	11	1	4	4		0	7	1
1989	8	7	1	5	3		3	4	1
1990	11	5		6	2		5	3	
1991	10	6		6	2		4	4	
1992	10	6		7	1		3	5	
1993	11	5		7	1		4	4	
1994	9	7		5	3		4	4	
1995	13	3		8	0		5	3	
1996	9	7		5	3		4	4	
1997	13	3		8	0		5	3	
1998	7	9		5	3		2	6	
	306	262	12	179	106	4	127	156	8

includes Dallas Texans (1960-62).

MIAMI DOLPHINS

	All Games			Home Games			Road Games		
Season	W	L	T	W	L	T	W	L	T
1966	3	11		2	5		1	6	
1967	4	10		4	3		0	7	
1968	5	8	1	1	5	1	4	3	
1969	3	10	1	2	4	1	1	6	
1970	10	4		6	1		4	3	
1971	10	3	1	6	1		4	2	1
1972	14	0		7	0		7	0	
1973	12	2		7	0		5	2	
1974	11	3		7	0		4	3	
1975	10	4		5	2		5	2	
1976	6	8		3	4		3	4	
1977	10	4		6	1		4	3	
1978	11	5		7	1		4	4	
1979	10	6		6	2		4	4	
1980	8	8		5	3		3	5	
1981	11	4	1	6	1	1	5	3	
1982	7	2		4	0		3	2	
1983	12	4		7	1		5	3	
1984	14	2		7	1		7	1	
1985	12	4		8	0		4	4	
1986	8	8		4	4		4	4	
1987	8	7		4	3		4	4	
1988	6	10		4	4		2	6	
1989	8	8		4	4		4	4	
1990	12	4		7	1		5	3	
1991	8	8		5	3		3	5	
1992	11	5		6	2		5	3	
1993	9	7		4	4		5	3	
1994	10	6		6	2		4	4	
1995	9	7		5	3		4	4	
1996	8	8		4	4		4	4	
1997	9	7		6	2		3	5	
1998	10	6		7	1		3	5	
	299	193	4	172	72	3	127	121	1

NEW ENGLAND PATRIOTS*

	All Games			Home Games			Road Games		
Season	W	L	T	W	L	T	W	L	T
1960	5	9		3	4		2	5	
1961	9	4	1	4	2	1	5	2	
1962	9	4	1	6	1		3	3	1
1963	7	6	1	5	1	1	2	5	
1964	10	3	1	4	2	1	6	1	
1965	4	8	2	1	4	2	3	4	
1966	8	4	2	4	2	1	4	2	1
1967	3	10	1	2	4		1	6	1
1968	4	10		2	5		2	5	
1969	4	10		2	5		2	5	
1970	2	12		1	6		1	6	
1971	6	8		5	2		1	6	
1972	3	11		2	5		1	6	
1973	5	9		3	4		2	5	
1974	7	7		3	4		4	3	
1975	3	11		2	5		1	6	
1976	11	3		6	1		5	2	
1977	9	5		6	1		3	4	
1978	11	5		5	3		6	2	
1979	9	7		6	2		3	5	
1980	10	6		6	2		4	4	
1981	2	14		2	6		0	8	
1982	5	4		3	1		2	3	
1983	8	8		5	3		3	5	
1984	9	7		5	3		4	4	
1985	11	5		7	1		4	4	
1986	11	5		4	4		7	1	
1987	8	7		5	3		3	4	
1988	9	7		7	1		2	6	
1989	5	11		3	5		2	6	
1990	1	15		0	8		1	7	
1991	6	10		4	4		2	6	
1992	2	14		1	7		1	7	
1993	5	11		3	5		2	6	
1994	10	6		5	3		5	3	
1995	6	10		3	5		3	5	
1996	11	5		6	2		5	3	
1997	10	6		6	2		4	4	
1998	9	7		6	2		3	5	
	267	304	9	153	130	6	114	174	3

includes Boston Patriots (1960-70).

NEW YORK JETS*

	All Games			Home Games			Road Games		
Season	W	L	T	W	L	T	W	L	T
1960	7	7		3	4		4	3	
1961	7	7		5	2		2	5	
1962	5	9		2	5		3	4	
1963	5	8	1	4	2	1	1	6	
1964	5	8	1	5	1	1	0	7	
1965	5	8	1	3	3	1	2	5	
1966	6	6	2	4	3		2	3	2
1967	8	5	1	4	2	1	4	3	
1968	11	3		6	1		5	2	
1969	10	4		5	2		5	2	
1970	4	10		2	5		2	5	
1971	6	8		4	3		2	5	
1972	7	7		4	3		3	4	
1973	4	10		2	4		2	6	
1974	7	7		3	4		4	3	
1975	3	11		1	6		2	5	
1976	3	11		2	5		1	6	
1977	3	11		1	6		2	5	
1978	8	8		4	4		4	4	
1979	8	8		6	2		2	6	
1980	4	12		2	6		2	6	
1981	10	5	1	6	2		4	3	1
1982	6	3		3	1		3	2	
1983	7	9		2	6		5	3	
1984	7	9		3	5		4	4	
1985	11	5		7	1		4	4	
1986	10	6		5	3		5	3	
1987	6	9		4	4		2	5	
1988	8	7	1	5	2	1	3	5	
1989	4	12		1	7		3	5	
1990	6	10		3	5		3	5	
1991	8	8		4	4		4	4	
1992	4	12		3	5		1	7	
1993	8	8		3	5		5	3	
1994	6	10		4	4		2	6	
1995	3	13		2	6		1	7	
1996	1	15		0	8		1	7	
1997	9	7		5	3		4	4	
1998	12	4		7	1		5	3	
	252	320	8	139	145	5	113	175	3

includes New York Titans (1960-62).

OAKLAND RAIDERS*

	All Games			Home Games			Road Games		
Season	W	L	T	W	L	T	W	L	T
1960	6	8		3	4		3	4	
1961	2	12		1	6		1	6	
1962	1	13		1	6		0	7	
1963	10	4		6	1		4	3	
1964	5	7	2	5	2		0	5	2
1965	8	5	1	5	2		3	3	1
1966	8	5	1	3	3	1	5	2	
1967	13	1		7	0		6	1	
1968	12	2		6	1		6	1	
1969	12	1	1	7	0		5	1	1
1970	8	4	2	6	1		2	3	2
1971	8	4	2	5	1	1	3	3	1
1972	10	3	1	5	1	1	5	2	
1973	9	4	1	5	2		4	2	1
1974	12	2		6	1		6	1	
1975	11	3		6	1		5	2	
1976	13	1		7	0		6	1	
1977	11	3		6	1		5	2	
1978	9	7		4	4		5	3	
1979	9	7		6	2		3	5	
1980	11	5		6	2		5	3	
1981	7	9		4	4		3	5	
1982	8	1		4	0		4	1	
1983	12	4		6	2		6	2	
1984	11	5		6	2		5	3	
1985	12	4		7	1		5	3	
1986	8	8		3	5		5	3	
1987	5	10		3	5		2	5	
1988	7	9		3	5		4	4	
1989	8	8		7	1		1	7	
1990	12	4		6	2		6	2	
1991	9	7		5	3		4	4	
1992	7	9		5	3		2	6	
1993	10	6		5	3		5	3	
1994	9	7		4	4		5	3	
1995	8	8		4	4		4	4	
1996	7	9		4	4		3	5	
1997	4	12		2	6		2	6	
1998	8	8		4	4		4	4	
	340	229	11	188	99	3	152	130	8

includes Los Angeles Raiders (1982-94).

PITTSBURGH STEELERS*

	All Games			Home Games			Road Games		
Season	W	L	T	W	L	T	W	L	T
1933	3	6	2	2	3		1	3	2
1934	2	10		1	5		1	5	
1935	4	8		2	5		2	3	
1936	6	6		4	1		2	5	
1937	4	7		2	4		2	3	
1938	2	9		0	5		2	4	
1939	1	9	1	1	4		0	5	1
1940	2	7	2	1	2	2	1	5	
1941	1	9	1	1	4		0	5	1
1942	7	4		3	2		4	2	
1945	2	8		1	4		1	4	
1946	5	5	1	4	1		1	4	1
1947	8	4		5	1		3	3	
1948	4	8		4	2		0	6	
1949	6	5	1	3	2	1	3	3	
1950	6	6		2	4		4	2	
1951	4	7	1	1	4	1	3	3	
1952	5	7		2	4		3	3	
1953	6	6		3	3		3	3	
1954	5	7		4	2		1	5	
1955	4	8		3	2		1	6	
1956	5	7		3	3		2	4	
1957	6	6		4	2		2	4	
1958	7	4	1	5	1		2	3	1
1959	6	5	1	3	2	1	3	3	
1960	5	6	1	4	2		1	4	1
1961	6	8		4	3		2	5	
1962	9	5		4	3		5	2	
1963	7	4	3	5	0	2	2	4	1
1964	5	9		2	5		3	4	
1965	2	12		1	6		1	6	
1966	5	8	1	3	3	1	2	5	
1967	4	9	1	1	6		3	3	1
1968	2	11	1	1	6		1	5	1
1969	1	13		1	6		0	7	
1970	5	9		4	3		1	6	
1971	6	8		5	2		1	6	
1972	11	3		7	0		4	3	
1973	10	4		7	1		3	3	
1974	10	3	1	5	2		5	1	1
1975	12	2		6	1		6	1	
1976	10	4		6	1		4	3	
1977	9	5		6	1		3	4	
1978	14	2		7	1		7	1	

	All Games			Home Games			Road Games		
Season	W	L	T	W	L	T	W	L	T
1979	12	4		8	0		4	4	
1980	9	7		6	2		3	5	
1981	8	8		5	3		3	5	
1982	6	3		4	0		2	3	
1983	10	6		4	4		6	2	
1984	9	7		6	2		3	5	
1985	7	9		5	3		2	6	
1986	6	10		4	4		2	6	
1987	8	7		4	3		4	4	
1988	5	11		4	4		1	7	
1989	9	7		4	4		5	3	
1990	9	7		6	2		3	5	
1991	7	9		5	3		2	6	
1992	11	5		7	1		4	4	
1993	9	7		6	2		3	5	
1994	12	4		7	1		5	3	
1995	11	5		6	2		5	3	
1996	10	6		7	1		3	5	
1997	11	5		7	1		4	4	
1998	7	9		5	3		2	6	
	420	429	19	253	169	8	167	260	11

**includes Pittsburgh Pirates (1933-40).*

SAN DIEGO CHARGERS*

	All Games			Home Games			Road Games		
Season	W	L	T	W	L	T	W	L	T
1960	10	4		5	2		5	2	
1961	12	2		6	1		6	1	
1962	4	10		3	4		1	6	
1963	11	3		6	1		5	2	
1964	8	5	1	4	3		4	2	1
1965	9	2	3	4	1	2	5	1	1
1966	7	6	1	5	2		2	4	1
1967	8	5	1	5	2	1	3	3	
1968	9	5		4	3		5	2	
1969	8	6		5	2		3	4	
1970	5	6	3	2	3	2	3	3	1
1971	6	8		6	1		0	7	
1972	4	9	1	2	5		2	4	1
1973	2	11	1	2	5		0	6	1
1974	5	9		3	4		2	5	
1975	2	12		1	6		1	6	
1976	6	8		3	4		3	4	
1977	7	7		3	4		4	3	
1978	9	7		5	3		4	4	
1979	12	4		7	1		5	3	
1980	11	5		6	2		5	3	
1981	10	6		5	3		5	3	
1982	6	3		3	1		3	2	
1983	6	10		4	4		2	6	
1984	7	9		4	4		3	5	
1985	8	8		6	2		2	6	
1986	4	12		2	6		2	6	
1987	8	7		4	3		4	4	
1988	6	10		3	5		3	5	
1989	6	10		4	4		2	6	
1990	6	10		3	5		3	5	
1991	4	12		3	5		1	7	
1992	11	5		6	2		5	3	
1993	8	8		4	4		4	4	
1994	11	5		5	3		6	2	
1995	9	7		5	3		4	4	
1996	8	8		5	3		3	5	
1997	4	12		2	6		2	6	
1998	5	11		4	4		1	7	
	282	287	11	159	126	5	123	161	6

**includes Los Angeles Chargers (1960).*

SEATTLE SEAHAWKS

	All Games			Home Games			Road Games		
Season	W	L	T	W	L	T	W	L	T
1976	2	12		1	6		1	6	
1977	5	9		3	4		2	5	
1978	9	7		5	3		4	4	
1979	9	7		5	3		4	4	
1980	4	12		0	8		4	4	
1981	6	10		5	3		1	7	
1982	4	5		3	2		1	3	
1983	9	7		5	3		4	4	
1984	12	4		7	1		5	3	
1985	8	8		5	3		3	5	
1986	10	6		7	1		3	5	
1987	9	6		6	2		3	4	
1988	9	7		5	3		4	4	
1989	7	9		3	5		4	4	
1990	9	7		5	3		4	4	
1991	7	9		5	3		2	6	
1992	2	14		1	7		1	7	
1993	6	10		4	4		2	6	
1994	6	10		3	5		3	5	
1995	8	8		5	3		3	5	
1996	7	9		4	4		3	5	
1997	8	8		4	4		4	4	
1998	8	8		6	2		2	6	
	164	192		97	82		67	110	

TENNESSEE TITANS*

	All Games			Home Games			Road Games		
Season	W	L	T	W	L	T	W	L	T
1960	10	4		6	1		4	3	
1961	10	3	1	6	1		4	2	1
1962	11	3		6	1		5	2	
1963	6	8		4	3		2	5	
1964	4	10		3	4		1	6	
1965	4	10		3	4		1	6	
1966	3	11		3	4		0	7	
1967	9	4	1	5	2		4	2	1
1968	7	7		3	4		4	3	
1969	6	6	2	4	2	1	2	4	1
1970	3	10	1	1	6		2	4	1
1971	4	9	1	3	3	1	1	6	
1972	1	13		1	6		0	7	
1973	1	13		0	7		1	6	
1974	7	7		3	4		4	3	
1975	10	4		5	2		5	2	
1976	5	9		3	4		2	5	
1977	8	6		5	2		3	4	
1978	10	6		5	3		5	3	
1979	11	5		6	2		5	3	
1980	11	5		6	2		5	3	
1981	7	9		5	3		2	6	
1982	1	8		1	4		0	4	
1983	2	14		2	6		0	8	
1984	3	13		2	6		1	7	
1985	5	11		4	4		1	7	
1986	5	11		4	4		1	7	
1987	9	6		5	2		4	4	
1988	10	6		7	1		3	5	
1989	9	7		6	2		3	5	
1990	9	7		6	2		3	5	
1991	11	5		7	1		4	4	
1992	10	6		5	3		5	3	
1993	12	4		7	1		5	3	
1994	2	14		2	6		0	8	
1995	7	9		3	5		4	4	
1996	8	8		2	6		6	2	
1997	8	8		6	2		2	6	
1998	8	8		3	5		5	3	
	267	307	6	158	130	2	109	177	4

**includes Houston Oilers (1960-96) and Tennessee Oilers (1997-98).*

NFC

ARIZONA CARDINALS*

	All Games			Home Games			Road Games		
Season	W	L	T	W	L	T	W	L	T
1920	6	2	2	5	1	1	1	1	1
1921	3	3	2	3	3	1	0	0	1
1922	8	3		8	3		0	0	
1923	8	4		8	3		0	1	
1924	5	4	1	5	3	1	0	1	
1925	11	2	1	11	2		0	0	1
1926	5	6	1	3	3		2	3	1
1927	3	7	1	2	3	1	1	4	
1928	1	5		1	1		0	4	
1929	6	6	1	3	2		3	4	1
1930	5	6	2	3	2		2	4	2
1931	5	4		3	0		2	4	
1932	2	6	2	1	2	1	1	4	1
1933	1	9	1	0	4	1	1	5	
1934	5	6		2	2		3	4	
1935	6	4	2	2	2		4	2	2
1936	3	8	1	3	1	1	0	7	
1937	5	5	1	1	3		4	2	1
1938	2	9		1	4		1	5	
1939	1	10		0	4		1	6	
1940	2	7	2	2	1	1	0	6	1
1941	3	7	1	0	3	1	3	4	
1942	3	8		2	2		1	6	
1943	0	10		0	3		0	7	
1945	1	9		0	3		1	6	
1946	6	5		2	2		4	3	
1947	9	3		5	0		4	3	
1948	11	1		5	1		6	0	
1949	6	5	1	2	3	1	4	2	
1950	5	7		3	3		2	4	
1951	3	9		1	5		2	4	
1952	4	8		2	4		2	4	
1953	1	10	1	0	5	1	1	5	
1954	2	10		2	4		0	6	
1955	4	7	1	3	2	1	1	5	
1956	7	5		4	2		3	3	
1957	3	9		0	6		3	3	
1958	2	9	1	1	4	1	1	5	
1959	2	10		2	4		0	6	
1960	6	5	1	3	2	1	3	3	
1961	7	7		3	4		4	3	
1962	4	9	1	2	4	1	2	5	
1963	9	5		3	4		6	1	
1964	9	3	2	4	1	1	5	2	1
1965	5	9		2	5		3	4	
1966	8	5	1	5	1	1	3	4	
1967	6	7	1	3	3	1	3	4	
1968	9	4	1	4	2	1	5	2	
1969	4	9	1	3	4		1	5	1
1970	8	5	1	6	1		2	4	1
1971	4	9	1	1	5	1	3	4	
1972	4	9	1	2	5		2	4	1
1973	4	9	1	2	4	1	2	5	
1974	10	4		5	2		5	2	
1975	11	3		6	1		5	2	
1976	10	4		6	1		4	3	
1977	7	7		4	3		3	4	
1978	6	10		3	5		3	5	
1979	5	11		3	5		2	6	
1980	5	11		2	6		3	5	
1981	7	9		5	3		2	6	
1982	5	4		1	3		4	1	
1983	8	7	1	4	3	1	4	4	
1984	9	7		5	3		4	4	
1985	5	11		4	4		1	7	
1986	4	11	1	3	5		1	6	1
1987	7	8		4	3		3	5	
1988	7	9		4	4		3	5	
1989	5	11		2	6		3	5	
1990	5	11		3	5		2	6	
1991	4	12		2	6		2	6	
1992	4	12		3	5		1	7	
1993	7	9		4	4		3	5	
1994	8	8		5	3		3	5	
1995	4	12		3	5		1	7	
1996	7	9		5	3		2	6	
1997	4	12		3	5		1	7	
1998	9	7		5	3		4	4	
	415	562	39	238	246	22	177	316	17

**includes Chicago Cardinals (1920-59), St. Louis Cardinals (1960-87), and Phoenix Cardinals (1988-93).*

ATLANTA FALCONS

	All Games			Home Games			Road Games		
Season	W	L	T	W	L	T	W	L	T
1966	3	11		1	6		2	5	
1967	1	12	1	1	5	1	0	7	
1968	2	12		1	6		1	6	
1969	6	8		4	3		2	5	
1970	4	8	2	3	4		1	4	2
1971	7	6	1	4	3		3	3	1
1972	7	7		4	3		3	4	
1973	9	5		4	3		5	2	
1974	3	11		2	5		1	6	
1975	4	10		3	4		1	6	
1976	4	10		3	4		1	6	

	All Games			Home Games			Road Games		
Season	W	L	T	W	L	T	W	L	T
1977	7	7		4	3		3	4	
1978	9	7		7	1		2	6	
1979	6	10		3	5		3	5	
1980	12	4		6	2		6	2	
1981	7	9		4	4		3	5	
1982	5	4		2	3		3	1	
1983	7	9		4	4		3	5	
1984	4	12		2	6		2	6	
1985	4	12		3	5		1	7	
1986	7	8	1	2	5	1	5	3	
1987	3	12		2	6		1	6	
1988	5	11		2	6		3	5	
1989	3	13		3	5		0	8	
1990	5	11		5	3		0	8	
1991	10	6		6	2		4	4	
1992	6	10		5	3		1	7	
1993	6	10		4	4		2	6	
1994	7	9		5	3		2	6	
1995	9	7		7	1		2	6	
1996	3	13		2	6		1	7	
1997	7	9		3	5		4	4	
1998	14	2		8	0		6	2	
	196	295	5	119	128	2	77	167	3

CAROLINA PANTHERS

Season	W	L	T	W	L	T	W	L	T
1995	7	9		5	3		2	6	
1996	12	4		8	0		4	4	
1997	7	9		2	6		5	3	
1998	4	12		2	6		2	6	
	30	34		17	15		13	19	

CHICAGO BEARS*

	All Games			Home Games			Road Games		
Season	W	L	T	W	L	T	W	L	T
1920	10	1	2	6	0	1	4	1	1
1921	9	1	1	9	1	1	0	0	
1922	9	3		7	1		2	2	
1923	9	2	1	7	1	1	2	1	
1924	6	1	4	5	0	3	1	1	1
1925	9	5	3	7	1	1	2	4	2
1926	12	1	3	10	0	2	2	1	1
1927	9	3	2	7	1	1	2	2	1
1928	7	5	1	6	3		1	2	1
1929	4	9	2	1	5	2	3	4	
1930	9	4	1	5	2	1	4	2	
1931	8	5		6	3		2	2	
1932	7	1	6	6	1	1	1	0	5
1933	10	2	1	6	0		4	2	1
1934	13	0		5	0		8	0	
1935	6	4	2	1	2	2	5	2	
1936	9	3		3	1		6	2	
1937	9	1	1	4	1		5	0	1
1938	6	5		2	3		4	2	
1939	8	3		4	1		4	2	
1940	8	3		5	0		3	3	
1941	10	1		5	1		5	0	
1942	11	0		6	0		5	0	
1943	8	1	1	5	0		3	1	1
1944	6	3	1	4	0	1	2	3	
1945	3	7		2	3		1	4	
1946	8	2	1	4	1	1	4	1	
1947	8	4		4	2		4	2	
1948	10	2		5	1		5	1	
1949	9	3		5	1		4	2	
1950	9	3		6	0		3	3	
1951	7	5		3	3		4	2	
1952	5	7		3	3		2	4	
1953	3	8	1	1	4	1	2	4	
1954	8	4		4	2		4	2	
1955	8	4		5	1		3	3	
1956	9	2	1	6	0		3	2	1
1957	5	7		2	4		3	3	
1958	8	4		5	1		3	3	
1959	8	4		4	2		4	2	
1960	5	6	1	4	2		1	4	1
1961	8	6		5	2		3	4	
1962	9	5		4	3		5	2	
1963	11	1	2	6	0	1	5	1	1
1964	5	9		2	5		3	4	
1965	9	5		5	2		4	3	
1966	5	7	2	4	1	2	1	6	
1967	7	6	1	3	3	1	4	3	
1968	7	7		2	5		5	2	
1969	1	13		1	6		0	7	
1970	6	8		3	4		3	4	
1971	6	8		4	3		2	5	
1972	4	9	1	1	5	1	3	4	
1973	3	11		1	6		2	5	
1974	4	10		4	3		0	7	
1975	4	10		3	4		1	6	
1976	7	7		4	3		3	4	
1977	9	5		5	2		4	3	
1978	7	9		4	4		3	5	
1979	10	6		6	2		4	4	
1980	7	9		5	3		2	6	
1981	6	10		4	4		2	6	
1982	3	6		2	2		1	4	
1983	8	8		5	3		3	5	
1984	10	6		6	2		4	4	
1985	15	1		8	0		7	1	
1986	14	2		7	1		7	1	
1987	11	4		6	2		5	2	
1988	12	4		7	1		5	3	
1989	6	10		4	4		2	6	
1990	11	5		7	1		4	4	
1991	11	5		6	2		5	3	
1992	5	11		4	4		1	7	
1993	7	9		3	5		4	4	
1994	9	7		5	3		4	4	
1995	9	7		5	3		4	4	
1996	7	9		6	2		1	7	
1997	4	12		2	6		2	6	
1998	4	12		3	5		1	7	
	606	418	42	357	174	24	249	244	18

**includes Decatur Staleys (1920) and Chicago Staleys (1921).*

DALLAS COWBOYS

	All Games			Home Games			Road Games		
Season	W	L	T	W	L	T	W	L	T
1960	0	11	1	0	6		0	5	1
1961	4	9	1	2	4	1	2	5	
1962	5	8	1	2	4	1	3	4	
1963	4	10		3	4		1	6	
1964	5	8	1	2	4	1	3	4	
1965	7	7		5	2		2	5	
1966	10	3	1	6	1		4	2	1
1967	9	5		5	2		4	3	
1968	12	2		5	2		7	0	
1969	11	2	1	6	0	1	5	2	
1970	10	4		6	1		4	3	
1971	11	3		6	1		5	2	
1972	10	4		5	2		5	2	
1973	10	4		6	1		4	3	
1974	8	6		5	2		3	4	
1975	10	4		5	2		5	2	
1976	11	3		6	1		5	2	
1977	12	2		6	1		6	1	
1978	12	4		7	1		5	3	
1979	11	5		6	2		5	3	
1980	12	4		8	0		4	4	
1981	12	4		8	0		4	4	
1982	6	3		3	2		3	1	
1983	12	4		6	2		6	2	
1984	9	7		5	3		4	4	
1985	10	6		7	1		3	5	
1986	7	9		3	5		4	4	
1987	7	8		3	4		4	4	
1988	3	13		1	7		2	6	
1989	1	15		0	8		1	7	
1990	7	9		5	3		2	6	
1991	11	5		6	2		5	3	
1992	13	3		7	1		6	2	
1993	12	4		6	2		6	2	
1994	12	4		6	2		6	2	
1995	12	4		6	2		6	2	
1996	10	6		6	2		4	4	
1997	6	10		5	3		1	7	
1998	10	6		6	2		4	4	
	344	228	6	191	94	4	153	134	2

DETROIT LIONS*

	All Games			Home Games			Road Games		
Season	W	L	T	W	L	T	W	L	T
1930	5	6	3	5	1	2	0	5	1
1931	11	3		8	0		3	3	
1932	6	2	4	3	0	2	3	2	2
1933	6	5		4	1		2	4	
1934	10	3		6	2		4	1	
1935	7	3	2	5	0	1	2	3	1
1936	8	4		5	1		3	3	
1937	7	4		4	2		3	2	
1938	7	4		4	3		3	1	
1939	6	5		4	2		2	3	
1940	5	5	1	3	3		2	2	1
1941	4	6	1	3	2		1	4	1
1942	0	11		0	7		0	4	
1943	3	6	1	2	2	1	1	4	
1944	6	3	1	4	2		2	1	1
1945	7	3		4	1		3	2	
1946	1	10		1	5		0	5	
1947	3	9		2	4		1	5	
1948	2	10		2	4		0	6	
1949	4	8		2	4		2	4	
1950	6	6		4	2		2	4	
1951	7	4	1	3	3	1	4	1	
1952	9	3		6	1		3	2	
1953	10	2		5	1		5	1	
1954	9	2	1	5	0	1	4	2	
1955	3	9		3	4		0	5	
1956	9	3		5	1		4	2	
1957	8	4		5	1		3	3	
1958	4	7	1	2	4		2	3	1
1959	3	8	1	2	4		1	4	1
1960	7	5		5	1		2	4	
1961	8	5	1	2	5		6	0	1
1962	11	3		7	0		4	3	
1963	5	8	1	3	3	1	2	5	
1964	7	5	2	3	3	1	4	2	1
1965	6	7	1	2	4	1	4	3	
1966	4	9	1	3	4		1	5	1
1967	5	7	2	3	4		2	3	2
1968	4	8	2	1	4	2	3	4	
1969	9	4	1	5	2		4	2	1
1970	10	4		6	1		4	3	
1971	7	6	1	3	4		4	2	1
1972	8	5	1	5	2		3	3	1
1973	6	7	1	4	3		2	4	1
1974	7	7		5	2		2	5	
1975	7	7		4	3		3	4	
1976	6	8		5	2		1	6	
1977	6	8		5	2		1	6	
1978	7	9		5	3		2	6	
1979	2	14		2	6		0	8	
1980	9	7		6	2		3	5	
1981	8	8		7	1		1	7	
1982	4	5		2	3		2	2	
1983	9	7		6	2		3	5	
1984	4	11	1	2	5	1	2	6	
1985	7	9		6	2		1	7	
1986	5	11		1	7		4	4	
1987	4	11		1	6		3	5	
1988	4	12		2	6		2	6	
1989	7	9		4	4		3	5	
1990	6	10		3	5		3	5	
1991	12	4		8	0		4	4	
1992	5	11		3	5		2	6	
1993	10	6		5	3		5	3	
1994	9	7		6	2		3	5	
1995	10	6		7	1		3	5	
1996	5	11		4	4		1	7	
1997	9	7		6	2		3	5	
1998	5	11		4	4		1	7	
	440	457	32	272	189	14	168	268	18

**includes Portsmouth Spartans (1930-33).*

GREEN BAY PACKERS

	All Games			Home Games			Road Games		
Season	W	L	T	W	L	T	W	L	T
1921	3	2	1	2	1		1	1	1
1922	4	3	3	4	1	1	0	2	2
1923	7	2	1	4	2	1	3	0	
1924	7	4		5	0		2	4	
1925	8	5		6	0		2	5	

	All Games			Home Games			Road Games		
Season	W	L	T	W	L	T	W	L	T
1926	7	3	3	4	1	2	3	2	1
1927	7	2	1	6	1		1	1	1
1928	6	4	3	2	2	2	4	2	1
1929	12	0	1	5	0		7	0	1
1930	10	3	1	6	0		4	3	1
1931	12	2		8	0		4	2	
1932	10	3	1	5	0	1	5	3	
1933	5	7	1	3	2	1	2	5	
1934	7	6		4	2		3	4	
1935	8	4		5	2		3	2	
1936	10	1	1	5	1		5	0	1
1937	7	4		3	2		4	2	
1938	8	3		4	2		4	1	
1939	9	2		4	1		5	1	
1940	6	4	1	4	2		2	2	1
1941	10	1		4	1		6	0	
1942	8	2	1	4	1		4	1	1
1943	7	2	1	2	1	1	5	1	
1944	8	2		5	0		3	2	
1945	6	4		4	1		2	3	
1946	6	5		2	3		4	2	
1947	6	5	1	4	2		2	3	1
1948	3	9		2	4		1	5	
1949	2	10		1	5		1	5	
1950	3	9		3	3		0	6	
1951	3	9		2	4		1	5	
1952	6	6		3	3		3	3	
1953	2	9	1	1	5		1	4	1
1954	4	8		2	4		2	4	
1955	6	6		5	1		1	5	
1956	4	8		2	4		2	4	
1957	3	9		1	5		2	4	
1958	1	10	1	1	4	1	0	6	
1959	7	5		4	2		3	3	
1960	8	4		4	2		4	2	
1961	11	3		6	1		5	2	
1962	13	1		7	0		6	1	
1963	11	2	1	6	1		5	1	1
1964	8	5	1	4	3		4	2	1
1965	10	3	1	6	1		4	2	1
1966	12	2		6	1		6	1	
1967	9	4	1	4	2	1	5	2	
1968	6	7	1	2	5		4	2	1
1969	8	6		5	2		3	4	
1970	6	8		4	3		2	5	
1971	4	8	2	3	3	1	1	5	1
1972	10	4		4	3		6	1	
1973	5	7	2	3	2	2	2	5	
1974	6	8		4	3		2	5	
1975	4	10		3	4		1	6	
1976	5	9		4	3		1	6	
1977	4	10		2	5		2	5	
1978	8	7	1	5	2	1	3	5	
1979	5	11		4	4		1	7	
1980	5	10	1	4	4		1	6	1
1981	8	8		4	4		4	4	
1982	5	3	1	3	1		2	2	1
1983	8	8		5	3		3	5	
1984	8	8		5	3		3	5	
1985	8	8		5	3		3	5	
1986	4	12		1	7		3	5	
1987	5	9	1	2	5	1	3	4	
1988	4	12		2	6		2	6	
1989	10	6		6	2		4	4	
1990	6	10		3	5		3	5	
1991	4	12		2	6		2	6	
1992	9	7		6	2		3	5	
1993	9	7		6	2		3	5	
1994	9	7		7	1		2	6	
1995	11	5		7	1		4	4	
1996	13	3		8	0		5	3	
1997	13	3		8	0		5	3	
1998	11	5		7	1		4	4	
	551	445	36	318	181	16	233	264	20

MINNESOTA VIKINGS

	All Games			Home Games			Road Games		
Season	W	L	T	W	L	T	W	L	T
1961	3	11		3	4		0	7	
1962	2	11	1	1	5	1	1	6	
1963	5	8	1	3	4		2	4	1

	All Games			Home Games			Road Games		
Season	W	L	T	W	L	T	W	L	T
1964	8	5	1	4	3		4	2	1
1965	7	7		2	5		5	2	
1966	4	9	1	2	5		2	4	1
1967	3	8	3	1	4	2	2	4	1
1968	8	6		4	3		4	3	
1969	12	2		7	0		5	2	
1970	12	2		7	0		5	2	
1971	11	3		5	2		6	1	
1972	7	7		3	4		4	3	
1973	12	2		7	0		5	2	
1974	10	4		4	3		6	1	
1975	12	2		7	0		5	2	
1976	11	2	1	6	0	1	5	2	
1977	9	5		5	2		4	3	
1978	8	7	1	5	3		3	4	1
1979	7	9		5	3		2	6	
1980	9	7		5	3		4	4	
1981	7	9		5	3		2	6	
1982	5	4		4	1		1	3	
1983	8	8		3	5		5	3	
1984	3	13		2	6		1	7	
1985	7	9		4	4		3	5	
1986	9	7		5	3		4	4	
1987	8	7		5	3		3	4	
1988	11	5		7	1		4	4	
1989	10	6		8	0		2	6	
1990	6	10		4	4		2	6	
1991	8	8		4	4		4	4	
1992	11	5		5	3		6	2	
1993	9	7		4	4		5	3	
1994	10	6		6	2		4	4	
1995	8	8		6	2		2	6	
1996	9	7		5	3		4	4	
1997	9	7		5	3		4	4	
1998	15	1		8	0		7	1	
	313	244	9	176	104	4	137	140	5

NEW ORLEANS SAINTS

	All Games			Home Games			Road Games		
Season	W	L	T	W	L	T	W	L	T
1967	3	11		2	5		1	6	
1968	4	9	1	3	4		1	5	1
1969	5	9		3	4		2	5	
1970	2	11	1	2	5		0	6	1
1971	4	8	2	2	4	1	2	4	1
1972	2	11	1	2	5		0	6	1
1973	5	9		5	2		0	7	
1974	5	9		4	3		1	6	
1975	2	12		2	5		0	7	
1976	4	10		2	5		2	5	
1977	3	11		2	5		1	6	
1978	7	9		3	5		4	4	
1979	8	8		3	5		5	3	
1980	1	15		0	8		1	7	
1981	4	12		2	6		2	6	
1982	4	5		2	3		2	2	
1983	8	8		5	3		3	5	
1984	7	9		3	5		4	4	
1985	5	11		3	5		2	6	
1986	7	9		4	4		3	5	
1987	12	3		6	1		6	2	
1988	10	6		5	3		5	3	
1989	9	7		5	3		4	4	
1990	8	8		5	3		3	5	
1991	11	5		6	2		5	3	
1992	12	4		6	2		6	2	
1993	8	8		4	4		4	4	
1994	7	9		3	5		4	4	
1995	7	9		4	4		3	5	
1996	3	13		2	6		1	7	
1997	6	10		3	5		3	5	
1998	6	10		4	4		2	6	
	189	288	5	107	133	1	82	155	4

NEW YORK GIANTS

	All Games			Home Games			Road Games		
Season	W	L	T	W	L	T	W	L	T
1925	8	4		7	2		1	2	
1926	8	4	1	5	2	1	3	2	
1927	11	1	1	7	1		4	0	1
1928	4	7	2	1	2	2	3	5	

	All Games			Home Games			Road Games		
Season	W	L	T	W	L	T	W	L	T
1929	13	1	1	7	1		6	0	1
1930	13	4		6	2		7	2	
1931	7	6	1	4	2	1	3	4	
1932	4	6	2	3	2	1	1	4	1
1933	11	3		7	0		4	3	
1934	8	5		5	1		3	4	
1935	9	3		4	2		5	1	
1936	5	6	1	3	3	1	2	3	
1937	6	3	2	4	2	1	2	1	1
1938	8	2	1	6	1		2	1	1
1939	9	1	1	6	0		3	1	1
1940	6	4	1	4	3		2	1	1
1941	8	3		5	2		3	1	
1942	5	5	1	3	2	1	2	3	
1943	6	3	1	4	2		2	1	1
1944	8	1	1	5	1		3	0	1
1945	3	6	1	2	4		1	2	1
1946	7	3	1	5	1	1	2	2	
1947	2	8	2	2	3	1	0	5	1
1948	4	8		2	4		2	4	
1949	6	6		2	4		4	2	
1950	10	2		5	1		5	1	
1951	9	2	1	5	1		4	1	1
1952	7	5		2	4		5	1	
1953	3	9		2	4		1	5	
1954	7	5		4	2		3	3	
1955	6	5	1	4	1	1	2	4	
1956	8	3	1	4	1	1	4	2	
1957	7	5		3	3		4	2	
1958	9	3		5	1		4	2	
1959	10	2		5	1		5	1	
1960	6	4	2	1	3	2	5	1	
1961	10	3	1	4	2	1	6	1	
1962	12	2		6	1		6	1	
1963	11	3		5	2		6	1	
1964	2	10	2	2	5		0	5	2
1965	7	7		3	4		4	3	
1966	1	12	1	1	6		0	6	1
1967	7	7		5	2		2	5	
1968	7	7		3	4		4	3	
1969	6	8		5	2		1	6	
1970	9	5		5	2		4	3	
1971	4	10		1	6		3	4	
1972	8	6		4	3		4	3	
1973	2	11	1	2	4	1	0	7	
1974	2	12		0	7		2	5	
1975	5	9		2	5		3	4	
1976	3	11		3	4		0	7	
1977	5	9		3	4		2	5	
1978	6	10		5	3		1	7	
1979	6	10		4	4		2	6	
1980	4	12		2	6		2	6	
1981	9	7		4	4		5	3	
1982	4	5		2	3		2	2	
1983	3	12	1	1	7		2	5	1
1984	9	7		6	2		3	5	
1985	10	6		6	2		4	4	
1986	14	2		8	0		6	2	
1987	6	9		5	3		1	6	
1988	10	6		5	3		5	3	
1989	12	4		7	1		5	3	
1990	13	3		7	1		6	2	
1991	8	8		5	3		3	5	
1992	6	10		4	4		2	6	
1993	11	5		6	2		5	3	
1994	9	7		4	4		5	3	
1995	5	11		3	5		2	6	
1996	6	10		3	5		3	5	
1997	10	5	1	6	2		4	3	1
1998	8	8		5	3		3	5	
	531	437	33	301	201	16	230	236	17

PHILADELPHIA EAGLES

	All Games			Home Games			Road Games		
Season	W	L	T	W	L	T	W	L	T
1933	3	5	1	2	3	1	1	2	
1934	4	7		2	4		2	3	
1935	2	9		0	5		2	4	
1936	1	11		1	6		0	5	
1937	2	8	1	0	5	1	2	3	
1938	5	6		2	3		3	3	

Season	All Games W	L	T	Home Games W	L	T	Road Games W	L	T
1939	1	9	1	1	3	1	0	6	
1940	1	10		1	4		0	6	
1941	2	8	1	1	4	1	1	4	
1942	2	9		0	5		2	4	
1944	7	1	2	3	1	2	4	0	
1945	7	3		6	0		1	3	
1946	6	5		3	2		3	3	
1947	8	4		6	1		2	3	
1948	9	2	1	6	0		3	2	1
1949	11	1		6	0		5	1	
1950	6	6		2	4		4	2	
1951	4	8		1	5		3	3	
1952	7	5		4	2		3	3	
1953	7	4	1	5	0	1	2	4	
1954	7	4	1	5	1		2	3	1
1955	4	7	1	4	2		0	5	1
1956	3	8	1	2	3	1	1	5	
1957	4	8		3	3		1	5	
1958	2	9	1	2	4		0	5	1
1959	7	5		5	1		2	4	
1960	10	2		5	1		5	1	
1961	10	4		5	2		5	2	
1962	3	10	1	2	5		1	5	1
1963	2	10	2	1	5	1	1	5	1
1964	6	8		3	4		3	4	
1965	5	9		2	5		3	4	
1966	9	5		5	2		4	3	
1967	6	7	1	5	2		1	5	1
1968	2	12		1	6		1	6	
1969	4	9	1	2	5		2	4	1
1970	3	10	1	3	3	1	0	7	
1971	6	7	1	3	4		3	3	1
1972	2	11	1	0	6	1	2	5	
1973	5	8	1	4	3		1	5	1
1974	7	7		5	2		2	5	
1975	4	10		2	5		2	5	
1976	4	10		2	5		2	5	
1977	5	9		4	3		1	6	
1978	9	7		5	3		4	4	
1979	11	5		5	3		6	2	
1980	12	4		7	1		5	3	
1981	10	6		6	2		4	4	
1982	3	6		1	4		2	2	
1983	5	11		1	7		4	4	
1984	6	9	1	5	3		1	6	1
1985	7	9		4	4		3	5	
1986	5	10	1	2	5	1	3	5	
1987	7	8		4	4		3	4	
1988	10	6		5	3		5	3	
1989	11	5		6	2		5	3	
1990	10	6		6	2		4	4	
1991	10	6		4	4		6	2	
1992	11	5		8	0		3	5	
1993	8	8		3	5		5	3	
1994	7	9		5	3		2	6	
1995	10	6		6	2		4	4	
1996	10	6		5	3		5	3	
1997	6	9	1	6	2		0	7	1
1998	3	13		3	5		0	8	
	386	464	24	224	206	12	162	258	12

ST. LOUIS RAMS*

Season	All Games W	L	T	Home Games W	L	T	Road Games W	L	T
1937	1	10		0	5		1	5	
1938	4	7		2	2		2	5	
1939	5	5	1	3	2	1	2	3	
1940	4	6	1	3	1	1	1	5	
1941	2	9		1	4		1	5	
1942	5	6		3	2		2	4	
1944	4	6		1	2		3	4	
1945	9	1		4	0		5	1	
1946	6	4	1	3	2		3	2	1
1947	6	6		3	3		3	3	
1948	6	5	1	3	2	1	3	3	
1949	8	2	2	5	1		3	1	2
1950	9	3		5	1		4	2	
1951	8	4		5	2		3	2	
1952	9	3		5	1		4	2	
1953	8	3	1	5	1		3	2	1
1954	6	5	1	3	2	1	3	3	
1955	8	3	1	5	1		3	2	1
1956	4	8		4	2		0	6	
1957	6	6		5	1		1	5	
1958	8	4		4	2		4	2	
1959	2	10		0	6		2	4	
1960	4	7	1	2	3	1	2	4	
1961	4	10		4	3		0	7	
1962	1	12	1	0	7		1	5	1
1963	5	9		3	4		2	5	
1964	5	7	2	3	2	2	2	5	
1965	4	10		3	4		1	6	
1966	8	6		5	2		3	4	
1967	11	1	2	5	1	1	6	0	1
1968	10	3	1	5	2		5	1	1
1969	11	3		5	2		6	1	
1970	9	4	1	3	3	1	6	1	
1971	8	5	1	4	2	1	4	3	
1972	6	7	1	4	3		2	4	1
1973	12	2		7	0		5	2	
1974	10	4		6	1		4	3	
1975	12	2		6	1		6	1	
1976	10	3	1	5	2		5	1	1
1977	10	4		7	0		3	4	
1978	12	4		6	2		6	2	
1979	9	7		4	4		5	3	
1980	11	5		6	2		5	3	
1981	6	10		4	4		2	6	
1982	2	7		1	4		1	3	
1983	9	7		5	3		4	4	
1984	10	6		5	3		5	3	
1985	11	5		6	2		5	3	
1986	10	6		6	2		4	4	
1987	6	9		3	4		3	5	
1988	10	6		4	4		6	2	
1989	11	5		6	2		5	3	
1990	5	11		2	6		3	5	
1991	3	13		2	6		1	7	
1992	6	10		4	4		2	6	
1993	5	11		3	5		2	6	
1994	4	12		3	5		1	7	
1995	7	9		4	4		3	5	
1996	6	10		4	4		2	6	
1997	5	11		2	6		3	5	
1998	4	12		2	6		2	6	
	420	391	20	231	169	10	189	222	10

includes Cleveland Rams (1937-42, 1944-45) and Los Angeles Rams (1946-94).

SAN FRANCISCO 49ERS

Season	All Games W	L	T	Home Games W	L	T	Road Games W	L	T
1950	3	9		3	3		0	6	
1951	7	4	1	5	1		2	3	1
1952	7	5		3	3		4	2	
1953	9	3		5	1		4	2	
1954	7	4	1	4	2		3	2	1
1955	4	8		2	4		2	4	
1956	5	6	1	3	3		2	3	1
1957	8	4		5	1		3	3	
1958	6	6		4	2		2	4	
1959	7	5		4	2		3	3	
1960	7	5		3	3		4	2	
1961	7	6	1	5	1	1	2	5	
1962	6	8		1	6		5	2	
1963	2	12		2	5		0	7	
1964	4	10		3	4		1	6	
1965	7	6	1	4	2	1	3	4	
1966	6	6	2	4	2	1	2	4	1
1967	7	7		3	4		4	3	
1968	7	6	1	3	3	1	4	3	
1969	4	8	2	3	3	1	1	5	1
1970	10	3	1	5	1	1	5	2	
1971	9	5		4	3		5	2	
1972	8	5	1	4	2	1	4	3	
1973	5	9		3	4		2	5	
1974	6	8		3	4		3	4	
1975	5	9		2	5		3	4	
1976	8	6		4	3		4	3	
1977	5	9		3	4		2	5	
1978	2	14		2	6		0	8	
1979	2	14		2	6		0	8	
1980	6	10		4	4		2	6	
1981	13	3		7	1		6	2	
1982	3	6		0	5		3	1	
1983	10	6		4	4		6	2	
1984	15	1		7	1		8	0	
1985	10	6		5	3		5	3	
1986	10	5	1	6	2		4	3	1
1987	13	2		6	1		7	1	
1988	10	6		4	4		6	2	
1989	14	2		6	2		8	0	
1990	14	2		6	2		8	0	
1991	10	6		7	1		3	5	
1992	14	2		7	1		7	1	
1993	10	6		6	2		4	4	
1994	13	3		7	1		6	2	
1995	11	5		6	2		5	3	
1996	12	4		6	2		6	2	
1997	13	3		8	0		5	3	
1998	12	4		8	0		4	4	
	393	292	13	211	131	7	182	161	6

TAMPA BAY BUCCANEERS

Season	All Games W	L	T	Home Games W	L	T	Road Games W	L	T
1976	0	14		0	7		0	7	
1977	2	12		1	6		1	6	
1978	5	11		3	5		2	6	
1979	10	6		5	3		5	3	
1980	5	10	1	2	5	1	3	5	
1981	9	7		6	2		3	5	
1982	5	4		4	1		1	3	
1983	2	14		1	7		1	7	
1984	6	10		6	2		0	8	
1985	2	14		2	6		0	8	
1986	2	14		1	7		1	7	
1987	4	11		2	5		2	6	
1988	5	11		3	5		2	6	
1989	5	11		2	6		3	5	
1990	6	10		4	4		2	6	
1991	3	13		3	5		0	8	
1992	5	11		3	5		2	6	
1993	5	11		3	5		2	6	
1994	6	10		4	4		2	6	
1995	7	9		5	3		2	6	
1996	6	10		5	3		1	7	
1997	10	6		5	3		5	3	
1998	8	8		6	2		2	6	
	118	237	1	76	101	1	42	136	

WASHINGTON REDSKINS*

Season	All Games W	L	T	Home Games W	L	T	Road Games W	L	T
1932	4	4	2	2	3	1	2	1	1
1933	5	5	2	4	2		1	3	2
1934	6	6		4	3		2	3	
1935	2	8	1	2	5		0	3	1
1936	7	5		4	3		3	2	
1937	8	3		4	2		4	1	
1938	6	3	2	3	1	1	3	2	1
1939	8	2	1	5	0	1	3	2	
1940	9	2		6	0		3	2	
1941	6	5		4	2		2	3	
1942	10	1		5	1		5	0	
1943	6	3	1	4	2		2	1	1
1944	6	3	1	4	2		2	1	1
1945	8	2		6	0		2	2	
1946	5	5	1	3	2	1	2	3	
1947	4	8		4	2		0	6	
1948	7	5		4	2		3	3	
1949	4	7	1	3	3		1	4	1
1950	3	9		1	5		2	4	
1951	5	7		2	4		3	3	
1952	4	8		1	5		3	3	
1953	6	5	1	3	3		3	2	1
1954	3	9		3	3		0	6	
1955	8	4		3	3		5	1	
1956	6	6		4	2		2	4	
1957	5	6	1	2	3	1	3	3	
1958	4	7	1	3	2	1	1	5	
1959	3	9		2	4		1	5	
1960	1	9	2	1	4	1	0	5	1
1961	1	12	1	1	6		0	6	1
1962	5	7	2	3	4		2	3	2
1963	3	11		1	6		2	5	
1964	6	8		4	3		2	5	
1965	6	8		3	4		3	4	

	All Games			Home Games			Road Games		
Season	**W**	**L**	**T**	**W**	**L**	**T**	**W**	**L**	**T**
1966	7	7		4	3		3	4	
1967	5	6	3	2	4	1	3	2	2
1968	5	9		3	4		2	5	
1969	7	5	2	4	2	1	3	3	1
1970	6	8		4	3		2	5	
1971	9	4	1	4	2	1	5	2	
1972	11	3		6	1		5	2	
1973	10	4		7	0		3	4	
1974	10	4		6	1		4	3	
1975	8	6		5	2		3	4	
1976	10	4		5	2		5	2	
1977	9	5		5	2		4	3	
1978	8	8		5	3		3	5	
1979	10	6		6	2		4	4	
1980	6	10		4	4		2	6	
1981	8	8		5	3		3	5	
1982	8	1		3	1		5	0	
1983	14	2		7	1		7	1	
1984	11	5		7	1		4	4	
1985	10	6		5	3		5	3	
1986	12	4		7	1		5	3	
1987	11	4		6	1		5	3	
1988	7	9		4	4		3	5	
1989	10	6		4	4		6	2	
1990	10	6		7	1		3	5	
1991	14	2		7	1		7	1	
1992	9	7		6	2		3	5	
1993	4	12		3	5		1	7	
1994	3	13		0	8		3	5	
1995	6	10		4	4		2	6	
1996	9	7		5	3		4	4	
1997	8	7	1	5	2	1	3	5	
1998	6	10		4	4		2	6	
	461	410	27	267	180	11	194	230	16

**includes Boston Braves (1932) and Boston Redskins (1933-36).*

History

PRO FOOTBALL HALL OF FAME

The Professional Football Hall of Fame is located in Canton, Ohio, site of the organizational meeting on September 17, 1920, from which the National Football League evolved. The NFL recognized Canton as the Hall of Fame site on April 27, 1961. Canton area individuals, foundations, and companies donated almost $400,000 in cash and services to provide funds for the construction of the original two-building complex, which was dedicated on September 7, 1963. Since that time, the Hall added three buildings with major expansion projects in 1971, 1978, and 1995. The Hall's largest-ever expansion, a $9.2 million project, was completed in early fall 1995. With the new fifth building, the Hall's size is now 82,307-square feet, more than four times its original size.

The expanded Hall represents the sport of pro football in many ways—through (1) GameDay Stadium, a dynamic two-part turntable theater featuring NFL action in Cinemascope for the first time, (2) a standard theater showing NFL films hourly, (3) six large exhibition areas where the history of pro football is detailed in memento, picture, and story form, (4) an extensive library and research center, and (5) a new and enlarged museum store.

In recent years, the Pro Football Hall of Fame has become an extremely popular tourist attraction. At the end of 1998, a total of 6,507,923 fans had visited the Hall of Fame.

New members of the Pro Football Hall of Fame are elected annually by a 36-member National Board of Selectors, made up of media representatives from every league city, five at-large representatives, and a representative of the Pro Football Writers of America. Between four and seven new members are elected each year. An affirmative vote of approximately 80 percent is needed for election.

Any fan may nominate any eligible player or contributor simply by writing to the Pro Football Hall of Fame. Players must be retired five years to be eligible, while a coach need only to be retired with no time limit specified. Contributors (administrators, owners, *et al.*) may be elected while they are still active.

The charter class of 17 enshrinees was elected in 1963 and the honor roll now stands at 199 with the election of a five-man class in 1999. That class consists of Eric Dickerson, Tom Mack, Ozzie Newsome, Billy Shaw, and Lawrence Taylor.

ROSTER OF MEMBERS

HERB ADDERLEY
Defensive back. 6-1, 200. Born in Philadelphia, Pennsylvania, June 8, 1939. Michigan State. Inducted in 1980. 1961-69 Green Bay Packers, 1970-72 Dallas Cowboys. **Highlights:** 48 interceptions, 7 touchdowns. Played in four Super Bowls, five Pro Bowls.

LANCE ALWORTH
Wide receiver. 6-0, 184. Born in Houston, Texas, August 3, 1940. Arkansas. Inducted in 1978. 1962-70 San Diego Chargers, 1971-72 Dallas Cowboys. **Highlights:** 542 receptions for 10,266 yards, 85 touchdowns. All-AFL seven times, seven All-Star games.

DOUG ATKINS
Defensive end. 6-8, 275. Born in Humboldt, Tennessee, May 8, 1930. Tennessee. Inducted in 1982. 1953-54 Cleveland Browns, 1955-66 Chicago Bears, 1967-69 New Orleans Saints. **Highlights:** Eight Pro Bowls, All-NFL four times. Played for 17 years, 205 games.

MORRIS (RED) BADGRO
End. 6-0, 190. Born in Orilla, Washington, December 1, 1902. Died July 13, 1998. Southern California. Inducted in 1981. 1927 New York Yankees, 1930-35 New York Giants, 1936 Brooklyn Dodgers. **Highlights:** All-NFL three times. Scored first touchdown in NFL Championship Game series.

LEM BARNEY
Cornerback. 6-0, 190. Born in Gulfport, Mississippi, September 8, 1945. Jackson State. Inducted in 1992. 1967-77 Detroit Lions. **Highlights:** 56 interceptions for 1,077 yards, 11 touchdowns (7 defensive, 4 special teams). Seven Pro Bowls, All-NFL/NFC four times.

CLIFF BATTLES
Halfback. 6-1, 201. Born in Akron, Ohio, May 1, 1910. Died April 28, 1981. West Virginia Wesleyan. Inducted in 1968. 1932 Boston Braves, 1933-36 Boston Redskins, 1937 Washington Redskins. **Highlights:** NFL rushing champion 1932, 1937. First to gain more than 200 yards in a game, 1933.

SAMMY BAUGH
Quarterback. 6-2, 180. Born in Temple, Texas, March 17, 1914. Texas Christian. Inducted in 1963. 1937-52 Washington Redskins. **Highlights:** Charter enshrinee. Six-time NFL passing leader. NFL passing, punting, interception champ, 1943.

CHUCK BEDNARIK
Center-linebacker. 6-3, 230. Born in Bethlehem, Pennsylvania, May 1, 1925. Pennsylvania. Inducted in 1967. 1949-62 Philadelphia Eagles. **Highlights:** Eight Pro Bowls. Missed three games in 14 years. Named NFL all-time center, 1969.

BERT BELL
Team owner. Commissioner. Born in Philadelphia, Pennsylvania, February 25, 1895. Died October 11, 1959. Pennsylvania. Inducted in 1963. 1933-40 Philadelphia Eagles, 1941-42 Pittsburgh Steelers, 1943 Phil-Pitt, 1944 Card-Pitt, 1945-46 Pittsburgh Steelers. Commissioner, 1946-59. **Highlights:** Charter enshrinee. Built NFL image as commissioner, 1946-1959. Set up long-term television policies.

BOBBY BELL
Linebacker. 6-4, 225. Born in Shelby, North Carolina, June 17, 1940. Minnesota. Inducted in 1983. 1963-74 Kansas City Chiefs. **Highlights:** 26 interceptions. All-AFL/AFC eight times. Nine career touchdowns, 1 on onside kick return.

RAYMOND BERRY
End. 6-2, 187. Born in Corpus Christi, Texas, February 27, 1933. Southern Methodist. Inducted in 1973. 1955-67 Baltimore Colts. **Highlights:** 631 receptions for 9,275 yards, 68 touchdowns. Set NFL title game mark with 12 catches for 178 yards, 1958.

CHARLES W. BIDWILL, SR.
Team owner. Born in Chicago, Illinois, September 16, 1895. Died April 19, 1947. Loyola of Chicago. Inducted in 1967. 1933-43 Chicago Cardinals, 1944 Card-Pitt, 1945-47 Chicago Cardinals. **Highlights:** Guiding light for NFL during depression years. Built famous "Dream Backfield."

FRED BILETNIKOFF
Wide receiver. 6-1, 190. Born in Erie, Pennsylvania, February 23, 1943. Florida State. Inducted in 1988. 1965-78 Oakland Raiders. **Highlights:** 589 receptions for 8,974 yards, 76 touchdowns. 40 catches 10 straight years. MVP, Super Bowl XI.

GEORGE BLANDA
Quarterback-kicker. 6-2, 215. Born in Youngwood, Pennsylvania, September 17, 1927. Kentucky. Inducted in 1981. 1949-58 Chicago Bears, 1950 Baltimore Colts, 1960-66 Houston Oilers, 1967-75 Oakland Raiders. **Highlights:** Record 2,002 career points. 26-season, 340-game career longest in NFL history.

MEL BLOUNT
Cornerback. 6-3, 205. Born in Vidalia, Georgia, April 10, 1948. Southern University. Inducted in 1989. 1970-83 Pittsburgh Steelers. **Highlights:** 57 interceptions for 736 yards. NFL defensive MVP, 1975. Played in five Pro Bowls.

TERRY BRADSHAW
Quarterback. 6-3, 210. Born in Shreveport, Louisiana, September 2, 1948. Louisiana Tech. Inducted in 1989. 1970-83 Pittsburgh Steelers. **Highlights:** 27,989 yards passing, 212 touchdowns. MVP in Super Bowls XIII, XIV.

JIM BROWN
Fullback. 6-2, 228. Born in St. Simons, Georgia, February 17, 1936. Syracuse. Inducted in 1971. 1957-65 Cleveland Browns. **Highlights:** 12,312 yards rushing, 756 points. Led NFL rushers eight years. Nine consecutive Pro Bowls.

PAUL BROWN
Coach. Born in Norwalk, Ohio, September 7, 1908. Died August 5, 1991. Miami (Ohio). Inducted in 1967. 1946-49 Cleveland Browns (AAFC), 1950-62 Cleveland Browns. **Highlights:** Built Cleveland dynasty with 167-53-8 record, four AAFC titles, three NFL crowns. Returned to coaching with Cincinnati Bengals after induction, 1968-1975.

ROOSEVELT BROWN
Tackle. 6-3, 255. Born in Charlottesville, Virginia, October 20, 1932. Morgan State. Inducted in 1975. 1953-65 New York Giants. **Highlights:** All-NFL eight consecutive years, nine Pro Bowls. NFL's lineman of year, 1956.

WILLIE BROWN
Cornerback. 6-1, 210. Born in Yazoo City, Mississippi, December 2, 1940. Grambling. Inducted in 1984. 1963-66 Denver Broncos, 1967-78 Oakland Raiders. **Highlights:** 54 interceptions for 472 yards. Scored on 75-yard interception in Super Bowl XI.

BUCK BUCHANAN
Defensive tackle. 6-7, 274. Born in Gainesville, Alabama, September 10, 1940. Died July 16, 1992. Grambling. Inducted in 1990. 1963-75 Kansas City Chiefs. **Highlights:** Led Chiefs defensive efforts in Super Bowl I, IV. Did not miss a game in 13 years.

DICK BUTKUS
Linebacker. 6-3, 245. Born in Chicago, Illinois, December 9, 1942. Illinois. Inducted in 1979. 1965-73 Chicago Bears. **Highlights:** All-NFL six years, eight consecutive Pro Bowls. 25 fumble recoveries.

EARL CAMPBELL
Running back. 5-11, 233. Born in Tyler, Texas, March 29, 1955. Texas. Inducted in 1991. 1978-84 Houston Oilers, 1984-85 New Orleans Saints. **Highlights:** 9,407 yards rushing, 74 touchdowns. 1,934 yards rushing in 1980, including four games with at least 200 yards.

TONY CANADEO
Halfback. 5-11, 195. Born in Chicago, Illinois, May 5, 1919. Gonzaga. Inducted in 1974. 1941-44, 1946-52 Green Bay Packers. **Highlights:** Two-way player. Third player to rush for 1,000 yards in single season, 1949.

JOE CARR
NFL president. Born in Columbus, Ohio, October 22, 1880. Died May 20, 1939. Did not attend college. Inducted in 1963. President, 1921-39 National Football League. **Highlights:** Charter enshrinee. NFL co-organizer, 1920. Introduced standard player's contract.

GUY CHAMBERLIN
End. Coach. 6-2, 210. Born in Blue Springs, Nebraska, January 16, 1894. Died April 4, 1967. Nebraska. Inducted in 1965. 1919 Canton Bulldogs, 1920 Decatur Staleys, 1921 Chicago Staleys, player-coach 1922-23 Canton Bulldogs, 1924 Cleveland Bulldogs, 1925-26 Frankford Yellow Jackets, 1927-28 Chicago Cardinals. **Highlights:** Player-coach of four NFL championship teams. Six-year coaching record 58-16-7.

JACK CHRISTIANSEN
Safety. 6-1, 185. Born in Sublette, Kansas, December 20, 1928. Died June 29, 1986. Colorado State. Inducted in 1970. 1951-58 Detroit Lions. **Highlights:** 46 interceptions. NFL interception leader, 1953, 1957. Eight punt returns for touchdowns.

EARL (DUTCH) CLARK
Quarterback. 6-0, 185. Born in Fowler, Colorado, October 11, 1906. Died August 5, 1978. Colorado College.

Inducted in 1963. 1931-32 Portsmouth Spartans, 1934-38 Detroit Lions. **Highlights:** Charter enshrinee. NFL scoring champion three years. Led Lions to 1935 NFL title.

GEORGE CONNOR
Tackle-linebacker. 6-3, 240. Born in Chicago, Illinois, January 21, 1925. Holy Cross, Notre Dame. Inducted in 1975. 1948-55 Chicago Bears. **Highlights:** All-NFL at three positions—T, DT, LB. All-NFL five years. Played in first four Pro Bowls.

JIMMY CONZELMAN
Quarterback. Coach. Team owner. 6-0, 180. Born in St. Louis, Missouri, March 6, 1898. Died July 31, 1970. Washington of St. Louis. Inducted in 1964. 1920 Decatur Staleys, 1921-22 Rock Island Independents, 1923-24 Milwaukee Badgers; owner-coach 1925-26 Detroit Panthers; player-coach 1927-29, coach 1930 Providence Steam Roller; coach 1940-42, 1946-48 Chicago Cardinals. **Highlights:** Player-coach of four NFL teams in 1920's. Coached Cardinals to 1947 NFL crown.

LOU CREEKMUR
Tackle-guard. 6-4, 255. Born in Hopelawn, New Jersey. January 22, 1927. William & Mary. Inducted in 1996. 1950-59 Detroit Lions. **Highlights:** All-NFL six times, twice at guard and four times at tackle. Selected to eight Pro Bowls and played on three NFL championship teams.

LARRY CSONKA
Running back. 6-3, 235. Born in Stow, Ohio, December 25, 1946. Syracuse. Inducted in 1987. 1968-74, 1979 Miami Dolphins, 1976-78 New York Giants. **Highlights:** 8,081 yards rushing, 68 touchdowns. MVP Super Bowl VIII. Only 21 fumbles in 1,891 carries and 106 receptions.

AL DAVIS
Team, League Administrator. Born in Brockton, Massachusetts, July 4, 1929. Wittenberg, Syracuse. Inducted in 1992. 1963-81, 1995-present Oakland Raiders, 1982-94 Los Angeles Raiders, 1966 American Football League. **Highlights:** Only person to serve in pros as personnel assistant, scout, assistant coach, head coach, general manager, commissioner, team owner/CEO.

WILLIE DAVIS
Defensive end. 6-3, 245. Born in Lisbon, Louisiana, July 24, 1934. Grambling. Inducted in 1981. 1958-59 Cleveland Browns, 1960-69 Green Bay Packers. **Highlights:** All-NFL five seasons, five Pro Bowls. Did not miss game in 12-year career.

LEN DAWSON
Quarterback. 6-0, 190. Born in Alliance, Ohio, June 20, 1935. Purdue. Inducted in 1987. 1957-59 Pittsburgh Steelers, 1960-61 Cleveland Browns, 1962 Dallas Texans, 1963-75 Kansas City Chiefs. **Highlights:** 28,711 yards passing, 239 touchdowns. Four AFL passing crowns. MVP, Super Bowl IV.

ERIC DICKERSON
Running back. 6-3, 220. Born in Sealy, Texas, September 2, 1960. Southern Methodist. Inducted in 1999. 1983-87 Los Angeles Rams, 1987-91 Indianapolis Colts, 1992 Los Angeles Raiders, 1993 Atlanta Falcons. **Highlights:** Rushed for 13,259 career yards, including an NFL record 2,105 yards in 1984. All-Pro five times, six Pro Bowls.

DAN DIERDORF
Tackle. 6-3, 290. Born in Canton, Ohio, June 29, 1949. Michigan. Inducted in 1996. 1971-83 St. Louis Cardinals. **Highlights:** All-Pro five times, played in six Pro Bowls, named NFL's best blocker three times.

MIKE DITKA
Tight end. 6-3, 225. Born in Carnegie, Pennsylvania, October 18, 1939. Pittsburgh. Inducted in 1988. 1961-66 Chicago Bears, 1967-68 Philadelphia Eagles, 1969-72 Dallas Cowboys. **Highlights:** 427 receptions for 5,812 yards, 43 touchdowns. First tight end selected to Hall of Fame. Five consecutive Pro Bowls.

ART DONOVAN
Defensive tackle. 6-3, 265. Born in Bronx, New York, June 5, 1925. Boston College. Inducted in 1968. 1950 Baltimore Colts, 1951 New York Yanks, 1952 Dallas Texans, 1953-61 Baltimore Colts. **Highlights:** Five Pro Bowls. Vital part of Baltimore's climb to powerhouse status in 1950s.

TONY DORSETT
Running back. 5-11, 184. Born in Rochester, Pennsylvania, April 7, 1954. Pittsburgh. Inducted in 1994. 1977-87 Dallas Cowboys, 1988 Denver Broncos. **Highlights:** 12,739 yards rushing, 398 receptions, 91 touchdowns. Ran record 99 yards for touchdown vs. Minnesota, January, 1983.

JOHN (PADDY) DRISCOLL
Quarterback. 5-11, 160. Born in Evanston, Illinois, January 11, 1896. Died June 29, 1968. Northwestern. Inducted in 1965. 1919 Hammond Pros, 1920 Decatur Staleys, 1920-25 Chicago Cardinals, 1926-29 Chicago Bears. **Highlights:** All-NFL seven times. Dropkicked record 4 field goals in one game, 1925.

BILL DUDLEY
Halfback. 5-10, 176. Born in Bluefield, Virginia, December 24, 1921. Virginia. Inducted in 1966. 1942, 1945-46 Pittsburgh Steelers, 1947-49 Detroit Lions, 1950-51, 1953 Washington Redskins. **Highlights:** Won NFL rushing, interception, punt return titles, 1946. All-NFL 1942, 1946, and 1947.

ALBERT GLEN (TURK) EDWARDS
Tackle. 6-2, 260. Born in Mold, Washington, September 28, 1907. Died January 12, 1973. Washington State. Inducted in 1969. 1932 Boston Braves, 1933-36 Boston Redskins, 1937-40 Washington Redskins. **Highlights:** All-NFL 1932-34, 1936, 1937. Steamrolling blocker, smothering tackler.

WEEB EWBANK
Coach. Born in Richmond, Indiana, May 6, 1907. Died November 17, 1998. Miami (Ohio). Inducted in 1978. 1954-62 Baltimore Colts, 1963-73 New York Jets. **Highlights:** Only coach to win championships in both NFL, AFL. Led both Colts (1958) and Jets (1968) to championships.

TOM FEARS
End. 6-2, 215. Born in Los Angeles, California, December 3, 1923. Santa Clara, UCLA. Inducted in 1970. 1948-56 Los Angeles Rams. **Highlights:** 400 receptions for 5,397 yards, 38 touchdowns. Led NFL receivers first three seasons. Record 18 receptions in single game.

JIM FINKS
Administrator. Born in St. Louis, Missouri, August 31, 1927. Died May 8, 1994. Tulsa. Inducted 1995. 1964-73 Minnesota Vikings, 1974-82 Chicago Bears, 1986-93 New Orleans Saints. **Highlights:** Developed Vikings, Bears, Saints—all teams with losing records—into winners.

RAY FLAHERTY
Coach. Born in Spokane, Washington, September 1, 1903. Died July 19, 1994. Gonzaga. Inducted in 1976. 1936 Boston Redskins, 1937-42 Washington Redskins, 1946-48 New York Yankees (AAFC), 1949 Chicago Hornets (AAFC). **Highlights:** 82-41-5 coaching record. Introduced screen pass in 1937 title game and platoon system.

LEN FORD
Defensive end. 6-5, 260. Born in Washington, D.C., February 18, 1926. Died March 14, 1972. Morgan State, Michigan. Inducted in 1976. 1948-49 Los Angeles Dons (AAFC), 1950-57 Cleveland Browns, 1958 Green Bay Packers. **Highlights:** All-NFL five times, four Pro Bowls. Recovered 20 opponents' fumbles.

DAN FORTMANN
Guard. 6-0, 210. Born in Pearl River, New York, April 11, 1916. Died May 24, 1995. Colgate. Inducted in 1965. 1936-43 Chicago Bears. **Highlights:** At 20, became youngest starter in NFL. All-NFL six consecutive years.

DAN FOUTS
Quarterback. 6-3, 210. Born in San Francisco, California, June 10, 1951. Oregon. Inducted in 1993. 1973-1987 San Diego Chargers. **Highlights:** 43,040 passing yards, 254 touchdowns. Six Pro Bowls, NFL MVP, 1982.

FRANK GATSKI
Center. 6-3, 240. Born in Farmington, West Virginia, March 18, 1922. Marshall, Auburn. Inducted in 1985. 1946-49 Cleveland Browns (AAFC), 1950-56 Cleveland Browns, 1957 Detroit Lions. **Highlights:** Never missed game in high school, college, or pro football. Played 11 championship games, winning eight.

BILL GEORGE
Linebacker. 6-2, 230. Born in Waynesburg, Pennsylvania, October 27, 1930. Died September 30, 1982. Wake Forest. Inducted in 1974. 1952-65 Chicago Bears, 1966 Los Angeles Rams. **Highlights:** All-NFL eight years, eight consecutive Pro Bowls. 14 years of service, longest of any Bears player.

JOE GIBBS
Coach. Born in Mocksville, North Carolina, November 25, 1940. Cerritos (Calif.) J.C., San Diego State. Inducted in 1996. 1981-92 Washington Redskins. **Highlights:** 124-60-0 record in regular season, 16-5 in postseason, including four Super Bowl appearances—winning three. Won 10 or more games eight times.

FRANK GIFFORD
Halfback. 6-1, 195. Born in Santa Monica, California, August 16, 1930. Southern California. Inducted in 1977. 1952-60, 1962-64 New York Giants. **Highlights:** Starred on both offense and defense. Seven Pro Bowls, 1956 NFL player of the year.

SID GILLMAN
Coach. Born in Minneapolis, Minnesota, October 26, 1911. Ohio State. Inducted in 1983. 1955-59 Los Angeles Rams, 1960 Los Angeles Chargers, 1961-69, 1971 San Diego Chargers, 1973-74 Houston Oilers. **Highlights:** 123-104-7 coaching record. First to win division titles in both NFL, AFL.

OTTO GRAHAM
Quarterback. 6-1, 195. Born in Waukegan, Illinois, December 6, 1921. Northwestern. Inducted in 1965. 1946-49 Cleveland Browns (AAFC), 1950-55 Cleveland Browns. **Highlights:** 23,584 passing yards, 174 touchdowns. Guided Browns to 10 division or league crowns in 10 years.

HAROLD (RED) GRANGE
Halfback. 6-0, 185. Born in Forksville, Pennsylvania, June 13, 1903. Died January 28, 1991. Illinois. Inducted in 1963. 1925 Chicago Bears, 1926 New York Yankees (AFL), 1927 New York Yankees, 1929-34 Chicago Bears. **Highlights:** Nicknamed "Galloping Ghost." Name produced first huge pro football crowds.

BUD GRANT
Coach. Born in Superior, Wisconsin, May 20, 1927. Minnesota. Inducted in 1994. 1967-83, 1985 Minnesota Vikings. **Highlights:** 168-108-5 coaching record. Led Vikings to 11 division championships, four Super Bowls.

JOE GREENE
Defensive tackle. 6-4, 260. Born in Temple, Texas, September 24, 1946. North Texas State. Inducted in 1987. 1969-81 Pittsburgh Steelers. **Highlights:** NFL defensive player of the year, 1972, 1974. Four-time Super Bowl champion, 10 Pro Bowls.

FORREST GREGG
Tackle. 6-4, 250. Born in Birthright, Texas, October 18, 1933. Southern Methodist. Inducted in 1977. 1956, 1958-70 Green Bay Packers, 1971 Dallas Cowboys. **Highlights:** Played 188 consecutive games. Nine Pro Bowls. Played on six NFL champi-

onship teams, three Super Bowl winners.

BOB GRIESE
Quarterback. 6-1, 190. Born in Evansville, Indiana, February 3, 1945. Purdue. Inducted in 1990. 1967-80 Miami Dolphins. **Highlights:** 25,092 passing yards, 192 touchdowns. Led Miami to three AFC titles, Super Bowl VII, VIII wins.

LOU GROZA
Tackle-kicker. 6-3, 250. Born in Martins Ferry, Ohio, January 25, 1924. Ohio State. Inducted in 1974. 1946-49 Cleveland Browns (AAFC), 1950-59, 1961-67 Cleveland Browns. **Highlights:** 1,608 points in 21 years. Nine Pro Bowls, All-NFL six years. NFL player of the year, 1954.

JOE GUYON
Halfback. 6-1, 180. Born on White Earth Indian Reservation, Minnesota, November 26, 1892. Died November 27, 1971. Carlisle, Georgia Tech. Inducted in 1966. 1919-20 Canton Bulldogs, 1921 Cleveland Indians, 1922-23 Oorang Indians, 1924 Rock Island Independents, 1924-25 Kansas City Cowboys, 1927 New York Giants. **Highlights:** Touchdown pass gave Giants victory over Bears to win 1927 championship.

GEORGE HALAS
End. Coach. Team owner. Born in Chicago, Illinois, February 2, 1895. Died October 31, 1983. Illinois. Inducted in 1963. Player-coach 1920 Decatur Staleys, 1921 Chicago Staleys, 1922-29 Chicago Bears; coach 1933-42, 1946-55, 1958-67 Chicago Bears. **Highlights:** Charter enshrinee. 324 coaching wins. Only person associated with NFL throughout first 50 years. Coached Bears 40 seasons, won six NFL titles.

JACK HAM
Linebacker. 6-1, 225. Born in Johnstown, Pennsylvania, December 23, 1948. Penn State. Inducted in 1988. 1971-82 Pittsburgh Steelers. **Highlights:** Won four Super Bowls, 21 opponents' fumbles recovered, 32 interceptions. Eight consecutive Pro Bowls.

JOHN HANNAH
Guard. 6-3, 265. Born in Canton, Georgia, April 4, 1951. Alabama. Inducted in 1991. 1973-85 New England Patriots. **Highlights:** Renowned as premier guard of era. All-Pro 10 years, nine Pro Bowls.

FRANCO HARRIS
Running back. 6-2, 225. Born in Fort Dix, New Jersey, March 7, 1950. Penn State. Inducted in 1990. 1972-83 Pittsburgh Steelers, 1984 Seattle Seahawks. **Highlights:** 12,120 rushing yards, 100 total touchdowns. 1,556 rushing yards in 19 postseason games. MVP in Super Bowl IX.

MIKE HAYNES
Cornerback. 6-2, 195. Born in Denison, Texas, July 1, 1953. Arizona State. Inducted in 1997. 1976-82 New England Patriots, 1983-89 Los Angeles Raiders. **Highlights:** Defensive rookie of the year. Selected to nine Pro Bowls and intercepted 46 passes, plus one pick in Super Bowl XVIII.

ED HEALEY
Tackle. 6-3, 220. Born in Indian Orchard, Massachusetts, December 28, 1894. Died December 9, 1978. Dartmouth. Inducted in 1964. 1920-22 Rock Island Independents, 1922-27 Chicago Bears. **Highlights:** Two-way star. Perennial all-pro with Bears.

MEL HEIN
Center. 6-2, 225. Born in Redding, California, August 22, 1909. Died January 31, 1992. Washington State. Inducted in 1963. 1931-45 New York Giants. **Highlights:** Charter enshrinee. 60-minute regular for 15 years. All-NFL eight consecutive years.

TED HENDRICKS
Linebacker. 6-7, 235. Born in Guatemala City, Guatemala, November 1, 1947. Miami. Inducted in 1990. 1969-73 Baltimore Colts, 1974 Green Bay Packers, 1975-81 Oakland Raiders, 1982-83 Los Angeles Raiders. **Highlights:** 25 blocked field goals, extra points, and punts, 26 interceptions. Played in 215 consecutive games.

WILBUR (PETE) HENRY
Tackle. 6-0, 250. Born in Mansfield, Ohio, October 31, 1897. Died February 7, 1952. Washington & Jefferson. Inducted in 1963. 1920-23, 1925-26 Canton Bulldogs, 1927 New York Giants, 1927-28 Pottsville Maroons. **Highlights:** Largest player of his time at 250 pounds. Bulwark of Canton's championship lines.

ARNIE HERBER
Quarterback. 6-0, 200. Born in Green Bay, Wisconsin, April 2, 1910. Died October 14, 1969. Wisconsin, Regis College. Inducted in 1966. 1930-40 Green Bay Packers, 1944-45 New York Giants. **Highlights:** NFL passing leader 1932, 1934, 1936. Came out of retirement to lead 1944 Giants to NFL Eastern crown.

BILL HEWITT
End. 5-11, 191. Born in Bay City, Michigan, October 8, 1909. Died January 14, 1947. Michigan. Inducted in 1971. 1932-36 Chicago Bears, 1937-39 Philadelphia Eagles, 1943 Phil-Pitt. **Highlights:** First to be named all-NFL with two teams—1933, 1934, 1936 Bears; 1937 Eagles.

CLARKE HINKLE
Fullback. 5-11, 201. Born in Toronto, Ohio, April 10, 1909. Died November 9, 1988. Bucknell. Inducted in 1964. 1932-41 Green Bay Packers. **Highlights:** 3,860 yards rushing, 379 points. Fullback on offense, linebacker on defense.

ELROY (CRAZYLEGS) HIRSCH
Halfback-end. 6-2, 190. Born in Wausau, Wisconsin, June 17, 1923. Wisconsin, Michigan. Inducted in 1968. 1946-48 Chicago Rockets (AAFC), 1949-57 Los Angeles Rams. **Highlights:** 387 receptions for 7,029 yards, 60 touchdowns. Key part of Rams' revolutionary "three end" offense, 1949.

PAUL HORNUNG
Halfback. 6-2, 220. Born in Louisville, Kentucky, December 23, 1935. Notre Dame. Inducted in 1986. 1957-62, 1964-66 Green Bay Packers. **Highlights:** 760 points. Led NFL scorers three years, including record 176 points, 1960. Record 19 points scored in 1961 NFL title game.

KEN HOUSTON
Safety. 6-3, 198. Born in Lufkin, Texas, November 12, 1944. Prairie View A&M. Inducted in 1986. 1967-72 Houston Oilers, 1973-80 Washington Redskins. **Highlights:** 49 interceptions, 898 yards, 9 touchdowns. NFL's premier strong safety of 1970s. 12 Pro Bowls.

ROBERT (CAL) HUBBARD
Tackle. 6-5, 250. Born in Keytesville, Missouri, October 31, 1900. Died October 17, 1977. Centenary, Geneva. Inducted in 1963. 1927-28 New York Giants, 1929-33, 1935 Green Bay Packers, 1936 New York Giants, 1936 Pittsburgh Pirates. **Highlights:** Charter enshrinee. Most feared lineman of his time. All-NFL six years, 1927-29, 1931-33.

SAM HUFF
Linebacker. 6-1, 230. Born in Morgantown, West Virginia, October 4, 1934. West Virginia. Inducted in 1982. 1956-63 New York Giants, 1964-67, 1969 Washington Redskins. **Highlights:** 30 interceptions. Played in six NFL title games, five Pro Bowls. Redskins player-coach, 1969.

LAMAR HUNT
Team owner. Born in El Dorado, Arkansas, August 2, 1932. Southern Methodist. Inducted in 1972. 1960-62 Dallas Texans, 1963-present Kansas City Chiefs. **Highlights:** Driving force behind organization of AFL. Spearheaded merger negotiations with NFL, 1966.

DON HUTSON
End. 6-1, 180. Born in Pine Bluff, Arkansas, January 31, 1913. Died June 26, 1997. Alabama. Inducted in 1963. 1935-45 Green Bay Packers. **Highlights:** 488 receptions for 7,991 yards, 99 touchdowns. NFL receiving champion eight years. NFL MVP, 1941, 1942.

JIMMY JOHNSON
Cornerback. 6-2, 187. Born in Dallas, Texas, March 31, 1938. UCLA. Inducted in 1994. 1961-76 San Francisco 49ers. **Highlights:** 47 interceptions for 615 yards. Five Pro Bowls. Opposing passers avoided throwing in his area.

JOHN HENRY JOHNSON
Fullback. 6-2, 225. Born in Waterproof, Louisiana, November 24, 1929. St. Mary's, Arizona State. Inducted in 1987. 1954-56 San Francisco 49ers, 1957-59 Detroit Lions, 1960-65 Pittsburgh Steelers, 1966 Houston Oilers. **Highlights:** 6,803 yards rushing, 55 total touchdowns. Member of San Francisco's "Fabulous Foursome" backfield.

CHARLIE JOINER
Wide receiver. 5-11, 180. Born in Many, Louisiana, October 14, 1947. Grambling. Inducted in 1996. 1969-72 Houston Oilers, 1972-75 Cincinnati Bengals, 1976-86 San Diego Chargers. **Highlights:** 750 receptions for 12,146 yards and 65 touchdowns. Played 18 seasons, 239 games, most ever for wide receiver.

DAVID (DEACON) JONES
Defensive end. 6-5, 260. Born in Eatonville, Florida, December 9, 1938. South Carolina State, Mississippi Vocational. Inducted in 1980. 1961-71 Los Angeles Rams, 1972-73 San Diego Chargers, 1974 Washington Redskins. **Highlights:** Specialized in quarterback 'sacks,' a term he invented. Unanimous all-league five consecutive years.

STAN JONES
Guard-defensive tackle. 6-1, 250. Born in Altoona, Pennsylvania, November 24, 1931. Maryland. Inducted in 1991. 1954-65 Chicago Bears, 1966 Washington Redskins. **Highlights:** Seven consecutive Pro Bowls. First to rely on weightlifting for football preparation.

HENRY JORDAN
Defensive tackle, 6-3, 240. Born in Emporia, Virginia, January 26, 1935. Died February 21, 1977. Virginia. Inducted in 1995. 1957-58 Cleveland Browns, 1959-69 Green Bay Packers. **Highlights:** Fixture at DT during Packers' dynasty. Played in four Pro Bowls, seven NFL title games, Super Bowls I, II.

SONNY JURGENSEN
Quarterback. 6-0, 203. Born in Wilmington, North Carolina, August 23, 1934. Duke. Inducted in 1983. 1957-63 Philadelphia Eagles, 1964-74 Washington Redskins. **Highlights:** 32,224 yards passing, 255 touchdowns, 82.63 passer rating. Surpassed 3,000 yards passing in five seasons.

LEROY KELLY
Running back. 6-0, 205. Born in Philadelphia, Pennsylvania, May 20, 1942. Morgan State. Inducted in 1994. 1964-73 Cleveland Browns. **Highlights:** 7,274 yards rushing, 90 total touchdowns, 1,000-yard rusher first three years as starter. Punt return champion, 1965.

WALT KIESLING
Guard. Coach. 6-2, 245. Born in St. Paul, Minnesota, March 27, 1903. Died March 2, 1962. St. Thomas (Minnesota). Inducted in 1966. 1926-27 Duluth Eskimos, 1928 Pottsville Maroons, 1929-33 Chicago Cardinals, 1934 Chicago Bears, 1935-36 Green Bay Packers, 1937-38 Pittsburgh Pirates; coach, 1939 Pittsburgh Pirates, 1940-42 Pittsburgh Steelers; co-coach, 1943 Phil-Pitt, 1944 Card-Pitt; coach, 1954-56 Pittsburgh Steelers. **Highlights:** 34-year career as pro player, assistant coach, head coach. Led Steelers to first winning season, 1942.

FRANK (BRUISER) KINARD
Tackle. 6-1, 210. Born in Pelahatchie, Mississippi, October 23, 1914. Died September 7, 1985. Mississippi. Inducted in 1971. 1938-43 Brooklyn Dodgers, 1944 Brooklyn Tigers, 1946-47 New York Yankees (AAFC). **Highlights:** First man to earn both All-NFL, All-AAFC honors. Out because of injury only once.

PAUL KRAUSE
Safety. 6-3, 200. Born in Flint, Michigan, February 19, 1942. Iowa. Inducted in 1998. 1964-67 Washington Redskins, 1968-79 Minnesota Vikings. **Highlights:** NFL all-time leader with 81 interceptions. Played in eight Pro Bowls. Starting safety in four Super Bowls.

EARL (CURLY) LAMBEAU
Coach. Born in Green Bay, Wisconsin, April 9, 1898. Died June 1, 1965. Notre Dame. Inducted in 1963. 1919-49 Green Bay Packers, 1950-51 Chicago Cardinals, 1952-53 Washington Redskins. **Highlights:** 229-134-22 coaching record with six NFL championships. Founded pre-NFL Packers, 1919.

JACK LAMBERT
Linebacker. 6-4, 220. Born in Mantua, Ohio, July 8, 1952. Kent State. Inducted in 1990. 1974-84 Pittsburgh Steelers. **Highlights:** Leader of 'Steel Curtain.' NFL defensive player of year in 1976, nine Pro Bowls.

TOM LANDRY
Coach. Born in Mission, Texas, September 11, 1924. Texas. Inducted in 1990. 1960-88 Dallas Cowboys. **Highlights:** 270-178-6 coaching record. 20 consecutive winning seasons. Innovator on offense and defense.

DICK (NIGHT TRAIN) LANE
Cornerback. 6-2, 210. Born in Austin, Texas, April 16, 1928. Scottsbluff Junior College. Inducted in 1974. 1952-53 Los Angeles Rams, 1954-59 Chicago Cardinals, 1960-65 Detroit Lions. **Highlights:** 68 interceptions for 1,207 yards, 5 touchdowns. Record 14 interceptions as rookie. Seven Pro Bowls.

JIM LANGER
Center. 6-2, 255. Born in Little Falls, Minnesota, May 16, 1948. South Dakota State. Inducted in 1987. 1970-79 Miami Dolphins, 1980-81 Minnesota Vikings. **Highlights:** Played every offensive down in Dolphins' perfect 1972 season. Six Pro Bowls.

WILLIE LANIER
Linebacker. 6-1, 245. Born in Clover, Virginia, August 21, 1945. Morgan State. Inducted in 1986. 1967-77 Kansas City Chiefs. **Highlights:** 27 interceptions. Defensive star in Super Bowl IV upset. Nicknamed 'Contact' for ferocious tackling.

STEVE LARGENT
Wide receiver. 5-11, 191. Born in Tulsa, Oklahoma, September 28, 1954, Tulsa. Inducted in 1995. 1976-89 Seattle Seahawks. **Highlights:** 819 receptions for 13,089 yards, 100 touchdowns. Receptions in 177 consecutive games.

YALE LARY
Defensive back-punter. 5-11, 189. Born in Fort Worth, Texas, November 24, 1930. Texas A&M. Inducted in 1979. 1952-53, 1956-64 Detroit Lions. **Highlights:** 50 interceptions. Three NFL punting crowns, three touchdowns on punt returns. Nine Pro Bowls.

DANTE LAVELLI
End. 6-0, 199. Born in Hudson, Ohio, February 23, 1923. Ohio State. Inducted in 1975. 1946-49 Cleveland Browns (AAFC), 1950-56 Cleveland Browns. **Highlights:** 386 receptions for 6,488 yards, 62 touchdowns. 24 catches in six NFL title games.

BOBBY LAYNE
Quarterback. 6-2, 190. Born in Santa Ana, Texas, December 19, 1926. Died December 1, 1986. Texas. Inducted in 1967. 1948 Chicago Bears, 1949 New York Bulldogs, 1950-58 Detroit Lions, 1958-62 Pittsburgh Steelers. **Highlights:** 26,768 yards passing, 196 touchdowns, 2,451 yards rushing. Late touchdown pass won 1953 NFL title game.

ALPHONSE (TUFFY) LEEMANS
Fullback. 6-0, 200. Born in Superior, Wisconsin, November 12, 1912. Died January 19, 1979. Oregon, George Washington. Inducted in 1978. 1936-43 New York Giants. **Highlights:** 3,132 yards rushing, 2,324 yards passing, 422 yards receiving. Led NFL rushers as rookie, 1936.

BOB LILLY
Defensive tackle. 6-5, 260. Born in Olney, Texas, July 26, 1939. Texas Christian. Inducted in 1980. 1961-74 Dallas Cowboys. **Highlights:** Eleven Pro Bowls. Played 196 consecutive games. Foundation of great Dallas defensive units.

LARRY LITTLE
Guard. 6-1, 265. Born in Groveland, Georgia, November 2, 1945. Bethune-Cookman. Inducted in 1993. 1967-68 San Diego Chargers, 1969-80 Miami Dolphins. **Highlights:** Five Pro Bowls, started in three Super Bowls. Epitome of powerful Dolphins rushing game of 1970s.

VINCE LOMBARDI
Coach. Born in Brooklyn, New York, June 11, 1913. Died September 3, 1970. Fordham. Inducted in 1971. 1959-67 Green Bay Packers, 1969 Washington Redskins. **Highlights:** 105-35-6 coaching record in 10 years, including five NFL titles and victories in Super Bowls I and II.

SID LUCKMAN
Quarterback. 6-0, 195. Born in Brooklyn, New York, November 21, 1916. Died July 5, 1998. Columbia. Inducted in 1965. 1939-50 Chicago Bears. **Highlights:** 137 touchdown passes. All-NFL five times. League MVP in 1943.

WILLIAM ROY (LINK) LYMAN
Tackle. 6-2, 252. Born in Table Rock, Nebraska, November 30, 1898. Died December 16, 1972. Nebraska. Inducted in 1964. 1922-23, 1925 Canton Bulldogs, 1924 Cleveland Bulldogs, 1925 Frankford Yellow Jackets, 1926-28, 1930-31, 1933-34 Chicago Bears. **Highlights:** Played for four NFL champions. In 16 seasons of college and pro football, played on one losing team.

TOM MACK
Guard. 6-3, 250. Born in Cleveland, Ohio, November 1, 1943. Michigan. Inducted in 1999. 1966-78 Los Angeles Rams. **Highlights:** Never missed a game in entire 184-game career. Elected to 11 Pro Bowls.

JOHN MACKEY
Tight end. 6-2, 224. Born in New York, New York, September 24, 1941. Syracuse. Inducted in 1992. 1963-71 Baltimore Colts, 1972 San Diego Chargers. **Highlights:** 331 receptions for 5,236 yards, 38 touchdowns. Second tight end to enter Hall of Fame.

TIM MARA
Team owner. Born in New York, New York, July 29, 1887. Died February 17, 1959. Did not attend college. Inducted in 1963. 1925-59 New York Giants. **Highlights:** Charter enshrinee. Founder of New York Giants. Built team into powerhouse winning four NFL titles, 10 division titles.

WELLINGTON MARA
Team owner. Born in New York, New York, August 14, 1916. Fordham. Inducted in 1997. 1937-present New York Giants. **Highlights:** Lifetime contributor to NFL and New York Giants. Worked as Giants' ballboy, secretary, vice-president, president and co-CEO. NFC president 1984-present.

GINO MARCHETTI
Defensive end. 6-4, 245. Born in Smithers, West Virginia, January 2, 1927. San Francisco. Inducted in 1972. 1952 Dallas Texans, 1953-64, 1966 Baltimore Colts. **Highlights:** Named top defensive end of NFL's first 50 years. 10 consecutive Pro Bowls. All-NFL seven times.

GEORGE PRESTON MARSHALL
Team owner. Born in Grafton, West Virginia, October 11, 1897. Died August 9, 1969. Randolph-Macon. Inducted in 1963. 1932 Boston Braves, 1933-36 Boston Redskins, 1937-69 Washington Redskins. **Highlights:** Charter enshrinee. Sponsored progressive rules changes. Organized first team band, pioneered halftime shows.

OLLIE MATSON
Halfback. 6-2, 220. Born in Trinity, Texas, May 1, 1930. San Francisco. Inducted in 1972. 1952, 1954-58 Chicago Cardinals, 1959-62 Los Angeles Rams, 1963 Detroit Lions, 1964-66 Philadelphia Eagles. **Highlights:** Nine touchdowns on kickoff, punt returns. Traded for nine players in 1959.

DON MAYNARD
Wide receiver. 6-1, 185. Born in Crosbyton, Texas, January 25, 1935. Texas Western. Inducted in 1987. 1958 New York Giants, 1960-62 New York Titans, 1963-72 New York Jets, 1973 St. Louis Cardinals. **Highlights:** 633 receptions for 11,834 yards, 88 touchdowns. At least 50 catches and 1,000 yards in five different seasons.

GEORGE McAFEE
Halfback. 6-0, 177. Born in Corbin, Kentucky, March 13, 1918. Duke. Inducted in 1966. 1940-41, 1945-50 Chicago Bears. **Highlights:** Two-way star. 25 interceptions, 234 points. Career punt-return average of 12.78 yards per return.

MIKE McCORMACK
Tackle. 6-4, 250. Born in Chicago, Illinois, June 21, 1930. Kansas. Inducted in 1984. 1951 New York Yanks, 1954-62 Cleveland Browns. **Highlights:** Excelled as offensive right tackle for eight years. Six Pro Bowls.

TOMMY McDONALD
Wide receiver. 5-9, 175. Born in Roy, New Mexico, July 26, 1934. Oklahoma. Inducted in 1998. 1957-63 Philadelphia Eagles, 1964 Dallas Cowboys, 1965-66 Los Angeles Rams, 1967 Atlanta Falcons, 1968 Cleveland Browns. **Highlights:** Recorded 495 receptions for 8,410 yards, 84 touchdowns.

HUGH McELHENNY
Halfback. 6-1, 198. Born in Los Angeles, California, December 31, 1928. Washington. Inducted in 1970. 1952-60 San Francisco 49ers, 1961-62 Minnesota Vikings, 1963 New York Giants, 1964 Detroit Lions. **Highlights:** 5,281 rushing yards, 360 points. Totaled 11,369 yards rushing, receiving, and returning kicks.

JOHNNY (BLOOD) McNALLY
Halfback. 6-0, 185. Born in New Richmond, Wisconsin, November 27, 1903. Died November 28, 1985. Notre Dame, St. John's (Minnesota). Inducted in 1963. 1925-26 Milwaukee Badgers, 1926-27 Duluth Eskimos, 1928 Pottsville Maroons, 1929-33, 1935-36 Green Bay Packers, 1934 Pittsburgh Pirates; player-coach, 1937-38 Pittsburgh Pirates. **Highlights:** 49 touchdowns, 296 points in 14 seasons with five teams.

MIKE MICHALSKE
Guard. 6-0, 209. Born in Cleveland, Ohio, April 24, 1903. Died October 26, 1983. Penn State. Inducted in 1964. 1926 New York Yankees (AFL), 1927-28 New York Yankees, 1929-35, 1937 Green Bay Packers. **Highlights:** Anchored Packers' championship lines, 1929-1931. First guard enshrined in Canton.

WAYNE MILLNER
End. 6-0, 191. Born in Roxbury, Massachusetts, January 31, 1913. Died November 19, 1976. Notre Dame. Inducted in 1968. 1936 Boston Redskins, 1937-41, 1945 Washington Redskins. **Highlights:** Redskins' all-time leader with 124 catches when

retired. 55- and 78-yard touchdown receptions in 1937 NFL Championship Game.

BOBBY MITCHELL
Running back-wide receiver. 6-0, 195. Born in Hot Springs, Arkansas, June 6, 1935. Illinois. Inducted in 1983. 1958-61 Cleveland Browns, 1962-68 Washington Redskins. **Highlights:** 91 touchdowns, including 8 on kickoff and punt returns. 14,078 combined yards.

RON MIX
Tackle. 6-4, 255. Born in Los Angeles, California, March 10, 1938. Southern California. Inducted in 1979. 1960 Los Angeles Chargers, 1961-69 San Diego Chargers, 1971 Oakland Raiders. **Highlights:** All-AFL nine times. Only two holding penalties in 10 years with the Chargers.

LENNY MOORE
Flanker-running back. 6-1, 198. Born in Reading, Pennsylvania, November 25, 1933. Penn State. Inducted in 1975. 1956-67 Baltimore Colts. **Highlights:** From 1963-65, scored touchdowns in record 18 consecutive games. 113 career touchdowns, 12,451 combined net yards.

MARION MOTLEY
Fullback. 6-1, 238. Born in Leesburg, Georgia, June 5, 1920. South Carolina State, Nevada. Inducted in 1968. 1946-49 Cleveland Browns (AAFC), 1950-53 Cleveland Browns, 1955 Pittsburgh Steelers. **Highlights:** AAFC's all-time rushing champion. Led league in rushing in first NFL season.

ANTHONY MUÑOZ
Tackle. 6-6, 278. Born in Ontario, California, August 19, 1958. Southern California. Inducted in 1998. 1980-92 Cincinnati Bengals. **Highlights:** All-Pro choice 11 consecutive years, 1981-91. Selected to 11 straight Pro Bowls.

GEORGE MUSSO
Guard-tackle. 6-2, 270. Born in Collinsville, Illinois. April 8, 1910. Millikin. Inducted in 1982. 1933-44 Chicago Bears. **Highlights:** First player to achieve All-NFL status at two positions—tackle in 1935 and guard in 1937.

BRONKO NAGURSKI
Fullback. 6-2, 225. Born in Rainy River, Ontario, Canada, November 3, 1908. Died January 7, 1990. Minnesota. Inducted in 1963. 1930-37, 1943 Chicago Bears. **Highlights:** Charter enshrinee. 2,778 rushing yards in nine seasons. All-NFL three times.

JOE NAMATH
Quarterback. 6-2, 200. Born in Beaver Falls, Pennsylvania, May 31, 1943. Alabama. Inducted in 1985. 1965-76 New York Jets, 1977 Los Angeles Rams. **Highlights:** First quarterback to pass for more than 4,000 yards in season, 1967. Guaranteed, delivered victory over Colts in Super Bowl III.

EARLE (GREASY) NEALE
Coach. Born in Parkersburg, West Virginia, November 5, 1891. Died November 2, 1973. West Virginia Wesleyan. Inducted in 1969. 1941-42, 1944-50 Philadelphia Eagles; co-coach, 1943 Phil-Pitt. **Highlights:** Turned Eagles into winners with three consecutive division crowns, NFL championships in 1948 and 1949.

ERNIE NEVERS
Fullback. 6-1, 205. Born in Willow River, Minnesota, June 11, 1903. Died May 3, 1976. Stanford. Inducted in 1963. 1926-27 Duluth Eskimos, 1929-31 Chicago Cardinals. **Highlights:** Charter enshrinee. Holds NFL's longest-standing record, 40 points in one game in 1929.

OZZIE NEWSOME
Tight end. 6-2, 232. Born in Muscle Shoals, Alabama, March 16, 1956. Alabama. Inducted in 1999. 1978-90 Cleveland Browns. **Highlights:** Leading tight end receiver in NFL history with 662 receptions for 7,980 yards.

RAY NITSCHKE
Linebacker. 6-3, 235. Born in Elmwood Park, Illinois, December 29, 1936. Died March 8, 1998. Illinois. Inducted in 1978. 1958-72 Green Bay Packers. **Highlights:** MVP of 1962 title game. Named NFL's all-time linebacker in 1969.

CHUCK NOLL
Coach. Born in Cleveland, Ohio, January 5, 1932. Dayton. Inducted in 1993. 1969-91 Pittsburgh Steelers. **Highlights:** Coached for 23 years. Only coach to win four Super Bowl titles (IX, X, XIII, XIV).

LEO NOMELLINI
Defensive tackle. 6-3, 264. Born in Lucca, Italy, June 19, 1924. Minnesota. Inducted in 1969. 1950-63 San Francisco 49ers. **Highlights:** Played every 49ers game for 14 seasons. 10 Pro Bowls.

MERLIN OLSEN
Defensive tackle. 6-5, 270. Born in Logan, Utah, September 15, 1940. Utah State. Inducted in 1982. 1962-76 Los Angeles Rams. **Highlights:** Member of the Fearsome Foursome. Named to 14 consecutive Pro Bowls, Rams' all-time team.

JIM OTTO
Center. 6-2, 255. Born in Wausau, Wisconsin, January 5, 1938. Miami. Inducted in 1980. 1960-74 Oakland Raiders. **Highlights:** Named AFL's all-time center. Played in 210 games, 12 AFL All-Star Games or Pro Bowls, six AFL/AFC title games.

STEVE OWEN
Tackle. Coach. 6-2, 235. Born in Cleo Springs, Oklahoma, April 21, 1898. Died May 17, 1964. Phillips. Inducted in 1966. 1924-25 Kansas City Cowboys, 1925 Cleveland Bulldogs, 1926-31, 1933 New York Giants; coach, 1931-53 New York Giants. **Highlights:** Both player and coach. Coached Giants to record of 153-108-17, eight divisional titles, two NFL championships.

ALAN PAGE
Defensive tackle. 6-4, 225. Born in Canton, Ohio, August 7, 1945. Notre Dame. Inducted in 1988. 1967-78 Minnesota Vikings, 1978-81 Chicago Bears. **Highlights:** Dominating defensive tackle played in 218 consecutive games, four Super Bowls. Won league MVP honors in 1971.

CLARENCE (ACE) PARKER
Quarterback. 5-11, 168. Born in Portsmouth, Virginia, May 17, 1912. Duke. Inducted in 1972. 1937-41 Brooklyn Dodgers, 1945 Boston Yanks, 1946 New York Yankees (AAFC). **Highlights:** Two-way threat. Two-time All-NFL performer, league MVP in 1940.

JIM PARKER
Guard-tackle. 6-3, 273. Born in Macon, Georgia, April 3, 1934. Ohio State. Inducted in 1973. 1957-67 Baltimore Colts. **Highlights:** First full-time offensive lineman elected to Hall of Fame. All-NFL eight consecutive years, eight Pro Bowls.

WALTER PAYTON
Running back. 5-10, 202. Born in Columbia, Mississippi, July 25, 1954. Jackson State. Inducted in 1993. 1975-87 Chicago Bears. **Highlights:** NFL's all-time leading rusher with 16,726 yards. Holds single-game rushing record of 275 yards.

JOE PERRY
Fullback. 6-0, 200. Born in Stevens, Arkansas, January 22, 1927. Compton Junior College. Inducted in 1969. 1948-49 San Francisco 49ers (AAFC), 1950-60, 1963 San Francisco 49ers, 1961-62 Baltimore Colts. **Highlights:** First player in NFL history to gain 1,000 yards two consecutive seasons. 12,505 combined yards.

PETE PIHOS
End. 6-1, 210. Born in Orlando, Florida, October 22, 1923. Indiana. Inducted in 1970. 1947-55 Philadelphia Eagles. **Highlights:** Three-time NFL receiving champion. Caught winning touchdown in 1949 NFL Championship Game.

HUGH (SHORTY) RAY
Supervisor of officials 1938-52. Born in Highland Park, Illinois, September 21, 1884. Died September 16, 1956. Illinois. Inducted in 1966. **Highlights:** Supervisor of Officials, 1938-1952. Streamlined rules to improve game tempo, player safety.

DAN REEVES
Team owner. Born in New York, New York, June 30, 1912. Died April 15, 1971. Georgetown. Inducted in 1967. 1941-45 Cleveland Rams, 1946-71 Los Angeles Rams. **Highlights:** Moved Rams to Los Angeles in 1946 and opened up West Coast to pro football. First postwar owner to sign African-American player.

MEL RENFRO
Cornerback-safety. 6-0, 192. Born in Houston, Texas, December 30, 1941. Oregon. Inducted in 1996. 1964-77 Dallas Cowboys. **Highlights:** 52 interceptions for 626 yards and 3 touchdowns. Also added 842 yards on punt returns, 2,246 yards on kickoff returns. Elected to Pro Bowl first 10 seasons.

JOHN RIGGINS
Running back. 6-2, 240. Born in Seneca, Kansas, August 4, 1949. Kansas. Inducted in 1992. 1971-75 New York Jets, 1976-79, 1981-85 Washington Redskins. **Highlights:** 11,352 rushing yards, 116 total touchdowns. MVP of Super Bowl XVII with 166 rushing yards including game-winning 43-yard touchdown.

JIM RINGO
Center. 6-2, 230. Born in Orange, New Jersey, November 21, 1931. Syracuse. Inducted in 1981. 1953-63 Green Bay Packers, 1964-67 Philadelphia Eagles. **Highlights:** Ten-time Pro Bowl selection, six-time All-NFL selection. Started in then-record 182 consecutive games.

ANDY ROBUSTELLI
Defensive end. 6-0, 230. Born in Stamford, Connecticut, December 6, 1925. Arnold College. Inducted in 1971. 1951-55 Los Angeles Rams, 1956-64 New York Giants. **Highlights:** Anchored defense in eight championship games. Named NFL's top player in 1962.

ART ROONEY
Team owner. Born in Coulterville, Pennsylvania, January 27, 1901. Died August 25, 1988. Georgetown, Duquesne. Inducted in 1964. 1933-39 Pittsburgh Pirates, 1940-42, 1945-88 Pittsburgh Steelers, 1943 Phil-Pitt, 1944 Card-Pitt. **Highlights:** Founded Pittsburgh Pirates in 1933 and renamed them Steelers in 1940. Team won four Super Bowls in 1970s.

PETE ROZELLE
Commissioner. Born in South Gate, California, March 1, 1926. Died December 6, 1996. Compton Junior College, San Francisco. Inducted in 1985. Commissioner, 1960-89. **Highlights:** Negotiated first league-wide television contract in 1962. Generally recognized as premiere commissioner in all of sports. Credited with making NFL the nation's most popular sport.

BOB ST. CLAIR
Tackle. 6-9, 265. Born in San Francisco, California, February 18, 1931. San Francisco, Tulsa. Inducted in 1990. 1953-63 San Francisco 49ers. **Highlights:** Exceptional offensive lineman. Also played goal-line defense and had 10 blocked field goals, 1956.

GALE SAYERS
Running back. 6-0, 200. Born in Wichita, Kansas, May 30, 1943. Kansas. Inducted in 1977. 1965-71 Chicago Bears. **Highlights:** Broke into league by scoring rookie-record 22 touchdowns. Led league in rushing in 1966, 1969. MVP of three Pro Bowls.

JOE SCHMIDT
Linebacker. 6-0, 222. Born in Pittsburgh, Pennsylvania, January 18, 1932. Pittsburgh. Inducted in 1973.

1953-65 Detroit Lions. **Highlights:** 24 interceptions. Lions' team captain for nine years. Mastered middle linebacker position that evolved in 1950s.

TEX SCHRAMM
Team president-general manager. Born in San Gabriel, California, June 2, 1920. Texas. Inducted in 1991. 1947-56 Los Angeles Rams. 1960-89 Dallas Cowboys. **Highlights:** Played prominent role in AFL-NFL merger. Chairman of Competition Committee from 1966-1988.

LEE ROY SELMON
Defensive end. 6-3, 250. Born in Eufaula, Oklahoma, October 20, 1954. Oklahoma. Inducted in 1995. 1976-84 Tampa Bay Buccaneers. **Highlights:** 78½ sacks, 380 quarterback pressures, forced 28 fumbles. Six consecutive Pro Bowl selections.

BILLY SHAW
Guard. 6-2, 258. Born in Natchez, Mississippi, December 15, 1938. Georgia Tech. Inducted in 1999. 1961-69 Buffalo Bills. **Highlights:** First player who played entire career in AFL to be elected to Hall of Fame. Named to AFL's all-time team.

ART SHELL
Tackle. 6-5, 285. Born in Charleston, South Carolina, November 26, 1946. Maryland State-Eastern Shore. Inducted in 1989. 1968-81 Oakland Raiders, 1982 Los Angeles Raiders. **Highlights:** Cornerstone of Raiders' offensive line in 1970s. 207 regular-season games, 24 postseason games, eight Pro Bowls.

DON SHULA
Coach. Born in Painesville, Ohio, January 4, 1930. John Carroll. Inducted in 1997. 1963-69 Baltimore Colts, 1970-1995 Miami Dolphins. **Highlights:** Won more games (347) than any coach in NFL history. Won two Super Bowl titles, including Super Bowl VII when Dolphins recorded NFL's only perfect season (17-0).

O.J. SIMPSON
Running back. 6-1, 212. Born in San Francisco, California, July 9, 1947. City College (San Francisco), Southern California. Inducted in 1985. 1969-77 Buffalo Bills, 1978-79 San Francisco 49ers. **Highlights:** In 1973, became first player to rush for 2,000 yards in season. Finished career with four rushing titles, 11,236 yards.

MIKE SINGLETARY
Linebacker. 6-0, 230. Born in Houston, Texas, October 9, 1958. Baylor. Inducted in 1998. 1981-92 Chicago Bears. **Highlights:** All-Pro choice eight times and All-NFC nine consecutive seasons. Selected to 10 Pro Bowls.

JACKIE SMITH
Tight end. 6-4, 232. Born in Columbia, Mississippi, February 23, 1940. Northwestern State (Louisiana). Inducted in 1994. 1963-77 St. Louis Cardinals, 1978 Dallas Cowboys. **Highlights:** 480 receptions for 7,918 yards, 40 touchdowns. Third tight end to be elected to Hall of Fame.

BART STARR
Quarterback. 6-1, 200. Born in Montgomery, Alabama, January 9, 1934. Alabama. Inducted in 1977. 1956-71 Green Bay Packers. **Highlights:** Quarterbacked Packers to six division titles, five NFL titles, and first two Super Bowls in which he was MVP.

ROGER STAUBACH
Quarterback. 6-3, 202. Born in Cincinnati, Ohio, February 5, 1942. New Mexico Military Institute, Navy. Inducted in 1985. 1969-79 Dallas Cowboys. **Highlights:** Led Cowboys to four NFC titles and victories in Super Bowls VI, XII. When retired, 83.4 career passer rating was best of all time.

ERNIE STAUTNER
Defensive tackle. 6-2, 235. Born in Prinzing-by-Cham, Bavaria, April 20, 1925. Boston College. Inducted in 1969. 1950-63 Pittsburgh Steelers. **Highlights:** Played in nine Pro Bowls and won the best lineman award in 1957. Recorded 3 safeties.

JAN STENERUD
Kicker. 6-2, 190. Born in Fetsund, Norway, November 26, 1942. Montana State. Inducted in 1991. 1967-79 Kansas City Chiefs, 1980-83 Green Bay Packers, 1984-85 Minnesota Vikings. **Highlights:** 1,699 points on 580 extra points, 373 field goals. First pure placekicker to enter Hall of Fame.

DWIGHT STEPHENSON
Center. 6-2, 255. Born in Murfreesboro, North Carolina, November 20, 1957. Alabama. Inducted in 1998. 1980-87 Miami Dolphins. **Highlights:** Recognized as premier center of his time. All-Pro, All-AFC five straight years. Selected to five Pro Bowls.

KEN STRONG
Halfback. 5-11, 210. Born in West Haven, Connecticut, August 6, 1906. Died October 5, 1979. New York University. Inducted in 1967. 1929-32 Staten Island Stapletons, 1933-35, 1939, 1944-47 New York Giants, 1936-37 New York Yanks (AFL). **Highlights:** Scored 17 points to lead Giants to victory in 1934 'Sneakers' game, led NFL with 64 points, 1933.

JOE STYDAHAR
Tackle. 6-4, 230. Born in Kaylor, Pennsylvania, March 17, 1912. Died March 23, 1977. West Virginia. Inducted in 1967. 1936-42, 1945-46 Chicago Bears. **Highlights:** One of stalwarts of Bears' 'Monsters of the Midway.' Played on five divisional, three NFL championship teams.

FRAN TARKENTON
Quarterback. 6-0, 185. Born in Richmond, Virginia, February 3, 1940. Georgia. Inducted in 1986. 1961-66, 1972-78 Minnesota Vikings, 1967-71 New York Giants. **Highlights:** At retirement, held NFL records for attempts (6,467), completions (3,686), yards (47,003), and touchdowns (342). Four touchdowns passes in first NFL game.

CHARLEY TAYLOR
Running back-wide receiver. 6-3, 210. Born in Grand Prairie, Texas, September 28, 1941. Arizona State. Inducted in 1984. 1964-75, 1977 Washington Redskins. **Highlights:** Won rookie of year honors as running back. Switched to wide receiver and won receiving titles in 1966, 1967.

JIM TAYLOR
Fullback. 6-0, 216. Born in Baton Rouge, Louisiana, September 20, 1935. Louisiana State. Inducted in 1976. 1958-66 Green Bay Packers, 1967 New Orleans Saints. **Highlights:** 8,597 rushing yards, 558 points. In 1962, led league in rushing and scoring with 19 touchdowns.

LAWRENCE TAYLOR
Linebacker. 6-3, 237. Born in Williamsburg, Virginia, February 4, 1959. North Carolina. Inducted in 1999. 1981-93 New York Giants. **Highlights:** Redefined the position of outside linebacker. All-Pro nine times, 10 Pro Bowls. NFL MVP in 1986.

JIM THORPE
Halfback. 6-1, 190. Born in Prague, Oklahoma, May 28, 1888. Died March 28, 1953. Carlisle. Inducted in 1963. 1915-17, 1919-20, 1926 Canton Bulldogs, 1921 Cleveland Indians, 1922-23 Oorang Indians, 1924 Rock Island Independents, 1925 New York Giants, 1928 Chicago Cardinals. **Highlights:** Charter enshrinee. First president of American Professional Football Association, 1920. Played for 12 seasons.

Y.A. TITTLE
Quarterback. 6-0, 200. Born in Marshall, Texas, October 24, 1926. Louisiana State. Inducted in 1971. 1948-49 Baltimore Colts (AAFC), 1950 Baltimore Colts, 1951-60 San Francisco 49ers, 1961-64 New York Giants. **Highlights:** 33,070 yards, 242 touchdowns. 33 touchdown passes in 1962 and 36 in 1963. Two-time league MVP.

GEORGE TRAFTON
Center. 6-2, 235. Born in Chicago, Illinois, December 6, 1896. Died September 5, 1971. Notre Dame. Inducted in 1964. 1920 Decatur Staleys, 1921 Chicago Staleys, 1922-32 Chicago Bears. **Highlights:** First center to snap with one hand. Named top NFL center of 1920s.

CHARLEY TRIPPI
Halfback-quarterback. 6-0, 185. Born in Pittston, Pennsylvania, December 14, 1922. Georgia. Inducted in 1968. 1947-55 Chicago Cardinals. **Highlights:** One of football's most versatile performers. Played halfback five years, quarterback for two, defense for two.

EMLEN TUNNELL
Safety. 6-1, 200. Born in Bryn Mawr, Pennsylvania, March 29, 1925. Died July 22, 1975. Toledo, Iowa. Inducted in 1967. 1948-58 New York Giants, 1959-61 Green Bay Packers. **Highlights:** 79 interceptions. Gained more yards on kickoff, punt, and interception returns (924) in 1952 than that season's NFL rushing leader.

CLYDE (BULLDOG) TURNER
Center. 6-2, 235. Born in Plains, Texas, March 10, 1919. Died October 30, 1998. Hardin-Simmons. Inducted in 1966. 1940-52 Chicago Bears. **Highlights:** Anchored defense for four NFL championship teams, including 4 interceptions in five title games.

JOHNNY UNITAS
Quarterback. 6-1, 195. Born in Pittsburgh, Pennsylvania, May 7, 1933. Louisville. Inducted in 1979. 1956-72 Baltimore Colts, 1973 San Diego Chargers. **Highlights:** 40,239 passing yards, 290 touchdowns. Led Colts to two NFL championships. Passed for at least one touchdown in 47 consecutive games.

GENE UPSHAW
Guard. 6-5, 255. Born in Robstown, Texas, August 15, 1945. Texas A & I. Inducted in 1987. 1967-81 Oakland Raiders. **Highlights:** Premier guard of his era played in 10 AFL/AFC Championship Games, three Super Bowls, seven Pro Bowls.

NORM VAN BROCKLIN
Quarterback. 6-1, 190. Born in Eagle Butte, South Dakota, March 15, 1926. Died May 2, 1983. Oregon. Inducted in 1971. 1949-57 Los Angeles Rams, 1958-60 Philadelphia Eagles. **Highlights:** NFL-record 554 yards passing in 1951 season opener. Guided Eagles to NFL crown as league MVP in 1960.

STEVE VAN BUREN
Halfback. 6-1, 200. Born in La Ceiba, Honduras, December 28, 1920. Louisiana State. Inducted in 1965. 1944-51 Philadelphia Eagles. **Highlights:** Four-time rushing champion. Won 1944 punt-return title and was 1945 kickoff-return champion.

DOAK WALKER
Halfback. 5-11, 173. Born in Dallas, Texas, January 1, 1927. Died September 27, 1998. Southern Methodist. Inducted in 1986. 1950-55 Detroit Lions. **Highlights:** 534 points. Won two NFL scoring titles. Had winning 67-yard scoring run in 1952 title game.

BILL WALSH
Coach. Born in Los Angeles, California, November 30, 1931. San Jose State. Inducted in 1993. 1979-88 San Francisco 49ers. **Highlights:** 102-63-1 coaching record. Guided 49ers to three Super Bowl titles (XVI, XIX, XXIII) in 10 years.

PAUL WARFIELD
Wide receiver. 6-0, 188. Born in Warren, Ohio, November 28, 1942. Ohio State. Inducted in 1983. 1964-69, 1976-77 Cleveland Browns, 1970-74 Miami Dolphins. **Highlights:** 8,565 yards receiving, 85 touchdowns. Eight-time Pro Bowl player. Key to both Cleveland and Miami offenses.

BOB WATERFIELD
Quarterback. 6-2, 200. Born in Elmira, New York, July 26, 1920. Died March 25, 1983. UCLA. Inducted in 1965. 1945 Cleveland Rams, 1946-52 Los Angeles Rams. **Highlights:** NFL MVP as rookie in 1945 and led Rams to

NFL title. Grabbed 20 interceptions in limited defensive duties.

MIKE WEBSTER
Center. 6-2, 260. Born in Tomahawk, Wisconsin, March 18, 1952. Wisconsin. Inducted in 1997. 1974-88 Pittsburgh Steelers, 1989-90 Kansas City Chiefs. **Highlights:** Played in 245 games, nine Pro Bowls, and won four Super Bowls during 17-year career.

ARNIE WEINMEISTER
Defensive tackle. 6-4, 235. Born in Rhein, Saskatchewan, Canada, March 23, 1923. Washington. Inducted in 1984. 1948-49 New York Yankees (AAFC), 1950-53 New York Giants. **Highlights:** Dominant defensive tackle of his time. Four-time All-NFL selection, four Pro Bowls.

RANDY WHITE
Defensive tackle. 6-4, 265. Born in Pittsburgh, Pennsylvania, January 15, 1953. Maryland. Inducted in 1994. 1975-88 Dallas Cowboys. **Highlights:** Missed only one game in 14 seasons. Co-MVP of Super Bowl XII. Nine-time Pro Bowl selection.

BILL WILLIS
Guard. 6-2, 215. Born in Columbus, Ohio, October 5, 1921. Ohio State. Inducted in 1977. 1946-49 Cleveland Browns (AAFC), 1950-53 Cleveland Browns. **Highlights:** Two-way player who excelled on defense. Four-time All-NFL player, played in three Pro Bowls.

LARRY WILSON
Safety. 6-0, 190. Born in Rigby, Idaho, March 24, 1938. Utah. Inducted in 1978. 1960-72 St. Louis Cardinals. **Highlights:** 52 interceptions. Had interception in seven consecutive games in 1966. Made "safety blitz" famous.

KELLEN WINSLOW
Tight end. 6-5, 250. Born in St. Louis, Missouri, November 5, 1957. Missouri. Inducted in 1995. 1979-87 San Diego Chargers **Highlights:** 541 receptions for 6,741 yards, 45 touchdowns. 13 catches, blocked field goal in 1981 playoff win over Miami.

ALEX WOJCIECHOWICZ
Center. 6-0, 235. Born in South River, New Jersey, August 12, 1915. Died July 13, 1992. Fordham. Inducted in 1968. 1938-46 Detroit Lions, 1946-50 Philadelphia Eagles. **Highlights:** One of league's first iron men. Played both ways for eight years with Lions.

WILLIE WOOD
Safety. 5-10, 190. Born in Washington, D.C., December 23, 1936. Southern California. Inducted in 1989. 1960-71 Green Bay Packers. **Highlights:** 48 interceptions. Competed in six NFL Championship Games and Super Bowls I and II.

ENSHRINEES BY YEAR OF INDUCTION

**Deceased*
(Date of enshrinement in parentheses)

1963 CHARTER CLASS
(September 7, 1963)
Sammy Baugh
Bert Bell*
Joe Carr*
Earl (Dutch) Clark*
Harold (Red) Grange*
George Halas*
Mel Hein*
Wilbur (Pete) Henry*
Robert (Cal) Hubbard*
Don Hutson*
Earl (Curly) Lambeau*
Tim Mara*
George Preston Marshall*
John (Blood) McNally*
Bronko Nagurski*
Ernie Nevers*
Jim Thorpe*

CLASS OF 1964
(September 6, 1964)
Jimmy Conzelman*
Ed Healey*
Clarke Hinkle*
William Roy (Link) Lyman*
Mike Michalske*
Art Rooney*
George Trafton*

CLASS OF 1965
(September 12, 1965)
Guy Chamberlin*
John (Paddy) Driscoll*
Dan Fortmann*
Otto Graham
Sid Luckman*
Steve Van Buren
Bob Waterfield*

CLASS OF 1966
(September 17, 1966)
BIll Dudley
Joe Guyon*
Arnie Herber*
Walt Kiesling*
George McAfee
Steve Owen*
Hugh (Shorty) Ray*
Clyde (Bulldog) Turner*

CLASS OF 1967
(August 5, 1967)
Chuck Bednarik
Charles W. Bidwill, Sr.*
Paul Brown*
Bobby Layne*
Dan Reeves*
Ken Strong*
Joe Stydahar*
Emlen Tunnell*

CLASS OF 1968
(August 3, 1968)
Cliff Battles*
Art Donovan
Elroy (Crazylegs) Hirsch
Wayne Millner*
Marion Motley
Charley Trippi
Alex Wojciechowicz*

CLASS OF 1969
(September 13, 1969)
Albert Glen (Turk) Edwards*
Earle (Greasy) Neale*
Leo Nomellini
Joe Perry
Ernie Stautner

CLASS OF 1970
(August 8, 1970)
Jack Christiansen*
Tom Fears
Hugh McElhenny
Pete Pihos

CLASS OF 1971
(July 31, 1971)
Jim Brown
Bill Hewitt*
Frank (Bruiser) Kinard*
Vince Lombardi*
Andy Robustelli
Y. A. Tittle
Norm Van Brocklin*

CLASS OF 1972
(July 29, 1972)
Lamar Hunt
Gino Marchetti
Ollie Matson
Clarence (Ace) Parker

CLASS OF 1973
(July 28, 1973)
Raymond Berry
Jim Parker
Joe Schmidt

CLASS OF 1974
(July 27, 1974)
Tony Canadeo
Bill George*
Lou Groza
Dick (Night Train) Lane

CLASS OF 1975
(August 2, 1975)
Roosevelt Brown
George Connor
Dante Lavelli
Lenny Moore

CLASS OF 1976
(July 24, 1976)
Ray Flaherty*
Len Ford*
Jim Taylor

CLASS OF 1977
(July 30, 1977)
Frank Gifford
Forrest Gregg
Gale Sayers
Bart Starr
Bill Willis

CLASS OF 1978
(July 29, 1978)
Lance Alworth
Weeb Ewbank*
Alphonse (Tuffy) Leemans*
Ray Nitschke*
Larry Wilson

CLASS OF 1979
(July 28, 1979)
Dick Butkus
Yale Lary
Ron Mix
Johnny Unitas

CLASS OF 1980
(August 2, 1980)
Herb Adderley
David (Deacon) Jones
Bob Lilly
Jim Otto

CLASS OF 1981
(August 1, 1981)
Morris (Red) Badgro*
George Blanda
Willie Davis
Jim Ringo

CLASS OF 1982
(August 7, 1982)
Doug Atkins
Sam Huff
George Musso
Merlin Olsen

CLASS OF 1983
(July 30, 1983)
Bobby Bell
Sid Gillman
Sonny Jurgensen
Bobby Mitchell
Paul Warfield

CLASS OF 1984
(July 28, 1984)
Willie Brown
Mike McCormack
Charley Taylor
Arnie Weinmeister

CLASS OF 1985
(August 3, 1985)
Frank Gatski
Joe Namath
Pete Rozelle*
O. J. Simpson
Roger Staubach

CLASS OF 1986
(August 2, 1986)
Paul Hornung
Ken Houston
Willie Lanier
Fran Tarkenton
Doak Walker*

CLASS OF 1987
(August 8, 1987)
Larry Csonka
Len Dawson
Joe Greene
John Henry Johnson
Jim Langer
Don Maynard
Gene Upshaw

CLASS OF 1988
(July 30, 1988)
Fred Biletnikoff
Mike Ditka
Jack Ham
Alan Page

CLASS OF 1989
(August 5, 1989)
Mel Blount
Terry Bradshaw
Art Shell
Willie Wood

CLASS OF 1990
(August 4, 1990)
Buck Buchanan*
Bob Griese
Franco Harris
Ted Hendricks
Jack Lambert
Tom Landry
Bob St. Clair

CLASS OF 1991
(July 27, 1991)
Earl Campbell
John Hannah
Stan Jones
Tex Schramm
Jan Stenerud

CLASS OF 1992
(August 1, 1992)
Lem Barney
Al Davis
John Mackey
John Riggins

CLASS OF 1993
(July 31, 1993)
Dan Fouts
Larry Little
Chuck Noll
Walter Payton
Bill Walsh

CLASS OF 1994
(July 30, 1994)
Tony Dorsett
Bud Grant
Jimmy Johnson
Leroy Kelly
Jackie Smith
Randy White

CLASS OF 1995
(July 29, 1995)
Jim Finks*
Henry Jordan*
Steve Largent
Lee Roy Selmon
Kellen Winslow

CLASS OF 1996
(July 27, 1996)
Lou Creekmur
Dan Dierdorf
Joe Gibbs
Charlie Joiner
Mel Renfro

CLASS OF 1997
(July 26, 1997)
Mike Haynes
Wellington Mara
Don Shula
Mike Webster

CLASS OF 1998
(August 1, 1998)
Paul Krause
Tommy McDonald
Anthony Muñoz
Mike Singletary
Dwight Stephenson

CLASS OF 1999
(August 7, 1999)
Eric Dickerson
Tom Mack
Ozzie Newsome
Billy Shaw
Lawrence Taylor

CHRONOLOGY OF PROFESSIONAL FOOTBALL

1869
Rutgers and Princeton played a college soccer football game, the first ever, November 6. The game used modified London Football Association rules. During the next seven years, rugby gained favor with the major eastern schools over soccer, and modern football began to develop from rugby.

1876
At the Massasoit convention, the first rules for American football were written. Walter Camp, who would become known as the father of American football, first became involved with the game.

1892
In an era in which football was a major attraction of local athletic clubs, an intense competition between two Pittsburgh-area clubs, the Allegheny Athletic Association (AAA) and the Pittsburgh Athletic Club (PAC), led to the making of the first professional football player. Former Yale All-America guard William (Pudge) Heffelfinger was paid $500 by the AAA to play in a game against the PAC, becoming the first person to be paid to play football, November 12. The AAA won the game 4-0 when Heffelfinger picked up a PAC fumble and ran 25 yards for a touchdown.

1893
The Pittsburgh Athletic Club signed one of its players, probably halfback Grant Dibert, to the first known pro football contract, which covered all of the PAC's games for the year.

1895
John Brallier became the first football player to openly turn pro, accepting $10 and expenses to play for the Latrobe YMCA against the Jeannette Athletic Club.

1896
The Allegheny Athletic Association team fielded the first completely professional team for its abbreviated two-game season.

1897
The Latrobe Athletic Association football team went entirely professional, becoming the first team to play a full season with only professionals.

1898
A touchdown was changed from four points to five.

1899
Chris O'Brien formed a neighborhood team, which played under the name the Morgan Athletic Club, on the south side of Chicago. The team later became known as the Normals, then the Racine (for a street in Chicago) Cardinals, the Chicago Cardinals, the St. Louis Cardinals, the Phoenix Cardinals, and, in 1994, the Arizona Cardinals. The team remains the oldest continuing operation in pro football.

1900
William C. Temple took over the team payments for the Duquesne Country and Athletic Club, becoming the first known individual club owner.

1902
Baseball's Philadelphia Athletics, managed by Connie Mack, and the Philadelphia Phillies formed professional football teams, joining the Pittsburgh Stars in the first attempt at a pro football league, named the National Football League. The Athletics won the first night football game ever played, 39-0 over Kanaweola AC at Elmira, New York, November 21.

All three teams claimed the pro championship for the year, but the league president, Dave Berry, named the Stars the champions. Pitcher Rube Waddell was with the Athletics, and pitcher Christy Mathewson a fullback for Pittsburgh.

The first World Series of pro football, actually a five-team tournament, was played among a team made up of players from both the Athletics and the Phillies, but simply named New York; the New York Knickerbockers; the Syracuse AC; the Warlow AC; and the Orange (New Jersey) AC at New York's original Madison Square Garden. New York and Syracuse played the first indoor football game before 3,000, December 28. Syracuse, with Glen (Pop) Warner at guard, won 6-0 and went on to win the tournament.

1903
The Franklin (Pa.) Athletic Club won the second and last World Series of pro football over the Oreos AC of Asbury Park, New Jersey; the Watertown Red and Blacks; and the Orange AC.

Pro football was popularized in Ohio when the Massillon Tigers, a strong amateur team, hired four Pittsburgh pros to play in the season-ending game against Akron. At the same time, pro football declined in the Pittsburgh area, and the emphasis on the pro game moved west from Pennsylvania to Ohio.

1904
A field goal was changed from five points to four.

Ohio had at least seven pro teams, with Massillon winning the Ohio Independent Championship, that is, the pro title. Talk surfaced about forming a state-wide league to end spiraling salaries brought about by constant bidding for players and to write universal rules for the game. The feeble attempt to start the league failed.

Halfback Charles Follis signed a contract with the Shelby (Ohio) AC, making him the first known black pro football player.

1905
The Canton AC, later to become known as the Bulldogs, became a professional team. Massillon again won the Ohio League championship.

1906
The forward pass was legalized. The first authenticated pass completion in a pro game came on October 27, when George (Peggy) Parratt of Massillon threw a completion to Dan (Bullet) Riley in a victory over a combined Benwood-Moundsville team.

Arch-rivals Canton and Massillon, the two best pro teams in America, played twice, with Canton winning the first game but Massillon winning the second and the Ohio League championship. A betting scandal and the financial disaster wrought upon the two clubs by paying huge salaries caused a temporary decline in interest in pro football in the two cities and, somewhat, throughout Ohio.

1909
A field goal dropped from four points to three.

1912
A touchdown was increased from five points to six.

Jack Cusack revived a strong pro team in Canton.

1913
Jim Thorpe, a former football and track star at the Carlisle Indian School (Pa.) and a double gold medal winner at the 1912 Olympics in Stockholm, played for the Pine Village Pros in Indiana.

1915
Massillon again fielded a major team, reviving the old rivalry with Canton. Cusack signed Thorpe to play for Canton for $250 a game.

1916
With Thorpe and former Carlisle teammate Pete Calac starring, Canton went 9-0-1, won the Ohio League championship, and was acclaimed the pro football champion.

1917
Despite an upset by Massillon, Canton again won the Ohio League championship.

1919
Canton again won the Ohio League championship, despite the team having been turned over from Cusack to Ralph Hay. Thorpe and Calac were joined in the backfield by Joe Guyon.

Earl (Curly) Lambeau and George Calhoun organized the Green Bay Packers. Lambeau's employer at the Indian Packing Company provided $500 for equipment and allowed the team to use the company field for practices. The Packers went 10-1.

1920
Pro football was in a state of confusion due to three major problems: dramatically rising salaries; players continually jumping from one team to another following the highest offer; and the use of college players still enrolled in school. A league in which all the members would follow the same rules seemed the answer. An organizational meeting, at which the Akron Pros, Canton Bulldogs, Cleveland Indians, and Dayton Triangles were represented, was held at the Jordan and Hupmobile auto showroom in Canton, Ohio, August 20. This meeting resulted in the formation of the American Professional Football Conference.

A second organizational meeting was held in Canton, September 17. The teams were from four states—Akron, Canton, Cleveland, and Dayton from Ohio; the Hammond Pros and Muncie Flyers from Indiana; the Rochester Jeffersons from New York; and the Rock Island Independents, Decatur Staleys, and Racine Cardinals from Illinois. The name of the league was changed to the American Professional Football Association. Hoping to capitalize on his fame, the members elected Thorpe president; Stanley Cofall of Cleveland was elected vice president. A membership fee of $100 per team was charged to give an appearance of respectability, but no team ever paid it. Scheduling was left up to the teams, and there were wide variations, both in the overall number of games played and in the number played against APFA member teams.

Four other teams—the Buffalo All-Americans, Chicago Tigers, Columbus Panhandles, and Detroit Heralds—joined the league sometime during the year. On September 26, the first game featuring an APFA team was played at Rock Island's Douglas Park. A crowd of 800 watched the Independents defeat the St. Paul Ideals 48-0. A week later, October 3, the first game matching two APFA teams was held. At Triangle Park, Dayton defeated Columbus 14-0, with Lou Partlow of Dayton scoring the first touchdown in a game between Association teams. The same day, Rock Island defeated Muncie 45-0.

By the beginning of December, most of the teams in the APFA had abandoned their hopes for a championship, and some of them, including the Chicago Tigers and the Detroit Heralds, had finished their seasons, disbanded, and had their franchises canceled by the Association. Four teams—Akron, Buffalo, Canton, and Decatur—still had championship aspirations, but a series of late-season games among them left Akron as the only undefeated team in the Association. At one of these games, Akron sold tackle Bob Nash to Buffalo for $300 and five percent of the gate receipts—the first APFA player deal.

1921
At the league meeting in Akron, April 30, the championship of the 1920 season was awarded to the Akron Pros. The APFA was reorganized, with Joe Carr of the Columbus Panhandles named president and Carl Storck of Dayton secretary-treasurer. Carr moved the Association's headquarters to Columbus, drafted a league constitution and by-laws, gave teams territorial rights, restricted player movements, developed membership criteria for the franchises, and issued standings for the first time, so that the APFA would have a clear champion.

The Association's membership increased to 22 teams, including the Green Bay Packers, who were awarded to John Clair of the Acme Packing Company.

Thorpe moved from Canton to the Cleveland Indians, but he was hurt early in the season and played very little.

A.E. Staley turned the Decatur Staleys over to player-coach George Halas, who moved the team to Cubs Park in Chicago. Staley paid Halas

$5,000 to keep the name Staleys for one more year. Halas made halfback Ed (Dutch) Sternaman his partner.

Player-coach Fritz Pollard of the Akron Pros became the first black head coach.

The Staleys claimed the APFA championship with a 9-1-1 record, as did Buffalo at 9-1-2. Carr ruled in favor of the Staleys, giving Halas his first championship.

1922
After admitting the use of players who had college eligibility remaining during the 1921 season, Clair and the Green Bay management withdrew from the APFA, January 28. Curly Lambeau promised to obey league rules and then used $50 of his own money to buy back the franchise. Bad weather and low attendance plagued the Packers, and Lambeau went broke, but local merchants arranged a $2,500 loan for the club. A public nonprofit corporation was set up to operate the team, with Lambeau as head coach and manager.

The American Professional Football Association changed its name to the National Football League, June 24. The Chicago Staleys became the Chicago Bears.

The NFL fielded 18 teams, including the new Oorang Indians of Marion, Ohio, an all-Indian team featuring Thorpe, Joe Guyon, and Pete Calac, and sponsored by the Oorang dog kennels.

Canton, led by player-coach Guy Chamberlin and tackles Link Lyman and Wilbur (Pete) Henry, emerged as the league's first true powerhouse, going 10-0-2.

1923
For the first time, all of the franchises considered to be part of the NFL fielded teams. Thorpe played first for Oorang, then for the Toledo Maroons. Against the Bears, Thorpe fumbled, and Halas picked up the ball and returned it 98 yards for a touchdown, a record that would last until 1972.

Canton had its second consecutive undefeated season, going 11-0-1 for the NFL title.

1924
The league had 18 franchises, including new ones in Kansas City, Kenosha, and Frankford, a section of Philadelphia. League champion Canton, successful on the field but not at the box office, was purchased by the owner of the Cleveland franchise, who kept the Canton franchise inactive, while using the best players for his Cleveland team, which he renamed the Bulldogs. Cleveland won the title with a 7-1-1 record.

1925
Five new franchises were admitted to the NFL—the New York Giants, who were awarded to Tim Mara and Billy Gibson for $500; the Detroit Panthers, featuring Jimmy Conzelman as owner, coach, and tailback; the Providence Steam Roller; a new Canton Bulldogs team; and the Pottsville Maroons, who had been perhaps the most successful independent pro team. The NFL established its first player limit, at 16 players.

Late in the season, the NFL made its greatest coup in gaining national recognition. Shortly after the University of Illinois season ended in November, All-America halfback Harold (Red) Grange signed a contract to play with the Chicago Bears. On Thanksgiving Day, a crowd of 36,000—the largest in pro football history—watched Grange and the Bears play the Chicago Cardinals to a scoreless tie at Wrigley Field. At the beginning of December, the Bears left on a barnstorming tour that saw them play eight games in 12 days, in St. Louis, Philadelphia, New York City, Washington, Boston, Pittsburgh, Detroit, and Chicago. A crowd of 73,000 watched the game against the Giants at the Polo Grounds, helping assure the future of the troubled NFL franchise in New York. The Bears then played nine more games in the South and West, including a game in Los Angeles, in which 75,000 fans watched them defeat the Los Angeles Tigers in the Los Angeles Memorial Coliseum.

Pottsville and the Chicago Cardinals were the top contenders for the league title, with Pottsville winning a late-season meeting 21-7. Pottsville scheduled a game against a team of former Notre Dame players for Shibe Park in Philadelphia. Frankford lodged a protest not only because the game was in Frankford's protected territory, but because it was being played the same day as a Yellow Jackets home game. Carr gave three different notices forbidding Pottsville to play the game, but Pottsville played anyway, December 12. That day, Carr fined the club, suspended it from all rights and privileges (including the right to play for the NFL championship), and returned its franchise to the league. The Cardinals, who ended the season with the best record in the league, were named the 1925 champions.

1926
Grange's manager, C.C. Pyle, told the Bears that Grange wouldn't play for them unless he was paid a five-figure salary and given one-third ownership of the team. The Bears refused. Pyle leased Yankee Stadium in New York City, then petitioned for an NFL franchise. After he was refused, he started the first American Football League. It lasted one season and included Grange's New York Yankees and eight other teams. The AFL champion Philadelphia Quakers played a December game against the New York Giants, seventh in the NFL, and the Giants won 31-0. At the end of the season, the AFL folded.

Halas pushed through a rule that prohibited any team from signing a player whose college class had not graduated.

The NFL grew to 22 teams, including the Duluth Eskimos, who signed All-America fullback Ernie Nevers of Stanford, giving the league a gate attraction to rival Grange. The 15-member Eskimos, dubbed the Iron Men of the North, played 29 exhibition and league games, 28 on the road, and Nevers played in all but 29 minutes of them.

Frankford edged the Bears for the championship, despite Halas having obtained John (Paddy) Driscoll from the Cardinals. On December 4, the Yellow Jackets scored in the final two minutes to defeat the Bears 7-6 and move ahead of them in the standings.

1927
At a special meeting in Cleveland, April 23, Carr decided to secure the NFL's future by eliminating the financially weaker teams and consolidating the quality players onto a limited number of more successful teams. The new-look NFL dropped to 12 teams, and the center of gravity of the league left the Midwest, where the NFL had started, and began to emerge in the large cities of the East. One of the new teams was Grange's New York Yankees, but Grange suffered a knee injury and the Yankees finished in the middle of the pack. The NFL championship was won by the cross-town rival New York Giants, who posted 10 shutouts in 13 games.

1928
Grange and Nevers both retired from pro football, and Duluth disbanded, as the NFL was reduced to only 10 teams. The Providence Steam Roller of Jimmy Conzelman and Pearce Johnson won the championship, playing in the Cycledrome, a 10,000-seat oval that had been built for bicycle races.

1929
Chris O'Brien sold the Chicago Cardinals to David Jones, July 27.

The NFL added a fourth official, the field judge, July 28.

Grange and Nevers returned to the NFL. Nevers scored six rushing touchdowns and four extra points as the Cardinals beat Grange's Bears 40-6, November 28. The 40 points set a record that remains the NFL's oldest.

Providence became the first NFL team to host a game at night under floodlights, against the Cardinals, November 3.

The Packers added back Johnny Blood (McNally), tackle Cal Hubbard, and guard Mike Michalske, and won their first NFL championship, edging the Giants, who featured quarterback Benny Friedman.

1930
Dayton, the last of the NFL's original franchises, was purchased by William B. Dwyer and John C. Depler, moved to Brooklyn, and renamed the Dodgers. The Portsmouth, Ohio, Spartans entered the league.

The Packers edged the Giants for the title, but the most improved team was the Bears. Halas retired as a player and replaced himself as coach of the Bears with Ralph Jones, who refined the T-formation by introducing wide ends and a halfback in motion. Jones also introduced rookie All-America fullback-tackle Bronko Nagurski.

The Giants defeated a team of former Notre Dame players coached by Knute Rockne 22-0 before 55,000 at the Polo Grounds, December 14. The proceeds went to the New York Unemployment Fund to help those suffering because of the Great Depression, and the easy victory helped give the NFL credibility with the press and the public.

1931
The NFL decreased to 10 teams, and halfway through the season the Frankford franchise folded. Carr fined the Bears, Packers, and Portsmouth $1,000 each for using players whose college classes had not graduated.

The Packers won an unprecedented third consecutive title, beating out the Spartans, who were led by rookie backs Earl (Dutch) Clark and Glenn Presnell.

1932
George Preston Marshall, Vincent Bendix, Jay O'Brien, and M. Dorland Doyle were awarded a franchise for Boston, July 9. Despite the presence of two rookies—halfback Cliff Battles and tackle Glen (Turk) Edwards—the new team, named the Braves, lost money and Marshall was left as the sole owner at the end of the year.

NFL membership dropped to eight teams, the lowest in history. Official statistics were kept for the first time. The Bears and the Spartans finished the season in the first-ever tie for first place. After the season finale, the league office arranged for an additional regular-season game to determine the league champion. The game was moved indoors to Chicago Stad-ium because of bitter cold and heavy snow. The arena allowed only an 80-yard field that came right to the walls. The goal posts were moved from the end lines to the goal lines and, for safety, inbounds lines or hashmarks where the ball would be put in play were drawn 10 yards from the walls that butted against the sidelines. The Bears won 9-0, December 18, scoring the winning touchdown on a two-yard pass from Nagurski to Grange. The Spartans claimed Nagurski's pass was thrown from less than five yards behind the line of scrimmage, violating the existing passing rule, but the play stood.

1933
The NFL, which long had followed the rules of college football, made a number of significant changes from the college game for the first time and began to develop rules serving its needs and the style of play it preferred. The innovations from the 1932 championship game—inbounds line or hashmarks and goal posts on the goal lines—were adopted. Also the forward pass was legalized from anywhere behind the line of scrimmage, February 25.

Marshall and Halas pushed through a proposal that divided the NFL into two divisions, with the winners to meet in an annual championship game, July 8.

Three new franchises joined the league—the Pittsburgh Pirates of Art Rooney, the Philadelphia Eagles of Bert Bell and Lud Wray, and the Cincinnati Reds. The Staten Island Stapletons suspended operations for a year, but never returned to the league.

Halas bought out Sternaman, became sole owner of the Bears, and reinstated himself as head coach. Marshall changed the name of the Boston Braves to the Redskins. David Jones sold the Chicago Cardinals to Charles W. Bidwill.

In the first NFL Championship Game scheduled before the season, the Western Division champion Bears defeated the Eastern Division champion Giants 23-21 at Wrigley Field, December 17.

1934
G.A. (Dick) Richards purchased the Portsmouth Spartans, moved them to Detroit, and renamed them the Lions.

Professional football gained new prestige when the Bears were matched against the best college football players in the first Chicago College All-Star Game, August 31. The game ended in a scoreless tie before 79,432 at Soldier Field.

The Cincinnati Reds lost their first eight games, then were suspended from the league for defaulting on payments. The St. Louis Gunners, an independent team, joined the NFL by buying the Cincinnati franchise and went 1-2 the last three weeks.

Rookie Beattie Feathers of the Bears became the NFL's first 1,000-yard rusher, gaining 1,004 on 101 carries. The Thanksgiving Day game between the Bears and the Lions became the first NFL game broadcast nationally, with Graham McNamee the announcer for NBC radio.

In the championship game, on an extremely cold and icy day at the Polo Grounds, the Giants trailed the Bears 13-3 in the third quarter before changing to basketball shoes for better footing. The Giants won 30-13 in what has come to be known as the Sneakers Game, December 9.

The player waiver rule was adopted, December 10.

1935
The NFL adopted Bert Bell's proposal to hold an annual draft of college players, to begin in 1936, with teams selecting in an inverse order of finish, May 19. The inbounds line or hashmarks were moved nearer the center of the field, 15 yards from the sidelines.

All-America end Don Hutson of Alabama joined Green Bay. The Lions defeated the Giants 26-7 in the NFL Championship Game, December 15.

1936
There were no franchise transactions for the first year since the formation of the NFL. It also was the first year in which all member teams played the same number of games.

The Eagles made University of Chicago halfback and Heisman Trophy winner Jay Berwanger the first player ever selected in the NFL draft, February 8. The Eagles traded his rights to the Bears, but Berwanger never played pro football. The first player selected to actually sign was the number-two pick, Riley Smith of Alabama, who was selected by Boston.

A rival league was formed, and it became the second to call itself the American Football League. The Boston Shamrocks were its champions.

Because of poor attendance, Marshall, the owner of the host team, moved the Championship Game from Boston to the Polo Grounds in New York. Green Bay defeated the Redskins 21-6, December 13.

1937
Homer Marshman was granted a Cleveland franchise, named the Rams, February 12. Marshall moved the Redskins to Washington, D.C., February 13. The Redskins signed TCU All-America tailback Sammy Baugh, who led them to a 28-21 victory over the Bears in the NFL Championship Game, December 12.

The Los Angeles Bulldogs had an 8-0 record to win the AFL title, but then the 2-year-old league folded.

1938
At the suggestion of Halas, Hugh (Shorty) Ray became a technical advisor on rules and officiating to the NFL. A new rule called for a 15-yard penalty for roughing the passer.

Rookie Byron (Whizzer) White of the Pittsburgh Pirates led the NFL in rushing. The Giants defeated the Packers 23-17 for the NFL title, December 11.

Marshall, *Los Angeles Times* sports editor Bill Henry, and promoter Tom Gallery established the Pro Bowl game between the NFL champion and a team of pro all-stars.

1939
The New York Giants defeated the Pro All-Stars 13-10 in the first Pro Bowl, at Wrigley Field, Los Angeles, January 15.

Carr, NFL president since 1921, died in Columbus, May 20. Carl Storck was named acting president, May 25.

An NFL game was televised for the first time when NBC broadcast the Brooklyn Dodgers-Philadelphia Eagles game from Ebbets Field to the approximately 1,000 sets then in New York.

Green Bay defeated New York 27-0 in the NFL Championship Game, December 10 at Milwaukee. NFL attendance exceeded 1 million in a season for the first time, reaching 1,071,200.

1940
A six-team rival league, the third to call itself the American Football League, was formed, and the Columbus Bullies won its championship.

Halas's Bears, with additional coaching by Clark Shaughnessy of Stanford, defeated the Redskins 73-0 in the NFL Championship Game, December 8. The game, which was the most decisive victory in NFL history, popularized the Bears' T-formation with a man-in-motion. It was the first championship carried on network radio, broadcast by Red Barber to 120 stations of the Mutual Broadcasting System, which paid $2,500 for the rights.

Art Rooney sold the Pittsburgh franchise to Alexis Thompson, December 9, then bought part interest in the Philadelphia Eagles.

1941
Elmer Layden was named the first Commissioner of the NFL, March 1; Storck, the acting president, resigned, April 5. NFL headquarters were moved to Chicago.

Bell and Rooney traded the Eagles to Thompson for the Pirates, then re-named their new team the Steelers. Homer Marshman sold the Rams to Daniel F. Reeves and Fred Levy, Jr.

The league by-laws were revised to provide for playoffs in case there were ties in division races, and sudden-death overtimes in case a playoff game was tied after four quarters. An official *NFL Record Manual* was published for the first time.

Columbus again won the championship of the AFL, but the two-year-old league then folded.

The Bears and the Packers finished in a tie for the Western Division championship, setting up the first divisional playoff game in league history. The Bears won 33-14, then defeated the Giants 37-9 for the NFL championship, December 21.

1942
Players departing for service in World War II depleted the rosters of NFL teams. Halas left the Bears in midseason to join the Navy, and Luke Johnsos and Heartley (Hunk) Anderson served as co-coaches as the Bears went 11-0 in the regular season. The Redskins defeated the Bears 14-6 in the NFL Championship Game, December 13.

1943
The Cleveland Rams, with co-owners Reeves and Levy in the service, were granted permission to suspend operations for one season, April 6. Levy transferred his stock in the team to Reeves, April 16.

The NFL adopted free substitution, April 7. The league also made the wearing of helmets mandatory and approved a 10-game schedule for all teams.

Philadelphia and Pittsburgh were granted permission to merge for one season, June 19. The team, known as Phil-Pitt (and called the Steagles by fans), divided home games between the two cities, and Earle (Greasy) Neale of Philadelphia and Walt Kiesling of Pittsburgh served as co-coaches. The merger automatically dissolved the last day of the season, December 5.

Ted Collins was granted a franchise for Boston, to become active in 1944.

Sammy Baugh led the league in passing, punting, and interceptions. He led the Redskins to a tie with the Giants for the Eastern Division title, and then to a 28-0 victory in a divisional playoff game. The Bears beat the Redskins 41-21 in the NFL Championship Game, December 26.

1944
Collins, who had wanted a franchise in Yankee Stadium in New York, named his new team in Boston the Yanks. Cleveland resumed operations. The Brooklyn Dodgers changed their name to the Tigers.

Coaching from the bench was legalized, April 20.

The Cardinals and the Steelers were granted permission to merge for one year under the name Card-Pitt, April 21. Phil Handler of the Cardinals and Walt Kiesling of the Steelers served as co-coaches. The merger automatically dissolved the last day of the season, December 3.

In the NFL Championship Game, Green Bay defeated the New York Giants 14-7, December 17.

1945
The inbounds lines or hashmarks were moved from 15 yards away from the sidelines to nearer the center of the field—20 yards from the sidelines.

Brooklyn and Boston merged into a team that played home games in both cities and was known simply as The Yanks. The team was coached by former Boston head coach Herb Kopf. In December, the Brooklyn franchise withdrew from the NFL to join the new All-America Football Conference; all the players on its active and reserve lists were assigned to The Yanks, who once again became the Boston Yanks.

Halas rejoined the Bears late in the season after service with the U.S. Navy. Although Halas took over much of the coaching duties, Anderson and Johnsos remained the coaches of record throughout the season.

Steve Van Buren of Philadelphia led the NFL in rushing, kickoff returns, and scoring.

After the Japanese surrendered ending World War II, a count showed that the NFL service roster, limited to men who had played in league games, totaled 638, 21 of whom had died in action.

Rookie quarterback Bob Waterfield led Cleveland to a 15-14 victory over Washington in the NFL Championship Game, December 16.

1946
The contract of Commissioner Layden was not renewed, and Bert Bell, the co-owner of the Steelers, replaced him, January 11. Bell moved the league headquarters from Chicago to the Philadelphia suburb of Bala-Cynwyd.

Free substitution was withdrawn and substitutions were limited to no more than three men at a time. Forward passes were made automatically incomplete upon striking the goal posts, January 11.

The NFL took on a truly national appearance for the first time when Reeves was granted permission by the league to move his NFL champion Rams to Los Angeles.

Halfback Kenny Washington (March 21) and end Woody Strode (May 7) signed with the Los Angeles Rams to become the first African-Americans to play in the NFL in the modern era. Guard Bill Willis (August 6) and running back Marion Motley (August 9) joined the AAFC with the Cleveland Browns.

The rival All-America Football Conference began play with eight teams. The Cleveland Browns, coached by Paul Brown, won the AAFC's first championship, defeating the New York Yankees 14-9.

Bill Dudley of the Steelers led the NFL in rushing, interceptions, and punt returns, and won the league's most valuable player award.

Backs Frank Filchock and Merle Hapes of the Giants were questioned about an attempt by a New York man to fix the championship game with the Bears. Bell suspended Hapes but allowed Filchock to play; he played well, but Chicago won 24-14, December 15.

1947
The NFL added a fifth official, the back judge.

A bonus choice was made for the first time in the NFL draft. One team each year would select the special choice before the first round began. The Chicago Bears won a lottery and the rights to the first choice and drafted back Bob Fenimore of Oklahoma A&M.

The Cleveland Browns again won the AAFC title, defeating the New York Yankees 14-3.

Charles Bidwill, Sr., owner of the Cardinals, died April 19, but his wife and sons retained ownership of the team. On December 28, the Cardinals won the NFL Championship Game 28-21 over the Philadelphia Eagles, who had beaten Pittsburgh 21-0 in a playoff.

1948
Plastic helmets were prohibited. A flexible artificial tee was permitted at the kickoff. Officials other than the referee were equipped with whistles, not horns, January 14.

Fred Mandel sold the Detroit Lions to a syndicate headed by D. Lyle Fife, January 15.

Halfback Fred Gehrke of the Los Angeles Rams painted horns on the Rams' helmets, the first modern helmet emblems in pro football.

The Cleveland Browns won their third straight championship in the AAFC, going 14-0 and then defeating the Buffalo Bills 49-7.

In a blizzard, the Eagles defeated the Cardinals 7-0 in the NFL Championship Game, December 19.

1949
Alexis Thompson sold the champion Eagles to a syndicate headed by James P. Clark, January 15. The Boston Yanks became the New York Bulldogs, sharing the Polo Grounds with the Giants.

Free substitution was adopted for one year, January 20.

The NFL had two 1,000-yard rushers in the same season for the first time—Steve Van Buren of Philadelphia and Tony Canadeo of Green Bay.

The AAFC played its season with a one-division, seven-team format. On December 9, Bell announced a merger agreement in which three AAFC franchises—Cleveland, San Francisco, and Baltimore—would join the NFL in 1950. The Browns won their fourth consecutive AAFC title, defeating the 49ers 21-7, December 11.

In a heavy rain, the Eagles defeated the Rams 14-0 in the NFL Championship Game, December 18.

1950
Unlimited free substitution was restored, opening the way for the era of two platoons and specialization in pro football, January 20.

Curly Lambeau, founder of the franchise and Green Bay's head coach since 1921, resigned under fire, February 1.

The name National Football League was restored after about three months as the National-American Football League. The American and National conferences were created to replace the Eastern and Western divisions, March 3.

The New York Bulldogs became the Yanks and divided the players of the former AAFC Yankees with the Giants. A special allocation draft was held in which the 13 teams drafted the remaining AAFC players, with special consideration for Baltimore, which received 15 choices compared to 10 for other teams.

The Los Angeles Rams became the first NFL team to have all of its games—both home and away—televised. The Washington Redskins followed the Rams in arranging to televise their games; other teams made deals to put selected games on television.

In the first game of the season, former AAFC champion Cleveland defeated NFL champion Philadelphia 35-10. For the first time, deadlocks occurred in both conferences and playoffs were necessary. The Browns defeated the Giants in the American and the Rams defeated the Bears in the National. Cleveland defeated Los Angeles 30-28 in the NFL Championship Game, December 24.

1951
The Pro Bowl game, dormant since 1942, was revived under a new format matching the all-stars of each conference at the Los Angeles Memorial Coliseum. The American Conference defeated the National Conference 28-27, January 14.

Abraham Watner returned the Baltimore franchise and its player contracts back to the NFL for $50,000. Baltimore's former players were made available for drafting at the same time as college players, January 18.

A rule was passed that no tackle, guard, or center would be eligible to catch a forward pass, January 18.

The Rams reversed their television policy and televised only road games.

The NFL Championship Game was televised coast-to-coast for the first time, December 23. The DuMont Network paid $75,000 for the rights to the game, in which the Rams defeated the Browns 24-17.

1952
Ted Collins sold the New York Yanks' franchise back to the NFL, January 19. A new franchise was awarded to a group in Dallas after it purchased the assets of the Yanks, January 24. The new Texans went 1-11, with the owners turning the franchise back to the league in midseason. For the last five games of the season, the commissioner's office operated the Texans as a road team, using Hershey, Pennsylvania, as a home base. At the end of the season the franchise was canceled, the last time an NFL team failed.

The Pittsburgh Steelers abandoned the Single-Wing for the T-formation, the last pro team to do so.

The Detroit Lions won their first NFL championship in 17 years, defeating the Browns 17-7 in the title game, December 28.

1953
A Baltimore group headed by Carroll Rosenbloom was granted a franchise and was awarded the holdings of the defunct Dallas organization, January 23. The team, named the Colts, put together the largest trade in league history, acquiring 10 players from Cleveland in exchange for five.

The names of the American and National conferences were changed to the Eastern and Western conferences, January 24.

Jim Thorpe died, March 28.

Mickey McBride, founder of the Cleveland Browns, sold the franchise to a syndicate headed by Dave R. Jones, June 10.

The NFL policy of blacking out home games was upheld by Judge Allan K. Grim of the U.S. District Court in Philadelphia, November 12.

The Lions again defeated the Browns in the NFL Championship Game, winning 17-16, December 27.

1954
The Canadian Football League began a series of raids on NFL teams, signing quarterback Eddie LeBaron and defensive end Gene Brito of Washington and defensive tackle Arnie Weinmeister of the Giants, among others.

Fullback Joe Perry of the 49ers became the first player in league history to gain 1,000 yards rushing in consecutive seasons.

Cleveland defeated Detroit 56-10 in the NFL Championship Game, December 26.

1955
The sudden-death overtime rule was used for the first time in a preseason game between the Rams and Giants at Portland, Oregon, August 28. The Rams won 23-17 three minutes into overtime.

A rule change declared the ball dead immediately if the ball carrier touched the ground with any part of his body except his hands or feet while in the grasp of an opponent.

The Baltimore Colts made an 80-cent phone call to Johnny Unitas and signed him as a free agent. Another quarterback, Otto Graham, played his last game as the Browns defeated the Rams 38-14 in the NFL Championship Game, December 26. Graham had quarterbacked the Browns to 10 championship-game appearances in 10 years.

NBC replaced DuMont as the network for the title game, paying a rights fee of $100,000.

1956
The NFL Players Association was founded.

Grabbing an opponent's facemask (other than the ball carrier) was made illegal. Using radio receivers to communicate with players on the field was prohibited. A natural leather ball with white end stripes replaced the white ball with black stripes for night games.

The Giants moved from the Polo Grounds to Yankee Stadium.

Halas retired as coach of the Bears, and was replaced by Paddy Driscoll.

CBS became the first network to broadcast some NFL regular-season games to selected television markets across the nation.

The Giants routed the Bears 47-7 in the NFL Championship Game, December 30.

1957
Pete Rozelle was named general manager of the Rams. Anthony J. Morabito, founder and co-owner of the 49ers, died of a heart attack during a game against the Bears at Kezar Stadium, October 28. An NFL-record crowd of 102,368 saw the 49ers-Rams game at the Los Angeles Memorial Coliseum, November 10.

The Lions came from 20 points down to post a 31-27 playoff victory over the 49ers, December 22. Detroit defeated Cleveland 59-14 in the NFL Championship Game, December 29.

1958
The bonus selection in the draft was eliminated, January 29. The last selection was quarterback King Hill of Rice by the Chicago Cardinals.

Halas reinstated himself as coach of the Bears.

Jim Brown of Cleveland gained an NFL-record 1,527 yards rushing. In a divisional playoff game, the Giants held Brown to eight yards and defeated Cleveland 10-0.

Baltimore, coached by Weeb Ewbank, defeated the Giants 23-17 in the first sudden-death overtime in an NFL Championship Game, December 28. The game ended when Colts fullback Alan Ameche scored on a one-yard touchdown run after 8:15 of overtime.

1959
Vince Lombardi was named head coach of the Green Bay Packers, January 28. Tim Mara, the co-founder of the Giants, died, February 17.

Lamar Hunt of Dallas announced his intentions to form a second pro football league. The first meeting was held in Chicago, August 14, and consisted of Hunt representing Dallas; Bob Howsam, Denver; K.S. (Bud) Adams, Houston; Barron Hilton, Los Angeles; Max Winter and Bill Boyer, Minneapolis; and Harry Wismer, New York City. They made plans to begin play in 1960.

The new league was named the American Football League, August 22. Buffalo, owned by Ralph Wilson, became the seventh franchise, October 28. Boston, owned by William H. Sullivan, became the eighth team, November 22. The first AFL draft, lasting 33 rounds, was held, November 22. Joe Foss was named AFL Commissioner, November 30. An additional draft of 20 rounds was held by the AFL, December 2.

NFL Commissioner Bert Bell died of a heart attack suffered at Franklin

Field, Philadelphia, during the last two minutes of a game between the Eagles and the Steelers, October 11. Treasurer Austin Gunsel was named president in the office of the commissioner, October 14.

The Colts again defeated the Giants in the NFL Championship Game, 31-16, December 27.

1960

Pete Rozelle was elected NFL Commissioner as a compromise choice on the twenty-third ballot, January 26. Rozelle moved the league offices to New York City.

Hunt was elected AFL president for 1960, January 26. Minneapolis withdrew from the AFL, January 27, and the same ownership was given an NFL franchise for Minnesota (to start in 1961), January 28. Dallas received an NFL franchise for 1960, January 28. Oakland received an AFL franchise, January 30.

The AFL adopted the two-point option on points after touchdown, January 28. A no-tampering verbal pact, relative to players' contracts, was agreed to between the NFL and AFL, February 9.

The NFL owners voted to allow the transfer of the Chicago Cardinals to St. Louis, March 13.

The AFL signed a five-year television contract with ABC, June 9.

The Boston Patriots defeated the Buffalo Bills 28-7 before 16,000 at Buffalo in the first AFL preseason game, July 30. The Denver Broncos defeated the Patriots 13-10 before 21,597 at Boston in the first AFL regular-season game, September 9.

Philadelphia defeated Green Bay 17-13 in the NFL Championship Game, December 26.

1961

The Houston Oilers defeated the Los Angeles Chargers 24-16 before 32,183 in the first AFL Championship Game, January 1.

Detroit defeated Cleveland 17-16 in the first Playoff Bowl, or Bert Bell Benefit Bowl, between second-place teams in each conference in Miami, January 7.

End Willard Dewveall of the Bears played out his option and joined the Oilers, becoming the first player to move deliberately from one league to the other, January 14.

Ed McGah, Wayne Valley, and Robert Osborne bought out their partners in the ownership of the Raiders, January 17. The Chargers were transferred to San Diego, February 10. Dave R. Jones sold the Browns to a group headed by Arthur B. Modell, March 22. The Howsam brothers sold the Broncos to a group headed by Calvin Kunz and Gerry Phipps, May 26.

NBC was awarded a two-year contract for radio and television rights to the NFL Championship Game for $615,000 annually, $300,000 of which was to go directly into the NFL Player Benefit Plan, April 5.

Canton, Ohio, where the league that became the NFL was formed in 1920, was chosen as the site of the Pro Football Hall of Fame, April 27. Dick McCann, a former Redskins executive, was named executive director.

A bill legalizing single-network television contracts by professional sports leagues was introduced in Congress by Representative Emanuel Celler. It passed the House and Senate and was signed into law by President John F. Kennedy, September 30.

Houston defeated San Diego 10-3 for the AFL championship, December 24. Green Bay won its first NFL championship since 1944, defeating the New York Giants 37-0, December 31.

1962

The Western Division defeated the Eastern Division 47-27 in the first AFL All-Star Game, played before 20,973 in San Diego, January 7.

Both leagues prohibited grabbing any player's facemask. The AFL voted to make the scoreboard clock the official timer of the game.

The NFL entered into a single-network agreement with CBS for telecasting all regular-season games for $4.65 million annually, January 10.

Judge Roszel Thompson of the U.S. District Court in Baltimore ruled against the AFL in its antitrust suit against the NFL, May 21. The AFL had charged the NFL with monopoly and conspiracy in areas of expansion, television, and player signings. The case lasted two and a half years, the trial two months.

McGah and Valley acquired controlling interest in the Raiders, May 24. The AFL assumed financial responsibility for the New York Titans, November 8. With Commissioner Rozelle as referee, Daniel F. Reeves regained the ownership of the Rams, outbidding his partners in sealed-envelope bidding for the team, November 27.

The Dallas Texans defeated the Oilers 20-17 for the AFL championship at Houston after 17 minutes, 54 seconds of overtime on a 25-yard field goal by Tommy Brooker, December 23. The game lasted a record 77 minutes, 54 seconds.

Judge Edward Weinfeld of the U.S. District Court in New York City upheld the legality of the NFL's television blackout within a 75-mile radius of home games and denied an injunction that would have forced the championship game between the Giants and the Packers to be televised in the New York City area, December 28. The Packers beat the Giants 16-7 for the NFL title, December 30.

1963

The Dallas Texans transferred to Kansas City, becoming the Chiefs, February 8. The New York Titans were sold to a five-man syndicate headed by David (Sonny) Werblin, March 28. Weeb Ewbank became the Titans' new head coach and the team's name was changed to the Jets, April 15. They began play in Shea Stadium.

NFL Properties, Inc., was founded to serve as the licensing arm of the NFL.

Rozelle indefinitely suspended Green Bay halfback Paul Hornung and Detroit defensive tackle Alex Karras for placing bets on their own teams and on other NFL games; he also fined five other Detroit players $2,000 each for betting on one game in which they did not participate, and the Detroit Lions Football Company $2,000 on each of two counts for failure to report information promptly and for lack of sideline supervision.

Paul Brown, head coach of the Browns since their inception, was fired and replaced by Blanton Collier. Don Shula replaced Weeb Ewbank as head coach of the Colts.

The AFL allowed the Jets and Raiders to select players from other franchises in hopes of giving the league more competitive balance, May 11.

NBC was awarded exclusive network broadcasting rights for the 1963 AFL Championship Game for $926,000, May 23.

The Pro Football Hall of Fame was dedicated at Canton, Ohio, September 7.

The U.S. Fourth Circuit Court of Appeals reaffirmed the lower court's finding for the NFL in the $10-million suit brought by the AFL, ending three and a half years of litigation, November 21.

Jim Brown of Cleveland rushed for an NFL single-season record 1,863 yards.

Boston defeated Buffalo 26-8 in the first divisional playoff game in AFL history, December 28.

The Bears defeated the Giants 14-10 in the NFL Championship Game, a record sixth and last title for Halas in his thirty-sixth season as the Bears' coach, December 29.

1964

The Chargers defeated the Patriots 51-10 in the AFL Championship Game, January 5.

William Clay Ford, the Lions' president since 1961, purchased the team, January 10. A group representing the late James P. Clark sold the Eagles to a group headed by Jerry Wolman, January 21. Carroll Rosenbloom, the majority owner of the Colts since 1953, acquired complete ownership of the team, January 23.

The AFL signed a five-year, $36-million television contract with NBC to begin with the 1965 season, January 29.

Commissioner Rozelle negotiated an agreement on behalf of the NFL clubs to purchase Ed Sabol's Blair Motion Pictures, which was renamed NFL Films, March 5.

Hornung and Karras were reinstated by Rozelle, March 16.

CBS submitted the winning bid of $14.1 million per year for the NFL regular-season television rights for 1964 and 1965, January 24. CBS acquired the rights to the championship games for 1964 and 1965 for $1.8 million per game, April 17.

Pete Gogolak of Cornell signed a contract with Buffalo, becoming the first soccer-style kicker in pro football.

Buffalo defeated San Diego 20-7 in the AFL Championship Game, December 26. Cleveland defeated Baltimore 27-0 in the NFL Championship Game, December 27.

1965

The NFL teams pledged not to sign college seniors until completion of all their games, including bowl games, and empowered the Commissioner to discipline the clubs up to as much as the loss of an entire draft list for a violation of the pledge, February 15.

The NFL added a sixth official, the line judge, February 19. The color of the officials' penalty flags was changed from white to bright gold, April 5.

Atlanta was awarded an NFL franchise for 1966, with Rankin Smith, Sr., as owner, June 30. Miami was awarded an AFL franchise for 1966, with Joe Robbie and Danny Thomas as owners, August 16.

Field Judge Burl Toler became the first black official in NFL history, September 19.

According to a Harris survey, sports fans chose professional football (41 percent) as their favorite sport, overtaking baseball (38 percent) for the first time, October.

Green Bay defeated Baltimore 13-10 in sudden-death overtime in a Western Conference playoff game. Don Chandler kicked a 25-yard field goal for the Packers after 13 minutes, 39 seconds of overtime, December 26. The Packers then defeated the Browns 23-12 in the NFL Championship Game, January 2.

In the AFL Championship Game, the Bills again defeated the Chargers, 23-0, December 26.

CBS acquired the rights to the NFL regular-season games in 1966 and 1967, with an option for 1968, for $18.8 million per year, December 29.

1966

The AFL-NFL war reached its peak, as the leagues spent a combined $7 million to sign their 1966 draft choices. The NFL signed 75 percent of its 232 draftees, the AFL 46 percent of its 181. Of the 111 common draft choices, 79 signed with the NFL, 28 with the AFL, and 4 went unsigned.

Buddy Young became the first African-American to work in the league office when Commissioner Rozelle named him director of player relations, February 1.

The rights to the 1966 and 1967 NFL Championship Games were sold to CBS for $2 million per game, February 14.

Foss resigned as AFL Commissioner, April 7. Al Davis, the head coach and general manager of the Raiders, was named to replace him, April 8.

Goal posts offset from the goal line, painted bright yellow, and with uprights 20 feet above the cross-bar were made standard in the NFL, May 16.

A series of secret meetings regarding a possible AFL-NFL merger were held in the spring between Hunt of Kansas City and Tex Schramm of Dallas. Rozelle announced the merger, June 8. Under the agreement, the two leagues would combine to form an expanded league with 24 teams, to be increased to 26 in 1968 and to 28 by 1970 or soon thereafter. All existing franchises would be retained, and no franchises would be transferred outside their metropolitan areas. While maintaining separate schedules through 1969, the leagues agreed to play an annual AFL-NFL World Championship Game beginning in January, 1967, and to hold a combined draft, also beginning in 1967. Preseason games would be held between teams of each league starting in 1967. Official regular-season play would start in 1970 when the two leagues would officially merge to form one league with two conferences. Rozelle was named Commissioner of the expanded league setup.

Davis rejoined the Raiders, and Milt Woodard was named president of the AFL, July 25.

The St. Louis Cardinals moved into newly constructed Busch Memorial Stadium.

Barron Hilton sold the Chargers to a group headed by Eugene Klein and Sam Schulman, August 25.

Congress approved the AFL-NFL merger, passing legislation exempting the agreement itself from antitrust action, October 21.

New Orleans was awarded an NFL franchise to begin play in 1967, November 1. John Mecom, Jr., of Houston was designated majority stockholder and president of the franchise, December 15.

The NFL was realigned for the 1967-69 seasons into the Capitol and Century Divisions in the Eastern Conference and the Central and Coastal Divisions in the Western Conference, December 2. New Orleans and the New York Giants agreed to switch divisions in 1968 and return to the 1967 alignment in 1969.

The rights to the Super Bowl for four years were sold to CBS and NBC for $9.5 million, December 13.

1967

Green Bay earned the right to represent the NFL in the first AFL-NFL World Championship Game by defeating Dallas 34-27, January 1. The same day, Kansas City defeated Buffalo 31-7 to represent the AFL. The Packers defeated the Chiefs 35-10 before 61,946 fans at the Los Angeles Memorial Coliseum in the first game between AFL and NFL teams, January 15. The winning players' share for the Packers was $15,000 each, and the losing players' share for the Chiefs was $7,500 each. The game was televised by both CBS and NBC.

The "sling-shot" goal post and a six-foot-wide border around the field were made standard in the NFL, February 22.

Baltimore made Bubba Smith, a Michigan State defensive lineman, the first choice in the first combined AFL-NFL draft, March 14.

The AFL awarded a franchise to begin play in 1968 to Cincinnati, May 24. A group with Paul Brown as part owner, general manager, and head coach, was awarded the Cincinnati franchise, September 27.

Arthur B. Modell, the president of the Cleveland Browns, was elected president of the NFL, May 28.

Defensive back Emlen Tunnell of the New York Giants became the first black player to enter the Pro Football Hall of Fame, August 5.

An AFL team defeated an NFL team for the first time, when Denver beat Detroit 13-7 in a preseason game, August 5.

Green Bay defeated Dallas 21-17 for the NFL championship on a last-minute 1-yard quarterback sneak by Bart Starr in 13-below-zero temperature at Green Bay, December 31. The same day, Oakland defeated Houston 40-7 for the AFL championship.

1968

Green Bay defeated Oakland 33-14 in Super Bowl II at Miami, January 14. The game had the first $3-million gate in pro football history.

Vince Lombardi resigned as head coach of the Packers, but remained as general manager, January 28.

Werblin sold his shares in the Jets to his partners Don Lillis, Leon Hess, Townsend Martin, and Phil Iselin, May 21. Lillis assumed the presidency of the club, but then died July 23. Iselin was appointed president, August 6.

Halas retired for the fourth and last time as head coach of the Bears, May 27.

The Oilers left Rice Stadium for the Astrodome and became the first NFL team to play its home games in a domed stadium.

The movie *Heidi* became a footnote in sports history when NBC didn't show the last :50 of the Jets-Raiders game in order to permit the children's special to begin on time. The Raiders scored two touchdowns in the last 42 seconds to win 43-32, November 17.

Ewbank became the first coach to win titles in both the NFL and AFL when his Jets defeated the Raiders 27-23 for the AFL championship, December 29. The same day, Baltimore defeated Cleveland 34-0.

1969

The AFL established a playoff format for the 1969 season, with the winner in one division playing the runner-up in the other, January 11.

An AFL team won the Super Bowl for the first time, as the Jets defeated the Colts 16-7 at Miami, January 12 in Super Bowl III. The title Super Bowl was recognized by the NFL for the first time.

Vince Lombardi became part owner, executive vice-president, and head coach of the Washington Redskins, February 7.

Wolman sold the Eagles to Leonard Tose, May 1.

Baltimore, Cleveland, and Pittsburgh agreed to join the AFL teams to form the 13-team American Football Conference of the NFL in 1970, May 17. The NFL also agreed on a playoff format that would include one "wild-card" team per conference—the second-place team with the best record.

Monday Night Football was signed for 1970. ABC acquired the rights to televise 13 NFL regular-season Monday night games in 1970, 1971, and 1972.

George Preston Marshall, president emeritus of the Redskins, died at 72, August 9.

The NFL marked its fiftieth year by the wearing of a special patch by each of the 16 teams.

1970

Kansas City defeated Minnesota 23-7 in Super Bowl IV at New Orleans, January 11. The gross receipts of approximately $3.8 million were the largest ever for a one-day sports event.

Four-year television contracts, under which CBS would televise all NFC games and NBC all AFC games (except Monday night games) and the two would divide televising the Super Bowl and AFC-NFC Pro Bowl games, were announced, January 26.

Art Modell resigned as president of the NFL, March 12. Milt Woodard resigned as president of the AFL, March 13. Lamar Hunt was elected president of the AFC and George Halas was elected president of the NFC, March 19.

The merged 26-team league adopted rules changes putting names on the backs of players' jerseys, making a point after touchdown worth only one point, and making the scoreboard clock the official timing device of the game, March 18.

The Players Negotiating Committee and the NFL Players Association announced a four-year agreement guaranteeing approximately $4,535,000 annually to player pension and insurance benefits, August 3. The owners also agreed to contribute $250,000 annually to improve or implement items such as disability payments, widows' benefits, maternity benefits, and dental benefits. The agreement also provided for increased preseason game and per diem payments, averaging approximately $2.6 million annually.

The Pittsburgh Steelers moved into Three Rivers Stadium. The Cincinnati Bengals moved to Riverfront Stadium.

Lombardi died of cancer at 57, September 3.

Tom Dempsey of New Orleans kicked a game-winning NFL-record 63-yard field goal against Detroit, November 8.

1971

Baltimore defeated Dallas 16-13 on Jim O'Brien's 32-yard field goal with five seconds to go in Super Bowl V at Miami, January 17. The NBC telecast was viewed in an estimated 23,980,000 homes, the largest audience ever for a one-day sports event.

The NFC defeated the AFC 27-6 in the first AFC-NFC Pro Bowl at Los Angeles, January 24.

The Boston Patriots changed their name to the New England Patriots, March 25. Their new stadium, Schaefer Stadium, was dedicated in a 20-14 preseason victory over the Giants.

The Philadelphia Eagles left Franklin Field and played their games at the new Veterans Stadium.

The San Francisco 49ers left Kezar Stadium and moved their games to Candlestick Park.

Daniel F. Reeves, the president and general manager of the Rams, died at 58, April 15.

The Dallas Cowboys moved from the Cotton Bowl into their new home, Texas Stadium, October 24.

Miami defeated Kansas City 27-24 in sudden-death overtime in an AFC Divisional Playoff Game, December 25. Garo Yepremian kicked a 37-yard field goal for the Dolphins after 22 minutes, 40 seconds of overtime, as the game lasted 82 minutes, 40 seconds overall, making it the longest game in history.

1972

Dallas defeated Miami 24-3 in Super Bowl VI at New Orleans, January 16. The CBS telecast was viewed in an estimated 27,450,000 homes, the top-rated one-day telecast ever.

The inbounds lines or hashmarks were moved nearer the center of the field, 23 yards, 1 foot, 9 inches from the sidelines, March 23. The method of determining won-lost percentage in standings changed. Tie games, previously not counted in the standings, were made equal to a half-game won and a half-game lost, May 24.

Robert Irsay purchased the Los Angeles Rams and transferred ownership of the club to Carroll Rosenbloom in exchange for the Baltimore Colts, July 13.

William V. Bidwill purchased the stock of his brother Charles (Stormy) Bidwill to become the sole owner of the St. Louis Cardinals, September 2.

The National District Attorneys Association endorsed the position of professional leagues in opposing proposed legalization of gambling on professional team sports, September 28.

Franco Harris's "Immaculate Reception" gave the Steelers their first postseason win ever, 13-7 over the Raiders, December 23.

1973

Rozelle announced that all Super Bowl VII tickets were sold and that the game would be telecast in Los Angeles, the site of the game, on an experimental basis, January 3.

Miami defeated Washington 14-7 in Super Bowl VII at Los Angeles, completing a 17-0 season, the first perfect-record regular-season and postseason mark in NFL history, January 14. The NBC telecast was viewed by approximately 75 million people.

The AFC defeated the NFC 33-28 in the Pro Bowl in Dallas, the first time since 1942 that the game was played outside Los Angeles, January 21.

A jersey numbering system was adopted, April 5: 1-19 for quarterbacks and specialists, 20-49 for running backs and defensive backs, 50-59 for centers and linebackers, 60-79 for defensive linemen and interior offensive linemen other than centers, and 80-89 for wide receivers and tight ends. Players who had been in the NFL in 1972 could continue to use old numbers.

NFL Charities, a nonprofit organization, was created to derive an income from monies generated from NFL Properties' licensing of NFL trademarks and team names, June 26. NFL Charities was set up to support education and charitable activities and to supply economic support to persons formerly associated with professional football who were no longer able to support themselves.

Congress adopted experimental legislation (for three years) requiring any NFL game that had been declared a sellout 72 hours prior to kickoff to be made available for local televising, September 14. The legislation provided for an annual review to be made by the Federal Communications Commission.

The Buffalo Bills moved their home games from War Memorial Stadium to Rich Stadium in nearby Orchard Park. The Giants tied the Eagles 23-23 in the final game in Yankee Stadium, September 23. The Giants played the rest of their home games at the Yale Bowl in New Haven, Connecticut.

A rival league, the World Football League, was formed and was reported in operation, October 2. It had plans to start play in 1974.

O.J. Simpson of Buffalo became the first player to rush for more than 2,000 yards in a season, gaining 2,003.

1974
Miami defeated Minnesota 24-7 in Super Bowl VIII at Houston, the second consecutive Super Bowl championship for the Dolphins, January 13. The CBS telecast was viewed by approximately 75 million people.

Rozelle was given a 10-year contract effective January 1, 1973, February 27.

Tampa Bay was awarded a franchise to begin operation in 1976, April 24.

Sweeping rules changes were adopted to add action and tempo to games: one sudden-death overtime period was added for preseason and regular-season games; the goal posts were moved from the goal line to the end lines; kickoffs were moved from the 40- to the 35-yard line; after missed field goals from beyond the 20, the ball was to be returned to the line of scrimmage; restrictions were placed on members of the punting team to open up return possibilities; roll-blocking and cutting of wide receivers was eliminated; the extent of downfield contact a defender could have with an eligible receiver was restricted; the penalties for offensive holding, illegal use of the hands, and tripping were reduced from 15 to 10 yards; wide receivers blocking back toward the ball within three yards of the line of scrimmage were prevented from blocking below the waist, April 25.

Seattle was awarded an NFL franchise to begin play in 1976, June 4. Lloyd W. Nordstrom, president of the Seattle Seahawks, and Hugh Culverhouse, president of the Tampa Bay Buccaneers, signed franchise agreements, December 5.

The Birmingham Americans defeated the Florida Blazers 22-21 in the WFL World Bowl, winning the league championship, December 5.

1975
Pittsburgh defeated Minnesota 16-6 in Super Bowl IX at New Orleans, the Steelers' first championship since entering the NFL in 1933. The NBC telecast was viewed by approximately 78 million people.

The Memphis Southmen of the WFL signed Larry Csonka, Jim Kiick, and Paul Warfield of Miami, March 31.

The divisional winners with the highest won-loss percentage were made the home team for the divisional playoffs, and the surviving winners with the highest percentage made home teams for the championship games, June 26.

Referees were equipped with wireless microphones for all preseason, regular-season, and playoff games.

The Lions moved to the new Pontiac Silverdome. The Giants played their home games in Shea Stadium. The Saints moved into the Louisiana Superdome.

The World Football League folded, October 22.

1976
Pittsburgh defeated Dallas 21-17 in Super Bowl X in Miami. The Steelers joined Green Bay and Miami as the only teams to win two Super Bowls; the Cowboys became the first wild-card team to play in the Super Bowl. The CBS telecast was viewed by an estimated 80 million people, the largest television audience in history.

Lloyd Nordstrom, the president of the Seahawks, died at 66, January 20. His brother Elmer succeeded him as majority representative of the team.

The owners awarded Super Bowl XII, to be played on January 15, 1978, to New Orleans. They also adopted the use of two 30-second clocks for all games, visible to both players and fans to note the official time between the ready-for-play signal and snap of the ball, March 16.

A veteran player allocation was held to stock the Seattle and Tampa Bay franchises with 39 players each, March 30-31. In the college draft, Seattle and Tampa Bay each received eight extra choices, April 8-9.

The Giants moved into new Giants Stadium in East Rutherford, New Jersey.

The Steelers defeated the College All-Stars in a storm-shortened Chicago College All-Star Game, the last of the series, July 23. St. Louis defeated San Diego 20-10 in a preseason game before 38,000 in Korakuen Stadium, Tokyo, in the first NFL game outside of North America, August 16.

1977
Oakland defeated Minnesota 32-14 in Super Bowl XI at Pasadena, January 9. The paid attendance was a pro record 103,438. The NBC telecast was viewed by 81.9 million people, the largest ever to view a sports event. The victory was the fifth consecutive for the AFC in the Super Bowl.

The NFL Players Association and the NFL Management Council ratified a collective bargaining agreement extending until 1982, covering five football seasons while continuing the pension plan—including years 1974, 1975, and 1976—with contributions totaling more than $55 million. The total cost of the agreement was estimated at $107 million. The agreement called for a college draft at least through 1986; contained a no-strike, no-suit clause; established a 43-man active player limit; reduced pension vesting to four years; provided for increases in minimum salaries and preseason and postseason pay; improved insurance, medical, and dental benefits; modified previous practices in player movement and control; and reaffirmed the NFL Commissioner's disciplinary authority. Additionally, the agreement called for the NFL member clubs to make payments totaling $16 million the next 10 years to settle various legal disputes, February 25.

The San Francisco 49ers were sold to Edward J. DeBartolo, Jr., March 28.

A 16-game regular season, 4-game preseason was adopted to begin in 1978, March 29. A second wild-card team was adopted for the playoffs beginning in 1978, with the wild-card teams to play each other and the winners advancing to a round of eight postseason series.

The Seahawks were permanently aligned in the AFC Western Division and the Buccaneers in the NFC Central Division, March 31.

The owners awarded Super Bowl XIII, to be played on January 21, 1979, to Miami, to be played in the Orange Bowl; Super Bowl XIV, to be played January 20, 1980, was awarded to Pasadena, to be played in the Rose Bowl, June 14.

Rules changes were adopted to open up the passing game and to cut down on injuries. Defenders were permitted to make contact with eligible receivers only once; the head slap was outlawed; offensive linemen were prohibited from thrusting their hands to an opponent's neck, face, or head; and wide receivers were prohibited from clipping, even in the legal clipping zone.

Rozelle negotiated contracts with the three television networks to televise all NFL regular-season and postseason games, plus selected preseason games, for four years beginning with the 1978 season. ABC was awarded yearly rights to 16 Monday night games, four prime-time games, the AFC-NFC Pro Bowl, and the Hall of Fame games. CBS received the rights to all NFC regular-season and postseason games (except those in the ABC package) and to Super Bowls XIV and XVI. NBC received the rights to all AFC regular-season and postseason games (except those in the ABC package) and to Super Bowls XIII and XV. Industry sources considered it the largest single television package ever negotiated, October 12.

Chicago's Walter Payton set a single-game rushing record with 275 yards (40 carries) against Minnesota, November 20.

1978
Dallas defeated Denver 27-10 in Super Bowl XII, held indoors for the first time, at the Louisiana Superdome in New Orleans, January 15. The CBS telecast was viewed by more than 102 million people, meaning the game was watched by more viewers than any other show of any kind in the history of television. Dallas's victory was the first for the NFC in six years.

According to a Louis Harris Sports Survey, 70 percent of the nation's sports fans said they followed football, compared to 54 percent who followed baseball. Football increased its lead as the country's favorite, 26 percent to 16 percent for baseball, January 19.

A seventh official, the side judge, was added to the officiating crew, March 14.

The NFL continued a trend toward opening up the game. Rules changes permitted a defender to maintain contact with a receiver within five yards of the line of scrimmage, but restricted contact beyond that point. The pass-blocking rule was interpreted to permit the extending of arms and open hands, March 17.

A study on the use of instant replay as an officiating aid was made during seven nationally televised preseason games.

The NFL played for the first time in Mexico City, with the Saints defeating the Eagles 14-7 in a preseason game, August 5.

Bolstered by the expansion of the regular-season schedule from 14 to 16 weeks, NFL paid attendance exceeded 12 million (12,771,800) for the first time. The per-game average of 57,017 was the third-highest in league history and the most since 1973.

1979
Pittsburgh defeated Dallas 35-31 in Super Bowl XIII at Miami to become the first team ever to win three Super Bowls, January 21. The NBC telecast was viewed in 35,090,000 homes, by an estimated 96.6 million fans.

The owners awarded three future Super Bowl sites: Super Bowl XV to the Louisiana Superdome in New Orleans, to be played on January 25, 1981; Super Bowl XVI to the Pontiac Silverdome in Pontiac, Michigan, to be played on January 24, 1982; and Super Bowl XVII to Pasadena's Rose Bowl, to be played on January 30, 1983, March 13.

NFL rules changes emphasized additional player safety. The changes prohibited players on the receiving team from blocking below the waist during kickoffs, punts, and field-goal attempts; prohibited the wearing of torn or altered equipment and exposed pads that could be hazardous; extended the zone in which there could be no crackback blocks; and instructed officials to quickly whistle a play dead when a quarterback was clearly in the grasp of a tackler, March 16.

Rosenbloom, the president of the Rams, drowned at 72, April 2. His widow, Georgia, assumed control of the club.

1980
Pittsburgh defeated the Los Angeles Rams 31-19 in Super Bowl XIV at Pasadena to become the first team to win four Super Bowls, January 20. The game was viewed in a record 35,330,000 homes.

The AFC-NFC Pro Bowl, won 37-27 by the NFC, was played before 48,060 fans at Aloha Stadium in Honolulu, Hawaii. It was the first time in the 30-year history of the Pro Bowl that the game was played in a non-NFL city.

Rules changes placed greater restrictions on contact in the area of the head, neck, and face. Under the heading of "personal foul," players were prohibited from directly striking, swinging, or clubbing on the head, neck, or face. Starting in 1980, a penalty could be called for such contact whether or not the initial contact was made below the neck area.

CBS, with a record bid of $12 million, won the national radio rights to 26 NFL regular-season games, including Monday Night Football, and all 10 postseason games for the 1980-83 seasons.

The Los Angeles Rams moved their home games to Anaheim Stadium in nearby Orange County, California.

The Oakland Raiders joined the Los Angeles Coliseum Commission's antitrust suit against the NFL. The suit contended the league violated antitrust laws in declining to approve a proposed move by the Raiders from Oakland to Los Angeles.

NFL regular-season attendance of nearly 13.4 million set a record for the third year in a row. The average paid attendance for the 224-game 1980 regular season was 59,787, the highest in the league's 61-year history. NFL games in 1980 were played before 92.4 percent of total stadium capacity.

Television ratings in 1980 were the second-best in NFL history, trailing only the combined ratings of the 1976 season. All three networks posted gains, and NBC's 15.0 rating was its best ever. CBS and ABC had their best ratings since 1977, with 15.3 and 20.8 ratings, respectively. CBS Radio reported a record audience of 7 million for Monday night and special games.

1981

Oakland defeated Philadelphia 27-10 in Super Bowl XV at the Louisiana Superdome In New Orleans, to become the first wild-card team to win a Super Bowl, January 25.

Edgar F. Kaiser, Jr., purchased the Denver Broncos from Gerald and Allan Phipps, February 26.

The owners adopted a disaster plan for re-stocking a team should the club be involved in a fatal accident, March 20.

The owners awarded Super Bowl XVIII to Tampa, to be played in Tampa Stadium on January 22, 1984, June 3.

A CBS-New York Times poll showed that 48 percent of sports fans preferred football to 31 percent for baseball.

The NFL teams hosted 167 representatives from 44 predominantly black colleges during training camps for a total of 289 days. The program was adopted for renewal during each training camp period.

NFL regular-season attendance—13.6 million for an average of 60,745—set a record for the fourth year in a row. It also was the first time the per-game average exceeded 60,000. NFL games in 1981 were played before 93.8 percent of total stadium capacity.

ABC and CBS set all-time rating highs. ABC finished with a 21.7 rating and CBS with a 17.5 rating. NBC was down slightly to 13.9.

1982

San Francisco defeated Cincinnati 26-21 in Super Bowl XVI at the Pontiac Silverdome, in the first Super Bowl held in the North, January 24. The CBS telecast achieved the highest rating of any televised sports event ever, 49.1 with a 73.0 share. The game was viewed by a record 110.2 million fans. CBS Radio reported a record 14 million listeners for the game.

The NFL signed a five-year contract with the three television networks (ABC, CBS, and NBC) to televise all NFL regular-season and postseason games starting with the 1982 season.

The owners awarded the 1983, 1984, and 1985 AFC-NFC Pro Bowls to Honolulu's Aloha Stadium.

A jury ruled against the NFL in the antitrust trial brought by the Los Angeles Coliseum Commission and the Oakland Raiders, May 7. The verdict cleared the way for the Raiders to move to Los Angeles, where they defeated Green Bay 24-3 in their first preseason game, August 29.

The 1982 season was reduced from a 16-game schedule to nine as the result of a 57-day players' strike. The strike was called by the NFLPA at midnight on Monday, September 20, following the Green Bay at New York Giants game. Play resumed November 21-22 following ratification of the Collective Bargaining Agreement by NFL owners, November 17 in New York.

Under the Collective Bargaining Agreement, which was to run through the 1986 season, the NFL draft was extended through 1992 and the veteran free-agent system was left basically unchanged. A minimum salary schedule for years of experience was established; training camp and postseason pay were increased; players' medical, insurance, and retirement benefits were increased; and a severance-pay system was introduced to aid in career transition, a first in professional sports.

Despite the players' strike, the average paid attendance in 1982 was 58,472, the fifth-highest in league history.

The owners awarded the sites of two Super Bowls, December 14: Super Bowl XIX, to be played on January 20, 1985, to Stanford University Stadium in Stanford, California, with San Francisco as host team; and Super Bowl XX, to be played on January 26, 1986, to the Louisiana Superdome in New Orleans.

1983

Because of the shortened season, the NFL adopted a format of 16 teams competing in a Super Bowl Tournament for the 1982 playoffs. The NFC's number-one seed, Washington, defeated the AFC's number-two seed, Miami, 27-17 in Super Bowl XVII at the Rose Bowl in Pasadena, January 30.

Super Bowl XVII was the second-highest rated live television program of all time, giving the NFL a sweep of the top 10 live programs in television history. The game was viewed in more than 40 million homes, the largest ever for a live telecast.

Halas, the owner of the Bears and the last surviving member of the NFL's second organizational meeting, died at 88, October 31.

1984

The Los Angeles Raiders defeated Washington 38-9 in Super Bowl XVIII at Tampa Stadium, January 22. The game achieved a 46.4 rating and 71.0 share.

An 11-man group headed by H.R. (Bum) Bright purchased the Dallas Cowboys from Clint Murchison, Jr., March 20. Club president Tex Schramm was designated as managing general partner.

Patrick Bowlen purchased a majority interest in the Denver Broncos from Edgar Kaiser, Jr., March 21.

The Colts relocated to Indianapolis, March 28. Their new home became the Hoosier Dome.

The owners awarded two Super Bowl sites at their May 23-25 meetings: Super Bowl XXI, to be played on January 25, 1987, to the Rose Bowl in Pasadena; and Super Bowl XXII, to be played on January 31, 1988, to San Diego Jack Murphy Stadium.

The New York Jets moved their home games to Giants Stadium in East Rutherford, New Jersey.

Alex G. Spanos purchased a majority interest in the San Diego Chargers from Eugene V. Klein, August 28.

Houston defeated Pittsburgh 23-20 to mark the one-hundredth overtime game in regular-season play since overtime was adopted in 1974, December 2.

On the field, many all-time records were set: Dan Marino of Miami passed for 5,084 yards and 48 touchdowns; Eric Dickerson of the Los Angeles Rams rushed for 2,105 yards; Art Monk of Washington caught 106 passes; and Walter Payton of Chicago broke Jim Brown's career rushing mark, finishing the season with 13,309 yards.

According to a CBS Sports/*New York Times* survey, 53 percent of the nation's sports fans said they most enjoyed watching football, compared to 18 percent for baseball, December 2-4.

NFL paid attendance exceeded 13 million for the fifth consecutive complete regular season when 13,398,112, an average of 59,813, attended games. The figure was the second-highest in league history. Teams averaged 42.4 points per game, the second-highest total since the 1970 merger.

1985

San Francisco defeated Miami 38-16 in Super Bowl XIX at Stanford Stadium in Stanford, California, January 20. The game was viewed on television by more people than any other live event in history. President Ronald Reagan, who took his second oath of office before tossing the coin for the game, was one of 115,936,000 viewers. The game drew a 46.4 rating and a 63.0 share. In addition, 6 million people watched the Super Bowl in the United Kingdom and a similar number in Italy. Super Bowl XIX had a direct economic impact of $113.5 million on the San Francisco Bay area.

NBC Radio and the NFL entered into a two-year agreement granting NBC the radio rights to a 37-game package in each of the 1985-86 seasons, March 6. The package included 27 regular-season games and 10 postseason games.

The owners awarded two Super Bowl sites at their annual meeting, March 10-15: Super Bowl XXIII, to be played on January 22, 1989, to the proposed Dolphins Stadium in Miami; and Super Bowl XXIV, to be played on January 28, 1990, to the Louisiana Superdome in New Orleans.

Norman Braman, in partnership with Edward Leibowitz, bought the Philadelphia Eagles from Leonard Tose, April 29.

Bruce Smith, a Virginia Tech defensive lineman selected by Buffalo, was the first player chosen in the fiftieth NFL draft, April 30.

A group headed by Tom Benson, Jr., was approved to purchase the New Orleans Saints from John W. Mecom, Jr., June 3.

The NFL owners adopted a resolution calling for a series of overseas preseason games, beginning in 1986, with one game to be played in England/Europe and/or one game in Japan each year. The game would be a fifth preseason game for the clubs involved and all arrangements and selection of the clubs would be under the control of the Commissioner, May 23.

The league-wide conversion to videotape from movie film for coaching study was approved.

Commissioner Rozelle was authorized to extend the commitment to Honolulu's Aloha Stadium for the AFC-NFC Pro Bowl for 1988, 1989, and 1990, October 15.

The NFL set a single-weekend paid attendance record when 902,657 tickets were sold for the weekend of October 27-28.

A Louis Harris poll in December revealed that pro football remained the sport most followed by Americans. Fifty-nine percent of those surveyed followed pro football, compared with 54 percent who followed baseball.

The Chicago-Miami Monday game had the highest rating, 29.6, and share, 46.0, of any prime-time game in NFL history, December 2. The game was viewed in more than 25 million homes.

The NFL showed a ratings increase on all three networks for the season, gaining 4 percent on NBC, 10 on CBS, and 16 on ABC.

1986

Chicago defeated New England 46-10 in Super Bowl XX at the Louisiana Superdome, January 26. The Patriots had earned the right to play the Bears by becoming the first wild-card team to win three consecutive games on the road. The NBC telecast replaced the final episode of *M*A*S*H* as the most-viewed television program in history, with an audience of 127 million viewers, according to A.C. Nielsen figures. In addition to drawing a 48.3 rating and a 70 percent share in the United States, Super Bowl XX was televised to 59 foreign countries and beamed via satellite to the QE II. An estimated 300 million Chinese viewed a tape delay of the game in March. NBC Radio figures indicated an audience of 10 million for the game.

Super Bowl XX injected more than $100 million into the New Orleans-area economy, and fans spent $250 per day and a record $17.69 per person on game day.

The owners adopted limited use of instant replay as an officiating aid, prohibited players from wearing or otherwise displaying equipment, apparel, or other items that carry commercial names, names of organizations, or personal messages of any type, March 11.

After an 11-week trial, a jury in U.S. District Court in New York awarded the United States Football League one dollar in its $1.7 billion antitrust suit against the NFL. The jury rejected all of the USFL's television-related claims, which were the self-proclaimed heart of the USFL's case, July 29.

Chicago defeated Dallas 17-6 at Wembley Stadium in London in the first American Bowl. The game drew a sellout crowd of 82,699 and the NBC national telecast in this country produced a 12.4 rating and 36 percent share, making it the second-highest-rated daytime preseason game and highest daytime preseason television audience ever with 10.65-million viewers, August 3.

Monday Night Football became the longest-running prime-time series in the history of the ABC network.

Instant replay was used to reverse two plays in 31 preseason games. During the regular season, 374 plays were closely reviewed by replay officials, leading to 38 reversals in 224 games. Eighteen plays were closely reviewed by instant replay in 10 postseason games with three reversals.

1987

The New York Giants defeated Denver 39-20 in Super Bowl XXI and captured their first NFL title since 1956. The game, played in Pasadena's Rose Bowl, drew a sellout crowd of 101,063. According to A.C. Nielsen figures, the CBS broadcast of the game was viewed in the U.S. on television by 122.64-million people, making the telecast the second most-watched television show of all-time behind Super Bowl XX. The game was watched live or on tape in 55 foreign countries and NBC Radio's broadcast of the game was heard by a record 10.1 million people.

The NFL set an all-time paid attendance mark of 17,304,463 for all games, including preseason, regular-season, and postseason. Average regular-season game attendance (60,663) exceeded the 60,000 figure for only the second time in league history.

New three-year TV contracts with ABC, CBS, and NBC were announced for 1987-89 at the NFL annual meeting in Maui, Hawaii, March 15. Commissioner Rozelle and Broadcast Committee Chairman Art Modell also announced a three-year contract with ESPN to televise 13 prime-time games each season. The ESPN contract was the first with a cable network. However, NFL games on ESPN also were scheduled for regular television in the city of the visiting team and in the home city if the game was sold out 72 hours in advance.

Owners also voted to continue in effect for one year the instant replay system used during the 1986 season.

A special payment program was adopted to benefit nearly 1,000 former NFL players who participated in the League before the current Bert Bell NFL Pension Plan was created and made retroactive to the 1959 season. Players covered by the new program spent at least five years in the League and played all or part of their career prior to 1959. Each vested player would receive $60 per month for each year of service in the League for life.

Possible sites for Super Bowl XXV were reduced to five locations by the NFL Super Bowl XXV Site Selection Committee: Anaheim Stadium, Los Angeles Memorial Coliseum, Joe Robbie Stadium, San Diego Jack Murphy Stadium, and Tampa Stadium.

NFL and CBS Radio jointly announced agreement granting CBS the radio rights to a 40-game package in each of the next three NFL seasons, 1987-89, April 7.

NFL owners awarded Super Bowl XXV, to be played on January 27, 1991, to Tampa Stadium, May 20.

Over 400 former NFL players from the pre-1959 era received first payments from NFL owners, July 1.

The NFL's debut on ESPN produced the two highest-rated and most-watched sports programs in basic cable history. The Chicago at Miami game on August 16 drew an 8.9 rating in 3.81 million homes. Those records fell two weeks later when the Los Angeles Raiders at Dallas game achieved a 10.2 cable rating in 4.36 million homes.

Fifty-eight preseason games drew a record paid attendance of 3,116,870.

The 1987 season was reduced from a 16-game season to 15 as the result of a 24-day players' strike. The strike was called by the NFLPA on Tuesday, September 22, following the New England at New York Jets game. Games scheduled for the third weekend were canceled but the games of weeks four, five, and six were played with replacement teams. Striking players returned for the seventh week of the season, October 25.

In a three-team deal involving 10 players and/or draft choices, the Los Angeles Rams traded running back Eric Dickerson to the Indianapolis Colts for six draft choices and two players. Buffalo obtained the rights to linebacker Cornelius Bennett from Indianapolis, sending Greg Bell and three draft choices to the Rams. The Colts added Owen Gill and three draft choices of their own to complete the deal with the Rams, October 31.

The Chicago at Minnesota game became the highest-rated and most-watched sports program in basic cable history when it drew a 14.4 cable rating in 6.5 million homes, December 6.

Instant replay was used to reverse eight plays in 52 preseason games. During the strike-shortened 210-game regular season, 490 plays were closely reviewed by replay officials, leading to 57 reversals. Eighteen plays were closely reviewed by instant replay in 10 postseason games, with three reversals.

1988

Washington defeated Denver 42-10 in Super Bowl XXII to earn its second victory this decade in the NFL Championship Game. The game, played for the first time in San Diego Jack Murphy Stadium, drew a sellout crowd of 73,302. According to A.C. Nielsen figures, the ABC broadcast of the game was viewed in the U.S. on television by 115,000,000 people. The game was seen live or on tape in 60 foreign countries, including the People's Republic of China, and CBS's radio broadcast of the game was heard by 13.7 million people.

A total of 811 players shared in the postseason pool of $16.9 million, the most ever distributed in a single season.

In a unanimous 3-0 decision, the 2nd Circuit Court of Appeals in New York upheld the verdict of the jury that in July, 1986, had awarded the United States Football League one dollar in its $1.7 billion antitrust suit against the NFL. In a 91-page opinion, Judge Ralph K. Winter said the USFL sought through court decree the success it failed to gain among football fans, March 10.

By a 23-5 margin, owners voted to continue the instant replay system for the third consecutive season with the Instant Replay Official to be assigned to a regular seven-man, on-the-field crew. At the NFL annual meeting in Phoenix, Arizona, a 45-second clock was also approved to replace the 30-second clock. For a normal sequence of plays, the interval between plays was changed to 45 seconds from the time the ball is signaled dead until it is snapped on the succeeding play.

NFL owners approved the transfer of the Cardinals' franchise from St. Louis to Phoenix; approved two supplemental drafts each year—one prior to training camp and one prior to the regular season; and voted to initiate an annual series of games in Japan/Asia as early as the 1989 preseason, March 14-18.

The NFL Annual Selection Meeting returned to a separate two-day format and for the first time originated on a Sunday. ESPN drew a 3.6 rating during their seven-hour coverage of the draft, which was viewed in 1.6 million homes, April 24-25.

Art Rooney, founder and owner of the Steelers, died at 87, August 25.

Johnny Grier became the first African-American referee in NFL history, September 4.

Paid and average attendance of 934,271 and 66,734 at 14 games on October 16-17 set single weekend records.

Commissioner Rozelle announced that two teams would play a preseason game as part of the American Bowl series on August 6, 1989, in the Korakuen Tokyo Dome in Japan, December 16.

NFL regular-season paid attendance of 13,535,335 and the average of 60,427 was the third highest all-time. Buffalo set an NFL team single-season, in-house attendance mark of 622,793.

1989

San Francisco defeated Cincinnati 20-16 in Super Bowl XXIII. The game, played for the first time at Joe Robbie Stadium in Miami, was attended by a sellout crowd of 75,129. NBC's telecast of the game was watched by an estimated 110,780,000 viewers, according to A.C. Nielsen, making it the sixth most-watched program in television history. The game was seen live or on tape in 60 foreign countries, including an estimated 300 million in China. The CBS Radio broadcast of the game was heard by 11.2 million people.

Commissioner Rozelle announced his retirement, pending the naming of a successor, March 22 at the NFL annual meeting in Palm Desert, California.

Following the announcement, AFC president Lamar Hunt and NFC president Wellington Mara announced the formation of a six-man search committee composed of Art Modell, Robert Parins, Dan Rooney, and Ralph Wilson. Hunt and Mara served as co-chairmen.

By a 24-4 margin, owners voted to continue the instant replay system for the fourth straight season. A strengthened policy regarding anabolic steroids and masking agents was announced by Commissioner Rozelle. NFL clubs called for strong disciplinary measures in cases of feigned injuries and adopted a joint proposal by the Long-Range Planning and Finance committees regarding player personnel rules, March 19-23.

Two hundred twenty-nine unconditional free agents signed with new teams under management's Plan B system, April 1.

Jerry Jones purchased a majority interest in the Dallas Cowboys from H.R. (Bum) Bright, April 18.

Tex Schramm was named president of the new World League of American Football to work with a six-man committee of Dan Rooney, chairman; Norman Braman, Lamar Hunt, Victor Kiam, Mike Lynn, and Bill Walsh, April 18.

NFL and CBS Radio jointly announced agreement extending CBS's radio rights to an annual 40-game package through the 1994 season, April 18.

NFL owners awarded Super Bowl XXVI, to be played on January 26, 1992, to Minneapolis, May 24.

As of opening day, September 10, of the 229 Plan B free agents, 111 were active and 23 others were on teams' reserve lists. Ninety-two others were waived and three retired.

Art Shell was named head coach of the Los Angeles Raiders making him the NFL's first black head coach since Fritz Pollard coached the Akron Pros in 1921, October 3.

The site of the New England Patriots at San Francisco 49ers game scheduled for Candlestick Park on October 22 was switched to Stanford Stadium in the aftermath of the Bay Area Earthquake of October 17. The change was announced on October 19.

Paul Tagliabue became the seventh chief executive of the NFL on October 26 when he was chosen to succeed Commissioner Pete Rozelle on the sixth ballot of a three-day meeting in Cleveland, Ohio.

In all, 12 ballots were required to select Tagliabue. Two were conducted at a meeting in Chicago on July 6, and four at a meeting in Dallas on October 10-11. On the twelfth ballot, with Seattle absent, Tagliabue received more than the 19 affirmative votes required for election from among the 27 clubs present.

The transfer from Commissioner Rozelle to Commissioner Tagliabue took place at 12:01 A.M. on Sunday, November 5.

NFL Charities donated $1 million through United Way to benefit Bay Area earthquake victims, November 6.

NFL paid attendance of 17,399,538 was the highest total in league history. This included a total of 13,625,662 for an average of 60,829—both NFL records—for the 224-game regular season.

1990

San Francisco defeated Denver 55-10 in Super Bowl XXIV at the Louisiana Superdome, January 28. San Francisco joined Pittsburgh as the NFL's only teams to win four Super Bowls.

The NFL announced revisions in its 1990 draft eligibility rules. College juniors became eligible but must renounce their collegiate football eligibility before applying for the NFL Draft, February 16.

Commissioner Tagliabue announced NFL teams will play their 16-game schedule over 17 weeks in 1990 and 1991 and 16 games over 18 weeks in 1992 and 1993, February 27.

The NFL revised its playoff format to include two additional wild-card teams (one per conference).

Commissioner Tagliabue and Broadcast Committee Chairman Art Modell announced a four-year contract with Turner Broadcasting to televise nine Sunday-night games.

New four-year TV agreements were ratified for 1990-93 for ABC, CBS, NBC, ESPN, and TNT at the NFL annual meeting in Orlando, Florida, March 12. The contracts totaled $3.6 billion, the largest in TV history.

The NFL announced plans to expand its American Bowl series of preseason games. In addition to games in London and Tokyo, American Bowl games were scheduled for Berlin, Germany, and Montreal, Canada, in 1990.

For the fifth straight year, NFL owners voted to continue a limited system of Instant Replay. Beginning in 1990, the replay official will have a two-minute time limit to make a decision. The vote was 21-7, March 12.

Commissioner Tagliabue announced the formation of a Committee on Expansion and Realignment, March 13. He also named a Player Advisory Council, comprised of 12 former NFL players, March 14.

One-hundred eighty-four Plan B unconditional free agents signed with new teams, April 2.

Commissioner Tagliabue appointed Dr. John Lombardo as the League's Drug Advisor for Anabolic Steroids, April 25 and named Dr. Lawrence Brown as the League's Advisor for Drugs of Abuse, May 17.

NFL owners awarded Super Bowl XXVIII, to be played in 1994, to the proposed Georgia Dome, May 23.

Commissioner Tagliabue named NFL referee Jerry Seeman as NFL Director of Officiating, replacing Art McNally, who announced his retirement after 31 years on the field and at the league office, July 12.

NFL International Week was celebrated with four preseason games in seven days in Tokyo, London, Berlin, and Montreal. More than 200,000 fans on three continents attended the four games, August 4-11.

Commissioner Tagliabue announced the NFL Teacher of the Month program in which the League furnishes grants and scholarships in recognition of teachers who provided a positive influence upon NFL players in elementary and secondary schools, September 20.

For the first time since 1957, every NFL club won at least one of its first four games, October 1.

NFL total paid attendance of 17,665,671 was the highest total in League history. The regular-season total paid attendance of 13,959,896 and average of 62,321 for 224 games were the highest ever, surpassing the previous records set in the 1989 season.

1991

The New York Giants defeated Buffalo 20-19 in Super Bowl XXV to capture their second title in five years. The game was played before a sellout crowd of 73,813 at Tampa Stadium and became the first Super Bowl decided by one point, January 26. The ABC broadcast of the game was seen by more than 112-million people in the United States and was seen live or taped in 60 other countries.

NFL playoff games earned the top television rating spot of the week for each week of the month-long playoffs, January 29.

A total of 693 players shared in the postseason pool of $14.9 million.

New York businessman Robert Tisch purchased a 50 percent interest in the New York Giants from Mrs. Helen Mara Nugent and her children, Tim Mara and Maura Mara Concannon, February 2.

Commissioner Tagliabue named Neil Austrian to the newly created position of President of the NFL to be chief operating officer for League-wide business and financial operations, February 27.

NFL clubs voted to continue a limited system of Instant Replay for the sixth consecutive year. The vote was 21-7, March 19.

The NFL launched the World League of American Football, the first sports league to operate on a weekly basis on two separate continents, March 23.

NFL Charities presented a $250,000 donation to the United Service Organization. The donation was the second largest single grant ever by NFL Charities, April 5.

Commissioner Tagliabue named Harold Henderson as Executive Vice President for Labor Relations and Chairman of the NFL Management Council Executive Committee, April 8.

Russell Maryland, a University of Miami defensive lineman, was selected by Dallas, becoming the first player chosen in the 1991 NFL draft, April 21.

NFL clubs approved a recommendation by the Expansion and Realignment Committee to add two teams for the 1994 season, resulting in six divisions of five teams each, May 22.

NFL clubs awarded Super Bowl XXIX, to be played on January 29, 1995, to Miami, May 23.

"NFL International Week" featured six 1990 playoff teams playing nationally televised games in London, Berlin, and Tokyo on July 28 and August 3-4. The games drew more than 150,000 fans.

Paul Brown, founder of the Cleveland Browns and Cincinnati Bengals, died at age 82, August 5.

NFL clubs approved a resolution establishing an international division, reporting to the President of the NFL. A three-year financial plan for the World League was approved by NFL clubs at a meeting in Dallas, October 23.

1992

The NFL agreed to provide a minimum of $2.5 million in financial support to the NFL Alumni Association and assistance to NFL Alumni-related programs. The agreement included contributions from NFL Charities to the Pre-59ers and Dire Need Programs for former players, January 25.

The Washington Redskins defeated the Buffalo Bills 37-24 in Super Bowl XXVI to capture their third world championship in 10 years, January 26. The game was played before a sellout crowd of 63,130 at the Hubert H. Humphrey Metrodome in Minneapolis and attracted the second largest television audience in Super Bowl history. The CBS broadcast was seen by more than 123 million people nationally, second only to the 127 million who viewed Super Bowl XX.

For the third consecutive season, NFL total paid attendance reached a record level. Total paid attendance was 17,752,139 for the 296 preseason, regular-season, and postseason games, February 3.

The use in officiating of a limited system of Instant Replay for a seventh consecutive year was not approved. The vote was 17-11 in favor of approval (21 votes were required), March 18.

Steve Emtman, a University of Washington defensive lineman, was selected by Indianapolis, becoming the first player chosen in the 1992 NFL draft, April 26.

St. Louis businessman James Orthwein purchased controlling interest in the New England Patriots from Victor Kiam, May 11.

In a Harris Poll taken during the NFL offseason, professional football again was declared the nation's most popular sport. Professional football finished atop similar surveys conducted by Harris in 1985 and 1989, May 23.

NFL clubs accepted the report of the Expansion Committee at a league meeting in Pasadena. The report names five cities as finalists for the two expansion teams—Baltimore, Charlotte, Jacksonville, Memphis, and St. Louis, May 19.

At a league meeting in Dallas, NFL clubs approved a proposal by the World League Board of Directors to restructure the World League and place future emphasis on its international success, September 17.

1993

The NFL and lawyers for the players announced a settlement of various lawsuits and an agreement on the terms of a seven-year deal that included a new player system to be in place through the 1999 season, January 6.

Commissioner Tagliabue announced the establishment of the "NFL World Partnership Program" to develop amateur football internationally through a series of clinics conducted by former NFL players and coaches, January 14.

As part of Super Bowl XXVII, the NFL announced the creation of the first NFL Youth Education Town, a facility located in south central Los Angeles for inner city youth. January 25.

The Dallas Cowboys defeated the Buffalo Bills 52-17 in Super Bowl XXVII to capture their first NFL title since 1978. The game was played before a crowd of 98,374 at the Rose Bowl in Pasadena, California. The NBC broadcast of the game was the most watched program in television history and was seen by 133,400,000 people in the United States. The game also was seen live or taped in 101 other countries. The rating for the game was 45.1, the tenth highest for any televised sports event, January 31.

A total of 695 players shared in the postseason pool of $14.9 million, February 15.

For the fourth consecutive season, the NFL total paid attendance reached a record level. Total paid attendance was 17,784,354 for the 296 preseason, regular-season, and postseason games, March 4.

NFL clubs awarded Super Bowl XXX to the city of Phoenix, to be played on January 28, 1996, at Sun Devil Stadium, March 23.

Drew Bledsoe, a quarterback from Washington State, was selected by New England, becoming the first player chosen in the 1993 NFL draft, April 25.

The NFL and the NFL Players Association officially signed a 7-year Collective Bargaining Agreement in Washington, D.C., which guarantees more than $1 billion in pension, health, and post-career benefits for current and retired players—the most extensive benefits plan in pro sports. It was the NFL's first CBA since the 1982 agreement expired in 1987, June 29.

Ron Bernard was named president of NFL Enterprises, a newly formed division of the NFL responsible for NFL Films, home video, and special domestic and international television programming, August 19.

NFL announced plans to allow fans, for the first time ever, to join players and coaches in selecting the annual

AFC and NFC Pro Bowl teams, October 12.

NFL clubs unanimously awarded the league's twenty-ninth franchise to the Carolina Panthers at a meeting in Chicago. NFL clubs also awarded Super Bowl XXXI to New Orleans and Super Bowl XXXII to San Diego, October 26.

At the same meeting in Chicago, NFL clubs approved a plan to form a European league with joint venture partners, October 27.

Don Shula became the winningest coach in NFL history when Miami beat Philadelphia to give Shula his 325th victory, one more than George Halas, November 14.

NFL clubs awarded the league's thirtieth franchise to the Jacksonville Jaguars at a meeting in Chicago, November 30.

The NFL announced new 4-year television agreements with ABC, ESPN, TNT, and NFL newcomer FOX, which took over the NFC package from CBS, December 18.

The NFL completed its new TV agreements by announcing that NBC would retain the rights to the AFC package, December 20.

1994

The NFL announced that a regular-season paid attendance record was set in 1993. Attendance averaged 62,354, topping the previous record of 62,321 set in 1990, January 6.

The Dallas Cowboys defeated the Buffalo Bills 30-13 in Super Bowl XXVIII to become the fifth team to win back-to-back Super Bowl titles. The game was viewed by the largest U.S. audience in television history—134.8 million people. The game's 45.5 rating was the highest for a Super Bowl since 1987 and the tenth highest-rated Super Bowl ever, January 30.

NFL clubs unanimously approved the transfer of the New England Patriots from James Orthwein to Robert Kraft at a meeting in Orlando, February 22.

In an effort to increase offensive production, NFL clubs at the league's annual meeting in Orlando adopted a package of changes, including modifications in line play, chucking rules, and the roughing-the-passer rule, plus the adoption of the two-point conversion and moving the spot of the kickoff back to the 30-yard line, March 22.

NFL clubs approved the transfer of the majority interest in the Miami Dolphins from the Robbie family to H. Wayne Huizenga, March 23.

The NFL and FOX announced the formation of a joint venture to create a six-team World League to begin play in Europe in April, 1995, March 23.

The NFL announced a total paid attendance record for the fifth consecutive year, with 17,951,831 in paid attendance for all 1993 games, March 23.

Dan Wilkinson, a defensive tackle from Ohio State, was selected by Cincinnati as the first overall selection in the draft, April 24.

The Carolina Panthers earned the right to select first in the 1995 NFL draft by winning a coin toss with the Jacksonville Jaguars. The Jaguars received the second selection in the 1995 draft, April 24.

NFL clubs approved the transfer of the Philadelphia Eagles from Norman Braman to Jeffrey Lurie, May 6.

The NFL launched "NFL Sunday Ticket," a new season subscription service for satellite television dish owners, June 1.

Sara Levinson, president/business director of MTV, was named president of NFL Properties, July 12.

An all-time NFL record crowd of 112,376 attended the American Bowl game between Dallas and Houston in Mexico City. It concluded the biggest American Bowl series in NFL history with four games attracting a record 256,666 fans, August 15.

The NFL 75th Anniversary All-Time Team was announced at a press conference at Radio City Music Hall, August 30.

The NFL reached agreement on a new seven-year contract with its game officials, September 22.

The NFL Management Council and the NFL Players Association announced an agreement on the formulation and implementation of the most comprehensive drug and alcohol policy in sports, October 28.

At an NFL meeting in Chicago, Commissioner Tagliabue slotted the two new expansion teams into the AFC Central (Jacksonville Jaguars) and NFC West (Carolina Panthers) for the 1995 season only. He also appointed a special committee on realignment to make recommendations on the 1996 season and beyond, November 2.

The NFL set a regular-season paid attendance record for the second consecutive year, topping 14 million for the first time (14,034,977), December 27.

1995

The San Francisco 49ers became the first team to win five Super Bowls when they defeated the San Diego Chargers 49-26 in Super Bowl XXIX at Joe Robbie Stadium in Miami, January 29.

Carolina and Jacksonville stocked their expansion rosters with a total of 66 players from other NFL teams in a veteran player allocation draft in New York, February 16.

CBS Radio and the NFL agreed to a new four-year contract for an annual 53-game package of games, continuing a relationship that spanned 15 of the past 17 years, February 22.

NFL total paid attendance for all 1994 season games reached a record level for the sixth consecutive year, exceeding 18 million for the first time (18,010,264), March 9.

NFL clubs approved the transfer of the Tampa Bay Buccaneers from the estate of the late Hugh Culverhouse to South Florida businessman Malcolm Glazer, March 13.

A total of $20.3 million, the largest NFL postseason pool ever, was divided among 729 players who participated in the 1994 playoffs, March 13.

A series of safety-related rules changes were adopted at a league meeting in Phoenix, primarily related to the use of the helmet against defenseless players, March 14.

After a two-year hiatus, the World League of American Football returned to action with six teams in Europe, April 8.

The NFL became the first major sports league to establish a site on the Internet system of on-line computer communication, April 10.

The transfer of the Rams from Los Angeles to St. Louis was approved by a vote of the NFL clubs at a meeting in Dallas, April 12.

ABC's *NFL Monday Night Football* finished the 1994-95 television season as the fifth highest-rated show out of 146 with a 17.8 average rating, the highest finish in the 25-year history of the series, April 18.

Ki-Jana Carter, a running back from Penn State, was selected by the Cincinnati Bengals as the first overall selection in the draft, April 22.

In an ABC News Poll taken during the NFL offseason, America's sports fans chose football as their favorite spectator sport by more than a 2-to-1 margin over basketball and baseball (35%-16%-12%), April 26.

The Frankfurt Galaxy defeated the Amsterdam Admirals 26-22 to win the 1995 World Bowl before a crowd of 23,847 in Amsterdam's Olympic Stadium, June 23.

Former NFL quarterback and Rhein Fire general manager Oliver Luck was named President of the World League, July 13.

The transfer of the Raiders from Los Angeles to Oakland was approved by a vote of the NFL clubs at a meeting in Chicago, July 22.

Jacksonville Municipal Stadium opened before a sold-out crowd of more than 70,000 for the first preseason game in Jaguars history, August 18.

NFL Charities and 50 NFL players donated $1 million to the United Negro College Fund in honor of the fiftieth anniversary of the UNCF and the integration of the modern NFL, September 15.

The Pro Football Hall Of Fame in Canton, Ohio, completed an $8.9 million expansion including a $4 million contribution by the NFL clubs, October 14.

The Trans World Dome opened in St. Louis before a sold-out crowd of 65,598 as the Rams defeated the Carolina Panthers 28-17, November 12.

NFL paid attendance totaled 963,521 for 15 games in Week 12, the highest weekend total in the league's 76-year history, November 19-20.

On the field, many significant records and milestones were achieved: Miami's Dan Marino surpassed Pro Football Hall of Famer Fran Tarkenton in four major passing categories—attempts, completions, yards, and touchdowns—to become the NFL's all-time career leader. San Francisco's Jerry Rice became the all-time reception and receiving-yardage leader with career totals of 942 catches and 15,123 yards. Dallas' Emmitt Smith scored 25 touchdowns, breaking the season record of 24 set by Washington's John Riggins in 1983.

1996

The Dallas Cowboys won their third Super Bowl title in four years when they defeated the Pittsburgh Steelers 27-17 in Super Bowl XXX at Sun Devil Stadium in Tempe, Arizona. The game was viewed by the largest audience in U.S. television history—138.5 million people, January 28.

An agreement between the NFL and the city of Cleveland regarding the Cleveland Browns' relocation was approved by a vote of the NFL clubs, February 9. According to the agreement, the city of Cleveland retained the Browns' heritage and records, including the name, logo, colors, history, playing records, trophies, and memorabilia, and committed to building a new 72,000-seat stadium for a reactivated Browns' franchise to begin play there no later than 1999. Art Modell received approval to move his franchise to Baltimore and rename it.

NFL total paid attendance for all 1995 games reached a record level for the seventh consecutive year, exceeding 19 million for the first time (19,202,757), March 7.

A total of $21.5 million, the largest NFL postseason pool ever, was divided among 717 players who participated in the 1995 playoffs, March 11.

Keyshawn Johnson, a wide receiver from Southern California, was selected by the New York Jets as the first overall selection in the draft, April 20.

The transfer of the Oilers from Houston to Nashville for the 1998 season was approved by a vote of the NFL clubs at a meeting in Atlanta, April 30.

The Scottish Claymores defeated the Frankfurt Galaxy 32-27 to win the 1996 World Bowl in front of 38,982 at Murrayfield Stadium in Edinburgh, Scotland, June 23.

The NFL returned to Baltimore when the new Baltimore Ravens defeated the Philadelphia Eagles 17-9 in a preseason game before a crowd of 63,804 at Memorial Stadium, August 3.

Ericsson Stadium opened in Charlotte, North Carolina before a crowd of 65,350 as the Carolina Panthers defeated the Chicago Bears 30-12 in a preseason game, August 3.

Points scored totaled 762 and NFL paid attendance totaled 964,079 for 15 games in Week 11, the highest weekend totals in either category in the league's 77-year history, November 10-11.

Former NFL Commissioner Pete Rozelle died at his home in Rancho Santa Fe, California. Rozelle, regarded as the premiere commissioner in sports history, led the NFL for 29 years, from 1960-1989, December 6.

1997

Indianapolis Colts owner Robert Irsay died from complications related to a stroke he suffered in 1995. Irsay acquired the club in 1972 when he traded his Los Angeles Rams to Carrol Rosenbloom for the Colts. He later moved the Colts from Baltimore to Indianapolis in 1984, January 14.

The Green Bay Packers won their first NFL title in 29 years by defeating the New England Patriots 35-21 in Super Bowl XXXI at the Louisiana Superdome in New Orleans. The game was viewed by the fourth-largest audience in U.S. television history—128 million people, January 26.

A total of $24.3 million, the largest NFL postseason pool ever, was divided among 730 players who participated in the 1996 playoffs, March 11.

The rules governing cross-ownership were modified, permitting NFL club owners to also own teams in other sports in their home market or markets without NFL teams. The vote was 24-5 (one abstention) in favor of approval, March 11.

Washington Redskins owner Jack Kent Cooke died at his home in Washington, D.C. Cooke became majority owner in 1974 and the Redskins won three Super Bowls under his leadership, April 6.

Orlando Pace, an offensive tackle from Ohio State, was selected by the St. Louis Rams as the first overall selection in the draft, April 19.

The Barcelona Dragons defeated the Rhein Fire 38-24 to win the 1997 World Bowl in front of 31,100 fans at Estadi Olimpic de Montjuic in Barcelona, Spain, June 22.

NFL clubs approved the transfer of the Seattle Seahawks from Ken Behring to Paul Allen, August 19.

Jack Kent Cooke Stadium opened in Raljon, Maryland before a crowd of 78,270 as the Washington Redskins defeated the Arizona Cardinals 19-13, September 14.

The 10,000th regular-season game in NFL history was played when the Seattle Seahawks defeated the Tennessee Oilers 16-13 at the Kingdome in Seattle, October 5.

Atlanta Falcons owner Rankin Smith died of heart failure three days prior to his seventy-third birthday. Smith was the founder of the Falcons and was instrumental in bringing Super Bowls XXVIII and XXXIV to Atlanta, October 26.

NFL paid attendance totaled 999,778 for 15 games in Week 12, the highest weekend total in league history, November 16-17.

Regular-season paid attendance in 1997 rose to 14,967,314 for an average of 62,364 per game. That total was the second-highest all-time, behind the 15,043,562 of 1995, December 23.

1998

The NFL reached agreement on record eight-year television contracts with four networks. ABC (*Monday Night Football*) and FOX (NFC) retained their previous rights, CBS took over the AFC package from NBC, and ESPN won the right to broadcast the entire Sunday night cable package, January 13.

The World League was renamed the NFL Europe League, January 22.

The Denver Broncos won their first Super Bowl by defeating the defending champion Green Bay Packers 31-24 in Super Bowl XXXII at Qualcomm Stadium in San Diego. The game tied Super Bowl XXVII for the third-largest audience in U.S. television history with 133.4 million viewers, January 25.

The NFL clubs approved a six-year extension of the Collective Bargaining Agreement through 2003. The extended CBA also created a $100 million fund for youth football, March 22.

The NFL clubs unanimously approved an expansion team for Cleveland to fulfill the commitment to return the Browns to the field in 1999, March 23.

NFL paid attendance of 19,049,886 for all games played during the 1997 season was the second highest in league history. In 1995, 19,202,757 fans paid to attend games, March 23.

A total of $25.1 million, the largest NFL postseason pool ever, was divided among 737 players who participated in the 1997 playoffs, March 24.

Peyton Manning, a quarterback from Tennessee, was selected by the Indianapolis Colts as the first overall selection in the draft, April 18.

The Rhein Fire defeated the Frankfurt Galaxy 34-10 to win the 1998 World Bowl in front of 47,846 fans in Frankfurt's Waldstadion—the biggest crowd to witness a World Bowl since 1991, June 14.

NFL clubs approved the transfer of the Minnesota Vikings from a 10-man ownership group to Red McCombs, July 28.

The NFL Stadium at Camden Yards opened in Baltimore, Maryland before a crowd of 65,938 as the Baltimore Ravens defeated the Chicago Bears 19-14 in a preseason game, August 8.

Raymond James Stadium opened in Tampa, Florida before a crowd of 62,410 as the Tampa Bay Buccaneers defeated the Chicago Bears 27-15, September 20.

NFL paid attendance totaled 997,835 for 15 games in Week 1, the highest opening weekend total in league history and the second-highest total ever. In 1997, paid attendance totaled 999,778 for 15 games in Week 12, September 6-7.

A Harris Poll says 55 percent of adults follow professional football, up 4 percent from 1997 and 6 percent from 1992, October 15.

Tennessee Oilers owner Bud Adams announced the team will change its name to the Tennessee Titans following the 1998 season. The NFL announced that the name Oilers will be retired–a first in league history, November 14.

1999

The Denver Broncos won their second consecutive Super Bowl title by defeating the NFC champion Atlanta Falcons 34-19 in Super Bowl XXXIII at Pro Player Stadium in Miami. The game was viewed by 127.5 million viewers, the sixth most-watched program in U.S. television history, January 31.

Jim Pyne, a center allocated by the Detroit Lions, was the first selection of the Cleveland Browns in the 1999 NFL Expansion Draft. The Browns eventually selected 37 players, February 9.

CBS Radio/Westwood One agreed to a 3-year extension of their exclusive national radio rights to NFL games, March 11.

NFL paid attendance of 19,741,493 for all games played during the 1998 season was the highest in league history, topping the 19,202,757 fans who paid to attend games in 1995. The 1998 regular-season total paid attendance of 15,364,873 for an average of 64,020 were also records, March 15.

By a vote of 28-3, the owners adopted an instant replay system as an officiating aid for the 1999 season, March 17.

Tim Couch, a quarterback from Kentucky, was selected by the Cleveland Browns as the first overall selection in the draft, April 17.

New York Jets owner Leon Hess died from complications of a blood disease. Hess had been involved in the ownership of the Jets since 1963 and was sole owner of the club since 1984, May 9.

A group led by Washington area businessman Daniel Snyder is approved by NFL clubs as the new owner of the Washington Redskins at a league meeting in Atlanta, May 25.

NFL COMMISSIONERS AND PRESIDENTS*

1920 ....Jim Thorpe, President
1921-39.................Joe Carr, President
1939-41 ....Carl Storck, President
1941-46 ....Elmer Layden, Commissioner
1946-59 ....Bert Bell, Commissioner
1960-89 ....Pete Rozelle, Commissioner
1989-present...............Paul Tagliabue, Commissioner

**NFL treasurer Austin Gunsel served as president in the office of the commissioner following the death of Bert Bell (Oct. 11, 1959) until the election of Pete Rozelle (Jan. 26, 1960).*

PAST STANDINGS

1998

AMERICAN CONFERENCE

Eastern Division

	W	L	T	Pct.	Pts.	OP
N.Y. Jets	12	4	0	.750	416	266
Miami*	10	6	0	.625	321	265
Buffalo*	10	6	0	.625	400	333
New England*	9	7	0	.563	337	329
Indianapolis	3	13	0	.188	310	444

Central Division

	W	L	T	Pct.	Pts.	OP
Jacksonville	11	5	0	.688	392	338
Tennessee	8	8	0	.500	330	320
Pittsburgh	7	9	0	.438	263	303
Baltimore	6	10	0	.375	269	335
Cincinnati	3	13	0	.188	268	452

Western Division

	W	L	T	Pct.	Pts.	OP
Denver	14	2	0	.875	501	309
Oakland	8	8	0	.500	288	356
Seattle	8	8	0	.500	372	310
Kansas City	7	9	0	.438	327	363
San Diego	5	11	0	.313	241	342

NATIONAL CONFERENCE

Eastern Division

	W	L	T	Pct.	Pts.	OP
Dallas	10	6	0	.625	381	275
Arizona*	9	7	0	.563	325	378
N.Y. Giants	8	8	0	.500	287	309
Washington	6	10	0	.375	319	421
Philadelphia	3	13	0	.188	161	344

Central Division

	W	L	T	Pct.	Pts.	OP
Minnesota	15	1	0	.938	556	296
Green Bay*	11	5	0	.688	408	319
Tampa Bay	8	8	0	.500	314	295
Detroit	5	11	0	.313	306	378
Chicago	4	12	0	.250	276	368

Western Division

	W	L	T	Pct.	Pts.	OP
Atlanta	14	2	0	.875	442	289
San Francisco*	12	4	0	.750	479	328
New Orleans	6	10	0	.375	305	359
Carolina	4	12	0	.250	336	413
St. Louis	4	12	0	.250	285	378

**Wild-Card qualifier for playoffs*

Miami finished ahead of Buffalo based on better net division points (6 to Bills' 0). Oakland finished ahead of Seattle based on head-to-head sweep (2-0). Carolina finished ahead of St. Louis based on head-to-head sweep (2-0).

AFC Wild Card Playoff: MIAMI 24, Buffalo 17; JACKSONVILLE 25, New England 10
NFC Wild Card Playoff: Arizona 20, DALLAS 7; SAN FRANCISCO 30, Green Bay 27
AFC Divisional Playoff: DENVER 38, Miami 3; N.Y. JETS 34, Jacksonville 24
NFC Divisional Playoff: ATLANTA 20, San Francisco 18; MINNESOTA 41, Arizona 21
AFC Championship: DENVER 23, N.Y. Jets 10
NFC Championship: ATLANTA 30, Minnesota 27 (OT)
Super Bowl XXXIII: Denver (AFC) 34, Atlanta (NFC) 19, at Pro Player Stadium, Miami, Florida

In Past Standings section, home teams in playoff games are indicated by capital letters.

1997

AMERICAN CONFERENCE

Eastern Division

	W	L	T	Pct.	Pts.	OP
New England	10	6	0	.625	369	289
Miami*	9	7	0	.563	339	327
N.Y. Jets	9	7	0	.563	348	287
Buffalo	6	10	0	.375	255	367
Indianapolis	3	13	0	.188	313	401

Central Division

	W	L	T	Pct.	Pts.	OP
Pittsburgh	11	5	0	.688	372	307
Jacksonville*	11	5	0	.688	394	318
Tennessee	8	8	0	.500	333	310
Cincinnati	7	9	0	.438	355	405
Baltimore	6	9	1	.406	326	345

Western Division

	W	L	T	Pct.	Pts.	OP
Kansas City	13	3	0	.813	375	232
Denver*	12	4	0	.750	472	287
Seattle	8	8	0	.500	365	362
Oakland	4	12	0	.250	324	419
San Diego	4	12	0	.250	266	425

NATIONAL CONFERENCE

Eastern Division

	W	L	T	Pct.	Pts.	OP
N.Y. Giants	10	5	1	.656	307	265
Washington	8	7	1	.531	327	289
Philadelphia	6	9	1	.406	317	372
Dallas	6	10	0	.375	304	314
Arizona	4	12	0	.250	283	379

Central Division

	W	L	T	Pct.	Pts.	OP
Green Bay	13	3	0	.813	422	282
Tampa Bay*	10	6	0	.625	299	263
Detroit*	9	7	0	.563	379	306
Minnesota*	9	7	0	.563	354	359
Chicago	4	12	0	.250	263	421

Western Division

	W	L	T	Pct.	Pts.	OP
San Francisco	13	3	0	.813	375	265
Carolina	7	9	0	.438	265	314
Atlanta	7	9	0	.438	320	361
New Orleans	6	10	0	.375	237	327
St. Louis	5	11	0	.313	299	359

**Wild-Card qualifier for playoffs*

Miami finished ahead of New York Jets based on head-to-head sweep (2-0). Pittsburgh finished ahead of Jacksonville based on better net division points (78 to Jaguars' 23). Oakland finished ahead of San Diego based on better division record (2-6 to Chargers' 1-7). Detroit finished ahead of Minnesota based on head-to-head sweep (2-0). Carolina finished ahead of Atlanta based on head-to-head sweep (2-0).

Wild-Card playoffs: DENVER 42, Jacksonville 17; NEW ENGLAND 17, Miami 3
Divisional playoffs: PITTSBURGH 7, New England 6; Denver 14, KANSAS CITY 10
AFC championship: Denver 24, PITTSBURGH 21
Wild-Card playoffs: Minnesota 23, N.Y. GIANTS 22; TAMPA BAY 20, Detroit 10
Divisional playoffs: SAN FRANCISCO 38, Minnesota 22; GREEN BAY 21, Tampa Bay 7
NFC championship: Green Bay 23, SAN FRANCISCO 10
Super Bowl XXXII: Denver (AFC) 31, Green Bay (NFC) 24, at Qualcomm Stadium, San Diego, California

1996

AMERICAN CONFERENCE

Eastern Division

	W	L	T	Pct.	Pts.	OP
New England	11	5	0	.688	418	313
Buffalo*	10	6	0	.625	319	266
Indianapolis*	9	7	0	.563	317	334
Miami	8	8	0	.500	339	325
N.Y. Jets	1	15	0	.063	279	454

Central Division

	W	L	T	Pct.	Pts.	OP
Pittsburgh	10	6	0	.625	344	257
Jacksonville*	9	7	0	.563	325	335
Cincinnati	8	8	0	.500	372	369
Houston	8	8	0	.500	345	319
Baltimore	4	12	0	.250	371	441

Western Division

	W	L	T	Pct.	Pts.	OP
Denver	13	3	0	.813	391	275
Kansas City	9	7	0	.563	297	300
San Diego	8	8	0	.500	310	376
Oakland	7	9	0	.438	340	293
Seattle	7	9	0	.438	317	376

NATIONAL CONFERENCE

Eastern Division

	W	L	T	Pct.	Pts.	OP
Dallas	10	6	0	.625	286	250
Philadelphia*	10	6	0	.625	363	341
Washington	9	7	0	.563	364	312
Arizona	7	9	0	.438	300	397
N.Y. Giants	6	10	0	.375	242	297

Central Division

	W	L	T	Pct.	Pts.	OP
Green Bay	13	3	0	.813	456	210
Minnesota*	9	7	0	.563	298	315
Chicago	7	9	0	.438	283	305
Tampa Bay	6	10	0	.375	221	293
Detroit	5	11	0	.313	302	368

Western Division

	W	L	T	Pct.	Pts.	OP
Carolina	12	4	0	.750	367	218
San Francisco*	12	4	0	.750	398	257
St. Louis	6	10	0	.375	303	409
Atlanta	3	13	0	.188	309	461
New Orleans	3	13	0	.188	229	339

**Wild-Card qualifier for playoffs*

Jacksonville finished ahead of Indianapolis and Kansas City based on better conference record (7-5 to Colts' 6-6 and Chiefs' 5-7). Indianapolis was third Wild Card based on head-to-head victory over Kansas City (1-0). Cincinnati finished ahead of Houston based on better net division points (19 to Oilers' 11). Oakland finished ahead of Seattle based on better division record (3-5 to Seahawks' 2-6). Dallas finished ahead of Philadelphia based on better record against common opponents (8-5 to Eagles' 7-6). Minnesota was third Wild Card based on better conference record than Washington (8-4 to Redskins' 6-6). Carolina finished ahead of San Francisco based on head-to-head sweep (2-0). Atlanta finished ahead of New Orleans based on head-to-head sweep (2-0).

Wild-Card playoffs: Jacksonville 30, BUFFALO 27; PITTSBURGH 42, Indianapolis 14
Divisional playoffs: Jacksonville 30, DENVER 27; NEW ENGLAND 28, Pittsburgh 3
AFC championship: NEW ENGLAND 20, Jacksonville 6
Wild-Card playoffs: DALLAS 40, Minnesota 15; SAN FRANCISCO 14, Philadelphia 0
Divisional playoffs: GREEN BAY 35, San Francisco 14; CAROLINA 26, Dallas 17
NFC championship: GREEN BAY 30, Carolina 13
Super Bowl XXXI: Green Bay (NFC) 35, New England (AFC) 21, at Louisiana Superdome, New Orleans, Louisiana

1995

AMERICAN CONFERENCE

Eastern Division

	W	L	T	Pct.	Pts.	OP
Buffalo	10	6	0	.625	350	335
Indianapolis*	9	7	0	.563	331	316
Miami*	9	7	0	.563	398	332
New England	6	10	0	.375	294	377
N.Y. Jets	3	13	0	.188	233	384

Central Division

	W	L	T	Pct.	Pts.	OP
Pittsburgh	11	5	0	.688	407	327
Cincinnati	7	9	0	.438	349	374
Houston	7	9	0	.438	348	324
Cleveland	5	11	0	.313	289	356
Jacksonville	4	12	0	.250	275	404

Western Division

	W	L	T	Pct.	Pts.	OP
Kansas City	13	3	0	.813	358	241
San Diego*	9	7	0	.563	321	323
Seattle	8	8	0	.500	363	366
Denver	8	8	0	.500	388	345
Oakland	8	8	0	.500	348	332

NATIONAL CONFERENCE

Eastern Division

	W	L	T	Pct.	Pts.	OP
Dallas	12	4	0	.750	435	291
Philadelphia*	10	6	0	.625	318	338
Washington	6	10	0	.375	326	359
N.Y. Giants	5	11	0	.313	290	340
Arizona	4	12	0	.250	275	422

Central Division

	W	L	T	Pct.	Pts.	OP
Green Bay	11	5	0	.688	404	314
Detroit*	10	6	0	.625	436	336
Chicago	9	7	0	.563	392	360
Minnesota	8	8	0	.500	412	385
Tampa Bay	7	9	0	.438	238	335

Western Division

	W	L	T	Pct.	Pts.	OP
San Francisco	11	5	0	.688	457	258
Atlanta*	9	7	0	.563	362	349
St. Louis	7	9	0	.438	309	418
Carolina	7	9	0	.438	289	325
New Orleans	7	9	0	.438	319	348

**Wild-Card qualifier for playoffs*

Indianapolis finished ahead of Miami based on head-to-head sweep (2-0). San Diego was first Wild Card based on head-to-head victory over Indianapolis (1-0). Cincinnati finished ahead of Houston based on better division record (4-4 to Oilers' 3-5). Seattle finished ahead of Denver and Oakland based on best head-to-head record (3-1 to Broncos' 2-2 and Raiders' 1-3). Denver finished ahead of Oakland based on head-to-head sweep (2-0). Philadelphia was first Wild Card ahead of Detroit based on better conference record (9-3 to Lions' 7-5). Atlanta was third Wild Card ahead of Chicago based on better record against common opponents (4-2 to Bears' 3-3). St. Louis finished ahead of Carolina and New Orleans based on best head-to-head record (3-1 to Panthers' 1-3 and Saints' 2-2). Carolina finished ahead of New Orleans based on better conference record (4-8 to 3-9).

Wild-Card playoffs: BUFFALO 37, Miami 22; Indianapolis 35, SAN DIEGO 20
Divisional playoffs: PITTSBURGH 40, Buffalo 21; Indianapolis 10, KANSAS CITY 7
AFC championship: PITTSBURGH 20, Indianapolis 16
Wild-Card playoffs: PHILADELPHIA 58, Detroit 37; GREEN BAY 37, Atlanta 20
Divisional playoffs: Green Bay 27, SAN FRANCISCO 17; DALLAS 30, Philadelphia 11
NFC championship: DALLAS 38, Green Bay 27
Super Bowl XXX: Dallas (NFC) 27, Pittsburgh (AFC)17, at Sun Devil Stadium, Tempe, Arizona

1994

AMERICAN CONFERENCE

Eastern Division

	W	L	T	Pct.	Pts.	OP
Miami	10	6	0	.625	389	327
New England*	10	6	0	.625	351	312
Indianapolis	8	8	0	.500	307	320
Buffalo	7	9	0	.438	340	356
N.Y. Jets	6	10	0	.375	264	320

Central Division

	W	L	T	Pct.	Pts.	OP
Pittsburgh	12	4	0	.750	316	234
Cleveland*	11	5	0	.688	340	204
Cincinnati	3	13	0	.188	276	406
Houston	2	14	0	.125	226	352

Western Division

	W	L	T	Pct.	Pts.	OP
San Diego	11	5	0	.688	381	306
Kansas City*	9	7	0	.563	319	298
L.A. Raiders	9	7	0	.563	303	327
Denver	7	9	0	.438	347	396
Seattle	6	10	0	.375	287	323

NATIONAL CONFERENCE

Eastern Division

	W	L	T	Pct.	Pts.	OP
Dallas	12	4	0	.750	414	248
N.Y. Giants	9	7	0	.563	279	305
Arizona	8	8	0	.500	235	267
Philadelphia	7	9	0	.438	308	308
Washington	3	13	0	.188	320	412

Central Division

	W	L	T	Pct.	Pts.	OP
Minnesota	10	6	0	.625	356	314
Green Bay*	9	7	0	.563	382	287
Detroit*	9	7	0	.563	357	342
Chicago*	9	7	0	.563	271	307
Tampa Bay	6	10	0	.375	251	351

Western Division

	W	L	T	Pct.	Pts.	OP
San Francisco	13	3	0	.813	505	296
New Orleans	7	9	0	.438	348	407
Atlanta	7	9	0	.438	317	385
L.A. Rams	4	12	0	.250	286	365

**Wild-Card qualifier for playoffs*

Miami finished ahead of New England based on a head-to-head sweep (2-0). Kansas City finished ahead of L.A. Raiders based on a head-to-head sweep (2-0). Green Bay was first Wild Card based on best head-to-head record (3-1) vs. Detroit (2-2) and Chicago (1-3) and better conference record (8-4) than N.Y. Giants (6-6). Detroit was second Wild Card based on better division record (4-4) than Chicago (3-5) and head-to-head sweep of N.Y. Giants (1-0). Chicago was third Wild Card based on better record vs. common opponents (4-4) than N.Y. Giants (3-5). New Orleans finished ahead of Atlanta based on a head-to-head sweep (2-0).

Wild-Card playoffs: MIAMI 27, Kansas City 17; CLEVELAND 20, New England 13

Divisional playoffs: PITTSBURGH 29, Cleveland 9; SAN DIEGO 22, Miami 21

AFC championship: San Diego 17, PITTSBURGH 13

Wild-Card playoffs: GREEN BAY 16, Detroit 12; Chicago 35, MINNESOTA 18

Divisional playoffs: SAN FRANCISCO 44, Chicago 15; DALLAS 35, Green Bay 9

NFC championship: SAN FRANCISCO 38, Dallas 28

Super Bowl XXIX: San Francisco (NFC) 49, San Diego (AFC) 26, at Joe Robbie Stadium, Miami, Florida

1993

AMERICAN CONFERENCE

Eastern Division

	W	L	T	Pct.	Pts.	OP
Buffalo	12	4	0	.750	329	242
Miami	9	7	0	.563	349	351
N.Y. Jets	8	8	0	.500	270	247
New England	5	11	0	.313	238	286
Indianapolis	4	12	0	.250	189	378

Central Division

	W	L	T	Pct.	Pts.	OP
Houston	12	4	0	.750	368	238
Pittsburgh*	9	7	0	.563	308	281
Cleveland	7	9	0	.438	304	307
Cincinnati	3	13	0	.188	187	319

Western Division

	W	L	T	Pct.	Pts.	OP
Kansas City	11	5	0	.688	328	291
L.A. Raiders*	10	6	0	.625	306	326
Denver*	9	7	0	.563	373	284
San Diego	8	8	0	.500	322	290
Seattle	6	10	0	.375	280	314

NATIONAL CONFERENCE

Eastern Division

	W	L	T	Pct.	Pts.	OP
Dallas	12	4	0	.750	376	229
N.Y. Giants*	11	5	0	.688	288	205
Philadelphia	8	8	0	.500	293	315
Phoenix	7	9	0	.438	326	269
Washington	4	12	0	.250	230	345

Central Division

	W	L	T	Pct.	Pts.	OP
Detroit	10	6	0	.625	298	292
Minnesota*	9	7	0	.563	277	290
Green Bay*	9	7	0	.563	340	282
Chicago	7	9	0	.438	234	230
Tampa Bay	5	11	0	.313	237	376

Western Division

	W	L	T	Pct.	Pts.	OP
San Francisco	10	6	0	.625	473	295
New Orleans	8	8	0	.500	317	343
Atlanta	6	10	0	.375	316	385
L.A. Rams	5	11	0	.313	221	367

**Wild-Card qualifier for playoffs*

Minnesota finished ahead of Green Bay based on a head-to-head sweep (2-0).

Wild-Card playoffs: KANSAS CITY 27, Pittsburgh 24 (OT); L.A. RAIDERS 42, Denver 24

Divisional playoffs: BUFFALO 29, L.A. Raiders 23; Kansas City 28, HOUSTON 20

AFC championship: BUFFALO 30, Kansas City 13

Wild-Card playoffs: Green Bay 28, DETROIT 24; N.Y. GIANTS 17, Minnesota 10

Divisional playoffs: SAN FRANCISCO 44, N.Y. Giants 3; DALLAS 27, Green Bay 17

NFC championship: DALLAS 38, San Francisco 21

Super Bowl XXVIII: Dallas (NFC) 30, Buffalo (AFC) 13, at Georgia Dome, Atlanta, Georgia

1992

AMERICAN CONFERENCE

Eastern Division

	W	L	T	Pct.	Pts.	OP
Miami	11	5	0	.688	340	281
Buffalo*	11	5	0	.688	381	283
Indianapolis	9	7	0	.563	216	302
N.Y. Jets	4	12	0	.250	220	315
New England	2	14	0	.125	205	363

Central Division

	W	L	T	Pct.	Pts.	OP
Pittsburgh	11	5	0	.688	299	225
Houston*	10	6	0	.625	352	258
Cleveland	7	9	0	.438	272	275
Cincinnati	5	11	0	.313	274	364

Western Division

	W	L	T	Pct.	Pts.	OP
San Diego	11	5	0	.688	335	241
Kansas City*	10	6	0	.625	348	282
Denver	8	8	0	.500	262	329
L.A. Raiders	7	9	0	.438	249	281
Seattle	2	14	0	.125	140	312

NATIONAL CONFERENCE

Eastern Division

	W	L	T	Pct.	Pts.	OP
Dallas	13	3	0	.813	409	243
Philadelphia*	11	5	0	.688	354	245
Washington*	9	7	0	.563	300	255
N.Y. Giants	6	10	0	.375	306	367
Phoenix	4	12	0	.250	243	332

Central Division

	W	L	T	Pct.	Pts.	OP
Minnesota	11	5	0	.688	374	249
Green Bay	9	7	0	.563	276	296
Tampa Bay	5	11	0	.313	267	365
Chicago	5	11	0	.313	295	361
Detroit	5	11	0	.313	273	332

Western Division

	W	L	T	Pct.	Pts.	OP
San Francisco	14	2	0	.875	431	236
New Orleans*	12	4	0	.750	330	202
Atlanta	6	10	0	.375	327	414
L.A. Rams	6	10	0	.375	313	383

**Wild-Card qualifier for playoffs*

Miami finished ahead of Buffalo based on better conference record (9-3 to 7-5). Tampa Bay finished ahead of Chicago and Detroit based on better conference record (5-9 to Bears' 4-8 and Lions' 3-9). Atlanta finished ahead of L.A. Rams based on better record versus common opponents (5-7 to 4-8).

Wild-Card playoffs: SAN DIEGO 17, Kansas City 0; BUFFALO 41, Houston 38 (OT)

Divisional playoffs: Buffalo 24, PITTSBURGH 3; MIAMI 31, San Diego 0

AFC championship: Buffalo 29, MIAMI 10

Wild-Card playoffs: Washington 24, MINNESOTA 7; Philadelphia 36, NEW ORLEANS 20

Divisional playoffs: SAN FRANCISCO 20, Washington 13; DALLAS 34, Philadelphia 10

NFC championship: Dallas 30, SAN FRANCISCO 20

Super Bowl XXVII: Dallas (NFC) 52, Buffalo (AFC) 17, at Rose Bowl, Pasadena, California

1991

AMERICAN CONFERENCE

Eastern Division

	W	L	T	Pct.	Pts.	OP
Buffalo	13	3	0	.813	458	318
N.Y. Jets*	8	8	0	.500	314	293
Miami	8	8	0	.500	343	349
New England	6	10	0	.375	211	305
Indianapolis	1	15	0	.063	143	381

Central Division

	W	L	T	Pct.	Pts.	OP
Houston	11	5	0	.688	386	251
Pittsburgh	7	9	0	.438	292	344
Cleveland	6	10	0	.375	293	298
Cincinnati	3	13	0	.188	263	435

Western Division

	W	L	T	Pct.	Pts.	OP
Denver	12	4	0	.750	304	235
Kansas City*	10	6	0	.625	322	252
L.A. Raiders*	9	7	0	.563	298	297
Seattle	7	9	0	.438	276	261
San Diego	4	12	0	.250	274	342

NATIONAL CONFERENCE

Eastern Division

	W	L	T	Pct.	Pts.	OP
Washington	14	2	0	.875	485	224
Dallas*	11	5	0	.688	342	310
Philadelphia	10	6	0	.625	285	244
N.Y. Giants	8	8	0	.500	281	297
Phoenix	4	12	0	.250	196	344

Central Division

	W	L	T	Pct.	Pts.	OP
Detroit	12	4	0	.750	339	295
Chicago*	11	5	0	.688	299	269
Minnesota	8	8	0	.500	301	306
Green Bay	4	12	0	.250	273	313
Tampa Bay	3	13	0	.188	199	365

Western Division

	W	L	T	Pct.	Pts.	OP
New Orleans	11	5	0	.688	341	211
Atlanta*	10	6	0	.625	361	338
San Francisco	10	6	0	.625	393	239
L.A. Rams	3	13	0	.188	234	390

**Wild-Card qualifiers for playoffs*

New York Jets finished ahead of Miami based on head-to-head sweep (2-0). Atlanta finished ahead of San Francisco based on head-to-head sweep (2-0).

Wild-Card playoffs: KANSAS CITY 10, L.A. Raiders 6; HOUSTON 17, N.Y. Jets 10

Divisional playoffs: DENVER 26, Houston 24; BUFFALO 37, Kansas City 14

AFC championship: BUFFALO 10, Denver 7

Wild-Card playoffs: Atlanta 27, NEW ORLEANS 20; Dallas 17, CHICAGO 13

Divisional playoffs: WASHINGTON 24, Atlanta 7; DETROIT 38, Dallas 6

NFC championship: WASHINGTON 41, Detroit 10

Super Bowl XXVI: Washington (NFC) 37, Buffalo (AFC) 24, at Hubert H. Humphrey Metrodome, Minneapolis, Minnesota

PAST STANDINGS

1990

AMERICAN CONFERENCE

Eastern Division

	W	L	T	Pct.	Pts.	OP
Buffalo	13	3	0	.813	428	263
Miami*	12	4	0	.750	336	242
Indianapolis	7	9	0	.438	281	353
N.Y. Jets	6	10	0	.375	295	345
New England	1	15	0	.063	181	446

Central Division

	W	L	T	Pct.	Pts.	OP
Cincinnati	9	7	0	.563	360	352
Houston*	9	7	0	.563	405	307
Pittsburgh	9	7	0	.563	292	240
Cleveland	3	13	0	.188	228	462

Western Division

	W	L	T	Pct.	Pts.	OP
L.A. Raiders	12	4	0	.750	337	268
Kansas City*	11	5	0	.688	369	257
Seattle	9	7	0	.563	306	286
San Diego	6	10	0	.375	315	281
Denver	5	11	0	.313	331	374

NATIONAL CONFERENCE

Eastern Division

	W	L	T	Pct.	Pts.	OP
N.Y. Giants	13	3	0	.813	335	211
Philadelphia*	10	6	0	.625	396	299
Washington*	10	6	0	.625	381	301
Dallas	7	9	0	.438	244	308
Phoenix	5	11	0	.313	268	396

Central Division

	W	L	T	Pct.	Pts.	OP
Chicago	11	5	0	.688	348	280
Tampa Bay	6	10	0	.375	264	367
Detroit	6	10	0	.375	373	413
Green Bay	6	10	0	.375	271	347
Minnesota	6	10	0	.375	351	326

Western Division

	W	L	T	Pct.	Pts.	OP
San Francisco	14	2	0	.875	353	239
New Orleans*	8	8	0	.500	274	275
L.A. Rams	5	11	0	.313	345	412
Atlanta	5	11	0	.313	348	365

**Wild-Card qualifiers for playoffs*

Cincinnati won AFC Central title based on best head-to-head record (3-1) vs. Houston (2-2) and Pittsburgh (1-3). Houston was Wild Card based on better conference record (8-4) than Seattle (7-5) and Pittsburgh (6-6). Philadelphia finished second in the NFC East based on better division record (5-3) than Washington (4-4). Tampa Bay was second in NFC Central based on 5-1 record vs. Detroit, Green Bay, and Minnesota. Detroit finished third based on best net division points (minus 8) vs. Green Bay (minus 40) in fourth. Minnesota was fifth based on 4-8 conference record. The Los Angeles Rams finished third in NFC West based on net points in division (plus 1) vs. Atlanta (minus 31).

Wild-Card playoffs: MIAMI 17, Kansas City 16; CINCINNATI 41, Houston 14
Divisional playoffs: BUFFALO 44, Miami 34; L.A. RAIDERS 20, Cincinnati 10
AFC championship: BUFFALO 51, L.A. Raiders 3
Wild-Card playoffs: Washington 20, PHILADELPHIA 6; CHICAGO 16, New Orleans 6
Divisional playoffs: SAN FRANCISCO 28, Washington 10; N.Y. GIANTS 31, Chicago 3
NFC championship: N.Y. Giants 15, SAN FRANCISCO 13
Super Bowl XXV: N.Y. Giants (NFC) 20, Buffalo (AFC) 19, at Tampa Stadium, Tampa, Florida

1989

AMERICAN CONFERENCE

Eastern Division

	W	L	T	Pct.	Pts.	OP
Buffalo	9	7	0	.563	409	317
Indianapolis	8	8	0	.500	298	301
Miami	8	8	0	.500	331	379
New England	5	11	0	.313	297	391
N.Y. Jets	4	12	0	.250	253	411

Central Division

	W	L	T	Pct.	Pts.	OP
Cleveland	9	6	1	.594	334	254
Houston*	9	7	0	.563	365	412
Pittsburgh*	9	7	0	.563	265	326
Cincinnati	8	8	0	.500	404	285

Western Division

	W	L	T	Pct.	Pts.	OP
Denver	11	5	0	.688	362	226
Kansas City	8	7	1	.531	318	286
L.A. Raiders	8	8	0	.500	315	297
Seattle	7	9	0	.438	241	327
San Diego	6	10	0	.375	266	290

NATIONAL CONFERENCE

Eastern Division

	W	L	T	Pct.	Pts.	OP
N.Y. Giants	12	4	0	.750	348	252
Philadelphia*	11	5	0	.688	342	274
Washington	10	6	0	.625	386	308
Phoenix	5	11	0	.313	258	377
Dallas	1	15	0	.063	204	393

Central Division

	W	L	T	Pct.	Pts.	OP
Minnesota	10	6	0	.625	351	275
Green Bay	10	6	0	.625	362	356
Detroit	7	9	0	.438	312	364
Chicago	6	10	0	.375	358	377
Tampa Bay	5	11	0	.313	320	419

Western Division

	W	L	T	Pct.	Pts.	OP
San Francisco	14	2	0	.875	442	253
L.A. Rams*	11	5	0	.688	426	344
New Orleans	9	7	0	.563	386	301
Atlanta	3	13	0	.188	279	437

**Wild-Card qualifiers for playoffs*

Indianapolis finished ahead of Miami in AFC East because of better conference record (7-5 vs. 6-8). Houston finished ahead of Pittsburgh in AFC Central because of head-to-head sweep (2-0). Minnesota finished ahead of Green Bay in NFC Central because of better division record (6-2 vs. 5-3).

Wild-Card playoff: Pittsburgh 26, HOUSTON 23 (OT)
Divisional playoffs: CLEVELAND 34, Buffalo 30; DENVER 24, Pittsburgh 23
AFC championship: DENVER 37, Cleveland 21
Wild-Card playoff: L.A. Rams 21, PHILADELPHIA 7
Divisional playoffs: L.A. Rams 19, N.Y. GIANTS 13 (OT); SAN FRANCISCO 41, Minnesota 13
NFC championship: SAN FRANCISCO 30, L.A. Rams 3
Super Bowl XXIV: San Francisco (NFC) 55, Denver (AFC) 10, at Louisiana Superdome, New Orleans, Louisiana

1988

AMERICAN CONFERENCE

Eastern Division

	W	L	T	Pct.	Pts.	OP
Buffalo	12	4	0	.750	329	237
Indianapolis	9	7	0	.563	354	315
New England	9	7	0	.563	250	284
N.Y. Jets	8	7	1	.531	372	354
Miami	6	10	0	.375	319	380

Central Division

	W	L	T	Pct.	Pts.	OP
Cincinnati	12	4	0	.750	448	329
Cleveland*	10	6	0	.625	304	288
Houston*	10	6	0	.625	424	365
Pittsburgh	5	11	0	.313	336	421

Western Division

	W	L	T	Pct.	Pts.	OP
Seattle	9	7	0	.563	339	329
Denver	8	8	0	.500	327	352
L.A. Raiders	7	9	0	.438	325	369
San Diego	6	10	0	.375	231	332
Kansas City	4	11	1	.281	254	320

NATIONAL CONFERENCE

Eastern Division

	W	L	T	Pct.	Pts.	OP
Philadelphia	10	6	0	.625	379	319
N.Y. Giants	10	6	0	.625	359	304
Washington	7	9	0	.438	345	387
Phoenix	7	9	0	.438	344	398
Dallas	3	13	0	.188	265	381

Central Division

	W	L	T	Pct.	Pts.	OP
Chicago	12	4	0	.750	312	215
Minnesota*	11	5	0	.688	406	233
Tampa Bay	5	11	0	.313	261	350
Detroit	4	12	0	.250	220	313
Green Bay	4	12	0	.250	240	315

Western Division

	W	L	T	Pct.	Pts.	OP
San Francisco	10	6	0	.625	369	294
L.A. Rams*	10	6	0	.625	407	293
New Orleans	10	6	0	.625	312	283
Atlanta	5	11	0	.313	244	315

**Wild-Card qualifiers for playoffs*

Indianapolis finished second in AFC East on basis of better record versus common opponents (7-5) over New England (6-6). Cleveland gained first AFC Wild-Card position based on better division record (4-2) over Houston (3-3). Philadelphia finished first in NFC East on basis of head-to-head sweep over New York Giants. Washington finished third in NFC East on basis of better division record (4-4) over Phoenix (3-5). Detroit finished fourth in NFC Central on basis of head-to-head sweep over Green Bay. San Francisco finished first in NFC West based on better head-to-head record (3-1) over Los Angeles Rams (2-2) and New Orleans (1-3). Los Angeles Rams finished second in NFC West on basis of better division record (4-2) over New Orleans (3-3) and earned Wild-Card position based on better conference record (8-4) over New York Giants (9-5) and New Orleans (6-6).

Wild-Card playoff: Houston 24, CLEVELAND 23
Divisional playoffs: CINCINNATI 21, Seattle 13; BUFFALO 17, Houston 10
AFC championship: CINCINNATI 21, Buffalo 10
Wild-Card playoff: MINNESOTA 28, Los Angeles Rams 17
Divisional playoffs: CHICAGO 20, Philadelphia 12; SAN FRANCISCO 34, Minnesota 9
NFC championship: San Francisco 28, CHICAGO 3
Super Bowl XXIII: San Francisco (NFC) 20, Cincinnati (AFC) 16, at Joe Robbie Stadium, Miami, Florida

1987

AMERICAN CONFERENCE

Eastern Division

	W	L	T	Pct.	Pts.	OP
Indianapolis	9	6	0	.600	300	238
New England	8	7	0	.533	320	293
Miami	8	7	0	.533	362	335
Buffalo	7	8	0	.467	270	305
N.Y. Jets	6	9	0	.400	334	360

Central Division

	W	L	T	Pct.	Pts.	OP
Cleveland	10	5	0	.667	390	239
Houston*	9	6	0	.600	345	349
Pittsburgh	8	7	0	.533	285	299
Cincinnati	4	11	0	.267	285	370

Western Division

	W	L	T	Pct.	Pts.	OP
Denver	10	4	1	.700	379	288
Seattle*	9	6	0	.600	371	314
San Diego	8	7	0	.533	253	317
L.A. Raiders	5	10	0	.333	301	289
Kansas City	4	11	0	.267	273	388

NATIONAL CONFERENCE

Eastern Division

	W	L	T	Pct.	Pts.	OP
Washington	11	4	0	.733	379	285
Dallas	7	8	0	.467	340	348
St. Louis	7	8	0	.467	362	368
Philadelphia	7	8	0	.467	337	380
N.Y. Giants	6	9	0	.400	280	312

Central Division

	W	L	T	Pct.	Pts.	OP
Chicago	11	4	0	.733	356	282
Minnesota*	8	7	0	.533	336	335
Green Bay	5	9	1	.367	255	300
Tampa Bay	4	11	0	.267	286	360
Detroit	4	11	0	.267	269	384

Western Division

	W	L	T	Pct.	Pts.	OP
San Francisco	13	2	0	.867	459	253
New Orleans*	12	3	0	.800	422	283
L.A. Rams	6	9	0	.400	317	361
Atlanta	3	12	0	.200	205	436

**Wild-Card qualifiers for playoffs*

Houston gained first AFC Wild-Card position on better conference record (7-4) over Seattle (5-6).

Wild-Card playoff: HOUSTON 23, Seattle 20 (OT)
Divisional playoffs: CLEVELAND 38, Indianapolis 21; DENVER 34, Houston 10
AFC championship: DENVER 38, Cleveland 33
Wild-Card playoff: Minnesota 44, NEW ORLEANS 10
Divisional playoffs: Minnesota 36, SAN FRANCISCO 24; Washington 21, CHICAGO 17
NFC championship: WASHINGTON 17, Minnesota 10
Super Bowl XXII: Washington (NFC) 42, Denver (AFC) 10, at San Diego Jack Murphy Stadium, San Diego, California

Note: 1987 regular season was reduced from 16 to 15 games for each team due to players' strike.

1986

AMERICAN CONFERENCE

Eastern Division

	W	L	T	Pct.	Pts.	OP
New England	11	5	0	.688	412	307
N.Y. Jets*	10	6	0	.625	364	386
Miami	8	8	0	.500	430	405
Buffalo	4	12	0	.250	287	348
Indianapolis	3	13	0	.188	229	400

Central Division

	W	L	T	Pct.	Pts.	OP
Cleveland	12	4	0	.750	391	310
Cincinnati	10	6	0	.625	409	394
Pittsburgh	6	10	0	.375	307	336
Houston	5	11	0	.313	274	329

Western Division

	W	L	T	Pct.	Pts.	OP
Denver	11	5	0	.688	378	327
Kansas City*	10	6	0	.625	358	326
Seattle	10	6	0	.625	366	293
L.A. Raiders	8	8	0	.500	323	346
San Diego	4	12	0	.250	335	396

NATIONAL CONFERENCE

Eastern Division

	W	L	T	Pct.	Pts.	OP
N.Y. Giants	14	2	0	.875	371	236
Washington*	12	4	0	.750	368	296
Dallas	7	9	0	.438	346	337
Philadelphia	5	10	1	.344	256	312
St. Louis	4	11	1	.281	218	351

Central Division

	W	L	T	Pct.	Pts.	OP
Chicago	14	2	0	.875	352	187
Minnesota	9	7	0	.563	398	273
Detroit	5	11	0	.313	277	326
Green Bay	4	12	0	.250	254	418
Tampa Bay	2	14	0	.125	239	473

Western Division

	W	L	T	Pct.	Pts.	OP
San Francisco	10	5	1	.656	374	247
L.A. Rams*	10	6	0	.625	309	267
Atlanta	7	8	1	.469	280	280
New Orleans	7	9	0	.438	288	287

**Wild-Card qualifiers for playoffs*

New York Jets gained first AFC Wild-Card position on better conference record (8-4) over Kansas City (9-5), Seattle (7-5), and Cincinnati (7-5). Kansas City gained second Wild Card based on better conference record (9-5) over Seattle (7-5) and Cincinnati (7-5).

Wild-Card playoff: NEW YORK JETS 35, Kansas City 15

Divisional playoffs: CLEVELAND 23, New York Jets 20 (OT); DENVER 22, New England 17

AFC championship: Denver 23, CLEVELAND 20 (OT)

Wild-Card playoff: WASHINGTON 19, Los Angeles Rams 7

Divisional playoffs: Washington 27, CHICAGO 13 NEW YORK GIANTS 49, San Francisco 3

NFC championship: NEW YORK GIANTS 17, Washington 0

Super Bowl XXI: New York Giants (NFC) 39, Denver (AFC) 20, at Rose Bowl, Pasadena, California

1985

AMERICAN CONFERENCE

Eastern Division

	W	L	T	Pct.	Pts.	OP
Miami	12	4	0	.750	428	320
N.Y. Jets*	11	5	0	.688	393	264
New England*	11	5	0	.688	362	290
Indianapolis	5	11	0	.313	320	386
Buffalo	2	14	0	.125	200	381

Central Division

	W	L	T	Pct.	Pts.	OP
Cleveland	8	8	0	.500	287	294
Cincinnati	7	9	0	.438	441	437
Pittsburgh	7	9	0	.438	379	355
Houston	5	11	0	.313	284	412

Western Division

	W	L	T	Pct.	Pts.	OP
L.A. Raiders	12	4	0	.750	354	308
Denver	11	5	0	.688	380	329
Seattle	8	8	0	.500	349	303
San Diego	8	8	0	.500	467	435
Kansas City	6	10	0	.375	317	360

NATIONAL CONFERENCE

Eastern Division

	W	L	T	Pct.	Pts.	OP
Dallas	10	6	0	.625	357	333
N.Y. Giants*	10	6	0	.625	399	283
Washington	10	6	0	.625	297	312
Philadelphia	7	9	0	.438	286	310
St. Louis	5	11	0	.313	278	414

Central Division

	W	L	T	Pct.	Pts.	OP
Chicago	15	1	0	.938	456	198
Green Bay	8	8	0	.500	337	355
Minnesota	7	9	0	.438	346	359
Detroit	7	9	0	.438	307	366
Tampa Bay	2	14	0	.125	294	448

Western Division

	W	L	T	Pct.	Pts.	OP
L.A. Rams	11	5	0	.688	340	277
San Francisco*	10	6	0	.625	411	263
New Orleans	5	11	0	.313	294	401
Atlanta	4	12	0	.250	282	452

**Wild-Card qualifiers for playoffs*

New York Jets gained first AFC Wild-Card position on better conference record (9-3) over New England (8-4) and Denver (8-4). New England gained second AFC Wild-Card position based on better record vs. common opponents (4-2) than Denver (3-3). Dallas won NFC Eastern Division title based on better record (4-0) vs. New York Giants (1-3) and Washington (1-3). New York Giants gained first NFC Wild Card position based on better conference record (8-4) over San Francisco (7-5) and Washington (6-6). San Francisco gained second NFC Wild-Card position based on head-to-head victory over Washington.

Wild-Card playoff: New England 26, NEW YORK JETS 14

Divisional playoffs: MIAMI 24, Cleveland 21; New England 27, LOS ANGELES RAIDERS 20

AFC championship: New England 31, MIAMI 14

Wild-Card playoff: NEW YORK GIANTS 17, San Francisco 3

Divisional playoffs: LOS ANGELES RAMS 20, Dallas 0; CHICAGO 21, New York Giants 0

NFC championship: CHICAGO 24, Los Angeles Rams 0

Super Bowl XX: Chicago (NFC) 46, New England (AFC) 10, at Louisiana Superdome, New Orleans, Louisiana

1984

AMERICAN CONFERENCE

Eastern Division

	W	L	T	Pct.	Pts.	OP
Miami	14	2	0	.875	513	298
New England	9	7	0	.563	362	352
N.Y. Jets	7	9	0	.438	332	364
Indianapolis	4	12	0	.250	239	414
Buffalo	2	14	0	.125	250	454

Central Division

	W	L	T	Pct.	Pts.	OP
Pittsburgh	9	7	0	.563	387	310
Cincinnati	8	8	0	.500	339	339
Cleveland	5	11	0	.313	250	297
Houston	3	13	0	.188	240	437

Western Division

	W	L	T	Pct.	Pts.	OP
Denver	13	3	0	.813	353	241
Seattle*	12	4	0	.750	418	282
L.A. Raiders*	11	5	0	.688	368	278
Kansas City	8	8	0	.500	314	324
San Diego	7	9	0	.438	394	413

NATIONAL CONFERENCE

Eastern Division

	W	L	T	Pct.	Pts.	OP
Washington	11	5	0	.688	426	310
N.Y. Giants*	9	7	0	.563	299	301
St. Louis	9	7	0	.563	423	345
Dallas	9	7	0	.563	308	308
Philadelphia	6	9	1	.406	278	320

Central Division

	W	L	T	Pct.	Pts.	OP
Chicago	10	6	0	.625	325	248
Green Bay	8	8	0	.500	390	309
Tampa Bay	6	10	0	.375	335	380
Detroit	4	11	1	.281	283	408
Minnesota	3	13	0	.188	276	484

Western Division

	W	L	T	Pct.	Pts.	OP
San Francisco	15	1	0	.938	475	227
L.A. Rams*	10	6	0	.625	346	316
New Orleans	7	9	0	.438	298	361
Atlanta	4	12	0	.250	281	382

**Wild-Card qualifiers for playoffs*

New York Giants clinched Wild-Card berth based on 3-1 record vs. St. Louis's 2-2 and Dallas's 1-3. St. Louis finished ahead of Dallas based on better division record (5-3 to 3-5).

Wild-Card playoff: SEATTLE 13, Los Angeles Raiders 7

Divisional playoffs: MIAMI 31, Seattle 10; Pittsburgh 24, DENVER 17

AFC championship: MIAMI 45, Pittsburgh 28

Wild-Card playoff: New York Giants 16, LOS ANGELES RAMS 13

Divisional playoffs: SAN FRANCISCO 21, New York Giants 10; Chicago 23, WASHINGTON 19

NFC championship: SAN FRANCISCO 23, Chicago 0

Super Bowl XIX: San Francisco (NFC) 38, Miami (AFC) 16, at Stanford Stadium, Stanford, California

1983

AMERICAN CONFERENCE

Eastern Division

	W	L	T	Pct.	Pts.	OP
Miami	12	4	0	.750	389	250
New England	8	8	0	.500	274	289
Buffalo	8	8	0	.500	283	351
Baltimore	7	9	0	.438	264	354
N.Y. Jets	7	9	0	.438	313	331

Central Division

	W	L	T	Pct.	Pts.	OP
Pittsburgh	10	6	0	.625	355	303
Cleveland	9	7	0	.563	356	342
Cincinnati	7	9	0	.438	346	302
Houston	2	14	0	.125	288	460

Western Division

	W	L	T	Pct.	Pts.	OP
L.A. Raiders	12	4	0	.750	442	338
Seattle*	9	7	0	.563	403	397
Denver*	9	7	0	.563	302	327
San Diego	6	10	0	.375	358	462
Kansas City	6	10	0	.375	386	367

NATIONAL CONFERENCE

Eastern Division

	W	L	T	Pct.	Pts.	OP
Washington	14	2	0	.875	541	332
Dallas*	12	4	0	.750	479	360
St. Louis	8	7	1	.531	374	428
Philadelphia	5	11	0	.313	233	322
N.Y. Giants	3	12	1	.219	267	347

Central Division

	W	L	T	Pct.	Pts.	OP
Detroit	9	7	0	.563	347	286
Green Bay	8	8	0	.500	429	439
Chicago	8	8	0	.500	311	301
Minnesota	8	8	0	.500	316	348
Tampa Bay	2	14	0	.125	241	380

Western Division

	W	L	T	Pct.	Pts.	OP
San Francisco	10	6	0	.625	432	293
L.A. Rams*	9	7	0	.563	361	344
New Orleans	8	8	0	.500	319	337
Atlanta	7	9	0	.438	370	389

**Wild-Card qualifiers for playoffs*

Seattle and Denver gained Wild-Card berths over Cleveland because of their victories over the Browns.

Wild-Card playoff: SEATTLE 31, Denver 7

Divisional playoffs: Seattle 27, MIAMI 20; LOS ANGELES RAIDERS 38, Pittsburgh 10

AFC championship: LOS ANGELES RAIDERS 30, Seattle 14

Wild-Card playoff: Los Angeles Rams 24, DALLAS 17

Divisional playoffs: SAN FRANCISCO 24, Detroit 23; WASHINGTON 51, L.A. Rams 7

NFC championship: WASHINGTON 24, San Francisco 21

Super Bowl XVIII: Los Angeles Raiders (AFC) 38, Washington (NFC) 9, at Tampa Stadium, Tampa, Florida

PAST STANDINGS

1982

AMERICAN CONFERENCE

	W	L	T	Pct.	Pts.	OP
L.A. Raiders	8	1	0	.889	260	200
Miami	7	2	0	.778	198	131
Cincinnati	7	2	0	.778	232	177
Pittsburgh	6	3	0	.667	204	146
San Diego	6	3	0	.667	288	221
N.Y. Jets	6	3	0	.667	245	166
New England	5	4	0	.556	143	157
Cleveland	4	5	0	.444	140	182
Buffalo	4	5	0	.444	150	154
Seattle	4	5	0	.444	127	147
Kansas City	3	6	0	.333	176	184
Denver	2	7	0	.222	148	226
Houston	1	8	0	.111	136	245
Baltimore	0	8	1	.056	113	236

NATIONAL CONFERENCE

	W	L	T	Pct.	Pts.	OP
Washington	8	1	0	.889	190	128
Dallas	6	3	0	.667	226	145
Green Bay	5	3	1	.611	226	169
Minnesota	5	4	0	.556	187	198
Atlanta	5	4	0	.556	183	199
St. Louis	5	4	0	.556	135	170
Tampa Bay	5	4	0	.556	158	178
Detroit	4	5	0	.444	181	176
New Orleans	4	5	0	.444	129	160
N.Y. Giants	4	5	0	.444	164	160
San Francisco	3	6	0	.333	209	206
Chicago	3	6	0	.333	141	174
Philadelphia	3	6	0	.333	191	195
L.A. Rams	2	7	0	.222	200	250

As the result of a 57-day players' strike, the 1982 NFL regular season schedule was reduced from 16 weeks to 9. At the conclusion of the regular season, the NFL conducted a 16-team postseason Super Bowl Tournament. Eight teams from each conference were seeded 1-8 based on their records during the season.

Miami finished ahead of Cincinnati based on better conference record (6-1 to 6-2). Pittsburgh won common games tie-breaker with San Diego (3-1 to 2-1) after New York Jets were eliminated from three-way tie based on conference record (Pittsburgh and San Diego 5-3 vs. Jets 2-3). Cleveland finished ahead of Buffalo and Seattle based on better conference record (4-3 to 3-3 to 3-5). Minnesota (4-1), Atlanta (4-3), St. Louis (5-4), Tampa Bay (3-3) seeds were determined by best won-lost record in conference games. Detroit finished ahead of New Orleans and the New York Giants based on better conference record (4-4 to 3-5 to 3-5).

First round playoff: MIAMI 28, New England 13
LOS ANGELES RAIDERS 27, Cleveland 10
New York Jets 44, CINCINNATI 17
San Diego 31, PITTSBURGH 28
Second round playoff: New York Jets 17, LOS ANGELES RAIDERS 14
MIAMI 34, San Diego 13
AFC championship: MIAMI 14, New York Jets 0
First round playoff: WASHINGTON 31, Detroit 7
GREEN BAY 41, St. Louis 16
MINNESOTA 30, Atlanta 24
DALLAS 30, Tampa Bay 17
Second round playoff: WASHINGTON 21, Minnesota 7
DALLAS 37, Green Bay 26
NFC championship: WASHINGTON 31, Dallas 17
Super Bowl XVII: Washington (NFC) 27, Miami (AFC) 17, at Rose Bowl, Pasadena, California

1981

AMERICAN CONFERENCE

Eastern Division	W	L	T	Pct.	Pts.	OP
Miami	11	4	1	.719	345	275
N.Y. Jets*	10	5	1	.656	355	287
Buffalo*	10	6	0	.625	311	276
Baltimore	2	14	0	.125	259	533
New England	2	14	0	.125	322	370
Central Division	**W**	**L**	**T**	**Pct.**	**Pts.**	**OP**
Cincinnati	12	4	0	.750	421	304
Pittsburgh	8	8	0	.500	356	297
Houston	7	9	0	.438	281	355
Cleveland	5	11	0	.313	276	375
Western Division	**W**	**L**	**T**	**Pct.**	**Pts.**	**OP**
San Diego	10	6	0	.625	478	390
Denver	10	6	0	.625	321	289
Kansas City	9	7	0	.563	343	290
Oakland	7	9	0	.438	273	343
Seattle	6	10	0	.375	322	388

NATIONAL CONFERENCE

Eastern Division	W	L	T	Pct.	Pts.	OP
Dallas	12	4	0	.750	367	277
Philadelphia*	10	6	0	.625	368	221
N.Y. Giants*	9	7	0	.563	295	257
Washington	8	8	0	.500	347	349
St. Louis	7	9	0	.438	315	408
Central Division	**W**	**L**	**T**	**Pct.**	**Pts.**	**OP**
Tampa Bay	9	7	0	.563	315	268
Detroit	8	8	0	.500	397	322
Green Bay	8	8	0	.500	324	361
Minnesota	7	9	0	.438	325	369
Chicago	6	10	0	.375	253	324
Western Division	**W**	**L**	**T**	**Pct.**	**Pts.**	**OP**
San Francisco	13	3	0	.813	357	250
Atlanta	7	9	0	.438	426	355
Los Angeles	6	10	0	.375	303	351
New Orleans	4	12	0	.250	207	378

**Wild-Card qualifiers for playoffs*

San Diego won AFC Western title over Denver on the basis of a better division record (6-2 to 5-3). Buffalo won a Wild-Card playoff berth over Denver as the result of a 9-7 victory in head-to-head competition.

Wild-Card playoff: Buffalo 31, NEW YORK JETS 27
Divisional playoffs: San Diego 41, MIAMI 38 (OT); CINCINNATI 28, Buffalo 21
AFC championship: CINCINNATI 27, San Diego 7
Wild-Card playoff: New York Giants 27, PHILADELPHIA 21
Divisional playoffs: DALLAS 38, Tampa Bay 0; SAN FRANCISCO 38, New York Giants 24
NFC championship: SAN FRANCISCO 28, Dallas 27
Super Bowl XVI: San Francisco (NFC) 26, Cincinnati (AFC) 21, at Silverdome, Pontiac, Michigan

1980

AMERICAN CONFERENCE

Eastern Division	W	L	T	Pct.	Pts.	OP
Buffalo	11	5	0	.688	320	260
New England	10	6	0	.625	441	325
Miami	8	8	0	.500	266	305
Baltimore	7	9	0	.438	355	387
N.Y. Jets	4	12	0	.250	302	395
Central Division	**W**	**L**	**T**	**Pct.**	**Pts.**	**OP**
Cleveland	11	5	0	.688	357	310
Houston*	11	5	0	.688	295	251
Pittsburgh	9	7	0	.563	352	313
Cincinnati	6	10	0	.375	244	312
Western Division	**W**	**L**	**T**	**Pct.**	**Pts.**	**OP**
San Diego	11	5	0	.688	418	327
Oakland*	11	5	0	.688	364	306
Kansas City	8	8	0	.500	319	336
Denver	8	8	0	.500	310	323
Seattle	4	12	0	.250	291	408

NATIONAL CONFERENCE

Eastern Division	W	L	T	Pct.	Pts.	OP
Philadelphia	12	4	0	.750	384	222
Dallas*	12	4	0	.750	454	311
Washington	6	10	0	.375	261	293
St. Louis	5	11	0	.313	299	350
N.Y. Giants	4	12	0	.250	249	425
Central Division	**W**	**L**	**T**	**Pct.**	**Pts.**	**OP**
Minnesota	9	7	0	.563	317	308
Detroit	9	7	0	.563	334	272
Chicago	7	9	0	.438	304	264
Tampa Bay	5	10	1	.344	271	341
Green Bay	5	10	1	.344	231	371
Western Division	**W**	**L**	**T**	**Pct.**	**Pts.**	**OP**
Atlanta	12	4	0	.750	405	272
Los Angeles*	11	5	0	.688	424	289
San Francisco	6	10	0	.375	320	415
New Orleans	1	15	0	.063	291	487

**Wild-Card qualifiers for playoffs*

Philadelphia won division title over Dallas on the basis of best net points in division games (plus 84 net points to plus 50). Minnesota won division title because of a better conference record than Detroit (8-4 to 9-5). Cleveland won division title because of a better conference record than Houston (8-4 to 7-5). San Diego won division title over Oakland on the basis of best net points in division games (plus 60 net points to plus 37).

Wild-Card playoff: OAKLAND 27, Houston 7
Divisional playoffs: SAN DIEGO 20, Buffalo 14; Oakland 14, CLEVELAND 12
AFC championship: Oakland 34, SAN DIEGO 27
Wild-Card playoff: DALLAS 34, Los Angeles 13
Divisional playoffs: PHILADELPHIA 31, Minnesota 16; Dallas 30, ATLANTA 27
NFC championship: PHILADELPHIA 20, Dallas 7
Super Bowl XV: Oakland (AFC) 27, Philadelphia (NFC) 10, at Louisiana Superdome, New Orleans, Louisiana

1979

AMERICAN CONFERENCE

Eastern Division	W	L	T	Pct.	Pts.	OP
Miami	10	6	0	.625	341	257
New England	9	7	0	.563	411	326
N.Y. Jets	8	8	0	.500	337	383
Buffalo	7	9	0	.438	268	279
Baltimore	5	11	0	.313	271	351
Central Division	**W**	**L**	**T**	**Pct.**	**Pts.**	**OP**
Pittsburgh	12	4	0	.750	416	262
Houston*	11	5	0	.688	362	331
Cleveland	9	7	0	.563	359	352
Cincinnati	4	12	0	.250	337	421
Western Division	**W**	**L**	**T**	**Pct.**	**Pts.**	**OP**
San Diego	12	4	0	.750	411	246
Denver*	10	6	0	.625	289	262
Seattle	9	7	0	.563	378	372
Oakland	9	7	0	.563	365	337
Kansas City	7	9	0	.438	238	262

NATIONAL CONFERENCE

Eastern Division	W	L	T	Pct.	Pts.	OP
Dallas	11	5	0	.688	371	313
Philadelphia*	11	5	0	.688	339	282
Washington	10	6	0	.625	348	295
N.Y. Giants	6	10	0	.375	237	323
St. Louis	5	11	0	.313	307	358
Central Division	**W**	**L**	**T**	**Pct.**	**Pts.**	**OP**
Tampa Bay	10	6	0	.625	273	237
Chicago*	10	6	0	.625	306	249
Minnesota	7	9	0	.438	259	337
Green Bay	5	11	0	.313	246	316
Detroit	2	14	0	.125	219	365
Western Division	**W**	**L**	**T**	**Pct.**	**Pts.**	**OP**
Los Angeles	9	7	0	.563	323	309
New Orleans	8	8	0	.500	370	360
Atlanta	6	10	0	.375	300	388
San Francisco	2	14	0	.125	308	416

**Wild-Card qualifiers for playoffs*

Dallas won division title because of a better conference record than Philadelphia (10-2 to 9-3). Tampa Bay won division title because of a better division record than Chicago (6-2 to 5-3). Chicago won a Wild-Card berth over Washington on the basis of best net points in all games (plus 57 net points to plus 53).

Wild-Card playoff: HOUSTON 13, Denver 7
Divisional playoffs: Houston 17, SAN DIEGO 14; PITTSBURGH 34, Miami 14
AFC championship: PITTSBURGH 27, Houston 13
Wild-Card playoff: PHILADELPHIA 27, Chicago 17
Divisional playoffs: TAMPA BAY 24, Philadelphia 17; Los Angeles 21, DALLAS 19
NFC championship: Los Angeles 9, TAMPA BAY 0
Super Bowl XIV: Pittsburgh (AFC) 31, Los Angeles (NFC) 19, at Rose Bowl, Pasadena, California

1978

AMERICAN CONFERENCE

Eastern Division

	W	L	T	Pct.	Pts.	OP
New England	11	5	0	.688	358	286
Miami*	11	5	0	.688	372	254
N.Y. Jets	8	8	0	.500	359	364
Buffalo	5	11	0	.313	302	354
Baltimore	5	11	0	.313	239	421

Central Division

	W	L	T	Pct.	Pts.	OP
Pittsburgh	14	2	0	.875	356	195
Houston*	10	6	0	.625	283	298
Cleveland	8	8	0	.500	334	356
Cincinnati	4	12	0	.250	252	284

Western Division

	W	L	T	Pct.	Pts.	OP
Denver	10	6	0	.625	282	198
Oakland	9	7	0	.563	311	283
Seattle	9	7	0	.563	345	358
San Diego	9	7	0	.563	355	309
Kansas City	4	12	0	.250	243	327

NATIONAL CONFERENCE

Eastern Division

	W	L	T	Pct.	Pts.	OP
Dallas	12	4	0	.750	384	208
Philadelphia*	9	7	0	.563	270	250
Washington	8	8	0	.500	273	283
St. Louis	6	10	0	.375	248	296
N.Y. Giants	6	10	0	.375	264	298

Central Division

	W	L	T	Pct.	Pts.	OP
Minnesota	8	7	1	.531	294	306
Green Bay	8	7	1	.531	249	269
Detroit	7	9	0	.438	290	300
Chicago	7	9	0	.438	253	274
Tampa Bay	5	11	0	.313	241	259

Western Division

	W	L	T	Pct.	Pts.	OP
Los Angeles	12	4	0	.750	316	245
Atlanta*	9	7	0	.563	240	290
New Orleans	7	9	0	.438	281	298
San Francisco	2	14	0	.125	219	350

**Wild-Card qualifiers for playoffs*

New England won division title on the basis of a better division record than Miami (6-2 to 5-3). Minnesota won division title because of a better head-to-head record against Green Bay (1-0-1).

Wild-Card playoff: Houston 17, MIAMI 9

Divisional playoffs: Houston 31, NEW ENGLAND 14; PITTSBURGH 33, Denver 10

AFC championship: PITTSBURGH 34, Houston 5

Wild-Card playoff: ATLANTA 14, Philadelphia 13

Divisional playoffs: DALLAS 27, Atlanta 20; LOS ANGELES 34, Minnesota 10

NFC championship: Dallas 28, LOS ANGELES 0

Super Bowl XIII: Pittsburgh (AFC) 35, Dallas (NFC) 31, at Orange Bowl, Miami, Florida

1977

AMERICAN CONFERENCE

Eastern Division

	W	L	T	Pct.	Pts.	OP
Baltimore	10	4	0	.714	295	221
Miami	10	4	0	.714	313	197
New England	9	5	0	.643	278	217
N.Y. Jets	3	11	0	.214	191	300
Buffalo	3	11	0	.214	160	313

Central Division

	W	L	T	Pct.	Pts.	OP
Pittsburgh	9	5	0	.643	283	243
Houston	8	6	0	.571	299	230
Cincinnati	8	6	0	.571	238	235
Cleveland	6	8	0	.429	269	267

Western Division

	W	L	T	Pct.	Pts.	OP
Denver	12	2	0	.857	274	148
Oakland*	11	3	0	.786	351	230
San Diego	7	7	0	.500	222	205
Seattle	5	9	0	.357	282	373
Kansas City	2	12	0	.143	225	349

NATIONAL CONFERENCE

Eastern Division

	W	L	T	Pct.	Pts.	OP
Dallas	12	2	0	.857	345	212
Washington	9	5	0	.643	196	189
St. Louis	7	7	0	.500	272	287
Philadelphia	5	9	0	.357	220	207
N.Y. Giants	5	9	0	.357	181	265

Central Division

	W	L	T	Pct.	Pts.	OP
Minnesota	9	5	0	.643	231	227
Chicago*	9	5	0	.643	255	253
Detroit	6	8	0	.429	183	252
Green Bay	4	10	0	.286	134	219
Tampa Bay	2	12	0	.143	103	223

Western Division

	W	L	T	Pct.	Pts.	OP
Los Angeles	10	4	0	.714	302	146
Atlanta	7	7	0	.500	179	129
San Francisco	5	9	0	.357	220	260
New Orleans	3	11	0	.214	232	336

**Wild-Card qualifier for playoffs*

Baltimore won division title on the basis of a better conference record than Miami (9-3 to 8-4). Chicago won a Wild-Card berth over Washington on the basis of best net points in conference games (plus 48 net points to plus 4).

Divisional playoffs: DENVER 34, Pittsburgh 21; Oakland 37, BALTIMORE 31 (OT)

AFC championship: DENVER 20, Oakland 17

Divisional playoffs: DALLAS 37, Chicago 7; Minnesota 14, LOS ANGELES 7

NFC championship: DALLAS 23, Minnesota 6

Super Bowl XII: Dallas (NFC) 27, Denver (AFC) 10, at Louisiana Superdome, New Orleans, Louisiana

1976

AMERICAN CONFERENCE

Eastern Division

	W	L	T	Pct.	Pts.	OP
Baltimore	11	3	0	.786	417	246
New England*	11	3	0	.786	376	236
Miami	6	8	0	.429	263	264
N.Y. Jets	3	11	0	.214	169	383
Buffalo	2	12	0	.143	245	363

Central Division

	W	L	T	Pct.	Pts.	OP
Pittsburgh	10	4	0	.714	342	138
Cincinnati	10	4	0	.714	335	210
Cleveland	9	5	0	.643	267	287
Houston	5	9	0	.357	222	273

Western Division

	W	L	T	Pct.	Pts.	OP
Oakland	13	1	0	.929	350	237
Denver	9	5	0	.643	315	206
San Diego	6	8	0	.429	248	285
Kansas City	5	9	0	.357	290	376
Tampa Bay	0	14	0	.000	125	412

NATIONAL CONFERENCE

Eastern Division

	W	L	T	Pct.	Pts.	OP
Dallas	11	3	0	.786	296	194
Washington*	10	4	0	.714	291	217
St. Louis	10	4	0	.714	309	267
Philadelphia	4	10	0	.286	165	286
N.Y. Giants	3	11	0	.214	170	250

Central Division

	W	L	T	Pct.	Pts.	OP
Minnesota	11	2	1	.821	305	176
Chicago	7	7	0	.500	253	216
Detroit	6	8	0	.429	262	220
Green Bay	5	9	0	.357	218	299

Western Division

	W	L	T	Pct.	Pts.	OP
Los Angeles	10	3	1	.750	351	190
San Francisco	8	6	0	.571	270	190
Atlanta	4	10	0	.286	172	312
New Orleans	4	10	0	.286	253	346
Seattle	2	12	0	.143	229	429

**Wild-Card qualifier for playoffs*

Baltimore won division title on the basis of a better division record than New England (7-1 to 6-2). Pittsburgh won division title because of a two-game sweep over Cincinnati. Washington won Wild-Card berth over St. Louis because of a two-game sweep over Cardinals.

Divisional playoffs: OAKLAND 24, New England 21; Pittsburgh 40, BALTIMORE 14

AFC championship: OAKLAND 24, Pittsburgh 7

Divisional playoffs: MINNESOTA 35, Washington 20; Los Angeles 14, DALLAS 12

NFC championship: MINNESOTA 24, Los Angeles 13

Super Bowl XI: Oakland (AFC) 32, Minnesota (NFC) 14, at Rose Bowl, Pasadena, California

1975

AMERICAN CONFERENCE

Eastern Division

	W	L	T	Pct.	Pts.	OP
Baltimore	10	4	0	.714	395	269
Miami	10	4	0	.714	357	222
Buffalo	8	6	0	.571	420	355
New England	3	11	0	.214	258	358
N.Y. Jets	3	11	0	.214	258	433

Central Division

	W	L	T	Pct.	Pts.	OP
Pittsburgh	12	2	0	.857	373	162
Cincinnati*	11	3	0	.786	340	246
Houston	10	4	0	.714	293	226
Cleveland	3	11	0	.214	218	372

Western Division

	W	L	T	Pct.	Pts.	OP
Oakland	11	3	0	.786	375	255
Denver	6	8	0	.429	254	307
Kansas City	5	9	0	.357	282	341
San Diego	2	12	0	.143	189	345

NATIONAL CONFERENCE

Eastern Division

	W	L	T	Pct.	Pts.	OP
St. Louis	11	3	0	.786	356	276
Dallas*	10	4	0	.714	350	268
Washington	8	6	0	.571	325	276
N.Y. Giants	5	9	0	.357	216	306
Philadelphia	4	10	0	.286	225	302

Central Division

	W	L	T	Pct.	Pts.	OP
Minnesota	12	2	0	.857	377	180
Detroit	7	7	0	.500	245	262
Chicago	4	10	0	.286	191	379
Green Bay	4	10	0	.286	226	285

Western Division

	W	L	T	Pct.	Pts.	OP
Los Angeles	12	2	0	.857	312	135
San Francisco	5	9	0	.357	255	286
Atlanta	4	10	0	.286	240	289
New Orleans	2	12	0	.143	165	360

**Wild-Card qualifier for playoffs*

Baltimore won division title on the basis of a two-game sweep over Miami.

Divisional playoffs: PITTSBURGH 28, Baltimore 10; OAKLAND 31, Cincinnati 28

AFC championship: PITTSBURGH 16, Oakland 10

Divisional playoffs: LOS ANGELES 35, St. Louis 23; Dallas 17, MINNESOTA 14

NFC championship: Dallas 37, LOS ANGELES 7

Super Bowl X: Pittsburgh (AFC) 21, Dallas (NFC) 17, at Orange Bowl, Miami, Florida

PAST STANDINGS

1974

AMERICAN CONFERENCE

Eastern Division

	W	L	T	Pct.	Pts.	OP
Miami	11	3	0	.786	327	216
Buffalo*	9	5	0	.643	264	244
New England	7	7	0	.500	348	289
N.Y. Jets	7	7	0	.500	279	300
Baltimore	2	12	0	.143	190	329

Central Division

	W	L	T	Pct.	Pts.	OP
Pittsburgh	10	3	1	.750	305	189
Cincinnati	7	7	0	.500	283	259
Houston	7	7	0	.500	236	282
Cleveland	4	10	0	.286	251	344

Western Division

	W	L	T	Pct.	Pts.	OP
Oakland	12	2	0	.857	355	228
Denver	7	6	1	.536	302	294
Kansas City	5	9	0	.357	233	293
San Diego	5	9	0	.357	212	285

NATIONAL CONFERENCE

Eastern Division

	W	L	T	Pct.	Pts.	OP
St. Louis	10	4	0	.714	285	218
Washington*	10	4	0	.714	320	196
Dallas	8	6	0	.571	297	235
Philadelphia	7	7	0	.500	242	217
N.Y. Giants	2	12	0	.143	195	299

Central Division

	W	L	T	Pct.	Pts.	OP
Minnesota	10	4	0	.714	310	195
Detroit	7	7	0	.500	256	270
Green Bay	6	8	0	.429	210	206
Chicago	4	10	0	.286	152	279

Western Division

	W	L	T	Pct.	Pts.	OP
Los Angeles	10	4	0	.714	263	181
San Francisco	6	8	0	.429	226	236
New Orleans	5	9	0	.357	166	263
Atlanta	3	11	0	.214	111	271

**Wild-Card qualifier for playoffs*

St. Louis won division title because of a two-game sweep over Washington.

Divisional playoffs: OAKLAND 28, Miami 26; PITTSBURGH 32, Buffalo 14

AFC championship: Pittsburgh 24, OAKLAND 13

Divisional playoffs: MINNESOTA 30, St. Louis 14; LOS ANGELES 19, Washington 10

NFC championship: MINNESOTA 14, Los Angeles 10

Super Bowl IX: Pittsburgh (AFC) 16, Minnesota (NFC) 6, at Tulane Stadium, New Orleans, Louisiana

1973

AMERICAN CONFERENCE

Eastern Division

	W	L	T	Pct.	Pts.	OP
Miami	12	2	0	.857	343	150
Buffalo	9	5	0	.643	259	230
New England	5	9	0	.357	258	300
Baltimore	4	10	0	.286	226	341
N.Y. Jets	4	10	0	.286	240	306

Central Division

	W	L	T	Pct.	Pts.	OP
Cincinnati	10	4	0	.714	286	231
Pittsburgh*	10	4	0	.714	347	210
Cleveland	7	5	2	.571	234	255
Houston	1	13	0	.071	199	447

Western Division

	W	L	T	Pct.	Pts.	OP
Oakland	9	4	1	.679	292	175
Denver	7	5	2	.571	354	296
Kansas City	7	5	2	.571	231	192
San Diego	2	11	1	.179	188	386

NATIONAL CONFERENCE

Eastern Division

	W	L	T	Pct.	Pts.	OP
Dallas	10	4	0	.714	382	203
Washington*	10	4	0	.714	325	198
Philadelphia	5	8	1	.393	310	393
St. Louis	4	9	1	.321	286	365
N.Y. Giants	2	11	1	.179	226	362

Central Division

	W	L	T	Pct.	Pts.	OP
Minnesota	12	2	0	.857	296	168
Detroit	6	7	1	.464	271	247
Green Bay	5	7	2	.429	202	259
Chicago	3	11	0	.214	195	334

Western Division

	W	L	T	Pct.	Pts.	OP
Los Angeles	12	2	0	.857	388	178
Atlanta	9	5	0	.643	318	224
New Orleans	5	9	0	.357	163	312
San Francisco	5	9	0	.357	262	319

**Wild-Card qualifier for playoffs*

Cincinnati won division title on the basis of a better conference record than Pittsburgh (8-3 to 7-4). Dallas won division title on the basis of a better point differential vs. Washington (net 13 points).

Divisional playoffs: OAKLAND 33, Pittsburgh 14; MIAMI 34, Cincinnati 16

AFC championship: MIAMI 27, Oakland 10

Divisional playoffs: MINNESOTA 27, Washington 20; DALLAS 27, Los Angeles 16

NFC championship: Minnesota 27, DALLAS 10

Super Bowl VIII: Miami (AFC) 24, Minnesota (NFC) 7, at Rice Stadium, Houston, Texas

1972

AMERICAN CONFERENCE

Eastern Division

	W	L	T	Pct.	Pts.	OP
Miami	14	0	0	1.000	385	171
N.Y. Jets	7	7	0	.500	367	324
Baltimore	5	9	0	.357	235	252
Buffalo	4	9	1	.321	257	377
New England	3	11	0	.214	192	446

Central Division

	W	L	T	Pct.	Pts.	OP
Pittsburgh	11	3	0	.786	343	175
Cleveland*	10	4	0	.714	268	249
Cincinnati	8	6	0	.571	299	229
Houston	1	13	0	.071	164	380

Western Division

	W	L	T	Pct.	Pts.	OP
Oakland	10	3	1	.750	365	248
Kansas City	8	6	0	.571	287	254
Denver	5	9	0	.357	325	350
San Diego	4	9	1	.321	264	344

NATIONAL CONFERENCE

Eastern Division

	W	L	T	Pct.	Pts.	OP
Washington	11	3	0	.786	336	218
Dallas*	10	4	0	.714	319	240
N.Y. Giants	8	6	0	.571	331	247
St. Louis	4	9	1	.321	193	303
Philadelphia	2	11	1	.179	145	352

Central Division

	W	L	T	Pct.	Pts.	OP
Green Bay	10	4	0	.714	304	226
Detroit	8	5	1	.607	339	290
Minnesota	7	7	0	.500	301	252
Chicago	4	9	1	.321	225	275

Western Division

	W	L	T	Pct.	Pts.	OP
San Francisco	8	5	1	.607	353	249
Atlanta	7	7	0	.500	269	274
Los Angeles	6	7	1	.464	291	286
New Orleans	2	11	1	.179	215	361

**Wild-Card qualifier for playoffs*

Divisional playoffs: PITTSBURGH 13, Oakland 7; MIAMI 20, Cleveland 14

AFC championship: Miami 21, PITTSBURGH 17

Divisional playoffs: Dallas 30, SAN FRANCISCO 28; WASHINGTON 16, Green Bay 3

NFC championship: WASHINGTON 26, Dallas 3

Super Bowl VII: Miami (AFC) 14, Washington (NFC) 7, at Memorial Coliseum, Los Angeles, California

1971

AMERICAN CONFERENCE

Eastern Division

	W	L	T	Pct.	Pts.	OP
Miami	10	3	1	.769	315	174
Baltimore*	10	4	0	.714	313	140
New England	6	8	0	.429	238	325
N.Y. Jets	6	8	0	.429	212	299
Buffalo	1	13	0	.071	184	394

Central Division

	W	L	T	Pct.	Pts.	OP
Cleveland	9	5	0	.643	285	273
Pittsburgh	6	8	0	.429	246	292
Houston	4	9	1	.308	251	330
Cincinnati	4	10	0	.286	284	265

Western Division

	W	L	T	Pct.	Pts.	OP
Kansas City	10	3	1	.769	302	208
Oakland	8	4	2	.667	344	278
San Diego	6	8	0	.429	311	341
Denver	4	9	1	.308	203	275

NATIONAL CONFERENCE

Eastern Division

	W	L	T	Pct.	Pts.	OP
Dallas	11	3	0	.786	406	222
Washington*	9	4	1	.692	276	190
Philadelphia	6	7	1	.462	221	302
St. Louis	4	9	1	.308	231	279
N.Y. Giants	4	10	0	.286	228	362

Central Division

	W	L	T	Pct.	Pts.	OP
Minnesota	11	3	0	.786	245	139
Detroit	7	6	1	.538	341	286
Chicago	6	8	0	.429	185	276
Green Bay	4	8	2	.333	274	298

Western Division

	W	L	T	Pct.	Pts.	OP
San Francisco	9	5	0	.643	300	216
Los Angeles	8	5	1	.615	313	260
Atlanta	7	6	1	.538	274	277
New Orleans	4	8	2	.333	266	347

**Wild-Card qualifier for playoffs*

Divisional playoffs: Miami 27, KANSAS CITY 24 (OT); Baltimore 20, CLEVELAND 3

AFC championship: MIAMI 21, Baltimore 0

Divisional playoffs: Dallas 20, MINNESOTA 12; SAN FRANCISCO 24, Washington 20

NFC championship: DALLAS 14, San Francisco 3

Super Bowl VI: Dallas (NFC) 24, Miami (AFC) 3, at Tulane Stadium, New Orleans, Louisiana

1970

AMERICAN CONFERENCE

Eastern Division

	W	L	T	Pct.	Pts.	OP
Baltimore	11	2	1	.846	321	234
Miami*	10	4	0	.714	297	228
N.Y. Jets	4	10	0	.286	255	286
Buffalo	3	10	1	.231	204	337
Boston Patriots	2	12	0	.143	149	361

Central Division

	W	L	T	Pct.	Pts.	OP
Cincinnati	8	6	0	.571	312	255
Cleveland	7	7	0	.500	286	265
Pittsburgh	5	9	0	.357	210	272
Houston	3	10	1	.231	217	352

Western Division

	W	L	T	Pct.	Pts.	OP
Oakland	8	4	2	.667	300	293
Kansas City	7	5	2	.583	272	244
San Diego	5	6	3	.455	282	278
Denver	5	8	1	.385	253	264

NATIONAL CONFERENCE

Eastern Division

	W	L	T	Pct.	Pts.	OP
Dallas	10	4	0	.714	299	221
N.Y. Giants	9	5	0	.643	301	270
St. Louis	8	5	1	.615	325	228
Washington	6	8	0	.429	297	314
Philadelphia	3	10	1	.231	241	332

Central Division

	W	L	T	Pct.	Pts.	OP
Minnesota	12	2	0	.857	335	143
Detroit*	10	4	0	.714	347	202
Chicago	6	8	0	.429	256	261
Green Bay	6	8	0	.429	196	293

Western Division

	W	L	T	Pct.	Pts.	OP
San Francisco	10	3	1	.769	352	267
Los Angeles	9	4	1	.692	325	202
Atlanta	4	8	2	.333	206	261
New Orleans	2	11	1	.154	172	347

**Wild-Card qualifier for playoffs*

Divisional playoffs: BALTIMORE 17, Cincinnati 0; OAKLAND 21, Miami 14
AFC championship: BALTIMORE 27, Oakland 17
Divisional playoffs: DALLAS 5, Detroit 0; San Francisco 17, MINNESOTA 14
NFC championship: Dallas 17, SAN FRANCISCO 10
Super Bowl V: Baltimore (AFC) 16, Dallas (NFC) 13, at Orange Bowl, Miami, Florida

1969 NFL

EASTERN CONFERENCE

Capitol Division

	W	L	T	Pct.	Pts.	OP
Dallas	11	2	1	.846	369	223
Washington	7	5	2	.583	307	319
New Orleans	5	9	0	.357	311	393
Philadelphia	4	9	1	.308	279	377

Century Division

	W	L	T	Pct.	Pts.	OP
Cleveland	10	3	1	.769	351	300
N.Y. Giants	6	8	0	.429	264	298
St. Louis	4	9	1	.308	314	389
Pittsburgh	1	13	0	.071	218	404

WESTERN CONFERENCE

Coastal Division

	W	L	T	Pct.	Pts.	OP
Los Angeles	11	3	0	.786	320	243
Baltimore	8	5	1	.615	279	268
Atlanta	6	8	0	.429	276	268
San Francisco	4	8	2	.333	277	319

Central Division

	W	L	T	Pct.	Pts.	OP
Minnesota	12	2	0	.857	379	133
Detroit	9	4	1	.692	259	188
Green Bay	8	6	0	.571	269	221
Chicago	1	13	0	.071	210	339

Conference championships: Cleveland 38, DALLAS 14; MINNESOTA 23, Los Angeles 20
NFL championship: MINNESOTA 27, Cleveland 7
Super Bowl IV: Kansas City (AFL) 23, Minnesota (NFL) 7, at Tulane Stadium, New Orleans, Louisiana

1969 AFL

EASTERN DIVISION

	W	L	T	Pct.	Pts.	OP
N.Y. Jets	10	4	0	.714	353	269
Houston	6	6	2	.500	278	279
Boston Patriots	4	10	0	.286	266	316
Buffalo	4	10	0	.286	230	359
Miami	3	10	1	.231	233	332

WESTERN DIVISION

	W	L	T	Pct.	Pts.	OP
Oakland	12	1	1	.923	377	242
Kansas City	11	3	0	.786	359	177
San Diego	8	6	0	.571	288	276
Denver	5	8	1	.385	297	344
Cincinnati	4	9	1	.308	280	367

Divisional playoffs: Kansas City 13, N.Y. JETS 6; OAKLAND 56, Houston 7
AFL championship: Kansas City 17, OAKLAND 7

1968 NFL

EASTERN CONFERENCE

Capitol Division

	W	L	T	Pct.	Pts.	OP
Dallas	12	2	0	.857	431	186
N.Y. Giants	7	7	0	.500	294	325
Washington	5	9	0	.357	249	358
Philadelphia	2	12	0	.143	202	351

Century Division

	W	L	T	Pct.	Pts.	OP
Cleveland	10	4	0	.714	394	273
St. Louis	9	4	1	.692	325	289
New Orleans	4	9	1	.308	246	327
Pittsburgh	2	11	1	.154	244	397

WESTERN CONFERENCE

Coastal Division

	W	L	T	Pct.	Pts.	OP
Baltimore	13	1	0	.929	402	144
Los Angeles	10	3	1	.769	312	200
San Francisco	7	6	1	.538	303	310
Atlanta	2	12	0	.143	170	389

Central Division

	W	L	T	Pct.	Pts.	OP
Minnesota	8	6	0	.571	282	242
Chicago	7	7	0	.500	250	333
Green Bay	6	7	1	.462	281	227
Detroit	4	8	2	.333	207	241

Conference championships: CLEVELAND 31, Dallas 20; BALTIMORE 24, Minnesota 14
NFL championship: Baltimore 34, CLEVELAND 0
Super Bowl III: N.Y. Jets (AFL) 16, Baltimore (NFL) 7, at Orange Bowl, Miami, Florida

1968 AFL

EASTERN DIVISION

	W	L	T	Pct.	Pts.	OP
N.Y. Jets	11	3	0	.786	419	280
Houston	7	7	0	.500	303	248
Miami	5	8	1	.385	276	355
Boston Patriots	4	10	0	.286	229	406
Buffalo	1	12	1	.077	199	367

WESTERN DIVISION

	W	L	T	Pct.	Pts.	OP
Oakland	12	2	0	.857	453	233
Kansas City	12	2	0	.857	371	170
San Diego	9	5	0	.643	382	310
Denver	5	9	0	.357	255	404
Cincinnati	3	11	0	.214	215	329

Western Division playoff: OAKLAND 41, Kansas City 6
AFL championship: N.Y. JETS 27, Oakland 23

1967 NFL

EASTERN CONFERENCE

Capitol Division

	W	L	T	Pct.	Pts.	OP
Dallas	9	5	0	.643	342	268
Philadelphia	6	7	1	.462	351	409
Washington	5	6	3	.455	347	353
New Orleans	3	11	0	.214	233	379

Century Division

	W	L	T	Pct.	Pts.	OP
Cleveland	9	5	0	.643	334	297
N.Y. Giants	7	7	0	.500	369	379
St. Louis	6	7	1	.462	333	356
Pittsburgh	4	9	1	.308	281	320

WESTERN CONFERENCE

Coastal Division

	W	L	T	Pct.	Pts.	OP
Los Angeles	11	1	2	.917	398	196
Baltimore	11	1	2	.917	394	198
San Francisco	7	7	0	.500	273	337
Atlanta	1	12	1	.077	175	422

Central Division

	W	L	T	Pct.	Pts.	OP
Green Bay	9	4	1	.692	332	209
Chicago	7	6	1	.538	239	218
Detroit	5	7	2	.417	260	259
Minnesota	3	8	3	.273	233	294

Los Angeles won division title on the basis of advantage in points (58-34) in two games vs. Baltimore.

Conference championships: DALLAS 52, Cleveland 14; GREEN BAY 28, Los Angeles 7
NFL championship: GREEN BAY 21, Dallas 17
Super Bowl II: Green Bay (NFL) 33, Oakland (AFL) 14, at Orange Bowl, Miami, Florida

1967 AFL

EASTERN DIVISION

	W	L	T	Pct.	Pts.	OP
Houston	9	4	1	.692	258	199
N.Y. Jets	8	5	1	.615	371	329
Buffalo	4	10	0	.286	237	285
Miami	4	10	0	.286	219	407
Boston Patriots	3	10	1	.231	280	389

WESTERN DIVISION

	W	L	T	Pct.	Pts.	OP
Oakland	13	1	0	.929	468	233
Kansas City	9	5	0	.643	408	254
San Diego	8	5	1	.615	360	352
Denver	3	11	0	.214	256	409

AFL championship: OAKLAND 40, Houston 7

1966 NFL

EASTERN CONFERENCE

	W	L	T	Pct.	Pts.	OP
Dallas	10	3	1	.769	445	239
Cleveland	9	5	0	.643	403	259
Philadelphia	9	5	0	.643	326	340
St. Louis	8	5	1	.615	264	265
Washington	7	7	0	.500	351	355
Pittsburgh	5	8	1	.385	316	347
Atlanta	3	11	0	.214	204	437
N.Y. Giants	1	12	1	.077	263	501

WESTERN CONFERENCE

	W	L	T	Pct.	Pts.	OP
Green Bay	12	2	0	.857	335	163
Baltimore	9	5	0	.643	314	226
Los Angeles	8	6	0	.571	289	212
San Francisco	6	6	2	.500	320	325
Chicago	5	7	2	.417	234	272
Detroit	4	9	1	.308	206	317
Minnesota	4	9	1	.308	292	304

NFL championship: Green Bay 34, DALLAS 27
Super Bowl I: Green Bay (NFL) 35, Kansas City (AFL) 10, at Memorial Coliseum, Los Angeles, California

1966 AFL

EASTERN DIVISION

	W	L	T	Pct.	Pts.	OP
Buffalo	9	4	1	.692	358	255
Boston Patriots	8	4	2	.677	315	283
N.Y. Jets	6	6	2	.500	322	312
Houston	3	11	0	.214	335	396
Miami	3	11	0	.214	213	362

WESTERN DIVISION

	W	L	T	Pct.	Pts.	OP
Kansas City	11	2	1	.846	448	276
Oakland	8	5	1	.615	315	288
San Diego	7	6	1	.538	335	284
Denver	4	10	0	.286	196	381

AFL championship: Kansas City 31, BUFFALO 7

1965 NFL

EASTERN CONFERENCE

	W	L	T	Pct.	Pts.	OP
Cleveland	11	3	0	.786	363	325
Dallas	7	7	0	.500	325	280
N.Y. Giants	7	7	0	.500	270	338
Washington	6	8	0	.429	257	301
Philadelphia	5	9	0	.357	363	359
St. Louis	5	9	0	.357	296	309
Pittsburgh	2	12	0	.143	202	397

WESTERN CONFERENCE

	W	L	T	Pct.	Pts.	OP
Green Bay	10	3	1	.769	316	224
Baltimore	10	3	1	.769	389	284
Chicago	9	5	0	.643	409	275
San Francisco	7	6	1	.538	421	402
Minnesota	7	7	0	.500	383	403
Detroit	6	7	1	.462	257	295
Los Angeles	4	10	0	.286	269	328

Western Conference playoff: GREEN BAY 13, Baltimore 10 (OT)
NFL championship: GREEN BAY 23, Cleveland 12

PAST STANDINGS

1965 AFL

EASTERN DIVISION

	W	L	T	Pct.	Pts.	OP
Buffalo	10	3	1	.769	313	226
N.Y. Jets	5	8	1	.385	285	303
Boston Patriots	4	8	2	.333	244	302
Houston	4	10	0	.286	298	429

WESTERN DIVISION

	W	L	T	Pct.	Pts.	OP
San Diego	9	2	3	.818	340	227
Oakland	8	5	1	.615	298	239
Kansas City	7	5	2	.583	322	285
Denver	4	10	0	.286	303	392

AFL championship: Buffalo 23, SAN DIEGO 0

1964 NFL

EASTERN CONFERENCE

	W	L	T	Pct.	Pts.	OP
Cleveland	10	3	1	.769	415	293
St. Louis	9	3	2	.750	357	331
Philadelphia	6	8	0	.429	312	313
Washington	6	8	0	.429	307	305
Dallas	5	8	1	.385	250	289
Pittsburgh	5	9	0	.357	253	315
N.Y. Giants	2	10	2	.167	241	399

WESTERN CONFERENCE

	W	L	T	Pct.	Pts.	OP
Baltimore	12	2	0	.857	428	225
Green Bay	8	5	1	.615	342	245
Minnesota	8	5	1	.615	355	296
Detroit	7	5	2	.583	280	260
Los Angeles	5	7	2	.417	283	339
Chicago	5	9	0	.357	260	379
San Francisco	4	10	0	.286	236	330

NFL championship: CLEVELAND 27, Baltimore 0

1964 AFL

EASTERN DIVISION

	W	L	T	Pct.	Pts.	OP
Buffalo	12	2	0	.857	400	242
Boston Patriots	10	3	1	.769	365	297
N.Y. Jets	5	8	1	.385	278	315
Houston	4	10	0	.286	310	355

WESTERN DIVISION

	W	L	T	Pct.	Pts.	OP
San Diego	8	5	1	.615	341	300
Kansas City	7	7	0	.500	366	306
Oakland	5	7	2	.417	303	350
Denver	2	11	1	.154	240	438

AFL championship: BUFFALO 20, San Diego 7

1963 NFL

EASTERN CONFERENCE

	W	L	T	Pct.	Pts.	OP
N.Y. Giants	11	3	0	.786	448	280
Cleveland	10	4	0	.714	343	262
St. Louis	9	5	0	.643	341	283
Pittsburgh	7	4	3	.636	321	295
Dallas	4	10	0	.286	305	378
Washington	3	11	0	.214	279	398
Philadelphia	2	10	2	.167	242	381

WESTERN CONFERENCE

	W	L	T	Pct.	Pts.	OP
Chicago	11	1	2	.917	301	144
Green Bay	11	2	1	.846	369	206
Baltimore	8	6	0	.571	316	285
Detroit	5	8	1	.385	326	265
Minnesota	5	8	1	.385	309	390
Los Angeles	5	9	0	.357	210	350
San Francisco	2	12	0	.143	198	391

NFL championship: CHICAGO 14, N.Y. Giants 10

1963 AFL

EASTERN DIVISION

	W	L	T	Pct.	Pts.	OP
Boston Patriots	7	6	1	.538	327	257
Buffalo	7	6	1	.538	304	291
Houston	6	8	0	.429	302	372
N.Y. Jets	5	8	1	.385	249	399

WESTERN DIVISION

	W	L	T	Pct.	Pts.	OP
San Diego	11	3	0	.786	399	255
Oakland	10	4	0	.714	363	282
Kansas City	5	7	2	.417	347	263
Denver	2	11	1	.154	301	473

Eastern Division playoff: Boston 26, BUFFALO 8
AFL championship: SAN DIEGO 51, Boston 10

1962 NFL

EASTERN CONFERENCE

	W	L	T	Pct.	Pts.	OP
N.Y. Giants	12	2	0	.857	398	283
Pittsburgh	9	5	0	.643	312	363
Cleveland	7	6	1	.538	291	257
Washington	5	7	2	.417	305	376
Dallas Cowboys	5	8	1	.385	398	402
St. Louis	4	9	1	.308	287	361
Philadelphia	3	10	1	.231	282	356

WESTERN CONFERENCE

	W	L	T	Pct.	Pts.	OP
Green Bay	13	1	0	.929	415	148
Detroit	11	3	0	.786	315	177
Chicago	9	5	0	.643	321	287
Baltimore	7	7	0	.500	293	288
San Francisco	6	8	0	.429	282	331
Minnesota	2	11	1	.154	254	410
Los Angeles	1	12	1	.077	220	334

NFL championship: Green Bay 16, N.Y. GIANTS 7

1962 AFL

EASTERN DIVISION

	W	L	T	Pct.	Pts.	OP
Houston	11	3	0	.786	387	270
Boston Patriots	9	4	1	.692	346	295
Buffalo	7	6	1	.538	309	272
N.Y. Titans	5	9	0	.357	278	423

WESTERN DIVISION

	W	L	T	Pct.	Pts.	OP
Dallas Texans	11	3	0	.786	389	233
Denver	7	7	0	.500	353	334
San Diego	4	10	0	.286	314	392
Oakland	1	13	0	.071	213	370

AFL championship: Dallas Texans 20, HOUSTON 17 (OT)

1961 NFL

EASTERN CONFERENCE

	W	L	T	Pct.	Pts.	OP
N.Y. Giants	10	3	1	.769	368	220
Philadelphia	10	4	0	.714	361	297
Cleveland	8	5	1	.615	319	270
St. Louis	7	7	0	.500	279	267
Pittsburgh	6	8	0	.429	295	287
Dallas Cowboys	4	9	1	.308	236	380
Washington	1	12	1	.077	174	392

WESTERN CONFERENCE

	W	L	T	Pct.	Pts.	OP
Green Bay	11	3	0	.786	391	223
Detroit	8	5	1	.615	270	258
Baltimore	8	6	0	.571	302	307
Chicago	8	6	0	.571	326	302
San Francisco	7	6	1	.538	346	272
Los Angeles	4	10	0	.286	263	333
Minnesota	3	11	0	.214	285	407

NFL championship: GREEN BAY 37, N.Y. Giants 0

1961 AFL

EASTERN DIVISION

	W	L	T	Pct.	Pts.	OP
Houston	10	3	1	.769	513	242
Boston Patriots	9	4	1	.692	413	313
N.Y. Titans	7	7	0	.500	301	390
Buffalo	6	8	0	.429	294	342

WESTERN DIVISION

	W	L	T	Pct.	Pts.	OP
San Diego	12	2	0	.857	396	219
Dallas Texans	6	8	0	.429	334	343
Denver	3	11	0	.214	251	432
Oakland	2	12	0	.143	237	458

AFL championship: Houston 10, SAN DIEGO 3

1960 NFL

EASTERN CONFERENCE

	W	L	T	Pct.	Pts.	OP
Philadelphia	10	2	0	.833	321	246
Cleveland	8	3	1	.727	362	217
N.Y. Giants	6	4	2	.600	271	261
St. Louis	6	5	1	.545	288	230
Pittsburgh	5	6	1	.455	240	275
Washington	1	9	2	.100	178	309

WESTERN CONFERENCE

	W	L	T	Pct.	Pts.	OP
Green Bay	8	4	0	.667	332	209
Detroit	7	5	0	.583	239	212
San Francisco	7	5	0	.583	208	205
Baltimore	6	6	0	.500	288	234
Chicago	5	6	1	.455	194	299
L.A. Rams	4	7	1	.364	265	297
Dallas Cowboys	0	11	1	.000	177	369

NFL championship: PHILADELPHIA 17, Green Bay 13

1960 AFL

EASTERN CONFERENCE

	W	L	T	Pct.	Pts.	OP
Houston	10	4	0	.714	379	285
N.Y. Titans	7	7	0	.500	382	399
Buffalo	5	8	1	.385	296	303
Boston	5	9	0	.357	286	349

WESTERN CONFERENCE

	W	L	T	Pct.	Pts.	OP
L.A. Chargers	10	4	0	.714	373	336
Dallas Texans	8	6	0	.571	362	253
Oakland	6	8	0	.429	319	388
Denver	4	9	1	.308	309	393

AFL championship: HOUSTON 24, L.A. Chargers 16

1959

EASTERN CONFERENCE

	W	L	T	Pct.	Pts.	OP
N.Y. Giants	10	2	0	.833	284	170
Cleveland	7	5	0	.583	270	214
Philadelphia	7	5	0	.583	268	278
Pittsburgh	6	5	1	.545	257	216
Washington	3	9	0	.250	185	350
Chi. Cardinals	2	10	0	.167	234	324

WESTERN CONFERENCE

	W	L	T	Pct.	Pts.	OP
Baltimore	9	3	0	.750	374	251
Chi. Bears	8	4	0	.667	252	196
Green Bay	7	5	0	.583	248	246
San Francisco	7	5	0	.583	255	237
Detroit	3	8	1	.273	203	275
Los Angeles	2	10	0	.167	242	315

NFL championship: BALTIMORE 31, N.Y. Giants 16

1958

EASTERN CONFERENCE

	W	L	T	Pct.	Pts.	OP
N.Y. Giants	9	3	0	.750	246	183
Cleveland	9	3	0	.750	302	217
Pittsburgh	7	4	1	.636	261	230
Washington	4	7	1	.364	214	268
Chi. Cardinals	2	9	1	.182	261	356
Philadelphia	2	9	1	.182	235	306

WESTERN CONFERENCE

	W	L	T	Pct.	Pts.	OP
Baltimore	9	3	0	.750	381	203
Chi. Bears	8	4	0	.667	298	230
Los Angeles	8	4	0	.667	344	278
San Francisco	6	6	0	.500	257	324
Detroit	4	7	1	.364	261	276
Green Bay	1	10	1	.091	193	382

Eastern Conference playoff: N.Y. GIANTS 10, Cleveland 0
NFL championship: Baltimore 23, N.Y. GIANTS 17 (OT)

1957

EASTERN CONFERENCE

	W	L	T	Pct.	Pts.	OP
Cleveland	9	2	1	.818	269	172
N.Y. Giants	7	5	0	.583	254	211
Pittsburgh	6	6	0	.500	161	178
Washington	5	6	1	.455	251	230
Philadelphia	4	8	0	.333	173	230
Chi. Cardinals	3	9	0	.250	200	299

WESTERN CONFERENCE

	W	L	T	Pct.	Pts.	OP
Detroit	8	4	0	.667	251	231
San Francisco	8	4	0	.667	260	264
Baltimore	7	5	0	.583	303	235
Los Angeles	6	6	0	.500	307	278
Chi. Bears	5	7	0	.417	203	211
Green Bay	3	9	0	.250	218	311

Western Conference playoff: Detroit 31, SAN FRANCISCO 27
NFL championship: DETROIT 59, Cleveland 14

1956

EASTERN CONFERENCE

	W	L	T	Pct.	Pts.	OP
N.Y. Giants	8	3	1	.727	264	197
Chi. Cardinals	7	5	0	.583	240	182
Washington	6	6	0	.500	183	225
Cleveland	5	7	0	.417	167	177
Pittsburgh	5	7	0	.417	217	250
Philadelphia	3	8	1	.273	143	215

WESTERN CONFERENCE

	W	L	T	Pct.	Pts.	OP
Chi. Bears	9	2	1	.818	363	246
Detroit	9	3	0	.750	300	188
San Francisco	5	6	1	.455	233	284
Baltimore	5	7	0	.417	270	322
Green Bay	4	8	0	.333	264	342
Los Angeles	4	8	0	.333	291	307

NFL championship: N.Y. GIANTS 47, Chi. Bears 7

1955

EASTERN CONFERENCE

	W	L	T	Pct.	Pts.	OP
Cleveland	9	2	1	.818	349	218
Washington	8	4	0	.667	246	222
N.Y. Giants	6	5	1	.545	267	223
Chi. Cardinals	4	7	1	.364	224	252
Philadelphia	4	7	1	.364	248	231
Pittsburgh	4	8	0	.333	195	285

WESTERN CONFERENCE

	W	L	T	Pct.	Pts.	OP
Los Angeles	8	3	1	.727	260	231
Chi. Bears	8	4	0	.667	294	251
Green Bay	6	6	0	.500	258	276
Baltimore	5	6	1	.455	214	239
San Francisco	4	8	0	.333	216	298
Detroit	3	9	0	.250	230	275

NFL championship: Cleveland 38, LOS ANGELES 14

1954

EASTERN CONFERENCE

	W	L	T	Pct.	Pts.	OP
Cleveland	9	3	0	.750	336	162
Philadelphia	7	4	1	.636	284	230
N.Y. Giants	7	5	0	.583	293	184
Pittsburgh	5	7	0	.417	219	263
Washington	3	9	0	.250	207	432
Chi. Cardinals	2	10	0	.167	183	347

WESTERN CONFERENCE

	W	L	T	Pct.	Pts.	OP
Detroit	9	2	1	.818	337	189
Chi. Bears	8	4	0	.667	301	279
San Francisco	7	4	1	.636	313	251
Los Angeles	6	5	1	.545	314	285
Green Bay	4	8	0	.333	234	251
Baltimore	3	9	0	.250	131	279

NFL championship: CLEVELAND 56, Detroit 10

1953

EASTERN CONFERENCE

	W	L	T	Pct.	Pts.	OP
Cleveland	11	1	0	.917	348	162
Philadelphia	7	4	1	.636	352	215
Washington	6	5	1	.545	208	215
Pittsburgh	6	6	0	.500	211	263
N.Y. Giants	3	9	0	.250	179	277
Chi. Cardinals	1	10	1	.091	190	337

WESTERN CONFERENCE

	W	L	T	Pct.	Pts.	OP
Detroit	10	2	0	.833	271	205
San Francisco	9	3	0	.750	372	237
Los Angeles	8	3	1	.727	366	236
Chi. Bears	3	8	1	.273	218	262
Baltimore	3	9	0	.250	182	350
Green Bay	2	9	1	.182	200	338

NFL championship: DETROIT 17, Cleveland 16

1952

AMERICAN CONFERENCE

	W	L	T	Pct.	Pts.	OP
Cleveland	8	4	0	.667	310	213
N.Y. Giants	7	5	0	.583	234	231
Philadelphia	7	5	0	.583	252	271
Pittsburgh	5	7	0	.417	300	273
Chi. Cardinals	4	8	0	.333	172	221
Washington	4	8	0	.333	240	287

NATIONAL CONFERENCE

	W	L	T	Pct.	Pts.	OP
Detroit	9	3	0	.750	344	192
Los Angeles	9	3	0	.750	349	234
San Francisco	7	5	0	.583	285	221
Green Bay	6	6	0	.500	295	312
Chi. Bears	5	7	0	.417	245	326
Dallas Texans	1	11	0	.083	182	427

National Conference playoff: DETROIT 31, Los Angeles 21
NFL championship: Detroit 17, CLEVELAND 7

1951

AMERICAN CONFERENCE

	W	L	T	Pct.	Pts.	OP
Cleveland	11	1	0	.917	331	152
N.Y. Giants	9	2	1	.818	254	161
Washington	5	7	0	.417	183	296
Pittsburgh	4	7	1	.364	183	235
Philadelphia	4	8	0	.333	234	264
Chi. Cardinals	3	9	0	.250	210	287

NATIONAL CONFERENCE

	W	L	T	Pct.	Pts.	OP
Los Angeles	8	4	0	.667	392	261
Detroit	7	4	1	.636	336	259
San Francisco	7	4	1	.636	255	205
Chi. Bears	7	5	0	.583	286	282
Green Bay	3	9	0	.250	254	375
N.Y. Yanks	1	9	2	.100	241	382

NFL championship: LOS ANGELES 24, Cleveland 17

1950

AMERICAN CONFERENCE

	W	L	T	Pct.	Pts.	OP
Cleveland	10	2	0	.833	310	144
N.Y. Giants	10	2	0	.833	268	150
Philadelphia	6	6	0	.500	254	141
Pittsburgh	6	6	0	.500	180	195
Chi. Cardinals	5	7	0	.417	233	287
Washington	3	9	0	.250	232	326

NATIONAL CONFERENCE

	W	L	T	Pct.	Pts.	OP
Los Angeles	9	3	0	.750	466	309
Chi. Bears	9	3	0	.750	279	207
N.Y. Yanks	7	5	0	.583	366	367
Detroit	6	6	0	.500	321	285
Green Bay	3	9	0	.250	244	406
San Francisco	3	9	0	.250	213	300
Baltimore	1	11	0	.083	213	462

American Conference playoff: CLEVELAND 8, N.Y. Giants 3
National Conference playoff: LOS ANGELES 24, Chi. Bears 14
NFL championship: CLEVELAND 30, Los Angeles 28

1949

EASTERN DIVISION

	W	L	T	Pct.	Pts.	OP
Philadelphia	11	1	0	.917	364	134
Pittsburgh	6	5	1	.545	224	214
N.Y. Giants	6	6	0	.500	287	298
Washington	4	7	1	.364	268	339
N.Y. Bulldogs	1	10	1	.091	153	368

WESTERN DIVISION

	W	L	T	Pct.	Pts.	OP
Los Angeles	8	2	2	.800	360	239
Chi. Bears	9	3	0	.750	332	218
Chi. Cardinals	6	5	1	.545	360	301
Detroit	4	8	0	.333	237	259
Green Bay	2	10	0	.167	114	329

NFL championship: Philadelphia 14, LOS ANGELES 0

1948

EASTERN DIVISION

	W	L	T	Pct.	Pts.	OP
Philadelphia	9	2	1	.818	376	156
Washington	7	5	0	.583	291	287
N.Y. Giants	4	8	0	.333	297	388
Pittsburgh	4	8	0	.333	200	243
Boston	3	9	0	.250	174	372

WESTERN DIVISION

	W	L	T	Pct.	Pts.	OP
Chi. Cardinals	11	1	0	.917	395	226
Chi. Bears	10	2	0	.833	375	151
Los Angeles	6	5	1	.545	327	269
Green Bay	3	9	0	.250	154	290
Detroit	2	10	0	.167	200	407

NFL championship: PHILADELPHIA 7, Chi. Cardinals 0

1947

EASTERN DIVISION

	W	L	T	Pct.	Pts.	OP
Philadelphia	8	4	0	.667	308	242
Pittsburgh	8	4	0	.667	240	259
Boston	4	7	1	.364	168	256
Washington	4	8	0	.333	295	367
N.Y. Giants	2	8	2	.200	190	309

WESTERN DIVISION

	W	L	T	Pct.	Pts.	OP
Chi. Cardinals	9	3	0	.750	306	231
Chi. Bears	8	4	0	.667	363	241
Green Bay	6	5	1	.545	274	210
Los Angeles	6	6	0	.500	259	214
Detroit	3	9	0	.250	231	305

Eastern Division playoff: Philadelphia 21, PITTSBURGH 0
NFL championship: CHI. CARDINALS 28, Philadelphia 21

1946

EASTERN DIVISION

	W	L	T	Pct.	Pts.	OP
N.Y. Giants	7	3	1	.700	236	162
Philadelphia	6	5	0	.545	231	220
Washington	5	5	1	.500	171	191
Pittsburgh	5	5	1	.500	136	117
Boston	2	8	1	.200	189	273

WESTERN DIVISION

	W	L	T	Pct.	Pts.	OP
Chi. Bears	8	2	1	.800	289	193
Los Angeles	6	4	1	.600	277	257
Green Bay	6	5	0	.545	148	158
Chi. Cardinals	6	5	0	.545	260	198
Detroit	1	10	0	.091	142	310

NFL championship: Chi. Bears 24, N.Y. GIANTS 14

1945

EASTERN DIVISION

	W	L	T	Pct.	Pts.	OP
Washington	8	2	0	.800	209	121
Philadelphia	7	3	0	.700	272	133
N.Y. Giants	3	6	1	.333	179	198
Boston	3	6	1	.333	123	211
Pittsburgh	2	8	0	.200	79	220

WESTERN DIVISION

	W	L	T	Pct.	Pts.	OP
Cleveland	9	1	0	.900	244	136
Detroit	7	3	0	.700	195	194
Green Bay	6	4	0	.600	258	173
Chi. Bears	3	7	0	.300	192	235
Chi. Cardinals	1	9	0	.100	98	228

NFL championship: CLEVELAND 15, Washington 14

1944

EASTERN DIVISION

	W	L	T	Pct.	Pts.	OP
N.Y. Giants	8	1	1	.889	206	75
Philadelphia	7	1	2	.875	267	131
Washington	6	3	1	.667	169	180
Boston	2	8	0	.200	82	233
Brooklyn	0	10	0	.000	69	166

WESTERN DIVISION

	W	L	T	Pct.	Pts.	OP
Green Bay	8	2	0	.800	238	141
Chi. Bears	6	3	1	.667	258	172
Detroit	6	3	1	.667	216	151
Cleveland	4	6	0	.400	188	224
Card-Pitt	0	10	0	.000	108	328

NFL championship: Green Bay 14, N.Y. GIANTS 7

1943

EASTERN DIVISION

	W	L	T	Pct.	Pts.	OP
Washington	6	3	1	.667	229	137
N.Y. Giants	6	3	1	.667	197	170
Phil-Pitt	5	4	1	.556	225	230
Brooklyn	2	8	0	.200	65	234

WESTERN DIVISION

	W	L	T	Pct.	Pts.	OP
Chi. Bears	8	1	1	.889	303	157
Green Bay	7	2	1	.778	264	172
Detroit	3	6	1	.333	178	218
Chi. Cardinals	0	10	0	.000	95	238

Eastern Division playoff: Washington 28, N.Y. GIANTS 0
NFL championship: CHI. BEARS 41, Washington 21

1942

EASTERN DIVISION

	W	L	T	Pct.	Pts.	OP
Washington	10	1	0	.909	227	102
Pittsburgh	7	4	0	.636	167	119
N.Y. Giants	5	5	1	.500	155	139
Brooklyn	3	8	0	.273	100	168
Philadelphia	2	9	0	.182	134	239

WESTERN DIVISION

	W	L	T	Pct.	Pts.	OP
Chi. Bears	11	0	0	1.000	376	84
Green Bay	8	2	1	.800	300	215
Cleveland	5	6	0	.455	150	207
Chi. Cardinals	3	8	0	.273	98	209
Detroit	0	11	0	.000	38	263

NFL championship: WASHINGTON 14, Chi. Bears 6

PAST STANDINGS

1941

EASTERN DIVISION

	W	L	T	Pct.	Pts.	OP
N.Y. Giants	8	3	0	.727	238	114
Brooklyn	7	4	0	.636	158	127
Washington	6	5	0	.545	176	174
Philadelphia	2	8	1	.200	119	218
Pittsburgh	1	9	1	.100	103	276

WESTERN DIVISION

	W	L	T	Pct.	Pts.	OP
Chi. Bears	10	1	0	.909	396	147
Green Bay	10	1	0	.909	258	120
Detroit	4	6	1	.400	121	195
Chi. Cardinals	3	7	1	.300	127	197
Cleveland	2	9	0	.182	116	244

Western Division playoff: CHI. BEARS 33, Green Bay 14
NFL championship: CHI. BEARS 37, N.Y. Giants 9

1940

EASTERN DIVISION

	W	L	T	Pct.	Pts.	OP
Washington	9	2	0	.818	245	142
Brooklyn	8	3	0	.727	186	120
N.Y. Giants	6	4	1	.600	131	133
Pittsburgh	2	7	2	.222	60	178
Philadelphia	1	10	0	.091	111	211

WESTERN DIVISION

	W	L	T	Pct.	Pts.	OP
Chi. Bears	8	3	0	.727	238	152
Green Bay	6	4	1	.600	238	155
Detroit	5	5	1	.500	138	153
Cleveland	4	6	1	.400	171	191
Chi. Cardinals	2	7	2	.222	139	222

NFL championship: Chi. Bears 73, WASHINGTON 0

1939

EASTERN DIVISION

	W	L	T	Pct.	Pts.	OP
N.Y. Giants	9	1	1	.900	168	85
Washington	8	2	1	.800	242	94
Brooklyn	4	6	1	.400	108	219
Philadelphia	1	9	1	.100	105	200
Pittsburgh	1	9	1	.100	114	216

WESTERN DIVISION

	W	L	T	Pct.	Pts.	OP
Green Bay	9	2	0	.818	233	153
Chi. Bears	8	3	0	.727	298	157
Detroit	6	5	0	.545	145	150
Cleveland	5	5	1	.500	195	164
Chi. Cardinals	1	10	0	.091	84	254

NFL championship: GREEN BAY 27, N.Y. Giants 0

1938

EASTERN DIVISION

	W	L	T	Pct.	Pts.	OP
N.Y. Giants	8	2	1	.800	194	79
Washington	6	3	2	.667	148	154
Brooklyn	4	4	3	.500	131	161
Philadelphia	5	6	0	.455	154	164
Pittsburgh	2	9	0	.182	79	169

WESTERN DIVISION

	W	L	T	Pct.	Pts.	OP
Green Bay	8	3	0	.727	223	118
Detroit	7	4	0	.636	119	108
Chi. Bears	6	5	0	.545	194	148
Cleveland	4	7	0	.364	131	215
Chi. Cardinals	2	9	0	.182	111	168

NFL championship: N.Y. GIANTS 23, Green Bay 17

1937

EASTERN DIVISION

	W	L	T	Pct.	Pts.	OP
Washington	8	3	0	.727	195	120
N.Y. Giants	6	3	2	.667	128	109
Pittsburgh	4	7	0	.364	122	145
Brooklyn	3	7	1	.300	82	174
Philadelphia	2	8	1	.200	86	177

WESTERN DIVISION

	W	L	T	Pct.	Pts.	OP
Chi. Bears	9	1	1	.900	201	100
Green Bay	7	4	0	.636	220	122
Detroit	7	4	0	.636	180	105
Chi. Cardinals	5	5	1	.500	135	165
Cleveland	1	10	0	.091	75	207

NFL championship: Washington 28, CHI. BEARS 21

1936

EASTERN DIVISION

	W	L	T	Pct.	Pts.	OP
Boston	7	5	0	.583	149	110
Pittsburgh	6	6	0	.500	98	187
N.Y. Giants	5	6	1	.455	115	163
Brooklyn	3	8	1	.273	92	161
Philadelphia	1	11	0	.083	51	206

WESTERN DIVISION

	W	L	T	Pct.	Pts.	OP
Green Bay	10	1	1	.909	248	118
Chi. Bears	9	3	0	.750	222	94
Detroit	8	4	0	.667	235	102
Chi. Cardinals	3	8	1	.273	74	143

NFL championship: Green Bay 21, Boston 6, at Polo Grounds, N.Y.

1935

EASTERN DIVISION

	W	L	T	Pct.	Pts.	OP
N.Y. Giants	9	3	0	.750	180	96
Brooklyn	5	6	1	.455	90	141
Pittsburgh	4	8	0	.333	100	209
Boston	2	8	1	.200	65	123
Philadelphia	2	9	0	.182	60	179

WESTERN DIVISION

	W	L	T	Pct.	Pts.	OP
Detroit	7	3	2	.700	191	111
Green Bay	8	4	0	.667	181	96
Chi. Bears	6	4	2	.600	192	106
Chi. Cardinals	6	4	2	.600	99	97

NFL championship: DETROIT 26, N.Y. Giants 7
One game between Boston and Philadelphia was canceled.

1934

EASTERN DIVISION

	W	L	T	Pct.	Pts.	OP
N.Y. Giants	8	5	0	.615	147	107
Boston	6	6	0	.500	107	94
Brooklyn	4	7	0	.364	61	153
Philadelphia	4	7	0	.364	127	85
Pittsburgh	2	10	0	.167	51	206

WESTERN DIVISION

	W	L	T	Pct.	Pts.	OP
Chi. Bears	13	0	0	1.000	286	86
Detroit	10	3	0	.769	238	59
Green Bay	7	6	0	.538	156	112
Chi. Cardinals	5	6	0	.455	80	84
St. Louis	1	2	0	.333	27	61
Cincinnati	0	8	0	.000	10	243

NFL championship: N.Y. GIANTS 30, Chi. Bears 13

1933

EASTERN DIVISION

	W	L	T	Pct.	Pts.	OP
N.Y. Giants	11	3	0	.786	244	101
Brooklyn	5	4	1	.556	93	54
Boston	5	5	2	.500	103	97
Philadelphia	3	5	1	.375	77	158
Pittsburgh	3	6	2	.333	67	208

WESTERN DIVISION

	W	L	T	Pct.	Pts.	OP
Chi. Bears	10	2	1	.833	133	82
Portsmouth	6	5	0	.545	128	87
Green Bay	5	7	1	.417	170	107
Cincinnati	3	6	1	.333	38	110
Chi. Cardinals	1	9	1	.100	52	101

NFL championship: CHI. BEARS 23, N.Y. Giants 21

1932

	W	L	T	Pct.
Chicago Bears	7	1	6	.875
Green Bay Packers	10	3	1	.769
Portsmouth Spartans	6	2	4	.750
Boston Braves	4	4	2	.500
New York Giants	4	6	2	.400
Brooklyn Dodgers	3	9	0	.250
Chicago Cardinals	2	6	2	.250
Staten Island Stapletons	2	7	3	.222

Chicago Bears and Portsmouth finished regularly scheduled games tied for first place. Bears won playoff game, which counted in standings, 9-0.

1931

	W	L	T	Pct.
Green Bay Packers	12	2	0	.857
Portsmouth Spartans	11	3	0	.786
Chicago Bears	8	5	0	.615
Chicago Cardinals	5	4	0	.556
New York Giants	7	6	1	.538
Providence Steam Roller	4	4	3	.500
Staten Island Stapletons	4	6	1	.400
Cleveland Indians	2	8	0	.200
Brooklyn Dodgers	2	12	0	.143
Frankford Yellow Jackets	1	6	1	.143

1930

	W	L	T	Pct.
Green Bay Packers	10	3	1	.769
New York Giants	13	4	0	.765
Chicago Bears	9	4	1	.692
Brooklyn Dodgers	7	4	1	.636
Providence Steam Roller	6	4	1	.600
Staten Island Stapletons	5	5	2	.500
Chicago Cardinals	5	6	2	.455
Portsmouth Spartans	5	6	3	.455
Frankford Yellow Jackets	4	13	1	.222
Minneapolis Red Jackets	1	7	1	.125
Newark Tornadoes	1	10	1	.091

1929

	W	L	T	Pct.
Green Bay Packers	12	0	1	1.000
New York Giants	13	1	1	.929
Frankford Yellow Jackets	10	4	5	.714
Chicago Cardinals	6	6	1	.500
Boston Bulldogs	4	4	0	.500
Staten Island Stapletons	3	4	3	.429
Providence Steam Roller	4	6	2	.400
Orange Tornadoes	3	5	4	.375
Chicago Bears	4	9	2	.308
Buffalo Bisons	1	7	1	.125
Minneapolis Red Jackets	1	9	0	.100
Dayton Triangles	0	6	0	.000

1928

	W	L	T	Pct.
Providence Steam Roller	8	1	2	.889
Frankford Yellow Jackets	11	3	2	.786
Detroit Wolverines	7	2	1	.778
Green Bay Packers	6	4	3	.600
Chicago Bears	7	5	1	.583
New York Giants	4	7	2	.364
New York Yankees	4	8	1	.333
Pottsville Maroons	2	8	0	.200
Chicago Cardinals	1	5	0	.167
Dayton Triangles	0	7	0	.000

1927

	W	L	T	Pct.
New York Giants	11	1	1	.917
Green Bay Packers	7	2	1	.778
Chicago Bears	9	3	2	.750
Cleveland Bulldogs	8	4	1	.667
Providence Steam Roller	8	5	1	.615
New York Yankees	7	8	1	.467
Frankford Yellow Jackets	6	9	3	.400
Pottsville Maroons	5	8	0	.385
Chicago Cardinals	3	7	1	.300
Dayton Triangles	1	6	1	.143
Duluth Eskimos	1	8	0	.111
Buffalo Bisons	0	5	0	.000

1926

	W	L	T	Pct.
Frankford Yellow Jackets	14	1	2	.933
Chicago Bears	12	1	3	.923
Pottsville Maroons	10	2	2	.833
Kansas City Cowboys	8	3	0	.727
Green Bay Packers	7	3	3	.700
Los Angeles Buccaneers	6	3	1	.667
New York Giants	8	4	1	.667
Duluth Eskimos	6	5	3	.545
Buffalo Rangers	4	4	2	.500
Chicago Cardinals	5	6	1	.455
Providence Steam Roller	5	7	1	.417
Detroit Panthers	4	6	2	.400
Hartford Blues	3	7	0	.300
Brooklyn Lions	3	8	0	.273
Milwaukee Badgers	2	7	0	.222
Akron Pros	1	4	3	.200
Dayton Triangles	1	4	1	.200
Racine Tornadoes	1	4	0	.200
Columbus Tigers	1	6	0	.143
Canton Bulldogs	1	9	3	.100
Hammond Pros	0	4	0	.000
Louisville Colonels	0	4	0	.000

1925

	W	L	T	Pct.
Chicago Cardinals	11	2	1	.846
Pottsville Maroons	10	2	0	.833
Detroit Panthers	8	2	2	.800
New York Giants	8	4	0	.667
Akron Indians	4	2	2	.667
Frankford Yellow Jackets	13	7	0	.650
Chicago Bears	9	5	3	.643
Rock Island Independents	5	3	3	.625
Green Bay Packers	8	5	0	.615
Providence Steam Roller	6	5	1	.545
Canton Bulldogs	4	4	0	.500
Cleveland Bulldogs	5	8	1	.385
Kansas City Cowboys	2	5	1	.286
Hammond Pros	1	4	0	.200
Buffalo Bisons	1	6	2	.143
Duluth Kelleys	0	3	0	.000
Rochester Jeffersons	0	6	1	.000
Milwaukee Badgers	0	6	0	.000
Dayton Triangles	0	7	1	.000
Columbus Tigers	0	9	0	.000

1924

	W	L	T	Pct.
Cleveland Bulldogs	7	1	1	.875
Chicago Bears	6	1	4	.857
Frankford Yellow Jackets	11	2	1	.846
Duluth Kelleys	5	1	0	.833
Rock Island Independents	5	2	2	.714
Green Bay Packers	7	4	0	.636
Racine Legion	4	3	3	.571
Chicago Cardinals	5	4	1	.556
Buffalo Bisons	6	5	0	.545
Columbus Tigers	4	4	0	.500
Hammond Pros	2	2	1	.500
Milwaukee Badgers	5	8	0	.385
Akron Indians	2	6	0	.250
Dayton Triangles	2	6	0	.250
Kansas City Blues	2	7	0	.222
Kenosha Maroons	0	4	1	.000
Minneapolis Marines	0	6	0	.000
Rochester Jeffersons	0	7	0	.000

1923

	W	L	T	Pct.
Canton Bulldogs	11	0	1	1.000
Chicago Bears	9	2	1	.818
Green Bay Packers	7	2	1	.778
Milwaukee Badgers	7	2	3	.778
Cleveland Indians	3	1	3	.750
Chicago Cardinals	8	4	0	.667
Duluth Kelleys	4	3	0	.571
Buffalo All-Americans	5	4	3	.556
Columbus Tigers	5	4	1	.556
Racine Legion	4	4	2	.500
Toledo Maroons	3	3	2	.500
Rock Island Independents	2	3	3	.400
Minneapolis Marines	2	5	2	.286
St. Louis All-Stars	1	4	2	.200
Hammond Pros	1	5	1	.167
Dayton Triangles	1	6	1	.143
Akron Indians	1	6	0	.143
Oorang Indians	1	10	0	.091
Louisville Brecks	0	3	0	.000
Rochester Jeffersons	0	4	0	.000

1922

	W	L	T	Pct.
Canton Bulldogs	10	0	2	1.000
Chicago Bears	9	3	0	.750
Chicago Cardinals	8	3	0	.727
Toledo Maroons	5	2	2	.714
Rock Island Independents	4	2	1	.667
Racine Legion	6	4	1	.600
Dayton Triangles	4	3	1	.571
Green Bay Packers	4	3	3	.571
Buffalo All-Americans	5	4	1	.556
Akron Pros	3	5	2	.375
Milwaukee Badgers	2	4	3	.333
Oorang Indians	3	6	0	.333
Minneapolis Marines	1	3	0	.250
Louisville Brecks	1	3	0	.250
Evansville Crimson Giants	0	3	0	.000
Rochester Jeffersons	0	4	1	.000
Hammond Pros	0	5	1	.000
Columbus Panhandles	0	8	0	.000

1921

	W	L	T	Pct.
Chicago Staleys	9	1	1	.900
Buffalo All-Americans	9	1	2	.900
Akron Pros	8	3	1	.727
Canton Bulldogs	5	2	3	.714
Rock Island Independents	4	2	1	.667
Evansville Crimson Giants	3	2	0	.600
Green Bay Packers	3	2	1	.600
Dayton Triangles	4	4	1	.500
Chicago Cardinals	3	3	2	.500
Rochester Jeffersons	2	3	0	.400
Cleveland Indians	3	5	0	.375
Washington Senators	1	2	0	.333
Cincinnati Celts	1	3	0	.250
Hammond Pros	1	3	1	.250
Minneapolis Marines	1	3	0	.250
Detroit Heralds	1	5	1	.167
Columbus Panhandles	1	8	0	.111
Tonawanda Kardex	0	1	0	.000
Muncie Flyers	0	2	0	.000
Louisville Brecks	0	2	0	.000
New York Giants	0	2	0	.000

1920*

	W	L	T	Pct.
Akron Pros	8	0	3	1.000
Decatur Staleys	10	1	2	.909
Buffalo All-Americans	9	1	1	.900
Chicago Cardinals	6	2	2	.750
Rock Island Independents	6	2	2	.750
Dayton Triangles	5	2	2	.714
Rochester Jeffersons	6	3	2	.667
Canton Bulldogs	7	4	2	.636
Detroit Heralds	2	3	3	.400
Cleveland Tigers	2	4	2	.333
Chicago Tigers	2	5	1	.286
Hammond Pros	2	5	0	.286
Columbus Panhandles	2	6	2	.250
Muncie Flyers	0	1	0	.000

**No official standing was maintained for the 1920 season, and the championship was awarded to the Akron Pros in a League meeting on April 30, 1921. Clubs played schedules which included games against non-league opponents.*

ALL-TIME TEAM VS. TEAM RESULTS

RS=REGULAR SEASON
PS=POSTSEASON

***ARIZONA vs. ATLANTA**
RS: Cardinals lead series, 13-6
1966—Falcons, 16-10 (A)
1968—Cardinals, 17-12 (StL)
1971—Cardinals, 26-9 (A)
1973—Cardinals, 32-10 (A)
1975—Cardinals, 23-20 (StL)
1978—Cardinals, 42-21 (StL)
1980—Falcons, 33-27 (StL) OT
1981—Falcons, 41-20 (A)
1982—Cardinals, 23-20 (A)
1986—Falcons, 33-13 (A)
1987—Cardinals, 34-21 (A)
1989—Cardinals, 34-20 (P)
1990—Cardinals, 24-13 (A)
1991—Cardinals, 16-10 (P)
1992—Falcons, 20-17 (A)
1993—Cardinals, 27-10 (A)
1994—Falcons, 10-6 (Atl)
1995—Cardinals, 40-37 (Ariz) OT
1997—Cardinals, 29-26 (Ariz)
(RS Pts.—Cardinals 460, Falcons 382)
**Franchise known as Phoenix prior to 1994 and in St. Louis prior to 1988*

***ARIZONA vs. BALTIMORE**
RS: Cardinals lead series, 1-0
1997—Cardinals, 16-13 (B)
(RS Pts.—Cardinals 16, Ravens 13)

***ARIZONA vs. BUFFALO**
RS: Series tied, 3-3
1971—Cardinals, 28-23 (B)
1975—Bills, 32-14 (StL)
1981—Cardinals, 24-0 (StL)
1984—Cardinals, 37-7 (StL)
1986—Bills, 17-10 (B)
1990—Bills, 45-14 (B)
(RS Pts.—Cardinals 127, Bills 124)
**Franchise known as Phoenix prior to 1994 and in St. Louis prior to 1988*

ARIZONA vs. CAROLINA
RS: Panthers lead series, 1-0
1995—Panthers, 27-7 (C)
(RS Pts.—Panthers 27, Cardinals 7)

***ARIZONA vs. **CHICAGO**
RS: Bears lead series, 52-26-6
(NP denotes Normal Park;
Wr denotes Wrigley Field;
Co denotes Comiskey Park;
So denotes Soldier Field;
all Chicago)
1920—Cardinals, 7-6 (NP)
Staleys, 10-0 (Wr)
1921—Tie, 0-0 (Wr)
1922—Cardinals, 6-0 (Co)
Cardinals, 9-0 (Co)
1923—Bears, 3-0 (Wr)
1924—Bears, 6-0 (Wr)
Bears, 21-0 (Co)
1925—Cardinals, 9-0 (Co)
Tie, 0-0 (Wr)
1926—Bears, 16-0 (Wr)
Bears, 10-0 (So)
Tie, 0-0 (Wr)
1927—Bears, 9-0 (NP)
Cardinals, 3-0 (Wr)
1928—Bears, 15-0 (NP)
Bears, 34-0 (Wr)
1929—Tie, 0-0 (Wr)
Cardinals, 40-6 (Co)
1930—Bears, 32-6 (Co)
Bears, 6-0 (Wr)
1931—Bears, 26-13 (Wr)
Bears, 18-7 (Wr)
1932—Tie, 0-0 (Wr)
Bears, 34-0 (Wr)
1933—Bears, 12-9 (Wr)
Bears, 22-6 (Wr)
1934—Bears, 20-0 (Wr)
Bears, 17-6 (Wr)
1935—Tie, 7-7 (Wr)
Bears, 13-0 (Wr)
1936—Bears, 7-3 (Wr)
Cardinals, 14-7 (Wr)
1937—Bears, 16-7 (Wr)
Bears, 42-28 (Wr)
1938—Bears, 16-13 (So)
Bears, 34-28 (Wr)
1939—Bears, 44-7 (Wr)
Bears, 48-7 (Co)
1940—Cardinals, 21-7 (Co)
Bears, 31-23 (Wr)
1941—Bears, 53-7 (Wr)
Bears, 34-24 (Co)
1942—Bears, 41-14 (Wr)
Bears, 21-7 (Co)
1943—Bears, 20-0 (Wr)
Bears, 35-24 (Co)
1945—Cardinals, 16-7 (Wr)
Bears, 28-20 (Co)
1946—Bears, 34-17 (Co)
Cardinals, 35-28 (Wr)
1947—Cardinals, 31-7 (Co)
Cardinals, 30-21 (Wr)
1948—Bears, 28-17 (Co)
Cardinals, 24-21 (Wr)
1949—Bears, 17-7 (Co)
Bears, 52-21 (Wr)
1950—Bears, 27-6 (Wr)
Cardinals, 20-10 (Co)
1951—Cardinals, 28-14 (Co)
Cardinals, 24-14 (Wr)
1952—Cardinals, 21-10 (Co)
Bears, 10-7 (Wr)
1953—Cardinals, 24-17 (Wr)
1954—Bears, 29-7 (Co)
1955—Cardinals, 53-14 (Co)
1956—Bears, 10-3 (Wr)
1957—Bears, 14-6 (Co)
1958—Bears, 30-14 (Wr)
1959—Bears, 31-7 (So)
1965—Bears, 34-13 (Wr)
1966—Cardinals, 24-17 (StL)
1967—Bears, 30-3 (Wr)
1969—Cardinals, 20-17 (StL)
1972—Bears, 27-10 (StL)
1975—Cardinals, 34-20 (So)
1977—Cardinals, 16-13 (StL)
1978—Bears, 17-10 (So)
1979—Bears, 42-6 (So)
1982—Cardinals, 10-7 (So)
1984—Cardinals, 38-21 (StL)
1990—Bears, 31-21 (P)
1994—Bears, 19-16 (A) OT
1998—Cardinals, 20-7 (A)
(RS Pts.—Bears 1,574, Cardinals 1,034)
**Franchise known as Phoenix prior to 1994, in St. Louis prior to 1988, and in Chicago prior to 1960*
***Franchise in Decatur prior to 1921 and known as Staleys prior to 1922*

***ARIZONA vs. CINCINNATI**
RS: Bengals lead series, 4-2
1973—Bengals, 42-24 (C)
1979—Bengals, 34-28 (C)
1985—Cardinals, 41-27 (StL)
1988—Bengals, 21-14 (C)
1994—Cardinals, 28-7 (A)
1997—Bengals, 24-21 (C)
(RS Pts.—Cardinals 156, Bengals 155)
**Franchise known as Phoenix prior to 1994 and in St. Louis prior to 1988*

***ARIZONA vs. CLEVELAND**
RS: Browns lead series, 32-10-3
1950—Browns, 34-24 (Cle)
Browns, 10-7 (Chi)
1951—Browns, 34-17 (Chi)
Browns, 49-28 (Cle)
1952—Browns, 28-13 (Cle)
Browns, 10-0 (Chi)
1953—Browns, 27-7 (Chi)
Browns, 27-16 (Cle)
1954—Browns, 31-7 (Cle)
Browns, 35-3 (Chi)
1955—Browns, 26-20 (Chi)
Browns, 35-24 (Cle)
1956—Cardinals, 9-7 (Chi)
Cardinals, 24-7 (Cle)
1957—Browns, 17-7 (Chi)
Browns, 31-0 (Cle)
1958—Browns, 35-28 (Cle)
Browns, 38-24 (Chi)
1959—Browns, 34-7 (Chi)
Browns, 17-7 (Cle)
1960—Browns, 28-27 (Cle)
Tie, 17-17 (StL)
1961—Browns, 20-17 (Cle)
Browns, 21-10 (StL)
1962—Browns, 34-7 (StL)
Browns, 38-14 (Cle)
1963—Cardinals, 20-14 (Cle)
Browns, 24-10 (StL)
1964—Tie, 33-33 (Cle)
Cardinals, 28-19 (StL)
1965—Cardinals, 49-13 (Cle)
Browns, 27-24 (StL)
1966—Cardinals, 34-28 (Cle)
Browns, 38-10 (StL)
1967—Browns, 20-16 (Cle)
Browns, 20-16 (StL)
1968—Cardinals, 27-21 (Cle)
Cardinals, 27-16 (StL)
1969—Tie, 21-21 (Cle)
Browns, 27-21 (StL)
1974—Cardinals, 29-7 (StL)
1979—Browns, 38-20 (StL)
1985—Cardinals, 27-24 (Cle) OT
1988—Browns, 29-21 (P)
1994—Browns, 32-0 (Cle)
(RS Pts.—Browns 1,141, Cardinals 797)
**Franchise known as Phoenix prior to 1994, in St. Louis prior to 1988, and in Chicago prior to 1960*

***ARIZONA vs. DALLAS**
RS: Cowboys lead series, 49-23-1
PS: Cardinals lead series, 1-0
1960—Cardinals, 12-10 (StL)
1961—Cardinals, 31-17 (D)
Cardinals, 31-13 (StL)
1962—Cardinals, 28-24 (D)
Cardinals, 52-20 (StL)
1963—Cardinals, 34-7 (D)
Cowboys, 28-24 (StL)
1964—Cardinals, 16-6 (D)
Cowboys, 31-13 (StL)
1965—Cardinals, 20-13 (StL)
Cowboys, 27-13 (D)
1966—Tie, 10-10 (StL)
Cowboys, 31-17 (D)
1967—Cowboys, 46-21 (D)
1968—Cowboys, 27-10 (StL)
1969—Cowboys, 24-3 (D)
1970—Cardinals, 20-7 (StL)
Cardinals, 38-0 (D)
1971—Cowboys, 16-13 (StL)
Cowboys, 31-12 (D)
1972—Cowboys, 33-24 (D)
Cowboys, 27-6 (StL)
1973—Cowboys, 45-10 (D)
Cowboys, 30-3 (StL)
1974—Cardinals, 31-28 (StL)
Cowboys, 17-14 (D)
1975—Cowboys, 37-31 (D) OT
Cardinals, 31-17 (StL)
1976—Cardinals, 21-17 (StL)
Cowboys, 19-14 (D)
1977—Cowboys, 30-24 (StL)
Cardinals, 24-17 (D)
1978—Cowboys, 21-12 (D)
Cowboys, 24-21 (StL) OT
1979—Cowboys, 22-21 (StL)
Cowboys, 22-13 (D)
1980—Cowboys, 27-24 (StL)
Cowboys, 31-21 (D)
1981—Cowboys, 30-17 (D)
Cardinals, 20-17 (StL)
1982—Cowboys, 24-7 (StL)
1983—Cowboys, 34-17 (StL)
Cowboys, 35-17 (D)
1984—Cardinals, 31-20 (D)
Cowboys, 24-17 (StL)
1985—Cardinals, 21-10 (StL)
Cowboys, 35-17 (D)
1986—Cowboys, 31-7 (StL)
Cowboys, 37-6 (D)
1987—Cardinals, 24-13 (StL)
Cowboys, 21-16 (D)
1988—Cowboys, 17-14 (P)
Cardinals, 16-10 (D)
1989—Cardinals, 19-10 (D)
Cardinals, 24-20 (P)
1990—Cardinals, 20-3 (P)
Cowboys, 41-10 (D)
1991—Cowboys, 17-9 (P)
Cowboys, 27-7 (D)
1992—Cowboys, 31-20 (D)
Cowboys, 16-10 (P)
1993—Cowboys, 17-10 (P)
Cowboys, 20-15 (D)
1994—Cowboys, 38-3 (D)
Cowboys, 28-21 (A)
1995—Cowboys, 34-20 (D)
Cowboys, 37-13 (A)
1996—Cowboys, 17-3 (D)
Cowboys, 10-6 (A)
1997—Cardinals, 25-22 (A) OT
Cowboys, 24-6 (D)
1998—Cowboys, 38-10 (D)
Cowboys, 35-28 (A)
**Cardinals, 20-7 (D)
(RS Pts.—Cowboys 1,695, Cardinals 1,289)
(PS Pts.—Cardinals 20, Cowboys 7)
**Franchise known as Phoenix prior to 1994 and in St. Louis prior to 1988*
***NFC First-Round Playoff*

***ARIZONA vs. DENVER**
RS: Broncos lead series, 4-0-1
1973—Tie, 17-17 (StL)
1977—Broncos, 7-0 (D)
1989—Broncos, 37-0 (P)
1991—Broncos, 24-19 (D)
1995—Broncos, 38-6 (D)
(RS Pts.—Broncos 123, Cardinals 42)
**Franchise known as Phoenix prior to 1994 and in St. Louis prior to 1988*

***ARIZONA vs. **DETROIT**
RS: Lions lead series, 27-18-5
1930—Tie, 0-0 (Port)
Cardinals, 23-0 (C)
1931—Cardinals, 20-19 (C)
1932—Tie, 7-7 (Port)
1933—Spartans, 7-6 (Port)
1934—Lions, 6-0 (D)
Lions, 17-13 (C)
1935—Tie, 10-10 (D)
Lions, 7-6 (C)
1936—Lions, 39-0 (D)
Lions, 14-7 (C)
1937—Lions, 16-7 (C)
Lions, 16-7 (D)
1938—Lions, 10-0 (D)
Lions, 7-3 (C)
1939—Lions, 21-3 (D)
Lions, 17-3 (C)
1940—Tie, 0-0 (Buffalo)
Lions, 43-14 (C)
1941—Tie, 14-14 (C)
Lions, 21-3 (D)
1942—Cardinals, 13-0 (C)
Cardinals, 7-0 (D)
1943—Lions, 35-17 (D)
Lions, 7-0 (Buffalo)
1945—Lions, 10-0 (Milwaukee)
Lions, 26-0 (D)
1946—Cardinals, 34-14 (C)
Cardinals, 36-14 (D)
1947—Cardinals, 45-21 (C)
Cardinals, 17-7 (D)
1948—Cardinals, 56-20 (C)
Cardinals, 28-14 (D)
1949—Lions, 24-7 (C)

Cardinals, 42-19 (D)
1959—Lions, 45-21 (D)
1961—Lions, 45-14 (StL)
1967—Cardinals, 38-28 (StL)
1969—Lions, 20-0 (D)
1970—Lions, 16-3 (D)
1973—Lions, 20-16 (StL)
1975—Cardinals, 24-13 (D)
1978—Cardinals, 21-14 (StL)
1980—Lions, 20-7 (D)
Cardinals, 24-23 (StL)
1989—Cardinals, 16-13 (D)
1993—Lions, 26-20 (D)
Lions, 21-14 (Phx)
1995—Cardinals, 20-17 (D)
1998—Cardinals, 17-15 (D)
(RS Pts.—Lions 838, Cardinals 713)
Franchise known as Phoenix prior to 1994, in St. Louis prior to 1988, and in Chicago prior to 1960
***Franchise in Portsmouth prior to 1934 and known as the Spartans*

***ARIZONA vs. GREEN BAY**
RS: Packers lead series, 39-21-4
PS: Packers lead series, 1-0
1921—Tie, 3-3 (C)
1922—Cardinals, 16-3 (C)
1924—Cardinals, 3-0 (C)
1925—Cardinals, 9-6 (C)
1926—Cardinals, 13-7 (GB)
Packers, 3-0 (C)
1927—Packers, 13-0 (GB)
Tie, 6-6 (C)
1928—Packers, 20-0 (GB)
1929—Packers, 9-2 (GB)
Packers, 7-6 (C)
Packers, 12-0 (C)
1930—Packers, 14-0 (GB)
Cardinals, 13-6 (C)
1931—Packers, 26-7 (GB)
Cardinals, 21-13 (C)
1932—Packers, 15-7 (GB)
Packers, 19-9 (C)
1933—Packers, 14-6 (C)
1934—Packers, 15-0 (GB)
Cardinals, 9-0 (Mil)
Cardinals, 6-0 (C)
1935—Cardinals, 7-6 (GB)
Cardinals, 3-0 (Mil)
Cardinals, 9-7 (C)
1936—Packers, 10-7 (GB)
Packers, 24-0 (Mil)
Tie, 0-0 (C)
1937—Cardinals, 14-7 (GB)
Packers, 34-13 (Mil)
1938—Packers, 28-7 (Mil)
Packers, 24-22 (Buffalo)
1939—Packers, 14-10 (GB)
Packers, 27-20 (Mil)
1940—Packers, 31-6 (Mil)
Packers, 28-7 (C)
1941—Packers, 14-13 (Mil)
Packers, 17-9 (GB)
1942—Packers, 17-13 (C)
Packers, 55-24 (GB)
1943—Packers, 28-7 (C)
Packers, 35-14 (Mil)
1945—Packers, 33-14 (GB)
1946—Packers, 19-7 (C)
Cardinals, 24-6 (GB)
1947—Cardinals, 14-10 (GB)
Cardinals, 21-20 (C)
1948—Cardinals, 17-7 (Mil)
Cardinals, 42-7 (C)
1949—Cardinals, 39-17 (Mil)
Cardinals, 41-21 (C)
1955—Packers, 31-14 (GB)
1956—Packers, 24-21 (C)
1962—Packers, 17-0 (Mil)
1963—Packers, 30-7 (StL)
1967—Packers, 31-23 (StL)
1969—Packers, 45-28 (GB)
1971—Tie, 16-16 (StL)
1973—Packers, 25-21 (GB)
1976—Cardinals, 29-0 (StL)
1982—**Packers, 41-16 (GB)
1984—Packers, 24-23 (GB)
1985—Cardinals, 43-28 (StL)
1988—Packers, 26-17 (P)
1990—Packers, 24-21 (P)
(RS Pts.—Packers 1,078, Cardinals 823)
(PS Pts.—Packers 41, Cardinals 16)
Franchise known as Phoenix prior to 1994, in St. Louis prior to 1988, and in Chicago prior to 1960
***NFC First-Round Playoff*

***ARIZONA vs. **INDIANAPOLIS**
RS: Series tied, 6-6
1961—Colts, 16-0 (B)
1964—Colts, 47-27 (B)
1968—Colts, 27-0 (B)
1972—Cardinals, 10-3 (B)
1976—Cardinals, 24-17 (StL)
1978—Colts, 30-17 (StL)
1980—Cardinals, 17-10 (B)
1981—Cardinals, 35-24 (B)
1984—Cardinals, 34-33 (I)
1990—Cardinals, 20-17 (P)
1992—Colts, 16-13 (I)
1996—Colts, 20-13 (I)
(RS Pts.—Colts 260, Cardinals 210)
Franchise known as Phoenix prior to 1994 and in St. Louis prior to 1988
***Franchise in Baltimore prior to 1984*

***ARIZONA vs. KANSAS CITY**
RS: Chiefs lead series, 5-1-1
1970—Tie, 6-6 (KC)
1974—Chiefs, 17-13 (StL)
1980—Chiefs, 21-13 (StL)
1983—Chiefs, 38-14 (KC)
1986—Cardinals, 23-14 (StL)
1995—Chiefs, 24-3 (A)
1998—Chiefs, 34-24 (KC)
(RS Pts.—Chiefs 154, Cardinals 96)
Franchise known as Phoenix prior to 1994 and in St. Louis prior to 1988

***ARIZONA vs. MIAMI**
RS: Dolphins lead series, 7-0
1972—Dolphins, 31-10 (M)
1977—Dolphins, 55-14 (StL)
1978—Dolphins, 24-10 (M)
1981—Dolphins, 20-7 (StL)
1984—Dolphins, 36-28 (StL)
1990—Dolphins, 23-3 (M)
1996—Dolphins, 38-10 (A)
(RS Pts.—Dolphins 227, Cardinals 82)
Franchise known as Phoenix prior to 1994 and in St. Louis prior to 1988

***ARIZONA vs. MINNESOTA**
RS: Cardinals lead series, 8-7
PS: Vikings lead series, 2-0
1963—Cardinals, 56-14 (M)
1967—Cardinals, 34-24 (M)
1969—Vikings, 27-10 (StL)
1972—Cardinals, 19-17 (M)
1974—Vikings, 28-24 (StL)
**Vikings, 30-14 (M)
1977—Cardinals, 27-7 (M)
1979—Cardinals, 37-7 (StL)
1981—Cardinals, 30-17 (StL)
1983—Cardinals, 41-31 (StL)
1991—Vikings, 34-7 (M)
Vikings, 28-0 (P)
1994—Cardinals, 17-7 (A)
1995—Vikings, 30-24 (A) OT
1996—Vikings, 41-17 (M)
1997—Vikings, 20-19 (A)
1998—**Vikings, 41-21 (M)
(RS Pts.—Cardinals 362, Vikings 332)
(PS Pts.—Vikings 71, Cardinals 35)
Franchise known as Phoenix prior to 1994 and in St. Louis prior to 1988
***NFC Divisional Playoff*

***ARIZONA vs. **NEW ENGLAND**
RS: Cardinals lead series, 6-3
1970—Cardinals, 31-0 (StL)
1975—Cardinals, 24-17 (StL)
1978—Patriots, 16-6 (StL)
1981—Cardinals, 27-20 (NE)
1984—Cardinals, 33-10 (NE)
1990—Cardinals, 34-14 (P)
1991—Cardinals, 24-10 (P)
1993—Patriots, 23-21 (P)
1996—Patriots, 31-0 (NE)
(RS Pts.—Cardinals 200, Patriots 141)
Franchise known as Phoenix prior to 1994 and in St. Louis prior to 1988
***Franchise in Boston prior to 1971*

***ARIZONA vs. NEW ORLEANS**
RS: Cardinals lead series, 12-10
1967—Cardinals, 31-20 (StL)
1968—Cardinals, 21-20 (NO)
Cardinals, 31-17 (StL)
1969—Saints, 51-42 (StL)
1970—Cardinals, 24-17 (StL)
1974—Saints, 14-0 (NO)
1977—Cardinals, 49-31 (StL)
1980—Cardinals, 40-7 (NO)
1981—Cardinals, 30-3 (StL)
1982—Cardinals, 21-7 (NO)
1983—Saints, 28-17 (NO)
1984—Saints, 34-24 (NO)
1985—Cardinals, 28-16 (StL)
1986—Saints, 16-7 (StL)
1987—Cardinals, 24-19 (StL)
1990—Saints, 28-7 (NO)
1991—Saints, 27-3 (P)
1992—Saints, 30-21 (P)
1993—Saints, 20-17 (P)
1996—Cardinals, 28-14 (NO)
1997—Saints, 27-10 (NO)
1998—Cardinals, 19-17 (A)
(RS Pts.—Cardinals 494, Saints 463)
Franchise known as Phoenix prior to 1994 and in St. Louis prior to 1988

***ARIZONA vs. N.Y. GIANTS**
RS: Giants lead series, 73-37-2
1926—Giants, 20-0 (NY)
1927—Giants, 28-7 (NY)
1929—Giants, 24-21 (NY)
1930—Giants, 25-12 (NY)
Giants, 13-7 (C)
1935—Cardinals, 14-13 (NY)
1936—Giants, 14-6 (NY)
1938—Giants, 6-0 (NY)
1939—Giants, 17-7 (NY)
1941—Cardinals, 10-7 (NY)
1942—Giants, 21-7 (NY)
1943—Giants, 24-13 (NY)
1946—Giants, 28-24 (NY)
1947—Giants, 35-31 (NY)
1948—Cardinals, 63-35 (NY)
1949—Giants, 41-38 (C)
1950—Cardinals, 17-3 (C)
Giants, 51-21 (NY)
1951—Giants, 28-17 (NY)
Giants, 10-0 (C)
1952—Cardinals, 24-23 (NY)
Giants, 28-6 (C)
1953—Giants, 21-7 (NY)
Giants, 23-20 (C)
1954—Giants, 41-10 (C)
Giants, 31-17 (NY)
1955—Cardinals, 28-17 (C)
Giants, 10-0 (NY)
1956—Cardinals, 35-27 (C)
Giants, 23-10 (NY)
1957—Giants, 27-14 (NY)
Giants, 28-21 (C)
1958—Giants, 37-7 (Buffalo)
Cardinals, 23-6 (NY)
1959—Giants, 9-3 (NY)
Giants, 30-20 (Minn)
1960—Giants, 35-14 (StL)
Cardinals, 20-13 (NY)
1961—Cardinals, 21-10 (NY)
Giants, 24-9 (StL)
1962—Giants, 31-14 (StL)
Giants, 31-28 (NY)
1963—Giants, 38-21 (StL)
Cardinals, 24-17 (NY)
1964—Giants, 34-17 (NY)
Tie, 10-10 (StL)
1965—Giants, 14-10 (NY)
Giants, 28-15 (StL)
1966—Cardinals, 24-19 (StL)
Cardinals, 20-17 (NY)
1967—Giants, 37-20 (StL)
Giants, 37-14 (NY)
1968—Cardinals, 28-21 (NY)
1969—Cardinals, 42-17 (StL)
Giants, 49-6 (NY)
1970—Giants, 35-17 (NY)
Giants, 34-17 (StL)
1971—Giants, 21-20 (StL)
Cardinals, 24-7 (NY)
1972—Giants, 27-21 (NY)
Giants, 13-7 (StL)
1973—Cardinals, 35-27 (StL)
Giants, 24-13 (New Haven)
1974—Cardinals, 23-21 (New Haven)
Cardinals, 26-14 (StL)
1975—Cardinals, 26-14 (StL)
Cardinals, 20-13 (NY)
1976—Cardinals, 27-21 (StL)
Cardinals, 17-14 (NY)
1977—Cardinals, 28-0 (StL)
Giants, 27-7 (NY)
1978—Cardinals, 20-10 (StL)
Giants, 17-0 (NY)
1979—Cardinals, 27-14 (NY)
Cardinals, 29-20 (StL)
1980—Giants, 41-35 (StL)
Cardinals, 23-7 (NY)
1981—Giants, 34-14 (NY)
Giants, 20-10 (StL)
1982—Cardinals, 24-21 (StL)
1983—Tie, 20-20 (StL) OT
Cardinals, 10-6 (NY)
1984—Giants, 16-10 (NY)
Cardinals, 31-21 (StL)
1985—Giants, 27-17 (NY)
Giants, 34-3 (StL)
1986—Giants, 13-6 (StL)
Giants, 27-7 (NY)
1987—Giants, 30-7 (NY)
Cardinals, 27-24 (StL)
1988—Cardinals, 24-17 (P)
Giants, 44-7 (NY)
1989—Giants, 35-7 (NY)
Giants, 20-13 (P)
1990—Giants, 20-19 (NY)
Giants, 24-21 (P)
1991—Giants, 20-9 (NY)
Giants, 21-14 (P)
1992—Giants, 31-21 (NY)
Cardinals, 19-0 (P)
1993—Giants, 19-17 (NY)
Cardinals, 17-6 (P)
1994—Giants, 20-17 (A)
Cardinals, 10-9 (NY)
1995—Giants, 27-21 (NY) OT
Giants, 10-6 (A)
1996—Giants, 16-8 (NY)
Cardinals, 31-23 (A)
1997—Giants, 27-13 (A)
Giants, 19-10 (NY)
1998—Giants, 34-7 (NY)
Giants, 23-19 (A)
(RS Pts.—Giants 2,485, Cardinals 1,895)
Franchise known as Phoenix prior to 1994, in St. Louis prior to 1988, and in Chicago prior to 1960

***ARIZONA vs. N.Y. JETS**
RS: Series tied, 2-2
1971—Cardinals, 17-10 (StL)
1975—Cardinals, 37-6 (NY)
1978—Jets, 23-10 (NY)
1996—Jets, 31-21 (A)
(RS Pts.—Cardinals 85, Jets 70)
Franchise known as Phoenix prior to 1994 and in St. Louis prior to 1988

ALL-TIME TEAM VS. TEAM RESULTS

***ARIZONA vs. **OAKLAND**
RS: Raiders lead series, 3-1
1973—Raiders, 17-10 (StL)
1983—Cardinals, 34-24 (LA)
1989—Raiders, 16-14 (LA)
1998—Raiders, 23-20 (A)
(RS Pts.—Raiders 80, Cardinals 78)
**Franchise known as Phoenix prior to 1994 and in St. Louis prior to 1988*
***Franchise in Los Angeles from 1982-1994*

***ARIZONA vs. PHILADELPHIA**
RS: Cardinals lead series, 49-48-5
PS: Series tied, 1-1
1935—Cardinals, 12-3 (C)
1936—Cardinals, 13-0 (C)
1937—Tie, 6-6 (P)
1938—Eagles, 7-0 (Erie, Pa.)
1941—Eagles, 21-14 (P)
1945—Eagles, 21-6 (P)
1947—Cardinals, 45-21 (P)
**Cardinals, 28-21 (C)
1948—Cardinals, 21-14 (C)
**Eagles, 7-0 (P)
1949—Eagles, 28-3 (P)
1950—Eagles, 45-7 (C)
Cardinals, 14-10 (P)
1951—Eagles, 17-14 (C)
1952—Eagles, 10-7 (P)
Cardinals, 28-22 (C)
1953—Eagles, 56-17 (C)
Eagles, 38-0 (P)
1954—Eagles, 35-16 (C)
Eagles, 30-14 (P)
1955—Tie, 24-24 (C)
Eagles, 27-3 (P)
1956—Cardinals, 20-6 (P)
Cardinals, 28-17 (C)
1957—Eagles, 38-21 (C)
Cardinals, 31-27 (P)
1958—Tie, 21-21 (C)
Eagles, 49-21 (P)
1959—Eagles, 28-24 (Minn)
Eagles, 27-17 (P)
1960—Eagles, 31-27 (P)
Eagles, 20-6 (StL)
1961—Cardinals, 30-27 (P)
Eagles, 20-7 (StL)
1962—Cardinals, 27-21 (P)
Cardinals, 45-35 (StL)
1963—Cardinals, 28-24 (P)
Cardinals, 38-14 (StL)
1964—Cardinals, 38-13 (P)
Cardinals, 36-34 (StL)
1965—Eagles, 34-27 (P)
Eagles, 28-24 (StL)
1966—Cardinals, 16-13 (StL)
Cardinals, 41-10 (P)
1967—Cardinals, 48-14 (StL)
1968—Cardinals, 45-17 (P)
1969—Eagles, 34-30 (StL)
1970—Cardinals, 35-20 (P)
Cardinals, 23-14 (StL)
1971—Eagles, 37-20 (StL)
Eagles, 19-7 (P)
1972—Tie, 6-6 (P)
Cardinals, 24-23 (StL)
1973—Cardinals, 34-23 (P)
Eagles, 27-24 (StL)
1974—Cardinals, 7-3 (StL)
Cardinals, 13-3 (P)
1975—Cardinals, 31-20 (StL)
Cardinals, 24-23 (P)
1976—Cardinals, 33-14 (StL)
Cardinals, 17-14 (P)
1977—Cardinals, 21-17 (P)
Cardinals, 21-16 (StL)
1978—Cardinals, 16-10 (P)
Eagles, 14-10 (StL)
1979—Eagles, 24-20 (StL)
Eagles, 16-13 (P)
1980—Cardinals, 24-14 (StL)
Eagles, 17-3 (P)
1981—Eagles, 52-10 (StL)
Eagles, 38-0 (P)
1982—Cardinals, 23-20 (P)
1983—Cardinals, 14-11 (P)
Cardinals, 31-7 (StL)
1984—Cardinals, 34-14 (P)
Cardinals, 17-16 (StL)
1985—Eagles, 30-7 (P)
Eagles, 24-14 (StL)
1986—Cardinals, 13-10 (StL)
Tie, 10-10 (P) OT
1987—Eagles, 28-23 (StL)
Cardinals, 31-19 (P)
1988—Eagles, 31-21 (P)
Eagles, 23-17 (Phx)
1989—Eagles, 17-5 (Phx)
Eagles, 31-14 (P)
1990—Cardinals, 23-21 (P)
Eagles, 23-21 (Phx)
1991—Cardinals, 26-10 (P)
Eagles, 34-14 (Phx)
1992—Eagles, 31-14 (Phx)
Eagles, 7-3 (P)
1993—Eagles, 23-17 (P)
Cardinals, 16-3 (Phx)
1994—Eagles, 17-7 (P)
Cardinals, 12-6 (A)
1995—Eagles, 31-19 (A)
Eagles, 21-20 (P)
1996—Cardinals, 36-30 (A)
Eagles, 29-19 (P)
1997—Eagles, 13-10 (P) OT
Cardinals, 31-21 (A)
1998—Cardinals, 17-3 (A)
Cardinals, 20-17 (P) OT
(RS Pts.—Eagles 2,132, Cardinals 1,995)
(PS Pts.—Eagles 28, Cardinals 28)
**Franchise known as Phoenix prior to 1994, in St. Louis prior to 1988, and in Chicago prior to 1960*
***NFL Championship*

***ARIZONA vs. **PITTSBURGH**
RS: Steelers lead series, 30-22-3
1933—Pirates, 14-13 (C)
1935—Pirates, 17-13 (P)
1936—Cardinals, 14-6 (C)
1937—Cardinals, 13-7 (P)
1939—Cardinals, 10-0 (P)
1940—Tie, 7-7 (P)
1942—Steelers, 19-3 (P)
1945—Steelers, 23-0 (P)
1946—Steelers, 14-7 (P)
1948—Cardinals, 24-7 (P)
1950—Steelers, 28-17 (C)
Steelers, 28-7 (P)
1951—Steelers, 28-14 (C)
1952—Steelers, 34-28 (C)
Steelers, 17-14 (P)
1953—Steelers, 31-28 (P)
Steelers, 21-17 (C)
1954—Cardinals, 17-14 (C)
Steelers, 20-17 (P)
1955—Steelers, 14-7 (P)
Cardinals, 27-13 (C)
1956—Steelers, 14-7 (P)
Cardinals, 38-27 (C)
1957—Steelers, 29-20 (P)
Steelers, 27-2 (C)
1958—Steelers, 27-20 (C)
Steelers, 38-21 (P)
1959—Cardinals, 45-24 (C)
Steelers, 35-20 (P)
1960—Steelers, 27-14 (P)
Cardinals, 38-7 (StL)
1961—Steelers, 30-27 (P)
Cardinals, 20-0 (StL)
1962—Steelers, 26-17 (StL)
Steelers, 19-7 (P)
1963—Steelers, 23-10 (P)
Cardinals, 24-23 (StL)
1964—Cardinals, 34-30 (StL)
Cardinals, 21-20 (P)
1965—Cardinals, 20-7 (P)
Cardinals, 21-17 (StL)
1966—Steelers, 30-9 (P)
Cardinals, 6-3 (StL)
1967—Cardinals, 28-14 (P)
Tie, 14-14 (StL)
1968—Tie, 28-28 (StL)
Cardinals, 20-10 (P)
1969—Cardinals, 27-14 (P)
Cardinals, 47-10 (StL)
1972—Steelers, 25-19 (StL)
1979—Steelers, 24-21 (StL)
1985—Steelers, 23-10 (P)
1988—Cardinals, 31-14 (Phx)
1994—Cardinals, 20-17 (A) OT
1997—Steelers, 26-20 (A) OT
(RS Pts.—Steelers 1,064, Cardinals 1,023)
**Franchise known as Phoenix prior to 1994, in St. Louis prior to 1988, and in Chicago prior to 1960*
***Steelers known as Pirates prior to 1941*

***ARIZONA vs. **ST. LOUIS**
RS: Rams lead series, 23-21-2
PS: Rams lead series, 1-0
1937—Cardinals, 6-0 (Clev)
Cardinals, 13-7 (Chi)
1938—Cardinals, 7-6 (Clev)
Cardinals, 31-17 (Chi)
1939—Rams, 24-0 (Chi)
Rams, 14-0 (Clev)
1940—Rams, 26-14 (Clev)
Cardinals, 17-7 (Chi)
1941—Rams, 10-6 (Clev)
Cardinals, 7-0 (Chi)
1942—Cardinals, 7-0 (Buffalo)
Rams, 7-3 (Clev)
1945—Rams, 21-0 (Clev)
Rams, 35-21 (Chi)
1946—Cardinals, 34-10 (Chi)
Rams, 17-14 (LA)
1947—Rams, 27-7 (LA)
Cardinals, 17-10 (Chi)
1948—Cardinals, 27-22 (LA)
Cardinals, 27-24 (Chi)
1949—Tie, 28-28 (Chi)
Cardinals, 31-27 (LA)
1951—Rams, 45-21 (LA)
1953—Tie, 24-24 (Chi)
1954—Rams, 28-17 (LA)
1958—Rams, 20-14 (Chi)
1960—Cardinals, 43-21 (LA)
1965—Rams, 27-3 (StL)
1968—Rams, 24-13 (StL)
1970—Rams, 34-13 (LA)
1972—Cardinals, 24-14 (StL)
1975—***Rams, 35-23 (LA)
1976—Cardinals, 30-28 (LA)
1979—Rams, 21-0 (LA)
1980—Rams, 21-13 (StL)
1984—Rams, 16-13 (StL)
1985—Rams, 46-14 (LA)
1986—Rams, 16-10 (StL)
1987—Rams, 27-24 (StL)
1988—Cardinals, 41-27 (LA)
1989—Rams, 37-14 (LA)
1991—Cardinals, 24-14 (LA)
1992—Cardinals, 20-14 (LA)
1993—Cardinals, 38-10 (P)
1994—Rams, 14-12 (LA)
1996—Cardinals, 31-28 (A) OT
1998—Cardinals, 20-17 (StL)
(RS Pts.—Rams 912, Cardinals 793)
(PS Pts.—Rams 35, Cardinals 23)
**Franchise known as Phoenix prior to 1994, in St. Louis prior to 1988, and in Chicago prior to 1960*
***Franchise in Los Angeles prior to 1995 and in Cleveland prior to 1946*
****NFC Divisional Playoff*

***ARIZONA vs. SAN DIEGO**
RS: Chargers lead series, 6-2
1971—Chargers, 20-17 (SD)
1976—Chargers, 43-24 (SD)
1983—Cardinals, 44-14 (StL)
1987—Chargers, 28-24 (SD)
1989—Chargers, 24-13 (P)
1992—Chargers, 27-21 (P)
1995—Chargers, 28-25 (SD)
1998—Cardinals, 16-13 (A)
(RS Pts.—Chargers 197, Cardinals 184)
**Franchise known as Phoenix prior to 1994, in St. Louis prior to 1988,*

***ARIZONA vs. SAN FRANCISCO**
RS: 49ers lead series, 10-9
1951—Cardinals, 27-21 (SF)
1957—Cardinals, 20-10 (SF)
1962—49ers, 24-17 (StL)
1964—Cardinals, 23-13 (SF)
1968—49ers, 35-17 (SF)
1971—49ers, 26-14 (StL)
1974—Cardinals, 34-9 (SF)
1976—Cardinals, 23-20 (StL) OT
1978—Cardinals, 16-10 (SF)
1979—Cardinals, 13-10 (StL)
1980—49ers, 24-21 (SF) OT
1982—49ers, 31-20 (StL)
1983—49ers, 42-27 (StL)
1986—49ers, 43-17 (SF)
1987—49ers, 34-28 (SF)
1988—Cardinals, 24-23 (P)
1991—49ers, 14-10 (SF)
1992—Cardinals, 24-14 (P)
1993—49ers, 28-14 (SF)
(RS Pts.—49ers 431, Cardinals 389)
**Franchise known as Phoenix prior to 1994, in St. Louis prior to 1988, and in Chicago prior to 1960*

***ARIZONA vs. SEATTLE**
RS: Cardinals lead series, 5-1
1976—Cardinals, 30-24 (S)
1983—Cardinals, 33-28 (StL)
1989—Cardinals, 34-24 (S)
1993—Cardinals, 30-27 (S) OT
1995—Cardinals, 20-14 (A) OT
1998—Seahawks, 33-14 (S)
(RS Pts.—Cardinals 161, Seahawks 150)
**Franchise known as Phoenix prior to 1994 and in St. Louis prior to 1988*

***ARIZONA vs. TAMPA BAY**
RS: Series tied, 7-7
1977—Buccaneers, 17-7 (TB)
1981—Buccaneers, 20-10 (TB)
1983—Cardinals, 34-27 (TB)
1985—Buccaneers, 16-0 (TB)
1986—Cardinals, 30-19 (TB)
Cardinals, 21-17 (StL)
1987—Cardinals, 31-28 (StL)
Cardinals, 31-14 (TB)
1988—Cardinals, 30-24 (TB)
1989—Buccaneers, 14-13 (P)
1992—Buccaneers, 23-7 (TB)
Buccaneers, 7-3 (P)
1996—Cardinals, 13-9 (A)
1997—Buccaneers, 19-18 (TB)
(RS Pts.—Buccaneers 254, Cardinals 248)
**Franchise known as Phoenix prior to 1994 and in St. Louis prior to 1988*

***ARIZONA vs. **TENNESSEE**
RS: Cardinals lead series, 4-3
1970—Cardinals, 44-0 (StL)
1974—Cardinals, 31-27 (H)
1979—Cardinals, 24-17 (H)
1985—Oilers, 20-10 (StL)
1988—Oilers, 38-20 (H)
1994—Cardinals, 30-12 (H)
1997—Oilers, 41-14 (T)
(RS Pts.—Cardinals 173, Titans 155)
**Franchise known as Phoenix prior to 1994 and in St. Louis prior to 1988*
***Franchise in Houston prior to 1997; known as Oilers prior to 1999*

***ARIZONA vs. **WASHINGTON**
RS: Redskins lead series, 64-43-2
1932—Cardinals, 9-0 (B)
Braves, 8-6 (C)
1933—Redskins, 10-0 (C)
Tie, 0-0 (B)

1934—Redskins, 9-0 (B)
1935—Cardinals, 6-0 (B)
1936—Redskins, 13-10 (B)
1937—Cardinals, 21-14 (W)
1939—Redskins, 28-7 (W)
1940—Redskins, 28-21 (W)
1942—Redskins, 28-0 (W)
1943—Redskins, 13-7 (W)
1945—Redskins, 24-21 (W)
1947—Redskins, 45-21 (W)
1949—Cardinals, 38-7 (C)
1950—Cardinals, 38-28 (W)
1951—Redskins, 7-3 (C)
Redskins, 20-17 (W)
1952—Redskins, 23-7 (C)
Cardinals, 17-6 (W)
1953—Redskins, 24-13 (C)
Redskins, 28-17 (W)
1954—Cardinals, 38-16 (C)
Redskins, 37-20 (W)
1955—Cardinals, 24-10 (W)
Redskins, 31-0 (C)
1956—Cardinals, 31-3 (W)
Redskins, 17-14 (C)
1957—Redskins, 37-14 (C)
Cardinals, 44-14 (W)
1958—Cardinals, 37-10 (C)
Redskins, 45-31 (W)
1959—Cardinals, 49-21 (C)
Redskins, 23-14 (W)
1960—Cardinals, 44-7 (StL)
Cardinals, 26-14 (W)
1961—Cardinals, 24-0 (W)
Cardinals, 38-24 (StL)
1962—Redskins, 24-14 (W)
Tie, 17-17 (StL)
1963—Cardinals, 21-7 (W)
Cardinals, 24-20 (StL)
1964—Cardinals, 23-17 (W)
Cardinals, 38-24 (StL)
1965—Cardinals, 37-16 (W)
Redskins, 24-20 (StL)
1966—Cardinals, 23-7 (StL)
Redskins, 26-20 (W)
1967—Cardinals, 27-21 (W)
1968—Cardinals, 41-14 (StL)
1969—Redskins, 33-17 (W)
1970—Cardinals, 27-17 (StL)
Redskins, 28-27 (W)
1971—Redskins, 24-17 (StL)
Redskins, 20-0 (W)
1972—Redskins, 24-10 (W)
Redskins, 33-3 (StL)
1973—Cardinals, 34-27 (StL)
Redskins, 31-13 (W)
1974—Cardinals, 17-10 (W)
Cardinals, 23-20 (StL)
1975—Redskins, 27-17 (W)
Cardinals, 20-17 (StL) OT
1976—Redskins, 20-10 (W)
Redskins, 16-10 (StL)
1977—Redskins, 24-14 (W)
Redskins, 26-20 (StL)
1978—Redskins, 28-10 (StL)
Cardinals, 27-17 (W)
1979—Redskins, 17-7 (StL)
Redskins, 30-28 (W)
1980—Redskins, 23-0 (W)
Redskins, 31-7 (StL)
1981—Cardinals, 40-30 (StL)
Redskins, 42-21 (W)
1982—Redskins, 12-7 (StL)
Redskins, 28-0 (W)
1983—Redskins, 38-14 (StL)
Redskins, 45-7 (W)
1984—Cardinals, 26-24 (StL)
Redskins, 29-27 (W)
1985—Redskins, 27-10 (W)
Redskins, 27-16 (StL)
1986—Redskins, 28-21 (W)
Redskins, 20-17 (StL)
1987—Redskins, 28-21 (W)
Redskins, 34-17 (StL)
1988—Cardinals, 30-21 (P)
Redskins, 33-17 (W)
1989—Redskins, 30-28 (W)
Redskins, 29-10 (P)
1990—Redskins, 31-0 (W)
Redskins, 38-10 (P)
1991—Redskins, 34-0 (W)
Redskins, 20-14 (P)
1992—Cardinals, 27-24 (P)
Redskins, 41-3 (W)
1993—Cardinals, 17-10 (W)
Cardinals, 36-6 (P)
1994—Cardinals, 19-16 (W) OT
Cardinals, 17-15 (A)
1995—Redskins, 27-7 (W)
Cardinals, 24-20 (A)
1996—Cardinals, 37-34 (W) OT
Cardinals, 27-26 (A)
1997—Redskins, 19-13 (W) OT
Redskins, 38-28 (A)
1998—Cardinals, 29-27 (A)
Cardinals, 45-42 (W)
(RS Pts.—Redskins 2,425, Cardinals 2,072)
Franchise known as Phoenix prior to 1994, in St. Louis prior to 1988, and in Chicago prior to 1960
***Franchise in Boston prior to 1937 and known as Braves prior to 1933*

ATLANTA vs. ARIZONA
RS: Cardinals lead series, 13-6;
See Arizona vs. Atlanta

ATLANTA vs. BUFFALO
RS: Bills lead series, 4-3
1973—Bills, 17-6 (A)
1977—Bills, 3-0 (B)
1980—Falcons, 30-14 (B)
1983—Falcons, 31-14 (A)
1989—Falcons, 30-28 (A)
1992—Bills, 41-14 (B)
1995—Bills, 23-17 (B)
(RS Pts.—Bills 140, Falcons 128)

ATLANTA vs. CAROLINA
RS: Series tied 4-4
1995—Falcons, 23-20 (A) OT
Panthers, 21-17 (C)
1996—Panthers, 29-6 (C)
Falcons, 20-17 (A)
1997—Panthers, 9-6 (A)
Panthers, 21-12 (C)
1998—Falcons, 19-14 (C)
Falcons, 51-23 (A)
(RS Pts.—Panthers 154, Falcons 154)

ATLANTA vs. CHICAGO
RS: Falcons lead series, 10-9
1966—Bears, 23-6 (C)
1967—Bears, 23-14 (A)
1968—Falcons, 16-13 (C)
1969—Falcons, 48-31 (A)
1970—Bears, 23-14 (A)
1972—Falcons, 37-21 (C)
1973—Falcons, 46-6 (A)
1974—Falcons, 13-10 (A)
1976—Falcons, 10-0 (C)
1977—Falcons, 16-10 (C)
1978—Bears, 13-7 (C)
1980—Falcons, 28-17 (A)
1983—Falcons, 20-17 (C)
1985—Bears, 36-0 (C)
1986—Bears, 13-10 (A)
1990—Bears, 30-24 (C)
1992—Bears, 41-31 (C)
1993—Bears, 6-0 (C)
1998—Falcons, 20-13 (A)
(RS Pts.—Falcons 360, Bears 346)

ATLANTA vs. CINCINNATI
RS: Bengals lead series, 7-2
1971—Falcons, 9-6 (C)
1975—Bengals, 21-14 (A)
1978—Bengals, 37-7 (C)
1981—Bengals, 30-28 (A)
1984—Bengals, 35-14 (C)
1987—Bengals, 16-10 (A)
1990—Falcons, 38-17 (A)
1993—Bengals, 21-17 (C)
1996—Bengals, 41-31 (C)
(RS Pts.—Bengals 224, Falcons 168)

ATLANTA vs. CLEVELAND
RS: Browns lead series, 8-2
1966—Browns, 49-17 (A)
1968—Browns, 30-7 (C)
1971—Falcons, 31-14 (C)
1976—Browns, 20-17 (A)
1978—Browns, 24-16 (A)
1981—Browns, 28-17 (C)
1984—Browns, 23-7 (A)
1987—Browns, 38-3 (C)
1990—Browns, 13-10 (C)
1993—Falcons, 17-14 (A)
(RS Pts.—Browns 253, Falcons 142)

ATLANTA vs. DALLAS
RS: Cowboys lead series, 11-6
PS: Cowboys lead series, 2-0
1966—Cowboys, 47-14 (A)
1967—Cowboys, 37-7 (D)
1969—Cowboys, 24-17 (A)
1970—Cowboys, 13-0 (D)
1974—Cowboys, 24-0 (A)
1976—Falcons, 17-10 (A)
1978—*Cowboys, 27-20 (D)
1980—*Cowboys, 30-27 (A)
1985—Cowboys, 24-10 (D)
1986—Falcons, 37-35 (D)
1987—Falcons, 21-10 (D)
1988—Cowboys, 26-20 (D)
1989—Falcons 27-21 (A)
1990—Falcons, 26-7 (A)
1991—Cowboys, 31-27 (D)
1992—Cowboys, 41-17 (A)
1993—Falcons, 27-14 (A)
1995—Cowboys, 28-13 (A)
1996—Cowboys, 32-28 (D)
(RS Pts.—Cowboys 424, Falcons 308)
(PS Pts.—Cowboys 57, Falcons 47)
**NFC Divisional Playoff*

ATLANTA vs. DENVER
RS: Broncos lead series, 6-3
PS: Broncos lead series, 1-0
1970—Broncos, 24-10 (D)
1972—Falcons, 23-20 (A)
1975—Falcons, 35-21 (A)
1979—Broncos, 20-17 (A) OT
1982—Falcons, 34-27 (D)
1985—Broncos, 44-28 (A)
1988—Broncos, 30-14 (D)
1994—Broncos, 32-28 (D)
1997—Broncos, 29-21 (A)
1998—*Broncos, 34-19 (Miami)
(RS Pts.—Broncos 247, Falcons 210)
(PS Pts.—Broncos 34, Falcons 19)
*Super Bowl XXXIII

ATLANTA vs. DETROIT
RS: Lions lead series, 20-7
1966—Lions, 28-10 (D)
1967—Lions, 24-3 (D)
1968—Lions, 24-7 (A)
1969—Lions, 27-21 (D)
1971—Lions, 41-38 (D)
1972—Lions, 26-23 (A)
1973—Lions, 31-6 (D)
1975—Lions, 17-14 (A)
1976—Lions, 24-10 (D)
1977—Falcons, 17-6 (A)
1978—Falcons, 14-0 (A)
1979—Lions, 24-23 (D)
1980—Falcons, 43-28 (A)
1983—Falcons, 30-14 (D)
1984—Lions, 27-24 (A) OT
1985—Lions, 28-27 (A)
1986—Falcons, 20-6 (D)
1987—Lions, 30-13 (A)
1988—Lions, 31-17 (D)
1989—Lions, 31-24 (A)
1990—Lions, 21-14 (D)
1993—Lions, 30-13 (D)
1994—Lions, 31-28 (D) OT
1995—Falcons, 34-22 (A)
1996—Lions, 28-24 (D)
1997—Lions, 28-17 (D)
1998—Falcons, 24-17 (D)
(RS Pts.—Lions 644, Falcons 538)

ATLANTA vs. GREEN BAY
RS: Packers lead series, 10-9
PS: Packers lead series, 1-0
1966—Packers, 56-3 (Mil)
1967—Packers, 23-0 (Mil)
1968—Packers, 38-7 (A)
1969—Packers, 28-10 (GB)
1970—Packers, 27-24 (GB)
1971—Falcons, 28-21 (A)
1972—Falcons, 10-9 (Mil)
1974—Falcons, 10-3 (A)
1975—Packers, 22-13 (GB)
1976—Packers, 24-20 (A)
1979—Falcons, 25-7 (A)
1981—Falcons, 31-17 (GB)
1982—Packers, 38-7 (A)
1983—Falcons, 47-41 (A) OT
1988—Falcons, 20-0 (A)
1989—Packers, 23-21 (Mil)
1991—Falcons, 35-31 (A)
1992—Falcons, 24-10 (A)
1994—Packers, 21-17 (Mil)
1995—*Packers, 37-20 (GB)
(RS Pts.—Packers 439, Falcons 352)
(PS Pts.—Packers 37, Falcons 20)
**NFC First-Round Playoff*

ATLANTA vs. *INDIANAPOLIS
RS: Colts lead series, 10-1
1966—Colts, 19-7 (A)
1967—Colts, 38-31 (B)
Colts, 49-7 (A)
1968—Colts, 28-20 (A)
Colts, 44-0 (B)
1969—Colts, 21-14 (A)
Colts, 13-6 (B)
1974—Colts, 17-7 (A)
1986—Colts, 28-23 (A)
1989—Colts, 13-9 (I)
1998—Falcons, 28-21 (A)
(RS Pts.—Colts 291, Falcons 152)
**Franchise in Baltimore prior to 1984*

ATLANTA vs. JACKSONVILLE
RS: Jaguars lead series, 1-0
1996—Jaguars, 19-17 (J)
(RS Pts.—Jaguars, 19, Falcons 17)

ATLANTA vs. KANSAS CITY
RS: Chiefs lead series, 4-0
1972—Chiefs, 17-14 (A)
1985—Chiefs, 38-10 (KC)
1991—Chiefs, 14-3 (KC)
1994—Chiefs, 30-10 (A)
(RS Pts.—Chiefs 99, Falcons 37)

ATLANTA vs. MIAMI
RS: Dolphins lead series, 6-2
1970—Dolphins, 20-7 (A)
1974—Dolphins, 42-7 (M)
1980—Dolphins, 20-17 (A)
1983—Dolphins, 31-24 (M)
1986—Falcons, 20-14 (M)
1992—Dolphins, 21-17 (M)
1995—Dolphins, 21-20 (M)
1998—Falcons, 38-16 (A)
(RS Pts.—Dolphins 185, Falcons 150)

ATLANTA vs. MINNESOTA
RS: Vikings lead series, 12-6
PS: Series tied, 1-1
1966—Falcons, 20-13 (M)
1967—Falcons, 21-20 (A)
1968—Vikings, 47-7 (M)
1969—Falcons, 10-3 (A)
1970—Vikings, 37-7 (A)
1971—Vikings, 24-7 (M)
1973—Falcons, 20-14 (A)
1974—Vikings, 23-10 (M)
1975—Vikings, 38-0 (M)
1977—Vikings, 14-7 (A)
1980—Vikings, 24-23 (M)
1981—Falcons, 31-30 (A)

ALL-TIME TEAM VS. TEAM RESULTS

1982—*Vikings, 30-24 (M)
1984—Vikings, 27-20 (M)
1985—Falcons, 14-13 (A)
1987—Vikings, 24-13 (M)
1989—Vikings, 43-17 (M)
1991—Vikings, 20-19 (A)
1996—Vikings, 23-17 (A)
1998—**Falcons, 30-27 (M) OT
(RS Pts.—Vikings 437, Falcons 263)
(PS Pts.—Vikings 57, Falcons 54)
NFC First-Round Playoff
***NFC Championship*

ATLANTA vs. NEW ENGLAND
RS: Falcons lead series, 6-3
1972—Patriots, 21-20 (NE)
1977—Patriots, 16-10 (A)
1980—Falcons, 37-21 (NE)
1983—Falcons, 24-13 (A)
1986—Patriots, 25-17 (NE)
1989—Falcons, 16-15 (A)
1992—Falcons, 34-0 (A)
1995—Falcons, 30-17 (A)
1998—Falcons, 41-10 (NE)
(RS Pts.—Falcons 229, Patriots 138)

ATLANTA vs. NEW ORLEANS
RS: Falcons lead series, 35-24
PS: Falcons lead series, 1-0
1967—Saints, 27-24 (NO)
1969—Falcons, 45-17 (A)
1970—Falcons, 14-3 (NO)
Falcons, 32-14 (A)
1971—Falcons, 28-6 (A)
Falcons, 24-20 (NO)
1972—Falcons, 21-14 (NO)
Falcons, 36-20 (A)
1973—Falcons, 62-7 (NO)
Falcons, 14-10 (A)
1974—Saints, 14-13 (NO)
Saints, 13-3 (A)
1975—Falcons, 14-7 (A)
Saints, 23-7 (NO)
1976—Saints, 30-0 (NO)
Falcons, 23-20 (A)
1977—Saints, 21-20 (NO)
Falcons, 35-7 (A)
1978—Falcons, 20-17 (NO)
Falcons, 20-17 (A)
1979—Falcons, 40-34 (NO) OT
Saints, 37-6 (A)
1980—Falcons, 41-14 (NO)
Falcons, 31-13 (A)
1981—Falcons, 27-0 (A)
Falcons, 41-10 (NO)
1982—Falcons, 35-0 (A)
Saints, 35-6 (NO)
1983—Saints, 19-17 (A)
Saints, 27-10 (NO)
1984—Falcons, 36-28 (NO)
Saints, 17-13 (A)
1985—Falcons, 31-24 (A)
Falcons, 16-10 (NO)
1986—Falcons, 31-10 (NO)
Saints, 14-9 (A)
1987—Saints, 38-0 (A)
1988—Saints, 29-21 (A)
Saints, 10-9 (NO)
1989—Saints, 20-13 (NO)
Saints, 26-17 (A)
1990—Falcons, 28-27 (A)
Saints, 10-7 (NO)
1991—Saints, 27-6 (A)
Falcons, 23-20 (NO) OT
*Falcons, 27-20 (NO)
1992—Saints, 10-7 (A)
Saints, 22-14 (NO)
1993—Saints, 34-31 (A)
Falcons, 26-15 (NO)
1994—Saints, 33-32 (NO)
Saints, 29-20 (A)
1995—Falcons, 27-24 (NO) OT
Falcons, 19-14 (A)
1996—Falcons, 17-15 (A)
Falcons, 31-15 (NO)
1997—Falcons, 23-17 (NO)
Falcons, 20-3 (A)
1998—Falcons, 31-23 (A)
Falcons, 27-17 (NO)
(RS Pts.—Falcons 1,294, Saints 1,077)
(PS Pts.—Falcons 27, Saints 20)
NFC First-Round Playoff

ATLANTA vs. N.Y. GIANTS
RS: Falcons lead series, 7-6
1966—Falcons, 27-16 (NY)
1968—Falcons, 24-21 (A)
1971—Giants, 21-17 (A)
1974—Falcons, 14-7 (New Haven)
1977—Falcons, 17-3 (A)
1978—Falcons, 23-20 (A)
1979—Giants, 24-3 (NY)
1981—Giants, 27-24 (A) OT
1982—Falcons, 16-14 (NY)
1983—Giants, 16-13 (A) OT
1984—Giants, 19-7 (A)
1988—Giants, 23-16 (A)
1998—Falcons, 34-20 (NY)
(RS Pts.—Falcons 235, Giants 231)

ATLANTA vs. N.Y. JETS
RS: Series tied, 4-4
1973—Falcons, 28-20 (NY)
1980—Jets, 14-7 (A)
1983—Falcons, 27-21 (NY)
1986—Jets, 28-14 (A)
1989—Jets, 27-7 (NY)
1992—Falcons, 20-17 (A)
1995—Falcons, 13-3 (A)
1998—Jets, 28-3 (NY)
(RS Pts.—Jets 158, Falcons 119)

ATLANTA vs. *OAKLAND
RS: Raiders lead series, 6-3
1971—Falcons, 24-13 (A)
1975—Raiders, 37-34 (O) OT
1979—Raiders, 50-19 (O)
1982—Raiders, 38-14 (A)
1985—Raiders, 34-24 (A)
1988—Falcons, 12-6 (LA)
1991—Falcons, 21-17 (A)
1994—Raiders, 30-17 (LA)
1997—Raiders, 36-31 (A)
(RS Pts.—Raiders 261, Falcons 196)
Franchise in Los Angeles from 1982-1994

ATLANTA vs. PHILADELPHIA
RS: Series tied, 9-9-1
PS: Falcons lead series, 1-0
1966—Eagles, 23-10 (P)
1967—Eagles, 38-7 (A)
1969—Falcons, 27-3 (P)
1970—Tie, 13-13 (P)
1973—Falcons, 44-27 (P)
1976—Eagles, 14-13 (A)
1978—*Falcons, 14-13 (A)
1979—Falcons, 14-10 (P)
1980—Falcons, 20-17 (P)
1981—Eagles, 16-13 (P)
1983—Eagles, 28-24 (A)
1984—Falcons, 26-10 (A)
1985—Eagles, 23-17 (P) OT
1986—Eagles, 16-0 (A)
1988—Falcons, 27-24 (P)
1990—Eagles, 24-23 (A)
1994—Falcons, 28-21 (A)
1996—Eagles, 33-18 (A)
1997—Falcons, 20-17 (A)
1998—Falcons, 17-12 (A)
(RS Pts.—Eagles 369, Falcons 361)
(PS Pts.—Falcons 14, Eagles 13)
NFC First-Round Playoff

ATLANTA vs. PITTSBURGH
RS: Steelers lead series, 10-1
1966—Steelers, 57-33 (A)
1968—Steelers, 41-21 (A)
1970—Falcons, 27-16 (A)
1974—Steelers, 24-17 (P)
1978—Steelers, 31-7 (P)
1981—Steelers, 34-20 (A)
1984—Steelers, 35-10 (P)
1987—Steelers, 28-12 (A)
1990—Steelers, 21-9 (P)
1993—Steelers, 45-17 (A)
1996—Steelers, 20-17 (A)
(RS Pts.—Steelers 352, Falcons 190)

ATLANTA vs. *ST. LOUIS
RS: Rams lead series, 39-23-2
1966—Rams, 19-14 (A)
1967—Rams, 31-3 (A)
Rams, 20-3 (LA)
1968—Rams, 27-14 (LA)
Rams, 17-10 (A)
1969—Rams, 17-7 (LA)
Rams, 38-6 (A)
1970—Tie, 10-10 (LA)
Rams, 17-7 (A)
1971—Tie, 20-20 (LA)
Rams, 24-16 (A)
1972—Falcons, 31-3 (A)
Rams, 20-7 (LA)
1973—Rams, 31-0 (LA)
Falcons, 15-13 (A)
1974—Rams, 21-0 (LA)
Rams, 30-7 (A)
1975—Rams, 22-7 (LA)
Rams, 16-7 (A)
1976—Rams, 30-14 (A)
Rams, 59-0 (LA)
1977—Falcons, 17-6 (A)
Rams, 23-7 (LA)
1978—Rams, 10-0 (LA)
Falcons, 15-7 (A)
1979—Rams, 20-14 (LA)
Rams, 34-13 (A)
1980—Falcons, 13-10 (A)
Rams, 20-17 (LA) OT
1981—Rams, 37-35 (A)
Rams, 21-16 (LA)
1982—Falcons, 34-17 (A)
1983—Rams, 27-21 (LA)
Rams, 36-13 (A)
1984—Falcons, 30-28 (LA)
Rams, 24-10 (A)
1985—Rams, 17-6 (LA)
Falcons, 30-14 (A)
1986—Falcons, 26-14 (A)
Rams, 14-7 (LA)
1987—Falcons, 24-20 (A)
Rams, 33-0 (LA)
1988—Rams, 33-0 (A)
Rams, 22-7 (LA)
1989—Rams, 31-21 (A)
Rams, 26-14 (LA)
1990—Rams, 44-24 (LA)
Falcons, 20-13 (A)
1991—Falcons, 31-14 (A)
Falcons, 31-14 (LA)
1992—Falcons, 30-28 (A)
Rams, 38-27 (LA)
1993—Falcons, 30-24 (A)
Falcons, 13-0 (LA)
1994—Falcons, 31-13 (A)
Falcons, 8-5 (LA)
1995—Rams, 21-19 (StL)
Falcons, 31-6 (A)
1996—Rams, 59-16 (StL)
Rams, 34-27 (A)
1997—Falcons, 34-31 (A)
Falcons, 27-21 (StL)
1998—Falcons, 37-15 (A)
Falcons, 21-10 (StL)
(RS Pts.—Rams 1,419, Falcons 1,045)
Franchise in Los Angeles prior to 1995

ATLANTA vs. SAN DIEGO
RS: Falcons lead series, 5-1
1973—Falcons, 41-0 (SD)
1979—Falcons, 28-26 (SD)
1988—Chargers, 10-7 (A)
1991—Falcons, 13-10 (SD)
1994—Falcons, 10-9 (A)
1997—Falcons, 14-3 (SD)
(RS Pts.—Falcons 113, Chargers 58)

ATLANTA vs. SAN FRANCISCO
RS: 49ers lead series, 40-23-1
PS: Falcons lead series, 1-0
1966—49ers, 44-7 (A)
1967—49ers, 38-7 (SF)
49ers, 34-28 (A)
1968—49ers, 28-13 (SF)
49ers, 14-12 (A)
1969—Falcons, 24-12 (A)
Falcons, 21-7 (SF)
1970—Falcons, 21-20 (A)
49ers, 24-20 (SF)
1971—Falcons, 20-17 (A)
49ers, 24-3 (SF)
1972—49ers, 49-14 (A)
49ers, 20-0 (SF)
1973—49ers, 13-9 (A)
Falcons, 17-3 (SF)
1974—49ers, 16-10 (A)
49ers, 27-0 (SF)
1975—Falcons, 17-3 (SF)
Falcons, 31-9 (A)
1976—49ers, 15-0 (SF)
Falcons, 21-16 (A)
1977—Falcons, 7-0 (SF)
49ers, 10-3 (A)
1978—Falcons, 20-17 (SF)
Falcons, 21-10 (A)
1979—49ers, 20-15 (SF)
Falcons, 31-21 (A)
1980—Falcons, 20-17 (SF)
Falcons, 35-10 (A)
1981—Falcons, 34-17 (A)
49ers, 17-14 (SF)
1982—Falcons, 17-7 (SF)
1983—49ers, 24-20 (SF)
Falcons, 28-24 (A)
1984—49ers, 14-5 (SF)
49ers, 35-17 (A)
1985—49ers, 35-16 (SF)
49ers, 38-17 (A)
1986—Tie, 10-10 (A) OT
49ers, 20-0 (SF)
1987—49ers, 25-17 (A)
49ers, 35-7 (SF)
1988—Falcons, 34-17 (SF)
49ers, 13-3 (A)
1989—49ers, 45-3 (SF)
49ers, 23-10 (A)
1990—49ers, 19-13 (SF)
49ers, 45-35 (A)
1991—Falcons, 39-34 (SF)
Falcons, 17-14 (A)
1992—49ers, 56-17 (SF)
49ers, 41-3 (A)
1993—49ers, 37-30 (SF)
Falcons, 27-24 (A)
1994—49ers, 42-3 (A)
49ers, 50-14 (SF)
1995—49ers, 41-10 (SF)
Falcons, 28-27 (A)
1996—49ers, 39-17 (SF)
49ers, 34-10 (A)
1997—49ers, 34-7 (SF)
49ers, 35-28 (A)
1998—49ers, 31-20 (SF)
Falcons, 31-19 (A)
*Falcons, 20-18 (A)
(RS Pts.—49ers 1,559, Falcons 1,048)
(PS Pts.—Falcons 20, 49ers 18)
NFC Divisional Playoff

ATLANTA vs. SEATTLE
RS: Seahawks lead series, 4-2
1976—Seahawks, 30-13 (S)
1979—Seahawks, 31-28 (A)
1985—Seahawks, 30-26 (S)
1988—Seahawks, 31-20 (A)
1991—Falcons, 26-13 (A)
1997—Falcons, 24-17 (S)
(RS Pts.—Seahawks 152, Falcons 137)

ATLANTA vs. TAMPA BAY
RS: Falcons lead series, 8-7
1977—Falcons, 17-0 (TB)

1978—Buccaneers, 14-9 (TB)
1979—Falcons, 17-14 (A)
1981—Buccaneers, 24-23 (TB)
1984—Buccaneers, 23-6 (TB)
1986—Falcons, 23-20 (TB) OT
1987—Buccaneers, 48-10 (TB)
1988—Falcons, 17-10 (A)
1990—Buccaneers, 23-17 (TB)
1991—Falcons, 43-7 (A)
1992—Falcons, 35-7 (TB)
1993—Buccaneers, 31-24 (A)
1994—Falcons, 34-13 (A)
1995—Falcons, 24-21 (TB)
1997—Buccaneers, 31-10 (A)
(RS Pts.—Falcons 309, Buccaneers 286)

ATLANTA vs. *TENNESSEE
RS: Falcons lead series, 5-4
1972—Falcons, 20-10 (A)
1976—Oilers, 20-14 (H)
1978—Falcons, 20-14 (A)
1981—Falcons, 31-27 (H)
1984—Falcons, 42-10 (A)
1987—Oilers, 37-33 (H)
1990—Falcons, 47-27 (A)
1993—Oilers, 33-17 (H)
1996—Oilers, 23-13 (A)
(RS Pts.—Falcons 237, Titans 201)
Franchise in Houston prior to 1997; known as Oilers prior to 1999

ATLANTA vs. WASHINGTON
RS: Redskins lead series, 13-4-1
PS: Redskins lead series, 1-0
1966—Redskins, 33-20 (W)
1967—Tie, 20-20 (A)
1969—Redskins, 27-20 (W)
1972—Redskins, 24-13 (W)
1975—Redskins, 30-27 (A)
1977—Redskins, 10-6 (W)
1978—Falcons, 20-17 (A)
1979—Redskins, 16-7 (A)
1980—Falcons, 10-6 (A)
1983—Redskins, 37-21 (W)
1984—Redskins, 27-14 (W)
1985—Redskins, 44-10 (A)
1987—Falcons, 21-20 (A)
1989—Redskins, 31-30 (A)
1991—Redskins, 56-17 (W)
*Redskins, 24-7 (W)
1992—Redskins, 24-17 (W)
1993—Redskins, 30-17 (W)
1994—Falcons, 27-20 (W)
(RS Pts.—Redskins 472, Falcons 317)
(PS Pts.—Redskins 24, Falcons 7)
**NFC Divisional Playoff*

BALTIMORE vs. ARIZONA
RS: Cardinals lead series, 1-0;
See Arizona vs. Baltimore

BALTIMORE vs. CAROLINA
RS: Panthers lead series, 1-0
1996—Panthers, 27-16 (C)
(RS Pts.—Panthers 27, Ravens 16)

BALTIMORE vs. CHICAGO
RS: Bears lead series, 1-0
1998—Bears, 24-3 (C)
(RS Pts.—Bears 24, Ravens 3)

BALTIMORE vs. CINCINNATI
RS: Series tied, 3-3
1996—Bengals, 24-21 (B)
Bengals, 21-14 (C)
1997—Ravens, 23-10 (B)
Bengals, 16-14 (C)
1998—Ravens, 31-24 (B)
Ravens, 20-13 (C)
(RS Pts.—Ravens 123, Bengals 108)

BALTIMORE vs. DENVER
RS: Broncos lead series, 1-0
1996—Broncos, 45-34 (D)
(RS Pts.—Broncos 45, Ravens 34)

BALTIMORE vs. DETROIT
RS: Ravens lead series, 1-0
1998—Ravens, 19-10 (B)
(RS Pts.—Ravens 19, Lions 10)

BALTIMORE vs. GREEN BAY
RS: Packers lead series, 1-0
1998—Packers, 28-10 (GB)
(RS Pts.—Packers 28, Ravens 10)

BALTIMORE vs. INDIANAPOLIS
RS: Series tied, 1-1
1996—Colts, 26-21 (I)
1998—Ravens, 38-31 (B)
(RS Pts.—Ravens 59, Colts 57)

BALTIMORE vs. JACKSONVILLE
RS: Jaguars lead series, 6-0
1996—Jaguars, 30-27 (J)
Jaguars, 28-25 (B) OT
1997—Jaguars, 28-27 (B)
Jaguars, 29-27 (J)
1998—Jaguars, 24-10 (J)
Jaguars, 45-19 (B)
(RS Pts.—Jaguars 184, Ravens 135)

BALTIMORE vs. MIAMI
RS: Dolphins lead series, 1-0
1997—Dolphins, 24-13 (B)
(RS Pts.—Dolphins 24, Ravens 13)

BALTIMORE vs. MINNESOTA
RS: Vikings lead series, 1-0
1998—Vikings, 38-28 (B)
(RS Pts.—Vikings 38, Ravens 28)

BALTIMORE vs. NEW ENGLAND
RS: Patriots lead series, 1-0
1996—Patriots, 46-38 (B)
(RS Pts.—Patriots 46, Ravens 38)

BALTIMORE vs. NEW ORLEANS
RS: Ravens lead series, 1-0
1996—Ravens, 17-10 (B)
(RS Pts.—Ravens 17, Saints 10)

BALTIMORE vs. N.Y. GIANTS
RS: Ravens lead series, 1-0
1997—Ravens, 24-23 (NY)
(RS Pts.—Ravens 24, Giants 23)

BALTIMORE vs. N.Y. JETS
RS: Series tied, 1-1
1997—Jets, 19-16 (NY) OT
1998—Ravens, 24-10 (NY)
(RS Pts.—Ravens 40, Jets 29)

BALTIMORE vs. OAKLAND
RS: Ravens lead series, 2-0
1996—Ravens, 19-14 (B)
1998—Ravens, 13-10 (B)
(RS Pts.—Ravens 32, Raiders 24)

BALTIMORE vs. PHILADELPHIA
RS: Series tied, 0-0-1
1997—Tie, 10-10 (B) OT
(RS Pts.—Ravens 10, Eagles 10)

BALTIMORE vs. PITTSBURGH
RS: Steelers lead series, 5-1
1996—Steelers, 31-17 (P)
Ravens, 31-17 (B)
1997—Steelers, 42-34 (B)
Steelers, 37-0 (P)
1998—Steelers, 20-13 (B)
Steelers, 16-6 (P)
(RS Pts.—Steelers 163, Ravens 101)

BALTIMORE vs. ST. LOUIS
RS: Ravens lead series, 1-0
1996—Ravens, 37-31 (B) OT
(RS Pts.—Ravens 37, Rams 31)

BALTIMORE vs. SAN DIEGO
RS: Chargers lead series, 2-0
1997—Chargers, 21-17 (SD)
1998—Chargers, 14-13 (SD)
(RS Pts.—Chargers 35, Ravens 30)

BALTIMORE vs. SAN FRANCISCO
RS: 49ers lead series, 1-0
1996—49ers, 38-20 (SF)
(RS Pts.—49ers 38, Ravens 20)

BALTIMORE vs. SEATTLE
RS: Ravens lead series, 1-0
1997—Ravens, 31-24 (B)
(RS Pts.—Ravens 31, Seahawks 24)

BALTIMORE vs. *TENNESSEE
RS: Titans lead series, 4-2
1996—Oilers, 29-13 (H)
Oilers, 24-21 (B)
1997—Ravens, 36-10 (T)
Ravens, 21-19 (B)
1998—Oilers, 12-8 (B)
Oilers, 16-14 (T)
(RS Pts.—Ravens 113, Titans 110)
Franchise in Houston prior to 1997; known as Oilers prior to 1999

BALTIMORE vs. WASHINGTON
RS: Ravens lead series, 1-0
1997—Ravens, 20-17 (W)
(RS Pts.—Ravens 20, Redskins 17)

BUFFALO vs. ARIZONA
RS: Series tied, 3-3;
See Arizona vs. Buffalo

BUFFALO vs. ATLANTA
RS: Bills lead series, 4-3;
See Atlanta vs. Buffalo

BUFFALO vs. CAROLINA
RS: Bills lead series, 2-0
1995—Bills, 31-9 (B)
1998—Bills, 30-14 (C)
(RS Pts.—Bills 61, Panthers 23)

BUFFALO vs. CHICAGO
RS: Bears lead series, 5-2
1970—Bears, 31-13 (C)
1974—Bills, 16-6 (B)
1979—Bears, 7-0 (B)
1988—Bears, 24-3 (C)
1991—Bills, 35-20 (B)
1994—Bears, 20-13 (C)
1997—Bears, 20-3 (C)
(RS Pts.—Bears 128, Bills 83)

BUFFALO vs. CINCINNATI
RS: Series tied, 9-9
PS: Bengals lead series, 2-0
1968—Bengals, 34-23 (C)
1969—Bills, 16-13 (B)
1970—Bengals, 43-14 (B)
1973—Bengals, 16-13 (B)
1975—Bengals, 33-24 (C)
1978—Bills, 5-0 (B)
1979—Bills, 51-24 (B)
1980—Bills, 14-0 (C)
1981—Bengals, 27-24 (C) OT
*Bengals, 28-21 (C)
1983—Bills, 10-6 (C)
1984—Bengals, 52-21 (C)
1985—Bengals, 23-17 (B)
1986—Bengals, 36-33 (C) OT
1988—Bengals, 35-21 (C)
**Bengals, 21-10 (C)
1989—Bills, 24-7 (B)
1991—Bills, 35-16 (B)
1996—Bills, 31-17 (B)
1998—Bills, 33-20 (C)
(RS Pts.—Bills 409, Bengals 402)
(PS Pts.—Bengals 49, Bills 31)
**AFC Divisional Playoff*
***AFC Championship*

BUFFALO vs. CLEVELAND
RS: Browns lead series, 7-4
PS: Browns lead series, 1-0
1972—Browns, 27-10 (C)
1974—Bills, 15-10 (C)
1977—Browns, 27-16 (B)
1978—Browns, 41-20 (C)
1981—Bills, 22-13 (B)
1984—Browns, 13-10 (B)
1985—Browns, 17-7 (C)
1986—Browns, 21-17 (B)
1987—Browns, 27-21 (C)
1989—*Browns, 34-30 (C)
1990—Bills, 42-0 (C)
1995—Bills, 22-19 (C)
(RS Pts.—Browns 215, Bills 202)
(PS Pts.—Browns 34, Bills 30)
**AFC Divisional Playoff*

BUFFALO vs. DALLAS
RS: Series tied, 3-3
PS: Cowboys lead series, 2-0
1971—Cowboys, 49-37 (B)
1976—Cowboys, 17-10 (D)
1981—Cowboys, 27-14 (D)
1984—Bills, 14-3 (B)
1992—*Cowboys, 52-17 (Pasadena)
1993—Bills, 13-10 (D)
**Cowboys, 30-13 (Atlanta)
1996—Bills, 10-7 (B)
(RS Pts.—Cowboys 113, Bills 98)
(PS Pts.—Cowboys 82, Bills 30)
**Super Bowl XXVII*
***Super Bowl XXVIII*

BUFFALO vs. DENVER
RS: Bills lead series, 17-12-1
PS: Bills lead series, 1-0
1960—Broncos, 27-21 (B)
Tie, 38-38 (D)
1961—Broncos, 22-10 (B)
Bills, 23-10 (D)
1962—Broncos, 23-20 (B)
Bills, 45-38 (D)
1963—Bills, 30-28 (D)
Bills, 27-17 (B)
1964—Bills, 30-13 (B)
Bills, 30-19 (D)
1965—Bills, 30-15 (D)
Bills, 31-13 (B)
1966—Bills, 38-21 (B)
1967—Bills, 17-16 (D)
Broncos, 21-20 (B)
1968—Broncos, 34-32 (D)
1969—Bills, 41-28 (B)
1970—Broncos, 25-10 (B)
1975—Bills, 38-14 (B)
1977—Broncos, 26-6 (D)
1979—Broncos, 19-16 (B)
1981—Bills, 9-7 (B)
1984—Broncos, 37-7 (B)
1987—Bills, 21-14 (B)
1989—Broncos, 28-14 (B)
1990—Bills, 29-28 (B)
1991—*Bills, 10-7 (B)
1992—Bills, 27-17 (B)
1994—Bills, 27-20 (B)
1995—Broncos, 22-7 (D)
1997—Broncos, 23-20 (B) OT
(RS Pts.—Bills 714, Broncos 663)
(PS Pts.—Bills 10, Broncos 7)
*AFC Championship

BUFFALO vs. DETROIT
RS: Lions lead series, 3-2-1
1972—Tie, 21-21 (B)
1976—Lions, 27-14 (D)
1979—Bills, 20-17 (D)
1991—Lions, 17-14 (B) OT
1994—Lions, 35-21 (D)
1997—Bills, 22-13 (B)
(RS Pts.—Lions 130, Bills 112)

BUFFALO vs. GREEN BAY
RS: Bills lead series, 5-2
1974—Bills, 27-7 (GB)
1979—Bills, 19-12 (B)
1982—Packers, 33-21 (Mil)
1988—Bills, 28-0 (B)
1991—Bills, 34-24 (Mil)
1994—Bills 29-20 (B)
1997—Packers, 31-21 (GB)
(RS Pts.—Bills 179, Packers 127)

BUFFALO vs. *INDIANAPOLIS
RS: Bills lead series, 33-23-1
1970—Tie, 17-17 (Balt)
Colts, 20-14 (Buff)
1971—Colts, 43-0 (Buff)
Colts, 24-0 (Balt)
1972—Colts, 17-0 (Buff)
Colts, 35-7 (Balt)
1973—Bills, 31-13 (Buff)
Bills, 24-17 (Balt)
1974—Bills, 27-14 (Balt)
Bills, 6-0 (Buff)
1975—Bills, 38-31 (Balt)
Colts, 42-35 (Buff)
1976—Colts, 31-13 (Buff)
Colts, 58-20 (Balt)
1977—Colts, 17-14 (Balt)
Colts, 31-13 (Buff)

ALL-TIME TEAM VS. TEAM RESULTS

1978—Bills, 24-17 (Buff)
Bills, 21-14 (Balt)
1979—Bills, 31-13 (Balt)
Colts, 14-13 (Buff)
1980—Colts, 17-12 (Buff)
Colts, 28-24 (Balt)
1981—Bills, 35-3 (Balt)
Bills, 23-17 (Buff)
1982—Bills, 20-0 (Buff)
1983—Bills, 28-23 (Buff)
Bills, 30-7 (Balt)
1984—Colts, 31-17 (I)
Bills, 21-15 (Buff)
1985—Colts, 49-17 (I)
Bills, 21-9 (Buff)
1986—Bills, 24-13 (Buff)
Colts, 24-14 (I)
1987—Colts, 47-6 (Buff)
Bills, 27-3 (I)
1988—Bills, 34-23 (Buff)
Colts, 17-14 (I)
1989—Colts, 37-14 (I)
Bills, 30-7 (Buff)
1990—Bills, 26-10 (Buff)
Bills, 31-7 (I)
1991—Bills, 42-6 (Buff)
Bills, 35-7 (I)
1992—Bills, 38-0 (Buff)
Colts, 16-13 (I) OT
1993—Bills, 23-9 (Buff)
Bills, 30-10 (I)
1994—Colts, 27-17 (Buff)
Colts, 10-9 (I)
1995—Bills, 20-14 (Buff)
Bills, 16-10 (I)
1996—Bills, 16-13 (Buff) OT
Colts, 13-10 (I) OT
1997—Bills, 37-35 (B)
Bills, 9-6 (I)
1998—Bills, 31-24 (I)
Bills, 34-11 (B)
(RS Pts.—Bills 1,196, Colts 1,066)
Franchise in Baltimore prior to 1984

BUFFALO vs. JACKSONVILLE
RS: Series tied, 1-1
PS: Jaguars lead series, 1-0
1996—*Jaguars, 30-27 (B)
1997—Jaguars, 20-14 (B)
1998—Bills, 17-16 (B)
(RS Pts.—Jaguars 36, Bills 31)
(PS Pts.—Jaguars 30, Bills 27)
*AFC First-Round Playoff

BUFFALO vs. *KANSAS CITY
RS: Bills lead series, 17-14-1
PS: Bills lead series, 2-1
1960—Texans, 45-28 (B)
Texans, 24-7 (D)
1961—Bills, 27-24 (B)
Bills, 30-20 (D)
1962—Texans, 41-21 (D)
Bills, 23-14 (B)
1963—Tie, 27-27 (B)
Bills, 35-26 (KC)
1964—Bills, 34-17 (B)
Bills, 35-22 (KC)
1965—Bills, 23-7 (KC)
Bills, 34-25 (B)
1966—Chiefs, 42-20 (B)
Bills, 29-14 (KC)
**Chiefs, 31-7 (B)
1967—Chiefs, 23-13 (KC)
1968—Chiefs, 18-7 (B)
1969—Chiefs, 29-7 (B)
Chiefs, 22-19 (KC)
1971—Chiefs, 22-9 (KC)
1973—Bills, 23-14 (B)
1976—Bills, 50-17 (B)
1978—Bills, 28-13 (B)
Chiefs, 14-10 (KC)
1982—Bills, 14-9 (B)
1983—Bills, 14-9 (KC)
1986—Chiefs, 20-17 (B)
Bills, 17-14 (KC)
1991—Chiefs, 33-6 (KC)
***Bills, 37-14 (B)
1993—Chiefs, 23-7 (KC)
****Bills, 30-13 (B)
1994—Bills, 44-10 (B)
1996—Bills, 20-9 (B)
1997—Chiefs, 22-16 (KC)
(RS Pts.—Bills 694, Chiefs 669)
(PS Pts.—Bills 74, Chiefs 58)
Franchise in Dallas prior to 1963 and known as Texans
**AFL Championship*
***AFC Divisional Playoff*
****AFC Championship*

BUFFALO vs. MIAMI
RS: Dolphins lead series, 42-23-1
PS: Bills lead series, 3-1
1966—Bills, 58-24 (B)
Bills, 29-0 (M)
1967—Bills, 35-13 (B)
Dolphins, 17-14 (M)
1968—Tie, 14-14 (M)
Dolphins, 21-17 (B)
1969—Dolphins, 24-6 (M)
Bills, 28-3 (B)
1970—Dolphins, 33-14 (B)
Dolphins, 45-7 (M)
1971—Dolphins, 29-14 (B)
Dolphins, 34-0 (M)
1972—Dolphins, 24-23 (M)
Dolphins, 30-16 (B)
1973—Dolphins, 27-6 (M)
Dolphins, 17-0 (B)
1974—Dolphins, 24-16 (B)
Dolphins, 35-28 (M)
1975—Dolphins, 35-30 (B)
Dolphins, 31-21 (M)
1976—Dolphins, 30-21 (B)
Dolphins, 45-27 (M)
1977—Dolphins, 13-0 (B)
Dolphins, 31-14 (M)
1978—Dolphins, 31-24 (M)
Dolphins, 25-24 (B)
1979—Dolphins, 9-7 (B)
Dolphins, 17-7 (M)
1980—Bills, 17-7 (B)
Dolphins, 17-14 (M)
1981—Bills, 31-21 (B)
Dolphins, 16-6 (M)
1982—Dolphins, 9-7 (B)
Dolphins, 27-10 (M)
1983—Dolphins, 12-0 (B)
Bills, 38-35 (M) OT
1984—Dolphins, 21-17 (B)
Dolphins, 38-7 (M)
1985—Dolphins, 23-14 (B)
Dolphins, 28-0 (M)
1986—Dolphins, 27-14 (M)
Dolphins, 34-24 (B)
1987—Bills, 34-31 (M) OT
Bills, 27-0 (B)
1988—Bills, 9-6 (B)
Bills, 31-6 (M)
1989—Bills, 27-24 (M)
Bills, 31-17 (B)
1990—Dolphins, 30-7 (M)
Bills, 24-14 (B)
*Bills, 44-34 (B)
1991—Bills, 35-31 (B)
Bills, 41-27 (M)
1992—Dolphins, 37-10 (B)
Bills, 26-20 (M)
**Bills, 29-10 (M)
1993—Dolphins, 22-13 (B)
Bills, 47-34 (M)
1994—Bills, 21-11 (B)
Bills, 42-31 (M)
1995—Dolphins, 23-6 (M)
Bills, 23-20 (B)
***Bills, 37-22 (B)
1996—Dolphins, 21-7 (B)
Dolphins, 16-14 (M)
1997—Bills, 9-6 (B)
Dolphins, 30-13 (M)
1998—Dolphins, 13-7 (M)
Bills, 30-24 (B)
***Dolphins, 24-17 (M)
(RS Pts.—Dolphins 1,490, Bills 1,233)
(PS Pts.—Bills 127, Dolphins 90)
*AFC Divisional Playoff
**AFC Championship*
***AFC First-Round Playoff*

BUFFALO vs. MINNESOTA
RS: Vikings lead series, 6-2
1971—Vikings, 19-0 (M)
1975—Vikings, 35-13 (B)
1979—Vikings, 10-3 (M)
1982—Bills, 23-22 (B)
1985—Vikings, 27-20 (B)
1988—Bills, 13-10 (B)
1994—Vikings, 21-17 (B)
1997—Vikings, 34-13 (B)
(RS Pts.—Vikings 178, Bills 102)

BUFFALO vs. *NEW ENGLAND
RS: Patriots lead series, 40-36-1
PS: Patriots lead series, 1-0
1960—Bills, 13-0 (Bos)
Bills, 38-14 (Buff)
1961—Patriots, 23-21 (Buff)
Patriots, 52-21 (Bos)
1962—Tie, 28-28 (Buff)
Patriots, 21-10 (Bos)
1963—Bills, 28-21 (Buff)
Patriots, 17-7 (Bos)
**Patriots, 26-8 (Buff)
1964—Patriots, 36-28 (Buff)
Bills, 24-14 (Bos)
1965—Bills, 24-7 (Buff)
Bills, 23-7 (Bos)
1966—Patriots, 20-10 (Buff)
Patriots, 14-3 (Bos)
1967—Patriots, 23-0 (Buff)
Bills, 44-16 (Bos)
1968—Patriots, 16-7 (Buff)
Patriots, 23-6 (Bos)
1969—Bills, 23-16 (Buff)
Patriots, 35-21 (Bos)
1970—Bills, 45-10 (Bos)
Patriots, 14-10 (Buff)
1971—Patriots, 38-33 (NE)
Bills, 27-20 (Buff)
1972—Bills, 38-14 (Buff)
Bills, 27-24 (NE)
1973—Bills, 31-13 (NE)
Bills, 37-13 (Buff)
1974—Bills, 30-28 (Buff)
Bills, 29-28 (NE)
1975—Bills, 45-31 (Buff)
Bills, 34-14 (NE)
1976—Patriots, 26-22 (Buff)
Patriots, 20-10 (NE)
1977—Bills, 24-14 (NE)
Patriots, 20-7 (Buff)
1978—Patriots, 14-10 (Buff)
Patriots, 26-24 (NE)
1979—Patriots, 26-6 (Buff)
Bills, 16-13 (NE) OT
1980—Bills, 31-13 (Buff)
Patriots, 24-2 (NE)
1981—Bills, 20-17 (Buff)
Bills, 19-10 (NE)
1982—Patriots, 30-19 (NE)
1983—Patriots, 31-0 (Buff)
Patriots, 21-7 (NE)
1984—Patriots, 21-17 (Buff)
Patriots, 38-10 (NE)
1985—Patriots, 17-14 (Buff)
Patriots, 14-3 (NE)
1986—Patriots, 23-3 (Buff)
Patriots, 22-19 (NE)
1987—Patriots, 14-7 (NE)
Patriots, 13-7 (Buff)
1988—Bills, 16-14 (NE)
Bills, 23-20 (Buff)
1989—Bills, 31-10 (Buff)
Patriots, 33-24 (NE)
1990—Bills, 27-10 (NE)
Bills, 14-0 (Buff)
1991—Bills, 22-17 (Buff)
Patriots, 16-13 (NE)
1992—Bills, 41-7 (NE)
Bills, 16-7 (Buff)
1993—Bills, 38-14 (Buff)
Bills, 13-10 (NE) OT
1994—Bills, 38-35 (NE)
Patriots, 41-17 (Buff)
1995—Patriots, 27-14 (NE)
Patriots, 35-25 (Buff)
1996—Bills, 17-10 (Buff)
Patriots, 28-25 (NE)
1997—Patriots, 33-6 (NE)
Patriots, 31-10 (B)
1998—Bills, 13-10 (B)
Patriots, 25-21 (NE)
(RS Pts.—Patriots 1,550, Bills 1,526)
(PS Pts.—Patriots 26, Bills 8)
*Franchise in Boston prior to 1971
**Division Playoff*

BUFFALO vs. NEW ORLEANS
RS: Bills lead series, 4-2
1973—Saints, 13-0 (NO)
1980—Bills, 35-26 (NO)
1983—Bills, 27-21 (B)
1989—Saints, 22-19 (B)
1992—Bills, 20-16 (NO)
1998—Bills, 45-33 (NO)
(RS Pts.—Bills 146, Saints 131)

BUFFALO vs. N.Y. GIANTS
RS: Bills lead series, 5-2
PS: Giants lead series, 1-0
1970—Giants, 20-6 (NY)
1975—Giants, 17-14 (B)
1978—Bills, 41-17 (B)
1987—Bills, 6-3 (B) OT
1990—Bills, 17-13 (NY)
*Giants, 20-19 (Tampa)
1993—Bills, 17-14 (B)
1996—Bills, 23-20 (NY) OT
(RS Pts.—Bills 124, Giants 104)
(PS Pts.—Giants 20, Bills 19)
*Super Bowl XXV

BUFFALO vs. *N.Y. JETS
RS: Bills lead series, 43-33
PS: Bills lead series, 1-0
1960—Titans, 27-3 (NY)
Titans, 17-13 (B)
1961—Bills, 41-31 (B)
Titans, 21-14 (NY)
1962—Titans, 17-6 (B)
Bills, 20-3 (NY)
1963—Bills, 45-14 (B)
Bills, 19-10 (NY)
1964—Bills, 34-24 (B)
Bills, 20-7 (NY)
1965—Bills, 33-21 (B)
Jets, 14-12 (NY)
1966—Bills, 33-23 (NY)
Bills, 14-3 (B)
1967—Bills, 20-17 (B)
Jets, 20-10 (NY)
1968—Bills, 37-35 (B)
Jets, 25-21 (NY)
1969—Jets, 33-19 (B)
Jets, 16-6 (NY)
1970—Bills, 34-31 (B)
Bills, 10-6 (NY)
1971—Jets, 28-17 (NY)
Jets, 20-7 (B)
1972—Jets, 41-24 (B)
Jets, 41-3 (NY)
1973—Bills, 9-7 (B)
Bills, 34-14 (NY)
1974—Bills, 16-12 (B)
Jets, 20-10 (NY)
1975—Bills, 42-14 (B)
Bills, 24-23 (NY)
1976—Jets, 17-14 (NY)
Jets, 19-14 (B)
1977—Jets, 24-19 (B)

Bills, 14-10 (NY)
1978—Jets, 21-20 (B)
Jets, 45-14 (NY)
1979—Bills, 46-31 (B)
Bills, 14-12 (NY)
1980—Bills, 20-10 (B)
Bills, 31-24 (NY)
1981—Bills, 31-0 (B)
Jets, 33-14 (NY)
**Bills, 31-27 (NY)
1983—Jets, 34-10 (B)
Bills, 24-17 (NY)
1984—Jets, 28-26 (B)
Jets, 21-17 (NY)
1985—Jets, 42-3 (NY)
Jets, 27-7 (B)
1986—Jets, 28-24 (B)
Jets, 14-13 (NY)
1987—Jets, 31-28 (B)
Bills, 17-14 (NY)
1988—Bills, 37-14 (NY)
Bills, 9-6 (B) OT
1989—Bills, 34-3 (B)
Bills, 37-0 (NY)
1990—Bills, 30-7 (NY)
Bills, 30-27 (B)
1991—Bills, 23-20 (NY)
Bills, 24-13 (B)
1992—Bills, 24-20 (NY)
Jets, 24-17 (B)
1993—Bills, 19-10 (NY)
Bills, 16-14 (B)
1994—Jets, 23-3 (B)
Jets, 22-17 (NY)
1995—Bills, 29-10 (B)
Bills, 28-26 (NY)
1996—Bills, 25-22 (NY)
Bills, 35-10 (B)
1997—Bills, 28-22 (NY)
Bills, 20-10 (B)
1998—Jets, 34-12 (NY)
Jets, 17-10 (B)
(RS Pts.—Bills 1,577, Jets 1,491)
(PS Pts.—Bills 31, Jets 27)
Jets known as Titans prior to 1963
***AFC First-Round Playoff*

BUFFALO vs. *OAKLAND
RS: Series tied, 15-15
PS: Bills lead series, 2-0
1960—Bills, 38-9 (B)
Raiders, 20-7 (O)
1961—Raiders, 31-22 (B)
Bills, 26-21 (O)
1962—Bills, 14-6 (B)
Bills, 10-6 (O)
1963—Raiders, 35-17 (O)
Bills, 12-0 (B)
1964—Bills, 23-20 (B)
Raiders, 16-13 (O)
1965—Bills, 17-12 (B)
Bills, 17-14 (O)
1966—Bills, 31-10 (O)
1967—Raiders, 24-20 (B)
Raiders, 28-21 (O)
1968—Raiders, 48-6 (B)
Raiders, 13-10 (O)
1969—Raiders, 50-21 (O)
1972—Raiders, 28-16 (O)
1974—Bills, 21-20 (B)
1977—Raiders, 34-13 (O)
1980—Bills, 24-7 (B)
1983—Raiders, 27-24 (B)
1987—Raiders, 34-21 (LA)
1988—Bills, 37-21 (B)
1990—Bills, 38-24 (B)
**Bills, 51-3 (B)
1991—Bills, 30-27 (LA) OT
1992—Raiders, 20-3 (LA)
1993—Raiders, 25-24 (B)
***Bills, 29-23 (B)
1998—Bills, 44-21 (B)
(RS Pts.—Raiders 651, Bills 620)
(PS Pts.—Bills 80, Raiders 26)
Franchise in Los Angeles from 1982-1994
***AFC Championship*
****AFC Divisional Playoff*

BUFFALO vs. PHILADELPHIA
RS: Series tied, 4-4
1973—Bills, 27-26 (B)
1981—Eagles, 20-14 (B)
1984—Eagles, 27-17 (B)
1985—Eagles, 21-17 (P)
1987—Eagles, 17-7 (P)
1990—Bills, 30-23 (B)
1993—Bills, 10-7 (P)
1996—Bills, 24-17 (P)
(RS Pts.—Eagles 158, Bills 146)

BUFFALO vs. PITTSBURGH
RS: Steelers lead series, 8-7
PS: Steelers lead series, 2-1
1970—Steelers, 23-10 (P)
1972—Steelers, 38-21 (B)
1974—*Steelers, 32-14 (P)
1975—Bills, 30-21 (P)
1978—Steelers, 28-17 (B)
1979—Steelers, 28-0 (P)
1980—Bills, 28-13 (B)
1982—Bills, 13-0 (B)
1985—Steelers, 30-24 (P)
1986—Bills, 16-12 (B)
1988—Bills, 36-28 (B)
1991—Bills, 52-34 (B)
1992—Bills, 28-20 (B)
*Bills, 24-3 (P)
1993—Steelers, 23-0 (P)
1994—Steelers, 23-10 (P)
1995—*Steelers, 40-21 (P)
1996—Steelers, 24-6 (P)
(RS Pts.—Steelers 345, Bills 291)
(PS Pts.—Steelers 75, Bills 59)
AFC Divisional Playoff

BUFFALO vs. *ST. LOUIS
RS: Series tied, 4-4
1970—Rams, 19-0 (B)
1974—Rams, 19-14 (LA)
1980—Bills, 10-7 (B) OT
1983—Rams, 41-17 (LA)
1989—Bills, 23-20 (B)
1992—Bills, 40-7 (B)
1995—Bills, 45-27 (StL)
1998—Rams, 34-33 (B)
(RS Pts.—Bills 182, Rams 174)
Franchise in Los Angeles prior to 1995

BUFFALO vs. *SAN DIEGO
RS: Chargers lead series, 17-7-2
PS: Bills lead series, 2-1
1960—Chargers, 24-10 (B)
Bills, 32-3 (LA)
1961—Chargers, 19-11 (B)
Chargers, 28-10 (SD)
1962—Bills, 35-10 (B)
Bills, 40-20 (SD)
1963—Chargers, 14-10 (SD)
Chargers, 23-13 (B)
1964—Bills, 30-3 (B)
Bills, 27-24 (SD)
**Bills, 20-7 (B)
1965—Chargers, 34-3 (B)
Tie, 20-20 (SD)
**Bills, 23-0 (SD)
1966—Chargers, 27-7 (SD)
Tie, 17-17 (B)
1967—Chargers, 37-17 (B)
1968—Chargers, 21-6 (B)
1969—Chargers, 45-6 (SD)
1971—Chargers, 20-3 (SD)
1973—Chargers, 34-7 (SD)
1976—Chargers, 34-13 (B)
1979—Chargers, 27-19 (SD)
1980—Bills, 26-24 (SD)
***Chargers, 20-14 (SD)
1981—Bills, 28-27 (SD)
1985—Chargers, 14-9 (B)
Chargers, 40-7 (SD)
1998—Chargers, 16-14 (SD)
(RS Pts.—Chargers 605, Bills 420)
(PS Pts.—Bills 57, Chargers 27)
Franchise in Los Angeles prior to 1961
***AFL Championship*
****AFC Divisional Playoff*

BUFFALO vs. SAN FRANCISCO
RS: Bills lead series, 4-3
1972—Bills, 27-20 (B)
1980—Bills, 18-13 (SF)
1983—49ers, 23-10 (B)
1989—49ers, 21-10 (SF)
1992—Bills, 34-31 (SF)
1995—49ers, 27-17 (SF)
1998—Bills, 26-21 (B)
(RS Pts.—49ers 156, Bills 142)

BUFFALO vs. SEATTLE
RS: Seahawks lead series, 4-2
1977—Seahawks, 56-17 (S)
1984—Seahawks, 31-28 (S)
1988—Bills, 13-3 (S)
1989—Seahawks, 17-16 (S)
1995—Bills, 27-21 (B)
1996—Seahawks, 26-18 (S)
(RS Pts.—Seahawks 154, Bills 119)

BUFFALO vs. TAMPA BAY
RS: Buccaneers lead series, 4-2
1976—Bills, 14-9 (TB)
1978—Buccaneers, 31-10 (TB)
1982—Buccaneers, 24-23 (TB)
1986—Buccaneers, 34-28 (TB)
1988—Buccaneers, 10-5 (TB)
1991—Bills, 17-10 (TB)
(RS Pts.—Buccaneers 118, Bills 97)

BUFFALO vs. *TENNESSEE
RS: Titans lead series, 22-13
PS: Bills lead series, 2-0
1960—Bills, 25-24 (B)
Oilers, 31-23 (H)
1961—Bills, 22-12 (H)
Oilers, 28-16 (B)
1962—Oilers, 28-23 (B)
Oilers, 17-14 (H)
1963—Oilers, 31-20 (B)
Oilers, 28-14 (H)
1964—Bills, 48-17 (H)
Bills, 24-10 (B)
1965—Oilers, 19-17 (B)
Bills, 29-18 (H)
1966—Bills, 27-20 (B)
Bills, 42-20 (H)
1967—Oilers, 20-3 (B)
Oilers, 10-3 (H)
1968—Oilers, 30-7 (B)
Oilers, 35-6 (H)
1969—Oilers, 17-3 (B)
Oilers, 28-14 (H)
1971—Oilers, 20-14 (B)
1974—Oilers, 21-9 (B)
1976—Oilers, 13-3 (B)
1978—Oilers, 17-10 (H)
1983—Bills, 30-13 (B)
1985—Bills, 20-0 (B)
1986—Oilers, 16-7 (H)
1987—Bills, 34-30 (B)
1988—**Bills, 17-10 (B)
1989—Bills, 47-41 (H) OT
1990—Oilers, 27-24 (H)
1992—Oilers, 27-3 (H)
***Bills, 41-38 (B) OT
1993—Bills, 35-7 (B)
1994—Bills, 15-7 (H)
1995—Oilers, 28-17 (B)
1997—Oilers, 31-14 (T)
(RS Pts.—Titans 741, Bills 662)
(PS Pts.—Bills 58, Titans 48)
Franchise in Houston prior to 1997; known as Oilers prior to 1999
***AFC Divisional Playoff*
****AFC First-Round Playoff*

BUFFALO vs. WASHINGTON
RS: Series tied, 4-4
PS: Redskins lead series, 1-0
1972—Bills, 24-17 (W)
1977—Redskins, 10-0 (B)
1981—Bills, 21-14 (B)
1984—Redskins, 41-14 (W)
1987—Redskins, 27-7 (B)
1990—Redskins, 29-14 (W)
1991—*Redskins, 37-24 (Minneapolis)
1993—Bills, 24-10 (B)
1996—Bills, 38-13 (B)
(RS Pts.—Redskins 161, Bills 142)
(PS Pts.—Redskins 37, Bills 24)
Super Bowl XXVI

CAROLINA vs. ARIZONA
RS: Panthers lead series, 1-0;
See Arizona vs. Carolina

CAROLINA vs. ATLANTA
RS: Series tied, 4-4;
See Atlanta vs. Carolina

CAROLINA vs. BALTIMORE
RS: Panthers lead series, 1-0
See Baltimore vs. Carolina

CAROLINA vs. BUFFALO
RS: Bills lead series, 2-0;
See Buffalo vs. Carolina

CAROLINA vs. CHICAGO
RS: Bears lead series, 1-0
1995—Bears, 31-27 (Chi)
(RS Pts.—Bears 31, Panthers 27)

CAROLINA vs. DALLAS
RS: Series tied, 1-1
PS: Panthers lead series, 1-0
1996—*Panthers, 26-17 (C)
1997—Panthers, 23-13 (D)
1998—Cowboys, 27-20 (D)
(RS Pts.—Panthers 43, Cowboys 40)
(PS Pts.—Panthers 26, Cowboys 17)
NFC Divisional Playoff

CAROLINA vs. DENVER
RS: Broncos lead series, 1-0
1997—Broncos, 34-0 (D)
(RS Pts.—Broncos 34, Panthers 0)

CAROLINA vs. GREEN BAY
RS: Packers lead series, 2-0
PS: Packers lead series, 1-0
1996—*Packers, 30-13 (GB)
1997—Packers, 31-10 (C)
1998—Packers, 37-30 (C)
(RS Pts.—Packers 68, Panthers 40)
(PS Pts.—Packers 30, Panthers 13)
NFC Championship

CAROLINA vs. INDIANAPOLIS
RS: Panthers lead series, 2-0
1995—Panthers, 13-10 (C)
1998—Panthers, 27-19 (I)
(RS Pts.—Panthers 40, Colts 29)

CAROLINA vs. JACKSONVILLE
RS: Jaguars lead series, 1-0
1996—Jaguars, 24-14 (J)
(RS Pts.—Jaguars 24, Panthers 14)

CAROLINA vs. KANSAS CITY
RS: Chiefs lead series, 1-0
1997—Chiefs, 35-14 (C)
(RS Pts.—Chiefs 35, Panthers 14)

CAROLINA vs. MIAMI
RS: Dolphins lead series, 1-0
1998—Dolphins, 13-9 (C)
(RS Pts.—Dolphins 13, Panthers 9)

CAROLINA vs. MINNESOTA
RS: Vikings lead series, 2-0
1996—Vikings, 14-12 (M)
1997—Vikings, 21-14 (M)
(RS Pts.—Vikings 35, Panthers 26)

CAROLINA vs. NEW ENGLAND
RS: Panthers lead series, 1-0
1995—Panthers, 20-17 (NE) OT
(RS Pts.—Panthers 20, Patriots 17)

CAROLINA vs. NEW ORLEANS
RS: Panthers lead series, 5-3
1995—Panthers, 20-3 (C)
Saints, 34-26 (NO)
1996—Panthers, 22-20 (NO)
Panthers, 19-7 (C)
1997—Panthers, 13-0 (NO)

ALL-TIME TEAM VS. TEAM RESULTS

Saints, 16-13 (C)
1998—Saints, 19-14 (NO)
Panthers, 31-17 (C)
(RS Pts.—Panthers 158, Saints 116)
CAROLINA vs. N.Y. GIANTS
RS: Panthers lead series, 1-0
1995—Panthers, 27-17 (C)
(RS Pts.—Panthers 27, Giants 17)
CAROLINA vs. N.Y. JETS
RS: Series tied, 1-1
1995—Panthers, 26-15 (C)
1998—Jets, 48-21 (NY)
(RS Pts.—Jets 63, Panthers 47)
CAROLINA vs. OAKLAND
RS: Panthers lead series, 1-0
1997—Panthers, 38-14 (C)
(RS Pts.—Panthers 38, Raiders 14)
CAROLINA vs. PHILADELPHIA
RS: Eagles lead series, 1-0
1996—Eagles, 20-9 (P)
(RS Pts.—Eagles 20, Panthers 9)
CAROLINA vs. PITTSBURGH
RS: Panthers lead series, 1-0
1996—Panthers, 18-14 (C)
(RS Pts.—Panthers 18, Steelers 14)
CAROLINA vs. ST. LOUIS
RS: Series tied, 3-3
1995—Rams, 31-10 (C)
Rams, 28-17 (StL)
1996—Panthers, 45-13 (C)
Panthers, 20-10 (StL)
1997—Panthers, 16-10 (StL)
Rams, 30-18 (C)
1998—Panthers, 24-20 (StL)
Panthers, 20-13 (C)
(RS Pts.—Panthers 170, Rams 155)
CAROLINA vs. SAN DIEGO
RS: Panthers lead series, 1-0
1997—Panthers, 26-7 (SD)
(RS Pts.—Panthers 26, Chargers 7)
CAROLINA vs. SAN FRANCISCO
RS: 49ers lead series, 5-3
1995—Panthers, 13-7 (SF)
49ers, 31-10 (C)
1996—Panthers, 23-7 (C)
Panthers, 30-24 (SF)
1997—49ers, 34-21 (C)
49ers, 27-19 (SF)
1998—49ers, 25-23 (SF)
49ers, 31-28 (C) OT
(RS Pts.—49ers 186, Panthers 167)
CAROLINA vs. TAMPA BAY
RS: Buccaneers lead series, 2-1
1995—Buccaneers, 20-13 (C)
1996—Panthers, 24-0 (C)
1998—Buccaneers, 16-13 (TB)
(RS Pts.—Panthers 50, Buccaneers 36)
CAROLINA vs. *TENNESSEE
RS: Panthers lead series, 1-0
1996—Panthers, 31-6 (H)
(RS Pts.—Panthers 31, Titans 6)
**Franchise in Houston prior to 1997; known as Oilers prior to 1999*
CAROLINA vs. WASHINGTON
RS: Redskins lead series, 3-0
1995—Redskins, 20-17 (W)
1997—Redskins, 24-10 (C)
1998—Redskins, 28-25 (C)
(RS Pts.—Redskins 72, Panthers 52)

CHICAGO vs. ARIZONA
RS: Bears lead series, 52-26-6;
See Arizona vs. Chicago
CHICAGO vs. ATLANTA
RS: Falcons lead series, 10-9;
See Atlanta vs. Chicago
CHICAGO vs. BALTIMORE
RS: Bears lead series, 1-0;
See Baltimore vs. Chicago
CHICAGO vs. BUFFALO
RS: Bears lead series, 5-2;
See Buffalo vs. Chicago
CHICAGO vs. CAROLINA
RS: Bears lead series, 1-0;
See Carolina vs. Chicago
CHICAGO vs. CINCINNATI
RS: Bengals lead series, 4-2
1972—Bengals, 13-3 (Chi)
1980—Bengals, 17-14 (Chi) OT
1986—Bears, 44-7 (Cin)
1989—Bears, 17-14 (Chi)
1992—Bengals, 31-28 (Chi) OT
1995—Bengals, 16-10 (Cin)
(RS Pts.—Bears 116, Bengals 98)
CHICAGO vs. CLEVELAND
RS: Browns lead series, 8-3
1951—Browns, 42-21 (Cle)
1954—Browns, 39-10 (Chi)
1960—Browns, 42-0 (Cle)
1961—Bears, 17-14 (Chi)
1967—Browns, 24-0 (Cle)
1969—Browns, 28-24 (Chi)
1972—Bears, 17-0 (Cle)
1980—Browns, 27-21 (Cle)
1986—Bears, 41-31 (Chi)
1989—Browns, 27-7 (Cle)
1992—Browns, 27-14 (Cle)
(RS Pts.—Browns 301, Bears 172)
CHICAGO vs. DALLAS
RS: Cowboys lead series, 9-8
PS: Cowboys lead series, 2-0
1960—Bears, 17-7 (C)
1962—Bears, 34-33 (D)
1964—Cowboys, 24-10 (C)
1968—Cowboys, 34-3 (C)
1971—Bears, 23-19 (C)
1973—Cowboys, 20-17 (C)
1976—Cowboys, 31-21 (D)
1977—*Cowboys, 37-7 (D)
1979—Cowboys, 24-20 (D)
1981—Cowboys, 10-9 (D)
1984—Cowboys, 23-14 (C)
1985—Bears, 44-0 (D)
1986—Bears, 24-10 (D)
1988—Bears, 17-7 (C)
1991—**Cowboys, 17-13 (C)
1992—Cowboys, 27-14 (D)
1996—Bears, 22-6 (C)
1997—Cowboys, 27-3 (D)
1998—Bears, 13-12 (C)
(RS Pts.—Cowboys 314, Bears 305)
(PS Pts.—Cowboys 54, Bears 20)
**NFC Divisional Playoff*
***NFC First-Round Playoff*
CHICAGO vs. DENVER
RS: Broncos lead series, 6-5
1971—Broncos, 6-3 (D)
1973—Bears, 33-14 (D)
1976—Broncos, 28-14 (C)
1978—Broncos, 16-7 (D)
1981—Bears, 35-24 (C)
1983—Bears, 31-14 (C)
1984—Bears, 27-0 (C)
1987—Broncos, 31-29 (D)
1990—Bears, 16-13 (D) OT
1993—Broncos, 13-3 (C)
1996—Broncos, 17-12 (D)
(RS Pts.—Bears 210, Broncos 176)
CHICAGO vs. *DETROIT
RS: Bears lead series, 77-56-5
1930—Spartans, 7-6 (P)
Bears, 14-6 (C)
1931—Bears, 9-6 (C)
Spartans, 3-0 (P)
1932—Tie, 13-13 (C)
Tie, 7-7 (P)
Bears, 9-0 (C)
1933—Bears, 17-14 (C)
Bears, 17-7 (P)
1934—Bears, 19-16 (D)
Bears, 10-7 (C)
1935—Tie, 20-20 (C)
Lions, 14-2 (D)
1936—Bears, 12-10 (C)
Lions, 13-7 (D)
1937—Bears, 28-20 (C)
Bears, 13-0 (D)
1938—Lions, 13-7 (C)
Lions, 14-7 (D)
1939—Lions, 10-0 (C)
Bears, 23-13 (D)
1940—Bears, 7-0 (C)
Lions, 17-14 (D)
1941—Bears, 49-0 (C)
Bears, 24-7 (D)
1942—Bears, 16-0 (C)
Bears, 42-0 (D)
1943—Bears, 27-21 (D)
Bears, 35-14 (C)
1944—Tie, 21-21 (C)
Lions, 41-21 (D)
1945—Lions, 16-10 (D)
Lions, 35-28 (C)
1946—Bears, 42-6 (C)
Bears, 45-24 (D)
1947—Bears, 33-24 (C)
Bears, 34-14 (D)
1948—Bears, 28-0 (C)
Bears, 42-14 (D)
1949—Bears, 27-24 (C)
Bears, 28-7 (D)
1950—Bears, 35-21 (D)
Bears, 6-3 (C)
1951—Bears, 28-23 (D)
Lions, 41-28 (C)
1952—Bears, 24-23 (C)
Lions, 45-21 (D)
1953—Lions, 20-16 (C)
Lions, 13-7 (D)
1954—Lions, 48-23 (D)
Bears, 28-24 (C)
1955—Bears, 24-14 (D)
Bears, 21-20 (C)
1956—Lions, 42-10 (D)
Bears, 38-21 (C)
1957—Bears, 27-7 (D)
Lions, 21-13 (C)
1958—Bears, 20-7 (D)
Bears, 21-16 (C)
1959—Bears, 24-14 (D)
Bears, 25-14 (C)
1960—Bears, 28-7 (C)
Lions, 36-0 (D)
1961—Bears, 31-17 (D)
Lions, 16-15 (C)
1962—Lions, 11-3 (D)
Bears, 3-0 (C)
1963—Bears, 37-21 (D)
Bears, 24-14 (C)
1964—Lions, 10-0 (C)
Bears, 27-24 (D)
1965—Bears, 38-10 (C)
Bears, 17-10 (D)
1966—Lions, 14-3 (D)
Tie, 10-10 (C)
1967—Bears, 14-3 (C)
Bears, 27-13 (D)
1968—Lions, 42-0 (D)
Lions, 28-10 (C)
1969—Lions, 13-7 (D)
Lions, 20-3 (C)
1970—Lions, 28-14 (D)
Lions, 16-10 (C)
1971—Bears, 28-23 (D)
Lions, 28-3 (C)
1972—Lions, 38-24 (C)
Lions, 14-0 (D)
1973—Lions, 30-7 (C)
Lions, 40-7 (D)
1974—Bears, 17-9 (C)
Lions, 34-17 (D)
1975—Lions, 27-7 (D)
Bears, 25-21 (C)
1976—Bears, 10-3 (C)
Lions, 14-10 (D)
1977—Bears, 30-20 (C)
Bears, 31-14 (D)
1978—Bears, 19-0 (D)
Lions, 21-17 (C)
1979—Bears, 35-7 (C)
Lions, 20-0 (D)
1980—Bears, 24-7 (C)
Bears, 23-17 (D) OT
1981—Lions, 48-17 (D)
Lions, 23-7 (C)
1982—Lions, 17-10 (D)
Bears, 20-17 (C)
1983—Lions, 31-17 (D)
Lions, 38-17 (C)
1984—Bears, 16-14 (C)
Bears, 30-13 (D)
1985—Bears, 24-3 (C)
Bears, 37-17 (D)
1986—Bears, 13-7 (C)
Bears, 16-13 (D)
1987—Bears, 30-10 (C)
1988—Bears, 24-7 (D)
Bears, 13-12 (C)
1989—Bears, 47-27 (D)
Lions, 27-17 (C)
1990—Bears, 23-17 (C) OT
Lions, 38-21 (D)
1991—Bears, 20-10 (C)
Lions, 16-6 (D)
1992—Bears, 27-24 (C)
Lions, 16-3 (D)
1993—Bears, 10-6 (D)
Lions, 20-14 (C)
1994—Lions, 21-16 (D)
Bears, 20-10 (C)
1995—Lions, 24-17 (C)
Lions, 27-7 (D)
1996—Lions, 35-16 (D)
Bears, 31-14 (C)
1997—Lions, 32-7 (C)
Lions, 55-20 (D)
1998—Bears, 31-27 (C)
Lions, 26-3 (D)
(RS Pts.—Bears 2,554, Lions 2,427)
**Franchise in Portsmouth prior to 1934 and known as the Spartans*
***CHICAGO vs. GREEN BAY**
RS: Bears lead series, 81-69-6
PS: Bears lead series, 1-0
1921—Staleys, 20-0 (C)
1923—Bears, 3-0 (GB)
1924—Bears, 3-0 (C)
1925—Packers, 14-10 (GB)
Bears, 21-0 (C)
1926—Tie, 6-6 (GB)
Bears, 19-13 (C)
Tie, 3-3 (C)
1927—Bears, 7-6 (GB)
Bears, 14-6 (C)
1928—Tie, 12-12 (GB)
Packers, 16-6 (C)
Packers, 6-0 (C)
1929—Packers, 23-0 (GB)
Packers, 14-0 (C)
Packers, 25-0 (C)
1930—Packers, 7-0 (GB)
Packers, 13-12 (C)
Bears, 21-0 (C)
1931—Packers, 7-0 (GB)
Packers, 6-2 (C)
Bears, 7-6 (C)
1932—Tie, 0-0 (GB)
Packers, 2-0 (C)
Bears, 9-0 (C)
1933—Bears, 14-7 (GB)
Bears, 10-7 (C)
Bears, 7-6 (C)
1934—Bears, 24-10 (GB)
Bears, 27-14 (C)
1935—Packers, 7-0 (GB)
Packers, 17-14 (C)
1936—Bears, 30-3 (GB)
Packers, 21-10 (C)
1937—Bears, 14-2 (GB)
Packers, 24-14 (C)
1938—Bears, 2-0 (GB)
Packers, 24-17 (C)

1939—Packers, 21-16 (GB)
Bears, 30-27 (C)
1940—Bears, 41-10 (GB)
Bears, 14-7 (C)
1941—Bears, 25-17 (GB)
Packers, 16-14 (C)
**Bears, 33-14 (C)
1942—Bears, 44-28 (GB)
Bears, 38-7 (C)
1943—Tie, 21-21 (GB)
Bears, 21-7 (C)
1944—Packers, 42-28 (GB)
Bears, 21-0 (C)
1945—Packers, 31-21 (GB)
Bears, 28-24 (C)
1946—Bears, 30-7 (GB)
Bears, 10-7 (C)
1947—Packers, 29-20 (GB)
Bears, 20-17 (C)
1948—Bears, 45-7 (GB)
Bears, 7-6 (C)
1949—Bears, 17-0 (GB)
Bears, 24-3 (C)
1950—Packers, 31-21 (GB)
Bears, 28-14 (C)
1951—Bears, 31-20 (GB)
Bears, 24-13 (C)
1952—Bears, 24-14 (GB)
Packers, 41-28 (C)
1953—Bears, 17-13 (GB)
Tie, 21-21 (C)
1954—Bears, 10-3 (GB)
Bears, 28-23 (C)
1955—Packers, 24-3 (GB)
Bears, 52-31 (C)
1956—Bears, 37-21 (GB)
Bears, 38-14 (C)
1957—Packers, 21-17 (GB)
Bears, 21-14 (C)
1958—Bears, 34-20 (GB)
Bears, 24-10 (C)
1959—Packers, 9-6 (GB)
Bears, 28-17 (C)
1960—Bears, 17-14 (GB)
Packers, 41-13 (C)
1961—Packers, 24-0 (GB)
Packers, 31-28 (C)
1962—Packers, 49-0 (GB)
Packers, 38-7 (C)
1963—Bears, 10-3 (GB)
Bears, 26-7 (C)
1964—Packers, 23-12 (GB)
Packers, 17-3 (C)
1965—Packers, 23-14 (GB)
Bears, 31-10 (C)
1966—Packers, 17-0 (C)
Packers, 13-6 (GB)
1967—Packers, 13-10 (GB)
Packers, 17-13 (C)
1968—Bears, 13-10 (GB)
Packers, 28-27 (C)
1969—Packers, 17-0 (GB)
Packers, 21-3 (C)
1970—Packers, 20-19 (GB)
Bears, 35-17 (C)
1971—Packers, 17-14 (C)
Packers, 31-10 (GB)
1972—Packers, 20-17 (GB)
Packers, 23-17 (C)
1973—Bears, 31-17 (GB)
Packers, 21-0 (C)
1974—Bears, 10-9 (C)
Packers, 20-3 (Mil)
1975—Bears, 27-14 (C)
Packers, 28-7 (GB)
1976—Bears, 24-13 (C)
Bears, 16-10 (GB)
1977—Bears, 26-0 (GB)
Bears, 21-10 (C)
1978—Packers, 24-14 (GB)
Bears, 14-0 (C)
1979—Bears, 6-3 (C)
Bears, 15-14 (GB)
1980—Packers, 12-6 (GB) OT
Bears, 61-7 (C)
1981—Packers, 16-9 (C)
Packers, 21-17 (GB)
1983—Packers, 31-28 (GB)
Bears, 23-21 (C)
1984—Bears, 9-7 (GB)
Packers, 20-14 (C)
1985—Bears, 23-7 (C)
Bears, 16-10 (GB)
1986—Bears, 25-12 (GB)
Bears, 12-10 (C)
1987—Bears, 26-24 (GB)
Bears, 23-10 (C)
1988—Bears, 24-6 (GB)
Bears, 16-0 (C)
1989—Packers, 14-13 (GB)
Packers, 40-28 (C)
1990—Bears, 31-13 (GB)
Bears, 27-13 (C)
1991—Bears, 10-0 (GB)
Bears, 27-13 (C)
1992—Bears, 30-10 (GB)
Packers, 17-3 (C)
1993—Packers, 17-3 (GB)
Bears, 30-17 (C)
1994—Packers, 33-6 (C)
Packers, 40-3 (GB)
1995—Packers, 27-24 (C)
Packers, 35-28 (GB)
1996—Packers, 37-6 (C)
Packers, 28-17 (GB)
1997—Packers, 38-24 (GB)
Packers, 24-23 (C)
1998—Packers, 26-20 (GB)
Packers, 16-13 (C)
(RS Pts.—Bears 2,642, Packers 2,434)
(PS Pts.—Bears 33, Packers 14)
Bears known as Staleys prior to 1922
***Division Playoff*

CHICAGO vs. *INDIANAPOLIS
RS: Colts lead series, 21-16
1953—Colts, 13-9 (B)
Colts, 16-14 (C)
1954—Bears, 28-9 (C)
Bears, 28-13 (B)
1955—Colts, 23-17 (B)
Bears, 38-10 (C)
1956—Colts, 28-21 (B)
Bears, 58-27 (C)
1957—Colts, 21-10 (B)
Colts, 29-14 (C)
1958—Colts, 51-38 (B)
Colts, 17-0 (C)
1959—Bears, 26-21 (B)
Colts, 21-7 (C)
1960—Colts, 42-7 (B)
Colts, 24-20 (C)
1961—Bears, 24-10 (C)
Bears, 21-20 (B)
1962—Bears, 35-15 (C)
Bears, 57-0 (B)
1963—Bears, 10-3 (C)
Bears, 17-7 (B)
1964—Colts, 52-0 (B)
Colts, 40-24 (C)
1965—Colts, 26-21 (C)
Bears, 13-0 (B)
1966—Bears, 27-17 (C)
Colts, 21-16 (B)
1967—Colts, 24-3 (C)
1968—Colts, 28-7 (B)
1969—Colts, 24-21 (C)
1970—Colts, 21-20 (B)
1975—Colts, 35-7 (C)
1983—Colts, 22-19 (B) OT
1985—Bears, 17-10 (C)
1988—Bears, 17-13 (I)
1991—Bears, 31-17 (I)
(RS Pts.—Colts 770, Bears 742)
**Franchise in Baltimore prior to 1984*

CHICAGO vs. JACKSONVILLE
RS: Series tied, 1-1
1995—Bears, 30-27 (J)
1998—Jaguars, 24-23 (C)
(RS Pts.—Bears 53, Jaguars 51)

CHICAGO vs. KANSAS CITY
RS: Bears lead series, 4-3
1973—Chiefs, 19-7 (KC)
1977—Bears, 28-27 (C)
1981—Bears, 16-13 (KC) OT
1987—Bears, 31-28 (C)
1990—Chiefs, 21-10 (C)
1993—Bears, 19-17 (KC)
1996—Chiefs, 14-10 (KC)
(RS Pts.—Chiefs 139, Bears 121)

CHICAGO vs. MIAMI
RS: Dolphins lead series, 5-3
1971—Dolphins, 34-3 (M)
1975—Dolphins, 46-13 (C)
1979—Dolphins, 31-16 (M)
1985—Dolphins, 38-24 (M)
1988—Bears, 34-7 (C)
1991—Dolphins, 16-13 (C) OT
1994—Bears, 17-14 (M)
1997—Bears, 36-33 (M) OT
(RS Pts.—Dolphins 219, Bears 156)

CHICAGO vs. MINNESOTA
RS: Vikings lead series, 41-32-2
PS: Bears lead series, 1-0
1961—Vikings, 37-13 (M)
Bears, 52-35 (C)
1962—Bears, 13-0 (M)
Bears, 31-30 (C)
1963—Bears, 28-7 (M)
Tie, 17-17 (C)
1964—Bears, 34-28 (M)
Vikings, 41-14 (C)
1965—Bears, 45-37 (M)
Vikings, 24-17 (C)
1966—Bears, 13-10 (M)
Bears, 41-28 (C)
1967—Bears, 17-7 (M)
Tie, 10-10 (C)
1968—Bears, 27-17 (M)
Bears, 26-24 (C)
1969—Vikings, 31-0 (C)
Vikings, 31-14 (M)
1970—Vikings, 24-0 (C)
Vikings, 16-13 (M)
1971—Bears, 20-17 (M)
Vikings, 27-10 (C)
1972—Bears, 13-10 (C)
Vikings, 23-10 (M)
1973—Vikings, 22-13 (C)
Vikings, 31-13 (M)
1974—Vikings, 11-7 (M)
Vikings, 17-0 (C)
1975—Vikings, 28-3 (M)
Vikings, 13-9 (C)
1976—Vikings, 20-19 (M)
Bears, 14-13 (C)
1977—Vikings, 22-16 (M) OT
Bears, 10-7 (C)
1978—Vikings, 24-20 (C)
Vikings, 17-14 (M)
1979—Bears, 26-7 (C)
Vikings, 30-27 (M)
1980—Vikings, 34-14 (C)
Vikings, 13-7 (M)
1981—Vikings, 24-21 (M)
Bears, 10-9 (C)
1982—Vikings, 35-7 (M)
1983—Vikings, 23-14 (C)
Bears, 19-13 (M)
1984—Bears, 16-7 (C)
Bears, 34-3 (M)
1985—Bears, 33-24 (M)
Bears, 27-9 (C)
1986—Bears, 23-0 (C)
Vikings, 23-7 (M)
1987—Bears, 27-7 (C)
Bears, 30-24 (M)
1988—Vikings, 31-7 (C)
Vikings, 28-27 (M)
1989—Bears, 38-7 (C)
Vikings, 27-16 (M)
1990—Bears, 19-16 (C)
Vikings, 41-13 (M)
1991—Bears, 10-6 (C)
Bears, 34-17 (M)
1992—Vikings, 21-20 (M)
Vikings, 38-10 (C)
1993—Vikings, 10-7 (M)
Vikings, 19-12 (C)
1994—Vikings, 42-14 (C)
Vikings, 33-27 (M) OT
*Bears, 35-18 (M)
1995—Bears, 31-14 (C)
Bears, 14-6 (M)
1996—Vikings, 20-14 (C)
Bears, 15-13 (M)
1997—Vikings, 27-24 (C)
Vikings, 29-22 (M)
1998—Vikings, 31-28 (C)
Vikings, 48-22 (M)
(RS Pts.—Vikings 1,565, Bears 1,382)
(PS Pts.—Bears 35, Vikings 18)
**NFC First-Round Playoff*

CHICAGO vs. NEW ENGLAND
RS: Patriots lead series, 5-2
PS: Bears lead series, 1-0
1973—Patriots, 13-10 (C)
1979—Patriots, 27-7 (C)
1982—Bears, 26-13 (C)
1985—Bears, 20-7 (C)
*Bears, 46-10 (New Orleans)
1988—Patriots, 30-7 (NE)
1994—Patriots, 13-3 (C)
1997—Patriots, 31-3 (NE)
(RS Pts.—Patriots 134, Bears 76)
(PS Pts.—Bears 46, Patriots 10)
**Super Bowl XX*

CHICAGO vs. NEW ORLEANS
RS: Bears lead series, 9-8
PS: Bears lead series, 1-0
1968—Bears, 23-17 (NO)
1970—Bears, 24-3 (NO)
1971—Bears, 35-14 (C)
1973—Saints, 21-16 (NO)
1974—Bears, 24-10 (C)
1975—Bears, 42-17 (NO)
1977—Saints, 42-24 (C)
1980—Bears, 22-3 (C)
1982—Saints, 10-0 (C)
1983—Saints, 34-31 (NO) OT
1984—Bears, 20-7 (C)
1987—Saints, 19-17 (C)
1990—*Bears, 16-6 (C)
1991—Bears, 20-17 (NO)
1992—Saints, 28-6 (NO)
1994—Bears, 17-7 (C)
1996—Saints, 27-24 (NO)
1997—Saints, 20-17 (C)
(RS Pts.—Bears 362, Saints 296)
(PS Pts.—Bears 16, Saints 6)
**NFC First-Round Playoff*

CHICAGO vs. N.Y. GIANTS
RS: Bears lead series, 25-16-2
PS: Bears lead series, 5-3
1925—Bears, 19-7 (NY)
Giants, 9-0 (C)
1926—Bears, 7-0 (C)
1927—Giants, 13-7 (NY)
1928—Bears, 13-0 (C)
1929—Giants, 26-14 (C)
Giants, 34-0 (NY)
Giants, 14-9 (C)
1930—Giants, 12-0 (C)
Bears, 12-0 (NY)
1931—Bears, 6-0 (C)
Bears, 12-6 (NY)
Giants, 25-6 (C)
1932—Bears, 28-8 (NY)
Bears, 6-0 (C)
1933—Bears, 14-10 (C)
Giants, 3-0 (NY)
*Bears, 23-21 (C)
1934—Bears, 27-7 (C)

ALL-TIME TEAM VS. TEAM RESULTS

Bears, 10-9 (NY)
*Giants, 30-13 (NY)
1935—Bears, 20-3 (NY)
Giants, 3-0 (C)
1936—Bears, 25-7 (NY)
1937—Tie, 3-3 (NY)
1939—Giants, 16-13 (NY)
1940—Bears, 37-21 (NY)
1941—*Bears, 37-9 (C)
1942—Bears, 26-7 (NY)
1943—Bears, 56-7 (NY)
1946—Giants, 14-0 (NY)
*Bears, 24-14 (NY)
1948—Bears, 35-14 (C)
1949—Giants, 35-28 (NY)
1956—Tie, 17-17 (NY)
*Giants, 47-7 (NY)
1962—Giants, 26-24 (C)
1963—*Bears, 14-10 (C)
1965—Bears, 35-14 (NY)
1967—Bears, 34-7 (C)
1969—Giants, 28-24 (NY)
1970—Bears, 24-16 (NY)
1974—Bears, 16-13 (C)
1977—Bears, 12-9 (NY) OT
1985—**Bears, 21-0 (C)
1987—Bears, 34-19 (C)
1990—**Giants, 31-3 (NY)
1991—Bears, 20-17 (C)
1992—Giants, 27-14 (C)
1993—Giants, 26-20 (C)
1995—Bears, 27-24 (NY)
(RS Pts.—Bears 734, Giants 556)
(PS Pts.—Giants 162, Bears 142)
NFL Championship
**NFC Divisional Playoff*

CHICAGO vs. N.Y. JETS
RS: Bears lead series, 4-2
1974—Jets, 23-21 (C)
1979—Bears, 23-13 (C)
1985—Bears, 19-6 (NY)
1991—Bears, 19-13 (C) OT
1994—Bears, 19-7 (NY)
1997—Jets, 23-15 (C)
(RS Pts.—Bears 116, Jets 85)

CHICAGO vs. *OAKLAND
RS: Raiders lead series, 5-4
1972—Raiders, 28-21 (O)
1976—Raiders, 28-27 (C)
1978—Raiders, 25-19 (C) OT
1981—Bears, 23-6 (O)
1984—Bears, 17-6 (C)
1987—Bears, 6-3 (LA)
1990—Raiders, 24-10 (LA)
1993—Raiders, 16-14 (C)
1996—Bears, 19-17 (C)
(RS Pts.—Bears 156, Raiders 153)
Franchise in Los Angeles from 1982-1994

CHICAGO vs. PHILADELPHIA
RS: Bears lead series, 24-4-1
PS: Series tied, 1-1
1933—Tie, 3-3 (P)
1935—Bears, 39-0 (P)
1936—Bears, 17-0 (P)
Bears, 28-7 (P)
1938—Bears, 28-6 (P)
1939—Bears, 27-14 (C)
1941—Bears, 49-14 (P)
1942—Bears, 45-14 (C)
1944—Bears, 28-7 (P)
1946—Bears, 21-14 (C)
1947—Bears, 40-7 (C)
1948—Eagles, 12-7 (P)
1949—Bears, 38-21 (C)
1955—Bears, 17-10 (C)
1961—Eagles, 16-14 (P)
1963—Bears, 16-7 (C)
1968—Bears, 29-16 (P)
1970—Bears, 20-16 (C)
1972—Bears, 21-12 (P)
1975—Bears, 15-13 (C)
1979—*Eagles, 27-17 (P)
1980—Eagles, 17-14 (P)
1983—Bears, 7-6 (P)
Bears, 17-14 (C)
1986—Bears, 13-10 (C) OT
1987—Bears, 35-3 (P)
1988—**Bears, 20-12 (C)
1989—Bears, 27-13 (C)
1993—Bears, 17-6 (P)
1994—Eagles, 30-22 (P)
1995—Bears, 20-14 (C)
(RS Pts.—Bears 674, Eagles 322)
(PS Pts.—Eagles 39, Bears 37)
NFC First-Round Playoff
**NFC Divisional Playoff*

CHICAGO vs. *PITTSBURGH
RS: Bears lead series, 16-6-1
1934—Bears, 28-0 (P)
1935—Bears, 23-7 (P)
1936—Bears, 27-9 (P)
Bears, 26-6 (C)
1937—Bears, 7-0 (P)
1939—Bears, 32-0 (P)
1941—Bears, 34-7 (C)
1945—Bears, 28-7 (C)
1947—Bears, 49-7 (C)
1949—Bears, 30-21 (C)
1958—Steelers, 24-10 (P)
1959—Bears, 27-21 (C)
1963—Tie, 17-17 (P)
1967—Steelers, 41-13 (P)
1969—Bears, 38-7 (C)
1971—Bears, 17-15 (C)
1975—Steelers, 34-3 (P)
1980—Steelers, 38-3 (P)
1986—Bears, 13-10 (C) OT
1989—Bears, 20-0 (P)
1992—Bears, 30-6 (C)
1995—Steelers, 37-34 (C) OT
1998—Steelers, 17-12 (P)
(RS Pts.—Bears 521, Steelers 331)
Steelers known as Pirates prior to 1941

CHICAGO vs. *ST. LOUIS
RS: Bears lead series, 47-31-3
PS: Series tied, 1-1
1937—Bears, 20-2 (Clev)
Bears, 15-7 (C)
1938—Rams, 14-7 (C)
Rams, 23-21 (Clev)
1939—Bears, 30-21 (Clev)
Bears, 35-21 (C)
1940—Bears, 21-14 (Clev)
Bears, 47-25 (C)
1941—Bears, 48-21 (Clev)
Bears, 31-13 (C)
1942—Bears, 21-7 (Clev)
Bears, 47-0 (C)
1944—Rams, 19-7 (Clev)
Bears, 28-21 (C)
1945—Rams, 17-0 (Clev)
Rams, 41-21 (C)
1946—Tie, 28-28 (C)
Bears, 27-21 (LA)
1947—Bears, 41-21 (LA)
Rams, 17-14 (C)
1948—Bears, 42-21 (C)
Bears, 21-6 (LA)
1949—Rams, 31-16 (C)
Rams, 27-24 (LA)
1950—Bears, 24-20 (LA)
Bears, 24-14 (C)
**Rams, 24-14 (LA)
1951—Rams, 42-17 (C)
1952—Rams, 31-7 (LA)
Rams, 40-24 (C)
1953—Rams, 38-24 (LA)
Bears, 24-21 (C)
1954—Rams, 42-38 (LA)
Bears, 24-13 (C)
1955—Bears, 31-20 (LA)
Bears, 24-3 (C)
1956—Bears, 35-24 (LA)
Bears, 30-21 (C)
1957—Bears, 34-26 (C)
Bears, 16-10 (LA)
1958—Bears, 31-10 (C)
Rams, 41-35 (LA)
1959—Rams, 28-21 (C)
Bears, 26-21 (LA)
1960—Bears, 34-27 (C)
Tie, 24-24 (LA)
1961—Bears, 21-17 (LA)
Bears, 28-24 (C)
1962—Bears, 27-23 (LA)
Bears, 30-14 (C)
1963—Bears, 52-14 (LA)
Bears, 6-0 (C)
1964—Bears, 38-17 (C)
Bears, 34-24 (LA)
1965—Rams, 30-28 (LA)
Bears, 31-6 (C)
1966—Rams, 31-17 (LA)
Bears, 17-10 (C)
1967—Rams, 28-17 (C)
1968—Bears, 17-16 (LA)
1969—Rams, 9-7 (C)
1971—Rams, 17-3 (LA)
1972—Tie, 13-13 (C)
1973—Rams, 26-0 (C)
1975—Rams, 38-10 (LA)
1976—Rams, 20-12 (LA)
1977—Bears, 24-23 (C)
1979—Bears, 27-23 (C)
1981—Rams, 24-7 (C)
1982—Bears, 34-26 (LA)
1983—Rams, 21-14 (LA)
1984—Rams, 29-13 (LA)
1985—***Bears, 24-0 (C)
1986—Rams, 20-17 (C)
1988—Rams, 23-3 (LA)
1989—Bears, 20-10 (C)
1990—Bears, 38-9 (C)
1993—Rams, 20-6 (LA)
1994—Bears, 27-13 (C)
1995—Rams, 34-28 (StL)
1996—Bears, 35-9 (C)
1997—Bears, 13-10 (StL)
1998—Rams, 20-12 (C)
(RS Pts.—Bears 1,885, Rams 1,645)
(PS Pts.—Bears 38, Rams 24)
Franchise in Los Angeles prior to 1995 and in Cleveland prior to 1946
**Conference Playoff*
***NFC Championship*

CHICAGO vs. SAN DIEGO
RS: Chargers lead series, 4-3
1970—Chargers, 20-7 (C)
1974—Chargers, 28-21 (SD)
1978—Chargers, 40-7 (SD)
1981—Bears, 20-17 (C) OT
1984—Chargers, 20-7 (SD)
1993—Bears, 16-13 (SD)
1996—Bears, 27-14 (C)
(RS Pts.—Chargers 152, Bears 105)

CHICAGO vs. SAN FRANCISCO
RS: Series tied, 25-25-1
PS: 49ers lead series, 3-0
1950—Bears, 32-20 (SF)
Bears, 17-0 (C)
1951—Bears, 13-7 (C)
1952—49ers, 40-16 (C)
Bears, 20-17 (SF)
1953—49ers, 35-28 (C)
49ers, 24-14 (SF)
1954—49ers, 31-24 (C)
Bears, 31-27 (SF)
1955—49ers, 20-19 (C)
Bears, 34-23 (SF)
1956—Bears, 31-7 (C)
Bears, 38-21 (SF)
1957—49ers, 21-17 (C)
49ers, 21-17 (SF)
1958—Bears, 28-6 (C)
Bears, 27-14 (SF)
1959—49ers, 20-17 (SF)
Bears, 14-3 (C)
1960—Bears, 27-10 (C)
49ers, 25-7 (SF)
1961—Bears, 31-0 (C)
49ers, 41-31 (SF)
1962—Bears, 30-14 (SF)
49ers, 34-27 (C)
1963—49ers, 20-14 (SF)
Bears, 27-7 (C)
1964—49ers, 31-21 (SF)
Bears, 23-21 (C)
1965—49ers, 52-24 (SF)
Bears, 61-20 (C)
1966—Tie, 30-30 (C)
49ers, 41-14 (SF)
1967—Bears, 28-14 (SF)
1968—Bears, 27-19 (C)
1969—49ers, 42-21 (SF)
1970—49ers, 37-16 (C)
1971—49ers, 13-0 (SF)
1972—49ers, 34-21 (C)
1974—49ers, 34-0 (C)
1975—49ers, 31-3 (SF)
1976—Bears, 19-12 (SF)
1978—Bears, 16-13 (SF)
1979—Bears, 28-27 (SF)
1981—49ers, 28-17 (SF)
1983—Bears, 13-3 (C)
1984—*49ers, 23-0 (SF)
1985—Bears, 26-10 (SF)
1987—49ers, 41-0 (SF)
1988—Bears, 10-9 (C)
*49ers, 28-3 (C)
1989—49ers, 26-0 (SF)
1991—49ers, 52-14 (SF)
1994—**49ers, 44-15 (SF)
(RS Pts.—49ers 1,148, Bears 1,063)
(PS Pts.—49ers 95, Bears 18)
NFC Championship
**NFC Divisional Playoff*

CHICAGO vs. SEATTLE
RS: Seahawks lead series, 4-2
1976—Bears, 34-7 (S)
1978—Seahawks, 31-29 (C)
1982—Seahawks, 20-14 (S)
1984—Seahawks, 38-9 (S)
1987—Seahawks, 34-21 (C)
1990—Bears, 17-0 (C)
(RS Pts.—Seahawks 130, Bears 124)

CHICAGO vs. TAMPA BAY
RS: Bears lead series, 30-12
1977—Bears, 10-0 (TB)
1978—Buccaneers, 33-19 (TB)
Bears, 14-3 (C)
1979—Buccaneers, 17-13 (C)
Bears, 14-0 (TB)
1980—Bears, 23-0 (C)
Bears, 14-13 (TB)
1981—Bears, 28-17 (C)
Buccaneers, 20-10 (TB)
1982—Buccaneers, 26-23 (TB) OT
1983—Bears, 17-10 (C)
Bears, 27-0 (TB)
1984—Bears, 34-14 (C)
Bears, 44-9 (TB)
1985—Bears, 38-28 (C)
Bears, 27-19 (TB)
1986—Bears, 23-3 (TB)
Bears, 48-14 (C)
1987—Bears, 20-3 (C)
Bears, 27-26 (TB)
1988—Bears, 28-10 (C)
Bears, 27-15 (TB)
1989—Buccaneers, 42-35 (TB)
Buccaneers, 32-31 (C)
1990—Bears, 26-6 (TB)
Bears, 27-14 (C)
1991—Bears, 21-20 (TB)
Bears, 27-0 (C)
1992—Bears, 31-14 (C)
Buccaneers, 20-17 (TB)
1993—Bears, 47-17 (C)
Buccaneers, 13-10 (TB)
1994—Bears, 21-9 (C)
Bears, 20-6 (TB)

1995—Bears, 25-6 (TB)
Bears, 31-10 (C)
1996—Bears, 13-10 (C)
Buccaneers, 34-19 (TB)
1997—Bears, 13-7 (C)
Buccaneers, 31-15 (TB)
1998—Buccaneers, 27-15 (TB)
Buccaneers, 31-17 (C)
(RS Pts.—Bears 989, Buccaneers 629)

CHICAGO vs. *TENNESSEE
RS: Series tied, 4-4
1973—Bears, 35-14 (C)
1977—Oilers, 47-0 (H)
1980—Oilers, 10-6 (C)
1986—Bears, 20-7 (H)
1989—Oilers, 33-28 (C)
1992—Oilers, 24-7 (H)
1995—Bears, 35-32 (C)
1998—Bears, 23-20 (T)
(RS Pts.—Titans 187, Bears 154)
**Franchise in Houston prior to 1997; known as Oilers prior to 1999*

CHICAGO vs. *WASHINGTON
RS: Bears lead series, 18-14-1
PS: Redskins lead series, 4-3
1932—Tie, 7-7 (B)
1933—Bears, 7-0 (C)
Redskins, 10-0 (B)
1934—Bears, 21-0 (B)
1935—Bears, 30-14 (B)
1936—Bears, 26-0 (B)
1937—**Redskins, 28-21 (C)
1938—Bears, 31-7 (C)
1940—Redskins, 7-3 (W)
**Bears, 73-0 (W)
1941—Bears, 35-21 (C)
1942—**Redskins, 14-6 (W)
1943—Redskins, 21-7 (W)
**Bears, 41-21 (C)
1945—Redskins, 28-21 (W)
1946—Bears, 24-20 (C)
1947—Bears, 56-20 (W)
1948—Bears, 48-13 (C)
1949—Bears, 31-21 (W)
1951—Bears, 27-0 (W)
1953—Bears, 27-24 (W)
1957—Redskins, 14-3 (C)
1964—Redskins, 27-20 (W)
1968—Redskins, 38-28 (C)
1971—Bears, 16-15 (C)
1974—Redskins, 42-0 (W)
1976—Bears, 33-7 (C)
1978—Bears, 14-10 (W)
1980—Bears, 35-21 (C)
1981—Redskins, 24-7 (C)
1984—***Bears, 23-19 (W)
1985—Bears, 45-10 (C)
1986—***Redskins, 27-13 (C)
1987—***Redskins, 21-17 (C)
1988—Bears, 34-14 (W)
1989—Redskins, 38-14 (W)
1990—Redskins, 10-9 (W)
1991—Redskins, 20-7 (C)
1996—Redskins, 10-3 (W)
1997—Redskins, 31-8 (C)
(RS Pts.—Bears 677, Redskins 544)
(PS Pts.—Bears 194, Redskins 130)
**Franchise in Boston prior to 1937 and known as Braves prior to 1933*
***NFL Championship*
****NFC Divisional Playoff*

CINCINNATI vs. ARIZONA
RS: Bengals lead series, 4-2;
See Arizona vs. Cincinnati

CINCINNATI vs. ATLANTA
RS: Bengals lead series, 7-2;
See Atlanta vs. Cincinnati

CINCINNATI vs. BALTIMORE
RS: Series tied, 3-3;
See Baltimore vs. Cincinnati

CINCINNATI vs. BUFFALO
RS: Series tied, 9-9
PS: Bengals lead series, 2-0;
See Buffalo vs. Cincinnati

CINCINNATI vs. CHICAGO
RS: Bengals lead series, 4-2;
See Chicago vs. Cincinnati

CINCINNATI vs. CLEVELAND
RS: Browns lead series, 27-24
1970—Browns, 30-27 (Cle)
Bengals, 14-10 (Cin)
1971—Browns, 27-24 (Cin)
Browns, 31-27 (Cle)
1972—Browns, 27-6 (Cle)
Browns, 27-24 (Cin)
1973—Browns, 17-10 (Cle)
Bengals, 34-17 (Cin)
1974—Bengals, 33-7 (Cin)
Bengals, 34-24 (Cle)
1975—Bengals, 24-17 (Cin)
Browns, 35-23 (Cle)
1976—Bengals, 45-24 (Cle)
Bengals, 21-6 (Cin)
1977—Browns, 13-3 (Cin)
Bengals, 10-7 (Cle)
1978—Browns, 13-10 (Cle) OT
Bengals, 48-16 (Cin)
1979—Browns, 28-27 (Cle)
Bengals, 16-12 (Cin)
1980—Browns, 31-7 (Cle)
Browns, 27-24 (Cin)
1981—Browns, 20-17 (Cin)
Bengals, 41-21 (Cle)
1982—Bengals, 23-10 (Cin)
1983—Browns, 17-7 (Cle)
Bengals, 28-21 (Cin)
1984—Bengals, 12-9 (Cin)
Bengals, 20-17 (Cle) OT
1985—Bengals, 27-10 (Cin)
Browns, 24-6 (Cle)
1986—Bengals, 30-13 (Cle)
Browns, 34-3 (Cin)
1987—Browns, 34-0 (Cin)
Browns, 38-24 (Cle)
1988—Bengals, 24-17 (Cin)
Browns, 23-16 (Cle)
1989—Bengals, 21-14 (Cin)
Bengals, 21-0 (Cle)
1990—Bengals, 34-13 (Cle)
Bengals, 21-14 (Cin)
1991—Browns, 14-13 (Cle)
Bengals, 23-21 (Cin)
1992—Bengals, 30-10 (Cin)
Browns, 37-21 (Cle)
1993—Browns, 27-14 (Cle)
Browns, 28-17 (Cin)
1994—Browns, 28-20 (Cin)
Browns, 37-13 (Cle)
1995—Browns, 29-26 (Cin) OT
Browns, 26-10 (Cle)
(RS Pts.—Bengals 1,053, Browns 1,052)

CINCINNATI vs. DALLAS
RS: Cowboys lead series, 4-3
1973—Cowboys, 38-10 (D)
1979—Cowboys, 38-13 (D)
1985—Bengals, 50-24 (C)
1988—Bengals, 38-24 (D)
1991—Cowboys, 35-23 (D)
1994—Cowboys, 23-20 (C)
1997—Bengals, 31-24 (C)
(RS Pts.—Cowboys 206, Bengals 185)

CINCINNATI vs. DENVER
RS: Broncos lead series, 14-6
1968—Bengals, 24-10 (C)
Broncos, 10-7 (D)
1969—Broncos, 30-23 (C)
Broncos, 27-16 (D)
1971—Bengals, 24-10 (D)
1972—Bengals, 21-10 (C)
1973—Broncos, 28-10 (D)
1975—Bengals, 17-16 (D)
1976—Bengals, 17-7 (C)
1977—Broncos, 24-13 (C)
1979—Broncos, 10-0 (D)
1981—Bengals, 38-21 (C)
1983—Broncos, 24-17 (D)
1984—Broncos, 20-17 (D)
1986—Broncos, 34-28 (D)
1991—Broncos, 45-14 (D)
1994—Broncos, 15-13 (D)
1996—Broncos, 14-10 (C)
1997—Broncos, 38-20 (D)
1998—Broncos, 33-26 (C)
(RS Pts.—Broncos 426, Bengals 355)

CINCINNATI vs. DETROIT
RS: Bengals lead series, 4-3
1970—Lions, 38-3 (D)
1974—Lions, 23-19 (C)
1983—Bengals, 17-9 (C)
1986—Bengals, 24-17 (D)
1989—Bengals, 42-7 (C)
1992—Lions, 19-13 (C)
1998—Bengals, 34-28 (D) OT
(RS Pts.—Bengals 152, Lions 141)

CINCINNATI vs. GREEN BAY
RS: Packers lead series, 5-4
1971—Packers, 20-17 (GB)
1976—Bengals, 28-7 (C)
1977—Bengals, 17-7 (Mil)
1980—Packers, 14-9 (GB)
1983—Bengals, 34-14 (C)
1986—Bengals, 34-28 (Mil)
1992—Packers, 24-23 (GB)
1995—Packers, 24-10 (GB)
1998—Packers, 13-6 (C)
(RS Pts.—Bengals 178, Packers 151)

CINCINNATI vs. *INDIANAPOLIS
RS: Colts lead series, 10-8
PS: Colts lead series, 1-0
1970—**Colts, 17-0 (B)
1972—Colts, 20-19 (C)
1974—Bengals, 24-14 (B)
1976—Colts, 28-27 (B)
1979—Colts, 38-28 (B)
1980—Bengals, 34-33 (C)
1981—Bengals, 41-19 (B)
1982—Bengals, 20-17 (B)
1983—Colts, 34-31 (C)
1987—Bengals, 23-21 (I)
1989—Colts, 23-12 (C)
1990—Colts, 34-20 (C)
1992—Colts, 21-17 (C)
1993—Colts, 9-6 (C)
1994—Colts, 17-13 (C)
1995—Bengals, 24-21 (I) OT
1996—Bengals, 31-24 (C)
1997—Bengals, 28-13 (I)
1998—Colts, 39-26 (I)
(RS Pts.—Colts 425, Bengals 424)
(PS Pts.—Colts 17, Bengals 0)
**Franchise in Baltimore prior to 1984*
***AFC Divisional Playoff*

CINCINNATI vs. JACKSONVILLE
RS: Series tied, 4-4
1995—Bengals, 24-17 (C)
Bengals, 17-13 (J)
1996—Bengals, 28-21 (C)
Jaguars, 30-27 (J)
1997—Jaguars, 21-13 (J)
Bengals, 31-26 (C)
1998—Jaguars, 24-11 (J)
Jaguars, 34-17 (C)
(RS Pts.—Jaguars 186, Bengals 168)

CINCINNATI vs. KANSAS CITY
RS: Chiefs lead series, 11-9
1968—Chiefs, 13-3 (KC)
Chiefs, 16-9 (C)
1969—Bengals, 24-19 (C)
Chiefs, 42-22 (KC)
1970—Chiefs, 27-19 (C)
1972—Bengals, 23-16 (KC)
1973—Bengals, 14-6 (C)
1974—Bengals, 33-6 (C)
1976—Bengals, 27-24 (KC)
1977—Bengals, 27-7 (KC)
1978—Chiefs, 24-23 (C)
1979—Chiefs, 10-7 (C)
1980—Bengals, 20-6 (KC)
1983—Chiefs, 20-15 (KC)
1984—Chiefs, 27-22 (C)
1986—Chiefs, 24-14 (KC)
1987—Bengals, 30-27 (C) OT
1988—Chiefs, 31-28 (KC)
1989—Bengals, 21-17 (KC)
1993—Chiefs, 17-15 (KC)
(RS Pts.—Bengals 396, Chiefs 379)

CINCINNATI vs. MIAMI
RS: Dolphins lead series, 11-3
PS: Dolphins lead series, 1-0
1968—Dolphins, 24-22 (C)
Bengals, 38-21 (M)
1969—Bengals, 27-21 (C)
1971—Dolphins, 23-13 (C)
1973—*Dolphins, 34-16 (M)
1974—Dolphins, 24-3 (M)
1977—Bengals, 23-17 (C)
1978—Dolphins, 21-0 (M)
1980—Dolphins, 17-16 (M)
1983—Dolphins, 38-14 (M)
1987—Dolphins, 20-14 (C)
1989—Dolphins, 20-13 (C)
1991—Dolphins, 37-13 (M)
1994—Dolphins, 23-7 (C)
1995—Dolphins, 26-23 (C)
(RS Pts.—Dolphins 332, Bengals 226)
(PS Pts.—Dolphins 34, Bengals 16)
**AFC Divisional Playoff*

CINCINNATI vs. MINNESOTA
RS: Vikings lead series, 5-4
1973—Bengals, 27-0 (C)
1977—Vikings, 42-10 (M)
1980—Bengals, 14-0 (C)
1983—Vikings, 20-14 (M)
1986—Bengals, 24-20 (C)
1989—Vikings, 29-21 (M)
1992—Vikings, 42-7 (C)
1995—Bengals, 27-24 (C)
1998—Vikings, 24-3 (M)
(RS Pts.—Vikings 201, Bengals 147)

CINCINNATI vs. *NEW ENGLAND
RS: Patriots lead series, 9-7
1968—Patriots, 33-14 (B)
1969—Patriots, 25-14 (C)
1970—Bengals, 45-7 (C)
1972—Bengals, 31-7 (NE)
1975—Bengals, 27-10 (C)
1978—Patriots, 10-3 (C)
1979—Patriots, 20-14 (C)
1984—Patriots, 20-14 (NE)
1985—Patriots, 34-23 (NE)
1986—Bengals, 31-7 (NE)
1988—Patriots, 27-21 (NE)
1990—Bengals, 41-7 (C)
1991—Bengals, 29-7 (C)
1992—Bengals, 20-10 (C)
1993—Patriots, 7-2 (NE)
1994—Patriots, 31-28 (C)
(RS Pts.—Bengals 357, Patriots 262)
**Franchise in Boston prior to 1971*

CINCINNATI vs. NEW ORLEANS
RS: Saints lead series, 5-4
1970—Bengals, 26-6 (C)
1975—Bengals, 21-0 (NO)
1978—Saints, 20-18 (C)
1981—Saints, 17-7 (NO)
1984—Bengals, 24-21 (NO)
1987—Saints, 41-24 (C)
1990—Saints, 21-7 (C)
1993—Saints, 20-13 (NO)
1996—Bengals, 30-15 (C))
(RS Pts.—Bengals 170, Saints 161)

CINCINNATI vs. N.Y. GIANTS
RS: Bengals lead series, 4-2
1972—Bengals, 13-10 (C)
1977—Bengals, 30-13 (C)
1985—Bengals, 35-30 (C)
1991—Bengals, 27-24 (C)
1994—Giants, 27-20 (NY)
1997—Giants, 29-27 (NY)
(RS Pts.—Bengals 152, Giants 133)

ALL-TIME TEAM VS. TEAM RESULTS

CINCINNATI vs. N.Y. JETS
RS: Jets lead series, 10-6
PS: Jets lead series, 1-0
1968—Jets, 27-14 (NY)
1969—Jets, 21-7 (C)
Jets, 40-7 (NY)
1971—Jets, 35-21 (NY)
1973—Bengals, 20-14 (C)
1976—Bengals, 42-3 (NY)
1981—Bengals, 31-30 (NY)
1982—*Jets, 44-17 (C)
1984—Jets, 43-23 (NY)
1985—Jets, 29-20 (C)
1986—Bengals, 52-21 (C)
1987—Jets, 27-20 (NY)
1988—Bengals, 36-19 (C)
1990—Bengals, 25-20 (C)
1992—Jets, 17-14 (NY)
1993—Jets, 17-12 (NY)
1997—Jets, 31-14 (C)
(RS Pts.—Jets 394, Bengals 358)
(PS Pts.—Jets 44, Bengals 17)
**AFC First-Round Playoff*
CINCINNATI vs. *OAKLAND
RS: Raiders lead series, 16-7
PS: Raiders lead series, 2-0
1968—Raiders, 31-10 (O)
Raiders, 34-0 (C)
1969—Bengals, 31-17 (C)
Raiders, 37-17 (O)
1970—Bengals, 31-21 (C)
1971—Raiders, 31-27 (O)
1972—Raiders, 20-14 (C)
1974—Raiders, 30-27 (O)
1975—Bengals, 14-10 (C)
**Raiders, 31-28 (O)
1976—Raiders, 35-20 (O)
1978—Raiders, 34-21 (C)
1980—Raiders, 28-17 (O)
1982—Bengals, 31-17 (C)
1983—Raiders, 20-10 (C)
1985—Raiders, 13-6 (LA)
1988—Bengals, 45-21 (LA)
1989—Raiders, 28-7 (LA)
1990—Raiders, 24-7 (LA)
**Raiders, 20-10 (LA)
1991—Raiders, 38-14 (C)
1992—Bengals, 24-21 (C) OT
1993—Bengals, 16-10 (C)
1995—Raiders, 20-17 (C)
1998—Raiders, 27-10 (O)
(RS Pts.—Raiders 567, Bengals 416)
(PS Pts.—Raiders 51, Bengals 38)
**Franchise in Los Angeles from 1982-1994*
***AFC Divisional Playoff*
CINCINNATI vs. PHILADELPHIA
RS: Bengals lead series, 6-2
1971—Bengals, 37-14 (C)
1975—Bengals, 31-0 (P)
1979—Bengals, 37-13 (C)
1982—Bengals, 18-14 (P)
1988—Bengals, 28-24 (P)
1991—Eagles, 17-10 (P)
1994—Bengals, 33-30 (C)
1997—Eagles, 44-42 (P)
(RS Pts.—Bengals 236, Eagles 156)
CINCINNATI vs. PITTSBURGH
RS: Steelers lead series, 32-25
1970—Steelers, 21-10 (P)
Bengals, 34-7 (C)
1971—Steelers, 21-10 (P)
Steelers, 21-13 (C)
1972—Bengals, 15-10 (C)
Steelers, 40-17 (P)
1973—Bengals, 19-7 (C)
Steelers, 20-13 (P)
1974—Bengals, 17-10 (C)
Steelers, 27-3 (P)
1975—Steelers, 30-24 (C)
Steelers, 35-14 (P)
1976—Steelers, 23-6 (P)
Steelers, 7-3 (C)
1977—Steelers, 20-14 (P)
Bengals, 17-10 (C)
1978—Steelers, 28-3 (C)
Steelers, 7-6 (P)
1979—Bengals, 34-10 (C)
Steelers, 37-17 (P)
1980—Bengals, 30-28 (C)
Bengals, 17-16 (P)
1981—Bengals, 34-7 (C)
Bengals, 17-10 (P)
1982—Steelers, 26-20 (P) OT
1983—Steelers, 24-14 (C)
Bengals, 23-10 (P)
1984—Steelers, 38-17 (P)
Bengals, 22-20 (C)
1985—Bengals, 37-24 (P)
Bengals, 26-21 (C)
1986—Bengals, 24-22 (C)
Steelers, 30-9 (P)
1987—Steelers, 23-20 (P)
Steelers, 30-16 (C)
1988—Bengals, 17-12 (P)
Bengals, 42-7 (C)
1989—Bengals, 41-10 (C)
Bengals, 26-16 (P)
1990—Bengals, 27-3 (C)
Bengals, 16-12 (P)
1991—Steelers, 33-27 (C) OT
Steelers, 17-10 (P)
1992—Steelers, 20-0 (P)
Steelers, 21-9 (C)
1993—Steelers, 34-7 (P)
Steelers, 24-16 (C)
1994—Steelers, 14-10 (P)
Steelers, 38-15 (C)
1995—Bengals, 27-9 (P)
Steelers, 49-31 (C)
1996—Steelers, 20-10 (P)
Bengals, 34-24 (C)
1997—Steelers, 26-10 (C)
Steelers, 20-3 (P)
1998—Bengals, 25-20 (C)
Bengals, 25-24 (P)
(RS Pts.—Steelers 1,173, Bengals 1,043)
CINCINNATI vs. *ST. LOUIS
RS: Bengals lead series, 5-3
1972—Rams, 15-12 (LA)
1976—Bengals, 20-12 (C)
1978—Bengals, 20-19 (LA)
1981—Bengals, 24-10 (C)
1984—Rams, 24-14 (C)
1990—Bengals, 34-31 (LA) OT
1993—Bengals, 15-3 (C)
1996—Rams, 26-16 (StL)
(RS Pts.—Bengals 155, Rams 140)
**Franchise in Los Angeles prior to 1995*
CINCINNATI vs. SAN DIEGO
RS: Chargers lead series, 14-9
PS: Bengals lead series, 1-0
1968—Chargers, 29-13 (SD)
Chargers, 31-10 (C)
1969—Bengals, 34-20 (C)
Chargers, 21-14 (SD)
1970—Bengals, 17-14 (SD)
1971—Bengals, 31-0 (C)
1973—Bengals, 20-13 (SD)
1974—Chargers, 20-17 (C)
1975—Bengals, 47-17 (C)
1977—Chargers, 24-3 (SD)
1978—Chargers, 22-13 (SD)
1979—Chargers, 26-24 (C)
1980—Chargers, 31-14 (C)
1981—Bengals, 40-17 (SD)
*Bengals, 27-7 (C)
1982—Chargers, 50-34 (SD)
1985—Chargers, 44-41 (C)
1987—Chargers, 10-9 (C)
1988—Bengals, 27-10 (C)
1990—Bengals, 21-16 (SD)
1992—Chargers, 27-10 (SD)
1994—Chargers, 27-10 (SD)
1996—Chargers, 27-14 (SD)
1997—Bengals, 38-31 (C)
(RS Pts.—Chargers 527, Bengals 501)
(PS Pts.—Bengals 27, Chargers 7)
**AFC Championship*
CINCINNATI vs. SAN FRANCISCO
RS: 49ers lead series, 7-1
PS: 49ers lead series, 2-0
1974—Bengals, 21-3 (SF)
1978—49ers, 28-12 (SF)
1981—49ers, 21-3 (C)
*49ers, 26-21 (Detroit)
1984—49ers, 23-17 (SF)
1987—49ers, 27-26 (C)
1988—**49ers, 20-16 (Miami)
1990—49ers, 20-17 (C) OT
1993—49ers, 21-8 (SF)
1996—49ers, 28-21 (SF)
(RS Pts.—49ers 171, Bengals 125)
(PS Pts.—49ers 46, Bengals 37)
**Super Bowl XVI*
***Super Bowl XXIII*
CINCINNATI vs. SEATTLE
RS: Series tied, 7-7
PS: Bengals lead series, 1-0
1977—Bengals, 42-20 (C)
1981—Bengals, 27-21 (C)
1982—Bengals, 24-10 (C)
1984—Seahawks, 26-6 (C)
1985—Seahawks, 28-24 (C)
1986—Bengals, 34-7 (C)
1987—Bengals, 17-10 (S)
1988—*Bengals, 21-13 (C)
1989—Seahawks, 24-17 (C)
1990—Seahawks, 31-16 (S)
1991—Seahawks, 13-7 (C)
1992—Bengals, 21-3 (S)
1993—Seahawks, 19-10 (C)
1994—Bengals, 20-17 (S) OT
1995—Seahawks, 24-21 (S)
(RS Pts.—Bengals 286, Seahawks 253)
(PS Pts.—Bengals 21, Seahawks 13)
**AFC Divisional Playoff*
CINCINNATI vs. TAMPA BAY
RS: Series tied, 3-3
1976—Bengals, 21-0 (C)
1980—Buccaneers, 17-12 (C)
1983—Bengals, 23-17 (TB)
1989—Bengals, 56-23 (C)
1995—Buccaneers, 19-16 (TB)
1998—Buccaneers, 35-0 (C)
(RS Pts.—Bengals 128, Buccaneers 111)
CINCINNATI vs. *TENNESSEE
RS: Titans lead series, 31-28-1
PS: Bengals lead series, 1-0
1968—Oilers, 27-17 (C)
1969—Tie, 31-31 (H)
1970—Oilers, 20-13 (C)
Bengals, 30-20 (H)
1971—Oilers, 10-6 (H)
Bengals, 28-13 (C)
1972—Bengals, 30-7 (C)
Bengals, 61-17 (H)
1973—Bengals, 24-10 (C)
Bengals, 27-24 (H)
1974—Oilers, 34-21 (C)
Oilers, 20-3 (H)
1975—Bengals, 21-19 (H)
Bengals, 23-19 (C)
1976—Bengals, 27-7 (H)
Bengals, 31-27 (C)
1977—Bengals, 13-10 (C) OT
Oilers, 21-16 (H)
1978—Bengals, 28-13 (C)
Oilers, 17-10 (H)
1979—Oilers, 30-27 (C) OT
Oilers, 42-21 (H)
1980—Oilers, 13-10 (C)
Oilers, 23-3 (H)
1981—Oilers, 17-10 (H)
Bengals, 34-21 (C)
1982—Bengals, 27-6 (C)
Bengals, 35-27 (H)
1983—Bengals, 55-14 (H)
Bengals, 38-10 (C)
1984—Bengals, 13-3 (C)
Bengals, 31-13 (H)
1985—Oilers, 44-27 (H)
Bengals, 45-27 (C)
1986—Bengals, 31-28 (C)
Oilers, 32-28 (H)
1987—Oilers, 31-29 (C)
Oilers, 21-17 (H)
1988—Bengals, 44-21 (C)
Oilers, 41-6 (H)
1989—Oilers, 26-24 (H)
Bengals, 61-7 (C)
1990—Oilers, 48-17 (H)
Bengals, 40-20 (C)
**Bengals, 41-14 (C)
1991—Oilers, 30-7 (C)
Oilers, 35-3 (H)
1992—Oilers, 38-24 (C)
Oilers, 26-10 (H)
1993—Oilers, 28-12 (H)
Oilers, 38-3 (C)
1994—Oilers, 20-13 (H)
Bengals, 34-31 (C)
1995—Oilers, 38-28 (C)
Bengals, 32-25 (H)
1996—Oilers, 30-27 (C) OT
Bengals, 21-13 (H)
1997—Oilers, 30-7 (T)
Bengals, 41-14 (C)
1998—Oilers, 23-14 (C)
Oilers, 44-14 (T)
(RS Pts.—Bengals 1,423, Titans 1,394)
(PS Pts.—Bengals 41, Titans 14)
**Franchise in Houston prior to 1997; known as Oilers prior to 1999*
***AFC First-Round Playoff*
CINCINNATI vs. WASHINGTON
RS: Redskins lead series, 4-2
1970—Redskins, 20-0 (W)
1974—Bengals, 28-17 (C)
1979—Redskins, 28-14 (W)
1985—Redskins, 27-24 (W)
1988—Bengals, 20-17 (C) OT
1991—Redskins, 34-27 (C)
(RS Pts.—Redskins 143, Bengals 113)

CLEVELAND vs. ARIZONA
RS: Browns lead series, 32-10-3;
See Arizona vs. Cleveland
CLEVELAND vs. ATLANTA
RS: Browns lead series, 8-2;
See Atlanta vs. Cleveland
CLEVELAND vs. BUFFALO
RS: Browns lead series, 7-4
PS: Browns lead series, 1-0;
See Buffalo vs. Cleveland
CLEVELAND vs. CHICAGO
RS: Browns lead series, 8-3;
See Chicago vs. Cleveland
CLEVELAND vs. CINCINNATI
RS: Browns lead series, 27-24;
See Cincinnati vs. Cleveland
CLEVELAND vs. DALLAS
RS: Browns lead series, 15-9
PS: Browns lead series, 2-1
1960—Browns, 48-7 (D)
1961—Browns, 25-7 (C)
Browns, 38-17 (D)
1962—Browns, 19-10 (C)
Cowboys, 45-21 (D)
1963—Browns, 41-24 (D)
Browns, 27-17 (C)
1964—Browns, 27-6 (C)
Browns, 20-16 (D)
1965—Browns, 23-17 (C)
Browns, 24-17 (D)
1966—Browns, 30-21 (C)
Cowboys, 26-14 (D)
1967—Cowboys, 21-14 (C)
*Cowboys, 52-14 (D)
1968—Cowboys, 28-7 (C)
*Browns, 31-20 (C)
1969—Browns, 42-10 (C)

*Browns, 38-14 (D)
1970—Cowboys, 6-2 (C)
1974—Cowboys, 41-17 (D)
1979—Browns, 26-7 (C)
1982—Cowboys, 31-14 (D)
1985—Cowboys, 20-7 (D)
1988—Browns, 24-21 (C)
1991—Cowboys, 26-14 (C)
1994—Browns, 19-14 (D)
(RS Pts.—Browns 543, Cowboys 455)
(PS Pts.—Cowboys 86, Browns 83)
*Conference Championship

CLEVELAND vs. DENVER
RS: Broncos lead series, 13-5
PS: Broncos lead series, 3-0
1970—Browns, 27-13 (D)
1971—Broncos, 27-0 (C)
1972—Browns, 27-20 (D)
1974—Browns, 23-21 (C)
1975—Broncos, 16-15 (D)
1976—Broncos, 44-13 (D)
1978—Broncos, 19-7 (C)
1980—Broncos, 19-16 (C)
1981—Broncos, 23-20 (D) OT
1983—Broncos, 27-6 (D)
1984—Broncos, 24-14 (C)
1986—*Broncos, 23-20 (C) OT
1987—*Broncos, 38-33 (D)
1988—Broncos, 30-7 (D)
1989—Browns, 16-13 (C)
*Broncos, 37-21 (D)
1990—Browns, 30-29 (D)
1991—Broncos, 17-7 (C)
1992—Broncos, 12-0 (C)
1993—Broncos, 29-14 (C)
1994—Broncos, 26-14 (D)
(RS Pts.—Broncos 409, Browns 256)
(PS Pts.—Broncos 98, Browns 74)
*AFC Championship

CLEVELAND vs. DETROIT
RS: Lions lead series, 12-3
PS: Lions lead series, 3-1
1952—Lions, 17-6 (D)
*Lions, 17-7 (C)
1953—*Lions, 17-16 (D)
1954—Lions, 14-10 (C)
*Browns, 56-10 (C)
1957—Lions, 20-7 (D)
*Lions, 59-14 (D)
1958—Lions, 30-10 (C)
1963—Lions, 38-10 (D)
1964—Browns, 37-21 (C)
1967—Lions, 31-14 (D)
1969—Lions, 28-21 (C)
1970—Lions, 41-24 (C)
1975—Lions, 21-10 (D)
1983—Browns, 31-26 (D)
1986—Browns, 24-21 (C)
1989—Lions, 13-10 (D)
1992—Lions, 24-14 (D)
1995—Lions, 38-20 (D)
(RS Pts.—Lions 383, Browns 248)
(PS Pts.—Lions 103, Browns 93)
*NFL Championship

CLEVELAND vs. GREEN BAY
RS: Packers lead series, 8-6
PS: Packers lead series, 1-0
1953—Browns, 27-0 (Mil)
1955—Browns, 41-10 (C)
1956—Browns, 24-7 (Mil)
1961—Packers, 49-17 (C)
1964—Packers, 28-21 (Mil)
1965—*Packers, 23-12 (GB)
1966—Packers, 21-20 (C)
1967—Packers, 55-7 (Mil)
1969—Browns, 20-7 (C)
1972—Packers, 26-10 (C)
1980—Browns, 26-21 (C)
1983—Packers, 35-21 (Mil)
1986—Packers, 17-14 (C)
1992—Browns, 17-6 (C)
1995—Packers, 31-20 (C)
(RS Pts.—Packers 313, Browns 285)
(PS Pts.—Packers 23, Browns 12)
*NFL Championship

CLEVELAND vs. *INDIANAPOLIS
RS: Browns lead series, 13-7
PS: Series tied, 2-2
1956—Colts, 21-7 (C)
1959—Browns, 38-31 (B)
1962—Colts, 36-14 (C)
1964—**Browns, 27-0 (C)
1968—Browns, 30-20 (B)
**Colts, 34-0 (C)
1971—Browns, 14-13 (B)
***Colts, 20-3 (C)
1973—Browns, 24-14 (C)
1975—Colts, 21-7 (B)
1978—Browns, 45-24 (B)
1979—Browns, 13-10 (C)
1980—Browns, 28-27 (B)
1981—Browns, 42-28 (C)
1983—Browns, 41-23 (C)
1986—Browns, 24-9 (I)
1987—Colts, 9-7 (C)
***Browns, 38-21 (C)
1988—Browns, 23-17 (C)
1989—Colts, 23-17 (I) OT
1991—Browns, 31-0 (I)
1992—Colts, 14-3 (I)
1993—Colts, 23-10 (I)
1994—Browns, 21-14 (I)
(RS Pts.—Browns 439, Colts 377)
(PS Pts.—Colts 75, Browns 68)
*Franchise in Baltimore prior to 1984
**NFL Championship
***AFC Divisional Playoff

CLEVELAND vs. JACKSONVILLE
RS: Jaguars lead series, 2-0
1995—Jaguars, 23-15 (C)
Jaguars, 24-21 (J)
(RS Pts.—Jaguars 47, Browns 36)

CLEVELAND vs. KANSAS CITY
RS: Browns lead series, 8-7-2
1971—Chiefs, 13-7 (KC)
1972—Chiefs, 31-7 (C)
1973—Tie, 20-20 (KC)
1975—Browns, 40-14 (C)
1976—Chiefs, 39-14 (KC)
1977—Browns, 44-7 (C)
1978—Chiefs, 17-3 (KC)
1979—Browns, 27-24 (KC)
1980—Browns, 20-13 (C)
1984—Chiefs, 10-6 (KC)
1986—Browns, 20-7 (C)
1988—Browns, 6-3 (KC)
1989—Tie, 10-10 (C) OT
1990—Chiefs, 34-0 (KC)
1991—Browns, 20-15 (C)
1994—Chiefs, 20-13 (KC)
1995—Browns, 35-17 (C)
(RS Pts.—Chiefs 294, Browns 292)

CLEVELAND vs. MIAMI
RS: Dolphins lead series, 6-4
PS: Dolphins lead series, 2-0
1970—Browns, 28-0 (M)
1972—*Dolphins, 20-14 (M)
1973—Dolphins, 17-9 (C)
1976—Browns, 17-13 (C)
1979—Browns, 30-24 (C) OT
1985—*Dolphins, 24-21 (M)
1986—Browns, 26-16 (C)
1988—Dolphins, 38-31 (M)
1989—Dolphins, 13-10 (M) OT
1990—Dolphins, 30-13 (C)
1992—Dolphins, 27-23 (C)
1993—Dolphins, 24-14 (C)
(RS Pts.—Dolphins 202, Browns 201)
(PS Pts.—Dolphins 44, Browns 35)
*AFC Divisional Playoff

CLEVELAND vs. MINNESOTA
RS: Vikings lead series, 8-3
PS: Vikings lead series, 1-0
1965—Vikings, 27-17 (C)
1967—Browns, 14-10 (C)
1969—Vikings, 51-3 (M)
*Vikings, 27-7 (M)
1973—Vikings, 26-3 (M)
1975—Vikings, 42-10 (C)
1980—Vikings, 28-23 (M)
1983—Vikings, 27-21 (C)
1986—Browns, 23-20 (M)
1989—Browns, 23-17 (C) OT
1992—Vikings, 17-13 (M)
1995—Vikings, 27-11 (M)
(RS Pts.—Vikings 292, Browns 161)
(PS Pts.—Vikings 27, Browns 7)
*NFL Championship

CLEVELAND vs. NEW ENGLAND
RS: Browns lead series, 10-4
PS: Browns lead series, 1-0
1971—Browns, 27-7 (C)
1974—Browns, 21-14 (NE)
1977—Browns, 30-27 (C) OT
1980—Patriots, 34-17 (NE)
1982—Browns, 10-7 (C)
1983—Browns, 30-0 (NE)
1984—Patriots, 17-16 (C)
1985—Browns, 24-20 (C)
1987—Browns, 20-10 (NE)
1991—Browns, 20-0 (NE)
1992—Browns, 19-17 (NE)
1993—Patriots, 20-17 (C)
1994—Browns, 13-6 (C)
*Browns, 20-13 (C)
1995—Patriots, 17-14 (NE)
(RS Pts.—Browns 278, Patriots 196)
(PS Pts.—Browns 20, Patriots 13)
*AFC First-Round Playoff

CLEVELAND vs. NEW ORLEANS
RS: Browns lead series, 9-3
1967—Browns, 42-7 (NO)
1968—Browns, 24-10 (NO)
Browns, 35-17 (C)
1969—Browns, 27-17 (NO)
1971—Browns, 21-17 (NO)
1975—Browns, 17-16 (C)
1978—Browns, 24-16 (NO)
1981—Browns, 20-17 (C)
1984—Saints, 16-14 (C)
1987—Saints, 28-21 (NO)
1990—Saints, 25-20 (NO)
1993—Browns, 17-13 (C)
(RS Pts.—Browns 282, Saints 199)

CLEVELAND vs. N.Y. GIANTS
RS: Browns lead series, 25-17-2
PS: Series tied, 1-1
1950—Giants, 6-0 (C)
Giants, 17-13 (NY)
*Browns, 8-3 (C)
1951—Browns, 14-13 (C)
Browns, 10-0 (NY)
1952—Giants, 17-9 (C)
Giants, 37-34 (NY)
1953—Browns, 7-0 (NY)
Browns, 62-14 (C)
1954—Browns, 24-14 (C)
Browns, 16-7 (NY)
1955—Browns, 24-14 (C)
Tie, 35-35 (NY)
1956—Giants, 21-9 (C)
Browns, 24-7 (NY)
1957—Browns, 6-3 (C)
Browns, 34-28 (NY)
1958—Giants, 21-17 (C)
Giants, 13-10 (NY)
*Giants, 10-0 (NY)
1959—Giants, 10-6 (C)
Giants, 48-7 (NY)
1960—Giants, 17-13 (C)
Browns, 48-34 (NY)
1961—Giants, 37-21 (C)
Tie, 7-7 (NY)
1962—Browns, 17-7 (C)
Giants, 17-13 (NY)
1963—Browns, 35-24 (NY)
Giants, 33-6 (C)
1964—Browns, 42-20 (C)
Browns, 52-20 (NY)
1965—Browns, 38-14 (NY)
Browns, 34-21 (C)
1966—Browns, 28-7 (NY)
Browns, 49-40 (C)
1967—Giants, 38-34 (NY)
Browns, 24-14 (C)
1968—Browns, 45-10 (C)
1969—Browns, 28-17 (C)
Giants, 27-14 (NY)
1973—Browns, 12-10 (C)
1977—Browns, 21-7 (NY)
1985—Browns, 35-33 (NY)
1991—Giants, 13-10 (NY)
1994—Giants, 16-13 (C)
(RS Pts.—Browns 1,000, Giants 808)
(PS Pts.—Giants 13, Browns 8)
*Conference Playoff

CLEVELAND vs. N.Y. JETS
RS: Browns lead series, 9-6
PS: Browns lead series, 1-0
1970—Browns, 31-21 (C)
1972—Browns, 26-10 (NY)
1976—Browns, 38-17 (C)
1978—Browns, 37-34 (C) OT
1979—Browns, 25-22 (NY) OT
1980—Browns, 17-14 (C)
1981—Jets, 14-13 (C)
1983—Browns, 10-7 (C)
1984—Jets, 24-20 (C)
1985—Jets, 37-10 (NY)
1986—*Browns, 23-20 (C) OT
1988—Jets, 23-3 (C)
1989—Browns, 38-24 (C)
1990—Jets, 24-21 (NY)
1991—Jets, 17-14 (C)
1994—Browns, 27-7 (C)
(RS Pts.—Browns 330, Jets 295)
(PS Pts.—Browns 23, Jets 20)
*AFC Divisional Playoff

CLEVELAND vs. *OAKLAND
RS: Raiders lead series, 8-4
PS: Raiders lead series, 2-0
1970—Raiders, 23-20 (O)
1971—Raiders, 34-20 (C)
1973—Browns, 7-3 (O)
1974—Raiders, 40-24 (C)
1975—Raiders, 38-17 (O)
1977—Raiders, 26-10 (C)
1979—Raiders, 19-14 (O)
1980—**Raiders, 14-12 (C)
1982—***Raiders, 27-10 (LA)
1985—Raiders, 21-20 (C)
1986—Raiders, 27-14 (LA)
1987—Browns, 24-17 (LA)
1992—Browns, 28-16 (LA)
1993—Browns, 19-16 (LA)
(RS Pts.—Raiders 280, Browns 217)
(PS Pts.—Raiders 41, Browns 22)
*Franchise in Los Angeles from 1982-1994
**AFC Divisional Playoff
***AFC First-Round Playoff

CLEVELAND vs. PHILADELPHIA
RS: Browns lead series, 31-12-1
1950—Browns, 35-10 (P)
Browns, 13-7 (C)
1951—Browns, 20-17 (C)
Browns, 24-9 (P)
1952—Browns, 49-7 (P)
Eagles, 28-20 (C)
1953—Browns, 37-13 (C)
Eagles, 42-27 (P)
1954—Eagles, 28-10 (P)
Browns, 6-0 (C)
1955—Browns, 21-17 (C)
Eagles, 33-17 (P)
1956—Browns, 16-0 (P)
Browns, 17-14 (C)
1957—Browns, 24-7 (C)
Eagles, 17-7 (P)
1958—Browns, 28-14 (C)
Browns, 21-14 (P)
1959—Browns, 28-7 (C)

ALL-TIME TEAM VS. TEAM RESULTS

Browns, 28-21 (P)
1960—Browns, 41-24 (P)
Eagles, 31-29 (C)
1961—Eagles, 27-20 (P)
Browns, 45-24 (C)
1962—Eagles, 35-7 (P)
Tie, 14-14 (C)
1963—Browns, 37-7 (C)
Browns, 23-17 (P)
1964—Browns, 28-20 (P)
Browns, 38-24 (C)
1965—Browns, 35-17 (P)
Browns, 38-34 (C)
1966—Browns, 27-7 (C)
Eagles, 33-21 (P)
1967—Eagles, 28-24 (P)
1968—Browns, 47-13 (C)
1969—Browns, 27-20 (P)
1972—Browns, 27-17 (P)
1976—Browns, 24-3 (C)
1979—Browns, 24-19 (P)
1982—Eagles, 24-21 (C)
1988—Browns, 19-3 (C)
1991—Eagles, 32-30 (C)
1994—Browns, 26-7 (P)
(RS Pts.—Browns 1,120, Eagles 785)

CLEVELAND vs. PITTSBURGH
RS: Browns lead series, 52-40
PS: Steelers lead series, 1-0
1950—Browns, 30-17 (P)
Browns, 45-7 (C)
1951—Browns, 17-0 (C)
Browns, 28-0 (P)
1952—Browns, 21-20 (P)
Browns, 29-28 (C)
1953—Browns, 34-16 (C)
Browns, 20-16 (P)
1954—Steelers, 55-27 (P)
Browns, 42-7 (C)
1955—Browns, 41-14 (C)
Browns, 30-7 (P)
1956—Browns, 14-10 (P)
Steelers, 24-16 (C)
1957—Browns, 23-12 (P)
Browns, 24-0 (C)
1958—Browns, 45-12 (P)
Browns, 27-10 (C)
1959—Steelers, 17-7 (P)
Steelers, 21-20 (C)
1960—Browns, 28-20 (C)
Steelers, 14-10 (P)
1961—Browns, 30-28 (P)
Steelers, 17-13 (C)
1962—Browns, 41-14 (P)
Browns, 35-14 (C)
1963—Browns, 35-23 (C)
Steelers, 9-7 (P)
1964—Steelers, 23-7 (C)
Browns, 30-17 (P)
1965—Browns, 24-19 (C)
Browns, 42-21 (P)
1966—Browns, 41-10 (C)
Steelers, 16-6 (P)
1967—Browns, 21-10 (C)
Browns, 34-14 (P)
1968—Browns, 31-24 (C)
Browns, 45-24 (P)
1969—Browns, 42-31 (C)
Browns, 24-3 (P)
1970—Browns, 15-7 (C)
Steelers, 28-9 (P)
1971—Browns, 27-17 (C)
Steelers, 26-9 (P)
1972—Browns, 26-24 (C)
Steelers, 30-0 (P)
1973—Steelers, 33-6 (P)
Browns, 21-16 (C)
1974—Steelers, 20-16 (P)
Steelers, 26-16 (C)
1975—Steelers, 42-6 (C)
Steelers, 31-17 (P)
1976—Steelers, 31-14 (P)
Browns, 18-16 (C)
1977—Steelers, 28-14 (C)
Steelers, 35-31 (P)
1978—Steelers, 15-9 (P) OT
Steelers, 34-14 (C)
1979—Steelers, 51-35 (C)
Steelers, 33-30 (P) OT
1980—Browns, 27-26 (C)
Steelers, 16-13 (P)
1981—Steelers, 13-7 (P)
Steelers, 32-10 (C)
1982—Browns, 10-9 (C)
Steelers, 37-21 (P)
1983—Steelers, 44-17 (P)
Browns, 30-17 (C)
1984—Browns, 20-10 (C)
Steelers, 23-20 (P)
1985—Browns, 17-7 (C)
Steelers, 10-9 (P)
1986—Browns, 27-24 (P)
Browns, 37-31 (C) OT
1987—Browns, 34-10 (C)
Browns, 19-13 (P)
1988—Browns, 23-9 (P)
Browns, 27-7 (C)
1989—Browns, 51-0 (P)
Steelers, 17-7 (C)
1990—Browns, 13-3 (C)
Steelers, 35-0 (P)
1991—Browns, 17-14 (C)
Steelers, 17-10 (P)
1992—Browns, 17-9 (C)
Steelers, 23-13 (P)
1993—Browns, 28-23 (C)
Steelers, 16-9 (P)
1994—Steelers, 17-10 (C)
Steelers, 17-7 (P)
*Steelers, 29-9 (P)
1995—Steelers, 20-3 (P)
Steelers, 20-17 (C)
(RS Pts.—Browns 1,989, Steelers 1,756)
(PS Pts.—Steelers 29, Browns 9)
**AFC Divisional Playoff*

CLEVELAND vs. *ST. LOUIS
RS: Browns lead series, 8-7
PS: Browns lead series, 2-1
1950—**Browns, 30-28 (C)
1951—Browns, 38-23 (LA)
**Rams, 24-17 (LA)
1952—Browns, 37-7 (C)
1955—**Browns, 38-14 (LA)
1957—Browns, 45-31 (C)
1958—Browns, 30-27 (LA)
1963—Browns, 20-6 (C)
1965—Rams, 42-7 (LA)
1968—Rams, 24-6 (C)
1973—Rams, 30-17 (LA)
1977—Rams, 9-0 (C)
1978—Browns, 30-19 (C)
1981—Rams, 27-16 (LA)
1984—Rams, 20-17 (LA)
1987—Browns, 30-17 (C)
1990—Rams, 38-23 (C)
1993—Browns, 42-14 (LA)
(RS Pts.—Browns 358, Rams 334)
(PS Pts.—Browns 85, Rams 66)
**Franchise in Los Angeles prior to 1995*
***NFL Championship*

CLEVELAND vs. SAN DIEGO
RS: Chargers lead series, 9-6-1
1970—Chargers, 27-10 (C)
1972—Browns, 21-17 (SD)
1973—Tie, 16-16 (C)
1974—Chargers, 36-35 (SD)
1976—Browns, 21-17 (C)
1977—Chargers, 37-14 (SD)
1981—Chargers, 44-14 (C)
1982—Chargers, 30-13 (C)
1983—Browns, 30-24 (SD) OT
1985—Browns, 21-7 (SD)
1986—Browns, 47-17 (C)
1987—Chargers, 27-24 (SD) OT
1990—Chargers, 24-14 (C)
1991—Browns, 30-24 (SD) OT
1992—Chargers, 14-13 (C)
1995—Chargers, 31-13 (SD)
(RS Pts.—Chargers 392, Browns 336)

CLEVELAND vs. SAN FRANCISCO
RS: Browns lead series, 9-6
1950—Browns, 34-14 (C)
1951—49ers, 24-10 (SF)
1953—Browns, 23-21 (C)
1955—Browns, 38-3 (SF)
1959—49ers, 21-20 (C)
1962—Browns, 13-10 (SF)
1968—Browns, 33-21 (SF)
1970—49ers, 34-31 (SF)
1974—Browns, 7-0 (C)
1978—Browns, 24-7 (C)
1981—Browns, 15-12 (SF)
1984—49ers, 41-7 (C)
1987—49ers, 38-24 (SF)
1990—49ers, 20-17 (SF)
1993—Browns, 23-13 (C)
(RS Pts.—Browns 319, 49ers 279)

CLEVELAND vs. SEATTLE
RS: Seahawks lead series, 9-4
1977—Seahawks, 20-19 (S)
1978—Seahawks, 47-24 (S)
1979—Seahawks, 29-24 (C)
1980—Browns, 27-3 (S)
1981—Seahawks, 42-21 (S)
1982—Browns, 21-7 (S)
1983—Seahawks, 24-9 (C)
1984—Seahawks, 33-0 (S)
1985—Seahawks, 31-13 (S)
1988—Seahawks, 16-10 (C)
1989—Browns, 17-7 (S)
1993—Seahawks, 22-5 (S)
1994—Browns, 35-9 (C)
(RS Pts.—Seahawks 290, Browns 225)

CLEVELAND vs. TAMPA BAY
RS: Browns lead series, 5-0
1976—Browns, 24-7 (TB)
1980—Browns, 34-27 (TB)
1983—Browns, 20-0 (C)
1989—Browns, 42-31 (TB)
1995—Browns, 22-6 (C)
(RS Pts.—Browns 142, Buccaneers 71)

CLEVELAND vs. *TENNESSEE
RS: Browns lead series, 30-21
PS: Titans lead series, 1-0
1970—Browns, 28-14 (C)
Browns, 21-10 (H)
1971—Browns, 31-0 (C)
Browns, 37-24 (H)
1972—Browns, 23-17 (H)
Browns, 20-0 (C)
1973—Browns, 42-13 (C)
Browns, 23-13 (H)
1974—Browns, 20-7 (C)
Oilers, 28-24 (H)
1975—Oilers, 40-10 (C)
Oilers, 21-10 (H)
1976—Browns, 21-7 (H)
Browns, 13-10 (C)
1977—Browns, 24-23 (H)
Oilers, 19-15 (C)
1978—Oilers, 16-13 (C)
Oilers, 14-10 (H)
1979—Oilers, 31-10 (H)
Browns, 14-7 (C)
1980—Oilers, 16-7 (C)
Browns, 17-14 (H)
1981—Oilers, 9-3 (C)
Oilers, 17-13 (H)
1982—Browns, 20-14 (H)
1983—Browns, 25-19 (C) OT
Oilers, 34-27 (H)
1984—Browns, 27-10 (C)
Browns, 27-20 (H)
1985—Browns, 21-6 (H)
Browns, 28-21 (C)
1986—Browns, 23-20 (H)
Browns, 13-10 (C) OT
1987—Oilers, 15-10 (C)
Browns, 40-7 (H)
1988—Oilers, 24-17 (H)
Browns, 28-23 (C)
**Oilers, 24-23 (C)
1989—Browns, 28-17 (C)
Browns, 24-20 (H)
1990—Oilers, 35-23 (C)
Oilers, 58-14 (H)
1991—Oilers, 28-24 (H)
Oilers, 17-14 (C)
1992—Browns, 24-14 (H)
Oilers, 17-14 (C)
1993—Oilers, 27-20 (C)
Oilers, 19-17 (H)
1994—Browns, 11-8 (H)
Browns, 34-10 (C)
1995—Browns, 14-7 (H)
Oilers, 37-10 (C)
(RS Pts.—Browns 1,026, Titans 907)
(PS Pts.—Titans 24, Browns 23)
**Franchise in Houston prior to 1997; known as Oilers prior to 1999*
***AFC First-Round Playoff*

CLEVELAND vs. WASHINGTON
RS: Browns lead series, 32-9-1
1950—Browns, 20-14 (C)
Browns, 45-21 (W)
1951—Browns, 45-0 (C)
1952—Browns, 19-15 (C)
Browns, 48-24 (W)
1953—Browns, 30-14 (W)
Browns, 27-3 (C)
1954—Browns, 62-3 (C)
Browns, 34-14 (W)
1955—Redskins, 27-17 (C)
Browns, 24-14 (W)
1956—Redskins, 20-9 (W)
Redskins, 20-17 (C)
1957—Browns, 21-17 (C)
Tie, 30-30 (W)
1958—Browns, 20-10 (W)
Browns, 21-14 (C)
1959—Browns, 34-7 (C)
Browns, 31-17 (W)
1960—Browns, 31-10 (W)
Browns, 27-16 (C)
1961—Browns, 31-7 (C)
Browns, 17-6 (W)
1962—Redskins, 17-16 (C)
Redskins, 17-9 (W)
1963—Browns, 37-14 (C)
Browns, 27-20 (W)
1964—Browns, 27-13 (W)
Browns, 34-24 (C)
1965—Browns, 17-7 (W)
Browns, 24-16 (C)
1966—Browns, 38-14 (W)
Browns, 14-3 (C)
1967—Browns, 42-37 (C)
1968—Browns, 24-21 (W)
1969—Browns, 27-23 (C)
1971—Browns, 20-13 (W)
1975—Redskins, 23-7 (C)
1979—Redskins, 13-9 (C)
1985—Redskins, 14-7 (C)
1988—Browns, 17-13 (W)
1991—Redskins, 42-17 (W)
(RS Pts.—Browns 1,073, Redskins 667)

DALLAS vs. ARIZONA
RS: Cowboys lead series, 49-23-1
PS: Cardinals lead series, 1-0;
See Arizona vs. Dallas

DALLAS vs. ATLANTA
RS: Cowboys lead series, 11-6
PS: Cowboys lead series, 2-0;
See Atlanta vs. Dallas

DALLAS vs. BUFFALO
RS: Series tied, 3-3
PS: Cowboys lead series, 2-0;
See Buffalo vs. Dallas

DALLAS vs. CAROLINA
RS: Series tied, 1-1
PS: Panthers lead series, 1-0;

See Carolina vs. Dallas
DALLAS vs. CHICAGO
RS: Cowboys lead series, 9-8
PS: Cowboys lead series, 2-0;
See Chicago vs. Dallas
DALLAS vs. CINCINNATI
RS: Cowboys lead series, 4-3;
See Cincinnati vs. Dallas
DALLAS vs. CLEVELAND
RS: Browns lead series, 15-9
PS: Browns lead series, 2-1;
See Cleveland vs. Dallas
DALLAS vs. DENVER
RS: Cowboys lead series, 4-3
PS: Cowboys lead series, 1-0
1973—Cowboys, 22-10 (Den)
1977—Cowboys, 14-6 (Dal)
*Cowboys, 27-10 (New Orleans)
1980—Broncos, 41-20 (Den)
1986—Broncos, 29-14 (Den)
1992—Cowboys, 31-27 (Den)
1995—Cowboys, 31-21 (Dal)
1998—Broncos, 42-23 (Den)
(RS Pts.—Broncos 176, Cowboys 155)
(PS Pts.—Cowboys 27, Broncos 10)
**Super Bowl XII*
DALLAS vs. DETROIT
RS: Cowboys lead series, 7-6
PS: Series tied, 1-1
1960—Lions, 23-14 (Det)
1963—Cowboys, 17-14 (Dal)
1968—Cowboys, 59-13 (Dal)
1970—*Cowboys, 5-0 (Dal)
1972—Cowboys, 28-24 (Dal)
1975—Cowboys, 36-10 (Det)
1977—Cowboys, 37-0 (Dal)
1981—Lions, 27-24 (Det)
1985—Lions, 26-21 (Det)
1986—Cowboys, 31-7 (Det)
1987—Lions, 27-17 (Det)
1991—Lions, 34-10 (Det)
*Lions, 38-6 (Det)
1992—Cowboys, 37-3 (Det)
1994—Lions, 20-17 (Dal) OT
(RS Pts.—Cowboys 348, Lions 228)
(PS Pts.—Lions 38, Cowboys 11)
**NFC Divisional Playoff*
DALLAS vs. GREEN BAY
RS: Series tied, 9-9
PS: Cowboys lead series, 4-2
1960—Packers, 41-7 (GB)
1964—Packers, 45-21 (D)
1965—Packers, 13-3 (Mil)
1966—*Packers, 34-27 (D)
1967—*Packers, 21-17 (GB)
1968—Packers, 28-17 (D)
1970—Cowboys, 16-3 (D)
1972—Packers, 16-13 (Mil)
1975—Packers, 19-17 (D)
1978—Cowboys, 42-14 (Mil)
1980—Cowboys, 28-7 (Mil)
1982—**Cowboys, 37-26 (D)
1984—Cowboys, 20-6 (D)
1989—Packers, 31-13 (GB)
Packers, 20-10 (D)
1991—Cowboys, 20-17 (Mil)
1993—Cowboys, 36-14 (D)
***Cowboys, 27-17 (D)
1994—Cowboys, 42-31 (D)
***Cowboys, 35-9 (D)
1995—Cowboys, 34-24 (D)
****Cowboys, 38-27 (D)
1996—Cowboys, 21-6 (D)
1997—Packers, 45-17 (GB)
(RS Pts.—Packers 380, Cowboys 377)
(PS Pts.—Cowboys 181, Packers 134)
**NFL Championship*
***NFC Second-Round Playoff*
****NFC Divisional Playoff*
*****NFC Championship*
DALLAS vs. *INDIANAPOLIS
RS: Cowboys lead series, 7-3
PS: Colts lead series, 1-0
1960—Colts, 45-7 (D)
1967—Colts, 23-17 (B)
1969—Cowboys, 27-10 (D)
1970—**Colts, 16-13 (Miami)
1972—Cowboys, 21-0 (B)
1976—Cowboys, 30-27 (D)
1978—Cowboys, 38-0 (D)
1981—Cowboys, 37-13 (B)
1984—Cowboys, 22-3 (D)
1993—Cowboys, 27-3 (I)
1996—Colts, 25-24 (D)
(RS Pts.—Cowboys 250, Colts 149)
(PS Pts.—Colts 16, Cowboys 13)
**Franchise in Baltimore prior to 1984*
***Super Bowl V*
DALLAS VS. JACKSONVILLE
RS: Cowboys lead series, 1-0
1997—Cowboys, 26-22 (D)
(RS Pts.—Cowboys 26, Jaguars 22)
DALLAS vs. KANSAS CITY
RS: Cowboys lead series, 4-3
1970—Cowboys, 27-16 (KC)
1975—Chiefs, 34-31 (D)
1983—Cowboys, 41-21 (D)
1989—Chiefs, 36-28 (KC)
1992—Cowboys, 17-10 (D)
1995—Cowboys, 24-12 (D)
1998—Chiefs, 20-17 (KC)
(RS Pts.—Cowboys 185, Chiefs 149)
DALLAS vs. MIAMI
RS: Dolphins lead series, 6-2
PS: Cowboys lead series, 1-0
1971—*Cowboys, 24-3 (New Orleans)
1973—Dolphins, 14-7 (D)
1978—Dolphins, 23-16 (M)
1981—Cowboys, 28-27 (D)
1984—Dolphins, 28-21 (M)
1987—Dolphins, 20-14 (D)
1989—Dolphins, 17-14 (D)
1993—Dolphins, 16-14 (D)
1996—Cowboys, 29-10 (M)
(RS Pts.—Dolphins 155, Cowboys 143)
(PS Pts.—Cowboys 24, Dolphins 3)
**Super Bowl VI*
DALLAS vs. MINNESOTA
RS: Cowboys lead series, 9-7
PS: Cowboys lead series, 4-1
1961—Cowboys, 21-7 (D)
Cowboys, 28-0 (M)
1966—Cowboys, 28-17 (D)
1968—Cowboys, 20-7 (M)
1970—Vikings, 54-13 (M)
1971—*Cowboys, 20-12 (M)
1973—**Vikings, 27-10 (D)
1974—Vikings, 23-21 (D)
1975—*Cowboys, 17-14 (M)
1977—Cowboys, 16-10 (M) OT
**Cowboys, 23-6 (D)
1978—Vikings, 21-10 (D)
1979—Cowboys, 36-20 (M)
1982—Vikings, 31-27 (M)
1983—Cowboys, 37-24 (M)
1987—Vikings, 44-38 (D) OT
1988—Vikings, 43-3 (D)
1993—Cowboys, 37-20 (M)
1995—Cowboys, 23-17 (M) OT
1996—***Cowboys, 40-15 (D)
1998—Vikings, 46-36 (D)
(RS Pts.—Cowboys 394, Vikings 384)
(PS Pts.—Cowboys 110, Vikings 74)
**NFC Divisional Playoff*
***NFC Championship*
****NFC First-Round Playoff*
DALLAS vs. NEW ENGLAND
RS: Cowboys lead series, 7-0
1971—Cowboys, 44-21 (D)
1975—Cowboys, 34-31 (NE)
1978—Cowboys, 17-10 (D)
1981—Cowboys, 35-21 (NE)
1984—Cowboys, 20-17 (D)
1987—Cowboys, 23-17 (NE) OT
1996—Cowboys, 12-6 (D)
(RS Pts.—Cowboys 185, Patriots 123)
DALLAS vs. NEW ORLEANS
RS: Cowboys lead series, 14-4
1967—Cowboys, 14-10 (D)
Cowboys, 27-10 (NO)
1968—Cowboys, 17-3 (NO)
1969—Cowboys, 21-17 (NO)
Cowboys, 33-17 (D)
1971—Saints, 24-14 (NO)
1973—Cowboys, 40-3 (D)
1976—Cowboys, 24-6 (NO)
1978—Cowboys, 27-7 (D)
1982—Cowboys, 21-7 (D)
1983—Cowboys, 21-20 (D)
1984—Cowboys, 30-27 (D) OT
1988—Saints, 20-17 (NO)
1989—Saints, 28-0 (NO)
1990—Cowboys, 17-13 (D)
1991—Cowboys, 23-14 (D)
1994—Cowboys, 24-16 (NO)
1998—Saints, 22-3 (NO)
(RS Pts.—Cowboys 373, Saints 264)
DALLAS vs. N.Y. GIANTS
RS: Cowboys lead series, 46-25-2
1960—Tie, 31-31 (NY)
1961—Giants, 31-10 (D)
Cowboys, 17-16 (NY)
1962—Giants, 41-10 (D)
Giants, 41-31 (NY)
1963—Giants, 37-21 (NY)
Giants, 34-27 (D)
1964—Tie, 13-13 (D)
Cowboys, 31-21 (NY)
1965—Cowboys, 31-2 (D)
Cowboys, 38-20 (NY)
1966—Cowboys, 52-7 (D)
Cowboys, 17-7 (NY)
1967—Cowboys, 38-24 (D)
1968—Giants, 27-21 (D)
Cowboys, 28-10 (NY)
1969—Cowboys, 25-3 (D)
1970—Cowboys, 28-10 (D)
Giants, 23-20 (NY)
1971—Cowboys, 20-13 (D)
Cowboys, 42-14 (NY)
1972—Cowboys, 23-14 (NY)
Giants, 23-3 (D)
1973—Cowboys, 45-28 (D)
Cowboys, 23-10 (New Haven)
1974—Giants, 14-6 (D)
Cowboys, 21-7 (New Haven)
1975—Cowboys, 13-7 (NY)
Cowboys, 14-3 (D)
1976—Cowboys, 24-14 (NY)
Cowboys, 9-3 (D)
1977—Cowboys, 41-21 (D)
Cowboys, 24-10 (NY)
1978—Cowboys, 34-24 (NY)
Cowboys, 24-3 (D)
1979—Cowboys, 16-14 (NY)
Cowboys, 28-7 (D)
1980—Cowboys, 24-3 (D)
Giants, 38-35 (NY)
1981—Cowboys, 18-10 (D)
Giants, 13-10 (NY) OT
1983—Cowboys, 28-13 (D)
Cowboys, 38-20 (NY)
1984—Giants, 28-7 (NY)
Giants, 19-7 (D)
1985—Cowboys, 30-29 (NY)
Cowboys, 28-21 (D)
1986—Cowboys, 31-28 (D)
Giants, 17-14 (NY)
1987—Cowboys, 16-14 (NY)
Cowboys, 33-24 (D)
1988—Giants, 12-10 (D)
Giants, 29-21 (NY)
1989—Giants, 30-13 (D)
Giants, 15-0 (NY)
1990—Giants, 28-7 (D)
Giants, 31-17 (NY)
1991—Cowboys, 21-16 (D)
Giants, 22-9 (NY)
1992—Cowboys, 34-28 (NY)
Cowboys, 30-3 (D)
1993—Cowboys, 31-9 (D)
Cowboys, 16-13 (NY) OT
1994—Cowboys, 38-10 (D)
Giants, 15-10 (NY)
1995—Cowboys, 35-0 (NY)
Cowboys, 21-20 (D)
1996—Cowboys, 27-0 (D)
Giants, 20-6 (NY)
1997—Giants, 20-17 (NY)
Giants, 20-7 (D)
1998—Cowboys, 31-7 (NY)
Cowboys, 16-6 (D)
(RS Pts.—Cowboys 1,635, Giants 1,258)
DALLAS vs. N.Y. JETS
RS: Cowboys lead series, 5-1
1971—Cowboys, 52-10 (D)
1975—Cowboys, 31-21 (NY)
1978—Cowboys, 30-7 (NY)
1987—Cowboys, 38-24 (NY)
1990—Jets, 24-9 (NY)
1993—Cowboys, 28-7 (NY)
(RS Pts.—Cowboys 188, Jets 93)
DALLAS vs. *OAKLAND
RS: Raiders lead series, 4-3
1974—Raiders, 27-23 (O)
1980—Cowboys, 19-13 (O)
1983—Raiders, 40-38 (D)
1986—Raiders, 17-13 (D)
1992—Cowboys, 28-13 (LA)
1995—Cowboys, 34-21 (O)
1998—Raiders, 13-12 (D)
(RS Pts.—Cowboys 167, Raiders 144)
**Franchise in Los Angeles from 1982-1994*
DALLAS vs. PHILADELPHIA
RS: Cowboys lead series, 47-29
PS: Cowboys lead series, 2-1
1960—Eagles, 27-25 (D)
1961—Eagles, 43-7 (D)
Eagles, 35-13 (P)
1962—Cowboys, 41-19 (D)
Eagles, 28-14 (P)
1963—Eagles, 24-21 (P)
Cowboys, 27-20 (D)
1964—Eagles, 17-14 (D)
Eagles, 24-14 (P)
1965—Eagles, 35-24 (D)
Cowboys, 21-19 (P)
1966—Cowboys, 56-7 (D)
Eagles, 24-23 (P)
1967—Eagles, 21-14 (P)
Cowboys, 38-17 (D)
1968—Cowboys, 45-13 (P)
Cowboys, 34-14 (D)
1969—Cowboys, 38-7 (P)
Cowboys, 49-14 (D)
1970—Cowboys, 17-7 (P)
Cowboys, 21-17 (D)
1971—Cowboys, 42-7 (P)
Cowboys, 20-7 (D)
1972—Cowboys, 28-6 (D)
Cowboys, 28-7 (P)
1973—Eagles, 30-16 (P)
Cowboys, 31-10 (D)
1974—Eagles, 13-10 (P)
Cowboys, 31-24 (D)
1975—Cowboys, 20-17 (P)
Cowboys, 27-17 (D)
1976—Cowboys, 27-7 (D)
Cowboys, 26-7 (P)
1977—Cowboys, 16-10 (P)
Cowboys, 24-14 (D)
1978—Cowboys, 14-7 (D)
Cowboys, 31-13 (P)
1979—Eagles, 31-21 (D)
Cowboys, 24-17 (P)
1980—Eagles, 17-10 (P)
Cowboys, 35-27 (D)
*Eagles, 20-7 (P)
1981—Cowboys, 17-14 (P)
Cowboys, 21-10 (D)
1982—Eagles, 24-20 (D)

ALL-TIME TEAM VS. TEAM RESULTS

1983—Cowboys, 37-7 (D)
Cowboys, 27-20 (P)
1984—Cowboys, 23-17 (D)
Cowboys, 26-10 (P)
1985—Eagles, 16-14 (P)
Cowboys, 34-17 (D)
1986—Cowboys, 17-14 (P)
Eagles, 23-21 (D)
1987—Cowboys, 41-22 (D)
Eagles, 37-20 (P)
1988—Eagles, 24-23 (P)
Eagles, 23-7 (D)
1989—Eagles, 27-0 (D)
Eagles, 20-10 (P)
1990—Eagles, 21-20 (D)
Eagles, 17-3 (P)
1991—Eagles, 24-0 (D)
Cowboys, 25-13 (P)
1992—Eagles, 31-7 (P)
Cowboys, 20-10 (D)
**Cowboys, 34-10 (D)
1993—Cowboys, 23-10 (P)
Cowboys, 23-17 (D)
1994—Cowboys, 24-13 (D)
Cowboys, 31-19 (P)
1995—Cowboys, 34-12 (D)
Eagles, 20-17 (P)
**Cowboys, 30-11 (D)
1996—Cowboys, 23-19 (P)
Eagles, 31-21 (D)
1997—Cowboys, 21-20 (D)
Eagles, 13-12 (P)
1998—Cowboys, 34-0 (P)
Cowboys, 13-9 (D)
(RS Pts.—Cowboys 1,746, Eagles 1,344)
(PS Pts.—Cowboys 71, Eagles 41)
NFC Championship
***NFC Divisional Playoff*

DALLAS vs. PITTSBURGH
RS: Cowboys lead series, 14-11
PS: Steelers lead series, 2-1
1960—Steelers, 35-28 (D)
1961—Cowboys, 27-24 (D)
Steelers, 37-7 (P)
1962—Steelers, 30-28 (D)
Cowboys, 42-27 (P)
1963—Steelers, 27-21 (P)
Steelers, 24-19 (D)
1964—Steelers, 23-17 (P)
Cowboys, 17-14 (D)
1965—Steelers, 22-13 (P)
Cowboys, 24-17 (D)
1966—Cowboys, 52-21 (D)
Cowboys, 20-7 (P)
1967—Cowboys, 24-21 (P)
1968—Cowboys, 28-7 (D)
1969—Cowboys, 10-7 (P)
1972—Cowboys, 17-13 (D)
1975—*Steelers, 21-17 (Miami)
1977—Steelers, 28-13 (P)
1978—**Steelers, 35-31 (Miami)
1979—Steelers, 14-3 (P)
1982—Steelers, 36-28 (D)
1985—Cowboys, 27-13 (D)
1988—Steelers, 24-21 (P)
1991—Cowboys, 20-10 (D)
1994—Cowboys, 26-9 (P)
1995—***Cowboys, 27-17 (Tempe)
1997—Cowboys, 37-7 (P)
(RS Pts.—Cowboys 569, Steelers 497)
(PS Pts.—Cowboys 75, Steelers 73)
Super Bowl X
***Super Bowl XIII*
****Super Bowl XXX*

DALLAS vs. *ST. LOUIS
RS: Rams lead series, 9-8
PS: Series tied, 4-4
1960—Rams, 38-13 (D)
1962—Cowboys, 27-17 (LA)
1967—Rams, 35-13 (D)
1969—Rams, 24-23 (LA)
1971—Cowboys, 28-21 (D)
1973—Rams, 37-31 (LA)
**Cowboys, 27-16 (D)
1975—Cowboys, 18-7 (D)
***Cowboys, 37-7 (LA)
1976—**Rams, 14-12 (D)
1978—Rams, 27-14 (LA)
***Cowboys, 28-0 (LA)
1979—Cowboys, 30-6 (D)
**Rams, 21-19 (D)
1980—Rams, 38-14 (LA)
****Cowboys, 34-13 (D)
1981—Cowboys, 29-17 (D)
1983—****Rams, 24-17 (D)
1984—Cowboys, 20-13 (LA)
1985—**Rams, 20-0 (LA)
1986—Rams, 29-10 (LA)
1987—Cowboys, 29-21 (LA)
1989—Rams, 35-31 (D)
1990—Cowboys, 24-21 (LA)
1992—Rams, 27-23 (D)
(RS Pts.—Rams 413, Cowboys 377)
(PS Pts.—Cowboys 174, Rams 115)
Franchise in Los Angeles prior to 1995
***NFC Divisional Playoff*
****NFC Championship*
*****NFC First-Round Playoff*

DALLAS vs. SAN DIEGO
RS: Cowboys lead series, 5-1
1972—Cowboys, 34-28 (SD)
1980—Cowboys, 42-31 (D)
1983—Chargers, 24-23 (SD)
1986—Cowboys, 24-21 (SD)
1990—Cowboys, 17-14 (D)
1995—Cowboys, 23-9 (SD)
(RS Pts.—Cowboys 163, Chargers 127)

DALLAS vs. SAN FRANCISCO
RS: 49ers lead series, 12-7-1
PS: Cowboys lead series, 5-2
1960—49ers, 26-14 (D)
1963—49ers, 31-24 (SF)
1965—Cowboys, 39-31 (D)
1967—49ers, 24-16 (SF)
1969—Tie, 24-24 (D)
1970—*Cowboys, 17-10 (SF)
1971—*Cowboys, 14-3 (D)
1972—49ers, 31-10 (D)
**Cowboys, 30-28 (SF)
1974—Cowboys, 20-14 (D)
1977—Cowboys, 42-35 (SF)
1979—Cowboys, 21-13 (SF)
1980—Cowboys, 59-14 (D)
1981—49ers, 45-14 (SF)
*49ers, 28-27 (SF)
1983—49ers, 42-17 (SF)
1985—49ers, 31-16 (SF)
1989—49ers, 31-14 (D)
1990—49ers, 24-6 (D)
1992—*Cowboys, 30-20 (SF)
1993—Cowboys, 26-17 (D)
*Cowboys, 38-21 (D)
1994—49ers, 21-14 (SF)
*49ers, 38-28 (SF)
1995—49ers, 38-20 (D)
1996—Cowboys, 20-17 (SF) OT
1997—49ers, 17-10 (SF)
(RS Pts.—49ers 526, Cowboys 426)
(PS Pts.—Cowboys 184, 49ers 148)
NFC Championship
***NFC Divisional Playoff*

DALLAS vs. SEATTLE
RS: Cowboys lead series, 5-1
1976—Cowboys, 28-13 (S)
1980—Cowboys, 51-7 (D)
1983—Cowboys, 35-10 (S)
1986—Seahawks, 31-14 (D)
1992—Cowboys, 27-0 (D)
1998—Cowboys, 30-22 (D)
(RS Pts.—Cowboys 185, Seahawks 83)

DALLAS vs. TAMPA BAY
RS: Cowboys lead series, 6-0
PS: Cowboys lead series, 2-0
1977—Cowboys, 23-7 (D)
1980—Cowboys, 28-17 (D)
1981—*Cowboys, 38-0 (D)
1982—Cowboys, 14-9 (D)
**Cowboys, 30-17 (D)
1983—Cowboys, 27-24 (D) OT
1990—Cowboys, 14-10 (D)
Cowboys, 17-13 (TB)
(RS Pts.—Cowboys 123, Buccaneers 80)
(PS Pts.—Cowboys 68, Buccaneers 17)
NFC Divisional Playoff
***NFC First-Round Playoff*

DALLAS vs. *TENNESSEE
RS: Cowboys lead series, 5-4
1970—Cowboys, 52-10 (D)
1974—Cowboys, 10-0 (H)
1979—Oilers, 30-24 (D)
1982—Cowboys, 37-7 (H)
1985—Cowboys, 17-10 (H)
1988—Oilers, 25-17 (D)
1991—Oilers, 26-23 (H) OT
1994—Cowboys, 20-17 (D)
1997—Oilers, 27-14 (D)
(RS Pts.—Cowboys 214, Titans 152)
Franchise in Houston prior to 1997; known as Oilers prior to 1999

DALLAS vs. WASHINGTON
RS: Cowboys lead series, 43-31-2
PS: Redskins lead series, 2-0
1960—Redskins, 26-14 (W)
1961—Tie, 28-28 (D)
Redskins, 34-24 (W)
1962—Tie, 35-35 (D)
Cowboys, 38-10 (W)
1963—Redskins, 21-17 (W)
Cowboys, 35-20 (D)
1964—Cowboys, 24-18 (D)
Redskins, 28-16 (W)
1965—Cowboys, 27-7 (D)
Redskins, 34-31 (W)
1966—Cowboys, 31-30 (W)
Redskins, 34-31 (D)
1967—Cowboys, 17-14 (W)
Redskins, 27-20 (D)
1968—Cowboys, 44-24 (W)
Cowboys, 29-20 (D)
1969—Cowboys, 41-28 (W)
Cowboys, 20-10 (D)
1970—Cowboys, 45-21 (W)
Cowboys, 34-0 (D)
1971—Redskins, 20-16 (D)
Cowboys, 13-0 (W)
1972—Redskins, 24-20 (W)
Cowboys, 34-24 (D)
*Redskins, 26-3 (W)
1973—Redskins, 14-7 (W)
Cowboys, 27-7 (D)
1974—Redskins, 28-21 (W)
Cowboys, 24-23 (D)
1975—Redskins, 30-24 (W) OT
Cowboys, 31-10 (D)
1976—Cowboys, 20-7 (W)
Redskins, 27-14 (D)
1977—Cowboys, 34-16 (D)
Cowboys, 14-7 (W)
1978—Redskins, 9-5 (W)
Cowboys, 37-10 (D)
1979—Redskins, 34-20 (W)
Cowboys, 35-34 (D)
1980—Cowboys, 17-3 (W)
Cowboys, 14-10 (D)
1981—Cowboys, 26-10 (W)
Cowboys, 24-10 (D)
1982—Cowboys, 24-10 (W)
*Redskins, 31-17 (W)
1983—Cowboys, 31-30 (W)
Redskins, 31-10 (D)
1984—Redskins, 34-14 (W)
Redskins, 30-28 (D)
1985—Cowboys, 44-14 (D)
Cowboys, 13-7 (W)
1986—Cowboys, 30-6 (D)
Redskins, 41-14 (W)
1987—Redskins, 13-7 (D)
Redskins, 24-20 (W)
1988—Redskins, 35-17 (D)
Cowboys, 24-17 (W)
1989—Redskins, 30-7 (D)
Cowboys, 13-3 (W)
1990—Redskins, 19-15 (W)
Cowboys, 27-17 (D)
1991—Redskins, 33-31 (D)
Cowboys, 24-21 (W)
1992—Cowboys, 23-10 (D)
Redskins, 20-17 (W)
1993—Redskins, 35-16 (W)
Cowboys, 38-3 (D)
1994—Cowboys, 34-7 (W)
Cowboys, 31-7 (D)
1995—Redskins, 27-23 (W)
Redskins, 24-17 (D)
1996—Cowboys, 21-10 (D)
Redskins, 37-10 (W)
1997—Redskins, 21-16 (W)
Cowboys, 17-14 (D)
1998—Cowboys, 31-10 (W)
Cowboys, 23-7 (D)
(RS Pts.—Cowboys 1,788, Redskins 1,473)
(PS Pts.—Redskins 57, Cowboys 20)
NFC Championship

DENVER vs. ARIZONA
RS: Broncos lead series, 4-0-1;
See Arizona vs. Denver

DENVER vs. ATLANTA
RS: Broncos lead series, 6-3
PS: Broncos lead series, 1-0;
See Atlanta vs. Denver

DENVER vs. BALTIMORE
RS: Broncos lead series, 1-0;
See Baltimore vs. Denver

DENVER vs. BUFFALO
RS: Bills lead series, 17-12-1
PS: Bills lead series, 1-0;
See Buffalo vs. Denver

DENVER vs. CAROLINA
RS: Broncos lead series, 1-0;
See Carolina vs. Denver

DENVER vs. CHICAGO
RS: Broncos lead series, 6-5;
See Chicago vs. Denver

DENVER vs. CINCINNATI
Broncos lead series, 14-6;
See Cincinnati vs. Denver

DENVER vs. CLEVELAND
RS: Broncos lead series, 13-5
PS: Broncos lead series, 3-0;
See Cleveland vs. Denver

DENVER vs. DALLAS
RS: Cowboys lead series, 4-3
PS: Cowboys lead series, 1-0;
See Dallas vs. Denver

DENVER vs. DETROIT
RS: Broncos lead series, 4-3
1971—Lions, 24-20 (Den)
1974—Broncos, 31-27 (Det)
1978—Lions, 17-14 (Det)
1981—Broncos, 27-21 (Den)
1984—Broncos, 28-7 (Det)
1987—Broncos, 34-0 (Den)
1990—Lions, 40-27 (Det)
(RS Pts.—Broncos 181, Lions 136)

DENVER vs. GREEN BAY
RS: Broncos lead series, 4-3-1
PS: Broncos lead series, 1-0
1971—Packers, 34-13 (Mil)
1975—Broncos, 23-13 (D)
1978—Broncos, 16-3 (D)
1984—Broncos, 17-14 (D)
1987—Tie, 17-17 (Mil) OT
1990—Broncos, 22-13 (D)
1993—Packers, 30-27 (GB)
1996—Packers, 41-6 (GB)
1997—*Broncos, 31-24 (San Diego)
(RS Pts.—Packers 165, Broncos 141)
(PS Pts.—Broncos 31, Packers 24)
Super Bowl XXXII

DENVER vs. *INDIANAPOLIS
RS: Broncos lead series, 9-2

1974—Broncos, 17-6 (B)
1977—Broncos, 27-13 (D)
1978—Colts, 7-6 (B)
1981—Broncos, 28-10 (D)
1983—Broncos, 17-10 (B)
Broncos, 21-19 (D)
1985—Broncos, 15-10 (I)
1988—Colts, 55-23 (I)
1989—Broncos, 14-3 (D)
1990—Broncos, 27-17 (I)
1993—Broncos, 35-13 (D)
(RS Pts.—Broncos 230, Colts 163)
Franchise in Baltimore prior to 1984

DENVER vs. JACKSONVILLE
RS: Broncos lead series, 2-0
PS: Series tied, 1-1
1995—Broncos, 31-23 (D)
1996—*Jaguars, 30-27 (D)
1997—**Broncos, 42-17 (D)
1998—Broncos, 37-24 (D)
(RS Pts.—Broncos 68, Jaguars 47)
(PS Pts.—Broncos 69, Jaguars 47)
**AFC Divisional Playoff*
***AFC First-Round Playoff*

DENVER vs. *KANSAS CITY
RS: Chiefs lead series, 43-34
PS: Broncos lead series, 1-0
1960—Texans, 17-14 (D)
Texans, 34-7 (Dal)
1961—Texans, 19-12 (D)
Texans, 49-21 (Dal)
1962—Texans, 24-3 (D)
Texans, 17-10 (Dal)
1963—Chiefs, 59-7 (D)
Chiefs, 52-21 (KC)
1964—Broncos, 33-27 (D)
Chiefs, 49-39 (KC)
1965—Chiefs, 31-23 (D)
Chiefs, 45-35 (KC)
1966—Chiefs, 37-10 (KC)
Chiefs, 56-10 (D)
1967—Chiefs, 52-9 (KC)
Chiefs, 38-24 (D)
1968—Chiefs, 34-2 (KC)
Chiefs, 30-7 (D)
1969—Chiefs, 26-13 (D)
Chiefs, 31-17 (KC)
1970—Broncos, 26-13 (D)
Chiefs, 16-0 (KC)
1971—Chiefs, 16-3 (D)
Chiefs, 28-10 (KC)
1972—Chiefs, 45-24 (D)
Chiefs, 24-21 (KC)
1973—Chiefs, 16-14 (KC)
Broncos, 14-10 (D)
1974—Broncos, 17-14 (KC)
Chiefs, 42-34 (D)
1975—Broncos, 37-33 (D)
Chiefs, 26-13 (KC)
1976—Broncos, 35-26 (KC)
Broncos, 17-16 (D)
1977—Broncos, 23-7 (D)
Broncos, 14-7 (KC)
1978—Broncos, 23-17 (KC) OT
Broncos, 24-3 (D)
1979—Broncos, 24-10 (KC)
Broncos, 20-3 (D)
1980—Chiefs, 23-17 (D)
Chiefs, 31-14 (KC)
1981—Chiefs, 28-14 (KC)
Broncos, 16-13 (D)
1982—Chiefs, 37-16 (D)
1983—Broncos, 27-24 (D)
Chiefs, 48-17 (KC)
1984—Broncos, 21-0 (D)
Chiefs, 16-13 (KC)
1985—Broncos, 30-10 (KC)
Broncos, 14-13 (D)
1986—Broncos, 38-17 (D)
Chiefs, 37-10 (KC)
1987—Broncos, 26-17 (KC)
Broncos, 20-17 (D)
1988—Chiefs, 20-13 (KC)
Broncos, 17-11 (D)
1989—Broncos, 34-20 (D)
Broncos, 16-13 (KC)
1990—Broncos, 24-23 (D)
Chiefs, 31-20 (KC)
1991—Broncos, 19-16 (D)
Broncos, 24-20 (KC)
1992—Broncos, 20-19 (D)
Chiefs, 42-20 (KC)
1993—Chiefs, 15-7 (KC)
Broncos, 27-21 (D)
1994—Chiefs, 31-28 (D)
Broncos, 20-17 (KC) OT
1995—Chiefs, 21-7 (D)
Chiefs, 20-17 (KC)
1996—Chiefs, 17-14 (KC)
Broncos, 34-7 (D)
1997—Broncos, 19-3 (D)
Chiefs, 24-22 (KC)
**Broncos, 14-10 (KC)
1998—Broncos, 30-7 (KC)
Broncos, 35-31 (D)
(RS Pts.—Chiefs 1,859, Broncos 1,470)
(PS Pts.—Broncos 14, Chiefs 10)
**Franchise in Dallas prior to 1963 and known as Texans*
***AFC Divisional Playoff*

DENVER vs. MIAMI
RS: Dolphins lead series, 6-2-1
PS: Broncos lead series, 1-0
1966—Dolphins, 24-7 (M)
Broncos, 17-7 (D)
1967—Dolphins, 35-21 (M)
1968—Broncos, 21-14 (D)
1969—Dolphins, 27-24 (M)
1971—Tie, 10-10 (D)
1975—Dolphins, 14-13 (M)
1985—Dolphins, 30-26 (D)
1998—Dolphins, 31-21 (M)
*Broncos, 38-3 (D)
(RS Pts.—Dolphins 192, Broncos 160)
(PS Pts.—Broncos 38, Dolphins 3)
**AFC Divisonal Playoff*

DENVER vs. MINNESOTA
RS: Vikings lead series, 5-4
1972—Vikings, 23-20 (D)
1978—Vikings, 12-9 (M) OT
1981—Broncos, 19-17 (D)
1984—Broncos, 42-21 (D)
1987—Vikings, 34-27 (M)
1990—Vikings, 27-22 (M)
1991—Broncos, 13-6 (M)
1993—Vikings, 26-23 (D)
1996—Broncos, 21-17 (M)
(RS Pts.—Broncos 196, Vikings 183)

DENVER vs. *NEW ENGLAND
RS: Broncos lead series, 20-12
PS: Broncos lead series, 1-0
1960—Broncos, 13-10 (B)
Broncos, 31-24 (D)
1961—Patriots, 45-17 (B)
Patriots, 28-24 (D)
1962—Patriots, 41-16 (B)
Patriots, 33-29 (D)
1963—Broncos, 14-10 (D)
Patriots, 40-21 (B)
1964—Patriots, 39-10 (D)
Patriots, 12-7 (B)
1965—Broncos, 27-10 (B)
Patriots, 28-20 (D)
1966—Patriots, 24-10 (D)
Broncos, 17-10 (B)
1967—Broncos, 26-21 (D)
1968—Patriots, 20-17 (D)
Broncos, 35-14 (B)
1969—Broncos, 35-7 (D)
1972—Broncos, 45-21 (D)
1976—Patriots, 38-14 (NE)
1979—Broncos, 45-10 (D)
1980—Patriots, 23-14 (NE)
1984—Broncos, 26-19 (D)
1986—Broncos, 27-20 (D)
**Broncos, 22-17 (D)
1987—Broncos, 31-20 (D)
1988—Broncos, 21-10 (D)
1991—Broncos, 9-6 (NE)
Broncos, 20-3 (D)
1995—Broncos, 37-3 (NE)
1996—Broncos, 34-8 (NE)
1997—Broncos, 34-13 (D)
1998—Broncos, 27-21 (D)
(RS Pts.—Broncos 753, Patriots 631)
(PS Pts.—Broncos 22, Patriots 17)
**Franchise in Boston prior to 1971*
***AFC Divisional Playoff*

DENVER vs. NEW ORLEANS
RS: Broncos lead series, 4-2
1970—Broncos, 31-6 (NO)
1974—Broncos, 33-17 (D)
1979—Broncos, 10-3 (D)
1985—Broncos, 34-23 (D)
1988—Saints, 42-0 (NO)
1994—Saints, 30-28 (D)
(RS Pts.—Broncos 136, Saints 121)

DENVER vs. N.Y. GIANTS
RS: Giants lead series, 4-3
PS: Giants lead series, 1-0
1972—Giants, 29-17 (NY)
1976—Broncos, 14-13 (D)
1980—Broncos, 14-9 (NY)
1986—Giants, 19-16 (NY)
*Giants, 39-20 (Pasadena)
1989—Giants, 14-7 (D)
1992—Broncos, 27-13 (D)
1998—Giants, 20-16 (NY)
(RS Pts.—Giants 117, Broncos 111)
(PS Pts.—Giants 39, Broncos 20)
**Super Bowl XXI*

DENVER vs. *N.Y. JETS
RS: Broncos lead series, 13-12-1
PS: Broncos lead series, 1-0
1960—Titans, 28-24 (NY)
Titans, 30-27 (D)
1961—Titans, 35-28 (NY)
Broncos, 27-10 (D)
1962—Broncos, 32-10 (NY)
Titans, 46-45 (D)
1963—Tie, 35-35 (NY)
Jets, 14-9 (D)
1964—Jets, 30-6 (NY)
Broncos, 20-16 (D)
1965—Broncos, 16-13 (D)
Jets, 45-10 (NY)
1966—Jets, 16-7 (D)
1967—Jets, 38-24 (D)
Broncos, 33-24 (NY)
1968—Broncos, 21-13 (NY)
1969—Broncos, 21-19 (D)
1973—Broncos, 40-28 (NY)
1976—Broncos, 46-3 (D)
1978—Jets, 31-28 (D)
1980—Broncos, 31-24 (D)
1986—Jets, 22-10 (NY)
1992—Broncos, 27-16 (D)
1993—Broncos, 26-20 (NY)
1994—Jets, 25-22 (NY) OT
1996—Broncos, 31-6 (D)
1998—**Broncos, 23-10 (D)
(RS Pts.—Broncos 646, Jets 597)
(PS Pts.—Broncos 23, Jets 10)
**Jets known as Titans prior to 1963*
***AFC Championship*

DENVER vs. *OAKLAND
RS: Raiders lead series, 49-26-2
PS: Series tied, 1-1
1960—Broncos, 31-14 (D)
Raiders, 48-10 (O)
1961—Raiders, 33-19 (O)
Broncos, 27-24 (D)
1962—Broncos, 44-7 (D)
Broncos, 23-6 (O)
1963—Raiders, 26-10 (D)
Raiders, 35-31 (O)
1964—Raiders, 40-7 (O)
Tie, 20-20 (D)
1965—Raiders, 28-20 (D)
Raiders, 24-13 (O)
1966—Raiders, 17-3 (D)
Raiders, 28-10 (O)
1967—Raiders, 51-0 (O)
Raiders, 21-17 (D)
1968—Raiders, 43-7 (D)
Raiders, 33-27 (O)
1969—Raiders, 24-14 (D)
Raiders, 41-10 (O)
1970—Raiders, 35-23 (O)
Raiders, 24-19 (D)
1971—Raiders, 27-16 (D)
Raiders, 21-13 (O)
1972—Broncos, 30-23 (O)
Raiders, 37-20 (D)
1973—Tie, 23-23 (D)
Raiders, 21-17 (O)
1974—Raiders, 28-17 (D)
Broncos, 20-17 (O)
1975—Raiders, 42-17 (D)
Raiders, 17-10 (O)
1976—Raiders, 17-10 (D)
Raiders, 19-6 (O)
1977—Broncos, 30-7 (O)
Raiders, 24-14 (D)
**Broncos, 20-17 (D)
1978—Broncos, 14-6 (D)
Broncos, 21-6 (O)
1979—Raiders, 27-3 (O)
Raiders, 14-10 (D)
1980—Raiders, 9-3 (O)
Raiders, 24-21 (D)
1981—Broncos, 9-7 (D)
Broncos, 17-0 (O)
1982—Raiders, 27-10 (LA)
1983—Raiders, 22-7 (D)
Raiders, 22-20 (LA)
1984—Broncos, 16-13 (D)
Broncos, 22-19 (LA) OT
1985—Raiders, 31-28 (LA) OT
Raiders, 17-14 (D) OT
1986—Broncos, 38-36 (D)
Broncos, 21-10 (LA)
1987—Broncos, 30-14 (D)
Broncos, 23-17 (LA)
1988—Raiders, 30-27 (D) OT
Raiders, 21-20 (LA)
1989—Broncos, 31-21 (D)
Raiders, 16-13 (LA) OT
1990—Raiders, 14-9 (LA)
Raiders, 23-20 (D)
1991—Raiders, 16-13 (LA)
Raiders, 17-16 (D)
1992—Broncos, 17-13 (D)
Raiders, 24-0 (LA)
1993—Raiders, 23-20 (D)
Raiders, 33-30 (LA) OT
***Raiders, 42-24 (LA)
1994—Raiders, 48-16 (D)
Raiders, 23-13 (LA)
1995—Broncos, 27-0 (D)
Broncos, 31-28 (O)
1996—Broncos, 22-21 (O)
Broncos, 24-19 (D)
1997—Raiders, 28-25 (O)
Broncos, 31-3 (D)
1998—Broncos, 34-17 (O)
Broncos, 40-14 (D)
(RS Pts.—Raiders 1,718, Broncos 1,434)
(PS Pts.—Raiders 59, Broncos 44)
**Franchise in Los Angeles from 1982-1994*
***AFC Championship*
****AFC First-Round Playoff*

DENVER vs. PHILADELPHIA
RS: Eagles lead series, 6-3
1971—Eagles, 17-16 (P)
1975—Broncos, 25-10 (D)
1980—Eagles, 27-6 (P)
1983—Eagles, 13-10 (D)
1986—Broncos, 33-7 (P)
1989—Eagles, 28-24 (D)
1992—Eagles, 30-0 (P)

ALL-TIME TEAM VS. TEAM RESULTS

1995—Eagles, 31-13 (P)
1998—Broncos, 41-16 (D)
(RS Pts.—Eagles 179, Broncos 168)

DENVER vs. PITTSBURGH
RS: Broncos lead series, 10-6-1
PS: Broncos lead series, 3-2
1970—Broncos, 16-13 (D)
1971—Broncos, 22-10 (P)
1973—Broncos, 23-13 (P)
1974—Tie, 35-35 (D) OT
1975—Steelers, 20-9 (P)
1977—Broncos, 21-7 (D)
*Broncos, 34-21 (D)
1978—Steelers, 21-17 (D)
*Steelers, 33-10 (P)
1979—Steelers, 42-7 (P)
1983—Broncos, 14-10 (P)
1984—*Steelers, 24-17 (D)
1985—Broncos, 31-23 (P)
1986—Broncos, 21-10 (P)
1988—Steelers, 39-21 (P)
1989—Broncos, 34-7 (D)
*Broncos, 24-23 (D)
1990—Steelers, 34-17 (D)
1991—Broncos, 20-13 (D)
1993—Broncos, 37-13 (D)
1997—Steelers, 35-24 (P)
**Broncos, 24-21 (P)
(RS Pts.—Broncos 369, Steelers 345)
(PS Pts.—Steelers 122, Broncos 109)
AFC Divisional Playoff
***AFC Championship*

DENVER vs. *ST. LOUIS
RS: Series tied, 4-4
1972—Broncos, 16-10 (LA)
1974—Rams, 17-10 (D)
1979—Rams, 13-9 (D)
1982—Broncos, 27-24 (LA)
1985—Rams, 20-16 (LA)
1988—Broncos, 35-24 (D)
1994—Rams, 27-21 (LA)
1997—Broncos, 35-14 (D)
(RS Pts.—Broncos 169, Rams 149)
Franchise in Los Angeles prior to 1995

DENVER vs. *SAN DIEGO
RS: Broncos lead series, 42-35-1
1960—Chargers, 23-19 (D)
Chargers, 41-33 (LA)
1961—Chargers, 37-0 (SD)
Chargers, 19-16 (D)
1962—Broncos, 30-21 (D)
Broncos, 23-20 (SD)
1963—Broncos, 50-34 (D)
Chargers, 58-20 (SD)
1964—Chargers, 42-14 (SD)
Chargers, 31-20 (D)
1965—Chargers, 34-31 (SD)
Chargers, 33-21 (D)
1966—Chargers, 24-17 (SD)
Broncos, 20-17 (D)
1967—Chargers, 38-21 (D)
Chargers, 24-20 (SD)
1968—Chargers, 55-24 (SD)
Chargers, 47-23 (D)
1969—Broncos, 13-0 (D)
Chargers, 45-24 (SD)
1970—Chargers, 24-21 (SD)
Tie, 17-17 (D)
1971—Broncos, 20-16 (D)
Chargers, 45-17 (SD)
1972—Chargers, 37-14 (SD)
Broncos, 38-13 (D)
1973—Broncos, 30-19 (D)
Broncos, 42-28 (SD)
1974—Broncos, 27-7 (D)
Chargers, 17-0 (SD)
1975—Broncos, 27-17 (SD)
Broncos, 13-10 (D) OT
1976—Broncos, 26-0 (D)
Broncos, 17-0 (SD)
1977—Broncos, 17-14 (SD)
Broncos, 17-9 (D)
1978—Broncos, 27-14 (D)
Chargers, 23-0 (SD)
1979—Broncos, 7-0 (D)
Chargers, 17-7 (SD)
1980—Chargers, 30-13 (D)
Broncos, 20-13 (SD)
1981—Broncos, 42-24 (D)
Chargers, 34-17 (SD)
1982—Chargers, 23-3 (D)
Chargers, 30-20 (SD)
1983—Broncos, 14-6 (D)
Chargers, 31-7 (SD)
1984—Broncos, 16-13 (SD)
Broncos, 16-13 (D)
1985—Chargers, 30-10 (SD)
Broncos, 30-24 (D) OT
1986—Broncos, 31-14 (SD)
Chargers, 9-3 (D)
1987—Broncos, 31-17 (SD)
Broncos, 24-0 (D)
1988—Broncos, 34-3 (D)
Broncos, 12-0 (SD)
1989—Broncos, 16-10 (D)
Chargers, 19-16 (SD)
1990—Chargers, 19-7 (SD)
Broncos, 20-10 (D)
1991—Broncos, 27-19 (D)
Broncos, 17-14 (SD)
1992—Broncos, 21-13 (D)
Chargers, 24-21 (SD)
1993—Broncos, 34-17 (D)
Chargers, 13-10 (SD)
1994—Chargers, 37-34 (D)
Broncos, 20-15 (SD)
1995—Chargers, 17-6 (SD)
Broncos, 30-27 (D)
1996—Broncos, 28-17 (D)
Chargers, 16-10 (SD)
1997—Broncos, 38-28 (SD)
Broncos, 38-3 (D)
1998—Broncos, 27-10 (D)
Broncos, 31-16 (SD)
(RS Pts.—Chargers 1,630, Broncos 1,617)
Franchise in Los Angeles prior to 1961

DENVER vs. SAN FRANCISCO
RS: Series tied, 4-4
PS: 49ers lead series, 1-0
1970—49ers, 19-14 (SF)
1973—49ers, 36-34 (D)
1979—Broncos, 38-28 (SF)
1982—Broncos, 24-21 (D)
1985—Broncos, 17-16 (D)
1988—Broncos, 16-13 (SF) OT
1989—*49ers, 55-10 (New Orleans)
1994—49ers, 42-19 (SF)
1997—49ers, 34-17 (SF)
(RS Pts.—49ers 209, Broncos 179)
(PS Pts.—49ers 55, Broncos 10)
Super Bowl XXIV

DENVER vs. SEATTLE
RS: Broncos lead series, 28-15
PS: Seahawks lead series, 1-0
1977—Broncos, 24-13 (S)
1978—Broncos, 28-7 (D)
Broncos, 20-17 (S) OT
1979—Broncos, 37-34 (D)
Seahawks, 28-23 (S)
1980—Broncos, 36-20 (D)
Broncos, 25-17 (S)
1981—Seahawks, 13-10 (S)
Broncos, 23-13 (D)
1982—Seahawks, 17-10 (D)
Seahawks, 13-11 (S)
1983—Seahawks, 27-19 (S)
Broncos, 38-27 (D)
*Seahawks, 31-7 (S)
1984—Seahawks, 27-24 (D)
Broncos, 31-14 (S)
1985—Broncos, 13-10 (D) OT
Broncos, 27-24 (S)
1986—Broncos, 20-13 (D)
Seahawks, 41-16 (S)
1987—Broncos, 40-17 (D)
Seahawks, 28-21 (S)
1988—Seahawks, 21-14 (D)
Seahawks, 42-14 (S)
1989—Broncos, 24-21 (S) OT
Broncos, 41-14 (D)
1990—Broncos, 34-31 (D) OT
Seahawks, 17-12 (S)
1991—Broncos, 16-10 (D)
Seahawks, 13-10 (S)
1992—Seahawks, 16-13 (S) OT
Broncos, 10-6 (D)
1993—Broncos, 28-17 (D)
Broncos, 17-9 (S)
1994—Broncos, 16-9 (S)
Broncos, 17-10 (D)
1995—Seahawks, 27-10 (S)
Seahawks, 31-27 (D)
1996—Broncos, 30-20 (S)
Broncos, 34-7 (D)
1997—Broncos, 35-14 (S)
Broncos, 30-27 (D)
1998—Broncos, 21-16 (S)
Broncos, 28-21 (D)
(RS Pts.—Broncos 977, Seahawks 819)
(PS Pts.—Seahawks 31, Broncos 7)
AFC First-Round Playoff

DENVER vs. TAMPA BAY
RS: Broncos lead series, 3-1
1976—Broncos, 48-13 (D)
1981—Broncos, 24-7 (TB)
1993—Buccaneers, 17-10 (D)
1996—Broncos, 27-23 (D)
(RS Pts.—Broncos 109, Buccaneers 60)

DENVER vs. *TENNESSEE
RS: Titans lead series, 20-11-1
PS: Broncos lead series, 2-1
1960—Oilers, 45-25 (D)
Oilers, 20-10 (H)
1961—Oilers, 55-14 (D)
Oilers, 45-14 (H)
1962—Broncos, 20-10 (D)
Oilers, 34-17 (H)
1963—Oilers, 20-14 (H)
Oilers, 33-24 (D)
1964—Oilers, 38-17 (D)
Oilers, 34-15 (H)
1965—Broncos, 28-17 (D)
Broncos, 31-21 (H)
1966—Oilers, 45-7 (H)
Broncos, 40-38 (D)
1967—Oilers, 10-6 (H)
Oilers, 20-18 (D)
1968—Oilers, 38-17 (H)
1969—Oilers, 24-21 (H)
Tie, 20-20 (D)
1970—Oilers, 31-21 (H)
1972—Broncos, 30-17 (D)
1973—Broncos, 48-20 (H)
1974—Broncos, 37-14 (D)
1976—Oilers, 17-3 (H)
1977—Broncos, 24-14 (H)
1979—**Oilers, 13-7 (H)
1980—Oilers, 20-16 (D)
1983—Broncos, 26-14 (H)
1985—Broncos, 31-20 (D)
1987—Oilers, 40-10 (D)
***Broncos, 34-10 (D)
1991—Oilers, 42-14 (H)
***Broncos, 26-24 (D)
1992—Broncos, 27-21 (D)
1995—Oilers, 42-33 (H)
(RS Pts.—Titans 879, Broncos 678)
(PS Pts.—Broncos 67, Titans 47)
Franchise in Houston prior to 1997; known as the Oilers prior to 1999
***AFC First-Round Playoff*
****AFC Divisional Playoff*

DENVER vs. WASHINGTON
RS: Broncos lead series, 5-3
PS: Redskins lead series, 1-0
1970—Redskins, 19-3 (D)
1974—Redskins, 30-3 (W)
1980—Broncos, 20-17 (D)
1986—Broncos, 31-30 (D)
1987—*Redskins, 42-10 (San Diego)
1989—Broncos, 14-10 (W)
1992—Redskins, 34-3 (W)
1995—Broncos, 38-31 (D)
1998—Broncos, 38-16 (W)
(RS Pts.—Redskins 187, Broncos 150)
(PS Pts.—Redskins 42, Broncos 10)
Super Bowl XXII

DETROIT vs. ARIZONA
RS: Lions lead series, 27-18-5;
See Arizona vs. Detroit

DETROIT vs. ATLANTA
RS: Lions lead series, 20-7;
See Atlanta vs. Detroit

DETROIT vs. BALTIMORE
RS: Ravens lead series, 1-0;
See Baltimore vs. Detroit

DETROIT vs. BUFFALO
RS: Lions lead series, 3-2-1;
See Buffalo vs. Detroit

DETROIT vs. CHICAGO
RS: Bears lead series, 77-56-5;
See Chicago vs. Detroit

DETROIT vs. CINCINNATI
RS: Bengals lead series, 4-3;
See Cincinnati vs. Detroit

DETROIT vs. CLEVELAND
RS: Lions lead series, 12-3
PS: Lions lead series, 3-1;
See Cleveland vs. Detroit

DETROIT vs. DALLAS
RS: Cowboys lead series, 7-6
PS: Series tied, 1-1;
See Dallas vs. Detroit

DETROIT vs. DENVER
RS: Broncos lead series, 4-3;
See Denver vs. Detroit

***DETROIT vs. GREEN BAY**
RS: Packers lead series, 70-60-7
PS: Packers lead series, 2-0
1930—Packers, 47-13 (GB)
Tie, 6-6 (P)
1932—Packers, 15-10 (GB)
Spartans, 19-0 (P)
1933—Packers, 17-0 (GB)
Spartans, 7-0 (P)
1934—Lions, 3-0 (GB)
Packers, 3-0 (D)
1935—Packers, 13-9 (Mil)
Packers, 31-7 (GB)
Lions, 20-10 (D)
1936—Packers, 20-18 (GB)
Packers, 26-17 (D)
1937—Packers, 26-6 (GB)
Packers, 14-13 (D)
1938—Lions, 17-7 (GB)
Packers, 28-7 (D)
1939—Packers, 26-7 (GB)
Packers, 12-7 (D)
1940—Lions, 23-14 (GB)
Packers, 50-7 (D)
1941—Packers, 23-0 (GB)
Packers, 24-7 (D)
1942—Packers, 38-7 (Mil)
Packers, 28-7 (D)
1943—Packers, 35-14 (GB)
Packers, 27-6 (D)
1944—Packers, 27-6 (Mil)
Packers, 14-0 (D)
1945—Packers, 57-21 (Mil)
Lions, 14-3 (D)
1946—Packers, 10-7 (Mil)
Packers, 9-0 (D)
1947—Packers, 34-17 (GB)
Packers, 35-14 (D)
1948—Packers, 33-21 (GB)
Lions, 24-20 (D)
1949—Packers, 16-14 (Mil)
Lions, 21-7 (D)
1950—Lions, 45-7 (GB)
Lions, 24-21 (D)
1951—Lions, 24-17 (GB)

Lions, 52-35 (D)
1952—Lions, 52-17 (GB)
Lions, 48-24 (D)
1953—Lions, 14-7 (GB)
Lions, 34-15 (D)
1954—Lions, 21-17 (GB)
Lions, 28-24 (D)
1955—Packers, 20-17 (GB)
Lions, 24-10 (D)
1956—Lions, 20-16 (GB)
Packers, 24-20 (D)
1957—Lions, 24-14 (GB)
Lions, 18-6 (D)
1958—Tie, 13-13 (GB)
Lions, 24-14 (D)
1959—Packers, 28-10 (GB)
Packers, 24-17 (D)
1960—Packers, 28-9 (GB)
Lions, 23-10 (D)
1961—Lions, 17-13 (Mil)
Packers, 17-9 (D)
1962—Packers, 9-7 (GB)
Lions, 26-14 (D)
1963—Packers, 31-10 (Mil)
Tie, 13-13 (D)
1964—Packers, 14-10 (D)
Packers, 30-7 (GB)
1965—Packers, 31-21 (D)
Lions, 12-7 (GB)
1966—Packers, 23-14 (GB)
Packers, 31-7 (D)
1967—Tie, 17-17 (GB)
Packers, 27-17 (D)
1968—Lions, 23-17 (GB)
Tie, 14-14 (D)
1969—Packers, 28-17 (D)
Lions, 16-10 (GB)
1970—Lions, 40-0 (GB)
Lions, 20-0 (D)
1971—Lions, 31-28 (D)
Tie, 14-14 (Mil)
1972—Packers, 24-23 (D)
Packers, 33-7 (GB)
1973—Tie, 13-13 (GB)
Lions, 34-0 (D)
1974—Packers, 21-19 (Mil)
Lions, 19-17 (D)
1975—Lions, 30-16 (Mil)
Lions, 13-10 (D)
1976—Packers, 24-14 (GB)
Lions, 27-6 (D)
1977—Lions, 10-6 (D)
Packers, 10-9 (GB)
1978—Packers, 13-7 (D)
Packers, 35-14 (Mil)
1979—Packers, 24-16 (Mil)
Packers, 18-13 (D)
1980—Lions, 29-7 (Mil)
Lions, 24-3 (D)
1981—Lions, 31-27 (D)
Packers, 31-17 (GB)
1982—Lions, 30-10 (GB)
Lions, 27-24 (D)
1983—Lions, 38-14 (D)
Lions, 23-20 (Mil) OT
1984—Packers, 41-9 (GB)
Lions, 31-28 (D)
1985—Packers, 43-10 (GB)
Packers, 26-23 (D)
1986—Lions, 21-14 (GB)
Packers, 44-40 (D)
1987—Lions, 19-16 (GB) OT
Packers, 34-33 (D)
1988—Lions, 19-9 (Mil)
Lions, 30-14 (D)
1989—Packers, 23-20 (Mil) OT
Lions, 31-22 (D)
1990—Packers, 24-21 (D)
Lions, 24-17 (GB)
1991—Lions, 23-14 (D)
Lions, 21-17 (GB)
1992—Packers, 27-13 (D)
Packers, 38-10 (Mil)
1993—Packers, 26-17 (Mil)
Lions, 30-20 (D)
**Packers, 28-24 (D)
1994—Packers, 38-30 (Mil)
Lions, 34-31 (D)
**Packers, 16-12 (GB)
1995—Packers, 30-21 (GB)
Lions, 24-16 (D)
1996—Packers, 28-18 (GB)
Packers, 31-3 (D)
1997—Lions, 26-15 (D)
Packers, 20-10 (GB)
1998—Packers, 38-19 (GB)
Lions, 27-20 (D)
(RS: Pts.—Packers 2,754, Lions 2,483)
(PS Pts.—Packers 44, Lions 36)
Franchise in Portsmouth prior to 1934 and known as the Spartans
***NFC First-Round Playoff*

DETROIT vs. *INDIANAPOLIS
RS: Lions lead series, 18-17-2
1953—Lions, 27-17 (B)
Lions, 17-7 (D)
1954—Lions, 35-0 (D)
Lions, 27-3 (B)
1955—Colts, 28-13 (B)
Lions, 24-14 (D)
1956—Lions, 31-14 (B)
Lions, 27-3 (D)
1957—Colts, 34-14 (B)
Lions, 31-27 (D)
1958—Colts, 28-15 (B)
Colts, 40-14 (D)
1959—Colts, 21-9 (B)
Colts, 31-24 (D)
1960—Lions, 30-17 (D)
Lions, 20-15 (B)
1961—Lions, 16-15 (B)
Colts, 17-14 (D)
1962—Lions, 29-20 (B)
Lions, 21-14 (D)
1963—Colts, 25-21 (D)
Colts, 24-21 (B)
1964—Colts, 34-0 (D)
Lions, 31-14 (B)
1965—Colts, 31-7 (B)
Tie, 24-24 (D)
1966—Colts, 45-14 (B)
Lions, 20-14 (D)
1967—Colts, 41-7 (B)
1968—Colts, 27-10 (D)
1969—Tie, 17-17 (B)
1973—Colts, 29-27 (D)
1977—Lions, 13-10 (B)
1980—Colts, 10-9 (D)
1985—Colts, 14-6 (I)
1991—Lions, 33-24 (I)
1997—Lions, 32-10 (D)
(RS Pts.—Colts 758, Lions 730)
Franchise in Baltimore prior to 1984

DETROIT vs. JACKSONVILLE
RS: Series tied, 1-1
1995—Lions, 44-0 (D)
1998—Jaguars, 37-22 (J)
(RS Pts.—Lions 66, Jaguars 37)

DETROIT vs. KANSAS CITY
RS: Chiefs lead series, 5-3
1971—Lions, 32-21 (D)
1975—Chiefs, 24-21 (KC) OT
1980—Chiefs, 20-17 (KC)
1981—Lions, 27-10 (D)
1987—Chiefs, 27-20 (D)
1988—Lions, 7-6 (KC)
1990—Chiefs, 43-24 (KC)
1996—Chiefs, 28-24 (D)
(RS Pts.—Chiefs 179, Lions 172)

DETROIT vs. MIAMI
RS: Dolphins lead series, 4-2
1973—Dolphins, 34-7 (M)
1979—Dolphins, 28-10 (D)
1985—Lions, 31-21 (D)
1991—Lions, 17-13 (D)
1994—Dolphins, 27-20 (M)
1997—Dolphins, 33-30 (M)
(RS Pts.—Dolphins 156, Lions 115)

DETROIT vs. MINNESOTA
RS: Vikings lead series, 46-27-2
1961—Lions, 37-10 (M)
Lions, 13-7 (D)
1962—Lions, 17-6 (M)
Lions, 37-23 (D)
1963—Lions, 28-10 (D)
Vikings, 34-31 (M)
1964—Lions, 24-20 (M)
Tie, 23-23 (D)
1965—Lions, 31-29 (M)
Vikings, 29-7 (D)
1966—Lions, 32-31 (M)
Vikings, 28-16 (D)
1967—Tie, 10-10 (M)
Lions, 14-3 (D)
1968—Vikings, 24-10 (M)
Vikings, 13-6 (D)
1969—Vikings, 24-10 (M)
Vikings, 27-0 (D)
1970—Vikings, 30-17 (D)
Vikings, 24-20 (M)
1971—Vikings, 16-13 (D)
Vikings, 29-10 (M)
1972—Vikings, 34-10 (D)
Vikings, 16-14 (M)
1973—Vikings, 23-9 (D)
Vikings, 28-7 (M)
1974—Vikings, 7-6 (D)
Lions, 20-16 (M)
1975—Vikings, 25-19 (M)
Lions, 17-10 (D)
1976—Vikings, 10-9 (D)
Vikings, 31-23 (M)
1977—Vikings, 14-7 (M)
Vikings, 30-21 (D)
1978—Vikings, 17-7 (M)
Lions, 45-14 (D)
1979—Vikings, 13-10 (D)
Vikings, 14-7 (M)
1980—Lions, 27-7 (D)
Vikings, 34-0 (M)
1981—Vikings, 26-24 (M)
Lions, 45-7 (D)
1982—Vikings, 34-31 (D)
1983—Vikings, 20-17 (M)
Lions, 13-2 (D)
1984—Vikings, 29-28 (D)
Lions, 16-14 (M)
1985—Vikings, 16-13 (M)
Lions, 41-21 (D)
1986—Lions, 13-10 (M)
Vikings, 24-10 (D)
1987—Vikings, 34-19 (M)
Vikings, 17-14 (D)
1988—Vikings, 44-17 (M)
Vikings, 23-0 (D)
1989—Vikings, 24-17 (M)
Vikings, 20-7 (D)
1990—Lions, 34-27 (M)
Vikings, 17-7 (D)
1991—Lions, 24-20 (D)
Lions, 34-14 (M)
1992—Lions, 31-17 (D)
Vikings, 31-14 (M)
1993—Lions, 30-27 (M)
Vikings, 13-0 (D)
1994—Vikings, 10-3 (M)
Lions, 41-19 (D)
1995—Vikings, 20-10 (M)
Lions, 44-38 (D)
1996—Vikings, 17-13 (M)
Vikings, 24-22 (D)
1997—Lions, 38-15 (D)
Lions, 14-13 (M)
1998—Vikings, 29-6 (M)
Vikings, 34-13 (D)
(RS Pts.—Vikings 1,543, Llons 1,367)

DETROIT vs. NEW ENGLAND
RS: Series tied, 3-3
1971—Lions, 34-7 (NE)
1976—Lions, 30-10 (D)
1979—Patriots, 24-17 (NE)
1985—Patriots, 23-6 (NE)
1993—Lions, 19-16 (NE) OT
1994—Patriots, 23-17 (D)
(RS Pts.—Lions 123, Patriots 103)

DETROIT vs. NEW ORLEANS
RS: Saints lead series, 8-6-1
1968—Tie, 20-20 (D)
1970—Saints, 19-17 (NO)
1972—Lions, 27-14 (D)
1973—Saints, 20-13 (NO)
1974—Lions, 19-14 (D)
1976—Saints, 17-16 (NO)
1977—Lions, 23-19 (D)
1979—Saints, 17-7 (NO)
1980—Lions, 24-13 (D)
1988—Saints, 22-14 (D)
1989—Lions, 21-14 (D)
1990—Lions, 27-10 (NO)
1992—Saints, 13-7 (D)
1993—Saints, 14-3 (NO)
1997—Saints, 35-17 (NO)
(RS Pts.—Saints 261, Lions 255)

***DETROIT vs. N.Y. GIANTS**
RS: Lions lead series, 18-17-1
PS: Lions lead series, 1-0
1930—Giants, 19-6 (P)
1931—Spartans, 14-6 (P)
Giants, 14-0 (NY)
1932—Spartans, 7-0 (P)
Spartans, 6-0 (NY)
1933—Spartans, 17-7 (P)
Giants, 13-10 (NY)
1934—Lions, 9-0 (D)
1935—**Lions, 26-7 (D)
1936—Giants, 14-7 (NY)
Lions, 38-0 (D)
1937—Lions, 17-0 (NY)
1939—Lions, 18-14 (D)
1941—Giants, 20-13 (NY)
1943—Tie, 0-0 (D)
1945—Giants, 35-14 (NY)
1947—Lions, 35-7 (D)
1949—Lions, 45-21 (NY)
1953—Lions, 27-16 (NY)
1955—Giants, 24-19 (D)
1958—Giants, 19-17 (D)
1962—Giants, 17-14 (NY)
1964—Lions, 26-3 (D)
1967—Lions, 30-7 (NY)
1969—Lions, 24-0 (D)
1972—Lions, 30-16 (D)
1974—Lions, 20-19 (D)
1976—Giants, 24-10 (NY)
1982—Giants, 13-6 (D)
1983—Lions, 15-9 (D)
1988—Giants, 30-10 (NY)
Giants, 13-10 (D) OT
1989—Giants, 24-14 (NY)
1990—Giants, 20-0 (NY)
1994—Lions, 28-25 (NY) OT
1996—Giants, 35-7 (D)
1997—Giants, 26-20 (D) OT
(RS Pts.—Lions 583, Giants 510)
(PS Pts.—Lions 26, Giants 7)
Franchise in Portsmouth prior to 1934 and known as the Spartans
***NFL Championship*

DETROIT vs. N.Y. JETS
RS: Lions lead series, 5-3
1972—Lions, 37-20 (D)
1979—Jets, 31-10 (NY)
1982—Jets, 28-13 (D)
1985—Lions, 31-20 (D)
1988—Jets, 17-10 (D)
1991—Lions, 34-20 (D)
1994—Lions, 18-7 (NY)
1997—Lions, 13-10 (D)
(RS Pts.—Lions 166, Jets 153)

DETROIT vs. *OAKLAND
RS: Raiders lead series, 6-2
1970—Lions, 28-14 (D)

ALL-TIME TEAM VS. TEAM RESULTS

1974—Raiders, 35-13 (O)
1978—Raiders, 29-17 (O)
1981—Lions, 16-0 (D)
1984—Raiders, 24-3 (D)
1987—Raiders, 27-7 (LA)
1990—Raiders, 38-31 (D)
1996—Raiders, 37-21 (O)
(RS Pts.—Raiders 204, Lions 136)
Franchise in Los Angeles from 1982-1994

***DETROIT vs. PHILADELPHIA**
RS: Lions lead series, 12-11-2
PS: Eagles lead series, 1-0
1933—Spartans, 25-0 (P)
1934—Lions, 10-0 (P)
1935—Lions, 35-0 (D)
1936—Lions, 23-0 (P)
1938—Eagles, 21-7 (D)
1940—Lions, 21-0 (P)
1941—Lions, 21-17 (D)
1945—Lions, 28-24 (D)
1948—Eagles, 45-21 (P)
1949—Eagles, 22-14 (D)
1951—Lions, 28-10 (P)
1954—Tie, 13-13 (D)
1957—Lions, 27-16 (P)
1960—Eagles, 28-10 (P)
1961—Eagles, 27-24 (D)
1965—Lions, 35-28 (P)
1968—Eagles, 12-0 (D)
1971—Eagles, 23-20 (D)
1974—Eagles, 28-17 (P)
1977—Lions, 17-13 (D)
1979—Eagles, 44-7 (P)
1984—Tie, 23-23 (D) OT
1986—Lions, 13-11 (P)
1995—**Eagles, 58-37 (P)
1996—Eagles, 24-17 (P)
1998—Eagles, 10-9 (P)
(RS Pts.—Lions 465, Eagles 439)
(PS Pts.—Eagles 58, Lions 37)
**Franchise in Portsmouth prior to 1934 and known as the Spartans*
***NFC First-Round Playoff*

DETROIT vs. *PITTSBURGH
RS: Lions lead series, 14-12-1
1934—Lions, 40-7 (D)
1936—Lions, 28-3 (D)
1937—Lions, 7-3 (D)
1938—Lions, 16-7 (D)
1940—Pirates, 10-7 (D)
1942—Steelers, 35-7 (D)
1946—Lions, 17-7 (D)
1947—Steelers, 17-10 (P)
1948—Lions, 17-14 (D)
1949—Steelers, 14-7 (P)
1950—Lions, 10-7 (D)
1952—Lions, 31-6 (P)
1953—Lions, 38-21 (D)
1955—Lions, 31-28 (P)
1956—Lions, 45-7 (D)
1959—Tie, 10-10 (P)
1962—Lions, 45-7 (D)
1966—Steelers, 17-3 (P)
1967—Steelers, 24-14 (D)
1969—Steelers, 16-13 (P)
1973—Steelers, 24-10 (P)
1983—Lions, 45-3 (D)
1986—Steelers, 27-17 (P)
1989—Steelers, 23-3 (D)
1992—Steelers, 17-14 (P)
1995—Steelers, 23-20 (P)
1998—Lions, 19-16 (D) OT
(RS Pts.—Lions 524, Steelers 393)
**Steelers known as Pirates prior to 1941*

DETROIT vs. *ST. LOUIS
RS: Rams lead series, 39-35-1
PS: Lions lead series, 1-0
1937—Lions, 28-0 (C)
Lions, 27-7 (D)
1938—Rams, 21-17 (C)
Lions, 6-0 (D)
1939—Lions, 15-7 (D)
Rams, 14-3 (C)
1940—Lions, 6-0 (D)
Rams, 24-0 (C)
1941—Lions, 17-7 (D)
Lions, 14-0 (C)
1942—Rams, 14-0 (D)
Rams, 27-7 (C)
1944—Rams, 20-17 (D)
Lions, 26-14 (C)
1945—Rams, 28-21 (D)
1946—Rams, 35-14 (LA)
Rams, 41-20 (D)
1947—Rams, 27-13 (D)
Rams, 28-17 (LA)
1948—Rams, 44-7 (LA)
Rams, 34-27 (D)
1949—Rams, 27-24 (LA)
Rams, 21-10 (D)
1950—Rams, 30-28 (D)
Rams, 65-24 (LA)
1951—Rams, 27-21 (D)
Lions, 24-22 (LA)
1952—Lions, 17-14 (LA)
Lions, 24-16 (D)
**Lions, 31-21 (D)
1953—Rams, 31-19 (D)
Rams, 37-24 (LA)
1954—Lions, 21-3 (D)
Lions, 27-24 (LA)
1955—Rams, 17-10 (D)
Rams, 24-13 (LA)
1956—Lions, 24-21 (D)
Lions, 16-7 (LA)
1957—Lions, 10-7 (D)
Rams, 35-17 (LA)
1958—Rams, 42-28 (D)
Lions, 41-24 (LA)
1959—Lions, 17-7 (LA)
Lions, 23-17 (D)
1960—Rams, 48-35 (LA)
Lions, 12-10 (D)
1961—Lions, 14-13 (D)
Lions, 28-10 (LA)
1962—Lions, 13-10 (D)
Lions, 12-3 (LA)
1963—Lions, 23-2 (LA)
Rams, 28-21 (D)
1964—Tie, 17-17 (LA)
Lions, 37-17 (D)
1965—Lions, 20-0 (D)
Lions, 31-7 (LA)
1966—Rams, 14-7 (D)
Rams, 23-3 (LA)
1967—Rams, 31-7 (D)
1968—Rams, 10-7 (LA)
1969—Lions, 28-0 (D)
1970—Lions, 28-23 (LA)
1971—Rams, 21-13 (D)
1972—Lions, 34-17 (LA)
1974—Rams, 16-13 (LA)
1975—Rams, 20-0 (D)
1976—Rams, 20-17 (D)
1980—Lions, 41-20 (LA)
1981—Rams, 20-13 (LA)
1982—Lions, 19-14 (LA)
1983—Rams, 21-10 (LA)
1986—Rams, 14-10 (LA)
1987—Rams, 37-16 (D)
1988—Rams, 17-10 (LA)
1991—Lions, 21-10 (D)
1993—Lions, 16-13 (LA)
(RS Pts.—Rams 1,436, Lions 1,340)
(PS Pts.—Lions 31, Rams 21)
**Franchise in Los Angeles prior to 1995 and in Cleveland prior to 1946*
***Conference Playoff*

DETROIT vs. SAN DIEGO
RS: Series tied, 3-3
1972—Lions, 34-20 (D)
1977—Lions, 20-0 (D)
1978—Lions, 31-14 (D)
1981—Chargers, 28-23 (SD)
1984—Chargers, 27-24 (SD)
1996—Chargers, 27-21 (SD)
(RS Pts.—Lions 153, Chargers 116)

DETROIT vs. SAN FRANCISCO
RS: 49ers lead series, 29-26-1
PS: Series tied, 1-1
1950—Lions, 24-7 (D)
49ers, 28-27 (SF)
1951—49ers, 20-10 (D)
49ers, 21-17 (SF)
1952—49ers, 17-3 (SF)
49ers, 28-0 (D)
1953—Lions, 24-21 (D)
Lions, 14-10 (SF)
1954—49ers, 37-31 (SF)
Lions, 48-7 (D)
1955—49ers, 27-24 (D)
49ers, 38-21 (SF)
1956—Lions, 20-17 (D)
Lions, 17-13 (SF)
1957—49ers, 35-31 (SF)
Lions, 31-10 (D)
*Lions, 31-27 (SF)
1958—49ers, 24-21 (SF)
Lions, 35-21 (D)
1959—49ers, 34-13 (D)
49ers, 33-7 (SF)
1960—49ers, 14-10 (D)
Lions, 24-0 (SF)
1961—49ers, 49-0 (D)
Tie, 20-20 (SF)
1962—Lions, 45-24 (D)
Lions, 38-24 (SF)
1963—Lions, 26-3 (D)
Lions, 45-7 (SF)
1964—Lions, 26-17 (SF)
Lions, 24-7 (D)
1965—49ers, 27-21 (D)
49ers, 17-14 (SF)
1966—49ers, 27-24 (SF)
49ers, 41-14 (D)
1967—Lions, 45-3 (SF)
1968—49ers, 14-7 (D)
1969—Lions, 26-14 (SF)
1970—Lions, 28-7 (D)
1971—49ers, 31-27 (SF)
1973—Lions, 30-20 (D)
1974—Lions, 17-13 (D)
1975—Lions, 28-17 (SF)
1977—49ers, 28-7 (SF)
1978—Lions, 33-14 (D)
1980—Lions, 17-13 (D)
1981—Lions, 24-17 (D)
1983—**49ers, 24-23 (SF)
1984—49ers, 30-27 (D)
1985—Lions, 23-21 (D)
1988—49ers, 20-13 (SF)
1991—49ers, 35-3 (SF)
1992—49ers, 24-6 (SF)
1993—49ers, 55-17 (D)
1994—49ers, 27-21 (D)
1995—Lions, 27-24 (D)
1996—49ers, 24-14 (SF)
1998—49ers, 35-13 (SF)
(RS Pts.—49ers 1,211, Lions 1,202)
(PS Pts.—Lions 54, 49ers 51)
**Conference Playoff*
***NFC Divisional Playoff*

DETROIT vs. SEATTLE
RS: Seahawks lead series, 4-3
1976—Lions, 41-14 (S)
1978—Seahawks, 28-16 (S)
1984—Seahawks, 38-17 (S)
1987—Seahawks, 37-14 (D)
1990—Seahawks, 30-10 (S)
1993—Lions, 30-10 (D)
1996—Lions, 17-16 (D)
(RS Pts.—Seahawks 173, Lions 145)

DETROIT vs. TAMPA BAY
RS: Lions lead series, 24-18
PS: Buccaneers lead series, 1-0
1977—Lions, 16-7 (D)
1978—Lions, 15-7 (TB)
Lions, 34-23 (D)
1979—Buccaneers, 31-16 (TB)
Buccaneers, 16-14 (D)
1980—Lions, 24-10 (TB)
Lions, 27-14 (D)
1981—Buccaneers, 28-10 (TB)
Buccaneers, 20-17 (D)
1982—Buccaneers, 23-21 (TB)
1983—Lions, 11-0 (TB)
Lions, 23-20 (D)
1984—Buccaneers, 21-17 (TB)
Lions, 13-7 (D) OT
1985—Lions, 30-9 (D)
Buccaneers, 19-16 (TB) OT
1986—Buccaneers, 24-20 (D)
Lions, 38-17 (TB)
1987—Buccaneers, 31-27 (D)
Lions, 20-10 (TB)
1988—Buccaneers, 23-20 (D)
Buccaneers, 21-10 (TB)
1989—Lions, 17-16 (TB)
Lions, 33-7 (D)
1990—Buccaneers, 38-21 (D)
Buccaneers, 23-20 (TB)
1991—Lions, 31-3 (D)
Buccaneers, 30-21 (TB)
1992—Buccaneers, 27-23 (D)
Lions, 38-7 (TB)
1993—Buccaneers, 27-10 (TB)
Lions, 23-0 (D)
1994—Buccaneers, 24-14 (TB)
Lions, 14-9 (D)
1995—Lions, 27-24 (D)
Lions, 37-10 (TB)
1996—Lions, 21-6 (D)
Lions, 27-0 (TB)
1997—Buccaneers, 24-17 (D)
Lions, 27-9 (TB)
*Buccaneers, 20-10 (TB)
1998—Lions, 27-6 (D)
Lions, 28-25 (TB)
(RS Pts—Lions 915, Buccaneers 696)
(PS Pts.—Buccaneers 20, Lions 10)
**NFC First-Round Playoff*

DETROIT vs. *TENNESSEE
RS: Titans lead series, 4-3
1971—Lions, 31-7 (H)
1975—Oilers, 24-8 (H)
1983—Oilers, 27-17 (H)
1986—Lions, 24-13 (D)
1989—Oilers, 35-31 (H)
1992—Oilers, 24-21 (D)
1995—Lions, 24-17 (H)
(RS Pts.—Lions 156, Titans 147)
**Franchise in Houston prior to 1997; known as Oilers prior to 1999*

***DETROIT vs. **WASHINGTON**
RS: Redskins lead series, 24-8
PS: Redskins lead series, 2-0
1932—Spartans, 10-0 (P)
1933—Spartans, 13-0 (B)
1934—Lions, 24-0 (D)
1935—Lions, 17-7 (B)
Lions, 14-0 (D)
1938—Redskins, 7-5 (D)
1939—Redskins, 31-7 (W)
1940—Redskins, 20-14 (D)
1942—Redskins, 15-3 (D)
1943—Redskins, 42-20 (W)
1946—Redskins, 17-16 (W)
1947—Lions, 38-21 (D)
1948—Redskins, 46-21 (W)
1951—Lions, 35-17 (D)
1956—Redskins, 18-17 (W)
1965—Lions, 14-10 (D)
1968—Redskins, 14-3 (W)
1970—Redskins, 31-10 (W)
1973—Redskins, 20-0 (D)
1976—Redskins, 20-7 (W)
1978—Redskins, 21-19 (D)
1979—Redskins, 27-24 (D)
1981—Redskins, 33-31 (W)
1982—***Redskins, 31-7 (W)
1983—Redskins, 38-17 (W)

1984—Redskins, 28-14 (W)
1985—Redskins, 24-3 (W)
1987—Redskins, 20-13 (W)
1990—Redskins, 41-38 (D)
1991—Redskins, 45-0 (W)
****Redskins, 41-10 (W)
1992—Redskins, 13-10 (W)
1995—Redskins, 36-30 (W) OT
1997—Redskins, 30-7 (W)
(RS Pts.—Redskins 692, Lions 494)
(PS Pts.—Redskins 72, Lions 17)
Franchise in Portsmouth prior to 1934 and known as the Spartans.
***Franchise in Boston prior to 1937*
****NFC First-Round Playoff*
*****NFC Championship*

GREEN BAY vs. ARIZONA
RS: Packers lead series, 39-21-4
PS: Packers lead series, 1-0;
See Arizona vs. Green Bay

GREEN BAY vs. ATLANTA
RS: Packers lead series, 10-9
PS: Packers lead series, 1-0;
See Atlanta vs. Green Bay

GREEN BAY vs. BALTIMORE
RS: Packers lead series, 1-0;
See Baltimore vs. Green Bay

GREEN BAY vs. BUFFALO
RS: Bills lead series, 5-2
See Buffalo vs. Green Bay

GREEN BAY vs. CAROLINA
RS: Packers lead series, 2-0
PS: Packers lead series, 1-0;
See Carolina vs. Green Bay

GREEN BAY vs. CHICAGO
RS: Bears lead series, 81-69-6
PS: Bears lead series, 1-0;
See Chicago vs. Green Bay

GREEN BAY vs. CINCINNATI
RS: Packers lead series, 5-4;
See Cincinnati vs. Green Bay

GREEN BAY vs. CLEVELAND
RS: Packers lead series, 8-6
PS: Packers lead series, 1-0;
See Cleveland vs. Green Bay

GREEN BAY vs. DALLAS
RS: Series tied, 9-9
PS: Cowboys lead series, 4-2;
See Dallas vs. Green Bay

GREEN BAY vs. DENVER
RS: Broncos lead series, 4-3-1
PS: Broncos lead series, 1-0;
See Denver vs. Green Bay

GREEN BAY vs. DETROIT
RS: Packers lead series, 70-60-7
PS: Packers lead series, 2-0;
See Detroit vs. Green Bay

GREEN BAY vs. *INDIANAPOLIS
RS: Colts lead series, 19-18-1
PS: Packers lead series, 1-0
1953—Packers, 37-14 (GB)
Packers, 35-24 (B)
1954—Packers, 7-6 (B)
Packers, 24-13 (Mil)
1955—Colts, 24-20 (Mil)
Colts, 14-10 (B)
1956—Packers, 38-33 (Mil)
Colts, 28-21 (B)
1957—Colts, 45-17 (Mil)
Packers, 24-21 (B)
1958—Colts, 24-17 (Mil)
Colts, 56-0 (B)
1959—Colts, 38-21 (B)
Colts, 28-24 (Mil)
1960—Packers, 35-21 (GB)
Colts, 38-24 (B)
1961—Packers, 45-7 (GB)
Colts, 45-21 (B)
1962—Packers, 17-6 (B)
Packers, 17-13 (GB)
1963—Packers, 31-20 (GB)
Packers, 34-20 (B)
1964—Colts, 21-20 (GB)
Colts, 24-21 (B)
1965—Packers, 20-17 (Mil)
Packers, 42-27 (B)
**Packers, 13-10 (GB) OT
1966—Packers, 24-3 (Mil)
Packers, 14-10 (B)
1967—Colts, 13-10 (B)
1968—Colts, 16-3 (GB)
1969—Colts, 14-6 (B)
1970—Colts, 13-10 (Mil)
1974—Packers, 20-13 (B)
1982—Tie, 20-20 (B) OT
1985—Colts, 37-10 (I)
1988—Colts, 20-13 (GB)
1991—Packers, 14-10 (Mil)
1997—Colts, 41-38 (I)
(RS Pts.—Colts 837, Packers 804)
(PS Pts.—Packers 13, Colts 10)
**Franchise in Baltimore prior to 1984*
***Conference Playoff*

GREEN BAY vs. JACKSONVILLE
RS: Packers lead series, 1-0
1995—Packers, 24-14 (J)
(RS Pts.—Packers 24, Jaguars 14)

GREEN BAY vs. KANSAS CITY
RS: Chiefs lead series, 5-1-1
PS: Packers lead series, 1-0
1966—*Packers, 35-10 (Los Angeles)
1973—Tie, 10-10 (Mil)
1977—Chiefs, 20-10 (KC)
1987—Packers, 23-3 (KC)
1989—Chiefs, 21-3 (GB)
1990—Chiefs, 17-3 (GB)
1993—Chiefs, 23-16 (KC)
1996—Chiefs, 27-20 (KC)
(RS Pts.—Chiefs 121, Packers 85)
(PS Pts.—Packers 35, Chiefs 10)
**Super Bowl I*

GREEN BAY vs. MIAMI
RS: Dolphins lead series, 8-1
1971—Dolphins, 27-6 (Mia)
1975—Dolphins, 31-7 (GB)
1979—Dolphins, 27-7 (Mia)
1985—Dolphins, 34-24 (GB)
1988—Dolphins, 24-17 (Mia)
1989—Dolphins, 23-20 (Mia)
1991—Dolphins, 16-13 (Mia)
1994—Dolphins, 24-14 (Mil)
1997—Packers, 23-18 (GB)
(RS Pts.—Dolphins 224, Packers 131)

GREEN BAY vs. MINNESOTA
RS: Vikings lead series, 38-36-1
1961—Packers, 33-7 (Minn)
Packers, 28-10 (Mil)
1962—Packers, 34-7 (GB)
Packers, 48-21 (Minn)
1963—Packers, 37-28 (Minn)
Packers, 28-7 (GB)
1964—Vikings, 24-23 (GB)
Packers, 42-13 (Minn)
1965—Packers, 38-13 (Minn)
Packers, 24-19 (GB)
1966—Vikings, 20-17 (GB)
Packers, 28-16 (Minn)
1967—Vikings, 10-7 (Mil)
Packers, 30-27 (Minn)
1968—Vikings, 26-13 (Mil)
Vikings, 14-10 (Minn)
1969—Vikings, 19-7 (Minn)
Vikings, 9-7 (Mil)
1970—Packers, 13-10 (Mil)
Vikings, 10-3 (Minn)
1971—Vikings, 24-13 (GB)
Vikings, 3-0 (Minn)
1972—Vikings, 27-13 (GB)
Packers, 23-7 (Minn)
1973—Vikings, 11-3 (Minn)
Vikings, 31-7 (GB)
1974—Vikings, 32-17 (GB)
Packers, 19-7 (Minn)
1975—Vikings, 28-17 (GB)
Vikings, 24-3 (Minn)
1976—Vikings, 17-10 (Mil)
Vikings, 20-9 (Minn)
1977—Vikings, 19-7 (Minn)
Vikings, 13-6 (GB)
1978—Vikings, 21-7 (Minn)
Tie, 10-10 (GB) OT
1979—Vikings, 27-21 (Minn) OT
Packers, 19-7 (Mil)
1980—Packers, 16-3 (GB)
Packers, 25-13 (Minn)
1981—Vikings, 30-13 (Mil)
Packers, 35-23 (Minn)
1982—Packers, 26-7 (Mil)
1983—Vikings, 20-17 (GB) OT
Packers, 29-21 (Minn)
1984—Packers, 45-17 (Mil)
Packers, 38-14 (Minn)
1985—Packers, 20-17 (Mil)
Packers, 27-17 (Minn)
1986—Vikings, 42-7 (Minn)
Vikings, 32-6 (GB)
1987—Packers, 23-16 (Minn)
Packers, 16-10 (Mil)
1988—Packers, 34-14 (Minn)
Packers, 18-6 (GB)
1989—Vikings, 26-14 (Minn)
Packers, 20-19 (Mil)
1990—Packers, 24-10 (Mil)
Vikings, 23-7 (Minn)
1991—Vikings, 35-21 (GB)
Packers, 27-7 (Minn)
1992—Vikings, 23-20 (GB) OT
Vikings, 27-7 (Minn)
1993—Vikings, 15-13 (Minn)
Vikings, 21-17 (Mil)
1994—Packers, 16-10 (GB)
Vikings, 13-10 (M) OT
1995—Packers, 38-21 (GB)
Vikings, 27-24 (M)
1996—Vikings, 30-21 (M)
Packers, 38-10 (GB)
1997—Packers, 38-32 (GB)
Packers, 27-11 (M)
1998—Vikings, 37-24 (GB)
Vikings, 28-14 (M)
(RS Pts.—Packers 1,409, Vikings 1,365)

GREEN BAY vs. NEW ENGLAND
RS: Series tied, 3-3
PS: Packers lead series, 1-0
1973—Patriots, 33-24 (NE)
1979—Packers, 27-14 (GB)
1985—Patriots, 26-20 (NE)
1988—Packers, 45-3 (Mil)
1994—Patriots, 17-16 (NE)
1996—*Packers, 35-21 (New Orleans)
1997—Packers, 28-10 (NE)
(RS Pts.—Packers 160, Patriots 103)
(PS Pts.—Packers 35, Patriots 21)
**Super Bowl XXXI*

GREEN BAY vs. NEW ORLEANS
RS: Packers lead series, 13-4
1968—Packers, 29-7 (Mil)
1971—Saints, 29-21 (Mil)
1972—Packers, 30-20 (NO)
1973—Packers, 30-10 (Mil)
1975—Saints, 20-19 (NO)
1976—Packers, 32-27 (Mil)
1977—Packers, 24-20 (NO)
1978—Packers, 28-17 (Mil)
1979—Packers, 28-19 (Mil)
1981—Packers, 35-7 (NO)
1984—Packers, 23-13 (NO)
1985—Packers, 38-14 (Mil)
1986—Saints, 24-10 (NO)
1987—Saints, 33-24 (NO)
1989—Packers, 35-34 (GB)
1993—Packers, 19-17 (NO)
1995—Packers, 34-23 (NO)
(RS Pts.—Packers 459, Saints 334)

GREEN BAY vs. N.Y. GIANTS
RS: Packers lead series, 23-20-2
PS: Packers lead series, 4-1
1928—Giants, 6-0 (GB)
Packers, 7-0 (NY)
1929—Packers, 20-6 (NY)
1930—Packers, 14-7 (GB)
Giants, 13-6 (NY)
1931—Packers, 27-7 (GB)
Packers, 14-10 (NY)
1932—Packers, 13-0 (GB)
Giants, 6-0 (NY)
1933—Giants, 10-7 (Mil)
Giants, 17-6 (NY)
1934—Packers, 20-6 (Mil)
Giants, 17-3 (NY)
1935—Packers, 16-7 (GB)
1936—Packers, 26-14 (NY)
1937—Giants, 10-0 (NY)
1938—Giants, 15-3 (NY)
*Giants, 23-17 (NY)
1939—*Packers, 27-0 (Mil)
1940—Giants, 7-3 (NY)
1942—Tie, 21-21 (NY)
1943—Packers, 35-21 (NY)
1944—Giants, 24-0 (NY)
*Packers, 14-7 (NY)
1945—Packers, 23-14 (NY)
1947—Tie, 24-24 (NY)
1948—Giants, 49-3 (Mil)
1949—Giants, 30-10 (GB)
1952—Packers, 17-3 (NY)
1957—Giants, 31-17 (GB)
1959—Giants, 20-3 (NY)
1961—Packers, 20-17 (Mil)
*Packers, 37-0 (GB)
1962—*Packers, 16-7 (NY)
1967—Packers, 48-21 (NY)
1969—Packers, 20-10 (Mil)
1971—Giants, 42-40 (GB)
1973—Packers, 16-14 (New Haven)
1975—Packers, 40-14 (Mil)
1980—Giants, 27-21 (NY)
1981—Packers, 27-14 (NY)
Packers, 26-24 (Mil)
1982—Packers, 27-19 (NY)
1983—Giants, 27-3 (NY)
1985—Packers, 23-20 (GB)
1986—Giants, 55-24 (NY)
1987—Giants, 20-10 (NY)
1992—Giants, 27-7 (NY)
1995—Packers, 14-6 (GB)
1998—Packers, 37-3 (NY)
(RS Pts.—Giants 755, Packers 741)
(PS Pts.—Packers 111, Giants 37)
**NFL Championship*

GREEN BAY vs. N.Y. JETS
RS: Jets lead series, 5-2
1973—Packers, 23-7 (Mil)
1979—Jets, 27-22 (GB)
1981—Jets, 28-3 (NY)
1982—Jets, 15-13 (NY)
1985—Jets, 24-3 (Mil)
1991—Jets, 19-16 (NY) OT
1994—Packers, 17-10 (GB)
(RS Pts.—Jets 130, Packers 97)

GREEN BAY vs. *OAKLAND
RS: Raiders lead series, 5-2
PS: Packers lead series, 1-0
1967—**Packers, 33-14 (Miami)
1972—Raiders, 20-14 (GB)
1976—Raiders, 18-14 (O)
1978—Raiders, 28-3 (GB)
1984—Raiders, 28-7 (LA)
1987—Raiders, 20-0 (GB)
1990—Packers, 29-16 (LA)
1993—Packers, 28-0 (GB)
(RS Pts.—Raiders 130, Packers 95)
(PS Pts.—Packers 33, Raiders 14)
**Franchise in Los Angeles from 1982-1994*
***Super Bowl II*

GREEN BAY vs. PHILADELPHIA
RS: Packers lead series, 21-9
PS: Eagles lead series, 1-0
1933—Packers, 35-9 (GB)
Packers, 10-0 (P)

1934—Packers, 19-6 (GB)
1935—Packers, 13-6 (P)
1937—Packers, 37-7 (Mil)
1939—Packers, 23-16 (P)
1940—Packers, 27-20 (GB)
1942—Packers, 7-0 (P)
1946—Packers, 19-7 (P)
1947—Eagles, 28-14 (P)
1951—Packers, 37-24 (GB)
1952—Packers, 12-10 (Mil)
1954—Packers, 37-14 (P)
1958—Packers, 38-35 (GB)
1960—*Eagles, 17-13 (P)
1962—Packers, 49-0 (P)
1968—Packers, 30-13 (GB)
1970—Packers, 30-17 (Mil)
1974—Eagles, 36-14 (P)
1976—Packers, 28-13 (GB)
1978—Eagles, 10-3 (P)
1979—Eagles, 21-10 (GB)
1987—Packers, 16-10 (GB) OT
1990—Eagles, 31-0 (P)
1991—Eagles, 20-3 (GB)
1992—Packers, 27-24 (Mil)
1993—Eagles, 20-17 (GB)
1994—Eagles, 13-7 (P)
1996—Packers, 39-13 (GB)
1997—Eagles, 10-9 (P)
1998—Packers, 24-16 (GB)
(RS Pts.—Packers 634, Eagles 449)
(PS Pts.—Eagles 17, Packers 13)
NFL Championship

GREEN BAY vs. *PITTSBURGH
RS: Packers lead series, 18-12
1933—Packers, 47-0 (GB)
1935—Packers, 27-0 (GB)
Packers, 34-14 (P)
1936—Packers, 42-10 (Mil)
1938—Packers, 20-0 (GB)
1940—Packers, 24-3 (Mil)
1941—Packers, 54-7 (P)
1942—Packers, 24-21 (Mil)
1946—Packers, 17-7 (GB)
1947—Steelers, 18-17 (Mil)
1948—Steelers, 38-7 (P)
1949—Steelers, 30-7 (Mil)
1951—Packers, 35-33 (Mil)
Steelers, 28-7 (P)
1953—Steelers, 31-14 (P)
1954—Steelers, 21-20 (GB)
1957—Packers, 27-10 (P)
1960—Packers, 19-13 (P)
1963—Packers, 33-14 (Mil)
1965—Packers, 41-9 (P)
1967—Steelers, 24-17 (GB)
1969—Packers, 38-34 (P)
1970—Packers, 20-12 (P)
1975—Steelers, 16-13 (Mil)
1980—Steelers, 22-20 (P)
1983—Steelers, 25-21 (GB)
1986—Steelers, 27-3 (P)
1992—Packers, 17-3 (GB)
1995—Packers, 24-19 (GB)
1998—Steelers, 27-20 (P)
(RS Pts.—Packers 709, Steelers 516)
Steelers known as Pirates prior to 1941

GREEN BAY vs. *ST. LOUIS
RS: Rams lead series, 43-39-2
PS: Packers lead series, 1-0
1937—Packers, 35-10 (C)
Packers, 35-7 (GB)
1938—Packers, 26-17 (GB)
Packers, 28-7 (C)
1939—Rams, 27-24 (GB)
Packers, 7-6 (C)
1940—Packers, 31-14 (GB)
Tie, 13-13 (C)
1941—Packers, 24-7 (Mil)
Packers, 17-14 (C)
1942—Packers, 45-28 (GB)
Packers, 30-12 (C)
1944—Packers, 30-21 (GB)
Packers, 42-7 (C)
1945—Rams, 27-14 (GB)
Rams, 20-7 (C)
1946—Rams, 21-17 (Mil)
Rams, 38-17 (LA)
1947—Packers, 17-14 (Mil)
Packers, 30-10 (LA)
1948—Packers, 16-0 (GB)
Rams, 24-10 (LA)
1949—Rams, 48-7 (GB)
Rams, 35-7 (LA)
1950—Rams, 45-14 (Mil)
Rams, 51-14 (LA)
1951—Rams, 28-0 (Mil)
Rams, 42-14 (LA)
1952—Rams, 30-28 (Mil)
Rams, 45-27 (LA)
1953—Rams, 38-20 (Mil)
Rams, 33-17 (LA)
1954—Packers, 35-17 (Mil)
Rams, 35-27 (LA)
1955—Packers, 30-28 (Mil)
Rams, 31-17 (LA)
1956—Packers, 42-17 (Mil)
Rams, 49-21 (LA)
1957—Rams, 31-27 (Mil)
Rams, 42-17 (LA)
1958—Rams, 20-7 (GB)
Rams, 34-20 (LA)
1959—Rams, 45-6 (Mil)
Packers, 38-20 (LA)
1960—Rams, 33-31 (Mil)
Packers, 35-21 (LA)
1961—Packers, 35-17 (GB)
Packers, 24-17 (LA)
1962—Packers, 41-10 (Mil)
Packers, 20-17 (LA)
1963—Packers, 42-10 (GB)
Packers, 31-14 (LA)
1964—Rams, 27-17 (Mil)
Tie, 24-24 (LA)
1965—Packers, 6-3 (Mil)
Rams, 21-10 (LA)
1966—Packers, 24-13 (GB)
Packers, 27-23 (LA)
1967—Rams, 27-24 (LA)
**Packers, 28-7 (Mil)
1968—Rams, 16-14 (Mil)
1969—Rams, 34-21 (LA)
1970—Rams, 31-21 (GB)
1971—Rams, 30-13 (LA)
1973—Rams, 24-7 (LA)
1974—Packers, 17-6 (Mil)
1975—Rams, 22-5 (LA)
1977—Rams, 24-6 (Mil)
1978—Rams, 31-14 (LA)
1980—Rams, 51-21 (LA)
1981—Rams, 35-23 (LA)
1982—Packers, 35-23 (Mil)
1983—Packers, 27-24 (Mil)
1984—Packers, 31-6 (Mil)
1985—Rams, 34-17 (LA)
1988—Rams, 34-7 (GB)
1989—Rams, 41-38 (LA)
1990—Packers, 36-24 (GB)
1991—Rams, 23-21 (LA)
1992—Packers, 28-13 (GB)
1993—Packers, 36-6 (Mil)
1994—Packers, 24-17 (GB)
1995—Rams, 17-14 (GB)
1996—Packers, 24-9 (StL)
1997—Packers, 17-7 (GB)
(RS Pts.—Rams 1,967, Packers 1,858)
(PS Pts.—Packers 28, Rams 7)
Franchise in Los Angeles prior to 1995 and in Cleveland prior to 1946
***Conference Championship*

GREEN BAY vs. SAN DIEGO
RS: Packers lead series, 5-1
1970—Packers, 22-20 (SD)
1974—Packers, 34-0 (GB)
1978—Packers, 24-3 (SD)
1984—Chargers, 34-28 (GB)
1993—Packers, 20-13 (SD)
1996—Packers, 42-10 (GB)
(RS Pts.—Packers 170, Chargers 80)

GREEN BAY vs. SAN FRANCISCO
RS: 49ers lead series, 25-23-1
PS: Packers lead series, 3-1
1950—Packers, 25-21 (GB)
49ers, 30-14 (SF)
1951—49ers, 31-19 (SF)
1952—49ers, 24-14 (SF)
1953—49ers, 37-7 (Mil)
49ers, 48-14 (SF)
1954—49ers, 23-17 (Mil)
49ers, 35-0 (SF)
1955—Packers, 27-21 (Mil)
Packers, 28-7 (SF)
1956—49ers, 17-16 (GB)
49ers, 38-20 (SF)
1957—49ers, 24-14 (Mil)
49ers, 27-20 (SF)
1958—49ers, 33-12 (Mil)
49ers, 48-21 (SF)
1959—Packers, 21-20 (GB)
Packers, 36-14 (SF)
1960—Packers, 41-14 (Mil)
Packers, 13-0 (SF)
1961—Packers, 30-10 (GB)
49ers, 22-21 (SF)
1962—Packers, 31-13 (Mil)
Packers, 31-21 (SF)
1963—Packers, 28-10 (Mil)
Packers, 21-17 (SF)
1964—Packers, 24-14 (Mil)
49ers, 24-14 (SF)
1965—Packers, 27-10 (GB)
Tie, 24-24 (SF)
1966—49ers, 21-20 (SF)
Packers, 20-7 (Mil)
1967—Packers, 13-0 (GB)
1968—49ers, 27-20 (SF)
1969—Packers, 14-7 (Mil)
1970—49ers, 26-10 (SF)
1972—Packers, 34-24 (Mil)
1973—49ers, 20-6 (SF)
1974—49ers, 7-6 (SF)
1976—49ers, 26-14 (GB)
1977—Packers, 16-14 (Mil)
1980—Packers, 23-16 (Mil)
1981—49ers, 13-3 (Mil)
1986—49ers, 31-17 (Mil)
1987—49ers, 23-12 (GB)
1989—Packers, 21-17 (SF)
1990—49ers, 24-20 (GB)
1995—*Packers, 27-17 (SF)
1996—Packers, 23-20 (GB) OT
*Packers, 35-14 (GB)
1997—**Packers, 23-10 (SF)
1998—Packers, 36-22 (GB)
***49ers, 30-27 (SF)
(RS Pts.—49ers 1,022, Packers 958)
(PS Pts.—Packers 112, 49ers 71)
NFC Divisional Playoff
***NFC Championship*
****NFC First-Round Playoff*

GREEN BAY vs. SEATTLE
RS: Packers lead series, 4-3
1976—Packers, 27-20 (Mil)
1978—Packers, 45-28 (Mil)
1981—Packers, 34-24 (GB)
1984—Seahawks, 30-24 (Mil)
1987—Seahawks, 24-13 (S)
1990—Seahawks, 20-14 (Mil)
1996—Packers, 31-10 (S)
(RS Pts.—Packers 188, Seahawks 156)

GREEN BAY vs. TAMPA BAY
RS: Packers lead series, 25-14-1
PS: Packers lead series, 1-0
1977—Packers, 13-0 (TB)
1978—Packers, 9-7 (GB)
Packers, 17-7 (TB)
1979—Buccaneers, 21-10 (GB)
Buccaneers, 21-3 (TB)
1980—Tie, 14-14 (TB) OT
Buccaneers, 20-17 (Mil)
1981—Buccaneers, 21-10 (GB)
Buccaneers, 37-3 (TB)
1983—Packers, 55-14 (GB)
Packers, 12-9 (TB) OT
1984—Buccaneers, 30-27 (TB) OT
Packers, 27-14 (GB)
1985—Packers, 21-0 (GB)
Packers, 20-17 (TB)
1986—Packers, 31-7 (Mil)
Packers, 21-7 (TB)
1987—Buccaneers, 23-17 (Mil)
1988—Buccaneers, 13-10 (GB)
Buccaneers, 27-24 (TB)
1989—Buccaneers, 23-21 (GB)
Packers, 17-16 (TB)
1990—Buccaneers, 26-14 (TB)
Packers, 20-10 (Mil)
1991—Packers, 15-13 (GB)
Packers, 27-0 (TB)
1992—Buccaneers, 31-3 (TB)
Packers, 19-14 (Mil)
1993—Packers, 37-14 (TB)
Packers, 13-10 (GB)
1994—Packers, 30-3 (GB)
Packers, 34-19 (TB)
1995—Packers, 35-13 (GB)
Buccaneers, 13-10 (TB) OT
1996—Packers, 34-3 (TB)
Packers, 13-7 (GB)
1997—Packers, 21-16 (GB)
Packers, 17-6 (TB)
*Packers, 21-7 (GB)
1998—Packers, 23-15 (GB)
Buccaneers, 24-22 (TB)
(RS Pts.—Packers 786, Buccaneers 585)
(PS Pts.—Packers 21, Buccaneers 7)
NFC Divisional Playoff

GREEN BAY vs. *TENNESSEE
RS: Packers lead series, 4-3
1972—Packers, 23-10 (H)
1977—Oilers, 16-10 (GB)
1980—Oilers, 22-3 (GB)
1983—Packers, 41-38 (H) OT
1986—Oilers, 31-3 (GB)
1992—Packers, 16-14 (H)
1998—Packers, 30-22 (GB)
(RS Pts.—Titans 153, Packers 126)
Franchise in Houston prior to 1997; known as Oilers prior to 1999

GREEN BAY vs. *WASHINGTON
RS: Packers lead series, 13-12-1
PS: Series tied, 1-1
1932—Packers, 21-0 (B)
1933—Tie, 7-7 (GB)
Redskins, 20-7 (B)
1934—Packers, 10-0 (B)
1936—Packers, 31-2 (GB)
Packers, 7-3 (B)
**Packers, 21-6 (New York)
1937—Redskins, 14-6 (W)
1939—Packers, 24-14 (Mil)
1941—Packers, 22-17 (W)
1943—Redskins, 33-7 (Mil)
1946—Packers, 20-7 (W)
1947—Packers, 27-10 (Mil)
1948—Redskins, 23-7 (Mil)
1949—Redskins, 30-0 (W)
1950—Packers, 35-21 (Mil)
1952—Packers, 35-20 (Mil)
1958—Redskins, 37-21 (W)
1959—Packers, 21-0 (GB)
1968—Packers, 27-7 (W)
1972—Redskins, 21-16 (W)
***Redskins, 16-3 (W)
1974—Redskins, 17-6 (GB)
1977—Redskins, 10-9 (W)
1979—Redskins, 38-21 (W)
1983—Packers, 48-47 (GB)
1986—Redskins, 16-7 (GB)
1988—Redskins, 20-17 (Mil)
(RS Pts.—Packers 459, Redskins 434)
(PS Pts.—Packers 24, Redskins 22)
Franchise in Boston prior to 1937 and

known as Braves prior to 1933
***NFL Championship*
****NFC Divisional Playoff*

INDIANAPOLIS vs. ARIZONA
RS: Series tied, 6-6;
See Arizona vs. Indianapolis
INDIANAPOLIS vs. ATLANTA
RS: Colts lead series, 10-1;
See Atlanta vs. Indianapolis
INDIANAPOLIS vs. BALTIMORE
RS: Series tied, 1-1;
See Baltimore vs. Indianapolis
INDIANAPOLIS vs. BUFFALO
RS: Bills lead series, 33-23-1;
See Buffalo vs. Indianapolis
INDIANAPOLIS vs. CAROLINA
RS: Panthers lead series, 2-0;
See Carolina vs. Indianapolis
INDIANAPOLIS vs. CHICAGO
RS: Colts lead series, 21-16;
See Chicago vs. Indianapolis
INDIANAPOLIS vs. CINCINNATI
RS: Colts lead series, 10-8
PS: Colts lead series, 1-0;
See Cincinnati vs. Indianapolis
INDIANAPOLIS vs. CLEVELAND
RS: Browns lead series, 13-7
PS: Series tied, 2-2;
See Cleveland vs. Indianapolis
INDIANAPOLIS vs. DALLAS
RS: Cowboys lead series, 7-3
PS: Colts lead series, 1-0;
See Dallas vs. Indianapolis
INDIANAPOLIS vs. DENVER
RS: Broncos lead series, 9-2;
See Denver vs. Indianapolis
INDIANAPOLIS vs. DETROIT
RS: Lions lead series, 18-17-2;
See Detroit vs. Indianapolis
INDIANAPOLIS vs. GREEN BAY
RS: Colts lead series, 19-18-1
PS: Packers lead series, 1-0;
See Green Bay vs. Indianapolis
INDIANAPOLIS vs. JACKSONVILLE
RS: Colts lead series, 1-0
1995—Colts, 41-31 (J)
(RS Pts.—Colts 41, Jaguars 31)
***INDIANAPOLIS vs. KANSAS CITY**
RS: Chiefs lead series, 6-5
PS: Colts lead series, 1-0
1970—Chiefs, 44-24 (B)
1972—Chiefs, 24-10 (KC)
1975—Colts, 28-14 (B)
1977—Colts, 17-6 (KC)
1979—Chiefs, 14-0 (KC)
Chiefs, 10-7 (B)
1980—Colts, 31-24 (KC)
Chiefs, 38-28 (B)
1985—Chiefs, 20-7 (KC)
1990—Colts, 23-19 (I)
1995—**Colts, 10-7 (KC)
1996—Colts, 24-19 (KC)
(RS Pts.—Chiefs 232, Colts 199)
(PS Pts.—Colts 10, Chiefs 7)
**Franchise in Baltimore prior to 1984*
***AFC Divisional Playoff*
***INDIANAPOLIS vs. MIAMI**
RS: Dolphins lead series, 39-19
PS: Dolphins lead series, 1-0
1970—Colts, 35-0 (B)
Dolphins, 34-17 (M)
1971—Dolphins, 17-14 (M)
Colts, 14-3 (B)
**Dolphins, 21-0 (M)
1972—Dolphins, 23-0 (B)
Dolphins, 16-0 (M)
1973—Dolphins, 44-0 (M)
Colts, 16-3 (B)
1974—Dolphins, 17-7 (M)
Dolphins, 17-16 (B)
1975—Colts, 33-17 (M)
Colts, 10-7 (B) OT
1976—Colts, 28-14 (B)
Colts, 17-16 (M)
1977—Colts, 45-28 (B)
Dolphins, 17-6 (M)
1978—Dolphins, 42-0 (B)
Dolphins, 26-8 (M)
1979—Dolphins, 19-0 (M)
Dolphins, 28-24 (B)
1980—Colts, 30-17 (M)
Dolphins, 24-14 (B)
1981—Dolphins, 31-28 (B)
Dolphins, 27-10 (M)
1982—Dolphins, 24-20 (M)
Dolphins, 34-7 (B)
1983—Dolphins, 21-7 (B)
Dolphins, 37-0 (M)
1984—Dolphins, 44-7 (M)
Dolphins, 35-17 (I)
1985—Dolphins, 30-13 (M)
Dolphins, 34-20 (I)
1986—Dolphins, 30-10 (M)
Dolphins, 17-13 (I)
1987—Dolphins, 23-10 (I)
Colts, 40-21 (M)
1988—Colts, 15-13 (I)
Colts, 31-28 (M)
1989—Dolphins, 19-13 (M)
Colts, 42-13 (I)
1990—Dolphins, 27-7 (I)
Dolphins, 23-17 (M)
1991—Dolphins, 17-6 (M)
Dolphins, 10-6 (I)
1992—Colts, 31-20 (M)
Dolphins, 28-0 (I)
1993—Dolphins, 24-20 (I)
Dolphins, 41-27 (M)
1994—Dolphins, 22-21 (M)
Colts, 10-6 (I)
1995—Colts, 27-24 (M) OT
Colts, 36-28 (I)
1996—Colts, 10-6 (I)
Dolphins, 37-13 (M)
1997—Dolphins, 16-10 (M)
Colts, 41-0 (I)
1998—Dolphins, 24-15 (I)
Dolphins, 27-14 (M)
(RS Pts.—Dolphins 1,290, Colts 948)
(PS Pts.—Dolphins 21, Colts 0)
**Franchise in Baltimore prior to 1984*
***AFC Championship*
***INDIANAPOLIS vs. MINNESOTA**
RS: Colts lead series, 11-7-1
PS: Colts lead series, 1-0
1961—Colts, 34-33 (B)
Vikings, 28-20 (M)
1962—Colts, 34-7 (M)
Colts, 42-17 (B)
1963—Colts, 37-34 (M)
Colts, 41-10 (B)
1964—Vikings, 34-24 (M)
Colts, 17-14 (B)
1965—Colts, 35-16 (B)
Colts, 41-21 (M)
1966—Colts, 38-23 (M)
Colts, 20-17 (B)
1967—Tie, 20-20 (M)
1968—Colts, 21-9 (B)
**Colts, 24-14 (B)
1969—Vikings, 52-14 (M)
1971—Vikings, 10-3 (M)
1982—Vikings, 13-10 (M)
1988—Vikings, 12-3 (M)
1997—Vikings, 39-28 (M)
(RS Pts.—Colts 482, Vikings 409)
(PS Pts.—Colts 24, Vikings 14)
**Franchise in Baltimore prior to 1984*
***Conference Championship*
***INDIANAPOLIS vs. **NEW ENGLAND**
RS: Patriots lead series, 35-22
1970—Colts, 14-6 (Bos)
Colts, 27-3 (Balt)
1971—Colts, 23-3 (NE)
Patriots, 21-17 (Balt)
1972—Colts, 24-17 (NE)
Colts, 31-0 (Balt)
1973—Patriots, 24-16 (NE)
Colts, 18-13 (Balt)
1974—Patriots, 42-3 (NE)
Patriots, 27-17 (Balt)
1975—Patriots, 21-10 (NE)
Colts, 34-21 (Balt)
1976—Colts, 27-13 (NE)
Patriots, 21-14 (Balt)
1977—Patriots, 17-3 (NE)
Colts, 30-24 (Balt)
1978—Colts, 34-27 (NE)
Patriots, 35-14 (Balt)
1979—Colts, 31-26 (Balt)
Patriots, 50-21 (NE)
1980—Patriots, 37-21 (Balt)
Patriots, 47-21 (NE)
1981—Colts, 29-28 (NE)
Colts, 23-21 (Balt)
1982—Patriots, 24-13 (Balt)
1983—Colts, 29-23 (NE) OT
Colts, 12-7 (Balt)
1984—Patriots, 50-17 (I)
Patriots, 16-10 (NE)
1985—Patriots, 34-15 (NE)
Patriots, 38-31 (I)
1986—Patriots, 33-3 (NE)
Patriots, 30-21 (I)
1987—Colts, 30-16 (I)
Patriots, 24-0 (NE)
1988—Patriots, 21-17 (NE)
Colts, 24-21 (I)
1989—Patriots, 23-20 (I) OT
Patriots, 22-16 (NE)
1990—Patriots, 16-14 (I)
Colts, 13-10 (NE)
1991—Patriots, 16-7 (I)
Patriots, 23-17 (NE) OT
1992—Patriots, 37-34 (I) OT
Colts, 6-0 (NE)
1993—Colts, 9-6 (I)
Patriots, 38-0 (NE)
1994—Patriots, 12-10 (I)
Patriots, 28-13 (NE)
1995—Colts, 24-10 (NE)
Colts, 10-7 (I)
1996—Patriots, 27-9 (I)
Patriots, 27-13 (NE)
1997—Patriots, 31-6 (I)
Patriots, 20-17 (NE)
1998—Patriots, 29-6 (NE)
Patriots, 21-16 (I)
(RS Pts.—Patriots 1,284, Colts 984)
**Franchise in Baltimore prior to 1984*
***Franchise in Boston prior to 1971*
***INDIANAPOLIS vs. NEW ORLEANS**
RS: Saints lead series, 4-3
1967—Colts, 30-10 (B)
1969—Colts, 30-10 (NO)
1973—Colts, 14-10 (B)
1986—Saints, 17-14 (I)
1989—Saints, 41-6 (NO)
1995—Saints, 17-14 (NO)
1998—Saints, 19-13 (I) OT
(RS Pts.—Colts 124, Saints 121)
**Franchise in Baltimore prior to 1984*
***INDIANAPOLIS vs. N.Y. GIANTS**
RS: Series tied, 5-5
PS: Colts lead series, 2-0
1954—Colts, 20-14 (B)
1955—Giants, 17-7 (NY)
1958—Giants, 24-21 (NY)
**Colts, 23-17 (NY) OT
1959—**Colts, 31-16 (B)
1963—Giants, 37-28 (B)
1968—Colts, 26-0 (NY)
1971—Colts, 31-7 (NY)
1975—Colts, 21-0 (NY)
1979—Colts, 31-7 (NY)
1990—Giants, 24-7 (I)
1993—Giants, 20-6 (NY)
(RS Pts.—Colts 198, Giants 150)
(PS Pts.—Colts 54, Giants 33)
**Franchise in Baltimore prior to 1984*
***NFL Championship*
***INDIANAPOLIS vs. N.Y. JETS**
RS: Colts lead series, 34-23
PS: Jets lead series, 1-0
1968—**Jets 16-7 (Miami)
1970—Colts, 29-22 (NY)
Colts, 35-20 (B)
1971—Colts, 22-0 (B)
Colts, 14-13 (NY)
1972—Jets, 44-34 (B)
Jets, 24-20 (NY)
1973—Jets, 34-10 (B)
Jets, 20-17 (NY)
1974—Colts, 35-20 (NY)
Jets, 45-38 (B)
1975—Colts, 45-28 (NY)
Colts, 52-19 (B)
1976—Colts, 20-0 (NY)
Colts, 33-16 (B)
1977—Colts, 20-12 (NY)
Colts, 33-12 (B)
1978—Jets, 33-10 (B)
Jets, 24-16 (NY)
1979—Colts, 10-8 (B)
Jets, 30-17 (NY)
1980—Colts, 17-14 (NY)
Colts, 35-21 (B)
1981—Jets, 41-14 (B)
Jets, 25-0 (NY)
1982—Jets, 37-0 (NY)
1983—Colts, 17-14 (NY)
Jets, 10-6 (B)
1984—Jets, 23-14 (I)
Colts, 9-5 (NY)
1985—Jets, 25-20 (NY)
Jets, 35-17 (I)
1986—Jets, 26-7 (I)
Jets, 31-16 (NY)
1987—Colts, 6-0 (I)
Colts, 19-14 (NY)
1988—Colts, 38-14 (I)
Jets, 34-16 (NY)
1989—Colts, 17-10 (NY)
Colts, 27-10 (I)
1990—Colts, 17-14 (I)
Colts, 29-21 (NY)
1991—Jets, 17-6 (I)
Colts, 28-27 (NY)
1992—Colts, 6-3 (I) OT
Colts, 10-6 (NY)
1993—Jets, 31-17 (I)
Colts, 9-6 (NY)
1994—Jets, 16-6 (NY)
Colts, 28-25 (I)
1995—Colts, 27-24 (NY) OT
Colts, 17-10 (I)
1996—Colts, 21-7 (NY)
Colts, 34-29 (I)
1997—Jets, 16-12 (I)
Colts, 22-14 (NY)
1998—Jets, 44-6 (NY)
Colts, 24-23 (I)
(RS Pts.—Jets 1,146, Colts 1,124)
(PS Pts.—Jets 16, Colts 7)
**Franchise in Baltimore prior to 1984*
***Super Bowl III*
***INDIANAPOLIS vs **OAKLAND**
RS: Raiders lead series, 5-2
PS: Series tied, 1-1
1970—***Colts, 27-17 (B)
1971—Colts, 37-14 (O)
1973—Raiders, 34-21 (B)
1975—Raiders, 31-20 (B)
1977—****Raiders, 37-31 (B) OT
1984—Raiders, 21-7 (LA)
1986—Colts, 30-24 (LA)
1991—Raiders, 16-0 (LA)
1995—Raiders, 30-17 (O)
(RS Pts.—Raiders 170, Colts 132)
(PS Pts.—Colts 58, Raiders 54)
**Franchise in Baltimore prior to 1984*

ALL-TIME TEAM VS. TEAM RESULTS

***Franchise in Los Angeles from 1982-1994*
****AFC Championship*
*****AFC Divisional Playoff*

***INDIANAPOLIS vs. PHILADELPHIA**
RS: Colts lead series, 7-6
1953—Eagles, 45-14 (P)
1965—Colts, 34-24 (B)
1967—Colts, 38-6 (P)
1969—Colts, 24-20 (B)
1970—Colts, 29-10 (B)
1974—Eagles, 30-10 (P)
1978—Eagles, 17-14 (B)
1981—Eagles, 38-13 (P)
1983—Colts, 22-21 (P)
1984—Eagles, 16-7 (P)
1990—Colts, 24-23 (P)
1993—Eagles, 20-10 (I)
1996—Colts, 37-10 (I)
(RS Pts.—Eagles 280, Colts 276)
**Franchise in Baltimore prior to 1984*

***INDIANAPOLIS vs. PITTSBURGH**
RS: Steelers lead series, 12-4
PS: Steelers lead series, 4-0
1957—Steelers, 19-13 (B)
1968—Colts, 41-7 (P)
1971—Colts, 34-21 (B)
1974—Steelers, 30-0 (P)
1975—**Steelers, 28-10 (P)
1976—**Steelers, 40-14 (B)
1977—Colts, 31-21 (B)
1978—Steelers, 35-13 (P)
1979—Steelers, 17-13 (P)
1980—Steelers, 20-17 (B)
1983—Steelers, 24-13 (B)
1984—Colts, 17-16 (I)
1985—Steelers, 45-3 (P)
1987—Steelers, 21-7 (P)
1991—Steelers, 21-3 (I)
1992—Steelers, 30-14 (P)
1994—Steelers, 31-21 (P)
1995—***Steelers, 20-16 (P)
1996—****Steelers, 42-14 (P)
1997—Steelers, 24-22 (P)
(RS Pts.—Steelers 382, Colts 262)
(PS Pts.—Steelers 130, Colts 54)
**Franchise in Baltimore prior to 1984*
***AFC Divisional Playoff*
****AFC Championship*
*****AFC First-Round Playoff*

***INDIANAPOLIS vs. **ST. LOUIS**
RS: Colts lead series, 21-16-2
1953—Rams, 21-13 (B)
Rams, 45-2 (LA)
1954—Rams, 48-0 (B)
Colts, 22-21 (LA)
1955—Tie, 17-17 (B)
Rams, 20-14 (LA)
1956—Colts, 56-21 (B)
Rams, 31-7 (LA)
1957—Colts, 31-14 (B)
Rams, 37-21 (LA)
1958—Colts, 34-7 (B)
Rams, 30-28 (LA)
1959—Colts, 35-21 (B)
Colts, 45-26 (LA)
1960—Colts, 31-17 (B)
Rams, 10-3 (LA)
1961—Colts, 27-24 (B)
Rams, 34-17 (LA)
1962—Colts, 30-27 (B)
Colts, 14-2 (LA)
1963—Rams, 17-16 (LA)
Colts, 19-16 (B)
1964—Colts, 35-20 (B)
Colts, 24-7 (LA)
1965—Colts, 35-20 (B)
Colts, 20-17 (LA)
1966—Colts, 17-3 (LA)
Rams, 23-7 (B)
1967—Tie, 24-24 (B)
Rams, 34-10 (LA)
1968—Colts, 27-10 (B)
Colts, 28-24 (LA)
1969—Rams, 27-20 (B)
Colts, 13-7 (LA)
1971—Colts, 24-17 (B)
1975—Rams, 24-13 (LA)
1986—Rams, 24-7 (I)
1989—Rams, 31-17 (LA)
1995—Colts, 21-18 (I)
(RS Pts.—Rams 836, Colts 824)
**Franchise in Baltimore prior to 1984*
***Franchise in Los Angeles prior to 1995*

***INDIANAPOLIS vs. SAN DIEGO**
RS: Chargers lead series, 12-6
PS: Colts lead series, 1-0
1970—Colts, 16-14 (SD)
1972—Chargers, 23-20 (B)
1976—Colts, 37-21 (SD)
1981—Chargers, 43-14 (B)
1982—Chargers, 44-26 (SD)
1984—Chargers, 38-10 (I)
1986—Chargers, 17-3 (I)
1987—Chargers, 16-13 (I)
Colts, 20-7 (SD)
1988—Colts, 16-0 (SD)
1989—Colts, 10-6 (I)
1992—Chargers, 34-14 (I)
Chargers, 26-0 (SD)
1993—Chargers, 31-0 (I)
1995—Chargers, 27-24 (I)
**Colts, 35-20 (SD)
1996—Chargers, 26-19 (I)
1997—Chargers, 35-19 (SD)
1998—Colts, 17-12 (I)
(RS Pts.—Chargers 420, Colts 278)
(PS Pts.—Colts 35, Chargers 20)
**Franchise in Baltimore prior to 1984*
***AFC First-Round Playoff*

***INDIANAPOLIS vs. SAN FRANCISCO**
RS: Colts lead series, 22-17
1953—49ers, 38-21 (B)
49ers, 45-14 (SF)
1954—Colts, 17-13 (B)
49ers, 10-7 (SF)
1955—Colts, 26-14 (B)
49ers, 35-24 (SF)
1956—49ers, 20-17 (B)
49ers, 30-17 (SF)
1957—Colts, 27-21 (B)
49ers, 17-13 (SF)
1958—Colts, 35-27 (B)
49ers, 21-12 (SF)
1959—Colts, 45-14 (B)
Colts, 34-14 (SF)
1960—49ers, 30-22 (B)
49ers, 34-10 (SF)
1961—Colts, 20-17 (B)
Colts, 27-24 (SF)
1962—49ers, 21-13 (B)
Colts, 22-3 (SF)
1963—Colts, 20-14 (SF)
Colts, 20-3 (B)
1964—Colts, 37-7 (B)
Colts, 14-3 (SF)
1965—Colts, 27-24 (B)
Colts, 34-28 (SF)
1966—Colts, 36-14 (B)
Colts, 30-14 (SF)
1967—Colts, 41-7 (B)
Colts, 26-9 (SF)
1968—Colts, 27-10 (B)
Colts, 42-14 (SF)
1969—49ers, 24-21 (B)
49ers, 20-17 (SF)
1972—49ers, 24-21 (SF)
1986—49ers, 35-14 (SF)
1989—49ers, 30-24 (I)
1995—Colts, 18-17 (I)
1998—49ers, 34-31 (SF)
(RS Pts.—Colts 923, 49ers 779)
**Franchise in Baltimore prior to 1984*

***INDIANAPOLIS vs. SEATTLE**
RS: Colts lead series, 4-3
1977—Colts, 29-14 (S)
1978—Colts, 17-14 (S)
1991—Seahawks, 31-3 (S)
1994—Colts, 17-15 (I)
Colts, 31-19 (S)
1997—Seahawks, 31-3 (I)
1998—Seahawks, 27-23 (S)
(RS Pts.—Seahawks 151, Colts 123)
**Franchise in Baltimore prior to 1984*

***INDIANAPOLIS vs. TAMPA BAY**
RS: Colts lead series, 5-4
1976—Colts, 42-17 (B)
1979—Buccaneers, 29-26 (B) OT
1985—Colts, 31-23 (TB)
1987—Colts, 24-6 (I)
1988—Colts, 35-31 (I)
1991—Buccaneers, 17-3 (TB)
1992—Colts, 24-14 (TB)
1994—Buccaneers, 24-10 (TB)
1997—Buccaneers, 31-28 (I)
(RS Pts.—Colts 223, Buccaneers 192)
**Franchise in Baltimore prior to 1984*

***INDIANAPOLIS vs. **TENNESSEE**
RS: Series tied, 7-7
1970—Colts, 24-20 (H)
1973—Oilers, 31-27 (B)
1976—Colts, 38-14 (B)
1979—Oilers, 28-16 (B)
1980—Oilers, 21-16 (H)
1983—Colts, 20-10 (B)
1984—Colts, 35-21 (H)
1985—Colts, 34-16 (I)
1986—Oilers, 31-17 (H)
1987—Colts, 51-27 (I)
1988—Oilers, 17-14 (I) OT
1990—Oilers, 24-10 (H)
1992—Oilers, 20-10 (I)
1994—Colts, 45-21 (I)
(RS Pts.—Colts 357, Titans 301)
**Franchise in Baltimore prior to 1984*
***Franchise in Houston prior to 1997; known as Oilers prior to 1999*

***INDIANAPOLIS vs. WASHINGTON**
RS: Colts lead series, 16-9
1953—Colts, 27-17 (B)
1954—Redskins, 24-21 (W)
1955—Redskins, 14-13 (B)
1956—Colts, 19-17 (B)
1957—Colts, 21-17 (W)
1958—Colts, 35-10 (B)
1959—Redskins, 27-24 (W)
1960—Colts, 20-0 (B)
1961—Colts, 27-6 (W)
1962—Colts, 34-21 (B)
1963—Colts, 36-20 (W)
1964—Colts, 45-17 (B)
1965—Colts, 38-7 (W)
1966—Colts, 37-10 (B)
1967—Colts, 17-13 (W)
1969—Colts, 41-17 (B)
1973—Redskins, 22-14 (W)
1977—Colts, 10-3 (B)
1978—Colts, 21-17 (B)
1981—Redskins, 38-14 (W)
1984—Redskins, 35-7 (I)
1990—Colts, 35-28 (I)
1993—Redskins, 30-24 (W)
1994—Redskins, 41-27 (I)
1996—Redskins, 31-16 (W)
(RS Pts.—Colts 623, Redskins 482)
**Franchise in Baltimore prior to 1984*

JACKSONVILLE vs. ATLANTA
RS: Jaguars lead series, 1-0;
See Atlanta vs. Jacksonville

JACKSONVILLE vs. BALTIMORE
RS: Jaguars lead series, 6-0;
See Baltimore vs. Jacksonville

JACKSONVILLE vs. BUFFALO
RS: Series tied, 1-1
PS: Jaguars lead series, 1-0;
See Buffalo vs. Jacksonville

JACKSONVILLE vs. CAROLINA
RS: Jaguars lead series, 1-0;
See Carolina vs. Jacksonville

JACKSONVILLE vs. CHICAGO
RS: Series tied, 1-1;
See Chicago vs. Jacksonville

JACKSONVILLE vs. CINCINNATI
RS: Series tied, 4-4;
See Cincinnati vs. Jacksonville

JACKSONVILLE vs. CLEVELAND
RS: Jaguars lead series, 2-0;
See Cleveland vs. Jacksonville

JACKSONVILLE vs. DALLAS
RS: Cowboys lead series, 1-0;
See Dallas vs. Jacksonville

JACKSONVILLE vs. DENVER
RS: Broncos lead series, 2-0
PS: Series tied, 1-1;
See Denver vs. Jacksonville

JACKSONVILLE vs. DETROIT
RS: Series tied, 1-1;
See Detroit vs. Jacksonville

JACKSONVILLE vs. GREEN BAY
RS: Packers lead series, 1-0;
See Green Bay vs. Jacksonville

JACKSONVILLE vs. INDIANAPOLIS
RS: Colts lead series, 1-0;
See Indianapolis vs. Jacksonville

JACKSONVILLE vs. KANSAS CITY
RS: Jaguars lead series, 2-0
1997—Jaguars, 24-10 (J)
1998—Jaguars, 21-16 (J)
(RS Pts.—Jaguars 45, Chiefs 26)

JACKSONVILLE vs. MIAMI
RS: Jaguars lead series, 1-0
1998—Jaguars, 28-21 (J)
(RS Pts.—Jaguars 28, Dolphins 21)

JACKSONVILLE vs. MINNESOTA
RS: Vikings lead series, 1-0
1998—Vikings, 50-10 (M)
(RS Pts.—Vikings 50, Jaguars 10)

JACKSONVILLE vs. NEW ENGLAND
RS: Patriots lead series, 2-0
PS: Series tied, 1-1
1996—Patriots, 28-25 (NE) OT
*Patriots, 20-6 (NE)
1997—Patriots, 26-20 (J)
1998—**Jaguars, 25-10 (J)
(RS Pts.—Patriots 54, Jaguars 45)
(PS Pts.—Jaguars 31, Patriots 30)
**AFC Championship*
***AFC First-Round Playoff*

JACKSONVILLE vs. NEW ORLEANS
RS: Saints lead series, 1-0
1996—Saints, 17-13 (NO)
(RS Pts.—Saints 17, Jaguars 13)

JACKSONVILLE vs. N.Y. GIANTS
RS: Jaguars lead series, 1-0
1997—Jaguars, 40-13 (J)
(RS Pts.—Jaguars 40, Giants 13)

JACKSONVILLE vs. N.Y. JETS
RS: Series tied, 1-1
PS: Jets lead series, 1-0
1995—Jets, 27-10 (NY)
1996—Jaguars, 21-17 (J)
1998—*Jets, 34-24 (NY)
(RS Pts.—Jets 44, Jaguars 31)
(PS Pts.—Jets 34, Jaguars 24
**AFC Divisional Playoff*

JACKSONVILLE vs. OAKLAND
RS: Series tied, 1-1
1996—Raiders, 17-3 (O)
1997—Jaguars, 20-9 (O)
(RS Pts.—Raiders 26, Jaguars 23)

JACKSONVILLE vs. PHILADELPHIA
RS: Jaguars lead series, 1-0
1997—Jaguars, 38-21 (J)
(RS Pts.—Jaguars 38, Eagles 21)

JACKSONVILLE vs. PITTSBURGH
RS: Series tied, 4-4
1995—Jaguars, 20-16 (J)
Steelers, 24-7 (P)
1996—Jaguars, 24-9 (J)
Steelers, 28-3 (P)
1997—Jaguars, 30-21 (J)

Steelers, 23-17 (P) OT
1998—Steelers, 30-15 (P)
Jaguars, 21-3 (J)
(RS Pts.—Steelers 154, Jaguars 137)
JACKSONVILLE vs. ST. LOUIS
RS: Rams lead series, 1-0
1996—Rams, 17-14 (StL)
(RS Pts.—Rams 17, Jaguars 14)
JACKSONVILLE vs. SEATTLE
RS: Series tied, 1-1
1995—Seahawks, 47-30 (J)
1996—Jaguars, 20-13 (J)
(RS Pts.—Seahawks 60, Jaguars 50)
JACKSONVILLE vs. TAMPA BAY
RS: Series tied, 1-1
1995—Buccaneers, 17-16 (TB)
1998—Jaguars, 29-24 (J)
(RS Pts.—Jaguars 45, Buccaneers 41)
JACKSONVILLE vs. *TENNESSEE
RS: Jaguars lead series, 5-3
1995—Oilers, 10-3 (J)
Jaguars, 17-16 (H)
1996—Oilers, 34-27 (J)
Jaguars, 23-17 (H)
1997—Jaguars, 30-24 (T)
Jaguars, 17-9 (J)
1998—Jaguars, 27-22 (T)
Titans, 16-13 (J)
(RS Pts.—Jaguars 157, Titans 148)
**Franchise in Houston prior to 1997; known as Oilers prior to 1999*
JACKSONVILLE vs. WASHINGTON
RS: Redskins lead series, 1-0
1997—Redskins, 24-12 (W)
(RS Pts.—Redskins 24, Jaguars 12)

KANSAS CITY vs. ARIZONA
RS: Chiefs lead series, 5-1-1;
See Arizona vs. Kansas City
KANSAS CITY vs. ATLANTA
RS: Chiefs lead series, 4-0;
See Atlanta vs. Kansas City
KANSAS CITY vs. BUFFALO
RS: Bills lead series, 17-14-1
PS: Bills lead series, 2-1;
See Buffalo vs. Kansas City
KANSAS CITY vs. CARLOINA
RS: Chiefs lead series, 1-0;
See Carolina vs. Kansas City
KANSAS CITY vs. CHICAGO
RS: Bears lead series, 4-3;
See Chicago vs. Kansas City
KANSAS CITY vs. CINCINNATI
RS: Chiefs lead series, 11-9;
See Cincinnati vs. Kansas City
KANSAS CITY vs. CLEVELAND
RS: Browns lead series, 8-7-2;
See Cleveland vs. Kansas City
KANSAS CITY vs. DALLAS
RS: Cowboys lead series, 4-3;
See Dallas vs. Kansas City
KANSAS CITY vs. DENVER
RS: Chiefs lead series, 43-34
PS: Broncos lead series, 1-0;
See Denver vs. Kansas City
KANSAS CITY vs. DETROIT
RS: Chiefs lead series, 5-3;
See Detroit vs. Kansas City
KANSAS CITY vs. GREEN BAY
RS: Chiefs lead series, 5-1-1
PS: Packers lead series, 1-0;
See Green Bay vs. Kansas City
KANSAS CITY vs. INDIANAPOLIS
RS: Chiefs lead series, 6-5
PS: Colts lead series, 1-0;
See Indianapolis vs. Kansas City
KANSAS CITY vs. JACKSONVILLE
RS: Jaguars lead series, 2-0;
See Jacksonville vs. Kansas City
KANSAS CITY vs. MIAMI
RS: Series tied, 10-10
PS: Dolphins lead series, 3-0
1966—Chiefs, 34-16 (KC)
Chiefs, 19-18 (M)
1967—Chiefs, 24-0 (M)
Chiefs, 41-0 (KC)
1968—Chiefs, 48-3 (M)
1969—Chiefs, 17-10 (KC)
1971—*Dolphins, 27-24 (KC) OT
1972—Dolphins, 20-10 (KC)
1974—Dolphins, 9-3 (M)
1976—Chiefs, 20-17 (M) OT
1981—Dolphins, 17-7 (KC)
1983—Dolphins, 14-6 (M)
1985—Dolphins, 31-0 (M)
1987—Dolphins, 42-0 (M)
1989—Chiefs, 26-21 (KC)
Chiefs, 27-24 (M)
1990—**Dolphins, 17-16 (M)
1991—Chiefs, 42-7 (KC)
1993—Dolphins, 30-10 (M)
1994—Dolphins, 45-28 (M)
**Dolphins, 27-17 (M)
1995—Dolphins, 13-6 (M)
1997—Dolphins, 17-14 (M)
(RS Pts.—Chiefs 382, Dolphins 354)
(PS Pts.—Dolphins 71, Chiefs 57)
**AFC Divisional Playoff*
***AFC First-Round Playoff*
KANSAS CITY vs. MINNESOTA
RS: Series tied, 3-3
PS: Chiefs lead series, 1-0
1969—*Chiefs, 23-7 (New Orleans)
1970—Vikings, 27-10 (M)
1974—Vikings, 35-15 (KC)
1981—Chiefs, 10-6 (M)
1990—Chiefs, 24-21 (KC)
1993—Vikings, 30-10 (M)
1996—Chiefs, 21-6 (M)
(RS Pts.—Vikings 125, Chiefs 90)
(PS Pts.—Chiefs 23, Vikings 7)
**Super Bowl IV*
***KANSAS CITY vs. **NEW ENGLAND**
RS: Chiefs lead series, 14-8-3
1960—Patriots, 42-14 (B)
Texans, 34-0 (D)
1961—Patriots, 18-17 (D)
Patriots, 28-21 (B)
1962—Texans, 42-28 (D)
Texans, 27-7 (B)
1963—Tie, 24-24 (B)
Chiefs, 35-3 (KC)
1964—Patriots, 24-7 (B)
Patriots, 31-24 (KC)
1965—Chiefs, 27-17 (KC)
Tie, 10-10 (B)
1966—Chiefs, 43-24 (B)
Tie, 27-27 (KC)
1967—Chiefs, 33-10 (B)
1968—Chiefs, 31-17 (KC)
1969—Chiefs, 31-0 (B)
1970—Chiefs, 23-10 (KC)
1973—Chiefs, 10-7 (NE)
1977—Patriots, 21-17 (NE)
1981—Patriots, 33-17 (NE)
1990—Chiefs, 37-7 (NE)
1992—Chiefs, 27-20 (KC)
1995—Chiefs, 31-26 (KC)
1998—Patriots, 40-10 (NE)
(RS Pts.—Chiefs 619, Patriots 474)
**Franchise located in Dallas prior to 1963 and known as Texans*
***Franchise in Boston prior to 1971*
KANSAS CITY vs. NEW ORLEANS
RS: Chiefs lead series, 4-3
1972—Chiefs, 20-17 (NO)
1976—Saints, 27-17 (KC)
1982—Saints, 27-17 (NO)
1985—Chiefs, 47-27 (NO)
1991—Saints, 17-10 (KC)
1994—Chiefs, 30-17 (NO)
1997—Chiefs, 25-13 (KC)
(RS Pts.—Chiefs 166, Saints 145)
KANSAS CITY vs. N.Y. GIANTS
RS: Giants lead series, 7-2
1974—Giants, 33-27 (KC)
1978—Giants, 26-10 (NY)
1979—Giants, 21-17 (KC)
1983—Chiefs, 38-17 (KC)
1984—Giants, 28-27 (NY)
1988—Giants, 28-12 (NY)
1992—Giants, 35-21 (NY)
1995—Chiefs, 20-17 (KC) OT
1998—Giants, 28-7 (NY)
(RS Pts.—Giants 233, Chiefs 179)
***KANSAS CITY vs. **N.Y. JETS**
RS: Chiefs lead series, 14-13-1
PS: Series tied, 1-1
1960—Titans, 37-35 (D)
Titans, 41-35 (NY)
1961—Titans, 28-7 (NY)
Texans, 35-24 (D)
1962—Texans, 20-17 (D)
Texans, 52-31 (NY)
1963—Jets, 17-0 (NY)
Chiefs, 48-0 (KC)
1964—Jets, 27-14 (NY)
Chiefs, 24-7 (KC)
1965—Chiefs, 14-10 (NY)
Jets, 13-10 (KC)
1966—Chiefs, 32-24 (NY)
1967—Chiefs, 42-18 (KC)
Chiefs, 21-7 (NY)
1968—Jets, 20-19 (KC)
1969—Chiefs, 34-16 (NY)
***Chiefs, 13-6 (NY)
1971—Jets, 13-10 (NY)
1974—Chiefs, 24-16 (KC)
1975—Jets, 30-24 (KC)
1982—Chiefs, 37-13 (KC)
1984—Jets, 17-16 (KC)
Jets, 28-7 (NY)
1986—****Jets, 35-15 (NY)
1987—Jets, 16-9 (KC)
1988—Tie, 17-17 (NY)
Chiefs, 38-34 (KC)
1992—Chiefs, 23-7 (NY)
1998—Jets, 20-17 (KC)
(RS Pts.—Chiefs 664, Jets 548)
(PS Pts.—Jets 41, Chiefs 28)
**Franchise in Dallas prior to 1963 and known as Texans*
***Jets known as Titans prior to 1963*
****Inter-Divisional Playoff*
*****AFC First-Round Playoff*
***KANSAS CITY vs. **OAKLAND**
RS: Chiefs lead series, 39-36-2
PS: Chiefs lead series, 2-1
1960—Texans, 34-16 (O)
Raiders, 20-19 (D)
1961—Texans, 42-35 (O)
Texans, 43-11 (D)
1962—Texans, 26-16 (O)
Texans, 35-7 (D)
1963—Raiders, 10-7 (O)
Raiders, 22-7 (KC)
1964—Chiefs, 21-9 (O)
Chiefs, 42-7 (KC)
1965—Raiders, 37-10 (O)
Chiefs, 14-7 (KC)
1966—Chiefs, 32-10 (O)
Raiders, 34-13 (KC)
1967—Raiders, 23-21 (O)
Raiders, 44-22 (KC)
1968—Chiefs, 24-10 (KC)
Raiders, 38-21 (O)
***Raiders, 41-6 (O)
1969—Raiders, 27-24 (KC)
Raiders, 10-6 (O)
****Chiefs, 17-7 (O)
1970—Tie, 17-17 (KC)
Raiders, 20-6 (O)
1971—Tie, 20-20 (O)
Chiefs, 16-14 (KC)
1972—Chiefs, 27-14 (KC)
Raiders, 26-3 (O)
1973—Chiefs, 16-3 (KC)
Raiders, 37-7 (O)
1974—Raiders, 27-7 (O)
Raiders, 7-6 (KC)
1975—Chiefs, 42-10 (KC)
Raiders, 28-20 (O)
1976—Raiders, 24-21 (KC)
Raiders, 21-10 (O)
1977—Raiders, 37-28 (KC)
Raiders, 21-20 (O)
1978—Raiders, 28-6 (O)
Raiders, 20-10 (KC)
1979—Chiefs, 35-7 (KC)
Chiefs, 24-21 (O)
1980—Raiders, 27-14 (KC)
Chiefs, 31-17 (O)
1981—Chiefs, 27-0 (KC)
Chiefs, 28-17 (O)
1982—Raiders, 21-16 (KC)
1983—Raiders, 21-20 (LA)
Raiders, 28-20 (KC)
1984—Raiders, 22-20 (KC)
Raiders, 17-7 (LA)
1985—Chiefs, 36-20 (KC)
Raiders, 19-10 (LA)
1986—Raiders, 24-17 (KC)
Chiefs, 20-17 (LA)
1987—Raiders, 35-17 (LA)
Chiefs, 16-10 (KC)
1988—Raiders, 27-17 (KC)
Raiders, 17-10 (LA)
1989—Chiefs, 24-19 (KC)
Raiders, 20-14 (LA)
1990—Chiefs, 9-7 (KC)
Chiefs, 27-24 (LA)
1991—Chiefs, 24-21 (KC)
Chiefs, 27-21 (LA)
*****Chiefs, 10-6 (KC)
1992—Chiefs, 27-7 (KC)
Raiders, 28-7 (LA)
1993—Chiefs, 24-9 (KC)
Chiefs, 31-20 (LA)
1994—Chiefs, 13-3 (KC)
Chiefs, 19-9 (LA)
1995—Chiefs, 23-17 (KC) OT
Chiefs, 29-23 (O)
1996—Chiefs, 19-3 (KC)
Raiders, 26-7 (O)
1997—Chiefs, 28-27 (O)
Chiefs, 30-0 (KC)
1998—Chiefs, 28-8 (KC)
Chiefs, 31-24 (O)
(RS Pts.—Chiefs 1,571, Raiders 1,450)
(PS Pts.—Raiders 54, Chiefs 33)
**Franchise in Dallas prior to 1963 and known as Texans*
***Franchise in Los Angeles from 1982-1994*
****Division Playoff*
*****AFL Championship*
******AFC First-Round Playoff*
KANSAS CITY vs. PHILADELPHIA
RS: Chiefs lead series, 2-1
1972—Eagles, 21-20 (KC)
1992—Chiefs, 24-17 (KC)
1998—Chiefs, 24-21 (P)
(RS Pts.—Chiefs 68, Eagles 59)
KANSAS CITY vs. PITTSBURGH
RS: Steelers lead series, 15-6
PS: Chiefs lead series, 1-0
1970—Chiefs, 31-14 (P)
1971—Chiefs, 38-16 (KC)
1972—Steelers, 16-7 (P)
1974—Steelers, 34-24 (KC)
1975—Steelers, 28-3 (P)
1976—Steelers, 45-0 (KC)
1978—Steelers, 27-24 (P)
1979—Steelers, 30-3 (KC)
1980—Steelers, 21-16 (P)
1981—Chiefs, 37-33 (P)
1982—Steelers, 35-14 (P)
1984—Chiefs, 37-27 (P)
1985—Steelers, 36-28 (KC)
1986—Chiefs, 24-19 (P)
1987—Steelers, 17-16 (KC)
1988—Steelers, 16-10 (P)

ALL-TIME TEAM VS. TEAM RESULTS

1989—Steelers, 23-17 (P)
1992—Steelers, 27-3 (KC)
1993—*Chiefs, 27-24 (KC) OT
1996—Steelers, 17-7 (KC)
1997—Chiefs, 13-10 (KC)
1998—Steelers, 20-13 (KC)
(RS Pts.—Steelers 511, Chiefs 365)
(PS Pts.—Chiefs 27, Steelers 24)
AFC First-Round Playoff

KANSAS CITY vs. *ST. LOUIS
RS: Rams lead series, 4-2
1973—Rams, 23-13 (KC)
1982—Rams, 20-14 (LA)
1985—Rams, 16-0 (KC)
1991—Chiefs, 27-20 (LA)
1994—Rams, 16-0 (KC)
1997—Chiefs, 28-20 (StL)
(RS Pts.—Rams 115, Chiefs 82)
Franchise in Los Angeles prior to 1995

***KANSAS CITY vs. **SAN DIEGO**
RS: Chiefs lead series, 40-36-1
PS: Chargers lead series, 1-0
1960—Chargers, 21-20 (LA)
Texans, 17-0 (D)
1961—Chargers, 26-10 (D)
Chargers, 24-14 (SD)
1962—Chargers, 32-28 (SD)
Texans, 26-17 (D)
1963—Chargers, 24-10 (SD)
Chargers, 38-17 (KC)
1964—Chargers, 28-14 (KC)
Chiefs, 49-6 (SD)
1965—Tie, 10-10 (SD)
Chiefs, 31-7 (KC)
1966—Chiefs, 24-14 (KC)
Chiefs, 27-17 (SD)
1967—Chargers, 45-31 (SD)
Chargers, 17-16 (KC)
1968—Chiefs, 27-20 (KC)
Chiefs, 40-3 (SD)
1969—Chiefs, 27-9 (SD)
Chiefs, 27-3 (KC)
1970—Chiefs, 26-14 (KC)
Chargers, 31-13 (SD)
1971—Chargers, 21-14 (SD)
Chiefs, 31-10 (KC)
1972—Chiefs, 26-14 (SD)
Chargers, 27-17 (KC)
1973—Chiefs, 19-0 (SD)
Chiefs, 33-6 (KC)
1974—Chiefs, 24-14 (SD)
Chargers, 14-7 (KC)
1975—Chiefs, 12-10 (SD)
Chargers, 28-20 (KC)
1976—Chargers, 30-16 (KC)
Chiefs, 23-20 (SD)
1977—Chargers, 23-7 (KC)
Chiefs, 21-16 (SD)
1978—Chargers, 29-23 (SD) OT
Chiefs, 23-0 (KC)
1979—Chargers, 20-14 (KC)
Chargers, 28-7 (SD)
1980—Chargers, 24-7 (KC)
Chargers, 20-7 (SD)
1981—Chargers, 42-31 (KC)
Chargers, 22-20 (SD)
1982—Chiefs, 19-12 (KC)
1983—Chargers, 17-14 (KC)
Chargers, 41-38 (SD)
1984—Chiefs, 31-13 (KC)
Chiefs, 42-21 (SD)
1985—Chargers, 31-20 (SD)
Chiefs, 38-34 (KC)
1986—Chiefs, 42-41 (KC)
Chiefs, 24-23 (SD)
1987—Chiefs, 20-13 (KC)
Chargers, 42-21 (SD)
1988—Chargers, 24-23 (KC)
Chargers, 24-13 (SD)
1989—Chargers, 21-6 (SD)
Chargers, 20-13 (KC)
1990—Chiefs, 27-10 (KC)
Chiefs, 24-21 (SD)
1991—Chiefs, 14-13 (SD)
Chiefs, 20-17 (KC) OT
1992—Chiefs, 24-10 (SD)
Chiefs, 16-14 (KC)
***Chargers, 17-0 (SD)
1993—Chiefs, 17-14 (SD)
Chiefs, 28-24 (KC)
1994—Chargers, 20-6 (SD)
Chargers, 14-13 (KC)
1995—Chiefs, 29-23 (KC) OT
Chiefs, 22-7 (SD)
1996—Chargers, 22-19 (SD)
Chargers, 28-14 (KC)
1997—Chiefs, 31-3 (KC)
Chiefs, 29-7 (SD)
1998—Chiefs, 23-7 (KC)
Chargers, 38-37 (SD)
(RS Pts.—Chiefs 1,663, Chargers 1,493)
(PS Pts.—Chargers 17, Chiefs 0)
Franchise in Dallas prior to 1963 and known as Texans
***Franchise in Los Angeles prior to 1961*
****AFC First-Round Playoff*

KANSAS CITY vs. SAN FRANCISCO
RS: 49ers lead series, 4-3
1971—Chiefs, 26-17 (SF)
1975—49ers, 20-3 (KC)
1982—49ers, 26-13 (KC)
1985—49ers, 31-3 (SF)
1991—49ers, 28-14 (SF)
1994—Chiefs, 24-17 (KC)
1997—Chiefs, 44-9 (KC)
(PS Pts.—49ers 148, Chiefs 127)

KANSAS CITY vs. SEATTLE
RS: Chiefs lead series, 27-14
1977—Seahawks, 34-31 (KC)
1978—Seahawks, 13-10 (KC)
Seahawks, 23-19 (S)
1979—Chiefs, 24-6 (S)
Chiefs, 37-21 (KC)
1980—Seahawks, 17-16 (KC)
Chiefs, 31-30 (S)
1981—Chiefs, 20-14 (S)
Chiefs, 40-13 (KC)
1983—Chiefs, 17-13 (KC)
Seahawks, 51-48 (S) OT
1984—Seahawks, 45-0 (S)
Chiefs, 34-7 (KC)
1985—Chiefs, 28-7 (KC)
Seahawks, 24-6 (S)
1986—Seahawks, 23-17 (S)
Chiefs, 27-7 (KC)
1987—Seahawks, 43-14 (S)
Chiefs, 41-20 (KC)
1988—Seahawks, 31-10 (S)
Chiefs, 27-24 (KC)
1989—Chiefs, 20-16 (S)
Chiefs, 20-10 (KC)
1990—Seahawks, 19-7 (S)
Seahawks, 17-16 (KC)
1991—Chiefs, 20-13 (KC)
Chiefs, 19-6 (S)
1992—Chiefs, 26-7 (KC)
Chiefs, 24-14 (S)
1993—Chiefs, 31-16 (S)
Chiefs, 34-24 (KC)
1994—Chiefs, 38-23 (KC)
Seahawks, 10-9 (S)
1995—Chiefs, 34-10 (S)
Chiefs, 26-3 (KC)
1996—Chiefs, 35-17 (S)
Chiefs, 34-16 (KC)
1997—Chiefs, 20-17 (KC) OT
Chiefs, 19-14 (S)
1998—Chiefs, 17-6 (KC)
Seahawks, 24-12 (S)
(RS Pts.—Chiefs 958, Seahawks 748)

KANSAS CITY vs. TAMPA BAY
RS: Chiefs lead series, 5-2
1976—Chiefs, 28-19 (TB)
1978—Buccaneers, 30-13 (KC)
1979—Buccaneers, 3-0 (TB)
1981—Chiefs, 19-10 (KC)
1984—Chiefs, 24-20 (KC)
1986—Chiefs, 27-20 (KC)
1993—Chiefs, 27-3 (TB)
(RS Pts.—Chiefs 138, Buccaneers 105)

***KANSAS CITY vs. **TENNESSEE**
RS: Chiefs lead series, 24-17
PS: Chiefs lead series, 2-0
1960—Oilers, 20-10 (H)
Texans, 24-0 (D)
1961—Texans, 26-21 (D)
Oilers, 38-7 (H)
1962—Texans, 31-7 (H)
Oilers, 14-6 (D)
***Texans, 20-17 (H) OT
1963—Chiefs, 28-7 (KC)
Oilers, 28-7 (H)
1964—Chiefs, 28-7 (KC)
Chiefs, 28-19 (H)
1965—Chiefs, 52-21 (KC)
Oilers, 38-36 (H)
1966—Chiefs, 48-23 (KC)
1967—Chiefs, 25-20 (H)
Oilers, 24-19 (KC)
1968—Chiefs, 26-21 (H)
Chiefs, 24-10 (KC)
1969—Chiefs, 24-0 (KC)
1970—Chiefs, 24-9 (KC)
1971—Chiefs, 20-16 (H)
1973—Chiefs, 38-14 (KC)
1974—Chiefs, 17-7 (H)
1975—Oilers, 17-13 (KC)
1977—Oilers, 34-20 (H)
1978—Oilers, 20-17 (KC)
1979—Oilers, 20-6 (H)
1980—Chiefs, 21-20 (KC)
1981—Chiefs, 23-10 (KC)
1983—Chiefs, 13-10 (H) OT
1984—Oilers, 17-16 (KC)
1985—Oilers, 23-20 (H)
1986—Chiefs, 27-13 (KC)
1988—Oilers, 7-6 (H)
1989—Chiefs, 34-0 (KC)
1990—Oilers, 27-10 (KC)
1991—Oilers, 17-7 (H)
1992—Oilers, 23-20 (H) OT
1993—Oilers, 30-0 (H)
****Chiefs, 28-20 (H)
1994—Chiefs, 31-9 (KC)
1995—Chiefs, 20-13 (KC)
1996—Chiefs, 20-19 (H)
(RS Pts.—Chiefs 872, Titans 693)
(PS Pts.—Chiefs 48, Titans 37)
Franchise in Dallas prior to 1963 and known as Texans
***Franchise in Houston prior to 1997; known as Oilers prior to 1999*
****AFL Championship*
*****AFC Divisional Playoff*

KANSAS CITY vs. WASHINGTON
RS: Chiefs lead series, 4-1
1971—Chiefs, 27-20 (KC)
1976—Chiefs, 33-30 (W)
1983—Redskins, 27-12 (W)
1992—Chiefs, 35-16 (KC)
1995—Chiefs, 24-3 (KC)
(RS Pts.—Chiefs 131, Redskins 96)

MIAMI vs. ARIZONA
RS: Dolphins lead series, 7-0;
See Arizona vs. Miami

MIAMI vs. ATLANTA
RS: Dolphins lead series, 6-2;
See Atlanta vs. Miami

MIAMI vs. BALTIMORE
RS: Dolphins lead series, 1-0;
See Baltimore vs. Miami

MIAMI vs. BUFFALO
RS: Dolphins lead series, 42-23-1
PS: Bills lead series, 3-1;
See Buffalo vs. Miami

MIAMI vs. CAROLINA
RS: Dolphins lead series, 1-0;
See Carolina vs. Miami

MIAMI vs. CHICAGO
RS: Dolphins lead series, 5-3;
See Chicago vs. Miami

MIAMI vs. CINCINNATI
RS: Dolphins lead series, 11-3
PS: Dolphins lead series, 1-0;
See Cincinnati vs. Miami

MIAMI vs. CLEVELAND
RS: Dolphins lead series, 6-4
PS: Dolphins lead series, 2-0;
See Cleveland vs. Miami

MIAMI vs. DALLAS
RS: Dolphins lead series, 6-2
PS: Cowboys lead series, 1-0;
See Dallas vs. Miami

MIAMI vs. DENVER
RS: Dolphins lead series, 6-2-1
PS: Broncos lead series, 1-0;
See Denver vs. Miami

MIAMI vs. DETROIT
RS: Dolphins lead series, 4-2;
See Detroit vs. Miami

MIAMI vs. GREEN BAY
RS: Dolphins lead series, 8-1;
See Green Bay vs. Miami

MIAMI vs. INDIANAPOLIS
RS: Dolphins lead series, 39-19
PS: Dolphins lead series, 1-0;
See Indianapolis vs. Miami

MIAMI vs. JACKSONVILLE
RS: Jaguars lead series, 1-0;
See Jacksonville vs. Miami

MIAMI vs. KANSAS CITY
RS: Series tied, 10-10
PS: Dolphins lead series, 3-0;
See Kansas City vs. Miami

MIAMI vs. MINNESOTA
RS: Dolphins lead series, 4-2
PS: Dolphins lead series, 1-0
1972—Dolphins, 16-14 (Minn)
1973—*Dolphins, 24-7 (Houston)
1976—Vikings, 29-7 (Mia)
1979—Dolphins, 27-12 (Minn)
1982—Dolphins, 22-14 (Mia)
1988—Dolphins, 24-7 (Mia)
1994—Vikings, 38-35 (M)
(RS Pts.—Dolphins 131, Vikings 114)
(PS Pts.—Dolphins 24, Vikings 7)
Super Bowl VIII

MIAMI vs. *NEW ENGLAND
RS: Dolphins lead series, 38-26
PS: Patriots lead series, 2-1
1966—Patriots, 20-14 (M)
1967—Patriots, 41-10 (B)
Dolphins, 41-32 (M)
1968—Dolphins, 34-10 (B)
Dolphins, 38-7 (M)
1969—Dolphins, 17-16 (B)
Patriots, 38-23 (Tampa)
1970—Patriots, 27-14 (B)
Dolphins, 37-20 (M)
1971—Dolphins, 41-3 (M)
Patriots, 34-13 (NE)
1972—Dolphins, 52-0 (M)
Dolphins, 37-21 (NE)
1973—Dolphins, 44-23 (M)
Dolphins, 30-14 (NE)
1974—Patriots, 34-24 (NE)
Dolphins, 34-27 (M)
1975—Dolphins, 22-14 (NE)
Dolphins, 20-7 (M)
1976—Patriots, 30-14 (NE)
Dolphins, 10-3 (M)
1977—Dolphins, 17-5 (M)
Patriots, 14-10 (NE)
1978—Patriots, 33-24 (NE)
Dolphins, 23-3 (M)
1979—Patriots, 28-13 (NE)
Dolphins, 39-24 (M)
1980—Patriots, 34-0 (NE)
Dolphins, 16-13 (M) OT
1981—Dolphins, 30-27 (NE) OT
Dolphins, 24-14 (M)

1982—Patriots, 3-0 (NE)
**Dolphins, 28-13 (M)
1983—Dolphins, 34-24 (M)
Patriots, 17-6 (NE)
1984—Dolphins, 28-7 (M)
Dolphins, 44-24 (NE)
1985—Patriots, 17-13 (NE)
Dolphins, 30-27 (M)
***Patriots, 31-14 (M)
1986—Patriots, 34-7 (NE)
Patriots, 34-27 (M)
1987—Patriots, 28-21 (NE)
Patriots, 24-10 (M)
1988—Patriots, 21-10 (NE)
Patriots, 6-3 (M)
1989—Dolphins, 24-10 (NE)
Dolphins, 31-10 (M)
1990—Dolphins, 27-24 (NE)
Dolphins, 17-10 (M)
1991—Dolphins, 20-10 (NE)
Dolphins, 30-20 (M)
1992—Dolphins, 38-17 (M)
Dolphins, 16-13 (NE) OT
1993—Dolphins, 17-13 (M)
Patriots, 33-27 (NE) OT
1994—Dolphins, 39-35 (M)
Dolphins, 23-3 (NE)
1995—Dolphins, 20-3 (NE)
Patriots, 34-17 (M)
1996—Dolphins, 24-10 (M)
Patriots, 42-23 (NE)
1997—Patriots, 27-24 (NE)
Patriots, 14-12 (M)
**Patriots, 17-3 (NE)
1998—Dolphins, 12-9 (M) OT
Patriots, 26-23 (NE)
(RS Pts.—Dolphins 1,462, Patriots 1,245)
(PS Pts.—Patriots 61, Dolphins 45)
Franchise in Boston prior to 1971
***AFC First-Round Playoff*
****AFC Championship*

MIAMI vs. NEW ORLEANS
RS: Dolphins lead series, 5-3
1970—Dolphins, 21-10 (M)
1974—Dolphins, 21-0 (NO)
1980—Dolphins, 21-16 (M)
1983—Saints, 17-7 (NO)
1986—Dolphins, 31-27 (NO)
1992—Saints, 24-13 (NO)
1995—Saints, 33-30 (NO)
1998—Dolphins, 30-10 (M)
(RS Pts.—Dolphins 174, Saints 137)

MIAMI vs. N.Y. GIANTS
RS: Giants lead series, 3-1
1972—Dolphins, 23-13 (NY)
1990—Giants, 20-3 (NY)
1993—Giants, 19-14 (M)
1996—Giants, 17-7 (M)
(RS Pts.—Giants 69, Dolphins 47)

MIAMI vs. N.Y. JETS
RS: Dolphins lead series, 34-31-1
PS: Dolphins lead series, 1-0
1966—Jets, 19-14 (M)
Jets, 30-13 (NY)
1967—Jets, 29-7 (NY)
Jets, 33-14 (M)
1968—Jets, 35-17 (NY)
Jets, 31-7 (M)
1969—Jets, 34-31 (NY)
Jets, 27-9 (M)
1970—Dolphins, 20-6 (NY)
Dolphins, 16-10 (M)
1971—Jets, 14-10 (M)
Dolphins, 30-14 (NY)
1972—Dolphins, 27-17 (NY)
Dolphins, 28-24 (M)
1973—Dolphins, 31-3 (M)
Dolphins, 24-14 (NY)
1974—Dolphins, 21-17 (M)
Jets, 17-14 (NY)
1975—Dolphins, 43-0 (NY)
Dolphins, 27-7 (M)
1976—Dolphins, 16-0 (M)
Dolphins, 27-7 (NY)
1977—Dolphins, 21-17 (M)
Dolphins, 14-10 (NY)
1978—Jets, 33-20 (NY)
Jets, 24-13 (M)
1979—Jets, 33-27 (NY)
Jets, 27-24 (M)
1980—Jets, 17-14 (NY)
Jets, 24-17 (M)
1981—Tie, 28-28 (M) OT
Jets, 16-15 (NY)
1982—Dolphins, 45-28 (NY)
Dolphins, 20-19 (M)
*Dolphins, 14-0 (M)
1983—Dolphins, 32-14 (NY)
Dolphins, 34-14 (M)
1984—Dolphins, 31-17 (NY)
Dolphins, 28-17 (M)
1985—Jets, 23-7 (NY)
Dolphins, 21-17 (M)
1986—Jets, 51-45 (NY) OT
Dolphins, 45-3 (M)
1987—Jets, 37-31 (NY) OT
Dolphins, 37-28 (M)
1988—Jets, 44-30 (M)
Jets, 38-34 (NY)
1989—Jets, 40-33 (M)
Dolphins, 31-23 (NY)
1990—Dolphins, 20-16 (M)
Dolphins, 17-3 (NY)
1991—Jets, 41-23 (NY)
Jets, 23-20 (M) OT
1992—Jets, 26-14 (NY)
Dolphins, 19-17 (M)
1993—Jets, 24-14 (M)
Jets, 27-10 (NY)
1994—Dolphins, 28-14 (M)
Dolphins, 28-24 (NY)
1995—Dolphins, 52-14 (M)
Jets, 17-16 (NY)
1996—Dolphins, 36-27 (M)
Dolphins, 31-28 (NY)
1997—Dolphins, 31-20 (NY)
Dolphins, 24-17 (M)
1998—Jets, 20-9 (NY)
Jets, 21-16 (M)
(RS Pts.—Dolphins 1,551, Jets 1,409)
(PS Pts.—Dolphins 14, Jets 0)
**AFC Championship*

MIAMI vs. *OAKLAND
RS: Raiders lead series, 15-7-1
PS: Raiders lead series, 2-1
1966—Raiders, 23-14 (M)
Raiders, 21-10 (O)
1967—Raiders, 31-17 (O)
1968—Raiders, 47-21 (M)
1969—Raiders, 20-17 (O)
Tie, 20-20 (M)
1970—Dolphins, 20-13 (M)
**Raiders, 21-14 (O)
1973—Raiders, 12-7 (O)
***Dolphins, 27-10 (M)
1974—**Raiders, 28-26 (O)
1975—Raiders, 31-21 (M)
1978—Dolphins, 23-6 (M)
1979—Raiders, 13-3 (O)
1980—Raiders, 16-10 (O)
1981—Raiders, 33-17 (M)
1983—Raiders, 27-14 (LA)
1984—Raiders, 45-34 (M)
1986—Raiders, 30-28 (M)
1988—Dolphins, 24-14 (LA)
1990—Raiders, 13-10 (M)
1992—Dolphins, 20-7 (M)
1994—Dolphins, 20-17 (M) OT
1996—Raiders, 17-7 (O)
1997—Dolphins, 34-16 (O)
1998—Dolphins, 27-17 (O)
(RS Pts.—Raiders 489, Dolphins 418)
(PS Pts.—Dolphins 67, Raiders 59)
**Franchise in Los Angeles from 1982-1994*
***AFC Divisional Playoff*
****AFC Championship*

MIAMI vs. PHILADELPHIA
RS: Dolphins lead series, 6-3
1970—Eagles, 24-17 (P)
1975—Dolphins, 24-16 (M)
1978—Eagles, 17-3 (P)
1981—Dolphins, 13-10 (M)
1984—Dolphins, 24-23 (M)
1987—Dolphins, 28-10 (P)
1990—Dolphins, 23-20 (M) OT
1993—Dolphins, 19-14 (P)
1996—Eagles, 35-28 (P)
(RS Pts.—Dolphins 179, Eagles 169)

MIAMI vs. PITTSBURGH
RS: Dolphins lead series, 9-7
PS: Dolphins lead series, 2-1
1971—Dolphins, 24-21 (M)
1972—*Dolphins, 21-17 (P)
1973—Dolphins, 30-26 (M)
1976—Steelers, 14-3 (P)
1979—**Steelers, 34-14 (P)
1980—Steelers, 23-10 (P)
1981—Dolphins, 30-10 (M)
1984—Dolphins, 31-7 (P)
*Dolphins, 45-28 (M)
1985—Dolphins, 24-20 (M)
1987—Dolphins, 35-24 (M)
1988—Steelers, 40-24 (P)
1989—Steelers, 34-14 (M)
1990—Dolphins, 28-6 (P)
1993—Steelers, 21-20 (M)
1994—Steelers, 16-13 (P) OT
1995—Dolphins, 23-10 (M)
1996—Steelers, 24-17 (M)
1998—Dolphins, 21-0 (M)
(RS Pts.—Dolphins 347, Steelers 296)
(PS Pts.—Dolphins 80, Steelers 79)
**AFC Championship*
***AFC Divisional Playoff*

MIAMI vs. *ST. LOUIS
RS: Dolphins lead series, 7-1
1971—Dolphins, 20-14 (LA)
1976—Rams, 31-28 (M)
1980—Dolphins, 35-14 (LA)
1983—Dolphins, 30-14 (M)
1986—Dolphins, 37-31 (LA) OT
1992—Dolphins, 26-10 (M)
1995—Dolphins, 41-22 (StL)
1998—Dolphins, 14-0 (M)
(RS Pts.—Dolphins 231, Rams 136)
**Franchise in Los Angeles prior to 1995*

MIAMI vs. SAN DIEGO
RS: Chargers lead series, 10-6
PS: Series tied, 2-2
1966—Chargers, 44-10 (SD)
1967—Chargers, 24-0 (SD)
Dolphins, 41-24 (M)
1968—Chargers, 34-28 (SD)
1969—Chargers, 21-14 (M)
1972—Dolphins, 24-10 (M)
1974—Dolphins, 28-21 (SD)
1977—Chargers, 14-13 (M)
1978—Dolphins, 28-21 (SD)
1980—Chargers, 27-24 (M) OT
1981—*Chargers, 41-38 (M) OT
1982—**Dolphins, 34-13 (M)
1984—Chargers, 34-28 (SD) OT
1986—Chargers, 50-28 (SD)
1988—Dolphins, 31-28 (M)
1991—Chargers, 38-30 (SD)
1992—*Dolphins, 31-0 (M)
1993—Chargers, 45-20 (SD)
1994—*Chargers, 22-21 (SD)
1995—Dolphins, 24-14 (SD)
(RS Pts.—Chargers 449, Dolphins 371)
(PS Pts.—Dolphins 124, Chargers 76)
**AFC Divisional Playoff*
***AFC Second-Round Playoff*

MIAMI vs. SAN FRANCISCO
RS: Dolphins lead series, 4-3
PS: 49ers lead series, 1-0
1973—Dolphins, 21-13 (M)
1977—Dolphins, 19-15 (SF)
1980—Dolphins, 17-13 (M)
1983—Dolphins, 20-17 (SF)
1984—*49ers, 38-16 (Stanford)
1986—49ers, 31-16 (M)
1992—49ers, 27-3 (SF)
1995—49ers, 44-20 (M)
(RS Pts.—49ers 160, Dolphins 116)
(PS Pts.—49ers 38, Dolphins 16)
**Super Bowl XIX*

MIAMI vs. SEATTLE
RS: Dolphins lead series, 4-2
PS: Series tied, 1-1
1977—Dolphins, 31-13 (M)
1979—Dolphins, 19-10 (M)
1983—*Seahawks, 27-20 (M)
1984—*Dolphins, 31-10 (M)
1987—Seahawks, 24-20 (S)
1990—Dolphins, 24-17 (M)
1992—Dolphins, 19-17 (S)
1996—Seahawks, 22-15 (M)
(RS Pts.—Dolphins 128, Seahawks 103)
(PS Pts.—Dolphins 51, Seahawks 37)
**AFC Divisional Playoff*

MIAMI vs. TAMPA BAY
RS: Dolphins lead series, 4-2
1976—Dolphins, 23-20 (TB)
1982—Buccaneers, 23-17 (TB)
1985—Dolphins, 41-38 (M)
1988—Dolphins, 17-14 (TB)
1991—Dolphins, 33-14 (M)
1997—Buccaneers, 31-21 (TB)
(RS Pts.—Dolphins 152, Buccaneers 140)

MIAMI vs. *TENNESSEE
RS: Dolphins lead series, 13-11
PS: Titans lead series, 1-0
1966—Dolphins, 20-13 (H)
Dolphins, 29-28 (M)
1967—Oilers, 17-14 (H)
Oilers, 41-10 (M)
1968—Oilers, 24-10 (M)
Dolphins, 24-7 (H)
1969—Oilers, 22-10 (H)
Oilers, 32-7 (M)
1970—Dolphins, 20-10 (H)
1972—Dolphins, 34-13 (M)
1975—Oilers, 20-19 (H)
1977—Dolphins, 27-7 (M)
1978—Oilers, 35-30 (H)
**Oilers, 17-9 (M)
1979—Oilers, 9-6 (M)
1981—Dolphins, 16-10 (H)
1983—Dolphins, 24-17 (H)
1984—Dolphins, 28-10 (M)
1985—Oilers, 26-23 (H)
1986—Dolphins, 28-7 (M)
1989—Oilers, 39-7 (H)
1991—Oilers, 17-13 (M)
1992—Dolphins, 19-16 (M)
1996—Dolphins, 23-20 (H)
1997—Dolphins, 16-13 (M) OT
(RS Pts.—Dolphins 457, Titans 453)
(PS Pts.—Titans 17, Dolphins 9)
**Franchise in Houston prior to 1997; known as Oilers prior to 1999*
***AFC First-Round Playoff*

MIAMI vs. WASHINGTON
RS: Dolphins lead series, 5-2
PS: Series tied, 1-1
1972—*Dolphins, 14-7 (Los Angeles)
1974—Redskins, 20-17 (W)
1978—Dolphins, 16-0 (W)
1981—Dolphins, 13-10 (M)
1982—**Redskins, 27-17 (Pasadena)
1984—Dolphins, 35-17 (W)
1987—Dolphins, 23-21 (M)
1990—Redskins, 42-20 (W)
1993—Dolphins, 17-10 (M)
(RS Pts.—Dolphins 141, Redskins 120)
(PS Pts.—Redskins 34, Dolphins 31)
**Super Bowl VII*
***Super Bowl XVII*

ALL-TIME TEAM VS. TEAM RESULTS

MINNESOTA vs. ARIZONA
RS: Cardinals lead series, 8-7
PS: Vikings lead series, 2-0;
See Arizona vs. Minnesota
MINNESOTA vs. ATLANTA
RS: Vikings lead series, 12-6
PS: Series tied, 1-1;
See Atlanta vs. Minnesota
MINNESOTA vs. BALTIMORE
RS: Vikings lead series, 1-0;
See Baltimore vs. Minnesota
MINNESOTA vs. BUFFALO
RS: Vikings lead series, 6-2;
See Buffalo vs. Minnesota
MINNESOTA vs. CAROLINA
RS: Vikings lead series, 2-0;
See Carolina vs. Minnesota
MINNESOTA vs. CHICAGO
RS: Vikings lead series, 41-32-2
PS: Bears lead series, 1-0;
See Chicago vs. Minnesota
MINNESOTA vs. CINCINNATI
RS: Vikings lead series, 5-4;
See Cincinnati vs. Minnesota
MINNESOTA vs. CLEVELAND
RS: Vikings lead series, 8-3
PS: Vikings lead series, 1-0;
See Cleveland vs. Minnesota
MINNESOTA vs. DALLAS
RS: Cowboys lead series, 9-7
PS: Cowboys lead series, 4-1;
See Dallas vs. Minnesota
MINNESOTA vs. DENVER
RS: Vikings lead series, 5-4;
See Denver vs. Minnesota
MINNESOTA vs. DETROIT
RS: Vikings lead series, 46-27-2;
See Detroit vs. Minnesota
MINNESOTA vs. GREEN BAY
RS: Vikings lead series, 38-36-1;
See Green Bay vs. Minnesota
MINNESOTA vs. INDIANAPOLIS
RS: Colts lead series, 11-7-1
PS: Colts lead series, 1-0;
See Indianapolis vs. Minnesota
MINNESOTA vs. JACKSONVILLE
RS: Vikings lead series, 1-0;
See Jacksonville vs. Minnesota
MINNESOTA vs. KANSAS CITY
RS: Series tied, 3-3
PS: Chiefs lead series, 1-0;
See Kansas City vs. Minnesota
MINNESOTA vs. MIAMI
RS: Dolphins lead series, 4-2
PS: Dolphins lead series, 1-0;
See Miami vs. Minnesota
MINNESOTA vs. *NEW ENGLAND
RS: Patriots lead series, 4-3
1970—Vikings, 35-14 (B)
1974—Patriots, 17-14 (M)
1979—Patriots, 27-23 (NE)
1988—Vikings, 36-6 (M)
1991—Patriots, 26-23 (NE) OT
1994—Patriots, 26-20 (NE) OT
1997—Vikings, 23-18 (M)
(RS Pts.—Vikings 174, Patriots 134)
**Franchise in Boston prior to 1971*
MINNESOTA vs. NEW ORLEANS
RS: Vikings lead series, 14-6
PS: Vikings lead series, 1-0
1968—Saints, 20-17 (NO)
1970—Vikings, 26-0 (M)
1971—Vikings, 23-10 (NO)
1972—Vikings, 37-6 (M)
1974—Vikings, 29-9 (M)
1975—Vikings, 20-7 (NO)
1976—Vikings, 40-9 (NO)
1978—Saints, 31-24 (NO)
1980—Vikings, 23-20 (NO)
1981—Vikings, 20-10 (M)
1983—Saints, 17-16 (NO)
1985—Saints, 30-23 (M)
1986—Vikings, 33-17 (M)
1987—*Vikings, 44-10 (NO)
1988—Vikings, 45-3 (M)
1990—Vikings, 32-3 (M)
1991—Saints, 26-0 (NO)
1993—Saints, 17-14 (M)
1994—Vikings, 21-20 (M)
1995—Vikings, 43-24 (M)
1998—Vikings, 31-24 (M)
(RS Pts.—Vikings 517, Saints 303)
(PS Pts.—Vikings 44, Saints 10)
**NFC First-Round Playoff*
MINNESOTA vs. N.Y. GIANTS
RS: Vikings lead series, 7-5
PS: Series tied, 1-1
1964—Vikings, 30-21 (NY)
1965—Vikings, 40-14 (M)
1967—Vikings, 27-24 (M)
1969—Giants, 24-23 (NY)
1971—Vikings, 17-10 (NY)
1973—Vikings, 31-7 (New Haven)
1976—Vikings, 24-7 (M)
1986—Giants, 22-20 (M)
1989—Giants, 24-14 (NY)
1990—Giants, 23-15 (NY)
1993—*Giants, 17-10 (NY)
1994—Vikings, 27-10 (NY)
1996—Giants, 15-10 (NY)
1997—*Vikings, 23-22 (NY)
(RS Pts.—Vikings 278, Giants 201)
(PS Pts.—Giants 39, Vikings 33)
**NFC First-Round Playoff*
MINNESOTA vs. N.Y. JETS
RS: Jets lead series, 5-1
1970—Jets, 20-10 (NY)
1975—Vikings, 29-21 (M)
1979—Jets, 14-7 (NY)
1982—Jets, 42-14 (M)
1994—Jets, 31-21 (M)
1997—Jets, 23-21 (NY)
(RS Pts.—Jets 151, Vikings 102)
MINNESOTA vs. *OAKLAND
RS: Raiders lead series, 6-3
PS: Raiders lead series, 1-0
1973—Vikings, 24-16 (M)
1976—**Raiders, 32-14 (Pasadena)
1977—Raiders, 35-13 (O)
1978—Raiders, 27-20 (O)
1981—Raiders, 36-10 (M)
1984—Raiders, 23-20 (LA)
1987—Vikings, 31-20 (M)
1990—Raiders, 28-24 (M)
1993—Raiders, 24-7 (LA)
1996—Vikings, 16-13 (O) OT
(RS Pts.—Raiders 222, Vikings 165)
(PS Pts.—Raiders 32, Vikings 14)
**Franchise in Los Angeles from 1982-1994*
***Super Bowl XI*
MINNESOTA vs. PHILADELPHIA
RS: Vikings lead series, 11-6
PS: Eagles lead series, 1-0
1962—Vikings, 31-21 (M)
1963—Vikings, 34-13 (P)
1968—Vikings, 24-17 (P)
1971—Vikings, 13-0 (P)
1973—Vikings, 28-21 (M)
1976—Vikings, 31-12 (P)
1978—Vikings, 28-27 (M)
1980—Eagles, 42-7 (M)
*Eagles, 31-16 (P)
1981—Vikings, 35-23 (M)
1984—Eagles, 19-17 (P)
1985—Vikings, 28-23 (P)
Eagles, 37-35 (M)
1988—Vikings, 23-21 (M)
1989—Eagles, 10-9 (P)
1990—Eagles, 32-24 (P)
1992—Eagles, 28-17 (P)
1997—Vikings, 28-19 (M)
(RS Pts.—Vikings 412, Eagles 365)
(PS Pts.—Eagles 31, Vikings 16)
**NFC Divisional Playoff*
MINNESOTA vs. PITTSBURGH
RS: Vikings lead series, 8-4
PS: Steelers lead series, 1-0
1962—Steelers, 39-31 (P)
1964—Vikings, 30-10 (M)
1967—Vikings, 41-27 (P)
1969—Vikings, 52-14 (M)
1972—Steelers, 23-10 (P)
1974—*Steelers, 16-6 (New Orleans)
1976—Vikings, 17-6 (M)
1980—Steelers, 23-17 (M)
1983—Vikings, 17-14 (P)
1986—Vikings, 31-7 (M)
1989—Steelers, 27-14 (P)
1992—Vikings, 6-3 (P)
1995—Vikings, 44-24 (P)
(RS Pts.—Vikings 310, Steelers 217)
(PS Pts.—Steelers 16, Vikings 6)
**Super Bowl IX*
MINNESOTA vs. *ST. LOUIS
RS: Vikings lead series, 16-11-2
PS: Vikings lead series, 5-1
1961—Rams, 31-17 (LA)
Vikings, 42-21 (M)
1962—Vikings, 38-14 (LA)
Tie, 24-24 (M)
1963—Rams, 27-24 (LA)
Vikings, 21-13 (M)
1964—Rams, 22-13 (LA)
Vikings, 34-13 (M)
1965—Vikings, 38-35 (LA)
Vikings, 24-13 (M)
1966—Vikings, 35-7 (M)
Rams, 21-6 (LA)
1967—Rams, 39-3 (LA)
1968—Rams, 31-3 (M)
1969—Vikings, 20-13 (LA)
**Vikings, 23-20 (M)
1970—Vikings, 13-3 (M)
1972—Vikings, 45-41 (LA)
1973—Vikings, 10-9 (M)
1974—Rams, 20-17 (LA)
***Vikings, 14-10 (M)
1976—Tie, 10-10 (M) OT
***Vikings, 24-13 (M)
1977—Rams, 35-3 (LA)
****Vikings, 14-7 (LA)
1978—Rams, 34-17 (M)
****Rams, 34-10 (LA)
1979—Rams, 27-21 (LA) OT
1985—Rams, 13-10 (LA)
1987—Vikings, 21-16 (LA)
1988—*****Vikings, 28-17 (M)
1989—Vikings, 23-21 (M) OT
1991—Vikings, 20-14 (M)
1992—Vikings, 31-17 (LA)
1998—Vikings, 38-31 (StL)
(RS Pts.—Vikings 621, Rams 615)
(PS Pts.—Vikings 113, Rams 101)
**Franchise in Los Angeles prior to 1995*
***Conference Championship*
****NFC Championship*
*****NFC Divisional Playoff*
******NFC First-Round Playoff*
MINNESOTA vs. SAN DIEGO
RS: Chargers lead series, 4-3
1971—Chargers, 30-14 (SD)
1975—Vikings, 28-13 (M)
1978—Chargers, 13-7 (M)
1981—Vikings, 33-31 (SD)
1984—Chargers, 42-13 (M)
1985—Vikings, 21-17 (M)
1993—Chargers, 30-17 (M)
(RS Pts.—Chargers 176, Vikings 133)
MINNESOTA vs. SAN FRANCISCO
RS: 49ers lead series, 17-16-1
PS: 49ers lead series, 4-1
1961—49ers, 38-24 (M)
49ers, 38-28 (SF)
1962—49ers, 21-7 (SF)
49ers, 35-12 (M)
1963—Vikings, 24-20 (SF)
Vikings, 45-14 (M)
1964—Vikings, 27-22 (SF)
Vikings, 24-7 (M)
1965—Vikings, 42-41 (SF)
49ers, 45-24 (M)
1966—Tie, 20-20 (SF)
Vikings, 28-3 (SF)
1967—49ers, 27-21 (M)
1968—Vikings, 30-20 (SF)
1969—Vikings, 10-7 (M)
1970—*49ers, 17-14 (M)
1971—49ers, 13-9 (M)
1972—49ers, 20-17 (SF)
1973—Vikings, 17-13 (SF)
1975—Vikings, 27-17 (M)
1976—49ers, 20-16 (SF)
1977—Vikings, 28-27 (M)
1979—Vikings, 28-22 (M)
1983—49ers, 48-17 (M)
1984—49ers, 51-7 (SF)
1985—Vikings, 28-21 (M)
1986—Vikings, 27-24 (SF) OT
1987—*Vikings, 36-24 (SF)
1988—49ers, 24-21 (SF)
*49ers, 34-9 (SF)
1989—*49ers, 41-13 (SF)
1990—49ers, 20-17 (M)
1991—Vikings, 17-14 (M)
1992—49ers, 20-17 (M)
1993—49ers, 38-19 (SF)
1994—Vikings, 21-14 (M)
1995—49ers, 37-30 (SF)
1997—49ers, 28-17 (SF)
*49ers, 38-22 (SF)
(RS Pts.—49ers 829, Vikings 746)
(PS Pts.—49ers 154, Vikings 94)
**NFC Divisional Playoff*
MINNESOTA vs. SEATTLE
RS: Seahawks lead series, 4-2
1976—Vikings, 27-21 (M)
1978—Seahawks, 29-28 (S)
1984—Seahawks, 20-12 (M)
1987—Seahawks, 28-17 (S)
1990—Vikings, 24-21 (S)
1996—Seahawks, 42-23 (S)
(RS Pts.—Seahawks 161, Vikings 131)
MINNESOTA vs. TAMPA BAY
RS: Vikings lead series, 28-14
1977—Vikings, 9-3 (TB)
1978—Buccaneers, 16-10 (M)
Vikings, 24-7 (TB)
1979—Buccaneers, 12-10 (M)
Vikings, 23-22 (TB)
1980—Vikings, 38-30 (M)
Vikings, 21-10 (TB)
1981—Buccaneers, 21-13 (TB)
Vikings, 25-10 (M)
1982—Vikings, 17-10 (M)
1983—Vikings, 19-16 (TB) OT
Buccaneers, 17-12 (M)
1984—Buccaneers, 35-31 (TB)
Vikings, 27-24 (M)
1985—Vikings, 31-16 (TB)
Vikings, 26-7 (M)
1986—Vikings, 23-10 (TB)
Vikings, 45-13 (M)
1987—Buccaneers, 20-10 (TB)
Vikings, 23-17 (M)
1988—Vikings, 14-13 (M)
Vikings, 49-20 (TB)
1989—Vikings, 17-3 (M)
Vikings, 24-10 (TB)
1990—Buccaneers, 23-20 (M) OT
Buccaneers, 26-13 (TB)
1991—Vikings, 28-13 (M)
Vikings, 26-24 (TB)
1992—Vikings, 26-20 (M)
Vikings, 35-7 (TB)
1993—Vikings, 15-0 (M)
Buccaneers, 23-10 (TB)
1994—Vikings, 36-13 (TB)
Buccaneers, 20-17 (M) OT
1995—Buccaneers, 20-17 (TB) OT
Vikings, 31-17 (M)

1996—Buccaneers, 24-13 (TB)
Vikings, 21-10 (M)
1997—Buccaneers, 28-14 (M)
Vikings, 10-6 (TB)
1998—Vikings, 31-7 (M)
Buccaneers, 27-24 (TB)
(RS Pts.—Vikings 928, Buccaneers 670)

MINNESOTA vs. *TENNESSEE
RS: Vikings lead series, 5-3
1974—Vikings, 51-10 (M)
1980—Oilers, 20-16 (H)
1983—Vikings, 34-14 (M)
1986—Oilers, 23-10 (H)
1989—Vikings, 38-7 (M)
1992—Oilers, 17-13 (M)
1995—Vikings, 23-17 (M) OT
1998—Vikings, 26-16 (T)
(RS Pts.—Vikings 211, Titans 124)
**Franchise in Houston prior to 1997; known as Oilers prior to 1999*

MINNESOTA vs. WASHINGTON
RS: Redskins lead series, 6-5
PS: Redskins lead series, 3-2
1968—Vikings, 27-14 (M)
1970—Vikings, 19-10 (W)
1972—Redskins, 24-21 (M)
1973—*Vikings, 27-20 (M)
1975—Redskins, 31-30 (W)
1976—*Vikings, 35-20 (M)
1980—Vikings, 39-14 (W)
1982—**Redskins, 21-7 (W)
1984—Redskins, 31-17 (M)
1986—Redskins, 44-38 (W) OT
1987—Redskins, 27-24 (M) OT
***Redskins, 17-10 (W)
1992—Redskins, 15-13 (M)
****Redskins, 24-7 (M)
1993—Vikings, 14-9 (W)
1998—Vikings, 41-7 (M)
(RS Pts.—Vikings 283, Redskins 226)
(PS Pts.—Redskins 102, Vikings 86)
**NFC Divisional Playoff*
***NFC Second-Round Playoff*
****NFC Championship*
*****NFC First-Round Playoff*

NEW ENGLAND vs. ARIZONA
RS: Cardinals lead series, 6-3;
See Arizona vs. New England

NEW ENGLAND vs. ATLANTA
RS: Falcons lead series, 6-3;
See Atlanta vs. New England

NEW ENGLAND vs. BALTIMORE
RS: Patriots lead series, 1-0;
See Baltimore vs. New England

NEW ENGLAND vs. BUFFALO
RS: Patriots lead series, 40-36-1
PS: Patriots lead series, 1-0;
See Buffalo vs. New England

NEW ENGLAND vs. CAROLINA
RS: Panthers lead series, 1-0;
See Carolina vs. New England

NEW ENGLAND vs. CHICAGO
RS: Patriots lead series, 5-2
PS: Bears lead series, 1-0;
See Chicago vs. New England

NEW ENGLAND vs. CINCINNATI
RS: Patriots lead series, 9-7;
See Cincinnati vs. New England

NEW ENGLAND vs. CLEVELAND
RS: Browns lead series, 10-4
PS: Browns lead series, 1-0;
See Cleveland vs. New England

NEW ENGLAND vs. DALLAS
RS: Cowboys lead series, 7-0;
See Dallas vs. New England

NEW ENGLAND vs. DENVER
RS: Broncos lead series, 20-12
PS: Broncos lead series, 1-0;
See Denver vs. New England

NEW ENGLAND vs. DETROIT
RS: Series tied, 3-3;
See Detroit vs. New England

NEW ENGLAND vs. GREEN BAY
RS: Series tied, 3-3
PS: Packers lead series, 1-0;
See Green Bay vs. New England

NEW ENGLAND vs. INDIANAPOLIS
RS: Patriots lead series, 35-22;
See Indianapolis vs. New England

NEW ENGLAND vs. JACKSONVILLE
RS: Patriots lead series, 2-0
PS: Series tied, 1-1;
See Jacksonville vs. New England

NEW ENGLAND vs. KANSAS CITY
RS: Chiefs lead series, 14-8-3;
See Kansas City vs. New England

NEW ENGLAND vs. MIAMI
RS: Dolphins lead series, 38-26
PS: Patriots lead series, 2-1;
See Miami vs. New England

NEW ENGLAND vs. MINNESOTA
RS: Patriots lead series, 4-3;
See Minnesota vs. New England

NEW ENGLAND vs. NEW ORLEANS
RS: Patriots lead series, 6-3
1972—Patriots, 17-10 (NO)
1976—Patriots, 27-6 (NE)
1980—Patriots, 38-27 (NO)
1983—Patriots, 7-0 (NE)
1986—Patriots, 21-20 (NO)
1989—Saints, 28-24 (NE)
1992—Saints, 31-14 (NE)
1995—Saints, 31-17 (NE)
1998—Patriots, 30-27 (NO)
(RS Pts.—Patriots 195, Saints 180)

***NEW ENGLAND vs. N.Y. GIANTS**
RS: Giants lead series, 3-2
1970—Giants, 16-0 (B)
1974—Patriots, 28-20 (New Haven)
1987—Giants, 17-10 (NY)
1990—Giants, 13-10 (NE)
1996—Patriots, 23-22 (NY)
(RS Pts.—Giants 88, Patriots 71)
**Franchise in Boston prior to 1971*

***NEW ENGLAND vs. **N.Y. JETS**
RS: Jets lead series, 42-34-1
PS: Patriots lead series, 1-0
1960—Patriots, 28-24 (NY)
Patriots, 38-21 (B)
1961—Titans, 21-20 (B)
Titans, 37-30 (NY)
1962—Patriots, 43-14 (NY)
Patriots, 24-17 (B)
1963—Patriots, 38-14 (B)
Jets, 31-24 (NY)
1964—Patriots, 26-10 (B)
Jets, 35-14 (NY)
1965—Jets, 30-20 (B)
Patriots, 27-23 (NY)
1966—Tie, 24-24 (B)
Jets, 38-28 (NY)
1967—Jets, 30-23 (NY)
Jets, 29-24 (B)
1968—Jets, 47-31 (Birmingham)
Jets, 48-14 (NY)
1969—Jets, 23-14 (B)
Jets, 23-17 (NY)
1970—Jets, 31-21 (B)
Jets, 17-3 (NY)
1971—Patriots, 20-0 (NE)
Jets, 13-6 (NY)
1972—Jets, 41-13 (NE)
Jets, 34-10 (NY)
1973—Jets, 9-7 (NE)
Jets, 33-13 (NY)
1974—Patriots, 24-0 (NY)
Jets, 21-16 (NE)
1975—Jets, 36-7 (NY)
Jets, 30-28 (NE)
1976—Patriots, 41-7 (NE)
Patriots, 38-24 (NY)
1977—Jets, 30-27 (NY)
Patriots, 24-13 (NE)
1978—Patriots, 55-21 (NE)
Patriots, 19-17 (NY)
1979—Patriots, 56-3 (NE)
Jets, 27-26 (NY)
1980—Patriots, 21-11 (NY)
Patriots, 34-21 (NE)
1981—Jets, 28-24 (NY)
Jets, 17-6 (NE)
1982—Jets, 31-7 (NE)
1983—Patriots, 23-13 (NE)
Jets, 26-3 (NY)
1984—Patriots, 28-21 (NY)
Patriots, 30-20 (NE)
1985—Patriots, 20-13 (NE)
Jets, 16-13 (NY) OT
***Patriots, 26-14 (NY)
1986—Patriots, 20-6 (NY)
Jets, 31-24 (NE)
1987—Jets, 43-24 (NY)
Patriots, 42-20 (NE)
1988—Patriots, 28-3 (NE)
Patriots, 14-13 (NY)
1989—Patriots, 27-24 (NY)
Jets, 27-26 (NE)
1990—Jets, 37-13 (NE)
Jets, 42-7 (NY)
1991—Jets, 28-21 (NE)
Patriots, 6-3 (NY)
1992—Jets, 30-21 (NY)
Patriots, 24-3 (NE)
1993—Jets, 45-7 (NY)
Jets, 6-0 (NE)
1994—Jets, 24-17 (NY)
Patriots, 24-13 (NE)
1995—Patriots, 20-7 (NY)
Patriots, 31-28 (NE)
1996—Patriots, 31-27 (NY)
Patriots, 34-10 (NE)
1997—Patriots, 27-24 (NE) OT
Jets, 24-19 (NY)
1998—Jets, 24-14 (NE)
Jets, 31-10 (NY)
(RS Pts.—Jets 1,736, Patriots 1,701)
(PS Pts.—Patriots 26, Jets 14)
**Franchise in Boston prior to 1971*
***Jets known as Titans prior to 1963*
****AFC First-Round Playoff*

***NEW ENGLAND vs. **OAKLAND**
RS: Raiders lead series, 13-12-1
PS: Series tied, 1-1
1960—Raiders, 27-14 (O)
Patriots, 34-28 (B)
1961—Patriots, 20-17 (B)
Patriots, 35-21 (O)
1962—Patriots, 26-16 (B)
Raiders, 20-0 (O)
1963—Patriots, 20-14 (O)
Patriots, 20-14 (B)
1964—Patriots, 17-14 (O)
Tie, 43-43 (B)
1965—Raiders, 24-10 (B)
Raiders, 30-21 (O)
1966—Patriots, 24-21 (B)
1967—Raiders, 35-7 (O)
Raiders, 48-14 (B)
1968—Raiders, 41-10 (O)
1969—Raiders, 38-23 (B)
1971—Patriots, 20-6 (NE)
1974—Raiders, 41-26 (O)
1976—Patriots, 48-17 (NE)
***Raiders, 24-21 (O)
1978—Patriots, 21-14 (O)
1981—Raiders, 27-17 (O)
1985—Raiders, 35-20 (NE)
***Patriots, 27-20 (LA)
1987—Patriots, 26-23 (NE)
1989—Raiders, 24-21 (LA)
1994—Raiders, 21-17 (NE)
(RS Pts.—Raiders 659, Patriots 554)
(PS Pts.—Patriots 48, Raiders 44)
**Franchise in Boston prior to 1971*
***Franchise in Los Angeles from 1982-1994*
****AFC Divisional Playoff*

NEW ENGLAND vs. PHILADELPHIA
RS: Eagles lead series, 5-2
1973—Eagles, 24-23 (P)
1977—Patriots, 14-6 (NE)
1978—Patriots, 24-14 (NE)
1981—Eagles, 13-3 (P)
1984—Eagles, 27-17 (P)
1987—Eagles, 34-31 (NE) OT
1990—Eagles, 48-20 (P)
(RS Pts.—Eagles 166, Patriots 132)

NEW ENGLAND vs. PITTSBURGH
RS: Steelers lead series, 11-4
PS: Series tied, 1-1
1972—Steelers, 33-3 (P)
1974—Steelers, 21-17 (NE)
1976—Patriots, 30-27 (P)
1979—Steelers, 16-13 (NE) OT
1981—Steelers, 27-21 (P) OT
1982—Steelers, 37-14 (P)
1983—Patriots, 28-23 (P)
1986—Patriots, 34-0 (P)
1989—Steelers, 28-10 (P)
1990—Steelers, 24-3 (P)
1991—Steelers, 20-6 (P)
1993—Steelers, 17-14 (P)
1995—Steelers, 41-27 (P)
1996—*Patriots, 28-3 (NE)
1997—Steelers, 24-21 (NE) OT
*Steelers, 7-6 (P)
1998—Patriots, 23-9 (P)
(RS Pts.—Steelers 347, Patriots 264)
(PS Pts.—Patriots 34, Steelers 10)
**AFC Divisional Playoff*

NEW ENGLAND vs. *ST. LOUIS
RS: Rams lead series, 4-3
1974—Patriots, 20-14 (NE)
1980—Rams, 17-14 (NE)
1983—Patriots, 21-7 (LA)
1986—Patriots, 30-28 (LA)
1989—Rams, 24-20 (NE)
1992—Rams, 14-0 (LA)
1998—Rams, 32-18 (StL)
(RS Pts.—Rams 136, Patriots 123)
**Franchise in Los Angeles prior to 1995*

***NEW ENGLAND vs. **SAN DIEGO**
RS: Patriots lead series, 16-11-2
PS: Chargers lead series, 1-0
1960—Patriots, 35-0 (LA)
Chargers, 45-16 (B)
1961—Chargers, 38-27 (B)
Patriots, 41-0 (SD)
1962—Patriots, 24-20 (B)
Patriots, 20-14 (SD)
1963—Chargers, 17-13 (SD)
Chargers, 7-6 (B)
***Chargers, 51-10 (SD)
1964—Patriots, 33-28 (SD)
Chargers, 26-17 (B)
1965—Tie, 10-10 (B)
Patriots, 22-6 (SD)
1966—Chargers, 24-0 (SD)
Patriots, 35-17 (B)
1967—Chargers, 28-14 (SD)
Tie, 31-31 (SD)
1968—Chargers, 27-17 (B)
1969—Chargers, 13-10 (B)
Chargers, 28-18 (SD)
1970—Chargers, 16-14 (B)
1973—Patriots, 30-14 (NE)
1975—Patriots, 33-19 (SD)
1977—Patriots, 24-20 (SD)
1978—Patriots, 28-23 (NE)
1979—Patriots, 27-21 (NE)
1983—Patriots, 37-21 (NE)
1994—Patriots, 23-17 (NE)
1996—Patriots, 45-7 (SD)
1997—Patriots, 41-7 (NE)
(RS Pts.—Patriots 691, Chargers 544)
(PS Pts.—Chargers 51, Patriots 10)
**Franchise in Boston prior to 1971*
***Franchise in Los Angeles prior to 1961*
****AFL Championship*

ALL-TIME TEAM VS. TEAM RESULTS

NEW ENGLAND vs. SAN FRANCISCO
RS: 49ers lead series, 7-2
1971—49ers, 27-10 (SF)
1975—Patriots, 24-16 (NE)
1980—49ers, 21-17 (SF)
1983—49ers, 33-13 (NE)
1986—49ers, 29-24 (NE)
1989—49ers, 37-20 (SF)
1992—49ers, 24-12 (NE)
1995—49ers, 28-3 (SF)
1998—Patriots, 24-21 (NE)
(RS Pts.—49ers 236, Patriots 147)
NEW ENGLAND vs. SEATTLE
RS: Seahawks lead series, 7-6
1977—Patriots, 31-0 (NE)
1980—Patriots, 37-31 (S)
1982—Patriots, 16-0 (S)
1983—Seahawks, 24-6 (S)
1984—Patriots, 38-23 (NE)
1985—Patriots, 20-13 (S)
1986—Seahawks, 38-31 (NE)
1988—Patriots, 13-7 (NE)
1989—Seahawks, 24-3 (NE)
1990—Seahawks, 33-20 (NE)
1992—Seahawks, 10-6 (NE)
1993—Seahawks, 17-14 (NE)
Seahawks, 10-9 (S)
(RS Pts.—Patriots 244, Seahawks 230)
NEW ENGLAND vs. TAMPA BAY
RS: Patriots lead series, 3-1
1976—Patriots, 31-14 (TB)
1985—Patriots, 32-14 (TB)
1988—Patriots, 10-7 (NE) OT
1997—Buccaneers, 27-7 (TB)
(RS Pts.—Patriots 80, Buccaneers 62)
***NEW ENGLAND vs. **TENNESSEE**
RS: Patriots lead series, 18-14-1
PS: Titans lead series, 1-0
1960—Oilers, 24-10 (B)
Oilers, 37-21 (H)
1961—Tie, 31-31 (B)
Oilers, 27-15 (H)
1962—Patriots, 34-21 (B)
Oilers, 21-17 (H)
1963—Patriots, 45-3 (B)
Patriots, 46-28 (H)
1964—Patriots, 25-24 (B)
Patriots, 34-17 (H)
1965—Oilers, 31-10 (H)
Patriots, 42-14 (B)
1966—Patriots, 27-21 (B)
Patriots, 38-14 (H)
1967—Patriots, 18-7 (B)
Oilers, 27-6 (H)
1968—Oilers, 16-0 (B)
Oilers, 45-17 (H)
1969—Patriots, 24-0 (B)
Oilers, 27-23 (H)
1971—Patriots, 28-20 (NE)
1973—Patriots, 32-0 (H)
1975—Oilers, 7-0 (NE)
1978—Oilers, 26-23 (NE)
***Oilers, 31-14 (NE)
1980—Oilers, 38-34 (H)
1981—Patriots, 38-10 (NE)
1982—Patriots, 29-21 (NE)
1987—Patriots, 21-7 (H)
1988—Oilers, 31-6 (H)
1989—Patriots, 23-13 (NE)
1991—Patriots, 24-20 (NE)
1993—Oilers, 28-14 (NE)
1998—Patriots, 27-16 (NE)
(RS Pts.—Patriots 782, Titans 672)
(PS Pts.—Titans 31, Patriots 14)
**Franchise in Boston prior to 1971*
***Franchise in Houston prior to 1997; known as Oilers prior to 1999*
****AFC Divisional Playoff*
NEW ENGLAND vs. WASHINGTON
RS: Redskins lead series, 5-1
1972—Patriots, 24-23 (NE)
1978—Redskins, 16-14 (NE)
1981—Redskins, 24-22 (W)
1984—Redskins, 26-10 (NE)
1990—Redskins, 25-10 (NE)
1996—Redskins, 27-22 (NE)
(RS Pts.—Redskins 141, Patriots 102)

NEW ORLEANS vs. ARIZONA
RS: Cardinals lead series, 12-10;
See Arizona vs. New Orleans
NEW ORLEANS vs. ATLANTA
RS: Falcons lead series, 35-24
PS: Falcons lead series, 1-0;
See Atlanta vs. New Orleans
NEW ORLEANS vs. BALTIMORE
RS: Ravens lead series, 1-0;
See Baltimore vs. New Orleans
NEW ORLEANS vs. BUFFALO
RS: Bills lead series, 4-2;
See Buffalo vs. New Orleans
NEW ORLEANS vs. CAROLINA
RS: Panthers lead series, 5-3;
See Carolina vs. New Orleans
NEW ORLEANS vs. CHICAGO
RS: Bears lead series, 9-8
PS: Bears lead series, 1-0;
See Chicago vs. New Orleans
NEW ORLEANS vs. CINCINNATI
RS: Saints lead series, 5-4;
See Cincinnati vs. New Orleans
NEW ORLEANS vs. CLEVELAND
RS: Browns lead series, 9-3;
See Cleveland vs. New Orleans
NEW ORLEANS vs. DALLAS
RS: Cowboys lead series, 14-4;
See Dallas vs. New Orleans
NEW ORLEANS vs. DENVER
RS: Broncos lead series, 4-2;
See Denver vs. New Orleans
NEW ORLEANS vs. DETROIT
RS: Saints lead series, 8-6-1;
See Detroit vs. New Orleans
NEW ORLEANS vs. GREEN BAY
RS: Packers lead series, 13-4;
See Green Bay vs. New Orleans
NEW ORLEANS vs. INDIANAPOLIS
RS: Saints lead series, 4-3;
See Indianapolis vs. New Orleans
NEW ORLEANS vs. JACKSONVILLE
RS: Saints lead series, 1-0;
See Jacksonville vs. New Orleans
NEW ORLEANS vs. KANSAS CITY
RS: Chiefs lead series, 4-3;
See Kansas City vs. New Orleans
NEW ORLEANS vs. MIAMI
RS: Dolphins lead series, 5-3;
See Miami vs. New Orleans
NEW ORLEANS vs. MINNESOTA
RS: Vikings lead series, 14-6
PS: Vikings lead series, 1-0;
See Minnesota vs. New Orleans
NEW ORLEANS vs. NEW ENGLAND
RS: Patriots lead series, 6-3;
See New England vs. New Orleans
NEW ORLEANS vs. N.Y. GIANTS
RS: Giants lead series, 11-8
1967—Giants, 27-21 (NY)
1968—Giants, 38-21 (NY)
1969—Saints, 25-24 (NY)
1970—Saints, 14-10 (NO)
1972—Giants, 45-21 (NY)
1975—Giants, 28-14 (NY)
1978—Saints, 28-17 (NO)
1979—Saints, 24-14 (NO)
1981—Giants, 20-7 (NY)
1984—Saints, 10-3 (NY)
1985—Giants, 21-13 (NO)
1986—Giants, 20-17 (NY)
1987—Saints, 23-14 (NO)
1988—Giants, 13-12 (NO)
1993—Giants, 24-14 (NO)
1994—Saints, 27-22 (NO)
1995—Giants, 45-29 (NY)
1996—Saints 17-3 (NY)
1997—Giants, 14-9 (NY)
(RS Pts.—Giants 402, Saints 346)
NEW ORLEANS vs. N.Y. JETS
RS: Series tied, 4-4
1972—Jets, 18-17 (NY)
1977—Jets, 16-13 (NO)
1980—Saints, 21-20 (NY)
1983—Jets, 31-28 (NO)
1986—Jets, 28-23 (NY)
1989—Saints, 29-14 (NO)
1992—Saints, 20-0 (NY)
1995—Saints, 12-0 (NY)
(RS Pts.—Saints 163, Jets 127)
NEW ORLEANS vs. *OAKLAND
RS: Raiders lead series, 4-3-1
1971—Tie, 21-21 (NO)
1975—Raiders, 48-10 (O)
1979—Raiders, 42-35 (NO)
1985—Raiders, 23-13 (LA)
1988—Saints, 20-6 (NO)
1991—Saints, 27-0 (NO)
1994—Raiders, 24-19 (LA)
1997—Saints, 13-10 (O)
(RS Pts.—Raiders 174, Saints 158)
**Franchise in Los Angeles from 1982-1994*
NEW ORLEANS vs. PHILADELPHIA
RS: Eagles lead series, 12-8
PS: Eagles lead series, 1-0
1967—Saints, 31-24 (NO)
Eagles, 48-21 (P)
1968—Eagles, 29-17 (P)
1969—Eagles, 13-10 (P)
Saints, 26-17 (NO)
1972—Saints, 21-3 (NO)
1974—Saints, 14-10 (NO)
1977—Eagles, 28-7 (P)
1978—Eagles, 24-17 (NO)
1979—Eagles, 26-14 (NO)
1980—Eagles, 34-21 (NO)
1981—Eagles, 31-14 (NO)
1983—Saints, 20-17 (P) OT
1985—Saints, 23-21 (NO)
1987—Eagles, 27-17 (P)
1989—Saints, 30-20 (NO)
1991—Saints, 13-6 (P)
1992—Eagles, 15-13 (P)
*Eagles, 36-20 (NO)
1993—Eagles, 37-26 (P)
1995—Eagles, 15-10 (NO)
(RS Pts.—Eagles 445, Saints 365)
(PS Pts.—Eagles 36, Saints 20)
**NFC First-Round Playoff*
NEW ORLEANS vs. PITTSBURGH
RS: Steelers lead series, 6-5
1967—Steelers, 14-10 (NO)
1968—Saints, 16-12 (P)
Saints, 24-14 (NO)
1969—Saints, 27-24 (NO)
1974—Steelers, 28-7 (NO)
1978—Steelers, 20-14 (P)
1981—Steelers, 20-6 (NO)
1984—Saints, 27-24 (NO)
1987—Saints, 20-16 (P)
1990—Steelers, 9-6 (NO)
1993—Steelers, 37-14 (P)
(RS Pts.—Steelers 218, Saints 171)
NEW ORLEANS vs. *ST. LOUIS
RS: Rams lead series, 32-26
1967—Rams, 27-13 (NO)
1969—Rams, 36-17 (LA)
1970—Rams, 30-17 (NO)
Rams, 34-16 (LA)
1971—Saints, 24-20 (NO)
Rams, 45-28 (LA)
1972—Rams, 34-14 (LA)
Saints, 19-16 (NO)
1973—Rams, 29-7 (LA)
Rams, 24-13 (NO)
1974—Rams, 24-0 (LA)
Saints, 20-7 (NO)
1975—Rams, 38-14 (LA)
Rams, 14-7 (NO)
1976—Rams, 16-10 (NO)
Rams, 33-14 (LA)
1977—Rams, 14-7 (LA)
Saints, 27-26 (NO)
1978—Rams, 26-20 (NO)
Saints, 10-3 (LA)
1979—Rams, 35-17 (NO)
Saints, 29-14 (LA)
1980—Rams, 45-31 (LA)
Rams, 27-7 (NO)
1981—Saints, 23-17 (NO)
Saints, 21-13 (LA)
1983—Rams, 30-27 (LA)
Rams, 26-24 (NO)
1984—Rams, 28-10 (NO)
Rams, 34-21 (LA)
1985—Rams, 28-10 (LA)
Saints, 29-3 (NO)
1986—Saints, 6-0 (NO)
Rams, 26-13 (LA)
1987—Saints, 37-10 (NO)
Saints, 31-14 (LA)
1988—Rams, 12-10 (NO)
Saints, 14-10 (LA)
1989—Saints, 40-21 (LA)
Rams, 20-17 (NO) OT
1990—Saints, 24-20 (LA)
Saints, 20-17 (NO)
1991—Saints, 24-7 (NO)
Saints, 24-17 (LA)
1992—Saints, 13-10 (NO)
Saints, 37-14 (LA)
1993—Saints, 37-6 (LA)
Rams, 23-20 (NO)
1994—Saints, 37-34 (NO)
Saints, 31-15 (LA)
1995—Rams, 17-13 (StL)
Saints, 19-10 (NO)
1996—Rams, 26-10 (NO)
Rams, 14-13 (StL)
1997—Rams, 38-24 (StL)
Rams, 34-27 (NO)
1998—Saints, 24-17 (StL)
Saints, 24-3 (NO)
(RS Pts.—Rams 1,231, Saints 1,135)
**Franchise in Los Angeles prior to 1995*
NEW ORLEANS vs. SAN DIEGO
RS: Chargers lead series, 6-1
1973—Chargers, 17-14 (SD)
1977—Chargers, 14-0 (NO)
1979—Chargers, 35-0 (NO)
1988—Saints, 23-17 (SD)
1991—Chargers, 24-21 (SD)
1994—Chargers, 36-22 (NO)
1997—Chargers, 20-6 (NO)
(RS Pts.—Chargers 163, Saints 86)
NEW ORLEANS vs. SAN FRANCISCO
RS: 49ers lead series, 42-15-2
1967—49ers, 27-13 (SF)
1969—Saints, 43-38 (NO)
1970—Tie, 20-20 (SF)
49ers, 38-27 (NO)
1971—49ers, 38-20 (NO)
Saints, 26-20 (SF)
1972—49ers, 37-2 (NO)
Tie, 20-20 (SF)
1973—49ers, 40-0 (SF)
Saints, 16-10 (NO)
1974—49ers, 17-13 (NO)
49ers, 35-21 (SF)
1975—49ers, 35-21 (SF)
49ers, 16-6 (NO)
1976—49ers, 33-3 (SF)
49ers, 27-7 (NO)
1977—49ers, 10-7 (NO) OT
49ers, 20-17 (SF)
1978—Saints, 14-7 (SF)
Saints, 24-13 (NO)
1979—Saints, 30-21 (SF)
Saints, 31-20 (NO)
1980—49ers, 26-23 (NO)
49ers, 38-35 (SF) OT
1981—49ers, 21-14 (SF)
49ers, 21-17 (NO)

1982—Saints, 23-20 (SF)
1983—49ers, 32-13 (NO)
49ers, 27-0 (SF)
1984—49ers, 30-20 (SF)
49ers, 35-3 (NO)
1985—Saints, 20-17 (SF)
49ers, 31-19 (NO)
1986—49ers, 26-17 (SF)
Saints, 23-10 (NO)
1987—49ers, 24-22 (NO)
Saints, 26-24 (SF)
1988—49ers, 34-33 (NO)
49ers, 30-17 (SF)
1989—49ers, 24-20 (NO)
49ers, 31-13 (SF)
1990—49ers, 13-12 (NO)
Saints, 13-10 (SF)
1991—Saints, 10-3 (NO)
49ers, 38-24 (SF)
1992—49ers, 16-10 (NO)
49ers, 21-20 (SF)
1993—Saints, 16-13 (NO)
49ers, 42-7 (SF)
1994—49ers, 24-13 (SF)
49ers, 35-14 (NO)
1995—49ers, 24-22 (NO)
Saints, 11-7 (SF)
1996—49ers, 27-11 (SF)
49ers, 24-17 (NO)
1997—49ers, 33-7 (SF)
49ers, 23-0 (NO)
1998—49ers, 31-0 (NO)
49ers, 31-20 (SF)
(RS Pts.—49ers 1,458, Saints 966)

NEW ORLEANS vs. SEATTLE
RS: Saints lead series, 4-2
1976—Saints, 51-27 (S)
1979—Seahawks, 38-24 (S)
1985—Seahawks, 27-3 (NO)
1988—Saints, 20-19 (S)
1991—Saints, 27-24 (NO)
1997—Saints, 20-17 (NO) OT
(RS Pts.—Seahawks 152, Saints 145)

NEW ORLEANS vs. TAMPA BAY
RS: Saints lead series, 13-5
1977—Buccaneers, 33-14 (NO)
1978—Saints, 17-10 (TB)
1979—Saints, 42-14 (TB)
1981—Buccaneers, 31-14 (NO)
1982—Buccaneers, 13-10 (NO)
1983—Saints, 24-21 (TB)
1984—Saints, 17-13 (NO)
1985—Saints, 20-13 (NO)
1986—Saints, 38-7 (NO)
1987—Saints, 44-34 (NO)
1988—Saints, 13-9 (NO)
1989—Buccaneers, 20-10 (TB)
1990—Saints, 35-7 (NO)
1991—Saints, 23-7 (NO)
1992—Saints, 23-21 (NO)
1994—Saints, 9-7 (TB)
1996—Buccaneers, 13-7 (TB)
1998—Saints, 9-3 (NO)
(RS Pts.—Saints 369, Buccaneers 276)

NEW ORLEANS vs. *TENNESSEE
RS: Series tied, 4-4-1
1971—Tie, 13-13 (H)
1976—Oilers, 31-26 (NO)
1978—Oilers, 17-12 (NO)
1981—Saints, 27-24 (H)
1984—Saints, 27-10 (H)
1987—Saints, 24-10 (NO)
1990—Oilers, 23-10 (H)
1993—Saints, 33-21 (NO)
1996—Oilers, 31-14 (NO)
(RS Pts.—Saints 186, Titans 180)
**Franchise in Houston prior to 1997; known as Oilers prior to 1999*

NEW ORLEANS vs. WASHINGTON
RS: Redskins lead series, 12-5
1967—Redskins, 30-10 (NO)
Saints, 30-14 (W)
1968—Saints, 37-17 (NO)
1969—Redskins, 26-20 (NO)
Redskins, 17-14 (W)
1971—Redskins, 24-14 (W)
1973—Saints, 19-3 (NO)
1975—Redskins, 41-3 (W)
1979—Saints, 14-10 (W)
1980—Redskins, 22-14 (W)
1982—Redskins, 27-10 (NO)
1986—Redskins, 14-6 (NO)
1988—Redskins, 27-24 (W)
1989—Redskins, 16-14 (NO)
1990—Redskins, 31-17 (W)
1992—Saints, 20-3 (NO)
1994—Redskins, 38-24 (NO)
(RS Pts.—Redskins 360, Saints 290)

N.Y. GIANTS vs. ARIZONA
RS: Giants lead series, 73-37-2;
See Arizona vs. N.Y. Giants

N.Y. GIANTS vs. ATLANTA
RS: Falcons lead series, 7-6;
See Atlanta vs. N.Y. Giants

N.Y. GIANTS vs. BALTIMORE
RS: Ravens lead series, 1-0;
See Baltimore vs. N.Y. Giants

N.Y. GIANTS vs. BUFFALO
RS: Bills lead series, 5-2
PS: Giants lead series, 1-0;
See Buffalo vs. N.Y. Giants

N.Y. GIANTS vs. CAROLINA
RS: Panthers lead series, 1-0;
See Carolina vs. N.Y. Giants

N.Y. GIANTS vs. CHICAGO
RS: Bears lead series, 25-16-2
PS: Bears lead series, 5-3;
See Chicago vs. N.Y. Giants

N.Y. GIANTS vs. CINCINNATI
RS: Bengals lead series, 4-2;
See Cincinnati vs. N.Y. Giants

N.Y. GIANTS vs. CLEVELAND
RS: Browns lead series, 25-17-2
PS: Series tied, 1-1;
See Cleveland vs. N.Y. Giants

N.Y. GIANTS vs. DALLAS
RS: Cowboys lead series, 46-25-2;
See Dallas vs. N.Y. Giants

N.Y. GIANTS vs. DENVER
RS: Giants lead series, 4-3
PS: Giants lead series, 1-0;
See Denver vs. N.Y. Giants

N.Y. GIANTS vs. DETROIT
RS: Lions lead series, 18-17-1
PS: Lions lead series, 1-0;
See Detroit vs. N.Y. Giants

N.Y. GIANTS vs. GREEN BAY
RS: Packers lead series, 23-20-2
PS: Packers lead series, 4-1;
See Green Bay vs. N.Y. Giants

N.Y. GIANTS vs. INDIANAPOLIS
RS: Series tied, 5-5
PS: Colts lead series, 2-0;
See Indianapolis vs. N.Y. Giants

N.Y. GIANTS vs. JACKSONVILLE
RS: Jaguars lead series, 1-0;
See Jacksonville vs. N.Y. Giants

N.Y. GIANTS vs. KANSAS CITY
RS: Giants lead series, 7-2;
See Kansas City vs. N.Y. Giants

N.Y. GIANTS vs. MIAMI
RS: Giants lead series, 3-1;
See Miami vs. N.Y. Giants

N.Y. GIANTS vs. MINNESOTA
RS: Vikings lead series, 7-5
PS: Series tied, 1-1;
See Minnesota vs. N.Y. Giants

N.Y. GIANTS vs. NEW ENGLAND
RS: Giants lead series, 3-2;
See New England vs. N.Y. Giants

N.Y. GIANTS vs. NEW ORLEANS
RS: Giants lead series, 11-8;
See New Orleans vs. N.Y. Giants

N.Y. GIANTS vs. N.Y. JETS
RS: Series tied, 4-4
1970—Giants, 22-10 (NYJ)
1974—Jets, 26-20 (New Haven) OT
1981—Jets, 26-7 (NYG)
1984—Giants, 20-10 (NYJ)
1987—Giants, 20-7 (NYG)
1988—Jets, 27-21 (NYJ)
1993—Jets, 10-6 (NYG)
1996—Giants, 13-6 (NYJ)
(RS Pts.—Giants 129, Jets 122)

N.Y. GIANTS vs. *OAKLAND
RS: Raiders lead series, 6-2
1973—Raiders, 42-0 (O)
1980—Raiders, 33-17 (NY)
1983—Raiders, 27-12 (LA)
1986—Giants, 14-9 (LA)
1989—Giants, 34-17 (NY)
1992—Raiders, 13-10 (LA)
1995—Raiders, 17-13 (NY)
1998—Raiders, 20-17 (O)
(RS Pts.—Raiders 178, Giants 117)
**Franchise in Los Angeles from 1982-1994*

N.Y. GIANTS vs. PHILADELPHIA
RS: Giants lead series, 68-58-2
PS: Giants lead series, 1-0
1933—Giants, 56-0 (NY)
Giants, 20-14 (P)
1934—Giants, 17-0 (NY)
Eagles, 6-0 (P)
1935—Giants, 10-0 (NY)
Giants, 21-14 (P)
1936—Eagles, 10-7 (P)
Giants, 21-17 (NY)
1937—Giants, 16-7 (P)
Giants, 21-0 (NY)
1938—Eagles, 14-10 (P)
Giants, 17-7 (NY)
1939—Giants, 13-3 (P)
Giants, 27-10 (NY)
1940—Giants, 20-14 (P)
Giants, 17-7 (NY)
1941—Giants, 24-0 (P)
Giants, 16-0 (NY)
1942—Giants, 35-17 (NY)
Giants, 14-0 (P)
1944—Eagles, 24-17 (NY)
Tie, 21-21 (P)
1945—Eagles, 38-17 (P)
Giants, 28-21 (NY)
1946—Eagles, 24-14 (P)
Giants, 45-17 (NY)
1947—Eagles, 23-0 (P)
Eagles, 41-24 (NY)
1948—Eagles, 45-0 (P)
Eagles, 35-14 (NY)
1949—Eagles, 24-3 (NY)
Eagles, 17-3 (P)
1950—Giants, 7-3 (NY)
Giants, 9-7 (P)
1951—Giants, 26-24 (NY)
Giants, 23-7 (P)
1952—Giants, 31-7 (P)
Eagles, 14-10 (NY)
1953—Eagles, 30-7 (P)
Giants, 37-28 (NY)
1954—Giants, 27-14 (NY)
Eagles, 29-14 (P)
1955—Eagles, 27-17 (P)
Giants, 31-7 (NY)
1956—Giants, 20-3 (NY)
Giants, 21-7 (P)
1957—Giants, 24-20 (P)
Giants, 13-0 (NY)
1958—Eagles, 27-24 (P)
Giants, 24-10 (NY)
1959—Eagles, 49-21 (P)
Giants, 24-7 (NY)
1960—Eagles, 17-10 (NY)
Eagles, 31-23 (P)
1961—Giants, 38-21 (NY)
Giants, 28-24 (P)
1962—Giants, 29-13 (P)
Giants, 19-14 (NY)
1963—Giants, 37-14 (P)
Giants, 42-14 (NY)
1964—Eagles, 38-7 (P)
Eagles, 23-17 (NY)
1965—Giants, 16-14 (P)
Giants, 35-27 (NY)
1966—Eagles, 35-17 (P)
Eagles, 31-3 (NY)
1967—Giants, 44-7 (NY)
1968—Giants, 34-25 (P)
Giants, 7-6 (NY)
1969—Eagles, 23-20 (NY)
1970—Giants, 30-23 (NY)
Eagles, 23-20 (P)
1971—Eagles, 23-7 (P)
Eagles, 41-28 (NY)
1972—Giants, 27-12 (P)
Giants, 62-10 (NY)
1973—Tie, 23-23 (NY)
Eagles, 20-16 (P)
1974—Eagles, 35-7 (P)
Eagles, 20-7 (New Haven)
1975—Giants, 23-14 (P)
Eagles, 13-10 (NY)
1976—Eagles, 20-7 (P)
Eagles, 10-0 (NY)
1977—Eagles, 28-10 (NY)
Eagles, 17-14 (P)
1978—Eagles, 19-17 (NY)
Eagles, 20-3 (P)
1979—Eagles, 23-17 (P)
Eagles, 17-13 (NY)
1980—Eagles, 35-3 (P)
Eagles, 31-16 (NY)
1981—Eagles, 24-10 (NY)
Giants, 20-10 (P)
*Giants, 27-21 (P)
1982—Giants, 23-7 (NY)
Giants, 26-24 (P)
1983—Eagles, 17-13 (NY)
Giants, 23-0 (P)
1984—Giants, 28-27 (NY)
Eagles, 24-10 (P)
1985—Giants, 21-0 (NY)
Giants, 16-10 (P) OT
1986—Giants, 35-3 (NY)
Giants, 17-14 (P)
1987—Giants, 20-17 (P)
Giants, 23-20 (NY) OT
1988—Eagles, 24-13 (P)
Eagles, 23-17 (NY) OT
1989—Eagles, 21-19 (P)
Eagles, 24-17 (NY)
1990—Giants, 27-20 (NY)
Eagles, 31-13 (P)
1991—Eagles, 30-7 (P)
Eagles, 19-14 (NY)
1992—Eagles, 47-34 (NY)
Eagles, 20-10 (P)
1993—Giants, 21-10 (NY)
Giants, 7-3 (P)
1994—Giants, 28-23 (NY)
Giants, 16-13 (P)
1995—Eagles, 17-14 (NY)
Eagles, 28-19 (P)
1996—Eagles, 19-10 (NY)
Eagles, 24-0 (P)
1997—Giants, 31-17 (NY)
Giants, 31-21 (P)
1998—Giants, 20-0 (NY)
Giants, 20-10 (P)
(RS Pts.—Giants 2,437, Eagles 2,285)
(PS Pts.—Giants 27, Eagles 21)
**NFC First-Round Playoff*

N.Y. GIANTS vs. *PITTSBURGH
RS: Giants lead series, 42-27-3
1933—Giants, 23-2 (P)
Giants, 27-3 (NY)
1934—Giants, 14-12 (P)
Giants, 17-7 (NY)
1935—Giants, 42-7 (P)
Giants, 13-0 (NY)
1936—Pirates, 10-7 (P)

ALL-TIME TEAM VS. TEAM RESULTS

1937—Giants, 10-7 (P)
Giants, 17-0 (NY)
1938—Giants, 27-14 (P)
Pirates, 13-10 (NY)
1939—Giants, 14-7 (P)
Giants, 23-7 (NY)
1940—Tie, 10-10 (P)
Giants, 12-0 (NY)
1941—Giants, 37-10 (P)
Giants, 28-7 (NY)
1942—Steelers, 13-10 (P)
Steelers, 17-9 (NY)
1945—Giants, 34-6 (P)
Steelers, 21-7 (NY)
1946—Giants, 17-14 (P)
Giants, 7-0 (NY)
1947—Steelers, 38-21 (NY)
Steelers, 24-7 (P)
1948—Giants, 34-27 (NY)
Steelers, 38-28 (P)
1949—Steelers, 28-7 (P)
Steelers, 21-17 (NY)
1950—Giants, 18-7 (P)
Steelers, 17-6 (NY)
1951—Tie, 13-13 (P)
Giants, 14-0 (NY)
1952—Steelers, 63-7 (P)
1953—Steelers, 24-14 (P)
Steelers, 14-10 (NY)
1954—Giants, 30-6 (P)
Giants, 24-3 (NY)
1955—Steelers, 30-23 (P)
Steelers, 19-17 (NY)
1956—Giants, 38-10 (NY)
Giants, 17-14 (P)
1957—Giants, 35-0 (NY)
Steelers, 21-10 (P)
1958—Giants, 17-6 (NY)
Steelers, 31-10 (P)
1959—Giants, 21-16 (P)
Steelers, 14-9 (NY)
1960—Giants, 19-17 (P)
Giants, 27-24 (NY)
1961—Giants, 17-14 (P)
Giants, 42-21 (NY)
1962—Giants, 31-27 (P)
Steelers, 20-17 (NY)
1963—Steelers, 31-0 (P)
Giants, 33-17 (NY)
1964—Steelers, 27-24 (P)
Steelers, 44-17 (NY)
1965—Giants, 23-13 (P)
Giants, 35-10 (NY)
1966—Tie, 34-34 (P)
Steelers, 47-28 (NY)
1967—Giants, 27-24 (P)
Giants, 28-20 (NY)
1968—Giants, 34-20 (P)
1969—Giants, 10-7 (NY)
Giants, 21-17 (P)
1971—Steelers, 17-13 (P)
1976—Steelers, 27-0 (NY)
1985—Giants, 28-10 (NY)
1991—Giants, 23-20 (P)
1994—Steelers, 10-6 (NY)
(RS Pts.—Giants 1,399, Steelers 1,189)
**Steelers known as Pirates prior to 1941*

N.Y. GIANTS vs. *ST. LOUIS
RS: Rams lead series, 22-9
PS: Series tied, 1-1
1938—Giants, 28-0 (NY)
1940—Rams, 13-0 (NY)
1941—Giants, 49-14 (NY)
1945—Rams, 21-17 (NY)
1946—Rams, 31-21 (NY)
1947—Rams, 34-10 (LA)
1948—Rams, 52-37 (NY)
1953—Rams, 21-7 (LA)
1954—Rams, 17-16 (NY)
1959—Giants, 23-21 (LA)
1961—Giants, 24-14 (NY)
1966—Rams, 55-14 (LA)
1968—Rams, 24-21 (LA)
1970—Rams, 31-3 (NY)
1973—Rams, 40-6 (LA)
1976—Rams, 24-10 (LA)
1978—Rams, 20-17 (NY)
1979—Giants, 20-14 (LA)
1980—Rams, 28-7 (NY)
1981—Giants, 10-7 (NY)
1983—Rams, 16-6 (NY)
1984—Rams, 33-12 (LA)
**Giants, 16-13 (LA)
1985—Giants, 24-19 (NY)
1988—Rams, 45-31 (NY)
1989—Rams, 31-10 (LA)
***Rams, 19-13 (NY) OT
1990—Giants, 31-7 (LA)
1991—Rams, 19-13 (NY)
1992—Rams, 38-17 (LA)
1993—Giants, 20-10 (NY)
1994—Rams, 17-10 (LA)
1997—Rams, 13-3 (StL)
(RS Pts.—Rams 729, Giants 517)
(PS Pts.—Rams 32, Giants 29)
**Franchise in Los Angeles prior to 1995 and in Cleveland prior to 1946*
***NFC First-Round Playoff*
****NFC Divisional Playoff*

N.Y. GIANTS vs. SAN DIEGO
RS: Giants lead series, 5-3
1971—Giants, 35-17 (NY)
1975—Giants, 35-24 (NY)
1980—Chargers, 44-7 (SD)
1983—Chargers, 41-34 (NY)
1986—Giants, 20-7 (NY)
1989—Giants, 20-13 (SD)
1995—Chargers, 27-17 (NY)
1998—Giants, 34-16 (SD)
(RS Pts.—Giants 202, Chargers 189)

N.Y. GIANTS vs. SAN FRANCISCO
RS: 49ers lead series, 12-11
PS: Series tied, 3-3
1952—Giants, 23-14 (NY)
1956—Giants, 38-21 (SF)
1957—49ers, 27-17 (NY)
1960—Giants, 21-19 (SF)
1963—Giants, 48-14 (NY)
1968—49ers, 26-10 (NY)
1972—Giants, 23-17 (SF)
1975—Giants, 26-23 (SF)
1977—Giants, 20-17 (NY)
1978—Giants, 27-10 (NY)
1979—Giants, 32-16 (NY)
1980—49ers, 12-0 (SF)
1981—49ers, 17-10 (SF)
*49ers, 38-24 (SF)
1984—49ers, 31-10 (NY)
*49ers, 21-10 (SF)
1985—**Giants, 17-3 (NY)
1986—Giants, 21-17 (SF)
*Giants, 49-3 (NY)
1987—49ers, 41-21 (NY)
1988—49ers, 20-17 (NY)
1989—49ers, 34-24 (SF)
1990—49ers, 7-3 (SF)
***Giants, 15-13 (SF)
1991—Giants, 16-14 (NY)
1992—49ers, 31-14 (NY)
1993—*49ers, 44-3 (SF)
1995—49ers, 20-6 (SF)
1998—49ers, 31-7 (SF)
(RS Pts.—49ers 479, Giants 434)
(PS Pts.—49ers 122, Giants 118)
**NFC Divisional Playoff*
***NFC First-Round Playoff*
****NFC Championship*

N.Y. GIANTS vs. SEATTLE
RS: Giants lead series, 5-3
1976—Giants, 28-16 (NY)
1980—Giants, 27-21 (S)
1981—Giants, 32-0 (S)
1983—Seahawks, 17-12 (NY)
1986—Seahawks, 17-12 (S)
1989—Giants, 15-3 (NY)
1992—Giants, 23-10 (NY)
1995—Seahawks, 30-28 (S)
(RS Pts.—Giants 177, Seahawks 114)

N.Y. GIANTS vs. TAMPA BAY
RS: Giants lead series, 8-5
1977—Giants, 10-0 (TB)
1978—Giants, 19-13 (TB)
Giants, 17-14 (NY)
1979—Giants, 17-14 (NY)
Buccaneers, 31-3 (TB)
1980—Buccaneers, 30-13 (TB)
1984—Giants, 17-14 (NY)
Buccaneers, 20-17 (TB)
1985—Giants, 22-20 (NY)
1991—Giants, 21-14 (TB)
1993—Giants, 23-7 (NY)
1997—Buccaneers, 20-8 (NY)
1998—Buccaneers, 20-3 (TB)
(RS Pts.—Buccaneers 217, Giants 190)

N.Y. GIANTS vs. *TENNESSEE
RS: Giants lead series, 5-1
1973—Giants, 34-14 (NY)
1982—Giants, 17-14 (NY)
1985—Giants, 35-14 (H)
1991—Giants, 24-20 (NY)
1994—Giants, 13-10 (H)
1997—Oilers, 10-6 (T)
(RS Pts.—Giants 129, Titans 82)
**Franchise in Houston prior to 1997; known as Oilers prior to 1999*

N.Y. GIANTS vs. *WASHINGTON
RS: Giants lead series, 75-53-4
PS: Series tied, 1-1
1932—Braves, 14-6 (B)
Tie, 0-0 (NY)
1933—Redskins, 21-20 (B)
Giants, 7-0 (NY)
1934—Giants, 16-13 (B)
Giants, 3-0 (NY)
1935—Giants, 20-12 (B)
Giants, 17-6 (NY)
1936—Giants, 7-0 (B)
Redskins, 14-0 (NY)
1937—Redskins, 13-3 (W)
Redskins, 49-14 (NY)
1938—Giants, 10-7 (W)
Giants, 36-0 (NY)
1939—Tie, 0-0 (W)
Giants, 9-7 (NY)
1940—Redskins, 21-7 (W)
Giants, 21-7 (NY)
1941—Giants, 17-10 (W)
Giants, 20-13 (NY)
1942—Giants, 14-7 (W)
Redskins, 14-7 (NY)
1943—Giants, 14-10 (NY)
Giants, 31-7 (W)
**Redskins, 28-0 (NY)
1944—Giants, 16-13 (NY)
Giants, 31-0 (W)
1945—Redskins, 24-14 (NY)
Redskins, 17-0 (W)
1946—Redskins, 24-14 (W)
Giants, 31-0 (NY)
1947—Redskins, 28-20 (W)
Giants, 35-10 (NY)
1948—Redskins, 41-10 (W)
Redskins, 28-21 (NY)
1949—Giants, 45-35 (W)
Giants, 23-7 (NY)
1950—Giants, 21-17 (W)
Giants, 24-21 (NY)
1951—Giants, 35-14 (W)
Giants, 28-14 (NY)
1952—Giants, 14-10 (W)
Redskins, 27-17 (NY)
1953—Redskins, 13-9 (W)
Redskins, 24-21 (NY)
1954—Giants, 51-21 (W)
Giants, 24-7 (NY)
1955—Giants, 35-7 (NY)
Giants, 27-20 (W)
1956—Redskins, 33-7 (W)
Giants, 28-14 (NY)
1957—Giants, 24-20 (W)
Redskins, 31-14 (NY)
1958—Giants, 21-14 (W)
Giants, 30-0 (NY)
1959—Giants, 45-14 (NY)
Giants, 24-10 (W)
1960—Tie, 24-24 (NY)
Giants, 17-3 (W)
1961—Giants, 24-21 (W)
Giants, 53-0 (NY)
1962—Giants, 49-34 (NY)
Giants, 42-24 (W)
1963—Giants, 24-14 (W)
Giants, 44-14 (NY)
1964—Giants, 13-10 (NY)
Redskins, 36-21 (W)
1965—Redskins, 23-7 (NY)
Giants, 27-10 (W)
1966—Giants, 13-10 (NY)
Redskins, 72-41 (W)
1967—Redskins, 38-34 (W)
1968—Giants, 48-21 (NY)
Giants, 13-10 (W)
1969—Redskins, 20-14 (W)
1970—Giants, 35-33 (NY)
Giants, 27-24 (W)
1971—Redskins, 30-3 (NY)
Redskins, 23-7 (W)
1972—Redskins, 23-16 (NY)
Redskins, 27-13 (W)
1973—Redskins, 21-3 (New Haven)
Redskins, 27-24 (W)
1974—Redskins, 13-10 (New Haven)
Redskins, 24-3 (W)
1975—Redskins, 49-13 (W)
Redskins, 21-13 (NY)
1976—Redskins, 19-17 (W)
Giants, 12-9 (NY)
1977—Giants, 20-17 (NY)
Giants, 17-6 (W)
1978—Giants, 17-6 (NY)
Redskins, 16-13 (W) OT
1979—Redskins, 27-0 (W)
Giants, 14-6 (NY)
1980—Redskins, 23-21 (NY)
Redskins, 16-13 (W)
1981—Giants, 17-7 (W)
Redskins, 30-27 (NY) OT
1982—Redskins, 27-17 (NY)
Redskins, 15-14 (W)
1983—Redskins, 33-17 (NY)
Redskins, 31-22 (W)
1984—Redskins, 30-14 (W)
Giants, 37-13 (NY)
1985—Giants, 17-3 (NY)
Redskins, 23-21 (W)
1986—Giants, 27-20 (NY)
Giants, 24-14 (W)
***Giants, 17-0 (NY)
1987—Redskins, 38-12 (NY)
Redskins, 23-19 (W)
1988—Giants, 27-20 (NY)
Giants, 24-23 (W)
1989—Giants, 27-24 (W)
Giants, 20-17 (NY)
1990—Giants, 24-20 (W)
Giants, 21-10 (NY)
1991—Redskins, 17-13 (NY)
Redskins, 34-17 (W)
1992—Giants, 24-7 (W)
Redskins, 28-10 (NY)
1993—Giants, 41-7 (W)
Giants, 20-6 (NY)
1994—Giants, 31-23 (NY)
Giants, 21-19 (W)
1995—Giants, 24-15 (W)
Giants, 20-13 (NY)
1996—Redskins, 31-10 (NY)
Redskins, 31-21 (W)
1997—Tie, 7-7 (W) OT
Giants, 30-10 (NY)
1998—Giants, 31-24 (NY)
Redskins, 21-14 (W)

(RS Pts.—Giants 2,639, Redskins 2,361)
(PS Pts.—Redskins 28, Giants 17)
Franchise in Boston prior to 1937 and known as Braves prior to 1933
***Division Playoff*
****NFC Championship*

N.Y. JETS vs. ARIZONA
RS: Series tied, 2-2;
See Arizona vs. N.Y. Jets

N.Y. JETS vs. ATLANTA
RS: Series tied, 4-4;
See Atlanta vs. N.Y. Jets

N.Y. JETS vs BALTIMORE
RS: Series tied, 1-1;
See Baltimore vs. N.Y. Jets

N.Y. JETS vs. BUFFALO
RS: Bills lead series, 43-33
PS: Bills lead series, 1-0;
See Buffalo vs. N.Y. Jets

N.Y. JETS vs. CAROLINA
RS: Series tied, 1-1;
See Carolina vs. N.Y. Jets

N.Y. JETS vs. CHICAGO
RS: Bears lead series, 4-2;
See Chicago vs. N.Y. Jets

N.Y. JETS vs. CINCINNATI
RS: Jets lead series, 10-6
PS: Jets lead series, 1-0;
See Cincinnati vs. N.Y. Jets

N.Y. JETS vs. CLEVELAND
RS: Browns lead series, 9-6
PS: Browns lead series, 1-0;
See Cleveland vs. N.Y. Jets

N.Y. JETS vs. DALLAS
RS: Cowboys lead series, 5-1;
See Dallas vs. N.Y. Jets

N.Y. JETS vs. DENVER
RS: Broncos lead series, 13-12-1
PS: Broncos lead series, 1-0;
See Denver vs. N.Y. Jets

N.Y. JETS vs. DETROIT
RS: Lions lead series, 5-3;
See Detroit vs. N.Y. Jets

N.Y. JETS vs. GREEN BAY
RS: Jets lead series, 5-2;
See Green Bay vs. N.Y. Jets

N.Y. JETS vs. INDIANAPOLIS
RS: Colts lead series, 34-23
PS: Jets lead series, 1-0;
See Indianapolis vs. N.Y. Jets

N.Y. JETS vs. JACKSONVILLE
RS: Series tied, 1-1
PS: Jets lead series, 1-0;
See Jacksonville vs. N.Y. Jets

N.Y. JETS vs. KANSAS CITY
RS: Chiefs lead series, 14-13-1
PS: Series tied, 1-1;
See Kansas City vs. N.Y. Jets

N.Y. JETS vs. MIAMI
RS: Dolphins lead series, 34-31-1
PS: Dolphins lead series, 1-0;
See Miami vs. N.Y. Jets

N.Y. JETS vs. MINNESOTA
RS: Jets lead series, 5-1;
See Minnesota vs. N.Y. Jets

N.Y. JETS vs. NEW ENGLAND
RS: Jets lead series, 42-34-1
PS: Patriots lead series, 1-0;
See New England vs. N.Y. Jets

N.Y. JETS vs. NEW ORLEANS
RS: Series tied, 4-4;
See New Orleans vs. N.Y. Jets

N.Y. JETS vs. N.Y. GIANTS
RS: Series tied, 4-4;
See N.Y. Giants vs. N.Y. Jets

***N.Y. JETS vs. **OAKLAND**
RS: Raiders lead series, 16-10-2
PS: Jets lead series, 2-0
1960—Raiders, 28-27 (NY)
Titans, 31-28 (O)
1961—Titans, 14-6 (O)
Titans, 23-12 (NY)
1962—Titans, 28-17 (O)
Titans, 31-21 (NY)
1963—Jets, 10-7 (NY)
Raiders, 49-26 (O)
1964—Jets, 35-13 (NY)
Raiders, 35-26 (O)
1965—Tie, 24-24 (NY)
Raiders, 24-14 (O)
1966—Raiders, 24-21 (NY)
Tie, 28-28 (O)
1967—Jets, 27-14 (NY)
Raiders, 38-29 (O)
1968—Raiders, 43-32 (O)
***Jets, 27-23 (NY)
1969—Raiders, 27-14 (NY)
1970—Raiders, 14-13 (NY)
1972—Raiders, 24-16 (O)
1977—Raiders, 28-27 (NY)
1979—Jets, 28-19 (NY)
1982—****Jets, 17-14 (LA)
1985—Raiders, 31-0 (LA)
1989—Raiders, 14-7 (NY)
1993—Raiders, 24-20 (LA)
1995—Raiders, 47-10 (NY)
1996—Raiders, 34-13 (NY)
1997—Jets 23-22 (NY)
(RS Pts.—Raiders 695, Jets 597)
(PS Pts.—Jets 44, Raiders 37)
**Jets known as Titans prior to 1963*
***Franchise in Los Angeles from 1982-1994*
****AFL Championship*
*****AFC Second-Round Playoff*

N.Y. JETS vs. PHILADELPHIA
RS: Eagles lead series, 6-0
1973—Eagles, 24-23 (P)
1977—Eagles, 27-0 (P)
1978—Eagles, 17-9 (P)
1987—Eagles, 38-27 (NY)
1993—Eagles, 35-30 (NY)
1996—Eagles, 21-20 (NY)
(RS Pts.—Eagles 162, Jets 109)

N.Y. JETS vs. PITTSBURGH
RS: Steelers lead series, 12-1
1970—Steelers, 21-17 (P)
1973—Steelers, 26-14 (P)
1975—Steelers, 20-7 (NY)
1977—Steelers, 23-20 (NY)
1978—Steelers, 28-17 (NY)
1981—Steelers, 38-10 (P)
1983—Steelers, 34-7 (NY)
1984—Steelers, 23-17 (NY)
1986—Steelers, 45-24 (NY)
1988—Jets, 24-20 (NY)
1989—Steelers, 13-0 (NY)
1990—Steelers, 24-7 (NY)
1992—Steelers, 27-10 (P)
(RS Pts.—Steelers 342, Jets 174)

N.Y. JETS vs. *ST. LOUIS
RS: Rams lead series, 7-2
1970—Jets, 31-20 (LA)
1974—Rams, 20-13 (NY)
1980—Rams, 38-13 (LA)
1983—Jets, 27-24 (NY) OT
1986—Rams, 17-3 (NY)
1989—Rams, 38-14 (LA)
1992—Rams, 18-10 (LA)
1995—Rams, 23-20 (NY)
1998—Rams, 30-10 (StL)
(RS Pts.—Rams 228, Jets 141)
**Franchise in Los Angeles prior to 1995*

***N.Y. JETS vs. **SAN DIEGO**
RS: Chargers lead series, 17-9-1
1960—Chargers, 21-7 (NY)
Chargers, 50-43 (LA)
1961—Chargers, 25-10 (NY)
Chargers, 48-13 (SD)
1962—Chargers, 40-14 (SD)
Titans, 23-3 (NY)
1963—Chargers, 24-20 (SD)
Chargers, 53-7 (NY)
1964—Tie, 17-17 (NY)
Chargers, 38-3 (SD)
1965—Chargers, 34-9 (NY)
Chargers, 38-7 (SD)
1966—Jets, 17-16 (NY)
Chargers, 42-27 (SD)
1967—Jets, 42-31 (SD)
1968—Jets, 23-20 (NY)
Jets, 37-15 (SD)
1969—Chargers, 34-27 (SD)
1971—Chargers, 49-21 (SD)
1974—Jets, 27-14 (NY)
1975—Chargers, 24-16 (SD)
1983—Jets, 41-29 (SD)
1989—Jets, 20-17 (SD)
1990—Chargers, 39-3 (NY)
Chargers, 38-17 (SD)
1991—Jets, 24-3 (NY)
1994—Chargers, 21-6 (NY)
(RS Pts.—Chargers 783, Jets 521)
**Jets known as Titans prior to 1963*
***Franchise in Los Angeles prior to 1961*

N.Y. JETS vs. SAN FRANCISCO
RS: 49ers lead series, 7-1
1971—49ers, 24-21 (NY)
1976—49ers, 17-6 (SF)
1980—49ers, 37-27 (NY)
1983—Jets, 27-13 (SF)
1986—49ers, 24-10 (SF)
1989—49ers, 23-10 (NY)
1992—49ers, 31-14 (NY)
1998—49ers, 36-30 (SF) OT
(RS Pts.—49ers 205, Jets 145)

N.Y. JETS vs. SEATTLE
RS: Seahawks lead series, 8-6
1977—Seahawks, 17-0 (NY)
1978—Seahawks, 24-17 (NY)
1979—Seahawks, 30-7 (S)
1980—Seahawks, 27-17 (NY)
1981—Seahawks, 19-3 (NY)
Seahawks, 27-23 (S)
1983—Seahawks, 17-10 (NY)
1985—Jets, 17-14 (NY)
1986—Jets, 38-7 (S)
1987—Jets, 30-14 (NY)
1991—Seahawks, 20-13 (S)
1995—Jets, 16-10 (S)
1997—Jets, 41-3 (S)
1998—Jets, 32-31 (NY)
(RS Pts.—Jets 264, Seahawks 260)

N.Y. JETS vs. TAMPA BAY
RS: Jets lead series, 6-1
1976—Jets, 34-0 (NY)
1982—Jets, 32-17 (NY)
1984—Buccaneers, 41-21 (TB)
1985—Jets, 62-28 (NY)
1990—Jets, 16-14 (TB)
1991—Jets, 16-13 (NY)
1997—Jets, 31-0 (NY)
(RS Pts.—Jets 212, Buccaneers 113)

***N.Y. JETS vs. **TENNESSEE**
RS: Titans lead series, 20-13-1
PS: Titans lead series, 1-0
1960—Oilers, 27-21 (H)
Oilers, 42-28 (NY)
1961—Oilers, 49-13 (H)
Oilers, 48-21 (NY)
1962—Oilers, 56-17 (H)
Oilers, 44-10 (NY)
1963—Jets, 24-17 (NY)
Oilers, 31-27 (H)
1964—Jets, 24-21 (NY)
Oilers, 33-17 (H)
1965—Oilers, 27-21 (H)
Jets, 41-14 (NY)
1966—Jets, 52-13 (NY)
Oilers, 24-0 (H)
1967—Tie, 28-28 (NY)
1968—Jets, 20-14 (H)
Jets, 26-7 (NY)
1969—Jets, 26-17 (NY)
Jets, 34-26 (H)
1972—Oilers, 26-20 (H)
1974—Oilers, 27-22 (NY)
1977—Oilers, 20-0 (H)
1979—Oilers, 27-24 (H) OT
1980—Jets, 31-28 (NY) OT
1981—Jets, 33-17 (NY)
1984—Oilers, 31-20 (H)
1988—Jets, 45-3 (NY)
1990—Jets, 17-12 (H)
1991—Oilers, 23-20 (NY)
***Oilers, 17-10 (H)
1993—Oilers, 24-0 (H)
1994—Oilers, 24-10 (H)
1995—Oilers, 23-6 (H)
1996—Oilers, 35-10 (NY)
1998—Jets, 24-3 (T)
(RS Pts.—Titans 861, Jets 732)
(PS Pts.—Titans 17, Jets 10)
**Jets known as Titans prior to 1963*
***Franchise in Houston prior to 1997; known as Oilers prior to 1999*
****AFC First-Round Playoff*

N.Y. JETS vs. WASHINGTON
RS: Redskins lead series, 5-1
1972—Redskins, 35-17 (NY)
1976—Redskins, 37-16 (NY)
1978—Redskins, 23-3 (W)
1987—Redskins, 17-16 (W)
1993—Jets, 3-0 (W)
1996—Redskins, 31-16 (W)
(RS Pts.—Redskins 143, Jets 71)

OAKLAND vs. ARIZONA
RS: Raiders lead series, 3-1;
See Arizona vs. Oakland

OAKLAND vs. ATLANTA
RS: Raiders lead series, 6-3;
See Atlanta vs. Oakland

OAKLAND vs. BALTIMORE
RS: Ravens lead series, 2-0;
See Baltimore vs. Oakland

OAKLAND vs. BUFFALO
RS: Series tied, 15-15
PS: Bills lead series, 2-0;
See Buffalo vs. Oakland

OAKLAND vs CAROLINA
RS: Panthers lead series, 1-0;
See Carolina vs Oakland

OAKLAND vs. CHICAGO
RS: Raiders lead series, 5-4;
See Chicago vs. Oakland

OAKLAND vs. CINCINNATI
RS: Raiders lead series, 16-7
PS: Raiders lead series, 2-0;
See Cincinnati vs. Oakland

OAKLAND vs. CLEVELAND
RS: Raiders lead series, 8-4
PS: Raiders lead series, 2-0;
See Cleveland vs. Oakland

OAKLAND vs. DALLAS
RS: Raiders lead series, 4-3;
See Dallas vs. Oakland

OAKLAND vs. DENVER
RS: Raiders lead series, 49-26-2
PS: Series tied, 1-1;
See Denver vs. Oakland

OAKLAND vs. DETROIT
RS: Raiders lead series, 6-2;
See Detroit vs. Oakland

OAKLAND vs. GREEN BAY
RS: Raiders lead series, 5-2
PS: Packers lead series, 1-0;
See Green Bay vs. Oakland

OAKLAND vs. INDIANAPOLIS
RS: Raiders lead series, 5-2
PS: Series tied, 1-1;
See Indianapolis vs. Oakland

OAKLAND vs. JACKSONVILLE
RS: Series tied, 1-1;
See Jacksonville vs. Oakland

OAKLAND vs. KANSAS CITY
RS: Chiefs lead series, 39-36-2
PS: Chiefs lead series, 2-1;
See Kansas City vs. Oakland

OAKLAND vs. MIAMI
RS: Raiders lead series, 15-7-1

ALL-TIME TEAM VS. TEAM RESULTS

PS: Raiders lead series, 2-1;
See Miami vs. Oakland
OAKLAND vs. MINNESOTA
RS: Raiders lead series, 6-3
PS: Raiders lead series, 1-0;
See Minnesota vs. Oakland
OAKLAND vs. NEW ENGLAND
RS: Raiders lead series, 13-12-1
PS: Series tied, 1-1;
See New England vs. Oakland
OAKLAND vs. NEW ORLEANS
RS: Raiders lead series, 4-3-1;
See New Orleans vs. Oakland
OAKLAND vs. N.Y. GIANTS
RS: Raiders lead series, 6-2;
See N.Y. Giants vs. Oakland
OAKLAND vs. N.Y. JETS
RS: Raiders lead series, 16-10-2
PS: Jets lead series, 2-0;
See N.Y. Jets vs. Oakland
***OAKLAND vs. PHILADELPHIA**
RS: Eagles lead series, 4-3
PS: Raiders lead series, 1-0
1971—Raiders, 34-10 (O)
1976—Raiders, 26-7 (P)
1980—Eagles, 10-7 (P)
**Raiders, 27-10 (New Orleans)
1986—Eagles, 33-27 (LA) OT
1989—Eagles, 10-7 (P)
1992—Eagles, 31-10 (P)
1995—Raiders, 48-17 (O)
(RS Pts.—Raiders 159, Eagles 118)
(PS Pts.—Raiders 27, Eagles 10)
Franchise in Los Angeles from 1982-1994
***Super Bowl XV*
***OAKLAND vs. PITTSBURGH**
RS: Raiders lead series, 7-5
PS: Series tied, 3-3
1970—Raiders, 31-14 (O)
1972—Steelers, 34-28 (P)
**Steelers, 13-7 (P)
1973—Steelers, 17-9 (O)
**Raiders, 33-14 (O)
1974—Raiders, 17-0 (P)
***Steelers, 24-13 (O)
1975—***Steelers, 16-10 (P)
1976—Raiders, 31-28 (O)
***Raiders, 24-7 (O)
1977—Raiders, 16-7 (P)
1980—Raiders, 45-34 (P)
1981—Raiders, 30-27 (O)
1983—**Raiders, 38-10 (LA)
1984—Steelers, 13-7 (LA)
1990—Raiders, 20-3 (LA)
1994—Steelers, 21-3 (LA)
1995—Steelers, 29-10 (O)
(RS Pts.—Raiders 247, Steelers 227)
(PS Pts.—Raiders 125, Steelers 84)
Franchise in Los Angeles from 1982-1994
***AFC Divisional Playoff*
****AFC Championship*
***OAKLAND vs. **ST. LOUIS**
RS: Raiders lead series, 7-2
1972—Raiders, 45-17 (O)
1977—Rams, 20-14 (LA)
1979—Raiders, 24-17 (LA)
1982—Raiders, 37-31 (LA Raiders)
1985—Raiders, 16-6 (LA Rams)
1988—Rams, 22-17 (LA Raiders)
1991—Raiders, 20-17 (LA Raiders)
1994—Raiders, 20-17 (LA Rams)
1997—Raiders, 35-17 (O)
(RS Pts.—Raiders 228, Rams 164)
Franchise in Los Angeles from 1982-1994
***Franchise in Los Angeles prior to 1995*
***OAKLAND vs. **SAN DIEGO**
RS: Raiders lead series, 47-29-2
PS: Raiders lead series, 1-0
1960—Chargers, 52-28 (LA)
Chargers, 41-17 (O)
1961—Chargers, 44-0 (SD)
Chargers, 41-10 (O)
1962—Chargers, 42-33 (O)
Chargers, 31-21 (SD)
1963—Raiders, 34-33 (SD)
Raiders, 41-27 (O)
1964—Chargers, 31-17 (SD)
Raiders, 21-20 (O)
1965—Chargers, 17-6 (O)
Chargers, 24-14 (SD)
1966—Chargers, 29-20 (O)
Raiders, 41-19 (SD)
1967—Raiders, 51-10 (O)
Raiders, 41-21 (SD)
1968—Chargers, 23-14 (O)
Raiders, 34-27 (SD)
1969—Raiders, 24-12 (SD)
Raiders, 21-16 (O)
1970—Tie, 27-27 (SD)
Raiders, 20-17 (O)
1971—Raiders, 34-0 (SD)
Raiders, 34-33 (O)
1972—Tie, 17-17 (O)
Raiders, 21-19 (SD)
1973—Raiders, 27-17 (SD)
Raiders, 31-3 (O)
1974—Raiders, 14-10 (SD)
Raiders, 17-10 (O)
1975—Raiders, 6-0 (SD)
Raiders, 25-0 (O)
1976—Raiders, 27-17 (SD)
Raiders, 24-0 (O)
1977—Raiders, 24-0 (O)
Chargers, 12-7 (SD)
1978—Raiders, 21-20 (SD)
Chargers, 27-23 (O)
1979—Chargers, 30-10 (SD)
Raiders, 45-22 (O)
1980—Chargers, 30-24 (SD) OT
Raiders, 38-24 (O)
***Raiders, 34-27 (SD)
1981—Chargers, 55-21 (O)
Chargers, 23-10 (SD)
1982—Raiders, 28-24 (LA)
Raiders, 41-34 (SD)
1983—Raiders, 42-10 (SD)
Raiders, 30-14 (LA)
1984—Raiders, 33-30 (LA)
Raiders, 44-37 (SD)
1985—Raiders, 34-21 (LA)
Chargers, 40-34 (SD) OT
1986—Raiders, 17-13 (LA)
Raiders, 37-31 (SD) OT
1987—Chargers, 23-17 (LA)
Chargers, 16-14 (SD)
1988—Raiders, 24-13 (LA)
Raiders, 13-3 (SD)
1989—Raiders, 40-14 (LA)
Chargers, 14-12 (SD)
1990—Raiders, 24-9 (SD)
Raiders, 17-12 (LA)
1991—Chargers, 21-13 (LA)
Raiders, 9-7 (SD)
1992—Chargers, 27-3 (SD)
Chargers, 36-14 (LA)
1993—Chargers, 30-23 (LA)
Raiders, 12-7 (SD)
1994—Chargers, 26-24 (LA)
Raiders, 24-17 (SD)
1995—Raiders, 17-7 (O)
Chargers, 12-6 (SD)
1996—Chargers, 40-34 (O)
Raiders, 23-14 (SD)
1997—Chargers, 25-10 (O)
Raiders, 38-13 (SD)
1998—Raiders, 7-6 (O)
Raiders, 17-10 (SD)
(RS Pts.—Raiders 1,810, Chargers 1,629)
(PS Pts.—Raiders 34, Chargers 27)
Franchise in Los Angeles from 1982-1994
***Franchise in Los Angeles prior to 1961*
****AFC Championship*
***OAKLAND vs. SAN FRANCISCO**
RS: Raiders lead series, 5-3
1970—49ers, 38-7 (O)
1974—Raiders, 35-24 (SF)
1979—Raiders, 23-10 (O)
1982—Raiders, 23-17 (SF)
1985—49ers, 34-10 (LA)
1988—Raiders, 9-3 (SF)
1991—Raiders, 12-6 (LA)
1994—49ers, 44-14 (SF)
(RS Pts.—49ers 176, Raiders 133)
Franchise in Los Angeles from 1982-1994
***OAKLAND vs. SEATTLE**
RS: Raiders lead series, 23-19
PS: Series tied, 1-1
1977—Raiders, 44-7 (O)
1978—Seahawks, 27-7 (S)
Seahawks, 17-16 (O)
1979—Seahawks, 27-10 (S)
Seahawks, 29-24 (O)
1980—Raiders, 33-14 (O)
Raiders, 19-17 (S)
1981—Raiders, 20-10 (O)
Raiders, 32-31 (S)
1982—Raiders, 28-23 (LA)
1983—Seahawks, 38-36 (S)
Seahawks, 34-21 (LA)
**Raiders, 30-14 (LA)
1984—Raiders, 28-14 (LA)
Seahawks, 17-14 (S)
***Seahawks, 13-7 (S)
1985—Seahawks, 33-3 (S)
Raiders, 13-3 (LA)
1986—Raiders, 14-10 (LA)
Seahawks, 37-0 (S)
1987—Seahawks, 35-13 (LA)
Raiders, 37-14 (S)
1988—Seahawks, 35-27 (S)
Seahawks, 43-37 (LA)
1989—Seahawks, 24-20 (LA)
Seahawks, 23-17 (S)
1990—Raiders, 17-13 (S)
Raiders, 24-17 (LA)
1991—Raiders, 23-20 (S) OT
Raiders, 31-7 (LA)
1992—Raiders, 19-0 (S)
Raiders, 20-3 (LA)
1993—Raiders, 17-13 (S)
Raiders, 27-23 (LA)
1994—Seahawks, 38-9 (LA)
Raiders, 17-16 (S)
1995—Raiders, 34-14 (O)
Seahawks, 44-10 (S)
1996—Raiders, 27-21 (S)
Seahawks, 28-21 (O)
1997—Seahawks, 45-34 (S)
Seahawks, 22-21 (O)
1998—Raiders, 31-18 (S)
Raiders, 20-17 (O)
(RS Pts.—Seahawks 921, Raiders 915)
(PS Pts.—Raiders 37, Seahawks 27)
Franchise in Los Angeles from 1982-1994
***AFC Championship*
****AFC First-Round Playoff*
***OAKLAND vs. TAMPA BAY**
RS: Raiders lead series, 3-1
1976—Raiders, 49-16 (O)
1981—Raiders, 18-16 (O)
1993—Raiders, 27-20 (LA)
1996—Buccaneers, 20-17 (TB) OT
(RS Pts.—Raiders 111, Buccaneers 72)
Franchise in Los Angeles from 1982-1994
***OAKLAND vs. **TENNESSEE**
RS: Raiders lead series, 20-14
PS: Raiders lead series, 3-0
1960—Oilers, 37-22 (O)
Raiders, 14-13 (H)
1961—Oilers, 55-0 (H)
Oilers, 47-16 (O)
1962—Oilers, 28-20 (O)
Oilers, 32-17 (H)
1963—Raiders, 24-13 (H)
Raiders, 52-49 (O)
1964—Oilers, 42-28 (H)
Raiders, 20-10 (O)
1965—Raiders, 21-17 (O)
Raiders, 33-21 (H)
1966—Oilers, 31-0 (H)
Raiders, 38-23 (O)
1967—Raiders, 19-7 (H)
***Raiders, 40-7 (O)
1968—Raiders, 24-15 (H)
1969—Raiders, 21-17 (O)
****Raiders, 56-7 (O)
1971—Raiders, 41-21 (O)
1972—Raiders, 34-0 (H)
1973—Raiders, 17-6 (H)
1975—Oilers, 27-26 (O)
1976—Raiders, 14-13 (H)
1977—Raiders, 34-29 (O)
1978—Raiders, 21-17 (O)
1979—Oilers, 31-17 (H)
1980—*****Raiders, 27-7 (O)
1981—Oilers, 17-16 (H)
1983—Raiders, 20-6 (LA)
1984—Raiders, 24-14 (H)
1986—Raiders, 28-17 (H)
1988—Oilers, 38-35 (H)
1989—Oilers, 23-7 (H)
1991—Oilers, 47-17 (H)
1994—Raiders, 17-14 (LA)
1997—Oilers, 24-21 (T) OT
(RS Pts.—Titans 801, Raiders 758)
(PS Pts.—Raiders 123, Titans 21)
Franchise in Los Angeles from 1982-1994
***Franchise in Houston prior to 1997; known as Oilers prior to 1999*
****AFL Championship*
*****Inter-Divisional Playoff*
******AFC First-Round Playoff*
***OAKLAND vs. WASHINGTON**
RS: Raiders lead series, 6-3
PS: Raiders lead series, 1-0
1970—Raiders, 34-20 (O)
1975—Raiders, 26-23 (W) OT
1980—Raiders, 24-21 (O)
1983—Redskins, 37-35 (W)
**Raiders, 38-9 (Tampa)
1986—Redskins, 10-6 (W)
1989—Raiders, 37-24 (LA)
1992—Raiders, 21-20 (W)
1995—Raiders, 20-8 (W)
1998—Redskins, 29-19 (O)
(RS Pts.—Raiders 222, Redskins 192)
(PS Pts.—Raiders 38, Redskins 9)
Franchise in Los Angeles from 1982-1994
***Super Bowl XVIII*

PHILADELPHIA vs. ARIZONA
RS: Cardinals lead series, 49-48-5
PS: Series tied, 1-1;
See Arizona vs. Philadelphia
PHILADELPHIA vs. ATLANTA
RS: Series tied, 9-9-1
PS: Falcons lead series, 1-0;
See Atlanta vs. Philadelphia
PHILADELPHIA vs. BALTIMORE
RS: Series tied, 0-0-1;
See Baltimore vs. Philadelphia
PHILADELPHIA vs. BUFFALO
RS: Series tied, 4-4;
See Buffalo vs. Philadelphia
PHILADELPHIA vs. CAROLINA
RS: Eagles lead series, 1-0;
See Carolina vs. Philadelphia
PHILADELPHIA vs. CHICAGO
RS: Bears lead series, 24-4-1
PS: Series tied, 1-1;
See Chicago vs. Philadelphia

PHILADELPHIA vs. CINCINNATI
RS: Bengals lead series, 6-2;
See Cincinnati vs. Philadelphia
PHILADELPHIA vs. CLEVELAND
RS: Browns lead series, 31-12-1;
See Cleveland vs. Philadelphia
PHILADELPHIA vs. DALLAS
RS: Cowboys lead series, 47-29
PS: Cowboys lead series, 2-1;
See Dallas vs. Philadelphia
PHILADELPHIA vs. DENVER
RS: Eagles lead series, 6-3;
See Denver vs. Philadelphia
PHILADELPHIA vs. DETROIT
RS: Lions lead series, 12-11-2
PS: Eagles lead series, 1-0;
See Detroit vs. Philadelphia
PHILADELPHIA vs. GREEN BAY
RS: Packers lead series, 21-9
PS: Eagles lead series, 1-0;
See Green Bay vs. Philadelphia
PHILADELPHIA vs. INDIANAPOLIS
RS: Colts lead series, 7-6;
See Indianapolis vs. Philadelphia
PHILADELPHIA vs. JACKSONVILLE
RS: Jaguars lead series, 1-0;
See Jacksonville vs. Philadelphia
PHILADELPHIA vs. KANSAS CITY
RS: Chiefs lead series, 2-1;
See Kansas City vs. Philadelphia
PHILADELPHIA vs. MIAMI
RS: Dolphins lead series, 6-3;
See Miami vs. Philadelphia
PHILADELPHIA vs. MINNESOTA
RS: Vikings lead series, 11-6
PS: Eagles lead series, 1-0;
See Minnesota vs. Philadelphia
PHILADELPHIA vs. NEW ENGLAND
RS: Eagles lead series, 5-2;
See New England vs. Philadelphia
PHILADELPHIA vs. NEW ORLEANS
RS: Eagles lead series, 12-8
PS; Eagles lead series, 1-0;
See New Orleans vs. Philadelphia
PHILADELPHIA vs. N.Y. GIANTS
RS: Giants lead series, 68-58-2
PS: Giants lead series, 1-0;
See N.Y. Giants vs. Philadelphia
PHILADELPHIA vs. N.Y. JETS
RS: Eagles lead series, 6-0;
See N.Y. Jets vs. Philadelphia
PHILADELPHIA vs. OAKLAND
RS: Eagles lead series, 4-3
PS: Raiders lead series, 1-0;
See Oakland vs. Philadelphia
PHILADELPHIA vs. *PITTSBURGH
RS: Eagles lead series, 44-26-3
PS: Eagles lead series, 1-0
1933—Eagles, 25-6 (Phila)
1934—Eagles, 17-0 (Pitt)
Pirates, 9-7 (Phila)
1935—Pirates, 17-7 (Phila)
Eagles, 17-6 (Pitt)
1936—Pirates, 17-0 (Pitt)
Pirates, 6-0 (Johnstown, Pa.)
1937—Pirates, 27-14 (Pitt)
Pirates, 16-7 (Pitt)
1938—Eagles, 27-7 (Buffalo)
Eagles, 14-7 (Charleston, W. Va.)
1939—Eagles, 17-14 (Phila)
Pirates, 24-12 (Pitt)
1940—Pirates, 7-3 (Pitt)
Eagles, 7-0 (Phila)
1941—Eagles, 10-7 (Pitt)
Tie, 7-7 (Phila)
1942—Eagles, 24-14 (Pitt)
Steelers, 14-0 (Phila)
1945—Eagles, 45-3 (Pitt)
Eagles, 30-6 (Phila)
1946—Steelers, 10-7 (Pitt)
Eagles, 10-7 (Phila)
1947—Steelers, 35-24 (Pitt)
Eagles, 21-0 (Phila)
**Eagles, 21-0 (Pitt)
1948—Eagles, 34-7 (Pitt)
Eagles, 17-0 (Phila)
1949—Eagles, 38-7 (Pitt)
Eagles, 34-17 (Phila)
1950—Eagles, 17-10 (Pitt)
Steelers, 9-7 (Phila)
1951—Eagles, 34-13 (Pitt)
Steelers, 17-13 (Phila)
1952—Eagles, 31-25 (Pitt)
Eagles, 26-21 (Phila)
1953—Eagles, 23-17 (Phila)
Eagles, 35-7 (Pitt)
1954—Eagles, 24-22 (Phila)
Steelers, 17-7 (Pitt)
1955—Steelers, 13-7 (Pitt)
Eagles, 24-0 (Phila)
1956—Eagles, 35-21 (Pitt)
Eagles, 14-7 (Phila)
1957—Steelers, 6-0 (Pitt)
Eagles, 7-6 (Phila)
1958—Steelers, 24-3 (Pitt)
Steelers, 31-24 (Phila)
1959—Eagles, 28-24 (Phila)
Steelers, 31-0 (Pitt)
1960—Eagles, 34-7 (Phila)
Steelers, 27-21 (Pitt)
1961—Eagles, 21-16 (Phila)
Eagles, 35-24 (Pitt)
1962—Steelers, 13-7 (Pitt)
Steelers, 26-17 (Phila)
1963—Tie, 21-21 (Phila)
Tie, 20-20 (Pitt)
1964—Eagles, 21-7 (Phila)
Eagles, 34-10 (Pitt)
1965—Steelers, 20-14 (Phila)
Eagles, 47-13 (Pitt)
1966—Eagles, 31-14 (Pitt)
Eagles, 27-23 (Phila)
1967—Eagles, 34-24 (Phila)
1968—Steelers, 6-3 (Pitt)
1969—Eagles, 41-27 (Phila)
1970—Eagles, 30-20 (Phila)
1974—Steelers, 27-0 (Pitt)
1979—Eagles, 17-14 (Phila)
1988—Eagles, 27-26 (Pitt)
1991—Eagles, 23-14 (Phila)
1994—Steelers, 14-3 (Pitt)
1997—Eagles, 23-20 (Phila)
(RS Pts.—Eagles 1,385, Steelers 1,041)
(PS Pts.—Eagles 21, Steelers 0)
Steelers known as Pirates prior to 1941
***Division Playoff*
PHILADELPHIA vs. *ST. LOUIS
RS: Rams lead series, 15-13-1
PS: Series tied, 1-1
1937—Rams, 21-3 (P)
1939—Rams, 35-13 (Colorado Springs)
1940—Rams, 21-13 (C)
1942—Rams, 24-14 (Akron)
1944—Eagles, 26-13 (P)
1945—Eagles, 28-14 (P)
1946—Eagles, 25-14 (LA)
1947—Eagles, 14-7 (P)
1948—Tie, 28-28 (LA)
1949—Eagles, 38-14 (P)
**Eagles, 14-0 (LA)
1950—Eagles, 56-20 (P)
1955—Rams, 23-21 (P)
1956—Rams, 27-7 (LA)
1957—Rams, 17-13 (LA)
1959—Eagles, 23-20 (P)
1964—Rams, 20-10 (LA)
1967—Rams, 33-17 (LA)
1969—Rams, 23-17 (P)
1972—Rams, 34-3 (P)
1975—Rams, 42-3 (P)
1977—Rams, 20-0 (LA)
1978—Rams, 16-14 (P)
1983—Eagles, 13-9 (P)
1985—Rams, 17-6 (P)
1986—Eagles, 34-20 (P)
1988—Eagles, 30-24 (P)
1989—***Rams, 21-7 (P)
1990—Eagles, 27-21 (LA)
1995—Eagles, 20-9 (P)
1998—Eagles, 17-14 (P)
(RS Pts.—Rams 600, Eagles 533)
(PS Pts.—Rams 21, Eagles 21)
Franchise in Los Angeles prior to 1995 and in Cleveland prior to 1946
***NFL Championship*
****NFC First-Round Playoff*
PHILADELPHIA vs. SAN DIEGO
RS: Chargers lead series, 5-2
1974—Eagles, 13-7 (SD)
1980—Chargers, 22-21 (SD)
1985—Chargers, 20-14 (SD)
1986—Eagles, 23-7 (P)
1989—Chargers, 20-17 (SD)
1995—Chargers, 27-21 (P)
1998—Chargers, 13-10 (SD)
(RS Pts.—Eagles 119, Chargers 116)
PHILADELPHIA vs. SAN FRANCISCO
RS: 49ers lead series, 14-6-1
PS: 49ers lead series, 1-0
1951—Eagles, 21-14 (P)
1953—49ers, 31-21 (SF)
1956—Tie, 10-10 (P)
1958—49ers, 30-24 (P)
1959—49ers, 24-14 (SF)
1964—49ers, 28-24 (P)
1966—Eagles, 35-34 (SF)
1967—49ers, 28-27 (P)
1969—49ers, 14-13 (SF)
1971—49ers, 31-3 (P)
1973—49ers, 38-28 (SF)
1975—Eagles, 27-17 (P)
1983—Eagles, 22-17 (SF)
1984—49ers, 21-9 (P)
1985—49ers, 24-13 (SF)
1989—49ers, 38-28 (P)
1991—49ers, 23-7 (P)
1992—49ers, 20-14 (SF)
1993—Eagles, 37-34 (SF) OT
1994—Eagles, 40-8 (SF)
1996—*49ers, 14-0 (SF)
1997—49ers, 24-12 (P)
(RS Pts.—49ers 508, Eagles 429)
(PS Pts.—49ers 14, Eagles 0)
**NFC First-Round Playoff*
PHILADELPHIA vs. SEATTLE
RS: Eagles lead series, 4-3
1976—Eagles, 27-10 (P)
1980—Eagles, 27-20 (S)
1986—Seahawks, 24-20 (S)
1989—Eagles, 31-7 (P)
1992—Eagles, 20-17 (S) OT
1995—Seahawks, 26-14 (S)
1998—Seahawks, 38-0 (P)
(RS Pts.—Seahawks 142, Eagles 139)
PHILADELPHIA vs. TAMPA BAY
RS: Eagles lead series, 3-2
PS: Buccaneers lead series, 1-0
1977—Eagles, 13-3 (P)
1979—*Buccaneers, 24-17 (TB)
1981—Eagles, 20-10 (P)
1988—Eagles, 41-14 (TB)
1991—Buccaneers, 14-13 (TB)
1995—Buccaneers, 21-6 (P)
(RS Pts.—Eagles 93, Buccaneers 62)
(PS Pts.—Buccaneers 24, Eagles 17)
**NFC Divisional Playoff*
PHILADELPHIA vs. *TENNESSEE
RS: Eagles lead series, 6-0
1972—Eagles, 18-17 (H)
1979—Eagles, 26-20 (H)
1982—Eagles, 35-14 (P)
1988—Eagles, 32-23 (P)
1991—Eagles, 13-6 (H)
1994—Eagles, 21-6 (P)
(RS Pts.—Eagles 145, Titans 86)
Franchise in Houston prior to 1997; known as Oilers prior to 1999
PHILADELPHIA vs. *WASHINGTON
RS: Redskins lead series, 69-53-5
PS: Redskins lead series, 1-0
1934—Redskins, 6-0 (B)
Redskins, 14-7 (P)
1935—Eagles, 7-6 (B)
1936—Redskins, 26-3 (P)
Redskins, 17-7 (B)
1937—Eagles, 14-0 (W)
Redskins, 10-7 (P)
1938—Redskins, 26-23 (P)
Redskins, 20-14 (W)
1939—Redskins, 7-0 (P)
Redskins, 7-6 (W)
1940—Redskins, 34-17 (P)
Redskins, 13-6 (W)
1941—Redskins, 21-17 (P)
Redskins, 20-14 (W)
1942—Redskins, 14-10 (P)
Redskins, 30-27 (W)
1944—Tie, 31-31 (P)
Eagles, 37-7 (W)
1945—Redskins, 24-14 (W)
Eagles, 16-0 (P)
1946—Eagles, 28-24 (W)
Redskins, 27-10 (P)
1947—Eagles, 45-42 (P)
Eagles, 38-14 (W)
1948—Eagles, 45-0 (W)
Eagles, 42-21 (P)
1949—Eagles, 49-14 (P)
Eagles, 44-21 (W)
1950—Eagles, 35-3 (P)
Eagles, 33-0 (W)
1951—Redskins, 27-23 (P)
Eagles, 35-21 (W)
1952—Eagles, 38-20 (P)
Redskins, 27-21 (W)
1953—Tie, 21-21 (P)
Redskins, 10-0 (W)
1954—Eagles, 49-21 (W)
Eagles, 41-33 (P)
1955—Redskins, 31-30 (P)
Redskins, 34-21 (W)
1956—Eagles, 13-9 (P)
Redskins, 19-17 (W)
1957—Eagles, 21-12 (P)
Redskins, 42-7 (W)
1958—Redskins, 24-14 (P)
Redskins, 20-0 (W)
1959—Eagles, 30-23 (P)
Eagles, 34-14 (W)
1960—Eagles, 19-13 (P)
Eagles, 38-28 (W)
1961—Eagles, 14-7 (P)
Eagles, 27-24 (W)
1962—Redskins, 27-21 (P)
Eagles, 37-14 (W)
1963—Eagles, 37-24 (W)
Redskins, 13-10 (P)
1964—Redskins, 35-20 (W)
Redskins, 21-10 (P)
1965—Redskins, 23-21 (W)
Eagles, 21-14 (P)
1966—Redskins, 27-13 (P)
Eagles, 37-28 (W)
1967—Eagles, 35-24 (P)
Tie, 35-35 (W)
1968—Redskins, 17-14 (W)
Redskins, 16-10 (P)
1969—Tie, 28-28 (W)
Redskins, 34-29 (P)
1970—Redskins, 33-21 (P)
Redskins, 24-6 (W)
1971—Tie, 7-7 (W)
Redskins, 20-13 (P)
1972—Redskins, 14-0 (W)
Redskins, 23-7 (P)
1973—Redskins, 28-7 (P)
Redskins, 38-20 (W)
1974—Redskins, 27-20 (P)
Redskins, 26-7 (W)
1975—Eagles, 26-10 (P)
Eagles, 26-3 (W)
1976—Redskins, 20-17 (P) OT

ALL-TIME TEAM VS. TEAM RESULTS

Redskins, 24-0 (W)
1977—Redskins, 23-17 (W)
Redskins, 17-14 (P)
1978—Redskins, 35-30 (W)
Eagles, 17-10 (P)
1979—Eagles, 28-17 (P)
Redskins, 17-7 (W)
1980—Eagles, 24-14 (P)
Eagles, 24-0 (W)
1981—Eagles, 36-13 (P)
Redskins, 15-13 (W)
1982—Redskins, 37-34 (P) OT
Redskins, 13-9 (W)
1983—Redskins, 23-13 (P)
Redskins, 28-24 (W)
1984—Redskins, 20-0 (W)
Eagles, 16-10 (P)
1985—Eagles, 19-6 (W)
Redskins, 17-12 (P)
1986—Redskins, 41-14 (W)
Redskins, 21-14 (P)
1987—Redskins, 34-24 (W)
Eagles, 31-27 (P)
1988—Redskins, 17-10 (W)
Redskins, 20-19 (P)
1989—Eagles, 42-37 (W)
Redskins, 10-3 (P)
1990—Redskins, 13-7 (W)
Eagles, 28-14 (P)
**Redskins, 20-6 (P)
1991—Redskins, 23-0 (W)
Eagles, 24-22 (P)
1992—Redskins, 16-12 (W)
Eagles, 17-13 (P)
1993—Eagles, 34-31 (P)
Eagles, 17-14 (W)
1994—Eagles, 21-17 (P)
Eagles, 31-29 (W)
1995—Eagles, 37-34 (P) (OT)
Eagles, 14-7 (W)
1996—Eagles, 17-14 (W)
Redskins, 26-21 (P)
1997—Eagles, 24-10 (P)
Redskins, 35-32 (W)
1998—Eagles, 17-12 (P)
Redskins, 28-3 (W)
(RS Pts.—Eagles 2,564, Redskins 2,536)
(PS Pts.—Redskins 20, Eagles 6)
Franchise in Boston prior to 1937
***NFC First-Round Playoff*

PITTSBURGH vs. ARIZONA
RS: Steelers lead series, 30-22-3;
See Arizona vs. Pittsburgh
PITTSBURGH vs. ATLANTA
RS: Steelers lead series, 10-1;
See Atlanta vs. Pittsburgh
PITTSBURGH vs. BALTIMORE
RS: Steelers lead series, 5-1;
See Baltimore vs. Pittsburgh
PITTSBURGH vs. BUFFALO
RS: Steelers lead series, 8-7
PS: Steelers lead series, 2-1;
See Buffalo vs. Pittsburgh
PITTSBURGH vs. CAROLINA
RS: Panthers lead series, 1-0;
See Carolina vs. Pittsburgh
PITTSBURGH vs. CHICAGO
RS: Bears lead series, 16-6-1;
See Chicago vs. Pittsburgh
PITTSBURGH vs. CINCINNATI
RS: Steelers lead series, 32-25;
See Cincinnati vs. Pittsburgh
PITTSBURGH vs. CLEVELAND
RS: Browns lead series, 52-40
PS: Steelers lead series, 1-0;
See Cleveland vs. Pittsburgh
PITTSBURGH vs. DALLAS
RS: Cowboys lead series, 14-11
PS: Steelers lead series, 2-1;
See Dallas vs. Pittsburgh
PITTSBURGH vs. DENVER
RS: Broncos lead series, 10-6-1
PS: Broncos lead series, 3-2;
See Denver vs. Pittsburgh
PITTSBURGH vs. DETROIT
RS: Lions lead series, 14-12-1;
See Detroit vs. Pittsburgh
PITTSBURGH vs. GREEN BAY
RS: Packers lead series, 18-12;
See Green Bay vs. Pittsburgh
PITTSBURGH vs. INDIANAPOLIS
RS: Steelers lead series, 12-4
PS: Steelers lead series, 4-0;
See Indianapolis vs. Pittsburgh
PITTSBURGH vs. JACKSONVILLE
RS: Series tied, 4-4;
See Jacksonville vs. Pittsburgh
PITTSBURGH vs. KANSAS CITY
RS: Steelers lead series, 15-6
PS: Chiefs lead series, 1-0;
See Kansas City vs. Pittsburgh
PITTSBURGH vs. MIAMI
RS: Dolphins lead series, 9-7
PS: Dolphins lead series, 2-1;
See Miami vs. Pittsburgh
PITTSBURGH vs. MINNESOTA
RS: Vikings lead series, 8-4
PS: Steelers lead series, 1-0;
See Minnesota vs. Pittsburgh
PITTSBURGH vs. NEW ENGLAND
RS: Steelers lead series, 11-4
PS: Series tied, 1-1;
See New England vs. Pittsburgh
PITTSBURGH vs. NEW ORLEANS
RS: Steelers lead series, 6-5;
See New Orleans vs. Pittsburgh
PITTSBURGH vs. N.Y. GIANTS
RS: Giants lead series, 42-27-3;
See N.Y. Giants vs. Pittsburgh
PITTSBURGH vs. N.Y. JETS
RS: Steelers lead series, 12-1;
See N.Y. Jets vs. Pittsburgh
PITTSBURGH vs. OAKLAND
RS: Raiders lead series, 7-5
PS: Series tied, 3-3;
See Oakland vs. Pittsburgh
PITTSBURGH vs. PHILADELPHIA
RS: Eagles lead series, 44-26-3
PS: Eagles lead series, 1-0;
See Philadelphia vs. Pittsburgh
***PITTSBURGH vs. **ST. LOUIS**
RS: Rams lead series, 14-5-2
PS: Steelers lead series, 1-0
1938—Rams, 13-7 (New Orleans)
1939—Tie, 14-14 (C)
1941—Rams, 17-14 (Akron)
1947—Rams, 48-7 (P)
1948—Rams, 31-14 (LA)
1949—Tie, 7-7 (P)
1952—Rams, 28-14 (LA)
1955—Rams, 27-26 (LA)
1956—Steelers, 30-13 (P)
1961—Rams, 24-14 (LA)
1964—Rams, 26-14 (P)
1968—Rams, 45-10 (LA)
1971—Rams, 23-14 (P)
1975—Rams, 10-3 (LA)
1978—Rams, 10-7 (LA)
1979—***Steelers, 31-19 (Pasadena)
1981—Steelers, 24-0 (P)
1984—Steelers, 24-14 (P)
1987—Rams, 31-21 (LA)
1990—Steelers, 41-10 (P)
1993—Rams, 27-0 (LA)
1996—Steelers, 42-6 (P)
(RS Pts.—Rams 424, Steelers 347)
(PS Pts.—Steelers 31, Rams 19)
Steelers known as Pirates prior to 1941
***Franchise in Los Angeles prior to 1995 and in Cleveland prior to 1946*
****Super Bowl XIV*
PITTSBURGH vs. SAN DIEGO
RS: Steelers lead series, 16-5
PS: Chargers lead series, 2-0
1971—Steelers, 21-17 (P)
1972—Steelers, 24-2 (SD)
1973—Steelers, 38-21 (P)
1975—Steelers, 37-0 (SD)
1976—Steelers, 23-0 (P)
1977—Steelers, 10-9 (SD)
1979—Chargers, 35-7 (SD)
1980—Chargers, 26-17 (SD)
1982—*Chargers, 31-28 (P)
1983—Steelers, 26-3 (P)
1984—Steelers, 52-24 (P)
1985—Chargers, 54-44 (SD)
1987—Steelers, 20-16 (SD)
1988—Chargers, 20-14 (SD)
1989—Steelers, 20-17 (P)
1990—Steelers, 36-14 (P)
1991—Steelers, 26-20 (P)
1992—Steelers, 23-6 (SD)
1993—Steelers,.16-3 (P)
1994—Chargers, 37-34 (SD)
**Chargers, 17-13 (P)
1995—Steelers, 31-16 (P)
1996—Steelers, 16-3 (P)
(RS Pts.—Steelers 535, Chargers 343)
(PS Pts.—Chargers 48, Steelers 41)
**AFC First-Round Playoff*
***AFC Championship*
PITTSBURGH vs. SAN FRANCISCO
RS: 49ers lead series, 9-7
1951—49ers, 28-24 (P)
1952—Steelers, 24-7 (SF)
1954—49ers, 31-3 (SF)
1958—49ers, 23-20 (SF)
1961—Steelers, 20-10 (P)
1965—49ers, 27-17 (SF)
1968—49ers, 45-28 (P)
1973—Steelers, 37-14 (SF)
1977—Steelers, 27-0 (P)
1978—Steelers, 24-7 (SF)
1981—49ers, 17-14 (P)
1984—Steelers, 20-17 (SF)
1987—Steelers, 30-17 (P)
1990—49ers, 27-7 (SF)
1993—49ers, 24-13 (P)
1996—49ers, 25-15 (P)
(RS Pts.—Steelers 323, 49ers 319)
PITTSBURGH vs. SEATTLE
RS: Series tied, 6-6
1977—Steelers, 30-20 (P)
1978—Steelers, 21-10 (P)
1981—Seahawks, 24-21 (S)
1982—Seahawks, 16-0 (S)
1983—Steelers, 27-21 (S)
1986—Seahawks, 30-0 (S)
1987—Steelers, 13-9 (P)
1991—Seahawks, 27-7 (P)
1992—Steelers, 20-14 (P)
1993—Seahawks, 16-6 (S)
1994—Seahawks, 30-13 (S)
1998—Steelers, 13-10 (P)
(RS Pts.—Seahawks 227, Steelers 171)
PITTSBURGH vs. TAMPA BAY
RS: Steelers lead series, 4-1
1976—Steelers, 42-0 (P)
1980—Steelers, 24-21 (TB)
1983—Steelers, 17-12 (P)
1989—Steelers, 31-22 (TB)
1998—Buccaneers, 16-3 (TB)
(RS Pts.—Steelers 117, Buccaneers 71)
PITTSBURGH vs. *TENNESSEE
RS: Steelers lead series, 35-22
PS: Steelers lead series, 3-0
1970—Oilers, 19-7 (P)
Steelers, 7-3 (H)
1971—Steelers, 23-16 (P)
Oilers, 29-3 (H)
1972—Steelers, 24-7 (P)
Steelers, 9-3 (H)
1973—Steelers, 36-7 (H)
Steelers, 33-7 (P)
1974—Steelers, 13-7 (H)
Oilers, 13-10 (P)
1975—Steelers, 24-17 (P)
Steelers, 32-9 (H)
1976—Steelers, 32-16 (P)
Steelers, 21-0 (H)
1977—Oilers, 27-10 (H)
Steelers, 27-10 (P)
1978—Oilers, 24-17 (P)
Steelers, 13-3 (H)
**Steelers, 34-5 (P)
1979—Steelers, 38-7 (P)
Oilers, 20-17 (H)
**Steelers, 27-13 (P)
1980—Steelers, 31-17 (P)
Oilers, 6-0 (H)
1981—Steelers, 26-13 (P)
Oilers, 21-20 (H)
1982—Steelers, 24-10 (H)
1983—Steelers, 40-28 (H)
Steelers, 17-10 (P)
1984—Steelers, 35-7 (P)
Oilers, 23-20 (H) OT
1985—Steelers, 20-0 (P)
Steelers, 30-7 (H)
1986—Steelers, 22-16 (H) OT
Steelers, 21-10 (P)
1987—Oilers, 23-3 (P)
Oilers, 24-16 (H)
1988—Oilers, 34-14 (P)
Steelers, 37-34 (H)
1989—Oilers, 27-0 (H)
Oilers, 23-16 (P)
***Steelers, 26-23 (H) OT
1990—Steelers, 20-9 (P)
Oilers, 34-14 (H)
1991—Steelers, 26-14 (P)
Oilers, 31-6 (H)
1992—Steelers, 29-24 (H)
Steelers, 21-20 (P)
1993—Oilers, 23-3 (H)
Oilers, 26-17 (P)
1994—Steelers, 30-14 (P)
Steelers, 12-9 (H) OT
1995—Steelers, 34-17 (H)
Steelers, 21-7 (P)
1996—Steelers, 30-16 (P)
Oilers, 23-13 (H)
1997—Steelers, 37-24 (P)
Oilers, 16-6 (T)
1998—Oilers, 41-31 (P)
Oilers, 23-14 (T)
(RS Pts.—Steelers 1,152, Titans 948)
(PS Pts.—Steelers 87, Titans 41)
**Franchise in Houston prior to 1997; known as Oilers prior to 1999*
***AFC Championship*
****AFC First-Round Playoff*
***PITTSBURGH vs. **WASHINGTON**
RS: Redskins lead series, 42-28-3
1933—Redskins, 21-6 (P)
Pirates, 16-14 (B)
1934—Redskins, 7-0 (P)
Redskins, 39-0 (B)
1935—Pirates, 6-0 (P)
Redskins, 13-3 (B)
1936—Pirates, 10-0 (P)
Redskins, 30-0 (B)
1937—Redskins, 34-20 (W)
Pirates, 21-13 (P)
1938—Redskins, 7-0 (P)
Redskins, 15-0 (W)
1939—Redskins, 44-14 (W)
Redskins, 21-14 (P)
1940—Redskins, 40-10 (P)
Redskins, 37-10 (W)
1941—Redskins, 24-20 (P)
Redskins, 23-3 (W)
1942—Redskins, 28-14 (W)
Redskins, 14-0 (P)
1945—Redskins, 14-0 (P)
Redskins, 24-0 (W)
1946—Tie, 14-14 (W)
Steelers, 14-7 (P)
1947—Redskins, 27-26 (W)
Steelers, 21-14 (P)
1948—Redskins, 17-14 (W)

Steelers, 10-7 (P)
1949—Redskins, 27-14 (P)
Redskins, 27-14 (W)
1950—Steelers, 26-7 (W)
Redskins, 24-7 (P)
1951—Redskins, 22-7 (P)
Steelers, 20-10 (W)
1952—Redskins, 28-24 (P)
Steelers, 24-23 (W)
1953—Redskins, 17-9 (P)
Steelers, 14-13 (W)
1954—Steelers, 37-7 (P)
Redskins, 17-14 (W)
1955—Redskins, 23-14 (P)
Redskins, 28-17 (W)
1956—Steelers, 30-13 (P)
Steelers, 23-0 (W)
1957—Steelers, 28-7 (P)
Redskins, 10-3 (W)
1958—Steelers, 24-16 (P)
Tie, 14-14 (W)
1959—Redskins, 23-17 (P)
Steelers, 27-6 (W)
1960—Tie, 27-27 (W)
Steelers, 22-10 (P)
1961—Steelers, 20-0 (P)
Steelers, 30-14 (W)
1962—Steelers, 23-21 (P)
Steelers, 27-24 (W)
1963—Steelers, 38-27 (P)
Steelers, 34-28 (W)
1964—Redskins, 30-0 (P)
Steelers, 14-7 (W)
1965—Redskins, 31-3 (P)
Redskins, 35-14 (W)
1966—Redskins, 33-27 (P)
Redskins, 24-10 (W)
1967—Redskins, 15-10 (P)
1968—Redskins, 16-13 (W)
1969—Redskins, 14-7 (P)
1973—Steelers, 21-16 (P)
1979—Steelers, 38-7 (P)
1985—Redskins, 30-23 (P)
1988—Redskins, 30-29 (W)
1991—Redskins, 41-14 (P)
1997—Steelers, 14-13 (P)
(RS Pts.—Redskins 1,403, Steelers 1,131)
Steelers known as Pirates prior to 1941
***Franchise in Boston prior to 1937*

ST. LOUIS vs. ARIZONA
RS: Rams lead series, 23-21-2
PS: Rams lead series, 1-0;
See Arizona vs. St. Louis
ST. LOUIS vs. ATLANTA
RS: Rams lead series, 39-23-2;
See Atlanta vs. St. Louis
ST. LOUIS vs. BALTIMORE
RS: Ravens lead series, 1-0;
See Baltimore vs. St. Louis
ST. LOUIS vs. BUFFALO
RS: Series tied, 4-4;
See Buffalo vs. St. Louis
ST. LOUIS vs. CAROLINA
RS: Panthers lead series, 5-3;
See Carolina vs. St. Louis
ST. LOUIS vs. CHICAGO
RS: Bears lead series, 47-31-3
PS: Series tied, 1-1;
See Chicago vs. St. Louis
ST. LOUIS vs. CINCINNATI
RS: Bengals lead series, 5-3;
See Cincinnati vs. St. Louis
ST. LOUIS vs. CLEVELAND
RS: Browns lead series, 8-7
PS: Browns lead series, 2-1;
See Cleveland vs. St. Louis
ST. LOUIS vs. DALLAS
RS: Rams lead series, 9-8
PS: Series tied, 4-4;
See Dallas vs. St. Louis
ST. LOUIS vs. DENVER
RS: Series tied, 4-4;
See Denver vs. St. Louis
ST. LOUIS vs. DETROIT
RS: Rams lead series, 39-35-1
PS: Lions lead series, 1-0;
See Detroit vs. St. Louis
ST. LOUIS vs. GREEN BAY
RS: Rams lead series, 43-39-2
PS: Packers lead series, 1-0;
See Green Bay vs. St. Louis
ST. LOUIS vs. INDIANAPOLIS
RS: Colts lead series, 21-16-2;
See Indianapolis vs. St. Louis
ST. LOUIS vs. JACKSONVILLE
RS: Rams lead series, 1-0;
See Jacksonville vs. St. Louis
ST. LOUIS vs. KANSAS CITY
RS: Rams lead series, 4-2;
See Kansas City vs. St. Louis
ST. LOUIS vs. MIAMI
RS: Dolphins lead series, 7-1;
See Miami vs. St. Louis
ST. LOUIS vs. MINNESOTA
RS: Vikings lead series, 16-11-2
PS: Vikings lead series, 5-1;
See Minnesota vs. St. Louis
ST. LOUIS vs. NEW ENGLAND
RS: Rams lead series, 4-3;
See New England vs. St. Louis
ST. LOUIS vs. NEW ORLEANS
RS: Rams lead series, 32-26;
See New Orleans vs. St. Louis
ST. LOUIS vs. N.Y. GIANTS
RS: Rams lead series, 22-9
PS: Series tied, 1-1;
See N.Y. Giants vs. St. Louis
ST. LOUIS vs. N.Y. JETS
RS: Rams lead series, 7-2;
See N.Y. Jets vs. St. Louis
ST. LOUIS vs. OAKLAND
RS: Raiders lead series, 7-2;
See Oakland vs. St. Louis
ST. LOUIS vs. PHILADELPHIA
RS: Rams lead series, 15-13-1
PS: Series tied, 1-1;
See Philadelphia vs. St. Louis
ST. LOUIS vs. PITTSBURGH
RS: Rams lead series, 14-5-2
PS: Steelers lead series, 1-0;
See Pittsburgh vs. St. Louis
***ST. LOUIS vs. SAN DIEGO**
RS: Series tied, 3-3
1970—Rams, 37-10 (LA)
1975—Rams, 13-10 (SD) OT
1979—Chargers, 40-16 (LA)
1988—Chargers, 38-24 (LA)
1991—Rams, 30-24 (LA)
1994—Chargers, 31-17 (SD)
(RS Pts.—Chargers 153, Rams 137)
**Franchise in Los Angeles prior to 1995*
***ST. LOUIS vs. SAN FRANCISCO**
RS: Series tied, 48-48-2
PS: 49ers lead series, 1-0
1950—Rams, 35-14 (SF)
Rams, 28-21 (LA)
1951—49ers, 44-17 (SF)
Rams, 23-16 (LA)
1952—Rams, 35-9 (LA)
Rams, 34-21 (SF)
1953—49ers, 31-30 (SF)
49ers, 31-27 (LA)
1954—Tie, 24-24 (LA)
Rams, 42-34 (SF)
1955—Rams, 23-14 (SF)
Rams, 27-14 (LA)
1956—49ers, 33-30 (SF)
Rams, 30-6 (LA)
1957—49ers, 23-20 (SF)
Rams, 37-24 (LA)
1958—Rams, 33-3 (SF)
Rams, 56-7 (LA)
1959—49ers, 34-0 (SF)
49ers, 24-16 (LA)
1960—49ers, 13-9 (SF)
49ers, 23-7 (LA)
1961—49ers, 35-0 (SF)
Rams, 17-7 (LA)
1962—Rams, 28-14 (SF)
49ers, 24-17 (LA)
1963—Rams, 28-21 (LA)
Rams, 21-17 (SF)
1964—Rams, 42-14 (LA)
49ers, 28-7 (SF)
1965—49ers, 45-21 (LA)
49ers, 30-27 (SF)
1966—Rams, 34-3 (LA)
49ers, 21-13 (SF)
1967—49ers, 27-24 (LA)
Rams, 17-7 (SF)
1968—Rams, 24-10 (LA)
Tie, 20-20 (SF)
1969—Rams, 27-21 (SF)
Rams, 41-30 (LA)
1970—49ers, 20-6 (LA)
Rams, 30-13 (SF)
1971—Rams, 20-13 (SF)
Rams, 17-6 (LA)
1972—Rams, 31-7 (LA)
Rams, 26-16 (SF)
1973—Rams, 40-20 (SF)
Rams, 31-13 (LA)
1974—Rams, 37-14 (LA)
Rams, 15-13 (SF)
1975—Rams, 23-14 (SF)
49ers, 24-23 (LA)
1976—49ers, 16-0 (LA)
Rams, 23-3 (SF)
1977—Rams, 34-14 (LA)
Rams, 23-10 (SF)
1978—Rams, 27-10 (LA)
Rams, 31-28 (SF)
1979—Rams, 27-24 (LA)
Rams, 26-20 (SF)
1980—Rams, 48-26 (LA)
Rams, 31-17 (SF)
1981—49ers, 20-17 (SF)
49ers, 33-31 (LA)
1982—49ers, 30-24 (LA)
Rams, 21-20 (SF)
1983—Rams, 10-7 (SF)
49ers, 45-35 (LA)
1984—49ers, 33-0 (LA)
49ers, 19-16 (SF)
1985—49ers, 28-14 (LA)
Rams, 27-20 (SF)
1986—Rams, 16-13 (LA)
49ers, 24-14 (SF)
1987—49ers, 31-10 (LA)
49ers, 48-0 (SF)
1988—49ers, 24-21 (LA)
Rams, 38-16 (SF)
1989—Rams, 13-12 (SF)
49ers, 30-27 (LA)
**49ers, 30-3 (SF)
1990—Rams, 28-17 (SF)
49ers, 26-10 (LA)
1991—49ers, 27-10 (SF)
49ers, 33-10 (LA)
1992—49ers, 27-24 (SF)
49ers, 27-10 (LA)
1993—49ers, 40-17 (SF)
49ers, 35-10 (LA)
1994—49ers, 34-19 (LA)
49ers, 31-27 (SF)
1995—49ers, 44-10 (StL)
49ers, 41-13 (SF)
1996—49ers, 34-0 (SF)
49ers, 28-11 (StL)
1997—49ers, 15-12 (StL)
49ers, 30-10 (SF)
1998—49ers, 28-10 (StL)
49ers, 38-19 (SF)
(RS Pts.—49ers 2,186, Rams 2,144)
(PS Pts.—49ers 30, Rams 3)
**Franchise in Los Angeles prior to 1995*
***NFC Championship*
***ST. LOUIS vs. SEATTLE**
RS: Rams lead series, 4-2
1976—Rams, 45-6 (LA)
1979—Rams, 24-0 (S)
1985—Rams, 35-24 (S)
1988—Rams, 31-10 (LA)
1991—Seahawks, 23-9 (S)
1997—Seahawks, 17-9 (StL)
(RS Pts.—Rams 153, Seahawks 80)
**Franchise in Los Angeles prior to 1995*
***ST. LOUIS vs. TAMPA BAY**
RS: Rams lead series, 8-3
PS: Rams lead series, 1-0
1977—Rams, 31-0 (LA)
1978—Rams, 26-23 (LA)
1979—Buccaneers, 21-6 (TB)
**Rams, 9-0 (TB)
1980—Buccaneers, 10-9 (TB)
1984—Rams, 34-33 (TB)
1985—Rams, 31-27 (TB)
1986—Rams, 26-20 (LA) OT
1987—Rams, 35-3 (LA)
1990—Rams, 35-14 (TB)
1992—Rams, 31-27 (TB)
1994—Buccaneers, 24-14 (TB)
(RS Pts.—Rams 278, Buccaneers 202)
(PS Pts.—Rams 9, Buccaneers 0)
**Franchise in Los Angeles prior to 1995*
***NFC Championship*
***ST. LOUIS vs. **TENNESSEE**
RS: Rams lead series, 5-2
1973—Rams, 31-26 (H)
1978—Rams, 10-6 (H)
1981—Oilers, 27-20 (LA)
1984—Rams, 27-16 (LA)
1987—Oilers, 20-16 (H)
1990—Rams, 17-13 (LA)
1993—Rams, 28-13 (H)
(RS Pts.—Rams 149, Titans 121)
**Franchise in Los Angeles prior to 1995*
***Franchise in Houston prior to 1997; known as Oilers prior to 1999*
***ST. LOUIS vs. WASHINGTON**
RS: Redskins lead series, 17-6-1
PS: Series tied, 2-2
1937—Redskins, 16-7 (C)
1938—Redskins, 37-13 (W)
1941—Redskins, 17-13 (W)
1942—Redskins, 33-14 (W)
1944—Redskins, 14-10 (W)
1945—**Rams, 15-14 (C)
1948—Rams, 41-13 (W)
1949—Rams, 53-27 (LA)
1951—Redskins, 31-21 (W)
1962—Redskins, 20-14 (W)
1963—Redskins, 37-14 (LA)
1967—Tie, 28-28 (LA)
1969—Rams, 24-13 (W)
1971—Redskins, 38-24 (LA)
1974—Redskins, 23-17 (LA)
***Rams, 19-10 (LA)
1977—Redskins, 17-14 (W)
1981—Redskins, 30-7 (LA)
1983—Redskins, 42-20 (LA)
***Redskins, 51-7 (W)
1986—****Redskins, 19-7 (W)
1987—Rams, 30-26 (W)
1991—Redskins, 27-6 (LA)
1993—Rams, 10-6 (LA)
1994—Redskins, 24-21 (LA)
1995—Redskins, 35-23 (StL)
1996—Redskins, 17-10 (StL)
1997—Rams, 23-20 (W)
(RS Pts.—Redskins 591, Rams 457)
(PS Pts.—Redskins 94, Rams 48)
**Franchise in Los Angeles prior to 1995 and in Cleveland prior to 1946*
***NFL Championship*
****NFC Divisional Playoff*
*****NFC First-Round Playoff*

SAN DIEGO vs. ARIZONA
RS: Chargers lead series, 6-2;

ALL-TIME TEAM VS. TEAM RESULTS

See Arizona vs. San Diego
SAN DIEGO vs. ATLANTA
RS: Falcons lead series, 5-1;
See Atlanta vs. San Diego
SAN DIEGO vs BALTIMORE
RS: Chargers lead series, 2-0;
See Baltimore vs. San Diego
SAN DIEGO vs. BUFFALO
RS: Chargers lead series, 17-7-2
PS: Bills lead series, 2-1;
See Buffalo vs. San Diego
SAN DIEGO vs. CAROLINA
RS: Panthers lead series, 1-0;
See Carolina vs. San Diego
SAN DIEGO vs. CHICAGO
RS: Chargers lead series, 4-3;
See Chicago vs. San Diego
SAN DIEGO vs. CINCINNATI
RS: Chargers lead series, 14-9
PS: Bengals lead series, 1-0;
See Cincinnati vs. San Diego
SAN DIEGO vs. CLEVELAND
RS: Chargers lead series, 9-6-1;
See Cleveland vs. San Diego
SAN DIEGO vs. DALLAS
RS: Cowboys lead series, 5-1;
See Dallas vs. San Diego
SAN DIEGO vs. DENVER
RS: Broncos lead series, 42-35-1;
See Denver vs. San Diego
SAN DIEGO vs. DETROIT
RS: Series tied, 3-3;
See Detroit vs. San Diego
SAN DIEGO vs. GREEN BAY
RS: Packers lead series, 5-1;
See Green Bay vs. San Diego
SAN DIEGO vs. INDIANAPOLIS
RS: Chargers lead series, 12-6
PS: Colts lead series, 1-0;
See Indianapolis vs. San Diego
SAN DIEGO vs. KANSAS CITY
RS: Chiefs lead series, 40-36-1
PS: Chargers lead series, 1-0;
See Kansas City vs. San Diego
SAN DIEGO vs. MIAMI
RS: Chargers lead series, 10-6
PS: Series tied, 2-2;
See Miami vs. San Diego
SAN DIEGO vs. MINNESOTA
RS: Chargers lead series, 4-3;
See Minnesota vs. San Diego
SAN DIEGO vs. NEW ENGLAND
RS: Patriots lead series, 16-11-2
PS: Chargers lead series, 1-0;
See New England vs. San Diego
SAN DIEGO vs. NEW ORLEANS
RS: Chargers lead series, 6-1;
See New Orleans vs. San Diego
SAN DIEGO vs. N.Y. GIANTS
RS: Giants lead series, 5-3;
See N.Y. Giants vs. San Diego
SAN DIEGO vs. N.Y. JETS
RS: Chargers lead series, 17-9-1;
See N.Y. Jets vs. San Diego
SAN DIEGO vs. OAKLAND
RS: Raiders lead series, 47-29-2
PS: Raiders lead series, 1-0;
See Oakland vs. San Diego
SAN DIEGO vs. PHILADELPHIA
RS: Chargers lead series, 5-2;
See Philadelphia vs. San Diego
SAN DIEGO vs. PITTSBURGH
RS: Steelers lead series, 16-5
PS: Chargers lead series, 2-0;
See Pittsburgh vs. San Diego
SAN DIEGO vs. ST. LOUIS
RS: Series tied, 3-3
See St. Louis vs. San Diego
SAN DIEGO vs. SAN FRANCISCO
RS: 49ers lead series, 5-3
PS: 49ers lead series, 1-0
1972—49ers, 34-3 (SF)
1976—Chargers, 13-7 (SD) OT
1979—Chargers, 31-9 (SD)
1982—Chargers, 41-37 (SF)
1988—49ers, 48-10 (SD)
1991—49ers, 34-14 (SF)
1994—49ers, 38-15 (SD)
*49ers, 49-26 (Miami)
1997—49ers, 17-10 (SF)
(RS Pts.—49ers 224, Chargers 137)
(PS Pts.—49ers 49, Chargers 26)
**Super Bowl XXIX*
SAN DIEGO vs. SEATTLE
RS: Series tied, 20-20
1977—Chargers, 30-28 (S)
1978—Chargers, 24-20 (S)
Chargers, 37-10 (SD)
1979—Chargers, 33-16 (S)
Chargers, 20-10 (SD)
1980—Chargers, 34-13 (S)
Chargers, 21-14 (SD)
1981—Chargers, 24-10 (SD)
Seahawks, 44-23 (S)
1983—Seahawks, 34-31 (S)
Chargers, 28-21 (SD)
1984—Seahawks, 31-17 (S)
Seahawks, 24-0 (SD)
1985—Seahawks, 49-35 (SD)
Seahawks, 26-21 (S)
1986—Seahawks, 33-7 (S)
Seahawks, 34-24 (SD)
1987—Seahawks, 34-3 (S)
1988—Chargers, 17-6 (SD)
Seahawks, 17-14 (S)
1989—Seahawks, 17-16 (SD)
Seahawks, 10-7 (S)
1990—Chargers, 31-14 (S)
Seahawks, 13-10 (SD) OT
1991—Seahawks, 20-9 (S)
Chargers, 17-14 (SD)
1992—Chargers, 17-6 (SD)
Chargers, 31-14 (S)
1993—Chargers, 18-12 (SD)
Seahawks, 31-14 (S)
1994—Chargers, 24-10 (S)
Chargers, 35-15 (SD)
1995—Chargers, 14-10 (SD)
Chargers, 35-25 (S)
1996—Chargers, 29-7 (SD)
Seahawks, 32-13 (S)
1997—Seahawks, 26-22 (S)
Seahawks, 37-31 (SD)
1998—Seahawks, 27-20 (SD)
Seahawks, 38-17 (S)
(RS Pts.—Chargers 853, Seahawks 852)
SAN DIEGO vs. TAMPA BAY
RS: Chargers lead series, 6-1
1976—Chargers, 23-0 (TB)
1981—Chargers, 24-23 (TB)
1987—Chargers, 17-13 (TB)
1990—Chargers, 41-10 (SD)
1992—Chargers, 29-14 (SD)
1993—Chargers, 32-17 (TB)
1996—Buccaneers, 25-17 (SD)
(RS Pts.—Chargers 183, Buccaneers 102)
***SAN DIEGO vs. **TENNESSEE**
RS: Chargers lead series, 19-13-1
PS: Titans lead series, 3-0
1960—Oilers, 38-28 (H)
Chargers, 24-21 (LA)
***Oilers, 24-16 (H)
1961—Chargers, 34-24 (SD)
Oilers, 33-13 (H)
***Oilers, 10-3 (SD)
1962—Oilers, 42-17 (SD)
Oilers, 33-27 (H)
1963—Chargers, 27-0 (SD)
Chargers 20-14 (H)
1964—Chargers, 27-21 (SD)
Chargers, 20-17 (H)
1965—Chargers, 31-14 (SD)
Chargers, 37-26 (H)
1966—Chargers, 28-22 (H)
1967—Chargers, 13-3 (SD)
Oilers, 24-17 (H)
1968—Chargers, 30-14 (SD)
1969—Chargers, 21-17 (H)
1970—Tie, 31-31 (SD)
1971—Oilers, 49-33 (H)
1972—Chargers, 34-20 (SD)
1974—Oilers, 21-14 (H)
1975—Oilers, 33-17 (H)
1976—Chargers, 30-27 (SD)
1978—Chargers, 45-24 (H)
1979—****Oilers, 17-14 (SD)
1984—Chargers, 31-14 (SD)
1985—Oilers, 37-35 (H)
1986—Chargers, 27-0 (SD)
1987—Oilers, 33-18 (H)
1989—Oilers, 34-27 (SD)
1990—Oilers, 17-7 (SD)
1992—Oilers, 27-0 (H)
1993—Chargers, 18-17 (SD)
1998—Chargers, 13-7 (T)
(RS Pts.—Chargers 794, Titans 754)
(PS Pts.—Titans 51, Chargers 33)
**Franchise in Los Angeles prior to 1961*
***Franchise in Houston prior to 1997; known as Oilers prior to 1999*
****AFL Championship*
*****AFC Divisional Playoff*
SAN DIEGO vs. WASHINGTON
RS: Redskins lead series, 6-0
1973—Redskins, 38-0 (W)
1980—Redskins, 40-17 (W)
1983—Redskins, 27-24 (SD)
1986—Redskins, 30-27 (SD)
1989—Redskins, 26-21 (W)
1998—Redskins, 24-20 (W)
(RS Pts.—Redskins 185, Chargers 109)

SAN FRANCISCO vs. ARIZONA
RS: 49ers lead series, 10-9;
See Arizona vs. San Francisco
SAN FRANCISCO vs. ATLANTA
RS: 49ers lead series, 40-23-1
PS: Falcons lead series, 1-0;
See Atlanta vs. San Francisco
SAN FRANCISCO vs. BALTIMORE
RS: 49ers lead series, 1-0;
See Baltimore vs. San Francisco
SAN FRANCISCO vs. BUFFALO
RS: Bills lead series, 4-3;
See Buffalo vs. San Francisco
SAN FRANCISCO vs. CAROLINA
RS: 49ers lead series, 5-3;
See Carolina vs. San Francisco
SAN FRANCISCO vs. CHICAGO
RS: Series tied, 25-25-1
PS: 49ers lead series, 3-0;
See Chicago vs. San Francisco
SAN FRANCISCO vs. CINCINNATI
RS: 49ers lead series, 7-1
PS: 49ers lead series, 2-0;
See Cincinnati vs. San Francisco
SAN FRANCISCO vs. CLEVELAND
RS: Browns lead series, 9-6;
See Cleveland vs. San Francisco
SAN FRANCISCO vs. DALLAS
RS: 49ers lead series, 12-7-1
PS: Cowboys lead series, 5-2;
See Dallas vs. San Francisco
SAN FRANCISCO vs. DENVER
RS: Series tied, 4-4
PS: 49ers lead series, 1-0;
See Denver vs. San Francisco
SAN FRANCISCO vs. DETROIT
RS: 49ers lead series, 29-26-1
PS: Series tied, 1-1;
See Detroit vs. San Francisco
SAN FRANCISCO vs. GREEN BAY
RS: 49ers lead series, 25-23-1
PS: Packers lead series, 3-1;
See Green Bay vs. San Francisco
SAN FRANCISCO vs. INDIANAPOLIS
RS: Colts lead series, 22-17;
See Indianapolis vs. San Francisco
SAN FRANCISCO vs. KANSAS CITY
RS: 49ers lead series, 4-3;
See Kansas City vs. San Francisco
SAN FRANCISCO vs. MIAMI
RS: Dolphins lead series, 4-3
PS: 49ers lead series, 1-0;
See Miami vs. San Francisco
SAN FRANCISCO vs. MINNESOTA
RS: 49ers lead series, 17-16-1
PS: 49ers lead series, 4-1;
See Minnesota vs. San Francisco
SAN FRANCISCO vs. NEW ENGLAND
RS: 49ers lead series, 7-2;
See New England vs. San Francisco
SAN FRANCISCO vs. NEW ORLEANS
RS: 49ers lead series, 42-15-2;
See New Orleans vs. San Francisco
SAN FRANCISCO vs. N.Y. GIANTS
RS: 49ers lead series, 12-11
PS: Series tied, 3-3;
See N.Y. Giants vs. San Francisco
SAN FRANCISCO vs. N.Y. JETS
RS: 49ers lead series, 7-1;
See N.Y. Jets vs. San Francisco
SAN FRANCISCO vs. OAKLAND
RS: Raiders lead series, 5-3;
See Oakland vs. San Francisco
SAN FRANCISCO vs. PHILADELPHIA
RS: 49ers lead series, 14-6-1
PS: 49ers lead series, 1-0;
See Philadelphia vs. San Francisco
SAN FRANCISCO vs. PITTSBURGH
RS: 49ers lead series, 9-7;
See Pittsburgh vs. San Francisco
SAN FRANCISCO vs. ST. LOUIS
RS: Series tied, 48-48-2
PS: 49ers lead series, 1-0;
See St. Louis vs. San Francisco
SAN FRANCISCO vs. SAN DIEGO
RS: 49ers lead series, 5-3
PS: 49ers lead series, 1-0;
See San Diego vs. San Francisco
SAN FRANCISCO vs. SEATTLE
RS: 49ers lead series, 4-2
1976—49ers, 37-21 (S)
1979—Seahawks, 35-24 (SF)
1985—49ers, 19-6 (SF)
1988—49ers, 38-7 (S)
1991—49ers, 24-22 (S)
1997—Seahawks, 38-9 (S)
(RS Pts.—49ers 151, Seahawks 129)
SAN FRANCISCO vs. TAMPA BAY
RS: 49ers lead series, 12-2
1977—49ers, 20-10 (SF)
1978—49ers, 6-3 (SF)
1979—49ers, 23-7 (SF)
1980—Buccaneers, 24-23 (SF)
1983—49ers, 35-21 (SF)
1984—49ers, 24-17 (SF)
1986—49ers, 31-7 (TB)
1987—49ers, 24-10 (TB)
1989—49ers, 20-16 (TB)
1990—49ers, 31-7 (SF)
1992—49ers, 21-14 (SF)
1993—49ers, 45-21 (TB)
1994—49ers, 41-16 (SF)
1997—Buccaneers, 13-6 (TB)
(RS Pts.—49ers 350, Buccaneers 186)
SAN FRANCISCO vs. *TENNESSEE
RS: 49ers lead series, 6-3
1970—49ers, 30-20 (H)
1975—Oilers, 27-13 (SF)
1978—Oilers, 20-19 (H)
1981—49ers, 28-6 (SF)
1984—49ers, 34-21 (H)
1987—49ers, 27-20 (SF)
1990—49ers, 24-21 (H)
1993—Oilers, 10-7 (SF)
1996—49ers, 10-9 (H)
(RS Pts.—49ers 192, Titans 154)
**Franchise in Houston prior to 1997; known as Oilers prior to 1999*

SAN FRANCISCO vs. WASHINGTON
RS: 49ers lead series, 12-6-1
PS: 49ers lead series, 3-1
1952—49ers, 23-17 (W)
1954—49ers, 41-7 (SF)
1955—Redskins, 7-0 (W)
1961—49ers, 35-3 (SF)
1967—Redskins, 31-28 (W)
1969—Tie, 17-17 (SF)
1970—49ers, 26-17 (SF)
1971—*49ers, 24-20 (SF)
1973—Redskins, 33-9 (W)
1976—Redskins, 24-21 (SF)
1978—Redskins, 38-20 (W)
1981—49ers, 30-17 (W)
1983—**Redskins, 24-21 (W)
1984—49ers, 37-31 (SF)
1985—49ers, 35-8 (W)
1986—Redskins, 14-6 (W)
1988—49ers, 37-21 (SF)
1990—49ers, 26-13 (SF)
*49ers, 28-10 (SF)
1992—*49ers, 20-13 (SF)
1994—49ers, 37-22 (W)
1996—49ers, 19-16 (W) OT
1998—49ers, 45-10 (W)
(RS Pts.—49ers 492, Redskins 346)
(PS Pts.—49ers 93, Redskins 67)
NFC Divisional Playoff
***NFC Championship*

SEATTLE vs. ARIZONA
RS: Cardinals lead series, 5-1;
See Arizona vs. Seattle
SEATTLE vs. ATLANTA
RS: Seahawks lead series, 4-2;
See Atlanta vs. Seattle
SEATTLE vs. BALTIMORE
RS: Ravens lead series, 1-0;
See Baltimore vs. Seattle
SEATTLE vs. BUFFALO
RS: Seahawks lead series, 4-2;
See Buffalo vs. Seattle
SEATTLE vs. CHICAGO
RS: Seahawks lead series, 4-2;
See Chicago vs. Seattle
SEATTLE vs. CINCINNATI
RS: Series tied, 7-7
PS: Bengals lead series, 1-0;
See Cincinnati vs. Seattle
SEATTLE vs. CLEVELAND
RS: Seahawks lead series, 9-4;
See Cleveland vs. Seattle
SEATTLE vs. DALLAS
RS: Cowboys lead series, 5-1;
See Dallas vs. Seattle
SEATTLE vs. DENVER
RS: Broncos lead series, 28-15
PS: Seahawks lead series, 1-0;
See Denver vs. Seattle
SEATTLE vs. DETROIT
RS: Seahawks lead series, 4-3;
See Detroit vs. Seattle
SEATTLE vs. GREEN BAY
RS: Packers lead series, 4-3;
See Green Bay vs. Seattle
SEATTLE vs. INDIANAPOLIS
RS: Colts lead series, 4-3;
See Indianapolis vs. Seattle
SEATTLE vs. JACKSONVILLE
RS: Series tied, 1-1;
See Jacksonville vs. Seattle
SEATTLE vs. KANSAS CITY
RS: Chiefs lead series, 27-14;
See Kansas City vs. Seattle
SEATTLE vs. MIAMI
RS: Dolphins lead series, 4-2
PS: Series tied, 1-1;
See Miami vs. Seattle
SEATTLE vs. MINNESOTA
RS: Seahawks lead series, 4-2;
See Minnesota vs. Seattle
SEATTLE vs. NEW ENGLAND
RS: Seahawks lead series, 7-6;
See New England vs. Seattle
SEATTLE vs. NEW ORLEANS
RS: Saints lead series, 4-2;
See New Orleans vs. Seattle
SEATTLE vs. N.Y. GIANTS
RS: Giants lead series, 5-3;
See N.Y. Giants vs. Seattle
SEATTLE vs. N.Y. JETS
RS: Seahawks lead series, 8-6;
See N.Y. Jets vs. Seattle
SEATTLE vs. OAKLAND
RS: Raiders lead series, 23-19
PS: Series tied, 1-1;
See Oakland vs. Seattle
SEATTLE vs. PHILADELPHIA
RS: Eagles lead series, 4-3;
See Philadelphia vs. Seattle
SEATTLE vs. PITTSBURGH
RS: Series tied, 6-6;
See Pittsburgh vs. Seattle
SEATTLE vs. ST. LOUIS
RS: Rams lead series, 4-2;
See St. Louis vs. Seattle
SEATTLE vs. SAN DIEGO
RS: Series tied, 20-20;
See San Diego vs. Seattle
SEATTLE vs. SAN FRANCISCO
RS: 49ers lead series, 4-2;
See San Francisco vs. Seattle
SEATTLE vs. TAMPA BAY
RS: Seahawks lead series, 4-0
1976—Seahawks, 13-10 (TB)
1977—Seahawks, 30-23 (S)
1994—Seahawks, 22-21 (S)
1996—Seahawks, 17-13 (TB)
(RS Pts.—Seahawks 82, Buccaneers 67)
SEATTLE vs. *TENNESSEE
RS: Seahawks lead series, 8-4
PS: Titans lead series, 1-0
1977—Oilers, 22-10 (S)
1979—Seahawks, 34-14 (S)
1980—Seahawks, 26-7 (H)
1981—Oilers, 35-17 (H)
1982—Oilers, 23-21 (H)
1987—**Oilers, 23-20 (H) OT
1988—Seahawks, 27-24 (S)
1990—Seahawks, 13-10 (S) OT
1993—Oilers, 24-14 (H)
1994—Seahawks, 16-14 (H)
1996—Seahawks, 23-16 (S)
1997—Seahawks, 16-13 (S)
1998—Seahawks, 20-18 (S)
(RS Pts.—Seahawks 237, Titans 220)
(PS Pts.—Titans 23, Seahawks 20)
Franchise in Houston prior to 1997; known as Oilers prior to 1999
***AFC First-Round Playoff*
SEATTLE vs. WASHINGTON
RS: Redskins lead series, 5-4
1976—Redskins, 31-7 (W)
1980—Seahawks, 14-0 (W)
1983—Redskins, 27-17 (S)
1986—Redskins, 19-14 (W)
1989—Redskins, 29-0 (S)
1992—Redskins, 16-3 (S)
1994—Seahawks, 28-7 (W)
1995—Seahawks, 27-20 (W)
1998—Seahawks, 24-14 (S)
(RS Pts.—Redskins 163, Seahawks 134)

TAMPA BAY vs. ARIZONA
RS: Series tied, 7-7;
See Arizona vs. Tampa Bay
TAMPA BAY vs. ATLANTA
RS: Falcons lead series, 8-7;
See Atlanta vs. Tampa Bay
TAMPA BAY vs. BUFFALO
RS: Buccaneers lead series, 4-2;
See Buffalo vs. Tampa Bay
TAMPA BAY vs. CAROLINA
RS: Buccaneers lead series, 2-1;
See Carolina vs. Tampa Bay
TAMPA BAY vs. CHICAGO
RS: Bears lead series, 30-12;
See Chicago vs. Tampa Bay
TAMPA BAY vs. CINCINNATI
RS: Series tied, 3-3;
See Cincinnati vs. Tampa Bay
TAMPA BAY vs. CLEVELAND
RS: Browns lead series, 5-0;
See Cleveland vs. Tampa Bay
TAMPA BAY vs. DALLAS
RS: Cowboys lead series, 6-0
PS: Cowboys lead series, 2-0;
See Dallas vs. Tampa Bay
TAMPA BAY vs. DENVER
RS: Broncos lead series, 3-1;
See Denver vs. Tampa Bay
TAMPA BAY vs. DETROIT
RS: Lions lead series, 24-18
PS: Buccaneers lead series, 1-0;
See Detroit vs. Tampa Bay
TAMPA BAY vs. GREEN BAY
RS: Packers lead series, 25-14-1
PS: Packers lead series, 1-1;
See Green Bay vs. Tampa Bay
TAMPA BAY vs. INDIANAPOLIS
RS: Colts lead series, 5-4;
See Indianapolis vs. Tampa Bay
TAMPA BAY vs. JACKSONVILLE
RS: Series tied, 1-1;
See Jacksonville vs. Tampa Bay
TAMPA BAY vs. KANSAS CITY
RS: Chiefs lead series, 5-2;
See Kansas City vs. Tampa Bay
TAMPA BAY vs. MIAMI
RS: Dolphins lead series, 4-2;
See Miami vs. Tampa Bay
TAMPA BAY vs. MINNESOTA
RS: Vikings lead series, 28-14;
See Minnesota vs. Tampa Bay
TAMPA BAY vs. NEW ENGLAND
RS: Patriots lead series, 3-1;
See New England vs. Tampa Bay
TAMPA BAY vs. NEW ORLEANS
RS: Saints lead series, 13-5,
See New Orleans vs. Tampa Bay
TAMPA BAY vs. N.Y. GIANTS
RS: Giants lead series, 8-5;
See N.Y. Giants vs. Tampa Bay
TAMPA BAY vs. N.Y. JETS
RS: Jets lead series, 6-1;
See N.Y. Jets vs. Tampa Bay
TAMPA BAY vs. OAKLAND
RS: Raiders lead series, 3-1;
See Oakland vs. Tampa Bay
TAMPA BAY vs. PHILADELPHIA
RS: Eagles lead series, 3-2
PS: Buccaneers lead series, 1-0;
See Philadelphia vs. Tampa Bay
TAMPA BAY vs. PITTSBURGH
RS: Steelers lead series, 4-1;
See Pittsburgh vs. Tampa Bay
TAMPA BAY vs. ST. LOUIS
RS: Rams lead series, 8-3
PS: Rams lead series, 1-0;
See St. Louis vs. Tampa Bay
TAMPA BAY vs. SAN DIEGO
RS: Chargers lead series, 6-1;
See San Diego vs. Tampa Bay
TAMPA BAY vs. SAN FRANCISCO
RS: 49ers lead series, 12-2;
See San Francisco vs. Tampa Bay
TAMPA BAY vs. SEATTLE
RS: Seahawks lead series, 4-0;
See Seattle vs. Tampa Bay
TAMPA BAY vs. *TENNESSEE
RS: Titans lead series, 5-1
1976—Oilers, 20-0 (H)
1980—Oilers, 20-14 (H)
1983—Buccaneers, 33-24 (TB)
1989—Oilers, 20-17 (H)
1995—Oilers, 19-7 (H)
1998—Oilers, 31-22 (TB)
(RS Pts.—Titans 134, Buccaneers 93)
Franchise in Houston prior to 1997; known as Oilers prior to 1999
TAMPA BAY vs. WASHINGTON
RS: Redskins lead series, 5-4
1977—Redskins, 10-0 (TB)
1982—Redskins, 21-13 (TB)
1989—Redskins, 32-28 (W)
1993—Redskins, 23-17 (TB)
1994—Buccaneers, 26-21 (TB)
Buccaneers, 17-14 (W)
1995—Buccaneers, 14-6 (TB)
1996—Buccaneers, 24-10 (TB)
1998—Redskins, 20-16 (W)
(RS Pts.—Redskins 157, Buccaneers 155)

TENNESSEE VS. ARIZONA
RS: Cardinals lead series, 4-3;
See Arizona vs. Tennessee
TENNESSEE vs. ATLANTA
RS: Falcons lead series, 5-4;
See Atlanta vs. Tennessee
TENNESSEE vs. BALTIMORE
RS: Titans lead series, 4-2;
See Baltimore vs. Tennessee
TENNESSEE vs. BUFFALO
RS: Titans lead series, 22-13
PS: Bills lead series, 2-0;
See Buffalo vs. Tennessee
TENNESSEE vs. CAROLINA
RS: Panthers lead series, 1-0;
See Carolina vs. Tennessee
TENNESSEE vs. CHICAGO
RS: Series tied, 4-4;
See Chicago vs. Tennessee
TENNESSEE vs. CINCINNATI
RS: Titans lead series, 31-28-1
PS: Bengals lead series, 1-0;
See Cincinnati vs. Tennessee
TENNESSEE vs. CLEVELAND
RS: Browns lead series, 30-21
PS: Titans lead series, 1-0;
See Cleveland vs. Tennessee
TENNESSEE vs. DALLAS
RS: Cowboys lead series, 5-4
See Dallas vs. Tennessee
TENNESSEE vs. DENVER
RS: Titans lead series, 20-11-1
PS: Broncos lead series, 2-1;
See Denver vs. Tennessee
TENNESSEE vs. DETROIT
RS: Titans lead series, 4-3;
See Detroit vs. Tennessee
TENNESSEE vs. GREEN BAY
RS: Packers lead series, 4-3;
See Green Bay vs. Tennessee
TENNESSEE vs. INDIANAPOLIS
RS: Series tied, 7-7;
See Indianapolis vs. Tennessee
TENNESSEE vs. JACKSONVILLE
RS: Jaguars lead series, 5-3;
See Jacksonville vs. Tennessee
TENNESSEE vs. KANSAS CITY
RS: Chiefs lead series, 24-17
PS: Chiefs lead series, 2-0;
See Kansas City vs. Tennessee
TENNESSEE vs. MIAMI
RS: Dolphins lead series, 13-11
PS: Titans lead series, 1-0;
See Miami vs. Tennessee
TENNESSEE vs. MINNESOTA
RS: Vikings lead series, 5-3;
See Minnesota vs. Tennessee
TENNESSEE vs. NEW ENGLAND
RS: Patriots lead series, 18-14-1
PS: Titans lead series, 1-0;
See New England vs. Tennessee
TENNESSEE vs. NEW ORLEANS
RS: Series tied, 4-4-1;
See New Orleans vs. Tennessee
TENNESSEE vs. N.Y. GIANTS
RS: Giants lead series, 5-1;
See N.Y. Giants vs. Tennessee

ALL-TIME TEAM VS. TEAM RESULTS

TENNESSEE vs. N.Y. JETS
RS: Titans lead series, 20-13-1
PS: Titans lead series, 1-0;
See N.Y. Jets vs. Tennessee
TENNESSEE vs. OAKLAND
RS: Raiders lead series, 20-14
PS: Raiders lead series, 3-0;
See Oakland vs. Tennessee
TENNESSEE vs. PHILADELPHIA
RS: Eagles lead series, 6-0;
See Philadelphia vs. Tennessee
TENNESSEE vs. PITTSBURGH
RS: Steelers lead series, 35-22
PS: Steelers lead series, 3-0;
See Pittsburgh vs. Tennessee
TENNESSEE vs. ST. LOUIS
RS: Rams lead series, 5-2;
See St. Louis vs. Tennessee
TENNESSEE vs. SAN DIEGO
RS: Chargers lead series, 19-13-1
PS: Titans lead series, 3-0;
See San Diego vs. Tennessee
TENNESSEE vs. SAN FRANCISCO
RS: 49ers lead series, 6-3;
See San Francisco vs. Tennessee
TENNESSEE vs. SEATTLE
RS: Seahawks lead series, 8-4
PS: Titans lead series, 1-0;
See Seattle vs. Tennessee
TENNESSEE vs. TAMPA BAY
RS: Titans lead series, 5-1;
See Tampa Bay vs. Tennessee
***TENNESSEE vs. WASHINGTON**
RS: Titans lead series, 4-3
1971—Redskins, 22-13 (W)
1975—Oilers, 13-10 (H)
1979—Oilers, 29-27 (W)
1985—Redskins, 16-13 (W)
1988—Oilers, 41-17 (H)
1991—Redskins, 16-13 (W) OT
1997—Oilers, 28-14 (T)
(RS—Titans 150, Redskins 122)
**Franchise in Houston prior to 1997; known as Oilers prior to 1999*

WASHINGTON vs. ARIZONA
RS: Redskins lead series, 64-43-2;
See Arizona vs. Washington
WASHINGTON vs. ATLANTA
RS: Redskins lead series, 13-4-1
PS: Redskins lead series, 1-0;
See Atlanta vs. Washington
WASHINGTON vs BALTIMORE
RS: Ravens lead series, 1-0;
See Baltimore vs. Washington
WASHINGTON vs. BUFFALO
RS: Series tied, 4-4
PS: Redskins lead series, 1-0;
See Buffalo vs. Washington
WASHINGTON vs. CAROLINA
RS: Redskins lead series, 3-0;
See Carolina vs. Washington
WASHINGTON vs. CHICAGO
RS: Bears lead series, 18-14-1
PS: Redskins lead series, 4-3;
See Chicago vs. Washington
WASHINGTON vs. CINCINNATI
RS: Redskins lead series, 4-2;
See Cincinnati vs. Washington
WASHINGTON vs. CLEVELAND
RS: Browns lead series, 32-9-1;
See Cleveland vs. Washington
WASHINGTON vs. DALLAS
RS: Cowboys lead series, 43-31-2
PS: Redskins lead series, 2-0;
See Dallas vs. Washington
WASHINGTON vs. DENVER
RS: Broncos lead series, 5-3
PS: Redskins lead series, 1-0;
See Denver vs. Washington
WASHINGTON vs. DETROIT
RS: Redskins lead series, 24-8
PS: Redskins lead series, 2-0;
See Detroit vs. Washington
WASHINGTON vs. GREEN BAY
RS: Packers lead series, 13-12-1
PS: Series tied, 1-1;
See Green Bay vs. Washington
WASHINGTON vs. INDIANAPOLIS
RS: Colts lead series, 16-9;
See Indianapolis vs. Washington
WASHINGTON vs. JACKSONVILLE
RS: Redskins lead series, 1-0;
See Jacksonville vs. Washington
WASHINGTON vs. KANSAS CITY
RS: Chiefs lead series, 4-1;
See Kansas City vs. Washington
WASHINGTON vs. MIAMI
RS: Dolphins lead series, 5-2
PS: Series tied, 1-1;
See Miami vs. Washington
WASHINGTON vs. MINNESOTA
RS: Redskins lead series, 6-5
PS: Redskins lead series, 3-2;
See Minnesota vs. Washington
WASHINGTON vs. NEW ENGLAND
RS: Redskins lead series, 5-1;
See New England vs. Washington
WASHINGTON vs. NEW ORLEANS
RS: Redskins lead series, 12-5;
See New Orleans vs. Washington
WASHINGTON vs. N.Y. GIANTS
RS: Giants lead series, 75-53-4
PS: Series tied, 1-1;
See N.Y. Giants vs. Washington
WASHINGTON vs. N.Y. JETS
RS: Redskins lead series, 5-1;
See N.Y. Jets vs. Washington
WASHINGTON vs. OAKLAND
RS: Raiders lead series, 6-3
PS: Raiders lead series, 1-0;
See Oakland vs. Washington
WASHINGTON vs. PHILADELPHIA
RS: Redskins lead series, 69-53-5
PS: Redskins lead series, 1-0;
See Philadelphia vs. Washington
WASHINGTON vs. PITTSBURGH
RS: Redskins lead series, 42-28-3;
See Pittsburgh vs. Washington
WASHINGTON vs. ST. LOUIS
RS: Redskins lead series, 17-6-1
PS: Series tied, 2-2;
See St. Louis vs. Washington
WASHINGTON vs. SAN DIEGO
RS: Redskins lead series, 6-0;
See San Diego vs. Washington
WASHINGTON vs. SAN FRANCISCO
RS: 49ers lead series, 12-6-1
PS: 49ers lead series, 3-1;
See San Francisco vs. Washington
WASHINGTON vs. SEATTLE
RS: Redskins lead series, 5-4;
See Seattle vs. Washington
WASHINGTON vs. TAMPA BAY
RS: Redskins lead series, 5-4;
See Tampa Bay vs. Washington
WASHINGTON vs. TENNESSEE
RS: Titans lead series, 4-3;
See Tennessee vs. Washington

RESULTS

Super Bowl	Date	Winner (Share)	Loser (Share)	Score	Site	Attendance
XXXIII	1-31-99	Denver ($53,000)	Atlanta ($32,500)	34-19	Miami	74,803
XXXII	1-25-98	Denver ($48,000)	Green Bay ($29,000)	31-24	San Diego	68,912
XXXI	1-26-97	Green Bay ($48,000)	New England ($29,000)	35-21	New Orleans	72,301
XXX	1-28-96	Dallas ($42,000)	Pittsburgh ($27,000)	27-17	Tempe	76,347
XXIX	1-29-95	San Francisco ($42,000)	San Diego ($26,000)	49-26	Miami	74,107
XXVIII	1-30-94	Dallas ($38,000)	Buffalo ($23,500)	30-13	Atlanta	72,817
XXVII	1-31-93	Dallas ($36,000)	Buffalo ($18,000)	52-17	Pasadena	98,374
XXVI	1-26-92	Washington ($36,000)	Buffalo ($18,000)	37-24	Minneapolis	63,130
XXV	1-27-91	N.Y. Giants ($36,000)	Buffalo ($18,000)	20-19	Tampa	73,813
XXIV	1-28-90	San Francisco ($36,000)	Denver ($18,000)	55-10	New Orleans	72,919
XXIII	1-22-89	San Francisco ($36,000)	Cincinnati ($18,000)	20-16	Miami	75,129
XXII	1-31-88	Washington ($36,000)	Denver ($18,000)	42-10	San Diego	73,302
XXI	1-25-87	N.Y. Giants ($36,000)	Denver ($18,000)	39-20	Pasadena	101,063
XX	1-26-86	Chicago ($36,000)	New England ($18,000)	46-10	New Orleans	73,818
XIX	1-20-85	San Francisco ($36,000)	Miami ($18,000)	38-16	Stanford	84,059
XVIII	1-22-84	L.A. Raiders ($36,000)	Washington ($18,000)	38-9	Tampa	72,920
XVII	1-30-83	Washington ($36,000)	Miami ($18,000)	27-17	Pasadena	103,667
XVI	1-24-82	San Francisco ($18,000)	Cincinnati ($9,000)	26-21	Pontiac	81,270
XV	1-25-81	Oakland ($18,000)	Philadelphia ($9,000)	27-10	New Orleans	76,135
XIV	1-20-80	Pittsburgh ($18,000)	Los Angeles ($9,000)	31-19	Pasadena	103,985
XIII	1-21-79	Pittsburgh ($18,000)	Dallas ($9,000)	35-31	Miami	79,484
XII	1-15-78	Dallas ($18,000)	Denver ($9,000)	27-10	New Orleans	75,583
XI	1-9-77	Oakland ($15,000)	Minnesota ($7,500)	32-14	Pasadena	103,438
X	1-18-76	Pittsburgh ($15,000)	Dallas ($7,500)	21-17	Miami	80,187
IX	1-12-75	Pittsburgh ($15,000)	Minnesota ($7,500)	16-6	New Orleans	80,997
VIII	1-13-74	Miami ($15,000)	Minnesota ($7,500)	24-7	Houston	71,882
VII	1-14-73	Miami ($15,000)	Washington ($7,500)	14-7	Los Angeles	90,182
VI	1-16-72	Dallas ($15,000)	Miami ($7,500)	24-3	New Orleans	81,023
V	1-17-71	Baltimore ($15,000)	Dallas ($7,500)	16-13	Miami	79,204
IV	1-11-70	Kansas City ($15,000)	Minnesota ($7,500)	23-7	New Orleans	80,562
III	1-12-69	N.Y. Jets ($15,000)	Baltimore ($7,500)	16-7	Miami	75,389
II	1-14-68	Green Bay ($15,000)	Oakland ($7,500)	33-14	Miami	75,546
I	1-15-67	Green Bay ($15,000)	Kansas City ($7,500)	35-10	Los Angeles	61,946

SUPER BOWL COMPOSITE STANDINGS

	W	L	Pct.	Pts.	OP
San Francisco 49ers	5	0	1.000	188	89
New York Giants	2	0	1.000	59	39
Chicago Bears	1	0	1.000	46	10
New York Jets	1	0	1.000	16	7
Pittsburgh Steelers	4	1	.800	120	100
Green Bay Packers	3	1	.750	127	76
Oakland/L.A. Raiders	3	1	.750	111	66
Dallas Cowboys	5	3	.625	221	132
Washington Redskins	3	2	.600	122	103
Baltimore Colts	1	1	.500	23	29
Kansas City Chiefs	1	1	.500	33	42
Miami Dolphins	2	3	.400	74	103
Denver Broncos	2	4	.333	115	206
Atlanta Falcons	0	1	.000	19	34
Los Angeles Rams	0	1	.000	19	31
Philadelphia Eagles	0	1	.000	10	27
San Diego Chargers	0	1	.000	26	49
Cincinnati Bengals	0	2	.000	37	46
New England Patriots	0	2	.000	31	81
Buffalo Bills	0	4	.000	73	139
Minnesota Vikings	0	4	.000	34	95

SUPER BOWL MOST VALUABLE PLAYERS*

Super Bowl I — QB Bart Starr, Green Bay
Super Bowl II — QB Bart Starr, Green Bay
Super Bowl III — QB Joe Namath, N.Y. Jets
Super Bowl IV — QB Len Dawson, Kansas City
Super Bowl V — LB Chuck Howley, Dallas
Super Bowl VI — QB Roger Staubach, Dallas
Super Bowl VII — S Jake Scott, Miami
Super Bowl VIII — RB Larry Csonka, Miami
Super Bowl IX — RB Franco Harris, Pittsburgh
Super Bowl X — WR Lynn Swann, Pittsburgh
Super Bowl XI — WR Fred Biletnikoff, Oakland
Super Bowl XII — DT Randy White and DE Harvey Martin, Dallas
Super Bowl XIII — QB Terry Bradshaw, Pittsburgh
Super Bowl XIV — QB Terry Bradshaw, Pittsburgh
Super Bowl XV — QB Jim Plunkett, Oakland
Super Bowl XVI — QB Joe Montana, San Francisco
Super Bowl XVII — RB John Riggins, Washington
Super Bowl XVIII — RB Marcus Allen, L.A. Raiders
Super Bowl XIX — QB Joe Montana, San Francisco
Super Bowl XX — DE Richard Dent, Chicago
Super Bowl XXI — QB Phil Simms, N.Y. Giants
Super Bowl XXII — QB Doug Williams, Washington
Super Bowl XXIII — WR Jerry Rice, San Francisco
Super Bowl XXIV — QB Joe Montana, San Francisco
Super Bowl XXV — RB Ottis Anderson, N.Y. Giants
Super Bowl XXVI — QB Mark Rypien, Washington
Super Bowl XXVII — QB Troy Aikman, Dallas
Super Bowl XXVIII — RB Emmitt Smith, Dallas
Super Bowl XXIX — QB Steve Young, San Francisco
Super Bowl XXX — CB Larry Brown, Dallas
Super Bowl XXXI — KR-PR Desmond Howard, Green Bay
Super Bowl XXXII — RB Terrell Davis, Denver
Super Bowl XXXIII — QB John Elway, Denver

* Award named Pete Rozelle Trophy since Super Bowl XXV.

SUPER BOWL XXXIII

Pro Player Stadium, Miami, Florida
January 31, 1999, Attendance: 74,803

DENVER 34, ATLANTA 19—John Elway, in his last game, passed for 336 yards and ran for a touchdown to earn most valuable player honors as the Broncos became the first AFC team to win consecutive Super Bowls since the Steelers won XIII and XIV. A 25-yard pass interference penalty on Ray Crockett assisted the Falcons' nine-play, 48-yard game-opening drive that was capped by Morten Andersen's 32-yard field goal. Elway's 41-yard pass to Rod Smith kept alive Denver's ensuing drive and led to Howard Griffith's 1-yard touchdown run. Ronnie Bradford's interception and return to the Broncos' 35 late in the first quarter gave Atlanta excellent field position. However, Jamal Anderson was stopped for no gain on third-and-1 and thrown for a 2-yard loss on fourth down. Denver capitalized on its defensive effort with Jason Elam's 26-yard field goal. The Falcons responded by driving to the Broncos' 8, but Andersen's 26-yard field-goal attempt sailed wide right and on the next play, Elway fired an 80-yard touchdown pass to Smith to turn a possible 10-6 game into a 17-3 Broncos lead. Andersen's 28-yard field goal and 2 misses by Elam on the Broncos' first two second-half possessions gave Atlanta an opportunity to climb back into the game. However, Darrien Gordon dashed the Falcons' hopes with interceptions on consecutive possessions inside the Broncos' 20 to stop drives and set up Broncos touchdowns. Gordon returned the first interception, on a tipped pass, 58 yards to the Falcons' 24 to set up Griffith's second touchdown five plays later, and picked the second pass off at the Broncos' 2 and returned it 50 yards. Terrell Davis turned a short pass into a 39-yard gain, and Elway scored two plays later to give Denver a 31-6 lead. Tim Dwight returned the ensuing kickoff for a touchdown, and, after a field goal by Elam, the Falcons' offense scored with 2:04 remaining on Chandler's 3-yard pass to Tony Martin. Byron Chamberlain recovered the ensuing onside kick, but Tyrone Braxton recovered Anderson's fumble at the Falcons' 33 with 1:30 remaining to ice the game. The Falcons drove inside the Broncos' 30 seven times, but tallied just 1 touchdown and 2 field goals, throwing 2 interceptions, missing 1 field goal, and turning the ball over 1 time on downs during the other possessions. Elway was 18 of 29 for 336 yards and 1 touchdown, with 1 interception. Davis had 25 carries for 102 yards. Smith had 5 receptions for 152 yards. Chandler was 19 of 35 for 219 yards and 1 touchdown, with 3 interceptions.

Denver (34)	Offense	Atlanta (19)
Rod Smith	WR	Tony Martin
Tony Jones	LT	Bob Whitfield
Mark Schlereth	LG	Calvin Collins
Tom Nalen	C	Robbie Tobeck
Dan Neil	RG	Gene Williams
Harry Swayne	RT	Ephraim Salaam
Shannon Sharpe	TE	O.J. Santiago
Ed McCaffrey	WR	Terance Mathis
John Elway	QB	Chris Chandler
Terrell Davis	RB	Jamal Anderson
Howard Griffith	FB	Brian Kozlowski
	Defense	
Harald Hasselbach	LE	Lester Archambeau
Keith Traylor	LT	Travis Hall
Trevor Pryce	RT	Shane Dronett

Maa Tanuvasa	RE	Chuck Smith
John Mobley	LLB	Cornelius Bennett
Glenn Cadrez	MLB	Jessie Tuggle
Bill Romanowski	RLB	Henri Crockett
Ray Crockett	LCB	Ray Buchanan
Darrien Gordon	RCB	Ronnie Bradford
Tyrone Braxton	SS	William White
Steve Atwater	FS	Eugene Robinson

SUBSTITUTIONS

DENVER—Offense: K—Jason Elam. P—Tom Rouen. QB—Bubby Brister. RB—Vaughn Hebron, Derek Loville. FB—Anthony Lynn, Detron Smith. WR—Willie Green, Marcus Nash. TE—Dwayne Carswell, Byron Chamberlain. T—Matt Lepsis. G/C—David Diaz-Infante. Defense: DE—Neil Smith, Alfred Williams. DT—Mike Lodish, Marvin Washington. LB—Keith Burns, Seth Joyner. CB—Tory James, Darrius Johnson, Tito Paul. S—George Coghill. Inactive: QB—Brian Griese. WR—Justin Armour. T—Trey Teague. G—Chris Banks. C—K.C. Jones. DE—Cyron Brown. LB—Nate Wayne. S—Eric Brown.

ATLANTA—Offense: K—Morten Andersen. P—Dan Stryzinski. RB—Harold Green. FB—Gary Downs. WR—Tim Dwight, Ronnie Harris. TE—Ed Smith. T—Jose Portilla. G—Bob Hallen. C—Adam Schreiber. Defense: DT—Esera Tuaolo. DE—John Burrough, Antonio Edwards. LB—Keith Brooking, Ruffin Hamilton, Craig Sauer, Ben Talley. CB—Michael Booker, Randy Fuller, Elijah Williams. S—Devin Bush. DNP: QB—Steve DeBerg. RB—Ken Oxendine. Inactive: QB—Tony Graziani. WR—Todd Kinchen. TE—Rod Monroe. G—Dave Widell. DE—Shawn Swayda. CB—Darren Anderson. S—Chris Bayne, Omar Brown.

OFFICIALS

Referee—Bernie Kukar. Umpire—Jim Daopoulos. Line Judge—Ron Baynes. Side Judge—Gary Lane. Head Linesman—Sanford Rivers. Back Judge—Don Hakes. Field Judge—Tim Millis.

SCORING

Denver (AFC)	7	10	0	17	—	34
Atlanta (NFC)	3	3	0	13	—	19

Atl — FG Andersen 32 (5:25)
Den — Griffith 1 run (Elam kick) (11:05)
Den — FG Elam 26 (5:43)
Den — R. Smith 80 pass from Elway (Elam kick) (10:06)
Atl — FG Andersen 28 (12:35)
Den — Griffith 1 run (Elam kick) (:04)
Den — Elway 3 run (Elam kick) (3:40)
Atl — Dwight 94 kickoff return (Andersen kick) (3:59)
Den — FG Elam 37 (7:52)
Atl — Mathis 3 pass from Chandler (pass failed) (12:56)

TEAM STATISTICS	**DEN.**	**ATL.**
Total First Downs	22	21
Rushing	8	8
Passing	14	12
Penalty	0	1
Total Net Yardage	457	337
Total Offensive Plays	65	60
Average Gain Per Offensive Play	7.0	5.6
Rushes	36	23
Yards Gained Rushing (Net)	121	131
Average Yards per Rush	3.4	5.7
Passes Attempted	29	35
Passes Completed	18	19
Had Intercepted	1	3
Tackled Attempting to Pass	0	2
Yards Lost Attempting to Pass	0	13
Yards Gained Passing (Net)	336	206
Punts	1	1
Average Distance	35.0	39.0
Punt Returns	0	0
Punt Return Yardage	0	0
Kickoff Returns	3	7
Kickoff Return Yardage	44	227
Interception Return Yardage	136	1
Total Return Yardage	180	228
Fumbles	0	1
Fumbles Lost	0	1
Own Fumbles Recovered	0	0
Opponent Fumbles Recovered	1	0
Penalties	4	0
Yards Penalized	61	0
Field Goals	2	2
Field Goals Attempted	4	3
Third-Down Efficiency	6/13	5/11
Fourth-Down Efficiency	0/1	1/2
Time of Possession	31:23	28:37

INDIVIDUAL STATISTICS

RUSHING: DEN: Davis 25-102, Griffith 4-9, Loville 2-8, Elway 3-2, R. Smith 1-1, Brister 1-(-1). ATL: J. Anderson 18-96, Chandler 4-30, Dwight 1-5.

PASSING: DEN: Elway 18-29-336-1. ATL: Chandler 19-35-219-1.

RECEIVING: DEN: R. Smith 5-152, McCaffrey 5-72, Chamberlain 3-29, Davis 2-50, Sharpe 2-26, Griffith 1-7. ATL: Mathis 7-85, Martin 5-79, J. Anderson 3-16, Harris 2-21, Santiago 1-13, Kozlowski 1-5.

KICKOFF RETURNS: DEN: Hebron 2-42, Chamberlain 1-2. ATL: Dwight 5-210, Kozlowski 2-17.

PUNTING: DEN: Rouen 1-35-35-0. ATL: Stryzinski 1-39-39-0.

INTERCEPTIONS: DEN: Gordon 2-108-58-0, Johnson 1-28-28-0. ATL: Bradford 1-1-1-0.

SUPER BOWL XXXII

Qualcomm Stadium, San Diego, California
January 25, 1998, Attendance: 68,912

DENVER 31, GREEN BAY 24—Terrell Davis rushed for 157 yards and a Super Bowl-record 3 touchdowns to lead the Broncos to their first NFL championship and break the NFC's streak of Super Bowl victories at 13. The defending Super Bowl champion Packers took the opening kickoff and marched 76 yards in just over four minutes, scoring the first points on Brett Favre's 22-yard touchdown pass to Antonio Freeman. The Broncos responded with a 10-play, 58-yard drive capped by Davis's 1-yard run to tie the game. Tyrone Braxton intercepted Favre two plays later, and John Elway scored on a third-and-goal play to begin the second quarter. Steve Atwater forced Favre to fumble three plays later, and Neil Smith recovered at the Packers' 33. Jason Elam converted a 51-yard field goal, the second longest in Super Bowl history, to give the Broncos a 17-7 lead with 12:21 left in the half. After an exchange of punts, the Packers produced a 17-play, 95-yard drive that consumed 7:26 and finished with Favre's 6-yard touchdown pass to Mark Chmura on third-and-5 with 12 seconds left in the half. Tyrone Williams forced and recovered Davis's fumble at the Broncos' 26 on the first play from scrimmage in the second half. However, the Broncos' defense kept the Packers out of the end zone as Ryan Longwell's 27-yard field goal tied the game with 11:59 left in the third quarter. After another exchange of punts, Elway's 36-yard pass to Ed McCaffrey keyed a 13-play, 92-yard drive capped by Davis's 1-yard touchdown run with 34 seconds left in the third quarter. Tim McKyer recovered Freeman's fumble at the Packers' 22 on the ensuing kickoff return, giving the Broncos a golden opportunity, but Eugene Robinson intercepted Elway's pass in the end zone on the next play. Sparked by Robinson's play, the Packers took just four plays, three on passes to Freeman, to score the tying touchdown with 13:32 remaining. Each defense stiffened, forcing two punts, but the Broncos got great field position following Craig Hentrich's 39-yard punt to the Packers' 49 with 3:27 left and the score tied 24-24. Davis rushed for 2 yards on the first play, but Darrius Holland's 15-yard facemask penalty moved the ball to the Packers' 32. Elway threw a 23-yard pass to Howard Griffith two plays later, and after a holding penalty, Davis rushed 17 yards to the Packers' 1 with 1:47 left. After a timeout, Davis waltzed into the end zone to give Denver a 31-24 lead with 1:45 remaining. Freeman returned the kickoff 22 yards to the Broncos' 30, and Favre completed 22- and 13-yard screen passes to Dorsey Levens to reach the Broncos' 35 with 1:04 left. But after a 4-yard pass to Levens and incompletions to Freeman and Brooks, John Mobley knocked away Favre's pass to Chmura with 32 seconds left to give the Broncos the Vince Lombardi Trophy. Elway was 12 of 22 for 123 yards, with 1 interception. Favre was 25 of 42 for 256 yards and 1 touchdown, with 1 interception. Freeman had 9 receptions for 126 yards. Davis was named the game's most valuable player.

Green Bay (NFC)	7	7	3	7	—	24
Denver (AFC)	7	10	7	7	—	31

GB — Freeman 22 pass from Favre (Longwell kick) (4:02)
Den — Davis 1 run (Elam kick) (9:21)
Den — Elway 1 run (Elam kick) (:05)
Den — FG Elam 51 (2:39)
GB — Chmura 6 pass from Favre (Longwell kick) (14:48)
GB — FG Longwell 27 (3:01)
Den — Davis 1 run (Elam kick) (14:26)
GB — Freeman 13 pass from Favre (Longwell kick) (1:28)
Den — Davis 1 run (Elam kick) (13:15)

SUPER BOWL XXXI

Louisiana Superdome, New Orleans, Louisiana
January 26, 1997, Attendance: 72,301

GREEN BAY 35, NEW ENGLAND 21— Desmond Howard returned a kickoff 99 yards for a touchdown and Brett Favre passed for 2 touchdowns and ran for a score as the Packers won their first Super Bowl in twenty-nine years. Howard, en route to garnering the MVP trophy, equaled a Super Bowl record with 244 total return yards. It was Favre's arm that struck first, as he hit Andre Rison for a 54-yard touchdown pass on the Packers' second play from scrimmage to take a 7-0 lead. Two plays later Doug Evans made a diving interception of Drew Bledsoe's pass at the 28-yard line, setting up Chris Jacke's field goal and giving the Packers a 10-0 lead just 6:18 into the Super Bowl. The Patriots answered with touchdowns on their next two possessions. Craig Newsome's pass interference penalty set up the first touchdown and a 44-yard completion from Bledsoe to Terry Glenn preceeding Ben Coates's touchdown gave New England its first and only lead. The 24 combined first quarter points were the most in Super Bowl history. Green Bay struck again 56 seconds into the second quarter as Favre hit Antonio Freeman with a Super Bowl-record 81-yard touchdown bomb. Jacke booted his second field goal on Green Bay's next possession. After a Mike Prior interception, Favre orchestrated a 74-yard, nearly 6-minute drive that concluded with a diving Favre touching the ball against the pylon to give Green Bay a 27-14 halftime lead. Curtis Martin brought the Patriots to within a score by running in from 18 yards out with 3:27 left in the third quarter. But Howard broke the Patriots' spirit by returning the ensuing kickoff a Super Bowl-record 99 yards. Favre found Mark Chmura for the 2-point conversion to finish the scoring. Bledsoe was intercepted twice in the fourth quarter as the Patriots never crossed midfield in 4 fourth-quarter possessions. Reggie White set a Super Bowl record with 3 sacks. Favre completed 14 of 27 passes for 246 yards, with no interceptions. Bledsoe completed 11 more passes than Favre, but for just 7 more yards, and threw 4 interceptions.

New England (AFC)	14	0	7	0	—	21
Green Bay (NFC)	10	17	8	0	—	35

GB — Rison 54 pass from Favre (Jacke kick) (3:32)
GB — FG Jacke 37 (6:18)
NE — Byars 1 pass from Bledsoe (Vinatieri kick) (8:25)
NE — Coates 4 pass from Bledsoe (Vinatieri kick) (12:27)
GB — Freeman 81 pass from Favre (Jacke kick) (0:56)
GB — FG Jacke 31 (6:45)
GB — Favre 2 run (Jacke kick) (13:49)
NE — Martin 18 run (Vinatieri kick) (11:33)
GB — Howard 99 kickoff return (Chmura pass from Favre) (11:50)

SUPER BOWL XXX

Sun Devil Stadium, Tempe, Arizona
January 28, 1996, Attendance: 76,347

DALLAS 27, PITTSBURGH 17—Cornerback Larry Brown's 2 interceptions led to 14 second-half points and helped lift the Cowboys to their third Super Bowl victory in the last four seasons and their record-tying fifth title overall. Brown's interceptions foiled the comeback efforts of the Steelers, and earned him the Pete Rozelle Trophy as the game's most valuable player. Dallas scored on each of its first three possessions, taking a 13-0 lead on Troy Aikman's 3-yard touchdown pass to Jay Novacek and a pair of field goals by Chris Boniol. Neil O'Donnell's 6-yard touchdown pass to Yancey Thigpen 13 seconds before halftime pulled Pittsburgh within 6 points, and the Steelers had the ball near midfield midway through the third quarter. But O'Donnell's third-down pass was intercepted by Brown at the Cowboys' 38-yard line, and his 44-yard return carried to Pittsburgh's 18. After Aikman's 17-yard completion to Michael Irvin, Emmitt Smith ran 1 yard for the touchdown that put Dallas ahead again by 13 points. The Steelers rallied, though, behind Norm Johnson's 46-yard field goal, a successful surprise onside kick, and Byron (Bam) Morris's 1-yard touchdown run with 6:36 to play in the game. And when they forced a punt and took possession at their own 32-yard line trailing only 20-17 with 4:15 remaining, it appeared they might have a chance to break the NFC's recent domination in the Super Bowl. But on second down, Brown struck again, intercepting O'Donnell's pass at the 39 and returning it 33 yards to the 6. Two plays later, Smith barreled over from 4 yards out for the clinching touchdown with 3:43 to go. Pittsburgh limited the Cowboys' powerful running game to only 56 yards and enjoyed a whopping 201-61 advantage in total yards in the second half, but could not overcome the 3 interceptions (another came on the game's final play) thrown by O'Donnell, the NFL's career leader for fewest interceptions per pass attempt. In all, O'Donnell completed 28 of 49 passes for 239 yards. Morris rushed for a game-high 73 yards on 19 carries. For Dallas, Aikman completed 15 of 23 pass attempts for 209 yards. The Cowboys' victory was the twelfth in a row for NFC teams over AFC teams in the Super Bowl.

Dallas (NFC)	10	3	7	7	—	27
Pittsburgh (AFC)	0	7	0	10	—	17

Dall — FG Boniol 42 (2:55)
Dall — Novacek 3 pass from Aikman (Boniol kick) (9:37)
Dall — FG Boniol 35 (8:57)
Pitt — Thigpen 6 pass from O'Donnell (N. Johnson kick) (14:47)
Dall — E. Smith 1 run (Boniol kick) (8:18)
Pitt — FG N. Johnson 46 (3:40)
Pitt — Morris 1 run (N. Johnson kick) (8:24)
Dall — E. Smith 4 run (Boniol kick) (11:17)

SUPER BOWL XXIX

Joe Robbie Stadium, Miami, Florida
January 29, 1995, Attendance: 74,107

SAN FRANCISCO 49, SAN DIEGO 26—Steve Young passed for a record 6 touchdowns, and the 49ers became the first team to win five Super Bowls when they routed the Chargers. Young, the game's most valuable player, directed an explosive offense that generated 7 touchdowns, 28 first downs, and 455 total yards. He completed 24 of 36 passes for 325 yards, and broke the record of 5 touchdown passes set by fromer 49ers quarterback Joe Montana in Super Bowl XXIV. San Francisco wasted little time scoring, taking the lead for good on Young's 44-yard touchdown pass to Jerry Rice only three plays and 1:24 into the game. The next time they had the ball, the 49ers marched 79 yards in four plays, taking a 14-0 lead when Young teamed with running back Ricky Watters on a 51-yard touchdown pass with 10:05 still to play in the opening period. San Diego then put together its most impressive possession of the game, a 13-play, 78-yard drive that consumed more than 7 minutes and was capped by Natrone Means's 1-yard touchdown run, to cut its deficit to 14-7 late in the quarter. But San Francisco countered with a 70-yard drive of its own, and Young's 5-yard touchdown pass to fullback William Floyd made it 21-7. Young's fourth touchdown pass of the half, 8 yards to Watters 4:44 before halftime, increased the advantage to 28-7, and the Chargers could get no closer than 18 points after that. Watters, who ran 9 yards for a touchdown in the third quarter, equaled the Super Bowl record with 3 touchdowns. Rice also scored 3 touchdowns (the second time in his career he'd done that in a Super Bowl) while catching 10 passes for 149 yards. He established career records for receptions, yards, and touchdowns in a Super Bowl. Young, who scrambled 21 yards and 15 yards to set up touchdowns in the first half, was the game's leading rusher with 49 yards on 5 carries. San Diego's Means, who rushed for 1,350 yards during the regular season, was limited to 33 yards on 13 attempts. Chargers quarterback Stan Humphries completed 24 of 49 passes for 275 yards. Rookie Andre Coleman became only the third player in Super Bowl history to return a kickoff for a touchdown, going 98 yards in the third quarter. The 75 points scored by the two teams established another record, breaking the previous mark of 69 set in Dallas's 52-17 victory over Buffalo in XXVII. The 49ers' victory was the eleventh straight for NFC teams over AFC teams in the Super Bowl.

San Diego (AFC)	7	3	8	8	—	26
San Francisco (NFC)	14	14	14	7	—	49

SF — Rice 44 pass from S. Young (Brien kick) (1:24)
SF — Watters 51 pass from S. Young (Brien kick) (4:55)
SD — Means 1 run (Carney kick) (12:16)
SF — Floyd 5 pass from S. Young (Brien kick) (1:58)
SF — Watters 8 pass from S. Young (Brien kick) (10:16)
SD — FG Carney 31 (13:16)
SF — Watters 9 run (Brien kick) (5:25)
SF — Rice 15 pass from S. Young (Brien kick) (11:42)
SD — Coleman 98 kickoff return (Seay pass from Humphries) (11:59)
SF — Rice 7 pass from S. Young (Brien kick) (1:11)
SD — Martin 30 pass from Humphries (Pupunu pass from Humphries) (12:35)

SUPER BOWL XXVIII

Georgia Dome, Atlanta, Georgia
January 30, 1994, Attendance: 72,817

DALLAS 30, BUFFALO 13—Emmitt Smith rushed for 132 yards and 2 second-half touchdowns to power the Cowboys to their second consecutive NFL title. By winning, Dallas joined San Francisco and Pittsburgh as the only franchises with four Super Bowl victories. The Bills, meanwhile, extended a dubious string by losing in the Super Bowl for the fourth consecutive year. To win, the Cowboys had to rally from a 13-6 halftime deficit. Buffalo had forged its lead on Thurman Thomas's 4-yard touchdown run and a pair of field goals by Steve Christie, including a 54-yard kick, the longest in Super Bowl history. But just 55 seconds into the second half, Thomas was stripped of the ball by Dallas defensive tackle Leon Lett. Safety James Washington recovered and weaved his way 46 yards for a touchdown to tie the game at 13-13. After forcing the Bills to punt, the Cowboys began their next possession on their 36-yard line and Smith, the game's most valuable player, took over. He carried 7 times for 61 yards on the ensuing 8-play, 64-yard drive, capping the march with a 15-yard touchdown run to give Dallas the lead for good with 8:42 remaining in the third quarter. Early in the fourth quarter, Washington intercepted Jim Kelly's pass and returned it 12 yards to Buffalo's 34. A penalty moved the ball back to the 39, but Smith carried twice for 10 yards and caught a screen pass for 9, and quarterback Troy Aikman completed a 16-yard pass to Alvin Harper to give the Cowboys a first-and-goal at the 6. Smith took it from there, cracking the end zone on fourth-and-goal from the 1 to put Dallas ahead 27-13 with 9:50 remaining. Eddie Murray's third field goal, from 20 yards with 2:50 left, ended any doubt about the game's outcome. Smith had 30 carries in all, with 19 of his attempts and 92 yards coming after intermission. Washington, normally a reserve who played most of the game because the Cowboys used five defensive backs to combat the Bills' No-Huddle offense, had 11 tackles and forced another fumble by Thomas in the first quarter. Aikman completed 19 of 27 passes for 207 yards. Buffalo's Kelly completed a Super Bowl-record 31 passes in 50 attempts for 260 yards. Dallas, the first team in NFL history to begin the regular season 0-2 and go on to win the Super Bowl, also became the fifth to win back-to-back titles, following Green Bay, Miami, Pittsburgh (the Steelers did it twice), and San Francisco. Buffalo became the third team, along with Minnesota and Denver, to lose four Super Bowls. The Cowboys' victory was the tenth in succession for the NFC over the AFC.

Dallas (NFC)	6	0	14	10	—	30
Buffalo (AFC)	3	10	0	0	—	13

Dall — FG Murray 41 (2:19)
Buff — FG Christie 54 (4:41)
Dall — FG Murray 24 (11:05)
Buff — Thomas 4 run (Christie kick) (2:34)
Buff — FG Christie 28 (15:00)
Dall — Washington 46 fumble return (Murray kick) (0:55)
Dall — E. Smith 15 run (Murray kick) (6:18)
Dall — E. Smith 1 run (Murray kick) (5:10)
Dall — FG Murray 20 (12:10)

SUPER BOWL XXVII

Rose Bowl, Pasadena, California
January 31, 1993, Attendance: 98,374

DALLAS 52, BUFFALO 17—Troy Aikman passed for 4 touchdowns, Emmitt Smith rushed for 108 yards, and the Cowboys converted 9 turnovers into 35 points while coasting to the victory. Dallas's win was its third in its record sixth Super Bowl appearance; the Bills became the first team to drop three in succession. Buffalo led 7-0 until the first 2 of its record number of turnovers helped the Cowboys take the lead for good late in the opening quarter. First, Dallas safety James Washington intercepted Jim Kelly's pass and returned it 13 yards to the Bills' 47, setting up Aikman's 23-yard touchdown pass to tight end Jay Novacek with 1:36 remaining in the period. On the next play from scrimmage, Kelly was sacked by Charles Haley and fumbled at the Bills' 2-yard line where the Cowboys' Jimmie Jones picked up the loose ball and ran 2 yards for a touchdown. Dallas, which recovered 5 fumbles and intercepted 4 passes, struck just as quickly late in the first half, when Aikman tossed 19- and 18-yard touchdown passes to Michael Irvin 18 seconds apart to give the Cowboys a 28-10 lead at intermission. The second score was set up when Bills running back Thurman Thomas lost a fumble at his 19-yard line. Buffalo scored for the last time when backup quarterback Frank Reich, playing because Kelly was injured while attempting to pass midway through the second quarter, threw a 40-yard touchdown pass to Don Beebe on the final play of the third period to trim the deficit to 31-17. But Dallas put the game out of reach by scoring three times in a span of 2:33 of the fourth quarter. Aikman, the game's most valuable player, completed 22 of 30 passes for 273 yards. The victory was the ninth in succession for the NFC over the AFC.

Buffalo (AFC)	7	3	7	0	—	17
Dallas (NFC)	14	14	3	21	—	52

Buff — Thomas 2 run (Christie kick) (5:00)
Dall — Novacek 23 pass from Aikman (Elliott kick) (13:24)
Dall — J. Jones 2 fumble recovery return (Elliott kick) (13:39)
Buff — FG Christie 21 (11:36)
Dall — Irvin 19 pass from Aikman (Elliott kick) (13:06)
Dall — Irvin 18 pass from Aikman (Elliott kick) (13:24)
Dall — FG Elliott 20 (6:39)

Buff — Beebe 40 pass from Reich (Christie kick) (15:00)
Dall — Harper 45 pass from Aikman (Elliott kick) (4:56)
Dall — E. Smith 10 run (Elliott kick) (6:48)
Dall — Norton 9 fumble recovery return (Elliott kick) (7:29)

SUPER BOWL XXVI

Metrodome, Minneapolis, Minnesota
January 26, 1992, Attendance: 63,130

WASHINGTON 37, BUFFALO 24—Mark Rypien passed for 292 yards and 2 touchdowns as the Redskins overwhelmed the Bills to win their third Super Bowl in the past 10 years. Rypien, the game's most valuable player, completed 18 of 33 passes, including a 10-yard scoring strike to Earnest Byner and a 30-yard touchdown to Gary Clark. The latter came late in the third quarter after Buffalo had trimmed a 24-0 deficit to 24-10, and effectively put the game out of reach. Washington went on to lead by as much as 37-10 before the Bills made it close wih a pair of touchdowns in the final six minutes. Though the Redskins struggled early, converting their first three drives inside the Bills' 20-yard line into only 3 points, they built a 17-0 halftime lead. And they made it 24-0 just 16 seconds into the second half, after Kurt Gouveia intercepted Buffalo quarterback Jim Kelly's pass on the first play of the third quarter and returned it 23 yards to the Bills' 2. One play later, Gerald Riggs scored his second touchdown of the game to make it 24-0. Kelly, forced to bring Buffalo from behind, completed 28 of a Super Bowl-record 58 passes for 275 yards and 2 touchdowns, but was intercepted 4 times. Bills running back Thurman Thomas, who had an AFC-high 1,407 yards rushing and an NFL-best 2,038 total yards from scrimmage during the regular season, ran for only 13 yards on 10 carries and was limited to 27 yards on 4 receptions. Clark had 7 catches for 114 yards and Art Monk added 7 for 113 for the Redskins, who amassed 417 yards of total offense while limiting the explosive Bills to 283. Washington's Joe Gibbs became only the third head coach to win three Super Bowls.

Washington (NFC)	0	17	14	6	—	37
Buffalo (AFC)	0	0	10	14	—	24

Wash — FG Lohmiller 34 (1:58)
Wash — Byner 10 pass from Rypien (Lohmiller kick) (5:06)
Wash — Riggs 1 run (Lohmiller kick) (7:43)
Wash — Riggs 2 run (Lohmiller kick) (0:16)
Buff — FG Norwood 21 (3:01)
Buff — Thomas 1 run (Norwood kick) (9:02)
Wash — Clark 30 pass from Rypien (Lohmiller kick) (13:36)
Wash — FG Lohmiller 25 (0:06)
Wash — FG Lohmiller 39 (3:24)
Buff — Metzelaars 2 pass from Kelly (Norwood kick) (9:01)
Buff — Beebe 4 pass from Kelly (Norwood kick) (11:05)

SUPER BOWL XXV

Tampa Stadium, Tampa, Florida
January 27, 1991, Attendance: 73,813

NEW YORK GIANTS 20, BUFFALO 19—The NFC champion New York Giants won their second Super Bowl in five years with a 20-19 victory over AFC titlist Buffalo. New York, employing its ball-control offense, had possession for 40 minutes, 33 seconds, a Super Bowl record. The Bills, who scored 95 points in their previous two playoff games leading to Super Bowl XXV, had the ball for less than eight minutes in the second half and just 19:27 for the game. Fourteen of New York's 73 plays came on its initial drive of the third quarter, which covered 75 yards and consumed a Super Bowl-record 9:29 before running back Ottis Anderson ran 1 yard for a touchdown. Giants quarterback Jeff Hostetler kept the long drive going by converting three third-down plays—an 11-yard pass to running back David Meggett on third-and-eight, a 14-yard toss to wide receiver Mark Ingram on third-and-13, and a 9-yard pass to Howard Cross on third-and-four—to give New York a 17-12 lead in the third quarter. Buffalo jumped to a 12-3 lead midway through the second quarter before Hostetler completed a 14-yard scoring strike to wide receiver Stephen Baker to close the score to 12-10 at halftime. Buffalo's Thurman Thomas ran 31 yards for a touchdown on the opening play of the fourth quarter to help Buffalo recapture the lead 19-17. Matt Bahr's 21-yard field goal gave the Giants a 20-19 lead, but Buffalo's Scott Norwood had a chance to win the game with seconds remaining before his 47-yard field-goal attempt sailed wide right. Hostetler completed 20 of 32 passes for 222 yards and 1 touchdown. Anderson rushed 21 times for 102 yards and 1 touchdown to capture most-valuable-player honors. Thomas totaled 190 scrimmage yards, rushing 15 times for 135 yards and catching 5 passes for 55 yards.

Buffalo (AFC)	3	9	0	7	—	19
N.Y. Giants (NFC)	3	7	7	3	—	20

NYG — FG Bahr 28 (7:46)
Buff — FG Norwood 23 (9:09)
Buff — D. Smith 1 run (Norwood kick) (2:30)
Buff — Safety, B. Smith tackled Hostetler in end zone (6:33)
NYG — Baker 14 pass from Hostetler (Bahr kick) (14:35)
NYG — Anderson 1 run (Bahr kick) (9:29)
Buff — Thomas 31 run (Norwood kick) (0:08)
NYG — FG Bahr 21 (7:40)

SUPER BOWL XXIV

Louisiana Superdome, New Orleans, Louisiana
January 28, 1990, Attendance: 72,919

SAN FRANCISCO 55, DENVER 10—NFC titlist San Francisco won its fourth Super Bowl championship with a 55-10 victory over AFC champion Denver. The 49ers, who also won Super Bowls XVI, XIX, and XXIII, tied the Pittsburgh Steelers for most Super Bowl victories. The Steelers captured Super Bowls IX, X, XIII, and XIV. San Francisco's 55 points broke the previous Super Bowl scoring mark of 46 points by Chicago in Super Bowl XX. San Francisco scored touchdowns on four of its six first-half possessions to hold a 27-3 lead at halftime. Interceptions by Michael Walter and Chet Brooks ended the Broncos' first two possessions of the second half. San Francisco quarterback Joe Montana was named the Super Bowl most valuable player for a record third time. Montana completed 22 of 29 passes for 297 yards and a Super Bowl-record 5 touchdowns. Jerry Rice, Super Bowl XXIII most valuable player, caught 7 passes for 148 yards and 3 touchdowns. The 49ers' domination included first downs (28 to 12), net yards (461 to 167), and time of possession (39:31 to 20:29).

San Francisco (NFC)	13	14	14	14	—	55
Denver (AFC)	3	0	7	0	—	10

SF — Rice 20 pass from Montana (Cofer kick) (4:54)
Den — FG Treadwell 42 (8:13)
SF — Jones 7 pass from Montana (kick failed) (14:57)
SF — Rathman 1 run (Cofer kick) (7:45)
SF — Rice 38 pass from Montana (Cofer kick) (14:26)
SF — Rice 28 pass from Montana (Cofer kick) (2:12)
SF — Taylor 35 pass from Montana (Cofer kick) (5:16)
Den — Elway 3 run (Treadwell kick) (8:07)
SF — Rathman 3 run (Cofer kick) (0:03)
SF — Craig 1 run (Cofer kick) (1:13)

SUPER BOWL XXIII

Joe Robbie Stadium, Miami, Florida
January 22, 1989, Attendance: 75,129

SAN FRANCISCO 20, CINCINNATI 16—NFC champion San Francisco captured its third Super Bowl of the 1980s by defeating AFC champion Cincinnati 20-16. The 49ers, who also won Super Bowls XVI and XIX, became the first NFC team to win three Super Bowls. Pittsburgh, with four Super Bowl titles (IX, X, XIII, and XIV), and the Oakland/Los Angeles Raiders, with three (XI, XV, and XVIII), lead AFC franchises. Even though San Francisco held an advantage in total net yards (453 to 229), the 49ers found themselves trailing the Bengals late in the game. With the score 13-13, Cincinnati took a 16-13 lead on Jim Breech's 40-yard field goal with 3:20 remaining. It was Breech's third field goal of the day, following earlier successes from 34 and 43 yards. The 49ers started their winning drive at their 8-yard line. Over the next 11 plays, San Francisco covered 92 yards with the decisive score coming on a 10-yard pass from quarterback Joe Montana to wide receiver John Taylor with 34 seconds remaining. At halftime, the score was 3-3, the first time in Super Bowl history the game was tied at intermission. After the teams traded third-period field goals, the Bengals jumped ahead 13-6 on Stanford Jennings's 93-yard kickoff return for a touchdown with 34 seconds remaining in the quarter. The 49ers didn't waste any time coming back as they covered 85 yards in four plays, concluding with Montana's 14-yard scoring pass to Jerry Rice 57 seconds into the final stanza. Rice was named the game's most valuable player after compiling 11 catches for a Super Bowl-record 215 yards. Montana completed 23 of 36 passes for a Super Bowl-record 357 yards and 2 touchdowns.

Cincinnati (AFC)	0	3	10	3	—	16
San Francisco (NFC)	3	0	3	14	—	20

SF — FG Cofer 41 (11:46)
Cin — FG Breech 34 (13:45)
Cin — FG Breech 43 (9:21)
SF — FG Cofer 32 (14:10)
Cin — Jennings 93 kickoff return (Breech kick) (14:26)
SF — Rice 14 pass from Montana (Cofer kick) (0:57)
Cin — FG Breech 40 (11:40)
SF — Taylor 10 pass from Montana (Cofer kick) (14:26)

SUPER BOWL XXII

San Diego Jack Murphy Stadium, San Diego, California
January 31, 1988, Attendance: 73,302

WASHINGTON 42, DENVER 10—NFC champion Washington won Super Bowl XXII and its second NFL championship of the 1980s with a 42-10 decision over AFC champion Denver. The Redskins, who also won Super Bowl XVII, enjoyed a record-setting second quarter en route to the victory. The Broncos broke in front 10-0 when quarterback John Elway threw a 56-yard touchdown pass to wide receiver Ricky Nattiel on the Broncos' first play from scrimmage. Following a Washington punt, Denver's Rich Karlis kicked a 24-yard field goal to cap a seven-play, 61-yard scoring drive. The Redskins then erupted for 35 points on five straight possessions in the second period and coasted thereafter. The 35 points established an NFL postseason mark for most points in a period. Redskins quarterback Doug Williams led the second-period explosion by passing for a Super Bowl record-tying 4 touchdowns, including 80- and 50-yard passes to wide receiver Ricky Sanders, a 27-yard toss to wide receiver Gary Clark, and an 8-yard pass to tight end Clint Didier. Washington scored 5 touchdowns in 18 plays with total time of possession of only 5:47. Overall, Williams completed 18 of 29 passes for 340 yards and was named the game's most valuable player. His pass-yardage total eclipsed the Super Bowl record of 331 yards by Joe Montana of San Francisco in Super Bowl XIX. Sanders ended with 193 yards on 8 catches, breaking the previous Super Bowl yardage record of 161 yards by Lynn Swann of Pittsburgh in Game X. Rookie running back Timmy Smith was the game's leading rusher with 22 carries for a Super Bowl-record 204 yards, breaking the previous mark of 191 yards by Marcus Allen of the Raiders in Game XVIII. Smith also scored twice on runs of 58 and 4 yards. Washington's 6 touchdowns and 602 total yards gained also set Super Bowl records. Redskins cornerback Barry Wilburn had 2 of the team's 3 interceptions, and strong safety Alvin Walton had 2 of Washington's 5 sacks.

Washington (NFC)	0	35	0	7 —	42
Denver (AFC)	10	0	0	0 —	10

Den — Nattiel 56 pass from Elway (Karlis kick) (1:57)
Den — FG Karlis 24 (5:51)
Wash — Sanders 80 pass from Williams (Haji-Sheikh kick) (0:53)
Wash — Clark 27 pass from Williams (Haji-Sheikh kick) (4:45)
Wash — Smith 58 run (Haji-Sheikh kick) (8:33)
Wash — Sanders 50 pass from Williams (Haji-Sheikh kick) (11:18)
Wash — Didier 8 pass from Williams (Haji-Sheikh kick) (13:56)
Wash — Smith 4 run (Haji-Sheikh kick) (1:51)

SUPER BOWL XXI

Rose Bowl, Pasadena, California
January 25, 1987, Attendance: 101,063

NEW YORK GIANTS 39, DENVER 20—The NFC champion New York Giants captured their first NFL title since 1956 when they downed the AFC champion Denver Broncos 39-20 in Super Bowl XXI. The victory marked the NFC's fifth NFL title in the past six seasons. The Broncos, behind the passing of quarterback John Elway, who was 13 of 20 for 187 yards in the first half, held a 10-9 lead at intermission, the narrowest halftime margin in Super Bowl history. Denver's Rich Karlis opened the scoring with a Super Bowl record-tying 48-yard field goal. New York drove 78 yards in nine plays on the next series to take a 7-3 lead on quarterback Phil Simms's 6-yard touchdown pass to tight end Zeke Mowatt. The Broncos came right back with a 58-yard scoring drive on six plays capped by Elway's 4-yard touchdown run. The only scoring in the second period was the sack of Elway in the end zone by defensive end George Martin for a New York safety. The Giants produced a key defensive stand early in the second quarter when the Broncos had a first down at the New York 1-yard line, but failed to score on three running plays and Karlis's 23-yard missed field-goal attempt. The Giants took command of the game in the third period en route to a 30-point second half, the most ever scored in one half of Super Bowl play. New York took the lead for good on tight end Mark Bavaro's 13-yard touchdown catch 4:52 into the third period. The nine-play, 63-yard scoring drive included the successful conversion of a fourth-and-1 play on the New York 46-yard line. Denver was limited to only 2 net yards on 10 offensive plays in the third period. Simms set Super Bowl records for most consecutive completions (10) and highest completion percentage (88 percent on 22 completions in 25 attempts). He also passed for 268 yards and 3 touchdowns and was named the game's most valuable player. New York running back Joe Morris was the game's leading rusher with 20 carries for 67 yards. Denver wide receiver Vance Johnson led all receivers with 5 catches for 121 yards.

Denver (AFC)	10	0	0	10 —	20
N.Y. Giants (NFC)	7	2	17	13 —	39

Den — FG Karlis 48 (4:09)
NYG — Mowatt 6 pass from Simms (Allegre kick) (9:33)
Den — Elway 4 run (Karlis kick) (12:54)
NYG — Safety, Martin tackled Elway in end zone (12:14)
NYG — Bavaro 13 pass from Simms (Allegre kick) (4:52)
NYG — FG Allegre 21 (11:06)
NYG — Morris 1 run (Allegre kick) (14:36)
NYG — McConkey 6 pass from Simms (Allegre kick) (4:04)
Den — FG Karlis 28 (8:59)
NYG — Anderson 2 run (kick failed) (10:42)
Den — V. Johnson 47 pass from Elway (Karlis kick) (12:54)

SUPER BOWL XX

Louisiana Superdome, New Orleans, Louisiana
January 26, 1986, Attendance: 73,818

CHICAGO 46, NEW ENGLAND 10—The NFC champion Chicago Bears, seeking their first NFL title since 1963, scored a Super Bowl-record 46 points in downing AFC champion New England 46-10 in Super Bowl XX. The previous record for most points in a Super Bowl was 38, shared by San Francisco in XIX and the Los Angeles Raiders in XVIII. The Bears' league-leading defense tied the Super Bowl record for sacks (7) and limited the Patriots to a record-low 7 rushing yards. New England took the quickest lead in Super Bowl history when Tony Franklin kicked a 36-yard field goal with 1:19 elapsed in the first period. The score came about because of Larry McGrew's fumble recovery at the Chicago 19-yard line. However, the Bears rebounded for a 23-3 first-half lead, while building a yardage advantage of 236 total yards to New England's minus 19. Running back Matt Suhey rushed 8 times for 37 yards, including an 11-yard touchdown run, and caught 1 pass for 24 yards in the first half. After the Patriot's first drive of the second half ended with a punt to the Bears' 4-yard line, Chicago marched 96 yards in nine plays with quarterback Jim McMahon's 1-yard scoring run capping the drive. McMahon became the first quarterback in Super Bowl history to rush for a pair of touchdowns. The Bears completed their scoring via a 28-yard interception return by reserve cornerback Reggie Phillips, a 1-yard run by defensive tackle/fullback William Perry, and a safety when defensive end Henry Waechter tackled Patriots quarterback Steve Grogan in the end zone. Bears defensive end Richard Dent became the fourth defender to be named the game's most valuable player after contributing 1½ sacks. The Bears' victory margin of 36 points was the largest in Super Bowl history, bettering the previous mark of 29 by the Los Angeles Raiders when they topped Washington 38-9 in Game XVIII. McMahon completed 12 of 20 passes for 256 yards before leaving the game in the fourth period with a wrist injury. The NFL's all-time leading rusher, Bears running back Walter Payton, carried 22 times for 61 yards. Wide receiver Willie Gault caught 4 passes for 129 yards, the fourth-most receiving yards in a Super Bowl. Chicago coach Mike Ditka became the second man (Tom Flores of Raiders was the other) to win a Super Bowl ring as a player and as a coach.

Chicago (NFC)	13	10	21	2 —	46
New England (AFC)	3	0	0	7 —	10

NE — FG Franklin 36 (1:19)
Chi — FG Butler 28 (5:40)
Chi — FG Butler 24 (13:34)
Chi — Suhey 11 run (Butler kick) (14:37)
Chi — McMahon 2 run (Butler kick) (7:36)
Chi — FG Butler 24 (15:00)
Chi — McMahon 1 run (Butler kick) (7:38)
Chi — Phillips 28 interception return (Butler kick) (8:44)
Chi — Perry 1 run (Butler kick) (11:38)
NE — Fryar 8 pass from Grogan (Franklin kick) (1:46)
Chi — Safety, Waechter tackled Grogan in end zone (9:24)

SUPER BOWL XIX

Stanford Stadium, Stanford, California
January 20, 1985, Attendance: 84,059

SAN FRANCISCO 38, MIAMI 16—The San Francisco 49ers captured their second Super Bowl title with a dominating offense and a defense that tamed Miami's explosive passing attack. The Dolphins held a 10-7 lead at the end of the first period, which represented the most points scored by two teams in an opening quarter of a Super Bowl. However, the 49ers used excellent field position in the second period to build a 28-16 halftime lead. Running back Roger Craig set a Super Bowl record by scoring 3 touchdowns on pass receptions of 8 and 16 yards and a run of 2 yards. San Francisco's Joe Montana was voted the game's most valuable player. He joined Green Bay's Bart Starr and Pittsburgh's Terry Bradshaw as the only two-time Super Bowl most valuable players. Montana completed 24 of 35 passes for a Super Bowl-record 331 yards and 3 touchdowns, and rushed 5 times for 59 yards, including a 6-yard touchdown. Craig had 58 yards on 15 carries and caught 7 passes for 77 yards. Wendell Tyler rushed 13 times for 65 yards and had 4 catches for 70 yards. Dwight Clark had 6 receptions for 77 yards, while Russ Francis had 5 for 60. San Francisco's 537 total net yards bettered the previous Super Bowl record of 429 yards by Oakland in Super Bowl XI. The 49ers also held a time of possession advantage over the Dolphins of 37:11 to 22:49.

Miami (AFC)	10	6	0	0 —	16
San Francisco (NFC)	7	21	10	0 —	38

Mia — FG von Schamann 37 (7:36)
SF — Monroe 33 pass from Montana (Wersching kick) (11:48)
Mia — D. Johnson 2 pass from Marino (von Schamann kick) (14:15)
SF — Craig 8 pass from Montana (Wersching kick) (3:26)
SF — Montana 6 run (Wersching kick) (8:02)
SF — Craig 2 run (Wersching kick) (12:55)
Mia — FG von Schamann 31 (14:48)
Mia — FG von Schamann 30 (15:00)
SF — FG Wersching 27 (4:48)
SF — Craig 16 pass from Montana (Wersching kick) (8:42)

SUPER BOWL XVIII

Tampa Stadium, Tampa, Florida
January 22, 1984, Attendance: 72,920

LOS ANGELES RAIDERS 38, WASHINGTON 9—The Los Angeles Raiders dominated the Washington Redskins from the beginning in Super Bowl XVIII and achieved the most lopsided victory in Super Bowl history, surpassing Green Bay's 35-10 win over Kansas City in Super Bowl I. The Raiders took a 7-0 lead 4:52 into the game when Derrick Jensen blocked Jeff Hayes's punt and recovered it in the end zone for a touchdown. With 9:14 remaining in the first half, Raiders quarterback Jim Plunkett fired a 12-yard touchdown pass to wide receiver Cliff Branch to complete a three-play, 65-yard drive. Washington cut the Raiders' lead to 14-3 on a 24-yard field goal by Mark Moseley. With seven seconds left in the first half, Raiders linebacker Jack Squirek intercepted Joe Theismann's pass at the Redskins' 5-yard line and ran it in for a touchdown to give Los Angeles a 21-3 halftime lead. In the third period, running back Marcus Allen, who rushed for a Super Bowl-record 191 yards on 20 carries, increased the Raiders' lead to 35-9 on touchdown runs of 5 and 74 yards, the latter erasing the Super Bowl record of 58 yards set by Baltimore's Tom Matte in Game III. Allen was named the game's most valuable player. The victory over Washington raised Raiders coach Tom Flores' playoff record to 8-1, including a 27-10 win against Philadelphia in Super Bowl XV. The 38 points scored by the Raiders were the highest total by a Super Bowl team. The previous high was 35 points by Green Bay in Game I.

Washington (NFC)	0	3	6	0 —	9
L.A. Raiders (AFC)	7	14	14	3 —	38

Raiders — Jensen recovered blocked punt in end zone (Bahr kick) (4:52)
Raiders — Branch 12 pass from Plunkett (Bahr kick) (5:46)
Wash — FG Moseley 24 (11:55)
Raiders — Squirek 5 interception return (Bahr kick) (14:53)
Wash — Riggins 1 run (kick blocked) (4:08)
Raiders — Allen 5 run (Bahr kick) (7:54)
Raiders — Allen 74 run (Bahr kick) (15:00)
Raiders — FG Bahr 21 (12:36)

SUPER BOWL XVII

Rose Bowl, Pasadena, California
January 30, 1983, Attendance: 103,667

WASHINGTON 27, MIAMI 17—Fullback John Riggins ran for a Super Bowl-record 166 yards on 38 carries to spark Washington to a 27-17 victory over AFC champion Miami. It was Riggins's fourth straight

100-yard rushing game during the playoffs, also a record. The win marked Washington's first NFL title since 1942, and was only the second time in Super Bowl history NFL/NFC teams scored consecutive victories (Green Bay did it in Super Bowls I and II and San Francisco won Super Bowl XVI). The Redskins, under second-year head coach Joe Gibbs, used a balanced offense that accounted for 400 total yards (a Super Bowl-record 276 yards rushing and 124 passing), second in Super Bowl history to 429 yards by Oakland in Super Bowl XI. The Dolphins built a 17-10 halftime lead on a 76-yard touchdown pass from quarterback David Woodley to wide receiver Jimmy Cefalo 6:49 into the first period, a 20-yard field goal by Uwe von Schamann with 6:00 left in the half, and a Super Bowl-record 98-yard kickoff return by Fulton Walker with 1:38 remaining. Washington had tied the score at 10-10 with 1:51 left on a 4-yard touchdown pass from Joe Theismann to wide receiver Alvin Garrett. Mark Moseley started the Redskins' scoring with a 31-yard field goal late in the first period, and added a 20-yard kick midway through the third period to cut the Dolphins' lead to 17-13. Riggins, who was voted the game's most valuable player, gave Washington its first lead of the game with 10:01 left when he ran 43 yards off left tackle for a touchdown in a fourth-and-1 situation. Wide receiver Charlie Brown caught a 6-yard scoring pass from Theismann with 1:55 left to complete the scoring. The Dolphins managed only 176 yards (142 in first half). Theismann completed 15 of 23 passes for 143 yards, with 2 touchdowns and 2 interceptions. For Miami, Woodley was 4 of 14 for 97 yards, with 1 touchdown, and 1 interception. Don Strock was 0 for 3 in relief.

Miami (AFC)	7	10	0	0	—	17
Washington (NFC)	0	10	3	14	—	27

Mia — Cefalo 76 pass from Woodley (von Schamann kick) (6:49)
Wash — FG Moseley 31 (0:21)
Mia — FG von Schamann 20 (9:00)
Wash — Garrett 4 pass from Theismann (Moseley kick) (13:09)
Mia — Walker 98 kickoff return (von Schamann kick) (13:22)
Wash — FG Moseley 20 (6:51)
Wash — Riggins 43 run (Moseley kick) (4:59)
Wash — Brown 6 pass from Theismann (Moseley kick) (13:05)

SUPER BOWL XVI

Pontiac Silverdome, Pontiac, Michigan
January 24, 1982, Attendance: 81,270

SAN FRANCISCO 26, CINCINNATI 21—Ray Wersching's Super Bowl record-tying 4 field goals and Joe Montana's controlled passing helped lift the San Francisco 49ers to their first NFL championship with a 26-21 victory over Cincinnati. The 49ers built a game-record 20-0 halftime lead via Montana's 1-yard touchdown run, which capped an 11-play, 68-yard drive; fullback Earl Cooper's 11-yard scoring pass from Montana, which climaxed a Super Bowl record 92-yard drive on 12 plays; and Wersching's 22- and 26-yard field goals. The Bengals rebounded in the second half, closing the gap to 20-14 on quarterback Ken Anderson's 5-yard run and Dan Ross's 4-yard reception from Anderson, who established Super Bowl passing records for completions (25) and completion percentage (73.5 percent on 25 of 34). Wersching added early fourth-period field goals of 40 and 23 yards to increase the 49ers' lead to 26-14. The Bengals managed to score on an Anderson-to-Ross 3-yard pass with only 16 seconds remaining. Ross set a Super Bowl record with 11 receptions for 104 yards. Montana, the game's most valuable player, completed 14 of 22 passes for 157 yards. Cincinnati compiled 356 yards to San Francisco's 275, which marked the first time in Super Bowl history that the team that gained the most yards from scrimmage lost the game.

San Francisco (NFC)	7	13	0	6	—	26
Cincinnati (AFC)	0	0	7	14	—	21

SF — Montana 1 run (Wersching kick) (9:08)
SF — Cooper 11 pass from Montana (Wersching kick) (8:07)
SF — FG Wersching 22 (14:45)
SF — FG Wersching 26 (14:58)
Cin — Anderson 5 run (Breech kick) (3:35)
Cin — Ross 4 pass from Anderson (Breech kick) (4:54)
SF — FG Wersching 40 (9:35)
SF — FG Wersching 23 (13:03)
Cin — Ross 3 pass from Anderson (Breech kick) (14:44)

SUPER BOWL XV

Louisiana Superdome, New Orleans, Louisiana
January 25, 1981, Attendance: 76,135

OAKLAND 27, PHILADELPHIA 10—Jim Plunkett passed for 3 touchdowns, including an 80-yard strike to Kenny King, as the Raiders became the first wild-card team to win the Super Bowl. Plunkett's touchdown bomb to King—the longest play in Super Bowl history—gave Oakland a decisive 14-0 lead with nine seconds left in the first period. Linebacker Rod Martin had set up Oakland's first touchdown, a 2-yard reception by Cliff Branch, with a 17-yard interception return to the Eagles' 30-yard line. The Eagles never recovered from that early deficit, managing only Tony Franklin's field goal (30 yards) and an 8-yard touchdown pass from Ron Jaworski to Keith Krepfle. Plunkett, who became a starter in the sixth game of the season, completed 13 of 21 for 261 yards and was named the game's most valuable player. Oakland won 9 of 11 games with Plunkett starting, but that was good enough only for second place in the AFC West, although they tied division winner San Diego with an 11-5 record. The Raiders, who had previously won Super Bowl XI over Minnesota, had to win three playoff games to get to the championship game. Oakland defeated Houston 27-7 at home followed by road victories over Cleveland (14-12) and San Diego (34-27). Oakland's Mark van Eeghen was the game's leading rusher with 75 yards on 18 carries. Philadelphia's Wilbert Montgomery led all receivers with 6 receptions for 91 yards. Branch had 5 for 67 and Harold Carmichael of Philadelphia 5 for 83. Martin finished the game with 3 interceptions, a Super Bowl record.

Oakland (AFC)	14	0	10	3	—	27
Philadelphia (NFC)	0	3	0	7	—	10

Oak — Branch 2 pass from Plunkett (Bahr kick) (6:04)
Oak — King 80 pass from Plunkett (Bahr kick) (14:51)
Phil — FG Franklin 30 (4:32)
Oak — Branch 29 pass from Plunkett (Bahr kick) (2:36)
Oak — FG Bahr 46 (10:25)
Phil — Krepfle 8 pass from Jaworski (Franklin kick) (1:01)
Oak — FG Bahr 35 (6:31)

SUPER BOWL XIV

Rose Bowl, Pasadena, California
January 20, 1980, Attendance: 103,985

PITTSBURGH 31, LOS ANGELES 19—Terry Bradshaw completed 14 of 21 passes for 309 yards and set two passing records as the Steelers became the first team to win four Super Bowls. Despite 3 interceptions by the Rams, Bradshaw kept his poise and brought the Steelers from behind twice in the second half. Trailing 13-10 at halftime, Pittsburgh went ahead 17-13 when Bradshaw hit Lynn Swann with a 47-yard touchdown pass after 2:48 of the third quarter. On the Rams' next possession Vince Ferragamo, who completed 15 of 25 passes for 212 yards, responded with a 50-yard pass to Billy Waddy that moved Los Angeles from its 26 to the Steelers' 24. On the following play, Lawrence McCutcheon connected with Ron Smith on a halfback option pass that gave the Rams a 19-17 lead. On Pittsburgh's initial possession of the final period, Bradshaw lofted a 73-yard scoring pass to John Stallworth to put the Steelers in front to stay 24-19. Franco Harris scored on a 1-yard run later in the quarter to seal the verdict. A 45-yard pass from Bradshaw to Stallworth was the key play in the drive to Harris's score. Bradshaw, the game's most valuable player for the second straight year, set career Super Bowl records for most touchdown passes (9) and most passing yards (932). Larry Anderson gave the Steelers excellent field position throughout the game with 5 kickoff returns for a record 162 yards.

Los Angeles (NFC)	7	6	6	0	—	19
Pittsburgh (AFC)	3	7	7	14	—	31

Pitt — FG Bahr 41 (7:29)
LA — Bryant 1 run (Corral kick) (12:16)
Pitt — Harris 1 run (Bahr kick) (2:08)
LA — FG Corral 31 (7:39)
LA — FG Corral 45 (14:46)
Pitt — Swann 47 pass from Bradshaw (Bahr kick) (2:48)
LA — Smith 24 pass from McCutcheon (kick failed) (4:45)
Pitt — Stallworth 73 pass from Bradshaw (Bahr kick) (2:56)
Pitt — Harris 1 run (Bahr kick) (13:11)

SUPER BOWL XIII

Orange Bowl, Miami, Florida
January 21, 1979, Attendance: 79,484

PITTSBURGH 35, DALLAS 31—Terry Bradshaw passed for a record 4 touchdowns to lead the Steelers to victory. The Steelers became the first team to win three Super Bowls, mostly because of Bradshaw's accurate arm. Bradshaw, voted the game's most valuable player, completed 17 of 30 passes for 318 yards, a personal high. Four of those passes went for touchdowns—2 to John Stallworth and the third, with 26 seconds remaining in the second period, to Rocky Bleier for a 21-14 halftime lead. The Cowboys scored twice before intermission on Roger Staubach's 39-yard pass to Tony Hill and a 37-yard fumble return by linebacker Mike Hegman, who stole the ball from Bradshaw. The Steelers broke open the contest with 2 touchdowns in a span of 19 seconds midway through the final period. Franco Harris rambled 22 yards up the middle to give the Steelers a 28-17 lead with 7:10 left. Pittsburgh got the ball right back when Randy White fumbled the kickoff and Dennis Winston recovered for the Steelers. On first down, Bradshaw fired his fourth touchdown pass, an 18-yard pass to Lynn Swann to boost the Steelers' lead to 35-17 with 6:51 to play. The Cowboys refused to let the Steelers run away with the contest. Staubach connected with Billy Joe DuPree on a 7-yard scoring pass with 2:23 left. Then the Cowboys recovered an onside kick and Staubach took them in for another score, passing 4 yards to Butch Johnson with 22 seconds remaining. Bleier recovered another onside kick with 17 seconds left to seal the victory for the Steelers.

Pittsburgh (AFC)	7	14	0	14	—	35
Dallas (NFC)	7	7	3	14	—	31

Pitt — Stallworth 28 pass from Bradshaw (Gerela kick) (5:13)
Dall — Hill 39 pass from Staubach (Septien kick) (15:00)
Dall — Hegman 37 fumble recovery return (Septien kick) (2:52)
Pitt — Stallworth 75 pass from Bradshaw (Gerela kick) (4:35)
Pitt — Bleier 7 pass from Bradshaw (Gerela kick) (14:34)
Dall — FG Septien 27 (12:24)
Pitt — Harris 22 run (Gerela kick) (7:50)
Pitt — Swann 18 pass from Bradshaw (Gerela kick) (8:09)
Dall — DuPree 7 pass from Staubach (Septien kick) (12:37)
Dall — B. Johnson 4 pass from Staubach (Septien kick) (14:38)

SUPER BOWL XII

Louisiana Superdome, New Orleans, Louisiana
January 15, 1978, Attendance: 75,583

DALLAS 27, DENVER 10—The Cowboys evened their Super Bowl record at 2-2 by defeating Denver before a sellout crowd of 75,583, plus 102,010,000 television viewers, the largest audience ever to watch a sporting event. Dallas converted 2 interceptions into 10 points and Efren Herrera added a 35-yard field goal for a 13-0 halftime advantage. In the third period Craig Morton engineered a drive to the Cowboys' 30 and Jim Turner's 47-yard field goal made the score 13-3. After an exchange of punts, Butch Johnson made a spectacular diving catch in the end zone to complete a 45-yard pass from Roger Staubach and put the Cowboys ahead 20-3. Following Rick Upchurch's 67-yard kickoff return, Norris Weese guided the Broncos to a touchdown to cut the Dallas lead to 20-10. Dallas clinched the victory when running back Robert Newhouse tossed a 29-yard touchdown pass to Golden Richards with 7:04 remaining in the game. It was the first pass thrown by Newhouse since 1975. Harvey Martin and Randy White, who were named co-most valuable players, led the Cowboys' defense, which recovered 4 fumbles and intercepted 4 passes.

Dallas (NFC)	10	3	7	7	—	27
Denver (AFC)	0	0	10	0	—	10

Dall — Dorsett 3 run (Herrera kick) (10:31)
Dall — FG Herrera 35 (13:29)
Dall — FG Herrera 43 (3:44)
Den — FG Turner 47 (2:28)
Dall — Johnson 45 pass from Staubach (Herrera kick) (8:01)
Den — Lytle 1 run (Turner kick) (9:21)
Dall — Richards 29 pass from Newhouse (Herrera kick) (7:56)

SUPER BOWL XI

Rose Bowl, Pasadena, California
January 9, 1977, Attendance: 103,438

OAKLAND 32, MINNESOTA 14—The Raiders won their first NFL championship before a record Super Bowl crowd plus 81 million television viewers, the largest audience ever to watch a sporting event. The Raiders gained a record-breaking 429 yards, including running back Clarence Davis's 137 rushing yards. Wide receiver Fred Biletnikoff made 4 key receptions, which earned him the game's most valuable player trophy. Oakland scored on three successive possessions in the second quarter to build a 16-0 halftime lead. Errol Mann's 24-yard field goal opened the scoring, then the AFC champions put together drives of 64 and 35 yards, scoring on a 1-yard pass from Ken Stabler to Dave Casper and a 1-yard run by Pete Banaszak. The Raiders increased their lead to 19-0 on a 40-yard field goal in the third quarter, but Minnesota responded with a 12-play, 58-yard drive late in the period, with Fran Tarkenton passing 8 yards to wide receiver Sammy White to cut the deficit to 19-7. Two fourth-quarter interceptions clinched the title for the Raiders. One set up Banaszak's second touchdown run, the other resulted in cornerback Willie Brown's Super Bowl-record 75-yard interception return.

Oakland (AFC)	0	16	3	13	—	32
Minnesota (NFC)	0	0	7	7	—	14

Oak — FG Mann 24 (0:48)
Oak — Casper 1 pass from Stabler (Mann kick) (7:50)
Oak — Banaszak 1 run (kick failed) (11:27)
Oak — FG Mann 40 (9:44)
Minn — S. White 8 pass from Tarkenton (Cox kick) (14:13)
Oak — Banaszak 2 run (Mann kick) (7:21)
Oak — Brown 75 interception return (kick failed) (9:17)
Minn — Voigt 13 pass from Lee (Cox kick) (14:35)

SUPER BOWL X

Orange Bowl, Miami, Florida
January 18, 1976, Attendance: 80,187

PITTSBURGH 21, DALLAS 17—The Steelers won the Super Bowl for the second year in a row on Terry Bradshaw's 64-yard touchdown pass to Lynn Swann and an aggressive defense that snuffed out a late rally by the Cowboys with an end-zone interception on the final play of the game. In the fourth quarter, Pittsburgh ran on fourth down and gave up the ball on the Cowboys' 39 with 1:22 to play. Roger Staubach ran and passed for 2 first downs but his last desperation pass was picked off by Glen Edwards. Dallas's scoring was the result of 2 touchdown passes by Staubach, one to Drew Pearson for 29 yards and the other to Percy Howard for 34 yards. Toni Fritsch had a 36-yard field goal. The Steelers scored on 2 touchdown passes by Bradshaw, 1 to Randy Grossman for 7 yards and the long bomb to Swann. Roy Gerela had 36- and 18-yard field goals. Reggie Harrison blocked a punt through the end zone for a safety. Swann set a Super Bowl record by gaining 161 yards on his 4 receptions.

Dallas (NFC)	7	3	0	7	—	17
Pittsburgh (AFC)	7	0	0	14	—	21

Dall — D. Pearson 29 pass from Staubach (Fritsch kick) (4:36)
Pitt — Grossman 7 pass from Bradshaw (Gerela kick) (9:03)
Dall — FG Fritsch 36 (0:15)
Pitt — Safety, Harrison blocked Hoopes's punt through end zone (3:32)
Pitt — FG Gerela 36 (6:19)
Pitt — FG Gerela 18 (8:23)
Pitt — Swann 64 pass from Bradshaw (kick failed) (11:58)
Dall — P. Howard 34 pass from Staubach (Fritsch kick) (13:12)

SUPER BOWL IX

Tulane Stadium, New Orleans, Louisiana
January 12, 1975, Attendance: 80,997

PITTSBURGH 16, MINNESOTA 6—AFC champion Pittsburgh, in its initial Super Bowl appearance, and NFC champion Minnesota, making a third bid for its first Super Bowl title, struggled through a first half in which the only score was produced by the Steelers' defense when Dwight White downed Vikings' quarterback Fran Tarkenton in the end zone for a safety 7:49 into the second period. The Steelers forced another break and took advantage on the second-half kickoff when Minnesota's Bill Brown fumbled and Marv Kellum recovered for Pittsburgh on the Vikings' 30. After Rocky Bleier failed to gain on first down, Franco Harris carried 3 consecutive times for 24 yards, a loss of 3, and a 9-yard touchdown and a 9-0 lead. Though its offense was completely stymied by Pittsburgh's defense, Minnesota managed to move into a threatening position after 4:27 of the final period when Matt Blair blocked Bobby Walden's punt and Terry Brown recovered the ball in the end zone for a touchdown. Fred Cox's kick failed and the Steelers led 9-6. Pittsburgh wasted no time putting the victory away. The Steelers took the ensuing kickoff and marched 66 yards in 11 plays, climaxed by Terry Bradshaw's 4-yard scoring pass to Larry Brown with 3:31 left. Pittsburgh's defense permitted Minnesota only 119 yards total offense, including a Super Bowl low of 17 rushing yards. The Steelers, meanwhile, gained 333 yards, including Harris's record 158 yards on 34 carries.

Pittsburgh (AFC)	0	2	7	7	—	16
Minnesota (NFC)	0	0	0	6	—	6

Pitt — Safety, White downed Tarkenton in end zone (7:49)
Pitt — Harris 9 run (Gerela kick) (1:35)
Minn — T. Brown recovered blocked punt in end zone (kick failed) (4:27)
Pitt — L. Brown 4 pass from Bradshaw (Gerela kick) (11:29)

SUPER BOWL VIII

Rice Stadium, Houston, Texas
January 13, 1974, Attendance: 71,882

MIAMI 24, MINNESOTA 7—The defending NFL champion Dolphins, representing the AFC for the third straight year, scored the first two times they had possession on marches of 62 and 56 yards while the Miami defense limited the Vikings to only seven plays in the first period. Larry Csonka climaxed the initial 10-play drive with a 5-yard touchdown bolt through right guard after 5:27 had elapsed. Four plays later, Miami began another 10-play scoring drive, which ended with Jim Kiick bursting 1 yard through the middle for another touchdown after 13:38 of the period. Garo Yepremian added a 28-yard field goal midway in the second period for a 17-0 Miami lead. Minnesota then drove from its 20 to a second-and-2 situation on the Miami 7 yard line with 1:18 left in the half. But on two plays, Miami limited Oscar Reed to 1 yard. On fourth-and-1 from the 6, Reed went over right tackle, but Dolphins middle linebacker Nick Buoniconti jarred the ball loose and Jake Scott recovered for Miami to halt the Minnesota threat. The Vikings were unable to muster enough offense in the second half to threaten the Dolphins. Csonka rushed 33 times for a Super Bowl-record 145 yards. Bob Griese of Miami completed 6 of 7 passes for 73 yards.

Minnesota (NFC)	0	0	0	7	—	7
Miami (AFC)	14	3	7	0	—	24

Mia — Csonka 5 run (Yepremian kick) (9:33)
Mia — Kiick 1 run (Yepremian kick) (13:38)
Mia — FG Yepremian 28 (8:58)
Mia — Csonka 2 run (Yepremian kick) (6:16)
Minn — Tarkenton 4 run (Cox kick) (1:35)

SUPER BOWL VII

Memorial Coliseum, Los Angeles, California
January 14, 1973, Attendance: 90,182

MIAMI 14, WASHINGTON 7—The Dolphins played virtually perfect football in the first half as their defense permitted the Redskins to cross midfield only once and their offense turned good field position into 2 touchdowns. On its third possession, Miami opened its first scoring drive from the Dolphins' 37 yard line. An 18-yard pass from Bob Griese to Paul Warfield preceded by three plays Griese's 28-yard touchdown pass to Howard Twilley. After Washington moved from its 17 to the Miami 48 with two minutes remaining in the first half, Dolphins linebacker Nick Buoniconti intercepted Billy Kilmer's pass at the Miami 41 and returned it to the Washington 27. Jim Kiick ran for 3 yards, Larry Csonka for 3, Griese passed to Jim Mandich for 19, and Kiick gained 1 to the 1-yard line. With 18 seconds left until intermission, Kiick scored from the 1. Washington's only touchdown came with 2:07 left in the game and resulted from a misplayed field-goal attempt and fumble by Garo Yepremian, with the Redskins' Mike Bass picking the ball out of the air and running 49 yards for the score. Dolphins safety Jake Scott, who had 2 interceptions, including 1 in the end zone to kill a Redskins' drive, was voted the game's most valuable player.

Miami (AFC)	7	7	0	0	—	14
Washington (NFC)	0	0	0	7	—	7

Mia — Twilley 28 pass from Griese (Yepremian kick) (14:59)
Mia — Kiick 1 run (Yepremian kick) (14:42)
Wash — Bass 49 fumble recovery return (Knight kick) (12:53)

SUPER BOWL VI

Tulane Stadium, New Orleans, Louisiana
January 16, 1972, Attendance: 81,023

DALLAS 24, MIAMI 3—The Cowboys rushed for a record 252 yards and their defense limited the Dolphins to a low of 185 yards while not permitting a touchdown for the first time in Super Bowl history. Dallas converted Chuck Howley's recovery of Larry Csonka's first fumble of the season into a 3-0 advantage and led at halftime 10-3. After Dallas received the second-half kickoff, Duane Thomas led a 71-yard march in eight plays for a 17-

3 margin. Howley intercepted Bob Griese's pass at the 50 and returned it to the Miami 9 early in the fourth period, and three plays later Roger Staubach passed 7 yards to Mike Ditka for the final touchdown. Thomas rushed for 95 yards and Walt Garrison gained 74. Staubach, voted the game's most valuable player, completed 12 of 19 passes for 119 yards and 2 touchdowns.

Dallas (NFC)	3	7	7	7	— 24
Miami (AFC)	0	3	0	0	— 3

Dall — FG Clark 9 (13:37)
Dall — Alworth 7 pass from Staubach (Clark kick) (13:45)
Mia — FG Yepremian 31 (14:56)
Dall — D. Thomas 3 run (Clark kick) (5:17)
Dall — Ditka 7 pass from Staubach (Clark kick) (3:18)

SUPER BOWL V

Orange Bowl, Miami, Florida
January 17, 1971, Attendance: 79,204

BALTIMORE 16, DALLAS 13—A 32-yard field goal by rookie kicker Jim O'Brien brought the Baltimore Colts a victory over the Dallas Cowboys in the final five seconds of Super Bowl V. The game between the champions of the AFC and NFC was played on artificial turf for the first time. Dallas led 13-6 at the half but interceptions by Rick Volk and Mike Curtis set up a Baltimore touchdown and O'Brien's decisive kick in the fourth period. Earl Morrall relieved an injured Johnny Unitas late in the first half, although Unitas completed the Colts' only scoring pass. It caromed off receiver Eddie Hinton's fingertips, off Dallas defensive back Mel Renfro, and finally settled into the grasp of John Mackey, who went 45 yards to score on a 75-yard play.

Baltimore (AFC)	0	6	0	10	— 16
Dallas (NFC)	3	10	0	0	— 13

Dall — FG Clark 14 (9:28)
Dall — FG Clark 30 (0:08)
Balt — Mackey 75 pass from Unitas (kick blocked) (0:05)
Dall — Thomas 7 pass from Morton (Clark kick) (7:07)
Balt — Nowatzke 2 run (O'Brien kick) (7:25)
Balt — FG O'Brien 32 (14:55)

SUPER BOWL IV

Tulane Stadium, New Orleans, Louisiana
January 11, 1970, Attendance: 80,562

KANSAS CITY 23, MINNESOTA 7—The AFL squared the Super Bowl at two games apiece with the NFL, building a 16-0 halftime lead behind Len Dawson's superb quarterbacking and a powerful defense. Dawson, the fourth consecutive quarterback to be chosen the Super Bowl's top player, called an almost flawless game, completing 12 of 17 passes and hitting Otis Taylor on a 46-yard play for the final Chiefs touchdown. The Kansas City defense limited Minnesota's strong rushing game to 67 yards and had 3 interceptions and 2 fumble recoveries. The crowd of 80,562 set a Super Bowl record, as did the gross receipts of $3,817,872.69.

Minnesota (NFL)	0	0	7	0	— 7
Kansas City (AFL)	3	13	7	0	— 23

KC — FG Stenerud 48 (8:08)
KC — FG Stenerud 32 (1:40)
KC — FG Stenerud 25 (7:08)
KC — Garrett 5 run (Stenerud kick) (9:26)
Minn — Osborn 4 run (Cox kick) (10:28)
KC — Taylor 46 pass from Dawson (Stenerud kick) (13:38)

SUPER BOWL III

Orange Bowl, Miami, Florida
January 12, 1969, Attendance: 75,389

NEW YORK JETS 16, BALTIMORE 7—Jets quarterback Joe Namath "guaranteed" victory on the Thursday before the game, then went out and led the AFL to its first Super Bowl victory over a Baltimore team that had lost only once in 16 games all season. Namath, chosen the outstanding player, completed 17 of 28 passes for 206 yards and directed a steady attack that dominated the NFL champions after the Jets' defense had intercepted Colts quarterback Earl Morrall 3 times in the first half. The Jets had 337 total yards, including 121 rushing yards by Matt Snell. Johnny Unitas, who had missed most of the season with a sore elbow, came off the bench and led Baltimore to its only touchdown late in the fourth quarter after New York led 16-0.

New York Jets (AFL)	0	7	6	3	— 16
Baltimore (NFL)	0	0	0	7	— 7

NYJ — Snell 4 run (Turner kick) (5:57)
NYJ — FG Turner 32 (4:52)
NYJ — FG Turner 30 (11:02)
NYJ — FG Turner 9 (1:34)
Balt — Hill 1 run (Michaels kick) (11:41)

SUPER BOWL II

Orange Bowl, Miami, Florida
January 14, 1968, Attendance: 75,546

GREEN BAY 33, OAKLAND 14—Green Bay, after winning its third consecutive NFL championship, won the Super Bowl title for the second straight year, defeating the AFL champion Raiders in a game that drew the first $3-million gate in football history. Bart Starr again was chosen the game's most valuable player as he completed 13 of 24 passes for 202 yards and 1 touchdown and directed a Packers' attack that was in control all the way after building a 16-7 halftime lead. Don Chandler kicked 4 field goals and all-pro cornerback Herb Adderley capped the Green Bay scoring with a 60-yard interception return. The game marked the last for Vince Lombardi as Packers coach, ending nine years at Green Bay in which he won six Western Conference championships, five NFL championships, and two Super Bowls.

Green Bay (NFL)	3	13	10	7	— 33
Oakland (AFL)	0	7	0	7	— 14

GB — FG Chandler 39 (5:07)
GB — FG Chandler 20 (3:08)
GB — Dowler 62 pass from Starr (Chandler kick) (4:10)
Oak — Miller 23 pass from Lamonica (Blanda kick) (8:45)
GB — FG Chandler 43 (14:59)
GB — Anderson 2 run (Chandler kick) (9:06)
GB — FG Chandler 31 (14:58)
GB — Adderley 60 interception return (Chandler kick) (3:57)
Oak — Miller 23 pass from Lamonica (Blanda kick) (5:47)

SUPER BOWL I

Memorial Coliseum, Los Angeles, California
January 15, 1967, Attendance: 61,946

GREEN BAY 35, KANSAS CITY 10—The Green Bay Packers opened the Super Bowl series by defeating the AFL champion Chiefs behind the passing of Bart Starr, the receiving of Max McGee, and a key interception by all-pro safety Willie Wood. Green Bay broke open the game with 3 second-half touchdowns, the first of which was set up by Wood's 50-yard return of an interception. McGee, filling in for ailing Boyd Dowler after having caught only 4 passes all season, caught 7 from Starr for 138 yards and 2 touchdowns. Elijah Pitts ran for 2 other scores. The Chiefs' 10 points came in the second quarter, the only touchdown on a 7-yard pass from Len Dawson to Curtis McClinton. Starr completed 16 of 23 passes for 250 yards and 2 touchdowns and was chosen the most valuable player. The Packers collected $15,000 per man and the Chiefs $7,500—the largest single-game shares in the history of team sports.

Kansas City (AFL)	0	10	0	0	— 10
Green Bay (NFL)	7	7	14	7	— 35

GB — McGee 37 pass from Starr (Chandler kick) (8:56)
KC — McClinton 7 pass from Dawson (Mercer kick) (4:20)
GB — Taylor 14 run (Chandler kick) (10:23)
KC — FG Mercer 31 (14:06)
GB — Pitts 5 run (Chandler kick) (2:27)
GB — McGee 13 pass from Starr (Chandler kick) (14:09)
GB — Pitts 1 run (Chandler kick) (8:25)

AFC CHAMPIONSHIP GAME RESULTS

Includes AFL Championship Games (1960-69)

Season	Date	Winner (Share)	Loser (Share)	Score	Site	Attendance
1998	Jan. 17	Denver ($32,500)	N.Y. Jets ($32,500)	23-10	Denver	75,482
1997	Jan. 11	Denver ($30,000)	Pittsburgh ($30,000)	24-21	Pittsburgh	61,382
1996	Jan. 12	New England ($29,000)	Jacksonville ($29,000)	20-6	New England	60,190
1995	Jan. 14	Pittsburgh ($27,000)	Indianapolis ($27,000)	20-16	Pittsburgh	61,062
1994	Jan. 15	San Diego ($26,000)	Pittsburgh ($26,000)	17-13	Pittsburgh	61,545
1993	Jan. 23	Buffalo ($23,500)	Kansas City ($23,500)	30-13	Buffalo	76,642
1992	Jan. 17	Buffalo ($18,000)	Miami ($18,000)	29-10	Miami	72,703
1991	Jan. 12	Buffalo ($18,000)	Denver ($18,000)	10-7	Buffalo	80,272
1990	Jan. 20	Buffalo ($18,000)	L.A. Raiders ($18,000)	51-3	Buffalo	80,325
1989	Jan. 14	Denver ($18,000)	Cleveland ($18,000)	37-21	Denver	76,046
1988	Jan. 8	Cincinnati ($18,000)	Buffalo ($18,000)	21-10	Cincinnati	59,747
1987	Jan. 17	Denver ($18,000)	Cleveland ($18,000)	38-33	Denver	76,197
1986	Jan. 11	Denver ($18,000)	Cleveland ($18,000)	23-20*	Cleveland	79,973
1985	Jan. 12	New England ($18,000)	Miami ($18,000)	31-14	Miami	75,662
1984	Jan. 6	Miami ($18,000)	Pittsburgh ($18,000)	45-28	Miami	76,029
1983	Jan. 8	L.A. Raiders ($18,000)	Seattle ($18,000)	30-14	Los Angeles	91,445
1982	Jan. 23	Miami ($18,000)	N.Y. Jets ($18,000)	14-0	Miami	67,396
1981	Jan. 10	Cincinnati ($9,000)	San Diego ($9,000)	27-7	Cincinnati	46,302
1980	Jan. 11	Oakland ($9,000)	San Diego ($9,000)	34-27	San Diego	52,675
1979	Jan. 6	Pittsburgh ($9,000)	Houston ($9,000)	27-13	Pittsburgh	50,475
1978	Jan. 7	Pittsburgh ($9,000)	Houston ($9,000)	34-5	Pittsburgh	50,725
1977	Jan. 1	Denver ($9,000)	Oakland ($9,000)	20-17	Denver	75,044
1976	Dec. 26	Oakland ($8,500)	Pittsburgh ($5,500)	24-7	Oakland	53,821
1975	Jan. 4	Pittsburgh ($8,500)	Oakland ($5,500)	16-10	Pittsburgh	50,609
1974	Dec. 29	Pittsburgh ($8,500)	Oakland ($5,500)	24-13	Oakland	53,800
1973	Dec. 30	Miami ($8,500)	Oakland ($5,500)	27-10	Miami	79,325
1972	Dec. 31	Miami ($8,500)	Pittsburgh ($5,500)	21-17	Pittsburgh	50,845
1971	Jan. 2	Miami ($8,500)	Baltimore ($5,500)	21-0	Miami	76,622
1970	Jan. 3	Baltimore ($8,500)	Oakland ($5,500)	27-17	Baltimore	54,799
1969	Jan. 4	Kansas City ($7,755)	Oakland ($6,252)	17-7	Oakland	53,564
1968	Dec. 29	N.Y. Jets ($7,007)	Oakland ($5,349)	27-23	New York	62,627
1967	Dec. 31	Oakland ($6,321)	Houston ($4,996)	40-7	Oakland	53,330
1966	Jan. 1	Kansas City ($5,309)	Buffalo ($3,799)	31-7	Buffalo	42,080
1965	Dec. 26	Buffalo ($5,189)	San Diego ($3,447)	23-0	San Diego	30,361
1964	Dec. 26	Buffalo ($2,668)	San Diego ($1,738)	20-7	Buffalo	40,242
1963	Jan. 5	San Diego ($2,498)	Boston ($1,596)	51-10	San Diego	30,127
1962	Dec. 23	Dallas ($2,206)	Houston ($1,471)	20-17*	Houston	37,981
1961	Dec. 24	Houston ($1,792)	San Diego ($1,111)	10-3	San Diego	29,556
1960	Jan. 1	Houston ($1,025)	L.A. Chargers ($718)	24-16	Houston	32,183

**Sudden death overtime.*

AFC CHAMPIONSHIP GAME COMPOSITE STANDINGS

	W	L	Pct.	Pts.	OP
Cincinnati Bengals	2	0	1.000	48	17
Denver Broncos	6	1	.857	172	132
Buffalo Bills	6	2	.750	180	92
Kansas City Chiefs*	3	1	.750	81	61
Miami Dolphins	5	2	.714	152	115
New England Patriots**	2	1	.667	61	71
Pittsburgh Steelers	5	5	.500	207	188
Tennessee Titans##	2	4	.333	76	140
Indianapolis Colts#	1	2	.333	43	58
New York Jets	1	2	.333	37	60
Oakland/L.A. Raiders	4	8	.333	228	264
San Diego Chargers***	2	6	.250	128	161
Jacksonville Jaguars	0	1	.000	6	20
Seattle Seahawks	0	1	.000	14	30
Cleveland Browns	0	3	.000	74	98

**One game played when franchise was in Dallas (Texans). (Won 20-17)*
***One game played when franchise was in Boston. (Lost 51-10)*
****One game played when franchise was in Los Angeles. (Lost 24-16)*
#Two games played when franchise was in Baltimore. (Won 27-17, lost 21-0)
##Six games played when franchise was in Houston and known as Oilers. (Won 2, lost 4)

1998 AFC CHAMPIONSHIP GAME

Mile High Stadium, Denver, Colorado
January 17, 1999, Attendance: 75,482

DENVER 23, N.Y. JETS 10—In John Elway's final game in Denver, Terrell Davis rushed for 167 yards, and the Broncos forced 6 Jets' turnovers en route to scoring the game's final 23 points to capture their second consecutive AFC title. The game was played in a strong wind, with the wind chill dipping to 18 degrees and causing special teams problems for both sides. John Hall missed a 42-yard field goal on the game's opening drive, but the Jets kept the game scoreless by forcing Elway to throw an incomplete pass on fourth-and-goal from the Jets' 1 late in the first quarter. Tom Rouen dropped the ball while attempting to punt early in the second quarter, resulting in a 9-yard loss and giving the Jets the ball at the Broncos' 43. However, Keith Byars fumbled on the ensuing possession. Hall ended the half with a 32-yard field goal to give the Jets a 3-0 lead going into the locker room. Blake Spence blocked Rouen's punt early in the second half, and Fred Baxter recovered the ball at the Broncos' 1. Curtis Martin crashed into the end zone on the next play to give the Jets a 10-0 lead with 11:56 left in the third quarter. Elway, who had passed for just 33 yards in the first half, completed a 47-yard pass to Ed McCaffrey on the first play of the next drive, and then found Howard Griffith two plays later for a touchdown. A strong wind knocked Jason Elam's next kickoff to the ground near the Jets' 25. James Farrior momentarily recovered the bouncing ball, but he fumbled and Keith Burns's recovery gave the Broncos the ball at the Jets' 31. Elam's field goal tied the game with 8:23 left, and, after forcing a punt, Elam gave the Broncos the lead with 2:58 left in the quarter. The Broncos' defense forced another punt, and Darrien Gordon returned it 36 yards, setting up Davis's 31-yard touchdown run to give the Broncos 20 points in a span of 11:38. Gordon intercepted Vinny Testaverde twice in the final five minutes, the first of which led to Elam's final field goal. Elway was 13 of 34 for 173 yards and 1 touchdown. Testaverde was 31 of 52 for 356 yards, with 2 interceptions. Wayne Chrebet had 8 receptions for 121 yards.

N.Y. Jets (10)	Offense	Denver (23)
Keyshawn Johnson	WR	Rod Smith
John Elliott	LT	Tony Jones
Todd Burger	LG	Mark Schlereth
Kevin Mawae	C	Tom Nalen
Matt O'Dwyer	RG	Dan Neil
Jason Fabini	RT	Harry Swayne
Kyle Brady	TE	Shannon Sharpe
Wayne Chrebet	WR	Ed McCaffrey
Vinny Testaverde	QB	John Elway
Curtis Martin	RB	Terrell Davis
Keith Byars	FB	Howard Griffith
	Defense	
Rick Lyle	LE	Harald Hasselbach
Jason Ferguson	LT	Keith Traylor
Chad Cascadden	RT	Trevor Pryce
Anthony Pleasant	RE	Maa Tanuvasa
Mo Lewis	LLB-WLB	John Mobley
Pepper Johnson	MLB	Glenn Cadrez
Bryan Cox	RLB-SLB	Bill Romanowski
Ray Mickens	LCB	Ray Crockett
Otis Smith	RCB	Darrien Gordon
Victor Green	SS	Darrius Johnson
Corwin Brown	FS	Steve Atwater

SUBSTITUTIONS

N.Y. Jets—Offense: C-G—Mike Gisler, John Hudson. T-G—Kerry Jenkins. TE—Fred Baxter, Blake Spence. WR—Alex Van Dyke, Dedric Ward. RB—David Meggett. P—John Kidd. K—John Hall. Defense: DT-DE—Ernie Logan. DE-DT—Bobby Hamilton. DE—Eric Ogbogu. LB—James Farrior, Dwayne Gordon, Rob Holmberg. DB—Marcus Coleman, Scott Frost, Aaron Glenn, Chris Hayes, Kevin Williams. DNP—Richie Anderson, Ray Lucas.

Denver—Offense: G—David Diaz-Infante. T—Matt Lepsis. TE—Dwayne Carswell, Byron Chamberlain. TE/RB—Anthony Lynn. WR—Willie Green, Marcus Nash. RB—Vaughn Hebron, Derek Loville, Detron Smith. P—Tom Rouen. K—Jason Elam. Defense: DT—Mark Lodish. DE—Neil Smith, Marvin Washington, Alfred Williams. LB—Keith Burns, Seth Joyner. DB—Tyrone Braxton, George Coghill, Tory James, Tito Paul. DNP—Bubby Brister.

PLAYOFF GAMES SUMMARIES

OFFICIALS
Referee—Ed Hochuli. Umpire—Chad Brown. Line Judge—Tom Barnes. Side Judge—Doug Toole. Head Linesman—George Hayward. Back Judge—Richard Reels. Field Judge— Tom Sifferman.

SCORING

N.Y. Jets	0	3	7	0	—	10
Denver	0	0	20	3	—	23

NYJ — FG Hall 32
NYJ — Martin 1 run (Hall kick)
Den — Griffith 11 pass from Elway (Elam kick)
Den — FG Elam 44
Den — FG Elam 48
Den — Davis 31 run (Elam kick)
Den — FG Elam 35

TEAM STATISTICS	**NYJ**	**Den**
Total First Downs	18	14
Rushing	1	8
Passing	17	6
Penalty	0	0
Total Net Yardage	370	331
Total Offensive Plays	65	75
Average Gain Per Offensive Play	5.7	4.4
Rushes	13	38
Yards Gained Rushing (Net)	14	178
Average Yards per Rush	1.1	4.7
Passes Attempted	52	34
Passes Completed	31	13
Had Intercepted	2	0
Tackled Attempting to Pass	0	3
Yards Lost Attempting to Pass	0	20
Yards Gained Passing (Net)	356	153
Punts	7	8
Average Distance	47.9	39.6
Punt Returns	3	5
Punt Return Yardage	43	79
Kickoff Returns	5	1
Kickoff Return Yardage	46	28
Interception Return Yardage	0	48
Total Return Yardage	89	155
Fumbles	4	2
Fumbles Lost	4	0
Own Fumbles Recovered	0	2
Opponent Fumbles Recovered	0	4
Penalties	6	6
Yards Penalized	49	47
Field Goals	1	3
Field Goals Attempted	2	3
Third-Down Efficiency	3/12	4/19
Fourth-Down Efficiency	1/1	1/4
Time of Possession	27:00	33:00

INDIVIDUAL STATISTICS
RUSHING: NYJ: Martin 13-14. DEN: Davis 32-167, Elway 3-13, Loville 2-7, Rouen 1-(-9).
PASSING: NYJ: Testavede 31-52-356-2. DEN: Elway 13-34-173-0.
RECEIVING: NYJ: Chrebet 8-121, K. Johnson 7-73, Ward 5-61, Martin 4-39, Byars 3-33, Brady 2-11, Van Dyke 1-16, Meggett 1-2. DEN: McCaffrey 3-66, R. Smith 3-37, Chamberlain 2-26, Sharpe 2-14, Davis 1-12, Griffith 1-11, Carswell 1-7.
KICKOFF RETURNS: NYJ: Meggett 3-32, Hamilton 1-14, Farrior 1-0. DEN: Hebron 1-28.
PUNT RETURNS: NYJ: Meggett 3-43. DEN: Gordon 5-79.
PUNTING: NYJ: Kidd 7-335-47.9 DEN: Rouen 7-317-45.3.
INTERCEPTIONS: DEN: Gordon 2-48.
SACKS: NYJ: Cascadden 2, Farrior 1.

NFC CHAMPIONSHIP GAME RESULTS

Includes NFL Championship Games (1933-69)

Season	Date	Winner (Share)	Loser (Share)	Score	Site	Attendance
1998	Jan. 17	Atlanta ($32,500)	Minnesota ($32,500)	30-27*	Minnesota	64,060
1997	Jan. 11	Green Bay ($30,000)	San Francisco ($30,000)	23-10	San Francisco	68,987
1996	Jan. 12	Green Bay ($29,000)	Carolina ($29,000)	30-13	Green Bay	60,216
1995	Jan. 14	Dallas ($27,000)	Green Bay ($27,000)	38-27	Dallas	65,135
1994	Jan. 15	San Francisco ($26,000)	Dallas ($26,000)	38-28	San Francisco	69,125
1993	Jan. 23	Dallas ($23,500)	San Francisco ($23,500)	38-21	Dallas	64,902
1992	Jan. 17	Dallas ($18,000)	San Francisco ($18,000)	30-20	San Francisco	64,920
1991	Jan. 12	Washington ($18,000)	Detroit ($18,000)	41-10	Washington	55,585
1990	Jan. 20	N.Y. Giants ($18,000)	San Francisco ($18,000)	15-13	San Francisco	65,750
1989	Jan. 14	San Francisco ($18,000)	L.A. Rams ($18,000)	30-3	San Francisco	65,634
1988	Jan. 8	San Francisco ($18,000)	Chicago ($18,000)	28-3	Chicago	66,946
1987	Jan. 17	Washington ($18,000)	Minnesota ($18,000)	17-10	Washington	55,212
1986	Jan. 11	New York Giants ($18,000)	Washington ($18,000)	17-0	East Rutherford	76,891
1985	Jan. 12	Chicago ($18,000)	L.A. Rams ($18,000)	24-0	Chicago	66,030
1984	Jan. 6	San Francisco ($18,000)	Chicago ($18,000)	23-0	San Francisco	61,336
1983	Jan. 8	Washington ($18,000)	San Francisco ($18,000)	24-21	Washington	55,363
1982	Jan. 22	Washington ($18,000)	Dallas ($18,000)	31-17	Washington	55,045
1981	Jan. 10	San Francisco ($9,000)	Dallas ($9,000)	28-27	San Francisco	60,525
1980	Jan. 11	Philadelphia ($9,000)	Dallas ($9,000)	20-7	Philadelphia	71,522
1979	Jan. 6	Los Angeles ($9,000)	Tampa Bay ($9,000)	9-0	Tampa Bay	72,033
1978	Jan. 7	Dallas ($9,000)	Los Angeles ($9,000)	28-0	Los Angeles	71,086
1977	Jan. 1	Dallas ($9,000)	Minnesota ($9,000)	23-6	Dallas	64,293
1976	Dec. 26	Minnesota ($8,500)	Los Angeles ($5,500)	24-13	Minnesota	48,379
1975	Jan. 4	Dallas ($8,500)	Los Angeles ($5,500)	37-7	Los Angeles	88,919
1974	Dec. 29	Minnesota ($8,500)	Los Angeles ($5,500)	14-10	Minnesota	48,444
1973	Dec. 30	Minnesota ($8,500)	Dallas ($5,500)	27-10	Dallas	64,422
1972	Dec. 31	Washington ($8,500)	Dallas ($5,500)	26-3	Washington	53,129
1971	Jan. 2	Dallas ($8,500)	San Francisco ($5,500)	14-3	Dallas	63,409
1970	Jan. 3	Dallas ($8,500)	San Francisco ($5,500)	17-10	San Francisco	59,364
1969	Jan. 4	Minnesota ($7,930)	Cleveland ($5,118)	27-7	Minnesota	46,503
1968	Dec. 29	Baltimore ($9,306)	Cleveland ($5,963)	34-0	Cleveland	78,410
1967	Dec. 31	Green Bay ($7,950)	Dallas ($5,299)	21-17	Green Bay	50,861
1966	Jan. 1	Green Bay ($9,813)	Dallas ($6,527)	34-27	Dallas	74,152
1965	Jan. 2	Green Bay ($7,819)	Cleveland ($5,288)	23-12	Green Bay	50,777
1964	Dec. 27	Cleveland ($8,052)	Baltimore ($5,571)	27-0	Cleveland	79,544
1963	Dec. 29	Chicago ($5,899)	New York ($4,218)	14-10	Chicago	45,801
1962	Dec. 30	Green Bay ($5,888)	New York ($4,166)	16-7	New York	64,892
1961	Dec. 31	Green Bay ($5,195)	New York ($3,339)	37-0	Green Bay	39,029
1960	Dec. 26	Philadelphia ($5,116)	Green Bay ($3,105)	17-13	Philadelphia	67,325
1959	Dec. 27	Baltimore ($4,674)	New York ($3,083)	31-16	Baltimore	57,545
1958	Dec. 28	Baltimore ($4,718)	New York ($3,111)	23-17*	New York	64,185
1957	Dec. 29	Detroit ($4,295)	Cleveland ($2,750)	59-14	Detroit	55,263
1956	Dec. 30	New York ($3,779)	Chi. Bears ($2,485)	47-7	New York	56,836
1955	Dec. 26	Cleveland ($3,508)	Los Angeles ($2,316)	38-14	Los Angeles	85,693
1954	Dec. 26	Cleveland ($2,478)	Detroit ($1,585)	56-10	Cleveland	43,827
1953	Dec. 27	Detroit ($2,424)	Cleveland ($1,654)	17-16	Detroit	54,577
1952	Dec. 28	Detroit ($2,274)	Cleveland ($1,712)	17-7	Cleveland	50,934
1951	Dec. 23	Los Angeles ($2,108)	Cleveland ($1,483)	24-17	Los Angeles	57,522
1950	Dec. 24	Cleveland ($1,113)	Los Angeles ($686)	30-28	Cleveland	29,751
1949	Dec. 18	Philadelphia ($1,094)	Los Angeles ($739)	14-0	Los Angeles	27,980
1948	Dec. 19	Philadelphia ($1,540)	Chi. Cardinals ($874)	7-0	Philadelphia	36,309
1947	Dec. 28	Chi. Cardinals ($1,132)	Philadelphia ($754)	28-21	Chicago	30,759
1946	Dec. 15	Chi. Bears ($1,975)	New York ($1,295)	24-14	New York	58,346
1945	Dec. 16	Cleveland ($1,469)	Washington ($902)	15-14	Cleveland	32,178
1944	Dec. 17	Green Bay ($1,449)	New York ($814)	14-7	New York	46,016

Season	Date	Winner (Share)	Loser (Share)	Score	Site	Attendance
1943	Dec. 26	Chi. Bears ($1,146)	Washington ($765)	41-21	Chicago	34,320
1942	Dec. 13	Washington ($965)	Chi. Bears ($637)	14-6	Washington	36,006
1941	Dec. 21	Chi. Bears ($430)	New York ($288)	37-9	Chicago	13,341
1940	Dec. 8	Chi. Bears ($873)	Washington ($606)	73-0	Washington	36,034
1939	Dec. 10	Green Bay ($703.97)	New York ($455.57)	27-0	Milwaukee	32,279
1938	Dec. 11	New York ($504.45)	Green Bay ($368.81)	23-17	New York	48,120
1937	Dec. 12	Washington ($225.90)	Chi. Bears ($127.78)	28-21	Chicago	15,870
1936	Dec. 13	Green Bay ($250)	Boston ($180)	21-6	New York	29,545
1935	Dec. 15	Detroit ($313.35)	New York ($200.20)	26-7	Detroit	15,000
1934	Dec. 9	New York ($621)	Chi. Bears ($414.02)	30-13	New York	35,059
1933	Dec. 17	Chi. Bears ($210.34)	New York ($140.22)	23-21	Chicago	26,000

**Sudden death overtime.*

NFC CHAMPIONSHIP GAME COMPOSITE STANDINGS

	W	L	Pct.	Pts.	OP
Atlanta Falcons	1	0	1.000	30	27
Philadelphia Eagles	4	1	.800	79	48
Green Bay Packers	10	3	.769	303	177
Baltimore Colts	3	1	.750	88	60
Detroit Lions	4	2	.667	139	141
Washington Redskins*	7	5	.583	222	255
Minnesota Vikings	4	3	.571	135	110
Chicago Bears	7	6	.538	286	245
Dallas Cowboys	8	8	.500	361	319
Arizona Cardinals**	1	1	.500	28	28
San Francisco 49ers	5	7	.417	245	222
Cleveland Browns	4	7	.364	224	253
New York Giants	5	11	.313	240	322
St. Louis Rams***	3	9	.250	123	270
Carolina Panthers	0	1	.000	13	30
Tampa Bay Buccaneers	0	1	.000	0	9

**One game played when franchise was in Boston. (Lost 21-6)*
***Both games played when franchise was in Chicago. (Won 28-21, lost 7-0)*
****One game played when franchise was in Cleveland (Won 15-14), and 11 games when franchise was in Los Angeles (Won 2, lost 9, scored 108 points, allowed 256 points).*

1998 NFC CHAMPIONSHIP GAME

Metrodome, Minneapolis, Minnesota
January 17, 1999, Attendance: 64,060

ATLANTA 30, MINNESOTA 27 (OT)—Chris Chandler passed for 3 touchdowns, and Morten Andersen made a 38-yard field goal 11:52 into overtime to catapult the Falcons into their first Super Bowl. The Falcons drove 12 plays to score on their opening possession, but Minnesota retaliated by scoring on their first four possessions. First, Randall Cunningham capped a 5-play drive with a 31-yard touchdown pass to Randy Moss. Fumbles by Harold Green and O.J. Santiago led to Gary Anderson's 29-yard field goal and Cunningham's 1-yard sneak. Following a punt, Anderson, who did not miss a field-goal or extra-point attempt all season, made a 35-yard field goal to give the Vikings a 20-7 lead with 2:45 left in the half. The Vikings' defense forced another punt and started at their 18 with 1:17 left in the half. After 2 incompletions, Chuck Smith stripped Cunningham of the ball, and Travis Hall recovered. Chandler fired a 14-yard scoring strike to Terance Mathis on the next play to cut the deficit to 20-14 at halftime. Andersen's field goal cut the Vikings' lead to three points midway through the third quarter, but the Vikings used a 15-play, 82-yard drive, culminated by Cunningham's 5-yard touchdown pass to Matthew Hatchette, to take a 27-17 lead with 13:41 left. Chandler's 70-yard pass to Tony Martin set up Andersen's second field goal with 11:02 left, and Cunningham's fumble, recovered by Shane Dronett at the Vikings' 30, kept the Falcons' hopes alive. However, trailing 27-20 and faced with fourth-and-4 from the Vikings' 24 with 6:13 left, Chandler threw an incomplete pass. The Vikings held onto the ball for the next four minutes, but Anderson's 38-yard field-goal attempt failed, his first miss in 122 attempts. Chandler promptly drove the Falcons downfield, with the big play being a 29-yard pass to Ronnie Harris, and on second-and-10 from the Vikings' 16 with 57 seconds left, Chandler found Mathis just beyond the goal line for the game-tying touchdown. After a scramble and incomplete pass, Cunningham took a knee and the game went to overtime. Minnesota won the toss, but could not move beyond midfield with either of its two possessions. Following the second overtime punt, the Falcons began at the their 9, and Chandler found Santiago for 15- and 26-yard gains to move into Vikings' territory. A scramble by Chandler and a 9-yard run by Jamal Anderson set up Andersen's winning kick. Chandler was 27 of 43 for 340 yards and 3 touchdowns. Martin had 5 catches for 129 yards. Cunningham was 29 of 48 for 266 yards and 2 touchdowns. This was the first championship game to go to overtime since the 1986 AFC Championship Game.

Atlanta (30)	Offense	Minnesota (27)
Tony Martin	WR	Randy Moss
Bob Whitfield	LT	Todd Steussie
Calvin Collins	LG	Randall McDaniel
Robbie Tobeck	C	Jeff Christy
Gene Williams	RG	David Dixon
Ephraim Salaam	RT	Korey Stringer
O.J. Santiago	TE	Greg DeLong
Terance Mathis	WR	Cris Carter
Chris Chandler	QB	Randall Cunningham
Bob Kozlowski	FB-RB	Robert Smith
Jamal Anderson	RB-TE	Hunter Goodwin
	Defense	
Lester Archambeau	LE	Derrick Alexander
Travis Hall	LT-NT	Jerry Ball
Shane Dronett	RT-UT	Tony Williams
Chuck Smith	RE	John Randle
Cornelius Bennett	WLB	Dwayne Rudd
Jessie Tuggle	MLB	Ed McDaniel
Henri Crockett	SLB	Dixon Edwards
Ray Buchanan	LCB	Corey Fuller
Michael Booker	RCB	Jimmy Hitchcock
William White	SS	Richard Griffith
Eugene Robinson	FS	Orlando Thomas

SUBSTITUTIONS

Atlanta—Offense: C—Bob Hallen, Adam Schreiber. T—Jose Portilla. TE—Ed Smith. WR—Tim Dwight, Ronnie Harris. RB—Gary Downs, Harold Green, Ken Oxendine. P—Dan Stryzinski. K—Morten Andersen. Defense: DT—Esera Tuaolo. DE—John Burrough, Antonio Edwards. LB—Keith Brooking, Ruffin Hamilton, Craig Sauer. DB—Chris Bayne, Ronnie Bradford, Randy Fuller, Elijah Williams. DNP—Steve DeBerg, Ben Talley.

Minnesota—Offense: C—Everett Lindsay, Mike Morris. TE—Andrew Glover. WR—Matthew Hatchette, Chris Walsh. RB—Charles Evans, Leroy Hoard, Harold Morrow, David Palmer. P—Mitch Berger. K—Gary Anderson. Defense: DT—Jason Fisk. DE—Duane Clemons, Stalin Colinet. LB—Pete Bercich, Bobby Houston. DB—Antonio Banks, Anthony Bass, Greg Briggs, Duane Butler, Ramos McDonald. DNP—Matt Birk, Brad Johnson.

OFFICIALS

Referee—Walt Coleman. Umpire—Ron Botchan. Line Judge—Byron Boston. Side Judge—Neeley Dunn. Head Linesman—Mark Baltz. Back Judge—Billy Smith. Field Judge—Bill Lovett.

SCORING

Atlanta	7	7	3	10	3	—	30
Minnesota	7	13	0	7	0	—	27

Atl — J. Anderson 5 pass from Chandler (Andersen kick)
Minn — Moss 31 pass from Cunningham (G. Anderson kick)
Minn — FG G. Anderson 29
Minn — Cunningham 1 run (Anderson kick)
Minn — FG G. Anderson 35
Atl — Mathis 14 pass from Chandler (Andersen kick)
Atl — FG Andersen 27
Minn — Hatchette 5 pass from Cunningham (G. Anderson kick)
Atl — FG Andersen 24
Atl — Mathis 16 pass from Chandler (Andersen kick)
Atl — FG Andersen 38

TEAM STATISTICS	ATL	MINN
Total First Downs	25	26
Rushing	6	4
Passing	17	19
Penalty	2	3
Total Net Yardage	427	356
Total Offensive Plays	75	85
Average Gain Per Offensive Play	5.7	4.2
Rushes	29	34
Yards Gained Rushing (Net)	110	102
Average Yards per Rush	3.8	3.0
Passes Attempted	43	48
Passes Completed	27	29
Had Intercepted	0	0
Tackled Attempting to Pass	3	3
Yards Lost Attempting to Pass	23	12
Yards Gained Passing (Net)	317	254
Punts	4	4
Average Distance	44.8	50.8
Punt Returns	2	0
Punt Return Yardage	35	0
Kickoff Returns	4	3
Kickoff Return Yardage	110	75
Interception Return Yardage	0	0
Total Return Yardage	145	75
Fumbles	2	3
Fumbles Lost	2	2
Own Fumbles Recovered	0	1
Opponent Fumbles Recovered	2	2
Penalties	4	6
Yards Penalized	65	30
Field Goals	3	2
Field Goals Attempted	3	3
Third-Down Efficiency	5/13	9/18
Fourth-Down Efficiency	0/1	0/0
Time of Possession	35:04	36:48

INDIVIDUAL STATISTICS

RUSHING: ATL: J. Anderson 23-67, Dwight 3-28, Chandler 2-15, Oxendine 1-0. MINN: R. Smith 21-71, Cunningham 6-13, Hoard 6-10, Evans 1-8.

PASSING: ATL: Chandler 27-43-340-0. MINN: Cunningham 29-48-266-0.

RECEIVING: ATL: Mathis 6-73, J. Anderson 6-33, Martin 5-129, Santiago 3-54, Kozlowski 3-11, Green 2-9, Harris 1-29, E. Smith 1-2. MINN: Moss 6-75, Carter 6-67, Glover 4-34, Hatchette 4-34, Hoard 3-23, DeLong 2-17, Palmer 2-9, Evans 1-8, R. Smith 1-(-1).

KICKOFF RETURNS: ATL: Dwight 4-10. MINN: Palmer 3-75.

PUNT RETURNS: ATL: Dwight 2-35.

PUNTING: ATL: Stryzinski: 4-179-44.8. MINN: Berger 4-203-50.8

SACKS: ATL: R. Fuller 1, C. Smith 1, Archambeau 1. MINN: Fisk 2, T. Williams 1.

PLAYOFF GAMES SUMMARIES

AFC DIVISIONAL PLAYOFFS RESULTS

Includes Second-Round Playoff Games (1982), AFC Inter-Divisional Games (1969), and special playoff games to break ties for AFL Division Championships (1963, 1968)

Season	Date	Winner (Share)	Loser (Share)	Score	Site	Attendance
1998	Jan. 10	N.Y. Jets ($15,000)	Jacksonville ($15,000)	34-24	East Rutherford	78,817
	Jan. 9	Denver ($15,000)	Miami ($15,000)	38-3	Denver	75,729
1997	Jan. 4	Denver ($15,000)	Kansas City ($15,000)	14-10	Kansas City	76,965
	Jan. 3	Pittsburgh ($15,000)	New England ($15,000)	7-6	Pittsburgh	61,228
1996	Jan. 5	New England ($14,000)	Pittsburgh ($14,000)	28-3	New England	60,188
	Jan. 4	Jacksonville ($14,000)	Denver ($14,000)	30-27	Denver	75,678
1995	Jan. 7	Indianapolis ($13,000)	Kansas City ($13,000)	10-7	Kansas City	77,594
	Jan. 6	Pittsburgh ($13,000)	Buffalo ($13,000)	40-21	Pittsburgh	59,072
1994	Jan. 8	San Diego ($12,000)	Miami ($12,000)	22-21	San Diego	63,381
	Jan. 7	Pittsburgh ($12,000)	Cleveland ($12,000)	29-9	Pittsburgh	58,185
1993	Jan. 16	Kansas City ($12,000)	Houston ($12,000)	28-20	Houston	64,011
	Jan. 15	Buffalo ($12,000)	L.A. Raiders ($12,000)	29-23	Buffalo	61,923
1992	Jan. 10	Miami ($10,000)	San Diego ($10,000)	31-0	Miami	71,224
	Jan. 9	Buffalo ($10,000)	Pittsburgh ($10,000)	24-3	Pittsburgh	60,407
1991	Jan. 5	Buffalo ($10,000)	Kansas City ($10,000)	37-14	Buffalo	80,182
	Jan. 4	Denver ($10,000)	Houston ($10,000)	26-24	Denver	75,301
1990	Jan. 13	L.A. Raiders ($10,000)	Cincinnati ($10,000)	20-10	Los Angeles	92,045
	Jan. 12	Buffalo ($10,000)	Miami ($10,000)	44-34	Buffalo	77,087
1989	Jan. 7	Denver ($10,000)	Pittsburgh ($10,000)	24-23	Denver	75,477
	Jan. 6	Cleveland ($10,000)	Buffalo ($10,000)	34-30	Cleveland	78,921
1988	Jan. 1	Buffalo ($10,000)	Houston ($10,000)	17-10	Buffalo	79,532
	Dec. 31	Cincinnati ($10,000)	Seattle ($10,000)	21-13	Cincinnati	58,560
1987	Jan. 10	Denver ($10,000)	Houston ($10,000)	34-10	Denver	75,440
	Jan. 9	Cleveland ($10,000)	Indianapolis ($10,000)	38-21	Cleveland	79,372
1986	Jan. 4	Denver ($10,000)	New England ($10,000)	22-17	Denver	75,262
	Jan. 3	Cleveland ($10,000)	N.Y. Jets ($10,000)	23-20*	Cleveland	79,720
1985	Jan. 5	New England ($10,000)	L.A. Raiders ($10,000)	27-20	Los Angeles	87,163
	Jan. 4	Miami ($10,000)	Cleveland ($10,000)	24-21	Miami	74,667
1984	Dec. 30	Pittsburgh ($10,000)	Denver ($10,000)	24-17	Denver	74,981
	Dec. 29	Miami ($10,000)	Seattle ($10,000)	31-10	Miami	73,469
1983	Jan. 1	L.A. Raiders ($10,000)	Pittsburgh ($10,000)	38-10	Los Angeles	90,380
	Dec. 31	Seattle ($10,000)	Miami ($10,000)	27-20	Miami	74,136
1982	Jan. 16	Miami ($10,000)	San Diego ($10,000)	34-13	Miami	71,383
	Jan. 15	N.Y. Jets ($10,000)	L.A. Raiders ($10,000)	17-14	Los Angeles	90,038
1981	Jan. 3	Cincinnati ($5,000)	Buffalo ($5,000)	28-21	Cincinnati	55,420
	Jan. 2	San Diego ($5,000)	Miami ($5,000)	41-38*	Miami	73,735
1980	Jan. 4	Oakland ($5,000)	Cleveland ($5,000)	14-12	Cleveland	78,245
	Jan. 3	San Diego ($5,000)	Buffalo ($5,000)	20-14	San Diego	52,253
1979	Dec. 30	Pittsburgh ($5,000)	Miami ($5,000)	34-14	Pittsburgh	50,214
	Dec. 29	Houston ($5,000)	San Diego ($5,000)	17-14	San Diego	51,192
1978	Dec. 31	Houston ($5,000)	New England ($5,000)	31-14	New England	60,735
	Dec. 30	Pittsburgh ($5,000)	Denver ($5,000)	33-10	Pittsburgh	50,230
1977	Dec. 24	Oakland ($5,000)	Baltimore ($5,000)	37-31*	Baltimore	59,925
	Dec. 24	Denver ($5,000)	Pittsburgh ($5,000)	34-21	Denver	75,059
1976	Dec. 19	Pittsburgh [$]	Baltimore [$]	40-14	Baltimore	59,296
	Dec. 18	Oakland [$]	New England [$]	24-21	Oakland	53,050
1975	Dec. 28	Oakland [$]	Cincinnati [$]	31-28	Oakland	53,030
	Dec. 27	Pittsburgh [$]	Baltimore [$]	28-10	Pittsburgh	49,557
1974	Dec. 22	Pittsburgh [$]	Buffalo [$]	32-14	Pittsburgh	49,841
	Dec. 21	Oakland [$]	Miami [$]	28-26	Oakland	53,023
1973	Dec. 23	Miami [$]	Cincinnati [$]	34-16	Miami	78,928
	Dec. 22	Oakland [$]	Pittsburgh [$]	33-14	Oakland	52,646
1972	Dec. 24	Miami [$]	Cleveland [$]	20-14	Miami	78,916
	Dec. 23	Pittsburgh [$]	Oakland [$]	13-7	Pittsburgh	50,327
1971	Dec. 26	Baltimore [$]	Cleveland [$]	20-3	Cleveland	70,734
	Dec. 25	Miami [$]	Kansas City [$]	27-24*	Kansas City	45,822
1970	Dec. 27	Oakland [$]	Miami [$]	21-14	Oakland	52,594
	Dec. 26	Baltimore [$]	Cincinnati [$]	17-0	Baltimore	49,694
1969	Dec. 21	Oakland [$]	Houston [$]	56-7	Oakland	53,539
	Dec. 20	Kansas City [$]	N.Y. Jets [$]	13-6	New York	62,977
1968	Dec. 22	Oakland [$]	Kansas City [$]	41-6	Oakland	53,605
1963	Dec. 28	Boston [$]	Buffalo [$]	26-8	Buffalo	33,044

**Sudden Death Overtime.*

$ Players received 1/14 of annual salary for playoff appearances.

1998 AFC DIVISIONAL PLAYOFF GAMES

Giants Stadium, East Rutherford, New Jersey
January 10, 1999, Attendance: 78,817

N.Y. JETS 34, JACKSONVILLE 24—Keyshawn Johnson caught a touchdown pass, rushed for a touchdown, and intercepted a pass to seal the Jets' first postseason victory since 1986. The Jets needed just seven plays on the game's opening drive to reach the end zone, courtesy of Vinny Testaverde's 21-yard pass to Johnson, to take a 7-0 lead. A 13-play drive set up John Hall's 52-yard field goal to give the Jets a 10-0 lead, and Otis Smith's interception on the Jaguars' first play after the field goal gave the Jets the ball at their 40. Ten plays later, from the Jaguars' 22, Curtis Martin fumbled, and Chris Hudson recovered the ball. Hudson ran into Jets' territory and attempted a lateral, recovered by Johnson at the Jets' 35. The Jets then took 11 plays to march 65 yards, capped by Johnson's 10-yard reverse run to take a 17-0 lead with 33 seconds left in the half. The Jets had run 34 of the last 35 plays from scrimmage. The Jaguars got on the scoreboard, as Jimmy Smith caught Mark Brunell's 52-yard bomb as the half expired. Corwin Brown's interception in the opening minutes of the second half set up Martin's 1-yard touchdown run, but Reggie Barlow's 88-yard kickoff return led to Brunell's 3-yard touchdown pass to Keenan McCardell to cut the deficit to 24-10. Martin scored again on the next drive, but the Jaguars used Brunell's second touchdown pass to Smith to cut the lead to 31-21, and then used Wayne Chrebet's fumble to set up Mike Hollis's 37-yard field goal with 6:38 left. Donovin Darius halted the Jets' next drive with an interception in the end zone, but he stepped out and was tackled at the Jets' 1 with 2:24 left. The Jaguars failed to get a first down, and Hall iced the game with a 30-yard field goal with 24 seconds left. In the final seconds, Brunell's Hail Mary pass was picked off by Johnson, who finished with 9 receptions for 121 yards, with a touchdown, interception, and fumble recovery. Testaverde was 24 of 36 for 284 yards and 1 touchdown, with 1 interception. Martin rushed 36 times for 124 yards, while Johnson had 9 receptions for 121 yards. Brunell was 12 of 31 for 156 yards and 3 touchdowns, with 3 interceptions. Smith had 5 catches for 104 yards.

Jacksonville	0	7	7	10	—	24
N.Y. Jets	7	10	14	3	—	34

NYJ — K. Johnson 21 pass from Testaverde (Hall kick)
NYJ — FG Hall 52
NYJ — K. Johnson 10 run (Hall kick)
Jac — Smith 52 pass from Brunell (Hollis kick)
NYJ — Martin 1 run (Hall kick)
Jac — McCardell 3 pass from Brunell (Hollis kick)
NYJ — Martin 1 run (Hall kick)
Jac — Smith 19 pass from Brunell (Hollis kick)
Jac — FG Hollis 37
NYJ — FG Hall 30

Mile High Stadium, Denver, Colorado
January 9, 1999, Attendance: 75,729

DENVER 38, MIAMI 3—Terrell Davis rushed for 199 yards and 2 touchdowns and the Broncos' defense limited Miami to just 14 rushing yards as Denver began its postseason bid to repeat as Super Bowl champions. The Broncos scored on their first three possessions, driving 92 and 66 yards in the first quarter and, following an Olindo Mare field goal, marching 87 yards to a third touchdown in the second quarter to take a 21-3 lead at halftime. Davis rushed for more yards (129) than the Dolphins had gained (119) at intermission. Davis scampered 62 yards on the first play of the second half to set up Jason Elam's field goal to give Denver a 24-3 lead. The Dolphins drove into Broncos' territory three times in the second half, but Bill Romanowski and Darrius Johnson each recorded interceptions and Neil Smith recovered Oronde Gadsden's fumble and rumbled 79 yards for the game's final points. John Elway was 14 of 23 for 182 yards and 1 touchdown. Dan Marino was 26 of 37 for 243 yards, with 2 interceptions. O.J. McDuffie had 9 receptions for 118 yards.

Miami	0	3	0	0	—	3
Denver	14	7	3	14	—	38

Den — Davis 1 run (Elam kick)
Den — Davis 20 run (Elam kick)
Mia — FG Mare 22
Den — Loville 11 run (Elam kick)
Den — FG Elam 32
Den — R. Smith 28 pass from Elway (Elam kick)
Den — N. Smith 79 fumble return (Elam kick)

NFC DIVISIONAL PLAYOFFS RESULTS

Includes Second-Round Playoff Games (1982), NFL Conference Championship Games (1967-69), and special playoff games to break ties for NFL Division or Conference Championships (1941, 1943, 1947, 1950, 1952, 1957, 1958, 1965)

Season	Date	Winner (Share)	Loser (Share)	Score	Site	Attendance
1998	Jan. 10	Minnesota ($15,000)	Arizona ($15,000)	41-21	Minnesota	63,760
	Jan. 9	Atlanta ($15,000)	San Francisco ($15,000)	20-18	Atlanta	70,262
1997	Jan. 4	Green Bay ($15,000)	Tampa Bay ($15,000)	21-7	Green Bay	60,327
	Jan. 3	San Francisco ($15,000)	Minnesota ($15,000)	38-22	San Francisco	65,018
1996	Jan. 5	Carolina ($14,000)	Dallas ($14,000)	26-17	Carolina	72,808
	Jan. 4	Green Bay ($14,000)	San Francisco ($14,000)	35-14	Green Bay	60,787
1995	Jan. 7	Dallas ($13,000)	Philadelphia ($13,000)	30-11	Dallas	64,371
	Jan. 6	Green Bay ($13,000)	San Francisco ($13,000)	27-17	San Francisco	69,311
1994	Jan. 8	Dallas ($12,000)	Green Bay ($12,000)	35-9	Dallas	64,745
	Jan. 7	San Francisco ($12,000)	Chicago ($12,000)	44-15	San Francisco	64,644
1993	Jan. 16	Dallas ($12,000)	Green Bay ($12,000)	27-17	Dallas	64,790
	Jan. 15	San Francisco ($12,000)	N.Y. Giants ($12,000)	44-3	San Francisco	67,143
1992	Jan. 10	Dallas ($10,000)	Philadelphia ($10,000)	34-10	Dallas	63,721
	Jan. 9	San Francisco ($10,000)	Washington ($10,000)	20-13	San Francisco	64,991
1991	Jan. 5	Detroit ($10,000)	Dallas ($10,000)	38-6	Detroit	78,290
	Jan. 4	Washington ($10,000)	Atlanta ($10,000)	24-7	Washington	55,181
1990	Jan. 13	N.Y. Giants ($10,000)	Chicago ($10,000)	31-3	East Rutherford	77,025
	Jan. 12	San Francisco ($10,000)	Washington ($10,000)	28-10	San Francisco	65,292
1989	Jan. 7	L.A. Rams ($10,000)	N.Y. Giants ($10,000)	19-13*	East Rutherford	76,526
	Jan. 6	San Francisco ($10,000)	Minnesota ($10,000)	41-13	San Francisco	64,918
1988	Jan. 1	San Francisco ($10,000)	Minnesota ($10,000)	34-9	San Francisco	61,848
	Dec. 31	Chicago ($10,000)	Philadelphia ($10,000)	20-12	Chicago	65,534
1987	Jan. 10	Washington ($10,000)	Chicago ($10,000)	21-17	Chicago	65,268
	Jan. 9	Minnesota ($10,000)	San Francisco ($10,000)	36-24	San Francisco	63,008
1986	Jan. 4	N.Y. Giants ($10,000)	San Francisco ($10,000)	49-3	East Rutherford	75,691
	Jan. 3	Washington ($10,000)	Chicago ($10,000)	27-13	Chicago	65,524
1985	Jan. 5	Chicago ($10,000)	N.Y. Giants ($10,000)	21-0	Chicago	65,670
	Jan. 4	L.A. Rams ($10,000)	Dallas ($10,000)	20-0	Anaheim	66,581
1984	Dec. 30	Chicago ($10,000)	Washington ($10,000)	23-19	Washington	55,431
	Dec. 29	San Francisco ($10,000)	N.Y. Giants ($10,000)	21-10	San Francisco	60,303
1983	Jan. 1	Washington ($10,000)	L.A. Rams ($10,000)	51-7	Washington	54,440
	Dec. 31	San Francisco ($10,000)	Detroit ($10,000)	24-23	San Francisco	59,979
1982	Jan. 16	Dallas ($10,000)	Green Bay ($10,000)	37-26	Dallas	63,972
	Jan. 15	Washington ($10,000)	Minnesota ($10,000)	21-7	Washington	54,593
1981	Jan. 3	San Francisco ($5,000)	N.Y. Giants ($5,000)	38-24	San Francisco	58,360
	Jan. 2	Dallas ($5,000)	Tampa Bay ($5,000)	38-0	Dallas	64,848
1980	Jan. 4	Dallas ($5,000)	Atlanta ($5,000)	30-27	Atlanta	59,793
	Jan. 3	Philadelphia ($5,000)	Minnesota ($5,000)	31-16	Philadelphia	70,178
1979	Dec. 30	Los Angeles ($5,000)	Dallas ($5,000)	21-19	Dallas	64,792
	Dec. 29	Tampa Bay ($5,000)	Philadelphia ($5,000)	24-17	Tampa Bay	71,402
1978	Dec. 31	Los Angeles ($5,000)	Minnesota ($5,000)	34-10	Los Angeles	70,436
	Dec. 30	Dallas ($5,000)	Atlanta ($5,000)	27-20	Dallas	63,406
1977	Dec. 26	Dallas ($5,000)	Chicago ($5,000)	37-7	Dallas	63,260
	Dec. 26	Minnesota ($5,000)	Los Angeles ($5,000)	14-7	Los Angeles	70,203
1976	Dec. 19	Los Angeles [$]	Dallas [$]	14-12	Dallas	63,283
	Dec. 18	Minnesota [$]	Washington [$]	35-20	Minnesota	47,466
1975	Dec. 28	Dallas [$]	Minnesota [$]	17-14	Minnesota	48,050
	Dec. 27	Los Angeles [$]	St. Louis [$]	35-23	Los Angeles	73,459
1974	Dec. 22	Los Angeles [$]	Washington [$]	19-10	Los Angeles	77,925
	Dec. 21	Minnesota [$]	St. Louis [$]	30-14	Minnesota	48,150
1973	Dec. 23	Dallas [$]	Los Angeles [$]	27-16	Dallas	63,272
	Dec. 22	Minnesota [$]	Washington [$]	27-20	Minnesota	48,040
1972	Dec. 24	Washington [$]	Green Bay [$]	16-3	Washington	52,321
	Dec. 23	Dallas [$]	San Francisco [$]	30-28	San Francisco	59,746
1971	Dec. 26	San Francisco [$]	Washington [$]	24-20	San Francisco	45,327
	Dec. 25	Dallas [$]	Minnesota [$]	20-12	Minnesota	47,307
1970	Dec. 27	San Francisco [$]	Minnesota [$]	17-14	Minnesota	45,103
	Dec. 26	Dallas [$]	Detroit [$]	5-0	Dallas	69,613
1969	Dec. 28	Cleveland [$]	Dallas [$]	38-14	Dallas	69,321
	Dec. 27	Minnesota [$]	Los Angeles [$]	23-20	Minnesota	47,900

1968	Dec. 22	Baltimore [$]	Minnesota [$]	24-14	Baltimore	60,238
	Dec. 21	Cleveland [$]	Dallas [$]	31-20	Cleveland	81,497
1967	Dec. 24	Dallas [$]	Cleveland [$]	52-14	Dallas	70,786
	Dec. 23	Green Bay [$]	Los Angeles [$]	28-7	Milwaukee	49,861
1965	Dec. 26	Green Bay [$]	Baltimore [$]	13-10*	Green Bay	50,484
1958	Dec. 21	N.Y. Giants (#)	Cleveland (#)	10-0	New York	61,274
1957	Dec. 22	Detroit (#)	San Francisco (#)	31-27	San Francisco	60,118
1952	Dec. 21	Detroit (#)	Los Angeles (#)	31-21	Detroit	47,645
1950	Dec. 17	Los Angeles (#)	Chicago Bears (#)	24-14	Los Angeles	83,501
	Dec. 17	Cleveland (#)	N.Y. Giants (#)	8-3	Cleveland	33,054
1947	Dec. 21	Philadelphia (#)	Pittsburgh (#)	21-0	Pittsburgh	35,729
1943	Dec. 19	Washington (¢)	N.Y. Giants (¢)	28-0	New York	42,800
1941	Dec. 14	Chicago Bears (¢)	Green Bay (¢)	33-14	Chicago	43,425

* *Sudden Death Overtime.*
[$] Players received 1/14 of annual salary for playoff appearances.
 # Players received 1/12 of annual salary for playoff appearances.
¢ Players received 1/10 of annual salary for playoff appearances.

1998 NFC DIVISIONAL PLAYOFF GAMES

Metrodome, Minneapolis, Minnesota
January 10, 1999, Attendance: 63,760

MINNESOTA 41, ARIZONA 21—Randall Cunningham passed for 3 touchdowns, and Leroy Hoard scored 3 times, as the Vikings reached the NFC Championship Game for the first time since 1987. The Vikings consumed nearly half of the first quarter during a 13-play, 80-yard game-opening drive capped by Hoard's 1-yard plunge. After a Cardinals' punt, the Vikings were set to score again, but Aeneas Williams intercepted a pass in the end zone. However, Jake Plummer threw interceptions on consecutive plays, leading to a Vikings' touchdown and a field goal. The Vikings led 17-0 before the Cardinals recorded a first down. The clubs exchanged touchdowns, with Hoard's second coming with just 24 seconds left in the half, as Minnesota took a 24-7 lead into the locker room. The Cardinals used the first 7:35 of the third quarter to drive 80 yards, capped by Mario Bates's second touchdown run. However, David Palmer's 38-yard kickoff return set up Gary Anderson's 20-yard field goal and, after Antonio Banks recovered Plummer's fumble at the Cardinals' 10, Cunningham completed a 2-yard scoring pass to Randy Moss to give Minnesota a 34-14 lead late in the third quarter. Eric Metcalf's 36-yard punt return set up Bates's third touchdown, with 11:45 left, but the Vikings went on a 12-play, 73-yard drive that consumed more than seven minutes and culminated with Hoard's third touchdown with 4:23 left. Cunningham was 17 of 27 for 236 yards and 3 touchdowns, with 1 interception. Robert Smith had 19 carries for 124 yards. Plummer was 23 of 41 for 242 yards, with 2 interceptions.

Arizona	0	7	7	7	— 21
Minnesota	7	17	10	7	— 41

Minn — Hoard 1 run (Anderson kick)
Minn — Glover 15 pass from Cunningham (Anderson kick)
Minn — FG Anderson 34
Ariz — Bates 1 run (Jacke kick)
Minn — Hoard 16 pass from Cunningham (Anderson kick)
Ariz — Bates 1 run (Jacke kick)
Minn — FG Anderson 20
Minn — Moss 2 pass from Cunningham (Anderson kick)
Ariz — Bates 1 run (Jacke kick)
Minn — Hoard 6 run (Anderson kick)

Georgia Dome, Atlanta, Georgia
January 9, 1999, Attendance: 70,262

ATLANTA 20, SAN FRANCISCO 18—Jamal Anderson rushed for 113 yards and 2 touchdowns as the Falcons won just their third playoff game in club history. Tim Dwight's 36-yard punt return midway through the first quarter set up Anderson's first touchdown run, and Anderson carried 4 times for 52 yards on a 7-play, 82-yard second-quarter drive, capped by a 34-yard scamper, to give Atlanta a 14-0 lead. The 49ers scored twice in the final 1:10 of the half, with Steve Young's 34-yard pass to Chuck Levy on third-and-23 setting up Jerry Rice's 17-yard touchdown catch, and Junior Bryant's interception leading to Wade Richey's 36-yard field goal as the half expired. Eugene Robinson stopped a 49ers' drive late in the third quarter by intercepting a pass at the Falcons' 3 and returning it 77 yards, being denied a touchdown by Terry Kirby's tackle. Atlanta settled for Morten Andersen's 29-yard field goal, and Andersen tacked three more points on the board less than six minutes later following William White's interception. The 49ers responded with a 13-play, 87-yard drive, capped by Young's 8-yard run with 2:57 remaining. A high snap on the extra-point attempt prompted holder Ty Detmer to roll out and throw a 2-point conversion pass to Greg Clark to cut the deficit to 20-18. The 49ers' onside kick hopped out of bounds, and San Francisco did not gain possession until getting the ball on their own 4-yard line with 38 seconds left. The 49ers' hopes ended when White intercepted Young at the 49ers' 35 as time expired. Chris Chandler was 13 of 19 for 169 yards, with 1 interception. Young was 23 of 37 for 289 yards and 1 touchdown, with 3 interceptions.

San Francisco	0	10	0	8	— 18
Atlanta	7	7	3	3	— 20

Atl — Anderson 2 run (Andersen kick)
Atl — Anderson 34 run (Andersen kick)
SF — Rice 17 pass from Young (Richey kick)
SF — FG Richey 36
Atl — FG Andersen 29
Atl — FG Andersen 32
SF — Young 8 run (Clark pass from Detmer)

AFC WILD CARD PLAYOFF GAMES RESULTS

Season	Date	Winner (Share)	Loser (Share)	Score	Site	Attendance
1998	Jan. 3	Jacksonville ($15,000)	New England ($10,000)	25-10	Jacksonville	71,139
	Jan. 2	Miami ($10,000)	Buffalo ($10,000)	24-17	Miami	72,698
1997	Dec. 28	New England ($15,000)	Miami ($10,000)	17-3	New England	60,041
	Dec. 27	Denver ($10,000)	Jacksonville ($10,000)	42-17	Denver	74,481
1996	Dec. 29	Pittsburgh ($14,000)	Indianapolis ($10,000)	42-14	Pittsburgh	58,078
	Dec. 28	Jacksonville ($10,000)	Buffalo ($10,000)	30-27	Buffalo	70,213
1995	Dec. 31	Indianapolis ($7,500)	San Diego ($7,500)	35-20	San Diego	61,182
	Dec. 30	Buffalo ($13,000)	Miami ($7,500)	37-22	Buffalo	73,103
1994	Jan. 1	Cleveland ($7,500)	New England ($7,500)	20-13	Cleveland	77,452
	Dec. 31	Miami ($12,000)	Kansas City ($7,500)	27-17	Miami	67,487
1993	Jan. 9	L.A. Raiders ($7,500)	Denver ($7,500)	42-24	Los Angeles	65,314
	Jan. 8	Kansas City ($12,000)	Pittsburgh ($7,500)	27-24*	Kansas City	74,515
1992	Jan. 3	Buffalo ($6,000)	Houston ($6,000)	41-38*	Buffalo	75,141
	Jan. 2	San Diego ($10,000)	Kansas City ($6,000)	17-0	San Diego	58,278
1991	Dec. 29	Houston ($10,000)	N.Y. Jets ($6,000)	17-10	Houston	61,485
	Dec. 28	Kansas City ($6,000)	L.A. Raiders ($6,000)	10-6	Kansas City	75,827
1990	Jan. 6	Cincinnati ($10,000)	Houston ($6,000)	41-14	Cincinnati	60,012
	Jan. 5	Miami ($6,000)	Kansas City ($6,000)	17-16	Miami	67,276
1989	Dec. 31	Pittsburgh ($6,000)	Houston ($6,000)	26-23*	Houston	59,406
1988	Dec. 26	Houston ($6,000)	Cleveland ($6,000)	24-23	Cleveland	75,896
1987	Jan. 3	Houston ($6,000)	Seattle ($6,000)	23-20*	Houston	50,519
1986	Dec. 28	N.Y. Jets ($6,000)	Kansas City ($6,000)	35-15	East Rutherford	75,210
1985	Dec. 28	New England ($6,000)	N.Y. Jets ($6,000)	26-14	East Rutherford	75,945
1984	Dec. 22	Seattle ($6,000)	L.A. Raiders ($6,000)	13-7	Seattle	62,049
1983	Dec. 24	Seattle ($6,000)	Denver ($6,000)	31-7	Seattle	64,275
1982	Jan. 9	N.Y. Jets ($6,000)	Cincinnati ($6,000)	44-17	Cincinnati	57,560
	Jan. 9	San Diego ($6,000)	Pittsburgh ($6,000)	31-28	Pittsburgh	53,546
	Jan. 8	L.A. Raiders ($6,000)	Cleveland ($6,000)	27-10	Los Angeles	56,555
	Jan. 8	Miami ($6,000)	New England ($6,000)	28-13	Miami	68,842
1981	Dec. 27	Buffalo ($3,000)	N.Y. Jets ($3,000)	31-27	New York	57,050

1980	Dec. 28	Oakland ($3,000)	Houston ($3,000)	27-7	Oakland	53,333
1979	Dec. 23	Houston ($3,000)	Denver ($3,000)	13-7	Houston	48,776
1978	Dec. 24	Houston ($3,000)	Miami ($3,000)	17-9	Miami	72,445

*Sudden death overtime.

1998 AFC WILD CARD PLAYOFF GAMES

ALLTEL Stadium, Jacksonville, Florida
January 3, 1999, Attendance: 71,139

JACKSONVILLE 25, NEW ENGLAND 10—Fred Taylor rushed for 162 yards, the most in the postseason by a rookie since Timmy Smith in Super Bowl XXII, and scored a touchdown as the Jaguars reached the divisional playoffs for the second time in the franchise's four seasons. The Jaguars scored on two of their first three possessions, the second keyed by Taylor's 46-yard run, to take a 6-0 lead. Taylor reversed field on a 21-yard gain before sprinting 13 yards for a touchdown in the second quarter to give the Jaguars a 12-0 halftime lead. The Jaguars' defense forced 7 punts in the first half, as Jacksonville had more first downs (12-1) and total yards (199-54). The Patriots retaliated with a 17-play, 85-yard scoring drive that took 8:48 off the clock on their first possession of the second half, capped by Robert Edwards's 1-yard run. Adam Vinatieri's field goal on the next drive cut the deficit to 12-10, but Mark Brunell, who missed the previous three games with an ankle injury, needed just six plays to respond, lofting a 37-yard touchdown pass to a diving Jimmy Smith to give the Jaguars a 19-10 lead with 12:24 remaining in the game. Tony Brackens recovered a fumble and sacked Scott Zolak on fourth down to set up 2 late Mike Hollis field goals as the Patriots never crossed midfield the remainder of the game. Brunell was 14 of 34 for 161 yards and 1 touchdown. Zolak, who started in place of injured Drew Bledsoe, was 21 of 44 for 190 yards, with 1 interception. The Jaguars' defense limited the Patriots to 35 rushing yards on 19 carries.

New England	0	0	7	3	—	10
Jacksonville	6	6	0	13	—	25

Jac — FG Hollis 35
Jac — FG Hollis 24
Jac — Taylor 13 run (run failed)
NE — Edwards 1 run (Vinatieri kick)
NE — FG Vinatieri 27
Jac — Smith 37 pass from Brunell (Hollis kick)
Jac — FG Hollis 34
Jac — FG Hollis 21

Pro Player Stadium, Miami, Florida
January 2, 1999, Attendance: 72,698

MIAMI 24, BUFFALO 17—Trace Armstrong sacked Doug Flutie and forced him to fumble at the Dolphins' 3-yard line with nine seconds left to preserve Miami's first postseason victory in four seasons. Flutie completed a 65-yard pass to Eric Moulds on the game's first play, but Terrell Buckley stripped Moulds and Brock Marion recovered. Olindo Mare kicked field goals to finish each of the Dolphins' first 2 possessions. Following the second score, Mare attempted an onside kick, but Buffalo's Dan Brandenburg recovered the ball. Flutie's 37-yard pass to Moulds set up Thurman Thomas's touchdown run to give Buffalo a 7-6 lead. The Bills drove to the Dolphins' 6 late in the half, but Marion intercepted Flutie's pass in the end zone. Dan Marino's 52-yard Hail Mary pass was caught by Oronde Gadsden at the Bills' 9 with six seconds left, but Mare's 26-yard field-goal attempt hit the right upright as the half expired. Karim Abdul-Jabbar's 3-yard run, and Stanley Pritchett's 2-point conversion jaunt, gave the Dolphins a 14-7 lead with 2:32 left in the quarter. However, Flutie's 23-yard pass to Moulds set up the pair's 32-yard touchdown connection to tie the game in the quarter's final minute. Mare's 23-yard field goal gave the Dolphins a 17-14 lead with 9:45 left, and Jerry Wilson forced Andre Reed to fumble and Buckley recovered at the Dolphins' 44 with 8:02 left. The Dolphins burned 4:20 off the clock and scored on Marino's 11-yard touchdown pass to Lamar Thomas. On the following drive, Buffalo reached the Dolphins' 1, but a personal foul penalty on Reed pushed the Bills back and they settled for Steve Christie's field goal with 1:33 left to cut the deficit to 24-17. Sam Madison bobbled the ensuing onside kick, and Buffalo's Curt Schulz recovered at the Bills' 31. The Bills drove to the Dolphins' 5 with 17 seconds left before Shane Burton recovered the fumble that Armstrong forced. Marino was 23 of 34 for 235 yards and 1 touchdown, with 1 interception. Flutie was 21 of 36 for 360 yards and 1 touchdown, with 1 interception. Moulds, who had 9 catches, set an NFL playoff record with 240 receiving yards.

Buffalo	0	7	7	3	—	17
Miami	3	3	8	10	—	24

Mia — FG Mare 31
Mia — FG Mare 40
Buff — Thomas 1 run (Christie kick)
Mia — Abdul-Jabbar 3 run (Pritchett run)
Buff — Moulds 32 pass from Flutie (Christie kick)
Mia — FG Mare 23
Mia — Thomas 12 pass from Marino (Mare kick)
Buff — FG Christie 33

NFC WILD CARD PLAYOFF GAMES RESULTS

Season	Date	Winner (Share)	Loser (Share)	Score	Site	Attendance
1998	Jan. 3	San Francisco ($10,000)	Green Bay ($10,000)	30-27	San Francisco	66,506
	Jan. 2	Arizona ($10,000)	Dallas ($15,000)	20-7	Dallas	62,969
1997	Dec. 28	Tampa Bay ($10,000)	Detroit ($10,000)	20-10	Tampa Bay	73,361
	Dec. 27	Minnesota ($10,000)	N.Y. Giants ($15,000)	23-22	East Rutherford	77,497
1996	Dec. 29	San Francisco ($10,000)	Philadelphia ($10,000)	14-0	San Francisco	56,460
	Dec. 28	Dallas ($14,000)	Minnesota ($10,000)	40-15	Dallas	64,682
1995	Dec. 31	Green Bay ($13,000)	Atlanta ($7,500)	37-20	Green Bay	60,453
	Dec. 30	Philadelphia ($7,500)	Detroit ($7,500)	58-37	Philadelphia	66,099
1994	Jan. 1	Chicago ($7,500)	Minnesota ($12,000)	35-18	Minnesota	60,347
	Dec. 31	Green Bay ($7,500)	Detroit ($7,500)	16-12	Green Bay	58,125
1993	Jan. 9	N.Y. Giants ($7,500)	Minnesota ($7,500)	17-10	East Rutherford	75,089
	Jan. 8	Green Bay ($7,500)	Detroit ($12,000)	28-24	Detroit	68,479
1992	Jan. 3	Philadelphia ($6,000)	New Orleans ($6,000)	36-20	New Orleans	68,893
	Jan. 2	Washington ($6,000)	Minnesota ($10,000)	24-7	Minnesota	57,353
1991	Dec. 29	Dallas ($6,000)	Chicago ($6,000)	17-13	Chicago	62,594
	Dec. 28	Atlanta ($6,000)	New Orleans ($10,000)	27-20	New Orleans	68,794
1990	Jan. 6	Chicago ($10,000)	New Orleans ($6,000)	16-6	Chicago	60,767
	Jan. 5	Washington ($6,000)	Philadelphia ($6,000)	20-6	Philadelphia	65,287
1989	Dec. 31	L.A. Rams ($6,000)	Philadelphia ($6,000)	21-7	Philadelphia	65,479
1988	Dec. 26	Minnesota ($6,000)	L.A. Rams ($6,000)	28-17	Minnesota	61,204
1987	Jan. 3	Minnesota ($6,000)	New Orleans ($6,000)	44-10	New Orleans	68,546
1986	Dec. 28	Washington ($6,000)	L.A. Rams ($6,000)	19-7	Washington	54,567
1985	Dec. 29	N.Y. Giants ($6,000)	San Francisco ($6,000)	17-3	East Rutherford	75,131
1984	Dec. 23	N.Y. Giants ($6,000)	L.A. Rams ($6,000)	16-3	Anaheim	67,037
1983	Dec. 26	L.A. Rams ($6,000)	Dallas ($6,000)	24-17	Dallas	62,118
1982	Jan. 9	Dallas ($6,000)	Tampa Bay ($6,000)	30-17	Dallas	65,042
	Jan. 9	Minnesota ($6,000)	Atlanta ($6,000)	30-24	Minnesota	60,560
	Jan. 8	Green Bay ($6,000)	St. Louis ($6,000)	41-16	Green Bay	54,282
	Jan. 8	Washington ($6,000)	Detroit ($6,000)	31-7	Washington	55,045
1981	Dec. 27	N.Y. Giants ($3,000)	Philadelphia ($3,000)	27-21	Philadelphia	71,611
1980	Dec. 28	Dallas ($3,000)	Los Angeles ($3,000)	34-13	Dallas	63,052
1979	Dec. 23	Philadelphia ($3,000)	Chicago ($3,000)	27-17	Philadelphia	69,397
1978	Dec. 24	Atlanta ($3,000)	Philadelphia ($3,000)	14-13	Atlanta	59,403

1998 NFC WILD CARD PLAYOFF GAMES

3COM Park, San Francisco, California
January 3, 1999, Attendance: 66,506

SAN FRANCISCO 30, GREEN BAY 27—With eight seconds left and no timeouts remaining, Steve Young fired a 25-yard strike to Terrell Owens to give the 49ers a victory against the Packers in stunning fashion. Darren Sharper forced Owens to fumble at the Packers' 47 on the game's third play. Pat Terrell recovered the ball, leading to Ryan Longwell's first field goal. Merton Hanks forced Dorsey Levens to fumble later in the quarter, and Chris Doleman recovered. Greg Clark caught a touchdown pass from Steve Young three plays later to give the 49ers a 7-3 lead. Brett Favre threw a 2-yard touchdown pass to Antonio Freeman on the next drive, but R.W. McQuarter's 19-yard punt return set up Wade Richey's tying field goal midway through the second quarter. Randy Kirk recovered Roell Preston's muffed punt at the 49ers' 18, but George Koonce intercepted Young's pass two plays later and the Packers proceeded to drive 83 yards to take a 17-10 lead on Levens's touchdown run. Recently signed free-agent Charles Haley pressured Favre into throwing an early second-half interception, which Lee Woodall returned 17 yards to the Packers' 33. From there, Young tossed his second touchdown pass of the game to Clark to tie the score. Three field goals on successive possessions, 2 by Richey and 1 by Longwell, gave the 49ers a 23-20 lead with 6:12 to play. Darnell Walker intercepted Favre at the Packers' 43, but the 49ers were forced to punt giving Green Bay the ball at their own 11 with 4:19 remaining. Favre completed a 47-yard pass to Corey Bradford, and a few plays later lofted a 15-yard scoring pass to Freeman to give the Packers a 27-23 lead with 1:56 to play. The 49ers drove to the Packers' 25 with eight seconds left and no timeouts, when Young fired a 25-yard strike to Owens, who was belted by Terrell and Sharper but held on for the winning points. Young, who completed 7 of 9 passes on the game-winning 76-yard drive, was 18 of 32 for 182 yards and 3 touchdowns, with 2 interceptions. Garrison Hearst had 22 carries for 128 yards. Favre was 20 of 35 for 292 yards and 2 touchdowns, with 2 interceptions. Levens had 27 carries for 116 yards.

Green Bay	3	14	0	10	—	27
San Francisco	7	3	10	10	—	30

GB — FG Longwell 23
SF — Clark 1 pass from Young (Richey kick)
GB — Freeman 2 pass from Favre (Longwell kick)
SF — FG Richey 34
GB — Levens 2 run (Longwell kick)
SF — Clark 8 pass from Young (Richey kick)
SF — FG Richey 48
GB — FG Longwell 37
SF — FG Richey 40
GB — Freeman 15 pass from Favre (Longwell kick)
SF — Owens 25 pass from Young (Richey kick)

Texas Stadium, Dallas, Texas
January 2, 1999, Attendance: 62,969

ARIZONA 20, DALLAS 7—Jake Plummer passed for 2 touchdowns and Aeneas Williams had 2 interceptions as the Cardinals won a postseason game for the first time since 1947. Richie Cunningham missed a 36-yard field goal in the latter part of the first quarter, and Plummer immediately seized the opportunity, firing a 59-yard pass to Frank Sanders. Three plays later, Plummer flipped a shovel pass to Adrian Murrell, who scooted into the end zone to give Arizona a 7-0 lead. The Cowboys drove deep into Cardinals' territory, but Mark Maddox stopped Emmitt Smith on fourth-and-1 at the Cardinals' 7. Chris Jacke kicked a field goal 19 seconds before halftime, and Murrell raced 74 yards on the second play of the second half, setting up Plummer's 3-yard toss to Larry Centers to give the Cardinals a 17-0 lead 1:16 into the third quarter. Williams's second interception at the Cowboys' 37 set up Jacke's second field goal 2:05 into the final quarter. The Cardinals' defense twice stopped Dallas on fourth-down attempts before Troy Aikman's 6-yard pass to Billy Davis averted the shutout with 3:33 remaining. Larry Centers recovered the ensuing onsides kick, and Tommy Bennett intercepted a pass from Aikman with 48 seconds remaining to secure the victory. Plummer was 19 of 36 for 213 yards, 2 touchdowns, with 2 interceptions. Aikman was 22 of 49 for 191 yards, 1 touchdown, with 3 interceptions.

Arizona	7	3	7	3	—	20
Dallas	0	0	0	7	—	7

Ariz — Murrell 12 pass from Plummer (Jacke kick)
Ariz — FG Jacke 37
Ariz — Centers 3 pass from Plummer (Jacke kick)
Ariz — FG Jacke 46
Dall — Davis 6 pass from Aikman (Cunningham kick)

AFC-NFC PRO BOWL AT A GLANCE RESULTS (1971-1999)

NFC leads series, 15-14

Year	Date	Winner (Share)	Loser (Share)	Score	Site	Attendance
1999	Feb. 7	AFC ($25,000)	NFC ($12,500)	23-10	Honolulu	50,075
1998	Feb. 1	AFC ($25,000)	NFC ($12,500)	29-24	Honolulu	49,995
1997	Feb. 2	AFC ($20,000)	NFC ($10,000)	26-23 (OT)	Honolulu	50,031
1996	Feb. 4	NFC ($20,000)	AFC ($10,000)	20-13	Honolulu	50,034
1995	Feb. 5	AFC ($20,000)	NFC ($10,000)	41-13	Honolulu	49,121
1994	Feb. 6	NFC ($20,000)	AFC ($10,000)	17-3	Honolulu	50,026
1993	Feb. 7	AFC ($10,000)	NFC ($5,000)	23-20 (OT)	Honolulu	50,007
1992	Feb. 2	NFC ($10,000)	AFC ($5,000)	21-15	Honolulu	50,209
1991	Feb. 3	AFC ($10,000)	NFC ($5,000)	23-21	Honolulu	50,345
1990	Feb. 4	NFC ($10,000)	AFC ($5,000)	27-21	Honolulu	50,445
1989	Jan. 29	NFC ($10,000)	AFC ($5,000)	34-3	Honolulu	50,113
1988	Feb. 7	AFC ($10,000)	NFC ($5,000)	15-6	Honolulu	50,113
1987	Feb. 1	AFC ($10,000)	NFC ($5,000)	10-6	Honolulu	50,101
1986	Feb. 2	NFC ($10,000)	AFC ($5,000)	28-24	Honolulu	50,101
1985	Jan. 27	AFC ($10,000)	NFC ($5,000)	22-14	Honolulu	50,385
1984	Jan. 29	NFC ($10,000)	AFC ($5,000)	45-3	Honolulu	50,445
1983	Feb. 6	NFC ($10,000)	AFC ($5,000)	20-19	Honolulu	49,883
1982	Jan. 31	AFC ($5,000)	NFC ($2,500)	16-13	Honolulu	50,402
1981	Feb. 1	NFC ($5,000)	AFC ($2,500)	21-7	Honolulu	50,360
1980	Jan. 27	NFC ($5,000)	AFC ($2,500)	37-27	Honolulu	49,800
1979	Jan. 29	NFC ($5,000)	AFC ($2,500)	13-7	Los Angeles	46,281
1978	Jan. 23	NFC ($5,000)	AFC ($2,500)	14-13	Tampa	51,337
1977	Jan. 17	AFC ($2,000)	NFC ($1,500)	24-14	Seattle	64,752
1976	Jan. 26	NFC ($2,000)	AFC ($1,500)	23-20	New Orleans	30,546
1975	Jan. 20	NFC ($2,000)	AFC ($1,500)	17-10	Miami	26,484
1974	Jan. 20	AFC ($2,000)	NFC ($1,500)	15-13	Kansas City	66,918
1973	Jan. 21	AFC ($2,000)	NFC ($1,500)	33-28	Dallas	37,091
1972	Jan. 23	AFC ($2,000)	NFC ($1,500)	26-13	Los Angeles	53,647
1971	Jan. 24	NFC ($2,000)	AFC ($1,500)	27-6	Los Angeles	48,222

1999 AFC-NFC PRO BOWL

Aloha Stadium, Honolulu, Hawaii
February 7, 1999, Attendance: 50,075

AFC 23, NFC 10—John Elway, appearing in uniform on a football field for the final time, drove the AFC to its initial touchdown and then watched a strong defensive effort as the AFC won the Pro Bowl for the third consecutive season. Elway capped a game-opening 61-yard drive with a touchdown pass to Sam Gash. The AFC led 10-3 late in the first half when Deion Sanders intercepted a Vinny Testaverde pass at the NFC's 10 and raced downfield, only to be caught by Ed McCaffrey at the AFC 3-yard line as the half expired. The NFC drove into AFC territory early in the second half, but Ty Law thwarted the NFC's spirits with a 67-yard interception return for a touchdown to give the AFC a 17-3 lead with 9:42 left in the third quarter. The NFC reached the end zone three minutes later as Emmitt Smith scored, but the AFC responded with a field goal on its ensuing possession. Jason Elam's third field goal with 1:02 remaining finished the scoring. Elway played just one drive and was 4 of 5 for 55 yards and 1 touchdown. Keyshawn Johnson had 7 catches for 87 yards and shared player-of-the-game honors with Law. Chandler completed 9 of 25 passes for 133 yards en route to leading the NFC to its only touchdown. Randy Moss had 7 catches for 108 yards.

AFC (23)	Offense	NFC (10)
Jimmy Smith (Jacksonville)	WR	Randy Moss (Minnesota)
Tony Boselli (Jacksonville)	LT	Larry Allen (Dallas)
Ruben Brown (Buffalo)	LG	Randall McDaniel (Minnesota)
Dermontti Dawson (Pittsburgh)	C	Jeff Christy (Minnesota)
Will Shields (Kansas City)	RG	Kevin Gogan (San Francisco)
Jonathan Ogden (Baltimore)	RT	Todd Steussie (Minnesota)
Ben Coates (New England)	TE	Mark Chmura (Green Bay)
Ed McCaffrey (Denver)	WR	Antonio Freeman (Green Bay)
John Elway (Denver)	QB	Steve Young (San Francisco)
Sam Gash (Buffalo)	RB	Mike Alstott (Tampa Bay)
Marshall Faulk (Indianapolis)	RB	Jamal Anderson (Atlanta)
	Defense	
Michael McCrary (Baltimore)	LE	Reggie White (Green Bay)
Darrell Russell (Oakland)	IL	John Randle (Minnesota)
Ted Washington (Buffalo)	IL	Warren Sapp (Tampa Bay)
Bruce Smith (Buffalo)	RE	Michael Strahan (N.Y. Giants)
Chad Brown (Seattle)	LOLB	Derrick Brooks (Tampa Bay)
Junior Seau (San Diego)	ILB	Jessie Tuggle (Atlanta)
Mo Lewis (N.Y. Jets)	ROLB	Kevin Greene (Carolina)
Ty Law (New England)	LCB	Deion Sanders (Dallas)
Shawn Springs (Seattle)	RCB	Ray Buchanan (Atlanta)
Rodney Harrison (San Diego)	SS	LeRoy Butler (Green Bay)
Steve Atwater (Denver)	FS	Eugene Robinson (Atlanta)

SUBSTITUTIONS

AFC—Offense: G—Mark Schlereth (Denver). T—Tony Jones (Denver). C—Tom Nalen (Denver). TE—Frank Wycheck (Tennessee). WR—Keyshawn Johnson (N.Y. Jets), Jermaine Lewis (Baltimore), Eric Moulds (Buffalo). RB—Eddie George (Tennessee), Curtis Martin (N.Y. Jets). QB—Doug Flutie (Buffalo), Vinny Testaverde (N.Y. Jets). P—Craig Hentrich (Tennessee). K—Jason Elam (Denver). Defense: IL—Cortez Kennedy (Seattle). DE—Michael Sinclair (Seattle). LB—Peter Boulware (Baltimore), Ray Lewis (Baltimore), Bill Romanowski (Denver). DB—Lawyer Milloy (New England), Bennie Thompson (Baltimore), Charles Woodson (Oakland).

NFC—Offense: G—Nate Newton (Dallas). T—Bob Whitfield (Atlanta). C—Tony Mayberry (Tampa Bay). TE—Wesley Walls (Carolina). WR—Michael Bates (Carolina), Cris Carter (Minnesota), Roell Preston (Green Bay), Jerry Rice (San Francisco). RB—Emmitt Smith (Dallas), Robert Smith (Minnesota). QB—Chris Chandler (Atlanta), Randall Cunningham (Minnesota). P—Matt Turk (Washington). K—Gary Anderson (Minnesota). Defense: IL—Leon Lett (Dallas). DE—Joe Johnson (New Orleans). LB—Jessie Armstead (N.Y. Giants), Hardy Nickerson (Tampa Bay), Winfred Tubbs (San Francisco). DB—Aeneas Williams (Arizona), Darren Woodson (Dallas).

HEAD COACHES

AFC—Bill Belichick (N.Y. Jets assistant head coach)*
NFC—Dennis Green (Minnesota)
**N.Y. Jets head coach Bill Parcells was excused for medical reasons.*

OFFICIALS

Referee—Dick Hantak. Umpire—Carl Madsen. Side Judge—Tommy Moore. Linesman—John Schleyer. Back Judge—Bob Lawing. Field Judge—Lloyd McPeters. Line Judge—Dale Orem.

SCORING

NFC	3	0	7	0	—	10
AFC	7	3	10	3	—	23

AFC — Gash 3 pass from Elway (Elam kick)
NFC — FG Anderson 23
AFC — FG Elam 23
AFC — Law 67 interception return (Elam kick)
NFC — E. Smith 3 run (Anderson kick)
AFC — FG Elam 46
AFC — FG Elam 26

TEAM STATISTICS	NFC	AFC
Total First Downs	17	19
Rushing	4	7
Passing	10	11
Penalty	3	1
Total Net Yardage	278	330
Total Offensive Plays	67	68
Average Gain Per Offensive Play	4.1	4.9
Rushes	18	33
Yards Gained Rushing (Net)	55	108
Average Yards per Rush	3.1	3.3
Passes Attempted	46	35
Passes Completed	19	18
Had Intercepted	3	3
Tackled Attempting to Pass	3	0
Yards Lost Attempting to Pass	16	0
Yards Gained Passing (Net)	223	222
Punts	4	4
Average Distance	52.0	47.8

Punt Returns	4	3
Punt Return Yardage	32	20
Kickoff Returns	5	3
Kickoff Return Yardage	100	40
Interception Return Yardage	102	70
Total Return Yardage	234	130
Fumbles	2	1
Fumbles Lost	0	1
Own Fumbles Recovered	2	0
Opponent Fumbles Recovered	1	0
Penalties	5	10
Yards Penalized	28	80
Field Goals	1	3
Field Goals Attempted	1	3
Third-Down Efficiency	4/16	5/14
Fourth-Down Efficiency	1/5	0/0
Time of Possession	27:52	32:08

INDIVIDUAL STATISTICS

RUSHING: NFC: J. Anderson 4-21-0; E. Smith 8-19-1; Alstott 3-10-0; R. Smith 2-7-0; Chandler 1-0-0. AFC: George 12-33-0; Faulk 7-33-0; Martin 8-29-0; Gash 3-14-0; J. Lewis 1-1-0; Flutie 2-(-2)-0.

PASSING: NFC: Chandler 25-9-133-0-1; Cunningham 8-5-71-0-2; Young 12-5-35-0-0; Turk 1-0-0-0-0. AFC: Testaverde 16-10-87-0-3; Flutie 14-4-80-0-0; Elway 5-4-55-1-0.

RECEIVING: NFC: Moss 7-108-0; Rice 5-60-0; Alstott 3-31-0; Bates 1-18-0; Carter 2-16-0; Walls 1-6-0. AFC: Johnson 7-87-0; Moulds 1-39-0; Coates 1-36-0; George 1-23-0; McCaffrey 1-17-0; Faulk 3-12-0; Gash 3-8-1; Martin 1-0-0.

KICKOFF RETURNS: NFC: Preston 4-86, Bates 1-14. AFC: J. Lewis is 3-40.

PUNT RETURNS: NFC: Preston 1-11, Sanders 1-11, Moss 1-10. AFC: J. Lewis 2-9, Woodson 1-11.

PUNTING: NFC: Turk 4-208-52.0. AFC: Hentrich 4-191-47.8.

SACKS: AFC: McCrary 2, Russell 1.

1998 AFC-NFC PRO BOWL

Aloha Stadium, Honolulu, Hawaii
February 1, 1998, Attendance: 49,995

AFC 29, NFC 24—Warren Moon guided the AFC to points on all three of his drives, including the winning touchdown from 1 yard with 1:49 left as the AFC scored the game's final 15 points to beat the NFC. Steve Young threw a 22-yard touchdown pass to Herman Moore to cap the game's opening drive and give the NFC a 7-0 lead. Late in the first quarter, Mark Brunell threw a 17-yard touchdown pass to Andre Rison to tie the game. Both touchdown passes came on third-and-8 plays. The NFC responded with a 7-play, 71-yard drive capped by Young's 36-yard touchdown pass to Rob Moore. Trent Dilfer guided the NFC to its third touchdown, keyed by a 21-yard pass to Irving Fryar and 23-yard pass to Mike Alstott, and capped by Dorsey Levens's 12-yard touchdown run with 1:36 left in the half to give the NFC a 21-7 lead. The NFC had a chance to pad its lead on its first possession of the second half, but Jason Hanson missed a 44-yard field goal. The AFC bounced back with a 10-play, 65-yard drive that culminated with Drew Bledsoe's 14-yard touchdown pass to Jimmy Smith late in the third quarter. After Hanson's 35-yard field goal gave the NFC a 24-14 lead with 13:42 left, Moon entered the game and drove the AFC into field-goal range, where Mike Hollis drilled a 48-yard attempt with 8:51 left. Attempting to grind out the clock, Warrick Dunn fumbled, and Darryl Williams recovered at the AFC's 49 with 3:03 remaining. After a holding penalty moved the AFC back 10 yards, Moon fired a 57-yard pass to Tim Brown to set up Eddie George's 4-yard run with 2:31 left. The AFC went for the lead instead of a tie, but Moon's pass to Rison fell incomplete. However, the AFC got the ball back when Chris Chandler fumbled the snap on the NFC's first play, and Michael Sinclair recovered at the NFC's 16 with 2:19 left. Three runs by George set up Moon's winning sneak with 1:49 remaining. Moon's 2-point conversion pass to Brown was incomplete, keeping the AFC's lead at 29-24. The NFC was unable to move beyond its own 31-yard line in the final moments, and the AFC prevailed. Tim Brown had 5 receptions for 129 yards. Moon, who was 4 of 8 for 89 yards, earned player of the game honors.

AFC	7	0	7	15	—	29
NFC	7	14	0	3	—	24

NFC —H. Moore 22 pass from Young (Hanson kick)
AFC —Rison 17 pass from Brunell (Hollis kick)
NFC —R. Moore 36 pass from Young (Hanson kick)
NFC —Levens 12 run (Hanson kick)
AFC —J. Smith 14 pass from Bledsoe (Hollis kick)
NFC —FG Hanson 35
AFC —FG Hollis 48
AFC —George 4 run (pass failed)
AFC —Moon 1 run (pass failed)

1997 AFC-NFC PRO BOWL

Aloha Stadium, Honolulu, Hawaii
February 2, 1997, Attendance: 50,031

AFC 26, NFC 23 (OT)—Cary Blanchard's 37-yard field goal 8:16 into overtime gave the AFC a 26-23 victory. The field goal was an ironic ending to a game that saw Blanchard and NFC kicker John Kasay, who each broke the previous single-season record of 35 field goals, combine to miss 5 of 8 field-goal attempts. The NFC scored on its first two possessions, with Vikings guard Randall McDaniel, who lined up as a fullback, scoring his first professional touchdown to give the NFC a 9-0 lead. However, the follies of the kicking unit began as holder Matt Turk muffed the snap on the extra point attempt. Blanchard booted a 28-yard field goal with 27 seconds left in the half to cut the NFC's lead to 9-3. In the third quarter, Barry Sanders scored from 6 yards out, but Kerry Collins was sacked on the 2-point attempt. A 41-yard pass from Drew Bledsoe to Tony Martin led to Curtis Martin's 3-yard run, and after Ashley Ambrose ran an interception back 54 yards for a touchdown 11 seconds into the fourth quarter, the AFC found itself with a 16-15 lead. The NFC drove for more than six minutes, only to have Kasay miss a 40-yard field goal attempt. After an AFC punt, Cris Carter caught a 47-yard touchdown bomb from Gus Frerotte to put the NFC ahead 23-16. After each team punted, the AFC got the ball on its own 20-yard line with 55 seconds left. Mark Brunell hit Tim Brown with an 80-yard bomb down the right sideline to tie the game with 44 seconds left. Wesley Walls caught a 33-yard pass to give the NFC a chance to win in regulation, but Kasay missed a 39-yard attempt and the game went to overtime. The AFC won the overtime toss, but Blanchard missed a 41-yard field goal attempt. The NFC had to punt after three plays, and Brunell hit Ben Coates with a 43-yard pass on the AFC's first play. After three running plays failed to gain a first down, Blanchard trotted onto the field and made the game-winning kick. The teams combined for a Pro Bowl record 962 total yards. Brunell, who completed 12 of 22 pass attempts for 236 yards, was selected as the player of the game.

AFC	0	3	7	13	3	— 26
NFC	9	0	6	8	0	— 23

NFC — FG Kasay 20
NFC — R. McDaniel 5 pass from Favre (muffed snap)
AFC — FG Blanchard 28
NFC — Sanders 6 run (pass failed)
AFC — Martin 3 run (Blanchard kick)
AFC — Ambrose 54 interception return (pass failed)
NFC — Carter 53 pass from Frerotte (Walls pass from Frerotte)
AFC — T. Brown 80 pass from Brunell (Blanchard kick)
AFC — FG Blanchard 37

1996 AFC-NFC PRO BOWL

Aloha Stadium, Honolulu, Hawaii
February 4, 1996, Attendance: 50,034

NFC 20, AFC 13—Jerry Rice had 6 receptions for 82 yards and 1 touchdown to earn player of the game honors in the NFC's victory. The 49ers' wide receiver, who was named to the Pro Bowl for the tenth consecutive year, caught a 1-yard touchdown pass from Packers quarterback Brett Favre 1:41 into the second quarter to cap an 80-yard drive and give the NFC the lead for good at 10-7. The AFC had taken a 7-0 lead 2:26 into the game when Bengals quarterback Jeff Blake connected with Steelers wide receiver Yancey Thigpen on a Pro Bowl-record 93-yard touchdown pass. The NFC increased its advantage to 20-7 at halftime on Redskins linebacker Ken Harvey's 36-yard interception return for a touchdown and Falcons kicker Morten Andersen's 24-yard field goal. The AFC trimmed its deficit to 20-13 when Colts quarterback Jim Harbaugh teamed with Patriots running back Curtis Martin on a 17-yard touchdown pass in the final minute of the third quarter, but its bid to win or tie was rebuffed twice in the final minutes of the fourth quarter. First, 49ers safety Tim McDonald intercepted Harbaugh's pass in the end zone with 1:50 remaining. Then, after the AFC forced a punt and got the ball back near midfield, Harbaugh drove his team to the NFC's 9-yard line in the closing seconds. But he spiked the ball once to stop the clock and threw 3 consecutive incompletions as time ran out. The AFC outgained the NFC 390 total yards to 287, but its quarterbacks suffered 4 interceptions, including 3 off Harbaugh, the NFL's leading passer during the regular season. The NFC raised its edge to 15-11 in Pro Bowl games since the AFL-NFL merger in 1970.

NFC	3	17	0	0	—	20
AFC	7	0	6	0	—	13

AFC — Thigpen 93 pass from Blake (Elam kick)
NFC — FG Andersen 36
NFC — Rice 1 pass from Favre (Andersen kick)
NFC — Harvey 36 interception return (Andersen kick)
NFC — FG Andersen 24
AFC — Martin 17 pass from Harbaugh (kick failed)

1995 AFC-NFC PRO BOWL

Aloha Stadium, Honolulu, Hawaii
February 5, 1995, Attendance: 49,121

AFC 41, NFC 13—Colts rookie Marshall Faulk rushed for a Pro Bowl-record 180 yards to key the AFC's rout of the NFC. Faulk, who earned the Dan McGuire Trophy as the player of the game, averaged nearly 14 yards on his 13 carries and shattered the previous rushing mark of 112 yards set by O.J. Simpson in the 1973 game. Faulk's 49-yard touchdown run from punt formation in the fourth quarter was the longest in Pro Bowl history. The Seahawks' Chris Warren added 127 yards on 14 carries as the AFC amassed records for rushing yards (400) and total yards (552). Steelers tight end Eric Green caught 2 touchdown passes for the victors. The NFC managed only 196 total yards, a large chunk coming when 49ers quarterback Steve Young and Vikings wide receiver Cris Carter teamed on a 51-yard touchdown pass in the first quarter. That gave the NFC a 10-0 advantage, but the AFC rallied in the second quarter and took the lead for good when the Browns' Leroy Hoard scored on a 4-yard touchdown run 2:07 before halftime.

AFC	0	17	3	21	—	41
NFC	10	0	3	0	—	13

NFC — FG Reveiz 28
NFC — Carter 51 pass from Young (Reveiz kick)
AFC — Green 22 pass from Elway (Carney kick)
AFC — FG Carney 22
AFC — Hoard 4 run (Carney kick)
NFC — FG Reveiz 49
AFC — FG Carney 23
AFC — Warren 11 run (Carney kick)
AFC — Green 16 pass from Hostetler (Carney kick)
AFC — Faulk 49 run (Carney kick)

1994 AFC-NFC PRO BOWL

Aloha Stadium, Honolulu, Hawaii
February 6, 1994, Attendance: 50,026

NFC 17, AFC 3—The NFC converted a blocked punt and a fumble recovery into touchdowns just 2:20 apart in the second half of its victory over the AFC. With the score tied 3-3 late in the third quarter, Saints linebacker Renaldo Turnbull deflected a punt by the Oilers' Greg Montgomery, and the NFC took possession at the AFC's 48-yard line. A 32-yard pass from Bobby Hebert to Falcons teammate Andre Rison positioned Rams running back Jerome Bettis for a 4-yard touchdown run with 1:27 left in the third quarter. Moments later, Rams defensive tackle Sean

Gilbert recovered a fumble by Oilers quarterback Warren Moon at the AFC's 19. Hebert then teamed with the Vikings' Cris Carter on a 15-yard touchdown pass 53 seconds into the fourth period. The NFC kept the AFC out of the end zone by maintaining possession for more than 38 minutes and forcing 6 turnovers. Rison earned the Dan McGuire Trophy as the player of the game by catching 6 passes for 86 yards. The victory was the fourth in the last six years for the NFC, which leads the series 14-10.

NFC	3	0	7	7	—	17
AFC	0	3	0	0	—	3

NFC — FG Johnson 35
AFC — FG Anderson 25
NFC — Bettis 4 run (Johnson kick)
NFC — Carter 15 pass from Hebert (Johnson kick)

1993 AFC-NFC PRO BOWL

Aloha Stadium, Honolulu, Hawaii
February 7, 1993, Attendance: 50,007

AFC 23, NFC 20—Nick Lowery's 33-yard field goal 4:09 into overtime gave the American Conference all-stars an unlikely 23-20 victory over the National Conference. Despite being overwhelmed by the NFC in first downs (30-9), and total yards (471-114), the AFC won because it forced 6 turnovers, blocked a pair of field goals (1 of which was returned for a touchdown), and returned an interception for a score. Special-teams star Steve Tasker of the Bills earned the Dan McGuire Trophy as the player of the game for making 4 tackles, forcing a fumble, and blocking a field goal. The block came with eight minutes left in regulation and the game tied at 13-13. The Raiders' Terry McDaniel picked up the loose ball and ran 28 yards for a touchdown and a 20-13 AFC lead. The NFC rallied behind 49ers quarterback Steve Young, whose fourth-down, 23-yard touchdown pass to Giants running back Rodney Hampton tied the game at 20-20 with 10 seconds left in regulation. Young completed 18 of 32 passes for 196 yards but was intercepted 3 times and lost a fumble when sacked in overtime. Raiders defensive end Howie Long fell on that fumble at the NFC 28-yard line, and five plays later, Lowery converted the winning field goal.

AFC	0	10	3	7	3	— 23
NFC	3	10	0	7	0	— 20

NFC — FG Andersen 27
AFC — Seau 31 interception return (Lowery kick)
NFC — FG Andersen 37
NFC — Irvin 9 pass from Aikman (Andersen kick)
AFC — FG Lowery 42
AFC — FG Lowery 29
AFC — McDaniel 28 blocked field goal return (Lowery kick)
NFC — Hampton 23 pass from Young (Andersen kick)
AFC — FG Lowery 33

1992 AFC-NFC PRO BOWL

Aloha Stadium, Honolulu, Hawaii
February 2, 1992, Attendance: 50,209

NFC 21, AFC 15—Atlanta's Chris Miller threw an 11-yard touchdown pass to San Francisco's Jerry Rice with 4:04 remaining in the game to lift the NFC over the AFC. It was the NFC's thirteenth win in the 22-game series. The AFC had taken a 15-14 lead when the Raiders' Jeff Jaeger kicked a 27-yard field goal 1:49 into the fourth quarter. But the NFC, aided by a key roughing-the-passer penalty on a third-down incompletion from the AFC 24-yard line, drove 85 yards to the winning score. The Cowboys' Michael Irvin, playing in his first Pro Bowl, caught 8 passes for 125 yards, including a 13-yard touchdown in the first quarter, and was named the player of the game. Rice had 7 catches for 77 yards. Mark Rypien of Washington, the Super Bowl most valuable player one week earlier, completed 11 of 18 passes for 165 yards and 2 touchdowns for the NFC, including a 35-yard pass to Redskins teammate Gary Clark just 26 seconds before halftime. Miller completed 7 of his 10 attempts for 85 yards.

NFC	7	7	0	7	—	21
AFC	7	5	0	3	—	15

AFC — Clayton 4 pass from Kelly (Jaeger kick)
NFC — Irvin 13 pass from Rypien (Lohmiller kick)
AFC — Safety, Townsend tackled Byner in end zone
AFC — FG Jaeger 48
NFC — Clark 35 pass from Rypien (Lohmiller kick)
AFC — FG Jaeger 27
NFC — Rice 11 pass from Miller (Lohmiller kick)

1991 AFC-NFC PRO BOWL

Aloha Stadium, Honolulu, Hawaii
February 3, 1991, Attendance: 50,345

AFC 23, NFC 21—Buffalo's Jim Kelly and Houston's Ernest Givins combined for a 13-yard scoring pass late in the fourth quarter to rally the AFC over the NFC. Phoenix rookie Johnny Johnson scored on runs of 1 and 9 yards to put the NFC ahead 14-3 in the third quarter. Buffalo's Andre Reed, who led all receivers with 4 catches for 80 yards, caught a 20-yard scoring reception from Kelly early in the fourth quarter to move the AFC to within 1 point. Barry Sanders ran 22 yards for a touchdown to increase the NFC's lead to 21-13. Miami's Jeff Cross blocked a 46-yard field-goal attempt by New Orleans's Morten Andersen with seven seconds remaining to preserve the win. Buffalo's Bruce Smith recorded 3 sacks and also had a blocked field goal. Kelly, who completed 13 of 19 passes for 210 yards and 2 touchdowns, was presented the Dan McGuire Award as player of the game. The AFC's victory narrowed the NFC's Pro Bowl series lead to 12-9.

AFC	3	0	3	17	—	23
NFC	0	7	7	7	—	21

AFC — FG Lowery 26
NFC — J. Johnson 1 run (Andersen kick)
AFC — FG Lowery 43
NFC — J. Johnson 9 run (Andersen kick)
AFC — Reed 20 pass from Kelly (Lowery kick)
NFC — Sanders 22 run (Andersen kick)
AFC — FG Lowery 34
AFC — Givins 13 pass from Kelly (Lowery kick)

1990 AFC-NFC PRO BOWL

Aloha Stadium, Honolulu, Hawaii
February 4, 1990, Attendance: 50,445

NFC 27, AFC 21—The NFC captured its second straight Pro Bowl as the defense accounted for a pair of touchdowns and forced 5 turnovers before the eleventh consecutive sellout crowd at Aloha Stadium. The AFC held a 7-6 halftime edge on a 1-yard scoring run by Christian Okoye of the Chiefs. The NFC then rallied with 21 unanswered points in the third quarter. David Meggett of the Giants began the comeback with an 11-yard touchdown reception from Philadelphia's Randall Cunningham. The Rams' Jerry Gray followed with a 51-yard interception return for a score and the Vikings' Keith Millard added an 8-yard fumble return for a touchdown four minutes later to give the NFC a commanding 27-7 lead. Seattle's Dave Krieg rallied the AFC with a 5-yard touchdown pass to Miami's Ferrell Edmunds. Cleveland's Mike Johnson then returned an interception 22 yards for a score to pull the AFC to within 27-21. Gray, who was credited with 7 tackles, was given the Dan McGuire Award as player of the game. Krieg led all quarterbacks by completing 15 of 23 for 148 yards and 1 touchdown. Buffalo's Thurman Thomas topped all receivers with 5 catches for 47 yards, while Indianapolis's Eric Dickerson led all rushers with 46 yards on 15 carries. The win gave the NFC a 12-8 advantage in Pro Bowl games since 1971.

NFC	3	3	21	0	—	27
AFC	0	7	0	14	—	21

NFC — FG Murray 23
NFC — FG Murray 41
AFC — Okoye 1 run (Treadwell kick)
NFC — Meggett 11 pass from Cunningham (Murray kick)
NFC — Gray 51 interception return (Murray kick)
NFC — Millard 8 fumble recovery return (Murray kick)
AFC — Edmunds 5 pass from Krieg (Treadwell kick)
AFC — M. Johnson 22 interception return (Treadwell kick)

1989 AFC-NFC PRO BOWL

Aloha Stadium, Honolulu, Hawaii
January 29, 1989, Attendance: 50,113

NFC 34, AFC 3—The NFC scored 34 unanswered points to snap a two-game losing streak to the AFC before the tenth straight sellout crowd in Honolulu's Aloha Stadium. Bills kicker Scott Norwood provided the AFC's only points on a 38-yard field goal 6:23 into the game. Touchdown runs by Dallas's Herschel Walker (4 yards) and Atlanta's John Settle (1) brought the NFC a 14-3 halftime lead. Walker added a 7-yard scoring run, the Saints' Morten Andersen kicked field goals of 27 and 51 yards, and Los Angeles Rams' wide receiver Henry Ellard caught an 8-yard scoring pass from Minnesota quarterback Wade Wilson in the second half to complete the scoring. Chicago running back Neal Anderson and Philadelphia quarterback Randall Cunningham, who were both appearing in their first Pro Bowl, also played major roles in the NFC's victory. Anderson rushed 13 times for 85 yards and had 2 receptions for 17. Cunningham, who was voted the game's outstanding player, completed 10 of 14 passes for 63 yards and rushed for 49 yards. The NFC, which had 5 takeaways, outgained the AFC 355 yards to 167 and held a time-of-possession advantage of 35:18 to 24:42. Houston quarterback Warren Moon completed 13 of 20 passes for 134 yards for the AFC. The win gave the NFC an 11-8 advantage in Pro Bowl games.

AFC	3	0	0	0	—	3
NFC	7	7	10	10	—	34

AFC — FG Norwood 38
NFC — Walker 4 run (Andersen kick)
NFC — Settle 1 run (Andersen kick)
NFC — FG Andersen 27
NFC — Walker 7 run (Andersen kick)
NFC — FG Andersen 51
NFC — Ellard 8 pass from Wilson (Andersen kick)

1988 AFC-NFC PRO BOWL

Aloha Stadium, Honolulu, Hawaii
February 7, 1988, Attendance: 50,113

AFC 15, NFC 6—Led by a tenacious pass rush, the AFC defeated the NFC for the second consecutive year before the ninth straight sellout crowd in Honolulu's Aloha Stadium. Buffalo quarterback Jim Kelly scored the game's lone touchdown on a 1-yard run for a 7-6 halftime lead. Colts kicker Dean Biasucci added field goals from 37 and 30 yards to complete the AFC's scoring. Saints kicker Morten Andersen had 25- and 36-yard field goals to account for the NFC's points. AFC defenders held the NFC to 213 yards and recorded 8 sacks. Bills defensive end Bruce Smith, who had 2 sacks among his 5 tackles, was voted the game's outstanding player. Oilers running back Mike Rozier led all rushers with 49 yards on 9 carries. Jets wide receiver Al Toon had 5 receptions for 75 yards. The AFC generated 341 yards total offense and held a time-of-possession advantage of 34:14 to 25:46. By winning, the AFC cut the NFC's lead in the Pro Bowl series to 10-8.

NFC	0	6	0	0	—	6
AFC	0	7	6	2	—	15

NFC — FG Andersen 25
AFC — Kelly 1 run (Biasucci kick)
NFC — FG Andersen 36
AFC — FG Biasucci 37
AFC — FG Biasucci 30
AFC — Safety, Montana forced out of end zone

1987 AFC-NFC PRO BOWL

Aloha Stadium, Honolulu, Hawaii
February 1, 1987, Attendance: 50,101

AFC 10, NFC 6—The AFC defeated the NFC in the lowest-scoring game in AFC-NFC Pro Bowl history. The AFC took a 10-0 halftime lead on Broncos quarterback John Elway's 10-yard touchdown pass to Raiders tight end Todd Christensen and Patriots kicker Tony Franklin's 26-yard field goal. The AFC defense made the lead stand by forcing the NFC to settle for a pair of field goals from 38 and 19 yards by Saints kicker Morten Andersen after the NFC had first downs at the AFC 31-, 7-, 16-, 15-, 5-, and 7-yard lines. Both AFC scores were set up by fumble recoveries by Seahawks linebacker Fredd Young and Dolphins linebacker John Offerdahl, respectively. Eagles defensive end Reggie White, who tied a Pro Bowl record with 4 sacks among his 7 solo tackles, was voted the game's outstanding player. The AFC victory cut the NFC's lead in the Pro Bowl series to 10-7.

AFC	7	3	0	0	—	10
NFC	0	0	3	3	—	6

AFC — Christensen 10 pass from Elway (Franklin kick)
AFC — FG Franklin 26
NFC — FG Andersen 38
NFC — FG Andersen 19

1986 AFC-NFC PRO BOWL

Aloha Stadium, Honolulu, Hawaii
February 2, 1986, Attendance: 50,101

NFC 28, AFC 24—New York Giants quarterback Phil Simms brought the NFC back from a 24-7 halftime deficit to defeat the AFC. Simms, who completed 15 of 27 passes for 212 yards and 3 touchdowns, was named the most valuable player of the game. The AFC had taken its first-half lead behind a 2-yard run by Los Angeles Raiders running back Marcus Allen, who also threw a 51-yard scoring pass to San Diego wide receiver Wes Chandler, an 11-yard touchdown catch by Pittsburgh wide receiver Louis Lipps, and a 34-yard field goal by Steelers kicker Gary Anderson. Minnesota's Joey Browner accounted for the NFC's only score before halftime with a 48-yard interception return. After intermission, the NFC blanked the AFC while scoring 3 touchdowns via a 15-yard catch by Washington wide receiver Art Monk, a 2-yard reception by Dallas tight end Doug Cosbie, and a 15-yard catch by Tampa Bay tight end Jimmie Giles with 2:47 remaining in the game. The victory gave the NFC a 10-6 Pro Bowl record against the AFC.

NFC	0	7	7	14	—	28
AFC	7	17	0	0	—	24

AFC — Allen 2 run (Anderson kick)
NFC — Browner 48 interception return (Andersen kick)
AFC — Chandler 51 pass from Allen (Anderson kick)
AFC — FG Anderson 34
AFC — Lipps 11 pass from O'Brien (Anderson kick)
NFC — Monk 15 pass from Simms (Andersen kick)
NFC — Cosbie 2 pass from Simms (Andersen kick)
NFC — Giles 15 pass from Simms (Andersen kick)

1985 AFC-NFC PRO BOWL

Aloha Stadium, Honolulu, Hawaii
January 27, 1985, Attendance: 50,385

AFC 22, NFC 14—Defensive end Art Still of the Kansas City Chiefs recovered a fumble and returned it 83 yards for a touchdown to clinch the AFC's victory over the NFC. Still's touchdown came in the fourth period with the AFC trailing 14-12 and was one of several outstanding defensive plays in a Pro Bowl dominated by two record-breaking defenses. The teams combined for a Pro Bowl-record 17 sacks, including 4 by New York Jets defensive end Mark Gastineau, who was named the game's outstanding player. The AFC's first score came on a safety when Gastineau tackled running back Eric Dickerson of the Los Angeles Rams in the end zone. The AFC's second score, a 6-yard pass from Miami's Dan Marino to Los Angeles Raiders running back Marcus Allen, was set up by a partial block of a punt by Seahawks linebacker Fredd Young. The NFC leads the series 9-6.

AFC	0	9	0	13	—	22
NFC	0	0	7	7	—	14

AFC — Safety, Gastineau tackled Dickerson in end zone
AFC — Allen 6 pass from Marino (Johnson kick)
NFC — Lofton 13 pass from Montana (Stenerud kick)
NFC — Payton 1 run (Stenerud kick)
AFC — FG Johnson 33
AFC — Still 83 fumble recovery return (Johnson kick)
AFC — FG Johnson 22

1984 AFC-NFC PRO BOWL

Aloha Stadium, Honolulu, Hawaii
January 29, 1984, Attendance: 50,445

NFC 45, AFC 3—The NFC won its sixth Pro Bowl in the last seven seasons by routing the AFC. The NFC was led by the passing of most valuable player Joe Theismann of Washington, who completed 21 of 27 passes for 242 yards and 3 touchdowns. Theismann set Pro Bowl records for completions and touchdown passes. The NFC established Pro Bowl marks for most points scored and fewest points allowed. Running back William Andrews of Atlanta had 6 carries for 43 yards and caught 4 passes for 49 yards, including scoring receptions of 16 and 2 yards. Los Angeles Rams rookie Eric Dickerson gained 46 yards on 11 carries, including a 14-yard touchdown run, and had 45 yards on 5 catches. Rams safety Nolan Cromwell had a 44-yard interception return for a touchdown early in the third period to give the NFC a commanding 24-3 lead. Green Bay wide receiver James Lofton caught an 8-yard touchdown pass, while tight end teammate Paul Coffman had a 6-yard scoring catch.

NFC	3	14	14	14	—	45
AFC	0	3	0	0	—	3

NFC — FG Haji-Sheikh 23
NFC — Andrews 16 pass from Theismann (Haji-Sheikh kick)
NFC — Andrews 2 pass from Montana (Haji-Sheikh kick)
AFC — FG Anderson 43
NFC — Cromwell 44 interception return (Haji-Sheikh kick)
NFC — Lofton 8 pass from Theismann (Haji-Sheikh kick)
NFC — Coffman 6 pass from Theismann (Haji-Sheikh kick)
NFC — Dickerson 14 run (Haji-Sheikh kick)

1983 AFC-NFC PRO BOWL

Aloha Stadium, Honolulu, Hawaii
February 6, 1983, Attendance: 49,883

NFC 20, AFC 19—Dallas's Danny White threw an 11-yard touchdown pass to the Packers' John Jefferson with 35 seconds remaining to rally the NFC over the AFC. White, who completed 14 of 26 passes for 162 yards, kept the winning 65-yard drive alive with a 14-yard completion to Jefferson on a fourth-and-7 play at the AFC 25. The AFC was ahead 12-10 at halftime and increased the lead to 19-10 in the third period, when Marcus Allen scored on a 1-yard run. San Diego's Dan Fouts, who attempted 30 passes, set Pro Bowl records for most completions (17) and yards (274). Pittsburgh's John Stallworth was the AFC's leading receiver with 7 catches for 67 yards. William Andrews topped the NFC with 5 receptions for 48 yards. Fouts and Jefferson were co-winners of the player of the game award.

AFC	9	3	7	0	—	19
NFC	0	10	0	10	—	20

AFC — Walker 34 pass from Fouts (Benirschke kick)
AFC — Safety, Still tackled Theismann in end zone
NFC — Andrews 3 run (Moseley kick)
NFC — FG Moseley 35
AFC — FG Benirschke 29
AFC — Allen 1 run (Benirschke kick)
NFC — FG Moseley 41
NFC — Jefferson 11 pass from D. White (Moseley kick)

1982 AFC-NFC PRO BOWL

Aloha Stadium, Honolulu, Hawaii
January 31, 1982, Attendance: 50,402

AFC 16, NFC 13—Nick Lowery of Kansas City kicked a 23-yard field goal with three seconds remaining to give the AFC a last-second victory over the NFC. Lowery's kick climaxed a 69-yard drive directed by quarterback Dan Fouts. The NFC gained a 13-13 tie with 2:43 to go when Dallas's Tony Dorsett ran 4 yards for a touchdown. In the drive to the winning field goal, Fouts completed 3 passes, including a 23-yard toss to San Diego teammate Kellen Winslow that put the ball on the NFC's 5-yard line. Two plays later, Lowery kicked the field goal. Winslow, who caught 6 passes for 86 yards, was named co-player of the game along with Tampa Bay defensive end Lee Roy Selmon.

NFC	0	6	0	7	—	13
AFC	0	0	13	3	—	16

NFC — Giles 4 pass from Montana (kick blocked)
AFC — Muncie 2 run (kick failed)
AFC — Campbell 1 run (Lowery kick)
NFC — Dorsett 4 run (Septien kick)
AFC — FG Lowery 23

1981 AFC-NFC PRO BOWL

Aloha Stadium, Honolulu, Hawaii
February 1, 1981, Attendance: 50,360

NFC 21, AFC 7—Eddie Murray kicked 4 field goals and Steve Bartkowski fired a 55-yard scoring pass to Alfred Jenkins to lead the NFC to its fourth straight victory over the AFC and a 7-4 edge in the series. Murray was named the game's most valuable player and missed tying Garo Yepremian's Pro Bowl record of 5 field goals when a 37-yard attempt hit the crossbar with 22 seconds remaining. The AFC's only score came on a 9-yard pass from Brian Sipe to Stanley Morgan in the second period. Bartkowski completed 9 of 21 passes for 173 yards, while Sipe connected on 10 of 15 for 142 yards. Ottis Anderson led all rushers with 70 yards on 10 carries. Earl Campbell, the NFL's leading rusher in 1980, was limited to 24 yards on 8 attempts.

AFC	0	7	0	0	—	7
NFC	3	6	0	12	—	21

NFC — FG Murray 31
AFC — Morgan 9 pass from Sipe (J. Smith kick)
NFC — FG Murray 31
NFC — FG Murray 34
NFC — Jenkins 55 pass from Bartkowski (Murray kick)
NFC — FG Murray 36
NFC — Safety, Shell called for holding in end zone

1980 AFC-NFC PRO BOWL

Aloha Stadium, Honolulu, Hawaii
January 27, 1980, Attendance: 49,800

NFC 37, AFC 27—Running back Chuck Muncie of New Orleans ran for 2 touchdowns and threw a 25-yard option pass for another score to give the NFC its third consecutive victory over the AFC. Muncie, who was selected the game's most valuable player, snapped a 3-3 tie on a 1-yard touchdown run at 1:41 of the second quarter, then scored on an 11-yard run in the fourth quarter for the NFC's final touchdown. Two scoring records were set in the game— 37 points by the NFC, eclipsing the 33 by the AFC in 1973, and the 64 points by both teams, surpassing the 61 scored in 1973.

NFC	3	20	7	7	—	37
AFC	3	7	10	7	—	27

NFC — FG Moseley 37
AFC — FG Fritsch 19
NFC — Muncie 1 run (Moseley kick)
AFC — Pruitt 1 pass from Bradshaw (Fritsch kick)
NFC — D. Hill 13 pass from Manning (kick failed)
NFC — T. Hill 25 pass from Muncie (Moseley kick)
NFC — Henry 86 punt return (Moseley kick)
AFC — Campbell 2 run (Fritsch kick)
AFC — FG Fritsch 29
NFC — Muncie 11 run (Moseley kick)
AFC — Campbell 1 run (Fritsch kick)

1979 AFC-NFC PRO BOWL
Memorial Coliseum, Los Angeles, California
January 29, 1979, Attendance: 46,281

NFC 13, AFC 7—Roger Staubach completed 9 of 15 passes for 125 yards, including the winning touchdown on a 19-yard strike to Dallas Cowboys teammate Tony Hill in the third period. The winning drive began at the AFC's 45-yard line after a shanked punt. Staubach hit Ahmad Rashad with passes of 15 and 17 yards to set up Hill's decisive catch. The victory gave the NFC a 5-4 advantage in Pro Bowl games. Rashad, who accounted for 89 yards on 5 receptions, was named the player of the game. The AFC led 7-6 at halftime on Bob Griese's 8-yard scoring toss to Steve Largent late in the second quarter. Largent finished the game with 5 receptions for 75 yards. The NFC scored first as Archie Manning marched his team 70 yards in 11 plays, capped by Wilbert Montgomery's 2-yard touchdown run. The AFC's Earl Campbell was the game's leading rusher with 66 yards on 12 carries.

AFC	0	7	0	0	—	7
NFC	0	6	7	0	—	13

NFC — Montgomery 2 run (kick failed)
AFC — Largent 8 pass from Griese (Yepremian kick)
NFC — T. Hill 19 pass from Staubach (Corral kick)

1978 AFC-NFC PRO BOWL
Tampa Stadium, Tampa, Florida
January 23, 1978, Attendance: 51,337

NFC 14, AFC 13—Walter Payton, the NFL's leading rusher in 1977, sparked a second-half comeback to give the NFC the win and tie the series between the two conferences at four victories each. Payton, who was the game's most valuable player, gained 77 yards on 13 carries and scored the tying touchdown on a 1-yard burst with 7:37 left in the game. Efren Herrera kicked the winning extra point. The AFC dominated the first half of the game, taking a 13-0 lead on field goals of 21 and 39 yards by Toni Linhart and a 10-yard touchdown pass from Ken Stabler to Oakland teammate Cliff Branch. On the NFC's first possession of the second half, Pat Haden put together the first touchdown drive after Eddie Brown returned Ray Guy's punt to the AFC 46-yard line. Haden connected on all 4 of his passes on that drive, finally hitting Terry Metcalf with a 4-yard scoring toss. The NFC continued to rally and, with Jim Hart at quarterback, moved 63 yards in 12 plays for the go-ahead score. During the winning drive, Hart completed 5 of 6 passes for 38 yards and Payton picked up 20 more on the ground.

AFC	3	10	0	0	—	13
NFC	0	0	7	7	—	14

AFC — FG Linhart 21
AFC — Branch 10 pass from Stabler (Linhart kick)
AFC — FG Linhart 39
NFC — Metcalf 4 pass from Haden (Herrera kick)
NFC — Payton 1 run (Herrera kick)

1977 AFC-NFC PRO BOWL
Kingdome, Seattle, Washington
January 17, 1977, Attendance: 64,752

AFC 24, NFC 14—O.J. Simpson's 3-yard touchdown burst at 7:03 of the first quarter gave the AFC a lead it would not surrender, breaking a two-game NFC win streak and giving the American Conference stars a 4-3 series lead. The AFC took a 17-7 lead midway through the second period on the first of 2 Ken Anderson touchdown passes, a 12-yard toss to Charlie Joiner. But the NFC mounted a 73-yard drive capped by Lawrence McCutcheon's 1-yard touchdown plunge to pull within 17-14 at the half. Following a scoreless third quarter, player of the game Mel Blount thwarted a possible NFC score when he intercepted Jim Hart's pass in the end zone. Less than three minutes later, Blount again picked off a Hart pass. That set up Anderson's 27-yard touchdown strike to the Raiders' Cliff Branch for the final score.

NFC	0	14	0	0	—	14
AFC	10	7	0	7	—	24

AFC — Simpson 3 run (Linhart kick)
AFC — FG Linhart 31
NFC — Thomas 15 run (Bakken kick)
AFC — Joiner 12 pass from Anderson (Linhart kick)
NFC — McCutcheon 1 run (Bakken kick)
AFC — Branch 27 pass from Anderson (Linhart kick)

1976 AFC-NFC PRO BOWL
Superdome, New Orleans, Louisiana
January 26, 1976, Attendance: 30,546

NFC 23, AFC 20—Mike Boryla, a late substitute who did not enter the game until 5:39 remained, lifted the National Football Conference to the victory over the American Football Conference with 2 touchdown passes in the final minutes. It was the second straight NFC win, squaring the series at 3-3. Until Boryla started firing the ball the AFC was in control, leading 13-0 at the half. Boryla entered the game after Billy Johnson had raced 90 yards with a punt to make the score 20-9 in favor of the AFC. He floated a 14-yard touchdown pass to Terry Metcalf and later fired an 8-yard scoring pass to Mel Gray for the winner.

AFC	0	13	0	7	—	20
NFC	0	0	9	14	—	23

AFC — FG Stenerud 20
AFC — FG Stenerud 35
AFC — Burrough 64 pass from Pastorini (Stenerud kick)
NFC — FG Bakken 42
NFC — Foreman 4 pass from Hart (kick blocked)
AFC — Johnson 90 punt return (Stenerud kick)
NFC — Metcalf 14 pass from Boryla (Bakken kick)
NFC — Gray 8 pass from Boryla (Bakken kick)

1975 AFC-NFC PRO BOWL
Orange Bowl, Miami, Florida
January 20, 1975, Attendance: 26,484

NFC 17, AFC 10—Los Angeles quarterback James Harris, who took over the NFC offense after Jim Hart of St. Louis suffered a laceration above his right eye in the second period, threw 2 touchdown passes early in the fourth period to pace the NFC to its second victory in the five-game Pro Bowl series. The NFC win snapped a three-game AFC victory string. Harris, who was named the player of the game, connected with St. Louis's Mel Gray for an 8-yard touchdown 2:03 into the final period. One minute and 24 seconds later, following a fumble recovery by Washington's Ken Houston, Harris tossed another 8-yard scoring pass to Washington's Charley Taylor for the decisive points.

NFC	0	3	0	14	—	17
AFC	0	0	10	0	—	10

NFC — FG Marcol 33
AFC — Warfield 32 pass from Griese (Gerela kick)
AFC — FG Gerela 33
NFC — Gray 8 pass from J. Harris (Marcol kick)
NFC — Taylor 8 pass from J. Harris (Marcol kick)

1974 AFC-NFC PRO BOWL
Arrowhead Stadium, Kansas City, Missouri
January 20, 1974, Attendance: 66,918

AFC 15, NFC 13—Miami's Garo Yepremian's fifth field goal—a 42-yard kick with 21 seconds remaining—gave the AFC its third straight victory since the NFC won the inaugural game following the 1970 season. The field goal by Yepremian, who was voted the game's outstanding player, offset a 21-yard field goal by Atlanta's Nick Mike-Mayer that had given the NFC a 13-12 advantage with 1:41 remaining. The only touchdown in the game was scored by the NFC on a 14-yard pass from Philadelphia's Roman Gabriel to Lawrence McCutcheon of the Los Angeles Rams.

NFC	0	10	0	3	—	13
AFC	3	3	3	6	—	15

AFC — FG Yepremian 16
NFC — FG Mike-Mayer 27
NFC — McCutcheon 14 pass from Gabriel (Mike-Mayer kick)
AFC — FG Yepremian 37
AFC — FG Yepremian 27
AFC — FG Yepremian 41
NFC — FG Mike-Mayer 21
AFC — FG Yepremian 42

1973 AFC-NFC PRO BOWL
Texas Stadium, Irving, Texas
January 21, 1973, Attendance: 37,091

AFC 33, NFC 28—Paced by the rushing and receiving of player of the game O.J. Simpson, the AFC erased a 14-0 first period deficit and built a commanding 33-14 lead midway through the fourth period before the NFC managed 2 touchdowns in the final minute of play. Simpson rushed for 112 yards and caught 3 passes for 58 more to gain unanimous recognition in the balloting for player of the game. John Brockington scored 3 touchdowns for the NFC.

AFC	0	10	10	13	—	33
NFC	14	0	0	14	—	28

NFC — Brockington 1 run (Marcol kick)
NFC — Brockington 3 pass from Kilmer (Marcol kick)
AFC — Simpson 7 run (Gerela kick)
AFC — FG Gerela 18
AFC — FG Gerela 22
AFC — Hubbard 11 run (Gerela kick)
AFC — O. Taylor 5 pass from Lamonica (kick failed)
AFC — Bell 12 interception return (Gerela kick)
NFC — Brockington 1 run (Marcol kick)
NFC — Kwalick 12 pass from Snead (Marcol kick)

1972 AFC-NFC PRO BOWL
Memorial Coliseum, Los Angeles, California
January 23, 1972, Attendance: 53,647

AFC 26, NFC 13—Kansas City's Jan Stenerud kicked 4 field goals to lead the AFC from a 6-0 deficit to victory. The AFC defense picked off 3 passes. Stenerud was selected as the outstanding offensive player and his Kansas City teammate, linebacker Willie Lanier, was the game's outstanding defensive player.

AFC	0	3	13	10	—	26
NFC	0	6	0	7	—	13

NFC — Grim 50 pass from Landry (kick failed)
AFC — FG Stenerud 25
AFC — FG Stenerud 23
AFC — FG Stenerud 48
AFC — Morin 5 pass from Dawson (Stenerud kick)
AFC — FG Stenerud 42
NFC — V. Washington 2 run (Knight kick)
AFC — F. Little 6 run (Stenerud kick)

1971 AFC-NFC PRO BOWL
Memorial Coliseum, Los Angeles, California
January 24, 1971, Attendance: 48,222

NFC 27, AFC 6—Mel Renfro of Dallas broke open the first meeting between the American Football Conference and National Football Conference all-star teams as he returned a pair of punts 82 and 56 yards for touchdowns in the final period to clinch the NFC victory over the AFC. Renfro was voted the game's outstanding back and linebacker Fred Carr of Green Bay the outstanding lineman.

AFC	0	3	3	0	—	6
NFC	0	3	10	14	—	27

AFC — FG Stenerud 37
NFC — FG Cox 13
NFC — Osborn 23 pass from Brodie (Cox kick)
NFC — FG Cox 35
AFC — FG Stenerud 16
NFC — Renfro 82 punt return (Cox kick)
NFC — Renfro 56 punt return (Cox kick)

PRO BOWL ALL-TIME RESULTS

Date	Result	Site (attendance)	Honored players
Jan. 15, 1939	New York Giants 13, Pro All-Stars 10	Wrigley Field, Los Angeles (20,000)	
Jan. 14, 1940	Green Bay 16, NFL All-Stars 7	Gilmore Stadium, Los Angeles (18,000)	
Dec. 29, 1940	Chicago Bears 28, NFL All-Stars 14	Gilmore Stadium, Los Angeles (21,624)	
Jan. 4, 1942	Chicago Bears 35, NFL All-Stars 24	Polo Grounds, New York (17,725)	
Dec. 27, 1942	NFL All-Stars 17, Washington 14	Shibe Park, Philadelphia (18,671)	
Jan. 14, 1951	American Conf. 28, National Conf. 27	Los Angeles Memorial Coliseum (53,676)	Otto Graham, Cleveland, player of the game
Jan. 12, 1952	National Conf. 30, American Conf. 13	Los Angeles Memorial Coliseum (19,400)	Dan Towler, Los Angeles, player of the game
Jan. 10, 1953	National Conf. 27, American Conf. 7	Los Angeles Memorial Coliseum (34,208)	Don Doll, Detroit, player of the game
Jan. 17, 1954	East 20, West 9	Los Angeles Memorial Coliseum (44,214)	Chuck Bednarik, Philadelphia, player of the game
Jan. 16, 1955	West 26, East 19	Los Angeles Memorial Coliseum (43,972)	Billy Wilson, San Francisco, player of the game
Jan. 15, 1956	East 31, West 30	Los Angeles Memorial Coliseum (37,867)	Ollie Matson, Chi. Cardinals, player of the game
Jan. 13, 1957	West 19, East 10	Los Angeles Memorial Coliseum (44,177)	Bert Rechichar, Baltimore, outstanding back Ernie Stautner, Pittsburgh, outstanding lineman
Jan. 12, 1958	West 26, East 7	Los Angeles Memorial Coliseum (66,634)	Hugh McElhenny, San Francisco, outstanding back Gene Brito, Washington, outstanding lineman
Jan. 11, 1959	East 28, West 21	Los Angeles Memorial Coliseum (72,250)	Frank Gifford, N.Y. Giants, outstanding back Doug Atkins, Chi. Bears, outstanding lineman
Jan. 17, 1960	West 38, East 21	Los Angeles Memorial Coliseum (56,876)	Johnny Unitas, Baltimore, outstanding back Gene (Big Daddy) Lipscomb, Baltimore, outstanding lineman
Jan. 15, 1961	West 35, East 31	Los Angeles Memorial Coliseum (62,971)	Johnny Unitas, Baltimore, outstanding back Sam Huff, N.Y. Giants, outstanding lineman
Jan. 7, 1962	AFL West 47, East 27	Balboa Stadium, San Diego (20,973)	Cotton Davidson, Dallas Texans, player of the game
Jan. 14, 1962	NFL West 31, East 30	Los Angeles Memorial Coliseum (57,409)	Jim Brown, Cleveland, outstanding back Henry Jordan, Green Bay, outstanding lineman
Jan. 13, 1963	AFL West 21, East 14	Balboa Stadium, San Diego (27,641)	Curtis McClinton, Dallas Texans, outstanding offensive player Earl Faison, San Diego, outstanding defensive player
Jan. 13, 1963	NFL East 30, West 20	Los Angeles Memorial Coliseum (61,374)	Jim Brown, Cleveland, outstanding back Gene (Big Daddy) Lipscomb, Pittsburgh, outstanding lineman
Jan. 12, 1964	NFL West 31, East 17	Los Angeles Memorial Coliseum (67,242)	Johnny Unitas, Baltimore, player of the game Gino Marchetti, Baltimore, outstanding lineman
Jan. 19, 1964	AFL West 27, East 24	Balboa Stadium, San Diego (20,016)	Keith Lincoln, San Diego, outstanding offensive player Archie Matsos, Oakland, outstanding defensive player
Jan. 10, 1965	NFL West 34, East 14	Los Angeles Memorial Coliseum (60,598)	Fran Tarkenton, Minnesota, outstanding back Terry Barr, Detroit, outstanding lineman
Jan. 16, 1965	AFL West 38, East 14	Jeppesen Stadium, Houston (15,446)	Keith Lincoln, San Diego, outstanding offensive player Willie Brown, Denver, outstanding defensive player
Jan. 15, 1966	AFL All-Stars 30, Buffalo 19	Rice Stadium, Houston (35,572)	Joe Namath, N.Y. Jets, most valuable player, offense Frank Buncom, San Diego, most valuable player, defense
Jan. 15, 1966	NFL East 36, West 7	Los Angeles Memorial Coliseum (60,124)	Jim Brown, Cleveland, outstanding back Dale Meinert, St. Louis, outstanding lineman
Jan. 21, 1967	AFL East 30, West 23	Oakland-Alameda County Coliseum (18,876)	Babe Parilli, Boston, outstanding offensive player Verlon Biggs, N.Y. Jets, outstanding defensive player
Jan. 22, 1967	NFL East 20, West 10	Los Angeles Memorial Coliseum (15,062)	Gale Sayers, Chicago, outstanding back Floyd Peters, Philadelphia, outstanding lineman
Jan. 21, 1968	AFL East 25, West 24	Gator Bowl, Jacksonville, Fla. (40,103)	Joe Namath and Don Maynard, N.Y. Jets, out. off. players Leslie (Speedy) Duncan, San Diego, out. def. player
Jan. 21, 1968	NFL West 38, East 20	Los Angeles Memorial Coliseum (53,289)	Gale Sayers, Chicago, outstanding back Dave Robinson, Green Bay, outstanding lineman
Jan. 19, 1969	AFL West 38, East 25	Gator Bowl, Jacksonville, Fla. (41,058)	Len Dawson, Kansas City, outstanding offensive player George Webster, Houston, outstanding defensive player
Jan. 19, 1969	NFL West 10, East 7	Los Angeles Memorial Coliseum (32,050)	Roman Gabriel, Los Angeles, outstanding back Merlin Olsen, Los Angeles, outstanding lineman
Jan. 17, 1970	AFL West 26, East 3	Astrodome, Houston (30,170)	John Hadl, San Diego, player of the game
Jan. 18, 1970	NFL West 16, East 13	Los Angeles Memorial Coliseum (57,786)	Gale Sayers, Chicago, outstanding back George Andrie, Dallas, outstanding lineman
Jan. 24, 1971	NFC 27, AFC 6	Los Angeles Memorial Coliseum (48,222)	Mel Renfro, Dallas, outstanding back Fred Carr, Green Bay, outstanding lineman
Jan. 23, 1972	AFC 26, NFC 13	Los Angeles Memorial Coliseum (53,647)	Jan Stenerud, Kansas City, outstanding offensive player Willie Lanier, Kansas City, outstanding defensive player
Jan. 21, 1973	AFC 33, NFC 28	Texas Stadium, Irving (37,091)	O.J. Simpson, Buffalo, player of the game
Jan. 20, 1974	AFC 15, NFC 13	Arrowhead Stadium, Kansas City (66,918)	Garo Yepremian, Miami, player of the game
Jan. 20, 1975	NFC 17, AFC 10	Orange Bowl, Miami (26,484)	James Harris, Los Angeles, player of the game
Jan. 26, 1976	NFC 23, AFC 20	Louisiana Superdome, New Orleans (30,546)	Billy Johnson, Houston, player of the game
Jan. 17, 1977	AFC 24, NFC 14	Kingdome, Seattle (64,752)	Mel Blount, Pittsburgh, player of the game
Jan. 23, 1978	NFC 14, AFC 13	Tampa Stadium (51,337)	Walter Payton, Chicago, player of the game
Jan. 29, 1979	NFC 13, AFC 7	Los Angeles Memorial Coliseum (46,281)	Ahmad Rashad, Minnesota, player of the game
Jan. 27, 1980	NFC 37, AFC 27	Aloha Stadium, Honolulu (49,800)	Chuck Muncie, New Orleans, player of the game
Feb. 1, 1981	NFC 21, AFC 7	Aloha Stadium, Honolulu (50,360)	Eddie Murray, Detroit, player of the game
Jan. 31, 1982	AFC 16, NFC 13	Aloha Stadium, Honolulu (50,402)	Kellen Winslow, San Diego, and Lee Roy Selmon, Tampa Bay, players of the game
Feb. 6, 1983	NFC 20, AFC 19	Aloha Stadium, Honolulu (49,883)	Dan Fouts, San Diego, and John Jefferson, Green Bay, players of the game
Jan. 29, 1984	NFC 45, AFC 3	Aloha Stadium, Honolulu (50,445)	Joe Theismann, Washington, player of the game
Jan. 27, 1985	AFC 22, NFC 14	Aloha Stadium, Honolulu (50,385)	Mark Gastineau, N.Y. Jets, player of the game
Feb. 2, 1986	NFC 28, AFC 24	Aloha Stadium, Honolulu (50,101)	Phil Simms, N.Y. Giants, player of the game
Feb. 1, 1987	AFC 10, NFC 6	Aloha Stadium, Honolulu (50,101)	Reggie White, Philadelphia, player of the game
Feb. 7, 1988	AFC 15, NFC 6	Aloha Stadium, Honolulu (50,113)	Bruce Smith, Buffalo, player of the game
Jan. 29, 1989	NFC 34, AFC 3	Aloha Stadium, Honolulu (50,113)	Randall Cunningham, Philadelphia, player of the game
Feb. 4, 1990	NFC 27, AFC 21	Aloha Stadium, Honolulu (50,445)	Jerry Gray, L.A. Rams, player of the game
Feb. 3, 1991	AFC 23, NFC 21	Aloha Stadium, Honolulu (50,345)	Jim Kelly, Buffalo, player of the game
Feb. 2, 1992	NFC 21, AFC 15	Aloha Stadium, Honolulu (50,209)	Michael Irvin, Dallas, player of the game
Feb. 7, 1993	AFC 23, NFC 20 (OT)	Aloha Stadium, Honolulu (50,007)	Steve Tasker, Buffalo, player of the game
Feb. 6, 1994	NFC 17, AFC 3	Aloha Stadium, Honolulu (50,026)	Andre Rison, Atlanta, player of the game
Feb. 5, 1995	AFC 41, NFC 13	Aloha Stadium, Honolulu (49,121)	Marshall Faulk, Indianapolis, player of the game
Feb. 4, 1996	NFC 20, AFC 13	Aloha Stadium, Honolulu (50,034)	Jerry Rice, San Francisco, player of the game
Feb. 2, 1997	AFC 26, NFC 23 (OT)	Aloha Stadium, Honolulu (50,031)	Mark Brunell, Jacksonville, player of the game
Feb. 1, 1998	AFC 29, NFC 24	Aloha Stadium, Honolulu (49,995)	Warren Moon, Seattle, player of the game
Feb. 7, 1999	AFC 23, NFC 10	Aloha Stadium, Honolulu (50,075)	Keyshawn Johnson, N.Y. Jets and Ty Law, New England, co-players of the game

PRO FOOTBALL HALL OF FAME GAME

1962	New York Giants 21, St. Louis Cardinals 21
1963	Pittsburgh Steelers 16, Cleveland Browns 7
1964	Baltimore Colts 48, Pittsburgh Steelers 17
1965	Washington Redskins 20, Detroit Lions 3
1966	No game
1967	Philadelphia Eagles 28, Cleveland Browns 13
1968	Chicago Bears 30, Dallas Cowboys 24
1969	Green Bay Packers 38, Atlanta Falcons 24
1970	New Orleans Saints 14, Minnesota Vikings 13
1971	Los Angeles Rams (NFC) 17, Houston Oilers (AFC) 6
1972	Kansas City Chiefs (AFC) 23, New York Giants (NFC) 17
1973	San Francisco 49ers (NFC) 20, New England Patriots (AFC) 7
1974	St. Louis Cardinals (NFC) 21, Buffalo Bills (AFC) 13
1975	Washington Redskins (NFC) 17, Cincinnati Bengals (AFC) 9
1976	Denver Broncos (AFC) 10, Detroit Lions (NFC) 7
1977	Chicago Bears (NFC) 20, New York Jets (AFC) 6
1978	Philadelphia Eagles (NFC) 17, Miami Dolphins (AFC) 3
1979	Oakland Raiders (AFC) 20, Dallas Cowboys (NFC) 13
1980*	San Diego Chargers (AFC) 0, Green Bay Packers (NFC) 0
1981	Cleveland Browns (AFC) 24, Atlanta Falcons (NFC) 10
1982	Minnesota Vikings (NFC) 30, Baltimore Colts (AFC) 14
1983	Pittsburgh Steelers (AFC) 27, New Orleans Saints (NFC) 14
1984	Seattle Seahawks (AFC) 38, Tampa Bay Buccaneers (NFC) 0
1985	New York Giants (NFC) 21, Houston Oilers (AFC) 20
1986	New England Patriots (AFC) 21, St. Louis Cardinals (NFC) 16
1987	San Francisco 49ers (NFC) 20, Kansas City Chiefs (AFC) 7
1988	Cincinnati Bengals (AFC) 14, Los Angeles Rams (NFC) 7
1989	Washington Redskins (NFC) 31, Buffalo Bills (AFC) 6
1990	Chicago Bears (NFC) 13, Cleveland Browns (AFC) 0
1991	Detroit Lions (NFC) 14, Denver Broncos (AFC) 3
1992	New York Jets (AFC) 41, Philadelphia Eagles (NFC) 14
1993	Los Angeles Raiders (AFC) 19, Green Bay Packers (NFC) 3
1994	Atlanta Falcons (NFC) 21, San Diego Chargers (AFC) 17
1995	Carolina Panthers (NFC) 20, Jacksonville Jaguars (AFC) 14
1996	Indianapolis Colts (AFC) 10, New Orleans Saints (NFC) 3
1997	Minnesota Vikings (NFC) 28, Seattle Seahawks (AFC) 26
1998	Tampa Bay Buccaneers (NFC) 30, Pittsburgh Steelers (AFC) 6

Game called with 5:29 remaining because of severe thunder and lightning.

NFL INTERNATIONAL GAMES

Date	Site	Teams
Aug. 12, 1950	Ottawa, Canada	N.Y. Giants 27, Ottawa Rough Riders 6
Aug. 11, 1951	Ottawa, Canada	N.Y. Giants 41, Ottawa Rough Riders 18
Aug. 5, 1959	Toronto, Canada	Chi. Cardinals 55, Tor. Argonauts 26
Aug. 3, 1960	Toronto, Canada	Pittsburgh 43, Toronto Argonauts 16
Aug. 15, 1960	Toronto, Canada	Chicago 16, N.Y. Giants 7
Aug. 2, 1961	Toronto, Canada	St. Louis 36, Toronto Argonauts 7
Aug. 5, 1961	Montreal, Canada	Chicago 34, Montreal Allouettes 16
Aug. 8, 1961	Hamilton, Canada	Hamilton Tiger-Cats 38, Buffalo 21
Sept. 11, 1969	Montreal, Canada	Pittsburgh 17, N.Y. Giants 13
Aug. 25, 1969	Montreal, Canada	Detroit 22, Boston 9
Aug. 16, 1976	Tokyo, Japan	St. Louis 20, San Diego 10
Aug. 5, 1978	Mexico City, Mexico	New Orleans 14, Philadelphia 7
Aug. 6, 1983	London, England	Minnesota 28, St. Louis 10
*Aug. 3, 1986	London, England	Chicago 17, Dallas 6
*Aug. 9, 1987	London, England	L.A. Rams 28, Denver 27
*July 31, 1988	London, England	Miami 27, San Francisco 21
Aug. 14, 1988	Goteborg, Sweden	Minnesota 28, Chicago 21
Aug. 18, 1988	Montreal, Canada	N.Y. Jets 11, Cleveland 7
*Aug. 5, 1989	Tokyo, Japan	L.A. Rams 16, San Francisco 13 (OT)
*Aug. 6, 1989	London, England	Philadelphia 17, Cleveland 13
*Aug. 4, 1990	Tokyo, Japan	Denver 10, Seattle 7
*Aug. 5, 1990	London, England	New Orleans 17, L.A. Raiders 10
*Aug. 9, 1990	Montreal, Canada	Pittsburgh 30, New England 14
*Aug. 11, 1990	Berlin, Germany	L.A. Rams 19, Kansas City 3
*July 28, 1991	London, England	Buffalo 17, Philadelphia 13
*Aug. 3, 1991	Berlin, Germany	San Francisco 21, Chicago 7
*Aug. 3, 1991	Tokyo, Japan	Miami 19, L.A. Raiders 17
*Aug. 1, 1992	Tokyo, Japan	Houston 34, Dallas 23
*Aug. 15, 1992	Berlin, Germany	Miami 31, Denver 27
*Aug. 16, 1992	London, England	San Francisco 17, Washington 15
*July 31, 1993	Tokyo, Japan	New Orleans 28, Philadelphia 16
*Aug. 1, 1993	Barcelona, Spain	San Francisco 21, Pittsburgh 14
*Aug. 7, 1993	Berlin, Germany	Minnesota 20, Buffalo 6
*Aug. 8, 1993	London, England	Dallas 13, Detroit 13 (OT)
Aug. 14, 1993	Toronto, Canada	Cleveland 12, New England 9
*July 31, 1994	Barcelona, Spain	L.A. Raiders 25, Denver 22
*Aug. 6, 1994	Tokyo, Japan	Minnesota 17, Kansas City 9
*Aug. 13, 1994	Berlin, Germany	N.Y. Giants 28, San Diego 20
*Aug. 15, 1994	Mexico City, Mexico	Houston 6, Dallas 0
*Aug. 5, 1995	Tokyo, Japan	Denver 24, San Francisco 10
*Aug. 12, 1995	Toronto, Canada	Buffalo 9, Dallas 7
*July 27, 1996	Tokyo, Japan	San Diego 20, Pittsburgh 10
*Aug. 5, 1996	Monterrey, Mexico	Kansas City 32, Dallas 6
*July 27, 1997	Dublin, Ireland	Pittsburgh 30, Chicago 17
*Aug. 4, 1997	Mexico City, Mexico	Miami 38, Denver 19
*Aug. 1, 1998	Tokyo, Japan	Green Bay 27, Kansas City 24 (OT)
*Aug. 15, 1998	Vancouver, Canada	San Francisco 24, Seattle 21
*Aug. 17, 1998	Mexico City, Mexico	New England 21, Dallas 3

**American Bowl Game*

CHICAGO ALL-STAR GAME

Pro teams won 31, lost 9, and tied 2. The game was discontinued after 1976.

Year	Date	Winner	Loser	Attendance
1976*	July 23	Pittsburgh 24	All-Stars 0	52,895
1975	Aug. 1	Pittsburgh 21	All-Stars 14	54,103
1974		No game was played		
1973	July 27	Miami 14	All-Stars 3	54,103
1972	July 28	Dallas 20	All-Stars 7	54,162
1971	July 30	Baltimore 24	All-Stars 17	52,289
1970	July 31	Kansas City 24	All-Stars 3	69,940
1969	Aug. 1	N.Y. Jets 26	All-Stars 24	74,208
1968	Aug. 2	Green Bay 34	All-Stars 17	69,917
1967	Aug. 4	Green Bay 27	All-Stars 0	70,934
1966	Aug. 5	Green Bay 38	All-Stars 0	72,000
1965	Aug. 6	Cleveland 24	All-Stars 16	68,000
1964	Aug. 7	Chicago 28	All-Stars 17	65,000
1963	Aug. 2	All-Stars 20	Green Bay 17	65,000
1962	Aug. 3	Green Bay 42	All-Stars 20	65,000
1961	Aug. 4	Philadelphia 28	All-Stars 14	66,000
1960	Aug. 12	Baltimore 32	All-Stars 7	70,000
1959	Aug. 14	Baltimore 29	All-Stars 0	70,000
1958	Aug. 15	All-Stars 35	Detroit 19	70,000
1957	Aug. 9	N.Y. Giants 22	All-Stars 12	75,000
1956	Aug. 10	Cleveland 26	All-Stars 0	75,000
1955	Aug. 12	All-Stars 30	Cleveland 27	75,000
1954	Aug. 13	Detroit 31	All-Stars 6	93,470
1953	Aug. 14	Detroit 24	All-Stars 10	93,818
1952	Aug. 15	Los Angeles 10	All-Stars 7	88,316
1951	Aug. 17	Cleveland 33	All-Stars 0	92,180
1950	Aug. 11	All-Stars 17	Philadelphia 7	88,885
1949	Aug. 12	Philadelphia 38	All-Stars 0	93,780
1948	Aug. 20	Chi. Cardinals 28	All-Stars 0	101,220
1947	Aug. 22	All-Stars 16	Chi. Bears 0	105,840
1946	Aug. 23	All-Stars 16	Los Angeles 0	97,380
1945	Aug. 30	Green Bay 19	All-Stars 7	92,753
1944	Aug. 30	Chi. Bears 24	All-Stars 21	48,769
1943	Aug. 25	All-Stars 27	Washington 7	48,471
1942	Aug. 28	Chi. Bears 21	All-Stars 0	101,100
1941	Aug. 28	Chi. Bears 37	All-Stars 13	98,203
1940	Aug. 29	Green Bay 45	All-Stars 28	84,567
1939	Aug. 30	N.Y. Giants 9	All-Stars 0	81,456
1938	Aug. 31	All-Stars 28	Washington 16	74,250
1937	Sept. 1	All-Stars 6	Green Bay 0	84,560
1936	Sept. 3	Detroit 7	All-Stars 7 (tie)	76,000
1935	Aug. 29	Chi. Bears 5	All-Stars 0	77,450
1934	Aug. 31	Chi. Bears 0	All-Stars 0 (tie)	79,432

**Game shortened due to thunderstorms.*

NFL PLAYOFF BOWL

Western Conference won 8, Eastern Conference won 2.
All games played at Miami's Orange Bowl.

1970	Los Angeles Rams 31, Dallas Cowboys 0
1969	Dallas Cowboys 17, Minnesota Vikings 13
1968	Los Angeles Rams 30, Cleveland Browns 6
1967	Baltimore Colts 20, Philadelphia Eagles 14
1966	Baltimore Colts 35, Dallas Cowboys 3
1965	St. Louis Cardinals 24, Green Bay Packers 17
1964	Green Bay Packers 40, Cleveland Browns 23
1963	Detroit Lions 17, Pittsburgh Steelers 10
1962	Detroit Lions 28, Philadelphia Eagles 10
1961	Detroit Lions 17, Cleveland Browns 16

INTERCONFERENCE GAMES

AFC VS. NFC (REGULAR SEASON), 1970-1998

	1970	1971	1972	1973	1974	1975	1976	1977	1978	1979	1980	1981	1982	1983	1984
Miami	2-1	3-0	3-0	3-0	2-1	3-0	0-2	2-0	3-1	4-0	4-0	3-1	1-1	3-1	4-0
Oakland	1-2	1-1-1	3-0	2-1	3-0	3-0	3-0	1-1	4-0	4-0	2-2	2-2	3-0	2-2	3-1
Kansas City	0-2-1	2-1	2-1	1-1-1	1-2	2-1	1-1	1-1	0-2	0-2	2-0	2-2	0-3	2-2	1-1
Pittsburgh	0-3	1-2	2-1	3-0	3-0	2-1	1-1	2-0	3-1	3-1	4-0	3-1	1-0	2-2	3-1
Denver	2-2	1-3	1-3	0-3-1	2-2	2-1	2-0	1-1	2-2	3-1	3-1	3-1	2-1	0-2	3-1
Cincinnati	1-2	1-2	2-1	2-1	2-1	3-0	2-0	2-1	2-2	2-2	2-2	2-2	1-0	3-1	2-2
Seattle								1-0	3-1	3-1	1-3	0-2	1-0	1-3	4-0
Cleveland	0-3	2-1	1-2	1-2	1-2	1-3	2-0	1-1	4-0	3-1	3-1	3-1	0-2	2-2	1-3
Buffalo	0-3	0-3	2-0-1	2-1	2-1	1-2	0-2	1-1	1-1	2-2	3-1	1-3	1-2	1-3	1-3
San Diego	1-2	2-1	0-3	1-2	1-2	0-3	2-0	1-1	2-2	3-1	2-2	2-2	1-0	2-2	4-0
Baltimore															
Jacksonville															
Tennessee	0-3	0-2-1	0-3	0-3	0-3	3-0	2-0	2-0	2-2	2-2	4-0	1-3	0-3	1-3	0-4
N.Y. Jets	2-1	0-3	1-2	0-3	2-1	0-3	0-2	1-1	1-3	3-1	1-3	2-0	4-0	3-1	0-2
New England	0-3	0-3	3-0	2-1	3-0	1-2	1-1	2-0	2-2	3-1	1-3	0-4	0-1	2-2	0-4
Indianapolis	3-0	2-1	0-3	2-1	1-2	2-1	0-2	1-1	2-2	1-1	1-1	0-4	0-1-1	2-0	0-4
Tampa Bay							0-1								
TOTALS	12-27-1	15-23-2	20-19-1	19-19-2	23-17	23-17	16-12	19-9	31-21	36-16	33-19	24-28	15-14-1	26-26	26-26

	1985	1986	1987	1988	1989	1990	1991	1992	1993	1994	1995	1996	1997	1998	Totals
Miami	3-1	2-2	3-0	3-1	2-0	2-2	3-1	2-2	3-1	2-2	2-2	1-3	1-3	3-1	72-29
Oakland	3-1	1-3	2-2	1-3	2-2	3-1	2-2	2-2	3-1	3-1	3-1	1-3	2-2	3-1	68-37-1
Kansas City	2-2	1-1	1-2	0-2	2-0	4-0	2-2	2-2	2-2	3-1	3-1	4-0	4-0	3-1	50-38-2
Pittsburgh	1-3	2-2	2-2	1-3	3-1	3-1	0-4	1-3	2-2	2-2	2-2	2-2	2-2	2-2	58-45
Denver	3-1	3-1	2-1-1	3-1	2-2	1-3	2-0	1-3	1-3	1-3	2-2	3-1	3-1	3-1	57-47-2
Cincinnati	2-2	3-1	1-2	4-0	2-2	1-3	1-3	1-3	2-2	1-3	2-2	2-2	2-2	1-3	54-49
Seattle	2-2	3-1	4-0	1-3	0-4	2-2	1-3	0-4	0-2	2-0	3-1	2-2	2-2	3-1	39-37
Cleveland	1-3	2-2	2-2	4-0	3-1	1-3	0-4	2-2	3-1	3-1	1-3				47-46
Buffalo	0-2	1-1	1-2	2-2	1-3	3-1	3-1	4-0	4-0	1-3	3-1	4-0	1-3	3-1	49-48-1
San Diego	1-1	0-4	2-0	2-2	2-2	1-1	1-3	2-0	2-2	2-2	3-1	1-3	1-3	1-3	45-50
Baltimore												2-2	2-1-1	1-3	5-6-1
Jacksonville											0-4	2-2	2-2	3-1	7-9
Tennessee	1-3	2-2	2-2	3-1	3-1	1-3	1-3	3-1	2-2	0-4	1-3	2-2	4-0	1-3	43-61-1
N.Y. Jets	2-2	2-2	0-4	2-0	1-3	2-0	2-2	0-4	2-2	1-3	0-4	1-3	3-1	2-2	40-58
New England	3-1	3-1	0-3	2-2	0-4	0-4	1-1	0-4	1-1	4-0	0-4	2-2	1-3	2-2	39-59
Indianapolis	3-1	1-3	1-0	2-2	1-3	2-2	0-4	2-0	0-4	0-2	2-2	3-1	1-3	0-4	35-55-1
Tampa Bay															0-1
TOTALS	27-25	26-26	23-22-1	30-22	24-28	26-26	19-33	22-30	27-25	25-27	27-33	32-28	31-28-1	31-29	708-675-9

NFC VS. AFC (REGULAR SEASON), 1970-1998

	1970	1971	1972	1973	1974	1975	1976	1977	1978	1979	1980	1981	1982	1983	1984
Dallas	3-0	3-0	3-0	2-1	2-1	2-1	2-0	1-1	3-1	1-3	3-1	4-0	2-1	2-2	2-2
San Francisco	4-0	2-1	2-1	1-2	0-3	1-2	1-1	0-2	1-3	0-4	2-2	3-1	1-3	2-2	3-1
Carolina															
Washington	2-1	1-2	1-2	2-1	2-1	1-2	1-1	1-1	2-2	2-2	1-3	2-2		4-0	3-1
Philadelphia	2-1	1-2	2-1	2-1	2-1	0-3	0-2	1-1	3-1	2-2	3-1	3-1	2-1	1-1	3-1
Minnesota	2-1	2-1	1-2	2-1	2-1	4-0	2-0	1-1	1-3	1-3	1-3	1-3	1-3	4-0	0-4
St. Louis	2-1	1-2	1-2	3-0	3-1	3-0	1-1	2-0	2-2	2-2	2-2	1-3	1-2	1-3	3-1
N.Y. Giants	3-0	1-2	1-2	1-2	1-2	2-1	0-2	0-2	1-1	1-1	1-3	1-1	1-0	0-4	2-0
Chicago	1-2	1-2	1-2	2-2	0-3	0-3	0-2	1-1	0-4	2-2	0-4	4-0	1-1	1-1	2-2
Detroit	3-0	4-0	2-0-1	0-3	1-2	1-2	2-0	2-0	2-2	0-4	0-2	2-2	0-1	1-3	0-4
Green Bay	2-1	2-1	2-1	1-1-1	2-1	0-3	0-2	0-3	2-2	1-3	1-3	1-1	1-1-1	2-2	0-4
New Orleans	0-3	0-1-2	0-3	1-2	0-3	0-3	1-2	0-2	1-3	0-4	1-3	2-2	1-0	1-3	3-1
Arizona	2-0-1	2-1	1-2	0-2-1	2-1	2-1	1-1	0-2	0-4	1-3	1-1	3-1		3-1	3-1
Atlanta	1-2	3-0	2-2	2-1	0-3	1-2	0-2	0-2	1-3	1-3	2-2	1-3	1-1	3-1	1-3
Tampa Bay								0-1	2-0	2-0	1-3	0-4	2-1	1-3	1-1
Seattle							1-0								
TOTALS	27-12-1	23-15-2	19-20-1	19-19-2	17-23	17-23	12-16	9-19	21-31	16-36	19-33	28-24	14-15-1	26-26	26-26

	1985	1986	1987	1988	1989	1990	1991	1992	1993	1994	1995	1996	1997	1998	Totals
Dallas	3-1	1-3	2-1	0-4	0-2	1-1	3-1	4-0	2-2	3-1	4-0	2-2	2-2	1-3	63-37
San Francisco	3-1	4-0	3-1	2-2	4-0	4-0	3-1	3-1	2-2	3-1	3-1	4-0	2-2	2-2	65-42
Carolina											3-1	3-1	2-2	1-3	9-7
Washington	4-0	3-1	2-1	1-3	2-2	3-1	4-0	2-2	1-3	1-1	0-4	3-1	1-3	2-2	54-45
Philadelphia	1-1	2-2	3-1	2-2	3-1	1-3	4-0	3-1	2-2	1-3	1-3	2-2	2-1-1	0-4	54-46-1
Minnesota	2-0	1-3	2-1	2-2	2-2	2-2	0-2	3-1	2-2	2-2	3-1	1-3	3-1	4-0	54-48
St. Louis	3-1	2-2	1-2	2-2	3-1	2-2	1-3	2-2	2-2	2-2	1-3	2-2	0-4	3-1	54-51
N.Y. Giants	2-2	3-1	2-1	1-1	4-0	3-1	3-1	2-2	2-2	3-1	0-4	2-2	1-3	3-1	47-45
Chicago	3-1	4-0	2-2	3-1	2-2	2-2	2-2	1-3	2-2	3-1	2-2	2-2	2-2	2-2	48-55
Detroit	2-2	1-3	0-4	1-1	1-3	1-3	4-0	2-2	2-0	2-2	3-1	1-3	2-2	1-3	43-54-1
Green Bay	0-4	1-3	1-2-1	1-3	0-2	1-3	1-3	3-1	3-1	1-3	4-0	3-1	3-1	3-1	42-57-3
New Orleans	0-4	1-3	4-0	4-0	4-0	2-2	3-1	3-1	2-2	1-3	4-0	1-3	2-2	1-3	43-59-2
Arizona	2-2	1-1	0-1	1-3	1-3	2-2	1-1	0-2	1-1	3-1	1-3	0-4	1-3	1-3	36-51-2
Atlanta	0-4	1-3	0-4	1-3	2-2	2-2	3-1	2-2	1-3	1-3	2-2	0-4	2-2	3-1	39-66
Tampa Bay	0-4	1-1	0-2	1-3	0-4	0-2	1-3	0-2	1-3	1-1	2-2	2-2	3-1	2-2	23-45
Seattle															1-0
TOTALS	25-27	26-26	22-23-1	22-30	28-24	26-26	33-19	30-22	25-27	27-25	33-27	28-32	28-31-1	29-31	675-708-9

INTERCONFERENCE GAMES

1998 INTERCONFERENCE GAMES

(Home Team in capital letters)

AFC 31, NFC 29

AFC Victories

Jacksonville 24, CHICAGO 23
Seattle 38, PHILADELPHIA 0
SEATTLE 33, Arizona 14
PITTSBURGH 17, Chicago 12
Cincinnati 34, DETROIT 28 (OT)
DENVER 42, Dallas 23
OAKLAND 20, New York Giants 17
SEATTLE 24, Washington 14
Denver 38, WASHINGTON 16
Kansas City 24, PHILADELPHIA 21
Oakland 13, DALLAS 12
DENVER 41, Philadelphia 16
New England 30, NEW ORLEANS 27
Oakland 23, ARIZONA 20
BUFFALO 26, San Francisco 21
SAN DIEGO 13, Philadelphia 10
MIAMI 14, St. Louis 0
NEW YORK JETS 28, Atlanta 3
Buffalo 30, CAROLINA 14
PITTSBURGH 27, Green Bay 20
Tennessee 31, TAMPA BAY 22
Miami 13, CAROLINA 9
JACKSONVILLE 29, Tampa Bay 24
KANSAS CITY 34, Arizona 24
NEW YORK JETS 48, Carolina 21
MIAMI 30, New Orleans 10
JACKSONVILLE 37, Detroit 22
KANSAS CITY 20, Dallas 17
NEW ENGLAND 24, San Francisco 21
Buffalo 45, NEW ORLEANS 33
BALTIMORE 19, Detroit 10

NFC Victories

SAN FRANCISCO 36, New York Jets 30 (OT)
Green Bay 13, CINCINNATI 6
St. Louis 34, BUFFALO 33
NEW ORLEANS 19, Indianapolis 13 (OT)
New York Giants 34, SAN DIEGO 16
ST. LOUIS 30, New York Jets 10
SAN FRANCISCO 34, Indianapolis 31
GREEN BAY 28, Baltimore 10
Chicago 23, TENNESSEE 20
Atlanta 41, NEW ENGLAND 10
MINNESOTA 24, Cincinnati 3
DALLAS 30, Seattle 22
DETROIT 19, Pittsburgh 16 (OT)
Washington 29, OAKLAND 19
ATLANTA 28, Indianapolis 21
WASHINGTON 24, San Diego 20
NEW YORK GIANTS 20, Denver 16
Minnesota 38, BALTIMORE 28
ST. LOUIS 32, New England 18
TAMPA BAY 16, Pittsburgh 3
CHICAGO 24, Baltimore 3
MINNESOTA 50, Jacksonville 10
NEW YORK GIANTS 28, Kansas City 7
GREEN BAY 30, Tennessee 22
Carolina 27, INDIANAPOLIS 19
ATLANTA 38, Miami 16
MINNESOTA 26, Tennessee 16
ARIZONA 16, San Diego 13
Tampa Bay 35, CINCINNATI 0

REGULAR SEASON INTERCONFERENCE RECORDS, 1970-1998

AMERICAN FOOTBALL CONFERENCE

Eastern Division	W	L	T	Pct.
Miami	72	29	0	.713
Buffalo	49	48	1	.505
New York Jets	40	58	0	.408
New England	39	59	0	.398
Indianapolis	35	55	1	.390
Central Division				
Pittsburgh	58	45	0	.563
Cincinnati	54	49	0	.524
Cleveland	47	46	0	.505
Baltimore	5	6	1	.458
Jacksonville	7	9	0	.438
Tennessee	43	61	1	.414
Western Division				
Oakland	68	37	1	.642
Kansas City	50	38	2	.567
Denver	57	47	2	.547
Seattle*	39	37	0	.513
San Diego	45	50	0	.474

NATIONAL FOOTBALL CONFERENCE

Eastern Division	W	L	T	Pct.
Dallas	63	37	0	.630
Washington	54	45	0	.545
Philadelphia	54	46	1	.540
New York Giants	47	45	0	.511
Arizona	36	51	2	.412
Central Division				
Minnesota	54	48	0	.529
Chicago	48	55	0	.466
Detroit	43	54	1	.444
Green Bay	42	57	3	.426
Tampa Bay*	23	46	0	.333
Western Division				
San Francisco	65	42	0	.601
Carolina	9	7	0	.563
St. Louis	54	51	0	.514
New Orleans	43	59	2	.423
Atlanta	39	66	0	.371

**Records include one game played between Seattle and Tampa Bay, won by the Seahwaks 13-10, in their inaugural season (1976) when Seattle competed in the NFC and Tampa Bay in the AFC.*

INTERCONFERENCE VICTORIES, 1970-1998

REGULAR SEASON

	AFC	NFC	Tie
1970	12	27	1
1971	15	23	2
1972	20	19	1
1973	19	19	2
1974	23	17	0
1975	23	17	0
1976	16	12	0
1977	19	9	0
1978	31	21	0
1979	36	16	0
1980	33	19	0
1981	24	28	0
1982	15	14	1
1983	26	26	0
1984	26	26	0
1985	27	25	0
1986	26	26	0
1987	23	22	1
1988	30	22	0
1989	24	28	0
1990	26	26	0
1991	19	33	0
1992	22	30	0
1993	27	25	0
1994	25	27	0
1995	27	33	0
1996	32	28	0
1997	31	28	1
1998	31	29	0
Total	708	675	9

PRESEASON

	AFC	NFC	Tie
1970	21	28	1
1971	28	28	3
1972	27	25	4
1973	23	35	2
1974	35	25	0
1975	30	26	1
1976	30	31	0
1977	38	25	0
1978	20	19	0
1979	25	18	0
1980	22	20	1
1981	18	19	0
1982	25	16	0
1983	15	24	0
1984	16	19	0
1985	10	22	1
1986	22	17	0
1987	22	22	0
1988	23	16	1
1989	16	27	0
1990	15	29	0
1991	19	27	0
1992	30	22	0
1993	17	22	0
1994	22	16	0
1995	19	26	0
1996	27	19	0
1997	26	17	0
1998	34	16	0
Total	675	656	14

RECORDS AFTER BYE WEEKS, 1990-98

AFC

Baltimore	1-2	Miami	8-2
Buffalo	9-1	New England	4-6
Cincinnati	3-7	N.Y. Jets	4-6
Cleveland	2-5	Oakland	5-5
Denver	8-2	Pittsburgh	5-5
Indianapolis	4-6	San Diego	4-6
Jacksonville	3-1	Seattle	3-7
Kansas City	7-3	Tennessee	5-5

RECORDS AFTER BYE WEEKS, 1990-98

NFC

Arizona	5-5	New Orleans	5-5
Atlanta	7-3	N.Y. Giants	2-8
Carolina	1-3	Philadelphia	6-4
Chicago	7-3	St. Louis	4-6
Dallas	8-2	San Francisco	5-5
Detroit	5-5	Tampa Bay	3-7
Green Bay	4-6	Washington	4-6
Minnesota	8-2		

MONDAY NIGHT FOOTBALL, 1970-1998

(Home Team in capitals, games listed in chronological order.)

1998
DENVER 27, New England 21
San Francisco 45, WASHINGTON 10
Dallas 31, NEW YORK GIANTS 7
DETROIT 27, Tampa Bay 6
Minnesota 37, GREEN BAY 24
JACKSONVILLE 28, Miami 21
New York Jets 24, NEW ENGLAND 14
Pittsburgh 20, KANSAS CITY 13
Dallas 34, PHILADELPHIA 0
PITTSBURGH 27, Green Bay 20
Denver 30, KANSAS CITY 7
NEW ENGLAND 26, Miami 23
SAN FRANCISCO 35, New York Giants 7
TAMPA BAY 24, Green Bay 22
SAN FRANCISCO 35, Detroit 13
MIAMI 31, Denver 21
JACKSONVILLE 21, Pittsburgh 3

1997
GREEN BAY 38, Chicago 24
Kansas City 28, OAKLAND 27
DALLAS 21, Philadelphia 20
JACKSONVILLE 30, Pittsburgh 21
San Francisco 34, CAROLINA 21
DENVER 34, New England 13
WASHINGTON 21, Dallas 16
Buffalo 9, INDIANAPOLIS 6
Green Bay 28, NEW ENGLAND 10
Chicago 36, MIAMI 33 (OT)
KANSAS CITY 13, Pittsburgh 10
San Francisco 24, PHILADELPHIA 12
MIAMI 30, Buffalo 13
DENVER 31, Oakland 3
Green Bay 27, MINNESOTA 11
Carolina 23, DALLAS 13
SAN FRANCISCO 34, Denver 17
New England 14, MIAMI 12

1996
CHICAGO 22, Dallas 6
GREEN BAY 39, Philadelphia 13
PITTSBURGH 24, Buffalo 6
INDIANAPOLIS 10, Miami 6
Dallas 23, PHILADELPHIA 19
Pittsburgh 17, KANSAS CITY 7
GREEN BAY 23, San Francisco 20 (OT)
Oakland 23, SAN DIEGO 14
Chicago 15, MINNESOTA 13
Denver 22, OAKLAND 21
SAN DIEGO 27, Detroit 21
DALLAS 21, Green Bay 6
Pittsburgh 24, MIAMI 17
San Francisco 34, ATLANTA 10
OAKLAND 26, Kansas City 7
MIAMI 16, Buffalo 14
SAN FRANCISCO 24, Detroit 14

1995
Dallas 35, NEW YORK GIANTS 0
Green Bay 27, CHICAGO 24
MIAMI 23, Pittsburgh 10
DETROIT 27, San Francisco 24
Buffalo 22, CLEVELAND 19
KANSAS CITY 29, San Diego 23 (OT)
DENVER 27, Oakland 0
NEW ENGLAND 27, Buffalo 14
Chicago 14, MINNESOTA 6
DALLAS 34, Philadelphia 12
PITTSBURGH 20, Cleveland 3
San Francisco 44, MIAMI 20
SAN DIEGO 12, Oakland 6
DETROIT 27, Chicago 7
MIAMI 13, Kansas City 6
SAN FRANCISCO 37, Minnesota 30
Dallas 37, ARIZONA 13

1994
SAN FRANCISCO 44, Los Angeles Raiders 14
PHILADELPHIA 30, Chicago 22
Detroit 20, DALLAS 17 (OT)
BUFFALO 27, Denver 20
PITTSBURGH 30, Houston 14
Minnesota 27, NEW YORK GIANTS 10
Kansas City 31, DENVER 28
PHILADELPHIA 21, Houston 6
Green Bay 33, CHICAGO 6
DALLAS 38, New York Giants 10
PITTSBURGH 23, Buffalo 10
New York Giants 13, HOUSTON 10
San Francisco 35, NEW ORLEANS 14
Los Angeles Raiders 24, SAN DIEGO 17
MIAMI 45, Kansas City 28
Dallas 24, NEW ORLEANS 16
MINNESOTA 21, San Francisco 14

1993
WASHINGTON 35, Dallas 16
CLEVELAND 23, San Francisco 13
KANSAS CITY 15, Denver 7
Pittsburgh 45, ATLANTA 17
MIAMI 17, Washington 10
BUFFALO 35, Houston 7
Los Angeles Raiders 23, DENVER 20
Minnesota 19, CHICAGO 12
BUFFALO 24, Washington 10
KANSAS CITY 23, Green Bay 16
PITTSBURGH 23, Buffalo 0
SAN FRANCISCO 42, New Orleans 7
San Diego 31, INDIANAPOLIS 0
DALLAS 23, Philadelphia 17
Pittsburgh 21, MIAMI 20
New York Giants 24, NEW ORLEANS 14
SAN DIEGO 45, Miami 20
Philadelphia 37, SAN FRANCISCO 34 (OT)

1992
DALLAS 23, Washington 10
Miami 27, CLEVELAND 23
New York Giants 27, CHICAGO 14
KANSAS CITY 27, Los Angeles Raiders 7
PHILADELPHIA 31, Dallas 7
WASHINGTON 34, Denver 3
PITTSBURGH 20, Cincinnati 0
Buffalo 24, NEW YORK JETS 20
Minnesota 38, CHICAGO 10
San Francisco 41, ATLANTA 3
Buffalo 26, MIAMI 20
NEW ORLEANS 20, Washington 3
SEATTLE 16, Denver 13 (OT)
HOUSTON 24, Chicago 7
MIAMI 20, Los Angeles Raiders 7
Dallas 41, ATLANTA 17
SAN FRANCISCO 24, Detroit 6

1991
NEW YORK GIANTS 16, San Francisco 14
Washington 33, DALLAS 31
HOUSTON 17, Kansas City 7
CHICAGO 19, New York Jets 13 (OT)
WASHINGTON 23, Philadelphia 0
KANSAS CITY 33, Buffalo 6
New York Giants 23, PITTSBURGH 20
BUFFALO 35, Cincinnati 16
KANSAS CITY 24, Los Angeles Raiders 21
PHILADELPHIA 30, New York Giants 7
Chicago 34, MINNESOTA 17
Buffalo 41, MIAMI 27
San Francisco 33, LOS ANGELES RAMS 10
Philadelphia 13, HOUSTON 6
MIAMI 37, Cincinnati 13
NEW ORLEANS 27, Los Angeles Raiders 0
SAN FRANCISCO 52, Chicago 14

1990
San Francisco 13, NEW ORLEANS 12
DENVER 24, Kansas City 23
Buffalo 30, NEW YORK JETS 7
SEATTLE 31, Cincinnati 16
Cleveland 30, DENVER 29
PHILADELPHIA 32, Minnesota 24
Cincinnati 34, CLEVELAND 13
PITTSBURGH 41, Los Angeles Rams 10
New York Giants 24, INDIANAPOLIS 7
PHILADELPHIA 28, Washington 14
Los Angeles Raiders 13, MIAMI 10
HOUSTON 27, Buffalo 24
SAN FRANCISCO 7, New York Giants 3
Los Angeles Raiders 38, DETROIT 31
San Francisco 26, LOS ANGELES RAMS 10
NEW ORLEANS 20, Los Angeles Rams 17

1989
New York Giants 27, WASHINGTON 24
Denver 28, BUFFALO 14
CINCINNATI 21, Cleveland 14
CHICAGO 27, Philadelphia 13
Los Angeles Raiders 14, NEW YORK JETS 7
BUFFALO 23, Los Angeles Rams 20
CLEVELAND 27, Chicago 7
NEW YORK GIANTS 24, Minnesota 14
SAN FRANCISCO 31, New Orleans 13
HOUSTON 26, Cincinnati 24
Denver 14, WASHINGTON 10
SAN FRANCISCO 34, New York Giants 24
SEATTLE 17, Buffalo 16
San Francisco 30, LOS ANGELES RAMS 27
NEW ORLEANS 30, Philadelphia 20
MINNESOTA 29, Cincinnati 21

1988
NEW YORK GIANTS 27, Washington 20
Dallas 17, PHOENIX 14
CLEVELAND 23, Indianapolis 17
Los Angeles Raiders 30, DENVER 27 (OT)
NEW ORLEANS 20, Dallas 17
PHILADELPHIA 24, New York Giants 13
Buffalo 37, NEW YORK JETS 14
CHICAGO 10, San Francisco 9
INDIANAPOLIS 55, Denver 23
HOUSTON 24, Cleveland 17
Buffalo 31, MIAMI 6
SAN FRANCISCO 37, Washington 21
SEATTLE 35, Los Angeles Raiders 27
LOS ANGELES RAMS 23, Chicago 3
MIAMI 38, Cleveland 31
MINNESOTA 28, Chicago 27

1987
CHICAGO 34, New York Giants 19
NEW YORK JETS 43, New England 24
San Francisco 41, NEW YORK GIANTS 21
DENVER 30, Los Angeles Raiders 14
Washington 13, DALLAS 7
CLEVELAND 30, Los Angeles Rams 17
MINNESOTA 34, Denver 27
DALLAS 33, New York Giants 24
NEW YORK JETS 30, Seattle 14
DENVER 31, Chicago 29
Los Angeles Rams 30, WASHINGTON 26
Los Angeles Raiders 37, SEATTLE 14
MIAMI 37, New York Jets 28
SAN FRANCISCO 41, Chicago 0
Dallas 29, LOS ANGELES RAMS 21
New England 24, MIAMI 10

MONDAY NIGHT FOOTBALL

1986
DALLAS 31, New York Giants 28
Denver 21, PITTSBURGH 10
Chicago 25, GREEN BAY 12
Dallas 31, ST. LOUIS 7
SEATTLE 33, San Diego 7
CINCINNATI 24, Pittsburgh 22
NEW YORK JETS 22, Denver 10
NEW YORK GIANTS 27, Washington 20
Los Angeles Rams 20, CHICAGO 17
CLEVELAND 26, Miami 16
WASHINGTON 14, San Francisco 6
MIAMI 45, New York Jets 3
New York Giants 21, SAN FRANCISCO 17
SEATTLE 37, Los Angeles Raiders 0
Chicago 16, DETROIT 13
New England 34, MIAMI 27

1985
DALLAS 44, Washington 14
CLEVELAND 17, Pittsburgh 7
Los Angeles Rams 35, SEATTLE 24
Cincinnati 37, PITTSBURGH 24
WASHINGTON 27, St. Louis 10
NEW YORK JETS 23, Miami 7
CHICAGO 23, Green Bay 7
LOS ANGELES RAIDERS 34, San Diego 21
ST. LOUIS 21, Dallas 10
DENVER 17, San Francisco 16
WASHINGTON 23, New York Giants 21
SAN FRANCISCO 19, Seattle 6
MIAMI 38, Chicago 24
Los Angeles Rams 27, SAN FRANCISCO 20
MIAMI 30, New England 27
L.A. Raiders 16, L.A. RAMS 6

1984
Dallas 20, LOS ANGELES RAMS 13
SAN FRANCISCO 37, Washington 31
Miami 21, BUFFALO 17
LOS ANGELES RAIDERS 33, San Diego 30
PITTSBURGH 38, Cincinnati 17
San Francisco 31, NEW YORK GIANTS 10
DENVER 17, Green Bay 14
Los Angeles Rams 24, ATLANTA 10
Seattle 24, SAN DIEGO 0
WASHINGTON 27, Atlanta 14
SEATTLE 17, Los Angeles Raiders 14
NEW ORLEANS 27, Pittsburgh 24
MIAMI 28, New York Jets 17
SAN DIEGO 20, Chicago 7
Los Angeles Raiders 24, DETROIT 3
MIAMI 28, Dallas 21

1983
Dallas 31, WASHINGTON 30
San Diego 17, KANSAS CITY 14
LOS ANGELES RAIDERS 27, Miami 14
NEW YORK GIANTS 27, Green Bay 3
New York Jets 34, BUFFALO 10
Pittsburgh 24, CINCINNATI 14
GREEN BAY 48, Washington 47
ST. LOUIS 20, New York Giants 20 (OT)
Washington 27, SAN DIEGO 24
DETROIT 15, New York Giants 9
Los Angeles Rams 36, ATLANTA 13
New York Jets 31, NEW ORLEANS 28
MIAMI 38, Cincinnati 14
DETROIT 13, Minnesota 2
Green Bay 12, TAMPA BAY 9 (OT)
SAN FRANCISCO 42, Dallas 17

1982
Pittsburgh 36, DALLAS 28
Green Bay 27, NEW YORK GIANTS 19
LOS ANGELES RAIDERS 28, San Diego 24
TAMPA BAY 23, Miami 17
New York Jets 28, DETROIT 13
Dallas 37, HOUSTON 7
SAN DIEGO 50, Cincinnati 34
MIAMI 27, Buffalo 10
MINNESOTA 31, Dallas 27

1981
San Diego 44, CLEVELAND 14
Oakland 36, MINNESOTA 10
Dallas 35, NEW ENGLAND 21
Los Angeles 24, CHICAGO 7
PHILADELPHIA 16, Atlanta 13
BUFFALO 31, Miami 21
DETROIT 48, Chicago 17
PITTSBURGH 26, Houston 13
DENVER 19, Minnesota 17
DALLAS 27, Buffalo 14
SEATTLE 44, San Diego 23
ATLANTA 31, Minnesota 30
MIAMI 13, Philadelphia 10
OAKLAND 30, Pittsburgh 27
LOS ANGELES 21, Atlanta 16
SAN DIEGO 23, Oakland 10

1980
Dallas 17, WASHINGTON 3
Houston 16, CLEVELAND 7
PHILADELPHIA 35, New York Giants 3
NEW ENGLAND 23, Denver 14
CHICAGO 23, Tampa Bay 0
DENVER 20, Washington 17
Oakland 45, PITTSBURGH 34
NEW YORK JETS 17, Miami 14
CLEVELAND 27, Chicago 21
HOUSTON 38, New England 34
Oakland 19, SEATTLE 17
Los Angeles 27, NEW ORLEANS 7
OAKLAND 9, Denver 3
MIAMI 16, New England 13 (OT)
LOS ANGELES 38, Dallas 14
SAN DIEGO 26, Pittsburgh 17

1979
Pittsburgh 16, NEW ENGLAND 13 (OT)
Atlanta 14, PHILADELPHIA 10
WASHINGTON 27, New York Giants 0
CLEVELAND 26, Dallas 7
GREEN BAY 27, New England 14
OAKLAND 13, Miami 3
NEW YORK JETS 14, Minnesota 7
PITTSBURGH 42, Denver 7
Seattle 31, ATLANTA 28
Houston 9, MIAMI 6
Philadelphia 31, DALLAS 21
LOS ANGELES 20, Atlanta 14
SEATTLE 30, New York Jets 7
Oakland 42, NEW ORLEANS 35
HOUSTON 20, Pittsburgh 17
SAN DIEGO 17, Denver 7

1978
DALLAS 38, Baltimore 0
MINNESOTA 12, Denver 9 (OT)
Baltimore 34, NEW ENGLAND 27
Minnesota 24, CHICAGO 20
WASHINGTON 9, Dallas 5
MIAMI 21, Cincinnati 0
DENVER 16, Chicago 7
Houston 24, PITTSBURGH 17
ATLANTA 15, Los Angeles 7
BALTIMORE 21, Washington 17
Oakland 34, CINCINNATI 21
HOUSTON 35, Miami 30
Pittsburgh 24, SAN FRANCISCO 7
SAN DIEGO 40, Chicago 7
Cincinnati 20, LOS ANGELES 19
MIAMI 23, New England 3

1977
PITTSBURGH 27, San Francisco 0
CLEVELAND 30, New England 27 (OT)
Oakland 37, KANSAS CITY 28
CHICAGO 24, Los Angeles 23
PITTSBURGH 20, Cincinnati 14
LOS ANGELES 35, Minnesota 3
ST. LOUIS 28, New York Giants 0
BALTIMORE 10, Washington 3
St. Louis 24, DALLAS 17
WASHINGTON 10, Green Bay 9
OAKLAND 34, Buffalo 13
MIAMI 17, Baltimore 6
Dallas 42, SAN FRANCISCO 35

1976
Miami 30, BUFFALO 21
Oakland 24, KANSAS CITY 21
Washington 20, PHILADELPHIA 17 (OT)
MINNESOTA 17, Pittsburgh 6
San Francisco 16, LOS ANGELES 0
NEW ENGLAND 41, New York Jets 7
WASHINGTON 20, St. Louis 10
BALTIMORE 38, Houston 14
CINCINNATI 20, Los Angeles 12
DALLAS 17, Buffalo 10
Baltimore 17, MIAMI 16
SAN FRANCISCO 20, Minnesota 16
OAKLAND 35, Cincinnati 20

1975
Oakland 31, MIAMI 21
DENVER 23, Green Bay 13
Dallas 36, DETROIT 10
WASHINGTON 27, St. Louis 17
New York Giants 17, BUFFALO 14
Minnesota 13, CHICAGO 9
Los Angeles 42, PHILADELPHIA 3
Kansas City 34, DALLAS 31
CINCINNATI 33, Buffalo 24
Pittsburgh 32, HOUSTON 9
MIAMI 20, New England 7
OAKLAND 17, Denver 10
SAN DIEGO 24, New York Jets 16

1974
BUFFALO 21, Oakland 20
PHILADELPHIA 13, Dallas 10
WASHINGTON 30, Denver 3
MIAMI 21, New York Jets 17
DETROIT 17, San Francisco 13
CHICAGO 10, Green Bay 9
PITTSBURGH 24, Atlanta 17
Los Angeles 15, SAN FRANCISCO 13
Minnesota 28, ST. LOUIS 24
Kansas City 42, DENVER 34
Pittsburgh 28, NEW ORLEANS 7
MIAMI 24, Cincinnati 3
Washington 23, LOS ANGELES 17

1973
GREEN BAY 23, New York Jets 7
DALLAS 40, New Orleans 3
DETROIT 31, Atlanta 6
WASHINGTON 14, Dallas 7
Miami 17, CLEVELAND 9
DENVER 23, Oakland 23
BUFFALO 23, Kansas City 14
PITTSBURGH 21, Washington 16
KANSAS CITY 19, Chicago 7
ATLANTA 20, Minnesota 14
SAN FRANCISCO 20, Green Bay 6
MIAMI 30, Pittsburgh 26
LOS ANGELES 40, New York Giants 6

1972
Washington 24, MINNESOTA 21
Kansas City 20, NEW ORLEANS 17
New York Giants 27, PHILADELPHIA 12
Oakland 34, HOUSTON 0
Green Bay 24, DETROIT 23
CHICAGO 13, Minnesota 10
DALLAS 28, Detroit 24
Baltimore 24, NEW ENGLAND 17
Cleveland 21, SAN DIEGO 17
WASHINGTON 24, Atlanta 13
MIAMI 31, St. Louis 10
Los Angeles 26, SAN FRANCISCO 16
OAKLAND 24, New York Jets 16

1971
Minnesota 16, DETROIT 13
ST. LOUIS 17, New York Jets 10
Oakland 34, CLEVELAND 20
DALLAS 20, New York Giants 13
KANSAS CITY 38, Pittsburgh 16
MINNESOTA 10, Baltimore 3
GREEN BAY 14, Detroit 14
BALTIMORE 24, Los Angeles 17
SAN DIEGO 20, St. Louis 17
ATLANTA 28, Green Bay 21
MIAMI 34, Chicago 3
Kansas City 26, SAN FRANCISCO 17
Washington 38, LOS ANGELES 24

1970
CLEVELAND 31, New York Jets 21
Kansas City 44, BALTIMORE 24
DETROIT 28, Chicago 14
Green Bay 22, SAN DIEGO 20
OAKLAND 34, Washington 20
MINNESOTA 13, Los Angeles 3
PITTSBURGH 21, Cincinnati 10
Baltimore 13, GREEN BAY 10
St. Louis 38, DALLAS 0
PHILADELPHIA 23, New York Giants 20
Miami 20, ATLANTA 7
Cleveland 21, HOUSTON 10
Detroit 28, LOS ANGELES 23

MONDAY NIGHT WON-LOST RECORDS, 1970-1998

AMERICAN FOOTBALL CONFERENCE

	Balt.	Buff.	Cin.	Clev.	Den.	Ind.	Jax.	K.C.	Mia.	N.E.	N.Y.J.	Oak.	Pitt.	S.D.	Sea.	Tenn.
Total	0-0	16-19	7-16	13-11	18-21-1	10-8	3-0	16-12	34-26	7-16	10-16	33-16-1	27-18	14-12	11-5	11-11
1998					2-1		2-0	0-2	1-2	1-2	1-0		2-1			
1997		1-1			2-1	0-1	1-0	2-0	1-2	1-2		0-2	0-2			
1996		0-2			1-0	1-0		0-2	1-2			2-1	3-0	1-1		
1995		1-1		0-2	1-0			1-1	2-1	1-0		0-2	1-1	1-1		
1994		1-1			0-2			1-1	1-0			1-1	2-0	0-1		0-3
1993		2-1		1-0	0-2	0-1		2-0	1-2			1-0	3-0	2-0		0-1
1992		2-0	0-1	0-1	0-2			1-0	2-1		0-1	0-2	1-0		1-0	1-0
1991		2-1	0-2					2-1	1-1		0-1	0-2	0-1			1-1
1990		1-1	1-1	1-1	1-1	0-1		0-1	0-1		0-1	2-0	1-0		1-0	1-0
1989		1-2	1-2	1-1	2-0						0-1	1-0			1-0	1-0
1988		2-0		1-2	0-2	1-1			1-1		0-1	1-1			1-0	1-0
1987				1-0	2-1				1-1	1-1	2-1	1-1			0-2	
1986			1-0	1-0	1-1				1-2	1-0	1-1	0-1	0-2	0-1	2-0	
1985			1-0	1-0	1-0				2-1	0-1	1-0	2-0	0-2	0-1	0-2	
1984		0-1	0-1		1-0				3-0		0-1	2-1	1-1	1-2	2-0	
1983		0-1	0-2					0-1	1-1		2-0	1-0	1-0	1-1		
1982		0-1	0-1		0-1				1-1		1-0	1-0	1-0	1-1		0-1
1981		1-1		0-1	1-0				1-1	0-1		2-1	1-1	2-1	1-0	0-1
1980				1-1	1-2				1-1	1-2	1-0	3-0	0-2	1-0	0-1	2-0
1979				1-0	0-2				0-2	0-2	1-1	2-0	2-1	1-0	2-0	2-0
1978			1-2		1-1	2-1			2-1	0-2		1-0	1-1	1-0		2-0
1977		0-1	0-1	1-0		1-1		0-1	1-0	0-1		2-0	2-0			
1976		0-2	1-1			2-0		0-1	1-1	1-0	0-1	2-0	0-1			0-1
1975		0-2	1-0		1-1			1-0	1-1	0-1	0-1	2-0	1-0	1-0		0-1
1974		1-0	0-1		0-2			1-0	2-0		0-1	0-1	2-0			
1973		1-0		0-1	0-0-1			1-1	2-0		0-1	0-0-1	1-1			
1972				1-0		1-0		1-0	1-0	0-1	0-1	2-0		0-1		0-1
1971				0-1		1-1		2-0	1-0		0-1	1-0	0-1	1-0		
1970			0-1	2-0		1-1		1-0	1-0		0-1	1-0	1-0	0-1		0-1

NATIONAL FOOTBALL CONFERENCE

	Ariz.	Atl.	Car.	Chi.	Dall.	Det.	G.B.	Minn.	N.O.	N.Y.G.	Phil.	St. L.	S.F.	T.B.	Wash.
Total	5-9-1	5-15	1-1	16-28	32-23	11-12-1	14-15-1	17-17	6-12	14-22-1	14-16	17-20	33-18	2-3	23-22
1998					2-0	1-1	0-3	1-0		0-2	0-1		3-0	1-1	0-1
1997			1-1	1-1	1-2		3-0	0-1			0-2		3-0		1-0
1996		0-1		2-0	2-1	0-2	2-1	0-1			0-2		2-1		
1995	0-1			1-2	3-0	2-0	1-0	0-2		0-1	0-1		2-1		
1994				0-2	2-1	1-0	1-0	2-0	0-2	1-2	2-0		2-1		
1993		0-1		0-1	1-1		0-1	1-0	0-2	1-0	1-1		1-2		1-2
1992		0-2		0-3	2-1	0-1		1-0	1-0	1-0	1-0		2-0		1-2
1991				2-1	0-1			0-1	1-0	2-1	2-1	0-1	2-1		2-0
1990						0-1		0-1	1-1	1-1	2-0	0-3	3-0		0-1
1989				1-1				1-1	1-1	2-1	0-2	0-2	3-0		0-2
1988	0-1			1-2	1-1			1-0	1-0	1-0	1-1	1-0	1-1		0-2
1987				1-2	2-1			1-0		0-3		1-2	2-0		1-1
1986	0-1			2-1	2-0	0-1	0-1			2-1		1-0	0-2		1-1
1985	1-1			1-1	1-1		0-1			0-1		2-1	1-2		2-1
1984		0-2		0-1	1-1	0-1	0-1		1-0	0-1		1-1	2-0		1-1
1983	0-0-1	0-1			1-1	2-0	2-1	0-1	0-1	1-1-1		1-0	1-0	0-1	1-2
1982					1-2	0-1	1-0	1-0		0-1				1-0	
1981		1-2		0-2	2-0	1-0		0-3			1-1	2-0			
1980				1-1	1-1				0-1	0-1	1-0	2-0		0-1	0-2
1979		1-2			0-2		1-0	0-1	0-1	0-1	1-1	1-0			1-0
1978		1-0		0-3	1-1			2-0				0-2	0-1		1-1
1977	2-0			1-0	1-1		0-1	0-1		0-1		1-1	0-2		1-1
1976	0-1				1-0			1-1			0-1	0-2	2-0		2-0
1975	0-1			0-1	1-1	0-1	0-1	1-0		1-0	0-1	1-0			1-0
1974	0-1	0-1		1-0	0-1	1-0	0-1	1-0	0-1		1-0	1-1	0-2		2-0
1973		1-1		0-1	1-1	1-0	1-1	0-1	0-1	0-1		1-0	1-0		1-1
1972	0-1	0-1		1-0	1-0	0-2	1-0	0-2	0-1	1-0	0-1	1-0	0-1		2-0
1971	1-1	1-0		0-1	1-0	0-1-1	0-1-1	2-0		0-1		0-2	0-1		1-0
1970	1-0	0-1		0-1	0-1	2-0	1-1	1-0		0-1	1-0	0-2			0-1

Compiled by Elias Sports Bureau
*Set or tied NFL all-time record.

MONDAY NIGHT RECORDS

SCORING
TOUCHDOWNS
Most Touchdowns, Game
4 Ron Johnson, N.Y. Giants at Philadelphia, Oct. 2, 1972
4 Earl Campbell, Houston vs. Miami, Nov. 20, 1978
4 Marcus Allen, L.A. Raiders vs. San Diego, Sept. 24, 1984
4 Eric Dickerson, Indianapolis vs. Denver, Oct. 31, 1988
4 Emmitt Smith, Dallas at N.Y. Giants, Sept. 4. 1995
FIELD GOALS
Most Field Goals, Game
7 Chris Boniol, Dallas vs. Green Bay, Nov. 18, 1996*
5 Tim Mazzetti, Atlanta vs. Los Angeles, Oct. 30, 1978
5 Roger Ruzek, Dallas at L.A. Rams, Dec. 21, 1987
5 Rich Karlis, Minnesota vs. Cincinnati, Dec. 25, 1989
5 Nick Lowery, Kansas City vs. Denver, Sept. 20, 1993
5 Chris Jacke, Green Bay vs. San Francisco, Oct. 14, 1996 (OT)
5 Richie Cunningham, Dallas vs. Philadelphia, Sept. 15, 1997

RUSHING
YARDS GAINED
Most Yards Rushing, Game
221 Bo Jackson, L.A. Raiders at Seattle, Nov. 30, 1987
214 Thurman Thomas, Buffalo at N.Y. Jets, Sept. 24, 1990
199 Earl Campbell, Houston vs. Miami, Nov. 20, 1978
Longest Run From Scrimage, Game
99 Tony Dorsett, Dallas at Minnesota, Jan. 3, 1983 (TD)*
91 Bo Jackson, L.A. Raiders at Seattle, Nov. 30, 1987 (TD)
83 James Lofton, Green Bay at N.Y. Giants, Sept. 20, 1982 (TD)
TOUCHDOWNS
Most Rushing Touchdowns, Game
4 Earl Campbell, Houston vs. Miami, Nov. 20, 1978
4 Eric Dickerson, Indianapolis vs. Denver, Oct. 31, 1988
4 Emmitt Smith, Dallas at N.Y. Giants, Sept. 4, 1995

PASSING
YARDS GAINED
Most Yards Passing, Game
458 Joe Montana, San Francisco at L.A. Rams, Dec. 11, 1989
447 Ken Anderson, Cincinnati vs. Buffalo, Nov. 17, 1975
445 Charley Johnson, Denver vs. Kansas City, Nov. 18, 1974
Longest Pass Play
99 Brett Favre to Robert Brooks, Green Bay at Chicago, Sept. 11, 1995 (TD)*
97 Bernie Kosar to Webster Slaughter, Cleveland vs. Chicago, Oct. 23, 1989 (TD)
95 Joe Montana to John Taylor, San Francisco at L.A. Rams, Dec. 11, 1989 (TD)
TOUCHDOWNS
Most Touchdown Passes, Game
5 Dave Krieg, Seattle vs. L.A. Raiders, Nov. 28, 1988
5 Jim Kelly, Buffalo vs. Cincinnati, Oct. 21, 1991

PASS RECEIVING
RECEPTIONS
Most Pass Receptions, Game
14 Herman Moore, Detroit vs. Chicago, Dec. 4, 1995
14 Jerry Rice, San Francisco vs. Minnesota, Dec. 18, 1995
13 Andre Reed, Buffalo vs. Denver, Sept. 18, 1989
YARDS GAINED
Most Yards on Pass Receptions, Game
289 Jerry Rice, San Francisco vs. Minnesota, Dec. 18, 1995
286 John Taylor, San Francisco at L.A. Rams, Dec. 11, 1989
260 Wes Chandler, San Diego vs. Cincinnati, Dec. 20, 1982
TOUCHDOWNS
Most Touchdown Pass Receptions, Game
3 Ron Johnson, N.Y. Giants at Philadelphia, Oct. 2, 1972
3 Wesley Walker, N.Y. Jets at Detroit, Dec. 6, 1982
3 Steve Largent, Seattle at San Diego, Oct. 29, 1984
3 Mark Clayton, Miami vs. Dallas, Dec. 17, 1984
3 Jerry Rice, San Francisco vs. Chicago, Dec. 14, 1987
3 Jerry Rice, San Francisco vs. Minnesota, Dec. 18, 1995
3 Lamar Thomas, Miami vs. Denver, Dec. 21, 1998

INTERCEPTIONS BY
Most Interceptions, Game
4 Dick Anderson, Miami vs. Pittsburgh, Dec. 3, 1973*
3 Johnny Robinson, Kansas City at Baltimore, Sept. 28, 1970
3 Charlie Babb, Miami vs. Oakland, Sept. 22, 1975
3 Charles Phillips, Oakland vs. Denver, Dec. 8, 1975
3 Mark Murphy, Washington at San Diego, Oct. 31, 1983
3 Ken Easley, Seattle at San Diego, Oct. 29, 1984
3 Dwayne Harper, San Diego vs. Oakland, Nov. 27, 1995
Longest Interception Return
102 Eddie Anderson, L.A. Raiders at Miami, Dec. 14, 1992 (TD)
94 Nolan Cromwell, L.A. Rams vs. Atlanta, Dec. 14, 1981
94 Walker Lee Ashley, Minnesota vs. Chicago, Dec. 19, 1988 (TD)

PUNTING
Longest Punt
74 Craig Colquitt, Pittsburgh vs. Oakland, Dec. 7, 1981
73 Tom Tupa, New England at Denver, Oct. 6, 1997
72 Bill Van Heusen, Denver at Oakland, Oct. 22, 1973

PUNT RETURNS
Longest Punt Return
95 John Taylor, San Francisco vs. Washington, Nov. 21, 1988 (TD)
94 Dennis McKinnon, Chicago vs. N.Y. Giants, Sept. 14, 1987 (TD)
91 JoJo Townsell, N.Y. Jets vs. Seattle, Nov. 9, 1987 (TD)

KICKOFF RETURNS
Longest Kickoff Return
105 Terry Fair, Detroit vs. Tampa Bay, Sept. 28, 1998 (TD)
102 Harold Hart, Oakland at Miami, Sept. 22, 1975 (TD)
101 Roell Preston, Green Bay vs. Minnesota, Oct. 5, 1998 (TD)

FUMBLES
Longest Fumble Return
99 Don Griffin, San Francisco vs. Chicago, Dec. 23, 1991 (TD)
96 Joe Lavender, Philadelphia vs. Dallas, Sept. 23, 1974 (TD)
88 Keith McKenzie, Pittsburgh vs. Green Bay, Nov. 9, 1998 (TD)

THANKSGIVING DAY RECORDS

SCORING
Most Touchdowns, Game
6 Ernie Nevers, Chi. Cardinals vs. Chi. Bears, Nov. 28, 1929*
4 Sterling Sharpe, Green Bay at Dallas, Nov. 24, 1994
3 By many players

RUSHING
Most Yards Rushing, Game
273 O.J. Simpson, Buffalo at Detroit, Nov. 25, 1976
198 Bob Hoernschemeyer, Detroit vs. N.Y. Yankees, Nov. 23, 1950
195 Earl Campbell, Houston at Dallas, Nov. 22, 1979

PASSING
Most Yards Passing, Game
455 Troy Aikman, Dallas vs. Minnesota, Nov. 26, 1998
410 Scott Mitchell, Detroit vs. Minnesota, Nov. 23, 1995
384 Warren Moon, Minnesota at Detroit, Nov. 23, 1995

PASS RECEIVING
RECEPTIONS
Most Pass Receptions, Game
12 Brett Perriman, Detroit vs. Minnesota, Nov. 23, 1995
11 Daryl Johnston, Dallas vs. Miami, Nov. 25, 1993
Michael Irvin, Dallas vs Kansas City, Nov. 23 1995
YARDS GAINED
Most Yards on Pass Receptions, Game
303 Jim Benton, Cleveland at Detroit, Nov. 22, 1945
185 Lance Alworth, San Diego vs. Buffalo, Nov. 26, 1964
184 Anthony Carter, Minnesota at Dallas, Nov. 26, 1987 (OT)

THURSDAY-SUNDAY NIGHT FOOTBALL

THURSDAY-SUNDAY NIGHT FOOTBALL, 1974-1998

(Home Team in capitals, games listed in chronological order.)

1998
KANSAS CITY 28, Oakland 8 (Sun.)
NEW ENGLAND 29, Indianapolis 6 (Sun.)
ARIZONA 17, Philadelphia 3 (Sun.)
BALTIMORE 31, Cincinnati 24 (Sun.)
KANSAS CITY 17, Seattle 6 (Sun.)
Atlanta 34, NEW YORK GIANTS 20 (Sun.)
DETROIT 27, Green Bay 20 (Thurs.)
Buffalo 30, CAROLINA 14 (Sun.)
Oakland 31, SEATTLE 18 (Sun.)
Tennessee 31, TAMPA BAY 22 (Sun.)
DETROIT 26, Chicago 3 (Sun.)
SAN FRANCISCO 31, New Orleans 20 (Sun.)
Denver 31, SAN DIEGO 16 (Sun.)
PHILADELPHIA 17, St. Louis 14 (Thurs.)
MINNESOTA 48, Chicago 22 (Sun.)
New York Jets 21, MIAMI 16 (Sun.)
MINNESOTA 50, Jacksonville 10 (Sun.)
Dallas 23, WASHINGTON 7 (Sun.)

1997
Washington 24, CAROLINA 10 (Sun.)
ARIZONA 25, Dallas 22 (OT) (Sun.)
NEW ENGLAND 27, New York Jets 24 (OT) (Sun.)
TAMPA BAY 31, Miami 21 (Sun.)
MINNESOTA 28, Philadelphia 19 (Sun.)
New Orleans 20, CHICAGO 17 (Sun.)
PITTSBURGH 24, Indianapolis 22 (Sun.)
KANSAS CITY 31, San Diego 3 (Thurs.)
CAROLINA 21, Atlanta 12 (Sun.)
GREEN BAY 20, Detroit 10 (Sun.)
PITTSBURGH 37, Baltimore 0 (Sun.)
Oakland 38, SAN DIEGO 13 (Sun.)
WASHINGTON 7, New York Giants 7 (OT) (Sun.)
Denver 38, SAN DIEGO 28 (Sun.)
CINCINNATI 41, Tennessee 14 (Thurs.)
MIAMI 33, Detroit 30 (Sun.)
Chicago 13, ST. LOUIS 10 (Sun.)
SEATTLE 38, San Francisco 9 (Sun.)

1996
Buffalo 23, NEW YORK GIANTS 20 (OT) (Sun.)
Miami 38, ARIZONA 10 (Sun.)
DENVER 27, Tampa Bay 23 (Sun.)
Philadelphia 33, ATLANTA 18 (Sun.)
WASHINGTON 31, New York Jets 16 (Sun.)
Houston 30, CINCINNATI 27 (OT) (Sun.)
INDIANAPOLIS 26, Baltimore 21 (Sun.)
KANSAS CITY 34, Seattle 16 (Thurs.)
NEW ENGLAND 28, Buffalo 25 (Sun.)
San Francisco 24, NEW ORLEANS 17 (Sun.)
CAROLINA 27, New York Giants 17 (Sun.)
Minnesota 16, OAKLAND 13 (OT) (Sun.)
Green Bay 24, ST. LOUIS 9 (Sun.)
New England 45, SAN DIEGO 7 (Sun.)
INDIANAPOLIS 37, Philadelphia 10 (Thurs.)
Minnesota 24, DETROIT 22 (Sun.)
JACKSONVILLE 20, Seattle 13 (Sun.)
SAN DIEGO 16, Denver 10 (Sun.)

1995
DENVER 22, Buffalo 7 (Sun.)
Philadelphia 31, ARIZONA 19 (Sun.)
Dallas 23, MINNESOTA 17 (OT) (Sun.)
Green Bay 24, JACKSONVILLE 14 (Sun.)
Oakland 47, NEW YORK JETS 10 (Sun.)
Denver 37, NEW ENGLAND 3 (Sun.)
ST. LOUIS 21, Atlanta 19 (Thurs.)
Cincinnati 27, PITTSBURGH 9 (Thurs.)
New York Giants 24, WASHINGTON 15 (Sun.)
Miami 24, SAN DIEGO 14 (Sun.)
PHILADELPHIA 31, Denver 13 (Sun.)
KANSAS CITY 20, Houston 13 (Sun.)
NEW ORLEANS 34, Carolina 26 (Sun.)
New York Giants 10, ARIZONA 6 (Thurs.)
SAN FRANCISCO 27, Buffalo 17 (Sun.)
TAMPA BAY 13, Green Bay 10 (OT) (Sun.)
SEATTLE 44, Oakland 10 (Sun.)
INDIANAPOLIS 10, New England 7 (Sat.)

1994
San Diego 17, DENVER 34 (Sun.)
New York Giants 20, ARIZONA 17 (Sun.)
Kansas City 30, ATLANTA 10 (Sun.)
Chicago 19, NEW YORK JETS 7 (Sun.)
Miami 23, CINCINNATI 7 (Sun.)
PHILADELPHIA 21, Washington 17 (Sun.)
Cleveland 11, HOUSTON 8 (Thurs.)
MINNESOTA 13, Green Bay 10 (OT) (Thurs.)
ARIZONA 20, Pittsburgh 17 (OT) (Sun.)
KANSAS CITY 13, Los Angeles Raiders 3 (Sun.)
DETROIT 14, Tampa Bay 9 (Sun.)
SAN FRANCISCO 31, Los Angeles Rams 27 (Sun.)
New England 12, INDIANAPOLIS 10 (Sun.)
MINNESOTA 33, Chicago 27 (OT) (Thurs.)
Buffalo 42, MIAMI 31 (Sun.)
New Orleans 29, ATLANTA 20 (Sun.)
Los Angeles Raiders 17, SEATTLE 16 (Sun.)
MIAMI 27, Detroit 20 (Sun.)

1993
NEW ORLEANS 33, Houston 21 (Sun.)
Los Angeles Raiders 17, SEATTLE 13 (Sun.)
Dallas 17, PHOENIX 10 (Sun.)
NEW YORK JETS 45, New England 7 (Sun.)
BUFFALO 17, New York Giants 14 (Sun.)
GREEN BAY 30, Denver 27 (Sun.)
ATLANTA 30, Los Angeles Rams 24 (Thurs.)
MIAMI 41, Indianapolis 27 (Sun.)
Detroit 30, MINNESOTA 27 (Sun.)
WASHINGTON 30, Indianapolis 24 (Sun.)
Chicago 16, SAN DIEGO 13 (Sun.)
TAMPA BAY 23, Minnesota 10 (Sun.)
HOUSTON 23, Pittsburgh 3 (Sun.)
SAN FRANCISCO 21, Cincinnati 8 (Sun.)
Green Bay 20, SAN DIEGO 13 (Sun.)
Philadelphia 20, INDIANAPOLIS 10 (Sun.)
MINNESOTA 30, Kansas City 10 (Sun.)
HOUSTON 24, New York Jets 0 (Sun.)

1992
DENVER 17, Los Angeles Raiders 13 (Sun.)
Philadelphia 31, PHOENIX 14 (Sun.)
BUFFALO 38, Indianapolis 0 (Sun.)
San Francisco 16, NEW ORLEANS 10 (Sun.)
NEW YORK JETS 30, New England 21 (Sun.)
NEW ORLEANS 13, Los Angeles Rams 10 (Sun.)
MINNESOTA 31, Detroit 14 (Thurs.)
Pittsburgh 27, KANSAS CITY 3 (Sun.)
New York Giants 24, WASHINGTON 7 (Sun.)
Cincinnati 31, CHICAGO 28 (OT) (Sun.)
DENVER 27, New York Giants 13 (Sun.)
Kansas City 24, SEATTLE 14 (Sun.)
SAN DIEGO 27, Los Angeles Raiders 3 (Sun.)
NEW ORLEANS 22, Atlanta 14 (Thurs.)
Los Angeles Rams 31, TAMPA BAY 27 (Sun.)
Green Bay 16, HOUSTON 14 (Sun.)
MIAMI 19, New York Jets 17 (Sun.)
HOUSTON 27, Buffalo 3 (Sun.)

1991
WASHINGTON 45, Detroit 0 (Sun.)
Houston 30, CINCINNATI 7 (Sun.)
NEW ORLEANS 24, Los Angeles Rams 7 (Sun.)
Dallas 17, PHOENIX 9 (Sun.)
Denver 13, MINNESOTA 6 (Sun.)
Pittsburgh 21, INDIANAPOLIS 3 (Sun.)
Los Angeles Raiders 23, SEATTLE 20 (Sun.)
Chicago 10, GREEN BAY 0 (Thurs.)
Washington 17, NEW YORK GIANTS 13 (Sun.)
DENVER 20, Pittsburgh 13 (Sun.)
MIAMI 30, New England 20 (Sun.)
HOUSTON 28, Cleveland 24 (Sun.)
Atlanta 23, NEW ORLEANS 20 (OT) (Sun.)
Los Angeles Raiders 9, SAN DIEGO 7 (Sun.)
Minnesota 26, TAMPA BAY 24 (Sun.)
Buffalo 35, INDIANAPOLIS 7 (Sun.)
SEATTLE 23, Los Angeles Rams 9 (Sun.)

1990
NEW YORK GIANTS 27, Philadelphia 20 (Sun.)
PITTSBURGH 20, Houston 9 (Sun.)
TAMPA BAY 23, Detroit 20 (Sun.)
Washington 38, PHOENIX 10 (Sun.)
BUFFALO 38, Los Angeles Raiders 24 (Sun.)
CHICAGO 38, Los Angeles Rams 9 (Sun.)
MIAMI 17, New England 10 (Thurs.)
ATLANTA 38, Cincinnati 17 (Sun.)
MINNESOTA 27, Denver 22 (Sun.)
San Francisco 24, DALLAS 6 (Sun.)
CINCINNATI 27, Pittsburgh 3 (Sun.)
Seattle 13, SAN DIEGO 10 (Sun.)
MINNESOTA 23, Green Bay 7 (Sun.)
MIAMI 23, Philadelphia 20 (Sun.)
DETROIT 38, Chicago 21 (Sun.)
INDIANAPOLIS 35, Washington 28 (Sat.)
SEATTLE 17, Denver 12 (Sun.)
HOUSTON 34, Pittsburgh 14 (Sun.)

1989
Dallas 13, WASHINGTON 3 (Sun.)
SAN DIEGO 14, Los Angeles Raiders 12 (Sun.)
INDIANAPOLIS 27, New York Jets 10 (Sun.)
Los Angeles Rams 20, NEW ORLEANS 17 (Sun.)
MINNESOTA 27, Chicago 16 (Sun.)
MIAMI 31, New England 10 (Sun.)
SEATTLE 23, Los Angeles Raiders 17 (Sun.)
Cleveland 24, HOUSTON 20 (Sat.)

1988
HOUSTON 41, Washington 17 (Sun.)
Los Angeles Raiders 13, SAN DIEGO 3 (Sun.)
Minnesota 43, DALLAS 3 (Sun.)
New England 6, MIAMI 3 (Sun.)
New York Giants 13, NEW ORLEANS 12 (Sun.)
Pittsburgh 37, HOUSTON 34 (Sun.)
SEATTLE 42, Denver 14 (Sun.)
Los Angeles Rams 38, SAN FRANCISCO 16 (Sun.)

1987
NEW YORK GIANTS 17, New England 10 (Sun.)
SAN DIEGO 16, Los Angeles Raiders 14 (Sun.)
Miami 20, DALLAS 14 (Sun.)
SAN FRANCISCO 38, Cleveland 24 (Sun.)
Chicago 30, MINNESOTA 24 (Sun.)
SEATTLE 28, Denver 21 (Sun.)
MIAMI 23, Washington 21 (Sun.)
SAN FRANCISCO 48, Los Angeles Rams 0 (Sun.)

1986
New England 20, NEW YORK JETS 6 (Thurs.)
Cincinnati 30, CLEVELAND 13 (Thurs.)
Los Angeles Raiders 37, SAN DIEGO 31 (OT) (Thurs.)
LOS ANGELES RAMS 29, Dallas 10 (Sun.)
SAN FRANCISCO 24, Los Angeles Rams 14 (Fri.)

1985
KANSAS CITY 36, Los Angeles Raiders 20 (Thurs.)
Chicago 33, MINNESOTA 24 (Thurs.)
Dallas 30, NEW YORK GIANTS 29 (Sun.)
SAN DIEGO 54, Pittsburgh 44 (Sun.)
Denver 27, SEATTLE 24 (Fri.)

1984
Pittsburgh 23, NEW YORK JETS 17 (Thurs.)
Denver 24, CLEVELAND 14 (Sun.)
DALLAS 30, New Orleans 27 (Sun.)
Washington 31, MINNESOTA 17 (Thurs.)
SAN FRANCISCO 19, Los Angeles Rams 16 (Fri.)

1983
San Francisco 48, MINNESOTA 17 (Thurs.)
CLEVELAND 17, Cincinnati 7 (Thurs.)
Los Angeles Raiders 40, DALLAS 38 (Sun.)
Los Angeles Raiders 42, SAN DIEGO 10 (Thurs.)
MIAMI 34, New York Jets 14 (Fri.)

1982
BUFFALO 23, Minnesota 22 (Thurs.)
SAN FRANCISCO 30, Los Angeles Rams 24 (Thurs.)
ATLANTA 17, San Francisco 7 (Sun.)

1981
MIAMI 30, Pittsburgh 10 (Thurs.)
Philadelphia 20, BUFFALO 14 (Thurs.)
DALLAS 29, Los Angeles 17 (Sun.)
HOUSTON 17, Cleveland 13 (Thurs.)

1980
TAMPA BAY 10, Los Angeles 9 (Thurs.)
DALLAS 42, San Diego 31 (Sun.)
San Diego 27, MIAMI 24 (OT) (Thurs.)
HOUSTON 6, Pittsburgh 0 (Thurs.)

1979
Los Angeles 13, DENVER 9 (Thurs.)
DALLAS 30, Los Angeles 6 (Sun.)
OAKLAND 45, San Diego 22 (Thurs.)
MIAMI 39, New England 24 (Thurs.)

1978
New England 21, OAKLAND 14 (Sun.)
Minnesota 21, DALLAS 10 (Thurs.)
LOS ANGELES 10, Pittsburgh 7 (Sun.)
Denver 21, OAKLAND 6 (Sun.)

1977
Minnesota 30, DETROIT 21 (Sat.)

1976
Los Angeles 20, DETROIT 17 (Sat.)

1975
LOS ANGELES 10, Pittsburgh 3 (Sat.)

1974
OAKLAND 27, Dallas 23 (Sat.)

OVERTIME GAMES

HISTORY OF OVERTIME GAMES

PRESEASON

Aug. 28, 1955	Los Angeles 23, New York Giants 17, at Portland, Oregon
Aug. 24, 1962	Denver 27, Dallas Texans 24, at Fort Worth, Texas
Aug. 10, 1974	San Diego 20, New York Jets 14, at San Diego
Aug. 17, 1974	Pittsburgh 33, Philadelphia 30, at Philadelphia
Aug. 17, 1974	Dallas 19, Houston 13, at Dallas
Aug. 17, 1974	Cincinnati 13, Atlanta 7, at Atlanta
Sept. 6, 1974	Buffalo 23, New York Giants 17, at Buffalo
Aug. 9, 1975	Baltimore 23, Denver 20, at Denver
Aug. 30, 1975	New England 20, Green Bay 17, at Milwaukee
Sept. 13, 1975	Minnesota 14, San Diego 14, at San Diego
Aug. 1, 1976	New England 13, New York Giants 7, at New England
Aug. 2, 1976	Kansas City 9, Houston 3, at Kansas City
Aug. 20, 1976	New Orleans 26, Baltimore 20, at Baltimore
Sept. 4, 1976	Dallas 26, Houston 20, at Dallas
Aug. 13, 1977	Seattle 23, Dallas 17, at Seattle
Aug. 28, 1977	New England 13, Pittsburgh 10, at New England
Aug. 28, 1977	New York Giants 24, Buffalo 21, at East Rutherford, N.J.
Aug. 2, 1979	Seattle 12, Minnesota 9, at Minnesota
Aug. 4, 1979	Los Angeles 20, Oakland 14, at Los Angeles
Aug. 24, 1979	Denver 20, New England 17, at Denver
Aug. 23, 1980	Tampa Bay 20, Cincinnati 14, at Tampa Bay
Aug. 5, 1981	San Francisco 27, Seattle 24, at Seattle
Aug. 29, 1981	New Orleans 20, Detroit 17, at New Orleans
Aug. 28, 1982	Miami 17, Kansas City 17, at Kansas City
Sept. 3, 1982	Miami 16, New York Giants 13, at Miami
Aug. 6, 1983	L.A. Raiders 26, San Francisco 23, at Los Angeles
Aug. 6, 1983	Atlanta 13, Washington 10, at Atlanta
Aug. 13, 1983	St. Louis 27, Chicago 24, at St. Louis
Aug. 18, 1983	New York Jets 20, Cincinnati 17, at Cincinnati
Aug. 27, 1983	Chicago 20, Kansas City 17, at Chicago
Aug. 11, 1984	Pittsburgh 20, Philadelphia 17, at Pittsburgh
Aug. 9, 1985	Buffalo 10, Detroit 10, at Pontiac, Mich.
Aug. 10, 1985	Minnesota 16, Miami 13, at Miami
Aug. 17, 1985	Dallas 27, San Diego 24, at San Diego
Aug. 24, 1985	N.Y. Giants 34, N.Y. Jets 31, at East Rutherford, N.J.
Aug. 15, 1986	Washington 27, Pittsburgh 24, at Washington
Aug. 15, 1986	Detroit 30, Seattle 27, at Detroit
Aug. 23, 1986	Los Angeles Rams 20, San Diego 17, at Anaheim
Aug. 30, 1986	Minnesota 23, Indianapolis 20, at Indianapolis
Aug. 23, 1987	Philadelphia 19, New England 13, at New England
Sept. 5, 1987	Cleveland 30, Green Bay 24, at Milwaukee
Sept. 6, 1987	Kansas City 13, St. Louis 10, at Memphis, Tenn.
Aug. 11, 1988	Seattle 16, Detroit 13, at Detroit
Aug. 19, 1988	Miami 16, Denver 13, at Miami
Aug. 19, 1988	Green Bay 21, Kansas City 21, at Milwaukee
Aug. 20, 1988	Houston 20, Los Angeles Rams 17, at Anaheim
Aug. 21, 1988	Minnesota 19, Phoenix 16, at Phoenix
Aug. 5, 1989	Los Angeles Rams 16, San Francisco 13, at Tokyo, Japan
Aug. 26, 1989	Denver 24, Dallas 21, at Denver
Sept. 1, 1989	N.Y. Jets 15, Kansas City 13, at Kansas City
Aug. 24, 1990	Cincinnati 13, New England 10, at New England
Aug. 16, 1991	Cleveland 24, Washington 21, at Washington
Aug. 17, 1991	Cincinnati 27, Minnesota 24, at Cincinnati
Aug. 23, 1991	Dallas 20, Atlanta 17, at Dallas
Aug. 24, 1991	Cincinnati 19, Green Bay 16, at Green Bay
Aug. 22, 1992	Los Angeles Rams 16, Green Bay 13, at Anaheim
Aug. 8, 1993	Dallas 13, Detroit 13, at London, England
Aug. 12, 1995	Washington 16, Houston 13, at Knoxville, Tenn.
Aug. 19, 1995	Indianapolis 20, Green Bay 17, at Green Bay
Aug. 3, 1996	Minnesota 23, San Diego 20, at Minnesota
Aug. 10, 1996	San Francisco 16, San Diego 13, at San Francisco
Aug. 1, 1998	Green Bay 27, Kansas City 24, at Tokyo, Japan
Aug. 7, 1998	Detroit 13, Arizona 10, at Pontiac, Mich.
Aug. 22, 1998	Minnesota 25, Carolina 22, at Charlotte, N.C.

REGULAR SEASON

Sept. 22, 1974—Pittsburgh 35, Denver 35, at Denver; Steelers win toss. Gilliam's pass intercepted and returned by Rowser to Denver's 42. Turner misses 41-yard field goal. Walden punts and Greer returns to Broncos' 39. Van Heusen punts and Edwards returns to Steelers' 16. Game ends with Steelers on own 26.

Nov. 10, 1974—New York Jets 26, New York Giants 20, at New Haven, Conn.; Giants win toss. Gogolak misses 42-yard field goal. Namath passes to Boozer for five yards and touchdown at 6:53.

Sept. 28, 1975—Dallas 37, St. Louis 31, at Dallas; Cardinals win toss. Hart's pass intercepted and returned by Jordan to Cardinals' 37. Staubach passes to DuPree for three yards and touchdown at 7:53.

Oct. 12, 1975—Los Angeles 13, San Diego 10, at San Diego; Chargers win toss. Partee punts to Rams' 14. Dempsey kicks 22-yard field goal at 9:27.

Nov. 2, 1975—Washington 30, Dallas 24, at Washington; Cowboys win toss. Staubach's pass intercepted and returned by Houston to Cowboys' 35. Kilmer runs one yard for touchdown at 6:34.

Nov. 16, 1975—St. Louis 20, Washington 17, at St. Louis; Cardinals win toss. Bakken kicks 37-yard field goal at 7:00.

Nov. 23, 1975—Kansas City 24, Detroit 21, at Kansas City; Lions win toss. Chiefs take over on downs at own 38. Stenerud kicks 26-yard field goal at 6:44.

Nov. 23, 1975—Oakland 26, Washington 23, at Washington; Redskins win toss. Bragg punts to Raiders' 42. Blanda kicks 27-yard field goal at 7:13.

Nov. 30, 1975—Denver 13, San Diego 10, at Denver; Broncos win toss. Turner kicks 25-yard field goal at 4:13.

Nov. 30, 1975—Oakland 37, Atlanta 34, at Oakland; Falcons win toss. James punts to Raiders' 16. Guy punts and Herron returns to Falcons' 41. Nick Mike-Mayer misses 45-yard field goal. Guy punts into Falcons' end zone. James punts to Raiders' 39. Blanda kicks 36-yard field goal at 15:00.

Dec. 14, 1975—Baltimore 10, Miami 7, at Baltimore; Dolphins win toss. Seiple punts to Colts' 4. Linhart kicks 31-yard field goal at 12:44.

Sept. 19, 1976—Minnesota 10, Los Angeles 10, at Minnesota; Vikings win toss. Tarkenton's pass intercepted by Monte Jackson and returned to Minnesota 16. Allen blocks Dempsey's 30-yard field goal attempt, ball rolls into end zone for touchback. Clabo punts and Scribner returns to Rams' 20. Rusty Jackson punts to Vikings' 35. Tarkenton's pass intercepted by Kay at Rams' 1, no return. Game ends with Rams on own 3.

***Sept. 27, 1976—Washington 20, Philadelphia 17,** at Philadelphia; Eagles win toss. Jones punts and E. Brown loses one yard on return to Redskins' 40. Bragg punts 51 yards into end zone for touchback. Jones punts and E. Brown returns to Redskins' 42. Bragg punts and Marshall returns to Eagles' 41. Boryla's pass intercepted by Dusek at Redskins' 37, no return. Bragg punts and Bradley returns. Philadelphia holding penalty moves ball back to Eagles' 8. Boryla pass intercepted by E. Brown and returned to Eagles' 22. Moseley kicks 29-yard field goal at 12:49.

Oct. 17, 1976—Kansas City 20, Miami 17, at Miami; Chiefs win toss. Wilson punts into end zone for touchback. Bulaich fumbles into Kansas City end zone, Collier recovers for touchback. Stenerud kicks 34-yard field goal at 14:48.

Oct. 31, 1976—St. Louis 23, San Francisco 20, at St. Louis; Cardinals win toss. Joyce punts and Leonard fumbles on return, Jones recovers at 49ers' 43. Bakken kicks 21-yard field goal at 6:42.

Dec. 5, 1976—San Diego 13, San Francisco 7, at San Diego; Chargers win toss. Morris runs 13 yards for touchdown at 5:12.

Sept. 18, 1977—Dallas 16, Minnesota 10, at Minnesota; Vikings win toss. Dallas starts on Vikings' 47 after a punt early in the overtime period. Staubach scores seven plays later on a four-yard run at 6:14.

***Sept. 26, 1977—Cleveland 30, New England 27,** at Cleveland; Browns win toss. Sipe throws a 22-yard pass to Logan at Patriots' 19. Cockroft kicks 35-yard field goal at 4:45.

Oct. 16, 1977—Minnesota 22, Chicago 16, at Minnesota; Bears win toss. Parsons punts 53 yards to Vikings' 18. Minnesota drives to Bears' 11. On a first-and-10, Vikings fake a field goal and holder Krause hits Voigt with a touchdown pass at 6:45.

Oct. 30, 1977—Cincinnati 13, Houston 10, at Cincinnati; Bengals win toss. Bahr kicks a 22-yard field goal at 5:51.

Nov. 13, 1977—San Francisco 10, New Orleans 7, at New Orleans; Saints win toss. Saints fail to move ball and Blanchard punts to 49ers' 41. Wersching kicks a 33-yard field goal at 6:33.

Dec. 18, 1977—Chicago 12, New York Giants 9, at East Rutherford, N.J.; Giants win toss. The ball changes hands eight times before Thomas kicks a 28-yard field goal at 14:51.

Sept. 10, 1978—Cleveland 13, Cincinnati 10, at Cleveland; Browns win toss. Collins returns kickoff 41 yards to Browns' 47. Cockroft kicks 27-yard field goal at 4:30.

***Sept. 11, 1978—Minnesota 12, Denver 9,** at Minnesota; Vikings win toss. Danmeier kicks 44-yard field goal at 2:56.

Sept. 24, 1978—Pittsburgh 15, Cleveland 9, at Pittsburgh; Steelers win toss. Cunningham scores on a 37-yard "gadget" pass from Bradshaw at 3:43. Steelers start winning drive on their 21.

Sept. 24, 1978—Denver 23, Kansas City 17, at Kansas City; Broncos win toss. Dilts punts to Kansas City. Chiefs advance to Broncos' 40 where Reed fails to make first down on fourth-and-one situation. Broncos march downfield. Preston scores two-yard touchdown at 10:28.

Oct. 1, 1978—Oakland 25, Chicago 19, at Chicago; Bears win toss. Both teams punt on first possession. On Chicago's second offensive series, Colzie intercepts Avellini's pass and returns it to Bears' 3. Three plays later, Whittington runs two yards for a touchdown at 5:19.

Oct. 15, 1978—Dallas 24, St. Louis 21, at St. Louis; Cowboys win toss. Dallas drives from its 23 into field goal range. Septien kicks 27-yard field goal at 3:28.

Oct. 29, 1978—Denver 20, Seattle 17, at Seattle; Broncos win toss. Ball changes hands four times before Turner kicks 18-yard field goal at 12:59.

Nov. 12, 1978—San Diego 29, Kansas City 23, at San Diego; Chiefs win toss. Fouts hits Jefferson for decisive 14-yard touchdown pass on the last play (15:00) of overtime period.

Nov. 12, 1978—Washington 16, New York Giants 13, at Washington; Redskins win toss. Moseley kicks winning 45-yard field goal at 8:32 after missing first down field goal attempt of 35 yards at 4:50.

Nov. 26, 1978—Green Bay 10, Minnesota 10, at Green Bay; Packers win toss. Both teams have possession of the ball four times.

Dec. 9, 1978—Cleveland 37, New York Jets 34, at Cleveland; Browns win toss. Cockroft kicks 22-yard field goal at 3:07.

Sept. 2, 1979—Atlanta 40, New Orleans 34, at New Orleans; Falcons win toss. Bartkowski's pass intercepted by Myers and returned to Falcons' 46. Erxleben punts to Falcons' 4. James punts to Chandler on Saints' 43. Erxleben punts and Ryckman returns to Falcons' 28. James punts and Chandler returns to Saints' 36. Erxleben retrieves punt snap on Saints' 1 and attempts pass. Mayberry intercepts and returns six yards for touchdown at 8:22.

Sept. 2, 1979—Cleveland 25, New York Jets 22, at New York; Jets win toss. Leahy's 43-yard field goal attempt goes wide right at 4:41. Evans's punt blocked by Dykes is recovered by Newton. Ramsey punts into end zone for touchback. Evans punts and Harper returns to Jets' 24. Robinson's pass intercepted by Davis and returned 33 yards to Jets' 31. Cockroft kicks 27-yard field goal at 14:45.

***Sept. 3, 1979—Pittsburgh 16, New England 13,** at Foxboro; Patriots win toss. Hare punts to Swann at Steelers' 31. Bahr kicks 41-yard field goal at 5:10.

Sept. 9, 1979—Tampa Bay 29, Baltimore 26, at Baltimore; Colts win toss. Landry fumbles, recovered by Kollar at Colts' 14. O'Donoghue kicks 31-yard, first-down field goal at 1:41.

Sept. 16, 1979—Denver 20, Atlanta 17, at Atlanta; Broncos win toss. Broncos march 65 yards to Falcons' 7. Turner kicks 24-yard field goal at 6:15.

Sept. 23, 1979—Houston 30, Cincinnati 27, at Cincinnati; Oilers win toss. Parsley punts and Lusby returns to Bengals' 33. Bahr's 32-yard field goal attempt is wide right at 8:05. Parsley's punt downed on Bengals' 5. McInally punts and Ellender returns to Bengals' 42. Fritsch's third down, 29-yard field goal attempt hits left upright and bounces through at 14:28.

Sept. 23, 1979—Minnesota 27, Green Bay 21, at Minnesota; Vikings win toss. Kramer throws 50-yard touchdown pass to Rashad at 3:18.

Oct. 28, 1979—Houston 27, New York Jets 24, at Houston; Oilers win toss. Oilers march 58 yards to Jets' 18. Fritsch kicks 35-yard field goal at 5:10.

Nov. 18, 1979—Cleveland 30, Miami 24, at Cleveland; Browns win toss. Sipe passes 39 yards to Rucker for touchdown at 1:59.

Nov. 25, 1979—Pittsburgh 33, Cleveland 30, at Pittsburgh; Browns win toss. Sipe's pass intercepted by Blount on Steelers' 4. Bradshaw pass intercepted by Bolton on Browns' 12. Evans punts and Bell returns to Steelers' 17. Bahr kicks 37-yard field goal at 14:51.

Nov. 25, 1979—Buffalo 16, New England 13, at Foxboro; Patriots win toss. Hare's punt downed on Bills' 38. Jackson punts and Morgan returns to Patriots' 20. Grogan's pass intercepted by Haslett and returned to Bills' 42. Ferguson's 51-yard pass to Butler sets up N. Mike-Mayer's 29-yard field goal at 9:15.

Dec. 2, 1979—Los Angeles 27, Minnesota 21, at Los Angeles; Rams win toss. Clark punts and Miller returns to Vikings' 25. Kramer's pass intercepted by Brown and returned to Rams' 40. Cromwell, holding for 22-yard field goal attempt, runs around left end untouched for winning score at 6:53.

Sept. 7, 1980—Green Bay 12, Chicago 6, at Green Bay; Bears win toss. Parsons punts and Nixon returns 16 yards. Five plays later, Marcol returns own blocked field goal attempt 24 yards for touchdown at 6:00.

Sept. 14, 1980—San Diego 30, Oakland 24, at San Diego; Raiders win toss. Pastorini's first-down pass intercepted by Edwards. Millen intercepts Fouts' first-down pass and returns to San Diego 46. Bahr's 50-yard field goal attempt partially blocked by Williams and recovered on Chargers' 32. Eight plays later, Fouts throws 24-yard touchdown pass to Jefferson at 8:09.

Sept. 14, 1980—San Francisco 24, St. Louis 21, at San Francisco; Cardinals win toss. Swider punts and Robinson returns to 49ers' 32. San Francisco drives 52 yards to St. Louis 16, where Wersching kicks 33-yard field goal at 4:12.

Oct. 12, 1980—Green Bay 14, Tampa Bay 14, at Tampa Bay; Packers win toss. Teams trade punts twice. Lee returns second Tampa Bay punt to Green Bay 42. Dickey completes three passes to Buccaneers' 18, where Birney's 36-yard field goal attempt is wide right as time expires.

Nov. 9, 1980—Atlanta 33, St. Louis 27, at St. Louis; Falcons win toss. Strong runs 21 yards for touchdown at 4:20.

#Nov. 20, 1980—San Diego 27, Miami 24, at Miami; Chargers win toss. Partridge punts into end zone, Dolphins take over on their own 20. Woodley's pass for Nathan intercepted by Lowe and returned 28 yards to Dolphins' 12. Benirschke kicks 28-yard field goal at 7:14.

Nov. 23, 1980—New York Jets 31, Houston 28, at New York; Jets win toss. Leahy kicks 38-yard field goal at 3:58.

Nov. 27, 1980—Chicago 23, Detroit 17, at Detroit; Bears win toss. Williams returns kickoff 95 yards for touchdown at 0:21.

Dec. 7, 1980—Buffalo 10, Los Angeles 7, at Buffalo; Rams win toss. Corral punts and Hooks returns to Bills' 34. Ferguson's 30-yard pass to Lewis sets up N. Mike-Mayer's 30-yard field goal at 5:14.

Dec. 7, 1980—San Francisco 38, New Orleans 35, at San Francisco; Saints win toss. Erxleben's punt downed by Hardy on 49ers' 27. Wersching kicks 36-yard field goal at 7:40.

***Dec. 8, 1980—Miami 16, New England 13,** at Miami; Dolphins win toss. Von Schamann kicks 23-yard field goal at 3:20.

Dec. 14, 1980—Cincinnati 17, Chicago 14, at Chicago; Bengals win toss. Breech kicks 28-yard field goal at 4:23.

Dec. 21, 1980—Los Angeles 20, Atlanta 17, at Los Angeles; Rams win toss. Corral's punt downed at Rams' 37. James punts into end zone for touchback. Corral's punt downed on Falcons' 17. Bartkowski fumbles when hit by Harris, recovered by Delaney. Corral kicks 23-yard field goal on first play of possession at 7:00.

Sept. 27, 1981—Cincinnati 27, Buffalo 24, at Cincinnati; Bills win toss. Cater punts into end zone for touchback. Bengals drive to the Bills' 10 where Breech kicks 28-yard field goal at 9:33.

Sept. 27, 1981—Pittsburgh 27, New England 21, at Pittsburgh; Patriots win toss. Hubach punts and Smith returns five yards to midfield. Four plays later Bradshaw throws 24-yard touchdown pass to Swann at 3:19.

Oct. 4, 1981—Miami 28, New York Jets 28, at Miami; Jets win toss. Teams trade punts twice. Leahy's 48-yard field goal attempt is wide right as time expires.

Oct. 25, 1981—New York Giants 27, Atlanta 24, at Atlanta; Giants win toss. Jennings' punt goes out of bounds at New York 47. Bright returns Atlanta punt to Giants' 14. Woerner fair catches punt at own 28. Andrews fumbles on first play, recovered by Van Pelt. Danelo kicks 40-yard field goal four plays later at 9:20.

Oct. 25, 1981—Chicago 20, San Diego 17, at Chicago; Bears win toss. Teams trade punts. Bears' second punt returned by Brooks to Chargers' 33. Fouts pass intercepted by Fencik and returned 32 yards to San Diego 27. Roveto kicks 27-yard field goal seven plays later at 9:30.

Nov. 8, 1981—Chicago 16, Kansas City 13, at Kansas City; Bears win toss. Teams trade punts. Kansas City takes over on downs on its own 38. Fuller's fumble recovered by Harris on Chicago 36. Roveto's 37-yard field goal wide, but Chiefs penalized for leverage. Roveto's 22-yard field goal attempt three plays later is good at 13:07.

Nov. 8, 1981—Denver 23, Cleveland 20, at Denver; Browns win toss. D. Smith recovers Hill's fumble at Denver 48. Morton's 33-yard pass to Upchurch and 6-yard run by Preston set up Steinfort's 30-yard field goal at 4:10.

Nov. 8, 1981—Miami 30, New England 27, at New England; Dolphins win toss. Orosz punts and Morgan returns six yards to New England 26. Grogan's pass intercepted by Brudzinski who returns 19 yards to Patriots' 26. Von Schamann kicks 30-yard field goal on first down at 7:09.

Nov. 15, 1981—Washington 30, New York Giants 27, at New York; Giants win toss. Nelms returns Giants' punt 26 yards to New York 47. Five plays later Moseley kicks 48-yard field goal at 3:44.

Dec. 20, 1981—New York Giants 13, Dallas 10, at New York; Cowboys win toss and kick off. Jennings punts to Dallas 40. Taylor recovers Dorsett's fumble on second down. Danelo's 33-yard field goal attempt hits right upright and bounces back. White's pass for Pearson intercepted by Hunt and returned seven yards to Dallas 24. Four plays later Danelo kicks 35-yard field goal at 6:19.

Sept. 12, 1982—Washington 37, Philadelphia 34, at Philadelphia; Redskins win toss. Theismann completes five passes for 63 yards to set up Moseley's 26-yard field goal at 4:47.

Sept. 19, 1982—Pittsburgh 26, Cincinnati 20, at Pittsburgh; Bengals win toss. Anderson's pass intended for Kreider intercepted by Woodruff and returned 30 yards to Cincinnati 2. Bradshaw completes two-yard touchdown pass to Stallworth on first down at 1:08.

Dec. 19, 1982—Baltimore 20, Green Bay 20, at Baltimore; Packers win toss. K. Anderson intercepts Dickey's first-down pass and returns to Packers' 42. Miller's 44-yard field goal attempt blocked by G. Lewis. Teams trade punts before Stenerud's 47-yard field goal attempt is wide right. Teams trade punts again before time expires in Colts possession.

Jan. 2, 1983—Tampa Bay 26, Chicago 23, at Tampa; Bears win toss. Parsons punts to T. Bell at Buccaneers' 40. Capece kicks 33-yard field goal at 3:14.

Sept. 4, 1983—Baltimore 29, New England 23, at New England; Patriots win toss. Cooks runs 52 yards with fumble recovery three plays into overtime at 0:30.

Sept. 4, 1983—Green Bay 41, Houston 38, at Houston; Packers win toss. Stenerud kicks 42-yard field goal at 5:55.

Sept. 11, 1983—New York Giants 16, Atlanta 13, at Atlanta; Giants win toss. Dennis returns kickoff 54 yards to Atlanta 41. Haji-Sheikh kicks 30-yard field goal at 3:38.

Sept. 18, 1983—New Orleans 34, Chicago 31, at New Orleans; Bears win toss. Parsons punts and Groth returns five yards to New Orleans 34. Stabler pass intercepted by Schmidt at Chicago 47. Parsons punt downed by Gentry at New Orleans 2. Stabler gains 36 yards in four passes; Wilson 38 on six carries. Andersen kicks 41-yard field goal at 10:57.

Sept. 18, 1983—Minnesota 19, Tampa Bay 16, at Tampa; Vikings win toss. Coleman punts and Bell returns eight yards to Tampa Bay 47. Capece's 33-yard field goal attempt sails wide at 7:26. Dils and Young combine for 48-yard gain to Tampa Bay 27. Ricardo kicks 42-yard field goal at 9:27.

Sept. 25, 1983—Baltimore 22, Chicago 19, at Baltimore; Colts win toss. Allegre kicks 33-yard field goal nine plays later at 4:51.

Sept. 25, 1983—Cleveland 30, San Diego 24, at San Diego; Browns win toss. Walker returns kickoff 33 yards to Cleveland 37. Sipe completes 48-yard touchdown pass to Holt four plays later at 1:53.

Sept. 25, 1983—New York Jets 27, Los Angeles Rams 24, at New York; Jets win toss. Ramsey punts to Irvin who returns to 25 but penalty puts Rams on own 13. Holmes 30-yard interception return sets up Leahy's 26-yard field goal at 3:22.

Oct. 9, 1983—Buffalo 38, Miami 35, at Miami; Dolphins win toss. Von Schamann's 52-yard field goal attempt goes wide at 12:36. Cater punts to Clayton who loses 11 to own 13. Von Schamann's 43-yard field goal attempt sails wide at 5:15. Danelo kicks 36-yard field goal nine plays later at 13:58.

Oct. 9, 1983—Dallas 27, Tampa Bay 24, at Dallas; Cowboys win toss. Septien's 51-yard field goal attempt goes wide but Buccaneers penalized for roughing kicker. Septien kicks 42-yard field goal at 4:38.

OVERTIME GAMES

Oct. 23, 1983—Kansas City 13, Houston 10, at Houston; Chiefs win toss. Lowery kicks 41-yard field goal 13 plays later at 7:41.

Oct. 23, 1983—Minnesota 20, Green Bay 17, at Green Bay; Packers win toss. Scribner's punt downed on Vikings' 42. Ricardo kicks 32-yard field goal eight plays later at 5:05.

***Oct. 24, 1983—New York Giants 20, St. Louis 20,** at St. Louis; Cardinals win toss. Teams trade punts before O'Donoghue's 44-yard field goal attempt is wide left. Jennings' punt returned by Bird to St. Louis 21. Lomax pass intercepted by Haynes who loses six yards to New York 33. Jennings' punt downed on St. Louis 17. O'Donoghue's 19-yard field goal attempt is wide right. Rutledge's pass intercepted by L. Washington who returns 25 yards to New York 25. O'Donoghue's 42-yard field goal attempt is wide right. Rutledge's pass intercepted by W. Smith at St. Louis 33 to end game.

Oct. 30, 1983—Cleveland 25, Houston 19, at Cleveland; Oilers win toss. Teams trade punts. Nielsen's pass intercepted by Whitwell who returns to Houston 20. Green runs 20 yards for touchdown on first down at 6:34.

Nov. 20, 1983—Detroit 23, Green Bay 20, at Milwaukee; Packers win toss. Scribner punts and Jenkins returns 14 yards to Green Bay 45. Murray's 33-yard field goal attempt is wide left at 9:32. Whitehurst's pass intercepted by Watkins and returned to Green Bay 27. Murray kicks 37-yard field goal four plays later at 8:30.

Nov. 27, 1983—Atlanta 47, Green Bay 41, at Atlanta; Packers win toss. K. Johnson returns interception 31 yards for touchdown at 2:13.

Nov. 27, 1983—Seattle 51, Kansas City 48, at Seattle; Seahawks win toss. Dixon's 47-yard kickoff return sets up N. Johnson's 42-yard field goal at 1:36.

Dec. 11, 1983—New Orleans 20, Philadelphia 17, at Philadelphia; Eagles win toss. Runager punts to Groth who fair catches on New Orleans 32. Stabler completes two passes for 36 yards to Goodlow to set up Andersen's 50-yard field goal at 5:30.

***Dec. 12, 1983—Green Bay 12, Tampa Bay 9,** at Tampa; Packers win toss. Stenerud kicks 23-yard field goal 11 plays later at 4:07.

Sept. 9, 1984—Detroit 27, Atlanta 24, at Atlanta; Lions win toss. Murray kicks 48-yard field goal nine plays later at 5:06.

Sept. 30, 1984—Tampa Bay 30, Green Bay 27, at Tampa; Packers win toss. Scribner punts 44 yards to Tampa Bay 2. Epps returns Garcia's punt three yards to Green Bay 27. Scribner's punt downed on Buccaneers' 33. Ariri kicks 46-yard field goal 11 plays later at 10:32.

Oct. 14, 1984—Detroit 13, Tampa Bay 7, at Detroit; Buccaneers win toss. Tampa Bay drives to Lions' 39 before Wilder fumbles. Five plays later Danielson hits Thompson with 37-yard touchdown pass at 4:34.

Oct. 21, 1984—Dallas 30, New Orleans 27, at Dallas; Cowboys win toss. Septien kicks 41-yard field goal eight plays later at 3:42.

Oct. 28, 1984—Denver 22, Los Angeles Raiders 19, at Los Angeles; Raiders win toss. Hawkins fumble recovered by Foley at Denver 7. Teams trade punts. Karlis's 42-yard field goal attempt is wide left. Teams trade punts. Wilson pass intercepted by R. Jackson at Los Angeles 45, returned 23 yards to Los Angeles 22. Karlis kicks 35-yard field goal two plays later at 15:00.

Nov. 4, 1984—Philadelphia 23, Detroit 23, at Detroit; Lions win toss. Lions drive to Eagles' 3 in eight plays. Murray's 21-yard field goal attempt hits right upright and bounces back. Jaworski's pass intercepted by Watkins at Detroit 5. Teams trade punts. Cooper returns Black's punt five yards to Eagles' 14. Time expires four plays later with Eagles on own 21.

Nov. 18, 1984—San Diego 34, Miami 28, at San Diego; Chargers win toss. McGee scores eight plays later on a 25-yard run at 3:17.

Dec. 2, 1984—Cincinnati 20, Cleveland 17, at Cleveland; Browns win toss. Simmons returns Cox's punt 30 yards to Cleveland 35. Breech kicks 35-yard field goal seven plays later at 4:34.

Dec. 2, 1984—Houston 23, Pittsburgh 20, at Houston; Oilers win toss. Cooper kicks 30-yard field goal 16 plays later at 5:53.

Sept. 8, 1985—St. Louis 27, Cleveland 24, at Cleveland; Cardinals win toss. O'Donoghue kicks 35-yard field goal nine plays later at 5:27.

Sept. 29, 1985—New York Giants 16, Philadelphia 10, at Philadelphia; Eagles win toss. Jaworski's pass tipped by Quick and intercepted by Patterson who returns 29 yards for touchdown at 0:55.

Oct. 20, 1985—Denver 13, Seattle 10, at Denver; Seahawks win toss. Teams trade punts twice. Krieg's pass intercepted by Hunter and returned to Seahawks' 15. Karlis kicks 24-yard field goal four plays later at 9:19.

Nov. 10, 1985—Philadelphia 23, Atlanta 17, at Philadelphia; Falcons win toss. Donnelly's 62-yard punt goes out of bounds at Eagles' 1. Jaworski completes 99-yard touchdown pass to Quick two plays later at 1:49.

Nov. 10, 1985—San Diego 40, Los Angeles Raiders 34, at San Diego; Chargers win toss. James scores on 17-yard run seven plays later at 3:44.

Nov. 17, 1985—Denver 30, San Diego 24, at Denver; Chargers win toss. Thomas' 40-yard field goal attempt blocked by Smith and returned 60 yards by Wright for touchdown at 4:45.

Nov. 24, 1985—New York Jets 16, New England 13, at New York; Jets win toss. Teams trade punts twice. Patriots' second punt returned 46 yards by Sohn to Patriots' 15. Leahy kicks 32-yard field goal one play later at 10:05.

Nov. 24, 1985—Tampa Bay 19, Detroit 16, at Tampa; Lions win toss. Teams trade punts. Lions' punt downed on Buccaneers' 38. Igwebuike kicks 24-yard field goal 11 plays later at 12:31.

Nov. 24, 1985—Los Angeles Raiders 31, Denver 28, at Los Angeles; Raiders win toss. Bahr kicks 32-yard field goal six plays later at 2:42.

Dec. 8, 1985—Los Angeles Raiders 17, Denver 14, at Denver; Broncos win toss. Teams trade punts twice. Elway's fumble recovered by Townsend at Broncos' 8. Bahr kicks 26-yard field goal one play later at 4:55.

Sept. 14, 1986—Chicago 13, Philadelphia 10, at Chicago; Eagles win toss. Crawford's fumble of kickoff recovered by Jackson at Eagles' 35. Butler kicks 23-yard field goal 10 plays later at 5:56.

Sept. 14, 1986—Cincinnati 36, Buffalo 33, at Cincinnati; Bills win toss. Zander intercepts Kelly's first-down pass and returns it to Bills' 17. Breech kicks 20-yard field goal two plays later at 0:56.

Sept. 21, 1986—New York Jets 51, Miami 45, at New York; Jets win toss. O'Brien completes 43-yard touchdown pass to Walker five plays later at 2:35.

Sept. 28, 1986—Pittsburgh 22, Houston 16, at Houston; Oilers win toss. Johnson's punt returned 41 yards by Woods to Oilers' 15. Abercrombie scores on three-yard run three plays later at 2:35.

Sept. 28, 1986—Atlanta 23, Tampa Bay 20, at Tampa; Falcons win toss. Teams trade punts. Luckhurst kicks 34-yard field goal 10 plays later at 12:35.

Oct. 5, 1986—Los Angeles Rams 26, Tampa Bay 20, at Anaheim; Rams win toss. Dickerson scores four plays later on 42-yard run at 2:16.

Oct. 12, 1986—Minnesota 27, San Francisco 24, at San Francisco; Vikings win toss. C. Nelson kicks 28-yard field goal nine plays later at 4:27.

Oct. 19, 1986—San Francisco 10, Atlanta 10, at Atlanta; Falcons win toss. Teams trade punts twice. Donnelly punts to 49ers' 27. The following play Wilson recovers Rice's fumble at 49ers' 46 as time expires.

Nov. 2, 1986—Washington 44, Minnesota 38, at Washington; Redskins win toss. Schroeder completes 38-yard touchdown pass to Clark four plays later at 1:46.

Nov. 20, 1986—Los Angeles Raiders 37, San Diego 31, at San Diego; Raiders win toss. Teams trade punts. Allen scores five plays later on 28-yard run at 8:33.

Nov. 23, 1986—Cleveland 37, Pittsburgh 31, at Cleveland; Browns win toss. Teams trade punts. Six plays later Kosar hits Slaughter with 36-yard touchdown pass at 6:37.

Nov. 30, 1986—Chicago 13, Pittsburgh 10, at Chicago; Bears win toss and kick off. Newsome's punt returned by Barnes to Chicago 49. Butler kicks 42-yard field goal five plays later at 3:55.

Nov. 30, 1986—Philadelphia 33, Los Angeles Raiders 27, at Los Angeles; Eagles win toss. Teams trade punts. Long recovers Cunningham's fumble at Philadelphia 42. Waters returns Allen's fumble 81 yards to Los Angeles 4. Cunningham scores on one-yard run two plays later at 6:53.

Nov. 30, 1986—Cleveland 13, Houston 10, at Cleveland; Oilers win toss and kick off. Gossett punts to Houston 39. Luck's pass intercepted by Minnifield at Cleveland 21. Gossett punts to Houston 34. Luck's pass intercepted by Minnifield at Cleveland 43 who returns 20 yards to Houston 37. Moseley kicks 29-yard field goal nine plays later at 14:44.

Dec. 7, 1986—St. Louis 10, Philadelphia 10, at Philadelphia; Cardinals win toss. White blocks Schubert's 40-yard field goal attempt. Teams trade punts. McFadden's 43-yard field goal attempt is wide left. Schubert's 37-yard field goal attempt is wide right. Cavanaugh's pass intercepted by Carter and returned to Eagles' 48 to end game.

Dec. 14, 1986—Miami 37, Los Angeles Rams 31, at Anaheim; Dolphins win toss. Marino completes 20-yard touchdown pass to Duper six plays later at 3:04.

Sept. 20, 1987—Denver 17, Green Bay 17, at Milwaukee; Packers win toss. Del Greco's 47-yard field goal attempt is short. Teams trade punts. Elway intercepted by Noble who returns 10 yards to Green Bay 34. Davis fumbles on next play and Smith recovers. Two plays later, Karlis's 40-yard field goal attempt is wide left. Time expires two plays later with Packers on own 23.

Oct. 11, 1987—Detroit 19, Green Bay 16, at Green Bay; Lions win toss. Prindle's 42-yard field goal attempt is wide left. Packers punt downed on Detroit 17. Prindle kicks 31-yard field goal 16 plays later at 12:26.

Oct. 18, 1987—New York Jets 37, Miami 31, at New York; Jets win toss. Teams trade punts. Ryan intercepted by Hooper at Jets' 47 who returns 11 yards. Mackey intercepted by Haslett at Jets' 37 who returns 9 yards. Jets punt. Mackey intercepted by Radachowsky who returns 45 yards to Miami 24. Ryan completes eight-yard touchdown pass to Hunter five plays later at 14:26.

Oct. 18, 1987—Green Bay 16, Philadelphia 10, at Green Bay; Packers win toss. Hargrove scores on seven-yard run 10 plays later at 5:04.

Oct. 18, 1987—Buffalo 6, New York Giants 3, at Buffalo; Bills win toss. Schlopy's 28-yard field goal attempt is wide left. Teams trade punts. Rutledge intercepted by Clark who returns 23 yards to Buffalo 40. Schlopy kicks 27-yard field goal nine plays later at 14:41.

Oct. 25, 1987—Buffalo 34, Miami 31, at Miami; Bills win toss. Norwood kicks 27-yard field goal seven plays later at 4:12.

Nov. 1, 1987—San Diego 27, Cleveland 24, at San Diego; Browns win toss. Kosar intercepted by Glenn who returns 20 yards to Browns' 25. Abbott kicks 33-yard field goal three plays later at 2:16.

Nov. 15, 1987—Dallas 23, New England 17, at New England; Cowboys win toss. Walker scores on 60-yard run four plays later at 1:50.

Nov. 26, 1987—Minnesota 44, Dallas 38, at Dallas; Vikings win toss. Coleman's punt downed by Hilton at Cowboys' 37. White intercepted by Studwell who returns 12 yards to Vikings' 37. D. Nelson scores on 24-yard run seven plays later at 7:51.

Nov. 29, 1987—Philadelphia 34, New England 31, at New England; Patriots win toss. Ramsey intercepted by Joyner who returns 29 yards to Eagles' 32. Fryar fair catches Teltschik's punt at Patriots' 13. Franklin's 46-yard field goal attempt is short. McFadden's 39-yard field goal attempt is wide left. Tatupu fumbles on next play and Cobb recovers. McFadden kicks 38-yard field goal

four plays later at 12:16.
Dec. 6, 1987—New York Giants 23, Philadelphia 20, at New York; Giants win toss and kick off. Teams trade punts twice. Teltschik's punt is returned 16 yards by McConkey to Eagles' 33. Three plays later, Allegre's 50-yard field goal attempt is blocked by Joyner and returned 25 yards by Hoage to Eagles' 30. McConkey returns Teltschik's punt four yards to Giants' 44. Allegre kicks 28-yard field goal four plays later at 10:42.
Dec. 6, 1987—Cincinnati 30, Kansas City 27, at Cincinnati; Bengals win toss. Teams trade punts. Breech kicks 32-yard field goal 16 plays later at 9:44.
Dec. 26, 1987—Washington 27, Minnesota 24, at Minnesota; Redskins win toss. Haji-Sheikh kicks 26-yard field goal six plays later at 2:09.
Sept. 4, 1988—Houston 17, Indianapolis 14, at Indianapolis; Colts win toss. Dickerson fumble recovered by Lyles who returns six yards to Colts' 42. Zendejas kicks 35-yard field goal six plays later at 3:51.
***Sept. 26, 1988—Los Angeles Raiders 30, Denver 27,** at Denver; Broncos win toss. Teams trade punts twice. Elway intercepted by Lee who returns 20 yards to Broncos' 31. Bahr kicks 35-yard field goal four plays later at 12:35.
Oct. 2, 1988—New York Jets 17, Kansas City 17, at New York; Chiefs win toss. Chiefs punt goes into end zone for touchback. Leahy's 44-yard field goal attempt is wide right. Chiefs punt is returned by Townsell to Jets' 26. Burruss recovers McNeil's fumble at Chiefs' 11. DeBerg intercepted by Humphery at Jets' 49. Three plays later, time expires.
Oct. 9, 1988—Denver 16, San Francisco 13, at San Francisco; Broncos win toss and kick off. Young intercepted by Haynes at Broncos' 32. Denver punt downed at 49ers' 5. Young intercepted by Wilson who returns seven yards to 49ers' 5. Karlis kicks 22-yard field goal two plays later at 8:11.
Oct. 30, 1988—New York Giants 13, Detroit 10, at Detroit; Lions win toss. James's fumble recovered by Taylor at Lions' 22. Three plays later, McFadden kicks 33-yard field goal at 1:13.
Nov. 20, 1988—Buffalo 9, New York Jets 6, at Buffalo; Jets win toss. Vick's fumble recovered by Bennett at Bills' 32. Norwood kicks 30-yard field goal five plays later at 3:47.
Nov. 20, 1988—Philadelphia 23, New York Giants 17, at New York; Eagles win toss. Philadelphia's punt goes into end zone for touchback. Hostetler intercepted by Hoage who returns 11 yards to Giants' 41. Six plays later, Zendejas's 30-yard field-goal attempt is blocked and ball is recovered behind line of scrimmage by Eagles' Simmons, who runs 15 yards for touchdown at 3:09.
Dec. 11, 1988—New England 10, Tampa Bay 7, at New England; Buccaneers win toss and kick off. Staurovsky kicks 27-yard field goal six plays later at 3:08.
Dec. 17, 1988—Cincinnati 20, Washington 17, at Cincinnati; Bengals win toss. Cincinnati's punt returned by Oliphant to Redskins' 16. Grant recovers Williams's fumble at Redskins' 17. Breech kicks 20-yard field goal three plays later at 7:01.
Sept. 24, 1989—Buffalo 47, Houston 41, at Houston; Oilers win toss. Johnson returns Brady's kickoff 17 yards to Oilers' 19. Oilers drive to Buffalo 25, Zendejas's 37-yard field goal blocked, but Bills offsides and Zendejas's second attempt is wide left. Bills' ball and Kelly completes series of passes, including 28-yard game-winner to Andre Reed, at 8:42.
Oct. 8, 1989—Miami 13, Cleveland 10, at Miami; Browns win toss. Metcalf returns Stoyanovich's kickoff 20 yards to Browns' 28. Browns drive ball 46 yards in eight plays; Bahr wide left on 44-yard field goal attempt. Dolphins ball. Browns called for pass interference on Marino pass to Banks at Cleveland 47. Two plays later, Banks's 20-yard reception at Browns' 23 sets up winning 35-yard field goal by Stoyanovich at 6:23.
Oct. 22, 1989—Denver 24, Seattle 21, at Seattle; Seahawks win toss. Treadwell's 56-yard kickoff returned 18 yards by Jefferson to Seahawks' 27. Seahawks drive to Broncos' 22 in 10 plays, but Johnson's 40-yard field goal attempt wide left. Smith intercepts a Krieg pass and returns it 28 yards to Seahawks' 10. Treadwell kicks winning 27-yard field goal at 7:46.
Oct. 29, 1989—New England 23, Indianapolis 20, at Indianapolis; Patriots win toss. Biasucci kickoff returned 13 yards to Patriots' 23 by Martin. Holding penalty brings ball back to Patriots' 13. After six plays, Feagles punt returned 11 yards by Verdin to Colts' 28. Six plays later, Colts punt to Martin at Patriots' 12. Grogan completes three straight passes to Patriots' 44. Five consecutive runs put New England on Colts' 33. Davis kicks a 51-yard winning field goal for Patriots at 9:46.
Oct. 29, 1989—Green Bay 23, Detroit 20, at Milwaukee; Lions win toss. Sanders touchback on Jacke kickoff. On first play, Murphy intercepts Lions' Peete and returns it three yards to Lions' 26. Fullwood gains five yards on three plays to set up Jacke's 38-yard field goal at 2:14.
Nov. 5, 1989—Minnesota 23, Los Angeles Rams 21, at Minneapolis; Rams win toss. Karlis's kick returned 18 yards by Delpino to Rams' 19. Drive stops at Rams' 28. Merriweather blocks Hatcher's punt at 12. Ball rolls out of end zone for safety.
Nov. 19, 1989—Cleveland 10, Kansas City 10, at Cleveland; Browns win toss. Browns punt three times; Chiefs twice; before Kansas City's Lowery misses 47-yard field goal with 17 seconds remaining in overtime. Kosar's pass intercepted as time expired.
Nov. 26, 1989—Los Angeles Rams 20, New Orleans 17, at New Orleans; Saints win toss. Lansford's kickoff returned 27 yards to Saints' 30. After four plays, Barnhardt punts to Rams' 15. Saints penalized 35 yards for interference to Rams' 43. Three plays later, Everett hits Anderson with 14-yard pass to Saints' 40, then 26-yarder to put Rams in field goal position. Lansford kicks 31-yard field goal at 6:38.
Dec. 3, 1989—Los Angeles Raiders 16, Denver 13, at Los Angeles; Broncos win toss. Bell returns Jaeger kickoff 14 yards to Broncos' 18. Broncos' penalized for illegal block to Broncos' 9. Elway completes three passes for two first downs. On third and eight Elway sacked for 10-yard loss. Horan punts, Adams calls for fair catch at Raiders' 29. Dyal's 26-yard reception moves Raiders to Denver 43. Raiders move ball 34 yards in three plays to set up Jaeger's 26-yard field goal at 7:02.
Dec. 10, 1989—Indianapolis 23, Cleveland 17, at Indianapolis; Browns win toss. Teams trade punts. McNeil returns Colts' punt 42 yards to 42. Seven plays later, Bahr misses 35-yard field goal attempt. Three plays later, Stark punts and McNeil returns ball to 50-yard line. Two plays later, Prior intercepts Kosar's pass at Colts' 42 and returns it 58 yards for touchdown at 10:54.
Dec. 17, 1989—Cleveland 23, Minnesota 17, at Cleveland; Browns win toss. Browns punt to Vikings' 18. Six plays later, Vikings punt to Browns' 22. Nine plays later, Bahr lines up to attempt 31-yard field goal. Holder Pagel takes snap and passes 14 yards to Waiters for touchdown at 9:30.
Sept. 23, 1990—Denver 34, Seattle 31, at Denver; Seahawks win toss. Loville returns kickoff 19 yards to Seahawks' 27. Seahawks drive to Broncos' 26, where Johnson misses 44-yard field goal wide right. Broncos take over and Elway completes series of passes to set up Treadwell's 25-yard field goal at 9:14.
Sept. 30, 1990—Tampa Bay 23, Minnesota 20, at Minnesota; Vikings win toss. Vikings drive to Buccaneers' 31; Igwebuike's 48-yard field goal attempt wide left. Buccaneers drive to Vikings' 43 and punt. Gannon's pass is intercepted at Vikings' 26 by Wayne Haddix. Buccaneers drive to Vikings' 19 to set up Christie's 36-yard field goal at 9:11.
Oct. 7, 1990—Cincinnati 34, Los Angeles Rams 31, at Anaheim; Rams win toss. Berry returns kickoff to Rams' 21. After 3 plays, English punts and Green downs ball at Bengals' 25. After 3 plays, Johnson punts and Sutton downs ball at Rams' 29-yard line. After 3 plays, English punts and Price signals fair catch at Bengals' 47. Esiason completes series of passes to 26-yard line to set up Breech's 44-yard field goal at 11:56.
Nov. 4, 1990—Washington 41, Detroit 38, at Detroit; Redskins win toss. Howard downs kickoff on Redskins' 15. After 3 plays, Mojsiejenko punts to Redskins' 45. After 3 plays, Arnold punts to Redskins' 10. Rutledge completes series of passes to set up Lohmiller's 34-yard field goal at 9:10.
Nov. 18, 1990—Chicago 16, Denver 13, at Denver; Broncos win toss. Ezor returns kickoff to Broncos' 12. Both teams have ball twice and have to punt after each possession. Broncos punt after third possession of overtime and Bailey returns 20 yards to Broncos' 34. Harbaugh completes 10-yard pass to Thornton to set up Butler's 44-yard field goal at 13:14.
Nov. 25, 1990—Seattle 13, San Diego 10, at San Diego; Chargers win toss. Lewis returns kickoff to Chargers' 22. After 2 plays, Cox fumbles and ball is recovered by Porter at Chargers' 23. After two plays, Johnson kicks 40-yard field goal at 3:01.
Dec. 2, 1990—Chicago 23, Detroit 17, at Chicago; Lions win toss. Gray returns kickoff to Lions' 35. After 10 plays, Murray misses 35-yard field goal. Bears take possession at Chicago 20. Harbaugh completes 50-yard game-winning pass to Anderson at 10:57.
Dec. 2, 1990—Seattle 13, Houston 10, at Seattle; Seahawks win toss. Warren returns kickoff to Seahawks' 13. After 5 plays, Donnelly punts to Oilers' 23-yard line. Ford's fumble recovered by Wyman. Seahawks take possession at Oilers' 27. After 2 plays, Johnson kicks 42-yard field goal at 4:25.
Dec. 9, 1990—Miami 23, Philadelphia 20, at Miami; Eagles win toss. After 11 plays, Feagles punts to Dolphins' 26. After 6 plays, Roby punts to Eagles' 14 and Harris returns to 25. After 3 plays, Feagles punts to Dolphins' 43. Marino completes series of passes to Eagles' 22. Stoyanovich kicks 39-yard field goal at 12:32.
Dec. 9, 1990—San Francisco 20, Cincinnati 17, at Cincinnati; 49ers win toss. Carter returns kickoff to 49ers' 19. After 10 plays, Cofer kicks 23-yard field goal at 6:12.
Sept. 23, 1991—Chicago 19, New York Jets 13, at Chicago; Jets win toss. Mathis returns kickoff seven yards to New York's 12. Jets drive to New York 26; Bailey returns punt to Chicago 39. Bears drive to Jets' 44-yard line and punt into the end zone. Jets drive to Bears' 11 where Leahy's 28-yard field goal attempt is wide left. Bears drive from 20 to Jets' 1 where Harbaugh runs for touchdown at 14:42.
Oct. 13, 1991—Los Angeles Raiders 23, Seattle 20, at Seattle. Seahawks win toss. Seahawks begin on 20. After 5 plays, Tuten punts and Brown signals fair catch at Raiders' 24. After 3 plays, Gossett punts and Land downs ball at Seattle 9. After 1 play, Lott intercepts at Seahawks' 19 to set up Jaeger's game-winning 37-yard field goal at 6:37.
Oct. 20, 1991—Cleveland 30, San Diego 24, at San Diego; Chargers win toss. After kickoff, Chargers drive to Browns' 45 and punt to Browns' 6 where Hendrickson downs ball. Browns drive to 38 and punt; Taylor fair catches on Chargers' 14. After 3 plays, Brandon intercepts at Chargers' 30 and scores at 5:58.
Oct. 20, 1991—New England 26, Minnesota 23, at New England; Patriots win toss. Martin returns kickoff 18 yards to New England 22. Patriots drive to Minnesota 19. Staurovsky's 36-yard field goal attempt is wide left. Minnesota drives to the 50 where Newsome punts into end zone. On first play, McMillian intercepts at the 40 for Minnesota. After 2 plays, Marion causes Jordan fumble and Pool recovers at New England 20. New England drives to Minnesota 24 where Staurovsky kicks 42-yard field goal as time expires.
Nov. 3, 1991—New York Jets 19, Green Bay 16, at New York; Packers win toss. Thompson returns kickoff 30 yards to Packers' 39. Green Bay drives to New York 24 where Jacke's 42-yard field goal attempt is wide right. Jets drive to 50. Aguiar's punt is fumbled by Sikahema and recovered by New York at Packers' 23. After 2 plays, Leahy kicks 37-yard field goal at 9:40.

OVERTIME GAMES

Nov. 3, 1991—Washington 16, Houston 13, at Washington; Redskins win toss. Mitchell returns kickoff 9 yards to Washington 14. After 4 plays, Goodburn punts and Givins returns to Houston 31. After 1 play, Moon's pass is intercepted by Green at Oilers' 35. After 3 plays, Lohmiller kicks 41-yard field goal at 4:01.

Nov. 10, 1991—Houston 26, Dallas 23, at Houston; Oilers win toss. Pinkett returns kickoff 20 yards to Houston 24. After 6 plays, Montgomery punts and Martin returns to Dallas 24. Cowboys drive to Oilers' 24 where Smith fumbles and McDowell recovers at Oilers' 15. Houston drives to Dallas 5 where Del Greco kicks 23-yard field goal at 14:31.

Nov. 10, 1991—Pittsburgh 33, Cincinnati 27, at Cincinnati; Pittsburgh wins toss. Woodson downs kickoff for touchback. After 3 plays, Stryzinski punts and Barber returns 7 yards to Cincinnati 38. Bengals drive to Pittsburgh 37 where Woods fumbles and Lloyd returns recovery to Cincinnati 44. After 2 plays, O'Donnell passes to Green for 26-yard touchdown at 6:32.

Nov. 24, 1991—Atlanta 23, New Orleans 20, at New Orleans; Atlanta wins toss. Falcons begin at 20. After 3 plays, Fulhage punts and Fenerty signals fair catch at New Orleans 43. After 3 plays, Barnhardt punts and Thompson downs ball at Atlanta 23. After 3 plays, Fulhage punts and Fenerty fair catches at New Orleans 25. Saints drive to Atlanta 38 where Andersen misses 55-yard field-goal attempt. After 1 play, Rozier fumbles and Martin recovers on 50. Saints drive to Atlanta 38 where Barnhardt punts to Falcons' 2. Atlanta drives to New Orleans 33 where Johnson kicks 50-yard field goal at 13:03.

Nov. 24, 1991—Miami 16, Chicago 13, at Chicago; Miami wins toss. Butler kicks to Miami 20 where Paige returns kickoff 15 yards to 35. Miami drives to Chicago 9 where Stoyanovich kicks 27-yard field goal at 4:11.

Dec. 8, 1991—Buffalo 30, Los Angeles Raiders 27, at Los Angeles; Raiders win toss. Daluiso kicks into end zone for touchback. On third play, Kelso intercepts for Buffalo and returns ball to Bills' 36. Bills drive to Los Angeles 24 where Norwood kicks 42-yard field goal at 2:34.

Dec. 8, 1991—Kansas City 20, San Diego 17, at Kansas City; Chiefs win toss. Carney kicks to Kansas City 10 where Stradford returns 23 yards to 33. After 3 plays, Barker punts to San Diego 4. Chargers drive to 40 where Kidd punts 60 yards into end zone for touchback. Kansas City drives to San Diego 39 where Barker punts 38 yards to 1. After 3 plays, Kidd punts 41 yards to San Diego 42 where Stradford returns 12 yards to 30. Chiefs drive to San Diego 1 where Lowery kicks 18-yard field goal at 11:26.

Dec. 8, 1991—New England 23, Indianapolis 17, at New England; Indianapolis wins toss. Baumann kicks off to Indianapolis 2 where Martin returns 23 yards to 25. After 3 downs, Stark punts to New England 17 where Henderson returns 8 yards to 25. New England drives to 50 where McCarthy punts and Prior signals fair catch at Indianapolis 15. After 3 plays, Stark punts to New England 40 where Henderson returns 7 yards to 47. After 2 plays, Millen passes to Timpson for 45-yard touchdown at 8:55.

Dec. 22, 1991—Detroit 17, Buffalo 14, at Buffalo; Detroit wins toss. Daluiso kicks off to Detroit 20 where Dozier returns 15 yards to Lions 35. Lions drive to Bills' 3 where Murray kicks 21-yard field goal at 4:23.

Dec. 22, 1991—New York Jets 23, Miami 20, at Miami; Jets win toss. Aguiar kicks to Miami's 30 where Logan returns 3 yards to the 33. After 4 downs, Stoyanovich punts to Jets' 15 where Baty returns 8 yards to 23. Jets drive to Miami 12 where Allegre kicks 30-yard field goal at 6:33.

Sept. 6, 1992—Minnesota 23, Green Bay 20, at Green Bay. Vikings win toss. Nelson returns kickoff 14 yards to the Minnesota 23. After 5 plays, Newsome punts 49 yards to Green Bay 21 where Brooks returns 12 yards to the 33. After 2 plays, Glenn intercepts pass at the Vikings' 48. On first play, Allen fumbles and Billups recovers at Green Bay 35. After 3 plays, McJulien punts 33 yards to Vikings' 35. Vikings drive to Minnesota 48; Newsome punts 52 yards for touchback. After 3 plays, McJulien punts and Parker returns 10 yards to Green Bay 48. Vikings drive to Packers' 9 where Reveiz kicks 26-yard field goal at 10:20.

Sept. 13, 1992—Cincinnati 24, Los Angeles Raiders 21, at Cincinnati. Raiders win toss. Land returns kickoff 13 yards but fumbles at Los Angeles's 20; ball recovered by Bengals' Bennett at Raiders' 21. After 1 play, Breech kicks 34-yard field goal at 1:01.

Sept. 20, 1992—Houston 23, Kansas City 20, at Houston. Chiefs win toss. Carter returns kickoff 25 yards to Kansas City 28. On third play of drive, Birden fumbles at Kansas City 34; ball recovered by Houston's D. Smith at Chiefs' 23. After one play, Del Greco kicks 39-yard field goal at 1:55.

Oct. 11, 1992—Indianapolis 6, New York Jets 3, at Indianapolis. Colts win toss. Verdin returns kickoff 33 yards to Colts' 36. Colts drive to Jets' 30 where Biasucci kicks 47-yard field goal at 3:01.

Nov. 8, 1992—Cincinnati 31, Chicago 28, at Chicago. Bears win toss. Lewis returns kickoff 22 yards to Chicago's 29. Bears drive to Chicago's 46 where Gardocki punts; fair catch by Wright at the Cincinnati 17. Bengals drive to Bears' 18 where Breech kicks 36-yard field goal at 8:39.

Nov. 15, 1992—New England 37, Indianapolis 34, at Indianapolis. Colts win toss. Verdin returns kickoff 10 yards to Colts' 20; holding penalty brings ball back to Colts' 10. After two plays, Henderson intercepts pass at Colts' 38 and returns it 9 yards to the 29. In three plays, Patriots drive to 1 where Baumann kicks 18-yard field goal at 3:25.

Nov. 29, 1992—Indianapolis 16, Buffalo 13, at Indianapolis. Colts win toss. Verdin returns kickoff 24 yards to Colts' 22. Colts drive to Buffalo 22 where Biasucci kicks 40-yard field goal at 3:51.

***Nov. 30, 1992—Seattle 16, Denver 13,** at Seattle. Seahawks win toss. Daluiso kicks through end zone for touchback. After three plays, Tuten punts 53 yards to Denver 18 where Marshall returns for no gain. After three plays, Rodriguez punts 29 yards to Seattle 45 where Warren signals fair catch. Seahawks drive to Denver 15 where Kasay's 33-yard field goal attempt misses. Broncos take over at Denver 20. After three plays, Rodriguez punts 43 yards to Seattle 38 where Warren signals for fair catch. After four plays, Tuten punts 39 yards to Denver 4 where Daniels downs punt. After three plays, Rodriguez punts 46 yards to Denver 48 where Warren returns 10 yards to the 38. Seahawks drive to Denver 14 where Kasay kicks 32-yard field goal at 11:10.

Dec. 13, 1992—Philadelphia 20, Seattle 17, at Seattle. Eagles win toss. Sydner returns kick 12 yards to Eagles' 16; illegal block penalty brings ball back to 8. Eagles drive to Philadelphia 45 where Feagles punts for a touchback. After 6 plays, Tuten punts 45 yards to Philadelphia 22 where Sydner returns 7 yards to 29. After 6 plays, Feagles punts 44 yards to Seattle 26 where Warren returns 5 yards to 31. After 5 plays, Tuten punts 32 yards to Philadelphia 20 where Sydner signals for fair catch. Eagles drive to Seattle 27 where Ruzek kicks 44-yard field goal with no time remaining.

Dec. 27, 1992—Miami 16, New England 13, at New England. Patriots win toss. Lockwood returns kickoff 15 yards to Patriots' 21. After three plays, McCarthy punts 39 yards to Miami 33 where Miller returns 2 yards to the 35. Miami drives to New England 18 where Stoyanovich kicks 35-yard field goal at 8:17.

Sept. 12, 1993—Detroit 19, New England 16, at New England. Patriots win toss. Patriots begin at 20. After 3 plays, Saxon punts 42 yards to Detroit 29 where Gray returns 12 yards to the 41. After 3 plays, Arnold punts 41 yards to New England 12 where Brown returns 16 yards to the 28. Patriots drive to Detroit 44 where Saxon punts into the end zone for a touchback. Detroit drives to New England 20 where Hanson kicks 38-yard field goal at 11:04.

Nov. 7, 1993—Buffalo 13, New England 10, at New England. Patriots win toss. T. Brown returns kickoff 27 yards to Patriots 30. Patriots drive to Buffalo 48 where Bills take over on downs. Bills drive to New England 25 where Metzelaars fumbles, and C. Brown recovers. After 3 plays, Saxon punts 46 yards to Buffalo 24 where Copeland returns 11 yards to the 35. Bills drive to New England 14 where Christie kicks 32-yard field goal at 9:22.

Dec. 19, 1993—Phoenix 30, Seattle 27, at Seattle. Cardinals win toss. Bailey returns kickoff 14 yards to Cardinals 20. Cardinals drive to Seattle 23 where Davis kicks 41-yard field goal at 6:45.

Jan. 2, 1994—Dallas 16, New York Giants 13, at New York. Giants win toss. Meggett returns kickoff 19 yards to Giants 19. After 6 plays, Horan punts 45 yards to Cowboys 25 where Widmer downs punt. Cowboys drive to Giants' 23 where Murray kicks 41-yard field goal at 10:44.

Jan. 2, 1994—New England 33, Miami 27, at New England. Dolphins win toss. McDuffie returns kickoff 21 yards to Miami 27. After 3 plays, Hatcher punts 43 yards to New England 29 where Harris returns 6 yards to the 35. After 2 plays, Brown intercepts pass from Bledsoe and returns 3 yards to Miami 49. After 3 plays, Hatcher punts 37 yards to New England 14 where Harris returns 18 yards to the 32. After 2 plays, Bledsoe passes 36 yards to Timpson for touchdown at 4:44.

Jan. 2, 1994—Los Angeles Raiders 33, Denver 30, at Los Angeles. Broncos win toss. Delpino returns kickoff 12 yards to Denver 25. Broncos drive to Los Angeles 22 where Elam's 40-yard field goal attempt is wide left. Raiders drive to Denver 29 where Jaeger kicks 47-yard field goal at 7:10.

***Jan. 3, 1994—Philadelphia 37, San Francisco 34,** at San Francisco. 49ers win toss. Walker returns kickoff, 19 yards to San Francisco 27. 49ers drive to Philadelphia 14 where Cofer misses 32-yard field goal. Eagles start at their 20-yard line, and, after 3 plays, Feagles punts 48 yards to San Francisco 36 where Carter fumbles and 49ers recover. After 7 plays, Wilmsmeyer punts 57 yards to Philadelphia 6 where Sikahema returns 16 yards to the 22. Eagles drive to San Francisco 10 where Ruzek kicks 28-yard field goal with no time remaining.

Sept. 4, 1994—Detroit 31, Atlanta 28, at Detroit. Falcons win toss. Falcons start at their own 16 after holding penalty on kickoff. After 3 plays, Alexander punts 41 yards to Detroit 39 where Clay returns 12 yards to Atlanta 49. Detroit drives to Atlanta 20 where Hanson kicks 37-yard field goal with 9:46 remaining.

Sept. 11, 1994—New York Jets 25, Denver 22, at New York. Jets win toss. Murrell returns kickoff 24 yards to New York 33. Jets drive to Denver 22 where Lowery kicks 39-yard field goal with 11:03 remaining.

***Sept. 19, 1994—Detroit 20, Dallas 17,** at Dallas. Lions win toss. Gray returns kickoff 24 yards to Detroit 32. Lions drive to Dallas 34 where Hanson's 51-yard field-goal attempt is blocked by Lett. Cowboys take possession at Dallas 42. Cowboys drive to Detroit 37 where Kennard fumbles and Swilling recovers. Lions take possession at Detroit 45. After 6 plays, Montgomery punts 31 yards to Dallas 16. Cowboys drive to Dallas 49 where Aikman fumbles and Thomas recovers at Dallas 43. Lions drive to Dallas 26 where Hanson kicks 44-yard field goal with 27 seconds remaining.

Oct. 16, 1994—Arizona 19, Washington 16, at Washington. Redskins win toss. Mitchell returns kickoff 27 yards to Washington 41. Redskins drive to Arizona 34 where Lohmiller's 51-yard field-goal attempt is blocked by Joyner and recovered by Williams who returns it to the Washington 37. After 5 plays, Peterson's 45-yard field-goal attempt is wide right. Redskins take possession at the Washington 36. After 3 plays, Roby punts 36 yards to the Arizona 37 where Robinson returns 3 yards to the 40. After 3 plays, Feagles punts 51 yards for a touchback. After 1 play, Shuler's pass is intercepted by Hoage who returns it to the Washington 12. Peterson kicks 29-yard field goal with 5:00 remaining.

Oct. 16, 1994—Miami 20, Los Angeles Raiders 17, at Miami. Dolphins win toss. McDuffie returns kickoff 19 yards to Miami 23. Dolphins drive to Los Angeles 12 where Stoyanovich kicks 29-yard field goal with 9:14 remaining.

#**Oct. 20, 1994—Minnesota 13, Green Bay 10,** at Minnesota. Vikings win toss. Ismail returns kickoff 22 yards to Minnesota 29. Vikings drive to Green Bay 9 where Fuad Reveiz kicks 27-yard field goal with 10:34 remaining.

Oct. 30, 1994—Detroit 28, New York Giants 25, at New York. Giants win toss. Lewis returns kickoff 16 yards to New York 27. After 3 plays, Horan punts 42 yards to Detroit 24 where Gray calls for fair catch. Detroit drives to New York 6 where Hanson kicks 24-yard field goal with 8:17 remaining.

Oct. 30, 1994—Arizona 20, Pittsburgh 17, at Arizona. Steelers win toss. Johnson returns kickoff 24 yards to Pittsburgh 30 where he fumbles and Arizona's Merritt recovers at Pittsburgh 32. After 3 plays, Davis kicks 51-yard field goal with 13:20 remaining.

Nov. 6, 1994—Cincinnati 20, Seattle 17, at Seattle. Seahawks win toss. Warren returns kickoff 32 yards to Seattle 33. After 3 plays, Tuten punts 37 yards to Cincinnati 28 where Sawyer calls for fair catch. After 3 plays, Johnson punts 64 yards to Seattle 2 where Truitt downs ball. Seahawks drive to Seattle 38 where Tuten punts 50 yards to Cincinnati 12 and Sawyer returns 5 yards to 17. Blake passes to Scott for 76 yards to Seattle 7. Pelfrey kicks 26-yard field goal with 6:46 remaining.

Nov. 6, 1994—Pittsburgh 12, Houston 9, at Houston. Steelers win toss. Stone returns kickoff 15 yards to Pittsburgh 28. After 3 plays, Royals punts 53 yards to Houston 13 where Givins downs ball. After 3 plays, Camarillo punts 57 yards to Pittsburgh 31 where Woodson returns 20 yards to Houston 49. After 3 plays, Royals punts 43 yards to Houston 15 where Coleman returns 3 yards to 18. After 5 plays, Camarillo punts 57 yards to Pittsburgh 12 where Hastings returns 12 yards to 24. Steelers drive to Houston 41 where Royals punts 29 yards to Houston 12, and Coleman calls for fair catch. Brown fumbles on first play and Jones recovers at Houston 22. After 1 play, Anderson kicks 40-yard field goal with 3:36 remaining.

Nov. 13, 1994—New England 26, Minnesota 20, at New England. Patriots win toss. Thompson returns kickoff 27 yards to New England 33. Patriots drive to Minnesota 14 where Bledsoe passes 14 yards to Turner for touchdown with 10:50 remaining.

Nov. 20, 1994—Pittsburgh 16, Miami 13, at Pittsburgh. Steelers win toss. Stone returns kickoff 15 yards to Pittsburgh 16. Steelers drive to Miami 39 where they lose possession on downs. Dolphins drive to Pittsburgh 47 where Arnold punts 35 yards to Pittsburgh 12 and Oliver downs ball. Steelers drive to Miami 21 where Anderson kicks 39-yard field goal with 4:41 remaining.

Nov. 27, 1994—Chicago 19, Arizona 16, at Arizona. Cardinals win toss. Levy returns kickoff 31 yards to Arizona 45. After 5 plays, Feagles punts 38 yards to the end zone for a touchback. Bears drive to Arizona 10 where Butler kicks 27-yard field goal with 6:49 remaining.

Nov. 27, 1994—Tampa Bay 20, Minnesota 17, at Minnesota. Buccaneers win toss. Harris returns kickoff 12 yards to Tampa Bay 38. After 6 plays, Stryzinski punts 40 yards to Minnesota 4 where Guliford muffs punt and Buccaneers' Brady recovers. Husted kicks 22-yard field goal with 12:52 remaining.

#**Dec. 1, 1994—Minnesota 33, Chicago 27,** at Minnesota. Bears win toss. Lewis returns kickoff 23 yards to Chicago 33. Bears drive to Minnesota 22 where Butler's 40-yard field goal attempt is wide left. After 1 play, Moon passes 65 yards to Carter for touchdown with 9:14 remaining.

Dec. 4, 1994—Denver 20, Kansas City 17, at Kansas City. Broncos win toss. Milburn returns kickoff 24 yards to Denver 29. After 3 plays, Millen fumbles and Phillips recovers at Denver 35. After 4 plays, Allen fumbles and Smith recovers at Denver 27. After 6 plays, Rouen punts 45 yards to Kansas City 25 where Hughes calls for fair catch. After 3 plays, Aguiar punts 33 yards to Denver 42 where Chiefs down ball. Broncos drive to Kansas City 17 where Elam kicks 34-yard field goal with 2:48 remaining.

Sept. 3, 1995—Cincinnati 24, Indianapolis 21, at Indianapolis. Bengals win toss. Dunn returns kickoff 15 yards to Bengals' 17. Cincinnati drives to Indianapolis 29 where Pelfrey kicks 47-yard field goal with 12:24 remaining.

Sept. 3, 1995—Atlanta 23, Carolina 20, at Atlanta. Panthers win toss. Baldwin downs kickoff for touchback. Panthers drive to Carolina 42 where Reich fumbles and ball is recovered by Archambeau at Carolina 31. Falcons drive to Panthers' 16 where Andersen kicks 35-yard field goal with 8:43 remaining.

Sept. 10, 1995—Indianapolis 27, New York Jets 24, at New York. Jets win toss. Carter downs kickoff for touchback. Jets punt downed at Colts' 37. Colts drive to Jets' 35 where Cofer kicks 52-yard field goal with 10:33 remaining.

Sept. 10, 1995—Kansas City 20, New York Giants 17, at Kansas City. Chiefs win toss. Vanover returns kickoff 30 yards to Chiefs' 28. Aguiar punts to Giants' 3. Horan punts to Chiefs' 49. Chiefs drive to Giants' 6 where Elliott kicks 23-yard field goal with 7:11 left.

Sept. 17, 1995—Dallas 23, Minnesota 17, at Minnesota. Cowboys win toss. K. Williams returns kickoff 23 yards to Cowboys' 27. E. Smith scores on 31-yard run with 12:34 left.

Sept. 17, 1995—Kansas City 23, Oakland 17, at Kansas City. Chiefs win toss. Vanover returns kickoff 28 yards to Chiefs' 41. M. Allen fumbles, ball recovered by Robbins at Raiders' 38. Hasty intercepts pass at Chiefs' 36 and returns it 64 yards for touchdown with 10:33 left.

Sept. 17, 1995—Atlanta 27, New Orleans 24, at Atlanta. Saints win toss. Hughes returns kickoff 21 yards to Saints' 17. Metcalf returns Wilmsmeyer's punt 18 yards to Saints' 39. Stryzinski punts, fair catch by Hughes at Saints' 14. Wilmsmeyer punt downed at Falcons' 6. Falcons drive to Saints' 3 where Andersen kicks 21-yard field goal with 7:02 left.

Oct. 8, 1995—Indianapolis 27, Miami 24, at Miami. Colts win toss. Warren returns kickoff 25 yards to Colts' 33. Colts drive to Dolphins' 10 where Blanchard kicks 27-yard field goal with 10:02 left.

Oct. 8, 1995—New York Giants 27, Arizona 21, at New York. Cardinals win toss. Terry returns kickoff 20 yards to Cardinals' 23. Hamilton recovers Krieg's fumble at Cardinals' 36. Lynch recovers Brown's fumble at Cardinals' 38. Armstead intercepts pass at Giants' 42 and returns it 58 yards for touchdown with 10:55 left.

Oct. 8, 1995—Minnesota 23, Houston 17, at Minnesota. Vikings win toss. Palmer returns kickoff 10 yards to Vikings' 15. Saxon's punt downed at Oilers' 8. Washington intercepts pass at Vikings' 47 and returns it 25 yards to Oilers' 28. R. Smith scores on 20-yard run with 7:50 left.

Oct. 8, 1995—Philadelphia 37, Washington 34, at Philadelphia. Redskins win toss. Redskins take possession at their 20 after touchback. Turk punt out of bounds at Eagles' 9. Eagles drive to Redskins' 18 where Anderson kicks 35-yard field goal with 4:54 left.

* **Oct. 9, 1995—Kansas City 29, San Diego 23,** at Kansas City. Chargers win toss. Coleman returns kickoff 24 yards to Chargers' 28. Vanover makes fair catch of Bennett's punt at Chiefs' 15. Coleman makes fair catch of Aguiar's punt at Chargers' 43. Vanover returns Bennett's punt 86 yards for a touchdown with 7:33 left.

Oct. 15, 1995—Tampa Bay 20, Minnesota 17, at Tampa Bay. Buccaneers win toss. Edmonds returns kickoff 19 yards to Buccaneers' 22. A. Lee returns Roby's punt to Vikings' 48. Vikings drive to Tampa Bays' 35 where Reveiz's 53-yard field-goal attempt is wide right. Buccaneers take over at own 43 and drive to Vikings' 33 where Husted kicks 51-yard field goal with 8:37 left.

Oct. 22, 1995—Washington 36, Detroit 30, at Washington. Redskins win toss. B. Mitchell returns kickoff 16 yards to Redskins' 27. Turk's punt downed at Lions' 4. D. Green intercepts S. Mitchell's pass and returns it 7 yards for touchdown with 11:19 left.

Oct. 29, 1995—Carolina 20, New England 17, at New England. Panthers win toss. Baldwin returns kickoff 22 yards to Panthers' 25. Meggett makes fair catch of Barnhardt's punt at Patriots' 9. Guliford returns O'Neill's punt 9 yards to Patriots' 32. Panthers drive to Patriots' 12 where Kasay kicks 29-yard field goal with 7:52 left.

Oct. 29, 1995—Cleveland 29, Cincinnati 26, at Cincinnati. Browns win toss. Hunter returns kickoff 31 yards to Browns' 31. Bieniemy returns Tupa's punt 9 yards to Bengals' 37. McCardell makes fair catch of Johnson's punt at Browns' 12. Bieniemy returns Tupa's punt 0 yards to Bengals' 38. Hall intercepts Blake's pass and returns it 5 yards to Bengals' 45. Browns drive to Bengals' 11 where Stover kicks 28-yard field goal with 8:30 left.

Oct. 29, 1995—Arizona 20, Seattle 14, at Arizona. Cardinals win toss. Dowdell returns kickoff 16 yards to Cardinals' 25. Cardinals drive to Seahawks' 10 where G. Davis' 27-yard field goal attempt is blocked. L. Lynch intercepts Friesz's pass at Cardinals' 28 and returns it 72 yards for a touchdown with 3:44 left.

Nov. 5, 1995—Pittsburgh 37, Chicago 34, at Chicago. Bears win toss. Timpson returns kickoff 23 yards to Bears' 33. Hastings returns Sauerbrun's punt 2 yards to Steelers' 31. Steelers drive to Bears' 6 where N. Johnson kicks 24-yard field goal with 6:41 left.

Nov. 12, 1995—Minnesota 30, Arizona 24, at Arizona. Vikings win toss. A. Lee returns kickoff 20 yards to Vikings' 25. Moon throws 50-yard touchdown pass to Ismail with 12:44 left.

Nov. 26, 1995—Arizona 40, Atlanta 37, at Arizona. Falcons win toss. J. Anderson returns kickoff 20 yards to Falcons' 20. Stryzinski fumbles punt snap. Recovered by England at Falcons' 10 where G. Davis kicks 28-yard field goal with 13:17 left.

Dec. 10, 1995—Tampa Bay 13, Green Bay 10, at Tampa Bay. Buccaneers win toss. Edmonds returns kickoff 24 yards to Buccaneers' 23. Tampa Bay drives to Packers' 29 where Husted kicks 47-yard field goal with 11:14 remaining.

Sept. 1, 1996—Buffalo 23, New York Giants 20, at New York. Bills win toss. Daluiso kick is a touchback. Bills drive to Buffalo 46. Toomer returns Mohr's punt to Giants' 16. Dave Brown's fumble recovered by Spielman at Giants' 33. Bills drive to Giants' 16 where Christie kicks 34-yard field goal with 5:52 remaining.

Sept. 22, 1996—New England 28, Jacksonville 25, at New England. Patriots win toss. T. Brown returns kickoff 18 yards to Patriots' 29. Patriots drive to Jaguars' 22 where Vinatieri kicks 40-yard field goal with 12:24 remaining.

Sept. 29, 1996—Arizona 31, St. Louis 28, at Arizona. Cardinals win toss. Lohmiller kick is a touchback. Cardinals drive to Rams' 7 where G. Davis kicks 24-yard field goal with 13:06 remaining.

Oct. 6, 1996—Buffalo 16, Indianapolis 13, at Buffalo. Colts win toss. Christie kick is a touchback. Colts drive to Indianapolis 32. Burris returns Gardocki's punt to Bills' 35. Bills drive to Colts' 48. Mohr punts out of bounds at Colts' 14. Colts drive to Indianapolis 9. Burris returns Gardocki's punt to Colts' 48. Bills drive to Colts' 22 where Christie kicks 39-yard field goal with 5:38 remaining.

Oct. 6, 1996—Houston 30, Cincinnati 27, at Cincinnati. Bengals win toss. Dunn returns kickoff 23 yards to Bengals' 34. Bengals drive to Cincinnati 36. Floyd returns L. Johnson's punt to Oilers' 18. Oilers drive to Bengals' 31 where Del Greco kicks 49-yard field goal with 7:53 remaining.

* **Oct. 14, 1996—Green Bay 23, San Francisco 20,** at Green Bay. 49ers win toss. D. Carter returns kickoff 23 yards to 49ers' 22. 49ers' drive to San Francisco 25. Howard makes fair catch of Thompson's punt at Packers' 44. Packers drive to 49ers' 35 where Jacke kicks 53-yard field goal with 11:19 remaining.

Oct. 27, 1996—Baltimore 37, St. Louis 31, at Baltimore. Rams win toss. J. Thomas returns kickoff 17 yard to Rams' 17. Rams drive to Ravens' 15. F. Miller fumble in field goal formation recovered by S. Moore at Ravens' 17. Ravens drive to Baltimore 49 and turn ball over on downs. Rams drive to Ravens' 40 and turn

ball over on downs. Testaverde throws 22-yard scoring pass to M. Jackson with 10 seconds remaining.
Nov. 10, 1996—Dallas 20, San Francisco 17, at San Francisco. Cowboys win toss. H. Walker returns kickoff 10 yards to Cowboys' 23. Cowboys drive to 49ers' 11 where Boniol kicks 29-yard field goal with 8:43 remaining.
Nov. 10, 1996—Arizona 37, Washington 34, at Washington. Arizona wins toss. Blanton's kickoff is a touchback. Cardinals drive to Redskins' 15 where Butler misses 32-yard field goal. Redskins drive to Cardinals' 43 where Turk punts for touchback. L. Johnson fumble returned by Morrison to Cardinals' 27. Redskins drive to Cardinals' 31 where Blanton misses 48-yard field goal. Cardinals drive to Redskins' 15 where Butler kicks 32-yard field goal with 33 seconds remaining.
Nov. 10, 1996—Tampa Bay 20, Oakland 17, at Tampa Bay. Tampa Bay wins toss. M. Marshall returns kickoff 15 yards to Bucs' 17. Bucs drive to Tampa Bay 36. T. Brown returns Barnhardt's punt four yards to Raiders' 22. Raiders drive to Oakland 25. M. Marshall returns Gossett's punt nine yards to Bucs' 39. Bucs drive to Raiders' 4 where Husted kicks 23-yard field goal with 3:04 remaining.
Nov. 17, 1996—Minnesota 16, Oakland 13, at Oakland. Oakland wins toss. Kaufman returns kickoff 32 yards to Raiders' 27. Raiders drive to Oakland 46 where Gossett punts to Vikings' 17. Vikings drive to Raiders' 12 where Sisson kicks 31-yard field goal with 3:07 remaining.
Nov. 24, 1996—Jacksonville 28, Baltimore 25, at Baltimore. Jacksonville wins toss. Jordon returns kickoff 16 yards to Jaguars' 30. Jaguars drive to Jacksonville 37. Barker's punt is downed at Ravens' 6. Ravens drive to Jaguars' 37 where Pritchett recovers Byner's fumble. Jaguars drive to Ravens' 15 where Hollis kicks 34-yard field goal with 5:54 remaining.
Nov. 24, 1996—San Francisco 19, Washington 16, at Washington. San Francisco wins toss. D. Carter returns kickoff 20 yards to 49ers' 32. 49ers drive to Redskins' 20 where Wilkins kicks 38-yard field goal with 11:36 remaining.
Dec. 1, 1996—Indianapolis 13, Buffalo 10, at Indianapolis. Buffalo wins toss. Moulds returns kickoff 26 yards to Bills' 25. Bills drive to Buffalo 49. Stock returns Mohr's punt one yard to Colts' 16. Colts drive to Bills' 32 where Blanchard kicks 49-yard field goal with 4:14 remaining.
Aug. 31, 1997—Tennessee 24, Oakland 21, at Tennessee. Oilers win toss. Gray returns kickoff 32 yards to Tennessee 33. Oilers drive to Tennessee 38. Roby's punt is downed at the Oakland 33. Raiders drive to Oakland 32. Gray returns Araguz punt to Tennessee 35. Oilers drive to Oakland 15 where Del Greco kicks 33-yard field goal with 8:03 remaining.
Sept. 7, 1997—Miami 16, Tennessee 13, at Miami. Dolphins win toss. Spikes returns kickoff 48 yards to Tennessee 45. Dolphins drive to Tennessee 11 where Mare kicks 29-yard field goal with 12:45 remaining.
Sept. 7, 1997— Arizona 25, Dallas 22, at Arizona. Cowboys win toss. Walker returns kickoff 21 yards to Dallas 25. Cowboys drive to Arizona 43. Gowin punts 43 yards for a touchback. Cardinals drive to Dallas 44. Graham fumbles. Cowboys drive to Arizona 42. Williams fumbles. Cardinals drive to Dallas 3 where Butler kicks 20-yard field goal with 6:30 remaining.
Sept. 14, 1997—Washington 19, Arizona 13, at Washington. Cardinals win toss. K. Williams returns kickoff 27 yards to Arizona 34. Cardinals drive to Arizona 40. McElroy fumbles. Redskins drive to Arizona 40. Westbrook catches 40-yard touchdown pass from Frerotte with 13:24 remaining.
Sept. 14, 1997—New England 27, New York Jets 24, at New England. Patriots win toss. Hall's kickoff is a touchback. Patriots drive to New England 15. Bledsoe pass intercepted by O. Smith. Jets drive to New York 46. Hansen punts 47 yards. Meggett returns to New England 21. Patriots drive to New York 17 where Vinatieri kicks 34-yard field goal with 6:57 remaining.
Sept. 28, 1997—Kansas City 20, Seattle 17, at Kansas City. Seahawks win toss. Broussard returns kickoff 12 yards to Seattle 14. Seahawks drive to Seattle 17. Vanover returns Tuten punt 8 yards to Kansas City 26. Chiefs drive to Seattle 44. Aguiar punt downed at Seattle 11. Seahawks drive to Seattle 26. Moon pass intercepted by Woods and returned 13 yards to 50. Chiefs drive to Seattle 23 where Stoyanovich kicks 41-yard field goal with 1:56 remaining.
Oct. 20, 1997—Philadelphia 13, Arizona 10, at Philadelphia. Cardinals win toss. K. Williams returns kickoff 28 yards to Arizona 42. Cardinals drive to Philadelphia 48. Feagles punts 48 yards for touchback. Eagles drive to Arizona 7 where Boniol kicks 24-yard field goal with 10:58 remaining.
Oct. 20, 1997—New York Giants 26, Detroit 20, at Detroit. Giants win toss. Pegram returns kickoff 16 yards to New York 18. Giants drive to New York 32. Calloway catches 68-yard touchdown pass from Kanell with 13:20 remaining.
Oct. 26, 1997—Denver 23, Buffalo 20, at Buffalo. Denver wins toss and elects to kickoff. Holmes returns kickoff 20 yards to Buffalo 25. Bills drive to Buffalo 23. Mohr punt downed at Denver 40. Broncos drive to Buffalo 48. Rouen punt downed at Buffalo 1. Bills drive to Buffalo 20. Gordon returns Mohr punt to Denver 42. Broncos drive to Buffalo 15 where Elam kicks 33-yard field goal with 1:56 remaining.
Oct. 26, 1997—Pittsburgh 23, Jacksonville 17, at Pittsburgh. Pittsburgh wins toss. Coleman returns kickoff 23 yards to Pittsburgh 23. Steelers drive to Jacksonville 17. Bettis catches 17-yard touchdown pass from Stewart with 11:13 remaining.
Oct. 27, 1997—Chicago 36, Miami 33, at Miami. Miami wins toss. McPhail returns kickoff 23 yards to Miami 27. Dolphins drive to Miami 36. Kidd punts out of bounds at Chicago 10. Bears drive to the Chicago 39. Sauerbrun punt out of bounds at Miami 27. Reeves recovers Marino fumble at Miami 17. Bears drive to Miami 17 where Jaeger kicks 35-yard field goal with 5:35 remaining.
Nov. 2, 1997—New York Jets 19, Baltimore 16, at New York. New York wins toss. Stover's kickoff is a touchback. Jets drive to Baltimore 20 where Hall kicks 37-yard field goal with 10:02 remaining.
Nov. 16, 1997—Philadelphia 10, Baltimore 10, at Baltimore. Philadelphia wins toss. Stover's kickoff is a touchback. Eagles drive to Philadelphia 19. Hutton punts 36 yards to Baltimore 45. Ravens drive to Baltimore 36 where Eagles take over on downs. Eagles drive to Baltimore 33 where Ravens take over on downs. Ravens drive to Baltimore 37. Montgomery punts 55 yards, and Solomon returns to Philadelphia 22. Eagles drive to Philadelphia 16. Hutton punts 41 yards, and Roe returns to Baltimore 46. Ravens drive to Philadelphia 35 where Stover's 53-yard field-goal attempt is no good. Eagles drive to Baltimore 22 where Boniol's 40-yard field-goal is no good as time expires.
Nov. 16, 1997—New Orleans 20, Seattle 17, at New Orleans. Seattle wins toss. Brien's kickoff is a touchback. Seahawks start at Seattle 20 where Moon's pass intercepted by Tubbs who returns 15 yards to Seattle 20. Saints Brien kicks 38-yard field goal with 14:43 remaining.
Nov. 23, 1997—New York Giants 7, Washington 7, at Washington. Washington wins toss. Davis returns kickoff 28 yards to Washington 39. Redskins drive to Washington 36 where Hostetler's pass intercepted by Sehorn who returns minus-2 yards before lateralling to Wooten who returns 5 yards to New York 41. Giants drive to New York 26 where Maynard punts 37 yards to Washington 37. Redskins drive to New York 39 where Hostetler fumble is recovered by Harris at New York 40. Giants drive to New York 43 where Maynard punts 57 yards for a touchback. Washington drives to New York 41. Giants take over on downs at New York 40. Giants drive to Washington 36 where Daluiso's 54-yard field-goal attempt is no good. Redskins drive to Washington 45 where Hostetler's pass intercepted by Sparks at New York 49. Giants drive to Washington 36 where Maynard punts 36 yards for a touchback. Redskins drive to New York 36 where Blanton's 54-yard field-goal attempt is no good. Giants drive to New York 45 where Kanell's pass intercepted by Patton who laterals to Pounds who returns 11 yards to Washington 24 as time expires.
Nov. 30, 1997—Pittsburgh 26, Arizona 20, at Arizona. Arizona wins toss. K. Williams returns kickoff 11 yards to Arizona 23. Cardinals drive to Arizona 18 where Feagles punts 43 yards. Hawkins returns punt 9 yards to Pittsburgh 48. Steelers drive to Arizona 10 where Bettis scores on a 10-yard touchdown run with 9:26 remaining.
Dec. 13, 1997—Pittsburgh 24, New England 21, at New England. Pittsburgh wins toss. Coleman returns kickoff 19 yards to Pittsburgh 26. Steelers drive to New England 13 where Johnson kicks a 31-yard field goal with 10:17 remaining.
Sept. 6, 1998—San Francisco 36, New York Jets 30, at San Francisco. Jets win toss. Richey's kickoff is a touchback. Jets drive to New York 11. Gallery punts 48 yards. McQuarters returns to New York 43. 49ers drive to New York 44. Howard punts 23 yards to New York 21. Johnson calls fair catch. Jets drive to New York 47. Gallery's 49-yard punt downed at San Francisco 4. Hearst runs for a 96-yard touchdown with 10:52 remaining.
Sept. 13, 1998—Cincinnati 34, Detroit 28, at Detroit. Lions win toss. Johnson's kickoff is a touchback. Lions drive to Detroit 47 where Mitchell's pass is intercepted by Sawyer and returned for a 58-yard touchdown with 12:54 remaining.
Sept. 27, 1998—New Orleans 19, Indianapolis 13, at Indianapolis. Saints win toss. Gardocki's kickoff is returned by Ismail to New Orleans 28. Saints drive to New Orleans 30. Royals punts 64 yards. Poole returns to Indianapolis 12. Colts drive to Indianapolis 20. Gardocki punts 58 yards. Hastings returns to New Orleans 29. Saints drive to New Orleans 32. Royals punts 59 yards. Punt downed at Indianapolis 9. Colts drive to Indianapolis 44 where Manning's pass is intercepted by Drakeford and returned to Indianapolis 36. Saints drive to Indianapolis 33. Wuerffel throws 33-yard touchdown pass to Cleeland with 8:50 remaining.
Oct. 25, 1998—Miami 12, New England 9, at Miami. Dolphins win toss. Vinatieri's kickoff is returned by Avery to Miami 15. Dolphins drive to New England 26 where Mare kicks 43-yard field goal with 10:24 remaining.
Nov. 26, 1998—Detroit 19, Pittsburgh 16, at Detroit. Lions win toss. Johnson's kickoff is returned by Fair to Detroit 35. Lions drive to Pittsburgh 24 where Hanson kicks 42-yard field goal with 12:08 remaining.
Dec. 6, 1998—San Francisco 31, Carolina 28, at Carolina. Panthers win toss. Richey's kickoff is returned by Floyd to Carolina 36. Panthers drive to Carolina 38 where Beuerlein's fumble is recovered by Doleman at Carolina 30. 49ers drive to Carolina 5 where Richey kicks 23-yard field goal with 10:44 remaining.
Dec. 13, 1998—Arizona 20, Philadelphia 17, at Philadelphia. Cardinals win toss. Boniol's kickoff is returned by Metcalf to Arizona 28. Cardinals drive to Philadelphia 15 where Jacke kicks 32-yard field goal with 10:30 remaining.
**indicates Monday night game*
#indicates Thursday night game

POSTSEASON

Dec. 28, 1958—Baltimore 23, New York Giants 17, at New York in NFL Championship Game. Giants win toss. Maynard returns kickoff to Giants' 20. Chandler punts and Taseff returns one yard to Colts' 20. Colts win at 8:15 on a 1-yard run by Ameche.
Dec. 23, 1962—Dallas Texans 20, Houston Oilers 17, at Houston in AFL Championship Game. Texans win toss and kick off. Jancik returns kickoff to Oilers' 33. Norton punts and Jackson makes fair catch on Texans' 22. Wilson punts and Jancik makes fair catch on Oilers' 45. Robinson intercepts Blanda's

pass and returns 13 yards to Oilers' 47. Wilson's punt rolls dead at Oilers' 12. Hull intercepts Blanda's pass and returns 23 yards to midfield. Texans win at 17:54 on a 25-yard field goal by Brooker.

Dec. 26, 1965—Green Bay 13, Baltimore 10, at Green Bay in NFL Divisional Playoff Game. Packers win toss. Moore returns kickoff to Packers' 22. Chandler punts and Haymond returns nine yards to Colts' 41. Gilburg punts and Wood makes fair catch at Packers' 21. Chandler punts and Haymond returns one yard to Colts' 41. Michaels misses 47-yard field goal. Packers win at 13:39 on 25-yard field goal by Chandler.

Dec. 25, 1971—Miami 27, Kansas City 24, at Kansas City in AFC Divisional Playoff Game. Chiefs win toss. Podolak, after a lateral from Buchanan, returns kickoff to Chiefs' 46. Stenerud's 42-yard field goal is blocked. Seiple punts and Podolak makes fair catch at Chiefs' 17. Wilson punts and Scott returns 18 yards to Dolphins' 39. Yepremian misses 62-yard field goal. Scott intercepts Dawson's pass and returns 13 yards to Dolphins' 46. Seiple punts and Podolak loses one yard to Chiefs' 15. Wilson punts and Scott makes fair catch on Dolphins' 30. Dolphins win at 22:40 on a 37-yard field goal by Yepremian.

Dec. 24, 1977—Oakland 37, Baltimore 31, at Baltimore in AFC Divisional Playoff Game. Colts win toss. Raiders start on own 42 following a punt late in the first overtime. Oakland works way into field-goal range on Stabler's 19-yard pass to Branch at Colts' 26. Four plays later, on the second play of the second overtime, Stabler hits Casper with a 10-yard touchdown pass at 15:43.

Jan. 2, 1982—San Diego 41, Miami 38, at Miami in AFC Divisional Playoff Game. Chargers win toss. San Diego drives from its 13 to Miami 8. On second-and-goal, Benirschke misses 27-yard field goal attempt wide left at 9:15. Miami has the ball twice and San Diego twice more before the Dolphins get their third possession. Miami drives from the San Diego 46 to Chargers' 17 and on fourth-and-two, von Schamann's 34-yard field goal attempt is blocked by San Diego's Winslow after 11:27. Fouts then completes four of five passes, including a 39-yarder to Joiner that puts the ball on Dolphins' 10. On first down, Benirschke kicks a 29-yard field goal at 13:52. San Diego's winning drive covered 74 yards in six plays.

Jan. 3, 1987—Cleveland 23, New York Jets 20, at Cleveland in AFC Divisional Playoff Game. Jets win toss. Jets' punt downed at Browns' 26. Moseley's 23-yard field goal attempt is wide right. Teams trade punts. Jets' second punt downed at Browns' 31. First overtime period expires eight plays later with Browns in possession at Jets' 42. Moseley kicks 27-yard field goal four plays into second overtime at 17:02.

Jan. 11, 1987—Denver 23, Cleveland 20, at Cleveland in AFC Championship Game. Browns win toss. Broncos hold Browns on four downs. Browns' punt returned four yards to Denver's 25. Elway completes 22- and 28-yard passes to set up Karlis's 33-yard field goal nine plays into drive at 5:38.

Jan. 3, 1988—Houston 23, Seattle 20, at Houston in AFC Wild Card Game. Seahawks win toss. Rodriguez punts to K. Johnson who returns one yard to Houston 15. Zendejas kicks 32-yard field goal 12 plays later at 8:05.

Dec. 31, 1989—Pittsburgh 26, Houston 23, at Houston in AFC Wild Card Playoff Game. Steelers win toss. Steelers punt to Oilers. Oilers' fumble recovered by Woodson and returned three yards. Four plays and 13 yards later, Anderson kicks a 50-yard field goal at 3:26.

Jan. 7, 1990—Los Angeles Rams 19, New York Giants 13, at New York in NFC Divisional Game. Rams win toss. Everett completes two passes to move ball to Giants' 48. White called for pass interference; ball spotted on Giants' 25. Everett hits Anderson with a 30-yard touchdown pass at 1:06.

Jan. 3, 1993—Buffalo 41, Houston 38, at Buffalo in AFC Wild Card Game. Houston wins toss. Oilers begin at 20. After 2 plays, Moon's pass is intercepted by Odomes who returns ball 2 yards to Houston 35. After 2 plays, Christie kicks 32-yard field goal at 3:06.

Jan. 8, 1994—Kansas City 27, Pittsburgh 24, at Kansas City in AFC Wild Card Game. Kansas City wins toss. Hughes returns kickoff 20 yards to Kansas City 25. After 3 plays, Barker punts 48 yards to Pittsburgh 18 where Woodson returns 8 yards to the 26. After 6 plays, Royals punts 30 yards to Kansas City 20. Kansas City drives to Pittsburgh 14 where Lowery kicks 32-yard field goal at 11:03.

Jan. 17, 1999—Atlanta 30, Minnesota 27, at Minnesota in NFC Championship Game. Minnesota wins toss. Palmer returns kickoff 30 yards to Minnesota 29. After four plays, Berger punts 51 yards to Atlanta 7 where Dwight returns 8 yards to Atlanta 15. Falcons drive to Atlanta 36. Stryzinski punts 37 yards to Vikings' 27. Palmer calls fair catch. Vikings drive to Minnesota 39. Berger punts 52 yards to Atlanta 9. Downed by Vikings. Atlanta drives to Minnesota 21 where Andersen kicks 38-yard field goal at 11:52.

NFL POSTSEASON OVERTIME GAMES

(BY LENGTH OF GAME)

Date	Game	Length
Dec. 25, 1971	Miami 27, KANSAS CITY 24	82:40
Dec. 23, 1962	Dallas Texans 20, HOUSTON 17	77:54
Jan. 3, 1987	CLEVELAND 23, New York Jets 20	77:02
Dec. 24, 1977	Oakland 37, BALTIMORE 31	75:43
Jan. 2, 1982	San Diego 41, MIAMI 38	73:52
Dec. 26, 1965	GREEN BAY 13, Baltimore 10	73:39
Jan. 17, 1999	Atlanta 30, MINNESOTA 27	71:52
Jan. 8, 1994	KANSAS CITY 27, Pittsburgh 24	71:03
Dec. 28, 1958	Baltimore 23, N.Y. GIANTS 17	68:15
Jan. 3, 1988	HOUSTON 23, Seattle 20	68:05
Jan. 11, 1987	Denver 23, CLEVELAND 20	65:38
Dec. 31, 1989	Pittsburgh 26, HOUSTON 23	63:26
Jan. 3, 1993	BUFFALO 41, Houston 38	63:06
Jan. 7, 1990	Los Angeles Rams 19, N.Y. GIANTS 13	61:06

Home team in CAPS

There have been 14 overtime postseason games dating back to 1958. In 13 cases, both teams had at least one possession. Last time: 1/17/99, Atlanta 30, MINNESOTA 27.

OVERTIME WON-LOST RECORDS, 1974-1998

(REGULAR SEASON)

AFC	W	L	T	Pct.
Baltimore	1	2	1	.375
Buffalo	11	6	0	.647
Cincinnati	13	7	0	.650
Cleveland	12	8	1	.595
Denver	13	9	2	.583
Indianapolis	9	8	1	.528
Jacksonville	1	2	0	.333
Kansas City	8	7	2	.529
Miami	10	14	1	.420
New England	9	16	0	.360
New York Jets	10	9	2	.524
Oakland	10	11	0	.476
Pittsburgh	13	5	1	.711
San Diego	7	10	0	.412
Seattle	4	11	0	.267
Tennessee	8	13	0	.380

NFC	W	L	T	Pct.
Arizona	12	10	2	.542
Atlanta	7	9	1	.441
Carolina	1	2	0	.333
Chicago	11	11	0	.500
Dallas	9	6	0	.600
Detroit	10	10	1	.500
Green Bay	6	10	4	.400
Minnesota	13	12	2	.519
New Orleans	4	7	0	.364
New York Giants	8	10	2	.450
Philadelphia	8	9	3	.475
St. Louis	6	7	1	.464
San Francisco	7	7	1	.500
Tampa Bay	9	7	1	.559
Washington	11	7	1	.605

OVERTIME GAMES BY YEAR

(REGULAR SEASON)

1998-7	1991-15	1984- 9	1977- 6
1997-17	1990-10	1983-19	1976- 5
1996-14	1989-11	1982- 4	1975- 9
1995-21	1988- 9	1981-10	1974- 2
1994-16	1987-13	1980-13	
1993-7	1986-16	1979-12	
1992-10	1985-10	1978-11	

OVERTIME GAMES

OVERTIME GAME SUMMARY—1974-1998

There have been 276 overtime games in regular-season play since the rule was adopted in 1974 (7 in 1998 season). Breakdown follows:

204(4) times both teams had at least one possession (74%)
136(4) times the team which won the toss won the game (49%)
125(3) times the team which lost the toss won the game (45%)
15(0) games ended tied (5%). Last time: Nov. 23, 1997, N.Y. Giants 7, at Washington 7.
72(3) times the team which won the toss drove for winning score (52 FG, 20 TD) (26%)
190(4) games were decided by a field goal (69%)
70(3) games were decided by a touchdown (25%)
1(0) games were decided by a safety (.4%)

Note: The number in parentheses represents the 1998 season total in each category.

MOST OVERTIME GAMES, SEASON

5 Green Bay Packers, 1983
4 Denver Broncos, 1985
Cleveland Browns, 1989
Minnesota Vikings, 1994
Arizona Cardinals, 1995
Minnesota Vikings, 1995
Arizona Cardinals, 1997
3 By many teams, last time: Pittsburgh Steelers, 1997

LONGEST CONSECUTIVE GAME STREAKS WITHOUT OVERTIME (Current)

51 Denver Broncos (last OT game, 12/4/94 at Kansas City)
(Record: 110, Phoenix Cardinals, 12/7/86-12/19/93)

SHORTEST OVERTIME GAMES

0:17 New Orleans 20, Seattle 17; 11/16/97
0:21 Chicago 23, Detroit 17; 11/27/80—only kickoff return for TD
0:30 Baltimore 29, New England 23; 9/4/83

LONGEST OVERTIME GAMES

(ALL POSTSEASON GAMES)

22:40 Miami 27, Kansas City 24; 12/25/71
17:54 Dallas Texans 20, Houston 17; 12/23/62
17:02 Cleveland 23, New York Jets 20; 1/3/87

OVERTIME SCORING SUMMARY

190 were decided by a field goal
30 were decided by a touchdown pass
21 were decided by a touchdown run
10 were decided by interceptions (Atlanta 40, New Orleans 34, 9/2/79; Atlanta 47, Green Bay 41, 11/27/83; New York Giants 16, Philadelphia 10, 9/29/85; Indianapolis 23, Cleveland 17, 12/10/89; Cleveland 30, San Diego 24, 10/20/91; Kansas City 23, Oakland 17, 9/17/95; New York Giants 27, Arizona 21, 10/8/95; Washington 36, Detroit 30, 10/22/95; Arizona 20, Seattle 14, 10/29/95; Cincinnati 34, Detroit 28, 9/13/98)
2 were decided on a fake field goal/touchdown pass (Minnesota 22, Chicago 16, 10/16/77; Cleveland 23, Minnesota 17, 12/17/89)
1 was decided by a kickoff return (Chicago 23, Detroit 17, 11/27/80)
1 was decided by a punt return (Kansas City 29, San Diego 23, 10/9/95)
1 was decided by a fumble recovery (Baltimore 29, New England 23, 9/4/83)
1 was decided on a fake field goal/touchdown run (Los Angeles Rams 27, Minnesota 21, 12/2/79)
1 was decided on a blocked field goal (Denver 30, San Diego 24, 11/17/85)
1 was decided on a blocked field goal/recovery by kicker (Green Bay 12, Chicago 6, 9/7/80)
1 was decided on a blocked field goal/recovery by kicking team (Philadelphia 23, New York Giants 17, 11/20/88)
1 was decided by a safety (Minnesota 23, Los Angeles Rams 21, 11/5/89)
15 ended tied

OVERTIME RECORDS

Longest Touchdown Pass

99 Yards — Ron Jaworski to Mike Quick, Philadelphia 23, Atlanta 17 (11/10/85)
68 Yards — Danny Kanell to Chris Calloway, New York Giants 26, Detroit 20 (10/20/97)
65 Yards — Warren Moon to Cris Carter, Minnesota 33, Chicago 27 (12/1/94)

Longest Touchdown Run

96 Yards — Garrison Hearst, San Francisco 36, N.Y. Jets 30 (9/6/98)
60 Yards — Herschel Walker, Dallas 23, New England 17 (11/15/87)
42 Yards — Eric Dickerson, Los Angeles Rams 26, Tampa Bay 20 (10/5/86)

Longest Field Goal

53 Yards — Chris Jacke, Green Bay 23, San Francisco 20 (10/4/96)
52 Yards — Mike Cofer, Indianapolis 27, N.Y. Jets 24 (9/10/95)
51 Yards — Greg Davis, New England 23, Indianapolis 20 (10/29/89)
Greg Davis, Arizona 20, Pittsburgh 17 (10/30/94)
Michael Husted, Tampa Bay 20, Minnesota 17 (10/15/95)

Longest Touchdown Plays

99 Yards — (Pass) Ron Jaworski to Mike Quick, Philadelphia 23, Atlanta 17 (11/10/85)
96 Yards — (Run) Garrison Hearst, San Francisco 36, N.Y. Jets 30 (9/6/98)
95 Yards — (Kickoff return) Dave Williams, Chicago 23, Detroit 17 (11/27/80)
86 Yards — (Punt return) Tamarick Vanover, Kansas City 29, San Diego 23 (10/9/95)
72 Yards — (Interception return) Lorenzo Lynch, Arizona 20, Seattle 14 (10/29/95)

NFL PAID ATTENDANCE

For detailed 1998 attendance, see page 242.

Year	Regular Season		Average	Postseason	Total
1998	#15,364,873	(240 games)	#64,020	822,885 (12)	#16,187,758
1997	14,967,314	(240 games)	62,364	801,879 (12)	15,769,193
1996	14,612,417	(240 games)	60,885	769,310 (12)	15,381,727
1995	15,043,562	(240 games)	62,682	790,906 (12)	15,834,468
1994	14,030,435	(224 games)	62,636	779,738 (12)	14,810,173
1993	13,966,843	(224 games)	62,352	814,607 (12)	14,781,450
1992	13,828,887	(224 games)	61,736	815,910 (12)	14,644,797
1991	13,841,459	(224 games)	61,792	813,247 (12)	14,654,706
1990	13,959,896	(224 games)	62,321	847,543 (12)	14,807,439
1989	13,625,662	(224 games)	60,829	685,771 (10)	14,311,433
1988	13,539,848	(224 games)	60,446	658,317 (10)	14,198,165
1987	*11,406,166	(210 games)	54,315	656,977 (10)	12,063,143
1986	13,588,551	(224 games)	60,663	734,002 (10)	14,322,553
1985	13,345,047	(224 games)	59,567	710,768 (10)	14,055,815
1984	13,398,112	(224 games)	59,813	665,194 (10)	14,063,306
1983	13,277,222	(224 games)	59,273	675,513 (10)	13,952,735
1982	**7,367,438	(126 games)	58,472	1,033,153 (16)	8,400,591
1981	13,606,990	(224 games)	60,745	637,763 (10)	14,244,753
1980	13,392,230	(224 games)	59,787	624,430 (10)	14,016,660
1979	13,182,039	(224 games)	58,848	630,326 (10)	13,812,365
1978	12,771,800	(224 games)	57,017	624,388 (10)	13,396,188
1977	11,018,632	(196 games)	56,218	534,925 (8)	11,553,557
1976	11,070,543	(196 games)	56,482	492,884 (8)	11,563,427
1975	10,213,193	(182 games)	56,116	475,919 (8)	10,689,112
1974	10,236,322	(182 games)	56,244	438,664 (8)	10,674,986
1973	10,730,933	(182 games)	58,961	525,433 (8)	11,256,366
1972	10,445,827	(182 games)	57,395	483,345 (8)	10,929,172
1971	10,076,035	(182 games)	55,363	483,891 (8)	10,559,926
1970	9,533,333	(182 games)	52,381	458,493 (8)	9,991,826
1969	6,096,127	(112 games) NFL	54,430	162,279 (3)	6,258,406
	2,843,373	(70 games) AFL	40,620	167,088 (3)	3,010,461
1968	5,882,313	(112 games) NFL	52,521	215,902 (3)	6,098,215
	2,635,004	(70 games) AFL	37,643	114,438 (2)	2,749,442
1967	5,938,924	(112 games) NFL	53,026	166,208 (3)	6,105,132
	2,295,697	(63 games) AFL	36,439	53,330 (1)	2,349,027
1966	5,337,044	(105 games) NFL	50,829	74,152 (1)	5,411,196
	2,160,369	(63 games) AFL	34,291	42,080 (1)	2,202,449
1965	4,634,021	(98 games) NFL	47,286	100,304 (2)	4,734,325
	1,782,384	(56 games) AFL	31,828	30,361 (1)	1,812,745
1964	4,563,049	(98 games) NFL	46,562	79,544 (1)	4,642,593
	1,447,875	(56 games) AFL	25,855	40,242 (1)	1,488,117
1963	4,163,643	(98 games) NFL	42,486	45,801 (1)	4,209,444
	1,208,697	(56 games) AFL	21,584	63,171 (2)	1,271,868
1962	4,003,421	(98 games) NFL	40,851	64,892 (1)	4,068,313
	1,147,302	(56 games) AFL	20,487	37,981 (1)	1,185,283
1961	3,986,159	(98 games) NFL	40,675	39,029 (1)	4,025,188
	1,002,657	(56 games) AFL	17,904	29,556 (1)	1,032,213
1960	3,128,296	(78 games) NFL	40,106	67,325 (1)	3,195,621
	926,156	(56 games) AFL	16,538	32,183 (1)	958,339
1959	3,140,000	(72 games)	43,617	57,545 (1)	3,197,545
1958	3,006,124	(72 games)	41,752	123,659 (2)	3,129,783
1957	2,836,318	(72 games)	39,393	119,579 (2)	2,955,897
1956	2,551,263	(72 games)	35,434	56,836 (1)	2,608,099
1955	2,521,836	(72 games)	35,026	85,693 (1)	2,607,529
1954	2,190,571	(72 games)	30,425	43,827 (1)	2,234,398
1953	2,164,585	(72 games)	30,064	54,577 (1)	2,219,162
1952	2,052,126	(72 games)	28,502	97,507 (2)	2,149,633
1951	1,913,019	(72 games)	26,570	57,522 (1)	1,970,541
1950	1,977,753	(78 games)	25,356	136,647 (3)	2,114,400
1949	1,391,735	(60 games)	23,196	27,980 (1)	1,419,715
1948	1,525,243	(60 games)	25,421	36,309 (1)	1,561,552
1947	1,837,437	(60 games)	30,624	66,268 (2)	1,903,705
1946	1,732,135	(55 games)	31,493	58,346 (1)	1,790,481
1945	1,270,401	(50 games)	25,408	32,178 (1)	1,302,579
1944	1,019,649	(50 games)	20,393	46,016 (1)	1,065,665
1943	969,128	(40 games)	24,228	71,315 (2)	1,040,443
1942	887,920	(55 games)	16,144	36,006 (1)	923,926
1941	1,108,615	(55 games)	20,157	55,870 (2)	1,164,485
1940	1,063,025	(55 games)	19,328	36,034 (1)	1,099,059
1939	1,071,200	(55 games)	19,476	32,279 (1)	1,103,479
1938	937,197	(55 games)	17,040	48,120 (1)	985,317
1937	963,039	(55 games)	17,510	15,878 (1)	978,917
1936	816,007	(54 games)	15,111	29,545 (1)	845,552
1935	638,178	(53 games)	12,041	15,000 (1)	653,178
1934	492,684	(60 games)	8,211	35,059 (1)	527,743

 # Record

**Players' 24-day strike reduced 224-game schedule to 210 games.*

***Players' 57-day strike reduced 224-game schedule to 126 games.*

ATTENDANCE/TV RATINGS

NFL'S TOP 10 PAID ATTENDANCE WEEKENDS

Weekend	Games	Attendance
November 23-24, 1997	15	999,778
September 6-7, 1998	15	997,835
December 13-14, 1998	15	992,659
December 20-21, 1998	15	987,518
November 8-9, 1998	15	984,630
December 4, 7-8, 1997	15	983,684
November 15-16, 1998	15	970,800
November 10-11, 1996	15	964,079
December 9-11, 1995	15	963,512
November 19-20 1995	15	962,523

NFL'S 10 HIGHEST SCORING WEEKENDS

Point Total	Date	Weekend
762	November 10-11, 1996	11th
761	October 16-17, 1983	7th
740	November 29-30, 1998	13th
739	November 23, 26-27, 1995	13th
736	October 25-26, 1987	7th
734	November 19-20, 1995	12th
732	November 9-10, 1980	10th
725	November 24, 27-28, 1983	13th
719	November 27, 30-December 1, 1997	14th
714	September 17-18, 1989	2nd

TOP 10 TELEVISED SPORTS EVENTS OF ALL-TIME

(Based on A.C. Nielsen Figures)

Program	Date	Network	Share	Rating
Super Bowl XVI	1/24/82	CBS	73.0	49.1
Super Bowl XVII	1/30/83	NBC	69.0	48.6
Winter Olympics	2/23/94	CBS	64.0	48.5
Super Bowl XX	1/26/86	NBC	70.0	48.3
Super Bowl XII	1/15/78	CBS	67.0	47.2
Super Bowl XIII	1/21/79	NBC	74.0	47.1
Super Bowl XVIII	1/22/84	CBS	71.0	46.4
Super Bowl XIX	1/20/85	ABC	63.0	46.4
Super Bowl XIV	1/20/80	CBS	67.0	46.3
Super Bowl XXX	1/28/96	NBC	68.0	46.0

TEN MOST WATCHED TV PROGRAMS & ESTIMATED TOTAL NUMBER OF VIEWERS

(Based on A.C. Nielsen Figures)

Program	Date	Network	*Total Viewers
Super Bowl XXX	Jan. 28, 1996	NBC	138,488,000
Super Bowl XXVIII	Jan. 30, 1994	NBC	134,800,000
Super Bowl XXXII	Jan. 25, 1998	NBC	133,400,000
Super Bowl XXVII	Jan. 31, 1993	NBC	133,400,000
Super Bowl XXXI	Jan. 26, 1997	FOX	128,900,000
Super Bowl XXXIII	Jan. 31, 1999	FOX	127,500,000
Super Bowl XX	Jan. 26, 1986	NBC	127,000,000
Winter Olympics	Feb. 23, 1994	CBS	126,686,000
Super Bowl XXIX	Jan. 29, 1995	ABC	125,216,000
Super Bowl XXI	Jan. 25, 1987	CBS	122,640,000

**Watched some portion of the broadcast*

NFL'S TOP 10 TEAM SINGLE-SEASON HOME PAID ATTENDANCE TOTALS

Year	Club	Games	Attendance
1980	Detroit Lions	8	634,204
1988	Buffalo Bills	8	631,818
1991	Buffalo Bills	8	631,786
1992	Buffalo Bills	8	630,978
1997	Kansas City Chiefs	8	629,763
1998	Kansas City Chiefs	8	629,209
1996	Kansas City Chiefs	8	628,460
1994	Kansas City Chiefs	8	626,612
1989	Buffalo Bills	8	626,399
1995	Kansas City Chiefs	8	625,936

NFL'S TOP FIVE PAID ATTENDANCE TOTALS FOR ALL GAMES

Year	Preseason	Regular Season	Postseason	All Games
1998	3,553,735	15,364,873	822,885	19,741,493
1995	3,368,289	15,043,562	790,906	19,202,757
1997	3,280,693	14,967,314	801,879	19,049,886
1996	3,267,254	14,612,417	769,310	18,648,981
1994	3,200,091	14,030,435	779,738	18,010,264

TEN HIGHEST-RATED ABC NFL MONDAY NIGHT FOOTBALL GAMES OF ALL-TIME

(Based on A.C. Nielsen Figures)

Game	Date	Share	Rating
Chicago at Miami	12/2/85	46.0	29.6
N.Y. Giants at San Francisco	12/3/90	42.0	26.9
Dallas at Washington	10/2/78	43.0	26.8
Pittsburgh at San Diego	12/22/80	40.0	25.3
Philadelphia at Miami	11/30/81	40.0	25.3
Pittsburgh at Houston	12/10/79	40.0	25.1
Dallas at Miami	12/17/84	40.0	25.1
Pittsburgh at Dallas	9/13/82	42.0	24.9
Cincinnati at Oakland	12/6/76	40.0	24.7
Dallas at Washington	10/8/73	40.0	24.6
Minnesota at Atlanta	11/19/73	40.0	24.6

NFL'S 10 BIGGEST SINGLE-GAME ATTENDANCE TOTALS

Date	Site	Game	Teams	Attendance
August 15, 1994	Azteca Stadium	American Bowl (Mexico City)	Cowboys vs. Oilers	112,376
August 17, 1998	Azteca Stadium	American Bowl (Mexico City)	Cowboys vs. Patriots	106,424
August 22, 1947	Soldier Field	College All-Star	Bears vs. All-Stars	105,840
August 4, 1997	Estadio Guillermo Canedo	American Bowl (Mexico City)	Broncos vs. Dolphins	104,629
January 20, 1980	Rose Bowl	Super Bowl XIV	Steelers vs. Rams	103,985
January 30, 1983	Rose Bowl	Super Bowl XVII	Redskins vs. Dolphins	103,667
January 9, 1977	Rose Bowl	Super Bowl XI	Raiders vs. Vikings	103,438
November 10, 1957	L.A. Coliseum	Regular Season	49ers at Rams	102,368
January 25, 1987	Rose Bowl	Super Bowl XXI	Giants vs. Broncos	101,643
August 20, 1948	Soldier Field	College All-Star	Cardinals vs. All-Stars	101,220

NUMBER-ONE DRAFT CHOICES

Season	Date	Team	Player	Position	College
1999	April 17-18	Cleveland	Tim Couch	QB	Kentucky
1998	April 18-19	Indianapolis	Peyton Manning	QB	Tennessee
1997	April 19-20	St. Louis	Orlando Pace	T	Ohio State
1996	April 20-21	New York Jets	Keyshawn Johnson	WR	Southern California
1995	April 22-23	Cincinnati	Ki-Jana Carter	RB	Penn State
1994	April 24-25	Cincinnati	Dan Wilkinson	DT	Ohio State
1993	April 25-26	New England	Drew Bledsoe	QB	Washington State
1992	April 26-27	Indianapolis	Steve Emtman	DT	Washington
1991	April 21-22	Dallas	Russell Maryland	DT	Miami
1990	April 22-23	Indianapolis	Jeff George	QB	Illinois
1989	April 23-24	Dallas	Troy Aikman	QB	UCLA
1988	April 24-25	Atlanta	Aundray Bruce	LB	Auburn
1987	April 28-29	Tampa Bay	Vinny Testaverde	QB	Miami
1986	April 29-30	Tampa Bay	Bo Jackson	RB	Auburn
1985	April 30-May 1	Buffalo	Bruce Smith	DE	Virginia Tech
1984	May 1-2	New England	Irving Fryar	WR	Nebraska
1983	April 26-27	Baltimore	John Elway	QB	Stanford
1982	April 27-28	New England	Kenneth Sims	DT	Texas
1981	April 28-29	New Orleans	George Rogers	RB	South Carolina
1980	April 29-30	Detroit	Billy Sims	RB	Oklahoma
1979	May 3-4	Buffalo	Tom Cousineau	LB	Ohio State
1978	May 2-3	Houston	Earl Campbell	RB	Texas
1977	May 3-4	Tampa Bay	Ricky Bell	RB	Southern California
1976	April 8-9	Tampa Bay	Lee Roy Selmon	DE	Oklahoma
1975	January 28-29	Atlanta	Steve Bartkowski	QB	California
1974	January 29-30	Dallas	Ed Jones	DE	Tennessee State
1973	January 30-31	Houston	John Matuszak	DE	Tampa
1972	February 1-2	Buffalo	Walt Patulski	DE	Notre Dame
1971	January 28-29	New England	Jim Plunkett	QB	Stanford
1970	January 27-28	Pittsburgh	Terry Bradshaw	QB	Louisiana Tech
1969	January 28-29	Buffalo (AFL)	O.J. Simpson	RB	Southern California
1968	January 30-31	Minnesota	Ron Yary	T	Southern California
1967	March 14	Baltimore	Bubba Smith	DT	Michigan State
1966	November 27, 1965	Atlanta	Tommy Nobis	LB	Texas
	November 28, 1965	Miami (AFL)	Jim Grabowski	RB	Illinois
1965	November 28, 1964	New York Giants	Tucker Frederickson	RB	Auburn
	November 28, 1964	Houston (AFL)	Lawrence Elkins	E	Baylor
1964	December 2, 1963	San Francisco	Dave Parks	E	Texas Tech
	November 30, 1963	Boston (AFL)	Jack Concannon	QB	Boston College
1963	December 3, 1962	Los Angeles	Terry Baker	QB	Oregon State
	December 1, 1962	Kansas City (AFL)	Buck Buchanan	DT	Grambling
1962	December 4, 1961	Washington	Ernie Davis	RB	Syracuse
	December 2, 1961	Oakland (AFL)	Roman Gabriel	QB	North Carolina State
1961	December 27-28, 1960	Minnesota	Tommy Mason	RB	Tulane
	November 23, 1960	Buffalo (AFL)	Ken Rice	G	Auburn
1960	Secret Draft	Los Angeles	Billy Cannon	RB	Louisiana State
	November 22, December 2, 1959	(AFL had no formal first pick)			
1959	December 2, 1958	Green Bay	Randy Duncan	QB	Iowa
1958	December 2, 1957	Chicago Cardinals	King Hill	QB	Rice
1957	November 27, 1956	Green Bay	Paul Hornung	HB	Notre Dame
1956	November 29, 1955	Pittsburgh	Gary Glick	DB	Colorado A&M
1955	January 27-28	Baltimore	George Shaw	QB	Oregon
1954	January 28	Cleveland	Bobby Garrett	QB	Stanford
1953	January 22	San Francisco	Harry Babcock	E	Georgia
1952	January 17	Los Angeles	Bill Wade	QB	Vanderbilt
1951	January 18-19	New York Giants	Kyle Rote	HB	Southern Methodist
1950	January 21-22	Detroit	Leon Hart	E	Notre Dame
1949	December 21, 1948	Philadelphia	Chuck Bednarik	C	Pennsylvania
1948	December 19, 1947	Washington	Harry Gilmer	QB	Alabama
1947	December 16, 1946	Chicago Bears	Bob Fenimore	HB	Oklahoma A&M
1946	January 14	Boston	Frank Dancewicz	QB	Notre Dame
1945	April 6	Chicago Cardinals	Charley Trippi	HB	Georgia
1944	April 19	Boston	Angelo Bertelli	QB	Notre Dame
1943	April 8	Detroit	Frank Sinkwich	HB	Georgia
1942	December 22, 1941	Pittsburgh	Bill Dudley	HB	Virginia
1941	December 10, 1940	Chicago Bears	Tom Harmon	HB	Michigan
1940	December 9, 1939	Chicago Cardinals	George Cafego	HB	Tennessee
1939	December 8, 1938	Chicago Cardinals	Ki Aldrich	C	Texas Christian
1938	December 12, 1937	Cleveland	Corbett Davis	FB	Indiana
1937	December 12, 1936	Philadelphia	Sam Francis	FB	Nebraska
1936	February 8	Philadelphia	Jay Berwanger	HB	Chicago

Note: From 1947 through 1958, the first selection in the draft was a Bonus pick, awarded to the winner of a random draw. That club, in turn, forfeited its last-round draft choice. The winner of the Bonus choice was eliminated from future draws. The system was abolished after 1958, by which time all clubs had received a Bonus choice.

FIRST-ROUND SELECTIONS

FIRST-ROUND SELECTIONS

If club had no first-round selection, first player drafted is listed with round in parentheses.

ARIZONA CARDINALS

Year	Player, College, Position
1936	Jim Lawrence, Texas Christian, B
1937	Ray Buivid, Marquette, B
1938	Jack Robbins, Arkansas, B
1939	Charles (Ki) Aldrich, Texas Christian, C
1940	George Cafego, Tennessee, B
1941	John Kimbrough, Texas A&M, B
1942	Steve Lach, Duke, B
1943	Glenn Dobbs, Tulsa, B
1944	Pat Harder, Wisconsin, B
1945	Charley Trippi, Georgia, B
1946	Dub Jones, Louisiana State, B
1947	DeWitt (Tex) Coulter, Army, T
1948	Jim Spavital, Oklahoma A&M, B
1949	Bill Fischer, Notre Dame, G
1950	Jack Jennings, Ohio State, T (2)
1951	Jerry Groom, Notre Dame, C
1952	Ollie Matson, San Francisco, B
1953	Johnny Olszewski, California, B
1954	Lamar McHan, Arkansas, B
1955	Max Boydston, Oklahoma, E
1956	Joe Childress, Auburn, B
1957	Jerry Tubbs, Oklahoma, C
1958	King Hill, Rice, B
	John David Crow, Texas A&M, B
1959	Bill Stacy, Mississippi State, B
1960	George Izo, Notre Dame, QB
1961	Ken Rice, Auburn, T
1962	Fate Echols, Northwestern, DT
	Irv Goode, Kentucky, C
1963	Jerry Stovall, Louisiana State, S
	Don Brumm, Purdue, DE
1964	Ken Kortas, Louisville, DT
1965	Joe Namath, Alabama, QB
1966	Carl McAdams, Oklahoma, LB
1967	Dave Williams, Washington, WR
1968	MacArthur Lane, Utah State, RB
1969	Roger Wehrli, Missouri, DB
1970	Larry Stegent, Texas A&M, RB
1971	Norm Thompson, Utah, CB
1972	Bobby Moore, Oregon, RB-WR
1973	Dave Butz, Purdue, DT
1974	J.V. Cain, Colorado, TE
1975	Tim Gray, Texas A&M, DB
1976	Mike Dawson, Arizona, DT
1977	Steve Pisarkiewicz, Missouri, QB
1978	Steve Little, Arkansas, K
	Ken Greene, Washington State, DB
1979	Ottis Anderson, Miami, RB
1980	Curtis Greer, Michigan, DE
1981	E.J. Junior, Alabama, LB
1982	Luis Sharpe, UCLA, T
1983	Leonard Smith, McNeese State, DB
1984	Clyde Duncan, Tennessee, WR
1985	Freddie Joe Nunn, Mississippi, LB
1986	Anthony Bell, Michigan State, LB
1987	Kelly Stouffer, Colorado State, QB
1988	Ken Harvey, California, LB
1989	Eric Hill, Louisiana State, LB
	Joe Wolf, Boston College, G
1990	Anthony Thompson, Indiana, RB (2)
1991	Eric Swann, No College, DE
1992	Tony Sacca, Penn State, QB (2)
1993	Garrison Hearst, Georgia, RB
	Ernest Dye, South Carolina, T
1994	Jamir Miller, UCLA, LB
1995	Frank Sanders, Auburn, WR (2)
1996	Simeon Rice, Illinois, DE
1997	Tom Knight, Iowa, DB
1998	Andre Wadsworth, Florida State, DE
1999	David Boston, Ohio State, WR
	L.J. Shelton, Eastern Michigan, T

ATLANTA FALCONS

Year	Player, College, Position
1966	Tommy Nobis, Texas, LB
	Randy Johnson, Texas A&I, QB
1967	Leo Carroll, San Diego State, DE (2)
1968	Claude Humphrey, Tennessee State, DE
1969	George Kunz, Notre Dame, T
1970	John Small, Citadel, LB
1971	Joe Profit, Northeast Louisiana, RB
1972	Clarence Ellis, Notre Dame, DB
1973	Greg Marx, Notre Dame, DT (2)
1974	Gerald Tinker, Kent State, WR (2)
1975	Steve Bartkowski, California, QB
1976	Bubba Bean, Texas A&M, RB
1977	Warren Bryant, Kentucky, T
	Wilson Faumuina, San Jose State, DT
1978	Mike Kenn, Michigan, T
1979	Don Smith, Miami, DE
1980	Junior Miller, Nebraska, TE
1981	Bobby Butler, Florida State, DB
1982	Gerald Riggs, Arizona State, RB
1983	Mike Pitts, Alabama, DE
1984	Rick Bryan, Oklahoma, DT
1985	Bill Fralic, Pittsburgh, T
1986	Tony Casillas, Oklahoma, NT
	Tim Green, Syracuse, LB
1987	Chris Miller, Oregon, QB
1988	Aundray Bruce, Auburn, LB
1989	Deion Sanders, Florida State, DB
	Shawn Collins, Northern Arizona, WR
1990	Steve Broussard, Washington State, RB
1991	Bruce Pickens, Nebraska, DB
	Mike Pritchard, Colorado, WR
1992	Bob Whitfield, Stanford, T
	Tony Smith, Southern Mississippi, RB
1993	Lincoln Kennedy, Washington, T
1994	Bert Emanuel, Rice, WR (2)
1995	Devin Bush, Florida State, DB
1996	Shannon Brown, Alabama, DT (3)
1997	Michael Booker, Nebraska, DB
1998	Keith Brooking, Georgia Tech, LB
1999	Patrick Kerney, Virginia, DE

BALTIMORE RAVENS

Year	Player, College, Position
1996	Jonathan Ogden, UCLA, T
	Ray Lewis, Miami, LB
1997	Peter Boulware, Florida State, DE
1998	Duane Starks, Miami, DB
1999	Chris McAlister, Arizona, DB

BUFFALO BILLS

Year	Player, College, Position
1960	Richie Lucas, Penn State, QB
1961	Ken Rice, Auburn, T
1962	Ernie Davis, Syracuse, RB
1963	Dave Behrman, Michigan State, C
1964	Carl Eller, Minnesota, DE
1965	Jim Davidson, Ohio State, T
1966	Mike Dennis, Mississippi, RB
1967	John Pitts, Arizona State, S
1968	Haven Moses, San Diego State, WR
1969	O.J. Simpson, Southern California, RB
1970	Al Cowlings, Southern California, DE
1971	J.D. Hill, Arizona State, WR
1972	Walt Patulski, Notre Dame, DE
1973	Paul Seymour, Michigan, TE
	Joe DeLamielleure, Michigan State, G
1974	Reuben Gant, Oklahoma State, TE
1975	Tom Ruud, Nebraska, LB
1976	Mario Clark, Oregon, DB
1977	Phil Dokes, Oklahoma State, DT
1978	Terry Miller, Oklahoma State, RB
1979	Tom Cousineau, Ohio State, LB
	Jerry Butler, Clemson, WR
1980	Jim Ritcher, North Carolina State, C
1981	Booker Moore, Penn State, RB
1982	Perry Tuttle, Clemson, WR
1983	Tony Hunter, Notre Dame, TE
	Jim Kelly, Miami, QB
1984	Greg Bell, Notre Dame, RB
1985	Bruce Smith, Virginia Tech, DE
	Derrick Burroughs, Memphis State, DB
1986	Ronnie Harmon, Iowa, RB
	Will Wolford, Vanderbilt, T
1987	Shane Conlan, Penn State, LB
1988	Thurman Thomas, Oklahoma State, RB (2)
1989	Don Beebe, Chadron, Neb., WR (3)
1990	James Williams, Fresno State, DB
1991	Henry Jones, Illinois, DB
1992	John Fina, Arizona, T
1993	Thomas Smith, North Carolina, DB
1994	Jeff Burris, Notre Dame, DB
1995	Ruben Brown, Pittsburgh, G
1996	Eric Moulds, Mississippi State, WR
1997	Antowain Smith, Houston, RB
1998	Sam Cowart, Florida State, LB (2)
1999	Antoine Winfield, Ohio State, DB

CAROLINA PANTHERS

Year	Player, College, Position
1995	Kerry Collins, Penn State, QB
	Tyrone Poole, Ft. Valley State, DB
	Blake Brockermeyer, Texas, T
1996	Tim Biakabutuka, Michigan, RB
1997	Rae Carruth, Colorado, WR
1998	Jason Peter, Nebraska, DT
1999	Chris Terry, Georgia, T (2)

CHICAGO BEARS

Year	Player, College, Position
1936	Joe Stydahar, West Virginia, T
1937	Les McDonald, Nebraska, E
1938	Joe Gray, Oregon State, B
1939	Sid Luckman, Columbia, QB
	Bill Osmanski, Holy Cross, B
1940	Clyde (Bulldog) Turner, Hardin-Simmons, C
1941	Tom Harmon, Michigan, B
	Norm Standlee, Stanford, B
	Don Scott, Ohio State, B
1942	Frankie Albert, Stanford, B
1943	Bob Steber, Missouri, B
1944	Ray Evans, Kansas, B
1945	Don Lund, Michigan, B
1946	Johnny Lujack, Notre Dame, QB
1947	Bob Fenimore, Oklahoma State, B
	Don Kindt, Wisconsin, B
1948	Bobby Layne, Texas, QB
	Max Bumgardner, Texas, E
1949	Dick Harris, Texas, C
1950	Chuck Hunsinger, Florida, B
	Fred Morrison, Ohio State, B
1951	Bob Williams, Notre Dame, B
	Billy Stone, Bradley, B
	Gene Schroeder, Virginia, E
1952	Jim Dooley, Miami, B
1953	Billy Anderson, Compton (Calif.) J.C., B
1954	Stan Wallace, Illinois, B
1955	Ron Drzewiecki, Marquette, B
1956	Menan (Tex) Schriewer, Texas, E
1957	Earl Leggett, Louisiana State, T
1958	Chuck Howley, West Virginia, G
1959	Don Clark, Ohio State, B
1960	Roger Davis, Syracuse, G
1961	Mike Ditka, Pittsburgh, E
1962	Ronnie Bull, Baylor, RB
1963	Dave Behrman, Michigan State, C
1964	Dick Evey, Tennessee, DT
1965	Dick Butkus, Illinois, LB
	Gale Sayers, Kansas, RB
	Steve DeLong, Tennessee, T
1966	George Rice, Louisiana State, DT
1967	Loyd Phillips, Arkansas, DE
1968	Mike Hull, Southern California, RB
1969	Rufus Mayes, Ohio State, T
1970	George Farmer, UCLA, WR (3)
1971	Joe Moore, Missouri, RB
1972	Lionel Antoine, Southern Illinois, T
	Craig Clemons, Iowa, DB
1973	Wally Chambers, Eastern Kentucky, DE
1974	Waymond Bryant, Tennessee State, LB
	Dave Gallagher, Michigan, DT
1975	Walter Payton, Jackson State, RB
1976	Dennis Lick, Wisconsin, T
1977	Ted Albrecht, California, T
1978	Brad Shearer, Texas, DT (3)
1979	Dan Hampton, Arkansas, DT
	Al Harris, Arizona State, DE
1980	Otis Wilson, Louisville, LB
1981	Keith Van Horne, Southern California, T

1982 Jim McMahon, Brigham Young, QB
1983 Jim Covert, Pittsburgh, T
Willie Gault, Tennessee, WR
1984 Wilber Marshall, Florida, LB
1985 William Perry, Clemson, DT
1986 Neal Anderson, Florida, RB
1987 Jim Harbaugh, Michigan, QB
1988 Brad Muster, Stanford, RB
Wendell Davis, Louisiana State, WR
1989 Donnell Woolford, Clemson, DB
Trace Armstrong, Florida, DE
1990 Mark Carrier, Southern California, DB
1991 Stan Thomas, Texas, T
1992 Alonzo Spellman, Ohio State, DE
1993 Curtis Conway, Southern California, WR
1994 John Thierry, Alcorn State, DE
1995 Rashaan Salaam, Colorado, RB
1996 Walt Harris, Mississippi State, DB
1997 John Allred, Southern California, TE (2)
1998 Curtis Enis, Penn State, RB
1999 Cade McNown, UCLA, QB

CINCINNATI BENGALS

Year Player, College, Position
1968 Bob Johnson, Tennessee, C
1969 Greg Cook, Cincinnati, QB
1970 Mike Reid, Penn State, DT
1971 Vernon Holland, Tennessee State, T
1972 Sherman White, California, DE
1973 Isaac Curtis, San Diego State, WR
1974 Bill Kollar, Montana State, DT
1975 Glenn Cameron, Florida, LB
1976 Billy Brooks, Oklahoma, WR
Archie Griffin, Ohio State, RB
1977 Eddie Edwards, Miami, DT
Wilson Whitley, Houston, DT
Mike Cobb, Michigan State, TE
1978 Ross Browner, Notre Dame, DT
Blair Bush, Washington, C
1979 Jack Thompson, Washington State, QB
Charles Alexander, Louisiana State, RB
1980 Anthony Muñoz, Southern California, T
1981 David Verser, Kansas, WR
1982 Glen Collins, Mississippi State, DE
1983 Dave Rimington, Nebraska, C
1984 Ricky Hunley, Arizona, LB
Pete Koch, Maryland, DE
Brian Blados, North Carolina, T
1985 Eddie Brown, Miami, WR
Emanuel King, Alabama, LB
1986 Joe Kelly, Washington, LB
Tim McGee, Tennessee, WR
1987 Jason Buck, Brigham Young, DE
1988 Rickey Dixon, Oklahoma, DB
1989 Eric Ball, UCLA, RB (2)
1990 James Francis, Baylor, LB
1991 Alfred Williams, Colorado, LB
1992 David Klingler, Houston, QB
Darryl Williams, Miami, DB
1993 John Copeland, Alabama, DE
1994 Dan Wilkinson, Ohio State, DT
1995 Ki-Jana Carter, Penn State, RB
1996 Willie Anderson, Auburn, T
1997 Reinard Wilson, Florida State, LB
1998 Takeo Spikes, Cincinnati, LB
Brian Simmons, North Carolina, LB
1999 Akili Smith, Oregon, QB

CLEVELAND BROWNS

Year Player, College, Position
1950 Ken Carpenter, Oregon State, B
1951 Ken Konz, Louisiana State, B
1952 Bert Rechichar, Tennessee, DB
Harry Agganis, Boston U., QB
1953 Doug Atkins, Tennessee, DE
1954 Bobby Garrett, Stanford, QB
John Bauer, Illinois, G
1955 Kurt Burris, Oklahoma, C
1956 Preston Carpenter, Arkansas, B
1957 Jim Brown, Syracuse, RB
1958 Jim Shofner, Texas Christian, DB
1959 Rich Kreitling, Illinois, DE
1960 Jim Houston, Ohio State, DE
1961 Bobby Crespino, Mississippi, TE
1962 Gary Collins, Maryland, WR
Leroy Jackson, Western Illinois, RB
1963 Tom Hutchinson, Kentucky, WR
1964 Paul Warfield, Ohio State, WR
1965 James Garcia, Purdue, T (2)
1966 Milt Morin, Massachusetts, TE
1967 Bob Matheson, Duke, LB
1968 Marvin Upshaw, Trinity, Tex., DT-DE
1969 Ron Johnson, Michigan, RB
1970 Mike Phipps, Purdue, QB
Bob McKay, Texas, T
1971 Clarence Scott, Kansas State, CB
1972 Thom Darden, Michigan, DB
1973 Steve Holden, Arizona State, WR
Pete Adams, Southern California, T
1974 Billy Corbett, Johnson C. Smith, T (2)
1975 Mack Mitchell, Houston, DE
1976 Mike Pruitt, Purdue, RB
1977 Robert Jackson, Texas A&M, LB
1978 Clay Matthews, Southern California, LB
Ozzie Newsome, Alabama, TE
1979 Willis Adams, Houston, WR
1980 Charles White, Southern California, RB
1981 Hanford Dixon, Southern Mississippi, DB
1982 Chip Banks, Southern California, LB
1983 Ron Brown, Arizona State, WR (2)
1984 Don Rogers, UCLA, DB
1985 Greg Allen, Florida State, RB (2)
1986 Webster Slaughter, San Diego State, WR (2)
1987 Mike Junkin, Duke, LB
1988 Clifford Charlton, Florida, LB
1989 Eric Metcalf, Texas, RB
1990 Leroy Hoard, Michigan, RB (2)
1991 Eric Turner, UCLA, DB
1992 Tommy Vardell, Stanford, RB
1993 Steve Everitt, Michigan, C
1994 Antonio Langham, Alabama, DB
Derrick Alexander, Michigan, WR
1995 Craig Powell, Ohio State, LB
1999 Tim Couch, Kentucky, QB

DALLAS COWBOYS

Year Player, College, Position
1960 None
1961 Bob Lilly, Texas Christian, DT
1962 Sonny Gibbs, Texas Christian, QB (2)
1963 Lee Roy Jordan, Alabama, LB
1964 Scott Appleton, Texas, DT
1965 Craig Morton, California, QB
1966 John Niland, Iowa, G
1967 Phil Clark, Northwestern, DB (3)
1968 Dennis Homan, Alabama, WR
1969 Calvin Hill, Yale, RB
1970 Duane Thomas, West Texas State, RB
1971 Tody Smith, Southern California, DE
1972 Bill Thomas, Boston College, RB
1973 Billy Joe DuPree, Michigan State, TE
1974 Ed (Too Tall) Jones, Tennessee State, DE
Charley Young, North Carolina State, RB
1975 Randy White, Maryland, LB
Thomas Henderson, Langston, LB
1976 Aaron Kyle, Wyoming, DB
1977 Tony Dorsett, Pittsburgh, RB
1978 Larry Bethea, Michigan State, DE
1979 Robert Shaw, Tennessee, C
1980 Bill Roe, Colorado, LB (3)
1981 Howard Richards, Missouri, T
1982 Rod Hill, Kentucky State, DB
1983 Jim Jeffcoat, Arizona State, DE
1984 Billy Cannon, Jr., Texas A&M, LB
1985 Kevin Brooks, Michigan, DE
1986 Mike Sherrard, UCLA, WR
1987 Danny Noonan, Nebraska, DT
1988 Michael Irvin, Miami, WR
1989 Troy Aikman, UCLA, QB
1990 Emmitt Smith, Florida, RB
1991 Russell Maryland, Miami, DT
Alvin Harper, Tennessee, WR
Kelvin Pritchett, Mississippi, DT
1992 Kevin Smith, Texas A&M, DB
Robert Jones, East Carolina, LB
1993 Kevin Williams, Miami, WR (2)
1994 Shante Carver, Arizona State, DE
1995 Sherman Williams, Alabama, RB (2)
1996 Kavika Pittman, McNeese State, DE (2)
1997 David LaFleur, Louisiana State, TE
1998 Greg Ellis, North Carolina, DE
1999 Ebenezer Ekuban, North Carolina, DE

DENVER BRONCOS

Year Player, College, Position
1960 Roger LeClerc, Trinity, Conn., C
1961 Bob Gaiters, New Mexico State, RB
1962 Merlin Olsen, Utah State, DT
1963 Kermit Alexander, UCLA, CB
1964 Bob Brown, Nebraska, T
1965 Dick Butkus, Illinois, LB (2)
1966 Jerry Shay, Purdue, DT
1967 Floyd Little, Syracuse, RB
1968 Curley Culp, Arizona State, DE (2)
1969 Grady Cavness, Texas-El Paso, DB (2)
1970 Bob Anderson, Colorado, RB
1971 Marv Montgomery, Southern California, T
1972 Riley Odoms, Houston, TE
1973 Otis Armstrong, Purdue, RB
1974 Randy Gradishar, Ohio State, LB
1975 Louis Wright, San Jose State, DB
1976 Tom Glassic, Virginia, G
1977 Steve Schindler, Boston College, G
1978 Don Latimer, Miami, DT
1979 Kelvin Clark, Nebraska, T
1980 Rulon Jones, Utah State, DE (2)
1981 Dennis Smith, Southern California, DB
1982 Gerald Willhite, San Jose State, RB
1983 Chris Hinton, Northwestern, G
1984 Andre Townsend, Mississippi, DE (2)
1985 Steve Sewell, Oklahoma, RB
1986 Jim Juriga, Illinois, T (4)
1987 Ricky Nattiel, Florida, WR
1988 Ted Gregory, Syracuse, NT
1989 Steve Atwater, Arkansas, DB
1990 Alton Montgomery, Houston, DB (2)
1991 Mike Croel, Nebraska, LB
1992 Tommy Maddox, UCLA, QB
1993 Dan Williams, Toledo, DE
1994 Allen Aldridge, Houston, LB (2)
1995 Jamie Brown, Florida A&M, T (4)
1996 John Mobley, Kutztown, LB
1997 Trevor Pryce, Clemson, DT
1998 Marcus Nash, Tennessee, WR
1999 Al Wilson, Tennessee, LB

DETROIT LIONS

Year Player, College, Position
1936 Sid Wagner, Michigan State, G
1937 Lloyd Cardwell, Nebraska, B
1938 Alex Wojciechowicz, Fordham, C
1939 John Pingel, Michigan State, B
1940 Doyle Nave, Southern California, B
1941 Jim Thomason, Texas A&M, B
1942 Bob Westfall, Michigan, B
1943 Frank Sinkwich, Georgia, B
1944 Otto Graham, Northwestern, B
1945 Frank Szymanski, Notre Dame, C
1946 Bill Dellastatious, Missouri, B
1947 Glenn Davis, Army, B
1948 Y.A. Tittle, Louisiana State, B
1949 John Rauch, Georgia, B
1950 Leon Hart, Notre Dame, E
Joe Watson, Rice, C
1951 Dick Stanfel, San Francisco, G (2)
1952 Yale Lary, Texas A&M, B (3)
1953 Harley Sewell, Texas, G
1954 Dick Chapman, Rice, T
1955 Dave Middleton, Auburn, B
1956 Hopalong Cassady, Ohio State, B
1957 Bill Glass, Baylor, G
1958 Alex Karras, Iowa, T
1959 Nick Pietrosante, Notre Dame, B
1960 John Robinson, Louisiana State, S
1961 Danny LaRose, Missouri, T (2)
1962 John Hadl, Kansas, QB
1963 Daryl Sanders, Ohio State, T
1964 Pete Beathard, Southern California, QB
1965 Tom Nowatzke, Indiana, RB

FIRST-ROUND SELECTIONS

1966 Nick Eddy, Notre Dame, RB (2)
1967 Mel Farr, UCLA, RB
1968 Greg Landry, Massachusetts, QB
Earl McCullouch, Southern California, WR
1969 Altie Taylor, Utah State, RB (2)
1970 Steve Owens, Oklahoma, RB
1971 Bob Bell, Cincinnati, DT
1972 Herb Orvis, Colorado, DE
1973 Ernie Price, Texas A&I, DE
1974 Ed O'Neil, Penn State, LB
1975 Lynn Boden, South Dakota State, G
1976 James Hunter, Grambling, DB
Lawrence Gaines, Wyoming, RB
1977 Walt Williams, New Mexico State, DB (2)
1978 Luther Bradley, Notre Dame, DB
1979 Keith Dorney, Penn State, T
1980 Billy Sims, Oklahoma, RB
1981 Mark Nichols, San Jose State, WR
1982 Jimmy Williams, Nebraska, LB
1983 James Jones, Florida, RB
1984 David Lewis, California, TE
1985 Lomas Brown, Florida, T
1986 Chuck Long, Iowa, QB
1987 Reggie Rogers, Washington, DE
1988 Bennie Blades, Miami, DB
1989 Barry Sanders, Oklahoma State, RB
1990 Andre Ware, Houston, QB
1991 Herman Moore, Virginia, WR
1992 Robert Porcher, South Carolina State, DE
1993 Ryan McNeil, Miami, DB (2)
1994 Johnnie Morton, Southern California, WR
1995 Luther Elliss, Utah, DT
1996 Reggie Brown, Texas A&M, LB
Jeff Hartings, Penn State, G
1997 Bryant Westbrook, Texas, DB
1998 Terry Fair, Tennessee, DB
1999 Chris Claiborne, Southern California, LB
Aaron Gibson, Wisconsin, T

GREEN BAY PACKERS

Year	Player, College, Position
1936	Russ Letlow, San Francisco, G
1937	Eddie Jankowski, Wisconsin, B
1938	Cecil Isbell, Purdue, B
1939	Larry Buhler, Minnesota, B
1940	Harold Van Every, Minnesota, B
1941	George Paskvan, Wisconsin, B
1942	Urban Odson, Minnesota, T
1943	Dick Wildung, Minnesota, T
1944	Merv Pregulman, Michigan, G
1945	Walt Schlinkman, Texas Tech, B
1946	Johnny (Strike) Strzykalski, Marquette, B
1947	Ernie Case, UCLA, B
1948	Earl (Jug) Girard, Wisconsin, B
1949	Stan Heath, Nevada, B
1950	Clayton Tonnemaker, Minnesota, C
1951	Bob Gain, Kentucky, T
1952	Babe Parilli, Kentucky, QB
1953	Al Carmichael, Southern California, B
1954	Art Hunter, Notre Dame, T
	Veryl Switzer, Kansas State, B
1955	Tom Bettis, Purdue, G
1956	Jack Losch, Miami, B
1957	Paul Hornung, Notre Dame, B
	Ron Kramer, Michigan, E
1958	Dan Currie, Michigan State, C
1959	Randy Duncan, Iowa, B
1960	Tom Moore, Vanderbilt, RB
1961	Herb Adderley, Michigan State, CB
1962	Earl Gros, Louisiana State, RB
1963	Dave Robinson, Penn State, LB
1964	Lloyd Voss, Nebraska, DT
1965	Donny Anderson, Texas Tech, RB
	Lawrence Elkins, Baylor, E
1966	Jim Grabowski, Illinois, RB
	Gale Gillingham, Minnesota, T
1967	Bob Hyland, Boston College, C
	Don Horn, San Diego State, QB
1968	Fred Carr, Texas-El Paso, LB
	Bill Lueck, Arizona, G
1969	Rich Moore, Villanova, DT
1970	Mike McCoy, Notre Dame, DT
	Rich McGeorge, Elon, TE
1971	John Brockington, Ohio State, RB
1972	Willie Buchanon, San Diego State, DB
	Jerry Tagge, Nebraska, QB
1973	Barry Smith, Florida State, WR
1974	Barty Smith, Richmond, RB
1975	Bill Bain, Southern California, G (2)
1976	Mark Koncar, Colorado, T
1977	Mike Butler, Kansas, DE
	Ezra Johnson, Morris Brown, DE
1978	James Lofton, Stanford, WR
	John Anderson, Michigan, LB
1979	Eddie Lee Ivery, Georgia Tech, RB
1980	Bruce Clark, Penn State, DE
	George Cumby, Oklahoma, LB
1981	Rich Campbell, California, QB
1982	Ron Hallstrom, Iowa, G
1983	Tim Lewis, Pittsburgh, DB
1984	Alphonso Carreker, Florida State, DE
1985	Ken Ruettgers, Southern California, T
1986	Kenneth Davis, Texas Christian, RB (2)
1987	Brent Fullwood, Auburn, RB
1988	Sterling Sharpe, South Carolina, WR
1989	Tony Mandarich, Michigan State, T
1990	Tony Bennett, Mississippi, LB
	Darrell Thompson, Minnesota, RB
1991	Vinnie Clark, Ohio State, DB
1992	Terrell Buckley, Florida State, DB
1993	Wayne Simmons, Clemson, LB
	George Teague, Alabama, DB
1994	Aaron Taylor, Notre Dame, T
1995	Craig Newsome, Arizona State, DB
1996	John Michels, Southern California, T
1997	Ross Verba, Iowa, T
1998	Vonnie Holliday, North Carolina, DT
1999	Antuan Edwards, Clemson, DB

INDIANAPOLIS COLTS

Year	Player, College, Position
1953	Billy Vessels, Oklahoma, B
1954	Cotton Davidson, Baylor, B
1955	George Shaw, Oregon, B
	Alan Ameche, Wisconsin, FB
1956	Lenny Moore, Penn State, B
1957	Jim Parker, Ohio State, G
1958	Lenny Lyles, Louisville, B
1959	Jackie Burkett, Auburn, C
1960	Ron Mix, Southern California, T
1961	Tom Matte, Ohio State, RB
1962	Wendell Harris, Louisiana State, S
1963	Bob Vogel, Ohio State, T
1964	Marv Woodson, Indiana, CB
1965	Mike Curtis, Duke, LB
1966	Sam Ball, Kentucky, T
1967	Bubba Smith, Michigan State, DT
	Jim Detwiler, Michigan, RB
1968	John Williams, Minnesota, G
1969	Eddie Hinton, Oklahoma, WR
1970	Norman Bulaich, Texas Christian, RB
1971	Don McCauley, North Carolina, RB
	Leonard Dunlap, North Texas State, DB
1972	Tom Drougas, Oregon, T
1973	Bert Jones, Louisiana State, QB
	Joe Ehrmann, Syracuse, DT
1974	John Dutton, Nebraska, DE
	Roger Carr, Louisiana Tech, WR
1975	Ken Huff, North Carolina, G
1976	Ken Novak, Purdue, DT
1977	Randy Burke, Kentucky, WR
1978	Reese McCall, Auburn, TE
1979	Barry Krauss, Alabama, LB
1980	Curtis Dickey, Texas A&M, RB
	Derrick Hatchett, Texas, DB
1981	Randy McMillan, Pittsburgh, RB
	Donnell Thompson, North Carolina, DT
1982	Johnie Cooks, Mississippi State, LB
	Art Schlichter, Ohio State, QB
1983	John Elway, Stanford, QB
1984	Leonard Coleman, Vanderbilt, DB
	Ron Solt, Maryland, G
1985	Duane Bickett, Southern California, LB
1986	Jon Hand, Alabama, DE
1987	Cornelius Bennett, Alabama, LB
1988	Chris Chandler, Washington, QB (3)
1989	Andre Rison, Michigan State, WR
1990	Jeff George, Illinois, QB
1991	Shane Curry, Miami, DE (2)
1992	Steve Emtman, Washington, DT
	Quentin Coryatt, Texas A&M, LB
1993	Sean Dawkins, California, WR
1994	Marshall Faulk, San Diego State, RB
	Trev Alberts, Nebraska, LB
1995	Ellis Johnson, Florida, DT
1996	Marvin Harrison, Syracuse, WR
1997	Tarik Glenn, California, T
1998	Peyton Manning, Tennessee, QB
1999	Edgerrin James, Miami, RB

JACKSONVILLE JAGUARS

Year	Player, College, Position
1995	Tony Boselli, Southern California, T
	James Stewart, Tennessee, RB
1996	Kevin Hardy, Illinois, LB
1997	Renaldo Wynn, Notre Dame, DT
1998	Fred Taylor, Florida, RB
	Donovin Darius, Syracuse, DB
1999	Fernando Bryant, Alabama, DB

KANSAS CITY CHIEFS

Year	Player, College, Position
1960	Don Meredith, Southern Methodist, QB
1961	E.J. Holub, Texas Tech, C
1962	Ronnie Bull, Baylor, RB
1963	Buck Buchanan, Grambling, DT
	Ed Budde, Michigan State, G
1964	Pete Beathard, Southern California, QB
1965	Gale Sayers, Kansas, RB
1966	Aaron Brown, Minnesota, DE
1967	Gene Trosch, Miami, DE-DT
1968	Mo Moorman, Texas A&M, G
	George Daney, Texas-El Paso, G
1969	Jim Marsalis, Tennessee State, CB
1970	Sid Smith, Southern California, T
1971	Elmo Wright, Houston, WR
1972	Jeff Kinney, Nebraska, RB
1973	Gary Butler, Rice, TE (2)
1974	Woody Green, Arizona State, RB
1975	Elmore Stephens, Kentucky, TE (2)
1976	Rod Walters, Iowa, G
1977	Gary Green, Baylor, DB
1978	Art Still, Kentucky, DE
1979	Mike Bell, Colorado State, DE
	Steve Fuller, Clemson, QB
1980	Brad Budde, Southern California, G
1981	Willie Scott, South Carolina, TE
1982	Anthony Hancock, Tennessee, WR
1983	Todd Blackledge, Penn State, QB
1984	Bill Maas, Pittsburgh, DT
	John Alt, Iowa, T
1985	Ethan Horton, North Carolina, RB
1986	Brian Jozwiak, West Virginia, T
1987	Paul Palmer, Temple, RB
1988	Neil Smith, Nebraska, DE
1989	Derrick Thomas, Alabama, LB
1990	Percy Snow, Michigan State, LB
1991	Harvey Williams, Louisiana State, RB
1992	Dale Carter, Tennessee, DB
1993	Will Shields, Nebraska, G (3)
1994	Greg Hill, Texas A&M, RB
1995	Trezelle Jenkins, Michigan, T
1996	Jerome Woods, Memphis, DB
1997	Tony Gonzalez, California, TE
1998	Victor Riley, Auburn, T
1999	John Tait, Brigham Young, T

MIAMI DOLPHINS

Year	Player, College, Position
1966	Jim Grabowski, Illinois, RB
	Rick Norton, Kentucky, QB
1967	Bob Griese, Purdue, QB
1968	Larry Csonka, Syracuse, RB
	Doug Crusan, Indiana, T
1969	Bill Stanfill, Georgia, DE
1970	Jim Mandich, Michigan, TE (2)
1971	Otto Stowe, Iowa State, WR (2)
1972	Mike Kadish, Notre Dame, DT
1973	Chuck Bradley, Oregon, C (2)

1974 Donald Reese, Jackson State, DE
1975 Darryl Carlton, Tampa, T
1976 Larry Gordon, Arizona State, LB
Kim Bokamper, San Jose State, LB
1977 A.J. Duhe, Louisiana State, DT
1978 Guy Benjamin, Stanford, QB (2)
1979 Jon Giesler, Michigan, T
1980 Don McNeal, Alabama, DB
1981 David Overstreet, Oklahoma, RB
1982 Roy Foster, Southern California, G
1983 Dan Marino, Pittsburgh, QB
1984 Jackie Shipp, Oklahoma, LB
1985 Lorenzo Hampton, Florida, RB
1986 John Offerdahl, Western Michigan, LB (2)
1987 John Bosa, Boston College, DE
1988 Eric Kumerow, Ohio State, DE
1989 Sammie Smith, Florida State, RB
Louis Oliver, Florida, DB
1990 Richmond Webb, Texas A&M, T
1991 Randal Hill, Miami, WR
1992 Troy Vincent, Wisconsin, DB
Marco Coleman, Georgia Tech, LB
1993 O.J. McDuffie, Penn State, WR
1994 Tim Bowens, Mississippi, DT
1995 Billy Milner, Houston, T
1996 Daryl Gardener, Baylor, DT
1997 Yatil Green, Miami, WR
1998 John Avery, Mississippi, RB
1999 James Johnson, Mississippi State, RB (2)

MINNESOTA VIKINGS

Year Player, College, Position

1961 Tommy Mason, Tulane, RB
1962 Bill Miller, Miami, WR (3)
1963 Jim Dunaway, Mississippi, T
1964 Carl Eller, Minnesota, DE
1965 Jack Snow, Notre Dame, WR
1966 Jerry Shay, Purdue, DT
1967 Clint Jones, Michigan State, RB
Gene Washington, Michigan State, WR
Alan Page, Notre Dame, DT
1968 Ron Yary, Southern California, T
1969 Ed White, California, G (2)
1970 John Ward, Oklahoma State, DT
1971 Leo Hayden, Ohio State, RB
1972 Jeff Siemon, Stanford, LB
1973 Chuck Foreman, Miami, RB
1974 Fred McNeill, UCLA, LB
Steve Riley, Southern California, T
1975 Mark Mullaney, Colorado State, DE
1976 James White, Oklahoma State, DT
1977 Tommy Kramer, Rice, QB
1978 Randy Holloway, Pittsburgh, DE
1979 Ted Brown, North Carolina State, RB
1980 Doug Martin, Washington, DT
1981 Mardye McDole, Mississippi State, WR (2)
1982 Darrin Nelson, Stanford, RB
1983 Joey Browner, Southern California, DB
1984 Keith Millard, Washington State, DE
1985 Chris Doleman, Pittsburgh, LB
1986 Gerald Robinson, Auburn, DE
1987 D.J. Dozier, Penn State, RB
1988 Randall McDaniel, Arizona State, G
1989 David Braxton, Wake Forest, LB (2)
1990 Mike Jones, Texas A&M, TE (3)
1991 Carlos Jenkins, Michigan State, LB (3)
1992 Robert Harris, Southern University, DE (2)
1993 Robert Smith, Ohio State, RB
1994 DeWayne Washington, N. Carolina St., DB
Todd Steussie, California, T
1995 Derrick Alexander, Florida State, DE
Korey Stringer, Ohio State, T
1996 Duane Clemons, California, DE
1997 Dwayne Rudd, Alabama, LB
1998 Randy Moss, Marshall, WR
1999 Daunte Culpepper, Central Florida, QB
Dimitrius Underwood, Michigan State, DE

NEW ENGLAND PATRIOTS

Year Player, College, Position

1960 Ron Burton, Northwestern, RB
1961 Tommy Mason, Tulane, RB
1962 Gary Collins, Maryland, WR
1963 Art Graham, Boston College, WR
1964 Jack Concannon, Boston College, QB
1965 Jerry Rush, Michigan State, DE
1966 Karl Singer, Purdue, T
1967 John Charles, Purdue, S
1968 Dennis Byrd, North Carolina State, DE
1969 Ron Sellers, Florida State, WR
1970 Phil Olsen, Utah State, DE
1971 Jim Plunkett, Stanford, QB
1972 Tom Reynolds, San Diego State, WR (2)
1973 John Hannah, Alabama, G
Sam Cunningham, So. California, RB
Darryl Stingley, Purdue, WR
1974 Steve Corbett, Boston College, G (2)
1975 Russ Francis, Oregon, TE
1976 Mike Haynes, Arizona State, DB
Pete Brock, Colorado, C
Tim Fox, Ohio State, DB
1977 Raymond Clayborn, Texas, DB
Stanley Morgan, Tennessee, WR
1978 Bob Cryder, Alabama, G
1979 Rick Sanford, South Carolina, DB
1980 Roland James, Tennessee, DB
Vagas Ferguson, Notre Dame, RB
1981 Brian Holloway, Stanford, T
1982 Kenneth Sims, Texas, DT
Lester Williams, Miami, DT
1983 Tony Eason, Illinois, QB
1984 Irving Fryar, Nebraska, WR
1985 Trevor Matich, Brigham Young, C
1986 Reggie Dupard, Southern Methodist, RB
1987 Bruce Armstrong, Louisville, T
1988 John Stephens, Northwestern St., La., RB
1989 Hart Lee Dykes, Oklahoma State, WR
1990 Chris Singleton, Arizona, LB
Ray Agnew, North Carolina State, DE
1991 Pat Harlow, Southern California, T
Leonard Russell, Arizona State, RB
1992 Eugene Chung, Virginia Tech, T
1993 Drew Bledsoe, Washington State, QB
1994 Willie McGinest, Southern California, DE
1995 Ty Law, Michigan, DB
1996 Terry Glenn, Ohio State, WR
1997 Chris Canty, Kansas State, DB
1998 Robert Edwards, Georgia, RB
Tebucky Jones, Syracuse, DB
1999 Damien Woody, Boston College, C
Andy Katzenmoyer, Ohio State, LB

NEW ORLEANS SAINTS

Year Player, College, Position

1967 Les Kelley, Alabama, RB
1968 Kevin Hardy, Notre Dame, DE
1969 John Shinners, Xavier, G
1970 Ken Burrough, Texas Southern, WR
1971 Archie Manning, Mississippi, QB
1972 Royce Smith, Georgia, G
1973 Derland Moore, Oklahoma, DE (2)
1974 Rick Middleton, Ohio State, LB
1975 Larry Burton, Purdue, WR
Kurt Schumacher, Ohio State, T
1976 Chuck Muncie, California, RB
1977 Joe Campbell, Maryland, DE
1978 Wes Chandler, Florida, WR
1979 Russell Erxleben, Texas, P-K
1980 Stan Brock, Colorado, T
1981 George Rogers, South Carolina, RB
1982 Lindsay Scott, Georgia, WR
1983 Steve Korte, Arkansas, G (2)
1984 James Geathers, Wichita State, DE
1985 Alvin Toles, Tennessee, LB
1986 Jim Dombrowski, Virginia, T
1987 Shawn Knight, Brigham Young, DT
1988 Craig Heyward, Pittsburgh, RB
1989 Wayne Martin, Arkansas, DE
1990 Renaldo Turnbull, West Virginia, DE
1991 Wesley Carroll, Miami, WR (2)
1992 Vaughn Dunbar, Indiana, RB
1993 Willie Roaf, Louisiana Tech, T
Irv Smith, Notre Dame, TE
1994 Joe Johnson, Louisville, DE
1995 Mark Fields, Washington State, LB
1996 Alex Molden, Oregon, DB
1997 Chris Naeole, Colorado, G
1998 Kyle Turley, San Diego State, T
1999 Ricky Williams, Texas, RB

NEW YORK GIANTS

Year Player, College, Position

1936 Art Lewis, Ohio U., T
1937 Ed Widseth, Minnesota, T
1938 George Karamatic, Gonzaga, B
1939 Walt Neilson, Arizona, B
1940 Grenville Lansdell, Southern California, B
1941 George Franck, Minnesota, B
1942 Merle Hapes, Mississippi, B
1943 Steve Filipowicz, Fordham, B
1944 Billy Hillenbrand, Indiana, B
1945 Elmer Barbour, Wake Forest, B
1946 George Connor, Notre Dame, T
1947 Vic Schwall, Northwestern, B
1948 Tony Minisi, Pennsylvania, B
1949 Paul Page, Southern Methodist, B
1950 Travis Tidwell, Auburn, B
1951 Kyle Rote, Southern Methodist, B
Jim Spavital, Oklahoma A&M, B
1952 Frank Gifford, Southern California, B
1953 Bobby Marlow, Alabama, B
1954 Ken Buck, Pacific, C (2)
1955 Joe Heap, Notre Dame, B
1956 Henry Moore, Arkansas, B (2)
1957 Sam DeLuca, South Carolina, T (2)
1958 Phil King, Vanderbilt, B
1959 Lee Grosscup, Utah, B
1960 Lou Cordileone, Clemson, G
1961 Bruce Tarbox, Syracuse, G (2)
1962 Jerry Hillebrand, Colorado, LB
1963 Frank Lasky, Florida, T (2)
1964 Joe Don Looney, Oklahoma, RB
1965 Tucker Frederickson, Auburn, RB
1966 Francis Peay, Missouri, T
1967 Louis Thompson, Alabama, DT (4)
1968 Dick Buzin, Penn State, T (2)
1969 Fred Dryer, San Diego State, DE
1970 Jim Files, Oklahoma, LB
1971 Rocky Thompson, West Texas State, WR
1972 Eldridge Small, Texas A&I, DB
Larry Jacobson, Nebraska, DE
1973 Brad Van Pelt, Michigan State, LB (2)
1974 John Hicks, Ohio State, G
1975 Al Simpson, Colorado State, T (2)
1976 Troy Archer, Colorado, DE
1977 Gary Jeter, Southern California, DT
1978 Gordon King, Stanford, T
1979 Phil Simms, Morehead State, QB
1980 Mark Haynes, Colorado, DB
1981 Lawrence Taylor, North Carolina, LB
1982 Butch Woolfolk, Michigan, RB
1983 Terry Kinard, Clemson, DB
1984 Carl Banks, Michigan State, LB
William Roberts, Ohio State, T
1985 George Adams, Kentucky, RB
1986 Eric Dorsey, Notre Dame, DE
1987 Mark Ingram, Michigan State, WR
1988 Eric Moore, Indiana, T
1989 Brian Williams, Minnesota, C-G
1990 Rodney Hampton, Georgia, RB
1991 Jarrod Bunch, Michigan, RB
1992 Derek Brown, Notre Dame, TE
1993 Michael Strahan, Texas Southern, DE (2)
1994 Thomas Lewis, Indiana, WR
1995 Tyrone Wheatley, Michigan, RB
1996 Cedric Jones, Oklahoma, DE
1997 Ike Hilliard, Florida, WR
1998 Shaun Williams, UCLA, DB
1999 Luke Petitgout, Notre Dame, T

NEW YORK JETS

Year Player, College, Position

1960 George Izo, Notre Dame, QB
1961 Tom Brown, Minnesota, G
1962 Sandy Stephens, Minnesota, QB
1963 Jerry Stovall, Louisiana State, S
1964 Matt Snell, Ohio State, RB
1965 Joe Namath, Alabama, QB
Tom Nowatzke, Indiana, RB

FIRST-ROUND SELECTIONS

1966 Bill Yearby, Michigan, DT
1967 Paul Seiler, Notre Dame, T
1968 Lee White, Weber State, RB
1969 Dave Foley, Ohio State, T
1970 Steve Tannen, Florida, CB
1971 John Riggins, Kansas, RB
1972 Jerome Barkum, Jackson State, WR
Mike Taylor, Michigan, LB
1973 Burgess Owens, Miami, DB
1974 Carl Barzilauskas, Indiana, DT
1975 Anthony Davis, Southern California, RB (2)
1976 Richard Todd, Alabama, QB
1977 Marvin Powell, Southern California, T
1978 Chris Ward, Ohio State, T
1979 Marty Lyons, Alabama, DE
1980 Johnny (Lam) Jones, Texas, WR
1981 Freeman McNeil, UCLA, RB
1982 Bob Crable, Notre Dame, LB
1983 Ken O'Brien, Cal-Davis, QB
1984 Russell Carter, Southern Methodist, DB
Ron Faurot, Arkansas, DE
1985 Al Toon, Wisconsin, WR
1986 Mike Haight, Iowa, T
1987 Roger Vick, Texas A&M, RB
1988 Dave Cadigan, Southern California, T
1989 Jeff Lageman, Virginia, LB
1990 Blair Thomas, Penn State, RB
1991 Browning Nagle, Louisville, QB (2)
1992 Johnny Mitchell, Nebraska, TE
1993 Marvin Jones, Florida State, LB
1994 Aaron Glenn, Texas A&M, DB
1995 Kyle Brady, Penn State, TE
Hugh Douglas, Central State, Ohio, DE
1996 Keyshawn Johnson, Southern California, WR
1997 James Farrior, Virginia, LB
1998 Dorian Boose, Washington State, DE (2)
1999 Randy Thomas, Mississippi State, G (2)

OAKLAND RAIDERS

Year Player, College, Position
1960 Dale Hackbart, Wisconsin, CB
1961 Joe Rutgens, Illinois, DT
1962 Roman Gabriel, North Carolina State, QB
1963 George Wilson, Alabama, RB (6)
1964 Tony Lorick, Arizona State, RB
1965 Harry Schuh, Memphis State, T
1966 Rodger Bird, Kentucky, S
1967 Gene Upshaw, Texas A&I, G
1968 Eldridge Dickey, Tennessee State, QB
1969 Art Thoms, Syracuse, DT
1970 Raymond Chester, Morgan State, TE
1971 Jack Tatum, Ohio State, S
1972 Mike Siani, Villanova, WR
1973 Ray Guy, Southern Mississippi, P
1974 Henry Lawrence, Florida A&M, T
1975 Neal Colzie, Ohio State, DB
1976 Charles Philyaw, Texas Southern, DT (2)
1977 Mike Davis, Colorado, DB (2)
1978 Dave Browning, Washington, DE (2)
1979 Willie Jones, Florida State, DE (2)
1980 Marc Wilson, Brigham Young, QB
1981 Ted Watts, Texas Tech, DB
Curt Marsh, Washington, T
1982 Marcus Allen, Southern California, RB
1983 Don Mosebar, Southern California, T
1984 Sean Jones, Northeastern, DE (2)
1985 Jessie Hester, Florida State, WR
1986 Bob Buczkowski, Pittsburgh, DE
1987 John Clay, Missouri, T
1988 Tim Brown, Notre Dame, WR
Terry McDaniel, Tennessee, DB
Scott Davis, Illinois, DE
1989 Jeff Francis, Tennessee, QB (6)
1990 Anthony Smith, Arizona, DE
1991 Todd Marinovich, Southern California, QB
1992 Chester McGlockton, Clemson, DE
1993 Patrick Bates, Texas A&M, DB
1994 Rob Fredrickson, Michigan State, LB
1995 Napoleon Kaufman, Washington, RB
1996 Rickey Dudley, Ohio State, TE
1997 Darrell Russell, Southern California, DT
1998 Charles Woodson, Michigan, DB
Mo Collins, Florida, T
1999 Matt Stinchcomb, Georgia, T

PHILADELPHIA EAGLES

Year Player, College, Position
1936 Jay Berwanger, Chicago, B
1937 Sam Francis, Nebraska, B
1938 Jim McDonald, Ohio State, B
1939 Davey O'Brien, Texas Christian, B
1940 George McAfee, Duke, B
1941 Art Jones, Richmond, B (2)
1942 Pete Kmetovic, Stanford, B
1943 Joe Muha, Virginia Military, B
1944 Steve Van Buren, Louisiana State, B
1945 John Yonaker, Notre Dame, E
1946 Leo Riggs, Southern California, B
1947 Neill Armstrong, Oklahoma A&M, E
1948 Clyde (Smackover) Scott, Arkansas, B
1949 Chuck Bednarik, Pennsylvania, C
Frank Tripucka, Notre Dame, B
1950 Harry (Bud) Grant, Minnesota, E
1951 Ebert Van Buren, Louisiana State, B
Chet Mutryn, Xavier, B
1952 Johnny Bright, Drake, B
1953 Al Conway, Army, B (2)
1954 Neil Worden, Notre Dame, B
1955 Dick Bielski, Maryland, B
1956 Bob Pellegrini, Maryland, C
1957 Clarence Peaks, Michigan State, B
1958 Walt Kowalczyk, Michigan State, B
1959 J.D. Smith, Rice, T (2)
1960 Ron Burton, Northwestern, RB
1961 Art Baker, Syracuse, RB
1962 Pete Case, Georgia, G (2)
1963 Ed Budde, Michigan State, G
1964 Bob Brown, Nebraska, T
1965 Ray Rissmiller, Georgia, T (2)
1966 Randy Beisler, Indiana, DE
1967 Harry Jones, Arkansas, RB
1968 Tim Rossovich, Southern California, DE
1969 Leroy Keyes, Purdue, RB
1970 Steve Zabel, Oklahoma, TE
1971 Richard Harris, Grambling, DE
1972 John Reaves, Florida, QB
1973 Jerry Sisemore, Texas, T
Charle Young, Southern California, TE
1974 Mitch Sutton, Kansas, DT (3)
1975 Bill Capraun, Miami, T (7)
1976 Mike Smith, Florida, DE (4)
1977 Skip Sharp, Kansas, DB (5)
1978 Reggie Wilkes, Georgia Tech, LB (3)
1979 Jerry Robinson, UCLA, LB
1980 Roynell Young, Alcorn State, DB
1981 Leonard Mitchell, Houston, DE
1982 Mike Quick, North Carolina State, WR
1983 Michael Haddix, Mississippi State, RB
1984 Kenny Jackson, Penn State, WR
1985 Kevin Allen, Indiana, T
1986 Keith Byars, Ohio State, RB
1987 Jerome Brown, Miami, DT
1988 Keith Jackson, Oklahoma, TE
1989 Jessie Small, Eastern Kentucky, LB (2)
1990 Ben Smith, Georgia, DB
1991 Antone Davis, Tennessee, T
1992 Siran Stacy, Alabama, RB (2)
1993 Lester Holmes, Jackson State, T
Leonard Renfro, Colorado, DT
1994 Bernard Williams, Georgia, T
1995 Mike Mamula, Boston College, DE
1996 Jermane Mayberry, Texas A&M-Kingsville, T
1997 Jon Harris, Virginia, DE
1998 Tra Thomas, Florida State, T
1999 Donovan McNabb, Syracuse, QB

PITTSBURGH STEELERS

Year Player, College, Position
1936 Bill Shakespeare, Notre Dame, B
1937 Mike Basrak, Duquesne, C
1938 Byron (Whizzer) White, Colorado, B
1939 Bill Patterson, Baylor, B (3)
1940 Kay Eakin, Arkansas, B
1941 Chet Gladchuk, Boston College, C (2)
1942 Bill Dudley, Virginia, B
1943 Bill Daley, Minnesota, B
1944 Johnny Podesto, St. Mary's, Calif., B
1945 Paul Duhart, Florida, B
1946 Felix (Doc) Blanchard, Army, B
1947 Hub Bechtol, Texas, E
1948 Dan Edwards, Georgia, E
1949 Bobby Gage, Clemson, B
1950 Lynn Chandnois, Michigan State, B
1951 Butch Avinger, Alabama, B
1952 Ed Modzelewski, Maryland, B
1953 Ted Marchibroda, St. Bonaventure, B
1954 Johnny Lattner, Notre Dame, B
1955 Frank Varrichione, Notre Dame, T
1956 Gary Glick, Colorado A&M, B
Art Davis, Mississippi State, B
1957 Len Dawson, Purdue, B
1958 Larry Krutko, West Virginia, B (2)
1959 Tom Barnett, Purdue, B (8)
1960 Jack Spikes, Texas Christian, RB
1961 Myron Pottios, Notre Dame, LB (2)
1962 Bob Ferguson, Ohio State, RB
1963 Frank Atkinson, Stanford, T (8)
1964 Paul Martha, Pittsburgh, S
1965 Roy Jefferson, Utah, WR (2)
1966 Dick Leftridge, West Virginia, RB
1967 Don Shy, San Diego State, RB (2)
1968 Mike Taylor, Southern California, T
1969 Joe Greene, North Texas State, DT
1970 Terry Bradshaw, Louisiana Tech, QB
1971 Frank Lewis, Grambling, WR
1972 Franco Harris, Penn State, RB
1973 J.T. Thomas, Florida State, DB
1974 Lynn Swann, Southern California, WR
1975 Dave Brown, Michigan, DB
1976 Bennie Cunningham, Clemson, TE
1977 Robin Cole, New Mexico, LB
1978 Ron Johnson, Eastern Michigan, DB
1979 Greg Hawthorne, Baylor, RB
1980 Mark Malone, Arizona State, QB
1981 Keith Gary, Oklahoma, DE
1982 Walter Abercrombie, Baylor, RB
1983 Gabriel Rivera, Texas Tech, DT
1984 Louis Lipps, Southern Mississippi, WR
1985 Darryl Sims, Wisconsin, DE
1986 John Rienstra, Temple, G
1987 Rod Woodson, Purdue, DB
1988 Aaron Jones, Eastern Kentucky, DE
1989 Tim Worley, Georgia, RB
Tom Ricketts, Pittsburgh, T
1990 Eric Green, Liberty, TE
1991 Huey Richardson, Florida, DE
1992 Leon Searcy, Miami, T
1993 Deon Figures, Colorado, DB
1994 Charles Johnson, Colorado, WR
1995 Mark Bruener, Washington, TE
1996 Jamain Stephens, North Carolina A&T, T
1997 Chad Scott, Maryland, DB
1998 Alan Faneca, Louisiana State, G
1999 Troy Edwards, Lousiana Tech, WR

ST. LOUIS RAMS

Year Player, College, Position
1937 Johnny Drake, Purdue, B
1938 Corbett Davis, Indiana, B
1939 Parker Hall, Mississippi, B
1940 Ollie Cordill, Rice, B
1941 Rudy Mucha, Washington, C
1942 Jack Wilson, Baylor, B
1943 Mike Holovak, Boston College, B
1944 Tony Butkovich, Illinois, B
1945 Elroy (Crazylegs) Hirsch, Wisconsin, B
1946 Emil Sitko, Notre Dame, B
1947 Herman Wedemeyer, St. Mary's, Calif., B
1948 Tom Keane, West Virginia, B (2)
1949 Bobby Thomason, Virginia Military, B
1950 Ralph Pasquariello, Villanova, B
Stan West, Oklahoma, G
1951 Bud McFadin, Texas, G
1952 Bill Wade, Vanderbilt, QB
Bob Carey, Michigan State, E
1953 Donn Moomaw, UCLA, C
Ed Barker, Washington State, E
1954 Ed Beatty, Cincinnati, C
1955 Larry Morris, Georgia Tech, C

1956	Joe Marconi, West Virginia, B
	Charles Horton, Vanderbilt, B
1957	Jon Arnett, Southern California, B
	Del Shofner, Baylor, E
1958	Lou Michaels, Kentucky, T
	Jim Phillips, Auburn, E
1959	Dick Bass, Pacific, B
	Paul Dickson, Baylor, T
1960	Billy Cannon, Louisiana State, RB
1961	Marlin McKeever, Southern California, E-LB
1962	Roman Gabriel, North Carolina State, QB
	Merlin Olsen, Utah State, DT
1963	Terry Baker, Oregon State, QB
	Rufus Guthrie, Georgia Tech, G
1964	Bill Munson, Utah State, QB
1965	Clancy Williams, Washington State, CB
1966	Tom Mack, Michigan, G
1967	Willie Ellison, Texas Southern, RB (2)
1968	Gary Beban, UCLA, QB (2)
1969	Larry Smith, Florida, RB
	Jim Seymour, Notre Dame, WR
	Bob Klein, Southern California, TE
1970	Jack Reynolds, Tennessee, LB
1971	Isiah Robertson, Southern, LB
	Jack Youngblood, Florida, DE
1972	Jim Bertelsen, Texas, RB (2)
1973	Cullen Bryant, Colorado, DB (2)
1974	John Cappelletti, Penn State, RB
1975	Mike Fanning, Notre Dame, DT
	Dennis Harrah, Miami, T
	Doug France, Ohio State, T
1976	Kevin McLain, Colorado State, LB
1977	Bob Brudzinski, Ohio State, LB
1978	Elvis Peacock, Oklahoma, RB
1979	George Andrews, Nebraska, LB
	Kent Hill, Georgia Tech, T
1980	Johnnie Johnson, Texas, DB
1981	Mel Owens, Michigan, LB
1982	Barry Redden, Richmond, RB
1983	Eric Dickerson, Southern Methodist, RB
1984	Hal Stephens, East Carolina, DE (5)
1985	Jerry Gray, Texas, DB
1986	Mike Schad, Queen's University, Canada, T
1987	Donald Evans, Winston-Salem, DE (2)
1988	Gaston Green, UCLA, RB
	Aaron Cox, Arizona State, WR
1989	Bill Hawkins, Miami, DE
	Cleveland Gary, Miami, RB
1990	Bern Brostek, Washington, C
1991	Todd Lyght, Notre Dame, DB
1992	Sean Gilbert, Pittsburgh, DE
1993	Jerome Bettis, Notre Dame, RB
1994	Wayne Gandy, Auburn, T
1995	Kevin Carter, Florida, DE
1996	Lawrence Phillips, Nebraska, RB
	Eddie Kennison, Louisiana State, WR
1997	Orlando Pace, Ohio State, T
1998	Grant Wistrom, Nebraska, DE
1999	Torry Holt, North Carolina State, WR

SAN DIEGO CHARGERS

Year	Player, College, Position
1960	Monty Stickles, Notre Dame, E
1961	Earl Faison, Indiana, DE
1962	Bob Ferguson, Ohio State, RB
1963	Walt Sweeney, Syracuse, G
1964	Ted Davis, Georgia Tech, LB
1965	Steve DeLong, Tennessee, DE
1966	Don Davis, Cal State-Los Angeles, DT
1967	Ron Billingsley, Wyoming, DE
1968	Russ Washington, Missouri, DT
	Jimmy Hill, Texas A&I, DB
1969	Marty Domres, Columbia, QB
	Bob Babich, Miami, Ohio, LB
1970	Walker Gillette, Richmond, WR
1971	Leon Burns, Long Beach State, RB
1972	Pete Lazetich, Stanford, DE (2)
1973	Johnny Rodgers, Nebraska, WR
1974	Bo Matthews, Colorado, RB
	Don Goode, Kansas, LB
1975	Gary Johnson, Grambling, DT
	Mike Williams, Louisiana State, DB
1976	Joe Washington, Oklahoma, RB
1977	Bob Rush, Memphis State, C
1978	John Jefferson, Arizona State, WR
1979	Kellen Winslow, Missouri, TE
1980	Ed Luther, San Jose State, QB (4)
1981	James Brooks, Auburn, RB
1982	Hollis Hall, Clemson, DB (7)
1983	Billy Ray Smith, Arkansas, LB
	Gary Anderson, Arkansas, WR
	Gill Byrd, San Jose State, DB
1984	Mossy Cade, Texas, DB
1985	Jim Lachey, Ohio State, G
1986	Leslie O'Neal, Oklahoma State, DE
	James FitzPatrick, Southern California, T
1987	Rod Bernstine, Texas A&M, TE
1988	Anthony Miller, Tennessee, WR
1989	Burt Grossman, Pittsburgh, DE
1990	Junior Seau, Southern California, LB
1991	Stanley Richard, Texas, DB
1992	Chris Mims, Tennessee, DE
1993	Darrien Gordon, Stanford, DB
1994	Isaac Davis, Arkansas, G (2)
1995	Terrance Shaw, Stephen F. Austin, DB (2)
1996	Bryan Still, Virginia Tech, WR (2)
1997	Freddie Jones, North Carolina, TE (2)
1998	Ryan Leaf, Washington State, QB
1999	Jermaine Fazande, Oklahoma, RB (2)

SAN FRANCISCO 49ERS

Year	Player, College, Position
1950	Leo Nomellini, Minnesota, T
1951	Y.A. Tittle, Louisiana State, B
1952	Hugh McElhenny, Washington, B
1953	Harry Babcock, Georgia, E
	Tom Stolhandske, Texas, E
1954	Bernie Faloney, Maryland, B
1955	Dickie Moegle, Rice, B
1956	Earl Morrall, Michigan State, B
1957	John Brodie, Stanford, B
1958	Jim Pace, Michigan, B
	Charlie Krueger, Texas A&M, T
1959	Dave Baker, Oklahoma, B
	Dan James, Ohio State, C
1960	Monty Stickles, Notre Dame, E
1961	Jimmy Johnson, UCLA, CB
	Bernie Casey, Bowling Green, WR
	Bill Kilmer, UCLA, QB
1962	Lance Alworth, Arkansas, WR
1963	Kermit Alexander, UCLA, CB
1964	Dave Parks, Texas Tech, WR
1965	Ken Willard, North Carolina, RB
	George Donnelly, Illinois, DB
1966	Stan Hindman, Mississippi, DE
1967	Steve Spurrier, Florida, QB
	Cas Banaszek, Northwestern, T
1968	Forrest Blue, Auburn, C
1969	Ted Kwalick, Penn State, TE
	Gene Washington, Stanford, WR
1970	Cedrick Hardman, North Texas State, DE
	Bruce Taylor, Boston U., DB
1971	Tim Anderson, Ohio State, DB
1972	Terry Beasley, Auburn, WR
1973	Mike Holmes, Texas Southern, DB
1974	Wilbur Jackson, Alabama, RB
	Bill Sandifer, UCLA, DT
1975	Jimmy Webb, Mississippi State, DT
1976	Randy Cross, UCLA, C (2)
1977	Elmo Boyd, Eastern Kentucky, WR (3)
1978	Ken MacAfee, Notre Dame, TE
	Dan Bunz, Cal State-Long Beach, LB
1979	James Owens, UCLA, WR (2)
1980	Earl Cooper, Rice, RB
	Jim Stuckey, Clemson, DT
1981	Ronnie Lott, Southern California, DB
1982	Bubba Paris, Michigan, T (2)
1983	Roger Craig, Nebraska, RB (2)
1984	Todd Shell, Brigham Young, LB
1985	Jerry Rice, Mississippi Valley State, WR
1986	Larry Roberts, Alabama, DE (2)
1987	Harris Barton, North Carolina, T
	Terrence Flagler, Clemson, RB
1988	Danny Stubbs, Miami, DE (2)
1989	Keith DeLong, Tennessee, LB
1990	Dexter Carter, Florida State, RB
1991	Ted Washington, Louisville, DT
1992	Dana Hall, Washington, DB
1993	Dana Stubblefield, Kansas, DT
	Todd Kelly, Tennessee, DE
1994	Bryant Young, Notre Dame, DT
	William Floyd, Florida State, RB
1995	J.J. Stokes, UCLA, WR
1996	Israel Ifeanyi, Southern California, DE (2)
1997	Jim Druckenmiller, Virginia Tech, QB
1998	R.W. McQuarters, Oklahoma State, DB
1999	Reggie McGrew, Florida, DT

SEATTLE SEAHAWKS

Year	Player, College, Position
1976	Steve Niehaus, Notre Dame, DT
1977	Steve August, Tulsa, G
1978	Keith Simpson, Memphis State, DB
1979	Manu Tuiasosopo, UCLA, DT
1980	Jacob Green, Texas A&M, DE
1981	Ken Easley, UCLA, DB
1982	Jeff Bryant, Clemson, DE
1983	Curt Warner, Penn State, RB
1984	Terry Taylor, Southern Illinois, DB
1985	Owen Gill, Iowa, RB (2)
1986	John L. Williams, Florida, RB
1987	Tony Woods, Pittsburgh, LB
1988	Brian Blades, Miami, WR (2)
1989	Andy Heck, Notre Dame, T
1990	Cortez Kennedy, Miami, DT
1991	Dan McGwire, San Diego State, QB
1992	Ray Roberts, Virginia, T
1993	Rick Mirer, Notre Dame, QB
1994	Sam Adams, Texas A&M, DT
1995	Joey Galloway, Ohio State, WR
1996	Pete Kendall, Boston College, T
1997	Shawn Springs, Ohio State, DB
	Walter Jones, Florida State, T
1998	Anthony Simmons, Clemson, LB
1999	Lamar King, Saginaw Valley, DE

TAMPA BAY BUCCANEERS

Year	Player, College, Position
1976	Lee Roy Selmon, Oklahoma, DT
1977	Ricky Bell, Southern California, RB
1978	Doug Williams, Grambling, QB
1979	Greg Roberts, Oklahoma, G (2)
1980	Ray Snell, Wisconsin, G
1981	Hugh Green, Pittsburgh, LB
1982	Sean Farrell, Penn State, G
1983	Randy Grimes, Baylor, C (2)
1984	Keith Browner, Southern California, LB (2)
1985	Ron Holmes, Washington, DE
1986	Bo Jackson, Auburn, RB
	Roderick Jones, Southern Methodist, DB
1987	Vinny Testaverde, Miami, QB
1988	Paul Gruber, Wisconsin, T
1989	Broderick Thomas, Nebraska, LB
1990	Keith McCants, Alabama, LB
1991	Charles McRae, Tennessee, T
1992	Courtney Hawkins, Michigan State, WR (2)
1993	Eric Curry, Alabama, DE
1994	Trent Dilfer, Fresno State, QB
1995	Warren Sapp, Miami, DT
	Derrick Brooks, Florida State, LB
1996	Regan Upshaw, California, DE
	Marcus Jones, North Carolina, DT
1997	Warrick Dunn, Florida State, RB
	Reidel Anthony, Florida, WR
1998	Jacquez Green, Florida, WR (2)
1999	Anthony McFarland, Louisiana State, DT

TENNESSEE TITANS

Year	Player, College, Position
1960	Billy Cannon, Louisiana State, RB
1961	Mike Ditka, Pittsburgh, E
1962	Ray Jacobs, Howard Payne, DT
1963	Danny Brabham, Arkansas, LB
1964	Scott Appleton, Texas, DT
1965	Lawrence Elkins, Baylor, WR
1966	Tommy Nobis, Texas, LB
1967	George Webster, Michigan State, LB
	Tom Regner, Notre Dame, G
1968	Mac Haik, Mississippi, WR (2)

FIRST-ROUND SELECTIONS

1969 Ron Pritchard, Arizona State, LB
1970 Doug Wilkerson, N. Carolina Central, G
1971 Dan Pastorini, Santa Clara, QB
1972 Greg Sampson, Stanford, DE
1973 John Matuszak, Tampa, DE
George Amundson, Iowa State, RB
1974 Steve Manstedt, Nebraska, LB (4)
1975 Robert Brazile, Jackson State, LB
Don Hardeman, Texas A&I, RB
1976 Mike Barber, Louisiana Tech, TE (2)
1977 Morris Towns, Missouri, T
1978 Earl Campbell, Texas, RB
1979 Mike Stensrud, Iowa State, DE (2)
1980 Angelo Fields, Michigan State, T (2)
1981 Michael Holston, Morgan State, WR (3)
1982 Mike Munchak, Penn State, G
1983 Bruce Matthews, Southern California, T
1984 Dean Steinkuhler, Nebraska, T
1985 Ray Childress, Texas A&M, DE
Richard Johnson, Wisconsin, DB
1986 Jim Everett, Purdue, QB
1987 Alonzo Highsmith, Miami, RB
Haywood Jeffires, North Carolina St., WR
1988 Lorenzo White, Michigan State, RB
1989 David Williams, Florida, T
1990 Lamar Lathon, Houston, LB
1991 Mike Dumas, Indiana, DB (2)
1992 Eddie Robinson, Alabama State, LB (2)
1993 Brad Hopkins, Illinois, T
1994 Henry Ford, Arkansas, DE
1995 Steve McNair, Alcorn State, QB
1996 Eddie George, Ohio State, RB
1997 Kenny Holmes, Miami, DE
1998 Kevin Dyson, Utah, WR
1999 Jevon Kearse, Florida, DE

WASHINGTON REDSKINS

Year Player, College, Position
1936 Riley Smith, Alabama, B
1937 Sammy Baugh, Texas Christian, B
1938 Andy Farkas, Detroit, B
1939 I.B. Hale, Texas Christian, T
1940 Ed Boell, New York U., B
1941 Forest Evashevski, Michigan, B
1942 Orban (Spec) Sanders, Texas, B
1943 Jack Jenkins, Missouri, B
1944 Mike Micka, Colgate, B
1945 Jim Hardy, Southern California, B
1946 Casl Rossi, UCLA, B*
1947 Casl Rossi, UCLA, B
1948 Harry Gilmer, Alabama, B
Lowell Tew, Alabama, B
1949 Rob Goode, Texas A&M, B
1950 George Thomas, Oklahoma, B
1951 Leon Heath, Oklahoma, B
1952 Larry Isbell, Baylor, B
1953 Jack Scarbath, Maryland, B
1954 Steve Meilinger, Kentucky, E
1955 Ralph Guglielmi, Notre Dame, B
1956 Ed Vereb, Maryland, B
1957 Don Bosseler, Miami, B
1958 Mike Sommer, George Washington, B (2)
1959 Don Allard, Boston College, B
1960 Richie Lucas, Penn State, QB
1961 Norman Snead, Wake Forest, QB
Joe Rutgens, Illinois, DT
1962 Ernie Davis, Syracuse, RB
1963 Pat Richter, Wisconsin, TE
1964 Charley Taylor, Arizona State, RB-WR
1965 Bob Breitenstein, Tulsa, T (2)
1966 Charlie Gogolak, Princeton, K
1967 Ray McDonald, Idaho, RB
1968 Jim Smith, Oregon, DB
1969 Eugene Epps, Texas-El Paso, DB (2)
1970 Bill Bundige, Colorado, DT (2)
1971 Cotton Speyrer, Texas, WR (2)
1972 Moses Denson, Maryland State, RB (8)
1973 Charles Cantrell, Lamar, G (5)
1974 Jon Keyworth, Colorado, TE (6)
1975 Mike Thomas, Nevada-Las Vegas, RB (6)
1976 Mike Hughes, Baylor, G (5)
1977 Duncan McColl, Stanford, DE (4)
1978 Tony Green, Florida, RB (6)
1979 Don Warren, San Diego State, TE (4)
1980 Art Monk, Syracuse, WR
1981 Mark May, Pittsburgh, T
1982 Vernon Dean, San Diego State, DB (2)
1983 Darrell Green, Texas A&I, DB
1984 Bob Slater, Oklahoma, DT (2)
1985 Tory Nixon, San Diego State, DB (2)
1986 Markus Koch, Boise State, DE (2)
1987 Brian Davis, Nebraska, DB (2)
1988 Chip Lohmiller, Minnesota, K (2)
1989 Tracy Rocker, Auburn, DT (3)
1990 Andre Collins, Penn State, LB (2)
1991 Bobby Wilson, Michigan State, DT
1992 Desmond Howard, Michigan, WR
1993 Tom Carter, Notre Dame, DB
1994 Heath Shuler, Tennessee, QB
1995 Michael Westbrook, Colorado, WR
1996 Andre Johnson, Penn State, T
1997 Kenard Lang, Miami, DE
1998 Stephen Alexander, Oklahoma, TE (2)
1999 Champ Bailey, Georgia, DB

**Choice lost because of ineligibility*

ASSOCIATED PRESS NFL MOST VALUABLE PLAYERS

NFL MOST VALUABLE PLAYERS NAMED BY *ASSOCIATED PRESS* IN BALLOTING BY A NATIONWIDE PANEL OF MEDIA:

YEAR	PLAYER	POS.	TEAM	ACCOMPLISHMENTS
1957	Jim Brown	RB	Cleveland Browns	Rushed for league-leading 942 yards and added 9 TDs as a rookie.
1958	Gino Marchetti	DE	Baltimore Colts	Leader of defense that permitted league-low 1,291 rushing yards and division-low 203 points.
1959	Charley Conerly	QB	New York Giants	Passed for 14 TDs vs. 4 interceptions. Led offense to division-leading 284 points.
1960	Norm Van Brocklin	QB	Philadelphia Eagles	Guided Eagles to first division title since 1949. Passed for 2,471 yards and 24 TDs.
	Joe Schmidt	LB	Detroit Lions	Team went 7-2 after 0-3 start when he returned from injury. Scored 2 defensive TDs.
1961	Paul Hornung	RB	Green Bay Packers	Led league in scoring for second straight season with 146 points (10 TD, 15 FG, 41 PAT).
1962	Jim Taylor	RB	Green Bay Packers	League rushing champion with 1,474 yards. Scored then all-time record 19 touchdowns.
1963	Y.A. Tittle	QB	New York Giants	Set then all-time season record with 36 TD passes. Guided league's top offense (5,024 yards).
1964	Johnny Unitas	QB	Baltimore Colts	Guided Colts to NFL's best record (12-2) and league's top offensive attack (4,779 yards).
1965	Jim Brown	RB	Cleveland Browns	Leader of NFL's top rushing attack. Led league with 1,544 yards, added 21 total TDs.
1966	Bart Starr	QB	Green Bay Packers	Passed for 14 touchdowns vs. 3 interceptions. Led Packers to league-best 12-2 record.
1967	Johnny Unitas	QB	Baltimore Colts	Passed for 3,428 yards and 20 touchdowns. Led Colts to 11-1-2 record.
1968	Earl Morrall	QB	Baltimore Colts	Guided Colts to NFL-best 13-1 record. Led league with 26 touchdown passes.
1969	Roman Gabriel	QB	Los Angeles Rams	Led NFL with 24 touchdown passes. Guided Rams to 11-3 record.
1970	John Brodie	QB	San Francisco 49ers	Took 49ers to first-ever division title. Threw NFL-best 24 TD passes.
1971	Alan Page	DT	Minnesota Vikings	Led defense that allowed NFL-low 139 points. Vikings won fourth straight NFC Central title.
1972	Larry Brown	RB	Washington Redskins	Led conference with 1,216 rushing yards. Redskins had NFC-best 11-3 record.
1973	O.J. Simpson	RB	Buffalo Bills	Rushed for then all-time record 2,003 yards, including three 200-yard performances.
1974	Ken Stabler	QB	Oakland Raiders	Led league with 26 touchdown passes vs. 12 interceptions. Raiders had NFL-best 12-2 record.
1975	Fran Tarkenton	QB	Minnesota Vikings	Tied for league-best 12-2 record. Led NFC with 91.7 passer rating.
1976	Bert Jones	QB	Baltimore Colts	Threw 24 touchdowns vs. 9 interceptions for 102.5 passer rating.
1977	Walter Payton	RB	Chicago Bears	Rushed for league-leading 1,852 yards and 16 total touchdowns.
1978	Terry Bradshaw	QB	Pittsburgh Steelers	Led Steelers to league-leading 14-2 mark. Set team record with 28 TD passes.
1979	Earl Campbell	RB	Houston Oilers	Led league with 1,697 rushing yards and 19 touchdowns.
1980	Brian Sipe	QB	Cleveland Browns	NFL-best 91.4 passer rating. Set Browns' records with 30 TD passes and 4,132 yards.
1981	Ken Anderson	QB	Cincinnati Bengals	Led Bengals to first division title since 1973. NFL-high 98.5 passer rating.
1982	Mark Moseley	K	Washington Redskins	Converted 20 of 21 FGs. Set then consecutive field-goal record at 23 (including last three in '81).
1983	Joe Theismann	QB	Washington Redskins	Leader of offense that scored NFL record 541 points. Redskins had NFL-best 14-2 record.
1984	Dan Marino	QB	Miami Dolphins	Set NFL records with 5,084 yards and 48 TD passes. Led Dolphins to AFC-best 14-2 mark.
1985	Marcus Allen	RB	Los Angeles Raiders	Rushed for league-leading 1,759 yards. Tied for AFC lead with 11 rushing touchdowns.
1986	Lawrence Taylor	LB	New York Giants	Recorded league-high 20.5 sacks, and led Giants' second-ranked defense (297.3).
1987	John Elway	QB	Denver Broncos	In 12 games, passed for 19 TDs and 3,198 yards, including four 300-yard games.
1988	Boomer Esiason	QB	Cincinnati Bengals	Led NFL with 97.4 passer rating. Tied for AFC lead with 28 TD passes.
1989	Joe Montana	QB	San Francisco 49ers	Set then NFL record with 112.4 passer rating, including 70.2 completion percentage.
1990	Joe Montana	QB	San Francisco 49ers	Led 49ers to league-best 14-2 record. Completed NFC-high 61.7 percent of passes.
1991	Thurman Thomas	RB	Buffalo Bills	Recorded league-high 2,038 yards from scrimmage (1,407 rushing, 631 receiving).
1992	Steve Young	QB	San Francisco 49ers	NFL's top passer with 107.0 rating. Led 49ers to league-best 14-2 record.
1993	Emmitt Smith	RB	Dallas Cowboys	Led league in rushing (1,486 yards) for third straight year despite missing first two games.
1994	Steve Young	QB	San Francisco 49ers	Compiled NFL all-time best 112.8 passer rating. Completed more than 70 percent of his passes.
1995	Brett Favre	QB	Green Bay Packers	Led league with 38 touchdown passes and NFC with 99.5 passer rating.
1996	Brett Favre	QB	Green Bay Packers	Led Packers to top conference record (13-3). Threw NFL-best 39 TD passes.
1997	Brett Favre	QB	Green Bay Packers	Led league with 35 touchdown passes. Led NFC with 3,867 passing yards
	Barry Sanders	RB	Detroit Lions	Rushed for all-time second-best 2,053 yards, including record 14 straight 100-yard games.
1998	Terrell Davis	RB	Denver Broncos	Rushed for 2,008 yards and scored league-best 23 total touchdowns.

Total *Associated Press* NFL MVPs: 44
Two-time Winners: Jim Brown, Brett Favre (3), Joe Montana, Johnny Unitas, Steve Young

ASSOCIATED PRESS NFL MVP BY POSITION

Quarterback:	26	**Defensive End:**	1
Running Back:	13	**Defensive Tackle:**	1
Linebacker:	2	**Kicker:**	1

ASSOCIATED PRESS MVPs WHO WON SUPER BOWL/NFL CHAMPIONSHIP IN SAME SEASON: 13

1958	Gino Marchetti	Baltimore Colts
1960	Norm Van Brocklin	Philadelphia Eagles
1961	Paul Hornung	Green Bay Packers
1962	Jim Taylor	Green Bay Packers
1966	Bart Starr	Green Bay Packers
1978	Terry Bradshaw	Pittsburgh Steelers
1982	Mark Moseley	Washington Redskins
1986	Lawrence Taylor	New York Giants
1989	Joe Montana	San Francisco 49ers
1993	Emmitt Smith	Dallas Cowboys
1994	Steve Young	San Francisco 49ers
1996	Brett Favre	Green Bay Packers
1998	Terrell Davis	Denver Broncos

ASSOCIATED PRESS MVPs BY TEAM

6	Green Bay Packers
5	Baltimore Colts San Francisco 49ers
3	Cleveland Browns New York Giants Washington Redskins
2	Buffalo Bills Cincinnati Bengals Denver Broncos Detroit Lions Minnesota Vikings Oakland/Los Angeles Raiders
1	Chicago Bears Dallas Cowboys Houston Oilers Los Angeles Rams Miami Dolphins Philadelphia Eagles Pittsburgh Steelers

MILLER LITE PLAYERS OF THE YEAR

YEAR	PLAYER	POS.	TEAM
1989	Joe Montana	QB	San Francisco 49ers
1990	Joe Montana	QB	San Francisco 49ers
1991	Thurman Thomas	RB	Buffalo Bills
1992	Steve Young	QB	San Francisco 49ers
1993	Emmitt Smith	RB	Dallas Cowboys
1994	Steve Young	QB	San Francisco 49ers
1995	Brett Favre	QB	Green Bay Packers
1996	Brett Favre	QB	Green Bay Packers
1997	Barry Sanders	RB	Detroit Lions
1998	Randall Cunningham	QB	Minnesota Vikings

ALL-TIME NFL TEAMS

75TH ANNIVERSARY ALL-TIME TEAM

Chosen by a selection committee of media and league personnel in 1994.

Position	Name	Team(s)	Ht.	Wt.	College
OFFENSE					
QB	Sammy Baugh	Washington Redskins (1937-52)	6-2	180	Texas Christian
QB	Otto Graham	Cleveland Browns (1946-55)	6-1	195	Northwestern
QB	Joe Montana	San Francisco 49ers (1979-92), Kansas City Chiefs (1993-94)	6-2	195	Notre Dame
QB	Johnny Unitas	Baltimore Colts (1956-72), San Diego Chargers (1973)	6-1	195	Louisville
RB	Jim Brown	Cleveland Browns (1957-65)	6-2	232	Syracuse
RB	Marion Motley	Cleveland Browns (1946-53), Pittsburgh Steelers (1955)	6-1	238	Nevada-Reno
RB	Bronko Nagurski	Chicago Bears (1930-37, 1943)	6-2	225	Minnesota
RB	Walter Payton	Chicago Bears (1975-87)	5-10	202	Jackson State
RB	Gale Sayers	Chicago Bears (1965-71)	6-0	200	Kansas
RB	O.J. Simpson	Buffalo Bills (1969-77), San Francisco 49ers (1978-79)	6-1	212	Southern California
RB	Steve Van Buren	Philadelphia Eagles (1944-51)	6-1	200	Louisiana State
WR	Lance Alworth	San Diego Chargers (1962-70), Dallas Cowboys (1971-72)	6-0	184	Arkansas
WR	Raymond Berry	Baltimore Colts (1955-67)	6-2	187	Southern Methodist
WR	Don Hutson	Green Bay Packers (1935-45)	6-1	180	Alabama
WR	Jerry Rice	San Francisco 49ers (1985-present)	6-2	200	Miss. Valley State
TE	Mike Ditka	Chicago Bears (1961-66), Philadelphia Eagles (1967-68), Dallas Cowboys (1969-72)	6-3	225	Pittsburgh
TE	Kellen Winslow	San Diego Chargers (1979-87)	6-5	250	Missouri
T	Roosevelt Brown	New York Giants (1953-65)	6-3	255	Morgan State
T	Forrest Gregg	Green Bay Packers (1956, 1958-70)	6-4	250	Southern Methodist
T	Anthony Muñoz	Cincinnati Bengals (1980-92)	6-6	285	Southern California
G	John Hannah	New England Patriots (1973-85)	6-3	265	Alabama
G	Jim Parker	Baltimore Colts (1957-67)	6-3	273	Ohio State
G	Gene Upshaw	Oakland Raiders (1967-81)	6-5	255	Texas A&I
C	Mel Hein	New York Giants (1931-45)	6-2	225	Washington State
C	Mike Webster	Pittsburgh Steelers (1974-88), Kansas City Chiefs (1989-90)	6-2	250	Wisconsin
DEFENSE					
DE	David (Deacon) Jones	Los Angeles Rams (1961-71), San Diego Chargers (1972-73), Washington Redskins (1974)	6-5	250	Miss. Vocational
DE	Gino Marchetti	Dallas Texans (1952), Baltimore Colts (1953-64,1966)	6-4	245	San Francisco
DE	Reggie White	Philadelphia Eagles (1985-95), Green Bay Packers (1993-present)	6-5	290	Tennessee
DT	Joe Greene	Pittsburgh Steelers (1969-81)	6-4	260	North Texas State
DT	Bob Lilly	Dallas Cowboys (1961-74)	6-5	260	Texas Christian
DT	Merlin Olsen	Los Angeles Rams (1962-76)	6-5	270	Utah State
LB	Dick Butkus	Chicago Bears (1965-73)	6-3	245	Illinois
LB	Jack Ham	Pittsburgh Steelers (1971-82)	6-1	225	Penn State
LB	Ted Hendricks	Baltimore Colts (1969-73), Green Bay Packers (1974), Oakland/L.A. Raiders (1975-83)	6-7	235	Miami
LB	Jack Lambert	Pittsburgh Steelers (1974-84)	6-4	220	Kent State
LB	Willie Lanier	Kansas City Chiefs (1967-77)	6-1	245	Morgan State
LB	Ray Nitschke	Green Bay Packers (1958-72)	6-3	235	Illinois
LB	Lawrence Taylor	New York Giants (1981-93)	6-3	243	North Carolina
CB	Mel Blount	Pittsburgh Steelers (1970-83)	6-3	205	Southern
CB	Mike Haynes	New England Patriots (1976-82), Los Angeles Raiders (1983-89)	6-2	190	Arizona State
CB	Dick (Night Train) Lane	Los Angeles Rams (1952-53), Chicago Cardinals (1954-59), Detroit Lions (1960-65)	6-2	210	Scottsbluff JC
CB	Rod Woodson	Pittsburgh Steelers (1987-96), San Francisco 49ers (1997)	6-0	200	Purdue
S	Ken Houston	Houston Oilers (1967-72), Washington Redskins (1973-80)	6-3	198	Prairie View A&M
S	Ronnie Lott	San Francisco 49ers (1981-90), Los Angeles Raiders (1991-92), New York Jets (1993-94)	6-0	200	Southern California
S	Larry Wilson	St. Louis Cardinals (1960-72)	6-0	190	Utah
SPECIAL TEAMS					
P	Ray Guy	Oakland/L.A. Raiders (1973-86)	6-3	190	Southern Miss.
K	Jan Stenerud	Kansas City Chiefs (1967-79), Green Bay Packers (1980-83), Minnesota Vikings (1984-85)	6-2	190	Montana State
PR	Billy (White Shoes) Johnson	Houston Oilers (1974-80), Atlanta Falcons (1982-87), Washington Redskins (1988)	5-9	170	Widener
KR	Gale Sayers	Chicago Bears (1965-71)	6-0	200	Kansas

75TH ANNIVERSARY ALL-TWO-WAY TEAM

Positions	
Quarterback, Defensive Halfback, Punter	Sammy Baugh
Center, Linebacker	Chuck Bednarik
Quarterback, Defensive Halfback, Punter	Earl (Dutch) Clark
Tackle, Defensive Tackle	George Connor
Guard, Defensive Tackle	Danny Fortmann
Center, Defensive Tackle	Mel Hein
Tackle, Defensive Tackle, Punter	Wilbur (Pete) Henry
Back, Defensive Halfback	Bill Hewitt
Fullback, Linebacker, Kicker	Clarke Hinkle
Tackle, Defensive Tackle	Cal Hubbard
End, Defensive Halfback	Don Hutson
Back, Defensive Back	George McAfee
Fullback, Linebacker	Marion Motley
Guard-Tackle, Defensive Tackle	George Musso
Fullback, Linebacker	Bronko Nagurski
Halfback, Defensive Halfback	Ernie Nevers
End, Defensive Back	Pete Pihos
Tackle, Defensive Tackle	Joe Stydahar
Running Back, Defensive Back	Steve Van Buren

50TH ANNIVERSARY TEAM

Chosen by the Hall of Fame Selection Committee in 1969.

Offense

Split End	Don Hutson
Tight End	John Mackey
Tackle	Cal Hubbard
Guard	Jerry Kramer
Center	Chuck Bednarik
Flanker	Elroy Hirsch
Quarterback	Johnny Unitas
Halfback	Jim Thorpe
Halfback	Gale Sayers
Fullback	Jim Brown
Kicker	Lou Groza

Defense

End	Gino Marchetti
Tackle	Leo Nomellini
Linebacker	Ray Nitschke
Cornerback	Dick (Night Train) Lane
Safety	Emlen Tunnell

ALL-TIME AFL TEAM

Chosen by 1969 AFL Hall of Fame Selection Committee members.

Offense

Flanker	Lance Alworth
End	Don Maynard
Tight End	Fred Arbanas
Tackle	Ron Mix
Tackle	Jim Tyrer
Guard	Ed Budde
Guard	Billy Shaw
Center	Jim Otto
Quarterback	Joe Namath
Running Back	Clemon Daniels
Running Back	Paul Lowe

Defense

End	Jerry Mays
End	Gerry Philbin
Tackle	Houston Antwine
Tackle	Tom Sestak
Linebacker	Bobby Bell
Linebacker	George Webster
Linebacker	Nick Buoniconti
Cornerback	Willie Brown
Cornerback	Dave Grayson
Safety	Johnny Robinson
Safety	George Saimes

Special Teams

Kicker	George Blanda
Punter	Jerrel Wilson

SUPER BOWL SILVER ANNIVERSARY TEAM

Chosen by the fans prior to Super Bowl XXV in 1990.

Head Coach Vince Lombardi

Offense

Quarterback	Joe Montana
Running Back	Franco Harris
Running Back	Larry Csonka
Wide Receiver	Lynn Swann
Wide Receiver	Jerry Rice
Tight End	Dave Casper
Tackle	Art Shell
Tackle	Forrest Gregg
Guard	Gene Upshaw
Guard	Jerry Kramer
Center	Mike Webster

Defense

Defensive End	L.C. Greenwood
Defensive End	Ed (Too Tall) Jones
Defensive Tackle	Joe Greene
Defensive Tackle	Randy White
Inside Linebacker	Jack Lambert
Inside Linebacker	Mike Singletary
Outside Linebacker	Jack Ham
Outside Linebacker	Ted Hendricks
Cornerback	Ronnie Lott
Cornerback	Mel Blount
Safety	Donnie Shell
Safety	Willie Wood

Special Teams

Punter	Ray Guy
Kicker	Jan Stenerud
Kick Returner	John Taylor

ALL-TIME NFL TEAMS

All-Decade teams chosen by the Hall of Fame Selection Committee Members.

1920's ALL-DECADE TEAM

End	Guy Chamberlin
End	Lavern Dilweg
End	George Halas
Tackle	Ed Healey
Tackle	Wilbur (Pete) Henry
Tackle	Cal Hubbard
Tackle	Steve Owen
Guard	Hunk Anderson
Guard	Walt Kiesling
Guard	Mike Michalske
Center	George Trafton
Quarterback	Jimmy Conzelman
Quarterback	John (Paddy) Driscoll
Halfback	Harold (Red) Grange
Halfback	Joe Guyon
Halfback	Earl (Curly) Lambeau
Halfback	Jim Thorpe
Fullback	Ernie Nevers

1930's ALL-DECADE TEAM

End	Bill Hewitt
End	Don Hutson
End	Wayne Millner
End	Gaynell Tinsley
Tackle	George Christensen
Tackle	Frank Cope
Tackle	Glen (Turk) Edwards
Tackle	Bill Lee
Tackle	Joe Stydahar
Guard	Grover (Ox) Emerson
Guard	Dan Fortmann
Guard	Charles (Buckets) Goldenberg
Guard	Russ Letlow
Center	Mel Hein
Center	George Svendsen
Quarterback	Earl (Dutch) Clark
Quarterback	Arnie Herber
Quarterback	Cecil Isbell
Halfback	Cliff Battles
Halfback	Johnny (Blood) McNally
Halfback	Beattie Feathers
Halfback	Alphonse (Tuffy) Leemans
Halfback	Ken Strong
Fullback	Clarke Hinkle
Fullback	Bronko Nagurski

1940's ALL-DECADE TEAM

End	Jim Benton
End	Jack Ferrante
End	Ken Kavanaugh
End	Dante Lavelli
End	Pete Pihos
End	Mac Speedie
End	Ed Sprinkle
Tackle	Al Blozis
Tackle	George Connor
Tackle	Frank (Bucko) Kilroy
Tackle	Buford (Baby) Ray
Tackle	Vic Sears
Tackle	Al Wistert
Guard	Bruno Banducci
Guard	Bill Edwards
Guard	Garrard (Buster) Ramsey
Guard	Bill Willis
Guard	Len Younce
Center	Charley Brock
Center	Clyde (Bulldog) Turner
Center	Alex Wojciechowicz
Quarterback	Sammy Baugh
Quarterback	Sid Luckman
Quarterback	Bob Waterfield
Halfback	Tony Canadeo
Halfback	Bill Dudley
Halfback	George McAfee
Halfback	Charley Trippi
Halfback	Steve Van Buren
Halfback	Byron (Whizzer) White
Fullback	Pat Harder
Fullback	Marion Motley
Fullback	Bill Osmanski

1950's ALL-DECADE TEAM

Offense

End	Raymond Berry
End	Tom Fears
End	Bobby Walston
Halfback-End	Elroy (Crazylegs) Hirsch
Tackle	Roosevelt Brown
Tackle	Bob St. Clair
Guard	Dick Barwegan
Guard	Jim Parker
Guard	Dick Stanfel
Center	Chuck Bednarik
Quarterback	Otto Graham
Quarterback	Bobby Layne
Quarterback	Norm Van Brocklin
Halfback	Frank Gifford
Halfback	Ollie Matson
Halfback	Hugh McElhenny
Halfback	Lenny Moore
Fullback	Alan Ameche
Fullback	Joe Perry
Kicker	Lou Groza

Defense

End	Len Ford
End	Gino Marchetti
Tackle	Art Donovan
Tackle	Leo Nomellini
Tackle	Ernie Stautner
Linebacker	Joe Fortunato
Linebacker	Bill George
Linebacker	Sam Huff
Linebacker	Joe Schmidt
Halfback	Jack Butler
Halfback	Dick (Night Train) Lane
Safety	Jack Christiansen
Safety	Yale Lary
Safety	Emlen Tunnell

1960's ALL-DECADE TEAM

Offense

Split End	Del Shofner
Split End	Charley Taylor
Flanker	Gary Collins
Flanker	Boyd Dowler
Tight End	John Mackey
Tackle	Bob Brown
Tackle	Forrest Gregg
Tackle	Ralph Neely
Guard	Gene Hickerson
Guard	Jerry Kramer
Guard	Howard Mudd
Center	Jim Ringo
Quarterback	Sonny Jurgensen
Quarterback	Bart Starr
Quarterback	Johnny Unitas
Halfback	John David Crow
Halfback	Paul Hornung
Halfback	Leroy Kelly
Halfback	Gale Sayers
Fullback	Jim Brown
Fullback	Jim Taylor
Kicker	Jim Bakken

Defense

End	Doug Atkins
End	Willie Davis
End	David (Deacon) Jones
Tackle	Alex Karras
Tackle	Bob Lilly
Tackle	Merlin Olsen
Linebacker	Dick Butkus
Linebacker	Larry Morris
Linebacker	Ray Nitschke
Linebacker	Tommy Nobis
Linebacker	Dave Robinson
Cornerback	Herb Adderley
Cornerback	Lem Barney
Cornerback	Bobby Boyd
Safety	Eddie Meador
Safety	Larry Wilson
Safety	Willie Wood
Punter	Don Chandler

1970's ALL-DECADE TEAM

Offense

Wide Receiver	Harold Carmichael
Wide Receiver	Drew Pearson
Wide Receiver	Lynn Swann
Wide Receiver	Paul Warfield
Tight End	Dave Casper
Tight End	Charlie Sanders
Tackle	Dan Dierdorf
Tackle	Art Shell
Tackle	Rayfield Wright
Tackle	Ron Yary
Guard	Joe DeLamielleure
Guard	John Hannah
Guard	Larry Little
Guard	Gene Upshaw
Center	Jim Langer
Center	Mike Webster
Quarterback	Terry Bradshaw
Quarterback	Ken Stabler
Quarterback	Roger Staubach
Running Back	Earl Campbell
Running Back	Franco Harris
Running Back	Walter Payton
Running Back	O.J. Simpson
Kicker	Garo Yepremian

Defense

End	Carl Eller
End	L.C. Greenwood
End	Harvey Martin
End	Jack Youngblood
Tackle	Joe Greene
Tackle	Bob Lilly
Tackle	Merlin Olsen
Tackle	Alan Page
Linebacker	Bobby Bell
Linebacker	Robert Brazile
Linebacker	Dick Butkus
Linebacker	Jack Ham
Linebacker	Ted Hendricks
Linebacker	Jack Lambert
Cornerback	Willie Brown
Cornerback	Jimmy Johnson
Cornerback	Roger Wehrli
Cornerback	Louis Wright
Safety	Dick Anderson
Safety	Cliff Harris
Safety	Ken Houston
Safety	Larry Wilson
Punter	Ray Guy

1980's ALL-DECADE TEAM

Offense

Wide Receiver	Jerry Rice
Wide Receiver	Steve Largent
Wide Receiver	James Lofton
Wide Receiver	Art Monk
Tight End	Kellen Winslow
Tight End	Ozzie Newsome
Tackle	Anthony Munoz
Tackle	Jim Covert
Tackle	Gary Zimmerman
Tackle	Joe Jacoby
Guard	John Hannah
Guard	Russ Grimm
Guard	Bill Fralic
Guard	Mike Munchak
Center	Dwight Stephenson
Center	Mike Webster
Quarterback	Joe Montana
Quarterback	Dan Fouts
Running Back	Walter Payton
Running Back	Eric Dickerson
Running Back	Roger Craig
Running Back	John Riggins

Defense

End	Reggie White
End	Howie Long
End	Lee Roy Selmon
End	Bruce Smith
Tackle	Randy White
Tackle	Dan Hampton
Tackle	Keith Millard
Tackle	Dave Butz
Linebacker	Mike Singletary
Linebacker	Lawrence Taylor
Linebacker	Ted Hendricks
Linebacker	Jack Lambert
Linebacker	Andre Tippett
Linebacker	John Anderson
Linebacker	Carl Banks
Cornerback	Mike Haynes
Cornerback	Mel Blount
Cornerback	Frank Minnifield
Cornerback	Lester Hayes
Safety	Ronnie Lott
Safety	Kenny Easley
Safety	Deron Cherry
Safety	Joey Browner
Safety	Nolan Cromwell

Specialists

Punter	Sean Landeta
Punter	Reggie Roby
Kicker	Morten Andersen
Kicker	Gary Anderson
Kicker	Eddie Murray
Punt Returner	Billy (White Shoes) Johnson
Punt Returner	John Taylor
Kick Returner	Mike Nelms
Kick Returner	Rick Upchurch
Coach	Bill Walsh
Coach	Chuck Noll

Records

ALL-TIME RECORDS

Compiled by Elias Sports Bureau

The following records reflect all available official information on the National Football League from its formation in 1920 to date. Also included are all applicable records from the American Football League, 1960-69.

Individuals eligible for Rookie records are players who were in their first season of professional football and had not been on the roster of another professional football team, including teams in other leagues, for any regular-season or postseason games in a previous season. Eligible players, therefore, include those who were under contract to a National Football League club for a previous season but were terminated prior to their club's first regular-season game and not re-signed, or who were placed on Reserve/Injured (or another category of the Reserve List) prior to their club's first regular-season game and were not activated during the rest of the regular season or postseason.

INDIVIDUAL RECORDS

SERVICE

Most Seasons

26 George Blanda, Chi. Bears, 1949, 1950-58; Baltimore, 1950; Houston, 1960-66; Oakland, 1967-75
21 Earl Morrall, San Francisco, 1956; Pittsburgh, 1957-58; Detroit, 1958-64; N.Y. Giants, 1965-67; Baltimore, 1968-71; Miami, 1972-76
20 Jim Marshall, Cleveland, 1960; Minnesota, 1961-79
Jackie Slater, L.A. Rams, 1976-94; St. Louis, 1995

Most Seasons, One Club

20 Jackie Slater, L.A. Rams, 1976-94; St. Louis, 1995
19 Jim Marshall, Minnesota, 1961-79
18 Jim Hart, St. Louis, 1966-83
Jeff Van Note, Atlanta, 1969-86
Pat Leahy, N.Y. Jets, 1974-91

Most Games Played, Career

340 George Blanda, Chi. Bears, 1949, 1950-58; Baltimore, 1950; Houston, 1960-66; Oakland, 1967-75
282 Jim Marshall, Cleveland, 1960; Minnesota, 1961-79
278 Clay Matthews, Cleveland, 1978-93; Atlanta, 1994-96

Most Consecutive Games Played, Career

282 Jim Marshall, Cleveland, 1960; Minnesota, 1961-79
240 Mick Tingelhoff, Minnesota, 1962-78
234 Jim Bakken, St. Louis, 1962-78

SCORING

Most Seasons Leading League

5 Don Hutson, Green Bay, 1940-44
Gino Cappelletti, Boston, 1961, 1963-66
3 Earl (Dutch) Clark, Portsmouth, 1932; Detroit, 1935-36
Pat Harder, Chi. Cardinals, 1947-49
Paul Hornung, Green Bay, 1959-61
2 Jack Manders, Chi. Bears, 1934, 1937
Gordy Soltau, San Francisco, 1952-53
Doak Walker, Detroit, 1950, 1955
Gene Mingo, Denver, 1960, 1962
Jim Turner, N.Y. Jets, 1968-69
Fred Cox, Minnesota, 1969-70
Chester Marcol, Green Bay, 1972, 1974
John Smith, New England, 1979-80

Most Consecutive Seasons Leading League

5 Don Hutson, Green Bay, 1940-44
4 Gino Cappelletti, Boston, 1963-66
3 Pat Harder, Chi. Cardinals, 1947-49
Paul Hornung, Green Bay, 1959-61

POINTS

Most Points, Career

2,002 George Blanda, Chi. Bears, 1949, 1950-58; Baltimore, 1950; Houston, 1960-66; Oakland, 1967-75 (9-td, 943-pat, 335-fg)
1,845 Gary Anderson, Pittsburgh, 1982-94; Philadelphia, 1995-96; San Francisco, 1997; Minnesota, 1998
1,761 Morten Andersen, New Orleans, 1982-94; Atlanta, 1995-98

Most Points, Season

176 Paul Hornung, Green Bay, 1960 (15-td, 41-pat, 15-fg)
164 Gary Anderson, Minnesota, 1998 (59-pat, 35-fg)
161 Mark Moseley, Washington, 1983 (62-pat, 33-fg)

Most Points, No Touchdowns, Season

164 Gary Anderson, Minnesota, 1998 (59-pat, 35-fg)
161 Mark Moseley, Washington, 1983 (62-pat, 33-fg)
149 Chip Lohmiller, Washington, 1991 (56-pat, 31-fg)

Most Seasons, 100 or More Points

12 Morten Andersen, New Orleans, 1985-89, 1991-94; Atlanta, 1995, 1997-98
11 Nick Lowery, Kansas City, 1981, 1983-86, 1988-93
Gary Anderson, Pittsburgh, 1983-85, 1988, 1991-94; Philadelphia, 1996; San Francisco, 1997; Minnesota, 1998
9 Norm Johnson, Seattle, 1983-84, 1986, 1988, 1990; Atlanta, 1993; Pittsburgh, 1995-97

Most Points, Rookie, Season

144 Kevin Butler, Chicago, 1985 (51-pat, 31-fg)
132 Gale Sayers, Chicago, 1965 (22-td)
128 Doak Walker, Detroit, 1950 (11-td, 38-pat, 8-fg)
Chester Marcol, Green Bay, 1972 (29-pat, 33-fg)

Most Points, Game

40 Ernie Nevers, Chi. Cardinals vs. Chi. Bears, Nov. 28, 1929 (6-td, 4-pat)
36 Dub Jones, Cleveland vs. Chi. Bears, Nov. 25, 1951 (6-td)
Gale Sayers, Chicago vs. San Francisco, Dec. 12, 1965 (6-td)
33 Paul Hornung, Green Bay vs. Baltimore, Oct. 8, 1961 (4-td, 6-pat, 1-fg)

Most Consecutive Games Scoring

238 Morten Andersen, New Orleans, 1982-94; Atlanta, 1995-98 (current)
186 Jim Breech, Oakland, 1979; Cincinnati, 1980-92
155 Ray Wersching, San Francisco, 1977-87

TOUCHDOWNS

Most Seasons Leading League

8 Don Hutson, Green Bay, 1935-38, 1941-44
3 Jim Brown, Cleveland, 1958-59, 1963
Lance Alworth, San Diego, 1964-66
Emmitt Smith, Dallas, 1992, 1994-95
2 By many players

Most Consecutive Seasons Leading League

4 Don Hutson, Green Bay, 1935-38, 1941-44
3 Lance Alworth, San Diego, 1964-66
2 By many players

Most Touchdowns, Career

175 Jerry Rice, San Francisco, 1985-98 (10-r, 164-p, 1-ret)
145 Marcus Allen, L.A. Raiders, 1982-92; Kansas City, 1993-97 (123-r, 21-p, 1-ret)
134 Emmitt Smith, Dallas, 1990-98 (125-r, 9-p)

Most Touchdowns, Season

25 Emmitt Smith, Dallas, 1995 (25-r)
24 John Riggins, Washington, 1983 (24-r)
23 O.J. Simpson, Buffalo, 1975 (16-r, 7-p)
Jerry Rice, San Francisco, 1987 (1-r, 22-p)
Terrell Davis, Denver, 1998 (21-r, 2-p)

Most Touchdowns, Rookie, Season

22 Gale Sayers, Chicago, 1965 (14-r, 6-p, 2-ret)
20 Eric Dickerson, L.A. Rams, 1983 (18-r, 2-p)
17 Randy Moss, Minnesota, 1998 (17-p)
Fred Taylor, Jacksonville, 1998 (14-r, 3-p)

Most Touchdowns, Game

6 Ernie Nevers, Chi. Cardinals vs. Chi. Bears, Nov. 28, 1929 (6-r)
Dub Jones, Cleveland vs. Chi. Bears, Nov. 25, 1951 (4-r, 2-p)
Gale Sayers, Chicago vs. San Francisco, Dec. 12, 1965 (4-r, 1-p, 1-ret)
5 Bob Shaw, Chi. Cardinals vs. Baltimore, Oct. 2, 1950 (5-p)
Jim Brown, Cleveland vs. Baltimore, Nov. 1, 1959 (5-r)
Abner Haynes, Dall. Texans vs. Oakland, Nov. 26, 1961 (4-r, 1-p)
Billy Cannon, Houston vs. N.Y. Titans, Dec. 10, 1961 (3-r, 2-p)
Cookie Gilchrist, Buffalo vs. N.Y. Jets, Dec. 8, 1963 (5-r)
Paul Hornung, Green Bay vs. Baltimore, Dec. 12, 1965 (3-r, 2-p)
Kellen Winslow, San Diego vs. Oakland, Nov. 22, 1981 (5-p)
Jerry Rice, San Francisco vs. Atlanta, Oct. 14, 1990 (5-p)
James Stewart, Jacksonville vs. Pittsburgh, Oct. 12, 1997 (5-r)
4 By many players. Last time: Corey Dillon, Cincinnati vs. Tennessee, Dec. 4, 1997 (4-r)

Most Consecutive Games Scoring Touchdowns

18 Lenny Moore, Baltimore, 1963-65
14 O.J. Simpson, Buffalo, 1975
13 John Riggins, Washington, 1982-83
George Rogers, Washington, 1985-86
Jerry Rice, San Francisco, 1986-87

POINTS AFTER TOUCHDOWN

Most Seasons Leading League

8 George Blanda, Chi. Bears, 1956; Houston, 1961-62; Oakland, 1967-69, 1972, 1974
4 Bob Waterfield, Cleveland, 1945; Los Angeles, 1946, 1950, 1952
3 Earl (Dutch) Clark, Portsmouth, 1932; Detroit, 1935-36
Jack Manders, Chi. Bears, 1933-35
Don Hutson, Green Bay, 1941-42, 1945

Most (Kicking) Points After Touchdown Attempted, Career

959 George Blanda, Chi. Bears, 1949, 1950-58; Baltimore, 1950; Houston, 1960-66; Oakland, 1967-75
657 Lou Groza, Cleveland, 1950-59, 1961-67
620 Norm Johnson, Seattle, 1982-90; Atlanta, 1991-94; Pittsburgh, 1995-98

Most (Kicking) Points After Touchdown Attempted, Season

70 Uwe von Schamann, Miami, 1984
65 George Blanda, Houston, 1961

63 Mark Moseley, Washington, 1983

Most (Kicking) Points After Touchdown Attempted, Game

10 Charlie Gogolak, Washington vs. N.Y. Giants, Nov. 27, 1966
9 Pat Harder, Chi. Cardinals vs. N.Y. Giants, Oct. 17, 1948; vs. N.Y. Bulldogs, Nov. 13, 1949
Bob Waterfield, Los Angeles vs. Baltimore, Oct. 22, 1950
Bob Thomas, Chicago vs. Green Bay, Dec. 7, 1980
8 By many players

Most (One-Point) Points After Touchdown, Career

943 George Blanda, Chi. Bears, 1949, 1950-58; Baltimore, 1950; Houston, 1960-66; Oakland, 1967-75
641 Lou Groza, Cleveland, 1950-59, 1961-67
613 Norm Johnson, Seattle, 1982-90; Atlanta, 1991-94; Pittsburgh, 1995-98

Most (One-Point) Points After Touchdown, Season

66 Uwe von Schamann, Miami, 1984
64 George Blanda, Houston, 1961
62 Mark Moseley, Washington, 1983

Most (One-Point) Points After Touchdown, Game

9 Pat Harder, Chi. Cardinals vs. N.Y. Giants, Oct. 17, 1948
Bob Waterfield, Los Angeles vs. Baltimore, Oct. 22, 1950
Charlie Gogolak, Washington vs. N.Y. Giants, Nov. 27, 1966
8 By many players

Most Consecutive (Kicking) Points After Touchdown

276 Norm Johnson, Atlanta, 1991-94; Pittsburgh, 1995-98 (current)
250 Eddie Murray, Detroit, 1988-91; Kansas City, 1992; Tampa Bay, 1992; Dallas, 1993; Philadelphia, 1994; Washington, 1995; Minnesota, 1997
235 Jason Elam, Denver, 1993-98 (current)

Highest (Kicking) Points After Touchdown Percentage, Career (200 points after touchdown)

99.62 Jason Elam, Denver, 1993-98 (260-259)
99.43 Tommy Davis, San Francisco, 1959-69 (350-348)
99.15 Gary Anderson, Pittsburgh, 1982-94; Philadelphia, 1995-96; San Francisco, 1997; Minnesota, 1998 (590-585)

Most (Kicking) Points After Touchdown, No Misses, Season

59 Gary Anderson, Minnesota, 1998
58 Jason Elam, Denver, 1998
56 Danny Villanueva, Dallas, 1966
Ray Wersching, San Francisco, 1984
Chip Lohmiller, Washington, 1991

Most (Kicking) Points After Touchdown, No Misses, Game

9 Pat Harder, Chi. Cardinals vs. N.Y. Giants, Oct. 17, 1948
Bob Waterfield, Los Angeles vs. Baltimore, Oct. 22, 1950
8 By many players

Most Two-Point Conversions, Career

6 Terance Mathis, Atlanta, 1994-98
5 Cris Carter, Minnesota, 1994-98
Rob Moore, N.Y. Jets, 1994; Arizona, 1995-98
4 Gino Cappelletti, Boston, 1960-69
Jerry Rice, San Francisco, 1994-98
Lamar Smith, Seattle, 1994-97; New Orleans, 1998
Floyd Turner, Indianapolis, 1994-95; Baltimore, 1996, 1998

Most Two-Point Conversions, Season

3 Gino Cappelletti, Boston, 1960
Richie Lucas, Buffalo, 1961
Ronnie Harmon, San Diego, 1994
Haywood Jeffires, Houston, 1994
Tom Tupa, Cleveland, 1994
Terance Mathis, Atlanta, 1995
Lamar Smith, Seattle, 1996
Cris Carter, Minnesota, 1997
Terrell Davis, Denver, 1997
2 By many players

Most Two-Point Conversions, Game

2 Brett Perriman, Detroit vs. Green Bay, Nov. 6, 1994
Michael Jackson, Baltimore vs. New England, Oct. 6, 1996
Terrell Davis, Denver vs. Atlanta, Sept. 28, 1997
Charles Johnson, Pittsburgh vs. Tennessee, Nov. 1, 1998

FIELD GOALS

Most Seasons Leading League

5 Lou Groza, Cleveland, 1950, 1952-54, 1957
4 Jack Manders, Chi. Bears, 1933-34, 1936-37
Ward Cuff, N.Y. Giants, 1938-39, 1943; Green Bay, 1947
Mark Moseley, Washington, 1976-77, 1979, 1982
3 Bob Waterfield, Los Angeles, 1947, 1949, 1951
Gino Cappelletti, Boston, 1961, 1963-64
Fred Cox, Minnesota, 1965, 1969-70
Jan Stenerud, Kansas City, 1967, 1970, 1975

Most Consecutive Seasons Leading League

3 Lou Groza, Cleveland, 1952-54
2 Jack Manders, Chi. Bears, 1933-34
Armand Niccolai, Pittsburgh, 1935-36
Jack Manders, Chi. Bears, 1936-37
Ward Cuff, N.Y. Giants, 1938-39
Clark Hinkle, Green Bay, 1940-41
Cliff Patton, Philadelphia, 1948-49
Gino Cappelletti, Boston, 1963-64
Jim Turner, N.Y. Jets, 1968-69
Fred Cox, Minnesota, 1969-70
Mark Moseley, Washington, 1976-77
Chip Lohmiller, Washington, 1991-92
Pete Stoyanovich, Miami, 1991-92

Most Field Goals Attempted, Career

637 George Blanda, Chi. Bears, 1949, 1950-58; Baltimore, 1950; Houston, 1960-66; Oakland, 1967-75
558 Jan Stenerud, Kansas City, 1967-79; Green Bay, 1980-83; Minnesota, 1984-85
525 Gary Anderson, Pittsburgh, 1982-94; Philadelphia, 1995-96; San Francisco, 1997; Minnesota, 1998

Most Field Goals Attempted, Season

49 Bruce Gossett, Los Angeles, 1966
Curt Knight, Washington, 1971
48 Chester Marcol, Green Bay, 1972
47 Jim Turner, N.Y. Jets, 1969
David Ray, Los Angeles, 1973
Mark Moseley, Washington, 1983

Most Field Goals Attempted, Game

9 Jim Bakken, St. Louis vs. Pittsburgh, Sept. 24, 1967
8 Lou Michaels, Pittsburgh vs. St. Louis, Dec. 2, 1962
Garo Yepremian, Detroit vs. Minnesota, Nov. 13, 1966
Jim Turner, N.Y. Jets vs. Buffalo, Nov. 3, 1968
7 By many players

Most Field Goals, Career

420 Gary Anderson, Pittsburgh, 1982-94; Philadelphia, 1995-96; San Francisco, 1997; Minnesota, 1998
401 Morten Andersen, New Orleans, 1982-94; Atlanta, 1995-98
383 Nick Lowery, New England, 1978; Kansas City, 1980-93; N.Y. Jets, 1994-96

Most Field Goals, Season

37 John Kasay, Carolina, 1996
36 Cary Blanchard, Indianapolis, 1996
Al Del Greco, Tennessee, 1998
35 Ali Haji-Sheikh, N.Y. Giants, 1983
Jeff Jaeger, L.A. Raiders, 1993
Gary Anderson, Minnesota, 1998

Most Field Goals, Rookie, Season

35 Ali Haji-Sheikh, N.Y. Giants, 1983
34 Richie Cunningham, Dallas, 1997
33 Chester Marcol, Green Bay, 1972

Most Field Goals, Game

7 Jim Bakken, St. Louis vs. Pittsburgh, Sept. 24, 1967
Rich Karlis, Minnesota vs. L.A. Rams, Nov. 5, 1989 (OT)
Chris Boniol, Dallas vs. Green Bay, Nov. 18, 1996
6 Gino Cappelletti, Boston vs. Denver, Oct. 4, 1964
Garo Yepremian, Detroit vs. Minnesota, Nov. 13, 1966
Jim Turner, N.Y. Jets vs. Buffalo, Nov. 3, 1968
Tom Dempsey, Philadelphia vs. Houston, Nov. 12, 1972
Bobby Howfield, N.Y. Jets vs. New Orleans, Dec. 3, 1972
Jim Bakken, St. Louis vs. Atlanta, Dec. 9, 1973
Joe Danelo, N.Y. Giants vs. Seattle, Oct. 18, 1981
Ray Wersching, San Francisco vs. New Orleans, Oct. 16, 1983
Gary Anderson, Pittsburgh vs. Denver, Oct. 23, 1988
John Carney, San Diego vs. Seattle, Sept. 5, 1993
John Carney, San Diego vs. Houston, Sept. 19, 1993
Doug Pelfrey, Cincinnati vs. Seattle, Nov. 6, 1994 (OT)
Norm Johnson, Atlanta vs. New Orleans, Nov. 13, 1994
Jeff Wilkins, San Francisco vs. Atlanta, Sept. 29, 1996
Steve Christie, Buffalo vs. N.Y. Jets, Oct. 20, 1996
Greg Davis, San Diego vs. Oakland, Oct. 5, 1997
Gary Anderson, Minnesota vs. Baltimore, Dec. 13, 1998
5 By many players

Most Field Goals, One Quarter

4 Garo Yepremian, Detroit vs. Minnesota, Nov. 13, 1966 (second quarter)
Curt Knight, Washington vs. N.Y. Giants, Nov. 15, 1970 (second quarter)
Roger Ruzek, Dallas vs. N.Y. Giants, Nov. 2, 1987 (fourth quarter)
Cary Blanchard, Indianapolis vs. Buffalo, Sept. 21 1997 (second quarter)
3 By many players

Most Consecutive Games Scoring Field Goals

31 Fred Cox, Minnesota, 1968-70
28 Jim Turner, N.Y. Jets, 1970; Denver, 1971-72
Chip Lohmiller, Washington, 1988-90
23 Morten Andersen, New Orleans, 1986-88

ALL-TIME RECORDS

Most Consecutive Field Goals
40 Gary Anderson, San Francisco, 1997; Minnesota, 1998 (current)
31 Fuad Reveiz, Minnesota, 1994-95
29 John Carney, San Diego, 1992-93

Longest Field Goal
63 Tom Dempsey, New Orleans vs. Detroit, Nov. 8, 1970
Jason Elam, Denver vs. Jacksonville, Oct. 25, 1998
60 Steve Cox, Cleveland vs. Cincinnati, Oct. 21, 1984
Morten Andersen, New Orleans vs. Chicago, Oct. 27, 1991
59 Tony Franklin, Philadelphia vs. Dallas, Nov. 12, 1979
Pete Stoyanovich, Miami vs. N.Y. Jets, Nov. 12, 1989
Steve Christie, Buffalo vs. Miami, Sept. 26, 1993
Morten Andersen, Atlanta vs. San Francisco, Dec. 24, 1995

Highest Field Goal Percentage, Career (100 field goals)
81.60 Mike Hollis, Jacksonville, 1995-98 (125-102)
81.06 John Carney, Tampa Bay, 1988-89; L.A. Rams, 1990; San Diego, 1990-98 (264-214)
80.69 Chris Boniol, Dallas, 1994-96; Philadelphia, 1997-98 (145-117)

Highest Field Goal Percentage, Season (Qualifiers)
100.00 Tony Zendejas, L.A. Rams, 1991 (17-17)
Gary Anderson, Minnesota, 1998 (35-35)
96.43 Chris Boniol, Dallas, 1995 (28-27)
96.30 Norm Johnson, Atlanta, 1993 (27-26)
Pete Stoyanovich, Kansas City, 1997 (27-26)

Most Field Goals, No Misses, Game
7 Rich Karlis, Minnesota vs. L.A. Rams, Nov. 5, 1989 (OT)
Chris Boniol, Dallas vs. Green Bay, Nov. 18, 1996
6 Gino Cappelletti, Boston vs. Denver, Oct. 4, 1964
Joe Danelo, N.Y. Giants vs. Seattle, Oct. 18, 1981
Ray Wersching, San Francisco vs. New Orleans, Oct. 16, 1983
Gary Anderson, Pittsburgh vs. Denver, Oct. 23, 1988
John Carney, San Diego vs. Seattle, Sept. 5, 1993
John Carney, San Diego vs. Houston, Sept. 19, 1993
Doug Pelfrey, Cincinnati vs. Seattle, Nov. 6, 1994 (OT)
Norm Johnson, Atlanta vs. New Orleans, Nov. 13, 1994
Jeff Wilkins, San Francisco vs. Atlanta, Sept. 29, 1996
Greg Davis, San Diego vs. Oakland, Oct. 5, 1997
Gary Anderson, Minnesota vs. Baltimore, Dec. 13, 1998
5 By many players

Most Field Goals, 50 or More Yards, Career
35 Morten Andersen, New Orleans, 1982-94; Atlanta, 1995-98
22 Nick Lowery, New England, 1978; Kansas City, 1980-93; N.Y. Jets, 1994-96
21 Eddie Murray, Detroit, 1980-91; Kansas City, 1992; Tampa Bay, 1992; Dallas, 1993; Philadelphia, 1994; Washington, 1995; Minnesota, 1997

Most Field Goals, 50 or More Yards, Season
8 Morten Andersen, Atlanta, 1995
6 Dean Biasucci, Indianapolis, 1988
Chris Jacke, Green Bay, 1993
Tony Zendejas, L.A. Rams, 1993
Mike Vanderjagt, Indianapolis, 1998
5 Fred Steinfort, Denver, 1980
Norm Johnson, Seattle, 1986
Kevin Butler, Chicago, 1993
Jason Elam, Denver, 1995
Cary Blanchard, Indianapolis, 1996

Most Field Goals, 50 or More Yards, Game
3 Morten Andersen, Atlanta vs. New Orleans, Dec. 10, 1995
2 By many players. Last time:
Doug Brien, New Orleans vs. Dallas, Dec. 6, 1998

SAFETIES

Most Safeties, Career
4 Ted Hendricks, Baltimore, 1969-73; Green Bay, 1974; Oakland, 1975-81; L.A. Raiders, 1982-83
Doug English, Detroit, 1975-79, 1981-85
3 Bill McPeak, Pittsburgh, 1949-57
Charlie Krueger, San Francisco, 1959-73
Ernie Stautner, Pittsburgh, 1950-63
Jim Katcavage, N.Y. Giants, 1956-68
Roger Brown, Detroit, 1960-66; Los Angeles, 1967-69
Bruce Maher, Detroit, 1960-67; N.Y. Giants, 1968-69
Ron McDole, St. Louis, 1961; Houston, 1962; Buffalo, 1963-70; Washington, 1971-78
Alan Page, Minnesota, 1967-78; Chicago, 1979-81
Lyle Alzado, Denver, 1971-78; Cleveland, 1979-81; L.A. Raiders, 1982-85
Rulon Jones, Denver, 1980-88
Steve McMichael, New England, 1980; Chicago, 1981-93; Green Bay, 1994
Kevin Greene, L.A. Rams, 1985-92; Pittsburgh, 1993-95; Carolina, 1996, 1998; San Francisco, 1997
Burt Grossman, San Diego, 1989-93; Philadelphia, 1994
Eric Swann, Phoenix, 1991-93; Arizona, 1994-98
Dan Saleaumua, Detroit, 1987-88; Kansas City, 1989-96; Seattle, 1997-98
Derrick Thomas, Kansas City, 1989-98
2 By many players

Most Safeties, Season
2 Tom Nash, Green Bay, 1932
Roger Brown, Detroit, 1962
Ron McDole, Buffalo, 1964
Alan Page, Minnesota, 1971
Fred Dryer, Los Angeles, 1973
Benny Barnes, Dallas, 1973
James Young, Houston, 1977
Doug English, Detroit, 1983
Don Blackmon, New England, 1985
Tim Harris, Green Bay, 1988
Brian Jordan, Atlanta, 1991
Burt Grossman, San Diego, 1992
Rod Stephens, Seattle, 1993
Bryant Young, San Francisco, 1996

Most Safeties, Game
2 Fred Dryer, Los Angeles vs. Green Bay, Oct. 21, 1973

RUSHING

Most Seasons Leading League
8 Jim Brown, Cleveland, 1957-61, 1963-65
4 Steve Van Buren, Philadelphia, 1945, 1947-49
O.J. Simpson, Buffalo, 1972-73, 1975-76
Eric Dickerson, L.A. Rams, 1983-84, 1986; Indianapolis, 1988
Emmitt Smith, Dallas, 1991-93, 1995
Barry Sanders, Detroit, 1990, 1994, 1996-97
3 Earl Campbell, Houston, 1978-80

Most Consecutive Seasons Leading League
5 Jim Brown, Cleveland, 1957-61
3 Steve Van Buren, Philadelphia, 1947-49
Jim Brown, Cleveland, 1963-65
Earl Campbell, Houston, 1978-80
Emmitt Smith, Dallas, 1991-93
2 Bill Paschal, N.Y. Giants, 1943-44
Joe Perry, San Francisco, 1953-54
Jim Nance, Boston, 1966-67
Leroy Kelly, Cleveland, 1967-68
O.J. Simpson, Buffalo, 1972-73; 1975-76
Eric Dickerson, L.A. Rams, 1983-84
Barry Sanders, Detroit, 1996-97

ATTEMPTS

Most Seasons Leading League
6 Jim Brown, Cleveland, 1958-59, 1961, 1963-65
4 Steve Van Buren, Philadelphia, 1947-50
Walter Payton, Chicago, 1976-79
3 Cookie Gilchrist, Buffalo, 1963-64; Denver, 1965
Jim Nance, Boston, 1966-67, 1969
O.J. Simpson, Buffalo, 1973-75
Eric Dickerson, L.A. Rams, 1983, 1986; Indianapolis, 1988
Emmitt Smith, Dallas, 1991, 1994-95

Most Consecutive Seasons Leading League
4 Steve Van Buren, Philadelphia, 1947-50
Walter Payton, Chicago, 1976-79
3 Jim Brown, Cleveland, 1963-65
Cookie Gilchrist, Buffalo, 1963-64; Denver, 1965
O.J. Simpson, Buffalo, 1973-75
2 By many players

Most Attempts, Career
3,838 Walter Payton, Chicago, 1975-87
3,062 Barry Sanders, Detroit, 1989-98
3,022 Marcus Allen, L.A. Raiders, 1982-92; Kansas City, 1993-97

Most Attempts, Season
410 Jamal Anderson, Atlanta, 1998
407 James Wilder, Tampa Bay, 1984
404 Eric Dickerson, L.A. Rams, 1986

Most Attempts, Rookie, Season
390 Eric Dickerson, L.A. Rams, 1983
378 George Rogers, New Orleans, 1981
368 Curtis Martin, New England, 1995

Most Attempts, Game
45 Jamie Morris, Washington vs. Cincinnati, Dec. 17, 1988 (OT)
43 Butch Woolfolk, N.Y. Giants vs. Philadelphia, Nov. 20, 1983
James Wilder, Tampa Bay vs. Green Bay, Sept. 30, 1984 (OT)
42 James Wilder, Tampa Bay vs. Pittsburgh, Oct. 30, 1983
Terrell Davis, Denver vs. Buffalo, Oct. 26, 1997 (OT)

YARDS GAINED

Most Yards Gained, Career
16,726 Walter Payton, Chicago, 1975-87
15,269 Barry Sanders, Detroit, 1989-98
13,259 Eric Dickerson, L.A. Rams, 1983-87; Indianapolis, 1987-91; L.A. Raiders, 1992; Atlanta, 1993

Most Seasons, 1,000 or More Yards Rushing
10 Walter Payton, Chicago, 1976-81, 1983-86
Barry Sanders, Detroit, 1989-98
8 Franco Harris, Pittsburgh, 1972, 1974-79, 1983
Tony Dorsett, Dallas, 1977-81, 1983-85
Thurman Thomas, Buffalo, 1989-96
Emmitt Smith, Dallas, 1991-98
7 Jim Brown, Cleveland, 1958-61, 1963-65
Eric Dickerson, L.A. Rams, 1983-86; L.A. Rams-Indianapolis, 1987; Indianapolis, 1988-89

Most Consecutive Seasons, 1,000 or More Yards Rushing
10 Barry Sanders, Detroit, 1989-98 (current)
8 Thurman Thomas, Buffalo, 1989-96
Emmitt Smith, Dallas, 1991-98 (current)
7 Eric Dickerson, L.A. Rams, 1983-86; L.A. Rams-Indianapolis, 1987; Indianapolis, 1988-89

Most Yards Gained, Season
2,105 Eric Dickerson, L.A. Rams, 1984
2,053 Barry Sanders, Detroit, 1997
2,008 Terrell Davis, Denver, 1998

Most Yards Gained, Rookie, Season
1,808 Eric Dickerson, L.A. Rams, 1983
1,674 George Rogers, New Orleans, 1981
1,605 Ottis Anderson, St. Louis, 1979

Most Yards Gained, Game
275 Walter Payton, Chicago vs. Minnesota, Nov. 20, 1977
273 O.J. Simpson, Buffalo vs. Detroit, Nov. 25, 1976
250 O.J. Simpson, Buffalo vs. New England, Sept. 16, 1973

Most Games, 200 or More Yards Rushing, Career
6 O.J. Simpson, Buffalo, 1969-77; San Francisco, 1978-79
4 Jim Brown, Cleveland, 1957-65
Earl Campbell, Houston, 1978-84; New Orleans, 1984-85
Barry Sanders, Detroit, 1989-98
3 Eric Dickerson, L.A. Rams, 1983-87; Indianapolis, 1987-91; L.A. Raiders, 1992; Atlanta, 1993
Greg Bell, Buffalo, 1984-87; L.A. Rams, 1987-89; L.A. Raiders, 1990
Terrell Davis, Denver, 1995-98

Most Games, 200 or More Yards Rushing, Season
4 Earl Campbell, Houston, 1980
3 O.J. Simpson, Buffalo, 1973
2 Jim Brown, Cleveland, 1963
O.J. Simpson, Buffalo, 1976
Walter Payton, Chicago, 1977
Eric Dickerson, L.A. Rams, 1984
Greg Bell, L.A. Rams, 1989
Terrell Davis, Denver, 1997
Barry Sanders, Detroit, 1997

Most Consecutive Games, 200 or More Yards Rushing
2 O.J. Simpson, Buffalo, 1973, 1976
Earl Campbell, Houston, 1980

Most Games, 100 or More Yards Rushing, Career
77 Walter Payton, Chicago, 1975-87
76 Barry Sanders, Detroit, 1989-98
64 Eric Dickerson, L.A. Rams, 1983-87; Indianapolis, 1987-91; L.A. Raiders, 1992; Atlanta, 1993

Most Games, 100 or More Yards Rushing, Season
14 Barry Sanders, Detroit, 1997
12 Eric Dickerson, L.A. Rams, 1984
Barry Foster, Pittsburgh, 1992
Jamal Anderson, Atlanta, 1998
11 O.J. Simpson, Buffalo, 1973
Earl Campbell, Houston, 1979
Marcus Allen, L.A. Raiders, 1985
Eric Dickerson, L.A. Rams, 1986
Emmitt Smith, Dallas, 1995
Terrell Davis, Denver, 1998

Most Consecutive Games, 100 or More Yards Rushing
14 Barry Sanders, Detroit, 1997
11 Marcus Allen, L.A. Raiders, 1985-86
9 Walter Payton, Chicago, 1985

Longest Run From Scrimmage
99 Tony Dorsett, Dallas vs. Minnesota, Jan. 3, 1983 (TD)
97 Andy Uram, Green Bay vs. Chi. Cardinals, Oct. 8, 1939 (TD)
Bob Gage, Pittsburgh vs. Chi. Bears, Dec. 4, 1949 (TD)
96 Jim Spavital, Baltimore vs. Green Bay, Nov. 5, 1950 (TD)
Bob Hoernschemeyer, Detroit vs. N.Y. Yanks, Nov. 23, 1950 (TD)
Garrison Hearst, San Francisco vs. N.Y. Jets, Sept. 6, 1998 (TD)

AVERAGE GAIN

Highest Average Gain, Career (750 attempts)
5.22 Jim Brown, Cleveland, 1957-65 (2,359-12,312)
5.14 Eugene (Mercury) Morris, Miami, 1969-75; San Diego, 1976 (804-4,133)
5.00 Gale Sayers, Chicago, 1965-71 (991-4,956)

Highest Average Gain, Season (Qualifiers)
8.44 Beattie Feathers, Chi. Bears, 1934 (119-1,004)
7.98 Randall Cunningham, Philadelphia 1990 (118-942)
6.87 Bobby Douglass, Chicago, 1972 (141-968)

Highest Average Gain, Game (10 attempts)
17.09 Marion Motley, Cleveland vs. Pittsburgh, Oct. 29, 1950 (11-188)
16.70 Bill Grimes, Green Bay vs. N.Y. Yanks, Oct. 8, 1950 (10-167)
16.57 Bobby Mitchell, Cleveland vs. Washington, Nov. 15, 1959 (14-232)

TOUCHDOWNS

Most Seasons Leading League
5 Jim Brown, Cleveland, 1957-59, 1963, 1965
4 Steve Van Buren, Philadelphia, 1945, 1947-49
3 Abner Haynes, Dall. Texans, 1960-62
Cookie Gilchrist, Buffalo, 1962-64
Paul Lowe, L.A. Chargers, 1960; San Diego, 1961, 1965
Leroy Kelly, Cleveland, 1966-68
Emmitt Smith, Dallas, 1992, 1994-95

Most Consecutive Seasons Leading League
3 Steve Van Buren, Philadelphia, 1947-49
Jim Brown, Cleveland, 1957-59
Abner Haynes, Dall. Texans, 1960-62
Cookie Gilchrist, Buffalo, 1962-64
Leroy Kelly, Cleveland, 1966-68

Most Touchdowns, Career
125 Emmitt Smith, Dallas, 1990-98
123 Marcus Allen, L.A. Raiders, 1982-92; Kansas City, 1993-97
110 Walter Payton, Chicago, 1975-87

Most Touchdowns, Season
25 Emmitt Smith, Dallas, 1995
24 John Riggins, Washington, 1983
21 Joe Morris, N.Y. Giants, 1985
Emmitt Smith, Dallas, 1994
Terry Allen, Washington, 1996
Terrell Davis, Denver, 1998

Most Touchdowns, Rookie, Season
18 Eric Dickerson, L.A. Rams, 1983
15 Ickey Woods, Cincinnati, 1988
14 Gale Sayers, Chicago, 1965
Barry Sanders, Detroit, 1989
Curtis Martin, New England, 1995
Fred Taylor, Jacksonville, 1998

Most Touchdowns, Game
6 Ernie Nevers, Chi. Cardinals vs. Chi. Bears, Nov. 28, 1929
5 Jim Brown, Cleveland vs. Baltimore, Nov. 1, 1959
Cookie Gilchrist, Buffalo vs. N.Y. Jets, Dec. 8, 1963
James Stewart, Jacksonville vs. Philadelphia, Oct. 12, 1997
4 By many players

Most Consecutive Games Rushing for Touchdowns
13 John Riggins, Washington, 1982-83
George Rogers, Washington, 1985-86
11 Lenny Moore, Baltimore, 1963-64
Emmitt Smith, Dallas, 1994-95
Emmitt Smith, Dallas, 1995
10 Greg Bell, L.A. Rams, 1988-89
Terry Allen, Washington, 1995-96

PASSING

Most Seasons Leading League
6 Sammy Baugh, Washington, 1937, 1940, 1943, 1945, 1947, 1949
Steve Young San Francisco, 1991-94, 1996-97
4 Len Dawson, Dall. Texans; 1962; Kansas City, 1964, 1966, 1968
Roger Staubach, Dallas, 1971, 1973, 1978-79
Ken Anderson, Cincinnati, 1974-75, 1981-82
3 Arnie Herber, Green Bay, 1932, 1934, 1936
Norm Van Brocklin, Los Angeles, 1950, 1952, 1954
Bart Starr, Green Bay, 1962, 1964, 1966

Most Consecutive Seasons Leading League
4 Steve Young, San Francisco, 1991-94
2 Cecil Isbell, Green Bay, 1941-42
Milt Plum, Cleveland, 1960-61
Ken Anderson, Cincinnati, 1974-75, 1981-82
Roger Staubach, Dallas, 1978-79
Steve Young, San Francisco, 1996-97

ALL-TIME RECORDS

PASS RATING

Highest Passer Rating, Career (1,500 attempts)
97.6 Steve Young, Tampa Bay, 1985-86; San Francisco, 1987-98
92.3 Joe Montana, San Francisco, 1979-90, 1992; Kansas City, 1993-94
89.0 Brett Favre, Atlanta, 1991; Green Bay, 1992-98

Highest Passer Rating, Season (Qualifiers)
112.8 Steve Young, San Francisco, 1994
112.4 Joe Montana, San Francisco, 1989
110.4 Milt Plum, Cleveland, 1960

Highest Passer Rating, Rookie, Season (Qualifiers)
96.0 Dan Marino, Miami, 1983
88.2 Greg Cook, Cincinnati, 1969
84.0 Charlie Conerly, N.Y. Giants, 1948

ATTEMPTS

Most Seasons Leading League
5 Dan Marino, Miami, 1984, 1986, 1988, 1992, 1997
4 Sammy Baugh, Washington, 1937, 1943, 1947-48
Johnny Unitas, Baltimore, 1957, 1959-61
George Blanda, Chi. Bears, 1953; Houston, 1963-65
3 Arnie Herber, Green Bay, 1932, 1934, 1936
Sonny Jurgensen, Washington, 1966-67, 1969
Drew Bledsoe, New England, 1994-96

Most Consecutive Seasons Leading League
3 Johnny Unitas, Baltimore, 1959-61
George Blanda, Houston, 1963-65
Drew Bledsoe, New England, 1994-96
2 By many players

Most Passes Attempted, Career
7,989 Dan Marino, Miami, 1983-98
7,250 John Elway, Denver, 1983-98
6,786 Warren Moon, Houston, 1984-93; Minnesota, 1994-96; Seattle, 1997-98

Most Passes Attempted, Season
691 Drew Bledsoe, New England, 1994
655 Warren Moon, Houston, 1991
636 Drew Bledsoe, New England, 1995

Most Passes Attempted, Rookie, Season
575 Peyton Manning, Indianapolis, 1998
486 Rick Mirer, Seattle, 1993
439 Jim Zorn, Seattle, 1976

Most Passes Attempted, Game
70 Drew Bledsoe, New England vs. Minnesota, Nov. 13, 1994 (OT)
68 George Blanda, Houston vs. Buffalo, Nov. 1, 1964
66 Chris Miller, Atlanta vs. Detroit, Dec. 24, 1989

COMPLETIONS

Most Seasons Leading League
6 Dan Marino, Miami, 1984-86, 1988, 1992, 1997
5 Sammy Baugh, Washington, 1937, 1943, 1945, 1947-48
4 George Blanda, Chi. Bears, 1953; Houston, 1963-65
Sonny Jurgensen, Philadelphia, 1961; Washington, 1966-67, 1969

Most Consecutive Seasons Leading League
3 George Blanda, Houston, 1963-65
Dan Marino, Miami, 1984-86
2 By many players

Most Passes Completed, Career
4,763 Dan Marino, Miami, 1983-98
4,123 John Elway, Denver, 1983-98
3,972 Warren Moon, Houston, 1984-93; Minnesota, 1994-96; Seattle, 1997-98

Most Passes Completed, Season
404 Warren Moon, Houston, 1991
400 Drew Bledsoe, New England, 1994
385 Dan Marino, Miami, 1994

Most Passes Completed, Rookie, Season
326 Peyton Manning, Indianapolis, 1998
274 Rick Mirer, Seattle, 1993
214 Drew Bledsoe, New England, 1993
Kerry Collins, Carolina, 1995

Most Passes Completed, Game
45 Drew Bledsoe, New England vs. Minnesota, Nov. 13, 1994 (OT)
42 Richard Todd, N.Y. Jets vs. San Francisco, Sept. 21, 1980
Vinny Testaverde, N.Y. Jets vs. Seattle, Dec. 6, 1998
41 Warren Moon, Houston vs. Dallas, Nov. 10, 1991 (OT)

Most Consecutive Passes Completed
22 Joe Montana, San Francisco vs. Cleveland (5), Nov. 29, 1987; vs. Green Bay (17), Dec. 6, 1987
20 Ken Anderson, Cincinnati vs. Houston, Jan. 2, 1983
Hugh Millen, Denver vs. L.A. Raiders (7), Dec. 11, 1994; vs. San Francisco (13), Dec. 17, 1994
Steve Young, San Francisco vs. Washington, Nov. 24, 1996
18 Steve DeBerg, Denver vs. L.A. Rams (17), Dec. 12, 1982; vs. Kansas City (1), Dec. 19, 1982
Lynn Dickey, Green Bay vs. Houston, Sept. 4, 1983
Joe Montana, San Francisco vs. L.A. Rams (13), Oct. 28, 1984; vs. Cincinnati (5), Nov. 4, 1984
Don Majkowski, Green Bay vs. New Orleans, Sept. 18, 1989
Boomer Esiason, N.Y. Jets vs. Miami (5), Sept. 12, 1993; vs. New England (13), Sept. 26, 1993

COMPLETION PERCENTAGE

Most Seasons Leading League
8 Len Dawson, Dall. Texans, 1962; Kansas City, 1964-69, 1975
7 Sammy Baugh, Washington, 1940, 1942-43, 1945, 1947-49
5 Joe Montana, San Francisco, 1980-81, 1985, 1987, 1989
Steve Young, San Francisco, 1992, 1994-97

Most Consecutive Seasons Leading League
6 Len Dawson, Kansas City, 1964-69
4 Steve Young, San Francisco, 1994-97
3 Sammy Baugh, Washington, 1947-49
Otto Graham, Cleveland, 1953-55
Milt Plum, Cleveland, 1959-61

Highest Completion Percentage, Career (1,500 attempts)
64.50 Steve Young, Tampa Bay, 1985-86; San Francisco, 1987-98 (4,065-2,622)
63.24 Joe Montana, San Francisco, 1979-90, 1992; Kansas City, 1993-94 (5,391-3,409)
61.81 Troy Aikman, Dallas, 1989-98 (4,011-2,479)

Highest Completion Percentage, Season (Qualifiers)
70.55 Ken Anderson, Cincinnati, 1982 (309-218)
70.33 Sammy Baugh, Washington, 1945 (182-128)
70.28 Steve Young, San Francisco, 1994 (461-324)

Highest Completion Percentage, Rookie, Season (Qualifiers)
58.45 Dan Marino, Miami, 1983 (296-173)
57.14 Jim McMahon, Chicago, 1982 (210-120)
57.10 Charlie Batch, Detroit, 1998 (303-173)

Highest Completion Percentage, Game (20 attempts)
91.30 Vinny Testaverde, Cleveland vs. L.A. Rams, Dec. 26, 1993 (23-21)
90.91 Ken Anderson, Cincinnati vs. Pittsburgh, Nov. 10, 1974 (22-20)
90.48 Lynn Dickey, Green Bay vs. New Orleans, Dec. 13, 1981 (21-19)

YARDS GAINED

Most Seasons Leading League
5 Sonny Jurgensen, Philadelphia, 1961-62; Washington, 1966-67, 1969
Dan Marino, Miami, 1984-86, 1988, 1992
4 Sammy Baugh, Washington, 1937, 1940, 1947-48
Johnny Unitas, Baltimore, 1957, 1959-60, 1963
Dan Fouts, San Diego, 1979-82
3 Arnie Herber, Green Bay, 1932, 1934, 1936
Sid Luckman, Chi. Bears, 1943, 1945-46
John Brodie, San Francisco, 1965, 1968, 1970
John Hadl, San Diego, 1965, 1968, 1971
Joe Namath, N.Y. Jets, 1966-67, 1972

Most Consecutive Seasons Leading League
4 Dan Fouts, San Diego, 1979-82
3 Dan Marino, Miami, 1984-86
2 By many players

Most Yards Gained, Career
58,913 Dan Marino, Miami, 1983-98
51,475 John Elway, Denver, 1983-98
49,097 Warren Moon, Houston, 1984-93; Minnesota, 1994-96; Seattle, 1997-98

Most Seasons, 3,000 or More Yards Passing
13 Dan Marino, Miami, 1984-92, 1994-95, 1997-98
12 John Elway, Denver, 1985-91, 1993-97
9 Warren Moon, Houston, 1984, 1986, 1989-91, 1993; Minnesota, 1994-95; Seattle, 1997

Most Yards Gained, Season
5,084 Dan Marino, Miami, 1984
4,802 Dan Fouts, San Diego, 1981
4,746 Dan Marino, Miami, 1986

Most Yards Gained, Rookie, Season
3,739 Peyton Manning, Indianapolis, 1998
2,833 Rick Mirer, Seattle, 1993
2,717 Kerry Collins, Carolina, 1995

Most Yards Gained, Game
554 Norm Van Brocklin, Los Angeles vs. N.Y. Yanks, Sept. 28, 1951
527 Warren Moon, Houston vs. Kansas City, Dec. 16, 1990
522 Boomer Esiason, Arizona vs. Washington, Nov. 10, 1996

Most Games, 400 or More Yards Passing, Career
13 Dan Marino, Miami, 1983-98
7 Joe Montana, San Francisco, 1979-90, 1992; Kansas City, 1993-94
Warren Moon, Houston, 1984-93; Minnesota, 1994-96; Seattle, 1997-98
6 Dan Fouts, San Diego, 1973-87

Most Games, 400 or More Yards Passing, Season
4 Dan Marino, Miami, 1984
3 Dan Marino, Miami, 1986
2 By many players

Most Consecutive Games, 400 or More Yards Passing
2 Dan Fouts, San Diego, 1982
Dan Marino, Miami, 1984
Phil Simms, N.Y. Giants, 1985

Most Games, 300 or More Yards Passing, Career
60 Dan Marino, Miami, 1983-98
51 Dan Fouts, San Diego, 1973-87
49 Warren Moon, Houston, 1984-93; Minnesota, 1994-96; Seattle, 1997-98

Most Games, 300 or More Yards Passing, Season
9 Dan Marino, Miami, 1984
Warren Moon, Houston, 1990
8 Dan Fouts, San Diego, 1980
7 Dan Fouts, San Diego, 1981
Bill Kenney, Kansas City, 1983
Neil Lomax, St. Louis, 1984
Dan Fouts, San Diego, 1985
Brett Favre, Green Bay, 1995
Steve Young, San Francisco, 1998

Most Consecutive Games, 300 or More Yards Passing
6 Steve Young, San Francisco, 1998
5 Joe Montana, San Francisco, 1982
4 Dan Fouts, San Diego, 1979
Dan Fouts, San Diego, 1980-81
Bill Kenney, Kansas City, 1983
Joe Montana, San Francisco, 1985-86
Joe Montana, San Francisco, 1990
Warren Moon, Houston, 1990
Drew Bledsoe, New England, 1993-94

Longest Pass Completion (All TDs except as noted)
99 Frank Filchock (to Farkas), Washington vs. Pittsburgh, Oct. 15, 1939
George Izo (to Mitchell), Washington vs. Cleveland, Sept. 15, 1963
Karl Sweetan (to Studstill), Detroit vs. Baltimore, Oct. 16, 1966
Sonny Jurgensen (to Allen), Washington vs. Chicago, Sept. 15, 1968
Jim Plunkett (to Branch), L.A. Raiders vs. Washington, Oct. 2, 1983
Ron Jaworski (to Quick), Philadelphia vs. Atlanta, Nov. 10, 1985
Stan Humphries (to Martin), San Diego vs. Seattle, Sept. 18, 1994
Brett Favre (to Brooks), Green Bay vs. Chicago, Sept. 11, 1995
98 Doug Russell (to Tinsley), Chi. Cardinals vs. Cleveland, Nov. 27, 1938
Ogden Compton (to Lane), Chi. Cardinals vs. Green Bay, Nov. 13, 1955
Bill Wade (to Farrington), Chicago Bears vs. Detroit, Oct. 8, 1961
Jacky Lee (to Dewveall), Houston vs. San Diego, Nov. 25, 1962
Earl Morrall (to Jones), N.Y. Giants vs. Pittsburgh, Sept. 11, 1966
Jim Hart (to Moore), St. Louis vs. Los Angeles, Dec. 10, 1972 (no TD)
Bobby Hebert (to Haynes), Atlanta vs. New Orleans, Sept. 12, 1993
Charlie Batch (to Morton), Detroit vs. Chicago, Oct. 4, 1998
97 Pat Coffee (to Tinsley), Chi. Cardinals vs. Chi. Bears, Dec. 5, 1937
Bobby Layne (to Box), Detroit vs. Green Bay, Nov. 26, 1953
George Shaw (to Tarr), Denver vs. Boston, Sept. 21, 1962
Bernie Kosar (to Slaughter), Cleveland vs. Chicago, Oct. 23, 1989
Steve Young (to Taylor), San Francisco vs. Atlanta, Nov. 3, 1991

AVERAGE GAIN

Most Seasons Leading League
7 Sid Luckman, Chi. Bears, 1939-43, 1946-47
5 Steve Young, San Francisco, 1991-94, 1997
3 Arnie Herber, Green Bay, 1932, 1934, 1936
Norm Van Brocklin, Los Angeles, 1950, 1952, 1954
Len Dawson, Dall. Texans, 1962; Kansas City, 1966, 1968
Bart Starr, Green Bay, 1966-68

Most Consecutive Seasons Leading League
5 Sid Luckman, Chi. Bears, 1939-43
4 Steve Young, San Francisco, 1991-94
3 Bart Starr, Green Bay, 1966-68

Highest Average Gain, Career (1,500 attempts)
8.63 Otto Graham, Cleveland, 1950-55 (1,565-13,499)
8.42 Sid Luckman, Chi. Bears, 1939-50 (1,744-14,686)
8.16 Norm Van Brocklin, Los Angeles, 1949-57; Philadelphia, 1958-60 (2,895-23,611)

Highest Average Gain, Season (Qualifiers)
11.17 Tommy O'Connell, Cleveland, 1957 (110-1,229)
10.86 Sid Luckman, Chi. Bears, 1943 (202-2,194)
10.55 Otto Graham, Cleveland, 1953 (258-2,722)

Highest Average Gain, Rookie, Season (Qualifiers)
9.411 Greg Cook, Cincinnati, 1969 (197-1,854)
9.409 Bob Waterfield, Cleveland, 1945 (171-1,609)
8.36 Zeke Bratkowski, Chi. Bears, 1954 (130-1,087)

Highest Average Gain, Game (20 attempts)
18.58 Sammy Baugh, Washington vs. Boston, Oct. 31, 1948 (24-446)
18.50 Johnny Unitas, Baltimore vs. Atlanta, Nov. 12, 1967 (20-370)
17.71 Joe Namath, N.Y. Jets vs. Baltimore, Sept. 24, 1972 (28-496)

TOUCHDOWNS

Most Seasons Leading League
4 Johnny Unitas, Baltimore, 1957-60
Len Dawson, Dall. Texans, 1962; Kansas City, 1963, 1965-66
Steve Young, San Francisco, 1992-94, 1998
3 Arnie Herber, Green Bay, 1932, 1934, 1936
Sid Luckman, Chi. Bears, 1943, 1945-46
Y.A. Tittle, San Francisco, 1955; N.Y. Giants, 1962-63
Dan Marino, Miami, 1984-86
Brett Favre, Green Bay, 1995-97
2 By many players

Most Consecutive Seasons Leading League
4 Johnny Unitas, Baltimore, 1957-60
3 Dan Marino, Miami, 1984-86
Steve Young, San Francisco, 1992-94
Brett Favre, Green Bay, 1995-97
2 By many players

Most Touchdown Passes, Career
408 Dan Marino, Miami, 1983-98
342 Fran Tarkenton, Minnesota, 1961-66, 1972-78; N.Y. Giants, 1967-71
300 John Elway, Denver, 1983-98

Most Touchdown Passes, Season
48 Dan Marino, Miami, 1984
44 Dan Marino, Miami, 1986
39 Brett Favre, Green Bay, 1996

Most Touchdown Passes, Rookie, Season
26 Peyton Manning, Indianapolis, 1998
22 Charlie Conerly, N.Y. Giants, 1948
20 Dan Marino, Miami, 1983

Most Touchdown Passes, Game
7 Sid Luckman, Chi. Bears vs. N.Y. Giants, Nov. 14, 1943
Adrian Burk, Philadelphia vs. Washington, Oct. 17, 1954
George Blanda, Houston vs. N.Y. Titans, Nov. 19, 1961
Y.A. Tittle, N.Y. Giants vs. Washington, Oct. 28, 1962
Joe Kapp, Minnesota vs. Baltimore, Sept. 28, 1969
6 By many players. Last time:
Mark Rypien, Washington vs. Atlanta, Nov. 10, 1991

Most Games, Four or More Touchdown Passes, Career
21 Dan Marino, Miami, 1983-98
17 Johnny Unitas, Baltimore, 1956-72; San Diego, 1973
13 George Blanda, Chi. Bears, 1949, 1950-58; Baltimore, 1950; Houston, 1960-66; Oakland, 1967-75
Brett Favre, Atlanta, 1991; Green Bay, 1992-98

Most Games, Four or More Touchdown Passes, Season
6 Dan Marino, Miami, 1984
5 Dan Marino, Miami, 1986
Brett Favre, Green Bay, 1996
4 George Blanda, Houston, 1961
Vince Ferragamo, Los Angeles, 1980
Randall Cunningham, Minnesota, 1998

Most Consecutive Games, Four or More Touchdown Passes
4 Dan Marino, Miami, 1984
2 By many players

Most Consecutive Games, Touchdown Passes
47 Johnny Unitas, Baltimore, 1956-60
30 Dan Marino, Miami, 1985-87
28 Dave Krieg, Seattle, 1983-85

HAD INTERCEPTED

Most Consecutive Passes Attempted, None Intercepted
308 Bernie Kosar, Cleveland, 1990-91
294 Bart Starr, Green Bay, 1964-65
279 Jeff George, Indianapolis, 1993; Atlanta, 1994

Most Passes Had Intercepted, Career
277 George Blanda, Chi. Bears, 1949, 1950-58; Baltimore, 1950; Houston, 1960-66; Oakland, 1967-75
268 John Hadl, San Diego, 1962-72; Los Angeles, 1973-74; Green Bay, 1974-75; Houston, 1976-77
266 Fran Tarkenton, Minnesota, 1961-66, 1972-78; N.Y. Giants, 1967-71

Most Passes Had Intercepted, Season
42 George Blanda, Houston, 1962
35 Vinny Testaverde, Tampa Bay, 1988
34 Frank Tripucka, Denver, 1960

Most Passes Had Intercepted, Game
8 Jim Hardy, Chi. Cardinals vs. Philadelphia, Sept. 24, 1950
7 Parker Hall, Cleveland vs. Green Bay, Nov. 8, 1942
Frank Sinkwich, Detroit vs. Green Bay, Oct. 24, 1943
Bob Waterfield, Los Angeles vs. Green Bay, Oct. 17, 1948
Zeke Bratkowski, Chicago vs. Baltimore, Oct. 2, 1960

Tommy Wade, Pittsburgh vs. Philadelphia, Dec. 12, 1965
Ken Stabler, Oakland vs. Denver, Oct. 16, 1977
Steve DeBerg, Tampa Bay vs. San Francisco, Sept. 7, 1986
6 By many players

Most Attempts, No Interceptions, Game
70 Drew Bledsoe, New England vs. Minnesota, Nov. 13, 1994 (OT)
63 Rich Gannon, Minnesota vs. New England, Oct. 20, 1991 (OT)
60 Davey O'Brien, Philadelphia vs. Washington, Dec. 1, 1940

LOWEST PERCENTAGE, PASSES HAD INTERCEPTED

Most Seasons Leading League, Lowest Percentage, Passes Had Intercepted
5 Sammy Baugh, Washington, 1940, 1942, 1944-45, 1947
3 Charlie Conerly, N.Y. Giants, 1950, 1956, 1959
Bart Starr, Green Bay, 1962, 1964, 1966
Roger Staubach, Dallas, 1971, 1977, 1979
Ken Anderson, Cincinnati, 1972, 1981-82
Ken O'Brien, N.Y. Jets, 1985, 1987-88
2 By many players

Lowest Percentage, Passes Had Intercepted, Career (1,500 attempts)
1.99 Neil O'Donnell, Pittsburgh, 1991-95; N.Y. Jets, 1996-97; Cincinnati, 1998 (2,862-57)
2.47 Steve Bono, Minnesota, 1985-86; Pittsburgh, 1987-88; San Francisco, 1989, 1991-93; Kansas City, 1994-96; Green Bay, 1997; St. Louis, 1998 (1,700-42)
2.50 Mark Brunell, Green Bay, 1994; Jacksonville, 1995-98 (1,719-43)

Lowest Percentage, Passes Had Intercepted, Season (Qualifiers)
0.66 Joe Ferguson, Buffalo, 1976 (151-1)
0.90 Steve DeBerg, Kansas City, 1990 (444-4)
1.16 Steve Bartkowski, Atlanta, 1983 (432-5)

Lowest Percentage, Passes Had Intercepted, Rookie, Season (Qualifiers)
1.98 Charlie Batch, Detroit, 1998 (303-6)
2.03 Dan Marino, Miami, 1983 (296-6)
2.10 Gary Wood, N.Y. Giants, 1964 (143-3)

TIMES SACKED

Times Sacked has been compiled since 1963.

Most Times Sacked, Career
516 John Elway, Denver, 1983-98
494 Dave Krieg, Seattle, 1980-91; Kansas City, 1992-93; Detroit, 1994; Arizona, 1995; Chicago, 1996; Tennessee, 1997-98
483 Fran Tarkenton, Minnesota, 1963-66, 1972-78; N.Y. Giants, 1967-71

Most Times Sacked, Season
72 Randall Cunningham, Philadelphia, 1986
62 Ken O'Brien, N.Y. Jets, 1985
61 Neil Lomax, St. Louis, 1985

Most Times Sacked, Game
12 Bert Jones, Baltimore vs. St. Louis, Oct. 26, 1980
Warren Moon, Houston vs. Dallas, Sept. 29, 1985
11 Charley Johnson, St. Louis vs. N.Y. Giants, Nov. 1, 1964
Bart Starr, Green Bay vs. Detroit, Nov. 7, 1965
Jack Kemp, Buffalo vs. Oakland, Oct. 15, 1967
Bob Berry, Atlanta vs. St. Louis, Nov. 24, 1968
Greg Landry, Detroit vs. Dallas, Oct. 6, 1975
Ron Jaworski, Philadelphia vs. St. Louis, Dec. 18, 1983
Paul McDonald, Cleveland vs. Kansas City, Sept. 30, 1984
Archie Manning, Minnesota vs. Chicago, Oct. 28, 1984
Steve Pelluer, Dallas vs. San Diego, Nov. 16, 1986
Randall Cunningham, Philadelphia vs. L.A. Raiders, Nov. 30, 1986 (OT)
David Norrie, N.Y. Jets vs. Dallas, Oct. 4, 1987
Troy Aikman, Dallas vs. Philadelphia, Sept. 15, 1991
Bernie Kosar, Cleveland vs. Indianapolis, Sept. 6, 1992
10 By many players

PASS RECEIVING

Most Seasons Leading League
8 Don Hutson, Green Bay, 1936-37, 1939, 1941-45
5 Lionel Taylor, Denver, 1960-63, 1965
3 Tom Fears, Los Angeles, 1948-50
Pete Pihos, Philadelphia, 1953-55
Billy Wilson, San Francisco, 1954, 1956-57
Raymond Berry, Baltimore, 1958-60
Lance Alworth, San Diego, 1966, 1968-69
Sterling Sharpe, Green Bay, 1989, 1992-93

Most Consecutive Seasons Leading League
5 Don Hutson, Green Bay, 1941-45
4 Lionel Taylor, Denver, 1960-63
3 Tom Fears, Los Angeles, 1948-50
Pete Pihos, Philadelphia, 1953-55
Raymond Berry, Baltimore, 1958-60

Most Pass Receptions, Career
1,139 Jerry Rice, San Francisco, 1985-98
940 Art Monk, Washington, 1980-93; N.Y. Jets, 1994; Philadelphia, 1995
889 Andre Reed, Buffalo, 1985-98

Most Seasons, 50 or More Pass Receptions
12 Jerry Rice, San Francisco, 1986-96, 1998
Andre Reed, Buffalo, 1986-94, 1996-98
10 Steve Largent, Seattle, 1976, 1978-81, 1983-87
Gary Clark, Washington, 1985-92; Phoenix, 1993; Arizona, 1994
Henry Ellard, L.A. Rams, 1985, 1987-91, 1993; Washington, 1994-96
9 Art Monk, Washington, 1980-81, 1984-86, 1988-91
James Lofton, Green Bay, 1979-81, 1983-86; Buffalo, 1991-92

Most Pass Receptions, Season
123 Herman Moore, Detroit, 1995
122 Cris Carter, Minnesota, 1994
Cris Carter, Minnesota, 1995
Jerry Rice, San Francisco, 1995
119 Isaac Bruce, St. Louis, 1995

Most Pass Receptions, Rookie, Season
90 Terry Glenn, New England, 1996
83 Earl Cooper, San Francisco, 1980
81 Keith Jackson, Philadelphia, 1988

Most Pass Receptions, Game
18 Tom Fears, Los Angeles vs. Green Bay, Dec. 3, 1950
17 Clark Gaines, N.Y. Jets vs. San Francisco, Sept. 21, 1980
16 Sonny Randle, St. Louis vs. N.Y. Giants, Nov. 4, 1962
Jerry Rice, San Francisco vs. L.A. Rams, Nov. 20, 1994
Keenan McCardell, Jacksonville vs. St. Louis, Oct. 20, 1996

Most Consecutive Games, Pass Receptions
193 Jerry Rice, San Francisco, 1985-98 (current)
183 Art Monk, Washington, 1980-93; N.Y. Jets, 1994; Philadelphia, 1995
177 Steve Largent, Seattle, 1977-89

YARDS GAINED

Most Seasons Leading League
7 Don Hutson, Green Bay, 1936, 1938-39, 1941-44
6 Jerry Rice, San Francisco, 1986, 1989-90, 1993-95
3 Raymond Berry, Baltimore, 1957, 1959-60
Lance Alworth, San Diego, 1965-66, 1968

Most Consecutive Seasons Leading League
4 Don Hutson, Green Bay, 1941-44
3 Jerry Rice, San Francisco, 1993-95
2 By many players

Most Yards Gained, Career
17,612 Jerry Rice, San Francisco, 1985-98
14,004 James Lofton, Green Bay, 1978-86; L.A. Raiders, 1987-88; Buffalo, 1989-92; L.A. Rams, 1993; Philadelphia, 1993
13,777 Henry Ellard, L.A. Rams, 1983-1993; Washington, 1994-97; New England-Washington, 1998

Most Seasons, 1,000 or More Yards, Pass Receiving
12 Jerry Rice, San Francisco, 1986-96, 1998
8 Steve Largent, Seattle, 1978-81, 1983-86
7 Lance Alworth, San Diego, 1963-69
Henry Ellard, L.A. Rams, 1988-91; Washington 1994-96
Michael Irvin, Dallas, 1991-95, 1997-98

Most Yards Gained, Season
1,848 Jerry Rice, San Francisco, 1995
1,781 Isaac Bruce, St. Louis, 1995
1,746 Charley Hennigan, Houston, 1961

Most Yards Gained, Rookie, Season
1,473 Bill Groman, Houston, 1960
1,313 Randy Moss, Minnesota, 1998
1,231 Bill Howton, Green Bay, 1952

Most Yards Gained, Game
336 Willie Anderson, L.A. Rams vs. New Orleans, Nov. 26, 1989 (OT)
309 Stephone Paige, Kansas City vs. San Diego, Dec. 22, 1985
303 Jim Benton, Cleveland vs. Detroit, Nov. 22, 1945

Most Games, 200 or More Yards Pass Receiving, Career
5 Lance Alworth, San Diego, 1962-70; Dallas, 1971-72
4 Don Hutson, Green Bay, 1935-45
Charley Hennigan, Houston, 1960-66
Jerry Rice, San Francisco, 1985-98
3 Don Maynard, N.Y. Giants, 1958; N.Y. Jets, 1960-72; St. Louis, 1973
Wes Chandler, New Orleans, 1978-81; San Diego, 1981-87; San Francisco, 1988
Isaac Bruce, L.A. Rams, 1994; St. Louis, 1995-98

Most Games, 200 or More Yards Pass Receiving, Season
3 Charley Hennigan, Houston, 1961
2 Don Hutson, Green Bay, 1942
Gene Roberts, N.Y. Giants, 1949
Lance Alworth, San Diego, 1963
Don Maynard, N.Y. Jets, 1968

Most Games, 100 or More Yards Pass Receiving, Career
64 Jerry Rice, San Francisco, 1985-98
50 Don Maynard, N.Y. Giants, 1958; N.Y. Jets, 1960-72; St. Louis, 1973
46 Michael Irvin, Dallas, 1988-98

Most Games, 100 or More Yards Pass Receiving, Season
11 Michael Irvin, Dallas, 1995
10 Charley Hennigan, Houston, 1961
Herman Moore, Detroit, 1995
9 Elroy (Crazylegs) Hirsch, Los Angeles, 1951
Bill Groman, Houston, 1960
Lance Alworth, San Diego, 1965
Don Maynard, N.Y. Jets, 1967
Stanley Morgan, New England, 1986
Mark Carrier, Tampa Bay, 1989
Robert Brooks, Green Bay, 1995
Isaac Bruce, St. Louis, 1995
Jerry Rice, San Francisco, 1995

Most Consecutive Games, 100 or More Yards Pass Receiving
7 Charley Hennigan, Houston, 1961
Bill Groman, Houston, 1961
Michael Irvin, Dallas, 1995
6 Raymond Berry, Baltimore, 1960
Pat Studstill, Detroit, 1966
Isaac Bruce, St. Louis, 1995
5 Elroy (Crazylegs) Hirsch, Los Angeles, 1951
Bob Boyd, Los Angeles, 1954
Terry Barr, Detroit, 1963
Lance Alworth, San Diego, 1966
Don Maynard, N.Y. Jets, 1968-69
Harold Jackson, Philadelphia, 1971-72

Longest Pass Reception (All TDs except as noted)
99 Andy Farkas (from Filchock), Washington vs. Pittsburgh, Oct. 15, 1939
Bobby Mitchell (from Izo), Washington vs. Cleveland, Sept. 15, 1963
Pat Studstill (from Sweetan), Detroit vs. Baltimore, Oct. 16, 1966
Gerry Allen (from Jurgensen), Washington vs. Chicago, Sept. 15, 1968
Cliff Branch (from Plunkett), L.A. Raiders vs. Washington, Oct. 2, 1983
Mike Quick (from Jaworski), Philadelphia vs. Atlanta, Nov. 10, 1985
Tony Martin (from Humphries), San Diego vs. Seattle, Sept. 18, 1994
Robert Brooks (from Favre), Green Bay vs. Chicago, Sept. 11, 1995
98 Gaynell Tinsley (from Russell), Chi. Cardinals vs. Cleveland, Nov. 17, 1938
Dick (Night Train) Lane (from Compton), Chi. Cardinals vs. Green Bay, Nov. 13, 1955
John Farrington (from Wade), Chicago vs. Detroit, Oct. 8, 1961
Willard Dewveall (from Lee), Houston vs. San Diego, Nov. 25, 1962
Homer Jones (from Morrall), N.Y. Giants vs. Pittsburgh, Sept. 11, 1966
Bobby Moore (from Hart), St. Louis vs. Los Angeles, Dec. 10, 1972 (no TD)
Michael Haynes (from Hebert), Atlanta vs. New Orleans, Sept. 12, 1993
Johnnie Morton (from Batch), Detroit vs. Chicago, Oct. 4, 1998
97 Gaynell Tinsley (from Coffee), Chi. Cardinals vs. Chi. Bears, Dec. 5, 1937
Cloyce Box (from Layne), Detroit vs. Green Bay, Nov. 26, 1953
Jerry Tarr (from Shaw), Denver vs. Boston, Sept. 21, 1962
Webster Slaughter (from Kosar), Cleveland vs. Chicago, Oct. 23, 1989
John Taylor (from Young), San Francisco vs. Atlanta, Nov. 3, 1991

AVERAGE GAIN

Highest Average Gain, Career (200 receptions)
22.26 Homer Jones, N.Y. Giants, 1964-69; Cleveland, 1970 (224-4,986)
20.83 Buddy Dial, Pittsburgh, 1959-63; Dallas, 1964-66 (261-5,436)
20.24 Harlon Hill, Chi. Bears, 1954-61; Pittsburgh, 1962; Detroit, 1962 (233-4,717)

Highest Average Gain, Season (24 receptions)
32.58 Don Currivan, Boston, 1947 (24-782)
31.44 Bucky Pope, Los Angeles, 1964 (25-786)
28.60 Bobby Duckworth, San Diego, 1984 (25-715)

Highest Average Gain, Game (3 receptions)
60.67 Bill Groman, Houston vs. Denver, Nov. 20, 1960 (3-182)
Homer Jones, N.Y. Giants vs. Washington, Dec. 12, 1965 (3-182)
60.33 Don Currivan, Boston vs. Washington, Nov. 30, 1947 (3-181)
59.67 Bobby Duckworth, San Diego vs. Chicago, Dec. 3, 1984 (3-179)

TOUCHDOWNS

Most Seasons Leading League
9 Don Hutson, Green Bay, 1935-38, 1940-44
6 Jerry Rice, San Francisco, 1986-87, 1989-91, 1993
3 Lance Alworth, San Diego, 1964-66

Most Consecutive Seasons Leading League
5 Don Hutson, Green Bay, 1940-44
4 Don Hutson, Green Bay, 1935-38
3 Lance Alworth, San Diego, 1964-66
Jerry Rice, San Francisco, 1989-91

Most Touchdowns, Career
164 Jerry Rice, San Francisco, 1985-98
101 Cris Carter, Philadelphia, 1987-89; Minnesota, 1990-98
100 Steve Largent, Seattle, 1976-89

Most Touchdowns, Season
22 Jerry Rice, San Francisco, 1987
18 Mark Clayton, Miami, 1984
Sterling Sharpe, Green Bay, 1994
17 Don Hutson, Green Bay, 1942
Elroy (Crazylegs) Hirsch, Los Angeles, 1951
Bill Groman, Houston, 1961
Jerry Rice, San Francisco, 1989
Cris Carter, Minnesota, 1995
Carl Pickens, Cincinnati, 1995
Randy Moss, Minnesota, 1998

Most Touchdowns, Rookie, Season
17 Randy Moss, Minnesota, 1998
13 Bill Howton, Green Bay, 1952
John Jefferson, San Diego, 1978
12 Harlon Hill, Chi. Bears, 1954
Bill Groman, Houston, 1960
Mike Ditka, Chicago, 1961
Bob Hayes, Dallas, 1965

Most Touchdowns, Game
5 Bob Shaw, Chi. Cardinals vs. Baltimore, Oct. 2, 1950
Kellen Winslow, San Diego vs. Oakland, Nov. 22, 1981
Jerry Rice, San Francisco vs. Atlanta, Oct. 14, 1990
4 By many players. Last time:
Irving Fryar, Philadelphia vs. Miami, Oct. 20, 1996

Most Consecutive Games, Touchdowns
13 Jerry Rice, San Francisco, 1986-87
11 Elroy (Crazylegs) Hirsch, Los Angeles, 1950-51
Buddy Dial, Pittsburgh, 1959-60
10 Carl Pickens, Cincinnati, 1994-95

INTERCEPTIONS BY

Most Seasons Leading League
3 Everson Walls, Dallas, 1981-82, 1985
2 Dick (Night Train) Lane, Los Angeles, 1952; Chi. Cardinals, 1954
Jack Christiansen, Detroit, 1953, 1957
Milt Davis, Baltimore, 1957, 1959
Dick Lynch, N.Y. Giants, 1961, 1963
Johnny Robinson, Kansas City, 1966, 1970
Bill Bradley, Philadelphia, 1971-72
Emmitt Thomas, Kansas City, 1969, 1974
Ronnie Lott, San Francisco, 1986; L.A. Raiders, 1991

Most Interceptions By, Career
81 Paul Krause, Washington, 1964-67; Minnesota, 1968-79
79 Emlen Tunnell, N.Y. Giants, 1948-58; Green Bay, 1959-61
68 Dick (Night Train) Lane, Los Angeles, 1952-53; Chi. Cardinals, 1954-59; Detroit, 1960-65

Most Interceptions By, Season
14 Dick (Night Train) Lane, Los Angeles, 1952
13 Dan Sandifer, Washington, 1948
Orban (Spec) Sanders, N.Y. Yanks, 1950
Lester Hayes, Oakland, 1980
12 By nine players

Most Interceptions By, Rookie, Season
14 Dick (Night Train) Lane, Los Angeles, 1952
13 Dan Sandifer, Washington, 1948
12 Woodley Lewis, Los Angeles, 1950
Paul Krause, Washington, 1964

Most Interceptions By, Game
4 Sammy Baugh, Washington vs. Detroit, Nov. 14, 1943
Dan Sandifer, Washington vs. Boston, Oct. 31, 1948
Don Doll, Detroit vs. Chi. Cardinals, Oct. 23, 1949
Bob Nussbaumer, Chi. Cardinals vs. N.Y. Bulldogs, Nov. 13, 1949
Russ Craft, Philadelphia vs. Chi. Cardinals, Sept. 24, 1950
Bobby Dillon, Green Bay vs. Detroit, Nov. 26, 1953
Jack Butler, Pittsburgh vs. Washington, Dec. 13, 1953
Austin (Goose) Gonsoulin, Denver vs. Buffalo, Sept. 18, 1960
Jerry Norton, St. Louis vs. Washington, Nov. 20, 1960; vs. Pittsburgh, Nov. 26, 1961
Dave Baker, San Francisco vs. L.A. Rams, Dec. 4, 1960
Bobby Ply, Dall. Texans vs. San Diego, Dec. 16, 1962
Bobby Hunt, Kansas City vs. Houston, Oct. 4, 1964
Willie Brown, Denver vs. N.Y. Jets, Nov. 15, 1964
Dick Anderson, Miami vs. Pittsburgh, Dec. 3, 1973
Willie Buchanon, Green Bay vs. San Diego, Sept. 24, 1978
Deron Cherry, Kansas City vs. Seattle, Sept. 29, 1985
Kwamie Lassiter, Arizona vs. San Diego, Dec. 27, 1998

Most Consecutive Games, Passes Intercepted By
8 Tom Morrow, Oakland, 1962-63
7 Paul Krause, Washington, 1964
Larry Wilson, St. Louis, 1966
Ben Davis, Cleveland, 1968

6 Dick (Night Train) Lane, Chi. Cardinals, 1954-55
Will Sherman, Los Angeles, 1954-55
Jim Shofner, Cleveland, 1960
Paul Krause, Minnesota, 1968
Willie Williams, N.Y. Giants, 1968
Kermit Alexander, San Francisco, 1968-69
Mel Blount, Pittsburgh, 1975
Lemar Parrish, Washington, 1978-79
Eric Harris, Kansas City, 1980
Lester Hayes, Oakland, 1980
Barry Wilburn, Washington, 1987

YARDS GAINED

Most Seasons Leading League
2 Dick (Night Train) Lane, Los Angeles, 1952; Chi. Cardinals, 1954
Herb Adderley, Green Bay, 1965, 1969
Dick Anderson, Miami, 1968, 1970

Most Yards Gained, Career
1,282 Emlen Tunnell, N.Y. Giants, 1948-58; Green Bay, 1959-61
1,207 Dick (Night Train) Lane, Los Angeles, 1952-53; Chi. Cardinals, 1954-59; Detroit, 1960-65
1,185 Paul Krause, Washington, 1964-67; Minnesota, 1968-79

Most Yards Gained, Season
349 Charlie McNeil, San Diego, 1961
303 Deion Sanders, San Francisco, 1994
301 Don Doll, Detroit, 1949

Most Yards Gained, Rookie, Season
301 Don Doll, Detroit, 1949
298 Dick (Night Train) Lane, Los Angeles, 1952
275 Woodley Lewis, Los Angeles, 1950

Most Yards Gained, Game
177 Charlie McNeil, San Diego vs. Houston, Sept. 24, 1961
170 Louis Oliver, Miami vs. Buffalo, Oct. 4, 1992
167 Dick Jauron, Detroit vs. Chicago, Nov. 18, 1973

Longest Return (All TDs)
103 Vencie Glenn, San Diego vs. Denver, Nov. 29, 1987
Louis Oliver, Miami vs. Buffalo, Oct. 4, 1992
102 Bob Smith, Detroit vs. Chi. Bears, Nov. 24, 1949
Erich Barnes, N.Y. Giants vs. Dall. Cowboys, Oct. 15, 1961
Gary Barbaro, Kansas City vs. Seattle, Dec. 11, 1977
Louis Breeden, Cincinnati vs. San Diego, Nov. 8, 1981
Eddie Anderson, L.A. Raiders vs. Miami, Dec. 14, 1992
Donald Frank, San Diego vs. L.A. Raiders, Oct. 31, 1993
101 Richie Petitbon, Chicago vs Los Angeles, Dec. 9, 1962
Henry Carr, N.Y. Giants vs. Los Angeles, Nov. 13, 1966
Tony Greene, Buffalo vs. Kansas City, Oct. 3, 1976
Tom Pridemore, Atlanta vs. San Francisco, Sept. 20, 1981

TOUCHDOWNS

Most Touchdowns, Career
9 Ken Houston, Houston, 1967-72; Washington, 1973-80
8 Deion Sanders, Atlanta, 1989-93; San Francisco, 1994; Dallas, 1995-98
7 Herb Adderley, Green Bay, 1961-69; Dallas, 1970-72
Erich Barnes, Chi. Bears, 1958-60; N.Y. Giants, 1961-64; Cleveland, 1965-70
Lem Barney, Detroit, 1967-77
Rod Woodson, Pittsburgh, 1987-96; San Francisco, 1997; Baltimore, 1998

Most Touchdowns, Season
4 Ken Houston, Houston, 1971
Jim Kearney, Kansas City, 1972
Eric Allen, Philadelphia, 1993
3 Dick Harris, San Diego, 1961
Dick Lynch, N.Y. Giants, 1963
Herb Adderley, Green Bay, 1965
Lem Barney, Detroit, 1967
Miller Farr, Houston, 1967
Monte Jackson, Los Angeles, 1976
Rod Perry, Los Angeles, 1978
Ronnie Lott, San Francisco, 1981
Lloyd Burruss, Kansas City, 1986
Wayne Haddix, Tampa Bay, 1990
Robert Massey, Phoenix, 1992
Ray Buchanan, Indianapolis, 1994
Deion Sanders, San Francisco, 1994
Mark McMillian, Kansas City, 1997
Otis Smith, N.Y. Jets, 1997
Jimmy Hitchcock, Minnesota, 1998
2 By many players

Most Touchdowns, Rookie, Season
3 Lem Barney, Detroit, 1967
Ronnie Lott, San Francisco, 1981
2 By many players

Most Touchdowns, Game
2 Bill Blackburn, Chi. Cardinals vs. Boston, Oct. 24, 1948
Dan Sandifer, Washington vs. Boston, Oct. 31, 1948
Bob Franklin, Cleveland vs. Chicago, Dec. 11, 1960
Bill Stacy, St. Louis vs. Dall. Cowboys, Nov. 5, 1961
Jerry Norton, St. Louis vs. Pittsburgh, Nov. 26, 1961
Miller Farr, Houston vs. Buffalo, Dec. 7, 1968
Ken Houston, Houston vs. San Diego, Dec. 19, 1971
Jim Kearney, Kansas City vs. Denver, Oct. 1, 1972
Lemar Parrish, Cincinnati vs. Houston, Dec. 17, 1972
Dick Anderson, Miami vs. Pittsburgh, Dec. 3, 1973
Prentice McCray, New England vs. N.Y. Jets, Nov. 21, 1976
Kenny Johnson, Atlanta vs. Green Bay, Nov. 27, 1983 (OT)
Mike Kozlowski, Miami vs. N.Y. Jets, Dec. 16, 1983
Dave Brown, Seattle vs. Kansas City, Nov. 4, 1984
Lloyd Burruss, Kansas City vs. San Diego, Oct. 19, 1986
Henry Jones, Buffalo vs. Indianapolis, Sept. 20, 1992
Robert Massey, Phoenix vs. Washington, Oct. 4, 1992
Eric Allen, Philadelphia vs. New Orleans, Dec. 26, 1993
Ken Norton, San Francisco vs. St. Louis, Oct. 22, 1995
Otis Smith, N.Y. Jets vs. Tampa Bay, Dec. 14, 1997
Dewayne Washington, Pittsburgh vs. Jacksonville, Nov. 22, 1998

PUNTING

Most Seasons Leading League
4 Sammy Baugh, Washington, 1940-43
Jerrel Wilson, Kansas City, 1965, 1968, 1972-73
3 Yale Lary, Detroit, 1959, 1961, 1963
Jim Fraser, Denver, 1962-64
Ray Guy, Oakland, 1974-75, 1977
Rohn Stark, Baltimore, 1983; Indianapolis, 1985-86
2 By many players

Most Consecutive Seasons Leading League
4 Sammy Baugh, Washington, 1940-43
3 Jim Fraser, Denver, 1962-64
2 By many players

PUNTS

Most Punts, Career
1,154 Dave Jennings, N.Y. Giants, 1974-84; N.Y. Jets, 1985-87
1,141 Rohn Stark, Baltimore, 1982-83; Indianapolis, 1984-94; Pittsburgh, 1995; Carolina, 1996; Seattle, 1997
1,083 John James, Atlanta, 1972-81; Detroit, 1982, Houston, 1982-84

Most Punts, Season
114 Bob Parsons, Chicago, 1981
111 Brad Maynard, N.Y. Giants, 1997
109 John James, Atlanta, 1978

Most Punts, Rookie, Season
111 Brad Maynard, N.Y. Giants, 1997
108 John Teltschik, Philadelphia, 1986
99 Lewis Colbert, Kansas City, 1986

Most Punts, Game
16 Leo Araguz, Oakland vs. San Diego, Oct. 11, 1998
15 John Teltschik, Philadelphia vs. N.Y. Giants, Dec. 6, 1987 (OT)
14 Dick Nesbitt, Chi. Cardinals vs. Chi. Bears, Nov. 30, 1933
Keith Molesworth, Chi. Bears vs. Green Bay, Dec. 10, 1933
Sammy Baugh, Washington vs. Philadelphia, Nov. 5, 1939
Carl Kinscherf, N.Y. Giants vs. Detroit, Nov. 7, 1943
George Taliaferro, N.Y. Yanks vs. Los Angeles, Sept. 28, 1951

Longest Punt
98 Steve O'Neal, N.Y. Jets vs. Denver, Sept. 21, 1969
94 Joe Lintzenich, Chi. Bears vs. N.Y. Giants, Nov. 16, 1931
93 Shawn McCarthy, New England vs. Buffalo, Nov. 3, 1991

AVERAGE YARDAGE

Highest Average, Punting, Career (250 punts)
45.10 Sammy Baugh, Washington, 1937-52 (338-15,245)
44.71 Darren Bennett, San Diego, 1995-98 (343-15,334)
44.68 Tommy Davis, San Francisco, 1959-69 (511-22,833)

Highest Average, Punting, Season (Qualifiers)
51.40 Sammy Baugh, Washington, 1940 (35-1,799)
48.94 Yale Lary, Detroit, 1963 (35-1,713)
48.73 Sammy Baugh, Washington, 1941 (30-1,462)

Highest Average, Punting, Rookie, Season (Qualifiers)
45.92 Frank Sinkwich, Detroit, 1943 (12-551)
45.66 Tommy Davis, San Francisco, 1959 (59-2,694)
45.57 David Lee, Baltimore, 1966 (49-2,233)

Highest Average, Punting, Game (4 punts)
61.75 Bob Cifers, Detroit vs. Chi. Bears, Nov. 24, 1946 (4-247)
61.60 Roy McKay, Green Bay vs. Chi. Cardinals, Oct. 28, 1945 (5-308)
59.50 Darren Bennett, San Diego vs. Pittsburgh, Oct. 1, 1995 (4-238)

PUNTS HAD BLOCKED
Most Consecutive Punts, None Blocked
623 Dave Jennings, N.Y. Giants, 1976-83
619 Ray Guy, Oakland, 1979-81; L.A. Raiders, 1982-86
578 Bobby Walden, Minnesota, 1964-67; Pittsburgh, 1968-72
Most Punts Had Blocked, Career
14 Herman Weaver, Detroit, 1970-76; Seattle, 1977-80
Harry Newsome, Pittsburgh, 1985-89; Minnesota, 1990-93
12 Jerrel Wilson, Kansas City, 1963-77; New England, 1978
Tom Blanchard, N.Y. Giants, 1971-73; New Orleans, 1974-78; Tampa Bay, 1979-81
11 David Lee, Baltimore, 1966-78
Most Punts Had Blocked, Season
6 Harry Newsome, Pittsburgh, 1988
4 Bryan Wagner, Cleveland, 1990
3 By many players

PUNT RETURNS
Most Seasons Leading League
3 Les (Speedy) Duncan, San Diego, 1965-66; Washington, 1971
Rick Upchurch, Denver, 1976, 1978, 1982
2 Dick Christy, N.Y. Titans, 1961-62
Claude Gibson, Oakland, 1963-64
Billy (White Shoes) Johnson, Houston, 1975, 1977
Mel Gray, New Orleans, 1987; Detroit, 1991

PUNT RETURNS
Most Punt Returns, Career
349 David Meggett, N.Y. Giants, 1989-94; New England, 1995-97; N.Y. Jets, 1998
304 Tim Brown, L.A. Raiders, 1989-94; Oakland, 1995-98
292 Vai Sikahema, St. Louis, 1986-87; Phoenix, 1988-90; Green Bay, 1991; Philadelphia, 1992-93
Most Punt Returns, Season
70 Danny Reece, Tampa Bay, 1979
62 Fulton Walker, Miami-L.A. Raiders, 1985
58 J.T. Smith, Kansas City, 1979
Greg Pruitt, L.A. Raiders, 1983
Leo Lewis, Minnesota, 1988
Desmond Howard, Green Bay, 1996
Most Punt Returns, Rookie, Season
57 Lew Barnes, Chicago, 1986
54 James Jones, Dallas, 1980
53 Louis Lipps, Pittsburgh, 1984
Most Punt Returns, Game
11 Eddie Brown, Washington vs. Tampa Bay, Oct. 9, 1977
10 Theo Bell, Pittsburgh vs. Buffalo, Dec. 16, 1979
Mike Nelms, Washington vs. New Orleans, Dec. 26, 1982
Ronnie Harris, New England vs. Pittsburgh, Dec. 5, 1993
9 Rodger Bird, Oakland vs. Denver, Sept. 10, 1967
Ralph McGill, San Francisco vs. Atlanta, Oct. 29, 1972
Ed Podolak, Kansas City vs. San Diego, Nov. 10, 1974
Anthony Leonard, San Francisco vs. New Orleans, Oct. 17, 1976
Butch Johnson, Dallas vs. Buffalo, Nov. 15, 1976
Larry Marshall, Philadelphia vs. Tampa Bay, Sept. 18, 1977
Nesby Glasgow, Baltimore vs. Kansas City, Sept. 2, 1979
Mike Nelms, Washington vs. St. Louis, Dec. 21, 1980
Leon Bright, N.Y. Giants vs. Philadelphia, Dec. 11, 1982
Pete Shaw, N.Y. Giants vs. Philadelphia, Nov. 20, 1983
Cleotha Montgomery, L.A. Raiders vs. Detroit, Dec. 10, 1984
Phil McConkey, N.Y. Giants vs. Philadelphia, Dec. 6, 1987 (OT)
Andre Hastings, Pittsburgh vs. Cleveland, Nov. 13, 1995

FAIR CATCHES
Most Fair Catches, Career
137 Brian Mitchell, Washington, 1990-98
121 Mel Gray, New Orleans, 1986-88; Detroit, 1989-94; Houston, 1995-96; Tennessee, 1997; Philadelphia, 1997
114 David Meggett, N.Y. Giants, 1989-94; New England, 1995-97; N.Y. Jets, 1998
Most Fair Catches, Season
27 Leo Lewis, Minnesota, 1989
26 Eric Guliford, New Orleans, 1997
Glyn Milburn, Detroit, 1997
25 Mark Konecny, Philadelphia, 1988
Phil McConkey, N.Y. Giants, 1988
Chris Warren, Seattle, 1992
Eddie Kennison, St. Louis, 1998
Most Fair Catches, Game
7 Lem Barney, Detroit vs. Chicago, Nov. 21, 1976
Bobby Morse, Philadelphia vs. Buffalo, Dec. 27, 1987
6 Jake Scott, Miami vs. Buffalo, Dec. 20, 1970
Greg Pruitt, L.A. Raiders vs. Seattle, Oct. 7, 1984
Phil McConkey, San Diego vs. Kansas City, Dec. 17, 1989
Gerald McNeil, Houston vs. Pittsburgh, Sept. 16, 1990
Bobby Engram, Chicago vs. Minnesota, Sept. 15, 1996
5 By many players

YARDS GAINED
Most Seasons Leading League
3 Alvin Haymond, Baltimore, 1965-66; Los Angeles, 1969
2 Bill Dudley, Pittsburgh, 1942, 1946
Emlen Tunnell, N.Y. Giants, 1951-52
Dick Christy, N.Y. Titans, 1961-62
Claude Gibson, Oakland, 1963-64
Rodger Bird, Oakland, 1966-67
J.T. Smith, Kansas City, 1979-80
Vai Sikahema, St. Louis, 1986-87
David Meggett, N.Y. Giants, 1989-90
Most Yards Gained, Career
3,708 David Meggett, N.Y. Giants, 1989-94; New England, 1995-97; N.Y. Jets, 1998
3,317 Billy (White Shoes) Johnson, Houston, 1974-80; Atlanta, 1982-87; Washington, 1988
3,169 Vai Sikahema, St. Louis, 1986-87; Phoenix, 1988-90; Green Bay, 1991; Philadelphia, 1992-93
Most Yards Gained, Season
875 Desmond Howard, Green Bay, 1996
692 Fulton Walker, Miami-L.A. Raiders, 1985
666 Greg Pruitt, L.A. Raiders, 1983
Most Yards Gained, Rookie, Season
656 Louis Lipps, Pittsburgh, 1984
655 Neal Colzie, Oakland, 1975
619 Leon Johnson, N.Y. Jets, 1997
Most Yards Gained, Game
207 LeRoy Irvin, Los Angeles vs. Atlanta, Oct. 11, 1981
205 George Atkinson, Oakland vs. Buffalo, Sept. 15, 1968
184 Tom Watkins, Detroit vs. San Francisco, Oct. 6, 1963
Jermaine Lewis, Baltimore vs. Seattle, Dec. 7, 1997
Longest Punt Return (All TDs)
103 Robert Bailey, L.A. Rams vs. New Orleans, Oct. 23, 1994
98 Gil LeFebvre, Cincinnati vs. Brooklyn, Dec. 3, 1933
Charlie West, Minnesota vs. Washington, Nov. 3, 1968
Dennis Morgan, Dallas vs. St. Louis, Oct. 13, 1974
Terance Mathis, N.Y. Jets vs. Dallas, Nov. 4, 1990
97 Greg Pruitt, L.A. Raiders vs. Washington, Oct. 2, 1983

AVERAGE YARDAGE
Highest Average, Career (75 returns)
13.16 Darrien Gordon, San Diego, 1993-94, 1996; Denver, 1997-98 (177-2,329)
12.78 George McAfee, Chi. Bears, 1940-41, 1945-50 (112-1,431)
12.75 Jack Christiansen, Detroit, 1951-58 (85-1,084)
Highest Average, Season (Qualifiers)
23.00 Herb Rich, Baltimore, 1950 (12-276)
21.47 Jack Christiansen, Detroit, 1952 (15-322)
21.28 Dick Christy, N.Y. Titans, 1961 (18-383)
Highest Average, Rookie, Season (Qualifiers)
23.00 Herb Rich, Baltimore, 1950 (12-276)
20.88 Jerry Davis, Chi. Cardinals, 1948 (16-334)
20.73 Frank Sinkwich, Detroit, 1943 (11-228)
Highest Average, Game (3 returns)
47.67 Chuck Latourette, St. Louis vs. New Orleans, Sept. 29, 1968 (3-143)
47.33 Johnny Roland, St. Louis vs. Philadelphia, Oct. 2, 1966 (3-142)
45.67 Dick Christy, N.Y. Titans vs. Denver, Sept. 24, 1961 (3-137)

TOUCHDOWNS
Most Touchdowns, Career
9 Eric Metcalf, Cleveland, 1989-94; Atlanta, 1995-96; San Diego, 1997; Arizona, 1998
8 Jack Christiansen, Detroit, 1951-58
Rick Upchurch, Denver, 1975-83
7 David Meggett, N.Y. Giants, 1989-94; New England, 1995-97; N.Y. Jets, 1998
Brian Mitchell, Washington, 1990-98
Most Touchdowns, Season
4 Jack Christiansen, Detroit, 1951
Rick Upchurch, Denver, 1976
3 Emlen Tunnell, N.Y. Giants, 1951
Billy (White Shoes) Johnson, Houston, 1975
LeRoy Irvin, Los Angeles, 1981
Desmond Howard, Green Bay, 1996
Darrien Gordon, Denver, 1997
Eric Metcalf, San Diego, 1997
2 By many players

Most Touchdowns, Rookie, Season
4 Jack Christiansen, Detroit, 1951
2 By many players

Most Touchdowns, Game
2 Jack Christiansen, Detroit vs. Los Angeles, Oct. 14, 1951; vs. Green Bay, Nov. 22, 1951
Dick Christy, N.Y. Titans vs. Denver, Sept. 24, 1961
Rick Upchurch, Denver vs. Cleveland, Sept. 26, 1976
LeRoy Irvin, Los Angeles vs. Atlanta, Oct. 11, 1981
Vai Sikahema, St. Louis vs. Tampa Bay, Dec. 21, 1986
Todd Kinchen, L.A. Rams vs. Atlanta, Dec. 27, 1992
Eric Metcalf, Cleveland vs. Pittsburgh, Oct. 24, 1993; San Diego vs. Cincinnati, Nov. 2, 1997
Darrien Gordon, Denver vs. Carolina, Nov. 9, 1997
Jermaine Lewis, Baltimore vs. Seattle, Dec. 7, 1997

KICKOFF RETURNS

Most Seasons Leading League
3 Abe Woodson, San Francisco, 1959, 1962-63
2 Lynn Chandnois, Pittsburgh, 1951-52
Bobby Jancik, Houston, 1962-63
Travis Williams, Green Bay, 1967; Los Angeles, 1971
Mel Gray, Detroit, 1991, 1994
Michael Bates, Carolina, 1996-97

KICKOFF RETURNS

Most Kickoff Returns, Career
421 Mel Gray, New Orleans, 1986-88; Detroit, 1989-94; Houston, 1995-96; Tennessee, 1997; Philadelphia, 1997
378 Brian Mitchell, Washington, 1990-98
283 Tyrone Hughes, New Orleans, 1993-96; Chicago, 1997; Dallas, 1998

Most Kickoff Returns, Season
70 Tyrone Hughes, New Orleans, 1996
66 Tyrone Hughes, New Orleans, 1995
64 Glyn Milburn, Detroit, 1996

Most Kickoff Returns, Rookie, Season
56 Tony Horne, St. Louis, 1998
55 Stump Mitchell, St. Louis, 1981
54 Leeland McElroy, Arizona, 1996

Most Kickoff Returns, Game
10 Desmond Howard, Oakland vs. Seattle, Oct. 26, 1997
9 Noland Smith, Kansas City vs. Oakland, Nov. 23, 1967
Dino Hall, Cleveland vs. Pittsburgh, Oct. 7, 1979
Paul Palmer, Kansas City vs. Seattle, Sept. 20, 1987
Eric Metcalf, Atlanta vs. San Francisco, Sept. 29, 1996; vs. St. Louis, Nov. 10, 1996
Michael Bates, Carolina vs. Atlanta, Oct. 4, 1998
8 By many players

YARDS GAINED

Most Seasons Leading League
3 Bruce Harper, N.Y. Jets, 1977-79
Tyrone Hughes, New Orleans, 1994-96
2 Marshall Goldberg, Chi. Cardinals, 1941-42
Woodley Lewis, Los Angeles, 1953-54
Al Carmichael, Green Bay, 1956-57
Timmy Brown, Philadelphia, 1961, 1963
Bobby Jancik, Houston, 1963, 1966
Ron Smith, Atlanta, 1966-67

Most Yards Gained, Career
10,250 Mel Gray, New Orleans, 1986-88; Detroit, 1989-94; Houston, 1995-96; Tennessee, 1997; Philadelphia, 1997
8,693 Brian Mitchell, Washington, 1990-98
6,999 Tyrone Hughes, New Orleans, 1993-96; Chicago, 1997; Dallas, 1998

Most Yards Gained, Season
1,791 Tyrone Hughes, New Orleans, 1996
1,627 Glyn Milburn, Detroit, 1996
1,617 Tyrone Hughes, New Orleans, 1995

Most Yards Gained, Rookie, Season
1,428 Terry Fair, Detroit, 1998
1,345 Buster Rhymes, Minnesota, 1985
1,306 Tony Horne, St. Louis, 1998

Most Yards Gained, Game
304 Tyrone Hughes, New Orleans vs. L.A. Rams, Oct. 23, 1994
294 Wally Triplett, Detroit vs. Los Angeles, Oct. 29, 1950
256 Roell Preston, Green Bay vs. Minnesota, Oct. 5, 1998

Longest Kickoff Return (All TDs)
106 Al Carmichael, Green Bay vs. Chi. Bears, Oct. 7, 1956
Noland Smith, Kansas City vs. Denver, Dec. 17, 1967
Roy Green, St. Louis vs. Dallas, Oct. 21, 1979
105 Frank Seno, Chi. Cardinals vs. N.Y. Giants, Oct. 20, 1946
Ollie Matson, Chi. Cardinals vs. Washington, Oct. 14, 1956
Abe Woodson, San Francisco vs. Los Angeles, Nov. 8, 1959
Timmy Brown, Philadelphia vs. Cleveland, Sept. 17, 1961
Jon Arnett, Los Angeles vs. Detroit, Oct. 29, 1961
Eugene (Mercury) Morris, Miami vs. Cincinnati, Sept. 14, 1969
Travis Williams, Los Angeles vs. New Orleans, Dec. 5, 1971
Terry Fair, Detroit vs. Tampa Bay, Sept. 28, 1998
104 By many players

AVERAGE YARDAGE

Highest Average, Career (75 returns)
30.56 Gale Sayers, Chicago, 1965-71 (91-2,781)
29.57 Lynn Chandnois, Pittsburgh, 1950-56 (92-2,720)
28.69 Abe Woodson, San Francisco, 1958-64; St. Louis, 1965-66 (193-5,538)

Highest Average, Season (Qualifiers)
41.06 Travis Williams, Green Bay, 1967 (18-739)
37.69 Gale Sayers, Chicago, 1967 (16-603)
35.50 Ollie Matson, Chi. Cardinals, 1958 (14-497)

Highest Average, Rookie, Season (Qualifiers)
41.06 Travis Williams, Green Bay, 1967 (18-739)
33.08 Tom Moore, Green Bay, 1960 (12-397)
32.88 Duriel Harris, Miami, 1976 (17-559)

Highest Average, Game (3 returns)
73.50 Wally Triplett, Detroit vs. Los Angeles, Oct. 29, 1950 (4-294)
67.33 Lenny Lyles, San Francisco vs. Baltimore, Dec. 18, 1960 (3-202)
65.33 Ken Hall, Houston vs. N.Y. Titans, Oct. 23, 1960 (3-196)

TOUCHDOWNS

Most Touchdowns, Career
6 Ollie Matson, Chi. Cardinals, 1952, 1954-58; L.A. Rams, 1959-62; Detroit, 1963; Philadelphia, 1964
Gale Sayers, Chicago, 1965-71
Travis Williams, Green Bay, 1967-70; Los Angeles, 1971
Mel Gray, New Orleans, 1986-88; Detroit, 1989-94; Houston, 1995-96; Tennessee, 1997; Philadelphia, 1997
5 Bobby Mitchell, Cleveland, 1958-61; Washington, 1962-68
Abe Woodson, San Francisco, 1958-64; St. Louis, 1965-66
Timmy Brown, Green Bay, 1959; Philadelphia, 1960-67; Baltimore, 1968
4 Cecil Turner, Chicago, 1968-73
Ron Brown, L.A. Rams, 1984-89, 1991; L.A. Raiders, 1990
Jon Vaughn, New England, 1991-92; Seattle, 1993-94; Kansas City, 1994
Andre Coleman, San Diego, 1994-96; Seattle, 1997; Pittsburgh, 1997-98
Tamarick Vanover, Kansas City, 1995-98

Most Touchdowns, Season
4 Travis Williams, Green Bay, 1967
Cecil Turner, Chicago, 1970
3 Verda (Vitamin T) Smith, Los Angeles, 1950
Abe Woodson, San Francisco, 1963
Gale Sayers, Chicago, 1967
Raymond Clayborn, New England, 1977
Ron Brown, L.A. Rams, 1985
Mel Gray, Detroit, 1994
2 By many players

Most Touchdowns, Rookie, Season
4 Travis Williams, Green Bay, 1967
3 Raymond Clayborn, New England, 1977
2 By many players

Most Touchdowns, Game
2 Timmy Brown, Philadelphia vs. Dallas, Nov. 6, 1966
Travis Williams, Green Bay vs. Cleveland, Nov. 12, 1967
Ron Brown, L.A. Rams vs. Green Bay, Nov. 24, 1985
Tyrone Hughes, New Orleans vs. L.A. Rams, Oct. 23, 1994

COMBINED KICK RETURNS

Most Combined Kick Returns, Career
673 Mel Gray, New Orleans, 1986-88; Detroit, 1989-94; Houston, 1995-96; Tennessee, 1997; Philadelphia, 1997 (p-252, k-421)
655 Brian Mitchell, Washington, 1990-98 (p-277; k-378)
601 David Meggett, N.Y. Giants, 1989-94; New England, 1995-97; N.Y. Jets, 1998 (p-349; k-252)

Most Combined Kick Returns, Season
103 Brian Mitchell, Washington, 1998 (p-44; k-59)
102 Glyn Milburn, Detroit, 1997 (p-47, k-55)
101 Roell Preston, Green Bay, 1998 (p-44; k-57)

Most Combined Kick Returns, Game
13 Stump Mitchell, St. Louis vs. Atlanta, Oct. 18, 1981 (p-6, k-7)
Ronnie Harris, New England vs. Pittsburgh, Dec. 5, 1993 (p-10, k-3)
12 Mel Renfro, Dallas vs. Green Bay, Nov. 29, 1964 (p-4, k-8)
Larry Jones, Washington vs. Dallas, Dec. 13, 1975 (p-6, k-6)
Eddie Brown, Washington vs. Tampa Bay, Oct. 9, 1977 (p-11, k-1)
Nesby Glasgow, Baltimore vs. Denver, Sept. 2, 1979 (p-9, k-3)
11 By many players

YARDS GAINED

Most Yards Returned, Career

13,003 Mel Gray, New Orleans, 1986-88; Detroit, 1989-94; Houston, 1995-96; Tennessee, 1997; Philadelphia, 1997 (p-2,753, k-10,250)
11,837 Brian Mitchell, Washington, 1990-98 (p-3,144, k-8,693)
9,274 David Meggett, N.Y. Giants, 1989-94; New England, 1995-97; N.Y. Jets, 1998 (p-3,708; k-5,566)

Most Yards Returned, Season

1,943 Tyrone Hughes, New Orleans, 1996 (p-152, k-1,791)
1,930 Brian Mitchell, Washington, 1994 (p-452, k-1,478)
1,920 Kevin Williams, Arizona, 1997 (p-462, k-1,458)

Most Yards Returned, Game

347 Tyrone Hughes, New Orleans vs. L.A. Rams, Oct. 23, 1994 (p-43, k-304)
294 Wally Triplett, Detroit vs. Los Angeles, Oct. 29, 1950 (k-294)
Woodley Lewis, Los Angeles vs. Detroit, Oct. 18, 1953 (p-120, k-174)
289 Eddie Payton, Detroit vs. Minnesota, Dec. 17, 1977 (p-105, k-184)

TOUCHDOWNS

Most Touchdowns, Career

11 Eric Metcalf, Cleveland, 1989-94; Atlanta, 1995-96; San Diego, 1997; Arizona, 1998 (p-9; k-2)
9 Ollie Matson, Chi. Cardinals, 1952, 1954-58; Los Angeles, 1959-62; Detroit, 1963; Philadelphia, 1964-66 (p-3, k-6)
Mel Gray, New Orleans, 1986-88; Detroit, 1989-94; Houston, 1995-96; Tennessee, 1997; Philadelphia, 1997 (p-3, k-6)
Brian Mitchell, Washington, 1990-98 (p-7; k-2)
8 Jack Christiansen, Detroit, 1951-58 (p-8)
Bobby Mitchell, Cleveland, 1958-61; Washington, 1962-68 (p-3, k-5)
Gale Sayers, Chicago, 1965-71 (p-2, k-6)
Rick Upchurch, Denver, 1975-83 (p-8)
Billy (White Shoes) Johnson, Houston, 1974-80; Atlanta, 1982-87; Washington, 1988 (p-6, k-2)
David Meggett, N.Y. Giants, 1989-94; New England, 1995-97; N.Y. Jets, 1998 (p-7; k-1)
Deion Sanders, Atlanta, 1989-93; San Francisco, 1994; Dallas, 1995-98 (p-5; k-3)

Most Touchdowns, Season

4 Jack Christiansen, Detroit, 1951 (p-4)
Emlen Tunnell, N.Y. Giants, 1951 (p-3, k-1)
Gale Sayers, Chicago, 1967 (p-1, k-3)
Travis Williams, Green Bay, 1967 (k-4)
Cecil Turner, Chicago, 1970 (k-4)
Billy Johnson, Houston, 1975 (p-3, k-1)
Rick Upchurch, Denver, 1976 (p-4)
3 Verda (Vitamin T) Smith, Los Angeles, 1950 (k-3)
Abe Woodson, San Francisco, 1963 (k-3)
Raymond Clayborn, New England, 1977 (k-3)
Billy Johnson, Houston, 1977 (p-2, k-1)
LeRoy Irvin, Los Angeles, 1981 (p-3)
Ron Brown, L.A. Rams, 1985 (k-3)
Tyrone Hughes, New Orleans, 1993 (p-2, k-1)
Mel Gray, Detroit, 1994 (k-3)
Andre Coleman, San Diego, 1995 (p-2; k-1)
Tamarick Vanover, Kansas City, 1995 (p-1, k-2)
Desmond Howard, Green Bay, 1996 (p-3)
Darrien Gordon, Denver, 1997 (p-3)
Eric Metcalf, San Diego, 1997 (p-3)
Glyn Milburn, Chicago, 1998 (p-2; k-1)
Roell Preston, Green Bay, 1998 (p-2; k-1)
2 By many players

Most Touchdowns, Game

2 Jack Christiansen, Detroit vs. Los Angeles, Oct. 14, 1951 (p-2); vs. Green Bay, Nov. 22, 1951 (p-2)
Jim Patton, N.Y. Giants vs. Washington, Oct. 30, 1955 (p-1, k-1)
Bobby Mitchell, Cleveland vs. Philadelphia, Nov. 23, 1958 (p-1, k-1)
Dick Christy, N.Y. Titans vs. Denver, Sept. 24, 1961 (p-2)
Al Frazier, Denver vs. Boston, Dec. 3, 1961 (p-1, k-1)
Timmy Brown, Philadelphia vs. Dallas, Nov. 6, 1966 (k-2)
Travis Williams, Green Bay vs. Cleveland, Nov. 12, 1967 (k-2); vs. Pittsburgh, Nov. 2, 1969 (p-1, k-1)
Gale Sayers, Chicago vs. San Francisco, Dec. 3, 1967 (p-1, k-1)
Rick Upchurch, Denver vs. Cleveland, Sept. 26, 1976 (p-2)
Eddie Payton, Detroit vs. Minnesota, Dec. 17, 1977 (p-1, k-1)
LeRoy Irvin, Los Angeles vs. Atlanta, Oct. 11, 1981 (p-2)
Ron Brown, L.A. Rams vs. Green Bay, Nov. 24, 1985 (k-2)
Vai Sikahema, St. Louis vs. Tampa Bay, Dec. 21, 1986 (p-2)
Todd Kinchen, L.A. Rams vs. Atlanta, Dec. 27, 1992 (p-2)
Eric Metcalf, Cleveland vs. Pittsburgh, Oct. 24, 1993 (p-2); San Diego vs. Cincinnati, Nov. 2, 1997 (p-2)
Tyrone Hughes, New Orleans vs. L.A. Rams, Oct. 23, 1994 (k-2)
Darrien Gordon, Denver vs. Carolina, Nov. 9, 1997 (p-2)
Jermaine Lewis, Baltimore vs. Seattle, Dec. 7, 1997 (p-2)

FUMBLES

Most Fumbles, Career

160 Warren Moon, Houston, 1984-93; Minnesota, 1994-96; Seattle, 1997-98
153 Dave Krieg, Seattle, 1980-91; Kansas City, 1992-93; Detroit, 1994; Arizona, 1995; Chicago, 1996; Tennessee, 1997-98
137 John Elway, Denver, 1983-98

Most Fumbles, Season

21 Tony Banks, St. Louis, 1996
18 Dave Krieg, Seattle, 1989
Warren Moon, Houston, 1990
17 Dan Pastorini, Houston, 1973
Warren Moon, Houston, 1984
Randall Cunningham, Philadelphia, 1989

Most Fumbles, Game

7 Len Dawson, Kansas City vs. San Diego, Nov. 15, 1964
6 Sam Etcheverry, St. Louis vs. N.Y. Giants, Sept, 17, 1961
Dave Krieg, Seattle vs. Kansas City, Nov. 5, 1989
Brett Favre, Green Bay vs. Tampa Bay, Dec. 7, 1998
5 Paul Christman, Chi. Cardinals vs. Green Bay, Nov. 10, 1946
Charlie Conerly, N.Y. Giants vs. San Francisco, Dec. 1, 1957
Jack Kemp, Buffalo vs. Houston, Oct. 29, 1967
Roman Gabriel, Philadelphia vs. Oakland, Nov. 21, 1976
Randall Cunningham, Philadelphia vs. L.A. Raiders, Nov. 30, 1986 (OT)
Willie Totten, Buffalo vs. Indianapolis, Oct. 4, 1987
Dave Walter, Cincinnati vs. Seattle, Oct. 11, 1987
Dave Krieg, Seattle vs. San Diego, Nov. 25, 1990 (OT)
Andre Ware, Detroit vs. Green Bay, Dec. 6, 1992
Steve Beuerlein, Carolina vs. San Francisco, Nov. 8, 1998

FUMBLES RECOVERED

Most Fumbles Recovered, Career, Own and Opponents'

55 Warren Moon, Houston, 1984-93, Minnesota, 1994-96; Seattle, 1997-98 (55 own)
47 Dave Krieg, Seattle, 1980-91; Kansas City, 1992-93; Detroit, 1994; Arizona, 1995; Chicago, 1996; Tennessee, 1997-98 (47 own)
45 Boomer Esiason, Cincinnati, 1984-92, 1997; N.Y. Jets, 1993-95; Arizona, 1996 (45 own)

Most Fumbles Recovered, Season, Own and Opponents'

9 Don Hultz, Minnesota, 1963 (9 opp)
Dave Krieg, Seattle, 1989 (9 own)
8 Paul Christman, Chi. Cardinals, 1945 (8 own)
Joe Schmidt, Detroit, 1955 (8 opp)
Bill Butler, Minnesota, 1963 (8 own)
Kermit Alexander, San Francisco, 1965 (4 own, 4 opp)
Jack Lambert, Pittsburgh, 1976 (1 own, 7 opp)
Danny White, Dallas, 1981 (8 own)
Dan Marino, Miami, 1988 (7 own, 1 opp)
Tony Banks, St. Louis, 1998 (8 own)
7 By many players

Most Fumbles Recovered, Game, Own and Opponents'

4 Otto Graham, Cleveland vs. N.Y. Giants, Oct. 25, 1953 (4 own)
Sam Etcheverry, St. Louis vs. N.Y. Giants, Sept. 17, 1961 (4 own)
Roman Gabriel, Los Angeles vs. San Francisco, Oct. 12, 1969 (4 own)
Joe Ferguson, Buffalo vs. Miami, Sept. 18, 1977 (4 own)
Randall Cunningham, Philadelphia vs. L.A. Raiders, Nov. 30, 1986 (OT) (4 own)
3 By many players

OWN FUMBLES RECOVERED

Most Own Fumbles Recovered, Career

55 Warren Moon, Houston, 1984-93; Minnesota, 1994-96; Seattle, 1997-98 (55 own)
47 Dave Krieg, Seattle, 1980-91; Kansas City, 1992-93; Detroit, 1994; Arizona, 1995; Chicago, 1996; Tennessee, 1997-98 (47 own)
45 Boomer Esiason, Cincinnati, 1984-92, 1997; N.Y. Jets, 1993-95; Arizona, 1996 (45 own)

Most Own Fumbles Recovered, Season

9 Dave Krieg, Seattle, 1989
8 Paul Christman, Chi. Cardinals, 1945
Bill Butler, Minnesota, 1963
Danny White, Dallas, 1981
Tony Banks, St. Louis, 1998
7 By many players

Most Own Fumbles Recovered, Game

4 Otto Graham, Cleveland vs. N.Y. Giants, Oct. 25, 1953
Sam Etcheverry, St. Louis vs. N.Y. Giants, Sept. 17, 1961
Roman Gabriel, Los Angeles vs. San Francisco, Oct. 12, 1969
Joe Ferguson, Buffalo vs. Miami, Sept. 18, 1977
Randall Cunningham, Philadelphia vs. L.A. Raiders, Nov. 30, 1986 (OT)
3 By many players

ALL-TIME RECORDS

OPPONENTS' FUMBLES RECOVERED

Most Opponents' Fumbles Recovered, Career

29 Jim Marshall, Cleveland, 1960; Minnesota, 1961-79
28 Rickey Jackson, New Orleans, 1981-93; San Francisco, 1994-95
25 Dick Butkus, Chicago, 1965-73

Most Opponents' Fumbles Recovered, Season

9 Don Hultz, Minnesota, 1963
8 Joe Schmidt, Detroit, 1955
7 Alan Page, Minnesota, 1970
Jack Lambert, Pittsburgh, 1976
Ray Childress, Houston, 1988
Rickey Jackson, New Orleans, 1990

Most Opponents' Fumbles Recovered, Game

3 Corwin Clatt, Chi. Cardinals vs. Detroit, Nov. 6, 1949
Vic Sears, Philadelphia vs. Green Bay, Nov. 2, 1952
Ed Beatty, San Francisco vs. Los Angeles, Oct. 7, 1956
Ron Carroll, Houston vs. Cincinnati, Oct. 27, 1974
Maurice Spencer, New Orleans vs. Atlanta, Oct. 10, 1976
Steve Nelson, New England vs. Philadelphia, Oct. 8, 1978
Charles Jackson, Kansas City vs. Pittsburgh, Sept. 6, 1981
Willie Buchanon, San Diego vs. Denver, Sept. 27, 1981
Joey Browner, Minnesota vs. San Francisco, Sept. 8, 1985
Ray Childress, Houston vs. Washington, Oct. 30, 1988
John Thierry, Chicago vs. Houston, Oct. 22, 1995
Stephen Boyd, Detroit vs. Chicago, Oct. 4, 1998
Darryl Williams, Seattle vs. Kansas City, Oct. 4, 1998
2 By many players

YARDS RETURNING FUMBLES

Longest Fumble Run (All TDs)

104 Jack Tatum, Oakland vs. Green Bay, Sept. 24, 1972
100 Chris Martin, Kansas City vs. Miami, Oct. 13, 1991
99 Don Griffin, San Francisco vs. Chicago, Dec. 23, 1991

TOUCHDOWNS

Most Touchdowns, Career (Total)

5 Jessie Tuggle, Atlanta, 1987-98
4 Bill Thompson, Denver, 1969-81
Derrick Thomas, Kansas City, 1989-98
3 By many players

Most Touchdowns, Season (Total)

2 Harold McPhail, Boston, 1934
Harry Ebding, Detroit, 1937
John Morelli, Boston, 1944
Frank Maznicki, Boston, 1947
Fred (Dippy) Evans, Chi. Bears, 1948
Ralph Heywood, Boston, 1948
Art Tait, N.Y. Yanks, 1951
John Dwyer, Los Angeles, 1952
Leo Sugar, Chi. Cardinals, 1957
Doug Cline, Houston, 1961
Jim Bradshaw, Pittsburgh, 1964
Royce Berry, Cincinnati, 1970
Ahmad Rashad, Buffalo, 1974
Tim Gray, Kansas City, 1977
Charles Phillips, Oakland, 1978
Kenny Johnson, Atlanta, 1981
George Martin, N.Y. Giants, 1981
Del Rodgers, Green Bay, 1982
Mike Douglass, Green Bay, 1983
Shelton Robinson, Seattle, 1983
Erik McMillan, N.Y. Jets, 1989
Les Miller, San Diego, 1990
Seth Joyner, Philadelphia, 1991
Robert Goff, New Orleans, 1992
Willie Clay, Detroit, 1993
Tyrone Hughes, New Orleans, 1994
Chad Brown, Seattle, 1997
Marcus Robertson, Tennessee, 1997
Dwayne Rudd, Minnesota, 1998

Most Touchdowns, Career (Own recovered)

2 Ken Kavanaugh, Chi. Bears, 1940-41, 1945-50
Mike Ditka, Chicago, 1961-66; Philadelphia, 1967-68; Dallas, 1969-72
Gail Cogdill, Detroit, 1960-68; Baltimore, 1968; Atlanta, 1969-70
Ahmad Rashad, St. Louis, 1972-73; Buffalo, 1974; Minnesota, 1976-82
Jim Mitchell, Atlanta, 1969-79
Drew Pearson, Dallas, 1973-83
Del Rodgers, Green Bay, 1982, 1984; San Francisco, 1987-88

Most Touchdowns, Season (Own recovered)

2 Ahmad Rashad, Buffalo, 1974
Del Rodgers, Green Bay, 1982
1 By many players

Most Touchdowns, Career (Opponents' recovered)

5 Jessie Tuggle, Atlanta, 1987-98
4 Derrick Thomas, Kansas City, 1989-98
3 By many players

Most Touchdowns, Season (Opponents' recovered)

2 Harold McPhail, Boston, 1934
Harry Ebding, Detroit, 1937
John Morelli, Boston, 1944
Frank Maznicki, Boston, 1947
Fred (Dippy) Evans, Chi. Bears, 1948
Ralph Heywood, Boston, 1948
Art Tait, N.Y. Yanks, 1951
John Dwyer, Los Angeles, 1952
Leo Sugar, Chi. Cardinals, 1957
Doug Cline, Houston, 1961
Jim Bradshaw, Pittsburgh, 1964
Royce Berry, Cincinnati, 1970
Tim Gray, Kansas City, 1977
Charles Phillips, Oakland, 1978
Kenny Johnson, Atlanta, 1981
George Martin, N.Y. Giants, 1981
Mike Douglass, Green Bay, 1983
Shelton Robinson, Seattle, 1983
Erik McMillan, N.Y. Jets, 1989
Les Miller, San Diego, 1990
Seth Joyner, Philadelphia, 1991
Robert Goff, New Orleans, 1992
Willie Clay, Detroit, 1993
Tyrone Hughes, New Orleans, 1994
Chad Brown, Seattle, 1997
Marcus Robertson, Tennessee, 1997
Dwayne Rudd, Minnesota, 1998

Most Touchdowns, Game (Opponents' recovered)

2 Fred (Dippy) Evans, Chi. Bears vs. Washington, Nov. 28, 1948

COMBINED NET YARDS GAINED

Rushing, receiving, interception returns, punt returns, kickoff returns, and fumble returns

Most Seasons Leading League

5 Jim Brown, Cleveland, 1958-61, 1964
4 Brian Mitchell, Washington, 1994-96, 1998
3 Cliff Battles, Boston, 1932-33; Washington, 1937
Gale Sayers, Chicago, 1965-67
Eric Dickerson, L.A. Rams, 1983-84, 1986
Thurman Thomas, Buffalo, 1989, 1991-92

Most Consecutive Seasons Leading League

4 Jim Brown, Cleveland, 1958-61
3 Gale Sayers, Chicago, 1965-67
Brian Mitchell, Washington, 1994-96
2 Cliff Battles, Boston, 1932-33
Charley Trippi, Chi. Cardinals, 1948-49
Timmy Brown, Philadelphia, 1962-63
Floyd Little, Denver, 1967-68
James Brooks, San Diego, 1981-82
Eric Dickerson, L.A. Rams, 1983-84
Thurman Thomas, Buffalo, 1991-92

ATTEMPTS

Most Attempts, Career

4,368 Walter Payton, Chicago, 1975-87
3,624 Marcus Allen, L.A. Raiders, 1982-92; Kansas City, 1993-97
3,432 Barry Sanders, Detroit, 1989-98

Most Attempts, Season

496 James Wilder, Tampa Bay, 1984
449 Marcus Allen, L.A. Raiders, 1985
442 Eric Dickerson, L.A. Rams, 1983

Most Attempts, Rookie, Season

442 Eric Dickerson, L.A. Rams, 1983
401 Curtis Martin, New England, 1995
395 George Rogers, New Orleans, 1981

Most Attempts, Game

48 James Wilder, Tampa Bay vs. Pittsburgh, Oct. 30, 1983
47 James Wilder, Tampa Bay vs. Green Bay, Sept. 30, 1984 (OT)
Terrell Davis, Denver vs. Buffalo, Oct. 26, 1997 (OT)
46 Gerald Riggs, Atlanta vs. L.A. Rams, Nov. 17, 1985

YARDS GAINED

Most Yards Gained, Career

21,803 Walter Payton, Chicago, 1975-87
18,308 Barry Sanders, Detroit, 1989-98
18,232 Jerry Rice, San Francisco, 1985-98

Most Yards Gained, Season
2,535 Lionel James, San Diego, 1985
2,477 Brian Mitchell, Washington, 1994
2,462 Terry Metcalf, St. Louis, 1975
Most Yards Gained, Rookie, Season
2,317 Tim Brown, L.A. Raiders, 1988
2,272 Gale Sayers, Chicago, 1965
2,212 Eric Dickerson, L.A. Rams, 1983
Most Yards Gained, Game
404 Glyn Milburn, Denver vs. Seattle, Dec. 10, 1995
373 Billy Cannon, Houston vs. N.Y. Titans, Dec. 10, 1961
347 Tyrone Hughes, New Orleans vs. L.A. Rams, Oct. 23, 1994

SACKS

Sacks have been compiled since 1982.
Most Seasons Leading League
2 Mark Gastineau, N.Y. Jets, 1983-84
Reggie White, Philadelphia, 1987-88
Kevin Greene, Pittsburgh, 1994; Carolina, 1996
Most Sacks, Career
192.5 Reggie White, Philadelphia, 1985-92; Green Bay, 1993-98
164.0 Bruce Smith, Buffalo, 1985-98
148.0 Kevin Greene, L.A. Rams, 1985-92; Pittsburgh, 1993-95; Carolina, 1996, 1998; San Francisco, 1997
Most Sacks, Season
22 Mark Gastineau, N.Y. Jets, 1984
21 Reggie White, Philadelphia, 1987
Chris Doleman, Minnesota, 1989
20.5 Lawrence Taylor, N.Y. Giants, 1986
Most Sacks, Rookie, Season
12.5 Leslie O'Neal, San Diego, 1986
Simeon Rice, Arizona, 1996
12 Charles Haley, San Francisco, 1986
11.5 Peter Boulware, Baltimore, 1997
Most Sacks, Game
7 Derrick Thomas, Kansas City vs. Seattle, Nov. 11, 1990
6 Fred Dean, San Francisco vs. New Orleans, Nov. 13, 1983
Derrick Thomas, Kansas City vs. Oakland, Sept. 6, 1998
5.5 William Gay, Detroit vs. Tampa Bay, Sept. 4, 1983
Most Seasons, 10 or More Sacks
12 Reggie White, Philadelphia, 1985-92; Green Bay, 1993, 1995, 1997-98
Bruce Smith, Buffalo, 1986-90, 1992-98
9 Kevin Greene, L.A. Rams, 1988-90, 1992; Pittsburgh, 1993-94; Carolina, 1996, 1998; San Francisco, 1997
8 Richard Dent, Chicago, 1984-88, 1990-91, 1993
Leslie O'Neal, San Diego, 1986, 1989-90, 1992-95; St. Louis, 1997
Chris Doleman, Minnesota, 1987, 1989-90, 1992-93; San Francisco, 1996-98
Most Consecutive Seasons, 10 or More Sacks
9 Reggie White, Philadelphia, 1985-92; Green Bay, 1993
7 Lawrence Taylor, N.Y. Giants, 1984-1990
John Randle, Minnesota, 1992-98 (current)
Bruce Smith, Buffalo, 1992-98 (current)
5 Richard Dent, Chicago, 1984-88
Bruce Smith, Buffalo, 1986-90
Simon Fletcher, Denver, 1989-93

MISCELLANEOUS

Longest Return of Missed Field Goal (All TDs)
104 Aaron Glenn, N.Y. Jets vs. Indianapolis, Nov. 15, 1998
101 Al Nelson, Philadelphia vs. Dallas, Sept. 26, 1971
100 Al Nelson, Philadelphia vs. Cleveland, Dec. 11, 1966
Ken Ellis, Green Bay vs. N.Y. Giants, Sept. 19, 1971

TEAM RECORDS

CHAMPIONSHIPS

Most Seasons League Champion
12 Green Bay, 1929-31, 1936, 1939, 1944, 1961-62, 1965-67, 1996
9 Chi. Bears, 1921, 1932-33, 1940-41, 1943, 1946, 1963, 1985
6 N.Y. Giants, 1927, 1934, 1938, 1956, 1986, 1990
Most Consecutive Seasons League Champion
3 Green Bay, 1929-31
Green Bay, 1965-67
2 Canton, 1922-23
Chi. Bears, 1932-33
Chi. Bears, 1940-41
Philadelphia, 1948-49
Detroit, 1952-53
Cleveland, 1954-55
Baltimore, 1958-59
Houston, 1960-61
Green Bay, 1961-62
Buffalo, 1964-65
Miami, 1972-73
Pittsburgh, 1974-75
Pittsburgh, 1978-79
San Francisco, 1988-89
Dallas, 1992-93
Denver, 1997-98
Most Times Finishing First, Regular Season
19 N.Y. Giants, 1927, 1933-35, 1938-39, 1941, 1944, 1946, 1956, 1958-59, 1961-63, 1986, 1989-90, 1997
Dallas, 1966-71, 1973, 1976-79, 1981, 1985, 1992-96, 1998
18 Clev. Browns, 1950-55, 1957, 1964-65, 1967-69, 1971, 1980, 1985-87, 1989
Chi. Bears, 1921, 1932-34, 1937, 1940-43, 1946, 1956, 1963, 1984-88, 1990
17 Green Bay, 1929-31, 1936, 1938-39, 1944, 1960-62, 1965-67, 1972, 1995-97
Most Consecutive Times Finishing First, Regular Season
7 Los Angeles, 1973-79
6 Cleveland, 1950-55
Dallas, 1966-71
Minnesota, 1973-78
Pittsburgh, 1974-79
5 Oakland, 1972-76
Chicago, 1984-88
San Francisco, 1986-90
Dallas, 1992-96

GAMES WON

Most Consecutive Games Won
17 Chi. Bears, 1933-34
16 Chi. Bears, 1941-42
Miami, 1971-73
Miami, 1983-84
15 L.A. Chargers/San Diego, 1960-61
San Francisco, 1989-90
Most Consecutive Games Without Defeat
25 Canton, 1921-23 (won 22, tied 3)
24 Chi. Bears, 1941-43 (won 23, tied 1)
23 Green Bay, 1928-30 (won 21, tied 2)
Most Games Won, Season
15 San Francisco, 1984
Chicago, 1985
Minnesota, 1998
14 Frankford, 1926
Miami, 1972
Pittsburgh, 1978
Washington, 1983
Miami, 1984
Chicago, 1986
N.Y. Giants, 1986
San Francisco, 1989
San Francisco, 1990
Washington, 1991
San Francisco, 1992
Atlanta, 1998
Denver, 1998
13 By many teams
Most Consecutive Games Won, Season
14 Miami, 1972
13 Chi. Bears, 1934
Denver, 1998
12 Minnesota, 1969
Chicago, 1985
Most Consecutive Games Won, Start of Season
14 Miami, 1972, entire season
13 Chi. Bears, 1934, entire season
Denver, 1998
12 Chicago, 1985
Most Consecutive Games Won, End of Season
14 Miami, 1972, entire season
13 Chi. Bears, 1934, entire season
11 Chi. Bears, 1942, entire season
Cleveland, 1951
Houston, 1993
Most Consecutive Games Without Defeat, Season
14 Miami, 1972 (won 14)
13 Chi. Bears, 1926 (won 11, tied 2)
Green Bay, 1929 (won 12, tied 1)
Chi. Bears, 1934 (won 13)
Baltimore, 1967 (won 11, tied 2)
Denver, 1998 (won 13)

12 Canton, 1922 (won 10, tied 2)
Canton, 1923 (won 11, tied 1)
Minnesota, 1969 (won 12)
Chicago, 1985 (won 12)

Most Consecutive Games Without Defeat, Start of Season
14 Miami, 1972 (won 14), entire season
13 Chi. Bears, 1926 (won 11, tied 2)
Green Bay, 1929 (won 12, tied 1), entire season
Chi. Bears, 1934 (won 13), entire season
Baltimore, 1967 (won 11, tied 2)
Denver, 1998 (won 13)
12 Canton, 1922 (won 10, tied 2), entire season
Canton, 1923 (won 11, tied 1), entire season
Chicago, 1985 (won 12)

Most Consecutive Games Without Defeat, End of Season
14 Miami, 1972 (won 14), entire season
13 Green Bay, 1929 (won 12, tied 1), entire season
Chi. Bears, 1934 (won 13), entire season
12 Canton, 1922 (won 10, tied 2), entire season
Canton, 1923 (won 11, tied 1), entire season

Most Consecutive Home Games Won
27 Miami, 1971-74
25 Green Bay, 1995-98
24 Denver, 1996-98 (current)

Most Consecutive Home Games Without Defeat
30 Green Bay, 1928-33 (won 27, tied 3)
27 Miami, 1971-74 (won 27)
25 Chi. Bears, 1923-25 (won 19, tied 6)
Green Bay, 1995-98 (won 25)

Most Consecutive Road Games Won
18 San Francisco, 1988-90
11 L.A. Chargers/San Diego, 1960-61
San Francisco, 1987-88
10 Chi. Bears, 1941-42
Dallas, 1968-69
New Orleans, 1987-88

Most Consecutive Road Games Without Defeat
18 San Francisco, 1988-90 (won 18)
13 Chi. Bears, 1941-43 (won 12, tied 1)
12 Green Bay, 1928-30 (won 10, tied 2)

Most Shutout Games Won or Tied, Season
10 Pottsville, 1926 (won 9, tied 1)
N.Y. Giants, 1927 (won 9, tied 1)
9 Akron, 1921 (won 8, tied 1)
Canton, 1922 (won 7, tied 2)
Frankford, 1926 (won 9)
Frankford, 1929 (won 6, tied 3)
8 By many teams

Most Consecutive Shutout Games Won or Tied
13 Akron, 1920-21 (won 10, tied 3)
7 Pottsville, 1926 (won 6, tied 1)
Detroit, 1934 (won 7)
6 Buffalo, 1920-21 (won 5, tied 1)
Frankford, 1926 (won 6)
Detroit, 1926 (won 4, tied 2)
N.Y. Giants, 1926-27 (won 5, tied 1)

GAMES LOST

Most Consecutive Games Lost
26 Tampa Bay, 1976-77
19 Chi. Cardinals, 1942-43, 1945
Oakland, 1961-62
18 Houston, 1972-73

Most Consecutive Games Without Victory
26 Tampa Bay, 1976-77 (lost 26)
23 Rochester, 1922-25 (lost 21, tied 2)
Washington, 1960-61 (lost 20, tied 3)
19 Dayton, 1927-29 (lost 18, tied 1)
Chi. Cardinals, 1942-43, 1945 (lost 19)
Oakland, 1961-62 (lost 19)

Most Games Lost, Season
15 New Orleans, 1980
Dallas, 1989
New England, 1990
Indianapolis, 1991
N.Y. Jets, 1996
14 By many teams

Most Consecutive Games Lost, Season
14 Tampa Bay, 1976
New Orleans, 1980
Baltimore, 1981
New England, 1990
13 Oakland, 1962
Pittsburgh, 1969
Indianapolis, 1986
12 Tampa Bay, 1977

Most Consecutive Games Lost, Start of Season
14 Tampa Bay, 1976, entire season
New Orleans, 1980
13 Oakland, 1962
Indianapolis, 1986
12 Tampa Bay, 1977

Most Consecutive Games Lost, End of Season
14 Tampa Bay, 1976, entire season
New England, 1990
13 Pittsburgh, 1969
11 Philadelphia, 1936
Detroit, 1942, entire season
Houston, 1972

Most Consecutive Games Without Victory, Season
14 Tampa Bay, 1976 (lost 14), entire season
New Orleans, 1980 (lost 14)
Baltimore, 1981 (lost 14)
New England, 1990 (lost 14)
13 Washington, 1961 (lost 12, tied 1)
Oakland, 1962 (lost 13)
Pittsburgh, 1969 (lost 13)
Indianapolis, 1986 (lost 13)
12 Dall. Cowboys, 1960 (lost 11, tied 1), entire season
Tampa Bay, 1977 (lost 12)

Most Consecutive Games Without Victory, Start of Season
14 Tampa Bay, 1976 (lost 14), entire season
New Orleans, 1980 (lost 14)
13 Washington, 1961 (lost 12, tied 1)
Oakland, 1962 (lost 13)
Indianapolis, 1986 (lost 13)
12 Dall. Cowboys, 1960 (lost 11, tied 1), entire season
Tampa Bay, 1977 (lost 12)

Most Consecutive Games Without Victory, End of Season
14 Tampa Bay, 1976, (lost 14), entire season
New England, 1990 (lost 14)
13 Pittsburgh, 1969 (lost 13)
12 Dall. Cowboys, 1960 (lost 11, tied 1), entire season

Most Consecutive Home Games Lost
14 Dallas, 1988-89
13 Houston, 1972-73
Tampa Bay, 1976-77
N.Y. Jets, 1995-97
11 Oakland, 1961-62
Los Angeles, 1961-63

Most Consecutive Home Games Without Victory
14 Dallas, 1988-89 (lost 14)
13 Houston, 1972-73 (lost 13)
Tampa Bay, 1976-77 (lost 13)
N.Y. Jets, 1995-97 (lost 13)
12 Philadelphia, 1936-38 (lost 11, tied 1)

Most Consecutive Road Games Lost
23 Houston, 1981-84
22 Buffalo, 1983-86
19 Tampa Bay, 1983-85
Atlanta, 1988-91

Most Consecutive Road Games Without Victory
23 Houston, 1981-84 (lost 23)
22 Buffalo, 1983-86 (lost 22)
19 Tampa Bay, 1983-85 (lost 19)
Atlanta, 1988-91 (lost 19)

Most Shutout Games Lost or Tied, Season
8 Frankford, 1927 (lost 6, tied 2)
Brooklyn, 1931 (lost 8)
7 Dayton, 1925 (lost 6, tied 1)
Orange, 1929 (lost 4, tied 3)
Frankford, 1931 (lost 6, tied 1)
6 By many teams

Most Consecutive Shutout Games Lost or Tied
8 Rochester, 1922-24 (lost 8)
7 Hammond, 1922-23 (lost 6, tied 1)
6 Providence, 1926-27 (lost 5, tied 1)
Brooklyn, 1942-43 (lost 6)

TIE GAMES

Most Tie Games, Season
6 Chi. Bears, 1932
5 Frankford, 1929
4 Chi. Bears, 1924
Orange, 1929
Portsmouth, 1932

Most Consecutive Tie Games
3 Chi. Bears, 1932
2 By many teams

SCORING

Most Seasons Leading League
10 Chi. Bears, 1932, 1934-35, 1939, 1941-43, 1946-47, 1956
9 San Francisco, 1953, 1965, 1970, 1987, 1989, 1992-95
7 Green Bay, 1931, 1936-38, 1961-62, 1996

Most Consecutive Seasons Leading League
4 San Francisco, 1992-1995
3 Green Bay, 1936-38
Chi. Bears, 1941-43
Los Angeles, 1950-52
Oakland, 1967-69
2 By many teams

POINTS

Most Points, Season
556 Minnesota, 1998
541 Washington, 1983
513 Houston, 1961
Miami, 1984

Fewest Points, Season (Since 1932)
37 Cincinnati/St. Louis, 1934
38 Cincinnati, 1933
Detroit, 1942
51 Pittsburgh, 1934
Philadelphia, 1936

Most Points, Game
72 Washington vs. N.Y. Giants, Nov. 27, 1966
70 Los Angeles vs. Baltimore, Oct. 22, 1950
65 Chi. Cardinals vs. N.Y. Bulldogs, Nov. 13, 1949
Los Angeles vs. Detroit, Oct. 29, 1950

Most Points, Both Teams, Game
113 Washington (72) vs. N.Y. Giants (41), Nov. 27, 1966
101 Oakland (52) vs. Houston (49), Dec. 22, 1963
99 Seattle (51) vs. Kansas City (48), Nov. 27, 1983 (OT)

Fewest Points, Both Teams, Game
0 In many games. Last time: N.Y. Giants vs. Detroit, Nov. 7, 1943

Most Points, Shutout Victory, Game
64 Philadelphia vs. Cincinnati, Nov. 6, 1934
62 Akron vs. Oorang, Oct. 29, 1922
60 Rock Island vs. Evansville, Oct. 15, 1922
Chi. Cardinals vs. Rochester, Oct. 7, 1923

Fewest Points, Shutout Victory, Game
2 Green Bay vs. Chi. Bears, Oct. 16, 1932
Chi. Bears vs. Green Bay, Sept. 18, 1938

Most Points Overcome to Win Game
28 San Francisco vs. New Orleans, Dec. 7, 1980 (OT) (trailed 7-35, won 38-35)
26 Buffalo vs. Indianapolis, Sept., 21, 1997 (trailed 26-0, won 37-35)
25 St. Louis vs. Tampa Bay, Nov. 8, 1987 (trailed 3-28, won 31-28)

Most Points Overcome to Tie Game
31 Denver vs. Buffalo, Nov. 27, 1960 (trailed 7-38, tied 38-38)
28 Los Angeles vs. Philadelphia, Oct. 3, 1948 (trailed 0-28, tied 28-28)

Most Points, Each Half
1st: 49 Green Bay vs. Tampa Bay, Oct. 2, 1983
48 Buffalo vs. Miami, Sept. 18, 1966
45 Green Bay vs. Cleveland, Nov. 12, 1967
Indianapolis vs. Denver, Oct. 31, 1988
Houston vs. Cleveland, Dec. 9, 1990
2nd: 49 Chi. Bears vs. Philadelphia, Nov. 30, 1941
48 Chi. Cardinals vs. Baltimore, Oct. 2, 1950
N.Y. Giants vs. Baltimore, Nov. 19, 1950
45 Cincinnati vs. Houston, Dec. 17, 1972

Most Points, Both Teams, Each Half
1st: 70 Houston (35) vs. Oakland (35), Dec. 22, 1963
62 N.Y. Jets (41) vs. Tampa Bay (21), Nov. 17, 1985
59 St. Louis (31) vs. Philadelphia (28), Dec. 16, 1962
2nd: 65 Washington (38) vs. N.Y. Giants (27), Nov. 27, 1966
62 L.A. Raiders (31) vs. San Diego (31), Jan. 2, 1983
58 New England (37) vs. Baltimore (21), Nov. 23, 1980
N.Y. Jets (37) vs. New England (21), Sept. 21, 1987

Most Points, One Quarter
41 Green Bay vs. Detroit, Oct. 7, 1945 (second quarter)
Los Angeles vs. Detroit, Oct. 29, 1950 (third quarter)
37 Los Angeles vs. Green Bay, Sept. 21, 1980 (second quarter)
35 Chi. Cardinals vs. Boston, Oct. 24, 1948 (third quarter)
Green Bay vs. Cleveland, Nov. 12, 1967 (first quarter)
Green Bay vs. Tampa Bay, Oct. 2, 1983 (second quarter)

Most Points, Both Teams, One Quarter
49 Oakland (28) vs. Houston (21), Dec. 22, 1963 (second quarter)
48 Green Bay (41) vs. Detroit (7), Oct. 7, 1945 (second quarter)
Los Angeles (41) vs. Detroit (7), Oct. 29, 1950 (third quarter)
47 St. Louis (27) vs. Philadelphia (20), Dec. 13, 1964 (second quarter)

Most Points, Each Quarter
1st: 35 Green Bay vs. Cleveland, Nov. 12, 1967
31 Buffalo vs. Kansas City, Sept. 13, 1964
28 By eight teams
2nd: 41 Green Bay vs. Detroit, Oct. 7, 1945
37 Los Angeles vs. Green Bay, Sept. 21, 1980
35 Green Bay vs. Tampa Bay, Oct. 2, 1983
3rd: 41 Los Angeles vs. Detroit, Oct. 29, 1950
35 Chi. Cardinals vs. Boston, Oct. 24, 1948
28 By 10 teams
4th: 31 Oakland vs. Denver, Dec. 17, 1960
Oakland vs. San Diego, Dec. 8, 1963
Atlanta vs. Green Bay, Sept. 13, 1981
28 By many teams

Most Points, Both Teams, Each Quarter
1st: 42 Green Bay (35) vs. Cleveland (7), Nov. 12, 1967
35 Dall. Texans (21) vs. N.Y. Titans (14), Nov. 11, 1962
Dallas (28) vs. Philadelphia (7), Oct. 19, 1969
Kansas City (21) vs. Seattle (14), Dec. 11, 1977
Detroit (21) vs. L.A. Raiders (14), Dec. 10, 1990
Dallas (21) vs. Atlanta (14), Dec. 22, 1991
34 Los Angeles (21) vs. Baltimore (13), Oct. 22, 1950
Oakland (21) vs. Atlanta (13), Nov. 30, 1975
2nd: 49 Oakland (28) vs. Houston (21), Dec. 22, 1963
48 Green Bay (41) vs. Detroit (7), Oct. 7, 1945
47 St. Louis (27) vs. Philadelphia (20), Dec. 13, 1964
3rd: 48 Los Angeles (41) vs. Detroit (7), Oct. 29, 1950
42 Washington (28) vs. Philadelphia (14), Oct. 1, 1955
41 Green Bay (21) vs. N.Y. Yanks (20), Oct. 8, 1950
4th: 42 Chi. Cardinals (28) vs. Philadelphia (14), Dec. 7, 1947
Green Bay (28) vs. Chi. Bears (14), Nov. 6, 1955
N.Y. Jets (28) vs. Boston (14), Oct. 27, 1968
Pittsburgh (21) vs. Cleveland (21), Oct. 18, 1969
41 Baltimore (27) vs. New England (14), Sept. 18, 1978
New England (27) vs. Baltimore (14), Nov. 23, 1980
40 Chicago (21) vs. Tampa Bay (19), Nov. 19, 1989

Most Consecutive Games Scoring
338 San Francisco, 1977-98 (current)
274 Cleveland, 1950-71
218 Dallas, 1970-85

TOUCHDOWNS

Most Seasons Leading League, Touchdowns
13 Chi. Bears, 1932, 1934-35, 1939, 1941-44, 1946-48, 1956, 1965
7 Dallas, 1966, 1968, 1971, 1973, 1977-78, 1980
San Francisco, 1953, 1970, 1987, 1992-95
6 Oakland, 1967-69, 1972, 1974, 1977
San Diego, 1963, 1965, 1979, 1981-82, 1985
Green Bay, 1932, 1937-38, 1961-62, 1996

Most Consecutive Seasons Leading League, Touchdowns
4 Chi. Bears, 1941-44
Los Angeles, 1949-52
San Francisco, 1992-95
3 Chi. Bears, 1946-48
Baltimore, 1957-59
Oakland, 1967-69
2 By many teams

Most Touchdowns, Season
70 Miami, 1984
66 Houston, 1961
San Francisco, 1994
64 Los Angeles, 1950
Minnesota, 1998

Fewest Touchdowns, Season (Since 1932)
3 Cincinnati, 1933
4 Cincinnati/St. Louis, 1934
5 Detroit, 1942

Most Touchdowns, Game
10 Philadelphia vs. Cincinnati, Nov. 6, 1934
Los Angeles vs. Baltimore, Oct. 22, 1950
Washington vs. N.Y. Giants, Nov. 27, 1966
9 Chi. Cardinals vs. Rochester, Oct. 7, 1923
Chi. Cardinals vs. N.Y. Giants, Oct. 17, 1948
Chi. Cardinals vs. N.Y. Bulldogs, Nov. 13, 1949
Los Angeles vs. Detroit, Oct. 29, 1950
Pittsburgh vs. N.Y. Giants, Nov. 30, 1952
Chicago vs. San Francisco, Dec. 12, 1965
Chicago vs. Green Bay, Dec. 7, 1980
8 By many teams.

Most Touchdowns, Both Teams, Game
16 Washington (10) vs. N.Y. Giants (6), Nov. 27, 1966
14 Chi. Cardinals (9) vs. N.Y. Giants (5), Oct. 17, 1948
Los Angeles (10) vs. Baltimore (4), Oct. 22, 1950
Houston (7) vs. Oakland (7), Dec. 22, 1963
13 New Orleans (7) vs. St. Louis (6), Nov. 2, 1969
Kansas City (7) vs. Seattle (6), Nov. 27, 1983 (OT)
San Diego (8) vs. Pittsburgh (5), Dec. 8, 1985
N.Y. Jets (7) vs. Miami (6), Sept. 21, 1986 (OT)
Most Consecutive Games Scoring Touchdowns
166 Cleveland, 1957-69
97 Oakland, 1966-73
96 Kansas City, 1963-70

POINTS AFTER TOUCHDOWN
Most (One-Point) Points After Touchdown, Season
66 Miami, 1984
65 Houston, 1961
62 Washington, 1983
Fewest (One-Point) Points After Touchdown, Season
2 Chi. Cardinals, 1933
3 Cincinnati, 1933
Pittsburgh, 1934
4 Cincinnati/St. Louis, 1934
Most (One-Point) Points After Touchdown, Game
10 Los Angeles vs. Baltimore, Oct. 22, 1950
9 Chi. Cardinals vs. N.Y. Giants, Oct. 17, 1948
Pittsburgh vs. N.Y. Giants, Nov. 30, 1952
Washington vs. N.Y. Giants, Nov. 27, 1966
8 By many teams
Most (One-Point) Points After Touchdown, Both Teams, Game
14 Chi. Cardinals (9) vs. N.Y. Giants (5), Oct. 17, 1948
Houston (7) vs. Oakland (7), Dec. 22, 1963
Washington (9) vs. N.Y. Giants (5), Nov. 27, 1966
13 Los Angeles (10) vs. Baltimore (3), Oct. 22, 1950
12 In many games
Most Two-Point Conversions, Season
6 Miami, 1994
Minnesota, 1997
5 Arizona, 1995
Baltimore, 1996
Jacksonville, 1996
Chicago, 1997
San Francisco, 1998
4 By many teams
Most Two-Point Conversions, Game
3 Baltimore vs. New England, Oct. 6, 1996
Pittsburgh vs. Tennessee, Nov. 1, 1998
2 Denver vs. Oakland, Oct. 1, 1961
Oakland vs. San Diego, Sept. 30, 1962
Kansas City vs. Houston, Oct. 24, 1965
Houston vs. N.Y. Jets, Dec. 6, 1969
Seattle vs. Kansas City, Oct. 23, 1994
Tampa Bay vs. San Francisco, Oct. 23, 1994
Detroit vs. Green Bay, Nov. 6, 1994
Washington vs. San Francisco, Nov. 6, 1994
Carolina vs. New Orleans, Nov. 26, 1995
Miami vs. Indianapolis, Nov. 26, 1995
New England vs. Baltimore, Oct. 6, 1996
Minnesota vs. Seattle, Nov. 10, 1996
Denver vs. Atlanta, Sept. 28, 1997
Kansas City vs. St. Louis, Oct. 26, 1997
Indianapolis vs. Green Bay, Nov. 16, 1997
Carolina vs. St. Louis, Dec. 20, 1997
Most Two-Point Conversions, Both Teams, Game
5 Baltimore (3) vs. New England (2), Oct. 6, 1996
3 Seattle (2) vs. Kansas City (1), Oct. 23, 1994
Minnesota (2) vs. Seattle (1), Nov. 10, 1996
Pittsburgh (3) vs. Tennessee (0), Nov. 1, 1998
2 In many games

FIELD GOALS
Most Seasons Leading League, Field Goals
11 Green Bay, 1935-36, 1940-43, 1946-47, 1955, 1972, 1974
8 Washington, 1945, 1956, 1971, 1976-77, 1979, 1982, 1992
7 N.Y. Giants, 1933, 1937, 1939, 1941, 1944, 1959, 1983
Most Consecutive Seasons Leading League, Field Goals
4 Green Bay, 1940-43
3 Cleveland, 1952-54
2 By many teams
Most Field Goals Attempted, Season
49 Los Angeles, 1966
Washington, 1971
48 Green Bay, 1972
47 N.Y. Jets, 1969
Los Angeles, 1973
Washington, 1983
Fewest Field Goals Attempted, Season (Since 1938)
0 Chi. Bears, 1944
2 Cleveland, 1939
Card-Pitt, 1944
Boston, 1946
Chi. Bears, 1947
3 Chi. Bears, 1945
Cleveland, 1945
Most Field Goals Attempted, Game
9 St. Louis vs. Pittsburgh, Sept. 24, 1967
8 Pittsburgh vs. St. Louis, Dec. 2, 1962
Detroit vs. Minnesota, Nov. 13, 1966
N.Y. Jets vs. Buffalo, Nov. 3, 1968
7 By many teams
Most Field Goals Attempted, Both Teams, Game
11 St. Louis (6) vs. Pittsburgh (5), Nov. 13, 1966
Washington (6) vs. Chicago (5), Nov. 14, 1971
Green Bay (6) vs. Detroit (5), Sept. 29, 1974
Washington (6) vs. N.Y. Giants (5), Nov. 14, 1976
10 In many games
Most Field Goals, Season
37 Carolina, 1996
36 Indianapolis, 1996
Tennessee, 1998
35 N.Y. Giants, 1983
L.A. Raiders, 1993
Minnesota, 1998
Fewest Field Goals, Season (Since 1932)
0 Boston, 1932, 1935
Chi. Cardinals, 1932, 1945
Green Bay, 1932, 1944
N.Y. Giants, 1932
Brooklyn, 1944
Card-Pitt, 1944
Chi. Bears, 1944, 1947
Boston, 1946
Baltimore, 1950
Dallas, 1952
Most Field Goals, Game
7 St. Louis vs. Pittsburgh, Sept. 24, 1967
Minnesota vs. L.A. Rams, Nov. 5, 1989 (OT)
Dallas vs. Green Bay, Nov. 18, 1996
6 Boston vs. Denver, Oct. 4, 1964
Detroit vs. Minnesota, Nov. 13, 1966
N.Y. Jets vs. Buffalo, Nov. 3, 1968
Philadelphia vs. Houston, Nov. 12, 1972
N.Y. Jets vs. New Orleans, Dec. 3, 1972
St. Louis vs. Atlanta, Dec. 9, 1973
N.Y. Giants vs. Seattle, Oct. 18, 1981
San Francisco vs. New Orleans, Oct. 16, 1983
Pittsburgh vs. Denver, Oct. 23, 1988
San Diego vs. Seattle, Sept. 5, 1993
San Diego vs. Houston, Sept. 19, 1993
Cincinnati vs. Seattle, Nov. 6, 1994
Atlanta vs. New Orleans, Nov. 13, 1994
San Francisco vs. Atlanta, Sept. 29, 1996
Buffalo vs. N.Y. Jets, Oct. 20, 1996
San Diego vs. Oakland, Oct. 5, 1997
Minnesota vs. Baltimore, Dec. 13, 1998
5 By many teams
Most Field Goals, Both Teams, Game
9 San Diego (5) vs. Kansas City (4), Sept. 29, 1996
8 Cleveland (4) vs. St. Louis (4), Sept. 20, 1964
Chicago (5) vs. Philadelphia (3), Oct. 20, 1968
Washington (5) vs. Chicago (3), Nov. 14, 1971
Kansas City (5) vs. Buffalo (3), Dec. 19, 1971
Detroit (4) vs. Green Bay (4), Sept. 29, 1974
Cleveland (5) vs. Denver (3), Oct. 19, 1975
New England (4) vs. San Diego (4), Nov. 9, 1975
San Francisco (6) vs. New Orleans (2), Oct. 16, 1983
Seattle (5) vs. L.A. Raiders (3), Dec. 18, 1988
Atlanta (6) vs. New Orleans (2), Nov. 13, 1994
Indianapolis (4) vs. San Diego (4), Nov. 3, 1996
7 In many games
Most Consecutive Games Scoring Field Goals
31 Minnesota, 1968-70
28 Washington, 1988-90
22 San Francisco, 1988-89

SAFETIES

Most Safeties, Season

4 Cleveland, 1927
Detroit, 1962
Seattle, 1993
San Francisco, 1996
3 By many teams

Most Safeties, Game

3 L.A. Rams vs. N.Y. Giants, Sept. 30, 1984
2 N.Y. Giants vs. Pottsville, Oct. 30, 1927
Chi. Bears vs. Pottsville, Nov. 13, 1927
Detroit vs. Brooklyn, Dec. 1, 1935
N.Y. Giants vs. Pittsburgh, Sept. 17, 1950
N.Y. Giants vs. Washington, Nov. 5, 1961
Chicago vs. Pittsburgh, Nov. 9, 1969
Dallas vs. Philadelphia, Nov. 19, 1972
Los Angeles vs. Green Bay, Oct. 21, 1973
Oakland vs. San Diego, Oct. 26, 1975
Denver vs. Seattle, Jan. 2, 1983
New Orleans vs. Cleveland, Sept. 13, 1987
Buffalo vs. Denver, Nov. 8, 1987
San Francisco vs. St. Louis, Sept. 8, 1996

Most Safeties, Both Teams, Game

3 L.A. Rams (3) vs. N.Y. Giants (0), Sept. 30, 1984
2 Chi. Cardinals (1) vs. Frankford (1), Nov. 19, 1927
Chi. Cardinals (1) vs. Cincinnati (1), Nov. 12, 1933
Chi. Bears (1) vs. San Francisco (1), Oct. 19, 1952
Cincinnati (1) vs. Los Angeles (1), Oct. 22, 1972
Chi. Bears (1) vs. San Francisco (1), Sept. 19, 1976
Baltimore (1) vs. Miami (1), Oct. 29, 1978
Atlanta (1) vs. Detroit (1), Oct. 5, 1980
Houston (1) vs. Philadelphia (1), Oct. 2, 1988
Cleveland (1) vs. Seattle (1), Nov. 14, 1993
Arizona (1) vs. Houston (1), Dec. 4, 1994
(Also see previous record)

FIRST DOWNS

Most Seasons Leading League

9 Chi. Bears, 1935, 1939, 1941, 1943, 1945, 1947-49, 1955
7 San Diego, 1965, 1969, 1980-83, 1985
6 L.A. Rams, 1946, 1950-51, 1954, 1957, 1973
San Francisco, 1965, 1987, 1989, 1993-94, 1998

Most Consecutive Seasons Leading League

4 San Diego, 1980-83
3 Chi. Bears, 1947-49
2 By many teams

Most First Downs, Season

387 Miami, 1984
381 San Francisco, 1998
380 San Diego, 1985

Fewest First Downs, Season

51 Cincinnati, 1933
64 Pittsburgh, 1935
67 Philadelphia, 1937

Most First Downs, Game

39 N.Y. Jets vs. Miami, Nov. 27, 1988
Washington vs. Detroit, Nov. 4, 1990 (OT)
38 Los Angeles vs. N.Y. Giants, Nov. 13, 1966
37 Green Bay vs. Philadelphia, Nov. 11, 1962

Fewest First Downs, Game

0 N.Y. Giants vs. Green Bay, Oct. 1, 1933
Pittsburgh vs. Boston, Oct. 29, 1933
Philadelphia vs. Detroit, Sept. 20, 1935
N.Y. Giants vs. Washington, Sept. 27, 1942
Denver vs. Houston, Sept. 3, 1966

Most First Downs, Both Teams, Game

62 San Diego (32) vs. Seattle (30), Sept. 15, 1985
59 Miami (31) vs. Buffalo (28), Oct. 9, 1983 (OT)
Seattle (33) vs. Kansas City (26), Nov. 27, 1983 (OT)
N.Y. Jets (32) vs. Miami (27), Sept. 21, 1986 (OT)
N.Y. Jets (39) vs. Miami (20), Nov. 27, 1988
58 Los Angeles (30) vs. Chi. Bears (28), Oct. 24, 1954
Denver (34) vs. Kansas City (24), Nov. 18, 1974
Atlanta (35) vs. New Orleans (23), Sept. 2, 1979 (OT)
Pittsburgh (36) vs. Cleveland (22), Nov. 25, 1979 (OT)
San Diego (34) vs. Miami (24), Nov. 18, 1984 (OT)
Cincinnati (32) vs. San Diego (26), Sept. 22, 1985

Fewest First Downs, Both Teams, Game

7 Chi. Cardinals (2) vs. Detroit (5), Sept. 15, 1940
9 Pittsburgh (1) vs. Boston (8), Oct. 27, 1935
Boston (4) vs. Brooklyn (5), Nov. 24, 1935
N.Y. Giants (3) vs. Detroit (6), Nov. 7, 1943
Pittsburgh (4) vs. Chi. Cardinals (5), Nov. 11, 1945
N.Y. Bulldogs (1) vs. Philadelphia (8), Sept. 22, 1949
10 N.Y. Giants (4) vs. Washington (6), Dec. 11, 1960

Most First Downs, Rushing, Season

181 New England, 1978
177 Los Angeles, 1973
176 Chicago, 1985

Fewest First Downs, Rushing, Season

36 Cleveland, 1942
Boston, 1944
39 Brooklyn, 1943
40 Philadelphia, 1940
Detroit, 1945

Most First Downs, Rushing, Game

25 Philadelphia vs. Washington, Dec. 2, 1951
23 St. Louis vs. New Orleans, Oct. 5, 1980
21 Cleveland vs. Philadelphia, Dec. 13, 1959
Green Bay vs. Philadelphia, Nov. 11, 1962
Los Angeles vs. New Orleans, Nov. 25, 1973
Pittsburgh vs. Kansas City, Nov. 7, 1976
New England vs. Denver, Nov. 28, 1976
Oakland vs. Green Bay, Sept. 17, 1978
Buffalo vs. Washington, Nov. 3, 1996
San Francisco vs. Detroit, Dec. 14, 1998

Fewest First Downs, Rushing, Game

0 By many teams. Last time: Washington vs. N.Y. Giants, Dec. 13, 1997

Most First Downs, Rushing, Both Teams, Game

36 Philadelphia (25) vs. Washington (11), Dec. 2, 1951
31 Detroit (18) vs. Washington (13), Sept. 30, 1951
30 Los Angeles (17) vs. Minnesota (13), Nov. 5, 1961
New Orleans (17) vs. Green Bay (13), Sept. 9, 1979
New Orleans (16) vs. San Francisco (14), Nov. 11, 1979
New England (16) vs. Kansas City (14), Oct. 4, 1981

Fewest First Downs, Rushing, Both Teams, Game

2 Houston (0) vs. Denver (2), Dec. 2, 1962
N.Y. Jets, (1) vs. St. Louis (1), Dec. 3, 1995
3 Philadelphia (1) vs. Pittsburgh (2), Oct. 27, 1957
Boston (1) vs. Buffalo (2), Nov. 15, 1964
Los Angeles (0) vs. San Francisco (3), Dec. 6, 1964
Pittsburgh (1) vs. St. Louis (2), Nov. 13, 1966
Seattle (1) vs. New Orleans (2), Sept. 1, 1991
New Orleans (0) vs. N.Y. Jets (3), Dec. 24, 1995
Philadelphia (1) vs. Carolina (2), Oct. 27, 1996
San Diego (1) vs. New Orleans (2), Sept. 7, 1997
New Orleans (1) vs. Tampa Bay (2), Oct, 25, 1998
New England (1) vs. Miami (2), Oct. 25, 1998 (OT)
Miami (1) vs. New England (2), Nov. 23, 1998
4 In many games

Most First Downs, Passing, Season

259 San Diego, 1985
251 Houston, 1990
250 Miami, 1986

Fewest First Downs, Passing, Season

18 Pittsburgh, 1941
23 Brooklyn, 1942
N.Y. Giants, 1944
24 N.Y. Giants, 1943

Most First Downs, Passing, Game

29 N.Y. Giants vs. Cincinnati, Oct. 13, 1985
27 San Diego vs. Seattle, Sept. 15, 1985
26 Miami vs. Cleveland, Dec. 12, 1988

Fewest First Downs, Passing, Game

0 By many teams. Last time:
San Diego vs. Kansas City, Sept. 20, 1998

Most First Downs, Passing, Both Teams, Game

43 San Diego (23) vs. Cincinnati (20), Dec. 20, 1982
Miami (24) vs. N.Y. Jets (19), Sept. 21, 1986 (OT)
42 San Francisco (22) vs. San Diego (20), Dec. 11, 1982
41 San Diego (27) vs. Seattle (14), Sept. 15, 1985
Miami (26) vs. Cleveland (15), Dec. 12, 1988

Fewest First Downs, Passing, Both Teams, Game

0 Brooklyn vs. Pittsburgh, Nov. 29, 1942
1 Green Bay (0) vs. Cleveland (1), Sept. 21, 1941
Pittsburgh (0) vs. Brooklyn (1), Oct. 11, 1942
N.Y. Giants (0) vs. Detroit (1), Nov. 7, 1943
Pittsburgh (0) vs. Chi. Cardinals (1), Nov. 11, 1945
N.Y. Bulldogs (0) vs. Philadelphia (1), Sept. 22, 1949
Chicago (0) vs. Buffalo (1), Oct. 7, 1979
2 In many games

Most First Downs, Penalty, Season

43 Denver, 1994
42 Chicago, 1987
41 Denver, 1986

Fewest First Downs, Penalty, Season
2 Brooklyn, 1940
4 Chi. Cardinals, 1940
N.Y. Giants, 1942, 1944
Washington, 1944
Cleveland, 1952
Kansas City, 1969
5 Brooklyn, 1939
Chi. Bears, 1939
Detroit, 1953
Los Angeles, 1953
Houston, 1982

Most First Downs, Penalty, Game
11 Denver vs. Houston, Oct. 6, 1985
9 Chi. Bears vs. Cleveland, Nov. 25, 1951
Baltimore vs. Pittsburgh, Oct. 30, 1977
N.Y. Jets vs. Houston, Sept. 18, 1988
8 Philadelphia vs. Detroit, Dec. 2, 1979
Cincinnati vs. N.Y. Jets, Oct. 6, 1985
Buffalo vs. Houston, Sept. 20, 1987
Houston vs. Atlanta, Sept. 9, 1990
Kansas City vs. L.A. Raiders, Oct. 3, 1993
San Francisco vs. New Orleans, Oct. 11, 1998

Most First Downs, Penalty, Both Teams, Game
12 Buffalo (7) vs. San Francisco (5), Oct. 4, 1998
11 Chi. Bears (9) vs. Cleveland (2), Nov. 25, 1951
Cincinnati (8) vs. N.Y. Jets (3), Oct. 6, 1985
Denver (11) vs. Houston (0), Oct. 6, 1985
Detroit (6) vs. Dallas (5), Nov. 8, 1987
N.Y. Jets (9) vs. Houston (2), Sept. 18, 1988
Kansas City (8) vs. L.A. Raiders (3), Oct. 3, 1993
Detroit (6) vs. San Diego (5), Nov. 11, 1996
10 In many games

NET YARDS GAINED RUSHING AND PASSING

Most Seasons Leading League
12 Chi. Bears, 1932, 1934-35, 1939, 1941-44, 1947, 1949, 1955-56
7 San Diego, 1963, 1965, 1980-83, 1985
6 L.A. Rams, 1946, 1950-51, 1954, 1957, 1973
Baltimore, 1958-60, 1964, 1967, 1976
Dall. Cowboys, 1966, 1968-69, 1971, 1974, 1977
San Francisco, 1965, 1987, 1989, 1992-93, 1998

Most Consecutive Seasons Leading League
4 Chi. Bears, 1941-44
San Diego, 1980-83
3 Baltimore, 1958-60
Houston, 1960-62
Oakland, 1968-70
2 By many teams

Most Yards Gained, Season
6,936 Miami, 1984
6,800 San Francisco, 1998
6,744 San Diego, 1981

Fewest Yards Gained, Season
1,150 Cincinnati, 1933
1,443 Chi. Cardinals, 1934
1,486 Chi. Cardinals, 1933

Most Yards Gained, Game
735 Los Angeles vs. N.Y. Yanks, Sept. 28, 1951
683 Pittsburgh vs. Chi. Cardinals, Dec. 13, 1958
682 Chi. Bears vs. N.Y. Giants, Nov. 14, 1943

Fewest Yards Gained, Game
–7 Seattle vs. Los Angeles, Nov. 4, 1979
–5 Denver vs. Oakland, Sept. 10, 1967
14 Chi. Cardinals vs. Detroit, Sept. 15, 1940

Most Yards Gained, Both Teams, Game
1,133 Los Angeles (636) vs. N.Y. Yanks (497), Nov. 19, 1950
1,102 San Diego (661) vs. Cincinnati (441), Dec. 20, 1982
1,087 St. Louis (589) vs. Philadelphia (498), Dec. 16, 1962

Fewest Yards Gained, Both Teams, Game
30 Chi. Cardinals (14) vs. Detroit (16), Sept. 15, 1940
136 Chi. Cardinals (50) vs. Green Bay (86), Nov. 18, 1934
154 N.Y. Giants (51) vs. Washington (103), Dec. 11, 1960

Most Consecutive Games, 400 or More Yards Gained
11 San Diego, 1982-83
6 Houston, 1961-62
San Diego, 1981
San Francisco, 1987
5 Chi. Bears, 1947
Philadelphia, 1953
Chi. Bears, 1955
Oakland, 1968
New England, 1981
Cincinnati, 1986
San Francisco, 1994
San Francisco, 1998

Most Consecutive Games, 300 or More Yards Gained
29 Los Angeles, 1949-51
26 Miami, 1983-85
25 Miami, 1993-95

RUSHING

Most Seasons Leading League
16 Chi. Bears, 1932, 1934-35, 1939-42, 1951, 1955-56, 1968, 1977, 1983-86
7 Buffalo, 1962, 1964, 1973, 1975, 1982, 1991-92
6 Cleveland, 1958-59, 1963, 1965-67

Most Consecutive Seasons Leading League
4 Chi. Bears, 1939-42
Chi. Bears, 1983-86
3 Detroit, 1936-38
San Francisco, 1952-54
Cleveland, 1965-67
2 By many teams

ATTEMPTS

Most Rushing Attempts, Season
681 Oakland, 1977
674 Chicago, 1984
671 New England, 1978

Fewest Rushing Attempts, Season
211 Philadelphia, 1982
219 San Francisco, 1982
225 Houston, 1982

Most Rushing Attempts, Game
72 Chi. Bears vs. Brooklyn, Oct. 20, 1935
70 Chi. Cardinals vs. Green Bay, Dec. 5, 1948
69 Chi. Cardinals vs. Green Bay, Dec. 6, 1936
Kansas City vs. Cincinnati, Sept. 3, 1978

Fewest Rushing Attempts, Game
6 Chi. Cardinals vs. Boston, Oct. 29, 1933
7 Oakland vs. Buffalo, Oct. 15, 1963
Houston vs. N.Y. Giants, Dec. 8, 1985
Seattle vs. L.A. Raiders, Nov. 17, 1991
Green Bay vs. Miami, Sept. 11, 1994
8 Denver vs. Oakland, Dec. 17, 1960
Buffalo vs. St. Louis, Sept. 9, 1984
Detroit vs. San Francisco, Oct. 20, 1991
Atlanta vs. Detroit, Sept. 5, 1993

Most Rushing Attempts, Both Teams, Game
108 Chi. Cardinals (70) vs. Green Bay (38), Dec. 5, 1948
105 Oakland (62) vs. Atlanta (43), Nov. 30, 1975 (OT)
104 Chi. Bears (64) vs. Pittsburgh (40), Oct. 18, 1936

Fewest Rushing Attempts, Both Teams, Game
34 Atlanta (12) vs. Houston (22), Dec. 5, 1993
Atlanta (15) vs. San Francisco (19), Dec. 24, 1995
35 Seattle (15) vs. New Orleans (20), Sept. 1, 1991
36 Houston (15) vs. N.Y. Jets (21), Oct. 13, 1991

YARDS GAINED

Most Yards Gained Rushing, Season
3,165 New England, 1978
3,088 Buffalo, 1973
2,986 Kansas City, 1978

Fewest Yards Gained Rushing, Season
298 Philadelphia, 1940
467 Detroit, 1946
471 Boston, 1944

Most Yards Gained Rushing, Game
426 Detroit vs. Pittsburgh, Nov. 4, 1934
423 N.Y. Giants vs. Baltimore, Nov. 19, 1950
420 Boston vs. N.Y. Giants, Oct. 8, 1933

Fewest Yards Gained Rushing, Game
–53 Detroit vs. Chi. Cardinals, Oct. 17, 1943
–36 Philadelphia vs. Chi. Bears, Nov. 19, 1939
–33 Phil-Pitt vs. Brooklyn, Oct. 2, 1943

Most Yards Gained Rushing, Both Teams, Game
595 Los Angeles (371) vs. N.Y. Yanks (224), Nov. 18, 1951
574 Chi. Bears (396) vs. Pittsburgh (178), Oct. 10, 1934
558 Boston (420) vs. N.Y. Giants (138), Oct. 8, 1933

Fewest Yards Gained Rushing, Both Teams, Game
–15 Detroit (–53) vs. Chi. Cardinals (38), Oct. 17, 1943
4 Detroit (–10) vs. Chi. Cardinals (14), Sept. 15, 1940
62 L.A. Rams (15) vs. San Francisco (47), Dec. 6, 1964

AVERAGE GAIN
Highest Average Gain, Rushing, Season
5.74 Cleveland, 1963
5.65 San Francisco, 1954
5.56 San Diego, 1963
Lowest Average Gain, Rushing, Season
0.94 Philadelphia, 1940
1.45 Boston, 1944
1.55 Pittsburgh, 1935

TOUCHDOWNS
Most Touchdowns, Rushing, Season
36 Green Bay, 1962
33 Pittsburgh, 1976
30 Chi. Bears, 1941
New England, 1978
Washington, 1983
Fewest Touchdowns, Rushing, Season
1 Brooklyn, 1934
2 Chi. Cardinals, 1933
Cincinnati, 1933
Pittsburgh, 1934
Philadelphia, 1935
Philadelphia, 1936
Philadelphia, 1937
Philadelphia, 1938
Pittsburgh, 1940
Philadelphia, 1972
N.Y. Jets, 1995
3 By many teams
Most Touchdowns, Rushing, Game
7 Los Angeles vs. Atlanta, Dec. 4, 1976
6 By many teams
Most Touchdowns, Rushing, Both Teams, Game
8 Los Angeles (6) vs. N.Y. Yanks (2), Nov. 18, 1951
Chi. Bears (5) vs. Green Bay (3), Nov. 6, 1955
Cleveland (6) vs. Los Angeles (2), Nov. 24, 1957
7 In many games

PASSING
ATTEMPTS
Most Passes Attempted, Season
709 Minnesota, 1981
699 New England, 1994
686 New England, 1995
Fewest Passes Attempted, Season
102 Cincinnati, 1933
106 Boston, 1933
120 Detroit, 1937
Most Passes Attempted, Game
70 New England vs. Minnesota, Nov. 13, 1994
68 Houston vs. Buffalo, Nov 1, 1964
66 Atlanta vs. Detroit, Dec. 24, 1989
Fewest Passes Attempted, Game
0 Green Bay vs. Portsmouth, Oct. 8, 1933
Detroit vs. Cleveland, Sept. 10, 1937
Pittsburgh vs. Brooklyn, Nov. 16, 1941
Pittsburgh vs. Los Angeles, Nov. 13, 1949
Cleveland vs. Philadelphia, Dec. 3, 1950
Most Passes Attempted, Both Teams, Game
112 New England (70) vs. Minnesota (42), Nov. 13, 1994
104 Miami (55) vs. N.Y. Jets (49), Oct. 18, 1987 (OT)
N.Y. Jets (58) vs. San Francisco (46), Sept. 6, 1998 (OT)
102 San Francisco (57) vs. Atlanta (45), Oct. 6, 1985
Fewest Passes Attempted, Both Teams, Game
4 Chi. Cardinals (1) vs. Detroit (3), Nov. 3, 1935
Detroit (0) vs. Cleveland (4), Sept. 10, 1937
6 Chi. Cardinals (2) vs. Detroit (4), Sept. 15, 1940
8 Brooklyn (2) vs. Philadelphia (6), Oct. 1, 1939

COMPLETIONS
Most Passes Completed, Season
432 San Francisco, 1995
411 Houston, 1991
409 Minnesota, 1994
Fewest Passes Completed, Season
25 Cincinnati, 1933
33 Boston, 1933
34 Chi. Cardinals, 1934
Detroit, 1934
Most Passes Completed, Game
45 New England vs. Minnesota, Nov. 13, 1994 (OT)
43 Washington vs. Detroit, Nov. 4, 1990 (OT)
42 N.Y. Jets vs. San Francisco, Sept. 21, 1980
N.Y. Jets vs. Seattle, Dec. 6, 1998
Fewest Passes Completed, Game
0 By many teams. Last time: Buffalo vs. N.Y. Jets, Sept. 29, 1974
Most Passes Completed, Both Teams, Game
71 New England (45) vs. Minnesota (26), Nov. 13, 1994
68 San Francisco (37) vs. Atlanta (31), Oct. 6, 1985
66 Cincinnati (40) vs. San Diego (26), Dec. 20, 1982
Fewest Passes Completed, Both Teams, Game
1 Chi. Cardinals (0) vs. Philadelphia (1), Nov. 8, 1936
Detroit (0) vs. Cleveland (1), Sept. 10, 1937
Chi. Cardinals (0) vs. Detroit (1), Sept. 15, 1940
Brooklyn (0) vs. Pittsburgh (1), Nov. 29, 1942
2 Chi. Cardinals (0) vs. Detroit (2), Nov. 3, 1935
Buffalo (0) vs. N.Y. Jets (2), Sept. 29, 1974
Chi. Cardinals (0) vs. Green Bay (2), Nov. 18, 1934
3 In seven games

YARDS GAINED
Most Seasons Leading League, Passing Yardage
10 San Diego, 1965, 1968, 1971, 1978-83, 1985
8 Chi. Bears, 1932, 1939, 1941, 1943, 1945, 1949, 1954, 1964
Washington, 1938, 1940, 1944, 1947-48, 1967, 1974, 1989
7 Houston, 1960-61, 1963-64, 1990-92
Most Consecutive Seasons Leading League, Passing Yardage
6 San Diego, 1978-83
4 Green Bay, 1934-37
3 Miami, 1986-88
Houston, 1990-92
Most Yards Gained, Passing, Season
5,018 Miami, 1984
4,870 San Diego, 1985
4,805 Houston, 1990
Fewest Yards Gained, Passing, Season
302 Chi. Cardinals, 1934
357 Cincinnati, 1933
459 Boston, 1934
Most Yards Gained, Passing, Game
554 Los Angeles vs. N.Y. Yanks, Sept. 28, 1951
530 Minnesota vs. Baltimore, Sept. 28, 1969
521 Miami vs. N.Y. Jets, Oct. 23, 1988
Fewest Yards Gained, Passing, Game
–53 Denver vs. Oakland, Sept. 10, 1967
–52 Cincinnati vs. Houston, Oct. 31, 1971
–39 Atlanta vs. San Francisco, Oct. 23, 1976
Most Yards Gained, Passing, Both Teams, Game
884 N.Y. Jets (449) vs. Miami (435), Sept. 21, 1986 (OT)
883 San Diego (486) vs. Cincinnati (397), Dec. 20, 1982
874 Miami (456) vs. New England (418), Sept. 4, 1994
Fewest Yards Gained, Passing, Both Teams, Game
–11 Green Bay (–10) vs. Dallas (–1), Oct. 24, 1965
1 Chi. Cardinals (0) vs. Philadelphia (1), Nov. 8, 1936
7 Brooklyn (0) vs. Pittsburgh (7), Nov. 29, 1942

TIMES SACKED
Most Seasons Leading League, Fewest Times Sacked
10 Miami, 1973, 1982-90
4 San Diego, 1963-64, 1967-68
San Francisco, 1964-65, 1970-71
N.Y. Jets, 1965-66, 1968, 1993
3 Houston, 1961-62, 1978
St. Louis, 1974-76
Washington, 1966-67, 1991
Most Consecutive Seasons Leading League, Fewest Times Sacked
9 Miami, 1982-90
3 St. Louis, 1974-76
2 By many teams
Most Times Sacked, Season
104 Philadelphia, 1986
78 Arizona, 1997
72 Philadelphia, 1987
Fewest Times Sacked, Season
7 Miami, 1988
8 San Francisco, 1970
St. Louis, 1975
9 N.Y. Jets, 1966
Washington, 1991
Most Times Sacked, Game
12 Pittsburgh vs. Dallas, Nov. 20, 1966
Baltimore vs. St. Louis, Oct. 26, 1980
Detroit vs. Chicago, Dec. 16, 1984
Houston vs. Dallas, Sept. 29, 1985
11 St. Louis vs. N.Y. Giants, Nov. 1, 1964

Los Angeles vs. Baltimore, Nov. 22, 1964
Denver vs. Buffalo, Dec. 13, 1964
Green Bay vs. Detroit, Nov. 7, 1965
Buffalo vs. Oakland, Oct. 15, 1967
Denver vs. Oakland, Nov. 5, 1967
Atlanta vs. St. Louis, Nov. 24, 1968
Detroit vs. Dallas, Oct. 6, 1975
Philadelphia vs. St. Louis, Dec. 18, 1983
Cleveland vs. Kansas City, Sept. 30, 1984
Minnesota vs. Chicago, Oct. 28, 1984
Atlanta vs. Cleveland, Nov. 18, 1984
Dallas vs. San Diego, Nov. 16, 1986
Philadelphia vs. Detroit, Nov. 16, 1986
Philadelphia vs. L.A. Raiders, Nov. 30, 1986 (OT)
L.A. Raiders vs. Seattle, Dec. 8, 1986
N.Y. Jets vs. Dallas, Oct. 4, 1987
Philadelphia vs. Chicago, Oct. 4, 1987
Dallas vs. Philadelphia, Sept. 15, 1991
Cleveland vs. Indianapolis, Sept. 6, 1992
10 By many teams

Most Times Sacked, Both Teams, Game
18 Green Bay (10) vs. San Diego (8), Sept. 24, 1978
17 Buffalo (10) vs. N.Y. Titans (7), Nov. 23, 1961
Pittsburgh (12) vs. Dallas (5), Nov. 20, 1966
Atlanta (9) vs. Philadelphia (8), Dec. 16, 1984
Philadelphia (11) vs. L.A. Raiders (6), Nov. 30, 1986 (OT)
16 Los Angeles (11) vs. Baltimore (5), Nov. 22, 1964
Buffalo (11) vs. Oakland (5), Oct. 15, 1967

COMPLETION PERCENTAGE

Most Seasons Leading League, Completion Percentage
14 San Francisco, 1952, 1957-58, 1965, 1981, 1983, 1987, 1989, 1992-97
11 Washington, 1937, 1939-40, 1942-45, 1947-48, 1969-70
8 Green Bay, 1936, 1941, 1961-62, 1964, 1966, 1968, 1998

Most Consecutive Seasons Leading League, Completion Percentage
6 San Francisco, 1992-97
4 Washington, 1942-45
Kansas City, 1966-69
3 Cleveland, 1953-55

Highest Completion Percentage, Season
70.65 Cincinnati, 1982 (310-219)
70.25 San Francisco, 1994 (511-359)
70.19 San Francisco, 1989 (483-339)

Lowest Completion Percentage, Season
22.9 Philadelphia, 1936 (170-39)
24.5 Cincinnati, 1933 (102-25)
25.0 Pittsburgh, 1941 (168-42)

TOUCHDOWNS

Most Touchdowns, Passing, Season
49 Miami, 1984
48 Houston, 1961
46 Miami, 1986

Fewest Touchdowns, Passing, Season
0 Cincinnati, 1933
Pittsburgh, 1945
1 Boston, 1932
Boston, 1933
Chi. Cardinals, 1934
Cincinnati/St. Louis, 1934
Detroit, 1942
2 Chi. Cardinals, 1932
Stapleton, 1932
Chi. Cardinals, 1935
Brooklyn, 1936
Pittsburgh, 1942

Most Touchdowns, Passing, Game
7 Chi. Bears vs. N.Y. Giants, Nov. 14, 1943
Philadelphia vs. Washington, Oct. 17, 1954
Houston vs. N.Y. Titans, Nov. 19, 1961
Houston vs. N.Y. Titans, Oct. 14, 1962
N.Y. Giants vs. Washington, Oct. 28, 1962
Minnesota vs. Baltimore, Sept. 28, 1969
San Diego vs. Oakland, Nov. 22, 1981
6 By many teams

Most Touchdowns, Passing, Both Teams, Game
12 New Orleans (6) vs. St. Louis (6), Nov. 2, 1969
11 N.Y. Giants (7) vs. Washington (4), Oct. 28, 1962
Oakland (6) vs. Houston (5), Dec. 22, 1963
10 San Diego (5) vs. Seattle (5), Sept. 15, 1985
Miami (6) vs. N.Y. Jets (4), Sept. 21, 1986 (OT)
San Francisco (6) vs. Atlanta (4), Oct. 14, 1990

PASSES HAD INTERCEPTED

Most Passes Had Intercepted, Season
48 Houston, 1962
45 Denver, 1961
41 Card-Pitt, 1944

Fewest Passes Had Intercepted, Season
5 Cleveland, 1960
Green Bay, 1966
Kansas City, 1990
N.Y. Giants, 1990
6 Green Bay, 1964
St. Louis, 1982
Dallas, 1993
7 Los Angeles, 1969

Most Passes Had Intercepted, Game
9 Detroit vs. Green Bay, Oct. 24, 1943
Pittsburgh vs. Philadelphia, Dec. 12, 1965
8 Green Bay vs. N.Y. Giants, Nov. 21, 1948
Chi. Cardinals vs. Philadelphia, Sept. 24, 1950
N.Y. Yanks vs. N.Y. Giants, Dec. 16, 1951
Denver vs. Houston, Dec. 2, 1962
Chi. Bears vs. Detroit, Sept. 22, 1968
Baltimore vs. N.Y. Jets, Sept. 23, 1973
7 By many teams. Last time:
San Diego vs. Seattle, Dec. 13, 1998

Most Passes Had Intercepted, Both Teams, Game
13 Denver (8) vs. Houston (5), Dec. 2, 1962
11 Philadelphia (7) vs. Boston (4), Nov. 3, 1935
Boston (6) vs. Pittsburgh (5), Dec. 1, 1935
Cleveland (7) vs. Green Bay (4), Oct. 30, 1938
Green Bay (7) vs. Detroit (4), Oct. 20, 1940
Detroit (7) vs. Chi. Bears (4), Nov. 22, 1942
Detroit (7) vs. Cleveland (4), Nov. 26, 1944
Chi. Cardinals (8) vs. Philadelphia (3), Sept. 24, 1950
Washington (7) vs. N.Y. Giants (4), Dec. 8, 1963
Pittsburgh (9) vs. Philadelphia (2), Dec 12, 1965
10 In many games

PUNTING

Most Seasons Leading League (Average Distance)
6 Washington, 1940-43, 1945, 1958
Denver, 1962-64, 1966-67, 1982
Kansas City, 1968, 1971-73, 1979, 1984
5 L.A. Rams, 1946, 1949, 1955-56, 1994

Most Consecutive Seasons Leading League (Average Distance)
4 Washington, 1940-43
3 Cleveland, 1950-52
Denver, 1962-64
Kansas City, 1971-73

Most Punts, Season
114 Chicago, 1981
113 Boston, 1934
Brooklyn, 1934
112 Boston, 1935
N.Y. Giants, 1997

Fewest Punts, Season
23 San Diego, 1982
31 Cincinnati, 1982
32 Chi. Bears, 1941

Most Punts, Game
17 Chi. Bears vs. Green Bay, Oct. 22, 1933
Cincinnati vs. Pittsburgh, Oct. 22, 1933
16 Cincinnati vs. Portsmouth, Sept. 17, 1933
Chi. Cardinals vs. Chi. Bears, Nov. 30, 1933
Chi. Cardinals vs. Detroit, Sept. 15, 1940
Oakland vs. San Diego, Oct. 11, 1998
15 N.Y. Giants vs. Chi. Bears, Nov. 17, 1935
Philadelphia vs. N.Y. Giants, Dec. 6, 1987 (OT)

Fewest Punts, Game
0 By many teams. Last time: Tampa Bay vs. Minnesota, Nov. 1, 1998

Most Punts, Both Teams, Game
31 Chi. Bears (17) vs. Green Bay (14), Oct. 22, 1933
Cincinnati (17), vs. Pittsburgh (14), Oct. 22, 1933
29 Chi. Cardinals (15) vs. Cincinnati (14), Nov. 12, 1933
Chi. Cardinals (16) vs. Chi. Bears (13), Nov. 30, 1933
Chi. Cardinals (16) vs. Detroit (13), Sept. 15, 1940
28 Philadelphia (14) vs. Washington (14), Nov. 5, 1939

Fewest Punts, Both Teams, Game
0 Buffalo vs. San Francisco, Sept. 13, 1992
1 Baltimore (0) vs. Cleveland (1), Nov. 1, 1959
Dall. Cowboys (0) vs. Cleveland (1), Dec. 3, 1961
Chicago (0) vs. Detroit (1), Oct. 1, 1972
San Francisco (0) vs. N.Y. Giants (1), Oct. 15, 1972

Green Bay (0) vs. Buffalo (1), Dec. 5, 1982
Miami (0) vs. Buffalo (1), Oct. 12, 1986
Green Bay (0) vs. Chicago (1), Dec. 17, 1989
2 In many games

AVERAGE YARDAGE

Highest Average Distance, Punting, Season
47.6 Detroit, 1961 (56-2,664)
47.2 Tennessee, 1998 (69-3,258)
47.0 Pittsburgh, 1961 (73-3,431)

Lowest Average Distance, Punting, Season
32.7 Card-Pitt, 1944 (60-1,964)
33.8 Cincinnati, 1986 (59-1,996)
33.9 Detroit, 1969 (74-2,510)

PUNT RETURNS

Most Seasons Leading League (Average Return)
9 Detroit, 1943-45, 1951-52, 1962, 1966, 1969, 1991
7 Chi. Cardinals/St. Louis, 1948-49, 1955-56, 1959, 1986-87
6 Green Bay, 1950, 1953-54, 1961, 1972, 1996

Most Consecutive Seasons Leading League (Average Return)
3 Detroit, 1943-45
2 By many teams

Most Punt Returns, Season
71 Pittsburgh, 1976
Tampa Bay, 1979
L.A. Raiders, 1985
67 Pittsburgh, 1974
Los Angeles, 1978
L.A. Raiders, 1984
65 San Francisco, 1976

Fewest Punt Returns, Season
12 Baltimore, 1981
San Diego, 1982
14 Los Angeles, 1961
Philadelphia, 1962
Baltimore, 1982
15 Houston, 1960
Washington, 1960
Oakland, 1961
N.Y. Giants, 1969
Philadelphia, 1973
Kansas City, 1982

Most Punt Returns, Game
12 Philadelphia vs. Cleveland, Dec. 3, 1950
11 Chi. Bears vs. Chi. Cardinals, Oct. 8, 1950
Washington vs. Tampa Bay, Oct. 9, 1977
10 Philadelphia vs. N.Y. Giants, Nov. 26, 1950
Philadelphia vs. Tampa Bay, Sept. 18, 1977
Pittsburgh vs. Buffalo, Dec. 16, 1979
Washington vs. New Orleans, Dec. 26, 1982
Philadelphia vs. Seattle, Dec. 13, 1992 (OT)
New England vs. Pittsburgh, Dec. 5, 1993

Most Punt Returns, Both Teams, Game
17 Philadelphia (12) vs. Cleveland (5), Dec. 3, 1950
16 N.Y. Giants (9) vs. Philadelphia (7), Dec. 12, 1954
Washington (11) vs. Tampa Bay (5), Oct. 9, 1977
Oakland (8) vs. San Diego (8), Oct. 11, 1998
15 Detroit (8) vs. Cleveland (7), Sept. 27, 1942
Los Angeles (8) vs. Baltimore (7), Nov. 27, 1966
Pittsburgh (8) vs. Houston (7), Dec. 1, 1974
Philadelphia (10) vs. Tampa Bay (5), Sept. 18, 1977
Baltimore (9) vs. Kansas City (6), Sept. 2, 1979
Washington (10) vs. New Orleans (5), Dec. 26, 1982
L.A. Raiders (8) vs. Cleveland (7), Nov. 16, 1986

FAIR CATCHES

Most Fair Catches, Season
34 Baltimore, 1971
32 San Diego, 1969
31 Minnesota, 1996

Fewest Fair Catches, Season
0 San Diego, 1975
New England, 1976
Tampa Bay, 1976
Pittsburgh, 1977
Dallas, 1982
1 Cleveland, 1974
San Francisco, 1975
Kansas City, 1976
St. Louis, 1976
San Diego, 1976
L.A. Rams, 1982
St. Louis, 1982
Tampa Bay, 1982
2 By many teams

Most Fair Catches, Game
7 Minnesota vs. Dallas, Sept. 25, 1966
Detroit vs. Chicago, Nov. 21, 1976
Philadelphia vs. Buffalo, Dec. 27, 1987
6 By many teams

YARDS GAINED

Most Yards, Punt Returns, Season
875 Green Bay, 1996
785 L.A. Raiders, 1985
781 Chi. Bears, 1948

Fewest Yards, Punt Returns, Season
27 St. Louis, 1965
35 N.Y. Giants, 1965
37 New England, 1972

Most Yards, Punt Returns, Game
231 Detroit vs. San Francisco, Oct. 6, 1963
225 Oakland vs. Buffalo, Sept. 15, 1968
219 Los Angeles vs. Atlanta, Oct. 11, 1981

Fewest Yards, Punt Returns, Game
-28 Washington vs. Dallas, Dec. 11, 1966
-23 N.Y. Giants vs. Buffalo, Oct. 20, 1975
Pittsburgh vs. Houston, Sept. 20, 1970
-20 New Orleans vs. Pittsburgh, Oct. 20, 1968

Most Yards, Punt Returns, Both Teams, Game
282 Los Angeles (219) vs. Atlanta (63), Oct. 11, 1981
245 Detroit (231) vs. San Francisco (14), Oct. 6, 1963
244 Oakland (225) vs. Buffalo (19), Sept. 15, 1968

Fewest Yards, Punt Returns, Both Teams, Game
-18 Buffalo (-18) vs. Pittsburgh (0), Oct. 29, 1972
-14 Miami (-14) vs. Boston (0), Nov. 30, 1969
-13 N.Y. Giants (-13) vs. Cleveland (0), Nov. 14, 1965

AVERAGE YARDS RETURNING PUNTS

Highest Average, Punt Returns, Season
20.2 Chi. Bears, 1941 (27-546)
19.1 Chi. Cardinals, 1948 (35-669)
18.2 Chi. Cardinals, 1949 (30-546)

Lowest Average, Punt Returns, Season
1.2 St. Louis, 1965 (23-27)
1.5 N.Y. Giants, 1965 (24-35)
1.7 Washington, 1970 (27-45)

TOUCHDOWNS RETURNING PUNTS

Most Touchdowns, Punt Returns, Season
5 Chi. Cardinals, 1959
4 Chi. Cardinals, 1948
Detroit, 1951
N.Y. Giants, 1951
Denver, 1976
3 Washington, 1941
Detroit, 1952
Pittsburgh, 1952
Houston, 1975
Los Angeles, 1981
Cleveland, 1993
Green Bay, 1996
Denver, 1997
San Diego, 1997

Most Touchdowns, Punt Returns, Game
2 Detroit vs. Los Angeles, Oct. 14, 1951
Detroit vs. Green Bay, Nov. 22, 1951
Chi. Cardinals vs. Pittsburgh, Nov. 1, 1959
Chi. Cardinals vs. N.Y. Giants, Nov. 22, 1959
N.Y. Titans vs. Denver, Sept. 24, 1961
Denver vs. Cleveland, Sept. 26, 1976
Los Angeles vs. Atlanta, Oct. 11, 1981
St. Louis vs. Tampa Bay, Dec. 21, 1986
L.A. Rams vs. Atlanta, Dec. 27, 1992
Cleveland vs. Pittsburgh, Oct. 24, 1993
San Diego vs. Cincinnati, Nov. 2, 1997
Denver vs. Carolina, Nov. 9, 1997
Baltimore vs. Seattle, Dec. 7, 1997

Most Touchdowns, Punt Returns, Both Teams, Game
2 Philadelphia (1) vs. Washington (1), Nov. 9, 1952
Kansas City (1) vs. Buffalo (1), Sept. 11, 1966
Baltimore (1) vs. New England (1), Nov. 18, 1979
L.A. Raiders (1) vs. Philadelphia (1), Nov. 30, 1986 (OT)
Cincinnati (1) vs. Green Bay (1), Sept. 20, 1992
Oakland (1) vs. Seattle (1), Nov. 15, 1998

ALL-TIME RECORDS

(Also see previous record)

KICKOFF RETURNS

Most Seasons Leading League (Average Return)
8 Washington, 1942, 1947, 1962-63, 1973-74, 1981, 1995
6 Chicago Bears, 1943, 1948, 1958, 1966, 1972, 1985
5 N.Y. Giants, 1944, 1946, 1949, 1951, 1953

Most Consecutive Seasons Leading League (Average Return)
3 Denver, 1965-67
2 By many teams

Most Kickoff Returns, Season
88 New Orleans, 1980
87 Atlanta, 1996
86 Minnesota, 1984
Cincinnati, 1994
Baltimore, 1996

Fewest Kickoff Returns, Season
17 N.Y. Giants, 1944
20 N.Y. Giants, 1941, 1943
Chi. Bears, 1942
23 Washington, 1942

Most Kickoff Returns, Game
12 N.Y. Giants vs. Washington, Nov. 27, 1966
10 By many teams

Most Kickoff Returns, Both Teams, Game
19 N.Y. Giants (12) vs. Washington (7), Nov. 27, 1966
18 Houston (10) vs. Oakland (8), Dec. 22, 1963
17 Washington (9) vs. Green Bay (8), Oct. 17, 1983
San Diego (9) vs. Pittsburgh (8), Dec. 8, 1985
Detroit (9) vs. Green Bay (8), Nov. 27, 1986
L.A. Raiders (9) vs. Seattle (8), Dec. 18, 1988
Oakland (10) vs. Seattle (7), Oct. 26, 1997

YARDS GAINED

Most Yards, Kickoff Returns, Season
1,973 New Orleans, 1980
1,899 New Orleans, 1996
1,840 New Orleans, 1994

Fewest Yards, Kickoff Returns, Season
282 N.Y. Giants, 1940
381 Green Bay, 1940
424 Chicago, 1963

Most Yards, Kickoff Returns, Game
367 Baltimore vs. Minnesota, Dec. 13, 1998
362 Detroit vs. Los Angeles, Oct. 29, 1950
304 Chi. Bears vs. Green Bay, Nov. 9, 1952
New Orleans vs. L.A. Rams, Oct. 23, 1994

Most Yards, Kickoff Returns, Both Teams, Game
560 Detroit (362) vs. Los Angeles (198), Oct. 29, 1950
511 Baltimore (367) vs. Minnesota (144), Dec. 13, 1998
501 New Orleans (304) vs. L.A. Rams (197), Oct. 23, 1994

AVERAGE YARDAGE

Highest Average, Kickoff Returns, Season
29.4 Chicago, 1972 (52-1,528)
28.9 Pittsburgh, 1952 (39-1,128)
28.2 Washington, 1962 (61-1,720)

Lowest Average, Kickoff Returns, Season
14.7 N.Y. Jets, 1993 (46-675)
15.8 N.Y. Giants, 1993 (32-507)
15.9 Tampa Bay, 1993 (58-922)

TOUCHDOWNS

Most Touchdowns, Kickoff Returns, Season
4 Green Bay, 1967
Chicago, 1970
Detroit, 1994
3 Los Angeles, 1950
Chi. Cardinals, 1954
San Francisco, 1963
Denver, 1966
Chicago, 1967
New England, 1977
L.A. Rams, 1985
2 By many teams

Most Touchdowns, Kickoff Returns, Game
2 Chi. Bears vs. Green Bay, Sept. 22, 1940
Chi. Bears vs. Green Bay, Nov. 9, 1952
Philadelphia vs. Dallas, Nov. 6, 1966
Green Bay vs. Cleveland, Nov. 12, 1967
L.A. Rams vs. Green Bay, Nov. 24, 1985
New Orleans vs. L.A. Rams, Oct. 23, 1994
Baltimore vs. Minnesota, Dec. 13, 1998

Most Touchdowns, Kickoff Returns, Both Teams, Game
3 Baltimore (2) vs. Minnesota (1), Dec. 13, 1998
2 In many games

FUMBLES

Most Fumbles, Season
56 Chi. Bears, 1938
San Francisco, 1978
54 Philadelphia, 1946
51 New England, 1973

Fewest Fumbles, Season
8 Cleveland, 1959
10 Indianapolis, 1998
Minnesota, 1998
11 Green Bay, 1944

Most Fumbles, Game
10 Phil-Pitt vs. N.Y. Giants, Oct. 9, 1943
Detroit vs. Minnesota, Nov. 12, 1967
Kansas City vs. Houston, Oct. 12, 1969
San Francisco vs. Detroit, Dec. 17, 1978
9 Philadelphia vs. Green Bay, Oct. 13, 1946
Kansas City vs. San Diego, Nov. 15, 1964
N.Y. Giants vs. Buffalo, Oct. 20, 1975
St. Louis vs. Washington, Oct. 25, 1976
San Diego vs. Green Bay, Sept. 24, 1978
Pittsburgh vs. Cincinnati, Oct. 14, 1979
Cleveland vs. Seattle, Dec. 20, 1981
Cleveland vs. Pittsburgh, Dec. 23, 1990
Oakland vs. Seattle, Dec. 22, 1996
8 By many teams

Most Fumbles, Both Teams, Game
14 Washington (8) vs. Pittsburgh (6), Nov. 14, 1937
Chi. Bears (7) vs. Cleveland (7), Nov. 24, 1940
St. Louis (8) vs. N.Y. Giants (6), Sept. 17, 1961
Kansas City (10) vs. Houston (4), Oct. 12, 1969
13 Washington (8) vs. Pittsburgh (5), Nov. 14, 1937
Philadelphia (7) vs. Boston (6), Dec. 8, 1946
N.Y. Giants (7) vs. Washington (6), Nov. 5, 1950
Kansas City (9) vs. San Diego (4), Nov. 15, 1964
Buffalo (7) vs. Denver (6), Dec. 13, 1964
N.Y. Jets (7) vs. Houston (6), Sept. 12, 1965
Houston (8) vs. Pittsburgh (5), Dec. 9, 1973
St. Louis (9) vs. Washington (4), Oct. 25, 1976
Cleveland (9) vs. Seattle (4), Dec. 20, 1981
Green Bay (7) vs. Detroit (6), Oct. 6, 1985
12 In many games

FUMBLES LOST

Most Fumbles Lost, Season
36 Chi. Cardinals, 1959
31 Green Bay, 1952
29 Chi. Cardinals, 1946
Pittsburgh, 1950

Fewest Fumbles Lost, Season
3 Philadelphia, 1938
Minnesota, 1980
4 San Francisco, 1960
Kansas City, 1982
Minnesota, 1998
5 Chi. Cardinals, 1943
Detroit, 1943
N.Y. Giants, 1943
Cleveland, 1959
Minnesota, 1982
San Diego, 1993
Detroit, 1996
Indianapolis, 1998

Most Fumbles Lost, Game
8 St. Louis vs. Washington, Oct. 25, 1976
Cleveland vs. Pittsburgh, Dec. 23, 1990
7 Cincinnati vs. Buffalo, Nov. 30, 1969
Pittsburgh vs. Cincinnati, Oct. 14, 1979
Cleveland vs. Seattle, Dec. 20, 1981
6 By many teams

FUMBLES RECOVERED

Most Fumbles Recovered, Season, Own and Opponents'
58 Minnesota, 1963 (27 own, 31 opp)
51 Chi. Bears, 1938 (37 own, 14 opp)
San Francisco, 1978 (24 own, 27 opp)
50 Philadelphia, 1987 (23 own, 27 opp)

Fewest Fumbles Recovered, Season, Own and Opponents'
9 San Francisco, 1982 (5 own, 4 opp)

11 Cincinnati, 1982 (5 own, 6 opp)
12 Washington, 1994 (6 own, 6 opp)
Arizona, 1997 (7 own, 5 opp)

Most Fumbles Recovered, Game, Own and Opponents'
10 Denver vs. Buffalo, Dec. 13, 1964 (5 own, 5 opp)
Pittsburgh vs. Houston, Dec. 9, 1973 (5 own, 5 opp)
Washington vs. St. Louis, Oct. 25, 1976 (2 own, 8 opp)
9 St. Louis vs. N.Y. Giants, Sept. 17, 1961 (6 own, 3 opp)
Houston vs. Cincinnati, Oct. 27, 1974 (4 own, 5 opp)
Kansas City vs. Dallas, Nov. 10, 1975 (4 own, 5 opp)
Green Bay vs. Detroit, Oct. 6, 1985 (5 own, 4 opp)
Pittsburgh vs. Cleveland, Dec. 23, 1990 (1 own, 8 opp)
8 By many teams

Most Own Fumbles Recovered, Season
37 Chi. Bears, 1938
28 Pittsburgh, 1987
27 Philadelphia, 1946
Minnesota, 1963

Fewest Own Fumbles Recovered, Season
2 Washington, 1958
3 Detroit, 1956
Cleveland, 1959
Houston, 1982
4 By many teams

Most Opponents' Fumbles Recovered, Season
31 Minnesota, 1963
29 Cleveland, 1951
28 Green Bay, 1946
Houston, 1977
Seattle, 1983

Fewest Opponents' Fumbles Recovered, Season
3 Los Angeles, 1974
Green Bay, 1995
4 Philadelphia, 1944
San Francisco, 1982
5 Baltimore, 1982
Arizona, 1997
Baltimore, 1998

Most Opponents' Fumbles Recovered, Game
8 Washington vs. St. Louis, Oct. 25, 1976
Pittsburgh vs. Cleveland, Dec. 23, 1990
7 Buffalo vs. Cincinnati, Nov. 30, 1969
Cincinnati vs. Pittsburgh, Oct. 14, 1979
Seattle vs. Cleveland, Dec. 20, 1981
6 By many teams

TOUCHDOWNS

Most Touchdowns, Fumbles Recovered, Season, Own and Opponents'
5 Chi. Bears, 1942 (1 own, 4 opp)
Los Angeles, 1952 (1 own, 4 opp)
San Francisco, 1965 (1 own, 4 opp)
Oakland, 1978 (2 own, 3 opp)
4 Chi. Bears, 1948 (1 own, 3 opp)
Boston, 1948 (4 opp)
Denver, 1979 (1 own, 3 opp)
Atlanta, 1981 (1 own, 3 opp)
Denver, 1984 (4 opp)
St. Louis, 1987 (4 opp)
Minnesota, 1989 (4 opp)
Atlanta, 1991 (4 opp)
Philadelphia, 1995 (4 opp)
Atlanta, 1998 (4 opp)
New Orleans, 1998 (4 opp)
3 By many teams

Most Touchdowns, Own Fumbles Recovered, Season
2 Chi. Bears, 1953
New England, 1973
Buffalo, 1974
Denver, 1975
Oakland, 1978
Green Bay, 1982
New Orleans, 1983
Cleveland, 1986
Green Bay, 1989
Miami, 1996

Most Touchdowns, Opponents' Fumbles Recovered, Season
4 Detroit, 1937
Chi. Bears, 1942
Boston, 1948
Los Angeles, 1952
San Francisco, 1965
Denver, 1984
St. Louis, 1987
Minnesota, 1989
Atlanta, 1991
Philadelphia, 1995
Atlanta, 1998
New Orleans, 1998
3 By many teams

Most Touchdowns, Fumbles Recovered, Game, Own and Opponents'
2 By many teams

Most Touchdowns, Fumbled Recovered, Game, Both Teams, Own and Opponents'
3 Detroit (2) vs. Minnesota (1), Dec. 9, 1962 (2 own, 1 opp)
Green Bay (2) vs. Dallas (1), Nov. 29, 1964 (3 opp)
Oakland (2) vs. Buffalo (1), Dec. 24, 1967 (3 opp)
Oakland (2) vs. Philadelphia (1), Sept. 24, 1995 (3 opp)

Most Touchdowns, Own Fumbles Recovered, Game
2 Miami vs. New England, Sept.1, 1996

Most Touchdowns, Opponents' Fumbles Recovered, Game
2 Detroit vs. Cleveland, Nov. 7, 1937
Philadelphia vs. N.Y. Giants, Sept. 25, 1938
Chi. Bears vs. Washington, Nov. 28, 1948
N.Y. Giants vs. Pittsburgh, Sept. 17, 1950
Cleveland vs. Dall. Cowboys, Dec. 3, 1961
Cleveland vs. N.Y. Giants, Oct. 25, 1964
Green Bay vs. Dallas, Nov. 29, 1964
San Francisco vs. Detroit, Nov. 14, 1965
Oakland vs. Buffalo, Dec. 24, 1967
N.Y. Giants vs. Green Bay, Sept. 19, 1971
Washington vs. San Diego, Sept. 16, 1973
New Orleans vs. San Francisco, Oct. 19, 1975
Cincinnati vs. Pittsburgh, Oct. 14, 1979
Atlanta vs. Detroit, Oct. 5, 1980
Kansas City vs. Oakland, Oct. 5, 1980
New England vs. Baltimore, Nov. 23, 1980
Denver vs. Green Bay, Oct. 15, 1984
Miami vs. Kansas City, Oct. 11, 1987
St. Louis vs. New Orleans, Oct. 11, 1987
Minnesota vs. Atlanta, Dec. 10, 1989
Atlanta vs. Houston, Dec. 9, 1990
Philadelphia vs. Phoenix, Nov. 24, 1991
Cincinnati vs. Seattle, Sept. 6, 1992
Oakland vs. Philadelphia, Sept. 24, 1995
Pittsburgh vs. New England, Dec. 16, 1995
New England vs. San Diego, Dec.1, 1996

Most Touchdowns, Opponents' Fumbled Recovered, Game, Both Teams
3 Green Bay (2) vs. Dallas (1), Nov. 29, 1964
Oakland (2) vs. Buffalo (1), Dec. 24, 1967
Oakland (2) vs. Philadelphia (1), Sept. 24, 1995

TURNOVERS

(Number of times losing the ball on interceptions and fumbles.)

Most Turnovers, Season
63 San Francisco, 1978
58 Chi. Bears, 1947
Pittsburgh, 1950
N.Y. Giants, 1983
57 Green Bay, 1950
Houston, 1962, 1963
Pittsburgh, 1965

Fewest Turnovers, Season
12 Kansas City, 1982
14 N.Y. Giants, 1943
Cleveland, 1959
N.Y. Giants, 1990
15 Dallas, 1998

Most Turnovers, Game
12 Detroit vs. Chi. Bears, Nov. 22, 1942
Chi. Cardinals vs. Philadelphia, Sept. 24, 1950
Pittsburgh vs. Philadelphia, Dec. 12, 1965
11 San Diego vs. Green Bay, Sept. 24, 1978
10 Washington vs. N.Y. Giants, Dec. 4, 1938
Pittsburgh vs. Green Bay, Nov. 23, 1941
Detroit vs. Green Bay, Oct. 24, 1943
Chi. Cardinals vs. Green Bay, Nov. 10, 1946
Chi. Cardinals vs. N.Y. Giants, Nov. 2, 1952
Minnesota vs. Detroit, Dec. 9, 1962
Houston vs. Oakland, Sept. 7, 1963
Washington vs. N.Y. Giants, Dec. 8, 1963
Chicago vs. Detroit, Sept. 22, 1968
St. Louis vs. Washington, Oct. 25, 1976
N.Y. Jets vs. New England, Nov. 21, 1976
San Francisco vs. Dallas, Oct. 12, 1980
Cleveland vs. Seattle, Dec. 20, 1981
Detroit vs. Denver, Oct. 7, 1984

Most Turnovers, Both Teams, Game

17 Detroit (12) vs. Chi. Bears (5), Nov. 22, 1942
Boston (9) vs. Philadelphia (8), Dec. 8, 1946
16 Chi. Cardinals (12) vs. Philadelphia (4), Sept. 24, 1950
Chi. Cardinals (8) vs. Chi. Bears (8), Dec. 7, 1958
Minnesota (10) vs. Detroit (6), Dec. 9, 1962
Houston (9) vs. Kansas City (7), Oct. 12, 1969
15 Philadelphia (8) vs. Chi. Cardinals (7), Oct. 3, 1954
Denver (9) vs. Houston (6), Dec. 2, 1962
Washington (10) vs. N.Y. Giants (5), Dec. 8, 1963
St. Louis (9) vs. Kansas City (6), Oct. 2, 1983

PENALTIES

Most Seasons Leading League, Fewest Penalties

13 Miami, 1968, 1976-84, 1986, 1990-91
9 Pittsburgh, 1946-47, 1950-52, 1954, 1963, 1965, 1968
7 Boston/New England, 1962, 1964-65, 1973, 1987, 1989, 1993

Most Consecutive Seasons Leading League, Fewest Penalties

9 Miami, 1976-84
3 Pittsburgh, 1950-52
2 By many teams

Most Seasons Leading League, Most Penalties

16 Chi. Bears, 1941-44, 1946-49, 1951, 1959-61, 1963, 1965, 1968, 1976
12 Oakland/L.A. Raiders, 1963, 1966, 1968-69, 1975, 1982, 1984, 1991, 1993-96
7 L.A./St. Louis Rams, 1950, 1952, 1962, 1969, 1978, 1980, 1997

Most Consecutive Seasons Leading League, Most Penalties

4 Chi. Bears, 1941-44, 1946-49
L.A./Oakland Raiders, 1993-96
3 Chi. Cardinals, 1954-56
Chi. Bears, 1959-61
Houston, 1988-90

Fewest Penalties, Season

19 Detroit, 1937
21 Boston, 1935
24 Philadelphia, 1936

Most Penalties, Season

158 Kansas City, 1998
156 L.A. Raiders, 1994
Oakland, 1996
149 Houston, 1989

Fewest Penalties, Game

0 By many teams. Last time:
Philadelphia vs. N.Y. Giants, Dec. 27, 1998

Most Penalties, Game

22 Brooklyn vs. Green Bay, Sept. 17, 1944
Chi. Bears vs. Philadelphia, Nov. 26, 1944
San Francisco vs. Buffalo, Oct. 4, 1998
21 Cleveland vs. Chi. Bears, Nov. 25, 1951
20 Tampa Bay vs. Seattle, Oct. 17, 1976
Oakland vs. Denver, Dec. 15, 1996

Fewest Penalties, Both Teams, Game

0 Brooklyn vs. Pittsburgh, Oct. 28, 1934
Brooklyn vs. Boston, Sept. 28, 1936
Cleveland vs. Chi. Bears, Oct. 9, 1938
Pittsburgh vs. Philadelphia, Nov. 10, 1940

Most Penalties, Both Teams, Game

37 Cleveland (21) vs. Chi. Bears (16), Nov. 25, 1951
35 Tampa Bay (20) vs. Seattle (15), Oct. 17, 1976
34 San Francisco (22) vs. Buffalo (12), Oct. 4, 1998

YARDS PENALIZED

Most Seasons Leading League, Fewest Yards Penalized

13 Miami, 1967-68, 1973, 1977-84, 1990-91
10 Boston/Washington, 1935, 1953-54, 1956-58, 1970, 1985, 1995, 1997
7 Pittsburgh, 1946-47, 1950, 1952, 1962, 1965, 1968
Boston/New England, 1962, 1964-66, 1987, 1989, 1993

Most Consecutive Seasons Leading League, Fewest Yards Penalized

8 Miami, 1977-84
3 Washington, 1956-58
Boston, 1964-66
2 By many teams

Most Seasons Leading League, Most Yards Penalized

15 Chi. Bears, 1935, 1937, 1939-44, 1946-47, 1949, 1951, 1961-62, 1968
12 Oakland/L.A. Raiders, 1963-64, 1968-69, 1975, 1982, 1984, 1991, 1993-94, 1996
6 Buffalo, 1962, 1967, 1970, 1972, 1981, 1983
Houston, 1961, 1985-86, 1988-90

Most Consecutive Seasons Leading League, Most Yards Penalized

6 Chi. Bears, 1939-44
3 Cleveland, 1976-78
Houston, 1988-90
2 By many teams

Fewest Yards Penalized, Season

139 Detroit, 1937
146 Philadelphia, 1937
159 Philadelphia, 1936

Most Yards Penalized, Season

1,304 Kansas City, 1998
1,274 Oakland, 1969
1,266 Oakland, 1996

Fewest Yards Penalized, Game

0 By many teams. Last time:
Philadelphia vs. N.Y. Giants, Dec. 27, 1998

Most Yards Penalized, Game

209 Cleveland vs. Chi. Bears, Nov. 25, 1951
191 Philadelphia vs. Seattle, Dec. 13, 1992 (OT)
190 Tampa Bay vs. Seattle, Oct. 17, 1976

Fewest Yards Penalized, Both Teams, Game

0 Brooklyn vs. Pittsburgh, Oct. 28, 1934
Brooklyn vs. Boston, Sept. 28, 1936
Cleveland vs. Chi. Bears, Oct. 9, 1938
Pittsburgh vs. Philadelphia, Nov. 10, 1940

Most Yards Penalized, Both Teams, Game

374 Cleveland (209) vs. Chi. Bears (165), Nov. 25, 1951
310 Tampa Bay (190) vs. Seattle (120), Oct. 17, 1976
309 Green Bay (184) vs. Boston (125), Oct. 21, 1945

DEFENSE

SCORING

Most Seasons Leading League, Fewest Points Allowed

11 N.Y. Giants, 1927, 1935, 1938-39, 1941, 1944, 1958-59, 1961, 1990, 1993
9 Chi. Bears, 1932, 1936-37, 1942, 1948, 1963, 1985-86, 1988
7 Cleveland, 1951, 1953-57, 1994
Green Bay, 1929, 1935, 1947, 1962, 1965-66, 1996

Most Consecutive Seasons Leading League, Fewest Points Allowed

5 Cleveland, 1953-57
3 Buffalo, 1964-66
Minnesota, 1969-71
2 By many teams

Fewest Points Allowed, Season (Since 1932)

44 Chi. Bears, 1932
54 Brooklyn, 1933
59 Detroit, 1934

Most Points Allowed, Season

533 Baltimore, 1981
501 N.Y. Giants, 1966
487 New Orleans, 1980

Fewest Touchdowns Allowed, Season (Since 1932)

6 Chi. Bears, 1932
Brooklyn, 1933
7 Detroit, 1934
8 Green Bay, 1932

Most Touchdowns Allowed, Season

68 Baltimore, 1981
66 N.Y. Giants, 1966
63 Baltimore, 1950

FIRST DOWNS

Fewest First Downs Allowed Season

77 Detroit, 1935
79 Boston, 1935
82 Washington, 1937

Most First Downs Allowed, Season

406 Baltimore, 1981
371 Seattle, 1981
366 Green Bay, 1983

Fewest First Downs Allowed, Rushing, Season

35 Chi. Bears, 1942
40 Green Bay, 1939
41 Brooklyn, 1944

Most First Downs Allowed, Rushing, Season

179 Detroit, 1985
178 New Orleans, 1980
175 Seattle, 1981

Fewest First Downs Allowed, Passing, Season

33 Chi. Bears, 1943
34 Pittsburgh, 1941
Washington, 1943
35 Detroit, 1940
Philadelphia, 1940, 1944

Most First Downs Allowed, Passing, Season

230 Atlanta, 1995
218 San Diego, 1985

216 San Diego, 1981
N.Y. Jets, 1986

Fewest First Downs Allowed, Penalty, Season
1 Boston, 1944
3 Philadelphia, 1940
Pittsburgh, 1945
Washington, 1957
4 Cleveland, 1940
Green Bay, 1943
N.Y. Giants, 1943

Most First Downs Allowed, Penalty, Season
56 Kansas City, 1998
48 Houston, 1985
46 Houston, 1986

NET YARDS ALLOWED RUSHING AND PASSING

Most Seasons Leading League, Fewest Yards Allowed
8 Chi. Bears, 1942-43, 1948, 1958, 1963, 1984-86
6 N.Y. Giants, 1938, 1940-41, 1951, 1956, 1959
Philadelphia, 1944-45, 1949, 1953, 1981, 1991
Minnesota, 1969-70, 1975, 1988-89, 1993
5 Boston/Washington, 1935-37, 1939, 1946

Most Consecutive Seasons Leading League, Fewest Yards Allowed
3 Boston/Washington, 1935-37
Chicago, 1984-86
2 By many teams

Fewest Yards Allowed, Season
1,539 Chi. Cardinals, 1934
1,703 Chi. Bears, 1942
1,789 Brooklyn, 1933

Most Yards Allowed, Season
6,793 Baltimore, 1981
6,403 Green Bay, 1983
6,352 Minnesota, 1984

RUSHING

Most Seasons Leading League, Fewest Yards Allowed
10 Chi. Bears, 1937, 1939, 1942, 1946, 1949, 1963, 1984-85, 1987-88
7 Detroit, 1938, 1950, 1952, 1962, 1970, 1980-81
Philadelphia, 1944-45, 1947-48, 1953, 1990-91
Dallas, 1966-69, 1972, 1978, 1992
5 N.Y. Giants, 1940, 1951, 1956, 1959, 1986

Most Consecutive Seasons Leading League, Fewest Yards Allowed
4 Dallas, 1966-69
2 By many teams

Fewest Yards Allowed, Rushing, Season
519 Chi. Bears, 1942
558 Philadelphia, 1944
762 Pittsburgh, 1982

Most Yards Allowed, Rushing, Season
3,228 Buffalo, 1978
3,106 New Orleans, 1980
3,010 Baltimore, 1978

Fewest Touchdowns Allowed, Rushing, Season
2 Detroit, 1934
Dallas, 1968
Minnesota, 1971
3 By many teams

Most Touchdowns Allowed, Rushing, Season
36 Oakland, 1961
31 N.Y. Giants, 1980
Tampa Bay, 1986
30 Baltimore, 1981

PASSING

Most Seasons Leading League, Fewest Yards Allowed
9 Green Bay, 1947-48, 1962, 1964-68, 1996
7 Washington, 1939, 1942, 1945, 1952-53, 1980, 1985
Philadelphia 1934, 1936, 1940, 1949, 1981, 1991, 1998
6 Chi. Bears, 1938, 1943-44, 1958, 1960, 1963
Minnesota, 1969-70, 1972, 1975-76, 1989
Pittsburgh, 1941, 1946, 1951, 1955, 1974, 1990

Most Consecutive Seasons Leading League, Fewest Yards Allowed
5 Green Bay, 1964-68
2 By many teams

Fewest Yards Allowed, Passing, Season
545 Philadelphia, 1934
558 Portsmouth, 1933
585 Chi. Cardinals, 1934

Most Yards Allowed, Passing, Season
4,541 Atlanta, 1995
4,389 N.Y. Jets, 1986
4,311 San Diego, 1981

Fewest Touchdowns Allowed, Passing, Season
1 Portsmouth, 1932
Philadelphia, 1934
2 Brooklyn, 1933
Chi. Bears, 1934
3 Chi. Bears, 1932
Green Bay, 1932
Green Bay, 1934
Chi. Bears, 1936
New York, 1939
New York, 1944

Most Touchdowns Allowed, Passing, Season
40 Denver, 1963
38 St. Louis, 1969
37 Washington, 1961
Baltimore, 1981

SACKS

Most Seasons Leading League
5 Oakland/L.A. Raiders, 1966-68, 1982, 1986
4 Boston/New England, 1961, 1963, 1977, 1979
Dallas, 1966, 1968-69, 1978
Dallas/Kansas City, 1960, 1965, 1969, 1990
3 San Francisco, 1967, 1972, 1976
L.A. Rams, 1968, 1970, 1988
N.Y. Giants, 1963, 1985, 1998

Most Consecutive Seasons Leading League
3 Oakland, 1966-68
2 Dallas, 1968-69

Most Sacks, Season
72 Chicago, 1984
71 Minnesota, 1989
70 Chicago, 1987

Fewest Sacks, Season
11 Baltimore, 1982
12 Buffalo, 1982
13 Baltimore, 1981

Most Sacks, Game
12 Dallas vs. Pittsburgh, Nov. 20, 1966
St. Louis vs. Baltimore, Oct. 26, 1980
Chicago vs. Detroit, Dec. 16, 1984
Dallas vs. Houston, Sept. 29, 1985
11 N.Y. Giants vs. St. Louis, Nov. 1, 1964
Baltimore vs. Los Angeles, Nov. 22, 1964
Buffalo vs. Denver, Dec. 13, 1964
Detroit vs. Green Bay, Nov. 7, 1965
Oakland vs. Buffalo, Oct. 15, 1967
Oakland vs. Denver, Nov. 5, 1967
St. Louis vs. Atlanta, Nov. 24, 1968
Dallas vs. Detroit, Oct. 6, 1975
St. Louis vs. Philadelphia, Dec. 18, 1983
Kansas City vs. Cleveland, Sept. 30, 1984
Chicago vs. Minnesota, Oct. 28, 1984
Cleveland vs. Atlanta, Nov. 18, 1984
Detroit vs. Philadelphia, Nov. 16, 1986
San Diego vs. Dallas, Nov. 16, 1986
L.A. Raiders vs. Philadelphia, Nov. 30, 1986 (OT)
Seattle vs. L.A. Raiders, Dec. 8, 1986
Chicago vs. Philadelphia, Oct. 4, 1987
Dallas vs. N.Y. Jets, Oct. 4, 1987
Philadelphia vs. Dallas, Sept. 15, 1991
Indianapolis vs. Cleveland, Sept. 6, 1992
10 By many teams

Most Opponents Yards Lost Attempting to Pass, Season
666 Oakland, 1967
583 Chicago, 1984
573 San Francisco, 1976

Fewest Opponents Yards Lost Attempting to Pass, Season
72 Jacksonville, 1995
75 Green Bay, 1956
77 N.Y. Bulldogs, 1949

INTERCEPTIONS BY

Most Seasons Leading League
10 N.Y. Giants, 1933, 1937-39, 1944, 1948, 1951, 1954, 1961, 1997
8 Green Bay, 1940, 1942-43, 1947, 1955, 1957, 1962, 1965
Chi. Bears, 1935-36, 1941-42, 1946, 1963, 1985, 1990
6 Kansas City, 1966-70, 1974

Most Consecutive Seasons Leading League
5 Kansas City, 1966-70
3 N.Y. Giants, 1937-39
2 By many teams

Most Passes Intercepted By, Season
49 San Diego, 1961
42 Green Bay, 1943
41 N.Y. Giants, 1951

Fewest Passes Intercepted By, Season
3 Houston, 1982
5 Baltimore, 1982
6 Houston, 1972
St. Louis, 1982
Atlanta, 1996

Most Passes Intercepted By, Game
9 Green Bay vs. Detroit, Oct. 24, 1943
Philadelphia vs. Pittsburgh, Dec. 12, 1965
8 N.Y. Giants vs. Green Bay, Nov. 21, 1948
Philadelphia vs. Chi. Cardinals, Sept. 24, 1950
N.Y. Giants vs. N.Y. Yanks, Dec. 16, 1951
Houston vs. Denver, Dec. 2, 1962
Detroit vs. Chicago, Sept. 22, 1968
N.Y. Jets vs. Baltimore, Sept. 23, 1973
7 By many teams. Last time:
Seattle vs. San Diego, Dec. 13, 1998

Most Consecutive Games, One or More Interceptions By
46 L.A. Chargers/San Diego, 1960-63
37 Detroit, 1960-63
36 Boston, 1944-47

Most Yards Returning Interceptions, Season
929 San Diego, 1961
712 Los Angeles, 1952
697 Seattle, 1984

Fewest Yards Returning Interceptions, Season
5 Los Angeles, 1959
37 Dallas, 1989
41 Atlanta, 1996

Most Yards Returning Interceptions, Game
325 Seattle vs. Kansas City, Nov. 4, 1984
314 Los Angeles vs. San Francisco, Oct. 18, 1964
245 Houston vs. N.Y. Jets, Oct. 15, 1967

Most Yards Returning Interceptions, Both Teams, Game
356 Seattle (325) vs. Kansas City (31), Nov. 4, 1984
338 Los Angeles (314) vs. San Francisco (24), Oct. 18, 1964
308 Dallas (182) vs. Los Angeles (126), Nov. 2, 1952

Most Touchdowns, Returning Interceptions, Season
9 San Diego, 1961
8 Seattle, 1998
7 Seattle, 1984

Most Touchdowns Returning Interceptions, Game
4 Seattle vs. Kansas City, Nov. 4, 1984
3 Baltimore vs. Green Bay, Nov. 5, 1950
Cleveland vs. Chicago, Dec. 11, 1960
Philadelphia vs. Pittsburgh, Dec. 12, 1965
Baltimore vs. Pittsburgh, Sept. 29, 1968
Buffalo vs. N.Y. Jets, Sept. 29, 1968
Houston vs. San Diego, Dec. 19, 1971
Cincinnati vs. Houston, Dec. 17, 1972
Tampa Bay vs. New Orleans, Dec. 11, 1977
2 By many teams

Most Touchdown Returning Interceptions, Both Teams, Game
4 Philadelphia (3) vs. Pittsburgh (1), Dec. 12, 1965
Seattle (4) vs. Kansas City (0), Nov. 4, 1984
3 Los Angeles (2) vs. Detroit (1), Nov. 1, 1953
Cleveland (2) vs. N.Y. Giants (1), Dec. 18, 1960
Pittsburgh (2) vs. Cincinnati (1), Oct. 10, 1983
Kansas City (2) vs. San Diego (1), Oct. 19, 1986
(Also see previous record)

PUNT RETURNS

Fewest Opponents Punt Returns, Season
7 Washington, 1962
San Diego, 1982
10 Buffalo, 1982
11 Boston, 1962

Most Opponents Punt Returns, Season
71 Tampa Bay, 1976, 1977
69 N.Y. Giants, 1953
68 Cleveland, 1974

Fewest Yards Allowed, Punt Returns, Season
22 Green Bay, 1967
34 Washington, 1962
39 Cleveland, 1959
Washington, 1972

Most Yards Allowed, Punt Returns, Season
932 Green Bay, 1949
913 Boston, 1947
906 New Orleans, 1974

Lowest Average Allowed, Punt Returns, Season
1.20 Chi. Cardinals, 1954 (46-55)
1.22 Cleveland, 1959 (32-39)
1.55 Chi. Cardinals, 1953 (44-68)

Highest Average Allowed, Punt Returns, Season
18.6 Green Bay, 1949 (50-932)
18.0 Cleveland, 1977 (31-558)
17.9 Boston, 1960 (20-357)

Most Touchdowns Allowed, Punt Returns, Season
4 New York, 1959
Atlanta, 1992
3 Green Bay, 1949
Chi. Cardinals, 1951
L.A. Rams, 1951, 1994
Washington, 1952
Dallas, 1952
Pittsburgh, 1959, 1993
N.Y. Jets, 1968
Cleveland, 1977
Atlanta, 1986
Tampa Bay, 1986
2 By many teams

KICKOFF RETURNS

Fewest Opponents Kickoff Returns, Season
10 Brooklyn, 1943
13 Denver, 1992
15 Detroit, 1942
Brooklyn, 1944

Most Opponents Kickoff Returns, Season
91 Washington, 1983
89 New England, 1980
San Francisco, 1994
Denver, 1997
Denver, 1998
88 San Diego, 1981
Pittsburgh, 1995

Fewest Yards Allowed, Kickoff Returns, Season
225 Brooklyn, 1943
254 Denver, 1992
293 Brooklyn, 1944

Most Yards Allowed, Kickoff Returns, Season
2,045 Kansas City, 1966
2,008 Minnesota, 1998
2,006 Denver, 1998

Lowest Average Allowed, Kickoff Returns, Season
14.3 Cleveland, 1980 (71-1,018)
14.9 Indianapolis, 1993 (37-551)
15.0 Seattle, 1982 (24-361)

Highest Average Allowed, Kickoff Returns, Season
29.5 N.Y. Jets, 1972 (47-1,386)
29.4 Los Angeles, 1950 (48-1,411)
29.1 New England, 1971 (49-1,427)

Most Touchdowns Allowed, Kickoff Returns, Season
4 Minnesota, 1998
3 Minnesota, 1963, 1970
Dallas, 1966
Detroit, 1980
Pittsburgh, 1986
Buffalo, 1997
2 By many teams

FUMBLES

Fewest Opponents Fumbles, Season
11 Cleveland, 1956
Baltimore, 1982
Tennessee, 1998
12 Green Bay, 1995
Cincinnati, 1998
13 Los Angeles, 1956
Chicago, 1960
Cleveland, 1963
Cleveland, 1965
Detroit, 1967
San Diego, 1969

Most Opponents Fumbles, Season
50 Minnesota, 1963
San Francisco, 1978
48 N.Y. Giants, 1980
N.Y. Jets, 1986
47 N.Y. Giants, 1977
Seattle, 1984

TURNOVERS

(Number of times losing the ball on interceptions and fumbles.)

Fewest Opponents Turnovers, Season

11 Baltimore, 1982
13 San Francisco, 1982
15 St. Louis, 1982

Most Opponents Turnovers, Season

66 San Diego, 1961
63 Seattle, 1984
61 Washington, 1983

Most Opponents Turnovers, Game

12 Chi. Bears vs. Detroit, Nov. 22, 1942
Philadelphia vs. Chi. Cardinals, Sept. 24, 1950
Philadelphia vs. Pittsburgh, Dec. 12, 1965
11 Green Bay vs. San Diego, Sept. 24, 1978
10 By 14 teams

OUTSTANDING PERFORMERS

1,000 YARDS RUSHING IN A SEASON

Year	Player, Team	Att.	Yards	Avg.	Long	TD
1998	Terrell Davis, Denver[4]	392	2,008	5.1	70	21
	Jamal Anderson, Atlanta[3]	410	1,846	4.5	48	14
	Garrison Hearst, San Francisco[3]	310	1,570	5.1	96	7
	Barry Sanders, Detroit[10]	343	1,491	4.3	73	4
	Emmitt Smith, Dallas[8]	319	1,332	4.2	32	13
	Marshall Faulk, Indianapolis[4]	324	1,319	4.1	68	6
	Eddie George, Tennessee[3]	348	1,294	3.7	37	5
	Curtis Martin, N.Y. Jets[4]	369	1,287	3.5	60	8
	Ricky Watters, Seattle[5]	319	1,239	3.9	39	9
	*Fred Taylor, Jacksonville	264	1,223	4.6	77	14
	Robert Smith, Minnesota[2]	249	1,187	4.8	74	6
	Jerome Bettis, Pittsburgh[5]	316	1,185	3.8	42	3
	Corey Dillon, Cincinnati[2]	262	1,130	4.3	66	4
	Antowain Smith, Buffalo	300	1,124	3.7	30	8
	*Robert Edwards, New England	291	1,115	3.8	53	9
	Duce Staley, Philadelphia	258	1,065	4.1	64	5
	Gary Brown, N.Y. Giants[2]	247	1,063	4.3	45	5
	Adrian Murrell, Arizona[3]	274	1,042	3.8	32	8
	Warrick Dunn, Tampa Bay	245	1,026	4.2	50	2
	Priest Holmes, Baltimore	233	1,008	4.3	56	7
1997	Barry Sanders, Detroit[9]	335	2,053	6.1	82	11
	Terrell Davis, Denver[3]	369	1,750	4.7	50	15
	Jerome Bettis, Pittsburgh[4]	375	1,665	4.4	34	7
	Dorsey Levens, Green Bay	329	1,435	4.4	52	7
	Eddie George, Tennessee[2]	357	1,399	3.9	30	6
	Napoleon Kaufman, Oakland	272	1,294	4.8	83	6
	Robert Smith, Minnesota	232	1,266	5.5	78	6
	Curtis Martin, New England[3]	274	1,160	4.2	70	4
	*Corey Dillon, Cincinnati	233	1,129	4.8	71	10
	Ricky Watters, Philadelphia[4]	285	1,110	3.9	28	7
	Adrian Murrell, N.Y. Jets[2]	300	1,086	3.6	43	7
	Emmitt Smith, Dallas[7]	261	1,074	4.1	44	4
	Marshall Faulk, Indianapolis[3]	264	1,054	4.0	45	7
	Raymont Harris, Chicago	275	1,033	3.8	68	10
	Garrison Hearst, San Francisco[2]	234	1,019	4.4	51	4
	Jamal Anderson, Atlanta[2]	290	1,002	3.5	39	7
1996	Barry Sanders, Detroit[8]	307	1,553	5.1	54	11
	Terrell Davis, Denver[2]	345	1,538	4.5	71	13
	Jerome Bettis, Pittsburgh[3]	320	1,431	4.5	50	11
	Ricky Watters, Philadelphia[3]	353	1,411	4.0	56	13
	*Eddie George, Houston	335	1,368	4.1	76	8
	Terry Allen, Washington[4]	347	1,353	3.9	49	21
	Adrian Murrell, N.Y. Jets	301	1,249	4.1	78	6
	Emmitt Smith, Dallas[6]	327	1,204	3.7	42	12
	Curtis Martin, New England[2]	316	1,152	3.6	57	14
	Anthony Johnson, Carolina	300	1,120	3.7	29	6
	*Karim Abdul-Jabbar, Miami	307	1,116	3.6	29	11
	Jamal Anderson, Atlanta	232	1,055	4.5	32	5
	Thurman Thomas, Buffalo[8]	281	1,033	3.7	36	8
1995	Emmitt Smith, Dallas[5]	377	1,773	4.7	60	25
	Barry Sanders, Detroit[7]	314	1,500	4.8	75	11
	*Curtis Martin, New England	368	1,487	4.0	49	14
	Chris Warren, Seattle[4]	310	1,346	4.3	52	15
	Terry Allen, Washington[3]	338	1,309	3.9	28	10
	Ricky Watters, Philadelphia[2]	337	1,273	3.8	57	11
	Errict Rhett, Tampa Bay[2]	332	1,207	3.6	21	11
	Rodney Hampton, N.Y. Giants[5]	306	1,182	3.9	32	10
	*Terrell Davis, Denver	237	1,117	4.7	60	7
	Harvey Williams, Oakland	255	1,114	4.4	60	9
	Craig Heyward, Atlanta	236	1,083	4.6	31	6
	Marshall Faulk, Indianapolis[2]	289	1,078	3.7	40	11
	*Rashaan Salaam, Chicago	296	1,074	3.6	42	10
	Garrison Hearst, Arizona	284	1,070	3.8	38	1
	Edgar Bennett, Green Bay	316	1,067	3.4	23	3
	Thurman Thomas, Buffalo[7]	267	1,005	3.8	49	6
1994	Barry Sanders, Detroit[6]	331	1,883	5.7	85	7
	Chris Warren, Seattle[3]	333	1,545	4.6	41	9
	Emmitt Smith, Dallas[4]	368	1,484	4.0	46	21
	Natrone Means, San Diego	343	1,350	3.9	25	12
	*Marshall Faulk, Indianapolis	314	1,282	4.1	52	11
	Thurman Thomas, Buffalo[6]	287	1,093	3.8	29	7
	Rodney Hampton, N.Y. Giants[4]	327	1,075	3.3	27	6
	Terry Allen, Minnesota[2]	255	1,031	4.0	45	8
	Jerome Bettis, L.A. Rams[2]	319	1,025	3.2	19	3
	*Errict Rhett, Tampa Bay	284	1,011	3.6	27	7
1993	Emmitt Smith, Dallas[3]	283	1,486	5.3	62	9
	*Jerome Bettis, L.A. Rams	294	1,429	4.9	71	7
	Thurman Thomas, Buffalo[5]	355	1,315	3.7	27	6
	Erric Pegram, Atlanta	292	1,185	4.1	29	3
	Barry Sanders, Detroit[5]	243	1,115	4.6	42	3
	Leonard Russell, New England	300	1,088	3.6	21	7
	Rodney Hampton, N.Y. Giants[3]	292	1,077	3.7	20	5
	Chris Warren, Seattle[2]	273	1,072	3.9	45	7
	*Reggie Brooks, Washington	223	1,063	4.8	85	3
	*Ron Moore, Phoenix	263	1,018	3.9	20	9
	Gary Brown, Houston	195	1,002	5.1	26	6
1992	Emmitt Smith, Dallas[2]	373	1,713	4.6	68	18
	Barry Foster, Pittsburgh	390	1,690	4.3	69	11
	Thurman Thomas, Buffalo[4]	312	1,487	4.8	44	[illegible]
	Barry Sanders, Detroit[4]	312	1,352	4.3	55	[illegible]
	Lorenzo White, Houston	265	1,226	4.6	44	7
	Terry Allen, Minnesota	266	1,201	4.5	51	13
	Reggie Cobb, Tampa Bay	310	1,171	3.8	25	9
	Harold Green, Cincinnati	265	1,170	4.4	53	2
	Rodney Hampton, N.Y. Giants[2]	257	1,141	4.4	63	14
	Cleveland Gary, L.A. Rams	279	1,125	4.0	63	7
	Herschel Walker, Philadelphia[2]	267	1,070	4.0	38	8
	Chris Warren, Seattle	223	1,017	4.6	52	3
	Ricky Watters, San Francisco	206	1,013	4.9	43	9
1991	Emmitt Smith, Dallas	365	1,563	4.3	75	12
	Barry Sanders, Detroit[3]	342	1,548	4.5	69	16
	Thurman Thomas, Buffalo[3]	288	1,407	4.9	33	7
	Rodney Hampton, N.Y. Giants	256	1,059	4.1	44	10
	Earnest Byner, Washington[3]	274	1,048	3.8	32	5
	Gaston Green, Denver	261	1,037	4.0	63	4
	Christian Okoye, Kansas City[2]	225	1,031	4.6	48	9
1990	Barry Sanders, Detroit[2]	255	1,304	5.1	45	13
	Thurman Thomas, Buffalo[2]	271	1,297	4.8	80	11
	Marion Butts, San Diego	265	1,225	4.6	52	8
	Earnest Byner, Washington[2]	297	1,219	4.1	22	6
	Bobby Humphrey, Denver[2]	288	1,202	4.2	37	7
	Neal Anderson, Chicago[3]	260	1,078	4.1	52	10
	Barry Word, Kansas City	204	1,015	5.0	53	4
	James Brooks, Cincinnati[3]	195	1,004	5.1	56	5
1989	Christian Okoye, Kansas City	370	1,480	4.0	59	12
	*Barry Sanders, Detroit	280	1,470	5.3	34	14
	Eric Dickerson, Indianapolis[7]	314	1,311	4.2	21	7
	Neal Anderson, Chicago[2]	274	1,275	4.7	73	11
	Dalton Hilliard, New Orleans	344	1,262	3.7	40	13
	Thurman Thomas, Buffalo	298	1,244	4.2	38	6
	James Brooks, Cincinnati[2]	221	1,239	5.6	65	7
	*Bobby Humphrey, Denver	294	1,151	3.9	40	7
	Greg Bell, L.A. Rams[3]	272	1,137	4.2	47	15
	Roger Craig, San Francisco[3]	271	1,054	3.9	27	6
	Ottis Anderson, N.Y. Giants[6]	325	1,023	3.1	36	14
1988	Eric Dickerson, Indianapolis[6]	388	1,659	4.3	41	14
	Herschel Walker, Dallas	361	1,514	4.2	38	5
	Roger Craig, San Francisco[2]	310	1,502	4.8	46	9
	Greg Bell, L.A. Rams[2]	288	1,212	4.2	44	16
	*John Stephens, New England	297	1,168	3.9	52	4
	Gary Anderson, San Diego	225	1,119	5.0	36	3
	Neal Anderson, Chicago	249	1,106	4.4	80	12
	Joe Morris, N.Y. Giants[3]	307	1,083	3.5	27	5
	*Ickey Woods, Cincinnati	203	1,066	5.3	56	15
	Curt Warner, Seattle[4]	266	1,025	3.9	29	10
	John Settle, Atlanta	232	1,024	4.4	62	7
	Mike Rozier, Houston	251	1,002	4.0	28	10
1987	Charles White, L.A. Rams	324	1,374	4.2	58	11
	Eric Dickerson, L.A. Rams-Indianapolis[5]	283	1,288	4.6	57	6
1986	Eric Dickerson, L.A. Rams[4]	404	1,821	4.5	42	11
	Joe Morris, N.Y. Giants[2]	341	1,516	4.4	54	14
	Curt Warner, Seattle[3]	319	1,481	4.6	60	13
	*Rueben Mayes, New Orleans	286	1,353	4.7	50	8
	Walter Payton, Chicago[10]	321	1,333	4.2	41	8
	Gerald Riggs, Atlanta[3]	343	1,327	3.9	31	9
	George Rogers, Washington[4]	303	1,203	4.0	42	18
	James Brooks, Cincinnati	205	1,087	5.3	56	5
1985	Marcus Allen, L.A. Raiders[3]	390	1,759	4.6	61	11
	Gerald Riggs, Atlanta[2]	397	1,719	4.3	50	10
	Walter Payton, Chicago[9]	324	1,551	4.8	40	9
	Joe Morris, N.Y. Giants	294	1,336	4.5	65	21
	Freeman McNeil, N.Y. Jets[2]	294	1,331	4.5	69	3
	Tony Dorsett, Dallas[8]	305	1,307	4.3	60	7
	James Wilder, Tampa Bay[2]	365	1,300	3.6	28	10
	Eric Dickerson, L.A. Rams[3]	292	1,234	4.2	43	12
	Craig James, New England	263	1,227	4.7	65	5
	Kevin Mack, Cleveland	222	1,104	5.0	61	7
	Curt Warner, Seattle[2]	291	1,094	3.8	38	8
	George Rogers, Washington[3]	231	1,093	4.7	35	7
	Roger Craig, San Francisco	214	1,050	4.9	62	9
	Earnest Jackson, Philadelphia[2]	282	1,028	3.6	59	5
	Stump Mitchell, St. Louis	183	1,006	5.5	64	7
	Earnest Byner, Cleveland	244	1,002	4.1	36	8
1984	Eric Dickerson, L.A. Rams[2]	379	2,105	5.6	66	14

	Walter Payton, Chicago[8]	381	1,684	4.4	72	11
	James Wilder, Tampa Bay	407	1,544	3.8	37	13
	Gerald Riggs, Atlanta	353	1,486	4.2	57	13
	Wendell Tyler, San Francisco[3]	246	1,262	5.1	40	7
	John Riggins, Washington[5]	327	1,239	3.8	24	14
	Tony Dorsett, Dallas[7]	302	1,189	3.9	31	6
	Earnest Jackson, San Diego	296	1,179	4.0	32	8
	Ottis Anderson, St. Louis[5]	289	1,174	4.1	24	6
	Marcus Allen, L.A. Raiders[2]	275	1,168	4.2	52	13
	Sammy Winder, Denver	296	1,153	3.9	24	4
	*Greg Bell, Buffalo	262	1,100	4.2	85	7
	Freeman McNeil, N.Y. Jets	229	1,070	4.7	53	5
1983	*Eric Dickerson, L.A. Rams	390	1,808	4.6	85	18
	William Andrews, Atlanta[4]	331	1,567	4.7	27	7
	*Curt Warner, Seattle	335	1,449	4.3	60	13
	Walter Payton, Chicago[7]	314	1,421	4.5	49	6
	John Riggins, Washington[4]	375	1,347	3.6	44	24
	Tony Dorsett, Dallas[6]	289	1,321	4.6	77	8
	Earl Campbell, Houston[5]	322	1,301	4.0	42	12
	Ottis Anderson, St. Louis[4]	296	1,270	4.3	43	5
	Mike Pruitt, Cleveland[4]	293	1,184	4.0	27	10
	George Rogers, New Orleans[2]	256	1,144	4.5	76	5
	Joe Cribbs, Buffalo[3]	263	1,131	4.3	45	3
	Curtis Dickey, Baltimore	254	1,122	4.4	56	4
	Tony Collins, New England	219	1,049	4.8	50	10
	Billy Sims, Detroit[3]	220	1,040	4.7	41	7
	Marcus Allen, L.A. Raiders	266	1,014	3.8	19	9
	Franco Harris, Pittsburgh[8]	279	1,007	3.6	19	5
1981	*George Rogers, New Orleans	378	1,674	4.4	79	13
	Tony Dorsett, Dallas[5]	342	1,646	4.8	75	4
	Billy Sims, Detroit[2]	296	1,437	4.9	51	13
	Wilbert Montgomery, Philadelphia[3]	286	1,402	4.9	41	8
	Ottis Anderson, St. Louis[3]	328	1,376	4.2	28	9
	Earl Campbell, Houston[4]	361	1,376	3.8	43	10
	William Andrews, Atlanta[3]	289	1,301	4.5	29	10
	Walter Payton, Chicago[6]	339	1,222	3.6	39	6
	Chuck Muncie, San Diego[2]	251	1,144	4.6	73	19
	*Joe Delaney, Kansas City	234	1,121	4.8	82	3
	Mike Pruitt, Cleveland[3]	247	1,103	4.5	21	7
	Joe Cribbs, Buffalo[2]	257	1,097	4.3	35	3
	Pete Johnson, Cincinnati	274	1,077	3.9	39	12
	Wendell Tyler, Los Angeles[2]	260	1,074	4.1	69	12
	Ted Brown, Minnesota	274	1,063	3.9	34	6
1980	Earl Campbell, Houston[3]	373	1,934	5.2	55	13
	Walter Payton, Chicago[5]	317	1,460	4.6	69	6
	Ottis Anderson, St. Louis[2]	301	1,352	4.5	52	9
	William Andrews, Atlanta[2]	265	1,308	4.9	33	4
	*Billy Sims, Detroit	313	1,303	4.2	52	13
	Tony Dorsett, Dallas[4]	278	1,185	4.3	56	11
	*Joe Cribbs, Buffalo	306	1,185	3.9	48	11
	Mike Pruitt, Cleveland[2]	249	1,034	4.2	56	6
1979	Earl Campbell, Houston[2]	368	1,697	4.6	61	19
	Walter Payton, Chicago[4]	369	1,610	4.4	43	14
	*Ottis Anderson, St. Louis	331	1,605	4.8	76	8
	Wilbert Montgomery, Philadelphia[2]	338	1,512	4.5	62	9
	Mike Pruitt, Cleveland	264	1,294	4.9	77	9
	Ricky Bell, Tampa Bay	283	1,263	4.5	49	7
	Chuck Muncie, New Orleans	238	1,198	5.0	69	11
	Franco Harris, Pittsburgh[7]	267	1,186	4.4	71	11
	John Riggins, Washington[3]	260	1,153	4.4	66	9
	Wendell Tyler, Los Angeles	218	1,109	5.1	63	9
	Tony Dorsett, Dallas[3]	250	1,107	4.4	41	6
	*William Andrews, Atlanta	239	1,023	4.3	23	3
1978	*Earl Campbell, Houston	302	1,450	4.8	81	13
	Walter Payton, Chicago[3]	333	1,395	4.2	76	11
	Tony Dorsett, Dallas[2]	290	1,325	4.6	63	7
	Delvin Williams, Miami[2]	272	1,258	4.6	58	8
	Wilbert Montgomery, Philadelphia	259	1,220	4.7	47	9
	Terdell Middleton, Green Bay	284	1,116	3.9	76	11
	Franco Harris, Pittsburgh[6]	310	1,082	3.5	37	8
	Mark van Eeghen, Oakland[3]	270	1,080	4.0	34	9
	*Terry Miller, Buffalo	238	1,060	4.5	60	7
	Tony Reed, Kansas City	206	1,053	5.1	62	5
	John Riggins, Washington[2]	248	1,014	4.1	31	5
1977	Walter Payton, Chicago[2]	339	1,852	5.5	73	14
	Mark van Eeghen, Oakland[2]	324	1,273	3.9	27	7
	Lawrence McCutcheon, Los Angeles[4]	294	1,238	4.2	48	7
	Franco Harris, Pittsburgh[5]	300	1,162	3.9	61	11
	Lydell Mitchell, Baltimore[3]	301	1,159	3.9	64	3
	Chuck Foreman, Minnesota[3]	270	1,112	4.1	51	6
	Greg Pruitt, Cleveland[3]	236	1,086	4.6	78	3
	Sam Cunningham, New England	270	1,015	3.8	31	4
	*Tony Dorsett, Dallas	208	1,007	4.8	84	12
1976	O.J. Simpson, Buffalo[5]	290	1,503	5.2	75	8
	Walter Payton, Chicago	311	1,390	4.5	60	13
	Delvin Williams, San Francisco	248	1,203	4.9	80	7
	Lydell Mitchell, Baltimore[2]	289	1,200	4.2	43	5
	Lawrence McCutcheon, Los Angeles[3]	291	1,168	4.0	40	9
	Chuck Foreman, Minnesota[2]	278	1,155	4.2	46	13
	Franco Harris, Pittsburgh[4]	289	1,128	3.9	30	14
	Mike Thomas, Washington	254	1,101	4.3	28	5
	Rocky Bleier, Pittsburgh	220	1,036	4.7	28	5
	Mark van Eeghen, Oakland	233	1,012	4.3	21	3
	Otis Armstrong, Denver[2]	247	1,008	4.1	31	5
	Greg Pruitt, Cleveland[2]	209	1,000	4.8	64	4
1975	O.J. Simpson, Buffalo[4]	329	1,817	5.5	88	16
	Franco Harris, Pittsburgh[3]	262	1,246	4.8	36	10
	Lydell Mitchell, Baltimore	289	1,193	4.1	70	11
	Jim Otis, St. Louis	269	1,076	4.0	30	5
	Chuck Foreman, Minnesota	280	1,070	3.8	31	13
	Greg Pruitt, Cleveland	217	1,067	4.9	50	8
	John Riggins, N.Y. Jets	238	1,005	4.2	42	8
	Dave Hampton, Atlanta	250	1,002	4.0	22	5
1974	Otis Armstrong, Denver	263	1,407	5.3	43	9
	*Don Woods, San Diego	227	1,162	5.1	56	7
	O.J. Simpson, Buffalo[3]	270	1,125	4.2	41	3
	Lawrence McCutcheon, Los Angeles[2]	236	1,109	4.7	23	3
	Franco Harris, Pittsburgh[2]	208	1,006	4.8	54	5
1973	O.J. Simpson, Buffalo[2]	332	2,003	6.0	80	12
	John Brockington, Green Bay[3]	265	1,144	4.3	53	3
	Calvin Hill, Dallas[2]	273	1,142	4.2	21	6
	Lawrence McCutcheon, Los Angeles	210	1,097	5.2	37	2
	Larry Csonka, Miami[3]	219	1,003	4.6	25	5
1972	O.J. Simpson, Buffalo	292	1,251	4.3	94	6
	Larry Brown, Washington[2]	285	1,216	4.3	38	8
	Ron Johnson, N.Y. Giants[2]	298	1,182	4.0	35	9
	Larry Csonka, Miami[2]	213	1,117	5.2	45	6
	Marv Hubbard, Oakland	219	1,100	5.0	39	4
	*Franco Harris, Pittsburgh	188	1,055	5.6	75	10
	Calvin Hill, Dallas	245	1,036	4.2	26	6
	Mike Garrett, San Diego[2]	272	1,031	3.8	41	6
	John Brockington, Green Bay[2]	274	1,027	3.7	30	8
	Eugene (Mercury) Morris, Miami	190	1,000	5.3	33	12
1971	Floyd Little, Denver	284	1,133	4.0	40	6
	*John Brockington, Green Bay	216	1,105	5.1	52	4
	Larry Csonka, Miami	195	1,051	5.4	28	7
	Steve Owens, Detroit	246	1,035	4.2	23	8
	Willie Ellison, Los Angeles	211	1,000	4.7	80	4
1970	Larry Brown, Washington	237	1,125	4.7	75	5
	Ron Johnson, N.Y. Giants	263	1,027	3.9	68	8
1969	Gale Sayers, Chicago[2]	236	1,032	4.4	28	8
1968	Leroy Kelly, Cleveland[3]	248	1,239	5.0	65	16
	*Paul Robinson, Cincinnati	238	1,023	4.3	87	8
1967	Jim Nance, Boston[2]	269	1,216	4.5	53	7
	Leroy Kelly, Cleveland[2]	235	1,205	5.1	42	11
	Hoyle Granger, Houston	236	1,194	5.1	67	6
	Mike Garrett, Kansas City	236	1,087	4.6	58	9
1966	Jim Nance, Boston	299	1,458	4.9	65	11
	Gale Sayers, Chicago	229	1,231	5.4	58	8
	Leroy Kelly, Cleveland	209	1,141	5.5	70	15
	Dick Bass, Los Angeles[2]	248	1,090	4.4	50	8
1965	Jim Brown, Cleveland[7]	289	1,544	5.3	67	17
	Paul Lowe, San Diego[2]	222	1,121	5.0	59	7
1964	Jim Brown, Cleveland[6]	280	1,446	5.2	71	7
	Jim Taylor, Green Bay[5]	235	1,169	5.0	84	12
	John Henry Johnson, Pittsburgh[2]	235	1,048	4.5	45	7
1963	Jim Brown, Cleveland[5]	291	1,863	6.4	80	12
	Clem Daniels, Oakland	215	1,099	5.1	74	3
	Jim Taylor, Green Bay[4]	248	1,018	4.1	40	9
	Paul Lowe, San Diego	177	1,010	5.7	66	8
1962	Jim Taylor, Green Bay[3]	272	1,474	5.4	51	19
	John Henry Johnson, Pittsburgh	251	1,141	4.5	40	7
	Cookie Gilchrist, Buffalo	214	1,096	5.1	44	13
	Abner Haynes, Dall. Texans	221	1,049	4.7	71	13
	Dick Bass, Los Angeles	196	1,033	5.3	57	6
	Charlie Tolar, Houston	244	1,012	4.1	25	7
1961	Jim Brown, Cleveland[4]	305	1,408	4.6	38	8
	Jim Taylor, Green Bay[2]	243	1,307	5.4	53	15
1960	Jim Brown, Cleveland[3]	215	1,257	5.8	71	9
	Jim Taylor, Green Bay	230	1,101	4.8	32	11
	John David Crow, St. Louis	183	1,071	5.9	57	6
1959	Jim Brown, Cleveland[2]	290	1,329	4.6	70	14
	J.D. Smith, San Francisco	207	1,036	5.0	73	10
1958	Jim Brown, Cleveland	257	1,527	5.9	65	17
1956	Rick Casares, Chi. Bears	234	1,126	4.8	68	12
1954	Joe Perry, San Francisco[2]	173	1,049	6.1	58	8

1953	Joe Perry, San Francisco	192	1,018	5.3	51	10
1949	Steve Van Buren, Philadelphia[2]	263	1,146	4.4	41	11
	Tony Canadeo, Green Bay	208	1,052	5.1	54	4
1947	Steve Van Buren, Philadelphia	217	1,008	4.6	45	13
1934	*Beattie Feathers, Chi. Bears	119	1,004	8.4	82	8

**First season of professional football.*

200 YARDS RUSHING IN A GAME

Date	Player, Team, Opponent	Att.	Yards	TD
Nov. 22, 1998	Priest Holmes, Baltimore vs. Cincinnati	36	227	1
Oct. 11, 1998	Terrell Davis, Denver vs Seattle	30	208	1
Dec. 4, 1997	*Corey Dillon, Cincinnati vs. Tennessee	39	246	4
Nov. 23, 1997	Barry Sanders, Detroit vs. Indianapolis	24	216	2
Oct. 26, 1997	Terrell Davis, Denver vs. Buffalo (OT)	42	207	1
Oct. 19, 1997	Napoleon Kaufman, Oakland vs. Denver	28	227	1
Oct. 12, 1997	Barry Sanders, Detroit vs. Tampa Bay	24	215	2
Sept. 21, 1997	Terrell Davis, Denver vs. Cincinnati	27	215	1
Aug. 31, 1997	Eddie George, Tennessee vs. Oakland (OT)	35	216	1
Sept. 22, 1996	LeShon Johnson, Arizona vs. New Orleans	21	214	2
Nov. 13, 1994	Barry Sanders, Detroit vs. Tampa Bay	26	237	0
Dec. 12, 1993	*Jerome Bettis, L.A. Rams vs. New Orleans	28	212	1
Oct. 31, 1993	Emmitt Smith, Dallas vs. Philadelphia	30	237	1
Nov. 24, 1991	Barry Sanders, Detroit vs. Minnesota	23	220	4
Dec. 23, 1990	James Brooks, Cincinnati vs. Houston	20	201	1
Oct. 14, 1990	Barry Word, Kansas City vs. Detroit	18	200	2
Sept. 24, 1990	Thurman Thomas, Buffalo vs. N.Y. Jets	18	214	0
Dec. 24, 1989	Greg Bell, L.A. Rams vs. New England	26	210	1
Sept. 24, 1989	Greg Bell, L.A. Rams vs. Green Bay	28	221	2
Sept. 17, 1989	Gerald Riggs, Washington vs. Philadelphia	29	221	1
Dec. 18, 1988	Gary Anderson, San Diego vs. Kansas City	34	217	1
Nov. 30, 1987	*Bo Jackson, L.A. Raiders vs. Seattle	18	221	2
Nov. 15, 1987	Charles White, L.A. Rams vs. St. Louis	34	213	1
Dec. 7, 1986	Rueben Mayes, New Orleans vs. Miami	28	203	2
Oct. 5, 1986	Eric Dickerson, L.A. Rams vs. Tampa Bay (OT)	30	207	2
Dec. 21, 1985	George Rogers, Washington vs. St. Louis	34	206	1
Dec. 21, 1985	Joe Morris, N.Y. Giants vs. Pittsburgh	36	202	3
Dec. 9, 1984	Eric Dickerson, L.A. Rams vs. Houston	27	215	2
Nov. 18, 1984	*Greg Bell, Buffalo vs. Dallas	27	206	1
Nov. 4, 1984	Eric Dickerson, L.A. Rams vs. St. Louis	21	208	0
Sept. 2, 1984	Gerald Riggs, Atlanta vs. New Orleans	35	202	2
Nov. 27, 1983	*Curt Warner, Seattle vs. Kansas City (OT)	32	207	3
Nov. 6, 1983	James Wilder, Tampa Bay vs. Minnesota	31	219	1
Sept. 18, 1983	Tony Collins, New England vs. N.Y. Jets	23	212	3
Sept. 4, 1983	George Rogers, New Orleans vs. St. Louis	24	206	2
Dec. 21, 1980	Earl Campbell, Houston vs. Minnesota	29	203	1
Nov. 16, 1980	Earl Campbell, Houston vs. Chicago	31	206	0
Oct. 26, 1980	Earl Campbell, Houston vs. Cincinnati	27	202	2
Oct. 19, 1980	Earl Campbell, Houston vs. Tampa Bay	33	203	0
Nov. 26, 1978	*Terry Miller, Buffalo vs. N.Y. Giants	21	208	2
Dec. 4, 1977	*Tony Dorsett, Dallas vs. Philadelphia	23	206	2
Nov. 20, 1977	Walter Payton, Chicago vs. Minnesota	40	275	1
Oct. 30, 1977	Walter Payton, Chicago vs. Green Bay	23	205	2
Dec. 5, 1976	O.J. Simpson, Buffalo vs. Miami	24	203	1
Nov. 25, 1976	O.J. Simpson, Buffalo vs. Detroit	29	273	2
Oct. 24, 1976	Chuck Foreman, Minnesota vs. Philadelphia	28	200	2
Dec. 14, 1975	Greg Pruitt, Cleveland vs. Kansas City	26	214	3
Sept. 28, 1975	O.J. Simpson, Buffalo vs. Pittsburgh	28	227	1
Dec. 16, 1973	O.J. Simpson, Buffalo vs. N.Y. Jets	34	200	1
Dec. 9, 1973	O.J. Simpson, Buffalo vs. New England	22	219	1
Sept. 16, 1973	O.J. Simpson, Buffalo vs. New England	29	250	2
Dec. 5, 1971	Willie Ellison, Los Angeles vs. New Orleans	26	247	1
Dec. 20, 1970	John (Frenchy) Fuqua, Pittsburgh vs. Philadelphia	20	218	2
Nov. 3, 1968	Gale Sayers, Chicago vs. Green Bay	24	205	0
Oct. 30, 1966	Jim Nance, Boston vs. Oakland	38	208	2
Oct. 10, 1964	John Henry Johnson, Pittsburgh vs. Cleveland	30	200	3
Dec. 8, 1963	Cookie Gilchrist, Buffalo vs. N.Y. Jets	36	243	5
Nov. 3, 1963	Jim Brown, Cleveland vs. Philadelphia	28	223	1
Oct. 20, 1963	Clem Daniels, Oakland vs. N.Y. Jets	27	200	2
Sept. 22, 1963	Jim Brown, Cleveland vs. Dallas	20	232	2
Dec. 10, 1961	Billy Cannon, Houston vs. N.Y. Titans	25	216	3
Nov. 19, 1961	Jim Brown, Cleveland vs. Philadelphia	34	237	4
Dec. 18, 1960	John David Crow, St. Louis vs. Pittsburgh	24	203	0
Nov. 15, 1959	Bobby Mitchell, Cleveland vs. Washington	14	232	3
Nov. 24, 1957	*Jim Brown, Cleveland vs. Los Angeles	31	237	4
Dec. 16, 1956	*Tom Wilson, Los Angeles vs. Green Bay	23	223	0
Nov. 22, 1953	Dan Towler, Los Angeles vs. Baltimore	14	205	1
Nov. 12, 1950	Gene Roberts, N.Y. Giants vs. Chi. Cardinals	26	218	2
Nov. 27, 1949	Steve Van Buren, Philadelphia vs. Pittsburgh	27	205	0
Oct. 8, 1933	Cliff Battles, Boston vs. N.Y. Giants	16	215	1

**First season of professional football.*

TIMES 200 OR MORE

70 times by 47 players...Simpson 6; Brown, Campbell, Sanders 4; Bell, Davis, Dickerson 3; Payton, Riggs, Rogers 2.

4,000 YARDS PASSING IN A SEASON

Year	Player, Team	Att.	Comp.	Pct.	Yards	TD	Int.
1998	Brett Favre, Green Bay[2]	551	347	63.0	4,212	31	23
	Steve Young, San Francisco[2]	517	322	62.3	4,170	36	12
1996	Mark Brunell, Jacksonville	557	353	63.4	4,367	19	20
	Vinny Testaverde, Baltimore	549	325	59.2	4,177	33	19
	Drew Bledsoe, New England[2]	623	373	59.9	4,086	27	15
1995	Brett Favre, Green Bay	570	359	63.0	4,413	38	13
	Scott Mitchell, Detroit	583	346	59.3	4,338	32	12
	Warren Moon, Minnesota[4]	606	377	62.2	4,228	33	14
	Jeff George, Atlanta	557	336	60.3	4,143	24	11
1994	Drew Bledsoe, New England	691	400	57.9	4,555	25	27
	Dan Marino, Miami[6]	615	385	62.6	4,453	30	17
	Warren Moon, Minnesota[3]	601	371	61.7	4,264	18	19
1993	John Elway, Denver	551	348	63.2	4,030	25	10
	Steve Young, San Francisco	462	314	68.0	4,023	29	16
1992	Dan Marino, Miami[5]	554	330	59.6	4,116	24	16
1991	Warren Moon, Houston[2]	655	404	61.7	4,690	23	21
1990	Warren Moon, Houston	584	362	62.0	4,689	33	13
1989	Don Majkowski, Green Bay	599	353	58.9	4,318	27	20
	Jim Everett, L.A. Rams	518	304	58.7	4,310	29	17
1988	Dan Marino, Miami[4]	606	354	58.4	4,434	28	23
1986	Dan Marino, Miami[3]	623	378	60.7	4,746	44	23
	Jay Schroeder, Washington	541	276	51.0	4,109	22	22
1985	Dan Marino, Miami[2]	567	336	59.3	4,137	30	21
1984	Dan Marino, Miami	564	362	64.2	5,084	48	17
	Neil Lomax, St. Louis	560	345	61.6	4,614	28	16
	Phil Simms, N.Y. Giants	533	286	53.7	4,044	22	18
1983	Lynn Dickey, Green Bay	484	289	59.7	4,458	32	29
	Bill Kenney, Kansas City	603	346	57.4	4,348	24	18
1981	Dan Fouts, San Diego[3]	609	360	59.1	4,802	33	17
1980	Dan Fouts, San Diego[2]	589	348	59.1	4,715	30	24
	Brian Sipe, Cleveland	554	337	60.8	4,132	30	14
1979	Dan Fouts, San Diego	530	332	62.6	4,082	24	24
1967	Joe Namath, N.Y. Jets	491	258	52.5	4,007	26	28

400 YARDS PASSING IN A GAME

Date	Player, Team, Opponent	Att.	Comp.	Yards	TD
Dec. 6, 1998	Vinny Testaverde, N.Y. Jets vs. Seattle	63	42	418	2
Dec. 6, 1998	John Elway, Denver vs. Kansas City	32	22	400	2
Nov. 26, 1998	Troy Aikman, Dallas vs. Minnesota	57	34	455	1
Nov. 23, 1998	Drew Bledsoe, New England vs. Miami	54	28	423	2
Nov. 15, 1998	Jake Plummer, Arizona vs. Dallas	56	31	465	3
Oct. 5, 1998	Randall Cunningham, Minnesota vs. Green Bay	32	20	442	4
Sept. 6, 1998	Glenn Foley, N.Y. Jets vs. San Francisco (OT)	58	30	415	3
Nov. 2, 1997	Tony Banks, St. Louis vs. Atlanta	34	23	401	2
Oct. 26, 1997	Warren Moon, Seattle vs. Oakland	44	28	409	5
Nov. 10, 1996	Boomer Esiason, Arizona vs. Washington (OT)	59	35	522	3
Nov. 3, 1996	Drew Bledsoe, New England vs. Miami	41	30	419	3
Oct. 27, 1996	Vinny Testaverde, Baltimore vs. St. Louis (OT)	51	31	429	3
Oct. 20, 1996	Mark Brunell, Jacksonville vs. St. Louis	52	37	421	0
Sept. 22, 1996	Mark Brunell, Jacksonville vs. New England (OT)	39	23	432	3
Dec. 18, 1995	Steve Young, San Francisco vs. Minnesota	49	30	425	3
Nov. 26, 1995	Dave Krieg, Arizona vs. Atlanta (OT)	43	27	413	4
Nov. 23, 1995	Scott Mitchell, Detroit vs. Minnesota	45	30	410	4
Oct. 1, 1995	Dan Marino, Miami vs. Cincinnati	48	33	450	2
Nov. 20, 1994	Warren Moon, Minnesota vs. N.Y. Jets	50	33	400	2
Nov. 13, 1994	Drew Bledsoe, New England vs. Minnesota (OT)	70	45	426	3
Nov. 6, 1994	Warren Moon, Minnesota vs. New Orleans	57	33	420	3
Sept. 25, 1994	Dan Marino, Miami vs. Minnesota	54	29	431	3
Sept. 4, 1994	Dan Marino, Miami vs. New England (OT)	42	23	473	5
Sept. 4, 1994	Drew Bledsoe, New England vs. Miami (OT)	51	32	421	4
Dec. 19, 1993	Steve Beuerlein, Phoenix vs. Seattle	53	34	431	3
Dec. 5, 1993	Brett Favre, Green Bay vs. Chicago	54	36	402	2
Nov. 28, 1993	Steve Young, San Francisco vs. L.A. Rams	32	26	462	4
Oct. 31, 1993	Jeff Hostetler, L.A. Raiders vs. San Diego	32	20	424	2
Sept. 13, 1992	Steve Young, San Francisco vs. Buffalo	37	26	449	3
Sept. 13, 1992	Jim Kelly, Buffalo vs. San Francisco	33	22	403	3
Nov. 10, 1991	Warren Moon, Houston vs. Dallas (OT)	56	41	432	0
Nov. 10, 1991	Mark Rypien, Washington vs. Atlanta	31	16	442	6
Oct. 13, 1991	Warren Moon, Houston vs. N.Y. Jets	50	35	423	2
Dec. 16, 1990	Warren Moon, Houston vs. Kansas City	45	27	527	3
Nov. 4, 1990	Joe Montana, San Francisco vs. Green Bay	40	25	411	3
Oct. 14, 1990	Joe Montana, San Francisco vs. Atlanta	49	32	476	6
Oct. 7, 1990	Boomer Esiason, Cincinnati vs. L.A. Rams (OT)	45	31	490	3
Dec. 23, 1989	Warren Moon, Houston vs. Cleveland	51	32	414	2
Dec. 11, 1989	Joe Montana, San Francisco vs. L.A. Rams	42	30	458	3

Nov. 26, 1989	Jim Everett, L.A. Rams vs. New Orleans (OT).51	29	454	1
Nov. 26, 1989	Mark Rypien, Washington vs. Chicago..........47	30	401	4
Oct. 2, 1989	Randall Cunningham, Philadelphia vs. Chicago..62	32	401	1
Sept. 24, 1989	Joe Montana, San Francisco vs. Philadelphia 34	25	428	5
Sept. 24, 1989	Dan Marino, Miami vs. N.Y. Jets.....................55	33	427	3
Sept. 17, 1989	Randall Cunningham, Phil. vs. Washington ...46	34	447	5
Dec. 18, 1988	Dave Krieg, Seattle vs. L.A. Raiders 32	19	410	4
Dec. 12, 1988	Dan Marino, Miami vs. Cleveland 50	30	404	4
Oct. 23, 1988	Dan Marino, Miami vs. N.Y. Jets.....................60	35	521	3
Oct. 16, 1988	Vinny Testaverde, Tampa Bay vs. Indianapolis..42	25	469	2
Sept. 11, 1988	Doug Williams, Washington vs. Pittsburgh.....52	30	430	2
Nov. 29, 1987	Tom Ramsey, New England vs. Philadelphia .53	34	402	3
Nov. 22, 1987	Boomer Esiason, Cincinnati vs. Pittsburgh 53	30	409	0
Sept. 20, 1987	Neil Lomax, St. Louis vs. San Diego...............61	32	457	3
Dec. 21, 1986	Boomer Esiason, Cincinnati vs. N.Y. Jets 30	23	425	5
Dec. 14, 1986	Dan Marino, Miami vs. L.A. Rams (OT) 46	29	403	5
Nov. 23, 1986	Bernie Kosar, Cleveland vs. Pittsburgh (OT) ..46	28	414	2
Nov. 17, 1986	Joe Montana, San Francisco vs. Washington....60	33	441	0
Nov. 16, 1986	Dan Marino, Miami vs. Buffalo 54	39	404	4
Nov. 10, 1986	Bernie Kosar, Cleveland vs. Miami..................50	32	401	0
Nov. 2, 1986	Tommy Kramer, Minnesota vs. Washington (OT).35	20	490	4
Nov. 2, 1986	Ken O'Brien, N.Y. Jets vs. Seattle 32	26	431	4
Oct. 27, 1986	Jay Schroeder, Washington vs. N.Y. Giants....40	22	420	1
Oct. 12, 1986	Steve Grogan, New England vs. N.Y. Jets......42	23	401	3
Sept. 21, 1986	Ken O'Brien, N.Y. Jets vs. Miami (OT).............43	29	479	4
Sept. 21, 1986	Dan Marino, Miami vs. N.Y. Jets (OT) 50	30	448	6
Sept. 21, 1986	Tony Eason, New England vs. Seattle............45	26	414	3
Dec. 20, 1985	John Elway, Denver vs. Seattle.......................42	24	432	1
Nov. 10, 1985	Dan Fouts, San Diego vs. L.A. Raiders (OT) ..41	26	436	4
Oct. 13, 1985	Phil Simms, N.Y. Giants vs. Cincinnati 62	40	513	1
Oct. 13, 1985	Dave Krieg, Seattle vs. Atlanta.......................51	33	405	4
Oct. 6, 1985	Phil Simms, N.Y. Giants vs. Dallas 36	18	432	3
Oct. 6, 1985	Joe Montana, San Francisco vs. Atlanta 57	37	429	5
Sept. 19, 1985	Tommy Kramer, Minnesota vs. Chicago 55	28	436	3
Sept. 15, 1985	Dan Fouts, San Diego vs. Seattle 43	29	440	4
Dec. 16, 1984	Neil Lomax, St. Louis vs. Washington 46	37	468	2
Dec. 9, 1984	Dan Marino, Miami vs. Indianapolis................41	29	404	4
Dec. 2, 1984	Dan Marino, Miami vs. L.A. Raiders................57	35	470	4
Nov. 25, 1984	Dave Krieg, Seattle vs. Denver 44	30	406	3
Nov. 4, 1984	Dan Marino, Miami vs. N.Y. Jets.....................42	23	422	2
Oct. 21, 1984	Dan Fouts, San Diego vs. L.A. Raiders 45	24	410	3
Sept. 30, 1984	Dan Marino, Miami vs. St. Louis 36	24	429	3
Sept. 2, 1984	Phil Simms, N.Y. Giants vs. Philadelphia 30	23	409	4
Dec. 11, 1983	Bill Kenney, Kansas City vs. San Diego..........41	31	411	4
Nov. 20, 1983	Dave Krieg, Seattle vs. Denver 42	31	418	3
Oct. 9, 1983	Joe Ferguson, Buffalo vs. Miami (OT) 55	38	419	5
Oct. 2, 1983	Joe Theismann, Washington vs. L.A. Raiders.39	23	417	3
Sept. 25, 1983	Richard Todd, N.Y. Jets vs. L.A. Rams (OT) ...50	37	446	2
Dec. 26, 1982	Vince Ferragamo, L.A. Rams vs. Chicago......46	30	509	3
Dec. 20, 1982	Dan Fouts, San Diego vs. Cincinnati 40	25	435	1
Dec. 20, 1982	Ken Anderson, Cincinnati vs. San Diego........56	40	416	2
Dec. 11, 1982	Dan Fouts, San Diego vs. San Francisco 48	33	444	5
Nov. 21, 1982	Joe Montana, San Francisco vs. St. Louis 39	26	408	3
Nov. 15, 1981	Steve Bartkowski, Atlanta vs. Pittsburgh 50	33	416	2
Oct. 25, 1981	Brian Sipe, Cleveland vs. Baltimore...............41	30	444	4
Oct. 25, 1981	David Woodley, Miami vs. Dallas 37	21	408	3
Oct. 11, 1981	Tommy Kramer, Minnesota vs. San Diego......43	27	444	4
Dec. 14, 1980	Tommy Kramer, Minnesota vs. Cleveland......49	38	456	4
Nov. 16, 1980	Doug Williams, Tampa Bay vs. Minnesota......55	30	486	4
Oct. 19, 1980	Dan Fouts, San Diego vs. N.Y. Giants............41	26	444	3
Oct. 12, 1980	Lynn Dickey, Green Bay vs. Tampa Bay (OT).51	35	418	1
Sept. 21, 1980	Richard Todd, N.Y. Jets vs. San Francisco 60	42	447	3
Oct. 3, 1976	James Harris, Los Angeles vs. Miami.............29	17	436	2
Nov. 17, 1975	Ken Anderson, Cincinnati vs. Buffalo 46	30	447	2
Nov. 18, 1974	Charley Johnson, Denver vs. Kansas City......42	28	445	2
Dec. 11, 1972	Joe Namath, N.Y. Jets vs. Oakland................46	25	403	1
Sept. 24, 1972	Joe Namath, N.Y. Jets vs. Baltimore..............28	15	496	6
Dec. 21, 1969	Don Horn, Green Bay vs. St. Louis.................31	22	410	5
Sept. 28, 1969	Joe Kapp, Minnesota vs. Baltimore................43	28	449	7
Sept. 9, 1968	Pete Beathard, Houston vs. Kansas City.......48	23	413	2
Nov. 26, 1967	Sonny Jurgensen, Washington vs. Cleveland .50	32	418	3
Oct. 1, 1967	Joe Namath, N.Y. Jets vs. Miami.....................39	23	415	3
Sept. 17, 1967	Johnny Unitas, Baltimore vs. Atlanta 32	22	401	2
Nov. 13, 1966	Don Meredith, Dallas vs. Washington............29	21	406	2
Nov. 28, 1965	Sonny Jurgensen, Washington vs. Dallas 43	26	411	3
Oct. 24, 1965	Fran Tarkenton, Minnesota vs. San Francisco .35	21	407	3
Nov. 1, 1964	Len Dawson, Kansas City vs. Denver............38	23	435	6
Oct. 25, 1964	Cotton Davidson, Oakland vs. Denver 36	23	427	5
Oct. 16, 1964	Babe Parilli, Boston vs. Oakland.....................47	25	422	4
Dec. 22, 1963	Tom Flores, Oakland vs. Houston...................29	17	407	6
Nov. 17, 1963	Norm Snead, Washington vs. Pittsburgh 40	23	424	2
Nov. 10, 1963	Don Meredith, Dallas vs. San Francisco.........48	30	460	3
Oct. 13, 1963	Charley Johnson, St. Louis vs. Pittsburgh......41	20	428	2
Dec. 16, 1962	Sonny Jurgensen, Philadelphia vs. St. Louis .34	15	419	5
Nov. 18, 1962	Bill Wade, Chicago vs. Dall. Cowboys...........46	28	466	2
Oct. 28, 1962	Y.A. Tittle, N.Y. Giants vs. Washington 39	27	505	7
Sept. 15, 1962	Frank Tripucka, Denver vs. Buffalo 56	29	447	2
Dec. 17, 1961	Sonny Jurgensen, Philadelphia vs. Detroit.....42	27	403	3
Nov. 19, 1961	George Blanda, Houston vs. N.Y. Titans.........32	20	418	7
Oct. 29, 1961	George Blanda, Houston vs. Buffalo 32	18	464	4
Oct. 29, 1961	Sonny Jurgensen, Philadelphia vs. Washington 41	27	436	3
Oct. 13, 1961	Jacky Lee, Houston vs. Boston 41	27	457	2
Dec. 13, 1958	Bobby Layne, Pittsburgh vs. Chi. Cardinals...49	23	409	2
Nov. 8, 1953	Bobby Thomason, Philadelphia vs. N.Y. Giants ..44	22	437	4
Oct. 4, 1952	Otto Graham, Cleveland vs. Pittsburgh 49	21	401	3
Sept. 28, 1951	Norm Van Brocklin, Los Angeles vs. N.Y. Yanks.41	27	554	5
Dec. 11, 1949	Johnny Lujack, Chi. Bears vs. Chi. Cardinals.39	24	468	6
Oct. 31, 1948	Sammy Baugh,Washington vs. Boston 24	17	446	4
Oct. 31, 1948	Jim Hardy, Los Angeles vs. Chi. Cardinals.....53	28	406	3
Nov. 14, 1943	Sid Luckman, Chi. Bears vs. N.Y. Giants 32	21	433	7

TIMES 400 OR MORE

137 times by 69 players. . .Marino 13; Montana, Moon 7; Fouts 6; Jurgensen, Krieg 5; Bledsoe, Esiason, Kramer 4; Cunningham, Namath, Simms, Testaverde, Young 3; Anderson, Blanda, Brunell, Elway, Johnson, Kosar, Lomax, Meredith, O'Brien, Rypien, Todd, Williams 2.

100 PASS RECEPTIONS IN A SEASON

Year	Player, Team	No.	Yards	Avg.	Long	TD
1997	Tim Brown, Oakland	104	1,408	13.5	59	5
	Herman Moore, Detroit[3]	104	1,293	12.4	79	8
1996	Jerry Rice, San Francisco[4]	108	1,254	11.6	39	8
	Herman Moore, Detroit[2]	106	1,296	12.2	50	9
	Carl Pickens, Cincinnati	100	1,180	11.8	61	12
1995	Herman Moore, Detroit	123	1,686	13.7	69	14
	Jerry Rice, San Francisco[3]	122	1,848	15.1	81	15
	Cris Carter, Minnesota[2]	122	1,371	11.2	60	17
	Isaac Bruce, St. Louis	119	1,781	15.0	72	13
	Michael Irvin, Dallas	111	1,603	14.4	50	10
	Brett Perriman, Detroit	108	1,488	13.8	91	9
	Eric Metcalf, Atlanta	104	1,189	11.4	62	8
	Robert Brooks, Green Bay	102	1,497	14.7	99	13
	Larry Centers, Arizona	101	962	9.5	32	2
1994	Cris Carter, Minnesota	122	1,256	10.3	65	7
	Jerry Rice, San Francisco[2]	112	1,499	13.4	69	13
	Terance Mathis, Atlanta	111	1,342	12.1	81	11
1993	Sterling Sharpe, Green Bay[2]	112	1,274	11.4	54	11
1992	Sterling Sharpe, Green Bay	108	1,461	13.5	76	13
1991	Haywood Jeffires, Houston	100	1,181	11.8	44	7
1990	Jerry Rice, San Francisco	100	1,502	15.0	64	13
1984	Art Monk, Washington	106	1,372	12.9	72	7
1964	Charley Hennigan, Houston	101	1,546	15.3	53	8
1961	Lionel Taylor, Denver	100	1,176	11.8	52	4

1,000 YARDS PASS RECEIVING IN A SEASON

Year	Player, Team	No.	Yards	Avg.	Long	TD
1998	Antonio Freeman, Green Bay[2]	84	1,424	17.0	84	14
	Eric Moulds, Buffalo	67	1,368	20.4	84	9
	*Randy Moss, Minnesota	69	1,313	19.0	61	17
	Rod Smith, Denver[2]	86	1,222	14.2	58	6
	Jimmy Smith, Jacksonville[3]	78	1,182	15.2	72	8
	Tony Martin, Atlanta[3]	66	1,181	17.9	62	6
	Jerry Rice, San Francisco[12]	82	1,157	14.1	75	9
	Frank Sanders, Arizona[2]	89	1,145	12.9	42	3
	Terance Mathis, Atlanta[3]	64	1,136	17.8	78	11
	Keyshawn Johnson, N.Y. Jets	83	1,131	13.6	41	10
	Terrell Owens, San Francisco	67	1,097	16.4	79	14
	Wayne Chrebet, N.Y. Jets	75	1,083	14.4	63	8
	Michael Irvin, Dallas[7]	74	1,057	14.3	51	1
	Ed McCaffrey, Denver	64	1,053	16.5	48	10
	O.J. McDuffie, Miami	90	1,050	11.7	61	7
	Joey Galloway, Seattle[3]	65	1,047	16.1	81	10
	Johnnie Morton, Detroit[2]	69	1,028	14.9	98	2
	Raghib Ismail, Carolina	69	1,024	14.8	62	8
	Carl Pickens, Cincinnati[4]	82	1,023	12.5	67	5
	Tim Brown, Oakland[6]	81	1,012	12.5	49	9
	Cris Carter, Minnesota[6]	78	1,011	13.0	54	12
1997	Rob Moore, Arizona[3]	97	1,584	16.3	47	8
	Tim Brown, Oakland[5]	104	1,408	13.5	59	5
	Yancey Thigpen, Pittsburgh[2]	79	1,398	17.7	69	7
	Jimmy Smith, Jacksonville[2]	82	1,324	16.1	75	4
	Irving Fryar, Philadelphia[5]	86	1,316	15.3	72	6
	Herman Moore, Detroit[4]	104	1,293	12.4	79	8
	Antonio Freeman, Green Bay	81	1,243	15.3	58	12

	Michael Irvin, Dallas[6]	75	1,180	15.7	55	9
	Rod Smith, Denver	70	1,180	16.9	78	12
	Keenan McCardell, Jacksonville[2]	85	1,164	13.7	60	5
	Jake Reed, Minnesota[4]	68	1,138	16.7	56	6
	Shannon Sharpe, Denver[3]	72	1,107	15.4	68	3
	Andre Rison, Kansas City[5]	72	1,092	15.2	45	7
	Cris Carter, Minnesota[5]	89	1,069	12.0	43	13
	Johnnie Morton, Detroit	80	1,057	13.2	73	6
	Joey Galloway, Seattle[2]	72	1,049	14.6	53	12
	Frank Sanders, Arizona	75	1,017	13.6	70	4
	Robert Brooks, Green Bay[2]	60	1,010	16.8	48	7
	Derrick Alexander, Baltimore[2]	65	1,009	15.5	92	9
1996	Isaac Bruce, St. Louis[2]	84	1,338	15.9	70	7
	Jake Reed, Minnesota[3]	72	1,320	18.3	82	7
	Herman Moore, Detroit[3]	106	1,296	12.2	50	9
	Jerry Rice, San Francisco[11]	108	1,254	11.6	39	8
	Jimmy Smith, Jacksonville	83	1,244	15.0	62	7
	Michael Jackson, Baltimore	76	1,201	15.8	86	14
	Irving Fryar, Philadelphia[4]	88	1,195	13.6	42	11
	Carl Pickens, Cincinnati[3]	100	1,180	11.8	61	12
	Tony Martin, San Diego[2]	85	1,171	13.8	55	14
	Cris Carter, Minnesota[4]	96	1,163	12.1	43	10
	*Terry Glenn, New England	90	1,132	12.6	37	6
	Keenan McCardell, Jacksonville	85	1,129	13.3	52	3
	Tim Brown, Oakland[4]	90	1,104	12.3	42	9
	Derrick Alexander, Baltimore	62	1,099	17.7	64	9
	Shannon Sharpe, Denver[2]	80	1,062	13.3	51	10
	Curtis Conway, Chicago[2]	81	1,049	13.0	58	7
	Andre Reed, Buffalo[4]	66	1,036	15.7	67	6
	Brett Perriman, Detroit[2]	94	1,021	10.9	44	5
	Rob Moore, Arizona[2]	58	1,016	17.5	69	4
	Henry Ellard, Washington[7]	52	1,014	19.5	51	2
	Charles Johnson, Pittsburgh	60	1,008	16.8	70	3
1995	Jerry Rice, San Francisco[10]	122	1,848	15.1	81	15
	Isaac Bruce, St. Louis	119	1,781	15.0	72	13
	Herman Moore, Detroit[2]	123	1,686	13.7	69	14
	Michael Irvin, Dallas[5]	111	1,603	14.4	50	10
	Robert Brooks, Green Bay	102	1,497	14.7	99	13
	Brett Perriman, Detroit	108	1,488	13.8	91	9
	Cris Carter, Minnesota[3]	122	1,371	11.2	60	17
	Tim Brown, Oakland[3]	89	1,342	15.1	80	10
	Yancey Thigpen, Pittsburgh	85	1,307	15.4	43	5
	Jeff Graham, Chicago	82	1,301	15.9	51	4
	Carl Pickens, Cincinnati[2]	99	1,234	12.5	68	17
	Tony Martin, San Diego	90	1,224	13.6	51	6
	Eric Metcalf, Atlanta	104	1,189	11.4	62	8
	Jake Reed, Minnesota[2]	72	1,167	16.2	55	9
	Quinn Early, New Orleans	81	1,087	13.4	70	8
	Anthony Miller, Denver[5]	59	1,079	18.3	62	14
	Bert Emanuel, Atlanta	74	1,039	14.0	52	5
	*Joey Galloway, Seattle	67	1,039	15.5	59	7
	Terance Mathis, Atlanta[2]	78	1,039	13.3	54	9
	Curtis Conway, Chicago	62	1,037	16.7	76	12
	Henry Ellard, Washington[6]	56	1,005	17.9	59	5
	Mark Carrier, Carolina[2]	66	1,002	15.2	66	3
	Brian Blades, Seattle[4]	77	1,001	13.0	49	4
1994	Jerry Rice, San Francisco[9]	112	1,499	13.4	69	13
	Henry Ellard, Washington[5]	74	1,397	18.9	73	6
	Terance Mathis, Atlanta	111	1,342	12.1	81	11
	Tim Brown, L.A. Raiders[2]	89	1,309	14.7	77	9
	Andre Reed, Buffalo[2]	90	1,303	14.5	83	8
	Irving Fryar, Miami[3]	73	1,270	17.4	54	7
	Cris Carter, Minnesota[2]	122	1,256	10.3	65	7
	Michael Irvin, Dallas[4]	79	1,241	15.7	65	6
	Jake Reed, Minnesota	85	1,175	13.8	59	4
	Ben Coates, New England	96	1,174	12.2	62	7
	Herman Moore, Detroit	72	1,173	16.3	51	11
	Fred Barnett, Philadelphia[2]	78	1,127	14.4	54	5
	Carl Pickens, Cincinnati	71	1,127	15.9	70	11
	Sterling Sharpe, Green Bay[4]	94	1,119	11.9	49	18
	Anthony Miller, Denver[4]	60	1,107	18.5	76	5
	Andre Rison, Atlanta[3]	81	1,088	13.4	69	8
	Brian Blades, Seattle[3]	81	1,088	13.4	45	4
	Rob Moore, N.Y. Jets	78	1,010	12.9	41	6
	Shannon Sharpe, Denver	87	1,010	11.6	44	4
1993	Jerry Rice, San Francisco[8]	98	1,503	15.3	80	15
	Michael Irvin, Dallas[3]	88	1,330	15.1	61	7
	Sterling Sharpe, Green Bay[4]	112	1,274	11.4	54	11
	Andre Rison, Atlanta[3]	86	1,242	14.4	53	15
	Tim Brown, L.A. Raiders	80	1,180	14.8	71	7
	Anthony Miller, San Diego[3]	84	1,162	13.8	66	7
	Cris Carter, Minnesota	86	1,071	12.5	58	9
	Reggie Langhorne, Indianapolis	85	1,038	12.2	72	3
	Irving Fryar, Miami[2]	64	1,010	15.8	65	5
1992	Sterling Sharpe, Green Bay[3]	108	1,461	13.5	76	13
	Michael Irvin, Dallas[2]	78	1,396	17.9	87	7
	Jerry Rice, San Francisco[7]	84	1,201	14.3	80	10
	Andre Rison, Atlanta[2]	93	1,119	12.0	71	11
	Fred Barnett, Philadelphia	67	1,083	16.2	71	6
	Anthony Miller, San Diego[2]	72	1,060	14.7	67	7
	Eric Martin, New Orleans[3]	68	1,041	15.3	52	5
1991	Michael Irvin, Dallas	93	1,523	16.4	66	8
	Gary Clark, Washington[5]	70	1,340	19.1	82	10
	Jerry Rice, San Francisco[6]	80	1,206	15.1	73	14
	Haywood Jeffires, Houston[2]	100	1,181	11.8	44	7
	Michael Haynes, Atlanta	50	1,122	22.4	80	11
	Andre Reed, Buffalo[2]	81	1,113	13.7	55	10
	Drew Hill, Houston[5]	90	1,109	12.3	61	4
	Mark Duper, Miami[4]	70	1,085	15.5	43	5
	James Lofton, Buffalo[6]	57	1,072	18.8	77	8
	Mark Clayton, Miami[5]	70	1,053	15.0	43	12
	Henry Ellard, L.A. Rams[4]	64	1,052	16.4	38	3
	Art Monk, Washington[5]	71	1,049	14.8	64	8
	Irving Fryar, New England	68	1,014	14.9	56	3
	John Taylor, San Francisco[2]	64	1,011	15.8	97	9
	Brian Blades, Seattle[2]	70	1,003	14.3	52	2
1990	Jerry Rice, San Francisco[5]	100	1,502	15.0	64	13
	Henry Ellard, L.A. Rams[3]	76	1,294	17.0	50	4
	Andre Rison, Atlanta	82	1,208	14.7	75	10
	Gary Clark, Washington[4]	75	1,112	14.8	53	8
	Sterling Sharpe, Green Bay[2]	67	1,105	16.5	76	6
	Willie Anderson, L.A. Rams[2]	51	1,097	21.5	55	4
	Haywood Jeffires, Houston	74	1,048	14.2	87	8
	Stephone Paige, Kansas City	65	1,021	15.7	86	5
	Drew Hill, Houston[4]	74	1,019	13.8	57	5
	Anthony Carter, Minnesota[3]	70	1,008	14.4	56	8
1989	Jerry Rice, San Francisco[4]	82	1,483	18.1	68	17
	Sterling Sharpe, Green Bay	90	1,423	15.8	79	12
	Mark Carrier, Tampa Bay	86	1,422	16.5	78	9
	Henry Ellard, L.A. Rams[2]	70	1,382	19.7	53	8
	Andre Reed, Buffalo	88	1,312	14.9	78	9
	Anthony Miller, San Diego	75	1,252	16.7	69	10
	Webster Slaughter, Cleveland	65	1,236	19.0	97	6
	Gary Clark, Washington[3]	79	1,229	15.6	80	9
	Tim McGee, Cincinnati	65	1,211	18.6	74	8
	Art Monk, Washington[4]	86	1,186	13.8	60	8
	Willie Anderson, L.A. Rams	44	1,146	26.0	78	5
	Ricky Sanders, Washington[2]	80	1,138	14.2	68	4
	Vance Johnson, Denver	76	1,095	14.4	69	7
	Richard Johnson, Detroit	70	1,091	15.6	75	8
	Eric Martin, New Orleans[2]	68	1,090	16.0	53	8
	John Taylor, San Francisco	60	1,077	18.0	95	10
	Mervyn Fernandez, L.A. Raiders	57	1,069	18.8	75	9
	Anthony Carter, Minnesota[2]	65	1,066	16.4	50	4
	Brian Blades, Seattle	77	1,063	13.8	60	5
	Mark Clayton, Miami[4]	64	1,011	15.8	78	9
1988	Henry Ellard, L.A. Rams	86	1,414	16.4	68	10
	Jerry Rice, San Francisco[3]	64	1,306	20.4	96	9
	Eddie Brown, Cincinnati	53	1,273	24.0	86	9
	Anthony Carter, Minnesota	72	1,225	17.0	67	6
	Ricky Sanders, Washington	73	1,148	15.7	55	12
	Drew Hill, Houston[3]	72	1,141	15.8	57	10
	Mark Clayton, Miami[3]	86	1,129	13.1	45	14
	Roy Green, Phoenix[3]	68	1,097	16.1	52	7
	Eric Martin, New Orleans	85	1,083	12.7	40	7
	Al Toon, N.Y. Jets[2]	93	1,067	11.5	42	5
	Bruce Hill, Tampa Bay	58	1,040	17.9	42	9
	Lionel Manuel, N.Y. Giants	65	1,029	15.8	46	4
1987	J.T. Smith, St. Louis[2]	91	1,117	12.3	38	8
	Jerry Rice, San Francisco[2]	65	1,078	16.6	57	22
	Gary Clark, Washington[2]	56	1,066	19.0	84	7
	Carlos Carson, Kansas City[3]	55	1,044	19.0	81	7
1986	Jerry Rice, San Francisco	86	1,570	18.3	66	15
	Stanley Morgan, New England[3]	84	1,491	17.8	44	10
	Mark Duper, Miami[3]	67	1,313	19.6	85	11
	Gary Clark, Washington	74	1,265	17.1	55	7
	Al Toon, N.Y. Jets	85	1,176	13.8	62	8
	Todd Christensen, L.A. Raiders[3]	95	1,153	12.1	35	8
	Mark Clayton, Miami[2]	60	1,150	19.2	68	10
	*Bill Brooks, Indianapolis	65	1,131	17.4	84	8
	Drew Hill, Houston[2]	65	1,112	17.1	81	5
	Steve Largent, Seattle[8]	70	1,070	15.3	38	9
	Art Monk, Washington[3]	73	1,068	14.6	69	4
	*Ernest Givins, Houston	61	1,062	17.4	60	3
	Cris Collinsworth, Cincinnati[4]	62	1,024	16.5	46	10
	Wesley Walker, N.Y. Jets[2]	49	1,016	20.7	83	12

	J.T. Smith, St. Louis	80	1,014	12.7	45	6
	Mark Bavaro, N.Y. Giants	66	1,001	15.2	41	4
1985	Steve Largent, Seattle[7]	79	1,287	16.3	43	6
	Mike Quick, Philadelphia[3]	73	1,247	17.1	99	11
	Art Monk, Washington[2]	91	1,226	13.5	53	2
	Wes Chandler, San Diego[4]	67	1,199	17.9	75	10
	Drew Hill, Houston	64	1,169	18.3	57	9
	James Lofton, Green Bay[5]	69	1,153	16.7	56	4
	Louis Lipps, Pittsburgh	59	1,134	19.2	51	12
	Cris Collinsworth, Cincinnati[3]	65	1,125	17.3	71	5
	Tony Hill, Dallas[3]	74	1,113	15.0	53	7
	Lionel James, San Diego	86	1,027	11.9	67	6
	Roger Craig, San Francisco	92	1,016	11.0	73	6
1984	Roy Green, St. Louis[2]	78	1,555	19.9	83	12
	John Stallworth, Pittsburgh[3]	80	1,395	17.4	51	11
	Mark Clayton, Miami	73	1,389	19.0	65	18
	Art Monk, Washington	106	1,372	12.9	72	7
	James Lofton, Green Bay[4]	62	1,361	22.0	79	7
	Mark Duper, Miami[2]	71	1,306	18.4	80	8
	Steve Watson, Denver[3]	69	1,170	17.0	73	7
	Steve Largent, Seattle[6]	74	1,164	15.7	65	12
	Tim Smith, Houston[2]	69	1,141	16.5	75	4
	Stacey Bailey, Atlanta	67	1,138	17.0	61	6
	Carlos Carson, Kansas City[2]	57	1,078	18.9	57	4
	Mike Quick, Philadelphia[2]	61	1,052	17.2	90	9
	Todd Christensen, L.A. Raiders[2]	80	1,007	12.6	38	7
	Kevin House, Tampa Bay[2]	76	1,005	13.2	55	5
	Ozzie Newsome, Cleveland[2]	89	1,001	11.2	52	5
1983	Mike Quick, Philadelphia	69	1,409	20.4	83	13
	Carlos Carson, Kansas City	80	1,351	16.9	50	7
	James Lofton, Green Bay[3]	58	1,300	22.4	74	8
	Todd Christensen, L.A. Raiders	92	1,247	13.6	45	12
	Roy Green, St. Louis	78	1,227	15.7	71	14
	Charlie Brown, Washington	78	1,225	15.7	75	8
	Tim Smith, Houston	83	1,176	14.2	47	6
	Kellen Winslow, San Diego[3]	88	1,172	13.3	46	8
	Earnest Gray, N.Y. Giants	78	1,139	14.6	62	5
	Steve Watson, Denver[2]	59	1,133	19.2	78	5
	Cris Collinsworth, Cincinnati[2]	66	1,130	17.1	63	5
	Steve Largent, Seattle[5]	72	1,074	14.9	46	11
	Mark Duper, Miami	51	1,003	19.7	85	10
1982	Wes Chandler, San Diego[3]	49	1,032	21.1	66	9
1981	Alfred Jenkins, Atlanta[2]	70	1,358	19.4	67	13
	James Lofton, Green Bay[2]	71	1,294	18.2	75	8
	Steve Watson, Denver	60	1,244	20.7	95	13
	Frank Lewis, Buffalo[2]	70	1,244	17.8	33	4
	Steve Largent, Seattle[4]	75	1,224	16.3	57	9
	Charlie Joiner, San Diego[4]	70	1,188	17.0	57	7
	Kevin House, Tampa Bay	56	1,176	21.0	84	9
	Wes Chandler, N.O.-San Diego[2]	69	1,142	16.6	51	6
	Dwight Clark, San Francisco	85	1,105	13.0	78	4
	John Stallworth, Pittsburgh[2]	63	1,098	17.4	55	5
	Kellen Winslow, San Diego[2]	88	1,075	12.2	67	10
	Pat Tilley, St. Louis	66	1,040	15.8	75	3
	Stanley Morgan, New England[2]	44	1,029	23.4	76	6
	Harold Carmichael, Philadelphia[3]	61	1,028	16.9	85	6
	Freddie Scott, Detroit	53	1,022	19.3	48	5
	*Cris Collinsworth, Cincinnati	67	1,009	15.1	74	8
	Joe Senser, Minnesota	79	1,004	12.7	53	8
	Ozzie Newsome, Cleveland	69	1,002	14.5	62	6
	Sammy White, Minnesota	66	1,001	15.2	53	3
1980	John Jefferson, San Diego[3]	82	1,340	16.3	58	13
	Kellen Winslow, San Diego	89	1,290	14.5	65	9
	James Lofton, Green Bay	71	1,226	17.3	47	4
	Charlie Joiner, San Diego[3]	71	1,132	15.9	51	4
	Ahmad Rashad, Minnesota[2]	69	1,095	15.9	76	5
	Steve Largent, Seattle[3]	66	1,064	16.1	67	6
	Tony Hill, Dallas[2]	60	1,055	17.6	58	8
	Alfred Jenkins, Atlanta	57	1,026	18.0	57	6
1979	Steve Largent, Seattle[2]	66	1,237	18.7	55	9
	John Stallworth, Pittsburgh	70	1,183	16.9	65	8
	Ahmad Rashad, Minnesota	80	1,156	14.5	52	9
	John Jefferson, San Diego[2]	61	1,090	17.9	65	10
	Frank Lewis, Buffalo	54	1,082	20.0	55	2
	Wes Chandler, New Orleans	65	1,069	16.4	85	6
	Tony Hill, Dallas	60	1,062	17.7	75	10
	Drew Pearson, Dallas[2]	55	1,026	18.7	56	8
	Wallace Francis, Atlanta	74	1,013	13.7	42	8
	Harold Jackson, New England[3]	45	1,013	22.5	59	7
	Charlie Joiner, San Diego[2]	72	1,008	14.0	39	4
	Stanley Morgan, New England	44	1,002	22.8	63	12
1978	Wesley Walker, N.Y. Jets	48	1,169	24.4	77	8
	Steve Largent, Seattle	71	1,168	16.5	57	8
	Harold Carmichael, Philadelphia[2]	55	1,072	19.5	56	8
	*John Jefferson, San Diego	56	1,001	17.9	46	13
1976	Roger Carr, Baltimore	43	1,112	25.9	79	11
	Cliff Branch, Oakland[2]	46	1,111	24.2	88	12
	Charlie Joiner, San Diego	50	1,056	21.1	81	7
1975	Ken Burrough, Houston	53	1,063	20.1	77	8
1974	Cliff Branch, Oakland	60	1,092	18.2	67	13
	Drew Pearson, Dallas	62	1,087	17.5	50	2
1973	Harold Carmichael, Philadelphia	67	1,116	16.7	73	9
1972	Harold Jackson, Philadelphia[2]	62	1,048	16.9	77	4
	John Gilliam, Minnesota	47	1,035	22.0	66	7
1971	Otis Taylor, Kansas City[2]	57	1,110	19.5	82	7
1970	Gene Washington, San Francisco	53	1,100	20.8	79	12
	Marlin Briscoe, Buffalo	57	1,036	18.2	48	8
	Dick Gordon, Chicago	71	1,026	14.5	69	13
	Gary Garrison, San Diego[2]	44	1,006	22.9	67	12
1969	Warren Wells, Oakland[2]	47	1,260	26.8	80	14
	Harold Jackson, Philadelphia	65	1,116	17.2	65	9
	Roy Jefferson, Pittsburgh[2]	67	1,079	16.1	63	9
	Dan Abramowicz, New Orleans	73	1,015	13.9	49	7
	Lance Alworth, San Diego[7]	64	1,003	15.7	76	4
1968	Lance Alworth, San Diego[6]	68	1,312	19.3	80	10
	Don Maynard, N.Y. Jets[5]	57	1,297	22.8	87	10
	George Sauer, N.Y. Jets[3]	66	1,141	17.3	43	3
	Warren Wells, Oakland	53	1,137	21.5	94	11
	Gary Garrison, San Diego	52	1,103	21.2	84	10
	Roy Jefferson, Pittsburgh	58	1,074	18.5	62	11
	Paul Warfield, Cleveland	50	1,067	21.3	65	12
	Homer Jones, N.Y. Giants[3]	45	1,057	23.5	84	7
	Fred Biletnikoff, Oakland	61	1,037	17.0	82	6
	Lance Rentzel, Dallas	54	1,009	18.7	65	6
1967	Don Maynard, N.Y. Jets[4]	71	1,434	20.2	75	10
	Ben Hawkins, Philadelphia	59	1,265	21.4	87	10
	Homer Jones, N.Y. Giants[2]	49	1,209	24.7	70	13
	Jackie Smith, St. Louis	56	1,205	21.5	76	9
	George Sauer, N.Y. Jets[2]	75	1,189	15.9	61	6
	Lance Alworth, San Diego[5]	52	1,010	19.4	71	9
1966	Lance Alworth, San Diego[4]	73	1,383	18.9	78	13
	Otis Taylor, Kansas City	58	1,297	22.4	89	8
	Pat Studstill, Detroit	67	1,266	18.9	99	5
	Bob Hayes, Dallas[2]	64	1,232	19.3	95	13
	Charlie Frazier, Houston	57	1,129	19.8	79	12
	Charley Taylor, Washington	72	1,119	15.5	86	12
	George Sauer, N.Y. Jets	63	1,081	17.2	77	5
	Homer Jones, N.Y. Giants	48	1,044	21.8	98	8
	Art Powell, Oakland[5]	53	1,026	19.4	46	11
1965	Lance Alworth, San Diego[3]	69	1,602	23.2	85	14
	Dave Parks, San Francisco	80	1,344	16.8	53	12
	Don Maynard, N.Y. Jets[3]	68	1,218	17.9	56	14
	Pete Retzlaff, Philadelphia	66	1,190	18.0	78	10
	Lionel Taylor, Denver[4]	85	1,131	13.3	63	6
	Tommy McDonald, Los Angeles[3]	67	1,036	15.5	51	9
	*Bob Hayes, Dallas	46	1,003	21.8	82	12
1964	Charley Hennigan, Houston[3]	101	1,546	15.3	53	8
	Art Powell, Oakland[4]	76	1,361	17.9	77	11
	Lance Alworth, San Diego[2]	61	1,235	20.2	82	13
	Johnny Morris, Chicago	93	1,200	12.9	63	10
	Elbert Dubenion, Buffalo	42	1,139	27.1	72	10
	Terry Barr, Detroit[2]	57	1,030	18.1	58	9
1963	Bobby Mitchell, Washington[2]	69	1,436	20.8	99	7
	Art Powell, Oakland[3]	73	1,304	17.9	85	16
	Buddy Dial, Pittsburgh[2]	60	1,295	21.6	83	9
	Lance Alworth, San Diego	61	1,205	19.8	85	11
	Del Shofner, N.Y. Giants[4]	64	1,181	18.5	70	9
	Lionel Taylor, Denver[3]	78	1,101	14.1	72	10
	Terry Barr, Detroit	66	1,086	16.5	75	13
	Charley Hennigan, Houston[2]	61	1,051	17.2	83	10
	Sonny Randle, St. Louis[2]	51	1,014	19.9	68	12
	Bake Turner, N.Y. Jets	71	1,009	14.2	53	6
1962	Bobby Mitchell, Washington	72	1,384	19.2	81	11
	Sonny Randle, St. Louis	63	1,158	18.4	86	7
	Tommy McDonald, Philadelphia[2]	58	1,146	19.8	60	10
	Del Shofner, N.Y. Giants[3]	53	1,133	21.4	69	12
	Art Powell, N.Y. Titans[2]	64	1,130	17.7	80	8
	Frank Clarke, Dall. Cowboys	47	1,043	22.2	66	14
	Don Maynard, N.Y. Titans[2]	56	1,041	18.6	86	8
1961	Charley Hennigan, Houston	82	1,746	21.3	80	12
	Lionel Taylor, Denver[2]	100	1,176	11.8	52	4
	Bill Groman, Houston[2]	50	1,175	23.5	80	17
	Tommy McDonald, Philadelphia	64	1,144	17.9	66	13
	Del Shofner, N.Y. Giants[2]	68	1,125	16.5	46	11
	Jim Phillips, Los Angeles	78	1,092	14.0	69	5
	*Mike Ditka, Chicago	56	1,076	19.2	76	12

	Dave Kocourek, San Diego	55	1,055	19.2	76	4
	Buddy Dial, Pittsburgh	53	1,047	19.8	88	12
	R.C. Owens, San Francisco	55	1,032	18.8	54	5
1960	*Bill Groman, Houston	72	1,473	20.5	92	12
	Raymond Berry, Baltimore	74	1,298	17.5	70	10
	Don Maynard, N.Y. Titans	72	1,265	17.6	65	6
	Lionel Taylor, Denver	92	1,235	13.4	80	12
	Art Powell, N.Y. Titans	69	1,167	16.9	76	14
1958	Del Shofner, Los Angeles	51	1,097	21.5	92	8
1956	Bill Howton, Green Bay[2]	55	1,188	21.6	66	12
	Harlon Hill, Chi. Bears[2]	47	1,128	24.0	79	11
1954	Bob Boyd, Los Angeles	53	1,212	22.9	80	6
	*Harlon Hill, Chi. Bears	45	1,124	25.0	76	12
1953	Pete Pihos, Philadelphia	63	1,049	16.7	59	10
1952	*Bill Howton, Green Bay	53	1,231	23.2	90	13
1951	Elroy (Crazylegs) Hirsch, Los Angeles	66	1,495	22.7	91	17
1950	Tom Fears, Los Angeles[2]	84	1,116	13.3	53	7
	Cloyce Box, Detroit	50	1,009	20.2	82	11
1949	Bob Mann, Detroit	66	1,014	15.4	64	4
	Tom Fears, Los Angeles	77	1,013	13.2	51	9
1945	Jim Benton, Cleveland	45	1,067	23.7	84	8
1942	Don Hutson, Green Bay	74	1,211	16.4	73	17

**First season of professional football.*

250 YARDS PASS RECEIVING IN A GAME

Date	Player, Team, Opponent	No.	Yards	TD
Dec. 18, 1995	Jerry Rice, San Francisco vs. Minnesota	14	289	3
Dec. 11, 1989	John Taylor, San Francisco vs. L.A. Rams	11	286	2
Nov. 26, 1989	Willie Anderson, L.A. Rams vs. New Orleans (OT)	15	336	1
Oct. 18, 1987	Steve Largent, Seattle vs. Detroit	15	261	3
Oct. 4, 1987	Anthony Allen, Washington vs. St. Louis	7	255	3
Dec. 22, 1985	Stephone Paige, Kansas City vs. San Diego	8	309	2
Dec. 20, 1982	Wes Chandler, San Diego vs. Cincinnati	10	260	2
Sept. 23, 1979	*Jerry Butler, Buffalo vs. N.Y. Jets	10	255	4
Nov. 4, 1962	Sonny Randle, St. Louis vs. N.Y. Giants	16	256	1
Oct. 28, 1962	Del Shofner, N.Y. Giants vs. Washington	11	269	1
Oct. 13, 1961	Charley Hennigan, Houston vs. Boston	13	272	1
Oct. 21, 1956	Billy Howton, Green Bay vs. Los Angeles	7	257	2
Dec. 3, 1950	Cloyce Box, Detroit vs. Baltimore	12	302	4
Nov. 22, 1945	Jim Benton, Cleveland vs. Detroit	10	303	1

**First season of professional football.*

2,000 COMBINED NET YARDS GAINED IN A SEASON

Year	Player, Team	Rushing Att.-Yds.	Pass Rec.	Punt Ret.	Kickoff Ret.	Fum. Ret.	Total Yds.
1998	Brian Mitchell, Washington	39-208	44-306	44-506	59-1,337	0-0	186-2,357
	Marshall Faulk, Indianapolis	324-1,319	86-908	0-0	0-0	2-13	412-2,240
	Terrell Davis, Denver	392-2,008	25-217	0-0	0-0	1-0	418-2,225
	Jamal Anderson, Atlanta	410-1,846	27-319	0-0	0-0	1-0	438-2,165
	Garrison Hearst, San Francisco	310-1,570	39-535	0-0	0-0	1-0	350-2,105
1997	Barry Sanders, Detroit	335-2,053	33-305	0-0	0-0	1-0	369-2,358
	Kevin Williams, Arizona	1-(-2)	20-273	40-462	59-1,458	1-0	121-2,191
	Brian Mitchell, Wash.	23-107	36-438	38-442	47-1,094	0-0	144-2,081
	Terrell Davis, Denver	369-1,750	42-287	0-0	0-0	2-(-7)	413-2,030
	Jermaine Lewis, Balt.	3-35	42-648	28-437	41-905	2-0	116-2,025
1995	Brian Mitchell, Wash.	46-301	38-324	25-315	55-1,408	0-0	164-2,348
	Emmitt Smith, Dallas	377-1,773	62-375	0-0	0-0	0-0	439-2,148
	Glyn Milburn, Denver	49-266	22-191	31-354	47-1,269	0-0	149-2,080
	Ernie Mills, Pittsburgh	5-39	39-679	0-0	54-1,306	0-0	98-2,024
1994	Brian Mitchell, Wash.	78-311	26-236	32-452	58-1,478	0-0	194-2,477
	Barry Sanders, Detroit	331-1,883	44-283	0-0	0-0	0-0	375-2,166
1992	Thurman Thomas, Buffalo	312-1,487	58-626	0-0	0-0	1-0	371-2,113
	Emmitt Smith, Dallas	373-1,713	59-335	0-0	0-0	1-0	433-2,048
	Barry Foster, Pittsburgh	390-1,690	36-344	0-0	0-0	2-(–20)	428-2,014
1991	Thurman Thomas, Buffalo	288-1,407	62-631	0-0	0-0	0-0	350-2,038
1990	Herschel Walker, Minnesota	184-770	35-315	0-0	44-966	4-0	267-2,051
1988	*Tim Brown, L.A. Raiders	14-50	43-725	49-444	41-1,098	7-0	154-2,317
	Roger Craig, San Fran.	310-1,502	76-534	0-0	2-32	2-0	390-2,068
	Eric Dickerson, Indianapolis	388-1,659	36-377	0-0	0-0	1-0	425-2,036
	Herschel Walker, Dallas	361-1,514	53-505	0-0	0-0	3-0	417-2,019
1986	Eric Dickerson, L.A. Rams	404-1,821	26-205	0-0	0-0	2-0	432-2,026
	Gary Anderson, San Diego	127-442	80-871	25-227	24-482	2-0	258-2,022
1985	Lionel James, San Diego	105-516	86-1,027	25-213	36-779	1-0	253-2,535
	Marcus Allen, L.A. Raiders	380-1,759	67-555	0-0	0-0	2-(–6)	449-2,308
	Roger Craig, San Fran.	214-1,050	92-1,016	0-0	0-0	0-0	306-2,066
	Walter Payton, Chicago	324-1,551	49-483	0-0	0-0	1-0	374-2,034
1984	Eric Dickerson, L.A. Rams	379-2,105	21-139	0-0	0-0	4-15	404-2,259
	James Wilder, Tampa Bay	407-1,544	85-685	0-0	0-0	4-0	496-2,229
	Walter Payton, Chicago	381-1,684	45-368	0-0	0-0	1-0	427-2,052
1983	*Eric Dickerson, L.A. Rams	390-1,808	51-404	0-0	0-0	1-0	442-2,212
	William Andrews, Atlanta	331-1,567	59-609	0-0	0-0	2-0	392-2,176
	Walter Payton, Chicago	314-1,421	53-607	0-0	0-0	2-0	369-2,028
1981	*James Brooks, San Diego	109-525	46-329	22-290	40-949	2-0	219-2,093
	William Andrews, Atlanta	289-1,301	81-735	0-0	0-0	0-0	370-2,036
1980	Bruce Harper, N.Y. Jets	45-126	50-634	28-242	49-1,070	3-0	175-2,072
1979	Wilbert Montgomery, Phil.	338-1,512	41-494	0-0	1-6	2-0	382-2,012
1978	Bruce Harper, N.Y. Jets	58-303	13-196	30-378	55-1,280	1-0	157-2,157
1977	Walter Payton, Chicago	339-1,852	27-269	0-0	2-95	5-0	373-2,216
	Terry Metcalf, St. Louis	149-739	34-403	14-108	32-772	1-0	230-2,022
1975	Terry Metcalf, St. Louis	165-816	43-378	23-285	35-960	2-23	268-2,462
	O.J. Simpson, Buffalo	329-1,817	28-426	0-0	0-0	1-0	358-2,243
1974	Mack Herron, New England	231-824	38-474	35-517	28-629	3-0	335-2,444
	Otis Armstrong, Denver	263-1,407	38-405	0-0	16-386	1-0	318-2,198
	Terry Metcalf, St. Louis	152-718	50-377	26-340	20-623	7-0	255-2,058
1973	O.J. Simpson, Buffalo	332-2,003	6-70	0-0	0-0	0-0	338-2,073
1966	Gale Sayers, Chicago	229-1,231	34-447	6-44	23-718	3-0	295-2,440
	Leroy Kelly, Cleveland	209-1,141	32-366	13-104	19-403	0-0	273-2,014
1965	*Gale Sayers, Chicago	166-867	29-507	16-238	21-660	4-0	236-2,272
1963	Timmy Brown, Philadelphia	192-841	36-487	16-152	33-945	2-3	279-2,428
	Jim Brown, Cleveland	291-1,863	24-268	0-0	0-0	0-0	315-2,131
1962	Timmy Brown, Philadelphia	137-545	52-849	6-81	30-831	4-0	229-2,306
	Dick Christy, N.Y. Titans	114-535	62-538	15-250	38-824	2-0	231-2,147
1961	Billy Cannon, Houston	200-948	43-586	9-70	18-439	2-0	272-2,043
1960	*Abner Haynes, Dall. Texans	156-875	55-576	14-215	19-434	4-0	248-2,100

**First season of professional football.*

300 COMBINED NET YARDS GAINED IN A GAME

Date	Player, Team, Opponent	No.	Yards	TD
Dec. 7, 1997	Jermaine Lewis, Baltimore vs. Seattle	10	308	3
Dec. 25, 1995	Kevin Williams, Dallas vs. Arizona	16	307	2
Dec. 10, 1995	Glyn Milburn, Denver vs. Seattle	33	404	0
Oct. 23, 1994	Tyrone Hughes, New Orleans vs. L.A. Rams	11	347	2
Dec. 11, 1989	John Taylor, San Francisco vs. L.A. Rams	14	321	2
Nov. 26, 1989	Willie Anderson, L.A. Rams vs. New Orleans (OT)	15	336	1
Nov. 28, 1988	*Tim Brown, L.A. Raiders vs. Seattle	12	308	1
Dec. 22, 1985	Stephone Paige, Kansas City vs. San Diego	8	309	2
Nov. 10, 1985	Lionel James, San Diego vs. L.A. Raiders (OT)	23	345	0
Sept. 22, 1985	Lionel James, San Diego vs. Cincinnati	20	316	2
Dec. 21, 1975	*Walter Payton, Chicago vs. New Orleans	32	300	1
Nov. 23, 1975	Greg Pruitt, Cleveland vs. Cincinnati	28	304	2
Nov. 1, 1970	Eugene (Mercury) Morris, Miami vs. Baltimore	17	302	0
Oct. 4, 1970	O.J. Simpson, Buffalo vs. N.Y. Jets	26	303	2
Dec. 6, 1969	Jerry LeVias, Houston vs. N.Y. Jets	18	329	1
Nov. 2, 1969	Travis Williams, Green Bay vs. Pittsburgh	11	314	3
Dec. 18, 1966	Gale Sayers, Chicago vs. Minnesota	20	339	2
Dec. 12, 1965	*Gale Sayers, Chicago vs. San Francisco	17	336	6
Nov. 17, 1963	Gary Ballman, Pittsburgh vs. Washington	12	320	2
Dec. 16, 1962	Timmy Brown, Philadelphia vs. St. Louis	19	341	2
Dec. 10, 1961	Billy Cannon, Houston vs. N.Y. Titans	32	373	5
Nov. 19, 1961	Jim Brown, Cleveland vs. Philadelphia	38	313	4
Dec. 3, 1950	Cloyce Box, Detroit vs. Baltimore	13	302	4
Oct. 29, 1950	Wally Triplett, Detroit vs. Los Angeles	11	331	1
Nov. 22, 1945	Jim Benton, Cleveland vs. Detroit	10	303	1

**First season of professional football.*

TOP 20 SCORERS

Player	Years	TD	FG	PAT	TP
George Blanda	26	9	335	943	2,002
Gary Anderson	17	0	420	585	1,845
Morten Andersen	17	0	401	558	1,761
Nick Lowery	18	0	383	562	1,711
Jan Stenerud	19	0	373	580	1,699
Norm Johnson	17	0	348	613	1,657
Eddie Murray	19	0	337	521	1,532
Pat Leahy	18	0	304	558	1,470
Jim Turner	16	1	304	521	1,439
Matt Bahr	17	0	300	522	1,422
Mark Moseley	16	0	300	482	1,382
Jim Bakken	17	0	282	534	1,380
Fred Cox	15	0	282	519	1,365
Al Del Greco	15	0	299	463	1,360
Lou Groza	17	1	234	641	1,349
Jim Breech	14	0	243	517	1,246
Chris Bahr	14	0	241	490	1,213
Kevin Butler	13	0	265	413	1,208
Gino Cappelletti	11	42	176	346	1,130
Ray Wersching	15	0	222	456	1,122

Cappelletti's total includes 4 two-point conversions.

TOP 20 TOUCHDOWN SCORERS

Player	Years	Rush	Rec.	Total Returns	TD
Jerry Rice	14	10	164	1	175
Marcus Allen	16	123	21	1	145
Emmitt Smith	9	125	9	0	134
Jim Brown	9	106	20	0	126

Walter Payton	13	110	15	0	125
John Riggins	14	104	12	0	116
Lenny Moore	12	63	48	2	113
Barry Sanders	10	99	10	0	109
Don Hutson	11	3	99	3	105
Cris Carter	12	0	101	1	102
Steve Largent	14	1	100	0	101
Franco Harris	13	91	9	0	100
Eric Dickerson	11	90	6	0	96
Jim Taylor	10	83	10	0	93
Tony Dorsett	12	77	13	1	91
Bobby Mitchell	11	18	65	8	91
Leroy Kelly	10	74	13	3	90
Charley Taylor	13	11	79	0	90
Don Maynard	15	0	88	0	88
Lance Alworth	11	2	85	0	87

TOP 20 RUSHERS

Player	Years	Att.	Yards	Avg.	Long	TD
Walter Payton	13	3,838	16,726	4.4	76	110
Barry Sanders	10	3,062	15,269	5.0	85	99
Eric Dickerson	11	2,996	13,259	4.4	85	90
Tony Dorsett	12	2,936	12,739	4.3	99	77
Emmitt Smith	9	2,914	12,566	4.3	75	125
Jim Brown	9	2,359	12,312	5.2	80	106
Marcus Allen	16	3,022	12,243	4.1	61	123
Franco Harris	13	2,949	12,120	4.1	75	91
Thurman Thomas	11	2,813	11,786	4.2	80	65
John Riggins	14	2,916	11,352	3.9	66	104
O.J. Simpson	11	2,404	11,236	4.7	94	61
Ottis Anderson	14	2,562	10,273	4.0	76	81
Earl Campbell	8	2,187	9,407	4.3	81	74
Jim Taylor	10	1,941	8,597	4.4	84	83
Joe Perry	14	1,737	8,378	4.8	78	53
Earnest Byner	14	2,095	8,261	3.9	54	56
Herschel Walker	12	1,954	8,225	4.2	91	61
Roger Craig	11	1,991	8,189	4.1	71	56
Gerald Riggs	10	1,989	8,188	4.1	58	69
Larry Csonka	11	1,891	8,081	4.3	54	64

TOP 20 COMBINED YARDS GAINED

	Years	Tot.	Rush.	Rec.	Int. Ret.	Punt Ret.	Kickoff Ret.	Fumble Ret.
Walter Payton	13	21,803	16,726	4,538	0	0	539	0
Barry Sanders	10	18,308	15,269	2,921	0	0	118	0
Jerry Rice	14	18,232	614	17,612	0	0	6	0
Herschel Walker	12	18,168	8,225	4,859	0	0	5,084	0
Marcus Allen	16	17,648	12,243	5,411	0	0	0	-6
Tony Dorsett	12	16,326	12,739	3,554	0	0	0	33
Eric Metcalf	10	16,280	2,365	5,420	0	2,804	5,691	0
Thruman Thomas	11	16,090	11,786	4,304	0	0	0	0
Henry Ellard	16	15,718	50	13,777	0	1,527	364	0
Jim Brown	10	16,280	2,365	5,420	0	2,804	5,691	0
Eric Dickerson	11	15,411	13,259	2,137	0	0	0	15
Emmitt Smith	9	15,175	12,566	2,609	0	0	0	0
Brian Mitchell	9	15,150	1,531	1,782	0	3,144	8,693	0
James Brooks	12	14,910	7,962	3,621	0	565	2,762	0
Irving Fryar	15	14,776	226	11,983	0	2,055	505	7
Franco Harris	13	14,622	12,120	2,287	0	0	233	–18
O.J. Simpson	11	14,368	11,236	2,142	0	0	990	0
James Lofton	16	14,277	246	14,004	0	0	0	27
Bobby Mitchell	11	14,078	2,735	7,954	0	699	2,690	0
Tim Brown	11	14,060	116	9,600	0	3,106	1,235	3

TOP 20 PASSERS

Player	Years	Att.	Comp.	Pct. Comp.	Yards	Avg. Gain	TD	Pct. TD	Int.	Pct. Int.	Rating
Steve Young	14	4,065	2,622	64.5	32,678	8.04	229	5.6	103	2.5	97.6
Joe Montana	15	5,391	3,409	63.2	40,551	7.52	273	5.1	139	2.6	92.3
Brett Favre	8	3,757	2,318	61.7	26,803	7.13	213	5.7	118	3.1	89.0
Dan Marino	16	7,989	4,763	59.6	58,913	7.37	408	5.1	235	2.9	87.3
Mark Brunell	5	1,719	1,038	60.4	12,512	7.28	72	4.2	43	2.5	86.3
Jim Kelly	11	4,779	2,874	60.1	35,467	7.42	237	5.0	175	3.7	84.4
R. Staubach	11	2,958	1,685	57.0	22,700	7.67	153	5.2	109	3.7	83.4
Troy Aikman	10	4,011	2,479	61.8	28,346	7.07	141	3.5	115	2.9	82.8
Neil Lomax	8	3,153	1,817	57.6	22,771	7.22	136	4.3	90	2.9	82.7
S. Jurgensen	18	4,262	2,433	57.1	32,224	7.56	255	6.0	189	4.4	82.6
Len Dawson	19	3,741	2,136	57.1	28,711	7.67	239	6.4	183	4.9	82.6
Ken Anderson	16	4,475	2,654	59.3	32,838	7.34	197	4.4	160	3.6	81.9
Bernie Kosar	12	3,365	1,994	59.3	23,301	6.92	124	3.7	87	2.6	81.8
Danny White	13	2,950	1,761	59.7	21,959	7.44	155	5.3	132	4.5	81.7
Neil O'Donnell	9	2,862	1,650	57.7	19,026	6.65	104	3.6	57	2.0	81.6
Randall Cunningham	13	3,875	2,177	56.2	27,082	6.99	190	4.9	119	3.1	81.6
Dave Krieg	19	5,311	3,105	58.5	38,147	7.18	261	4.9	199	3.7	81.5
Boomer Esiason	14	5,205	2,969	57.0	37,920	7.29	247	4.7	184	3.5	81.1
Warren Moon	15	6,786	3,972	58.5	49,097	7.24	290	4.3	232	3.4	81.0
Chris Chandler	11	2,587	1,494	57.8	18,526	7.16	119	4.6	90	3.5	80.9

1,500 or more attempts. The passing ratings are based on performance standards established for completion percentage, interception percentage, touchdown percentage, and average gain. Please consult page 16 for more information.

TOP 20 LEADERS IN PASSES COMPLETED

Dan Marino	4,763
John Elway	4,123
Warren Moon	3,972
Fran Tarkenton	3,686
Joe Montana	3,409
Dan Fouts	3,297
Dave Krieg	3,105
Boomer Esiason	2,969
Steve DeBerg	2,874
Jim Kelly	2,874
Jim Everett	2,841
Johnny Unitas	2,830
Ken Anderson	2,654
Steve Young	2,622
Jim Hart	2,593
Phil Simms	2,576
Vinny Testaverde	2,559
Troy Aikman	2,479
John Brodie	2,469
Sonny Jurgensen	2,433

TOP 20 LEADERS IN PASSING YARDS

Dan Marino	58,913
John Elway	51,475
Warren Moon	49,097
Fran Tarkenton	47,003
Dan Fouts	43,040
Joe Montana	40,551
Johnny Unitas	40,239
Dave Krieg	38,147
Boomer Esiason	37,920
Jim Kelly	35,467
Jim Everett	34,837
Jim Hart	34,665
Steve DeBerg	34,241
John Hadl	33,503
Phil Simms	33,462
Ken Anderson	32,838
Steve Young	32,678
Vinny Testaverde	32,479
Sonny Jurgensen	32,224
John Brodie	31,548

TOP 20 LEADERS IN TOUCHDOWN PASSES

Dan Marino	408
Fran Tarkenton	342
John Elway	300
Warren Moon	290
Johnny Unitas	290
Joe Montana	273
Dave Krieg	261
Sonny Jurgensen	255
Dan Fouts	254
Boomer Esiason	247
John Hadl	244
Len Dawson	239
Jim Kelly	237
George Blanda	236
Steve Young	229
John Brodie	214
Brett Favre	213
Terry Bradshaw	212
Y.A. Tittle	212
Jim Hart	209

TOP 20 PASS RECEIVERS

Player	Years	No.	Yards	Avg.	Long	TD
Jerry Rice	14	1,139	17,612	15.5	96	164
Art Monk	16	940	12,721	13.5	79	68
Andre Reed	14	889	12,559	14.1	83	85
Cris Carter	12	834	10,447	12.5	80	101
Steve Largent	14	819	13,089	16.0	74	100
Henry Ellard	16	814	13,777	16.9	81	65
Irving Fryar	15	784	11,983	15.3	80	77

OUTSTANDING PERFORMERS

James Lofton	16	764	14,004	18.3	80	75
Charlie Joiner	18	750	12,146	16.2	87	65
Michael Irvin	11	740	11,737	15.9	87	62
Gary Clark	11	699	10,856	15.5	84	65
Andre Rison	10	681	9,381	13.8	80	78
Tim Brown	11	680	9,600	14.1	80	69
Ozzie Newsome	13	662	7,980	12.1	74	47
Charley Taylor	13	649	9,110	14.0	88	79
Drew Hill	14	634	9,831	15.5	81	60
Don Maynard	15	633	11,834	18.7	87	88
Raymond Berry	13	631	9,275	14.7	70	68
Keith Byars	13	610	5,661	9.3	60	31
Herman Moore	8	610	8,467	13.9	93	57

TOP 20 LEADERS IN RECEPTION YARDS

Jerry Rice	17,612
James Lofton	14,004
Henry Ellard	13,777
Steve Largent	13,089
Art Monk	12,721
Andre Reed	12,559
Charlie Joiner	12,146
Irving Fryar	11,983
Don Maynard	11,834
Michael Irvin	11,737
Gary Clark	10,856
Stanley Morgan	10,716
Cris Carter	10,447
Harold Jackson	10,372
Lance Alworth	10,266
Drew Hill	9,831
Tim Brown	9,600
Andre Rison	9,381
Raymond Berry	9,275
Anthony Miller	9,148

TOP 20 INTERCEPTORS

Player	Years	No.	Yards	Avg.	Long	TD
Paul Krause	16	81	1,185	14.6	81	3
Emlen Tunnell	14	79	1,282	16.2	55	4
Dick (Night Train) Lane	14	68	1,207	17.8	80	5
Ken Riley	15	65	596	9.2	66	5
Ronnie Lott	14	63	730	11.6	83	5
Dick LeBeau	13	62	762	12.3	70	3
Dave Brown	15	62	698	11.3	90	5
Emmitt Thomas	13	58	937	16.2	73	5
Bobby Boyd	9	57	994	17.4	74	4
Johnny Robinson	12	57	741	13.0	57	1
Mel Blount	14	57	736	12.9	52	2
Everson Walls	13	57	504	8.8	40	1
Lem Barney	11	56	1,077	19.2	71	7
Pat Fischer	17	56	941	16.8	69	4
Willie Brown	16	54	472	8.7	45	2
Eugene Robinson	14	53	755	14.2	49	1
Bobby Dillon	8	52	976	18.8	61	5
Jack Butler	9	52	827	15.9	52	4
Larry Wilson	13	52	800	15.4	96	5
Jim Patton	12	52	712	13.7	51	2
Mel Renfro	14	52	626	12.0	90	3

TOP 20 PUNTERS

Player	Years	No.	Yards	Avg.	Long	Blk.
Sammy Baugh	16	338	15,245	45.1	85	9
Darren Bennett	4	343	15,334	44.7	66	1
Tommy Davis	11	511	22,833	44.7	82	2
Yale Lary	11	503	22,279	44.3	74	4
Matt Turk	4	326	14,417	44.2	69	2
Bob Scarpitto	8	283	12,408	43.8	87	4
Horace Gillom	7	385	16,872	43.8	80	5
Jerry Norton	11	358	15,671	43.8	78	2
Tom Rouen	6	386	16,876	43.7	76	3
David Lewis	4	285	12,447	43.7	63	0
Craig Hentrich	5	358	15,613	43.6	71	2
Sean Landeta	14	926	40,357	43.6	74	5
Greg Montgomery	9	524	22,831	43.6	77	8
Tom Tupa	10	366	15,924	43.5	73	1
Rick Tuten	10	709	30,831	43.5	73	2
Don Chandler	12	660	28,678	43.5	90	4
Rohn Stark	16	1,141	49,471	43.4	72	7
Reggie Roby	16	992	42,951	43.3	77	5
Jerrel Wilson	16	1,072	46,139	43.0	72	12
Norm Van Brocklin	12	523	22,413	42.9	72	3

250 or more punts.

TOP 20 PUNT RETURNERS

Player	Years	No.	Yards	Avg.	Long	TD
Darrien Gordon	6	177	2,329	13.2	94	6
George McAfee	8	112	1,431	12.8	74	2
Jack Christiansen	8	85	1,084	12.8	89	8
Claude Gibson	5	110	1,381	12.6	85	3
Jermaine Lewis	3	96	1,181	12.3	89	4
Reggie Barlow	3	79	967	12.2	85	1
Bill Dudley	9	124	1,515	12.2	96	3
Rick Upchurch	9	248	3,008	12.1	92	8
Desmond Howard	7	164	1,981	12.1	92	6
Billy Johnson	14	282	3,317	11.8	87	6
Mack Herron	3	84	982	11.7	66	0
Billy Thompson	13	157	1,814	11.6	60	0
Brian Mitchell	9	277	3,144	11.4	84	7
Henry Ellard	16	135	1,527	11.3	83	4
Rodger Bird	3	94	1,063	11.3	78	0
Bosh Pritchard	6	95	1,072	11.3	81	2
Terry Metcalf	6	84	936	11.1	69	1
Bob Hayes	11	104	1,158	11.1	90	3
Floyd Little	9	81	893	11.0	72	2
Louis Lipps	9	112	1,234	11.0	76	3

75 or more returns.

TOP 20 KICKOFF RETURNERS

Player	Years	No.	Yards	Avg.	Long	TD
Gale Sayers	7	91	2,781	30.6	103	6
Lynn Chandnois	7	92	2,720	29.6	93	3
Abe Woodson	9	193	5,538	28.7	105	5
Claude (Buddy) Young	6	90	2,514	27.9	104	2
Travis Williams	5	102	2,801	27.5	105	6
Joe Arenas	7	139	3,798	27.3	96	1
Clarence Davis	8	79	2,140	27.1	76	0
Steve Van Buren	8	76	2,030	26.7	98	3
Lenny Lyles	12	81	2,161	26.7	103	3
Eugene (Mercury) Morris	8	111	2,947	26.5	105	3
Bobby Jancik	6	158	4,185	26.5	61	0
Mel Renfro	14	85	2,246	26.4	100	2
Bobby Mitchell	11	102	2,690	26.4	98	5
Ollie Matson	14	143	3,746	26.2	105	6
Alvin Haymond	10	170	4,438	26.1	98	2
Noland Smith	3	82	2,137	26.1	106	1
Al Nelson	9	101	2,625	26.0	78	0
Tim Brown	11	184	4,781	26.0	105	5
Vic Washington	6	129	3,341	25.9	98	1
Dave Hampton	8	113	2,923	25.9	101	3

75 or more returns.

TOP 20 LEADERS IN SACKS

Player	*Years	No.
Reggie White	14	192.5
Bruce Smith	14	164.0
Kevin Greene	14	148.0
Chris Doleman	14	142.5
Richard Dent	15	137.5
Lawrence Taylor	12	132.5
Rickey Jackson	14	128.0
Leslie O'Neal	12	127.0
Derrick Thomas	10	119.5
Clyde Simmons	13	114.0
Sean Jones	13	113.0
Greg Townsend	13	109.5
Pat Swilling	12	107.5
Jim Jeffcoat	15	102.5
William Fuller	13	100.5
Andre Tippett	11	100.0
Neil Smith	11	98.0
Simon Fletcher	11	97.5
Jacob Green	11	97.5
Charles Haley	11	97.5
Dexter Manley	10	97.5

**Years played since 1982 when sacks became an official statistic.*

POSTSEASON LEADERS

TOP 10 RUSHERS

Player	Att.	Yards	Avg.	Long	TD
Franco Harris	400	1,556	3.9	50	16
Emmitt Smith	334	1,487	4.5	38	18
Thurman Thomas	334	1,432	4.3	40	16
Tony Dorsett	302	1,383	4.6	53	9
Marcus Allen	267	1,347	5.0	74	11
Terrell Davis	204	1,140	5.6	62	12
John Riggins	251	996	4.0	43	12
Larry Csonka	225	891	4.0	49	9
Chuck Foreman	229	860	3.8	62	7
Roger Craig	208	841	4.0	80	7

TOP 10 POSTSEASON PASSERS

Player	Att.	Comp.	Pct. Comp.	Yards	Avg. Gain	TD	Pct. TD	Int.	Pct. Int.	Rating
Bart Starr	213	130	61.0	1,753	8.23	15	7.0	3	1.4	104.8
Joe Montana	734	460	62.7	5,772	7.86	45	6.1	21	2.9	95.6
Ken Anderson	166	110	66.3	1,321	7.96	9	5.4	6	3.6	93.5
Joe Theismann	211	128	60.7	1,782	8.45	11	5.2	7	3.3	91.4
Brett Favre	449	270	60.1	3,390	7.55	25	5.6	12	2.7	91.1
Troy Aikman	464	298	64.2	3,563	7.68	23	5.0	16	3.4	89.8
Steve Young	471	292	62.0	3,326	7.06	20	4.2	13	2.8	85.8
Warren Moon	403	259	64.3	2,870	7.12	17	4.2	14	3.5	84.9
Ken Stabler	351	203	57.8	2,641	7.52	19	5.4	13	3.7	84.2
Bernie Kosar	270	152	56.3	1,953	7.23	16	5.9	10	3.7	83.5

150 or more attempts. The passing ratings are based on performance standards established for completion percentage, interception percentage, touchdown percentage, and average gain. Please consult page 16 for more information.

TOP 10 POSTSEASON PASS RECEIVERS

Player	No.	Yards	Avg.	Long	TD
Jerry Rice	124	1,811	14.6	72	19
Michael Irvin	87	1,315	15.1	53	8
Andre Reed	85	1,229	14.5	72	9
Thurman Thomas	76	672	8.8	27	5
Cliff Branch	73	1,289	17.7	72	5
Fred Biletnikoff	70	1,167	16.7	57	10
Art Monk	69	1,062	15.4	48	7
Drew Pearson	67	1,105	16.5	83	8
Tony Nathan	65	649	10.0	39	2
Roger Craig	63	606	9.6	40	2

TOP 10 POSTSEASON INTERCEPTION LEADERS

Player	Interceptions
Ronnie Lott	9
Bill Simpson	9
Charlie Waters	9
Lester Hayes	8
Willie Brown	7
Dennis Thurman	7
Bobby Bryant	6
Eric Davis	6
Glen Edwards	6
Cliff Harris	6
Vernon Perry	6

TOP 10 POSTSEASON SACK LEADERS

Player	Sacks
Bruce Smith	12.0
Reggie White	12.0
Charles Haley	11.0
Richard Dent	10.5
Charles Mann	10.0
Tony Tolbert	10.0
Neil Smith	9.5
Jeff Wright	9.0
Kevin Greene	8.5
Dexter Manley	8.0

YEARLY STATISTICAL LEADERS

ANNUAL SCORING LEADERS

Year	Player, Team	TD	FG	PAT	TP
1998	Gary Anderson, Minnesota, NFC	0	35	59	164
	Steve Christie, Buffalo, AFC	0	33	41	140
1997	Mike Hollis, Jacksonville, AFC	0	31	41	134
	Richie Cunningham, Dallas, NFC	0	34	24	126
1996	John Kasay, Carolina, NFC	0	37	34	145
	Cary Blanchard, Indianapolis, AFC	0	36	27	135
1995	Emmitt Smith, Dallas, NFC	25	0	0	150
	Norm Johnson, Pittsburgh, AFC	0	34	39	141
1994	John Carney, San Diego, AFC	0	34	33	135
	Fuad Reveiz, Minnesota, NFC	0	34	30	132
1993	Jeff Jaeger, L.A. Raiders, AFC	0	35	27	132
	Jason Hanson, Detroit, NFC	0	34	28	130
1992	Pete Stoyanovich, Miami, AFC	0	30	34	124
	Morten Andersen, New Orleans, NFC	0	29	33	120
	Chip Lohmiller, Washington, NFC	0	30	30	120
1991	Chip Lohmiller, Washington, NFC	0	31	56	149
	Pete Stoyanovich, Miami, AFC	0	31	28	121
1990	Nick Lowery, Kansas City, AFC	0	34	37	139
	Chip Lohmiller, Washington, NFC	0	30	41	131
1989	Mike Cofer, San Francisco, NFC	0	29	49	136
	*David Treadwell, Denver, AFC	0	27	39	120
1988	Scott Norwood, Buffalo, AFC	0	32	33	129
	Mike Cofer, San Francisco, NFC	0	27	40	121
1987	Jerry Rice, San Francisco, NFC	23	0	0	138
	Jim Breech, Cincinnati, AFC	0	24	25	97
1986	Tony Franklin, New England, AFC	0	32	44	140
	Kevin Butler, Chicago, NFC	0	28	36	120
1985	*Kevin Butler, Chicago, NFC	0	31	51	144
	Gary Anderson, Pittsburgh, AFC	0	33	40	139
1984	Ray Wersching, San Francisco, NFC	0	25	56	131
	Gary Anderson, Pittsburgh, AFC	0	24	45	117
1983	Mark Moseley, Washington, NFC	0	33	62	161
	Gary Anderson, Pittsburgh, AFC	0	27	38	119
1982	*Marcus Allen, L.A. Raiders, AFC	14	0	0	84
	Wendell Tyler, L.A. Rams, NFC	13	0	0	78
1981	Ed Murray, Detroit, NFC	0	25	46	121
	Rafael Septien, Dallas, NFC	0	27	40	121
	Jim Breech, Cincinnati, AFC	0	22	49	115
	Nick Lowery, Kansas City, AFC	0	26	37	115
1980	John Smith, New England, AFC	0	26	51	129
	*Ed Murray, Detroit, NFC	0	27	35	116
1979	John Smith, New England, AFC	0	23	46	115
	Mark Moseley, Washington, NFC	0	25	39	114
1978	*Frank Corral, Los Angeles, NFC	0	29	31	118
	Pat Leahy, N.Y. Jets, AFC	0	22	41	107
1977	Errol Mann, Oakland, AFC	0	20	39	99
	Walter Payton, Chicago, NFC	16	0	0	96
1976	Toni Linhart, Baltimore, AFC	0	20	49	109
	Mark Moseley, Washington, NFC	0	22	31	97
1975	O.J. Simpson, Buffalo, AFC	23	0	0	138
	Chuck Foreman, Minnesota, NFC	22	0	0	132
1974	Chester Marcol, Green Bay, NFC	0	25	19	94
	Roy Gerela, Pittsburgh, AFC	0	20	33	93
1973	David Ray, Los Angeles, NFC	0	30	40	130
	Roy Gerela, Pittsburgh, AFC	0	29	36	123
1972	*Chester Marcol, Green Bay, NFC	0	33	29	128
	Bobby Howfield, N.Y. Jets, AFC	0	27	40	121
1971	Garo Yepremian, Miami, AFC	0	28	33	117
	Curt Knight, Washington, NFC	0	29	27	114
1970	Fred Cox, Minnesota, NFC	0	30	35	125
	Jan Stenerud, Kansas City, AFC	0	30	26	116
1969	Jim Turner, N.Y. Jets, AFL	0	32	33	129
	Fred Cox, Minnesota, NFL	0	26	43	121
1968	Jim Turner, N.Y. Jets, AFL	0	34	43	145
	Leroy Kelly, Cleveland, NFL	20	0	0	120
1967	Jim Bakken, St. Louis, NFL	0	27	36	117
	George Blanda, Oakland, AFL	0	20	56	116
1966	Gino Cappelletti, Boston, AFL	6	16	35	119
	Bruce Gossett, Los Angeles, NFL	0	28	29	113
1965	*Gale Sayers, Chicago, NFL	22	0	0	132
	Gino Cappelletti, Boston, AFL	9	17	27	132
1964	Gino Cappelletti, Boston, AFL	7	25	36	#155
	Lenny Moore, Baltimore, NFL	20	0	0	120
1963	Gino Cappelletti, Boston, AFL	2	22	35	113
	Don Chandler, N.Y. Giants, NFL	0	18	52	106
1962	Gene Mingo, Denver, AFL	4	27	32	137
	Jim Taylor, Green Bay, NFL	19	0	0	114
1961	Gino Cappelletti, Boston, AFL	8	17	48	147
	Paul Hornung, Green Bay, NFL	10	15	41	146
1960	Paul Hornung, Green Bay, NFL	15	15	41	176
	*Gene Mingo, Denver, AFL	6	18	33	123
1959	Paul Hornung, Green Bay	7	7	31	94
1958	Jim Brown, Cleveland	18	0	0	108
1957	Sam Baker, Washington	1	14	29	77
	Lou Groza, Cleveland	0	15	32	77
1956	Bobby Layne, Detroit	5	12	33	99
1955	Doak Walker, Detroit	7	9	27	96
1954	Bobby Walston, Philadelphia	11	4	36	114
1953	Gordy Soltau, San Francisco	6	10	48	114
1952	Gordy Soltau, San Francisco	7	6	34	94
1951	Elroy (Crazylegs) Hirsch, Los Angeles	17	0	0	102
1950	*Doak Walker, Detroit	11	8	38	128
1949	Pat Harder, Chi. Cardinals	8	3	45	102
	Gene Roberts, N.Y. Giants	17	0	0	102
1948	Pat Harder, Chi. Cardinals	6	7	53	110
1947	Pat Harder, Chi. Cardinals	7	7	39	102
1946	Ted Fritsch, Green Bay	10	9	13	100
1945	Steve Van Buren, Philadelphia	18	0	2	110
1944	Don Hutson, Green Bay	9	0	31	85
1943	Don Hutson, Green Bay	12	3	36	117
1942	Don Hutson, Green Bay	17	1	33	138
1941	Don Hutson, Green Bay	12	1	20	95
1940	Don Hutson, Green Bay	7	0	15	57
1939	Andy Farkas, Washington	11	0	2	68
1938	Clarke Hinkle, Green Bay	7	3	7	58
1937	Jack Manders, Chi. Bears	5	8	15	69
1936	Earl (Dutch) Clark, Detroit	7	4	19	73
1935	Earl (Dutch) Clark, Detroit	6	1	16	55
1934	Jack Manders, Chi. Bears	3	10	31	79
1933	Ken Strong, N.Y. Giants	6	5	13	64
	Glenn Presnell, Portsmouth	6	6	10	64
1932	Earl (Dutch) Clark, Portsmouth	6	3	10	55

**First season of professional football.*

#Cappelletti's total includes a two-point conversion.

ANNUAL TOUCHDOWN LEADERS

Year	Player, Team	TD	Rush	Pass	Ret.
1998	Terrell Davis, Denver, AFC	23	21	2	0
	*Randy Moss, Minnesota, NFC	17	0	17	0
1997	Karim Abdul-Jabbar, Miami, AFC	16	15	1	0
	Barry Sanders, Detroit, NFC	14	11	3	0
1996	Terry Allen, Washington, NFC	21	21	0	0
	Curtis Martin, New England, AFC	17	14	3	0
1995	Emmitt Smith, Dallas, NFC	25	25	0	0
	Carl Pickens, Cincinnati, AFC	17	0	17	0
1994	Emmitt Smith, Dallas, NFC	22	21	1	0
	*Marshall Faulk, Indianapolis, AFC	12	11	1	0
	Natrone Means, San Diego, AFC	12	12	0	0
1993	Jerry Rice, San Francisco, NFC	16	1	15	0
	Marcus Allen, Kansas City, AFC	15	12	3	0
1992	Emmitt Smith, Dallas, NFC	19	18	1	0
	Thurman Thomas, Buffalo, AFC	12	9	3	0
1991	Barry Sanders, Detroit, NFC	17	16	1	0
	Mark Clayton, Miami, AFC	12	0	12	0
	Thurman Thomas, Buffalo, AFC	12	7	5	0
1990	Barry Sanders, Detroit, NFC	16	13	3	0
	Derrick Fenner, Seattle, AFC	15	14	1	0
1989	Dalton Hilliard, New Orleans, NFC	18	13	5	0
	Christian Okoye, Kansas City, AFC	12	12	0	0
	Thurman Thomas, Buffalo, AFC	12	6	6	0
1988	Greg Bell, L.A. Rams, NFC	18	16	2	0
	Eric Dickerson, Indianapolis, AFC	15	14	1	0
	*Ickey Woods, Cincinnati, AFC	15	15	0	0
1987	Jerry Rice, San Francisco, NFC	23	1	22	0
	Johnny Hector, N.Y. Jets, AFC	11	11	0	0
1986	George Rogers, Washington, NFC	18	18	0	0
	Sammy Winder, Denver, AFC	14	9	5	0
1985	Joe Morris, N.Y. Giants, NFC	21	21	0	0
	Louis Lipps, Pittsburgh, AFC	15	1	12	2
1984	Marcus Allen, L.A. Raiders, AFC	18	13	5	0
	Mark Clayton, Miami, AFC	18	0	18	0
	Eric Dickerson, L.A. Rams, NFC	14	14	0	0
	John Riggins, Washington, NFC	14	14	0	0
1983	John Riggins, Washington, NFC	24	24	0	0
	Pete Johnson, Cincinnati, AFC	14	14	0	0
	*Curt Warner, Seattle, AFC	14	13	1	0
1982	*Marcus Allen, L.A. Raiders, AFC	14	11	3	0
	Wendell Tyler, L.A. Rams, NFC	13	9	4	0
1981	Chuck Muncie, San Diego, AFC	19	19	0	0
	Wendell Tyler, Los Angeles, NFC	17	12	5	0
1980	*Billy Sims, Detroit, NFC	16	13	3	0
	Earl Campbell, Houston, AFC	13	13	0	0
	*Curtis Dickey, Baltimore, AFC	13	11	2	0
	John Jefferson, San Diego, AFC	13	0	13	0

1979	Earl Campbell, Houston, AFC	19	19	0	0
	Walter Payton, Chicago, NFC	16	14	2	0
1978	David Sims, Seattle, AFC	15	14	1	0
	Terdell Middleton, Green Bay, NFC	12	11	1	0
1977	Walter Payton, Chicago, NFC	16	14	2	0
	Nat Moore, Miami, AFC	13	1	12	0
1976	Chuck Foreman, Minnesota, NFC	14	13	1	0
	Franco Harris, Pittsburgh, AFC	14	14	0	0
1975	O.J. Simpson, Buffalo, AFC	23	16	7	0
	Chuck Foreman, Minnesota, NFC	22	13	9	0
1974	Chuck Foreman, Minnesota, NFC	15	9	6	0
	Cliff Branch, Oakland, AFC	13	0	13	0
1973	Larry Brown, Washington, NFC	14	8	6	0
	Floyd Little, Denver, AFC	13	12	1	0
1972	Emerson Boozer, N.Y. Jets, AFC	14	11	3	0
	Ron Johnson, N.Y. Giants, NFC	14	9	5	0
1971	Duane Thomas, Dallas, NFC	13	11	2	0
	Leroy Kelly, Cleveland, AFC	12	10	2	0
1970	Dick Gordon, Chicago, NFC	13	0	13	0
	MacArthur Lane, St. Louis, NFC	13	11	2	0
	Gary Garrison, San Diego, AFC	12	0	12	0
1969	Warren Wells, Oakland, AFL	14	0	14	0
	Tom Matte, Baltimore, NFL	13	11	2	0
	Lance Rentzel, Dallas, NFL	13	0	12	1
1968	Leroy Kelly, Cleveland, NFL	20	16	4	0
	Warren Wells, Oakland, AFL	12	1	11	0
1967	Homer Jones, N.Y. Giants, NFL	14	1	13	0
	Emerson Boozer, N.Y. Jets, AFL	13	10	3	0
1966	Leroy Kelly, Cleveland, NFL	16	15	1	0
	Dan Reeves, Dallas, NFL	16	8	8	0
	Lance Alworth, San Diego, AFL	13	0	13	0
1965	*Gale Sayers, Chicago, NFL	22	14	6	2
	Lance Alworth, San Diego, AFL	14	0	14	0
	Don Maynard, N.Y. Jets, AFL	14	0	14	0
1964	Lenny Moore, Baltimore, NFL	20	16	3	1
	Lance Alworth, San Diego, AFL	15	2	13	0
1963	Art Powell, Oakland, AFL	16	0	16	0
	Jim Brown, Cleveland, NFL	15	12	3	0
1962	Abner Haynes, Dallas, AFL	19	13	6	0
	Jim Taylor, Green Bay, NFL	19	19	0	0
1961	Bill Groman, Houston, AFL	18	1	17	0
	Jim Taylor, Green Bay, NFL	16	15	1	0
1960	Paul Hornung, Green Bay, NFL	15	13	2	0
	Sonny Randle, St. Louis, NFL	15	0	15	0
	Art Powell, N.Y. Titans, AFL	14	0	14	0
1959	Raymond Berry, Baltimore	14	0	14	0
	Jim Brown, Cleveland	14	14	0	0
1958	Jim Brown, Cleveland	18	17	1	0
1957	Lenny Moore, Baltimore	11	3	7	1
1956	Rick Casares, Chi. Bears	14	12	2	0
1955	*Alan Ameche, Baltimore	9	9	0	0
	Harlon Hill, Chi. Bears	9	0	9	0
1954	*Harlon Hill, Chi. Bears	12	0	12	0
1953	Joseph Perry, San Francisco	13	10	3	0
1952	Cloyce Box, Detroit	15	0	15	0
1951	Elroy (Crazylegs) Hirsch, Los Angeles	17	0	17	0
1950	Bob Shaw, Chi. Cardinals	12	0	12	0
1949	Gene Roberts, N.Y. Giants	17	9	8	0
1948	Mal Kutner, Chi. Cardinals	15	1	14	0
1947	Steve Van Buren, Philadelphia	14	13	0	1
1946	Ted Fritsch, Green Bay	10	9	1	0
1945	Steve Van Buren, Philadelphia	18	15	2	1
1944	Don Hutson, Green Bay	9	0	9	0
	Bill Paschal, N.Y. Giants	9	9	0	0
1943	Don Hutson, Green Bay	12	0	11	1
	*Bill Paschal, N.Y. Giants	12	10	2	0
1942	Don Hutson, Green Bay	17	0	17	0
1941	Don Hutson, Green Bay	12	2	10	0
	George McAfee, Chi. Bears	12	6	3	3
1940	John Drake, Cleveland	9	9	0	0
	Richard Todd, Washington	9	4	4	1
1939	Andrew Farkas, Washington	11	5	5	1
1938	Don Hutson, Green Bay	9	0	9	0
1937	Cliff Battles, Washington	7	5	1	1
	Clarke Hinkle, Green Bay	7	5	2	0
	Don Hutson, Green Bay	7	0	7	0
1936	Don Hutson, Green Bay	9	0	8	1
1935	*Don Hutson, Green Bay	7	0	6	1
1934	*Beattie Feathers, Chi. Bears	9	8	1	0
1933	*Charlie (Buckets) Goldenberg, Green Bay	7	4	1	2
	John (Shipwreck) Kelly, Brooklyn	7	2	3	2
	*Elvin (Kink) Richards, N.Y. Giants	7	4	3	0
1932	Earl (Dutch) Clark, Portsmouth	6	3	3	0
	Red Grange, Chi. Bears	6	3	3	0

**First season of professional football.*

ANNUAL LEADERS—MOST FIELD GOALS MADE

Year	Player, Team	Att.	Made	Pct.
1998	Al Del Greco, Tennessee, AFC	39	36	92.3
	Gary Anderson, Minnesota, NFC	35	35	100.0
1997	Richie Cunningham, Dallas, NFC	37	34	91.9
	Cary Blanchard, Indianapolis, AFC	41	32	78.1
1996	John Kasay, Carolina, NFC	45	37	82.2
	Cary Blanchard, Indianapolis, AFC	40	36	90.0
1995	Norm Johnson, Pittsburgh, AFC	41	34	82.9
	Morten Andersen, Atlanta, NFC	37	31	83.8
1994	John Carney, San Diego, AFC	38	34	89.5
	Fuad Reveiz, Minnesota, NFC	39	34	87.2
1993	Jeff Jaeger, L.A. Raiders, AFC	44	35	79.5
	Jason Hanson, Detroit, NFC	43	34	79.1
1992	Pete Stoyanovich, Miami, AFC	37	30	81.1
	Chip Lohmiller, Washington, NFC	40	30	75.0
1991	Pete Stoyanovich, Miami, AFC	37	31	83.8
	Chip Lohmiller, Washington, NFC	43	31	72.1
1990	Nick Lowery, Kansas City, AFC	37	34	91.9
	Chip Lohmiller, Washington, NFC	40	30	75.0
1989	Rich Karlis, Minnesota, NFC	39	31	79.5
	*David Treadwell, Denver, AFC	33	27	81.8
1988	Scott Norwood, Buffalo, AFC	37	32	86.5
	Mike Cofer, San Francisco, NFC	38	27	71.1
1987	Morten Andersen, New Orleans, NFC	36	28	77.8
	Dean Biasucci, Indianapolis, AFC	27	24	88.9
	Jim Breech, Cincinnati, AFC	30	24	80.0
1986	Tony Franklin, New England, AFC	41	32	78.0
	Kevin Butler, Chicago, NFC	41	28	68.3
1985	Gary Anderson, Pittsburgh, AFC	42	33	78.6
	Morten Andersen, New Orleans, NFC	35	31	88.6
	*Kevin Butler, Chicago, NFC	37	31	83.8
1984	*Paul McFadden, Philadelphia, NFC	37	30	81.1
	Gary Anderson, Pittsburgh, AFC	32	24	75.0
	Matt Bahr, Cleveland, AFC	32	24	75.0
1983	*Ali-Haji-Sheikh, N.Y. Giants, NFC	42	35	83.3
	*Raul Allegre, Baltimore, AFC	35	30	85.7
1982	Mark Moseley, Washington, NFC	21	20	95.2
	Nick Lowery, Kansas City, AFC	24	19	79.2
1981	Rafael Septien, Dallas, NFC	35	27	77.1
	Nick Lowery, Kansas City, AFC	36	26	72.2
1980	*Ed Murray, Detroit, NFC	42	27	64.3
	John Smith, New England, AFC	34	26	76.5
	Fred Steinfort, Denver, AFC	34	26	76.5
1979	Mark Moseley, Washington, NFC	33	25	75.8
	John Smith, New England, AFC	33	23	69.7
1978	*Frank Corral, Los Angeles, NFC	43	29	67.4
	Pat Leahy, N.Y. Jets, AFC	30	22	73.3
1977	Mark Moseley, Washington, NFC	37	21	56.8
	Errol Mann, Oakland, AFC	28	20	71.4
1976	Mark Moseley, Washington, NFC	34	22	64.7
	Jan Stenerud, Kansas City, AFC	38	21	55.3
1975	Jan Stenerud, Kansas City, AFC	32	22	68.8
	Toni Fritsch, Dallas, NFC	35	22	62.9
1974	Chester Marcol, Green Bay, NFC	39	25	64.1
	Roy Gerela, Pittsburgh, AFC	29	20	69.0
1973	David Ray, Los Angeles, NFC	47	30	63.8
	Roy Gerela, Pittsburgh, AFC	43	29	67.4
1972	*Chester Marcol, Green Bay, NFC	48	33	68.8
	Roy Gerela, Pittsburgh, AFC	41	28	68.3
1971	Curt Knight, Washington, NFC	49	29	59.2
	Garo Yepremian, Miami, AFC	40	28	70.0
1970	Jan Stenerud, Kansas City, AFC	42	30	71.4
	Fred Cox, Minnesota, NFC	46	30	65.2
1969	Jim Turner, N.Y. Jets, AFL	47	32	68.1
	Fred Cox, Minnesota, NFL	37	26	70.3
1968	Jim Turner, N.Y. Jets, AFL	46	34	73.9
	Mac Percival, Chicago, NFL	36	25	69.4
1967	Jim Bakken, St. Louis, NFL	39	27	69.2
	Jan Stenerud, Kansas City, AFL	36	21	58.3
1966	Bruce Gossett, Los Angeles, NFL	49	28	57.1
	Mike Mercer, Oakland-Kansas City, AFL	30	21	70.0
1965	Pete Gogolak, Buffalo, AFL	46	28	60.9
	Fred Cox, Minnesota, NFL	35	23	65.7
1964	Jim Bakken, St. Louis, NFL	38	25	65.8
	Gino Cappelletti, Boston, AFL	39	25	64.1
1963	Jim Martin, Baltimore, NFL	39	24	61.5
	Gino Cappelletti, Boston, AFL	38	22	57.9

Year	Player, Team			
1962	Gene Mingo, Denver, AFL	39	27	69.2
	Lou Michaels, Pittsburgh, NFL	42	26	61.9
1961	Steve Myhra, Baltimore, NFL	39	21	53.8
	Gino Cappelletti, Boston, AFL	32	17	53.1
1960	Tommy Davis, San Francisco, NFL	32	19	59.4
	*Gene Mingo, Denver, AFL	28	18	64.3
1959	Pat Summerall, N.Y. Giants	29	20	69.0
1958	Paige Cothren, Los Angeles	25	14	56.0
	*Tom Miner, Pittsburgh	28	14	50.0
1957	Lou Groza, Cleveland	22	15	68.2
1956	Sam Baker, Washington	25	17	68.0
1955	Fred Cone, Green Bay	24	16	66.7
1954	Lou Groza, Cleveland	24	16	66.7
1953	Lou Groza, Cleveland	26	23	88.5
1952	Lou Groza, Cleveland	33	19	57.6
1951	Bob Waterfield, Los Angeles	23	13	56.5
1950	Lou Groza, Cleveland	19	13	68.4
1949	Cliff Patton, Philadelphia	18	9	50.0
	Bob Waterfield, Los Angeles	16	9	56.3
1948	Cliff Patton, Philadelphia	12	8	66.7
1947	Ward Cuff, Green Bay	16	7	43.8
	Pat Harder, Chi. Cardinals	10	7	70.0
	Bob Waterfield, Los Angeles	16	7	43.8
1946	Ted Fritsch, Green Bay	17	9	52.9
1945	Joe Aguirre, Washington	13	7	53.8
1944	Ken Strong, N.Y. Giants	12	6	50.0
1943	Ward Cuff, N.Y. Giants	9	3	33.3
	Don Hutson, Green Bay	5	3	60.0
1942	Bill Daddio, Chi. Cardinals	10	5	50.0
1941	Clarke Hinkle, Green Bay	14	6	42.9
1940	Clarke Hinkle, Green Bay	14	9	64.3
1939	Ward Cuff, N.Y. Giants	16	7	43.8
1938	Ward Cuff, N.Y. Giants	9	5	55.6
	Ralph Kercheval, Brooklyn	13	5	38.5
1937	Jack Manders, Chi. Bears		8	
1936	Jack Manders, Chi. Bears		7	
	Armand Niccolai, Pittsburgh		7	
1935	Armand Niccolai, Pittsburgh		6	
	Bill Smith, Chi. Cardinals		6	
1934	Jack Manders, Chi. Bears		10	
1933	*Jack Manders, Chi. Bears		6	
	Glenn Presnell, Portsmouth		6	
1932	Earl (Dutch) Clark, Portsmouth		3	

First season of professional football.

ANNUAL RUSHING LEADERS

Year	Player, Team	Att.	Yards	Avg.	TD
1998	Terrell Davis, Denver, AFC	392	2,008	5.1	21
	Jamal Anderson, Atlanta, NFC	410	1,846	4.5	14
1997	Barry Sanders, Detroit, NFC	335	2,053	6.1	11
	Terrell Davis, Denver, AFC	369	1,750	4.7	15
1996	Barry Sanders, Detroit, NFC	307	1,553	5.1	11
	Terrell Davis, Denver, AFC	345	1,538	4.5	13
1995	Emmitt Smith, Dallas, NFC	377	1,773	4.7	25
	*Curtis Martin, New England, AFC	368	1,487	4.0	14
1994	Barry Sanders, Detroit, NFC	331	1,883	5.7	7
	Chris Warren, Seattle, AFC	333	1,545	4.6	9
1993	Emmitt Smith, Dallas, NFC	283	1,486	5.3	9
	Thurman Thomas, Buffalo, AFC	355	1,315	3.7	6
1992	Emmitt Smith, Dallas, NFC	373	1,713	4.6	18
	Barry Foster, Pittsburgh, AFC	390	1,690	4.3	11
1991	Emmitt Smith, Dallas, NFC	365	1,563	4.3	12
	Thurman Thomas, Buffalo, AFC	288	1,407	4.9	7
1990	Barry Sanders, Detroit, NFC	255	1,304	5.1	13
	Thurman Thomas, Buffalo, AFC	271	1,297	4.8	11
1989	Christian Okoye, Kansas City, AFC	370	1,480	4.0	12
	*Barry Sanders, Detroit, NFC	280	1,470	5.3	14
1988	Eric Dickerson, Indianapolis, AFC	388	1,659	4.3	14
	Herschel Walker, Dallas, NFC	361	1,514	4.2	5
1987	Charles White, L.A. Rams, NFC	324	1,374	4.2	11
	Eric Dickerson, Indianapolis, AFC	223	1,011	4.5	5
1986	Eric Dickerson, L.A. Rams, NFC	404	1,821	4.5	11
	Curt Warner, Seattle, AFC	319	1,481	4.6	13
1985	Marcus Allen, L.A. Raiders, AFC	380	1,759	4.6	11
	Gerald Riggs, Atlanta, NFC	397	1,719	4.3	10
1984	Eric Dickerson, L.A. Rams, NFC	379	2,105	5.6	14
	Earnest Jackson, San Diego, AFC	296	1,179	4.0	8
1983	*Eric Dickerson, L.A. Rams, NFC	390	1,808	4.6	18
	*Curt Warner, Seattle, AFC	335	1,449	4.3	13
1982	Freeman McNeil, N.Y. Jets, AFC	151	786	5.2	6
	Tony Dorsett, Dallas, NFC	177	745	4.2	5
1981	*George Rogers, New Orleans, NFC	378	1,674	4.4	13
	Earl Campbell, Houston, AFC	361	1,376	3.8	10
1980	Earl Campbell, Houston, AFC	373	1,934	5.2	13
	Walter Payton, Chicago, NFC	317	1,460	4.6	6
1979	Earl Campbell, Houston, AFC	368	1,697	4.6	19
	Walter Payton, Chicago, NFC	369	1,610	4.4	14
1978	*Earl Campbell, Houston, AFC	302	1,450	4.8	13
	Walter Payton, Chicago, NFC	333	1,395	4.2	11
1977	Walter Payton, Chicago, NFC	339	1,852	5.5	14
	Mark van Eeghen, Oakland, AFC	324	1,273	3.9	7
1976	O.J. Simpson, Buffalo, AFC	290	1,503	5.2	8
	Walter Payton, Chicago, NFC	311	1,390	4.5	13
1975	O.J. Simpson, Buffalo, AFC	329	1,817	5.5	16
	Jim Otis, St. Louis, NFC	269	1,076	4.0	5
1974	Otis Armstrong, Denver, AFC	263	1,407	5.3	9
	Lawrence McCutcheon, Los Angeles, NFC	236	1,109	4.7	3
1973	O.J. Simpson, Buffalo, AFC	332	2,003	6.0	12
	John Brockington, Green Bay, NFC	265	1,144	4.3	3
1972	O.J. Simpson, Buffalo, AFC	292	1,251	4.3	6
	Larry Brown, Washington, NFC	285	1,216	4.3	8
1971	Floyd Little, Denver, AFC	284	1,133	4.0	6
	*John Brockington, Green Bay, NFC	216	1,105	5.1	4
1970	Larry Brown, Washington, NFC	237	1,125	4.7	5
	Floyd Little, Denver, AFC	209	901	4.3	3
1969	Gale Sayers, Chicago, NFL	236	1,032	4.4	8
	Dickie Post, San Diego, AFL	182	873	4.8	6
1968	Leroy Kelly, Cleveland, NFL	248	1,239	5.0	16
	*Paul Robinson, Cincinnati, AFL	238	1,023	4.3	8
1967	Jim Nance, Boston, AFL	269	1,216	4.5	7
	Leroy Kelly, Cleveland, NFL	235	1,205	5.1	11
1966	Jim Nance, Boston, AFL	299	1,458	4.9	11
	Gale Sayers, Chicago, NFL	229	1,231	5.4	8
1965	Jim Brown, Cleveland, NFL	289	1,544	5.3	17
	Paul Lowe, San Diego, AFL	222	1,121	5.0	7
1964	Jim Brown, Cleveland, NFL	280	1,446	5.2	7
	Cookie Gilchrist, Buffalo, AFL	230	981	4.3	6
1963	Jim Brown, Cleveland, NFL	291	1,863	6.4	12
	Clem Daniels, Oakland, AFL	215	1,099	5.1	3
1962	Jim Taylor, Green Bay, NFL	272	1,474	5.4	19
	Cookie Gilchrist, Buffalo, AFL	214	1,096	5.1	13
1961	Jim Brown, Cleveland, NFL	305	1,408	4.6	8
	Billy Cannon, Houston, AFL	200	948	4.7	6
1960	Jim Brown, Cleveland, NFL	215	1,257	5.8	9
	*Abner Haynes, Dall. Texans, AFL	156	875	5.6	9
1959	Jim Brown, Cleveland	290	1,329	4.6	14
1958	Jim Brown, Cleveland	257	1,527	5.9	17
1957	*Jim Brown, Cleveland	202	942	4.7	9
1956	Rick Casares, Chi. Bears	234	1,126	4.8	12
1955	*Alan Ameche, Baltimore	213	961	4.5	9
1954	Joe Perry, San Francisco	173	1,049	6.1	8
1953	Joe Perry, San Francisco	192	1,018	5.3	10
1952	Dan Towler, Los Angeles	156	894	5.7	10
1951	Eddie Price, N.Y. Giants	271	971	3.6	7
1950	Marion Motley, Cleveland	140	810	5.8	3
1949	Steve Van Buren, Philadelphia	263	1,146	4.4	11
1948	Steve Van Buren, Philadelphia	201	945	4.7	10
1947	Steve Van Buren, Philadelphia	217	1,008	4.6	13
1946	Bill Dudley, Pittsburgh	146	604	4.1	3
1945	Steve Van Buren, Philadelphia	143	832	5.8	15
1944	Bill Paschal, N.Y. Giants	196	737	3.8	9
1943	*Bill Paschal, N.Y. Giants	147	572	3.9	10
1942	*Bill Dudley, Pittsburgh	162	696	4.3	5
1941	Clarence (Pug) Manders, Brooklyn	111	486	4.4	5
1940	Byron (Whizzer) White, Detroit	146	514	3.5	5
1939	*Bill Osmanski, Chicago	121	699	5.8	7
1938	*Byron (Whizzer) White, Pittsburgh	152	567	3.7	4
1937	Cliff Battles, Washington	216	874	4.0	5
1936	*Alphonse (Tuffy) Leemans, N.Y. Giants	206	830	4.0	2
1935	Doug Russell, Chi. Cardinals	140	499	3.6	0
1934	*Beattie Feathers, Chi. Bears	119	1,004	8.4	8
1933	Jim Musick, Boston	173	809	4.7	5
1932	*Cliff Battles, Boston	148	576	3.9	3

First season of professional football.

ANNUAL PASSING LEADERS

(Current rating system implemented in 1973)

Year	Player, Team	Att.	Comp.	Yards	TD	Int.	Rating
1998	Randall Cunningham, Minnesota, NFC	425	259	3,704	34	10	106.0
	Vinny Testaverde, NY Jets, AFC	421	259	3,256	29	7	101.6
1997	Steve Young, San Francisco, NFC	356	241	3,029	19	6	104.7
	Mark Brunell, Jacksonville, AFC	435	264	3,281	18	7	91.2
1996	Steve Young, San Francisco, NFC	316	214	2,410	14	6	97.2
	John Elway, Denver, AFC	466	287	3,328	26	14	89.2
1995	Jim Harbaugh, Indianapolis, AFC	314	200	2,575	17	5	100.7
	Brett Favre, Green Bay, NFC	570	359	4,413	38	13	99.5

1994	Steve Young, San Francisco, NFC	461	324	3,969	35	10	112.8
	Dan Marino, Miami, AFC	615	385	4,453	30	17	89.2
1993	Steve Young, San Francisco, NFC	462	314	4,023	29	16	101.5
	John Elway, Denver, AFC	551	348	4,030	25	10	92.8
1992	Steve Young, San Francisco, NFC	402	268	3,465	25	7	107.0
	Warren Moon, Houston, AFC	346	224	2,521	18	12	89.3
1991	Steve Young, San Francisco, NFC	279	180	2,517	17	8	101.8
	Jim Kelly, Buffalo, AFC	474	304	3,844	33	17	97.6
1990	Jim Kelly, Buffalo, AFC	346	219	2,829	24	9	101.2
	Phil Simms, N.Y. Giants, NFC	311	184	2,284	15	4	92.7
1989	Joe Montana, San Francisco, NFC	386	271	3,521	26	8	112.4
	Boomer Esiason, Cincinnati, AFC	455	258	3,525	28	11	92.1
1988	Boomer Esiason, Cincinnati, AFC	388	223	3,572	28	14	97.4
	Wade Wilson, Minnesota, NFC	332	204	2,746	15	9	91.5
1987	Joe Montana, San Francisco, NFC	398	266	3,054	31	13	102.1
	Bernie Kosar, Cleveland, AFC	389	241	3,033	22	9	95.4
1986	Tommy Kramer, Minnesota, NFC	372	208	3,000	24	10	92.6
	Dan Marino, Miami, AFC	623	378	4,746	44	23	92.5
1985	Ken O'Brien, N.Y. Jets, AFC	488	297	3,888	25	8	96.2
	Joe Montana, San Francisco, NFC	494	303	3,653	27	13	91.3
1984	Dan Marino, Miami, AFC	564	362	5,084	48	17	108.9
	Joe Montana, San Francisco, NFC	432	279	3,630	28	10	102.9
1983	Steve Bartkowski, Atlanta, NFC	432	274	3,167	22	5	97.6
	*Dan Marino, Miami, AFC	296	173	2,210	20	6	96.0
1982	Ken Anderson, Cincinnati, AFC	309	218	2,495	12	9	95.3
	Joe Theismann, Washington, NFC	252	161	2,033	13	9	91.3
1981	Ken Anderson, Cincinnati, AFC	479	300	3,754	29	10	98.4
	Joe Montana, San Francisco, NFC	488	311	3,565	19	12	88.4
1980	Brian Sipe, Cleveland, AFC	554	337	4,132	30	14	91.4
	Ron Jaworski, Philadelphia, NFC	451	257	3,529	27	12	91.0
1979	Roger Staubach, Dallas, NFC	461	267	3,586	27	11	92.3
	Dan Fouts, San Diego, AFC	530	332	4,082	24	24	82.6
1978	Roger Staubach, Dallas, NFC	413	231	3,190	25	16	84.9
	Terry Bradshaw, Pittsburgh, AFC	368	207	2,915	28	20	84.7
1977	Bob Griese, Miami, AFC	307	180	2,252	22	13	87.8
	Roger Staubach, Dallas, NFC	361	210	2,620	18	9	87.0
1976	Ken Stabler, Oakland, AFC	291	194	2,737	27	17	103.4
	James Harris, Los Angeles, NFC	158	91	1,460	8	6	89.6
1975	Ken Anderson, Cincinnati, AFC	377	228	3,169	21	11	93.9
	Fran Tarkenton, Minnesota, NFC	425	273	2,994	25	13	91.8
1974	Ken Anderson, Cincinnati, AFC	328	213	2,667	18	10	95.7
	Sonny Jurgensen, Washington, NFC	167	107	1,185	11	5	94.5
1973	Roger Staubach, Dallas, NFC	286	179	2,428	23	15	94.6
	Ken Stabler, Oakland, AFC	260	163	1,997	14	10	88.3
1972	Norm Snead, N.Y. Giants, NFC	325	196	2,307	17	12	
	Earl Morrall, Miami, AFC	150	83	1,360	11	7	
1971	Roger Staubach, Dallas, NFC	211	126	1,882	15	4	
	Bob Griese, Miami, AFC	263	145	2,089	19	9	
1970	John Brodie, San Francisco, NFC	378	223	2,941	24	10	
	Daryle Lamonica, Oakland, AFC	356	179	2,516	22	15	
1969	Sonny Jurgensen, Washington, NFL	442	274	3,102	22	15	
	*Greg Cook, Cincinnati, AFL	197	106	1,854	15	11	
1968	Len Dawson, Kansas City, AFL	224	131	2,109	17	9	
	Earl Morrall, Baltimore, NFL	317	182	2,909	26	17	
1967	Sonny Jurgensen, Washington, NFL	508	288	3,747	31	16	
	Daryle Lamonica, Oakland, AFL	425	220	3,228	30	20	
1966	Bart Starr, Green Bay, NFL	251	156	2,257	14	3	
	Len Dawson, Kansas City, AFL	284	159	2,527	26	10	
1965	Rudy Bukich, Chicago, NFL	312	176	2,641	20	9	
	John Hadl, San Diego, AFL	348	174	2,798	20	21	
1964	Len Dawson, Kansas City, AFL	354	199	2,879	30	18	
	Bart Starr, Green Bay, NFL	272	163	2,144	15	4	
1963	Y.A. Tittle, N.Y. Giants, NFL	367	221	3,145	36	14	
	Tobin Rote, San Diego, AFL	286	170	2,510	20	17	
1962	Len Dawson, Dall. Texans, AFL	310	189	2,759	29	17	
	Bart Starr, Green Bay, NFL	285	178	2,438	12	9	
1961	George Blanda, Houston, AFL	362	187	3,330	36	22	
	Milt Plum, Cleveland, NFL	302	177	2,416	18	10	
1960	Milt Plum, Cleveland, NFL	250	151	2,297	21	5	
	Jack Kemp, L.A. Chargers, AFL	406	211	3,018	20	25	
1959	Charlie Conerly, N.Y. Giants	194	113	1,706	14	4	
1958	Eddie LeBaron, Washington	145	79	1,365	11	10	
1957	Tommy O'Connell, Cleveland	110	63	1,229	9	8	
1956	Ed Brown, Chi. Bears	168	96	1,667	11	12	
1955	Otto Graham, Cleveland	185	98	1,721	15	8	
1954	Norm Van Brocklin, Los Angeles	260	139	2,637	13	21	
1953	Otto Graham, Cleveland	258	167	2,722	11	9	
1952	Norm Van Brocklin, Los Angeles	205	113	1,736	14	17	
1951	Bob Waterfield, Los Angeles	176	88	1,566	13	10	
1950	Norm Van Brocklin, Los Angeles	233	127	2,061	18	14	
1949	Sammy Baugh, Washington	255	145	1,903	18	14	
1948	Tommy Thompson, Philadelphia	246	141	1,965	25	11	
1947	Sammy Baugh, Washington	354	210	2,938	25	15	
1946	Bob Waterfield, Los Angeles	251	127	1,747	18	17	
1945	Sammy Baugh, Washington	182	128	1,669	11	4	
	Sid Luckman, Chi. Bears	217	117	1,725	14	10	
1944	Frank Filchock, Washington	147	84	1,139	13	9	
1943	Sammy Baugh, Washington	239	133	1,754	23	19	
1942	Cecil Isbell, Green Bay	268	146	2,021	24	14	
1941	Cecil Isbell, Green Bay	206	117	1,479	15	11	
1940	Sammy Baugh, Washington	177	111	1,367	12	10	
1939	*Parker Hall, Cleveland	208	106	1,227	9	13	
1938	Ed Danowski, N.Y. Giants	129	70	848	7	8	
1937	*Sammy Baugh, Washington	171	81	1,127	8	14	
1936	Arnie Herber, Green Bay	173	77	1,239	11	13	
1935	Ed Danowski, N.Y. Giants	113	57	794	10	9	
1934	Arnie Herber, Green Bay	115	42	799	8	12	
1933	*Harry Newman, N.Y. Giants	136	53	973	11	17	
1932	Arnie Herber, Green Bay	101	37	639	9	9	

**First season of professional football.*

ANNUAL PASSING TOUCHDOWN LEADERS

Year	Player, Team	TD
1998	Steve Young, San Francisco, NFC	36
	Vinny Testaverde, N.Y. Jets, AFC	29
1997	Brett Favre, Green Bay, NFC	35
	Jeff George, Oakland, AFC	29
1996	Brett Favre, Green Bay, NFC	39
	Vinny Testaverde, Baltimore, AFC	33
1995	Brett Favre, Green Bay, NFC	38
	Jeff Blake, Cincinnati, AFC	28
1994	Steve Young, San Francisco, NFC	35
	Dan Marino, Miami, AFC	30
1993	Steve Young, San Francisco, NFC	29
	John Elway, Denver, AFC	25
1992	Steve Young, San Francisco, NFC	25
	Dan Marino, Miami, AFC	24
1991	Jim Kelly, Buffalo, AFC	33
	Mark Rypien, Washington, NFC	28
1990	Warren Moon, Houston, AFC	33
	Randall Cunningham, Philadelphia, NFC	30
1989	Jim Everett, L.A. Rams, NFC	29
	Boomer Esiason, Cincinnati, AFC	28
1988	Jim Everett, L.A. Rams, NFC	31
	Boomer Esiason, Cincinnati, AFC	28
	Dan Marino, Miami, AFC	28
1987	Joe Montana, San Francisco, NFC	31
	Dan Marino, Miami, AFC	26
1986	Dan Marino, Miami, AFC	44
	Tommy Kramer, Minnesota, NFC	24
1985	Dan Marino, Miami, AFC	30
	Joe Montana, San Francisco, NFC	27
1984	Dan Marino, Miami, AFC	48
	Neil Lomax, St. Louis, NFC	28
	Joe Montana, San Francisco, NFC	28
1983	Lynn Dickey, Green Bay, NFC	32
	Joe Ferguson, Buffalo, AFC	26
	Brian Sipe, Cleveland, AFC	26
1982	Terry Bradshaw, Pittsburgh, AFC	17
	Dan Fouts, San Diego, AFC	17
	Joe Montana, San Francisco, NFC	17
1981	Dan Fouts, San Diego, AFC	33
	Steve Bartkowski, Atlanta, NFC	30
1980	Steve Bartkowski, Atlanta, NFC	31
	Dan Fouts, San Diego, AFC	30
	Brian Sipe, Cleveland, AFC	30
1979	Steve Grogan, New England, AFC	28
	Brian Sipe, Cleveland, AFC	28
	Roger Staubach, Dallas, NFC	27
1978	Terry Bradshaw, Pittsburgh, AFC	28
	Roger Staubach, Dallas, NFC	25
	Fran Tarkenton, Minnesota, NFC	25
1977	Bob Griese, Miami, AFC	22
	Ron Jaworski, Philadelphia, NFC	18
	Roger Staubach, Dallas, NFC	18
1976	Ken Stabler, Oakland, AFC	27
	Jim Hart, St. Louis, NFC	18
1975	Joe Ferguson, Buffalo, AFC	25
	Fran Tarkenton, Minnesota, NFC	25
1974	Ken Stabler, Oakland, AFC	26
	Jim Hart, St. Louis, NFC	20
1973	Roman Gabriel, Philadelphia, NFC	23
	Roger Staubach, Dallas, NFC	23
	Charley Johnson, Denver, AFC	20
1972	Billy Kilmer, Washington, NFC	19
	Joe Namath, N.Y. Jets, AFC	19

Year	Player, Team	
1971	John Hadl, San Diego, AFC	21
	John Brodie, San Francisco, NFC	18
1970	John Brodie, San Francisco, NFC	24
	John Hadl, San Diego, AFC	22
	Daryle Lamonica, Oakland, AFC	22
1969	Daryle Lamonica, Oakland, AFL	34
	Roman Gabriel, Los Angeles, NFL	24
1968	John Hadl, San Diego, AFL	27
	Earl Morrall, Baltimore, NFL	26
1967	Sonny Jurgensen, Washington, NFL	31
	Daryle Lamonica, Oakland, AFL	30
1966	Frank Ryan, Cleveland, NFL	29
	Len Dawson, Kansas City, AFL	26
1965	John Brodie, San Francisco, NFL	30
	Len Dawson, Kansas City, AFL	21
1964	Babe Parilli, Boston, AFL	31
	Frank Ryan, Cleveland, NFL	25
1963	Y.A. Tittle, N.Y. Giants, NFL	36
	Len Dawson, Kansas City, AFL	26
1962	Y.A. Tittle, N.Y. Giants, NFL	33
	Len Dawson, Dallas, AFL	29
1961	George Blanda, Houston, AFL	36
	Sonny Jurgensen, Philadelphia, NFL	32
1960	Al Dorow, N.Y. Titans, AFL	26
	Johnny Unitas, Baltimore, NFL	25
1959	Johnny Unitas, Baltimore	32
1958	Johnny Unitas, Baltimore	19
1957	Johnny Unitas, Baltimore	24
1956	Tobin Rote, Green Bay	18
1955	Tobin Rote, Green Bay	17
	Y.A. Tittle, San Francisco	17
1954	Adrian Burk, Philadelphia	23
1953	Robert Thomason, Philadelphia	21
1952	Jim Finks, Pittsburgh	20
	Otto Graham, Cleveland	20
1951	Bobby Layne, Detroit	26
1950	George Ratterman, N.Y. Yanks	22
1949	Johnny Lujack, Chi. Bears	23
1948	Tommy Thompson, Philadelphia	25
1947	Sammy Baugh, Washington	25
1946	Sid Luckman, Chi. Bears	17
	Bob Waterfield, Los Angeles	17
1945	Sid Luckman, Chi. Bears	14
	*Bob Waterfield, Cleveland	14
1944	Frank Filchock, Washington	13
1943	Sid Luckman, Chi. Bears	28
1942	Cecil Isbell, Green Bay	24
1941	Cecil Isbell, Green Bay	15
1940	Sammy Baugh, Washington	12
1939	Frank Filchock, Washington	11
1938	Bob Monnett, Green Bay	9
1937	Bernie Masterson, Chi. Bears	9
1936	Arnie Herber, Green Bay	11
1935	Ed Danowski, N.Y. Giants	10
1934	Arnie Herber, Green Bay	8
1933	*Harry Newman, N.Y. Giants	11
1932	Arnie Herber, Green Bay	9

First season of professional football.

ANNUAL PASS RECEIVING LEADERS

Year	Player, Team	No.	Yards	Avg.	TD
1998	O.J. McDuffie, Miami, AFC	90	1,050	11.7	7
	Frank Sanders, Arizona, NFC	89	1,145	12.9	3
1997	Tim Brown, Oakland, AFC	104	1,408	13.5	5
	Herman Moore, Detroit, NFC	104	1,293	12.4	8
1996	Jerry Rice, San Francisco, NFC	108	1,254	11.6	8
	Carl Pickens, Cincinnati, AFC	100	1,180	11.8	12
1995	Herman Moore, Detroit, NFC	123	1,686	13.7	14
	Carl Pickens, Cincinnati, AFC	99	1,234	12.5	17
1994	Cris Carter, Minnesota, NFC	122	1,256	10.3	7
	Ben Coates, New England, AFC	96	1,174	12.2	7
1993	Sterling Sharpe, Green Bay, NFC	112	1,274	11.4	11
	Reggie Langhorne, Indianapolis, AFC	85	1,038	12.2	3
1992	Sterling Sharpe, Green Bay, NFC	108	1,461	13.5	13
	Haywood Jeffires, Houston, AFC	90	913	10.1	9
1991	Haywood Jeffires, Houston, AFC	100	1,181	11.8	7
	Michael Irvin, Dallas, NFC	93	1,523	16.4	8
1990	Jerry Rice, San Francisco, NFC	100	1,502	15.0	13
	Haywood Jeffires, Houston, AFC	74	1,048	14.2	8
	Drew Hill, Houston, AFC	74	1,019	13.8	5
1989	Sterling Sharpe, Green Bay, NFC	90	1,423	15.8	12
	Andre Reed, Buffalo, AFC	88	1,312	14.9	9
1988	Al Toon, N.Y. Jets, AFC	93	1,067	11.5	5
	Henry Ellard, L.A. Rams, NFC	86	1,414	16.4	10
1987	J.T. Smith, St. Louis, NFC	91	1,117	12.3	8
	Al Toon, N.Y. Jets, AFC	68	976	14.4	5
1986	Todd Christensen, L.A. Raiders, AFC	95	1,153	12.1	8
	Jerry Rice, San Francisco, NFC	86	1,570	18.3	15
1985	Roger Craig, San Francisco, NFC	92	1,016	11.0	6
	Lionel James, San Diego, AFC	86	1,027	11.9	6
1984	Art Monk, Washington, NFC	106	1,372	12.9	7
	Ozzie Newsome, Cleveland, AFC	89	1,001	11.2	5
1983	Todd Christensen, L.A. Raiders, AFC	92	1,247	13.6	12
	Roy Green, St. Louis, NFC	78	1,227	15.7	14
	Charlie Brown, Washington, NFC	78	1,225	15.7	8
	Earnest Gray, N.Y. Giants, NFC	78	1,139	14.6	5
1982	Dwight Clark, San Francisco, NFC	60	913	15.2	5
	Kellen Winslow, San Diego, AFC	54	721	13.4	6
1981	Kellen Winslow, San Diego, AFC	88	1,075	12.2	10
	Dwight Clark, San Francisco, NFC	85	1,105	13.0	4
1980	Kellen Winslow, San Diego, AFC	89	1,290	14.5	9
	*Earl Cooper, San Francisco, NFC	83	567	6.8	4
1979	Joe Washington, Baltimore, AFC	82	750	9.1	3
	Ahmad Rashad, Minnesota, NFC	80	1,156	14.5	9
1978	Rickey Young, Minnesota, NFC	88	704	8.0	5
	Steve Largent, Seattle, AFC	71	1,168	16.5	8
1977	Lydell Mitchell, Baltimore, AFC	71	620	8.7	4
	Ahmad Rashad, Minnesota, NFC	51	681	13.4	2
1976	MacArthur Lane, Kansas City, AFC	66	686	10.4	1
	Drew Pearson, Dallas, NFC	58	806	13.9	6
1975	Chuck Foreman, Minnesota, NFC	73	691	9.5	9
	Reggie Rucker, Cleveland, AFC	60	770	12.8	3
	Lydell Mitchell, Baltimore, AFC	60	544	9.1	4
1974	Lydell Mitchell, Baltimore, AFC	72	544	7.6	2
	Charles Young, Philadelphia, NFC	63	696	11.0	3
1973	Harold Carmichael, Philadelphia, NFC	67	1,116	16.7	9
	Fred Willis, Houston, AFC	57	371	6.5	1
1972	Harold Jackson, Philadelphia, NFC	62	1,048	16.9	4
	Fred Biletnikoff, Oakland, AFC	58	802	13.8	7
1971	Fred Biletnikoff, Oakland, AFC	61	929	15.2	9
	Bob Tucker, N.Y. Giants, NFC	59	791	13.4	4
1970	Dick Gordon, Chicago, NFC	71	1,026	14.5	13
	Marlin Briscoe, Buffalo, AFC	57	1,036	18.2	8
1969	Dan Abramowicz, New Orleans, NFL	73	1,015	13.9	7
	Lance Alworth, San Diego, AFL	64	1,003	15.7	4
1968	Clifton McNeil, San Francisco, NFL	71	994	14.0	7
	Lance Alworth, San Diego, AFL	68	1,312	19.3	10
1967	George Sauer, N.Y. Jets, AFL	75	1,189	15.9	6
	Charley Taylor, Washington, NFL	70	990	14.1	9
1966	Lance Alworth, San Diego, AFL	73	1,383	18.9	13
	Charley Taylor, Washington, NFL	72	1,119	15.5	12
1965	Lionel Taylor, Denver, AFL	85	1,131	13.3	6
	Dave Parks, San Francisco, NFL	80	1,344	16.8	12
1964	Charley Hennigan, Houston, AFL	101	1,546	15.3	8
	Johnny Morris, Chicago, NFL	93	1,200	12.9	10
1963	Lionel Taylor, Denver, AFL	78	1,101	14.1	10
	Bobby Joe Conrad, St. Louis, NFL	73	967	13.2	10
1962	Lionel Taylor, Denver, AFL	77	908	11.8	4
	Bobby Mitchell, Washington, NFL	72	1,384	19.2	11
1961	Lionel Taylor, Denver, AFL	100	1,176	11.8	4
	Jim (Red) Phillips, Los Angeles, NFL	78	1,092	14.0	5
1960	Lionel Taylor, Denver, AFL	92	1,235	13.4	12
	Raymond Berry, Baltimore, NFL	74	1,298	17.5	10
1959	Raymond Berry, Baltimore	66	959	14.5	14
1958	Raymond Berry, Baltimore	56	794	14.2	9
	Pete Retzlaff, Philadelphia	56	766	13.7	2
1957	Billy Wilson, San Francisco	52	757	14.6	6
1956	Billy Wilson, San Francisco	60	889	14.8	5
1955	Pete Pihos, Philadelphia	62	864	13.9	7
1954	Pete Pihos, Philadelphia	60	872	14.5	10
	Billy Wilson, San Francisco	60	830	13.8	5
1953	Pete Pihos, Philadelphia	63	1,049	16.7	10
1952	Mac Speedie, Cleveland	62	911	14.7	5
1951	Elroy (Crazylegs) Hirsch, Los Angeles	66	1,495	22.7	17
1950	Tom Fears, Los Angeles	84	1,116	13.3	7
1949	Tom Fears, Los Angeles	77	1,013	13.2	9
1948	*Tom Fears, Los Angeles	51	698	13.7	4
1947	Jim Keane, Chi. Bears	64	910	14.2	10
1946	Jim Benton, Los Angeles	63	981	15.6	6
1945	Don Hutson, Green Bay	47	834	17.7	9
1944	Don Hutson, Green Bay	58	866	14.9	9
1943	Don Hutson, Green Bay	47	776	16.5	11
1942	Don Hutson, Green Bay	74	1,211	16.4	17
1941	Don Hutson, Green Bay	58	738	12.7	10
1940	*Don Looney, Philadelphia	58	707	12.2	4

Year	Player, Team	No.	Yards	Avg.	TD
1939	Don Hutson, Green Bay	34	846	24.9	6
1938	Gaynell Tinsley, Chi. Cardinals	41	516	12.6	1
1937	Don Hutson, Green Bay	41	552	13.5	7
1936	Don Hutson, Green Bay	34	536	15.8	8
1935	*Tod Goodwin, N.Y. Giants	26	432	16.6	4
1934	Joe Carter, Philadelphia	16	238	14.9	4
	Morris (Red) Badgro, N.Y. Giants	16	206	12.9	1
1933	John (Shipwreck) Kelly, Brooklyn	22	246	11.2	3
1932	Ray Flaherty, N.Y. Giants	21	350	16.7	3

First season of professional football.

ANNUAL PASS RECEIVING LEADERS (YARDS)

Year	Player, Team	No.	Yards	Avg.	TD
1998	Antonio Freeman, Green Bay, NFC	84	1,424	17.0	14
	Eric Moulds, Buffalo, AFC	67	1,368	20.4	9
1997	Rob Moore, Arizona, NFC	97	1,584	16.3	8
	Tim Brown, Oakland, AFC	104	1,408	13.5	5
1996	Isaac Bruce, St. Louis, NFC	84	1,338	15.9	7
	Jimmy Smith, Jacksonville, AFC	83	1,244	15.0	7
1995	Jerry Rice, San Francisco, NFC	122	1,848	15.1	15
	Tim Brown, Oakland, AFC	89	1,342	15.1	10
1994	Jerry Rice, San Francisco, NFC	112	1,499	13.4	13
	Tim Brown, L.A. Raiders, AFC	89	1,309	14.7	9
1993	Jerry Rice, San Francisco, NFC	98	1,503	15.3	15
	Tim Brown, L.A. Raiders, AFC	80	1,180	14.8	7
1992	Sterling Sharpe, Green Bay, NFC	108	1,461	13.5	13
	Anthony Miller, San Diego, AFC	72	1,060	14.7	7
1991	Michael Irvin, Dallas, NFC	93	1,523	16.4	8
	Haywood Jeffires, Houston, AFC	100	1,181	11.8	7
1990	Jerry Rice, San Francisco, NFC	100	1,502	15.0	13
	Haywood Jeffires, Houston, AFC	74	1,048	14.2	8
1989	Jerry Rice, San Francisco, NFC	82	1,483	18.1	17
	Andre Reed, Buffalo, AFC	88	1,312	14.9	9
1988	Henry Ellard, L.A. Rams, NFC	86	1,414	16.4	10
	Eddie Brown, Cincinnati, AFC	53	1,273	24.0	9
1987	J.T. Smith, St. Louis, NFC	91	1,117	12.3	8
	Carlos Carson, Kansas City, AFC	55	1,044	19.0	7
1986	Jerry Rice, San Francisco, NFC	86	1,570	18.3	15
	Stanley Morgan, New England, AFC	84	1,491	17.8	10
1985	Steve Largent, Seattle, AFC	79	1,287	16.3	6
	Mike Quick, Philadelphia, NFC	73	1,247	17.1	11
1984	Roy Green, St. Louis, NFC	78	1,555	19.9	12
	John Stallworth, Pittsburgh, AFC	80	1,395	17.4	11
1983	Mike Quick, Philadelphia, NFC	69	1,409	20.4	13
	Carlos Carson, Kansas City, AFC	80	1,351	16.9	7
1982	Wes Chandler, San Diego, AFC	49	1,032	21.1	9
	Dwight Clark, San Francisco, NFC	60	913	15.2	5
1981	Alfred Jenkins, Atlanta, NFC	70	1,358	19.4	13
	Frank Lewis, Buffalo, AFC	70	1,244	17.8	4
	Steve Watson, Denver, AFC	60	1,244	20.7	13
1980	John Jefferson, San Diego, AFC	82	1,340	16.3	13
	James Lofton, Green Bay, NFC	71	1,226	17.3	4
1979	Steve Largent, Seattle, AFC	66	1,237	18.7	9
	Ahmad Rashad, Minnesota, NFC	80	1,156	14.5	9
1978	Wesley Walker, N.Y. Jets, AFC	48	1,169	24.4	8
	Harold Carmichael, Philadelphia, NFC	55	1,072	19.5	8
1977	Drew Pearson, Dallas, NFC	48	870	18.1	2
	Ken Burrough, Houston, AFC	43	816	19.0	8
1976	Roger Carr, Baltimore, AFC	43	1,112	25.9	11
	*Sammy White, Minnesota, NFC	51	906	17.8	10
1975	Ken Burrough, Houston, AFC	53	1,063	20.1	8
	Mel Gray, St. Louis, NFC	48	926	19.3	11
1974	Cliff Branch, Oakland, AFC	60	1,092	18.2	13
	Drew Pearson, Dallas, NFC	62	1,087	17.5	2
1973	Harold Carmichael, Philadelphia, NFC	67	1,116	16.7	9
	*Isaac Curtis, Cincinnati, AFC	45	843	18.7	9
1972	Harold Jackson, Philadelphia, NFC	62	1,048	16.9	4
	Rich Caster, N.Y. Jets, AFC	39	833	21.4	10
1971	Otis Taylor, Kansas City, AFC	57	1,110	19.5	7
	Gene Washington, San Francisco, NFC	46	884	19.2	4
1970	Gene Washington, San Francisco, NFC	53	1,100	20.8	12
	Marlin Briscoe, Buffalo, AFC	57	1,036	18.2	8
1969	Warren Wells, Oakland, AFL	47	1,260	26.8	14
	Harold Jackson, Philadelphia, NFL	65	1,116	17.2	9
1968	Lance Alworth, San Diego, AFL	68	1,312	19.3	10
	Roy Jefferson, Pittsburgh, NFL	58	1,074	18.5	11
1967	Don Maynard, N.Y. Jets, AFL	71	1,434	20.3	10
	Ben Hawkins, Philadelphia, NFL	59	1,265	21.4	10
1966	Lance Alworth, San Diego, AFL	73	1,383	18.9	13
	Pat Studstill, Detroit, NFL	67	1,266	18.9	5
1965	Lance Alworth, San Diego, AFL	69	1,602	23.2	14
	Dave Parks, San Francisco, NFL	80	1,344	16.8	12
1964	Charley Hennigan, Houston, AFL	101	1,546	15.3	8
	Johnny Morris, Chicago, NFL	93	1,200	12.9	10
1963	Bobby Mitchell, Washington, NFL	69	1,436	20.8	7
	Art Powell, Oakland, AFL	73	1,304	17.8	16
1962	Bobby Mitchel, Washington, NFL	72	1,384	19.2	11
	Art Powell, N.Y. Titans, AFL	64	1,130	17.6	8
1961	Charley Hennigan, Houston, AFL	82	1,746	21.3	12
	Tommy McDonald, Philadelphia, NFL	64	1,144	17.9	13
1960	*Bill Groman, Houston, AFL	72	1,473	20.5	12
	Raymond Berry, Baltimore, NFL	74	1,298	17.5	10
1959	Raymond Berry, Baltimore	66	959	14.5	14
1958	Del Shofner, Los Angeles	51	1,097	21.5	8
1957	Raymond Berry, Baltimore	47	800	17.0	6
1956	Billy Howton, Green Bay	55	1,188	21.6	12
1955	Pete Pihos, Philadelphia	62	864	13.9	7
1954	Bob Boyd, Los Angeles	53	1,212	22.9	6
1953	Pete Pihos, Philadelphia	63	1,049	16.7	10
1952	*Bill Howton, Green Bay	53	1,231	23.2	13
1951	Elroy (Crazylegs) Hirsch, Los Angeles	66	1,495	22.7	17
1950	Tom Fears, Los Angeles	84	1,116	13.3	7
1949	Bob Mann, Detroit	66	1,014	15.4	4
1948	Mal Kutner, Chi. Cardinals	41	943	23.0	14
1947	Mal Kutner, Chi. Cardinals	43	944	21.9	7
1946	Jim Benton, Los Angeles	63	981	15.5	6
1945	Jim Benton, Cleveland	45	1,067	23.7	8
1944	Don Hutson, Green Bay	58	866	14.6	9
1943	Don Hutson, Green Bay	47	776	16.5	11
1942	Don Hutson, Green Bay	74	1,211	16.4	17
1941	Don Hutson, Green Bay	58	738	12.7	10
1940	*Don Looney, Philadelphia	58	707	12.2	4
1939	Don Hutson, Green Bay	34	846	24.9	6
1938	Don Hutson, Green Bay	32	548	17.1	9
1937	*Gaynell Tinsley, Chi. Cardinals	36	675	18.8	5
1936	Don Hutson, Green Bay	34	526	15.5	8
1935	Charley Malone, Boston	22	433	19.7	2
1934	Harry Ebding, Detroit	9	257	28.6	2
1933	*Paul Moss, Pittsburgh	18	383	21.3	2
1932	Johnny Blood (McNally), Green Bay	19	326	17.2	3

First season of professional football.

ANNUAL INTERCEPTION LEADERS

Year	Player, Team	No.	Yards	TD
1998	Ty Law, New England, AFC	9	133	1
	Kwamie Lassiter, Arizona, NFC	8	80	0
1997	Ryan McNeil, St. Louis, NFC	9	127	1
	Mark McMillian, Kansas City, AFC	8	274	3
	Darryl Williams, Seattle, AFC	8	172	1
1996	Tyrone Braxton, Denver, AFC	9	128	1
	Keith Lyle, St. Louis, NFC	9	152	0
1995	*Orlando Thomas, Minnesota, NFC	9	108	1
	Willie Williams, Pittsburgh, AFC	7	122	1
1994	Eric Turner, Cleveland, AFC	9	199	1
	Aeneas Williams, Arizona, NFC	9	89	0
1993	Eugene Robinson, Seattle, AFC	9	80	0
	Nate Odomes, Buffalo, AFC	9	65	0
	Deion Sanders, Atlanta, NFC	7	91	0
1992	Henry Jones, Buffalo, AFC	8	263	2
	Audray McMillian, Minnesota, NFC	8	157	2
1991	Ronnie Lott, L.A. Raiders, AFC	8	52	0
	Ray Crockett, Detroit, NFC	6	141	1
	Deion Sanders, Atlanta, NFC	6	119	1
	*Aeneas Williams, Phoenix, NFC	6	60	0
	Tim McKyer, Atlanta, NFC	6	24	0
1990	*Mark Carrier, Chicago, NFC	10	39	0
	Richard Johnson, Houston, AFC	8	100	1
1989	Felix Wright, Cleveland, AFC	9	91	1
	Eric Allen, Philadelphia, NFC	8	38	0
1988	Scott Case, Atlanta, NFC	10	47	0
	Erik McMillan, N.Y. Jets, AFC	8	168	2
1987	Barry Wilburn, Washington, NFC	9	135	1
	Mike Prior, Indianapolis, AFC	6	57	0
	Mark Kelso, Buffalo, AFC	6	25	0
	Keith Bostic, Houston, AFC	6	-14	0
1986	Ronnie Lott, San Francisco, NFC	10	134	1
	Deron Cherry, Kansas City, AFC	9	150	0
1985	Everson Walls, Dallas, NFC	9	31	0
	Albert Lewis, Kansas City, AFC	8	59	0
	Eugene Daniel, Indianapolis, AFC	8	53	0
1984	Ken Easley, Seattle, AFC	10	126	2
	*Tom Flynn, Green Bay, NFC	9	106	0
1983	Mark Murphy, Washington, NFC	9	127	0
	Ken Riley, Cincinnati, AFC	8	89	2
	Vann McElroy, L.A. Raiders, AFC	8	68	0

1982	Everson Walls, Dallas, NFC	7	61	0
	Ken Riley, Cincinnati, AFC	5	88	1
	Bobby Jackson, N.Y Jets, AFC	5	84	1
	Dwayne Woodruff, Pittsburgh, AFC	5	53	0
	Donnie Shell, Pittsburgh, AFC	5	27	0
1981	*Everson Walls, Dallas, NFC	11	133	0
	John Harris, Seattle, AFC	10	155	2
1980	Lester Hayes, Oakland, AFC	13	273	1
	Nolan Cromwell, Los Angeles, NFC	8	140	1
1979	Mike Reinfeldt, Houston, AFC	12	205	0
	Lemar Parrish, Washington, NFC	9	65	0
1978	Thom Darden, Cleveland, AFC	10	200	0
	Ken Stone, St. Louis, NFC	9	139	0
	Willie Buchanon, Green Bay, NFC	9	93	1
1977	Lyle Blackwood, Baltimore, AFC	10	163	0
	Rolland Lawrence, Atlanta, NFC	7	138	0
1976	Monte Jackson, Los Angeles, NFC	10	173	3
	Ken Riley, Cincinnati, AFC	9	141	1
1975	Mel Blount, Pittsburgh, AFC	11	121	0
	Paul Krause, Minnesota, NFC	10	201	0
1974	Emmitt Thomas, Kansas City, AFC	12	214	2
	Ray Brown, Atlanta, NFC	8	164	1
1973	Dick Anderson, Miami, AFC	8	163	2
	Mike Wagner, Pittsburgh, AFC	8	134	0
	Bobby Bryant, Minnesota, NFC	7	105	1
1972	Bill Bradley, Philadelphia, NFC	9	73	0
	Mike Sensibaugh, Kansas City, AFC	8	65	0
1971	Bill Bradley, Philadelphia, NFC	11	248	0
	Ken Houston, Houston, AFC	9	220	4
1970	Johnny Robinson, Kansas City, AFC	10	155	0
	Dick LeBeau, Detroit, NFC	9	96	0
1969	Mel Renfro, Dallas, NFL	10	118	0
	Emmitt Thomas, Kansas City, AFL	9	146	1
1968	Dave Grayson, Oakland, AFL	10	195	1
	Willie Williams, N.Y. Giants, NFL	10	103	0
1967	Miller Farr, Houston, AFL	10	264	3
	*Lem Barney, Detroit, NFL	10	232	3
	Tom Janik, Buffalo, AFL	10	222	2
	Dave Whitsell, New Orleans, NFL	10	178	2
	Dick Westmoreland, Miami, AFL	10	127	1
1966	Larry Wilson, St. Louis, NFL	10	180	2
	Johnny Robinson, Kansas City, AFL	10	136	1
	Bobby Hunt, Kansas City, AFL	10	113	0
1965	W.K. Hicks, Houston, AFL	9	156	0
	Bobby Boyd, Baltimore, NFL	9	78	1
1964	Dainard Paulson, N.Y. Jets, AFL	12	157	1
	*Paul Krause, Washington, NFL	12	140	1
1963	Fred Glick, Houston, AFL	12	180	1
	Dick Lynch, N.Y. Giants, NFL	9	251	3
	Roosevelt Taylor, Chicago, NFL	9	172	1
1962	Lee Riley, N.Y. Titans, AFL	11	122	0
	Willie Wood, Green Bay, NFL	9	132	0
1961	Billy Atkins, Buffalo, AFL	10	158	0
	Dick Lynch, N.Y. Giants, NFL	9	60	0
1960	*Austin (Goose) Gonsoulin, Denver, AFL	11	98	0
	Dave Baker, San Francisco, NFL	10	96	0
	Jerry Norton, St. Louis, NFL	10	96	0
1959	Dean Derby, Pittsburgh	7	127	0
	Milt Davis, Baltimore	7	119	1
	Don Shinnick, Baltimore	7	70	0
1958	Jim Patton, N.Y. Giants	11	183	0
1957	Milt Davis, Baltimore	10	219	2
	Jack Christiansen, Detroit	10	137	1
	Jack Butler, Pittsburgh	10	85	0
1956	Linden Crow, Chi. Cardinals	11	170	0
1955	Will Sherman, Los Angeles	11	101	0
1954	Dick (Night Train) Lane, Chi. Cardinals	10	181	0
1953	Jack Christiansen, Detroit	12	238	1
1952	*Dick (Night Train) Lane, Los Angeles	14	298	2
1951	Otto Schnellbacher, N.Y. Giants	11	194	2
1950	Orban (Spec) Sanders, N.Y. Yanks	13	199	0
1949	Bob Nussbaumer, Chi. Cardinals	12	157	0
1948	*Dan Sandifer, Washington	13	258	2
1947	Frank Reagan, N.Y. Giants	10	203	0
	Frank Seno, Boston	10	100	0
1946	Bill Dudley, Pittsburgh	10	242	1
1945	Roy Zimmerman, Philadelphia	7	90	0
1944	*Howard Livingston, N.Y. Giants	9	172	1
1943	Sammy Baugh, Washington	11	112	0
1942	Clyde (Bulldog) Turner, Chi. Bears	8	96	1
1941	Marshall Goldberg, Chi. Cardinals	7	54	0
	*Art Jones, Pittsburgh	7	35	0
1940	Clarence (Ace) Parker, Brooklyn	6	146	1
	Kent Ryan, Detroit	6	65	0
	Don Hutson, Green Bay	6	24	0

*First season of professional football.

ANNUAL PUNTING LEADERS

Year	Player, Team	No.	Avg.	Long
1998	Craig Hentrich, Tennessee, AFC	69	47.2	71
	Mark Royals, New Orleans, NFC	88	45.6	64
1997	Mark Royals, New Orleans, NFC	88	45.9	66
	Tom Tupa, New England, AFC	78	45.8	73
1996	John Kidd, Miami, AFC	78	46.3	63
	Matt Turk, Washington, NFC	75	45.1	63
1995	Rick Tuten, Seattle, AFC	83	45.0	73
	Sean Landeta, St. Louis, NFC	83	44.3	63
1994	Sean Landeta, L.A. Rams, NFC	78	44.8	62
	Jeff Gossett, L.A. Raiders, AFC	77	43.9	65
1993	Greg Montgomery, Houston, AFC	54	45.6	77
	Jim Arnold, Detroit, NFC	72	44.5	68
1992	Greg Montgomery, Houston, AFC	53	46.9	66
	Harry Newsome, Minnesota, NFC	72	45.0	84
1991	Reggie Roby, Miami, AFC	54	45.7	64
	Harry Newsome, Minnesota, AFC	68	45.5	65
1990	Mike Horan, Denver, AFC	58	44.4	67
	Sean Landeta, N.Y. Giants, NFC	75	44.1	67
1989	Rich Camarillo, Phoenix, NFC	76	43.4	58
	Greg Montgomery, Hounton, AFC	56	43.3	63
1988	Harry Newsome, Pittsburgh, AFC	65	45.4	62
	Jim Arnold, Detroit, NFC	97	42.4	69
1987	Rick Donnelly, Atlanta, NFC	61	44.0	62
	Ralf Mojsiejenko, San Diego, AFC	67	42.9	57
1986	Rohn Stark, Indianapolis, AFC	76	45.2	63
	Sean Landeta, N.Y. Giants, NFC	79	44.8	61
1985	Rohn Stark, Indianapolis, AFC	78	45.9	68
	*Rick Donnelly, Atlanta, NFC	59	43.6	68
1984	Jim Arnold, Kansas City, AFC	98	44.9	63
	*Brian Hansen, New Orleans, NFC	69	43.8	66
1983	Rohn Stark, Baltimore, AFC	91	45.3	68
	Frank Garcia, Tampa Bay, NFC	95	42.2	64
1982	Luke Prestridge, Denver, AFC	45	45.0	65
	Carl Birdsong, St. Louis, NFC	54	43.8	65
1981	Pat McInally, Cincinnati, AFC	72	45.4	62
	Tom Skladany, Detroit, NFC	64	43.5	74
1980	Dave Jennings, N.Y. Giants, NFC	94	44.8	63
	Luke Prestridge, Denver, AFC	70	43.9	57
1979	*Bob Grupp, Kansas City, AFC	89	43.6	74
	Dave Jennings, N.Y. Giants, NFC	104	42.7	72
1978	Pat McInally, Cincinnati, AFC	91	43.1	65
	*Tom Skladany, Detroit, NFC	86	42.5	63
1977	Ray Guy, Oakland, AFC	59	43.3	74
	Tom Blanchard, New Orleans, NFC	82	42.4	66
1976	Marv Bateman, Buffalo, AFC	86	42.8	78
	John James, Atlanta, NFC	101	42.1	67
1975	Ray Guy, Oakland, AFC	68	43.8	64
	Herman Weaver, Detroit, NFC	80	42.0	61
1974	Ray Guy, Oakland, AFC	74	42.2	66
	Tom Blanchard, New Orleans, NFC	88	42.1	71
1973	Jerrel Wilson, Kansas City, AFC	80	45.5	68
	*Tom Wittum, San Francisco, NFC	79	43.7	62
1972	Jerrel Wilson, Kansas City, AFC	66	44.8	69
	Dave Chapple, Los Angeles, NFC	53	44.2	70
1971	Dave Lewis, Cincinnati, AFC	72	44.8	56
	Tom McNeill, Philadelphia, NFC	73	42.0	64
1970	Dave Lewis, Cincinnati, AFC	79	46.2	63
	*Julian Fagan, New Orleans, NFC	77	42.5	64
1969	David Lee, Baltimore, NFL	57	45.3	66
	Dennis Partee, San Diego, AFL	71	44.6	62
1968	Jerrel Wilson, Kansas City, AFL	63	45.1	70
	Billy Lothridge, Atlanta, NFL	75	44.3	70
1967	Bob Scarpitto, Denver, AFL	105	44.9	73
	Billy Lothridge, Atlanta, NFL	87	43.7	62
1966	Bob Scarpitto, Denver, AFL	76	45.8	70
	*David Lee, Baltimore, NFL	49	45.6	64
1965	Gary Collins, Cleveland, NFL	65	46.7	71
	Jerrel Wilson, Kansas City, AFL	69	45.4	64
1964	Bobby Walden, Minnesota, NFL	72	46.4	73
	Jim Fraser, Denver, AFL	73	44.2	67
1963	Yale Lary, Detroit, NFL	35	48.9	73
	Jim Fraser, Denver, AFL	81	44.4	66
1962	Tommy Davis, San Francisco, NFL	48	45.6	82
	Jim Fraser, Denver, AFL	55	43.6	75
1961	Yale Lary, Detroit, NFL	52	48.4	71
	Billy Atkins, Buffalo, AFL	85	44.5	70

Year	Player, Team	No.	Avg.	Long
1960	Jerry Norton, St. Louis, NFL	39	45.6	62
	*Paul Maguire, L.A. Chargers, AFL	43	40.5	61
1959	Yale Lary, Detroit	45	47.1	67
1958	Sam Baker, Washington	48	45.4	64
1957	Don Chandler, N.Y. Giants	60	44.6	61
1956	Norm Van Brocklin, Los Angeles	48	43.1	72
1955	Norm Van Brocklin, Los Angeles	60	44.6	61
1954	Pat Brady, Pittsburgh	66	43.2	72
1953	Pat Brady, Pittsburgh	80	46.9	64
1952	Horace Gillom, Cleveland	61	45.7	73
1951	Horace Gillom, Cleveland	73	45.5	66
1950	*Fred (Curly) Morrison, Chi. Bears	57	43.3	65
1949	*Mike Boyda, N.Y. Bulldogs	56	44.2	61
1948	Joe Muha, Philadelphia	57	47.3	82
1947	Jack Jacobs, Green Bay	57	43.5	74
1946	Roy McKay, Green Bay	64	42.7	64
1945	Roy McKay, Green Bay	44	41.2	73
1944	Frank Sinkwich, Detroit	45	41.0	73
1943	Sammy Baugh, Washington	50	45.9	81
1942	Sammy Baugh, Washington	37	48.2	74
1941	Sammy Baugh, Washington	30	48.7	75
1940	Sammy Baugh, Washington	35	51.4	85
1939	*Parker Hall, Cleveland	58	40.8	80

**First season of professional football.*

ANNUAL PUNT RETURN LEADERS

Year	Player, Team	No.	Yards	Avg.	Long	TD
1998	Deion Sanders, Dallas, NFC	24	375	15.6	69	2
	Reggie Barlow, Jacksonville, AFC	43	555	12.9	85	1
1997	Jermaine Lewis, Baltimore, AFC	28	437	15.6	89	2
	David Palmer, Minnesota, NFC	34	444	13.1	57	0
1996	Desmond Howard, Green Bay, NFC	58	875	15.1	92	3
	Darrien Gordon, San Diego, AFC	36	537	14.9	81	1
1995	David Palmer, Minnesota, NFC	26	342	13.2	74	1
	Andre Coleman, San Diego, AFC	28	326	11.6	88	1
1994	Brian Mitchell, Washington, NFC	32	452	14.1	78	2
	Darrien Gordon, San Diego, AFC	36	475	13.2	90	2
1993	*Tyrone Hughes, New Orleans, NFC	37	503	13.6	83	2
	Eric Metcalf, Cleveland, AFC	36	464	12.9	91	2
1992	Johnny Bailey, Phoenix, NFC	20	263	13.2	65	0
	Rod Woodson, Pittsburgh, AFC	32	364	11.4	80	1
1991	Mel Gray, Detroit, NFC	25	385	15.4	78	1
	Rod Woodson, Pittsburgh, AFC	28	320	11.4	40	0
1990	Clarence Verdin, Indianapolis, AFC	31	396	12.8	36	0
	*Johnny Bailey, Chicago, NFC	36	399	11.1	95	1
1989	Walter Stanley, Detroit, NFC	36	496	13.8	74	0
	Clarence Verdin, Indianapolis, AFC	23	296	12.9	49	1
1988	John Taylor, San Francisco, NFC	44	556	12.6	95	2
	JoJo Townsell, N.Y. Jets, AFC	35	409	11.7	59	1
1987	Mel Gray, New Orleans, NFC	24	352	14.7	80	0
	Bobby Joe Edmonds, Seattle, AFC	20	251	12.6	40	0
1986	*Bobby Joe Edmonds, Seattle, AFC	34	419	12.3	75	1
	*Vai Sikahema, St. Louis, NFC	43	522	12.1	71	2
1985	Irving Fryar, New England, AFC	37	520	14.1	85	2
	Henry Ellard, L.A. Rams, NFC	37	501	13.5	80	1
1984	Mike Martin, Cincinnati, AFC	24	376	15.7	55	0
	Henry Ellard, L.A. Rams, NFC	30	403	13.4	83	2
1983	*Henry Ellard, L.A. Rams, NFC	16	217	13.6	72	1
	Kirk Springs, N.Y. Jets, AFC	23	287	12.5	76	1
1982	Rick Upchurch, Denver, AFC	15	242	16.1	78	2
	Billy Johnson, Atlanta, NFC	24	273	11.4	71	0
1981	LeRoy Irvin, Los Angeles, NFC	46	615	13.4	84	3
	*James Brooks, San Diego, AFC	22	290	13.2	42	0
1980	J.T. Smith, Kansas City, AFC	40	581	14.5	75	2
	*Kenny Johnson, Atlanta, NFC	23	281	12.2	56	0
1979	John Sciarra, Philadelphia, NFC	16	182	11.4	38	0
	*Tony Nathan, Miami, AFC	28	306	10.9	86	1
1978	Rick Upchurch, Denver, AFC	36	493	13.7	75	1
	Jackie Wallace, Los Angeles, NFC	52	618	11.9	58	0
1977	Billy Johnson, Houston, AFC	35	539	15.4	87	2
	Larry Marshall, Philadelphia, NFC	46	489	10.6	48	0
1976	Rick Upchurch, Denver, AFC	39	536	13.7	92	4
	Eddie Brown, Washington, NFC	48	646	13.5	71	1
1975	Billy Johnson, Houston, AFC	40	612	15.3	83	3
	Terry Metcalf, St. Louis, NFC	23	285	12.4	69	1
1974	Lemar Parrish, Cincinnati, AFC	18	338	18.8	90	2
	Dick Jauron, Detroit, NFC	17	286	16.8	58	0
1973	Bruce Taylor, San Francisco, NFC	15	207	13.8	61	0
	Ron Smith, San Diego, AFC	27	352	13.0	84	2
1972	Ken Ellis, Green Bay, NFC	14	215	15.4	80	1
	Chris Farasopoulos, N.Y. Jets, AFC	17	179	10.5	65	1
1971	Les (Speedy) Duncan, Washington, NFC	22	233	10.6	33	0
	Leroy Kelly, Cleveland, AFC	30	292	9.7	74	0
1970	Ed Podolak, Kansas City, AFC	23	311	13.5	60	0
	*Bruce Taylor, San Francisco, NFC	43	516	12.0	76	0
1969	Alvin Haymond, Los Angeles, NFL	33	435	13.2	52	0
	*Bill Thompson, Denver, AFL	25	288	11.5	40	0
1968	Bob Hayes, Dallas, NFL	15	312	20.8	90	2
	Noland Smith, Kansas City, AFL	18	270	15.0	80	1
1967	Floyd Little, Denver, AFL	16	270	16.9	72	1
	Ben Davis, Cleveland, NFL	18	229	12.7	52	1
1966	Les (Speedy) Duncan, San Diego, AFL	18	238	13.2	81	1
	Johnny Roland, St. Louis, NFL	20	221	11.1	86	1
1965	Leroy Kelly, Cleveland, NFL	17	265	15.6	67	2
	Les (Speedy) Duncan, San Diego, AFL	30	464	15.5	66	2
1964	Bobby Jancik, Houston, AFL	12	220	18.3	82	1
	Tommy Watkins, Detroit, NFL	16	238	14.9	68	2
1963	Dick James, Washington, NFL	16	214	13.4	39	0
	Claude (Hoot) Gibson, Oakland, AFL	26	307	11.8	85	2
1962	Dick Christy, N.Y. Titans, AFL	15	250	16.7	73	2
	Pat Studstill, Detroit, NFL	29	457	15.8	44	0
1961	Dick Christy, N.Y. Titans, AFL	18	383	21.3	70	2
	Willie Wood, Green Bay, NFL	14	225	16.1	72	2
1960	*Abner Haynes, Dall. Texans, AFL	14	215	15.4	46	0
	Abe Woodson, San Francisco, NFL	13	174	13.4	48	0
1959	Johnny Morris, Chi. Bears	14	171	12.2	78	1
1958	Jon Arnett, Los Angeles	18	223	12.4	58	0
1957	Bert Zagers, Washington	14	217	15.5	76	2
1956	Ken Konz, Cleveland	13	187	14.4	65	1
1955	Ollie Matson, Chi. Cardinals	13	245	18.8	78	2
1954	*Veryl Switzer, Green Bay	24	306	12.8	93	1
1953	Charley Trippi, Chi. Cardinals	21	239	11.4	38	0
1952	Jack Christiansen, Detroit	15	322	21.5	79	2
1951	Claude (Buddy) Young, N.Y. Yanks	12	231	19.3	79	1
1950	*Herb Rich, Baltimore	12	276	23.0	86	1
1949	Verda (Vitamin T) Smith, Los Angeles	27	427	15.8	85	1
1948	George McAfee, Chi. Bears	30	417	13.9	60	1
1947	*Walt Slater, Pittsburgh	28	435	15.5	33	0
1946	Bill Dudley, Pittsburgh	27	385	14.3	52	0
1945	*Dave Ryan, Detroit	15	220	14.7	56	0
1944	*Steve Van Buren, Philadelphia	15	230	15.3	55	1
1943	Andy Farkas, Washington	15	168	11.2	33	0
1942	Merlyn Condit, Brooklyn	21	210	10.0	23	0
1941	Byron (Whizzer) White, Detroit	19	262	13.8	64	0

**First season of professional football.*

ANNUAL KICKOFF RETURN LEADERS

Year	Player, Team	No.	Yards	Avg.	Long	TD
1998	*Terry Fair, Detroit, NFC	51	1,428	28.0	105	2
	Corey Harris, Baltimore, AFC	35	965	27.6	95	1
1997	Michael Bates, Carolina, NFC	47	1,281	27.3	56	0
	Aaron Glenn, N.Y. Jets, AFC	28	741	26.5	96	1
1996	Michael Bates, Carolina, NFC	33	998	30.2	93	1
	Tamarick Vanover, Kansas City, AFC	33	854	25.9	97	1
1995	Ron Carpenter, N.Y. Jets, AFC	20	553	27.7	58	0
	Brian Mitchell, Washington, NFC	55	1,408	25.6	59	0
1994	Mel Gray, Detroit, NFC	45	1,276	28.4	102	3
	Randy Baldwin, Cleveland, AFC	28	753	26.9	85	1
1993	Robert Brooks, Green Bay, NFC	23	611	26.6	95	1
	*Raghib Ismail, L.A. Raiders, AFC	25	605	24.2	66	0
1992	Jon Vaughn, New England, AFC	20	564	28.2	100	1
	Deion Sanders, Atlanta, NFC	40	1,067	26.7	99	2
1991	Mel Gray, Detroit, NFC	36	929	25.8	71	0
	Nate Lewis, San Diego, AFC	23	578	25.1	95	1
1990	Kevin Clark, Denver, AFC	20	505	25.3	75	0
	David Meggett, N.Y. Giants, NFC	21	492	23.4	58	0
1989	Rod Woodson, Pittsburgh, AFC	36	982	27.3	84	1
	Mel Gray, Detroit, NFC	24	640	26.7	57	0
1988	*Tim Brown, L.A. Raiders, AFC	41	1,098	26.8	97	1
	Donnie Elder, Tampa Bay, NFC	34	772	22.7	51	0
1987	Sylvester Stamps, Atlanta, NFC	24	660	27.5	97	1
	Paul Palmer, Kansas City, AFC	38	923	24.3	95	2
1986	Dennis Gentry, Chicago, NFC	20	576	28.8	91	1
	Lupe Sanchez, Pittsburgh, AFC	25	591	23.6	64	0
1985	Ron Brown, L.A. Rams, NFC	28	918	32.8	98	3
	Glen Young, Cleveland, AFC	35	898	25.7	63	0
1984	*Bobby Humphery, N.Y. Jets, AFC	22	675	30.7	97	1
	Barry Redden, L.A. Rams, NFC	23	530	23.0	40	0
1983	Fulton Walker, Miami, AFC	36	962	26.7	78	0
	Darrin Nelson, Minnesota, NFC	18	445	24.7	50	0
1982	*Mike Mosley, Buffalo, AFC	18	487	27.1	66	0
	Alvin Hall, Detroit, NFC	16	426	26.6	96	1
1981	Mike Nelms, Washington, NFC	37	1,099	29.7	84	0
	Carl Roaches, Houston, AFC	28	769	27.5	96	1
1980	Horace Ivory, New England, AFC	36	992	27.6	98	1
	Rich Mauti, New Orleans, NFC	31	798	25.7	52	0

YEARLY STATISTICAL LEADERS

1979	Larry Brunson, Oakland, AFC	17	441	25.9	89	0
	Jimmy Edwards, Minnesota, NFC	44	1,103	25.1	83	0
1978	Steve Odom, Green Bay, NFC	25	677	27.1	95	1
	*Keith Wright, Cleveland, AFC	30	789	26.3	86	0
1977	*Raymond Clayborn, New England, AFC	28	869	31.0	101	3
	*Wilbert Montgomery, Philadelphia, NFC	23	619	26.9	99	1
1976	*Duriel Harris, Miami, AFC	17	559	32.9	69	0
	Cullen Bryant, Los Angeles, NFC	16	459	28.7	90	1
1975	*Walter Payton, Chicago, NFC	14	444	31.7	70	0
	Harold Hart, Oakland, AFC	17	518	30.5	102	1
1974	Terry Metcalf, St. Louis, NFC	20	623	31.2	94	1
	Greg Pruitt, Cleveland, AFC	22	606	27.5	88	1
1973	Carl Garrett, Chicago, NFC	16	486	30.4	67	0
	*Wallace Francis, Buffalo, AFC	23	687	29.9	101	2
1972	Ron Smith, Chicago, NFC	30	924	30.8	94	1
	*Bruce Laird, Baltimore, AFC	29	843	29.1	73	0
1971	Travis Williams, Los Angeles, NFC	25	743	29.7	105	1
	Eugene (Mercury) Morris, Miami, AFC	15	423	28.2	94	1
1970	Jim Duncan, Baltimore, AFC	20	707	35.4	99	1
	Cecil Turner, Chicago, NFC	23	752	32.7	96	4
1969	Bobby Williams, Detroit, NFL	17	563	33.1	96	1
	*Bill Thompson, Denver, AFL	18	513	28.5	63	0
1968	Preston Pearson, Baltimore, NFL	15	527	35.1	102	2
	*George Atkinson, Oakland, AFL	32	802	25.1	60	0
1967	*Travis Williams, Green Bay, NFL	18	739	41.1	104	4
	*Zeke Moore, Houston, AFL	14	405	28.9	92	1
1966	Gale Sayers, Chicago, NFL	23	718	31.2	93	2
	*Goldie Sellers, Denver, AFL	19	541	28.5	100	2
1965	Tommy Watkins, Detroit, NFL	17	584	34.4	94	0
	Abner Haynes, Denver, AFL	34	901	26.5	60	0
1964	*Clarence Childs, N.Y. Giants, NFL	34	987	29.0	100	1
	Bo Roberson, Oakland, AFL	36	975	27.1	59	0
1963	Abe Woodson, San Francisco, NFL	29	935	32.2	103	3
	Bobby Jancik, Houston, AFL	45	1,317	29.3	53	0
1962	Abe Woodson, San Francisco, NFL	37	1,157	31.3	79	0
	*Bobby Jancik, Houston, AFL	24	826	30.3	61	0
1961	Dick Bass, Los Angeles, NFL	23	698	30.3	64	0
	*Dave Grayson, Dall. Texans, AFL	16	453	28.3	73	0
1960	*Tom Moore, Green Bay, NFL	12	397	33.1	84	0
	Ken Hall, Houston, AFL	19	594	31.3	104	1
1959	Abe Woodson, San Francisco	13	382	29.4	105	1
1958	Ollie Matson, Chi. Cardinals	14	497	35.5	101	2
1957	*Jon Arnett, Los Angeles	18	504	28.0	98	1
1956	*Tom Wilson, Los Angeles	15	477	31.8	103	1
1955	Al Carmichael, Green Bay	14	418	29.9	100	1
1954	Billy Reynolds, Cleveland	14	413	29.5	51	0
1953	Joe Arenas, San Francisco	16	551	34.4	82	0
1952	Lynn Chandnois, Pittsburgh	17	599	35.2	93	2
1951	Lynn Chandnois, Pittsburgh	12	390	32.5	55	0
1950	Verda (Vitamin T) Smith, Los Angeles	22	742	33.7	97	3
1949	*Don Doll, Detroit	21	536	25.5	56	0
1948	*Joe Scott, N.Y. Giants	20	569	28.5	99	1
1947	Eddie Saenz, Washington	29	797	27.5	94	2
1946	Abe Karnofsky, Boston	21	599	28.5	97	1
1945	Steve Van Buren, Philadelphia	13	373	28.7	98	1
1944	Bob Thurbon, Card.-Pitt.	12	291	24.3	55	0
1943	Ken Heineman, Brooklyn	16	444	27.8	69	0
1942	Marshall Goldberg, Chi. Cardinals	15	393	26.2	95	1
1941	Marshall Goldberg, Chi. Cardinals	12	290	24.2	41	0

**First season of professional football.*

ANNUAL LEADERS IN SACKS (SINCE 1982)

Year	Player, Team	Sacks
1998	Michael Sinclair, Seattle, AFC	16.5
	Reggie White, Green Bay, NFC	16
1997	John Randle, Minnesota, NFC	15.5
	Bruce Smith, Buffalo, AFC	14
1996	Kevin Greene, Carolina, NFC	14.5
	Michael McCrary, Seattle, AFC	13.5
	Bruce Smith, Buffalo, AFC	13.5
1995	Bryce Paup, Buffalo, AFC	17.5
	William Fuller, Philadelphia, NFC	13
	Wayne Martin, New Orleans, NFC	13
1994	Kevin Greene, Pittsburgh, AFC	14
	Ken Harvey, Washington, NFC	13.5
	John Randle, Minnesota, NFC	13.5
1993	Neil Smith, Kansas City, AFC	15
	Renaldo Turnbull, New Orleans, NFC	13
	Reggie White, Green Bay, NFC	13
1992	Clyde Simmons, Philadelphia, NFC	19
	Leslie O'Neal, San Diego, AFC	17
1991	Pat Swilling, New Orleans, NFC	17
	William Fuller, Houston, AFC	15
1990	Derrick Thomas, Kansas City, AFC	20
	Charles Haley, San Francisco, NFC	16
1989	Chris Doleman, Minnesota, NFC	21
	Lee Williams, San Diego, AFC	14
1988	Reggie White, Philadelphia, NFC	18
	G. Townsend, L.A. Raiders, AFC	11.5
1987	Reggie White, Philadelphia, NFC	21
	Andre Tippett, New England, AFC	12.5
1986	Lawrence Taylor, N.Y. Giants, NFC	20.5
	Sean Jones, L.A. Raiders, AFC	15.5
1985	Richard Dent, Chicago, NFC	17
	Andre Tippett, New England, AFC	16.5
1984	Mark Gastineau, N.Y. Jets, AFC	22
	Richard Dent, Chicago, NFC	17.5
1983	Mark Gastineau, N.Y. Jets, AFC	19
	Fred Dean, San Francisco, NFC	17.5
1982	Doug Martin, Minnesota, NFC	11.5
	Jesse Baker, Houston, AFC	7.5

POINTS SCORED

Year	Team	Points
1998	Minnesota, NFC	556
	Denver, AFC	501
1997	Denver, AFC	472
	Green Bay, NFC	422
1996	Green Bay, NFC	456
	New England, AFC	418
1995	San Francisco, NFC	457
	Pittsburgh, AFC	407
1994	San Francisco, NFC	505
	Miami, AFC	389
1993	San Francisco, NFC	473
	Denver, AFC	373
1992	San Francisco, NFC	431
	Buffalo, AFC	381
1991	Washington, NFC	485
	Buffalo, AFC	458
1990	Buffalo, AFC	428
	Philadelphia, NFC	396
1989	San Francisco, NFC	442
	Buffalo, AFC	409
1988	Cincinnati, AFC	448
	L.A. Rams, NFC	407
1987	San Francisco, NFC	459
	Cleveland, AFC	390
1986	Miami, AFC	430
	Minnesota, NFC	398
1985	San Diego, AFC	467
	Chicago, NFC	456
1984	Miami, AFC	513
	San Francisco, NFC	475
1983	Washington, NFC	541
	L.A. Raiders, AFC	442
1982	San Diego, AFC	288
	Dallas, NFC	226
	Green Bay, NFC	226
1981	San Diego, AFC	478
	Atlanta, NFC	426
1980	Dallas, NFC	454
	New England, AFC	441
1979	Pittsburgh, AFC	416
	Dallas, NFC	371
1978	Dallas, NFC	384
	Miami, AFC	372
1977	Oakland, AFC	351
	Dallas, NFC	345
1976	Baltimore, AFC	417
	Los Angeles, NFC	351
1975	Buffalo, AFC	420
	Minnesota, NFC	377
1974	Oakland, AFC	355
	Washington, NFC	320
1973	Los Angeles, NFC	388
	Denver, AFC	354
1972	Miami, AFC	385
	San Francisco, NFC	353
1971	Dallas, NFC	406
	Oakland, AFC	344
1970	San Francisco, NFC	352
	Baltimore, AFC	321
1969	Minnesota, NFL	379
	Oakland, AFL	377
1968	Oakland, AFL	453
	Dallas, NFL	431
1967	Oakland, AFL	468
	Los Angeles, NFL	398
1966	Kansas City, AFL	448
	Dallas, NFL	445
1965	San Francisco, NFL	421
	San Diego, AFL	340
1964	Baltimore, NFL	428
	Buffalo, AFL	400
1963	N.Y. Giants, NFL	448
	San Diego, AFL	399
1962	Green Bay, NFL	415
	Dall. Texans, AFL	389
1961	Houston, AFL	513
	Green Bay, NFL	391
1960	N.Y. Titans, AFL	382
	Cleveland, NFL	362
1959	Baltimore	374
1958	Baltimore	381
1957	Los Angeles	307
1956	Chi. Bears	363
1955	Cleveland	349
1954	Detroit	337
1953	San Francisco	372
1952	Los Angeles	349
1951	Los Angeles	392
1950	Los Angeles	466
1949	Philadelphia	364
1948	Chi. Cardinals	395
1947	Chi. Bears	363
1946	Chi. Bears	289
1945	Philadelphia	272
1944	Philadelphia	267
1943	Chi. Bears	303
1942	Chi. Bears	376
1941	Chi. Bears	396
1940	Washington	245
1939	Chi. Bears	298
1938	Green Bay	223
1937	Green Bay	220
1936	Green Bay	248
1935	Chi. Bears	192
1934	Chi. Bears	286
1933	N.Y. Giants	244
1932	Chicago Bears	160

TOTAL YARDS GAINED

Year	Team	Yards
1998	San Francisco, NFC	6,800
	Denver, AFC	6,092
1997	Denver, AFC	5,872
	Detroit, NFC	5,798
1996	Denver, AFC	5,791
	Philadelphia, NFC	5,627
1995	Detroit, NFC	6,113
	Denver, AFC	6,040
1994	Miami, AFC	6,078
	San Francisco, NFC	6,060
1993	San Francisco, NFC	6,435
	Miami, AFC	5,812
1992	San Francisco, NFC	6,195
	Buffalo, AFC	5,893

Year	Team	Yards
1991	Buffalo, AFC	6,252
	San Francisco, NFC	5,858
1990	Houston, AFC	6,222
	San Francisco, NFC	5,895
1989	San Francisco, NFC	6,268
	Cincinnati, AFC	6,101
1988	Cincinnati, AFC	6,057
	San Francisco, NFC	5,900
1987	San Francisco, NFC	5,987
	Denver, AFC	5,624
1986	Cincinnati, AFC	6,490
	San Francisco, NFC	6,082
1985	San Diego, AFC	6,535
	San Francisco, NFC	5,920
1984	Miami, AFC	6,936
	San Francisco, NFC	6,366
1983	San Diego, AFC	6,197
	Green Bay, NFC	6,172
1982	San Diego, AFC	4,048
	San Francisco, NFC	3,242
1981	San Diego, AFC	6,744
	Detroit, NFC	5,933
1980	San Diego, AFC	6,410
	Los Angeles, NFC	6,006
1979	Pittsburgh, AFC	6,258
	Dallas, NFC	5,968
1978	New England, AFC	5,965
	Dallas, NFC	5,959
1977	Dallas, NFC	4,812
	Oakland, AFC	4,736
1976	Baltimore, AFC	5,236
	St. Louis, NFC	5,136
1975	Buffalo, AFC	5,467
	Dallas, NFC	5,025
1974	Dallas, NFC	4,983
	Oakland, AFC	4,718
1973	Los Angeles, NFC	4,906
	Oakland, AFC	4,773
1972	Miami, AFC	5,036
	N.Y. Giants, NFC	4,483
1971	Dallas, NFC	5,035
	San Diego, AFC	4,738
1970	Oakland, AFC	4,829
	San Francisco, NFC	4,503
1969	Dallas, NFL	5,122
	Oakland, AFL	5,036
1968	Oakland, AFL	5,696
	Dallas, NFL	5,117
1967	N.Y. Jets, AFL	5,152
	Baltimore, NFL	5,008
1966	Dallas, NFL	5,145
	Kansas City, AFL	5,114
1965	San Francisco, NFL	5,270
	San Diego, AFL	5,188
1964	Buffalo, AFL	5,206
	Baltimore, NFL	4,779
1963	San Diego, AFL	5,153
	N.Y. Giants, NFL	5,024
1962	N.Y. Giants, NFL	5,005
	Houston, AFL	4,971
1961	Houston, AFL	6,288
	Philadelphia, NFL	5,112
1960	Houston, AFL	4,936
	Baltimore, NFL	4,245
1959	Baltimore	4,458
1958	Baltimore	4,539
1957	Los Angeles	4,143
1956	Chi. Bears	4,537
1955	Chi. Bears	4,316
1954	Los Angeles	5,187
1953	Philadelphia	4,811
1952	Cleveland	4,352
1951	Los Angeles	5,506
1950	Los Angeles	5,420
1949	Chi. Bears	4,873
1948	Chi. Cardinals	4,705
1947	Chi. Bears	5,053
1946	Los Angeles	3,793
1945	Washington	3,549
1944	Chi. Bears	3,239
1943	Chi. Bears	4,045
1942	Chi. Bears	3,900
1941	Chi. Bears	4,265
1940	Green Bay	3,400
1939	Chi. Bears	3,988
1938	Green Bay	3,037
1937	Green Bay	3,201
1936	Detroit	3,703
1935	Chi. Bears	3,454
1934	Chi. Bears	3,900
1933	N.Y. Giants	2,973
1932	Chi. Bears	2,755

YARDS RUSHING

Year	Team	Yards
1998	San Francisco, NFC	2,544
	Denver, AFC	2,468
1997	Pittsburgh, AFC	2,479
	Detroit, NFC	2,464
1996	Denver, AFC	2,362
	Washington, NFC	1,910
1995	Kansas City, AFC	2,222
	Dallas, NFC	2,201
1994	Pittsburgh, AFC	2,180
	Detroit, NFC	2,080
1993	N.Y. Giants, NFC	2,210
	Seattle, AFC	2,015
1992	Buffalo, AFC	2,436
	Philadelphia, NFC	2,388
1991	Buffalo, AFC	2,381
	Minnesota, NFC	2,201
1990	Philadelphia, NFC	2,556
	San Diego, AFC	2,257
1989	Cincinnati, AFC	2,483
	Chicago, NFC	2,287
1988	Cincinnati, AFC	2,710
	San Francisco, NFC	2,523
1987	San Francisco, NFC	2,237
	L.A. Raiders, AFC	2,197
1986	Chicago, NFC	2,700
	Cincinnati, AFC	2,533
1985	Chicago, NFC	2,761
	Indianapolis, AFC	2,439
1984	Chicago, NFC	2,974
	N.Y. Jets, AFC	2,189
1983	Chicago, NFC	2,727
	Baltimore, AFC	2,695
1982	Buffalo, AFC	1,371
	Dallas, NFC	1,313
1981	Detroit, NFC	2,795
	Kansas City, AFC	2,633
1980	Los Angeles, NFC	2,799
	Houston, AFC	2,635
1979	N.Y. Jets, AFC	2,646
	St. Louis, NFC	2,582
1978	New England, AFC	3,165
	Dallas, NFC	2,783
1977	Chicago, NFC	2,811
	Oakland, AFC	2,627
1976	Pittsburgh, AFC	2,971
	Los Angeles, NFC	2,528
1975	Buffalo, AFC	2,974
	Dallas, NFC	2,432
1974	Dallas, NFC	2,454
	Pittsburgh, AFC	2,417
1973	Buffalo, AFC	3,088
	Los Angeles, NFC	2,925
1972	Miami, AFC	2,960
	Chicago, NFC	2,360
1971	Miami, AFC	2,429
	Detroit, NFC	2,376
1970	Dallas, NFC	2,300
	Miami, AFC	2,082
1969	Dallas, NFL	2,276
	Kansas City, AFL	2,220
1968	Chicago, NFL	2,377
	Kansas City, AFL	2,227
1967	Cleveland, NFL	2,139
	Houston, AFL	2,122
1966	Kansas City, AFL	2,274
	Cleveland, NFL	2,166
1965	Cleveland, NFL	2,331
	San Diego, AFL	2,085
1964	Green Bay, NFL	2,276
	Buffalo, AFL	2,040
1963	Cleveland, NFL	2,639
	San Diego, AFL	2,203
1962	Buffalo, AFL	2,480
	Green Bay, NFL	2,460
1961	Green Bay, NFL	2,350
	Dall. Texans, AFL	2,189
1960	St. Louis, NFL	2,356
	Oakland, AFL	2,056
1959	Cleveland	2,149
1958	Cleveland	2,526
1957	Los Angeles	2,142
1956	Chi. Bears	2,468
1955	Chi. Bears	2,388
1954	San Francisco	2,498
1953	San Francisco	2,230
1952	San Francisco	1,905
1951	Chi. Bears	2,408
1950	N.Y. Giants	2,336
1949	Philadelphia	2,607
1948	Chi. Cardinals	2,560
1947	Los Angeles	2,171
1946	Green Bay	1,765
1945	Cleveland	1,714
1944	Philadelphia	1,661
1943	Phil-Pitt	1,730
1942	Chi. Bears	1,881
1941	Chi. Bears	2,263
1940	Chi. Bears	1,818
1939	Chi. Bears	2,043
1938	Detroit	1,893
1937	Detroit	2,074
1936	Detroit	2,885
1935	Chi. Bears	2,096
1934	Chi. Bears	2,847
1933	Boston	2,260
1932	Chi. Bears	1,770

YARDS PASSING

Leadership in this category has been based on net yards since 1952.

Year	Team	Yards
1998	Minnesota, NFC	4,328
	N.Y. Jets, AFC	3,836
1997	Seattle, AFC	3,959
	Green Bay, NFC	3,705
1996	Jacksonville, AFC	4,110
	Philadelphia, NFC	3,745
1995	San Francisco, NFC	4,608
	Miami, AFC	4,210
1994	New England, AFC	4,444
	Minnesota, NFC	4,324
1993	Miami, AFC	4,353
	San Francisco, NFC	4,302
1992	Houston, AFC	4,029
	San Francisco, NFC	3,880
1991	Houston, AFC	4,621
	San Francisco, NFC	3,997
1990	Houston, AFC	4,805
	San Francisco, NFC	4,177
1989	Washington, NFC	4,349
	Miami, AFC	4,216
1988	Miami, AFC	4,516
	Washington, NFC	4,136
1987	Miami, AFC	3,876
	San Francisco, NFC	3,750
1986	Miami, AFC	4,779
	San Francisco, NFC	4,096
1985	San Diego, AFC	4,870
	Dallas, NFC	3,861
1984	Miami, AFC	5,018
	St. Louis, NFC	4,257
1983	San Diego, AFC	4,661
	Green Bay, NFC	4,365
1982	San Diego, AFC	2,927
	San Francisco, NFC	2,502
1981	San Diego, AFC	4,739
	Minnesota, NFC	4,333
1980	San Diego, AFC	4,531
	Minnesota, NFC	3,688
1979	San Diego, AFC	3,915
	San Francisco, NFC	3,641
1978	San Diego, AFC	3,375
	Minnesota, NFC	3,243
1977	Buffalo, AFC	2,530
	St. Louis, NFC	2,499
1976	Baltimore, AFC	2,933
	Minnesota, NFC	2,855
1975	Cincinnati, AFC	3,241
	Washington, NFC	2,917
1974	Washington, NFC	2,978
	Cincinnati, AFC	2,804
1973	Philadelphia, NFC	2,998
	Denver, AFC	2,519
1972	N.Y. Jets, AFC	2,777
	San Francisco, NFC	2,735
1971	San Diego, AFC	3,134
	Dallas, NFC	2,786
1970	San Francisco, NFC	2,923
	Oakland, AFC	2,865
1969	Oakland, AFL	3,271
	San Francisco, NFL	3,158
1968	San Diego, AFL	3,623
	Dallas, NFL	3,026
1967	N.Y. Jets, AFL	3,845
	Washington, NFL	3,730
1966	N.Y. Jets, AFL	3,464
	Dallas, NFL	3,023
1965	San Francisco, NFL	3,487
	San Diego, AFL	3,103
1964	Houston, AFL	3,527
	Chicago, NFL	2,841
1963	Baltimore, NFL	3,296
	Houston, AFL	3,222
1962	Denver, AFL	3,404
	Philadelphia, NFL	3,385
1961	Houston, AFL	4,392
	Philadelphia, NFL	3,605
1960	Houston, AFL	3,203
	Baltimore, NFL	2,956
1959	Baltimore	2,753
1958	Pittsburgh	2,752
1957	Baltimore	2,388
1956	Los Angeles	2,419
1955	Philadelphia	2,472
1954	Chi. Bears	3,104
1953	Philadelphia	3,089
1952	Cleveland	2,566
1951	Los Angeles	3,296
1950	Los Angeles	3,709
1949	Chi. Bears	3,055
1948	Washington	2,861
1947	Washington	3,336
1946	Los Angeles	2,080
1945	Chi. Bears	1,857
1944	Washington	2,021
1943	Chi. Bears	2,310
1942	Green Bay	2,407
1941	Chi. Bears	2,002
1940	Washington	1,887
1939	Chi. Bears	1,965
1938	Washington	1,536
1937	Green Bay	1,398
1936	Green Bay	1,629
1935	Green Bay	1,449
1934	Green Bay	1,165
1933	N.Y. Giants	1,348
1932	Chi. Bears	1,013

FEWEST POINTS ALLOWED

Year	Team	Points
1998	Miami, AFC	265
	Dallas, NFC	275
1997	Kansas City, AFC	232
	Tampa Bay, NFC	263
1996	Green Bay, NFC	210
	Pittsburgh, AFC	257
1995	Kansas City, AFC	241
	San Francisco, NFC	258
1994	Cleveland, AFC	204
	Dallas, NFC	248
1993	N.Y. Giants, NFC	205
	Houston, AFC	238
1992	New Orleans, NFC	202
	Pittsburgh, AFC	225

Year	Team	Points
1991	New Orleans, NFC	211
	Denver, AFC	235
1990	N.Y. Giants, NFC	211
	Pittsburgh, AFC	240
1989	Denver, AFC	226
	N.Y. Giants, NFC	252
1988	Chicago, NFC	215
	Buffalo, AFC	237
1987	Indianapolis, AFC	238
	San Francisco, NFC	253
1986	Chicago, NFC	187
	Seattle, AFC	293
1985	Chicago, NFC	198
	N.Y. Jets, AFC	264
1984	San Francisco, NFC	227
	Denver, AFC	241
1983	Miami, AFC	250
	Detroit, NFC	286
1982	Washington, NFC	128
	Miami, AFC	131
1981	Philadelphia, NFC	221
	Miami, AFC	275
1980	Philadelphia, NFC	222
	Houston, AFC	251
1979	Tampa Bay, NFC	237
	San Diego, AFC	246
1978	Pittsburgh, AFC	195
	Dallas, NFC	208
1977	Atlanta, NFC	129
	Denver, AFC	148
1976	Pittsburgh, AFC	138
	Minnesota, NFC	176
1975	Los Angeles, NFC	135
	Pittsburgh, AFC	162
1974	Los Angeles, NFC	181
	Pittsburgh, AFC	189
1973	Miami, AFC	150
	Minnesota, NFC	168
1972	Miami, AFC	171
	Washington, NFC	218
1971	Minnesota, NFC	139
	Baltimore, AFC	140
1970	Minnesota, NFC	143
	Miami, AFC	228
1969	Minnesota, NFL	133
	Kansas City, AFL	177
1968	Baltimore, NFL	144
	Kansas City, AFL	170
1967	Los Angeles, NFL	196
	Houston, AFL	199
1966	Green Bay, NFL	163
	Buffalo, AFL	255
1965	Green Bay, NFL	224
	Buffalo, AFL	226
1964	Baltimore, NFL	225
	Buffalo, AFL	242
1963	Chicago, NFL	144
	San Diego, AFL	255
1962	Green Bay, NFL	148
	Dall. Texans, AFL	233
1961	San Diego, AFL	219
	N.Y. Giants, NFL	220
1960	San Francisco, NFL	205
	Dall. Texans, AFL	253
1959	N.Y. Giants	170
1958	N.Y. Giants	183
1957	Cleveland	172
1956	Cleveland	177
1955	Cleveland	218
1954	Cleveland	162
1953	Cleveland	162
1952	Detroit	192
1951	Cleveland	152
1950	Philadelphia	141
1949	Philadelphia	134
1948	Chi. Bears	151
1947	Green Bay	210
1946	Pittsburgh	117
1945	Washington	121
1944	N.Y. Giants	75
1943	Washington	137
1942	Chi. Bears	84
1941	N.Y. Giants	114
1940	Brooklyn	120
1939	N.Y. Giants	85
1938	N.Y. Giants	79
1937	Chi. Bears	100
1936	Chi. Bears	94
1935	Green Bay	96
	N.Y. Giants	96
1934	Detroit	59
1933	Brooklyn	54
1932	Chi. Bears	44

FEWEST TOTAL YARDS ALLOWED

Year	Team	Yards
1998	San Diego, AFC	4,208
	Tampa Bay, NFC	4,345
1997	San Francisco, NFC	4,013
	Denver, AFC	4,671
1996	Greem Bay, NFC	4,156
	Pittsburgh, AFC	4,362
1995	San Francisco, NFC	4,398
	Kansas City, AFC	4,549
1994	Dallas, NFC	4,313
	Pittsburgh, AFC	4,326
1993	Minnesota, NFC	4,406
	Pittsburgh, AFC	4,531
1992	Dallas, NFC	3,931
	Houston, AFC	4,211
1991	Philadelphia, NFC	3,549
	Denver, AFC	4,549
1990	Pittsburgh, AFC	4,115
	N.Y. Giants, NFC	4,206
1989	Minnesota, NFC	4,184
	Kansas City, AFC	4,293
1988	Minnesota, NFC	4,091
	Buffalo, AFC	4,578
1987	San Francisco, NFC	4,095
	Cleveland, AFC	4,264
1986	Chicago, NFC	4,130
	L.A. Raiders, AFC	4,804
1985	Chicago, NFC	4,135
	L.A. Raiders, AFC	4,603
1984	Chicago, NFC	3,863
	Cleveland, AFC	4,641
1983	Cincinnati, AFC	4,327
	New Orleans, NFC	4,691
1982	Miami, AFC	2,312
	Tampa Bay, NFC	2,442
1981	Philadelphia, NFC	4,447
	N.Y. Jets, AFC	4,871
1980	Buffalo, AFC	4,101
	Philadelphia, NFC	4,443
1979	Tampa Bay, NFC	3,949
	Pittsburgh, AFC	4,270
1978	Los Angeles, NFC	3,893
	Pittsburgh, AFC	4,168
1977	Dallas, NFC	3,213
	New England, AFC	3,638
1976	Pittsburgh, AFC	3,323
	San Francisco, NFC	3,562
1975	Minnesota, NFC	3,153
	Oakland, AFC	3,629
1974	Pittsburgh, AFC	3,074
	Washington, NFC	3,285
1973	Los Angeles, NFC	2,951
	Oakland, AFC	3,160
1972	Miami, AFC	3,297
	Green Bay, NFC	3,474
1971	Baltimore, AFC	2,852
	Minnesota, NFC	3,406
1970	Minnesota, NFC	2,803
	N.Y. Jets, AFC	3,655
1969	Minnesota, NFL	2,720
	Kansas City, AFL	3,163
1968	Los Angeles, NFL	3,118
	N.Y. Jets, AFL	3,363
1967	Oakland, AFL	3,294
	Green Bay, NFL	3,300
1966	St. Louis, NFL	3,492
	Oakland, AFL	3,910
1965	San Diego, AFL	3,262
	Detroit, NFL	3,557
1964	Green Bay, NFL	3,179
	Buffalo, AFL	3,878
1963	Chicago, NFL	3,176
	Boston, AFL	3,834
1962	Detroit, NFL	3,217
	Dall. Texans, AFL	3,951
1961	San Diego, AFL	3,726
	Baltimore, NFL	3,782
1960	St. Louis, NFL	3,029
	Buffalo, AFL	3,866
1959	N.Y. Giants	2,843
1958	Chi. Bears	3,066
1957	Pittsburgh	2,791
1956	N.Y. Giants	3,081
1955	Cleveland	2,841
1954	Cleveland	2,658
1953	Philadelphia	2,998
1952	Cleveland	3,075
1951	N.Y. Giants	3,250
1950	Cleveland	3,154
1949	Philadelphia	2,831
1948	Chi. Bears	2,931
1947	Green Bay	3,396
1946	Washington	2,451
1945	Philadelphia	2,073
1944	Philadelphia	1,943
1943	Chi. Bears	2,262
1942	Chi. Bears	1,703
1941	N.Y. Giants	2,368
1940	N.Y. Giants	2,219
1939	Washington	2,116
1938	N.Y. Giants	2,029
1937	Washington	2,123
1936	Boston	2,181
1935	Boston	1,996
1934	Chi. Cardinals	1,539
1933	Brooklyn	1,789

FEWEST RUSHING YARDS ALLOWED

Year	Team	Yards
1998	San Diego, AFC	1,140
	Atlanta, NFC	1,203
1997	Pittsburgh, AFC	1,318
	San Francisco, NFC	1,366
1996	Denver, AFC	1,331
	Green Bay, NFC	1,416
1995	San Francisco, NFC	1,061
	Pittsburgh, AFC	1,321
1994	Minnesota, NFC	1,090
	San Diego, AFC	1,404
1993	Houston, AFC	1,273
	Minnesota, NFC	1,536
1992	Dallas, NFC	1,244
	Buffalo, AFC	1,395
	San Diego, AFC	1,395
1991	Philadelphia, NFC	1,136
	N.Y. Jets, AFC	1,442
1990	Philadelphia, NFC	1,169
	San Diego, AFC	1,515
1989	New Orleans, NFC	1,326
	Denver, AFC	1,580
1988	Chicago, NFC	1,326
	Houston, AFC	1,592
1987	Chicago, NFC	1,413
	Cleveland, AFC	1,433
1986	N.Y. Giants, NFC	1,284
	Denver, AFC	1,651
1985	Chicago, NFC	1,319
	N.Y. Jets, AFC	1,516
1984	Chicago, NFC	1,377
	Pittsburgh, AFC	1,617
1983	Washington, NFC	1,289
	Cincinnati, AFC	1,499
1982	Pittsburgh, AFC	762
	Detroit, NFC	854
1981	Detroit, NFC	1,623
	Kansas City, AFC	1,747
1980	Detroit, NFC	1,599
	Cincinnati, AFC	1,680
1979	Denver, AFC	1,693
	Tampa Bay, NFC	1,873
1978	Dallas, NFC	1,721
	Pittsburgh, AFC	1,774
1977	Denver, AFC	1,531
	Dallas, NFC	1,651
1976	Pittsburgh, AFC	1,457
	Los Angeles, NFC	1,564
1975	Minnesota, NFC	1,532
	Houston, AFC	1,680
1974	Los Angeles, NFC	1,302
	New England, AFC	1,587
1973	Los Angeles, NFC	1,270
	Oakland, AFC	1,470
1972	Dallas, NFC	1,515
	Miami, AFC	1,548
1971	Baltimore, AFC	1,113
	Dallas, NFC	1,144
1970	Detroit, NFC	1,152
	N.Y. Jets, AFC	1,283
1969	Dallas, NFL	1,050
	Kansas City, AFL	1,091
1968	Dallas, NFL	1,195
	N.Y. Jets, AFL	1,195
1967	Dallas, NFL	1,081
	Oakland, AFL	1,129
1966	Buffalo, AFL	1,051
	Dallas, NFL	1,176
1965	San Diego, AFL	1,094
	Los Angeles, NFL	1,409
1964	Buffalo, AFL	913
	Los Angeles, NFL	1,501
1963	Boston, AFL	1,107
	Chicago, NFL	1,442
1962	Detroit, NFL	1,231
	Dall. Texans, AFL	1,250
1961	Boston, AFL	1,041
	Pittsburgh, NFL	1,463
1960	St. Louis, NFL	1,212
	Dall. Texans, AFL	1,338
1959	N.Y. Giants	1,261
1958	Baltimore	1,291
1957	Baltimore	1,174
1956	N.Y. Giants	1,443
1955	Cleveland	1,189
1954	Cleveland	1,050
1953	Philadelphia	1,117
1952	Detroit	1,145
1951	N.Y. Giants	913
1950	Detroit	1,367
1949	Chi. Bears	1,196
1948	Philadelphia	1,209
1947	Philadelphia	1,329
1946	Chi. Bears	1,060
1945	Philadelphia	817
1944	Philadelphia	558
1943	Phil-Pitt	793
1942	Chi. Bears	519
1941	Washington	1,042
1940	N.Y. Giants	977
1939	Chi. Bears	812
1938	Detroit	1,081
1937	Chi. Bears	933
1936	Boston	1,148
1935	Boston	998
1934	Chi. Cardinals	954
1933	Brooklyn	964

FEWEST PASSING YARDS ALLOWED

Leadership in this category has been based on net yards since 1952.

Year	Team	Yards
1998	Philadelphia, NFC	2,720
	Oakland, AFC	2,876
1997	Dallas, NFC	2,522
	Indianapolis, AFC	2,820
1996	Green Bay, NFC	2,740
	Pittsburgh, AFC	2,947
1995	N.Y. Jets, AFC	2,740
	Philadelphia, NFC	2,816
1994	Dallas, NFC	2,752
	Houston, AFC	2,795
1993	New Orleans, NFC	2,606
	Cincinnati, AFC	2,798

1992 New Orleans, NFC..........2,470
Kansas City, AFC............2,537
1991 Philadelphia, NFC...........2,413
Denver, AFC....................2,755
1990 Pittsburgh, AFC 2,500
Dallas, NFC.....................2,639
1989 Minnesota, NFC..............2,501
Kansas City, AFC............2,527
1988 Kansas City, AFC............2,434
Minnesota, NFC..............2,489
1987 San Francisco, NFC 2,484
L.A. Raiders, AFC...........2,727
1986 St. Louis, NFC 2,637
New England, AFC.........2,978
1985 Washington, NFC 2,746
Pittsburgh, AFC 2,783
1984 New Orleans, NFC..........2,453
Cleveland, AFC...............2,696
1983 New Orleans, NFC..........2,691
Cincinnati, AFC...............2,828
1982 Miami, AFC 1,027
Tampa Bay, NFC..............1,384
1981 Philadelphia, NFC...........2,696
Buffalo, AFC....................2,870
1980 Washington, NFC 2,171
Buffalo, AFC....................2,282
1979 Tampa Bay, NFC..............2,076
Buffalo, AFC....................2,530
1978 Buffalo, AFC....................1,960
Los Angeles, NFC...........2,048
1977 Atlanta, NFC 1,384
San Diego, AFC..............1,725
1976 Minnesota, NFC..............1,575
Cincinnati, AFC...............1,758
1975 Minnesota, NFC..............1,621
Cincinnati, AFC...............1,729
1974 Pittsburgh, AFC 1,466
Atlanta, NFC 1,572
1973 Miami, AFC 1,290
Atlanta, NFC 1,430
1972 Minnesota, NFC..............1,699
Cleveland, AFC...............1,736
1971 Atlanta, NFC 1,638
Baltimore, AFC 1,739
1970 Minnesota, NFC..............1,438
Kansas City, AFC............2,010
1969 Minnesota, NFL 1,631
Kansas City, AFL.............2,072
1968 Houston, AFL...................1,671
Green Bay, NFL 1,796
1967 Green Bay, NFL 1,377
Buffalo, AFL 1,825
1966 Green Bay, NFL 1,959
Oakland, AFL...................2,118
1965 Green Bay, NFL 1,981
San Diego, AFL...............2,168
1964 Green Bay, NFL 1,647
San Diego, AFL...............2,518
1963 Chicago, NFL...................1,734
Oakland, AFL...................2,589
1962 Green Bay, NFL 1,746
Oakland, AFL...................2,306
1961 Baltimore, NFL.................1,913
San Diego, AFL...............2,363
1960 Chicago, NFL...................1,388
Buffalo, AFL 2,124
1959 N.Y. Giants 1,582
1958 Chi. Bears 1,769
1957 Cleveland.........................1,300
1956 Cleveland.........................1,103
1955 Pittsburgh 1,295
1954 Cleveland.........................1,608
1953 Washington......................1,751
1952 Washington......................1,580
1951 Pittsburgh 1,687
1950 Cleveland.........................1,581
1949 Philadelphia.....................1,607
1948 Green Bay........................1,626
1947 Green Bay........................1,790
1946 Pittsburgh 939
1945 Washington......................1,121
1944 Chi. Bears 1,052
1943 Chi. Bears 980
1942 Washington......................1,093
1941 Pittsburgh 1,168
1940 Philadelphia.....................1,012
1939 Washington......................1,116
1938 Chi. Bears 897
1937 Detroit 804
1936 Philadelphia........................853
1935 Chi. Cardinals 793
1934 Philadelphia........................545
1933 Portsmouth 558

SUPER BOWL RECORDS

Compiled by Elias Sports Bureau

1967: Super Bowl I	1978: Super Bowl XII	1989: Super Bowl XXIII
1968: Super Bowl II	1979: Super Bowl XIII	1990: Super Bowl XXIV
1969: Super Bowl III	1980: Super Bowl XIV	1991: Super Bowl XXV
1970: Super Bowl IV	1981: Super Bowl XV	1992: Super Bowl XXVI
1971: Super Bowl V	1982: Super Bowl XVI	1993: Super Bowl XXVII
1972: Super Bowl VI	1983: Super Bowl XVII	1994: Super Bowl XXVIII
1973: Super Bowl VII	1984: Super Bowl XVIII	1995: Super Bowl XXIX
1974: Super Bowl VIII	1985: Super Bowl XIX	1996: Super Bowl XXX
1975: Super Bowl IX	1986: Super Bowl XX	1997: Super Bowl XXXI
1976: Super Bowl X	1987: Super Bowl XXI	1998: Super Bowl XXXII
1977: Super Bowl XI	1988: Super Bowl XXII	1999: Super Bowl XXXIII

INDIVIDUAL RECORDS

SERVICE

Most Games

6 Mike Lodish, Buffalo, 1991-94; Denver, 1998-99
5 Marv Fleming, Green Bay, 1967-68; Miami, 1972-74
Larry Cole, Dallas, 1971-72, 1976, 1978-79
Cliff Harris, Dallas, 1971-72, 1976, 1978-79
Charles Haley, San Francisco, 1989-90; Dallas, 1993-94, 1996
D.D. Lewis, Dallas, 1971-72, 1976, 1978-79
Preston Pearson, Baltimore, 1969; Pittsburgh, 1975; Dallas, 1976, 1978-79
Charlie Waters, Dallas, 1971-72, 1976, 1978-79
Rayfield Wright, Dallas, 1971-72, 1976, 1978-79
Cornelius Bennett, Buffalo, 1991-94; Atlanta, 1999
John Elway, Denver, 1987-88, 1990, 1998-99
4 By many players

Most Games, Winning Team

5 Charles Haley, San Francisco, 1989-90; Dallas, 1993-94, 1996
4 By many players

Most Games, Coach

6 Don Shula, Baltimore, 1969; Miami, 1972-74, 1983, 1985
5 Tom Landry, Dallas, 1971-72, 1976, 1978-79
4 Bud Grant, Minnesota, 1970, 1974-75, 1977
Chuck Noll, Pittsburgh, 1975-76, 1979-80
Joe Gibbs, Washington, 1983-84, 1988, 1992
Marv Levy, Buffalo, 1991-94
Dan Reeves, Denver, 1987-88, 1990; Atlanta, 1999

Most Games, Winning Team, Coach

4 Chuck Noll, Pittsburgh, 1975-76, 1979-80
3 Bill Walsh, San Francisco, 1982, 1985, 1989
Joe Gibbs, Washington, 1983, 1988, 1992
2 Vince Lombardi, Green Bay, 1967-68
Tom Landry, Dallas, 1972, 1978
Don Shula, Miami, 1973-74
Tom Flores, Oakland, 1981; L.A. Raiders, 1984
Bill Parcells, N.Y. Giants, 1987, 1991
Jimmy Johnson, Dallas, 1993-94
George Seifert, San Francisco, 1990, 1995
Mike Shanahan, Denver, 1998-99

Most Games, Losing Team, Coach

4 Bud Grant, Minnesota, 1970, 1974-75, 1977
Don Shula, Baltimore, 1969; Miami, 1972, 1983, 1985
Marv Levy, Buffalo, 1991-94
Dan Reeves, Denver, 1987-88, 1990; Atlanta, 1999
3 Tom Landry, Dallas, 1971, 1976, 1979

SCORING

POINTS

Most Points, Career

42 Jerry Rice, San Francisco, 3 games (7-td)
30 Emmitt Smith, Dallas, 3 games (5-td)
24 Franco Harris, Pittsburgh, 4 games (4-td)
Roger Craig, San Francisco, 3 games (4-td)
Thurman Thomas, Buffalo, 4 games (4-td)
John Elway, Denver, 5 games (4-td)

Most Points, Game

18 Roger Craig, San Francisco vs. Miami, 1985 (3-td)
Jerry Rice, San Francisco vs. Denver, 1990 (3-td); vs. San Diego, 1995 (3-td)
Ricky Watters, San Francisco vs. San Diego, 1995 (3-td)
Terrell Davis, Denver vs. Green Bay, 1998 (3-td)
15 Don Chandler, Green Bay vs. Oakland, 1968 (3-pat, 4-fg)
14 Ray Wersching, San Francisco vs. Cincinnati, 1982 (2-pat, 4-fg)
Kevin Butler, Chicago vs. New England, 1986 (5-pat, 3-fg)

TOUCHDOWNS

Most Touchdowns, Career

7 Jerry Rice, San Francisco, 3 games (7-p)
5 Emmitt Smith, Dallas, 3 games (5-r)
4 Franco Harris, Pittsburgh, 4 games (4-r)
Roger Craig, San Francisco, 3 games (2-r, 2-p)
Thurman Thomas, Buffalo, 4 games (4-r)
John Elway, Denver, 5 games (4-r)

Most Touchdowns, Game

3 Roger Craig, San Francisco vs. Miami, 1985 (1-r, 2-p)
Jerry Rice, San Francisco. vs. Denver, 1990 (3-p); vs. San Diego, 1995 (3-p)
Ricky Watters, San Francisco vs. San Diego, 1995 (1-r, 2-p)
Terrell Davis, Denver vs. Green Bay, 1998 (3-r)
2 Max McGee, Green Bay vs. Kansas City, 1967 (2-p)
Elijah Pitts, Green Bay vs. Kansas City, 1967 (2-r)
Bill Miller, Oakland vs. Green Bay, 1968 (2-p)
Larry Csonka, Miami vs. Minnesota, 1974 (2-r)
Pete Banaszak, Oakland vs. Minnesota, 1977 (2-r)
John Stallworth, Pittsburgh vs. Dallas, 1979 (2-p)
Franco Harris, Pittsburgh vs. Los Angeles, 1980 (2-r)
Cliff Branch, Oakland vs. Philadelphia, 1981 (2-p)
Dan Ross, Cincinnati vs. San Francisco, 1982 (2-p)
Marcus Allen, L.A. Raiders vs. Washington, 1984 (2-r)
Jim McMahon, Chicago vs. New England, 1986 (2-r)
Ricky Sanders, Washington vs. Denver, 1988 (2-p)
Timmy Smith, Washington vs. Denver, 1988 (2-r)
Tom Rathman, San Francisco vs. Denver, 1990 (2-r)
Gerald Riggs, Washington vs. Buffalo, 1992 (2-r)
Michael Irvin, Dallas vs. Buffalo, 1993 (2-p)
Emmitt Smith, Dallas vs. Buffalo, 1994 (2-r)
Emmitt Smith, Dallas vs. Pittsburgh, 1996 (2-r)
Antonio Freeman, Green Bay vs. Denver, 1998 (2-p)
Howard Griffith, Denver vs. Atlanta, 1999 (2-r)

POINTS AFTER TOUCHDOWN

Most (One-Point) Points After Touchdown, Career

9 Mike Cofer, San Francisco, 2 games (10 att)
8 Don Chandler, Green Bay, 2 games (8 att)
Roy Gerela, Pittsburgh, 3 games (9 att)
Chris Bahr, Oakland-L.A. Raiders, 2 games (8 att)
Jason Elam, Denver, 2 games (8 att)
7 Ray Wersching, San Francisco, 2 games (7 att)
Lin Elliott, Dallas, 1 game (7 att)
Doug Brien, San Francisco, 1 game (7 att)

Most (One-Point) Points After Touchdown, Game

7 Mike Cofer, San Francisco vs. Denver, 1990 (8 att)
Lin Elliott, Dallas vs. Buffalo, 1993 (7 att)
Doug Brien, San Francisco vs. San Diego, 1995 (7 att)
6 Ali Haji-Sheikh, Washington vs. Denver, 1988 (6 att)
5 Don Chandler, Green Bay vs. Kansas City, 1967 (5 att)
Roy Gerela, Pittsburgh vs. Dallas, 1979 (5 att)
Chris Bahr, L.A. Raiders vs. Washington, 1984 (5 att)
Ray Wersching, San Francisco vs. Miami, 1985 (5 att)
Kevin Butler, Chicago vs. New England, 1986 (5 att)

Most Two-Point Conversions, Game

1 Mark Seay, San Diego vs. San Francisco, 1995
Alfred Pupunu, San Diego vs. San Francisco, 1995
Mark Chmura, Green Bay vs. New England, 1997

FIELD GOALS

Field Goals Attempted, Career

6 Jim Turner, N.Y. Jets-Denver, 2 games
Roy Gerela, Pittsburgh, 3 games
Rich Karlis, Denver, 2 games
5 Efren Herrera, Dallas, 1 game
Ray Wersching, San Francisco, 2 games
Jason Elam, Denver, 2 games

Most Field Goals Attempted, Game

5 Jim Turner, N.Y. Jets vs. Baltimore, 1969
Efren Herrera, Dallas vs. Denver, 1978
4 Don Chandler, Green Bay vs. Oakland, 1968
Roy Gerela, Pittsburgh vs. Dallas, 1976
Ray Wersching, San Francisco vs. Cincinnati, 1982
Rich Karlis, Denver vs. N.Y. Giants, 1987
Mike Cofer, San Francisco vs. Cincinnati, 1989
Jason Elam, Denver vs. Atlanta, 1999

Most Field Goals, Career

5 Ray Wersching, San Francisco, 2 games (5 att)
4 Don Chandler, Green Bay, 2 games (4 att)
Jim Turner, N.Y. Jets-Denver, 2 games (6 att)
Uwe von Schamann, Miami, 2 games (4 att)
3 Mike Clark, Dallas, 2 games (3 att)
Jan Stenerud, Kansas City, 1 game (3 att)
Chris Bahr, Oakland-L.A. Raiders, 2 games (4 att)
Mark Moseley, Washington, 2 games (4 att)
Kevin Butler, Chicago, 1 game (3 att)

Rich Karlis, Denver, 2 games (6 att)
Jim Breech, Cincinnati, 2 games (3 att)
Matt Bahr, Pittsburgh-N.Y. Giants, 2 games (3 att)
Chip Lohmiller, Washington, 1 game (3 att)
Steve Christie, Buffalo, 2 games (3 att)
Eddie Murray, Dallas, 1 game (3 att)
Jason Elam, Denver, 2 games (5 att)

Most Field Goals, Game

4 Don Chandler, Green Bay vs. Oakland, 1968
Ray Wersching, San Francisco vs. Cincinnati, 1982
3 Jim Turner, N.Y. Jets vs. Baltimore, 1969
Jan Stenerud, Kansas City vs. Minnesota, 1970
Uwe von Schamann, Miami vs. San Francisco, 1985
Kevin Butler, Chicago vs. New England, 1986
Jim Breech, Cincinnati vs. San Francisco, 1989
Chip Lohmiller, Washington vs. Buffalo, 1992
Eddie Murray, Dallas vs. Buffalo, 1994

Longest Field Goal

54 Steve Christie, Buffalo vs. Dallas, 1994
51 Jason Elam, Denver vs. Green Bay, 1998
48 Jan Stenerud, Kansas City vs. Minnesota, 1970
Rich Karlis, Denver vs. N.Y. Giants, 1987

SAFETIES

Most Safeties, Game

1 Dwight White, Pittsburgh vs. Minnesota, 1975
Reggie Harrison, Pittsburgh vs. Dallas, 1976
Henry Waechter, Chicago vs. New England, 1986
George Martin, N.Y. Giants vs. Denver, 1987
Bruce Smith, Buffalo vs. N.Y. Giants, 1991

RUSHING

ATTEMPTS

Most Attempts, Career

101 Franco Harris, Pittsburgh, 4 games
70 Emmitt Smith, Dallas, 3 games
64 John Riggins, Washington, 2 games

Most Attempts, Game

38 John Riggins, Washington vs. Miami, 1983
34 Franco Harris, Pittsburgh vs. Minnesota, 1975
33 Larry Csonka, Miami vs. Minnesota, 1974

YARDS GAINED

Most Yards Gained, Career

354 Franco Harris, Pittsburgh, 4 games
297 Larry Csonka, Miami, 3 games
289 Emmitt Smith, Dallas, 3 games

Most Yards Gained, Game

204 Timmy Smith, Washington vs. Denver, 1988
191 Marcus Allen, L.A. Raiders vs. Washington, 1984
166 John Riggins, Washington vs. Miami, 1983

Longest Run From Scrimmage

74 Marcus Allen, L.A. Raiders vs. Washington, 1984 (TD)
58 Tom Matte, Baltimore vs. N.Y. Jets, 1969
Timmy Smith, Washington vs. Denver, 1988 (TD)
49 Larry Csonka, Miami vs. Washington, 1973

AVERAGE GAIN

Highest Average Gain, Career (20 attempts)

9.6 Marcus Allen, L.A. Raiders, 1 game (20-191)
9.3 Timmy Smith, Washington, 1 game (22-204)
5.3 Walt Garrison, Dallas, 2 games (26-139)

Highest Average Gain, Game (10 attempts)

10.5 Tom Matte, Baltimore vs. N.Y. Jets, 1969 (11-116)
9.6 Marcus Allen, L.A. Raiders vs. Washington, 1984 (20-191)
9.3 Timmy Smith, Washington vs. Denver, 1988 (22-204)

TOUCHDOWNS

Most Touchdowns, Career

5 Emmitt Smith, Dallas, 3 games
4 Franco Harris, Pittsburgh, 4 games
Thurman Thomas, Buffalo, 4 games
John Elway, Denver, 5 games
3 Terrell Davis, Denver, 2 games

Most Touchdowns, Game

3 Terrell Davis, Denver vs. Green Bay, 1998
2 Elijah Pitts, Green Bay vs. Kansas City, 1967
Larry Csonka, Miami vs. Minnesota, 1974
Pete Banaszak, Oakland vs. Minnesota, 1977
Franco Harris, Pittsburgh vs. Los Angeles, 1980
Marcus Allen, L.A. Raiders vs. Washington, 1984
Jim McMahon, Chicago vs. New England, 1986
Timmy Smith, Washington vs. Denver, 1988
Tom Rathman, San Francisco vs. Denver, 1990
Gerald Riggs, Washington vs. Buffalo, 1992
Emmitt Smith, Dallas vs. Buffalo, 1994
Emmitt Smith, Dallas vs. Pittsburgh, 1996
Howard Griffith, Denver vs. Atlanta, 1999

PASSING

PASSER RATING

Highest Passer Rating, Career (40 attempts)

127.8 Joe Montana, San Francisco, 4 games
122.8 Jim Plunkett, Oakland-L.A. Raiders, 2 games
112.8 Terry Bradshaw, Pittsburgh, 4 games

ATTEMPTS

Most Passes Attempted, Career

152 John Elway, Denver, 5 games
145 Jim Kelly, Buffalo, 4 games
122 Joe Montana, San Francisco, 4 games

Most Passes Attempted, Game

58 Jim Kelly, Buffalo vs. Washington, 1992
50 Dan Marino, Miami vs. San Francisco, 1985
Jim Kelly, Buffalo vs. Dallas, 1994
49 Stan Humphries, San Diego vs. San Francisco, 1995
Neil O'Donnell, Pittsburgh vs. Dallas, 1996

COMPLETIONS

Most Passes Completed, Career

83 Joe Montana, San Francisco, 4 games
81 Jim Kelly, Buffalo, 4 games
76 John Elway, Denver, 5 games

Most Passes Completed, Game

31 Jim Kelly, Buffalo vs. Dallas, 1994
29 Dan Marino, Miami vs. San Francisco, 1985
28 Jim Kelly, Buffalo vs. Washington, 1992
Neil O'Donnell, Pittsburgh vs. Dallas, 1996

Most Consecutive Completions, Game

13 Joe Montana, San Francisco vs. Denver, 1990
10 Phil Simms, N.Y. Giants vs. Denver, 1987
Troy Aikman, Dallas vs. Pittsburgh, 1996
9 Jim Kelly, Buffalo vs. Dallas, 1994
Neil O'Donnell, Pittsburgh vs. Dallas, 1996

COMPLETION PERCENTAGE

Highest Completion Percentage, Career (40 attempts)

70.0 Troy Aikman, Dallas, 3 games, (80-56)
68.0 Joe Montana, San Francisco, 4 games (122-83)
63.6 Len Dawson, Kansas City, 2 games (44-28)

Highest Completion Percentage, Game (20 attempts)

88.0 Phil Simms, N.Y. Giants vs. Denver, 1987 (25-22)
75.9 Joe Montana, San Francisco vs. Denver, 1990 (29-22)
73.5 Ken Anderson, Cincinnati vs. San Francisco, 1982 (34-25)

YARDS GAINED

Most Yards Gained, Career

1,142 Joe Montana, San Francisco, 4 games
1,128 John Elway, Denver, 5 games
932 Terry Bradshaw, Pittsburgh, 4 games

Most Yards Gained, Game

357 Joe Montana, San Francisco vs. Cincinnati, 1989
340 Doug Williams, Washington vs. Denver, 1988
336 John Elway, Denver vs. Atlanta, 1999

Longest Pass Completion

81 Brett Favre (to Freeman), Green Bay vs. New England, 1997 (TD)
80 Jim Plunkett (to King), Oakland vs. Philadelphia, 1981 (TD)
Doug Williams (to Sanders), Washington vs. Denver, 1988 (TD)
John Elway (to R. Smith), Denver vs. Atlanta, 1999 (TD)
76 David Woodley (to Cefalo), Miami vs. Washington, 1983 (TD)

AVERAGE GAIN

Highest Average Gain, Career (40 attempts)

11.10 Terry Bradshaw, Pittsburgh, 4 games (84-932)
9.62 Bart Starr, Green Bay, 2 games (47-452)
9.41 Jim Plunkett, Oakland-L.A. Raiders, 2 games (46-433)

Highest Average Gain, Game (20 attempts)

14.71 Terry Bradshaw, Pittsburgh vs. Los Angeles, 1980 (21-309)
12.80 Jim McMahon, Chicago vs. New England, 1986 (20-256)
12.43 Jim Plunkett, Oakland vs. Philadelphia, 1981 (21-261)

TOUCHDOWNS

Most Touchdown Passes, Career

11 Joe Montana, San Francisco, 4 games
9 Terry Bradshaw, Pittsburgh, 4 games
8 Roger Staubach, Dallas, 4 games

SUPER BOWL RECORDS

Most Touchdown Passes, Game
6 Steve Young, San Francisco vs. San Diego, 1995
5 Joe Montana, San Francisco vs. Denver, 1990
4 Terry Bradshaw, Pittsburgh vs. Dallas, 1979
Doug Williams, Washington vs. Denver, 1988
Troy Aikman, Dallas vs. Buffalo, 1993

HAD INTERCEPTED
Lowest Percentage, Passes Had Intercepted, Career (40 attempts)
0.00 Jim Plunkett, Oakland-L.A. Raiders, 2 games (46-0)
Joe Montana, San Francisco, 4 games (122-0)
1.25 Troy Aikman, Dallas, 3 games (80-1)
1.45 Brett Favre, Green Bay, 2 games (69-1)
Most Attempts, Without Interception, Game
36 Joe Montana, San Francisco vs. Cincinnati, 1989
Steve Young, San Francisco vs. San Diego, 1995
35 Joe Montana, San Francisco vs. Miami, 1985
32 Jeff Hostetler, N.Y. Giants vs. Buffalo, 1991
Most Passes Had Intercepted, Career
8 John Elway, Denver, 5 games
7 Craig Morton, Dallas-Denver, 2 games
Jim Kelly, Buffalo, 4 games
6 Fran Tarkenton, Minnesota, 3 games
Most Passes Had Intercepted, Game
4 Craig Morton, Denver vs. Dallas, 1978
Jim Kelly, Buffalo vs. Washington, 1992
Drew Bledsoe, New England vs. Green Bay, 1997
3 By ten players

PASS RECEIVING
RECEPTIONS
Most Receptions, Career
28 Jerry Rice, San Francisco, 3 games
27 Andre Reed, Buffalo, 4 games
20 Roger Craig, San Francisco, 3 games
Thurman Thomas, Buffalo, 4 games
Most Receptions, Game
11 Dan Ross, Cincinnati vs. San Francisco, 1982
Jerry Rice, San Francisco vs. Cincinnati, 1989
10 Tony Nathan, Miami vs. San Francisco, 1985
Jerry Rice, San Francisco vs. San Diego, 1995
Andre Hastings, Pittsburgh vs. Dallas, 1996
9 Ricky Sanders, Washington vs. Denver, 1988
Antonio Freeman, Green Bay vs. Denver, 1998

YARDS GAINED
Most Yards Gained, Career
512 Jerry Rice, San Francisco, 3 games
364 Lynn Swann, Pittsburgh, 4 games
323 Andre Reed, Buffalo, 4 games
Most Yards Gained, Game
215 Jerry Rice, San Francisco vs. Cincinnati, 1989
193 Ricky Sanders, Washington vs. Denver, 1988
161 Lynn Swann, Pittsburgh vs. Dallas, 1976
Longest Reception
81 Antonio Freeman (from Favre), Green Bay vs. New England, 1997 (TD)
80 Kenny King (from Plunkett), Oakland vs. Philadelphia, 1981 (TD)
Ricky Sanders (from Williams), Washington vs. Denver, 1988 (TD)
Rod Smith (from Elway), Denver vs. Atlanta, 1999
76 Jimmy Cefalo (from Woodley), Miami vs. Washington, 1983 (TD)

AVERAGE GAIN
Highest Average Gain, Career (8 receptions)
24.4 John Stallworth, Pittsburgh, 4 games (11-268)
23.4 Ricky Sanders, Washington, 2 games (10-234)
22.8 Lynn Swann, Pittsburgh, 4 games (16-364)
Highest Average Gain, Game (3 receptions)
40.33 John Stallworth, Pittsburgh vs. Los Angeles, 1980 (3-121)
40.25 Lynn Swann, Pittsburgh vs. Dallas, 1979 (4-161)
38.33 John Stallworth, Pittsburgh vs. Dallas, 1979 (3-115)

TOUCHDOWNS
Most Touchdowns, Career
7 Jerry Rice, San Francisco, 3 games
3 John Stallworth, Pittsburgh, 4 games
Lynn Swann, Pittsburgh, 4 games
Cliff Branch, Oakland-L.A. Raiders, 3 games
Antonio Freeman, Green Bay, 2 games
2 Max McGee, Green Bay, 2 games
Bill Miller, Oakland, 1 game
Butch Johnson, Dallas, 2 games
Dan Ross, Cincinnati, 1 game
Roger Craig, San Francisco, 3 games
Ricky Sanders, Washington, 2 games
John Taylor, San Francisco, 3 games
Gary Clark, Washington, 2 games
Don Beebe, Buffalo-Green Bay, 4 games
Michael Irvin, Dallas, 2 games
Ricky Watters, San Francisco, 1 game
Jay Novacek, Dallas, 3 games
Most Touchdowns, Game
3 Jerry Rice, San Francisco vs. San Diego, 1995; vs. Denver, 1990
2 Max McGee, Green Bay vs. Kansas City, 1967
Bill Miller, Oakland vs. Green Bay, 1968
John Stallworth, Pittsburgh vs. Dallas, 1979
Cliff Branch, Oakland vs. Philadelphia, 1981
Dan Ross, Cincinnati vs. San Francisco, 1982
Roger Craig, San Francisco vs. Miami, 1985
Ricky Sanders, Washington vs. Denver, 1988
Michael Irvin, Dallas vs. Buffalo, 1993
Ricky Watters, San Francisco vs. San Diego, 1995
Antonio Freeman, Green Bay vs. Denver, 1998

INTERCEPTIONS BY
Most Interceptions By, Career
3 Chuck Howley, Dallas, 2 games
Rod Martin, Oakland-L.A. Raiders, 2 games
Larry Brown, Dallas, 3 games
2 Randy Beverly, N.Y. Jets, 1 game
Jake Scott, Miami, 3 games
Mike Wagner, Pittsburgh, 3 games
Mel Blount, Pittsburgh, 4 games
Eric Wright, San Francisco, 4 games
Barry Wilburn, Washington, 1 game
Brad Edwards, Washington, 1 game
Thomas Everett, Dallas, 2 games
James Washington, Dallas, 2 games
Darrien Gordon, San Diego-Denver, 3 games
Most Interceptions By, Game
3 Rod Martin, Oakland vs. Philadelphia, 1981
2 Randy Beverly, N.Y. Jets vs. Baltimore, 1969
Chuck Howley, Dallas vs. Baltimore, 1971
Jake Scott, Miami vs. Washington, 1973
Barry Wilburn, Washington vs. Denver, 1988
Brad Edwards, Washington vs. Buffalo, 1992
Thomas Everett, Dallas vs. Buffalo, 1993
Larry Brown, Dallas vs. Pittsburgh, 1996
Darrien Gordon, Denver vs. Atlanta, 1999

YARDS GAINED
Most Yards Gained, Career
108 Darrien Gordon, San Diego-Denver, 3 games
77 Larry Brown, Dallas, 3 games
75 Willie Brown, Oakland, 2 games
Most Yards Gained, Game
108 Darrien Gordon, Denver vs. Atlanta, 1999
77 Larry Brown, Dallas vs. Pittsburgh, 1996
75 Willie Brown, Oakland vs. Minnesota, 1977
Longest Return
75 Willie Brown, Oakland vs. Minnesota, 1977 (TD)
60 Herb Adderley, Green Bay vs. Oakland, 1968 (TD)
58 Darrien Gordon, Denver vs. Atlanta, 1999

TOUCHDOWNS
Most Touchdowns, Game
1 Herb Adderley, Green Bay vs. Oakland, 1968
Willie Brown, Oakland vs. Minnesota, 1977
Jack Squirek, L.A. Raiders vs. Washington, 1984
Reggie Phillips, Chicago vs. New England, 1986

PUNTING
Most Punts, Career
17 Mike Eischeid, Oakland-Minnesota, 3 games
15 Larry Seiple, Miami, 3 games
Mike Horan, Denver, 3 games
14 Ron Widby, Dallas, 2 games
Ray Guy, Oakland-L.A. Raiders, 3 games
Chris Mohr, Buffalo, 3 games
Most Punts, Game
9 Ron Widby, Dallas vs. Baltimore, 1971
8 Tom Tupa, New England vs. Green Bay, 1997
7 By seven players
Longest Punt
63 Lee Johnson, Cincinnati vs. San Francisco, 1989
62 Rich Camarillo, New England vs. Chicago, 1986
61 Jerrel Wilson, Kansas City vs. Green Bay, 1967

AVERAGE YARDAGE

Highest Average, Punting, Career (10 punts)

46.5 Jerrel Wilson, Kansas City, 2 games (11-511)
41.9 Ray Guy, Oakland-L.A. Raiders, 3 games (14-587)
41.3 Larry Seiple, Miami, 3 games (15-620)

Highest Average, Punting, Game (4 punts)

48.8 Bryan Wagner, San Diego vs. San Francisco, 1995 (4-195)
48.5 Jerrel Wilson, Kansas City vs. Minnesota, 1970 (4-194)
46.3 Jim Miller, San Francisco vs. Cincinnati, 1982 (4-185)

PUNT RETURNS

Most Punt Returns, Career

6 Willie Wood, Green Bay, 2 games
Jake Scott, Miami, 3 games
Theo Bell, Pittsburgh, 2 games
Mike Nelms, Washington, 1 game
John Taylor, San Francisco, 3 games
Desmond Howard, Green Bay, 1 game
David Meggett, N.Y. Giants-New England, 2 games
5 Dana McLemore, San Francisco, 1 game
4 By eight players

Most Punt Returns, Game

6 Mike Nelms, Washington vs. Miami, 1983
Desmond Howard, Green Bay vs. New England, 1997
5 Willie Wood, Green Bay vs. Oakland, 1968
Dana McLemore, San Francisco vs. Miami, 1985
4 By seven players

Most Fair Catches, Game

3 Ron Gardin, Baltimore vs. Dallas, 1971
Golden Richards, Dallas vs. Pittsburgh, 1976
Greg Pruitt, L.A. Raiders vs. Washington, 1984
Al Edwards, Buffalo vs. N.Y. Giants, 1991
David Meggett, N.Y. Giants vs. Buffalo, 1991

YARDS GAINED

Most Yards Gained, Career

94 John Taylor, San Francisco, 3 games
90 Desmond Howard, Green Bay, 1 game
67 David Meggett, N.Y. Giants-New England, 2 games

Most Yards Gained, Game

90 Desmond Howard, Green Bay vs. New England, 1997
56 John Taylor, San Francisco vs. Cincinnati, 1989
52 Mike Nelms, Washington vs. Miami, 1983

Longest Return

45 John Taylor, San Francisco vs. Cincinnati, 1989
34 Darrell Green, Washington vs. L.A. Raiders, 1984
Desmond Howard, Green Bay vs. New England, 1997
32 Desmond Howard, Green Bay vs. New England, 1997

AVERAGE YARDAGE

Highest Average, Career (4 returns)

15.7 John Taylor, San Francisco, 3 games (6-94)
15.0 Desmond Howard, Green Bay, 1 game (6-90)
11.2 David Meggett, N.Y. Giants-New England, 2 games (6-67)

Highest Average, Game (3 returns)

18.7 John Taylor, San Francisco vs. Cincinnati, 1989 (3-56)
15.0 Desmond Howard, Green Bay vs. New England, 1997 (6-90)
12.7 John Taylor, San Francisco vs. Denver, 1990 (3-38)

TOUCHDOWNS

Most Touchdowns, Game

None

KICKOFF RETURNS

Most Kickoff Returns, Career

10 Ken Bell, Denver, 3 games
8 Larry Anderson, Pittsburgh, 2 games
Fulton Walker, Miami, 2 games
Andre Coleman, San Diego, 1 game
7 Preston Pearson, Baltimore-Pittsburgh-Dallas, 5 games
Stephen Starring, New England, 1 game
David Meggett, N.Y. Giants-New England, 2 games

Most Kickoff Returns, Game

8 Andre Coleman, San Diego vs. San Francisco, 1995
7 Stephen Starring, New England vs. Chicago, 1986
6 Darren Carrington, Denver vs. San Francisco, 1990
Antonio Freeman, Green Bay vs. Denver, 1998

YARDS GAINED

Most Yards Gained, Career

283 Fulton Walker, Miami, 2 games
244 Andre Coleman, San Diego, 1 game
210 Tim Dwight, Atlanta, 1 game

Most Yards Gained, Game

244 Andre Coleman, San Diego vs. San Francisco, 1995
210 Tim Dwight, Atlanta vs. Denver, 1999
190 Fulton Walker, Miami vs. Washington, 1983

Longest Return

99 Desmond Howard, Green Bay vs. New England, 1997 (TD)
98 Fulton Walker, Miami vs. Washington, 1983 (TD)
Andre Coleman, San Diego vs. San Francisco, 1995 (TD)
94 Tim Dwight, Atlanta vs. Denver, 1999 (TD)

AVERAGE YARDAGE

Highest Average, Career (4 returns)

42.0 Tim Dwight, Atlanta, 1 game (5-210)
38.5 Desmond Howard, Green Bay, 1 game (4-154)
35.4 Fulton Walker, Miami, 2 games (8-283)

Highest Average, Game (3 returns)

47.5 Fulton Walker, Miami vs. Washington, 1983 (4-190)
42.0 Tim Dwight, Atlanta vs. Denver, 1999 (5-210)
38.5 Desmond Howard, Green Bay vs. New England, 1997 (4-154)

TOUCHDOWNS

Most Touchdowns, Game

1 Fulton Walker, Miami vs. Washington, 1983
Stanford Jennings, Cincinnati vs. San Francisco, 1989
Andre Coleman, San Diego vs. San Francisco, 1995
Desmond Howard, Green Bay vs. New England, 1997
Tim Dwight, Atlanta vs. Denver, 1999

FUMBLES

Most Fumbles, Career

5 Roger Staubach, Dallas, 4 games
4 Jim Kelly, Buffalo, 4 games
3 Franco Harris, Pittsburgh, 4 games
Terry Bradshaw, Pittsburgh, 4 games
John Elway, Denver, 5 games
Frank Reich, Buffalo, 4 games
Thurman Thomas, Buffalo, 4 games

Most Fumbles, Game

3 Roger Staubach, Dallas vs. Pittsburgh, 1976
Jim Kelly, Buffalo vs. Washington, 1992
Frank Reich, Buffalo vs. Dallas, 1993
2 Franco Harris, Pittsburgh vs. Minnesota, 1975
Butch Johnson, Dallas vs. Denver, 1978
Terry Bradshaw, Pittsburgh vs. Dallas, 1979
Joe Montana, San Francisco vs. Cincinnati, 1989
John Elway, Denver vs. San Francisco, 1990
Thurman Thomas, Buffalo vs. Dallas, 1994

RECOVERIES

Most Fumbles Recovered, Career

2 Jake Scott, Miami, 3 games (1 own, 1 opp)
Fran Tarkenton, Minnesota, 3 games (2 own)
Franco Harris, Pittsburgh, 4 games (2 own)
Roger Staubach, Dallas, 4 games (2 own)
Bobby Walden, Pittsburgh, 2 games (2 own)
John Fitzgerald, Dallas, 4 games (2 own)
Randy Hughes, Dallas, 3 games (2 opp)
Butch Johnson, Dallas, 2 games (2 own)
Mike Singletary, Chicago, 1 game (2 opp)
John Elway, Denver, 5 games (2 own)
Jimmie Jones, Dallas, 2 games (2 opp)
Kenneth Davis, Buffalo, 4 games (2 own)

Most Fumbles Recovered, Game

2 Jake Scott, Miami vs. Minnesota, 1974 (1 own, 1 opp)
Roger Staubach, Dallas vs. Pittsburgh, 1976 (2 own)
Randy Hughes, Dallas vs. Denver, 1978 (2 opp)
Butch Johnson, Dallas vs. Denver, 1978 (2 own)
Mike Singletary, Chicago vs. New England, 1986 (2 opp)
Jimmie Jones, Dallas vs. Buffalo, 1993 (2 opp)

YARDS GAINED

Most Yards Gained, Game

64 Leon Lett, Dallas vs. Buffalo, 1993 (opp)
49 Mike Bass, Washington vs. Miami, 1973 (opp)
46 James Washington, Dallas vs. Buffalo, 1994 (opp)

SUPER BOWL RECORDS

Longest Return

64 Leon Lett, Dallas vs. Buffalo, 1993
49 Mike Bass, Washington vs. Miami, 1973 (TD)
46 James Washington, Dallas vs. Buffalo, 1994 (TD)

TOUCHDOWNS

Most Touchdowns, Game

1 Mike Bass, Washington vs. Miami, 1973 (opp 49 yds)
Mike Hegman, Dallas vs. Pittsburgh, 1979 (opp 37 yds)
Jimmie Jones, Dallas vs. Buffalo, 1993 (opp 2 yds)
Ken Norton, Dallas vs. Buffalo, 1993 (opp 9 yds)
James Washington, Dallas vs. Buffalo, 1994 (opp 46 yds)

COMBINED NET YARDS GAINED

(Rushing, receiving, interception returns, punt returns, kickoff returns, and fumble returns)

ATTEMPTS

Most Attempts, Career

108 Franco Harris, Pittsburgh, 4 games
81 Emmitt Smith, Dallas, 3 games
72 Roger Craig, San Francisco, 3 games
Thurman Thomas, Buffalo, 4 games

Most Attempts, Game

39 John Riggins, Washington vs. Miami, 1983
35 Franco Harris, Pittsburgh vs. Minnesota, 1975
34 Matt Snell, N.Y. Jets vs. Baltimore, 1969
Emmitt Smith, Dallas vs. Buffalo, 1994

YARDS GAINED

Most Yards Gained, Career

527 Jerry Rice, San Francisco, 3 games
468 Franco Harris, Pittsburgh, 4 games
410 Roger Craig, San Francisco, 3 games

Most Yards Gained, Game

244 Andre Coleman, San Diego vs. San Francisco, 1995
Desmond Howard, Green Bay vs. New England, 1997
235 Ricky Sanders, Washington vs. Denver, 1988
230 Antonio Freeman, Green Bay vs. Denver, 1998

SACKS

Sacks have been compiled since 1983.

Most Sacks, Career

4.5 Charles Haley, San Francisco-Dallas, 5 games
3 Danny Stubbs, San Francisco, 2 games
Leonard Marshall, N.Y. Giants, 2 games
Jeff Wright, Buffalo, 4 games
Reggie White, Green Bay, 2 games
2.5 Dexter Manley, Washington, 3 games

Most Sacks, Game

3 Reggie White, Green Bay vs. New England, 1997
2 Dwaine Board, San Francisco vs. Miami, 1985
Dennis Owens, New England vs. Chicago, 1986
Otis Wilson, Chicago vs. New England, 1986
Leonard Marshall, N.Y. Giants vs. Denver, 1987
Alvin Walton, Washington vs. Denver, 1988
Charles Haley, San Francisco vs. Cincinnati, 1989
Danny Stubbs, San Francisco vs. Denver, 1990
Jeff Wright, Buffalo vs. Dallas, 1994
Raylee Johnson, San Diego vs. San Francisco, 1995
Chad Hennings, Dallas vs. Pittsburgh, 1996
Tedy Bruschi, New England vs. Green Bay, 1997

TEAM RECORDS

GAMES, VICTORIES, DEFEATS

Most Games

8 Dallas, 1971-72, 1976, 1978-79, 1993-94, 1996
6 Denver, 1978, 1987-88, 1990, 1998-99
5 Miami, 1972-74, 1983, 1985
Washington, 1973, 1983-84, 1988, 1992
San Francisco, 1982, 1985, 1989-90, 1995
Pittsburgh, 1975-76, 1979-80, 1996

Most Consecutive Games

4 Buffalo, 1991-94
3 Miami, 1972-74
2 Green Bay, 1967-68; 1997-98
Dallas, 1971-72; 1978-79; 1993-94
Minnesota, 1974-75
Pittsburgh, 1975-76; 1979-80
Washington, 1983-84
Denver, 1987-88; 1998-99
San Francisco 1989-90

Most Games Won

5 San Francisco, 1982, 1985, 1989-90, 1995
Dallas, 1972, 1978, 1993-94, 1996
4 Pittsburgh, 1975-76, 1979-80
3 Oakland/L.A. Raiders, 1977, 1981, 1984
Washington, 1983, 1988, 1992
Green Bay, 1967-68, 1997

Most Consecutive Games Won

2 Green Bay, 1967-68
Miami, 1973-74
Pittsburgh, 1975-76, 1979-80
San Francisco, 1989-90
Dallas, 1993-94
Denver, 1998-99

Most Games Lost

4 Minnesota, 1970, 1974-75, 1977
Denver, 1978, 1987-88, 1990
Buffalo, 1991-94
3 Dallas, 1971, 1976, 1979
Miami, 1972, 1983, 1985
2 Washington, 1973, 1984
Cincinnati, 1982, 1989
New England, 1986, 1997

Most Consecutive Games Lost

4 Buffalo, 1991-94
2 Minnesota, 1974-75
Denver, 1987-88

SCORING

Most Points, Game

55 San Francisco vs. Denver, 1990
52 Dallas vs. Buffalo, 1993
49 San Francisco vs. San Diego, 1995

Fewest Points, Game

3 Miami vs. Dallas, 1972
6 Minnesota vs. Pittsburgh, 1975
7 By four teams

Most Points, Both Teams, Game

75 San Francisco (49) vs. San Diego (26), 1995
69 Dallas (52) vs. Buffalo (17), 1993
66 Pittsburgh (35) vs. Dallas (31), 1979

Fewest Points, Both Teams, Game

21 Washington (7) vs. Miami (14), 1973
22 Minnesota (6) vs. Pittsburgh (16), 1975
23 Baltimore (7) vs. N.Y. Jets (16), 1969

Largest Margin of Victory, Game

45 San Francisco vs. Denver, 1990 (55-10)
36 Chicago vs. New England, 1986 (46-10)
35 Dallas vs. Buffalo, 1993 (52-17)

Most Points, Each Half

1st: 35 Washington vs. Denver, 1988
2nd: 30 N.Y. Giants vs. Denver, 1987

Most Points, Each Quarter

1st: 14 Miami vs. Minnesota, 1974
Oakland vs. Philadelphia, 1981
Dallas vs. Buffalo, 1993
San Francisco vs. San Diego, 1995
New England vs. Green Bay, 1997
2nd: 35 Washington vs. Denver, 1988
3rd: 21 Chicago vs. New England, 1986
4th: 21 Dallas vs. Buffalo, 1993

Most Points, Both Teams, Each Half

1st: 45 Washington (35) vs. Denver (10), 1988
2nd: 44 Buffalo (24) vs. Washington (20), 1992

Fewest Points, Both Teams, Each Half

1st: 2 Minnesota (0) vs. Pittsburgh (2), 1975
2nd: 7 Miami (0) vs. Washington (7), 1973
Denver (0) vs. Washington (7), 1988

Most Points, Both Teams, Each Quarter

1st: 24 New England (14) vs. Green Bay (10), 1997
2nd: 35 Washington (35) vs. Denver (0), 1988
3rd: 24 Washington (14) vs. Buffalo (10), 1992
4th: 30 Denver (17) vs. Atlanta (13), 1999

TOUCHDOWNS

Most Touchdowns, Game

8 San Francisco vs. Denver, 1990
7 Dallas vs. Buffalo, 1993
San Francisco vs. San Diego, 1995
6 Washington vs. Denver, 1988

Fewest Touchdowns, Game
0 Miami vs. Dallas, 1972
1 By 17 teams

Most Touchdowns, Both Teams, Game
10 San Francisco (7) vs. San Diego (3), 1995
9 Pittsburgh (5) vs. Dallas (4), 1979
San Francisco (8) vs. Denver (1), 1990
Dallas (7) vs. Buffalo (2), 1993
7 N.Y. Giants (5) vs. Denver (2), 1987
Washington (6) vs. Denver (1), 1988
Washington (4) vs. Buffalo (3), 1992
Green Bay (4) vs. New England (3), 1997
Denver (4) vs. Green Bay (3), 1998

Fewest Touchdowns, Both Teams, Game
2 Baltimore (1) vs. N.Y. Jets (1), 1969
3 In six games

POINTS AFTER TOUCHDOWN

Most (One-Point) Points After Touchdown, Game
7 San Francisco vs. Denver, 1990
Dallas vs. Buffalo, 1993
San Francisco vs. San Diego, 1995
6 Washington vs. Denver, 1988
5 Green Bay vs. Kansas City, 1967
Pittsburgh vs. Dallas, 1979
L.A. Raiders vs. Washington, 1984
San Francisco vs. Miami, 1985
Chicago vs. New England, 1986

Most (One-Point) Points After Touchdown, Both Teams, Game
9 Pittsburgh (5) vs. Dallas (4), 1979
Dallas (7) vs. Buffalo (2), 1993
8 San Francisco (7) vs. Denver (1), 1990
San Francisco (7) vs. San Diego (1), 1995
7 Washington (6) vs. Denver (1), 1988
Washington (4) vs. Buffalo (3), 1992
Denver (4) vs. Green Bay (3), 1998

Fewest (One-Point) Points After Touchdown, Both Teams, Game
2 Baltimore (1) vs. N.Y. Jets (1), 1969
Baltimore (1) vs. Dallas (1), 1971
Minnesota (0) vs. Pittsburgh (2), 1975

Most Two-Point Conversions, Game
2 San Diego vs. San Francisco, 1995

Most Two-Point Conversions, Both Teams, Game
2 San Diego (2) vs. San Francisco (0), 1995

FIELD GOALS

Most Field Goals Attempted, Game
5 N.Y. Jets vs. Baltimore, 1969
Dallas vs. Denver, 1978
4 Green Bay vs. Oakland, 1968
Pittsburgh vs. Dallas, 1976
San Francisco vs. Cincinnati, 1982; 1989
Denver vs. N.Y. Giants, 1987
Denver vs. Atlanta, 1999

Most Field Goals Attempted, Both Teams, Game
7 N.Y. Jets (5) vs. Baltimore (2), 1969
San Francisco (4) vs. Cincinnati (3), 1989
Denver (4) vs. Atlanta (3), 1999
6 Dallas (5) vs. Denver (1), 1978
5 Green Bay (4) vs. Oakland (1), 1968
Pittsburgh (4) vs. Dallas (1), 1976
Oakland (3) vs. Philadelphia (2), 1981
Denver (4) vs. N.Y. Giants (1), 1987
Dallas (3) vs. Buffalo (2), 1994

Fewest Field Goals Attempted, Both Teams, Game
1 Minnesota (0) vs. Miami (1), 1974
San Francisco (0) vs. Denver (1), 1990
2 Green Bay (0) vs. Kansas City (2), 1967
Miami (1) vs. Washington (1), 1973
Dallas (1) vs. Pittsburgh (1), 1979
Dallas (1) vs. Buffalo (1), 1993
San Diego (1) vs. San Francisco (1), 1995
Denver (1) vs. Green Bay (1), 1998

Most Field Goals, Game
4 Green Bay vs. Oakland, 1968
San Francisco vs. Cincinnati, 1982
3 N.Y. Jets vs. Baltimore, 1969
Kansas City vs. Minnesota, 1970
Miami vs. San Francisco, 1985
Chicago vs. New England, 1986
Cincinnati vs. San Francisco, 1989
Washington vs. Buffalo, 1992
Dallas vs. Buffalo, 1994

Most Field Goals, Both Teams, Game
5 Cincinnati (3) vs. San Francisco (2), 1989
Dallas (3) vs. Buffalo (2), 1994
4 Green Bay (4) vs. Oakland (0), 1968
San Francisco (4) vs. Cincinnati (0), 1982
Miami (3) vs. San Francisco (1), 1985
Chicago (3) vs. New England (1), 1986
Washington (3) vs. Buffalo (1), 1992
Atlanta (2) vs. Denver (2), 1999
3 In eleven games

Fewest Field Goals, Both Teams, Game
0 Miami vs. Washington, 1973
Pittsburgh vs. Minnesota, 1975
1 Green Bay (0) vs. Kansas City (1), 1967
Minnesota (0) vs. Miami (1), 1974
Pittsburgh (0) vs. Dallas (1), 1979
Washington (0) vs. Denver (1), 1988
San Francisco (0) vs. Denver (1), 1990
San Francisco (0) vs. San Diego (1), 1995

SAFETIES

Most Safeties, Game
1 Pittsburgh vs. Minnesota, 1975; vs. Dallas, 1976
Chicago vs. New England, 1986
N.Y. Giants vs. Denver, 1987
Buffalo vs. N.Y. Giants, 1991

FIRST DOWNS

Most First Downs, Game
31 San Francisco vs. Miami, 1985
28 San Francisco vs. Denver, 1990
San Francisco vs. San Diego, 1995
25 Washington vs. Denver, 1988
Buffalo vs. Washington, 1992
Pittsburgh vs. Dallas, 1996

Fewest First Downs, Game
9 Minnesota vs. Pittsburgh, 1975
Miami vs. Washington, 1983
10 Dallas vs. Baltimore, 1971
Miami vs. Dallas, 1972
11 Denver vs. Dallas, 1978

Most First Downs, Both Teams, Game
50 San Francisco (31) vs. Miami (19), 1985
49 Buffalo (25) vs. Washington (24), 1992
48 San Francisco (28) vs. San Diego (20), 1995

Fewest First Downs, Both Teams, Game
24 Dallas (10) vs. Baltimore (14), 1971
26 Minnesota (9) vs. Pittsburgh (17), 1975
27 Pittsburgh (13) vs. Dallas (14), 1976

RUSHING

Most First Downs, Rushing, Game
16 San Francisco vs. Miami, 1985
15 Dallas vs. Miami, 1972
14 Washington vs. Miami, 1983
San Francisco vs. Denver, 1990
Denver vs. Green Bay, 1998

Fewest First Downs, Rushing, Game
1 New England vs. Chicago, 1986
2 Minnesota vs. Kansas City, 1970; vs. Pittsburgh, 1975; vs. Oakland, 1977
Pittsburgh vs. Dallas, 1979
Miami vs. San Francisco, 1985
3 Miami vs. Dallas, 1972
Philadelphia vs. Oakland, 1981
New England vs. Green Bay, 1997

Most First Downs, Rushing, Both Teams, Game
21 Washington (14) vs. Miami (7), 1983
19 Washington (13) vs. Denver (6), 1988
San Francisco (14) vs. Denver (5), 1990
18 Dallas (15) vs. Miami (3), 1972
Miami (13) vs. Minnesota (5), 1974
San Francisco (16) vs. Miami (2), 1985
N.Y. Giants (10) vs. Buffalo (8), 1991
Denver (14) vs. Green Bay (4), 1998

Fewest First Downs, Rushing, Both Teams, Game
8 Baltimore (4) vs. Dallas (4), 1971
Pittsburgh (2) vs. Dallas (6), 1979
9 Philadelphia (3) vs. Oakland (6), 1981
10 Minnesota (2) vs. Kansas City (8), 1970

SUPER BOWL RECORDS

PASSING

Most First Downs, Passing, Game

18 Buffalo vs. Washington, 1992
17 Miami vs. San Francisco, 1985
San Francisco vs. San Diego, 1995
16 Denver vs. N.Y. Giants, 1987
San Francisco vs. Cincinnati, 1989

Fewest First Downs, Passing, Game

1 Denver vs. Dallas, 1978
2 Miami vs. Washington, 1983
4 Miami vs. Minnesota, 1974

Most First Downs, Passing, Both Teams, Game

32 Miami (17) vs. San Francisco (15), 1985
31 San Francisco (17) vs. San Diego (14), 1995
30 Buffalo (18) vs. Washington (12), 1992

Fewest First Downs, Passing, Both Teams, Game

9 Denver (1) vs. Dallas (8), 1978
10 Minnesota (5) vs. Pittsburgh (5), 1975
11 Dallas (5) vs. Baltimore (6), 1971
Miami (2) vs. Washington (9), 1983

PENALTY

Most First Downs, Penalty, Game

4 Baltimore vs. Dallas, 1971
Miami vs. Minnesota, 1974
Cincinnati vs. San Francisco, 1982
Buffalo vs. Dallas, 1993
3 Kansas City vs. Minnesota, 1970
Minnesota vs. Oakland, 1977
Buffalo vs. Washington, 1992
Green Bay vs. Denver, 1998

Most First Downs, Penalty, Both Teams, Game

6 Cincinnati (4) vs. San Francisco (2), 1982
5 Baltimore (4) vs. Dallas (1), 1971
Miami (4) vs. Minnesota (1), 1974
Buffalo (3) vs. Washington (2), 1992
Green Bay (3) vs. Denver (2), 1998
4 Kansas City (3) vs. Minnesota (1), 1970
Buffalo (4) vs. Dallas (0), 1993

Fewest First Downs, Penalty, Both Teams, Game

0 Dallas vs. Miami, 1972
Miami vs. Washington, 1973
Dallas vs. Pittsburgh, 1976
Miami vs. San Francisco, 1985
1 Green Bay (0) vs. Kansas City (1), 1967
Miami (0) vs. Washington (1), 1983
Cincinnati (0) vs. San Francisco (1), 1989
San Francisco (0) vs. Denver (1), 1990
Dallas (0) vs. Buffalo (1), 1994
Dallas (0) vs. Pittsburgh (1), 1996
Denver (0) vs. Atlanta (1), 1999

NET YARDS GAINED RUSHING AND PASSING

Most Yards Gained, Game

602 Washington vs. Denver, 1988
537 San Francisco vs. Miami, 1985
461 San Francisco vs. Denver, 1990

Fewest Yards Gained, Game

119 Minnesota vs. Pittsburgh, 1975
123 New England vs. Chicago, 1986
156 Denver vs. Dallas, 1978

Most Yards Gained, Both Teams, Game

929 Washington (602) vs. Denver (327), 1988
851 San Francisco (537) vs. Miami (314), 1985
809 San Francisco (455) vs. San Diego (354), 1995

Fewest Yards Gained, Both Teams, Game

452 Minnesota (119) vs. Pittsburgh (333), 1975
481 Washington (228) vs. Miami (253), 1973
Denver (156) vs. Dallas (325), 1978
497 Minnesota (238) vs. Miami (259), 1974

RUSHING

ATTEMPTS

Most Attempts, Game

57 Pittsburgh vs. Minnesota, 1975
53 Miami vs. Minnesota, 1974
52 Oakland vs. Minnesota, 1977
Washington vs. Miami, 1983

Fewest Attempts, Game

9 Miami vs. San Francisco, 1985
11 New England vs. Chicago, 1986
13 New England vs. Green Bay, 1997

Most Attempts, Both Teams, Game

81 Washington (52) vs. Miami (29), 1983
78 Pittsburgh (57) vs. Minnesota (21), 1975
Oakland (52) vs. Minnesota (26), 1977
77 Miami (53) vs. Minnesota (24), 1974
Pittsburgh (46) vs. Dallas (31), 1976

Fewest Attempts, Both Teams, Game

49 Miami (9) vs. San Francisco (40), 1985
New England (13) vs. Green Bay (36), 1997
51 San Diego (19) vs. San Francisco (32), 1995
53 Kansas City (19) vs. Green Bay (34), 1967

YARDS GAINED

Most Yards Gained, Game

280 Washington vs. Denver, 1988
276 Washington vs. Miami, 1983
266 Oakland vs. Minnesota, 1977

Fewest Yards Gained, Game

7 New England vs. Chicago, 1986
17 Minnesota vs. Pittsburgh, 1975
25 Miami vs. San Francisco, 1985

Most Yards Gained, Both Teams, Game

377 Washington (280) vs. Denver (97), 1988
372 Washington (276) vs. Miami (96), 1983
338 N.Y. Giants (172) vs. Buffalo (166), 1991

Fewest Yards Gained, Both Teams, Game

158 New England (43) vs. Green Bay (115), 1997
159 Dallas (56) vs. Pittsburgh (103), 1996
168 Buffalo (43) vs. Washington (125), 1992

AVERAGE GAIN

Highest Average Gain, Game

7.00 L.A. Raiders vs. Washington, 1984 (33-231)
Washington vs. Denver, 1988 (40-280)
6.64 Buffalo vs. N.Y. Giants, 1991 (25-166)
6.22 Baltimore vs. N.Y. Jets, 1969 (23-143)

Lowest Average Gain, Game

0.64 New England vs. Chicago, 1986 (11-7)
0.81 Minnesota vs. Pittsburgh, 1975 (21-17)
2.23 Baltimore vs. Dallas, 1971 (31-69)

TOUCHDOWNS

Most Touchdowns, Game

4 Chicago vs. New England, 1986
Denver vs. Green Bay, 1998
3 Green Bay vs. Kansas City, 1967
Miami vs. Minnesota, 1974
San Francisco vs. Denver, 1990
Denver vs. Atlanta, 1999
2 Oakland vs. Minnesota, 1977
Pittsburgh vs. Los Angeles, 1980
L.A. Raiders vs. Washington, 1984
San Francisco vs. Miami, 1985
N.Y. Giants vs. Denver, 1987
Washington vs. Denver, 1988; vs. Buffalo, 1992
Buffalo vs. N.Y. Giants, 1991
Dallas vs. Buffalo, 1994; vs. Pittsburgh, 1996

Fewest Touchdowns, Game

0 By 20 teams

Most Touchdowns, Both Teams, Game

4 Miami (3) vs. Minnesota (1), 1974
Chicago (4) vs. New England (0), 1986
San Francisco (3) vs. Denver (1), 1990
Denver (4) vs. Green Bay (0), 1998
3 In nine games

Fewest Touchdowns, Both Teams, Game

0 Pittsburgh vs. Dallas, 1976
Oakland vs. Philadelphia, 1981
Cincinnati vs. San Francisco, 1989
1 In seven games

PASSING

ATTEMPTS

Most Passes Attempted, Game

59 Buffalo vs. Washington, 1992
55 San Diego vs. San Francisco, 1995
50 Miami vs. San Francisco, 1985
Buffalo vs. Dallas, 1994

Fewest Passes Attempted, Game

7 Miami vs. Minnesota, 1974
11 Miami vs. Washington, 1973
14 Pittsburgh vs. Minnesota, 1975

Most Passes Attempted, Both Teams, Game
93 San Diego (55) vs. San Francisco (38), 1995
92 Buffalo (59) vs. Washington (33), 1992
85 Miami (50) vs. San Francisco (35), 1985
Fewest Passes Attempted, Both Teams, Game
35 Miami (7) vs. Minnesota (28), 1974
39 Miami (11) vs. Washington (28), 1973
40 Pittsburgh (14) vs. Minnesota (26), 1975
Miami (17) vs. Washington (23), 1983

COMPLETIONS
Most Passes Completed, Game
31 Buffalo vs. Dallas, 1994
29 Miami vs. San Francisco, 1985
Buffalo vs. Washington, 1992
28 Pittsburgh vs. Dallas, 1996
Fewest Passes Completed, Game
4 Miami vs. Washington, 1983
6 Miami vs. Minnesota, 1974
8 Miami vs. Washington, 1973
Denver vs. Dallas, 1978
Most Passes Completed, Both Teams, Game
53 Miami (29) vs. San Francisco (24), 1985
52 San Diego (27) vs. San Francisco (25), 1995
50 Buffalo (31) vs. Dallas (19), 1994
Fewest Passes Completed, Both Teams, Game
19 Miami (4) vs. Washington (15), 1983
20 Pittsburgh (9) vs. Minnesota (11), 1975
22 Miami (8) vs. Washington (14), 1973

COMPLETION PERCENTAGE
Highest Completion Percentage, Game (20 attempts)
88.0 N.Y. Giants vs. Denver, 1987 (25-22)
75.0 San Francisco vs. Denver, 1990 (32-24)
73.5 Cincinnati vs. San Francisco, 1982 (34-25)
Lowest Completion Percentage, Game (20 attempts)
32.0 Denver vs. Dallas, 1978 (25-8)
37.9 Denver vs. San Francisco, 1990 (29-11)
38.5 Denver vs. Washington, 1988 (39-15)

YARDS GAINED
Most Yards Gained, Game
341 San Francisco vs. Cincinnati, 1989
336 Denver vs. Atlanta, 1999
326 San Francisco vs. Miami, 1985
Fewest Yards Gained, Game
35 Denver vs. Dallas, 1978
63 Miami vs. Minnesota, 1974
69 Miami vs. Washington, 1973
Most Yards Gained, Both Teams, Game
615 San Francisco (326) vs. Miami (289), 1985
603 San Francisco (316) vs. San Diego (287), 1995
583 Denver (320) vs. N.Y. Giants (263), 1987
Fewest Yards Gained, Both Teams, Game
156 Miami (69) vs. Washington (87), 1973
186 Pittsburgh (84) vs. Minnesota (102), 1975
204 Miami (80) vs. Washington (124), 1983

TIMES SACKED
Most Times Sacked, Game
7 Dallas vs. Pittsburgh, 1976
New England vs. Chicago, 1986
6 Kansas City vs. Green Bay, 1967
Washington vs. L.A. Raiders, 1984
Denver vs. San Francisco, 1990
5 Dallas vs. Denver, 1978; vs. Pittsburgh, 1979
Cincinnati vs. San Francisco, 1982; 1989
Denver vs. Washington, 1988
Buffalo vs. Washington, 1992
Green Bay vs. New England, 1997
New England vs. Green Bay, 1997
Fewest Times Sacked, Game
0 Baltimore vs. N.Y. Jets, 1969; vs. Dallas, 1971
Minnesota vs. Pittsburgh, 1975
Pittsburgh vs. Los Angeles, 1980
Philadelphia vs. Oakland, 1981
Washington vs. Buffalo, 1992
Denver vs. Green Bay, 1998
Denver vs. Atlanta, 1999
1 By 12 teams
Most Times Sacked, Both Teams, Game
10 New England (7) vs. Chicago (3), 1986
Green Bay (5) vs. New England (5), 1997
9 Kansas City (6) vs. Green Bay (3), 1967
Dallas (7) vs. Pittsburgh (2), 1976
Dallas (5) vs. Denver (4), 1978
Dallas (5) vs. Pittsburgh (4), 1979
Cincinnati (5) vs. San Francisco (4), 1989
8 Washington (6) vs. L.A. Raiders (2), 1984
Fewest Times Sacked, Both Teams, Game
1 Philadelphia (0) vs. Oakland (1), 1981
Denver (0) vs. Green Bay (1), 1998
2 Baltimore (0) vs. N.Y. Jets (2), 1969
Baltimore (0) vs. Dallas (2), 1971
Minnesota (0) vs. Pittsburgh (2), 1975
Denver (0) vs. Atlanta (2), 1999
3 In four games

TOUCHDOWNS
Most Touchdowns, Game
6 San Francisco vs. San Diego, 1995
5 San Francisco vs. Denver, 1990
4 Pittsburgh vs. Dallas, 1979
Washington vs. Denver, 1988
Dallas vs. Buffalo, 1993
Fewest Touchdowns, Game
0 By 17 teams
Most Touchdowns, Both Teams, Game
7 Pittsburgh (4) vs. Dallas (3), 1979
San Francisco (6) vs. San Diego (1), 1995
5 Washington (4) vs. Denver (1), 1988
San Francisco (5) vs. Denver (0), 1990
Dallas (4) vs. Buffalo (1), 1993
4 Dallas (2) vs. Pittsburgh (2), 1976
Oakland (3) vs. Philadelphia (1), 1981
San Francisco (3) vs. Miami (1), 1985
N.Y. Giants (3) vs. Denver (1), 1987
Washington (2) vs. Buffalo (2), 1992
Green Bay (2) vs. New England (2), 1997
Fewest Touchdowns, Both Teams, Game
0 N.Y. Jets vs. Baltimore, 1969
Miami vs. Minnesota, 1974
Buffalo vs. Dallas, 1994
1 In six games

INTERCEPTIONS BY
Most Interceptions By, Game
4 N.Y. Jets vs. Baltimore, 1969
Dallas vs. Denver, 1978
Washington vs. Buffalo, 1992
Dallas vs. Buffalo, 1993
Green Bay vs. New England, 1997
3 By 12 teams
Most Interceptions By, Both Teams, Game
6 Baltimore (3) vs. Dallas (3), 1971
5 Washington (4) vs. Buffalo (1), 1992
4 In nine games
Fewest Interceptions By, Both Teams, Game
0 Buffalo vs. N.Y. Giants, 1991
1 Oakland (0) vs. Green Bay (1), 1968
Miami (0) vs. Dallas (1), 1972
Minnesota (0) vs. Miami (1), 1974
N.Y. Giants (0) vs. Denver (1), 1987
Cincinnati (0) vs. San Francisco (1), 1989

YARDS GAINED
Most Yards Gained, Game
136 Denver vs. Atlanta, 1999
95 Miami vs. Washington, 1973
91 Oakland vs. Minnesota, 1977
Most Yards Gained, Both Teams, Game
137 Denver (136) vs. Atlanta (1), 1999
95 Miami (95) vs. Washington (0), 1973
91 Oakland (91) vs. Minnesota (0), 1977

TOUCHDOWNS
Most Touchdowns, Game
1 Green Bay vs. Oakland, 1968
Oakland vs. Minnesota, 1977
L.A. Raiders vs. Washington, 1984
Chicago vs. New England, 1986

PUNTING
Most Punts, Game
9 Dallas vs. Baltimore, 1971
8 Washington vs. L.A. Raiders, 1984

New England vs. Green Bay, 1997
7 By eight teams

Fewest Punts, Game
1 Atlanta vs. Denver, 1999
Denver vs. Atlanta, 1999
2 Pittsburgh vs. Los Angeles, 1980
Denver vs. N.Y. Giants, 1987
3 By 10 teams

Most Punts, Both Teams, Game
15 Washington (8) vs. L.A. Raiders (7), 1984
New England (8) vs. Green Bay (7), 1997
13 Dallas (9) vs. Baltimore (4), 1971
Pittsburgh (7) vs. Minnesota (6), 1975
12 In three games

Fewest Punts, Both Teams, Game
2 Atlanta (1) vs. Denver (1), 1999
5 Denver (2) vs. N.Y. Giants (3), 1987
6 Oakland (3) vs. Philadelphia (3), 1981

AVERAGE YARDAGE

Highest Average, Game (4 punts)
48.75 San Diego vs. San Francisco, 1995 (4-195)
48.50 Kansas City vs. Minnesota, 1970 (4-194)
46.25 San Francisco vs. Cincinnati, 1982 (4-185)

Lowest Average, Game (4 punts)
31.20 Washington vs. Miami, 1973 (5-156)
32.38 Washington vs. L.A. Raiders, 1984 (8-259)
32.40 Oakland vs. Minnesota, 1977 (5-162)

PUNT RETURNS

Most Punt Returns, Game
6 Washington vs. Miami, 1983
Green Bay vs. New England, 1997
5 By five teams

Fewest Punt Returns, Game
0 Minnesota vs. Miami, 1974
Buffalo vs. N.Y. Giants, 1991
Washington vs. Buffalo, 1992
Denver vs. Green Bay, 1998
Green Bay vs. Denver, 1998
Atlanta vs. Denver, 1999
Denver vs. Atlanta, 1999
1 By 15 teams

Most Punt Returns, Both Teams, Game
10 Green Bay (6) vs. New England (4), 1997
9 Pittsburgh (5) vs. Minnesota (4), 1975
8 Green Bay (5) vs. Oakland (3), 1968
Baltimore (5) vs. Dallas (3), 1971
Washington (6) vs. Miami (2), 1983

Fewest Punt Returns, Both Teams, Game
0 Denver vs. Green Bay, 1998
Atlanta vs. Denver, 1999
2 Dallas (1) vs. Miami (1), 1972
Denver (1) vs. N.Y. Giants (1), 1987
Buffalo (0) vs. N.Y. Giants (2), 1991
Buffalo (1) vs. Dallas (1), 1994
3 Kansas City (1) vs. Minnesota (2), 1970
Minnesota (0) vs. Miami (3), 1974
Washington (1) vs. Denver (2), 1988
Washington (0) vs. Buffalo (3), 1992
Dallas (1) vs. Pittsburgh (2), 1996

YARDS GAINED

Most Yards Gained, Game
90 Green Bay vs. New England, 1997
56 San Francisco vs. Cincinnati, 1989
52 Washington vs. Miami, 1983

Fewest Yards Gained, Game
–1 Dallas vs. Miami, 1972
0 By 12 teams

Most Yards Gained, Both Teams, Game
120 Green Bay (90) vs. New England (30), 1997
74 Washington (52) vs. Miami (22), 1983
66 San Francisco (51) vs. Miami (15), 1985

Fewest Yards Gained, Both Teams, Game
0 Denver vs. Green Bay, 1998
Atlanta vs. Denver, 1999
9 Washington (0) vs. Bufffalo (9), 1992
10 Buffalo (5) vs. Dallas (5), 1994

AVERAGE RETURN

Highest Average, Game (3 returns)
18.7 San Francisco vs. Cincinnati, 1989 (3-56)
15.0 Green Bay vs. New England, 1997 (6-90)
12.7 San Francisco vs. Denver, 1990 (3-38)

TOUCHDOWNS

Most Touchdowns, Game
None

KICKOFF RETURNS

Most Kickoff Returns, Game
9 Denver vs. San Francisco, 1990
8 San Diego vs. San Francisco, 1995
7 By seven teams

Fewest Kickoff Returns, Game
1 N.Y. Jets vs. Baltimore, 1969
L.A. Raiders vs. Washington, 1984
Washington vs. Buffalo, 1992
2 By seven teams

Most Kickoff Returns, Both Teams, Game
12 Denver (9) vs. San Francisco (3), 1990
San Diego (8) vs. San Francisco (4), 1995
11 Los Angeles (6) vs. Pittsburgh (5), 1980
Miami (7) vs. San Francisco (4), 1985
New England (7) vs. Chicago (4), 1986
Green Bay (6) vs. Denver (5), 1998
10 Oakland (7) vs. Green Bay (3), 1968
New England (6) vs. Green Bay (4), 1997
Atlanta (7) vs. Denver (3), 1999

Fewest Kickoff Returns, Both Teams, Game
5 N.Y. Jets (1) vs. Baltimore (4), 1969
Miami (2) vs. Washington (3), 1973
Washington (1) vs. Buffalo (4), 1992
6 In three games

YARDS GAINED

Most Yards Gained, Game
244 San Diego vs. San Francisco, 1995
227 Atlanta vs. Denver, 1999
222 Miami vs. Washington, 1983

Fewest Yards Gained, Game
16 Washington vs. Buffalo, 1992
17 L.A. Raiders vs. Washington, 1984
25 N.Y. Jets vs. Baltimore, 1969

Most Yards Gained, Both Teams, Game
292 San Diego (244) vs. San Francisco (480), 1995
289 Green Bay (154) vs. New England (135), 1997
279 Miami (222) vs. Washington (57), 1983

Fewest Yards Gained, Both Teams, Game
78 Miami (33) vs. Washington (45), 1973
82 Pittsburgh (32) vs. Minnesota (50), 1975
92 San Francisco (40) vs. Cincinnati (52), 1982

AVERAGE GAIN

Highest Average, Game (3 returns)
44.0 Cincinnati vs. San Francisco, 1989 (3-132)
38.5 Green Bay vs. New England, 1997 (4-154)
37.0 Miami vs. Washington, 1983 (6-222)

TOUCHDOWNS

Most Touchdowns, Game
1 Miami vs. Washington, 1983
Cincinnati vs. San Francisco, 1989
San Diego vs. San Francisco, 1995
Green Bay vs. New England, 1997
Atlanta vs. Denver, 1999

PENALTIES

Most Penalties, Game
12 Dallas vs. Denver, 1978
10 Dallas vs. Baltimore, 1971
9 Dallas vs. Pittsburgh, 1979
Green Bay vs. Denver, 1998

Fewest Penalties, Game
0 Miami vs. Dallas, 1972
Pittsburgh vs. Dallas, 1976
Denver vs. San Francisco, 1990
Atlanta vs. Denver, 1999
1 Green Bay vs. Oakland, 1968
Miami vs. Minnesota, 1974; vs. San Francisco, 1985
Buffalo vs. Dallas, 1994
2 By six teams

Most Penalties, Both Teams, Game
20 Dallas (12) vs. Denver (8), 1978
16 Cincinnati (8) vs. San Francisco (8), 1982

Green Bay (9) vs. Denver (7), 1998
14 Dallas (10) vs. Baltimore (4), 1971
Dallas (9) vs. Pittsburgh (5), 1979

Fewest Penalties, Both Teams, Game
2 Pittsburgh (0) vs. Dallas (2), 1976
3 Miami (0) vs. Dallas (3), 1972
Miami (1) vs. San Francisco (2), 1985
4 Denver (0) vs. San Francisco (4), 1990
Atlanta (0) vs. Denver (4), 1999

YARDS PENALIZED

Most Yards Penalized, Game
133 Dallas vs. Baltimore, 1971
122 Pittsburgh vs. Minnesota, 1975
94 Dallas vs. Denver, 1978

Fewest Yards Penalized, Game
0 Miami vs. Dallas, 1972
Pittsburgh vs. Dallas, 1976
Denver vs. San Francisco, 1990
Atlanta vs. Denver, 1999
4 Miami vs. Minnesota, 1974
10 Miami vs. San Francisco, 1985
San Francisco vs. Miami, 1985
Buffalo vs. Dallas, 1994

Most Yards Penalized, Both Teams, Game
164 Dallas (133) vs. Baltimore (31), 1971
154 Dallas (94) vs. Denver (60), 1978
140 Pittsburgh (122) vs. Minnesota (18), 1975

Fewest Yards Penalized, Both Teams, Game
15 Miami (0) vs. Dallas (15), 1972
20 Pittsburgh (0) vs. Dallas (20), 1976
Miami (10) vs. San Francisco (10), 1985
38 Denver (0) vs. San Francisco (38), 1990

FUMBLES

Most Fumbles, Game
8 Buffalo vs. Dallas, 1993
6 Dallas vs. Denver, 1978
Buffalo vs. Washington, 1992
5 Baltimore vs. Dallas, 1971

Fewest Fumbles, Game
0 By 16 teams

Most Fumbles, Both Teams, Game
12 Buffalo (8) vs. Dallas (4), 1993
10 Dallas (6) vs. Denver (4), 1978
8 Dallas (4) vs. Pittsburgh (4), 1976

Fewest Fumbles, Both Teams, Game
0 Los Angeles vs. Pittsburgh, 1980
Green Bay vs. New England, 1997
1 Oakland (0) vs. Minnesota (1), 1977
Oakland (0) vs. Philadelphia (1), 1981
Denver (0) vs. Washington (1), 1988
N.Y. Giants (0) vs. Buffalo (1), 1991
Denver (0) vs. Atlanta (1), 1999
2 In five games

Most Fumbles Lost, Game
5 Buffalo vs. Dallas, 1993
4 Baltimore vs. Dallas, 1971
Denver vs. Dallas, 1978
New England vs. Chicago, 1986
2 In many games

Most Fumbles Lost, Both Teams, Game
7 Buffalo (5) vs. Dallas (2), 1993
6 Denver (4) vs. Dallas (2), 1978
New England (4) vs. Chicago (2), 1986
5 Baltimore (4) vs. Dallas (1), 1971

Fewest Fumbles Lost, Both Teams, Game
0 Green Bay vs. Kansas City, 1967
Dallas vs. Pittsburgh, 1976
Los Angeles vs. Pittsburgh, 1980
Denver vs. N.Y. Giants, 1987
Denver vs. Washington, 1988
Buffalo vs. N.Y. Giants, 1991
San Diego vs. San Francisco, 1995
Dallas vs. Pittsburgh, 1996
Green Bay vs. New England, 1997

Most Fumbles Recovered, Game
8 Dallas vs. Denver, 1978 (4 own, 4 opp.)
6 Dallas vs. Buffalo, 1993 (1 own, 5 opp.)
5 Chicago vs. New England, 1986 (1 own, 4 opp.)

TURNOVERS

(Number of times losing the ball on interceptions and fumbles.)

Most Turnovers, Game
9 Buffalo vs. Dallas, 1993
8 Denver vs. Dallas, 1978
7 Baltimore vs. Dallas, 1971

Fewest Turnovers, Game
0 Green Bay vs. Oakland, 1968
Miami vs. Minnesota, 1974
Pittsburgh vs. Dallas, 1976
Oakland vs. Minnesota, 1977; vs. Philadelphia, 1981
N.Y. Giants vs. Denver, 1987; vs. Buffalo, 1991
San Francisco vs. Denver, 1990; vs. San Diego, 1995
Buffalo vs. N.Y. Giants, 1991
Dallas vs. Pittsburgh, 1996
Green Bay vs. New England, 1997
1 By many teams

Most Turnovers, Both Teams, Game
11 Baltimore (7) vs. Dallas (4), 1971
Buffalo (9) vs. Dallas (2), 1993
10 Denver (8) vs. Dallas (2), 1978
8 New England (6) vs. Chicago (2), 1986

Fewest Turnovers, Both Teams, Game
0 Buffalo vs. N.Y. Giants, 1991
1 N.Y. Giants (0) vs. Denver (1), 1987
2 Green Bay (1) vs. Kansas City (1), 1967
Miami (0) vs. Minnesota (2), 1974
Cincinnati (1) vs. San Francisco (1), 1989

POSTSEASON GAME RECORDS

Compiled by Elias Sports Bureau

Throughout this all-time postseason record section, the following abbreviations are used to indicate various levels of postseason games:

SB Super Bowl (1966 to date)
AFC AFC Championship Game (1970 to date) or AFL Championship Game (1960-69)
NFC NFC Championship Game (1970 to date) or NFL Championship Game (1933-69)
AFC-D AFC Divisional Playoff Game (1970 to date), AFC Second-Round Playoff Game (1982), AFL Inter-Divisional Playoff Game (1969), or special playoff game to break tie for AFL Division Championship (1963, 1968)
NFC-D NFC Divisional Playoff Game (1970 to date), NFC Second-Round Playoff Game (1982), NFL Conference Championship Game (1967-69), or special playoff game to break tie for NFL Division or Conference Championship (1941, 1943, 1947, 1950, 1952, 1957, 1958, 1965)
AFC-FR AFC First-Round Playoff Game (1978 to date)
NFC-FR NFC First-Round Playoff Game (1978 to date)

POSTSEASON GAME COMPOSITE STANDINGS

	W	L	PCT.	PTS.	OP
Green Bay Packers	22	10	.688	772	558
Dallas Cowboys	32	20	.615	1261	952
San Francisco 49ers	24	15	.615	984	759
Washington Redskins*	21	14	.600	738	615
Denver Broncos	16	11	.593	613	636
Oakland Raiders**	21	15	.583	855	659
Pittsburgh Steelers	21	15	.583	801	707
Miami Dolphins	18	16	.529	727	705
Buffalo Bills	14	14	.500	665	636
Carolina Panthers	1	1	.500	39	47
Chicago Bears	14	14	.500	579	552
Indianapolis Colts***	10	10	.500	360	389
Jacksonville Jaguars	3	3	.500	132	160
New York Jets	6	7	.462	260	247
Philadelphia Eagles	9	11	.450	359	369
Detroit Lions	7	9	.438	352	377
Seattle Seahawks	3	4	.429	128	139
New York Giants	14	19	.424	541	616
Kansas City Chiefs****	8	11	.421	301	384
Cincinnati Bengals	5	7	.417	246	257
Minnesota Vikings	15	21	.417	681	797
New England Patriots#	7	10	.412	310	357
Tennessee Titans†	9	13	.409	371	533
Atlanta Falcons	4	6	.400	208	260
St. Louis Rams††	13	20	.394	501	697
San Diego Chargers†††	7	11	.389	332	428
Cleveland Browns	11	19	.367	596	692
Tampa Bay Buccaneers	2	4	.333	68	125
Arizona Cardinals††††	2	5	.286	122	182
New Orleans Saints	0	4	.000	56	123

** One game played when franchise was in Boston (lost 21-6).*
*** 12 games played when franchise was in Los Angeles (won 6, lost 6, 268 points scored, 224 points allowed).*
**** 15 games played when franchise was in Baltimore (won 8, lost 7, 264 points scored, 262 points allowed).*
***** One game played when franchise was Dallas Texans (won 20-17).*
 # Two games played when franchise was in Boston (won 26-8, lost 51-10).
† 22 games played when franchise was in Houston and known as the Oilers (won 9, lost 13, 371 points scored, 533 points allowed).
†† One game played when franchise was in Cleveland (won 15-14), 32 games played when franchise was in Los Angeles (won 12, lost 20, 486 points scored, 683 points allowed).
††† One game played when franchise was in Los Angeles (lost 24-16).
†††† Two games played when franchise was in Chicago (won 28-21, lost 7-0), three games played when franchise was in St. Louis (lost 30-14, lost 35-23, lost 41-16).

INDIVIDUAL RECORDS

SERVICE

Most Games, Career
27 D.D. Lewis, Dallas (SB 5, NFC 9, NFC-D 12, NFC-FR 1)
26 Larry Cole, Dallas (SB 5, NFC 8, NFC-D 12, NFC-FR 1)
25 Charlie Waters, Dallas (SB 5, NFC 9, NFC-D 10, NFC-FR 1)

Most Games, Head Coach
36 Tom Landry, Dallas
Don Shula, Baltimore-Miami
24 Chuck Noll, Pittsburgh
22 Bud Grant, Minnesota

Most Games Won, Head Coach
20 Tom Landry, Dallas
19 Don Shula, Baltimore-Miami
16 Chuck Noll, Pittsburgh
Joe Gibbs, Washington

Most Games Lost, Head Coach
17 Don Shula, Baltimore-Miami
16 Tom Landry, Dallas
12 Bud Grant, Minnesota

SCORING

POINTS

Most Points, Career
126 Thurman Thomas, Buffalo, 20 games (21-td)
120 Emmitt Smith, Dallas, 16 games (20-td)
119 Gary Anderson, Pittsburgh-Philadelphia-San Francisco-Minnesota, 17 games (44-pat, 25-fg)

Most Points, Game
30 Ricky Watters, NFC-D:San Francisco vs. N.Y. Giants, 1993 (5-td)
19 Pat Harder, NFC-D: Detroit vs. Los Angeles, 1952 (2-td, 4-pat, 1-fg)
Paul Hornung, NFC: Green Bay vs. N.Y. Giants, 1961 (1-td, 4-pat, 3-fg)
18 By many players

Most Consecutive Games Scoring
19 George Blanda, Chi. Bears-Houston-Oakland, 1956-75
16 Norm Johnson, Seattle-Atlanta-Pittsburgh, 1983-97 (current)
15 Roy Gerela, Houston-Pittsburgh, 1969-78

TOUCHDOWNS

Most Touchdowns, Career
21 Thurman Thomas, Buffalo, 20 games (16-r, 5-p)
20 Emmitt Smith, Dallas, 16 games (18-r, 2-p)
19 Jerry Rice, San Francisco, 23 games (0-r, 19-p)

Most Touchdowns, Game
5 Ricky Watters, NFC-D:San Francisco vs. N.Y. Giants, 1993 (5-r)
3 Andy Farkas, NFC-D: Washington vs. N.Y. Giants, 1943 (3-r)
Tom Fears, NFC-D: Los Angeles vs. Chi. Bears, 1950 (3-p)
Otto Graham, NFC: Cleveland vs. Detroit, 1954 (3-r)
Gary Collins, NFC: Cleveland vs. Baltimore, 1964 (3-p)
Craig Baynham, NFC-D: Dallas vs. Cleveland, 1967 (2-r, 1-p)
Fred Biletnikoff, AFC-D: Oakland vs. Kansas City, 1968 (3-p)
Tom Matte, NFC: Baltimore vs. Cleveland, 1968 (3-r)
Larry Schreiber, NFC-D: San Francisco vs. Dallas, 1972 (3-r)
Larry Csonka, AFC: Miami vs. Oakland, 1973 (3-r)
Franco Harris, AFC-D: Pittsburgh vs. Buffalo, 1974 (3-r)
Preston Pearson, NFC: Dallas vs. Los Angeles, 1975 (3-p)
Dave Casper, AFC-D: Oakland vs. Baltimore, 1977 (OT) (3-p)
Alvin Garrett, NFC-FR: Washington vs. Detroit, 1982 (3-p)
John Riggins, NFC-D: Washington vs. L.A. Rams, 1983 (3-r)
Roger Craig, SB: San Francisco vs. Miami, 1984 (1-r, 2-p)
Jerry Rice, NFC-D: San Francisco vs. Minnesota, 1988 (3-p)
Jerry Rice, SB: San Francisco vs. Denver, 1989 (3-p)
Kenneth Davis, AFC: Buffalo vs. L.A. Raiders, 1990 (3-r)
Andre Reed, AFC-FR: Buffalo vs. Houston, 1992 (OT) (3-p)
Sterling Sharpe, NFC-FR: Green Bay vs. Detroit, 1993 (3-p)
Napoleon McCallum, AFC-FR: L.A. Raiders vs. Denver, 1993 (3-r)
Thurman Thomas, AFC: Buffalo vs. Kansas City, 1993 (3-r)
William Floyd, NFC-D: San Francisco vs. Chicago, 1994 (3-r)
Ricky Watters, SB: San Francisco vs. San Diego, 1994 (1-r, 2-p)
Jerry Rice, SB: San Francisco vs. San Diego, 1994 (3-p)
Emmitt Smith, NFC: Dallas vs. Green Bay, 1995 (3-r)
Curtis Martin, AFC-D: New England vs. Pittsburgh, 1996 (3-r)
Terrell Davis, SB: Denver vs. Green Bay, 1997 (3-r)
Mario Bates, NFC-D: Arizona vs. Minnesota, 1998 (3-r)
Leroy Hoard, NFC-D: Minnesota vs. Arizona, 1998 (2-r, 1-p)

Most Consecutive Games Scoring Touchdowns
9 Thurman Thomas, Buffalo, 1992-98 (current)
8 John Stallworth, Pittsburgh, 1978-83
Emmitt Smith, Dallas, 1993-96
7 John Riggins, Washington, 1982-84
Marcus Allen, L.A. Raiders, 1982-85
Terrell Davis, Denver, 1996-98

POINTS AFTER TOUCHDOWN

Most (One-Point) Points After Touchdown, Career
49 George Blanda, Chi. Bears-Houston-Oakland, 19 games (49 att)
44 Gary Anderson, Pittsburgh-Philadelphia-San Francisco-Minnesota, 17 games (44-att)
42 Mike Cofer, San Francisco, 12 games (46 att)

Most (One-Point) Points After Touchdown, Game
8 Lou Groza, NFC: Cleveland vs. Detroit, 1954 (8 att)
Jim Martin, NFC: Detroit vs. Cleveland, 1957 (8 att)
George Blanda, AFC-D: Oakland vs. Houston, 1969 (8 att)
7 Danny Villanueva, NFC-D: Dallas vs. Cleveland, 1967 (7 att)
Raul Allegre, NFC-D: N.Y. Giants vs. San Francisco, 1986 (7 att)
Mike Cofer, SB: San Francisco vs. Denver, 1989 (8 att)

Lin Elliott, SB: Dallas vs. Buffalo, 1992 (7 att)
Doug Brien, SB: San Francisco vs. San Diego, 1994 (7 att)
Gary Anderson, NFC-FR: Philadelphia vs. Detroit, 1995 (7 att)
6 George Blair, AFC: San Diego vs. Boston, 1963 (6 att)
Mark Moseley, NFC-D: Washington vs. L.A. Rams, 1983 (6 att)
Uwe von Schamann, AFC: Miami vs. Pittsburgh, 1984 (6 att)
Ali Haji-Sheikh, SB: Washington vs. Denver, 1987 (6 att)
Scott Norwood, AFC: Buffalo vs. L.A. Raiders, 1990 (7 att)
Jeff Jaeger, AFC-FR: L.A. Raiders vs. Denver, 1993 (6 att)
Jason Elam, AFC-FR: Denver vs. Jacksonville, 1997 (6 att)

Most (Kicking) Points After Touchdown, No Misses, Career
49 George Blanda, Chi. Bears-Houston-Oakland, 19 games
44 Gary Anderson, Pittsburgh-Philadelphia-San Francisco-Minnesota, 17 games
41 Rafael Septien, L.A. Rams-Dallas, 14 games

Most Two-Point Conversions, Career
1 By many players

Most Two-Point Conversions, Game
1 By many players

FIELD GOALS

Most Field Goals Attempted, Career
39 George Blanda, Chi. Bears-Houston-Oakland, 19 games
32 Gary Anderson, Pittsburgh-Philadelphia-San Francisco-Minnesota, 17 games
31 Mark Moseley, Washington-Cleveland, 11 games

Most Field Goals Attempted, Game
6 George Blanda, AFC: Oakland vs. Houston, 1967
David Ray, NFC-D: Los Angeles vs. Dallas, 1973
Mark Moseley, AFC-D: Cleveland vs. N.Y. Jets, 1986 (OT)
Matt Bahr, NFC: N.Y. Giants vs. San Francisco, 1990
Steve Christie, AFC: Buffalo vs. Miami, 1992
5 By many players

Most Field Goals, Career
25 Gary Anderson, Pittsburgh-Philadelphia-San Francisco-Minnesota, 17 games
22 George Blanda, Chi. Bears-Houston-Oakland, 19 games
21 Matt Bahr, Pittsburgh-Cleveland-N.Y. Giants-New England, 14 games
Steve Christie, Buffalo, 11 games

Most Field Goals, Game
5 Chuck Nelson, NFC-D: Minnesota vs. San Francisco, 1987
Matt Bahr, NFC: N.Y. Giants vs. San Francisco, 1990
Steve Christie, AFC: Buffalo vs. Miami, 1992
Brad Daluiso, NFC-FR: N.Y. Giants vs. Minnesota, 1997
4 Gino Cappelletti, AFC-D: Boston vs. Buffalo, 1963
George Blanda, AFC: Oakland vs. Houston, 1967
Don Chandler, SB: Green Bay vs. Oakland, 1967
Curt Knight, NFC: Washington vs. Dallas, 1972
George Blanda, AFC-D: Oakland vs. Pittsburgh, 1973
Ray Wersching, SB: San Francisco vs. Cincinnati, 1981
Tony Franklin, AFC-FR: New England vs. N.Y. Jets, 1985
Jess Atkinson, NFC-FR: Washington vs. L.A. Rams, 1986
Luis Zendejas, NFC-D: Philadelphia vs. Chicago, 1988
Gary Anderson, AFC-FR: Pittsburgh vs. Houston, 1989 (OT)
Norm Johnson, AFC-D: Pittsburgh vs. Buffalo, 1995
Chris Boniol, NFC-FR: Dallas vs. Minnesota, 1996
John Kasay, NFC-D: Carolina vs. Dallas, 1996
Mike Hollis, AFC-D: Jacksonville vs. New England, 1998
3 By many players

Most Consecutive Games Scoring Field Goals
13 Toni Fritsch, Dallas-Houston, 1972-79
9 Kevin Butler, Chicago, 1985-91
Scott Norwood, Buffalo, 1988-91
8 Mark Moseley, Washington-Cleveland, 1982-86
Rich Karlis, Denver-Minnesota, 1984-89
Steve Christie, Buffalo, 1993-95
Gary Anderson, Pittsburgh-Philadelphia, 1989-95
Morten Andersen, New Orleans-Atlanta, 1987-98 (current)

Most Consecutive Field Goals
16 Gary Anderson, Pittsburgh-Philadelphia, 1989-95
15 Rafael Septien, Dallas, 1978-82
13 Mike Hollis, Jacksonville, 1996-98 (current)
Morten Andersen, New Orleans-Atlanta, 1987-98

Longest Field Goal
58 Pete Stoyanovich, AFC-FR: Miami vs. Kansas City, 1990
54 Ed Murray, NFC-D: Detroit vs. San Francisco, 1983
Steve Christie, SB: Buffalo vs. Dallas, 1993
John Carney, AFC-FR: San Diego vs. Indianapolis, 1995
53 Al Del Greco, AFC-FR: Houston vs. N.Y. Jets, 1991

Highest Field Goal Percentage, Career (10 field goals)
93.3 Mike Hollis, Jacksonville, 6 games (15-14)
90.9 Chuck Nelson, L.A. Rams-Minnesota, 6 games (11-10)
87.5 Steve Christie, Buffalo, 11 games (24-21)

SAFETIES

Most Safeties, Game
1 Bill Willis, NFC-D: Cleveland vs. N.Y. Giants, 1950
Carl Eller, NFC-D: Minnesota vs. Los Angeles, 1969
George Andrie, NFC-D: Dallas vs. Detroit, 1970
Alan Page, NFC-D: Minnesota vs. Dallas, 1971
Dwight White, SB: Pittsburgh vs. Minnesota, 1974
Reggie Harrison, SB: Pittsburgh vs. Dallas, 1975
Jim Jensen, NFC-D: Dallas vs. Los Angeles, 1976
Ted Washington, AFC: Houston vs. Pittsburgh, 1978
Randy White, NFC-D: Dallas vs. Los Angeles, 1979
Henry Waechter, SB: Chicago vs. New England, 1985
Rulon Jones, AFC-FR: Denver vs. New England, 1986
George Martin, SB: N.Y. Giants vs. Denver, 1986
D.D. Hoggard, AFC: Cleveland vs. Denver, 1987
Bruce Smith, SB: Buffalo vs. N.Y. Giants, 1990
Reggie White, NFC-FR: Philadelphia vs. New Orleans, 1992
Willie Clay, NFC-FR: Detroit vs. Green Bay, 1994
Carnell Lake, AFC-D: Pittsburgh vs. Cleveland, 1994
Reuben Davis, AFC-D: San Diego vs. Miami, 1994

RUSHING

ATTEMPTS

Most Attempts, Career
400 Franco Harris, Pittsburgh, 19 games
334 Emmitt Smith, Dallas, 16 games
Thurman Thomas, Buffalo, 20 games
302 Tony Dorsett, Dallas, 17 games

Most Attempts, Game
38 Ricky Bell, NFC-D: Tampa Bay vs. Philadelphia, 1979
John Riggins, SB: Washington vs. Miami, 1982
37 Lawrence McCutcheon, NFC-D: Los Angeles vs. St. Louis, 1975
John Riggins, NFC-D: Washington vs. Minnesota, 1982
36 John Riggins, NFC: Washington vs. Dallas, 1982
John Riggins, NFC: Washington vs. San Francisco, 1983
Curtis Martin, AFC-D: N.Y. Jets vs. Jacksonville, 1998

YARDS GAINED

Most Yards Gained, Career
1,556 Franco Harris, Pittsburgh, 19 games
1,487 Emmitt Smith, Dallas, 16 games
1,432 Thurman Thomas, Buffalo, 20 games

Most Yards Gained, Game
248 Eric Dickerson, NFC-D: L.A. Rams vs. Dallas, 1985
206 Keith Lincoln, AFC: San Diego vs. Boston, 1963
204 Timmy Smith, SB: Washington vs. Denver, 1987

Most Games, 100 or More Yards Rushing, Career
7 Emmitt Smith, Dallas, 16 games
Terrell Davis, Denver, 8 games
6 John Riggins, Washington, 9 games
Thurman Thomas, Buffalo, 20 games
5 Franco Harris, Pittsburgh, 19 games
Marcus Allen, L.A. Raiders-Kansas City, 16 games

Most Consecutive Games, 100 or More Yards Rushing
7 Terrell Davis, Denver, 1997-98 (current)
6 John Riggins, Washington, 1982-83
4 Thurman Thomas, Buffalo, 1990-91

Longest Run From Scrimmage
80 Roger Craig, NFC-D: San Francisco vs. Minnesota, 1988 (TD)
78 Curtis Martin, AFC-D: New England vs. Pittsburgh, 1996 (TD)
74 Marcus Allen, SB: L.A. Raiders vs. Washington, 1983 (TD)
Adrian Murrell, NFC-FR: Arizona vs. Dallas, 1998

AVERAGE GAIN

Highest Average Gain, Career (100 attempts)
5.59 Terrell Davis, Denver, 8 games (204-1,140)
5.04 Marcus Allen, L.A. Raiders-Kansas City, 16 games (267-1,347)
4.89 Eric Dickerson, L.A. Rams-Indianapolis, 7 games (148-724)

Highest Average Gain, Game (10 attempts)
15.90 Elmer Angsman, NFC: Chi. Cardinals vs. Philadelphia, 1947 (10-159)
15.85 Keith Lincoln, AFC: San Diego vs. Boston, 1963 (13-206)
11.31 Zack Crockett, AFC-FR: Indianapolis vs. San Diego, 1995 (13-147)

TOUCHDOWNS

Most Touchdowns, Career
18 Emmitt Smith, Dallas, 16 games
16 Franco Harris, Pittsburgh, 19 games
Thurman Thomas, Buffalo, 20 games
12 John Riggins, Washington, 9 games
Terrell Davis, Denver, 8 games

Most Touchdowns, Game
5 Ricky Watters, NFC-D: San Francisco vs. N.Y. Giants, 1993
3 Andy Farkas, NFC-D: Washington vs. N.Y. Giants, 1943

Otto Graham, NFC: Cleveland vs. Detroit, 1954
Tom Matte, NFC: Baltimore vs. Cleveland, 1968
Larry Schreiber, NFC-D: San Francisco vs. Dallas, 1972
Larry Csonka, AFC: Miami vs. Oakland, 1973
Franco Harris, AFC-D: Pittsburgh vs. Buffalo, 1974
John Riggins, NFC-D: Washington vs. L.A. Rams, 1983
Kenneth Davis, AFC: Buffalo vs. L.A. Raiders, 1990
Napoleon McCallum, AFC-FR: L.A. Raiders vs. Denver, 1993
Thurman Thomas, AFC: Buffalo vs. Kansas City, 1993
William Floyd, NFC-D: San Francisco vs. Chicago, 1994
Emmitt Smith, NFC: Dallas vs. Green Bay, 1995
Curtis Martin, AFC-D: New England vs. Pittsburgh, 1996
Terrell Davis, SB: Denver vs. Green Bay, 1997
Mario Bates, NFC-D: Arizona vs. Minnesota, 1998

Most Consecutive Games Rushing for Touchdowns
8 Emmitt Smith, Dallas, 1993-96
Thurman Thomas, Buffalo, 1992-98 (current)
7 John Riggins, Washington, 1982-84
Terrell Davis, Denver, 1996-98
5 Franco Harris, Pittsburgh, 1974-75
Franco Harris, Pittsburgh, 1977-79
Curtis Martin, New England-N.Y. Jets, 1996-98 (current)

PASSING

PASSER RATING

Highest Passer Rating, Career (150 attempts)
104.8 Bart Starr, Green Bay, 10 games
95.6 Joe Montana, San Francisco-Kansas City, 23 games
93.5 Ken Anderson, Cincinnati, 6 games

ATTEMPTS

Most Passes Attempted, Career
734 Joe Montana, San Francisco-Kansas City, 23 games
651 John Elway, Denver, 22 games
632 Dan Marino, Miami, 16 games

Most Passes Attempted, Game
65 Steve Young, NFC-D: San Francisco vs. Green Bay, 1995
64 Bernie Kosar, AFC-D: Cleveland vs. N.Y. Jets, 1986 (OT)
Dan Marino, AFC-FR: Miami vs. Buffalo, 1995
58 Jim Kelly, SB: Buffalo vs. Washington, 1991

COMPLETIONS

Most Passes Completed, Career
460 Joe Montana, San Francisco-Kansas City, 23 games
357 Dan Marino, Miami, 16 games
355 John Elway, Denver, 22 games

Most Passes Completed, Game
36 Warren Moon, AFC-FR: Houston vs. Buffalo, 1992 (OT)
33 Dan Fouts, AFC-D: San Diego vs. Miami, 1981 (OT)
Bernie Kosar, AFC-D: Cleveland vs. N.Y. Jets, 1986 (OT)
Dan Marino, AFC-FR: Miami vs. Buffalo, 1995
32 Neil Lomax, NFC-FR: St. Louis vs. Green Bay, 1982
Danny White, NFC-FR: Dallas vs. L.A. Rams, 1983
Warren Moon, AFC-D: Houston vs. Kansas City, 1993
Neil O'Donnell, AFC: Pittsburgh vs. San Diego, 1994
Steve Young, NFC-D: San Francisco vs. Green Bay, 1995

COMPLETION PERCENTAGE

Highest Completion Percentage, Career (150 attempts)
66.3 Ken Anderson, Cincinnati, 6 games (166-110)
64.3 Warren Moon, Houston-Minnesota, 10 games (403-259)
64.2 Troy Aikman, Dallas, 15 games (464-298)

Highest Completion Percentage, Game (15 completions)
88.0 Phil Simms, SB: N.Y. Giants vs. Denver, 1986 (25-22)
86.7 Joe Montana, NFC: San Francisco vs. L.A. Rams, 1989 (30-26)
84.2 David Woodley, AFC-FR: Miami vs. New England, 1982 (19-16)

YARDS GAINED

Most Yards Gained, Career
5,772 Joe Montana, San Francisco-Kansas City, 23 games
4,964 John Elway, Denver, 22 games
4,219 Dan Marino, Miami, 16 games

Most Yards Gained, Game
489 Bernie Kosar, AFC-D: Cleveland vs. N.Y. Jets, 1986 (OT)
433 Dan Fouts, AFC-D: San Diego vs. Miami, 1981 (OT)
422 Dan Marino, AFC-FR: Miami vs. Buffalo, 1995

Most Games, 300 or More Yards Passing, Career
6 Joe Montana, San Francisco-Kansas City, 23 games
5 Dan Fouts, San Diego, 7 games
4 Warren Moon, Houston-Minnesota, 10 games
Troy Aikman, Dallas, 15 games
Dan Marino, Miami, 16 games
John Elway, Denver, 22 games

Most Consecutive Games, 300 or More Yards Passing
4 Dan Fouts, San Diego, 1979-81
3 Jim Kelly, Buffalo, 1989-90
Warren Moon, Houston, 1991-93
2 Daryle Lamonica, Oakland, 1968
Ken Anderson, Cincinnati, 1981-82
Terry Bradshaw, Pittsburgh, 1979-82
Joe Montana, San Francisco, 1983-84
Dan Marino, Miami, 1984
Troy Aikman, Dallas, 1994
Steve Young, San Francisco, 1994-95

Longest Pass Completion
94 Troy Aikman (to Harper), NFC-D: Dallas vs. Green Bay, 1994 (TD)
93 Daryle Lamonica (to Dubenion), AFC-D: Buffalo vs. Boston, 1963 (TD)
88 George Blanda (to Cannon), AFC: Houston vs. L.A. Chargers, 1960 (TD)

AVERAGE GAIN

Highest Average Gain, Career (150 attempts)
8.45 Joe Theismann, Washington, 10 games (211-1,782)
8.43 Jim Plunkett, Oakland/L.A.Raiders, 10 games (272-2,293)
8.41 Terry Bradshaw, Pittsburgh, 19 games (456-3,833)

Highest Average Gain, Game (20 attempts)
14.71 Terry Bradshaw, SB: Pittsburgh vs. Los Angeles, 1979 (21-309)
13.33 Bob Waterfield, NFC-D: Los Angeles vs. Chi. Bears, 1950 (21-280)
13.16 Dan Marino, AFC: Miami vs. Pittsburgh, 1984 (32-421)

TOUCHDOWNS

Most Touchdown Passes, Career
45 Joe Montana, San Francisco-Kansas City, 23 games
30 Terry Bradshaw, Pittsburgh, 19 games
Dan Marino, Miami, 16 games
27 John Elway, Denver, 22 games

Most Touchdown Passes, Game
6 Daryle Lamonica, AFC-D: Oakland vs. Houston, 1969
Steve Young, SB: San Francisco vs. San Diego, 1994
5 Sid Luckman, NFC: Chi. Bears vs. Washington, 1943
Daryle Lamonica, AFC-D: Oakland vs. Kansas City, 1968
Joe Montana, SB: San Francisco vs. Denver, 1989
4 Otto Graham, NFC: Cleveland vs. Los Angeles, 1950
Tobin Rote, NFC: Detroit vs. Cleveland, 1957
Bart Starr, NFC: Green Bay vs. Dallas, 1966
Ken Stabler, AFC-D: Oakland vs. Miami, 1974
Roger Staubach, NFC: Dallas vs. Los Angeles, 1975
Terry Bradshaw, SB: Pittsburgh vs. Dallas, 1978
Don Strock, AFC-D: Miami vs. San Diego, 1981 (OT)
Lynn Dickey, NFC-FR: Green Bay vs. St. Louis, 1982
Dan Marino, AFC: Miami vs. Pittsburgh, 1984
Phil Simms, NFC-D: N.Y. Giants vs. San Francisco, 1986
Doug Williams, SB: Washington vs. Denver, 1987
Jim Kelly, AFC-D: Buffalo vs. Cleveland, 1989
Joe Montana, NFC-D: San Francisco vs. Minnesota, 1989
Warren Moon, AFC-FR: Houston vs. Buffalo, 1992 (OT)
Frank Reich, AFC-FR: Buffalo vs. Houston, 1992 (OT)
Troy Aikman, SB: Dallas vs. Buffalo, 1992

Most Consecutive Games, Touchdown Passes
13 Dan Marino, Miami, 1983-95
10 Ken Stabler, Oakland, 1973-77
Joe Montana, San Francisco-Kansas City, 1988-93
Brett Favre, Green Bay, 1995-98 (current)
9 John Elway, Denver, 1984-89

HAD INTERCEPTED

Lowest Percentage, Passes Had Intercepted, Career (150 attempts)
1.41 Bart Starr, Green Bay, 10 games (213-3)
2.15 Phil Simms, N.Y. Giants, 10 games (279-6)
2.47 Randall Cunningham, Philadelphia-Minnesota, 11 games (365-9)

Most Attempts Without Interception, Game
54 Neil O'Donnell, AFC: Pittsburgh vs. San Diego, 1994
48 Warren Moon, AFC-FR: Houston vs. Pittsburgh, 1989 (OT)
Randall Cunningham, NFC: Minnesota vs. Atlanta, 1998
47 Daryle Lamonica, AFC: Oakland vs. N.Y. Jets, 1968

Most Passes Had Intercepted, Career
28 Jim Kelly, Buffalo, 17 games
26 Terry Bradshaw, Pittsburgh, 19 games
22 Dan Marino, Miami, 16 games

Most Passes Had Intercepted, Game
6 Frank Filchock, NFC: N.Y. Giants vs. Chi. Bears, 1946
Bobby Layne, NFC: Detroit vs. Cleveland, 1954
Norm Van Brocklin, NFC: Los Angeles vs. Cleveland, 1955
5 Frank Filchock, NFC: Washington vs. Chi. Bears, 1940
George Blanda, AFC: Houston vs. San Diego, 1961
George Blanda, AFC: Houston vs. Dall. Texans, 1962 (OT)
Y.A. Tittle, NFC: N.Y. Giants vs. Chicago, 1963

Mike Phipps, AFC-D: Cleveland vs. Miami, 1972
Dan Pastorini, AFC: Houston vs. Pittsburgh, 1978
Dan Fouts, AFC-D: San Diego vs. Houston, 1979
Tommy Kramer, NFC-D: Minnesota vs. Philadelphia, 1980
Dan Fouts, AFC-D: San Diego vs. Miami, 1982
Richard Todd, AFC: N.Y. Jets vs Miami, 1982
Gary Danielson, NFC-D: Detroit vs. San Francisco, 1983
Jay Schroeder, AFC: L.A. Raiders vs. Buffalo, 1990
4 By many players

PASS RECEIVING

RECEPTIONS

Most Receptions, Career
124 Jerry Rice, San Francisco, 23 games
87 Michael Irvin, Dallas, 16 games
85 Andre Reed, Buffalo, 20 games

Most Receptions, Game
13 Kellen Winslow, AFC-D: San Diego vs. Miami, 1981 (OT)
Thurman Thomas, AFC-D: Buffalo vs. Cleveland, 1989
Shannon Sharpe, AFC-FR: Denver vs. L.A. Raiders, 1993
12 Raymond Berry, NFC: Baltimore vs. N.Y. Giants, 1958
Michael Irvin, NFC: Dallas vs. San Francisco, 1994
11 Dante Lavelli, NFC: Cleveland vs. Los Angeles, 1950
Dan Ross, SB: Cincinnati vs. San Francisco, 1981
Franco Harris, AFC-FR: Pittsburgh vs. San Diego, 1982
Steve Watson, AFC-D: Denver vs. Pittsburgh, 1984
John L. Williams, AFC-D: Seattle vs. Cincinnati, 1988
Jerry Rice, SB: San Francisco vs. Cincinnati, 1988
Ernest Givins, AFC-FR: Houston vs. Pittsburgh, 1989 (OT)
Amp Lee, NFC-D: Minnesota vs. Chicago, 1994
Jay Novacek, NFC-D: Dallas vs. Green Bay, 1994
O.J. McDuffie, AFC-FR: Miami vs. Buffalo, 1995
Jerry Rice, NFC-C: San Francisco vs. Green Bay, 1995

Most Consecutive Games, Pass Receptions
23 Jerry Rice, San Francisco, 1985-98 (current)
22 Drew Pearson, Dallas, 1973-83
18 Paul Warfield, Cleveland-Miami, 1964-74
Cliff Branch, Oakland/L.A. Raiders, 1974-83
Thurman Thomas, Buffalo, 1989-98 (current)

YARDS GAINED

Most Yards Gained, Career
1,811 Jerry Rice, San Francisco, 23 games
1,315 Michael Irvin, Dallas, 16 games
1,289 Cliff Branch, Oakland/L.A. Raiders, 22 games

Most Yards Gained, Game
240 Eric Moulds, AFC-FR: Buffalo vs. Miami, 1998
227 Anthony Carter, NFC-D: Minnesota vs. San Francisco, 1987
215 Jerry Rice, SB: San Francisco vs. Cincinnati, 1988

Most Games, 100 or More Yards Receiving, Career
7 Jerry Rice, San Francisco, 23 games
6 Michael Irvin, Dallas, 16 games
5 John Stallworth, Pittsburgh, 18 games
Andre Reed, Buffalo, 20 games

Most Consecutive Games, 100 or More Yards Receiving, Career
3 Tom Fears, Los Angeles, 1950-51
Jerry Rice, San Francisco, 1988-89
2 By many players

Longest Reception
94 Alvin Harper (from Aikman), NFC-D: Dallas vs. Green Bay, 1994 (TD)
93 Elbert Dubenion (from Lamonica), AFC-D: Buffalo vs. Boston, 1963 (TD)
88 Billy Cannon (from Blanda), AFC: Houston vs. L.A. Chargers, 1960 (TD)

AVERAGE GAIN

Highest Average Gain, Career (20 receptions)
27.3 Alvin Harper, Dallas, 10 games (24-655)
23.7 Willie Gault, Chicago-L.A. Raiders, 12 games (21-497)
22.8 Harold Jackson, L.A. Rams-New England-Minnesota-Seattle, 14 games (24-548)

Highest Average Gain, Game (3 receptions)
46.3 Harold Jackson, NFC: Los Angeles vs. Minnesota, 1974 (3-139)
42.7 Billy Cannon, AFC: Houston vs. L.A. Chargers, 1960 (3-128)
42.0 Lenny Moore, NFC: Baltimore vs. N.Y. Giants, 1959 (3-126)

TOUCHDOWNS

Most Touchdowns, Career
19 Jerry Rice, San Francisco, 23 games
12 John Stallworth, Pittsburgh, 18 games
10 Fred Biletnikoff, Oakland, 19 games

Most Touchdowns, Game
3 Tom Fears, NFC-D: Los Angeles vs. Chi. Bears, 1950
Gary Collins, NFC: Cleveland vs. Baltimore, 1964
Fred Biletnikoff, AFC-D: Oakland vs. Kansas City, 1968
Preston Pearson, NFC: Dallas vs. Los Angeles, 1975
Dave Casper, AFC-D: Oakland vs. Baltimore, 1977 (OT)
Alvin Garrett, NFC-FR: Washington vs. Detroit, 1982
Jerry Rice, NFC-D: San Francisco vs. Minnesota, 1988
Jerry Rice, SB: San Francisco vs. Denver, 1989
Andre Reed, AFC-FR: Buffalo vs. Houston, 1992 (OT)
Sterling Sharpe, NFC-FR: Green Bay vs. Detroit, 1993
Jerry Rice, SB: San Francisco vs. San Diego, 1994

Most Consecutive Games, Touchdown Passes Caught
8 John Stallworth, Pittsburgh, 1978-83
5 James Lofton, Green Bay-Buffalo, 1982-90
4 Lynn Swann, Pittsburgh, 1978-79
Harold Carmichael, Philadelphia, 1978-80
Fred Solomon, San Francisco, 1983-84
Jerry Rice, San Francisco, 1988-89
John Taylor, San Francisco, 1988-89

INTERCEPTIONS BY

Most Interceptions, Career
9 Charlie Waters, Dallas, 25 games
Bill Simpson, Los Angeles-Buffalo, 11 games
Ronnie Lott, San Francisco-L.A. Raiders, 20 games
8 Lester Hayes, Oakland/L.A. Raiders, 13 games
7 Willie Brown, Oakland, 17 games
Dennis Thurman, Dallas, 14 games

Most Interceptions, Game
4 Vernon Perry, AFC-D: Houston vs. San Diego, 1979
3 Joe Laws, NFC: Green Bay vs. N.Y. Giants, 1944
Charlie Waters, NFC-D: Dallas vs. Chicago, 1977
Rod Martin, SB: Oakland vs. Philadelphia, 1980
Dennis Thurman, NFC-D: Dallas vs. Green Bay, 1982
A.J. Duhe, AFC: Miami vs. N.Y. Jets, 1982
2 By many players

Most Consecutive Games, Interceptions
3 Warren Lahr, Cleveland, 1950-51
Ken Gorgal, Cleveland, 1950-53
Joe Schmidt, Detroit, 1954-57
Emmitt Thomas, Kansas City, 1969
Mel Renfro, Dallas, 1970
Rick Volk, Baltimore, 1970-71
Mike Wagner, Pittsburgh, 1975-76
Randy Hughes, Dallas, 1977-78
Vernon Perry, Houston, 1979-80
Lester Hayes, Oakland, 1980
Gerald Small, Miami, 1982
Lester Hayes, L.A. Raiders, 1982-83
Fred Marion, New England, 1985
John Harris, Seattle-Minnesota, 1984-87
Felix Wright, Cleveland, 1987-88
Kurt Gouveia, Washington, 1991
Eric Davis, San Francisco, 1994
Deion Sanders, San Francisco-Dallas, 1994-95
Craig Newsome, Green Bay, 1996
Eugene Robinson, Green Bay-Atlanta, 1997-98

YARDS GAINED

Most Yards Gained, Career
196 Willie Brown, Oakland, 17 games
187 Ronnie Lott, San Francisco-L.A.-Raiders, 20 games
160 George Teague, Green Bay-Dallas-Miami-Dallas, 11 games

Most Yards Gained, Game
108 Darrien Gordon, SB: Denver vs. Atlanta, 1998
101 George Teague, NFC-FR: Green Bay vs. Detroit, 1993
98 Darrol Ray, AFC-FR: N.Y. Jets vs. Cincinnati, 1982

Longest Return
101 George Teague, NFC-FR: Green Bay vs. Detroit, 1993 (TD)
98 Darrol Ray, AFC-FR: N.Y. Jets vs. Cincinnati, 1982 (TD)
94 LeRoy Irvin, NFC-FR: L.A. Rams vs. Dallas, 1983

TOUCHDOWNS

Most Touchdowns, Career
3 Willie Brown, Oakland, 17 games
2 Lester Hayes, Oakland/L.A. Raiders, 13 games
Ronnie Lott, San Francisco-L.A. Raiders, 20 games
Darrell Green, Washington, 16 games
Melvin Jenkins, Seattle-Detroit, 5 games
George Teague, Green Bay-Dallas-Miami-Dallas, 11 games

Most Touchdowns, Game
1 By many players

PUNTING

Most Punts, Career
111 Ray Guy, Oakland/L.A. Raiders, 22 games

84 Danny White, Dallas, 18 games
73 Mike Eischeid, Oakland-Minnesota, 14 games

Most Punts, Game
14 Dave Jennings, AFC-D: N.Y. Jets vs. Cleveland, 1986 (OT)
12 David Lee, AFC-D: Baltimore vs. Oakland, 1977 (OT)
11 Ken Strong, NFC: N.Y. Giants vs. Chi. Bears, 1933
Jim Norton, AFC: Houston vs. Oakland, 1967
Ode Burrell, AFC-D: Houston vs. Oakland, 1969
Dale Hatcher, NFC: L.A. Rams vs. Chicago, 1985

Longest Punt
76 Ed Danowski, NFC: N.Y. Giants vs. Detroit, 1935
Mike Horan, AFC: Denver vs. Buffalo, 1991
72 Charlie Conerly, NFC-D: N.Y. Giants vs. Cleveland, 1950
Yale Lary, NFC: Detroit vs. Cleveland, 1953
71 Ray Guy, AFC: Oakland vs. San Diego, 1980

AVERAGE YARDAGE

Highest Average, Career (25 punts)
44.5 Rich Camarillo, New England, 6 games (35-1,559)
44.4 Lee Johnson, Cleveland-Cincinnati, 7 games (28-1,244)
43.4 Jerrel Wilson, Kansas City-New England, 8 games (43-1,866)

Highest Average, Game (4 punts)
56.0 Ray Guy, AFC: Oakland vs. San Diego, 1980 (4-224)
52.5 Sammy Baugh, NFC: Washington vs. Chi. Bears, 1942 (6-315)
51.6 Lee Johnson, AFC-D: Cincinnati vs. L.A. Raiders, 1990 (5-258)

PUNT RETURNS

Most Punt Returns, Career
34 David Meggett, N.Y. Giants-New England-N.Y. Jets, 13 games
25 Theo Bell, Pittsburgh-Tampa Bay, 10 games
21 Gerald McNeil, Cleveland-Houston, 8 games

Most Punt Returns, Game
7 Ron Gardin, AFC-D: Baltimore vs. Cincinnati, 1970
Carl Roaches, AFC-FR: Houston vs. Oakland, 1980
Gerald McNeil, AFC-D: Cleveland vs. N.Y. Jets, 1986 (OT)
Phil McConkey, NFC-D: N.Y. Giants vs. San Francisco, 1986
David Meggett, AFC-D: New England vs. Pittsburgh, 1996
Reggie Barlow, AFC-FR: Jacksonville vs. New England, 1998
6 George McAfee, NFC-D: Chi. Bears vs. Los Angeles, 1950
Eddie Brown, NFC-D: Washington vs. Minnesota, 1976
Theo Bell, AFC: Pittsburgh vs. Houston, 1978
Eddie Brown, NFC: Los Angeles vs. Tampa Bay, 1979
John Sciarra, NFC: Philadelphia vs. Dallas, 1980
Kurt Sohn, AFC: N.Y. Jets vs. Miami, 1982
Mike Nelms, SB: Washington vs. Miami, 1982
Anthony Carter, NFC-FR: Minnesota vs. New Orleans, 1987
Desmond Howard, SB: Green Bay vs.New England, 1996
5 By many players

YARDS GAINED

Most Yards Gained, Career
312 David Meggett, N.Y. Giants-New England-N.Y. Jets, 13 games
259 Anthony Carter, Minnesota-Detroit, 9 games
221 Neal Colzie, Oakland-Miami-Tampa Bay, 10 games

Most Yards Gained, Game
143 Anthony Carter, NFC-FR: Minnesota vs. New Orleans, 1987
141 Bob Hayes, NFC-D: Dallas vs. Cleveland, 1967
117 Desmond Howard, NFC-D: Green Bay vs. San Francisco, 1996

Longest Return
84 Anthony Carter, NFC-FR: Minnesota vs. New Orleans, 1987 (TD)
81 Hugh Gallarneau, NFC-D: Chi. Bears vs. Green Bay, 1941 (TD)
79 Bosh Pritchard, NFC-D: Philadelphia vs. Pittsburgh, 1947 (TD)

AVERAGE YARDAGE

Highest Average, Career (10 returns)
15.3 Robert Brooks, Green Bay, 11 games (14-214)
15.2 Anthony Carter, Minnesota-Detroit, 9 games (17-259)
14.3 Antonio Freeman, Green Bay, 10 games (10-143)

Highest Average Gain, Game (3 returns)
47.0 Bob Hayes, NFC-D: Dallas vs. Cleveland, 1967 (3-141)
29.0 George (Butch) Byrd, AFC: Buffalo vs. San Diego, 1965 (3-87)
25.3 Bosh Pritchard, NFC-D: Philadelphia vs. Pittsburgh, 1947 (4-101)

TOUCHDOWNS

Most Touchdowns
1 Hugh Gallarneau, NFC-D: Chicago Bears vs. Green Bay, 1941
Bosh Pritchard, NFC-D: Philadelphia vs. Pittsburgh, 1947
Charley Trippi, NFC: Chicago Cardinals vs. Philadelphia, 1947
Verda (Vitamin T) Smith, NFC-D: Los Angeles vs. Detroit, 1952
George (Butch) Byrd, AFC: Buffalo vs. San Diego, 1965
Golden Richards, NFC: Dallas vs. Minnesota, 1973
Wes Chandler, AFC-D: San Diego vs. Miami, 1981 (OT)
Shaun Gayle, NFC-D: Chicago vs. N.Y. Giants, 1985
Anthony Carter, NFC-FR: Minnesota vs. New Orleans, 1987
Darrell Green, NFC-D: Washington vs. Chicago, 1987
Antonio Freeman, NFC-FR: Green Bay vs. Atlanta, 1995
Desmond Howard, NFC-D: Green Bay vs. San Francisco, 1996

KICKOFF RETURNS

Most Kickoff Returns, Career
29 Fulton Walker, Miami-L.A. Raiders, 10 games
27 Kevin Williams, Dallas-Buffalo, 11 games
25 David Meggett, N.Y. Giants-New England-N.Y. Jets, 13 games
Eric Metcalf, Cleveland-Atlanta-Arizona, 7 games

Most Kickoff Returns, Game
8 Marc Logan, AFC-D: Miami vs. Buffalo, 1990
Andre Coleman, SB: San Diego vs. San Francisco, 1994
7 Don Bingham, NFC: Chi. Bears vs. N.Y. Giants, 1956
Reggie Brown, NFC-FR: Atlanta vs. Minnesota, 1982
David Verser, AFC-FR: Cincinnati vs. N.Y. Jets, 1982
Del Rodgers, NFC-D: Green Bay vs. Dallas, 1982
Henry Ellard, NFC-D: L.A. Rams vs. Washington, 1983
Stephen Starring, SB: New England vs. Chicago, 1985
Darick Holmes, AFC-D: Buffalo vs. Pittsburgh, 1995
Antonio Freeman, NFC: Green Bay vs. Dallas, 1995
Roell Preston, NFC-FR: Green Bay vs. San Francisco, 1998
6 By many players

YARDS GAINED

Most Yards Gained, Career
677 Fulton Walker, Miami-L.A. Raiders, 10 games
565 Eric Metcalf, Cleveland-Atlanta-Arizona, 7 games
559 Kevin Williams, Dallas-Buffalo, 11 games

Most Yards Gained, Game
244 Andre Coleman, SB: San Diego vs. San Francisco, 1994
210 Tim Dwight, SB: Atlanta vs. Denver, 1998
194 Roell Preston, NFC-FR: Green Bay vs. San Francisco, 1998

Longest Return
99 Desmond Howard, SB: Green Bay vs. New England, 1996 (TD)
98 Fulton Walker, SB: Miami vs. Washington, 1982 (TD)
Andre Coleman, SB: San Diego vs. San Francisco, 1994 (TD)
97 Vic Washington, NFC-D: San Francisco vs. Dallas, 1972 (TD)

AVERAGE YARDAGE

Highest Average, Career (10 returns)
34.3 Tim Dwight, Atlanta, 3 games (10-343)
30.1 Carl Garrett, Oakland, 5 games (16-481)
27.9 George Atkinson, Oakland, 16 games (12-335)

Highest Average, Game (3 returns)
56.7 Les (Speedy) Duncan, NFC-D: Washington vs. San Francisco, 1971 (3-170)
51.3 Ed Podolak, AFC-D: Kansas City vs. Miami, 1971 (OT) (3-154)
49.0 Les (Speedy) Duncan, AFC: San Diego vs. Buffalo, 1964 (3-147)

TOUCHDOWNS

Most Touchdowns
1 Vic Washington, NFC-D: San Francisco vs. Dallas, 1972
Nat Moore, AFC-D: Miami vs. Oakland, 1974
Marshall Johnson, AFC-D: Baltimore vs. Oakland, 1977 (OT)
Fulton Walker, SB: Miami vs. Washington, 1982
Stanford Jennings, SB: Cincinnati vs. San Francisco, 1988
Eric Metcalf, AFC-D: Cleveland vs. Buffalo, 1989
Andre Coleman, SB: San Diego vs. San Francisco, 1994
Desmond Howard, SB: Green Bay vs. New England, 1996
Chuck Levy, NFC: San Franisco vs. Green Bay, 1997
Tim Dwight, SB: Atlanta vs. Denver, 1998

FUMBLES

Most Fumbles, Career
16 Warren Moon, Houston-Minnesota, 10 games
14 John Elway, Denver, 22 games
13 Tony Dorsett, Dallas, 17 games

Most Fumbles, Game
5 Warren Moon, AFC-D: Houston vs. Kansas City, 1993
4 Brian Sipe, AFC-D: Cleveland vs. Oakland, 1980
Randall Cunningham, NFC-FR: Minnesota vs. N.Y. Giants, 1997
3 By many players

RECOVERIES

Most Own Fumbles Recovered, Career
8 Warren Moon, Houston-Minnesota, 10 games
7 John Elway, Denver, 22 games
6 Jim Kelly, Buffalo, 17 games

Most Opponents' Fumbles Recovered, Career
4 Cliff Harris, Dallas, 21 games
Harvey Martin, Dallas, 22 games
Ted Hendricks, Baltimore-Oakland/L.A. Raiders, 21 games

Alvin Walton, Washington, 9 games
Monte Coleman, Washington, 21 games
3 Paul Krause, Minnesota, 19 games
Jack Lambert, Pittsburgh, 18 games
Fred Dryer, Los Angeles, 14 games
Charlie Waters, Dallas, 25 games
Jack Ham, Pittsburgh, 16 games
Mike Hegman, Dallas, 16 games
Tom Jackson, Denver, 10 games
Rich Milot, Washington, 13 games
Mike Singletary, Chicago, 12 games
Darryl Grant, Washington, 16 games
Wes Hopkins, Philadelphia, 3 games
Wilber Marshall, Chicago-Washington, 15 games
Tyrone Braxton, Denver-Miami-Denver, 19 games
Neil Smith, Kansas City-Denver, 16 games
Dave Thomas, Dallas-Jacksonville, 8 games
2 By many players

Most Fumbles Recovered, Game, Own and Opponents'
3 Jack Lambert, AFC: Pittsburgh vs. Oakland, 1975 (3 opp)
Ron Jaworski, NFC-FR: Philadelphia vs. N.Y. Giants, 1981 (3 own)
2 By many players

YARDS GAINED
Longest Return
93 Andy Russell, AFC-D: Pittsburgh vs. Baltimore, 1975 (opp, TD)
79 Neil Smith, AFC-D: Denver vs. Miami, 1998 (opp, TD)
64 Leon Lett, SB: Dallas vs. Buffalo, 1992 (opp)

TOUCHDOWNS
Most Touchdowns
1 By many players

COMBINED NET YARDS GAINED
Rushing, receiving, interception returns, punt returns, kickoff returns, and fumble returns.

ATTEMPTS
Most Attempts, Career
454 Franco Harris, Pittsburgh, 19 games
412 Thurman Thomas, Buffalo, 20 games
381 Emmitt Smith, Dallas, 16 games

Most Attempts, Game
42 Curtis Martin, AFC-D: N.Y. Jets vs. Jacksonville, 1998
40 Lawrence McCutcheon, NFC-D: Los Angeles vs. St. Louis, 1975
39 John Riggins, SB: Washington vs. Miami, 1982
Rodney Hampton, NFC-FR: N.Y. Giants vs. Minnesota, 1993

YARDS GAINED
Most Yards Gained, Career
2,114 Thurman Thomas, Buffalo, 20 games
2,060 Franco Harris, Pittsburgh, 19 games
1,877 Marcus Allen, L.A. Raiders-Kansas City, 16 games

Most Yards Gained, Game
350 Ed Podolak, AFC-D: Kansas City vs. Miami, 1971 (OT)
329 Keith Lincoln, AFC: San Diego vs. Boston, 1963
285 Bob Hayes, NFC-D: Dallas vs. Cleveland, 1967

SACKS
Sacks have been compiled since 1982.

Most Sacks, Career
12 Bruce Smith, Buffalo, 19 games
Reggie White, Philadelphia-Green Bay, 19 games
11 Charles Haley, San Francisco-Dallas-San Francisco, 21 games
10.5 Richard Dent, Chicago-San Francisco-Indianapolis, 12 games

Most Sacks, Game
3.5 Rich Milot, NFC-D: Washington vs. Chicago, 1984
Richard Dent, NFC-D: Chicago vs. N.Y. Giants, 1985
3 Richard Dent, NFC-D: Chicago vs. Washington, 1984
Garin Veris, AFC-FR: New England vs. N.Y. Jets, 1985
Gary Jeter, NFC-D: L.A. Rams vs. Dallas, 1985
Carl Hairston, AFC-D: Cleveland vs. N.Y. Jets, 1986 (OT)
Charles Mann, NFC-D: Washington vs. Chicago, 1987
Kevin Greene, NFC-FR: L.A. Rams vs. Minnesota, 1988
Greg Townsend, AFC-D: L.A. Raiders vs. Cincinnati, 1990
Wilber Marshall, NFC: Washington vs. Detroit, 1991
Fred Stokes, NFC-FR: Washington vs. Minnesota, 1992
Pierce Holt, NFC-D: San Francisco vs. Washington, 1992
Tony Casillas, NFC: Dallas vs. San Francisco, 1992
Gerald Williams, AFC-FR: Pittsburgh vs. Kansas City, 1993
Chad Brown, AFC-FR: Pittsburgh vs. Indianapolis, 1996
Reggie White, SB: Green Bay vs. New England, 1996
Warren Sapp, NFC-D: Tampa Bay vs. Green Bay, 1997
2.5 Lyle Alzado, AFC-D: L.A. Raiders vs. Pittsburgh, 1983
Jacob Green, AFC-FR: Seattle vs. L.A. Raiders, 1984
Larry Roberts, NFC-D: San Francisco vs. Minnesota, 1988
Leslie O'Neal, AFC-FR: San Diego vs. Kansas City, 1992

TEAM RECORDS

GAMES, VICTORIES, DEFEATS
Most Seasons Participating in Postseason Games
25 Dallas, 1966-73, 1975-83, 1985, 1991-96, 1998
24 N.Y. Giants, 1933-35, 1938-39, 1941, 1943-44, 1946, 1950, 1956, 1958-59,1961-63, 1981, 1984-86, 1989-90, 1993, 1997
23 Cleveland, 1950-55, 1957-58, 1964-65, 1967-69, 1971-72, 1980, 1982, 1985-89, 1994

Most Consecutive Seasons Participating in Postseason Games
9 Dallas, 1975-83
8 Dallas, 1966-73
Pittsburgh, 1972-79
Los Angeles, 1973-80
San Francisco, 1983-90
7 Houston, 1987-93
San Francisco, 1992-98 (current)

Most Games
52 Dallas, 1966-73, 1975-83, 1985, 1991-96, 1998
39 San Francisco, 1957, 1970-72, 1981, 1983-90, 1992-98
36 Oakland/L.A. Raiders, 1967-70, 1973-77, 1980, 1982-85, 1990-91, 1993
Pittsburgh, 1947, 1972-79, 1982-84, 1989, 1992-97
Minnesota, 1968-71, 1973-78, 1980, 1982, 1987-89, 1992-94, 1996-98

Most Games Won
32 Dallas, 1967, 1970-73, 1975, 1977-78, 1980-82, 1991-96
24 San Francisco, 1970-71, 1981, 1983-84, 1988-90, 1992-94, 1996-98
22 Green Bay, 1936, 1939, 1944, 1961-62, 1965-67, 1982, 1993-97

Most Consecutive Games Won
9 Green Bay, 1961-62, 1965-67
7 Pittsburgh, 1974-76
San Francisco, 1988-90
Dallas, 1992-94
Denver, 1997-98 (current)
6 Miami, 1972-73
Pittsburgh, 1978-79
Washington, 1982-83

Most Games Lost
21 Minnesota, 1968-71, 1973-78, 1980, 1982, 1987-89, 1992-94, 1996-98
20 L.A. Rams, 1949-50, 1952, 1955, 1967, 1969, 1973-80, 1983-86, 1988-89
Dallas, 1966-70, 1972-73, 1975-76, 1978-83, 1985, 1991, 1994, 1996, 1998
19 Cleveland, 1951-53, 1957-58, 1965, 1967-69, 1971-72, 1980, 1982, 1985-89, 1994
N.Y. Giants, 1933, 1935, 1939, 1941, 1943-44, 1946, 1950, 1958-59, 1961-63, 1981, 1984-85, 1989, 1993, 1997

Most Consecutive Games Lost
6 N.Y. Giants, 1939, 1941, 1943-44, 1946, 1950
Cleveland, 1969, 1971-72, 1980, 1982, 1985
Minnesota, 1988-89, 1992-94, 1996
5 N.Y. Giants, 1958-59, 1961-63
Los Angeles, 1952, 1955, 1967, 1969, 1973
Denver, 1977-79, 1983-84
Baltimore/Indianapolis, 1971, 1975-77, 1987
Philadelphia, 1980-81, 1988-90
Detroit, 1991, 1993-95, 1997 (current)
4 Washington, 1972-74, 1976
Miami, 1974, 1978-79, 1981
Chi. Cardinals/St. Louis, 1948, 1974-75, 1982
Boston/New England, 1963, 1976, 1978, 1982
New Orleans, 1987, 1990-92 (current)
Kansas City, 1993-95, 1997 (current)

SCORING
Most Points, Game
73 NFC: Chi. Bears vs. Washington, 1940
59 NFC: Detroit vs. Cleveland, 1957
58 NFC-FR: Philadelphia vs. Detroit, 1995

Most Points, Both Teams, Game
95 NFC-FR: Philadelphia (58) vs. Detroit (37), 1995
79 AFC-D: San Diego (41) vs. Miami (38), 1981 (OT)
AFC-FR: Buffalo (41) vs. Houston (38), 1992 (OT)
78 AFC-D: Buffalo (44) vs. Miami (34), 1990

Fewest Points, Both Teams, Game
5 NFC-D: Detroit (0) vs. Dallas (5), 1970
7 NFC: Chi. Cardinals (0) vs. Philadelphia (7), 1948
9 NFC: Tampa Bay (0) vs. Los Angeles (9), 1979

POSTSEASON GAME RECORDS

Largest Margin of Victory, Game
73 NFC: Chi. Bears vs. Washington, 1940 (73-0)
49 AFC-D: Oakland vs. Houston, 1969 (56-7)
48 AFC: Buffalo vs. L.A. Raiders, 1990 (51-3)

Most Points, Shutout Victory, Game
73 NFC: Chi. Bears vs. Washington, 1940
38 NFC-D: Dallas vs. Tampa Bay, 1981
37 NFC: Green Bay vs. N.Y. Giants, 1961

Most Points Overcome to Win Game
32 AFC-FR: Buffalo vs. Houston, 1992 (trailed 3-35, won 41-38) (OT)
20 NFC-D: Detroit vs. San Francisco, 1957 (trailed 7-27, won 31-27)
18 NFC-D: Dallas vs. San Francisco, 1972 (trailed 3-21, won 30-28)
AFC-D: Miami vs. Cleveland, 1985 (trailed 3-21, won 24-21)

Most Points, Each Half
1st: 41 AFC: Buffalo vs. L.A. Raiders, 1990
38 NFC-D: Washington vs. L.A. Rams, 1983
NFC-FR: Philadelphia vs. Detroit, 1995
35 NFC: Cleveland vs. Detroit, 1954
AFC-D: Oakland vs. Houston, 1969
SB: Washington vs. Denver, 1987
2nd: 45 NFC: Chi. Bears vs. Washington, 1940
35 AFC-FR: Buffalo vs. Houston, 1992
30 SB: N.Y. Giants vs. Denver, 1986
AFC: Cleveland vs. Denver, 1987
NFC-FR: Detroit vs. Philadelphia, 1995

Most Points, Each Quarter
1st: 28 AFC-D: Oakland vs. Houston, 1969
24 AFC-D: San Diego vs. Miami, 1981
21 NFC: Chi. Bears vs. Washington, 1940
AFC: San Diego vs. Boston, 1963
AFC-D: Oakland vs. Kansas City, 1968
AFC: Oakland vs. San Diego, 1980
AFC: Buffalo vs. L.A. Raiders, 1990
NFC: San Francisco vs. Dallas, 1994
2nd: 35 SB: Washington vs. Denver, 1987
31 NFC-FR: Philadelphia vs. Detroit, 1995
26 AFC-D: Pittsburgh vs. Buffalo, 1974
3rd: 28 AFC-FR: Buffalo vs. Houston, 1992
26 NFC: Chi. Bears vs. Washington, 1940
21 NFC-D: Dallas vs. Cleveland, 1967
NFC-D: Dallas vs. Tampa Bay, 1981
AFC-D: L.A. Raiders vs. Pittsburgh, 1983
SB: Chicago vs. New England, 1985
NFC-D: N.Y. Giants vs. San Francisco, 1986
AFC: Cleveland vs. Denver, 1987
AFC: Cleveland vs. Denver, 1989
4th: 27 NFC: N.Y. Giants vs. Chi. Bears, 1934
26 NFC-FR: Philadelphia vs. New Orleans, 1992
24 NFC: Baltimore vs. N.Y. Giants, 1959
OT: 6 NFC: Baltimore vs. N.Y. Giants, 1958
AFC-D: Oakland vs. Baltimore, 1977
NFC-D: L.A. Rams vs. N.Y. Giants, 1989

TOUCHDOWNS

Most Touchdowns, Game
11 NFC: Chi. Bears vs. Washington, 1940
8 NFC: Cleveland vs. Detroit, 1954
NFC: Detroit vs. Cleveland, 1957
AFC-D: Oakland vs. Houston, 1969
SB: San Francisco vs. Denver, 1989
7 AFC: San Diego vs. Boston, 1963
NFC-D: Dallas vs. Cleveland, 1967
NFC-D: N.Y. Giants vs. San Francisco, 1986
AFC: Buffalo vs. L.A. Raiders, 1990
SB: Dallas vs. Buffalo, 1992
SB: San Francisco vs. San Diego, 1994
NFC-FR: Philadelphia vs. Detroit, 1995

Most Touchdowns, Both Teams, Game
12 NFC-FR: Philadelphia (7) vs. Detroit (5), 1995
11 NFC: Chi. Bears (11) vs. Washington (0), 1940
10 NFC: Detroit (8) vs. Cleveland (2), 1957
AFC-D: Miami (5) vs. San Diego (5), 1981 (OT)
AFC: Miami (6) vs. Pittsburgh (4), 1984
AFC-FR: Buffalo (5) vs. Houston (5), 1992 (OT)
SB: San Francisco (7) vs. San Diego (3), 1994

Fewest Touchdowns, Both Teams, Game
0 NFC-D: N.Y. Giants vs. Cleveland, 1950
NFC-D: Dallas vs. Detroit, 1970
NFC: Los Angeles vs. Tampa Bay, 1979
1 NFC: Chi. Cardinals (0) vs. Philadelphia (1), 1948
NFC-D: Cleveland (0) vs. N.Y. Giants (1), 1958
AFC: San Diego (0) vs. Houston (1), 1961
AFC-D: N.Y. Jets (0) vs. Kansas City (1), 1969
NFC-D: Green Bay (0) vs. Washington (1), 1972
NFC-FR: New Orleans (0) vs. Chicago (1), 1990
NFC: N.Y. Giants (0) vs. San Francisco (1), 1990
AFC-FR: L.A. Raiders (0) vs. Kansas City (1), 1991
AFC-D: New England (0) vs. Pittsburgh (1), 1997
2 In many games

POINTS AFTER TOUCHDOWN

Most (One-Point) Points After Touchdown, Game
8 NFC: Cleveland vs. Detroit, 1954
NFC: Detroit vs. Cleveland, 1957
AFC-D: Oakland vs. Houston, 1969
7 NFC: Chi. Bears vs. Washington, 1940
NFC-D: Dallas vs. Cleveland, 1967
NFC-D: N.Y. Giants vs. San Francisco, 1986
SB: San Francisco vs. Denver, 1989
SB: Dallas vs. Buffalo, 1992
SB: San Francisco vs. San Diego, 1994
NFC-FR: Philadelphia vs. Detroit, 1995
6 AFC: San Diego vs. Boston, 1963
NFC-D: Washington vs. L.A. Rams, 1983
AFC: Miami vs. Pittsburgh, 1984
SB: Washington vs. Denver, 1987
AFC: Buffalo vs. L.A. Raiders, 1990
AFC-FR: L.A. Raiders vs. Denver, 1993
AFC-FR: Denver vs. Jacksonville, 1997

Most (One-Point) Points After Touchdown, Both Teams, Game
10 NFC: Detroit (8) vs. Cleveland (2), 1957
AFC-D: Miami (5) vs. San Diego (5), 1981 (OT)
AFC: Miami (6) vs. Pittsburgh (4), 1984
AFC-FR: Buffalo (5) vs. Houston (5), 1992 (OT)
NFC-FR: Philadelphia (7) vs. Detroit (3), 1995
9 In many games

Fewest (One-Point) Points After Touchdown, Both Teams, Game
0 NFC-D: N.Y. Giants vs. Cleveland, 1950
NFC-D: Dallas vs. Detroit, 1970
NFC: Los Angeles vs. Tampa Bay, 1979

Most Two-Point Conversions, Game
2 SB: San Diego vs. San Francisco, 1994
NFC-FR: Detroit vs. Philadelphia, 1995
1 By many teams

FIELD GOALS

Most Field Goals, Game
5 NFC-D: Minnesota vs. San Francisco, 1987
NFC: N.Y. Giants vs. San Francisco, 1990
AFC: Buffalo vs. Miami, 1992
NFC-FR: N.Y. Giants vs. Minnesota, 1997
4 AFC-D: Boston vs. Buffalo, 1963
AFC: Oakland vs. Houston, 1967
SB: Green Bay vs. Oakland, 1967
NFC: Washington vs. Dallas, 1972
AFC-D: Oakland vs. Pittsburgh, 1973
SB: San Francisco vs. Cincinnati, 1981
AFC-FR: New England vs. N.Y. Jets, 1985
NFC-FR: Washington vs. L.A. Rams, 1986
NFC-D: Philadelphia vs. Chicago, 1988
AFC-FR: Pittsburgh vs. Houston, 1989 (OT)
AFC-D: Pittsburgh vs. Buffalo, 1995
NFC-FR: Dallas vs. Minnesota, 1996
NFC-D: Carolina vs. Dallas, 1996
AFC-FR: Jacksonville vs. New England, 1998
3 By many teams

Most Field Goals, Both Teams, Game
8 NFC-FR: N.Y. Giants (5) vs. Minnesota (3), 1997
7 AFC-FR: Pittsburgh (4) vs. Houston (3), 1989 (OT)
NFC: N.Y. Giants (5) vs. San Francisco (2), 1990
NFC-D: Carolina (4) vs. Dallas (3), 1996
6 NFC-D: Minnesota (5) vs. San Francisco (1), 1987
NFC-D: Philadelphia (4) vs. Chicago (2), 1988
AFC: Buffalo (5) vs. Miami (1), 1992

Most Field Goals Attempted, Game
6 AFC: Oakland vs. Houston, 1967
NFC-D: Los Angeles vs. Dallas, 1973
AFC-D: Cleveland vs. N.Y. Jets, 1986 (OT)
NFC: N.Y. Giants vs. San Francisco, 1990
AFC: Buffalo vs. Miami, 1992
5 By many teams

Most Field Goals Attempted, Both Teams, Game
9 NFC-D: Philadelphia (5) vs. Chicago (4), 1988
NFC-FR: N.Y. Giants (5) vs. Minnesota (4), 1997
8 NFC-D: Los Angeles (6) vs. Dallas (2), 1973
NFC-D: Detroit (5) vs. San Francisco (3), 1983

AFC-D: Cleveland (6) vs. N.Y. Jets (2), 1986 (OT)
NFC-D: Minnesota (5) vs. San Francisco (3), 1987
AFC-FR: Houston (4) vs. Pittsburgh (4), 1989 (OT)
NFC-FR: Chicago (4) vs. New Orleans (4), 1990
NFC: N.Y. Giants (6) vs. San Francisco (2), 1990
7 In many games

SAFETIES

Most Safeties, Game
1 By many teams

Most Safeties, Both Teams, Game
1 In many games

FIRST DOWNS

Most First Downs, Game
34 AFC-D: San Diego vs. Miami, 1981 (OT)
33 AFC-D: Cleveland vs. N.Y. Jets, 1986 (OT)
31 SB: San Francisco vs. Miami, 1984
NFC-D: San Francisco vs. Minnesota, 1997

Fewest First Downs, Game
6 NFC: N.Y. Giants vs. Green Bay, 1961
7 NFC: Green Bay vs. Boston, 1936
NFC-D: Pittsburgh vs. Philadelphia, 1947
NFC: Chi. Cardinals vs. Philadelphia, 1948
NFC: Los Angeles vs. Philadelphia, 1949
NFC-D: Cleveland vs. N.Y. Giants, 1958
AFC-D: Cincinnati vs. Baltimore, 1970
NFC-D: Detroit vs. Dallas, 1970
NFC: Tampa Bay vs. Los Angeles, 1979
8 By many teams

Most First Downs, Both Teams, Game
59 AFC-D: San Diego (34) vs. Miami (25), 1981 (OT)
55 AFC-FR: San Diego (29) vs. Pittsburgh (26), 1982
54 AFC-FR: Buffalo (28) vs. Miami (26), 1995

Fewest First Downs, Both Teams, Game
15 NFC: Green Bay (7) vs. Boston (8), 1936
19 NFC: N.Y. Giants (9) vs. Green Bay (10), 1939
NFC: Washington (9) vs. Chi. Bears (10), 1942
20 NFC-D: Cleveland (9) vs. N.Y. Giants (11), 1950

RUSHING

Most First Downs, Rushing, Game
19 NFC-FR: Dallas vs. Los Angeles, 1980
18 AFC-D: Miami vs. Cincinnati, 1973
AFC: Miami vs. Oakland, 1973
AFC-D: Pittsburgh vs. Buffalo, 1974
AFC-FR: Buffalo vs. Miami, 1995
AFC-FR: Denver vs. Jacksonville, 1997
17 AFC-D: Cincinnati vs. Seattle, 1988
AFC: Buffalo vs. Kansas City, 1993

Fewest First Downs, Rushing, Game
0 NFC: Los Angeles vs. Philadelphia, 1949
AFC-D: Buffalo vs. Boston, 1963
AFC: Oakland vs. Pittsburgh, 1974
NFC-FR: New Orleans vs. Minnesota, 1987
NFC: L.A. Rams vs. San Francisco, 1989
NFC-D: Chicago vs. N.Y. Giants, 1990
AFC-FR: Indianapolis vs. Pittsburgh, 1996
1 By many teams

Most First Downs, Rushing, Both Teams, Game
26 AFC: Buffalo (14) vs. L.A. Raiders (12), 1990
25 NFC-FR: Dallas (19) vs. Los Angeles (6), 1980
23 NFC: Cleveland (15) vs. Detroit (8), 1952
AFC-D: Miami (18) vs. Cincinnati (5), 1973
AFC-D: Pittsburgh (18) vs. Buffalo (5), 1974
AFC-FR: Buffalo (18) vs. Miami (5), 1995

Fewest First Downs, Rushing, Both Teams, Game
5 AFC-D: Buffalo (0) vs. Boston (5), 1963
6 NFC: Green Bay (2) vs. Boston (4), 1936
NFC-D: Baltimore (2) vs. Minnesota (4), 1968
AFC-D: Houston (1) vs. Oakland (5), 1969
AFC-FR: N.Y. Jets (1) vs. Houston (5), 1991
7 NFC-D: Washington (2) vs. N.Y. Giants (5), 1943
NFC: Baltimore (3) vs. N.Y. Giants (4), 1959
NFC: Washington (3) vs. Dallas (4), 1972
AFC-FR: N.Y. Jets (3) vs. Buffalo (4), 1981
NFC-D: Detroit (3) vs. Dallas (4), 1991
AFC-D: Kansas City (3) vs. Houston (4), 1993
NFC-FR: Detroit (1) vs. Green Bay (6), 1994
NFC-FR: Atlanta (1) vs. Green Bay (6), 1995
AFC-FR: New England (1) vs. Pittsburgh (6), 1997
NFC-FR: Arizona (2) vs. Dallas (5), 1998

PASSING

Most First Downs, Passing, Game
21 AFC-D: Miami vs. San Diego, 1981 (OT)
AFC-D: San Diego vs. Miami, 1981 (OT)
AFC-D: Cleveland vs. N.Y. Jets, 1986 (OT)
NFC-D: Philadelphia vs. Chicago, 1988
20 NFC-FR: Dallas vs. L.A. Rams, 1983
AFC-D: Buffalo vs. Cleveland, 1989
AFC-FR: Miami vs. Buffalo, 1995
NFC-FR: Detroit vs. Philadelphia, 1995
AFC-FR: San Diego vs. Indianapolis, 1995
19 NFC-FR: St. Louis vs. Green Bay, 1982
NFC-FR: Dallas vs. Tampa Bay, 1982
AFC-FR: Pittsburgh vs. San Diego, 1982
AFC-FR: San Diego vs. Pittsburgh, 1982
NFC: Dallas vs. Washington, 1982
NFC-D: Detroit vs. Dallas, 1991
AFC-FR: Kansas City vs. Pittsburgh, 1993 (OT)
NFC: Minnesota vs. Atlanta, 1998 (OT)

Fewest First Downs, Passing, Game
0 NFC: Philadelphia vs. Chi. Cardinals, 1948
1 NFC-D: N.Y. Giants vs. Washington, 1943
NFC: Cleveland vs. Detroit, 1953
SB: Denver vs. Dallas, 1977
2 By many teams

Most First Downs, Passing, Both Teams, Game
42 AFC-D: Miami (21) vs. San Diego (21), 1981 (OT)
38 AFC-FR: Pittsburgh (19) vs. San Diego (19), 1982
36 NFC: Minnesota (19) vs. Atlanta (17), 1998 (OT)

Fewest First Downs, Passing, Both Teams, Game
2 NFC: Philadelphia (0) vs. Chi. Cardinals (2), 1948
4 NFC-D: Cleveland (2) vs. N.Y. Giants (2), 1950
5 NFC: Detroit (2) vs. N.Y. Giants (3), 1935
NFC: Green Bay (2) vs. N.Y. Giants (3), 1939

PENALTY

Most First Downs, Penalty, Game
7 AFC-D: New England vs. Oakland, 1976
6 AFC-D: Cleveland vs. N.Y. Jets, 1986 (OT)
5 AFC-FR: Cleveland vs. L. A. Raiders, 1982
NFC-D: San Francisco vs. Minnesota, 1997
AFC-FR: Miami vs. Buffalo, 1998
NFC-D: Arizona vs. Minnesota, 1998

Most First Downs, Penalty, Both Teams, Game
9 AFC-D: New England (7) vs. Oakland (2), 1976
8 NFC-FR: Atlanta (4) vs. Minnesota (4), 1982
AFC-FR: Miami (5) vs. Buffalo (3), 1998
7 AFC-D: Baltimore (4) vs. Oakland (3), 1977 (OT)
AFC-FR: Denver (4) vs. L.A. Raiders (3), 1993
NFC-D: Dallas (4) vs. Carolina (3), 1996
AFC-D: Kansas City (4) vs. Denver (3), 1997

NET YARDS GAINED RUSHING AND PASSING

Most Yards Gained, Game
610 AFC: San Diego vs. Boston, 1963
602 SB: Washington vs. Denver, 1987
569 AFC: Miami vs. Pittsburgh, 1984

Fewest Yards Gained, Game
86 NFC-D: Cleveland vs. N.Y. Giants, 1958
99 NFC: Chi. Cardinals vs. Philadelphia, 1948
114 NFC-D: N.Y. Giants vs. Washington, 1943

Most Yards Gained, Both Teams, Game
1,038 AFC-FR: Buffalo (536) vs. Miami (502), 1995
1,036 AFC-D: San Diego (564) vs. Miami (472), 1981 (OT)
1,024 AFC: Miami (569) vs. Pittsburgh (455), 1984

Fewest Yards Gained, Both Teams, Game
331 NFC: Chi. Cardinals (99) vs. Philadelphia (232), 1948
332 NFC-D: N.Y. Giants (150) vs. Cleveland (182), 1950
336 NFC: Boston (116) vs. Green Bay (220), 1936

RUSHING

ATTEMPTS

Most Attempts, Game
65 NFC: Detroit vs. N.Y. Giants, 1935
61 NFC: Philadelphia vs. Los Angeles, 1949
59 AFC: New England vs. Miami, 1985

Fewest Attempts, Game
8 AFC-D: Miami vs. San Diego, 1994
9 SB: Miami vs. San Francisco, 1984
10 NFC: L.A. Rams vs. San Francisco, 1989
NFC-FR: Atlanta vs. Green Bay, 1995

Most Attempts, Both Teams, Game
109 NFC: Detroit (65) vs. N.Y. Giants (44), 1935

97 AFC-D: Baltimore (50) vs. Oakland (47), 1977 (OT)
91 NFC: Philadelphia (57) vs. Chi. Cardinals (34), 1948

Fewest Attempts, Both Teams, Game
32 AFC-D: Houston (14) vs. Kansas City (18), 1993
38 NFC-D: Detroit (16) vs. Dallas (22), 1991
39 NFC-FR: Atlanta (10) vs. Green Bay (29), 1995

YARDS GAINED

Most Yards Gained, Game
382 NFC: Chi. Bears vs. Washington, 1940
341 AFC-FR: Buffalo vs. Miami, 1995
338 NFC-FR: Dallas vs. Los Angeles, 1980

Fewest Yards Gained, Game
–4 NFC-FR: Detroit vs. Green Bay, 1994
7 AFC-D: Buffalo vs. Boston, 1963
SB: New England vs. Chicago, 1985
14 AFC-D: Miami vs. Denver, 1998
AFC: N.Y. Jets vs. Denver, 1998

Most Yards Gained, Both Teams, Game
430 NFC-FR: Dallas (338) vs. Los Angeles (92), 1980
426 NFC: Cleveland (227) vs. Detroit (199), 1952
411 AFC-FR: Buffalo (341) vs. Miami (70), 1995

Fewest Yards Gained, Both Teams, Game
77 NFC-FR: Detroit (–4) vs. Green Bay (81), 1994
90 AFC-D: Buffalo (7) vs. Boston (83), 1963
106 NFC: Boston (39) vs. Green Bay (67), 1936

AVERAGE GAIN

Highest Average Gain, Game
9.94 AFC: San Diego vs. Boston, 1963 (32-318)
9.29 NFC-D: Green Bay vs. Dallas, 1982 (17-158)
7.35 NFC-FR: Dallas vs. Los Angeles, 1980 (46-338)

Lowest Average Gain, Game
–0.27 NFC-FR: Detroit vs. Green Bay, 1994 (15-(–4))
0.58 AFC-D: Buffalo vs. Boston, 1963 (12-7)
0.64 SB: New England vs. Chicago, 1985 (11-7)

TOUCHDOWNS

Most Touchdowns, Game
7 NFC: Chi. Bears vs. Washington, 1940
6 NFC-D: San Francisco vs. N.Y. Giants, 1993
5 NFC: Cleveland vs. Detroit, 1954
NFC-D: San Francisco vs. Chicago, 1994
AFC-FR: Pittsburgh vs. Indianapolis, 1996
AFC-FR: Denver vs. Jacksonville, 1997

Most Touchdowns, Both Teams, Game
7 NFC: Chi. Bears (7) vs. Washington (0), 1940
6 NFC: Cleveland (5) vs. Detroit (1), 1954
NFC-D: San Francisco (6) vs. N.Y. Giants (0), 1993
NFC-D: San Francisco (5) vs. Chicago (1), 1994
AFC-FR: Denver (5) vs. Jacksonville (1), 1997
5 NFC: Chi. Cardinals (3) vs. Philadelphia (2), 1947
AFC: San Diego (4) vs. Boston (1), 1963
AFC-D: Cincinnati (3) vs. Buffalo (2), 1981
AFC-FR: Pittsburgh (5) vs. Indianapolis (0), 1996
NFC-D: Arizona (3) vs. Minnesota (2), 1998

PASSING

ATTEMPTS

Most Attempts, Game
66 AFC-FR: Miami vs. Buffalo, 1995
65 AFC-D: Cleveland vs. N.Y. Jets, 1986 (OT)
NFC-D: San Francisco vs. Green Bay, 1995
61 NFC-FR: Minnesota vs. Chicago, 1994

Fewest Attempts, Game
5 NFC: Detroit vs. N.Y. Giants, 1935
6 AFC: Miami vs. Oakland, 1973
7 SB: Miami vs. Minnesota, 1973

Most Attempts, Both Teams, Game
102 AFC-D: San Diego (54) vs. Miami (48), 1981 (OT)
96 AFC: N.Y. Jets (49) vs. Oakland (47), 1968
95 AFC-D: Cleveland (65) vs. N.Y. Jets (30), 1986 (OT)

Fewest Attempts, Both Teams, Game
18 NFC: Detroit (5) vs. N.Y. Giants (13), 1935
23 NFC: Chi. Cardinals (11) vs. Philadelphia (12), 1948
24 NFC-D: Cleveland (9) vs. N.Y. Giants (15), 1950

COMPLETIONS

Most Completions, Game
36 AFC-FR: Houston vs. Buffalo, 1992 (OT)
34 AFC-D: Cleveland vs. N.Y. Jets, 1986 (OT)
AFC-FR: Miami vs. Buffalo, 1995
33 AFC-D: San Diego vs. Miami, 1981 (OT)
NFC-FR: Minnesota vs. Chicago, 1994

Fewest Completions, Game
2 NFC: Detroit vs. N.Y. Giants, 1935
NFC: Philadelphia vs. Chi. Cardinals, 1948
3 NFC: N.Y. Giants vs. Chi. Bears, 1941
NFC: Green Bay vs. N.Y. Giants, 1944
NFC: Chi. Cardinals vs. Philadelphia, 1947
NFC: Chi. Cardinals vs. Philadelphia, 1948
NFC-D: Cleveland vs. N.Y. Giants, 1950
NFC-D: N.Y. Giants vs. Cleveland, 1950
NFC: Cleveland vs. Detroit, 1953
AFC: Miami vs. Oakland, 1973
4 NFC: N.Y. Giants vs. Detroit, 1935
NFC-D: N.Y. Giants vs. Washington, 1943
NFC-D: Pittsburgh vs. Philadelphia, 1947
NFC-D: Dallas vs. Detroit, 1970
AFC: Miami vs. Baltimore, 1971
SB: Miami vs. Washington, 1982
AFC-FR: Seattle vs. L.A. Raiders, 1984

Most Completions, Both Teams, Game
64 AFC-D: San Diego (33) vs. Miami (31), 1981 (OT)
57 AFC-FR: Houston (36) vs. Buffalo (21), 1992 (OT)
56 NFC-D: Dallas (28) vs. Green Bay (28), 1993
NFC: Minnesota (29) vs. Atlanta (27), 1998 (OT)

Fewest Completions, Both Teams, Game
5 NFC: Philadelphia (2) vs. Chi. Cardinals (3), 1948
6 NFC: Detroit (2) vs. N.Y. Giants (4), 1935
NFC-D: Cleveland (3) vs. N.Y. Giants (3), 1950
11 NFC: Green Bay (3) vs. N.Y. Giants (8), 1944
NFC-D: Dallas (4) vs. Detroit (7), 1970

COMPLETION PERCENTAGE

Highest Completion Percentage, Game (20 attempts)
88.0 SB: N.Y. Giants vs. Denver, 1986 (25-22)
87.1 NFC: San Francisco vs. L.A. Rams, 1989 (31-27)
80.0 NFC-D: Washington vs. L.A. Rams, 1983 (25-20)

Lowest Completion Percentage, Game (20 attempts)
18.5 NFC: Tampa Bay vs. Los Angeles, 1979 (27-5)
20.0 NFC-D: N.Y. Giants vs. Washington, 1943 (20-4)
25.8 NFC: Chi. Bears vs. Washington, 1937 (31-8)

YARDS GAINED

Most Yards Gained, Game
483 AFC-D: Cleveland vs. N.Y. Jets, 1986 (OT)
435 AFC: Miami vs. Pittsburgh, 1984
432 AFC-FR: Miami vs. Buffalo, 1995

Fewest Yards Gained, Game
3 NFC: Chi. Cardinals vs. Philadelphia, 1948
7 NFC: Philadelphia vs. Chi. Cardinals, 1948
9 NFC-D: N.Y. Giants vs. Cleveland, 1950
NFC: Cleveland vs. Detroit, 1953

Most Yards Gained, Both Teams, Game
809 AFC-D: San Diego (415) vs. Miami (394), 1981 (OT)
747 AFC: Miami (435) vs. Pittsburgh (312), 1984
666 AFC-D: Cleveland (483) vs. N.Y. Jets (183), 1986 (OT)

Fewest Yards Gained, Both Teams, Game
10 NFC: Chi. Cardinals (3) vs. Philadelphia (7), 1948
38 NFC-D: N.Y. Giants (9) vs. Cleveland (29), 1950
102 NFC-D: Dallas (22) vs. Detroit (80), 1970

TIMES SACKED

Most Times Sacked, Game
9 AFC: Kansas City vs. Buffalo, 1966
NFC: Chicago vs. San Francisco, 1984
AFC-D: N.Y. Jets vs. Cleveland, 1986 (OT)
AFC-D: Houston vs. Kansas City, 1993
8 NFC: Green Bay vs. Dallas, 1967
NFC: Minnesota vs. Washington, 1987
7 NFC-D: Dallas vs. Los Angeles, 1973
SB: Dallas vs. Pittsburgh, 1975
AFC-FR: Houston vs. Oakland, 1980
NFC-D: Washington vs. Chicago, 1984
SB: New England vs. Chicago, 1985
AFC-FR: Kansas City vs. San Diego, 1992
AFC-D: Pittsburgh vs. Buffalo, 1992

Most Times Sacked, Both Teams, Game
13 AFC: Kansas City (9) vs. Buffalo (4), 1966
AFC-D: N.Y. Jets (9) vs. Cleveland (4), 1986 (OT)
12 NFC-D: Dallas (7) vs. Los Angeles (5), 1973
NFC-D: Washington (7) vs. Chicago (5), 1984
NFC: Chicago (9) vs. San Francisco (3), 1984
AFC-FR: Kansas City (7) vs. San Diego (5), 1992
11 AFC-D: Houston (9) vs. Kansas City (2), 1993

Fewest Times Sacked, Both Teams, Game

0 AFC-D: Buffalo vs. Pittsburgh, 1974
AFC-FR: Pittsburgh vs. San Diego, 1982
AFC: Miami vs. Pittsburgh, 1984
AFC-D: Buffalo vs. Miami, 1990
AFC-D: Denver vs. Houston, 1991
AFC-FR: Buffalo vs. Miami, 1995
1 In many games

TOUCHDOWNS

Most Touchdowns, Game

6 AFC-D: Oakland vs. Houston, 1969
SB: San Francisco vs. San Diego, 1994
5 NFC: Chi. Bears vs. Washington, 1943
NFC: Detroit vs. Cleveland, 1957
AFC-D: Oakland vs. Kansas City, 1968
SB: San Francisco vs. Denver, 1989
4 By many teams

Most Touchdowns, Both Teams, Game

8 AFC-FR: Buffalo (4) vs. Houston (4), 1992 (OT)
7 NFC: Chi. Bears (5) vs. Washington (2), 1943
AFC-D: Oakland (6) vs. Houston (1), 1969
SB: Pittsburgh (4) vs. Dallas (3), 1978
AFC-D: Miami (4) vs. San Diego (3), 1981 (OT)
AFC: Miami (4) vs. Pittsburgh (3), 1984
AFC-D: Buffalo (4) vs. Cleveland (3), 1989
SB: San Francisco (6) vs. San Diego (1), 1994
NFC-FR: Detroit (4) vs. Philadelphia (3), 1995
6 NFC-FR: Green Bay (4) vs. St. Louis (2), 1982
AFC: Cleveland (3) vs. Denver (3), 1987
AFC-D: Buffalo (3) vs. Miami (3), 1990
AFC-FR: Denver (3) vs. L.A. Raiders (3), 1993

INTERCEPTIONS BY

Most Interceptions By, Game

8 NFC: Chi. Bears vs. Washington, 1940
7 NFC: Cleveland vs. Los Angeles, 1955
6 NFC: Green Bay vs. N.Y. Giants, 1939
NFC: Chi. Bears vs. N.Y. Giants, 1946
NFC: Cleveland vs. Detroit, 1954
AFC: San Diego vs. Houston, 1961
AFC: Buffalo vs. L.A. Raiders, 1990
NFC-FR: Philadelphia vs. Detroit, 1995

Most Interceptions By, Both Teams, Game

10 NFC: Cleveland (7) vs. Los Angeles (3), 1955
AFC: San Diego (6) vs. Houston (4), 1961
9 NFC: Green Bay (6) vs. N.Y. Giants (3), 1939
8 NFC: Chi. Bears (8) vs. Washington (0), 1940
NFC: Chi. Bears (6) vs. N.Y. Giants (2), 1946
NFC: Cleveland (6) vs. Detroit (2), 1954
AFC-FR: Buffalo (4) vs. N.Y. Jets (4), 1981
AFC: Miami (5) vs. N.Y. Jets (3), 1982

YARDS GAINED

Most Yards Gained, Game

138 AFC-FR: N.Y. Jets vs. Cincinnati, 1982
136 AFC: Dall. Texans vs. Houston, 1962 (OT)
SB: Denver vs. Atlanta, 1998
130 NFC-D: Los Angeles vs. St. Louis, 1975

Most Yards Gained, Both Teams, Game

156 NFC: Green Bay (123) vs. N.Y. Giants (33), 1939
149 NFC: Cleveland (103) vs. Los Angeles (46), 1955
141 AFC-FR: Buffalo (79) vs. N.Y. Jets (62), 1981

TOUCHDOWNS

Most Touchdowns, Game

3 NFC: Chi. Bears vs. Washington, 1940
2 NFC-D: Los Angeles vs. St. Louis, 1975
NFC-FR: Philadelphia vs. Detroit, 1995
1 In many games

Most Touchdowns, Both Teams, Game

3 NFC: Chi. Bears (3) vs. Washington (0), 1940
2 NFC-D: Los Angeles (2) vs. St. Louis(0), 1975
NFC-D: Dallas (1) vs. Green Bay (1), 1982
NFC-D: Minnesota (1) vs. San Francisco (1), 1987
NFC-FR: Detroit (1) vs. Green Bay (1), 1993
NFC-FR: Philadelphia (2) vs. Detroit (0), 1995
AFC-FR: Buffalo (1) vs. Jacksonville (1), 1996
1 In many games

PUNTING

Most Punts, Game

14 AFC-D: N.Y. Jets vs. Cleveland, 1986 (OT)
13 NFC: N.Y. Giants vs. Chi. Bears, 1933
AFC-D: Baltimore vs. Oakland, 1977 (OT)
11 AFC: Houston vs. Oakland, 1967
AFC-D: Houston vs. Oakland, 1969
NFC: L.A. Rams vs. Chicago, 1985

Fewest Punts, Game

0 NFC-FR: St. Louis vs. Green Bay, 1982
AFC-FR: N.Y. Jets vs. Cincinnati, 1982
1 By many teams

Most Punts, Both Teams, Game

23 NFC: N.Y. Giants (13) vs. Chi. Bears (10), 1933
22 AFC-D: N.Y. Jets (14) vs. Cleveland (8), 1986 (OT)
21 AFC-D: Baltimore (13) vs. Oakland (8), 1977 (OT)
NFC: L.A. Rams (11) vs. Chicago (10), 1985

Fewest Punts, Both Teams, Game

1 NFC-FR: St. Louis (0) vs. Green Bay (1), 1982
2 AFC-FR: N.Y. Jets (0) vs. Cincinnati (2), 1982
SB: Atlanta (1) vs. Denver (1), 1998
3 AFC: Miami (1) vs. Oakland (2), 1973
AFC-FR: San Diego (1) vs. Pittsburgh (2), 1982
AFC-D: Buffalo (1) vs. Miami (2), 1990
AFC-FR: L.A. Raiders (1) vs. Kansas City (2), 1991
AFC-D: Houston (1) vs. Denver (2), 1991
NFC-FR: Dallas (1) vs. Minnesota (2), 1996
AFC-FR: Miami (1) vs. Buffalo (2), 1998

AVERAGE YARDAGE

Highest Average, Punting, Game (4 punts)

56.0 AFC: Oakland vs. San Diego, 1980
52.5 NFC: Washington vs. Chi. Bears, 1942
51.6 AFC-D: Cincinnati vs. L.A. Raiders, 1990

Lowest Average, Punting, Game (4 punts)

24.9 NFC: Washington vs. Chi. Bears, 1937
25.3 AFC-FR: Pittsburgh vs. Houston, 1989
25.5 NFC: Green Bay vs. N.Y. Giants, 1962

PUNT RETURNS

Most Punt Returns, Game

8 NFC: Green Bay vs. N.Y. Giants, 1944
7 By many teams

Most Punt Returns, Both Teams, Game

13 AFC-FR: Houston (7) vs. Oakland (6), 1980
12 AFC-D: New England (7) vs. Pittsburgh (5), 1996
11 NFC: Green Bay (8) vs. N.Y. Giants (3), 1944
NFC-D: Green Bay (6) vs. Baltimore (5), 1965
AFC-FR: Jacksonville (7) vs. New England (4), 1998

Fewest Punt Returns, Both Teams, Game

0 NFC: Chi. Bears vs. N.Y. Giants, 1941
AFC: Boston vs. San Diego, 1963
NFC-FR: Green Bay vs. St. Louis, 1982
AFC-FR: Houston vs. N.Y. Jets, 1991
AFC-D: Denver vs. Houston, 1991
NFC-D: San Francisco vs. Washington, 1992
SB: Denver vs. Green Bay, 1997
SB: Atlanta vs. Denver, 1998
1 In many games

YARDS GAINED

Most Yards Gained, Game

155 NFC-D: Dallas vs. Cleveland, 1967
150 NFC: Chi. Cardinals vs. Philadelphia, 1947
143 NFC-FR: Minnesota vs. New Orleans, 1987

Fewest Yards Gained, Game

–10 NFC: Green Bay vs. Cleveland, 1965
–9 NFC: Dallas vs. Green Bay, 1966
AFC-D: Kansas City vs. Oakland, 1968
–7 NFC-D: San Francisco vs. Atlanta, 1998

Most Yards Gained, Both Teams, Game

166 NFC-D: Dallas (155) vs. Cleveland (11), 1967
160 NFC: Chi. Cardinals (150) vs. Philadelphia (10), 1947
146 NFC-D: Philadelphia (112) vs. Pittsburgh (34), 1947

Fewest Yards Gained, Both Teams, Game

–9 NFC: Dallas (–9) vs. Green Bay (0), 1966
–6 AFC-D: Miami (–5) vs. Oakland (–1), 1970
–3 NFC-D: San Francisco (–5) vs. Dallas (2), 1972

TOUCHDOWNS

Most Touchdowns, Game

1 By 12 teams

POSTSEASON GAME RECORDS

KICKOFF RETURNS

Most Kickoff Returns, Game

10 NFC-D: L.A. Rams vs. Washington, 1983
NFC-FR: Detroit vs. Philadelphia, 1995
9 NFC: Chi. Bears vs. N.Y. Giants, 1956
AFC: Boston vs. San Diego, 1963
AFC: Houston vs. Oakland, 1967
SB: Denver vs. San Francisco, 1989
AFC-D: Miami vs. Buffalo, 1990
AFC: L.A. Raiders vs. Buffalo, 1990
8 By many teams

Most Kickoff Returns, Both Teams, Game

15 AFC-D: Miami (9) vs. Buffalo (6), 1990
14 NFC-FR: Detroit (10) vs. Philadelphia (4), 1995
13 NFC-D: Green Bay (7) vs. Dallas (6), 1982
NFC-FR: Green Bay (7) vs. San Francisco (6), 1998

Fewest Kickoff Returns, Both Teams, Game

1 NFC: Green Bay (0) vs. Boston (1), 1936
AFC-FR: San Diego (0) vs. Kansas City (1), 1992
2 NFC-D: Los Angeles (0) vs. Chi. Bears (2), 1950
AFC: Houston (0) vs. San Diego (2), 1961
AFC-D: Oakland (1) vs. Pittsburgh (1), 1972
AFC-D: N.Y. Jets (0) vs. L.A. Raiders (2), 1982
AFC: Miami (1) vs. N.Y. Jets (1), 1982
NFC: N.Y. Giants (0) vs. Washington (2), 1986
3 In many games

YARDS GAINED

Most Yards Gained, Game

244 SB: San Diego vs. San Francisco, 1994
227 SB: Atlanta vs. Denver, 1998
225 NFC: Washington vs. Chi. Bears, 1940

Most Yards Gained, Both Teams, Game

379 AFC-D: Baltimore (193) vs. Oakland (186), 1977 (OT)
322 NFC-D: Green Bay (194) vs. San Francisco (128), 1998
321 NFC-D: Dallas (173) vs. Green Bay (148), 1982

Fewest Yards Gained, Both Teams, Game

5 AFC-FR: San Diego (0) vs. Kansas City (5), 1992
15 NFC: N.Y. Giants (0) vs. Washington (15), 1986
31 NFC-D: Los Angeles (0) vs. Chi. Bears (31), 1950

TOUCHDOWNS

Most Touchdowns, Game

1 NFC-D: San Francisco vs. Dallas, 1972
AFC-D: Miami vs. Oakland, 1974
AFC-D: Baltimore vs. Oakland, 1977 (OT)
SB: Miami vs. Washington, 1982
SB: Cincinnati vs. San Francisco, 1988
AFC-D: Cleveland vs. Buffalo, 1989
SB: San Diego vs. San Francisco, 1994
SB: Green Bay vs. New England, 1996
NFC: San Francisco vs. Green Bay, 1997
SB: Atlanta vs. Denver, 1998

PENALTIES

Most Penalties, Game

17 AFC-FR: L.A. Raiders vs. Denver, 1993
14 AFC-FR: Oakland vs. Houston, 1980
NFC-D: San Francisco vs. N.Y. Giants, 1981
13 AFC-FR: Houston vs. Cleveland, 1988
AFC-D: Houston vs. Denver, 1991
NFC-D: Arizona vs. Minnesota, 1998

Fewest Penalties, Game

0 NFC: Philadelphia vs. Green Bay, 1960
NFC-D: Detroit vs. Dallas, 1970
AFC-D: Miami vs. Oakland, 1970
SB: Miami vs. Dallas, 1971
NFC-D: Washington vs. Minnesota, 1973
SB: Pittsburgh vs. Dallas, 1975
NFC: San Francisco vs. Chicago, 1988
SB: Denver vs. San Francisco, 1989
AFC-D: L.A. Raiders vs. Cincinnati, 1990
AFC-D: Miami vs. San Diego, 1992
SB: Atlanta vs. Denver, 1998
1 By many teams

Most Penalties, Both Teams, Game

27 AFC-FR: L.A. Raiders (17) vs. Denver (10), 1993
22 AFC-FR: Oakland (14) vs. Houston (8), 1980
NFC-D: San Francisco (14) vs. N.Y. Giants (8), 1981
AFC-FR: Houston (13) vs. Cleveland (9), 1988
NFC-D: Arizona (13) vs. Minnesota (9), 1998
21 AFC-D: Oakland (11) vs. New England (10), 1976

Fewest Penalties, Both Teams, Game

1 AFC-D: L.A. Raiders (0) vs. Cincinnati (1), 1990
2 NFC: Washington (1) vs. Chi. Bears (1), 1937
NFC-D: Washington (0) vs. Minnesota (2), 1973
SB: Pittsburgh (0) vs. Dallas (2), 1975
3 AFC: Miami (1) vs. Baltimore (2), 1971
NFC: San Francisco (1) vs. Dallas (2), 1971
SB: Miami (0) vs. Dallas (3), 1971
AFC-D: Pittsburgh (1) vs. Oakland (2), 1972
AFC-D: Miami (1) vs. Cincinnati (2), 1973
SB: Miami (1) vs. San Francisco (2), 1984
NFC: San Francisco (0) vs. Chicago (3), 1988

YARDS PENALIZED

Most Yards Penalized, Game

145 NFC-D: San Francisco vs. N.Y. Giants, 1981
133 SB: Dallas vs. Baltimore, 1970
130 AFC-FR: L.A. Raiders vs. Denver, 1993

Fewest Yards Penalized, Game

0 By 11 teams

Most Yards Penalized, Both Teams, Game

227 AFC-FR: L.A. Raiders (130) vs. Denver (97), 1993
206 NFC-D: San Francisco (145) vs. N.Y. Giants (61), 1981
193 AFC-FR: Houston (118) vs. Cleveland (75), 1988

Fewest Yards Penalized, Both Teams, Game

5 AFC-D: L.A. Raiders (0) vs. Cincinnati (5), 1990
9 NFC-D: Washington (0) vs. Minnesota (9), 1973
15 SB: Miami (0) vs. Dallas (15), 1971

FUMBLES

Most Fumbles, Game

8 SB: Buffalo vs. Dallas, 1992
7 AFC-D: Houston vs. Kansas City, 1993
6 By 11 teams

Most Fumbles, Both Teams, Game

12 AFC: Houston (6) vs. Pittsburgh (6), 1978
SB: Buffalo (8) vs. Dallas (4), 1992
10 NFC: Chi. Bears (5) vs. N.Y. Giants (5), 1934
SB: Dallas (6) vs. Denver (4), 1977
9 NFC-D: San Francisco (6) vs. Detroit (3), 1957
NFC-D: San Francisco (5) vs. Dallas (4), 1972
NFC: Dallas (5) vs. Philadelphia (4), 1980

Most Fumbles Lost, Game

5 SB: Buffalo vs. Dallas, 1992
4 NFC: N.Y. Giants vs. Baltimore, 1958 (OT)
AFC: Kansas City vs. Oakland, 1969
SB: Baltimore vs. Dallas, 1970
AFC: Pittsburgh vs. Oakland, 1975
SB: Denver vs. Dallas, 1977
AFC: Houston vs. Pittsburgh, 1978
AFC: Miami vs. New England, 1985
SB: New England vs. Chicago, 1985
NFC-FR: L.A. Rams vs. Washington, 1986
NFC-FR: Minnesota vs. Dallas, 1996
AFC-FR: Buffalo vs. Miami, 1998
3 By many teams

Fewest Fumbles, Both Teams, Game

0 NFC: Green Bay vs. Cleveland, 1965
AFC-D: Houston vs. San Diego, 1979
NFC-D: Dallas vs. Los Angeles, 1979
SB: Los Angeles vs. Pittsburgh, 1979
AFC-D: Buffalo vs. Cincinnati, 1981
NFC: Minnesota vs. Washington, 1987
NFC-D: San Francisco vs. Washington, 1990
NFC: Dallas vs. Green Bay, 1995
AFC-D: New England vs. Pittsburgh, 1996
SB: Green Bay vs. New England., 1996
1 In many games

RECOVERIES

Most Total Fumbles Recovered, Game

8 SB: Dallas vs. Denver, 1977 (4 own, 4 opp)
7 NFC: Chi. Bears vs. N.Y. Giants, 1934 (5 own, 2 opp)
NFC-D: San Francisco vs. Detroit, 1957 (4 own, 3 opp)
NFC-D: San Francisco vs. Dallas, 1972 (4 own, 3 opp)
AFC: Pittsburgh vs. Houston, 1978 (3 own, 4 opp)
6 AFC: Houston vs. San Diego, 1961 (4 own, 2 opp)
AFC-D: Cleveland vs. Baltimore, 1971 (4 own, 2 opp)
AFC-D: Cleveland vs. Oakland, 1980 (5 own, 1 opp)
NFC: Philadelphia vs. Dallas, 1980 (3 own, 3 opp)
SB: Dallas vs. Buffalo, 1992 (1 own, 5 opp)
NFC-D: Green Bay vs. San Francisco, 1996 (4 own, 2 opp)
AFC: Denver vs. N.Y. Jets, 1998 (2 own, 4 opp)

Most Own Fumbles Recovered, Game

5 NFC: Chi. Bears vs. N.Y. Giants, 1934
AFC-D: Cleveland vs. Oakland, 1980
4 By many teams

TOUCHDOWNS

Most Touchdowns, Game

2 SB: Dallas vs. Buffalo, 1992

TURNOVERS

Numbers of times losing the ball on interceptions and fumbles.

Most Turnovers, Game

9 NFC: Washington vs. Chi. Bears, 1940
NFC: Detroit vs. Cleveland, 1954
AFC: Houston vs. Pittsburgh, 1978
SB: Buffalo vs. Dallas, 1992
8 NFC: N.Y. Giants vs. Chi. Bears, 1946
NFC: Los Angeles vs. Cleveland, 1955
NFC: Cleveland vs. Detroit, 1957
SB: Denver vs. Dallas, 1977
NFC-D: Minnesota vs. Philadelphia, 1980
7 In many games

Fewest Turnovers, Game

0 By many teams

Most Turnovers, Both Teams, Game

14 AFC: Houston (9) vs. Pittsburgh (5), 1978
13 NFC: Detroit (9) vs. Cleveland (4), 1954
AFC: Houston (7) vs. San Diego (6), 1961
12 AFC: Pittsburgh (7) vs. Oakland (5), 1975

Fewest Turnovers, Both Teams, Game

0 SB: Buffalo vs. N.Y. Giants, 1990
AFC-FR: Kansas City vs Pittsburgh, 1993 (OT)
NFC-FR: Detroit vs. Green Bay, 1994
AFC-FR:Denver vs. Jacksonville, 1996
1 AFC-D: Baltimore (0) vs. Cincinnati (1), 1970
AFC-D: Pittsburgh (0) vs. Buffalo (1), 1974
AFC: Oakland (0) vs. Pittsburgh (1), 1976
NFC-D: Minnesota (0) vs. Washington (1), 1982
NFC-D: Chicago (0) vs. N.Y. Giants (1), 1985
SB: N.Y. Giants (0) vs. Denver (1), 1986
NFC: Washington (0) vs. Minnesota (1), 1987
AFC-D: Cincinnati (0) vs. L.A. Raiders (1), 1990
NFC: N.Y. Giants (0) vs. San Francisco (1), 1990
NFC-FR: N.Y. Giants (0) vs. Minnesota (1), 1993
AFC-FR: L.A. Raiders (0) vs. Denver (1), 1993
NFC: Dallas (0) vs. San Francisco (1), 1993
AFC: Indianapolis (0) vs. Pittsburgh (1), 1995
NFC-D: San Francisco (0) vs. Minnesota (1), 1997
2 In many games

AFC-NFC PRO BOWL RECORDS

Includes records of AFC-NFC Pro Bowls, 1971-1998
Compiled by Elias Sports Bureau

INDIVIDUAL RECORDS

SERVICE

Most Games

11 ** Reggie White, Philadelphia, 1987-93; Green Bay, 1994, 1996-97, 1999
10 Lawrence Taylor, N.Y. Giants, 1982-91
Ronnie Lott, San Francisco, 1982-85, 1987-91; L.A. Raiders 1992
Mike Singletary, Chicago, 1984-93
Randall McDaniel, Minnesota, 1990-99
9 * Ken Houston, Houston, 1971-73; Washington, 1974-79
Joe Greene, Pittsburgh, 1971-77, 1979-80
Jack Lambert, Pittsburgh, 1976-84
Walter Payton, Chicago, 1977-81, 1984-87
Harry Carson, N.Y. Giants, 1979-80, 1982-88
Mike Webster, Pittsburgh, 1979-86, 1988
** Anthony Muñoz, Cincinnati, 1982-87, 1989-90, 1992
Warren Moon, Houston, 1989-94; Minnesota 1995-96; Seattle 1998
Derrick Thomas, Kansas City, 1990-98
*** Jerry Rice, San Francisco, 1987-88, 1990-94, 1996, 1999

**Also selected, but did not play, in one additional game*
***Also selected, but did not play, in two additional games*
****Also selected, but did not play, in three additional games*

SCORING

POINTS

Most Points, Career

45 Morten Andersen, New Orleans, 1986-89, 1991, 1993; Atlanta, 1996 (15-pat, 10-fg)
30 Jan Stenerud, Kansas City, 1971-72, 1976; Minnesota, 1985 (6-pat, 8-fg)
26 Nick Lowery, Kansas City, 1982, 1991, 1993 (5 pat, 7 fg)

Most Points, Game

18 John Brockington, Green Bay, 1973 (3-td)
15 Garo Yepremian, Miami, 1974 (5-fg)
14 Jan Stenerud, Kansas City, 1972 (2-pat, 4-fg)

TOUCHDOWNS

Most Touchdowns, Career

3 John Brockington, Green Bay, 1972-74 (2-r, 1-p)
Earl Campbell, Houston, 1979-82, 1984 (3-r)
Chuck Muncie, New Orleans, 1980; San Diego, 1982-83 (3-r)
William Andrews, Atlanta, 1981-84 (1-r, 2-p)
Marcus Allen, L.A. Raiders, 1983, 1985-86, 1988; Kansas City, 1994 (2-r, 1-p)
Cris Carter, Minnesota, 1994-99 (3-p)
2 By 17 players

Most Touchdowns, Game

3 John Brockington, Green Bay, 1973 (2-r, 1-p)
2 Mel Renfro, Dallas, 1971 (2-ret)
Earl Campbell, Houston, 1980 (2-r)
Chuck Muncie, New Orleans, 1980 (2-r)
William Andrews, Atlanta, 1984 (2-p)
Herschel Walker, Dallas, 1989 (2-r)
Johnny Johnson, Phoenix, 1991 (2-r)
Eric Green, Pittsburgh, 1995 (2-p)

POINTS AFTER TOUCHDOWN

Most Points After Touchdown, Career

15 Morten Andersen, New Orleans, 1986-89, 1991, 1993; Atlanta, 1996 (15 att)
6 Chester Marcol, Green Bay, 1973, 1975 (6 att)
Mark Moseley, Washington, 1980, 1983 (7 att)
Ali Haji-Sheikh, N.Y. Giants, 1984 (6 att)
Jan Stenerud, Kansas City, 1971-72, 1976; Green Bay, 1985 (6 att)
5 Nick Lowery, Kansas City, 1982, 1991, 1993 (5 att)
John Carney, San Diego, 1995 (5 att)

Most Points After Touchdown, Game

6 Ali Haji-Sheikh, N.Y. Giants, 1984 (6 att)
5 John Carney, San Diego, 1995 (5 att)
4 Chester Marcol, Green Bay, 1973 (4 att)
Mark Moseley, Washington, 1980 (5 att)
Morten Andersen, New Orleans, 1986 (4 att), 1989 (4 att)

FIELD GOALS

Most Field Goals Attempted, Career

18 Morten Andersen, New Orleans, 1986-89, 1991, 1993; Atlanta, 1996
15 Jan Stenerud, Kansas City, 1971-72, 1976; Minnesota, 1985
10 Nick Lowery, Kansas City, 1982, 1991, 1993

Most Field Goals Attempted, Game

6 Jan Stenerud, Kansas City, 1972
Eddie Murray, Detroit, 1981
Mark Moseley, Washington, 1983
5 Garo Yepremian, Miami, 1974
4 Jan Stenerud, Kansas City, 1976
Nick Lowery, Kansas City, 1991, 1993
Morten Andersen, New Orleans, 1993
Cary Blanchard, Indianapolis, 1997
John Kasay, Carolina, 1997

Most Field Goals, Career

10 Morten Andersen, New Orleans, 1986-89, 1991, 1993; Atlanta, 1996
8 Jan Stenerud, Kansas City, 1971-72, 1976; Minnesota, 1985
7 Nick Lowery, Kansas City, 1982, 1991, 1993

Most Field Goals, Game

5 Garo Yepremian, Miami, 1974 (5 att)
4 Jan Stenerud, Kansas City, 1972 (6 att)
Eddie Murray, Detroit, 1981 (6 att)
3 Nick Lowery, Kansas City, 1991 (4 att)
Nick Lowery, Kansas City, 1993 (4 att)
Jason Elam, Denver, 1999 (3 att)

Longest Field Goal

51 Morten Andersen, New Orleans, 1989
49 Fuad Reveiz, Minnesota, 1995
48 Jan Stenerud, Kansas City, 1972
Jeff Jaeger, L.A. Raiders, 1992
Mike Hollis, Jacksonville, 1998

SAFETIES

Most Safeties, Game

1 Art Still, Kansas City, 1983
Mark Gastineau, N.Y. Jets, 1985
Greg Townsend, L.A. Raiders, 1992

RUSHING

ATTEMPTS

Most Attempts, Career

81 Walter Payton, Chicago, 1977-81, 1984-87
68 O.J. Simpson, Buffalo, 1973-77
66 Barry Sanders, Detroit, 1990-93, 1995-98

Most Attempts, Game

19 O.J. Simpson, Buffalo, 1974
17 Marv Hubbard, Oakland, 1974
16 O.J. Simpson, Buffalo, 1973
Marcus Allen, L.A. Raiders, 1986

YARDS GAINED

Most Yards Gained, Career

368 Walter Payton, Chicago, 1977-81, 1984-87
356 O.J. Simpson, Buffalo, 1973-77
234 Chris Warren, Seattle, 1994-96

Most Yards Gained, Game

180 Marshall Faulk, Indianapolis, 1995
127 Chris Warren, Seattle, 1995
112 O. J. Simpson, Buffalo, 1973

Longest Run From Scrimmage

49 Marshall Faulk, Indianapolis, 1995 (TD)
41 Lawrence McCutcheon, Los Angeles, 1976
Natrone Means, San Diego, 1995
Marshall Faulk, Indianapolis, 1995
39 Chris Warren, Seattle, 1994

AVERAGE GAIN

Highest Average Gain, Career (20 attempts)

10.65 Marshall Faulk, Indianapolis, 1995-96, 1999 (20-213)
9.36 Chris Warren, Seattle, 1994-96, (25-234)
5.81 Marv Hubbard, Oakland, 1972-74 (36-209)

Highest Average Gain, Game (10 attempts)

13.85 Marshall Faulk, Indianapolis, 1995 (13-180)
9.07 Chris Warren, Seattle, 1995 (14-127)
7.00 O.J. Simpson, Buffalo, 1973 (16-112)
Ottis Anderson, St. Louis, 1981 (10-70)

TOUCHDOWNS

Most Touchdowns, Career

3 Earl Campbell, Houston, 1979-82, 1984
Chuck Muncie, New Orleans, 1980; San Diego, 1982-83
2 John Brockington, Green Bay, 1972-74
O.J. Simpson, Buffalo, 1973-77
Walter Payton, Chicago, 1977-81, 1984-87
Marcus Allen, L.A. Raiders, 1983, 1985-86, 1988; Kansas City, 1994
Herschel Walker, Dallas, 1988-89
Johnny Johnson, Phoenix, 1991

Barry Sanders, Detroit, 1990-93, 1995-98

Most Touchdowns, Game

2 John Brockington, Green Bay, 1973
Earl Campbell, Houston, 1980
Chuck Muncie, New Orleans, 1980
Herschel Walker, Dallas, 1989
Johnny Johnson, Phoenix, 1991

PASSING

ATTEMPTS

Most Attempts, Career

120 Dan Fouts, San Diego, 1980-84, 1986
101 Steve Young, San Francisco, 1993-96, 1998-99
90 Warren Moon, Houston, 1989-94; Minnesota, 1995-96; Seattle 1998

Most Attempts, Game

32 Bill Kenney, Kansas City, 1984
Steve Young, San Francisco, 1993
30 Dan Fouts, San Diego, 1983
28 Jim Hart, St. Louis, 1976

COMPLETIONS

Most Completions, Career

63 Dan Fouts, San Diego, 1980-84, 1986
48 Steve Young, San Francisco, 1993-96, 1998-99
45 Warren Moon, Houston, 1989-94; Minnesota, 1995-96; Seattle 1998

Most Completions, Game

21 Joe Theismann, Washington, 1984
18 Steve Young, San Francisco, 1993
17 Dan Fouts, San Diego, 1983

COMPLETION PERCENTAGE

Highest Completion Percentage, Career (40 attempts)

68.9 Joe Theismann, Washington, 1983-84 (45-31)
64.4 Jim Kelly, Buffalo, 1988, 1991-92 (45-29)
58.9 Ken Anderson, Cincinnati, 1976-77, 1982-83 (56-33)

Highest Completion Percentage, Game (10 attempts)

90.0 Archie Manning, New Orleans, 1980 (10-9)
77.8 Joe Theismann, Washington, 1984 (27-21)
72.2 Jim Everett, L.A. Rams, 1991 (18-13)

YARDS GAINED

Most Yards Gained, Career

890 Dan Fouts, San Diego, 1980-84, 1986
614 Steve Young, San Francisco, 1993-96, 1998-99
554 Bob Griese, Miami, 1971-72, 1974-75, 1977, 1979

Most Yards Gained, Game

274 Dan Fouts, San Diego, 1983
242 Joe Theismann, Washington, 1984
236 Mark Brunell, Jacksonville, 1997

Longest Completion

93 Jeff Blake, Cincinnati (to Thigpen, Pittsburgh), 1996 (TD)
80 Mark Brunell, Jacksonville (to Brown, Oakland), 1997 (TD)
64 Dan Pastorini, Houston (to Burrough, Houston), 1976 (TD)

AVERAGE GAIN

Highest Average Gain, Career (40 attempts)

8.12 Brett Favre, Green Bay, 1993-94, 1996-97 (57-463)
8.06 Randall Cunningham, Philadelphia, 1989-91; Minnesota, 1999 (52-419)
8.02 Jim Kelly, Buffalo, 1988, 1991-92 (45-361)

Highest Average Gain, Game (10 attempts)

15.27 Randall Cunningham, Philadelphia, 1991 (11-168)
13.00 Brett Favre, Green Bay, 1997 (11-143)
11.40 Ken Anderson, Cincinnati, 1977 (10-114)

TOUCHDOWNS

Most Touchdowns, Career

4 Steve Young, San Francisco, 1993-96, 1998-99
3 Joe Theismann, Washington, 1983-84
Joe Montana, San Francisco, 1982, 1984-85, 1988
Phil Simms, N.Y. Giants, 1986
Jim Kelly, Buffalo, 1988, 1991-92
John Elway, Denver, 1987-88, 1994-95, 1999
2 James Harris, Los Angeles, 1975
Mike Boryla, Philadelphia, 1976
Ken Anderson, Cincinnati, 1976-77, 1982-83
Bob Griese, Miami, 1971-72, 1974-75, 1977, 1979
Mark Rypien, Washington, 1990, 1992
Brett Favre, Green Bay, 1993-94, 1996-97
Mark Brunell, Jacksonville, 1997-98

Most Touchdowns, Game

3 Joe Theismann, Washington, 1984
Phil Simms, N.Y. Giants, 1986
2 James Harris, Los Angeles, 1975
Mike Boryla, Philadelphia, 1976
Ken Anderson, Cincinnati, 1977
Jim Kelly, Buffalo, 1991
Mark Rypien, Washington, 1992
Steve Young, San Francisco, 1998

HAD INTERCEPTED

Most Passes Had Intercepted, Career

8 Dan Fouts, San Diego, 1980-84, 1986
6 Jim Hart, St. Louis, 1975-78
5 Ken Stabler, Oakland, 1974-75, 1978

Most Passes Had Intercepted, Game

5 Jim Hart, St. Louis, 1977
4 Ken Stabler, Oakland, 1974
3 Dan Fouts, San Diego, 1986
Mark Rypien, Washington, 1990
Steve Young, San Francisco, 1993
Jim Harbaugh, Indianapolis, 1996
Vinny Testaverde, N.Y. Jets, 1999

Most Attempts, Without Interception, Game

27 Joe Theismann, Washington, 1984
Phil Simms, N.Y. Giants, 1986
26 John Brodie, San Francisco, 1971
Danny White, Dallas, 1983
23 Dave Krieg, Seattle, 1990

PERCENTAGE, PASSES HAD INTERCEPTED

Lowest Percentage, Passes Had Intercepted, Career (40 attempts)

0.00 Joe Theismann, Washington, 1983-84 (45-0)
2.13 Dave Krieg, Seattle, 1985, 1989-90 (47-1)
2.22 Jim Kelly, Buffalo, 1988, 1991-92 (45-1)

PASS RECEIVING

RECEPTIONS

Most Receptions, Career

33 Jerry Rice, San Francisco, 1987-88, 1990-94, 1996, 1999
23 Tim Brown, L.A. Raiders, 1989, 1992, 1994-95; Oakland 1996-98
18 Walter Payton, Chicago, 1977-81, 1984-87
Michael Irvin, Dallas, 1992-96

Most Receptions, Game

8 Steve Largent, Seattle, 1986
Michael Irvin, Dallas, 1992
Andre Rison, Atlanta, 1993
7 John Stallworth, Pittsburgh, 1983
Jerry Rice, San Francisco, 1992
Isaac Bruce, St. Louis, 1997
Keyshawn Johnson, N.Y. Jets, 1999
Randy Moss, Minnesota, 1999
6 John Stallworth, Pittsburgh, 1980
Kellen Winslow, San Diego, 1982
Gary Clark, Washington, 1991
Keith Byars, Miami, 1994
Andre Rison, Atlanta, 1994
Jerry Rice, San Francisco, 1996

YARDS GAINED

Most Yards Gained, Career

459 Jerry Rice, San Francisco, 1987-88, 1990-94, 1996, 1999
408 Tim Brown, L.A. Raiders, 1989, 1992, 1994-95; Oakland, 1996-98
274 Michael Irvin, Dallas, 1992-96

Most Yards Gained, Game

137 Tim Brown, Oakland, 1997
129 Tim Brown, Oakland, 1998
125 Michael Irvin, Dallas, 1992

Longest Reception

93 Yancey Thigpen, Pittsburgh (from Blake, Cincinnati), 1996 (TD)
80 Tim Brown, Oakland (from Brunell, Jacksonville), 1997 (TD)
64 Ken Burrough, Houston (from Pastorini, Houston), 1976 (TD)

TOUCHDOWNS

Most Touchdowns, Career

3 Cris Carter, Minnesota, 1994-99
2 Mel Gray, St. Louis, 1975-78
Cliff Branch, Oakland, 1975-78
Terry Metcalf, St. Louis, 1975-76, 1978
Tony Hill, Dallas, 1979-80, 1986
William Andrews, Atlanta, 1981-84
James Lofton, Green Bay, 1979, 1981-86; Buffalo 1992
Jimmie Giles, Tampa Bay, 1981-83, 1986
Michael Irvin, Dallas, 1992-95
Eric Green, Pittsburgh, 1994-95
Jerry Rice, San Francisco, 1987-88, 1990-94, 1996, 1999

Most Touchdowns, Game
2 William Andrews, Atlanta, 1984
Eric Green, Pittsburgh, 1995

INTERCEPTIONS BY

Most Interceptions By, Career
4 Everson Walls, Dallas, 1982-84, 1986
Deion Sanders, Atlanta, 1992-94; San Francisco, 1995; Dallas, 1999
3 Ken Houston, Houston, 1971-73; Washington, 1974-79
Jack Lambert, Pittsburgh, 1976-84
Ted Hendricks, Baltimore, 1972-74; Green Bay, 1975; Oakland, 1981-82; L.A. Raiders, 1983-84
Mike Haynes, New England, 1978-81, 1983; L.A. Raiders, 1985-87
2 By 11 players

Most Interceptions By, Game
2 Mel Blount, Pittsburgh, 1977
Everson Walls, Dallas, 1982, 1983
LeRoy Irvin, L.A. Rams, 1986
David Fulcher, Cincinnati, 1990

YARDS GAINED

Most Yards Gained, Career
103 Deion Sanders, Atlanta, 1992-94; San Francisco, 1995; Dallas, 1999
77 Ted Hendricks, Baltimore, 1972-74; Green Bay, 1975; Oakland, 1981-82; L.A. Raiders, 1983-84
73 Rod Woodson, Pittsburgh, 1990-95, 1997

Most Yards Gained, Game
87 Deion Sanders, Dallas, 1999
73 Rod Woodson, Pittsburgh, 1994
67 Ty Law, New England, 1999

Longest Gain
87 Deion Sanders, Dallas, 1999
73 Rod Woodson, Pittsburgh, 1994 (lateral)
67 Ty Law, New England, 1999 (TD)

TOUCHDOWNS

Most Touchdowns, Game
1 Bobby Bell, Kansas City, 1973
Nolan Cromwell, L.A. Rams, 1984
Joey Browner, Minnesota, 1986
Jerry Gray, L.A. Rams, 1990
Mike Johnson, Cleveland, 1990
Junior Seau, San Diego, 1993
Ken Harvey, Washington, 1996
Ashley Ambrose, Cincinnati, 1997
Ty Law, New England, 1999

PUNTING

Most Punts, Career
33 Ray Guy, Oakland, 1974-79, 1981
23 Rohn Stark, Indianapolis, 1986-87, 1991, 1993
22 Reggie Roby, Miami, 1985, 1990; Washington, 1995

Most Punts, Game
10 Reggie Roby, Miami, 1985
9 Tom Wittum, San Francisco, 1974
Rohn Stark, Indianapolis, 1987
8 Jerrel Wilson, Kansas City, 1971
Tom Skladany, Detroit, 1982
Reggie Roby, Washington, 1995

Longest Punt
64 Tom Wittum, San Francisco, 1974
Darren Bennett, San Diego, 1996
61 Reggie Roby, Miami, 1985
Jeff Feagles, Arizona, 1996
Matt Turk, Washington, 1997
60 Ron Widby, Dallas, 1972
Reggie Roby, Washington, 1995

AVERAGE YARDAGE

Highest Average, Career (10 punts)
46.73 Reggie Roby, Miami, 1985, 1990; Washington, 1995 (22-1,028)
45.27 Matt Turk, Washington, 1997-99 (15-679)
45.25 Jerrel Wilson, Kansas City, 1971-73 (16-724)

Highest Average, Game (4 punts)
55.50 Darren Bennett, San Diego, 1996 (4-222)
52.00 Matt Turk, Washington, 1999 (4-208)
50.13 Reggie Roby, Washington, 1995 (8-401)

PUNT RETURNS

Most Punt Returns, Career
13 Rick Upchurch, Denver, 1977, 1979-80, 1983
11 Vai Sikahema, St. Louis, 1987-88
Eric Metcalf, Cleveland 1994-95; San Diego 1998
10 Mike Nelms, Washington, 1981-83

Most Punt Returns, Game
7 Vai Sikahema, St. Louis, 1987
6 Henry Ellard, L.A. Rams, 1985
Gerald McNeil, Cleveland, 1988
Eric Metcalf, Cleveland, 1995
5 Rick Upchurch, Denver, 1980
Mike Nelms, Washington, 1981
Carl Roaches, Houston, 1982
Johnny Bailey, Phoenix, 1993

Most Fair Catches, Game
2 Jerry Logan, Baltimore, 1971
Dick Anderson, Miami, 1974
Henry Ellard, L.A. Rams, 1985
Isaac Bruce, St. Louis, 1997

YARDS GAINED

Most Yards Gained, Career
183 Billy Johnson, Houston, 1976, 1978; Atlanta, 1984
138 Mel Renfro, Dallas, 1971-72, 1974
Rick Upchurch, Denver, 1977, 1979-80, 1983
135 Eric Metcalf, Cleveland, 1994-95; San Diego 1998

Most Yards Gained, Game
159 Billy Johnson, Houston, 1976
138 Mel Renfro, Dallas, 1971
117 Wally Henry, Philadelphia, 1980

Longest Punt Return
90 Billy Johnson, Houston, 1976 (TD)
86 Wally Henry, Philadelphia, 1980 (TD)
82 Mel Renfro, Dallas, 1971 (TD)

AVERAGE YARDAGE

Highest Average, Career (4 returns)
22.88 Billy Johnson, Houston, 1976, 1978; Atlanta, 1984 (8-183)
21.50 Tony Green, Washington, 1979 (4-86)
15.67 David Meggett, N.Y. Giants, 1990; New England, 1997

Highest Average, Game (3 returns)
39.75 Billy Johnson, Houston, 1976 (4-159)
39.00 Wally Henry, Philadelphia, 1980 (3-117)
21.50 Tony Green, Washington, 1979 (4-86)

TOUCHDOWNS

Most Touchdowns, Game
2 Mel Renfro, Dallas, 1971
1 Billy Johnson, Houston, 1976
Wally Henry, Philadelphia, 1980

KICKOFF RETURNS

Most Kickoff Returns, Career
14 Mel Gray, Detroit, 1991-92, 1995
12 Michael Bates, Carolina, 1997-99
11 Eric Metcalf, Cleveland, 1994-95; San Diego, 1998

Most Kickoff Returns, Game
7 Mel Gray, Detroit, 1995
6 Greg Pruitt, L.A. Raiders, 1984
David Meggett, New England, 1997
Michael Bates, Carolina, 1998
5 By six players

YARDS GAINED

Most Yards Gained, Career
309 Greg Pruitt, Cleveland, 1974-75, 1977-78; L.A. Raiders, 1984
294 Mel Gray, Detroit, 1991-92, 1995
288 Michael Bates, Carolina, 1997-99

Most Yards Gained, Game
192 Greg Pruitt, L.A. Raiders, 1984
175 Les (Speedy) Duncan, Washington, 1972
173 David Meggett, New England, 1997

Longest Kickoff Return
62 Greg Pruitt, L.A. Raiders, 1984
61 Eugene (Mercury) Morris, Miami, 1972
55 Ron Smith, Chicago, 1973

AVERAGE YARDAGE

Highest Average, Career (4 returns)
35.00 Les (Speedy) Duncan, Washington, 1972 (5-175)
31.25 Eugene (Mercury) Morris, Miami, 1972 (3-93)
30.90 Greg Pruitt, Cleveland, 1974-75, 1977-78; L.A. Raiders, 1984 (6-192)

Highest Average, Game (3 returns)
35.00 Les (Speedy) Duncan, Washington, 1972 (5-175)
32.00 Greg Pruitt, L.A. Raiders, 1984 (6-192)
31.00 Eugene (Mercury) Morris, Miami, 1972 (3-93)

TOUCHDOWNS
Most Touchdowns, Game
None

FUMBLES
Most Fumbles, Career
6 Dan Fouts, San Diego, 1980-84, 1986
4 Lawrence McCutcheon, Los Angeles, 1974-78
Franco Harris, Pittsburgh, 1973-76, 1978-81
Jay Schroeder, Washington, 1987
Vai Sikahema, St. Louis, 1987-88
3 O.J. Simpson, Buffalo, 1973-77
William Andrews, Atlanta, 1981-84
Joe Montana, San Francisco, 1982, 1984-85, 1988
Walter Payton, Chicago, 1977-81, 1984-87
Neil Lomax, St. Louis, 1985, 1988
Jim Kelly, Buffalo, 1988, 1991-92
Chris Chandler, Atlanta, 1998-99
Most Fumbles, Game
4 Jay Schroeder, Washington, 1987
3 Dan Fouts, San Diego, 1982
Vai Sikahema, St. Louis, 1987
2 By 12 players

RECOVERIES
Most Fumbles Recovered, Career
3 Harold Jackson, Philadelphia, 1973; Los Angeles, 1974, 1976, 1978 (3-own)
Dan Fouts, San Diego, 1980-84, 1986 (3-own)
Randy White, Dallas, 1978, 1980-86 (3-opp)
2 By many players
Most Fumbles Recovered, Game
2 Dick Anderson, Miami, 1974 (1-own, 1-opp)
Harold Jackson, Los Angeles, 1974 (2-own)
Dan Fouts, San Diego, 1982 (2-own)
Joey Browner, Minnesota, 1990 (2-opp)
Jessie Armstead, N.Y. Giants, 1999 (1-own, 1-opp)

YARDAGE
Longest Fumble Return
83 Art Still, Kansas City, 1985 (TD, opp)
51 Phil Villapiano, Oakland, 1974 (opp)
37 Sam Mills, New Orleans, 1988 (opp)

TOUCHDOWNS
Most Touchdowns, Game
1 Art Still, Kansas City, 1985
Keith Millard, Minnesota, 1990

SACKS
Sacks have been compiled since 1983.
Most Sacks, Career
9.5 Reggie White, Philadelphia, 1987-93; Green Bay, 1994, 1996-97, 1999
9 Howie Long, L.A. Raiders, 1984-88, 1990, 1993-1994
7.5 Bruce Smith, Buffalo, 1988-91, 1995-96, 1998-99
Most Sacks, Game
4 Mark Gastineau, N.Y. Jets, 1985
Reggie White, Philadelphia, 1987
3 Richard Dent, Chicago, 1985
Bruce Smith, Buffalo, 1991
2.5 Bruce Smith, Buffalo, 1998

TEAM RECORDS

SCORING
Most Points, Game
45 NFC, 1984
Fewest Points, Game
3 AFC, 1984, 1989, 1994
Most Points, Both Teams, Game
64 NFC (37) vs. AFC (27), 1980
Fewest Points, Both Teams, Game
16 NFC (6) vs. AFC (10), 1987

TOUCHDOWNS
Most Touchdowns, Game
6 NFC, 1984
Fewest Touchdowns, Game
0 AFC, 1971, 1974, 1984, 1989, 1994
NFC, 1987, 1988
Most Touchdowns, Both Teams, Game
8 AFC (4) vs. NFC (4), 1973
NFC (5) vs. AFC (3), 1980
Fewest Touchdowns, Both Teams, Game
1 AFC (0) vs. NFC (1), 1974
NFC (0) vs. AFC (1), 1987
NFC (0) vs. AFC (1), 1988

POINTS AFTER TOUCHDOWN
Most Points After Touchdown, Game
6 NFC, 1984
Most Points After Touchdown, Both Teams, Game
7 NFC (4) vs. AFC (3), 1973
NFC (4) vs. AFC (3), 1980
NFC (4) vs. AFC (3), 1986

FIELD GOALS
Most Field Goals Attempted, Game
6 AFC, 1972
NFC, 1981, 1983
Most Field Goals Attempted, Both Teams, Game
9 NFC (6) vs. AFC (3), 1983
Most Field Goals, Game
5 AFC, 1974
Most Field Goals, Both Teams, Game
7 AFC (5) vs. NFC (2), 1974

NET YARDS GAINED RUSHING AND PASSING
Most Yards Gained, Game
552 AFC, 1995
Fewest Yards Gained, Game
114 AFC, 1993
Most Yards Gained, Both Teams, Game
962 NFC (496) vs. AFC (466), 1997
Fewest Yards Gained, Both Teams, Game
424 AFC (202) vs. NFC (222), 1987

RUSHING
ATTEMPTS
Most Attempts, Game
50 AFC, 1974
Fewest Attempts, Game
14 AFC, 1994
Most Attempts, Both Teams, Game
80 AFC (50) vs. NFC (30), 1974
Fewest Attempts, Both Teams, Game
47 NFC (22) vs. AFC (25), 1996

YARDS GAINED
Most Yards Gained, Game
400 AFC, 1995
Fewest Yards Gained, Game
28 NFC, 1992
Most Yards Gained, Both Teams, Game
441 AFC (400) vs. NFC (41), 1995
Fewest Yards Gained, Both Teams, Game
131 NFC (28) vs. AFC (103), 1992

TOUCHDOWNS
Most Touchdowns, Game
3 NFC, 1989, 1991
AFC, 1995
Most Touchdowns, Both Teams, Game
4 AFC (2) vs. NFC (2), 1973
AFC (2) vs. NFC (2), 1980

PASSING
ATTEMPTS
Most Attempts, Game
55 NFC, 1993
Fewest Attempts, Game
17 NFC, 1972
Most Attempts, Both Teams, Game
94 AFC (50) vs. NFC (44), 1983
Fewest Attempts, Both Teams, Game
42 NFC (17) vs. AFC (25), 1972

COMPLETIONS
Most Completions, Game
32 NFC, 1993
Fewest Completions, Game
7 NFC, 1972, 1982
Most Completions, Both Teams, Game
55 AFC (31) vs. NFC (24), 1983

AFC-NFC PRO BOWL RECORDS

Fewest Completions, Both Teams, Game
18 NFC (7) vs. AFC (11), 1972

YARDS GAINED

Most Yards Gained, Game
387 AFC, 1983
Fewest Yards Gained, Game
42 NFC, 1982
Most Yards Gained, Both Teams, Game
735 AFC (369) vs. NFC (366), 1997
Fewest Yards Gained, Both Teams, Game
215 NFC (89) vs. AFC (126), 1972

TIMES SACKED

Most Times Sacked, Game
9 NFC, 1985
Fewest Times Sacked, Game
0 AFC, 1998, 1999
NFC, 1971, 1997
Most Times Sacked, Both Teams, Game
17 NFC (9) vs. AFC (8), 1985
Fewest Times Sacked, Both Teams, Game
1 NFC (0) vs. AFC (1), 1997

TOUCHDOWNS

Most Touchdowns, Game
4 NFC, 1984
Most Touchdowns, Both Teams, Game
5 NFC (3) vs. AFC (2), 1986

INTERCEPTIONS BY

Most Interceptions By, Game
6 AFC, 1977
Most Interceptions By, Both Teams, Game
7 AFC (6) vs. NFC (1), 1977

YARDS GAINED

Most Yards Gained, Game
103 AFC, 1994
Most Yards Gained, Both Teams, Game
172 NFC (102) vs. AFC (70), 1999

TOUCHDOWNS

Most Touchdowns, Game
1 AFC, 1973, 1990, 1993, 1997, 1999
NFC, 1984, 1986, 1990, 1996

PUNTING

Most Punts, Game
10 AFC, 1985
Fewest Punts, Game
0 NFC, 1989
Most Punts, Both Teams, Game
16 AFC (10) vs. NFC (6), 1985
Fewest Punts, Both Teams, Game
4 NFC (1) vs. AFC (3), 1992

PUNT RETURNS

Most Punt Returns, Game
7 NFC, 1985, 1987
AFC, 1995
Fewest Punt Returns, Game
0 AFC, 1984, 1989
Most Punt Returns, Both Teams, Game
11 NFC (7) vs. AFC (4), 1985
Fewest Punt Returns, Both Teams, Game
2 AFC (1) vs. NFC (1), 1996

YARDS GAINED

Most Yards Gained, Game
177 AFC, 1976
Fewest Yards Gained, Game
–1 NFC, 1991
Most Yards Gained, Both Teams, Game
263 AFC (177) vs. NFC (86), 1976
Fewest Yards Gained, Both Teams, Game
16 AFC (0) vs. NFC (16), 1984

TOUCHDOWNS

Most Touchdowns, Game
2 NFC, 1971

KICKOFF RETURNS

Most Kickoff Returns, Game
8 NFC, 1995
Fewest Kickoff Returns, Game
1 NFC, 1971, 1984, 1994
AFC, 1988, 1991
Most Kickoff Returns, Both Teams, Game
12 NFC (8) vs. AFC (4), 1995
Fewest Kickoff Returns, Both Teams, Game
5 NFC (2) vs. AFC (3), 1979
AFC (1) vs. NFC (4), 1988
NFC (2) vs. AFC (3), 1992
NFC (1) vs. AFC (4), 1994

YARDS GAINED

Most Yards Gained, Game
215 AFC, 1984
Fewest Yards Gained, Game
6 NFC, 1971
Most Yards Gained, Both Teams, Game
325 AFC (173) vs. NFC (152), 1997
Fewest Yards Gained, Both Teams, Game
99 NFC (48) vs. AFC (51), 1987

TOUCHDOWNS

Most Touchdowns, Game
None

FUMBLES

Most Fumbles, Game
10 NFC, 1974
Most Fumbles, Both Teams, Game
15 NFC (10) vs. AFC (5), 1974

RECOVERIES

Most Fumbles Recovered, Game
10 NFC, 1974 (6 own, 4 opp)
Most Fumbles Lost, Game
4 AFC, 1974, 1988
NFC, 1974

YARDS GAINED

Most Yards Gained, Game
87 AFC, 1985

TOUCHDOWNS

Most Touchdowns, Game
1 AFC, 1985
NFC, 1990

TURNOVERS

(Number of times losing the ball on interceptions and fumbles.)
Most Turnovers, Game
8 AFC, 1974
Fewest Turnovers, Game
0 AFC, 1991, 1997
NFC, 1991, 1995, 1996
Most Turnovers, Both Teams, Game
12 AFC (8) vs. NFC (4), 1974
Fewest Turnovers, Both Teams, Game
0 AFC vs. NFC, 1991

Rules

OFFICIALS

1999 NFL ROSTER OF OFFICIALS

Jerry Seeman, Senior Director of Officiating
Larry Upson, Supervisor of Officials
Al Hynes, Supervisor of Officials
Mike Pereira, Supervisor of Officials
Ron DeSouza, Supervisor of Officials

No.	Name	Position	College
81	Anderson, Dave	Line Judge	Salem College
66	Anderson, Walt	Line Judge	Sam Houston State
108	Arthur, Gary	Line Judge	Wright State
34	Austin, Gerald	Referee	Western Carolina
22	Baetz, Paul	Field Judge	Heidelberg
91	Baker, Ken	Side Judge	Eastern Illinois
48	Balliet, Brian	Umpire	Lehigh
26	Baltz, Mark	Head Linesman	Ohio University
55	Barnes, Tom	Line Judge	Minnesota
56	Baynes, Ron	Line Judge	Auburn
32	Bergman, Jeff	Line Judge	Robert Morris
7	Blum, Ron	Referee	Marin College
18	Boston, Byron	Line Judge	Austin
110	Botchan, Ron	Umpire	Occidental
31	Brown, Chad	Umpire	East Texas State
126	Carey, Don	Back Judge	U.C. Riverside
94	Carey, Mike	Referee	Santa Clara
39	Carlsen, Don	Side Judge	Cal State-Chico
63	Carollo, Bill	Referee	Wisconsin-Milwaukee
11	Carroll, Duke	Field Judge	Ithaca
41	Cheek, Boris	Field Judge	Morgan State
65	Coleman, Walt	Referee	Arkansas
99	Corrente, Tony	Referee	Cal State-Fullerton
71	Coukart, Ed	Umpire	Northwestern
75	Daopoulos, Jim	Umpire	Kentucky
70	Dawson, Scott	Umpire	Virginia Tech
53	Defelice, Garth	Umpire	San Diego State
113	Dorkowski, Don	Back Judge	Cal State-Los Angeles
6	Dornan, Kirk	Back Judge	Central Washington
74	Duke, James	Umpire	Howard
89	Dunn, Neely	Side Judge	South Carolina State
3	Edwards, Scott	Field Judge	Alabama
47	Fincken, Tom	Side Judge	Kansas State
111	Frantz, Earnie	Head Linesman	No College
50	Gereb, Neil	Umpire	California
72	Gierke, Terry	Head Linesman	Portland State
19	Green, Scott	Back Judge	Delaware
23	Grier, Johnny	Referee	University of D.C.
40	Hannah, Charles	Umpire	Middle Tennessee State
104	Hamer, Dale	Head Linesman	California, Pa.
105	Hantak, Dick	Referee	Southeast Missouri
125	Hayes, Laird	Side Judge	Princeton
54	Hayward, George	Head Linesman	Missouri Western
97	Hill, Tom	Side Judge	Carson-Newman
28	Hittner, Mark	Head Linesman	Pittsburg State
82	Horton, Albert	Back Judge	Oregon State
85	Hochuli, Ed	Referee	Texas-El Paso
37	Howey, Jim	Back Judge	Erskine College
114	Johnson, Tom	Head Linesman	Miami, Ohio
106	Jury, Al	Field Judge	San Bernardino Valley
86	Kukar, Bernie	Referee	St. John's
120	Lane, Gary	Side Judge	Missouri
17	Lawing, Bob	Back Judge	North Carolina State
127	Leavy, Bill	Back Judge	San Jose State
130	Lewis, Darryll	Line Judge	Dartmouth
76	Liebsack, Ron	Side Judge	Regis
49	Look, Dean	Side Judge	Michigan State
98	Lovett, Bill	Field Judge	Maryland
59	Luckett, Phil	Referee	Texas-El Paso
102	Mack, Keven	Field Judge	Fort Valley State
92	Madsen, Carl	Umpire	Washington
107	Marinucci, Ron	Line Judge	Rowan State
38	Maurer, Bruce	Line Judge	Ohio State
77	McAulay, Terry	Side Judge	Louisiana State
95	McElwee, Bob	Referee	Navy
35	McGrath, Bob	Field Judge	Western Kentucky
64	McPeters, Lloyd	Field Judge	Oklahoma State
80	Millis, Timmie	Field Judge	Millsaps
117	Montgomery, Ben	Line Judge	Morehouse
60	Moore, Tommy	Side Judge	Stephen F. Austin
135	Morelli, Pete	Field Judge	St. Mary's
20	Nemmers, Larry	Referee	Upper Iowa
124	Paganelli, Carl	Umpire	Michigan State
46	Paganelli, Perry	Back Judge	Hope College
15	Patterson, Rick	Side Judge	Wofford
10	Phares, Ron	Line Judge	Virginia Tech
79	Pointer, Aaron	Line Judge	Pacific Lutheran
5	Quirk, Jim	Umpire	Delaware
83	Reels, Richard	Back Judge	Chicago State
44	Rice, Jeff	Umpire	Northwestern
121	Rivers, Sanford	Line Judge	Youngstown State
128	Rose, Larry	Side Judge	Florida
58	Saracino, Jim	Field Judge	Northern Colorado
21	Schleyer, John	Head Linesman	Millersville
122	Schmitz, Bill	Back Judge	Colorado State
109	Semon, Sid	Head Linesman	Southern California
118	Sifferman, Tom	Field Judge	Seattle
73	Skelton, Bobby	Back Judge	Alabama
30	Slaughter, Gary	Head Linesman	East Texas State
2	Smith, Billy	Back Judge	East Carolina
90	Spanier, Michael	Line Judge	St. Cloud State
119	Spitler, Ron	Back Judge	Panhandle State
12	Spyksma, Bill	Side Judge	South Dakota
24	Stabile, Tom	Head Linesman	Slippery Rock
88	Steenson, Scott	Field Judge	North Texas
84	Steinkerchner, Mark	Line Judge	Akron
62	Stewart, Charles	Line Judge	Long Beach State
4	Toole, Doug	Side Judge	Utah State
42	Triplette, Jeff	Referee	Wake Forest
93	Vaughan, Jack	Back Judge	Mississippi State
36	Veteri, Tony	Head Linesman	Manhattan College
25	Waggoner, Bob	Back Judge	Juniata College
100	Wagner, Bob	Umpire	Penn State
27	Warden, David	Field Judge	Oklahoma State
87	Weidner, Paul	Head Linesman	Cincinnati
123	White, Tom	Referee	Temple
8	Williams, Dale	Head Linesman	Cal State-Northridge
43	Wilson, James	Head Linesman	Eastern Kentucky
29	Wilson, Steve	Umpire	Whitworth College
14	Winter, Ron	Referee	Michigan State
16	Wyant, David	Side Judge	Virginia
33	Zimmer, Steve	Field Judge	Hofstra

NUMERICAL ROSTER

No.	Name	Position
2	Billy Smith	BJ
3	Scott Edwards	FJ
4	Doug Toole	SJ
5	Jim Quirk	U
6	Kirk Dornan	BJ
7	Ron Blum	R
8	Dale Williams	HL
10	Ron Phares	LJ
11	Duke Carroll	FJ
12	Bill Spyksma	SJ
14	Ron Winter	R
15	Rick Patterson	SJ
16	David Wyant	SJ
17	Bob Lawing	BJ
18	Byron Boston	LJ
19	Scott Green	BJ
20	Larry Nemmers	R
21	John Schleyer	HL
22	Paul Baetz	FJ
23	Johnny Grier	R
24	Tom Stabile	HL
25	Bob Waggoner	BJ
26	Mark Baltz	HL
27	David Warden	FJ
28	Mark Hittner	HL
29	Steve Wilson	U
30	Gary Slaughter	HL
31	Chad Brown	U
32	Jeff Bergman	LJ
33	Steve Zimmer	FJ
34	Gerry Austin	R
35	Bob McGrath	FJ
36	Tony Veteri	HL
37	Jim Howey	BJ
38	Bruce Maurer	LJ
39	Don Carlsen	SJ
40	Charles Hannah	U
41	Boris Cheek	FJ
42	Jeff Triplette	R
43	James Wilson	HL
44	Jeff Rice	U
46	Perry Paganelli	BJ
47	Tom Fincken	SJ
48	Brian Balliet	U
49	Dean Look	SJ
50	Neil Gereb	U
53	Garth Defelice	U
54	George Hayward	HL
55	Tom Barnes	LJ
56	Ron Baynes	LJ
58	Jim Saracino	FJ
59	Phil Luckett	R
60	Tommy Moore	SJ
62	Charles Stewart	LJ
63	Bill Carollo	R
64	Lloyd McPeters	FJ
65	Walt Coleman	R
66	Walt Anderson	LJ
70	Scott Dawson	U
71	Ed Coukart	U
72	Terry Gierke	HL
73	Bobby Skelton	BJ
74	James Duke	U
75	Jim Daopoulos	U
76	Ron Liebsack	SJ
77	Terry McAulay	SJ
79	Aaron Pointer	LJ
80	Timmie Millis	FJ
81	Dave Anderson	LJ
82	Albert Horton	BJ
83	Richard Reels	BJ
84	Mark Steinkerchner	LJ
85	Ed Hochuli	R
86	Bernie Kukar	R
87	Paul Weidner	HL
88	Scott Steenson	FJ
89	Neely Dunn	SJ
90	Michael Spanier	LJ
91	Ken Baker	SJ
92	Carl Madsen	U
93	Jack Vaughan	BJ
94	Mike Carey	R
95	Bob McElwee	R
97	Tom Hill	SJ
98	Bill Lovett	FJ
99	Tony Corrente	R
100	Bob Wagner	U
102	Keven Mack	FJ
104	Dale Hamer	HL
105	Dick Hantak	R
106	Al Jury	FJ
107	Ron Marinucci	LJ
108	Gary Arthur	LJ
109	Sid Semon	HL
110	Ron Botchan	U
111	Earnie Frantz	HL
113	Don Dorkowski	BJ
114	Tom Johnson	HL
117	Ben Montgomery	LJ
118	Tom Sifferman	FJ
119	Ron Spitler	BJ
120	Gary Lane	SJ
121	Sanford Rivers	HL
122	Bill Schmitz	BJ
123	Tom White	R
124	Carl Paganelli	U
125	Laird Hayes	SJ
126	Don Carey	BJ
127	Bill Leavy	BJ
128	Larry Rose	SJ
130	Darryll Lewis	LJ
135	Pete Morelli	FJ

1999 OFFICIALS AT A GLANCE

REFEREES

Gerry Austin, No. **34,** Western Carolina, president, leadership development group, 18th year.
Ron Blum, No. **7,** Marin College, professional golfer, 15th year.
Mike Carey, No. **94,** Santa Clara, owner, skiing accessories, 10th year.
Bill Carollo, No. **63,** Wisconsin-Milwaukee, marketing executive, 11th year.
Walt Coleman, No. **65,** Arkansas, president, dairy processor, 11th year.
Tony Corrente, No. **99,** Cal State-Fullerton, educator, 5th year.
Johnny Grier, No. **23,** University of D.C., planning engineer, 19th year.
Dick Hantak, No. **105,** Southeast Missouri, educator, 22nd year.
Ed Hochuli, No. **85,** Texas-El Paso, attorney, 10th year.
Bernie Kukar, No. **86,** St. John's, sales representative, employees benefit plan, 16th year.
Phil Luckett, No. **59,** Texas-El Paso, computer program analyst, federal civil services, 9th year.
Bob McElwee, No. **95,** Navy, owner, heavy construction firm, 24th year.
Larry Nemmers, No. **20,** Upper Iowa, motivational speaker, 15th year.
Jeff Triplette, No. **42,** Wake Forest, assistant treasurer, world-wide energy company, 4th year.
Tom White, No. **123,** Temple, president, athletic sportswear, 11th year.
Ron Winter, No. **14,** Michigan State, university professor, 5th year.

UMPIRES

Brian Balliet, No. **48,** Lehigh, sales engineer, 3rd year.
Ron Botchan, No. **110,** Occidental, college professor, former AFL player, 20th year.
Chad Brown, No. **31,** East Texas State, director, intramural/sports clubs, 8th year.
Ed Coukart, No. **71,** Northwestern, vice-president, commercial bank, 11th year.
Jim Daopoulos, No. **75,** Kentucky, mortgage broker, 11th year.
Scott Dawson, No. **70,** Virginia Tech, president/owner, commercial construction company, 5th year.
Garth Defelice, No. **53,** San Diego State, director of distributing, beverage company, 1st year.
James Duke, No. **74,** Howard, director of volunteer resources boys and girls clubs, 7th year.
Neil Gereb, No. **50,** California, project manager, aircraft company, 19th year.
Charles Hannah, No. **40,** Middle Tennessee State, federal probation officer, 1st year.
Carl Madsen, No. **92,** Washington, vice president of operations, 3rd year.
Carl Paganelli, No. **124,** Michigan State, federal probation officer, 1st year.
Jim Quirk, No. **5,** Delaware, senior vice-president, securities, 12th year.
Jeff Rice, No. **44,** Northwestern, attorney, 5th year.
Bob Wagner, No. **100,** Penn State, executive director, cardiovascular institute, 15th year.
Steve Wilson, No. **29,** Whitworth College, church administrator, 1st year.

HEAD LINESMEN

Mark Baltz, No. **26,** Ohio University, sales consultant, 11th year.
Earnie Frantz, No. **111,** no college, vice-president and manager, insurance company, 19th year.
Terry Gierke, No. **72,** Portland State, real estate broker, 19th year.
Dale Hamer, No. **104,** California Univ., Pa., consultant, 21st year.
George Hayward, No. **54,** Missouri Western, vice-president and manager, warehouse company, 9th year.
Mark Hittner, No. **28,** Pittsburg State, insurance sales, 3rd year.
Tom Johnson, No. **114,** Miami, Ohio, retired educator, president/owner, security company, 18th year.
Sanford Rivers, No. **121,** Youngstown State, assistant vice-president, school administration, 11th year.
John Schleyer, No. **21,** Millersville, medical sales, 10th year.
Sid Semon, No. **109,** Southern California, physical educational consultant, 22nd year.
Gary Slaughter, No. **30,** East Texas State, general manager, 4th year.
Tom Stabile, No. **24,** Slippery Rock, secondary educational administrator, 5th year.
Tony Veteri, No. **36,** Manhattan, director of athletics, 8th year.
Paul Weidner, No. **87,** Cincinnati, marketing manager, 14th year.
Dale Williams, No. **8,** Cal State-Northridge, sports official, 20th year.
James Wilson, No. **43,** Eastern Kentucky, area manager, 2nd year.

LINE JUDGES

Dave Anderson, No. **81,** Salem, insurance executive, 16th year.
Walt Anderson, No. **66,** Sam Houston, dentist, orthodontics, 4th year.
Gary Arthur, No. **108,** Wright State, commercial printing sales, 3rd year.
Tom Barnes, No. **55,** Minnesota, manufacturing representative, 14th year.
Ron Baynes, No. **56,** Auburn, school administrator, coach, 13th year.
Jeff Bergman, No. **32,** Robert Morris, president and chief executive officer, medical services, 8th year.
Byron Boston, No. **18,** Austin, tax consultant, 5th year.
Darryll Lewis, No. **130,** Dartmouth, associate professor, 3rd year.
Ron Marinucci, No. **107,** Glassboro State, vice president, novelty cone company, 3rd year.
Bruce Maurer, No. **38,** Ohio State, administrator/associate director, recreational sports, 13th year.
Ben Montgomery, No. **117,** Morehouse, school administrator, 18th year.
Ron Phares, No. **10,** Virginia Tech, president, construction company, 15th year.
Aaron Pointer, No. **79,** Pacific Lutheran, park department administrator, LOA, 12th year.
Michael Spanier, No. **90,** St. Cloud State, middle-school principal, 1st year.
Mark Steinkerchner, No. **84,** Akron, vice-president, 6th year.
Charles Stewart, No. **62,** Long Beach State, human services administrator, 8th year.

FIELD JUDGES

Paul Baetz, No. **22,** Heidelberg, financial consultant, 22nd year.
Duke Carroll, No. **11,** Ithaca, president, insurance agency, 5th year.
Boris Cheek, No. **41,** Morgan State, director of operations and management, 4th year.
Scott Edwards, No. **3,** Alabama, federal government program analyst, 1st year.
Al Jury, No. **106,** San Bernardino Valley, state traffic officer, 22nd year.
Bill Lovett, No. **98,** Maryland, managing partner, financial sales, 10th year.
Keven Mack, No. **102,** Ft. Valley State, economic development administrator, 3rd year.
Bob McGrath, No. **35,** Western Kentucky, sales representative, fund raiser, 7th year.
Lloyd McPeters, No. **64,** Oklahoma State, business insurance sales, 7th year.
Timmie Millis, No. **80,** Millsaps, financial investigative consultant, 11th year.
Pete Morelli, No. **135,** St. Mary's, high school principal, 3rd year.
Jim Saracino, No. **58,** Northern Colorado, secondary educator, 5th year.
Tom Sifferman, No. **118,** Seattle, manufacturer's representative, 14th year.
Scott Steenson, No. **88,** North Texas, commercial real estate broker, 9th year.
David Warden, No. **27,** Oklahoma State, dentist, 2nd year.
Steven Zimmer, No. **33,** Hofstra, attorney, 3rd year.

SIDE JUDGES

Ken Baker, No. **91,** Eastern Illinois, college educator, 9th year.
Don Carlsen, No. **39,** Cal State-Chico, assistant superintendent, county school, 11th year.
Neely Dunn, No. **89,** South Carolina State, principal, 5th year.
Tom Fincken, No. **47,** Emporia State, retired educational administrator, 16th year.
Laird Hayes, No. **125,** Princeton, professor, physical education & athletics, 5th year.
Tom Hill, No. **97,** Erskine College, teacher, 1st year.
Gary Lane, No. **120,** Missouri, owner hunting resort, former NFL player, 18th year.
Ron Liebsack, No. **76,** Regis, manager, telecommunications, 5th year.
Dean Look, No. **49,** Michigan State, consultant, medical manufacturing, former AFL player, 27th year.
Terry McAulay, No. **77,** Louisiana State, senior computer scientist, 2nd year.
Tommy Moore, No. **60,** Stephen F. Austin, marketing, manufacturing representative, 8th year.
Rick Patterson, No. **15,** Wofford, banker, 4th year.
Larry Rose, No. **128,** Florida, financial planner, 3rd year.
Bill Spyksma, No. **12,** South Dakota, commercial real estate, construction sales, 5th year.
Doug Toole, No. **4,** Utah State, physical therapist, 12th year.
David Wyant, No. **16,** Virginia, systems integration director, 9th year.

BACK JUDGES

Don Carey, No. **126,** California-Riverside, contract manager, 5th year.
Don Dorkowski, No. **113,** Cal State-Los Angeles, work experience coordinator, 14th year.
Kirk Dornan, No. **6,** Central Washington, industrial sales, 6th year.
Scott Green, No. **19,** Delaware, vice-president, government relations, 9th year.
Albert Horton, No. **82,** Oregon State, water service worker, 1st year.
Jim Howey, No. **37,** Erskine College, elemenatry school principal, 1st year.
Bob Lawing, No. **17,** North Carolina State, real estate management, 3rd year.
Bill Leavy, No. **127,** San Jose State, supervisor of officials, retired firefighter, 5th year.
Perry Paganelli, No. **46,** Hope College, high school administrator, 2nd year.
Richard Reels, No. **83,** Chicago State, director of security, court services, 7th year.
Bill Schmitz, No. **122,** Colorado State, general sales manager, 11th year.
Bobby Skelton, No. **73,** Alabama, industrial representative, 15th year.
Billy Smith, No. **2,** East Carolina, federal government, 6th year.
Ron Spitler, No. **119,** Panhandle State, owner, service center, 18th year.
Jack Vaughan, No. **93,** Mississippi State, marketing consultant, 23rd year.
Bob Waggoner, No. **25,** Juniata College, probation officer, 3rd year.

OFFICIAL SIGNALS

1

TOUCHDOWN, FIELD GOAL, or SUCCESSFUL TRY
Both arms extended above head.

2

SAFETY
Palms together above head.

3

FIRST DOWN
Arm pointed toward defensive team's goal.

4

CROWD NOISE, DEAD BALL, or NEUTRAL ZONE ESTABLISHED
One arm above head with an open hand.
With fist closed: **Fourth Down.**

5

BALL ILLEGALLY TOUCHED, KICKED, or BATTED
Fingertips tap both shoulders.

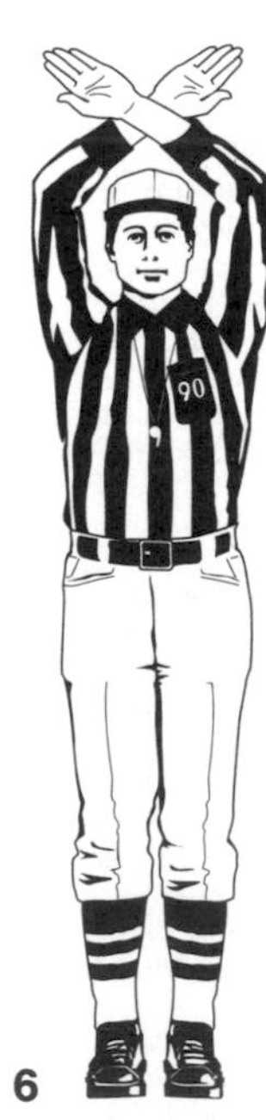

6

TIME OUT
Hands crisscrossed above head.

Same signal followed by placing one hand on top of cap: **Referee's Time Out.**

Same signal followed by arm swung at side: **Touchback.**

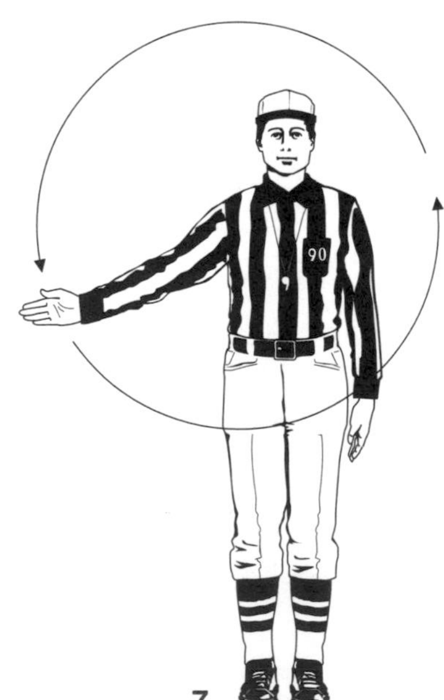

7

NO TIME OUT or TIME IN WITH WHISTLE
Full arm circled to simulate moving clock.

8

DELAY OF GAME or EXCESS TIME OUT
Folded arms.

9

FALSE START, ILLEGAL FORMATION, or KICKOFF or SAFETY KICK OUT OF BOUNDS or KICKING TEAM PLAYER VOLUNTARILY OUT OF BOUNDS DURING A PUNT
Forearms rotated over and over in front of body.

10

PERSONAL FOUL
One wrist striking the other above head.

Same signal followed by swinging leg: **Roughing the Kicker.**

Same signal followed by raised arm swinging forward: **Roughing the Passer.**

Same signal followed by grasping face mask: **Major Face Mask.**

11

HOLDING
Grasping one wrist, the fist clenched, in front of chest.

12

ILLEGAL USE OF HANDS, ARMS, or BODY
Grasping one wrist, the hand open and facing forward, in front of chest.

13

PENALTY REFUSED, INCOMPLETE PASS, PLAY OVER, or MISSED FIELD GOAL or EXTRA POINT
Hands shifted in horizontal plane.

14

PASS JUGGLED INBOUNDS AND CAUGHT OUT OF BOUNDS
Hands up and down in front of chest (following incomplete pass signal).

15

ILLEGAL FORWARD PASS
One hand waved behind back followed by loss of down signal (23), when appropriate.

16

INTENTIONAL GROUNDING OF PASS
Parallel arms waved in a diagonal plane across body. Followed by loss of down signal (23).

OFFICIAL SIGNALS

17

INTERFERENCE WITH FORWARD PASS or FAIR CATCH
Hands open and extended forward from shoulders with hands vertical.

18

INVALID FAIR-CATCH SIGNAL
One hand waved above head.

19

INELIGIBLE RECEIVER or INELIGIBLE MEMBER OF KICKING TEAM DOWNFIELD
Right hand touching top of cap.

20

ILLEGAL CONTACT
One open hand extended forward.

21

OFFSIDE, ENCROACHMENT, or NEUTRAL ZONE INFRACTION
Hands on hips.

22

ILLEGAL MOTION AT SNAP
Horizontal arc with one hand.

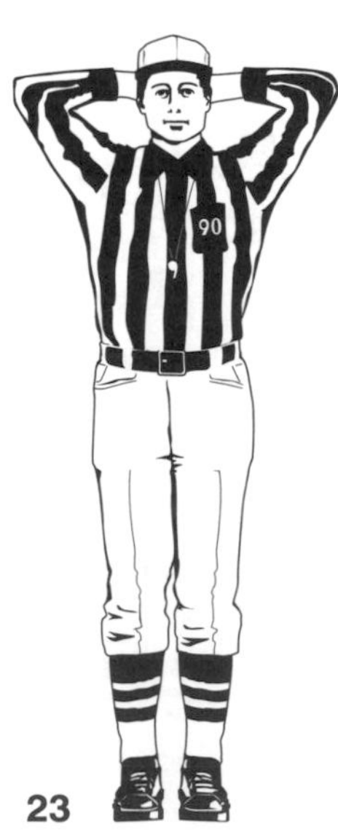

23

LOSS OF DOWN
Both hands held behind head.

24

INTERLOCKING INTERFERENCE, PUSHING, or HELPING RUNNER
Pushing movement of hands to front with arms downward.

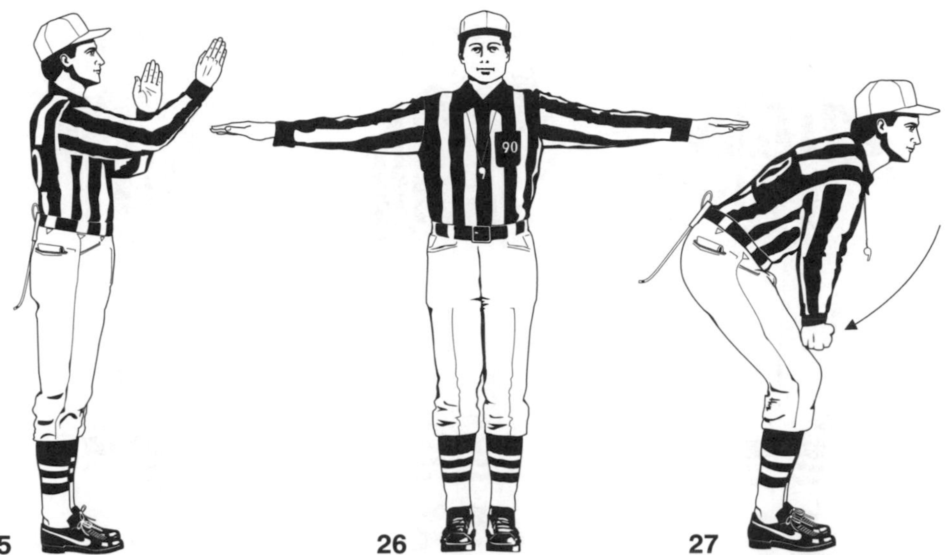

25

TOUCHING A FORWARD PASS or SCRIMMAGE KICK
Diagonal motion of one hand across another.

26

UNSPORTSMANLIKE CONDUCT
Arms outstretched, palms down.

27

ILLEGAL CUT
Hand striking front of thigh.
ILLEGAL BLOCK BELOW THE WAIST
One hand striking front of thigh preceded by personal-foul signal (10).
CHOP BLOCK
Both hands striking side of thighs preceded by personal-foul signal (10).
CLIPPING
One hand striking back of calf preceded by personal foul signal (10).

28

ILLEGAL CRACKBACK
Strike of an open right hand against the right mid-thigh preceded by personal foul signal (10).

29

PLAYER DISQUALIFIED
Ejection signal.

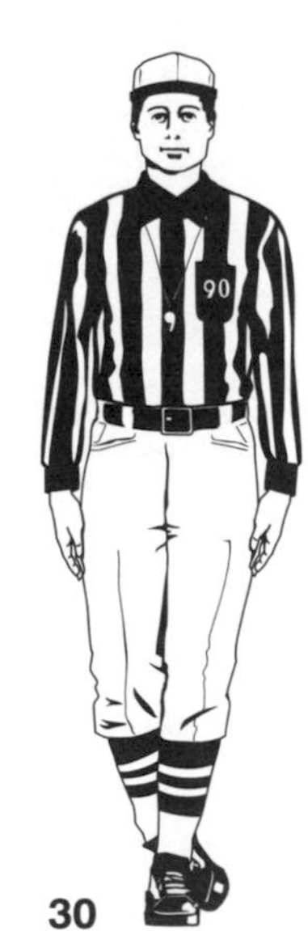

30

TRIPPING
Repeated action of right foot in back of left heel.

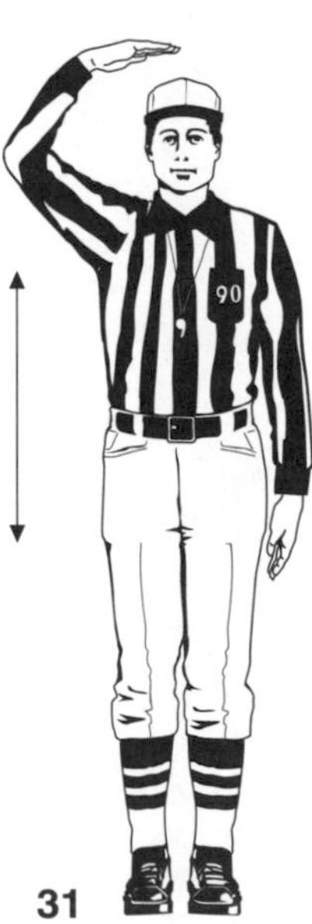

31

UNCATCHABLE FORWARD PASS
Palm of right hand held parallel to ground above head and moved back and forth.

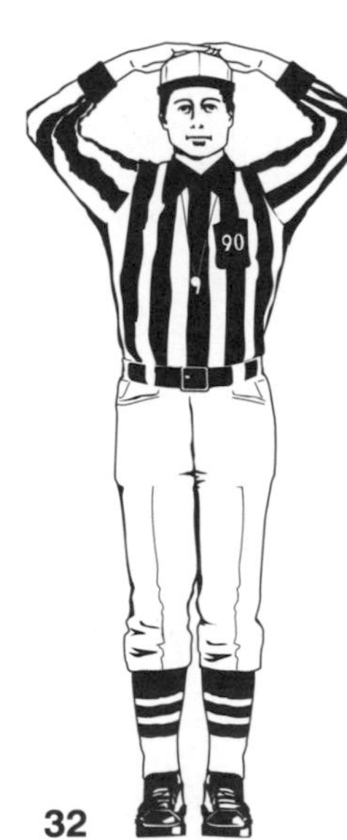

32

TWELVE MEN IN OFFENSIVE HUDDLE or TOO MANY MEN ON THE FIELD
Both hands on top of head.

OFFICIAL SIGNALS

33

FACE MASK
Grasping face mask with one hand.

34

ILLEGAL SHIFT
Horizontal arcs with two hands.

35

RESET PLAY CLOCK– 25 SECONDS
Pump one arm vertically.

36

RESET PLAY CLOCK– 40 SECONDS
Pump two arms vertically.

NFL DIGEST OF RULES

This Digest of Rules of the National Football League has been prepared to aid players, fans, and members of the press, radio, and television media in their understanding of the game.

It is not meant to be a substitute for the official rule book. In any case of conflict between these explanations and the official rules, the rules always have precedence.

In order to make it easier to coordinate the information in this digest, the topics discussed generally follow the order of the rule book.

OFFICIALS' JURISDICTIONS, POSITIONS, AND DUTIES

Referee—General oversight and control of game. Gives signals for all fouls and is final authority for rule interpretations. Takes a position in backfield 10 to 12 yards behind line of scrimmage, favors right side (if quarterback is right-handed passer). Determines legality of snap, observes deep back(s) for legal motion. On running play, observes quarterback during and after handoff, remains with him until action has cleared away, then proceeds downfield, checking on runner and contact behind him. When runner is downed, Referee determines forward progress from wing official and, if necessary, adjusts final position of ball.

On pass plays, drops back as quarterback begins to fade back, picks up legality of blocks by near linemen. Changes to complete concentration on quarterback as defenders approach. Primarily responsible to rule on possible roughing action on passer and if ball becomes loose, rules whether ball is free on a fumble or dead on an incomplete pass.

During kicking situations, Referee has primary responsibility to rule on kicker's actions and whether or not any subsequent contact by a defender is legal. The Referee will announce on the microphone when each period is ended.

Umpire—Primary responsibility to rule on players' equipment, as well as their conduct and actions on scrimmage line. Lines up approximately four to five yards downfield, varying position from in front of weakside tackle to strongside guard. Looks for possible false start by offensive linemen. Observes legality of contact by both offensive linemen while blocking and by defensive players while they attempt to ward off blockers. Is prepared to call rule infractions if they occur on offense or defense. Moves forward to line of scrimmage when pass play develops in order to insure that interior linemen do not move illegally downfield. If offensive linemen indicate screen pass is to be attempted, Umpire shifts his attention toward screen side, picks up potential receiver in order to insure that he will legally be permitted to run his pattern and continues to rule on action of blockers. Umpire is to assist in ruling on incomplete or trapped passes when ball is thrown overhead or short. On punt plays, Umpire positions himself opposite Referee in offensive backfield—5 yards from kicker and parallel.

Head Linesman—Primarily responsible for ruling on offside, encroachment, and actions pertaining to scrimmage line prior to or at snap. Keys on closest setback on his side of the field. On pass plays, Linesman is responsible to clear his receiver approximately seven yards downfield as he moves to a point five yards beyond the line. Linesman's secondary responsibility is to rule on any illegal action taken by defenders on any delay receiver moving downfield. Has full responsibility for ruling on sideline plays on his side, e.g., pass receiver or runner in or out of bounds. Together with Referee, Linesman is responsible for keeping track of number of downs and is in charge of mechanics of his chain crew in connection with its duties.

Linesman must be prepared to assist in determining forward progress by a runner on play directed toward middle or into his side zone. He, in turn, is to signal Referee or Umpire what forward point ball has reached. Linesman is also responsible to rule on legality of action involving any receiver who approaches his side zone. He is to call pass interference when the infraction occurs and is to rule on legality of blockers and defenders on plays involving ball carriers, whether it is entirely a running play, a combination pass and run, or a play involving a kick.

Line Judge—Straddles line of scrimmage on side of field opposite Linesman. Keeps time of game as a backup for clock operator. Along with Linesman is responsible for offside, encroachment, and actions pertaining to scrimmage line prior to or at snap. Line Judge keys on closest setback on his side of field. Line Judge is to observe his receiver until he moves at least seven yards downfield. He then moves toward backfield side, being especially alert to rule on any back in motion and on flight of ball when pass is made (he must rule whether forward or backward). Line Judge has primary responsibility to rule whether or not passer is behind or beyond line of scrimmage when pass is made. He also assists in observing actions by blockers and defenders who are on his side of field. After pass is thrown, Line Judge directs attention toward activities that occur in back of Umpire. During punting situations, Line Judge remains at line of scrimmage to be sure that only the end men move downfield until kick has been made. He also rules whether or not the kick crossed line and then observes action by members of the kicking team who are moving downfield to cover the kick. The Line Judge will advise the Referee when time has expired at the end of each period.

Field Judge—Operates on same side of field as Line Judge, 20 yards deep. Keys on wide receiver on his side. Concentrates on path of end or back, observing legality of his potential block(s) or of actions taken against him. Is prepared to rule from <u>deep</u> position on holding or illegal use of hands by end or back or on defensive infractions committed by player guarding him. Has primary responsibility to make decisions involving sideline on his side of field, e.g., pass receiver or runner in or out of bounds.

Field Judge makes decisions involving catching, recovery, or illegal touching of a loose ball beyond line of scrimmage; rules on plays involving pass receiver, including legality of catch or pass interference; assists in covering actions of runner, including blocks by teammates and that of defenders; calls clipping on punt returns; and, together with Back Judge, rules whether or not field goal attempts are successful.

Side Judge—Operates on same side of field as Linesman, 20 yards deep. Keys on wide receiver on his side. Concentrates on path of end or back, observing legality of his potential block(s) or of actions taken against him. Is prepared to rule from <u>deep</u> position on holding or illegal use of hands by end or back or on defensive infractions committed by player guarding him. Has primary responsibility to make decisions involving sideline on his side of field, e.g., pass receiver or runner in or out of bounds.

Side Judge makes decisions involving catching, recovery, or illegal touching of a loose ball beyond line of scrimmage; rules on plays involving pass receiver, including legality of catch or pass interference; assists in covering actions of runner, including blocks by teammates and that of defenders; and calls clipping on punt returns. On field goals and point after touchdown attempts, he becomes a double umpire.

Back Judge—Takes a position 25 yards downfield. In general, favors the tight end's side of field. Keys on tight end, concentrates on his path and observes legality of tight end's potential block(s) or of actions taken against him. Is prepared to rule from <u>deep</u> position on holding or illegal use of hands by end or back or on defensive infractions committed by player guarding him.

Back Judge times interval between plays on 40/25-second clock plus intermission between two periods of each half; makes decisions involving catching, recovery, or illegal touching of a loose ball beyond line of scrimmage; is responsible to rule on plays involving end line; calls pass interference, fair catch infractions, and clipping on kick returns; and, together with Field Judge, rules whether or not field goals and conversions are successful.

DEFINITIONS

1. **Chucking:** Warding off an opponent who is in front of a defender by contacting him with a quick extension of arm or arms, followed by the return of arm(s) to a flexed position, thereby breaking the original contact.
2. **Clipping:** Throwing the body across the back of an opponent's leg or hitting him from the back below the waist while moving up from behind unless the opponent is a runner or the action is in close line play.
3. **Close Line Play:** The area between the positions normally occupied by the offensive tackles, extending three yards on each side of the line of scrimmage. It is legal to clip above the knee.
4. **Crackback:** Eligible receivers who take or move to a position more than two yards outside the tackle may not block an opponent below the waist if they then move back inside to block.
5. **Dead Ball:** Ball not in play.
6. **Double Foul:** A foul by each team during the same down.
7. **Down:** The period of action that starts when the ball is put in play and ends when it is dead.
8. **Encroachment:** When a player enters the neutral zone and makes <u>contact</u> with an opponent before the ball is snapped.
9. **Fair Catch:** An unhindered catch of a kick by a member of the receiving team who must raise one arm a full length above his head while the kick is in flight.
10. **Foul:** Any violation of a playing rule.
11. **Free Kick:** A kickoff or safety kick. It may be a placekick, dropkick, or punt, except a punt may <u>not</u> be used on a kickoff following a touchdown, successful field goal, or to begin each half or overtime period. A tee cannot be used on a fair-catch or safety kick.
12. **Fumble:** The loss of possession of the ball.
13. **Game Clock:** Scoreboard game clock.
14. **Impetus:** The action of a player that gives momentum to the ball.
15. **Live Ball:** A ball legally free kicked or snapped. It continues in play until the down ends.
16. **Loose Ball:** A live ball not in possession of any player.
17. **Muff:** The touching of a loose ball by a player in an <u>unsuccessful</u> attempt to obtain possession.
18. **Neutral Zone:** The space the length of a ball between the two scrimmage lines. The offensive team and defensive team must remain behind their end of the ball.
    Exception: The offensive player who snaps the ball.
19. **Offside:** A player is offside when any part of his body is beyond his scrimmage or free kick line <u>when the ball is snapped.</u>
20. **Own Goal:** The goal a team is guarding.
21. **Play Clock:** 40/25 second clock.
22. **Pocket Area:** Applies from a point two yards outside of either offensive tackle and includes the tight end if he drops off the line of scrimmage to pass protect. Pocket extends longitudinally behind the line back to offensive team's own end line.
23. **Possession:** When a player controls the ball throughout the act of <u>clearly</u> touching both feet, or any other part of his body other than his hand(s), to the ground inbounds.
24. **Post-Possession Foul:** A foul by the receiving team that occurs after a ball is legally kicked from scrimmage prior to possession changing. The ball must cross the line of scrimmage and the receiving team must retain possession of the kicked ball.
25. **Punt:** A kick made when a player drops the ball and kicks it while it is in flight.

DIGEST OF RULES

26. **Safety:** The situation in which the ball is dead on or behind a team's own goal if the impetus comes from a player on that team. Two points are scored for the opposing team.
27. **Shift:** The movement of two or more offensive players at the same time before the snap.
28. **Striking:** The act of swinging, clubbing, or propelling the arm or forearm in contacting an opponent.
29. **Sudden Death:** The continuation of a tied game into sudden death overtime in which the team scoring first (by safety, field goal, or touchdown) wins.
30. **Touchback:** When a ball is dead on or behind a team's own goal line, provided the impetus came from an opponent and provided it is not a touchdown or a missed field goal.
31. **Touchdown:** When any part of the ball, legally in possession of a player inbounds, breaks the plane of the opponent's goal line, provided it is not a touchback.
32. **Unsportsmanlike Conduct:** Any act contrary to the generally understood principles of sportsmanship.

SUMMARY OF PENALTIES

Automatic First Down

1. Awarded to offensive team on all defensive fouls with these exceptions:
   (a) Offside.
   (b) Encroachment.
   (c) Delay of game.
   (d) Illegal substitution.
   (e) Excessive time out(s).
   (f) Incidental grasp of facemask.
   (g) Neutral zone infraction.
   (h) Running into the kicker.
   (i) More than 11 players on the field at the snap.

Five Yards

1. Defensive holding or illegal use of hands (automatic first down).
2. Delay of game on offense or defense.
3. Delay of kickoff.
4. Encroachment.
5. Excessive time out(s).
6. False start.
7. Illegal formation.
8. Illegal shift.
9. Illegal motion.
10. Illegal substitution.
11. First onside kickoff out of bounds between goal lines and not touched.
12. Invalid fair catch signal.
13. More than 11 players on the field at snap for either team.
14. Less than seven men on offensive line at snap.
15. Offside.
16. Failure to pause one second after shift or huddle.
17. Running into kicker.
18. More than one man in motion at snap.
19. Grasping facemask of the ball carrier or quarterback.
20. Player out of bounds at snap.
21. Ineligible member(s) of kicking team going beyond line of scrimmage before ball is kicked.
22. Illegal return.
23. Failure to report change of eligibility.
24. Neutral zone infraction.
25. Loss of team time out(s) or five-yard penalty on the defense for excessive crowd noise.
26. Ineligible player downfield during passing down.
27. Second forward pass behind the line.
28. Forward pass is first touched by eligible receiver who has gone out of bounds and returned.
29. Forward pass touches or is caught by an ineligible receiver on or behind line.
30. Forward pass thrown from behind line of scrimmage after ball once crossed the line.
31. Kicking team player voluntarily out of bounds during a punt.

10 Yards

1. Offensive pass interference.
2. Holding, illegal use of hands, arms, or body by offense.
3. Tripping by a member of either team.
4. Helping the runner.
5. Deliberately batting or punching a loose ball.
6. Deliberately kicking a loose ball.
7. Illegal block above the waist.

15 Yards

1. Chop block.
2. Clipping below the waist.
3. Fair catch interference.
4. Illegal crackback block by offense.
5. Piling on.
6. Roughing the kicker.
7. Roughing the passer.
8. Twisting, turning, or pulling an opponent by the facemask.
9. Unnecessary roughness.
10. Unsportsmanlike conduct.
11. Delay of game at start of either half.
12. Illegal low block.
13. A tackler using his helmet to butt, spear, or ram an opponent.
14. Any player who uses the top of his helmet unnecessarily.
15. A punter, placekicker, or holder who simulates being roughed by a defensive player.
16. A defender who takes a running start from beyond the line of scrimmage in an attempt to block a field goal or point after touchdown and lands on players at the line of scrimmage.

Five Yards and Loss of Down (Combination Penalty)

1. Forward pass thrown from beyond line of scrimmage.

10 Yards and Loss of Down (Combination Penalty)

1. Intentional grounding of forward pass (safety if passer is in own end zone). If foul occurs more than 10 yards behind line, play results in loss of down at spot of foul.

15 Yards and Loss of Coin Toss Option

1. Team's late arrival on the field prior to scheduled kickoff.
2. Captains not appearing for coin toss.

15 Yards (and disqualification if flagrant)

1. Striking opponent with fist.
2. Kicking or kneeing opponent.
3. Striking opponent on head or neck with forearm, elbow, or hands whether or not the initial contact is made below the neck area.
4. Roughing kicker.
5. Roughing passer.
6. Malicious unnecessary roughness.
7. Unsportsmanlike conduct.
8. Palpably unfair act. (Distance penalty determined by the Referee after consultation with other officials.)

15 Yards and Automatic Disqualification

1. Using a helmet (not worn) as a weapon.
2. Striking or purposely shoving a game official.

Suspension From Game For One Down

1. Illegal equipment. (Player may return after one down when legally equipped.)

Touchdown Awarded (Palpably Unfair Act)

1. When Referee determines a palpably unfair act deprived a team of a touchdown. (Example: Player comes off bench and tackles runner apparently en route to touchdown.)

FIELD

1. Sidelines and end lines are out of bounds. The goal line is actually in the end zone. A player with the ball in his possession scores when the ball is on, above, or over the goal line.
2. The field is rimmed by a white border, six feet wide, along the sidelines. All of this is out of bounds.
3. The hashmarks (inbound lines) are 70 feet, 9 inches from each sideline.
4. Goal posts must be single-standard type, offset from the end line and painted bright gold. The goal posts must be 18 feet, 6 inches wide and the top face of the crossbar must be 10 feet above the ground. Vertical posts extend at least 30 feet above the crossbar. A ribbon 4 inches by 42 inches long is to be attached to the top of each post. The actual goal is the plane extending indefinitely above the crossbar and between the outer edges of the posts.
5. The field is 360 feet long and 160 feet wide. The end zones are 30 feet deep. The line used in try-for-point plays is two yards out from the goal line.
6. Chain crew members and ball boys must be uniformly identifiable.
7. All clubs must use standardized sideline markers. Pylons must be used for goal line and end line markings.
8. End zone markings and club identification at 50 yard line must be approved by the Commissioner to avoid any confusion as to delineation of goal lines, sidelines, and end lines.

BALL

1. The home club shall have 24 balls available for testing with a pressure gauge by the referee two hours prior to the starting time of the game to meet with League requirements. Twelve (12) new footballs, sealed in a special box and shipped by the manufacturer, will be opened in the officials' locker room two hours prior to the starting time of the game. These balls are to be specially marked by the referee and used exclusively for the kicking game.

COIN TOSS

1. The toss of coin will take place within three minutes of kickoff in center of field. The toss will be called by the visiting captain before the coin is flipped. The winner may choose one of two privileges and the loser gets the other:
   (a) Receive or kick
   (b) Goal his team will defend
2. Immediately prior to the start of the second half, the captains of both teams must inform the officials of their respective choices. The loser of the original coin toss gets first choice.

TIMING

1. The stadium game clock is official. In case it stops or is operating incorrectly, the Line Judge takes over the official timing on the field.
2. Each period is 15 minutes. The intermission between the periods is two minutes. Halftime is 12 minutes, unless otherwise specified.

3. On charged team time outs, the Field Judge starts watch and blows whistle after 1 minute 50 seconds, unless television does not utilize the time for commercial. In this case the length of the time out is reduced to 40 seconds.
4. The Referee will allow necessary time to attend to an injured player, or repair a legal player's equipment.
5. Each team is allowed three time outs each half.
6. Time between plays will be 40 seconds from the end of a given play until the snap of the ball for the next play, or a 25-second interval after certain administrative stoppages and game delays.
7. Clock will start running when ball is snapped following all changes of team possession.
8. With the exception of the last two minutes of the first half and the last five minutes of the second half, the game clock will be restarted following a kickoff return, a player going out of bounds on a play from scrimmage, or after declined penalties when appropriate on the referee's signal.
9. Consecutive team time outs can be taken by opposing teams but the length of the second time out will be reduced to 40 seconds.
10. When, in the judgment of the Referee, the level of crowd noise prevents the offense from hearing its signals, he can institute a series of procedures which can result in a loss of team time outs or a five-yard penalty against the defensive team.

SUDDEN DEATH

1. The sudden death system of determining the winner shall prevail when score is tied at the end of the regulation playing time of all NFL games. The team scoring first during overtime play shall be the winner and the game automatically ends upon any score (by safety, field goal, or touchdown) or when a score is awarded by Referee for a palpably unfair act.
2. At the end of regulation time the Referee will immediately toss coin at center of field in accordance with rules pertaining to the usual pregame toss. The captain of the visiting team will call the toss prior to the coin being flipped.
3. Following a three-minute intermission after the end of the regulation game, play will be continued in 15-minute periods or until there is a score. There is a two-minute intermission between subsequent periods. The teams change goals at the start of each period. Each team has three time outs per half and all general timing provisions apply as during a regular game. Disqualified players are not allowed to return.
   Exception: In preseason and regular season games there shall be a maximum of 15 minutes of sudden death with two time outs instead of three. General provisions that apply for the fourth quarter will prevail. Try not attempted if touchdown scored.

TIMING IN FINAL TWO MINUTES OF EACH HALF

1. On kickoff, clock does not start until the ball has been legally touched by player of either team in the field of play. (In all other cases, clock starts with kickoff.)
2. A team cannot buy an excess time out for a penalty. However, a fourth time out is allowed without penalty for an injured player, who must be removed immediately. A fifth time out or more is allowed for an injury and a five-yard penalty is assessed if the clock was running. Additionally, if the clock was running and the score is tied or the team in possession is losing, the ball cannot be put in play for at least 10 seconds on the fourth or more time out. The half or game can end while those 10 seconds are run off on the clock.
3. If the defensive team is behind in the score and commits a foul when it has no time outs left in the final 30 seconds of either half, the offensive team can decline the penalty for the foul and have the time on the clock expire.
4. Fouls that occur in the last five minutes of the fourth quarter as well as the last two minutes of the first half will result in the clock starting on the snap.

TRY

1. After a touchdown, the scoring team is allowed a try during one scrimmage down. The ball may be spotted anywhere between the inbounds lines, two or more yards from the goal line. The successful conversion counts one point by kick; two points for a successful conversion by touchdown; or one point for a safety.
2. The defensive team never can score on a try. As soon as defense gets possession or the kick is blocked or a touchdown is not scored, the try is over.
3. Any distance penalty for fouls committed by the defense that prevent the try from being attempted can be enforced on the succeeding try or succeeding kickoff. Any foul committed on a successful try will result in a distance penalty being assessed on the ensuing kickoff.
4. Only the fumbling player can recover and advance a fumble during a try.

PLAYERS-SUBSTITUTIONS

1. Each team is permitted 11 men on the field at the snap.
2. Unlimited substitution is permitted. However, players may enter the field only when the ball is dead. Players who have been substituted for are not permitted to linger on the field. Such lingering will be interpreted as unsportsmanlike conduct.
3. Players leaving the game must be out of bounds on their own side, clearing the field between the end lines, before a snap or free kick. If player crosses end line leaving field, it is delay of game (five-yard penalty).
4. Offensive substitutes who remain in the game must move onto the field as far as the inside of the field numerals before moving to a wide position.
5. With the exception of the last two minutes of either half, the offensive team, while in the process of substitution or simulated substitution, is prohibited from rushing quickly to the line and snapping the ball with the obvious attempt to cause a defensive foul; i.e., too many men on the field.

KICKOFF

1. The kickoff shall be from the kicking team's 30-yard line at the start of each half and after a field goal and try. A kickoff is one type of free kick.
2. A one-inch tee may be used (no tee permitted for field goal or try attempt) on a kickoff. The ball is put in play by a placekick.
3. A kickoff may not score a field goal.
4. A kickoff is illegal unless it travels 10 yards OR is touched by the receiving team. Once the ball is touched by the receiving team or has gone 10 yards, it is a free ball. Receivers may recover and advance. Kicking team may recover but NOT advance UNLESS receiver had possession and lost the ball.
5. When a kickoff goes out of bounds between the goal lines without being touched by the receiving team, the ball belongs to the receivers 30 yards from the spot of the kick or at the out-of-bounds spot unless the ball went out-of-bounds the first time an onside kick was attempted. In this case, the kicking team is penalized five yards and the ball must be kicked again.
6. When a kickoff goes out of bounds between the goal lines and is touched last by receiving team, it is receiver's ball at out-of-bounds spot.
7. If the kicking team either illegally kicks off out of bounds or is guilty of a short free kick on two or more consecutive onside kicks, receivers may take possession of the ball at the dead ball spot, out-of-bounds spot, or spot of illegal touch.

SAFETY

1. In addition to a kickoff, the other free kick is a kick after a safety (safety kick). A punt may be used (a punt may not be used on a kickoff).
2. On a safety kick, the team scored upon puts ball in play by a punt, dropkick, or placekick without tee. No score can be made on a free kick following a safety, even if a series of penalties places team in position. (A field goal can be scored only on a play from scrimmage or a free kick after a fair catch.)

FAIR CATCH KICK

1. After a fair catch, the receiving team has the option to put the ball in play by a snap or a fair catch kick (field goal attempt), with fair catch kick lines established ten yards apart. All general rules apply as for a field goal attempt from scrimmage. The clock starts when the ball is kicked. (No tee permitted.)

FIELD GOAL

1. All field goals attempted (kicker) and missed from beyond the 20-yard line will result in the defensive team taking possession of the ball at the spot of the kick. On any field goal attempted and missed where the spot of the kick is on or inside the 20-yard line, ball will revert to defensive team at the 20-yard line.

SAFETY

1. The important factor in a safety is impetus. Two points are scored for the opposing team when the ball is dead on or behind a team's own goal line if the impetus came from a player on that team.

Examples of Safety:

(a) Blocked punt goes out of kicking team's end zone. Impetus was provided by punting team. The block only changes direction of ball, not impetus.
(b) Ball carrier retreats from field of play into his own end zone and is downed. Ball carrier provides impetus.
(c) Offensive team commits a foul and spot of enforcement is behind its own goal line.
(d) Player on receiving team muffs punt and, trying to get ball, forces or illegally kicks (creating new impetus) it into end zone where it goes out of the end zone or is recovered by a member of the receiving team in the end zone.

Examples of Non-Safety:

(a) Player intercepts a pass with both feet inbounds in the field of play and his momentum carries him into his own end zone. Ball is put in play at spot of interception.
(b) Player intercepts a pass in his own end zone and is downed in the end zone, even after recovering in the end zone. Impetus came from passing team, not from defense. (Touchback)
(c) Player passes from behind his own goal line. Opponent bats down ball in end zone. (Incomplete pass)

MEASURING

1. The forward point of the ball is used when measuring.

POSITION OF PLAYERS AT SNAP

1. Offensive team must have at least seven players on line.
2. Offensive players, not on line, must be at least one yard back at snap. **(Exception:** player who takes snap.)
3. No interior lineman may move abruptly after taking or simulating a three-point stance.

4. No player of either team may enter neutral zone before snap.
5. No player of offensive team may charge or move abruptly, after assuming set position, in such manner as to lead defense to believe snap has started. No player of the defensive team within one yard of the line of scrimmage may make an abrupt movement in an attempt to cause the offense to false start.
6. If a player changes his eligibility, the Referee must alert the defensive captain after player has reported to him.
7. All players of offensive team must be stationary at snap, except one back who may be in motion parallel to scrimmage line or backward (not forward).
8. After a shift or huddle all players on offensive team must come to an absolute stop for at least one second with no movement of hands, feet, head, or swaying of body.
9. Quarterbacks can be called for a false start penalty (five yards) if their actions are judged to be an obvious attempt to draw an opponent offside.
10. Offensive linemen are permitted to interlock legs.

USE OF HANDS, ARMS, AND BODY

1. No player on offense may assist a runner except by blocking for him. There shall be no interlocking interference.
2. A runner may ward off opponents with his hands and arms but no other player on offense may use hands or arms to obstruct an opponent by grasping with hands, pushing, or encircling any part of his body during a block. Hands (open or closed) can be thrust forward to initially contact an opponent on or outside the opponent's frame, but the blocker immediately must work to bring his hands on or inside the frame.
   Note: Pass blocking: Hand(s) thrust forward that slip outside the body of the defender will be legal if blocker immediately worked to bring them back inside. Hand(s) or arm(s) that encircle a defender—i.e., hook an opponent—are to be considered illegal and officials are to call a foul for holding.
   Blocker cannot use his hands or arms to push from behind, hang onto, or encircle an opponent in a manner that restricts his movement as the play develops.
3. Hands cannot be thrust forward above the frame to contact an opponent on the neck, face or head.
   Note: The frame is defined as the part of the opponent's body below the neck that is presented to the blocker.
4. A defensive player may not tackle or hold an opponent other than a runner. Otherwise, he may use his hands, arms, or body only:
   (a) To defend or protect himself against an obstructing opponent.
   Exception: An eligible receiver is considered to be an obstructing opponent ONLY to a point five yards beyond the line of scrimmage unless the player who receives the snap clearly demonstrates no further intention to pass the ball. Within this five-yard zone, a defensive player may check an eligible player in front of him. A defensive player is allowed to maintain continuous and unbroken contact within the five-yard zone until a point when the receiver is even with the defender. The defensive player cannot use his hands or arms to push from behind, hang onto, or encircle an eligible receiver in a manner that restricts movement as the play develops. Beyond this five-yard limitation, a defender may use his hands or arms ONLY to defend or protect himself against impending contact caused by a receiver. In such reaction, the defender may not contact a receiver who attempts to take a path to evade him.
   (b) To push or pull opponent out of the way on line of scrimmage.
   (c) In actual attempt to get at or tackle runner.
   (d) To push or pull opponent out of the way in a legal attempt to recover a loose ball.
   (e) During a legal block on an opponent who is not an eligible pass receiver.
   (f) When legally blocking an eligible pass receiver above the waist.
   Exception: Eligible receivers lined up within two yards of the tackle, whether on or immediately behind the line, may be blocked below the waist at or behind the line of scrimmage. NO eligible receiver may be blocked below the waist after he goes beyond the line. (Illegal cut)
   Note: Once the quarterback hands off or pitches the ball to a back, or if the quarterback leaves the pocket area, the restrictions (illegal chuck, illegal cut) on the defensive team relative to the offensive receivers will end, provided the ball is not in the air.
5. A defensive player may not contact an opponent above the shoulders with the palm of his hand except to ward him off on the line. This exception is permitted only if it is not a repeated act against the same opponent during any one contact. In all other cases the palms may be used on head, neck, or face only to ward off or push an opponent in legal attempt to get at the ball.
6. Any offensive player who pretends to possess the ball or to whom a teammate pretends to give the ball may be tackled provided he is crossing his scrimmage line between the ends of a normal tight offensive line.
7. An offensive player who lines up more than two yards outside his own tackle or a player who, at the snap, is in a backfield position and subsequently takes a position more than two yards outside a tackle may not clip an opponent anywhere nor may he contact an opponent below the waist if the blocker is moving toward the ball and if contact is made within an area five yards on either side of the line. (crackback)
8. A player of either team may block at any time provided it is not pass interference, fair catch interference, or unnecessary roughness.
9. A player may not bat or punch:
   (a) A loose ball (in field of play) toward his opponent's goal line or in any direction in either end zone.
   (b) A ball in player possession.
   Note: If there is any question as to whether a defender is stripping or batting a ball in player possession, the official(s) will rule the action as a legal act (stripping the ball).
   Exception: A forward or backward pass may be batted, tipped, or deflected in any direction at any time by either the offense or the defense.
   Note: A pass in flight that is controlled or caught may only be thrown backward, if it is thrown forward it is considered an illegal bat.
10. No player may deliberately kick any ball except as a punt, dropkick, or placekick.

FORWARD PASS

1. A forward pass may be touched or caught by any eligible receiver. All members of the defensive team are eligible. Eligible receivers on the offensive team are players on either end of line (other than center, guard, or tackle) or players at least one yard behind the line at the snap. A T-formation quarterback is not eligible to receive a forward pass during a play from scrimmage.
   Exception: T-formation quarterback becomes eligible if pass is previously touched by an eligible receiver.
2. An offensive team may make only one forward pass during each play from scrimmage (Loss of 5 yards).
3. The passer must be behind his line of scrimmage (Loss of down and five yards, enforced from the spot of pass).
4. Any eligible offensive player may catch a forward pass. If a pass is touched by one eligible offensive player and touched or caught by a second offensive player, pass completion is legal. Further, all offensive players become eligible once a pass is touched by an eligible receiver or any defensive player.
5. The rules concerning a forward pass and ineligible receivers:
   (a) If ball is touched accidentally by an ineligible receiver on or behind his line: loss of five yards.
   (b) If ineligible receiver is illegally downfield: loss of five yards.
   (c) If touched or caught (intentionally or accidentally) by ineligible receiver beyond the line: loss of 5 yards.
6. The player who first controls and continues to maintain control of a pass will be awarded the ball even though his opponent later establishes joint control of the ball.
7. Any forward pass becomes incomplete and ball is dead if:
   (a) Pass hits the ground or goes out of bounds.
   (b) Pass hits the goal post or the crossbar of either team.
   (c) Pass is caught by offensive player after touching ineligible receiver.
   (d) An illegal pass is caught by an offensive player.
8. A forward pass is complete when a receiver clearly possesses the pass and touches the ground with both feet inbounds while in possession of the ball. If a receiver would have landed inbounds with both feet but is carried or pushed out of bounds while maintaining possession of the ball, pass is complete at the out-of-bounds spot.
9. If an eligible receiver goes out of bounds accidentally or is legally forced out by a defender and returns to first touch and catch a pass, the play is regarded as an incomplete pass. Loss of 5 yards.
10. On a fourth down pass—when the offensive team is inside the opposition's 20-yard line—an incomplete pass results in a loss of down at the line of scrimmage.
11. If a personal foul is committed by the defense prior to the completion of a pass, the penalty is 15 yards from the spot where ball becomes dead.
12. If a personal foul is committed by the offense prior to the completion of a pass, the penalty is 15 yards from the previous line of scrimmage.

INTENTIONAL GROUNDING OF FORWARD PASS

1. Intentional grounding of a forward pass is a foul: loss of down and 10 yards from previous spot if passer is in the field of play or loss of down at the spot of the foul if it occurs more than 10 yards behind the line or safety if passer is in his own end zone when ball is released.
2. Intentional grounding will be called when a passer, facing an imminent loss of yardage due to pressure from the defense, throws a forward pass without a realistic chance of completion.
3. Intentional grounding will not be called when a passer, while out of the pocket and facing an imminent loss of yardage, throws a pass that lands at or beyond the line of scrimmage, even if no offensive player(s) have a realistic chance to catch the ball (including if the ball lands out of bounds over the sideline or end line).
4. Intentional gounding will not be called when a screen pass is developing and the quarterback throws the ball in the vicinity of the screen receiver.

PROTECTION OF PASSER

1. By interpretation, a pass begins when the passer—with possession of ball—starts to bring his hand forward. If ball strikes ground after this action has begun, play is ruled an incomplete pass. If passer loses control of ball prior to his bringing his hand forward, play is ruled a fumble.

2. No defensive player may run into a passer of a legal forward pass after the ball has left his hand (15 yards). The Referee must determine whether opponent had a reasonable chance to stop his momentum during an attempt to block the pass or tackle the passer while he still had the ball.
3. No defensive player who has an unrestricted path to the quarterback may hit him flagrantly in the area of the knee(s) or below when approaching in any direction.
4. Officials are to blow the play dead as soon as the quarterback is clearly in the grasp and control of any tackler, and his safety is in jeopardy.

PASS INTERFERENCE

1. There shall be no interference with a forward pass thrown from behind the line. The restriction for the passing team starts with the snap. The restriction on the defensive team starts when the ball leaves the passer's hand. Both restrictions end when the ball is touched by anyone.
2. The penalty for defensive pass interference is an automatic first down at the spot of the foul. If interference is in the end zone, it is first down for the offense on the defense's 1-yard line. If previous spot was inside the defense's 1-yard line, penalty is half the distance to the goal line.
3. The penalty for offensive pass interference is 10 yards from the previous spot.
4. It is pass interference by either team when any player movement beyond the line of scrimmage significantly hinders the progress of an eligible player of such player's opportunity to catch the ball. Offensive pass interference rules apply from the time the ball is snapped until the ball is touched. Defensive pass interference rules apply from the time the ball is thrown until the ball is touched. Actions that constitute defensive pass interference include but are not limited to:
   (a) Contact by a defender who is not playing the ball and such contact restricts the receiver's opportunity to make the catch.
   (b) Playing through the back of a receiver in an attempt to make a play on the ball.
   (c) Grabbing a receiver's arm(s) in such a manner that restricts his opportunity to catch a pass.
   (d) Extending an arm across the body of a receiver thus restricting his ability to catch a pass, regardless of whether the defender is playing the ball.
   (e) Cutting off the path of a receiver by making contact with him without playing the ball.
   (f) Hooking a receiver in an attempt to get to the ball in such a manner that it causes the receiver's body to turn prior to the ball arriving.

   Actions that do not constitute pass interference include but are not limited to:
   (a) Incidental contact by a defender's hands, arms, or body when both players are competing for the ball, or neither player is looking for the ball. If there is any question whether contact is incidental, the ruling shall be no interference.
   (b) Inadvertent tangling of feet when both players are playing the ball or neither player is playing the ball.
   (c) Contact that would normally be considered pass interference, but the pass is clearly uncatchable by the involved players.
   (d) Laying a hand on a receiver that does not restrict the receiver in an attempt to make a play on the ball.
   (e) Contact by a defender who has gained position on a receiver in an attempt to catch the ball.

   Actions that constitute offensive pass interference include but are not limited to:
   (a) Blocking downfield by an offensive player prior to the ball being touched.
   (b) Initiating contact with a defender by shoving or pushing off thus creating a separation in an attempt to catch a pass.
   (c) Driving through a defender who has established a position on the field.

   Actions that do not constitute offensive pass interference include but are not limited to:
   (a) Incidental contact by a receiver's hands, arms, or body when both players are competing for the ball or neither player is looking for the ball.
   (b) Inadvertent touching of feet when both players are playing the ball or neither player is playing the ball.
   (c) Contact that would normally be considered pass interference, but the ball is *clearly* uncatchable by involved players.

Note 1: If there is any question whether player contact is incidental, the ruling should be no interference.

Note 2: Defensive players have as much right to the path of the ball as eligible offensive players.

Note 3: Pass interference for both teams ends when the pass is touched.

Note 4: There can be no pass interference at or behind the line of scrimmage, but defensive actions such as tackling a receiver can still result in a 5-yard penalty for defensive holding, if accepted.

Note 5: Whenever a team presents an apparent punting formation, defensive pass interference is not to be called for action on the end man on the line of scrimmage, or an eligible receiver behind the line of scrimmage who is aligned or in motion more than one yard outside the end man on the line. Defensive holding, such as tackling a receiver, still can be called and result in a 5-yard penalty from the previous spot, if accepted. Offensive pass interference rules still apply.

BACKWARD PASS

1. Any pass not forward is regarded as a backward pass. A pass parallel to the line is a backward pass. A runner may pass backward at any time.
2. A backward pass that strikes the ground can be recovered and advanced by either team.
3. A backward pass caught in the air can be advanced by either team.
4. A backward pass in flight may not be batted forward by an offensive player.

FUMBLE

1. The distinction between a fumble and a muff should be kept in mind in considering rules about fumbles. A fumble is the loss of player possession of the ball. A muff is the touching of a loose ball by a player in an unsuccessful attempt to obtain possession.
2. A fumble may be advanced by any player on either team regardless of whether recovered before or after ball hits the ground.
3. A fumble that goes forward and out of bounds will return to the fumbling team at the spot of the fumble unless the ball goes out of bounds in the opponent's end zone. In this case, it is a touchback.
4. On a play from scrimmage, if an offensive player fumbles anywhere on the field during fourth down, only the fumbling player is permitted to recover and/or advance the ball. If any player fumbles after the two-minute warning in a half, only the fumbling player is permitted to recover and/or advance the ball. If recovered by any other offensive player, the ball is dead at the spot of the fumble unless it is recovered behind the spot of the fumble. In that case, the ball is dead at the spot of recovery. Any defensive player may recover and/or advance any fumble at any time.
5. A muffed hand-to-hand snap from center is treated as a fumble.

KICKS FROM SCRIMMAGE

1. Any kick from scrimmage must be made from behind the line to be legal.
2. Any punt or missed field goal that touches a goal post is dead.
3. During a kick from scrimmage, only the end men, as eligible receivers on the line of scrimmage at the time of the snap, are permitted to go beyond the line before the ball is kicked.
   Exception: An eligible receiver who, at the snap, is aligned or in motion behind the line and more than one yard outside the end man on his side of the line, clearly making him the outside receiver, replaces that end man as the player eligible to go downfield after the snap. All other members of the kicking team must remain at the line of scrimmage until the ball has been kicked.
4. Any punt that is blocked and does not cross the line of scrimmage can be recovered and advanced by either team. However, if offensive team recovers it must make the yardage necessary for its first down to retain possession if punt was on fourth down.
5. The kicking team may never advance its own kick even though legal recovery is made beyond the line of scrimmage. Possession only.
6. A member of the receiving team may not run into or rough a kicker who kicks from behind his line unless contact is:
   (a) Incidental to and after he had touched ball in flight.
   (b) Caused by kicker's own motions.
   (c) Occurs during a quick kick, or a kick made after a run behind the line, or after kicker recovers a loose ball on the ground. Ball is loose when kicker muffs snap or snap hits ground.
   (d) Defender is blocked into kicker.

   The penalty for running into the kicker is 5 yards. For roughing the kicker: 15 yards, an automatic first down and disqualification if flagrant.
7. If a member of the kicking team attempting to down the ball on or inside opponent's 5-yard line carries the ball into the end zone, it is a touchback.
8. Fouls during a punt are enforced from the previous spot (line of scrimmage).
   Exception: Illegal touching, fair-catch interference, invalid fair-catch signal, or personal foul (blocking after a fair-catch signal).
9. While the ball is in the air or rolling on the ground following a punt or field goal attempt and receiving team commits a foul before gaining possession, receiving team will retain possession and will be penalized for its foul.
10. It will be illegal for a defensive player to jump or stand on any player, or be picked up by a teammate or to use a hand or hands on a teammate to gain additional height in an attempt to block a kick (Penalty: 15 yards, unsportsmanlike conduct).
11. A punted ball remains a kicked ball until it is declared dead or in possession of either team.
12. Any member of the punting team may down the ball anywhere in the field of play. However, it is illegal touching (Official's time out and receiver's ball at spot of illegal touching). This foul does not offset any foul by receivers during the down.
13. Defensive team may advance all kicks from scrimmage (including unsuccessful field goal) whether or not ball crosses defensive team's goal line. Rules pertaining to kicks from scrimmage apply until defensive team gains possession.
14. When a team presents a punt formation, defensive pass interference is not to be called for actions on the widest player eligible to go beyond line. Defensive holding may be called.

DIGEST OF RULES

FAIR CATCH

1. The member of the receiving team must raise one arm a full length above his head and wave it from side to side while kick is in flight. (Failure to give proper sign: receivers' ball five yards behind spot of signal.) **Note:** It is legal for the receiver to shield his eyes from the sun by raising one hand no higher than the helmet.
2. No opponent may interfere with the fair catcher, the ball, or his path to the ball. Penalty: 15 yards from spot of foul and fair catch is awarded.
3. A player who signals for a fair catch is not required to catch the ball. However, if a player signals for a fair catch, he may not block or initiate contact with any player on the kicking team until the ball touches a player. Penalty: snap 15 yards behind spot of foul.
4. If ball hits ground or is touched by member of kicking team in flight, fair catch signal is off and all rules for a kicked ball apply.
5. Any undue advance by a fair catch receiver is delay of game. No specific distance is specified for undue advance as ball is dead at spot of catch. If player comes to a reasonable stop, no penalty. For violation, five yards.
6. If time expires while ball is in play and a fair catch is awarded, receiving team may choose to extend the period with one fair catch kick down. However, placekicker may not use tee.

FOUL ON LAST PLAY OF HALF OR GAME

1. On a foul by defense on last play of half or game, the down is replayed if penalty is accepted.
2. On a foul by the offense on last play of half or game, the down is not replayed and the play in which the foul is committed is nullified.
   Exception: Fair catch interference, foul following change of possession, illegal touching. No score by offense counts.

SPOT OF ENFORCEMENT OF FOUL

1. There are four basic spots at which a penalty for a foul is enforced:
   (a) Spot of foul: The spot where the foul is committed.
   (b) Previous spot: The spot where the ball was put in play.
   (c) Spot of snap, backward pass or fumble: The spot where the foul occurred or the spot where the penalty is to be enforced.
   (d) Succeeding spot: The spot where the ball next would be put in play if no distance penalty were to be enforced.
   Exception: If foul occurs after a touchdown and before the whistle for a try, succeeding spot is spot of next kickoff.
2. All fouls committed by offensive team behind the line of scrimmage (except in the end zone) shall be penalized from the previous spot. If the foul is in the end zone, it is a safety.
3. When spot of enforcement for fouls involving defensive holding or illegal use of hands by the defense is behind the line of scrimmage, any penalty yardage to be assessed on that play shall be measured from the line if the foul occurred beyond the line.

DOUBLE FOUL

1. If there is a double foul during a down in which there is a change of possession, the team last gaining possession may keep the ball unless its foul was committed prior to the change of possession.
2. If double foul occurs after a change of possession, the defensive team retains the ball at the spot of its foul or dead ball spot.
3. If one of the fouls of a double foul involves disqualification, that player must be removed, but no penalty yardage is to be assessed.
4. If the kickers foul during a kick before possession changes and the receivers foul after possession changes, the receivers will retain the ball after enforcement of its foul.

PENALTY ENFORCED ON FOLLOWING KICKOFF

1. When a team scores by touchdown, field goal, extra point, or safety and either team commits a personal foul, unsportsmanlike conduct, or obvious unfair act during the down, the penalty will be assessed on the following kickoff.

EMERGENCIES AND UNFAIR ACTS

Emergencies—Policy

The National Football League requires all League personnel, including game officials, League office employees, players, coaches, and other club employees to use best effort to see that each game—preseason, regular season, and postseason—is played to its conclusion. The League recognizes, however, that emergencies may arise that make a game's completion impossible or inadvisable. Such circumstances may include, but are not limited to, severely inclement weather, natural or manmade disaster, power failure, and spectator interference. Games should be suspended, cancelled, postponed, or terminated when circumstances exist such that comencement or continuation of play would pose a threat to the safety of participants or spectators.

Authority of Commissioner's Office

1. Authority to cancel, postpone, or terminate games is vested only in the Commissioner and the League President (other League office representatives and referees may suspend play temporarily; see point No. 3 under this section and point No. 1 under "Authority of Referee" below). The following definitions apply:
   - **Cancel.** To cancel a game is to nullify it either before or after it begins and to make no provision for rescheduling it or for including its score or other performance statistics in League records.
   - **Postpone.** To postpone a game is (a) to defer its starting time to a later date, or (b) to suspend it after play has begun and to make provision to resume at a later date with all scores and other performance statistics up to the point of postponement added to those achieved in the resumed portion of the game.
   - **Terminate.** To terminate a game is to end it short of a full 60 minutes of play, to record it officially as a completed game, and to make no provision to resume it at a later date. The Commissioner or League President may terminate a game in an emergency if, in his opinion, it is reasonable to project that its resumption (a) would not change its ultimate result or (b) would not adversely affect any other interteam competitive issue.
   - **Forfeit.** The Commissioner, (except in cases of disciplinary action; see last section on "Removing Team from Field"), League President, and their representatives, including referees, are not authorized unilaterally to declare forfeits. A forfeit occurs only when a game is not played because of the failure or refusal of *one* team to participate. In that event, the other team, if ready and willing to play, is the winner by a score of 2-0.
2. If an emergency arises that may require cancellation, postponement, or termination (see above), the highest ranking representative from the Commissioner's office working the game in a "control" capacity will consult with the Commissioner, League President, or game-day duty officer designated by the League (by telephone, if that person is not in attendance) concerning such decision. If circumstances warrant, the League representative should also attempt to consult with the weather bureau and with appropriate security personnel of the League, club, stadium, and local authorities. If no representative from the Commissioner's office is working the game in a "control" capacity, the referee will be in charge (see "Authority of Referee" below).
3. In circumstances where safety is of immediate concern, the Commissioner's-office representative may, after consulting with the referee, authorize a temporary suspension in play and, if warranted, removal of the participants from the playing field. The representative should be mindful of the safety of spectators, players, game officials, nonplayer personnel in the bench areas, and other field-level personnel such as photographers and cheerleaders.
4. If possible, the League-office representative should consult with authorized representatives of the two participating clubs before any decision involving cancellation, postponement, or termination is made by the Commissioner or League President.
5. If the Commissioner or League President decides to cancel, postpone, or terminate a game, his representative at the game or the game-day duty officer will then determine the method(s) for announcing such decision, e.g., by public-address announcement over referee's wireless microphone, by public-address announcement by home club, or by communication to radio, television, and other news media.

Authority of Referee

1. If a referee determines that an emergency warrants immediate removal of participants from the playing field for safety reasons, he may do so on his own authority. If, however, circumstances allow him the time, he must reach the highest ranking full-time League office representative working at the game in a "control" capacity or the game-day duty officer designated by the League (by telephone, if that person is not in attendance) and discuss the actual or potential emergency with such representative or duty officer. That representative or duty officer then will make the final decision on removal of participants from the field or obtain a decision from the Commissioner or League President.
2. If a referee removes participants from the playing field under No. 1 above, he may order them to their respective bench areas or to their locker rooms, whichever is appropriate in the circumstances.
3. After appropriate consultation under No. 1 above, the referee must advise the two participating head coaches of the nature of the emergency and the action contemplated (if the decision has not yet been reached) or of the final decision.
4. The referee must *not*, before a decision is reached, make an announcement on his microphone concerning the possibility of a cancellation, postponement, or termination unless instructed to do so by an appropriate representative of the Commissioner's office.
5. The referee must *not* discuss a forfeit with head coaches or club personnel and must *not* use that term over the referee's microphone (see definition of *forfeit* under No. 1 of "Authority of Commissioner's Office" above).
6. The referee must *not* assess an unsportsmanlike-conduct penalty on the home team for actions of fans that cause or contribute to an emergency.
7. The referee should be mindful of the safety of not only players and officials, but also of the spectators and other nonparticipants.
8. If an emergency involves spectator interference (for example, nonparticipants on the field or thrown objects), the referee immediately should contact the appropriate club or League representative for additional security assistance, including, if applicable, involvement of the League's security representative(s) assigned to the game.
9. The referee may order the resumption of play when he deems conditions safe for all concerned and, if circumstances warrant, after consultation with appropriate representatives of the Commissioner's office.
10. Under no circumstances is the referee authorized to cancel, postpone, terminate, or declare forfeiture of a game unilaterally.

Procedures for Starting and Resuming Games

Subject to the points of authority listed above, League personnel and referees will be guided by the following procedures for starting and resuming games that are affected by emergencies.

1. If, because of an emergency, a regular-season or postseason game is not started at its scheduled time and cannot be played at any later time that same day, the game nevertheless must be played on a subsequent date to be determined by the Commissioner.
2. If an emergency threatens to occur during the playing of a game (for example, an incoming tropical storm), the starting time of the game will not be moved to an earlier time unless there is clearly sufficient time to make an orderly change.
3. All games that are suspended temporarily and resumed on the same day, and all suspended games that are postponed to a later date, will be resumed at the point of suspension. On suspension, the referee will call timeout and make a record of the following: team possessing the ball, direction in which its offense was headed, position of the ball on the field, down, distance, period, time remaining in the period, and any other pertinent information required for an orderly and equitable resumption of play.
4. For regular-season postponements, the Commissioner will make every effort to set the game for no later than two days after its originally scheduled date and at the same site. If unable to schedule at the same site, he will select an appropriate alternative site. If it is impossible to schedule the game within two days after its original date, the Commissioner will attempt to schedule it on the Tuesday of the next calendar week. The Commissioner will keep in mind the potential for competitive inequities if one or both of the involved clubs has already been scheduled for a game close to the Tuesday of that week (for example, a Thursday game).
5. For postseason postponements, the Commissioner will make every effort to set the game as soon as possible after its originally scheduled date and at the same site. If unable to schedule at the same site, he will select an appropriate alternative site.
6. Whenever postponement is attributable to negligence by a club, the negligent club is responsible for all home club costs and expenses, including, subject to approval by the Commissioner, gate receipts and television-contract income. [See Section 19.11 (C) of the NFL Constitution and Bylaws.]
7. Each home club is strictly responsible for having the playing surface of its stadium well maintained and suitable for NFL play.

UNFAIR ACTS

Commissioner's Authority

The Commissioner has sole authority to investigate and to take appropriate disciplinary or corrective measures if any club action, nonparticipant interference, or emergency occurs in an NFL game which he deems so unfair or outside the accepted tactics encountered in professional football that such action has a major effect on the result of a game.

No Club Protests

The authority and measures provided for in this section (UNFAIR ACTS) do not constitute a protest machinery for NFL clubs to dispute the result of a game. The Commissioner will conduct an investigation under this section only to review an act or occurrence that he deems so unfair that the result of the game in question may be inequitable to one of the participating teams. The Commissioner will not apply his authority under this section when a club registers a complaint concerning judgmental errors or routine errors of omission by game officials. Games involving such complaints will continue to stand as completed.

Penalties for Unfair Acts

The Commissioner's powers under this section (UNFAIR ACTS) include the imposition of monetary fines and draft choice forfeitures, suspension of persons involved, and, if appropriate, the reversal of a game's result or the rescheduling of a game, either from the beginning or from the point at which the extraordinary act occurred. In the event of rescheduling a game, the Commissioner will be guided by the procedures specified above ("Procedures for Starting and Resuming Games" under EMERGENCIES). In all cases, the Commissioner will conduct a full investigation, including the opportunity for hearings, use of game videotape, and any other procedures he deems appropriate.

REMOVING TEAM FROM FIELD

No player, coach, or other person affiliated with a club may remove that club's team from the field during the playing of any game, including preseason, except at the direction of the referee. Any club violating this rule will be subject to disciplinary action by the Commissioner, including possible game forfeiture and sole liability for financial losses suffered by the opposing club and any other affected member clubs of the League. [See Section 9.1 (E) of the NFL Constitution and Bylaws.]

NATIONAL FOOTBALL LEAGUE, 1999

280 Park Avenue, New York, New York 10017 (212) 450-2000
NFL Internet Address: http://nfl.com

Commissioner: Paul Tagliabue
President: Neil Austrian

Executive Vice President-Labor Relations/Chairman NFLMC: Harold Henderson
Executive Vice President & League Counsel: Jeff Pash
Executive Vice President-League & Football Development: Roger Goodell
Executive Vice President and Chief Financial Officer: Tom Spock
Senior Vice President-Communications & Government Affairs: Joe Browne
Senior Vice President-Broadcasting & Network Television: Dennis Lewin
Senior Vice President-Football Operations: George Young

COMMUNICATIONS

Vice President of Public Relations: Greg Aiello
Director of International Public Affairs: Pete Abitante
Director of Community Affairs: Beth Colleton
Director of Media Services: Leslie Hammond
Director of Corporate Communications: Chris Widmaier

BROADCASTING

Senior Vice President of Programming and Sales: John Collins
Senior Director of Broadcast Planning and Scheduling: Joe Ferreira
Director of Broadcast Operations and Services: Dick Maxwell
Director of Sponsorship Sales: Peter Murray
Director of Programming: Constance Schwartz

LEAGUE AND FOOTBALL DEVELOPMENT

Senior Director of Security: Milt Ahlerich
Senior Director of Officiating: Jerry Seeman
Director of Security: Reuben Bradford
Director of Strategic Development: Neil Glat
Director of Game Operations: Peter Hadhazy
Director of Football Development: Gene Washington

SPECIAL EVENTS

Vice President of Special Events: Jim Steeg
Director of Special Events Operations: Don Renzulli
Director of Special Events Planning: Sue Robichek
Director of Corporate Services: Deborah Wardrop

MANAGEMENT COUNCIL

Senior Vice President-General Counsel: Dennis Curran
Senior Vice President-Labor Relations: Peter Ruocco
Vice President of Player & Employee Development: Lem Burnham
Senior Director of Player Personnel/ Football Operations: Joel Bussert
Director of Labor Administration and Information: Carol Constantine
Director of Compliance: Mike Keenan
Director of Labor Relations: Ed Tighe
Director of Player Programs: Guy Troupe

FINANCE AND ADMINISTRATION

Senior Vice President of Business Affairs: Frank Hawkins
Vice President of Systems & Information Processing: Mary Oliveti
Vice President and Treasurer: Joe Siclare
Vice President-Internal Audit: Tom Sullivan
Senior Director of Human Resources & Administration: John Buzzeo
Senior Director of Operating and Networking Systems: Joe Manto
Senior Director of Communications and Networking Technology: Dave Port
Controller: Peter Lops
Director of Business Planning: Dan Margoshes

NFL ENTERPRISES

President: Ron Bernard
Senior Vice President-International: Don Garber
Senior Vice President-Market Development: Tola Murphy-Baran
Vice President-International TV Distribution: Anne Murray
Vice President-International Marketing: Doug Quinn
President, NFL Europe: Oliver Luck
CFO/Chief Administration Officer, NFL Europe: Ken Saunders
Managing Director, NFL Europe: Chris Heyne
Managing Director, NFL Europe: Bill Peterson
Controller, NFL International: Dave Blasic

NFL FILMS

President: Steve Sabol
Senior Vice President-Finance & Operations: Barry Wolper
Vice President-Cinematography: Steve Andrich
Vice President-In Charge of Production: Bill Driber
Vice President-Video Operations: Jeff Howard
Vice President-Production Director: Hal Lipman
Vice President-Audio: Jerry Mahler
Vice President-Editor-in-Chief: Bob Ryan
Vice President-Special Projects: Phil Tuckett

NFL PROPERTIES

President: Sara Levinson
Senior Vice President-Finance/Administration: Ralph Carras
Senior Vice President-Business Affairs & General Counsel: Gary Gertzog
Senior Vice President-Marketing: Howard Handler
Senior Vice President-Club Services: Mark Holtzman
Senior Vice President-Corporate Sponsorships: Jim Schwebel
Senior Vice President-Consumer Products: Chuck Zona
Vice President-Club Marketing: Jesse Ewing
Vice President-Non-Apparel/Consumer Products: Gene Goldberg
Vice President-Marketing & Events: David Newman
Vice President-Corporate Sponsorship: Steve Phelps
Vice President-Publishing: John Wiebusch

NOTES

NOTES